CW00499255

Air-Britain

ERH 2017

European Registers Handbook 2017

Edited by David Partington

Part 1: CS- to F-

© Air-Britain Publishing 2017

Published by: Air-Britain Publishing
Sales Department: Unit 1A Munday Works, 58-66 Morley Road,
                     Tonbridge TN9 1RA, England
Membership Enquiries: 1 Rose Cottages, 179 Penn Road, Hazlemere,
                     Buckinghamshire HP15 7NE, England

Further information is available on our website: http://www.air-britain.co.uk

ISBN 978-0-85130-498-4   ISSN 0950-7477

COVER PHOTOS: PART 1

Front: *A regular visitor to many European events is the unique Verhees Delta F-PDHV. Here, having just arrived at the RSA Rally at Vichy on 8th July 2016, M. Verhees makes a call to confirm the end of another successful flight.*

Rear: Top - *The Humbert Moto-du-Ciel may not appear to be the most likely joy-riding aircraft but this young lady looks happy to take a trip around the bay in 50PS at Avranches on 25th August 2016.*

　　Centre - A very smart German-registered Breezer UL D-MJXC was one of a pair which visited the Swedish EAA Fly-in at Falköping on 4th June 2016.

　　Bottom - Fisheries Protection CASA 212 EC-HAP "Roche" returns to Tenerife-South on 13th March 2016 after a regular evening patrol around the island's coastal waters

(Photos: Dave Partington)

Printed by Bell & Bain Ltd, Glasgow G46 7UQ

Air-Britain supports the fight against terrorism and the efforts of the Police and other Authorities in protecting airports and airfields from criminal activity. If you see anything suspicious do not hesitate to call the
Anti-Terrorist Hotline 0800 789321
or alert a Police Officer.

EUROPEAN REGISTERS HANDBOOK 2017

CONTENTS:

EUROPEAN REGISTERS HANDBOOK 2017

INTRODUCTION

Welcome to the 32nd annual edition of European Registers Handbook, inevitably containing more entries than ever! The information within is that received up to mid-February 2017 and includes everything published in the "Overseas Registers" section of **Air-Britain News** up to the January 2017 issue together with some later additions already available from various reliable sources and contributors.

The continued growth of this publication has prompted a change this year, with the content divided into two separate parts. We hope that this will make them easier to handle and reduce the need for heavy-lifting gear when working through the contents. For the last eight years we have published a fully-searchable and illustrated CD containing all the traditional details to be found in this A4 book title. This time we have packaged the CD version, without photos, with the books so that rapid searches are available to all and users may select their preferred format for reference. As in recent years we now include all countries of continental Europe up to the Russian border, a total of 47 states currently.

It is worth mentioning that this is the only book with Europe-wide coverage which includes ALL the previous identities of each aircraft, adds details of aircraft known to be reserved or on permits which often do not appear in official lists, includes all gliders and balloons, and also makes an effort to identify and list all known microlights - especially in countries where their registers are not published. As in earlier years we have problems with the inaccessibility of data in several states but it is interesting to see that some countries are now calling for complete transparency and the availability of all civil registers on-line and now even paramotors and UAVs are joining in the fray. Meanwhile, Germany, the Netherlands, Finland and Turkey are among the larger countries to maintain restrictive data protection legislation. A further problem involves official admin standards that fail to keep abreast of changes, growth or even accuracy. Such problems rarely affect airliner and business jet entries where manufacturers' data and delivery information is generally more widely available; however, as by far the biggest growth sector in civil aviation is currently the microlight/ultralight area, we are clearly in need of more official data and would welcome observations and reports to help to update the German, French and Italian ULM sections in particular so please keep these coming in future. While we do not wish to expose private owners or clubs by publishing traditional registers with dates, owners and bases included (now often not available anyway) we do hope to provide a unique identification service to enthusiasts, photographers, pilots, historians and even manufacturers. There are known to be ATC control rooms where a copy of ERH is seen as a desirable asset!.

As ever, we are most grateful for the support of some very co-operative manufacturers of aircraft, gliders and balloons; and of course to the many enthusiasts in Britain and Europe who regularly send reports and observations. Why not join their number? Please send reports either to Ian Burnett as Editor of "Overseas Registers" in Air-Britain News (post to 'Briarwood', Swallowfield Street, Swallowfield, Reading, Berks RG7 1QX or e-mail **Ian.Burnett@air-britain.co.uk**) or to the ERH Editor at the address below - or preferably to both! It is useful to quote details such as names, c/ns or call-signs *actually seen* on the aircraft rather than quoting what is in this book - these things can change and we would like to know if they do. Reports including microlight registrations,call-signs and glider tail codes would also be particularly useful as these *do* often change. If you are unable to identify a new type or registration why not take a photo if possible and send it with your report - every little helps!

As usual this Editor's main task has been to work with material provided for use in "Overseas Registers", which is of course pre-processed with a massive input from the incomparable Ian Burnett, I can only really repeat here our joint thanks for the continued support of many contributors whether regular or infrequent, almost too numerous to name but they are all credited in each issue of News, Without them both our efforts would be so much poorer. This year the editor has personally handled most of the data in order to achieve earlier publication but grateful thanks are still due to all our previous 'updaters' and we hope that we can reconstruct the team to continue their earlier work in future editions. Additional volunteers are always welcome - please contact the editor for details.

As many readers will know, additions to all of the Registers in this volume are published regularly in the "Overseas Registers" section of the monthly **"Air-Britain News"**. Further details of Air-Britain membership may be found on our website **www.air-britain.co.uk**, alternatively anyone who is not already a member is invited to write to Barry Collman at 1,Rose Cottages, 179 Penn Road, Hazlemere, Bucks HP15 7NE for additional information. Full details of all our annual and non-annual publications may also be found on our welsite.

Any further comments, additions or amendments to this European Registers Handbook will as always be gratefully received by the Editor at the address below or by e-mail to: **Dave.Partington@air-britain.co.uk**

David Partington,   March 2017
"The Haven",
Nympsfield Road,
Nailsworth,
Gloucestershire   GL6 0EA
United Kingdom

IMPORTANT NOTE

The publication of these Registers should not be taken to imply that access to Civil Airfields is always permissable, or that photography of civil aircraft is authorised. Visitors should check these points beforehand as many states do not allow open access to civil airfields and an interest in aviation may not always be tolerated or understood.

USER'S GUIDE TO THE EUROPEAN REGISTERS HANDBOOK

The aim of this book is to identify the civil aircraft of Western Europe (except for the UK, published in a separate volume) including gliders, balloons and microlights. Four information 'fields' are available for each entry as follows:

REGISTRATION

The basic form of aircraft identification, usually painted on the aircraft itself (but not always as in the case of some microlights), which consists of the nationality prefix followed by the individual alphabetical or numerical identifier. Types such as gliders, balloons, ulms may be allocated separate blocks in some countries, in others they may be combined in the same sequence. In some countries the registration marks are allocated in strict alphabetical order, eg Spain, while others use blocks representing different classes, eg Germany, Switzerland, Austria, by weight, number of engines, etc, Sweden has separate blocks for jets, helicopters, etc, the former Czechoslovakia used the first letter to identify year of manufacture, Finland uses blocks for different manufacturers, while France has separate sections for vintage, homebuilt and overseas-based aircraft but registers microlights using only the number of the Département in which they are based. Other countries use completely unsequenced allocations, as in Italy, Belgium, Iceland, but may include blocks for particular operators. A brief study of any country's entries should quickly reveal the system adopted.

Where possible, if a registration has been used more than once, multiple use is indicated by a figure in brackets in the registration column, eg D-ABOM(2), LN-ORH(4). We must emphasise that these suffix marks are not carried on the aircraft themselves but are to assist in identifying different aircraft over a period of time. Austria has dropped a system which allows for multiple use of the same marks simultaneously for balloons registered to the same owner. In many countries gliders wear a one, two or even three-letter code/competition number which may not necessarilly be a part of the registration. Where known, these are added in the registration column thus: F-CFAN-J43, PH-754-YX, OO-ZSG-V. Icelandic aircraft are allocated a CofR number which is worn externally and is just as identifiable as the registration is.

Registrations known to have been reserved but not yet officially taken up or certificated (depending on national practice) are indicated as such in the second line of an entry beneath the type, the same location being used to identify aircraft known to be flying only on Permits or to 'flag-up' some particular problem or feature.

AIRCRAFT TYPE

The manufacturer or designer and actual model are quoted here, as far as possible using the official FAA designation. If the manufacturer has changed during the production run of a particular type this may be shown in cases where the date or unit of change can be clearly identified. In other cases we tend to adopt the original manufacturer's designation and only change this when a new model or type designation results. Thus de Havilland Tiger Moths will never be BAe Tiger Moths but the Learjet models produced entirely by Bombardier (eg. the 45 and 60) are listed as such. There are bound to be some anomalies in this system but the overall aim is to be both informative and accurate, even if these aims sometimes conflict.

Sometimes models may have changed names during a production run but retained the same designation (usually for ease of certification) which is the only part of the data to be published. Robin DR.400 production for example had the 400/120 Petit Prince replaced by the Dauphin 2+2 but during the transition period only by observing the name on the actual aircraft can the correct model be positively identified. We have now taken a cut-off date of the 1988 model to change the names listed for the DR.400/120 and DR.400/160 series, and 1991 for the DR.400/140. As this is fairly arbitrary any reports of actual names carried would still be most welcome! Meanwhile some types such as the Sportcruiser and the Bristell have quickly passed through a number of different manufacturers and designations..

In some countries the builder of a kit or home-built aircraft may be shown in front of the normal type or designer name, usually separated by an oblique. Any notable modifications to model or to engine, or other significant information about a particular aircraft may also be added in brackets in this column. With many weightshift ulms we attempt to list the trike type first followed by the wing designation.

CONSTRUCTOR'S NUMBER (C/n)

The constructor's number (also known as the manufacturer's serial number) is the only reliable permanent identification of each single airframe allocated at the time of building and remaining with the aircraft throughout any changes of owner or nationality. Specific changes may occur in the case of modification, rebuild, or the use of 'spare' fuselages. Such known cases are usually noted in column two. Users of this book may often find the fuselage or frame number (f/n) quoted in significant cases in order to clarify a particular identity - in the case of Piper Cubs and Super Cubs for example this number differs from the actual c/n but is often mistakenly quoted for it as the identification plate is in an accessible location! C/ns officially quoted, but known to be incorrect, are written between quotation marks and may merit further comment. A few aircraft may legitimately carry more than one c/n, as in the case of Cessna models built as 'knock-down' units in the US for assembly by Reims Aviation in France. Many aircraft carry the c/n on an external plate or have it painted on the rear fuselage or rudder. Specific numbering systems may also be used locally by certification authorities, particularly involving homebuilt or microlight aircraft as in Spain or Sweden for example.

PREVIOUS IDENTITY

Every time that an aircraft changes its country of registration a new identity will be allocated by the relevant authority. In Spain an internal change of owner is now sufficient to trigger a new identity! The immediate previous identity is given next to the aircraft c/n and if several identities are quoted the oldest is the last on the list. A basic history of each aircraft's past can thus be read from the listing. Registrations which have been allocated, but not taken up, are shown in brackets. Those which have been incorrectly applied or which are unofficial or unauthorised are shown in quotation marks. A question mark indicates that a particular identity is unconfirmed or incomplete.

Companion volumes to this publication covering the UK civil register, world airline fleets, business jets
and many other topicsare available by post-free mail order from

**Air-Britain Sales Department
Unit 1A Munday Works, 58-66 Morley Road,
Tonbridge, Kent TN9 1RA, UK**

For a full list of current titles and details of how to order, visit our e-commerce site at www.air-britain.co.uk
Visa / Mastercard / Delta / Switch accepted - please give full details of card number and expiry date.
Members of Air-Britain receive substantial discounts on the prices of all Air-Britain publications.

ABBREVIATIONS

The majority of the abbreviations listed below apply to the Previous Identity column where space is limited but a number also refer to manufacturers, names. As 'familiarity breeds contempt' we may have missed some examples - please let us know!

AAF	Austrian Air Force	LAAF	Libyan Arab Air Force
ALAT	Aviation Légère de l'Armée de Terre (French Army Aviation)	LSK	Luftstreitkrafte (The former East German Air Force)
BelAF	Belarus Air Force	MLD	Royal Netherlands Naval Air Service
BFAF	Burkina Faso Air Force	MM	Matricola Militare (Italian Air Force serial)
BGA	British Gliding Association	NEJSGSA	Near East Joint Services Gliding & Soaring Association (UK)
BulAF	Bulgarian Air Force	ntu	Not taken up
CAF	Canadian Armed Forces	OGMA	Oficinas Gerais de Material Aeronautico
CamAF	Cambodian Air Force		(Portuguese aircraft manufacturer)
CEA	Centre Est Aéronautique	PLAAF0C	People's Liberation Army Air Force of China
CEV	Centre d'Essais en Vol (French Flight Test Centre)	PLW	Polskie Lotnictwo Wosjkowe (Polish Air Force)
CofA	Certificate of Airworthiness	RAFGGA	Royal Air Force Germany Gliding Association (UK)
CPLAF	Chinese People's Liberation Air Force	RAFGSA	Royal Air Force Gliding & Soaring Association (UK)
CzAF	Czech Republic Air Force	RCAF	Royal Canadian Air Force - now CAF: Canadian Armed Forces
DOSAAF	Dobrovol'noe Obshchestvo Sodeistviya Armii, Aviasii i Flotu (Voluntary Society for Cooperation with the Army, Air Force and Navy - the Soviet youth and reserve training organisation)	RDAF	Royal Danish Air Force
		RHAF	Royal Hellenic (Greek) Air Force - now HAF
		RJAF	Royal Jordanian Air Force
EAF	Egyptian Air Force	RNoAF	Royal Norwegian Air Force
FAP	Forca Aérea Portuguesa (Portuguese Air Force)	RSrp	Republika Srpska (Serbian Republic military forces)
FLARF	Federatsiya Lyubitelei Aviatsii Rossiskoi Federatsii (Federation of Aviation Enthusiasts of the Russian Federation)	RusAF	Russian Air Force
		SAAF	South African Air Force
Fr.AF	French Air Force (the Armée de l'Air)	SEEMS	Société d'Exploitation des Etablissements Morane-Saulnier
Fr.Navy	French Navy (Aéronavale)	SLN-	'Serial' for aircraft at the former RCAF Solingen, Germany, Flying Club
Fr.Mil	One or more of the French forces		
Fv	Flygvapnet (Royal Swedish AF serial)	SOCATA	Société de Construction d'Avions de Tourisme et d'Affaires
GEMS	Gerance des Etablissements Morane-Saulnier	Sov.mil	Soviet military forces
HAF	Hellenic Air Force (Greece) , also Hungarian Air Force	SpAF	Spanish Air Force
HAFB	Hot Air Free Balloon	SwAF	Swiss Air Force
IAC	Irish Air Corps	TAF	Turkish Air Force
IAF	Iraqi Air Force	UAE	United Arab Emirates
IDFAF	Israeli Defence Force/Air Force	UkrAF	Ukraine Air Force
JRV	Jugoslovensko Ratno Vazduhoplovstvo (Yugoslav Air Force)	Wfu	Withdrawn from use
KLu	Koninklijke Nederlandse Luchtmacht (Royal Netherlands Air Force)	W/o	Written off
		. . + . . .	(in serial) German military serial with unit and identity

CS - PORTUGAL

Regn.	Type	C/n	Prev.Id.

The last official listing still suffered from many 'current' entries with CofAs which are long expired, have been withdrawn from use or written-off. Others known to be extant, together with some earlier expiries which may be candidates for rebuild or restoration, are indicated with an asterisk (*) but any recent reports would be welcome. Increasingly aircraft registered in other EU countries but based in Portugal continue to fly in their 'foreign' marks.

Regn.	Type	C/n	Prev.Id.
CS-AAP(*)	Piper J-3C-85 Cub	21984	G-AKBT
	(Under restoration - C/n suspect - 21984 was not built)		
CS-AAQ	Piper J-3C-65 Cub	22021	G-AKBU
	(C/n refers to spare frame built from spares 1947 - the real 22021 was current as N77531 until 1977)		
CS-ABA(*)	Piper PA-12 Super Cruiser	12-65	
	(Exp .72, for rebuild)		
CS-ABK	Piper J-3C-65 Cub	17674	
CS-ABO	Piper PA-25 Pawnee	25-646	N10F
CS-ABW	Piper J-3C-65 Cub	17242	
CS-ABY(*)	Piper J-3C-65 Cub	17243	
	(Stored, Torres Vedras)		
CS-ACE(*)	Piper PA-18 Super Cub 95	18-661	N10F
	(Exp 11.71)		
CS-ACF	Piper PA-18A-150 Super Cub	18-5414	(HK-939P), N10F
CS-ACH	Piper PA-18 Super Cub 95	18-6863	N10F
CS-ACY	Culver V	348	
CS-ADF	Cessna 150A	15059232	N7132X
	(Dam. 7.11.11, Cascais)		
CS-ADU(*)	Piper PA-18A-150 Super Cub	18-6715	N10F
	(Exp 7.62)		
CS-AEL(*)	OGMA/de Havilland DH.82 Tiger Moth	P-65	FAP1 . .
	(Under restoration, Alverca)		
CS-AFG	Beech A23-24 Musketeer Super III	MA-350	
CS-AFI	Piper PA-28-180 Cherokee D	28-5463	N2110R
CS-AFP	SEEMS MS.892A Rallye Commodore 150	10503	F-BMVR
CS-AFQ(*)	Piper PA-28-180 Cherokee E	28-5613	N11C
	(Stored)		
CS-AFR(*)	CEA Jodel DR.1050 Ambassadeur	39	F-BJQP
	(Stored)		
CS-AFU	Piper PA-28R-200 Cherokee Arrow	28R-35786	N5044S
CS-AGB(*)	American AA-1 Yankee	AA1-0377	N6177L
	(W/o 1988?)		
CS-AGI	SOCATA MS.893A Rallye Commodore 180	11782	
CS-AGK(*)	SOCATA MS.894A Minerva 220	11833	
	(Stored)		
CS-AGP	Rockwell Commander 112A	0192	N1192J
CS-AGW	Piper PA-23-250 Turbo Aztec E	27-4665	N14054
	(Stored engineless 4.11)		
CS-AGZ	SOCATA MS.894A Minerva 220	11940	
CS-AHE	Reims/Cessna F337F Super Skymaster	F33700037	
	(Reims-assembled Cessna 337F with US c/n 33701374)		
CS-AHG(*)	Grumman G.44 Widgeon	1242	FAP120
	(To Museu do Ar)		
CS-AHI	Reims/Cessna F150L	F15000759	
CS-AHO	Rockwell S.2R Thrush Commander	1610R	CR-LNO, CS-AHO, N5510X
CS-AHQ	Reims FR172H Rocket	FR17200318	
CS-AHS(*)	Cessna A188B Agwagon C	18800873	N4473Q
	(Wreck, Coimbra)		
CS-AHU	Wassmer WA.52 Europa	43	
CS-AHW	Cessna 414	414-0280	N1565T
CS-AHX	Reims FR172H Rocket	FR17200332	
CS-AIA	Piper PA-18 Super Cub 125	18-1295	CR-AKA, FAP3206, N10F
	(Dam. 2.8.15)		
CS-AIB(*)	Beagle A.109 Airedale	B-527	G-ASCB
	(Stored for Museu do Ar)		
CS-AIC	Piper PA-28-180 Cherokee C	28-4230	N4874L
	(Under restn)		
CS-AID	SOCATA MS.893A Rallye Commodore 180	10920	
CS-AIG	Alon A-2 Aircoupe	B-280	N5480F
	(W/o Ciborro 6.3.10)		
CS-AII	Piper PA-28-180 Cherokee D	28-4436	N5151L
CS-AIP	Piper PA-22-160 Tri-Pacer	22-7615	CR-LEM, G-ARGF, N10F
	(On rebuild .09)		
CS-AIQ	SOCATA MS.893A Rallye Commodore 180	11446	
CS-AIS(*)	Beech A23-24 Musketeer Super III	MA-106	HB-ENU
	(Exp 9.93)		
CS-AIW	SOCATA MS.880B Rallye Club	1348	
CS-AIY(*)	SOCATA MS.893A Rallye Commodore 180	11455	
	(W/o 1988?)		
CS-AJA	Wassmer Jodel D.120A Paris-Nice	338	
CS-AJB	SOCATA MS.893A Rallye Commodore 180	12034	
CS-AJD	Cessna 421B Golden Eagle	421B0270	N3395Q
CS-AJE	Helio H-295 Courier	1404	
	(Stored)		
CS-AJG	Reims FR172J Rocket	FR17200380	
CS-AJI (*)	Cessna A188B Agtruck	18801069T	N21840
	(Exp 5.89, dism)		
CS-AJN(*)	Slingsby T.66 Nipper Mk.III	1620/S.114	
	(For rebuild)		
CS-AJS	Rockwell S.2R Thrush Commander	1504R	CR-LNN, CS-AJS, N8804Q
CS-AKB	Cessna F172H	F172-0465	
CS-AKE	Cessna F172H	F172-0575	N14622
CS-AKF	Cessna 172C	17249439	N1839Y
CS-AKH	Cessna F172F	F172-0153	OE-DLB
	(Dam 19.12.14)		
CS-AKI	Cessna F172H	F172-0504	
CS-AKN(*)	Reims/Cessna F172H	F17200655	N10655
	(W/o 5.96, stored)		
CS-AKS	Cessna 150B	15059582	N1182Y
	(On rebuild .09)		
CS-AKV	Cessna F172G	F172-0303	
CS-AKX	Cessna 182M Skylane	18259880	N91710
CS-AKY	Cessna U206E Stationair	U20601678	N9478G
CS-AKZ	Reims FR172G Rocket	FR17200168	D-ECFM
CS-ALA	Piper PA-22-108 Colt	22-9749	N10F
CS-ALB	Paulistinha 56-C1	1162	PP-HME
	(W/o 18.8.12)		
CS-ALE(*)	Helio H-250 Courier	2502	(ET-ABN)
	(Exp 8.78)		
CS-ALF	Piper PA-32-260 Cherokee Six	32-631	N3718W
	(Stored)		
CS-ALI	Alpavia/ Fournier RF-3	72	
CS-ALM	Piper PA-23-160 Apache	23-1252	N3302P
	(Exp 1.94. For rebuild?)		
CS-ALP	Piper PA-22-108 Colt	22-9368	N10F
CS-ALS	Mooney M.20E Super 21	554	
CS-ALT	Piper PA-24-180 Comanche	24-3404	N8197P, N10F
CS-ALV(*)	Beagle A.109 Airedale	B-529	
	(W/o 16.3.97)		
CS-ALX	Piper PA-32-300 Cherokee Six	32-40154	N4157W
	(Dism.)		
CS-ALZ(*)	Piper PA-32-260 Cherokee Six	32-716	N3758W
	(Exp 12.74, std .98)		
CS-AMB(*)	Auster D4/108	3603	
	(Exp 5.66)		
CS-AMG(*)	OGMA/Auster D5/160	10	
	(Exp 5.73)		
CS-AMJ(*)	OGMA/Auster D4/108	36	
	(Exp 10.73)		
CS-AMX(*)	OGMA/Auster D5/160	81	
	(Preserved, Alverca)		
CS-AMZ	OGMA/Auster D5/160	99	
CS-ANB(*)	OGMA/Auster D5/160	101	
	(Exp 10.82, displayed Faro)		
CS-AND(*)	OGMA/Auster D5/160	108	
	(Exp 12.81)		
CS-ANF	OGMA/Auster D5/160	131	
CS-ANK(*)	OGMA/Auster D5/160	119	
	(Exp 10.73)		
CS-ANP(*)	OGMA/Auster D5/160	124	
	(Exp 3.72)		
CS-ANT(*)	OGMA/Auster D5/160	128	
	(Exp 12.81. Stored)		
CS-ANV(*)	OGMA/Auster D5/160	130	
	(Exp 2.74)		
CS-AOA(*)	Piper PA-34-200 Seneca	34-7350126	N15998
	(W/o 9.10.94)		
CS-AOB(*)	Reims FR172J Rocket	FR17200367	
	(W/o .93)		
CS-AOD	Cessna 210L Centurion	21059722	N22217
CS-AOE	Reims/Cessna F150L	F15000915	
CS-AOO	Piper PA-28-180 Cherokee Challenger	28-7305192	N11C
CS-AOT	Reims/Cessna F150L	F15000976	F-BRGV, (CN-TBD)
	(Dam 5.5.10)		
CS-APA	Reims/Cessna F150L	F15001068	F-BSGQ, (F-BVBD)
CS-APC	Piper PA-34-200 Seneca	34-7450080	N56539
CS-APN	Reims/Cessna F172M	F17201150	F-BRCR
CS-APQ(*)	Rockwell S.2R Thrush Commander	1823R	N5623X
	(For rebuild?)		
CS-APT	Piper PA-28-180 Cherokee Archer	28-7405105	EC-YYT, N9532N
CS-APU(*)	Piper PA-28-180 Cherokee Archer	28-7405109	EC-YYU, N9542N
	(Impounded in Morocco)		
CS-AQD	Rockwell S.2R Thrush Commander	1865R	CR-AQJ, N5665X
	(Wfu, stored 4.11)		
CS-AQE	Rockwell S.2RThrush Commander	1831R	CR-AQI, N5631X
CS-AQI (*)	Dornier Do.27A-3	350	FAP3339, QW+703, PL+427
	(To Museu do Ar)		
CS-AQM(*)	OGMA/DHC-1 Chipmunk T.20	OGMA-4	FAP1314
	(Stored)		
CS-AQN	Piper PA-18-150 Super Cub	18-7723	FAP ? , 61-2929
CS-AQQ(*)	Piper PA-18-135 Super Cub	18-2561	FAP ? , 52-6243
	(Exp 7.85, stored)		
CS-AQU(*)	Cessna A188B Agtruck	18803313T	N1978J
	(Reims-assembled with "c/n" 0029)		
CS-AQX	Reims/Cessna F172N	F17201903	
CS-AQY(*)	Piper PA-38-112 Tomahawk	38-79A0875	N9676N
	(W/o 1991)		
CS-ARA(*)	Aero Commander 100	084	
	(Exp 7.90)		
CS-ARB	Piper PA-28RT-201T Turbo Arrow IV	28R-8031171	N9602N, N82593
CS-ARC	Reims/Cessna F152	F15201790	F-WZIM
	(W/o 11.1.98)		
CS-ARD	Piper PA-31-325 Navajo C/R	31-7912102	N35379
CS-ARF(*)	Cessna A188B Agtruck	18803512T	N2779J
	(Exp 12.92, dismantled)		
CS-ARG	Cessna A188B Agtruck	18803531T	N2837J
CS-ARH(*)	Reims/Cessna F152	F15201837	F-WZIY
	(W/o 9.6.96)		
CS-ARJ (*)	Cessna 402B Utiliner	402B0119	PJ-SAA, HP-717, C9-ANL, CR-ANL, N7869Q
	(Exp 12.93)		
CS-ARK	SOCATA MS.893A Rallye Commodore 180	11432	CS-AIL
	(Wfu, stored 4.11)		
CS-ARL	Cessna 402B Utiliner	402B0318	PJ-SAB, HP-693, C9-AOT, CR-AOT, ZS-IUO, N1559T
CS-ARM(*)	Piper PA-34-220T Seneca III	34-8133112	N83934
	(W/o 24.7.91)		
CS-ARN(*)	Cessna 402B Utiliner	402B0443	PJ-SAC, HP-718, C9-AON, CR-AON, ZS-IVV, N69333
	(Exp 7.83, stored)		
CS-ARO(*)	Rockwell Commander 680FLP	1651-32	I-ZANU, N4598E
	(Exp 11.85, stored Alverca)		
CS-ARY	Piaggio FWP.149D	038	D-ENTL, 90+26, BF+403, BF+703
CS-ARZ(*)	Cessna A.152 Aerobat	A1521032	N758ZH
	(W/o 7.92)		
CS-ASH	Mooney M.20J Model 201	24-0998	N3974H
CS-ASI	Piper PA-36-375 Brave	36-8002031	N2456V
CS-ASM	Grumman G.164B Agcat	811B	
CS-ASO	Cessna 152	15282784	OY-CPN, N89553
CS-ASP	Cessna 152	15282439	N69020
CS-ASQ	Cessna 152	15281019	N48874
	(Damaged 20.8.11)		
CS-ASR	Cessna 152	15282999	N46113
CS-AST	Cessna 172N	17272060	N6735E
CS-ASW	Piper PA-36-285 Pawnee Brave	36-7660003	N57604
CS-ASX	Reims/Cessna F150M	F15001371	PH-BAR
CS-ASZ	Mooney M.20J Model 201	24-0958	G-BHRV, N3839H
CS-AUA	Piper PA-36-285 Pawnee Brave	36-7360027	N56070
CS-AUC	Piper PA-36-375 Brave	36-8202001	N2321X
	(W/o 18.6.15)		
CS-AUD	Reims/Cessna F172M	F17200983	D-EGJL
CS-AUF	Cessna TU206G Turbo Stationair II	U20603577	D-EHLK(2), N7240N

Reg	Type	c/n	Previous identities
CS-AUG	Cessna 150L	15074780	N10084
CS-AUH	Cessna 150L (Wreck stored)	15072396	EC-ECY(2), N6896G
CS-AUI	Cessna 152	15283688	N4876B
CS-AUJ	Cessna 152	15282656	N89162
CS-AUK	Cessna 152	15280376	N24783
CS-AUM	Beech F33A Bonanza	CE-763	N4214Q
CS-AUN	Cessna 152 (W/o)	15280040	N757VP
CS-AUP	Cessna 172C	17248845	N8345X
CS-AUR	Cessna 152 (W/o 26.6.12)	15283659	N4826B
CS-AUS	Cessna 152 (Dam. 23.8.98 nr Alfena)	15280296	N24507
CS-AUW	Cessna T210L Turbo Centurion	21060642	N1606X
CS-AVA	Cessna 152	15283295	G-BOBI, (G-BHJD), N48172
CS-AVB	Cessna 152	15279539	N714YN
CS-AVC	Cessna 152	15279621	N757BY
CS-AVD	Cessna 152	15279997	N757TS
CS-AVH	Piper PA-28RT-201 Arrow IV	28R-7918069	G-BORU, N1015S, N9614N
CS-AVJ (*)	Cessna 172N (W/o .95)	17269875	N738CQ
CS-AVK	Mooney M.20J Model 201	24-1384	N5648U
CS-AVL	Beech 76 Duchess	ME-332	N6718D
CS-AVM	Piper PA-31-350 Navajo Chieftain	31-7752159	N503SC, G-BFDB, N27339
CS-AVS	Cessna 182J Skylane	18257261	N3161F
CS-AVT	Cessna 172M	17261830	N12132
CS-AVV	Piper PA-38-112 Tomahawk	38-79A0588	N2358K
CS-AXA(*)	Jodel D.9 Bébé (To Museu do Ar, Alverca)	436	
CS-AXB(*)	Jurca MJ.2B Tempête (To Museu do Ar, Sintra)	9	
CS-AYC	Cessna R.172K Hawk XP	3056	N758FG
CS-AYG	Reims/Cessna F152	F15201573	G-BGHK
CS-AYH	Reims/Cessna F152 (Ditched off Sagres, 12.9.14)	F15201612	G-BGOF
CS-AYI	Cessna Turbo 310R	310R1408	N4943A
CS-AYJ	Reims/Cessna F150L (Dam 15.5.14)	F15000916	D-ECWL
CS-AYK	Cessna 152	15282482	G-BPBH, N69102
CS-AYL	Piper PA-28-140 Cherokee B	28-26315	N5585U
CS-AYM	Cessna A.152 Aerobat	A1520995	N761XR
CS-AYN	Cessna A.152 Aerobat	A1520990	N761VU
CS-AYR	Cessna 152	15281575	G-PACK, N65477
CS-AYT	Dornier 228-200	8084	VP-FBK, G-MAFS, D-ILAB, (D-CLAB)
CS-AYU	Cessna 152	15282355	N68749
CS-AYV	Cessna 172N	17273832	N5747J
CS-AYW	Cessna R.172K Hawk XP	3060	N758FL
CS-AYX	Cessna 152	15284658	N6296M
CS-AYY	Cessna 501 Citation I/SP	501-0183	ZS-KPA, N6777V
CS-AYZ	Cessna R.172K Hawk XP	3001	N758CZ
CS-AZA	Cessna 152	15282210	N68249
CS-AZB	Cessna 152	15281900	G-SACA, G-HOSE, N67538
CS-AZD	Cessna 172RG Cutlass RG	172RG0979	G-RGII, N9702B
CS-AZF	SOCATA TB-9 Tampico	1454	F-OHDC, F-WNGY
CS-AZG	SOCATA TB-9 Tampico	1455	F-OHDD
CS-AZI	Beech F33A Bonanza	CE-312	N9777S
CS-AZK	Mooney M.20J Model 201	24-1525	N57881
CS-AZQ	OGMA/DHC-1 Chipmunk T.20 (On rebuild)	OGMA-13	FAP-1323
CS-AZU	Piper PA-36-375 Brave (W/o 15.6.04)	36-8302015	VH-HSR, N82678
CS-AZV	Piper PA-32R-301 Saratoga	32R-8013038	G-BHNN, N3578C
CS-AZX	OGMA/DHC-1 Chipmunk T.20	OGMA-24	FAP-1334
CS-CHA	Bombardier BD-100-1A10 Challenger 350	20544	C-GOVY
CS-CHB	Bombardier BD-100-1A10 Challenger 350	20553	C-GOXR (2)
CS-CHC	Bombardier BD-100-1A10 Challenger 350	20572	C-GOXA
CS-CHD	Bombardier BD-100-1A10 Challenger 350	20584	C-GUGY
CS-CHE	Bombardier BD-100-1A10 Challenger 350	20623	C-GOXG
CS-DAA	SOCATA TB-9 Tampico	1553	F-OHDJ
CS-DAB	SOCATA TB-9 Tampico	1554	F-OHDK
CS-DAG	Cessna 172RG Cutlass RG (Reims-assembled with c/n 0003)	172RG0009	G-BHEP, N4668R
CS-DAJ	OGMA/DHC-1 Chipmunk T.20	OGMA-32	FAP1342
CS-DAK	Cessna 152	15284916	N5363M
CS-DAL	Cessna R.172K Hawk XP	3296	N758RH, V3-HEI, N758RH
CS-DAR(*)	OGMA/DHC-1 Chipmunk T.20 (Preserved, Alverca)	OGMA-66	FAP1376
CS-DAS	Cessna 152 (Dam 16.8.14)	15281047	N48916
CS-DAT	Cessna 152	15283914	N6258B
CS-DAY	Aviat Pitts S-2B	5282	
CS-DBA	Mooney M.20J Model 201	24-3100	G-MASL, N1012U
CS-DBC	Cessna 172N	17271143	N205JA, N2072E
CS-DBD	Reims/Cessna FTB337G Super Skymaster	0032	FAP3731, CS-ABR
CS-DBE	SOCATA MS.893A Rallye Commodore 180	10663	F-BODH
CS-DBF	Cessna 172M	17261139	N20263
CS-DBG	Piper PA-28-140 Cherokee F (Cr 15.5.99 Portimao, fuselage stored)	28-7325436	N55580
CS-DBH	Commander Aircraft 114B (Dismantled .06)	14591	N6015K
CS-DBN	Cessna 172N	17270051	N738LA
CS-DBO	Britten-Norman BN-2A-20 Islander	352	LN-FSK, F-OGNV, N352BN, C-GCXB, N24JA, G-BBJC
CS-DBR	Piper PA-23-250 Aztec D	27-4021	G-BCPF, N6748Y, N10F
CS-DBU	Piper PA-36-375 Brave	36-8302017	N90905
CS-DBW	Beech C24R Sierra	MC-660	N6042V
CS-DBX	Piper PA-36-375 Brave	36-7802033	N3881E
CS-DCF	Piper PA-31-350 Chieftain	31-8052174	PH-ECO, N4501Y
CS-DCH	SOCATA TB-10 Tobago	20	F-GBHJ
CS-DCJ	Piper PA-36-285 Pawnee Brave	36-7560076	N9965P
CS-DCK	Dassault Falcon 20E	297	"N297AG", PK-TIR, N121EU, (N370EU), N4443F, F-WMKF
CS-DCL	Reims FR172F Rocket	FR17200133	D-ECOR(2), F-WLIT
CS-DCN	Robin DR.400/180R Remo 180	1235	OE-DIN
CS-DCO	Cessna 152	15284611	N5548M, (N272SP), N5548M
CS-DCQ	Piper PA-28-140 Cherokee E	28-7225536	C-FBLD, CF-BLD
CS-DCR	Cessna T210N Turbo Centurion II	21063671	N4914C
CS-DCS	Beech 76 Duchess	ME-404	LX-TWN, F-GKDH, N771AW, EI-BKW, ST-AKB, EI-BKW, N3834Z
CS-DCU	Cessna 172N	17267812	N75563
CS-DCW	Piper PA-34-200T Seneca II	34-8170017	F-GFEM, N82772
CS-DCX	SOCATA MS.893A Rallye Commodore 180	11669	D-EGGD
CS-DCY	Piper PA-18-150 Super Cub (Dbr 14.1.14)	18-8479	SE-FAK, N4299Y
CS-DCZ	Cessna T210N Turbo Centurion II	21063239	N7581N
CS-DDD	SOCATA TB-10 Tobago	350	D-ESLX, LX-EUR
CS-DDG	Rockwell Commander 112	294	F-GMCC, N1294J
CS-DDH	SOCATA TB-10 Tobago	280	F-GDBH
CS-DDJ	Cessna 152	15283947	D-EPTL, N6547B
CS-DDK	SOCATA TB-20 Trinidad	1900	F-OIUM
CS-DDL	Piper PA-36-285 Pawnee Brave	36-7460017	N43706
CS-DDM	Cessna 182S	18280437	F-GUFA, N4219M
CS-DDO	Cessna A152 Aerobat	A1520804	CS-DDN, C-GVNC, N738SL
CS-DDP	Cessna 152	15285620	C-FFIP, N94198
CS-DDR	Cessna 172S	172S8760	N854SP
CS-DDS	Reims FR172J Rocket	FR17200409	F-BUMH
CS-DDT	SOCATA TB-10 Tobago	32	F-GBHR
CS-DDW	Cessna 152	15279470	N714VQ
CS-DDX	Robin ATL L	11	F-GFNK
CS-DDY	Cessna 152	15285474	N93370
CS-DDZ	Gates Learjet 31	31-034	N349SA, N45PK, N604LH, 9V-ATB, N5015U
CS-DED	SOCATA TB-200 Tobago XLS	2055	F-OJBD
CS-DEE	SOCATA TB-20 Trinidad	2080	F-OIUA
CS-DEG	SOCATA TB-200 Tobago XLS (Res. as SP-EXY 2013)	2067	F-OJBF
CS-DEH	SOCATA TB-200 Tobago XLS (W/o 5.9.12)	2068	F-OJBS
CS-DEI	SOCATA TB-200 Tobago XLS	2069	F-OJBT
CS-DEJ	SOCATA TB-200 Tobago XLS	2070	F-OJBU
CS-DEK	SOCATA TB-200 Tobago XLS	2071	F-OJBV
CS-DEM	SOCATA TB-200 Tobago XLS	2073	F-OJBY
CS-DEN	SOCATA TB-200 Tobago XLS	2079	F-OJBZ
CS-DEO	SOCATA TB-20 Trinidad	2085	F-OIUB
CS-DEP	SOCATA TB-20 Trinidad	2086	F-OIUC
CS-DEQ	Piper PA-34-220T Seneca V	3449233	N5341L, CS-DEQ, N5341L
CS-DER	Piper PA-34-220T Seneca V	3449236	N53422, CS-DER, N9528N
CS-DET	SOCATA TB-20 Trinidad	1859	PH-SXD, F-OIGK
CS-DEU	SOCATA TB-20 Trinidad	1857	PH-SXB, F-OIGI
CS-DEV	Piper PA-34-220T Seneca V (Dam. 4.2.11)	3449306	I-EMIC, N3091Y
CS-DFF	Dassault Falcon 2000EX	41	F-WWGW
CS-DFG	Dassault Falcon 2000EX	44	F-WWGA
CS-DFH	Dassault Falcon 900	91	N991EJ, CS-DFA, N91WF, A7-AAD, F-WWFH
CS-DFK	Dassault Falcon 2000EASy	65	F-WWMN
CS-DFZ	Hawker 800XP	258673	N673XP
CS-DGA(*)	Douglas C-47A (Exp 6.79) (Preserved as "CS-TDA" at Lisbon)	19503	4X-AOC, EI-ACK, 43-15037
CS-DGE	OGMA/Auster D5/180	132	
CS-DGF	OGMA/Auster D5/180	133	
CS-DGG(*)	OGMA/Auster D5/180 (Exp 11.79, stored)	110	
CS-DGH	Beech D55 Baron	TE-684	
CS-DGK	Rockwell Commander 114	14302	
CS-DGL	Beech P35 Bonanza	D-7230	N8605M
CS-DGM	Cessna 172R Skyhawk	17280548	N2616L
CS-DGN	Piper PA-44-180T Seminole (Dam. 19.8.10)	44-8107019	D-GLUT, N82556
CS-DGP	Cessna 172S Skyhawk SP	172S10325	N11364
CS-DGR	Cessna 650 Citation VII	650-7045	N745VP, CC-CPS, CC-PGL, N95CM, N12652
CS-DGS	Cessna 172R Skyhawk	17281169	OE-KNG, D-ERRP, N5358C
CS-DGT	Cessna 152	15282730	N89373
CS-DGU	Cessna 152	15284811	N4761P
CS-DGV	Cessna 152	15286025	N96846
CS-DGW	Cessna 525B CitationJet CJ3	525B-0235	N5174W
CS-DGX	Cessna 172R	17281460	N1739D
CS-DGY	Piper PA-28RT-201T Turbo Arrow IV	28R-8231053	PH-SIL, (PH-STI), N8392A, (HB-PGY)
CS-DHJ	Cessna 550 Citation Bravo	550-1082	N5180C
CS-DIA	Cessna 152	15284274	N5159L
CS-DIB	Cessna 152	15282845	G-BOIW, N89731
CS-DIC	PZL M-18B Dromader	1Z023-10	SP-FBT
CS-DID	Piper PA-34-220T Seneca V	3449229	SE-ITX, N9518N
CS-DIE	Piper J-3C-65 Cub	13950	N2075N, 45-55184
CS-DIF	Cessna 152	15281979	G-BPTF, N67715
CS-DIH	Cessna 172R	17280412	N972RA
CS-DII	Cessna 177 Cardinal	17700740	N3440T
CS-DIM	Piper PA-38-112 Tomahawk	38-78A0141	G-BTAP, N9603T
CS-DIN	Cessna 172N Skyhawk (Dbr 12.3.11)	17270671	EC-EKD, G-BNSK, N739NJ
CS-DIP	Cessna 150	15061698	N8098S
CS-DIS	SOCATA 880B Rallye Club	1295	F-BRDJ
CS-DIT	Reims Cessna FTB337G Milirole	FTB3370026	FAP-3725
CS-DIU	Cessna 185 Skywagon floatplane	185-0136	LN-DBG, N9936X
CS-DIV	SOCATA MS.893A Rallye Commodore 180	10688	F-BONH
CS-DIX	PZL M-18A Dromader	1Z022-26	EC-FDV, SP-DAE
CS-DIY	Cessna 525B CitationJet CJ3	525B-0146	
CS-DIZ	Diamond DA 42 Twin Star (Dam. 5.7.10)	42.171	OE-VPW, OE-VPI
CS-DJA	Aérospatiale/Alenia ATR-72-600	1294	PR-AKG, F-WWEX
CS-DJB	Aérospatiale/Alenia ATR-72-600	1305	PR-AKI, F-WWEK
CS-DJC	Aérospatiale/Alenia ATR-72-600	1232	PR-AQW, F-WWEG
CS-DJD	Aérospatiale/Alenia ATR-72-600	1233	PR-AQX, F-WWEH
CS-DJE	Aérospatiale/Alenia ATR-72-600	1236	PR-AQY, F-WWEK
CS-DJF	Aérospatiale/Alenia ATR-72-600	1241	PR-AQZ, F-WWEQ
CS-DJG	Aérospatiale/Alenia ATR-72-600	1316	F-WTDS, F-WWEW
CS-DJH	Aérospatiale/Alenia ATR-72-600	1323	F-WTDK, F-WWEF
CS-DKD	Gulfstream 550	5081	N581GA
CS-DKE	Gulfstream 550	5094	N594GA
CS-DKF	Gulfstream 550	5099	N699GA
CS-DKG	Gulfstream 550	5127	N527GA
CS-DKH	Gulfstream 550	5150	N43GA
CS-DKI	Gulfstream 550	5166	N966GA
CS-DKJ	Gulfstream 550	5174	N974GA
CS-DKK	Gulfstream 550	5201	N991GA
CS-DLB	Dassault Falcon 2000EASy	80	F-WWGQ
CS-DLC	Dassault Falcon 2000EASy	98	F-WWGP
CS-DLD	Dassault Falcon 2000EASy	109	F-WWGX

Reg	Type	Serial	Previous identities
CS-DLE	Dassault Falcon 2000EASy	127	F-WWGQ
CS-DLF	Dassault Falcon 2000EASy	134	F-WWGV
CS-DLG	Dassault Falcon 2000EASy	144	F-WWGW
CS-DLH	Dassault Falcon 2000EASy	149	F-WWGJ
CS-DMG	Beech 400A Beechjet	RK-417	N36907
CS-DMM	Beech 400A Beechjet	RK-472	N36632
CS-DMN	Beech 400A Beechjet	RK-475	N61675
CS-DMO	Beech 400A Beechjet	RK-494	N72594
CS-DNR	Dassault Falcon 2000	120	F-WWVP
CS-DOF	Canadair CL-600-2B16 Challenger 650	6079	C-FAUF
CS-DPA	Hawker 900XP	HA-0069	N3198V
CS-DPD	Cessna 152 (Dam 20.8.14, Evora)	15279563	G-BZAD, N303MA, N714ZN
CS-DPF	Dassault Falcon 900EASy	198	F-WWFF
CS-DPG	Cessna 172R Skyhawk	17281523	N6256F
CS-DPH	Cessna 172R Skyhawk	17281527	N6186Q
CS-DPI	Air Tractor AT-502B	502B-2587	
CS-DPL	Bombardier BD-700-1A10 Global 6000	9514	HB-JRM, C-GPYW
CS-DPM	Cessna 172R Skyhawk	17281536	N6308F
CS-DPR	Cessna 152	15279561	HA-ERD, N714ZL
CS-DPS	Cessna 402B	402B1040	N49JB, (N44TG), N49JB, N98673
CS-DPV	Cessna 510 Citation Mustang	510-0122	N230BF
CS-DQA	Cessna 560XLS Citation XLS	560-5798	N5157E
CS-DQB	Cessna 560XLS Citation XLS	560-5803	N50715
CS-DRA	Hawker 800XP	258686	N61746
CS-DRB	Hawker 800XP	258690	N36690
CS-DRH	Hawker 800XPi	258746	N6046J
CS-DRJ	Hawker 800XPi	258760	N37160
CS-DRL	Hawker 850XPi	258770	N36970
CS-DRN	Hawker 860XPi	258772	N672XP
CS-DRS	Hawker 800XPi	258795	N37295
CS-DRU	Hawker 800XPi	258821	N73721
CS-DRV	Hawker 800XPi	258825	N3725Z
CS-DRW	Hawker 800XPi	258829	N73729
CS-DRX	Hawker 800XPi	258834	N71934
CS-DRY	Hawker 800XPi	258840	N70040
CS-DRZ	Hawker 800XPi	258847	N74476
CS-DSB	Dassault Falcon 7X	43	F-WWVO
CS-DSE	Hawker 900XP	HA-204	N204XP
CS-DTB	Dassault Falcon 900EX	11	F-GOYA, F-WWFI
CS-DTC	Embraer EMB-500 Phenom 100	50000115	PT-TIT
CS-DTD	Dassault Falcon 7X	60	F-WWHC
CS-DTI	Beech 200 Super King Air	BB-681	F-GGPR, LN-AXA, (LN-AAX), N200NF, D-ILBO, N6751T
CS-DTN	Aérospatiale/Alenia ATR 42-320	093	F-GVZJ, F-WQNO, PH-XLK, TG-AGA, TG-MWA, F-WQCZ, N17810, F-WWES
CS-DTO	Aérospatiale/Alenia ATR 42-320	095	F-GKYN, (OY-FKA), F-GKYN, F-ODUL,
CS-DTP	Dassault Falcon 900	135	F-GYCP, VP-BPW, VR-BPW, F-WWFJ
CS-DTR	Dassault Falcon 2000	119	F-GESP, D-BDNL, F-WQBN, D-GXDP, F-WWVO
CS-DUA (2)	Hawker 750	HB-4	N804HB
CS-DUB	Hawker 750	HB-5	N31685, (CS-DUA(1))
CS-DUC	Hawker 750	HB-6	N3206V
CS-DUI	Hawker 750	HB-24	EC-KXS, N3417F
CS-DVF	Aérospatiale/Alenia ATR-72-202	350	SE-MGM, SX-BIK, F-WWEG
CS-DVH	Cessna 525B Citation CJ3	525B-0101	N511VP, PP-AVX, D-CTEC, N52113
CS-DVN	Cessna 650 Citation VII	650-7070	N556RA, OY-CKE, N654EJ, (N770VP), N322RG, N22RG, N95CM, N51176
CS-DVO	Aérospatiale/Alenia ATR-42-320	337	HR-AXA, D-BZZV, OY-EDH, SX-BIM, F-WQNQ, HC-CDC, F-WQNQ, TR-LFD, F-OGXO, (F-WQHC), N984MA, F-WWLB
CS-DVU	Dornier Do.228-201	8080	5Y-BUX, SX-BHI, D-COLE
CS-DVY	Embraer EMB-135BJ Legacy 600	14500979	N979PF, PH-ARO, VP-BVS, PT-SHQ
CS-DXC	Cessna 560XL Citation XLS	560-5559	N1281N, N5093L
CS-DXD	Cessna 560XL Citation XLS	560-5568	N6779D, N5197A
CS-DXE	Cessna 560XL Citation XLS	560-5578	N1299H
CS-DXF	Cessna 560XL Citation XLS	560-5586	N1299K, N5145V
CS-DXG	Cessna 560XL Citation XLS	550-5595	N5135K
CS-DXH	Cessna 560XL Citation XLS	560-5615	N5266F
CS-DXI	Cessna 560XL Citation XLS	560-5621	N1300J, N52683
CS-DXJ	Cessna 560XL Citation XLS	560-5627	N51396
CS-DXK	Cessna 560XL Citation XLS	560-5633	N13218, N5158J
CS-DXL	Cessna 560XL Citation XLS	560-5640	N1319X, N5188W
CS-DXM	Cessna 560XL Citation XLS	560-5683	N5256Z
CS-DXN	Cessna 560XL Citation XLS	560-5685	N5259Y
CS-DXO	Cessna 560XL Citation XLS	560-5692	N5026Q, N1198V
CS-DXP	Cessna 560XL Citation XLS	560-5702	N1275T
CS-DXQ	Cessna 560XL Citation XLS	560-5704	N1281R
CS-DXR	Cessna 560XL Citation XLS	560-5748	N585QS, N5246Z,N585QS
CS-DXS	Cessna 560XL Citation XLS	560-5754	N578QS, N51042
CS-DXT	Cessna 560XL Citation XLS	560-5765	N5233J
CS-DXU	Cessna 560XL Citation XLS	560-5775	N50522
CS-DXV	Cessna 560XL Citation XLS	560-5782	N5145P
CS-DXW	Cessna 560XL Citation XLS	560-5787	N5145V
CS-DXX	Cessna 560XL Citation XLS	560-5789	N5211Q
CS-DXY	Cessna 560XL Citation XLS	560-5791	N5268A
CS-DXZ	Cessna 560XL Citation XLS	560-5796	N5268E
CS-EAF	Cessna 152 (Damaged in transit?)	15281027	EC-IQI, N48884
CS-EAG	Cessna 152	15284065	EC-IQH, N5138H
CS-EAH	Cessna 152	15283177	EC-IQG, N47131
CS-EAI	OGMA/DHC-1 Chipmunk T.20 (Lyco)	OGMA-35	G-OACP, CS-DAO, FAP1345
CS-EAJ	Piper PA-32R-301T Saratoga II TC	3257413	OY-PKS, OM-GLB, G-ODRD, N3130G, N31248
CS-EAL	Air Tractor AT-401	401-1168	EC-JLM
CS-EAN	Cessna 172S Skyhawk SP	172S8683	N749SP
CS-EAQ	Tecnam P.2006T	046	
CS-EAR	Pacific Aerospace PAC 750XL	163	ZK-KAQ
CS-EAS	Cessna 152	15285289	EC-ELI, G-BNSJ, N65576
CS-EAT	Cessna 152	unkn	
CS-EAU	Cessna 150M	15075897	SX-KOS, G-BPMO, N66177
CS-EAV	Cessna 182	unkn	
CS-EAW	Cessna 182	unkn	
CS-EAX	Cessna TP206E Turbo Super Skylane	unkn	
CS-EAY	Air Tractor AT-802A Fire Boss	unkn	
CS-EBB	SOCATA MS.893A Rallye Commodore	unkn	
CS-EBD	Cessna 152	unkn	
CS-EBH	Cessna 182	unkn	
CS-FAF	Boeing 737-8FB	41159	
CS-GAA(*)	Beagle-Wallis WA.116 Series 1 (Exp 7.93)	B.202	G-ARZA, XR942, G-ARZA
CS-GLA	Bombardier BD-700-1A10 Global 6000	9478	C-GLKC
CS-GLB	Bombardier BD-700-1A10 Global 6000	9481	C-GMSO
CS-GLC	Bombardier BD-700-1A10 Global 6000	9533	C-GTUF
CS-GLD	Bombardier BD-700-1A10 Global 6000	9538	C-GTZN (2)
CS-GLE	Bombardier BD-700-1A10 Global 6000	9638	C-GZEB (2)
CS-GLF	Bombardier BD-700-1A10 Global 6000	9670	C-FEMF
CS-GLG	Bombardier BD-700-1A10 Global 6000	9757	C-FMYD
CS-HAA(*)	SNCASO SO.1221-S Djinn (Exp 9.67)	1013/FR46	F-BHOU, F-WHOU
CS-HAC(*)	SNCASO SO.1221-S Djinn (Exp 6.67)	1044/FR94	F-BJON
CS-HAJ(*)	Bell 47G-2 (H-13E conversion) (Exp 11.92)	738	N6398X, CF-NXP, N6398X, 51-13973
CS-HAM(*)	Bell 47D-1 (Barnes Conversion) (Exp 7.81)	SA2	N74090
CS-HAQ(*)	Bell 47G-2 (Exp 6.82)	2218	N6725D
CS-HAV	Hughes 269C	89-0826	G-HUSH
CS-HAZ	Hughes 269C (Dam. 10.9.10, rebt, cr 5.5.13)	1084	SE-HMI
CS-HBT	Bell UH-1E (204)	6167	N5010J, BuA154945
CS-HBU(*)	Bell UH-1E (204) (Exp 6.93)	6203	N48SS, BuA155348
CS-HBV	Bell TH-1L (204)	6426	N540GH, N540AH, N434RR, BuA157831
CS-HCH	Robinson R22 Beta	2038	
CS-HDD	Hughes 269B	16-0235	G-OHSD, N9457F
CS-HDM	Robinson R44 Astro	0183	
CS-HDS	Bell 222	47028	G-META, N5733H
CS-HED	Aérospatiale AS.350B2 Ecureuil	2669	D-HJOE, HB-XZY, D-HWPL
CS-HEE	Aérospatiale AS.355F1 Ecureuil 2	5006	F-W . . .
CS-HER	Agusta A.109E Power	11083	
CS-HES	Aérospatiale AS.350B2 Ecureuil	2224	F-GKAS
CS-HEU	Robinson R44 Clipper	0831	
CS-HEV	Robinson R44 Raven	0779	
CS-HEW	Schweizer 269C-1	0119	
CS-HEX	Eurocopter EC.120B Colibri (W/o 18.12.13)	1183	
CS-HEY	Aérospatiale AS.350B2 Ecureuil	9027	D-HXST
CS-HEZ	Bell 212	30557	EC-GHP, EC-256, EC-FYB, N83079, VH-HVX, ZK-HBK, LN-OQY, (G-BHAG), LN-OQY, N83072
CS-HFC	Bell 206L3 Long Ranger III	51358	D-HHTB, HB-XVS, N7133D, C-FIFV
CS-HFD	Schweizer 269C-1 (W/o 4.12.14)	0058	I-EAHS, HB-XJU
CS-HFF	Robinson R22B2 Beta	3431	
CS-HFI	Aérospatiale AS.350B2 Ecureuil	1216	PT-YJC, G-BXNI, C-GNML, F-WQDU
CS-HFJ	Bell 212 (Damaged 18.10.11)	30684	EC-GHO, EC-FYC, VH-NSU, G-BOOY, OY-HMA, LN-OSQ, EC-IEM, CS-HEJ
CS-HFK	Aérospatiale AS.350B3 Ecureuil	3223	LX-HDS, ZS-RLE
CS-HFN	Aérospatiale AS.350B2 Ecureuil	2437	D-HHWW
CS-HFO	Aérospatiale AS.350B2 Ecureuil	1824	F-GFDL, D-HHKK
CS-HFP	Eurocopter AS.350B2 Ecureuil (W/o 10.1.11)	4033	F-WQDB
CS-HFR	Aérospatiale AS.350B2 Ecureuil	9054	D-HHTA(2)
CS-HFT	Aérospatiale AS.350B2 Ecureuil	2097	I-FLAO
CS-HFU	Robinson R44 Raven II	11261	
CS-HFV	Aérospatiale AS.365N1 Dauphin 2	6338	N661ME, N365SC, N911UF, (N991UF), JA6600
CS-HFX	Aérospatiale AS.350B3 Ecureuil	4081	F-WWXD, F-GNOA
CS-HFZ	Aérospatiale AS.350B3 Ecureuil	9090	LN-OCR, F-WQEG
CS-HGA	Aérospatiale AS.365N1 Dauphin 2	6336	JA9978
CS-HGE	Robinson R22 Beta II	4123	N3016K
CS-HGF	Robinson R44 Raven II	11738	
CS-HGG	Aérospatiale AS.350B2 Ecureuil	9085	F-WQEH
CS-HGH	Agusta AW139	31115	
CS-HGI	Aérospatiale AS.365N1 Dauphin 2	6343	(F-OJTA), DU-133, G-BRVP
CS-HGJ	Aérospatiale AS.365N Dauphin 2	6205	N365NA, JA9648
CS-HGM	Aérospatiale AS.350B3 Ecureuil	3801	EC-IXK, F-WQDA
CS-HGO	Aérospatiale AS.350B3 Ecureuil	4521	
CS-HGQ	Agusta AW139	31057	N915DH
CS-HGU	Agusta AW139	31143	
CS-HGV	Aérospatiale AS.365N3 Dauphin 2	6829	
CS-HGW	Aérospatiale AS.365N3 Dauphin 2	6830	
CS-HGX	Aérospatiale AS.365N1 Dauphin 2	6138	5N-BIK, F-GNVS, JA9610
CS-HGY	Robinson R22 Beta II	4402	
CS-HGZ	Aérospatiale AS.350B3 Ecureuil	3785	EC-JFS, N18HX, N147AE
CS-HHA	Aérospatiale AS.350B2 Ecureuil	1845	CS-HEM, LN-OPC(2), OE-KXF, D-HHZZ
CS-HHB	Aérospatiale AS.350B3 Ecureuil	4790	
CS-HHD	Aérospatiale AS.350B2 Ecureuil	1871	5N-BHS, CS-HDK, D-HHFZ
CS-HHE	Agusta A.109E Power	11625	I-HDPR
CS-HHF	Aérospatiale AS.365N1 Dauphin 2	6128	5N-HGN, 5N-BHK, CS-HFH, HL9230, F-WYMP, D-HMKE
CS-HHG	Agusta A.109E Power	11759	EC-LBK, I-EASG
CS-HHH	Agusta A.109E Power	11729	EC-LAK, I-GIEC
CS-HHI	Aérospatiale SA.365N Dauphin 2	6089	F-OIBJ, N1UW, N5192E, C-GZPW, N365EM, G-BLRV
CS-HHN	Aérospatiale AS.350B3 Ecureuil	4974	
CS-HHO	Aérospatiale AS.350B3 Ecureuil	4888	
CS-HHP	Agusta A.109SP Grand	22214	
CS-HHQ	Aérospatiale AS.355N Ecureuil 2	unkn	
CS-HHR	Aérospatiale AS.365N3 Dauphin 2	6841	F-OJTU
CS-HHU	Schweizer 269C	S-1712	G-BWDV, N86G
CS-HHV	Schweizer 269C	S-1331	G-BPJB, N75065
CS-HHW	Aérospatiale AS.365N1 Dauphin 2	6307	G-DPHN, HB-ZBY, LX-HGR, JA9902
CS-HHX	Robinson R44 Clipper II	13472	
CS-HHY	Aérospatiale AS.350B2 Ecureuil	1222	5N-BHT, CS-HEO, RP-C8880, F-WQDS, C-GSBO, N144BH, N3609D
CS-HIA	Aérospatiale AS.350B3 Ecureuil (W/o 8.8.15)	3699	I-HORT
CS-HIB	Aérospatiale AS.350B3 Ecureuil	3702	I-HPLC
CS-HIC	Aérospatiale AS.350B3 Ecureuil	3940	I-HBLU, F-WWPE
CS-HID	Aérospatiale AS.350B3 Ecureuil	4243	I-DION, SE-JJP, F-WWXB

Reg	Type	Serial	Previous identities
CS-HIE	Aérospatiale AS.350B3 Ecureuil	3354	I-LIGU
CS-HIF	Aérospatiale AS.350B3 Ecureuil	4342	HB-ZIY, F-WQDB
CS-HIG	Aérospatiale AS.350B3 Ecureuil	3507	I-AMVN
CS-HIH	Guimbal Cabri G2	1053	
CS-HIL	Eurocopter EC.130T2	7985	
CS-HIM	Robinson R44 Raven II	13938	
CS-HMH	Aérospatiale AS.350B3 Ecureuil (Ditched 29.6.15)	4246	
CS-HMI	Aérospatiale AS.350B3 Ecureuil	4261	
CS-HMJ	Aérospatiale AS.350B3 Ecureuil	4269	
CS-HMK	Kamov Ka.32A11BC	9901	
CS-HML	Kamov Ka.32T	9902	
CS-HMM	Kamov Ka.32A11BC	9903	
CS-HMN	Kamov Ka.32A11BC	9904	
CS-HMO	Kamov Ka.32A11BC (W/o 3.9.12)	9905	
CS-HMP	Kamov Ka.32A11BC	9906	
CS-LAM	Bombardier BD-700-1A11 Global 5000	9602	C-GXAH(2)
CS-LSA	III Sky Arrow	L00203/00	
CS-PHA	Embraer EMB-505 Phenom 300	50500203	
CS-PHB	Embraer EMB-505 Phenom 300	50500209	
CS-PHC	Embraer EMB-505 Phenom 300	50500214	
CS-PHD	Embraer EMB-505 Phenom 300	50500225	
CS-PHE	Embraer EMB-505 Phenom 300	50500252	
CS-PHF	Embraer EMB-505 Phenom 300	50500260	
CS-PHG	Embraer EMB-505 Phenom 300	50500264	
CS-PHH	Embraer EMB-505 Phenom 300	50500270	
CS-TDI	Airbus A310-304	573	JY-AGK, A6-EKN, S7-RGA, LZ-JXC, CS-TEY, F-WWCG
CS-TEB	Lockheed 1011 Tristar 500	1240	V2-LEO, CS-TEB
CS-TEI	Airbus A310-304	495	F-WWCO
CS-TEX	Airbus A310-304	565	F-WWCC
CS-TFC	Beech 58 Baron	TH-524	N8130R
CS-TFJ	BAe. ATP	2018	(ES-NBB), G-MANG, G-LOGD, G-OLCD
CS-TFM	Boeing 777-212	28513	9V-SRA
CS-TFN	Dassault Falcon 900	66	CS-TMK, F-GJPM, F-WWFE
CS-TFQ	Bombardier Learjet 45	45-302	N99XR
CS-TFR	Bombardier Learjet 45	45-382	N40073
CS-TFT	Boeing 767-3Y0ER	26208	S9-DBY, PP-VTE, N639TW, EI-CKE, N6009F
CS-TFU	Airbus A319-115CJ	2440	I-ECJA, F-ONAS, I-ECJA, D-AVWZ
CS-TFV	Bombardier BD-100-1A10 Challenger 300	20252	C-FWRE
CS-TFW	Airbus A340-542 (Stored)	910	F-WJKH, (VT-VJD), F-WWTK
CS-TFX	Airbus A340-542	912	F-WJKI, (VT-VJE), F-WWTL
CS-TFY	Airbus A320-232	1868	N548JB, F-WWIQ
CS-TFZ	Airbus A330-243	1008	F-WWYD
CS-TGU	Airbus A310-304	571	F-GJKQ, TU-TAC, F-WWYM, F-GHYM
CS-TGV	Airbus A310-304	651	TU-TAD, F-WWCC
CS-TGX	BAe. ATP	2025	G-BRLY, TC-THP, G-BRLY
CS-TGY	BAe. ATP	2049	G-BTZJ, PK-MTY, (PK-MAE), G-BTZJ
CS-TJE	Airbus A321-211	1307	D-AVZM
CS-TJF	Airbus A321-211	1399	D-AVZI
CS-TJG	Airbus A321-211	1713	D-AVZS
CS-TKK	Airbus A320-214	2390	F-WWII
CS-TKN	Airbus A310-325	624	TF-ELR, OE-LAD, EC-HIF, OE-LAD, F-WWCE
CS-TKP	Airbus A320-214	2011	D-ALAC, EC-INZ, F-WWBR
CS-TKQ	Airbus A320-214	2325	EI-FMD, N204FR, N270AV, F-WWDY
CS-TKR	Boeing 767-36NER	30854	EI-FLV, 5Y-KQX
CS-TKS	Boeing 767-36NER	30841	EI-FKI, 5Y-KQY
CS-TKT	Boeing 767-36NER	30853	EI-FKJ, 5Y-KQZ
CS-TKV	Airbus A320-214	1422	SX-BDT, 4L-AJF, 9V-SLD, F-WWBK
CS-TLO	Boeing 767-383ER	24318	N318SR, LN-RCH, SE-DKO
CS-TLU	Airbus A319-133CJ	1256	F-GSVU, (F-GVBG), D-AVYZ, (VP-BCS), D-AVYZ, F-WWIF, D-AVYZ
CS-TLW	Bombardier Learjet 45	45-154	D-CEMM(2), N5011L
CS-TLY	Dassault Falcon 7X	15	F-WWUL
CS-TLZ	Boeing 767-375ERF	24086	N240LD, PP-VPV, N240SZ, PP-VPV, C-FCAJ, N6055X
CS-TMH	Short SD.3-60 Variant 100 (Stored)	SH.3694	G-BMNJ, N694PC, G-BMNJ, G-14-3694
CS-TMN	Short SD.3-60 Variant 100	SH.3638	G-ISLE, G-BLEG
CS-TMP	Lockheed 1011-500 Tristar	1248	SE-DVI, (9Y-BWC), V2-LEK, CS-TEG, JY-AGJ, N64959
CS-TMU	Beech 1900D	UE-335	N23269, EC-GZL, N23269
CS-TMV	Beech 1900D	UE-341	N23309, EC-HBG, N23309
CS-TMW	Airbus A320-214	1667	F-WWII
CS-TMY	Short SD.3-60	SH.3632	G-BLCP, OY-MMA, (SE-KSU), OY-MMA, EI-BYU, OY-MMA, G-BLCP
CS-TNG	Airbus A320-214	945	F-WWIX
CS-TNH	Airbus A320-214	960	F-WWBH
CS-TNI	Airbus A320-214	982	F-WWDF
CS-TNJ	Airbus A320-214	1181	F-WWDS
CS-TNK	Airbus A320-214	1206	F-WWIL
CS-TNL	Airbus A320-214	1231	F-WWIJ
CS-TNM	Airbus A320-214	1799	F-WWIF
CS-TNN	Airbus A320-214	1816	F-WWID
CS-TNP	Airbus A320-214	2178	9H-AER, (SU-LBF), F-WWIP
CS-TNQ	Airbus A320-214	3769	F-WWDQ
CS-TNR	Airbus A320-214	3883	F-WWIU
CS-TNS	Airbus A320-214	4021	F-WWDM
CS-TNT	Airbus A320-214	4095	F-WWDI
CS-TNU	Airbus A320-214	4106	F-WWDR
CS-TNV	Airbus A320-214	4145	F-WWIY
CS-TNW	Airbus A320-214	2792	9K-CAC, F-WWBM
CS-TNX	Airbus A320-214	2822	9K-CAD, F-WWDC
CS-TOA	Airbus A340-312	041	F-WWJB
CS-TOB	Airbus A340-312	044	F-WWJN
CS-TOC	Airbus A340-312	079	F-WWJS
CS-TOD	Airbus A340-312	091	F-WWJA
CS-TOE	Airbus A330-223	305	D-AXEL, D-AIMA, HB-IQL, F-WWYI
CS-TOF	Airbus A330-223	308	D-ARND, D-AIMB, HB-IQM, F-WWYK
CS-TOG	Airbus A330-223	312	D-ARNO, D-AIMC, HB-IQN, F-WWYO
CS-TOH	Airbus A330-223	181	OE-LAO, F-WWKA
CS-TOI	Airbus A330-223	195	OE-LAN, F-WWKJ
CS-TOJ	Airbus A330-223	223	OE-LAM, F-WWKQ
CS-TOK	Airbus A330-223	317	OE-LAP, F-WWYQ
CS-TOL	Airbus A330-202	877	F-WWKF
CS-TOM	Airbus A330-202	899	F-WWKN
CS-TON	Airbus A330-202	904	F-WWKT
CS-TOO	Airbus A330-202	914	F-WWTL
CS-TOP	Airbus A330-202	934	F-WWKZ
CS-TOQ	Airbus A330-203	477	PT-MVH, F-WWKS
CS-TOR	Airbus A330-203	486	PT-MVK, F-WWYL
CS-TOT	Airbus A330-243	372	PR-AIX, VH-XFB, A6-EAC, F-WWYQ
CS-TPA	Fokker F.28-0100	11257	(N208BN), PH-LMF, PH-EZA
CS-TPB	Fokker F.28-0100	11262	PH-EZE
CS-TPC	Fokker F.28-0100	11287	PH-LML
CS-TPD	Fokker F.28-0100	11317	PH-LNA, PH-EZU
CS-TPE	Fokker F.28-0100	11342	PH-LNJ
CS-TPF	Fokker F.28-0100	11258	PH-FZD, TR-LCR, PH-EZD
CS-TPG	Embraer EMB-145EP	145014	PT-SYK
CS-TPH	Embraer EMB-145EP	145017	PT-SYN
CS-TPI	Embraer EMB-145EP	145031	PT-SYZ
CS-TPJ	Embraer EMB-145EP	145036	PT-SZC
CS-TPK	Embraer EMB-145EP	145041	PT-SZG
CS-TPL	Embraer EMB-145EP	145051	PT-SZQ
CS-TPM	Embraer EMB-145EP	145095	PT-SBR
CS-TPN	Embraer EMB-145EP	145099	PT-SBV
CS-TPO	Embraer EMB-190-100LR	19000432	PP-PJM
CS-TPP	Embraer EMB-190-100LR	19000441	PP-PJN
CS-TPQ	Embraer EMB-190-100LR	19000450	PP-PJO
CS-TPR	Embraer EMB-190-100LR	19000460	PP-PJP
CS-TPS	Embraer EMB-190-100LR	19000493	PP-PJQ
CS-TPT	Embraer EMB-190-100LR	19000495	PP-PJR
CS-TPU	Embraer EMB-190-100LR	19000506	PP-PJT
CS-TPV	Embraer EMB-190-100LR	19000541	PP-PJU
CS-TPW	Embraer EMB-190-100LR	19000550	PP-PJV
CS-TQD	Airbus A320-214	870	HB-IJT, F-WWBX
CS-TQJ	Airbus A319-115CJ	2675	VP-BEY, D-AIJO, D-AVYP
CS-TQL	Airbus A340-312	133	M-YRGQ, A9C-LF, A40-LF, F-WWJP
CS-TQN	Airbus A340-313	450	OY-KBM, (SE-RED), F-WWJD
CS-TQP(2)	Airbus A330-202	211	N272LF, EC-KIM, EC-IYN, I-VLED, F-WQQN, C-GGWB, F-WWKL
CS-TQR	Boeing 737-301F	23258	OE-IAU, OO-TNK, N326AW, N579US, N306P
CS-TQU	Boeing 737-8K2	30646	PH-HZY, OY-TDA, PH-HZY, 9Y-TJQ, PH-HZY
CS-TQV	Airbus A310-304	494	PR-WTA, CS-TEJ, F-WWCM
CS-TQW	Airbus A330-223	262	VN-A370, 9M-MKT, HB-IQF, 9M-MKT, HB-IQF, F-WWKS
CS-TQX	Boeing 777-2FBLR	40668	3C-LLS
CS-TQY	Airbus A340-313X	190	A6-ERQ, D-AJGP, 9V-SJJ, F-WWJX
CS-TQZ	Airbus A340-313X	202	A6-ERR, D-ASID, 9V-SJK, F-WWJS
CS-TRB	DHC-8 Series 202	476	C-FXBX, N345PH, C-GFYI
CS-TRC	DHC-8 Series 202	480	C-FXBZ, N347PH, C-FWBB
CS-TRD	Bombardier DHC-8 Series 402Q	4291	C-GAUA(2)
CS-TRE	Bombardier DHC-8 Series 402Q	4295	C-GBIY(2)
CS-TRF	Bombardier DHC-8 Series 402Q	4297	C-GBJE
CS-TRG	Bombardier DHC-8 Series 402Q	4298	C-GBJF
CS-TRH	Airbus A330-343	833	EC-KCP
CS-TRI	Airbus A330-322	127	D-AERQ, F-WWKO
CS-TRJ	Airbus A321-231	1004	EI-FDP, TC-OAL, D-ALAK, D-AVZI
CS-TRL	Airbus A320-214	3758	EC-KYZ, F-WWBZ
CS-TRN	Boeing 767-33AER	25535	N535AW, S2-AFX, PH-MCJ, CS-TLM, N535AW, V5-NMB, VH-NOE, OO-VAS, F-GKAU, VH-NOE, N768TA, N6018N
CS-TRO	Airbus A320-214	548	PR-WTB, CS-TQO, F-GYFL, F-WQSZ, B-653L, B-2214, HB-IJC, F-WWIJ
CS-TRY	Airbus A330-223	970	EI-EJY, JY-AIE, EI-EJY, EC-KXB, F-WWYS
CS-TSL	Bombardier BD-700-1A11 Global 5000	9231	G-TSLS, D-AOTL, G-TSLS, VP-CAU, C-FJOK
CS-TSR	Airbus A318-112CJ	3932	D-ALHM, D-AYYB, D-AUAD
CS-TTA	Airbus A319-111	750	D-AVYO
CS-TTB	Airbus A319-111	755	D-AVYJ
CS-TTC	Airbus A319-111	763	D-AVYS
CS-TTD	Airbus A319-111	790	D-AVYC
CS-TTE	Airbus A319-111	821	D-AVYN
CS-TTF	Airbus A319-111	837	D-AVYL
CS-TTG	Airbus A319-111	906	D-AVYN
CS-TTH	Airbus A319-111	917	D-AVYJ
CS-TTI	Airbus A319-111	933	D-AVYP
CS-TTJ	Airbus A319-111	979	D-AVYM
CS-TTK	Airbus A319-111	1034	D-AVYL
CS-TTL	Airbus A319-111	1100	D-AVYX
CS-TTM	Airbus A319-111	1106	D-AVWR
CS-TTN	Airbus A319-111	1120	D-AVYI
CS-TTO	Airbus A319-111	1127	D-AVYH
CS-TTP	Airbus A319-111	1165	D-AVWV
CS-TTQ	Airbus A319-112	0629	SU-LBF, HB-IPZ, D-AVYR
CS-TTR	Airbus A319-111	1756	C-GJWE, D-AVYC
CS-TTS	Airbus A319-111	1765	C-GJWF, D-AVYO
CS-TTU	Airbus A319-112	1668	VT-SCD, C-GJTC, D-AVWA
CS-TTV	Airbus A319-112	1718	VT-SCE, C-GJVS, D-AVWO

Aircraft sold/delivered to Portugal for which no CS- marks are at present known, news of any sightings would be welcome:

Reg	Type	Serial	Previous identities
CS-H..	Aérospatiale AS.365N Dauphin 2	6147	F-GOTA, TN-AES
CS-H..	Agusta A.109E Power	11713	EC-KNH
CS-...	Air Tractor AT-400	400-0516	SE-IOE, SU-JAF, SE-IOE
CS-...	OGMA/Auster D.5/180	51	ZS-PRN, C9-AQQ, CR-AQQ, FAP3555
CS-...	Cassutt IIIM	C-879-F	N879BF
CS-...	Cessna 150H	15067284	N6484S
CS-...	Cessna 152	15280831	SP-KWS, N25872

Reg	Type	c/n	Identities
CS-E . .	Cessna 152	15283274	SP-IDB, N48049
CS-. . . .	Cessna 152	15284041	EC-HJG, N4948H
CS-. . . .	Cessna 172	unkn	HH-GLA
CS-. . . .	Cessna 172M	17263470	N5256R
CS-. . . .	Cessna 172N Skyhawk	17271181	N2184E
CS-. . . .	Reims/Cessna F172N	F17201879	N47PT, F-WBQT, F-GBQT
CS-. . . .	Cessna 172RG Cutlass RG	172RG0021	EC-HRN, D-EGIH(3), N4745R
CS-. . . .	Cessna 172RG Cutlass RG	172RG0780	EC-HOO, D-EMRK, N6610V
CS-D . .	Cessna 182D Skylane	18253391	F-BBOL, F-OBTL, N8991X
CS-. . . .	Cessna 182Q Skylane	18265935	I-EWAA, N182FM, (N759EM)
CS-. . . .	Cessna 210	57172	N210TM, N7472E
CS-. . . .	Cessna 337 Super Skymaster	337-0154	N415D, N200SV, N1SV, N2254X
CS-. . . .	Cessna 421B Golden Eagle	421B-0335	G-BBUJ, OY-RYD, (N6187Q)
CS-. . . .	Christen Eagle II	DHM001	N175DM
CS-. . . .	Dornier Do.27H-2	2013	D-EFQK(2), HB-HAC, V-606
CS-. . . .	Embraer EMB-500 Phenom 100	50000130	N600PB, PT-FQD
CS-. . . .	Grumman GA-7 Cougar	0057	LN-ALY, OY-GAV, N770GA
CS-. . . .	Piper PA-23-250 Aztec C	27-2545	N21922
CS-. . . .	Piper PA-31P-350 Mojave	31P-8414023	N684WB, N9238Y
CS-. . . .	Piper PA-34-200T Seneca II	34-7770403	EC-ISC, ZS-MFP, N47521
CS-. . . .	Piper PA-36-285 Pawnee Brave	36-7460022	N44118

HOMEBUILTS

Reg	Type	c/n	Identities
CS-XAA(*)	Evans VP-1 Volksplane (Exp 4.87)	V-1766	
CS-XAB	Taylor JT.1 Monoplane (Dam. 19.5.13 Lajes)	ASVP/JT1/1/P	
CS-XAC	Aero Designs Pulsar XP	292	
CS-XAD	Ultravia Pelican PL	503	
CS-XAF	Rans S-10 Sakota	0194169	
CS-XAG	Zenair CH-601HDS Zodiac	6-3238	
CS-XAJ	Rans S-6ES Coyote II	0893533	
CS-XAL	Arnet Pereyra Aventura II	AP-2A0053	
CS-XAM	Velocity XLRG Elite (Reported crashed & Dbf)	3RX055	
CS-XAN	Ultravia Pelican VS	0621	
CS-XAP	Alpi Aviation Pioneer 300S	28	
CS-XAQ	Van's RV-9A	90067	
CS-XAT	Jabiru J400	170	
CS-XAV	Rutan VariEze	1318	I-PINA
CS-XAX	Jabiru J450	240	
CS-XBA	ANAC Covilha	VF001	
CS-XBL	Van's RV-7A	unkn	
CS-XCA	Van's RV-9A	90464	
CS-XCB	Van's RV-7	70650	
CS-XCC	ICP MXP-740 Savannah	02-03-51-135	CS-XAU
CS-XCD	BRM Land Africa Impala	0148/K2/09-LA	
CS-XCE	Van's RV-7	71476	
CS-XCF	Van's RV-7 (Identity unconfirmed)	70520/PFA323-13897	G-RVMC
CS-XCH	Van's RV-7A	unkn	
CS-XCI	Rans S-10 Sakota	PFA/194-12044	G-BWIA
CS-XCJ	Rans S-10 Sakota	unkn	
CS-XCK	Van's RV-8A	82235	N158DL
CS-XHA	Rotorway Exec 162F	6102	N14897
CS-XHB	Rotorway Exec 162F	6103	
CS-XHC	Rotorway Exec 162F	6156	
CS-XHE	Rotorway Exec 162F	6273	
CS-XHF	Rotorway Exec 162F	6274	
CS-X . .	Rand-Robinson KR-2	PFA/129-11068	G-BSKR
CS-X . .	Dyn'Aéro MCR-4S 2002	07	F-PDOZ

BALLOONS

Reg	Type	c/n	Identities
CS-BAB(*)	Cameron O-105 HAFB (Exp 3.90)	1963	
CS-BAC(*)	Cameron N-65 HAFB (Exp 5.92)	1284	LX-HII
CS-BAE	Colt 90A HAFB	2355	
CS-BAF	Colt 90A HAFB	2522	
CS-BAG	Ultramagic M-77 HAFB	77/108	
CS-BAI	Cameron N-65 HAFB	3225	
CS-BAJ	Cameron C-80 HAFB	3834	
CS-BAK	Cameron N-77 HAFB	3841	
CS-BAL	Ultramagic M-105 HAFB	105/38	
CS-BAM	Cameron V-90 HAFB	3345	
CS-BAN	Cameron C-80 HAFB	3966	
CS-BAP	Sky Propane Cylinder SS HAFB	64	
CS-BAQ	Sky 65 HAFB	63	
CS-BAS	Cameron N-90 HAFB	4144	
CS-BAT	Sky 65 HAFB	095	
CS-BAU	Sky 65 HAFB	106	
CS-BAX	Ultramagic M-160 HAFB	160/19	
CS-BAY	Cameron N-77 HAFB	4356	
CS-BAZ	Cameron N-105 HAFB	4524	
CS-BBA	Cameron N-105 HAFB	4549	
CS-BBB	Ultramagic M-90 HAFB	90/31	
CS-BBC	Ultramagic M-65C HAFB	65/92	
CS-BBD	Cameron C-80 Concept HAFB	4897	
CS-BBE	Cameron C-80 Concept HAFB	10123	
CS-BBF	Ultramagic M-77 HAFB	77/206	
CS-BBG	Ultramagic M-77 HAFB	77/213	
CS-BBH	Ultramagic F-21 Gas Cylinder SS HAFB	F21/02	
CS-BBI	Ultramagic F-25 HAFB	F25/01	
CS-BBJ	Cameron Z-77 HAFB	10579	
CS-BBK	Ultramagic M-90 HAFB	90/71	
CS-BBL	Kubicek BB-30Z HAFB	329	
CS-BBM	Ultramagic M-90 HAFB	90/87	
CS-BBN	Ultramagic M-160 HAFB	160/47	
CS-BBO	Ultramagic M-77 HAFB	77/289	
CS-BBP	Ultramagic M-77 HAFB	77/293	
CS-BBQ	Ultramagic M-77 HAFB	77/299	
CS-BBT	Ultramagic SS HAFB	F32/01	
CS-BBU	Cameron Z-90 HAFB	6467	N40266
CS-BBV	Sky 77-24 HAFB	057	G-CDAM, CS-BAO
CS-BBY	Kubicek BB-34Z HAFB (Officially quoted as c/n 678 which is CN-CAJ)	676	

Reg	Type	c/n	Identities
CS-BBZ	Ultramagic M-77 HAFB	77/338	
CS-BCD	Ultramagic M-.. HAFB	unkn	

GLIDERS AND MOTOR-GLIDERS

Reg	Type	c/n	Identities
CS-PAE(*)	Grunau Baby IIb (To Museu do Ar, Alverca)	3567	
CS-PAM(*)	EoN Baby 1 (Exp 3.79, stored)	EON/B/035	
CS-PAP(*)	Grunau Baby III (Exp 9.81)	31-53	
CS-PAQ	Schleicher Rhönlerche II	381	
CS-PAR(*)	Schleicher Rhönlerche II (Exp 4.82)	382	
CS-PAS(*)	Schleicher Rhönlerche II (Stored)	802	
CS-PAV(*)	Schleicher Rhönlerche II (Exp 9.80)	820	
CS-PAZ	SZD-22C Mucha Standard	F-770	
CS-PBA	Schleicher Rhönlerche II	3087	
CS-PBB(*)	Scheibe Bergfalke II (Exp 12.86)	341	
CS-PBC(*)	Schleicher Rhönlerche II (Exp 5.89)	3084/Br	
CS-PBD	LET L-13 Blanik	173350	
CS-PBG	Scheibe SF 27M-A	6327	CS-AXC, D-KHOE
CS-PBH	Grob G 103A Twin II Acro	3733-K-48	D-6188
CS-PBJ	Centrair ASW 20FL	20154	F-CFLO
CS-PBL-C2	LAK-12 Lietuva	6231	
CS-PBM	LET L-13 Blanik	827421	OK-2730
CS-PBN-C3	PZL PW-5 Smyk (Crashed 24.4.03)	17.09.021	
CS-PBP	Grob G 103A Twin II Acro	3708-K-44	D-3789
CS-PBQ	LET L-13 Blanik	027325	DOSAAF
CS-PBU	Grob G 102 Astir CS Jeans	2155	D-4894
CS-PBY	LET L-13 Blanik (Wreck noted 5.00)	173220	
CS-PBZ	Schleicher ASK 21	21395	FAP10102, FAP1002
CS-PCA	LET L-13 Blanik	unkn	
CS-PCB-FZ	PZL PW-5 Smyk	unkn	
CS-PCC	Schleicher ASK 21	21410	FAP10104, FAP1004
CS-PRP	LET L-13 Blanik	174222	DOSAAF
CS-P . .	Grob/Schempp-Hirth CS-11 St.Cirrus	584G	F-CEMJ

MICROLIGHTS

Reg	Type	c/n	Identities
CS-UAA	Quicksilver MX-II HP	1265	
CS-UAB	Quicksilver MX-II HP	1266	
CS-UAC	Cosmos Bidulm 53	B0032	
CS-UAE	Quicksilver MX Sprint II	131	
CS-UAF	Quicksilver MXL-II	1291	
CS-UAH	Quicksilver MXL-II	1349	
CS-UAI	Quicksilver GT-400	1343	
CS-UAJ	Quicksilver MXL-II Sport	1697	
CS-UAK	Whittaker MW-5K Sorcerer	5K-0010-02	
CS-UAL	Whittaker MW-5K Sorcerer	5K-0013-02	
CS-UAO	Ferrari Tucano	0065	
CS-UAP	Quicksilver GTS-400	1287	
CS-UAT	Quicksilver MXL-II	1157	
CS-UAU	Quicksilver MXL-II Sport	165	
CS-UAW	Quicksilver MXL-II	1517	
CS-UAX	Quicksilver MXL-II	1452	
CS-UAY	Whittaker MW-5	5K-0016-02	
CS-UBA	Quicksilver MXL-II	191	
CS-UBB	Type unknown	unkn	
CS-UBF	Denney Kitfox	unkn	
CS-UBG	Ultralair Weedhopper JC-31 Premier AX3	0112856	
CS-UBH	Ultralair Weedhopper JC-31 Premier AX3	0112855	
CS-UBI	Cobra AJS-2000	R644988	
CS-UBJ	Quicksilver MX Sprint II	041	
CS-UBK	Quicksilver GTS-500	0030	
CS-UBL	Quicksilver MXL-II	189	
CS-UBX	Quicksilver GTS-400	1242	
CS-UBZ	Quicksilver MXL-II	2335	
CS-UCA	Ultralair Weedhopper AX3-503D (See CS-UDA, same c/n quoted)	B1112965	
CS-UCB	Ultralair Weedhopper AX-2	B1102953	
CS-UCC	Ultralair Weedhopper JC-24S	1101149	
CS-UCD	Air Création Safari GT BI / SX16	91-252	
CS-UCE	Air Création Safari GT BI / SX16	8-91-278	
CS-UCF	Air Création Safari GT BI 503	8-91-282	
CS-UCG	Air Création Safari GT BI 503	8-91-288	
CS-UCI	Quicksilver MXL-II Sport	82	
CS-UCJ	Quicksilver MXL-II Sport	255	
CS-UCK	Quicksilver MXL-II Sport	165	
CS-UCL	Quicksilver MXL-II Sport	1312	
CS-UCM	Air Création Safari GT BI 503/1	10-91-325	
CS-UCN	Air Création Safari GT BI 503/1	91-285	
CS-UCO	Air Création Safari GT BI 503/1	8-91-328	
CS-UCQ	Quicksilver GT-500	unkn	
CS-UCR	Cosmos Chronos	B-650	
CS-UCS	Cosmos Bidulm 53	unkn	
CS-UCT	Cosmos Bidulm 53	unkn	
CS-UCV	Cosmos Turbo 163	B-522	
CS-UCZ	Ferrari Tucano	0055	
CS-UDA	Ultralair Weedhopper Premier AX3 (See CS-UCA, same c/n quoted)	B1112965	
CS-UDC	Ultralair Weedhopper AX2-503	B1112963	
CS-UDD	Ultralair Weedhopper AX2	B1112964	
CS-UDE	Cosmos Chronos 14	B-731	
CS-UDG	Cosmos Chronos 16	B-725	
CS-UDJ	Kolb Twin Star Mk.II	TS-III	
CS-UDK	Ultralair Weedhopper AX-3	B2043007	
CS-UDL	Ultralair Weedhopper AX-3	B2033000	
CS-UDM	Ultralair Weedhopper JC-31 Premier AX3	B2032999	
CS-UDO	Ferrari Tucano	199	
CS-UDR	Cosmos Chronos 14	B-784	
CS-UDS	Cosmos Chronos	7794	
CS-UDT	Cosmos Chronos	780	
CS-UDU	Cosmos Chronos 16	781	

Reg	Type	C/n	Notes
CS-UDV	Cosmos Chronos 16	774	
CS-UDW	Epervier UL-582	6	
CS-UDX	Quicksilver MXL-II	unkn	
CS-UDZ	Daxiwings Falcon XP B2	01	
CS-UEC	Ultralair Weedhopper AX-3	B3023092	
CS-UED	Air Création GT BI / Quartz 18	04-92-105	
CS-UEE	Air Création GT BI / Quartz 18	03-02-95	
CS-UEG	Air Création Safari GT-BI / SX-16	10 92-264	
CS-UEH	Quicksilver MXL-II Sport	342	
CS-UEJ	Comco Ikarus Fox-C22	9211-3479	
CS-UEK	Daxiwings Falcon XP B2	600238	
CS-UEL	Volero Volero	V4924	
CS-UEM	Quicksilver GT-500	207	
CS-UEO	Quicksilver GT-500	200	
CS-UEP	Dynali Chickinox Kot Kot	2992-P4	
CS-UEQ	Dynali Chickinox Kot Kot	2992-P5	
CS-UES	Quicksilver MXL-II Sport	340	
CS-UEW	Cosmos Hermes 16	B-670	
CS-UEX	TLUltralight TL-32 Typhoon	93A001	
CS-UEZ	Quicksilver MXL-II Sport	303	
CS-UFA	Quicksilver MXL-II Sport	297	
CS-UFB	Quad City Challenger II	CH2-1092-894	
CS-UFC	Comco Ikarus Fox-C22	9306-3524	
CS-UFD	Comco Ikarus Fox-C22	4170-9983	
CS-UFE	Dallach Sunrise II	1	D-MXCL
CS-UFK	Quicksilver MXL-II Sport	488	
CS-UFL	Quicksilver MXL-II Sport	489	
	(Cr 27.11.04)		
CS-UFN	Euroala JF 91 JetFox	35	
CS-UFQ	Comco Ikarus Fox-C22	9311-3554	
CS-UFR	Quicksilver GT-500	232	
CS-UFS	Quicksilver GT-500	231	
CS-UFU	Rans S-6ES Coyote II	0792330	
CS-UFV	Cosmos Chronos 16	21012	
CS-UFW	Cosmos Chronos 16	unkn	
CS-UFY	Cosmos Chronos 16	21020	
CS-UFZ	Rans S-6ES Coyote II	0792331	
CS-UGA	Rans S-6ES Coyote II	0293448	
CS-UGB	Rans S-6ES Coyote II	0593501	
CS-UGC	Rans S-6ES Coyote II	0493479	
CS-UGD	Ultralair Weedhopper AX-3	C3113178	
CS-UGE	Quicksilver MXL-II	527	
CS-UGF	Rans S-6ES Coyote II	0493478	
CS-UGG	Tecnam P.92 Echo	2	
CS-UGH	Aviasud AE-209 Albatros	54	
CS-UGI	Chickinox Kot-Kot	4091-P3	
CS-UGJ	Chickinox Kot-Kot	4692-P10	
CS-UGK	Chickinox Kot-Kot	4692-P15	
CS-UGL	Ultralair Weedhopper AX-3	12595	
CS-UGM	Rans S-6ES Coyote II	0593506	
CS-UGN	Murphy Maverick	072M	
CS-UGO	Comco Ikarus Fox-C22	9408-3618	
CS-UGQ	Chickinox Kot-Kot	4692-P12	
CS-UGR	Rans S-6ES Coyote II	0494608	
CS-UGS	Ferrari Tucano	P305	
CS-UGT	Rans S-6ES Coyote II	0195722	
CS-UGU	Quicksilver MXL-II	1351	
CS-UGV	Rans S-6ES Coyote II	0493476	
	(Cr 5.7.98 Chaves)		
CS-UGW	SMAN Pétrel	11	
CS-UGY	Tecnam P.92 Echo	98	
CS-UGZ	Rans S-6XL Coyote II	0195727	
CS-UHB	Tecnam P.92 Echo	134	
CS-UHC	Tecnam P.92 Echo	135	
	(Same c/n as D-MOKS)		
CS-UHD	Ferrari Tucano	P-306	
CS-UHE	Tecnam P.92 Echo	146	
CS-UHF	Ultralair Weedhopper AX-3-16	E-4103227	
CS-UHG	Quicksilver MX-IISprint	273	
CS-UHH	Air Création Safari GT-BI	192026	
CS-UHI	Rans S-6ES Coyote II	0495800	
CS-UHJ	Ferrari Tucano	P-307	
CS-UHK	Quicksilver MX-IISprint	165	
CS-UHL	Quicksilver GT-400	1240	
CS-UHM	Campana AN-400	21	
CS-UHN	Rans S-6S Coyote II	1193558	
CS-UHO	Rans S-12XL Airaile	01960683	
CS-UHP	Rans S-6XL Coyote II	0495788	
CS-UHQ	Ultralair Weedhopper AX-3-16	E-4083220	
CS-UHR	Jabiru SK	0102	
CS-UHS	Comco Ikarus Fox-C22	9610-3719	
CS-UHT	Comco Ikarus Fox-C22 floatplane	9610-3718	
CS-UHU	Jabiru SK	P0103	
CS-UHV	Jabiru SK	P0104	
CS-UHW	Rans S-12XL Airaile	01960678	
CS-UHX	Comco Ikarus Fox-C22	9405-3604	
CS-UHY	Rans S-12XL Airaile	01960673	
CS-UHZ	Ultralair Weedhopper AX-3-16	E-4103219	
CS-UIA	Rans S-6ES Coyote II	1191236	
CS-UIB	Best Off Sky Ranger	0195	
CS-UIC	Ultravia Pelican VS	635	
CS-UID	Tecnam P.96 Golf	007	
CS-UIE	Jabiru SK	P-135	
CS-UIF	Jabiru SK	P-136	
	(Noted as Jabiru 400)		
CS-UIG	Jabiru SK	P-137	
CS-UII	Rans S-12XL Airaile	11960756	
CS-UIJ	Tecnam P.92 Echo	268	
CS-UIK	Best Off Sky Ranger	SK 0115497	
CS-UIL	Jabiru SK	P-149	
CS-UIN	Jabiru SK	P-153	
CS-UIO	Rans S-6ES Coyote IIXL	"11869061"	
	(C/n incorrect. Possibly 11961061 ex N7214W)		
CS-UIP	Quicksilver MXL-II Sport	773	
CS-UIQ	Jabiru SK	P-180	
CS-UIR	Raj Hamsa X'Air 502 TPE	363	
CS-UIS	Tecnam P.96 Golf	028	
CS-UIT	Tecnam P.96 Golf	029	
CS-UIU	Aviakit Hermes	"1-800-8"	
CS-UIW	Tecnam P.96 Golf Light	040	
CS-UIX	Aviatika MAI-890	0051	
CS-UIZ	Raj Hamsa X'Air	349	
CS-UJB	Jabiru SK	P-179	
	(Cr nr Lagos 1.5.03, wreck noted 4.11)		
CS-UJC	Jabiru SK	P-181	
CS-UJD	Jabiru SK	P-180	
CS-UJE	Quicksilver MXL-II Sport	772	
CS-UJF	Rans S-6ES Coyote IIXL	12961080	
	(W/o 1.15)		
CS-UJG	Rans S-6ES Coyote IIXL	10971083	
CS-UJH	Quicksilver GT-400	1436	
CS-UJJ	Tecnam P.96 Golf Light	073	
CS-UJK	Quicksilver MXL-II Sport	775	
CS-UJL	Raj Hamsa X'Air	398	
CS-UJM	Quicksilver "N/PT"	1290	
CS-UJN	Raj Hamsa X'Air 502 TPE	370	
CS-UJO	Raj Hamsa X'Air 502 TPE	376	
CS-UJP	Raj Hamsa X'Air 502 TPE	384	
CS-UJQ	SG Avn SG.2 Storm 300P	0012P	
CS-UJR	Tecnam P.96 Golf Light	085	
CS-UJS	DEA Yuma	11298 KS	
CS-UJT	Nando Groppo Groppino	058	
CS-UJU	Jabiru SK	P-182	
CS-UJV	Tecnam P.92 Echo	415	
CS-UJW	Tecnam P.96 Golf	084	
CS-UJX	Tecnam P.92 Echo	416	
	(Cr 15.3.09 Pista da Lezira)		
CS-UJY	Tecnam P.92 Echo	457	
CS-UJZ	TL Ultralight TL-96 Star	99S38	
CS-UKA	Best Off Sky Ranger	SKR 00.01.02	
CS-UKB	Microleve Corsario Mk.IV	203	
CS-UKD	Jabiru SK	P-271	
CS-UKE	Jabiru SK	P-276	
CS-UKF	TL Ultralight TL-96 Star	048	
CS-UKG	TL Ultralight TL-96 Star	058	
CS-UKH	Best Off Sky Ranger	SKR 00.06.049	
CS-UKI	Daxiwings Falcon XP B2	FW/82/04/00/001	
CS-UKJ	Air Création GT-BI / SX16	03-1991	
CS-UKK	Air Création GT-BI / XP15	123-9312	
CS-UKL	Best Off Sky Ranger	59	
CS-UKM	Quicksilver GT-500	500-0242	
CS-UKN	Best Off Sky Ranger	00.1060	
CS-UKO	Quicksilver MXL-II Sport	779	
CS-UKP	Raj Hamsa X'Air 602 TPE	593	
CS-UKQ	Air Création GT-BI / XP15	0293038	
CS-UKR	Tecnam P.92RG	009	
CS-UKS	Tecnam P.92 Echo	538	
CS-UKT	Tecnam P.96 Golf Light	4426806	
CS-UKU	ATEC Zephyr 2000	Z230600	
CS-UKV	Vol Mediterrani JL Esqual VM-1P	056	
CS-UKW	Best Off Sky Ranger	0104084	
	(W/o 29.8.10)		
CS-UKX	Tecnam P.96 Golf Light	174	
CS-UKY	Quicksilver MXL-II Sport	827	
CS-UKZ	Vol Mediterrani JL Esqual VM-1P	057	
CS-ULA	Loehle Sport Parasol	SP 0973263 LE	
CS-ULB	Best Off Sky Ranger	SKR 12081	
CS-ULC	Tecnam P.92 Echo	593	
CS-ULD	Raj Hamsa X'Air 602	591	
CS-ULE	Raj Hamsa X'Air 602	620	
CS-ULF	Tecnam P.92 Echo	592	
CS-ULG	Tecnam P.92 Echo	375	
CS-ULH	Quicksilver MXL-II Sport	780	
CS-ULI	Moyes Dragonfly	551	
CS-ULJ	Best Off Sky Ranger	SKR 0109138	
CS-ULK	Best Off Sky Ranger	SKR 0204189	
	(Dbr. 19.9.15)		
CS-ULL	Vol Mediterrani Esqual VM-1P	P-004	
	(W/o 4.6.12)		
CS-ULN	Best Off Sky Ranger	SKR 0205200	
CS-ULO	Best Off Sky Ranger	SKR 0205219	
CS-ULP	Rans S-6XL Coyote	0495790	
CS-ULQ	Vol Mediterrani Esqual VM-1P	P-061	
CS-ULR	Quicksilver MXL-II Sport	801	
CS-ULS	Jabiru SK	P475	
CS-ULT	ATEC Zephyr 2000	7641002A	
CS-ULV	Road Air Flamingo	044	
CS-ULW	Quicksilver MXL-II Sport	529	
CS-ULY	Best Off Sky Ranger	SKR 0209230	
CS-ULZ	Aerospool WT-9 Dynamic	DY 021/2002	
CS-UMB	Fantasy Air Allegro 2000P	02-607	
CS-UMC	Tecnam P.92 Echo	730	
CS-UMD	Aerospool WT-9 Dynamic	DY 024/2003	
CS-UME	Road Air Flamingo	035	
CS-UMG	Quicksilver MXL-II Sport	869	
CS-UMH	Best Off Sky Ranger	SKR 0204175	
CS-UMI	Aerospool WT-9 Dynamic	DY 031/2003	
CS-UMJ	Evektor EV-97 Eurostar	2003-1605	
CS-UMK	Aerospool WT-9 Dynamic	DY 030/2003	
CS-UML	Quicksilver MXL-II Sport	0861	
CS-UMM	Kappa 77 Sova	7993I	
CS-UMN	Quicksilver MXL-II Sport	879	
CS-UMO	Quicksilver MXL-II Sport	880	
CS-UMP	Alpha Bravo Funk FK-9	AB 09-101	
CS-UMQ	Raj Hamsa X'Air 602TPE	334	
CS-UMR	ATEC Zephyr 2000	Z 210500A	
CS-UMS	Moragón M-1	M1-03-001P	
CS-UMT	Evektor EV-97 Eurostar	2003-1615	
CS-UMV	Moragón M-1	M1-03-002P	
CS-UMW	TL Ultralight TL-2000 Sting	03ST52	
CS-UMX	ATEC Zephyr 2000	Z 8400903A	
CS-UMY	Tecnam P.92 Echo	65	
CS-UNA	EET/ Best Off Sky Ranger	SKR 0209239	
CS-UNB	Alpha Bravo Funk FK-9	AB 09-102	
CS-UNC	SG Aviation Storm RG-P	100122-P-01	
CS-UND	Tecnam P.2002 Sierra	017	
CS-UNE	SG Aviation Rally 105	R00904	
CS-UNF	Alpi Aviation Pioneer 200	049	
CS-UNG	ATEC Zephyr 2000	Z 950204A	
CS-UNH	ATEC Zephyr 2000	Z 1030604A	
CS-UNJ	Raj Hamsa X'Air 602 (f/p)	898	
CS-UNK	Road Air Flamingo	050	
CS-UNL	Alpha Bravo Funk FK-9	AB 09-103	
CS-UNM	Alpha Bravo Funk FK-9	AB 09-104	
CS-UNN	Pelicano Sea Max P22	010	
CS-UNO	ATEC Zephyr 2000	Z 940204	
CS-UNP	Pelicano Sea Max P22	011	
CS-UNR	Aerospool WT-9 Dynamic	DY087/2005	
CS-UNS	Evektor EV-97R Eurostar	2005-2512	
CS-UNT	Fantasy Air Allegro 2000P	04-712	
CS-UNU	Tecnam P.92 Echo	895	
CS-UNV	Best Off Sky Ranger	SKR 0502564	

CS-UNW	Tecnam P.92 Echo Super	731	
CS-UNX	Best Off Sky Ranger	SKR 0402441	
CS-UNY	Aerospool WT-9 Dynamic	DY025/2003	
CS-UNZ	Zenair CH-701 STOL	7-9562	
CS-UOA	Tecnam P.92 Echo	896	
CS-UOB	ATEC Zephyr 2000	Z1220605	
	(Dam. 7.7.10)		
CS-UOC	EDRA Super Petrel AV12A	S00160	
CS-UOD	Air Max Sea Max P22	015	
CS-UOE	ATEC Zephyr 2000	Z1240705A	
	(W/o 21.3.10)		
CS-UOF	Tecnam P.96 Golf	278	
CS-UOG	Evektor EV-97 Eurostar	2005-2602	
	(Same c/n as SE-VII)		
CS-UOH	Evektor EV-97 Eurostar	2005-2511	
	(W/o 5.1.13)		
CS-UOI	Air Max Sea Max P22	023	
CS-UOJ	BRM Land Africa Impala	0004/04	
CS-UOK	BRM Land Africa Impala	0005/04	
CS-UOL	BRM Land Africa Impala	0003/04	
CS-UON	Aerospool WT-9 Dynamic	DY108/2005	
CS-UOO	Tecnam P.96 Golf 100	285	
	(W/o 15.12.10)		
CS-UOQ	TL Ultralight TL-96 Star	02/01585	
CS-UOR	TL Ultralight TL-2000 Sting	06ST170	
CS-UOS	Aerospool WT-9 Dynamic	DYK06/2006	
CS-UOT	TL Ultralight TL-2000 Sting	06ST169	
CS-UOU	Air Max Sea Max P22	0031	
CS-UOV	Alpi Aviation Pioneer 300	109	
	(W/o 30.4.14)		
CS-UOW	Tecnam P.92 Echo	960	
CS-UOX	Alpi Aviation Pioneer 200	126	
CS-UOY	Alpi Aviation Pioneer 300	164	
CS-UOZ	Aerospool WT-9 Dynamic	DYK07/2006	
CS-UPA	Aerospool WT-9 Dynamic	DYK03/2006	
CS-UPD	Aeropro Eurofox Space Pro 3K	17705	OM-LEOS
CS-UPE	Tecnam P.92 Echo Super C Floatplane	958	
CS-UPF	Tecnam P.2002 Sierra	222	
CS-UPG	Tecnam P.92 Echo Super	999	
CS-UPH	Tecnam P.92 Echo Super	996	
	(W/o 1.15)		
CS-UPI	Tecnam P.2002 Sierra	218	
CS-UPK	Alpi Aviation Pioneer 200	139	
CS-UPL	CzAW Sportcruiser	06SC041	
CS-UPM	BRM Land Africa	0023/07	
	(Now believed to be EC-FS2)		
CS-UPN	CzAW Sportcruiser	07SC24	
CS-UPO	BRM Land Africa Impala	001/04	
CS-UPP	Aeropro Eurofox Space Pro 3K	22207	
CS-UPQ	CzAW Sportcruiser	07SC070	
CS-UPR	Aerospool WT-9 Dynamic	DY175/2007	
CS-UPS	TL Ultralight TL-2000 Sting	07ST233	
CS-UPT	BRM Land Africa Impala	0006/04	
CS-UPU	Urban Air UFM-13 Lambada	67-13	
CS-UPV	Urban Air Samba XXL	SAXL-34	
CS-UPW	CzAW Sportcruiser	07SC052	
CS-UPX	Tecnam P.2004 Bravo	112	
CS-UPY	Alpha Bravo Funk FK-9	AB09-106	
CS-UQA	CzAW Sportcruiser	07SC077	
CS-UQB	TL Ultralight TL-2000 Sting	5649279	
CS-UQC	CzAW Sportcruiser	07SC60	
CS-UQD	SG Avn Storm Century 04	S6-00S-0015	
CS-UQE	CzAW Sportcruiser	07SC069	
CS-UQF	CzAW Sportcruiser	07SC085	
CS-UQG	CzAW Sportcruiser	unkn	
CS-UQH	Urban Air Samba XXL	SAXL-51	
CS-UQI	Aerospool WT-9 Dynamic	DY218/2008	
CS-UQK	TL Ultralight TL-2000 Sting carbon	08ST268	
CS-UQL	TL Ultralight TL-2000 Sting carbon	08ST272	
	(W/o 3.4.12)		
CS-UQM	BRM Land Africa Impala	0103/08	
CS-UQN	Flyitalia MD-3 Rider	045/2008	
CS-UQO	Tecnam P.2002 Sierra	301	
CS-UQP	Tecnam P.2002 Sierra	308	
CS-UQQ	BRM Land Africa Impala	0113/08	
CS-UQR	Aerospool WT-9 Dynamic	DY244/2008	
CS-UQS	Monnet Sonex	883	
CS-UQT	BRM Land Africa Impala	0102/08	
CS-UQU	Air Max Sea Max P22	064	
CS-UQV	Aeropro Eurofox Space Pro 3K	26708	
	(To EC-GL8)		
CS-UQW	Avio Delta Swan 1 / Fun Cruiser	MK 05070601	
CS-UQX	Tecnam P.2002RG Sierra	323	
	(Dam. 16.8.09)		
CS-UQY	Aeropepe Flamingo	FL-007	
CS-UQZ	BRM Land Africa Impala	0124/08	
CS-URA	Tecnam P.92 Echo Super	1232	
CS-URB	TL Ultralight TL-2000 Sting carbon	09ST314	
CS-URD	Alpi Avn Pioneer 300S	14	
CS-URE	Aveko VL-3 Sprint	28	
CS-URF	Best Off Sky Ranger	SKR09853	
CS-URG	Ibis Magic GS-700LV	GS-01-09-700-784	
CS-URH	Jabiru J170	192	
CS-URI	Aerospool WT-9 Dynamic	DY323/2009	
CS-URJ	Alpi Avn Pioneer 300S	73S	
CS-URK	Roko Aero NG4 UL	18/2009	
CS-URL	CzAW Sportcruiser	09SC287	
CS-URN	Tecnam P.92 Echo Super	1260	
CS-URO	B&F Funk FK-14B Polaris	060	D-MISI(2)
	(W/o as D-MISI 6.2.15)		
CS-URQ	Jabiru J170	238	
CS-URR	Jihlavan KP-2U Skyleader 200	216818∅O	
CS-URS	Tecnam P.2002 Sierra	415	
CS-URT	Aeropro Eurofox Space Pro 3K	29209	
CS-URU	Best Off Sky Ranger	SKR0911984	
CS-URV	CzAW Sportcruiser	09SC100	
CS-URW	Tecnam P.2002 Sierra	411	
CS-URX	Tecnam P.92 Echo Super	1296	
CS-URY	BRM Land Africa Impala	0155/912ULS/10-LA	
CS-URZ	BRM Land Africa Impala	0167/912ULS/10-LA	
CS-USA	Aerospool WT-9 Dynamic	DY372/2010	
CS-USB	TL Ultralight TL-3000 Sirius	09SI04	
CS-USE	CzAW Sportcruiser	09SC165	
CS-USF	Aerospool WT-9 Dynamic	DY386/2010	
CS-USH	TL Ultralight TL-3000 Sirius	10SI30	

CS-USI	BRM Land Africa Impala	0154/912ULS/10-LA	
	(W/o 20.9.15)		
CS-USJ	TL Ultralight TL-3000 Sirius	10SI35	
CS-USK	Tomark SD-4 Viper	0029	
CS-USL	Light Aero Avid Flyer Mk.IV	1063D	
CS-USM	Aerospool WT-9 Dynamic	DY399/2010	
CS-USN	BRM Land Africa Impala	0165/912ULS/10-LA	
	(Same c/n quoted as CS-USC now EI-FBW)		
CS-USP	Roko Aero NG4 UL	"6776878"	
	(C/n is probably engine number)		
CS-USQ	Shark Aero Shark	001	OK-OUR 01
CS-USR	Tecnam P.2008	30	
	(Dam. 26.12.11 Pista do Cerval)		
CS-UST	Pipistrel Virus SW	unkn	
CS-USU	Best Off Nynja	SKR11074	
CS-USV	Pro Mecc. Sparviero 100R	PM64	
CS-USX	BRM Aero Bristell NG5	unkn	
CS-USZ	Alpi Pioneer 300	unkn	
CS-UTA	CzAW Sportcruiser	09SC311	OK-RAL ?
CS-UTB	ATEC 321 Faeta	unkn	
CS-UTD	BRM Land Africa	unkn	
CS-UTE	Tecnam P.2008	072	
	(W/o 10.6.14, Herdade da Lameira)		
CS-UTI	BRM Land Africa	0225/912ULS/13-LA	
CS-UTJ	Alpi Aviation Pioneer 300	unkn	
CS-UTK	BRM Land Africa	unkn	
CS-UTM	TL Ultralight TL-3000 Sirius	unkn	
CS-UTO	Zlin Savage Cub	unkn	
CS-UTP	Tecnam P.2002 Sierra	unkn	
CS-UTQ	Tecnam P.92 Eaglet LS	unkn	
CS-UTS	BRM Land Africa	unkn	
CS-UTT	BRM Land Africa	unkn	
CS-UTY	Aerospool WT-9 Dynamic	unkn	
CS-UTZ	BRM Land Africa	unkn	
CS-U . .	Aero Designs Pulsar 582-T	246	N8105X
CS-U . .	Aero Mirage TC2	AM0641285	N2062S
CS-U . .	CFM Streak Shadow	K 207	G-OTCH
CS-U . .	Dragon Fly 333	unkn	I-2692
CS-U . .	Light Aero Avid Flyer	329	G-BRNS
CS-U . .	Light Aero Avid Flyer	908/PFA/189-12023	G-BTMS
CS-U . .	Melvin/ Denney Kitfox II	615	N90EV
CS-U . .	Solar Wings Pegasus XL-R	SW-WA-1551	G-MYCH

D - GERMANY

Regn.	Type	C/n	Prev.Id.

CLASS A : Aircraft of over 20 metric tonnes (20,000 kgs)

Regn.	Type	C/n	Prev.Id.
D-AAAL(2)	Airbus A340-541	464	PT-MSL, C-GKOM, F-WWTJ
	(Permit 15.10.14)		
D-AAAX	Canadair CL-600-2B16 Challenger IV	5449	LX-SPK, VP-CCP, N604JR, N604GT, C-GLXF
D-AAAY	Canadair CL-600-2B16 Challenger IV	5602	LZ-YUP, HB-JRW, C-FDBJ, C-GLXD
D-AACM	Boeing 737-8JM	37663	N379BJ, N1796B
D-AAEA(2)	Airbus A330-322	116	SU-XXX, G-CIOH, 9M-MKI, F-WWKT
	(P. 7.16)		
D-AAEB(2)	Airbus A330-322	127	CS-TRI, D-AERQ, F-WWKO
	(Res.9.16)		
D-AAEC	Airbus A330-321	050	HS-TEA, F-WWKI
	(Res.2.16)		
D-AAED	Airbus A330-323X	346	HS-TEM, F-WWYE
	(Res.2.16)		
D-AAGF	Gulfstream IV	1159	HB-IKR, N458FA, 9K-AJB, N17583
	(Res.5.09)		
D-AAHB	Bombardier BD-700-1A10 Global Express	9011	HB-IHQ, VP-BJJ, N700KJ, C-GDGW
	(Res.9.16)		
D-AAHI	Bombardier BD.700-1A11 Global 5000	9170	OE-LAA, D-AAAZ, (VP-CKR), D-AAAZ, C-FCSY
	(Res. 8.12.14)		
D-AAIJ	Canadair CL-600-2B19 Challenger 850	8065	C-FJRN, C-FMMB
D-AALA	Boeing 777-FZN	36001	
D-AALB	Boeing 777-FZN	36002	N5017Q
D-AALC	Boeing 777-FZN	36003	
D-AALD	Boeing 777-FZN	36004	
D-AALE	Boeing 777-FZN	36198	
D-AALF	Boeing 777-FZN	36201	
D-AALG	Boeing 777-FZN	36199	
D-AALH	Boeing 777-FZN	36200	
D-AALI	Boeing 777-FZN	36202	
	(Res. 5.10)		
D-AALJ	Boeing 777-FZN	36203	
	(Res. 5.10)		
D-AALK	Boeing 777-FZN	36204	
	(Res. 5.10)		
D-AALL	Boeing 777-FZN	36205	
	(Res. 5.10)		
D-AALM	Boeing 777-FZN	36206	
	(Res. 5.10)		
D-AALN	Boeing 777-FZN	36207	
	(Res. 5.10)		
D-AALO	Boeing 777-FZN	36208	
	(Res. 5.10)		
D-AALP	Boeing 777-FZN	36209	
	(Res. 1.12)		
D-AALQ	Boeing 777-FZN	36210	
	(Res. 1.12)		
D-AALR	Boeing 777-FZN	36211	
	(Res. 1.12)		
D-AARK	Embraer EMB-190-100BJ Lineage 1000		
	(Res. 25.8.15)	19000109	A6-ARK, PP-XOL
D-ABAF(4)	Boeing 737-86J	30878	N1787B
D-ABAG(3)	Boeing 737-86J	30879	
D-ABBA(2)	Dassault Falcon 900LX	303	
	(Res.3.16)		
D-ABBD	Boeing 737-86J	30880	TC-IZF, D-ABBD
D-ABBK	Boeing 737-8BK	33013	
	(Res as ZS-ZWU 11.16)		
D-ABCA	Airbus A321-211	3708	D-AVZO
D-ABCB	Airbus A321-211	3749	D-AVZC
D-ABCC(2)	Airbus A321-211	4334	D-AZAK
D-ABCD	Canadair CL-600-2B16 Challenger IV	5565	N604KB, C-GLXS
D-ABCF	Airbus A321-211	1966	N221LF, 6Y-JMS, D-AVZH, F-WWIE, D-AVZH
D-ABCG	Airbus A321-211	1988	N341LF, 6Y-JMW, D-AVXH
D-ABCH	Airbus A321-211	4728	D-AVZF
D-ABCI(3)	Airbus A321-211	5038	D-AZAO
D-ABCJ(2)	Airbus A321-211	5126	D-AVZC
D-ABCK	Airbus A321-211	5133	D-AVZA
D-ABCL	Airbus A321-211	6168	D-AVXU
D-ABCM	Airbus A321-211	6432	D-AZAU
D-ABCN	Airbus A321-211	6454	D-AVZE
D-ABCO	Airbus A321-211	6501	D-AVZV
D-ABCP	Airbus A321-211	6629	D-AVXU
D-ABCQ	Airbus A321-211	6639	D-AVXY
D-ABCR	Airbus A321-211	6719	D-AYAA
D-ABCT	Airbus A321-211	7119	D-AZAR
	(For Pakistan 9.16)		
D-ABCV	Airbus A321-211	7260	D-AYAK
	(Stored)		
D-ABDB	Airbus A320-214	2619	SP-IAH, D-ABDB, F-WWDK
D-ABDO	Airbus A320-214	3055	HB-IOW, D-ABDO, F-WWDU
D-ABDQ	Airbus A320-214	3121	F-WWBD
	(Res as OE-LEK .16)		
D-ABDU	Airbus A320-214	3516	D-AVVC
D-ABDW	Airbus A320-214	3945	F-WWDX
D-ABDY	Airbus A320-214	4013	F-WWIG
D-ABEC(2)	Boeing 737-330	25149	
D-ABEY(2)	Canadair CL-600-2B16 Challenger V	5863	C-GJXY
D-ABFA(2)	Airbus A320-214	4101	D-AVVK
D-ABFC(2)	Airbus A320-214	4161	D-AVVP
D-ABFE(2)	Airbus A320-214	4269	D-AXAE
D-ABFF(2)	Airbus A320-214	4329	D-AXAP
D-ABFG	Airbus A320-214	4291	D-AXAG
D-ABFK	Airbus A320-214	4433	D-AVVQ
D-ABFN(2)	Airbus A320-214	4510	F-WWRK
D-ABFO	Airbus A320-214	4565	D-AVVA
D-ABGQ	Airbus A319-111	3700	EC-LRZ, D-ABGQ, D-AVVM
D-ABGR	Airbus A319-112	3704	EC-LRS, D-ABGR, D-AVVJ
D-ABGS	Airbus A319-112	3865	SP-IBA, D-ABGS, D-AVWD
D-ABHA(2)	Airbus A320-214	3540	PR-MHV, F-WWDG
D-ABHB(2)	Airbus A320-214	7312	D-AXAH
D-ABHC(2)	Airbus A320-214	3594	PR-MHY, F-WWDG
D-ABHD(2)	Airbus A320-214	7404	
D-ABHE(2)	Airbus A320-214	7474	D-AVVL
D-ABIA(2)	Boeing 737-530	24815	OK-SWY, D-ABIA(2), N3521N
	(Ground trainer with Lufthansa Technik, Hamburg)		
D-ABIG(2)	Canadair CL-600-2B16 Challenger 605	5950	(N605BE), C-GVWI(2)
	(Res. 7.9.15)		
D-ABKA(3)	Boeing 737-82R	29329	TC-APG, N1786B
D-ABKI(2)	Boeing 737-86J	37748	C-GBKI, D-ABKI, N1786B
D-ABKJ(2)	Boeing 737-86J	37749	N1786B
D-ABKM(3)	Boeing 737-86J	37755	N1796B
D-ABKN(3)	Boeing 737-86J	37756	
D-ABLA	Boeing 737-76J	36114	N1786B
D-ABMQ	Boeing 737-86J	37780	
D-ABMV	Boeing 737-86J	37785	
D-ABMW	Gulfstream 550	5336	N936GA
D-ABNE(2)	Airbus A320-214	2003	G-KKAZ, C-FZAZ, G-KKAZ, C-FZAZ, G-KKAZ, C-FZAZ, G-KKAZ, C-FZAZ, G-KKAZ, C-FZAZ, G-KKAZ, C-FZAZ, G-KKAZ, C-FZAZ, G-KKAZ, C-FZAZ, G-KKAZ, F-WWBN
D-ABNF(2)	Airbus A320-214	1961	G-SUEW, C-GUEW, G-SUEW, C-GUEW, G-SUEW, C-GUEW, G-SUEW, C-GUEW, G-SUEW, C-GUEW, G-SUEW, F-WWIX
D-ABNG	Airbus A320-214	4316	OE-LEC, D-AXAL
D-ABNH(2)	Airbus A320-214	1775	OE-IDF, PR-MHD, EC-JHJ, EI-LTE, EC-IEP, F-WWDL
D-ABNI(3)	Airbus A320-214	1717	OE-IDE, PR-MHC, EC-ICN, F-WWDC
D-ABNJ	Airbus A320-214	5522	OE-LER, D-AXAO
D-ABNK(2)	Airbus A320-214	1769	F-WTDO, B-6380, EC-JDK, 9H-ADY, F-WWDK
D-ABNL(2)	Airbus A320-214	1852	F-WTDP, B-6349, I-EEZC, F-WWIT
D-ABNM(2)	Airbus A320-214	6856	D-AXAW
D-ABNN(2)	Airbus A320-214	1889	OY-VKM, F-WWBV
D-ABNO(2)	Airbus A320-214	6831	D-AXAS
D-ABNP(2)	Bombardier BD-700-1A10 Global XRS	9339	VQ-BNP, C-GFRX, N112ZZ, C-FVGP
	(Res. 7.14)		
D-ABNQ	Airbus A320-214	6877	D-AXAZ
D-ABNR(2)	Airbus A320-214	6892	D-AUBC
D-ABNS(2)	Airbus A320-214	6902	D-AUBD
D-ABNT(2)	Airbus A320-214	2562	B-6259, F-WWIZ
D-ABNU	Airbus A320-214	2591	B-6260, F-WWDT
D-ABNV	Airbus A320-214	2606	B-6261, F-WWBR
D-ABNW	Airbus A320-214	2627	B-6262, F-WWDV
D-ABNX(2)	Airbus A320-214	6927	F-WWIF
D-ABNY(2)	Airbus A320-214	6966	D-AUBL
D-ABNZ(2)	Airbus A320-214	7224	D-AVVY
	(Stored, for China 9.16)		
D-ABOA	Boeing 757-330	29016	N757X
D-ABOB(2)	Boeing 757-330	29017	N6067B
D-ABOC(2)	Boeing 757-330	29015	N6069D
D-ABOE	Boeing 757-330	29012	N1012N
D-ABOF(2)	Boeing 757-330	29013	
D-ABOG(2)	Boeing 757-330	29014	N1786B
D-ABOH(2)	Boeing 757-330	30030	N1787B
D-ABOI	Boeing 757-330	29018	N1002R
D-ABOJ	Boeing 757-330	29019	
D-ABOK(2)	Boeing 757-330	29020	N1795B
D-ABOL(2)	Boeing 757-330	29021	
D-ABOM(2)	Boeing 757-330	29022	
D-ABON(2)	Boeing 757-330	29023	
D-ABQA	Bombardier DHC-8Q-402	4223	C-FTID
D-ABQB	Bombardier DHC-8Q-402	4226	C-FTUM
D-ABQC	Bombardier DHC-8Q-402	4231	C-FUCI
D-ABQD	Bombardier DHC-8Q-402	4234	C-FUCS
D-ABQE	Bombardier DHC-8Q-402	4239	C-FURQ
D-ABQF	Bombardier DHC-8Q-402	4245	C-FVGV
D-ABQG	Bombardier DHC-8Q-402	4250	C-FVUN
D-ABQH	Bombardier DHC-8Q-402	4256	C-FWGO
D-ABQI	Bombardier DHC-8Q-402	4264	C-FXIW
D-ABQJ	Bombardier DHC-8Q-402	4274	C-FYGN
D-ABQK	Bombardier DHC-8Q-402	4265	(D-AMHC), HB-JIK, C-GMRX, N511LX, C-FXJC
D-ABQL	Bombardier DHC-8Q-402	4184	(D-AMHA), HB-JIJ, C-GARX, N509LX, C-FNEI
D-ABQM(2)	Bombardier DHC-8Q-402	4119	N419KA, HK-4726, HL5251, C-FFCH
D-ABQN	Bombardier DHC-8Q-402	4124	C-FEUF, N464KA, HK-4725, HL5252, C-FFQF
D-ABQO	Bombardier DHC-8Q-402	4129	N129KA, HK-4727, HL5254, C-FGAJ
D-ABQP	Bombardier DHC-8Q-402	4137	C-FDLO, N137KA, HK-4724, HL5255, C-FHQL
D-ABQQ	Bombardier DHC-8Q-402	4198	HB-JGA, (D-AMHB), HB-JGA, C-FOKB
D-ABQR	Bombardier DHC-8Q-402	4538	C-FPTU
D-ABQS	Bombardier DHC-8Q-402	4539	
D-ABQT	Bombardier DHC-8Q-402	4541	
D-ABTA	Boeing 747-430	24285	
D-ABTK	Boeing 747-430	29871	(D-ABVI(2))
D-ABTL	Boeing 747-430	29872	(D-ABVG)
D-ABUA(2)	Boeing 767-330ER	26991	
D-ABUB(2)	Boeing 767-330ER	26987	
D-ABUC(2)	Boeing 767-330ER	26992	
D-ABUD(2)	Boeing 767-330ER	26983	
D-ABUE(2)	Boeing 767-330ER	26984	N1788B
D-ABUF(2)	Boeing 767-330ER	26985	
D-ABUH(2)	Boeing 767-330ER	26986	
D-ABUI (2)	Boeing 767-330ER	26988	
D-ABUK(2)	Boeing 767-343ER	30009	EI-CRM
D-ABUL(4)	Boeing 767-3B1ER	26259	EI-CRD, B-2565
D-ABUM(2)	Boeing 767-3B1ER	25170	EI-CRF, B-2566
D-ABUO(3)	Boeing 767-3Q8ER	29387	EI-RUY, EC-HSV
D-ABUP	Boeing 767-3Q8ER	30048	EI-RUZ, EC-HPU
D-ABUS	Boeing 767-38EER	30840	OO-JAP(2), N308MT, JA767F, N840MT, HL7595
D-ABUT	Boeing 767-3Q8ER	29383	EI-UNE, 5Y-KYY, EI-CRO
D-ABUZ	Boeing 767-330ER	25209	(N634TW), D-ABUZ
D-ABVL	Boeing 747-430	26425	N60659
D-ABVM(2)	Boeing 747-430	29101	(V8-AC2)
D-ABVN	Boeing 747-430	26427	
D-ABVO	Boeing 747-430	28086	
D-ABVP	Boeing 747-430	28284	
D-ABVR	Boeing 747-430	28285	
D-ABVS	Boeing 747-430	28286	
D-ABVT	Boeing 747-430	28287	
D-ABVU	Boeing 747-430	29492	
D-ABVW	Boeing 747-430	29493	

Reg	Type	Serial	Notes
D-ABVX	Boeing 747-430	29868	
D-ABVY	Boeing 747-430	29869	
D-ABVZ	Boeing 747-430	29870	
D-ABXA(2)	Airbus A330-223	288	HB-IQH, F-WWKK
D-ABXB(2)	Airbus A330-223	322	HB-IQQ, D-AIMD, F-WIHM, OO-SFT, F-WWYT
D-ABXC(2)	Airbus A330-223	665	I-EEZJ, F-WWKO
D-ABXD(2)	Airbus A330-223	822	EI-EZJ, I-EEZM, 4X-ABE, EC-KDF, (I-EEZM), F-WWKJ
D-ABXG	Airbus A330-223 (Res.2.16)	802	CS-TRX, EI-EZL, I-EEZL, F-WWYD
D-ABXP	Boeing 737-330	23874	
D-ABYA(2)	Boeing 747-830	37827	N5016R
D-ABYC(2)	Boeing 747-830	37828	
D-ABYD(2)	Boeing 747-830	37829	
D-ABYF(3)	Boeing 747-830	37830	
D-ABYG(3)	Boeing 747-830	37831	N5022E
D-ABYH(2)	Boeing 747-830	37832	
D-ABYI	Boeing 747-830	37833	
D-ABYJ(2)	Boeing 747-830	37834	
D-ABYK(2)	Boeing 747-830	37835	
D-ABYL(2)	Boeing 747-830	37836	
D-ABYM(2)	Boeing 747-830	37837	
D-ABYN(3)	Boeing 747-830	37838	
D-ABYO(2)	Boeing 747-830	37841	
D-ABYP(2)	Boeing 747-830	37839	
D-ABYQ(2)	Boeing 747-830	37840	
D-ABYR(2)	Boeing 747-830	37842	
D-ABYS(2)	Boeing 747-830	37843	
D-ABYT(2)	Boeing 747-830	37844	
D-ABYU(2)	Boeing 747-830	37845	
D-ABZA(2)	Airbus A320-216	3532	EI-DST, F-WWDY
D-ABZB(2)	Airbus A320-216	3515	EI-DSS, F-WWDP
D-ABZC(2)	Airbus A320-216	3502	EI-DSR, F-WWBR
D-ABZE(2)	Airbus A320-216	3464	EI-DSO, F-WWBM
D-ABZF(2)	Airbus A320-216	3482	EI-DSP, F-WWDM, (F-WWMA)
D-ABZH	Airbus A320-216 (Res. 9.10.14)	3343	EI-DSL, F-WWBO
D-ABZI(2)	Airbus A320-216	3328	EI-DSK, F-WWIX
D-ABZJ	Airbus A320-216	3295	EI-DSJ, F-WWDV
D-ABZK	Airbus A320-216	3213	EI-DSI, F-WWIU
D-ABZL(2)	Airbus A320-216	3178	EI-DSH, F-WWDS
D-ABZM	Airbus A320-216 (Res. 10.10.14)	3115	EI-DSG, F-WWIZ
D-ABZN	Airbus A320-216	3080	EI-DSF, F-WWIV
D-ACBN	Airbus A319-115X	3423	VP-CBN, F-WWBA, D-AVWD, (D-AVHD)
D-ACDE	Bombardier BD-700-1A11 Global 5000	9405	C-GEZJ(3)
D-ACKA(2)	Canadair CL-600-2D24 Regional Jet 900LR	15072	
D-ACKB(2)	Canadair CL-600-2D24 Regional Jet 900LR	15073	C-FJVT
D-ACKC	Canadair CL-600-2D24 Regional Jet 900LR	15078	
D-ACKD	Canadair CL-600-2D24 Regional Jet 900LR	15080	
D-ACKE	Canadair CL-600-2D24 Regional Jet 900LR	15081	
D-ACKF	Canadair CL-600-2D24 Regional Jet 900LR	15083	C-FJVR
D-ACKG	Canadair CL-600-2D24 Regional Jet 900LR	15084	C-GIAO
D-ACKH	Canadair CL-600-2D24 Regional Jet 900LR	15085	C-GICL
D-ACKI	Canadair CL-600-2D24 Regional Jet 900LR	15088	C-GIAP
D-ACKJ	Canadair CL-600-2D24 Regional Jet 900LR	15089	
D-ACKK	Canadair CL-600-2D24 Regional Jet 900LR	15094	
D-ACKL	Canadair CL-600-2D24 Regional Jet 900LR	15095	
D-ACNA(2)	Canadair CL-600-2D24 Regional Jet 900LR	15229	C-GZQA
D-ACNB	Canadair CL-600-2D24 Regional Jet 900LR	15230	C-GZQM
D-ACNC	Canadair CL-600-2D24 Regional Jet 900LR	15236	C-GIBO
D-ACND	Canadair CL-600-2D24 Regional Jet 900LR	15238	C-GIBT
D-ACNE	Canadair CL-600-2D24 Regional Jet 900LR	15241	C-GICL
D-ACNF	Canadair CL-600-2D24 Regional Jet 900LR	15243	C-GIAU
D-ACNG	Canadair CL-600-2D24 Regional Jet 900LR	15245	C-GZQF
D-ACNH	Canadair CL-600-2D24 Regional Jet 900LR	15247	C-GZQK
D-ACNI	Canadair CL-600-2D24 Regional Jet 900LR	15248	C-GHZV
D-ACNJ	Canadair CL-600-2D24 Regional Jet 900LR	15249	C-GZQX
D-ACNK	Canadair CL-600-2D24 Regional Jet 900LR	15251	C-GIBL
D-ACNL	Canadair CL-600-2D24 Regional Jet 900LR	15252	C-GZQA
D-ACNM	Canadair CL-600-2D24 Regional Jet 900LR	15253	C-GHZZ
D-ACNN	Canadair CL-600-2D24 Regional Jet 900LR	15254	C-GIAH
D-ACNO	Canadair CL-600-2D24 Regional Jet 900LR	15255	C-GIBN
D-ACNP	Canadair CL-600-2D24 Regional Jet 900LR	15259	C-GZQV
D-ACNQ	Canadair CL-600-2D24 Regional Jet 900LR	15260	C-GIBG
D-ACNR	Canadair CL-600-2D24 Regional Jet 900LR	15263	C-GIBT
D-ACNT	Canadair CL-600-2D24 Regional Jet 900LR	15264	C-GICB
D-ACNU	Canadair CL-600-2D24 Regional Jet 900LR	15267	C-GICP
D-ACNV	Canadair CL-600-2D24 Regional Jet 900LR	15268	C-GIAR
D-ACNW	Canadair CL-600-2D24 Regional Jet 900LR	15269	C-GIAU
D-ACNX	Canadair CL-600-2D24 Regional Jet 900LR	15270	C-GIAW
D-ADCL(2)	Gulfstream 550	5435	N435GA
D-ADCP	Embraer EMB-135BJ Legacy 600	14501067	PT-SES
D-ADDD(2)	Canadair CL-600-2B19 Regional Jet 200ER	7529	EC-HYG, C-GIXG, C-FMLI (Res. 12.5.15)
D-ADDI	Dassault Falcon 900DX	622	M-DADI, F-WWFD (Res. 7.12)
D-ADLD	Canadair CL-600-2B16 Challenger 604	5474	C-FBEM, C-FXCN, C-FXPB, N328FX, C-GLXM (Res. 8.9.15)
D-ADLR	Gulfstream 550 (For High Altitude Research)	5093	N593GA
D-ADNA	Airbus A319-133	1053	D-AVYN
D-ADSK(2)	Gulfstream 650	6143	N643GA
D-AEAA(3)	Airbus A300B4-622RF	743	EI-EYK, (TC-ACK), B-MAS, N221LF, B-18576, N88881, F-WWAH
D-AEAB(2)	Airbus A300B4-622RF	837	A6-HAZ, JA015D, F-WWAK
D-AEAC(2)	Airbus A300B4-622RF	602	N4602, JA8375, F-WWAT
D-AEAD(2)	Airbus A300B4-622RF	617	N2617, JA8376, F-WWAK
D-AEAE(2)	Airbus A300B4-622RF	753	N4753, JA8657, F-WWAK
D-AEAF(2)	Airbus A300B4-622RF	836	A6-SUL, JA014D, F-WWAF
D-AEAG	Airbus A300B4-622RF	621	N2621, JA8377, F-WWAA
D-AEAH(2)	Airbus A300B4-622RF	783	N5783, JA011D, F-WWAK
D-AEAI(2)	Airbus A300B4-622RF	637	N3740, JA8558, F-WWAX
D-AEAJ	Airbus A300B4-622R	641	(D-AEAI)(1), N5041, JA8550, F-WWAM
D-AEAK	Airbus A300B4-622RF	670	N2670, JA8561, F-WWAD
D-AEAL	Airbus A300B4-622RF	679	N4679, JA8562, F-WWAL
D-AEAM(2)	Airbus A300B4-622RF	797	A6-NIN, JA012D, F-WWAQ
D-AEAN(2)	Airbus A300B4-622RF	703	JA8564, F-WWAO
D-AEAO	Airbus A300B4-622RF	711	N7151, JA8565, F-WWAE
D-AEAP	Airbus A300B4-622RF	724	N1724, JA8527, F-WWAQ
D-AEAQ	Airbus A300B4-622RF	729	N3729, JA8529, F-WWAM
D-AEAR	Airbus A300B4-622RF	730	N4730, JA8566, F-WWAV
D-AEAS	Airbus A300B4-622RF	737	N4737, JA8573, F-WWAF
D-AEAT	Airbus A300B4-622RF	740	N3637, EI-EOT, JA8574, F-WWAG
D-AEBB	Embraer EMB-190-200LR	19000316	PT-TXE
D-AEBC	Embraer EMB-190-200LR	19000320	PT-TXI
D-AEBE	Embraer EMB-190-200LR	19000350	PT-XQQ
D-AEBG	Embraer EMB-190-200LR	19000423	PT-TBZ
D-AEBH	Embraer EMB-190-200LR	19000447	PT-TJI
D-AEBP	Embraer EMB-190-200LR	19000553	PT-TBZ
D-AEBQ	Embraer EMB-190-200LR	19000555	PT-TDJ
D-AEBR	Embraer EMB-190-200LR	19000558	PT-TDN
D-AEBS	Embraer EMB-190-200LR	19000565	PT-TDU
D-AECA	Embraer EMB-190-100LR	19000327	PT-TXP
D-AECB	Embraer EMB-190-100LR	19000332	PT-TXS
D-AECC	Embraer EMB-190-100LR	19000333	PT-TXT
D-AECD	Embraer EMB-190-100LR	19000337	PT-TXW
D-AECE	Embraer EMB-190-100LR	19000341	PT-XQI
D-AECF	Embraer EMB-190-100LR	19000359	PT-XNA
D-AECG(2)	Embraer EMB-190-100LR	19000368	PT-XNG
D-AECH	Embraer EMB-190-100LR	19000376	PT-XNM
D-AECI	Embraer EMB-190-100LR	19000381	PT-XNQ
D-AEMA	Embraer EMB-190-200LR	19000290	PT-TZE
D-AEMB	Embraer EMB-190-200LR	19000297	PT-TZL
D-AEMC	Embraer EMB-190-200LR	19000300	PT-TZO
D-AEMD	Embraer EMB-190-200LR	19000305	PT-TZT
D-AEME	Embraer EMB-190-200LR	19000308	PT-TZW
D-AENT	Canadair CL-600-2B19 CRJ-200LR	7534	N972EV, N65BR, C-FMMT
D-AERO(2)	Embraer EMB-135BJ Legacy 650	14501216	PR-LHD
D-AERQ	Airbus A330-322	127	F-WWKO
D-AETD	Dassault Falcon 900LX (Res. 5.14)	247	9H-GMT, F-WWFD
D-AEUK	Canadair CL-600-2B16 Challenger IV	5632	N604CG, C-GLXU
D-AEWC	Airbus A320-214	7012	D-AUBU
D-AEWD(2)	Airbus A320-214	7019	D-AVVR
D-AEWE(2)	Airbus A320-214	7056	D-AVVC
D-AEWF(2)	Airbus A320-214	7087	D-AVVH
D-AEWG(2)	Airbus A320-214	7121	D-AVVM
D-AEWH(2)	Airbus A320-214	7148	
D-AEWI(2)	Airbus A320-214	7210	D-AVVW
D-AFWJ(2)	Airbus A320-214	7216	D-AVVX
D-AEWK(2)	Airbus A320-214	7261	D-AXAC
D-AEWL(2)	Airbus A320-214	7263	D-AXAD
D-AEWM(2)	Airbus A320-214	7259	F-WWIO
D-AEWN(2)	Airbus A320-214	7393	D-AXAP
D-AEWO(2)	Airbus A320-214	7394	
D-AEWP(2)	Airbus A320-214	7377	D-AXAO
D-AEWQ(2)	Airbus A320-214	7398	
D-AEWR	Airbus A320-214	7412	
D-AEWS	Airbus A320-214	7439	
D-AEWT	Airbus A320-214	7534	
D-AEWU	Airbus A320-214	7513	
D-AEWV	Airbus A320-214	7545	
D-AEWW	Airbus A320-214	7615	
D-AFAA	Canadair CL-600-2B16 Challenger 604	5397	A6-PJA, VP-BJH, HB-IIV, VP-BCB, N605PA, C-GLXY
D-AFAB(2)	Canadair CL-600-2B16 Challenger 604	5378	D-ASTS(2), C-GDBZ
D-AFAC	Canadair CL-600-2B16 Challenger 604	5416	G-FTSL, N161MD, N161MN, N161MM, N604MG, C-GLXQ
D-AFAD	Canadair CL-600-2B16 Challenger 604	5348	N604NC, N881TW, C-GLWR
D-AFAI	Canadair CL-600-2B16 Challenger 604	5366	N906TF, C-GJFC, N604DD, RP-C1937, N604DD, C-066, N604DD, C-GLXO
D-AFAM	Bombardier BD-700-1A10 Global Express	9028	VP-BSE, N717TF, N117TF, C-GEZY
D-AFAU	Bombardier BD-700-1A10 Global Express	9013	LX-GEX, C-GZSM, HB-IUR, C-GDXU
D-AFPR	Dassault Falcon 7X	160	F-WWUQ
D-AFUN	Embraer EMB-135BJ Legacy 650	14501168	N650EE, PT-TFV
D-AGEC(2)	Boeing 737-76J	36118	(D-ABLE)
D-AGEL	Boeing 737-75B	28110	N1791B
D-AGEN	Boeing 737-75B	28100	N1786B
D-AGEP	Boeing 737-75B	28102	N5573B
D-AGEQ	Boeing 737-75B	28103	
D-AGER	Boeing 737-75B	28107	N1002R
D-AGES	Boeing 737-75B	28108	
D-AGET	Boeing 737-75B	28109	
D-AGEU	Boeing 737-75B	28104	
D-AGEX(2)	Bombardier BD-700-1A10 Global Express	9044	OE-IGS, I-MOVE, N700BP, C-GFXX
D-AGJP	Bombardier BD-700-1A10 Global 6000	9487	(D-ALUK), C-GMXY(3)
D-AGPH	Fokker F.28-0100	11308	PH-CXH, D-AGPH, PH-CXH, N865US, PH-EZI
D-AGVA	Gulfstream 550	5408	OH-GVA, N908GA
D-AGVI	Gulfstream 450	4243	OH-GIV, N943GA
D-AGVS	Gulfstream 450	4113	N913GA
D-AGWA(3)	Airbus A319-132	2813	D-AVWM
D-AGWB(2)	Airbus A319-132	2833	D-AVXI
D-AGWC(2)	Airbus A319-132	2976	D-AVYX
D-AGWD(2)	Airbus A319-132	3011	D-AVWB
D-AGWE(2)	Airbus A319-132	3128	D-AVXB
D-AGWF(2)	Airbus A319-132	3172	D-AVXG
D-AGWG	Airbus A319-132	3193	D-AVYS
D-AGWH	Airbus A319-132	3352	D-AVYX
D-AGWI	Airbus A319-132	3358	D-AVYZ
D-AGWJ	Airbus A319-132	3375	D-AVWB
D-AGWK	Airbus A319-132	3500	D-AVYW
D-AGWL	Airbus A319-132	3534	D-AVWB
D-AGWM(2)	Airbus A319-132	3839	D-AVYR
D-AGWN(2)	Airbus A319-132	3841	D-AVYS
D-AGWO	Airbus A319-132	4166	D-AVWH
D-AGWP	Airbus A319-132	4227	D-AVYK
D-AGWQ	Airbus A319-132	4256	D-AVYP
D-AGWR	Airbus A319-132	4285	D-AVWS
D-AGWS	Airbus A319-132	4998	D-AVYG
D-AGWT	Airbus A319-132	5043	D-AVYL
D-AGWU	Airbus A319-132	5457	D-AVYL
D-AGWV	Airbus A319-132	5467	D-AVYM
D-AGWW	Airbus A319-132	5535	D-AVYN,
D-AGWX	Airbus A319-132	5569	D-AVYO
D-AGWY	Airbus A319-132	5941	D-AVWG
D-AGWZ	Airbus A319-132	5978	D-AVWG
D-AHER(2)	Dassault Falcon 900EX	78	F-CXHG, D-AGSI, G-DAEX, F-WWFR
D-AHEX	Dassault Falcon 900LX	266	VP-CHG, F-WWFW
D-AHFT	Boeing 737-8K5	30413	N1015B
D-AHFV	Boeing 737-8K5	30415	

Reg	Type	c/n	Previous identities
D-AHFW	Boeing 737-8K5	30882	N1786B
D-AHFZ	Boeing 737-8K5	30883	
D-AHLK(3)	Boeing 737-8K5	35143	C-FTLK, D-AHLK, C-FTLK, D-AHLK, C-FTLK, D-AHLK
D-AHLO(2)	Boeing 737-4K5	24128	
D-AHOI(3)	Embraer EMB-135BJ Legacy 650	14501171	N671EE, (M-IRON), PT-TJX
D-AHOX	Embraer EMB-135BJ Legacy 650	14501213	PR-PIG
D-AHRN(2)	Dassault Falcon 900EX	96	HB-JSY, N900ZA, N93ZR, F-WWFP
D-AHXE	Boeing 737-7K5	35135	
D-AHXF	Boeing 737-7K5	35136	
D-AHXG	Boeing 737-7K5	35140	
D-AHXJ	Boeing 737-7K5	35277	
D-AIAA(2)	Airbus A321-211	1607	D-ALSD, I-PEKN, D-AVZN
D-AIAC(2)	Airbus A321-211	5969	D-AZAN
D-AIAD(2)	Airbus A321-211	6053	D-AVZR
D-AIAE(2)	Airbus A321-211	6376	D-AVXS
D-AIAF(2)	Airbus A321-211	6459	D-AVZF
D-AIAG	Airbus A321-211	6590	D-AVXJ
D-AIAH(2)	Airbus A321-211	6615	D-AVXP
D-AIBA(3)	Airbus A319-112	4141	D-AVWG
D-AIBB(3)	Airbus A319-112	4182	D-AVWK
D-AIBC(3)	Airbus A319-112	4332	D-AVXF
D-AIBD(3)	Airbus A319-112	4445	D-AVYC
D-AIBE(2)	Airbus A319-112	4511	D-AVYH
D-AIBF(3)	Airbus A319-112	4796	D-AVYZ
D-AIBG	Airbus A319-112	4841	D-AVWF
D-AIBH(2)	Airbus A319-112	5239	D-AVYA
D-AIBI	Airbus A319-112	5284	D-AVYY
D-AIBJ	Airbus A319-112	5293	D-AVWA
D-AICA(2)	Airbus A320-212	774	F-WWDN
D-AICC(2)	Airbus A320-212	809	F-WWIE
D-AICD(2)	Airbus A320-212	884	F-WWDE
D-AICE	Airbus A320-212	894	F-WWDI
D-AICF(2)	Airbus A320-212	905	F-WWDP
D-AICG	Airbus A320-212	957	F-WWBE
D-AICH(2)	Airbus A320-212	971	F-WWBY
D-AICK(2)	Airbus A320-212	1416	F-WWDZ
D-AICL	Airbus A320-212	1437	F-WWBG
D-AIDA(3)	Airbus A321-231	4360	D-AVZM
D-AIDB(2)	Airbus A321-231	4545	D-AVZZ
D-AIDC(2)	Airbus A321-231	4560	D-AZAB
D-AIDD(2)	Airbus A321-231	4585	D-AVZC
D-AIDE(2)	Airbus A321-231	4607	D-AZAK
D-AIDF(2)	Airbus A321-231	4626	D-AZAO
D-AIDG(2)	Airbus A321-231	4672	D-AZAF
D-AIDH(2)	Airbus A321-231	4710	D-AVZD
D-AIDI(2)	Airbus A321-231	4753	D-AVZI
D-AIDJ	Airbus A321-231	4792	D-AVZO
D-AIDK(2)	Airbus A321-231	4819	D-AVZQ
D-AIDL(2)	Airbus A321-231	4881	D-AVZC
D-AIDM(2)	Airbus A321-231	4916	D-AVZH
D-AIDN(3)	Airbus A321-231	4976	D-AZAI
D-AIDO	Airbus A321-231	4994	D-AZAJ
D-AIDP	Airbus A321-231	5049	D-AZAQ
D-AIDQ	Airbus A321-231	5028	D-AZAM
D-AIDT	Airbus A321-231	5087	D-AZAU
D-AIDU	Airbus A321-231	5186	D-AVZL
D-AIDV	Airbus A321-231	5413	D-AVZM
D-AIDW	Airbus A321-231	6415	D-AZAO
D-AIDX	Airbus A321-231	6451	D-AVZD
D-AIFA	Airbus A340-313X	352	F-WWJU
D-AIFC	Airbus A340-313X	379	F-WWJJ
D-AIFD	Airbus A340-313X	390	F-WWJE
D-AIFE	Airbus A340-313X	434	F-WWJT
D-AIFF	Airbus A340-313X	447	F-WWJB
D-AIGL	Airbus A340-313X	135	F-WWJS
D-AIGM	Airbus A340-313X	158	F-WWJN
D-AIGN	Airbus A340-313X	213	F-WWJM
D-AIGO	Airbus A340-313X	233	F-WWJJ
D-AIGP	Airbus A340-313X	252	F-WWJM
D-AIGS	Airbus A340-313X	297	F-WWJK
D-AIGT	Airbus A340-313X	304	F-WWJY
D-AIGU	Airbus A340-313X	321	F-WWJM
D-AIGV	Airbus A340-313X	325	F-WWJN
D-AIGW	Airbus A340-313X	327	F-WWJO
D-AIGX	Airbus A340-313X	354	F-WWJV
D-AIGY	Airbus A340-313X	335	F-WWJS
D-AIGZ	Airbus A340-313X	347	F-WWJT
D-AIHA	Airbus A340-642	482	F-WWCS
D-AIHB	Airbus A340-642	517	F-WWCR
D-AIHC	Airbus A340-642	523	F-WWCV
D-AIHD	Airbus A340-642	537	F-WWCZ
D-AIHE	Airbus A340-642	540	F-WWCF
D-AIHF	Airbus A340-642	543	F-WWCE
D-AIHH	Airbus A340-642	566	F-WWCJ
D-AIHI	Airbus A340-642	569	F-WWCB
D-AIHK	Airbus A340-642	580	F-WWCN
D-AIHL	Airbus A340-642	583	F-WWCQ
D-AIHM	Airbus A340-642	762	F-WWCI
D-AIHN	Airbus A340-642	763	F-WWCJ
D-AIHO	Airbus A340-642	767	F-WWCN
D-AIHP	Airbus A340-642	771	F-WWCQ
D-AIHQ	Airbus A340-642	790	F-WWCE
D-AIHR	Airbus A340-642	794	F-WWCF
D-AIHS	Airbus A340-642	812	F-WWCX
D-AIHT	Airbus A340-642	846	F-WWCH
D-AIHU	Airbus A340-642	848	F-WWCI
D-AIHV	Airbus A340-642	897	F-WWTI
D-AIHW	Airbus A340-642	972	F-WWCL
D-AIHX	Airbus A340-642	981	F-WWCN
D-AIHY	Airbus A340-642	987	F-WWCQ
D-AIHZ	Airbus A340-642	1005	F-WWCR
D-AIJW	Airbus A310-324 (Wfu, derelict)	501	VT-EVE, 9V-STS(1), F-WWCB
D-AIKA(2)	Airbus A330-343X	570	F-WWYV
D-AIKB	Airbus A330-343X	576	F-WWKN
D-AIKC	Airbus A330-343X	579	F-WWKG
D-AIKD	Airbus A330-343X	629	F-WWYF
D-AIKE	Airbus A330-343X	636	F-WWYL
D-AIKF	Airbus A330-343X	642	F-WWKV
D-AIKG	Airbus A330-343X	645	F-WWKE
D-AIKH	Airbus A330-343X	648	F-WWKG
D-AIKI	Dairbus A330-343X	687	F-WWYI
D-AIKJ	Airbus A330-343X	701	F-WWKD
D-AIKK	Airbus A330-343X	896	F-WWYX
D-AIKL	Airbus A330-343X	905	F-WWYC
D-AIKM	Airbus A330-343X	913	F-WWYJ
D-AIKN	Airbus A330-343X	922	F-WWYY
D-AIKO	Airbus A330-343X	989	F-WWKJ
D-AIKP(2)	Airbus A330-343X	1292	F-WWYQ
D-AIKQ	Airbus A330-343X	1305	F-WWYV
D-AIKR	Airbus A330-343X	1314	F-WWKD
D-AIKS	Airbus A330-343X	1497	F-WWTQ
D-AILA	Airbus A319-114	609	D-AVYF
D-AILB	Airbus A319-114	610	D-AVYG
D-AILC	Airbus A319-114	616	D-AVYI
D-AILD	Airbus A319-114	623	D-AVYL
D-AILE	Airbus A319-114	627	D-AVYO
D-AILF	Airbus A319-114	636	D-AVYS
D-AILH	Airbus A319-114	641	D-AVYV
D-AILI	Airbus A319-114	651	D-AVYY
D-AILK	Airbus A319-114	679	D-AVYG(2)
D-AILL	Airbus A319-114	689	D-AVYL(2)
D-AILM	Airbus A319-114	694	D-AVYR(2)
D-AILN	Airbus A319-114	700	D-AVYU(2)
D-AILP	Airbus A319-114	717	D-AVYA
D-AILR	Airbus A319-114	723	D-AVYD(3)
D-AILS	Airbus A319-114	729	D-AVYF(3)
D-AILT	Airbus A319-114	738	D-AVYN(3)
D-AILU	Airbus A319-114	744	D-AVYI (3)
D-AILW	Airbus A319-114	853	D-AVYO(4)
D-AILX	Airbus A319-114	860	D-AVYS(4)
D-AILY(2)	Airbus A319-114	875	D-AVYC(5)
D-AIMA(2)	Airbus A380-841	038	F-WWSH
D-AIMB(2)	Airbus A380-841	041	F-WWAF
D-AIMC(2)	Airbus A380-841	044	F-WWAJ
D-AIMD(2)	Airbus A380-841	048	F-WWAK
D-AIME(2)	Airbus A380-841	061	F-WWAV
D-AIMF(2)	Airbus A380-841	066	F-WWSN
D-AIMG(2)	Airbus A380-841	069	F-WWSO
D-AIMH	Airbus A380-841	070	F-WWSG
D-AIMI	Airbus A380-841	072	F-WWSR
D-AIMJ	Airbus A380-841	073	F-WWSP
D-AIMK	Airbus A380-841	146	F-WWAO
D-AIML	Airbus A380-841	149	F-WWSX
D-AIMM(6)	Airbus A380-841	175	F-WWSP
D-AIMN	Airbus A380-841	177	F-WWSR
D-AINA	Airbus A320-271N	6801	D-AXAQ
D-AINB	Airbus A320-271N	6864	D-AXAX
D-AINC	Airbus A320-271N	6920	D-AUBG
D-AIND(2)	Airbus A320-271N	7078	D-AVVG
D-AINE	Airbus A320-271N	7103	D-AVVJ
D-AIPA	Airbus A320-211	069	F-WWII
D-AIPB	Airbus A320-211	070	F-WWIJ
D-AIPC	Airbus A320-211	071	F-WWIO
D-AIPD	Airbus A320-211	072	F-WWIP
D-AIPE	Airbus A320-211	078	F-WWIU
D-AIPF	Airbus A320-211	083	F-WWDE
D-AIPH	Airbus A320-211	086	F-WWDJ
D-AIPK	Airbus A320-211	093	F-WWDQ
D-AIPL	Airbus A320-211	094	7T-VKO, D-AIPL, F-WWDR
D-AIPM	Airbus A320-211	104	F-WWIG
D-AIPP	Airbus A320-211	110	F-WWID
D-AIPR	Airbus A320-211	111	F-WWIE
D-AIPS	Airbus A320-211	116	F-WWIK
D-AIPT	Airbus A320-211	117	F-WWIL
D-AIPU	Airbus A320-211	135	F-WWDB
D-AIPW	Airbus A320-211	137	F-WWDD
D-AIPY	Airbus A320-211	161	F-WWIA
D-AIPZ	Airbus A320-211	162	F-WWDS
D-AIQA	Airbus A320-211	172	F-WWIK
D-AIQB	Airbus A320-211	200	F-WWDJ
D-AIQC	Airbus A320-211	201	F-WWDL
D-AIQD	Airbus A320-211	202	F-WWDM
D-AIQE	Airbus A320-211	209	F-WWDY
D-AIQF	Airbus A320-211	216	F-WWDR
D-AIQH	Airbus A320-211	217	F-WWDS
D-AIQK	Airbus A320-211	218	F-WWDX
D-AIQL	Airbus A320-211	267	F-WWDY
D-AIQM	Airbus A320-211	268	F-WWIB
D-AIQN	Airbus A320-211	269	F-WWIC
D-AIQP	Airbus A320-211	346	F-WWDX
D-AIQR	Airbus A320-211	382	F-WWIZ
D-AIQS	Airbus A320-211	401	F-WWDO
D-AIQT	Airbus A320-211	1337	F-WWDO
D-AIQU	Airbus A320-211	1365	F-WWIG
D-AIQW	Airbus A320-211	1367	F-WWIH
D-AIRA	Airbus A321-131	458	F-WWIQ
D-AIRB	Airbus A321-131	468	F-WWIS
D-AIRC	Airbus A321-131	473	D-AVZC
D-AIRD	Airbus A321-131	474	D-AVZD
D-AIRE	Airbus A321-131	484	D-AVZF
D-AIRF	Airbus A321-131	493	D-AVZH
D-AIRH	Airbus A321-131	412	D-AVZA, F-WWIC
D-AIRK	Airbus A321-131	502	D-AVZL
D-AIRL	Airbus A321-131	505	D-AVZM
D-AIRM	Airbus A321-131	518	D-AVZT
D-AIRN	Airbus A321-131	560	D-AVZK(2)
D-AIRO	Airbus A321-131	563	D-AVZN(2)
D-AIRP	Airbus A321-131	564	D-AVZL(2)
D-AIRR	Airbus A321-131	567	D-AVZM(2)
D-AIRS	Airbus A321-131	595	D-AVZX(2)
D-AIRT	Airbus A321-131	652	D-AVZI (3)
D-AIRU	Airbus A321-131	692	D-AVZT(3)
D-AIRW	Airbus A321-131	699	D-AVZY(3)
D-AIRX	Airbus A321-131	887	D-AVZI (5)
D-AIRY	Airbus A321-131	901	D-AVZK(5)
D-AISB	Airbus A321-231	1080	D-AVZP
D-AISC	Airbus A321-231	1161	D-AVZG
D-AISD	Airbus A321-231	1188	F-WWDD, D-AVZJ
D-AISE	Airbus A321-231	1214	D-AVZS
D-AISF	Airbus A321-231	1260	D-AVZI
D-AISG	Airbus A321-231	1273	D-AVZU
D-AISH	Airbus A321-231	3265	F-WWBS
D-AISI	Airbus A321-231	3339	D-AVZD
D-AISJ	Airbus A321-231	3360	D-AVZF
D-AISK	Airbus A321-231	3387	D-AVZO
D-AISL	Airbus A321-231	3434	D-AVZD
D-AISN	Airbus A321-231	3592	D-AZAA
D-AISO	Airbus A321-231	3625	D-AVZH
D-AISP	Airbus A321-231	3864	D-AVZK

Registration	Type	MSN	Previous identities
D-AISQ	Airbus A321-231	3936	D-AZAF
D-AISR	Airbus A321-231	3987	D-AZAN
D-AIST	Airbus A321-231	4005	D-AVZD
D-AISU	Airbus A321-231	4016	D-AVZF
D-AISV	Airbus A321-231	4047	D-AZAG
D-AISW	Airbus A321-231	4054	D-AZAR
D-AISX	Airbus A321-231	4073	D-AVZR
D-AISZ	Airbus A321-231	4085	D-AVZW
D-AIUA	Airbus A320-214	5935	D-AUBI
D-AIUB	Airbus A320-214	5972	D-AUBN
D-AIUC	Airbus A320-214	6006	D-AUBV
D-AIUD	Airbus A320-214	6033	D-AXAC
D-AIUE	Airbus A320-214	6092	D-AXAO
D-AIUF	Airbus A320-214	6141	D-AXAZ
D-AIUG	Airbus A320-214	6202	D-AVVH
D-AIUH	Airbus A320-214	6225	D-AVVM
D-AIUI	Airbus A320-214	6265	D-AVVS
D-AIUJ	Airbus A320-214	6301	D-AXAK
D-AIUK	Airbus A320-214	6423	D-AXAQ
D-AIUL	Airbus A320-214	6521	D-AXAZ
D-AIUM	Airbus A320-214	6577	D-AVVX
D-AIUN	Airbus A320-214	6549	D-AVVH
D-AIUO	Airbus A320-214	6636	D-AVVV
D-AIUP	Airbus A320-214	6807	D-AEWX, (OE-LCA(2)), (D-AIUP), D-AXAR
D-AIUR	Airbus A320-214	6947	D-AUBJ
D-AIUS	Airbus A320-214	6985	D-AUBQ
D-AIUS	Airbus A320-214	7024	D-AUBV
D-AIUT	Airbus A320-214	7115	D-AVVL
D-AIUU	Airbus A320-214	7158	D-AVVN
D-AIUV	Airbus A320-214	7174	D-AVVU
D-AIUW	Airbus A320-214	7251	F-WWBB
D-AIUX	Airbus A320-214	7256	F-WWBY
D-AIUY	Airbus A320-214	7355	D-AXAM
D-AIXA	Airbus A350-941	074	
D-AIXB	Airbus A350-941	080	
D-AIXC	Airbus A350-941	087	
D-AIZA	Airbus A320-214	4097	D-AVVF
D-AIZB	Airbus A320-214	4120	D-AVVV
D-AIZC	Airbus A320-214	4153	D-AVVL
D-AIZD	Airbus A320-214	4191	D-AVVD
D-AIZE	Airbus A320-214	4261	D-AXAC
D-AIZF	Airbus A320-214	4289	D-AXAF
D-AIZG	Airbus A320-214	4324	D-AXAO
D-AIZH(2)	Airbus A320-214	4363	D-AXAW
D-AIZI(2)	Airbus A320-214	4398	D-AVVL
D-AIZJ	Airbus A320-214	4449	D-AVVM
D-AIZK	Airbus A320-214	5122	D-AVVA
D-AIZM	Airbus A320-214	5203	D-AVVR
D-AIZN	Airbus A320-214	5425	D-AVVJ
D-AIZO	Airbus A320-214	5441	D-AVVP
D-AIZP	Airbus A320-214	5487	D-AXAA
D-AIZQ	Airbus A320-214	5497	D-AXAE
D-AIZR	Airbus A320-214	5525	D-AXAP
D-AIZS	Airbus A320-214	5557	D-AXAZ
D-AIZT	Airbus A320-214	5601	D-AUBL
D-AIZU	Airbus A320-214	5635	D-AUBR
D-AIZV	Airbus A320-214	5658	D-AUBY
D-AIZW	Airbus A320-214	5694	D-AVVH
D-AIZX	Airbus A320-214	5741	D-AVVT
D-AIZY	Airbus A320-214	5769	D-AVVX
D-AIZZ	Airbus A320-214	5831	D-AXAQ
D-AJAN	Canadair CL-600-2B16 Challenger 605	5798	VP-CBV, A7-RZA, N605RZ, C-FXQX
D-AJET(2)	Embraer EMB-135BJ Legacy 650	14501166	PT-TFK
D-AJOY	Canadair CL-600-2B19 Challenger 850	8069	A6-BNH, VP-BNH, C-FMGV
D-AKAT(2)	Embraer EMB-135BJ Legacy 600	14501038	(D-AFSD), N916LX, PT-SZH
D-AKNF	Airbus A319-112	0646	(I-LHKA), D-AVYB
D-AKNG	Airbus A319-112	0654	(I-LHKB), D-AVYX
D-AKNH	Airbus A319-112	0794	(I-LHKC), D-AVYD
D-AKNI	Airbus A319-112	1016	(I-LHKD), D-AVYK
D-AKNJ	Airbus A319-112	1172	(I-LHKE), D-AVWF
D-AKNK(2)	Airbus A319-112	1077	N718UW, D-AVWI
D-AKNL	Airbus A319-112	1084	N719US, D-AVWK
D-AKNM	Airbus A319-112	1089	N720US, D-AVYC
D-AKNN	Airbus A319-112	1136	N726US, D-AVYM
D-AKNO	Airbus A319-112	1147	N727UW, D-AVWI
D-AKNP	Airbus A319-112	1155	N728UW, D-AVYS
D-AKNQ	Airbus A319-112	1170	N729US, D-AVWQ
D-AKNR	Airbus A319-112	1209	N736US, D-AVYI
D-AKNS	Airbus A319-112	1277	N743UW, D-AVWJ
D-AKNT	Airbus A319-112	2607	D-AVXQ
D-AKNU	Airbus A319-112	2628	D-AVWB
D-AKNV	Airbus A319-112	2632	D-AVWE
D-ALAE(2)	Airbus A310-324	669	N819FD, VT-AIG(2), N230BA, 9V-STB, F-WWCC
D-ALAN(3)	Lockheed L-1649A-98 Starliner	1018	N7316C
D-ALCA	McDonnell-Douglas MD-11F	48781	N9020Q
D-ALCB	McDonnell-Douglas MD-11F	48782	N9166N
D-ALCC	McDonnell-Douglas MD-11F	48783	
D-ALCD	McDonnell-Douglas MD-11F	48784	
D-ALCE	McDonnell-Douglas MD-11F	48785	
D-ALCF	McDonnell-Douglas MD-11F	48798	
D-ALCG	McDonnell-Douglas MD-11F	48799	
D-ALCH	McDonnell-Douglas MD-11F	48801	
D-ALCI	McDonnell-Douglas MD-11F	48800	
D-ALCJ	McDonnell-Douglas MD-11F	48802	N9166N
D-ALCK	McDonnell-Douglas MD-11F	48803	
D-ALCL	McDonnell-Douglas MD-11F	48804	
D-ALCM	McDonnell-Douglas MD-11F	48805	N6069R
D-ALCN	McDonnell-Douglas MD-11F	48806	
D-ALEC(2)	Boeing 757-236SF	22175	OO-DLQ, G-BIKD
D-ALED	Boeing 757-236SF	22179	OO-DLP, G-BIKH, (G-BIKI)
D-ALEE	Boeing 757-236SF	22183	OO-DPB, G-BIKL, (G-BIKM)
D-ALEG	Boeing 757-236SF	23398	OO-DPO, G-BIKT
D-ALEH	Boeing 757-236SF	23492	OO-DPK, G-BIKW
D-ALEK	Boeing 757-236SF	23533	OO-DPN, G-BIKY
D-ALEN	Boeing 757-2Q8SF	29380	N380DH, VQ-BJK, N380RM, N405JS, N380RM, N1795B, N1799B
D-ALEO(2)	Boeing 757-2Q8SF	29443	N293DH, VQ-BDT, N763MX, N406JS, N763MX
D-ALEP	Boeing 757-2Q8SF	30046	N346DH, VQ-BHR, OH-LBV, N60668
D-ALEQ	Boeing 757-2Q8SF	26332	N332DH, VQ-BAK, N401JS, N101LF, LV-WMH
D-ALER(3)	Boeing 757-2Q8SF	27351	N273DH, VQ-BAL, N403JS, N764MX, N809AM, N756AT
D-ALES	Boeing 757-2Q8SF	29442	N294DH, VQ-BBU, N762MX, (N459JS), N762MX
D-ALEX(2)	Airbus A319-115CJ	5963	D-AVWF
D-ALFA(2)	Boeing 777-FBT	41674	
D-ALFB	Boeing 777-FBT	41675	
D-ALFC	Boeing 777-FBT	41676	
D-ALFD	Boeing 777-FBT	41677	
D-ALFE	Boeing 777-FBT	41678	
D-ALFX	Airbus A318-112CJ	4878	VP-BKG, F-WHUM, D-AUAC
D-ALIK	Canadair CL-600-2B19 Challenger 850	8066	G-SHAL, C-FLBV, (D-AKSA), C-FLBV, D-AMAC, C-FMML, C-FMML
D-ALIL	Dassault Falcon 7X	179	F-WWVM
D-ALIN(2)	BAe.146-Series 300	E-3142	EI-DEW, G-UKAC, G-5-142
D-ALOA(3)	Embraer EMB-135BJ Legacy 650	14501223	PR-LKS
D-ALPA	Airbus A330-223	403	F-WWKO
D-ALPB	Airbus A330-223	432	F-WWYG
D-ALPC	Airbus A330-223	444	F-WWKD
D-ALPD	Airbus A330-223	454	F-WWKG
D-ALPE	Airbus A330-223	469	F-WWKO
D-ALPF	Airbus A330-223	476	F-WWKT
D-ALPG	Airbus A330-223	493	F-WWKI
D-ALPH	Airbus A330-223	739	F-WWYD
D-ALPI	Airbus A330-223	828	F-WWKI
D-ALPJ	Airbus A330-223	911	F-WWYA
D-ALSA	Airbus A321-211	1629	D-AVZC
D-ALSB	Airbus A321-211	1994	D-AVZR
D-ALSC	Airbus A321-211	2005	D-AVXI
D-ALXX	Airbus A319-115CJ	4470	9H-ALX, D-AVYG
D-AMAJ	Bae.146-Series 200	E-2028	G-BZBA, G-DEBA, N171US, N351PS (Painted as D-NICE and used as a de-icing trainer at Frankfurt)
D-AMAX(3)	BAe.146-Series 300	E-3157	EI-DEX, G-UKID, G-6-157
D-AMGL	BAe.146-Series 200	E-2055	G-CBFL, SE-DRF, N697A, N145AC, G-5-055, N145AC, G-5-055
D-AMIA	Embraer EMB-135BJ Legacy 650	14501165	G-TCMC, N665PF, N912JC, PT-TFP
D-AMIB	Canadair CL-600-2B16 Challenger 604	5618	OE-IAA, D-ASIX, VP-CMB, C-FEYZ, C-GLXF (Res. 6.15)
D-AMOR(4)	Canadair CL-600-2B16 Challenger 605	5918	VP-BOR, C-GRYZ (Res. 9.9.15)
D-AMSC	Canadair CL-600-2B16 Challenger 604	5464	I-IRCS, (OE-IRJ), N326FX, C-GLWR
D-ANFE(2)	Aérospatiale/Alenia ATR-72-202	272	(D-ANFD)(2), SP-LFC(2), F-WWEN
D-ANGB	Canadair CL-600-2B16 Challenger 604	5541	N329FX, C-GLXO
D-ANMB	Bombardier BD-700-1A10 Global 6000	9723	C-FJXR
D-ANTE	Gulfstream V	572	OE-IIS, HB-IIS, P4-FAZ, N472GA, (N123SS), N472GA
D-ANTR	Canadair CL-600-2B16 Challenger 604	5616	LX-MDA, VP-CFD, C-FEXH, C-GLYO
D-AOLG	Fokker F.28-0100	11452	PH-RRN, EC-IVO, PH-RRN, PT-WHK, PH-RRN, PT-MCN, PH-EZU
D-AONE(3)	Canadair CL-600-2B16 Challenger 604	5430	OY-MMM, C-GFOE, N604MA, C-GLXS
D-APGS	Airbus A319-115CJ	3046	(D-ALGS), OE-LGS, D-AVYF
D-APLC	Dassault Falcon 7X	77	(D-ACGN), F-WWHS
D-APTA	Airbus A319-112	1263	LY-VEU, EI-EWA, N338MS, B-6151, N739US, D-AVYB
'D-AQUI'	*See D-CDLH*		
D-ARKO	Bombardier BD-700-1A10 Global XRS	9348	9H-BGL, C-FWGH
D-ARNI	Canadair Regional Jet CRJ-100LR	7086	OD-TAL, C-FLHQ, D-ACLR, C-FMLU (Res. 3.12)
D-ARYR	Bombardier BD-700-1A10 Global XRS	9419	C-GGUA

D-ASAA to D-ASAZ *Test registrations for Airbus A300 and A310 freighter conversions*

Registration	Type	MSN	Previous identities
D-ASAX	VFW-Fokker VFW-614	G-015	F-GATI, D-BABN (Advanced Technology Demonstrator) (Preserved at Bremen)
D-ASBG	Dassault Falcon 900EX EASy	141	F-HMCH, OE-IWG, HB-JSX, N141EX, F-WWFS
D-ASHY	Canadair CL-600-2B16 Challenger 605	5926	C-GUKT(2)
D-ASPA	Airbus A319-112	1598	N990TA, XA-UAQ, C-GJUK, C-GKZA, D-AVWV
D-ASPB	Airbus A319-112	1625	N991TA, N62TY, C-GKZC, D-AVYZ
D-ASPG	Airbus A320-214	2529	OE-LEA(3), F-WWID
D-ASPH	Airbus A320-214	2619	D-ABDB, SP-IAH, D-ABDB, F-WWDK (Res. .16)
D-ASTA	Airbus A319-113	4663	D-AVYF
D-ASTB	Airbus A319-112	4691	D-AVYO
D-ASTC(2)	Airbus A319-112	5085	D-AVYO
D-ASTE	Airbus A321-211	6005	D-AVZD
D-ASTF	Airbus A319-112	4268	F-HCZI, D-AVWP
D-ASTP	Airbus A321-211	0684	UR-WRP, OK-CED, C-GKOJ, D-AMTE, F-GTAC, D-AVZQ
D-ASTR	Airbus A319-112	3950	EI-FMB, A5-RGI, SX-OAG, D-AHIQ, D-AVWT
D-ASTT	Airbus A319-111	3560	D-AHHB, D-AHIK, D-AVWQ
D-ASTU	Airbus A319-113	3533	D-AHHA, D-AHIJ, D-AVYV
D-ASTV	Airbus A321-211	0995	TS-IQB, OO-SUB, D-AVZG
D-ASTW	Airbus A321-211	0970	TS-IQA, OO-SUA, D-AVZY
D-ASTX	Airbus A319-112	3202	HB-IOY, D-ABGG, D-AVWJ
D-ASTY	Airbus A319-112	3407	OE-LED, D-AVYC
D-ASTZ	Airbus A319-112	3019	OE-LEK, D-AVXM
D-ASUN	Boeing 737-8BK	33023	TC-SNM, VT-AXB(2),
N323CT,			N1786B
D-ASXA	Boeing 737-8Z9	28178	OE-LNK, N1784B, N1786B
D-ASXB	Boeing 737-8Z9	30420	OE-LNP
D-ASXC	Boeing 737-86N	30806	TC-SUY, G-OXLB, 5B-DBH
D-ASXD	Boeing 737-8AS	33562	EI-DCD
D-ASXE(2)	Boeing 737-86Q	32365	TC-SUG
D-ASXF	Boeing 737-8AS	33558	(TC-SNV), EI-DAY
D-ASXG	Boeing 737-8CX	32366	TC-SUH
D-ASXH	Boeing 737-8CX	32368	TC-SUJ
D-ASXI	Boeing 737-8CX	32367	TC-SUI
D-ASXJ	Boeing 737-86N	30807	TC-SUV, N50089, N1786B
D-ASXK	Boeing 737-86J	28070	D-ABAP(2)
D-ASXO	Boeing 737-8HX	29649	TC-SUZ, N1786B
D-ASXP	Boeing 737-8HX	29684	TC-SNF
D-ASXQ(2)	Boeing 737-8FH	30826	TC-SNH, EI-ECD, EC-JHV, (N3775)
D-ASXR(2)	Boeing 737-86J	30827	TC-SNJ, D-ABBO (Res. 3.16)
D-ASXS	Boeing 737-8AS	33563	EI-DCE

Reg	Type	c/n	Previous identities
D-ASXU	Boeing 737-8FH	29671	TC-SNI, EI-DMZ, EC-JGE
D-ATIM	Gulfstream 550	5354	(G-TIMA), N454GA
D-ATRA	Airbus A320-232	0659	F-WWDB, (D-ANNE), OE-LOE, D-ALAE, F-WWIV
D-ATRR	Aérospatiale/Alenia ATR-72-212 (Stored .15)	320	N322AC, N320AT, F-WWEM
D-ATRS	Aérospatiale/Alenia ATR-72-202 (P. 10.12, stored)	239	SE-MGH, SX-BIE, F-WWED
D-ATTT	Canadair CL-600-2B16 Challenger IV	5609	N604JC, C-FEFU, C-GLXS
D-ATUA(3)	Boeing 737-8K5	37245	
D-ATUB(3)	Boeing 737-8K5	37247	N1786B
D-ATUC	Boeing 737-8K5	34684	N1786B
D-ATUD	Boeing 737-8K5	34685	
D-ATUE	Boeing 737-8K5	34686	
D-ATUF	Boeing 737-8K5	34687	N1786B
D-ATUG	Boeing 737-8K5	34688	
D-ATUH D-ATUH	Boeing 737-8K5	34689	C-FYUH, D-ATUH, C-FYUH,
D-ATUI(2)	Boeing 737-8K5	37252	
D-ATUJ(3)	Boeing 737-8K5	39923	N1787B
D-ATUL(2)	Boeing 737-8K5	38820	C-GUUL(3), D-ATUL, C-GTUL(2), D-ATUL, C-GTUL(2), D-ATUL, (G-FDZX)
D-ATUM	Boeing 737-8K5	37240	(G-FDZY), N1796B
D-ATUN	Boeing 737-8K5	41660	
D-ATUO	Boeing 737-8K5	41661	
D-ATUP	Boeing 737-8K5	41662	
D-ATUQ	Boeing 737-8K5	41663	
D-ATUR	Boeing 737-8K5	41664	
D-ATUZ	Boeing 737-8K5	34691	OO-JPT, CN-RPF, G-FDZO, D-ATUA
D-ATWO(4)	Canadair CL-600-2B16 Challenger 604 (P. 8.16)	5539	HB-JFC, CS-DTJ, VP-CEO, VP-BDJ, PP-BIA, N539AB, C-GLXK
D-ATYF(2)	Boeing 767-304ER	28208	G-OBYF, D-AGYF, G-OBYF

D-AUAA to D-AUAZ   *Reserved for Airbus A318/A320 Test Registrations*

Reg	Type	c/n	Previous identities
D-AUCR	Dassault Falcon 900DX	606	F-WWFF
D-AUKE	Canadair CL-600-2B16 Challenger 604	5389	N604JE, C-GLXM
D-AUTO	Gulfstream 550	5171	N550BM, N971GA
D-AVAN	Embraer EMB-135BJ Legacy 600	14501092	PT-SMC
D-AVIB(2)	Embraer EMB-135BJ Legacy 600	14501109	PT-TKG
D-AVID	Aérospatiale/Alenia ATR-72-212 (Ntu, stored .15)	447	N447AM, F-WWEC
D-AVPB	Canadair CL-600-2B16 Challenger 605	5715	HB-JFA, CS-DTK, S5-ADB, C-FNIJ, (OE-IVB), C-FNIJ, C-GLXY

D-AVVA to D-AVVZ   *Reserved for Airbus A320 Test Registrations*

D-AVWA to D-AVWZ   *Reserved for Airbus A319 Test Registrations*

D-AVXA to D-AVXZ   *Reserved for Airbus A321 Test Registrations*

D-AVYA to D-AVYZ   *Reserved for Airbus A319 Test Registrations*

D-AVZA to D-AVZZ   *Reserved for Airbus A321 Test Registrations*

Reg	Type	c/n	Previous identities
D-AWBA	BAe.146 Series 300A	E-3134	ZK-NZF, G-5-134, G-11-134
D-AWBB	Boeing 737-7CN BBJ	30752	HB-IIQ, (D-APBA), HB-IIQ, N1026G, N1786B
D-AWKG	Dassault Falcon 900EX	20	(F-OIBE), F-WQBK, N158JA, N920EX
D-AWUE	BAe.146 Series 200	E-2050	PK-PJP, G-5-517, G-5-004

D-AXAA to D-AXAZ   *Reserved for Airbus A320 Test Registrations*

Reg	Type	c/n	Previous identities
D-AXGA	Airbus A330-203	530	B-16301, F-WWYA
D-AXGB	Airbus A330-202	684	A7-AFP, F-WWYG
D-AXGC	Airbus A330-203	555	B-16303, F-WWYL
D-AXGD	Airbus A330-203	573	B-16305, F-WWYP
D-AXGE	Airbus A330-202	612	A7-AFL, F-WWKZ
D-AXGF	Airbus A330-202	616	A7-AFM, F-WWKT
D-AXGG	Airbus A330-203 (Res. 2.3.15)	504	TC-JNG, A7-AFO, EI-DDV, I-VLEH, F-WWKL
D-AXTM	Bombardier BD-700-1A10 Global Express	9102	VP-CGS, HB-IGS, N700CY, C-GIXM
D-AXXX	Boeing 737-8LX BBJ2 (Res. 5.14)	39899	(D-ACSO), VP-BBZ
D-AYSM	Gulfstream 650	6146	N646GD

D-AYXA to D-AYXC   *Reserved for Testzwecke TFTS*

D-AZAA to D-AZAZ   *Reserved for Airbus A321 Test Registrations*

Reg	Type	c/n	Previous identities
D-AZEM	Dassault Falcon 900EASy	133	F-WQBK, F-WWFK
D-AZMO	Airbus A300F4-622R	872	N140MN, OD-TMA, N140MN, JA02GX, F-WWAI
D-AZUA	Boeing 767-33AER	27909	VQ-BUO, (LZ-AWB), ET-AMQ, PR-VAA, N279AN, B-2495, N279AN, VN-A766, N279AN, VH-NOA, N909SH, OE-LAS
D-AZUB	Boeing 767-33AER	28043	VQ-BUP, LZ-AWR, (CS-TKR), LZ-AWC, ET-ALC, (LZ-AWC), ET-ALC
D-AZUC	Boeing 767-3Y0ER	25411	N869TM, CS-TFS, S9-DBW, PP-VTC, N640TW, EI-CLR, SE-DKY, XA-EDE, XA-TJD, XA-EDE, SE-DKY, EI-CLR, XA-SKY, PT-TAF, EI-CEA
D-AZUR	Embraer EMB-135BJ Legacy 650	14501219	PR-LKC
D-AZZA(2)	Canadair CL-600-2B16 Challenger 605	5968	C-GYLP

CLASS B : Aircraft of between 14 and 20 Metric Tonnes

Reg	Type	c/n	Previous identities
D-BADA	Dornier 328-310	3224	D-BDXB
D-BADC	Dornier 328-310	3216	N328NP, D-BIUU, D-BDXD(5)
D-BADO	Bombardier BD-100-1A10 Challenger 300	20116	C-FIOC
D-BANN	Bombardier BD-100-1A10 Challenger 300	20221	C-FUBQ
D-BATR	Aérospatiale/Alenia ATR-42-300	042	UR-UTF, VP-BCD, I-ATRG, F-WWEW
D-BAVB	Bombardier BD-100-1A10 Challenger 300	20212	C-FTKC
D-BAVG	Cessna 750 Citation X	750-0227	(D-BTAG), EI-TEN, D-BAVG, (D-BTAG), EI-TEN, OH-DDI, M-DKDI, P4-LJG, N5267J
D-BDTB	Dornier 328-310 (P. 9.11) (Stored, then res. as D-BSUN 18.3.15)	3147	TF-MIK, (D-BAAB), N402FJ, D-BDXV(1)
D-BDTC	Dornier 328-310 (P. exp 12.11, since stored, D-BALU(2) ntu)	3149	TF-MIL, N403FJ, D-BDXY(1)

Reg	Type	c/n	Previous identities
D-BDTD	Dornier 328-300 (P. 9.11) (Stored)	3181	TF-MIO, N423FJ, D-BDXF(2)

D-BDXA to D-BDXZ   *Test Registrations for Dornier 328-300 production*

Reg	Type	c/n	Previous identities
D-BEAM	Bombardier BD-100-1A10 Challenger 300	20452	C-GOXB
D-BEAR	Cessna 750 Citation X	750-0085	D-BTEN, (N985QS), N5103J
D-BEEP	Cessna 750 Citation X	750-0107	N307RX, N520CM, (N332CM), N107CX, N5086W
D-BEJR	Dornier 328-300 (Preserved, Friedrichshafen)	3102	
D-BEKP	Bombardier BD-100-1A10 Challenger 300	20275	C-FZLX
D-BEKY	Dassault Falcon 2000LX	201	F-WWMG
D-BELO	Bombardier BD-100-1A10 Challenger 300	20402	YR-NVY, C-GOWQ
D-BERT(4)	Dassault Falcon 2000LX	271	F-WWJS
D-BEST	Dassault Falcon 2000	50	F-WWME
D-BETI	Dassault Falcon 50EX	267	F-OHFO, (D-BETI), F-WWHR
D-BFIL	Embraer EMB-545 Legacy 450	55010015	PR-LLQ
D-BGAB	Dornier 328-300 (Stored)	3134	D-BDXP
D-BGAS	Dornier 328-300	3139	D-BDXZ(1)
D-BGGM	Dassault Falcon 2000EX (Res. 8.6.15)	11	OE-HGM, I-NATS, F-WWGJ
D-BHGN	Bombardier BD-100-1A10 Challenger 350	20583	C-GOYL
D-BHHH	Aérospatiale/Alenia ATR-42-300	173	F-WWED
D-BIKA	Dassault Falcon 2000EX	76	F-WQBL, (D-BBED), A6-SMS, F-WWGM
D-BIRD(4)	Dornier 328-310	3180	N422FJ, D-BDX .
D-BJET(4)	Dornier 328-310	3207	D-BDXE, N328FG, (D-BCUU), D-BDXE
D-BJKP	Embraer EMB-550 Legacy 500	55000003	PR-LJN, PT-ZFV
D-BKAT	IAI Gulfstream 280	2070	N270GA, 4X-CVG
D-BLAU	Aérospatiale/Alenia ATR-42-300	068	UR-UTD, VP-BCF, I-ATRL, F-WWES
D-BLDI	Cessna 750 Citation X	750-0218	N5223X
D-BLTA	Dassault Falcon 2000LX	234	VP-CAM, F-WWJR
D-BMAD(2)	Dornier 328-300 (Res as OY-NCI, 2015)	3142	I-AIRX, D-BDXA
D-BMVV	Dassault Falcon 2000EX EASy	42	F-GUTC, F-WWGX
D-BNEW	Dornier 328-300	3141	5N-SPM, (D-BMAA), D-BDXK(2)
D-BOBI(2)	Dassault Falcon 2000LX	246	F-WWMF
D-BONN(2)	Dassault Falcon 2000EASy	118	F-WWGC
D-BOOC	Cessna 750 Citation X	750-0259	OE-HAL, N52114
D-BOOK(3)	Dassault Falcon 2000LX	277	F-WWGJ
D-BPWR	Bombardier BD-100-1A10 Challenger 300	20272	
D-BRAS	Aérospatiale/Alenia ATR-42-300	092	SP-KTR, D-BAAA, N92BN, 9J-AFC, F-WWER
D-BSUN	Dornier 328-310 (Res. 18.3.15)	3147	D-BDTB, TF-MIK, (D-BAAB), N402FJ, D-BDXV(1)
D-BTIG	Dassault Falcon 2000EX EASy (Res. 6.15)	75	F-GZLX, OO-GML, F-GUPH, F-WWGL
D-BTLT	Bombardier BD-100-1A10 Challenger 300	20042	(D-BHRN), M-BTLT, N550LF, A7-CEC, A7-AAN, C-FDSR, C-GZEH
D-BUBI	Bombardier BD-100-1A10 Challenger 300	20145	C-FLQG
D-BUZZ	Cessna 750 Citation X	750-0256	N756XJ
D-BVHA	Dassault Falcon 2000LX	263	F-WWMK
D-BVIP	Aérospatiale/Alenia ATR-42-320	333	F-WQNO, VP-BOG
D-B . . .	Aérospatiale/Alenia ATR-42-300	085	SP-KCA, F-WQNY, C-FLCP, F-WWEK

CLASS C : Aircraft of between 5.7 and 14 Metric Tonnes

Reg	Type	c/n	Previous identities
D-CAAA(4)	Cessna 560XL Citation XLS	560-6123	N5226B
D-CAAE	Gates Learjet 55	55-095	N55RT, N8565Z, N39398
D-CAAH(2)	Dornier 328-100	3010	N473PS, N332PH, D-CFFA
D-CAAL(3)	Dornier 228-212	8155	D-CALI(3), TR-LGM, PH-IOL, (TR-LGM), D-CALY, D-CBDU(8), D-CALY, D-CAOS(2), D-CBDG(2)
D-CAAM	Dornier 228-212	8205	D-CBDH(4)
D-CAAY(2)	Gates Learjet 55	55-087	N955NC, M-TNTJ, N1852, SE-RGU, N902RL, N554PF, N520SQ, N520SC, N103C, N8564Z, N1451B
D-CAHO	Cessna 560XL Citation XLS+	560-6165	
D-CAIR(3)	Cessna 560 Citation Excel	560-5620	N5264E
D-CALL(3)	Cessna 550 Citation II Bravo	550-0834	N834CB
D-CAPA(2)	Beech 1900C	UB-72	N504RH, OY-JRS, D-CAPA(2), OK-SEB, D-CAPA(2), N3076N
D-CAPB	Cessna 560 Citation Encore+	560-0806	N5196U
D-CAPO(2)	Gates Learjet 35A	35A-159	N93CK, N93C
D-CARL	Gates Learjet 35A	35A-387	
D-CARO(3)	Cessna 680 Citation Sovereign	680-0514	N683AB, N5085E
D-CAST	Cessna 525B CitationJet CJ3	525B-0330	
D-CATZ	Dornier 328-100	3090	N404SS, D-CDVY
D-CAUW	Cessna 560 Citation V	560-0578	(D-CSUN), N5264N
D-CAVA	Fairchild Swearingen SA.227AC Metro III	AC-758B	F-GPSN, N58NE
D-CAWA(2)	Dornier 328-110	3119	OE-LKC, D-CDXK(4)
D-CAWB	Cessna 680 Citation Sovereign	680-0319	N680AB, N5100J
D-CAWM	Cessna 560XL Citation XLS	560-6002	(D-CRUW), N502XL
D-CAWR	Cessna 560 Citation Encore+	560-0809	N196JP, N610BK, N5097H
D-CAWS	Cessna 680 Citation Sovereign	680-0328	N682AB, N5185J
D-CAWU(2)	Cessna 560XL Citation XLS	560-5797	N52061
D-CAWX	Cessna 680 Citation Sovereign +	680-0535	N684AB
D-CBAY(2)	Cessna 680 Citation Sovereign	680-0125	N666FH, N5053R
D-CBBB(4)	Cessna 560XL Citation XLS	560-6125	N5066U
D-CBBS	Embraer EMB-505 Phenom 300	50500343	PR-PGT
D-CBCT	Cessna 525C CitationJet CJ4	525C-0093	N5188A

D-CBDA to D-CBDZ   *Test Registrations for Dornier 228 production*

Reg	Type	c/n	Previous identities
D-CBEN(2)	Cessna 560XL Citation XLS+	560-6089	N52690
D-CBIN	Fairchild Swearingen SA.227AT Merlin IVC	AT-440B	I-FSAD, N36JP, N56TA
D-CBTA	Cessna 525C CitationJet CJ4	525C-0218	(D-CBRO), D-CBTA, N514KN
D-CCAA	Gates Learjet 35A	35A-315	N662AA, N927GL
D-CCAB	Cessna 550 Citation II Bravo	550-0827	
D-CCAS	Short SD.3-60 Variant 300	SH.3737	G-OLBA, G-BOFG
D-CCBH	Cessna 525B CitationJet CJ3	525B-0334	N5206T
D-CCCA	Gates Learjet 35A	35A-160	
D-CCCB	Gates Learjet 35A	35A-663	N91480
D-CCCC(2)	Fairchild Swearingen SA.227AT Merlin IVC	AT-511	N600N, N600L, N3108F

Registration	Type	C/N	Previous identities / Notes
D-CCCF	Cessna 550 Citation II	500-0189	HB-VGP, D-CAAT, N98601
D-CCGM	Embraer EMB-505 Phenom 300	50500359	
D-CCGN	Gates Learjet 55	55-017	N760AQ
D-CCHB	Gates Learjet 35A	35A-089	N3547F
D-CCSD	Cessna 650 Citation VI	650-0212	N651AR, N972VZ, N805GT, (N6820Y)
D-CCVD	Cessna 560XL Citation XLS	560-5784	N5264M
D-CCWD(3)	Cessna 560XL Citation XLS	560-6039	N50756
D-CCWM	Embraer EMB-505 Phenom 300	50500232	PR-PCS
D-CDAS(3)	Embraer EMB-505 Phenom 300	50500317	
D-CDAX(2)	Dornier 328-110	3087	N463PS, N329ML, F-GOFB, D-CDXK(3)
D-CDDD(4)	Cessna 560XL Citation XLS+	560-6166	
D-CDLH	Junkers Ju 52/3mg8e	130714	N52JU, N130LW, HC-ABS, LN-KAF, (LN-KAL), Luftwaffe
	(Painted as D-AQUI which was c/n 5489, later LN-DAH and Luftwaffe; regd LN-KAF 5.46 this was rebuilt with fuselage of c/n 130714 (LN-KAL ntu) in .47)		
D-CDLR	Grob G 850 Strato 2C	30001	
D-CDOC(2)	Bombardier Learjet 45	45-018	OO-LFS, N418LJ
D-CDTZ(2)	Embraer EMB-505 Phenom 300	50500198	PR-PBN
D-CDUS	Cessna 525C CitationJet CJ4	525C-0161	(D-CJUG(1))
D-CDXA to D-CDXZ *Test Registrations for Dornier 328-100 production*			
D-CEAC	Cessna 650 Citation VII	650-7117	PH-MYX, N135HC, N33D, N5263D
	(Res. 1.14)		
D-CEBM(3)	Cessna 560XL Citation XLS	560-5749	OE-GBR(2), N169SM, N5076L
	(Res. 9.12)		
D-CEBS	Embraer EMB-505 Phenom 300	50500343	
D-CECH	Cessna 560XL Citation XLS+	560-6140	(D-CZEC), UR-UQA, N51743
D-CEEE	Cessna 560XL Citation XLS	560-5630	N51612
D-CEER	Beech B200 King Air GT	BY-272	N272TA
D-CEFD	Cessna 525B CitationJet CJ3	525B-0120	N5211A
D-CEFE	Cessna 525C CitationJet CJ4	525C-0177	N51072
D-CEFO	Cessna 560XL Citation XLS	560-6082	(N282XL), N51817
D-CEHM	Cessna 560XL Citation XLS+	560-6021	(N941AA), HB-VWD, (HB-VWE), N5223X
D-CEIS(2)	Cessna 680 Citation Sovereign	680-0185	PH-CIJ, N50275
D-CELI(2)	Cessna 550 Citation II Bravo	550-0998	OE-GHP, (D-CGHP), OE-GHP, N5165P
D-CEMS	Cessna 525B CitationJet CJ3	525B-0107	D-COBO(1), N709PG
D-CESA(3)	Cessna 550 Citation II Bravo	550-1039	N139JA, OE-GRB, N511HA, N711HA, N320CS
D-CEUS	Cessna 525C CitationJet CJ4	525C-0233	N50820
D-CEXP	Gates Learjet 35A	35A-616	N876C, N876CS, N616LJ, PT-LQF, N8568Q, N3807G
D-CFAF	Bombardier Learjet 60	60-107	(EC-...), D-CFFB, N107LJ
D-CFAG(2)	Bombardier Learjet 60	60-281	ES-LVC, OH-GVE, D-CGTF, OE-GTF, "OE-GTS", N5013U
D-CFAJ	Bombardier Learjet 60	60-085	N814GF, N89KW, N99KW, N685LJ
D-CFAK(2)	Bombardier Learjet 60	60-300	OE-GSV, (D-CFAX(2)), OE-GSV, YL-ABA, EI-DXW, G-CJMC, OH-GEM, N4008
	(Res. 10.7.15)		
D-CFAN(3)	Bombardier Learjet 60	60-019	D-CRAN(5), HB-VKI, N40366, N50153
D-CFAX(3)	Bombardier Learjet 60	60-249	(D-CFAK(1)), EC-JYQ, D-CLUB(6), N4004Q, N50422
D-CFCF(2)	Gates Learjet 35A	35A-413	N27KG, N413MA, F-GHAE, N2637Z, HB-VHE
D-CFFF(2)	Cessna 560XL Citation XLS+	560-6170	N52691
D-CFFU	Dornier 228-212	8180	
D-CFGG	Gates Learjet 36A	36A-048	N32AJ, PT-WGM, N3NP, N24PT, N2FU, (N14FU), N3999B, HB-VHF
D-CFHZ	Embraer EMB-505 Phenom 300	50500413	
D-CFIV	Gates Learjet 35A	35A-385	N350EF, N535MC
D-CFLY(2)	Cessna 560XL Citation XLS	560-6014	N868JB
D-CFMD	Beech B300 King Air 350	FL-473	N37173
D-CFME	Beech B300 King Air 350	FL-627	N6127U
D-CFMI	Embraer EMB-505 Phenom 300	50500058	PT-TJR
D-CFOR(2)	Gates Learjet 35A	35A-656	G-ZMED, N356JW, N335SB, G-JETL, N3810G
	(P. 2.16)		
D-CFTG	Gates Learjet 35A	35A-204	(N277AM), N7PE, N99ME, N87MJ, D-COSY, N1466B
D-CGAA	Cessna 560XL Citation XLS+	560-6173	N5245L
D-CGBR	Gates Learjet 55	55-122	OE-GRO, C-FHJB, N99KV, N99KW, N18ZD, N8568P, N10870
D-CGEP(2)	Gulfstream 150	287	(D-CGPE), N487GA
D-CGFA	Gates Learjet 35A	35A-179	N801PF, C-FHLO, N718SW, (N696SC), N718SW, D-CAPD, (D-CCAR), N39412
D-CGFB	Gates Learjet 35A	35A-268	N2U, N510SG, (N286CP), N3857N, YV-286CP, N10870
D-CGFC	Gates Learjet 35A	35A-331	N435JW, N700NW, I-EJIB, HB-VGU, N1087D
D-CGFD	Gates Learjet 35A	35A-139	N15SC
D-CGFE	Gates Learjet 36A	36A-062	N4291N
D-CGFF	Gates Learjet 36A	36A-063	N1048X, N6340T
D-CGFG	Gates Learjet 35A	35A-222	N789KW, HB-VFZ, N90AL, I-EJID, HB-VFZ, N1468B
D-CGFH	Gates Learjet 35A	35A-607	N68MJ, PT-LIJ, N72614, N39399
D-CGFJ	Gates Learjet 35A	35A-643	N643MJ, G-LJET, (N35NK), G-LJET, N39418
D-CGFK	Gates Learjet 31A	31A-205	YR-TYC, N71FB, VP-CFB, N50153
D-CGFM	Gates Learjet 31A	31A-207	D-CSIE, N50126
D-CGFN	Gates Learjet 35A	35A-654	N770BM, N8189, B-98183, ZS-NSB, (B-98183), (N95EC), N600LF, N633WW, N4290K
D-CGFO	Gates Learjet 35A	35A-614	D-CFOR, N683EF, N683EL, N335EA, G-OCFR, G-VIPS, G-SOVN, HB-VJC, G-PJET, N3815G
D-CGFP	Gates Learjet 35A	35A-674	LV-BIE, N674LJ, N900JE, N22CN, N22SF
D-CGGG(2)	Gates Learjet 31A	31A-227	N40073, N30054
D-CGMR	Cessna 560XL Citation XLS	560-5593	D-CCEA, EC-JXI, N593XL, N559CS, N5152X
D-CGRC	Gates Learjet 35A	35A-223	N215JW
D-CHDC	Cessna 680 Citation Sovereign	680-0103	N5065G
D-CHDJ	Cessna 560XL Citation XLS	560-5744	N560QG, PR-MMV, N2003J
D-CHEC	Cessna 680 Citation Sovereign	680-0079	N680HC, N5172M
D-CHER(3)	Bombardier Learjet 60	60-148	HB-VOZ, N648TS, D-CETV, N80701
D-CHGS(2)	Embraer EMB-505 Phenom 300	50500150	(D-CAXO), PR-PBJ
D-CHIC(7)	Embraer EMB-505 Phenom 300	50500096	PT-TSV
D-CHIO	Cessna 525B CitationJet CJ3	525B-0378	N5117U
D-CHIP(2)	Cessna 525B CitationJet CJ3	525B-0498	N5233J
D-CHLR	Embraer EMB-505 Phenom 300	50500066	PT-TNB
D-CHMS(2)	Embraer EMB-505 Phenom 300	50500324	N60298
D-CHRA	Cessna 525C CitationJet CJ4	525C-0058	(D-CEFE), D-CHRA, N5185V
D-CHRB	Cessna 525C CitationJet CJ4	525C-0144	N5262W
D-CHRD	Cessna 680 Citation Sovereign	680-0142	N685CS, N51817
D-CHRE	Cessna 680 Citation Sovereign	680-0124	N622CS
D-CHZF	Cessna 550 Citation Bravo	550-0866	N866CB
D-CIAO(3)	Cessna 550 Citation II	550-0255	I-JESO, N28GA, I-DEAF, N6861L
D-CICR	Cessna 560XL Citation XL	560-5236	S5-ICR, S5-BAZ, N236LD, N51072
	(Res. 6.14)		
D-CIDO	Dornier Do 24TT	5345	RP-C2403, D-CATD(1), HD.5-4, HR.5-12, 65-12, KT+MY
D-CIFM(2)	Cessna 560 Citation XLS+	560-6178	
D-CINS	Bombardier Learjet 45	45-347	N40050
D-CIRI(4)	Dornier 328-110	3005	TF-CSC, HB-AEE, D-CITA(2)
D-CIRJ	Dornier 328-100	3035	N335LS, D-CDHU
D-CIRO(2)	Dornier 328-120	3025	N328LS, D-CDHK
	(Res.07; stored)		
D-CIRP(2)	Dornier 328-100	3006	TF-CSD, N470PS, N328PH, D-CDIY
D-CIRU(2)	Dornier 328-120	3033	N424JS, D-CDHS(3)
	(Res.07; stored)		
D-CITA(3)	Bombardier Learjet 60	60-069	N60CE, N50324
D-CITO(3)	Dornier 328-130	3063	CC-ACG, OE-LKE, D-CALP, F-GNPA, D-CDXK
D-CITY(2)	Gates Learjet 35A	35A-177	N174CP, N77CQ, N77CP, N1461B
D-CJAF	Bombardier Learjet 60	60-351	N5013Y
D-CJET(4)	Cessna 525B CitationJet CJ3	525B-0349	N5181U
D-CJOS	Cessna 525B CitationJet CJ3	525B-0367	D-CDTZ, N5247U
D-CJPD	Gates Learjet 31A	31A-057	D-CSAP, N9147Q
D-CJPG	Gates Learjet 35A	35A-108	N86PC, (N86PQ), N86PC, F-GCLE, D-COCO(2)
D-CJUG(2)	Cessna 560XL Citation XLS+	560-6206	D-CJUH, N7148J, N5257V
D-CKAZ	Beech B300 King Air 350	FL-216	N893MC, N898MC
D-CKHG	Cessna 560XL Citation XLS	560-5667	N128AW, XA-UGQ, N5192E
D-CKHK	Cessna 560XL Citation XLS+	560-6051	N651TK, PR-JSR, N912EL, N5157E
D-CKNA	Cessna 525C CitationJet CJ4	525C-0153	N5153K
D-CKPP	Fairchild SA.227DC Metro 23	DC-805B	N715MQ, XA-SFC, N3008L
D-CKWM	Beech B300 King Air 350	FL-756	N81026
D-CLAM	Embraer EMB-505 Phenom 300	50500108	PT-TOD
D-CLBM	Embraer EMB-505 Phenom 300	50500173	PR-PBX
D-CLDF(2)	Cessna 650 Citation VII	650-7085	N785CC, (N136WC), N785CS, N5112K
D-CLHS	Cessna 560XL Citation XLS+	560-6187	
D-CLMS	Bombardier Learjet 45	45-395	N40149
D-CLUE	Cessna 650 Citation III	650-0174	N674CC, (N1782E)
D-CLUZ(2)	Bombardier Learjet 60	60-386	D-CFAD, N812SD, OE-GVE, N60SJ, N40076
D-CMAN(2)	Cessna 525B CitationJet CJ3	525B-0215	OE-GBO, D-CTEC
D-CMDH	Cessna 680 Citation Sovereign	680-0322	M-DMMH, N50776
D-CMED	Gates Learjet 55	55-059	M-KRRR, OE-GRR, N59LJ, N50AF, D-CAEP, N211BY
D-CMEI	Cessna 560 Citation V	560-0117	N6804F
D-CMET	Dassault Falcon 20E-5	329/523	F-WRQV
D-CMHA(2)	Dornier 328-110	3023	G-BWIR, D-CDXF(2), N328DA, D-CDHH
D-CMHB(2)	Dornier 328-130	3110	OE-LKA, D-CDXI(3)
D-CMHC(2)	Dornier 328-110	3022	G-BWWT, D-CDXO(1), (VT-VIG), D-CDHG
D-CMHD(2)	Dornier 328-110	3088	G-BZOG, D-CDXN(5), F-GNPR, D-CDXU(2)
D-CMHS	Cessna 525B CitationJet CJ3	525B-0161	N5268M
D-CMMP(2)	Embraer EMB-505 Phenom 300	50500360	
D-CMOR	Embraer EMB-505 Phenom 300	50500373	PR-PHH
D-CMPD	Beech B200 King Air GT	BY-249	D-IMPD, N50494
D-CMSC	Bombardier Learjet 45	45-097	N5017J
D-CNAA	Fairchild SA.227DC Metro 23	DC-839B	VH-OYI, VH-DMI, N3022F
D-CNAB	Fairchild SA.227DC Metro 23	DC-848B	VH-OYB, N425LA, N3024U
D-CNAC	Fairchild SA.227DC Metro 23	DC-895B	N30384
D-CNAD	Fairchild SA.227DC Metro 23	DC-870B	VH-OYN, VH-DMO, N3030S
D-CNAE	Fairchild SA.227DC Metro 23	DC-875B	VH-OYG, VH-SWM, N3033B
D-CNAF	Fairchild Swearingen SA.227AC Metro III	AC-505B	TF-BBG, F-GHVC, HB-LND, EC-DXS, HB-LND, N31014
D-CNAG	Fairchild SA.227DC Metro 23	DC-893B	N3032A
D-CNAY	Fairchild Swearingen SA.227AT Merlin IVC	AT-493	PH-RAX, F-GGLG, N121FA, OY-CHC, N3075A, CP-2109, N3075A
D-CNCA(2)	Cessna 550 Citation II	550-0235	I-PNCA, N67SG, (N68035)
D-CNEU	Dornier 228-212	8206	PH-MNZ, D-CDOQ, D-CDIV
D-CNMB	Bombardier Learjet 45	45-024	C-FVSL, C-FBCL, N145ST
D-CNNN(2)	Cessna 560XL Citation XLS	560-6127	N5100J
D-CNOB	Cessna 525B CitationJet CJ3	525B-0119	N5257V
D-CNOC	Cessna 560XL Citation XLS	560-5814	D-CMIC(4), N5161J
D-CNUE	Bombardier Learjet 60	60-170	F-HAVB, 9H-AEE, D-COWS, N50154
D-COBI	Cessna 560XL Citation XLS	560-5645	N88SF, (D-CAFE(4)), N88SF, N5223X
D-COBO(2)	Cessna 525B CitationJet CJ3	525B-0414	D-COBC(3)
D-COCA(3)	Beech 1900D	UE-224	N224YV
D-CODE	Dornier 228-101	7083	(D-CEVA)
D-COKE	Gates Learjet 35A	35A-447	N300FN, N127K
D-COLT(3)	Embraer EMB-505 Phenom 300	50500207	
D-COMO(2)	Bombardier Learjet 60	60-169	OE-GII, N5014F
D-CONE(3)	Gates Learjet 35A	35A-111	I-LIAD, OE-GMA(1), (I-SIDU), N3815G
D-CONU(3)	Gates Learjet 55	55-124	SX-BTV, N58CQ, N58CG, N39391
D-COOL(2)	Gates Learjet 55	55-052	N58GF, N55GF, YV-292CP
D-COSY(3)	Dornier 328-110	3072	CC-AEY, OE-LKD, HS-PBB, D-CDXY(2)
D-COWB	Cessna 525B CitationJet CJ3	525B-0220	(D-CJVC), N52136
D-COXB	LET L-410-UVP Turbolet	820924	DDR-SXB
D-CPDA	PZL-Mielec M28-05 Skytruck	AJE003-45	SP-DGO(2)
	(Res. 17.8.15)		
D-CPDB	PZL-Mielec M28-05 Skytruck	AJE003-46	SP-DGU(3)
	(Res. 17.8.15)		
D-CPDR	Bombardier Learjet 40	45-2080	N40076
D-CPMI(2)	Cessna 560XL Citation XLS+	560-6121	N5227G

Registration	Type	Serial	Previous identities / Notes
D-CPMU	Bombardier Learjet 60	60-032	(D-CIFA), OE-GNL(2), N5013D
D-CPOS	Cessna 560XL Citation XLS+	560-6109	OY-GKC, N52141
D-CPRO(2)	Gates Learjet 31A	31A-155	N525GP
D-CPRS(2)	Beech B300 King Air 350	FL-631	G-KLNB, N60041
D-CPSW	Fairchild Swearingen SA.227AC Metro III	AC-757B	F-GJPN, N57NE
D-CPWF	Dornier 328-110	3112	D-CFWF, D-CGAN, D-CDXE(4)
D-CPWG	Dornier 328-120 (Permit 10.10.14; for spares?)	3012	N334PH, SE-LJU, D-CIRI(3), N334PH, D-CASI(2)
D-CQAJ	Gates Learjet 35A	35A-421	D-CDSF, I-VULC, N413JP, N3AH, (N88AH), N85QA, N85CA, N44MJ
D-CQQQ	Cessna 560XL Citation XLS+	560-6134	N52645
D-CRAH	Cessna 525B CitationJet CJ3	525B-0154	
D-CRAS	Short SD.3-60 Variant 300	SH.3744	N825BE, N744CC, G-14-3744
D-CRCR	Embraer EMB-505 Phenom 300	50500069	PT-TNF
D-CREW(2)	Dornier 328-110	3113	D-CGAO, D-CDXF(4)
D-CRON	Cessna 560XL Citation XLS	560-5762	N51780
D-CSAG(3)	Embraer EMB-505 Phenom 300	50500101	PT-TRJ
D-CSAL	Fairchild Swearingen SA.227AC Metro III	AC-601	I-FSAH, N90AG, OY-BPJ, N3117K
D-CSEB	Cessna 560XL Citation XLS+	560-6093	N5151D
D-CSFD	Cessna 560XL Citation XLS	560-5022	HZ-FYZ, N522XL
D-CSIM	Bombardier Learjet 60	60-274	N4003K
D-CSIX	Bombardier Learjet 60	60-120	(N141MB), D-CSIX, N120LJ
D-CSKY	Beech B300 King Air 350	FL-130	
D-CSLT	Bombardier Learjet 60	60-200	A6-EJA, (OY-LJK), (OY-TCG), N254FY, N254FX
D-CSMB	Cessna 550 Citation Bravo	550-1130	N5125J
D-CSOS(2)	Bombardier Learjet 45	45-161	SE-RKY, G-SOVC, N161AV, G-OLDR, N3000S
D-CSPG	Grob G 180A SPn Utility Jet	90004	
D-CSUE	Dornier 328-110	3019	N328DC, D-CDHD
D-CSUN(2)	Cessna 560XL Citation XLS+	560-6102	N51942
D-CTOP	Gates Learjet 35A	35A-440	N300SC, N917SC, (N354EM), N980HC, N903HC, N101PK, N101HK
D-CTRI	Gates Learjet 35A	35A-346	EC-IIC, (N34LZ), I-DLON, N35AJ, C-GMGA, N3803G
D-CTRJ	Dornier 328-110	3015	N339PH, D-CARR
D-CTTT	Cessna 560XL Citation XLS	560-5573	(OE-GAL), N51881
D-CTWO(2)	Gates Learjet 35A	35A-504	OE-GMJ, N505DH, G-RAFF, N8568B, N10871
D-CUBA	Cessna 525B CitationJet CJ3	525B-0169	N5250P
D-CUGF(2)	Cessna 525B CitationJet CJ3	525B-0479	N5165P
D-CULT	Dornier 228-212	8192	LN-BER(2), F-ODYC, D-CJKM, D-CBDB(4)
D-CURE	Bombardier Learjet 60XR	60-379	(D-CFAS), I-SDAG, N50154, (CS-DJA), N50154
D-CURT	Gates Learjet 31A	31A-042	D-CGGG(1)
D-CUTE(3)	Beech B300 King Air 350	FL-504	N553CL
D-CUUU(2)	Cessna 560XL Citation XLS+	560-6137	N52645
D-CVFL	Gates Learjet 35A	35A-405	N135DA, N442DM, N35FS, N35AS, N41MJ
D-CVGM	Cessna 550 Citation II	550-0492	I-AVGM, N1254G
D-CVHB(3)	Cessna 560XL Citation XLS+	560-6168	
D-CVMG	Beech B300 King Air 350	FL-857	RA-02778, N5057X
D-CVRM	Cessna 550 Citation II (Stored, Rome)	550-0491	I-AVRM, N1254D
D-CVVM	Cessna S550 Citation S/II (Stored, Rome)	S550-0062	I-AVVM, N12715
D-CWAY	Gates Learjet 55	55-107	PH-ABU, D-CWAY, N304AT, N155JT, N760G, N1466B
D-CWIR(2)	Cessna 525C CitationJet CJ4	525C-0118	
D-CWIT	Cessna 525C CitationJet CJ4	525C-0124	D-CVHA(3), N51055
D-CWWP(2)	Embraer EMB-505 Phenom 300 (P. 3.16)	50500333	N10139, N60318
D-CXLS	Cessna 560XL Citation XLS	560-6027	(G-GXLS), (D-CHAM), N5076J
D-CXNL	Hawker 800XP	258544	N799JC
D-CXXX	Douglas C-47B-30-DK (Crashed 19.6.10)	16124/32872	G-AMPZ, EI-BDT, G-AMPZ, TF-AIV, G-41-3-66, PH-RIC, G-AMPZ, OD-AEQ, G-AMPZ, KN442, 44-76540
D-CYES	Gates Learjet 35A	35A-676	N620MJ, N235AC, N35LJ
D-CYKP	Cessna 550 Citation Bravo	550-1017	N406CA, CS-DHD, N51666
D-CZZZ(2)	Cessna 560XL Citation XLS	560-6128	N50820
D-C . . .	Cessna 680 Citation Sovereign	680-0124	N622CS
D-C . . .	Dornier 328-100	3088	G-BZOG, D-CDXN(5), F-GNPR, D-CDXU

CLASS E : Single-Engined Aircraft under 2 Metric Tonnes

Registration	Type	Serial	Previous identities / Notes
D-EAAA	Bölkow BO.209 Monsun 150FF	161	
D-EAAB(3)	Piper PA-46-310P Malibu (JetProp DLX conversion # 165)	46-8608054	N719LR, N9539N, N9094Z
D-EAAC	Bölkow BO.209 Monsun 160RV	163	
D-EAAD(4)	Cessna 152	15281664	N65459
D-EAAE(2)	Mooney M.20F Executive	22-1345	N6983V
D-EAAF(3)	Diamond DA 20-A1 Katana	10197	N155SE, C-GKAH
D-EAAG	Bölkow B0.209 Monsun 160RV	167	
D-EAAH(2)	Cessna T182T Turbo Skylane	T18208735	HB-CZI, N22807
D-EAAI	Bölkow B0.209 Monsun 160RV	169	
D-EAAJ(2)	Eingartner/Brditschka HB-207 Alfa	207-006	
D-EAAK	Bölkow B0.209 Monsun 150FF	171	
D-EAAL(2)	Reims/Cessna F182Q Skylane	F18200059	
D-EAAM	Bölkow B0.209 Monsun 160RV	173	
D-EAAN	Bölkow B0.209 Monsun 160RV	174	
D-EAAO(2)	Reims/Cessna F182Q Skylane	F18200063	(D-EAAD)
D-EAAP	Bölkow B0.209 Monsun 160RV	176	
D-EAAQ(4)	Cessna 172S Skyhawk SP	172S10301	N1157B
D-EAAS(3)	Cessna T182T Turbo Skylane	T18209100	N910VB
D-EAAT	Bölkow B0.209 Monsun 150FF	179	
D-EAAU	Bölkow B0.209 Monsun 160FV	180	
D-EAAV	SOCATA MS.892A Rallye Commodore 150	11816	F-BSMT
D-EAAW	Bölkow B0.209 Monsun 160RV	181	
D-EABA	Aerostyle Breezer B600L (P .09)	009LSA	
D-EABB(2)	Piper PA-12 Super Cruiser	12-3115	N4219M, NC4219M
D-EABC(2)	Mooney M.20F Executive	690058	
D-EABD	Pipistrel Virus SW121 (P 8.7.14)	630SWN121	
D-EABF(3)	SOCATA TB-9 Tampico	1066	
D-EABG(2)	Reims FR172F Rocket	FR17200084	
D-EABH	Bölkow BO.208C Junior	694	
D-EABK	Bölkow BO.208C Junior	697	
D-EABL(2)	Piper PA-28R-200 Cherokee Arrow	28R-35131	N9419N
D-EABM(2)	SOCATA TB-10 Tobago	1043	
D-EABP(2)	Reims/Cessna F152 II	F15201575	
D-EABQ(2)	SIAI-Marchetti S.205/20R	4-242	
D-EABS(3)	Cessna 172P Skyhawk	17276179	N97325
D-EABT(2)	CEA Jodel DR.1050 Ambassadeur	209	F-BJUI
D-EABU(3)	Wassmer Jodel D.120A Paris-Nice	205	F-BKCU
D-EABV(2)	Cessna 150H	15068826	N23251
D-EABZ(3)	Cessna 152	15279736	N757GU
D-EACA(2)	Fuji FA-200-160 Aero Subaru	89	
D-EACB(2)	Bölkow BO.209 Monsun 150V	105A	HB-UEN, D-EBOJ(1)
D-EACC	SOCATA MS.880B Rallye Club	1334	
D-EACE(2)	Mooney M.20J Model 205 (Res. 11.5.15)	24-3175	I-MUGH, N1067L
D-EACF(2)	Robin DR.300/180R Remorqueur	625	
D-EACG	CEA DR.360 Chevalier	626	
D-EACH	Piper PA-28-151 Cherokee Warrior	28-7415065	N9610N
D-EACI	SAN Jodel D.117A Grand Tourisme	830	OE-ABI
D-EACJ	Reims FR172G Rocket	FR17200183	(D-EFHL)
D-EACK(4)	Cessna 172S Skyhawk SP	172S9969	N2301C
D-EACL(3)	Pale / TEAM F1 Rocket EVO	2002543	
D-EACM	Piper PA-24-260 Comanche C	24-4968	HB-OIW, D-EACM, N9460P
D-EACN	Piper PA-28-180 Cherokee F	28-7105041	N5187S
D-EACO(2)	Reims/Cessna FRA150M Aerobat	FRA1500330	PH-BER, N72567, F-WZDC, N81956
D-EACP	Wassmer WA.41 Baladou	155	F-BOYQ
D-EACQ	Partenavia P.66C Charlie	70	I-IACQ
D-EACS(7)	Sanders/ Van's RV-7	001	
D-EACT	CEA DR.253B Régent	192	
D-EACU	CEA DR.253B Régent	193	
D-EACV	Robin DR.300/125	633	
D-EACX	SOCATA TB-20 Trinidad	697	
D-EACZ	Champion 7GCBC Citabria	677-74	OE-AOA
D-EADA(2)	Diamond DA 20-A1 Katana	10265	C-FDVP
D-EADB(2)	Cessna P210N Pressurized Centurion II	P21000610	N2738C, N734QE
D-EADC(2)	Piper PA-46-310P Malibu (JetProp DLX conversion # 88)	46-8508005	(G-POCH), N4376B
D-EADE(3)	Maule MXT-7-180 Starcraft	14114C	D-ERCS
D-EADF(2)	Piper PA-28-235 Cherokee Pathfinder	28-7510048	N33580
D-EADI	Robin DR.400/180R Remorqueur	791	
D-EADJ	Cessna 150M	15078101	N9150U
D-EADL(2)	HOAC DV-20 Katana	20105	C-FVQB, N105DV
D-EADM	Cessna 182K Skylane	18257960	N2760Q
D-EADN	Piper PA-28-140 Cherokee Cruiser	28-7325358	N11C
D-EADO	Cessna F172H	F172-0445	
D-EADP(2)	Piaggio FWP.149D (Flies as "90+04")	009	90+04, BB+391
D-EADR	Cessna 210L Centurion	21060579	OO-ADR, N94276
D-EADU(2)	Cessna 152	15283229	N47477
D-EADW	Piper PA-28-180 Cherokee D (W/o 27.9.16)	28-5308	N7861N
D-EADY	Cessna 172N Skyhawk	17271568	N3491E
D-EAEA	Piper PA-28-151 Cherokee Warrior	28-7415319	N9568N
D-EAEB	Piper PA-18 Super Cub 95	18-3085	BAF: OL-L11, L-11, 53-4685
D-EAEC	Robin DR.300/180R Remorqueur	554	
D-EAEE	Fuji FA-200-180 Aero Subaru	91	
D-EAEF(3)	Cessna 152	15285296	N67394
D-EAEH(2)	Cessna 152	15285703	N94514
D-EAEI (2)	Cessna 172N Skyhawk	17273171	N6232F
D-EAEK(2)	Reims/Cessna FR182 Skylane RG	FR18200012	PH-ABK
D-EAEM	CEA DR.253B Régent	180	
D-EAEO(2)	Cessna 172P Skyhawk (Dbr 28.3.16)	17276044	N90ER, (N96223)
D-EAEP(2)	Robin DR.400/180S	1904	
D-EAER	Piper PA-18 Super Cub 95	18-1521	ALAT, 51-15521
D-EAES(2)	Cessna 172N Skyhawk	17269365	N62LA, N337ER
D-EAET	Piper PA-18 Super Cub 95	18-1571	ALAT, 51-15571
D-EAEU	Piper PA-18 Super Cub 95	18-1652	ALAT, 51-15652
D-EAEV	Robin DR.300/108 2+2	556	
D-EAEX	Reims/Cessna F172N	F17202027	HB-CFD, (D-EIZT)
D-EAFB(3)	Cessna 172S Skyhawk SP	172S8771	N390SP
D-EAFC	SAN Jodel DR.1050 Ambassadeur (Res. 31.3.15)	111	PH-ONE, (PH-ONO)
D-EAFE(2)	Mooney M.20K Model 231	25-0854	N5791R
D-EAFF(2)	Piper PA-28-140 Cherokee C	28-26920	N5287S
D-EAFH	SEEMS MS.892A Rallye Commodore 150	10480	F-BLSU
D-EAFI	Fuji FA-200-160 Aero Subaru	111	
D-EAFJ(2)	SOCATA TB-10 Tobago	894	
D-EAFK	Piper PA-28-180 Cherokee C	28-2509	N8329W
D-EAFL(3)	Aquila AT-01-100B	AT01-321	
D-EAFM(2)	Piper PA-28-180 Cherokee F	28-7105168	D-EAPD, N2148T
D-EAFN	Robin DR.300/180R Remorqueur	578	
D-EAFO(2)	Cessna 182Q Skylane	18267187	N97772
D-EAFP	CEA DR.253B Régent	183	
D-EAFQ	CEA DR.253B Régent	186	
D-EAFR	Gyroflug SC-01 Speed Canard	S-21	
D-EAFS(2)	SOCATA TB-20 Trinidad	918	
D-EAFU(2)	Cessna T.207A Turbo Stationair 8 (Robertson STOL) (Permit, for research use)	20700613	N73673
D-EAFW(2)	Piper PA-28RT-201T Turbo Arrow IV	28R-8331002	N8272B
D-EAFX(2)	Mooney M.20K Model 231 (P. 20.6.16)	25-0865	N5807X
D-EAFY	Beech C33A Debonair 285	CE-176	OH-BDC
D-EAFZ	SOCATA TB-20 Trinidad	924	
D-EAGA	Gardan GY-80 Horizon 180	245	
D-EAGC	Cessna F172H	F172-0637	(D-EBEB)
D-EAGF(3)	Cessna 150F	15063628	N7028F
D-EAGI	SOCATA MS.893A Rallye Commodore 180	11410	
D-EAGJ(2)	Diamond DA 20-A1 Katana	10115	N542SS, C-GKAN
D-EAGK	Cessna F150J	F150-0508	
D-EAGL(3)	Beierlein / Giles G202	007	
D-EAGN	SOCATA MS.883 Rallye 115	1383	
D-EAGP(3)	Xtreme Air Sbach XA-42	103	
D-EAGR	SOCATA MS.893A Rallye Commodore 180	11412	
D-EAGS(2)	Piper PA-28-181 Archer II	2890005	N9105V
D-EAGT(4)	American AG-5B Tiger	10131	OY-CKZ, (SE-KVA), N502IT
D-EAGV	Rockwell 114B Commander	14410	(D-EKCG)

Reg	Type	c/n	Previous identities
D-EAGW(4)	Piper PA-32RT-300T Turbo Lance II	32R-7887046	HB-PKU, G-WROY, G-WRAY, OY-BRD, "OY-BRO"
D-EAGY	SOCATA MS.883 Rallye 115	1365	
D-EAGZ	Robin DR.400/180 Régent	1414	I-SAGA
D-EAHA(2)	SOCATA MS.880B Rallye Club	1689	(D-EFHL)
D-EAHB	SOCATA MS.880B Rallye Club	1690	
D-EAHC(2)	Castermans/ Sequoia F.8LFalco	1728	
D-EAHD	SOCATA MS.880B Rallye Club	1787	
D-EAHF	SOCATA MS.893A Rallye Commodore 180	11708	
D-EAHG(2)	Grumman AA-5B Tiger	AA5B-0469	N6148A
D-EAHH(2)	Diamond DA 20-A1 Katana	10097	(D-ERKL), OE-VPZ, C-FDTI
D-EAHI (2)	Piper PA-28RT-201 Arrow IV	28R-7918222	N62TJ, N2925L
D-EAHK(2)	Robin DR.400/180R Remorqueur	1314	
D-EAHL(2)	SOCATA MS.894A Minerva 220	11836	(G-AYVW)
D-EAHM	Fuji FA-200-180 Aero Subaru	106	
D-EAHN(2)	Cessna 172N Skyhawk	17269925	N738ES
D-EAHO(2)	Cessna 172P Skyhawk	17274783	N53590
D-EAHP(3)	Maule MX-7-235 Star Rocket	10066C	HB-KDS, N90AG, HB-KER, D-EVAM(1), N6112Y
D-EAHR	SAN Jodel DR.1050 Ambassadeur	372	
D-EAHS	SOCATA MS.893E Rallye 180GT	12311	F-BUVC
D-EAHT	Cessna TU206F Turbo Stationair	U20602201	HB-CDT, N7431Q
D-EAHU(2)	Piper PA-28-181 Archer II	28-8190075	N82855
D-EAHX	Piper PA-18 Super Cub 95	18-3432	D-EAWK(1), 96+12, NL+109, AC+520, AA+520, AS+520, 54-732
D-EAHZ	Piper PA-38-112 Tomahawk II	38-81A0002	HB-PFN
D-EAIA(4)	Robin DR.400/135CDi	2592	
D-EAIB	Bölkow BO.209 Monsun 160FV	186	
D-EAIC(2)	Mooney M.20J Model 201	24-0399	
D-EAID(2)	Piper PA-28-181 Archer II	2890009	N9107J
D-EAIF(3)	Cessna 152 (P. 4.8.16)	15282287	N684Q, N68412
D-EAIG	Bölkow BO.209 Monsun 160RV	191	
D-EAIH(2)	Reims/Cessna F182P Skylane	F18200017	D-EATH
D-EAII (2)	Cessna 182P Skylane	18263683	N4682K
D-EAIK(2)	SOCATA MS.880B Rallye Club	1904	F-BSZZ
D-EAIM(2)	Fuji FA-200-160 Aero Subaru	173	
D-EAIN(3)	Aquila AT-01	AT01-115	
D-EAIO	Robin DR.300/180R Remorqueur	549	
D-EAIP	Fuji FA-200-180 Aero Subaru	92	
D-EAIQ	Fuji FA-200-180 Aero Subaru	100	
D-EAIR(2)	Bölkow BO.209 Monsun 160RV	199	
D-EAIS(2)	Beech F33A Bonanza	CE-1243	N3083K
D-EAIT	Mooney M.20K Model 231	25-0771	
D-EAIU	Cessna 150B	15059663	OE-AIU, N1263Y
D-EAIV	Piper PA-28RT-201T Turbo Arrow IV	28R-7931062	N3072N
D-EAIW(2)	SOCATA TB-9 Tampico	130	OO-TAB
D-EAIY(2)	Aquila AT-01	AT01-223	
D-EAJB(3)	SOCATA Rallye 100T	3042	OY-AJB, F-ODIH
D-EAJC	Dornier Do.27B-1	292	56+24, SE+534, SC+712
D-EAJF(2)	Tecnam P.2002-JF Sierra	088	
D-EAJG	Robin DR.300/180R Remorqueur	712	
D-EAJI	Robin DR.300/180R Remorqueur	722	
D-EAJJ	SOCATA MS.893A Rallye Commodore 180	10531	OO-SPD, F-BNBC
D-EAJM	Cessna R182 Skylane RG	R18200243	N3152C
D-EAJP(2)	Cessna TU206G Turbo Stationair 6-II	U20604465	N756YP
D-EAJR	Robin DR.400/180R Remorqueur	815	
D-EAJS	Extra EA.400	11	
D-EAJT(2)	Reims/Cessna F172P	F17202184	PH-AVA(2), PH-AXN, F-WZDD
D-EAJU	Bek Ju 87 replica (Permit expired 7.01)	1959	
D-EAJW	SOCATA TB-10 Tobago	147	
D-EAJZ	Robin DR.400/140B Dauphin 4	2671	
D-EAKA(2)	Cirrus SR22T	0015	N7800
D-EAKB	Reims/Cessna F150M	F15001158	
D-EAKC(2)	SOCATA TB-10 Tobago	1160	
D-EAKD(2)	SOCATA TB-10 Tobago	1161	
D-EAKE	Reims/Cessna F177RG Cardinal RG	F177RG0124	
D-EAKG(2)	Piper PA-28-236 Dakota	28-7911115	N3066T
D-EAKI (2)	Cessna 172R Skyhawk	17280111	N9859F
D-EAKJ	SOCATA TB-10 Tobago	1162	
D-EAKK	Piper PA-28-181 Archer II	28-7990417	N2125G
D-EAKL(2)	Robin DR.400/180R Remo 180	2228	
D-EAKM	SAN Jodel DR.1050 Ambassadeur	139	OE-AKM
D-EAKO(3)	Piper PA-28RT-201T Turbo Arrow IV	28R-8131146	N8401A
D-EAKP(2)	Piper PA-28-181 Archer II	28-8590048	N69093
D-EAKQ	OMF-100-160 Symphony	0005	
D-EAKR(2)	OMF-100-160 Symphony	0006	
D-EAKS(4)	Cessna 172S Skyhawk SP	172S10094	N23550
D-EAKT	Robin DR.400/180R Remorqueur	900	
D-EAKU(2)	Piper PA-28-181 Archer II	28-8590082	N2531X
D-EAKV	SOCATA TB-10 Tobago	1164	
D-EAKW(3)	Wolf/.Van's RV-7 (Permit 18.11.15)	72897	
D-EAKX	OMF-100-160 Symphony	0008	
D-EAKY(2)	Reims/Cessna F177RG Cardinal RG (Reims-assembled 177RG c/n 177RG0198)	F177RG0035	OE-DEE
D-EAKZ(2)	SOCATA TB-10 Tobago	1163	
D-EALB(2)	Bellanca 7ECA Citabria	1182-77	I-GALB
D-EALC	Piper PA-28-180 Cherokee G	28-7205311	N11C
D-EALD	SOCATA ST-10 Diplomate	128	
D-EALE	Cessna F172F	F172-0178	
D-EALF	Robin DR.400/180 Régent	976	(D-EOKC)
D-EALG	Lake LA-4-200 Buccaneer	558	N9972F, D-EALG, OY-DVN, N39794
D-EALH	Piper PA-28-181 Archer II	28-8090276	N8175N
D-EALI	Mooney M.20F Executive 21	680123	N3800N
D-EALL(3)	Piper PA-46-500TP Malibu Meridian	4697050	LX-FUN, N123SX, G-BZTP, N53308, G-BZTP, N9531N, N5020Y
D-EALM(3)	WACO YMF-F5C	F5C-8-123	N15WD
D-EALP	Reims/Cessna FRA150M Aerobat	FRA1500298	(G-BEOE), (5Y-AZY)
D-EALR	Reims FR172J Rocket	FR17200564	
D-EALS	Reims FR172J Rocket	FR17200577	
D-EALT(2)	Cessna 172S Skyhawk SP	172S11046	N52921
D-EALX(2)	Reims/Cessna F150L	F15000766	OE-ALX
D-EALY(2)	Commander Aircraft 114B	14585	
D-EALZ	Cessna P206D Super Skylane	P206-0603	N5703J
D-EAMA	Fuji FA-200-160 Aero Subaru	73	
D-EAMB(2)	Bölkow BO.208C Junior	597	OE-AMB, D-ECGE(1)
D-EAMC(4)	Sopport/ Dallach D4/E-BK/S Fascination	EB022	
D-EAMD(2)	Piper PA-28RT-201T Turbo Arrow IV	28R-8331042	N4308Z
D-EAMF	Fuji FA-200-180 Aero Subaru	81	
D-EAMG(2)	Reims/Cessna F182Q Skylane	F18200038	(D-EAMT), OE-DIP
D-EAMH(3)	SOCATA TB-10 Tobago	153	OE-DUZ
D-EAMI	Fuji FA-200-160 Aero Subaru	151	
D-EAMK	Cessna T210F Turbo-System Centurion	T210-0059	N6159R
D-EAML(2)	Cessna T206H Turbo Stationair	T20608348	N5146F
D-EAMM	Wassmer WA.52 Europa	88	
D-EAMN(2)	Piper PA-28-181 Cherokee Archer II	28-7890515	N36428
D-EAMO(2)	Brändli BX-2 Cherry (P 28.8.13)	21	(D-EYRS)
D-EAMP(4)	Cessna F150J	F150-0491	HB-CTW
D-EAMR(2)	Cessna 182J Skylane	18257493	N4786J, D-EHKN, N3493F
D-EAMS(2)	Piper PA-28-181 Archer II	28-8690046	N9085N, N9512N
D-EAMT(4)	Mooney M.20J Model 205	24-3084	9H-ACJ(2), SE-KYB, N5272N
D-EAMV	Fuji FA-200-160 Aero Subaru	177	
D-EAMW	Fuji FA-200-180 Aero Subaru	178	
D-EAMX(2)	Diamond DA 40D Star	D4.078	
D-EAMY	Piper PA-28-140 Cherokee Cruiser	28-7325212	N11C
D-EAMZ	Fuji FA-200-160 Aero Subaru	165	
D-EANA(3)	Aquila AT-01 100A (Res .16)	AT01-340	
D-EANB(2)	Hamacher / Flitzer Z-21	1	
D-EANE	Piper PA-28-151 Cherokee Warrior	28-7415155	N9515N
D-EANF	Reims/Cessna F172N	F17201684	
D-EANK(2)	Grob G 115A	8012	
D-EANM	PZL-110 Koliber 150	0389036	SP-ARY(2)
D-EANO	Piper PA-28-181 Cherokee Archer II	28-7890433	N9648C
D-EANQ	Wassmer WA.51A Pacific	28	F-BSNQ
D-EANS	Mooney M.20G Statesman	680008	N586MA
D-EANT	Reims FR172G Rocket	FR17200194	
D-EANU	Van's RV-8 (Res. .12)	83187	
D-EAOA	Piper PA-28-181 Archer II	2890052	N9133X
D-EAOD	Reims/Cessna F152	F15201910	
D-EAOE	Cessna 172RG Cutlass RG	172RG0380	N4795V
D-EAOJ	SOCATA TB-10 Tobago	995	
D-EAOK	Piper PA-28-160 Cherokee B	28-681	OY-AOK, N5577W
D-EAOM(2)	Bücker Bü 181 Bestmann (Res)	25115	D-EBOM(1), Fv25115
D-EAON	Piper PA-28R-200 Cherokee Arrow II	28R-7535273	N1408X
D-EAOO	Cessna T210N Turbo Centurion II	21063856	N6289C
D-EAOP	Beech K35 Bonanza	D-6028	D-ENOC
D-EAOR	Reims FR172F Rocket	FR17200071	
D-EAOT(2)	SAN Jodel DR.1050 Ambassadeur	147	OE-AOT
D-EAOU	SOCATA TB-20 Trinidad	999	
D-EAOV	Robin DR.400/180R Remorqueur	1959	
D-EAOY	SOCATA TB-10 Tobago	998	
D-EAOZ	SOCATA TB-21 Trinidad TC	632	
D-EAPA	Grumman AA-5 Traveler	AA5-0752	(N1352R)
D-EAPB	Robin DR.400/180R Remorqueur	1629	
D-EAPC(3)	Diamond DA 40D Star	D4.271	
D-EAPD(2)	Mooney M.20J Model 201	24-0520	HB-DFE
D-EAPE(2)	Cirrus SR22T	0984	N984JP
D-EAPF	Robin DR.400/180R Remorqueur	1630	
D-EAPG	Mooney M.20K Model 252 TSE	25-1147	
D-EAPH	Zlin Z.526AFS Akrobat	1230	
D-EAPJ(2)	Reims/Cessna F15M	F15001262	
D-EAPK	Cessna 182P Skylane (Reims-assembled with "c/n" 0026)	18263975	N9915E
D-EAPL(2)	Robin DR.400/180 Régent	1783	
D-EAPM(2)	Feichtinger/ Piel CP.301E Emeraude	065	OE-APR
D-EAPN(3)	Piper PA-32R-301 Saratoga II HP	3213088	TF-FAX, C-GIXL, N9251R
D-EAPO	Piper PA-28RT-201 Arrow IV	28R-8018033	N8149D
D-EAPS	Cessna 172L	17259327	N7627G
D-EAPW(3)	Piper PA-28-181 Archer II	28-8090298	N82018
D-EAPX	Piper PA-46-310P Malibu	4608051	N9092W
D-EAPZ	Cessna 172R Skyhawk	17280269	N427ES
D-EAQA	Test registration for Aquila AT-01 production		
D-EAQB	Aquila AT-01 (P .09)	AT01-103	PH-ANA, D-EANW(2)
D-EAQC	Aquila AT-01 (Res 29.8.16)	AT01-184	
D-EAQH	Piper PA-28-161 Cadet	2841116	N91716, N9647N
D-EAQJ	Aquila AT-01	AT01-213	
D-EAQK	Piper PA-28-140 Cherokee Cruiser	28-7625065	N9639N
D-EAQL(2)	Aquila AT-01	AT01-145	
D-EAQN	Aquila AT-01	AT01-140	OE-ASZ, (D-EAQN)
D-EAQR	Aquila AT-01	AT01-191	
D-EAQS	Aquila AT-01	AT01-201	
D-EAQT(2)	Aquila AT-01 (Res. .06)	AT01-144	
D-EAQU(3)	Aquila AT-01-100C	AT01-303	
D-EAQV	Aquila AT-01	AT01-173	
D-EAQX	Aquila AT-01	AT01-190	
D-EAQY	Aquila AT-01	AT01-166	
D-EARA(2)	Wohltmann / Hinz BL2 Ara (Permit to 17.2.17)	001/2002185	D-EAKW(2)
D-EARB(2)	Mooney M.20F Executive	22-1259	HB-DWG
D-EARC	Rockwell Commander 112A	468	OY-PRD, (SE-FLX), (N1468J)
D-EARF	Robin DR.400/180R Remorqueur	1718	
D-EARI	Beech S35 Bonanza	D-7386	
D-EARL(2)	Cessna T210M Turbo Centurion	21061747	N8719J, N732SW
D-EARM	Beech F35 Bonanza	D-4256	OO-JAO, OO-JAC
D-EARN(2)	Piper PA-28-161 Cadet	2841113	N9645N
D-EARO	Cessna 182N Skylane	18260106	N92237
D-EARP	SOCATA MS.880B Rallye Club	2054	F-BTRE
D-EARR	Beech C23 Sundowner 180	M-2275	
D-EART	Mooney M.20K Model 231	25-0376	
D-EARV(2)	Grob G 115C	82039/C	
D-EARY(3)	Piaggio FWP.149D	057	(D-EIJR), HB-EVU, 90+43, SB+212, SC+402, AS+484
D-EASB(3)	Cessna 172N Skyhawk	17272535	N5347D
D-EASC(2)	Piper PA-28-181 Archer II	28-8090212	N81418
D-EASD(2)	Grob G 115D	82067/D	OY-SKP(2), LN-TFX, N115MH, (D-EGVV)
D-EASE(3)	Cirrus SR20	1931	N648PG
D-EASF	Piper PA-28R-201 Cherokee Arrow III	28R-7737090	N38359
D-EASG(5)	Robin DR.400/180R Remorqueur	1529	HB-EQL, F-GCUX
D-EASH	Piper PA-28-180 Cherokee Archer	28-7505038	N9608N
D-EASJ	Bölkow BO.208C Junior	695	OE-ASR, D-EABI (1)
D-EASK	Sportavia-Pützer RF-6	6002	
D-EASL(2)	Mooney M.20K Model 231	25-0688	PH-WVR, N1167G, (PH-WVR), N1167G
D-EASM	Cessna 182M Skylane	18259654	(N71534)

Reg	Type	C/n	Previous identities
D-EASN	Mooney M.20J Model 201	24-1244	N1154Y
D-EASP	SOCATA MS.880B Rallye Club	1609	
D-EASS(5)	Cessna 172S Skyhawk SP	172S10405	N1355B
D-EAST(3)	HOAC DV-20 Katana	20027	OE-CDD(2), N27DV
D-EASU	SOCATA MS.893A Rallye Commodore 180	10988	
D-EASW	SAN Jodel DR.1050 Ambassadeur	131	F-BJJP
D-EASY(2)	Frenzel / Van's RV-10	40300	
D-EASZ	Evektor EV-97 SportStar MAX	20101303	
	(P 5.10)		
D-EATA(4)	Cessna 170A	18884	N9125A
D-EATB	SOCATA MS.892A Rallye Commodore 150	10953	
	(Permit 15.6.16)		
D-EATC	Cessna 150C	15059805	N2005Z
D-EATD(2)	Cessna 140	8784	(OY-RET), LN-RET, LN-TSI, N89735, NC89735
	(Res. 17.6.15)		
D-EATH(2)	Piper PA-28R-201T Turbo Arrow III	28R-7803346	
D-EATN	SAN Jodel DR.1050 Ambassadeur	451	
D-EATO	Wassmer CE.43 Guepard	438	
D-EATP(2)	RFB Fantrainer 400	011	98+77, D-EATP(2)
D-EATQ	Bellanca 7GCBC Citabria	835-75	OE-AOO
D-EATS(3)	Piper PA-18-135 Super Cub	18-3351	N4282V, EI-129, I-EIHD, 53-7751
D-EATT(2)	Piper PA-28-200 Cherokee Arrow	28R-35676	OO-JAE, D-EJAE(2), N4904S
D-EATV(2)	Piper PA-28R-201T Turbo Cherokee Arrow III	28R-7703303	N40435
D-EATW(2)	Diamond DA 20-A1 Katana	10141	C-FDVP
D-EATX(2)	Gyroflug SC-01B-160 Speed Canard	S-48	
D-EATY(2)	Piper PA-18 Super Cub 95	18-1511	OO-HBS, OO-SPK, ALAT, 51-15511
	(C/n officially quoted as 18-3080)		
D-EATZ	Cessna F150H	F150-0229	OE-AVV
D-EAUA	SOCATA TB-10 Tobago	1097	
D-EAUB(4)	Cessna 172N Skyhawk	17270150	N172TA, N738QG
D-EAUC	Grumman American AA-5A Cheetah	AA5A-0349	D-EOGN, HB-UCI
D-EAUD	Cessna 150G	15065230	ZS-ENR, 3D-AEY, ZS-ENR, N3930J
D-EAUF	SOCATA MS.893E Rallye 180GT	12267	F-BUJE
D-EAUI (2)	Piper PA-25-235 Pawnee	25-2179	EC-AUI, N6617Z, N10F
D-EAUO	Robin DR.400/180R Remo 180	2371	
D-EAUP(2)	Stemme ASP/S15-1	6.T.10.010	D-KOHC(2), (D-KCND)
	(Res. 30.4.15) (Converted from model S6 to airborne system platform)		
D-EAUS(2)	Gyroflug SC-01B-160 Speed Canard	S-10	
D-EAUT(3)	Piper PA-18-150 Super Cub	18-7909190	N9754N
D-EAUU(2)	Bücker Bü.133C Jungmeister	10	OE-AUU, D-EEEY(2), U-63
D-EAUW	Werner Rieseler R.III.22/K	1853	
	(Res)		
D-EAVA	Cessna 182M Skylane	18259806	N91525
D-EAVB	Beech F33A Bonanza	CE-1127	
D-EAVC	Reims/Cessna F172N	F17201728	N9900A
D-EAVE(2)	SOCATA TB-10 Tobago	930	
D-EAVG	Reims/Cessna F172M	F17201362	(D-EDRO)
D-EAVI (3)	Nachshon/ Velocity J-II	01	
	(Permit)		
D-EAVL	SAN Jodel DR.1050 Ambassadeur	360	
D-EAVM	AIAA/Stampe SV-4C	1134	F-BALM
D-EAVQ(2)	Robin DR.400/180R Remorqueur	1395	OE-DHN
D-EAVS	Robin DR.300/180R Remorqueur	706	
D-EAVT(2)	Piper PA-32-301T Saratoga II TC	3257399	(D-EPHE), PH-CON, N31166, PH-CON
D-EAVV	Bücker Bü.131B Jungmann	12	HB-UUB, A-5
D-EAVW	Aquila AT-01	AT01-229	
D-EAVX	Cessna 150M	15079321	N714PE
D-EAVY(2)	Piper PA-28R-201 Arrow	2844123	N3098E
D-EAVZ	Aquila AT-01-210	AT01-224	
D-EAWA	Gardan GY-80 Horizon 180	256	
D-EAWD(2)	Fieseler Fi.156C-3 Storch	5440	D-EBGY(1), Fv5825, PP+QA
	(C/n quoted as "2072-9")		
D-EAWF(2)	Cessna P210N Pressurized Centurion	P21000618	N734XN
D-EAWG	Cessna 182P Skylane	18264392	N1606M
	(Reims-assembled with "c/n" 0055)		
D-EAWH	Robin DR.400/180R Remorqueur	1440	
D-EAWI (4)	Extra EA.300/SC	SC033	
D-EAWJ	Robin R.3000/160	144	HB-KIE
D-EAWK(2)	Beech A36 Bonanza	E-2174	N184SB
D-EAWL(2)	Zlin Z.42M	0060	DDR-WNR, DM-WNR
D-EAWM	Grob G 115C	82035/C	OY-SKS, N115AZ
D-EAWP(3)	Mooney M.20K Model 231	25-0605	N1149E
D-EAWR(2)	Cirrus SR22	2759	HA-CIB, N753SR
D-EAWU(2)	Cessna 172S Skyhawk SP	172S8148	N53224
D-EAWW(2)	Piper PA-28R-201 Arrow III	28R-7837199	N9469C
D-EAWZ	Reims/Cessna F172M	F17201169	
D-EAXA	Grumman AA-5 Traveler	AA5-0497	(N7197L)
D-EAXB	Grumman AA-5 Traveler	AA5-0518	(N9518L)
D-EAXD	Grumman AA-5 Traveler	AA5-0545	(N9545L)
D-EAXE	Grumman AA-5 Traveler	AA5-0553	(N9553L)
D-EAXF(2)	Mooney M.20L PFM	26-0032	N152MP
	(Res. .10)		
D-EAXH	Grumman AA-1B Trainer	AA1B-0356	(N8856L)
D-EAXI (2)	Müller/ Denney Kitfox 4	C9909-0251	
D-EAXK(3)	Extra EA.300/LT	LT019	
D-EAXL	CASA C-1.131E Jungmann	2154	(D-EGXT), F-AZGH, E3B-538
D-EAXM	Aviat A-1B Husky	2438	G-DBLX, N117AA
D-EAXP	Korte/ Aero Designs Pulsar XP	1809	
D-EAXR	Cessna LC41-550FG Columbia	41720	N70TK
D-EAXT(2)	Piaggio FWP.149D	150	91+28, AC+464, AC+402, AS+084, KB+127
D-EAXX(2)	Piper PA-18-150 Super Cub	18-8209024	IDFAF114
	(Res. .15)		
D-EAXY(3)	Cessna 172S Skyhawk SP	172S10622	N12080
	(P .08)		
D-EAXZ	Cessna 175C Skylark	17557032	OE-DCH, N8332T
D-EAYB	Piper PA-28R-201 Cherokee Arrow III	28R-7737112	N38732
D-EAYP	Beech A36AT Bonanza	E-2656	
D-EAYV	Cessna F150H	F150-0301	G-EJMG, D-EJMG(2)
D-EAYX	Piper PA-32-301T Saratoga II TC	3257024	D-ESUV(2), N9295X
D-EAYY(2)	Cessna 172S Skyhawk SP	172S10229	N6042P
D-EAZA(2)	Macchi MB.308	19/5792	I-JOLE
	(Also wears original marks I-JOLE)		
D-EAZE	Focke-Wulf FW.44J Stieglitz	2779	OH-SZI, SZ-20, RNoAF 9, D-EXWP
D-EAZG(2)	Extra EA.200	02	(D-ETTW)
D-EAZL(3)	Cessna 172S Skyhawk SP	172S8299	N406SP
D-EAZR	FFA AS.202/18A4	0233	OH-NTN, G-BNTN
D-EAZS	FFA AS.202/18A4	0224	OH-NTE, G-BNTE
D-EAZT	SOCATA TB-9 Tampico Club	1113	
D-EAZU	FFA AS.202/18A4	0225	OH-NTF, G-BNTF
D-EAZV	FFA AS.202/18A4	0228	OH-NTI, G-BNTI
D-EAZW	Zech/ Neico Lancair 320	1700	
D-EAZY(2)	Rutan LongEz	1597	
	(Res)		
D-EBAA(3)	SOCATA TB-9 Tampico Club	1470	PH-BAW, OE-KMN
	(Res. .15)		
D-EBAB(2)	Piper PA-28-151 Cherokee Warrior	28-7415059	N9607N
D-EBAC(2)	Dornier Do.27A-4	381	56+76, PA+323, KD+ . . ., PG+102
D-EBAD(7)	Piper PA-18-95 Super Cub	18-3429	D-EJRR, 96+10, SB+220, AC+518, AS+518, 54-729
D-EBAE	CEA DR.253B Régent	147	(G-AXDG)
D-EBAF	Piper J-3C-65 Cub	13197	SL-AAR, F-BDTF, 45-4457
D-EBAG(2)	Reims/Cessna F172N	F17201655	
D-EBAH(3)	Echtle/ Brditschka HB-207A Alfa	207007	
D-EBAI	CEA DR.253B Régent	144	F-BRFZ
D-EBAJ(3)	Robin R.3000/140	102	D-EHIA(1)
D-EBAK(4)	Diamond DA 20-A1 Katana	10330	N330DA, C-GDMU
D-EBAL(2)	Piper PA-18-150 Super Cub	18-5364	N5884, ALAT, N10F
D-EBAM(2)	Cessna 210L Centurion II	21061120	N210GV, N210GM
D-EBAN(2)	SOCATA MS.883 Rallye 115	1586	
D-EBAO	CEA DR.253B Régent	151	
D-EBAP(3)	Mooney M.20M Model 257 TLS	27-0159	N30WA
D-EBAR(2)	SOCATA TB-9 Tampico	933	
D-EBAS(3)	Piper PA-28RT-201T Turbo Arrow IV	28R-8231024	N8062L
D-EBAT(3)	Dornier Do.27A-4	451	F-BSGK, 57+23, PB+223, PC+103, QM+007, KD+1
.D-EBAU	Taylorcraft 19 Sportsman 85	4-13107	
	(Permit 9.10)		
D-EBAV(2)	Wassmer WA.52 Europa	19	F-WSQG
D-EBAW(3)	Piper PA-18-150 Super Cub	18-5389	ALAT, N10F
D-EBAX(3)	Grumman AA-5 Traveler	AA5-0751	(N1351R)
D-EBAY	Robin DR.300/180R Remorqueur	595	
D-EBAZ(6)	Baaz/ Neico Lancair 320	489/1697	
D-EBBA(3)	Lang/ Aero Designs Pulsar XP	EB 432	
D-EBBB	Piper PA-18 Super Cub 95	18-3425	96+07, PZ+901, QZ+010, AC+514, AA+514, AS+514, 54-725
D-EBBC(2)	SOCATA TB-9 Tampico	1420	I-IAGU
D-EBBD	Reims FR172F Rocket	FR17200066	
D-EBBE(2)	SAN Jodel D.140C Mousquetaire III	119	F-BMBA
D-EBBI (5)	Cessna 150M	15075785	SP-KOD, N66027
D-EBBJ	Reims FR172F Rocket	FR17200119	
D-EBBK(2)	SOCATA TB-10 Tobago	399	F-OGKG
D-EBBM(3)	Cessna 172N Skyhawk	17268151	N733AU
D-EBBN(2)	Beech A36 Bonanza	E-2497	OH-BBN
D-EBBO(2)	Bölkow BO.207	291	D-EOXX, HB-UXX, (D-EJYR)
D-EBBR(2)	Winter LF-1 Zaunkönig V-4	5	D-EBCG(2), D-ECER(1)
	(Permit 26.1.12)		
D-EBBS(3)	Beech B36TC Bonanza	EA-457	N2749N
D-EBBV	Robin HR.100/285 Tiara	524	G-BGWD, F-BXRF
D-EBBW(2)	PZL-104 Wilga 35A	62167	DDR-WBW, DM-WBW
D-EBBY(2)	Reims/Cessna F172M	F17201337	
D-EBBZ	Beagle B.121 Pup 100	142	G-AXSE, G-35-142
D-EBCA(3)	Grumman American AA-5A Cheetah	AA5A-0733	G-BGFI, N6142A
D-EBCB(2)	Cessna R172K Hawk XP	R1722399	I-AMCB, N736BP
D-EBCC	SAN Jodel DR.1050M Excellence	488	
D-EBCD	Piper PA-28-161 Cherokee Warrior II	28-7816268	N9515N
D-EBCE(2)	Piper PA-28RT-201T Turbo Arrow IV	28R-8031093	N8190R
D-EBCF(2)	Beech B36TC Bonanza	EA-543	N534JS, F-GJIS, D-ECPK(2), N333PK
D-EBCI (2)	Piper PA-28-181 Cherokee Archer II	28-7690247	(D-EEEL), N9556N
D-EBCK	Procaer F15B Picchio	35	OE-DGE
D-EBCL	Reims/Cessna F150M	F15001405	
D-EBCM(3)	Cirrus SR22	0581	N1569C
D-EBCN	SNCAN/ Stampe SV.4C	543	F-BDCN, (OO-CDN), F-BDCN
D-EBCP	Beech C23 Sundowner 180	M-1948	
D-EBCR(3)	Piper PA-18-150 Super Cub	18-2032	D-EWDL, D-ENWO(2), R-35, 52-2432
D-EBCS(3)	Robin DR.500/200i Président	0005	
D-EBCT(2)	Cessna 152	15280950	N48746
D-EBCU(2)	Cessna F172H	F172-0642	
D-EBCV	HOAC DV-20 Katana	20018	N18DV
D-EBCW	Cessna R172K Hawk XP	R1722565	N736JN
D-EBCX	Cirrus SR22	0862	N5322A
D-EBDB	Piper PA-28-140 Cherokee B	28-26026	OY-BDD
D-EBDE	Piaggio FWP.149D	131	(91+10), D-EBDE, KB+108
D-EBDH(2)	Flight Design CT LS-ELA	12-08-05	
	(Permit 23.12.13)		
D-EBDJ	Volk/ Bede BD-5J/V	2055-J/V	
	(Permit 27.12.11)		
D-EBDL	Piper PA-46-310P Malibu	46-8608018	N9226M
D-EBDM	Cessna 172P Skyhawk	17276375	N98897
D-EBDO(4)	Oberbach/ Van's RV-4	01	
D-EBDR(2)	Dornier Do.27A-1	"272"	D-EBDR(1), 56+05, YA+014?, LC+158
	(True c/n either 260 or 507 or parts of both, each of which contained parts of c/n 272 which was D-EBDR(1) and is now "D-EPEA" in museum)		
D-EBDS	Diamond DA 40 Star	40247	N610DS
D-EBDT(2)	Mudry CAP.231	10	F-GGYH, F-WZCJ
D-EBDU(2)	Mooney M.20J Model 201	24-0880	(N4790H)
D-EBDW	HOAC DV-20 Katana	20050	
D-EBDX	Aerodifusión Jodel D.1190-S Compostela	E-95	OE-CFW, D-EBDX, EC-BDX
D-EBDZ	Christen A-1 Husky	1160	N8754J
D-EBEB(5)	CSA Sportcruiser (Piper Sport)	P1102021	
	(Permit 31.1.12)		
D-EBEC(3)	Diamond DA 20-A1 Katana	10331	N731DA, C-GKAN
D-EBEE(2)	SAN Jodel DR.1050 Ambassadeur	142	PH-ASE
	(P. 27.5.16)		
D-EBEF(2)	Beech C23 Sundowner 180	M-2195	
D-EBEG(2)	Piper PA-28R-201T Turbo Cherokee Arrow III	28R-7703064	N2401Q
D-EBEH(2)	Cessna 172C Skyhawk	17249296	N1596Y
D-EBEI (2)	Messerschmitt Bf 108D-1	2246	N108HP, N54208, NF+MAB
D-EBEJ(2)	Focke-Wulf FW.44J Stieglitz	1281	SZ-35
	(Res. 24.6.15) (c/n should be 2938 – to be confirmed)		
D-EBEK(2)	Piper PA-28-200 Cherokee Arrow II	28R-7335205	N55264
D-EBEM(2)	Piper PA-28-200 Cherokee Arrow II	28R-7335235	N55453

Reg	Type	C/n	Previous identities / notes
D-EBEN(2)	Mooney M.20L PFM	26-0013	
D-EBEP(4)	Piper PA-28RT-201T Turbo Arrow IV	28R-7931150	N2195Y
D-EBER(4)	HK Wega Ex	006	
	(Permit expired 7.04)		
D-EBES(2)	Piper PA-28R-201T Turbo Cherokee Arrow III	28R-7703063	N2295Q
D-EBET(3)	Cub Crafters CC11-160 Carbon Cub SS	CC11-00240	
	(Permit 19.4.13)		
D-EBEU	Piper PA-38-112 Tomahawk	38-79A0939	N9682N
D-EBEV(2)	Reims/Cessna F172N	F17202023	(PH-AYE)
D-EBEW(7)	Cirrus SR20	1203	S5-DKN, N274CD
D-EBEX	Cessna 140	10300	N73084
D-EBEY	Piper PA-28-161 Warrior II	28-7916441	N2815S
D-EBEZ(2)	Piper PA-28RT-201 Arrow IV	28R-7918208	N2895Y
D-EBFA(2)	Piper PA-28-236 Dakota	28-7911253	N2940N
D-EBFB	Piper PA-18 Super Cub 95	18-3217	OL-L43, L-143, 53-4817
D-EBFC	Piper PA-18 Super Cub 95	18-3161	OL-L83, L-83, 53-4761
D-EBFD	Piper PA-18 Super Cub 95	18-3197	OL-L02, L-123, 53-4797
D-EBFE	SAN Jodel DR.1050 Ambassadeur	276	
D-EBFF	Fritsch Albatros D-III Replica	253.24	
D-EBFH(2)	Robin DR.400/180 Régent	2570	
D-EBFI (2)	Wassmer Jodel D.120 Paris-Nice	82	F-BIKN
D-EBFJ	Piper PA-18 Super Cub 95	18-2044	(G-....), OO-NLG, PH-NLG, R-67, 52-2444
D-EBFK(2)	Robin DR.400/180R Remo 180	1960	
D-EBFM	Maier/ Van's RV-4	AB-01	
D-EBFN	Cessna 172N Skyhawk	17271227	N2306E
D-EBFR(2)	Piper PA-32-260 Cherokee Six	32-223	I-GOES, G-AVTK, (I-....),
	(P. 1.6.16)		G-AVTK, N3266W
D-EBFS	Robin DR.300/180R Remorqueur	667	
D-EBFT	Grob G 115B	8102	VH-AYB, D-ERFI, F-GGOR, (HB-...)
D-EBFU	Piper PA-18 Super Cub 95	18-3126	L-52, 53-4726
D-EBFW(3)	Messerschmitt Bf 108B Taifun	1561	OY-AIH, F-BBRH, Luftwaffe, D-IBHS
D-EBFY	Pützer Elster C	022	
D-EBGA(3)	Cessna 172S Skyhawk SP	172S9367	N53442
D-EBGB(2)	Piper PA-28-160 Cherokee	28-82	OO-RPC, D-EBRO, N11C, (N5073W)
D-EBGC(2)	Piper PA-18-135 Super Cub	18-2549	OL-L43, ALAI, 52-6231
D-EBGD(2)	Cessna F150J	F150-0511	(HB-CTY)
D-EBGE(2)	Piper PA-38-112 Tomahawk	38-79A0986	N9710N
D-EBGG(2)	Reims FR172G Rocket	FR17200151	
D-EBGH	Cessna F150J	F150-0528	HB-CUA, F-BRBU
D-EBGL	Great Lakes 2T-1A-1	0504	N504GL
D-EBGM(2)	Robin DR.400/180 Régent	2477	
D-EBGN	Piper PA-28R-201T Turbo Cherokee Arrow III	28R-7703232	N38504
D-EBGO(2)	Cessna 182J Skylane	18257497	N3497F
D-EBGP	Cessna 172S Skyhawk SP	172S10597	OO-FRF, N1023Q
D-EBGR	Rösinger/ Murphy Renegade Spirit RG90	001	
D-EBGS	Robin DR.400/180R Remorqueur	1438	
D-EBGT	Cessna F150J	F150-0462	
D-EBGW(3)	Cessna 172RG Cutlass RG	127RG0935	N9637B
D-EBGZ	Robin DR.400/180R Remorqueur	803	
D-EBHA(2)	Robin DR.400/RP Remorqueur	1784	
D-EBHB(3)	Robin DR.400/180 Régent	1311	
D-EBHC(2)	Dornier Do.27A-4	512	HB-HAI, D-EFMG(2), 57+58, MB+904, JC+904, JC+390, LB+163
D-EBHD(2)	Reims/Cessna F172P	F17202198	
D-EBHE(2)	Beech B36TC Bonanza	EA-669	OY-BVO(2), N4469S
D-EBHF	Cessna 152	15280844	N25902
D-EBHI (2)	Piper PA-28-161 Warrior II	28-7916284	N9601N
D-EBHJ(2)	SNCAN/ Stampe SV.4C	165	F-BBPH
D-EBHL(3)	SNCAN/ Stampe SV.4C	216	Fr.AF, (F-BNGC), Fr.Navy, Fr.AF
D-EBHM	Cessna 172M	17261888	N12216
D-EBHN(2)	Mooney M.20K Model 231	25-0316	OE-KPS, N231MX
D-EBHO(3)	Bellanca 7GCBC Citabria	759-74	OE-AOM
D-EBHP	Piper PA-22-150 Tri-Pacer	22-3141	HB-OPB
D-EBHS	Mooney M.20J Model 201	24-0019	
D-EBHT	Cessna 172S Skyhawk SP	172S10262	N6069U
D-EBHV	Piper PA-18 Super Cub 95	18-2058	PH-JKB, R-73, 52-2458
D-EBHX	Syrach Bearhawk	2002395	
	(Res. .12)		
D-EBHY(2)	Piper PA-18 Super Cub 95	18-2099	D-EBHL(1), ALAT, 52-2499
D-EBHZ	Beech A36AT Bonanza	E-2717	
D-EBIA	Binder CP.301S Smaragd	100	
D-EBID	Piper PA-18 Super Cub 95	18-5660	N10F
D-EBIE(2)	Mooney M.20K Model 231	25-0665	N11620
D-EBIF(2)	Piper PA-28R-200 Cherokee Arrow	B28R-7135194	N1973T
D-EBIG(3)	Diamond DA 20-A1 Katana	10033	N608F, C-GDMY
D-EBIH(2)	Robin HR.100/210D Safari	199	
D-EBII	Robin HR.100/210D Safari	200	
D-EBIK(4)	Reims/Cessna F150M	F15001256	PH-BIK, D-EIHC, (F-BJDK)
D-EBIL(2)	Piper PA-28-140 Cherokee Cruiser	28-7625104	N9507N
D-EBIM(3)	SIAI-Marchetti SF.260	2-48	I-CEMX
	(Res. .11)		
D-EBIO	Reims/Cessna F177RG Cardinal RG	F177RG0048	
D-EBIP(2)	Cessna F150F	F150-0048/15063375	(N6775F)
D-EBIQ(2)	Cessna 175B	17556814	OE-DCF, N8114T
D-EBIS(2)	Piper J-3C-65 Cub	12513	(D-EDUS), (Norway), 44-80217
D-EBIT	Piper PA-24-250 Comanche	24-393	N10F
D-EBIV(4)	Piper PA-28-161 Warrior II	28-7916175	N9558N
D-EBIW(3)	Cessna T206H Turbo Stationair	T20608262	N238ST
D-EBIX(3)	Mudry CAP.10B	220	OO-OFD
D-EBIY	Piper PA-28RT-201T Turbo Arrow IV	28R-7931320	N2858D
D-EBIZ(3)	Diamond DA 40 Star	40052	
D-EBJA(3)	Cessna 172N Skyhawk	17270249	N738UN
D-EBJB(2)	Piper PA-18-135 Super Cub	18-3922	N4282R, EI-226, I-EIJW, 54-2522
D-EBJF(2)	Tecnam P.2002-JF Sierra	239	
D-EBJG(3)	Piper PA-28-140 Cherokee	28-21500	OE-DPA, N11C
D-EBJK(3)	Aquila AT-01	AT01-165	G-UILA
D-EBJL(2)	Cessna P210N Pressurized Centurion II	P21000042	N116RS, G-IAIN, N3623P
D-EBJN	Bölkow BO.209 Monsun 150FF	154	
D-EBJO	Bölkow BO.209 Monsun 150FF	155	
D-EBJP	Bölkow BO.209 Monsun 160RV	156	
D-EBJQ	Bölkow BO.209 Monsun 150FF	157	
D-EBJR(2)	Cessna 182T Skylane	18281313	N21002
D-EBJS(2)	Dornier Do.27A-1	604	57+65, BD+398
	(Res)		
D-EBKA(2)	Aquila AT-01	AT01-257	
D-EBKC(2)	Cessna 172S Skyhawk SP	172S8364	N507SP
D-EBKD	Morane-Saulnier MS.880B Rallye Club	115	F-BKKH, (D-EMPY)
D-EBKF(3)	Remos GX	405	
	(Permit 29.3.12)		
D-EBKI (3)	Cessna 182S Skylane	18280493	N7269V
D-EBKJ	Diamond DA 40D Star	D4.236	OE-UDR
D-EBKK(2)	Piper PA-46-310P Malibu	4608120	N183WW, N133WW,
	(JetProp DLX conversion # 173)		N9136J
D-EBKL	Dornier Do.27B-1	363	56+68, LC+160, AS+942
D-EBKM(2)	Heliopolis Gomhouria Mk.6	187	SU-352, EAF 352
	(Permit 10.10.13) (C/n is believed correct, quoted officially as 352)		
D-EBKR	Gyroflug SC-01B-160i Speed Canard	S-13	
D-EBKT	de Havilland DH.82A Tiger Moth	85223/ E-13	(D-EAPN, OY-DYJ,
	(Cr 5.9.10, wfu?)		D-EDOM(1), DE153
D-EBKU(2)	Piper PA-28-161 Warrior II	28-7990543	N2903E
D-EBKW	Weiler/ Pottier P.180 S	155	
D-EBKY	Bölkow BO.207	234	
	(Permit 8.06)		
D-EBKZ	Robin DR.400/180 Régent	1055	
D-EBLC	Cessna F150J	F150-0495	
D-EBLD(2)	Cessna F172G	F172-0189	OE-DLD
D-EBLJ	Reims FR172G Rocket	FR17200148	
D-EBLK	Reims/Cessna F150K	F15000542	
D-EBLN(3)	Cirrus SR22T	0735	N177LN
D-EBLO	Bölkow BO.207	224	
D-EBLR	Reims/Cessna F150K	F15000576	
D-EBLS	Reims FR172G Rocket	FR17200207	
D-EBLT	Cessna 172B Skyhawk	17248473	N7973X
D-EBLW(2)	Piper PA-28RT-201 Arrow IV	28R-8118056	PH-SDE, OO-HKS, N83364
D-EBLX	SEEMS MS.892A Rallye Commodore 150	10449	F-BLSX
D-EBLY(2)	Bölkow BO.207	288	D-EUXY, HB-UXY, D-ENWE(1)
D-EBMA	Bölkow BO.207	235	
	(Res. 11.07)		
D-EBMB(5)	Fläming Air FA-04 Peregrine	026/11	
	(Permit 14.7.15)		
D-EBMC(2)	Cessna 172R Skyhawk	17281308	OE-KHS(2), N6008M
D-EBME(2)	Reims/Cessna F177RG Cardinal RG	F177RG0110	PH-OOG
D-EBMF	Cessna F172H	F172-0641	
D-EBMG	Reims FR172F Rocket	FR17200063	
D-EBMI	SAN Jodel DR.1050 Ambassadeur	353	
D-EBMK(2)	Beech B36TC Bonanza	EA-422	N6844L, N37PM, N6844L
D-EBMM(3)	HOAC DV-20 Katana	20137	
D-EBMN	Piper PA-38-112 Tomahawk	38-78A0397	(D-EOMN), N9705N
D-EBMR	Reims FR172F Rocket	FR17200123	(G-AXDA)
D-EBMS(2)	Maule MX7-235 Star Rocket	10067C	N6115Y
D-EBMT	Reims FR172F Rocket	FR17200112	
D-EBMU(2)	Beech C23 Sundowner	M-1467	OE-DMU, D-ENNQ
D-EBMW(4)	Cessna 207 Skywagon 207	20700088	OE-DEV, (N91138)
D-EBMX	Klemm L 25aVI	84	"D-1638", HB-UFA, CH-227
D-EBMZ	Reims FR172F Rocket	FR17200122	
D-EBNE	Cessna 182E Skylane	18253770	N9370X
D-EBNI	Cessna 182E Skylane	18254109	N3109Y
D-EBNK	Beech B24R Sierra 200	MC-222	
D-EBNL	Beech B24R Sierra 200	MC-233	
D-EBNN	Beech B24R Sierra 200	MC-260	
D-EBNO(2)	Beech F33A Bonanza	CE-484	
D-EBNQ	Beech V35B Bonanza	D-9602	
D-EBNS	Piper PA-18A-150 Super Cub	18-6117	G-JELY, PH-MAV, N8182D
D-EBNT	Berndt/ Jurca MJ-5 Sirocco	023	(D-EBTK(2))
D-EBNW	Robin DR.500/200i Président	0009	G-GSRV, F-GSRV
D-EBNY	Cessna 150D	15060497	N4497U
D-EBOA(2)	Haubensack/ Europa Avn Europa XS	161	
D-EBOB(2)	Piper PA-18-150 Super Cub	18-7501	N10F
D-EBOC(4)	Piper PA-28-181 Archer II	2890029	N9123N
D-EBOD(3)	Reims/Cessna F152	F15201618	
D-EBOE	Bölkow BO.209 Monsun 160RV	102	
D-EBOF(3)	Piaggio FWP.149D	109	90+89, AC+448, JC+390, AS+445
D-EBOG	Nitzsche/ Jodel D.9 Bébé	AB13	
	(Damaged 24.9.94, Res. 2.01 for rebuild)		
D-EBOI	Bölkow BO.209 Monsun 150FF	104	
D-EBOK(2)	Mooney M.20K Model 231	25-0256	N231HD
D-EBOL(5)	Piper PA-38-112 Tomahawk	38-78A0267	N9669N
D-EBOM(2)	Beech F33A Bonanza	CE-1147	
D-EBON(2)	Cessna 172P Skyhawk	17275093	PH-SCV, N54961
D-EBOO(3)	Reims FR172H Rocket	FR17200298	I-AMAI, D-ECRP
D-EBOQ(2)	Bölkow BO.209 Monsun 150FV	109	
D-EBOS	Bölkow BO.209 Monsun 150FV	110	
D-EBOT(3)	Aquila AT-01	AT01-142	
D-EBOU(2)	SNCAN/ Stampe SV.4C	326	OO-AKC, F-BCVS
D-EBOW(2)	Bölkow BO.209 Monsun 160RV	112	
D-EBOX	Cessna 150	17179	N5679E
D-EBOZ(2)	SNCAN/ Stampe SV.4C	297	F-BCGY
D-EBPA(4)	Piper PA-28-181 Archer III	2843596	N3093L
D-EBPC(3)	Cessna 152	15284716	N6414M
D-EBPE	Cessna 175C Skylark	17557085	N8385T
	(Franklin engine)		
D-EBPG(3)	Robin DR.400/120D Petit Prince	1432	HB-KAD
D-EBPH	Bölkow BO.209 Monsun 150FF	118	
D-EBPI	Bölkow BO.207	237	
D-EBPJ	Bölkow BO.209S Monsun 130FF	119	
D-EBPL	Cessna T182T Turbo Skylane	T18208753	N2355V
D-EBPM	Sportavia-Pützer RS-180 Sportsman	6011	
D-EBPO(2)	Sportavia-Pützer RS-180 Sportsman	6013	
D-EBPP	CASA C-1.131E Jungmann	2091	E3B-489
D-EBPR	Robin HR.200/120B	302	S5-DGR, D-EBPR
D-EBPS	Sueck/ Van's RV-7	0911	
D-EBPT	Bücker Bü.131 Jungmann	62	A-50
D-EBPY	Wassmer Jodel D.120 Paris-Nice	242	
D-EBQU	SEEMS MS.885 Super Rallye	5423	
D-EBRA	Erco 415CD Ercoupe	4833	OO-JDN, NC94722
D-EBRB(2)	SOCATA MS.880B Rallye Club	2951	OE-DRB
D-EBRD(2)	Cirrus SR22	2693	N979SR
D-EBRE(2)	Piper PA-28-181 Archer II	28-8090017	N2972V
D-EBRF	Piper PA-28R-200 Cherokee Arrow	28R-35658	N3034R
	(P 25.8.16)		
D-EBRH	Cessna P210N Pressurized Centurion II	P21000396	N6330K
D-EBRK(2)	Tecnam P.92J Echo-VLA	005	
D-EBRM(3)	Cessna 150C	150600006	OE-AYK, N7906Z
D-EBRO(4)	Cessna 172S Skyhawk SP	172S8175	N7256X

D-EBRP	Wassmer WA.81 Piranha	816	F-GAIR
D-EBRT	Reims/Cessna FR172K Hawk XP	FR17200610	G-BFRT, (LN-ALQ)
D-EBRU	Cessna 140	12604	OE-ABH(1), HB-CAE
D-EBRV	Servatius/ Van's RV-8	80303	
	(C/n officially quoted as 470 in error)		
D-EBRY	Cessna F172E	F172-0052	
D-EBSA(2)	Piper PA-28-180 Cherokee D	28-5329	N7918N
D-EBSB	Piper PA-28-140 Cherokee C	28-26566	N5901U
D-EBSC	Robin DR.400/180R Remorqueur	1310	
D-EBSD(2)	Cessna T.207A Turbo Stationair 8	20700644	N207PP, N75798
D-EBSF	Robin DR.400/180R Remorqueur	1041	
D-EBSG	SOCATA MS.894A Minerva 220	11828	F-BSMU
D-EBSH(2)	SNCAN/Stampe SV.4A	634	F-BUDY, F-BDMD
D-EBSI	Cessna 172B	17248089	N7589X
D-EBSK	Robin DR.400/180R Remorqueur	991	
D-EBSL	CEA DR.250/160 Capitaine	10	F-BMZI
D-EBSM	SOCATA MS.892A Rallye Commodore 150	11750	F-BSMF
D-EBSN(2)	Piper PA-28-181 Archer II	28-8190159	N8332K
D-EBSP	Cessna 182P Skylane	18263620	N6061J
D-EBSQ	Robin DR.400/180R Remorqueur	1802	
D-EBSR	Robin DR.400/RP	1766	(D-ELRA(2))
D-EBSS(3)	Aero-Jodel D.11A Club	604	OE-ASS
D-EBST	Robin DR.400/180R Remorqueur	876	
D-EBSU	Cessna 175B	17556862	N8162T
D-EBSV	Uetz Jodel D.11A Club	1021	HB-SVD
D-EBSX	Reims/Cessna F150M	F15001402	
D-EBSY(2)	Reims/Cessna F172N	F17201598	
D-EBSZ	Robin DR.400/180R Remorqueur	1854	
D-EBTA	Bölkow BO.207	239	
D-EBTB(2)	Cirrus SR22	3417	N65XP, S5-DJW, N110CK
D-EBTC	Piper PA-28-140 Cherokee B	28-25392	N8194N
D-EBTD	Piper PA-28R-200 Cherokee Arrow	28R-35065	N9358N
D-EBTG	Cessna TR182 Turbo Skylane RG	R18200866	OK-HBT, OE-DNI(2),
	(Res. .12)		OK-EIA
D-EBTJ(3)	Ulbrich / Van's RV-7	2002545	
	(Permit 14.7.15)		
D-EBTL(2)	Bellanca 7ECA Citabria	1198-77	OH-BCA, N4212Y
D-EBTM	Robin DR.400/180 Régent	1038	
D-EBTO(2)	Cessna 172S Skyhawk SP	172S9070	OK-RAK, D-EPCA(2),
			N2172W
D-EBTS(3)	Cirrus SR20	1026	(D-EPCD(2)), N132CD
D-EBTT	Reims/Cessna F172N	F17201877	
D-EBTU(3)	Grob G 115A	8028	D-EKVG
D-EBTX	Piper PA-18 Super Cub 95	18-3155	OO-KKK, D-EKKK(1),
			OL-L77, L-77, 53-4755
D-EBTY	Cessna 150D	15060459	N4459U
D-EBUA(3)	Cessna 182P Skylane	18263790	(9A-D . .), D-EBUA(3),
	(Reims-assembled with "c/n" 0004)		N6650M
D-EBUB	Cessna 170B	26934	HB-COX, N2991D
D-EBUC(4)	Piper J-3C-65 Cub	16217	N88591, NC88591
D-EBUF(3)	Piper PA-28-161 Warrior II	28-7916570	OO-SUF, N2942G
D-EBUG	Piper J-3C-90 Cub	12324	HB-OSB, 44-80028
D-EBUH(3)	Bücker Bü.181B-1 Bestmann (Sk25)	25076	(D-EBUM(4)),
			D-EBAM(1), Fv25076
D-EBUK(2)	Van's RV-7	"2002245"	
	(P .08)		
D-EBUL(2)	SOCATA MS.883 Rallye 115	1588	F-BTHL
D-EBUN(2)	Cessna T210N Turbo Centurion II	21063136	N6660N
	(Reims-assembled with c/n 0018)		
D-EBUR(2)	Piper J-3C-65 Cub	12408	HB-OEK, 44-80112
D-EBUS(2)	Piper PA-12 Super Cruiser	12-2857	N3973M, NC3973M
D-EBUT(4)	SNCAN/ Stampe SV.4C	304	F-BCLD
D-EBUU	SOCATA MS.893A Rallye Commodore 180	10981	F-BRJI
D-EBUY(2)	Cessna F150G	F150-0098	N246WA, N4232Y,
			D-EBYW(2)
D-EBUZ	Piper PA-18-150 Super Cub	18-6769	N3299P
D-EBVB(3)	Cessna 180H	18051589	D-EBCR(2), 5N-ADL,
			N2789X
D-EBVE	Aquila AT-01-100B	AT01-310	
D-EBVG	SIAT 223A-1 Flamingo	012	HB-EVG, D-EJDU(1)
D-EBVH	SOCATA MS.880B Rallye Club	1355	
D-EBVJ	Cessna 150F	15063532	N6932F
D-EBVL	Aerostyle Breezer B600	022LSA	
	(Permit 6.8.12)		
D-EBVM(2)	Piper PA-28-161 Cadet	2841143	N9184Q
D-EBVO(2)	Reims/Cessna F152	F15201767	
D-EBVP	SOCATA MS.894A Minerva 220	11056	
D-EBVR	Piper PA-28-161 Cadet	2841172	N9185N
D-EBVS(3)	Cessna A185F Skywagon	18503782	N102PM, N9636Q
D-EBVV	Stampe & Renard Stampe SV.4B	1200	OO-SVV, G-DANN,
			OO-SVV, V-58
D-EBVX	Piper PA-28-181 Archer III	2890223	(D-EKCF), D-EWWM,
			N9227R
D-EBVY	Luscombe 8F Silvaire	6211	N1584B
D-EBVZ	Beech F33A Bonanza	CE-1078	
D-EBWA	Piper PA-28-140 Cherokee	28-20209	N6185W
D-EBWF	Piper PA-28-140 Cherokee E	28-7225454	N11C
D-EBWG	SOCATA MS.893ED Rallye 180GT	12683	F-ODDM
D-EBWJ	SOCATA Rallye 150T-D	2660	F-ODDB
D-EBWO(2)	Robin DR.400/180R Remorqueur	1508	
D-EBWP	Piper PA-28R-200 Cherokee Arrow II	28R-7335224	N1776P
D-EBWQ	SOCATA MS.893E Rallye 180GT	12723	F-ODDQ
D-EBWR	SOCATA Rallye 100S-D Sport	2298	F-BULP
D-EBWT	SOCATA Rallye 100ST-D	2758	
D-EBWU	Piper PA-28-140 Cherokee	28-20377	N6321W
D-EBWV	SOCATA MS.893ED Rallye 180GT	12700	F-ODDT
D-EBWW	Piper PA-28-180 Cherokee D	28-4499	(D-EFWQ), N5208L
D-EBWX	SOCATA Rallye 235E-D	12771	
D-EBWY	Zlin Z.226T Trenér 6	870	F-BKRX, OO-AJT,
	(3rd prototype, conv from Z.126)		OK-JED, OK-JEB
D-EBWZ(3)	SOCATA Rallye 235E-D	12765	F-BNGU
D-EBXA	Reims FR172E Rocket	FR17200056	
D-EBXF	Piper PA-18 Super Cub 95	18-3456	96+32, NL+110, AC+528,
			AS+528, 54-756
D-EBXG	Wallerkowski Hornisse	01	
D-EBXI	Reims FR172E Rocket	FR17200053	
D-EBXM	Reims/Cessna F172N	F17201525	
D-EBXO(2)	Wallerkowski HW04 Tourist	01	
D-EBXQ	Reims/Cessna F172N	F17201759	
D-EBXT	Cessna 210K Centurion	21059455	OE-DSP, N8155G
D-EBXU	Reims FR172E Rocket	FR17200050	
D-EBXW	Reims/Cessna F150M	F15001407	
D-EBXX	Grumman AA-1B Trainer	AA1B-0334	G-BBWZ
D-EBXY(3)	Piper PA-18-150 Super Cub	18-7626	TC-CSS, TC-KPI, N10F
	(F/n 18-7813 officially quoted as c/n) (True identity unconfirmed) (P 8.09)		
D-EBYB	Piper PA-18 Super Cub 95	18-4648	N10F
	(F/n 18-7841 fitted)		
D-EBYC(2)	Beech V35B Bonanza	D-10033	
D-EBYE	Mooney M.20F Executive	670383	G-AYBF, N3290F
D-EBYF(2)	Simon/ Piel CP.301E Emeraude	AB.416	
D-EBYK(3)	Diamond DA 40 Star	40349	
	(Permit 8.06)		
D-EBYO(2)	Piper PA-18A-150 Super Cub	18-5859	OE-CPW , N7572D
	(Permit .06)		
D-EBYP(3)	Maule M6-235 Super Rocket	7402C	OH-MEN, N5652V
D-EBYQ(2)	Cessna 182P Skylane	18263886	OO-ADI , D-EEMK,
	(Reims-assembled with "c/n" 0009)		(SE-GKI), N6903M
D-EBYS(2)	Reims/Cessna F172N	F17201579	
D-EBYV(2)	Piper PA-38-112 Tomahawk	38-78A0560	N9691N
D-EBYX(3)	Piper PA-18 Super Cub 95	18-3450	96+26, NL+103, AC+535,
			AS+535, 54-750
D-EBYY	Extra EA.500	1007	
D-EBYZ	Scheibe SF.23A Sperling	2017	
D-EBZA(2)	Piper PA-28RT-201T Turbo Arrow IV	28R-8131160	N8406J
D-EBZE(2)	Bücker Bü.131B Jungmann	"25"	
	(Possibly CASA I-131E ex E3B-526 Air Classic exhibit)		
D-EBZH	SOCATA TB-10 Tobago	213	
D-EBZI	Cessna F150G	F150-0172	
D-EBZK	Reims/Cessna F172M	F17201458	
D-EBZM	Cessna T210L Turbo Centurion	21061425	N732DC
D-EBZP	Robin DR.400/180R Remorqueur	1418	
D-EBZR	Piper PA-18-135 Super Cub	18-4017	I-FADI, OO-LWA, EI-274,
	(Officially quoted with frame no. 18-5261)		I-EIVA, MM54-2617,
	(Permit 28.8.15)		54-2617
D-EBZU(2)	Evektor EV-97 SportStar RTC	2016-1907	
D-EBZV	Cirrus SR20	1245	N898CD
D-EBZW(2)	Mooney M.20K Model 231	25-0385	OE-DVU, N3981H
D-EBZZ	LET Z-37A-2 Cmelák	12-21	D-EOZL , DDR-SLL,
	(Res. .06 for restoration)		DM-SLL(2)
D-ECAA(2)	Tecnam P.2002-JF Sierra	266	
D-ECAB(2)	Klemm Kl.107C	154	
D-ECAD(4)	SOCATA MS.893A Rallye Commodore 180	12066	F-BTPZ
D-ECAE	Reims/Cessna FA150K Aerobat	FA1500057	
D-ECAF(3)	Piper PA-18-135 Super Cub	18-3862	PH-KNO, (PH-KNR),
	(Permit 5.06)		R-172, 54-2462
D-ECAG(3)	SOCATA TB-20 Trinidad	725	
D-ECAH	Klemm Kl.107B	126	
D-ECAI	Piper PA-18 Super Cub 95	18-1550	ALAT, 51-15550
D-ECAJ(2)	Diamond DA 20-A1 Katana	10018	C- . . . ., N605F, C-FDVP
D-ECAL(4)	Boeing Stearman E75	75-5535	N51RR, 42-17372
	(Permit 29.6.12)		
D-ECAM(3)	Cirrus SR22T	0837	N837EU
D-ECAN(5)	Diamond DA 20-A1 Katana	10146	C-FDVK
D-ECAO(3)	Cessna 172R Skyhawk	17280049	N9796F
D-ECAP(2)	Piper PA-28-180 Cherokee Challenger	28-7305172	N11C
D-ECAQ(2)	Bücker Bü.131 Jungmann	28	OE-AKW, HB-URC, A-19
D-ECAR(3)	Piper PA-46-350P Malibu Mirage	4636599	N599TN
D-ECAS	Piper J-3C-65 Cub	12989	HB-OGR , HB-ODF,
	(C/n officially quoted as 12809 in error)		44-80693
D-ECAT(3)	Piper PA-28-161 Cadet	2841112	N9646N, N9175Q
D-ECAV(3)	Diamond DA 40D Star	D4.116	
D-ECAW(3)	Gyroflug SC-01 Speed Canard	S-5	
D-ECAX(2)	Scheibe SF.23B Sperling	2011	
	(Mod from SF.23A-1, 9.07)		
D-ECAZ(5)	Zlin Z.526F Trenér Master	1128	N129F
D-ECBA(2)	Piper PA-28R-200 Cherokee Arrow II	28R-7635398	N4294F
D-ECBB(2)	Mooney M.20K Model 252 TSE	25-1002	N252AX
D-ECBE(4)	Piper PA-46-500TP Malibu Meridian	4697063	N253MM
D-ECBG(3)	Cirrus SR20	1551	N81452
D-ECBH(2)	SOCATA MS.893E Rallye 180GT	13231	F-GBSE
D-ECBK	Reims/Cessna F172H	F17200685	
D-ECBL(2)	Beech A36 Bonanza	E-1541	OY-CBI
D-ECBO	Bölkow BO.207	228	
D-ECBP	Reims/Cessna F150K	F15000609	
D-ECBS	Reims/Cessna F150K	F15000608	
D-ECBT	Reims/Cessna F150K	F15000605	
D-ECBV	Reims FR172G Rocket	FR17200175	
D-ECBW(2)	Piaggio P.149D	316	92+19, AC+467, AS+467
D-ECBX(4)	Reims/Cessna F150L	F15000685	
D-ECBY(2)	Reims/Cessna F172H	F17200717	
D-ECCA(3)	Fiat G.46-3B Series 2	44	G-BBII, I-AEHU,
	(Permit 22.8.14)		MM52801
D-ECCC(2)	CASA C-1.131E Jungmann	2230	E3B-630
	(Officially ex.E3B-619 but this is c/n 2219 / N72480)		
D-ECCD(4)	Cirrus SR22	3639	OH-GSC, N176CK
	(Res .16)		
D-ECCE(3)	Hille/ Impulse Excite	49	
D-ECCF(4)	Männich/ Rans S-7M Courier	01	
D-ECCI	Klemm Kl.35D	1904	SE-BHX, Fv5069
D-ECCJ(2)	Cirrus SR22	2706	N821P, D-EGGP(2),
			N930SR
D-ECCK(2)	Reims/Cessna FR172K Hawk XP	FR17200668	
D-ECCM	SOCATA MS.880B Rallye Club	1581	
D-ECCN(3)	Piper PA-28-161 Warrior II	2816093	N9183X
D-ECCO	Piper PA-28-140 Cherokee	28-20535	N6462W
D-ECCP	SOCATA MS.880B Rallye Club	1601	
D-ECCQ	SOCATA MS.893A Rallye Commodore 180	11456	
D-ECCR(2)	Cirrus SR20	1106	N747TG
D-ECCS	SOCATA MS.893A Rallye Commodore 180	11466	F-BNGU
D-ECCT(3)	CEA DR.221 Dauphin	97	F-BPCT
D-ECCU(3)	Heliopolis Gomhouria Mk.6	174	SU-337
D-ECCW(2)	Piper PA-18-150 Super Cub	18-7880	OE-ANE, N10F
D-ECCX(4)	Cessna 172S Skyhawk SP	172S10428	N1416A
D-ECCY	Cessna F172F	F172-0136	
D-ECDA(3)	HOAC DV-20 Katana	20150	OE-ADA
D-ECDB(2)	Aerospool WT-9 Dynamic LSA	DY466/2013	
	(Permit 26.4.13)		
D-ECDC(3)	Claren Ente Li 1	001	
	(Permit 8.10)		
D-ECDD	Reims FR172G Rocket	FR17200199	
D-ECDF(2)	Cessna 182S Skylane	18280008	
D-ECDI (4)	Robin DR.400/135cdi	2641	
D-ECDM	Reims/Cessna FA150K Aerobat	FA1500021	
D-ECDQ(2)	Reims/Cessna F172N	F17201646	
D-ECDS(2)	Cessna 172N Skyhawk	17271517	N5698
D-ECDT(2)	Piper PA-28R-201T Turbo Arrow III	28R-7803150	N2856M
D-ECDV	Reims/Cessna F150K	F15000599	
D-ECDW	Aero Commander 200D	368	N5565M
D-ECDZ(2)	Cessna P210N Pressurized Centurion II		
		P21000817	N888HG
D-ECEA	CEA Jodel DR.1050 Ambassadeur	620	

D-ECEB(2)	SAN Jodel DR.1050 Ambassadeur	174	
D-ECED(2)	Mooney M.20F Executive	670121	N9544M
D-ECEE	Reims/Cessna F150L	F15000729	
D-ECEF(3)	Cirrus SR20	1550	OK-KLM(1), N52697
D-ECEH	Klemm Kl.107C	127	
D-ECEI (2)	Reims/Cessna F150L	F15000733	
D-ECEJ	Reims/Cessna F172H	F17200693	
D-ECEL(2)	Cessna 182R Skylane	18268466	N9892E
D-ECEM(3)	Mooney M.20F Executive	22-1262	
D-ECEN(4)	HOAC DV-20 Katana	20039	N39DV
D-ECEO(3)	Piper PA-22-108 Colt	22-9144	OY-EAV, N10F
D-ECER(3)	Robin DR.400/180 Régent	1294	
D-ECET(3)	Cessna T182T Turbo Skylane	T18208918	(D-EZAA(3)), N5063A
D-ECEV(2)	Reims/Cessna F150K	F15000585	
D-ECEW(2)	Reims/Cessna F150K	F15000587	
D-ECEY(2)	Reims/Cessna F150L	F15000666	
D-ECFA(2)	Cessna T210K Turbo Centurion	21059212	N8212M
D-ECFB	Reims/Cessna F172H	F17200725	
D-ECFD(2)	Aquilla AT-01-100C	320	
D-ECFE	Oberlerchner JOB 15-150	058	OE-CAO
D-ECFF	Reims/Cessna F172L	F17200806	
D-ECFG	Piper PA-22-108 Colt	22-9591	OE-CFG, N5781Z
D-ECFH(3)	Cirrus SR20	1575	N53363
D-ECFI	Oberlerchner JOB 15-150	060	OE-CAR
D-ECFK(2)	Robin DR.400/140B Dauphin 4	2591	PH-JFK
D-ECFM(4)	Cirrus SR22T	1256	N143AF
D-ECFP	Cessna 172P Skyhawk	17274428	EI-CFP, N52178
D-ECFR	Reims/Cessna F150K	F15000596	
D-ECFT(2)	Piper PA-28-181 Archer II	2843616	EC-JNS, N31014
D-ECFW	Reims/Cessna F172H	F17200740	(G-AXUV)
D-ECFX	Reims/Cessna F150L	F15000709	
D-ECFZ	Reims/Cessna F172K	F17200801	
D-ECGB(2)	Cirrus SR22	2675	N171SU
D-ECGC(2)	Piper PA-12 Super Cruiser	12-3395	D-ELGD, N4443M,
			NC4443M
D-ECGH(2)	Piper PA-18 Super Cub 95	18-3449	96+25, NL+115, AC+534,
		(D-EMDY), AC+534, AA+534, AS+534, 54-749	
D-ECGI	Bölkow BO.208C Junior	598	
D-ECGK	Cessna 182N Skylane	18260407	N92876
D-ECGL	Reims/Cessna F150L	F15000680	
D-ECGM	Reims FR172H Rocket	FR17200239	
D-ECGN	Reims/Cessna FA150L Aerobat	FA1500116	
D-ECGR	Reims/Cessna F177RG Cardinal RG	F177RG0004	(N8090G)
	(Reims-assembled 177RG with c/n 177RG0090)		
D-ECGS	Reims/Cessna F177RG Cardinal RG	F177RG0005	(N8094G)
	(Reims-assembled 177RG with c/n 177RG0094)		
D-ECGT(2)	Reims/Cessna FRA150M Aerobat	FRA1500262	
D-ECGU(2)	Reims/Cessna FA150K Aerobat	FA1500068	
D-ECGW	Cessna 182N Skylane	18260460	N8920G
D-ECGX	Reims/Cessna F150L	F15000678	
D-ECGZ	Reims FR172H Rocket	FR17200238	
D-ECHA(3)	Christen A-1 Husky	1058	N29732
D-ECHB	Reims/Cessna F150K	F15000572	
D-ECHC(3)	Piper PA-32R-301 Saratoga SP	32R-8013011	G-EENA, C-GBBU
D-ECHD	Reims FR172G Rocket	FR17200173	
D-ECHE(2)	Reims/Cessna F172H	F17200733	
D-ECHF	Reims FR172H Rocket	FR17200252	
D-ECHG(2)	Cirrus SR20	1555	N50009
D-ECHH(2)	OMF-100-160 Symphony	0009	CC-PRD, (D-EAXK(2))
D-ECHK(4)	Cessna 172S Skyhawk SP	172S10846	N6344Z
D-ECHL(3)	Robin DR.400/180 Régent	497	
D-ECHP	Reims/Cessna F150L	F15000662	
D-ECHQ	Piper PA-28-181 Cherokee Archer II	28-7890505	N36321
D-ECHR	Reims/Cessna F177RG Cardinal RG	F177RG0008	(N8206G)
	(Reims-assembled 177RG with c/n 177RG0106)		
D-ECHS	Reims/Cessna F172K	F17200770	
D-ECHT(2)	Reims FR172H Rocket	FR17200251	
D-ECHU(2)	Reims/Cessna F150L	F15000681	
D-ECHW	Reims/Cessna F150L	F15000699	
D-ECHY(3)	Piper PA-28R-201T Turbo-Arrow III	28R-7803070	N9853K
D-ECIA(3)	Robin DR.400/180 Régent	1995	
D-ECIB(2)	Wassmer Jodel D.120 Paris-Nice	186	
D-ECIC	Klemm Kl.35D-160	2013	SE-BHU, Fv5064
D-ECIE	Reims/Cessna F172K	F17200795	
D-ECII (3)	Cessna L-19A Bird Dog (305A)	21510	OE-CCB , AAF: 3A-CB,
			51-4625
D-ECIJ	Reims/Cessna F172H	F17200708	(YU-BHJ)
D-ECIK(2)	Reims FR172H Rocket	FR17200240	
D-ECIM(4)	Piper PA-28-140 Cherokee E	28-7225596	C-FFQR, CF-FQR, N11C
D-ECIO	Reims/Cessna F177RG Cardinal RG	F177RG0013	(N8225G)
	(Reims-assembled 177RG with c/n 177RG0125)		
D-ECIP(3)	Robin R.3000/160	152	
D-ECIQ(2)	Piper J-3C-65 Cub	18167	N98024, NC98024
D-ECIR(4)	Cirrus SR20	1303	N806C
D-ECIS(3)	Cessna 150B	59433	OE-AIS, N7333X
D-ECIY	Reims/Cessna F150L	F15000731	
	(Permit 17.4.12)		
D-ECJA(2)	Diamond DA 40D Star	D4.123	OE-VPY
D-ECJB(3)	Robin DR.400/180 Régent	2291	
D-ECJC	Reims/Cessna F172H	F17200734	
D-ECJE	Reims/Cessna F172H	F17200737	
D-ECJF	Reims/Cessna F177RG Cardinal RG	F177RG0015	(N8230G)
	(Reims-assembled 177RG with c/n 177RG0130)		
D-ECJI (2)	Piper PA-28RT-201T Turbo Arrow IV	28R-8131192	EC-EJI, N8425D
D-ECJK	Reims FR172G Rocket	FR17200212	
D-ECJL	Reims/Cessna F172H	F17200742	
D-ECJM(2)	Reims/Cessna F172P	F17202091	
D-ECJN	Reims/Cessna F172H	F17200744	
D-ECJP(2)	SOCATA TB-20 Trinidad	292	
D-ECJR(2)	SOCATA MS.893E Rallye 180GT	12647	F-OBJR, F-BXMR
D-ECJT	Reims/Cessna F172H	F17200736	
D-ECJU	Reims/Cessna F172K	F17200804	
D-ECJV	Reims FR172H Rocket	FR17200269	
D-ECJX(2)	Reims FR172H Rocket	FR17200272	
D-ECJY(2)	Reims/Cessna F150L	F15000727	
D-ECKA	Beech P35 Bonanza	D-7194	
D-ECKB(2)	Beech F33A Bonanza	CE-1614	N8240X, (F-GIFM)
D-ECKC(2)	Aerotek Pitts S-2A	2127	G-SIIA, D-ECKC(2),
			N8073
D-ECKD	Reims FR172H Rocket	FR17200243	
D-ECKE(2)	Piper PA-28-160 Cherokee	28-372	N5316W
D-ECKF	Reims/Cessna F177RG Cardinal RG	F177RG0021	"PH-LTU" , (PH-LTT),
	(Reims-assembled 177RG with c/n 177RG0154)		D-ECKF, (N8254G)
D-ECKH(2)	Holtz/ Neico Lancair 235	362B	
D-ECKI (3)	Rockwell Commander 112A	298	N1298J
D-ECKK	Reims FR172H Rocket	FR17200259	
D-ECKL(2)	Robin DR.400/180R Remorqueur	1589	
D-ECKO(2)	Grumman AA-5 Traveler	AA5-0667	
D-ECKP	Reims/Cessna F172K	F17200768	
D-ECKR	Reims FR172H Rocket	FR17200249	
D-ECKS	Reims/Cessna F172H	F17200750	
D-ECKT	Reims FR172G Rocket	FR17200177	
D-ECKV	Reims FR172G Rocket	FR17200166	
D-ECKW	Cessna 182N Skylane	18260439	N92948
D-ECKY(3)	SOCATA MS.893E Rallye 180GT	13010	
D-ECLA(4)	Flight Design CT LS-ELA	F-12-02-06	
	(Permit 11.9.12)		
D-ECLB(3)	Reims/Cessna F172M	F17201358	I-CCAT
D-ECLC(2)	Mooney M.20K Model 252 TSE	25-1182	
D-ECLE(2)	Reims/Cessna F172N	F17201563	
D-ECLG(2)	Cessna 172RG Cutlass RG	172RG0767	N6544V
D-ECLH	Beech 35-C33 Debonair	CD-1016	
D-ECLI	Beech 35-C33 Debonair	CD-1017	
D-ECLK(2)	Piper PA-18-135 Super Cub	18-3321	EI-104, I-EIKD, 53-7721
D-ECLM(2)	Piper PA-28RT-201T Turbo Arrow IV	28R-8331046	N4322N, N9534N,
			N4312V
D-ECLO(3)	Reims/Cessna F182Q Skylane	F18200169	F-ODNO
D-ECLP(2)	Piper PA-28-180 Cherokee D	28-4404	N5121L
D-ECLR(2)	Piper PA-28-140 Cherokee	28-24130	N1718J
D-ECLT(2)	Cessna 182P Skylane	18264355	N1504M
	(Reims-assembled with "c/n" 0048)		
D-ECLU(2)	Diamond DA 20-A1 Katana	10271	(D-EYYE), D-EWDA,
			C-FDVT
D-ECLW(2)	Reims FR172E Rocket	FR17200052	
D-ECLX(2)	Reims FR172E Rocket	FR17200054	
D-ECMA(2)	Cessna 172M Skyhawk	17266437	N80195
D-ECMC	Reims/Cessna F172K	F17200780	(G-AYTI)
D-ECMD	Reims FR172H Rocket	FR17200261	
D-ECMF(2)	Mooney M.20J Model 201	24-1011	(N4005H)
D-ECMG	Reims/Cessna F177RG Cardinal RG	F177RG0009	(N8210G)
	(Reims-assembled 177RG with c/n 177RG0110)		
D-ECMH(3)	Piper PA-28-181 Archer II	2890068	N9138Z
D-ECMI (2)	Robin DR.400/180R Remo 180	2160	
D-ECMJ	Reims/Cessna F177RG Cardinal RG	F177RG0022	(N8256G)
	(Reims-assembled 177RG with c/n 177RG0156)		
D-ECMK(2)	Kritzinger/ Sequoia F.8L Falco	1730	
D-ECML	Reims/Cessna F150L	F15000717	
D-ECMM	SAN Jodel D.150 Rapid	17	
D-ECMN	Reims/Cessna F172K	F17200784	
D-ECMP(2)	Cessna 172N Skyhawk	17273915	N256FR, N256ER,
			N7557J
D-ECMQ	Reims FR172H Rocket	FR17200232	
D-ECMR(2)	Cirrus SR22	3075	OO-AND(2), N167CP
D-ECMS	Reims/Cessna F172K	F17200778	
D-ECMV	Cessna 172S Skyhawk SP	172S9056	N956BA
D-ECMX(3)	Reims/Cessna F150L	F15001413	OE-CMX
	(C/n officially quoted as 1412 in error)		
D-ECMY	Beech 35-C33A Debonair	CE-59	
D-ECMZ(2)	Piper PA-28-151 Cherokee Warrior	28-7415283	HB-OMZ, N9533N
D-ECNB(2)	Mooney M.20J Model 201	24-0059	
D-ECND	Bölkow B0.209 Monsun 160FV	128	(D-EFJF)
D-ECNG	Reims/Cessna F177RG Cardinal RG	F177RG0027	(N8282G)
	(Reims-assembled 177RG with c/n 177RG0182)		
D-ECNI	Cessna 150G	15066209	N8309J
D-ECNJ	Reims FR172H Rocket	FR17200226	
D-ECNL	Cessna 150J Commuter	15069649	N50927
D-ECNO	Cessna 150G	15066927	N3027S
D-ECNP(2)	Cessna T210K Turbo Centurion	21059456	N8156G
D-ECNS(2)	Piper PA-32-300 Cherokee Six	32-7840153	N31908
D-ECNW(2)	SOCATA MS.893ED Rallye 180GT	13009	
D-ECNZ	SIAI-Marchetti S.205-20/R	377	OO-JDC
D-ECOA(2)	Christen A-1 Husky	1142	
D-ECOC(3)	American Champion 7GCBC Explorer	1409-2006	G-GCBC
D-ECOE	Reims/Cessna F172K	F17200769	
D-ECOF(4)	American Champion 7GCBC Explorer	1447-2007	
D-ECOG(2)	Piper PA-28R-200 Cherokee Arrow II	28R-7635266	N75116
D-ECOH(2)	Mooney M.20J Model 205	24-3011	OE-KEC, N205ME
D-ECOL(3)	SOCATA TB-20 Trinidad	1749	
D-ECON(2)	Diamond DA 40D Star	D4.018	
D-ECOO(2)	Cessna 172RG Cutlass RG	172RG0060	N5464R
	(Reims-assembled with c/n 0001)		
D-ECOQ(3)	Cessna 172N Skyhawk	17269173	OY-AJL, N734WM
	(Res. 22.7.15)		
D-ECOR(4)	Diamond DA 40 Star	40228	EC-INE
	(Res .16)		
D-ECOS(3)	Piper PA-38-112 Tomahawk	38-79A1086	N24119
D-ECOT(3)	Beech F33A Bonanza	CE-1716	N8146T
D-ECOU	Reims/Cessna F172K	F17200797	
D-ECOV	Schwindt/ Jodel D.112 Club	278	SL-AAO
D-ECOW(2)	Reims/Cessna F177RG Cardinal RG	F177RG0028	(N8284G)
	(Reims-assembled 177RG with c/n 177RG0184)		
D-ECOX	Dornier Do.27Q-1	2018	
D-ECOY	Piaggio FWP.149D	020	90+11, AC+443, DB+394
D-ECOZ(4)	Reims FR172H Rocket	FR17200274	
D-ECPA(2)	Piper PA-28-181 Archer III	2843357	N4140L
D-ECPB(2)	Christen A-1 Husky	1107	
D-ECPC	Reims/Cessna FA150L Aerobat	FA1500097	
D-ECPD(2)	Piper PA-28R-200 Cherokee Arrow II	28R-7535180	N33697
D-ECPF	Reims/Cessna F150L	F15000663	
D-ECPH(2)	Mooney M.20J Model 201	24-0966	N3865H
D-ECPI (3)	Sonntag/ Sequoia F.8L Falco	1649	
D-ECPJ	Reims/Cessna F150L	F15000702	(D-ECMW)
D-ECPK(3)	OGMA/DHC-1 Chipmunk T.20	OGMA-35	G-OACP, (CS-DAO),
	(Res. .11, but ntu by 2016)		FAP-1345
D-ECPL(3)	SOCATA TB-10 Tobago	165	N662PL, D-EKWE(2),
			ZS-KWE, F-ODND
D-ECPM(3)	Cessna 182T Skylane	18282455	N7132F
D-ECPO	Reims/Cessna FA150L Aerobat	FA1500113	F-WLIP
D-ECPP	Reims/Cessna FA150L Aerobat	FA1500114	(OY-BYL), D-ECPP,
			(G-AYUZ)
D-ECPS(2)	SOCATA Rallye 180T-D Galérien	2975	
D-ECPT	Reims FR172H Rocket	FR17200284	
D-ECPU(4)	Diamond DA 20-A1 Katana	10002	OE-CPR, C-FTJD
D-ECPV	Reims FR172H Rocket	FR17200288	
D-ECPX	Reims/Cessna F172L	F17200820	
D-ECPY(2)	Orlican L-40 Meta-Sokol	150909	
D-ECPZ	Reims FR172H Rocket	FR17200282	
D-ECQA	Piper PA-18 Super Cub 95	18-3182	R-84, L-108, 53-4782
D-ECQC	Reims/Cessna FRA150L Aerobat	FRA1500124	
D-ECQD	Reims FR172H Rocket	FR17200286	
D-ECQH	Reims FR172H Rocket	FR17200283	
D-ECQL	Reims/Cessna F150L	F15000764	

Registration	Type	Serial	Previous identities
D-ECQO	Cessna F172H	F172-0347	
D-ECQP(2)	Grumman AA-5A Cheetah	AA5A-0187	
D-ECQQ	Reims/Cessna F150L	F15000768	
D-ECQS(2)	Robin DR.400/180 Régent	1252	D-ECOS(2)
D-ECQW	Reims/Cessna F172L	F17200826	
D-ECQX	Reims/Cessna F172L	F17200827	
D-ECRA	Reims FR172H Rocket	FR17200295	
D-ECRF(2)	Beech B36TC Bonanza	EA-299	N24RF, N6450A
D-ECRG(2)	Cirrus SR22	0557	N1638C
	(Res. .14)		
D-ECRH(2)	Reims/Cessna F150M	F15001233	N67266
D-ECRI	Mooney M.20C Mark 21	2176	N6429U
D-ECRK(2)	Robin DR.400/180 Régent	2387	
D-ECRL	Reims/Cessna F172L	F17200832	
D-ECRM	Reims FR172H Rocket	FR17200296	
D-ECRO	SIAT 223 V-1 Flamingo	001	"D-EDON"
	(Cld 2.03 but under rebuild)		
D-ECRP(3)	Cirrus SR22	3629	N867RP
D-ECRQ	Reims FR172H Rocket	FR17200299	
D-ECRR(2)	Riechers/ Aero Designs Pulsar XP	421 SB	
D-ECRS(2)	Cessna 182S Skylane	18280021	N97SD
D-ECRV	Reims/Cessna F150L	F15000758	
D-ECRW	Reims FR172H Rocket	FR17200306	
D-ECRX	Reims/Cessna F172L	F17200855	
D-ECRZ	Reims/Cessna F172L	F17200854	
D-ECSA(2)	Mooney M.20J Model 201	24-0086	
D-ECSB(2)	Piper PA-28-140 Cherokee B	28-25086	N7233F
D-ECSC	Reims FR172H Rocket	FR17200319	
D-ECSD(2)	Reims/Cessna FA150L Aerobat	FA1500120	PH-LUE, (LN-BEK)
D-ECSF	Piper PA-28-140 Cherokee	28-21121	HB-OYG, (N6941W)
D-ECSG	Reims/Cessna F172L	F17200813	
D-ECSI	Piper PA-28-180 Cherokee C	28-2325	N8197W
D-ECSJ	Reims/Cessna F150L	F15000780	
D-ECSK(2)	Piper PA-28RT-201T Turbo Arrow IV	28R-8131208	SE-KKV, N410FC, N8441P
D-ECSL	Reims/Cessna F172L	F17200837	
D-ECSM(2)	Robin DR.400/180 Régent	1957	
D-ECSO(2)	Boeing Stearman A75-N1	75-1391	OO-STM, N59257, (OO-JKT), N59257, BuA03614
D-ECSQ(2)	Sportavia-Pützer RS-180 Sportsman	6003	
D-ECSS	Reims/Cessna F172L	F17200844	
D-ECST	Gardan GY-80 Horizon 180	131	
D-ECSW	Reims/Cessna F172L	F17200846	
D-ECSX	Reims/Cessna F172L	F17200847	
D-ECSY(2)	Cessna 210N Centurion	21063434	N5432A
D-ECSZ	Reims/Cessna F172L	F17200848	
D-ECTC(2)	Reims/Cessna F172P	F17202105	
D-ECTE	Cessna F150H	F150-0275	
D-ECTH	Piper PA-28-140 Cherokee C	28-26676	N5845U
D-ECTI (2)	Pützer Elster B	018	OY-CTL, (OY-CYA), D-ECAY(2), 97+11, D-EDUF
	(Permit 20.4.11)		
D-ECTL	Reims FR172H Rocket	FR17200315	
D-ECTM(2)	de Havilland DH.82A Tiger Moth	83745	G-ANMV, F-BHAZ, G-ANMV, T7404
D-ECTN	CEA DR.340 Major	439	
D-ECTO(2)	Reims/Cessna F150L	F15000746	
D-ECTP(4)	Cessna T206H Turbo Stationair	T20608957	4L-GAM, D-EXAL(4), N2585F
	(Res .16)		
D-ECTR(2)	Cessna TR182 Turbo Skylane RG	R18201402	HB-CIN, D-EGPY(2), N4722S
	(Res .11)		
D-ECTS(2)	Beech F33A Bonanza	CE-1186	N3113T
D-ECTV	Piper PA-22-108 Colt	22-8861	HB-OTV, N10F
D-ECTW(2)	Zlin Z.143L	0024	
D-ECUA(2)	Piper PA-28-151 Cherokee Warrior	28-7415228	HB-PMX, D-EHRH(1), N9537N
D-ECUB(2)	Reims/Cessna F172N	F17201823	
D-ECUC(2)	Aeronca 7DC Champion (7AC convn)	7AC-3889	OO-SPA
D-ECUE	Reims/Cessna F150L	F15000901	
D-ECUJ	Reims/Cessna FRA150L Aerobat	FRA1500184	
D-ECUK	Jodel D.9 Bébé	AB-07	
D-ECUL(2)	Piper PA-28-161 Warrior II	28-8316010	N8292R
D-ECUN(2)	Ambrosini F.7 Rondone II	010	
D-ECUO	Reims/Cessna F172M	F17200921	
D-ECUP(3)	Piper J-3C-65 Cub	6334	G-BTBX, N35367, NC35367
D-ECUQ(2)	Reims/Cessna F172M	F17200925	
D-ECUS(4)	Piper PA-28R-200 Cherokee Arrow II	28R-7435104	N40742
D-ECUU	Reims/Cessna F172M	F17200932	
D-ECUZ	Auster Mk.5 Alpha	3414	G-APUL
D-ECVE	GEMS MS.892A Rallye Commodore 150	10536	
D-ECVF	Reims FR172J Rocket	FR17200378	
D-ECVJ	Reims FR172J Rocket	FR17200382	
D-ECVK(2)	Reims/Cessna F172M	F17201397	
D-ECVL	Cessna 182P Skylane	18261603	(N21389)
D-ECVR(2)	Cirrus SR22	0656	N6055H
D-ECVT	Reims/Cessna F150L	F15000904	
D-ECVU	Cessna F172G	F172-0182	
D-ECVY	Champion 7GCB Challenger	152	N9948Y
D-ECVZ(2)	Reims/Cessna F177RG Cardinal RG	F177RG074	
D-ECWB	Reims/Cessna F172M	F17200940	
D-ECWC(2)	SOCATA MS.893E Rallye 180GT	12639	F-BVNY
D-ECWJ(2)	Beech B36TC Bonanza	EA-517	F-GNMJ, D-ENMS(1), N8217W
D-ECWN(2)	Robin DR.400/180 Régent	2145	
D-ECWP	Reims/Cessna F172M	F17200948	
D-ECWQ	Reims/Cessna F172M	F17200950	
D-ECWR	Reims/Cessna F172M	F17200951	
D-ECWV	Cessna 182P Skylane	18261621	N21418
D-ECWX	Cessna 182P Skylane	18261823	N79461
D-ECWY	Beech V35 Bonanza	D-8079	
D-ECXA(2)	Xtreme Air XA-42	109	
	(For export to China 10.16)		
D-ECXB	Cessna 182P Skylane	18261668	N21492
D-ECXD	Cessna 182P Skylane	18261583	N21356
D-ECXI (2)	Reims/Cessna F150M	F15001249	HB-CXI, N31056
D-ECXJ	Reims/Cessna F172M	F17200974	
D-ECXK	Reims/Cessna F172M	F17200975	
D-ECXM	Reims FR172J Rocket	FR17200407	
D-ECXR	Reims/Cessna F177RG Cardinal RG	F177RG0076	
D-ECXS	Cessna 182P Skylane	18261750	N78101
D-ECXT	Cessna 182P Skylane	18261848	N79935
D-ECXU	Piper PA-18 Super Cub 95	18-1484	ALAT, 51-15484
D-ECYB(3)	Piper PA-28-140 Cherokee C	28-26721	SE-FHN
	(Res .13, ntu)		
D-ECYG(2)	Reims/Cessna F150L	F15000918	
D-ECYM(3)	Cessna 182P Skylane	18262593	N52417
D-ECYO	Reims/Cessna F150L	F15000934	
D-ECYS(2)	Scheibe SF-23C Sperling	3500	
D-ECYY	Wassmer WA.54 Atlantic	143	
D-ECZA	Procaer F.15B Picchio	24	
D-ECZB	Reims FR172F Rocket	FR17200107	
D-ECZC	CEA Jodel DR.1050 Ambassadeur	28	F-BJOY
D-ECZD	Piper PA-18-100 Super Cub	18-3196	OL-L22, L-122, 53-4796
	(PA-18 Super Cub 95 re-engined)		
D-ECZH	Reims/Cessna FR172K Hawk XP	FR17200672	I-ECZH, D-ECZH
D-ECZI	Piper J-3C-85 Cub	20488	N7224H, NC7224H
	(J-3C-65 convtd .99)		
D-ECZK	Reims/Cessna F172M	F17200968	
D-ECZL(3)	Mooney M.20J Model 205	24-3333	
D-ECZN	Reims FR172J Rocket	FR17200388	
D-ECZO(2)	Reims FR172J Rocket	FR17200389	
D-ECZR(2)	Flight Design CT LS-ELA	F-11-07-05	
	(Cr 16.5.13 Corlu, Turkey)		
D-ECZU	GEMS MS.892A Rallye Commodore 150	10504	
D-ECZV	Reims/Cessna F172M	F17201410	
D-ECZZ	Cirrus SR22	2966	N176CT
D-EDAA(3)	Grumman AA-5A Cheetah	AA5A-0347	EC-DAC
	(Res .15)		
D-EDAB(2)	Piper PA-28R-180 Cherokee Arrow	28R-30279	N3937T
D-EDAC(2)	Diamond DA 20-A1 Katana	10320	C-GKAC
D-EDAD(3)	Piper PA-28-180 Cherokee Archer	28-7405196	N43520, N9638N
D-EDAF(2)	Piper PA-22-160 Tri-Pacer	22-6869	OY-AEY
D-EDAH(4)	Beech 35-C33 Debonair	CD-918	N19J, N462KK, D-EMYU
D-EDAI	Cessna 182N Skylane	18260236	N92504
D-EDAJ	Cessna 172M	17261886	N12214
D-EDAK(3)	Cessna 172N Skyhawk	17268783	N734DW
D-EDAL(2)	Reims FR172J Rocket	FR17200366	
D-EDAN(3)	Lancair Legacy	unkn	
	(Res .09)		
D-EDAP(2)	Cessna 150L	15075118	N10898
D-EDAQ(2)	Bellanca 17-31ATC Turbo Viking	74-31100	N44313, D-EDAQ, N1HE
D-EDAR(3)	Cessna 150J	15071060	SP-KAV, D-EDAR(3), N5560G
D-EDAS(4)	Diamond DA 20-A1 Katana	10239	C-GKAX
D-EDAT(5)	Cessna 172S Skyhawk SP	172S8132	N871SP
D-EDAU	Piper PA-28-181 Cherokee Archer II	28-7890363	N6342C
D-EDAW(4)	Wördemann/ Pottier P.230S Panda	465	
D-EDAX(3)	Cessna 172M	17265372	N5199H
D-EDAY(2)	Cessna T210N Turbo Centurion II	21064305	N6240Y
D-EDBB(2)	Robin HR.100/210D Safari	213	
D-EDBD	SOCATA MS.880B Rallye Club	2372	F-BUXF
D-EDBF(3)	Robin DR.400/180RP Remorqueur	1857	
D-EDBG(3)	Piper PA-28-181 Archer II	2890150	N92104
D-EDBH(2)	Reims/Cessna FR182 Skylane RG	FR18200007	
D-EDBI (2)	CASA C-1.131E Jungmann	2085	E3B-374
D-EDBO(2)	Piper PA-32RT-300T Turbo Lance II	32R-7987061	N3057D
D-EDBP(2)	Robin DR.400/180 Régent	2178	
D-EDBQ	Reims/Cessna F172N	F17201569	PH-AXL, F-WZDD
D-EDBR	Reims/Cessna F172P	F17202082	
D-EDBS(2)	Beech F33A Bonanza	CE-1615	
D-EDBT(2)	CASA C-1.131E Jungmann	2083	E3B-479
D-EDBU(3)	Piper PA-46-310P Malibu	4608013	SE-IUM, N9084N
D-EDBV(2)	Piper PA-28-236 Dakota	28-8011131	N8247T
D-EDBW(3)	Piaggio FWP.149D	107	90+88, AC+438, CA+012, AS+426
D-EDBX	Cessna 182P Skylane	18263175	OY-RPN, D-EOQQ, N7392N
D-EDBY	Linzenkirchner/ Piel CP.301A Emeraude	AB.423	
D-EDBZ	Reims/Cessna F182Q Skylane	F18200090	
D-EDCA(2)	Beech V35B Bonanza	D-9131	N4262A
D-EDCB(2)	Piper PA-22-108 Colt	22-8719	D-EDCA, N10F
D-EDCE	Piper PA-22-108 Colt	22-8665	
D-EDCF	Wassmer WA.41 Baladou	157	F-BPTZ
D-EDCG	Dornier Do.27B-1	245	55+87, PA+316, PA+109, PG+107
D-EDCH(2)	Piper PA-22-160 Tri-Pacer	22-7419	OO-DLH, G-ARAL, N10F
D-EDCI	Piper PA-18 Super Cub 95	18-1976	L-5, 52-2376
D-EDCK(2)	SNCAN/ Stampe SV.4C	540	F-BDCK
D-EDCL	SIAT 223 A-1 Flamingo	052	EC-52A
D-EDCM(3)	Piper PA-28RT-201 Arrow IV	28R-8018103	N8259X
D-EDCN	Cessna TR182 Turbo Skylane RG	R18200742	N736MU
D-EDCP	Reims/Cessna F152	F15201507	
D-EDCQ	Reims/Cessna F172N Skyhawk II	F17201736	
D-EDCR(2)	Cessna TR182 Turbo Skylane RG	R18201099	(N756KY)
D-EDCT(3)	Piper PA-38-112 Tomahawk	38-78A0479	(D-EBYD(3)), S5-DCT, YU-DDO, N9732N
D-EDCV	Dornier Do.27A-4	390	56+82, PE+220, PP+104, PL+424
D-EDCW	Reims/Cessna F172N	F17201776	
	(Thielert Centurion Diesel engine installed .03)		
D-EDDA	Piper PA-18-150 Super Cub	18-7583	
D-EDDB(2)	Cessna 172P Skyhawk	17274499	N52352
D-EDDC(2)	Piper PA-28R-200 Cherokee Arrow II	28R-7535186	N33749
D-EDDD	CASA C-1.131E Jungmann	2223	E3B-604
D-EDDE	Wassmer Jodel D.120R Paris-Nice	20	F-BHTT
D-EDDF(3)	Van's RV-10	41733	
	(Res .16)		
D-EDDG(2)	Cessna 172S Skyhawk SP	172S9541	N2158Q
D-EDDH(5)	Cessna 172S Skyhawk SP	172S10393	N13470
D-EDDI (2)	CASA C-1.131E Jungmann	2172	E3B-552
	(Damaged 30.4.14 in f/l Scharding-Suben, Austria)		
D-EDDJ(3)	Gnad/ Brändli BX-2 Cherry	173SB	D-EPTI
	(Permit 3.6.13)		
D-EDDK	Piper PA-28R-200 Cherokee Arrow II	28R-7535189	N33760
D-EDDL(3)	Cessna R182 Skylane RG	R18201887	N5534T
D-EDDN	Mooney M.20C Mark 21	2595	(N6891U)
D-EDDO(3)	Aquila AT-01	AT01-242	
D-EDDP	Cessna 182L Skylane	18258765	(N3465R)
D-EDDR(2)	SOCATA TB-10 Tobago	1642	SP-KTD, D-EDDR
D-EDDS(4)	Piper PA-28RT-201T Turbo Arrow IV	28R-8231048	HB-PKH, (D-EURW), HB-PKH, N8205H
D-EDDU(5)	Piper PA-28R-201T Turbo Arrow III	28R-7803065	OY-BTK
D-EDDV(3)	Cessna 172S Skyhawk SP	172S8165	N7256C
D-EDDX	Cessna 172S Skyhawk SP	172S10124	N1700G
D-EDDY	Dornier Do.27Q-5	2096	
D-EDDZ	PZL-104 Wilga 35A	129453	
D-EDEB(5)	Cessna 172S Skyhawk SP	172S8558	N299ME
D-EDEC(5)	Robin DR.400/120D Petit Prince	1534	F-GDEC
D-EDED(3)	Mooney M.20J Model 201	24-1149	N1138Z
D-EDEE(3)	Cessna F172H	F172-0377	OY-III, SE-EXB, OH-CSQ
D-EDEF	Bücker Bü.131 Lerche R-180	63	HB-ESA, A-87, HB-ESA
D-EDEG(4)	Beech B36TC Bonanza	EA-447	N7243E

Regn	Type	C/n	Previous identities
D-EDEH(3)	Robin DR.400/180R Remorqueur	1429	
D-EDEL(5)	SIAI-Marchetti S.208 (Cvtd from 205-22/R)	4-231	OO-HEO, (OO-JNS)
D-EDEM(4)	de Havilland DH.82A Tiger Moth	86403	PH-III, D-EDEM(1), NL971
D-EDEN(4)	Bücker Bü181B-1 Bestmann (Sk25)	25080	D-EBEM(1), Fv25080
D-EDEO	Reims/Cessna F150L	F15000925	
D-EDES(5)	de Havilland DH.82A Tiger Moth	83458	D-EDES(1), T5823
D-EDEU	Reims/Cessna F172M	F17200958	
D-EDEW(4)	Cessna 172R Skyhawk	17281237	N66101
D-EDEX	Klemm Kl.35D Special (Permit 18.1.11)	1916	SE-BPI, Fv5027
D-EDEY	Reims/Cessna F172M	F17200973	F-WLIL
D-EDFA(2)	Robin DR.400/RP Remorqueur	1803	
D-EDFB(3)	Piper PA-28-181 Archer II	28-8190131	N8318S
D-EDFC	Cessna F150H	F150-0246	
D-EDFE(2)	Cessna 172R Skyhawk	17280109	N9869F
D-EDFF	Cessna F172H	F172-0463	
D-EDFG	Cessna F172H	F172-0481	
D-EDFH(2)	Zlin Z.142	0217	HA-SFH
D-EDFI (2)	Diamond DA 40D Star	D4.105	
D-EDFJ(2)	Cessna 150G	15066503	N8603J
D-EDFK	SOCATA MS.893A Rallye Commodore 180	11775	F-BSXX
D-EDFL	Dornier Do.27B-3	392	56+84, YA+913, D-EDFL, D-EBIV
D-EDFM	Robin DR.400/180 Régent	1326	
D-EDFN(4)	Diamond DA 40D Star	D4.109	
D-EDFO(2)	Reims/Cessna F172N	F17201558	
D-EDFR	Robin DR.400/180R Remorqueur	1334	
D-EDFS(2)	Cirrus SR22	0623	N6060Q
D-EDFT	Piper PA-18 Super Cub 95	18-3452	96+28, NL+119, AC+527, AS+527, 54-752
D-EDFU	Piper PA-22-108 Colt	22-8904	N10F
D-EDFW(2)	Mooney M.20K Model 231	25-0523	
D-EDFY	Cessna 182H Skylane	18256023	N1923X
D-EDFZ	Piper PA-18 Super Cub 95	18-3427	96+09, NL+1 . ., AC+516, AA+516, AS+516, 54-727
D-EDGD	Piper PA-18 Super Cub 95	18-1387	ALAT, 51-15387
D-EDGE(6)	Extra EA.300/L	1175	
D-EDGF	SIAI-Marchetti SF.260	2-38	OH-SRB, (OO-HEW)
D-EDGG	Reims/Cessna F152	F15201932	
D-EDGH	Gyroflug SC-01 Speed Canard	S-17	
D-EDGI (2)	Mooney M.20K Model 231	25-0193	N231CE
D-EDGM	Robin DR.400/180 Régent	2384	
D-EDGN(2)	Piper PA-18 Super Cub 95	18-3419	D-EDSN(1), 96+01, AC+510, AS+510, 54-719
D-EDGP(4)	Robin DR.400/140B Dauphin 4	2692	
D-EDGS(2)	Aquila AT-01 (Model A210)	AT01-102	
D-EDGV	Rockwell Commander 114A	14531	
D-EDGW	SOCATA MS.880B Rallye Club	2509	F-BVLS
D-EDGX(2)	Maule M-6-235 Super Rocket	7504C	N504CP
D-EDGY	Cessna F172H	F172-0451	
D-EDHA(2)	de Havilland DH.82A Tiger Moth	83105	G-AMIV, R5246
D-EDHB(3)	Piper PA-28-181 Archer II	28-8690038	N9091B, (N173AV), N9500N
D-EDHC	Beech 23 Musketeer	M-454	OE-DRK, SE-EEP, D-ENXI
D-EDHD	Cessna F172H	F172-0321	N17012
D-EDHF(2)	Mooney M.20J Model 201	24-0199	
D-EDHG	Robin DR.400/180 Régent	873	
D-EDHH	Piper PA-28R-200 Cherokee Arrow B	28R-7135063	N2118T
D-EDHI	Piper PA-28-180 Cherokee C	28-3149	N9107J
D-EDHK(2)	Beech F33A Bonanza	CE-1319	
D-EDHL(2)	Aero Designs Pulsar II (Permit .08)	P97120545	
D-EDHM	Robin DR.400/180 Régent	1574	
D-EDHN(2)	Cessna 172R Skyhawk	17280183	N9937F
D-EDHO	Piper PA-28-180 Cherokee C	28-3324	N9249J
D-EDHP(2)	Beech V35 Bonanza	D-8568	HB-EHC, N6207V
D-EDHQ	SOCATA MS.893A Rallye Commodore 180	11928	F-BTIY
D-EDHT	Winter/ Druine D.31 Turbulent KWSA	D31-01	ZS-UHT
D-EDHU	Cessna F150H	F150-0236	
D-EDHV	Piper PA-18 Super Cub 95	18-1514	(D-EEMV), ALAT, 51-15514
D-EDHW	Beech A36 Bonanza	E-1044	
D-EDHX(2)	Tank/ Van's RV-6 (Originally registered with c/n 2002208)	20892	
D-EDHZ(2)	Piper PA-18 Super Cub 95	18-3129	(OO-HBV), D-EHTR, OL-L55, L-55, 53-4729
D-EDIA	Piper PA-28R-200 Cherokee Arrow II	28R-7535038	N1058X
D-EDIB(2)	Reims/Cessna F172P	F17202131	
D-EDIC(2)	Reims/Cessna F150L	F15001264	
D-EDID(3)	Piper PA-32R-301T Saratoga IITC	3257164	PH-JRM, N41850, PH-JRM, N41850
D-EDIE(2)	Cessna 172RG Cutlass RG	172RG1058	N9856B
D-EDIF(3)	Robin DR.400/180 Régent	925	
D-EDIG(2)	SOCATA MS.893A Rallye Commodore 180	11971	F-BTJC
D-EDII (2)	Aviat Pitts S-2B	5209	
D-EDIJ	Reims/Cessna F172P	F17202174	
D-EDIK(2)	Piper PA-28R-200 Cherokee Arrow B	28R-7135202	N1974T
D-EDIL(2)	Reims/Cessna F172M	F17201418	
D-EDIN(2)	Reims/Cessna F150M	F15001267	
D-EDIO	SOCATA TB-10 Tobago	229	
D-EDIP(3)	Iren Dornier Libelle S-Ray 007	1	
D-EDIT	Piper J-3C-90 Cub (J-3C-65 convtd .99) (Officially quoted with the fuselage number 12552 as c/n)	12722	44-80426
D-EDIU	Bölkow BO.208C Junior	701	
D-EDIW(3)	Mooney M.20K Model 252 TSE	25-1173	
D-EDIX(2)	Cessna 175 Skylark	55114	N9314B
D-EDIZ(2)	Cessna F172G	F172-0219	
D-EDJC	Reims/Cessna F172M	F17201178	
D-EDJE	Reims/Cessna F177RG Cardinal RG	F177RG0108	
D-EDJF(2)	Mooney M.20K Model 231	25-0442	D-EKDW, (N3666H)
D-EDJG	Reims/Cessna F150L	F15001112	
D-EDJH	Reims/Cessna FRA150L Aerobat	FRA1500241	
D-EDJI	Reims/Cessna FRA150L Aerobat	FRA1500242	
D-EDJK	Reims/Cessna F172M Skyhawk II	F17201161	
D-EDJL	Reims/Cessna F172M	F17201162	
D-EDJM(2)	Cirrus SR22	3415	N447EQ, G-FIKI, N128CK
D-EDJN(2)	Piper PA-28R-200 Cherokee Arrow II	28R-7635264	HB-PAS, N75086
D-EDJP(2)	SOCATA Rallye 235E Gabier	13339	
D-EDJR	Reims/Cessna F172M	F17201176	
D-EDJW	Cessna 182P Skylane	18263107	N7323N
D-EDJY	Reims FR172J Rocket	FR17200503	
D-EDKA(2)	Cessna F172G	F172-0270	
D-EDKB	Piper PA-28-235 Cherokee C	28-11230	N9490W
D-EDKC	SOCATA MS.892A Rallye Commodore 150	10609	OY-DKB
D-EDKD	SOCATA TB-10 Tobago	230	
D-EDKE(2)	SOCATA TB-9 Tampico	231	
D-EDKH	Morane-Saulnier MS.880B Rallye Club	21	F-BKDJ
D-EDKK	SOCATA MS.893A Rallye Commodore 180	10934	F-BPYY
D-EDKL(3)	Lorenz / Van's RV-6 (Res. .14)	25632	
D-EDKN	Beech A36 Bonanza	E-1697	
D-EDKO	Cessna 172D	17249967	N2367U
D-EDKP(2)	Kaufhold / Van's RV-7	001/2002329	
D-EDKR(2)	Piaggio FWP.149D	093	90+75, BF+406, AS+412
D-EDKS(2)	Mooney M.20K Model 252 TSE	25-1223	
D-EDKU(2)	Piper PA-28-180 Cherokee Challenger	28-7305115	N11C
D-EDKV	Piper PA-28R-200 Cherokee Arrow	28R-35709	N4969S
D-EDKW(2)	Cessna 172S Skyhawk SP	172S8443	G-UFCD, G-OYZK, N7262C
D-EDKX	SOCATA TB-10 Tobago	215	
D-EDKY(2)	Diamond DA 40D Star	D4.325	
D-EDLB(2)	Cessna 172S Skyhawk SP	172S9339	N53300
D-EDLE(3)	Piper PA-28RT-201T Turbo Arrow IV	28R-8131027	N8298H
D-EDLF(2)	Robin DR.400/180 Régent	2115	
D-EDLK	Reims/Cessna FR172E Rocket	FR17200007	
D-EDLL(2)	Boeing Stearman A75N1	75-2764	C-FUCB, CF-UCB, N49948, 41-25275
D-EDLM(2)	Gyroflug SC-01B-160 Speed Canard	S-36	F-GGCA
D-EDLU(2)	Aerostyle Breezer B600L	011LSA	
D-EDLV	Reims FR172E Rocket	FR17200009	
D-EDLW(2)	Lang/ Brditschka HB-207R Alfa	207059	
D-EDLX	SOCATA Rallye 180T-D Galérien	3088	OE-DHL
D-EDLZ(2)	Reims FR172H Rocket	FR17200279	OE-DLZ
D-EDMA(4)	Dornier Do.27A-4	396	56+88, PS+716, QW+720, PL+426
D-EDMB(2)	SOCATA MS.880B Rallye Club	2510	F-BVLT
D-EDMF(2)	Piper PA-18-150 Super Cub	18-8780	OO-LAP, D-ECOL(2), N4444Z, N9659N
D-EDMG(2)	Cessna 152	15285279	N64830
D-EDMJ(3)	Cessna 152	15280019	OE-CEA, D-EBKF(1), N757US
D-EDMK(2)	Oberlerchner JOB 15-150	052	OE-CAM
D-EDML	SOCATA MS.893E Rallye 180GT	12183	F-BUCS
D-EDMM	Robin DR.400/180R Remorqueur	707	
D-EDMN	Piper PA-28R-200 Cherokee Arrow II	28R-7235240	N1218T
D-EDMO	Cessna 182H Skylane	18256158	N2058X
D-EDMR(2)	SOCATA TB-21 Trinidad TC	793	I-GLMC, F-ODSD
D-EDMS(2)	Diamond DA 40D Star	D4.024	
D-EDMT	Reims/Cessna F172N	F17201570	
D-EDMU	Piper J-3C-85 Cub	5082	N30744, NC30744
D-EDMV	SOCATA TB-10 Tobago	328	
D-EDMW	Piper PA-18 Super Cub 95	18-3426	96+08, SA+120, AC+515, AS+515, 54-726
D-EDMZ	SOCATA TB-10 Tobago	787	
D-EDNA	Bölkow BO.208C Junior	578	
D-EDNC	Wassmer WA.51 Pacific	08	
D-EDNE(2)	Robin DR.400/180 Régent	2667	
D-EDNL(2)	Piper PA-28R-200 Cherokee Arrow II	28R-7435240	OE-DRI, N42850
D-EDNM	Reims/Cessna F150M	F15001166	
D-EDNP	Zlin Z.43	0059	
D-EDNR	SOCATA TB-9 Tampico CS	211	
D-EDNT	Beech G35 Bonanza	D-4481	N174B
D-EDNU	Dornier Do.27B-3	401	56+92, MC+901, JB+901, AC+959
D-EDNW(2)	Dornier Do.27B-1	176	55+46, AS+902, AC+906, AS+906
D-EDNX(2)	Zlin Z.143L	0041	HB-TCR, OK-FAL
D-EDNY(2)	Grumman AA-5B Tiger	AA5B-1096	EC-DGF, N4527C
D-EDOA	Piper PA-28R-201 Arrow III	28R-7837298	N39474
D-EDOC(3)	Cessna T210M Turbo Centurion (Reims-assembled with "c/n" 0005)	21061910	PH-DOC , (PH-MDA), G-DAWN, (N732ZS)
D-EDOD(2)	SOCATA TB-9 Tampico	239	
D-EDOE(2)	Schmidt/ Denney Kitfox IV	1691	
D-EDOF(3)	Robin DR.400/180R Remorqueur	965	
D-EDOG(4)	Maule M-7-235C Super Rocket	25116C	N32536
D-EDOH	Piper J-3C-65 Cub (C/n unknown - officially registered as "43-79321")	unkn	SL-AAZ , F-BGQV, 43-. ?
D-EDOJ	Piper PA-18-150 Super Cub	18-7803	OE-AIN, OE-BIN, N10F
D-EDOL(2)	Wassmer Jodel D.120A Paris-Nice	179	
D-EDOM(2)	Robin HR.200/120B Super Club	61	(D-EHKW)
D-EDON(2)	Beech A36 Bonanza	E-2071	
D-EDOP(4)	WACO YMF-F5C	F5C-8-137	N337WC
D-EDOS(2)	Reims/Cessna F172P	F17202223	
D-EDOT(2)	Piper J-3C-65 Cub (Officially regd.with f/n 11671 as c/n)	11843	(D-EBOR(1)), 44-79547
D-EDOV(2)	Cessna F172G	F172-0227	
D-EDOY	Commander 114TC	20031	N115TB
D-EDPA(3)	de Havilland DH.82A Tiger Moth	85635	HB-UPY, G-ANOR, DE+894
D-EDPB(3)	Bunte/ Gyroflug SC-01B Speed Canard 160	S-62	N202FW
D-EDPC(2)	Cirrus SR22	3503	N440PK
D-EDPD	Piper PA-28R-200 Cherokee Arrow II	28R-7235056	N4456T
D-EDPF(2)	Piper PA-18 Super Cub 95	18-3423	96+05, NL+111, AC+503, AS+502, 54-723
D-EDPG	SOCATA TB-10 Tobago	243	
D-EDPI	Morane-Saulnier MS.885 Super Rallye	133	OY-AFY
D-EDPK	Robin DR.400/180R Remorqueur	994	
D-EDPL	Robin DR.400/180R Remorqueur	1004	
D-EDPM(2)	Robin DR.400/180R Remo 200	2209	HB-KDQ
D-EDPO(2)	Piaggio FWP.149D	168	91+46, JD+393, JE+393
D-EDPR	Dornier Do.27B-3	398	56+90, PX+221, PP+106, PC+224
D-EDPS(2)	Cessna 172RG Cutlass RG	172RG0114	N6204R
D-EDPU	Aeromere F.8L Falco III America	234	(D-ENSO)
D-EDPV	Cessna 172RG Cutlass RG	172RG0557	N5531V, (F-GCQJ)
D-EDPW(4)	Cessna 170B	25509	OO-GYM, D-EMIT, N4565C
D-EDPX	Reims/Cessna F152	F15201933	
D-EDPY	Weihermuller/ Binder CP.301S Smaragd	AB.701	
D-EDPZ	Dornier Do.27A-3	367	56+69, YA+908, AC+957
D-EDQA(2)	Cessna 172R Skyhawk	17280065	LN-ACU, (LN-KFK), N460ER
D-EDQB	Piper PA-28-161 Cherokee Warrior III	2842117	N5320X, N9511N
D-EDQC	Reims/Cessna F182Q Skylane	F18200026	
D-EDQE(2)	Robin DR.400/180R Remo 180	2193	
D-EDQI	Cessna F172H	F172-0520	
D-EDQK	Reims/Cessna F172M Skyhawk II	F17201338	
D-EDQR	Robin DR.400/180R Remorqueur	1047	

Reg	Type	c/n	Previous identities
D-EDQU	Reims FR172E Rocket	FR17200060	
D-EDQV	CEA DR.315 Petit Prince	477	
D-EDQW	Cessna 210D Centurion	21058342	HB-CMX, (D-ECMX), HB-CMX, N3842Y
D-EDRA	CEA DR.250/160 Capitaine	50	
D-EDRB(3)	Cessna 177B Cardinal	17701422	N30720
D-EDRD	SOCATA MS.893ED Rallye 180GT	12701	
D-EDRG	SOCATA Rallye 235E-D	12714	
D-EDRI (5)	Piper PA-28R-201T Turbo Cherokee Arrow III	28R-7703247	N38592
D-EDRJ	Cessna 182S Skylane	18280514	N7282D
D-EDRK(3)	Dieth/ Stephens Acro Sport II	1654	
D-EDRL(2)	Robin DR.400/180R Remorqueur	1391	OE-DRP
D-EDRM	Cessna P210N Pressurized Centurion II	P21000448	OE-DUK, N731EV
D-EDRN	Reims/Cessna F172M	F17201249	
D-EDRO(4)	Piper PA-28RT-201 Arrow IV	28R-8118021	N8287U
D-EDRP(2)	Reims/Cessna F172P	F17202179	
D-EDRQ	SOCATA Rallye 100ST-D	2910	
D-EDRR	Cessna 210B	21057992	OE-DKM, N9692X
D-EDRS(2)	Slingsby T-67C-3 Firefly	2083	PH-SGE, G-7-146, PH-SGE, G-7-140
D-EDRV(2)	Robin DR.400/180R Remorqueur	1446	D-EEKL(2), OE-DRV
D-EDRX	SOCATA Rallye 100ST-D	2911	
D-EDRY	Piper PA-18 Super Cub 95	18-7194	N3196Z
D-EDRZ(2)	Piper PA-28-181 Archer III	2843235	PH-LJM, N4126V
D-EDSA	Cessna 180F Skywagon	18051308	N4608U
D-EDSD	Robin DR.400/180R Remorqueur	1299	
D-EDSE	Cessna 205 (210-5)	205-0399	N8399Z
D-EDSG(2)	Reims/Cessna FR172K Hawk XP	FR17200665	
D-EDSJ	Reims/Cessna F152	F15201493	
D-EDSK	Reims/Cessna F172M	F17201269	
D-EDSL	Piper PA-18 Super Cub 95	18-3438	96+17, AC+506, AS+505, 54-738
D-EDSM	Dornier Do.27A-1	279	56+11, DB+901, GD+159, LB+159, CC+. . .
D-EDSN(2)	HOAC DV-20 Katana	20146	
D-EDSP	Dornier Do.27A-3 (Res 5.8.16)	465	57+36, MB+902, JC+902, AA+934 ?
D-EDSR(2)	Cessna 172P Skyhawk	17275353	N62896
D-EDST	Mooney M.20F Executive	22-1296	
D-EDSW(2)	Walker/ Stoddard-Hamilton Glasair IIS-RG	2179	
D-EDTA	Piper PA-28-180 Cherokee C	28-3631	N9510J
D-EDTC(2)	Reims/Cessna F172M	F17201323	(SE-GKG)
D-EDTE	Piper PA-18-150 Super Cub	18-7662	N10F
D-EDTG(3)	Yakovlev Yak-18T (Res. .14)	06-33	LY-PEP, DOSAAF
D-EDTJ	Cessna F172H	F172-0474	
D-EDTK	SAN Jodel D.117 Grand Tourisme	420	F-BHNE
D-EDTL(2)	Cessna A.152 Aerobat	A1521033	N758ZJ
D-EDTO	Cessna 150D	15060482	N4482U
D-EDTP	Zlin Z.526 Trenér Master	1048	
D-EDTR(2)	Cessna 182Q Skylane	18266467	LX-PCW, N94630
D-EDTS	Piper PA-28-181 Archer II	28-8090010	N8229E, N9611N
D-EDTW	Gyroflug SC-01B-160 Speed Canard	S-6	
D-EDTY(3)	Cessna 172S Skyhawk SP	172S9084	N5193C
D-EDUB(3)	SOCATA TB-10 Tobago (Res .16)	171	EC-DNO, ECT-040, F-ODNM
D-EDUC(3)	Piper PA-28-181 Archer II	2890170	N92327
D-EDUD(2)	Piper PA-28-181 Archer II	28-8090148	N81219
D-EDUF(3)	Cessna 172N Skyhawk	17272224	N9320E
D-EDUG(2)	SAN Jodel DR.1050 Ambassadeur	186	
D-EDUH(2)	Pützer Elster B	020	97+13, D-EDYM
D-EDUK(2)	Reims/Cessna F172M	F17201214	
D-EDUM(2)	Piper PA-28-181 Archer II	2890055	N9134R
D-EDUN(3)	Piper PA-18 Super Cub 95	18-1602	(D-ENCG), ALAT, 51-15602
D-EDUO	(Has f/n 18-1515 ex.51-15540, changed when in ALAT service) CEA DR.315 Petit Prince	481	
D-EDUP(2)	Piper PA-28-181 Archer II	28-8190081	N8289Y
D-EDUQ(2)	Piper PA-32-260 Cherokee Six	32-637	N11C
D-EDUR(2)	SIAI-Marchetti SF-260	1-10	OO-RUR, F-BRUR, OO-HAP
D-EDUS(3)	(Flies as 'ST-26' in Belgian AF colours) Cessna 172N Skyhawk	17270580	N739JM
D-EDUT	Piper J-3C-90 Cub	8962	HB-ODM, 42-38393
D-EDUU(2)	Piper PA-28-181 Archer II	2890100	N9158D
D-EDUV(2)	SAN Jodel DR.1050 Ambassadeur	187	
D-EDUW(2)	Piper PA-28-140 Cherokee	28-23243	N9759W, (G-AVKV), N9759W
D-EDUX(3)	Dallach/ Pitts S-1S Special	AB-K-025 (502)	
D-EDUY	Robin DR.300/180R Remorqueur	490	F-BSBU
D-EDVA(2)	SOCATA MS.880B Rallye-Club	2335	OO-LVA, F-BUVM
D-EDVC	Reims/Cessna F172M	F17201442	
D-EDVD	Reims/Cessna F172M	F17201452	
D-EDVE(3)	Robin DR.400/200R Remorqueur (DR.400/RP re-engined & type change 12.03)	1826	
D-EDVF(2)	Mooney M.20F Executive	670298	HB-DVF, N2904L
D-EDVH(2)	Christen A-1 Husky	1106	
D-EDVI (2)	Reims/Cessna F172M	F17201594	
D-EDVJ	Piper PA-28-140 Cherokee E	28-7225453	N11C
D-EDVK	Piper PA-28-180 Cherokee G	28-7205304	N11C
D-EDVM	SOCATA MS.893E Rallye 180GT	12788	
D-EDVN	SOCATA MS.893E Rallye 180GT (P 12.9.13)	12789	
D-EDVR	Reims/Cessna F150M	F15001363	
D-EDVS	Mooney M.20F Executive	670359	HB-DVS
D-EDVT(2)	Mooney M.20E Chaparral	690038	HB-DVT
D-EDVX	Mooney M.20E Chaparral	21-0017	HB-DVX
D-EDVY(4)	Cirrus SR22	1881	N128SR
D-EDVZ	Reims/Cessna F150L	F15001003	F-BUMR
D-EDWA	Pützer Elster C	034	
D-EDWB(2)	Cessna P210N Pressurized Centurion IIP	21000571	N732AC
D-EDWD	CASA C-1.131E Jungmann	2146	E3B-546
D-EDWF(2)	Cirrus SR20	1418	PH-PTS, N5338S
D-EDWG(3)	Piper PA-32-301 Saratoga II HP	3213063	N158VS, SE-KME, N9234Q
D-EDWH(2)	Piper PA-28R-201T Turbo Cherokee Arrow III	28R-7703266	N38722
D-EDWI (2)	Piper PA-32R-301T Saratoga IITC	3257226	OY-JPL, N9516N
D-EDWJ (2)	CASA C-1.131E Jungmann	2136	E3B-453
D-EDWK	CASA C-1.131E Jungmann	2080	E3B-470
D-EDWM(2)	Cessna 172N Skyhawk	17272618	N6180D
D-EDWN(2)	Robin DR.400/180 Régent	2193	
D-EDWO(4)	Cessna T206H Turbo Stationair	T20608839	D-EPWO, N62620
D-EDWP	Beech F33A Bonanza	CE-654	
D-EDWQ	Cessna 172R Skyhawk	17280536	N9552W
D-EDWR(2)	SIAI-Marchetti SF.260C	725/49-001	
D-EDWS(2)	Reims/Cessna F182Q Skylane	F18200034	
D-EDWV(2)	Degen/ Sea Rey C	1DK432C	
D-EDWW(2)	Piper PA-28R-200 Cherokee Arrow II	28R-7335436	N56438
D-EDWZ	CASA C-1.131E Jungmann	2015	E3B-411
D-EDXA	Reims/Cessna FA150K Aerobat	FA1500032	
D-EDXC(3)	Cessna 177RG Cardinal RG	177RG0890	EC-JAS, N90GS, N7609V
D-EDXD	Reims FR172G Rocket	FR17200211	
D-EDXE	Reims/Cessna F172H	F17200726	
D-EDXF	Reims FR172G Rocket	FR17200169	
D-EDXG(3)	Drescher/ Skystar Kitfox V	S 9508-0142	
D-EDXH(3)	Cessna 172S Skyhawk SP	172S9773	(D-EDDH(4)), N66011
D-EDXL	Reims/Cessna F172M	F17201098	
D-EDXM	Reims/Cessna F172M	F17201100	
D-EDXP	Reims/Cessna F172M	F17201106	
D-EDXQ	Piper PA-28RT-201T Turbo Arrow IV	28R-8031106	EC-JCA, D-EJKK, N8219N
D-EDXR	Reims/Cessna F172M	F17201034	F-BUMA
D-EDXT	Grumman AA-5A Cheetah	AA5A-0085	OY-GAK
D-EDXW	SOCATA TB-10 Tobago	462	
D-EDXY(2)	Cessna TR182 Turbo Skylane RG	R18200772	D-EFNT, OE-DNT, N736UQ
D-EDXZ	Aquila AT-01	AT01-239	
D-EDYA	Bölkow BO.207	286	HB-UYA, D-ENVY
D-EDYH	Piper PA-12 Super Cruiser	12-3480	SL-ABE, F-BEGP, NC4052H
D-EDYT	Piper J-3C-65 Cub	11771	HB-OEG, 43-30480
D-EDZI	Cessna F172E	F172-0023/17250578	OE-DEO, (N2978U)
D-EDZL	Cessna 182P Skylane (Reims-assembled with "c/n" 0001)	18263772	N6598M
D-EDZM	Cessna 182P Skylane (Reims-assembled with "c/n" 0002) (Status uncertain)	18263788	N6644M
D-EDZN	Reims/Cessna F150M	F15001168	
D-EDZO(2)	Cessna 182P Skylane	18263549	N5811J
D-EDZQ	Piper PA-28R-180 Cherokee Arrow	28R-31120	N3172R
D-EDZU	Cessna 182H Skylane	18256163	N2063X
D-EDZW	Piper PA-38-112 Tomahawk II	38-81A0103	N26022
D-EEAA(2)	Tecnam P.2008-JC (Permit 26.7.13) (Same c/n as D-EEEA)	1003	
D-EEAB	Bölkow BO.208C Junior	681	
D-EEAC	Bölkow BO.208C Junior	682	
D-EEAD	Stark/ Piel CP.301A Emeraude	101-052	OY-EAD
D-EEAE(3)	Beech B36TC Bonanza	EA-666	N432A
D-EEAF(3)	Dornier Do.27B-1	274	HB-HAF, D-EATA(1), 56+07, AC+926, AS+926
D-EEAG(2)	Oberlerchner JOB 15-180/2 (Conv from JOB 15-150)	053	OE-CAG
D-EEAH	Bölkow BO.208C Junior	658	(D-EJMH)
D-EEAI	Bölkow BO.208C Junior	686	
D-EEAL(2)	Piper PA-28-180 Cherokee D	28-4734	N6326J
D-EEAM(2)	Cessna 170B	25080	HB-COM, N8228A
D-EEAN(2)	Piper PA-28-181 Archer II	28-8390025	N8322X
D-EEAO(3)	PZL-104 Wilga 35A (Permit 16.8.11)	48037	SP-EAG
D-EEAP	Reims FR172F Rocket	FR17200067	
D-EEAR	SAN Jodel D.140C Mousquetaire III	143	
D-EEAT	Reims FR172F Rocket	FR17200062	(G-AXBT)
D-EEAU(3)	Robin HR.200/120B	274	
D-EEAV(2)	SOCATA TB-21 Trinidad TC	2124	
D-EEAY	Ruschmeyer R90-230RG	017	
D-EEAZ	Piaggio P.149D	323	92+25, AS+403, AS+473
D-EEBA(4)	Aerostyle Breezer	010E	
D-EEBB(2)	Diamond DA 40D Star (Res .16)	D4.263	HB-SDN, OE-VPT
D-EEBE(2)	Piper PA-38-112 Tomahawk	38-80A0112	N24817
D-EEBG	Reims/Cessna F152	F15201437	
D-EEBH(2)	Zlin Z.526F Trenér Master	1068	LZ-713
D-EEBI (2)	Cessna 172S Skyhawk SP	172S9115	N951SA
D-EEBK	Piper PA-28R-200 Cherokee Arrow II	28R-7435014	N56574
D-EEBM	Robin DR.400/180 Régent	929	
D-EEBO(2)	Reims/Cessna F150M	F15001273	
D-EEBP	Reims/Cessna F182Q Skylane	F18200041	
D-EEBS(2)	Zlin Z.526F Trenér Master	1151	(D-EJLL), SP-CDM
D-EEBT(2)	Beech F33A Bonanza	CE-1479	N44LR
D-EEBU	Piper PA-28-235 Cherokee B	28-10848	N9190W
D-EEBV	Ruschmeyer R90-230RG	011	
D-EEBW	Mooney M.20J Model 201	24-0424	
D-EEBY(4)	Zlin Z.526F Trenér Master	1087	LZ-720, LZ-020
D-EEBZ	SOCATA TB-10 Tobago	983	
D-EECA	Beech V35B Bonanza	D-9120	
D-EECB(2)	Piper PA-46-350P Malibu Mirage	4636549	N24750
D-EECC(3)	Cessna 172R Skyhawk (Thielert diesel)	17281213	N2121F
D-EECD(3)	Diamond DA 40 Star	40018	
D-EECE	Reims FR172J Rocket	FR17200495	
D-EECF	Cessna 182P Skylane	18262784	N52706
D-EECG(3)	Ruschmeyer R90-230G (Res)	023	N230S, D-EECC(2)
D-EECH	Cessna 182P Skylane	18262850	N52794
D-EECI (2)	Piper PA-46-350P Malibu	4622123	N312CC, JA4194, N111K, JA4194, N9208Z, (N444JM), N9208Z
D-EECK(2)	OMF-100-160 Symphony	0042	(D-EFEM(4)), (N420MF)
D-EECL(3)	Rockwell Commander 112TC	13039	N112FH
D-EECM(2)	Reims/Cessna F172M	F17201444	
D-EECN(2)	Cessna 172S Skyhawk SP	172S9701	(D-EEGE(3)), OY-FHV, N781MK
D-EECO	Beech V35B Bonanza	D-9229	
D-EECP(2)	Piper PA-28-161 Warrior II	28-8116242	N9543N
D-EECQ	Reims/Cessna F172M	F17201280	
D-EECR(2)	Ruschmeyer R90-230FG	030	(D-EEFX)
D-EECS(2)	Ruschmeyer R90-230RG	015	
D-EECT(4)	Flight Design CT LS-ELA (P 17.4.12)	F-11-11-08	
D-EECU(2)	Robin DR.400/180R Remorqueur	1215	
D-EECV	Reims/Cessna F172M	F17201634	(SU- . . .)
D-EEDA(4)	Diamond DA 40D Star	D4.001	
D-EEDB(3)	Cirrus SR20	2015	TC-AST, N737PG
D-EEDC(3)	Cessna 172S Skyhawk SP	172S9024	N5147V
D-EEDD(2)	Diamond DA 20-A1 Katana	10315	N315DA, C-GKAH
D-EEDE	SOCATA MS.883 Rallye 115	1573	F-BTHJ
D-EEDG	Reims/Cessna F172M	F17200906	
D-EEDH	Reims/Cessna F172M	F17200913	
D-EEDI (3)	Diamond DA 40D Star	D4.240	OE-VPU
D-EEDJ	Reims FR172J Rocket	FR17200355	
D-EEDK(2)	Reims/Cessna F150L	F15000941	(D-EGKD)
D-EEDL	Reims FR172J Rocket	FR17200359	

Registration	Type	c/n	Previous identities
D-EEDO(3)	Zlin Z.143LSi	0055	OK-STA
D-EEDP	Reims/Cessna F150L	F15000878	
D-EEDQ(3)	SNCAN/Stampe SV.4C (Res. 27.1.15)	58	F-BFCF(2), Fr.Navy, F-BDYN, ALAT
D-EEDR(2)	Ruschmeyer R90-230RG	024	D-EWWE(1), (D-EECY(2))
D-EEDS(2)	Beech A36AT Bonanza	E-2714	
D-EEDT	Reims/Cessna F172M	F17200919	
D-EEDU	Cessna 182P Skylane	18261537	N21284
D-EEDV	Cessna 182P Skylane	18261524	N21262
D-EEDW(2)	SNCAN/ Stampe SV.4C	245	F-BCKD
D-EEDZ(3)	SNCAN/Stampe SV.4C (Res. 27.1.15)	677	G-BZSY, N12426, F-BGGT, Fr.mil, (F-BDNV)
D-EEEA(2)	Tecnam P.2008-JC (Reported 4.13. Same c/n as D-EEAA)	1003	
D-EEEB(2)	Reims/Cessna F182Q Skylane	F18200112	OY-CBR, PH-AYD(2)
D-EEED(2)	Zlin Z.526M Trenér Master	1033	HB-TCI, D-EJAB(5), OO-YGO, (OO-UGO), YU-DIK, JRV41108, OK-XRC
D-EEEE(2)	SOCATA TB-20 Trinidad	300	
D-EEEF	Robin DR.400/160 Chevalier	883	
D-EEEH	SOCATA Rallye 180TS Galérien	3322	
D-EEEI	SOCATA Rallye 180TS Galérien	3321	
D-EEEJ(2)	Hartz/Aerostyle Breezer	009	
D-EEEK	CASA C-1.131E Jungmann	2056	E3B-455
D-EEEL(2)	Piper PA-28RT-201 Arrow IV	28R-8018055	N8178A
D-EEEM	SOCATA Rallye 235E-D	13155	
D-EEEN(2)	Gyroflug SC-01B Speed Canard	S-27	N190SC, HB-UCU, D-EEGX(1), (D-EAND(2))
D-EEEO(3)	Piper PA-46-350P Malibu Mirage (JetProp DLX conversion # 259)	4636425	N31112
D-EEEP(2)	Bücker Bü.133C Jungmeister (Res .16)	24	G-TAFI, N2210, HB-MIF, U-77
D-EEEQ(2)	SOCATA TB-200 Tobago XL	1760	
D-EEER	SOCATA TB-10 Tobago	137	
D-EEES(2)	Schlichtenhorst / Van's RV-4	4405	
D-EEET(2)	Memmingen / Van's RV-7/MM	2002467	
D-EEEU	Morane-Saulnier MS.885 Super Rallye	136	F-BKLL
D-EEEV(3)	Beech A36 Bonanza	E-1108	OO-JNS, C-GJLS, N18380
D-EEEW	Gyroflug SC-01B Speed Canard	A-3	
D-EEEX	Gyroflug SC-01B Speed Canard	A1-80	
D-EEEZ	Krauss/ Rutan VariEze VW-VP	A-0329	
D-EEFA	Piper PA-28-140 Cherokee C	28-26658	N5827U
D-EEFB(3)	AIAA/Stampe SV.4C	1077	N1322T, G-AXIJ, F-BJDV, Fr.AF
D-EEFC	Piper PA-24-260 Comanche C	24-4932	N9425P
D-EEFE	Reims/Cessna F172P	F17202168	
D-EEFF	Ficht/ Bölkow BO.209 Monsun 160RV (Built from MBB parts by Pneuma-Technik EFicht)	301	
D-EEFG(3)	Beech F33A Bonanza	CE-1626	N82689
D-EEFH	Piper PA-28-140 Cherokee C	28-26736	N5885U
D-EEFI(2)	Cessna 172S Skyhawk SP	172S11368	N698CS
D-EEFK(2)	Mooney M.20K Model 252 TSE	25-1175	
D-EEFL(2)	Beech F33A Bonanza	CE-1752	
D-EEFN(2)	Mooney M.20J Model 205	24-3215	
D-EEFO	Piper PA-28R-200 Cherokee Arrow	28R-35679	N4907S
D-EEFQ(2)	Cessna 172R Skyhawk	17280342	N9496F
D-EEFR	Reims/Cessna F172M	F17201246	
D-EEFS	Reims/Cessna F172P	F17202166	
D-EEFU(2)	SOCATA Rallye 235E-D Gabier	13329	
D-EEFV	Piper PA-28-180 Cherokee E	28-5757	N3655R
D-EEFW(2)	Cessna 172P Skyhawk	17275823	OE-KFW, N65701
D-EEFX(2)	Mooney M.20L Model PFM	26-0039	N1070S, (D-EFST(2)), N1070S
D-EEFY(2)	Reims/Cessna F172P	F17202229	
D-EEGA(2)	Gippsaero GA8 TC 320	GA8-TC 320-13-188	
D-EEGB	Beech B24R Sierra 200	MC-262	
D-EEGC	Robin DR.400/180R Remorqueur	1357	
D-EEGD	Piaggio P.149D	315	92+18, CA+478, AC+466, AS+466
D-EEGF	Robin DR.400/180 Régent	1013	
D-EEGG(2)	Mooney M.20J Model 205	24-3015	
D-EEGH(2)	Commander Aircraft 114B	14632	
D-EEGI	Piper PA-28-181 Cherokee Archer II	28-7790403	N2539Q
D-EEGJ	Piper PA-28-181 Archer II	2890066	N9137X
D-EEGK(2)	Cessna 182J Skylane	18256742	N2642F
D-EEGL	Reims/Cessna F172M	F17201335	
D-EEGN(2)	CASA C-1.131E Jungmann	2095	E3B-351
D-EEGO	Piper PA-28-140 Cherokee Cruiser	28-7725210	N9632N
D-EEGP	Reims/Cessna F172N	F17201981	
D-EEGQ(2)	Cirrus SR20 (Res. .13, ntu)	1506	OE-DDD, N61118
D-EEGR(3)	Cirrus SR22	1984	N993SR
D-EEGS(3)	Zlin Z.526F Trenér Master	1153	OK-ZLI, D-EFHZ, SP-CDO
D-EEGT(2)	Beech 77 Skipper (Res .16)	WA-117	OO-LDJ, (OO-DAL), N131DB, N3725Z
D-EEGU(2)	Diamond DA 40D Star	D4.350	I-AEBS, OE-VPU
D-EEGW(3)	Cessna TR182 Turbo Skylane RG	R18200667	OY-SFK, N9194R
D-EEHA	American AA-5 Traveler	AA5-0031	(N5831L)
D-EEHB	American AA-5 Traveler	AA5-0032	(N5832L)
D-EEHC	American AA-5 Traveler	AA5-0117	(N6017L)
D-EEHD	American AA-5 Traveler	AA5-0118	(N6018L)
D-EEHE(3)	Piper PA-32RT-300 Lance II	32R-7885004	N2204M
D-EEHF	American AA-5 Traveler	AA5-0136	(N6036L)
D-EEHG(2)	Cessna 182Q Skylane	18267235	N97871
D-EEHH(2)	Ruschmeyer R90-230RG	007	
D-EEHK(2)	Piper PA-28-161 Warrior II	28-8516012	F-GEEK(2), N4380F
D-EEHL(2)	Mooney M.20J Model 201	24-1612	
D-EEHM	American AA-5 Traveler	AA5-0318	(N5418L)
D-EEHN	American AA-5 Traveler	AA5-0345	(N5445L)
D-EEHO	Piper PA-28-140 Cherokee	28-20779	CF-RWL
D-EEHP(2)	Reims/Cessna F182Q Skylane	F18200165	OE-DOV
D-EEHR	Cessna 182P Skylane	18261008	OY-HER, D-EEHR, N7368Q
D-EEHS	American AA-5 Traveler	AA5-0411	
D-EEHT	American AA-5 Traveler	AA5-0412	
D-EEHW	Cessna P210N Pressurized Centurion II (Soloy conversion, 2.00)	P21000455	N731FX
D-EEHX	Ruschmeyer R90-230RG	008	
D-EEHY(2)	Ruschmeyer R90-230RG	029	(D-EEDZ(2))
D-EEHZ(2)	Ruschmeyer R90-230RG	009	
D-EEIA(3)	Robin DR.400/180R Remorqueur	1692	
D-EEIE	Reims/Cessna F177RG Cardinal RG	F177RG0117	
D-EEII (3)	Diamond DA 40D Star	D4.080	
D-EEIJ	Cessna T182T Turbo Skylane	T18208130	N5171X
D-EEIL(3)	Piper PA-18-150 Super Cub	18-7909091	N82295
D-EEIM	Robin DR.400/180R Remorqueur	849	
D-EEIN(3)	Robin DR.400/180R Remorqueur	1938	
D-EEIP(2)	Bölkow BO.209 Monsun 160RV	152	HB-UEP, D-EBJL
D-EEIR(2)	Diamond DA 40D Star	D4.336	OE-VPT
D-EEIS(2)	Cessna 150L	15075235	N11165
D-EEIT	SOCATA TB-200 Tobago XL	1625	
D-EEIU	Cessna F172H	F172-0512	PH-AAC
D-EEIV	Reims/Cessna F172M	F17201372	
D-EEIW	Reims/Cessna F172M	F17201371	
D-EEJA(2)	Yakovlev Yak-50	80-1705	DDR-WQO
D-EEJB	Robin DR.400/180R Remorqueur	968	
D-EEJD	Robin HR.200/100 Club	42	
D-EEJE	Robin DR.400/180S	1894	
D-EEJF	Piper PA-46-310P Malibu	4608135	OE-KEF, N67JB, N9145B
D-EEJJ(3)	Cessna 172R Skyhawk	17280813	N24056
D-EEJK	Cirrus SR22 (Res. 31.8.15)	2415	N153E
D-EEJL	Reims/Cessna F152	F15201545	
D-EEJM(2)	Cessna 172N Skyhawk	17270216	N7381C
D-EEJO	Robin HR.100/210D Safari	202	
D-EEJP(2)	Cessna F150G	F150-0175	OE-CMU, D-EFMU, (D-EHER)
D-EEJQ	Cessna 152	15283155	N46978
D-EEJR(2)	Ruschmeyer R90-230RG	020	
D-EEJW(3)	Yakovlev Yak-18T (Dbr 30.8.15 Itzehoe)	5201507	HA-CBD, RA-3025K, CCCP-81442
D-EEKD	Piper PA-28-180 Cherokee C	28-1999	N7952W, 6Y-JGM, N7952W
D-EEKE	Beech F33A Bonanza	CE-1145	N500TK, N500TL
D-EEKF	Reims/Cessna F172M	F17201260	
D-EEKI	Wassmer WA.54 Atlantic	123	
D-EEKL(3)	Cessna 172P Skyhawk	17274303	HB-CJR, N51370
D-EEKM(2)	SOCATA TB-21 Trinidad TC	2156	N923TT
D-EEKN	Cessna 172S Skyhawk SP	172S8308	N2431X
D-EEKO	Robin DR.400/180R Remorqueur	1350	I-ITAO
D-EEKP	SOCATA TB-20 Trinidad	324	
D-EEKR	Robin DR.400/180R Remorqueur	746	F-BTZA
D-EEKT(2)	Bode/ Van's RV-7 (c/n previously quoted as 001)	2002411	
D-EEKU(2)	Diamond DA 40D Star	40.DS002	OE-DXG
D-EEKW	Mraz M.1C Sokol	211	HB-TAD
D-EELA	Grumman AA-5 Traveler	AA5-0724	N5140A, (N1324R)
D-EELB	Robin DR.300/180R Remorqueur	534	LX-FIZ, F-BSLI
D-EELC(3)	Beech F33A Bonanza	CE-1589	N33PN, F-GIFJ
D-EELE	CASA C-1.131E Jungmann	2195	E3B-589
D-EELH(2)	Cessna 172N Skyhawk	17271463	N3192E
D-EELI	CEA DR.250/160 Capitaine	69	F-BNVG
D-EELK(2)	Focke-Wulf FW.44J Stieglitz (P. 2.8.16)	2924	D-ELFW, N212S, OH-SZM, SZ-21(Finn AF)
D-EELL(2)	Diamond DA 40D Star	D4.118	
D-EELM	Grumman AA-5B Tiger	AA5B-0151	
D-EELN	SOCATA Rallye 180TS Galérien	3359	
D-EELP(2)	Pipistrel Virus SW121 (Permit 1.7.14)	634SWN121	
D-EELQ	Robin DR.400/180R Remorqueur	944	
D-EELR	Robin DR.400/180R Remorqueur	950	
D-EELT	Cessna 172C Skyhawk	17248963	N8463X
D-EELU(2)	Mooney M.20E Chaparral	700002	N9332V
D-EELV	Cessna 172N Skyhawk	17273031	N1941F
D-EELW(3)	Beech F33A Bonanza	CE-1455	N5619D
D-EELY	Piper PA-28-161 Warrior II	28-8216121	N9636N
D-EELZ(2)	Gyroflug SC01B-160 Speed Canard	S-4	(D-EBDA)
D-EEMA	SOCATA MS.892A Rallye Commodore 150	11440	
D-EEMB(3)	Cirrus SR22T	1262	N141MB
D-EEMC	Piper PA-28-181 Archer III (Res. .15)	2843255	PH-RER, N41478, N9514N
D-EEME	Cessna T210N Turbo Centurion II	21064262	N6135Y
D-EEMF(3)	Cirrus SR22	3135	SP-KLS, N630CP
D-EEMG	Cessna 210C	21058150	HB-CMG, N3650Y
D-EEMH(2)	Cessna 172RG Cutlass RG	172RG1053	N9843B
D-EEMI	Piper PA-28-151 Cherokee Warrior	28-7415223	N9535N
D-EEMK(2)	Grumman-American AA-5B Tiger	AA5B-1014	OY-GAU
D-EEML	Robin HR.200/100 Club	101	
D-EEMM(N)	Sondermann/ Christen Eagle II	S-0470	
D-EEMN	Cessna FR.182 Skylane RG	0040	PH-AXB
D-EEMO	SOCATA MS.892E Rallye 150GT	12377	F-BVNO
D-EEMP	Reims/Cessna F150M	F15001247	
D-EEMR	Reims/Cessna F172M	F17201356	(F-BXZV), (D-EJTA)
D-EEMS	Piper PA-18 Super Cub 95	18-3229	OL-L52, L-155, 53-4829
D-EEMT(3)	Extra EA.200 (W/o 28.12.16)	1032	
D-EEMU	Robin DR.400/180 Régent	1036	
D-EEMV(3)	SIAI-Marchetti S.205-18/R (Res .16)	357	I-DERT
D-EEMW	Beech A36TC Bonanza	EA-190	
D-EEND	Cessna 182P Skylane	18262622	N52457
D-EENE	Reims/Cessna F150L	F15001073	
D-EENF	Reims/Cessna F150L	F15001075	
D-EENG	Reims/Cessna F150L	F15001076	
D-EENI (2)	Tecnam P.2002-JF Sierra	040	
D-EENK	Reims/Cessna F172M	F17201119	
D-EENN(2)	Champion 7GCB Challenger 180	53	OE-ADE
D-EENP	Reims FR172J Rocket	FR17200482	
D-EENR	Reims/Cessna F172M Skyhawk	F17201152	
D-EENU	Reims FR172J Rocket	FR17200474	
D-EENW	Reims/Cessna F150L	F15001089	
D-EENX	Reims/Cessna F150L	F15001059	
D-EENZ(2)	Piper PA-28-161 Warrior II	28-8016235	I-DENZ, PH-WVG, N8141R
D-EEOA(2)	Aquila AT-02	AT02-253	
D-EEOB(2)	Aviamilano F.8L Falco Srs II	114	G-OCDS, G-VEGL, OO-MEN, I-VEGL
D-EEOE(2)	Beech F33A Bonanza	CE-1647	N82627
D-EEOF	Robin DR.400/180 Régent	1435	
D-EEOH(2)	Diamond DA 40 Star	40014	
D-EEOK	Reims/Cessna F172M	F17201266	
D-EEOL(2)	Beech V35B Bonanza	D-9330	HB-EHK, D-EHKK(2)
D-EEOM	Reims/Cessna F172M	F17201295	
D-EEON(2)	Liberty XL-2	0070	YL-EON, N586XL
D-EEOO	Cessna 210M Centurion II (Reims-assembled with c/n 0013)	21062648	F-WZJE, N761ZL
D-EEOP	Robin DR.400/180R Remorqueur (W/o Backnang 9.9.12)	1434	
D-EEOR	Reims/Cessna FR172K Hawk XP	FR17200624	PH-JET
D-EEOS	Reims/Cessna F172P Skyhawk II	F17202078	
D-EEOV	Robin DR.400/180 Régent	1427	F-GCAP

Reg.	Type	Serial	Notes
D-EEPA(2)	Piper PA-28-181 Archer II	28-8690045	N9288Y
D-EEPD(2)	Piper PA-46R-350T Matrix	4692138	N138CM, N9541N
D-EEPE	Robin DR.400/180R Remorqueur	1222	
D-EEPF(2)	Robin DR.400/180S	1958	
D-EEPH	Reims/Cessna F172M	F17201216	(D-EOFY)
D-EEPJ	Dornier Do.27A-1	173	55+43, AC+923, AS+923
D-EEPK(2)	CASA C-1.131E Jungmann	2101	E3B-303
	(W/o Albstadt-Degerfield 23.8.12)		
D-EEPL	Reims/Cessna F172N	F17201539	
D-EEPM	Piper PA-28R-200 Cherokee Arrow II	28R-7435283	N43613
D-EEPN	Dornier Do.27A-4	395	56+87, QA+101, QW+709, PL+435, D-EJIG
D-EEPO(2)	WSK CSS-13	0430	OE-CPO, SE-XPP, SP-FZP, SP-AFC
	(P 14.1.13)		
D-EEPP	Beech B24R Sierra 200	MC-378	OE-DFP
	(Damaged 20.6.04)		
D-EEPQ	Robin DR.400/180 Régent	1234	
D-EEPR	Piper PA-38-112 Tomahawk	38-78A0292	N9676N
D-EEPU	Reims/Cessna F150M	F15001286	
D-EEPW	Reims/Cessna F182P Skylane	F18200003	
D-EEPY	Cessna TR182 Turbo Skylane RG	R18201431	N4796S
D-EEQH(2)	Reims/Cessna F182Q Skylane	F18200078	
	(Damaged 29.5.11)		
D-EEQI (2)	Piper PA-38-112 Tomahawk	38-79A0747	N9679N
D-EEQM(2)	CASA C-1.131E Jungmann	2221	E3B-621
	(P 3.12.13)		
D-EEQP	CASA C-1.131E Jungmann	2100	E3B-493
D-EEQQ(2)	Cessna 172S Skyhawk SP	172S9974	N1939S
D-EEQS	Reims/Cessna F172N	F17201909	(LN-HOJ)
D-EEQT	Reims/Cessna F172N	F17201920	
D-EEQW	Piper PA-18 Super Cub 95	18-3421	96+03, NL+106, AC+512, AA+512, AS+512, 54-721
D-EERA	Wassmer CE.43 Guepard	467	
D-EERC	Wassmer WA.54 Atlantic	154	
D-EERD	Piper PA-28-181 Cherokee Archer II	28-7790240	N9564N
D-EERF(2)	Wassmer WA.54 Atlantic	135	
D-EERG(2)	Beech F33A Bonanza	CE-1266	
D-EERH(3)	Diamond DA 40D Star	D4.124	OE-VPU
D-EERI (3)	Piper PA-28R-201T Turbo Arrow III	28R-7803273	N9691C
D-EERK(2)	Reims/Cessna FR182 Skylane RG	FR18200063	
D-EERM	Piper PA-28-180 Cherokee Archer	28-7405206	N9512N
D-EERN(2)	SOCATA TB-20 Trinidad	643	F-GENX
D-EERO(3)	Rockwell 114A	14532	HB-NCU
D-EERP	Piaggio P.149D	259	91+77, AC+410, AS+410
D-EERQ	Wassmer WA.81 Piranha	818	
D-EERR(2)	Cirrus SR22	0820	N301CD, N81404
	(P 21.9.16)		
D-EERT(2)	Reims/Cessna F172M	F17201416	
D-EERV	Wassmer WA.81 Piranha	823	
D-EESB(2)	Cessna 172P Skyhawk	17275461	N63648
D-EESC	Reims/Cessna F172M	F17201289	
D-EESG(2)	Reims/Cessna F172M	F17201315	
D-EESI	Reims/Cessna F172M	F17201322	
D-EESJ	Reims/Cessna F172M	F17201325	
D-EESL	Reims FR172J Rocket	FR17200549	
D-EESM	Reims/Cessna F172N	F17201547	
D-EESO	Piper PA-28-200 Cherokee Arrow II	28R-7435189	N41478
D-EEST(2)	Piper PA-28-200 Cherokee Arrow B	28R-35749	N5017S
D-EESW(2)	Evektor EV-97 SportStar RTC	2013 1603	
D-EESX	Cessna 172S Skyhawk SP	172S10382	N1327Z
D-EESY	Brand/ Rutan VariEze	1523/01E	
D-EETD	Cessna F150J	F150-0456	
D-EETE	Piper PA-28R-200 Cherokee Arrow	28R-35179	N9463N
D-EETH(2)	Diamond DA 40D Star	D4.196	
D-EETI	SOCATA MS.893A Rallye Commodore 180	11417	
D-EETK(3)	Cessna 170B	25390	D-EWOT, D-ERYS, D-EMEE(1), N3148B
D-EETL(3)	Diamond DA 20-A1 Katana	10321	C-GKAN
D-EETM(2)	Robin DR.400/180R Remorqueur	1230	
D-EETO	Cessna F172H	F172-0646	
D-EETP	Cessna F150J	F150-0433	
D-EETQ	Cessna F150J	F150-0435	
D-EETR	Piper PA-28-140 Cherokee B	28-25767	N5598F
D-EETS(2)	Cessna 172P Skyhawk	17275904	N65836
D-EETT	Piper PA-18-150 Super Cub	18-850	R-201, 51-15685
D-EETU(3)	Haubold/ Aero Designs Pulsar XP	1776SB	
D-EETW(2)	Diamond DA 20-A1 Katana	10253	
D-EETX	Cessna 182K Skylane	18258070	OE-DEB, N3070Q
D-EEUD(2)	SOCATA TB-20 Trinidad	275	
D-EEUE	SOCATA Rallye 180TS Galérien	3193	
D-EEUI	SOCATA Rallye 180T-D Galérien	3196	
D-EEUK(2)	SOCATA Rallye 150T-D	2971	F-GBCC
D-EEUO	SOCATA Rallye 180TS Galérien	3245	
D-EEUP	SOCATA Rallye 180TS Galérien	3246	
D-EEUQ	SOCATA Rallye 180TS Galérien	3247	
D-EEUR	SOCATA Rallye 180TS Galérien	3248	
D-EEUT	Piper PA-18-150 Super Cub	18-8726	N4395Z
	(Cr 8.6.13 Blumberg)		
D-EEUU(2)	Cessna 172P Skyhawk	17274551	N52538
D-EEUW	SOCATA Rallye 180TS Galérien	3252	
D-EEVA(3)	Robin DR.400/160D Major 80	1576	
D-EEVB	Reims/Cessna F172M	F17201209	
D-EEVD	Reims/Cessna F172M	F17201202	
D-EEVE(2)	Cessna 172M Skyhawk	17266168	OK-AKW, D-EEVE(2), N9467H
D-EEVH	Reims/Cessna F150M	F15001190	
D-EEVI (3)	Mooney M.20J Model 201	24-1648	
D-EEVJ	Reims/Cessna F172M	F17201270	
D-EEVK(2)	SIAT 223A-1 Flamingo	014	HB-EVK, D-ENBK(1)
D-EEVM	Reims/Cessna F172M	F17201291	
D-EEVN	Reims/Cessna F172M	F17201293	
D-EEVO(2)	Mooney M.20J Model 201	24-0829	N4735H
D-EEVQ(2)	Reims/Cessna F152	F15201655	N1662Q
D-EEVS(2)	CEA DR.315 Petit Prince	349	F-BRCR
D-EEVV	CASA C-1.131E Jungmann	2218	E3B-618
D-EEVX	American AG-5B Tiger	10144	
D-EEVZ	SOCATA TB-9 Tampico	895	
D-EEWA(3)	Beech F33A Bonanza	CE-1226	OE-KBE, N23EL
D-EEWB	Reims/Cessna F172L	F17200880	
D-EEWC	Cessna P210N Pressurized Centurion II	P21000542	N2108J, (N731SA)
D-EEWD	Beech F33A Bonanza	CE-905	
	(Dbr 17.3.10)		
D-EEWE(2)	Robin DR.400/180R Remorqueur	1973	
D-EEWF(3)	Cessna 172P Skyhawk	17275316	N62632
D-EEWG(2)	Cessna 172P Skyhawk	17274944	(D-EEAS), N54282
D-EEWI	Beech F33A Bonanza	CE-509	
D-EEWK	Robin HR.100/210D Safari	195	
D-EEWL	Piper PA-18 Super Cub 95	18-3448	96+24, NL+114, AC+533, AS+533, 54-748
D-EEWN	Beech A36 Bonanza	E-1823	
D-EEWO	Piper PA-18-150 Super Cub	18-554	R-202, 51-15668, N7183K
	(Dismantled 9.99, f/n 18-486)		
D-EEWP(3)	Ruschmeyer R90-230G	013	D-EEBY
D-EEWU	Diamond DA 40D Star	D4.210	
D-EEWW(2)	Piper PA-28RT-201T Turbo Arrow IV	28R-8031051	OE-KEN, S5-DDV, N74KG, N9169N
D-EEWX	Beech F33A Bonanza	CE-947	HB-EWX
D-EEWY	Reims/Cessna F172M	F17200956	
D-EEXA	Reims/Cessna F177RG Cardinal RG	F177RG0061	
D-EEXE(2)	Heliopolis Gomhouria Mk.6	148	SU-325, EAF-325
D-EEXG	Cessna T210L Turbo Centurion	21059508	N4608Q
D-EEXH	Reims/Cessna F150L	F15000795	
D-EEXI (3)	Van's RV-6	1949	
	(Permit 18.3.14)		
D-EEXL(2)	Piper PA-28-161 Warrior II	28-8116115	F-GFIG, N8316D
D-EEXN	Reims/Cessna F172L	F17200858	
D-EEXS	Reims/Cessna F172L	F17200840	
D-EEXX	Reims/Cessna F177RG Cardinal RG	F177RG0044	
D-EEXY(2)	Impulse 180TD	TD-5	
D-EEXZ	Cessna 182P Skylane	18261174	(N20745)
D-EEYD	Reims/Cessna F150L	F15000799	
D-EEYE	Reims/Cessna F150L	F15000805	
D-EEYI	Reims/Cessna F172L	F17200872	
D-EEYJ	Reims FR172H Rocket	FR17200322	
D-EEYN	Reims FR172H Rocket	FR17200329	
D-EEYO	Reims/Cessna F150L	F15000808	
D-EEYP	Reims/Cessna F150L	F15000811	
D-EEYS(2)	Stegner/ Pitts S-1-11B	479	
D-EEYU(2)	Cessna TU206F Turbo Stationair	U20602001	OO-ESC(2), PH-ESA, D-EEYU, N51404
D-EEYY	Reims/Cessna F172L	F17200876	
D-EEYZ	Reims/Cessna F177RG Cardinal RG	F177RG0045	N4939
D-EEZA	Reims/Cessna F177RG Cardinal RG	F177RG0062	
D-EEZB	Reims/Cessna F177RG Cardinal RG	F177RG0060	
D-EEZC	Reims/Cessna FRA150L Aerobat	FRA1500149	N150ZC, D-EEZC
D-EEZD	Reims/Cessna FRA150L Aerobat	FRA1500159	
D-EEZE	Reims/Cessna F172L	F17200875	
D-EEZH	Reims/Cessna F172L	F17200871	
D-EEZL	Cessna 182P Skylane	18261713	(N21555)
D-EEZM	Reims/Cessna F150L	F15000804	(G-AZKY)
D-EEZN(3)	Zlin Z.242L	0689	N242DK
	(Res. .13)		
D-EEZP(2)	Zuckschwerdt/ Rutan VariEze	1005	
D-EEZQ	Reims/Cessna F150L	F15000865	
D-EEZR	Reims/Cessna F150L	F15000868	
D-EEZT	Reims/Cessna F172L	F17200867	
D-EEZU	Reims FR172H Rocket	FR17200310	
D-EEZV	Reims FR172H Rocket	FR17200338	
D-EEZW	Reims/Cessna F172L	F17200884	
D-EEZX	Reims FR172H Rocket	FR17200339	
D-EEZY	Reims FR172H Rocket	FR17200340	
D-EEZZ(2)	Kämmerer/ Impulse 180TD	TD-4	
D-EFAB(3)	Diamond DA 40D Star	D4.153	OE-VPW
D-EFAC(4)	Robin DR.400/180R Remo 180	2333	
D-EFAD(3)	Mooney M.20K Model 252 TSE	25-1157	N252BW
D-EFAE	Robin DR.400/180R Remorqueur	798	
D-EFAF	Stark Turbulent D-1	111	
D-EFAG(3)	Piper PA-18 Super Cub 95	18-1543	D-EFTG(1), ALAT, 51-15543
D-EFAI	Zlin Z.326 Trenér Master	876	SE-CWK, D-EFAI, (D-ENQE)
D-EFAH	Klemm Kl.107C	136	
D-EFAK(5)	Cirrus SR20	1681	(D-EHEH(5)), (D-EDOP(4)), N938SR
D-EFAL(3)	Grob G 115A	8013	
D-EFAM(5)	Diamond DA 40F Star	40.575	N189DS
D-EFAN(5)	Piper PA-28-161 Cherokee Warrior II	28-7716163	N9647N
D-EFAO	Piper PA-18-150 Super Cub	18-5362	ALAT, N10F
D-EFAR(5)	Fürstenwalde Farman III (1910) replica	01	
	(Res)		
D-EFAS	Cessna 140	10463	N76069, NC76069
D-EFAT(3)	SOCATA MS.883 Rallye 115	1566	F-BTHI
D-EFAV(3)	Diamond DA 20-A1 Katana	10005	OE-AAQ, OE-VPZ, N847DF, C-FTJH
D-EFAW(2)	Mooney M.20K Model 252 TSE	25-1184	
D-EFAY	Piper PA-28-161 Warrior II	28-8516070	N2495X
D-EFBA(2)	Reims/Cessna F152	F15201845	PH-MJE, PH-AXH
D-EFBB	Beech 23 Musketeer	M-106	HB-ENB
D-EFBC	Robin DR.400/140 Major	884	
D-EFBE	Piper PA-18 Super Cub 95	18-6278	N8674D
D-EFBF	Sportavia RS-180 Sportsman	6014	
D-EFBH	Sportavia RS-180 Sportsman	6015	
D-EFBI (2)	Sportavia RS-180 Sportsman	6016	
D-EFBK(2)	Robin DR.400/180R Remorqueur	1535	
D-EFBL	Piper PA-28-180 Cherokee G	28-7205282	N11C
D-EFBM	Sportavia RS-180 Sportsman	6019	
D-EFBN	Sportavia RS-180 Sportsman	6020	
D-EFBO(2)	Cirrus SR22	3349	N793PG
D-EFBQ	Sportavia RS-180 Sportsman	6021	
D-EFBR	Piper PA-18 Super Cub 95	18-3457	96+33, NL+112, AC+539, AS+539, 54-757
D-EFBT(2)	Reims/Cessna F172N	F17201751	(D-EILW), PH-AXI, (D-EMSP)
D-EFBU	Piper PA-18-150 Super Cub	18-8062	N4068Z
D-EFBW	Robin R.2160D Acrobin	117	F-OCSK
D-EFBY(4)	Extra EA.300/S	1032	HA-RED
	(W/o 18.2.16 Valence, France)		
D-EFBZ	SOCATA TB-200 Tobago XL	1530	
D-EFCA	Cessna 172C	17249056	N1356Y
D-EFCB(2)	CASA C-1.131E Jungmann	2225	E3B-606
D-EFCC	Reims FR172F Rocket	FR17200089	
D-EFCD	Cirrus SR20	1136	N240CD
D-EFCE	Cessna 172C Skyhawk	17249065	N1365Y
D-EFCH(2)	Piper PA-46-310P Malibu	46-8608037	N9082E
	(JetProp DLX conversion # 57)		
D-EFCI (2)	Gulfstream American AA-5B Tiger	AA5B-1170	
D-EFCJ	Piper PA-28-180 Cherokee F	28-7105040	N5186S
D-EFCK	Piper PA-18 Super Cub 95	18-3436	96+15, NL+101, AC+504, AS+503, 54-736
D-EFCL(2)	Robin DR.400/180R Remorqueur	751	F-BTZD
D-EFCM(4)	Diamond DA 40 NG	40.N036	

D-EFCN	Piper PA-18 Super Cub 95	18-3439	96+18, NL+117, AC+524,
			AS+524, 54-739
D-EFCO(3)	Diamond DA 40 NG	40.N280	
D-EFCP	Aquila AT-01	AT-01-149	OO-NKE, D-EFVN
D-EFCR(2)	Piper PA-28-181 Archer II	2890013	N9108Q
D-EFCS(2)	Diamond DA 40 V1 Star	40001	OE-DEF(2), OE-VPC,
	(Permit .08)		"D-EDAI"
D-EFCT(3)	Cessna 172S Skyhawk SP	172S8186	N767KK
D-EFCU	SOCATA MS.893E Rallye 180GT	12604	TL-HCU
	(Res. 24.6.14)		
D-EFCV	Piper PA-28RT-201 Arrow IV	28R-8018048	N81677
D-EFCW(3)	Jodel D.20 Jubilé	07	F-WLRY
	(Res. .14)		
D-EFCX(2)	Piper PA-25-235 Pawnee	25-5334	N8825L
D-EFCY	Piper PA-18-150 Super Cub	18-7885	N6552Z
D-EFDA	Piper PA-24-250 Comanche	24-2977	N7850P, N10F
D-EFDB	Piper PA-18-135 Super Cub	18-3923	EI-227, I-EIJX, 54-2523
D-EFDC(2)	SOCATA MS.893A Rallye Commodore 180	11776	F-BSMJ
D-EFDD	SAN Jodel DR.1050 Sicile	486	
D-EFDE(2)	Cessna 177A Cardinal	17701273	N30466
D-EFDH	SOCATA TB-10 Tobago	716	
D-EFDI (3)	Piper PA-28-181 Archer II	28-8290111	N8180U
D-EFDK	Grumman AA-5 Traveler	AA5-0646	
D-EFDM(2)	Flight Design MC-ELA	A-09-01-31	
	(Res. 23.4.15)		
D-EFDN	Reims/Cessna F152 II	F15201721	
D-EFDQ	Reims/Cessna F172M	F17201298	
D-EFDR(2)	Piper PA-46-310P Malibu	4608061	N9124B
D-EFDU(2)	Reims/Cessna F152	F15201738	
D-EFEA(3)	Piper PA-28-181 Archer II	28-8290163	HB-PHF, (HB-PHC)
D-EFEB(2)	Reims/Cessna F172N	F17201737	
D-EFEC(2)	Cessna 140	14812	HB-CAM, N3540V
D-EFED(2)	Robin DR.400/180 Régent	1203	
D-EFEE(2)	Cessna 172M	17260996	G-BSAY, N20086
D-EFEF(2)	Aquila AT-01	AT01-170	(D-EAQU)
D-EFEG(2)	Reims/Cessna F172N	F17201734	
D-EFEH(3)	Cessna 172B	17248709	N8209X
D-EFEM(6)	SNCAN/ Stampe SV.4C	44	N10701, F-BFZI, Fr.AF
D-EFEP(2)	Cessna 172	36481	N8781B
D-EFER(3)	Piper PA-18-150 Super Cub	18-5347	F-BLCM, ALAT, N10F
D-EFES(2)	Piper PA-28-161 Warrior II	28-8316037	N9627N
D-EFEU	Burda/ Aero-Jodel D.11A Club	AB.6	
D-EFEW(4)	Fechner / Stoddard-Hamilton GlaStar GS-1	5923	
	(Res)		
D-EFEX	Piper PA-22-150 Tri-Pacer	22-4892	N10F
D-EFEY	Piper PA-28R-200 Cherokee Arrow	28R-35718	N4993S
D-EFEZ	Klemm Kl.107B	111	
D-EFFA(4)	Ruschmeyer R.90-230RG	018	D-ELVY(2), (D-EEBY(2))
D-EFFC	Jodel DR.250/160 Capitaine	49	
D-EFFD	Robin DR.400/125 Petit Prince	716	
D-EFFE(2)	Reims/Cessna F172M Skyhawk II	F17201394	
D-EFFF	Robin DR.400/180 Régent	721	
D-EFFG	CEA DR.253B Régent	171	
D-EFFI (3)	Hankers/ Van's RV-4	1588/V-1	
D-EFFJ(3)	Bellanca 8KCAB Decathlon	981-2005	G-EZPZ
D-EFFL(3)	Piper PA-28R-201 Arrow	2837034	N9187X
D-EFFM	SAN Jodel D.150 Rapid	59	
D-EFFN	Piper PA-28-180 Cherokee G	28-7205309	N1497T
D-EFFO(2)	Reims/Cessna F150M	F15001319	
D-EFFP	Piper PA-32-300 Cherokee Six	32-7440042	N57317
D-EFFQ(2)	SOCATA TB-20 Trinidad GT	2051	
D-EFFU	Berger/ Piel CP.301A Emeraude	AB-420	
D-EFFV(2)	Lake LA-4-250 Renegade	66	C-FFFV, N85JW
D-EFFW	Gardan GY-80 Horizon 160	43	OO-JON
D-EFGB	Cessna F150H	F150-0248	
D-EFGD	Mooney M.20C Mark 21	3393	HB-DWE, N3410X
D-EFGF(2)	Cessna 150M	15078657	N704JW
D-EFGG(2)	Robin R.2160 Alpha 160	275	
D-EFGH(2)	Robin DR.400/200R Remo 200	2433	
D-EFGJ	HOAC DV-20 Katana	20013	OE-CDD, C-FSLY
D-EFGL(2)	Reims/Cessna FR182 Skylane RG	FR18200032	
D-EFGO	Cessna 150	17640	N7840E
D-EFGS(4)	Commander Aircraft 114B	14607	A7-JBR, A6-RAK,
			N6030F
D-EFGU(3)	Cirrus SR20	2024	N104CS
D-EFGV	Robin DR.400/140 Major	816	
D-EFGX	Reims/Cessna F172N	F17201793	
D-EFGY(2)	Cessna F172E	F172-0069	
D-EFHA	Piper PA-28-160 Cherokee B	28-1293	N5724W
D-EFHB(4)	Robin R.3000/160	161	
D-EFHC	Cessna F172H	F172-0596	
D-EFHD(2)	Krasse Saita	1	
	(Res)		
D-EFHE(2)	Cessna F150G	F150-0093	
D-EFHF	Morane-Saulnier MS.885 Super Rallye	59	F-BKER
D-EFHG(2)	Robin HR.200/120B	264	
D-EFHJ	Piper J-3C-65 Cub	18970	N98739, NC98739
D-EFHK(2)	SOCATA MS.893A Rallye Commodore 180	11668	
D-EFHL(3)	Piper PA-28R-200 Cherokee Arrow II	28R-7435246	N43084
D-EFHM(2)	SOCATA TB-200 Tobago XL	1748	
D-EFHN(2)	Robin DR.400/180 Régent	1512	
D-EFHO(3)	Reims/Cessna F172N	F17201907	OE-DHO, LN-HOI
D-EFHS	Beech F33A Bonanza	CE-812	OE-DUB
D-EFHU(2)	Cirrus SR22	3364	N618CP
D-EFHV	Robin DR.400/180R Remorqueur	1452	
D-EFHW	Rockwell Commander 112A	402	N1402J
D-EFIA	Reims/Cessna F152	F15201755	
D-EFIC	Cessna 182J Skylane	18257150	N3050F
D-EFID(2)	Cessna F172H	F172-0537	
D-EFIE	Koller/ Aero-Jodel D11A Club	"Liz.639"	OE-ACX
D-EFIF(3)	Cessna P210N Pressurized Centurion	P21000440	PH-NIC, N210MJ,
			D-EDPW(3), HB-CCU, N213CC, N731CR
D-EFIG	Cessna 182J Skylane	18257180	N3080F
D-EFIH(2)	SOCATA TB-10 Tobago	470	
D-EFII	Piper PA-28-140 Cherokee E	28-7225106	N11C
D-EFIL(2)	Piper PA-38-112 Tomahawk	38-80A0100	D-EEIL(2), N9702N
D-EFIM(2)	Cessna 172M	17263568	N1423V
D-EFIN(3)	Cirrus SR22	2222	N151AL
D-EFIO	Grumman AA-5B Tiger	AA5B-0108	
D-EFIQ	Cessna F172G	F172-0271	
D-EFIS(3)	CSA PS-28 Cruiser	C0412	
D-EFIV(2)	Reims/Cessna F152	F15201769	
D-EFIX(2)	Tecnam P.2008-JC	1056	
D-EFIY	SNCAN/ Stampe SV.4C	136	F-BBIY, F-BBHY
D-EFJA(2)	Reims/Cessna F152	F15201778	
D-EFJB(2)	Böhm Starlite SL-1/B	001/1678	

D-EFJC	Bölkow BO.209 Monsun 160RV	125	
D-EFJE(3)	Reims/Cessna FRA150L Aerobat	FRA1500213	G-OISO, G-BBJW
D-EFJG	Bölkow BO.209 Monsun 160RV	129	
D-EFJH	Bölkow BO.209 Monsun 160RV	130	
D-EFJI	Bölkow BO.209 Monsun 160RV	131	(D-ELIE)
D-EFJJ	Bölkow BO.209 Monsun 160FV	132	
D-EFJK	Bölkow BO.209 Monsun 160RV	133	(D-EDAK(2))
D-EFJL	Bölkow BO.209 Monsun 160RV	134	
D-EFJM	Bölkow BO.209 Monsun 160FV	135	
D-EFJN	Bölkow BO.209 Monsun 150FF	136	I-SUDB, D-EFJN
D-EFJP	Bölkow BO.209 Monsun 150FF	138	(D-EFSG)
D-EFJR(2)	CASA C-1.131E Jungmann	2072	E3B-465
D-EFJV	Reims/Cessna F172N	F17201937	
D-EFJX	Reims/Cessna F172N	F17201962	
D-EFKA(3)	Piper PA-28R-201T Turbo Arrow III	28R-7803337	N36726
D-EFKB	Piper PA-18-180 Super Cub	18-5390	ALAT, N10F
D-EFKD	Reims/Cessna F172N	F17202000	
D-EFKF	Robin DR.400/180R Remorqueur	1550	
D-EFKG	Beech V35B Bonanza	D-9759	
D-EFKK	Mooney M.20F Executive	22-1202	
D-EFKL(2)	Klemm Kl.35D	1853	D-EFES(2), SE-BGI,
	(P 12.10)		Fv5019
D-EFKM	Reims/Cessna F172N	F17202004	
D-EFKN	Reims/Cessna F152	F15201713	
D-EFKO(2)	Piper PA-28-140 Cherokee	28-24639	
D-EFKP(2)	Piper PA-28-181 Cherokee Archer II	28-7890477	N31733
D-EFKR	Reims/Cessna FR172K Hawk XP II	FR17200635	PH-AXT
D-EFKS(3)	CSA PS-28 Cruiser	C0498	
D-EFKT(2)	Cessna 177RG Cardinal RG	177RG1341	N53081
D-EFKW(2)	Reims/Cessna F172P	F17202151	
D-EFKY	Robin HR.200/120B	260	D-EFKZ
D-EFLA(2)	SOCATA TB-10 Tobago	679	
D-EFLB	Cessna 172N Skyhawk	17271629	N4555E
D-EFLC	Piper PA-18 Super Cub 95	18-3422	96+04, NL+105, AC+513,
			AA+513, AS+513, 54-722
D-EFLE(2)	Piper PA-28-180 Cherokee Challenger	28-7305370	N55326
D-EFLF	Cessna 172N Skyhawk	17272217	N9303E
D-EFLG(3)	Cessna 172S Skyhawk SP	172S10178	N176MC
D-EFLH(2)	Flight Design CT LS-ELA	F-09-11-11	
D-EFLI (3)	Piper PA-28-181 Archer II	28-8190082	N82891
D-EFLJ	Cessna F172F	F172-0139	
D-EFLK(2)	Cessna 182T Skylane	18282311	N93227
D-EFLL	Cessna 172P Skyhawk	17275489	N63841
D-EFLM	Piaggio FWP.149D	082	90+64, GA+402, AS+491
D-EFLN(3)	Flight Design CT LS-ELA	F-09-11-12	
D-EFLO(3)	Cessna 182T Skylane	18282204	N5288F
D-EFLP	Piper PA-28-151 Cherokee Warrior	28-7415195	N9520N
D-EFLQ	Piper PA-28-140 Cherokee D	28-7125370	N8589N
D-EFLR	Reims/Cessna F177RG Cardinal RG	F177RG0055	
D-EFLS(2)	Piper PA-28RT-201T Turbo Arrow IV	28R-7931022	N2129K
D-EFLU(2)	Robin DR.300/180R Remoqueur	525	
D-EFLV	Piper PA-28-140 Cherokee D	28-7125248	N5082S
D-EFLX	Lauxen/ Denney Kitfox V Speedster S	94030004AB	
D-EFLY(2)	Robin DR.300/108 2+2	519	
D-EFLZ	SOCATA TB-10 Tobago	1067	
D-EFMB	Bölkow BO.208C Junior	632	
D-EFMC	Bölkow BO.208C Junior	633	
D-EFMD(2)	Robin DR.400/180 Régent	1477	
D-EFME	Bölkow BO.208C Junior	635	
D-EFMH(2)	CASA C-1.131E Jungmann (Lycoming)	2066	E3B-473
D-EFMI (2)	Gyroflug SC-01B-160 Speed Canard	S-28	(D-EAMT)
D-EFMJ(2)	Piper PA-28-140 Cherokee C	28-26832	N5933U
D-EFMK	CEA DR.253B Régent	123	
D-EFML	Fairchild F.24R-46A Argus III	947	HB-EIR, HB709,
			43-14983
D-EFMM	SOCATA MS.894A Minerva 220	11023	
D-EFMN(2)	Robin DR.400/180R Remorqueur	1460	
D-EFMO(3)	Cessna 172P Skyhawk	17275457	PH-TGH, OY-CPA,
			N63625
D-EFMP	Reims/Cessna F172N	F17202018	
D-EFMR	Reims/Cessna F172M	F17201378	
D-EFMS(3)	Maule MX-7-235 Star Rocket	4058C	N6119V, (D-EJSO)
D-EFMU(2)	Cessna 152	15283254	N47809
D-EFMV(3)	HOAC DV-20 Katana	20103	C-GFQW, N203DV
D-EFMY	Piper PA-28-140 Cherokee	28-20703	N6609W
D-EFMZ	Aviat A-1 Husky	1280	
D-EFNA	Oberlerchner JOB 15-180/2	063	OE-CAX
	(Originally built as -150)		
D-EFNB	SOCATA TB-10 Tobago	820	
D-EFNC	Cessna 172RG Cutlass RG	172RG0310	N5263U
D-EFNE(2)	Aerotek Pitts S-2B	5024	N20NE, (N5316C)
D-EFNI (2)	Oberlerchner JOB 15-150/2	067	OE-CAT
D-EFNL	Robin DR.400/180R Remorqueur	1551	
D-EFNN	Mooney M.20E Chaparral	21-1178	N6844V
D-EFNP(2)	Piper PA-28RT-201 Arrow IV	28R-7918018	N2125K
D-EFNS(2)	Piper PA-28-181 Archer II	28-8090282	N44WK, N8187Z
D-EFNW	Reims/Cessna FR182 Skylane RG	FR18200015	(D-EDBV)
D-EFNX	Reims/Cessna F152	F15201563	
D-EFNY	Bölkow BO.208C Junior	606	
D-EFNZ	Piper PA-28-181 Archer III	2843618	N31170, N53598
D-EFOB(2)	Dornier Do.27A-4	389	56+81, QW+111,
			QW+715, QM+615, PL+423
D-EFOD(2)	Piper PA-28-140 Cherokee	28-7325043	OY-DLZ, N15341
D-EFOF(2)	SOCATA TB-9 Tampico	108	
D-EFOG(3)	Maule MT-7-235 Super Rocket	18096C	
D-EFOH	Klemm Kl.107C	139	
D-EFOJ	Robin DR.400/120D Petit Prince	1565	
D-EFOK(2)	Piper PA-28-140 Cherokee F	28-7325289	N11C
D-EFOL(2)	Piper PA-28-140 Cherokee F	28-7325316	N11C
D-EFOM	DHC-1 Chipmunk 22 (Franklin)	C1/0248	G-AOJN, WD306
D-EFOP(2)	Cessna F172E	F172-0025/17250580	OE-DCO, (N2980U)
D-EFOQ	Scintex CP.301C Emeraude	542	
D-EFOR(2)	Binder CP.301S Smaragd	107	
D-EFOS(2)	Mooney M.20K Model 252 TSE	25-1090	N252YV
D-EFOU(2)	Dallach D4/E-BK/RS Fascination	1	
D-EFPA(3)	Piper PA-28-181 Archer II	2890077	N9143X
D-EFPB(3)	Cessna 172R Skyhawk	17200366	(N16606), N11C
D-EFPE(2)	Reims/Cessna F172P	F17202119	
D-EFPF(2)	Cessna 172RG Cutlass RG	172RG0484	N5248V
D-EFPJ	SOCATA TB-9 Tampico	107	
D-EFPK	SOCATA TB-10 Tobago	104	
D-EFPM	Cessna 182G Skylane	18255416	HB-CMP, N2316R
D-EFPN	Piper PA-28RT-201 Arrow IV	28R-7918143	N29699
D-EFPO	Bölkow BO.207	262	
D-EFPP	Cessna TR182 Turbo Skylane RG	R18201436	N4846S
D-EFPQ	Robin DR.400/180 Régent	1322	

Regn	Type	c/n	Previous identities / notes
D-EFPR	Pützer Elster C	042	97+19, D-ELBC
D-EFPS	SNCAN/ Stampe SV-4C	415	F-BCQY
D-EFPT(3)	Reims/Cessna F152	F15201617	D-EXIS, LX-AIS
D-EFPV(2)	Beech G36 Bonanza	E-3949	N6449R
D-EFQA	Bölkow BO.207	265	
D-EFQB	Robin DR.400/180R Remorqueur	1367	
D-EFQD	SOCATA TB-20 Trinidad	623	F-GHSA, N20EN
D-EFQE	Bölkow BO.207	266	
D-EFQN(2)	Robin DR.400/180 Régent	1744	(F-GNBJ), D-EFQN(2), F-GEKS
D-EFQO(2)	Grob G 115A	8018	F-GGOO, D-EANP
D-EFQP	CASA C-1.131E Jungmann	2046	E3B-442
D-EFQV	Dornier Do.27B-1	175	55+45, CC+053, AC+925 ?, AS+925 ?
D-EFRA	Cessna F172D	F172-0005/17250071	(N2471U)
D-EFRC	Cessna F172H	F172-0651	
D-EFRD	Cessna F172H	F172-0654	
D-EFRF	Reims FR172F Rocket	FR17200088	
D-EFRG	Cessna 172RG Cutlass RG	172RG0554	N5527V
D-EFRI (4)	Hüfner/ Votec 322	488	(Res. .04)
D-EFRJ(2)	Cirrus SR22	1187	N105DG
D-EFRK	Mooney M.20J Model 201	24-0730	(N4433H)
D-EFRL	Mooney M.20K Model 231	25-0153	
D-EFRN	SOCATA Rallye 180TS Galérien	3335	
D-EFRO(2)	CSA PS-28 Cruiser	C0452	
D-EFRP	Cessna 172P Skyhawk	17274657	N53001
D-EFRR(2)	American General AG-5B Tiger	10161	N1198N
D-EFRS	Robin DR.400/120D Dauphin	1714	
D-EFRT(2)	Cirrus SR20	1141	N1231G
D-EFRV	Reims/Cessna F172P	F17202096	
D-EFRW	Reims/Cessna F172P	F17202090	
D-EFRX	SOCATA Rallye 110ST Galopin	3333	
D-EFSA(3)	Diamond DA 40D Star	D.4.096	
D-EFSB(3)	Aquila AT-01	AT01-114	
D-EFSC(4)	Dornier Do.27A-4	2109	MAAW-16, D-EGVQ, D-12/OT-AMK, OL-D12, D-12
D-EFSE(3)	Cessna P210N Pressurized Centurion II	P21000814	N4680A
D-EFSI	Bölkow BO.207	213	HB-UXM, D-EFSI
D-EFSJ(2)	Tecnam P.2002-JF Sierra	004	HB-KOK (W/o Jesenwang 18.8.12)
D-EFSK(2)	Cessna 182T Skylane	18281232	N2128T
D-EFSL	Cessna 182Q Skylane	18265374	N735EV
D-EFSN	Cessna 172RG Cutlass RG	172RG1026	N9772B
D-EFSO(2)	Piper PA-28-140 Cherokee F	28-7325365	N11C
D-EFSP(3)	Cessna 172S Skyhawk SP	172S8986	N5114J
D-EFSR	Piper PA-28-181 Archer II	28-8190003	N8247E
D-EFSS(2)	Mooney M.20M Model 257 TLS	27-0129	N888JS, N230M
D-EFST(4)	Reims/Cessna FR172K Hawk XP	FR17200694	OE-DIX
D-EFSU(3)	Beech F33A Bonanza	CE-1519	
D-EFSV(3)	Cessna 172S Skyhawk SP	172S10720	PH-USB, N62446
D-EFSW(2)	Piper PA-18 Super Cub 100	18-3437	96+16, PX+901, QZ+030, AC+505, AS+504, 54-737 (Built as PA-18-95)
D-EFSY	Bölkow BO.207	216	
D-EFSZ	Mooney M.20K Model 231	25-0467	N277TA, N4090H
D-EFTA(4)	Aeronca 65C Super Chief	C-1288	N127KM, (D-EPKM), N127KM, N21323, NC21323 (Res. .14)
D-EFTB(2)	Piper PA-18 Super Cub 95	18-3455	96+31, NL+ . .., AC+537, AS+537, 54-755
D-EFTC	Bölkow BO.209 Monsun 150FF	172	G-AZTC, D-EAAL
D-EFTE(3)	Klemm L 25-1A	152	G-AAHW, D-ELFK, G-AAHW
D-EFTG(3)	Diamond DA 20-A1 Katana	10178	OK-BLC, C-GRUV
D-EFTH(2)	Cessna 195B	16087	N195MB, N2102C
D-EFTI	Bölkow BO.207	219	(W/o 15.4.15 near Moosburg)
D-EFTJ	Koch Fokker Dr.1 replica	003	G-BWRJ, D-EFTN(1)
D-EFTK	Reims/Cessna F172M	F17201265	
D-EFTM(2)	Morane-Saulnier MS.317	7603/345	F-BBQE (P. 15.10.14)
D-EFTN(2)	de Havilland DH.82A Tiger Moth	"84764"	G-ANIX, D-EFTF(2) (Composite rebuild - using identity of c/n 84764, ex T6390, D-ELOM, dbf 12.63)
D-EFTO(3)	Reims/Cessna F152	F15201958	(Cr 24.8.13 Aicach-Friedberg)
D-EFTP	Reims FR172H Rocket	FR17200276	
D-EFTQ	Robin DR.400/180R Remorqueur	1472	
D-EFTR(2)	SOCATA TB-10 Tobago	206	
D-EFTS	SAN Jodel DR.1050 Ambassadeur	397	
D-EFTT(4)	Cessna 172S Skyhawk SP	172S10408	N13912
D-EFTU(2)	Piaggio FWP.149D	091	90+73, AS+404
D-EFTW(2)	Robin DR.400/180 Régent	1274	
D-EFTX	Boeing Stearman A75N1 Kaydet	75-3475	G-BHUW , N474, N64639, BuA30038 (Wears code '475')
D-EFTY(3)	Klemm Kl.35D	1462	G-BWRD, D-EFTG(2), D-EHUX(2), SE-AIP, Fv5081, SE-AIP, Fv5086, SE-AIP (Painted as Luftwaffe '7')
D-EFUB	Klemm Kl.35D	1810	HB-UXC, SE-BGH, Fv5011
D-EFUF	Stark Turbulent D-1M	115	
D-EFUI	Reims/Cessna F152	F15201550	
D-EFUK(2)	Reims/Cessna F172N	F17201841	
D-EFUL	Piper J-3C-65 Cub	11313	HB-OAI, 43-30022
D-EFUM(2)	Piper PA-28-140 Cherokee Cruiser	28-7725080	N9530N
D-EFUN(4)	Cessna A152 Aerobat	A1520989	OE-AHK, N761VG
D-EFUS(2)	SOCATA MS.880B Rallye Club	2149	F-BUCA
D-EFUX(2)	Beech F33A Bonanza	CE-1150	
D-EFVA	FVA-18/3 Krähe V-1	01	
D-EFVB	Reims/Cessna FR172K Hawk	FR17200636	
D-EFVC	Piper PA-28-181 Archer III	2843570	N764C, N3038N, N9512N
D-EFVD	Cessna T210M Turbo Centurion	21062650	N761ZN (Reims-assembled with c/n 0012)
D-EFVF	Robin DR.400/180 Régent	1343	
D-EFVH(2)	Beech F33A Bonanza	CE-1770	N15229, N1529L, (D-EEJJ)
D-EFVI	Piaggio P.149D	254	(91+72), D-EFVI, AC+405, AS+405
D-EFVL(2)	Cirrus SR20	1403	N456CP
D-EFVM(2)	Ludwig/ Stark Turbulent D	AB-501	D-EGSU
D-EFVO(2)	Cessna F150G	F150-0159	
D-EFVP	Cessna 206H Stationair	20608300	D-ENDS, N6243M
D-EFVQ	Reims/Cessna F172P	F17202085	
D-EFVZ	Zendler Hina BL2-ARA	1777	
D-EFWA(2)	SOCATA Rallye 100ST-D	3043	OY-ARG, F-ODII
D-EFWB	Reims/Cessna F150M	F15001151	
D-EFWC(2)	Piper PA-24-250 Comanche	24-3294	OE-DST, N8139P, N10F, (N8049P)
D-EFWD	Beech V35B Bonanza	D-10347	
D-EFWE	Piper PA-28-140 Cherokee	28-20715	N6682W
D-EFWF	Piper PA-28R-200 Cherokee Arrow II	28R-7535170	(D-ILAX), N33651
D-EFWJ	Wassmer WA.54 Atlantic	109	(D-EAIJ)
D-EFWM	Piper PA-28-181 Cherokee Archer II	28-7790419	N2917Q
D-EFWO(3)	Robin DR.400/180R Remorqueur	1546	
D-EFWP(3)	Focke-Wulf Fw44J Stieglitz	2929	OE-AMC(2), D-EJOI, (D-EHDW), OH-SZA, SZ-26, D-EXWP
D-EFWS(2)	Cessna 172R Skyhawk	17280615	N95520
D-EFWT	SOCATA TB-10 Tobago	291	
D-EFWW	Piper PA-28-180 Cherokee Archer	28-7405075	N9648N
D-EFWZ	Piper PA-28-235 Cherokee	28-10207	N8676W
D-EFXB(3)	Aquila AT-01	AT01-222	
D-EFXC(2)	Piper PA-28-161 Cadet	2841051	N9632N, N9163K
D-EFXD(3)	Aquila AT-01	AT01-219	
D-EFXE(2)	Piper PA-28-161 Cadet	2841069	N9164Z
D-EFXF(2)	Piper PA-28-161 Cadet	2841082	N9167H, N9504N
D-EFXG	Piper PA-28-161 Cadet	2841087	N9170H
D-EFXH(2)	Aquila AT-01	AT01-220	
D-EFXI (2)	Piper PA-28-161 Cadet	2841118	N9649N
D-EFXJ(2)	Aquila AT-01	AT01-221	
D-EFXL	Piper PA-28-161 Cadet	2841126	N9181G
D-EFXM	Piper PA-28-161 Cadet	2841128	N9181J
D-EFXO	Robin DR.300/108 2+2	496	
D-EFXP(2)	Piper PA-28-161 Cadet	2841163	N9514N
D-EFXQ	Piper PA-28-161 Cadet	2841168	N9515N
D-EFXR	Piper PA-28-161 Cadet	2841201	N9189W
D-EFXS	Piper PA-28-161 Cadet	2841243	N9192P
D-EFXT	Piper PA-28-161 Cadet	2841244	N9192X
D-EFXU	Robin DR.300/180R Remorqueur	497	
D-EFXX(2)	Aquila AT-01	AT01-238	
D-EFYA	Reims/Cessna F182Q Skylane	F18200142	PH-AXZ
D-EFYB(2)	Piper PA-32-300 Cherokee Six	32-7340188	OY-DLK, CS-AOU, N56526
D-EFYC	Cessna F172G	F172-0223	
D-EFYF(2)	Piper PA-28RT-201 Arrow IV	28R-8118063	N83691
D-EFYH(2)	Cessna 152	15283107	N46802
D-EFYN(3)	Reims/Cessna F172P	F17202089	
D-EFYP	Pützer Elster C	002	
D-EFYQ	Cessna F172G	F172-0259	
D-EFYS(3)	Mudry CAP.231	16	F-GGYS
D-EFYY	Mooney M.20R Ovation	29-0452	N99YY (Res, still current in US)
D-EFYZ(2)	Piaggio FWP.149D	101	90+82, ND+103, D-EHUW, AS+403
D-EFZB(2)	Piper PA-28-161 Warrior II	28-8016233	N9608N
D-EFZC	SIAI-Marchetti S.208	2-18	
D-EFZF	Cessna 172N Skyhawk	17271249	N2360E
D-EFZG	Cessna 172RG Cutlass RG	172RG0559	N5533V
D-EFZH	Cessna 172RG Cutlass RG	17268307	N733HM
D-EFZI	Piper PA-18 Super Cub 95	18-6109	OE-AEE, N10F
D-EFZJ	Cessna 172RG Cutlass RG	172RG0046	N5204R
D-EFZM	Dornier Do.27A-4	483	57+48, GA+376, KD+141 ?
D-EFZO	Cessna F172F	F172-0156	
D-EFZR	Cessna 172N Skyhawk	17272920	N7398D
D-EFZS	Cessna 172N Skyhawk	17275531	N64189
D-EFZT	Cessna 182K Skylane	18258476	N2876R
D-EFZV	CEA DR.253B Régent	106	6V-ABU, F-OCKM
D-EFZW(2)	HOAC DV-20 Katana	20061	
D-EGAA(2)	Cessna F150H	F150-0359	
D-EGAB(2)	Cessna 182J Skylane	18256709	N2609F
D-EGAE	Fuji FA-200-180 Aero Subaru	114	
D-EGAF	Piper J-3C-65 Cub	12943	HB-ONI, 44-80647
D-EGAG(3)	Cessna TU206G Turbo Stationair 6-II	U20604336	OK-AAG, I-IPAP, N756TD
D-EGAH(2)	Cessna 182P Skylane	18263909	OO-GAI, OO-CKC, HB-CKC, OO-GAI, N6988M (Reims-assembled with "c/n" 0015)
D-EGAJ	Fuji FA-200-160 Aero Subaru	123	
D-EGAK(3)	Piper PA-28R-200 Cherokee Arrow II	28R-7635091	N7035C
D-EGAL(3)	Bölkow BO.208C Junior	641	
D-EGAM(3)	Fuji FA-200-180 Aero Subaru	117	(Marked FH20/180)
D-EGAN(2)	Piper PA-28-181 Archer II	28-8590023	N9514N
D-EGAO	Dornier Do.27B-3	2200	(D-EFKP)
D-EGAP(3)	Robin ATL L	41	F-GFOQ (Res. .13)
D-EGAS(4)	Mooney M.20J Model 205	24-3164	
D-EGAT(2)	Piper PA-28-151 Cherokee Warrior	28-7415083	N9623N
D-EGAU	Piper PA-28-181 Archer II	28-8090215	N8145Y
D-EGAV	Wassmer Jodel D.120 Paris-Nice	141	
D-EGAW(3)	Pilatus P.2-06	49	HB-RAW, U-132
D-EGAX(3)	Piper PA-28RT-201T Turbo Arrow IV	28R-7931187	N28529
D-EGAY(2)	Christen A-1 Husky	1113	
D-EGAZ(4)	Cessna 172RG Cutlass RG	172RG0531	OY-BNN, (D-EBNM), OY-BNN, N5435V
D-EGBA(2)	Heliopolis Gomhouria Mk.6	184	SU-346, EAF-346
D-EGBE(2)	Reims/Cessna F172M	F17200977	
D-EGBG	Reims/Cessna F172M	F17200979	
D-EGBH(2)	Robin DR.400/180R Remorqueur	1742	
D-EGBI (2)	PZL-104 Wilga 35A	61113	DDR-WBH, DM-WBH(2)
D-EGBK	Reims/Cessna F172M	F17200981	
D-EGBL(2)	Piper PA-28-161 Warrior II	28-8016345	PH-WLS, N8226X
D-EGBM(3)	CASA C-1.131E Jungmann	"2062"	E3B-415 (Same c/n quoted as HB-UVU. Previous identity confirmed correct)
D-EGBN	Reims/Cessna FRA150L Aerobat	FRA1500192	(OO-FCF)
D-EGBO	SAN Jodel DR.1050 Ambassadeur	367	(D-EDRO)
D-EGBP	Reims FR172J Rocket	FR17200417	
D-EGBQ	Reims FR172J Rocket	FR17200419	
D-EGBR(2)	Focke-Wulf FW.44J Stieglitz	2906	OH-SZK, SZ-9, D-EXWS(2) (Used parts of SZ-5 and SZ-21 in rebuild in Finland 1977-81)
D-EGBS(3)	Piper PA-28-140 Cherokee E	28-7225238	(D-EPHJ), LX-JHK, LX-OKC, HB-OKC, N11C
D-EGBV	Reims/Cessna F172M	F17200986	(On rebuild)
D-EGBW	Reims/Cessna F172M	F17200987	
D-EGBY	Bölkow BO.208A Junior	533	D-EGQA(1)
D-EGCA	Cessna F172H	F172-0425	
D-EGCB	Reims/Cessna F150L	F15000965	
D-EGCC	CEA DR.253B Régent	178	
D-EGCD	Cessna 172N Skyhawk	17268311	N733HR
D-EGCG	Robin DR.400/180R Remorqueur	1413	
D-EGCH	Bellanca 7GCBC Citabria	733-74	OE-AOH
D-EGCI (2)	Grob G 115A	8015	(D-EGRN(2))
D-EGCJ	Reims/Cessna F150L	F15000968	

Regn	Type	c/n	Previous identities
D-EGCK(2)	Grob G 115C1	82066	N115LR
D-EGCM	Reims/Cessna F150L	F15000972	
D-EGCN	Reims/Cessna FRA150L Aerobat	FRA1500211	
D-EGCO(2)	Reims/Cessna F172M	F17200988	
D-EGCP	Reims/Cessna F172M	F17200989	
D-EGCQ	Reims/Cessna F172M	F17200993	
D-EGCS	Reims/Cessna F172M	F17201001	
D-EGCT(2)	Reims/Cessna F152	F15201692	
D-EGCU	Cessna F172H	F172-0401	
D-EGCW(2)	Reims/Cessna F152	F15201691	
D-EGDA(2)	Robin DR.400/180 Régent	2293	
D-EGDB(2)	Grumman AA-5A Cheetah	AA5A-0551	
D-EGDC	Grumman AA-5B Tiger	AA5B-0728	
D-EGDD	Grumman AA-5B Tiger	AA5B-0827	
D-EGDE	Cessna F150G	F150-0114	
D-EGDF	Grumman AA-5B Tiger	AA5B-0776	
D-EGDH	Grumman AA-5B Tiger	AA5B-0932	
D-EGDI	SOCATA MS.892A Rallye Commodore 150	10550	
D-EGDL	Grumman AA-5B Tiger	AA5B-0779	
D-EGDN	Grumman AA-5B Tiger	AA5B-0750	
D-EGDO(2)	Reims/Cessna F172H	F172-0334	
D-EGDR	Grumman AA-5B Tiger	AA5B-1132	(N4527C)
D-EGDV(2)	Robin DR.400/180R Remorqueur	1578	
D-EGDX	Robin DR.400/180R Remorqueur	1588	
D-EGDY	Cessna F150G	F150-0086	
D-EGEB(2)	Cessna 172M	17263918	N21262
D-EGEE	SIAI-Marchetti S.205-22/R	4-130	
D-EGEF(2)	SOCATA MS.893ED Rallye 180GT Gaillard	13301	
D-EGEG(2)	Cessna 172B	17248683	N8183X
D-EGEI	Piaggio FWP.149D	121	91+01, D-ELHU, AS+410
D-EGEM(3)	Blume Bl 502 V-2 (Dam. 16.5.82, rebuilt 2015)	03	D-EGEM(1)
D-EGEP(2)	Wassmer CE.43 Guepard	435	
D-EGEQ(2)	Quast/ Van's RV-7 (P 16.8.11)	0710	
D-EGER(2)	Piper PA-28-235 Cherokee E	28-7110002	N8582N
D-EGET(2)	SOCATA MS.893ED Rallye 180GT Gaillard	13300	
D-EGEV(2)	Fuji FA-200-180 Aero Subaru	204	
D-EGFA(3)	Reims/Cessna F150M	F15001228	
D-EGFF(2)	Reims/Cessna F172K	F17200774	D-EYAM, D-ECGV
D-EGFG	Piper PA-18 Super Cub 95	18-3420	96+02, NL+107, AC+501, AS+509, 54-720
D-EGFH	Pützer Elster B	043	97+20, D-ELBD
D-EGFI	Bölkow BO.208C Junior	638	
D-EGFL(3)	Nowack Lightning XS/III (P. 2.16)	2002505	
D-EGFN	Robin DR.400/180R Remorqueur	1586	
D-EGFO	Bölkow BO.208C Junior	639	
D-EGFR	Dornier Do.27A-1	160	55+36, BD+9 .., SE+521, SC+718, QM+606, PC+113
D-EGFT(2)	Tecnam P.92J Echo VLA (Res .16)	002	I-TECK
D-EGFV	Robin R.3000/120D	116	
D-EGFW	Piper PA-38-112 Tomahawk	38-81A0005	N25460
D-EGGC	Cessna 172P Skyhawk	17274492	N52303
D-EGGE(2)	Zlin Z.526F Trenér Master	1062	HA-SAH
D-EGGF	Cessna 172RG Cutlass RG	172RG0301	N107JB, N5250U
D-EGGG(2)	Beech C24R Sierra 200	MC-626	N60137
D-EGGH	SOCATA MS.893A Rallye Commodore 180	11633	F-BSFV
D-EGGI (2)	Piper PA-28-235 Cherokee Pathfinder	28-7610074	N8361C
D-EGGJ	Cessna 172P Skyhawk	17274402	N52053
D-EGGM	Piper PA-18-150 Super Cub	18-5401	ALAT, N10F
D-EGGN	Gardan GY-80 Horizon 150	1	F-BLIB
D-EGGO(4)	Cessna U206F Stationair (Res .16)	U20602173	HA-SVU, HB-CZA, G-GNMG, F-GNMG, F-MJAE, F-BRGK, N7325Q
D-EGGR	Beech F33A Bonanza	CE-393	
D-EGGS	Bölkow BO.209 Monsun 160RV	175	HB-UEO, D-EAAO(1)
D-EGGT(3)	Cirrus SR22	0376	N427KW
D-EGGU	Cessna F172H	F172-0459	
D-EGGV	Cessna 182P Skylane	18262176	N58615
D-EGGW(2)	SOCATA TB-9 Tampico	261	
D-EGGX	Cessna 172RG Cutlass RG	172RG0307	N5260U
D-EGGY	Cessna F150H	F150-0237	
D-EGHA(3)	Piper PA-28R-201T Turbo Arrow III	28R-7803264	N9540C
D-EGHB	SAN Jodel D.140C Mousquetaire III	136	F-BMBU
D-EGHE	Piper PA-24-260 Comanche B	24-4473	N9012P
D-EGHF(2)	Cessna 172RG Cutlass RG	172RG0177	OE-KHF, F-GHXU, N6394R
D-EGHH(2)	Piper PA-28RT-201T Turbo Arrow IV	28R-8131003	N8271N
D-EGHL(2)	Cessna 182P Skylane	18261171	D-EEZF, (N20742)
D-EGHM	Cessna F150J	F150-0480	F-BRBT
D-EGHN	Cessna F172H	F172-0629	
D-EGHO(2)	Cessna 182P Skylane	18263484	N5667J
D-EGHP	Cessna 172RG Cutlass RG	172RG1155	N9423D
D-EGHQ	Robin DR.400/180R Remorqueur	1570	
D-EGHS	Robin DR.400/180R Remorqueur	893	
D-EGHT(2)	Beech F33A Bonanza	CE-1732	N80617
D-EGHV	Piper PA-28-181 Archer II	28-8090278	N8182D
D-EGHW(2)	Bölkow BO.209 Monsun 150FV	170	HB-UER, D-EAAJ
D-EGHX	Cirrus SR22	2672	N221CH
D-EGHY	Piper PA-28-180 Cherokee D	28-5473	N2158R
D-EGHZ	Beech V35B Bonanza	D-10024	
D-EGIC(2)	Bölkow BO.208C Junior	642	
D-EGID(2)	Wassmer WA.52 Europa	64	
D-EGIF(3)	Friedrich/ Brditschka HB-207VRG Alfa	207018	
D-EGIG	Luscombe 8A Silvaire	4252	OO-GMA, N1525K
D-EGII	Huschle/ Stephens Acro Sport II	388	
D-EGIL(2)	Piper PA-28R-200 Cherokee Arrow II	28R-7535218	N1018X
D-EGIM(2)	Piper PA-28R-200 Cherokee Arrow II	28R-7235304	N11C
D-EGIN	Piper PA-18 Super Cub 95	18-5652	N10F
D-EGIP(3)	Cessna P210R Pressurized Centurion II	P21000849	N5361A
D-EGIR(2)	Reims/Cessna F172M	F17201360	
D-EGIV(2)	Piper PA-28-181 Archer II	28-7990568	N2936A
D-EGIW(2)	Wassmer WA.52 Europa	63	
D-EGIX	Klemm Kl.107D	117	
D-EGIZ(2)	Robin DR.400/180R Remorqueur	1039	
D-EGJA	Reims/Cessna F172M (W/o 26.9.15 Sandstedt)	F17201003	
D-EGJC	Reims/Cessna F172M	F17201006	
D-EGJD	Reims FR172J Rocket	FR17200420	
D-EGJE	Reims FR172J Rocket	FR17200421	
D-EGJH(2)	Reims/Cessna F172N	F17201930	
D-EGJJ	Reims/Cessna F177RG Cardinal RG	F177RG0086	
D-EGJK	Cessna 182P Skylane	18262660	N52535
D-EGJM(2)	Robin DR.400/180 Régent	2296	
D-EGJN	Piper PA-18-150 Super Cub	18-564	R-210, 51-15678, N7193K
D-EGJO(2)	Cirrus SR20	1440	N497CD
D-EGJP(2)	Cessna 172S Skyhawk SP	172S8814	OE-KLP, N814LP
D-EGJS	Reims/Cessna F150L	F15001046	
D-EGJT(2)	Robin HR.200/120B Super Club	306	
D-EGJU	Cessna 182P Skylane	18262275	N58752
D-EGJX	Reims/Cessna F150L	F15000974	
D-EGKB	Reims FR172E Rocket	FR17200008	
D-EGKD(2)	Reims/Cessna F150L (Rotax 912S conv.)	F15000980	
D-EGKF(2)	SOCATA TB-10 Tobago	166	
D-EGKH(3)	SOCATA TB-10 Tobago	168	
D-EGKJ(2)	SOCATA TB-10 Tobago	170	
D-EGKK	Piper PA-28R-200 Cherokee Arrow II	28R-7335442	N56472
D-EGKL	Cessna 182J Skylane	18257059	N2959F
D-EGKM(2)	Robin ATL	119	F-GGHM
D-EGKN	SOCATA TB-10 Tobago	189	
D-EGKP	SOCATA TB-9 Tampico	195	
D-EGKQ	SOCATA TB-9 Tampico	196	
D-EGKR(2)	Cessna T210M Turbo Centurion (Reims-assembled with "c/n" 0006)	21061914	OO-BVC , D-EBVC, HB-CXR, (N732ZW)
D-EGKT	Reims/Cessna F172P	F17202058	
D-EGKU	Bölkow BO.207	252	
D-EGKV	Piper PA-38-112 Tomahawk	38-78A0123	N9519T
D-EGKW(2)	Klinke K1	001	
D-EGKY(2)	Reims/Cessna F150L	F15001051	
D-EGLA(3)	Piper PA-28-161 Warrior III	2842251	N31137
D-EGLB	Reims/Cessna F172N	F17201810	
D-EGLE	Bölkow BO.207	254	
D-EGLF	Reims/Cessna FR182 Skylane RG	FR18200034	
D-EGLG(2)	Reims/Cessna F152	F15201600	
D-EGLJ	Cessna 172P Skyhawk	17276144	N97005
D-EGLK(2)	Schwämmle HS-3 Motorlerche	844	
D-EGLM	Cessna 172N Skyhawk	17271780	N5224E
D-EGLO	Bölkow BO.207	256	(G-ASCW), D-EGLO
D-EGLP	Reims/Cessna FRA150M Aerobat	FRA1500319	
D-EGLQ	Robin DR.400/140 Major	858	
D-EGLR	Robin DR.400/180 Régent	857	
D-EGLT(2)	Cessna 172M	17262963	N13716
D-EGLU	Bölkow BO.207	257	G-ASAY, D-EGLU
D-EGLV	Piper PA-18-150 Super Cub	18-8009036	N6102A, N9760N
D-EGLW(2)	Cessna 172S Skyhawk SP	172S8731	N814SP
D-EGLX	Cessna 172N Skyhawk	17271099	LZ- . .., D-EGLX, N1697E
D-EGMA(2)	Beech F33A Bonanza	CE-903	N6746L
D-EGMB	Reims/Cessna F172P	F17202121	
D-EGMC	CEA DR.253B Régent	155	
D-EGMF	Diamond DA 20-A1 Katana (Res. 28.9.15)	10028	N128MF, C-GKAN
D-EGMG	Piper PA-46-350P Malibu Mirage	4636112	F-GSJR
D-EGMH	SOCATA MS.893E Rallye 180GT	12318	F-BUZF
D-EGML(4)	Gmelin / Glasair Sportsman 2+2 (P. 6.9.16)	(01)/7273	
D-EGMM(2)	Cessna 172S Skyhawk SP	172S11075	N9055S
D-EGMO(3)	Piper PA-18 Super Cub 95	18-3195	OL-L21, L-121, 53-4795
D-EGMP	Cirrus SR22	3647	N60AG
D-EGMR	SIAI-Marchetti SF.260	2-55	OY-BEA
D-EGMS(2)	Robin DR.400/180R Régent (Res. 22.9.15)	1844	F-GGHR
D-EGMT	Reims/Cessna F182Q (Porsche engine)	F18200057	
D-EGMU(3)	Piper PA-18 Super Cub (Painted as "96+18" "54-739")	18-426	TC-CCO, Turk AF: 50-1770
D-EGMV	Reims/Cessna F152	F15201762	
D-EGMW	Reims/Cessna F177RG Cardinal RG	F177RG0133	(D-EGWM)
D-EGMY(2)	Bölkow BO.208C Junior	644	
D-EGNB	SOCATA Rallye 150T-D	2805	
D-EGNC	SOCATA MS.893 Rallye 180GT	12847	
D-EGND	SOCATA Rallye 150T-D	2804	
D-EGNE	Bölkow BO.208A Junior	526	
D-EGNF	SOCATA Rallye 150T-D	2968	
D-EGNG	SOCATA MS.893ED Rallye 180GT	12825	
D-EGNH	SOCATA MS.893ED Rallye 180GT	12826	
D-EGNI (2)	Piper PA-28-140 Cherokee C	28-26712	N5936U
D-EGNJ	SOCATA Rallye 150T-D	2806	
D-EGNK	SOCATA MS.893ED Rallye 180GT	12827	
D-EGNM(2)	Piper PA-28-181 Archer II	28-8290010	N8438L
D-EGNO(2)	Cessna 172P Skyhawk	17275546	N64331
D-EGNP(2)	Diamond DA 40-180 Star	40015	
D-EGNS	SOCATA MS.893ED Rallye 180GT	12866	
D-EGNU(3)	Cessna F172H	F172-0379	
D-EGNY	Bölkow BO.208A Junior	530	
D-EGOA	Piper PA-28-181 Archer II	28-8190020	N8257V
D-EGOB(2)	Robin DR.300/125 Petit Prince	662	
D-EGOC(2)	Bölkow BO.208C Junior	646	
D-EGOE	Robin HR.100/210D Safari	166	F-BUPV
D-EGOF(3)	Piper PA-28-161 Warrior II	28-8216122	N9637N
D-EGOJ	Reims/Cessna F152	F15201647	
D-EGOK(3)	Piper PA-28-140 Cherokee	28-21724	N11C
D-EGOL(3)	Piper PA-28RT-201T Turbo Arrow IV	28R-7931197	N29322
D-EGOM(2)	Cessna 182P Skylane	18262263	CS-AOQ, N58733
D-EGON	Fieseler Fi.156C-3 Trop Storch	5987	PH-NEL, (PH-NDF), (PH-PBD), VN266, Luftwaffe
D-EGOP(5)	Cessna T206H Turbo Stationair (Soloy conversion)	T20608257	N583AD
D-EGOR(3)	Piper PA-18A-150 Super Cub floatplane	18-2632	OH-CPT, SE-BXW, N10F
D-EGOS	Piaggio FWP.149D	061	90+47, AC+406, DA+389
D-EGOT(2)	Grumman AA-5A Cheetah	AA5A-0032	PH-GOL, OO-HAH
D-EGOV(2)	Beech F33A Bonanza	CE-1576	N81863
D-EGOZ(2)	Beech F33A Bonanza	CE-959	OE-KEK, N1814D
D-EGPA(2)	Piper PA-28-181 Cherokee Archer II	28-7690189	N9529N
D-EGPB(3)	Diamond DA 20-A1 Katana	10016	SE-LYB, OE-VPZ, N125MF, N516WA, C-GKAN
D-EGPE(3)	CASA C-1.131E Jungmann	2092	D-EGRF, E3B-441
D-EGPF(2)	Reims/Cessna FA150L Aerobat	FA1500094	D-ECHQ
D-EGPG(2)	Robin DR.400/120D Petit Prince	1644	
D-EGPH	Bellanca 7GCBC Citabria	798-75	N8586V
D-EGPI (3)	Cessna F150G	F150-0169	
D-EGPL(2)	Piper PA-28-236 Dakota	28-8011103	N8197L
D-EGPM	Piper PA-28-140 Cherokee E	28-7225452	N11C
D-EGPO(2)	Reims/Cessna FR182 Skylane RG	FR18200043	HB-CHB, G-ILLI, (HB-CCU), N1660C
D-EGPP	Mooney M.20J Model 201	24-1644	
D-EGPR(2)	Piper PA-28-181 Archer II	28-8190292	N84196

Registration	Type	c/n	Previous identities / Notes
D-EGPS	Cessna 172S Skyhawk SP	172S9065	(OY-. . .), N5186R
D-EGPW	Great Lakes 2T-1A-1	0505	N505GL
D-EGPZ(2)	CSA PS-28 Cruiser	C0290	
D-EGQC	Reims/Cessna F172N	F17201618	
D-EGQF	Reims/Cessna F172N	F17201593	
D-EGRA(4)	SOCATA MS.894A Minerva 220	11835	F-BSMV
D-EGRB(2)	SOCATA TB-10 Tobago	2062	PH-DVT, F-WWRB, (D-EFFJ(2))
D-EGRC	SOCATA TB-10 Tobago	15	F-ODKD
D-EGRD	SOCATA TB-10 Tobago	46	F-ODMD
D-EGRE(4)	SOCATA TB-10 Tobago	119	
D-EGRF(4)	Diamond DA 40D Star	D4.107	
D-EGRG	Reims FR172F Rocket	FR17200120	
D-EGRK	Piper PA-28R-200 Cherokee Arrow II	28R-7235299	N11C
D-EGRM	CASA C-1.131E Jungmann	2143	E3B-543
D-EGRO(3)	Grobholz G-2000 Symphonie (Res. 22.3.13)	EB-01	
D-EGRP(3)	Piper PA-28-161 Cadet	2841207	N158ER
D-EGRT(2)	Beech C23 Sundowner	M-2358	N18355
D-EGRU	Oberlerchner JOB 15-180/2	055	OE-CAI
D-EGRV(3)	Piper PA-28-235 Cherokee C	28-11217	ZS-JWT, ZS-HSC, ZS-FVZ, N11C
D-EGRW	Piper PA-28-235 Cherokee C	28-11251	N8508N
D-EGRX	SOCATA TB-10 Tobago	47	F-ODMF
D-EGRZ	SOCATA TB-10 Tobago	65	
D-EGSA(2)	SOCATA TB-20 Trinidad	2148	
D-EGSC	Reims/Cessna F172N	F17201898	(PH-AXD)
D-EGSD(2)	Mooney M.20R Ovation	29-0073	
D-EGSE(2)	Piper PA-28R-200 Cherokee Arrow II	28R-7635272	N75170
D-EGSF	Reims/Cessna F172N	F17201711	
D-EGSH	Grumman AA-5A Cheetah	AA5A-0563	N26399
D-EGSI (2)	Cessna T210L Turbo Centurion II	21060057	N59058
D-EGSJ	CEA DR.253B Régent	199	
D-EGSL(3)	Cessna R182 Skylane RG II	R18201364	N4641S
D-EGSM(2)	Piper PA-28-180 Cherokee Challenger	28-7305506	D-EBFH, N55944
D-EGSN	Flight Design CT LS-ELA	F-10-07-06	
D-EGSO(2)	Strassburg/ Van's RV-9A	90888	D-EEGS(2)
D-EGSP(2)	Piper PA-28R-200 Cherokee Arrow II	28R-7535299	N1493X
D-EGSR	Reims/Cessna F172N	F17201857	
D-EGSS(2)	Seybold/ Impulse 180TD	TD-9	
D-EGST	Cessna F172F	F172-0141	
D-EGSU(2)	CEA Jodel DR.1050M Sicile Record	21	F-BJLQ
D-EGSY(3)	CASA C-1.131E Jungmann 180	2149	F-AZNB, E3B-533
D-EGTB(3)	Cessna 172S Skyhawk SP	172S9149	N991TB
D-EGTC(4)	Piper PA-46-350P Malibu Mirage	4636141	S5-CGS, N146GS, N4142P
D-EGTD	Reims/Cessna FR182 Skylane RG	FR18200003	
D-EGTE(2)	Robin DR.400/180 Régent	1953	F-GJQD
D-EGTG	Reims/Cessna FR182 Skylane RG	FR18200005	
D-EGTH	Reims/Cessna F172N	F17201516	F-WLIP
D-EGTJ	Cessna TR182 Turbo Skylane RG	R18201437	N4847S
D-EGTL	Grumman AA-5 Traveler	AA5-0602	
D-EGTP	Robin DR.400/180 Régent	1261	
D-EGTQ	Robin DR.400/180R Remorqueur	1264	
D-EGTR(2)	SOCATA TB-20 Trinidad	706	
D-EGTS(3)	Piper PA-28-181 Archer II	28-8290111	D-EFDI (3), N8180U
D-EGTT	SOCATA MS.893E Rallye 180GT	13084	SE-GTT
D-EGTU(2)	SOCATA MS.880B Rallye Club	1164	F-BPGE
D-EGTW(2)	Robin DR.400/180R Remorqueur	1260	
D-EGTY(2)	Morane-Saulnier MS.505 Criquet	73	G-BWRF, D-EFTY(2), F-BAUV, Fr.AF
D-EGTZ	Cessna 172N Skyhawk	17270995	N1428E
D-EGUB(3)	HOAC DV-20 Katana	20157	
D-EGUF(3)	Cessna U206G Stationair II seaplane	U20603596	SE-GUF, (D-ERPI), SE-GUF, N7272N
D-EGUG	Cessna 170B	26213	N2569C
D-EGUH(2)	Reims/Cessna F152	F15201590	
D-EGUJ	Cessna 172N Skyhawk II	17271599	N3591E
D-EGUK(2)	Cessna 172N Skyhawk	17269403	N737GH
D-EGUL(2)	Cessna T210N Turbo Centurion II	21063924	OE-DUL, (N6588C)
D-EGUM	Piper J-3C-65 Cub (P. 26.4.16)	12859	HB-OAF, 44-80563
D-EGUN(3)	Robin DR.400/180R Remorqueur	2472	
D-EGUQ(2)	Piper PA-28-140 Cherokee	28-21577	N11C
D-EGUS(2)	SOCATA TB-10 Tobago	714	
D-EGUT(3)	Cessna TR182 Turbo Skylane RG	R18200668	N9204R
D-EGUV(2)	Piper PA-28-140 Cherokee	28-21619	N11C
D-EGUY	Gyroflug SC-01B-160i Speed Canard	S-7	
D-EGVC	Dornier Do.27A-4	2059	OL-D03/OT-AMC, D-3/D-9506
D-EGVE	Bölkow BO.208C Junior	661	
D-EGVF(2)	Reims/Cessna F172N	F17201924	(PH-AXJ)
D-EGVG(2)	Reims/Cessna F172N	F17201933	(PH-AXK)
D-EGVH(2)	Robin R.2160D Acrobin	199	(C-GEMQ)
D-EGVI	Bölkow BO.208C Junior	662	
D-EGVK	Wassmer WA.54 Atlantic	127	
D-EGVM	SNCAN/ Stampe SV.4C	218	F-BCNZ, Fr.AF
D-EGVO(3)	Vosseler/ Steen Skybolt 200	HGV 001	
D-EGVS	Piper J-3L Cub	12769	D-EGYS, HB-OAA, 44-80473
D-EGVT	Beech C24R Sierra 200	MC-605	N2012Z
D-EGVV	*Test registration for Grob G 115 production*		
D-EGVW	Cessna F172G	F172-0209	D-EDOF
D-EGVX	*Test registration for Grob G 115 production*		
D-EGVZ	Robin DR.400/180R Remorqueur	1593	
D-EGWA(2)	Gardan GY-80 Horizon 180	203	OY-DTJ
D-EGWC	Piper J-3C-65 Cub	6679	D-ECWC, N37900, NC37900
D-EGWD	Pützer Elster B	030	97+18, D-ELBY
D-EGWE	Piper PA-28-180 Cherokee C	28-2043	
D-EGWF(2)	Reims/Cessna F182Q Skylane	F18200140	PH-AXX
D-EGWG(2)	Robin DR.400/180R Remorqueur	1214	
D-EGWH	Piper J-3C-90/SGAC Marabout	EN.1	F-BGKF
D-EGWK	Piaggio FWP.149D	174	91+52, SC+336, AS+415, KB+139
D-EGWM(2)	Beth/ Pitts S-1S Special (Res. 27.8.15)	AB-K-098	
D-EGWN	Fuji FA-200-160 Aero Subaru	227	
D-EGWO	Beech A-23 Musketeer II	M-771	
D-EGWP(2)	Mraz M.1D Sokol	304	G-BWRG, D-EGWP(2), (D-EFTB), HB-TBG, OK-DIX
D-EGWR	Piper PA-28-161 Cherokee Warrior II	28-7816670	N9630N
D-EGWS(2)	Mooney M.20J Model 201	24-0240	(N201HU)
D-EGWT	Robin R.2160D Acrobin	174	
D-EGWW(4)	Aquila AT-01	AT01-192	
D-EGWY	Bölkow BO.208C Junior	666	
D-EGWZ(3)	Gyroflug SC.01B-160 Speed Canard	S-38	
D-EGXI(2)	Grob G 115A	8029	
D-EGXO	Bölkow BO.208C Junior	669	
D-EGXY(2)	SNCAN/ Stampe SV.4C	651	F-BDMU
D-EGYA	Beech C23 Sundowner 180	M-1923	
D-EGYC(2)	Cessna F172H	F172-0328	
D-EGYD(2)	Beech C24R Sierra 200	MC-479	
D-EGYH(2)	SOCATA MS.893ED Rallye 180GT	12990	
D-EGYI	SOCATA Rallye 100ST-D	2956	
D-EGYJ	SOCATA MS.893ED Rallye 180GT	12992	
D-EGYK(2)	SOCATA MS.893ED Rallye 180GT	12991	
D-EGYM(2)	Reims/Cessna F172M	F17201344	
D-EGYN(2)	Reims/Cessna F172M	F17201241	
D-EGYQ	Cessna 182C Skylane	52862	N8962T
D-EGYU	SOCATA Rallye 180T-D Galérien	3024	
D-EGYX(4)	SOCATA MS.893A Rallye Commodore 180	10625	
D-EGYZ	SOCATA MS.893A Rallye Commodore 180	10615	
D-EGZA	Piper J-3C-90 Cub	10086	OE-AEW, NC60443, 43-1225
D-EGZB(3)	Cessna 172M	17265568	N444DA, N6754H
D-EGZC(3)	Cessna 172P Skyhawk	17274803	N53701
D-EGZE	Cessna F172F	F172-0120	
D-EGZM	Bölkow BO.208C Junior	679	
D-EGZO	Bölkow BO.208C Junior	575	
D-EGZQ	Piper PA-38-112 Tomahawk	38-79A0485	F-GGZQ, N2571F
D-EGZR	Heliopolis Gomhouria Mk.6	185	SU-347
D-EGZT	Reims/Cessna F172N	F17201891	(PH-AXG)
D-EGZU(2)	Cessna 210B	21057970	OE-DED(1), N9670X
D-EGZW	Piper PA-38-112 Tomahawk	38-81A0104	N26024
D-EGZY	Cessna 182H Skylane	18256276	N2376X
D-EGZZ	Diamond DA 40D Star	D4.195	OY-RBA, OE-VPU
D-EHAA	Robin DR.400/180R Remorqueur	1541	
D-EHAB(2)	Piper PA-28-181 Cherokee Archer II (Reserved as OY-ZMA 4.09)	28-7790293	(OY-ZMA), (OY-TBA), D-EHAB(2), N9587N
D-EHAC(2)	Bölkow BO.208C Junior	709	(D-ENVD)
D-EHAD	Cessna 172	29059	N6959A
D-EHAH(4)	Piper PA-32R-301T Saratoga IITC	3257103	OY-JAH, N9527N
D-EHAI(2)	Robin DR.400/180R Remorqueur	1547	
D-EHAJ	Fuji FA-200-160 Aero Subaru	88	
D-EHAK(2)	Piper PA-32R-300 Cherokee Lance	32R-7680154	(D-EFAN), N8616E
D-EHAL(4)	Extra EA.500	1005	(D-FXZJ)
D-EHAM(2)	Cessna 172B	17248415	N7915X
D-EHAN(3)	Mooney M.20C Mark 21	3314	N200EK, D-EHAH
D-EHAO(2)	Piper PA-28-151 Cherokee Warrior	28-7515278	OY-CBE, N32942
D-EHAP(3)	Piper PA-18 Super Cub 95	18-1530	D-EOCF, ALAT, 51-15530
D-EHAS	Piper PA-22-150 Tri-Pacer	22-5510	
D-EHAU(2)	Hauser/ Neico Lancair 235	1645	
D-EHAV(2)	Aviat Pitts S-2B	5302	N98AV
D-EHAW(2)	Fuji FA-200-160 Aero Subaru (Marked FH20/160)	120	
D-EHAY	CEA DR.253B Régent	190	
D-EHAZ(5)	Cessna 172S Skyhawk SP	172S9955	OY- . . ., N22757
D-EHBA(2)	Cessna F172G	F172-0319	
D-EHBB	SOCATA MS.893A Rallye Commodore 180	11777	F-BSXY
D-EHBC(2)	SIAI-Marchetti SF.260	2-59	OO-HOC
D-EHBH(2)	Cessna 172S Skyhawk SP	172S10460	N2164M
D-EHBI (3)	Reims/Cessna F152 (Dam 24.4.11)	F15201534	
D-EHBK(2)	Reims/Cessna FRA150L Aerobat	FRA1500218	EI-AYF
D-EHBL(2)	Cessna F172G	F172-0194	OO-HBF, OO-WIF, OO-SIF
D-EHBM(3)	Cessna 172R Skyhawk	17281211	N2117X
D-EHBN	Reims/Cessna F172N	F17201755	
D-EHBR(5)	Brunner/ Aerostyle Breezer (Res)	10	
D-EHBT(2)	Tennant/ Europa Avn Europa	SB193 formerly 1796	
D-EHBU	Wassmer Jodel D.112 Club (Wfu 12.05: then reservation)	1114	F-BKCX
D-EHBX	Piper PA-32-300 Lance (Res. .11, ntu by 2016)	32R-7780515	G-BHBG, N408RC, N9590N
D-EHBZ	Zlin Z.143L	0006	HB-TCE
D-EHCB	Piper PA-18 Super Cub 95 (Painted as OL-L45)	18-3219	OL-L45, L-145, 53-4819
D-EHCC(3)	Grob G 115A	8056	
D-EHCD	Piper PA-18 Super Cub 95	18-3137	OL-L63, L-63, 53-4737
D-EHCE(2)	Christen A-1 Husky	1148	
D-EHCF	Piper PA-18 Super Cub 95	18-3190	OL-L16, L-116, 53-4790
D-EHCK	Piper PA-18 Super Cub 95	18-1491	ALAT, 51-15491
D-EHCL	Piper PA-18 Super Cub 95	18-1436	ALAT, 51-15436
D-EHCM(2)	SOCATA MS.893A Rallye Commodore 180	11501	F-BSCR
D-EHCN(3)	Piper PA-28-161 Cadet	2841202	N91891
D-EHCO	Piper PA-18 Super Cub 95	18-1529	ALAT, 51-15529
D-EHCP(2)	Reims/Cessna F172N	F17201760	
D-EHCQ	Mooney M.20M Model 257 TLS	27-0205	N48CK, D-ELVY(3), G-BWIS
D-EHCR	Reims/Cessna F172N	F17201762	
D-EHCS	Robin DR.400/180 Régent	1628	
D-EHCT(3)	Flight Design CT LS-ELA (P .09)	F09-02-16	
D-EHCU	Piper PA-18 Super Cub 95	18-1447	N1156R, ALAT, 51-15447
D-EHCW(2)	Beech B36TC Bonanza	EA-412	N72319, N6866W
D-EHDA(2)	Müller/ Sequoia F.8L Falco (Built with parts of Laverda F.8L c/n 406 and Sequoia plans following w/o of c/n 406, 15.3.80. Sequoia c/n unknown)	406	D-EHDA(2)
D-EHDE(3)	Commander Aircraft 114B	14545	N132A
D-EHDF	Piaggio FWP.149D	170	91+48, EB+389, DA+387, KB+146
D-EHDG(2)	Robin HR.100/210D Safari	175	F-OCTY
D-EHDJ	Wassmer WA.52 Europa	68	
D-EHDO(3)	AIAA/Stampe SV.4A	1080	F-BCDO, Aéronavale
D-EHDQ(2)	Robin DR.400/180 Régent	1647	
D-EHDR(2)	Robin DR.400/180R Remorqueur	1646	
D-EHDT(2)	CASA C-1.131E Jungmann 180	2181	E3B-564
D-EHDW(1)	Hawickhorst/ Pitts S-1S Special	AB-K-O99	D-EKYH(1)
D-EHDZ(2)	Piper PA-28RT-201T Turbo Arrow IV	28R-7931142	N2081Y
D-EHEA	Piper PA-28-235 Cherokee D	28-11305	N8563N
D-EHEB(4)	Berger/ Jodel D.92 Bébé	AB18	D-EKYH(1)
D-EHEH(9)	Cirrus SR22T	0811	N258EH
D-EHEI	Piper PA-28R-200 Cherokee Arrow II	28R-7235040	N4415T
D-EHEK(2)	Piper PA-28RT-201 Arrow IV	28R-7918235	OE-DRA, N2954S
D-EHEL(3)	Piper PA-28-180 Cherokee Challenger	28-7305160	N11C
D-EHEM(5)	HOAC DV-20 Katana	20065	
D-EHEN(2)	Aerotek Pitts S-2A	2088	G-BCXD, N80044

D-EHEO	Robin DR.400/180 Régent	747	
D-EHEP(3)	Cirrus SR20	1486	N384CD
D-EHEQ	Focke-Wulf FW.44J Stieglitz	unkn	SE-BZI, Fv664
D-EHER(5)	Piper PA-28-181 Archer II	28-8390008	N8293L
D-EHEU(3)	Cessna 182S Skylane	18280155	
D-EHEX(3)	Beech H35 Bonanza	D-5105	EC-AUF, HB-EBA, D-EJIN(1), N12B
D-EHEY	Beech C23 Sundowner 180	M-2078	
D-EHEZ(2)	Robin DR.400/180 Régent	1080	
D-EHFA(2)	Piper PA-28-181 Cherokee Archer II	28-7790485	N5616V
D-EHFE(2)	Piper PA-28-180 Cherokee E	28-5658	(D-EKSY), N3322R
D-EHFF	Piper PA-28R-200 Cherokee Arrow II	28R-7335084	(D-EEPD), N11C
D-EHFG(2)	Beech F33A Bonanza	CE-730	
D-EHFH(2)	Robin DR.400/180R Remorqueur	1886	
D-EHFL	Piper PA-28R-200 Cherokee Arrow	28R-35245	N2674R
D-EHFM	Piper PA-28-180 Cherokee E	28-5610	N3687R
D-EHFN(3)	Robin DR.400/180R Remorqueur	1936	
D-EHFP	Piper PA-28-140 Cherokee B	28-25596	N98007
D-EHFR(2)	Cessna 172M Skyhawk	17265729	N9645Q
D-EHFS(2)	Reims/Cessna F172N	F17201944	D-EDXC(2), OE-DSV
D-EHFU	Cessna F172F	F172-0164	
D-EHFV(2)	Cessna T182T Turbo Skylane	T18208800	N1067P
D-EHFW	Piper PA-28R-180 Cherokee Arrow	28R-30405	N4544J
D-EHFZ	Piper PA-28R-200 Cherokee Arrow II	28R-7235279	N1405T
D-EHGA(2)	Grumman AA-5B Tiger	AA5B-0009	N1509R
D-EHGD	Robin DR.400/180 Régent	2159	
D-EHGE(2)	Rockwell Commander 114B	14385	
D-EHGG(2)	Gross/ Dallach D4/E Fascination	EB018	
D-EHGJ	Robin HR.200/120B	344	G-WAVN, G-VECA
D-EHGK	Piper PA-28-180 Cherokee Challenger	28-7305428	N15689
D-EHGM(3)	Piper PA-28-161 Cadet	2841084	N9169E
D-EHGO(2)	Rockwell Commander 114	14389	
D-EHGR	Piper PA-28RT-201T Turbo Arrow IV	28R-8231015	N80039
D-EHGS(2)	Cessna 172S Skyhawk SP	172S10119	N24468
D-EHGT	Beech F33A Bonanza	CE-1148	
D-EHGV	Robin DR.400/180 Régent	2248	
D-EHGW(2)	Piper PA-28-161 Cherokee Warrior II	28-7816073	N47430
D-EHGX	Cessna 182R Skylane	18268476	N9972E
D-EHGZ	Horstmann/ Jodel D.18	115	
D-EHHB(2)	Cessna 172S Skyhawk SP	172S8813	N3506Z
D-EHHC	Fuji FA-200-160 Aero Subaru	112	
D-EHHD(2)	Cessna 172S Skyhawk SP	172S8706	SE-LVS, (SE-LUT), N776SP
D-EHHE	Aeromere F.8L Falco III America	227	HB-UOI, D-EHHE
D-EHHF(3)	Piper PA-28RT-201 Arrow IV	28R-7918064	N3004T
D-EHHG(2)	Robin DR.400/180R Remorqueur	1972	
D-EHHH(2)	Kranz/ Steen Skybolt (C/n now quoted as 1729; P.20.6.16)	06/2002241	
D-EHHI (2)	Christen A-1 Husky	1080	N9594F
D-EHHJ	Beech E33 Bonanza	CD-1165	N8384N
D-EHHK	CEA Jodel DR.1050 Ambassadeur	47	HB-EBP
D-EHHL	Mooney M.20F Executive	670325	N2931L, (D-ECTJ), N2931L
D-EHHM	Cessna F172H	F172-0352	
D-EHHN	Wassmer Jodel D.112 Club	886	D-EJCS(1), F-PJCS
D-EHHP	Robin R.1180TD Aiglon	231	
D-EHHR(2)	Cessna T182T Turbo Skylane	T18208856	N6187Q
D-EHHS	Cessna 177A Cardinal	17701294	N30509
D-EHHT(2)	de Havilland DH.82A Tiger Moth	85478/E-3	D-EDAM(2), D-EDAN, DE482
	(Identity officially quoted as T6746 which was D-EDAM(1) c/n 85033 cr 4.58 and combined with D-EDAN to build D-EDAM(2) in 1972)		
D-EHHU	Cessna F172F	F172-0129	
D-EHHV	Piper PA-28-181 Archer II	28-8490064	N9580N
D-EHHW(2)	Piper PA-28-160 Cherokee	28-546	TJ-ADK, TU-TDG, D-EMBA, N11C, N5465W
D-EHHX	Cessna P210N Pressurized Centurion II	P21000679	N5379W
D-EHHY	CEA DR.220A 2+2	103	F-BPKA
D-EHHZ	Piaggio FWP.149D	063	90+49, DB+389
D-EHIA(2)	Robin R.3000/160	172	
D-EHIC(3)	Robin ATL L	107	HB-SCD
D-EHIF(2)	Cessna F172G	F172-0299	
D-EHIG(3)	Piper PA-28RT-201T Turbo Arrow IV	28R-7931114	N2153V
D-EHIH	Stark Turbulent D-1R	119	
D-EHIK(3)	Piper PA-28RT-201T Turbo Arrow IV	28R-8531013	N91082
D-EHIL(3)	Christen Pitts S-2B	5203	N317JK
D-EHIM	Beech 35 Bonanza	D-499	OO-NDH, D-EHIM, OO-ECI, HB-ECI, NC90580
D-EHIO	Robin DR.400/RP Remorqueur	1765	
D-EHIP(2)	Robin R.3000/160	138	
D-EHIS	Stark Turbulent D (V-4)	104	
D-EHIT(3)	Piper PA-32RT-300 Lance II	32R-7885061	PH-ADP, N9619C
D-EHIX(2)	Cessna 182J Skylane	18257185	N3085F
D-EHIY	Robin DR.400/180 Régent	1221	EC-EQS, D-EEIY
D-EHIZ	Bücker Bü.181B-1 Bestmann	FR.20	SL-ABI, F-BBLX, Luftwaffe
D-EHJA(2)	Cessna P210N Pressurized Centurion II	P21000016	3D-PJM, N210FW, N7581P
D-EHJC	Piper PA-18-150 Super Cub	18-5334	(D-EDBH), N5883, ALAT, N10F
D-EHJD	Piper PA-28-180 Cherokee F	28-7105090	N3986R
D-EHJG(2)	SOCATA TB-9 Tampico	751	
D-EHJH	SOCATA TB-9 Tampico	756	
D-EHJI	SOCATA TB-9 Tampico	757	
D-EHJJ	SOCATA TB-10 Tobago	768	
D-EHJK	Piaggio FWP.149D	031	90+21, AC+421, JA+393
D-EHJL	Piaggio FWP.149D	045	90+31, AC+441, AS+441, GA+394, D-EGEW, GA+394
D-EHJM	Mooney M.20J Model 201	24-0190	N201RM
D-EHJN	Piper PA-28-235 Cherokee Pathfinder	28-7410011	N56575
D-EHJO	SOCATA TB-10 Tobago	767	
D-EHJR(2)	Cessna T206H Turbo Stationair	T20608718	N921LK
D-EHJS	SAN Jodel DR.1050 Ambassadeur	358	
D-EHJT	SOCATA MS.880B Rallye Club	1178	F-BPGD
D-EHJV	Wassmer WA.51A Pacific	74	
D-EHKA	SAN Jodel DR.1050 Ambassadeur	476	
D-EHKB	Robin R.1180TD Aiglon	262	
D-EHKC(2)	Piper PA-28R-201T Turbo Cherokee Arrow III	28R-7703408	N47607
D-EHKD(2)	Cessna 182P Skylane (Reims-assembled with "c/n" 0063)	18264442	D-EJCD, OE-DIF, N1782M
D-EHKE(2)	Robin DR.400/180 Régent	2285	
D-EHKF(2)	Heigl / Denney Kitfox III (Permit exp 9.02 ?)	908	
D-EHKG	Piper PA-28R-200 Cherokee Arrow II	28R-7235267	N1353T
D-EHKH	Piper PA-28R-200 Cherokee Arrow	28R-35119	D-EHGM, N9407N
D-EHKL	Robin DR.400/180R Remorqueur	1209	
D-EHKO(3)	SEEMS MS.885 Super Rallye	5390	OO-MIL, F-BLSD
D-EHKP	Piper PA-28-151 Cherokee Warrior	28-7715088	N9508N
D-EHKR	CEA DR.340 Major	425	F-BRVF
D-EHKS	Piper PA-32-300 Cherokee Six E	32-7240038	N8691N
D-EHKT	Mooney M.20J Model 201	24-1550	N5808Y
D-EHKU(2)	Beech F33A Bonanza	CE-1474	OY-GEE
D-EHKW(3)	Weinerth/ Siebel Si 202/W (Res)	1	
D-EHKY	Bölkow BO.207	272	
D-EHLA	Bölkow BO.207	273	
D-EHLC	Cessna 182L Skylane	18258771	N3471R
D-EHLG(3)	Cessna 150L	15073550	N16217
D-EHLH	Cessna 182K Skylane	18258475	N2875R
D-EHLI (2)	Piper PA-28R-200 Cherokee Arrow II	28R-7435260	N43310
D-EHLJ	Piper PA-18 Super Cub 95	18-3440	QZ+020, AC+531, AS+531, 54-740
D-EHLL	Tecnam P.2002-JR Sierra	116	EC-LFI
D-EHLM(2)	Diamond DA 20-A1 Katana	10229	C-GKAC
D-EHLO(3)	Diamond DA 20-A1 Katana	10233	N223DA, C-GDMQ
D-EHLP	Aero Commander 100	10A-085	N5554M
D-EHLR	Robin DR.400/180R Remorqueur	1162	
D-EHLU	Bölkow BO.207	277	
D-EHLY(2)	Piper PA-28-181 Cherokee Archer II	28-7790224	N9557N
D-EHLZ(2)	Cessna T182T Turbo Skylane	T18208030	N3529M
D-EHMA(2)	Dornier Do.27A-4	388	56+80, QW+110, QW+701, QM+614, PL+422
D-EHMB(3)	Aerostyle Breezer B600 (P. 15.6.16)	033LSA	
D-EHMD(2)	Diamond DA 40 Star	40008	F-GNJY, OE-KPN, OE-VPN
D-EHME(2)	Robin DR.400/140 Major	879	
D-EHMG	Diamond DA 40D Star	D4.209	
D-EHMH	Piper PA-28-180 Cherokee F	28-7105180	N5143S
D-EHMI	Piper PA-18-150 Super Cub	18-6242	N8584D
D-EHMK	Piper PA-28-160 Cherokee	28-560	D-EMMJ, N11C
D-EHML(2)	PZL CSS-13 (Polikarpov PO-2) (P. 1.16) (Rebuilt at Jahnsdorf)	0408	DM-WAH, SP-ATA
D-EHMM(2)	Great Lakes 2T-1A-2	0762	N3767F
D-EHMN	Piper PA-28RT-201T Turbo Arrow IV	28R-7931158	N2128Z
D-EHMS(4)	Cirrus SR22T	0302	N720DE
D-EHMV	Piper PA-28-151 Cherokee Warrior	28-7415190	N9512N
D-EHMW(2)	Mooney M.20J Model 201	24-1394	
D-EHMY(2)	Cessna 195B	16047	N4462C
D-EHMZ	SAN Jodel DR.1050 Ambassadeur	485	
D-EHNA	Piper PA-22-108 Colt	22-9112	SE-CZX
D-EHNB	Piper PA-28-140 Cherokee	28-22717	N4341J
D-EHND	Reims/Cessna F152	F15201576	
D-EHNF	Reims/Cessna F152	F15201584	
D-EHNG	Reims/Cessna F152	F15201585	
D-EHNJ	Mooney M.20E Super 21	1151	OY-DDR, N3475X
D-EHNL(2)	Christen A-1 Husky	1178	
D-EHNS	SOCATA TB-21 Trinidad TC	554	
D-EHNW	Cessna T210L Turbo Centurion	21060771	N1750X
D-EHOA	Rockwell Commander 114A	14537	
D-EHOB(2)	Piper PA-28-180 Cherokee C	28-2941	N8931J
D-EHOD(3)	Beech V35B Bonanza	D-10149	
D-EHOG(2)	Commander Aircraft 114B	14592	N60132
D-EHOH(3)	HOAC DV-20 Katana	20044	N44DV, C-FSIQ
D-EHOK(2)	Piper PA-28-180 Cherokee C	28-2997	N8974J
D-EHOL(3)	Reims/Cessna F172M	F17201328	PH-JDB, D-EDZJ
D-EHOM(2)	Robin DR.400/180R Remorqueur	1204	
D-EHON(2)	Robin DR.400/180R Remorqueur	1205	
D-EHOP(2)	Bölkow BO.207	206	
D-EHOR(2)	Piper PA-28-180 Cherokee C	28-2965	N8947J
D-EHOS	Beech F33A Bonanza	CE-847	
D-EHOU	SOCATA MS.880B Rallye Club	1852	F-BSMY
D-EHOW(2)	Rockwell Commander 114A	14536	
D-EHOZ(2)	Reims/Cessna F152	F15201636	
D-EHPA(2)	Piper PA-46-350P Malibu Mirage	4622057	N9167H
D-EHPB	Piper PA-28RT-201T Turbo Arrow IV	28R-8131001	N8268T
D-EHPC	Reims/Cessna F182Q Skylane	F18200067	N70846
D-EHPF	Cessna 150M	15076751	N45140
D-EHPG	Cessna T210L Turbo Centurion II	21061020	N2053S
D-EHPH	Bellanca 7GCBC Citabria	734-74	OE-AOI
D-EHPI (2)	Piper PA-28-140 Cherokee B	28-25752	N8887N
D-EHPL(3)	Piper PA-46-350P Malibu Mirage	4636471	N770TK, N6105D
D-EHPM(2)	Mooney M.20L PFM	26-0032	(D-EAXF(2)), N152MP
D-EHPN	Cessna 172N Skyhawk	17272748	N6362D
D-EHPO	Cessna 172C	17249362	N1662Y
D-EHPP(2)	Timmermann/ Christen Eagle II	229	
D-EHPR	Piper PA-32R-301T Turbo Saratoga SP	32R-8129073	N959CJ, N326SP, N4446M, XB-CTR, N8393T
D-EHPS	Piper PA-28-180 Cherokee Challenger	28-7305424	N55609
D-EHPW(4)	Diamond DA 20-C1 Katana	C0122	N970CT, C-GKAT
D-EHPY(2)	Reims/Cessna F172N	F17201799	
D-EHPZ	Piper PA-32R-301 Saratoga SP	32R-8013078	N81751, N9535N
D-EHQT(2)	Reims/Cessna FR182 Skylane RG	FR18200011	HB-CHH, OE-DNG
D-EHRA(3)	Mooney M.20M Model 257 TLS	27-0190	OE-KTS, (OE-KID)
D-EHRC	Reims/Cessna F177RG Cardinal RG	F177RG0135	
D-EHRD(2)	SOCATA TB-21 Trinidad TC	698	
D-EHRF(2)	Cessna 172N Skyhawk	17272487	N5272D
D-EHRG(2)	Cirrus SR22	1866	N105SR
D-EHRH(2)	Hoffmann/ Aero Designs Pulsar XP	333/1805	
D-EHRI	Cessna 172A	47693	N9893T
D-EHRK(2)	Cessna 170A	18832	OY-EFR, D-EKIS(1), N9073A
D-EHRM	Mooney M.20F Executive	700044	N9476V
D-EHRN(2)	Cessna 210L Centurion	21060326	(F-BVVT), N93264
D-EHRO(2)	Piper PA-28-181 Cherokee Archer II	28-7790546	N38378
D-EHRP	SOCATA MS.893A Rallye Commodore 180	11778	F-BSXZ
D-EHRS(2)	Reims/Cessna FR172K Hawk XP	FR17200622	N70788
D-EHRT	Reims FR172H Rocket	FR17200270	(D-ECJX)
D-EHRV	Cessna 172RG Cutlass RG	172RG1048	N98238
D-EHRW	Piper PA-28-181 Archer II	28-8590060	N6917C
D-EHSA	Cessna 182F Skylane	18254655	N3255U
D-EHSC	Cessna 140	14442	N2211V
D-EHSE(3)	Robin DR.400/180 Régent	2579	
D-EHSF(2)	Wassmer WA.40 Super IV	25	F-BKAY
D-EHSG(2)	Piper PA-28R-200 Cherokee Arrow II	28R-7535346	N1595X
D-EHSI (2)	Piper PA-28R-200 Cherokee Arrow II	28R-7235092	N4564T
D-EHSK(2)	Robin ATL	48	F-GFOY
D-EHSN	SOCATA MS.880B Rallye Club	1256	
D-EHSO(2)	Piper PA-28-140 Cherokee Cruiser (Res. 26.6.15)	28-7625189	N9562N

D-EHSQ	SOCATA MS.893A Rallye Commodore 180	10828	
D-EHSR	SOCATA MS.893A Rallye Commodore 180	10823	
D-EHSS(2)	Reims/Cessna F172H (P 9.07)	F17200702	D-ECEZ(2)
D-EHST(2)	Cessna 210L Centurion	21061066	N2100S
D-EHSV(2)	Cirrus SR22	3500	N232KB
D-EHSX	SOCATA MS.893A Rallye Commodore 180	10829	
D-EHTA(2)	Tecnam P.2002-JF Sierra	106	
D-EHTB	CEA DR.360 Major	517	
D-EHTC	Robin R.2100A Club	139	
D-EHTL(2)	Langer/ Cozy BL	001	
D-EHTP	Robin DR.400/180R Remorqueur	1342	
D-EHTS(2)	Robin DR.400/180R Remorqueur	1631	
D-EHTU	Piper J-3C-65 Cub	12602	OE-ADV, OK-AOH, Czech.AF NZ-16, 44-80306
D-EHTW(4)	Zlin Z.526A Akrobat	1055	HA-SAF, N1189X, HA-SAF
D-EHUB(2)	Commander Aircraft 114B	14556	N6007S
D-EHUD(2)	Reims/Cessna FR172K Hawk XP	FR17200642	N1019Z
D-EHUE(2)	Cessna 152	15282964	N45966
D-EHUF(2)	Cessna 175A Skylark	56285	(D-EHUQ), N6785E
D-EHUG(4)	Hirsch/ Aero Designs Pulsar XP	1840	
D-EHUL(3)	Piper PA-28-181 Archer II	28-8290007	N84363
D-EHUN(2)	Auster J/1 Autocrat	2119	OY-DPE
D-EHUP(3)	Diamond DA 40D Star	D4.043	OH-DDS, D-EWSP(2)
D-EHUR(2)	Robin DR.300/108 2+2	529	
D-EHUS(2)	Reims FR172F Rocket	FR17200138	F-WLIT
D-EHUT(2)	Piper PA-28-181 Archer III	2890226	N9253X
D-EHUU	Robin DR.400/160 Chevalier	705	
D-EHUV(2)	Robin DR.400/180 Régent	1596	
D-EHUW(3)	Staub/ Binder CP.301S Smaragd	AB.703	
D-EHUX(3)	SOCATA TB-20 Trinidad	453	
D-EHUY	Piper PA-28-140 Cherokee Cruiser	28-7725073	N9527N
D-EHUZ(2)	Reims/Cessna F172N	F17201881	"D-EOSJ"
D-EHVA	Piper PA-22-108 Colt	22-9622	N10F
D-EHVC	Beech V35B Bonanza	D-10241	
D-EHVG	Robin DR.400/180R Remorqueur	1633	
D-EHVI	Piper PA-22-108 Colt	22-9510	
D-EHVL	Cessna 172C	17249517	N2017Y
D-EHVM(2)	Beech B36TC Bonanza	EA-315	N724T, N6511X
D-EHVN	Yakovlev Yak-18T	22202040425	RA-2933K, RA-02933, LY-AOO, CCCP81332
D-EHVO(2)	Piaggio FWP.149D	081	90+63, JA+391, AS+490
D-EHVR	Piaggio FWP.149D	054	90+40, SC+331, AS+481
D-EHVS	Reims/Cessna F172N	F17201693	
D-EHVT	Reims/Cessna F172N	F17201706	
D-EHVY	Mooney M.20D Master	165	N6739U
D-EHWA	Cessna 182G Skylane	18255467	N2367R
D-EHWC(2)	Wolfrum/ Stoddard-Hamilton Glasair IIRG	1039	
D-EHWD	Beech F33A Bonanza	CE-440	
D-EHWE(3)	Ehringhaus / Denney Kitfox II	472	
D-EHWF	Robin DR.400RP Remo 212	1800	
D-EHWG(2)	Robin DR.400/180S Régent	2026	
D-EHWH(2)	Zlin Z.50LS	0040/03	OK-PRH
D-EHWI (2)	Mooney M.20K Model 231	25-0221	N231FL
D-EHWJ	Beech C23 Sundowner 180	M-1479	
D-EHWK	Cessna 182G Skylane	18255475	N2375R
D-EHWL(3)	Dallach D4 Fascination VLA	1002	
D-EHWN(3)	Piper PA-28-181 Archer II	28-8590008	N144AV
D-EHWP(2)	Cessna 140	13721	N4250N, NC4250N
D-EHWR	Reims/Cessna FR182 Skylane RG	FR18200020	(G-BGAR)
D-EHWS(2)	Robin DR.400/180 Régent	1985	
D-EHWT	Gardan GY-80 Horizon 180	223	
D-EHWZ(2)	Reims/Cessna FR182 Skylane RG	FR18200022	(PH-ADM), PH-AXW
D-EHXI	Rockwell Commander 112	119	N1175J, (N1119J)
D-EHXK	Rockwell Commander 112	121	N1005J, (N1121J)
D-EHXL	Rockwell Commander 112A	129	N1176J, (N1129J)
D-EHXM	Rockwell Commander 112A	191	N1149J, (N1191J)
D-EHXN	Rockwell Commander 112A	209	N1209J
D-EHXO	Rockwell Commander 112A	214	N1214J
D-EHXR	Rockwell Commander 112A	324	N1324J
D-EHXS	Rockwell Commander 112A	357	N1357J
D-EHXU	Rockwell Commander 112A	467	N1467J
D-EHXW	Rockwell Commander 112A	475	(N1475J)
D-EHXX	Rockwell Commander 112A	279	N1279J
D-EHXY	Rockwell Commander 112A	489	(N1489J)
D-EHXZ	Bölkow BO.207	289	HB-UXZ, (D-ENWI)
D-EHYD	Aeronca 7AC Champion	3957	N85224
D-EHYG	Piper J-4A Cub Coupé	4-880	N26758, NC26758
D-EHYH	Ranz/ Jodel D.9 Bébé	AB.14 (Liz.225)	
D-EHYL(3)	Diamond DA 40D Star	D4.057	
D-EHYM	Piper J-3C-85 Cub	10776	D-EDIF, PH-NFI, PH-NAE, 43-29485
D-EHZK	Beech C24R Sierra 200 (W/o 10.9.15 near Könnern)	MC-648	N60181
D-EIAA	Reims/Cessna F152	F15201537	
D-EIAB(2)	Aerotek Pitts S-2A	2240	N31496
D-EIAE	CEA DR.220 2+2	42	F-BOKM
D-EIAF(3)	Piper PA-28-161 Cherokee Warrior II	28-7816424	N6460C
D-EIAG(3)	Piper PA-28-181 Cherokee Archer II	28-7890545	D-EDYP(2), N39625
D-EIAH(2)	Piper PA-46-310P Malibu	46-8508060	N4391V
D-EIAI	Piper PA-28-181 Archer II	28-8090365	N8240T
D-EIAJ	Karstens / Neico Lancair 360 (P. 9.3.16)	1894	
D-EIAL(2)	Piper PA-32-300 Cherokee Six (Damaged 29.8.15 after t/o from Latina, Italy)	32-7340119	(D-EOIL(3)), I-OBBY, N55463
D-EIAM	Piper PA-28-180 Cherokee F	28-7105141	N1687T
D-EIAN	Grob G 115A	8062	
D-EIAO	SOCATA MS.893E Rallye 180GT	12310	F-BUVB
D-EIAP(2)	Tecnam P.2008-JC	1060	
D-EIAS	Cessna TU206F Turbo Stationair	U20603187	N8326Q
D-EIAT	Piper PA-28R-200 Cherokee Arrow B	28R-7135210	N1975T
D-EIAW(3)	Beech V35B Bonanza	D-10289	N66648
D-EIAY	Grob G 115A	8050	
D-EIAZ	Rockwell Commander 112A	314	N1314J
D-EIBA	Piper PA-28-181 Cherokee Archer II	28-7690150	N9518N
D-EIBC(2)	Zlin Z.142	0227	SP-AZL
D-EIBD	Rockwell Commander 114B	14400	
D-EIBE	Dornier Do.27A-1	310	56+34, GD+154, LB+154, CC+ . . ., CB+002
D-EIBF	Reims/Cessna F152	F15201566	
D-EIBG	Reims/Cessna F152	F15201574	
D-EIBJ	Diamond DA 20-A1 Katana	10270	C-FDVK
D-EIBK	Piper PA-28-161 Warrior II	28-8116197	N83658
D-EIBL	Piper PA-18A-150 Super Cub	18-8009024	N63928
D-EIBN(2)	Cessna 172N Skyhawk	17271749	N5170E
D-EIBO(2)	Cessna P210N Pressurized Centurion II	P21000714	N6100W
D-EIBS(2)	Zlin Z.42M (Res. .10)	0081	SP-ADM(3)
D-EIBU(2)	Bücker Bü.133C Jungmeister (Res. .14; based Italy still UK regd 2016)	46	G-AXMT, N133SJ, N33SJ, G-AXMT, HB-MIY, U-99
D-EIBW	Piper PA-28RT-201T Turbo Arrow IV	28R-8131162	N8406V
D-EIBY	Robin HR.100/200B	126	F-BTBY
D-EICA	Mooney M.20F Executive	700035	N9446V
D-EICC	Robin DR.300/180R Remorqueur	727	
D-EICD(2)	Cessna 172S Skyhawk SP	172S9231	N52903
D-EICE	Piper PA-28R-201T Turbo Arrow III	28R-7803330	N36620
D-EICF	Cherdron/ Christen Eagle II	0162	
D-EICG	Piper PA-28R-200 Cherokee Arrow II	28R-7535128	N33162
D-EICH(4)	Beech F33A Bonanza	CE-1162	N3144W
D-EICI (2)	Aviat A-1 Husky	1296	
D-EICK	Piper PA-28R-200 Cherokee Arrow	28R-35601	N3046R
D-EICO(5)	Cirrus SR22T	1069	N108LR
D-EICR	Piper PA-28-181 Archer II	28-8490075	N4359T, (D-EFZN), N4359t
D-EICS	Cessna U206F Stationair II	U20603118	N8257Q
D-EICT	Piper PA-28RT-201T Turbo Arrow IV	28R-8231055	N8216J
D-EICV	Cirrus SR22	3594	N102TR
D-EICY	Reims/Cessna F177RG Cardinal RG	F177RG0167	(D-EIMP)
D-EIDA	Fuji FA-200-160 Aero Subaru	164	
D-EIDC	Fuji FA-200-180 Aero Subaru	223	
D-EIDG	Fuji FA-200-180AO Aero Subaru	270	
D-EIDI (3)	Van's RV-7 (Permit 20.12.13)	21565	
D-EIDJ	Fuji FA-200-160 Aero Subaru	267	
D-EIDL	Fuji FA-200-180 Aero Subaru	206	
D-EIDM	Fuji FA-200-160 Aero Subaru	221	
D-EIDO	Fuji FA-200-180AO Aero Subaru	248	
D-EIDP(2)	Beech F33A Bonanza	CE-1482	
D-EIDS	Fuji FA-200-180 Aero Subaru	273	
D-EIDT(3)	Columbia Lancair LC41-550FG	41734	N1568E
D-EIDU	Fuji FA-200-180AO Aero Subaru	274	
D-EIDV	Fuji FA-200-160 Aero Subaru	162	N73542
D-EIDY	Fuji FA-200-180AO Aero Subaru	275	
D-EIDZ	Fuji FA-200-180AO Aero Subaru	276	
D-EIEA	Reims/Cessna F152	F15201598	
D-EIEB	Reims/Cessna F152	F15201613	
D-EIED	Reims/Cessna F172N	F17201852	
D-EIEE	Reims/Cessna F172N Skyhawk II	F17201875	
D-EIEH	Robin DR.400/180R Remorqueur	1405	
D-EIEI (2)	Piper PA-18 Super Cub 95 (Fuselage of D-EKQH = c/n 18-1017 f/n 18-1087 confirmed, therefore ex (D-EKQH), ALAT, 51-15320; but uses paperwork of D-EKQJ as shown)	"18-1374"	D-EKQJ , ALAT, 51-15374
D-EIEL	Zlin Z.526 Trenér Master	1011	D-EIFL, OK-VRF
D-EIEM	SOCATA TB-20 Trinidad	311	
D-EIEN	SOCATA TB-9 Tampico	313	
D-EIEO	SOCATA TB-10 Tobago	314	
D-EIER(2)	Robin DR.400/180R Remorqueur	1198	
D-EIEW	Extra Pitts S-1E Special	8-9043	
D-EIFB(2)	SOCATA TB-21 Trinidad TC	717	
D-EIFC	Reims/Cessna FR182 Skylane RG	FR18200002	
D-EIFE	Piaggio FWP.149D	129	91+08, BF+417, AS+016, KB+106
D-EIFG	Piper PA-28R-200 Cherokee Arrow II	28R-7635161	N8442C
D-EIFH	Piper PA-38-112 Tomahawk	38-78A0414	N9679N
D-EIFI (2)	Cessna 210E Centurion	21058615	OE-DEI, N4915U
D-EIFJ	Mooney M.20K Model 231	25-0118	N231JJ
D-EIFK	Fuji FA-200-180 Aero Subaru	185	
D-EIFL(4)	Bölkow BO.209 Monsun 160FV	151	HB-UEC, D-EBJK(1)
D-EIFM	Reims/Cessna F152 II	F15201709	
D-EIFN	Piper PA-28-181 Archer III	2890229	N9255F
D-EIFO	Piper PA-28-181 Cherokee Archer II	28-7890548	N39645
D-EIFP(2)	Reims/Cessna F152	F15201961	SE-IPF
D-EIFS	Andres/ Binder CP.301S Passat	AB.01	
D-EIFT	Robin DR.400/180R Remorqueur	1014	
D-EIFV	Cessna 172R Skyhawk	17280898	N2150K
D-EIFW(2)	Heuer FW190 (Half-scale)	333AB	
D-EIGB	Mooney M.20E Chapparral	700031	N30PK, D-EIGB, N9443V
D-EIGC	Piper PA-28-236 Dakota	2811036	D-EMFI (2), N91855
D-EIGD	Gardan GY-80-160D Horizon	247	
D-EIGE	Reims/Cessna F172N	F17201808	
D-EIGF	Gardan GY-80 Horizon 160D	248	
D-EIGG(2)	Cessna T182T Turbo Skylane	T18208787	N2381W
D-EIGI	Piper PA-28-181 Archer II	28-8090279	
D-EIGK	Mudry CAP.10B	74	F-BXHM
D-EIGL	Piper PA-28-181 Archer II	28-8690009	N2608Y
D-EIGO(2)	Beech F33A Bonanza	CE-1720	OE-KSB
D-EIGS(2)	Cessna 172RG Cutlass RG	172RG0568	D-EKNK, N5550V
D-EIGW	Piper PA-28-181 Archer III	2843375	OY-LAD, N9526N
D-EIGZ	SOCATA TB-21 Trinidad TC	1478	
D-EIHA	Piper PA-28-161 Warrior II	28-7916296	N9609N
D-EIHD	Stampe & Renard/ Stampe SV.4B	1169	G-AZUL, V-27
D-EIHF	Evektor EV-97 SportStar Max	2010 1308	
D-EIHG(2)	Reims/Cessna FA150K Aerobat	FA1500064	D-ECAN(2)
D-EIHI	Reims/Cessna F152	F15201591	
D-EIHK(2)	Piper PA-28-161 Warrior II	2816002	N9089K
D-EIHL(2)	Piper PA-28-140 Cherokee F	28-7325400	D-EHWW(1), N11C
D-EIHM	Piper PA-28-181 Archer II	28-8290052	N8358F
D-EIHP	CessnaTR.182 Turbo Skylane RG	R18201982	N6326T
D-EIHQ	HOAC DV-20 Katana	20084	
D-EIHS	SOCATA MS.880B Rallye Club	2044	F-BTPO
D-EIHW	Cessna TU206G Turbo Stationair 6-II	U20606114	(N5443Z)
D-EIHY	Piper PA-28RT-201 Arrow IV	28R-8018068	
D-EIIB	Piper PA-28RT-201T Turbo Arrow IV	28R-7931275	N2957D
D-EIIC(4)	Piper PA-46-350P Malibu Mirage	4636504	N86MH, N9541N
D-EIID	Piper PA-28-181 Archer II	28-8090361	N8237Z
D-EIIE	Piper PA-28-235 Cherokee	28-10224	N8691W
D-EIIF(3)	Christen Pitts S-2B	5139	N15F
D-EIIG	Reims/Cessna F182Q Skylane	F18200069	
D-EIIH(3)	Reims/Cessna F172M	F17201248	D-EGYR(2)
D-EIII (3)	Bücker Bü.133C Jungmeister	1069	SpAF:E1-.?
D-EIIJ	Mooney M.20K Model 231	25-0830	N5764N
D-EIIK	Robin HR.200/100 Club	31	
D-EIIL	Robin HR.200/100 Club	34	
D-EIIM	Robin DR.400/180R Remorqueur	956	
D-EIIN	Robin DR.400/180 Régent	946	
D-EIIS(2)	Bücker Bü.133C Jungmeister	1013	SpAF:ES1-7, 35-7
D-EIIT(2)	Piper PA-28-161 Warrior II	2816011	N9118X
D-EIIU(2)	Zlin Z.142	0216	SP-AZK
D-EIIV(3)	Bücker Bü.133C Jungmeister (For export to USA 10.16)	35	N35133, HB-MKL, U-88

Reg	Type	C/N	Previous ID
D-EIIX	Aviat Pitts S-2B	5210	
D-EIIY	Mooney M.20J Model 201	24-1152	N1139L
D-EIIZ(3)	Möhlenkamp / Cassutt IIIM (Permit 28.5.13)	1967	
D-EIJH	Piper PA-28-181 Archer II	28-7990552	N2914N
D-EIJI	Robin DR.400/180 Régent	1029	
D-EIJJ	Cessna 152	15285216	N6273Q
D-EIJK(2)	Kurz Rieseler Ma.III	N01/1848	
D-EIJL	CASA C-1.131E Jungmann (Damaged 3.9.11)	2088	E3B-392
D-EIJN	Piper PA-28-181 Archer II	28-8190019	N8257H
D-EIJT(2)	Cirrus SR22	1942	EC-JZZ, N954SR
D-EIKA(3)	Mooney M.20K Model 252 TSE (Res. .14)	25-1164	N880RA
D-EIKB	Morane-Saulnier MS.885 Super Rallye	51	F-BKEX
D-EIKC(2)	Cessna P210N Pressurized Centurion II	P21000554	N731XF
D-EIKD	Reims/Cessna F172P	F17202107	
D-EIKE(2)	Mooney M.20J Model 205	24-3209	
D-EIKF	Reims/Cessna FR172K Hawk XP	FR17200675	
D-EIKG	Cessna 172S Skyhawk SP	172S10427	N14111
D-EIKH(2)	Grob G 115A	8077	
D-EIKI	SOCATA MS.893E Rallye 180GT	12182	F-BUCR
D-EIKK	Rans S-9KK Chaos	1109214	
D-EIKL	CEA DR.220 2+2	22	F-BOCP
D-EIKM	Beech V35B Bonanza	D-9919	N4KM
D-EIKN(2)	Cessna 172S Skyhawk SP	172S8126	N866SP
D-EIKO	Robin DR.400/180R Remorqueur	1130	(F-GABH)
D-EIKR(2)	Robin DR.400/180 Régent	1839	F-ODSI
D-EIKS(2)	Reims/Cessna F182Q Skylane	F18200075	
D-EIKT	Reims/Cessna F172N	F17202012	
D-EIKV(2)	Reims/Cessna FR172K Hawk XP	FR17200667	
D-EIKY	Bücker Bü.133D-1 Jungmeister (Res. 20.4.15)	2005	OE-AKE
D-EILB	PZL-104 Wilga 35A	62177	(D-EWBO), DDR-WBO, DM-WBO
D-EILE(3)	Commander Aircraft 114B	14549	D-EJKE(2), LX-BUG, D-ERPA(1), N172A
D-EILF(2)	Piper PA-28-160 Cherokee	28-368	C-GBBE, SLN-.., D-EJPI (1), N11C
D-EILH(2)	Robin DR.400/RP Remorqueur	1837	OE-KLH, D-ELSR
D-EILI (2)	Cessna 182R Skylane	18268449	N9810E
D-EILJ	SOCATA TB-9 Tampico	920	
D-EILK	Piper PA-28-181 Archer III	2843144	N4123Q
D-EILM	SOCATA MS.887 Rallye 125	2178	F-BVLN
D-EILO(2)	Piper PA-28-181 Archer II	28-7990379	N2163Y
D-EILR	Reims/Cessna F172P	F17202165	
D-EILS	Piper PA-28RT-201 Arrow IV	28R-7918126	N28409
D-EILT(2)	Mooney M.20F Executive	22-1343	
D-EILU	Piper PA-38-112 Tomahawk	38-79A0673	N9659N
D-EILX	Cessna 172RG Cutlass RG	172RG0817	D-EOCD, (N9417B)
D-EILY	Wassmer WA.52 Europa	49	
D-EIMB	Beech C24R Sierra 200	MC-603	
D-EIMC(2)	Grob G 115C2	82045	OO-GLB, D-EXGR
D-EIMD	Reims/Cessna F172P	F17202054	
D-EIME(3)	Aquila AT-01	AT01-171	
D-EIMF	Beech V35B Bonanza	D-9245	N9245Q
D-EIMG	Piper PA-28-181 Archer II	28-8090040	N4513L
D-EIMH	Reims/Cessna F172P	F17202147	
D-EIMI	Reims/Cessna F172N	F17201906	
D-EIMK(3)	Oberbach/ Van's RV-7DO	2002519	
D-EIML(2)	Reims/Cessna F172P	F17202252	
D-EIMM(2)	Cessna P210N Pressurized Centurion	P21000225	HB-CJT, N9FV, (N4588K)
D-EIMN	Reims/Cessna F172P Skyhawk II	F17202171	F-WZDT, (D-EGLK)
D-EIMO	Cessna T210G Turbo-System Centurion	T210-0276	N6876R
D-EIMS(2)	Cirrus SR20	1554	N81423
D-EIMT	Reims/Cessna F152	F15201941	
D-EIMU	Bellanca 7ECA Citabria	956-73	
D-EIMV	Reims/Cessna F172P	F17202143	
D-EIMW	Reims/Cessna F150K	F15000531	PH-ALF
D-EIMY	Reims/Cessna F172N	F17201908	
D-EIMZ	Reims/Cessna F172P	F17202226	F-WZIB
D-EINB	Navion Rangemaster H	NAV-4-2543	N600EJ, D-EINB, (N2543T)
D-EINC(2)	Cessna 172R Skyhawk	17280001	N172KS
D-EINE(2)	CASA C-1.131E Jungmann	2202	E3B-582
D-EINF	Navion Rangemaster H	NAV-4-2546	(N2546T)
D-EING	Navion Rangemaster H	NAV-4-2547	(N2547T)
D-EINH(2)	Robin DR.300/108 2+2	530	
D-EINK(2)	Piper PA-28RT-201 Turbo Arrow IV	28R-8331034	N4301K
D-EINN	SAN Jodel DR.1050 Ambassadeur	113	OO-OSM, D-EINN, F-BJJD
D-EINS(3)	Piper PA-46-310P Malibu	46-8508106	C-FCIR, (N743E), C-FCIR, N2603X
D-EINU	Stark Turbulent D	132	HB-SVF, D-EKEV
D-EINY	Wassmer WA.54 Atlantic	111	
D-EINZ	Piper PA-18-150 Super Cub	18-8310	N7443Z
D-EIOC	Cirrus SR22	2006	N946SR
D-EIOG(3)	Piper PA-16 Clipper	16-500	(D-ECES(3)), D-EIOG(1), HB-OOG
D-EIOH(3)	Cessna 172S Skyhawk SP	172S8190	OY-SSF, N369LP
D-EIOI(2)	Helselmann / Van's RV-7	21565	
D-EIOO	CASA C-1.131E Jungmann	2215	D-EDNN(1), E3B-615
D-EIOR	Mooney M.20J Model 201	24-0622	N102CK, N4106H
D-EIOU(2)	Piper PA-28RT-201T Turbo Arrow IV	28R-7931270	N2510U, N9597N
D-EIPA	Piper PA-28RT-201T Turbo Arrow IV	28R-7931242	N2874W
D-EIPB	Beech B24R Sierra 200 (CoA expired, status unknown)	MC-427	
D-EIPC	Beech C23 Sundowner 180	M-1835	
D-EIPF	Reims/Cessna F177RG Cardinal RG	F177RG0176	
D-EIPG	Mooney M.20E Chaparral	690017	N9089V
D-EIPI (2)	Flight Design CT LS-ELA	09-04-01	
D-EIPK	Mooney M.20F Executive	700036	N9451V
D-EIPL	Piaggio P.149D	279	OE-DKK, 91+93, AC+430, AS+430
D-EIPM	Reims/Cessna F152	F15201515	
D-EIPN	Cessna 182T Skylane	18281539	F-GPSJ, N1008U
D-EIPO	Reims/Cessna F152	F15201500	
D-EIPP	Christen A-1 Husky	1081	N9594P
D-EIPT	Reims/Cessna F172N	F17201721	
D-EIPV	SOCATA TB-20 Trinidad	443	
D-EIQD	Reims/Cessna FRA150L Aerobat	FRA1500216	
D-EIQI	Reims/Cessna F150L	F15001067	
D-EIQK	Reims/Cessna F172M	F17201052	
D-EIQO	Reims FR172J Rocket	FR17200447	
D-EIQQ	Reims FR172J Rocket	FR17200462	
D-EIQV	Reims/Cessna F150L	F15001054	
D-EIRA	Piper PA-28-180 Cherokee Archer	28-7505174	N9623N
D-EIRB	Reims/Cessna FR182 Skylane RG	FR18200023	PH-AXX
D-EIRC(2)	American AG-5B Tiger	10006	N1190N
D-EIRD	Reims/Cessna F172N	F17201935	
D-EIRE	Beech V35B Bonanza	D-9201	
D-EIRF(4)	SOCATA TB-20 Trinidad	583	F-GLPG, N102U
D-EIRH	Reims/Cessna F172N	F17202022	
D-EIRJ(2)	CEA DR.340 Major (P. 3.2.16)	320	I-MARJ, F-OCMG
D-EIRK(2)	SOCATA TB-20 Trinidad	386	D-EKTN
D-EIRL(2)	Robin DR.400/180 Régent	2191	
D-EIRN	Reims/Cessna F172P	F17202038	
D-EIRS	Cessna 180K Skywagon	18053164	
D-EIRT(2)	Robin DR.400/180 Régent	2412	
D-EIRV(2)	Aerotek Pitts S-1S	1-0045	PH-PUP, N3KZ, N9TH
D-EIRW(2)	Piper PA-32-300 Cherokee Six	32-40074	HB-OMC, N4052W
D-EIRX	Reims/Cessna F172P	F17202109	
D-EIRZ	Reims/Cessna F152	F15201844	
D-EISA	SAN Jodel D.140B Mousquetaire II	67	OE-DOP
D-EISB(2)	Grumman-American AA-5 Traveler (Res. 29.6.15)	AA5-0299	OY-AYY
D-EISC	Gyroflug SC-01B-160 Speed Canard	S-14	
D-EISD	Robin DR.400/180 Régent	1903	
D-EISE(3)	Mooney M.20K Model 252 TSE	25-1219	I-SESE, N1068G
D-EISF	Robin DR.400/180R Remorqueur	1115	
D-EISG	Robin DR.400/180R Remorqueur	1116	
D-EISH	Robin DR.400/180R Remorqueur	1117	
D-EISI	Robin DR.400/180R Remorqueur	1129	
D-EISK(2)	Cessna 172R Skyhawk	17280165	
D-EISM	Cessna 182Q Skylane	18265651	N735SQ
D-EISN	Cessna R172K Hawk XP	R1722969	PH-JBI, N758BR
D-EISO(2)	Piper PA-18-150 Super Cub	18-9000	I-CGAG, N9700N
D-EISQ	Cessna TU206F Turbo Stationair	U20602990	N2715Q, (D-ECBS(2)), N2715Q
D-EISR	Robin DR.400/180R Remorqueur	1650	
D-EISS	Piper PA-28R-200 Cherokee Arrow B	28R-7135079	N5077S
D-EIST	Piper PA-28-181 Archer II	28-8090041	N2317U
D-EISU	Piper PA-28-161 Warrior II	28-7916540	N2916Y
D-EITA(2)	Piper PA-28RT-201T Turbo Arrow IV	28R-8031086	N81837
D-EITB(2)	Cirrus SR22	3528	LX-YES, N158CK
D-EITD	Reims/Cessna F152	F15201759	
D-EITF(3)	SNCAN Stampe SV.4C1	517	F-GKGJ, F-BDIA
D-EITG	Reims/Cessna F172N	F17202002	
D-EITI (2)	Piper PA-28-181 Archer II	28-7990554	N2917X
D-EITJ	Zlin Z.142 (Res. .11)	0318	SP-ATS
D-EITK	Reims/Cessna F152	F15201896	
D-EITL	Piper PA-28R-200 Cherokee Arrow II	28R-7335018	N15085
D-EITN	Cessna 172E	17251442	D-EFGY, N5542T
D-EITO	SOCATA Rallye 100S-D Sport (Res. 3.5.11)	2345	I-RALQ
D-EITP(2)	Reims/Cessna F172P	F17202249	
D-EITR	Robin DR.400/180R Remorqueur	1651	
D-EITT(2)	Fuji FA-200-180 Aero Subaru	189	
D-EITX	Piper PA-18-150 Super Cub	18-7809033	I-BALN, N82951
D-EITY	Piper PA-28RT-201T Turbo Arrow IV	28R-8031063	N8156U
D-EIUA	SOCATA MS.893E Rallye 180GT (Cld 1.16 but reserved)	12496	F-BVNL
D-EIUB	SOCATA MS.880B Rallye Club	2541	F-BVZE
D-EIUL	Piper PA-18 Super Cub 95	18-3125	D-EETU, OL-L51, L-51, 53-4725
D-EIUW	Reims/Cessna FA152 Aerobat	0421	
D-EIVA	Piper PA-28RT-201T Turbo Arrow IV	28R-7931301	N8083N
D-EIVB	PZL-110 Koliber 150	03930049	
D-EIVD	PZL-110 Koliber 150	03930050	
D-EIVE	Dornier Do.27A-1	328	56+46, LC+161, JA+382
D-EIVI (3)	Cessna 172N Skyhawk	17271061	N1601E
D-EIVJ	PZL-110 Koliber 150	03940054	
D-EIVK	PZL-110 Koliber 150	03940055	
D-EIVL	SOCATA MS.894A Minerva 220	11881	F-BTHE
D-EIVM	Reims/Cessna F150M	F15001404	
D-EIVN	Reims/Cessna F150M	F15001392	
D-EIVS	PZL-110 Koliber 150	03900044	
D-EIVT(2)	PZL-110 Koliber 150	04950079	
D-EIVV	PZL-110 Koliber 150	03930047	
D-EIWB(2)	Piper PA-28-181 Archer II	2890119	N9179Z
D-EIWE(2)	Zlin Z.143L	0007	
D-EIWF	Beech K35 Bonanza	D-5969	HB-EGX
D-EIWJ	Yakovlev Yak-50	80-1704	DDR-WQN
D-EIWK(2)	Piper PA-28-236 Dakota	28-8011100	N81879
D-EIWL(2)	Robin DR.400/RP Remorqueur	1806	D-EIWP(2)
D-EIWM(3)	Cessna 172S Skyhawk SP	172S11104	N9173Z
D-EIWN	Robin DR.400/200R Remo 200	2268	
D-EIWO	Piper PA-28R-180 Cherokee Arrow	28R-30424	N4562J
D-EIWR	Robin R.2160D Acrobin	177	
D-EIWW(2)	CASA C-1.131E Jungmann	2028	D-ENHD, E3B-432
D-EIWZ	RFB Fantrainer 600 (Permit)	005	98+76, D-EIWZ
D-EIXA(2)	Xtreme Air Sbach 342	006	
D-EIXB	Rockwell Commander 114	14102	N4709W
D-EIXE	Rockwell Commander 114B	14200	(N4870W)
D-EIXI	Rockwell Commander 114B	14277	(N4957W)
D-EIXK	Rockwell Commander 112TC	13030	N1841J
D-EIXS	Rockwell Commander 114B	14248	
D-EIXT	Rockwell Commander 114B	14261	(N4939W)
D-EIXX	Aviat A-1 Husky	1295	
D-EIXY	Aviat A-1A Husky	1433	N4674L
D-EIYB	Reims/Cessna F152	F15201592	
D-EIYD	Reims/Cessna F152	F15201562	
D-EIYF	Reims/Cessna F152	F15201594	
D-EIYJ	Reims/Cessna F172N	F17201869	
D-EIYR	Reims/Cessna F172N	F17201838	
D-EIYS	Reims/Cessna F182Q Skylane	F18200123	
D-EIYT	Reims/Cessna F172N	F17201926	
D-EIYW	Reims/Cessna F172N	F17201943	
D-EIYY	Reims/Cessna F172N	F17201961	
D-EIZB	Reims/Cessna F172P	F17202079	
D-EIZC(2)	Reims/Cessna F172P	F17202154	
D-EIZD(2)	Beech F33A Bonanza	CE-1359	OY-GEY
D-EIZE	Beech F33A Bonanza	CE-774	
D-EIZF	Beech F33A Bonanza	CE-775	
D-EIZG	Beech F33A Bonanza	CE-779	
D-EIZJ	Beech F33A Bonanza	CE-788	
D-EIZK	Beech F33A Bonanza	CE-789	

Registration	Type	c/n	Previous identities / notes
D-EIZL	Beech F33A Bonanza	CE-791	
D-EIZM	Reims/Cessna F182Q Skyline	F18200138	
D-EIZN	Reims/Cessna FR182 Skyline RG II	FR18200055	
D-EIZP(2)	Reims/Cessna F152	F15201811	
D-EIZQ(2)	Beech F33A Bonanza	CE-1093	
D-EIZR(2)	Beech F33A Bonanza	CE-1094	
D-EIZT(2)	Beech F33A Bonanza	CE-1095	
D-EIZV	Cessna TR182 Turbo Skylane RG	R18201480	N4941S
D-EIZW	Reims/Cessna F152	F15201814	
D-EIZY	Cessna 172RG Cutlass RG	172RG0562	N5537V
D-EJAA(2)	Beech A36 Bonanza	E-990	OY-CPD, N17606
D-EJAB(6)	Kaiser / Jabiru SK	01	
	(P 8.07)		
D-EJAC(3)	Yakovlev Yak-18	"18-1432030"	N18YK, N7013S, PLAAF....
	(Res. 1.08 and 1.10; this c/n is actually a Nanchang CJ-5 c/n 14 320 30)		
D-EJAD(2)	Reims/Cessna F182Q Skyline	F18200163	
D-EJAE(2)	Wassmer WA.40 Super IV	30	D-EJAE(1)
D-EJAF(3)	Xtreme Air Angry Fish	2002455	
	(Permit 10.12) (Damaged 11.6.13 Cochstedt)		
D-EJAG(3)	Manhart/ Brditschka HB-207V RG Alpha	207024	
D-EJAH(2)	SOCATA TB-10 Tobago		
D-EJAJ(3)	Cirrus SR22	0166	N826CD
D-EJAK(2)	Piper PA-28-236 Dakota	28-7911242	N2909W
D-EJAN(3)	SOCATA TB-10 Tobago	580	
D-EJAP(2)	Cessna T182T Turbo Skylane	T18208725	N2189G
D-EJAR(3)	Diamond DA 20-A1 Katana	10133	N563SS, C-GKAX
D-EJAS(4)	Robin DR.400/180R Remorqueur	1266	
D-EJAY(2)	SOCATA TB-20 Trinidad	1611	
D-EJBA(2)	Robin DR.300/180R Remorqueur	589	
D-EJBC	Robin DR.300/180R Remorqueur	594	
D-EJBD	CEA DR.253B Régent	187	
D-EJBF	CEA DR.360 Major	598	
D-EJBG	Robin DR.300/108 2+2	592	
D-EJBH	Robin DR.300/108 2+2	593	
D-EJBK	Cessna 172N Skyhawk	17270466	N739DS
D-EJBM	Mooney M.20F Aerostar 220	700051	HB-DFV, D-EHOF(3), N9497V
D-EJBR	Mooney M.20J Model 201	24-1660	
D-EJBW(2)	Piper PA-28R-201T TurboCherokee Arrow III	28R-7703407	OE-KBW, D-EMOC(2), N47606
D-EJBY	Bölkow BO.207	245	
D-EJCA(3)	Commander Aircraft 114B	14544	N6007S
D-EJCB(2)	Extra EA.300/LT	LT025	
D-EJCC(2)	SOCATA TB-21 Trinidad TC	2064	N716TB
D-EJCF	Reims/Cessna F182P Skyline II	F18200011	
D-EJCH(2)	Macchi MB.308	71/5844	D-EJUP(1), I-NCOM
	(Also wears original marks I-NCOM)		
D-EJCI(2)	Reims/Cessna F182P Skyline	F18200019	
D-EJCK	Reims/Cessna F182P Skyline	F18200015	
D-EJCO(2)	Cessna 177B Cardinal	17702193	N35079
D-EJCP	Reims/Cessna F152	F15201632	
D-EJCR	Robin DR.400/180 Régent	2381	
D-EJCS(2)	SIAT 223A-1 Flamingo	016	HB-EVM, D-ENBM(1)
D-EJCT	Bücker Bü.131B Jungmann	61	HB-URH, A-49
D-EJCX	Jakobsen/ Thatcher CX4	2002360	
	(CX4 project number 67) (Res. .10)		
D-EJDB	Gyroflug SC-01B-160 Speed Canard	S-31	
D-EJDE(2)	Gyroflug SC-01B-160 Speed Canard	S-51	
D-EJDI	Cessna 150F	15061588	N6288R
D-EJDK	Cessna P210N Pressurized Centurion II	P21000808	N4598A
D-EJDL	Ruschmeyer R.90-230RG	010	PH-JDL, D-EEAU(2)
	(Res. 17.8.15)		
D-EJDR(2)	Cessna 170A	19370	D-EFAW(1), D-ERFA(1), N9273A
D-EJDT	Cessna 182T Skylane	18281758	OE-KHG, N24041
D-EJDZ	FFT Eurotrainer 2000A	A-1	
D-EJEB(2)	Mooney M.20A	1676	OE-DOM, N6080X
D-EJED(2)	Robin DR.400/180R Remorqueur	1317	
D-EJEE	SAN Jodel DR.1050M Excellence	487	
D-EJEF(4)	Feldmann/ Denney Kitfox IV	01/1745	
D-EJEG(2)	Beech F33A Bonanza	CE-723	
D-EJEJ	SOCATA TB-9 Tampico	1268	PH-RWL, F-GKVC
D-EJEK(2)	Robin DR.400/180R Remo 180	1141	F-GABX
D-EJEM(2)	Cessna F172G	F172-0261	
D-EJEN(2)	Piper PA-18 Super Cub 95	18-5644	OE-AEN, 2A-AS, N10F
D-EJER	Aeronca 11AC Chief	1609	OO-KER, OO-LUC
D-EJET(2)	Piper PA-28-200 Cherokee Arrow II	28R-7535325	N1559X
D-EJEV(2)	Cessna F150G	F150-0190	
D-EJEX	Dornier Do.27Q-1	2021	
D-EJFA(2)	Piper J-5A Cub Cruiser	5-529	N35021, NC35021
D-EJFD	Gyroflug SC-01B-160 Speed Canard	0527	
D-EJFF	Piper PA-28-200 Cherokee Arrow II	28R-7435285	N43642
D-EJFH	Fröhlich/ Van's RV-8	82639	
D-EJFL(2)	Beech V35B Bonanza	D-9717	(D-EANG(2)), ZS-JFI, N9377S
D-EJFN	Neumayer / Stoddard-Hamilton Glasair II-FT	1057AB	
	(W/o 22.3.14 Lanzen-Turnau, Austria)		
D-EJFR	CEA Jodel DR.1050 Ambassadeur	406	F-BLAG
D-EJFT	Diamond DA 20-C1 Katana	C0025	(SE-. . .), N125CL
D-EJFU(3)	Mooney M.20J Model 201	24-1617	
D-EJFW	Schöneseifen/ Jurca FW.190-A5	E-01/293	
	(Permit 4.99)		
D-EJGA	Cessna 172C	17249395	N1695Y
D-EJGB	Mooney M.20K Model 231	25-0711	(N1172G)
D-EJGD	Mooney M.20K Model 231	25-0703	(D-EJGO(3)), N231AV, (N1170X)
D-EJGF	Yakovlev Yak-18A	0527	DM-WGI, LSK-. . .
D-EJGG	Reims/Cessna FR172K Hawk XP	FR17200634	EC-JGG, D-EKAG(3)
D-EJGI	Piper J-3C-65 Cub	13204	(D-EIJG), D-EJGI, OE-ABD, HB-OVO, 45-4464
D-EJGO(5)	Aquila AT-01	AT01-198	
D-EJGR	Piper PA-18 Super Cub 95	18-3454	96+30, NL+116, AC+536, AS+536, 54-754
D-EJGS	Yakovlev Yak-50	791505	DDR-WQP, DM-WQP
D-EJGZ	Cessna 172N Skyhawk	17268340	N733JX
D-EJHA(2)	Stein/ Bf 109B-1 Scale Replica	BB1	
D-EJHB(2)	Beech A36 Bonanza	E-2286	N7205C
D-EJHE	Mooney M.20F Executive	670388	N3295F
D-EJHG	Gold/ Aero Designs Pulsar XP	P 001	
D-EJHH	SAN Jodel D.150 Mascaret	54	
D-EJHK	Wassmer WA.51 Pacific	05	
D-EJHL	Cessna 172N Skyhawk	17273730	N5204J
D-EJHM	Rockwell 114B Commander	14366	PH-CGY, (PH-CHI), OO-TRL, N5788N
D-EJHO	Oberlerchner JOB 15-150/2	062	OE-CAY
D-EJHW(2)	Robin DR.400/200R Remo 200	2389	
D-EJIA	Robin R.3000/160	157	
D-EJIB(2)	Piper PA-46-310P Malibu	4608095	N9122D
D-EJIC	SAN Jodel DR.1050 Ambassadeur	199	
D-EJIF(3)	SOCATA MS.893A Rallye Commodore 180	12030	OE-DIH, F-BTJD
D-EJII	Cessna P210N Pressurized Centurion II	P21000823	N4801A, (D-EVAL), N4801A, C-GEWN, N4801A, (N828VG), N4801A
D-EJIJ	PZL-104 Wilga 35A	74191	SP-HKM, SP-FKM, PLW-191
	(Res. .13)		
D-EJIM(3)	Piper PA-18 Super Cub 95	18-1531	OO-BLV, OO-HNC, ALAT, 51-15531
D-EJIN	Piper J-3C-65 Cub	12987	(OO-TIM), OY-ALR,
	(P. 2.8.16)		D-EDMA(2), D-ECYC, HB-OCL, 44-80691
D-EJIO	Macchi MB.308	122.5895	I-BIOI, MM53075
D-EJIP(2)	Iser/ Kelly Hatz CB-1	273	
D-EJIS(2)	SOCATA TB-10 Trinidad	2112	
D-EJIZ	Piper J-3C-65 Cub	3888	HB-OXH, N25939, NC25939
D-EJJA	Cirrus SR20	1544	N53302
D-EJJF	Tecnam P.2002-JF Sierra	257	
D-EJJG	Gralfs/ Europa Avn Europa	1781	
D-EJJI	Bücker Bü.133C Jungmeister	1006	
	(Res. .13)		
D-EJJJ	Dornier Do.27B-1	192	55+59, PF+219, PF+106, PD+107
D-EJJK	Pitts S-1S Special	AB-K-334-H	(D-ERIE)
D-EJJM	Robin DR.400/180R Remo 180	2346	
D-EJJO	SAN Jodel DR.1050 Ambassadeur	123	F-BJJO
D-EJKA(2)	SNCAN/ Stampe SV.4A	396	G-BWRE, D-EJKA(2), F-BDOT, Fr.AF
	(Flies in green camouflage Fr.AF c/s)		
D-EJKB	Bäuerle/ Neico Lancair IVB	IV-00-20	
	(Displayed in Deutsches Museum at Oberschleissheim)		
D-EJKC	SOCATA TB-9 Tampico	1374	I-IAFZ
D-EJKF	Sautter/ Denney Kitfox III	1641	
D-EJKG	Seufert Sisler Cygnet SF-2A	001	
D-EJKM	Piper PA-28-140 Cherokee E	28-7225449	N11C
D-EJKO	Cessna F172G	F172-0268	
D-EJKP	Piper J-3C-40 Cub	12473	SE-AHP, NC21517
	(Identity unconfirmed)		
D-EJKS(3)	Extra EA.300/S	010	
D-EJKT	Zlin Z.526F Trenér Master	1109	DDR-WKT, DM-WKT
D-EJKU	Piper PA-46-350P Malibu Mirage	4636319	OY-LTT, N5347A, OY-LTT, N9543N
D-EJKW	Piper PA-28RT-201 Arrow IV	28R-7918049	N2187P
D-EJLE	Bölkow BO.208C Junior	582	
D-EJLH(2)	Cirrus SR22	3022	(D-ELFL(1)), N997CT
D-EJLI	Bölkow BO.208C Junior	583	
D-EJLJ	Robin DR.400/135i	2617	F-HACO
D-EJLL(2)	Zlin Z.526F Trenér Master	1113	SP-CDK
D-EJLM	Piper PA-28-235 Cherokee Charger	28-7310117	N55141
D-EJLO(2)	Aquila AT-011	AT01-217	
D-EJLP	Cessna 150J	15069417	G-BNFI, N50588
D-EJLR	Robin DR.400/180 Régent	1762	
D-EJLS	PZL-104 Wilga 80	CF20890882	OK-UKB, SP-FWS
D-EJLT	Rockwell Commander 114B	14195	PH-VON, N4865W
D-EJLU	Bölkow BO.208A Junior	550	
D-EJLW	Beech F33A Bonanza	CE-1497	
D-EJLY	Cessna 182K Skylane	18257879	N2679Q
D-EJMA	Bölkow BO.208C Junior	651	
D-EJMB	Bölkow BO.208C Junior	652	
D-EJMC(3)	SAAB MFI-15-200 Safari	15004	Uganda AF-201, Sierra Leone GST-444, SE-FIZ
	(Res. .09; under resoration)		
D-EJMD(2)	Döring/ Van's RV-4	5549	
D-EJME(2)	Cessna 182K Skylane	18258194	N3194Q
D-EJMF	Bölkow BO.208C Junior	656	
D-EJMI (2)	CASA C-1.131E Jungmann	2194	I-OPEF, E3B-574
	(Painted as '781-34')		
D-EJMK(2)	Zlin Z.526AFS Akrobat	1228	SP-CSY
	(Res. .07)		
D-EJML	Wassmer/Jodel D.120A Paris-Nice	274	OO-FDR
	(Res. .12)		
D-EJMM	Zlin Z.526F Trenér Master	1280	SP-EMM
D-EJMO(3)	American AG-5B Tiger	10149	N1197Y
D-EJMP(2)	Cessna 182Q Skylane	18266213	N759SB
D-EJMR	Cessna 172S Skyhawk SP	172S9882	OY-ZZZ, N14019
	(Res. 24.9.15)		
D-EJMS(2)	Strauber/ Neico Lancair 360	394	
D-EJMT(2)	Cessna 172N Skyhawk	17273182	N6290F
D-EJMU	Bölkow BO.208C Junior	585	
D-EJMW	Piper PA-32R-301T Turbo Saratoga SP	32R-8329035	OE-KMW, N4314B
D-EJMZ	Beech F33A Bonanza	CE-962	HB-EJM
D-EJNA	Bölkow BO.208C Junior	587	
D-EJNB	Cessna U206G Stationair 6	U20606560	PH-JNB , OY-SUV, (SE-. . .), OY-SUV, N9597Z
	(Soloy conversion .00)		
D-EJNC	Extra EA.230	002	
D-EJNG	Cessna R182 Skylane RG	R18200337	N4182C
D-EJNI	Bölkow BO.208C Junior	589	
D-EJNY	Cessna F172H	F172-0558	
D-EJNZ	SAN Jodel DR.1050 Ambassadeur	169	F-BJNZ
D-EJOA	Bücker Bü.133C Jungmeister	48	HB-MIK, U-49
D-EJOB(2)	Oberlerchner JOB 15-150/2	070	OE-DOB, (D-EKEM)
D-EJOF(4)	Piper PA-28RT-201T Turbo Arrow IV	28R-7931257	N2920F
D-EJOG	Orlican L-40 Meta-Sokol	150402	OK-NMB
D-EJOH(4)	SOCATA TB-20 Trinidad	1627	
D-EJOL	Klemm L 25Ld VIIR	798	
D-EJON(4)	Commander Aircraft 114B	14547	HB-NDB
D-EJOO	Piper PA-28-181 Archer II	2890072	HB-PLS
D-EJOP(2)	Reims/Cessna F182Q Skyline	F18200164	
D-EJOR	Erco 415CD Ercoupe	4737	N9963F, HB-ERD, OO-EXE, (NC94630)
D-EJOT(3)	Cirrus SR22	1874	N119SR
D-EJPA(2)	Reims FR172J Rocket	FR17200429	HB-CFE, D-EGJT(1)
D-EJPB	Piper PA-28-235 Cherokee Charger	28-7310007	N11C
D-EJPC	Cessna 182P Skylane	18264106	N6091F
	(Reims-assembled with "c/n" 0037)		
D-EJPD(2)	Commander Aircraft 114B	14599	
D-EJPE(2)	Reims/Cessna F152	F15201577	(F-GBQC)
D-EJPG	SOCATA TB-10 Tobago	394	
D-EJPH	SOCATA TB-10 Tobago	396	
D-EJPJ	SOCATA TB-10 Tobago	398	
D-EJPK	SOCATA TB-10 Tobago	407	

D-EJPL	SOCATA TB-20 Trinidad	408	
D-EJPO	Piper PA-22-108 Colt	22-9330	N10F
D-EJPP	Jentsch/ Prescott Pusher	055	
D-EJPQ	SOCATA TB-10 Tobago	430	
D-EJPR	SOCATA TB-20 Trinidad	424	
D-EJPS(2)	Diamond DA 20-C1 Katana	C0286	N137PS
D-EJPT	Grumman AA-5B Tiger	AA5B-0416	
D-EJPU	Beech 35-B33 Debonair	CD-499	SE-CPP, D-EJPU
D-EJQF	Robin DR.400/180R Remorqueur	1617	
D-EJQO(2)	Piper PA-18 Super Cub 95	18-3206	OL-L32, L-132, 53-4806
D-EJRD	Robin DR.400/180R Remorqueur	1660	F-WZZU
D-EJRE(2)	Reims/Cessna F172M	F17201334	D-EFCM(2), HB-CWW,
			(OE-DTU)
D-EJRF(2)	Sportavia-Pützer RF-7	7001	G-LTRF, G-EHAP,
	(Permit 10.9.15)		(G-BGVC), D-EHAP(2), F-WPXV
D-EJRO(2)	Cessna P210N Pressurized Centurion II		
		P21000239	N4619K
D-EJRP	Bellanca 17-30A Viking	76-30818	C-GBDT
D-EJRV	SOCATA TB-9 Tampico	921	
D-EJRW	Cessna 172R Skyhawk	17280198	
D-EJSA(2)	Mooney M.20JModel 205	24-3348	ZS-NPF
D-EJSB	Piper PA-28-180 Cherokee G	28-7205086	N11C
D-EJSC	Robin R.3000/160	171	
D-EJSD	Robin DR.400/180R Remo 180	2011	
D-EJSG	Cessna 182Q Skylane	18265989	N759GT
D-EJSH	Robin DR.400/180R Remo 180	2348	
D-EJSM(3)	Piper PA-28RT-201T Turbo Arrow IV	28R-8031050	N8167B, N9618N
D-EJSN	Cessna 152	15282406	OO-KMS, N68927
	(Res. .15)		
D-EJSP(2)	Mooney M.20M Model 257 TLS	27-0055	
D-EJSR(2)	Robin DR.400/180S Régent	2085	
D-EJST	Piper PA-28R-201 Arrow III	28R-7837243	N31675
D-EJSW	Champion 7GCBC Citabria	110	N1845G
D-EJSY	Piper PA-28R-201T Turbo Cherokee Arrow III		
		28R-7703099	N106WC, N9643N
D-EJTA(2)	Robin DR.400/180 Régent	2184	
D-EJTC	Cessna 182P Skylane	18263630	N6090J
D-EJTD	Cessna 182P Skylane	18263779	N6615M
	(Reims-assembled with "c/n" 0003)		
D-EJTG	Piper PA-28-161 Cadet	2841306	N9263N, N9207Z
D-EJTH(2)	Cessna T210J Turbo Centurion	T210-0408	OK-RAY, D-ELRG,
			N2258R
D-EJTI	Piper PA-28-161 Cadet	2841308	N9265N, N9208X
D-EJTJ	Piper PA-46-310P Malibu	4608105	N68FB, D-ENFB(2),
			N9132B
D-EJTL	Piper PA-28-161 Cadet	2841313	N9270N, N9210N
D-EJTM(2)	Cessna 182P Skylane	18261338	G-EEZS, D-EEZS,
	(Res. 16.9.15)		N63054, D-EEZS, (N20981)
D-EJTN	Piper PA-28-161 Cadet	2841312	N9269N, N9210F
D-EJTR	Bücker Bü.131 Jungmann	49	HB-UTR, A-38
D-EJTT	Remos GX	408	
	(Permit 14.6.12)		
D-EJTU	Beech F33A Bonanza	CE-1381	N133EK, N5579Z
D-EJUD(2)	Jud/ Steen Skybolt	M212/M202/98	
D-EJUF(2)	Beech F33A Bonanza	CE-1247	
D-EJUG(2)	Däumer/ Van's RV-4	3394	
D-EJUI (2)	Junkers A50ce Junior	3517	VH-UCC, VH-MRR,
	(Res. .09; to Junkers Museum, Dessau)		VH-UCC
D-EJUK	Klemm Kl.107B	124	
D-EJUM(3)	Piper J-3C-65 Cub	1165	(D-EDIX), G-AFFJ
D-EJUN(2)	Bücker Bü.131B Jungmann	86	D-EEEQ(2), HB-URP,
	(Res. 27.1.15)		A-73
D-EJUR(2)	Robin R.1180TD Aiglon	267	OE-DRX
D-EJUT(3)	Piper PA-28-180 Cherokee B	28-904	HB-OVV, N7174W
D-EJUW	Orlican L-40 Meta-Sokol	150409	
D-EJVC	Christen Pitts S-2B	5141	SE-KOD, N6052U
D-EJVR(2)	Maule MXT-7-180 Starcraft	14115C	
D-EJVV	SOCATA MS.894A Minerva 220	11051	OO-CCB(2), F-BRJY
	(Res. 2.10 for restoration)		
D-EJWA(2)	Mooney M.20R Ovation	29-0322	N10412
D-EJWB(2)	Piper PA-28-161 Cadet	2841083	N9169B
D-EJWD	Döring/ Europa Aviation Europa	1854AB	
D-EJWF	Piper PA-28-181 Archer II	2890148	SE-KMV
D-EJWG	Mooney M.20K Model 231	25-0400	(N4047H)
D-EJWM	Reims/Cessna F172N	F17201874	
D-EJWO	Cessna F172H	F172-0411	
D-EJWP	SOCATA TB-20 Trinidad	1100	N2805V
D-EJWS(3)	Grumman AA-5 Traveler	AA5-0355	N5455L
D-EJWU	Cessna F172H	F172-0417	
D-EJWV	Piper PA-28R-201T Turbo Arrow III	28R-7803224	N6387C
D-EJWY	CEA Jodel DR.1050 Ambassadeur	208	F-BJZE
D-EJXA	Xtreme Air Sbach 342	005	
D-EJXC	Reims/Cessna F172M	F17201007	
D-EJXH	Reims/Cessna F150L	F15000985	
D-EJXO(2)	Reims/Cessna F172M	F17201174	
D-EJXQ	Reims/Cessna F172M	F17201020	
D-EJYC(2)	SIAI-Marchetti S.205-18/R	219	
D-EJYD	Piper J-3C-65 Cub	11658	G-AJDS, 43-30367
D-EJYF	Panholzer/ Aero-Jodel D.11A Club		
		AB.5 (Liz.228/625)	
D-EJYR(3)	SOCATA MS.880B Rallye Club	1105	
D-EJYT(2)	SAN Jodel DR.1050 Ambassadeur	200	(D-ELFI)
D-EJYZ	Cessna 175A Skylark	56267	N6767E
D-EKAB(2)	Piper PA-18A-135 Super Cub	18-2810	HB-OOW, N10F
D-EKAD(4)	Cessna P210N Pressurized Centurion II		
		P21000644	N27AM, N5139W
D-EKAE	Piper PA-28R-201 Arrow III	28R-7837253	N31882
D-EKAF(4)	Reims/Cessna F172M	F17201328	D-EHOL(3), PH-JDB,
			D-EDZJ
D-EKAH(2)	Beech F33A Bonanza	CE-757	N23791
D-EKAI (2)	Robin DR.400/180 Régent	1127	
D-EKAJ(2)	Cessna 182P Skylane	18264327	N1429M
	(Reims-assembled with "c/n" 0050)		
D-EKAL(2)	Piper PA-28R-200 Cherokee Arrow II	28R-7635198	N8726E
D-EKAM(2)	Piper PA-28-181 Archer II	2890129	N9187Q
D-EKAN(3)	Cirrus SR20	1214	N930CD
D-EKAO	Piper PA-28R-201 Arrow III	28R-7837212	N9632C
D-EKAP(3)	Piper PA-28R-200 Cherokee Arrow II	28R-7435178	N41403
D-EKAR(4)	Aerostyle Breezer	11	
D-EKAS(3)	Van's RV-4	001	
	(Permit 11.1.13)		
D-EKAT(3)	Piper PA-28RT-201T Turbo Arrow IV	28R-7931185	N28518
D-EKAU(2)	Piper PA-46-350P Malibu Mirage	4622100	N558RS, N9193V
	(JetProp DLX conversion #83)		
D-EKAV(3)	American AA-1A Trainer	AA1A-0448	OY-AYH, (N6248L)
D-EKAW	Beech 35-33 Debonair	CD-27	

D-EKAY	Piper PA-18 Super Cub 95	18-1340	D-ENLG, ALAT, 51-15340
D-EKAZ(2)	Piper PA-28-181 Archer III	2843141	N9293N
D-EKBA(2)	SOCATA TB-200 Tobago XL	1798	F-WWRB
D-EKBB(3)	Fuji FA-200-180 Aero Subaru	99	OY-FRI, LX-JFY,
			LX-MDM, D-EMYY
D-EKBC	Reims FR172G Rocket	FR17200205	
D-EKBD	Reims FR172G Rocket	FR17200174	
D-EKBF(2)	Piper PA-28R-200 Cherokee Arrow II	28R-7235310	N1517T
D-EKBG	Reims/Cessna FA150K Aerobat	FA1500052	
D-EKBJ	Robin R.3000/120D	129	HB-KBT
D-EKBK	Cessna P210N Pressurized Centurion II	P21000661	N5244W
	(STOL conversion)		
D-EKBL(2)	SOCATA TB-10 Tobago	732	HB-KBL
D-EKBM(3)	Müller/ Pitts S-1BM	"2254"	
D-EKBO(2)	Piper PA-18 Super Cub 95	18-3453	96+29, NL+120, AC+509,
			AS+508, 54-753
D-EKBR	Piper PA-28R-201T Turbo Cherokee Arrow III		
		28R-7703241	N38753
D-EKBT	Beech B36TC Bonanza	EA-514	
D-EKBW	Mooney M.20F Executive	670340	N2981L
D-EKCB	Reims/Cessna F172N	F17201739	
D-EKCC(2)	Piper PA-46-350P Malibu Mirage	4636590	SP-NSA, N25906,
	(Res .16)		(SP-NSA), N9549N
D-EKCD	SOCATA MS.893A Rallye Commodore 180	11434	F-BSAT
D-EKCE(2)	Cessna 172M	17263000	N13762
	(P. 28.1.16)		
D-EKCG(2)	Commander Aircraft 114B	14548	N162A
D-EKCH	Christen A-1 Husky	1087	N9596G
D-EKCI	Oberlerchner JOB 15-180/2	065	OE-CAV
D-EKCM(2)	Driessen/ Pottier P.220S Koala	1835	
D-EKCP	Reims/Cessna F150M	F15001395	
D-EKCR	Beech 35 Bonanza	D-686	HB-ECR, NC90573
D-EKCS	Cessna 182T Skylane	18282070	PH-SLK, N61831
D-EKCT	Robin DR.400/180R Remorqueur	1331	
D-EKCW	Piper PA-28-181 Archer II	28-8190018	N8257G
D-EKDB	Mooney M.20K Model 231	25-0565	N231BW
D-EKDC(2)	Diamond DA 20-C1 Katana	C0194	N494DC
D-EKDE(3)	Piper PA-28-235 Cherokee B	28-10961	N9285W
D-EKDF(2)	Akaflieg München Mü.30 Schlacro	001	
D-EKDG	Robin DR.400/180R Remorqueur	1638	
D-EKDH	Robin DR.400/120D Dauphin	1644	
D-EKDI	Bölkow BO.208C Junior	593	
D-EKDJ	Klemm L 25 Replica	1012	
	(Permit 12.9.14, was originally quoted as c/n 2002457)		
D-EKDL	Piper PA-28-161 Warrior II	28-7916562	N2941F
D-EKDS	Rockwell Commander 114	14206	N4876W
D-EKDT	Bähr/ Aero Designs Pulsar XP	EB 00	
	(C/n now quoted as "1822" which is type cert no)		
D-EKDU	Bölkow BO.208C Junior	595	(HB-UXW)
D-EKDV	HOAC DV-20 Katana	20075	
D-EKDY(2)	Reims/Cessna F172N	F17201939	
D-EKEA	Hinz BL1-KEA	1	
D-EKEB(3)	Mooney M.20J Model 205	24-3364	
D-EKEG(3)	Reims/Cessna FR172K Hawk XP	FR17200666	N8495B
D-EKEH(2)	Piper PA-28-181 Archer II	2890080	SE-KEH
D-EKEI	Piper PA-38-112 Tomahawk	38-80A0096	N9700N
D-EKEK	Klemm Kl.107C	132	
D-EKEL(3)	SOCATA MS.893E Rallye 180GT	12633	
D-EKEN(2)	Reims/Cessna F172N	F17201991	
D-EKEP(4)	Piper PA-28-181 Archer III	2843064	N516LZ, N9282K
D-EKEU	Piper PA-46-350P Malibu Mirage	4636110	OE-KEU, G-BXER
D-EKEW(5)	Extra EA.500	01	
	(Originally built as Extra EA.400T, N501EX, converted .03)		
D-EKEZ	Aeromere F.8L Falco III	210	
D-EKFA	Champion 7GCB Challenger	7GCB-159	
D-EKFB(2)	Piper PA-28RT-201T Turbo Arrow IV	28R-8131062	N83245
D-EKFC	Mooney M.20J Model 205	24-3083	
D-EKFD(3)	Piper PA-46-350P Malibu Mirage	4622008	OE-KFD, D-ENII (2),
	(JetProp DLX conversion #82)		N9151X
D-EKFE(2)	Cub Crafters CC11-160 Carbon Cub SS		
	(Permit 10.4.13)	CC11-000250	
D-EKFF	Piper PA-28RT-201T Turbo Arrow IV	28R-8131022	N8296P
D-EKFG	Dornier Do.27A-4	471	57+40, XB+901,
	(Wears Spanish Army "U.9-51" marks)		GA+374, KD+129
	(Res 17.5.16)		
D-EKFH	CSA Sportcruiser (PiperSport)	P1102009	
	(Permit 31.1.12)		
D-EKFI	Piper PA-12 Super Cruiser	12-1528	D-EMCO, N2413M,
			NC2413M
D-EKFK	Gyroflug SC-01B-160 Speed Canard	S-22	
D-EKFL	Piper PA-28-181 Archer II	28-8190110	N8309H
D-EKFM(2)	SOCATA TB-10 Tobago	760	OE-KFM
D-EKFN	CEA DR.250/160 Capitaine	36	PH-REN
D-EKFP	Cessna 182T Skylane	18282034	(D-EPHI), N1273F
D-EKFR	Cessna 172N Skyhawk	17271154	N2093E
D-EKFS(2)	Stuttgart FS-28 Avispa	V-1/1832	D-EAFS(1)
D-EKFT	Mooney M.20J Model 201	24-0834	(N4748H)
D-EKFW	Piper PA-28-181 Cherokee Archer II	28-7690339	N6108J, N9582N
D-EKGC	Zlin Z.43	0017	LSK-22
D-EKGE	SIAI-Marchetti S.205-18/R	358	
D-EKGI	SIAI-Marchetti S.205-18/R	365	
D-EKGK(2)	Piper PA-46-350P Malibu Mirage	4636010	N92562
D-EKGL	Mooney M.20J Model 205 MSE	24-3232	N91ZL
D-EKGM	Piper PA-18-100 Super Cub	18-1527	F-BOMR , ALAT,
	(Built as PA-18 Super Cub 95)		51-15527
D-EKGN	Zlin Z.43	0022	LSK-16
D-EKGS	Robin DR.400/180R Remorqueur	1092	
D-EKGW(2)	Cirrus SR22	2896	N106PG
D-EKHA(5)	Aquila AT-01	AT01-159	F-HARB
D-EKHB(2)	Mooney M.20E Super 21	1202	HB-DWA, N9255M
D-EKHD(2)	Focke-Wulf FW.44J Stieglitz	"648"	LX-OOI, HB-EBO,
			D-EBOB(1), SE-AYY, Fv648
D-EKHF(2)	Fahr/ Jurca MJ.2 Tempête	AB-01	
	(Permit exp 4.02)		
D-EKHG(2)	SOCATA MS.887 Rallye 125	2161	(D-EAPW), F-BUCF
D-EKHK	SOCATA MS.894E Minerva 220GT	12204	F-BULC
D-EKHL(2)	SOCATA MS.893E Rallye 180GT	12207	F-BUXJ
D-EKHM(2)	SOCATA MS.893E Rallye 180GT	12525	F-BVNS
D-EKHO(2)	Piper PA-18 Super Cub 95	18-1009	RHAF115312, 51-15312
D-EKHR	Cessna F172F	F172-0094	
D-EKHS(2)	Piper PA-32RT-300T Turbo Lance II	32R-7887160	N39755
D-EKHT	SOCATA MS.894E Minerva 220GT	12146	F-BUNY
D-EKHU	Laverda F.8L Falco IV	405	
D-EKHV	SOCATA MS.894E Minerva 220GT	12203	F-BULB
D-EKHW(2)	Piper PA-28RT-201T Turbo Arrow IV	28R-8031094	
D-EKHY(2)	SOCATA MS.893A Rallye Commodore 180	10723	

D-EKHZ	Cessna 182Q Skylane	18266466	OE-KHZ, N94628
D-EKIA	Robin DR.400/180S Régent	1893	
D-EKIB(2)	Piper PA-18-150 Super Cub	18-8321	N5736Y
D-EKIF	de Havilland DH.82A Tiger Moth	83091	G-AOED, R5216
D-EKIG	SAN Jodel DR.1050 Ambassadeur	108	
D-EKIH(3)	SOCATA MS.893A Rallye Commodore 180	12078	OE-KTH , HB-ETH,
	(Built as MS.894A Minerva 220, mod 7.99)		SE-FSX
D-EKII	Diamond DA 40 Star	40332	(D-EWEA), N137NK
D-EKIK(3)	Piper PA-28-181 Archer II	2890155	PH-KIK, D-ETAN, N92117
D-EKIL(2)	SOCATA MS.893A Rallye Commodore 180	10724	
D-EKIN(3)	Piper PA-28-181 Archer II	2890141	SE-KIZ
D-EKIO	Piper PA-28-161 Cadet	2841171	SE-KIO
D-EKIP	Piper J-3C-65 Cub	9086	N42033, NC42033
D-EKIR	Piper PA-18-150 Super Cub	18-3698	HB-OOY
D-EKIS(2)	Piper J-3C-65 Cub	20791	D-ECIS(1), N2024M,
			NC2024M
D-EKIT(2)	Reims/Cessna F172N	F17201994	
D-EKIW	Beech 35-33 Debonair	CD-180	
	(Accident 18.3.16)		
D-EKIZ(2)	Bellanca 8GCBC Scout 180	92-74	OE-AOG
D-EKJB	Robin DR.400/180R Remorqueur	1001	
D-EKJF	Piper PA-28-181 Archer II	2890070	YL-ELI, D-ENEE(2),
			N4311Z
D-EKJH(2)	Beech F33A Bonanza	CE-1125	N517RM
D-EKJL(2)	Cessna R182 Skylane RG	R18200529	N1712R
D-EKJM	Montjoje/ Denney Kitfox II	1625/528	
D-EKKA	Piper J-3C-65 Cub	6298	HB-OXB, N35331,
			NC35331
D-EKKB	Reims/Cessna F150K	F15000545	
D-EKKC	Reims FR172F Rocket	FR17200130	
D-EKKD	Reims/Cessna F172H	F17200665	(D-EKKR)
D-EKKF(3)	Piper PA-18 Super Cub 95	18-1418	ALAT, 51-15418
D-EKKG	Reims/Cessna F150K	F15000616	
D-EKKH(3)	Diamond DA 20-A1 Katana	10019	N606F, (N474F), N606F,
			C-GDMY
D-EKKI	Cessna 182F Skylane	18254908	N3508U
D-EKKJ(3)	Konzelmann/Kellner Kitfox S7KK	2002478	
D-EKKK(3)	Diamond DA 20-A1 Katana	10219	N697DA, C-GDMU
D-EKKL(3)	Diamond DA 40 Star	40072	
D-EKKM(2)	Evektor EV-97 SportStar MAX	2010 1302	
D-EKKN	Reims FR172G Rocket	FR17200149	
D-EKKO(2)	Reims FR172G Rocket	FR1720185	G-EKKC, D-EKKO
D-EKKP(3)	Piper PA-28-181 Archer III	2843816	N4434F, N9517N
D-EKKR(2)	Aeronca 65C Super Chief	C.1738	D-EKON(1), HB-UPI
D-EKKS(3)	Cessna 172N Skyhawk	17272162	N8275E
D-EKKU(2)	CEA DR.253B Régent	159	
D-EKKW(3)	Cessna T182T Turbo Skylane	T18208402	N542LB
D-EKKY(3)	Hankers/ Stephens Laser	1962	
D-EKKZ	Piper PA-28-180 Cherokee Challenger	28-7305446	N55690
D-EKLB(2)	Beech A36 Bonanza	E-2444	D-EKFJ
D-EKLC	Extra EA400	04	
D-EKLE(2)	Grob G 115A	8069	
D-EKLF(3)	Cirrus SR22	3140	N985CT
D-EKLH	Piper PA-28-161 Cadet	2841125	N9511N, N9181D
D-EKLI (3)	Diamond DA 20-C1 Katana	C0177	N977DC, C-GKAH
D-EKLM	Cessna T210M Turbo Centurion	21061592	(N732LG)
D-EKLO(2)	Piper PA-18-150 Super Cub	18-4263	I-VALO, N2487P
D-EKLS	Cessna 150F	15062405	PH-ALS, N8305G
D-EKLU	Fieseler Fi.156C-2 trop Storch	110061	Fv3809, D-EXWT
D-EKLW	Beech V35B Bonanza	D-9714	N7258R
D-EKLY	Piaggio FWP.149D	119	(90+99), D-EKLY, AS+461
D-EKMB(5)	SOCATA TB-10 Tobago	1133	OE-KMB
D-EKME(2)	SOCATA TB-200 Tobago XL	1446	
D-EKMF	Mooney M.20J Model 201	24-0429	
D-EKMG	Cessna 172N Skyhawk	17270868	N739WQ
D-EKMI (3)	Piper PA-32R-301T Saratoga II TC	3257251	PH-AEI, N53423, PH-AEI,
			N9516N
D-EKMJ	Zlin Z.43	0027	LSK-21
D-EKMK	Aeromere F.8L Falco III	232	
D-EKMM(3)	Aerotek Pitts S-2A	2106	N2CQ
D-EKMN	Zlin Z.43	0018	LSK-23
D-EKMO(3)	Zlin Z.43	0012	LSK-25
D-EKMQ	Zlin Z.43	0026	LSK-20
D-EKMS(2)	Cessna TR182 Turbo Skylane RG	R18200623	N4903R
D-EKMU(2)	Reims/Cessna FR182 Skylane RG	FR18200028	
D-EKMV	SOCATA TB-20 Trinidad	724	
D-EKMW(3)	Mair/ Neico Lancair IV-PT	M001	
D-EKMX	Zlin Z.43	0025	LSK-19
D-EKMY	Bölkow BO.208C Junior	514	G-ASAS, D-ENCY(1)
D-EKMZ	Zlin Z.43	0021	LSK-27
D-EKNA	Mooney M.20F Executive	670297	N9737M
D-EKNE(3)	Cessna TR182 Turbo Skylane RG	R18200854	N737MR
D-EKNI	SOCATA MS.892A Rallye Commodore 150	10551	
D-EKNM	Cessna R182 Skylane RG	R18200568	N1809R
D-EKNO(2)	Mooney M.20J Model 201	24-0045	
D-EKNR	Piper PA-28RT-201 Arrow IV	28R-7918187	I-NALD, N2873D
D-EKNS(2)	Cessna 177RG Cardinal RG	177RG1103	N45313
D-EKOA	Piper PA-28RT-201T Turbo Arrow IV	28R-8131112	N8364Z
D-EKOB(2)	Piper PA-28R-201 Cherokee Arrow III	28R-7737170	N47499
D-EKOC(3)	Mooney M.20J Model 205	24-3064	N5684D, (N205BG),
			N5684D
D-EKOD(4)	Aviat A-1B Husky	2292	G-CDOD, N322PA
D-EKOE(2)	Kögler/ Dallach D4/E-BK/S Fascination	EB024	
D-EKOH(2)	Piper PA-18-150 Super Cub	18-3224	OL-L50, L-150, 53-4824
D-EKOL	Piper PA-18-150 Super Cub	18-5612	N10F
D-EKOM(3)	Piper PA-28RT-201T Turbo Arrow IV	28R-8031034	N3563X
D-EKOQ	Cessna 172A	47504	N9704T
D-EKOR(3)	Cessna 172R Skyhawk	17281199	N21596
D-EKOS(2)	Aquila AT-01	AT01-147	
D-EKOT(2)	Cessna F172G	F172-0274	
D-EKOX(2)	Reims/Cessna F172N	F17201685	
D-EKPA	Cessna F172E	F172-0084	
D-EKPC(2)	Mooney M.20J Model 201	24-1625	
D-EKPE(3)	Reims/Cessna F152	F15201956	
D-EKPG	Cessna 172S Skyhawk SP	172S8469	N309ME
D-EKPH(2)	Pietsch/ Aero Designs Pulsar XP	403SB	
	(Originally reserved as c/n 1836)		
D-EKPL(2)	Cessna 172N Skyhawk	17273995	N5163K
D-EKPM(2)	Paul/ Van's RV-7A	71249	
	(Permit 27.8.15)		
D-EKPO(2)	Cessna 182J Skylane	18257303	N3303F
D-EKPP	Mooney M.20J Model 201	24-0268	
D-EKPR	Piper PA-28-181 Archer II	28-8190114	N8311A
D-EKQC	Piper PA-18 Super Cub 95	18-1461	ALAT, 51-15461
D-EKQD	Piper PA-18 Super Cub 95	18-1508	ALAT, 51-15508
D-EKQF	Piper PA-18 Super Cub 95	18-1621	ALAT, 51-15621

D-EKQI (2)	Reims/Cessna F150K	F15000600	
D-EKQM	Robin DR.400/180R Remorqueur	1482	OE-KAM, D-EKFM(1)
D-EKRB(3)	Cessna F150J	F150-0451	PH-VKB, D-EEBA(1)
D-EKRD	Piper PA-38-112 Tomahawk	38-79A0920	N9697N
D-EKRE(2)	Bücker Bü.133C Jungmeister	5	HB-MKF, U-58
D-EKRF	Robin HR.100/250TR Safari	551	
D-EKRI (2)	Mudry CAP.231	09	F-GUCF, CN-ABL
D-EKRK	Korff / Impulse 130	01	
D-EKRM(2)	Cessna 172P Skyhawk SP	17274481	SE-KRM, N52285
D-EKRO(2)	Focke-Wulf FW.44J Stieglitz	2549	D-EDYV, Fv5771
D-EKRS	Cessna T210L Turbo Centurion	21059569	N4669Q
D-EKRT	Diamond DA 40 Star	40050	
D-EKRV	Knost/ Van's RV-9A	2002210/91245	
D-EKSA(2)	Piper PA-28RT-201T Turbo Arrow IV	28R-8031096	N81981
D-EKSC	Gyroflug SC-01B-160 Speed Canard	S-20	
D-EKSD	Cessna 152	15283480	N49604
D-EKSE(2)	Robin DR.400/180R Remorqueur	1396	OE-KSE, D-EISE(2)
D-EKSF	Cessna P210N Pressurized Centurion II		
		P21000503	N731NF
D-EKSG(2)	Piper PA-28-181 Archer II	28-8290075	N8020K
D-EKSK	Cessna 172S Skyhawk SP	172S8571	N323ME
D-EKSL	Cessna T210N Turbo Centurion II	21064855	(N5254U)
D-EKSO(2)	Robin DR.400/180R Remorqueur	1708	OE-KBF, D-EEWF(2)
D-EKSR	Robin DR.400/180S Régent	2035	
D-EKSS	Mooney M.20J Model 205	24-3278	(PH-SXS), D-EKSS
D-EKSU	Cessna 150D	15060091	N7991Z
D-EKSV	Diamond DA 20-A1 Katana	10122	N549SS, C-GKAQ
D-EKSW	Robin DR.400/180R Remorqueur	844	
D-EKSY(2)	Piper PA-28-180 Cherokee C	28-3535	F-OCJU, N9424J
D-EKTB	SOCATA TB-10 Tobago	371	
D-EKTC	Piper PA-28R-201T Turbo Arrow III	28R-7803364	N21431
D-EKTD	SOCATA TB-10 Tobago	374	
D-EKTF	SOCATA TB-10 Tobago	375	
D-EKTG	SOCATA TB-10 Tobago	376	
D-EKTH	SOCATA TB-9 Tampico	387	
D-EKTI (2)	Beech A-36 Bonanza	E-1646	
D-EKTJ	SOCATA Rallye 180TS Galérien	3374	
D-EKTK	SOCATA TB-10 Tobago	366	
D-EKTL	Xtreme Air XA-41 Sbach 300	04	
	(P 30.8.11)		
D-EKTM	SOCATA TB-10 Tobago	367	
D-EKTN(3)	Cessna U206G Stationair	U20606768	N9949Z
D-EKTO	Cessna F172G	F172-0180	
D-EKTS(2)	Boeing Stearman B75N1	75-7319	N58756, BuA07715
	(P 11.7.13)		
D-EKTT(2)	Aerostyle Breezer B600	035LSA	
	(P. 14.6.16)		
D-EKTV	Cessna 182T Skylane	18282107	OE-KTV, N62849
D-EKUB(4)	Piper PA-18-150 Super Cub	18-7552	(D-EDDJ(3)), OE-COS,
			OE-BIM, N3814Z
D-EKUC(2)	Piper PA-28-180 Cherokee Challenger	28-7305470	N55791
D-EKUF	Beech G35 Bonanza	D-4713	N12B
D-EKUG	Cessna 150	17818	N6418T
D-EKUH(2)	Luscombe 8F Silvaire	6295	HB-DUC, NC1868B
D-EKUI	Dornier Do.27A-4	230	D-EKUT(2), D-EBAJ,
	(Damaged 27.8.16)		55+83, YA+907, D-EHYL
D-EKUJ(3)	Konzelmann/Kellner/ Denney Kitfox S7KK	2002478	
D-EKUL(2)	Piper PA-28-181 Archer II	28-8090042	N2322U
D-EKUM	Rhein RW-3-P75 Multoplan	2	
D-EKUN(3)	SOCATA MS.893E Rallye 180GT	12180	F-BUCN
D-EKUQ	Piper PA-18-100 Super Cub	18-6413	N8974D
	(Converted from PA-19 Super Cub 95)		
D-EKUR(2)	Mooney M.20K Model 231	25-0437	(N3655H)
D-EKUT(3)	Dornier Do.27Q-4	2024	HB-FAA
D-EKUW(2)	Piper PA-28RT-201T Turbo Arrow IV	28R-8031167	N82557
D-EKVA(2)	Beech A36 Bonanza	E-2328	N2644M
D-EKVF	Robin DR.400/180 Régent	1697	G-BLYS
D-EKVH	Piper PA-46-310P Malibu	46-8408041	(F-GTFM), D-EKVH,
			HB-PKB , (D-EIDN(2)), HB-PKB, D-ERAS,
			HB-PKB, (D-ERAS), HB-PKB, D-ELBU(3), N43467
D-EKVL	Robin DR.400/180R Remorqueur	1196	
D-EKVM(2)	Cessna U206G Stationair 6-II	U20605474	HB-CLK, N6394U
D-EKVW	Cessna P210N Pressurized Centurion	P21000579	N732GV
	(Robertson STOL conversion)		
D-EKWA(4)	Cessna 182P Skylane	18264136	N6234F
	(Reims-assembled with "c/n" 0041)		
D-EKWF	Piper PA-28-140 Cherokee E	28-7225456	N11C
D-EKWG(2)	Mooney M.20K Model 252 TSE	25-1091	N252YW
D-EKWM	Cessna 182E Skylane	18254307	OE-DDE, N3307Y
D-EKWP(2)	Robin DR.500/200i Président	0041	F-HBCI
	(Res .16)		
D-EKWR(2)	Robin DR.400/180 Régent	2327	
D-EKWS(2)	Robin DR.400/180RP Remorqueur	1790	
D-EKWT	Piper PA-24-260 Turbo Comanche C	24-4937	N9429P
D-EKXA	Beech F33C Bonanza	CJ-29	
D-EKXB	CEA DR.253B Régent	162	
D-EKXC	CEA DR.253B Régent	164	
D-EKXD	CEA DR.253B Régent	166	
D-EKXL	Piper PA-18-135 Super Cub	18-3131	PH-LRM, OO-GDH,
			OL-L57, 53-4731
D-EKYF	Bücker Bü181B-1	25016	Fv25016
D-EKYL	Piper PA-18 Super Cub 95	18-4462	N2872P
D-EKYM(2)	Scheibe SF.23B Sperling	2019	
D-EKYP	Scheibe SF.23A Sperling	2008	
D-EKYS(2)	Mooney M.20J Model 201	24-1095	
D-EKYT(3)	Piper PA-28-140 Cherokee C	28-26868	N5967U
D-EKYV(2)	Piper PA-28R-200 Cherokee Arrow	28R-35750	N5018S
D-EKYW(2)	Robin DR.400/180 Régent	1702	
D-EKZI	Piper PA-28-140 Cherokee	28-21427	N11C
D-EKZK	SEEMS MS.880B Rallye Club	371	F-BKZK
D-EKZO	Piper PA-28-140 Cherokee	28-21443	N11C
D-EKZY	Piper PA-28-140 Cherokee	28-21419	N11C
D-ELAA(2)	Flight Design MC-ELA	A-11-01-31	
	(Permit exp 25.5.13)		
D-ELAB(2)	Cessna 152	15280850	N25908
D-ELAD(2)	Reims/Cessna F172P	F17202232	
D-ELAE(2)	Flight Design CT LS-ELA	F-11-07-06	
	(Permit 28.11.11)		
D-ELAF(2)	Cirrus SR20	2055	N213CL
D-ELAH(2)	Gardan GY-80 Horizon 180	141	
D-ELAI (2)	Flight Design CT LS	F09-01-10	
D-ELAJ(2)	Stinson L-5C Sentinel	unkn	I-AEEP, MM52839
	(Permit 29.12.11) (Painted as '298491')		
D-ELAL(5)	American AG-5B Tiger	10143	PH-MLD
D-ELAM(2)	Piper PA-28RT-201 Arrow IV	28R-7918175	N2853L
D-ELAN(2)	Bramsche/ Piel CP.301 Emeraude	AB.419	

Regn	Type	c/n	Previous identities
D-ELAO(2)	Piper PA-46-310P Malibu (JetProp DLX conversion #141)	46-8608019	HB-POA, I-GHIO, G-BMMT, N9230T
D-ELAP(3)	Flight Design CT LS-ELA (Permit 14.5.12)	F-11-10-09	
D-ELAQ(2)	Piper PA-28-181 Cherokee Archer II	28-7890432	N9567N
D-ELAR(3)	Robin DR.400/RP Remorqueur	1793	
D-ELAS(2)	Zlin Z.126 Trenér 2	865	OE-AES, 2A-AN
D-ELAT(3)	Flight Design CT LS-ELA (Permit 5.7.11)	F-11-04-01	
D-ELAU	Piper PA-28-140 Cherokee Cruiser	28-7325296	N11C
D-ELAV(3)	Piper PA-28-181 Archer II	28-8190151	N8326B
D-ELAW(2)	Bölkow BO.208C Junior	627	
D-ELAX(2)	Flight Design CT LS-ELA (Permit 5.10)	F-10-03-01	
D-ELAY	Bellanca 17-31 ATC Turbo Viking	72-31034	
D-ELAZ(2)	Robin DR.300/108 2+2	542	
D-ELBA(3)	Diamond DA 20-A1 Katana	10276	C-GAHT, N576DA, C-GKAX
D-ELBB	SAN Jodel D.150 Mascaret	30	
D-ELBC(2)	Robin R.2160D Acrobin	121	(F-ODHO)
D-ELBD(3)	Piper PA-28-181 Archer III	2843079	N9273N
D-ELBE(4)	Cessna 182R Skylane	18268208	(N2499E)
D-ELBH(2)	SOCATA MS.880B Rallye Club	1372	F-BRRB
D-ELBL(2)	Piper PA-18-135 Super Cub	18-3944	(D-EBKP(1)), EI-245, I-EIQS, 54-2544
D-ELBM(2)	Beech A23-19 Musketeer Sport III	MB-35	HB-ENS
D-ELBO(2)	Piper PA-28-235 Cherokee D	28-11375	N8573N
D-ELBS(2)	Piper PA-28-181 Cherokee Archer II	28-7890317	OY-CBS, (N3614M), (D-EIIW), OY-CBS, N3614M
D-ELBT(2)	Robin DR.400/RP Remorqueur	1798	
D-ELBW(2)	Cirrus SR22T (Res. .12; still US-regd 4.16)	0166	N332BW
D-ELCA	Göbel/ Binder CP.301S Smaragd	AB.434	
D-ELCB	Fuji FA-200-180 Aero Subaru	272	
D-ELCC	Piper PA-38-112 Tomahawk	38-79A0672	N9697N
D-ELCD	Piper PA-38-112 Tomahawk	38-80A0095	N9689N
D-ELCE(3)	Cirrus SR22	1460	N372CD
D-ELCG	Reims/Cessna F172N Skyhawk II	F17201947	
D-ELCH(3)	Commander Aircraft 114B	14566	
D-ELCM	Piper PA-28-181 Archer II	28-8690043	N565DH, N9202C, N9274Y
D-ELCO(4)	Diamond DA 40 Star	40256	C-GDMQ
D-ELCP	Mooney M.20G Statesman	680070	N3969N
D-ELCQ	Piper PA-28-140 Cherokee	28-24206	N1783J
D-ELCR	SNCAN/ Stampe SV.4C	20	F-BLCO, Fr.AF
D-ELCS(2)	Cessna 182Q Skylane	18267140	N97586, D-ELCS, N97586
D-ELCT	Piper PA-28-181 Archer II	2890049	N9130X
D-ELCU	Piper PA-18 Super Cub 95	18-3114	L-40, 53-4714
D-ELCV	Piper PA-28-161 Warrior II	28-8216045	N9591N
D-ELCW	Piper PA-28R-201T Turbo Arrow	2803010	N9185X
D-ELCX(2)	Piper PA-28-161 Archer III	2842212	D-EZFV, D-EXPA(2), N30970
D-ELCY	CEA DR.250/160 Capitaine	93	
D-ELCZ	SOCATA Rallye 235E-D	12907	I-ALCH, F-GBXC, (YV-1445)
D-ELDA	Wassmer WA.52 Europa	61	"D-EFDA"
D-ELDB	Piper PA-28RT-201 Arrow IV	28R-8018067	N8198Z
D-ELDC(2)	Piper PA-28-181 Archer III	2890208	SE-KXF
D-ELDD	Beech F33A Bonanza	CE-869	
D-ELDI (2)	Piper PA-28-236 Dakota	28-7911065	N2151J
D-ELDK(2)	Mooney M.20M Model 257 TLS	27-0027	
D-ELDL	Fairchild F-24W-41A Argus 2	857	N24WM, D-EHUL(1), HB-EAB, HB620, 43-14893
D-ELDM(2)	SOCATA TB-20 Trinidad	860	OY-CDM
D-ELDO(3)	Piper PA-28-161 Cadet	2841340	N9215Q, OH-PFI, N128ND, (OH-PFI), (OH-PFA)
D-ELDP	Robin DR.400/180R Remorqueur	1461	
D-ELDS	Diamond DA 40D Star	D4.253	
D-ELDT(2)	Remos GX (Permit 10.10)	310	D-ERGX(1)
D-ELEA	Cessna F172H	F172-0394	
D-ELEB(2)	CASA C-1.131E Jungmann	2145	E3B-528
D-ELEC(2)	Piper PA-28-181 Archer III	2890214	N92513
D-ELED(2)	HOAC DV-20 Katana	20026	
D-ELEE(2)	Cessna 172S Skyhawk A1 (Centurion 2.0S engine)	172S10099	N23644
D-ELEF(3)	Robin DR.400/RP Remorqueur	1818	
D-ELEG(3)	Diamond DA 20-A1 Katana	10017	N126MF, N517WA, C-GKAC
D-ELEK(3)	SOCATA TB-10 Tobago	143	F-GCOH
D-ELEL(3)	Cessna 172S Skyhawk SP	172S10793	OO-GCF, N6202S
D-ELEN(2)	Piper PA-28-140 Cherokee D	28-7125103	N1788T
D-ELEO	Reims FR172H Rocket	FR17200228	N9448
D-ELEP	Diemer/ Piel CP.301A Emeraude	AB.404	
D-ELEQ	Klemm Kl.107C	148	
D-ELER(2)	Diamond DA 40D Star	D4.212	OE-VPU
D-ELES(4)	Bücker Bü.181B-1 Bestmann (Res .16)	25053	D-ELES(1), Fv25053
D-ELET(4)	Piper PA-32R-301T Saratoga II TC	3257056	N41257
D-ELEV(2)	Piaggio FWP.149D	144	91+22, GA+405, AS+079, (KB+121)
D-ELEW(3)	Benz Leonardo 2000 (Res. .10)	2002435	
D-ELEX(3)	Piper PA-46-350P Malibu Mirage (JetProp DLX conversion #80)	4636105	N92832
D-ELEY(2)	Mooney M.20J Model 201	24-0231	PH-IHD, N201HD
D-ELFB(2)	Cessna 172S Skyhawk SP	172S9837	N703FB
D-ELFC	Piper PA-28R-180 Cherokee Arrow	28R-30398	N4539J
D-ELFE(3)	Grob G 115A	8060	I-GROF
D-ELFF(2)	Piper PA-28-181 Archer II	28-8090068	N8077M
D-ELFG	Piper PA-28R-200 Cherokee Arrow II	28R-7335243	N55221
D-ELFH(2)	Aquila AT-01-100C	AT01-309	(D-EQIS)
D-ELFI (3)	Piper PA-28-140 Cherokee E	28-7225112	N11C
D-ELFK(2)	Robin DR.400/180R Remo 180	2513	
D-ELFL(2)	Cirrus SR22	3141	N983CT
D-ELFM(2)	Cirrus SR20	1444	SE-LUH, (D-EPMX), LN-MRO, N824JA
D-ELFN	Reims/Cessna F172M	F17201499	
D-ELFP	Cessna 182N Skylane	18260301	N92663
D-ELFR	Robin DR.400/180 Régent	1341	
D-ELFS(2)	Robin DR.400/180R Remorqueur	1875	
D-ELFT(2)	Piper PA-28-161 Cadet	2841287	N9526N, N92043
D-ELFU(2)	LFU 205	V-1	
D-ELFX	Cessna R182 Skylane RG	R18201823	(D-ERUL), PH-LFX, N5149T
D-ELFY(2)	SOCATA MS.894A Minerva 220	11626	
D-ELGA(2)	PZL-104 Wilga 35A	21930951	
D-ELGC	Piper PA-18 Super Cub 95	18-6456	N9084D
D-ELGD(2)	Cessna 182T Skylane	18282151	N5087G
D-ELGE(2)	Piper PA-38-112 Tomahawk	38-79A0447	N9729N
D-ELGG(2)	Cessna 172S Skyhawk SP	172S10218	N6049G
D-ELGH(2)	Piper PA-28R-200 Cherokee Arrow II	28R-7535150	N33426
D-ELGI(2)	Piper PA-28-151 Cherokee Warrior	28-7415150	N9513N
D-ELGK	Piper PA-12 Super Cruiser	12-2345	N3501M, NC3501M
D-ELGL(2)	Cessna 172N Skyhawk	17271825	N5297E
D-ELGM	Piper PA-24-250 Comanche	24-782	N5708P
D-ELGN	Cessna F172F	F172-0107	
D-ELGR(2)	Cessna 172N Skyhawk	17271094	N1687E
D-ELGS(2)	Cessna 182T Skylane	18282157	N5103L
D-ELGT(2)	Cessna 182R Skylane	18268360	N6349E
D-ELGV	CEA DR.315 Petit Prince	448	
D-ELGX	Cessna 182T Skylane	18282158	N5104H
D-ELGY(3)	Cessna 182T Skylane	18282304	N92978
D-ELGZ	Cessna 182T Skylane	18282165	N5238F
D-ELHC(2)	Piper PA-28-181 Archer III	2843356	N4136U
D-ELHF(2)	Mooney M.20J Model 201	24-1610	N5752E
D-ELHG(3)	Robin DR.400/180 Régent	1600	
D-ELHH(2)	Aerospool WT-9 Dynamic (Permit 12.3.12)	DY-429/2012	
D-ELHI (3)	Piper PA-28-181 Archer III	2843395	SP-KWR, N4185B, N9522N
D-ELHK	Beech V35B Bonanza	D-10020	
D-ELHL(2)	Piper PA-32R-301T Turbo Saratoga SP	32R-8429013	N4360H
D-ELHM	Piper PA-18 Super Cub 95	18-1336	ALAT, 51-15336
D-ELHN	Reims/Cessna F172M	F17201141	HB-CEG
D-ELHP(2)	Van's RV-7HM	2002553	
D-ELHQ	CEA DR.300/180R Remorqueur (Conv from DR.315)	479	
D-ELHS	Fuji FA-200-180 Aero Subaru	80	
D-ELHT	Piper PA-18 Super Cub 95 (Fuselage no. 18-1085)	18-1015	ALAT, 51-15318
D-ELHU(3)	de Havilland DH.82A Tiger Moth	83786	N82JH, N8052, D-EFPH, T7410
D-ELHY(2)	Grumman AA-5B Tiger	AA5B-0975	G-BLHP, OO-RTH, (OO-HRR)
D-ELIA(2)	CEA Jodel DR.1050 Ambassadeur	535	HB-KCC, D-EBEI (1), F-BLZF
D-ELIB(2)	Reims/Cessna F150M	F15001419	
D-ELIC(3)	Cessna TR182 Turbo Skylane RG II	R18201847	HB-CIC, (D-EITW), N5275T, (D-EITW)
D-ELID(3)	Beech C33A Debonair	CE-103	HB-EHF
D-ELIE(2)	Piper PA-32-300 Cherokee Six	32-7840182	G-KFRA, G-BGII, N20879
D-ELIF(4)	Reims/Cessna FR182 Skylane RG	FR1820029	N4102D, PH-CTM, SE-IBB
D-ELIG(3)	Piper PA-28-140 Cherokee Cruiser	28-7325309	N11C
D-ELII	Piper PA-28-140 Cherokee C	28-26664	N5833U
D-ELIL(4)	Piper PA-28-181 Archer II	28-7990114	N3020A
D-ELIO	CEA DR.253B Régent	172	
D-ELIP(4)	Aquila AT-01 100B	AT01-326	
D-ELIR(3)	Cessna 305C/L-19E Bird Dog (Res. .11)	24539	F-GFVD, ALAT
D-ELIT(2)	Piper PA-28R-201T Turbo Arrow III	28R-7803363	N21349
D-ELIV(4)	CEA DR.1051 Sicile (Res. .07 but still current in Italy 2014)	543	I-POBA
D-ELIY(2)	Nowack Lightning LS-1 (P 16.8.12)(W/o 12.11.12)	89	
D-ELIZ(2)	SOCATA ST-10 Diplomate	120	
D-ELJC	Piper PA-28-181 Archer III	2843439	N50104
D-ELJH	Hirt Starlite SL-1 (New Permit 7.08)	0001	
D-ELJI	Robin R.1180TD Aiglon	242	HB-EQI
D-ELJK(2)	Diamond DA 40D Star	D4.108	
D-ELJL	Piper PA-28R-200 Cherokee Arrow	28R-35233	F-BSEH, HB-OZS, N2628R
D-ELJM	Cessna F172G (Res .16)	F172-0249	I-ALJM
D-ELJP	Cessna F172G (Res. 27.5.15)	F172-0192	I-ALJP
D-ELJR	SAN Jodel DR.1050M-1 Excellence	468	(D-EHPL), F-BLJR
D-ELKA(3)	Piper PA-28R-201T Turbo Cherokee Arrow III	28R-7703174	N5982V
D-ELKC	Piper PA-28-181 Archer III	2843246	N4135Z
D-ELKE(2)	Piper PA-28-161 Warrior II	2816062	N9138N
D-ELKG(2)	Piper PA-18-150 Super Cub	18-7709056	D-EGFS, HB-PBM, N38524
D-ELKI (2)	Reims/Cessna F172N	F17201918	
D-ELKL	Remos GX (Permit 22.4.10)	362	
D-ELKN	Cessna 172R Skyhawk	17281208	N2109J
D-ELKO(5)	American Champion 7GCAA	502-2005	G-JOIE
D-ELKR(2)	Leverkusen/ Rand-Robinson KR-2/B	1808/002	
D-ELKS	Piaggio P.149D	256	91+74, D-EBCI, AC+407, AS+4-7
D-ELKU(2)	Reims/Cessna FR172K Hawk XP	FR17200656	
D-ELKW(2)	Piper PA-22-108 Colt (Res. .11)	22-9365	D-EFQI, N10F
D-ELKX	Piper PA-28-181 Archer III	2843605	(D-ESLH), N355SE, N31048
D-ELKY	Pützer Elster B	032	
D-ELLA(2)	SOCATA MS.894E Minerva 220GT	12198	F-BVZB
D-ELLB(2)	Piper PA-28-236 Dakota	2811024	N91637
D-ELLC	Piper PA-28-161 Warrior II	28-8116178	(N83514)
D-ELLD	Piper PA-28RT-201T Turbo Arrow IV	28R-7931303	N8090P
D-ELLE(2)	Neico Lancair IV Propjet (Permit 27.8.14)	2002219	
D-ELLF(2)	Colomban MC-100 Ban-bi	80	
D-ELLH	Piper PA-28-181 Archer II	2890134	N9190V
D-ELLI	Cessna 210	57339	N9539T
D-ELLJ(2)	Cirrus SR22 g3 (Res. .13, still US-regd 4.16)	2874	N387SR
D-ELLK	Piper PA-28-161 Cadet	2841288	N9527N, N92067
D-ELLL(2)	Robin HR.200/120B	44	HB-EXK
D-ELLM(2)	Nord 1002 Pingouin	88	N108U, F-BBBZ, Fr.AF
D-ELLN	Piper PA-28-161 Warrior II	2816058	N9132Z
D-ELLQ(2)	SOCATA MS.893A Rallye Commodore 180	11839	
D-ELLS	SOCATA MS.883 Rallye 115	1587	F-BTHK
D-ELLT(2)	Cirrus SR20	1011	N124CD
D-ELLU(2)	Piper PA-28-181 Archer II	28-8190271	N8408T
D-ELLV(2)	Rockwell Commander 112A	416	SE-FLV, (N1416J)
D-ELLX	Piper PA-28-181 Archer II	2890101	N9158Z

D-ELLY(3)	DHC-1 Chipmunk 22	C1/0584	G-JAKE, G-BBMY, WK565
D-ELLZ	Cessna 182R Skylane	18267974	(PH-AXO), N9650H
D-ELMA(2)	Piper PA-28-235 Cherokee Pathfinder	28-7510110	N1589X, N9584N
D-ELMC(2)	Mooney M.20K Model 252 TSE	25-1116	
D-ELMH	Grumman AA-5B Tiger	AA5B-0107	
D-ELMI (3)	Cessna 182J Skylane	18257426	N3426F
D-ELMK	Beech A36 Bonanza	E-1544	
D-ELMM(2)	Robin DR.400/180 Régent	2006	
D-ELMN(2)	Piper PA-28-181 Cherokee Archer II	28-7890456	SX-ABS, N30682
	(W/o 8.9.15 Toses, Girona, Spain)		
D-ELMO	CEA Jodel DR.1050 Ambassadeur	210	
D-ELMP	Aviat A-1 Husky	1282	N6091X
D-ELMR	Bareiss/ Brändli BX-2 Cherry	Eb 001/83	
D-ELMS(2)	Piper PA-28RT-201T Turbo Arrow IV	28R-8031133	N82377
D-ELMT	Cessna T210N Turbo Centurion II	21064530	N9507Y
	(Robertson STOL conversion)		
D-ELMW(2)	Aquila AT-01 100B	AT01-336	
D-ELMY(3)	Aviat A-1 Husky	1325	
D-ELMZ	Piper PA-28-180 Cherokee D	28-5156	LN-LMZ
D-ELNA(2)	Cessna F172G	F172-0238	
D-ELNB	Cessna F172H	F172-0530	
D-ELNC	Cessna F150H	F150-0357	
D-ELNF	Cessna F172H	F172-0540	
D-ELNI (2)	Piper PA-18 Super Cub 95 (L-18C)	18-456	RHAF 800, 50-1800
D-ELNN(2)	SOCATA Rallye 110ST Galopin	3383	F-GENN, F-OGMB
D-ELNY(2)	Beech F33A Bonanza	CE-787	
D-ELOA	Piper PA-28-161 Warrior II	28-8016239	N9613N
D-ELOB(3)	Reims/Cessna F172M	F17201103	
D-ELOC	Piper PA-18-150 Super Cub	18-6635	OO-CIP, N10F, N9370D
D-ELOF	Piper PA-18-135 Super Cub	18-2490	HB-OEC, N10F
D-ELOG(2)	Cessna F150G	F150-0096	
D-ELOH(3)	PZL-104 Wilga 80	CF15810612	YU-DHY
D-ELOK(2)	Piper PA-18-150 Super Cub	18-8797	N4450Z
D-ELOL(3)	Cessna F172G	F172-0207	
D-ELON(5)	Extra EA.300/S	004	OK-XJS, G-CCBD, OK-XTA, D-EBEW
D-ELOP(4)	Extra EA.300/200	023	C-GOEX, N32CP
D-ELOR(3)	Cessna T210N Turbo Centurion II	21064184	OH-ARI, OY-CKV, D-EHSD, (N5368Y)
D-ELOS(3)	Diamond DA 20-A1 Katana	10216	N691DA, C-GDMY
D-ELOT(3)	Reims/Cessna F152	F15201637	OY-BNC
D-ELOU	Beech A23A Musketeer	M-937	N2338W
D-ELOV(3)	Piper PA-32RT-300T Turbo Lance II	32R-7887155	N39728
D-ELOW	Piper PA-18-150 Super Cub	18-7095	
D-ELOX	Klemm Kl.35D	1959	LN-TAI, Fv5040
	(Res. .05, on rebuild)		
D-ELOY	Reims/Cessna F182Q Skylane	F18200073	
D-ELOZ(2)	Robin DR.300/108 2+2	526	
	(Dismantled)		
D-ELPA(3)	Piper PA-28-181 Archer III	2843590	N3043N
D-ELPC	Piper PA-28-181 Cherokee Archer II	28-7790292	N9586N
D-ELPD	Reims/Cessna F172N	F17201825	
D-ELPE(3)	Mooney M.20J Model 201	24-1280	N361SB, N201BQ
D-ELPF	SIAI-Marchetti SF.260C	715/ 47-004	I-ALPF
D-ELPG(3)	PZL-104 Wilga 35A	18840776	SE-IYT, SP-WDD
D-ELPH	Cessna 172P Skyhawk	17275583	YL-YES, N64569
D-ELPI (4)	Cessna 172S Skyhawk SP	172S9980	N2310W
D-ELPK	Mooney M.20C Ranger	20-1255	
D-ELPL	Cessna P210N Pressurized Centurion II	P21000535	N46932, D-ELPL, (N731QW)
D-ELPM(2)	Piper PA-28-161 Warrior II	28-8116298	N8427H
D-ELPN	HOAC DV-20 Katana	20023	
D-ELPP(2)	HOAC DV-20 Katana	20094	N194DV
D-ELPR	Hohenstein/ Europa Avn Europa	190SB	
	(Converted to tri-gear)		
D-ELPS(2)	Styrsky/ Neico Lancair 235 Pegasos	001/475	
D-ELPT	Fuji FA-200-180AO Aero Subaru	261	
D-ELPU(2)	Reims/Cessna F172P	F17202149	
D-ELPV	Piper PA-28-181 Archer III	2843666	N60853
D-ELPX	Piper PA-28-181 Archer III	2843675	N6092U, N9515N
D-ELPY(2)	SOCATA MS.893E Rallye 180GT	12315	F-GFVX, HB-ETG, F-BUZC
D-ELQC	Piper PA-28-181 Archer III	2843558	N53654, D-ELQC
D-ELQE	SEEMS MS.885 Super Rallye	5412	
D-ELQI	Cessna 172E	17251424	N5524T
D-ELQU	Mooney M.20A	1597	N6009X
D-ELQY	Piper PA-18 Super Cub 95	18-3083	L-9, 53-4683
D-ELRA(4)	Cessna T206H Turbo Stationair	T20608316	N3549Z
D-ELRB	Reims FR172F Rocket	FR17200096	
D-ELRD	Reims FR172F Rocket	FR17200095	
D-ELRE(2)	Reims/Cessna F152 II	F15201763	
D-ELRF(2)	Piper PA-28-140 Cherokee C	28-26670	N5839U
D-ELRI (3)	Hartz/ Piel CP.301E Emeraude	AB.405	D-ECAG(2)
D-ELRM(2)	Mudry CAP.231	11	HB-MSV, G-PELG, G-OPPS, F-GGYN, F-WZCI, G-OPPS
D-ELRO(2)	Beech B36TC Bonanza	EA-377	N67269
D-ELRP	Reims/Cessna F182Q Skylane	F18200056	
D-ELRS	Robin DR.400/180R Remorqueur	1231	
D-ELRT	SOCATA MS.894A Minerva 220	11075	HB-ERT, F-BRMF
D-ELRY	Gardan GY-80 Horizon 160	64	
D-ELSA(3)	Piper PA-28R-200 Cherokee Arrow II	28R-7535039	N9614N
D-ELSD	Cessna 152	15281427	N49987
D-ELSG	Robin DR.400/180R Remorqueur	1404	OO-KAC, OE-DKU
D-ELSI (2)	Piper PA-28-181 Cherokee Archer II	28-7790206	N9547N
D-ELSJ(2)	Beech F33A Bonanza	CE-1139	OY-BVU
D-ELSK	CASA C-1.131E Jungmann	2120	E3B-417
D-ELSM	SAN Jodel D.117A Grand Tourisme	839	F-BITL
D-ELSO	SAN Jodel DR.1050 Ambassadeur	396	
D-ELSP	Grob G 115A	8016	
D-ELSR(2)	Robin DR.400/180R Remo 180	2012	
D-ELSS	Zlin Z.50LA	0022	EC-DLV
	(Res .16)		
D-ELST(2)	Cessna 172N Skyhawk	17273727	(D-EGPB(2)), N5196J
D-ELSU(3)	Piper PA-32RT-301 Saratoga SP	32R-8013088	N8188M
D-ELSV(2)	Reims/Cessna F172P	F17202242	
D-ELSX	Piper PA-28-181 Archer III	2843674	N6092N
D-ELSZ	PZL-104 Wilga 80	CF15810604	YU-DHS
D-ELTA(2)	Reims/Cessna F172N	F17201940	EC-IYJ, D-EOVV(2)
D-ELTB(2)	Reims/Cessna F182Q Skylane II	F18200082	
D-ELTC(2)	Reims/Cessna F182Q Skylane	F18200139	
D-ELTE(2)	Piper PA-12 Super Cruiser	12-1874	N3204M, NC3204M
D-ELTG(2)	HOAC DV-20 Katana	20022	
D-ELTI (3)	Piper PA-12 Super Cruiser	12-3462	D-ELQB, D-ELOB, N4036H, NC4036H
D-ELTK(2)	Robin DR.400/135Tdi	2587	(D-EAIA)
	(Built as DR.400/140B, convtd .05) (W/o 1.9.16)		
D-ELTM	Mooney M.20F Executive	680147	
D-ELTO(2)	Schoon/TEAM MiniMax 1600R	1883	
	(C/n now MK118?) (Permit exp 6.01, believed to France as 57-UY later)		
D-ELTU(3)	Cessna 170B	20615	HB-CYV, N2463D, N550PB, OO-SPB, D-EMOX, N2463D
D-ELTV	Diamond DA 20-A1 Katana	10319	N202TB, N319DA, C-FDVP
D-ELTW	Diamond DA 20-A1 Katana	10324	C-FDVT
D-ELTY(2)	Pützer Elster B	008	97+06, D-EDEQ
D-ELTZ	Cessna T210N Turbo Centurion II	21064486	ZS-LTU, N9364Y
D-ELUC(2)	Piper PA-28R-201T Turbo Cherokee Arrow III		
	(Dam. 15.2.95; cld, rebt; restd. 2.06)	28R-7703370	N47401
D-ELUD	Zlin Z.126M	841	
	(Converted from Trenér 2,7.81, with M332 engine)		
D-ELUF(2)	Piper PA-18-180 Super Cub	18-2046	PH-LUF , PH-JWK, R-50, 52-2446
	(Originally built as Super Cub 95 / L-18C)		
D-ELUH(2)	Piper PA-28R-201T Turbo Cherokee Arrow III	28R-7703324	N43986
D-ELUI	Reims/Cessna F172N	F17201719	
D-ELUK(2)	Piper PA-18-150 Super Cub	18-7446	N6813P
D-ELUM	Piper J-3C-65 Cub	11005	HB-OFG, 43-29714
	(C/n officially listed as 13249 which was originally HB-OCK ex 45-4509. HB-OFG used the same paperwork on conversion but D-ELUM is definitely f/n 10830 = c/n 11005)		
D-ELUP(3)	Reims/Cessna F172N	F17201528	PH-SRO , OO-LWC, PH-SRO
	(Dam. 31.7.06)		
D-ELUV(2)	Cessna 170B	20471	D-ELIL, OO-SPA, N2319D
D-ELUW(2)	Aeromere F.8L Falco III	226	
D-ELUX(3)	Cirrus SR20	2035	N103CS
D-ELVA	Cessna F172E	F172-0067	
D-ELVB(2)	Hoffmann H-40-02	002	D-EABY(3)
D-ELVC(2)	Piper PA-28-181 Archer III	2943324	N41770, N9514N, N4171X
D-ELVD	Reims FR172F Rocket	FR17200085	
D-ELVE(2)	Piper PA-28R-200 Cherokee Arrow II	28R-7635327	N6255J
D-ELVG(2)	Robin DR.400/180R Remo 180	2383	
D-ELVH	Reims FR172F Rocket	FR17200117	
D-ELVI (3)	Reims/Cessna F182P Skylane	F18200002	D-ELLE(2)
D-ELVJ	Reims FR172F Rocket	FR17200118	
D-ELVL	Piper PA-46-350P Malibu Mirage	4636545	N24735, N9545N, (N24735)
D-ELVM(2)	Yakovlev Yak-18T	11-33	HA-CBA, RA-3305K, RA-44544
D-ELVO(2)	Cessna F172H	F172-0325	(D-EGDO)
D-ELVP	Gardan GY-80 Horizon 160	75	F-BLVP
D-ELVR	Piper PA-18-150 Super Cub	18-8083	OE-CBS, N4092Z, N10F
D-ELVS	PZL-104 Wilga 35A	19880863	SP-FWA
D-ELVW(2)	Cirrus SR22	1702	N583CD
D-ELWA(2)	SIAI-Marchetti SF.260	2-44	HB-EMK
D-ELWC(3)	Piper PA-28-181 Archer III	2943345	OY-PAW, N9513N
D-ELWD	Robin R.3000/160	145	
D-ELWE	Piper J-3C-65 Cub	15081	OE-AAZ, N42770
D-ELWF	Grob G 115A	8049	
D-ELWG	Reims/Cessna F150M	F15001308	
D-ELWK(2)	Mooney M.20K Model 231	25-0378	N231RN
D-ELWM(2)	Robin DR.400/180 Régent	2515	
D-ELWO	Piper PA-28-180 Cherokee B	28-1706	N7748W
D-ELWP	Hirt/ Denney Kitfox IV-1200	1733	
	(Permit) (C/n now quoted as DCU-025) (Presumed re-regd D-MLWP)		
D-ELWR	Cessna 172RG Cutlass RG	172RG0133	OE-DVR, N6271R
D-ELWS	Air Products F-1A Aircoupe	5752	G-AROR, N25B
D-ELWT	Grob G 115C	82040C	D-EXER
D-ELWU	Cessna 150	17833	OE-ADW, N6433T
D-ELWW	Piper PA-28-140 Cherokee Cruiser	28-7525259	N9640N
D-ELXC(2)	Cessna TR182 Turbo Skylane RG	R18201654	HB-CPJ, N6252S
D-ELXI	Cessna F172H	F172-0431	
D-ELXP	Cessna 172N Skyhawk	17271831	N5305E
D-ELYA	Maule MX.7-180 Star Rocket STOL	11042C	N6116E
D-ELYC(2)	Piper PA-28-181 Archer III	2943329	OY-JAT, N9519N
D-ELYD	Auster Mk.5	1790	G-ANKI, TW446
D-ELYF(3)	SOCATA MS.880B Rallye Club	1699	SE-LYF, D-ENAC(2), OE-DHC, D-EOVK, F-BSVK
D-ELYH	Piper PA-18 Super Cub 95	18-7069	
D-ELYK(2)	Cessna TU206G Turbo Stationair 6-II	U20606285	N6466Z
D-ELYN(3)	Aerotek Pitts S-2A	2005	N52SH, N919FC, N80000
D-ELYP(2)	Robin R.2160D	138	
	(Converted fron R.2100A .89)		
D-ELYQ	Klemm Kl.107C	152	
D-ELYR	Uetz Jodel D.11/85	400/3	HB-SUE
D-ELYS	Cessna 172	29353	N7253A
D-ELYT(2)	Piper PA-18-95 Super Cub	18-2013	PH-FLH, (PH-FLG), D-EANC, I-BDUE, I-EIPU/EI-83, MM52-2413, 52-2413
D-ELYW	Piper PA-18A-125 Super Cub	18-7096	
	(Built as PA-18-150)		
D-ELYX(2)	Cirrus SR22	0595	N897CD
D-ELYY(2)	Aquila AT-01	AT01-212	
D-ELYZ(2)	Rockwell Commander 112	53	D-EHXG, N1053J
D-ELZC	Piper PA-28-181 Archer III	2843548	N53662, D-ELZC, N53672, N5366W
D-ELZH	Grob G 115C	82020	
D-ELZU	Cessna F172E	F172-0051	
D-EMAA	Piper PA-28-180 Cherokee Archer	28-7405073	N9645N
D-EMAB(2)	Reims/Cessna F172P	F17202236	
D-EMAC(5)	Cirrus SR22	2383	D-EHEH(5), N565SR
D-EMAD(2)	Piper PA-18-100 Super Cub	18-2030	R-33, 52-2430
	(Built as PA-18-95)		
D-EMAE(2)	Mooney M.20F Executive	22-1211	
D-EMAF(3)	SOCATA MS.893A Rallye Commodore 180	10721	F-BPBU
D-EMAG(2)	Cessna 170B	27036	OE-DBO, HB-CPC, N3493D
D-EMAH	Orlican L-40 Meta-Sokol	150503	OK-NMF
D-EMAI	Piper PA-18-135 Super Cub	18-7180	N3185Z
	(Built as PA-18-95, then PA-18-105)		
D-EMAJ	Piper PA-28-181 Archer II	28-8190165	N83353
D-EMAK(3)	Beech F33A Bonanza	CE-1506	
D-EMAL(3)	Piper PA-18-150 Super Cub	1809023	OY-JEH
D-EMAM(2)	Piper PA-18 Super Cub 95	18-2037	R-39, 52-2437
D-EMAN(2)	CEA Jodel DR.1050 Ambassadeur	44	F-BJUC
	(On rebuild)		
D-EMAP(2)	Piper PA-28-181 Cherokee Archer II	28-7790453	N3345Q
D-EMAQ(3)	Cessna 182P	18264100	I-AMAD, D-EGWZ, PH-MYL, D-EJPD, N6085F
	(Reims-assembled with "c/n" 0036)		
	(Res. 24.11.15)		

Reg	Type	C/N	Previous identities
D-EMAR(2)	Piper PA-28R-200 Cherokee Arrow II	28R-7635372	N6990J
D-EMAS(2)	Hoyler/ Tomark SD-4 Viper (Permit 7.8.12')	0032	
D-EMAT(2)	Timmermann/ Christen Eagle II	02/1602-348	
D-EMAU(2)	Bücker Bü131B-1 Jungmann	82	N317BJ, N62200, HB-USC, A-69
D-EMAV(2)	Mraz K-65 Kap	475303	D-EKUS, HB-IKA, OK-DF
	(Officially regd.as a Fieseler Fi.156C-7 Storch, c/n 741 amended to 475303)		
D-EMAW	Scheibe SF.23A-1 Sperling	2500	
D-EMAX(3)	Focke-Wulf FW.44J Stieglitz	83	(D-EMIQ(2)), D-EMIL(3), D-EFUD, SE-AWT, Fv.631
D-EMAY(2)	Aerospool WT-9 Dynamic LSA (P 19.1.11)	DY395/2010	
D-EMAZ(4)	Mooney M.20M Model 257 TLS (W/o Egelsbach 17.9.12)	27-0273	N91706
D-EMBA(3)	Piaggio FWP.149D	055	90+41, ND+206, AS+482
D-EMBB	Dornier Do.27B-1	307	56+32, PA+319, PF+111, PL+414
D-EMBC	Cessna F150J	F150-0501	
D-EMBD(2)	Piper PA-28-180 Cherokee G	28-7205314	N11C
D-EMBE(2)	Cirrus SR20	1238	N323EM
D-EMBF	Fuji FA-200-160 Aero Subaru	152	
D-EMBG	Fuji FA-200-180 Aero Subaru	157	
D-EMBH	SOCATA MS.883 Rallye 115	1684	F-BTHR
D-EMBI (2)	Beech A36AT Bonanza	E-2710	N55764
D-EMBJ(2)	Maule MT-7-235 Super Rocket	18106C	
D-EMBK	Piper PA-46-500TP Malibu Meridian	4697113	N26KC, N6DM
	(Res .07 but still ntu)		
D-EMBL	Piper PA-28-180 Cherokee D	28-5315	N7950N
D-EMBM	Piper PA-28RT-201 Arrow IV	28R-7918173	N2845G
D-EMBN	Cessna 172S Skyhawk SP	172S9183	N5268C
D-EMBO(2)	Gardan GY-80 Horizon 180	157	
D-EMBP(2)	Beech G36 Bonanza	E-3910	N136EU
D-EMBR	Cessna TU206F Turbo Stationair	U20601761	(N9561G)
D-EMBS	Reims FR172H Rocket	FR17200275	
D-EMBT	HOAC DV-20 Katana	20136	HB-SCR
D-EMBU(2)	Piper PA-28RT-201T Turbo Arrow IV	28R-7931252	N2909N
D-EMBV	Fuji FA-200-180 Aero Subaru	242	
D-EMBW	Piper PA-28R-201T Turbo Cherokee Arrow III	28R-7703394	N47533
D-EMBZ	Piper PA-46-350P Malibu Mirage	4622148	S5-DGN, D-EMVF(2), N1221K, N9235X
	(JetProp DLX conversion # 225) (Dbr 15.1.15, Donaueschingen)		
D-EMCA(5)	Cessna T206H Turbo Stationair	T20608533	N2208U
D-EMCB	Piper PA-28-140 Cherokee D	28-7125520	N1849T
D-EMCC	Piper PA-28R-200 Cherokee Arrow II	28R-7235219	N5294T
D-EMCD	Piper PA-28R-200 Cherokee Arrow II	28R-7235150	N2872T
D-EMCG(2)	Reims/Cessna F172P	F17202206	
D-EMCH	Piper PA-28-180 Cherokee Challenger	28-7305375	N55404
D-EMCI	Piper PA-18-150 Super Cub	18-5549	N6968D
D-EMCL	Piper PA-28-151 Cherokee Warrior	28-7415086	N9626N
D-EMCM(2)	Reims/Cessna F172N	F17201556	PH-CIO, PH-AXU(1)
D-EMCN	Piper PA-38-112 Tomahawk	38-78A0324	N9693N
D-EMCO(2)	Piper PA-28-235 Cherokee	28-10365	N8817W
D-EMCP	Reims/Cessna F172N	F17201678	
D-EMCR(2)	Cirrus SR22	2287	PH-SFK, N626SM
D-EMCS	Piper PA-28-151 Cherokee Warrior	28-7415298	N9561N
D-EMCT	Cessna 182M Skylane	18259492	N71089
D-EMCU	Piper PA-28-235 Cherokee	28-10366	N8818W
D-EMCV	Cessna 182P Skylane	18263396	I-AMCW, N9471G
D-EMCW	Piper PA-28RT-201T Turbo Arrow IV	28R-7931285	N2967C
	(Open storage, Bonn since at least 2013)		
D-EMCX	Cessna 182P	18264380	HB-CXE, N1590M
	(Reims-assembled with "c/n" 0051) (Res .12)		
D-EMCY(2)	Cessna 205	205-0364	SE-EST, N8364Z
D-EMCZ	Cessna 182M Skylane	18259320	F-BRAH, N70598
D-EMDE	Cessna 172E	17250596	N2996U
D-EMDF	Reims/Cessna F172H	F17200715	
D-EMDG	Reims FR172G Rocket	FR17200201	
D-EMDI	Cessna F172E	F172-0022/17250577	(N2977U)
D-EMDK	Reims/Cessna F172H	F17200713	
D-EMDL	Reims FR172G Rocket	FR17200200	
D-EMDN(2)	SOCATA TB-9 Tampico	907	
D-EMDR(2)	Kurz/ Siebel Si202/K Replica	1	D-EPJK
	(Res. .07, status?)		
D-EMDS	Reims FR172H Rocket	FR17200290	
D-EMDT	Cessna P210N Pressurized Centurion II	P21000807	N6623W
D-EMDV	Boeing Stearman E75	75-5844	SE-KFT, N1723B, 41-17681
D-EMEB(3)	Cirrus SR20	1919	N148PG
D-EMEC(3)	Grob G 115B	8026	HB-UGE, (D-EGVV)
D-EMED(4)	Piper PA-28RT-201T Turbo Arrow IV	28R-8131138	N83890, (N21MH), N83890
D-EMEE(2)	Cessna 172N Skyhawk	17271788	N5236E
D-EMEI	Zlin Z.526L Trenér Master	1155	OE-AGA
D-EMEK(2)	Piper PA-18 Super Cub 95	18-3433	96+13, SC+340, AC+521, AA+521, AS+521, 54-733
D-EMEL(3)	Pützer Elster B	016	97+09, D-EDIF
D-EMEM(3)	Piper PA-28-181 Archer II	28-8290157	N82469, N9530N
D-EMEO	SIAI-Marchetti SF.260WL	407/29-227	9U-ZRD, LRAF 407, I-RAIT
D-EMEP(3)	Piper PA-38-112 Tomahawk	38-78A0620	N4469E
D-EMER	Piper J-3C-85 Cub	13210	HB-OCB, 45-4470
D-EMES(2)	Piper PA-28R-201T Turbo Arrow III	28R-7803214	N6258C
D-EMET(2)	HOAC DV-20 Katana	20115	HB-SCO
D-EMEX(2)	SOCATA MS.880B Rallye-Club	1921	F-BTIJ
D-EMEY	Piper PA-28-161 Cherokee Warrior II	28-7716166	N5612V
D-EMEZ(2)	Aquila AT-01	AT01-195	
D-EMFA	Morane-Saulnier MS.885 Super Rallye	5135	
D-EMFC(4)	Diamond DA 20-A1 Katana	10129	N558ND, N558SS, C-GKAN
D-EMFF	SOCATA MS.893E Rallye 180GT	12739	F-GAFL
D-EMFG(3)	Cessna P210N Pressurized Centurion II	P21000458	N731GW
D-EMFH(2)	Diamond DA 20-A1 Katana	10305	N605DA, C-GDMY
D-EMFJ	Piper PA-28-236 Dakota	28-8011027	N81170
D-EMFL(2)	Boeing Stearman E75N1	75-4695	OO-USN, N17PT, N37744, YS-272P, N54280, 42-16532
	(Coded '744')		
D-EMFM(2)	Cessna 152	15279655	N757DK
D-EMFN	Diamond DA 20-A1 Katana	10165	C-FDVA
D-EMFP	Piper PA-28RT-201 Arrow IV	28R-8118058	N8354A
D-EMFR	Cessna 172P Skyhawk	17274651	N52980
D-EMFT(2)	Piper PA-28R-201T Turbo Cherokee Arrow III	28R-7803313	9A-BMH, N36192
D-EMFU	Bölkow BO.208C Junior	574	
D-EMFW(2)	Mang/ Fw.190-M Replica (Permit 9.08)	1	
D-EMFX	SOCATA TB-9 Tampico Club	932	
D-EMFY(2)	Reims/Cessna F172N Skyhawk	F17201606	
D-EMGA	SAN Jodel D.140C Mousquetaire III	114	F-BKSZ
D-EMGC	Mooney M.20K Model 231	25-0409	
D-EMGD	Beech C24R Sierra	MC-507	F-GPHM, N18818
D-EMGH	SAN Jodel DR.1050 Sicile	480	
D-EMGK	HOAC DV-20 Katana	20140	
D-EMGM(2)	Procaer F-15B Picchio	12	F-BJOO, HB-EAW
	(Res .16)		
D-EMGO	Cessna F172H	F172-0440	
D-EMGP	CSA PS-28 Cruiser	C0457	
D-EMGS	Piper PA-28R-200 Cherokee Arrow II	28R-7335421	N56365
D-EMGT	Cirrus SR20	1951	N246DM
D-EMGV	Zlin Z.226MS Trenér	194	OK-MGV
	(Res. 26.6.15)		
D-EMGW	Reims/Cessna FR182 Skylane RG	FR18200024	
D-EMGX	Remos GX	337	
	(Permit .09)		
D-EMGZ	Cessna 172S Skyhawk SP	172S10407	N1380F
D-EMHB	Cessna F172F	F172-0152	N5054T, D-EMHB
D-EMHC	Piper PA-18 Super Cub 95	18-3430	96+11, AC+519, AA+519, AS+519, 54-730
D-EMHD	Bücker Bü.131 Jungmann	23	N131BJ, HB-USL, A-14
D-EMHF	Mooney M.20E Super 21	670004	
D-EMHG(2)	Piper J-3C-65 Cub	12308	SE-IMH, OY-AVD, D-EFQK, F-BFQK, OO-ZOU, 44-80012
D-EMHH(2)	Cessna 172RG Cutlass RG	172RG0198	G-OIFR, G-BHJG, N6529R
D-EMHI (2)	Piper PA-18-180 Super Cub	18-8245	N5995Z
D-EMHJ(2)	Reims/Cessna F172P Skyhawk II	F17202064	PH-WMA, D-EODP(2), (D-EJIM(2))
D-EMHL	Rockwell Commander 114B	14151	N4821W
D-EMHN	Klemm Kl.35D	1842	SE-BPL, Fv5065
D-EMHO(2)	Mooney M.20J Model 201	24-1002	(N3991H)
D-EMHP	Robin R.1180TD Aiglon	238	
D-EMHS(3)	Cessna 177B Cardinal	17701687	N34169
D-EMHV(2)	Piper PA-28-181 Archer II	28-7990253	VH-MHV, N9582N
D-EMHW(2)	Piper PA-28-161 Warrior III	2842176	(D-EASS(3)), N53642
D-EMIC(3)	OMF-100-160 Symphony	0003	
D-EMID(3)	Cirrus SR22	0178	G-SHMK, N125GB
D-EMIG	Focke-Wulf FW.44J Stieglitz	2293	SE-BXO, Fv625
D-EMIH	Dornier Do.27Q-5	2027	
D-EMII (2)	Fairchild F.24W-46A Argus III	'W46290'	N81390, NC81390
	(Res. 6.07; still current in US marks)		
D-EMIK(2)	Robin DR.400/140B Major	1107	
D-EMIL(4)	Focke-Wulf FW.44J Stieglitz	unkn	D-EMIL(2), (D-EKNE), (D-EKXG), SE-BXG, Fv662
D-EMIM(2)	Extra EA.300	03	G-OHIM, D-EBTS, G-OHIM, D-EBTS
D-EMIN(5)	Aquila AT-01 100A	AT01-341	
	(Res .16)		
D-EMIP(2)	Robin DR.400/180R Remorqueur	1375	
D-EMIR(3)	Beyer/ Klemm L.25d Replica	003	(D-ERNY)
	(Res. 4.08, nearing completion 2015)		
D-EMIS(2)	Cessna F172H	F172-0335	
D-EMIT(2)	Cessna 182P Skylane	18262063	N58439
D-EMIV(2)	Cirrus SR22	3607	N48CK
D-EMIW	Piper PA-24-250 Comanche	24-1017	N6892P, N10F
D-EMIX(2)	Van's RV-8/MIX	250854	
	(Permit 3.6.15)		
D-EMIY	Ströhle/ Aero Designs Pulsar XP	AB431	
	(C/n formerly quoted as 1839)		
D-EMIZ(3)	Aerotek Pitts S-1S	1-0028	YV-24P, YV-TAPA
D-EMJA(2)	Arau/ Dallach D4 E-BK 914F Fascination	EB023	
D-EMJB(2)	Cessna 172N Skyhawk	17269627	N737RY
D-EMJC(2)	SOCATA TB-20 Trinidad	1916	N445SD, F-GSZI, (N678TB)
D-EMJD(2)	Aquila AT-01	AT01-185	
D-EMJH(2)	Robin DR.400/180 Régent	2324	
D-EMJI	SOCATA MS.893A Rallye Commodore 180	12061	
D-EMJP	Piper PA-18 Super Cub 95	18-3199	D-EABS(2), OL-L03, L-125, 53-4799
D-EMJR	Great Lakes 2T-1A-2	0786	N3818F
D-EMJT	SOCATA TB-20 Trinidad	711	
D-EMKA(2)	Dornier Do.27B-1	152	55+32, PG+216, PF+108, PD+103
D-EMKB(2)	Eberl / Lancair 360	886-320-683SFB	
D-EMKC	Piper PA-28R-201T Turbo Cherokee Arrow III	28R-7703427	N47696
D-EMKE(3)	Reims/Cessna F182Q Skylane	F18200115	PH-AYN
D-EMKF(3)	Xtreme Air XA-41 Sbach 300	03	
	(Permit 19.1.11)		
D-EMKG	SOCATA TB-20 Trinidad	705	
D-EMKI (2)	Beech 77 Skipper	WA-94	
D-EMKJ	Mooney M.20C Mark 21	2550	HB-DEC, N6845U
D-EMKL	Robin DR.400/180R Remo 180	2187	F-WZZX
D-EMKM(2)	Cessna 182T Skylane	18281981	N1155X
D-EMKO(4)	SOCATA TB-9 Tampico	1110	I-TNAC, F-OGSA
D-EMKP(3)	Bücker Bü.133C Jungmeister	28	HB-MKP, (OO-ASA), HB-MKP, U-81
D-EMKR	Wassmer WA.52 Europa	59	
D-EMKS	Reims/Cessna F182Q Skylane II	F18200054	
D-EMKU	Binder CP.301S Smaragd	103	
D-EMKV	Reims/Cessna F172N	F17201559	
D-EMKX	Aviat A-1B Husky	2263	N173CA
D-EMKY	Binder CP.301S Smaragd	104	
D-EMLB	Reims/Cessna F172N	F17201580	
D-EMLD	Robin DR.400/180R Remorqueur	1494	
D-EMLE(2)	Piper PA-18-150 Super Cub	nil	(RBAF)
	(Built from spare fuselage no.18-4912)		
D-EMLG	Cessna F172H	F172-0565	D-EBCG, OY-AGJ
D-EMLH	Piper PA-28-181 Archer II	28-8090015	N2971Q
D-EMLI (2)	Cessna 182S Skylane	18280645	
D-EMLK	Diamond DA 40D Star	D4.092	G-CCPX
D-EMLL	Mooney M.20K Model 231	25-0699	N1169D
D-EMLN	Mooney M.20K Model 231	25-0636	LX-AGM, N1154P
D-EMLR	Pilatus P.2-05	25	U-105, A-105
D-EMLT	Cessna R172K Hawk XP	R1722495	N736FQ
D-EMLW	Beech A24R Sierra	MC-81	OY-AJD, N9729Q
D-EMLZ	Zeddies/ Skystar Kitfox V	S9502-0105	(D-ESLZ(3))
D-EMMA	Piper PA-18-150 Super Cub	18-6466	N10F
D-EMMB(2)	Piper PA-28-181 Archer II	2890051	N9133N
D-EMMD	SOCATA MS.893A Rallye Commodore 180	10930	
D-EMME	Piper PA-18-150 Super Cub	18-5107	N6985B

D-EMMF(3)	Piper PA-46-350P Malibu Mirage	4622103	OY-JEU, N9197F
D-EMMG	SAN Jodel DR.1050 Ambassadeur	371	
D-EMMH(2)	Robin DR.400/140B Dauphin 4	2666	(D-EDNE(2))
D-EMMI (3)	Focke-Wulf FW.44J Stieglitz	unkn	D-ECAN, SE-BWN, Fv667
D-EMMJ(2)	Piper PA-28R-180 Cherokee Arrow	28R-30580	D-ELRF, N4680J
D-EMMK(2)	Mooney M.20J Model 201	24-1260	N1157S
D-EMML(3)	Mooney M.20K Model 252 TSE	25-1153	HB-DHC
D-EMMM	Fuji FA-200-160 Aero Subaru	154	
D-EMMP	Morane-Saulnier MS.880B Rallye Club	72	F-BKDZ
D-EMMQ	Laverda F.8L Falco IV	415	
D-EMMR	Laverda F.8L Falco IV	420	
D-EMMS(3)	Beech G36 Bonanza	E-3970	N8150G
D-EMMT	Cessna F172F	F172-0148	
D-EMMU(2)	Piper PA-28-180 Cherokee F	28-7105056	N5196S
D-EMMV	Piper J-3C-90 Cub	12837	D-EHAC, HB-OGU, 44-80541
D-EMMW	Piper PA-32-300 Cherokee Six C	32-40922	N5225S
D-EMMX(2)	Maule MX.7-235 Star Rocket	10057C	N5GF
D-EMMY	Piper PA-18-150 Super Cub	18-7403	N10F
D-EMMZ(2)	Mooney M.20J Model 205	24-3367	
D-EMNA(3)	CSA PS28 Cruiser	C0459	
D-EMNC	Tecnam P.92J Echo-VLA	004	
D-EMND	CASA C-1.131E Jungmann	2017	D-EHMT, E3B-413
	(Res. .06, on rebuild ?)		
D-EMNH	Piper PA-38-112 Tomahawk	38-78A0355	N6249A
D-EMNI	Robin R.3000/140	118	HB-KBC
D-EMNN	Focke-Wulf FW.44J Stieglitz	1904	LN- . . ., SE-BRZ, Fv622
	(Res. .12; under restoration Old Warden, UK)		
D-EMNQ	Dornier Do.27B-1	305	56+30, EA+384, QM+613, PL+412
D-EMNU	Beech A23-24 Musketeer Super III	MA-36	
D-EMOA	Mooney M.20J Model 201	24-1652	
D-EMOB(2)	Cessna 172RG Cutlass RG	172RG0523	HB-CNW, (N5406V)
D-EMOC(3)	Mooney M.20J Model 205	24-3071	N205YY
D-EMOD(3)	Rockwell Commander 114	14421	(N5876N)
D-EMOE	Reims/Cessna F172N	F17201984	
D-EMOF	Focke-Wulf FW.44J Stieglitz	ASJA-82	SE-CBE, Fv630
D-EMOG(3)	Piper PA-28-140 Cherokee	28-22422	SE-EPL
D-EMOH(3)	Mooney M.20J Model 201	24-1599	
D-EMOI	Robin DR.400/180R Remorqueur	1392	
D-EMOJ	Mooney M.20J Model 205	24-3042	
D-EMOK	Höxter/ Aero-Jodel D.11A Club	AB.14	
	(W/o 5.5.90)		
D-EMOL(3)	Reims FR172F Rocket	FR17200079	
D-EMOM(2)	Mooney M.20J Model 201	24-0990	(N3947H)
D-EMON(6)	HOAC DV-20 Katana	20012	C-FSRX, N15DV, OE-CDV
D-EMOO(3)	Dallach/ Stevens Akro Diabolo 2	EB-002	
D-EMOP	Piper PA-22 Tri-Pacer 125	22-329	D-EMOL, N1416A
D-EMOR(3)	Mooney M.20J Model 205	24-3058	
D-EMOS(3)	Mosinger /Aerostyle Breezer	1	
	(Permit 24.6.09)		
D-EMOU(2)	Mooney M.20J Model 205	24-3172	
D-EMOW	Piper PA-18 Super Cub 105	18-7353	N10F
	(Built as PA-18 Super Cub 95)		
D-EMOX(2)	Beech F33A Bonanza	CE-875	
D-EMOY	Piper PA-28-161 Warrior II	28-8016365	N8240G
D-EMPB	Robin DR.400/180R Remorqueur	825	
D-EMPC	Reims/Cessna F152	F15201466	
D-EMPD(2)	Cessna 172N Skyhawk	17273543	D-EVOB, N5094G
D-EMPE(3)	Mooney M.20J Model 205	24-3186	N9118X
D-EMPF(2)	Cessna 177RG Cardinal RG	177RG1344	OO-RAD, N53096
D-EMPH	Cessna 180K Skywagon	18052979	N2537K
D-EMPI (3)	Piaggio FWP.149D	133	SE-XKM, OY-CPV, D-EFRB(2), 91+12, D-EBDO(1), (91+12), D-EBDO(1), KB+110
	(C/n quoted officially as 133-738 which includes Swedish EAA Project No 738)		
D-EMPJ	Diamond DA 20-C1 Katana	C0083	(SE- . . .), N157WC, N983CT, C-GKAC
D-EMPL(5)	SOCATA TB-10 Tobago	1239	EC-FGE, F-GKVF
D-EMPM	SNCAN/ Stampe SV.4C	159	F-BMKM, CEV, F-BFLH, CEV, F-BDKY
D-EMPN	Piper PA-28RT-201T Turbo Arrow IV	28R-7931254	N2915A
D-EMPO	Morane-Saulnier MS.885 Super Rallye	5143	(D-EMTO)
D-EMPR	Piper PA-28-181 Archer II	28-7990579	N2952N
D-EMPS(2)	Cirrus SR20	1491	F-GZPN, N520DR, N120SR, G-SRZO, N60524
D-EMPT	Reims/Cessna FR172K Hawk XP	FR17200629	
D-EMPU(3)	OMF-100-160 Symphony	0021	(N210MV)
D-EMPX	Xtreme Air XA-42	137	
D-EMPY(2)	Diamond DA 20-A1 Katana	10112	OE-AAD(2), N538FD, N538SS, C-GDMY
D-EMQA	Cessna F172E	F172-0037/17250707	(N3507S)
D-EMQI	Cessna 182G	18255129	(OY-BJI), D-EMQI, N3729U
	(W/o 27.7.08)		
D-EMRA(2)	Mooney M.20J Model 205	24-3195	
D-EMRB	Piper PA-38-112 Tomahawk	38-80A0008	(N70456), D-EMRB, N24810
D-EMRC	Cirrus SR22	2787	N277SR
D-EMRD	Beech V35B Bonanza	D-10138	
D-EMRE	Piper PA-18-150 Super Cub	18-6237	N8579D
	(Damaged 3.6.04)		
D-EMRF	Robin DR.400/180R Remo 180	2071	
D-EMRH	SOCATA TB-10 Tobago	14	HB-EYU, F-ODKC
D-EMRI	Cessna 172A	47638	N9838T
D-EMRJ	SIAI-Marchetti S.205/20R	4-113	I-ACMT
D-EMRK(4)	Yakovlev Yak-55	901110	LY-XRK
	(Permit 6.8.15)		
D-EMRP	Cessna 177B Cardinal	17702363	N11736
D-EMRS	Reims/Cessna F152	F15201511	
D-EMRT	SOCATA TB-20 Trinidad	452	
D-EMRV(2)	Van's RV-7A	72796	
	(Permit 2.9.11)		
D-EMRW	Piper PA-28R-200 Cherokee Arrow II	28R-7235213	N5275T
D-EMRY(2)	Piper PA-28R-201 Cherokee Arrow III	28R-7737066	N5617V
D-EMRZ	Robin DR.400/180 Régent	718	
D-EMSB	Cessna 152	15281418	N49969
D-EMSC	Cessna 152	15281440	N64829
D-EMSD	Reims/Cessna FR182 Skylane RG	FR18200053	(PH-AXP)
D-EMSE(2)	Cessna 172P Skyhawk	17276280	N98346
D-EMSF	Zlin Z.142	0001	OK-078
D-EMSG(3)	Grob G 115B	8020	HB-UGB, (D-EGVV)
D-EMSH(2)	Reims/Cessna F152	F15201935	
D-EMSI	Morane-Saulnier MS.885 Super Rallye	129	
D-EMSJ	Reims/Cessna F152-II	F15201787	PH-CBC
D-EMSK	Reims/Cessna F172M	F17201340	(SE-GKH)

D-EMSL	Robin DR.300/180R Remorqueur	464	F-BRZR
D-EMSN	Cessna 150M	15077564	N6164K
D-EMSO	Morane-Saulnier MS.885 Super Rallye	5127	
D-EMST	Piper PA-28-140 Cherokee D	28-7125141	N5587U
D-EMSW(2)	Stollenwerk/ Dallach D5/E-BK/S Evolution	1	
D-EMSX	Cessna 172P Skyhawk	17274630	N52893
D-EMSY	Morane-Saulnier MS.885 Super Rallye	165	(D-EMTU)
D-EMTA(2)	Grob G 115A	8057	
D-EMTB	Cessna F150H	F150-0329	
	(Rotax engine) (CofA reduced to permit 8.06)		
D-EMTD(2)	Mooney M.20J Model 205 MSE	24-3279	
D-EMTH	Piper PA-28-160 Cherokee	28-554	(D-EOTH), F-GOTH, HB-OVH, N5472W
D-EMTI (2)	SOCATA TB-10 Tobago	1608	
D-EMTK(2)	Piper PA-28RT-201T Turbo Arrow IV	28R-8131039	SE-KGI, N8305D
D-EMTN	Reims FR172G Rocket	FR17200147	
D-EMTO(2)	Piper PA-28-181 Cherokee Archer II	28-7890547	N39635
D-EMTP	Robin DR.400/180R Remorqueur	1328	F-GBII
D-EMTR	Cirrus SR22	0469	N716VR
D-EMTT	Fuji FA-200-180 Aero Subaru	190	(D-EITT(1))
D-EMTW	Piper PA-38-112 Tomahawk	38-78A0583	ZS-KHS, N4381E
D-EMTX(2)	Fläming-Air FA-02 Smaragd	23/05	
	(Permit .06)		
D-EMTY	Morane-Saulnier MS.885 Super Rallye	5169	
D-EMTZ	Robin DR.400/180R Remo 180	2020	I-ITBG
D-EMUA	CEA Jodel DR.1050M-1 Sicile Record	630	
D-EMUC	Tecnam P.2002-JF Sierra	198	SP-CPL, I-PDVF
D-EMUE	SAN Jodel DR.1050 Ambassadeur	359	
D-EMUF	Eichelsdörfer/ Piel CP.301A Emeraude	AB.412	
D-EMUG(2)	Gardan GY-80 Horizon 160	91	F-BMUG
D-EMUH	Bölkow BO.208C Junior	623	
D-EMUK(2)	Beech V35B Bonanza	D-9986	
D-EMUL(2)	Cessna 120	11226	N76794, NC76794
D-EMUM(2)	Piper PA-18-150 Super Cub	18-7709158	N82464
D-EMUP(2)	Piper PA-28-140 Cherokee D	28-7125047	N1731T
D-EMUR(2)	Sportavia-Pützer RS-180 Sportsman	6008	
D-EMUX(3)	Maule MXT-7-180A Starcraft	21021C	N1033Y
D-EMVA(2)	SOCATA TB-21 Trinidad TC	2015	
D-EMVB	Pützer Elster B	029	97+17, D-ELBU
D-EMVC	SIAI-Marchetti SF.260M	742/40-018	MM55016/"70-47"
	(Permit 7.5.11) (Coded '70-47')		
D-EMVG	Mroczeck/ Neico Lancair 320 II	1852	
	(Permit 11.10)		
D-EMVI	SEEMS MS.880B Rallye Club	5312	
D-EMVR	Cessna 182Q Skylane	18267132	N97560
D-EMVS(2)	Flight Design CT LS-ELA	09-04-10	
	(Permit 7.09)		
D-EMWC	Piper PA-28R-180 Cherokee Arrow	28R-30532	N4642J
D-EMWD	Piper PA-28R-180 Cherokee Arrow	28R-30648	N28WD, D-EMWD, N4927J
D-EMWE(2)	Cessna 172M Skyhawk	17266864	N1135U
D-EMWF(2)	Reims/Cessna F172N	F17201587	
D-EMWG(3)	SOCATA TB-200 Tobago XL	2195	N567GT
D-EMWH	Piper PA-28R-200 Cherokee Arrow	28R-35355	N3018R
D-EMWI	Cessna F172E	F172-0033/17250643	(N3043U)
D-EMWJ(3)	Cessna 172R Skyhawk	17280986	N7261S
D-EMWL	Piper PA-28R-200 Cherokee Arrow	28R-35706	N4986S
D-EMWM(2)	Mooney M.20J Model 201	24-0993	N3960H
D-EMWO	Oberlerchner JOB 15-150	056	OE-CAA(1)
D-EMWP	Piper PA-28-140 Cherokee C	28-26820	N11C
D-EMWQ	Piper PA-28-140 Cherokee C	28-26819	N5992U
D-EMWR(2)	Beech F33A Bonanza	CE-1554	N8105X
D-EMWS	Piper PA-28-140 Cherokee D	28-7125170	N11C
D-EMWT(2)	Beech F33A Bonanza	CE-1529	
D-EMWU	Cessna F172E	F172-0043	
	(W/o 17.9.06)		
D-EMWW	Piper PA-28R-200 Cherokee Arrow B	28R-7135166	N2203T
D-EMWX	Piper PA-28-140 Cherokee D	28-7125389	N8590N
D-EMWY	Cessna F172E	F172-0038/17250739	(N3539S)
D-EMXB	Cessna F172H	F172-0623	
D-EMXD	CEA DR.253B Régent	158	
D-EMXE	Cessna 177 Cardinal	17701149	N30249
D-EMXG	Cessna F172H	F172-0630	
D-EMXI	SIAT 223A-1 Flamingo	015	HB-EVL, D-ENBL
D-EMXL	Cessna 182T Skylane	18282052	N1312D
D-EMXR	SOCATA TB-200 Tobago XL	1632	G-MLLA, D-EREH
D-EMYC	Brillinger/ Jodel D.9 Bébé	AB.1	
D-EMYH	Mraz M.1D Sokol	350A	OK-CKP, OK-BXW
D-EMYK(3)	Diamond DV-20 Katana	20209	OE-VPX
D-EMYL	Piper J-3C-65 Cub	11740	HB-OSR, 43-30449
D-EMYP(2)	SOCATA MS.893A Rallye Commodore 180	10620	
D-EMYR(2)	Mooney M.20J Model 201	24-0527	
D-EMYS(3)	Mylius My.102 Tornado	V-1	
D-EMYZ(2)	SAN Jodel DR.1050M Excellence	191	F-BJNX
D-EMZA(2)	American AA-1A Trainer	AA1A-0353	HB-UBS
D-EMZD	Reims FR172G Rocket	FR17200157	
D-EMZE(2)	Piper PA-28-161 Archer III	2842206	N3092J
D-EMZF	Reims/Cessna F172H	F17200667	
D-EMZO	SOCATA MS.893A Rallye Commodore 180	10569	
D-EMZY(2)	Piper PA-28-161 Cherokee Warrior II	28-7816011	N40069
D-ENAB(2)	SOCATA MS.893A Rallye Commodore 180	11460	F-BSZE, OY-DJW, F-BNGV
D-ENAD	Wassmer Jodel D.120 Paris-Nice	138	
D-ENAF(2)	Piper PA-32R-300 Lance	32R-7780304	N3314Q
D-ENAH(3)	Cirrus SR22	1257	N203AH
D-ENAI	Reims/Cessna F152	F15201737	
D-ENAK(2)	Piper PA-28RT-201T Turbo Arrow IV	28R-7931097	N385A, N9615N
D-ENAL(2)	Reims/Cessna F152	F15201768	
D-ENAM(2)	Rockwell Commander 114	14008	N1908J
D-ENAN(2)	Piper PA-18 Super Cub 95	18-2072	R-61, 52-2472
D-ENAP	Mraz M.1D Sokol	274	OK-DHO
D-ENAQ	Piper PA-18 Super Cub 95	18-7397	N10F
D-ENAR(2)	Cessna TR182 Turbo Skylane RG	R18201433	C-GTSN, N4825S
D-ENAS(4)	Cessna 172S Skyhawk SP	172S8631	OE-DAL(2), N650SP
D-ENAV(2)	Piper PA-28-161 Cherokee Warrior II	28-7716106	(OO-FVP), D-ENAV(2), N9625N
D-ENAW(3)	Piper PA-28R-201 Arrow III	28R-7837143	N3947M
D-ENAY	Focke-Wulf FW.44J Stieglitz	unkn	D-EGAM, SE-BWH, Fv663
	(Flies as "NV+KG")		
D-ENAZ	Stark Turbulent D-1	125	
D-ENBA	Cessna 205	205-0075	N1875Z
D-ENBC	Cessna F172H	F172-0373	
D-ENBH	Piper PA-28R-180 Cherokee Arrow	28R-30556	N4660J
D-ENBL(2)	Piper PA-28R-200 Cherokee Arrow II	28R-7235235	N5494T
D-ENBM(2)	Piper PA-28R-180 Cherokee Arrow	28R-30678	N4941J
D-ENBO(2)	Piper PA-28RT-201T Turbo Arrow IV	28R-8031048	N3579K

D-ENBP(2)	Reims FR172F Rocket	FR17200068	
D-ENBR(3)	Ruschmeyer R.90-230RG	021	
D-ENBZ	Cessna F150J	F150-0429	
D-ENCC(2)	Piper PA-18-150 Super Cub	18-1483	ALAT, 51-15483
D-ENCD(3)	Reims/Cessna F172N Skyhawk II	F17201795	
D-ENCF(4)	Robin R.3000/160	150	HB-KIJ
D-ENCG(3)	Reims/Cessna FR172K Hawk XP	FR17200637	
D-ENCI	Bölkow BO.208 Junior	511	(CS-ALX)
D-ENCO(2)	Piper PA-28-140 Cherokee D	28-7125097	N1782T
D-ENCS	Diamond DA 40D Star	D4.213	
D-ENCT	Mooney M.20M Model 257 TLS	27-0313	N1020G
D-ENCU(2)	Cessna F172G	F172-0307	
D-ENCW	Piper PA-28-140 Cherokee E	28-7225455	N11C
D-ENCY(4)	Cessna 177RG Cardinal RG	177RG0069	N8069G
D-ENDA(2)	Ruschmeyer MF-85-NDAE	V001	D-EEHE(2), (D-EJHR)
D-ENDE(3)	Reims/Cessna F182Q Skylane	F18200146	
D-ENDI (3)	de Havilland DH.82A Tiger Moth	82335	G-ANDI, N40DH, G-ANDI, (G-ANDM), N9240
D-ENDK	Robin DR.400/180 Régent	1318	
D-ENDO(2)	Cessna F172G	F172-0289	
D-ENDR	Cessna 172N Skyhawk	17268804	N734EU
D-ENDS(2)	Cessna 206H Stationair	20608301	N1687L
D-ENDT	Reims/Cessna F150M	F15001171	
D-ENDW	Piper PA-46R-350T Matrix	4692125	SP-NDW, N525MM, N6072J
D-ENDY	Bölkow BO.208C Junior	520	
D-ENEB(2)	Cirrus SR22T	0469	N902JP
D-ENED	Wassmer Jodel D.120R Paris-Nice	139	
D-ENEF	Piper J-3C-90 Cub	6347	N35441, NC35441
D-ENEG	Cessna 180 Skywagon	31463	N4564B
D-ENEH(5)	SOCATA TB-10 Tobago	1136	
D-ENEJ	SOCATA MS.880B Rallye Club	1660	
D-ENEL(2)	Cessna T210N Turbo Centurion II	21064002	N4755Y
D-ENEN(2)	Robin R.3000/160	148	
D-ENER(4)	Piper PA-28-160 Cherokee C	28-2392	VH-NER, D-EMGU, N5877W
D-ENES(3)	Aquila AT-01	AT01-153	
D-ENET(3)	Beech B36TC Bonanza	EA-584	N44RN
D-ENEY	SAN Jodel DR.1050 Ambassadeur	145	F-BJNH
D-ENEZ(3)	Piper PA-28-161 Warrior II	28 8116207	N3998P, D-ENEZ(3), N8378B
D-ENFC	Piper PA-18-135 Super Cub	18-3830	R-140, 54-2430
D-ENFE	SAN Jodel DR.1050 Ambassadeur	381	
D-ENFF	Piper PA-28-161 Warrior II	28-8116075	N8291B
D-ENFH	SOCATA MS.893E Rallye 180GT	12988	
D-ENFK	Reims/Cessna F172M	F17201447	OE-KFK, D-EECZ
D-ENFL	Grumman AA-5B Tiger	AA5B-0310	
D-ENFR	Cessna 172P Skyhawk	17275499	N6286A, (N694), N63937
D-ENFS	Cessna 172M Skyhawk	17266396	N30MX, N30MP, (N80136)
D-ENFU	Piper PA-18-150 Super Cub	18-6588	N9282D
D-ENFV	Aerostyle Breezer B600	030LSA	
D-ENFY	Cessna F172D	F172-0018/17250303	(N2703U)
D-ENGB	Robin DR.400/180R Remorqueur	1735	
D-ENGD	Grob G 115D Acro	82018	
D-ENGI (2)	Reims/Cessna F150M	F15001314	
D-ENGK	Kälberer/ Viking Dragonfly Mk.II (Not completed, status unknown)	01	
D-ENGL(2)	Engel/ Van's RV-7	71487	
D-ENGM	Piper PA-28R-201T Turbo Arrow III	28R-7803327	N36515
D-ENGO(2)	SOCATA TB-10 Tobago	934	
D-ENGS(2)	Auster 5 Alpha	3406	D-ECUR
D-ENGU(3)	Piper PA-18-150 Super Cub	18-6696	I-PILA, N9453D
D-ENGV(2)	Piper PA-18-150 Super Cub (P. 25.4.16)	18-2546	EC-DLM, D-EMMX(1), (D-ELKF), ALAT, 52-6228
D-ENGW	SOCATA MS.880B Rallye Club	1127	F-BPBI
D-ENGY(2)	Piper PA-28-181 Cherokee Archer II	28-7690338	N6107J, N9581N
D-ENHB	Robin HR.100/210D Safari	212	
D-ENHG	Robin DR.400/180 Régent	2004	
D-ENHK(2)	Piper PA-28-181 Archer II	28-8290135	N8209B
D-ENHL	Reims/Cessna F150M	F15001258	
D-ENHM(2)	Cessna 182T Skylane	18281092	N5176D
D-ENHR	Robin HR.200/100 Club	98	
D-ENHS(2)	Piper PA-28-181 Archer II	28-8490032	N4332D
D-ENHU	Cessna 182G Skylane	18255099	N3699U
D-ENHV	Robin DR.400/180 Régent	2200	
D-ENIA	Cessna 150	17844	OE-AIP, N6444T
D-ENIB(2)	Aeromere F.8L Falco III (Res. .12, replacing original D-ENIB c/n 203)	201	D-ENEB
D-ENID	Champion 7FC Tri-Traveller	105	HB-UAG
D-ENIF(3)	Diamond DA 20-A1 Katana	10050	N108CM, C-GKAC
D-ENIG(2)	Diamond DA 20-A1 Katana	10329	N329DA, C-GDMY
D-ENIH(4)	Dornier Do.27A-4 (Res. .12)	450	5Y-JBA, 5Y-AYC, D-EOGM(1), 57+22, PJ+336, QO+603, QM+006, D-EBYQ, KD+117
D-ENII (3)	Diamond DA 20-A1 Katana	10053	N53MF, C-GDMQ
D-ENIK	Piper PA-12 Super Cruiser	12-1221	N2728M, NC2728M
D-ENIL(3)	Tecnam P.2002-JF Sierra	001	I-TEJF
D-ENIM(2)	Robin DR.400/RP Remorqueur	1827	
D-ENIN	Stark Turbulent D	122	
D-ENIR(2)	Beech F33C Bonanza	CJ-27	I-RAUL, HB-EKH
D-ENIS	Auster Mk.5	1812	TW473
D-ENIT(2)	Piper PA-18-150 Super Cub	18-7327	G-ARAO, N10F
D-ENIX(3)	Piper PA-28-140 Cherokee C	28-26640	N5811U
D-ENIY	Piper PA-28-161 Warrior II	28-8616026	N9095V, (N162AV), N9640N
D-ENJA	Piaggio FWP.149D	024	90+14, AC+434, DD+394
D-ENJD	Robin HR.100/200B	128	
D-ENJK	CEA DR.360 Chevalier	641	
D-ENJL	Wassmer WA.52 Europa	46	
D-ENJM	SOCATA MS.892A Rallye Commodore 150	11877	F-BTJB
D-ENJN	Robin DR.300/180R Remorqueur	708	
D-ENJQ	Piaggio FWP.149D	042	90+29, EA+391, GA+391
D-ENJR	Piper PA-18A-135 Super Cub (Quoted officially with f/n 18-3300 as c/n)	18-3345	EI-125, I-EIKX, MM537745, 53-7745
D-ENJU	SOCATA MS.893A Rallye Commodore 180	11970	F-BTJE
D-ENJZ	SEEMS MS.885 Super Rallye	5361	OE-CDM(1)
D-ENKA	Aquila AT-01	AT01-202	
D-ENKC(2)	Cessna 152	15283246	N47770
D-ENKE(2)	Dohmann/ Impulse Xtreme	41	
D-ENKK	Cessna T182T Turbo Skylane	T18208537	PH-PBW, (OO-...), N6028R
D-ENKL	Cessna LC41-550FG Columbia	411108	N106KL
D-ENKM	Heliopolis Gomhouria Mk.6	177	SU-341
D-ENKO	Cessna 150E	15061021	OE-AYU, N2521J
D-ENKR(2)	Aquila AT-01	AT01-189	
D-ENKS	Cessna 172R Skyhawk	17280136	(N150GM), N9347F
D-ENKT	Reims/Cessna F150M Commuter	F15001357	PH-ENK, D-EFAX, PH-AYF
D-ENKU	Aero Commander 100	10A-128	
D-ENLA	Reims/Cessna F150K	F15000575	
D-ENLB(3)	Piper PA-28R-200 Cherokee Arrow II	28R-7235261	N300LB
D-ENLC(2)	Piper PA-18 Super Cub 95	18-2033	R-36, 52-2433
D-ENLF	Piper PA-18 Super Cub 95	18-1337	(G-BERU), D-ENLF, ALAT, 51-15337
D-ENLH	Piper PA-18 Super Cub 95	18-1394	ALAT, 51-15394
D-ENLK(2)	Piper PA-18 Super Cub 95	18-1556	ALAT, 51-15556
D-ENLL	Piper PA-18 Super Cub 95	18-1578	ALAT, 51-15578
D-ENLM	Piper PA-18 Super Cub 95	18-1592	ALAT, 51-15592
D-ENLO(2)	Piper PA-18-150 Super Cub	18-7909137	(D-ELMG(2)), I-VORA, N9753N
D-ENLS	Robin DR.400/180 Régent	724	
D-ENLT	Robin DR.400/180R Remorqueur	725	
D-ENLU	Cessna F150H	F150-0220	N20220
D-ENLY	Piper PA-28R-201 Arrow III	28R-7837211	N9608C
D-ENMA(3)	Diamond DA 40 Star	40337	N319MA
D-ENMC(2)	Mooney M.20K Model 252 TSE	25-1195	
D-ENMD(3)	Diamond DA 20-A1 Katana	10062	C-FWNJ
D-ENMG(2)	Piper PA-38-112 Tomahawk	38-78A0603	N4436E
D-ENMI (2)	Piper PA-18 Super Cub 95	28-2023	I-NACA, EI-92, I-EITA, MM522423, 52-2423
D-ENMM(2)	Zlin Z.50LA	0027	HA-SIB
D-ENMO(2)	Grob G 115C (Originally built as G.115,wfu 4.90, conv. .02, listed as model "NMO-01")	8007	D-EGFB
D-ENMS(2)	HOAC DV-20 Katana	20145	OE-AGY, D-EDSV
D-ENMW	Cessna 150C	15059943	N150EK, D-ENMO, N78437
D-ENMY(3)	Mylius My 200	0104	
D-ENNA(4)	Beech F33A Bonanza	CE-650	(D-ENAA(2)), I-ANAG, D-ELKA(2)
D-ENNB	Cessna T206H Turbo Stationair	T20608949	N5266P
D-ENNE(3)	SOCATA TB-9 Tampico Club	1132	
D-ENNF	SOCATA TB-9 Tampico Club	1134	
D-ENNI (3)	Piper PA-22-135 Tri-Pacer	22-1618	HB-OOS
D-ENNN(2)	Cirrus SR22	0588	N876CD
D-ENNO(2)	Piper PA-28R-201 Arrow III	28R-7837056	N6188H
D-ENNP	Piper PA-28-180 Cherokee Challenger	28-7305403	N55861
D-ENNR	Beech F33A Bonanza	CE-428	
D-ENNU(2)	Piper PA-28-161 Cadet	2841085	N9505N, N9169Z
D-ENNY(2)	Piper PA-28-161 Warrior II	28-7716179	N9503N
D-ENOA	Evektor EV-97 Eurostar VLA (Permit 13.7.11)	2011 1409	D-MECH
D-ENOB	Aeromere F.8L Falco III	206	
D-ENOC(2)	Reims/Cessna F172N (Badly damaged 30.9.12)	F17201872	
D-ENOE	Diamond DA 40 Star	40359	
D-ENOH(3)	SNCAN/Stampe SV-4C (Res. .05; still on US register 2016)	383	N383DK, N48002, F-BCQI
D-ENOL(3)	Diamond DA 20-A1 Katana	10238	N238DA, C-GDMQ
D-ENOR	Cessna 140	11087	N76647
D-ENOS(2)	Piper PA-18 Super Cub 95	18-3156	OL-L78, L-78, 53-4756
D-ENOT(3)	SOCATA MS.883 Rallye 115	1390	F-BRYC
D-ENOU	Quist/ Neico Lancair 360	369	
D-ENOW(3)	Fieseler Fi.156C-3 Storch (Painted as "NO+OA")	1049	
D-ENOX(2)	Piper PA-28R-201T Turbo Cherokee Arrow III	28R-7703141	N5656V
D-ENOY	Focke-Wulf FW.44J Stieglitz	133	D-EMUT(3), LV-ZAV, LV-XCO, FAA143, D-EX ..
D-ENPA(2)	Piper PA-28-161 Warrior II	2816005	N9107R
D-ENPB	Cessna F172H	F172-0598	
D-ENPC	Cessna F172H	F172-0600	
D-ENPE(2)	Robin DR.400/180 Régent	1590	(D-EFDX)
D-ENPH	Pfeiffer/ Neico Lancair 320	1711	
D-ENPK	SOCATA MS.886 Rallye 160	1683	F-BTHQ
D-ENPL(2)	Rockwell Commander 114A (Built from Commander 114B airframe c/n 14441 ex N5896N)	14509	
D-ENPM(2)	Cessna 172S Skyhawk SP	172S9316	N5325J
D-ENPR	Piper PA-28-181 Archer II	28-8090016	N2972G
D-ENPS	Piper PA-28-151 Cherokee Warrior	28-7415324	N9571N
D-ENPT(3)	Cirrus SR20	1771	N696SR
D-ENPW	Piper PA-28R-201T Turbo Arrow	2803008	N91832
D-ENPY	Piper PA-28-180 Cherokee B	28-1088	N11C
D-ENQA	Cessna F172D	F172-0014/17250227	(N2627U)
D-ENQO	Piper PA-18-150 Super Cub	18-8202	N4135Z
D-ENQY	Piper PA-28R-180 Cherokee Arrow	28R-30677	N4940J
D-ENRA	Cessna 170B	26989	OE-DBB, HB-COY, N3446D
D-ENRC(2)	Cessna T182T Turbo Skylane	T18208194	N53374
D-ENRD	SOCATA TB-20 Trinidad	1253	
D-ENRE(2)	Piper PA-46-310P Malibu	46-8608004	N9104P, N9103M
D-ENRF(2)	Diamond DA 40 Star	40254	N254DS, C-FDVK
D-ENRG	Piper PA-32R-301T Turbo Saratoga SP	32R-8129088	N8416T
D-ENRI	Schriek/ Piel CP.301A Emeraude	AB.410	
D-ENRJ	Piper PA-18-150 Super Cub	18-7909080	I-AETB, N9753N
D-ENRK	Piper PA-28-161 Warrior II	28-8016234	N9609N
D-ENRR	Cessna 195	7358	OY-RUK, N117DH, N3888V
D-ENRS(2)	Cessna T206H Turbo Stationair	T20608378	SP-KKW, N403PW, C-GUSA(2), N52092
D-ENRV	Schiele/ Van's RV-4	2002463	
D-ENRW	Cessna TU206G Turbo Stationair II	U20604072	N756GD
D-ENSC	Gyroflug SC-01B Speed Canard	S-26	
D-ENSL(2)	Aquila AT-01	AT01-175	
D-ENSM	Aquila AT-01	AT01-129	
D-ENSO(2)	Cessna F172G	F172-0312	
D-ENSR	Mayer/ Stoddard-Hamilton Glasair II-SRG	2317	
D-ENST	Piper PA-28-140 Cherokee Cruiser	28-7725164	N9603N
D-ENSW	Piper PA-32R-301T Turbo Saratoga SP	32R-8129045	N8341A
D-ENSX	Piper PA-28-181 Archer III	2890220	N9250J
D-ENSY(2)	Piper PA-28-181 Cherokee Archer II	28-7790450	N3335Q
D-ENTA(2)	Cessna 172S Skyhawk SP	172S10157	N6027A
D-ENTB(2)	Piper PA-28R-201T Turbo Arrow III	28R-7803188	N3707M
D-ENTD(2)	Mooney M.20J Model 205	24-3048	
D-ENTE(6)	Dornier Do.27A-4	472	D-ENTF(2), P2-UIE, D-EAEI (1), 57+41, AC+912, LA+155, GA+375, KD+130
D-ENTG	Gschwind/ Brändli BX-2 Cherry (P 28.4.14) (Kit no.56)	2002432	
D-ENTI (2)	Pallaske/ Denney Kitfox 4-1200 Speedster	KCS-142/1029	

Registration	Type	c/n	Previous identities
D-ENTL(2)	Felshart/ Van's RV-12	120068	
	(P 12.6.12)		
D-ENTO(2)	American AG-5B Tiger	10166	N1198T
D-ENTP	Piaggio FWP.149D	027	90+17, AC+403, DE+393
D-ENTS(3)	SNCAN/ Stampe SV.4A	336	D-EOOS, F-BCGC
D-ENUA	Piper PA-18 Super Cub 95	18-1478	ALAT, 51-15478
D-ENUB(2)	Reims/Cessna F172M	F17201379	
D-ENUC(2)	Erco 415D Ercoupe	4718	OO-PTE, OO-FIL, OO-LXG, PH-NCG, NC94617
D-ENUE(2)	Piper PA-28-181 Archer III	2843660	N31144
D-ENUF(2)	Cessna 172R Skyhawk	17280002	N172SE
D-ENUI	Piper PA-18 Super Cub 95	18-2084	ALAT, 52-2484
D-ENUK	Cessna 172	28294	HB-CPF , N5694A
	(CoA exp .96, on rebuild)		
D-ENUP(2)	Piper PA-28-181 Archer III	2843658	G-WISE, N30910
D-ENUQ	Piper PA-18 Super Cub 95	18-7376	N10F
D-ENUT	Piper PA-18 Super Cub 95	18-7260	N3379Z
D-ENUU(2)	Cessna 152	15285116	SP-GML, N5527Q
D-ENVA(2)	Zlin Z.43	0023	D-ENDB(2), LSK-17
	(Flies in East German AF colour scheme)		
D-ENVF(2)	Cessna 182Q Skylane	18266288	N759VF
D-ENVI	Bölkow BO.207	283	
D-ENVR	CEA DR.250/160 Capitaine	77	F-BNVR
D-ENVU	Bölkow BO.207	285	
D-ENVY(3)	Extra EA.300/L	1205	
D-ENWA	Bölkow BO.207	287	
	(W/o 27.8.07)		
D-ENWE(2)	Cessna 182J Skylane	18257197	N3097F
D-ENWG	Gyroflug SC-01B-160 Speed Canard	S-40	PH-NWG, D-ENWG
D-ENWM(2)	Cirrus SR20	1040	N146CD
D-ENWQ	Diamond DA 40 Star	40039	
D-ENWR	Diamond DA 40 Star	40029	OE-DFG(2), D-ETFG, N429DS
D-ENWU(2)	Mooney M.20J Model 205	24-3099	
D-ENWW	SAN Jodel DR.1050 Ambassadeur	491	
D-ENXB	Piper PA-28-161 Cherokee Warrior II	28-7716035	N1658H
D-ENXM	Piper PA-28-161 Cadet	2841295	N9204X
D-ENYA(3)	Cirrus SR20	1810	N157JC
D-ENYC(3)	Cessna 172S Skyhawk SP	172S10233	N6043W
D-ENYR(2)	Cessna 172C	17249253	SE-EAB, N1553Y
	(Permit 1.08 but wfu since)		
D-ENYS	Aeronca 11BC Chief	1608	OO-TWM
D-ENYZ(2)	Gardan GY-80 Horizon 160D	151	F-BNQH
D-ENZA	Cessna 150C	15059757	N1957Z
D-ENZE	Scheibe SF.23C Sperling	3501	
D-ENZL	Piper PA-28-140 Cherokee Cruiser	28-7625216	N9577N
D-ENZM	Grob G 115B	8010	(F-GNBI), D-ENZM
D-ENZO(2)	SOCATA TB-10 Tobago	1060	
D-ENZU	Piper PA-22-108 Colt	22-9524	
D-ENZY(2)	SOCATA TB-20 Trinidad	1184	
D-EOAB(3)	Piper PA-28RT-201 Arrow IV	28R-8218013	OE-KAC, N8156L
D-EOAC	Dornier Do.27A-4	452	57+24, PG+218, PG+108, QM+008, KD+ . . . ?
D-EOAD	Dornier Do.27A-4	459	57+30, PK+222, PL+105, QM+015, KD+ . . . ?
D-EOAE(4)	Flight Design CT LS-ELA	F-11-04-05	HB-WYS
	(Permit 4.6.14)		
D-EOAG	Robin DR.300/180R Remorqueur	669	
D-EOAH	SOCATA MS.880B Rallye Club	1518	F-BRYI
D-EOAI (2)	Robin DR.400/140B Major	2673	
D-EOAJ	Piaggio FWP.149D	028	90+18, AC+409, DE+394
D-EOAK(2)	Dornier Do.27A-4	481	57+47, BF+951, GB+374, KD+139
D-EOAN(2)	Lancair Legacy 2000	T1610-0301N-07-0046	
D-EOAO	Piaggio FWP.149D	003	90+03, AC+426, DC+393, BA+393, AS+478
	(Built from Piaggio c/n 327)		
D-EOAP	SOCATA ST-10 Diplomate	146	F-BTIQ
D-EOAR(2)	Piper PA-18A-150 Super Cub	18-3875	PH-WAR, R-185, 54-2475
	(Officially quoted with f/n 18-3892 as c/n)		
D-EOAS(2)	Aquila AT-01	AT01-207	
D-EOAT	Dornier Do.27A-1	319	56+39, YA+903, YA+003
D-EOBA	Breezer B600	027LSA	
	(Permit 16.2.15)		
D-EOBC(3)	Reims/Cessna F172N	F17201828	OY-BNJ
D-EOBD	Fuji FA-200-180 Aero Subaru	119	
D-EOBE	SOCATA MS.880B Rallye Club	1865	
D-EOBF	SOCATA MS.880B Rallye Club	1866	
D-EOBG(3)	Aerospool WT-9 Dynamic LSA	DY449/2013	
	(Permit 18.2.13)		
D-EOBH	SOCATA MS.893A Rallye Commodore 180	11820	
D-EOBK	Reims/Cessna F177RG Cardinal RG	F177RG0036	(N . . . . .)
	(Reims-assembled 177RG with US c/n 177RG0200)		
D-EOBL(2)	Cessna 172N Skyhawk	17273840	N5809J
D-EOBM(2)	Robin HR.100/210D Safari	146	OE-DRE
D-EOBN	Fuji FA-200-180 Aero Subaru	125	
D-EOBP	Fuji FA-200-160 Aero Subaru	128	
D-EOBR	Robin DR.300/108 2+2	602	
D-EOBS	Robin DR.300/180R Remorqueur	606	
D-EOBU	Piaggio FWP.149D	138	91+17, BB+395, KB+115
D-EOBV(2)	Piper PA-46-310P Malibu	46-8508095	N662TC, D-EOBV(2), OE-KTA, (D-ELUZ), N9127Y, (SE-IOP)
	(Res. .10 but still ntu 2016)		
D-EOBW	Piaggio FWP.149D	158	91+36, AS+402, AS+O90, KB+135
D-EOBX(2)	Boeing Stearman E75	75-8232	N5729N, BuA43138, 42-109199
D-EOCA	Piper PA-18 Super Cub 95	18-1481	D-EHCN, ALAT, 51-15481
D-EOCB(2)	Cessna 152	15284798	N4673P
D-EOCC(2)	Cessna 172N Skyhawk	17270077	N738MD
D-EOCD(4)	Cessna 172S Skyhawk SP	172S9675	N61216
D-EOCF(2)	Diamond DA 40 Star	40058	N558DS
D-EOCH	Fuji FA-200-180 Aero Subaru	140	
D-EOCK	Cirrus SR22	3546	N238CK
D-EOCM(2)	Piper PA-28-181 Archer II	2890118	N9176P
D-EOCN(2)	Beech C24R Sierra	MC-770	N6188A
D-EOCO	SOCATA MS.893A Rallye Commodore 180	11843	F-BSZV
D-EOCS	Aero Z.131 (C-104)	213	HB-USY
D-EOCT(3)	Cessna 177RG Cardinal RG	177RG1309	N53078
D-EOCU	American AA-5 Traveler	AA5-0018	(N5818L)
D-EOCW	Robin DR.300/180R Remorqueur	639	
D-EOCX	Robin DR.400/180R Remorqueur	643	
D-EOCZ	CEA DR.253B Régent	194	
D-EODA(2)	SOCATA TB-20 Trinidad	2033	
D-EODB	SOCATA MS.892A Rallye Commodore 150	11845	F-BSZY
D-EODC	SOCATA MS.892A Rallye Commodore 150	10714	F-BOVF
D-EODD(2)	SOCATA MS.893A Rallye Commodore 180	10661	F-BODD
D-EODG	SIAI-Marchetti SF.260	111	OO-HID, OY-DND
D-EODH	SOCATA MS.880B Rallye Club	1920	
D-EODK	SOCATA MS.893A Rallye Commodore 180	11889	
D-EODM(2)	Robin DR.300/180R Remorqueur	547	
D-EODO	Robin DR.300/180R Remorqueur	645	
D-EODR	CEA DR.360 Chevalier	652	
D-EODT	CEA DR.253B Régent	198	
D-EODU	Robin DR.300/108 2+2	650	
D-EODV(2)	Reims/Cessna FR182 Skylane RG	FR18200069	
D-EODW(2)	Reims/Cessna FR182 Skylane RG II	FR18200070	
D-EODX(2)	Reims/Cessna F152	F15201794	D-EOOX(2)
D-EODY	Reims FR172H Rocket	FR17200308	
D-EOEA(2)	Mooney M.20K Model 231	25-0366	HB-DFY, N231QS
D-EOEC	Bölkow BO.209 Monsun 150FV	201	
D-EOEE(2)	SOCATA TB-9 Tampico	1834	PH-OHM, S5-DKR, 5N-CAP), F-OIDG
D-EOEG	Piper PA-28-235 Cherokee	28-10411	HB-OLG, N8857W
D-EOEI	HOAC DV-20 Katana	20102	C-FVOQ, N202DV
D-EOEN	CEA Jodel DR.1050M-1 Sicile Record	623	PH-PEN
D-EOEO	Piper PA-28R-201 Arrow III	28R-7837079	N2281M
D-EOES	SOCATA MS.894A Minerva 220	11873	F-BSXF
D-EOEU	Cessna 172R Skyhawk	17280200	N9949F
D-EOFA	Reims/Cessna F150L	F15001005	F-BURC
D-EOFC	Piper PA-28-180 Cherokee Challenger	28-7305332	N11C
D-EOFH	Reims/Cessna F172P	F17202071	
D-EOFP	Reims/Cessna F172P	F17202095	
D-EOFR	Cessna T206H Turbo Stationair	T20608781	N13265
D-EOFW	Piper PA-28-181 Archer II	2890096	N9154R
D-EOFX	Cessna A150M Aerobat	A1500678	G-BOFX, N9869J
D-EOGA	Reims/Cessna F172M	F17201317	
D-EOGB(2)	Piper PA-46-310P Malibu	4608070	N9131B, N9593N
D-EOGE(2)	Piaggio FWP.149D	125	91+04, BF+413, AS+012, KB+102
D-EOGI	Dornier Do.27A-4	473	57+42, EA+385, KD+131 ?
D-EOGK	Cessna 172N Skyhawk	17271511	N3338E
D-EOGM(2)	Meyer/ Neico Lancair 235	H447/235	
	(Res)		
D-EOGP	Cessna 172RG Cutlass RG	172RG0545	N5481V
D-EOGS(2)	Sukhoi SU-29	80-01	HA-HUO, RA-3352K, RA-44540, ZU-AXP
D-EOGT	Cirrus SR20	1865	N842SR
D-EOGU(2)	Reims/Cessna F172P	F17202194	HB-CGU, LX-III
D-EOGY(2)	Aviat A-1B Husky	2421	G-DOGY, N11UK
D-EOHB(3)	Stemme ASP/S15-1	ASP-31	
	(Res. 30.4.15)		
D-EOHC	Reims/Cessna F150M	F15001292	
D-EOHD	Piper PA-28-181 Archer II	2890116	N9152Q
D-EOHF	Robin DR.400/180 Regent	1397	
D-EOHG	Robin DR.400/180 Régent	1402	
D-EOHH	Reims/Cessna F172N	F17201804	
D-EOHK	Mooney M.20C Ranger	20-1230	
D-EOHP	SAN Jodel DR.1050 Ambassadeur	297	F-BKHB
D-EOHS	Schlüter Super Pulsar 100	2002125	
D-EOHT	SOCATA ST-10 Diplomate	145	OE-DHT, F-BTIP
D-EOIA(2)	Robin DR.400/180R Remo 180	2061	
D-EOIC(3)	Piper PA-28-181Archer III	2843049	N9272N
D-EOIO	Messerschmitt Bf.108B-1	2086	A-212, HB-HOL
	(P 22.9.16)		
D-EOIS(2)	Piper PA-38-112 Tomahawk	38-78A0264	D-EGIS(2), N9725N
D-EOIT	Piper PA-28-180 Cherokee E	28-5647	N2556R
D-EOJA	Reims/Cessna F172N	F17201534	
D-EOJC	Cessna 172P Skyhawk	17274457	SE-IPO, N52247
D-EOJE	Reims/Cessna F172N	F17201537	(F-GASO)
D-EOJH	Beech C23 Sundowner	M-2216	HB-EJH
D-EOJI	Reims/Cessna F172N	F17201628	
D-EOJM	Piper J-3C-90 Cub Special	22633	N4494M, NC4494M, NC3400N
D-EOJN	Piper PA-38-112 Tomahawk	38-79A0528	SE-ICD
D-EOJO	Reims/Cessna F172N	F17201551	
D-EOJT	Cessna 150L	15075013	N10759
D-EOJU	Reims/Cessna F172N	F17201635	
D-EOJX	Reims/Cessna F150L	F15000738	
D-EOKA	Robin HR.200/100 Club	49	
D-EOKB(2)	Mooney M.20R Ovation	29-0122	
D-EOKI	Reims FR172F Rocket	FR17200131	
D-EOKK	Cessna 152	15281132	N49068
D-EOKL	Gardan GY-80 Horizon 180	246	
D-EOKM(2)	Aquila AT-01	215	G-GAEB
D-EOKO(3)	Reims/Cessna F172N	F17201895	
D-EOKS	Christen A-1 Husky	1103	
D-EOLA	CEA DR.300/1255 Petit Prince	317	F-BPRD
	(Originally built as DR.315, modified 9.09)		
D-EOLB	Cessna 172N Skyhawk	17270813	N739UH
D-EOLC	Cessna 172RG Cutlass RG	172RG0208	N6606R
D-EOLD(3)	Taylorcraft BC-12D	10218	OE-AFV, D-EMAF(1), N44418, NC44418
D-EOLF(2)	Gippsland GA-8 Airvan	GA8-05-080	VH-IMI
D-EOLG	Cessna 182L Skylane	18258630	N3330R
D-EOLH	Cessna 210N Centurion II	21064220	N5479Y
D-EOLK	Robin DR.400/180 Régent	2434	
D-EOLM(3)	Cessna 172R Skyhawk	17280125	N9856F
D-EOLO(2)	Aero Designs Pulsar XP	EB433	
	(Also quoted as c/n1861/2004 = type cert and date) (P 15.8.11)		
D-EOLP	Reims/Cessna F182Q Skylane	F18200160	(OY-BNT)
D-EOLS	Robin DR.300/180R Remorqueur	555	
D-EOLT(2)	Beech B36TC Bonanza	EA-470	N2844B
D-EOLU	Reims/Cessna F182Q Skylane	F18200086	
D-EOLV	Cessna 172RG Cutlass RG	172RG0691	N6430V
D-EOLX(2)	Cessna 172R Skyhawk	17281332	D-EXAF, N6029G
D-EOLY(2)	Reims/Cessna F182Q Skylane	F18200079	
D-EOLZ	Cessna 172RG Cutlass RG	172RG0552	N5524V
D-EOMA(2)	Diamond DA 20-A1 Katana	10314	N644DA, C-GDMB
D-EOMB	Reims/Cessna F172P	F17202222	
D-EOMC	Reims/Cessna F172L	F17200900	F-BTUX
D-EOME(2)	Reims/Cessna F172N	F17201679	
D-EOMG(2)	Cessna 172N Skyhawk	17270151	N738QH
	(Dam. 9.5.89, not yet repaired)		
D-EOMI	Navion Rangemaster G	NAV-4-2479	HB-ESN, (D-EBMY), N2479T
	(Permit .07 after rebuild)		
D-EOMK	Robin DR.400/180 Régent	1267	G-EOMK, D-EOMK
D-EOML(2)	Cessna T182T Turbo Skylane	T18208814	N6170Z
D-EOMM	CASA C-1.131E Jungmann	2001	E3B-404
D-EOMN(2)	Cessna 172P Skyhawk	17276594	N9638L
D-EOMO	Cirrus SR22	3612	PH-DVD, N228CK
D-EOMQ	Piaggio FWP.149D	051	90+37, SB+211, SC+401, AS+478

Registration	Type	C/n	Previous identities
D-EOMS(2)	SOCATA MS.894A Minerva 220	11078	OO-CYF, F-BSCP
	(Res 5.8.16)		
D-EOMT	Cessna 152	15283960	N6617B
D-EOMV(2)	Cessna 172S Skyhawk SP	172S9076	N976TA
D-EOMX	Cessna 172P Skyhawk	17275304	N62587
D-EONA(2)	Piaggio P.149D	312	92+16, AC+463, AS+463
D-EONE(2)	Beech F33A Bonanza	CE-1106	SX-AML, N3021U
D-EONH	Stinson L-5C Sentinel	76-3615 ?	(G-BNUM), N8035H,
	(C/n unconfirmed, serial quoted as c/n)		N63485, 44-17328
D-EONS	Reims FR172H Rocket	FR17200273	OE-DNS, D-ECNS
D-EONU	Cessna F172H	F172-0583	
D-EONW	Reims/Cessna F182Q Skylane	F18200051	
D-EOOD	Reims/Cessna F172N	F17201958	
D-EOOE	CEA DR.250/160 Capitaine	84	F-BOCE
D-EOOG	Reims/Cessna F172N Skyhawk II	F17201952	
D-EOOI	Springer/ Neico Lancair 235	007	D-ESAR
D-EOOL(2)	Piper PA-28-236 Dakota	28-8311004	N8290Z
D-EOOM(2)	Cessna 172D	17249978	OO-MET, N2378U
D-EOON(3)	Cessna 172R Skyhawk	17280173	F-GJLS, N9893F
D-EOOO(2)	Cessna P210N Pressurized Centurion	P21000439	N731CM
	(Soloy conversion)		
D-EOOP	Reims/Cessna F152	F15201588	D-EOOO(1)
D-EOOR	Reims/Cessna F172N	F17201973	
D-EOOV(2)	Aerostyle Breezer	006	D-MOOW
D-EOOW	Reims/Cessna F172N	F17201971	
D-EOOY(2)	HOAC DV-20 Katana	20064	
D-EOOZ	SOCATA TB-200 Tobago XL	2067	SP-EXY, CS-DEG,
	(Res .16)		F-OJBF
D-EOPA	Piper PA-18 Super Cub 95	18-1523	N8944, D-ECEI, ALAT,
			51-15523
D-EOPB(2)	Bömer/ Thatcher CX4	196-1	
D-EOPC	Reims/Cessna F182Q Skylane	F18200159	
D-EOPD	Reims/Cessna F172N	F17201955	
D-EOPE	SOCATA ST-10 Diplomate	107	F-OCPE
D-EOPG(2)	Piper PA-46-350P Malibu Mirage	4622064	N255SW, N350KM,
	(JetProp DLX conversion # 67)		N350PM, N91782
D-EOPH	Cessna 172RG Cutlass RG	172RG0652	N6389V
D-EOPI	Erco 415D Ercoupe	541	(D-EBUY), D-EBUP,
			N87368
D-EOPK	Reims/Cessna F182Q Skylane	F18200044	OY-BUW
D-EOPL(3)	Cessna T206H Turbo Stationair	T20608907	N52273
D-EOPM	Piper PA-28-181 Cherokee Archer II	28-7790104	N5944F, N9516N
D-EOPR(2)	Cessna 182Q Skylane	18266605	N95709
	(Porsche engine)		
D-EOPS	Reims/Cessna F152	F15201670	
D-EOPT(3)	Fläming-Air FA-02 Smaragd 600	25/07	
	(Permit 5.10)		
D-EOPW(2)	Piper PA-46-350P Malibu Mirage	4622192	N369Z, (N695MA)
D-EOPX	Cessna 172P Skyhawk	17275187	LN-DBC(2), OY-CJC,
			N55471
D-EOPZ	Laubenthal/ Murphy Rebel R603	1926	
	(Amateur-built, c/n is type certificate no.)		
D-EOQE	Reims/Cessna F172M	F17201188	
D-EOQG	Reims/Cessna F172M	F17201191	
	(Cr 23.4.11)		
D-EOQK	Reims/Cessna F172M	F17201199	
D-EOQL	Reims/Cessna F172M	F17201203	
D-EOQM	Reims/Cessna F172M	F17201211	
D-EOQP	Cessna 182P Skylane	18263114	N7330N
	(Diesel engine)		
D-EOQY	SNCAN/ Stampe SV.4A	468	F-GCCY, EC-AYL,
			F-BDBE
D-EORA	Reims/Cessna F172M	F17201374	
D-EORC(2)	Piper PA-28-181 Archer II	2890132	SE-KIY, "SE-KIS"
D-EORD	Reims/Cessna F172N	F17201959	(D-EOOF)
D-EORF	Reims/Cessna F172N	F17201954	"D-EOCY"
D-EORK(2)	Piper PA-28RT-201T Turbo Arrow IV	28R-8131017	N8284H
D-EORO	Piper PA-28R-200 Cherokee Arrow II	28R-7335306	N55894
D-EORT	Cessna 172N Skyhawk	17270994	N1426E
D-EORV	Strassburg/ Van's RV-12	120584	
D-EORX	de Havilland DH.82A Tiger Moth	83866	N82DH, N82GS,
			HB-UBB, G-AORX, T7340
D-EOSB(2)	Grob G 115A	8037	HB-UGF, (D-EGVV)
D-EOSC(2)	Kurz/ Udet U12K Flamingo Replica	01	
D-EOSF	DHC-1 Chipmunk Mk.22	C1/0023	G-AOSF, D-EIIZ(2),
			G-AOSF, HB-TUA, G-AOSF, WB571
D-EOSG	Cessna 172R Skyhawk	17281200	N21379
D-EOSI	Wassmer WA.40A Super IV	27	HA-VEV, D-EOSI,
			HB-DCH, F-BKCC
D-EOSM	Seiss/ Udet U12a Flamingo	1785	
	(Painted as "D-1202") (Cr 24.8.13 Tannheim)		
D-EOSN(2)	Cirrus SR22T	0011	N411MX
D-EOSO	Reims/Cessna F182Q Skylane	F18200064	
D-EOSR	Robin DR.400/180R Remorqueur	1575	
D-EOSS(2)	Piper PA-18-150 Super Cub	18-7509122	I-ROYY, N40573
D-EOST	SOCATA MS.893A Rallye Commodore 180	12070	F-BUGA, (D-ENMD)
D-EOSU	Cessna TU206F Turbo Stationair	U20603298	N8439Q
D-EOSY	Cessna 182P Skylane	18263184	OY-BIT, SE-GGD,
			N7403N
D-EOTB	Robin DR.400/180 Régent	1607	
D-EOTC	SOCATA TB-10 Tobago	1115	
D-EOTE	Reims/Cessna F172N	F17201627	
D-EOTH	Aerostyle Breezer B600	LSA021	
	(Permit 20.6.12)		
D-EOTI	Reims/Cessna F172N	F17201538	
D-EOTK	Piper PA-22-150 Tri-Pacer	22-2752	HB-OTK, D-EFYV,
			N2341P
D-EOTL	Robin ATL L	83	F-GOTL, HB-SCC,
	(Permit 9.09)		F-WZZZ, HB-SCC
D-EOTO	Reims/Cessna F172N	F17201629	
D-EOTT	Reims/Cessna F172N	F17201816	
D-EOTY	Reims/Cessna F182Q	F18200052	CS-DBS, D-EOTY
D-EOTZ	Zlin Z.326 Trenér Master	902	HB-TCB
	(Res .14)		
D-EOUC	Cessna 172R Skyhawk	17280197	
D-EOUD	Piper J-3C-90 Cub	11854	HB-OUD, 44-79558
	(Res)		
D-EOUH	Cessna 182M Skylane	18259392	OE-DUH, OE-BUM,
			N70848
D-EOUI	LET Z-37A-2 Cmelák	20-02	DDR-SWI, DM-SWI
D-EOUK	Cessna 207 Skywagon 207	20700008	HB-CUK, N91009
D-EOUV	Becker/ Binder CP.301S Mistral	AB.01	
	(Permit exp 8.02)		
D-EOUW	SOCATA MS.893E Rallye 180GT	12845	OE-DUW
D-EOVA	Reims/Cessna F172N	F17201625	
D-EOVE	Reims/Cessna F172N	F17201636	
D-EOVL	SOCATA MS.893A Rallye Commodore 180	10717	F-BOVL
D-EOVO(2)	Reims/Cessna F150M	F15001411	
D-EOVU	Reims/Cessna F172N	F17201624	
D-EOVW	Cessna T182T Turbo Skylane	T18208987	N5275B
D-EOVY	Reims/Cessna F172N	F17201520	
D-EOWA	Reims/Cessna F172N	F17201724	
D-EOWB	Reims/Cessna F172N	F17201131	OY-AGW
D-EOWC	Piper PA-28RT-201T Turbo Arrow IV	28R-8231008	N8454T
D-EOWE	Reims/Cessna F172N	F17201729	
D-EOWG(2)	HOAC DV-20 Katana	20019	N19DV
D-EOWI (2)	Reims/Cessna F172N	F17201733	
D-EOWJ	SOCATA Rallye 180T-D	3135	F-GBCO
D-EOWM(2)	Maule MX.7-180 Star Rocket	11047C	N6121Q
D-EOWN	Cessna 172RG Cutlass RG	172RG0704	D-EIKP, N6443V
D-EOWO	Reims/Cessna F172M	F17201218	(SE-GKM)
D-EOWP	Piper PA-38-112 Tomahawk	38-79A0336	OY-BRR
D-EOWR	Cessna 210N Centurion II	21064234	N5516Y
D-EOWS(2)	Mooney M.20J Model 201	24-1227	N1151L
D-EOWV	Cessna 172RG Cutlass RG	172RG0675	N6413V
D-EOXC(2)	Piper PA-28-181 Archer III	2843149	PH-AEF, N9291S
D-EOXE(2)	LET Z-37A-2 Cmelák	16-01	DDR-SRE, DM-SRE
D-EOXI	Reims/Cessna F172M	F17201419	
D-EOXO	Reims/Cessna F172N	F17201708	
D-EOXQ	PZL-104 Wilga 35A	107336	DDR-WRK, DM-WRK
D-EOXR	PZL-104 Wilga 35A	96324	DDR-WRA, DM-WRA
D-EOXT	Bölkow BO.208C Junior	570	HB-UXT, D-EDMA(1)
D-EOXU	Reims/Cessna F172N	F17201714	
D-EOXX	Piper PA-46-310P Malibu	46-8408027	LY-MON, LY-STB,
			N43367
D-EOYE	Reims/Cessna F172N	F17201752	
D-EOYH	SOCATA TB-9 Tampico	272	OE-DYH
D-EOYS	Cessna 172N Skyhawk	17269857	N214FR, N214ER,
			N738BV
D-EOYU	Reims/Cessna F172N	F17201803	
D-EOYZ	LET Z-37-2 Cmelák	06-29	DDR-SNZ, DM-SNZ
D-EOZA	SEEMS MS.880B Rallye Club	326	F-BKZA
D-EOZC	SOCATA TB-21 Trinidad TC	806	SE-KBB
D-EOZE	Reims/Cessna F172N	F17201716	
D-EOZF	Piper PA-28-140 Cherokee	28-23088	HB-OZF, N9631W
D-EOZH	Piper PA-28R-180 Cherokee Arrow	28R-30695	HB-OZH, N4948J
D-EOZI	Reims/Cessna FRA150M Aerobat	FRA1500335	
D-EOZK(2)	Winkler/ EEL ULF-2	032	
	(Permit 7.05)		
D-EOZN	Piper PA-28-140 Cherokee B	28-25146	HB-OZN, N7234F
D-EOZW	Aermacchi AL.60B-2	6267/87	
	(For export to USA 8.16)		
D-EOZY	Dornier Do.27B-1	224	55+77, PD+334, PD+109,
			PF+106
D-EOZZ	Schacher/ Binder CP.301S Smaragd	AB.25	
D-EPAA	Piper PA-28-181 Archer II	28-8490074	PH-JVT, N43573
D-EPAB(2)	Flight Design CT LS-ELA	F-10-03-11	
	(Permit 8.10)		
D-EPAC(2)	Piper PA-20 Pacer 135	20-674	G-BFAO, ZS-CMH,
			ZS-CAH
D-EPAD	Cessna 172N Skyhawk	17269018	N734PY
D-EPAE	Maule MT-7-235 Super Rocket	18104C	
D-EPAF(2)	Piper PA-18-150 Super Cub	18-8006	I-EPVV, D-EPVV, I-PAVV,
	(Permit 9.9.15)		HB-OWK, N6785Z, N10F
D-EPAG	SOCATA TB-20 Trinidad	2118	
D-EPAH	Viere/ Van's RV-9A	91042	
D-EPAI	Piper PA-46-350P Malibu Mirage	4622122	N50MP, (N48CK),
			N9227R
D-EPAJ	Piper PA-18-150 Super Cub	18-3996	TC-EDA, TC-ECF,
			TurkAF, 54-2596
D-EPAK	DHC-1 Chipmunk 22	C1/0328	G-BDIC, WD388
D-EPAL	Piper PA-28-181 Cherokee Archer II	28-7890054	N47335
D-EPAM	Robin DR.400/135Cdi	2603	
D-EPAN	Cessna 172N Skyhawk	17273933	(YU-. . .), N9847J
D-EPAO	Piper PA-28-151 Cherokee Warrior	28-7615121	SE-GLX
D-EPAQ	Piper J-3C-90 Cub	12028	F-GJRC, (F-GJPR),
			HB-OUA, 44-79732
D-EPAR(2)	Cessna T182T Turbo Skylane	T18208942	N141RC
D-EPAS(2)	Piper PA-28-181 Archer III	2843080	N92854
D-EPAT	Piper PA-28-161 Warrior III	2842084	N41815
	(Diesel engine)		
D-EPAV	Cessna 182T Skylane	18282004	(D-ESEX(3)), N12224
D-EPAW(2)	Cessna 172RG Cutlass RG	172RG0757	I-ALEU, (D-EVKS),
	(Permit 19.7.13)		I-ALEU, N6532V
D-EPAX(2)	Bücker Bü.133C Jungmeister	'51'	OO-EII, D-EIII (2),
			Spanish AF
	(51 is the line number while the true c/n is between 1032 and 1050)		
D-EPAY	SIAI-Marchetti SF.260	2-26	I-CEMY
	(Res. .11)		
D-EPAZ	Piper PA-28-181 Archer III	2843632	N31349
D-EPBA	Aerostyle Breezer B600	020LSA	
	(Permit 19.5.14)		
D-EPBB	Cessna 150K	15071458	N5958G
D-EPBC	HOAC DV-20 Katana	20005	OE-CDI
D-EPBG(2)	Stemme ASP/S15-1	ASP-32	
	(Res. 21.5.15)		
D-EPBK	Piper PA-28RT-201T Turbo Arrow IV	28R-8031164	D-ELDW, N8253C,
			N9595N
D-EPBM	Miny/ Aero Designs Pulsar XP	420SB	
D-EPBN	Xtreme Air XA42	113	D-ETXA(3)
	(Res 9.16)		
D-EPBO	Cirrus SR22	1842	T7-AEA, D-ETEK,
			N794CD
D-EPBS(2)	Stemme ASP/S15-1	ASP-33	
	(Res. 21.5.15)		
D-EPBW(2)	Piper PA-28-160 Cherokee	28-337	N202W, D-EFRO, N11C
D-EPCA(3)	Yakovlev Yak-18T	08-34	G-RYAK, HA-YAF,
			RA-44480
D-EPCB	Diamond DA 20-C1 Katana	C0154	N85VS, C-GKAI
D-EPCC	Cessna T206H Turbo Stationair TC	T20608156	N2400U
	(Centurion diesel)		
D-EPCD	Cirrus SR22	2744	N550SR
D-EPCE	Cessna 172S Skyhawk SP	172S10958	LN-FTF, N5192P
D-EPCF	Schmidt/ Roloff-Unger RLU1 Breezy	1	
	(Res. .11)		
D-EPCG	Güthoff/ Brditschka HB-207 VRG Alfa	207013	
D-EPCH	Schneider/ Zenith CH-601 HD Zodiac	6-1724	
D-EPCI	Pilatus P.3-05	497-46	HB-RCB, LX-PAD,
	(Permit 21.9.15)		HB-RCB, A-859
D-EPCL	DHC-1 Chipmunk 22	C1/0137	OO-NCL, G-AOUN,
			WB689

48

Regn	Type	c/n	Previous identities
D-EPCM	Piper PA-28-161 Cadet	2841335	N92043, N92246, N125ND, N92246
D-EPCN	Piper PA-28-161 Warrior II	2816102	N9196X, (HB-PNN)
D-EPCO	Cessna R.172K Hawk XP	R1722439	N736DF
D-EPCR	Cessna 172S Skyhawk SP	172S9484	N298SP
D-EPCS	Cessna 172S Skyhawk SP	172S9491	N332SP
D-EPCT	Piper PA-22-108 Colt	22-9125	SE-CZE
D-EPCW	Cessna 172S Skyhawk SP	172S9550	N2161J
D-EPDA	Diamond DA 20-A1 Katana	10255	C-GKAT
D-EPDB	Diamond DA 20-A1 Katana	10166	C-GDMB
D-EPDC	Remos GX iS (P. 24.5.16)	444	
D-EPDD	Piper PA-28-181 Cherokee Archer II	28-7890528	HB-PDD, N36744
D-EPDF	Aerostyle Breezer B600 (P. 15.4.16)	031LSA	
D-EPDH	Grob G 115A	8022	LV-RTA, LV-DML
D-EPDR	HOAC DV-20 Katana	20091	
D-EPEA	Cirrus SR22	1025	N793CM
D-EPEB	Beech A36 Bonanza	E-2731	TC-SMS, N80287
D-EPED	Diamond DA 40D Star	D4.031	G-OTDI
D-EPEF	Stark Turbulent D-1	112	D-EFEF(1)
D-EPEG	Engmann/Slepcev Storch SS-4	SS4-051	
D-EPEK	Cirrus SR22	3351	OY-NBS, N582CP
D-EPEL	Balik Pelikan Sport 600S	752	
D-EPEP	Piper PA-28-181 Archer III	2890217	N92263
D-EPER	Diamond DA 40 Star	40321	N809ER
D-EPET(3)	Rospert/ Van's RV-6	25548	
D-EPEW	Mooney M.20K Model 231	25-0170	N231DN
D-EPEZ	American Champion 8KCAB Super Decathlon	1022-2006	
D-EPFA	Extra EA.300/L	1171	G-CCPI
D-EPFG	Cessna TR182 Turbo Skylane RG (Reims-assembled with 'c/n' 0001)	R18200794	D-EMCR, OO-ADM, PH-ADM, "PH-NEL", PH-ADM, PH-AYC, N736YX
D-EPFH	Cirrus SR22	3497	N93WR
D-EPFM	Robin DR.400/RP Remorqueur	1841	OE-KMP, D-EGMP(2)
D-EPFN	Neumayer/ Van's RV-7	4-10204	
D-EPFW	Cessna F150G (Permit 18.9.15)	F150-0151	D-ENYQ(2)
D-EPGA	Cirrus SR22	1474	N406AJ
D-EPGB(2)	Remos GX	375	
D-EPGC	Cessna TR182 Turbo Skylane RG	R18202018	OE-KEE, D-EFIB(3), N6423T
D-EPGL	Link/ Van's RV-7	0720	
D-EPGM	AIAA/Stampe SV-4C	1100	N97264, F-BASM, Fr.AF
D-EPGS	Robin DR.400/180R Remo 180	2167	
D-EPGT	Cirrus SR20	1966	N190PG
D-EPHA	Piper PA-28RT-201T Turbo Arrow IV	28R-8031151	N8245S
D-EPHB	Cessna TR182 Turbo Skylane RG	R18200858	(D-EVAS), N737NC
D-EPHG(2)	Aerospool WT-9 Dynamic (Permit 4.4.13)	DY-475/2013	
D-EPHH	Piper PA-46-350P Malibu Mirage (JetProp DLX conversion #248)	4636245	N13JC, N245MA, N4160N
D-EPHK	Piper PA-46-350P Malibu Mirage	4636163	D-EXPM, N234DZ, N313HP, N41266
D-EPHN	Robin DR.500/200i Président	007	
D-EPHP	Robin DR.400/180 Régent	2244	
D-EPHS	Hell / Denney Kitfox IV (Presumed re-regd D-MKIT)	1839	
D-EPIA(3)	Cirrus SR22	1610	N54KS
D-EPIC(3)	Van's RV-8	83036	
D-EPIE	Piper PA-28RT-201T Turbo Arrow IV	28R-7931119	N2102V
D-EPIG	Aquila AT-01	AT01-167	
D-EPIH	Piper PA-28RT-201T Turbo Arrow IV (Res. .14)	28R-8531012	OE-KIS, N2506V
D-EPII	Pilatus P.2-06	600-63	G-CJCI, U-143, U-114
D-EPIK	Piper PA-32R-300 Cherokee Lance	32R-7680107	N8352C
D-EPIL	Pilatus P.2-06	75	HB-RAP, U-155, I-126
D-EPIM	SOCATA TB-20 Trinidad	1116	
D-EPIP	Cessna 177RG Cardinal RG	177RG0362	N1962Q
D-EPIR	Maule MX-7-180 Star Rocket	20023C	N3104M
D-EPIT(2)	Cessna 172B	17248088	D-EBSE, N7588X
D-EPIX	Impulse 180 (Res)	TD-12	
D-EPIZ	Christen Pitts S-2B	5159	OH-TOM, N5342K
D-EPJB	Cirrus SR20	1244	N889CD
D-EPJC	Piper PA-18-150 Super Cub	18-8286	OO-VVC, N10F
D-EPJD	III Sky Arrow 650TC	C006	
D-EPJF	Tecnam P.2002-JF Sierra	068	
D-EPJH	Holland/ Aero Designs Pulsar XP	1799	
D-EPJN	Cirrus SR22	2028	N907SR
D-EPJO	Cirrus SR20	1992	N522PG
D-EPJP	Robin ATL L	99	F-GFSS
D-EPJR	Cessna 207 Skywagon 207	20700165	OK-DIB, OE-DIB(2), OE-BIB, OE-DEX, N1565U
D-EPJS	Beech A36 Bonanza Soloy	E-2997	N1067Z
D-EPKA(2)	Rockwell Commander 112TC	13085	N59FL, EC-FUR, N4593W
D-EPKB	Reims/Cessna F182Q Skylane .	F18200114	OY-BYA, SE-IBA
D-EPKL	Klink/ Europa Avn Europa	1	
D-EPKO	Piper PA-46-310P Malibu	4608017	N9101Z
D-EPKW	Flight Design CT LS-ELA (Permit 4.10)	F-10-01-17	
D-EPLA	Wassmer WA.52 Europa	62	OE-KLA, HB-DCG, (D-EGRJ(1))
D-EPLC	Cessna 172S Skyhawk SP	172S8585	N350ME
D-EPLD	Piper PA-46-310P Malibu	46-8608047	HB-PIU
D-EPLE	Cessna P210N Pressurised Centurion	P21000511	N900BC
D-EPLF	General Avia F22B Pinguino (Res. .11)	010	I-CARQ
D-EPLG	Aquila AT-01-100C	AT01-315	
D-EPLH	Cessna R182 Skylane RG	R18200063	N7572W, N84W, N7572W
D-EPLJ	SOCATA TB-10 Tobago	1069	PH-DFE, D-EBAP(2)
D-EPLM	Cessna 182P Skylane (Reims-assembled with "c/n" 0013)	18263892	D-EDQQ, N6929M
D-EPLP	Cessna 172S Skyhawk SP	172S9253	OH-KLE, N253FA
D-EPLR	Fuji FA.200-180AO Aero Subaru	246	HB-ETX
D-EPLT	Van's RV-7 (P. 12.8.16)	2002546	
D-EPMA	Mooney M.20M Model 257 TLS	27-0147	
D-EPMB	Piper PA-18-150 Super Cub	18-1591	D-EKQY, (D-EKQI), ALAT, 51-15591
D-EPMC	Pitzer/ Aero Designs Pulsar XP	1301	(D-EPMY)
D-EPME	Cessna 172S Skyhawk SP	172S10614	HA-BET(2), N16887
D-EPMI	Robin HR.200/120B	262	
D-EPMK(2)	Aquila AT-01	AT01-154	
D-EPML	Tecnam P.2008-JC	063	
D-EPMM	Piper PA-24-260 Comanche B	24-4456	N8995P
D-EPMP	Cirrus SR22	2588	N575CB
D-EPMR	Cirrus SR22	3112	D-EWGW, N179CP
D-EPMS	Cessna TU206F Turbo Stationair	U2060 2695	N33254
D-EPMT(3)	HOAC DV-20 Katana	20125	OE-CKL, OE-VPP, TF-FTZ, OY-JAK
D-EPNA	Piper PA-28-161 Archer II	2890185	HB-PNA
D-EPNE	Aquila AT-01-100C	327	
D-EPNH	Robin ATL	105	F-GFSY
D-EPNK	Piper PA-28-236 Dakota	28-7911324	CS-AUY, N80904
D-EPNL	Leis/ Pitts S-1E Special (Permit 17.12.13)	001	
D-EPOB	SOCATA TB-10 Tobago	172	F-GCOQ
D-EPOC	Zlin Z.526F Trenér Master	1146	LZ-. . .
D-EPOD	Cessna 177B Cardinal	17702729	EI-POD, N1444C
D-EPOH	Robin R.3000/160	153	LX-ROH, (D-EKKS)
D-EPOI	Extra EA.300	024	LN-CAN, D-EDCM
D-EPOM	Schulze/ Kitfox IV Speedster	1686	D-EPPM(1)
D-EPOP	Diamond DA 40 Star	40071	
D-EPOS(3)	Remos GX (Permit 4.10)	360	
D-EPOT	Piper PA-28-236 Dakota	28-7911108	(SE-LDT), OH-POT, N70WH, N2089R
D-EPOU	Koch HM-19C Himmelslaus (Permit 1.6.12)	001	HB-SPG
D-EPOZ	SOCATA MS.893E Rallye 150GT	13288	I-GBXK, F-GBXK
D-EPPC	Diamond DA 20-A1 Katana	10042	N442PC, C-GDMY
D-EPPD	SOCATA MS.880B Rallye Club	2406	OY-DZT, (F-BUZJ)
D-EPPG	Piper PA-46-500TP Malibu Meridian	4697158	N53667, (N117WT), N53667
D-EPPH	Van's RV-7	73054	
D-EPPI	Bohnhorst / Van's RV-4	1821	
D-EPPJ	Bohnhorst / Van's RV-4RS Harmon Rocket III (Permit 4.11.15)	2002542	
D-EPPK	Robin R.2160D Alpha Sport	150	OO-AYL, F-GAXL
D-EPPL	Piper PA-28-181 Archer III	2843044	N9268L
D-EPPM(2)	Cessna P210N Pressurised Centurion	P21000427	N62150, D-ELFM, N107TM, C-GDCB, N778SK
D-EPPN	Neumann/ Denney Kitfox IV-1200	KBS-081	
D-EPPO	Diamond DA 20-A1 Katana	10158	N280DA, C-GKAC
D-EPPP	Mooney M.20J Model 205	24-3292	
D-EPPR	Beech C23 Sundowner	M-2075	N2074K
D-EPPV	Diamond DA 20-A1 Katana	10138	HB-SCW, C-GKAQ
D-EPPW	Mooney M.20K Model 231	25-0624	N1150Z
D-EPPY	Piper PA-46-500TP Malibu Meridian	4697227	N771BL, (N9021A), N771BL, N9540N, N3113J
D-EPRB	Cirrus SR22T	0013	N864DF
D-EPRC	Pastötter/ Zenair CH-601XL Zodiac	6-9638	
D-EPRF(2)	Diamond DA 40 Star (Res .16)	40234	(D-EMPL(4)), OE-DHW, N609DS, C-GDMB
D-EPRH	Cessna 172S Skyhawk SP	172S9676	OK-MCP, N6124A
D-EPRI	Robin R.2160D	131	HB-EXZ
D-EPRK	Kehl/ Aero Designs Pulsar XP	01	
D-EPRL	Leveringhaus/ Capella XLS-TR	01	
D-EPRN	Polikarpov I-16 Rata Type 24	2421319	ZK-JIN, Soviet AF 5"
D-EPRO	Cessna 150M	15076080	(D-ERLE), N66493
D-EPRR	Cessna T206H Turbo Stationair (Soloy conversion)	T20608174	N206TL
D-EPRS(2)	Cirrus SR22T	0520	N770GC
D-EPRT	Cessna 172S Skyhawk SP	172S10495	N485MC
D-EPRV	Heigl/ Van's RV-7	73526	
D-EPRW	Beech B36TC Bonanza	EA-521	
D-EPSA	Piper PA-18-150 Super Cub	18-8503	HB-PSA, N3263D, C-FCIR, CF-CIR, N4260Z
D-EPSC	Reims/Cessna F182Q Skylane	F18200136	OE-DVO
D-EPSI	Robin DR.500/200i Président	0043	
D-EPSM(2)	Mooney M.20J Model 205	24-3429	(D-ESTC), G-DEST
D-EPSO	Sokolowski/ Neico Lancair 320 (Permit 5.8.14)	01	
D-EPSS	Cirrus SR22	1784	N683CD
D-EPST(2)	Cessna 172R Skyhawk	17280154	N715GT
D-EPSV	CSA Sportcruiser (Piper Sport)	P1001017	
D-EPSY	Aquila AT-01	AT01-197	
D-EPTA(2)	Robin DR.400/140B Dauphin 4	2652	(D-EYSS)
D-EPTB	Maule MX-7-235 Star Rocket	10004C	N39TB
D-EPTC	Piper PA-46-350P Malibu Mirage (JetProp DLX conversion #122)	4636012	N92575
D-EPTD	Boeing Stearman E75	75-5322	N131TP, N5272N, (BuA61200), 42-17159
D-EPTF	Flight Design CT LS (Permit .09)	F08-11-28	
D-EPTG	Flight Design CT LS-ELA (Permit 17.3.14)	F-08-10-20	I-9244, D-EPTG
D-EPTK	Cirrus SR22	3610	N220CK
D-EPTM	Beech B36TC Bonanza	EA-513	N8258F
D-EPTS	Aviat Pitts S-2B	5218	OK-PTS, G-SIIB, G-BUVY, N6073U
D-EPTU	Cessna 150M	15076423	N3214V
D-EPUD	Bölkow BO.209 Monsun 160FV	196	HB-UED, D-EAIL(1)
D-EPUL	Robin DR.300/180R Remorqueur	513	F-BSJO
D-EPUM	Brditschka HB-207VRG Alfa (Status unknown)	01/207023	
D-EPUP	HOAC DV-20 Katana	20154	OE-CDA
D-EPUR	Mudry CAP.10B	96	HB-SAY, F-BXHZ
D-EPUS	Piper PA-46-500TP Malibu Meridian	4697079	(D-EARG(2)), (D-EADK(3)), N5326C
D-EPUT	Cessna 172M	17262514	N13124
D-EPUZ	Diamond DA 40D Star	D4.337	OE-VPT
D-EPVA	Piper PA-28-180 Cherokee Challenger	28-7305352	N222MM, N35286
D-EPVS	Cirrus SR20	1719	N307SR
D-EPWB	Binder/Europa Avn Europa	1/149	
D-EPWE	Cessna 172N Skyhawk	17272533	N5345D
D-EPWF	Cessna TU206G Turbo Stationair II	U20603901	I- IPAE, N7363C
D-EPWG	Geradts/ Van's RV-9A	91432	
D-EPWH	Cessna 182T Skylane	18282088	N6245W
D-EPWL	Beech F33A Bonanza (Res. .11)	CE-1587	N100CH
D-EPWM	Beech F33A Bonanza	CE-1712	
D-EPWP	Beech F33A Bonanza	CE-1654	
D-EPWR	Extra EA.300/LC (Hybrid electric engine) (P.24.6.16)	LC053	
D-EPXA	Extreme Air Sbach 300	007	
D-EPXP	Baumgartner/ Aero Designs Pulsar XP	1776	
D-EPYN	Piper PA-46-350P Malibu Mirage	4636137	ZS-NZY, N123ZY, N123TF, N648DH, N41199

Reg	Type	c/n	Previous identities
D-EPYS	Cessna T182T Turbo Skylane	T18208558	N60325
D-EPZY	SOCATA TB-20 Trinidad	2139	TC-MRB, F-OIUU
D-EQAI	Diamond DA 40D Star	D4.023	
D-EQAL	Cessna T182T Turbo Skylane	T18208542	N60162
D-EQAM	Aquila AT-01-100A	AT01-300	
	(Exhibited at Oshkosh as "N211AU")		
D-EQAN	Storck/ Messerschmitt M35 replica	1	
	(Res .10)		
D-EQAP	Cessna TR182 Turbo Skylane RG	R18201179	SE-IXZ, N756WL
D-EQAS	Beech V35 Bonanza	D-8390	N3750Q
D-EQAT	Piper PA-32R-301T Saratoga II TC	3257151	SP-KRO, N8YG, OY-LAA, N9525N
D-EQAU	Aquila AT-01-100C	AT01-301	
	(Exhibited at Oshkosh as "N211AQ")		
D-EQAX(2)	Focke-Wulf FW.44J Stieglitz	1899	ZS-WRI, D-EFUR, Fv617
D-EQBB	Diamond DA 20-C1 Katana	C0126	N626DC, C-GKAC
D-EQCA	Commander Aircraft 114B	14565	
D-EQCC	Aquila AT-01	AT01-218	
D-EQCH	Cessna P210N Pressurized Centurion II	P21000704	N5526W
D-EQCS	Piper PA-28-181 Cherokee Archer II	28-7890512	N425AG, HB-PCY, N36375
D-EQCT	Schneider/ Denney Kitfox Vixen 1200	FCV 008	
D-EQDK	Aerostyle Breezer B600	037/LSA	
	(P. 26.9.16)		
D-EQER	Diamond DA 40D Star	D4.070	(OE-. . .), G-HASO, G-CCLZ
D-EQFA	Robin DR.400/180R Remorqueur	1470	HB-EQF
D-EQHS	Robin DR.400/180 Régent	758	G-BAJY
D-EQIA	Robin DR.500/200i Président	0003	
D-EQIL	Aquila AT-01	AT01-139	F-HCAR
D-EQIS	Aquila AT-01-300	AT01-318	
	(Permit 31.3.15)		
D-EQMA	Robin DR.400/140B Dauphin 4	2628	F-GXLM
D-EQMF	Cessna 182Q Skylane	18267051	HB-CCX, N97302
D-EQMM	SIAI-Marchetti SF.260D	566/41-002	I-LELC
D-EQOA	Bücker Bü.133CJungmeister	53	D-EIIH(2), SpanishAF
D-EQQE	Piper PA-28R-200 Cherokee Arrow II	28R-7335376	OE-DTZ, D-EAYE, N56185
D-EQQQ(2)	Diamond DA 40D Star	D4.115	
D-EQSH	Cessna 210M Centurion	21062785	HA-SKZ, N6554B
	(Res .16)		
D-EQTB	Aquila AT-01-200C	AT01-319	
	(Permit 2.4.14)		
D-EQTT	SOCATA ST-10 Diplomate	116	HB-EQT, D-ELEZ(2)
D-EQUA	Aerostyle Breezer B600	012LSA	
D-EQUI	Aquila AT-01 (A210)	AT01-100	
	(Formerly c/n A210-100)		
D-EQUO	SIAI-Marchetti SF.260TP	510/60-002	I-FAIR
	(Res .11)		
D-EQUP	Piper J-3C-65 Cub	6917	G-BVPN, G-TAFY, N31073, N38207, N38307, NC38307
	(Officially registered with c/n "5298")		
D-EQUS	Luscombe 8E Silvaire	5651	G-BSHJ, N2924K, NC2924K
D-EQWM	Maier FW.190 (Half-scale replica)	S-001	
	(Permit .02)		
D-EQWN	Mudry CAP.10B	185	HB-SAV, F-GDTE
D-EQXA	CASA C-1.131E Jungmann	1052	G-BXBD, E3B-117
	(Painted as Luftwaffe "CW+BG", "50")		
D-EQXB	AIAA/ Stampe SV.4C	1086	(D-ECLA(3)), OO-SVF, (OO-SVC), F-WLOZ, Fr.Navy
	(Flies as "86")		
D-EQXC	Bücker Bü.181B-1 Bestmann	331396/FR.11	(D-EBUC(4)), N9269Z, F-BBMI, VN174, Luftwaffe
	(Under rebuild, Paderborn)		
D-EQXD	Klemm Kl.35D	1979	(G-KLEM), N5050, N505Q, SE-BGD, Fv5050
	(Painted as "NQ+NR")		
D-EQXG	Dornier Do.27A-3	429	D-EMEJ, 57+03, GB+901, LC+155
	(Res. 20.5.15)		
D-EQXL	Boeing Stearman A75N1	75-658	N56457, 41-898
	(Painted as USNavy "787")		
D-ERAB	Piper PA-28RT-201T Turbo Arrow IV	28R-7931277	N2963A
D-ERAD	Remos GX	402	
	(Permit 14.2.12)		
D-ERAE	Cessna 172S Skyhawk SP	172S8015	S5-DGT, N23338
D-ERAF(2)	Grob G 115E	82085	
	(RAF Development a/c)		
D-ERAG	Kriwanek/ Dallach D4/E Fascination	EB010	
D-ERAI	Robin DR.400/180R Remorqueur	2189	F-GMKZ
D-ERAK	Kerschl/ Stoddard-Hamilton Glastar GS-1	5541	
	(Permit .10)		
D-ERAL	Cessna 172N Skyhawk	17271122	N2024E
D-ERAM	Mooney M.20M Model 257 TLS	27-0097	N712D
D-ERAN	Zlin Z.143L	0014	
D-ERAO	Cirrus SR22	0539	SP-CGT, N1378C
D-ERAP(3)	Peter/ Dallach D4/E-BK/S Fascination	EB020	
D-ERAR	Kitzenbauer Rocket VII	1	
	(Res .10)		
D-ERAS(2)	Piper PA-28-151 Cherokee Warrior	28-7415284	N41584
D-ERAT	SIAI-Marchetti S.208	2-25	I- LARS
D-ERAW	Mooney M.20M Model 257 TLS	27-0092	
D-ERAX	Boeing Stearman A75N1	75-7073	N64386, BuA07469
	(Code '333')		
D-ERAY	Mooney M.20J Model 205	24-3202	SE-LMA, D-EMON(5)
D-ERBA(2)	SIAI-Marchetti SF.260D	764	I-LELH
	(Res .11)		
D-ERBB	CASA C-1.131E Jungmann	unkn	E3B-347
D-ERBC	Kleitz/ Druine D.5 Turbi	85	
	(Rotax 912)		
D-ERBD	Cirrus SR22	2693	N979SR
D-ERBF	Reims/Cessna F172N	F17201904	G-MOGG, G-BHDY, (LN-HOH)
D-ERBG(2)	Maule MXT-7-180A Comet	21082C	N4247U
D-ERBH	SOCATA TB-10 Tobago	295	G-CIIG, (D-EHRX), EC-DRX, F-OGLP
D-ERBI (2)	Light Aero Avid Flyer Speedwing	1756	
	(Res)		
D-ERBJ	Bücker Bü.131 Jungmann	128	
	(Res. 3.4.07) (Presumed Polish-built T.131PA)		
D-ERBK	Aquila AT-01	AT01-165	G-UILA
D-ERBL	Blessing/ Van's RV-7	001	
	(Permit 18.8.11)		
D-ERBM	Jodel D.117	615	OE-ABM
	(Built as D.11A)		
D-ERBO	Diamond DA 40 Star	40257	N144BQ
D-ERBR	Beech C23 Sundowner 180	M-1484	OO-SUN, G-BBAT
D-ERBW	Piper PA-28-180 Cherokee D	28-4761	N6351J
D-ERCA	Rockwell Commander 114A	14500	N114BK, N5884N
D-ERCB	Diamond DA 40D Star	D4.027	OE-VPU
D-ERCC	Cessna 195B	7676	N1064D
	(Res .15)		
D-ERCD	Piper PA-28-140 Cherokee D	28-7125245	I-SCUD, N5079S
D-ERCE	Piper PA-28-181 Archer II	28-8590066	I-ANDY, N6920S
D-ERCF	SOCATA TB-20 Trinidad	1924	
D-ERCL	Caye/ Steen Skybolt	001	
	(Dam. 24.3.10, rebt 2012)		
D-ERCM	Diamond DA 20-A1 Katana	10243	C-FDVT
D-ERCO	HOAC DV-20 Katana	20116	
D-ERCP	Cirrus SR20	1930	N132PG
D-ERCR	Beech A36 Bonanza	E-1814	F-GIFG, N3825Z
D-ERCT	Diamond DA 20-C1 Katana	C0115	N895CT, C-GKAH
D-ERCW	Piper PA-46-350P Malibu Mirage	4636298	HB-PPC, N41864
D-ERDA	SNCAN/ Stampe SV.4C	599	D-EOWS(1), F-BDET
D-ERDB	Piper PA-28-180 Cherokee Challenger	28-7305284	N16563
D-ERDE(2)	SOCATA TB-9 Tampico	1273	OE-KME
D-ERDG	HOAC DV-20 Katana	20020	OE-V . .
D-ERDI	Cessna 170	18366	N2606V
D-ERDJ	Piper PA-18-150 Super Cub	18-2546	EC-DLM, D-EMMX(1), (D-ELKF), ALAT, 52-6228
D-ERDM	Ruschmeyer R90-230RG	027	N12AB, D-EFCT(2), (D-EEDO)
D-ERDP	Diamond DA 20-A1 Katana	10031	N331CH
D-ERDS	Diamond DA 40 Star	40.510	N810DS
D-ERDW	Klemm Kl.35D	1850	(D-EWRD(2)), SE-BPN, Fv5070
	(Res .16)		
D-ERDZ	American AG-5B Tiger	10159	N1198G
D-EREC	Diamond DA 20-A1 Katana	10317	HA-. . . , N303EC, C-GDMQ
D-ERED	SOCATA TB-9 Tampico Club	1609	
D-EREE	Cessna 172P Skyhawk	17274041	N5281K
D-EREG	Flight Design CT LS-ELA	F-14-04-03	
	(Permit 15.7.15)		
D-EREI	Reichart/ Brditschka HB-207VRG Alfa	207-028	
D-EREN	Cessna TR182 Turbo Skylane RG	R18201019	N182RH, N739ZJ
D-ERER(2)	Cirrus SR20	1608	(OY-. . .), N760MK
D-ERES	Hamann/ Dallach D5/E-BK/914 Evolution	D5/004	
	(Permit .05)		
D-EREW	Cessna P210N Pressurized Centurion II	P21000669	HB-CQG , N5284W
	(Soloy conversion)		
D-ERFA(2)	Diamond DA 40 Star	40020	
D-ERFB	Piper PA-28-181 Archer II	28-8490001	N4317M
D-ERFC	Piper PA-46-350P Malibu Mirage	4636091	G-PALL, G-RMST
	(JetProp DLX conversion #199)		
D-ERFD	Beech G35 Bonanza	D-4776	HB-EFD, F-DAFB
D-ERFH(2)	Diamond DA 20-A1 Katana	10304	N604DA, C-GDMQ
D-ERFI (2)	Diamond DA 40D Star	D4.127	
D-ERFK(2)	Piper PA-46-500TP Malibu Meridian	4697381	N19AG, HB-PRP, I-ROSM, N61106
D-ERFL	Mooney M.20J Model 205	24-3206	N91VR, N12WA, D-EKJH(1), N12WA
D-ERFM	Diamond DA 40D Star	D4.044	
D-ERFS	Mooney M.20J Model 201	24-1176	N1142U
D-ERFT(2)	Cessna 182T Skylane	18282148	N50983
D-ERFU	Mooney M.20M Model 257 TLS	27-0089	
D-ERFW	Karl/ FW.190A-1 Half Scale Replica	209	
	(Permit 28.7.15)		
D-ERGC	Piper PA-46-350P Malibu Mirage	4622200	N100VC, (N800RG), N100VC, N9258D
	(JetProp DLX conversion #144)		
D-ERGG	Cirrus SR22	2605	N265SR
D-ERGL(2)	Diamond DA 20-C1 Katana	C0305	N281DC
D-ERGN	Aquila AT-01	AT01-231	
D-ERGR	CASA C-1.131E Jungmann	2010	E3B-406
D-ERGS	Beech F33A Bonanza	CE-1758	N80639
D-ERGT	Reims FR172H Rocket	FR17200229	N229FL, D-ECOA(1)
D-ERGX(3)	Remos GX	418	
	(Permit 24.9.12)		
D-ERGY	Piper PA-22-160 Tripacer	22-7620	G-ARGY, G-JEST, G-ARGY, N10F
D-ERHA	Mooney M.20R Ovation	29-0054	
D-ERHB(2)	Mooney M.20E Super 21	344	HB-DEE, (N6984U)
D-ERHE	SOCATA TB-20 Trinidad	432	F-GDQK, F-ODQK
D-ERHG	Beech F33A Bonanza	CE-1507	N67HG, D-EARY(2)
D-ERHH	Piper J-3C-65 Cub	1997	OY-AIS , (SE-AIS)
	(Originally built as J-3F-50)		
D-ERHJ	Jud HRJ/ Zlin Savage AF Amphibian	2002469	
	(Permit 8.11.13)		
D-ERHK	Beech F33A Bonanza	CE-1608	N8235W
D-ERHM	SOCATA TB-10 Tobago	1747	
D-ERHN	Piper PA-28RT-201 Arrow IV	28R-8218007	N84571
D-ERHO	Grumman AA-5 Traveler	AA5-0507	OO-PAS
D-ERHS	SOCATA TB-20 Trinidad	584	F-GJAL, N103J
D-ERHV	Hassler/ Denney Kitfox III	758	
D-ERIA	Robin DR.400/200R Remo 200	2205	
D-ERIB	Remos GX	327	
	(Permit .09)		
D-ERIC	Piper PA-28-140 Cherokee	28-21907	C-GEXM, N7193R
D-ERIE(3)	Piper PA-28-181 Archer III	2843566	OK-MTT, N5232G, OK-MTT, N9527N
D-ERIF	Piper PA-28RT-201T Turbo Arrow IV	28R-8131163	N8411Y
	(W/o 3.4.15 en-route Niste – Kleinalmerode)		
D-ERIK	Auböck/ Jodel D.119	1243	OE-ACZ
D-ERIN	Piper PA-28R-201 Arrow	2844016	N4132U, SP-FEL, N4132U, (SP-FEL), N9529N
D-ERIO	Zlin Z.326 Trenér Master	902	(D-EOTZ), HB-TCB
D-ERIR	Renger/ Impulse 160TD	TD-7	
	(Formerly 120TD, conv 2004)		
D-ERIS	Aquila AT-01	AT01-161	
D-ERIT	Cessna F150J	F1500401	CS-AYA, D-EABB(1)
D-ERIZ	SOCATA MS.893E Rallye 180GT	13050	OE-DIZ
D-ERJA	Beech C23 Sundowner	M-2136	N6015W
D-ERJC	SOCATA TB-200 Tobago XL	1630	
D-ERJF	Grob G 115	8023	HB-UGD
D-ERJM	SOCATA TB-10 Tobago	1731	
D-ERJO	Cirrus SR22	3138	N229CP
D-ERJP	Cessna 172P Skyhawk	17274204	N177CB, N6507K
D-ERJS	SOCATA TB-9 Tampico	1165	F-GLAR
D-ERKA	Reims/Cessna F172N	F17201870	N5189D, D-EFOS(1)
D-ERKB	Piper PA-28-181 Archer II	28-8190204	OH-PDN, SE-ILC
D-ERKD	Robin DR.400/140B Dauphin 4	2626	
D-ERKF	Dudeck/ Denney Kitfox 4-1200	1757	
D-ERKH	Heumann/ Aero Designs Pulsar XP	001	
D-ERKK	Barland/ Murphy Rebel	1	
D-ERKL(2)	Diamond DA 20-A1 Katana	10058	N87MF, N198DA, C-FDVK

Registration	Type	C/n	Previous identities
D-ERKM	Zlin Z.142	0526	OK-VNG
D-ERKR	Roth/ Van's RV-4	3614	
D-ERKS	Cessna 172S Skyhawk SP	172S10190	N60313
D-ERKT	Cessna 172S Skyhawk SP	172S10078	N575TW
D-ERKV	Kersting/ Van's RV-9A	91395	
D-ERKW	Westermeier/ Aero Designs Pulsar XP	1907	
D-ERKY	Piper PA-28RT-201T Turbo Arrow IV	28R-8031068	LX-SKY, N81623
D-ERLA	SNCAN/ Stampe SV.4C	101	D-EBHL(2), F-BBVA
D-ERLB	Cessna T182 Turbo Skylane	18267773	(D-EGRR), SE-IHU, N5531N
D-ERLE(2)	Diamond DA 20-A1 Katana	10231	
D-ERLG	Cessna T206H Turbo Stationair	T20608896	N896JA
D-ERLH	Grob G 115C2	82058/C2	(D-EPST)
D-ERLI	Cessna 182T Skylane	18281307	N2096Q
D-ERLL	Aquila AT-01	AT01-200	
D-ERLM	Aquila AT-01	AT01-210	D-EAQQ
D-ERLO	Oberbach/ Van's RV-6	002	
	(C/n formerly quoted as 1871)		
D-ERLP	Funke/ Denney Kitfox III	1028	
D-ERLR	Beech F33A Bonanza	CE-1565	N8233X
D-ERLU	Mooney M.20J Model 201	24-1545	OY-NAJ, SX-AEM, N3KN, N2KN
D-ERLV	Diamond DA 20-A1 Katana	10318	N201TB, N318DA, C-GDMY
D-ERLZ	Flight Design CT LS LSA	F-10-07-07	
	(Res .16)		
D-ERMA(2)	Piper PA-18-135 Super Cub	18-3982	I-BUNO, I-EIUJ/E!-260, MM54-2582, 54-2582
	(Permit 5.4.13)		
D-ERMB	Beech F33A Bonanza	CE-1500	N150RM
D-ERME	Robin R.2160i	375	G-WAVT, G-CBLG
D-ERMF	American Champion 8KCAB Super Decathlon	1059-2008	
D-ERMG	SOCATA TB-10 Tobago	50	F-GCEB
D-ERMH(2)	Cessna T182T Turbo Skylane	T18208955	N5242F
D-ERMI	Piper PA-28R-201T Turbo Arrow III	28R-7803247	N9264C
D-ERMJ	Cessna 182J	18256707	HB-CBG, N2607F
D-ERMK	Oberbach/ Van's RV-7	003	
D-ERMM	Aquila AT-01	AT01-108	
D-ERMN	Extra EA.300/L	091	G-FIII, G-RGEE, D-ESEW(3)
	(Res .16)		
D-ERMO	Diamond DA 20-A1 Katana	10099	C-FDVK
D-ERMP	Grob G 115C	82036/C	N115SR
D-ERMR	Cessna 172P Skyhawk	17274404	N52066
D-ERMS(2)	Cirrus SR22T	0346	N170DE
D-ERNA	SOCATA TB-200 Tobago XL	1612	
D-ERNC	Piper PA-18-150 Super Cub	18-8777	SE-FYK, LN-BNY
D-ERNI (2)	SOCATA TB-9 Tampico Club	1647	
D-ERNS	Diamond DA 40 Star	40322	N89SE
D-ERNU	Piper PA-20 Pacer 135	20-971	N1922A
D-ERNY(2)	Aquila AT-01 100A	AT01-338	
D-EROA	Piper J-3C-65 Cub	20141	I-BOCA, N6910H, NC6910H
D-EROB	SNCAN/ Stampe SV.4C	151	D-ECDI (2), F-BNDI, Fr.AF/CEV
D-EROC	HOAC DV-20 Katana	20090	
D-EROE	Diamond DA 40D Star	D4.010	OY-TDI
D-EROG	American AG-5B Tiger	10115	N1196Z
D-EROH	Cessna 182R Skylane	18268155	OH-CTR, G-BOPF, N9984H
D-ERON	SOCATA TB-20 Trinidad	1441	F-GLFN
D-EROP	Amann/ Europa Avn Europa	1780	
	(Permit 10.10)		
D-EROQ	Cessna 172	46233	N6133E
D-EROR	Reims/Cessna F177RG Cardinal RG	F177RG0158	F-GAGE
D-EROS	Piper PA-28-161 Warrior II	28-8116181	N8352P
D-EROW	Cessna 172R Skyhawk	17280328	N9478F
D-EROY	Mooney M.20M Model 257 TLS	27-0154	
D-ERPC	Cessna 152	15280733	N25565
D-ERPD	Piper PA-28-140 Cherokee B	28-25740	F-BRPD, N8877N
D-ERPE	Reims/Cessna F172N	F17201979	D-EIYZ
D-ERPH	Cessna 172N Skyhawk	17271171	N2159E
D-ERPI (2)	Piper PA-22-108 Colt	22-9595	I-AIRP, N5753Z
	(Res .12)		
D-ERPK	Diamond DA 40D Star	D4.345	OE-VPT
D-ERPL	Cessna 172P Skyhawk II	17274722	N53328
D-ERPM	Diamond DA 40 Star	40062	G-CBFC
D-ERPR	Cirrus SR22	1852	N268RP
D-ERPS	Poth/ Pottier P.220S Koala	1849	
D-ERPW	Cessna 182Q Skylane	18267212	N61PG, N97827
D-ERRB	Cirrus SR22	2837	EC-KST, N851SR
	(Res. 22.9.15)		
D-ERRD	Bellanca 7GCBC Citabria	288-70	S5-DAP, SL-DAP, YU-CAN
D-ERRE	Rengers/ Aero Designs Pulsar XP	402	
D-ERRI (3)	Piper PA-28-180 Cherokee E	28-5843	I-ALPY, G-AYIE, N11C
D-ERRL	Aquila AT-01	AT01-177	G-DCHO
D-ERRN	Ripplinger/ Aero Designs Pulsar XP	432/007	
D-ERRO	Piper PA-28R-201 Arrow	2844005	N92698
D-ERRP(2)	Diamond DA 40D Star	D4.098	
D-ERRR	Mertensmeier/ Stoddard-Hamilton Glasair III		
	(Permit 19.11.15)	3095SB	D-ESEO(2)
D-ERRS	Bretzke/ Neico Lancair 360	3118	
D-ERRV(2)	Van's RV-7A	2002345	
D-ERRW	Cessna 172S Skyhawk SP	172S11039	N5284Y
D-ERSB	Piper PA-28-161 Warrior II	28-8016122	N8115V
D-ERSC	Cirrus SR20	1675	HB-KHF, N528AL
	(Res .14)		
D-ERSD	Piper PA-28-181 Archer III	2843075	OO-DSD, N92864
D-ERSE	Cessna 172P Skyhawk	17275559	OH-COB, N64422
D-ERSF	SIAI-Marchetti SF.260AM	689/40-012	MM54531/70-41
	(Res .11)		
D-ERSH	Diamond DA 20-A1 Katana	10004	OE-V . ., N848DF, C-FTJG
D-ERSL	Mooney M.20J Model 201	24-1049	D-EEGH(1), N4070H
D-ERSM	Bachmann/ Europa Avn Europa XS TG	542	
	(Permit 7.04)		
D-ERSO	Mooney M.20J Model 201	24-1672	N224DM
D-ERSP	Cessna 172S Skyhawk SP	172S8749	N843SP
D-ERSR	Alpi Aviation Pioneer 300	354	
	(Res .14)		
D-ERSS	Piper PA-28-181 Archer II	2890076	OH-PSS
D-ERST	SOCATA TB-9 Tampico Club	1295	
D-ERSV	Stinson 108-1 Voyager	2179	N9179K, NC9179K
	(Res .12)		
D-ERTA	Griener/Messerschmitt M17 replica	1994/1	
	(Wears "D-887")		
D-ERTB	Cessna 177RG Cardinal RG	177RG0962	N303RN, (N34079)
D-ERTC	Evektor EV-97 SportStar MAX	2011 1411	
D-ERTH(2)	Flight Design CT LS-ELA	F-10-04-04	
	(Permit 7.10)		
D-ERTI	Cessna 182Q Skylane	18266337	N759XH
D-ERTL	Diamond DA 20-A1 Katana	10326	HA-DAP, D-ENTF(3), N981FA, C-GKAX
D-ERTO	Cessna 182T Skylane	18282161	N5189N
D-ERTS	Rockwell Commander 112TC	13072	F-GMJR, N24WE
D-ERTT	Nord 1002 Pingouin	146	N108BW, N146MA, N5019K, F-BEOY
	(Registered as "Me 108B")		
	(P 23.3.16)		
D-ERTW	Twellmann/ Tri-R KIS TR-1C	104	
D-ERTY(2)	DHC-1 Chipmunk 22	C1/0718	G-BDCB, WP835
D-ERUD	Cessna R182 Skylane RG	R18200542	V5-RUD, N1739R
D-ERUG	PZL-110 Koliber 150	3900042	SE-KUG, (SE-KUO), (G-. . . .), PH-BIJ
D-ERUR	Cessna T206H Turbo Stationair	T20608131	N24479
	(Soloy conversion)		
D-ERUT	Diamond DA 20A-1 Katana	10181	N854DF, C-FDVA
D-ERVB	Zlin Z.143L	0012	
D-ERVE	Cessna T182T Turbo Skylane	T18208615	N6056X, (D-EXAJ)
D-ERVG	Strassburg/ Van's RV-8	82198	
	(C/n now quoted as 1 officially)		
D-ERVH	Höser/ Van's RV-7	72668	
D-ERVI	Strassburg/ Van's RV-8	82770	
D-ERVJ	Schubert / Van's RV-10	41608	
D-ERVK	König/ Van's RV-12	120318	
D-ERVP	Pohlmann/ Van's RV-9	91069	
	(Res. .13)		
D-ERVS(2)	Schröter/ Van's RV-7A	72626	
D-ERVT	Voussem/ Van's RV-10	2002424	
D-ERVX	Van's RV-4	4123	
D-ERWA	Piper PA-28-181 Archer II	28-8590078	N2491Y
D-ERWB	Piper PA-46-350P Malibu Mirage	4622125	N192PM, N9223R
D-ERWE	Mooney M.20R Ovation	29-0011	
D-ERWF	Commander Aircraft 114B	14580	
D-ERWH	Rall/ Europa Avn Europa	1889	
	(Permit .00)		
D-ERWJ	SOCATA TB-9 Tampico	1839	PH-RWJ, F-GSZZ, 5N-CAR, F-OIDI
D-ERWK	HOAC DV-20 Katana	20051	
D-ERWM	Cessna 172M	17264449	N9669V
D-ERWO	Aquila AT-01	AT01-248	
D-ERWP	Aquila AT-01	AT01-112	
D-ERWW	Mooney M.20K Model 231	25-0676	N1164A
D-ERXA(2)	Xtreme Air XA-42 Sbach 342	101	
D-ERXP	Meixner/ Aero Designs Pulsar XP	425	
D-ERYW	Mooney M.20L PFM	26-0035	P4-ING, G-RAAD, N160MP
D-ERZO	Cessna 182R Skylane	18267749	I-VOGH, N5480N
D-ESAA	Cessna 172S Skyhawk SP	172S8791	N2477B
D-ESAB	Lake LA-4-200 Buccaneer	975	EI-BSR, N3076P
D-ESAC(2)	Cessna 172P Skyhawk	17275141	F-GIMZ, N55241
	(Res .16)		
D-ESAD	Cessna 172R Skyhawk	17280149	
D-ESAE	Cessna 172SP Skyhawk SP	172S08118	
D-ESAG(2)	Aquila AT-01-100B	AT01-311	
D-ESAH(2)	Piper PA-28-181 Archer II	2890120	OH-PBM, OY-JEG
D-ESAI	Grob G 120A-1	85025	
D-ESAJ	Cessna F172G	F172-0251	D-ECGE(2)
D-ESAL	Cessna 172N Skyhawk	17272082	N7307E
D-ESAM(2)	Robin DR.400/180R Remo 180	2471	
D-ESAN(2)	Piper PA-28-181 Archer III	2843008	N9181J
D-ESAO	Piper PA-46-350P Malibu Mirage	4636282	D-EXED, OY-FIA
	(Res .16)		
D-ESAP	Cessna 182Q Skylane	18267138	N97582
D-ESAS(2)	Cessna 182T Skylane	18282303	OE-KMP(2)
D-ESAT	Commander Aircraft 114B	14551	N6000Z
D-ESAV	Reims/Cessna FRA150M Aerobat	FRA1500328	G-BFGX, F-BUDX
D-ESAW(2)	Diamond DA 20-A1 Katana	10232	N282DA, C-FDVT
D-ESAY	Cessna P210N Pressurized Centurion II		
		P21000629	HB-CQX, D-EMAZ(3), N4896W
D-ESBA(2)	Piper PA-46-500TP Malibu Meridian	4697291	EC-KDV, D-EAVK, N291ST, N1042H
D-ESBC(2)	Piper PA-28R-201T Turbo Cherokee Arrow III		
		28R-7803362	N20878
D-ESBD(2)	Piper PA-38-112 Tomahawk	38-79A0446	S5-DAS, SL-DAS, YU-DDR, N9683N
D-ESBF	Cirrus SR22T	0350	N281CD
D-ESBG(2)	Reims/Cessna F172P	F17202126	OO-LVD, D-EILV, (D-EDDL)
D-ESBH	Messerschmitt Bf.108B	370114	HB-ESM, G-AFZO, AW167, D-IJHW
D-ESBM	Cessna 172R Skyhawk	17280327	N9405Z
D-ESBO	Reims/Cessna F172P	F17202254	LN-RAW
D-ESBR	Robin R.2160D	275	F-WZZZ
D-ESBS	SOCATA TB-20 Trinidad	2026	PH-GTI, G-KUBB, F-OILS
D-ESBV	Piper PA-28RT-201T Turbo Arrow IV	28R-8031002	I-EJVA, D-EJVA(2), N81042
	(Permit 28.1.15)		
D-ESBW	Piper PA-28RT-201T Turbo Arrow IV	28R-7931251	OE-KBT, OY-PEE, N2904G
D-ESCB(2)	Cessna 170B	27167	LV-FZE, LV-PDF
D-ESCD	Cirrus SR22	0801	N125AL
D-ESCF	Piper PA-28-181 Archer III	2843436	N5319G
D-ESCH	Piper PA-28RT-201 Arrow IV	28R-7918093	N2147X
D-ESCI	Cessna 182S Skylane	18280387	OH-SIE, N2368B
	(Res .16)		
D-ESCN	Beech F33A Bonanza	CE-1466	N33VW, G-TERI, N5664X
D-ESCO	Cessna 172N Skyhawk	17273735	N5214J
D-ESCP	Diamond DA 20-A1 Katana	10107	N533SS, C-GKAN
D-ESCR(2)	Diamond DA 40TDI Star	D4.101	
D-ESCS	Diamond DA 40D Star	D4.194	OE-VPU
D-ESCW(2)	Cessna 182T Skylane	18281979	N1105T
D-ESDB	American AG-5B Tiger	10147	N1198A
D-ESDC	Diamond DA 20-C1 Katana	C0354	N335DC
D-ESDD	Cirrus SR22	0698	N8146S
D-ESDF	Piper PA-28R-201 Arrow III	28R-7837182	OE-DRT, N9237C
D-ESDJ	SOCATA TB-20 Trinidad GT	2029	
D-ESDS(2)	Piper PA-28RT-201 Arrow IV	28R-8018100	G-CEDD, N82507
D-ESDT(2)	Diamond DA 40D Star	D4.061	
D-ESEB	Piper PA-28R-200 Cherokee Arrow II	28R-7335155	I-CASP, N333RG
D-ESEC	SOCATA TB-20 Trinidad	1112	D-EANG(3)
D-ESED	Cessna 172S Skyhawk SP	172S10320	D-ESEX(4), N141RC
D-ESEE(2)	American AA-1A Trainer	AA1A-0167	HB-UBP, N9267L

Registration	Type	C/n	Previous identities
D-ESEF	Aquila AT-01	AT01-113	
D-ESEI	WACO YMF-F5C	F5C-107	N7022S
D-ESEK(2)	Mooney M.20R Ovation	29-0245	N10081
D-ESEL	Piper PA-28RT-201T Turbo Arrow IV	28R-8131010	G-BSZR, N8281B
D-ESEM	Cessna T182T Turbo Skylane	T18208967	N52532
D-ESEN	Aquila AT-01	AT01-233	
D-ESEO(2)	Mertensmeier/ Stoddard-Hamilton Glasair III	3095SB	
D-ESEP	Cessna 182P	18263998	OY-ARL, D-EATU(1),
	(Reims-assembled with "c/n" 0028)		N9938E
D-ESER(2)	SIAI-Marchetti SM.1019A	043	EI-442/MM57235
D-ESES	Cessna TR182 Turbo Skylane RG	R18201379	N4686S
D-ESET	Cirrus SR22T	0799	N256JP
D-ESEV	Mraz M.1C Sokol	110	OO-MAX, OO-PIM,
	(On rebuild) (C/n also quoted as 10)		OO-RDH, OO-AHU, OK-BHD
D-ESEW(4)	Brändli BX-2 Cherry	1666	
	(Kit no.66)		
D-ESEX(11)	Aquila AT-01 100C	AT01-0323	(D-EAQD)
D-ESFB	Cirrus SR20	1087	G-JOEW, N184CD
D-ESFC	Robin DR.400/180 Régent	2305	
D-ESFH	Diamond DA 40 Star	40055	
D-ESFK(2)	Fläming-Air FA-02 Smaragd	024/06	
D-ESFL	Christen A-1 Husky	1351	
D-ESFM	Cessna 172S Skyhawk SP	172S9804	N1006T
D-ESFN	Diamond DA 20-C1 Katana	C0253	N256DC
D-ESFO	Piper PA-28-181 Archer III	2843440	N5323G
D-ESFP	Piper PA-28-181 Archer III	2843455	(D-ELBG(2)), N5322L
D-ESFR	Beech F33A Bonanza	CE-1535	N81562, N4341J,
			(SE-KTL), N81562
D-ESFS	Cessna 172N Skyhawk	17268127	N76108
D-ESFW	HOAC DV-20 Katana	20056	
D-ESGA	Piper PA-32-300 Six	32-7940213	
D-ESGB	Bauernfeind/ S-H GlaStar GS-1	5448	
D-ESGC	Piper PA-28-180 Cherokee Archer	28-7405005	PH-SWD, OE-DML,
			N9558N
D-ESGE	Piper PA-46-350P Malibu Mirage	4636624	N4418X, N9534N
D-ESGH	Cessna 172S Skyhawk SP	172S10523	N32818
D-ESGJ	Cessna 172N Skyhawk	17271222	N2289E
D-ESGN	Aquila AT-01	AT01-234	
D-ESGO	Gyroflug SC-01B-160 Speed Canard	3-25	PH-TEY, D EOSC
	(Res. 9.12.15)		
D-ESGT	SOCATA TB-9 Tampico	1419	I-IAGT
D-ESGW	Cessna 172N Skyhawk	17273058	N1969F
D-ESHA	Schmaderer/ Aero Designs Pulsar XP	EB-001	
D-ESHB	Aquila AT-01-100A	AT01-316	
D-ESHG(2)	Zlin Z.50LX	0069	OK-SHG
D-ESHI	Cirrus SR20	2269	N502HJ
D-ESHK	Robin R.3000/160	162	
D-ESHM(2)	Diamond DA 20-A1 Katana	10191	N668DA, C-FDVK
D-ESHO	Robin DR.400/180 Régent	2245	
D-ESHP	Aeromere F.8L Falco III	205	LX-AIW, D-ENUB(1)
D-ESHS	Staltmeier / Pitts S-2S Special	AA/1/1980	G-SOLO
D-ESIA	Robin DR.400/200R Remo 200	2246	
D-ESIC	SIAI-Marchetti SF.260	102	(D-EGCL(2)), I-SIAW
D-ESID	Stemme S15-1	ASP-028	D-KLSA(3)
	(Res. .13) (under conversion from S6-RT)		
D-ESIH	CSA PS-28 Cruiser	C0447	OK-FED
D-ESII	Cessna 150J	15070110	D-EDAN(2), N60156
D-ESIM(2)	Mosinger/ Aerostyle Breezer	1218	
	(Serious damage 24.9.11)		
D-ESIR(3)	Diamond DA 20-A1 Katana	10106	N532SS, C-GDMY
D-ESIX	Dornier Do.27B-1	357	56+63, AC+936, AS+936
D-ESJA	Yakovlev Yak-18T	22202044785	N1876T, D-ESJA,
			HA-YAK, LY-AFS, DOSAAF
D-ESJD	Drumm/ Van's RV-6A	1689	
D-ESJG(2)	Cessna 172R Skyhawk	17281215	N21765
D-ESJN	Extra EA.200	1037	HB-MTF, N137EX
	(Res .16)		
D-ESJV	Cirrus SR20	1460	N71CV
D-ESJW	Weinert/ Van's RV-7	72080	
	(Permit 7.11.13)		
D-ESKA	Diamond DA 20-A1 Katana	10093	N195DA, C-GKAC
D-ESKB	Berger/ Rans S-9 Chaos	20023933	
	(Permit 9.1.14)		
D-ESKF	Cessna 172P Skyhawk	17275390	N63097
D-ESKG	Cessna 172P Skyhawk	17275228	SE-KKH, N62202
D-ESKJ	Cirrus SR22	1890	N133SR
D-ESKK	SIAI-Marchetti S.205-20/R	221	PH-RYK, (PH-NOW)
D-ESKM	Beech F33A Bonanza	CE-1184	N80990
D-ESKO	Maule MXT-7-180 Super Rocket	14008C	G-BSKO
D-ESKR	Roth/ Van's RV-4RG	4317	
D-ESKT	Diamond DA 40 Star	40351	
D-ESKY	Cessna R182 Skylane RG	R18200477	SE-KRY, N9874C
D-ESLB(2)	Cessna 182P Skylane	18263591	CS-DCG, HB-CWV,
			N5967J
D-ESLF	Ruschmeyer R90-230G	05	(D-EEHQ)
D-ESLG	SIAI-Marchetti SM.1019A	017	EI-417/MM57210
D-ESLI	SIAI-Marchetti SF-260	2-31	ZS-FZY
	(Cr.17.1.09)		
D-ESLM	Aerotek Pitts S-2A	2050	N70JJ
D-ESLO	Cirrus SR22	0023	N704CD
D-ESLT	Extra EA.300/LT	LT024	
D-ESMA	Bölkow BO.207	259	D-EGMA(1)
D-ESMB(2)	Cessna 182T Skylane	18282133	(D-EAMJ), N6328H
D-ESMC	SIAI-Marchetti SF.260C	737/40-015	MM55013
D-ESMD	Piper PA-28R-201T Turbo Cherokee Arrow III		
		28R-7703236	G-BSNP, N38537
D-ESMF	Diamond DA 40 Star	40077	
D-ESMG	Gess/ Van's RV-6	1692	
D-ESMH	Piper PA-28RT-201T Turbo Arrow IV	28R-8131006	N8277S
D-ESMI	Robin DR.400/180R Remo 180	2080	
D-ESMJ	Aquila AT-01	AT01-150	D-EAQA
D-ESMK(2)	Mooney M.20K Model 252 TSE	25-1185	N252TS
D-ESMM	Piper PA-28-181 Cherokee Archer II	28-7790091	N5336F
D-ESMN	Cessna 172N Skyhawk	17267981	N888TJ, N75526
D-ESMO	Cessna 172R Skyhawk	17281333	N6029H
D-ESMP	Reims/Cessna F172N	F17201633	G-BFKA
D-ESMR	Robin R.1180TD Aiglon	281	PH-RBA
D-ESMS	Cessna TR182 Turbo Skylane RG	R18201407	N4739S
D-ESMT	Mooney M.20R Ovation	29-0044	SE-LBL
D-ESMV	Piper PA-18-150 Super Cub	18-3854	PH-DKA, R-164, 54-2454
D-ESMW(3)	Piper PA-18 Super Cub 95	18-1522	D-EDGC(3), ALAT,
			51-15522
D-ESNA	Diamond DA 40 Star	40237	N65NA, C-FDVP
D-ESNB	Mooney M.20J Model 201	24-0426	OE-KFC, HB-DFC
D-ESNF	Cessna 152	15284468	OE-CFN, N6623L
D-ESNO	Reims/Cessna F172N	F17201521	D-EBXS
	(Res. .15)		
D-ESNQ	Zlin S.142	0234	OM-LNQ, OK-LNQ
D-ESNT(2)	Cirrus SR22T	0350	D-ESBF, N281CD
	(Res. 15.5.15)		
D-ESNX	Löffler/ Monnett Sonex	1965	
	(Res.)		
D-ESOA	Aquila AT-01	AT01-204	
D-ESOB	Piper PA-46-500TP Malibu Meridian	4697387	OY-PMM, N9533N
D-ESOC	SOCATA TB-10 Tobago	1794	
D-ESOF	Extra EA.300/L	1177	
D-ESOK	Mraz M.1D Sokol	281	D-ENEV, OK-DHU
D-ESOR	Piper PA-28R-201T Turbo Cherokee Arrow III		
		28R-7703254	N38637
D-ESOT(2)	Sotomayor / Van's RV-7A	1	
	(Res. .11)		
D-ESOX	Aquila AT-01-100B	AT01-317	
D-ESPA	Piper PA-28-181 Archer II	28-8490041	N4334Z
D-ESPH	Greuner/ Van's RV-6	001/1937	
D-ESPI (2)	Cirrus SR22	1581	N485CD
D-ESPJ	SOCATA TB-20 Trinidad	2140	M-GINZ, N565G
	(W/o 25.11.16)		
D-ESPL	Piper PA-28-180 Cherokee D	28-4500	OE-DPL, N5312L, N11C
	(Res. .14)		
D-ESPM	Impulse Aircraft Impulse 180TD	TD3	
D-ESPN	Extra EA.300/L	1257	
	(Damaged .16)		
D-ESPP	Hentzsche / Van's RV-9A	92225	
D-ESPR	Piper PA-28-151 Cherokee Warrior	28-7715284	OE-DKA, N9574N
D-ESPS(2)	Sukhoi SU-31	02-05	EC- . . ., ZU-AVG
	(Res. 18.8.16)		
D-ESPW	Cessna R172K Hawk XP	R1722890	N736YH
D-ESPX	Great Lakes 2T-1A-2	1006	N933EB, N5762N
D-ESPY	Cirrus SR20	1345	LX-TIM, N8124W
D-ESRA	SOCATA TB-10 Tobago	1369	SP-DSA
	(Assembled in Poland, PZL c/n P-001)		
D-ESRC	Cirrus SR20	1029	(D-EDWX(2)), N138CD
D-ESRE	Ehmann RE-4 Grasmücke	01	
D-ESRG(2)	Cessna 150M	15077275	N63385, (D-ECDR),
			N63385
D-ESRK(2)	Aquila AT-01	AT01-117	
D-ESRL(2)	Mooney M.20R Ovation	29-0064	
D-ESRM	Cirrus SR22	1926	T7-PAT, N179SR
D-ESRP(2)	Cessna 172R Skyhawk	17280360	N443ES
D-ESRR	Cessna 172R Skyhawk	17280212	
D-ESRT	Cessna 182P Skylane	18260834	N26561, D-ECRG,
			N9294G
D-ESRV(2)	Krups / Van's RV-6A	1208	
D-ESSB(2)	Cessna 172R Skyhawk	17280133	(N122GM), N9876F
D-ESSC(3)	Cessna 172S Skyhawk SP	172S9538	N2146W
D-ESSD(3)	American Champion 8KCAB Super Decathlon		
		1155-2015	
D-ESSE(2)	Cessna 182T Skylane	18282143	N6348U
D-ESSJ(2)	Mooney M.20K Model 231	25-0465	OE-KHS, N4088H
D-ESSM	Mooney M.20C Mark 21	2810	N7847V
D-ESSN(3)	Cirrus SR22	2718	SP-AVA, N452SR
D-ESSO(2)	Mooney M.20M Model 257 TLS	27-0204	
D-ESSP(2)	Extra EA.330LC	LC004	Fr AF/F-TGCI
D-ESSR(2)	Van's RV-14A	2002572	
	(Res .16)		
D-ESSS(3)	Cirrus SR20	1807	N747LD, N824SR
D-ESST	Cessna 172N Skyhawk	17271634	N4769E
D-ESSV(2)	Beech A36 Bonanza	E-2587	N58JM, N8094K
D-ESSW(2)	Piper PA-22-160 Tripacer	22-6797	G-APYN, N2804Z
D-ESSX	LET Z-37A Cmelák	17-26	OM-EJH, D-ENSH,
	(Reported as under rebuild 2015)		DDR-SSH, DM-SSH
D-ESSY(2)	Grob G 115A	8030	LX-ALF, (OO-PHD)
D-ESTA	SOCATA TB-20 Trinidad	1362	
D-ESTB	Piper PA-28-161 Cadet	2841333	N9216N
D-ESTC(3)	Robin DR.400/180 Régent	2505	G-CBBA
D-ESTD	SIAI-Marchetti SF.260C	570/42-006	HB-EZZ, I-SMAB, I-RAIB,
			(Zaire AF)
D-ESTE(3)	Aquila AT-01	AT01-256	
D-ESTF(2)	Tremmel/ Aerostyle Breezer	008	D-MAJH ?
D-ESTG(2)	Extra EA.200	1033	
D-ESTH(2)	Cessna 182T Skylane	18281174	N52975, (N385AV),
			N52975
D-ESTI	Piper PA-28-161 Cadet	2841350	N9233N
D-ESTK(2)	Cirrus SR22	2688	LX-NEU, N910SR
D-ESTL	Markett/ Neico Lancair 320	FB145AB	
D-ESTM(2)	Cessna 182Q Skylane	18267785	SE-LKM, OY-CKM,
			OH-CIU, N5551N
D-ESTN	Piper PA-28-161 Warrior II	2816101	N92333
D-ESTO	Piper PA-28-161 Cadet	2841304	N9261N, N9196X
D-ESTP	Cessna 195	7189	N3472V
	(Res. .09, not yet taken up 2016)		
D-ESTR	HOAC DV-20 Katana	20029	
D-ESTS	Piper PA-18-150 Super Cub	18-7893	I-ROBJ, N3977Z, N10F
D-ESTT(2)	Piper PA-46-350P Malibu Mirage	4636075	SE-LYL, N313BC,
	(Jet Prop DLX conversion #124)		N9281J
D-ESTW	Oberlerchner JOB 15-150/2	071	OE-DOC, D-EKEP(2)
D-ESUB(2)	Schreiber/ Neico Legacy 2000	L2K-183	
D-ESUE	Cessna 172S Skyhawk SP	172S10632	N1278L
D-ESUL	American Champion 7ECA Aurora	1396-2006	
D-ESUN	Cirrus SR20	1705	G-OUNI, (D-EBQS),
			G-OUNI, G-TABI, N950SR
D-ESUS(3)	Piper PA-18-150 Super Cub	18-611	S5-DAY, SL-DAY,
	(Res. .12 but ntu)		YU-DMG, D-EFGE, XB-PEF, N1039A
D-ESUW	Tecnam P.2002-JF Sierra	160	
D-ESVC	Cirrus SR20	1485	N54138
D-ESVI (3)	Piper PA-28RT-201T Turbo Arrow IV	28R-8131120	I-STEN, N8380Z
D-ESVL	LET Z-37A Cmelák	20-15	DDR-SVL, DM-SVL
D-ESVM(2)	Wahl/ Van's RV-9A	91371	
	(Permit 10.4.14)		
D-ESVO	LET Z-37A Cmelák	20-18	DDR-SVO, DM-SVO
D-ESVS	Cessna T206H Turbo Stationair	T20609000	N906CS
D-ESVV(2)	Piper PA-38-112 Tomahawk	38-79A1148	CS- . . ., F-GCFN,
			N9681N
D-ESWB(2)	Cirrus SR22	3227	N559PG
D-ESWE	LET Z-37A Cmelák	21-04	DDR-SWE, DM-SWE
D-ESWK	Kunert Buddy Baby	001	
D-ESWN	Cirrus SR22	0282	HB-KHM, N875CD
D-ESWO	LET Z-37A Cmelák	17-05	DDR-SWO, DM-SWO,
			SP-GDA
D-ESWP	Piper PA-20-135 Pacer	20-1053	N10339, N791
D-ESWS	Wegscheider/ Neico Lancair 320	1586	

Reg	Type	c/n	Previous identities
D-ESWT	Flight Design CT LS-ELA	F-10-12-12	(D-EWMD)
	(W/o 2.4.13 Uetersen)		
D-ESXA	Xtreme Air XP-30 Sbach 300	003	N143WP, D-ERXA(1)
D-ESXS	Piper PA-28-181 Cherokee Archer II	28-7990151	G-BSXS, N3055C
D-ESXT	Aquila AT-01	AT01-255	
D-ESXX	Beech A36 Bonanza	E-1749	N102FF
D-ESYK(2)	Orlican L-40 Meta-Sokol	150907	OK-NPM, G-ARSP
	(Res. .10)		
D-ESYL	Gyroflug SC-01B-160 Speed Canard	S-53	
D-ESYS	de Havilland DH.82A Tiger Moth	83900	I-RIAR, G-AJHU, T7471
D-ESYT	Cessna 172S Skyhawk SP	172S10524	N2291L
D-ESYY	Piper PA-25-235 Pawnee D	25-7756014	SE-KKC, G-BEOT, N82481
D-ESZN	Bitz/ Bücker Bü.133D-1 Jungmeister	2002	G-BSZN, N8103, D-ECAY(1)
D-ETAA(2)	Cessna 170A	19476	N5442C
	(Res .16)		
D-ETAB(2)	Pilatus P.2-06	77	HB-RBE, U-157, U-128
D-ETAD	Piper PA-38-112 Tomahawk	38-79A0220	N2534C
D-ETAE	Cessna 172N Skyhawk	17267614	N73701
D-ETAG	Cessna 182R Skylane	18267994	N9749H, (N182PW), N9749H
D-ETAI	Piper PA-28RT-201T Turbo.Arrow IV	28R-8131147	N8402H
D-ETAJ	Piper PA-28-181 Archer II	2890161	N9117Q, N91922, (F-GJOD)
D-ETAK	Piper PA-28-181 Archer II	2890162	N9212N, (SE-KME)
D-ETAM(2)	Robin HR.100/200B Royal	114	HB-EMW
D-ETAN(2)	HOAC DV-20 Katana	20122	
D-ETAO	Piper PA-46-350P Malibu Mirage	4636554	N546ST, N9541N
D-ETAP(2)	Piper PA-28-181 Archer III	2843254	N41330
D-ETAR	Cessna 182Q Skylane	18266456	N94597
D-ETAU(2)	Piper PA-18-150 Super Cub	18-7363	I-AVAM
D-ETAX	Mooney M.20J Model 201	24-1006	HB-DGA, N3997H
D-ETBA	Mooney M.20M Model 257 TLS	27-0006	N1036M
D-ETBB	Cessna 172M	17261629	N92818
D-ETBC(2)	SOCATA TB-200 Tobago XL	1811	EC-GYC, F-GRBQ
	(Res. .15)		
D-ETBD	SOCATA TB-20 Trinidad	989	HB-KCP
D-ETBG(2)	Cessna T182T Turbo Skylane	T18208231	I-GIBR, N2101Z
D-ETBH	SOCATA TB-10 Tobago	029	OH-TBA, F-GBHQ, (F-ODKM)
D-ETBJ	Cessna 182S Skylane	18280736	F-HPAP, EC-JSF, N341ME
D-ETBK	Cessna 152	15282677	G-BTBK, N89218
D-ETBO	Mooney M.20M Model 257 TLS	27-0032	F-GJMG
D-ETBR	Bek Me 109R4	002	
	(Permit expired 2004)		
D-ETBT	Piper PA-38-112 Tomahawk	38-79A0299	N2409D
D-ETBW	Wams/ Aero Designs Pulsar XP	413SB	
D-ETBX(2)	Reims/Cessna F150L	F15001043	CN-TBX
D-ETCB	Piper PA-28-181 Archer II	2890179	N9145B
D-ETCC	Piper PA-28-181 Archer II	2890180	N9145H
D-ETCH	Piper PA-28-181 Archer II	2890016	N9111F
D-ETCI	Cessna 172N Skyhawk	17270556	N739HM
D-ETCJ	Beech A23A Musketeer Custom	M-967	YR-ALX, D-EIPH
D-ETCM	Piper PA-28-181 Archer II	2890184	N9177J
D-ETCN	Piper PA-28-181 Archer II	2890186	N9178B
D-ETCP	Piper PA-28-181 Archer II	2890193	N9226Z
D-ETCR	Cessna 152	15279929	N757QW
D-ETCS	Diamond DA 20-C1 Katana	C0300	N286MA
	(Permit 2.3.11)		
D-ETCT	Flight Design CT LS-ELA	F-10-05-06	
	(Permit 8.10)		
D-ETCX	Piper PA-28-181 Archer II	2890195	N9234D
D-ETDA	Schroeder/ Jodel D.18	375	
D-ETDB	Bartling / Cozy BL	01, formerly 1608	(D-EEDB)
	(P 5.8.16)		
D-ETDF	Evers/Brditschka HB-207VRG Alpha	207-004	(PH-STP)
	(Permit expired .05)		
D-ETDI	Robin R.3000/160	159	
D-ETDK	Aerostyle Breezer B600	029LSA	
	(W/o 2.8.16)		
D-ETDP	Piper PA-28-181 Cherokee Archer II	28-7890043	G-BIDP, N44956
D-ETDS(2)	Diamond DA 40 Star	40065	N465DS
D-ETDT	Mooney M.20K Model 231	25-0109	N31PK, N231AV
D-ETEA(2)	Diamond DA 40 Star	D4.004	
D-ETED(2)	Cessna 182T Skylane	18282111	N6295T
D-ETEE	Marthiens/ Stoddard-Hamilton Glasair IIRG-S	V-1/2038	
	(CofA reduced to permit 10.4.07)		
D-ETEF	Pitts S-2A	2188	D-EDEE, G-FREE, LN-NAC
D-ETEG	Beech F33A Bonanza	CE-1440	N5541L
D-ETEL(2)	Diamond DA 20-A1 Katana	10241	C-FDVP
D-ETEN	SOCATA TB-21 Trinidad TC	1377	
D-ETEO	Robin DR.400/180R Remo 180	2347	
D-ETER(2)	Cirrus SR22T	0478	N192PR
D-ETES	SOCATA TB-10 Tobago	1667	
D-ETET	Cessna 150L	15073183	N5283Q
D-ETEX	Diamond DA 20-A1 Katana	10242	C-GDMU
D-ETFA	Piper PA-32RT-300 Lance II	32R-7985033	N2218D
D-ETFB(2)	SOCATA TB-10 Tobago	451	OE-KMF
D-ETFC(2)	Piper PA-28-181 Archer II	2843222	G-JACC, G-GIFT, G-IMVA, SE-KIH, N9524N, N4166F
D-ETFD	Beech F33A Bonanza	CE-1492	N15482
D-ETFE	Piper PA-28-181 Archer II	2843665	N60851
D-ETFF	Diamond DA 40NG Star	40.N030	
D-ETFH	Cessna 182T Skylane	18281564	N1036C
D-ETFL	Piper PA-28-181 Cherokee Archer II	28-7690058	N7145C
D-ETFT	Mooney M.20K Model 231	25-1227	G-GJKK, F-GJKK
D-ETFW	HOAC DV-20 Katana	20059	
D-ETGE(2)	Sukhoi SU-29M	76-021	HA-HUD, RA-3328K, RA-44672
D-ETGG	Grob G.115A	8066	OO-KMG, D-ENFM, F-BRUR, D-EHTA(3)
	(Res. .16)		
D-ETGK	Aquila AT-01	AT01-193	
D-ETGR	Grumman AA-5B Tiger	AA5B-0971	OO-GAZ(3), OO-HRD
D-ETGS	Rockwell Commander 112TCA	13177	N101GS, OE-KGS(2), (D-E . . .), ZS-MBF, N4647W
D-ETGZ	Cessna 172S Skyhawk SP	172S10350	EC-KHD, D-EPON, N22578
D-ETHA	Mooney M.20M Model 257 TLS	27-0082	N23WA, D-EEWA(2)
D-ETHB	Bücker/ Brändli BX-2 Cherry	101	
D-ETHC	de Havilland DH.82A Tiger Moth	82018	PH-CRO, G-AISY, VT-CZV, G-AISY, N6740
D-ETHF	Diamond DA 40D Star	40080D	OE-VTA, D-ETHF
	(Built as DA 40 c/n 40080, convtd 2004 to DA 40D)		
D-ETHG	Aquila AT-01 (Model A210)	AT01-101	(D-ECCX(2))
D-ETHH	Meier/ Rutan Long-Ez	1082	
D-ETHL	Mooney M.20M Model 257 TLS	27-0133	
D-ETHM	Beech A36 Bonanza	E-3023	N3267Q
D-ETHN	Pilatus P.2-05	27	HB-RAT, U-107, A-107
D-ETHO	Bücker Bü.131 Jungmann	60	HB-URM, A-48
D-ETHP	Pfeiffer/ Denney Kitfox IV-1200	JCU-113	
D-ETHS	Mooney M.20K Model 252 TSE	25-1123	HB-DGU
D-ETIB	Mooney M.20K Model 231	25-0397	N4042H
D-ETIC(2)	Cessna T182T Turbo Skylane	T18208367	OY-TAS, N66139
D-ETIG	American AG-5B Tiger	10139	N1197T
D-ETII	Lake LA-4-200 Buccaneer	921	N2820P
D-ETIK	Piper PA-28-161 Warrior II	2816116	N9254N
D-ETIL	Thiel Sky Princess	1	
	(Res. .09)		
D-ETIM(2)	Piper PA-18 Super Cub 95	18-1500	D-EOOF(2), D-EOCE, ALAT, 51-15500
D-ETIN	HOAC DV-20 Katana	20110	
D-ETIR	SOCATA Rallye 235E	12831	I-ETIK, F-GAKS
D-ETIS	Piper PA-28-181 Archer III	2843133	N41237
D-ETIT(2)	Beech S35 Bonanza	D-7617	I-STAS, N5686K
D-ETIV	Piper PA-28-181 Archer III	2843326	N4179R, N9518N
D-ETIX	Piper PA-28-161 Warrior III	2842001	N9217N
D-ETJA	Piper PA-28-181 Archer II	28-8690044	N9178Y
D-ETJD	Stark Turbulent D	133	D-ESMB(1), OY-AMB, OY-EAB, D-EKIV(1)
D-ETJG	Piper PA-46-350P Malibu Mirage	4622121	N91947, (N555PS), N9215Q
D-ETJK	Cessna 140	8216	G-BSYE, D-ESYE, (D-ETDS), G-BSYE, N89196, NC89196
D-ETJP	Cessna 172P Skyhawk	17274263	N51078
D-ETKA	Piper PA-28RT-201T Turbo Arrow IV	28R-8031173	OO-JJA, N82623
D-ETKB(2)	Cessna 172N Skyhawk	17270102	D-EJKL, N738NF
D-ETKD	Cessna 152	15285609	N94150
D-ETKE	Cessna 172N Skyhawk	17273452	N4905G
D-ETKF	Cirrus SR22	3063	N196CP
D-ETKG(2)	Cirrus SR22	2488	N666KG, G-ONEC, N686SR
	(Res. 16)		
D-ETKH	Aviat A-1 Husky	1281	
D-ETKJ	Cessna 172S Skyhawk SP	172S10678	D-EVCC, N6050C
	(Res. 16)		
D-ETKM	Cessna 172N Skyhawk II	17272198	N8425E
D-ETKN	Cessna 182T Skylane	18282129	EC-KYB, N63280
D-ETKP	Cessna 150L	15073727	(OY- . . .), G-BPWO, N18010
D-ETKR	Cessna 150M	15078318	(OY- . . .), G-BPUZ, N9369U
D-ETKS	Cessna TR182 Turbo Skylane RG	R18200937	G-GARY, N738KV
D-ETKT	Diamond DA 40 NG	40.N001	OE-DNG(2), OE-VPU
	(Res. .11, ntu)		
D-ETLA	Piper PA-28-181 Archer III	2843015	N9260J
D-ETLB	Cessna 172R Skyhawk	17281183	N2155A
D-ETLC	Aquila AT-01	AT01-241	
D-ETLE	Piper PA-32R-301T Saratoga II TC	3257458	OK-UAU, N1081P, OK-UAU, N1081P
	(Res. .13)		
D-ETLF	Robin DR.500/200i Président	0028	
D-ETLG	Cessna 172S Skyhawk SP	172S8561	EI-EDV, G-BZPM, N72760
D-ETLH(2)	Aquila AT-01	AT01-194	
D-ETLI	Hoffmann/ Denney Kitfox IV Speedster	1749/KBS-077	
D-ETLK(2)	Diamond DA 20-A1 Katana	10293	N293DA, C-GKAC
D-ETLL	Cessna 150M	15077050	N123WT, N63032
D-ETLN	Aquila AT-01	AT01-259	
D-ETLR	Piper PA-46-350P Malibu Mirage	4636258	SE-ILP
D-ETLS(2)	Mooney M.20M Model 257 TLS	27-0211	N281FH
D-ETLT	Aquila AT-01	AT01-116	
D-ETLU	Diamond DA 20-A1 Katana	10292	C-GSMR, C-FDVP
D-ETMA	Aviat A-1 Husky	1279	OY-TAW, D-EJHU(2)
D-ETMB	Stark Turbulent D-1	135	HB-SVG, D-EKUV
D-ETMC(2)	Cessna T182T Turbo Skylane	T18208586	N947MD
D-ETME	de Havilland DH.82A Tiger Moth	83228	G-AMIU, T5495
	(Res. 9.4.09)		
D-ETMF	Cessna 172N Skyhawk	17272290	SE-KTZ, N9927E
D-ETMG	Cirrus SR22T	0316	N150JP
D-ETMH	Cessna 172M Skyhawk	17266298	N9661H
D-ETMI	Robin DR.400/180R Remo 180	2144	
D-ETMM(2)	Cessna 172S Skyhawk SP	172S10436	N2120P
	(Reduced to Permit 4.07)		
D-ETMO	de Havilland DH.82A Tiger Moth	85652	D-EHXH(2), G-AIXH,
	(Flies as DE722)		N5445, VR-HFH, VR-HEL, G-AIXH, DE722
D-ETMP(1)	de Havilland DH.82A Tiger Moth	83683	D-ESPS(1), HB-UCX, D-EHAL, (D-EAKP), D-EKAL, G-ANGD, T7213
	(Under restoration, painted as T-7213) (Presumably alternative regn required)		
D-ETMP(2)	Tecnam P.2010	41	
D-ETMS	Stehr/ Denney Kitfox	681/1690	
D-ETMT	Beech F33A Bonanza	CE-1669	N8061P
D-ETMY	Mylius My-103 Mistral	V-1	
D-ETNA	SOCATA TB-200 Tobago XL	1656	
D-ETNC	Piper PA-28-161 Warrior II	28-8116312	N84324, (N99ES), N84234
D-ETNH	Cirrus SR22	2216	N920SE
D-ETNL	Cessna 172S Skyhawk SP	172S8874	OK-TWO, OM-FAB, N35587
D-ETNT	Cessna TR182 Turbo Skylane RG	R18201812	N4979T
D-ETOI	SAN Jodel DR.1050 Ambassadeur	483	D-EARL(1)
D-ETOJ(2)	Mudry CAP.232	38	F-GTOJ, F-WQOM
D-ETOL	Cessna 182Q Skylane	18267591	N5237N
D-ETOM	Cessna 152	15284787	N4629P
D-ETON	SOCATA TB-10 Tobago	1190	N55391
D-ETOR	Beech C33A Bonanza	CE-1050	N7214Z
D-ETOX	Cirrus SR22	1954	G-DUAL, N194SR
D-ETOY(2)	Xtreme 3000	2002299	
	(Permit .08)		
D-ETPA(2)	Piper PA-28-181 Archer III	2843553	N53596
D-ETPD	Piper PA-46-350P Malibu Mirage	4636217	G-EODE, N45YM, G-BYLM
D-ETPE	Piper PA-28-181 Archer III	2843003	N9256N
D-ETPG(3)	Grob G.120TP-A	11024	
	(Permit 14.11.13)		
D-ETPH	Piper PA-18 Super Cub 95	18-2006	SE-I MG, OY-DVV, EI-79/MM522406/I-EIFI, 52-2406
D-ETPK	Aquila AT-01	AT01-240	
D-ETPM	Piper PA-28-161 Cadet	2841363	N9234Q, (N629FT), (N9235D)
D-ETPO	Cessna 182T Skylane	18282134	PH-VDL, D-EAMP(3), N6336D

Reg	Type	c/n	Previous identities
D-ETPS	Piper PA-28-161 Cadet	2841364	N9237Q, (N630FT), (N9236J)
D-ETPX	Grob G.120TP-A	11001	(P 3.7.13) (Believed converted from D-ETPG(2) c/n 8502, see above)
D-ETPY	Piper PA-28-161 Cadet	2841365	N9250G, (N631FT), (N9228J)
D-ETPZ	CSA PS-28 Cruiser	C0322	
D-ETRA(2)	Extra EA.500	1002	(D-EHEW(2))
D-ETRE	Tecnam P.2002-JF Sierra	003	LX-TRE
D-ETRG	Cessna 152	15285109	N5410Q
D-ETRI (2)	Extra EA.300/LT	LT015	(Res .12)
D-ETRM	Cirrus SR22	2058	N297SR
D-ETRS	Robin DR.400/180S Régent	2095	
D-ETRV(2)	Vossler/ Van's RV-7A	73616	
D-ETRY(2)	Yakovlev Yak-52	900908	LY-TRY, DOSAAF (Res .16)
D-ETSA	Bölkow BO.209 Monsun 160FV	197	HB-UEI, D-EAIM(1)
D-ETSC	Cessna TU206F Turbo Stationair	U20602001	(D-EEYU(2)), PH-ESA, D-EEYU(2), N51404
D-ETSE	Beech K35 Bonanza	D-6113	N805R
D-ETSG	Beech A36TC Bonanza	EA-144	I-LSBV, HB-EJF
D-ETSM	Piper PA-28RT-201T Turbo Arrow IV	28R-7931200	N29580
D-ETSR	Robin DR.400/200R Remo 200	2243	
D-ETSS	Cirrus SR22	3472	N161CK
D-ETST	Cessna T182T Turbo Skylane	T18208888	N6194S
D-ETSW	Piper PA-32R-301 Saratoga IIHP	3213077	N9238Q
D-ETSY	Aviat A-1 Husky	1377	
D-ETTA	Van's RV-7A	2002494	(Permit 18.9.15)
D-ETTD	Cessna 172R Skyhawk	17281218	N2168Z
D-ETTG	Piper PA-46-310P Malibu	46-8508079	N6915P, (N88PL), N6915P
D-ETTH	Extra EA.400	21	
D-ETTJ	Cirrus SR22T	0148	D-EHEH(7), N318CH
D-ETTK	Cessna 172R Skyhawk	17281219	N2169M
D-ETTL	Cessna 172R Skyhawk	17281217	N21714
D-ETTM(2)	Cessna 182T Skylane	18281922	N22279
D-ETTR	Cessna 172R Skyhawk	17281221	N21703
D-ETTS	Cessna 172R Skyhawk	17281220	N2170D
D-ETTT(3)	Cessna A185F Skywagon	18504190	F-GCVS, N61440
D-ETTU	Cessna 172S Skyhawk SP	172S10081	N2472Z
D-ETTW(2)	Aquila AT-01-100A	AT01-322	
D-ETTY	Cirrus SR20	1212	PH-WGL, N270CD
D-ETUA	Cessna TU206G Turbo Stationair 6	U20606048	HB-CJP, N4914Z (Soloy conversion)
D-ETUC	SOCATA MS.893A Rallye Commodore 180	11487	F-BSAN
D-ETUF	Focke-Wulf FW.44J Stieglitz	154	LV-YZN, FA Argentina
D-ETUG	Piper PA-25-235 Pawnee	25-2235	SE-IZP, N6640Z
D-ETUI	Aeronca 65CA Super Chief	17951	N36894, NC36894
D-ETUK	Cirrus SR20	1866	N301PP
D-ETUR	Mudry CAP.10B	38	I-AVAA, F-BUDH
D-ETUS	Robin DR.400/180R Remo 180	2188	
D-ETUT	Aerospool WT-9 Dynamic LSA	DY-442/2012	(Permit 13.7.12)
D-ETUW	Beech C24R Sierra	MC-705	N6706D (Res; still US-regd 4.16)
D-ETVA(2)	Piper PA-32R-301T Saratoga II TC	3257155	G-VONS, N602MA (Res .16)
D-ETVG	SIAI-Marchetti SF.260WB	575/43-003	9U-ZRC
D-ETVH	Robin DR.400/180R Remo 180	2157	F-GLVH
D-ETVR	Impulse Xcite	unkn	
D-ETVV	SOCATA MS.893E Rallye 180GT	13104	I-CTVV, F-GBKJ
D-ETWA	Piper PA-46-310P Malibu	46-8408014	N4320E
D-ETWB	Cessna 172M	17264568	
D-ETWF	Frank/ Denney Kitfox II	597	
D-ETWH	Mooney M.20M Model 257 TLS	27-0140	
D-ETWK	Küster/ Denney Kitfox III	809/1765	
D-ETWL	Aquila AT-02	AT02-106	(D-ETLH(1))
D-ETWM(2)	Piper PA-28-181 Archer III	2843325	N41885
D-ETWN	SOCATA TB-200 Tobago XL	1445	PH-TFS, LX-FAR
D-ETWO(2)	Cirrus SR22	2627	G-WTEC, N819SR
D-ETWP	Cessna 172S Skyhawk SP	172S9374	N5347Q
D-ETWR	Diamond DA 20-A1 Katana	10128	OE-AMF, N557SS, C-GKAC
D-ETWS	SOCATA TB-9 Tampico	1793	OE-..., D-EMVZ
D-ETWW	Cessna 172N Skyhawk	17270981	N1383E
D-ETWZ	Christen A-1 Husky	1110	PH-TWZ
D-ETYP	Aquila AT-01	AT01-246	
D-ETYT	SOCATA MS.894E Minerva 220GT	12136	OO-TDF, F-BUGF
D-EUAC	Aquila AT-01	AT01-206	
D-EUAK	SOCATA TB-10 Tobago	630	SX-AMN, F-ODVV, (F-GFEI), (N20EX)
D-EUAP	Piper PA-28RT-201T Turbo Arrow IV	28R-8131166	N8412H
D-EUAS	Aquila AT-01	AT01-237	
D-EUAU(2)	Aquila A211	unkn	(Permit .16)
D-EUBA(2)	Aerostyle Breezer B600	015LSA	(Permit 31.3.11)
D-EUBL	Piper PA-18-150 Super Cub	18-5664	OE-CDP, D-EADP(1), OE-ADH, (D-ECEQ), N7196D
D-EUCA	Commander Aircraft 114B	14571	
D-EUCB(2)	Buchholz Rieseler R.III.22/K	1856	(Permit .01)
D-EUCD	Cirrus SR22	1320	N449CD
D-EUCE(2)	Cessna 172RG Cutlass RG	172RG0475	I-TYPE , N5219V
D-EUCH	HOAC DV-20 Katana	20083	
D-EUCI	Cessna U206D Skywagon 206	U206-1440	4X-CCQ, IDFAF045, N1703C, (N1040M)
D-EUCK	Cirrus SR22T	0156	N218CT
D-EUCO	Cessna 172N Skyhawk	17273373	N4825G
D-EUCP	Cessna 145 Airmaster	463	N19495, G-AFOH, N19495, NC19495
D-EUCR	Cessna LC41-550FG Columbia	411142	N10427
D-EUDA	Diamond DA 20-A1 Katana	10268	C-GDMU
D-EUDH	Yakovlev Yak-18T	22202034068	RA-3343K, LZ-CBL, LZ-TCB, CCCP44498 (Res .12) (Identity unconfirmed, c/n quoted above was w/o 4.93)
D-EUDI	Piper PA-32-300 Cherokee Six	32-7540169	I-GODF, N1524X
D-EUDO	Piper PA-28-236 Dakota	28-7911111	N333WE, N3022R
D-EUDR	Piper PA-46-310P Malibu	4608040	N54FM, N9111Z
D-EUEB	Bölkow BO.209 Monsun 160RV	124	(D-EXBJ), HB-UEB, D-EFJB(1)
D-EUFC	Cessna U206G Stationair 6	U20604101	HB-CJO, D-GJKD, N206DG, C-GBBV, N756HJ (Soloy conversion 4.91)
D-EUFD(2)	SOCATA TB-20 Trinidad GT	2019	
D-EUFK	Beech G36 Bonanza	E-3984	N136EU
D-EUFO	Cirrus SR22	3429	(D-EBBH(2)), N666LG
D-EUFR	Beech A36 Bonanza	E-3021	
D-EUGA	SOCATA TB-9 Tampico	299	CS-..., OO-ESX, D-EESX(1)
D-EUGC	Grob G 115A	8021	HB-UGC, (D-EGVV)
D-EUGD	Cessna 172H	17254949	N1454F
D-EUGS	HOAC DV-20 Katana	20034	
D-EUGW	Cessna 172N Skyhawk	17273046	N9877J
D-EUHF	Mooney M.20J Model 205	24-3360	
D-EUHU	SOCATA TB-20 Trinidad	1521	
D-EUHW	Beech A36 Bonanza	E-2990	N3218G
D-EUIB	Cessna P210N Pressurized Centurion II	P21000162	N6292P
D-EUIM	Cirrus SR22T	0566	N566AD
D-EUJF	Heimes/ Aero Designs Pulsar XP	01/1874	
D-EUJL	Lenhard/ Stoddard-Hamilton Glasair III	1943	(Res)
D-EUJS	Pitts S-2B Special	5240	N92AP
D-EUKA	Swoboda/ Europa Aviation Europa	1782	
D-EUKD	Grob G 115C	82071/C1	
D-EUKI	Kienle/ Brditschka HB-207VRG Alfa	207056	
D-EUKM	Cessna 182T Skylane	18281696	OO-FKG, N694MC
D-EULA	PZL-104 Wilga 35A	15800576	HA-SEW, DOSAAF-45
D-EULB	Schaller / Jabiru J400	176	
D-EULF	Cessna 150L	15074244	N19216 (W/o 27.4.10)
D-EULG	SIAI-Marchetti S.205/20R	215	I-BULG
D-EULI	Bronner / Rutan Long-Ez	1044	
D-EUMA(2)	Diamond DA 40 Star	40281	N186MA
D-EUMC(2)	Tecnam P.2002-JF Sierra	250	
D-EUMH	Cirrus SR22	1577	N478CD
D-EUMI	Robin R.2160D Acrobin	304	
D-EUMK	Cirrus SR22T	0025	(D-ESRW(2)), N123ZS
D-EUML(2)	Cessna 182T Skylane	18281478	OY-TLG, N134PB, N65796
D-EUMM	Diamond DA 20-A1 Katana	10250	C-GKAN
D-EUNA	Extra EA.300/L	1251	
D-EUNG	Piper PA-46-350P Malibu Mirage	4636393	N184BR
D-EUNO	Cirrus SR20	1358	N8152E
D-EUNP	Cessna T182T Turbo Skylane	T18208783	OK-AZZ, N1553S
D-EUOS	Cessna P210N Pressurized Centurion II	P21000368	N4918K (Permit 20.9.13)
D-EUPA	Hoffmann/ Europa Avn Europa	271/1843	
D-EUPC	Diamond DA 40 Star	D4.232	OE-VPU
D-EUPM(2)	Mooney M.20L PFM	26-0021	N141MP (Res .12, ntu, still current in US 4.16)
D-EURA	Jodel D.92 Bébé	216	D-ENIC(1), SL-AAM
D-EURF	Diamond DA 20-C1 Katana	C0082	N982CT, C-FDVA
D-EURI	Cessna 305C (L-19E) Bird Dog	305M-0033	I-EIAI, EI-20, MM61-2987, 61-2987 (Regal Air conversion) (Res .11, ntu by 6.15)
D-EURL	Robin DR.400/140B Dauphin 4	2629	
D-EURO	SOCATA TB-9 Tampico Club	1399	
D-EURS	Piper PA-46-310P Malibu	4608093	N9121N
D-EURU	Rupprecht/ Europa Aviation Europa	1954	
D-EUSA	Cessna 150H	15068758	N23154
D-EUSB	Cessna P210N Pressurized Centurion	P21000738	N6258W (Robertson STOL conversion) (Res .07, ntu still US-regd 4.16)
D-EUSD	Cessna 162 Skycatcher	16200043	N5215Q
D-EUSE	Diamond DA 40D Star	D4.214	
D-EUSM	Diamond DA 40 Star	40618	N518DS
D-EUST	Cirrus SR22	2745	T7-COM, N357SR
D-EUTA	Grob G 115C	82034/C	N115VA
D-EUTC	Cessna 172S Skyhawk SP	172S8810	N2726X
D-EUTE	American Champion 7GCBC Explorer	1443-2007	N261WM
D-EUTM(3)	Cirrus SR22T	0186	N105DE
D-EUTO	Bücker Bü.180B-1 Student	2115	(D-EFTO(2)), HB-UTO
D-EUTR	Piper PA-46-310P Malibu	4608045	N9113Z (Res .10; ntu, still US-regd 4.16)
D-EUTT	Diamond DA 20-A1 Katana	10246	(Dismantled)
D-EUTZ	Mooney M.20K Model 252 TSE	25-1056	N252DW
D-EUUH	Cessna 150M	15079342	PH-TXD, (PH-USB), N714QC
D-EUUT	Bücker Bü. APM 131-150 Jungmann	81	HB-UUT, A-68 (Res .14)
D-EUUU	Champion 7EC Traveler	7FC-404	D-EBMQ, N9829Y (Converted from 7FC Tri-Traveler)
D-EUUZ	Bücker Bü. APM 131-150 Jungmann	15	HB-UUZ, A-8
D-EUVH	Piper PA-46 Malibu Mirage	4636345	N708DP
D-EUVI	Mooney M.20M Model 257 TLS	27-0233	F=HABC, OE-KST, N10824
D-EUVM	Piper PA-28-161 Warrior II	28-7916119	N21619
D-EUWA	Aquila AT-01	AT01-178	
D-EUWC	CzAW Sportcruiser	09SC295	(Permit .10)
D-EUWE	Schirmer/Hinz BL2-ARA	1716	
D-EUWH	Extra EA.300/L	01	
D-EUWM	Beech F33A Bonanza	CE-1635	N82689
D-EUWN	Wagner/ Stoddard-Hamilton Glastar GS-1	5468	
D-EUWW	Robin DR.400/180 Régent	2249	
D-EUXA	Xtreme Air XA-42 Sbach 342	108	(Permit 5.8.11)
D-EUXL	Liberty XL-2	0047	N557XL
D-EUZZ	Boeing Stearman A75N1	75-4959	N399MB, N68484, BuA55722, 42-16796 (Permit 10.9.14)
D-EVAB(2)	HOAC DV-20 Katana	20025	
D-EVAC	Robin DR.400/180 Régent	2418	
D-EVAD(3)	Piper PA-28R-201T Turbo Arrow III	28R-7703231	HB-PMV, D-EKJW, N38503
D-EVAG	Piper PA-28RT-201T Turbo Arrow IV	28R-8131187	N82001, N9569N, N84209
D-EVAI(2)	Aero AT-3 R100	004	F-GURT, SP-TPF, (N55XT), (SP-TPF) (Res .16)
D-EVAJ	Geiser/ Van's RV-8	01/451	
D-EVAL(2)	Grob G 115C	82044/D2	
D-EVAM(2)	Cessna 172R Skyhawk	17280083	N382ES
D-EVAN	Cessna 152	15284234	N4826L
D-EVAO	Cessna 172R Skyhawk	17280395	
D-EVAR	Beech F33A Bonanza	CE-1651	N55389
D-EVAT	Piper PA-28-181 Archer II	28-8590057	N6915R
D-EVAU	SOCATA TB-20 Trinidad	1569	
D-EVBA(2)	Aerostyle Breezer BG600	032LSA	(P. 23.6.16)
D-EVBB(2)	Sauer/ Van's RV-4	4529	(Permit 2.5.11)

Reg	Type	S/N	Previous ID
D-EVBC	Cirrus SR22	3593	N345BY
D-EVBE	Cessna U206G Stationair 6-II (Soloy conversion)	U20606381	N7595Z
D-EVBH	HOAC DV-20 Katana	20138	OE-AHO
D-EVBM	Binder CP.301S Smaragd	106	OE-AGC, D-EFIR(2)
D-EVBO	HOAC DV-20 Katana	20060	OE-ADI (2), D-ENMH, OE-UDV
D-EVBS(2)	Evektor EV-97 SportStar RTC (For Turkey .9.16)	20141707	
D-EVCB	HOAC DV-20 Katana	20040	OE-AIB, N41DV
D-EVCD(2)	Cirrus SR22T	0708	N730DK
D-EVCL	Piper PA-28-181 Archer III	2843654	PH-OWL, I-MACA, N10733
D-EVCM	Cessna R172K Hawk XP	R1722972	N24CV, N58ER, (N758BU)
D-EVCX	Piper PA-18 Super Cub 125 (Officially quoted with f/n 18-939)	18-851	PH-VCX , (PH-VCH), R-205, 51-15686
D-EVDB	Morane Saulnier MS.505 Criquet (Regd as Fieseler Fi.156C-7 Storch c/n 2042) (P 5.08) (In Luftwaffe c/s with code "EV+DB")	269	OO-STO, F-BBUK, Fr.AF
D-EVDC	Piper PA-28R-200 Cherokee Arrow B	28R-7135126	VH-SLH, N8595N
D-EVDE	Cessna 182T Skylane	18281861	D-EXAK, N12383
D-EVDH	Tecnam P.2002-JF Sierra	085	
D-EVDI	Reims/Cessna F172M	F17201320	OE-DTU
D-EVDM	Aeronca 11AC Chief (Res. 13.5.15)	11AC-1598	OO-RIK
D-EVEB	Beech F33A Bonanza	CE-1380	N725MA, N1569F
D-EVEC	Piper PA-46-350P Malibu Mirage	4636266	N146PJ, D-ELRH, N41878
D-EVEE	Beech F33A Bonanza	CE-1354	N5583R
D-EVEI	Beech A36 Bonanza	E-2722	TC-ARZ, TC-ARI, N80225
D-EVEL	Cessna 172N Skyhawk	17273253	N333WB, N7364F
D-EVEM	Robin DR.400/140B Major	1398	PH-SRW
D-EVEN	SOCATA TB-9 Tampico Club	1320	
D-EVEO	CASA C-1.131E Jungmann (Res. .12)	unkn	N401J, N2304D, E3B-584
D-EVER(2)	Piper PA-46-500TP Malibu Meridian	4697105	N429MM
D-EVEV	Cessna T182T Skylane	T18208904	N6204M
D-EVEW	Beech C24R Sierra	MC-651	N6014Y
D-EVEZ	Resch/ Jodel D.18	104	
D-EVFG	Beech S35 Bonanza	D-7675	HB-EKN, I-FARE, HB-EKN
D-EVFH	Cessna 172N Skyhawk	17268918	N734KR
D-EVFM	Piper PA-28-181 Archer II	28-8290063	N8466W
D-EVGH	Piper PA-28RT-201T Turbo Arrow IV	28R-7931004	N44DY, N2079B
D-EVGI	Cessna 182T Skylane	18281500	N65901
D-EVGM	Robin DR.400/180R Remo 180	2143	
D-EVGP	Beech F33A Bonanza	CE-1183	N3081A
D-EVGR	Beech F33A Bonanza	CE-1494	N334MW
D-EVGS	Beech D35 Bonanza	D-3637	HB-EGS, PH-NFF
D-EVHB	Piper PA-38-112 Tomahawk	38-80A0012	N24849
D-EVHF	Diamond DV-20 Katana	20200	OE-VPX
D-EVHH	Robin DR.400/180 Régent	2449	
D-EVHL	Vicinius/ Europa Avn Europa (Permit 21.4.15)	150	
D-EVHM(3)	SOCATA TB-20 Trinidad	2144	D-EVHV(1)
D-EVHZ	Remos GX	326	
D-EVIA	Robin R.2160D Acrobin	289	
D-EVIB(2)	Piper PA-28-181 Archer III	2843043	N9274L
D-EVIC	Piper PA-28-181 Archer III	2843071	N9285N
D-EVID	Piper PA-28RT-201T Turbo Arrow IV	28R-8331045	N43081
D-EVIE	Aquila AT-01	AT01-205	
D-EVIG	Cessna LC41-550FG Columbia	41656	N1376C
D-EVII (2)	Aviat A-1 Husky	1241	
D-EVIJ	SOCATA TB-9 Tampico	1840	F-GTQA, (5N-CAS), F-OIDJ
D-EVIK	Beech A36 Bonanza (Allison 250-B17C turbine conversion)	E-2347	N900TT, N2611L
D-EVIL	Cessna 172N Skyhawk	17270159	N781MB
D-EVIM	HOAC DV-20 Katana	20033	
D-EVIN	SOCATA TB-10 Tobago	1476	
D-EVIP(2)	Cessna 172N Skyhawk	17272002	N6283E
D-EVIR	Reims/Cessna F177RG Cardinal RG	F177RG0089	F-BVIR, (D-EJXO(1))
D-EVIS	SOCATA TB-200 Tobago XL	1474	
D-EVIT	Cessna TU206F Turbo Stationair	U20602246	N1538U
D-EVIX	Extra EA.300/SC	SC029	D-EXTW
D-EVIY	Christen A-1 Husky	1156	HB-KIV, D-EHNP(3), N9609G
D-EVJO	Cessna 172P Skyhawk	17274591	N52715
D-EVKA	Zlin Z.42M	0166	D-EIIQ(2)), SP-WIB
D-EVKB	Piper PA-28-181 Archer II	28-8390054	N4300Z
D-EVKG	Piper PA-46-310P Malibu	4608022	N9094Z, N9103Q
D-EVKH	Cessna 182T Skylane	18281845	N6071U
D-EVKK	Krah/ Van's RV-8KK (Permit 20.7.15)	2002525	
D-EVKL	SOCATA Rallye 235E	13020	F-GBKL
D-EVKM(2)	Cessna 182T Skylane	18281931	N2179P
D-EVKO	Cessna 140	8936	G-BPKO, N89891, NC89891
D-EVKV	Diamond DA 40 Star	40350	
D-EVLA(2)	WDFL Dallach D4 Fascination VLA	1001	
D-EVLF	HOAC DV-20 Katana	20117	
D-EVLG	SIAI-Marchetti SM.1019A	035	EI- . . ./MM . . . .
D-EVLL	CEA DR.250/160 Capitaine	83	OY-DGD
D-EVLO	Piper PA-18-150 Super Cub	18-7809173	S5-DAR, SL-DAR, YU-DCG, N84222
D-EVLS	Diamond DA 20-A1 Katana	10244	C-GDMB
D-EVLX	Cessna 172R Skyhawk	17280984	N4361Y
D-EVMA(2)	Piper PA-46-310P Malibu	4608034	C-FTNM, N302H, N87WW, N121RP, N121RF, N9104Z
D-EVMC	Cessna 182P Skylane	18264653	N9034M
D-EVMG	Cessna 182T Skylane	18281775	N6012P
D-EVMH	SOCATA TB-200 Tobago XL	1629	
D-EVMI	Piper PA-28R-200 Cherokee Arrow II	28R-7535099	I-KIMI, N32914
D-EVMK(2)	Piper PA-28-181 Archer II	2843053	N9277Q
D-EVMO	Reims/Cessna F152	F15201517	D-EEJI
D-EVMT	Piper PA-46-350P Malibu Mirage (Res. .13)	4636204	N55WH
D-EVMU	Aquila AT-01	AT01-209	
D-EVNE	Cessna F150H	F150-0243	OY-LCF, D-ECNU
D-EVNM	SOCATA TB-200 Tobago XL	1439	D-EVHM, F-OHDA
D-EVNT	Van's RV-7 (Res. .10)	001	
D-EVOC	Cessna 172N Skyhawk	17271387	N2961E
D-EVOF	Piper PA-28-181 Archer III	2843671	N6002G
D-EVOG	Robin DR.500/200i Président	0019	
D-EVOI	HOAC DV-20 Katana	20130	
D-EVOK	SOCATA TB-20 Trinidad	2004	A7-MGK, F-OILL
D-EVOL	Cessna 172S Skyhawk SP	172S9984	N1229N
D-EVOM	Cessna 150M	15079122	N714EP
D-EVON	SOCATA TB-200 Tobago XL	1475	F-WNGZ
D-EVOO	HOAC DV-20 Katana	20042	
D-EVOP(2)	SIAT 223A-1 Flamingo	002	HB-EVO, D-EHQE, HB-EVO, D-EHQE
D-EVOR	HOAC DV-20 Katana	20017	
D-EVOS	Cessna 182Q Skylane	18266835	N96740
D-EVOT	Krüger/ Zenith CH-601 HD/S Zodiac	6-3102	
D-EVOX	HOAC DV-20 Katana	20038	
D-EVPA	Piper PA-46-350P Malibu Mirage	4622138	N9210P, (N9234Z)
D-EVPS	Cessna 172S Skyhawk SP	172S10411	N1401G
D-EVPW	Diamond DA 20-A1 Katana	10144	C-GKAN
D-EVQC	Diamond DA 20-C1 Katana	C0131	N631DC, C-GKAN
D-EVRA	SIAI-Marchetti SF.260 (Res. .11)	2-36	I-SYAI
D-EVRF	Falkenstein/ Van's RV-7	70151	
D-EVRP(2)	Evektor EV-97 SportStar RTC (W/o 8.9.16)	20121501	
D-EVRS	Ruttkay/ Aerospool WT-9 Dynamic	448/DB-01/02	
D-EVRV	Müller/ Van's RV-7 "MüBi"	2002374	
D-EVSA	Grob G 115D2 Bavarian	82002/D2	
D-EVSC	Cessna 172P Skyhawk	17276141	N96997, C-GSIU
D-EVSK	Diamond DA 40 Star	40021	OE-KSK
D-EVSL	Diamond DV 20 Katana	20201	OE-AEG
D-EVSM	Piper PA-46-350P Malibu Mirage (JetProp DLX conversion #180)	4622072	HB-PMO
D-EVSR	Robin DR.400/180 Régent	2066	
D-EVST	Robin DR.500/200i Président	0017	
D-EVTA	Piper PA-28-181 Archer II	2843033	N92703
D-EVTC	Cessna 172S Skyhawk SP	172S10037	N337TC
D-EVTE	Robin R.3000/160	168	
D-EVTP	Piper PA-46-500TP Malibu Meridian	4697325	N60419
D-EVTT	Lancair LC41-550FG Colombia 300	41639	N12747
D-EVUC	Grob G 115A	8100	G-BYFD, EI-CCN, G-BSGE
D-EVUG	Grünig/ Neico Lancair 360	1762	
D-EVUJ	Piper PA-28RT-201T Turbo Arrow IV	28R-7931134	N2124N, N2152X
D-EVUK	Koschel/ Van's RV-7A	2002353	
D-EVUW	Cessna 152	15282327	EC-LED, N68711
D-EVVA	Mooney M.20M Model 257 TLS	27-0002	N1002K
D-EVVB	Commander Aircraft 114B	14622	PH-VVB, N77HQ, N77HK, N500JR
D-EVVE	Beech A36 Bonanza	E-2200	F-GGGP, N216JP, N7212L
D-EVVT	Ruschmeyer R90-230RG	012	HB-DBC, D-EEBX
D-EVVV	Extra EA.300/S	006	
D-EVXA	Xtreme Air XA-41 (Permit 7.10)	01	
D-EVYY	Müller/ Van's RV-7	72892	
D-EWAA(2)	Cessna 172R Skyhawk	17280406	N9518Z
D-EWAC(2)	Zlin Z.126 Trenér 2 (Flies as "DM-WAC")	791	D-EJEW , OK-JGG
D-EWAD	Reims/Cessna F150L	F15000919	D-EGBC
D-EWAE	Cessna 172R Skyhawk	17280045	N352ES
D-EWAG	Diamond DA 20-A1 Katana	10163	C-GKAI
D-EWAI	Diamond DA 20-A1 Katana	10162	C-FDVT
D-EWAK	Kirchhof / Denney Kitfox IV-1200	1687/1744	
D-EWAL(2)	Diamond DA 40D Star	D4.064	
D-EWAM	Robin DR.400/180R Remo 180	2225	
D-EWAN	Grob G 115C	82041C	PH-SPX, D-EWAN
D-EWAO	HOAC DV-20 Katana	20085	(D-EWRD)
D-EWAP	Extra EA.300	034	D-EKFD(1)
D-EWAQ	Diamond DA 40D Star	D4.048	
D-EWAR	Piper PA-28-161 Warrior II	28-8616053	N9082X
D-EWAS(2)	Piper PA-18-150 Super Cub	18-8109006	I-LSBC, HB-PFV, SX-AJS, HB-PFV
D-EWAT	Commander Aircraft 114B	14564	(PH-WWW), D-EWAT
D-EWAU	Cessna 172R Skyhawk	17280329	N9502R, (D-ESKW)
D-EWAV	Diamond DA 20-A1 Katana	10164	C-GKAX
D-EWAW	Cessna 172P Skyhawk	17275329	N62709
D-EWAY	HOAC DV-20 Katana	20069	
D-EWAZ	SOCATA TB-200 Tobago XL	1628	
D-EWBA(2)	Zlin Z.526AFS Akrobat (Permit 11.07)	1301	SP-ENA
D-EWBC	Cessna R182 Skylane RG	R18200442	N9199C
D-EWBD	Flight Design CT LS-ELA (Permit 10.4.13) (See D-EWDB)	11-01-07	
D-EWBE	Cessna 172N Skyhawk II	17268608	N733WN
D-EWBG	PZL-104 Wilga 35A	61112	DDR-WBG, DM-WBG(2)
D-EWBI	Zlin Z.142	0270	SP-ATC
D-EWBK	Van's RV-7 (Permit 30.5.12)	1	
D-EWBM	Mooney M.20M Model 257 TLS	27-0225	
D-EWBQ	PZL-104 Wilga 35A	62179	DDR-WBQ, DM-WBQ(2)
D-EWBT	PZL-104 Wilga 35A	62182	DDR-WBT, DM-WBT (2)
D-EWBU	PZL-104 Wilga 35A	62183	DDR-WBU, DM-WBU(2)
D-EWBV	PZL-104 Wilga 35A	62166	DDR-WBV, DM-WBV(2)
D-EWBZ	PZL-104 Wilga 35A	140537	DDR-WBZ, DM-WBZ(2)
D-EWCB	Cessna 182Q Skylane	18265707	N735UZ
D-EWCC	Cessna 182T Skylane	18281819	D-EXAE, N60318
D-EWCD	Cirrus SR20	1875	N655SR
D-EWCN	Orlican L-40 Meta-Sokol	150511	DM-WCN
D-EWCS	SOCATA Rallye 235E-D Gabier	13395	SE-KNY
D-EWCT	Diamond DA 40 Star	40024	
D-EWDB	Flight Design CT LS-ELA (Permit 21.4.11) (Possible error for or re-regd D-EWBD)	11-01-07	
D-EWDC	Diamond DA 20-A1 Katana	10316	N646DA, C-GKAT
D-EWDH	Haag/Pitts M-12	202	
D-EWDI	Diamond DA 40D Star	D4.338	OK-JIP(2)
D-EWDL(2)	Zlin Z.242L	0657	E7-AAX, 9A-DBL, OK-YNC
D-EWDM	Aerotek Pitts S-2A	2046	OO-WDM, OO-XDM, D-EILH(1), YV-38P, YV-TAEF
D-EWEE	SOCATA TB-9 Tampico Club	919	PH-UUU, D-ENDU(2)
D-EWEF	Diamond DA 20-A1 Katana	10295	OE-VPZ, N44UV, N595DA, C-GDMU
D-EWEH	Diamond DA 40D Star	D4.058	OE-DXC(2), G-CCHG, OE-VPW
D-EWEI (2)	Mooney M.20M Model 257 TLS	27-0323	
D-EWEJ	Zlin Z.226T Trenér 6	243	DM-WEJ
D-EWEK	Piper PA-22-108 Colt	22-9654	N220EK, D-EKCE(1), N5830Z
D-EWEL	Ebel/ Zenair CH-601HDS Super Zodiac	6-8418	

Reg	Type	C/n	Previous identities
D-EWER	Aquila AT-01	AT01-188	(D-EAQQ)
D-EWES	SOCATA TB-21 Trinidad TC	963	HB-KDJ, D-EPRD, OE-KHG
D-EWET	Robin DR.400/180R Remo 180	2448	
D-EWEW	SOCATA TB-20 Trinidad GT	2012	(D-EUFD)
D-EWFA	Zlin Z.43	0038	DDR-WFA, DM-WFA(3)
D-EWFB	Zlin Z.43	0039/01	DDR-WFB, DM-WFB(2)
D-EWFC	Zlin Z.43	0040/01	DDR-WFC, DM-WFC(2)
D-EWFD	Zlin Z.43 (Res. .14)	0041/02	DDR-WFD, DM-WFD(2)
D-EWFE	Zlin Z.43	0042/02	DDR-WFE, DM-WFE(2)
D-EWFG	Zlin Z.43	0043/02	DDR-WFG, DM-WFG(2)
D-EWFH	Zlin Z.43	0044/02	DDR-WFH, DM-WFH(2)
D-EWFI	Zlin Z.43	0074	DDR-WFI, DM-WFI (2)
D-EWFK	Yakovlev Yak-50 (Permit 11.9.15)	791502	G-VLAD, D-EIVR, N51980, DDR-WQR, DM-WQR
D-EWFR	Flight Design CT LS-ELA (Permit 9.2.12)	F-11-09-04	
D-EWFU	Beech A23-19 Musketeer Sport III	MB-33	HB-ENP
D-EWGA(2)	Flight Design CT LS-ELA (Permit 4.10)	F-10-01-16	
D-EWGB	Piper PA-18-150 Super Cub	18-7442	D-EMFI (1), N4346P
D-EWGC	Commander 114TC	20032	N115PM
D-EWGL	Cirrus SR22	2536	N813SR
D-EWGO	Goldbrunner G8UL (Permit expired 5.03, status?)	1847	
D-EWGP	Robin ATL L	08	F-GFNH, F-WFNH
D-EWGR	Bücker Bü.131B-1 Jungmann	21	G-CCHY, I-CABI, HB-UTZ, A-12
D-EWGS	Diamond DA 20-A1 Katana	10171	C-FYVM
D-EWGV	Reims/Cessna F182Q Skylane	F18200168	PH-JMS, SX-AJR, F-WZIZ
D-EWHB	Cessna 172P Skyhawk	17275482	N63775
D-EWHC(2)	PZL-104 Wilga 80	CF15810602	(D-EWHZ), SP-AFK
D-EWHD(2)	American AA-5B Tiger	AA5B-0432	I-CLON, N81110
D-EWHF	PZL-104 Wilga 35A (Permit 3.3.11)	86227	DDR-WHF, DM-WHF(2)
D-EWHK	PZL-104 Wilga 35A	86230	DDR-WHK, DM-WHK
D-EWHL	PZL-104 Wilga 35A	86231	DDR-WHL, DM-WHL
D-EWHO	Beech A36AT Bonanza	E-2707	
D-EWHP	PZL-104 Wilga 35A	86264	DDR-WHP, DM-WHP
D-EWHR	PZL-104 Wilga 35A	86266	DDR-WHR, DM-WHR
D-EWHS	Cirrus SR22	0938	N141TS
D-EWHT	PZL-104 Wilga 35A	86268	DDR-WHT, DM-WHT
D-EWHV(3)	PZL-104 Wilga 35A	96319	D-EWHV(1), DDR-WHV, DM-WHV
D-EWHY(2)	PZL-104 Wilga 80	198800865	D-EWHV(2), HA-SEM
D-EWHZ	PZL-104 Wilga 35A	96323	DDR-WHZ, DM-WHZ
D-EWIA	Zlin Z.226T Trenér 6	353	DDR-WIA, DM-WIA
D-EWIC	Diamond DA 20-A1 Katana	10085	OE-CTB, N526SS, C-GKAX
D-EWIH	Rockwell Commander 114B	14153	N4823W
D-EWIK	Cessna 177B Cardinal	17702091	OE-DTS, (N34922)
D-EWIM	Beech F33A Bonanza	CE-1388	N5584N
D-EWIN	Grob G 115C	82053C	N115AH
D-EWIS	Schwarz / Van's RV-6	3921	
D-EWIT	Cessna 172S Skyhawk SP	172S10803	(PH-WIT), D-EWIT, N62036
D-EWJW	Wilkenloh/ Neico Lancair 360	382SB	
D-EWKA	Cessna 152	15281131	N47064
D-EWKE	Keiper/ Denney Kitfox III	1074	
D-EWKH	Buchs/ Neico Lancair 320	1737	
D-EWKI	Zlin Z.143L	0025	
D-EWKK	Cessna 152	15280245	N129SC, (N24380)
D-EWKT	Zlin Z.142	0214	SP-AZH(2)
D-EWKU	Kuche/ Stoddard-Hamilton Glasair II-SRG	2101 AB	
D-EWKX	Zlin Z.526A Akrobat (Now also flies as DM-WKX)	1041	DM-WKX
D-EWKY	Kynast / Van's RV-7A (P. 17.8.16) (C/n previously quoted as 20022436)	70359	(PH-SJP)
D-EWLA	Robin DR.400/180R Remo 180	2447	
D-EWLC	Zlin Z.143L	0009	OE-KGP, OK-AGP
D-EWLD	Zlin Z.143L	0038	OK-JPK, N143FS
D-EWLF	Bölkow BO.208C Junior	610	HB-UPC, D-EJUT(2)
D-EWLG	Maule MXT-7-180 Starcraft	14135C	
D-EWLH	Cessna 172S Skyhawk SP	172S8848	N35207
D-EWLL	Cessna T206H Turbo Stationair	T20608897	(D-EQSE), N6221N
D-EWLN	Wiebold/ Van's RV-9A	91041	
D-EWLU	Diamond DA 40D Star	D4.005	OE-VPW
D-EWMA	Zlin Z.42MU	0012	DDR-WMA, DM-WMA
D-EWMB	Diamond DA 20-A1 Katana	10248	C-GDMQ
D-EWMC(2)	Piper PA-32R-301 Saratoga II HP	3213081	F-GLGT, N9249G
D-EWME	Zlin Z.42MU	0069	DDR-WME, DM-WME
D-EWMF	Zlin Z.42MU	0017	DDR-WMF, DM-WMF
D-EWMH	Cessna 182S Skylane	18280293	N2385N
D-EWMI	Aviat A-1 Husky	1376	
D-EWMK	Zlin Z.42MU (Canx 20.6.12 as WFU, Res. for possible restoration)	0021	DDR-WMK, DM-WMK
D-EWML	Zlin Z.42MU	0022	DDR-WML, DM-WML
D-EWMM	Zlin Z.42MU	0023	DDR-WMM, DM-WMM
D-EWMN	Zlin Z.42MU	0024	DDR-WMN, DM-WMN
D-EWMO	Zlin Z.42MU	0025	DDR-WMO, DM-WMO
D-EWMQ	Zlin Z.42MU	0028	DDR-WMQ, DM-WMQ
D-EWMR	Zlin Z.42MU	0029	DDR-WMR, DM-WMR
D-EWMS	Zlin Z.42MU	0030	DDR-WMS, DM-WMS
D-EWMT	Zlin Z.42MU	0031	DDR-WMT, DM-WMT
D-EWMV	Zlin Z.42MU	0033	DDR-WMV, DM-WMV
D-EWMW	Zlin Z.42MU (Permit .08)	0034	DDR-WMW, DM-WMW
D-EWMZ	Zlin Z.42MU	0037	DDR-WMZ, DM-WMZ
D-EWNA	Zlin Z.42MU	0038	DDR-WNA, DM-WNA
D-EWND	Zlin Z.42MU	0041	DDR-WND, DM-WND
D-EWNE	Zlin Z.42MU	0042	DDR-WNE, DM-WNE
D-EWNG	Zlin Z.526F Trenér Master	1076	N3459, OK-YRC
D-EWNI	Zlin Z.142 (Res. .08, status?)	0246	SP-AZP
D-EWNK(2)	Zlin Z.142 (Res. .06, status?)	0354	SP-ASC(4)
D-EWNQ	Zlin Z.42MU	0051/02	DDR-WNQ, DM-WNQ
D-EWNT	Zlin Z.42MU	0062	DDR-WNT, DM-WNT
D-EWNU	Zlin Z.42M	0063	DDR-WNU, DM-WNU
D-EWOB	Zlin Z.42M	0084	DDR-WOB, DM-WOB
D-EWOC	Zlin Z.42M	0085	DDR-WOC, DM-WOC
D-EWOE	Zlin Z.42M	0087	DDR-WOE, DM-WOE
D-EWOF	Zlin Z.42M	0111	DDR-WOF, DM-WOF
D-EWOG	Zlin Z.42M	0112/04	DDR-WOG, DM-WOG
D-EWOH	Zlin Z.42M	0113	DDR-WOH, DM-WOH
D-EWOL	Zlin Z.42M	0130/05	DDR-WOL, DM-WOL
D-EWOM	Zlin Z.42M	0131	DDR-WOM, DM-WOM
D-EWON	Zlin Z.42M	0132	DDR-WON, DM-WON
D-EWOO	Aquila AT-01	AT01-208	
D-EWOP	Zlin Z.42M	0133/05	DDR-WOP, DM-WOP
D-EWOQ	Zlin Z.42M	0157	DDR-WOQ, DM-WOQ
D-EWOR(2)	Röhl / Brändli BX-2 Cherry (Permit)	313/38	
D-EWOW	Cirrus SR22	1526	N452CD
D-EWPB	Zlin Z.50LS	0064	OK-WRJ
D-EWPC	Piper PA-28-140 Cherokee C (Res. .13)	28-26721	(D-ECYB(2)), SE-FHN
D-EWPE	Beech F33A Bonanza	CE-1391	N5586M
D-EWPG	Robin R.3000/160	166	
D-EWPH	Held/ Brditschka HB-207VRG Alfa	207020	
D-EWPL	SOCATA TB-21 Trinidad TC	690	SP-KHT, SP-KPM, D-ESHG(1), HB-KBG
D-EWPM	Beech F33A Bonanza	CE-1774	N1551N
D-EWPR	Cessna 172N Skyhawk	17272032	N6539E
D-EWPS	Reims/Cessna F172M	F17201429	OE-DTV
D-EWPW	Cirrus SR22	0509	N1552C
D-EWQC	Zlin Z.526AFS Akrobat Special	1207	DDR-WQC, DM-WQC
D-EWQH	Zlin Z.526AFS Akrobat Special	1212	DDR-WQH, DM-WQH
D-EWQL	Zlin Z.526AFS Akrobat Special	1217	DDR-WQL, DM-WQL
D-EWRA(2)	Christen Pitts S-2B	5058	N260Z
D-EWRC	PZL-104 Wilga 35A	96326	DDR-WRC, DM-WRC
D-EWRD(2)	Klemm Kl.35D (Res. 31.3.15)	1850	SE-BPN, Fv5070
D-EWRE	PZL-104 Wilga 35A	96328	DDR-WRE, DM-WRE
D-EWRG	Dornier Do.27B-1	276	HB-HAG, D-EMAE(1), 56+09, BD+928, AC+928, AS+928
D-EWRJ	PZL-104 Wilga 35A	107338	DDR-WRJ, DM-WRJ
D-EWRL	PZL-104 Wilga 35A	118391	DDR-WRL, DM-WRL
D-EWRO	PZL-104 Wilga 35A	118394	DDR-WRO, DM-WRO
D-EWRR	Aerotechnik P.220S (For sale in Italy, 2016)	unkn	
D-EWRS	Diamond DA 20A-1 Katana	10328	N628DA, C-GKAT
D-EWRU	PZL-104 Wilga 35A	118399	DDR-WRU, DM-WRU
D-EWRV	PZL-104 Wilga 35A (Dbr 26.7.11)	118400	DDR-WRV, DM-WRV
D-EWRY	PZL-104 Wilga 35A	118409	DDR-WRY, DM-WRY
D-EWRZ	PZL-104 Wilga 35A	118410	DDR-WRZ, DM-WRZ
D-EWSH	Huber/ Colomban MC-100 Ban-bi	002	
D-EWSK	Spang/ Brändli BX-2 Cherry	159	
D-EWSM	HOAC DV-20 Katana	20043	
D-EWSN	Piper PA-32RT-300T Turbo Lance II (Res. 4.5.15)	32R-7987102	I-KORR, D-EIRR(1), N2209P
D-EWSR	Robin DR.400/180 Régent	2196	
D-EWSS	Robin DR.400/180 Régent	2079	
D-EWST	Cessna TR182 Turbo Skylane RG	R18201091	N756KE
D-EWTE	Cessna 182Q Skylane	18267125	N97536
D-EWTF	Aquila AT-01	AT01-225	
D-EWTG	Cirrus SR20	1518	N52709
D-EWTM	Onken/ Van's RV-6	1845	
D-EWTR	Zlin Z.326A Akrobat	555	DM-WKA
D-EWTT(2)	Cessna T182T Turbo Skylane	T18208877	N6306H
D-EWTW	Extra EA.300/SC	SC053	
D-EWUB	Cirrus SR20	1177	N100UH
D-EWUF	Cessna 172S Skyhawk SP	172S10080	N2473L
D-EWUG	Robin DR.400/180 Régent	1208	G-RTUG, D-ELHI (2)
D-EWUP	Cessna T206H Turbo Stationair	T20608576	S5-DHB, N24257
D-EWUT	CASA C-1.131E Jungmann (C/n officially quoted as "1136B")	1130	
D-EWUW	Cessna 140	8880	N89831, NC89831
D-EWUZ	Focke-Wulf FW.44J Stieglitz (Res. 17.8.15)	2896	SZ-5, D-EX..
D-EWVZ	SOCATA TB-20 Trinidad	1711	
D-EWWA	Diamond DA 20-A1 Katana	10120	N547SS, C-GDMB
D-EWWB	Boeing Stearman A75-N1 (PT-13D)	75-5659	(D-EQHB), SE-AMT, G-BAVN, 4X-AMT, 42-17496
D-EWWC	Cirrus SR20	1239	N942MA
D-EWWD	Cirrus SR22	1585	N139WD
D-EWWF	HOAC DV-20 Katana	20057	
D-EWWG	Diamond DA 40 Star	40027	
D-EWWH	Hohmann/ Neico Lancair 320	001	
D-EWWK	Cessna T182T Turbo Skylane	T18208940	N5194H
D-EWWL	Piper PA-46-350P Malibu Mirage	4636135	N37AT
D-EWWP	Cirrus SR22	2600	N261SR
D-EWWU	Cirrus SR22	2106	N961SR
D-EWWW(2)	Cessna 182Q Skylane	18266579	PH-MMA, (PH-GAC), (PH-MAD), (PH-ZAP), N95613, N684WB, N95613
D-EWXA	Zlin Z.526ASM Akrobat	1026	OK-WXA
D-EWYD	Cirrus SR22 (Res. still current on US register 4.16)	0600	N6051C
D-EWYL	SOCATA TB-20 Trinidad	1031	OO-VIA, F-GHZP
D-EWYP	Diamond DA 20-A1 Katana	10206	N187DA, C-FDVT
D-EWYS	Piper PA-28R-200 Cherokee Arrow II	28R-7635100	SP-KSD, F-BXSD, (F-OHCB), F-BXSD, N9642N
D-EWZA	Cessna L-19A Bird Dog (305A)	22245	EC-DQX, U.12-5, L.12-5, 51-11931
D-EXAA(2)	Cessna 182T Skylane	18281766	N2010H
D-EXAB(3)	Cessna 205	205-0294	OY-DPF, HB-CMW, N8294Z
D-EXAC(2)	Extra EA.400	18	
D-EXAD(2)	Flight Design CT LSi-LSA (Permit 19.3.14)	F-12-08-04	(D-EOAE(3))
D-EXAE	Extra EA.300/L	1213	
D-EXAG	Cessna T182T Turbo Skylane	T18208557	N60322
D-EXAI	Piper PA-18 Super Cub 95	18-3184	OE-ADM, D-EDVO, R-86, (OL-L110), 53-4784
D-EXAL	Cessna T206H Turbo Stationair (Permit 7.10)	T20608957	N5285F
D-EXAM	Mooney M.20R Ovation	29-0042	
D-EXAN	Cessna T210L Turbo Centurion	21060565	N849MD, (D-E. . .), N849MD, N94256
D-EXAO	Cessna 182T Skylane	18281932	N2183W
D-EXAS	Piper PA-38-112 Tomahawk	38-80A0071	HB-PFI, N9698N
D-EXAT	Piper PA-46-350P Malibu Mirage	4636368	N5370S, N3114P
D-EXAV	Cessna 172S Skyhawk SP	172S10953	N5153E
D-EXBA	Zlin Z.526F Trenér Master	1124	N29RW, N840C
D-EXBB	Reims/Cessna FR182 Skylane RG	FR18200026	OE-KUN, OE-BUN, (OE-DNI)
D-EXBC	Cessna 182S Skylane	18280113	HB-CIZ, N446ES

Registration	Type	c/n	Previous identities
D-EXBE	Extra EA.300/SC	SC023	
D-EXBH	Extra EA.300	057	G-EIII, G-HIII, D-ETYD
D-EXBL	Votec 221	1	
	(Permit 13.4.12)		
D-EXBR	Extra EA.300/LC	LC045	
D-EXBS	Cessna 172S Skyhawk SP	172S9416	(D-ELDT), N53637
D-EXBX	Extra EA.300/LC	LC052	
D-EXCA	Commander Aircraft 114B	14557	
D-EXCB(2)	Becker / Glasair II RG	2410	
D-EXCD	Cirrus SR22	2755	N646SR
D-EXCG	SOCATA TB-20 Trinidad	1898	G-OBGC, F-OIGT
D-EXCK	Cessna TP206D Super Skylane	P206-0522	SX-ACK, D-EETG, N8722Z
	(Res. .09, still current in Greece 2016)		
D-EXCL	Cessna 182P Skylane	18262271	OY-RYJ
D-EXCM	Cirrus SR22	2521	N922CE
D-EXDA	Diamond DA 20-A1 Katana	10275	C-GKAI
D-EXDB	Dörnemann/ Aero Designs Pulsar XP	410	
D-EXDD	Grob G 115A	8009	VH-YYX, D-EMFT, (D-EIEP)
D-EXDS	Diamond DA 40 Star	40211	N711DS, C-GDMQ
D-EXDW	Aerostyle Breezer B600L	010LSA	
	(Permit .09)		
D-EXEA	Extra EA.300/L	082	G-EXEA
	(Permit 29.6.12)		
D-EXEC	Diamond DA 40 Star	40.331	PH-CEC, N272DS
D-EXED	Piper PA-46-350P Malibu Mirage	4636282	OY-FIA
	(Res .16 as D-ESAO)		
D-EXEG	Piper PA-28-181 Archer II	28-7990445	PH-EAH, N29517
D-EXEK(2)	Kolb / Rans S-10EK Samota	1009216	(D-EREK(3))
D-EXEW	Extra EA.300/L	05	(D-ETYM(1))
D-EXEX	Bölkow BO.209 Monsun 160FV	103	HB-UEA, D-EBOF(2)
D-EXFB	Cirrus SR22T	0905	N227CL
D-EXFH	Reims/Cessna F172N	F17201567	D-EBJH(2)
	(Res .16)		
D-EXFK	B&F Funk FK-12 S2-X Comet	2002533	
	(Res. 1.6.15)		
D-EXFS	Cessna 172R Skyhawk	17281353	N12925
D-EXFT	Extra EA.200	025	
D-EXFX	Diamond DA 40 Star	40054	
D-EXGB	Extra EA.300/LC	LC047	
D-EXGF	Extra EA.300/L	1299	
D-EXGH	Extra EA.300/L	143	
D-EXGM	Gmachel/ Impulse 130NG	NG2	
D-EXGO	Extra EA.300/LT	LT018	G-ETXN, D-EAXN
	(Res .16)		
D-EXGR	Grob G 115C2	82045	
D-EXGS	Schiener/ Klemm Kl.25D Replica	01	
	(Res. .09, status?)		
D-EXGV	Robin HR.100/250TR Président	547	F-BXGV
D-EXGW	Welz/ Stoddard-Hamilton Glasair III	3256	
D-EXHA	Grob G 115D	82078	LN-TFW(2), (LN-RFK), (OY-SKN), (OY-SKP)
D-EXHB	Cessna 182P Skylane	18262472	N8505Z, N1279M, D-EENA, N52233
D-EXHG	Extra EA.300/L	03	
D-EXHH	Extra EA.300/SC	SC017	
D-EXHM	Cessna T182T Turbo Skylane	T18208806	N1274B
D-EXHP	Cirrus SR22	1553	N212CB
D-EXHQ	Extra EA.300/L	1317	
	(CofA for export to Russia 11.2.11)		
D-EXHT	Extra EA.300/SC	SC055	
D-EXHV	Piper PA-28-181 Archer III	2843554	G-VSPN, OY-PHC, N9521N
	(W/o 4.8.08)		
D-EXIA	Robin DR.500/200i Président	0024	
D-EXIB(2)	Reims/Cessna F182Q Skylane	F18200161	N232LY, OO-DEL, D-ENCK(2)
D-EXIE	Extra EA.300/L	121	G-IXTI, D-EXIE
D-EXII (2)	Xtreme Air XA-42	114	
D-EXIK	Extra EA.400	13	
D-EXIL	SOCATA TB-20 Trinidad	1298	
D-EXIQ	Reims/Cessna F152	F15201868	LX-AIQ
D-EXIS	Aerospool WT-9 Dynamic LSA	DY-433/2012	
	(Permit 22.5.12)		
D-EXIT	SOCATA TB-20 Trinidad	1299	
D-EXJD	Drummer Super Acro Sport	2002108	
	(Permit 17.10.12)		
D-EXJL	Piper PA-18-95 Super Cub	18-2083	OO-ALZ, ALAT, 52-2483
D-EXJM	SOCATA TB-20 Trinidad	1297	
D-EXJN	Flight Design CT LS-LSA	F-14-01-03	
	(Permit 24.11.15)		
D-EXJR	Fläming Air FA-02 Smaragd VLA	02-04	
D-EXKA	Piper PA-28-161 Cherokee Warrior II	28-7816601	N31967
D-EXKB	Aviat A-1 Husky	1244	
D-EXKG	Extra EA.400	26	
D-EXKH	Extra EA.300	039	JY-RND, D-ETXC
D-EXKJ	Jautz/ Dallach D4/E Fascination	EB019	
D-EXKK	Diamond DA 40D Star	D4.215	
D-EXKM	Cessna T206H Turbo Stationair	T20608822	N6189D
D-EXKP	Cirrus SR22	0879	N388CD
D-EXKS	Extra EA.300/L	1202	ES- . . ., N202FU
D-EXKT	Extra EA.300/L	1289	OM-BAT
D-EXKV	Extra EA.300/L	1204	D-EXTT
D-EXKW	Extra EA.300/LC	LC036	
D-EXLB(2)	Tecnam P.2002-JR Sierra	200	
D-EXLH	Extra EA.400	06	
D-EXLS(2)	Extra EA.300/SC	SC035	
	(Permit 17.4.13)		
D-EXLT	Extra EA.300/LT	LT001	
D-EXMA(2)	Extra EA.230	A001	
	(Permit 12.6.14)		
D-EXMB	Mooney M.20K Model 231	25-0813	N5744N
D-EXMD	Extra EA.300/SCE	SC002E	
D-EXME	Maule MX-7-180 Star Rocket	11037C	N5671N
D-EXMH	Heeren/ Van's RV-6	0001	
	(Permit 4.10)		
D-EXMI	Robin DR.400/180R Remo 180	2078	
D-EXMK	Extra EA.300/L	1310	
	(Permit 6.10)		
D-EXML	Extra EA.300/S	008	N8TH, F-GJRG, D-ETXF, D-EXML
D-EXMM	de Havilland DH.82A Tiger Moth	82814	G-ERTY, D-EFYZ(1), LX-JON, G-ANDC, R4897
D-EXMR	Extra EA.300/S	002	N300XX, D-ETEW(1)
D-EXMS(2)	Robin DR.400/140B Dauphin 4	2635	F-GXMS
D-EXMT(2)	Extra EA.300/SC	SC022	
D-EXNA	Extra EA.300/SCE	SC040E	
	(Permit 3.2.14)		
D-EXNI	Extra EA.300/S	1034	
D-EXNM	Beagle B.121 Pup 100	114	G-AXNM
D-EXON	Diamond DA 40D Star	D4.254	OE-VPT
D-EXOP	Cessna 140	12502	N418R, C-FJTN, CF-JTN, N2173N, NC2173N
D-EXOT	Piper PA-46-310P Malibu	46-8508010	N4378T, (N55BT), N4378T
D-EXPB	Christen A-1 Husky	1141	D-ENMA(2)
	(Res. 1.12.15)		
D-EXPC	Champion 8KCAB Super Decathlon	956-2004	
D-EXPD	Piper PA-46-350P Malibu Mirage	4636100	OY-JAM, D-EXPD, (D-ELVY(4))
D-EXPH	Aerotek Pitts S-2A	2015	N80007, (D-EPIT), N80007
D-EXPK	Kroker/ Van's RV-6A	1301	
D-EXPL	Mooney M.20R Ovation	29-0213	N2215V
D-EXPM(2)	Extra EA.300/L	1324	
D-EXPO	Piper PA-28-181 Archer III	2843083	N92876
D-EXPV	Vettel/ Van's RV-7	2002272	
	(Permit 17.12.12)		
D-EXPW	Extra EA.300/SCE	SC001E	
	(Permit 2.08)		
D-EXRA	Extra EA.300/L	1294	
D-EXRE	Piper PA-46-350P Malibu Mirage	4636211	XB-JYN, N31BG, N4134N
	(Jetprop DLX conversion #182)		
D-EXRH	Piper PA-28R-180 Cherokee Arrow	28R-30225	OH-PMI, LN-UXN
D-EXRI	Extra EA.300/SHP	1038E	D-EXMT, D-EXWB
D-EXRP	Extra EA.300/L	154	OK-EXT, N758KS, D-EXRP
D-EXRU	Beech C24R Sierra	MC-743	N3711B
D-EXRV	Hühn/ Van's RV-4	2849	
D-EXSH	Aerostyle Breezer B600	023LSA	
	(Permit 25.7.14)		
D-EXSL	Extra EA.300/L	08	
D-EXSR	Aquila AT-01	AT01-128	(D-EWPX)
D-EXSY	Robin R.3000/120	119	F-GEKJ
	(Permit 5.10)		
D-EXTA	Extra EA.500	1006	
D-EXTC	Fürle/ Denney Kitfox IV-1200	003	
	(Permit)		
D-EXTD	Extra EA.300/SC	SC032	
	(Permit 17.4.13)		
D-EXTH	Zlin Z.142	0292	SP-ATH
	(Res. .13)		
D-EXTL	Lukasczyk /Van's RV-4	495	
D-EXTM	Müller/ Van's RV-8	04-037	
	(Res. .04, status?)		
D-EXTO	Piper PA-25-235 Pawnee	25-3959	OH-PIG, N7766Z
	(Res. .11)		
D-EXTP	Extra EA.300/L	1285	EC-LAT, EC-KXH
D-EXTR(2)	Cirrus SR22	3032	4X-CWG, N743PG
D-EXTS	Cirrus SR22T	0305	N188DE
D-EXTT	*Test Registration for Extra EA.200/300 production*		
D-EXTW	Extra EA.300/SC	SC051	
D-EXTX/Y/Z	*Test Registrations for Extra EA.400 production*		
D-EXTX	Extra EA.300/SC	SC030	
	(Permit 22.12.11)		
D-EXUB	Fieseler Fi.156C-7 Storch	2466	
	(F/F 14.6.13 at Bonn after rebuild, destined for Spain)		
D-EXUG	Extra EA.300/L	152	
	(Damaged, Campo Maior, Portugal 6.8.13)		
D-EXUP	III Sky Arrow 650TCNS	CNS021	
D-EXUS(2)	Extra EA.200	022	N516HT
	(Res. .11)		
D-EXUW	Grumman-American AA-5B Tiger	AA5B-1135	OO-RTE, (OO-HRV)
	(P 12.9.16)		
D-EXVR	Aviat Pitts S-2B	5272	
D-EXWB	Berner/ Van's RV-9A	445	
D-EXWK	Extra EA.330/LC	LC002	
D-EXWL	Focke-Wulf FW.44J Stieglitz	2776	D-EXEK, OH-XEK, FinAF:SZ-14, RNorAF:3, D-EXWL
D-EXWM	Aviat A-1 Husky	1350	
D-EXWO	Focke-Wulf FW.44J Stieglitz	2778	SE-BSZ, FinAF:SZ-18, RNorAF:5, D-EXWO
	(Swedish EAA c/n 2778-1439)		
D-EXWP	American Champion 8KCAB Super Decathlon	930-2003	
D-EXWS	Aerotek Pitts S-2A	2269	OE-AHH, D-ELUP(2), N255CA
D-EXXA	Piper PA-28R-201 Arrow	2837033	N9185Z
D-EXXB	Piper PA-28R-201 Arrow	2837036	N91871
D-EXXC	Piper PA-28R-201 Arrow	2837037	N91886
D-EXXD	Piper PA-28R-201 Arrow	2837054	N9235F
D-EXXE	SOCATA TB-200 Tobago XL	1447	
D-EXXG	Aquila AT-01	AT01-236	
D-EXXI	SOCATA TB-20 Trinidad	1481	
D-EXXL	Richter/Dallach D4/E-BK/DZ Fascination XXL	1997	
D-EXXM	Mooney M.20R Ovation	29-0144	F-GMMS
D-EXXP	Müller/ Aero Designs Pulsar XP	1887	
D-EXXX	Mudry CAP.10B	259	
D-EXYY	Cirrus SR22	2969	N552CT
D-EXYC	Diamond DA 20-C1 Katana	C0021	N207ND
D-EXYY	HOAC DV-20 Katana	20037	
D-EXYX	Alpavia Jodel D.117A Grand Tourisme	1038	D-ENTI (1)
D-EXYZ	Christen A-1 Husky	1059	HB-KIR, D-ECHX(2), N2974C
D-EXZZ	Hamacher/ Van's RV-8	001	
D-EYAA	Robin DR.400/180R Remorqueur	1386	HB-EYA
D-EYAB	American Champion 8KCAB Super Decathlon	1107-2011	
	(Permit 12.5.11)		
D-EYAE	Diamond DA 20-A1 Katana	10082	N522SS, C-FDVK
D-EYAK	Nanchang CJ-5	13-320-07	PLAAFoC
	(Carries serial "1")		
D-EYAL	Cessna T182T Turbo Skylane	T18208095	N35520
D-EYAP(5)	Piper PA-46-350P Malibu Mirage	4636003	OE-KAP, (D-ESSN(2)), (D-ERAJ), OE-KAP, HB-PNH, N92575
D-EYAR	Cessna 172P Skyhawk	17274351	N999SW, N51804
D-EYAS	Siebenritt/ Jodel DR.1050M	AB 834-M	
D-EYAV	Cessna 172S Skyhawk SP	172S10999	N5272N
	(Res. .09, still current on US register 4.16)		

Registration	Type	C/n	Previous identities
D-EYAX	Yakovlev Yak-18T	22202034143	HA-HUF, RA-44536, LY-AMI, CCCP-44517
D-EYBH	Yakovlev Yak-18T	22202044595	LY-ALW, LY-XLW, LY-30
D-EYBK	Cirrus SR22	2955	N164CT
D-EYBL	Robin DR.400/140B Dauphin 4	2679	
D-EYCC	Boeing Stearman A75N1 (Res. .15)	75-2152	N53750, 41-8593
D-EYCD	Cirrus SR22	3615	N232CK
D-EYCG	Yakovlev Yak-50	781310	LY-GUY, DOSAAF
D-EYCM	Cessna 152	15280506	N25029
D-EYDS	Schwengels/ Van's RV-7A/DS	2002524	
D-EYDT	Piper PA-38-112 Tomahawk	38-82A0108	N9158A
D-EYEB	SIAI-Marchetti SM.1019A	079	EI-. . ./MM57 . . .
D-EYES	Diamond DA 20-A1 Katana	10137	C-GKAH
D-EYEW	Maule MX7-180 Star Rocket	11020C	S5-DDO, D-ESHH(1), PH-TZK, (PH-ZCT), N56633
D-EYFH	Reims/Cessna F172P	F17202245	D-EITE(2)
D-EYFI	Steen Skybolt RG3	2002322	
D-EYFP	Fuglsang-Petersen/ Rutan Cozy Mk.3 (Res. 17.12.15)	99	
D-EYGA	Gabbe/ Europa Avn Europa	1784	
D-EYGL	Zlin Z.126 Trenér 2	796	OK-IGL
D-EYGS	Cessna 172S Skyhawk SP	172S10653	N1285X
D-EYHB	Breit/ Brditschka HB-207 Alfa	207-025	
D-EYHL	Ruschmeyer R90-230RG	016	G-TTHL, G-TODE, D-EEAX
D-EYHP	Aquila AT-01	AT01-186	
D-EYHS	Reims/Cessna FR172K Hawk XP	FR17200661	OE-DBU(2), N988PK, (D-EBKP(2)), HB-CNU
D-EYHW	Stephens Akro Laser 260	2002240	
D-EYIA	Robin DR.400/200R Remo 200	2482	N24XX, F-WQOZ
D-EYKB	Reims/Cessna F152	F15201970	HB-CFG
D-EYLA	Cessna 182T Skylane	18281920	N21703
D-EYLE	PZL-104 Wilga 35A	20890888	SP-FWI
D-EYMA	Adenau/ Van's RV-7A	72847	
D-EYMB	Piper PA-28-161 Cadet (Res. .11)	2841081	D-EHLE(4), N91663
D-EYMC	Yakovlev Yak-18T	22202044533	ES-NYC, UR-BEM, DOSAAF
D EYMF	Classic Aircraft Waco YMF-5C	F5C-8-125	N825WC
D-EYMH	Grob G 115B	8109	VH-AYE(3), D-ELCF(2)
D-EYMI	Piper PA-18-150 Super Cub (Res. .14)	18-4649	G-BVMI, D-EIAC, (PH-WDP), D-EIAC, D-EKAF, N10F
	(C/n officially listed as 18-8482 from rebuild ex OH-PIN, N4262Z)		
D-EYML	Mooney M.20J Model 205	24-3249	SE-KUM
D-EYMM	SOCATA Rallye 100S-D Sport	2360	I-RALS
D-EYMW	Cessna T182T Turbo Skylane	T18208692	N1176K, (D-EXAP(3)), N1176K
D-EYMY	Cessna 182T Skylane	18282160	N51879
D-EYNA	Hohage/ Rans S-10PH Sakota	0505199	
D-EYOU	Pilatus P.3-05 (Permit 26.10.12)	490-39	HB-RCS, A-852
D-EYPA	Piper PA-28-181 Archer III	2843035	N9268B
D-EYPC	Cessna R182 Skylane RG	R18201822	N4407F, (C-GPGH), (N5138T)
D-EYPE	Reims/Cessna F152	F15201441	G-BFHT
D-EYPS	Extra EA.300/L	1190	
D-EYRM	Maule M-6-235 Super Rocket	7472C	N5665K
D-EYSA	SOCATA TB-20 Trinidad	654	D-ESTU, F-GFQR, (N20GN)
D-EYSY	Cessna 172R Skyhawk	17281214	N2183W
D-EYTB	Piper PA-28-181 Archer III	2843680	G-CGMY, N6104C, N9529N
D-EYTG	Yakovlev Yak-18A ("307") (Code "01")		G-BVVX, SovAF 307
D-EYTT	Zlin Z.226 Trenér 6	171-15	HB-TRT, D-EHSE(1), OK-MFZ
D-EYTZ	SOCATA MS.880B Rallye Club	1538	CS-AIT
D-EYUB	Reims/Cessna F172M	F17201420	D-EOHA
D-EYUG	Zlin Z.526M Trenér Master (Res. 30.6.15)	1031	OO-YUG, YU-DJX, JRV41106
D-EYWW	Cessna 210L Centurion	21060907	F-GHMA, N5319V
D-EYXA	Xtreme Air XA-41 (Permit 11.10) (Formerly Res. as c/n 107)	02	
D-EYXY	Robin DR.400/180R Remorqueur	1227	HB-EXY
D-EYYE(2)	Van's RV-9 (P. 8.8.16)	2002495	
D-EYYY	Piper PA-28RT-201 Arrow IV	28R-8018104	N8262V
D-EYYZ	Flight Design CT LS-ELA (Permit 10.4.13)	F-12-04-09	
D-EZAA(3)	CSA PS28 Cruiser	C0455	
D-EZAB(2)	Cessna T182T Turbo Skylane	T18208917	N917JA
D-EZAC	Diamond DA 20-A1 Katana	10089	D-EDAS(3), N189MF, C-FDVT
D-EZAG	Piper PA-28RT-201T Turbo Arrow IV	28R-8131058	N8320J
D-EZAI	HOAC DV-20 Katana	20121	
D-EZAK(2)	Reinsdorf 235 (Built from Xtreme Air Sbach 342S kit c/n 008) (P. 15.9.11)	001	
D-EZAM	Cessna T182T Turbo Skylane	T18208917	N5288V
D-EZAP	Cessna 152	15283078	N46598
D-EZAQ	SIAI-Marchetti S.205-20/R (Res. 28.5.15)	031/06-031	I-ICAQ
D-EZAR	Aviat A-1 Husky	1235	
D-EZAS(2)	Piper PA-28-181 Archer III	2843253	N4127N
D-EZAT	Aero AT-3-R100	003	SP-TPE
D-EZAW	Cirrus SR20	1669	N994SR
D-EZAY	Diamond DA 40D Star	D4.235	OE-UHK
D-EZBA	Reims/Cessna F152	F15201884	N3953A
D-EZBB	Aquila AT-01	AT01-160	F-HBUS
D-EZBI	Zlin Z.526F Trenér Master	1255	G-ZLYN, OK-CMC, YR-ZAB
D-EZBK	Mooney M.20K Model 252 TSE	25-1150	CS-TBB, N252AB, G-BREO, N252BX
D-EZBO	Beech 35-C33 Debonair	CD-876	I-ALBA, HB-EKO
D-EZCC	Cessna 150F	15062147	LN-IKD(2), (SE-ESP), N8847S
D-EZCJ	Zlin Z.526F Trenér Master	1174	N526SB
D-EZCS	Aquila AT-01	AT01-249	
D-EZDC	Diamond DA 40 Star	40019	
D-EZDG	Cirrus SR20	1426	OE-KSB, N514CD
D-EZDS	Zlin Z.526 Trenér Master (Originally Z.326, mod to Z.526 in 2000)	886	F-GNQN, F-BMQN
D-EZEB	Piper PA-28-181 Archer III	2843007	N9255N
D-EZEC	Diamond DA 40 Star	40.348	OE-KKS
D-EZEI (2)	Piper PA-28-181 Archer III	2843091	N92885, (N971PA)
D-EZEL	Robin DR.400/180R Remo 180	2345	

Registration	Type	C/n	Previous identities
D-EZEN	Piper PA-28-151 Cherokee Warrior	28-7615093	OO-DFM, N8336C
D-EZEW	Piper PA-28-181 Archer III (Permit 27.12.13)	2890228	N9251R
D-EZEZ	Mooney M.20J Model 201	24-0824	HB-DFS
D-EZFB	Cirrus SR20	1090	PH-MOM, N196CD
D-EZFD(2)	Flight Design C4 (Permit 2.4.15)	B-15-01-01	
D-EZFF	Robin DR.400/180R Remo 180	2113	
D-EZFS	HOAC DV-20 Katana	20045	N45DV, C-FSIU
D-EZFW	Hanusa/ Jurca MJ.8/FW.190A Replica (Permit 9.12.14)	1656	
D-EZGS	Diamond DV-20 Katana	20217	
D-EZHB	Robin DR.400/180 Régent	1450	F-GCID
D-EZHK	Aerostyle Breezer B600 (Permit 3.6.13)	024LSA	
D-EZHL	Robin DR.400/180RRemorqueur	1303	OE-KHL, D-EHWN(1)
D-EZIA	Robin DR.500/200i Président	0016	
D-EZIC	Diamond DA 20-A1 Katana	10054	N228P, C-GKAN
D-EZID	Cessna T182T Turbo Skylane	T18208686	(D-EZPD), N14685
D-EZIG	Extra EA.300/LC	LC030	
D-EZII	Erco 415D Ercoupe	1769	N99146, NC99146
D-EZIL	Zlin Z.142 (Res. .11)	0353	SP-ASB
D-EZIM	Cirrus SR20	1455	N357F
D-EZIN	Zlin Z.142 (Res. .11)	0081	(D-EIBS(2)), SP-ADM
D-EZIP	Piper PA-28-181 Archer III	2843013	N92580, D-ESAN(1)
D-EZIR	Piper PA-32R-301 Saratoga SP (Res. 24.3.15)	32R-8013120	F-GCPJ, N8252G, N9578N
D-EZIW	Wesemann Z1S Stummelflitzer (P 30.11.12. C/n now quoted as MGH049)	2002186	
D-EZJM	Focke-Wulf FW.44J Stieglitz (Res. .11; ntu by 5.16)	2782	F-AZMJ(2), OH-SZF, SZ-15, RNoAF 15, D-EXWS
D-EZJS	Aquila AT-01	AT01-235	
D-EZKA	Zlin Z.42M (Res. .13)	0093	SP-ADR
D-EZKB	Remos GX (Permit 8.10)	373	
D-EZKI	Van's RV-7WJ	2002536	
D-EZKK	Mooney M.20K Model 231	25-0128	N231KK
D-EZKM	SIAI-Marchetti SF.260C	563/41-001	I-LELB
D-EZKP	Diamond DV-20 Katana (Damaged 15.5.13 Kempten)	20206	OE-VPX
D-EZLI	Zlin Z.50LA (Permit 24.5.11)	0008	SP-AUA, OK-090
D-EZLL	Cessna 172S Skyhawk SP	172S9147	N52247
D-EZLN	Zlin Z.143L	0004	OK-ZOF
D-EZLS	HOAC DV-20 Katana	20092	N192DV
D-EZLX	Zlin Z.143LSi	0059	OK-ZLI
D-EZMA	Aviat A-1 Husky	1245	HB-KDZ, D-EXKL
D-EZMB	Cirrus SR22	3434	N859KD
D-EZMC	Beech C24R Sierra	MC-477	N24013
D-EZMH	Heeren/ Denney Kitfox Vixen 1200	JCV 021	
D-EZMM(2)	Cessna 182H	18256597	I-SKIM, N8497S
D-EZMR	Piper PA-28-180 Cherokee G	28-7305309	OE-DNK, N11C
D-EZMS	Fuji FA-200-160 Aero Subaru	86	HB-ESR
D-EZMT	Extra EA.200	1045	
D-EZMW	Mooney M.20K Model 231	25-0009	N225TB, D-EBML(3), N231HS
D-EZNL	Zlin Z.142 (Res. .12)	0323	SP-ATW
D-EZOE	Cessna R182 Skylane RG	R18200540	N1734R, (D-EASG(2)), N1734R
D-EZOF	Piper PA-28-181 Archer II	28-7990236	N2121K
D-EZOO	Extra EA.300/SC	SC025	
D-EZOP	Cessna 182K Skylane (Res. .12)	18257933	N2733Q
D-EZOR	Morane-Saulnier MS.317 (Permit 8.09)	6533/279	OO-MOR, N315MS, F-BGIL, Fr.AF
D-EZOT	Aquila AT-01	AT01-228	
D-EZOZ	Extra EA.300/L	029	(D-ETZJ)
D-EZPA	Piper PA-46-350P Malibu Mirage	4622184	N9251K
D-EZPM	Grob G 115D	82014	OY-SKO, LN-TFZ, D-EXEC(1)
D-EZPS	Cessna 172S Skyhawk SP	172S10768	N6306M
D-EZRA	Jülich/ Rans S-10 Supra	2002403	
D-EZRB	Rans S-10 Supra (Permit 25.7.13)	2002406	
D-EZRL	Laudenbach/ Zenair CH-601 Zodiac (Res. 6.99)	6-3666	
D-EZRP	Diamond DA 40 Star	40057	PH-USK
D-EZRS	Robin DR.400/180 Régent	2309	
D-EZRV	Albrecht/ Van's RV-7 (Permit 18.12.14)	SR-1	
D-EZSB	Reims/Cessna F172N	F17201607	N289YY, D-EOHI
D-EZTE	Cessna 172S Skyhawk SP	172S8433	N153ME
D-EZTJ	Beagle A.61 Terrier 2 (Permit 23.10.15)	B-604	F-AZTJ, G-ASAK, WE591
D-EZTL	Cirrus SR22	0365	N789RK, C-FBKR
D-EZTM	Robin DR.400/140B Major	2647	
D-EZTT	Zlin Z.526AFS Akrobat	1211	DDR-WQG, DM-WQG
D-EZUM(2)	Aquila AT-01 (Model A210)	AT01-107	
D-EZUP	HOAC DV-20 Katana	20008	
D-EZWA	Cessna 172S Skyhawk SP	172S9646	N2165T
D-EZWB	Cessna 172S Skyhawk SP	172S9529	N2162Y
D-EZWE	Zacheri/ Giles GB202 (Permit 24.4.12)	2002410	
D-EZWG	Commander Aircraft 114B	14620	N6035J
D-EZWO	Siek/ Funk FK-12 Comet	0037	
D-EZWW	Cirrus SR22	2346	N939SE
D-EZWZ	Morane-Saulnier MS.885 Super Rallye	82	HB-EDL
D-EZXA	Xtreme Air XA-42 (Permit 15.6.11)	107	
D-EZXL	Scheck/ Roland CH-601XL Zodiac (Built in 2012 as CH-605XLS c/n 1, permit re-issued 18.3.13)	6-9300	
D-EZXW	SNCAN/ Stampe SV-4C	530	CF-ZXW, F-BCXX
D-EZYA	Diamond DA 40 Star	40081	
D-EZYB	Diamond DA 40 Star	40082	OE-VPW
D-EZYC	Diamond DA 40 Star	40083	
D-EZYE	Diamond DA 40-180 Star	40268	9A-DAR, D-ETOW(2), C-FDVP
D-EZZA	Diamond DA 20-A1 Katana	10020	C-FZYU, N321FT, C-GDMQ
D-EZZB	Diamond DA 20-A1 Katana	10084	N524SS, C-GDMU
D-EZZC	Diamond DA 20-A1 Katana	10095	N529SS, C-GDMQ
D-EZZD	Diamond DA 20-A1 Katana	10103	N173AA, C-GKAC

D-EZZI	Maule M7-235C Super Rocket	25113C	
D-EZZL	Zlin Z.143L	0009	OE-KGP, OK-AGP
	(Res .13)		
D-EZZM	HOAC DV-20 Katana	20058	PH-ZZM
D-EZZO	Pitts S-2A	2199	I-CITU, G-BGSF
D-EZZZ	Fieseler Fi.156C-3 Storch	4370	D-EBGY(2), (D-EAXY),
	(C/n officially listed as 2543/13)		Fv3805, CK+KI

CLASS F : Single-Engined Aircraft of between 2 and 5.7 Metric Tonnes

D-FAAE	Cessna 208B Grand Caravan	208B1139	EC-JKU
D-FAAJ	Cessna 208B Grand Caravan	208B2003	N208AE
D-FABE	CCF/North American T-6H Harvard IV	CCF4-499	AA+624, 52-8578
D-FABS	Pilatus PC-12/47E	1585	HB-FQD(17)
D-FABZ	Cessna 208B Grand Caravan	208B1250	N950BZ
D-FACE(2)	Hawker Sea Fury T.11	ES3613	N51SF, N613RD, G-BCOV,
	(Res .12)		D-CACE, G-9-62, VX302
D-FAFA	Yakovlev Yak-9UM	0917918	VH-YXI
	(P. 4.08) (As SovAF '17' white)		
D-FAHH	Grob G 520 Strato 1	10005	D-FGRO
	(Res .16)		
D-FAIR	Antonov An-2	17205	(54+02), LSK-450
D-FALB	Cessna 208B Grand Caravan	208B0744	
D-FALF(2)	SOCATA TBM-700N	610	N426TB
D-FALK	Cessna 208 Caravan I	20800023	N9354F
D-FAME(2)	CCF Harvard Mk.4	CCF4-77	G-BKCK, N13631,
			RCAF20286
D-FAML	North American AT-6D Harvard III	88-15778	(D-FMDM), F-BJBH, Belg:
	(Possibly 88-17026, c/n listed as 41-34087)		H-16, EZ214, SAAF7578,
	(P.06)		(EZ214), (41-34087)
D-FAMT	Pilatus PC-9/B	164	HB-HQK(2)
D-FASS	North American AT-6D Harvard III	88-14383	SAAF7429, (EX847),
			41-33820
	(Officially listed incorrectly as 78-8177 and also previously as 88-13483)		
D-FAST(2)	Cessna 208 Caravan I	20800207	N208MC, N208MT
D-FAXI	Pilatus PC-6/B2-H4 Turbo Porter	862	(PH-AXI), D-FAXI,
			(F-GPGA), G-ITPS
D-FAYX	SOCATA TBM-700N	514	
D-FBAW	Antonov An-2TD	1G160-01	(54+13), LSK-804
	(Wears "LSK 804")		
D-FBMT	Pilatus PC-9/B	165	HB-HQL(2)
D-FBNG	Piper PA-46-500TP Malibu Meridian	4697152	D-EBNG, G-DERK,
			N165MA, N9533N
D-FBPS	Cessna 208B Grand Caravan	208B0494	LV-YJC, N208BA, N1219G
D-FBRS	Extra EA.500	1003	(D-ECBD(3))
D-FBSF	Cessna 208B Grand Caravan	208B2056	N51984
D-FBUN	North American P-51D Mustang	122-39270	N471R, N268BD,
	(P.11.07)		(N215RC), N268BD, 13 IDFAF, 44-72811
D-FBVB	Pilatus PC-12/47E	1555	HB-FRZ(16)
D-FCAE	Cessna 208B Grand Caravan	208B1296	N5202D
D-FCLG	Pilatus PC-6/B2-H4 Turbo-Porter	636	F-BOSZ
D-FCMT	Pilatus PC-9/B	166	
D-FCOM	Cessna 208B Grand Caravan	208B0933	N5265N
D-FCOR	Chance Vought F4U-7 Corsair	124541	F-AZYS, Argentine Navy
			0433
D-FCTP	Piper PA-46-500TP Malibu Meridian	4697070	D-ECTP(3), D-ESSS(3),
			D-FOXI, N53322, N9536N
D-FDHR	Pilatus PC-17/47E	1065	OH-GGO, D-FDHR,
			N184TH(2), HB-FRT(10)
D-FDLR	Cessna 208B Grand Caravan	208B0708	
D-FDME	Messerschmitt Bf.109G-10	151591	ZK-CIX, D-FEHD(2),
	(P. 11.10)		Luftwaffe
	(Identity in doubt. Fuselage may be HA.1112-MIL c/n 213		
	ex C.4K-141 fitted with wings of D-FEHD(1) ?)		
D-FDTZ	Pilatus PC-12/47E	1617	HB-FRJ
D-FEDY	Cessna 208B Grand Caravan	208B0059	N9347B, (N959FE)
D-FEFY	Pilatus PC-12/47E	1201	OK-PCA, HB-FTZ(11)
D-FEJE	Pilatus PC-6/B2-H4 Turbo Porter	941	HB-FMK
D-FELI	Pilatus PC-6/B2-H4 Turbo Porter	845	JA8223, HB-FAB
D-FEMT	Pilatus PC-9/B	168	
D-FEND	Pilatus PC-12/47E	1600	HB-FQS
D-FENK	Yakovlev Yak-9UM	0470403	F-AZYJ, N9250
	(P. 9.05) (Dam.16.7.08)		
D-FEPG	Pilatus PC-12/47E	1300	(D-FEBG), HB-FVL
D-FEUR	Vickers Supermarine 359 Spitfire HF.VIIIc		
		6S-583793	G-BKMI, A58-671, MV154
D-FFBZ(2)	Pilatus PC-6/B2-H4 Turbo Porter	869	
D-FFHZ	Pilatus PC-9/B	847	
D-FFMT	Pilatus PC-9/B	169	
D-FGAG	Pilatus PC-12/47	810	N184TH(1), HB-FRO(8)
D-FGMG	Pilatus PC-6/B2-H4 Turbo Porter	864	UAE-2216, UAE-322,
			Dubai 322, HB-FKK
D-FGMT	Pilatus PC-9/B	170	
D-FGOS	Pacific Aerospace PAC 750XL	113	ZK-JFI
	(Res. 11)		
D-FGWZ	SOCATA TBM-700N	394	N851WA
D-FGYY(2)	SOCATA TBM-700B	162	
D-FHBG	SOCATA TBM-700N	617	N850CK
D-FHEI	Piper PA-46-500TP Malibu Meridian	4697215	N31145
D-FHGK	Noorduyn/North American AT-16 Harvard IIb	14-324	G-AXCR, Swiss:U-322,
			FE590, (42-787)
D-FHGL	North American SNJ-5 Texan	51-819	N2965S, (D-FIII), N2965S,
			N467EW, SpAF C.6-162/793-15, "51819"
	(In 1953 regd with the documents of the genuine BuA51819 c/n 88-14713		
	which remained in the USA as N1143U, N7804B, N155DB and currently		
	N7804B. To avoid confusion the FAA allocated 'c/n' 51-819 to N467EW in .82)		
D-FHGV	North American NA-81 Harvard II	81-4038	N90541, C-FTSV, CF-TSV,
	(P. 4.13)		RCAF3771
D-FHHH	Grob G.520T Egrett	10200	VH-ARA, D-FARA,
	(P. 6.14)		D-FDST
D-FHKT	Piper PA-46-500TP Malibu Meridian	4697155	N338DB, N53677,
			N9534N, N53599
D-FHMT	Pilatus PC-9/B	171	HB-HQD
D-FHRB	SOCATA TBM-700N	551	N850RA, (D-FJJJ),
			N850RA, (D-FRAS)
D-FIAT	Fiat G.59-4B	179	VH-LIX, NX59B, MM53278
	(Res .16)		
D-FIBE	Pilatus PC-6/B2-H4 Turbo Porter	955	HB-FMY
D-FIBI	Pilatus PC-12/47	773	HB-FSX(7)
D-FICA	Pilatus PC-6/B2-H4 Turbo Porter	919	N919MA, HB-FLM,
			7T-WLA, HB-FLM
D-FIDT	Cessna 208B Grand Caravan	208B1197	N90646, N208ED,
			N208WE, N5262B
D-FINA	Cessna 208B Grand Caravan	208B0475	N1202D, 9M-PMT,
			N1220D, N5094D
D-FINK	Cessna 208B Grand Caravan	208B1259	N208WP
D-FIPO	Piper PA-46-500TP Malibu Meridian	4697060	C-FIPO, N5320A
D-FIPS	Pilatus PC-6/B2-H4 Turbo Porter	874	HB-FKO, V5-ODH,
			HB-FKO
D-FIRE	SOCATA TBM-700A	137	
D-FIST	Yakovlev Yak-9U-M	0470408	N908JW
D-FITE	North American NA-76 Harvard II	76-3556	N586AJ, N4657T, AJ586
D-FIVE	SOCATA TBM-700B	186	
D-FIXX(2)	Cessna 208B Grand Caravan	208B0760	N333FA
D-FJET(2)	Aero L-39ZO Albatros	731002	N139ZB, ES-YLL,
	(Res .13)		G-BWTS, 28+02, LSK-140
D-FJII	Yakovlev Yak-11	Y-5434	F-AZIO
D-FJJF	Antonov An-2T	1G108-70	DDR-WJF, DM-WJF
D-FJKA	Antonov An-2T	19318	DDR-WJP, LSK-839
D-FJMT	Pilatus PC-9/B	173	
D-FJNU	SOCATA TBM-700	327	(D-FJJJ), N300CX, N732C
D-FJOE	Piper PA-46-500TP Malibu Meridian	4697315	OK-NET, N31010
D-FKAE	SOCATA TBM-700N	428	PH-TJA
D-FKAI (3)	Pilatus PC-12/47E	1250	HB-FRR(12)
D-FKGF	Pilatus PC-12/47E	1080	D-FKGI(1), HB-FSI(10)
D-FKGI(2)	Pilatus PC-12/47E	1625	HB-FRR(17)
D-FKJM	Pilatus PC-12/47E	1461	HB-FVX
D-FKMB	Antonov An-2T	17308	(54+03), LSK-451
D-FKMC	Antonov An-2T	17612	(54+05), LSK-454
D-FKME	Antonov An-2T	17805	(54+08), LSK-457
D-FKMT	Pilatus PC-9/B	176	HB-HPE, D-FLFA,
			HB-HPE
D-FLAC	Pilatus PC-6/B2-H4 Turbo Porter	804	(D-FFOR), LV-MYZ
D-FLAT	Pilatus PC-12/47E	1487	(D-FHMS(3)), HB-FSI(15)
D-FLBK	Piper PA-46-500TP Malibu Meridian	4697031	ZS-ECO(2), N45PJ,
			N4182K
D-FLEC	Cessna 208 Caravan I	20800388	N68FE
D-FLEX	SOCATA TBM-700C2	321	F-HBCF, N700ZB
D-FLIC	Cessna 208 Caravan I	20800274	N12149, N52609
D-FLIP	Cessna 208B Grand Caravan	208B0331	N3331, 9M-PMO, N1036C
D-FLIR	Pilatus PC-12	128	TT-AAF, JA8599
D-FLIZ(2)	Cessna 208 Caravan 1	20800241	OO-NKA, N241KA, Peru
			EP857, N241KA, N1130K
D-FLOC	Cessna 208B Grand Caravan	208B0578	N555SA, N805TH
D-FLOH	Cessna 208B Grand Caravan	208B0576	N1041F
D-FLUC(2)	Cessna 208B Grand Caravan	208B0988	T7-VAL, LN-PBL, N52655
D-FLUG(2)	Yakovlev Yak-3M	0470105	
	(Res .10)		
D-FLUX	SOCATA TBM-700N	569	D-FRAS(2)
D-FLVL	Piper PA-46-500TP Malibu Meridian	4697574	N44307
D-FMAX	SPP Yakovlev C-11	171101	G-KYAK, F-AZQI, F-AZHQ,
			IDFAF, EAF-590, Czech AF 1701
D-FMBB(2)	Messerschmitt Bf 109G-6	156	C.4K-87
	(Constructed from a Hispano HA.1112-MIL airframe & parts from D-FMBB(1))		
D-FMCA	Holste MH.1521C-1 Broussard	185	F-GPRN, G-BWLR,
			F-GGKJ, F-WGKY, French AF
D-FMCP	SOCATA TBM-700N	475	G-KEMW
D-FMGZ(2)	Messerschmitt Me 109G-12	15208	D-FMVS, N109W, N9939,
	(Res 26.5.16)		G-AWHT, C4K-169
	(Originally Hispano HA.1112-MIL c/n 234. Flies as "Yellow 27")		
D-FMMM	Piper PA-46-500TP Malibu Meridian	4697524	N644MM, N9546N
	(Res 6.13, renewed 1.15)		
D-FMMT(2)	Pilatus PC-12/47	1263	N263NX, HB-FSD
	(Res 23.8.16)		
D-FMOR	Piper PA-46-500TP Malibu Meridian	4697299	N9544N
D-FNAH	Pilatus PC-12/47E	1160	HB-FSO(11)
D-FNEA	Cessna 208B Grand Caravan	208B0106	N106BZ, N979FE
	(Res 1.15)		
D-FNJP	Pilatus PC-12/47E	1590	HB-FQI(17)
D-FNVA	Antonov An-2T	19320	(D-FORK), (54+15),
			LSK-817
D-FOAA	PZL-106A Kruk	48039	DDR-TAA, DM-TAA
D-FOAB	PZL-106A Kruk	48040	DDR-TAB, DM-TAB
	(Painted as DDR-TAB, now single-seater again)		
D-FOBH	PZL-106 Kruk	60111	(N . . . . .), D-FOBH
	(Res 8.10, used as engine test-bed .13)		
D-FOFM	Antonov An-2T	12802	(54+11), LSK-802,
			SovAF 802
D-FOJB	Antonov An-2T	1G86-42	DDR-WJB, DM-WJB
D-FOJN	Antonov An-2T	1G166-39	DDR-WJN, DM-WJN
D-FOKE	Piper PA-46-500TP Malibu Meridian	4697470	N2453V
D-FOKK	Antonov An-2T	19504	DDR-SKK, DM-SKK
	(Wears DM-SKK)		
D-FOKY	Antonov An-2T	1G86-49	DDR-SKY, DM-SKY
D-FOLE(2)	Cessna 208B Grand Caravan	208B0523	N5197A
D-FOND	Antonov An-2P	19508	DDR-SKD(2), LSK-815
	(Wears DDR-SKD)		
D-FONE(2)	Antonov An-2P	17812	D-FKMD, (54+07),
			LSK-456
D-FONF	Antonov An-2P	117419	DDR-SKF(2), LSK-811
	(Painted as DDR-SKF)		
D-FONL	Antonov An-2T	17802	DDR-SKL(2), LSK-888
	(Painted as DM-SKL)		
D-FOOO	SOCATA TBM-700A	24	D-FTAN, PH-AJS, F-GLBD
D-FOTO(2)	Cessna 208 Caravan I	20800192	N9773F
D-FOUR(2)	SOCATA TBM-700N	1116	
D-FOXY(2)	Cessna 208 Caravan I Amphibian	20800303	I-SEAA, N984J, (N728CP),
			N984J, N984JD, N1260V
D-FPAE	North American T-6G Texan	168-587	LX-PAE, SpanAF E.16-106,
	(P. 26.7.16)		FrAF 93543, 49-3453
D-FPKD	Piper PA-46-500TP Malibu Meridian	4697019	D-EPKDOY-GPT,
			(OY-NEW), N519MM
D-FPMM	Piper PA-46-500TP Malibu Meridian	4697512	D-FSSS, N2586Y, N9544N
D-FPSI	North American P-51D Mustang	122-39232	G-CDHI, G-SUSY,
			N12066, FAN:GN120, 44-72773
D-FQOI	Stemme Q01-100 Observer	1	
	(P 25.11.15)		
D-FRAH	Piper PA-46-500TP Malibu Meridian	4697276	D-ERAH, N19563
D-FRBI	EKW C-3603-1	327	HB-RBI, SwissAF C-547
	(P. 06/13)		
D-FRCP	Noorduyn AT-16-ND Harvard IIB	14A-868	HB-RCP, G-BAFM,
			PH-SKL, Neth: B-104, FS728, (8104), FS728, (43-12569)
D-FRED	Cessna 208 Caravan I	20800293	G-ETHY, N1295M,
			G-ETHY
D-FREE	Pilatus PC-6/B1-H2 Turbo-Porter	731	C-GZCZ, VH-ZCZ,
			A14-705, A14-731, HB-FFS
D-FREI	Cessna 208B Grand Caravan	208B1024	N789JG
D-FROH	Pilatus PC-6/B2-H4 Turbo-Porter	654	HB-FDT, F-BSTF, HB-FDT

Reg	Type	c/n	Previous identities
D-FSAS(2)	Cessna 208B Grand Caravan	208B1238	N1156C
D-FSBG	SOCATA TBM-700N	1061	
D-FSCB	Pilatus PC-6/B2-H4 Turbo-Porter (W/o 19.6.16)	634	C-FPZB, ZK-FZB, VH-FZB, LN-VIJ, HB-FCU
D-FSFS	Piper PA-46-500TP Malibu Meridian	4697492	N2461T, N9541N
D-FSID	SOCATA TBM-700C1	288	D-FKAI(2)
D-FSJP	SOCATA TBM-700A	130	N38KJ, C-GSMO, N700AP, F-WWRM
D-FSKY	Pilatus PC-6/B2-H4 Turbo-Porter	878	
D-FSPG(2)	Cessna 208 Caravan I	20800584	
D-FSPT	Vickers Supermarine 394 Spitfire F.Mk XVIIIe	6S-676372-165	N280TP, G-BTXE, HS654, TP280
D-FSRT	Cessna 208B Grand Caravan	208B0358	PT-MEI
D-FSSS	SOCATA TBM-700N	1102	
D-FSTB	SOCATA TBM-700N	387	D-FBFS(2), F-WWRR
D-FSWW	Cessna 208B Grand Caravan	208B-0639	5H-TZU, ZS-PJJ, A6-MRM, N452NU, HR-IBJ, TI-LRB, N1132Y
D-FTAO	Pacific Aerospace PAC 750XL	182	ZK-KBT
D-FTBG	Grob G 160A (P. 3.04)	87001	
D-FTBM(4)	SOCATA TBM-700N	653	
D-FTDZ	Cessna 208B Grand Caravan	208B0726	F-OHQM(2)
D-FTOM	Pilatus PC-12/47E	1507	(D-FAAA(2)), HB-FQC(16)
D-FTRI	Pilatus PC-6/B2-H4 Turbo-Porter	791	LV-MCX
D-FTSI	North American P-51D Mustang	122-40411	NL7098V, RCAF9425, 44-73871
D-FTWO	Pilatus PC-6/B2-H4 Turbo-Porter	790	LV-MCW
D-FUDA	Pilatus PC-12/47E	1016	HB-FRH(10), (D-FEIA), HB-FRH(9)
D-FUEL	Pilatus PC-12/47E	1038	N227UT, OY-NUS, HB-FQR(10)
D-FUKK	CCF/North American T-6 Harvard IV	CCF4-46	N305GS, RCAF20256
D-FUKM	Antonov An-2T	17710	(D-FKMF), (54+06), LSK-455
D-FUMP	Cessna 208B Grand Caravan	208B0743	
D-FUMY	North American T-28C Trojan (Permit 22.11.12)	252-9	N2800M, BuA146246
D-FUNK	Cessna 208 Caravan I	20800407	N5262Z
D-FUNN	North American F-51D Mustang (P. 3.12)	122-31199	N551TF, N5437V, 44-63473
D-FUNY(2)	Cessna 208B Grand Caravan	208B0361	PT-MEL
D-FURY	North American AT-6D-NT Texan	88-18109	N7420C, 42-86328
D-FWAC	North American SNJ-5 Texan	121-42032	Sp.AF:C6-125, Sp.AF:421-43, BuA91036, (44-81310)
D-FWBC	North American T-28 Trojan (Res. pending)	unkn	
D-FWJD	Antonov An-2T	1G98-51	(D-FCJD), DDR-WJD, DM-WJD
D-FWJE	Antonov An-2T	1G108-69	(D-FCJE), DDR-WJE, DM-WJE
D-FWJG	Antonov An-2T	1G142-32	(D-FCJG), DDR-WJG, DM-WJG
D-FWJH	Antonov An-2T	1G142-33	(D-FIJH), DDR-WJH, DM-WJH
D-FWJK	Antonov An-2T (Damaged 6.9.15, Merseburg)	1G142-34	(D-FCJK), DDR-WJK, DM-WJK
D-FWJM	Antonov An-2T	1G166-38	DDR-WJM, DM-WJM
D-FWJO	Antonov An-2T	1G174-26	DDR-WJO, DM-WJO
D-FWJS	Flug Werk FW 190A-8/N (P. expired 18.1.12, for sale)	990016	
D-FWME	Hispano HA.1112-MIL Buchon (P. 2.08) (Flies as Bf 109G-6 "red 7")	139	
D-FWMV	Flug Werk FW 190A-2M (P. 7.11)	990009	G-FWAB
D-FWNC	North American P-51 Mustang (Res pending)	unkn	
D-FWSC	Flug Werk FW 190D-9 (Res pending)	unkn	
D-FWSE	Focke-Wulf FW.190A-8 (Res 10.15)	739137	Luftwaffe
D-FWUB	Bronner / Jurca MJ 80 (Focke-Wulf FW 190A-4 full-size replica) (P.8.06) (Accident 4.07)	1876	
D-FWZA	Cessna 208B Grand Caravan	208B1237	LN-AAZ(3), D-FIFA
D-FXXX	CCF Harvard IV	CCF4-164	N997RD, C-FNSN, CF-NSN, RCAF 20373
D-FYAC	Yakovlev Yak-3M	0470109	N234BJ
D-FYAG	Yakovlev Yak-3M (P. 5.06)	0470103	N42YK, ZU-STU, N494DJ
D-FYAK	LET/Yakovlev Yak-11 (Rebuild using parts of c/n 170103)	170102	G-DYAK, G-BWFU, OK-IIA
D-FYGJ	Yakovlev Yak-3M	0470204	N338Y
D-FYWM	SPP Yakovlev C-11 (P. 11.07)	171103	G-IYAK, 171103
D-FYYY	SOCATA TBM-700C2	314	N702MB
D-F . . .	Antonov An-2TD (Museum exhibit as fake "DM-SHL")	1G168-06	SP-EGA
D-F . . .	Cessna 208B Grand Caravan	208B1024	N789JG, (D-FREI), SU-KAH, G-WIKY, EC-JGQ, G-WIKY
D-F . . .	Fiat G.46-3B	44-MM-52-801	G-BBII, I-AEHU, MM52801
D-F . . .	Fiat G.59-4B	77	VH-LIX, NX59B, MM53278
D-F . . .	North American T-28A Fennec	174-228	C-GMWN, YN-BNM, Nicaragua AF FAS-164, N54612, CN-AET, French AF 42, 51-3690
D-F . . .	Pilatus P.2-06	77	N206KW, HB-RBE, U-157
D-F . . .	Pilatus P.2-06	600-58	N138U, HB-RBA, U-138, U-109

CLASS G : Twin-Engined Aircraft of below 2 Metric Tonnes

Reg	Type	c/n	Previous identities
D-GAAA(2)	Diamond DA 42 Twin Star	42.013	OE-VPY
D-GAAB	Piper PA-34-200T Seneca II	34-7670050	N139RJ, N4463X
D-GABO	LET Aero 145	19-020	OK- . . .?
D-GABT	Piper PA-34-220T Seneca III	34-8333098	N8210L, N9511N
D-GABY(2)	Piper PA-30 Twin Comanche B	30-1405	OE-FPG, N8397Y, N10F
D-GACR	Piper PA-34-220T Seneca III (Damaged 22.10.10, Bratislava)	34-8133215	N8429L
D-GADA	LET Aero 145 (Painted as DM-SGA)	15-018	OK-NHC
D-GADE	Cessna 336 Skymaster	336-0058	N1758Z
D-GAFC	Piper PA-44-180 Seminole	44-7995048	N21399
D-GAHB(2)	Piper PA-34-220T Seneca III	34-8233005	N84556
D-GAHM	Tecnam P.2006T	073	
D-GAHS	Piper PA-30 Turbo Twin Comanche C	30-1929	PH-ATV, N8773Y
D-GALE	LET L-200A Morava	170712	DDR-WLB, DM-WLB, OE-FTU, OK-PHA
D-GALF	Piper PA-30 Turbo Twin Comanche C	30-1966	HB-LFH, N8809Y
D-GAMA	Piper PA-44-180T Turbo Seminole	44-8207017	N8246S
D-GAMB	Piper PA-34-200T Seneca II	34-8070110	C-FSHC, N81404, N32DD, N81404
D-GAMU	Piper PA-44-180T Turbo Seminole	44-8107034	N8153H, ZP-PTV
D-GANA	Partenavia P.68B	117	
D-GAPA(2)	Piper PA34-220T Seneca V	3449313	N3103D
D-GAPP	Piper PA-44-180 Seminole	4496001	N9256R
D-GARE(2)	Piper PA-34-200T Seneca II	34-7870205	SE-GVN
D-GARP	Molck RP180 (Res 5.00)	01	
D-GASA(2)	LET Aero 145	19-014	G-AROE, (D-GONE), G-AROE, OK-NHF
D-GAST(2)	Piper PA-34-220T Seneca III	34-8233060	SP-UBU, G-BUBU, N8043B
D-GATA	Partenavia P.68B	82	
D-GATE(2)	Piper PA-34-220T Seneca V	3449007	N9285D
D-GAUL(2)	Piper PA-34-220T Seneca V	3449163	OK-OKR, N41770, (OK-OKR), N9527N
D-GAWA	Piper PA-34-200T Seneca II	34-7770298	N95G, N38353
D-GAWO	Piper PA-34-220T Seneca III	3433038	N9121K
D-GAXS	Piper PA-34-200T Seneca III (P.8.06)	34-8233175	I-SAXS, D-GENT, N8249Y
D-GAZE	Piper PA-30 Twin Comanche	30-681	N7646Y, N10F
D-GBAC	Piper PA-44-180T Turbo Seminole	44-8107017	N344D, G-IIBD, N180AP, N82554
D-GBAF	Piper PA-34-200T Seneca II	34-7970058	N2162F
D-GBAV	Piper PA-44-180T Turbo Seminole	44-8107051	N83709
D-GBBB	Diamond DA 42 Twin Star	42.055	OE-VPY, (D-GGWF)
D-GBCW	Piper PA-34-220T Seneca III	34-8233044	N8472E
D-GBFS	Diamond DA 42 Twin Star	42.349	OE-VPY
D-GBGK	Partenavia P.68C-TC	267-18-TC	N2958W
D-GBIG	Piper PA-34-200T Seneca II	34-8070018	N8110J
D-GBME	Piper PA-34-220T Seneca III (Res 12.15)	3433174	I-ACTD, N8242A
D-GBNI	Piper PA-30 Twin Comanche B (Exp 7.05, status unknown)	30-1462	EC-BNI, N8394Y
D-GBRS	Partenavia P.68B	34	HB-LHN
D-GBSK	Piper PA-44-180T Turbo Seminole	44-8107050	N0363D
D-GBVW	Piper PA-44-180 Seminole	4495004	C-GBVW, N192ND
D-GBWA	Piper PA-34-200T Seneca II	34-7670245	D-IAWA, N75375
D-GCAT	Piper PA-34-220T Seneca V	3449167	N4169Z
D-GCCC	Piper PA-34-220T Seneca III	34-8233108	N8161C
D-GCFM	Diamond DA 62 (Res .15)	62.0011	
D-GCMH	Piper PA-44-180 Seminole	44-7995306	N2916N
D-GCOB	Diamond DA 42 Twin Star	42.174	
D-GCPA(2)	Scheele/ Colomban MC-15 Cri-Cri	473-001 CS.PA	
D-GCUP	Diamond DA 42NG Twin Star	42.N007	OE-FYD, (SE-MBN), OE-VDK
D-GCWM	Tecnam P.2006T	02	3A-MTC
D-GDAU	Beech 95 Travel Air	TD-247	HB-GOD
D-GDDC	Piper PA-34-200T Seneca II	34-7770016	D-IMGU, N5401F
D-GDEF	Klein/ Rutan Defiant KII (W/o 15.9.07)	161-A	
D-GDIP	Piper PA-34-200T Seneca II (Res .16)	34-7670262	HB-LIG, N6146J
D-GDMF	Piper PA-34-220T Seneca III	34-8133113	N122RM, N8396L
D-GDON	Diamond DA 42 Twin Star	42.049	I-DADC
D-GDSA	Partenavia P.68C-TC	334-29-TC	N46810, YV-391P
D-GDTP	Piper PA-34-200T Seneca II	34-7970012	SE-IAZ
D-GDVK	Partenavia P.68C	212	EI-BWH, G-BHJP
D-GDWL	Piper PA-34-200T Seneca III	3448025	N9121G
D-GDWR	Piper PA-34-200T Seneca II	34-7970448	OY-CBJ, N2499U
D-GEBD	Piper PA-44-180T Turbo Seminole	44-8207018	N92PA, N9588N
D-GEDM	Piper PA-44-180 Seminole	44-7995232	N3042N
D-GEEK	Partenavia P.68C	218	PH-SOK, G-BJCR, OO-EEC
D-GEFI	Piper PA34-220T Seneca V	3449335	(D-GFGZ), OY-PHU, N9519N
D-GEHB	Piper PA-30 Twin Comanche B	30-1417	N8283Y
D-GEIL(2)	Piper PA-34-220T Seneca IV	3448065	I-KISE, N9251V, (N295PS), N9251R
D-GEJJ	Piper PA-34-220T Seneca III	3433123	N9143Z
D-GEJL	Piper PA-34-200T Seneca II	34-7870265	N31744
D-GEKW	Piper PA-34-220T Seneca III	34-8133140	D-IILY, N8403L
D-GELA	Partenavia P.68B	137	
D-GELB	PZL M-20-03 Mewa	1AH003-07	
D-GELD(2)	Piper PA-34-200T Seneca II	34-7670323	OE-FLH, N3899F
D-GELI	Partenavia P.68B	108	
D-GELR	Diamond DA 42 Twin Star	42.085	OE-VPY
D-GELX	Piper PA-34-220T Seneca V	3449059	N41184
D-GEMA(2)	Partenavia P.68B	175	(YV-1834P)
D-GEMB	Partenavia P.68B	188	
D-GEMC	Partenavia P.68B	200	
D-GEMF	Partenavia P.68C-TC	237-03-TC	
D-GEMI	Partenavia P.68C-TC	247-09-TC	
D-GERB	Partenavia P.68 Observer	173	
D-GERP(2)	Partenavia P.68B	25	ZK-LGO, HB-LGO
D-GERS	Piper PA-34-220T Seneca V	3449083	N61RC
D-GERT	Partenavia P.68B	47	
D-GERY	Partenavia P.68B	49	
D-GEST	Grumman GA-7 Cougar	0102	
D-GETT	Piper PA-34-200T Seneca II	34-7770376	D-IETT, N44924
D-GEWF	Diamond DA 42 Twin Star	42.014	OE-VPI
D-GFAS	Diamond DA 42 NG	42.294	OE-FJM, 3A-MWL, OE-FWA, OE-VPJ
D-GFGH	Piper PA-34-220T Seneca III	3447018	N9271L
D-GFHB	Piper PA-44-180 Seminole	4496166	PH-MLN, N53658, PH-MLN, N9511N
D-GFKH	Piper PA-34-220T Seneca III	3448028	N9155H
D-GFLY	Vulcanair P.68C	455	
D-GFPG	Partenavia P.68B	170	
D-GFPI	Partenavia P.68B	158	N146BK, (N2084J), D-GFPI
D-GGAB	Piper PA-34-220T Seneca IV	3447020	N9275C
D-GGER	Diamond DA 42NG	42.375	N42NG, OE-FYC, OE-VDP
D-GGGA	Piper PA-34-220T Seneca III	34-8533034	N2477Y, N9547N
D-GGGG	Piper PA-23-160 Apache	23-1579	G-IBA, N10F
D-GGLE	Piper PA-34-220T Seneca V	3449004	PH-FAC, N9282V
D-GGMD	Schlör/Colomban MC-15 Cri-Cri	279	D-GDSB
D-GGMM	Diamond DA42 NG Twin Star	42.034	OE-FKI(2)
D-GGOW	Piper PA-34-200 Seneca	34-7350225	N55521
D-GGRT	Piper PA-34-220T Seneca III	34-8333003	N8230S

Regn	Type	c/n	Previous identities
D-GGTT	Piper PA-34-220T Seneca III	34-8333115	N43129, N9535N, N43129, N9522N
D-GGUT	Tecnam P.2006T	105	
D-GGWB	Diamond DA 42 Twin Star	42.259	OE-VPY
D-GGWU	Diamond DA 42 Twin Star	42.220	OE-VPY
D-GHAN	Vulcanair P.68C	416	
D-GHBI	Piper PA-34-220T Seneca III (Res 11.15)	34-8133248	I-BEAS, N711KB, (D-GKBL), N711KB, N9589N
D-GHBN	Aero 45	51159	OK-HGD
D-GHCH	PZL M20-03 Mewa	1AH002-17	
D-GHEA	Vulcanair P.68 Observer 2	465-35/OB2	
D-GHEB	Piper PA-34-200T Seneca II	34-7870168	N9367C, N9550N
D-GHFW(2)	Piper PA-30 Twin Comanche B (Crashed 26.1.15)	30-1326	N8228Y, N10F
D-GHHP	Plogt/ Colomban MC-15 Cri-Cri (P 6.12)	2002387	
D-GHHZ	Zeiler/ Colomban MC-15 Cri-Cri	Z-01	
D-GHIK	Piper PA-39 Twin Comanche C/R	39-130	D-GHSH, G-AZNM, N8967Y
D-GHSB	Piper PA-34-220T Seneca V	3449182	N41825
D-GHWB	Huber/ Colomban MC-15 Cri-Cri	H/EB-01/149	
D-GHWW	Piper PA-23-160 Apache	23-1816	N4315P
D-GHYL(2)	Diamond DA 42 Twin Star	42.075	
D-GIAO	Piper PA-34-220T Seneca III	34-8133061	D-GJFN, SE-IYR, OY-CGI, N8371J
D-GICE	Piper PA-44-180 Seminole	4496128	N53518, N9512N
D-GICL	Piper PA-44-180 Seminole	4496221	N31248
D-GIDK	Vulcanair P.68C-TC	458/R	
D-GIES	Piper PA-34-220T Seneca III	34-8333020	F-GIES, D-GABU(2), N83010
D-GIFK	Piper PA-34-220T Seneca III (Formerly c/n 34-8233170)	34-8333028	N8291D, N9540N, N823IA
D-GIGY	Beech 76 Duchess	ME-80	
D-GIII(3)	Piper PA-34-200T Seneca II	34-7570249	OY-BYI, SE-ITG, (LN-PEK), SE-ITG, OY-BYI, PH-PEM, OO-HAM, N1452X
D-GINA(2)	Partenavia P.68B	59	
D-GIOW	Piper PA-34-200T Seneca II	34-7570270	D-IKOW, N1520X
D-GIPA(2)	Piper PA-34-220T Seneca IV	3449048	D-IOSK(2)
D-GIPC	Piper PA-34-220T Seneca IV	3448057	N92485
D-GISE	Piper PA-34-200T Seneca II	34-7870193	D-IHSE, N9508C
D-GITA	Partenavia P.68B	92	
D-GITY(2)	Partenavia P.68C-TC	360-41-TC	HB-LRK, D-GAHI, N360TC
D-GIWL	Piper PA-34-200T Seneca II	34-7570307	D-IFWL, N3903X
D-GJBA	Piper PA-34-200T Seneca II	34-8070116	N8149H
D-GJHO	Diamond DA 42 Twin Star	42.241	OE-VPW
D-GJNS	Piper PA-44-180 Seminole	44-8095001	N44ZS, F-GBOK, TR-LZE, N8087B
D-GJPA	Piper PA-44-180 Seminole	4496184	N3090K
D-GJPF	Piper PA-34-220T Seneca III	3433158	OE-FDO, N9176B
D-GJTL	Piper PA-34-220T Seneca III	34-8233147	N8207J
D-GKFE	Cessna 337A Super Skymaster	33700358	N958TM, N6358F
D-GKIM	Piper PA-34-220T Seneca III	34-7970228	N28710
D-GKKD(2)	Piper PA-44-180T Turbo Seminole	44-8207016	N94PA, N81419, N9550N, N82525
D-GKMI	Piper PA-34-200T Seneca II	34-8070290	I-ARMT, N8252D, N963PG
D-GKMP	Knittel/ Colomban MC-15 Cri-Cri	1569	
D-GKRE	Partenavia P.68C	285	EC-KBN, N344CC, N944CC, N3380P, YV-2380P, N39273
D-GLAC	Piper PA-34-220T Seneca V	3449338	N31403
D-GLAD	Piper PA-34-200T Seneca II	34-7970427	LX-YES, N2967X
D-GLAO	Piper PA-34-220T Seneca V	3449229	CS-DID, SE-ITX, N9518N
D-GLBA	Diamond DA 42 Twin Star	42.140	OE-VPY
D-GLGM	Tecnam P.2006T	036	
D-GLGN	Tecnam P.2006T	038	
D-GLIV	Piper PA-34-200T Seneca II	34-7870203	PH-FEJ, OO-FEJ, PH-FEJ, N9620C
D-GLLL	Diamond DA 42 Twin Star (W/o 15.4.08)	42.248	OE-VPI
D-GLLW	Piper PA-34-200T Seneca II (W/o 6.9.16)	34-8070170	HB-LLW, N8176T
D-GLMP	Piper PA-34-220T Seneca V	3449348	F-HEDP, S5-DHF, N10521
D-GLOC	Piper PA-34-200T Seneca II	34-7870093	OE-FTM, N2786M
D-GLUX(4)	Diamond DA 42NG Twin Star	42.N102	
D-GLUZ	Luz/ Colomban MC-15 Cri-Cri (P. 11.04)	1646-01	
D-GMAE	Diamond DA 42NG Twin Star	42.N038	OE-VDM
D-GMAI	Piper PA-39 Twin Comanche C/R	39-50	N8892Y
D-GMAJ	Piper PA-34-220T Seneca V	3449358	D-IMAJ, N10680
D-GMAX	Piper PA-44-180 Seminole (Res 11.15)	44-7995202	G-OACA, G-GSFT, EI-BYZ, N2193K
D-GMBH	Diamond DA 42 Twin Star	42.296	OE-VPI
D-GMBK	Piper PA-34-220T Seneca III	34-8233035	OE-FEK, N8467Z
D-GMCM	Reims/Cessna F337F Super Skymaster (Reims-assembled 337F with US c/n 33701401)	F33700047	D-IMCM, (D-GMCC), OO-GCM, N5443
D-GMFA	Piper PA-34-220T Seneca III	34-8233018	OY-RAS, I-CGAJ, S5-CAA, SL-CAA, YU-BPI, N8042M
D-GMJP	Tecnam P.2006T	161	
D-GMMM	Piper PA-34-200T Seneca II	34-7970022	N3040C
D-GMOF	Piper PA-34-200T Seneca II	34-7870301	D-IMOF, N36184
D-GMOH	Piper PA-34-200T Seneca II	34-7870281	D-IMOH, N31964
D-GMST	Piper PA-34-220T Seneca III	34-8433055	(HA-. . .), D-ILHW(3), D-GISY, N4365G
D-GMTP	Piper PA-34-200T Seneca II	34-7870037	9A-DOR, D-GAMM, D-IDMM, N9777K
D-GMUP	Tecnam P.2006T	014	
D-GMVF	Beech D95A Travel Air	TD-584	HB-GFF, SE-EWT, OH-BTA
D-GMWA	Piper PA-30 Twin Comanche B	30-1178	N8064Y
D-GMWF	Piper PA-34-200 Seneca	34-7250105	N4471T
D-GMYU	Beech 76 Duchess	ME-330	OE-FEW, D-GBTE
D-GMZE	Piper PA-34-200T Seneca II	34-7870452	OO-CFA, N21901
D-GNAA	Diamond DA 42NG Twin Star	42.N116	
D-GNAT	Piper PA-34-220T Seneca III	34-8133223	N8434P
D-GNJP	Diamond DA 62	62.009	D-GANM, (D-GGAA)
D-GNNN	Piper PA-34-220T Seneca III	3447017	N9272L
D-GNOM	Piper PA-34-220T Seneca III	34-8233022	N8460K
D-GNSL	Meinhardt/ Colomban MC-15 Cri-Cri (Res.5.99)	256AB	(D-GERM)
D-GOBB	Piper PA-34-200 Seneca	34-7350253	N55871
D-GOEL	Diamond DA 42 NG	42.N177	OE-VDO
D-GOFW	Piper PA-44-180 Seminole	44-7995123	N3011C
D-GOGO(2)	Partenavia P.68C-TC	343-31-TC	
D-GOKI	Piper PA-44-180T Turbo Seminole	44-8107005	N8226A
D-GOLD(2)	Piper PA-34-220T Seneca V	3449054	N9293W
D-GOLF	Piper PA-23-160 Apache	23-1361	N3398P, (D-GEKL), N3398P
D-GOMH	Diamond DA 42 Twin Star	42.276	
D-GOMS	Piper PA-44-180 Seminole	44-8095026	N8222C
D-GONG(2)	Partenavia P.68C-TC (Res .13)	346-32-TC	N288EH, (D-GMOT), YU-DSA, N43NR, N32PV
D-GOOO	Piper PA-34-200T Seneca II	34-7970360	OE-FBP, N19499, N9591N
D-GOPR	Piper PA-34-200T Seneca II	34-7970332	N274L, HB-LLI
D-GORK	Piper PA-34-220T Seneca III	34-8170053	I-MIRK, N8306P
D-GOSR	Piper PA-34-220T Seneca III	34-8133017	N8340S
D-GOST	Piper PA-34-220T Seneca III (P. 8.06)	3448039	N9208P
D-GOVA	Piper PA-34-200T Seneca II	34-8070209	PH-SYC, N81922
D-GPAN	Piper PA-34-220T Seneca III	3449208	N5320A
D-GPCS	Piper PA-34-200T Seneca II	34-8070261	N8231H
D-GPEZ	Piper PA-30 Twin Comanche C	30-1871	N8798Y, N9703N
D-GPJB	Piper PA-34-220T Seneca III	34-8133173	N84131
D-GPLA	Partenavia P.68B	10	EC-HYF, OH-PVA
D-GPTT	Piper PA-34-220T Seneca IV	3448043	N9245J
D-GRAF	Piper PA-44-180 Seminole	4496200	N938PR, N938ER
D-GREA	Piper PA-34-220T Seneca V	3449168	I-ILAB, OY-LAB, N9515N
D-GRIM	Diamond DA 42 Twin Star (Res.08)	42.335	OE-VPI
D-GRNG	Diamond DA 42 Twin Star (Res.07)	42.255	
D-GRRR	Piper PA-44-180T Turbo Seminole	44-8107038	N8332A
D-GRUS	Piper PA-34-220T Seneca V	3449161	N4174P
D-GTAC	Piper PA-34-200T Seneca V	3449385	N61071
D-GTFC	Piper PA-44-180 Seminole	4496238	N1075F, N9520N, N1032H
D-GTIM	Tecnam P.2006T	104	I-KERS
D-GUFI	Piper PA-34-220T Seneca V	3449225	OY-LAZ, N9528N
D-GUFM	Tecnam P.2006T (W/o 19.12.16)	166	
D-GULL	LET L.200D Morava	171407	OK-UHA
D-GURU	Kamenz/ Colomban MK17 Cri-Cri (Res .07)	1207	
D-GUST(2)	Grumman GA-7 Cougar (W/o 21.9.16)	GA7-0066	N779GA
D-GUTE	Piper PA-34-200T Seneca II	34-7770382	N44989
D-GVCC	Diamond DA 42 Twin Star	42.099	OE-VPI
D-GVIP	Diamond DA 42 Twin Star	42.257	
D-GVMD	Vulcanair P.68C	429	I-TOPZ
D-GWAW	Piper PA-34-200T Seneca II	34-7770298	N95G, N38353
D-GWFA	Kuhlmann/ Colomban MC-15 Cri-Cri	71	
D-GWIC	Partenavia P.68B	159	G-OLMA, G-BGBT
D-GWIT	Piper PA-34-220T Seneca V	3449132	N41488, N9530N
D-GWLB	LET L.200A Morava (P. 3.07)	170320	OK-OKZ, OM-OKZ, OK-OKZ, CzAF0320
D-GWPL	Piper PA-34-220T Seneca III	34-8433005	N4323Y, N9509N
D-GWTA	Tecnam P.2006T	051	HA-TEC
D-GWWW	Piper PA-34-220T Seneca V	3449021	N92882
D-GXXX	Piper PA-34-220T Seneca V	3449110	G-VDAC, N818JM, N9513N
D-GZOZ	Diamond DA 42 Twin Star	42.150	G-IANV, OE-VPI
D-GZXA	Piper PA-44-180 Seminole	4496136	N5352H
D-GZXC	Piper PA-44-180 Seminole	4496266	N6084A, D-GZXC, N6084A, N9520N
D-GZXD	Piper PA-44-180 Seminole	4496273	D-GPAZ, N6092C
D-G . . .	Cessna 337D Super Skymaster	33701076	OY-AKP, (G-AWYD), N86095
D-G . . .	Piper PA-34-220T Seneca III	34-8133004	I-AMCX, N83262

CLASS H : All Rotary-winged Aircraft without Weight Limit

Regn	Type	c/n	Previous identities
D-HAAA(3)	Westland-Bell 47G-3B1 /Soloy	WA/386	G-BHKB, XT227
D-HAAD(4)	Eurocopter EC.145T2 (BK.117D-2) (Res 2.15)	20021	LN-OOB, D-HCBS(2)
D-HAAE	Hiller UH-12E Soloy	2039	C-GMTF, N9060F, CF-OKC, CF-MHI
D-HAAG(3)	Robinson R44 Raven I	2072	PH-WMW
D-HAAH(5)	Robinson R44 Raven II	11491	OE-XGK
D-HAAI	Robinson R22 Beta	4380	N42243
D-HAAK(2)	Aérospatiale SA.365C3 Dauphin 2	5039	YR-DFD
D-HAAM	Aérospatiale AS.350B Ecureuil	1910	
D-HAAO	MBB Bö.105CBS-4	S-626	D-HTSD, D-HNWF, (D-HDSV)
D-HAAR(2)	Enstrom 280C Shark	1189	(D-HAAH), D-HGBX, SE-HKX
D-HABH	Eurocopter EC.145T2 (BK.117C-2)	9127	F-MJBI(2), D-HORN(4), F-MJBI(2), D-HMBQ(6)
D-HABM	Agusta A.109E Power	11080	
D-HABN	Hughes 269A (TH-55A)	105-0394	N62468, 64-18082
D-HABP	Heli-Sport CH-7 Kompress	unkn	
D-HABY(2)	Westland-Bell 47G-3B1/Soloy	WA/610	G-BHKD, XT848
D-HACK	Agusta-Bell 47J-2A	2071	5B-CAF, CR-1
D-HADA to HADY	Test registrations for Eurocopter /Airbus Helicopter EC.145 / H145 production		
D-HAEW	Enstrom F-28A-D	095	
D-HAFA(4)	Bell 206B Jet Ranger II	124	G-HELO, G-BAZN, 9J-RIN, ZS-HCJ
D-HAFB(2)	Westland-Bell 47G-3B1	WA/426	D-HAFW, (D-HAFN), XT514
D-HAFC(2)	Agusta-Bell 206B Jet Ranger 2	8323	OE-BXR(1)
D-HAFD(9)	Bell 412HP	36072	HZ-RC08, A6-BAE
D-HAFE(4)	Bell 412	36069	OY-HSJ, N412SX, OY-HSJ, N412SX, B-4369, (N128PA), B-4369, N70890, C-FOEP
D-HAFF(3)	Westland-Bell 47G-3B1	WA/705	G-BEGA, XW185
D-HAFH(3)	Bell 412	33211	PT-YXB, N412HS, PT-HVN, N3216N
D-HAFJ	Westland-Bell 47G-3B1	WA/701	XW181
D-HAFK	Westland-Bell 47G-3B1	WA/331	XT172
D-HAFL(4)	Bell 412EP	36133	(OY-HSR), N62734)
D-HAFM(4)	Agusta-Bell 412	25510	UgandaAF 402
D-HAFN(4)	Bell 412	36041	OE-XYY, A7-HAZ, N92801, D-HHTT, N3103K
D-HAFO(3)	Bell 412EP	36161	VT-AZC(2), N54169, C-GLZM
D-HAFP(3)	Agusta-Bell 206B Jet Ranger 2	8255	OM-SPP, D-HAFW(3), OE-BXO
D-HAFQ(5)	Agusta-Bell 412HP	25808	A6-DYR, OO-AAS, DU-321
D-HAFR(2)	Bell 205A-1	30318	N8227H, LN-OLM, C-GFHN

Reg	Type	c/n	Identities
D-HAFS(3)	Agusta-Bell 412	25514	Ug AF 406
D-HAFU(3)	Aérospatiale AS.350B Ecureuil (Res 28.9.16)	1788	
D-HAFW(8)	Bell 412SP	33178	VH-LLI(2), N556UH, N2024Z, JA9937, N32050
D-HAFX	Bell 206B Jet Ranger II	3419	N50Q, N700TU, N700TV
D-HAFY(2)	Agusta-Bell 206B Jet Ranger 3	8654	
D-HAGK	Bell 407	54323	N461ZB, C-GOGK, C-GLZC
D-HAHB	Bell 47G-2 (Res 8.15)	636	ST-AGQ, D-HAKE, CF-GXG
D-HAHN(4)	Aérospatiale AS.350B2 Ecureuil	9003	9N-AIW, D-HAHN(4)
D-HAIB	Robinson R44 Raven II	12060	LZ-RBV, D-HRBV
D-HAIC	Robinson R44 Clipper II	11533	G-OMKA
D-HAID	MBB-Kawasaki BK.117B-2	7018	OE-XAR, D-HDRG(3), PK-NZG, D-HBKT
D-HAIF	Aérospatiale AS.355N Ecureuil 2	5514	I-PFDC, F-WYMF, F-WYMB, F-WYMC
D-HAIH	Robinson R66	0691	N7092K
D-HAII	Aérospatiale AS.350B2 Ecureuil	9072	D-HPWF, G-CDTD, F-GUAZ, F-WQED
D-HAJH	Robinson R44 Raven	1354	D-HALM(3)
D-HAJO(4)	Bell 412HP	36050	C-GIHK(3), VT-HGG, VH-CFT(2), B-66188, VH-CFT(2), N4383D
D-HAKL	Robinson R44 Raven II	11679	D-HALV(3)
D-HALA(3)	Robinson R44 Raven II	11014	
D-HALB(4)	Robinson R44 Raven II	13194	
D-HALC(6)	Robinson R44 Raven II	1111	PH-FVZ, D-HALG(1)
D-HALD(4)	Robinson R44 Raven II	13066	
D-HALE(3)	Robinson R44 Raven	1707	
D-HALF(5)	Robinson R44 Raven II	12544	
D-HALG(2)	Robinson R44 Raven	1552	
D-HALH	Robinson R44 Raven II	10937	
D-HALJ	Robinson R44 Astro	0544	
D-HALK(2)	Eurocopter EC.120B Colibri	1278	
D-HALL(3)	Robinson R44 Astro	0578	
D-HALP	Robinson R44 Astro	0614	
D-HALQ(2)	Robinson R44 Raven	1939	
D-HALR(3)	Robinson R44 Raven II	12468	
D-HALS(2)	Robinson R44 Raven I	2374	
D-HALU(3)	Robinson R44 Raven	1310	
D-HALV(3)	Robinson R44 Raven I	2174	
D-HALW	Robinson R22 Beta II	3316	
D-HALX(2)	Robinson R66	0557	
D-HALZ(3)	Robinson R44 Raven I	2148	
D-HAMB	MBB Bö.105	S-205	HB-XFN, D-HDFT(2)
D-HAMM(2)	Agusta-Bell 206B Jet Ranger 3	8692	Dubai Air Wing DU-144
D-HAMV	Aérospatiale SA.365N Dauphin 2 (Correct c/n believed to be 6107)	6100	F-HIHI, YU-HCT
D-HANA(3)	Bell 427	56015	UR-IGA, UR-WIGA, N427TP, VH-JJS, N427RG, RP-C1608, N61044, C-GFNM
D-HAND(2)	Bell 412SP	33151	TR-KCV, N32055
D-HANK	Schweizer 269C	S-1811	
D-HANT	MBB Bö.105S	S-776	N8776, N829MB, D-HDYL
D-HAOD	Schweizer 269C	S-1544	JA7872
D-HAOE	MBB-Kawasaki BK.117C-1	7530	9A-HKB, D-HMBC, D-HBKA(2), D-HMBG
D-HAPE(2)	Bader/Canadian Home Rotors Safari (Permit)	2118	
D-HARE(2)	Eurocopter EC.120B Colibri	1552	
D-HARI (5)	Agusta A.109E Power	11708	D-HHHH(3)
D-HARK(3)	MBB-Kawasaki BK.117C-1	7542	I-AICO, D-HZBV, D-HMB .
D-HARO(2)	MBB Bö.105S	S-831	OE-XFS, HB-XXK, D-HFCO
D-HARZ	Bell 212	30598	
D-HASC	Bell 47G-5	7843	N1393X
D-HASI(5)	Robinson R44 Raven II	10229	(C-GELG). N19VB
D-HASW	Westland-Bell 47G-3B-1	WA/521	XT814
D-HATC	Guimbal G2 Cabri (Res as LN-OKR)	1016	F-WWHX
D-HATO(2)	Robinson R44 Raven	1054	OO-KND, D-HALI(2)
D-HAUA(2)	Aérospatiale AS.350B2 Ecureuil	2056	D-HAUN
D-HAUD(2)	Aérospatiale AS.355N Ecureuil 2	5538	F-WYMA, F-WZKL
D-HAUE(2)	Bell 206B Jet Ranger II	4195	
D-HAUF(3)	Aérospatiale AS.350B2 Ecureuil	2361	D-HECS, F-GGPY
D-HAUG	Sikorsky S-58C	58-836	R.Belg.AF B-15/OT-ZKP, OO-SHP, N869
D-HAUI(2)	MBB-Kawasaki BK.117C-2	9607	D-HMBF
D-HAUL(2)	Aérospatiale AS.355N Ecureuil 2	5742	G-NMEN, F-WQVX
D-HAUN(2)	MBB-Kawasaki BK.117C-2	9088	D-HMBO
D-HAUO(2)	Aérospatiale AS.350B3 Ecureuil	3342	F-WQDN
D-HAUP(2)	Aérospatiale AS.350B2 Ecureuil	1825	D-HHDD
D-HAUR	Aérospatiale AS.350B2 Ecureuil	2394	HB-XUY
D-HAUS(4)	Aérospatiale AS.350B Ecureuil	1730	CS-HCY, G-DSAM, D-HHGG(1)
D-HAUU	Aérospatiale AS.350B1 Ecureuil	2072	D-HAUZ, HB-XUK, I-ORTA
D-HAUW	Aérospatiale AS.350B3 Ecureuil	3170	
D-HAVA(3)	Aérospatiale AS.350B3 Ecureuil	3950	EC-JIJ
D-HAVE(2)	Guimbal G2 Cabri	1027	
D-HAVF	Guimbal G2 Cabri	1031	
D-HAVH	Guimbal G2 Cabri	1038	
D-HAVI(2)	Guimbal G2 Cabri	1061	
D-HAVJ	Guimbal G2 Cabri (Res .16)	1166	
D-HAVM	Robinson R22 Beta	1592	
D-HAVN	Agusta A.109S Grand	22039	
D-HAVU(2)	Aérospatiale AS.365N3 Dauphin 2	6884	G-REDF
D-HAVV	Eurocopter EC.155B Dauphin	6586	D-HBWB(2), F-WQDZ
D-HAVX	Eurocopter EC.155B Dauphin	6581	D-HBWA, F-WQDH
D-HAVY	Eurocopter EC.155B Dauphin	6557	(D-HLEW), PH-EQR, D-HLEW, (D-HOAT(2)), PH-EQR, D-HLEW, (VT-JUA), D-HLEW, ZS-RLI, (F-GJFJ), F-WJFJ
D-HAVZ	Aérospatiale AS.365N2 Dauphin 2	6478	EC-HIM, SE-JCE, F-WYMM
D-HAWF	Agusta-Bell 47G-2A-1	1620	MM80432 / EI-61
D-HAWK(2)	MBB-Kawasaki BK.117B-2	7225	D-HFDP
D-HAWR	Bell 407	53825	N136AW, C-FTJD, C-GAEP
D-HAXS(2)	Schweizer 269C	S-1745	OO-NQD
D-HBAD(4)	Bell 206B Jet Ranger II	3819	N3203Z
D-HBAM	Robinson R44 Raven I	2413	
D-HBAT(2)	Schneider Sch-2	AB 1	
D-HBAY(3)	MBB-Kawasaki BK.117B-2	7205	LN-OSY, D-HIMV
D-HBBA	Hughes 369HS (Res .16)	34-0574S	OE-XXL(3), D-HBBA, N5197Y, G-NUNK, G-BMSP, C-GOEA

Reg	Type	c/n	Identities
D-HBBB(3)	Robinson R44 Raven II	10266	(OY-HKS), OE-XTT, TC-HRS
D-HBBH	Blunck Invader Gyrocopter	BB1-3509	
D-HBBY	Eurocopter EC.135P2+	0262	D-HECJ
D-HBBZ(5)	Eurocopter EC.135P2+	0269	
D-HBDD	Robinson R22B2 Beta	3710	
D-HBEL(2)	Bell 407	53236	(N6375S)
D-HBFJ	Hughes 269C	100-0980	N1112P
D-HBFS	Agusta AW.109SP Nexus	22261	
D-HBGB	Elisport CH-7 Angel	136	(D-HBGF)
D-HBGL	Aérospatiale AS.332L Super Puma (Res 15.3.16)	2082	G-CIOI, LN-OLB, OY-HMJ, LN-OLB, F-WKQA
D-HBGR	Sikorsky S-76B	760320	
D-HBHB(3)	Agusta A.109E Power	11110	OE-XLH
D-HBHS(3)	Eurocopter EC.135P2+	0699	D-HECN
D-HBIN	Schweizer 269C	S-1639	N86G
D-HBIO	Eurocopter EC.120B Colibri	1201	
D-HBJR	Agusta A.109S Grand	22059	(D-HBRJ), G-MENY
D-HBKK	MBB-Kawasaki BK.117B-2	7009	
D-HBLA	Aérospatiale AS.350B3 Ecureuil	4267	N350AY, SE-HJB, F-WWPG
D-HBLN	Eurocopter EC.135P-1	0192	
D-HBMB(2)	Robinson R44 Raven II	10394	
D-HBMM(2)	Schweizer 269C-1	0283	
D-HBMS(2)	MBB-Kawasaki BK.117C-1	7531	I-HBMS, D-HMBB
D-HBNY(2)	Eurocopter EC.135T2	0473	F-HCDF, TC- . . ., D-HECL
D-HBOC	MBB Bö.105C	S-325	(D-HDJC)
D-HBPA(2)	Eurocopter EC.135P3	0831	D-HCBP
D-HBPB(2)	Eurocopter EC.135P3	0864	D-HCBQ
D-HBPC(2)	Eurocopter EC.135P2+	0870	
D-HBPD(2)	Eurocopter EC.135P2+	0882	D-HCBO
D-HBPE(2)	Eurocopter EC.135P3	0891	D-HTSK
D-HBPF(2)	Eurocopter EC.135P2+	0900	D-HCBP
D-HBPG(2)	Eurocopter EC.135P3	0902	D-HCBT
D-HBPH(2)	Eurocopter EC.135P3	0912	
D-HBPL(2)	Aérospatiale AS.350B3 Ecureuil	7650	F-WWXP
D-HBRM	Hughes 369HS	69-0101S	G-IDWR, N101LY, G-IDWR, G-AXEJ
	(Damaged 4.8.15)		
D-HBRO(2)	Robinson R22B2 Beta	unkn	
D-HBRU	Hughes 269B	44-0058	D-HCRA, N9376F
D-HBTJ(2)	Airbus H145 (BK.117D-2)	20047	
D-HBUR(2)	MBB-Kawasaki BK.117B-2	7007	D-HADZ, D-HBUR(2), D-HMBH(11), XA-TVP, D-HXXL(2), D-HMBB(4), F-GMBB, F-WMBB, D-HBKI
D-HBWH	MBB Bö.105S	S-929	D-HBOA(2)
D-HBWP	Bell 212	30645	N59586
D-HBWU	Eurocopter EC.145T2 (BK.117D-2)	20041	D-HCBV
D-HBWV	Eurocopter EC.145T2 (BK.117D-2)	20048	D-HBTS
D-HBWW	Eurocopter EC.145T2 (BK.117D-2)	20065	D-HMBB
D-HBWX	Eurocopter EC.145T2 (BK.117D-2)	20100	
D-HBWY	Eurocopter EC.145T2 (BK.117D-2)	20102	
D-HBWZ	Eurocopter EC.145T2 (BK.117D-2) (Res 22.2.16)	20106	
D-HBYA	Eurocopter EC.135P2	0057	
D-HBYB	Eurocopter EC.135P2	0059	D-HECR(3), D-HBYB
D-HBYD	Eurocopter EC.135P2	0061	
D-HBYE	Eurocopter EC.135P2	0075	D-HECG(3), D-HBYE
D-HBYF	Eurocopter EC.135P2	0078	
D-HBYH(2)	Eurocopter EC.135P2	0100	
D-HBZT	Bell 212	30943	HC-CHD, D-HBZT
D-HCAT(2)	Robinson R44 Astro	0180	

D-HCBA to HCBZ *Test registrations for Eurocopter EC.135 & Airbus H145 production*

Reg	Type	c/n	Identities
D-HCCC(4)	Robinson R44 Raven I	2325	
D-HCCH	Robinson R44 Clipper II	12323	G-OJCH
D-HCDL	Eurocopter EC.135P2/CPDS	0700	D-HECB(17)
D-HCFE	Robinson R44 Raven	0233	
D-HCIK	Aérospatiale AS.350B2 Ecureuil	4303	OO-STZ, G-HELM, (SE-HJE)
D-HCKJ	Hiller UH-12E (Soloy)	HA3035	D-HCCC(3), N135HA
D-HCLA	Aérospatiale AS.350B3 Ecureuil	3400	
D-HCLC	Eurocopter EC.120B Colibri	1442	G-LHMS, N120CL
D-HCMA	MBB-Kawasaki BK.117C-2 (Res 8.8.16)	9022	F-ZBPM, D-HMBE, D-HJFQ
D-HCMB	Robinson R44 Raven	1478	
D-HCMV	Eurocopter EC.120B Colibri	1375	YR-MBT, F-GZAS, F-WQDB
D-HCOL	Aérospatiale AS.350B2 Ecureuil	2814	F-WYMI
D-HCOR	Aérospatiale AS.350B Ecureuil	1601	
D-HCVG	Aérospatiale AS.355F2 Ecureuil 2	5504	
D-HDAC(2)	MBB-Kawasaki BK.117B-2	7005	D-HBKG
D-HDAN(4)	Aérospatiale AS.350B3 Ecureuil	3124	
D-HDDD(6)	MBB-Kawasaki BK.117B-2	7164	D-HMBB, I-HBHG, D-HBHG, Abu Dhabi S-716, D-HBHG
D-HDDL(3)	Eurocopter EC.135P2	1200	(D-HXDL(2))
D-HDDN(3)	MBB-Kawasaki BK.117C-2	9454	
D-HDDP	MBB Bö.105C	S-123	
D-HDEC(2)	Eurocopter EC.135P2	0321	
D-HDER(2)	MBB-Kawasaki BK.117C-2	9063	G-CDGM, D-HMB .
D-HDEY(2)	Robinson R44 Raven II	10618	G-RTWO
D-HDFU(2)	MBB Bö.105CBS-5	S-206	D-HTSC, D-HDFU(2), D-HMBO, D-HDFU(2)
D-HDHD(4)	Hughes 269C	98-0730	SpAF HE.20-08/"78-37"
D-HDHF(2)	Hughes 369E	0259E	OK-LES, D-HDHF(2), F-GOTM, C-FYTZ, N535JP, N1603K
D-HDHS(4)	Aérospatiale AS.350B2 Ecureuil	2379	I-RIEL, F-WYME
D-HDIK	Robinson R44 Raven II	12219	
D-HDJP(2)	Robinson R44 Raven II	11924	G-ZOOT
D-HDKW	Agusta-Bell 47G-2	238	74+07, AS+397
D-HDLH(4)	Robinson R44 Raven II	11915	OE-XSK, D-HMKV
D-HDMA(3)	Eurocopter EC.135P2	0239	
D-HDMB(3)	Guimbal G2 Cabri	1026	
D-HDML(3)	MBB Bö.105	S-438	
D-HDNK	American Sportscopter 496T	unkn	
D-HDNN(3)	MBB-Kawasaki BK.117C-1	7546	I-HDBX, D-HEEE(3), I-HDBX, D-HDBX(2)
D-HDNO(3)	MBB-Kawasaki BK.117C-1	7548	
D-HDOM	Eurocopter EC.145T2 (BK.117D-2)	20027	
D-HDON(2)	Eurocopter EC.145T2 (BK.117D-2) (P 17.8.16)	20093	D-HADK(9)
D-HDPP(3)	MBB-Kawasaki BK.117C-1	9055	9A-HKA, D-HMBC(7), 9A-HKA, D-HMBA(8), 9A-HKA, D-HMBO
D-HDPS(3)	MBB-Kawasaki BK.117B-2	7074	EC-EVT, D-HBNV
D-HDRA(3)	MBB Bö.105S	S-391	PK- . . ., D-HDRA(3), D-HBBB, D-HDLG

Reg	Type	C/n	Previous identities
D-HDRB(3)	Eurocopter EC.135P2	0233	
D-HDRC(3)	Eurocopter EC.135P2	0234	
D-HDRF(4)	MBB-Kawasaki BK.117B-2	7094	D-HMB . ., PT-HKF, N114AE, N214AE, N522MB, D-HBPO
D-HDRH(3)	MBB-Kawasaki BK.117B-2	7199	I-BKBO, D-HIMP(1), N54114, D-HIMP(1)
D-HDRK	Eurocopter EC.135P2	0477	
D-HDRL(3)	Eurocopter EC.135P2	0486	D-HECC
D-HDRM	Eurocopter EC.135P2	0503	
D-HDRN(4)	Eurocopter EC.135P2+	0639	D-HTSL
D-HDRO(4)	Eurocopter EC.135P2+	0657	
D-HDRP(2)	Eurocopter EC.135P2+	0556	
D-HDRQ	Eurocopter EC.135P2+	0566	
D-HDRR(2)	MBB-Kawasaki BK.117C-2 (EC.145)	9038	
D-HDRS(3)	Eurocopter EC.135P2+	0729	
D-HDRT(3)	Eurocopter EC.135P2+	0737	
D-HDRU(2)	Eurocopter EC.135P2+	0790	
D-HDRV(2)	Eurocopter EC.135P2+	0808	D-HECR(12)
D-HDRW(2)	Eurocopter EC.135P2+	0878	D-HECB(13)
D-HDRX(2)	Eurocopter EC.135P2+	0881	D-HCBT(3)
D-HDRY(3)	Eurocopter EC.135P2+	1029	D-HECT(11)
D-HDRZ(2)	MBB-Kawasaki BK.117C-2	9293	
D-HDSB(2)	MBB-Kawasaki BK.117C-2	9460	D-HADD(4)
D-HDSC(2)	MBB-Kawasaki BK.117C-2	9587	D-HADB(8)
D-HDSD(2)	Eurocopter EC.145T2 (BK.117D-2)	20004	D-HADT(3)
D-HDSE	Eurocopter EC.120B Colibri	1408	F-WQDA
D-HDSF(2)	Eurocopter EC.145T2 (BK.117D-2)	20010	D-HADO(6)
D-HDSG(2)	Eurocopter EC.145T2 (BK.117D-2)	20013	D-HADL(6)
D-HDSH(3)	Eurocopter EC.145T2 (BK.117D-2)	20032	D-HCBZ(3)
D-HDSI(2)	Eurocopter EC.145T2 (BK.117D-2)	20056	D-HADD(12)
D-HDSJ(2)	Eurocopter EC.145T2 (BK.117D-2)	20104	D-HADC(14)
D-HDSK(3)	Eurocopter EC.145T2 (BK.117D-2) (Res 7.4.16)	20118	
D-HDSR(2)	MBB-Kawasaki BK.117C-1	7545	D-HMBB
D-HDTZ(2)	Aérospatiale AS.350B2 Ecureuil	4958	D-HDIE(2), SE-JLV
D-HEAA	MBB Bö.105S	S-904	(RA-02534), D-HEAA
D-HEAB	Bell 407 (Damaged 26.6.16)	53605	RA-018 . ., N8061U, C-FBGO
D-HEAD(3)	Robinson R22 Beta	0988	OH-HAO, D-HHAI(2), G-HTRF
D-HEBE	Brantly B-2	40	N4998C
D-HEBM	Bell 206B Jet Ranger II	3533	I-MIBA, N2300H
D-HEBS	Bell 47J-2 Ranger	2855	N73291
D-HEBY	Eurocopter EC.135T2	0241	G-IWRC, D-HECA

D-HECA to HECZ *Test registrations for Eurocopter Deutschland for EC.135 production*

Reg	Type	C/n	Previous identities
D-HECE(2)	MBB-Kawasaki BK.117B-2	7244	I-HECE, D-HECE(2), D-HDDD(3), D-HECE(2), D-HMBH(4), (D-HFII)
D-HEDB	Bell 206B3 Jet Ranger III	4197	N206KV, N908CA, C-GLZA
D-HEEE(4)	Aérospatiale AS.350B3 Ecureuil	3362	D-HEHF(1), G-VKVK, G-XMEN, F-WQDG, G-ZWRC, F-GPNE
D-HEER(3)	MBB Bö.105CBS	S-827	N81992, D-HFCK
D-HEES	Rotorway Exec 90	3510	
D-HEEX	Eurocopter EC.135T-2 (H135)	0001	D-HECX, F-WQOI, D-HECX, D-HBOX
D-HEFA(2)	Robinson R44 Raven I	1357	G-EGTC, G-CCNK
D-HEFE(2)	Bell 206B Jet Ranger II	2631	(D-HXXH(2)), (N4380A), I-GRAO, N5016V
D-HEGA(2)	Aérospatiale AS.332L1 Super Puma	2234	
D-HEGC	Aérospatiale AS.332L1 Super Puma	2268	
D-HEGD	Aérospatiale AS.332L1 Super Puma	2018	G-PUMG, F-ODOS
D-HEGE	Aérospatiale AS.332L1 Super Puma	2355	HL9201, F-WYMF, F-WKQA
D-HEGF	Aérospatiale AS.332L Super Puma	2016	G-CDTN, N170EH, N170ED, C-GSLB, N6017L, C-GSLB, F-WXFB
D-HEGG	Aérospatiale AS.332L1 Super Puma	2101	G-PUMH
D-HEGH	Aérospatiale AS.332L2 Super Puma	2667	
D-HEGI	Aérospatiale AS.332L1 Super Puma	2073	G-PUML, LN-ODA, G-PUML, LN-OMG
D-HEGK	Aérospatiale AS.332L1 Super Puma	2720	
D-HEGL	Aérospatiale AS.332L1 Super Puma	2705	
D-HEGM	Aérospatiale AS.332L1 Super Puma	2774	
D-HEGO	Aérospatiale AS.332L1 Super Puma	2050	G-TIGL
D-HEGP	Aérospatiale AS.332L1 Super Puma	2115	G-TIGZ, C-GQKK, G-TIGZ
D-HEGS	Aérospatiale AS.332L1 Super Puma	2111	G-BLRY, LN-ONA, G-BLRY, LN-ONA, G-BLRY, P2-PHP, VR-BIJ, G-BLRY, C-GQGL, G-BLRY
D-HEGT	Aérospatiale AS.332L1 Super Puma	2071	(D-HEGQ), G-TIGR, F-WTNW
D-HEGU	Aérospatiale AS.332L1 Super Puma	2017	OY-HDT, G-BWHN, C-GSLC, HC-BQJ, C-GSLB, HC-BNC, C-GSLC
D-HEGW	Aérospatiale AS.332L1 Super Puma	2696	F-WQED
D-HEGY	Aérospatiale AS.332L1 Super Puma	2700	
D-HEGZ	Aérospatiale AS.332L1 Super Puma	2706	
D-HEHA	Eurocopter EC.120B Colibri	1292	
D-HEHB	Bell 206L Long Ranger	45011	
D-HEHF(2)	Eurocopter EC.130T2 Ecureuil	8195	
D-HEHH	Eurocopter EC.120B Colibri	1045	OE-XAA(2), D-HEHM, D-HEHH
D-HEHR	Ehringhaus/ Revolution Mini-500 (Permit)	100	
D-HEIA(2)	Bell 47G3B1 /Soloy	3433	N54SP, 64-17867
D-HEJJ	Robinson R22 Beta II	4140	N148SH
D-HELA	Robinson R44 Raven II	10446	D-HEJA
D-HELC	Popp HP-1 Gyrocopter	01	
D-HELD(3)	Enstrom 480 Turbine	5008	OO-VLW, G-BWHE
D-HELE	Robinson R44 Raven II	12454	
D-HELI (2)	Aérospatiale AS.350BA Ecureuil	1241	F-WZFL
D-HELL(3)	Robinson R44 Raven II	10358	
D-HELM(4)	Schweizer 269C-1	0277	F-GNOP, N86G
D-HELO(2)	Agusta-Bell 47G-2	228	D-HAUS(1), 74+04, AS+395
D-HELP(5)	Robinson R44 Clipper II	12500	I-AWAY
D-HELT	Agusta-Bell 47J	1058	G-APTH, 5N-ACP, G-APTH
D-HEMB	Hemberger TH-II	TH-II-01	
D-HEMS(3)	Eurocopter EC.145T2 (BK.117D-2)	20008	D-HADP(4)
D-HEMV	Eurocopter EC.120B Colibri	1327	F-GJIR(2)
D-HENA	Aérospatiale AS.350B Ecureuil	1781	OE-KXC, D-HENA
D-HEOE	MBB-Kawasaki BK.117B-2	7247	D-HBWF(2), (D-HFIL)
D-HEOP	Robinson R44 Astro	0008	N2361V
D-HEOY	Eurocopter EC.135T1	0035	I-HEMS, D-HEC .
D-HEPP	Bell 212	30650	
D-HEPT	Aérospatiale AS.350BA Ecureuil	1237	F-WYMG, N36062

Reg	Type	C/n	Previous identities
D-HERA	Bell 47G-4A	3368	ZS-HDH, 5R-MDM, N1194W
D-HERI (2)	Aérospatiale AS.350B2 Ecureuil	2827	N60972
D-HERR(2)	Bell 47G-4A	6685	F-GEDY, C-FXFX, CF-XFX
D-HERZ	Bell 47G-2	1992	74+36, AS+395, YA+031, PA+120
D-HESK	Robinson R22B2 Beta	2844	
D-HEVY	Aérospatiale AS.350B Ecureuil	1684	SE-JBN, JA9352
D-HEWA	Robinson R44 Raven II	11775	OY-HJV
D-HEWR	Aérospatiale AS.350B Ecureuil	1789	(F-GJPS), D-HEWR
D-HEXE(6)	Robinson R44 Raven II	11711	F-GXRP
D-HFAL	Robinson R44 Astro	0014	OH-HHT, SE-JDG, N144CH
D-HFAX(2)	Aérospatiale AS.350B2 Ecureuil	2585	HB-XZJ, F-WYMG
D-HFAY	Bell 206B Jet Ranger II	2776	N250TV, N2766L
D-HFCA(3)	Robinson R44 Astro	0260	SE-JFF
D-HFCB(2)	Robinson R44 Astro	0135	
D-HFCC(2)	Robinson R44 Raven II	10022	
D-HFCD(2)	Robinson R22B2 Beta	3634	
D-HFCE(2)	Aérospatiale AS.350BA Ecureuil	1669	F-GEJB, (JA9342)
D-HFCH(2)	Robinson R44 Raven	1588	
D-HFCM(2)	Robinson R44 Raven II	11810	N912TP
D-HFCO(2)	Robinson R44 Raven II	11200	EI-LAJ, N989Y
D-HFCQ(2)	Robinson R44 Raven II	12845	
D-HFCR(2)	Robinson R44 Raven II	12145	N67SA
D-HFCU(2)	Robinson R44 Raven I	1607	EI-DRN
D-HFCV(2)	Robinson R44 Raven II	1730	EI-EXH
D-HFCW(2)	Robinson R44 Raven II	12829	D-HSAD, N4385S
D-HFCY(2)	Robinson R44 Raven I	2015	SP-RAV
D-HFCZ(2)	Robinson R44 Astro	0463	PH-WSW, OO-JSY, D-HIBB(2)
D-HFEF	Robinson R22HP	0073	HB-XLN
D-HFEG	Eurocopter EC.120B Colibri	1402	SP-KFI, I-NBLU, F-WQDA
D-HFEM	Aérospatiale AS.350B Ecureuil	1322	TF-SYR, TR-GRO, D-HKHL
D-HFHG(2)	Robinson R22 Beta II	4286	LZ-HAR, OE-XPO
D-HFHS(2)	Eurocopter EC.135T2+	0028	D-HECV, D-HFHS(2), D-HECA(7)
D-HFIN(2)	Enstrom F-28A	176	G-BBPO
D-HFIX	Aérospatiale AS.350B2 Ecureuil	9010	
D-HFJM	Ellisport CH-7 Kompress (P .05)	0030	
D-HFKG	Aérospatiale AS.365N2 Dauphin 2	6419	LN-OKM, C-FYQC, 5N-BJF, EP-HCJ, PH-FMB, OY-HRH, SE-JFH, (OY-HJP), SE-JFH, JA6675, F-WYMC
D-HFLI	Hughes 269C	110-0988	N1108W
D-HFLO(3)	Robinson R22B2 Beta	2661	D-HFRH
D-HFMW(2)	Agusta A.109A-II	7307	G-JLCY, N109AB
D-HFOG(2)	Aérospatiale AS.365N3 Dauphin 2	6356	I-PATE
D-HFSG(2)	Aérospatiale AS.365N3 Dauphin 2	6649	I-ADDV
D-HFSO	Robinson R22B2 Beta	2882	OE-XPK, N7118Z
D-HFTD	Aérospatiale AS.350SD2 Ecureuil	1707	OE-XWA, HB-ZDN, D-HEND, F-OJJJ, F-WQDO(4), F-GIZC, F-WYMZ, CS-HBP, JA9355
D-HFUX	Robinson R22 Beta	1058	N8045X
D-HFVP	Aérospatiale AS.365N3 Dauphin 2	6352	N79MD
D-HGAR	Agusta-Bell 206B Jet Ranger 3	8735	HB-XZB, I-ATEA, HB-XZB
D-HGAS	Robinson R44 Astro	0864	
D-HGBW	Huschle/ Canadian Home Rotors Safari (P .05)	001	
D-HGGE	Hughes 269C	126-0567	D-HAES, JA7607
D-HGHS	Bell 412HP	36055	ZK-IKA, JA6710, (JA6709), N6162C, C-FOPX, (C-GADL)
D-HGPP(3)	Bell 212	30807	P2-DFA, D-HGPP(1)
D-HGRU	Bell 407	54008	N410NX, C-GFCP(2), C-GADL
D-HGSR	MBB Bö.105	S-925	
D-HGVB	Robinson R44 Raven II	12958	PH-SBH, (PH-SHB), D-HGVW, G-CGGR
D-HGWD	Eurocopter EC.135P2+	0875	
D-HGYN(2)	Eurocopter EC.135P2	0303	
D-HGYR	Schuffenhauer Gyrocopter	SG-3	
D-HHAA(4)	Agusta-Bell 412	25802	SE-JIV, Swed.Army;11332
D-HHAE(2)	Bell 206B Jet Ranger II	3590	N86CH, N48PD, OB-1681
D-HHAG(2)	Robinson R44 Raven	0852	YR-REA
D-HHBE(2)	Robinson R44 Raven I	1296	G-CCWD
D-HHBG(2)	Eurocopter EC.135P2+	0568	
D-HHBP	Aérospatiale AS.350B1 Ecureuil	1973	
D-HHBW	MBB Bö.105	S-346	N6170K, XC-CAR, N46981, D-HDJX
D-HHCC(2)	Bell 412	36066	N6227S
D-HHCF	Eurocopter EC.135P3	1067	D-HECH
D-HHDM	Bell 412EP	36355	N7008Q
D-HHDR	Agusta A.109A II	7318	N738GH, OE-XFH, VH-AUG, ZK-HXI, N109BL
D-HHEA	MBB-Kawasaki BK.117C-2	9004	D-HMBO, D-HHEA, D-HMBI(3), D-HDMG(3)
D-HHEB	MBB-Kawasaki BK.117C-2	9070	D-HMBF(9)
D-HHEC	MBB-Kawasaki BK.117C-2	9081	D-HMBB
D-HHED	Robinson R44 Raven	0803	N214BC
D-HHEL	Eurocopter EC.120B Colibri	1477	G-DLRH, F-HFLB
D-HHEM	Robinson R22B2 Beta	3602	N7529H
D-HHFB	Hughes 269C	90-0971	OE-CXD, D-HLUX, N1104U
D-HHFF(5)	Aérospatiale AS.355F2 Ecureuil 2	5155	OE-XJF, D-HIRK, D-HEUH, F-WQDB, D-HEUH, G-BPRK, N361E
D-HHFS (2)	Bell 206B Jet Ranger III	2757	YR- . ., D-HHFS(2), G-SHJJ, N220PJ, N27676
D-HHFW	Bell 206B Jet Ranger III	4257	
D-HHGB	Aérospatiale AS.350B Ecureuil	1708	
D-HHGR	Robinson R44 Raven II	12129	
D-HHHE	Eurocopter EC.120B Colibri	1098	OE-XOO, D-HHSR, F-WQDJ
D-HHHH(3)	Agusta A.109S Grand	22117	
D-HHHS(3)	Robinson R44 Clipper II	12420	OY-HLJ
D-HHIT(2)	Eurocopter EC.135P2	0380	
D-HHJS	Robinson R44 Raven II	13115	
D-HHKW	Bell 206B Jet Ranger II	3651	(N206AJ), N202WW, N2289T
D-HHLA	Robinson R44 Astro	0079	
D-HHLL(3)	Agusta-Bell 47G-2A-1	1625	MM80437/EI-66
D-HHMB	Robinson R44 Raven	1432	
D-HHMH	AgustaWestland AW139	31567	I-EASR
D-HHMP(2)	Bell 206B Jet Ranger II	3823	
D-HHMS(3)	Bell 407	53763	N51689, C-FNGJ
D-HHMV	Aérospatiale AS.350BA Ecureuil	9029	

Registration	Type	c/n	Previous identities
D-HHMW	Weber Rotorway A600 Talon (P. 8.13)	8086	
D-HHNH	Sikorsky S-76B	760395	N57RD, N908GM, N5QZ, N1HE, N1WL
D-HHOL	Schweizer 269C	S-1452	
D-HHOT	Schweizer 269C	S-1450	
D-HHPP(3)	Bell 412	33105	VH-ZZV, G-CDAF, PK-HMS
D-HHPR	Hughes 369HS	11-0270S	(D-HHII), G-HUES, G-GASC, G-WELD, G-FROG, OO-KAR
D-HHRM	Hughes 369E	0357E	G-MLSN, G-HMAC, HB-XUO
D-HHRO	Robinson R44 Raven II	12470	
D-HHSA(2)	Robinson R22 Beta II	3132	N585AB
D-HHSB(3)	Enstrom F-28C Turbo Shark	431	OE-XAM, G-SHDD, G-BNBS, SE-HIL
D-HHSH(3)	AgustaWestland AW139	31587	
D-HHTE	Eurocopter EC.120B Colibri	1299	SP-GRB, LN-ODN, (D-HAEC), D-HAUK
D-HHTF	HTM FJ-Sky-Trac	14	
D-HHTJ	AgustaWestland AW169	69033	I-EASV
D-HHTM(2)	Agusta A.109E Power	11014	D-HARI(4), G-POWR, G-BXUD
D-HHTP	Agusta-Bell 206B Jet Ranger 2	8549	SE-HGK
D-HHTS	Eurocopter EC.135P2	0381	
D-HHUD	Bell 206B Jet Ranger II	2327	N65CW, N700WD
D-HHVV(4)	Bell 412HP	36082	HZ-RC05, A6-BAF, C-GFNL
D-HHVZ	Robinson R44 Raven II (P .07)	11742	
D-HHWE	Ewig/ Elisport CH-7 Angel	035/3514	
D-HHWF	Bell 206B Jet Ranger II	2530	N5008Z
D-HHWS	Hughes 269C	80-0028	
D-HHWW(2)	Aérospatiale AS.355F2 Ecureuil 2	5429	OE-FXH, (D-HOLT), OE-FXH
D-HHXH	AgustaWestland AW139	31704	I-EASH
D-HIBT	Robinson R44 Raven II NewsCopter	10016	I-TVNW
D-HICA(3)	Bell 47G-4A	7637	N14SP
D-HICE(2)	Westland-Bell 47G-3B-1	WA/327	XT168
D-HIFI(3)	Eurocopter EC.135T2+	0672	
D-HIIX	Aérospatiale AS.350Ecureuil	9005	
D-HIKE	Hughes 369E	0148E	VH-JBE, N5229J
D-HIKO(2)	Hughes 269C	26-0469	JA7585
D-HIKS(2)	Robinson R22 Beta	2219	
D-HILF(5)	MBB-Kawasaki BK.117B-2	7096	D-HMB. , PT-HJM, N118MB, D-HBPQ
D-HILL(3)	Robinson R44 Raven I	2372	
D-HILV(2)	Hughes 369E	0323E	HB-XVF, N16030
D-HIMB	MBB-Kawasaki BK.117B-2	7185	JY-ACC, D-HIMB, (N5406V), D-HIMB
D-HIMP(2)	Robinson R44 Astro	0335	
D-HIOU	Bell 47G-4	3347	N1217W, CF-SCF
D-HIPO(2)	Bell 47G-4A	7661	G-OIBC, G-FORE, N1415W
D-HIPP(3)	Bell 412EP	36305	XC-GEP, N1082P
D-HIPY(2)	Bell 206B Jet Ranger II	4186	
D-HIRL(2)	MBB-Kawasaki BK.117C-2 (Res 4.15)	9031	F-ZBPQ, D-HJFV
D-HISA	Schweizer 269C	S-1425	F-GKJM
D-HISF	Bell 407	53039	C-FZIY, N97PM, N1164Z
D-HITE	Eurocopter EC.120B Colibri	1276	SP-KKO, D-HITE, F-WQDB
D-HITT(2)	Robinson R44 Raven	0966	OE-XKT
D-HJAN(2)	Aérospatiale SA.365N Dauphin 2 (P. 9.13)	6063	(OM-. . .), F-GVIF, XU-009, N21277, JA6665, N7138H, VR-BLI, XT-BBG, XT-MAO, F-WKQI
D-HJDS	Aérospatiale AS.350BA Ecureuil	1395	F-GLFM, F-WZJD, SE-HRR, G-PDCC, G-PORR, F-WZFF
D-HJES	Schweizer 269C	S-1448	F-GGVJ, D-HGUS
D-HJET(2)	Bell 206B Jet Ranger II	3777	HB-XSB, N3181G
	(W/o 7.1.08, rebt with parts of SU-BOX c/n 3665)		
D-HJJJ(2)	MBB-Kawasaki BK.117B-2	7251	I-HBHC, D-HITZ
D-HJMD	Eurocopter EC.135P2	0463	
D-HJMR	Bell 407	53085	TC-H..
D-HJOH	Aérospatiale AS.365N3 Dauphin 2	6650	N234JL
D-HJOY(2)	Robinson R44 Raven	0781	SP-SBK, SP-GSK
D-HJPF	Schweizer 269C	S-1229	HB-XPT
D-HJPH	Robinson R44 Astro	0196	
D-HJPW	Schweizer 269C	S-1394	HB-XUQ
D-HJSG	Bell 407GX (Res 14.1.16)	54651	N600FB
D-HJTS	Robinson R22 Beta	1867	OO-RJP, (OO-HIP), N4063C
D-HJUH	Aérospatiale AS.365N2 Dauphin 2	6131	G-BLEZ
D-HKAA(3)	Robinson R44 Raven II	11680	G-CEKX
D-HKAR	Robinson R44 Raven II	13211	G-MEHR
D-HKDV	Eurocopter EC.120B Colibri	1397	N526AG, (N313PM), N526AG, F-WWXK
D-HKEM(2)	Bell 47G-4A /Soloy	7635	N605
D-HKGD	Eurocopter EC.135P2+	1036	PH-FRL, D-HKGD
D-HKIS(2)	Rotorway Exec 162F	4125	
D-HKIT	Hughes 269C	77-0615	OY-HDR, D-HKIT, SE-HHK
D-HKIX	Aérospatiale AS.350B3 Ecureuil	7368	LN-OCN, F-WWXR
D-HKKO	Eurocopter EC.130B4 Ecureuil	7080	SP-RMR, SP-WIL
D-HKLE	Eurocopter EC.120B Colibri	1107	F-GSLH, HB-ZCK, F-WQDR
D-HKMB	Aérospatiale AS.350B3 Ecureuil	7682	F-WWXQ
D-HKMC	Aérospatiale AS.350B3 Ecureuil	3222	
D-HKMG	Aérospatiale AS.350BA Ecureuil	2650	
D-HKMM	Eurocopter EC.120B Colibri	1217	
D-HKMO	Aérospatiale AS.355N Ecureuil 2	5572	G-VONE, G-LCON
D-HKMS	Robinson R44 Raven II	11668	G-PYPA
D-HKMT	Aérospatiale AS.350B2 Ecureuil	9044	OH-HWI
D-HKTG	Agusta A.109S Grand	22047	N109GH, EI-NBG
D-HKUE	Eurocopter EC.135P2+	0527	
D-HKUP	Robinson R44 Clipper II	11450	
D-HLAA	MBB Bö.105C	S-266	RNethAF B-66, D-HDHZ(1)
D-HLCC	Agusta A.109A-II	7387	EI-ECA, N109RP, JA9662
D-HLCK	Eurocopter EC.135P2+	1003	
D-HLDM	Eurocopter EC.135P2	0392	
D-HLEA(2)	Aérospatiale AS.355F2 Ecureuil 2	5378	F-GTVE, DQ-FGH, F-WYMT
D-HLFM	Schweizer 269C	S-1748	
D-HLFR	Eurocopter EC.135P2	0447	
D-HLGB	Eurocopter EC.135P2	0488	

Registration	Type	c/n	Previous identities
D-HLGM(6)	Aérospatiale AS.355F2 Ecureuil 2	5439	G-CCWK, (LN-OES), N8066G, LN-OES, F-GGRS
D-HLIR	MBB-Kawasaki BK.117C-1	7500	I-HECD, D-HECD
D-HLIX	Aérospatiale AS.350BA Ecureuil	1525	F-GBMR
D-HLKB	Bell 206B Jet Ranger II	4209	
D-HLLL(2)	MBB Bö.105	S-875	N4345F, D-HMBM(2), (D-HSNG)
D-HLRG(2)	MBB-Kawasaki BK.117C-2	9029	
D-HLRZ	Eurocopter EC.155B Dauphin	6545	
D-HLTA	Eurocopter EC.155B Dauphin	6546	
D-HLTC	Eurocopter EC.155B Dauphin	6547	
D-HLTD(2)	Eurocopter EC.155B Dauphin	6558	
D-HLTE	Eurocopter EC.155B Dauphin	6559	
D-HLTF	Eurocopter EC.155B Dauphin	6562	
D-HLTG	Eurocopter EC.155B Dauphin	6569	F-WQDV
D-HLTH(2)	Eurocopter EC.155B Dauphin	6544	F-WQDA
D-HLTI (2)	Eurocopter EC.155B Dauphin	6576	
D-HLTJ(2)	Eurocopter EC.155B Dauphin	6577	F-WQDY
D-HLTK(2)	Eurocopter EC.155B Dauphin	6595	F-WQDT
D-HLTL	Eurocopter EC.155B Dauphin	6599	
D-HLTN	Eurocopter EC.155B1 Dauphin	6659	F-WWOE
D-HLTO	Eurocopter EC.155B1 Dauphin	6663	F-WWOV
D-HLTP	Eurocopter EC.155B1 Dauphin	6896	
D-HLTQ	Eurocopter EC.155B1 Dauphin	6920	F-WMXJ
D-HLTR	Eurocopter EC.155B1 Dauphin	6940	F-WMXK
D-HLTS	Eurocopter EC.155B1 Dauphin	6945	
D-HLTT	Eurocopter EC.155B1 Dauphin	6947	F-ZWBA
D-HMAX(4)	Robinson R44 Raven I	1850	N4148J
D-HMBA to HMBZ	Test registrations for Eurocopter Deutschland BK-117 production		
D-HMCD(2)	Bell 206B Jet Ranger II (Res .16)	2967	OE-XMD, D-HIEV, N2JC, N5434M
D-HMCP(2)	Schweizer 269C	S-1678	SP-FEM, D-HUFR, N69A
D-HMCR	Robinson R44 Raven II	12531	HB-ZPC, I-MGMG, N4181K
D-HMDR	MBB-Kawasaki BK.117B-2	7045	D-HMBD(3), D-HBKM(2), D-HBMT
D-HMDX(2)	McDonnell-Douglas MD-900 Explorer	00036	N9198Y
D-HMEB(2)	Robinson R44 Raven II	11818	N3033U
D-HMEG	Aérospatiale AS.350B2 Ecureuil (Soloy)	3066	OM-SIF, F-WPDS
D-HMEI	Bell 206B Jet Ranger II	2550	
D-HMGD	Hughes 369E	0556E	SE-JKL, N70526
D-HMGX	Sikorsky S-76C	760710	N2540D
D-HMIA(4)	Robinson R44 Raven II	13649	
D-HMIK	Hughes 369D	127-0251D	CS-HCX, D-HMIK, C-GSZV
D-HMIM	Schweizer 269C	S-1637	N86G
D-HMIT	Agusta-Bell 206A Jet Ranger 2	8256	F-GBRE, 3A-MCC, F-BSEG
D-HMKI	Eurocopter EC.120B Colibri	1190	
D-HMMC	Robinson R44 Raven II	11830	N44NR
D-HMMM(2)	MBB-Kawasaki BK.117B-2	7228	SE-JBC, D-HMBN(7), (D-HFDS)
D-HMMO	Robinson R44 Raven II	12846	
D-HMMW	Aérospatiale AS.350B2 Ecureuil	2727	F-WYMT
D-HMOH	Robinson R44 Raven II	12741	
D-HMOT(2)	Bell 206B Jet Ranger II	3947	
D-HMPJ	Robinson R22 Beta II	2476	N220WH
D-HMRA(2)	Aérospatiale AS.350B3 Ecureuil	4596	D-HMWS, F-WJXF
D-HMSB	Eurocopter EC.120B Colibri	1359	
D-HMSH	Robinson R44 Raven II	13160	
D-HMST	Hughes 369E	0282E	HB-XTI, N520WH, HB-XTI
D-HMTA(2)	Hughes 269C	120-1011	I-FVPD, N1107U
D-HMUG	MBB Bö.105C	S-121	D-HDDM, (D-HDDN)
D-HMVA	Eurocopter EC.135P1	0046	
D-HMVP	Eurocopter EC.135P2/CPDS	0030	D-HECM, F-WQEX, D-HETZ, D-HEC .
D-HMWP	Robinson R22B Beta	0686	
D-HNAH(2)	Robinson R44 Astro	0244	
D-HNAS	Robinson R44 Raven	1028	
D-HNCF	Henseleit /Elisport CH-7 Angel	007	D-HJAN
D-HNDL	Sikorsky S-76C	760437	N1055, HL9211
D-HNEL	Robinson R44 Raven II	12132	
D-HNEO	Jung Neo TwinChopper (Res .11; ff 31.10.11)	3520	
D-HNFC(3)	Fröhlich/ Heli-Sport CH-7 Kompress	0029	
D-HNFO	Molderings/ Elisport CH-7 Angel	094	D-HWMO
D-HNHA	Aérospatiale AS.365N3 Dauphin 2	6699	I-LOBE, (F-HELP), I-LOBE, F-WWOA, F-WQDK
D-HNHC	Aérospatiale SA.365C3 Dauphin 2	5017	EC-IEL, F-GHXF, F-ODJL, F-ODJL, F-GBGV, F-WTNW
		(F-GFIA), LV-BLA,	
D-HNNN(3)	MBB-Kawasaki BK.117B-2	7008	OE-XAS, D-HDDD, PK-NZH, (N39186), D-HBKJ
D-HNOF	Fröhlich/ Elisport CH-7 Angel	A068	
D-HNOW	Eurocopter EC.130B4 Ecureuil	3974	SP-NOW, JA130N, F-WQDC
D-HNPV	Agusta-Bell 206B Jet Ranger 2	8379	(D-HNPW), OE-XWW, D-HBLK
D-HNTE	Heli-Sport CH-7 Kompress	0028	
D-HNWA	MBB Bö.105S	S-398	D-HDLN
D-HNWE	MBB Bö.105S	S-456	D-HDNJ
D-HNWK	MBB-Kawasaki BK.117B-2	7200	(D-HIMQ)
D-HNWL	MBB-Kawasaki BK.117B-2	7212	(D-HFDC)
D-HNWM(2)	Eurocopter EC.155B Dauphin	6613	F-WQDN
D-HNWN	Eurocopter EC.155B Dauphin	6643	F-WQDY, F-WWOO
D-HNWO	MBB-Kawasaki BK.117C-1	7552	
D-HNWP	MBB-Kawasaki BK.117C-1	7553	
D-HNWQ	MBB-Kawasaki BK.117C-1	7554	D-HMBU, D-HNWQ
D-HNWR	Eurocopter EC.145T2 (BK.117D-2)	20071	D-HADY(4)
D-HNWS(3)	Eurocopter EC.145T2 (BK.117D-2)	20085	D-HADP(7)
D-HNWT	Eurocopter EC.145T2 (BK.117D-2) (Res 12.15)	20107	
D-HNWU	Eurocopter EC.145T2 (BK.117D-2) (Res 6.7.16)	20134	
D-HNWV	Eurocopter EC.145T2 (BK.117D-2) (Res 6.7.16)	20140	
D-HNWW	Eurocopter EC.145T2 (BK.117D-2) (Res 6.7.16)	20144	
D-HOAB	AgustaWestland AW139	31129	OY-HSN, D-HOAB, OY-HSN, I-EASY, (OH-HCR)
D-HOAC	AgustaWestland AW139	31424	I-AWTF, I-EAST
D-HOAD(2)	AgustaWestland AW139	41501	OY-HFP, (D-HOAD(2)), N268MM
D-HOAR	Aérospatiale AS.365N2 Dauphin 2	6446	LN-OCM(3), 5N-BJE, EP-HCK, 5N-BBR, OY-HMY, F-WYMN

Registration	Type	C/n	Previous/Notes
D-HOBB(3)	Bell 206B Jet Ranger II		"007"
D-HOBO(4)	Guimbal G2 Cabri	1030	
D-HOBS(3)	Hughes 269C	128-0755	SpAF HE.20-16/"78-45"
D-HOBV	Agusta A.109E Power	11146	
D-HOBY(2)	Hughes 369D	107-0215D	VH-HRJ, N8689F
D-HOCH(3)	Agusta-Bell 206B Jet Ranger 2	8405	SP-GAZ, D-HOCH(3), G-BHSM, EI-BHE, OO-MHS, F-BVEM
D-HOED	Agusta-Bell 47G-2	259	74+17, AS+059
D-HOEM	Eurocopter EC.135P2	0238	
D-HOFF(2)	Eurocopter EC.135P2	0260	
D-HOGE	Robinson R44 Raven II	10588	OO-KNC, D-HALN(2)
D-HOHL	Hughes 269C	88-0706	SpAF HE.20-09/"78-38"
D-HOHM	Robinson R44 Raven II	12680	OY-HEU
D-HOHO(2)	McDonnell-Douglas 369E	0240E	N1603L
D-HOLA	Enstrom F-28A-D	184	
D-HOLM(2)	Hughes 269C	98-0726	SpAF HE.20-04/"78-33"
D-HOLY(2)	Bell 206L-4 Long Ranger IV	52039	N206RT
D-HOLZ(2)	Hughes 369E	0146E	SE-HNT, LN-OUT, SE-HNT, LN-OMY, SE-HNT
D-HOME(4)	Hughes 369D	129-0628D	F-GFII, N58357
D-HONE(2)	Eurocopter EC.135P2	0338	
D-HONY(3)	Bell 206B Jet Ranger III	4256	OE-XCC
D-HOON	Agusta-Bell 206B Jet Ranger 2	8597	
D-HOPI(2)	Eurocopter EC.135P2	0323	
D-HOPP(3)	Bell 206A Jet Ranger	42	OE-DXM, D-HEAS(1), N9B
D-HORG	Agusta-Bell 206B Jet Ranger 2	8375	G-BBXN, HP-634, G-BBXN
D-HORS	Robinson R44 Raven II	10582	N74493
D-HOSB(2)	Sikorsky S-76A	760191	N15XW, D-HOSB(2)
D-HOSC(2)	Sikorsky S-76B	760391	N471NB, (N15NJ), N8NJ, N90151, G-HARH
D-HOSE(4)	Schweizer 269C-1	0047	
D-HOSF	Sikorsky S-76B	760413	N5006B
D-HOTT(2)	Bell 206L-3 Long Ranger III	51587	C-FNOQ
D-HOUV	Huschle/ Elisport CH-7 Angel	3511	
D-HOVY	Robinson R44 Raven I	2056	
D-HPEP	Robinson R22 Beta	2327	
D-HPET	Hughes 369D	37-0095D	OE-KXL, D-HMOL(1), C-GYUA
D-HPFA	Robinson R44 Astro	0096	
D-HPHP	Robinson R44 Raven II	13284	
D-HPIP	Robinson R22 Beta	2352	
D-HPIX	Aérospatiale AS.350B3 Ecureuil	3789	
D-HPMM	Eurocopter EC.135P2	0242	D-HECA
D-HPNA	McDonnell-Douglas MD-900 Explorer	00059	N9223K
D-HPNC	McDonnell-Douglas MD-900 Explorer	00062	N3064K
D-HPNE	Eurocopter EC.135P2+	1183	D-HCBK(7)
D-HPNF	Eurocopter EC.135P2+	1191	D-HCBF(8)
D-HQIX	Aérospatiale AS.350B3 Ecureuil	3479	
D-HQQQ(2)	MBB-Kawasaki BK.117B-2	7071	PT-YMD, D-HECC, SE-JBG, D-HMBG(1), N117VB, N117VU, N953MB, (N971US), N953MB, D-HBNS
D-HRAC	Eurocopter EC.135P2+	1047	
D-HRAD	Robinson R22 Beta II	3639	OE-XPH
D-HRAV	Robinson R44 Astro	0741	N7187H
D-HRBD	Robinson R66	0643	
D-HRED	Elisport CH-7 Angel	0052	
D-HRFA	Agusta-Bell 206B Jet Ranger 2	8693	F-GHDR
D-HRFF	Robinson R44 Raven II	13841	
D-HRFJ	Bell 206B Jet Ranger III	4440	OE-BXO(2), C-GLZU
D-HRGG	Robinson R66	0561	
D-HRGR	Eurocopter EC.135P2+	0893	D-HCBA
D-HRIC(2)	Schweizer 269C	S-1802	N41S
D-HRIK	Eurocopter EC.120B Colibri	1038	HB- . . . , D-HMHR, (VT-CHN)
D-HRIT	Schweizer 269C (Accident 26.8.02, current)	S-1799	N41S
D-HROB	Robinson R44 Raven	1465	
D-HROY	Robinson R44 Astro	0487	
D-HRPA	Eurocopter EC.135P2	0230	D-HECH
D-HRPB	Eurocopter EC.135P2	0318	
D-HRRR	Robinson R22 Beta	0754	G-MUSI
D-HRTA(2)	Eurocopter EC.135T3 (Res 24.8.16)	2017	
D-HRTB	Eurocopter EC.135T3 (Res 28.9.16)	2019	
D-HRUT	Schweizer 269C	S-1533	N69A
D-HRWI	Warnholz/ Elisport CH-7 Angel	CH-042	
D-HRWW	Wittman/ Elisport CH-7 Angel	A-141	
D-HRZZ	Robinson R22 Beta	2115	OH-HPH, OK-XIA
D-HSAA	Eurocopter EC.145T2 (BK.117D-2) (Res 12.15)	20127	
D-HSAB	MBB MBB Bö.105S	S-873	(D-HFNE)
D-HSAN(2)	Eurocopter EC.135P2	0276	
D-HSAS	MBB-Kawasaki BK.117B-2	7241	N3176Q, D-HMBO(2), D-HFIF
D-HSAT	MBB-Kawasaki BK.117B-2	7233	(D-HFDX)
D-HSCH	MBB Bö.105CBS-5	S-924	D-HGSQ
D-HSDM	MBB Bö.105C	S-126	D-HAYA, D-HDDS
D-HSEA	Schweizer 269C	S-1681	N69A
D-HSEP	Schweizer 269C	S-1451	F-GKAI, D-HLEX, N41S
D-HSFB	MBB-Kawasaki BK.117B-2	7240	D-HFIE
D-HSFF	Agusta-Bell 206B-1 Jet Ranger	9010	I-AGUN
D-HSGW	Eurocopter EC.120B Colibri	1604	
D-HSHB	Eurocopter EC.120B Colibri (Dam 29.1.08)	1514	
D-HSHC	Eurocopter EC.120B Colibri	1515	
D-HSHD	Eurocopter EC.120B Colibri	1527	
D-HSHE	Eurocopter EC.120B Colibri	1528	
D-HSHP	Eurocopter EC.135P2+	1014	D-HCBW(3)
D-HSHS	Eurocopter EC.120B Colibri	1500	
D-HSIX	Aérospatiale AS.350B3 Ecureuil	4811	
D-HSKG	Robinson R44 Raven II	12467	
D-HSKM	Agusta A.109S Grand	22101	
D-HSKY	Bell 407	53109	
D-HSLD	Agusta-Bell 204B	3031	N204NM, MM80285
D-HSMA	MBB-Kawasaki BK.117C-2	7073	XA-TRF, D-HMBJ, PT-HZM, CC-CSW, N12851, C-GJLE, D-HBNU
D-HSNC(2)	Eurocopter EC.135T2	0092	
D-HSND(2)	Eurocopter EC.135T2	0492	
D-HSNE(2)	Eurocopter EC.135T2+	1061	D-HCBY
D-HSOF	Aérospatiale AS.350B Ecureuil	1174	F-GJAB, N3599U
D-HSPA	Schweizer 269C (HKP 5B)	S-1189	Swed.Army : 05234
D-HSPE	Hughes 269C (HKP 5B)	31-1040	Swed.Army : 05230, SE-HKZ, N1099D
D-HSPH(2)	Robinson R66	0564	
D-HSPJ	Schweizer 269C (HKP 5B) (Cancelled and reserved .11)	S-1256	Swed.Army : 05239
D-HSPK	Schweizer 269C (HKP 5B)	S-1167	Swed.Army : 05231
D-HSPM	Hughes 269C (HKP 5B)	61-1053	Swed.Army : 05226, SE-HLO
D-HSPR(2)	Robinson R44 Clipper II	11378	G-XELA
D-HSPS	Hughes 269C (HKP 5B)	71-1069	Swed.Army : 05227, SE-HLU
D-HSPT	Schweizer 269C (HKP 5B)	S-1219	Swed.Army : 05238
D-HSPU	Schweizer 269C (HKP 5B)	S-1188	Swed.Army : 05233
D-HSPV	Schweizer 269C (HKP 5B)	S-1267	Swed.Army : 05242
D-HSTA	Bell 206B Jet Ranger II	2567	F-GJFV, N501WN, N5010N
D-HSUN(2)	Eurocopter EC.120B Colibri	1272	
D-HSWG	Eurocopter EC.135P2	0481	
D-HSYG	Gebel / Rotorway Exec 90 (Permit)	GE01 / 3508	
D-HTAC(3)	Guimbal G2 Cabri	1123	
D-HTAM	Guimbal G2 Cabri	1047	
D-HTAN	Guimbal G2 Cabri	1100	
D-HTAR	Agusta A.109S Grand	22065	N109GH, I-RMRM
D-HTAT	Guimbal G2 Cabri	1048	
D-HTAX	Guimbal G2 Cabri	1148	F-WWHX
D-HTCH	Robinson R22 Beta	2328	(D-HKAI), N2361K
D-HTCL	MBB-Kawasaki BK.117C-2 (EC.145)	9355	D-HMBO(17)
D-HTDM	MBB Bö.105C	S-140	D-HAYE, (D-HDEH)
D-HTEN	Bell 222UT	47549	EC-LHK, D-HTEN, OM- . . ., D-HTEN, LV- . . ., D-HTEN, JA9628
D-HTHA	MBB Bö.105S	S-858	(D-HFHP)
D-HTHC(2)	MBB-Kawasaki BK.117C-2	9117	D-HMBP
D-HTIK	Robinson R22 Beta	2135	
D-HTMA	Eurocopter EC.135P2+	0786	D-HECX
D-HTMB	Eurocopter EC.135P2	0060	D-HBYC
D-HTMC	Eurocopter EC.135P2	0096	D-HBYI(2)
D-HTMD	Eurocopter EC.135P2	0439	D-HAAT, OH-HMK
D-HTME	McDonnell-Douglas 369E	0479E	
D-HTMF	Eurocopter EC.135T3	1161	D-HECJ(25)
D-HTMG	Eurocopter EC.135P2+	0240	SE-HPX, D-HECA(18)
D-HTMH	Eurocopter EC.135P2+	0225	SE-HPU, D-HECH(7), D-HECN(9)
D-HTMI	Eurocopter EC.135P2+	0282	SE-HPZ, D-HECL(8)
D-HTMJ	Eurocopter EC.135P2+ (Res 11.15)	0237	SE-HPV, D-HECJ(9)
D-HTMK	Eurocopter EC.135P2+ (Res 11.15)	0265	SE-HPY, D-HECF(10)
D-HTML	Eurocopter EC.135P2+ (Res 11.15)	0207	SE-HPT, D-HECQ(2)
D-HTMM	Mahle/ Rotorway Exec 162F	7066	
D-HTOM	Bell 206B Jet Ranger II	2434	N4811E, PT-HPJ, N5002K
D-HTON	Eurocopter EC.225LP (P. 12/15)	2957	(PR-OTD)
D-HTOY	Guimbal G2 Cabri	1019	
D-HTPN	Eurocopter EC.225LP Super Puma II	2916	
D-HTPO	Eurocopter EC.225LP Super Puma II (Res 3.16)	2977	
D-HTPP	Eurocopter EC.225LP Super Puma II (Res 3.16)	2992	

D-HTSE to HTSZ *Test registrations for Eurocopter Deutschland EC-135 export production*

Registration	Type	C/n	Previous/Notes
D-HTTT	MBB-Kawasaki BK.117B-2	7246	D-HFIK
D-HTVU	Robinson R22 Beta	1937	G-BTVU
D-HTWO	Eurocopter EC.135P2	0343	D-HECN(11)
D-HUAB	MBB Bö.105C (Reservation)	S-203	D-HDFH(2), 98+25, D-HDFH(2)
D-HUAC	MBB Bö.105C (Reservation)	S-204	D-HDFS(2), 98+26, D-HDFS(2)
D-HUAH	Robinson R44 Astro	0279	
D-HUBA	Enstrom F-28A	281	G-BZHI, G-BPOZ, N246Q
D-HUBI(3)	Robinson R44 Astro (Res .16)	0725	LN-OGD, OH-HTH, FLARF 02748, N71877
D-HUBU	Revolution Mini-500	340	
D-HUBY(2)	Robinson R44 Raven	0988	
D-HUDM	MBB Bö.105S	S-883	D-HUBE, D-HMBT(2), D-HFNO
D-HUGO(3)	Sikorsky S-76C	760471	N165ML
D-HUKI	Robinson R22 Beta	2183	N2342W
D-HULI	Robinson R22 Beta	1879	
D-HULK	Sikorsky S-76A+	760282	SE-JUZ, N92RR, N92RP, N63WW
D-HUMS	MBB-Kawasaki BK.117C-2 (P. 9.15)	9021	F-ZBPL, D-HAAF, F-ZBPL, D-HMBQ, F-ZBPL, D-HJFP
D-HUND	Robinson R44 Astro	0126	
D-HUNT	Eurocopter EC.120B Colibri	1542	HB-ZJT
D-HUTE(2)	McDonnell-Douglas 369E	0203E	HA-MSB
D-HUTH	Eurocopter EC.135P2+	1000	D-HECD
D-HUTT	Robinson R44 Raven I	1462	OO-KKA
D-HVBA	Eurocopter EC.135T2+	0145	
D-HVBB	Eurocopter EC.135T1 (Crashed 25.2.16)	0146	
D-HVBC	Eurocopter EC.135T2+	0148	
D-HVBD	Eurocopter EC.135T2+	0150	D-HECW
D-HVBE	Eurocopter EC.135T1	0152	
D-HVBF	Eurocopter EC.135T1	0171	
D-HVBG	Eurocopter EC.135T2	0176	
D-HVBH	Eurocopter EC.135T1	0121	
D-HVBI	Eurocopter EC.135T1	0177	
D-HVBJ	Eurocopter EC.135T1	0211	
D-HVBK	Eurocopter EC.135T2+	0217	D-HTSJ, D-HVBK
D-HVBL	Eurocopter EC.135T2+	0256	
D-HVBM	Eurocopter EC.135T2+	0258	
D-HVBN	Eurocopter EC.135T2+	0261	
D-HVBO	Eurocopter EC.135T2+	0263	D-HTSH(2)
D-HVBP	Eurocopter EC.135T2+	0264	
D-HVBQ	Eurocopter EC.135T2+	0266	
D-HVBR	Eurocopter EC.135T2	0286	
D-HVBS	Eurocopter EC.135T2	0295	
D-HVBT	Eurocopter EC.135T2	0299	
D-HVBU	Eurocopter EC.135T2	0301	
D-HVBV	Eurocopter EC.135T2	0304	
D-HVBW	Eurocopter EC.135T2	0342	
D-HVBX	Eurocopter EC.135T2	0349	D-HECP(8)
D-HVBY	Eurocopter EC.135T2	0353	
D-HVIA	Aérospatiale AS.350BA Ecureuil	2551	G-PTFL, CS-HCP, F-WYMX
D-HVIC	Schweizer S.269C	S-1526	OO-HBM, D-HSPH

Registration	Type	C/N	Previous identities
D-HVIP(4)	Eurocopter EC.120B Colibri	1513	(D-HSHA), F-WWPR
D-HVWF	Horstmann/ Rotorway Exec 162F	6160	
D-HWAL(3)	Agusta-Bell 47G-4A	2519	G-BYCH, EC-BMB, EC-WMB, MM80504
	(P. 5.06)		
	(Rebuild using parts of c/n WA/719 ex D-HWAL(2), G-AXKN)		
D-HWBW	Wolf/ Rotorway Exec 90	5240	HB-YGR
D-HWEC	Agusta-Bell 206B Jet Ranger 2	8364	HB-XPA, D-HDIX(3), D-HDCS(3), HB-XPA, D-HHRT
D-HWEG	Aérospatiale AS.350B2 Ecureuil	9035	N130WE
D-HWEH	Weh/ Rotorway Exec 162F	6975	
D-HWFH	Eurocopter EC.135P2	0277	
D-HWFW	Bell 206B Jet Ranger II	4159	HB-XYF
D-HWIN	Hughes 269C	96-0542	F-GMIK, D-HGIS, SE-HNX, LN-OTX, SE-HNX, PH-HGH, N5083U, C-GGAN, N7426F
D-HWIT	Robinson R44 Astro	0147	
D-HWJW(2)	Wilkenloh/ Rotorway Exec 162F	6904	
	(P. 12.05; replaces c/n 96-01/16214 wfu)		
D-HWLL	Bell 206B Jet Ranger II	2359	N119AJ
D-HWOW	Robinson R44 Raven I	2219	
D-HWPY	Bell 206L-3 Long Ranger III	51491	N600TH, N4309M
D-HWVS	MBB-Kawasaki BK.117C-1 (EC.145)	9027	D-HMBX
D-HWWG(2)	Robinson R44 Raven II	12148	EI-DZG. N90815
D-HWWW	MBB-Kawasaki BK.117B-2	7248	D-HFIM
D-HXAB	Eurocopter EC.135P2+	1126	D-HECD
D-HXAC	Eurocopter EC.135P2+	1135	
D-HXAD	Eurocopter EC.135P2+	1138	
D-HXBA	Eurocopter EC.135P3/CPDS	1178	D-HECD
D-HXBB	Eurocopter EC.135P3/CPDS	1188	D-HECB
D-HXBC	Eurocopter EC.135P3/CPDS	1194	D-HCBE
D-HXGW	Rotorway Exec 162F	3003543	
D-HXKA	Aérospatiale AS.350B3 Ecureuil	7515	HB-ZPD
	(Res 17.3.16)		
D-HXRE	Agusta-Bell 206B-3 Jet Ranger III	8716	G-OMEC, G-OBLD
D-HXXL(3)	Bell 206B Jet Ranger III	4024	TC-HCC, C-FCYG
D-HXXR	Robinson R44 Raven II	10874	
D-HXXX	McDonnell-Douglas 369E	0322E	G-TUBE
D-HXYZ	Robinson R44 Raven II	11864	G-CEUX
D-HYAC	Eurocopter EC.145T2 (BK.117D-2)	20018	D-HCBP(5)
D-HYAE	Eurocopter EC.145T2 (BK.117D-2)	20035	D-HADU(3)
D-HYAF	Eurocopter EC.145T2 (BK.117D-2)	20043	D-HADJ(5)
D-HYAG	Eurocopter EC.145T2 (BK.117D-2)	20054	D-HMBF(21)
D-HYAH	Eurocopter EC.145T2 (BK.117D-2)	20079	D-HADC(13)
D-HYAI	Eurocopter EC.145T2 (BK.117D-2)	20082	D-HCBV(7)
D-HYAJ	Eurocopter EC.145T2 (BK.117D-2)	20103	
D-HYAK	Eurocopter EC.145T2 (BK.117D-2)	20121	
	(Res 9.8.16)		
D-HYAL	Eurocopter EC.145T2 (BK.117D-2)	20131	
	(Res 9.8.16)		
D-HYAM	Eurocopter EC.145T2 (BK.117D-2)	20142	
	(Res 16.8.16)		
D-HYES	Robinson R22 Beta	2167	
D-HYNO	Robinson R22 Beta	1707	N1707R, (D-H . . .), OY-HFH
D-HYPE	Robinson R44 Raven	0980	G-CRIB, G-JJWL
D-HYYY(2)	Eurocopter EC.135P2+	1030	
D-HZAR	Robinson R44 Raven I	2364	
D-HZIK	Robinson R22B2 Beta	2853	
D-HZSA	Eurocopter EC.135T2+	0508	D-HECC(13)
D-HZSB	Eurocopter EC.135T2+	0542	D-HECR(6)
D-HZSC	Eurocopter EC.135T2+	0549	D-HECH(18)
D-HZSD	Eurocopter EC.135T2+	0553	D-HECW(5)
D-HZSE	Eurocopter EC.135T2+	0558	D-HECH(19), D-HECJ(16)
D-HZSF	Eurocopter EC.135T2+	0560	
D-HZSG	Eurocopter EC.135T2+	0592	D-HTSF(4)
D-HZSH	Eurocopter EC.135T2+	0506	D-HECG(13)
D-HZSI	Eurocopter EC.135T2+	0594	D-HECJ(17)
D-HZSJ	Eurocopter EC.135T2+	0603	D-HECN(16)
D-HZSK	Eurocopter EC.135T2+	0617	D-HECD(5)
D-HZSL	Eurocopter EC.135T2+	0619	D-HECT(5)
D-HZSM	Eurocopter EC.135T2+	0621	D-HECU(15)
D-HZSN	Eurocopter EC.135T2+	0629	
D-HZSO	Eurocopter EC.135T2+	0644	D-HECR(9)
D-HZSP	Eurocopter EC.135T2+	0648	D-HECN(18)
D-HZXA	MBB Bö.105M	5016	80+16
D-HZXB	MBB Bö.105M	5074	80+74
D-HZXD	MBB Bö.105M	5025	80+25
D-HZXF	MBB Bö.105M	5057	80+57
D-HZXI	MBB Bö.105M	5014	80+14
D-HZYD(2)	MBB Bö.105M	5005	80+05
D-HZYE(2)	MBB Bö.105M	5054	80+54
D-HZYF(2)	MBB Bö.105M	5079	80+79
D-HZYG(2)	MBB Bö.105M	5091	80+91
D-HZYH(2)	MBB Bö.105M	5088	80+88
D-HZYI(2)	MBB Bö.105M	5090	80+90
D-HZYP	MBB Bö.105M	5041	80+41
D-HZYS	MBB Bö.105M	5056	80+56
D-HZYT	MBB Bö.105M	5060	80+60
D-HZYU	MBB Bö.105M	5037	80+37
D-HZYV	MBB Bö.105M	5095	80+95
D-HZYW	MBB Bö.105M	5053	80+53
D-HZYZ	MBB Bö.105M	5072	80+72
D-HZZZ	Robinson R22 Beta	2040	N2322B
D-H . . .	Aérospatiale AS.355N Ecureuil 2	5646	F-GSKI, SX-HEO, VP-B . ., F-GTJE
D-H . . .	Bell OH-58B	42156	N47VS, 73-21890
D-H . . .	Bell 412	33034	VH-UAH(2), N2141B
D-H . . .	Enstrom 280FX Shark	2082	G-HYST
D-H . . .	Eurocopter EC.635T2+	0858	ZS-RSN(2), YI-293, ZS-RSN(2), D-HCBU(2)
D-H . . .	Fussl Scorpion	1	N2232Y
D-H . . .	Hughes 269B	64-0111	N234JH, C-FRQA, CF-RQA
D-H . . .	MBB Bö.105DBS-4	S-416	G-NAAB, D-HDMO, D-HSTP, D-HDMO
D-H . . .	MBB Bö.105CBS	S-587	N26SE, N2909L, D-HDQJ(2)
D-H . . .	MBB Bö.105S	S-859	N3071K, D-HMBQ, D-HFHQ
D-H . . .	Robinson R22HP	0218	G-RALD, G-CHIL, (G-BMXI), N9074K
D-H . . .	Robinson R22 Beta	0769	F-GFEH
D-H . . .	Robinson R22 Beta	1379	F-GPCL, G-BSIN, N4015H
D-H . . .	Robinson R22 Beta II	4421	LN-OTB(5), OE-XRA(2)
D-H . . .	Robinson R44 Astro	0478	SE-JKX, G-TAND
D-H . . .	Robinson R44 Raven	0959	G-JILY
D-H . . .	Robinson R44 Raven	1232	G-LOTA
D-H . . .	Robinson R44 Raven	1302	F-GXRF, N71958
D-H . . .	Rotorway Exec 90	5118	G-CHTG, G-BVAJ
D-H . . .	Rotorway Exec 162F	6285	N728BG

CLASS I : Twin-Engined Aircraft of 2 to 5.7 Metric Tonnes

Registration	Type	C/N	Previous identities
D-IAAA(2)	Piper Aerostar 601P	62P-0924-8165048	N6896X
D-IAAB(3)	Embraer EMB-500 Phenom 100	50000180	N720MV, OE-FTF, PT-FYB
	(Res 29.8.16)		
D-IAAC	Cessna 441 Conquest II	441-0073	N88834
D-IAAD(3)	Embraer EMB-500 Phenom 100	50000215	PT-PYI
D-IAAE(3)	Piper PA-42-720 Cheyenne IIIA	42-5501047	I-TRER
D-IAAH(2)	Beech C90A King Air	LJ-1247	N5651J
D-IAAP	Cessna Turbo 310R	310R1348	(N3999A)
D-IAAR(2)	Embraer EMB-500 Phenom 100	50000127	PP-OVD, PT-TYD
	(Res 29.8.26)		
D-IAAT	Embraer EMB-500 Phenom 100	50000162	M-MACH, PT-FUJ
D-IAAW	Embraer EMB-500 Phenom 100	50000245	PT-TES
D-IAAY(2)	Embraer EMB-500 Phenom 100	50000243	OO-OTU(2), (OO-OUT), PT-TDR
D-IABB(4)	Aero Commander 680FL	1633-119	(D-IGCP), HB-GCP
D-IABD(2)	Aero Commander 680FL	1741-143	CN-TAU, N4669E
D-IABE(4)	Piper PA-42 Cheyenne III	42-8001037	N373CA, HK-3618W, N804CA, (N222RR), N804CA
D-IABF	Beech 65-B80 Queen Air	LD-410	CN-TKS, G-AZOH, N7891R
D-IABG	Cessna 501 Citation	501-0207	N207JF, VP-BHO, OE-FYC, N207CF, N968DM, N67839
D-IACC	Beech 95-B55 Baron	TC-173	OE-FME(1)
D-IACE(2)	Cessna 310Q	310Q0812	N69604
D-IADR(2)	Cessna 340 / RAMVI	340A0441	(N555HL), N6245X
D-IADV	Cessna 551 Citation II / SP	551-0552	OE-FPA
D-IAEB	Britten-Norman BN-2A-8 Islander	218	OH-BNB, G-51-218
D-IAFM(2)	Diamond DA 62	62.011	(D-GCFM)
	(P 26.2.16)		
D-IAFS	Beech 95-B55 Baron	TC-1796	N8773R
D-IAGC	Cessna 340/RAM	340-0109	N222BQ, N222BG, N222BC, N500TM, (N4559L)
D-IAHB	Cessna 414	414-0547	N1990G
D-IAHG	Cessna 525 CitationJet	525-0126	D-IMPC(2), D-IHGW, VP-CFP, D-IFUP(1), N14TV, N1264V, N5090Y
D-IAHT(3)	Mitsubishi MU-2B-26A	352SA	N41AD, N41WB, N978MA, N234BC, N737MA
D-IAHW	Cessna 340A	340A0355	N6LR, N37337
D-IAIB	Cessna 525 CitationJet	525-0615	(CS-DPU), N65EM, N5095N
D-IAIN	Cessna 340A	340A0921	N2741N, (N200MR), N2741N
D-IAJK (3)	Cessna 414 (RAM Srs VI)	414-0953	(D-IJAK), D-IDIT(2), N9KJ, (N11FX), N9KJ, N9KT, (N5401G)
D-IAKN	Cessna 525A CitationJet CJ2	525A-0367	N367CJ
D-IAMA	Piper PA-23-250 Aztec E	27-7305204	N40485
D-IAMI	Beech B200 King Air	BB-1874	F-HAMI, N6194V
	(Res 23.5.16)		
D-IAMR(2)	Cessna 414A Chancellor	414A0492	OE-FAA(3), N111KR, N36952
D-IANA(3)	Beech B200 Super King Air	BB-1517	N3217V
D-IAPD(3)	Cessna 404 Titan	404-0679	N679R, N6762R, (N3336K), N6762R
D-IARI	Cessna 525 CitationJet	525-0347	I-DAGF, N1133G
D-IARP	Cessna 340	340-0326	N69484
D-IASC(2)	Piper PA-31T Cheyenne	31T-7720066	N993RH, N888JM, N499EH, N15PJ, N70CW, N82189
D-IATE	Reims F406 Caravan II	F406-0007	(S9-KAW), TR-LEQ, LX-LMS, PH-FWC, EC-ESF, PH-FWC, OO-TIR, (OO-TIA), F-WZDT
D-IATS(3)	Cessna 425 Conquest I	425-0035	OE-FBH, N480EA, N402NG, N402NC, N6773F
D-IAVA(2)	Piper PA-23-250 Aztec E	27-7405378	G-HFTG, G-BSOB, G-BCJR, N54040
D-IAWB(2)	Piper PA-42-720 Cheyenne IIIA	42-5501054	B-3623, N92409
D-IAWE(2)	Cessna 425 Conquest I	425-0192	C-FSEA, N1221T
	(Res.07)		
D-IAWG(2)	Cessna 425 Corsair	425-0160	N505AK, N68865
D-IAWU(2)	Cessna 525 CitationJet	525-0435	G-CJAD, N525AD, N5244F
D-IBAD(4)	Beech B200 Super King Air	BB-1229	
D-IBAK(4)	Cessna 525 CitationJet	525-0499	F-HHSC, HB-VNP, N5200Z
D-IBAM(2)	Cessna 340A	340A0091	(N1392G)
D-IBAR(4)	Beech B200 Super King Air	BB-1280	
D-IBAU	Cessna 401A	410A-0101	(N6175Q)
	(Res 9.15)		
D-IBAZ	Piper PA-23-250 Aztec B	27-2221	N5193Y, N10F
D-IBBB(7)	Raytheon 390 Premier	RB-82	N61882
D-IBBH(3)	Cessna 414A Chancellor	414A0238	(N8846K)
D-IBBK	Cessna 340A	340A0338	LX-RST, F-GEJL, D-ILAK, N37310
D-IBBS	Cessna 525A CitationJet CJ2	525A-0313	N5157E
D-IBCT(2)	Cessna 525A CitationJet CJ2	525A-0328	N52352
D-IBFS(2)	Beech C90GTI King Air	LJ-1948	N6148Z
D-IBGC	Piper PA-31T2 Cheyenne IIXL	31T-8166047	XB-FSG, N457SR, N821SW
D-IBHE	Cessna 310R	310R0066	N3370Q
D-IBIE	Cessna 340A	340A0715	(PH-AXG), N98954
D-IBIS(5)	Cessna T303 Crusader	T30300024	SP-KKT, D-IKMA(2), N9545T
D-IBJH	Cessna T303 Crusader	T30300297	N5433V
D-IBJJ	Cessna 525A CitationJet CJ2	525A-0125	N525CG, N525CC, N125CE, N52038
D-IBMC(2)	Beech C90 King Air	LJ-931	HB-GIE, I-FIRS, N931KA, HB-GHB
D-IBMM	Cessna 310Q	310Q0905	N69638
D-IBON(3)	Cessna 340A	340A0603	N8612K
D-IBPW	Cessna 340A	340A0924	N39983, XB-BHW, (N2742A)
D-IBRO(2)	Cessna T303 Crusader	T30300215	HB-LRP, N9824C
D-IBSA	Piper PA-31T Cheyenne II	31T-8120033	N42TW, N2589Z
D-IBSF	Beech B60 Duke	P-536	N80WE
D-IBSL	Embraer EMB-500 Phenom 100	50000295	N100RY, N10160, N60237
D-IBTA	Beech B200GT King Air	BY-75	N61675
D-IBTI(2)	Cessna 525 CitationJet CJ1+	525-0684	D-IAMS, N5207A
D-IBUF(3)	Dornier Do.28D-6 Turbo Skyservant	4302	

Reg	Type	c/n	Identities
D-IBUR(4)	Cessna T303 Crusader	T30300079	N2255C
D-IBWA(2)	Cessna 525 CitationJet	525-0042	PH-MGT, N96GD, N3230M
D-IBWF	Cessna 402B	402B0221	(N7893Q)
D-ICAO(2)	Cessna 525 CitationJet CJ1+	525-0642	N466AE, N5151D
D-ICAR(3)	Diamond DA 62	62.036	(Res .16)
D-ICBB	Cessna 340A	340A0541	SE-KCA, D-ICBB, N1MT, (N4404A)
D-ICCC	Reims/Cessna F406 Caravan II	F406-0050	N406P, VH-RCA, VT-SAA, N7148T, F-WZDS
D-ICCP	Cessna 510 Citation Mustang	510-0375	N4086L
D-ICDE	Cessna T303 Crusader	T30300057	N1297C
D-ICDO	Dornier Do.228-200	4359	(P. 5.06)
D-ICDS(2)	Claudius Dornier CD-2 Seastar	1001	(Wfu 1991)
D-ICDY	Dornier Do.28D-2 Skyservant	4164	58+89
D-ICEE	Cessna 525 CitationJet CJ	525-0096	N5153X
D-ICEL(3)	Piper Aerostar 601P	61P-0577-7963252	N8091J, C-FDNJ, N8091J
D-ICEN(2)	Cessna 340A	340A0555	OE-FUA, N340GT, N340HB, N4584N
	(W/o 21.8.00)		
D-ICEY(2)	Cessna 525 CitationJet CJ	525-0611	N52645
D-ICGN	Piper PA-42-1000 Cheyenne 400LS	42-5527030	D-IUCN, D-IEXP, N41198, "HK-3320W", N41198
D-ICHG	Beech B200 Super King Air	BB-1400	N0085D
D-ICHO	Cessna T337GP Pressurized Skymaster	P3370288	N2QR
D-ICJL	Cessna T303 Crusader	T30300109	N7SX, N3681C
D-ICKE(3)	Beech B200GT King Air	BY-96	(D-CDKE), D-ICKE(3) G-OMSV, N6396H
D-ICKY	Beech B-60 Duke	P-342	
D-ICLM	Beech F90 King Air	LA-12	N19RK, N200E, N19RK, N19R, N66912
	(Res 6.13)		
D-ICLY	Cessna T303 Crusader	T30300159	N6588C
D-ICMF	Cessna 425 Corsair	425-0102	N151GA
D-ICMK	Beech C90GTI King Air	LJ-1928	N3188W
D-ICMS(2)	Cessna 525A CitationJet CJ2	525A-0108	N5136J
D-ICON	Piper PA-34-220T Seneca V	3449251	LN-AAY, OY-LAK, N33489, (N9511N)
D-ICOW	Mitsubishi MU-2B-60	1515SA	N50LY, LY-ZDV, OH-STA, N910DA
	(P 7.9.16)		
D-ICSB	Reims/Cessna FT337GP Super Skymaster	FP33700003	G-BAGP
	(Reims-assembled P337G Pressurized Skymaster with US c/n P3370047)		
D-ICSH	Embraer EMB-500 Phenom 100	50000143	N888PT, PT-FQQ
	(Res 9.9.16)		
D-ICSS	Cessna 525 CitationJet	525-0121	TC-EMA, N5264S
D-ICTA	Cessna 551 Citation II / SP	551-0011	(D-IHAT), N6863C
D-ICTR	Beech C90GTI King Air	LJ-2079	N279BC
D-ICVA	Beech 58P Baron	TJ-422	N6587M
D-ICVW(3)	Cessna 421C Golden Eagle	421C0260	N6146G
D-ICVY	Beech 95-58P Baron	TJ-46	N1546L
D-IDAK(4)	Beech C90 King Air	LJ-647	LX-DAK, N9075S
D-IDAS(5)	Embraer EMB-500 Phenom 100	50000365	PR-PAE
D-IDAZ	Cessna 525 CitationJet CJ1	525-0389	D-IDAS(3), N389CJ, N5156D
D-IDBA	Raytheon 390 Premier	RB-164	N36864
D-IDBB(2)	Dornier Do.28D-2 Skyservant	4080	58+05, D-9571
D-IDBH(2)	Dornier Do.28D-2 Skyservant	4167	58+92
	(Wfu .94)		
D-IDCA(2)	Beech 95-B55 Baron	TC-1942	
D-IDCV	Beech C90B King Air	LJ-1622	N4172Q
D-IDDD	Piper PA-31T1 Cheyenne I	31T-7820027	LX-RST, F-GGPJ, N61RA, N22CA, N82231
D-IDEE(3)	Piper PA-60-602P Aerostar	60-8365012	I-TOLA, N64716
D-IDEK(2)	Beech B60 Duke	P-306	N5403U, (N38EW), N5403U, YV-35CP, YV-TAKJ
D-IDES(2)	Dornier Do.28D-2 Skyservant	4187	59+12
D-IDIX(3)	Beech C90A King Air	LJ-1571	D-IKIA, D-IDIX(3), N90KA
D-IDKE	Beech C90GTI King Air	LJ-1865	D-ITDK, N34975
D-IDMR	Cessna 340A	340A0912	G-CCXJ, N25PJ, HB-LNM, LN-TEA, N27026
D-IDOS(2)	Cessna 404 Titan	404-0665	N5375C
D-IDOZ	Dornier Do.28D-2 Skyservant	4200	59+25
	(Permit)		
D-IDPL	Beech B100 King Air	BE-29	D-IZAC, D-IERI, N7729B, N333NB, N888RK, N18429
D-IDRB(2)	Cessna 421C Golden Eagle	unkn	
D-IDRH	Dornier Do.28D-2 Skyservant	4127	58+52
D-IDRR	Dornier Do.28D-2 Skyservant	4129	58+54
D-IDSM(2)	Beech B200GT King Air	BY-269	
	(P 14.9.16)		
D-IDTH	Cessna 421C Golden Eagle III	421C1062	N6865D
D-IEAG	Beech G58 Baron	TH-2267	N6377P
D-IEAH	Beech 65-C90A King Air	LJ-1216	N4HAH, N1562Z
D-IECS	Cessna 414	414-0023	OE-FMB, N8123Q
D-IEDO	Dornier Do.28G-92	4134	HA-ACM, D-IDRD, 58+59
	(Originally built as Do.28D-2)		
D-IEGA(2)	Cessna 500 Citation	500-0081	I-PEGA, HB-VDA, N5B, N581CC
D-IEHB(2)	Beech 95-B55 Baron	TC-1961	OE-FMF
D-IEIR	Cessna 501 Citation I SP	501-0259	N225WT, D-IEIR, N501MS
D-IEKU(2)	Cessna 525A CitationJet CJ2	525A-0043	N432CJ, N5148B
D-IEMC	Cessna 414A	414A-0282	I-NCCA, N2618C
D-IEMG	Cessna 510 Citation Mustang	510-0274	N713MD
D-IENE	Cessna 525A CitationJet CJ2+	525A-0501	D-DAGS, N5109W
D-IERF	Cessna 525 CitationJet	525-0310	OK-SLA, D-IIJS, (D-IVBG)
D-IESE	Piper PA-31 Navajo C	31-7812102	N27712
D-IESG	Beech B60 Duke	P-341	
D-IEST	Pilatus Britten-Norman BN-2B-26 Islander	2253	I-DEPE, G-BTLY
D-IEVE	Aero Commander 680FP	1431-150	N600EJ, N600BR, (OO-TCA), N600BR, N357CK, KAF-301, N6350U
D-IEVO(3)	Piaggio P.180 Avanti EVO	3004	(Res 8.15)
D-IEWR	Piper PA-23-250 Aztec D	27-4451	N13806
D-IEXF	Beech 99	U-62	LN-SAZ, OO-WAZ, F-BSUJ, N1178C VH-TMA, N6137U, N451MM
D-IFAP(2)	Raytheon Beech 390 Premier	RB-137	(D-ISMV), ZS-SHC,
	(Res 11.15)		
D-IFBN	Pilatus Britten-Norman BN-2B-26 Islander	2185	G-BLNF
D-IFBU	Piper PA-31 Navajo C	31-8012050	N3557W
D-IFCC	Fouga CM.170R Magister	079	93+02, SB+202, SC+603, (AA+179)
D-IFCS	Pilatus Britten-Norman BN-2B-20 Islander	2312	G-CIGM
D-IFDN	Cessna 525A CitationJet CJ2	525A-0343	N5108G
D-IFER	Cessna 510 Citation Mustang	510-0366	
D-IFFF(2)	Reims/Cessna F406 Caravan II	F406-0061	OO-SLX, F-ZBGE, F-GRAI, N406CT, F-GURA, F-OGVS, N3121X
D-IFFM	Cessna 414	414-0801	N1221G, (N15CT), N1221G
D-IFGN	Piper PA-31T1 Cheyenne I	31T-8120052	N67JG, D-IFGN, N43TW, N2519Y
D-IFGU	Cessna 425 Conquest I	425-0042	N1BM, N67735
D-IFHI	Beech C90 King Air	LJ-977	N1813P
D-IFIG	Ted Smith Aerostar 601P	61P-0183-012	OE-FIG, N246HG, N7467S
D-IFKU	Pilatus Britten-Norman BN-2B-20 Islander	2290	G-BVXY
D-IFLB(3)	Pilatus Britten-Norman BN-2B-20 Islander	2313	G-CJJO
	(Res 17.8.16)		
D-IFLN	Pilatus Britten-Norman BN-2B-20 Islander	2307	G-CEUC
D-IFMG	Raytheon 390 Premier	RB-109	N50078
D-IFMI	Beech C90A King Air	LJ-1101	N17EL, N17FL, N72206
D-IFRT	Beech C90A King Air	LJ-1284	OE-FHM(2), N25GA, OY-GEF
D-IFSA	de Havilland DH.104 Dove 7XC	04531	
D-IFSB(2)	Cessna 421B Golden Eagle	421B0561	N421SB, N8216Q
D-IFTI	Pilatus Britten-Norman BN-2B-20 Islander	2299	G-BWYY
D-IFUT	Pilatus Britten-Norman BN-2B-20 Islander	2300	G-OBNG, G-BWYZ
D-IGBB	Beech 58P Baron	TJ-193	N6030Q
D-IGCS	Beech C90GTI King Air	LJ-2009	OK-GIO, N8109K
D-IGCW	Cessna T303 Crusader	T30300177	N9457C
D-IGGG(3)	Cessna 501 Citation	501-0163	I-CIGB, (I-AGIK), N1354G
D-IGGW	Cessna 525 CitationJet	525-0322	F-HCPB, LX-YSL, N52LT
	(Res 7.15)		
D-IGIA	Cessna 421C Golden Eagle	421C0623	9H-GIA, (T7-GIA), OK-SMI, G-BLST, N88638
D-IGJC	Piper PA-23-250 Aztec D	27-4317	F-GZGC, G-BBCC, N6953Y
D-IGOB	Piaggio P.180 Avanti	1016	I-PJAT
D-IGPP	Cessna 421	421-0109	TC-DVK, YU-BEJ, N3128K
	(Permit expired)		
D-IGPS	Cessna T303 Crusader	T30300308	N303PK, N303ER, N6332V
D-IGRO	Cessna 525A CitationJet CJ2	525A-0230	N5136J
D-IGST	Raytheon 390 Premier	RB-152	N17EL, N3732Y
D-IHAG	Cessna 551 Citation II / SP	551-0180	N222VV, (N729MJ), N166MA, D-ICAB, N852WR, (D-CACS), N8520J
D-IHAH	Beech C90B King Air	LJ-1370	N1570C
D-IHBB(2)	Cessna 340A	340A0217	I-CCTT, N3880G
D-IHEB(4)	Cessna 525 CitationJet	525-0064	
D-IHEF	Cessna 414	414-0456	N1663T
D-IHHH(4)	Cessna 421B Golden Eagle	421B0512	G-TAMY, SE-FNS, N2BH, N69865
D-IHIT(2)	Beech 58P Baron	TJ-97	D-IIPW, 5N-ASG
D-IHKL	Cessna T303 Crusader	T30300135	N5423C
D-IHKW	Cessna 525 CitationJet	525-0677	N413CQ
D-IHLA(2)	Piper PA-42-720 Cheyenne IIIA	42-8301001	N842PC, JA8869, N842PC
D-IHLB(3)	Cessna 402B	402B1340	N6377X
D-IHLK	Cessna 421B Golden Eagle	421B0451	(N41101)
D-IHML	Cessna 421C Golden Eagle	421C1080	N25M, N68661
D-IHMW(2)	Piaggio P.180 Avanti II	1197	I-PJET, I-PDVS
	(Res 11.15)		
D-IHRG	Beech C90GT King Air	LJ-1845	N845KA
D-IHSI	Rockwell Commander 695	95039	N9790S
D-IHSW	Beech C90B King Air	LJ-1315	N8103E
D-IICE	Beech 200 Super King Air	BB-269	N269D, N180SN, N100SM, N18269
D-IIHS	Beech 58P Baron	TJ-345	N3839B
D-IIII()2	Piper PA-31T1 Cheyenne 1	31T-8004011	9A-BOR, D-IBIW, N76TG, (N803AW), N76TG, N707CM, N208SW, N2418W
D-IIIL	Cessna 421C Golden Eagle	421C0248	OE-FLX, (D-IBTU(1)), OE-FLX, D-IDEM, N5536G
	(P. 26.11.14)		
D-IIIV	Piper PA-34-220T Seneca V	3449332	I-VLMS, N31379
	(Res .13)		
D-IIKM	Beech C90A King Air	LJ-1120	N7237K
D-IIPN(3)	Piper PA-34-220T Seneca V	3449483	N4404L, N9527N
D-IITN	Piaggio P.180 Avanti	1188	(D-INWT), I-TIAF
D-IITS	Cessna 340	340-0068	HB-LGR, (I-MELE), N5916M, (I-ALBB)
D-IIVA	Piaggio P.180 Avanti	1125	
D-IIVK	Cessna T303 Crusader	T30300287	N5096V
D-IIWE	Aero Commander 500B	1301-116	OE-FAL
D-IJET(4)	Piaggio P.180 Avanti	1056	
D-IJGW	Cessna 425 Conquest I	425-0193	N1221X
D-IJHO	Cessna 510 Citation Mustang	510-0306	N146EP
D-IJOA	Cessna 525A CitationJet CJ2	525A-0034	N5211F
D-IJTT	Beech B60 Duke	P-440	N1TT
	(P. 11.05) (Converted to Thielert Centurion 4.0 diesel engines)		
D-IKAI	Piaggio P.180 Avanti	1014	I-ACTC
D-IKBO	Cessna 525A CitationJet CJ2	525A-0357	D-IVVB, N624PL, N50820
D-IKCS	Cessna 525 CitationJet CJ1	525-0396	D-IMAC(2), N51575
D-IKET	Piper PA-31T Cheyenne II	31T-8020017	N154CA, (N802SW), I-APIT, N802SW, (N100ES), N802SW, N2359W
D-IKEW	Piper PA-31T Cheyenne II	31T-7820066	N6108A
D-IKFG	de Havilland DH.89A Dragon Rapide	6853	ZK-SWR, BelgAF D.7, NR777
	(P 24.2.16)		
D-IKGT(2)	Raytheon Beech 390 Premier	RB-64	LX-PMR, N6164U
D-IKHS	Piper Aerostar 601P	61P-0542-231	N8059J
D-IKIM	Beech C90A King Air	LJ-1324	N82430
D-IKJH	Cessna T303 Crusader	T30300209	N9741C
D-IKKY	Mitsubishi MU-2B-40 Solitaire	420SA	I-SOLT, N5KD, N154MA
D-IKOB(2)	Beech B200 Super King Air	BB-921	N244JB, N76MP
D-IKOE	Cessna 510 Citation Mustang	510-0082	OE-FLR
D-IKOP	Cessna 525 CitationJet	525-0016	N216CJ, (N1328M)
D-IKOV	Cessna T310R	310R0276	HB-LSE, D-ICYF, (N5478J)
D-IKSI	Piaggio P.180 Avanti	1165	F-GPKP, I-PDVO
D-IKSW	Cessna T337GP Pressurized Skymaster	P3370124	N60E, N6CE
D-IKUB	Beech 95-55 Baron	TC-145	N55AW, D-IKUB
D-IKUM	Cessna T303 Crusader	T30300134	N303WW, D-IERS, N5409C
D-IKUR	de Havilland DH.104 Dove 2B	04296	HB-LAR, G-AMEI
D-ILAC(2)	Eclipse EA500	000177	N177EA
D-ILAH(2)	Beech B200GT King Air	BY-172	N172BY
D-ILAM	Cessna 525A CitationJet CJ2	525A-0070	N5157E
D-ILAP	Embraer EMB-500 Phenom 100	50000288	PT-TAR
D-ILAT(3)	Eclipse EA550	550-0269	N269EJ
D-ILAV	Eclipse EA500	550-1004	N170NE
D-ILCA(3)	Piper PA-31 Navajo C	31-7912035	N27923
D-ILCY	Beech A60 Duke	P-150	(OH-BDE)
D-ILDK	Cessna 340A	340A0972	HB-LMZ, OE-FCH, (N5703C)

Reg.	Type	Serial	Previous identities
D-ILDL	Cessna 525A CitationJet CJ2	525A-0167	N51806
D-ILFA(2)	Pilatus Britten-Norman BN-2B-26 Islander	2243	G-BSWO
D-ILFB	Pilatus Britten-Norman BN-2B-26 Islander (Dam. 3.3.07)	2271	G-BUBO
D-ILFD	Pilatus Britten-Norman BN-2B-26 Islander	2296	JA02TY, G-BWNF
D-ILFH(2)	Pilatus Britten-Norman BN-2B-26 Islander	2212	G-BPXS
D-ILGA(4)	Piper PA-31T1 Cheyenne 1A	31T-1104014	N9382T
D-ILHA(3)	Cessna 525 CitationJet CJ1+	525-0696	N51684
D-ILHB(3)	Cessna 525 CitationJet CJ1+	525-0675	(D-ILHA(1)), N41196, N5270E
D-ILHC(2)	Cessna 525 CitationJet CJ1+	525-0695	
D-ILHD(2)	Cessna 525 CitationJet CJ1+	525-0694	
D-ILHE(2)	Cessna 525 CitationJet CJ1+	525-0664	N88QG, N664CJ
D-ILHW(3)	Piper PA-34-220T Seneca III	34-8433055	G-GISY, N4356G
D-ILIT	de Havilland DH.89A Dragon Rapide (P. 12.99)	6879	G-AMAI,D-ILIT, "G-RCYR", EC-AGP, G-AMAI, NR803
D-ILKC	Beech 65-A90 King Air	LJ-211	N90JR, N76CV, N76CB, N553Z, N550Z, N867K
D-ILKY	Beech 95-B55 Baron	TC-1048	
D-ILLI (2)	Beech B60 Duke	P-537	(D-ILAH)
D-ILMC	Cessna 414	414-0906	N4635G, D-ILMC, N4635G
D-ILSA(2)	Piper PA-23-250 Aztec E	27-7305215	N40490
D-ILSE(4)	Beech 58 Baron	TH-539	F-GINJ, F-OANJ(2), 5T-CJS, F-BVUZ
D-ILUG	Cessna 525 CitationJet (Res 14.6.16)	525-0345	G-ZIZI, N5185V
D-ILWA	Cessna 340A (Robertson STOL)	340A0502	N6333X
D-ILWS	Dornier 228-200	8002	D-CBDU(6), OY-CHJ, 9M-AXB, D-IDCO, 9M-AXB, D-IDCO
D-IMAH	Cessna 525A CitationJet CJ2+	525A-0502	
D-IMAX(5)	Cessna 525A CitationJet CJ2	525A-0195	N51942
D-IMEL	Beech E55 Baron (Wfu, noted 9.16)	TE-855	N9443Q
D-IMEP	Beech C90GTI King Air	LJ-2026	N826MM
D-IMGW	Cessna 525A CitationJet CJ2+	525A-0498	N5296X
D-IMHA	Cessna 525A CitationJet CJ2	525A-0322	F-GMIR, (LX-WGR), N51575
D-IMHH	Piper PA-60-602P Aerostar	60-8365010	N6901D
D-IMHW(2)	Cessna 340A	340A1518	N6871C
D-IMIA	Piaggio P.180 Avanti	1212	
D-IMIC	Cessna 340A	340A1223	HB-LNW, N68279
D-IMKL	Cessna 340A	340A1279	N68692
D-IMME(3)	Cessna 551 Citation II /SP	551-0400	N280JS, N95CT, N550WR, (N67983)
D-IMMM(3)	Cessna 525A CitationJet CJ2+	525A-0400	N5235G
D-IMMO(3)	Piper PA-60-700P Aerostar	60-8423002	N700ET, N700AH, N9564N
D-IMOB	Dornier Do.28G-92	4199	HA-ACZ, D-IAAE, F-GHYI, Lw 59+24
D-IMOC(2)	Dornier Do.28D-2 (Operating on permit since 1993)	4107	Lw 58+32
D-IMOK(2)	Dornier Do.28G-92	4320	HA-ACY, Kenya AF-113, D-ILFL
D-IMOR	Embraer EMB-500 Phenom 100	50000281	PT-TUA
D-IMPC(3)	Cessna 525 CitationJet CJ1+	525-0639	(D-ICPO), N5201M
D-IMPD	Beech B200GT King Air (P. 15.1.16)	BY-249	N5049U
D-IMPO(2)	Beech C90A King Air	LJ-1718	PH-KBB, N720AF
D-IMRB	Beech C90GTI King Air	LJ-1900	F-HARC, N3400T
D-IMRT	Cessna T303 Crusader	T30300097	N2679C
D-IMTT(3)	Hammer/Messerschmitt Me.262B-1a (New build aircraft, 8.05) (P.4.06)	501244	N262MS
D-IMVC	Beech B200 Super King Air	BB-1741	OE-FOS, D-IIAH, N2341K
D-IMWK(2)	Fairchild Swearingen SA.227TT Merlin IIIC	TT-529A	N3109S
D-IMWM	Cessna 340	340-0095	N4507Q
D-IMWW	Beech E55 Baron	TE-930	(OH-BBW)
D-INAG	Beech 95-B55 Baron	TC-1550	
D-INCS	Cessna 525 CitationJet CJ1	525-0466	N119CS, (D-ILLL(3)), N119CS
D-INDI (2)	Cessna 421B Golden Eagle	421B0317	D-IJCZ, I-CLAA, N5945M
D-INDY(2)	Eclipse EA500	000246	N144EA
D-INEC	Beech B60 Duke	P-549	N614EC, N610PG, N742RH, N570U
D-INEW	Ted Smith Aerostar 601P	61P-0167-006	N7535S
D-INFO	Piper PA-31T-2 Cheyenne IIXL	31T-8166031	ZS-LSY, V5-LSY, ZS-LSY, N172CC
D-INFS	Cessna 525 CitationJet	525-0286	D-ICEY(1), N51666
D-INGE(3)	Cessna 340A	340A1258	N8841N, (N777TG), N8841N
D-INGI	Cessna 340A	340A0037	N98569
D-INGO(2)	Cessna 340A	340A1025	N340MM, N4756A
D-INGU	Piper Aerostar 601P	61P-0613-7963276	N8211J
D-INKA(8)	de Havilland DH.104 Dove 5	04266	G-BLRN, N531WB, G-BLRN, WB531
D-INKY	Piaggio P.180 Avanti	1162	
D-INMA	Beech C90A King Air	LJ-1566	N988XJ
D-INOB	Cessna 525A CitationJet CJ2	525A-0196	N5166T
D-INRR	Cessna 414A Chancellor	414A0097	PH-LTO, N4828A
D-INSP	Beech B60 Duke	P-554	N120SP, N99VT, N3699R
D-INWG(2)	Beech B60 Duke	P-446	N7860X
D-IOAK	Piper PA-34-200T Seneca II	34-7770167	D-GBPN, D-ILAC, N1066Q
D-IOBB(2)	Cessna 525 CitationJet CJ1+	525-0665	HB-VOX, N665CJ
D-IOBO(4)	Cessna 525 CitationJet CJ2	525A-0486	(D-IOBU(4)), (D-IOBC(2)), N5214L
D-IOFA	Cessna T303 Crusader	T30300038	N9690T
D-IOHL	Cessna 525A CitationJet CJ2	525A-0233	D-IBBE(3), N5236L
D-IOKE	Diamond DA 62	62.033	
D-IOLB	Cessna 404 Titan	404-0691	SE-IVG, VH-PVG, N67632
D-IOLK	Britten-Norman BN-2B-26 Islander	2306	G-CEUB
D-IOLM	Britten-Norman BN-2A-26 Islander	2037	ZK-MSF, OY-PPP, JA5284, G-BNEB
D-IOLN	Britten-Norman BN-2A-26 Islander	2043	ZK-TSS, RP-C693
D-IOLO	Britten-Norman BN-2B-20 Islander	2305	G-CEUA
D-IOLT(2)	Cessna T303 Crusader	T30300294	N5357V
D-IOSB	Piper PA-42-720 Cheyenne IIIA	42-5501042	
D-IOSD	Piper PA-42-720 Cheyenne IIIA	42-5501044	
D-IOSL	Piper PA-34-220T Seneca V	3449150	
D-IOTA	Beech 58P Baron	TJ-312	N3693L
D-IOTT(2)	Piper PA-31T Cheyenne II	31T-7920010	N6196A
D-IOVP	Piper PA-42-1000 Cheyenne IIIA	42-5501057	C-GWCA, C-GSAA, N120GA, OE-FAA
D-IOWA	Cessna 525 CitationJet CJ1+	525-0624	N5141F
D-IOVB	Cessna 421C Golden Eagle II	421C1061	N6798X
D-IPBB	Beech C90GTI King Air	LJ-2070	N5070A
D-IPCC(2)	Cessna 525A CitationJet CJ2	525A-0487	N5264N
D-IPCG	Cessna 425 Conquest I	425-0177	D-IAWG(1), C-GSFF, C-GSFI, C-GRJM, (N850GM), C-GRJM, N600TJ, TC-OPN, N414CW, (N435BC), N414CW, N6873X
D-IPCH	Cessna 525A CitationJet CJ2	525A-0347	M-ICRO(1), N5262X
D-IPEW	Piper PA-42-1000 Cheyenne IIIA	42-5527028	HB-LTM, N4119X
D-IPIT	Diamond DA 62	62.028	
D-IPOD	Cessna 525 CitationJet	525-0193	HB-VOX, D-ILCB, N193CJ, N5132T
D-IPRC	Cessna 340A	340A1248	TC- . . . , N87453, - ? - , (N87453)
D-IPVD	Cessna 525A CitationJet CJ2	525A-0218	
D-IPWA	Cessna 421B Golden Eagle	421B0632	N4939M, D-ILYR, (N1536G)
D-IQXX	Cessna 525 Citation M2	525-0854	N696MM
D-IRAR	Beech B200 Super King Air	BB-1957	N957BA, N104AG
D-IRAY	Diamond DA 62 (Res .16)	62.047	
D-IRBS	Piaggio P.180 Avanti	1221	
D-IRCB	Beech B55 Baron	TC-1513	N1835W, ZS-ING, N1835W
D-IRCP	Beech C90GTI King Air	LJ-1965	SP-NEO, N6015N
D-IRES	Dornier Do.28D-2 Skyservant	4186	59+11
D-IRIS	Beech F90 King Air	LA-229	N7209Z
D-IRIZ	Cessna 510 Citation Mustang (Res 5.1.16)	510-0410	N575SF
D-IRKE	Cessna 525 CitationJet	525-0123	N5223P
D-IROL	Dornier Do.228-100	7003	D-CBD . , SE-KHL, LN-HPA, D-
D-IROM	Beech E18S	BA-328	HB-GJG, N328N, N621AA, N729KB, N561FD, N5619D
D-IRON	Cessna 525 CitationJet	525-0168	
D-IRSB	Cessna 525 CitationJet CJ1	525-0476	N74PG, N50ET, N476CJ
D-IRTY(2)	Raytheon Beech 390 Premier (Res 3.5.16)	RB-201	M-ARIE, N390GW, D-ISGE, I-DMSA, N801BP
D-IRUN	Cessna 510 Citation Mustang	510-0424	
D-IRUP	Cessna 551 Citation II /SP	551-0572	N719EH, N193SS, N12992
D-IRVA(2)	Cessna T303 Crusader	T30300050	N2181W, D-INAA, (N9883T)
D-IRWP	Beech B60 Duke	P-581	D-IUTE, N39JT, N850YR
D-IRWR	Cessna 525 CitationJet	525-0118	N118AZ, (N61TF), N52178, N5203S
D-ISAA	Beech B55 Baron (Res 9.15)	TC-1351	N777QR, F-BTCR, HB-GES
D-ISAG(2)	Raytheon 390 Premier 1A	RB-221	N31921
D-ISAR(2)	Raytheon 390 Premier	RB-148	N6148Z
D-ISAV	Cessna 402B	402B0201	OY-SAV, N7873Q
D-ISAW	Beech B55 Baron	TC-1574	G-MDJN, G-SUZI, G-BAXR
D-ISBC	Beech C90GTI King Air	LJ-1935	N190EU
D-ISCA	Cessna T303 Crusader	T30300175	N9382C
D-ISCH(2)	Cessna 525A CitationJet CJ2	525A-0052	N51881
D-ISCO	Cessna 525A CitationJet CJ2 (P 1.4.16)	525A-0151	SP-KKB, (D-ISCO), N122SM
D-ISCV	Cessna 525A CitationJet CJ2+	525A-0429	N5048U
D-ISEA	Claudius Dornier CD2-02 Seastar	1002	D-IOKS, D-ICKS(2)
D-ISGS	Vulcanair AP.68TP-600 Viator	9010	HB-LRZ, VH-PNW
D-ISGW	Cessna 525 CitationJet CJ	525-0070	N70HW
D-ISHF	Piper PA-31T1 Cheyenne I	31T 8104029	OE-FKH, N803CA, (N90WA), N2484X
D-ISIG	Piper PA-31T1 Cheyenne I	31T 8104055	N123AT, N48TW, (N880WW), N48TW, N2491Y
D-ISIX	Beech C90B King Air	LJ-1355	N995PA, D-ISIX, N8105D
D-ISJA	Cessna 525A CitationJet CJ2	525A-0348	S5-BAS, N5076J
D-ISJM	Cessna 525 CitationJet CJ1+	525-0602	N74UK, N46JV, N602CJ, N5248V
D-ISJP	Cessna 525A CitationJet CJ2	525A-0030	N302DM, N5223Y
D-ISKO	Raytheon Beech 390 Premier (P 27.4.16)	RB-35	M-GDRS, D-IAGG, N435K
D-ISKY(4)	Beech B200 King Air	BB-2014	N6394Y
D-ISLA	Cessna T303 Crusader	T30300226	F-GFTP, N510TF, N9868C
D-ISMC	Cessna T303 Crusader	T30300245	G-OAPE, N303MF
D-ISMV	Raytheon 390 (Res 9.15)	RB-137	ZS-SHC, VH-TMA, N6137U, N451MM
D-ISPE	Cessna 340A	340A-0613	SE-IBO, N8674K
D-ISRM	Cessna 510 Citation Mustang	510-0035	N4202M
D-ISSS(3)	Cessna 510 Citation Mustang (Res 1.9.16)	510-0471	N4092E
D-ISTM	Piaggio P.180 Avanti (Res 3.15)	1238	
D-ISTP	Embraer EMB-500 Phenom 100	50000147	OO-GJP, PT-FQU
D-ISTT	Beech C90GTI King Air	LJ-1869	N31869
D-ISUN(2)	Cessna 525A CitationJet CJ2	525A-0143	
D-ISVK	Piper PA-31T1 Cheyenne I	31T-7904026	3A-MSI, N458SC, XC-CUA, N23447, N9746N
D-ISWA	Cessna 525 CitationJet CJ	525-0236	
D-ISXT	Cessna 510 Citation Mustang	510-0446	N422RR
D-ITAN	Cessna 525 CitationJet CJ	525-0399	(VP-CTN), N5135A
D-ITCH	Beech C90A King Air	LJ-1138	N17KA, XA-POK, N2706E
D-ITEM	Piper PA-31T2 Cheyenne IIXL	31T-1166003	EC-JRF, D-IXXX, D-ICDU, N2604R, (N68TW), N2604R
D-ITFA	Cessna 340A	340A-0546	OE-FLI, (D-IDDY), OE-FLI, PH-HNK, D-IFMY, PH-HNK, OO-DKE, D-IHAF, N4554N
D-ITFC	Beech B200 King Air	BB-1973	N74753
D-ITIP	Cessna 525 CitationJet CJ1	525-0494	N71HR
D-ITMA	Cessna 525A CitationJet CJ2	525A-0389	M-PSAC, N5153K
D-ITMS	Beech E50 Twin Bonanza	EH-56	N211EL, A-711, HB-HOU
D-ITOL	Cessna T303 Crusader	T30300048	G-BTDJ, I-BELT, N377CB, (N377GS), N377CB, N9839T
D-ITOR	Cessna 525A CitationJet CJ2+	525A-0364	N5090V
D-ITPI	Cessna 340A	340A0719	N63HC, N4DM, N78JD, N26663
D-ITPJ	Cessna T303 Crusader	T30300080	OE-FLI, OO-VJI, N2266C
D-ITPV	Piaggio P.180 Avanti	1012	N180TE
D-ITRA	Cessna 525 CitationJet CJ	525-0177	OE-FWM, F-HASC, G-OWRC, G-OCSB, N1280A, (RP-C7171), N1280A, N5163C
D-ITRI	Piper PA-42-720 Cheyenne IIIA	42-5501045	N56MV, D-ITRI, I-TREP
D-ITTO	Beech 58 Baron	TH-443	F-BVED
D-ITWL	Cessna 425 Conquest I	425-0048	N6774Z, (N425E), N6774Z
D-ITWO	Piper PA-42-720 Cheyenne IIIA	42-5501046	I-TREQ
D-IUCR(2)	Embraer EMB-500 Phenom 100	50000370	
D-IUDE	Beech C90A King Air	LJ-1323	N90KA
D-IURS	Cessna 525 CitationJet	525-0343	N5244F
D-IUSA	Beech B60 Duke	P-565	N3828L

D-IUTI	Beech B60 Duke	P-582	N518D
D-IUZI	Beech B55 Baron	TC-1279	SP-KTU, OH-BBX
D-IVAN	Beech B200 King Air	BB-1662	S5-CEC, N3262P
D-IVER	DHC-6-300 Twin Otter	411	SE-IYP, LN-FKG, CS-TFF, LN-FKC, C-FHBR, HK-2950X, C-FHBR
D-IVIA	Cessna 421B Golden Eagle (P 7.1.16)	421B0912	YA-. . ., N241DR
D-IVIN(3)	Piaggio P.180 Avanti	1159	I-FEMA, I-PDVO
D-IVIP	Beech B200 King Air	BB-1672	
D-IVIV	Cessna 525A CitationJet CJ2+	525A-0518	N51038
D-IVPD	Cessna 525 CitationJet	525-0181	SE-RIO, N88LD, N181CJ, N5180K
D-IVVB(2)	Cessna 525A CitationJet CJ2+	525A-0500	D-ILIB(3), N6061U
D-IVYA	Cessna T303 Crusader	T30300014	G-JUIN, OO-PEN, N9401T
D-IWAS	Cessna T303 Crusader	T30300111	N194W, D-IWAS, N3701C
D-IWAW	Beech 200 Super King Air	BB-526	OE-BBB
D-IWEL	Beech B60 Duke	P-431	N522V, N18286
D-IWID	Beech C90A King Air	LJ-1450	N3265K
D-IWIL	Cessna 525 CitationJet	525-0221	
D-IWIR	Cessna 525A CitationJet CJ2	525A-0102	N888KL
D-IWMS	Hispano HA.200 Saeta (Permit 15.8.13)	20/73	EC-FVU, EC-648, SpAF: A10B-67, C10B-67, E14B-67
D-IWPS(2)	Cessna 525A CitationJet CJ2 (Res 5.7.16)	525A-0496	M-IWPS, (D-IWPS), N52446
D-IWUT	Cessna 421B Golden Eagle	421B0832	G-BDCS, N1931G
D-IWWP	Cessna 525A CitationJet CJ2+	525A-0444	N20669
D-IWWW(2)	Raytheon 390 Premier	RB-89	N61589
D-IXAA(2)	Beech C90GTI King Air	LJ-1908	OE-FDY, N3208T
D-IXIE(3)	Beech 58P Pressurized Baron (Res. .14)	TJ-320	I-VVEE, N3707N
D-IXKJ	Piper PA-60 Aerostar 601P	61P-0607-7963272	D-IASS(2), N606AC, N60AC, G-SILK, N8207J
D-IXTT	High Performance Aircraft TT62 Alekto (P. 2.05)	PT1	
D-IXXX(5)	Cessna 525 CitationJet	525-0393	OE-FFK, OM-HLY, D-IBIT(2)
D-IZMM	Cessna 510 Citation Mustang	510-0386	N386TA
D-IZZY(2)	Piaggio P.180 Avanti	1034	N680JP, I-RAIH
D-IZZZ(2)	Cessna 525 CitationJet CJ1	525-0671	SE-RIX, N525AJ
D-I . . .	Beech H.18S	BA-716	N223JW, N23LT, N140QC, N140Q
D-I . . .	Cessna 340A RAM	340A0716	OO-EPM, OY-RAV, N98976, F-GCSQ, N98976
D-I . . .	Cessna 411A	411A0282	N850F, N3282R
D-I . . .	De Havilland DH.89A Dragon Rapide	6853	G-ZSWR, ZK-SWR, (D-IKFG), FAB D-7/OT-CZK, NR777
D-I . . .	Piper PA-34-220T Seneca III	34-8133248	I-BEAS, N711KB, (D-GKBL), N711KB, N9589N
D-I . . .	Piper PA-42-720 Cheyenne IIIA	42-5501050	G-GMED, N950TA, JA8873, N92275

CLASS K : Self-Launching and Winch-Launched Powered Gliders

D-KAAA	Sportavia/ Scheibe SF 25B Falke	4851	
D-KAAB(2)	Schleicher ASH 31Mi	31123	
D-KAAC(2)	Schleicher ASH 30Mi (P 5.13)	30004	(D-KLFU)
D-KAAE	Sportavia/ Scheibe SF 25B Falke	4855	
D-KAAF	Sportavia/ Scheibe SF 25B Falke	4856	
D-KAAH(2)	Glaser-Dirks DG-600M	6-72M23	
D-KAAJ(2)-AM	Schleicher ASH 31Mi	31119	
D-KAAL(4)	Sportavia-Pützer RF-5B Sperber	51075	PH-741, D-KAIT
D-KAAM(2)	Grob G 109B	6266	LX-CAM
D-KAAO(3)	Sportavia/ Fournier RF-4D	4040	OE-9055, D-KIRO
D-KAAS(2)	Scheibe SF 25C Falke 2000	44454	
D-KAAT(3)	Scheibe SF 25C Falke	46257C	
D-KAAV	Scheibe SF 25B Falke	46220	
D-KAAW	Scheibe SF 25C Falke	4406	
D-KAAX(3)-AT	Lange E1 Antares (P.2.08)	42E39	(D-KLDR(1))
D-KAAY(2)	Scheibe SF 25C Falke	4408	
D-KAAZ(3)	Eiriavion PIK-20E	20274	F-CAAZ, F-WAAZ
D-KABA(3)	Scheibe SF 25C Falke 2000	44311	
D-KABB(3)	HOAC HK 36R Super Dimona (Res. 11)	36316	HB-2191
D-KABC(2)-BC	Schempp-Hirth Discus-2cT	22	
D-KABE	Scheibe SF 24A/KM29	4002	
D-KABF(2)	HOAC HK-36R Super Dimona	36321	OE-9371
D-KABG(2)	Sportavia/ Fournier RF-5	5072	
D-KABH	Sportavia/ Fournier RF-4D	4152	
D-KABI (2)	Sportavia/ Fournier RF-5	5083	HB-2012
D-KABL(3)	Scheibe SF 25C Falke 2000	44505	
D-KABO(2)	Schempp-Hirth Janus CM	10	
D-KABR(2)	Scheibe SF 25C Falke 2000	44444	
D-KABT(3)-BT	Schempp-Hirth Arcus T	55	
D-KABU(2)	Scheibe SF 25C Falke	44128	(D-KLDE)
D-KABW	Scheibe SF 25B Falke	46123	
D-KABX	Scheibe SF 25D Falke	46124D	
D-KABY-BY	Schleicher ASW 22BLE	22044	
D-KACA	Sportavia-Pützer RF-5B Sperber	51076	HB-2345, D-KLEO
D-KACB(3)	DG Flugzeugbau DG-808C	8-411B310X71	
D-KACC	Scheibe SF 25B Falke	4660	
D-KACE(2)	Schempp-Hirth Ventus-2cM	113	
D-KACF	Scheibe SF 25B Falke	4663	
D-KACG(3)-CG	Schempp-Hirth Discus-2cT	124	(D-KACT)
D-KACH(5)	DG Flugzeugbau DG-1000T	10-118T38	HA-4530
D-KACI	Blessing Raab Krähe III V-6 (Quoted c/n is that of the builder - Raab c/n is 8)	5	
D-KACJ(3)	Scheibe SF 25C Rotax-Falke	44604	
D-KACL(2)	Diamond HK 36TTS Super Dimona (Res.3.00)	36514	OE-9454
D-KACM(5)	Schempp-Hirth Arcus M	150	
D-KACN(2)	Glaser-Dirks DG-500M	5E126M53	
D-KACO(3)	AVO 68v Samburo	008	OE-9118
D-KACP(3)	Nitsche AVO 68-R115 Samburo	006	
D-KACR(3)-ACR	Schempp-Hirth Arcus M	82	
D-KACS(2)	Scheibe SF 28A Tandem-Falke	5766	
D-KACT	IAR-Brasov IS-28M2/G (Permit 9.11.12)	70	HA-1005, D-KGBL
D-KACX-AC	Lange E1 Antares	60E50	D-KKGK
D-KACZ	Grob G 109	6112	OH-921, D-KIWO, OE-9203
D-KADC	Scheibe SF 25B Falke	46127	

D-KADE(3)	Stemme S10-VT	11-097	(D-KJGC)
D-KADF	Scheibe SF 25D Falke	46129D	
D-KADG(6)	Glaser-Dirks DG-800A	8-2A2	
D-KADI (4)	Glaser-Dirks DG-400	4-28	(F-WFVA)
D-KADK	Scheibe SF 25B Falke	46133	
D-KADL	Scheibe SF 25B Falke	46134	
D-KADO(4)	Schempp-Hirth Ventus-2cM	36/64	
D-KADP(2)-DP	Schempp-Hirth Janus CM	4	PH-1137, D-KKDR, (D-KJMC)
D-KADR(2)	Schempp-Hirth Duo Discus T	53/338	
D-KADT	Technoflug Piccolo	007	
D-KADU(2)	Scheibe SF 25C Falke	44193	
D-KADW	Diamond HK 36TTC Super Dimona	36537	
D-KADZ	Schempp-Hirth Ventus 2cT	213	
D-KAEB(2)	Schempp-Hirth Discus bT	153/547	
D-KAEC(2)-YES	Schleicher ASH 26E	26177	
D-KAEE	Sportavia/ Scheibe SF 25D Falke	4866D	(D-KAOA)
D-KAEJ(2)	Glaser-Dirks DG-400	4-171	
D-KAEK	Scheibe SFS-31 Milan	6610	
D-KAEM(2)	Lange E1 Antares (P.9.05)	18	
D-KAER	Scheibe SF 25C Falke	46229C	
D-KAET	Scheibe SF 25C Falke	4411	
D-KAEY(2)	Schempp-Hirth Discus-2cT	45	
D-KAFA(3)	Stemme S6/8 (P .08)	6.T.08.002	
D-KAFB(2)	Scheibe SF 25C Rotax-Falke	44698	
D-KAFL(2)-S6	Schempp-Hirth Discus-2T	38	
D-KAFM	Hoffmann H-36 Dimona	3693	
D-KAFO(2)	Sportavia/ Fournier RF-5	5090	
D-KAFR	Glaser-Dirks DG-400	4-105	(ZK-GPL)
D-KAFS	Schempp-Hirth Arcus M	146	
D-KAFT(3)	Schempp-Hirth Duo Discus XLT	272	
D-KAFV	Grob G 102 Astir CS77/TOP	1656	D-4824
D-KAFZ	Schleicher ASH 26E	26080	
D-KAGA(2)	Scheibe SF 25C Rotax-Falke	44632	
D-KAGB(3)	Scheibe SF 25C Rotax-Falke	44700	
D-KAGC	Scheibe SF 25C Rotax-Falke	44646	
D-KAGD	Schleicher ASH 26E	26100	
D-KAGF	Scheibe SF 25C Rotax-Falke	44658	
D-KAGG	Scheibe SF 25C Rotax-Falke	44670	
D-KAGH	Grob G 102 Astir CS Jeans/TOP	2213	D-3827
D-KAGJ(2)	Scheibe SF 25C Rotax-Falke	44678	
D-KAGK(2)	Scheibe SF 25C Rotax-Falke	44689	
D-KAGL(2)	HOAC HK 36R Super Dimona	36332	
D-KAGN(2)	Scheibe SF 25C Rotax-Falke	44714	
D-KAGO(4)	Hoffmann H-36 Dimona	3617	
D-KAGP(2)	Scheibe SF 25C Rotax-Falke	44715	
D-KAGQ	Scheibe SF 25C Falke	46183	
D-KAGR	Scheibe SF 25C Falke	46184	
D-KAGS(2)	Schleicher ASH 26E	26089	
D-KAGU(2)	Schempp-Hirth Discus-2T	25/163	
D-KAGV	Schempp-Hirth Ventus cM	29/462	
D-KAGW	Schleicher ASW 20L/TOP	20242	D-3182
D-KAGX	Scheibe SF 25C Heubacher-Falke	44721	
D-KAGY(2)-GY	Schleicher ASH 25E	25112	
D-KAGZ	Scheibe SF 25C Heubacher-Falke	44727	
D-KAHB(2)	Grob G 109B	6378	
D-KAHC	Sportavia/ Fournier RF-5	5018	
D-KAHD	Sportavia/ Fournier RF-5	5020	
D-KAHF(2)	Schempp-Hirth Discus bM	4/447	
D-KAHG(3)-1S	Schempp-Hirth Nimbus-4DM	17/26	
D-KAHH(2)-ET	Schleicher ASH 31Mi	31040	
D-KAHN(2)	Glaser-Dirks DG-500M	5E-25M13	HB-2180
D-KAHP(3)	Scheibe Bergfalke II/55M	277	?
D-KAHR	Sportavia/ Scheibe SF 25B Falke	4810	
D-KAHS	Schleicher ASW 20/TOP	20247	D-3376
D-KAHT	Technoflug Piccolo B	092	
D-KAHW-HW	Schempp-Hirth Ventus cM	34/466	
D-KAIB(3)-W	Lange E1 Antares 18T (P 1.09)	56T04	
D-KAIC(3)	Scheibe SF 25C Heubacher-Falke	44717	
D-KAID(2)	Hoffmann H-36 Dimona	3687	
D-KAIE(2)	Glaser-Dirks DG-400 (Res .08)	4-16	PH-994, D-KAIC
D-KAIF(2)	Lange E1 Antares	37E35	
D-KAIG	Sportavia/ Fournier RF-4D	4157	(PT-DVX)
D-KAIJ(2)-895	Lange E1 Antares 18T (P .08)	52T03	
D-KAIM(2)-IM	Schleicher ASH 25E	25069	G-CJCV, BGA 4415, D-KAIM
D-KAIN(2)	Scheibe SF 25C Falke	44270	
D-KAIP-IP2	Binder EB28	10	
D-KAIR	Stemme S6 (Res 4.15)	018	
D-KAIS(3)	Schleicher Ka 11 (P.4.12)	V-1	OE-9024, D-KAIS
D-KAIX(3)-4Y	Schempp-Hirth Nimbus-4DM	8/16	N142AB, D-KHIA
D-KAIZ	Glaser-Dirks DG-400	4-44	
D-KAJA(3)	Schleicher ASH 26E	26134	
D-KAJC	Sportavia/ Scheibe SF 25C Falke	4241	
D-KAJD(2)	DG Flugzeugbau DG-808C Competition	8-342B241X9	
D-KAJE(2)	Sportavia/ Scheibe SF 25C Falke	4243	
D-KAJH(2)	Glaser-Dirks DG-400	4-232	
D-KAJK(2)	Glaser-Dirks DG-400	4-158	
D-KAJM(2)-JM	Lange E1 Antares	08	
D-KAJO(2)	Glaser-Dirks DG-400	4-241	I-CAJO
D-KAJP	Valentin Taifun 17E-II	1135	
D-KAJR	Schempp-Hirth Ventus cT	113/384	
D-KAJT	Technoflug Piccolo B	95	D-KPIC(2), OE-9396, D-KIIC
D-KAJW-TM	Schempp-Hirth Discus bT	116/470	
D-KAKA(3)	Scheibe SF 25C Rotax-Falke	44641	ZS-GZL, D-KYGL
D-KAKE	Scheibe SF 25A Motorfalke	4525	
D-KAKG	Schleicher ASW 24E	24856	
D-KAKJ	DG Flugzeugbau DG-1000T (P. 8.11)	10-59T3	D-3543, D-KAKA(2)
D-KAKL-DM	Schempp-Hirth Ventus-2cT	173	
D-KAKM	DG Flugzeugbau DG-1000T	10-70T9	
D-KAKO(4)	Schleicher ASH 25M	25166	D-2715
D-KAKY(2)	Schleicher ASH 25E (P. 3.11)	25162	D-8122, OH-854, D-7021
D-KALB(2)	Sportavia/ Fournier RF-4D	4146	
D-KALC	Sportavia/ Fournier RF-4D	4102	
D-KALD(2)	HOAC HK 36R Super Dimona	36311	

Reg	Type	c/n	Prev id
D-KALE(3)	Schempp-Hirth Ventus-2cM	108/223	
D-KALF(2)	Lange Antares LF 20E (P.10.99)	1	
D-KALG	Sportavia/ Fournier RF-4D	4108	
D-KALH(3)-LH	Schempp-Hirth Arcus M	119	
D-KALI(2)	Schempp-Hirth Ventus-2cM	140	
D-KALK(3)-GE	Schempp-Hirth Ventus-2cxT	205	
D-KALL(2)	Scheibe SF 25B Falke	4634	
D-KALM(3)	Schempp-Hirth Ventus-2cxM	254	
D-KALN	Scheibe SF 25B Falke	4637	
D-KALO(2)	AVO 68v Samburo	029	
D-KALR	Ruppert Rhönlerche II (Constructed from Rhönlerche II c/n 3026 ex D-5301)	01	
D-KALT-LT	Schempp-Hirth Nimbus-3DT	22	
D-KALU(2)	Schempp-Hirth Arcus M	141	
D-KALZ	Schempp-Hirth Ventus-2cM	10/27	
D-KAMA	Scheibe SF 25A Motorfalke	4527	
D-KAMB(2)	Grob G 109/2400	6010	
D-KAMC(2)	Scheibe SF 25C Falke	44733	
D-KAME(4)-ME	Schleicher ASH-30Mi	30006	
D-KAMG(2)	Scheibe SF 27M-A	6319	OE-9034, D-KECJ(2)
D-KAMI (2)	Hoffmann H-36 Dimona II	36259	OE-9300
D-KAMK(2)-MK	Schleicher ASH 25M	25253	(D-KAYK), SE-UNU, (D-KHHH)
D-KAML(2)	Glaser-Dirks DG-400	4-186	
D-KAMN	Scheibe SF 25C Rotax-Falke	44519	
D-KAMQ	Scheibe SF 25C Rotax-Falke	44621	
D-KAMR	Schempp-Hirth Discus bT	42/355	
D-KAMS(2)	AMS Flight Carat A	CA004	
D-KAMT	Aeromot AMT-200 Super Ximango	200.060	
D-KAMU(2)	Grob G 109/2400	6138	
D-KAMW	Glaser-Dirks DG-500M	5E15M9	
D-KAMY(3)	Scheibe SF 25C Rotax-Falke	44547	
D-KANA(3)	Eiriavion PIK-20E	20204	OY-XJN, (OH-554)
D-KANC(3)	Grob G 109	6039	
D-KAND(2)	Glaser-Dirks DG-800LA	8-25A22	
D-KANE	Scheibe SF 27M-B	6330	
D-KANF(2)	Technoflug Piccolo	014	
D-KANG-NG	Schleicher ASW 28-18E	28730	
D-KANH-X7	Lange E1 Antares 18T (P 7.08) (Res as G-CKSF)	50T02	
D-KANI	Scheibe SF 25A Motorfalke	4543	
D-KANN(2)-NN	Schempp-Hirth Arcus M	11	
D-KANS	Schempp-Hirth Ventus-2cM (Res.06)	18/36	OH-962, D-KKJB
D-KANT(2)	Sportavia/ Fournier RF-4D	4086	F-BOXO
D-KANU(2)	Schleicher ASK 16	16023	
D-KANZ(3)	Schleicher ASW 28-18E	28739	
D-KAOB(3)	Schempp-Hirth Duo Discus XLT	254	
D-KAOC	Sportavia/ Scheibe SF 25B Falke	4868	
D-KAOD(2)	Sportavia/ Scheibe SF 25C Falke	4229	
D-KAOE(2)	Sportavia/ Scheibe SF 25C Falke	4230	
D-KAOG(2)	HOAC HK-36TTC Super Dimona	36701	SE-UDC, OY-STX
D-KAOL(2)-OL	Schempp-Hirth Nimbus-4M	17/41	
D-KAOM(2)	Otto Daidalos (P.09)	1	
D-KAOO	Scheibe SF 25C Falke	4419	
D-KAOR	Scheibe SF 25B Falke	AB.46306	
D-KAOS	Scheibe SF 28A Tandem-Falke	5703	
D-KAOT(2)	Alpavia/ Fournier RF-3	22	OE-9155, D-KEHL, F-BMDC
D-KAOU	Sportavia/ Scheibe SF 25C Falke	4234	
D-KAPA(2)	Sportavia/ Fournier RF-4D	4052	C-FAZO, CF-AZO, N2187,
D-KAQE			
D-KAPB(2)	DG Flugzeugbau DG-505MB	5E236B16	PH-1267
D-KAPC	Scheibe SF 25B Falke	4667	
D-KAPD(2)	Siren PIK-30	725	F-CFPI
D-KAPE(3)	Schleicher ASW 27-18E (ASG 29E)	29645	OH-1008
D-KAPF(2)	Schleicher ASH 26E	26070	
D-KAPG(2)	HOAC HK 36R Super Dimona	36389	
D-KAPH	Schleicher ASH 26E	26241	
D-KAPI (2)	Grob G 109/2400	6072	(VH- . . .)
D-KAPJ	Wezel Apis Jet (P. 12.11)	W010-GH01	
D-KAPL	Schleicher ASH 26E	26205	
D-KAPM	Schempp-Hirth Ventus cT	164/535	
D-KAPO(2)	Nitzsche AVo 68-R 115 Samburo	12	
D-KAPP(2)-App	Schleicher ASH 26E	26189	D-9922
D-KAPR	Glaser-Dirks DG-400	4-228	
D-KAPS(2)	Glaser-Dirks DG-800LA	8-62A37	
D-KAPT	Sportavia/ Fournier RF-4D	4083	PH-DYL, OO-WAD
D-KAPU(3)	Jonker Sailplanes JS/MD Single (P 4.15)	1C-079	
D-KAPW-PW	Lange E1 Antares	12	
D-KAPX	Schempp-Hirth Ventus-2cxM	194	
D-KAQA	Sportavia/ Fournier RF-4D	4038	
D-KAQB	Raab Krähe IV	AB 106	
D-KAQI	Sportavia/ Fournier RF-4D	4053	
D-KAQY(2)	Schleicher ASK 14	14022	HB-2002
D-KARA(4)	Scheibe SF 25C Rotax-Falke	44607	
D-KARB(2)	DG Flugzeugbau DG-808C	8-375B274X38	
D-KARC	Schempp-Hirth Arcus T	1	
D-KARF	Scheibe SF-25C Falke 2000	44268	
D-KARG	Hoffmann H-36 Dimona	36104	
D-KARH	Schempp-Hirth Ventus bT	13/148	D-KADR
D-KARJ	AVO-68S Samburo	012	HB-2039, OE-9140, OE-9117
D-KARL(2)	Sportavia/ Fournier RF-4D	4155	
D-KARO(3)	Sportine Aviacija LAK-17AT	176	HB-2425, LY-GQC
D-KARR(2)	Schempp-Hirth Discus bT	91/429	
D-KARS	ICA/Brasov IS-28M2/G	69	
D-KART(2)	Schempp-Hirth Arcus M	97	
D-KARU	Scheibe SF 25D Falke	4608D	
D-KARW	Glaser-Dirks DG-400	4-53	
D-KARX-2M	Schempp-Hirth Arcus M	36	
D-KARZ-IX	Glaser-Dirks DG-400	4-26	
D-KASB(3)-GPS	Schleicher ASW 27-18E (ASG 29E)	29716	
D-KASC(3)	Schempp-Hirth Ventus-2cM	155/. . .	
D-KASD(3)	HOAC HK 36R Super Dimona	36387	
D-KASG(2)	Schempp-Hirth Ventus-2cxM	232	
D-KASH(2)	Scheibe SF 25C Falke 2000	44411	
D-KASK	Scheibe SF 25B Falke	46196	
D-KASN(2)-7N	DG Flugzeugbau DG-1000S	10-60T4	D-7610
D-KASO	Scheibe SF 25B Falke (Res .13)	46200	
D-KASP(2)	Scheibe SF 25C Rotax-Falke	44539	
D-KASU(2)	Scheibe SF 25B Falke	46224	
D-KASV	Scheibe SF 25D Falke	46215D	
D-KASW(2)	Schleicher ASH 26E	26172	
D-KASX(2)	Schempp-Hirth Standard Cirrus B/TOP	685	D-6602
D-KASY(2)	Scheibe SF 25B Falke	46230	
D-KASZ	Scheibe SF 25C Falke 2000	44395	
D-KATA(2)	Aerotechnik L-13SDL Vivat	920419	OK-2102
D-KATC	Scheibe SF 25B Falke	4674	
D-KATD(2)	Technoflug Piccolo	009	
D-KATE(2)	Technoflug Piccolo B	091	
D-KATF	Sportavia/ Fournier RF-5	5050	
D-KATG	Glaser-Dirks DG-500M	5E90M38	(D-KCGM)
D-KATH	Technoflug Piccolo	017	
D-KATL(2)	Grob G 103C Twin IIISL	35005	
D-KATM(2)	Sportavia-Pützer RF-5B Sperber	51077	(VH-. . .)
D-KATO	Sportavia/ Fournier RF-5	5093	
D-KATP-C2	Schleicher ASH 26E	26032	
D-KATS	Glaser-Dirks DG-400	4-22	
D-KATT	Technoflug Piccolo	006	
D-KATV-70	Schleicher ASW 27-18E (ASG 29E)	29587	OM-2929
D-KATW	Grob G 109B	6313	G-BLMY
D-KATX	Diamond HK 36TTC Super Dimona (P.3.04)	36533	N533TT, C-GHUV, OE-9433
D-KATY(2)	Scheibe SF 25C Falke 2000	4446	OE-9084, D-KDAF
D-KATZ(2)	Sportavia/ Fournier RF-5	5122	
D-KAUB(2)	AVO 68s Samburo 2000	010	OE-9119
D-KAUC	Hoffmann H-36 Dimona	36256	
D-KAUE	Schleicher ASK 14 (P.12.06)	14002	D-KAUF(1)
D-KAUF(2)	Grob G 109B	6287	
D-KAUH	Schempp-Hirth Ventus cT	155/502	
D-KAUP	Sportavia/ Fournier RF-5 (Res.)	5118	
D-KAUW-1E	Glaser-Dirks DG-600/18M	6-70M17	
D-KAUZ	Scheibe SF 25C Falke	4455	(D-KOAB)
D-KAVC	Scheibe SF 25C Falke	46243C	
D-KAVF(2)	DG Flugzeugbau DG-800B	8-107B41	
D-KAVH	Scheibe SF 25B Falke	46248	
D-KAVM(2)	Schempp-Hirth Ventus-2cT	89	F-CJSD
D-KAVO(2)	Schleicher ASH 26E	26203	
D-KAVR	Schleicher ASK 16	16009	
D-KAVS	Schleicher ASK 16	16010	
D-KAVT	Schleicher ASK 16	16011	
D-KAVU	Schleicher ASK 16	16003	
D-KAVV	Lo 170-2M (Res .13)	V-1	D-0117
D-KAVY-VY	Jonker Sailplanes JS/MD Single (P. 5.4.16)	1C-100	
D-KAVZ	Diamond HK 36 TC Super Dimona	36821	
D-KAWA(2)	Scheibe SF 25C Rotax-Falke	44650	
D-KAWB(2)-26	Schleicher ASH 26E	26003	D-6161
D-KAWC(2)	Scheibe SF 25E Super-Falke (Res.12.99)	4307	OE-9163, D-KMTF, (D-KDDB)
D-KAWE(2)	Schempp-Hirth Ventus bT	8/133	
D-KAWG	Hoffmann H-36 Dimona	3520	
D-KAWI	Grob G 109B	6343	
D-KAWJ-8F	Glaser-Dirks DG-800A	8-21A18	
D-KAWK	Lange E1 Antares	21	
D-KAWL	Schempp-Hirth Ventus cM	18/447	HB-2164, D-KCPF(1)
D-KAWN-WN	Schleicher ASW 20L/TOP	20258	D-7647
D-KAWO	Hoffmann H-36 Dimona	3698	
D-KAWR	Technoflug Piccolo B	079	
D-KAWS	HOAC HK 36R Super Dimona	36336	
D-KAWT	Grob G 109B	6254	
D-KAWW-4T	Schempp-Hirth Nimbus-4T (P 3.10)	19	
D-KAXA	Schleicher ASK 16	16032	
D-KAXB(2)	Diamond HK 36 TC Super Dimona	36858	OE-9998
D-KAXD(2)	Schleicher ASW 24/TOP	24822	
D-KAXE	Schleicher ASK 16	16044	
D-KAXF(2)-XF	Schleicher ASW 28-18E (Res.06)	28722	D-6822
D-KAXG(2)	Scheibe SF 25C Rotax-Falke	44550	
D-KAXI	Schleicher ASW 24E	24823	
D-KAXK	Schleicher ASW 24E	24817	
D-KAXL-LW	Schleicher ASH 25E	25109	
D-KAXN	Schleicher ASW 22BE	22052	D-4942
D-KAXP-EY	Schleicher ASW 24E	24842	
D-KAXQ	Schleicher ASW 24/TOP	24847	
D-KAXR	Schleicher ASW 24E	24849	
D-KAXU	Schleicher ASH 25E	25142	
D-KAXV	Schleicher ASW 24E	24855	
D-KAXW	Schleicher ASW 22BE	22066	
D-KAXX	Schleicher ASW 24E	24829	
D-KAYA	Schempp-Hirth Ventus-2cxM	215	
D-KAYB	DG Flugzeugbau DG-1001M	10-161M10	
D-KAYC	Technoflug Piccolo B	121	
D-KAYK(2)	Schleicher ASK 16	16017	HB-2031, (D-KAAQ)
D-KAYV	Schempp-Hirth Ventus bT	16/154	
D-KAYX	Diamond HK 36TTC Super Dimona	36692	
D-KAYY(2)-YY	Schempp-Hirth Ventus-2cM	21/39	
D-KAZE(3)	Diamond HK 36TC Super Dimona	36695	
D-KAZF-4W	SZD-41AT Jantar Standard Turbo	B-749	D-4200
D-KAZS(2)	Lange E1 Antares 18T (P 4.13)	43T11	D-2022
D-KAZT(2)-SF	Lange E1 Antares	20	
D-KAZZ-X3	Schempp-Hirth Ventus bT	22/178	OY-HXX, D-KEVV
D-KBAA-V1	Schempp-Hirth Nimbus-4M	6/22	
D-KBAB(2)	Jonker JS/MD Single (P 22.6.16)	1C-102	
D-KBAC(2)	Sportavia-Pützer RF-5B Sperber	51009	OO-PLB, PL70, D-KAUA
D-KBAD(2)	Jonker JS-1C	unkn	
D-KBAE(2)	Sportavia-Pützer Fournier RF5	5062	OE-9251, D-KBAL
D-KBAF	Scheibe SF 25B Falke	4680	
D-KBAG(2)-N41	Schempp-Hirth Nimbus-3DT	55	F-CFUO
D-KBAI	Scheibe SF 25B Falke	4683	
D-KBAJ(2)	Schleicher ASH 26E	26152	
D-KBAK(2)	Hoffmann H-36 Dimona	3501	OE-9199
D-KBAL(2)	Schleicher ASH 25E	25058	D-1811
D-KBAM	Sportavia/ Fournier RF-5	5063	
D-KBAN	Sportavia/ Fournier RF-5	5064	
D-KBAP	Sportavia/ Scheibe SF 25B Falke	4802	
D-KBAS(2)-32	Schleicher ASG 32Mi (P. 5.14)	32001	
D-KBAU(2)	Schleicher ASH 26E	26130	
D-KBAX(2)-WB	Binder EB28 edition	32	

Reg	Type	Serial	Previous ids
D-KBAZ	Scheibe SF 25D Falke	4818D	
D-KBBA	Schleicher ASH 25E	25077	
D-KBBB	Grob G 109B	6301	
D-KBBE-BE	Schempp-Hirth Arcus T	63	
D-KBBF(3)	Binder EB28	7	F-CMBF, D-KMBF
D-KBBI	Schleicher ASH 25M	25171	V5-GAZ, HB-2253
(Res .06)			
D-KBBK(2)	DG Flugzeugbau DG-808C	8-420B319X79	
D-KBBN-BN	Schempp-Hirth Ventus-2cM	201	
D-KBBM	Schleicher ASH 26E	26255	
D-KBBO	Schleicher ASW 22M	22041M	OY-XOI, D-KBBO, OY-XOI,
D-KBBO			
D-KBBR-BR	Rolladen-Schneider LS8-t	8457	D-3344
D-KBBS	HOAC HK 36R Super Dimona	36306	
D-KBBT(2)	Schempp-Hirth Discus-2cT	18	
D-KBBU	Diamond HK 36TTC Super Dimona	36534	OE-9434
D-KBBW	Grob G 109B	6337	
D-KBBX-BX	Schempp-Hirth Ventus-2cxaj	21J	
(P 8.10)			
D-KBBY-CM	Schleicher ASW 22M	22023M	
D-KBBZ	AMS-Flight Carat A	CA14	N317JN
D-KBCA	Scheibe SF 25C Falke 2000	44410	
D-KBCB	Scheibe SF 25C Falke 2000	44579	
D-KBCD(2)	Scheibe SF 25C Falke	44702	
D-KBCE	Technoflug Piccolo	034	
D-KBCF	Scheibe SF 25C Falke 2000	44556	
D-KBCG	Scheibe SF 25C Falke 2000	44524	
D-KBCH	Schempp-Hirth Ventus cM	26/459	
D-KBCK	Scheibe SF 25C Falke	44686	
D-KBCN	Scheibe SF 25C Falke 2000	44633	
D-KBCP	Valentin Taifun 17E II	1109	
D-KBCR	Valentin Taifun 17E	1021	
D-KBCS	Schempp-Hirth Ventus-2cM	76/194	
D-KBCU	DG Flugzeugbau DG-808B	8-287B193	HB-2400
D-KBCW	Glaser-Dirks DG-600/18M	6-73M21	
D-KBCX-CX	Schempp-Hirth Discus-2cT	105	D-9460
D-KBDA	Sportavia/ Fournier RF-4D	4158	
D-KBDB-KR	Glaser-Dirks DG-600/18M	6-87M33	
D-KBDC	Glaser-Dirks DG-600/18M	6-62M13	
D-KBDD-3D	Eiriavion PIK-20E	20283	HB-2055
D-KBDE	Sportine Aviacija LAK-17AT	156	LY-GIX
D-KBDF	HOAC HK 36R Super Dimona	36397	
D-KBDG(4)	DG Flugzeugbau DG-800B	8-120B49	ZS-GVC, D-KBDG(4)
D-KBDI	Glaser-Dirks DG-600/18M	6-64M15	HB-2222
(Res .11)			
D-KBDP	Schleicher ASH 26E	26147	
D-KBDS	Technoflug Piccolo B	071	
D-KBDU-DU	Schempp-Hirth Duo Discus xT	176	
D-KBDV	Schempp-Hirth Ventus cM	110/611	
D-KBDW(2)-FUN	Schempp-Hirth Discus-2T	7/106	PH-1232, D-KBDW
D-KBEA(2)	Binder EB29D	33	
D-KBEB(3)-LF	Schleicher ASH 26E	26208	
D-KBEE-YT	Schleicher ASW 22M	22028M	
D-KBEI	Valentin Kiwi	3008	HB-2273, D-KBEI
D-KBEJ	Schleicher ASH 26E	26126	
D-KBEK(2)	Diamond HK 36TTC Super Dimona	36696	
D-KBEL	Technoflug Piccolo B	087	
D-KBEO	Sportavia-Pützer Fournier RF4D	4123	I-BPLG, F-BPLG
D-KBER	Grob G 109	6058	
D-KBES(2)	Technoflug Piccolo B	024	HB-2149, D-KCFA(1)
D-KBEW	Schempp-Hirth Discus bT	107/454	
D-KBFD-FD	Schleicher ASH 25Mi	25173	D-1724
D-KBFF	Diamond HK 36TS Super Dimona	36416	OE-9416
D-KBFG-4Z	Schempp-Hirth Nimbus-3DT	43	
D-KBFH	Schleicher ASH 25E	25059	
D-KBFM(2)-FM	Schempp-Hirth Duo Discus xT	129	
D-KBFO	Schempp-Hirth Nimbus-4T	15	
D-KBFR	Grob G 109B	6334	
D-KBFS	Schleicher ASH 26E	26257	
D-KBFU-FU	Schleicher ASH 25E	25168	
D-KBFV	Schempp-Hirth Duo Discus xT	155	
D-KBGA(2)-GA	Schleicher ASG 32Mi	32004	
D-KBGG-HP	Schempp-Hirth Nimbus-3DM	21/49	OY-XTU
D-KBGJ	Schleicher ASH 31Mi	31105	
D-KBGM	Valentin Taifun 17E	1023	
D-KBGN	Grob G 109B	6209	
D-KBGO(2)	DG Flugzeugbau DG-808B	8-336B235	
D-KBGR	Scheibe SF 25C Falke 2000	44363	
D-KBGS(2)	DG Flugzeugbau LS8-t	8524	
D-KBGV	Schempp-Hirth Discus bT	47/363	
D-KBGY-2i	Schempp-Hirth Nimbus-4M	20	
D-KBHA(2)	Schempp-Hirth Ventus-2cxT	210	
D-KBHB(2)	Jonker JS/MD Single	1C-089	
(P 5.4.16)			
D-KBHD	Schleicher ASW 22BLE	22058	
D-KBHE	Schleicher ASH 26E	26112	
D-KBHF	Schleicher ASH 26E	26029	
D-KBHG	Schempp-Hirth Ventus cM	13/437	
D-KBHH-S	Schempp-Hirth Ventus cT	115/386	D-5888
D-KBHI	Aerotechnik L-13SEH Vivat	940516	D-KOLB
D-KBHJ	Valentin Taifun 17E	1062	
D-KBHK(2)-HK	Schempp-Hirth Discus bT	21/311	
D-KBHM(2)	DG Flugzeugbau DG-808C	8-407B306X68	
D-KBHO-HO	Schempp-Hirth Ventus-2cM	78/161	OE-9411
D-KBHR	Schempp-Hirth Ventus cM	51/495	PH-1044, D-KBFL(1)
D-KBHS-MM	Schleicher ASW 22BLE	22061	
D-KBHT	Schempp-Hirth Ventus-2cT	168	
D-KBIA	Scheibe SF 25B Falke	46156	
D-KBIC	Scheibe SF 25B Falke	46158	
D-KBIG	Scheibe SF 25D Falke	46162D	
D-KBII (2)	Schempp-Hirth Ventus cM	3/403	
D-KBIL	Scheibe SF 25B Falke	46166	
D-KBIM(2)-PB	Schempp-Hirth Ventus bT	6/126	HA-4521, PH-925, (BGA2981), D-KMTL(1)
D-KBIP	Scheibe SF 25B Falke	46170	
D-KBIT(2)	Sportavia/ Fournier RF-5	5046	
D-KBIU	Scheibe SF 25D Falke	46174D	
D-KBIV(2)	Schempp-Hirth Duo Discus T	107/43	
D-KBIX(2)	Schempp-Hirth Ventus cM	88/571	
D-KBJA(2)	Schempp-Hirth Discus-2c-FES		
(Res .16)			
D-KBJB-2J	Schleicher ASW 27-18E (ASG 29E)	29548	
D-KBJF	Schempp-Hirth Ventus cT	178/583	
D-KBJJ	DG Flugzeugbau DG-1001M	10-167M16	
D-KBJK	AMS Flight Carat A	CA015	N567RL, HB-2410
(P.5.07)			
D-KBJL(2)-BC	Schempp-Hirth Nimbus-4DM	61	
D-KBJP-JP	Schempp-Hirth Ventus-2cxT	132	
D-KBKA-KA	Schempp-Hirth Discus bT	49/366	
D-KBKB	HOAC HK 36R Super Dimona	36323	
D-KBKD	Schempp-Hirth Discus bT	162/570	
D-KBKI(2)-KI	Schleicher Arcus M	110	
D-KBKJ-KJ	Schleicher ASH 26E	26067	
D-KBKM	Schleicher ASH 26E	26087	
D-KBKS-MC	Schleicher ASW 22BLE	22040	D-2322
D-KBKT-KT	Schleicher ASW 27-18E (ASG 29E)	29672	
D-KBKW-WO	Schempp-Hirth Duo Discus XLT	212	
D-KBLA	Schleicher ASK 16	16031	
D-KBLB	Valentin Taifun 17E	1104	
D-KBLE	DG Flugzeugbau DG-808C	8-351B250X15	PH-1369
D-KBLH	Schempp-Hirth Ventus-2cxM	253	
D-KBLL-JV	Glaser-Dirks DG-600/18M	6-105M47	HB-2216
D-KBLN	Diamond HK 36TTC Super Dimona	36601	
D-KBLS	Diamond HK 36TTC Super Dimona	36553	
D-KBLU	Glaser-Dirks DG-400	4-193	I-KCEO, D-KCEO
(Res 7.15)			
D-KBLV(3)	Schempp-Hirth Discus-2cT	126	
D-KBLW	Glaser-Dirks DG-600/18M	6-53M7	D-5807
D-KBLY	Schleicher ASH 25M	25261	
D-KBMA(2)	Lange E1 Antares	72E54	
D-KBMB	HB-Aircraft HB 23/2400SP	23027	OE-9296
D-KBMC(2)	Schempp-Hirth Arcus M	114	
D-KBMH	Hoffmann H-36 Dimona	36232	OE-9276
D-KBML	Schleicher ASH 26E	26013	D-0962, (D-KWML(1)), D-0962
D-KBMM	Schleicher ASW 24E	24814	
D-KBMP	Binder EB29	35	
(P 12.15)			
D-KBMR	Schleicher ASH 25Mi	25224	
D-KBMS	DG Flugzeugbau DG-800B	8-267B175	
D-KBMY	Schleicher ASK 14	14054	HB-2001, D-KISU(2)
D-KBNA	Grob G 109B	6441	
D-KBNG	Schleicher ASH 25M	25098M	OE-9347
D-KBNL-3W	Schleicher ASH 31Mi	31015	VH-IFA, D-KMFA
D-KBNO	Glaser-Dirks DG-500M	5E68M29	
D-KBNT	Schempp-Hirth Ventus cT	122/396	
D-KBOB	Hoffmann H-36 Dimona	3620	
D-KBOH-KB	Schleicher ASW 27-18E (ASG 29E)	29627	
D-KBOM	Diamond HK 36TC Super Dimona	36812	OE-9998
D-KBON	Diamond HK 36TTC Super Dimona	36521	
D-KBOR	DG Flugzeugbau DG-505MB	5E241MB18	SE-UOU, D-KBMC
D-KBOS(2)	Schleicher ASW 27-18E (ASG 29E)	29640	
D-KBOV	Schleicher ASW 24E	24825	
D-KBOX	IAR IS-28M2/GR	79	D-KUNT, YR-2511
D-KBOY	Technoflug Piccolo B	066	
D-KBPB	Glaser-Dirks DG-400	4-265	
D-KBPC	Schleicher ASH 25M	25200	(OO-WZW)
D-KBPE	Schleicher ASW 27-18E (ASG 29E)	29588	
D-KBPG	Schempp-Hirth Arcus M	101	
D-KBPK	HOAC HK 36R Super Dimona	36391	
D-KBPM(2)-AB	Schleicher ASW 28-18E	28711	(F-CJPM)
D-KBPP	Schempp-Hirth Ventus-2cxM	141	
(P.3.04)			
D-KBPT	Schleicher ASH 25M	25184	
D-KBRC-RC	Schleicher ASH 31Mi	31078	
D-KBRD	Schempp-Hirth Discus bT	103/445	
D-KBRE	Stemme S10	10-3	
D-KBRI-BRI	DG Flugzeugbau DG-1000T	10-90T26	
D-KBRO	Schleicher ASW 28-18E	28726	D-8728
D-KBRP	Schempp-Hirth Discus-2cT	51	
D-KBRZ	DG Flugzeugbau DG-1001M	10-217M24	
D-KBSA	DG Flugzeugbau DG-800B	8-205B127	
D-KBSD	Glaser-Dirks DG-800LA	8-16A13	
D-KBSH	Diamond HK 36TC Super Dimona	36651	
D-KBSK	Scheibe SF 25C Turbo-Falke	?	
D-KBSL	Schempp-Hirth Ventus-2cM	103/215	OY-SXL
D-KBSM	Scheibe SF 25B Falke	46105	D-KECS
D-KBSR	Schleicher ASH 26E	26114	
D-KBST(2)-ST	Schempp-Hirth Duo Discus XLT	264	
D-KBTB	Schempp-Hirth Nimbus-4DM	26/37	
D-KBTF	Technoflug Carat	003	
(P. 6.11)			
D-KBTL-TL	Schempp-Hirth Ventus-2cM	120/258	
D-KBTM	DG Flugzeugbau DG-808C	8-377B276	
D-KBTP-TP	Schleicher ASH 25 EB28	25255	
D-KBTR	Glaser-Dirks DG-500M	5E6M4	F-CHJA, D-KGBE
D-KBTS	Schempp-Hirth Discus bM	5/456	
D-KBTT	HOAC HK 36R Super Dimona	36357	OE-9375
D-KBUA	Scheibe SF 25C Falke 2000	44478	
D-KBUB	Scheibe SF 25C Falke 2000	44462	
D-KBUC	Scheibe SF 25C Falke 2000	44476	
D-KBUD	Scheibe SF 25C Falke 2000	44517	
D-KBUE	Scheibe SF 25C Rotax-Falke	44545	
D-KBUF	Scheibe SF 25C Rotax-Falke	44557	
(Tricycle u/c modification)			
D-KBUG	Scheibe SF 25C Falke 2000	44420	
D-KBUH	Scheibe SF 25C Rotax-Falke	44640	
D-KBUI	Scheibe SF 25C Falke 2000	44490	
D-KBUK	Scheibe SF 25C Rotax-Falke	44587	
D-KBUL	Scheibe SF 25C Rotax-Falke	44611	
D-KBUM	Scheibe SF 25C Rotax-Falke	44558	
D-KBUN	Scheibe SF 25C Rotax-Falke	44657	
D-KBUO	Scheibe SF 25C Rotax-Falke	44642	
D-KBUP	Scheibe SF 25C Rotax-Falke	44586	
D-KBUQ	Scheibe SF 25C Rotax-Falke	44625	
D-KBUR	Scheibe SF 25C Rotax-Falke	44631	
D-KBUS(2)	Scheibe SF 25C Rotax-Falke	44622	
D-KBUT	Scheibe SF 25C Rotax-Falke	44565	
D-KBUU	Scheibe SF 25C Rotax-Falke	44651	
D-KBUV	Scheibe SF 25C Rotax-Falke	44623	
D-KBUW	Scheibe SF 25C Rotax-Falke	44627	
D-KBUY	Scheibe SF 25C Rotax-Falke	44669	
D-KBUZ	Scheibe SF 25C Falke 2000	44616	
D-KBVB	Schempp-Hirth Ventus-2cM	39/69	
D-KBVG(2)-VG	Schempp-Hirth Ventus-2cM	175	
D-KBVH-VH	Schempp-Hirth Discus bT	125/483	
D-KBWA	Schempp-Hirth Ventus-2cxM	161	
D-KBWB(2)	Glaser-Dirks DG-800LA	8-1A1	D-KADG(5)
D-KBWC	Scheibe SF 25C Falke	44704	
D-KBWD-WD	Schempp-Hirth Duo Discus T	108	D-KEDD(3)
D-KBWF	Schleicher ASH 26E	26017	D-KRMA
(Res.05)			

Registration	Type	c/n	Previous identities / notes
D-KBWG	Schempp-Hirth Ventus cM	35/471	
D-KBWH-1E	Schleicher ASH 25E	25106	
D-KBWI-W1	Schleicher ASG 32Mi	32005	
D-KBWK	Schleicher ASH 26E	26075	
D-KBWL-V	Schempp-Hirth Nimbus-4DM	3/9	
D-KBWM	Schleicher ASW 20L/TOP	20409	OE-9368, OE-5368
D-KBWS(2)	Schleicher ASH 26E	26051	
D-KBWW	HOAC HK 36R Super Dimona	36310	
D-KBXG-XG	Schempp-Hirth Duo Discus XLT	263	
D-KBXH	Schempp-Hirth Ventus cM	72/537	
D-KBXN	Schleicher ASW 28-18E	28720	G-CKHX, BGA 5114, D-KAMF
D-KBXY-XY	Schempp-Hirth Duo Discus xT	137	
D-KBYT	Grob G 109	6025	
D-KBYY-Y	Kickert ETA	05	
D-KCAA(2)	Scheibe SF 25C Rotax-Falke	44620	
D-KCAB	Sportavia/ Scheibe SF 25B Falke	4820	
D-KCAC(2)	Schempp-Hirth Discus-2cT	10	(P.6.05)
D-KCAD(2)	Grob G 109B	6418	
D-KCAE-77	Schempp-Hirth Standard Cirrus/TOP	381	D-9226
D-KCAG	Scheibe SF 25D Falke	46140D	
D-KCAH(2)	Schleicher ASH 26E	26237	
D-KCAJ(2)	Scheibe SF 25B Falke	46207	(D-KASD)
D-KCAK(2)	Schempp-Hirth Ventus-2cM	63/125	
D-KCAM(2)	Schempp-Hirth Discus bT	157/558	HB-2277
D-KCAO	Scheibe SF 25D Falke	46149D	
D-KCAQ	Scheibe SF 25D Falke	46151D	
D-KCAR(2)	HOAC HK-36R Super Dimona	36396	
D-KCAS	Schempp-Hirth Ventus-2cM	94/195	
D-KCAT(2)	Schempp-Hirth Nimbus-4DM	48/65	
D-KCAX	Sportavia-Pützer RF-5B Sperber	51023	
D-KCBA(2)	Schleicher ASH 26E	26238	
D-KCBB	Eiriavion PIK-20E	20268	
D-KCBC	Schempp-Hirth Ventus cM	27/460	(OE-9340)
D-KCBO-LL	Schleicher ASW 24E	24824	
D-KCBP-BP	Schempp-Hirth Discus-2T	37/204	
D-KCBR	Schempp-Hirth Ventus-2cM	101/211	OO-HVD
D-KCBS-BS	DG Flugzeugbau DG-800B	8-264B172	
D-KCBW(2)	Schempp-Hirth Arcus M	51	
D-KCCA	Hoffmann H-36 Dimona	3606	
D-KCCB	Valentin Taifun 17E	1028	
D-KCCC(2)	Schempp-Hirth Ventus-2cxT	152	
D-KCCD	Schempp-Hirth Discus-2cT	39	
D-KCCH(2)	Schleicher ASH 26E	26060	
D-KCCL(2)	Schleicher ASH 31Mi	31041	
D-KCCN	Schleicher ASH 26E	26144	
D-KCCO	Diamond HK 36TTC Super Dimona	36563	
D-KCCP	Hoffmann H-36 Dimona	3521	
D-KCCW	Diamond HK 36TTC Super Dimona	36688	
D-KCDB	Schleicher ASW 28-18E	28719	
D-KCDG(3)	Glaser-Dirks DG-400	4-14	OO-CDG, LX-CDG, (D-KEBM(1))
D-KCEB-PWR	Schleicher ASH 25 EB28	25252	F-CCBF, (D-KBKF), D-KEWK(2)
D-KCEE	Schempp-Hirth Ventus cM	42/481	
D-KCEF	Glaser-Dirks DG-500M	5E40M18	LX-CPF
D-KCEH-B9	Schempp-Hirth Discus bT	36/347	
D-KCEI(2)-I	Schleicher ASW 27-18E (ASG 29E)	29650	
D-KCEK	Schempp-Hirth Ventus bT	24/182	
D-KCEL	Schempp-Hirth Discus bT	45/359	
D-KCEM(2)-ES	Schempp-Hirth Ventus-2cM	291	
D-KCES(2)	Stemme S10	10-2	D-KCHS (P.05)
D-KCFA	DG Flugzeugbau DG-808C	8-410B309X69	(Same c/n as HB-2449. Possibly' X70)
D-KCFB	Technoflug Piccolo	025	
D-KCFF	Technoflug Piccolo	029	
D-KCFI	Technoflug Piccolo	032	
D-KCFL-FL	Schempp-Hirth Discus bT	94/433	
D-KCFM	Schempp-Hirth Ventus-2cxM	167	
D-KCFT	Schleicher ASH 31Mi	31133	
D-KCFW-FW	Schempp-Hirth Arcus M	6	
D-KCGA-GA	Schempp-Hirth Ventus cM	62/519	
D-KCGB	Stemme S10	10-13	
D-KCGG(2)	Schempp-Hirth Arcus M	145	
D-KCHA(2)-HA	Schempp-Hirth Nimbus-4DM	56/76	
D-KCHB	Schempp-Hirth Ventus cT	128/402	
D-KCHC-9C	Rolladen-Schneider LS8-t	8458	D-3072
D-KCHD(2)	Schleicher ASH 31Mi	31140	
D-KCHF	Eiriavion PIK-20E	20205	
D-KCHG(2)-HG	Schleicher ASH 31Mi	31104	
D-KCHJ-FIX	Schempp-Hirth Nimbus-4DM	41	
D-KCHK-HK	Schempp-Hirth Ventus-2cxT	146	
D-KCHL	Schempp-Hirth Ventus cM	54/501	
D-KCHM-HM	Schleicher ASW 22BLE	22073	(Permit)
D-KCHR	Schempp-Hirth Discus 2cT	79	
D-KCHS(2)	Schempp-Hirth Ventus-2cT	40/131	
D-KCHT	HOAC HK 36R Super Dimona	36341	
D-KCIB(2)	Sportavia/ Fournier RF-5	5105	
D-KCIE	Sportavia/ Fournier RF-5	5103	
D-KCIF(2)	Glaser-Dirks DG-400	4-213	
D-KCII	Sportavia-Pützer RF-5B Sperber	51008	
D-KCIJ	Sportavia-Pützer RF-5B Sperber	51011	
D-KCIK	Sportavia-Pützer RF5B Sperber	51003	
D-KCIL(2)	Technoflug Piccolo B	104	
D-KCIN	Sportavia-Pützer RF-5B Sperber	51015	
D-KCIS(3)-IS	Schleicher ASH 31Mi	31020	
D-KCIT-PI	Schempp-Hirth Nimbus-4DM	52/71	OM-7777
D-KCJB-JB	Schempp-Hirth Ventus-2cxM	267	
D-KCJJ	Diamond HK 36TC Super Dimona	36565	OE-9450
D-KCJT-JT	Schempp-Hirth Ventus-2cM	52/106	
D-KCKA	DG Flugzeugbau DG-1000T	10-155T50	
D-KCKC	HOAC HK 36R Super Dimona	36394	PH-1135, HB-2259
D-KCKM-NH	Schleicher ASW 20CL TOP	20727	D-5360 (P.5.06) (AMT Draline Turbine jet conversion)
D-KCKN	Schempp-Hirth Discus-2cT	66	
D-KCKU	Stemme S6	6.T.09.008	(P.09)
D-KCKW	Schempp-Hirth Ventus-2cM	169	
D-KCLB(2)	Schleicher ASW 20CL/TOP	20738	D-3838
D-KCLD	Scheibe SF 28A Tandem-Falke	5774	
D-KCLE(2)	Nitzsche AVo 68-R115 Samburo	013	
D-KCLG(2)-LG	Schleicher ASH 31Mi	31008	
D-KCLI	Scheibe SF 28A Tandem-Falke	5779	
D-KCLL	DG Flugzeugbau DG-808C	8-385B284X46	
D-KCLO	Grob G 109B	6346	
D-KCMB(2)	Schempp-Hirth Arcus M	84	
D-KCMC	Schempp-Hirth Ventus-2cxM	184	
D-KCMD	DG Flugzeugbau DG-808C	8-338B237X6	OY-XUX, D-KSUN
D-KCMH	Schleicher ASH 26E	26024	
D-KCMI	Schempp-Hirth Ventus-2cxM	144	
D-KCML-ML	Lange E1 Antares	04	
D-KCMM-MM	Schempp-Hirth Nimbus-3DM	2/14	
D-KCMO-MC	Schempp-Hirth Ventus-2cxT	131	
D-KCMR	Schempp-Hirth Discus-2cT	86	
D-KCNO-A1	Schempp-Hirth Arcus T	16	
D-KCOK	Hoffmann H-36 Dimona	3623	
D-KCOL	AVO 68v Samburo	025R	
D-KCON	Stemme S6	6.T.09.007	(P. 7.09)
D-KCOR(2)	Schleicher ASH 25M	25222	D-1746
D-KCOT(2)	Jonker Sailplanes JS/MD Single	1C-087	(P 6.15)
D-KCPB	Schempp-Hirth Ventus cM	15/442	HB-2135, D-KCPB
D-KCPC	Sportavia/ Fournier RF-5	5124	
D-KCPE(2)	DG Flugzeugbau DG-800B	8-128B57	
D-KCPF(2)	Glaser-Dirks DG-500M	5E32M16	
D-KCPH-PH	Schleicher ASW 28-18E	28738	D-0186
D-KCPM	Schempp-Hirth Duo Discus T	128	
D-KCPS	Schempp-Hirth Ventus cM	52/498	
D-KCPT	Schempp-Hirth Ventus-2cxaj	7J	
D-KCPV	Stemme S6	6.T.09.011	(Res 4.15)
D-KCRA	Grob G 109B	6520	
D-KCRB	Schleicher ASW 27-18E (ASG 29E)	29700	
D-KCRE-RE	Glaser-Dirks DG-400	4-194	
D-KCRH	Schleicher ASH 25M	25245	
D-KCRS-RS	Schempp-Hirth Ventus-2cxT	216	
D-KCRT	Schempp-Hirth Janus CT	14/273	
D-KCSA(2)	Aerotechnik L-13SL Vivat	930511	
D-KCSC	Schempp-Hirth Ventus-2cT	175	
D-KCSE-DD	Schempp-Hirth Duo Discus XLT	219	
D-KCSF	Scheibe SF 25B Falke	4626	OE-9173, D-KIMA, (D-KIMG)
D-KCSG	Schleicher ASW 24E	24835	
D-KCSJ	DG Flugzeugbau DG-808C	8-437B336X96	
D-KCSM	Schleicher ASW 27-18E (ASG 29E)	29618	
D-KCSP-SP	Schleicher ASW 27-18E (ASG 29E)	29577	(W/o 9.8.16)
D-KCSS-TA2	Schleicher ASW 27-18E (ASG 29E)	29615	
D-KCSW	DG Flugzeugbau DG-800B	8-226B140	
D-KCSX	Schempp-Hirth Ventus-2cM	118/253	
D-KCTA(2)	Hoffmann H-36 Dimona	36103	OO-VIE, D-KFLG (P.2.00)
D-KCTB(2)	Hoffmann H 36 Dimona II	36235	PH-896, F-WGAO (Res .5.16)
D-KCTC(2)	Schleicher ASW 27-18E (ASG 29E)	29705	
D-KCTH-EV	Schempp-Hirth Discus-2cT	92	
D-KCTT	Schempp-Hirth Ventus cM	53/500	
D-KCTO-TO	Glaser-Dirks DG-800B	8-59B8	
D-KCTP	Binder EB28	09	
D-KCTS	Glaser-Dirks DG-600M	6-43M2	D-KMWS (Res.09)
D-KCUB-25	Schempp-Hirth Ventus-2cxT	193	
D-KCUF(2)	Schempp-Hirth Discus bT	54/372	HB-2198
D-KCUM	Stemme S10-VT	11-042	
D-KCUX	Stemme S6	6.T.09.006	(P.09) (Same c/n as D-KAZA, possibly should be 6.T.09.009 ?)
D-KCVH-VH	DG Flugzeugbau DG-808B	8-333B232	
D-KCVN	DG Flugzeugbau DG-808C	8-355B254X19	HB-2428
D-KCVV	Scheibe SF 25E Super Falke	4324	OO-CVV, D-KEFR
D-KCWB	Glaser-Dirks DG-400	4-267	
D-KCWD	Schleicher ASH 26E	26108	
D-KCWE-WE	Schempp-Hirth Discus bT	48/364	
D-KCWG	Lange E1 Antares	36E34	
D-KCWJ(2)-8F	Schempp-Hirth Arcus M	8/31	(D-KSMA(1))
D-KCWS	Schempp-Hirth Discus bT	63/387	
D-KCWW	Schleicher ASH 26E	26104	
D-KCXM-WB	Schempp-Hirth Ventus-2cxM	188	
D-KCYH-YV	Schempp-Hirth Ventus-2cxM	200	
D-KCYI	Schleicher ASK 16	16030	G-BCYI, D-KIWE(1)
D-KCYY-YY	Schempp-Hirth Ventus-2cxM	174	
D-KCZC-VP	Schempp-Hirth Duo Discus XLT	213	
D-KDAC(2)	Scheibe SF 25C Falke 2000	44265	(D-KDBX)
D-KDAE	Glaser-Dirks DG-400	4-202	F-CGRC
D-KDAG(2)	Schempp-Hirth Nimbus-4T	3/6	VH-YPM, BGA 3816, (BGA 3784)
D-KDAI	Scheibe SF 25C Falke	4449	
D-KDAL(3)-B7	Schempp-Hirth Discus-2T	34/191	
D-KDAM(3)	Schempp-Hirth Discus-2cT	112	
D-KDAN(2)	HOAC HK 36R Super Dimona	36337	
D-KDAO	Scheibe SF 28A Tandem-Falke	5715	
D-KDAR(2)	Technoflug Piccolo	047	
D-KDAS(2)	Schempp-Hirth Ventus cT	159/513	
D-KDAX	Schempp-Hirth Discus-2cT	42	
D-KDAY	Schempp-Hirth Arcus E	2/20	(P 7.10)
D-KDBA	Scheibe SF 25C Falke	44247	
D-KDBB	Scheibe SF 25C Falke	44246	
D-KDBD	Scheibe SF 25E Super-Falke	4343	
D-KDBG(2)	HOAC HK 36R Super Dimona	36392	OE-9392
D-KDBI (2)	Scheibe SF 25C Falke	44258	
D-KDBJ	Scheibe SF 25C Falke	44255	
D-KDBK	Scheibe SF 25K Falke	4901	
D-KDBL(2)	Scheibe SF 25C Falke 2000	44266	(ex Falke 1700)
D-KDBM(2)	Scheibe SF 25C Falke	44271	
D-KDBN(2)	Scheibe SF 25C Falke	44263	
D-KDBQ(2)	Scheibe SF 25C Falke 2000	44273	
D-KDBR(2)	Scheibe SF 25C Falke	44277	
D-KDBS(2)	Scheibe SF 25E Super-Falke	4347	
D-KDBU(3)	Scheibe SF 25C Falke	44279	
D-KDBW	Scheibe SF 25C Falke	44261	
D-KDCB(2)	Rolladen-Schneider LS9	9007	
D-KDCC(4)	Schempp-Hirth Discus-2cT	127	
D-KDCE(2)	Scheibe SF 25C Falke	44235	
D-KDCG	Scheibe SF 25C Falke 2000	44389	HB-2115, D-KNIE(2)
D-KDCH	Scheibe SF 25E Super-Falke	4337	
D-KDCK(2)	Scheibe SF 25C Falke	44243	
D-KDCL(2)	Schleicher ASG 32Mi	32003	

Reg	Type	Serial	Notes
D-KDCM	Schempp-Hirth Ventus-2cxM	233	
D-KDCN(2)	Scheibe SF 25C Falke	44242	
D-KDCO	Scheibe SF 25C Falke	44237	
D-KDCS	Scheibe SF 25C Falke	44245	
D-KDCT	Scheibe SF 25C Falke	44240	
D-KDDA(2)	Scheibe SF 25E Super-Falke	4311	
D-KDDC	Scheibe SF 25E Super-Falke	4308	
D-KDDD	Scheibe SF 25E Super-Falke	4309	
D-KDDF	Scheibe SF 25C Falke	44131	
D-KDDG	Scheibe SF 25C Falke	44132	
D-KDDK	Scheibe SF 25C Falke	44136	
D-KDDM(2)-DM	HpH Glasflügel 304MS	023-MS	
D-KDDP	Scheibe Bergfalke IVM	5901	
D-KDDT	Schempp-Hirth Duo Discus T	73/375	
D-KDDW	Glaser-Dirks DG-600M	6-91M37	
D-KDEB	Scheibe SF 25C Falke	44144	
D-KDEH(2)	Diamond HK 36TTC Super Dimona	36664	
D-KDEJ	Scheibe SF 25C Falke	44177	
D-KDEL(2)	DG Flugzeugbau DG-808C	8-396B295X57	
D-KDEU	Scheibe SF 25C Falke	44194	
D-KDEZ	Scheibe SF 25C Falke	44199	
D-KDFB(2)	Scheibe SF 25C Falke	44214	
D-KDFE(2)	Scheibe SF 25C Falke	44211	
D-KDFF(4)	Stemme S10-VT	11-029	
D-KDFI (2)	Scheibe SF 25C Falke	44217	
D-KDFJ(3)	Scheibe SF 25C Falke	44222	
D-KDFK(2)-AC	Schleicher ASH 26E	26018	
D-KDFL	Scheibe SF 25B Falke	46118	OE-9035, (D-KABQ)
D-KDFM(2)	Scheibe SF 25C Falke	44218	
D-KDFN(4)	Scheibe SF 25E Super-Falke	4335	
D-KDFT	Scheibe SF 25C Falke	44216	
D-KDFU(2)	Scheibe SF 25C Falke	44221	
D-KDGB	Scheibe SF 25C Falke 2000	44280	
D-KDGH(2)	Scheibe SF 25C Falke	44288	
D-KDGI (2)	Scheibe SF 25C Falke	44289	
D-KDGM	Scheibe SF 35	4701	
D-KDGN(2)	Scheibe SF 25C Falke	44293	
D-KDGP(2)	Scheibe SF 25C Falke	44295	
D-KDGS	Schempp-Hirth Ventus-2cxM	236	
D-KDGT(2)	Scheibe SF 25K Falke	4904	
D-KDGU(3)	Scheibe SF 25C Falke 2000	4356C	
D-KDGW(3)	Scheibe SF 25C Falke 2000	44303	
D-KDGX	Scheibe SF 25K Falke	4906	
D-KDHA	Diamond HK 36 TC (Res.07)	36.647	PH-1157
D-KDHB	Schleicher ASW 27-18E (ASG 29E)	29644	
D-KDHC	Sportine Aviacija LAK-17AT	198	
D-KDHD	DG Flugzeugbau LS8-t	8529	
D-KDHE	Lange E1 Antares	77T56	
D-KDHF	Schempp-Hirth Discus bT	58/380	
D-KDHG	Schempp-Hirth Ventus-2cM	168	
D-KDHH-IHH	Schempp-Hirth Ventus cM	50/494	
D-KDHL	Glaser-Dirks DG-600/18M	6-99M45	OO-IVC
D-KDHW	Schleicher ASH 31Mi	31055	
D-KDIB	Schempp-Hirth Arcus M (P.5.12)	33	
D-KDID-7D	Schempp-Hirth Ventus-2cxT	148	
D-KDIE	Schempp-Hirth Ventus bT	59/271	
D-KDIH	DG Flugzeugbau DG-808C	8-397B296X58	
D-KDIM	Hoffmann H-36 Dimona	3601	
D-KDIS-S7	Schempp-Hirth Discus-2T	39/212	
D-KDIT	Grob G 109B	6385	
D-KDIY	Stemme S10-VT	11-127	
D-KDJA	Diamond HK 36 TC Super Dimona	36.530	PH-1144
D-KDJH-A2	DG Flugzeugbau DG-808C	8-361B260X25	
D-KDJK	AVO-68R Samburu	028	OE-9165
D-KDJR-6V	Schempp-Hirth Ventus-2cM	65/133	
D-KDKD	HOAC HK 36R Super Dimona	36328	
D-KDKR	Diamond HK 36TTC Super Dimona	36690	
D-KDKT	Schempp-Hirth Discus-2cT	110	
D-KDKW	DG Flugzeugbau DG-800B	8-199B121	VH-XHG, (D-KIWA(2))
D-KDLA	Grob G 109B	6219	OY-XMG
D-KDLD-LD	Schleicher ASH 31Mi	31010	
D-KDLE	Sportavia-Pützer Fournier RF4D	4058	VH-TKD, N7720, D-KISI
D-KDLH	Schempp-Hirth Ventus-2cxM	196	
D-KDLQ-QD	Schempp-Hirth Duo Discus T	223	
D-KDLR(2)	Lange E1 Antares DLR-H2 (P.09)	901	
D-KDLV	Scheibe SF 25C Falke 2000	44325	HA-1267, SE-UBV, D-KOON
D-KDLY-BZ	Schempp-Hirth Duo Discus xLT	275	
D-KDMB(2)	Schleicher ASH 31Mi	31075	
D-KDMC	Schleicher ASW 27-18E (ASG 29E)	29576	
D-KDMD-VIN	DG Flugzeugbau DG-800B	8-224B138	
D-KDME-ME	Schleicher ASH 31Mi	31128	
D-KDMH	Lange E1 Antares 18T (P 7.14)	41T12	D-0380
D-KDMJ	Diamond HK 36TTC Super Dimona	36697	
D-KDMK-MK	Schempp-Hirth Arcus M	14	
D-KDML	Schempp-Hirth Ventus-2cxT (Res .15)	142	F-CAPY, OM-1802
D-KDMM	Lange E1 Antares	62E51	(D-KULS)
D-KDMO-MAX	Schleicher ASW 27-18E (ASG 29E)	29658	
D-KDMS	Grob G 109	6059	
D-KDNM	Grob G 109B	6373	OE-9258
D-KDOB	Fournier RF9	6	EC-DOB, F-ODNP, F-BZCX
D-KDOC-OC	Schempp-Hirth Duo Discus xT	150	
D-KDOL	Schleicher ASH 31Mi	31044	
D-KDOM	HOAC HK 36R Super Dimona	36313	
D-KDON	Glaser-Dirks DG-400	4-41	
D-KDOO	Schleicher ASW 27-18E (ASG 29E)	29519	G-CKOO, D-KAAD
D-KDOS-GB	Schempp-Hirth Discus bT	46/362	
D-KDOT	Diamond HK 36TTC Super Dimona	36603	
D-KDOV-OV	Schleicher ASH 25M	25143	D-7062
D-KDPB	HOAC HK 36R Super Dimona	36348	
D-KDPF-F2	Schempp-Hirth Ventus-2cxaJ (P 4.10)	J10/520	D-4670
D-KDPI	Glaser-Dirks DG-400	4-96	HB-2234, (D-KMOA), HB-2234, OO-DGI
D-KDPK	Stemme S6 (P.09)	6.T.09.003	
D-KDPR	HOAC HK 36R Super Dimona	36340	
D-KDPS	HOAC HK 36R Super Dimona	36361	
D-KDPT(2)	Schempp-Hirth Discus bT (Res .16)	65/391	G-CHJH, BGA3978, N224WT
D-KDPV	HOAC HK 36R Super Dimona	36364	
D-KDPZ-PZ	Schempp-Hirth Ventus cT	156/503	
D-KDRA	HOAC HK 36R Super Dimona	36334	
D-KDRD-RD	Stemme S10-VT	11-078	(D-KSMG)
D-KDRK	Diamond HK 36TTC Super Dimona (Res.08)	36804	
D-KDRM	Schleicher ASW 27J (P. 1.14)	27069	D-7716, OO-YYX, OE-5681, D-4427
D-KDRR	DG Flugzeugbau DG-808C	8-363B262Z1	
D-KDRS	Schleicher ASG 32Mi	32007	
D-KDRT	Glaser-Dirks DG-400	4-262	F-CGRJ
D-KDSA(2)	Glaser-Dirks DG-400	4-256	
D-KDSD	Schempp-Hirth Quintus M (P 5.13)	15	
D-KDSG(2)-30	Schleicher ASH 30Mi (P. 2.13)	30003	
D-KDSN(2)-LP	Schempp-Hirth Ventus 2cM	100/210	N70ZZ
D-KDSO(2)	Stemme S10-VT	11-111	
D-KDSP(2)	Schempp-Hirth Discus-2T	40	
D-KDSS(2)	Schempp-Hirth Ventus-2cxM	259	
D-KDST(2)	DG Flugzeugbau DG-800B	8-175B99	
D-KDTA	Grob G 109	6090	
D-KDTB	Grob G 109	6089	
D-KDTH	Grob G 109B	6415	N721DL
D-KDTI	Schempp-Hirth Nimbus-4DM	70	
D-KDTM-XM	Jonker Sailplanes JS1C Revelation (P 7.15)	1C-069	
D-KDTX	Schempp-Hirth Ventus-2cxM	190	(D-KXXC)
D-KDUA-UA	Schleicher ASW 27-18E (ASG 29E) (P.7.07)	29515	
D-KDUG	Schleicher ASH 26E	26040	
D-KDUI-AIR	DG Flugzeugbau DG-1000T	10-80T19	PH-1356
D-KDUL	Glaser-Dirks DG-500M	5E19M11	
D-KDUO-DDT	Schempp-Hirth Duo Discus T	116/448	G-RDDT, BGA 5150
D-KDUT-D8	Schempp-Hirth Discus bT	8/271	
D-KDWD	DG Flugzeugbau DG-800B	8-126B55	N98NL
D-KDWE-WE	Schempp-Hirth Ventus-2cxT	229	
D-KDWF-WF	Schempp-Hirth Duo Discus XLT	175	
D-KDWN	Grob G 109B	6221	
D-KDWR	Glaser-Dirks DG-400	4-97	
D-KDWS	Valentin Kiwi	K-3012	
D-KDXL	Schempp-Hirth Duo Discus XLT	234	
D-KDXT	Schempp-Hirth Duo Discus xT	154	
D-KEAA	Sportavia/ Fournier RF-5	5092	
D-KEAB(2)	Schleicher ASH 26E	26092	D-9461
D-KEAC(2)	Schempp-Hirth Discus-2cT	129	
D-KEAF	Sportavia/ Scheibe SF 25C Falke	4225	
D-KEAH	Sportavia/ Fournier RF-5	5110	
D-KEAJ(3)	DG Flugzeugbau DG-808C (W/o 4.5.16)	8-390B289X51	
D-KEAL	Sportavia-Pützer RF-5B Sperber	51028	
D-KEAP(4)	Schempp-Hirth Discus-2cT	97	
D-KEAS(2)	Schempp-Hirth Ventus cT	165/540	
D-KEAT	Scheibe SF 25B Falke	46253	
D-KEAZ(2)	Scheibe SF 25C Rotax-Falke	44578	
D-KEBD(2)	Schleicher ASW 22BLE	22249	N347KS
D-KEBF(2)-BV	Schempp-Hirth Discus-2cT (P.6.05)	9	
D-KEBG(3)	Schempp-Hirth Arcus M	140	
D-KEBH(3)	Diamond HK 36TC Super Dimona	36519	
D-KEBP	Glaser-Dirks DG-400	4-19	
D-KEBS	Scheibe SF 25C Falke 2000	44394	
D-KEBT(2)	Eiriavion PIK-20E	20210	
D-KEBU(3)-EB	Schleicher ASH 31Mi	31100	
D-KEBV	Schempp-Hirth Nimbus-3DM	16/39	
D-KEBW	Glaser-Dirks DG-400 (W/o 25.5.11)	4-79	
D-KEBY	Akaflieg München Mü 23 Saurier	V-1	
D-KECA(2)-AW	Eiriavion PIK-20E	20246	
D-KECB	Schleicher ASK 14	14014	
D-KECD(2)	Schempp-Hirth Ventus cT	111/379	
D-KECK(2)	Scheibe SF 25B Falke	4697	
D-KECM	Scheibe SF 25B Falke	46100	
D-KECN	Scheibe SF 25B Falke	46101	
D-KECP(2)	Glaser-Dirks DG-400	4-10	
D-KECT	Scheibe SF 27M-A	6318	
D-KECU	Scheibe SF 24B Motorspatz I (Permit)	4030	
D-KEDB(2)	Scheibe SF 25B Falke	4638	
D-KEDD(4)	Schempp-Hirth Arcus T	15	
D-KEDE(3)	Schleicher ASK 14	14016	
D-KEDG(2)	Scheibe SF 25B Falke	4642	
D-KEDI(3)	DG Flugzeugbau DG-800B	8-181B105	
D-KEDJ(2)	Schempp-Hirth Ventus cM	43/483	
D-KEDR	Schempp-Hirth Ventus-2cxT	167	
D-KEDX	Diamond HK 36 TTS Super Dimona	36855	OE-9998, OE-9997
D-KEDY(4)	DG Flugzeugbau DG-808XB Competition	8-331B230X3	
D-KEEB	Scheibe SF 25C Rotax-Falke	44535	
D-KEED	Schempp-Hirth Ventus-2cM (P.7.12)	125/274	D-KOFB
D-KEEE	Sportavia/ Fournier RF-4D	4039	OE-9020
D-KEEG	Scheibe SF 25C Rotax-Falke	44592	
D-KEEH	Scheibe SF 25C Rotax-Falke	44691	
D-KEEI	Schempp-Hirth Ventus-2cT	25/93	
D-KEEK	Stemme S10-VT	11-055	PT-PZF, PP-XXL
D-KEEM-E	Schempp-Hirth Duo Discus T	133	
D-KEEN	DG Flugzeugbau DG-800B	8-164B88	
D-KEES	Schleicher ASW 27-18E (ASG 29E)	29547	
D-KEEX-R1	Schempp-Hirth Ventus bT	31/202	F-CEDT, F-WEDT
D-KEFC	Scheibe SF 25C Falke	44153	
D-KEFG	Scheibe SF 25C Falke	44157	
D-KEFJ	Scheibe SF 25C Falke	44162	
D-KEFK	Scheibe SF 25E Super-Falke	4318	
D-KEFO	Scheibe SF 25C Falke	44163	
D-KEFS	Scheibe SF 25C Falke	44167	
D-KEFT	Scheibe SF 25C Falke	44170	
D-KEFW	Scheibe SF 25C Falke	44168	
D-KEFY(2)	Scheibe SF 25C Falke	44174	
D-KEGB	Scheibe SF 25C Rotax-Falke	44466	
D-KEGF	Schleicher ASH 26E	26046	D-8771
D-KEGG-GG	HpH Glasflügel 304MS	18-MS	OK-6404
D-KEGH	Diamond HK 36TTC Super Dimona	36.654	PH-1221, G-BYRL
D-KEGL(2)	Scheibe SF 25C Falke 2000	44525	
D-KEGM	Schleicher ASH 25E	25047	
D-KEGO(2)	Hoffmann H-36 Dimona	36261	OE-9308

Registration	Type	Serial	Notes
D-KEGP(2)-JM	Schempp-Hirth Arcus M	55	
D-KEGR	Glaser-Dirks DG-400	4-261	
D-KEGU(2)	Schleicher ASK 14 (P 10.15)	14013	
D-KEGY-OLC	Schempp-Hirth Discus-2cT	118	
D-KEHA	Eiriavion PIK-20E	20239	
D-KEHB(2)	Schleicher ASH 25Mi	25235	
D-KEHC	Glaser-Dirks DG-400	4-34	
D-KEHD-HD	HpH Glasflügel 304MS	015-MS	OK-3040
D-KEHE	Schleicher ASK 14	14017	
D-KEHF	Glaser-Dirks DG-400	4-163	I-KEHF, D-KEHF
D-KEHH-IHH	Schempp-Hirth Ventus bT	20/170	D-4110
D-KEHI(3)	Sportine Aviacija LAK-17B FES	236	
D-KEHK(2)-HK	Lange E1 Antares	02	(D-KKPB)
D-KEHL(2)-HL	Schempp-Hirth Discus-2cT	76	
D-KEHM	Technoflug Piccolo (Mod to Piccolo B, .07)	004	
D-KEHO(2)	Grob G 109	6022	
D-KEHU(2)	HOAC HK 36R Super Dimona	36315	
D-KEHW	Schleicher ASH 25Mi	25262	
D-KEHY(2)	Hoyer / Marco J-5/Ho	01	
D-KEHZ	Schempp-Hirth Nimbus-4M	15/38	
D-KEIC(2)	Schempp-Hirth Duo Discus T	134	
D-KEIE(2)	Scheibe SF 25C Falke	4494	
D-KEIH	Scheibe SF 25C Falke	4488	
D-KEII	Schempp-Hirth Discus-2cT	119	(D-KJMS)
D-KEIJ	Scheibe SF 25C Falke	4490	
D-KEIK	Schleicher ASK 16	16019	
D-KEIL	Sportavia/ Fournier RF-5	5066	F-BPLY
D-KEIM(2)	Hoffmann H-36 Dimona	36142	
D-KEIO(2)	Diamond HK 36TTC Super Dimona	36559	OE-9459
D-KEIS(3)	AMS Flight Carat A	CA009	
D-KEIZ(2)	Schleicher ASW 24E	24850	
D-KEJA-JA	Schempp-Hirth Ventus cM	24/457	
D-KEJC-JC	Schempp-Hirth Janus CT	1/167	
D-KEJD	Glaser-Dirks DG-400	4-131	
D-KEJE-JE	Glaser-Dirks DG-400	4-73	
D-KEJK	Schempp-Hirth Nimbus-3DM	11/29	
D-KEJS	Eiriavion PIK-20E	20244	OO-PCP, D-KEMA(1)
D-KEKB	Schempp-Hirth Ventus cT	97/350	
D-KEKE	Stemme S10-VT	11-009	D-KSTE(9)
D-KEKF	Glaser-Dirks DG-400	4-18	
D-KEKG	DG Flugzeugbau DG-808B	8-332B231	
D-KEKI(2)-IKI	Schempp-Hirth Ventus-2cxM	219	
D-KEKK	Hoffmann H-36 Dimona	36248	
D-KEKM	Grob G 109B	6427	
D-KEKS	Scheibe SF 25C Falke 2000	44391	
D-KEKW-2W	Schempp-Hirth Ventus 2cxT	156	HB-2416
D-KELA(2)	Scheibe SF 25C Falke 2000	44479	
D-KELE	Schleicher ASW 24E	24834	OE-9355
D-KELF-LF	Schleicher ASW 24E	24816	
D-KELG	Hoffmann H-36 Dimona	36257	
D-KELH-IHB	Schempp-Hirth Ventus cM	30/463	
D-KELI	Grob G 109	6013	
D-KELL	Sportavia-Pützer RF-5B Sperber	51079	
D-KELM	Hoffmann H-36 Dimona	3633	
D-KELN	Hoffmann H-36 Dimona	3697	
D-KELO	Eiriavion PIK-20E	20243	
D-KELS	Eiriavion PIK-20E	20261	
D-KELT(2)-LT	Schempp-Hirth Duo Discus xT	138	
D-KELV	Diamond HK 36TTC Super Dimona	36718	
D-KELZ(3)	Scheibe SF 25C Falke 2000	44451	
D-KEMA(2)	Glaser-Dirks DG-400	4-170	
D-KEMB	DG Flugzeugbau DG-800B	8-179B103	
D-KEMC(2)-MC	Schempp-Hirth Discus-2cT	113	
D-KEME-M	Schempp-Hirth Ventus bT	44/234	D-8898
D-KEMF-MF	Schleicher ASW 28-18E	28729	
D-KEMG	Glaser-Dirks DG-800B	8-47B2	D-KIPB
D-KEMH-KP	Schempp-Hirth Nimbus-3DM	12/34	
D-KEMI	Schleicher ASK 16	16040	
D-KEMJ-MJ	Schempp-Hirth Duo Discus T	23/284	(D-7605)
D-KEMK	Schempp-Hirth Discus bT	139/515	
D-KEMO	Schleicher ASK 16B	16039	N16KS, HB-2039
D-KEMP	Sportavia/ Fournier RF-5	5096	
D-KEMS	Hoffmann H-36 Dimona	3641	
D-KEMW-KR	Schleicher ASH 26E	26050	
D-KEMY(2)	DG Flugzeugbau LS8-t	8511	
D-KENC	Valentin Taifun 17E (Res.12.99)	1014	
D-KEND	Sportine Aviacija LAK-17AT	178	LY-GND
D-KENI(2)	Schleicher ASH 25M	25237	
D-KENJ	Technoflug Piccolo B	094	
D-KENO(3)	Rolladen-Schneider LS4 (P. 10.10)	4281	D-5025
D-KENV	Hoffmann H 36 Dimona	3603	PH-1257, D-KENI
D-KEOA	Grob G 109B	6281	
D-KEOC	Grob G 109B	6288	
D-KEOD	Grob G 109B	6294	
D-KEOF	Grob G 109B	6305	
D-KEOH	Grob G 109B	6312	
D-KEOI	Grob G 109B	6309	
D-KEOK	Grob G 109B	6328	
D-KEOM	Grob G 109B	6298	
D-KEOO	Schempp-Hirth Ventus-2cM	3/17	PH-1445, G-VENT, (BGA 4918), D-KBTL
D-KEOR	Scheibe SF 25C Rotax-Falke	44685	
D-KEOS	Scheibe SF 25C Rotax-Falke	44692	
D-KEOW	Grob G 109B	6306	
D-KEPA	Schleicher ASH 25E	25031	
D-KEPB	Grob G 109B	6347	
D-KEPC	Glaser-Dirks DG-400	4-66	
D-KEPG	Lange E1 Antares	22	
D-KEPH-AMI	Schleicher ASW 27-18E (ASG 29E)	29595	
D-KEPI	Grob G 109	6023	
D-KEPK	Glaser-Dirks DG-400	4-289	HB-2211
D-KEPM(2)-PM	Schempp-Hirth Ventus-2cxT	244	
D-KEPO	Hoffmann H-36 Dimona	3689	
D-KEPS-BL	Schempp-Hirth Discus bT	23/316	
D-KEPT	Diamond HK 36TTC Super Dimona	36544	F-CHQA, OE-9444
D-KEPW-PW	MAG Carat A	CA035	
D-KERA(2)	Glaser-Dirks DG-400	4-159	
D-KERB(2)	Scheibe SF 25C Rotax-Falke	44708	
D-KERC	Grob G 109	6102	
D-KERD	Glaser-Dirks DG-400	4-166	
D-KERF-RF	Schempp-Hirth Nimbus-3MR	1	
D-KERG(3)	DG Flugzeugbau DG-800B	8-309B209	
D-KERM-IT	Schleicher ASH 31Mi	31098	
D-KERN	Technoflug Piccolo B	080	
D-KERO(2)	DG Flugzeugbau DG-800B	8-233B147	
D-KERR	DG Flugzeugbau DG-800B	8-293B198	
D-KERW	Schleicher ASH 26E	26078	
D-KERY	Sportavia-Pützer RF5B Sperber	51010	HB-2018
D-KERZ-RZ	Schleicher ASH 26E	26245	N123RZ
D-KESA-PR	Schleicher ASW 27-18E (ASG 29E)	29582	
D-KESD	Diamond HK 36TTC Super Dimona	36556	
D-KESE	Sportavia-Pützer Fournier RF5	5008	(D-KIGY)
D-KESF	Schleicher ASK 21Mi	21880	
D-KESM	DG Flugzeugbau DG-1000S	10-82T21	D-5410
D-KESP(2)-ES	Schempp-Hirth Ventus-2cM	71/146	
D-KESS(2)	Scheibe SF 25C Falke	44110	
D-KEST	Glaser-Dirks DG-400	4-20	
D-KESU	Schempp-Hirth Ventus-2cM	56/110	
D-KETA	Kickert ETA	1	
D-KETB	Grob G 109B	6503	
D-KETE	HpH Glasflügel 304MS	032-MS	
D-KETF	Technoflug Carat	002	(D-KIZX)
D-KETL-4H	Grob G 102 Astir CS 77/TOP	1662	D-3873
D-KETS	Schleicher ASG 32Mi	32020	
D-KETT(3)	DG Flugzeugbau DG-800B	8-203B125	
D-KETU(2)	Schempp-Hirth Discus-2cT	12	
D-KETZ	Grob G 109B	6361	HB-2110, (EAF-672)
D-KEUB-B1	Schempp-Hirth Ventus-2cxT	153	
D-KEUL(2)	Schempp-Hirth Discus-2c FES (P 11.15)	2	
D-KEUN	Valentin Taifun 17E	1063	G-OFUN, D-KHVA(5)
D-KEUP	Schempp-Hirth Nimbus-3DT (Res. .13)	60	F-CFUP
D-KEUX	Fournier RF-9	10	
D-KEVA(2)	DG Flugzeugbau DG-800B	8-99B34	
D-KEVE	Grob G 109B	6397	G-LIVE
D-KEVI	Pfeifer C 10/85	1	
D-KEVK-VK	Schempp-Hirth Ventus-2cM	30/53	PH-1107, D-KTLL
D-KEVL	Schleicher ASH 26E (P.05)	26207	EC-INA
D-KEVT	Schempp-Hirth Ventus-2cxT	234	
D-KEVV	Sportavia-Pützer Fournier RF4D	4019	I-FEWW, F-BORF
D-KEWA	Hoffmann H-36 Dimona	3532	
D-KEWD	Grob G 109B	6431	
D-KEWE	Schempp-Hirth Ventus cT	109/372	
D-KEWI (3)-W1	Schleicher ASH 26E	26044	
D-KEWK(3)	Binder EB28	3	
D-KEWR	Glaser-Dirks DG-800A	8-49A33	
D-KEWS	Schempp-Hirth Ventus bT	2/101	
D-KEWW	Scheibe SF 25C Rotax-Falke	44608	
D-KEXI	Technoflug Piccolo	016	
D-KEXL	Schempp-Hirth Duo Discus T (Res .16)	166	OY-EXL, D-KEXL
D-KEXO	Hoffmann H-36 Dimona	36238	
D-KEXX-XXL	Schempp-Hirth Nimbus-3DT	2	
D-KEYX	Schempp-Hirth Ventus bT (Res.09)	30/199	PH-1395, N609Y, N49895
D-KEYY-YY	Schempp-Hirth Ventus cM	7/423	
D-KEZA	Grob G 109B	6259	
D-KEZF	Stemme S6 (P. 11.11)	017	
D-KEZL	Scheibe SF 25C Falke 2000	44485	
D-KEZW	Diamond HK 36 TC Super Dimona	36856	OE-9998
D-KEZZ	Technoflug Piccolo B	067	HB-2231, D-KAAL
D-KFAA	Schempp-Hirth Ventus-2cM	23/44	
D-KFAB	Schempp-Hirth Ventus-2cM	80/167	
D-KFAC(3)	Schempp-Hirth Ventus-2cM	68/140	D-KETU
D-KFAD	Schempp-Hirth Ventus cT	152/487	OO-ZLQ
D-KFAE	HB-Aircraft HB 23/2400	23034	OE-9348, HB-2143
D-KFAG(2)	Scheibe SF 25C Rotax-Falke	44618	
D-KFAI	Valentin Taifun 17E	1055	OO-TAI, D-KHVA(2)
D-KFAK-AK	Schleicher ASW 28-18E	28710	D-KTAK(2)
D-KFAL	Doppelraab IV MSR	EB-2	D-6207
D-KFAM-A2	Schempp-Hirth Ventus-2cxT	172	
D-KFAN(2)	Glaser-Dirks DG-500M (P.04)	5E95M41	HB-2239
D-KFAP(3)	MAG Carat A	CA033	
D-KFAR	Grob G 109B	6211	HB-2080
D-KFAS(2)	DG Flugzeugbau DG-800B	8-288B194	
D-KFAT	Scheibe SF 25C Rotax-Falke	44569	
D-KFAY	Scheibe SF 25C Falke	4201	SE-UAY, D-KAOF
D-KFBB	HOAC HK 36R Super Dimona	36356	
D-KFBE	Scheibe SF 25C Falke	44210	
D-KFBG	Eiriavion PIK-20E	20223	
D-KFBI	Diamond HK 36TTC Super Dimona	36525	OE-9425
D-KFBK	Valentin Taifun 17E-II	1118	OE-9313, D-KHVA(36)
D-KFBM-BM	Schleicher ASW 28-18E (P.5.04)	28708	
D-KFBO	Schleicher ASH 26E	26137	
D-KFBR-BR	Schempp-Hirth Duo Discus XLT	248	
D-KFBW	Aeromot AMT-200 Super Ximango	200.070	
D-KFBZ	Hoffmann H-36F Dimona (Modified by Frisch Engineering to Rotax 912)	3669	
D-KFCB	DG Flugzeugbau DG-800B	8-214B131	
D-KFCC	Schleicher ASK 21Mi	21857	
D-KFCD	HOAC HK 36R Super Dimona	36350	
D-KFCE	Scheibe SF 25C Rotax-Falke	44533	
D-KFCK	SZD-45A Ogar	B-649	DDR-3503, DM-3503
D-KFCL	Schempp-Hirth Duo Discus xT	131	
D-KFCN	Schempp-Hirth Discus-2cT	116	
D-KFCO	Grob G 109 (P .08)	6120	OE-9259, F-WAQL
D-KFCP	Glaser-Dirks DG-400	4-263	HB-2158
D-KFCR	DG Flugzeugbau DG-1001M	10-207M23	
D-KFCS	Schleicher ASH 25E (Res .16)	25019	HB-2318, D-KEMU
D-KFCT-PUR	Schempp-Hirth Discus 2cT	81	
D-KFCW	Grob G 109B	6249	
D-KFDG(3)-DG	DG Flugzeugbau DG-808B	8-219B133	
D-KFDH	Glaser-Dirks DG-400	4-49	HB-2074
D-KFDR	Schempp-Hirth Discus-2cT	70	
D-KFDS	Schempp-Hirth Duo Discus T (P.4.01)	17/269	
D-KFDT-D3	Schempp-Hirth Duo Discus T	224	
D-KFEB	Grob G 109B	6430	
D-KFEC	Scheibe SF 25C Rotax-Falke	44571	
D-KFEE	Hoffmann H-36 Dimona	36273	
D-KFEL	Scheibe SF 25C Falke 2000	44495	

Registration	Type	Serial	Previous identities
D-KFEM(2)	Kickert ETA	04	
D-KFEN-N	DG Flugzeugbau DG-808B	8-317B217	
D-KFES	Schempp-Hirth Discus-2c FES (P 10.15)	1	
D-KFFA(2)	Glaser-Dirks DG-400	4-220	D-KAHM(2)
D-KFFB(2)	Schempp-Hirth Discus bT	3/252	
D-KFFC-FC	Schempp-Hirth Discus-2T	26/166	
D-KFFG	Scheibe SF 25C Falke 2000	44457	
D-KFFK-FK	DG Flugzeugbau DG-800B	8-158B82	
D-KFFO-SD	Schempp-Hirth Duo Discus T	92/411	
D-KFFW-FW	Schempp-Hirth Ventus-2cT	48/149	D-4539
D-KFGB	DG Flugzeugbau DG-808B	8-319B219	
D-KFGD	Schempp-Hirth Nimbus-4DM	69	
D-KFGG	Schempp-Hirth Discus bT	134/508	
D-KFGH	Schempp-Hirth Janus CT	8/252	
D-KFGM	Scheibe SF 25C Falke 2000	44400	
D-KFGN	Nitsche AVO-68R Samburo	024R	OE-9166
D-KFGR-LG	Schempp-Hirth Ventus-2cxT	187	
D-KFGS	Schempp-Hirth Ventus-2cM	49/101	
D-KFGT(2)	Diamond HK 36TTC Super Dimona	36572	
D-KFGV	Schempp-Hirth Ventus-2cxT	217	
D-KFGW	Schempp-Hirth Ventus-2cT	6/14	
D-KFHA(2)-K4	Schempp-Hirth Nimbus-4DM	7/15	(D-9153)
D-KFHD	Schleicher ASH 26E	26165	
D-KFHG	DG Flugzeugbau DG-808C	8-395B294X56	
D-KFHI	Sportavia/ Fournier RF-4D	4090	SE-TGY
D-KFIF-IF	Schleicher ASW 22BLE (P. 4.14t)	22056	
D-KFIH	Valentin Taifun 17E	1057	SE-UBA, D-KHVA(4)
D-KFIL	Schleicher ASH 31Mi (P. 4.11)	31032	
D-KFIM	Schempp-Hirth Ventus-2cM	207	
D-KFIN-V8	Schempp-Hirth Arcus T	19	
D-KFIP	Binder EB29D (P 10.6.16)	38	
D-KFIR-56	Schempp-Hirth Ventus-2cxM (P.7.04)	147	
D-KFIS	Rolladen-Schneider LS8t (Res. 10)	8426	SE-UNX, D-3230
D-KFIT	Glaser-Dirks DG-400	4-23	OO-FIT, (OO-ZUD), (OO-PUD)
D-KFJA	Schleicher ASW 27-18E	29710	
D-KFJD	DG Flugzeugbau DG-808B	8-326B226	
D-KFJE	Binder EB29	14	
D-KFJS	Schempp-Hirth Ventus-2cxM	255	
D-KFJV	HOAC HK-36TTS Super Dimona	36624	OE-9424
D-KFKA	Schempp-Hirth Ventus bT	4/120	D-1137
D-KFKF	Hoffmann H-36 Dimona (Permit)	3511	
D-KFKL	Schempp-Hirth Duo Discus T	90/408	
D-KFKS	Eiriavion PIK-20E	20217	LN-GME, G-LYDE
D-KFLA-CS	Glaser-Dirks DG-800B	8-48B3	
D-KFLF	Lange E1 Antares	29	
D-KFLG(2)	Schempp-Hirth Arcus T	42	
D-KFLH	Schempp-Hirth Ventus-2cM	263	
D-KFLL-LL	Schempp-Hirth Duo Discus T	42/318	
D-KFLO	Glaser-Dirks DG-400	4-138	
D-KFLS	Stemme S10-VT	11-094	
D-KFLY	Valentin Kiwi	3007	
D-KFMB-MB	Schempp-Hirth Discus-2cT	72	
D-KFMD-A	Schempp-Hirth Discus-2cT (P.05)	3	
D-KFMF	Schempp-Hirth Discus bT	110/460	
D-KFMH	Schleicher ASH 26E	26035	
D-KFMI	DG Flugzeugbau DG-1001M	10-159M9	
D-KFMM	Stemme S10-VT	11-107	
D-KFMN-MN	Schempp-Hirth Ventus-2cM	121/264	
D-KFMO	Hoffmann H-36 Dimona	36227	OE-9269
D-KFMR	Schempp-Hirth Discus bT (P.6.06)	101/443	D-KICR
D-KFMS(2)	Schleicher ASH 26E	26250	
D-KFMW-MW	Schempp-Hirth Arcus M	58	
D-KFND	Schempp-Hirth Duo Discus T	105/431	
D-KFNH-NH	Schempp-Hirth Arcus T	44	
D-KFNM-NM	Schempp-Hirth Ventus-2cxM	216	
D-KFNT	Schempp-Hirth Discus bT	2/250	D-5070
D-KFNW-F6	Grob G 103C Twin IIISL	35045	
D-KFOG-OG	Schleicher ASW 28-18E	28715	D-6244
D-KFOR	Scheibe SF 25C Rotax-Falke	44563	
D-KFOW-OW	Schleicher ASH 25E	25025	
D-KFOX(2)	Schleicher ASH 26E	26057	HB-2266, D-KLEH
D-KFOZ	Glaser-Dirks DG-505M	5E148M60	HB-2271
D-KFPE	Schleicher ASH 31Mi	31086	
D-KFPF	Schempp-Hirth Ventus cT	176/577	OY-XTI
D-KFPI	Schempp-Hirth Nimbus-4DM	62	
D-KFPR-PR	Schempp-Hirth Arcus M	68	
D-KFPS	Aerotechnik L-13SDM Vivat	950607	
D-KFRA	Scheibe SF 25C Falke 2000	44441	
D-KFRB-RB	Schleicher ASH 26E	26240	
D-KFRR	Schempp-Hirth Nimbus-4DT (P .09)	16	
D-KFRW	DG Flugzeugbau DG-800B	8-97B32	PH-1109, D-KMAF
D-KFSC	Schleicher ASH 31Mi	31082	
D-KFSG	Scheibe SFS-31 Milan	6612	(D-KAUT)
D-KFSH-33	Schempp-Hirth Ventus-2cT	165	
D-KFSK	Diamond HK 36TTC Super Dimona	36577	
D-KFSM	Glaser-Dirks DG-400	4-245	
D-KFSN	AVO 68V Samburo 2000	019	
D-KFSP	Brditschka HB-21	21017	OE-9168
D-KFSS	Schleicher ASH 26E	26002	
D-KFST	Sportavia/ Fournier RF-4D	4151	OO-YES, PH-JFE
D-KFSV	Diamond HK 36R Super Dimona	36314	
D-KFTA	Diamond HK 36 TS Super Dimona	36512	
D-KFTR-FS	Eiriavion PIK-20E	20271	PH-693
D-KFTT	Schempp-Hirth Ventus-2cM	82/172	
D-KFUF	Schempp-Hirth Nimbus-3DM	47027	F-CFUF, D-KCUF
D-KFUN-WIN	Schleicher ASW 27-18E (ASG 29E)	29673	
D-KFUW	Scheibe SF 25C Falke 2000	44491	
D-KFVA	Sportavia/ Fournier RF-5	5099	
D-KFVC(2)-S2	Schleicher ASH 31Mi	31081	
D-KFVF	Schleicher ASH 31Mi	31107	
D-KFVS	Scheibe SF 25C Falke 2000	44515	
D-KFWA	Schempp-Hirth Arcus T	39	
D-KFWC	Hoffmann H-36 Dimona	3613	
D-KFWD(2)	DG Flugzeugbau DG-808B (P. 5.11)	8-271B179	D-KGHF
D-KFWE-AM	Schleicher ASW 22BLE	22055	
D-KFWH(2)-K1	Schempp-Hirth Ventus-2cT	29/100	
D-KFWI	HOAC HK 36R Super Dimona	36344	
D-KFWJ	Scheibe SF 25C Falke 2000	44267	
D-KFWP	Schleicher ASK 16	16036	
D-KFWS	Schempp-Hirth Ventus-2cM	66/135	
D-KFWW	Schempp-Hirth Ventus-2cM	204	
D-KFZA	Technoflug Piccolo B	097	
D-KFZW	HOAC HK 36R Super Dimona	36395	
D-KGAA	Sportavia/ Scheibe SF 25C Falke	4217	
D-KGAB(3)	DG Flugzeugbau DG-800B	8-157B81	D-KSPM
D-KGAC(2)	HOAC HK 36R Super Dimona	36319	I-NAOS, OE-9351
D-KGAD	Sportavia/ Scheibe SF 25C Falke 2000	4220	
D-KGAE	Sportavia/ Scheibe SF 25C Falke	4221	
D-KGAF	Hoffmann H-36 Dimona	3503	
D-KGAG(3)-AG	Schempp-Hirth Arcus M	50	
D-KGAH	Scheibe SF 25C Falke	44296	
D-KGAI(2)	Valentin Taifun 17E (R. 14)	1049	F-CGAD, F-WGAD, D-KDSO
D-KGAJ	Scheibe SF 25C Rotax-Falke	44606	
D-KGAK	Scheibe SF 25C Falke	44346	
D-KGAL	Scheibe SF 25C Falke	44310	
D-KGAN	Valentin Taifun 17E	1052	D-ECAN(3), D-KGAN
D-KGAO	Scheibe SF 25C Falke	44437	
D-KGAP	Scheibe SF 25C Falke	44326	
D-KGAQ	Scheibe SF 25C Rotax-Falke	44617	
D-KGAR	Scheibe SF 25C Falke	44340	
D-KGAS	Scheibe SF 25C Falke	44367	
D-KGAT(2)	Scheibe SF 25C Falke	44483	
D-KGAU	Scheibe SF 25C Falke 2000 (ex Falke 1700)	44527	
D-KGAV	Scheibe SF 25C Falke 2000 (ex Falke 1700)	44567	
D-KGAX	Scheibe SF 25C Falke	44585	
D-KGAY	Scheibe SF 25C Falke	44548	
D-KGBA	Valentin Taifun 17E-II	1108	
D-KGBI	Stemme S10-VT	11-030	
D-KGBL	Schempp-Hirth Ventus-2cxM	265	(D-KSEW)
D-KGBN	Scheibe SF 25C Rotax-Falke	44628	
D-KGBR(3)	Schempp-Hirth Ventus-2cxT	190	D-9517
D-KGBT	Schempp-Hirth Discus bT	136/511	
D-KGBS	Schempp-Hirth Ventus-2cM	28/50	OH-932, D-KGBS
D-KGCA	Stemme S10-V	14-019M	
D-KGCB(2)	Schleicher ASW 27-18E (ASG 29E)	29675	
D-KGCD(5)	Stemme S10	10-50	
D-KGCG-MO	Stemme S10-V	14-022M	
D-KGCH(3)	Stemme S10	10-52	
D-KGCI (6)	Stemme S10-V (Formerly c/n 14-003)	14-056M	OO-VCN, D-KGCI (4)
D-KGCL(2)	Stemme S10-V	14-007	
D-KGCM(2)	Schemp-Hirth Ventus 3T (Res .16)	8	(D-KEBE(3))
D-KGCN	Stemme S10-V (Permit)	14-031M	
D-KGCP	Stemme S10	10-36	
D-KGCQ	Stemme S10-V (Res .13)	14-038M	(D-KSTE)
D-KGCR(2)	Stemme S10-VT	11-001	
D-KGCT(2)	Sportine Aviacija LAK-19T	4	LN-GCT
D-KGCW	Stemme S10	10-40	
D-KGCY(3)	Stemme S10-V (Formerly c/n 14-004)	14-057M	
D-KGCZ(3)	Stemme S10-V	14-017	
D-KGDA(3)	Stemme S10-V	14-024	
D-KGDB(3)	Stemme S10-V	14-025	
D-KGDD(3)	Stemme S10-V	14-026	
D-KGDE	Grob G 109B	6341	OE-9250
D-KGDH	Schleicher ASW 27-18E (ASG 29E)	29679	
D-KGDS	Schleicher ASW 24E	24841	
D-KGEB(2)	Scheibe SF 25C Rotax-Falke	44595	HB-2280, D-KTIT
D-KGED	Stemme S10-V (Originally S-10 c/n 10-16)	14-016M	(D-KDKS), HB-2185, D-KGCD(1)
D-KGEN	Stuttgart e-Genius (P. 10.14.12)	001	N447KR, D-KGEN
D-KGEO-GEO	Schempp-Hirth Ventus cT	124/398	PH-1360, HB-2145
D-KGER-ER	Glaser-Dirks DG-800B	8-65B9	(D-KKER)
D-KGET-ET	Schempp-Hirth Ventus-2cM	173	
D-KGFB(2)	Stemme S10-VT	11-136	
D-KGFC	Grob G 109B	6207	
D-KGFD	Grob G 109B	6212	G-BNZF, D-KGFD
D-KGFE(2)-ME	Schleicher ASH 31Mi	31069	
D-KGFF(2)	Schempp-Hirth Nimbus-3DT	58	HB-2232
D-KGFH	Grob G 109	6080	F-WAQK
D-KGFL	Sportavia/ Fournier RF-5	5038	
D-KGFO(2)	Lange E1 Antares	05	
D-KGFR	Grob G 109B	6253	
D-KGFS	Grob G 109B	6226	
D-KGFT	Grob G 109B	6206	
D-KGFU	Grob G 109B	6264	
D-KGFW	Grob G 109B	6238	
D-KGFZ	Grob G 109B	6282	
D-KGGA-GA	Schleicher ASH 31Mi	31036	
D-KGGG-3W	Glaser-Dirks DG-300G Club Elan (GG300) (Solo 2350 engine) (P.1.05)	1 / 3E313C22	D-1930
D-KGGH	Schempp-Hirth Discus-2cT	109	
D-KGGK	DG Flugzeugbau DG-1000T	10-122T42	
D-KGGL-GL	Schleicher ASH 26E	26034	
D-KGGM-GM	Schempp-Hirth Ventus-2cxT	124	
D-KGGN	Schleicher ASW 27-18E (ASG 29E)	29609	
D-KGGO(2)	Schleicher ASH 25M (P.3.00)	25216	
D-KGGT	Schleicher ASW 27-18E (ASG 29E)	29685	
D-KGGX-GX	Schempp-Hirth Duo Discus T	110/ . . .	
D-KGHA	Schleicher ASH 26E	26239	
D-KGHB	Schempp-Hirth Nimbus-4DM	40/ . .	
D-KGHF(2)-HF	Lange E1 Antares	75E55	
D-KGHG-HG	Schleicher ASH 31Mi	31006	
D-KGHH(2)	DG Flugzeugbau DG-505MB	5E244B21	N505YB
D-KGHI	Schleicher ASK 21Mi	21827	
D-KGHL	Glaser-Dirks DG-400	4-72	EC-HYL, D-KLWM(1), HB-2095
D-KGHM	Stemme S10-VT	11-063	G-EXPD
D-KGHP	Schleicher ASH 25M	25203	
D-KGHS	Glaser-Dirks DG-400	4-236	OY-PVX
D-KGHW-HB	Schleicher ASH 25E	25014	
D-KGIL	DG Flugzeugbau DG-808C	8-423B322X82	

Reg	Type	c/n	Previous identities
D-KGIN(2)-UM	Glaser-Dirks DG-500M	5E92M39	
D-KGIT	Schempp-Hirth Ventus-2cM	107/220	D-KPYY
D-KGIU	DG Flugzeugbau DG-1000T	10-100T31	
D-KGJB	AMS Flight Carat A	CA010	
D-KGJM	Schleicher ASH 31Mi	31012	
D-KGKB	Schleicher ASH 26E	26148	
D-KGKG-TC	Schleicher ASW 22BE	22060	
D-KGKK-21	Schempp-Hirth Arcus M	4	
D-KGKS-V8	Schleicher ASH 26E	26014	D-5599
D-KGKW-T	DG Flugzeugbau DG-505MB	5E243MB20	
D-KGLA(2)-LA	Glaser-Dirks DG-800B	8-66B11	D-KUDS
D-KGLH	Grob G103C Twin III SL	35013	HB-2219
D-KGLO	Diamond HK 36TTC	36806	(D-KIBX(1))
D-KGLR	Stemme S10-VT	11-119	
D-KGLS-I	DG Flugzeugbau LS10-st	L10-007	(D-KALS)
D-KGLT	Stemme S10-VT	11-048	
D-KGLW	Diamond HK 36TTC Super Dimona	36667	
D-KGLX-PN	Schleicher ASH 25Mi	25241	ZS-GXL
D-KGMA(2)-MA	Schempp-Hirth Arcus M	44	
D-KGMB	DG Flugzeugbau DG-808B	8-303B203	
D-KGMD-MD	Schleicher ASH 26E	26121	
D-KGMF-MF	Schleicher ASH 25M	25248	D-8188
D-KGMH-MH	Schleicher ASH 31Mi	31056	
D-KGMI-13	Schleicher ASH 31Mi	31065	
D-KGMP	Schleicher ASH 31Mi	31076	HB-2501
(Res .16)			
D-KGMR(2)	Schleicher ASW 27-18E (ASG 29E)	29719	
D-KGMS	Schleicher ASW 24E	24828	G-BVUP, D-KEWI(2)
D-KGMW	Schempp-Hirth Nimbus-4DM	18/27	
D-KGMY-CY	Schempp-Hirth Ventus bT	3/116	
D-KGND	Stemme S10-V	14-026M	
(Originally built as Stemme S10 c/n 10-26)			
D-KGNS-GN	Schempp-Hirth Duo Discus XLT	228	
D-KGNY-NY	Schempp-Hirth Ventus-2cxT	238	
D-KGOC	Glaser-Dirks DG-400	4-46	(D-KLOC), D-KCHE
D-KGOD(2)	Schempp-Hirth Ventus cT	171/561	
D-KGOM	Hoffmann H-36 Dimona	3644	
D-KGON	Scheibe SF 28A Tandem-Falke	5704	HB-2048, D-KAVM
D-KGOR	Schleicher ASK 16	16020	I-AGOR, D-KGOR
D-KGOS	Valentin Taifun 17E	1024	
D-KGPB	Diamond HK 36TS Super Dimona	36586	
D-KGPC-PC	Sportine Aviacija LAK-17AT	195	
D-KGPF(3)-PF	Schempp-Hirth Arcus M	98	
D-KGPG-33	Glaser-Dirks DG-500M	5E72M30	(D-KGPL)
D-KGPI (2)	Glaser-Dirks DG-800B	8-53B6	
D-KGPL(2)	Schempp-Hirth Ventus-2cT	160	
D-KGPM	Schempp-Hirth Arcus M	60	
D-KGPR	Aerotechnik L-13SEH Vivat	940522	OK-4101
D-KGPS(2)	Schleicher ASH 31Mi	31097	
D-KGPW-GP	Schempp-Hirth Ventus-2cM	178	
D-KGRA(2)	Scheibe SF 24B Motorspatz	4035	D-KAHH, (D-KIBU)
D-KGRB	Scheibe SF 24A Motorspatz	4011	D-KADA(1)
(Res.12.99)			
D-KGRH	Scheibe SF 25C Rotax-Falke	44654	D-KIEO
D-KGRL	Glaser-Dirks DG-505MB	5E150B1	F-CHRD, D-KDTG
D-KGRM	Hoffmann H-36 Dimona	36193	OE-9245
D-KGRS	Sportavia/ Fournier RF-5	5068	OE-9033
(P.01)			
D-KGRU	Sportavia/ Fournier RF-4D	4132	OY-XBA, SE-TGU
D-KGSA(2)	Schleicher ASW 27-18E (ASG 29E)	29592	D-KKSW
D-KGSE-SE	Schempp-Hirth Ventus cT	107/370	D-KBEK
D-KGSF-7UP	Schempp-Hirth Duo Discus T	3/232	
D-KGSG	Diamond HK 36TTC Super Dimona	36631	N931TT
D-KGSL	Schleicher ASK 21Mi	21886	
D-KGSM-SM	Schleicher ASG 29E	29533	
D-KGSO	DG Flugzeugbau DG-800B	8-223B137	
D-KGST	Hoffmann H-36 Dimona	36100	
D-KGSU-SU	Schleicher ASW 27-18E (ASG 29E)	29674	
D-KGSW	Schempp-Hirth Ventus cM	59/514	
D-KGSX-SX	Schleicher ASH 31Mi	31099	SE-SSX
D-KGTB	HOAC HK-36R Super Dimona	36411	
D-KGTC	HOAC HK-36R Super Dimona	36414	
D-KGTD	Diamond HK 36TS Super Dimona	36508	
D-KGTE	Diamond HK 36TS Super Dimona	36510	
D-KGTF	Diamond HK 36TC Super Dimona	36605	
D-KGTG	Diamond HK 36TC Super Dimona	36517	OE-9417
(P.3.00)			
D-KGTH	Diamond HK 36TTC Super Dimona	36700	
(Res 3.00)			
D-KGTI	Diamond HK 36TTC Super Dimona	36689	
D-KGTJ	Diamond HK 36TTC Super Dimona	36723	
D-KGTK	Sportine Aviacija LAK-17AT	181	OK-9731, OH-973, LY-GNI
D-KGTT-2T	Schleicher ASW 27-18E (ASG 29E)	29551	OH-983
D-KGTW	Glaser-Dirks DG-400	4-235	(D-KLMH), SE-UUM, D-KGAB(3), I-ASAV, (D-KSAV), I-ASAV, D-KGAB(2)
D-KGUA	HOAC HK 36R Super Dimona	36381	
D-KGUB	HOAC HK 36R Super Dimona	36382	
D-KGUE	Schleicher ASH 25Mi	25256	G-CDPX, (D-KBTS)
D-KGUP	Diamond HK 36TTC Super Dimona	36822	(SE-URN), OE-9997
D-KGUT	Glaser-Dirks DG-400	4-29	PH-1098, D-KDAU
(Res. 11)			
D-KGUY-X	Schempp-Hirth Ventus-2cxM	149	
(P.05)			
D-KGVF	Schempp-Hirth Ventus-2cxM	182	
D-KGVM-VM	Schempp-Hirth Arcus M	92	(D-KMNM)
D-KGVP-VP	Lange E1 Antares	34E32	
D-KGVS	Schempp-Hirth Ventus cM	40/478	
D-KGVT	Stemme S10-VT	11-112	
D-KGVV-AR	DG Flugzeugbau DG-808B	8-311B211	
D-KGWB	Glaser-Dirks DG-400	4-95	
D-KGWG	Sportavia/ Fournier RF-4D	4020	F-BORG
D-KGWH	Grob G 109B	6511	
D-KGWL	Hoffmann H 36 Dimona	3514	OY-XZO, SE-UCK, N408DH
D-KGWS-OZ	Schempp-Hirth Ventus-2cM	13/30	
D-KGWX	DG Flugzeugbau DG-800B	8-231B145	
D-KGYY-YY	Glasfaser Nimeta	1	
(P.7.09; W/o 19.05.12)			
D-KGZT-99	Schempp-Hirth Nimbus-3DT	5	
D-KGZW-ZW	Schleicher ASH 31Mi	31045	
D-KGZZ-37	Lange E1 Antares 18T	31T10	D-9200, D-KHLF
(P 4.13)			
D-KHAA(2)	Technoflug Piccolo B	081	
D-KHAB(2)-AB	Schempp-Hirth Arcus T	64	
D-KHAG	Schempp-Hirth Nimbus-4DT	12/70	
(P.11.02)			
D-KHAH	Schempp-Hirth Ventus-2cxM	249	
D-KHAI(2)-E2	Schempp-Hirth Duo Discus XLT	214	
D-KHAK	Lange E1 Antares	E46	
(P.08) (Same c/n as D-KWWB)			
D-KHAL	Schleicher ASK 16B	16043	OE-9132, (D-KAXD)
D-KHAM	Schempp-Hirth Nimbus-4DM	19/28	
D-KHAN	Technoflug Piccolo	046	
D-KHAR	Schempp-Hirth Ventus-2cxa FES	151	
(P 10.15)			
D-KHAS(2)	Schleicher ASW 24E	24812	OE-9337
D-KHAT	Schempp-Hirth Ventus 3T	6	
(P 7.9.16)			
D-KHAU	Schleicher ASH 25E	25090	F-CHAU, F-WHAU
D-KHBA	Grob G 109B Turbo	6370	
D-KHBB(2)	Schleicher ASH 26E	26095	
D-KHBC	Schleicher ASW 24/TOP	24804	
D-KHBD	DG Flugzeugbau DG-800B	8-266B174	(D-KTEO)
D-KHBE(2)	Glaser-Dirks DG-400	4-279	
D-KHBG	Diamond HK 36TTC Super Dimona	36668	
D-KHBH	Schempp-Hirth Ventus-2cxM	162	
D-KHBI-E3	Schleicher ASW 27-18E (ASG 29E)	29678	
D-KHBS	Glaser-Dirks DG-400	4-290	
D-KHBX	Jonker JS/MD Single	1C-098	D-5525
(Res .16)			
D-KHCA	Diamond HK 36 TC Super Dimona	36813	OE-9997
D-KHCB	DG Flugzeugbau DG-505MB	5E206B10	PH-1215
D-KHCD-LN	Schempp-Hirth Discus bT	17/303	
D-KHCE	Schempp-Hirth Ventus cM	84/563	
D-KHCF	Schempp-Hirth Ventus-2cT	78	
D-KHCO	Valentin Taifun 17E-II	1110	
D-KHCQ-QQ	Binder EB28	6	
D-KHCT	Schempp-Hirth Duo Discus T	82	
D-KHDB-VG	Schempp-Hirth Ventus-2cxM	274	
D-KHDD	Schempp-Hirth Duo Discus XLT	269	
D-KHDF	Hoffmann H-36 Dimona	3656	
D-KHDH	Schleicher ASW 28-18E	28709	D-5718
D-KHDK-2J	Schempp-Hirth Discus bT	30/327	
D-KHDP	DG Flugzeugbau DG-808B	8-297B202	
D-KHDV	Glaser-Dirks DG-400	4-280	
D-KHDW	Schleicher ASH 25E	25150	G-CJDF, BGA 4425, D-KPAS
D-KHEB	Sportavia/ Scheibe SF 25B Falke	4822	
D-KHEC(2)	Scheibe SF 25C Falke 2000	44494	
D-KHEF(2)	Sportavia/ Scheibe SF 25C Falke	4244	(D-KAJF)
D-KHEL(2	Schempp-Hirth Arcus M	48	(D-KGMA(1))
D-KHEM(2)	Schempp-Hirth Ventus cT	135/415	
D-KHEN(2)	Scheibe SF 25C Rotax-Falke	44634	
D-KHEP	Sportavia/ Scheibe SF 25B Falke	4833	
D-KHES(2)	Schempp-Hirth Discus-2c/FES	4	
(P 4.4.16)			
D-KHEW	Sportavia/ Scheibe SF 25B Falke	4840	
D-KHEX	Sportavia/ Scheibe SF 25B Falke	4841	
D-KHEZ(2)	Valentin Taifun 17E	1072	F-WGAE, D-KHVA
D-KHFB(2)	HOAC HK 36R Super Dimona	36346	
D-KHFC(2)	Schempp-Hirth Ventus-2cM	157/...	
D-KHFD	Scheibe SF 25D Falke	4846D	
D-KHFE	Sportavia/ Scheibe SF 25B Falke	4847	
D-KHFG	Sportavia/ Scheibe SF 25B Falke	4849	
D-KHFM	Schleicher ASH 25Mi	25225	(D-KBEN)
(P.7.01)			
D-KHFN	Stemme S10-VT	11-067	
D-KHFP-JOY	Schleicher ASH 26E	26026	G-MORE, BGA4075/HNP
D-KHFR	Franke Doppelraab 7M (Hankur 1)	001	D-5626(1)
D-KHFW-H2	Schempp-Hirth Discus-2cT	49	
D-KHGA	Scheibe SF 25C Falke 2000	44358	
D-KHGG-XXL	Schleicher ASW 22BLE	22050	
D-KHGH	Scheibe SF 28A Tandem-Falke	57120	
D-KHGK	Schempp-Hirth Discus-2T	24/161	
D-KHGM	Schempp-Hirth Duo Discus XLT	206	
D-KHGO	Gomolzig RF-9-ABS	9021	(D-KABS)
D-KHGR-GR	Schleicher ASH 25E	25149	D-0825
D-KHGS	Schempp-Hirth Ventus bT	27/194	
D-KHGW(2)-GW	Schempp-Hirth Ventus-2cM	171	
D-KHHA	Valentin Taifun 17E-II	1126	
D-KHHB(2)	Binder EB29D	34	
D-KHHC(2)-9C	Schleicher ASW 27-18E (ASG 29E)	29647	
D-KHHD	Technoflug Piccolo	054	
(P.01)			
D-KHHG(2)	Schleicher ASH 25M	25174	D-5763
D-KHHH(5)	Schempp-Hirth Arcus M	131	(D-KRKA)
D-KHHL	Technoflug Piccolo	050	
D-KHHO-HO	Schleicher ASH 25M	25188	
D-KHHS	Technoflug Piccolo B	039	
(Res .13)			
D-KHHT	Scheibe SF 25C Falke 2000	44354	
D-KHHW-HW	Schleicher ASH 31Mi	31125	
D-KHIF-XZ	Schempp-Hirth Nimbus-3T	8/60	BGA 4263, D-KHIF
D-KHIK	Schempp-Hirth Janus CM	18/202	
D-KHIL(4)	Grob G 109B	6398	G-LLAN, OH-747
D-KHIM	Valentin Taifun 17E	1032	
D-KHIR	Hoffmann H-36 Dimona	3619	
D-KHIS	Valentin Kiwi	3005	
D-KHIT	Rolladen-Schneider LS8t	8448	D-2026
D-KHJC	Schempp-Hirth Discus bT	146/525	
D-KHJF	Glaser-Dirks DG-500M	5E83M35	F-CHJF
D-KHJG	Sportavia/ Fournier RF-4D	4129	F-BPLM
D-KHJH-JH	HpH Glasflügel 304MS	022-MS	
D-KHJM	DG Flugzeugbau DG-800B	8-125B54	
D-KHJO	Schleicher ASK 14	AB14061	(D-KICH)
D-KHJS-ZZ1	Schleicher ASK 21Mi	21806	
D-KHJT	Technoflug Piccolo	013	
D-KHKA-KC	Schempp-Hirth Nimbus-2M V-2	02	
D-KHKG	Grob G 103C Twin IIISL	35036	
D-KHKI	Technoflug Piccolo B	089	
D-KHKK-3K	Schempp-Hirth Discus-2T	6/96	
(P.4.01)			
D-KHKW	Glaser-Dirks DG-400	4-217	
D-KHLB(2)-HLB	Schempp-Hirth Arcus T	48	
D-KHLJ	Diamond HK 36TTC Super Dimona	36604	
D-KHLS	Schleicher ASH 26E	26224	
D-KHMA	Lange E1 Antares 18T	61T06	D-KMRB
(P 7.13)			
D-KHMB-LG	Schleicher ASH 26E	26007	
D-KHMC	Grob G 109B	6289	PH-1065, SE-UAA
D-KHMG	HOAC HK 36R Super Dimona	36318	
D-KHMI	DG Flugzeugbau DG-808B	8-248B161	N949AB

Reg	Type	Serial	Other
D-KHML	Rolladen-Schneider LS9	9003	
D-KHMM	Scheibe SF 25C Falke 2000	44384	
D-KHMN-11	Schempp-Hirth Discus-2cT	114	
D-KHMR-1R	DG Flugzeugbau DG-800B	8-123B52	HB-2323
D-KHMT-77	Schleicher ASW 27-18E (ASG 29E)	29649	
D-KHMV	Lange E1 Antares 23T	76B02	
	(P 8.15)		
D-KHMW-4C	Glaser-Dirks DG-600/18M	6-50M5	
	(Converted from DG-600M)		
D-KHMY-ET	Schleicher ASH 25M	25201	
D-KHND	Rolladen-Schneider LS8-t	8478	SE-USP
D-KHNG	AMS-Flight Carat A	CA024	OY-KLX
	(Res .16)		
D-KHNO	Schleicher ASW 27-18E (ASG 29E)	29540	D-KFVC
D-KHNZ	Schempp-Hirth Duo Discus T	273	
D-KHOA	Scheibe SF 27M-A	6323	
D-KHOB(3)-9A	Schempp-Hirth Ventus cM	80/553	
D-KHOC	Scheibe SF 27M-A	6325	
D-KHOE(2)	Diamond HK 36TTC Super Dimona	36575	
D-KHOF(2)	Scheibe SF 25C Falke 2000	44351	HB-2279, D-KNAI
	(Res .16)		
D-KHOI	Scheibe SF 25C Falke	4425	
D-KHOL(2)-3F	Schleicher ASH 25E	25135	
D-KHOM	Scheibe SF 25C Falke	4429	
D-KHOO(2)	Rolladen-Schneider LS9	9006	
D-KHOP(2)	Scheibe SF 28A Tandem-Falke	5706	
D-KHOR(2)	Stemme S10-VT	11-138	D-KSIO(4)
D-KHOX	HOAC HK 36R Super Dimona	36402	
D-KHOY	Technoflug Piccolo	002	
D-KHPB-WS	Schempp-Hirth Ventus-2cxM	176	
D-KHPC	Schempp-Hirth Ventus cM	48/489	
D-KHPE-AN	Glaser-Dirks DG-600M	6-55M9	
D-KHPG	Schempp-Hirth Ventus-2cxM	138/313	
D-KHPS	Glaser-Dirks DG-500M	5E4M3	ZS-GWU, D-KLAP
D-KHPT	Schleicher ASH 26E	26110	D-8326
	(Res.06)		
D-KHPU-HU	Schempp-Hirth Ventus-2cM	105/218	
D-KHQH	Diamond HK 36TC Super Dimona	36814	F-CHQH, OE-9997
D-KHRB	HOAC HK 36R Super Dimona	36376	
D-KHRD	Schempp-Hirth Arcus M	35	
D-KHRL-RL	Schleicher ASH 25M	25214	
	(P.1.00)		
D-KHRW	Schleicher ASW 22BE	22051	D-4753
	(Permit)		
D-KHSC-A	Schempp-Hirth Nimbus-2M	06	
D-KHSD	Lange E1 Antares	34	
	(Res.06, ntu)		
D-KHSF	Schempp-Hirth Ventus cT	125/399	HB-2128
D-KHSL-SL	Schempp-Hirth Arcus M	112	
D-KHSO(2)-5B	Sportine Aviacija LAK-17AT	187	OK-2222
D-KHSR-MK	Glaser-Dirks DG-600/18M	6-108M49	
D-KHSS-SS	Schempp-Hirth Nimbus-3T	24/90	
D-KHST	DG Flugzeugbau DG-808B	8-318B218	
D-KHSU	DG Flugzeugbau DG-808B	8-314B214	
D-KHSW	Valentin Mistral CM	MC-071/85	
D-KHSY	Schleicher ASH 26E	26230	
D-KHTA	Grob G 109B	6501	
D-KHTB	Grob G 109B	6543	
D-KHTI-TI	DG Flugzeugbau DG-808C Competition		
		8-357B256X21	OY-TIX, (D-KJIB)
D-KHTP	Schempp-Hirth Discus-2T	33	
D-KHUB	DG Flugzeugbau DG-800B	8-162B86	
D-KHUL	Hoffmann H-36 Dimona	3699	
D-KHVA(50)-JS	Schempp-Hirth Arcus M	22	
D-KHVG-TOY	Schleicher ASW 27-18E (ASG 29E)	29591	
D-KHVI	Grob G 102 Astir CS77/TOP	1797	D-7773
D-KHVL	Scheibe SF 25C Rotax-Falke	44554	
D-KHVS	Schempp-Hirth Ventus-2cxT	242	
D-KHWD	Sportavia/ Fournier RF-4D	4060	F-BOXH
	(Permit)		
D-KHWE	Brditschka HB-23/2400SP	23029-U	OE-9304
D-KHWF	Schleicher ASK 21Mi	21844	F-CLOP, D-KVVC
D-KHWG	AVO 68R Samburo	009R	OE-9121
	(Converted from AVO 68v c/n 009, 6.99)		
D-KHWH	Grob G 109B	6321	G-KIAM
D-KHWI	Schleicher ASH 31Mi	31011	
D-KHWL(2)	Schempp-Hirth Ventus-2cxT	185	
D-KHWM	Glaser-Dirks DG-400	4-255	
	(W/o 18.5.15)		
D-KHXY	Schempp-Hirth Ventus cM	107/606	
D-KHYL	DG Flugzeugbau DG-1000T	10-79T18	
D-KHYN	Schempp-Hirth Discus bT	117/473	
D-KHYU	Schempp-Hirth Discus-2T	41/246	
D-KHZZ	Grob G 103C Twin IIISL	35037	
D-KIAA(2)	Scheibe SF 25C Falke 2000	44438	
D-KIAC(2)	Scheibe SF 25C Falke 2100	44440	
D-KIAD	Scheibe SF 25C Falke 2000	44443	
D-KIAE(2)-50	DG Flugzeugbau DG-1000T	10-196T54	
D-KIAF	Scheibe SF 25C Falke 2000	44445	
D-KIAG	Scheibe SF 25C Falke 2000	44442	
D-KIAH(2)	Scheibe SF 25C Falke 2000	44456	
D-KIAI (2)	Scheibe SF 25C Falke 2000	44467	
D-KIAJ(3)-KAJ	Schempp-Hirth Ventus-2cT	86	G-CKAJ, BGA 4934
D-KIAK(2)	Scheibe SF 25C Falke 2000	44463	
D-KIAL	Scheibe SF 25C Falke 2000	44450	
D-KIAM	Scheibe SF 25C Falke 2000	44446	
D-KIAN	Scheibe SF 25C Falke 2000	44448	
D-KIAO(2)	Glaser-Dirks DG-400	4-130	I-GIOO, D-KERO
D-KIAP	Scheibe SF 25C Falke 2000	44465	
D-KIAR	Scheibe SF 25C Falke 2000	44458	
D-KIAS	Scheibe SF 25C Falke 2000	44470	
D-KIAT	Scheibe SF 25C Falke 2000	44472	
D-KIAV(2)	Scheibe SF 25E Super Falke	4334	G-BFHN, D-KDFW
D-KIAW	Scheibe SF 25C Falke 2000	44473	
D-KIAY(3)	Scheibe SF 25C Falke 2000	44482	
D-KIAZ	Scheibe SF 25C Falke 2000	44474	
D-KIBA(2)	Eiriavion PIK-20E	20207	
D-KIBB(2)-BB	Schempp-Hirth Duo Discus T	114/. . .	
D-KIBC(2)	HOAC HK-36R Super Dimona	36360	
D-KIBE(4)	Schempp-Hirth Nimbus-3DM	19/46	V5-GAK, G-MOAK
D-KIBN	Eiriavion PIK-20E	20251	OE-9255, D-KERH
D-KIBO(3)	Schempp-Hirth Janus BM	1/56	
D-KIBR-PAT	Sportine Aviacija LAK-17B FES	220	
D-KIBT-BT	Schempp-Hirth Discus bT	142/520	
D-KIBU(3)	Glaser-Dirks DG-400	4-204	
D-KICA(4)	Schempp-Hirth Ventus-2cM	124/273	
D-KICB(2)	DG Flugzeugbau DG-800B	8-124B53	
D-KICC(3)-CC	Schempp-Hirth Ventus-2cM	79/162	
D-KICD(2)	Schleicher ASK 14	14057	OO-ICD, D-KICD
D-KICE(3)	Schleicher ASK 14	14058	
D-KICF(2)	Schleicher ASK 14	14059	
D-KICG(3)	Schleicher ASK 14/KM29	14055	
D-KICH(3)	Schleicher ASK 16	16002	
D-KICI (3)	Hoffmann H-36 Dimona	3604	
D-KICK(2)	Schleicher ASH 26E	26085	
D-KICM	Schempp-Hirth Ventus cM	55/504	
D-KICO(2)	Valentin Taifun 17E-II	1121	
D-KICP	Schleicher ASW 24E	24860	
D-KICR(2)	Schempp-Hirth Ventus-2cT	80/245	
D-KICS	DG Flugzeugbau DG-800B	8-151B75	
D-KICX	Schempp-Hirth Ventus-2cT	121	
D-KIDA(2)	Hoffmann H-36 Dimona	3614	
D-KIDB	Eiri PIK-20E	20269	
D-KIDD(2)	Schempp-Hirth Discus bT	144/522	
D-KIDF-DF	Schleicher ASH 26E	26153	
D-KIDG-ML	DG Flugzeugbau DG-1000T	10-101T32	
D-KIDH	Schleicher ASH 26E	26031	D-1349
D-KIDI (2)	FBW Valentin Kiwi	K-3011	
D-KIDK	Schempp-Hirth Discus bT	6/264	
D-KIDL	Glaser-Dirks DG-500M	5E31M15	
D-KIDM(2)	Schleicher ASH 25M	25199	
D-KIDO(2)	Schleicher ASH 26E	26107	
D-KIDS	Glaser-Dirks DG-400	4-208	
D-KIDT-DT	Schempp-Hirth Discus-2cT	28	
D-KIDX	Schempp-Hirth Nimbus-4DM	54/74	
D-KIEA	Scheibe SF 25C Rotax-Falke	44648	
D-KIEB-E4	Schempp-Hirth Ventus cT	112/381	
D-KIEC	Scheibe SF 25C Rotax-Falke	44647	
D-KIED	Hoffmann H-36 Dimona	3651	
D-KIEE	Scheibe SF 25C Rotax-Falke	44644	
D-KIEF	Schempp-Hirth Janus CT	7/244	
D-KIEG	Glaser-Dirks DG-600M	6-84M30	
D-KIEH	Glaser-Dirks DG-600M	6-85M31	
D-KIEI (2)	Scheibe SF 25C Rotax-Falke	44674	
D-KIEJ(5)	Scheibe SF 25C Rotax-Falke	44687	
D-KIEK	Scheibe SF 25C Rotax-Falke	44638	
D-KIEL(4)-CP	Schempp-Hirth Duo Discus T	57/344	
D-KIEM	Schempp-Hirth Ventus bT	29/198	
D-KIEN	Scheibe SF 25C Rotax-Falke	44653	
D-KIEO(2)	Scheibe SF 25C Rotax-Falke	44671	
D-KIEP(2)	Scheibe SF 25C Rotax-Falke	44668	
D-KIEQ(3)	Scheibe SF 25C Rotax-Falke	44682	
D-KIER	Scheibe SF 25C Rotax-Falke	44637	
D-KIES(2)-ES	Schleicher ASH 31Mi	31108	
D-KIET(2)	Scheibe SF 25C Rotax-Falke	44672	
D-KIEU	Schleicher ASW 24E	24840	
D-KIEV(2)	Scheibe SF 25C Rotax-Falke	44679	
D-KIEW	Scheibe SF 25C Rotax-Falke	44629	
D-KIEX(2)	Schempp-Hirth Ventus cT	81/322	PH-1371, HA-4520, N201GF
D-KIEY	Scheibe SF 25C Rotax-Falke	44676	
D-KIEZ	Scheibe SF 25C Rotax-Falke	44639	
D-KIFA(3)	Eiriavion PIK-20E	20247	
	(Permit .09)		
D-KIFB(2)	Glaser-Dirks DG-400	4-205	
D-KIFC	Schempp-Hirth Nimbus-3DM	3/16	V5-GBA, HB-2218, D-KEML
	(Res.06)		
D-KIFE(2)	Scheibe SF 25C Heubacher-Falke	44726	
D-KIFF	Scheibe SFS-31 Milan	6604	
D-KIFH (2)	Schleicher ASH 26E	26163	
D-KIFI	Scheibe SF 25A Motorfalke	4505	
D-KIFM	Sportavia-Pützer RF-5B Sperber	51047	I-TILU, D-KITZ(1)
D-KIFO(2)-FO	Schempp-Hirth Duo Discus T	46/324	
D-KIFP	Sportavia/ Fournier RF-5	5088	
D-KIFR	Valentin Taifun 17E	1006	
D-KIFW	Glaser-Dirks DG-400	4-76	D-KOBI (3)
D-KIFZ	Schempp-Hirth Discus bT	59/381	
D-KIGA-GR	Schleicher ASW 22BLE	22067	
D-KIGB	Technoflug Piccolo B	082	
D-KIGC	Schempp-Hirth Ventus-2cxM	248	
D-KIGD	Scheibe SF 28A Tandem-Falke	5728	SE-TUR, OY-KEE, D-KAUN(2), (D-KOAQ)
D-KIGE(4)	Scheibe SF 25A Motorfalke	4548	OY-XJU, D-KOFE(1)
	(Res .16)		
D-KIGF-GF	Schleicher ASH 26E	26180	
D-KIGG-2G	Schempp-Hirth Arcus M	23	
D-KIGH	Schleicher ASH 25M	25189	
D-KIGI	Sportavia/ Fournier RF-5	5004	
D-KIGK	Schempp-Hirth Arcus M	80	
D-KIGM-GM	Schempp-Hirth Discus bT	7/269	
D-KIGP	Schleicher ASH 26E	26038	
D-KIGS	Grob G 102 Astir CS77/TOP	1717	D-2535
D-KIGT	Sportavia/ Fournier RF-4D	4154	OE-9029
D-KIGU	Sportavia/ Fournier RF-5	5006	
D-KIGV-GV	Schempp-Hirth Ventus bT	7/131	
D-KIGW	Grob G 109B	6573	
D-KIGY(2)-2i	Schleicher ASH 25EB	25243	
D-KIHB(2)	Schempp-Hirth Ventus cM	104/600	
D-KIHD(2)-HD	Schempp-Hirth Ventus cM	39/477	
D-KIHF-IHF	Schempp-Hirth Arcus M	18	(D-KRHP), (D-KRPH)
D-KIHG	Grob G 102 Astir CS/TOP	1305	D-7347
D-KIHH-HH	Glaser-Dirks DG-400	4-55	
D-KIHK	Glaser-Dirks DG-400	4-80	
D-KIHL(2)-KL	Kickert ETA	6	
D-KIHN	Schempp-Hirth Discus bT	4/257	
D-KIHO	Sportavia/ Fournier RF-5	5012	
D-KIHP(2)-HP	Schempp-Hirth Ventus cT	133/412	
D-KIHR	Glaser-Dirks DG-600/18M	6-110M51	PP-. . . ., D-KIHR, (D-KCWC)
D-KIHW(2)-IHW	Schempp-Hirth Duo Discus T	112	
D-KIIC-C	Schempp-Hirth Ventus-2cxM	180/438	
D-KIIF-W	Schleicher ASH 25Mi	25229	
D-KIII (2)-3I	Schempp-Hirth Ventus cM	14/441	HB-2166, D-KCPA
D-KIIJ	Schempp-Hirth Nimbus 3T	3	(D-KKYY(2))
D-KIIK-7K	Schempp-Hirth Ventus bT	25/189	D-1419
D-KIIL	Schempp-Hirth Discus bT	132/502	
D-KIIN	Schempp-Hirth Ventus cM	69/533	
D-KIIR-IR	Schleicher ASH 26E	26215	
D-KIIS(2)	Technoflug Piccolo B	101	HB-2268, D-KIKC
D-KIIT-IT	DG Flugzeugbau DG-1000T	10-28T1	
D-KIIV-TB	Schempp-Hirth Ventus aM	1/48	
D-KIIX-IX	Schempp-Hirth Ventus cT	66/286	

Registration	Type	Serial	Other
D-KIJC	Glaser-Dirks DG-600M	6-77M24	
D-KIJD	DG Flugzeugbau DG-808B	8-295B200	
D-KIJH	Schempp-Hirth Ventus-2cM	8/25	
D-KIJK	Lange Antares 23E	74A03	
	(P 9.3.16)		
D-KIJO	Glaser-Dirks DG-600/18M	6-97M43	
D-KIJR-DE	Schempp-Hirth Ventus-2cxM	181	F-CIJR
D-KIJT	DG Flugzeugbau DG-800B	8-178B102	
D-KIKA(2)-HI	Schleicher ASW 20L/TOP	20395	D-2694
D-KIKD	HOAC HK 36R Super Dimona	36303	
D-KIKE	Alpavia/ Fournier RF-3	42	
D-KIKI	Alpavia/ Fournier RF-3	38	
D-KIKK	Schempp-Hirth Ventus cT	146/452	
D-KIKL	Schleicher ASH 25M	25176	
D-KIKO(2)	Grob G 109	6017	
D-KIKR-KR	Schempp-Hirth Ventus cT	132/410	
D-KIKS	DG Flugzeugbau DG-800B	8-169B93	
D-KIKT	Glaser-Dirks DG-400	4-167	
D-KIKW	Schempp-Hirth Discus bT	149/539	
D-KILA(2)-A	Sportine Aviacija LAK-17AT	179T1	D-9717, LY-GNA
D-KILE(2)	Glaser-Dirks DG-600/18M	6-90M36	(PH-939)
D-KILH	Schempp-Hirth Ventus-2cM	12/29	
D-KILI(3)	Schempp-Hirth Arcus M	109	
D-KILK	Schleicher ASH 25E	25072	
D-KILL(3)	HpH Glasflügel 304MS	025-MS	
D-KILM	Glaser-Dirks DG-600M	6-57M11	
D-KILO(5)	Stemme S10-VT	11-100	
D-KILS	Rolladen-Schneider LS9	9000	
D-KILT	Sportavia/ Fournier RF-4D	4027	
D-KILU(2)-CD	Akaflieg Berlin B-13	001	
	(P.5.12)		
D-KILY(2)-LY	Schleicher ASW 27-18E (ASG 29E)	29623	
D-KILZ(2)	Schempp-Hirth Ventus-2cM	99/209	
D-KIMA(2)	Schempp-Hirth Ventus bT	39/229	
D-KIMB(2)	FFT Kiwi	K3013	HB-2163, D-KEGX
D-KIMC	Grob G 109	6093	
D-KIMD(2)	Schleicher ASG 32Mi	32024	
D-KIME(2)	Technoflug Piccolo B	058	
D-KIMG(2)	Technoflug Piccolo B	056	
D-KIMH-MH	Schleicher ASW 24E	24805	
D-KIMI	Grob G103C Twin III SL	35011	TF-SBT, N6062M,
	(Res .13)		ZS-GUG, HB-2242, D-KHEG
D-KIMJ(2)	Schempp-Hirth Discus bT	27/321	
D-KIML	Schempp-Hirth Ventus-2cM	25/47	(D-KKRB), OE-9501,
			N776MR
D-KIMM(3)	Schleicher ASK 21Mi	21840	
D-KIMO(2)-W	Schempp-Hirth Duo Discus T	9/254	
D-KIMP	Sportavia/ Fournier RF-5	5070	
D-KIMR(2)	Glaser-Dirks DG-400	4-231	
D-KIMS	Hoffmann H-36 Dimona	3665	
D-KIMT	DG Flugzeugbau LS10-st	L10-012	(D-KABJ)
D-KIMU	Schempp-Hirth Discus bT	62/386	
D-KIMW(3)	Schempp-Hirth Ventus-2cM	70/142	
D-KIMY(2)	Schempp-Hirth Arcus M	5	
D-KINA(2)	Scheibe SF 25C Falke 2000	44464	
D-KIND	Sportavia/ Fournier RF-5	5056	
D-KINE(2)	Grob G 109B	6423	
D-KING(2)	Diamond HK-36TTC Super Dimona	36691	
D-KINI (2)	Grob G 109	6029	
D-KINO	Alpavia/ Fournier RF-3	75	
D-KINT(2)	Scheibe SF 25C Rotax-Falke	44561	OE-9480, D-KWGB
D-KINY(2)	Schleicher ASW 27-18E (ASG 29E)	29611	
D-KIOB(2)	Scheibe SF 25C Falke 2000	44488	
D-KIOD(3)	Scheibe SF 25C Falke 2000	44496	
D-KIOE(2)	Scheibe SF 25C Falke 2000	44498	
D-KIOF(2)	Scheibe SF 25C Falke 2000	44493	
D-KIOG(3)	Scheibe SF 25C Falke 2000	44504	
D-KIOH(2)	Schleicher ASW 20/TOP	20038	D-7948
D-KIOI (2)	Scheibe SF 25C Falke 2000	44516	
D-KIOJ-110	Schempp-Hirth Nimbus-4M	3/14	G-IIOJ, D-KLXX
D-KIOM	Scheibe SF 25C Falke 2100	44521	
D-KION	Scheibe SF 25C Rotax-Falke	44526	
D-KIOO	Scheibe SF 25C Falke 2000	44528	
D-KIOP	Scheibe SF 25C Falke 2000	44523	
D-KIOQ	Scheibe SF 25C Rotax-Falke	44529	
D-KIOR	Scheibe SF 25C Falke 2000	44530	
D-KIOS	Scheibe SF 25C Rotax-Falke	44538	
D-KIOT	Scheibe SF 25C Falke 2000	44514	
D-KIOU(2)	Scheibe SF 25C Rotax-Falke	44551	
D-KIOV	Scheibe SF 25C Rotax-Falke	44541	
D-KIOW	Scheibe SF 25C Rotax-Falke	44537	
D-KIOX	Scheibe SF 25C Falke 2000	44507	
D-KIOY	Scheibe SF 25C Rotax-Falke	44596	
D-KIOZ	Scheibe SF 25C Rotax-Falke	44544	
D-KIPA	Scheibe SF 25C Falke	44111	
D-KIPC	Scheibe SF 25C Falke	44113	
D-KIPD	Scheibe SF 25C Falke	44114	
D-KIPE	Scheibe SF 25C Falke	44115	
D-KIPF	Stemme S10	10-10	
D-KIPH	Schempp-Hirth Ventus cT	116/390	
D-KIPI	Grob G 109	6068	
D-KIPL	Technoflug Piccolo	036	
D-KIPR	Valentin Taifun 17E	1083	I-KIPR, D-KIPR
D-KIPS	Hoffmann H-36 Dimona	36204	N89PS, OE-9264
D-KIPW	Schleicher ASH 26E	26143	
D-KIPZ-PZ	Schempp-Hirth Ventus-2cT	20/82	
D-KIQX-QX	Schleicher ASH 25E	25087	PH-969, D-KIQU
D-KIRA	Fournier RF-4	02	
D-KIRB	Binder EB28	5	N43EB, D-KIWW(2)
D-KIRF	Glaser-Dirks DG-400	4-94	
D-KIRI(3)-OG	Schempp-Hirth Ventus-2cxT	184	
D-KIRK	Sportavia-Pützer RF-5B Sperber	51063	
D-KIRL(2)	Schleicher ASH 25E	25034	OH-800
D-KIRO(2)	Grob G 109B	6200	
D-KIRP	DG Flugzeugbau DG-808C	8-366B265X29	
D-KIRR -RR	Glaser-Dirks DG-500M	5E30M14	
D-KIRS-RS	Schempp-Hirth Ventus-2cxT	196	
D-KIRW	Roth Moroee WR-II	364-58-2-89	D-4363
D-KISA(5)	HB-Aircraft HB 23/2400SP	23041	OE-9321
D-KISB	HOAC HK 36R Super Dimona	36345	
D-KISG	Schleicher ASH 25E	25084	
D-KISH	Schempp-Hirth Ventus cT	70/293	
D-KISI(4)-C	Schempp-Hirth Arcus M	147	
D-KISJ	Schempp-Hirth Janus CT	16/277	
D-KISK(3)-JOY	Schempp-Hirth Ventus-2cxT	125/. . .	
D-KISL	Schleicher ASK 14	14053	
D-KISN	Schleicher ASW 22BLE	22057	D-KIWW, F-WGKS
D-KISO(3)	Schleicher ASK 16 V-1	16001	
D-KISS	Schleicher ASK 14	14049	
	(Cld 3.8.12, now res. 24.11.14)		
D-KIST(2)	DG Flugzeugbau DG-1000T	10-78T17	
	(Res .06)		
D-KISV-JOY	Schempp-Hirth Duo Discus T	97/423	
D-KISW-IW	Glaser-Dirks DG-400	4-197	
D-KISY(3)-ISY	Schleicher ASH 25E	25145	
D-KITA	Alpavia/ Fournier RF-3	58	
D-KITB	Sportavia/ Fournier RF-5	5069	
D-KITE	Alpavia/ Fournier RF-3	65	
D-KITF	Technoflug Piccolo B	119	
D-KITH	Schempp-Hirth Discus bT	44/358	
D-KITI	Alpavia/ Fournier RF-3	57	
D-KITK	Binder EB29	24	
D-KITL-TL	Schempp-Hirth Ventus cT	86/331	
D-KITO(2)	DG Flugzeugbau DG-800B	8-166B90	N890LT
D-KITS	Glaser-Dirks DG-800B	8-51B5	HB-2278, D-KKDG,
			(D-KEBC(3))
D-KITT(4)-IYY	Schempp-Hirth Ventus-2cM	88/184	
D-KITY	Schleicher ASK 16	16028	
D-KITZ(3)	Schempp-Hirth Ventus cT	179/594	HB-2237
	(Res .16)		
D-KIUP	DG Flugzeugbau LS10-st	L10-022	(D-KJAP)
D-KIUT-UT	Schempp-Hirth Duo Discus XLT	251	
D-KIVA	Scheibe SF 25A Motorfalke	4503	
D-KIVE	Schleicher ASK 16	16013	
D-KIVO	Kaiser K 16X	002	
D-KIVP-MM	Schempp-Hirth Ventus cM	102/595	
D-KIVU(2)	Valentin Taifun 17E	1019	
D-KIVY	Schleicher ASK 16	16015	
D-KIWA(2)	DG Flugzeugbau DG-800B	8-196B118	
D-KIWC	Scheibe SF 25C Rotax-Falke	44589	
D-KIWE(3)	Schempp-Hirth Ventus-2cxM	269	
	(P 8.15)		
D-KIWG	Glaser-Dirks DG-600/18M	6-94M40	OE-9340
D-KIWK-WK	Schleicher ASH 25E	25079	
D-KIWM	Schempp-Hirth Ventus cT	154/497	
D-KIWP	Schleicher ASK 16B	16042	
D-KIWS	Glaser-Dirks DG-400	4-65	
D-KIWW(3)	Schempp-Hirth Arcus M	116	
D-KIWY	AVO 68v Samburo	015	
D-KIXI	Sportavia/ Fournier RF-4D	4153	OE-9028
D-KIXL(2)	Schempp-Hirth Duo Discus XLT	231	
D-KIXV-XV	Schleicher ASH 31Mi	31135	
D-KIXX(2)	Schleicher ASK 14	14032	F-CALA, D-KOHC
	(Res 6.15)		
D-KIXZ	Schempp-Hirth Discus-2cT	83	
D-KIYB-IYB	Schempp-Hirth Discus-2cT	62	
D-KIYL-PZ	DG Flugzeugbau DG-800B	8-192B114	
D-KIYY-YY	Schempp-Hirth Ventus bT	42/232	
D-KIYZ-YZ	Schleicher ASH 26E	26201	
D-KIZF-ZF	Schleicher ASH 31Mi	31110	
D-KIZY-ZY	DG Flugzeugbau DG-800B	8-94B29	
D-KIZZ	Schempp-Hirth Discus-2cT	34	
D-KJAA(2)	Schleicher ASH 25M	25192	
D-KJAB	Schempp-Hirth Discus-2cT	88	
D-KJAD	HOAC HK 36R Super Dimona	36358	
D-KJAG(2)	Schempp-Hirth Ventus cT	137/421	PH-1299, BGA 3472
D-KJAI	Sportavia-Pützer Fournier RF4D	4130	OE-9149, D-KALH
D-KJAK	Grob G 103C Twin IIISL	35040	
D-KJAN(2)-JAN	DG Flugzeugbau DG-800B	8-130B59	
D-KJAR	Schleicher ASW 28-18E	28753	
D-KJAS-26	Schleicher ASH 26E	26162	
D-KJAW	Schleicher ASW 27-18E (ASG 29E)	29556	
D-KJBA	Scheibe SF 25C Falke 2000	44399	
D-KJBB	Schempp-Hirth Duo Discus XT	199	
D-KJBC	DG Flugzeugbau DG-808C	8-434B333X93	
D-KJBO-WE	Schleicher ASW 27-18E (ASG 29E)	29553	
D-KJBW-BG	Glaser-Dirks DG-600/18M	6-81M27	
D-KJCB(2)	DG Flugzeugbau DG-808C	8-431B330X90	
D-KJCL-V7	Schleicher ASH 31Mi	31080	
D-KJCT	Schleicher ASH 26E	26132	
D-KJDM	HpH Glasflügel 304MS	062-MS	
	(Res .16)		
D-KJET(2)	Schleicher ASW 20CL-J	20557	D-0884
	(P.3.12)		
D-KJFJ-R8	Rolladen-Schneider LS8-t18	8423	OY-XXC, D-9027
D-KJFS-CH	Schempp-Hirth Discus bT	20/307	
D-KJFW-WK	Schleicher ASW 28-18E	28751	
D-KJGP	Lange E1 Antares	64E51	
D-KJHB-JHB	Schempp-Hirth Arcus M	72	
D-KJHE	Glaser-Dirks DG-400	4-154	HB-2112
D-KJHH-B2	Schempp-Hirth Discus bT	61/383	OO-ZXP, D-KHEI
D-KJHK	Schempp-Hirth Ventus bT	5/124	
D-KJHL-IKB	Schempp-Hirth Discus-2T	1/64	
	(P.2.00)		
D-KJHM(2)	Schleicher ASG 32Mi	32021	(D-KKHM)
	(Res 4.16)		
D-KJHO	Schempp-Hirth Duo Discus XLT	204	OH-987
	(P 4.15)		
D-KJHS	Binder EB29	31	
D-KJII	Schleicher ASW 27-18E (ASG 29E)	29680	
D-KJJI	Schempp-Hirth Ventus cM	92/580	
D-KJJJ	Schempp-Hirth Ventus bT	45/237	PH-1310, D-KGEB(1)
	(Res .16)		
D-KJJK-2K	Schempp-Hirth Discus-2cT	106	
D-KJJP	Schleicher ASW 24E	24809	
D-KJLH-ILH	Schempp-Hirth Ventus-2cM	206	
D-KJLU-MK	Schempp-Hirth Ventus-2cxM	238	OH-997, D-KOZZ
D-KJMA-MA	Schempp-Hirth Janus CM	2	
D-KJMB(2)	Glaser-Dirks DG-500M	5E-113M50	HB-2264, (D-KNDG)
	(Res. .12)		
D-KJMC(2)	Grob G 109B	6323	JA2343
	(Res 9.15)		
D-KJMF	Schleicher ASW 20CL-J	20721	D-9393
	(P. 3.10)		
D-KJMG-JM	Schleicher ASH 26E	26169	
D-KJMH-01	Schempp-Hirth Ventus-2cxaj	25J/559	D-4862
	(P. 3.11)		
D-KJMS(3)	Schempp-Hirth Discus-2cT	121	
D-KJMW	Schempp-Hirth Ventus 3T	4	
	(P 22.7.16)		
D-KJNK	Sportine Aviacija LAK-17AT	192	LN-GXO
D-KJMM	Schempp-Hirth Nimbus-4DM	29/43	

Registration	Type	Serial	Previous marks
D-KJNN	Sportavia/ Fournier RF-4D	4135	F-BPLP
D-KJNU-NU	Schempp-Hirth Discus-2T	35/200	D-1211
D-KJOH	Schleicher ASH 26E	26008	D-2603
D-KJOM	Stemme S10-VT	11-087	
D-KJOS	DG Flugzeugbau DG-800B	8-165B89	
D-KJOW-JO	Schleicher ASH 31Mi	31034	
D-KJOY-JOY	Schempp-Hirth Ventus-2cM	16/34	D-0575
D-KJPC-PC	HpH Glasflügel 304MS	026-MS	
	(P. 2.13)		
D-KJPE	Scheibe SF 25C Heubacher-Falke	44728	D-KSAH
D-KJPF	Schleicher ASH 31Mi	31093	
D-KJPG-PG	Schleicher ASH 31Mi	31111	
D-KJPH	DG Flugzeugbau DG-808C	8-432B331X91	
D-KJPL	Lange E1 Antares	900	
D-KJPT-PT	DG Flugzeugbau LS8-t	8528	
D-KJQA	Sportavia RF-5B Sperber	51067	
D-KJQT	Hoffman H36 Dimona II	36265	F-CGAV, F-WGAV
D-KJRA-RA	Schempp-Hirth Ventus cT	185/610	
D-KJRM-WA	Schempp-Hirth Arcus M	16	
D-KJRR	Schempp-Hirth Arcus M	20	
D-KJRS-RS	Jonker JS/MD Single	1C-101	
	(P 20.4.16)		
D-KJRX	Glaser-Dirks DG-400	4-195	C-GEOJ, D-KKPR
	(P.8.06)		
D-KJSA-SG	DG Flugzeugbau DG-808C	8-393B292X54	
D-KJSC	Jonker Sailplanes JS1C/MD Single	1C-078	
	(P 3.15)		
D-KJSI-SI	Schempp-Hirth Arcus T	54	
D-KJSM	Schempp-Hirth Discus-2T	21/157	
D-KJST	Technoflug Piccolo	005	HB-2131, D-KAFT
D-KJSW	Schempp-Hirth Ventus-2cT	135/. . .	
D-KJTN	Valentin Taifun 17E	1074	
D-KJTS	Schleicher ASH 31Mi	31124	
D-KJUL	Grob G 109	6018	
D-KJUN-HI	Schempp-Hirth Nimbus-3T	18/81	
D-KJVF	Schleicher ASW 27-18E (ASG 29E)	29659	
D-KJWE-L4	Schleicher ASH 26E	26200	(D-KKMK(1))
D-KJWL	Eiri PIK-20E	20249	LX-CAF
D-KJWM-WM	Schempp-Hirth Ventus-2cT	1J	D-9202
	(P .08)		
D-KJWT	Glaser-Dirks DG-800B	8-74B15	
D-KJYM	Stemme S10-VT	11-125	
D-KJZA-HZ	AMS-Flight Carat A	CA030	
D-KJZZ	Schleicher ASW 20BL-J	20695	(PH-1460), D-3738
	(P 5.10)		
D-KKAA	Schleicher ASH 26E	26214	
D-KKAB(2)	Rolladen-Schneider LS8-t	8509	
D-KKAC	Schempp-Hirth Ventus cM	74/541	N144AB, D-KKAB
D-KKAD	Scheibe SF 25C Falke 2000	44373	
D-KKAE-AE	Schempp-Hirth Ventus-2cT	5/13	
D-KKAF(2)	Eiriavion PIK-20E II	20295	(D-KGPE(2)), I-PIKE, OH-615
	(Res 6.6.16)		
D-KKAH(3)	Stemme S10-VT	11-093	
D-KKAI	Grob G 102 Astir CS/TOP	1303	D-7325
D-KKAJ(2)	Schempp-Hirth Ventus-2cM	128	D-5568
D-KKAN	Diamond HK 36TTC Super Dimona	36722	
D-KKAO(3)	Sportavia-Putzer Fournier RF-4D	4025	G-AVLW
D-KKAP	Schleicher ASH 26E	26249	
D-KKAR-U	Schempp-Hirth Ventus-2cT	100	
D-KKAY	DG Flugzeugbau DG-808B	8-251B164	S5-KAY
	(Dbf 15.8.16)		
D-KKAS-4X	Schleicher ASH 25E	25066	
D-KKBA	Glaser-Dirks DG-400	4-281	(D-KODM)
D-KKBB-4T	Schempp-Hirth Janus CT	22/300	
D-KKBE-BE	DG Flugzeugbau DG-808C	8-368B267X31	
D-KKBG	Schleicher ASW 27-18E (ASG 29E)	29634	
D-KKBK-BK	Schleicher ASW 27-18E (ASG 29E)	29539	
D-KKBL-B	Schleicher ASH 25M	25236	
D-KKBM	Schleicher ASW 24E	24858	
D-KKBR	Diamond HK 36TTC Super Dimona	36.853	
D-KKBS	Schempp-Hirth Ventus cM	10/426	
D-KKBX-BX	Schempp-Hirth Duo Discus XLT	244	
D-KKBY-BY	Schempp-Hirth Arcus T	53	
D-KKCB(2)	DG Flugzeugbau DG-808C Competition		
		8-345B244X11	
D-KKCC	Schleicher ASW 27-18E (ASG 29E)	29633	
D-KKCE-CE	DG Flugzeugbau LS8-st	8507	
D-KKCH	Schempp-Hirth Ventus cM	71/536	PH-900
D-KKCM-CM	Schempp-Hirth Nimbus-4DM	42	N13XC, D-KPAI, OO-PAA
D-KKCO-P	Schleicher ASH 25E	25117	
D-KKCW	Schleicher ASH 31Mi	31013	
D-KKDF-DF	Lange E1 Antares	03	
D-KKDG(2)	Schleicher ASW 24E	24848	I-DURT, (D-KAXS)
D-KKDH-KK	DG Flugzeugbau DG-800B	8-305B205	
D-KKDJ	Schempp-Hirth Discus bM	8/537	N98AS
D-KKDN	Diamond HK 36 TTC Super Dimona	36.838	PH-1453
D-KKDS	DG Flugzeugbau DG-808B	8-329B228	
D-KKDU	Schempp-Hirth Duo Discus T	58/345	
D-KKDV-M	Schempp-Hirth Ventus cM	12/434	OE-9334
D-KKEC	Scheibe SF 25C Falke	44368	
D-KKED	Lange E1 Antares	23	
	(Res 8.9.16)		
D-KKEE-EE	Schempp-Hirth Ventus-2cM	135	
D-KKEF	Lange E1 Antares 18T	54T.	D-1965, (D-KOLB(3))
	(W/o 18.5.15)		
D-KKEH	Scheibe SF 25C Rotax-Falke	44712	
D-KKEJ	Glaser-Dirks DG-600/18M	6-96M42	
D-KKEK-SH	Schleicher ASH 26E	26068	
D-KKEM	Schempp-Hirth Ventus cM	76/547	
D-KKET-ET	Schleicher ASH 31Mi	31028	(D-KENT(2))
D-KKEV-KEV	Eiriavion PIK-20E	20262	OO-FRI, D-KOSO
D-KKFC(2)-4E	Schempp-Hirth Discus-2cT	27	
D-KKFF-SKY	Schleicher ASH 26E	26202	
D-KKFK(2)	Schempp-Hirth Discus-2cT	11	
D-KKFL	Sportavia RF-5B Sperber	51021	(D-KCAV)
D-KKFM(2)	DG Flugzeugbau DG-800B	8-159B83	
D-KKFP-FP	HpH Glasflügel 304MS	033-MS	
D-KKFS-KK	Schempp-Hirth Duo Discus T	47/326	
D-KKFT	Schleicher ASH 26E	26212	
D-KKFW	DG Flugzeugbau DG-800B	8-127B56	
D-KKGD	Schempp-Hirth Discus bT	135/510	
D-KKGE-GE	Schleicher ASW 27-18E (ASG 29E)	29545	
D-KKGF-GF	Schempp-Hirth Arcus M	118	
D-KKGG	Valentin Taifun 17E	1008	HB-2076, D-KIHB(1)
D-KKGH-GH	Schempp-Hirth Discus bT	80/412	
D-KKGL	Schempp-Hirth Duo Discus T	33/307	
D-KKGN-GN	Schempp-Hirth Arcus T	31	
D-KKGR	Schempp-Hirth Ventus-2cT	57/187	
D-KKGS-GS	Schempp-Hirth Ventus cM	78/551	
D-KKGU	Schempp-Hirth Duo Discus T	115/. . .	
D-KKGW	Schempp-Hirth Arcus M	52	
D-KKGX-GX	Schempp-Hirth Arcus T	23	
D-KKHA(2)	Schempp-Hirth Discus-2cT	117	
D-KKHB(2)	Technoflug Piccolo B	084	HB-2252, (D-KIMZ)
D-KKHE	Schempp-Hirth Discus-2cT	102	
D-KKHF	Grob G 103C Twin IIISL	35010	N103SL, D-KOID(2)
D-KKHG	Schempp-Hirth Discus bT	98/440	
D-KKHH-2H	Schempp-Hirth Duo Discus XLT	190	
D-KKHI	Lange E1 Antares 23T	78B03	
	(P 12.5.16)		
D-KKHK	Schleicher ASH 31Mi	31018	
D-KKHL	Lange E1 Antares 23T	70B01	
	(P. 5.13)		
D-KKHR	Schleicher ASH 26E	26045	
D-KKHS	DG Flugzeugbau DG-808B	8-328B227	
D-KKHW	Akaflieg Darmstadt D-39HKW	01	
D-KKIA	Schleicher ASH 31Mi	31019	
D-KKII	Schempp-Hirth Ventus-2cM	2/16	
D-KKIK-IK	Schempp-Hirth Ventus-2cT	1/1	
D-KKIL-GW	Schempp-Hirth Ventus cM	75/544	
D-KKIS	DG Flugzeugbau DG-800B	8-106B40	
D-KKIX(2)-1X	Schempp-Hirth Ventus-2cT	81/247	SP-0059
D-KKJM-9X	Schleicher ASH 31Mi	31059	
D-KKJP-22	Schempp-Hirth ASW 22BLE	22042	
D-KKJS	Schempp-Hirth Ventus-2cM	117/251	
D-KKJT	Schempp-Hirth Ventus-2cT	164	
D-KKKA	Eiriavion PIK-20E	20277	OY-JRX, OE-9205, D-KIDM(1)
D-KKKB	Schleicher ASH 26E	26065	
D-KKKC-3KC	Schempp-Hirth Discus-2cT	44	
D-KKKG-G1	Eiriavion PIK-20E	20220	OE-9390, HB-2049
D-KKKH(2)-1H	Schempp-Hirth Discus-2cT	69	
D-KKKK(3)-V4	Schempp-Hirth Nimbus-4DM	43/60	JA24DM
D-KKKL(2)	Schleicher ASW 22BLE 50R	22076	
D-KKKO	Schempp-Hirth Arcus M	130	
D-KKKP	DG Flugzeugbau DG-505MB	5E185B2	HB-2334, D-KSGF
D-KKKW-KW	Schempp-Hirth Ventus-2cT	84/252	
D-KKLA(2)	Lange E1 Antares	48T01	
	(P.09)		
D-KKLB	Schleicher ASH 26E	26093	
D-KKLC	Schleicher ASW 27-18E (ASG 29E)	29597	
D-KKLD	Aerotechnik L-13SDM Vivat	970615	
D-KKLH	Schempp-Hirth Ventus cM	77/548	
D-KKLL	Grob G 109B	6271	
D-KKLM	Schempp-Hirth Ventus-2cT	13	
	(P. 4.11)		
D-KKMA	Hoffmann H-36 Dimona	36222	SE-UBR
D-KKMB-44	Schempp-Hirth Ventus-2cxT	211	
D-KKMH	Glaser-Dirks DG-400	4-203	F-CGRD
D-KKMK(2)	Schleicher ASH 26E	26010	D-0726
D-KKMM	Schempp-Hirth Janus CM	24/220	G-LIME
D-KKMO-MOI	Schempp-Hirth Ventus-2cxT	186	
D-KKMR	Schempp-Hirth Ventus-2cM	136	D-6268
	(P.8.08)		
D-KKMS-TOY	Schempp-Hirth Ventus-2cT	178	
D-KKMT	Schempp-Hirth Ventus-2cT	191	
D-KKMY-MY	Rolladen-Schneider LS8t	8419	D-6281, PH-1281, OY-TTX, D-5326
D-KKNA(2)	Schempp-Hirth Ventus-2cxT	221	
D-KKNZ-OG	Schleicher ASW 27-18E (ASG 29E)	29594	
D-KKOE	Schempp-Hirth Discus-2cT	53	
D-KKOK-OK	Schempp-Hirth Arcus M	81	
D-KKOP	Stemme S10-VT	11-086	
D-KKOR	Lange E1 Antares	14	
D-KKOV	Diamond HK-36TC Super Dimona	36.816	PH-1423
D-KKOY	Schempp-Hirth Arcus M	63	
D-KKPB-PB	Lange E1 Antares	07	
D-KKPC-PC	Schleicher ASH 25M	25218	
	(P.9.99)		
D-KKPE	Schempp-Hirth Nimbus-4DM	31/45	
D-KKPG-KPG	Schempp-Hirth Duo Discus XLT	200	T7-KPG, D-KKPG
D-KKPK-PK	Schempp-Hirth Ventus-2cxM	247	
D-KKPM	Schleicher ASH 26E	26072	D-5126
D-KKPO-Z3	Schempp-Hirth Discus bT	15/300	
D-KKPP	Schempp-Hirth Ventus cM	106/603	
D-KKPR(2)-H1	Schempp-Hirth Ventus-2cxT	113	HA-4517, D-KKAB
D-KKRG	Schempp-Hirth Discus-2cT	108	
D-KKRM	Glaser-Dirks DG-800LA	8-86A42	
D-KKRR-RR	Binder EB28	17	
D-KKSA	Schleicher ASW 24E	24819	
D-KKSC	Valentin Taifun 17E	1013	
D-KKSG	Rolladen-Schneider LS9	9002	
D-KKSH-H1	Schleicher ASK 21Mi	21838	
D-KKSI-S2	Schempp-Hirth Discus-2cT	46	
D-KKSL	Glaser-Dirks DG-400	4-288	JA00DG, ZS-GTL, (D-KIDG)
D-KKSM	Schempp-Hirth Duo Discus T	75/378	
D-KKSS-7	Binder EB28	13	
D-KKST(2)	DG Flugzeugbau DG-808C	8-403B302X64	
D-KKSW(3)-AK	Schleicher ASW 27-18E-t	29714	
D-KKSX	Rolladen-Schneider LS8-t	8416	D-4674
D-KKTB	Schempp-Hirth Ventus cM	79/552	
D-KKTE	Glaser-Dirks DG-400	4-4	
D-KKTH	Schleicher ASH 25Mi	25212	
	(P..99)		
D-KKTI	Schempp-Hirth Ventus-2cxM	268	
D-KKTK	Alpavia/ Fournier RF-3	68	OE-9159, D-KITO
D-KKTT	Schleicher ASW 24E	24806	
D-KKUA	Schleicher ASW 22BLE 50R	22086	
D-KKUB	DG Flugzeugbau DG-808B	8-321B221	
D-KKUJ	Glaser-Dirks DG-400	4-77	HA-4001, D-KHMZ
D-KKUP-KV	Schleicher ASW 22BLE	22043	
D-KKUR	Schleicher ASH 26E	26217	
D-KKUS-US	DG Flugzeugbau DG-808C	8-435B334X94	
D-KKVB-4U	Schempp-Hirth Nimbus-4DM	16/25	
D-KKVF	Schempp-Hirth Ventus cM	68/532	
D-KKVL-VT	Schempp-Hirth Ventus-2cxT	225	D-4948
	(P. 4.13)		
D-KKVO-2H	Schempp-Hirth Duo Discus T	122	
D-KKVR	DG Flugzeugbau LS10-st	L10-015	OY-RIX, (D-KZAA)
D-KKVV-VV	Schleicher ASH 31Mi	31139	
D-KKWD-WD	Schempp-Hirth Ventus-2cT	101/...	

Registration	Type	Serial	Previous/Notes
D-KKWE	Schempp-Hirth Ventus-2cM	4/18	
D-KKWH	Technoflug Piccolo B	125	HB-2388
D-KKWO-WO	Schempp-Hirth Ventus-2cT (P .09)	J2	D-1211
D-KKWW	Schempp-Hirth Discus bT	137/512	
D-KKXL	Schempp-Hirth Ventus-2cM	44/83	
D-KKXX	Schempp-Hirth Ventus-2cT (P .05)	138/. . .	
D-KKYD	Schleicher ASH 25M	25197	
D-KKZX-ZX	Schleicher ASH 31Mi	31033	
D-KKZZ-ZZ	Lange Antares 18T (P 9.6.16)	80T14	
D-KLAA(2)-AA	Schempp-Hirth Ventus-2cT	151	
D-KLAB(2)-AB	Jonker JS/MD Single (P 24.6.16)	1C-103	
D-KLAC(2)-4A	Schempp-Hirth Ventus-2cT	30/102	
D-KLAD(2)-FE	Schempp-Hirth Nimbus-4M	4/17	
D-KLAH-GC	Schempp-Hirth Ventus cT (W/o 19.6.16)	106/369	
D-KLAI	Diamond HK 36TTC Super Dimona	36567	
D-KLAK(3)-AK	Sportine Aviacija LAK-17AT	172	LY-GMY
D-KLAL-L7	Schempp-Hirth Discus-2cT	93	
D-KLAM	Sportavia/ Fournier RF-5	5123	
D-KLAN	Glaser-Dirks DG-400	4-234	
D-KLAQ-32	Sportine Aviacija LAK-17AT	177	LY-GNB
D-KLAP(3)	Schempp-Hirth Janus CM	37/290	F-CAOB, D-KAOK
D-KLAR	Schleicher ASK 14	14038	
D-KLAS(2)	Technoflug Piccolo B (Res.05)	20	
D-KLAT	Hoffmann H-36 Dimona	36246	
D-KLAU	Scheibe SF 25C Falke 2000	44481	
D-KLAX	Scheibe SF 25C Falke 2000	44428	
D-KLAY	Schempp-Hirth Janus CT	15/276	D-4530
D-KLBA	Scheibe SF 25B Falke	4621	OE-9341, D-KEGI
D-KLBB	Schleicher ASW 24E	24801	
D-KLBG	Schempp-Hirth Ventus cT	158/511	
D-KLBH	Schempp-Hirth Ventus-2cxM	278	
D-KLBI	Technoflug Piccolo	053	
D-KLBO	Schempp-Hirth Discus-2cT	89	
D-KLBP	Schleicher ASH 25M	25186	
D-KLBR	Glaser-Dirks DG-600/18M	6-104M38	OH-843
D-KLBS-BS	Schleicher ASW 27-18E (ASG 29E)	29625	
D-KLBW	Grob G 109B	6368	
D-KLBY	Klotz Moka 1	1	
D-KLCA	DG Flugzeugbau DG-800B	8-200B122	
D-KLCB	DG Flugzeugbau DG-800B	8-291B196	
D-KLCC(2)	Stemme S10-VT	11-072	
D-KLCH	Schempp-Hirth Discus bT	84/418	V5-GAB
D-KLCS-CS	Schempp-Hirth Arcus M	34	
D-KLDA	Scheibe SF 25C Falke	44124	
D-KLDG(2)-1V	DG Flugzeugbau DG-1000T	10-124T43	
D-KLDH	Schempp-Hirth Discus bT	1/245	(PH-1516), D-KLDH
D-KLDR(2)	Lange E1 Antares	44E41	
D-KLDT	Scheibe SF 25C Rotax-Falke	44636	
D-KLEB	Schempp-Hirth Ventus cT	177/581	
D-KLEC	Scheibe SF 25C Rotax-Falke	44546	
D-KLEE	Sportavia/ Fournier RF-5	5076	
D-KLEF	Diamond HK 36TC Super Dimona (Res.3.00)	36661	
D-KLEI(2)	Diamond HK 36TC Super Dimona	36679	PH-1209
D-KLEK	Schleicher ASH 31Mi	31039	
D-KLEM(2)	Diamond HK 36TTC Super Dimona	36657	
D-KLEO(3)-EO	Rolladen-Schneider LS8-t	8471	
D-KLEP	Lange E1 Antares	53E45	
D-KLER	Sportavia/ Fournier RF-5	5051	
D-KLEU	Glaser-Dirks DG-400	4-180	
D-KLEV-X7	Schempp-Hirth Duo Discus XT	168	
D-KLEX(2)	Scheibe SF 25C Falke 2000	44436	HB-2126, (D-KIAC)
D-KLEZ	DG Flugzeugbau DG-800B	8-98B33	HB-2313, D-KTAR
D-KLFA	Grob G 109B	6210	HB-2079
D-KLFB-FOX	Schempp-Hirth Duo Discus T	80/393	
D-KLFR	Schempp-Hirth Ventus-2cT	87/. . .	
D-KLFU	Binder EB29D	25	
D-KLFV	Schempp-Hirth Discus bM	9/542	
D-KLFW	Hoffmann H-36 Dimona	36249	OE-9290
D-KLGA	Schleicher ASH 26E	26058	
D-KLGB-GB	Schempp-Hirth Discus-2T	12/123	
D-KLGM-M2	Schempp-Hirth Ventus-2cxT	223	
D-KLGR	Glaser-Dirks DG-400	4-129	G-BUXG, D-KEHJ
D-KLGS	Schleicher ASH 26E	26077	
D-KLHA-HA	Schempp-Hirth Discus bT	79/411	
D-KLHG	Schleicher ASW 24/TOP	24821	
D-KLHH	Technoflug Piccolo	043	
D-KLHI-HI	Schempp-Hirth Discus-2T	32/181	F-CFDR
D-KLHJ-IKK	Schempp-Hirth Discus-2cT	71	
D-KLHL-HL	Schleicher ASW 22BLE	22070	
D-KLHM	Schempp-Hirth Nimbus-4DM	21/31	
D-KLHW	Schleicher ASH 25EB	25172	
D-KLIA	Schleicher ASH 26E	26081	
D-KLIB	Glasflügel H201BE Standard Libelle (Res .16)	276	OY-VXS, (BGA1520)
D-KLIC	Grob G 102 Astir CS77/TOP	1648	OE-9323, D-4823
D-KLID	Aerotechnik L-13SDM Vivat (Res .16)	970613	
D-KLIF	Diamond HK 36TC Super Dimona	36728	
D-KLII-FH	Schleicher ASW 24/TOP	24807	HB-2227, D-KCCL
D-KLIK	Sportavia/ Fournier RF-5	5125	
D-KLIL	Eiriavion PIK-20E	20224	
D-KLIM	Technoflug Piccolo	049	
D-KLIN(3)	Hoffmann H-36 Dimona	3616	HB-2066
D-KLIO	Scheibe SF 25A Motorfalke	4520	OE-9015, D-KAJE(1)
D-KLIP(2)	Schempp-Hirth Discus-2c-FES (Res .16)	8	
D-KLIR	Sportavia/ Fournier RF-5	5052	
D-KLIS-HR	Schempp-Hirth Ventus-2cT	36/124	
D-KLJC	Glaser-Dirks DG-400	4-114	
D-KLJM-66	Schempp-Hirth Ventus-2cxT	109/303	G-CEUR, BGA 5060, D-KKAO
D-KLJP	Schleicher ASH 25E	25082	
D-KLKA-M7	Schempp-Hirth Ventus cT	169/556	
D-KLKE	Diamond HK 36TC Super Dimona	36839	OE-9998
D-KLKG	Schleicher ASH 26E	26135	(D-KLUF)
D-KLKL-KL	Schleicher ASH 25E	25053	
D-KLKM	Eiriavion PIK-20E	20258	HB-2050
D-KLKS-Z4	Schempp-Hirth Discus-2cT	123	
D-KLLA-2L	Schleicher ASW 27-18E (ASG 29E)	29590	
D-KLLG(2)	Schleicher ASH 25Mi	25251	
D-KLLI (2)	Schleicher ASH 25E	25153	
D-KLLK	Schempp-Hirth Nimbus-4DM	63	
D-KLLL(2)-7L	Schempp-Hirth Ventus-2cT	68/207	
D-KLLS(2)-LS	DG Flugzeugbau LS10-st	L10-006	
D-KLLT	Schempp-Hirth Ventus-2cxM	214	
D-KLLW	Schempp-Hirth Ventus cM	58/508	
D-KLLX-CE	Schempp-Hirth Ventus-2cM	17/35	
D-KLLZ	Rolladen-Schneider LS9	9009	
D-KLMB-F	Schempp-Hirth Duo Discus T	93/413	
D-KLMC	Glaser-Dirks DG-600/18M	6-106M48	
D-KLMD-LM	Schleicher ASH 25E	25050	HB-2171, D-KCCH(1)
D-KLMI	HOAC HK 36R Super Dimona	36365	
D-KLMK	HOAC HK 36R Super Dimona	36367	
D-KLML	HOAC HK 36R Super Dimona	36368	
D-KLMM	HOAC HK 36R Super Dimona	36369	
D-KLMN	HOAC HK 36R Super Dimona	36370	
D-KLMS(2)-MS	Schempp-Hirth Discus-2cT	125	
D-KLOA-FT	Schleicher ASW 24E	24859	
D-KLOE(2)-CT	Schleicher ASW 27-18E (ASG 29E)	29600	
D-KLOF	Rolladen-Schneider LS9	9004	
D-KLOK-OK	Schempp-Hirth Ventus-2cxM	212	
D-KLON	Schleicher ASG 32Mi (For export to South Africa .16)	32014	
D-KLOR	Sportavia/ Fournier RF-5	5053	
D-KLOU(2)	Scheibe SF 25C Falke 2000	44508	
D-KLPA(3)	Schleicher ASW 27-18E (ASG 29E)	29696	
D-KLPC	Glaser-Dirks DG-400	4-190	
D-KLPH	HOAC HK 36R Super Dimona	36383	PH-1030, D-KMDD
D-KLPN-PN	Glaser-Dirks DG-400	4-251	
D-KLPP-PP	Glaser-Dirks DG-400	4-179	
D-KLPS	Diamond HK 36TC Super Dimona	36840	OE-9997
D-KLPW-HS	Schleicher ASH 26E	26113	
D-KLPY-PY	Schleicher ASH 26E	26079	
D-KLRD	SZD-45A Ogar	B-648	DDR-3502, DM-3502
D-KLRR	Glaser-Dirks DG-500M	5E33M17	VH-GKX, D-KLAF
D-KLRS(2)	Glaser-Dirks DG-400	4-81	
D-KLRW-KL	Schempp-Hirth Ventus-2cM	111/	
D-KLSB	Scheibe SF 25C Falke 2000	44503	
D-KLSC	Schleicher ASK 14	AB14066	
D-KLSE	Schempp-Hirth Ventus-2cM	106/219	
D-KLSG(2)-SG	Schempp-Hirth Arcus M	149	
D-KLSJ-Q	Schempp-Hirth Quintus M (P.3.12)	2	
D-KLSM	Schempp-Hirth Ventus-2cxM	148	
D-KLSR	Diamond HK 36TTC Super Dimona	36686	
D-KLST-8T	Rolladen-Schneider LS8-t	8400	
D-KLSU	Schempp-Hirth Ventus-2c-FES (P 29.7.16)	152	
D-KLSV(2)	Diamond HK 36TTC Super Dimona (Res.3.00)	36660	
D-KLSW(2)	Scheibe SF 25C Rotax-Falke	44580	
D-KLSX-SX	Schleicher ASH 26E	26097	D-6826
D-KLTB-TB	DG Flugzeugbau DG-800B	8-306B206	
D-KLTE	Valentin Taifun 17E	1077	(D-KLET)
D-KLTF	AMS Flight Carat A	CA006	
D-KLTI	DG Flugzeugbau DG-800B	8-238B152	
D-KLTM-MS	Schleicher ASW 27-18E (ASG 29E)	29614	
D-KLTS	Schleicher ASW 24E	24802	PH-1286, D-KLTS
D-KLUB(2)	Scheibe SF 25C Rotax-Falke	44543	
D-KLUC	Schempp-Hirth Ventus-2cxT	240	
D-KLUM	DG Flugzeugbau DG-1000T	10-127T45	
D-KLUT-8S	Schempp-Hirth Ventus-2cxT	228	
D-KLUW	Valentin Taifun 17E	1035	
D-KLUX(2)	Schempp-Hirth Ventus-2cM	58/114	
D-KLVA	Diamond HK 36 TC Super Dimona	36.714	G-HKSD, N105AM
D-KLVB-JOY	Schleicher ASH 31Mi	31017	
D-KLVD-3H	Schempp-Hirth Discus-2cT	87	
D-KLVF	Sportine Aviacija LAK-17B-FES (Res .16)	241	
D-KLVG	AVO 68v Samburo 2000	023	
D-KLVI	Grob G 109B	6230	(D-KIVI), OE-9247, D-KGFN
D-KLVO	Schleicher ASK 14	14019	(D-KEHO)
D-KLVR-VR	Schempp-Hirth Arcus T	10	
D-KLVT	Lange E1 Antares (P.8.05)	16	
D-KLVW	Diamond HK 36TTC Super Dimona	36662	
D-KLWA	DG Flugzeugbau DG-800B	8-96B31	
D-KLWH	DG Flugzeugbau LS8-t	8526	
D-KLWM	Scheibe SF 25C Rotax-Falke	44690	
D-KLWO-TWO	Schempp-Hirth Arcus M	138	
D-KLWS -WS	Schempp-Hirth Ventus cM	91/578	
D-KLWW	ICA/Brasov IS-28M2/G	71	
D-KLXH-XH	Schempp-Hirth Ventus-2cxT	204	
D-KLXL	Schleicher ASH 26E (Res. .13)	26188	SE-UTK, D-KSAB, D-KSAG
D-KLXV	Schleicher ASG 29Es	unkn	
D-KLYY-P2	Schempp-Hirth Ventus cM	28/461	D-2444
D-KLZM	Rolladen-Schneider LS9	9001	
D-KLZV(2)-ZV	HpH Glasflügel 304MS	041-MS	
D-KMAA(2)	Schempp-Hirth Ventus-2cxM	272	
D-KMAC(3)	DG Flugzeugbau DG-800B	8-262B170	
D-KMAF	Schempp-Hirth Ventus cM	38/474	I-KMAP, D-KMAP
D-KMAG	Scheibe SF 25B Falke	46112	
D-KMAH(2)	Schempp-Hirth Ventus-2cM	19/37	D-KNHC(1), D-3241
D-KMAI	Scheibe SF 25B Falke	46114	
D-KMAK(4)	Technoflug Piccolo B	102	HB-2272, D-KAIW
D-KMAL(2)	Diamond HK 36TTS Super Dimona	36585	
D-KMAM	Stemme S10-V	14-020	F-CGYO, (D-KGDC(2))
D-KMAN	Scheibe Bergfalke IVSM (Res 6.15)	5902	
D-KMAP(2)	Schempp-Hirth Ventus-2cxT	209	
D-KMAS(3)-30	Schleicher ASH 30Mi	30009	
D-KMAT(2)-M	Lange E1 Antares 18T (P. 5.11)	67T09	
D-KMAU-BM	DG Flugzeugbau DG-1001M	10-204M22	
D-KMAX	Scheibe SF 25C Falke 2000	44381	
D-KMBA	Schempp-Hirth Ventus-2cM	114/	
D-KMBD	Schempp-Hirth Arcus M	139	
D-KMBE-BE	Schempp-Hirth Ventus-2cM	116/248	
D-KMBG(2)	Grob G 109B	6558	
D-KMBL(2)	Diamond HK 36TTC Super Dimona	36617	N617TT
D-KMBP	Schleicher ASW 22BE	22045	VH-. . .
D-KMBR-IT	Schempp-Hirth Discus-2cT	65	
D-KMBS	Binder EB29	15	

Registration	Type	C/n	Previous identities
D-KMCA	Scheibe SF 25C Rotax-Falke	44605	
D-KMCB	Stemme S10	10-6	
D-KMCC	Schempp-Hirth Ventus-2cxM	257	
D-KMCD	DG Flugzeugbau DG-800B	8-180B104	
D-KMCE(2)	Schempp-Hirth Ventus-2cT	54/176	HB-2353
D-KMCH	Akaflieg Darmstadt D-39B	40	D-KIRI
D-KMCI	Stemme S10-VT	11-046	
D-KMCL	Technoflug Piccolo B	120	
D-KMCM-CM	Rolladen-Schneider LS8-t	8418	D-5984
D-KMCW	DG Flugzeugbau DG-800B	8-149B73	
D-KMDK	Schleicher ASH 25M	25182	
D-KMDO	Stemme S10-VT	11-069	
D-KMDS	Schempp-Hirth Discus bT (W/o 13.05.12)	72/400	
D-KMDZ	Alpavia/ Fournier RF-3	50	F-BMDZ
D-KMEA	Stemme S10-VT	11-080	
D-KMEB	Schleicher ASW 27-18E (ASG 29E)	29589	
D-KMEC	Nitzsche AVo 68-R 115 Samburo	011	
D-KMED	Grob G 109B	6291	
D-KMEE	Schempp-Hirth Arcus T	34	
D-KMEI	Technoflug Piccolo B	063	
D-KMEJ	DG Flugzeugbau DG-800B	8-134B63	
D-KMEM	Sportavia/ Fournier RF-4D	4037	G-BMEM, CN-TZZ
D-KMER	Valentin Taifun 17E	1018	
D-KMES	Schleicher ASK 16	16034	
D-KMET	Schleicher ASK 16	16007	
D-KMEU	Schempp-Hirth Nimbus 4DM	64	RF-00797, (D-KRVB)
D-KMEX	Schempp-Hirth Arcus M	86	
D-KMEY	Scheibe SF 25C Falke 2000	44484	
D-KMFB-FB	DG Flugzeugbau DG-808B	8-320B220	
D-KMFE	Schempp-Hirth Discus bT	26/319	
D-KMFF	Schleicher ASH 26E	26194	
D-KMFM-FM	Schempp-Hirth Duo Discus XLT	220	
D-KMFN-FN	Schempp-Hirth Ventus-2cT	33/115	
D-KMFS	Scheibe SF 25C Falke	44215	OO-VZA, D-KDFV(1)
D-KMFW(2)-EW	Stemme S10-VT	11-085	SE-UOY, D-KBBF
D-KMGA(2)	HOAC HK 36R Super Dimona	36322	(D-KBGA, OY-SXD, D-KMPC
D-KMGB	Scheibe SF 28A Tandem-Falke	5752	
D-KMGC	Scheibe SF 28A Tandem-Falke	5753	
D-KMGE(2)-GE	Schempp-Hirth Duo Discus T	18/271	
D-KMGG(2)	Schempp-Hirth Ventus-2cT	159	
D-KMGO	Diamond HK 36TTC Super Dimona	36568	
D-KMGR	Schempp-Hirth Ventus-2cT	18/76	
D-KMGS	Schleicher ASH 26E	26117	
D-KMHA	Valentin Taifun 17E (Repaired with new fuselage c/n 1105)	1061	HB-2113, D-KMHA
D-KMHB-HB	Valentin Kiwi	3006	
D-KMHD-HD	Schleicher ASW 27-18E (ASG 29E)	29624	
D-KMHF-EE	Schempp-Hirth Nimbus-3T	23/89	BGA 4932, D-KMHF
D-KMHG	Schleicher ASH 25M	25175	
D-KMHK	Technoflug Piccolo	052	
D-KMHP	Schempp-Hirth Ventus-2cxT	180	
D-KMHS	Schempp-Hirth Ventus-2cM	11/28	
D-KMHU	DG Flugzeugbau DG-808C	8-412B311X72	
D-KMHW	Glaser-Dirks DG-800LA	8-58A35	
D-KMIA-JOE	Schempp-Hirth Arcus M	91	
D-KMIB-CM	Schempp-Hirth Ventus-2cM	74/155	PH-1175
D-KMIC	Eiri PIK-20E	20285	HB-2057
D-KMII -CD	Schempp-Hirth Discus bT	33/208	
D-KMIK-M	HpH Glasflügel 304MS	016-MS	OK-3757
D-KMIL(2)	Schempp-Hirth Ventus bT	11/146	
D-KMIM-IM	Schempp-Hirth Janus CT	5/200	
D-KMIN	Schempp-Hirth Nimbus-3T	17/80	
D-KMIS	HOAC HK-36TTC Super Dimona	36.831	OE-9998
D-KMIX-IX	Schempp-Hirth Ventus-2cxT	158	
D-KMJE	Scheibe SF 25C Falke	44105	
D-KMJH	Scheibe SF 25C Falke	44108	
D-KMJI	Scheibe SF 25C Falke	44109	
D-KMJR	Schempp-Hirth Ventus-2cxT	237	
D-KMKH	Schempp-Hirth Ventus cTT (P.10.02)	290	D-2976
D-KMKL	Stemme S10-VT	11-040	OY-SAX, D-KAZT(1)
D-KMKM	Schleicher ASW 24E	24818	
D-KMKR	Hoffmann H-36 Dimona	36255	
D-KMKS	HOAC HK 36R Super Dimona	36409	
D-KMKW-AX	Schleicher ASH 25E	25151	D-6925
D-KMLA	DG Flugzeugbau DG-808B	8-296B201	
D-KMLI	Grob G 103C Twin IIISL	35024	D-KJHF
D-KMLL	Scheibe SF 25C Falke 2000	44510	
D-KMLM-MH	Schleicher ASH 25Mi	25266	
D-KMLN	Schempp-Hirth Ventus-2cM	7/24	F-CGLU, D-8137
D-KMLR	Glaser-Dirks DG-400	4-152	
D-KMLS	Schleicher ASH 31Mi	31095	
D-KMLV	Grob G 109B	6260	
D-KMMA	Schempp-Hirth Ventus-2cM	14/31	
D-KMMB-MB	Schempp-Hirth Duo Discus XT	142/491	G-CKNY, BGA 5226
D-KMMC-MC	Schempp-Hirth Discus bT	118/474	
D-KMMF	Stemme S6-RT	021	
D-KMMG	Scheibe SF 36B	4105	G-BKAH, (D-KOGF)
D-KMMK-SW	Schempp-Hirth Ventus cT	140/430	PH-872
D-KMML(3)	Diamond HK 36TTC Super Dimona	36573	
D-KMMM	Scheibe SF 25C Falke 2000	44502	
D-KMMO	Schleicher ASH 26E	26173	
D-KMMP	Scheibe SF 27M-B (P 11.15)	6302	(D-KRMR), D-KOLE
D-KMMR	Schempp-Hirth Discus bT	64/389	
D-KMMS	Schleicher ASW 24E	24820	HB-2192, D-KAXH
D-KMMV	Schempp-Hirth Ventus cT	110/377	I-EUGI
D-KMMW-PM	Schempp-Hirth Ventus cM	31/464	
D-KMNC-NC	Grob G 103C Twin IIISL	35023	
D-KMNM-MB	Schempp-Hirth Arcus M	93	
D-KMNN-NN	Schempp-Hirth Ventus-2c FES (P 5.15)	150	
D-KMNW	Glaser-Dirks DG-400	4-249	
D-KMOB	Grob G 103C Twin IIISL	35031	
D-KMOD	Scheibe SF 25C Rotax-Falke	44610	
D-KMOE	Schempp-Hirth Ventus cT	129/406	
D-KMOM	Stemme S10-VT	11-135	(D-KMCM)
D-KMON	Sportine Aviacija LAK-17B-FES	203	
D-KMOR	Scheibe SF 25C Falke 2000	44532	
D-KMOS(2)-AM	Schempp-Hirth Arcus T	6	
D-KMOT	Sportine Aviacija LAK-17AT	171T1	D-6369
D-KMPB(2)	Schempp-Hirth Ventus-2cM	46/95	
D-KMPE	Sportavia/ Scheibe SF 25C Falke	4253	
D-KMPF	Sportavia-Pützer RF-5B Sperber	51071	
D-KMPI(2)	Schleicher ASH 31Mi	31132	
D-KMPK	Schempp-Hirth Ventus-2cM	34/60	
D-KMPM	Schempp-Hirth Quintus M (P. 3.13)	14	
D-KMPP	Schleicher ASH 25M	25191	
D-KMPR	Schleicher ASH 26E	26056	
D-KMPS	Sportavia/ Scheibe SF 25C Falke	4255	
D-KMQB	Schempp-Hirth Nimbus-4DT	7	F-CIIT
D-KMRA	Glaser-Dirks DG-400	4-92	HB-2085
D-KMRD	Schleicher ASH 26E	26083	
D-KMRF-RF	Schempp-Hirth Duo Discus XLT	?	
D-KMRH	Scheibe SF 25C Rotax-Falke	44540	(D-KIOU)
D-KMRJ	Schleicher ASH 31Mi	31073	
D-KMRL	DG Flugzeugbau DG-800B	8-261B169	
D-KMRM	Grob G 109	6076	(D-KIRC)
D-KMRO-RO	Schleicher ASW 27-18E (ASG 29E)	29648	
D-KMRT	DG Flugzeugbau DG-808C	8-433B332X92	
D-KMRV-RV	Schempp-Hirth Ventus-2cM	54/108	
D-KMSA	Technoflug Piccolo B	090	
D-KMSB	Glaser-Dirks DG-400	4-48	G-DGLM, D-KMDH
D-KMSC	Scheibe SF 25C Rotax-Falke	44577	
D-KMSE	Reichelt Erpel	V-1	
D-KMSF-SF	Schempp-Hirth Ventus cT	100/357	
D-KMSH	Schleicher ASW 24E	24837	
D-KMSI-SI	Schempp-Hirth Ventus-2cxM	281	
D-KMSM-M	Schempp-Hirth Quintus M (P.5.12)	6	
D-KMSQ	Scheibe SF 25C Falke 2000	4435	
D-KMSP(2)-MF	Schempp-Hirth Ventus-2cxM	273	
D-KMSY	Schempp-Hirth Ventus-2cM	61/121	
D-KMTB	Glaser-Dirks DG-800LA	8-20A17	
D-KMTK	Technoflug Piccolo	031	HB-2156, D-KCFH
D-KMTL(2)	Schempp-Hirth Ventus cM	5/413	D-KLAZ
D-KMTO	Glaser-Dirks DG-800LA	8-17A14	
D-KMTT	Hoffmann H-36 Dimona	3630	
D-KMTW	DG Flugzeugbau DG-800B	8-275B183	
D-KMTX	DG Flugzeugbau DG-1000T	10-69T8	
D-KMTZ	Schempp-Hirth Ventus-2cxT	222	
D-KMUB-4S	Schempp-Hirth Ventus-2cxT	235	
D-KMUD	Nitzsche AVo 68-R 115 Samburo	009	
D-KMUE-12	Stemme S10	10-12	
D-KMUF-TM	DG Flugzeugbau DG-808C	8-358B257X22	
D-KMUH	Scheibe SF 25C Rotax-Falke	44707	PH-1324, D-KEOU
D-KMUW-UW	Schempp-Hirth Ventus-2cxT	224	
D-KMVC	Schempp-Hirth Ventus cT (Res .16)	179/594	(D-KITZ(3)), HB-2237
D-KMWA-UFO	Schempp-Hirth Ventus-2cM	95/200	N5FU
D-KMWD-WD	Schempp-Hirth Discus bT	86/421	
D-KMWH	Schempp-Hirth Ventus-2cxM	250	(D-KPGM)
D-KMWL-WL	Schempp-Hirth Ventus-2cM	290	
D-KMWM	DG Flugzeugbau DG-800B	8-193B115	
D-KMWT	Schempp-Hirth Arcus M	53	
D-KMWW	Glaser-Dirks DG-400	4-250	
D-KMXL-AG	Schleicher ASH 26E	26229	
D-KMYT	DG Flugzeugbau DG-808C	8-364B263X27	
D-KNAB	Scheibe SF 25C Falke 2000	44338	
D-KNAC	Scheibe SF 25C Falke 2000	44341	
D-KNAD	Scheibe SF 25C Falke 2000	44337	
D-KNAE(2)	Scheibe SF 25C Falke 2000	44345	
D-KNAG(2)	Scheibe SF 25C Falke 2000	44419	
D-KNAJ	Scheibe SF 25C Falke 2000 (W/o 28.5.10, noted 4.13)	44352	
D-KNAK(5)	Alpavia/ Fournier RF-3	88	OE-9102, D-KILE(1)
D-KNAL	Scheibe SF 25C Falke 2000 (Res .12)	44178	
D-KNAM(2)	Scheibe SF 25C Falke 2000	44356	
D-KNAO	Scheibe SF 25C Falke 2000	44361	
D-KNAP	Schleicher ASW 24E	24813	D-KGUI, F-CGKR, D-KAXF(2)
D-KNAQ(2)	Scheibe SF 25C Falke 2000	44366	
D-KNAR	Scheibe SF 25C Falke 2000	44359	
D-KNAS	Scheibe SF 25C Falke 2000	44365	
D-KNAT	Scheibe SF 25C Falke 2000	44364	
D-KNAU(2)	Scheibe SF 25E Super Falke	4363	
D-KNAW	Scheibe SF 25C Falke 2000	44372	
D-KNAX	Scheibe SF 25C Heubach-Falke	44719	
D-KNBB(3)-BB	Schempp-Hirth Discus-2cT	7	
D-KNBF-A25	Schleicher ASH 25E	25044	BGA 3341
D-KNBY	Schleicher ASH 25E	25111	
D-KNCB	DG Flugzeugbau DG-808C	8-401B300X62	
D-KNCL-CL	Schempp-Hirth Duo Discus T	11/257	D-2091
D-KNCM	Schempp-Hirth Ventus cM	98/589	
D-KNDS	Schempp-Hirth Discus-2T	36/201	
D-KNDY-A2	Schleicher ASW 27-18E (ASG 29E)	29676	
D-KNEB	Grob G 109B	6340	
D-KNED	Grob G 109B	6354	
D-KNEE	Grob G 109B	6351	
D-KNEF	Grob G 109B	6358	
D-KNEG	Grob G 109B	6359	
D-KNEI	Grob G 109B	6379	OH-747
D-KNEL	Grob G 109B	6426	
D-KNEM	Grob G 109B	6422	
D-KNEO	Grob G 109B	6439	
D-KNER	Grob G 109B	6551	
D-KNES	Grob G 109B	6421	
D-KNEV	Schleicher ASW 27-18E	29572	
D-KNEX	Grob G 109B	6402	
D-KNFA	Schempp-Hirth Discus bT	150/541	
D-KNFH	Stemme S10-VT (P. 2.11)	11-130	
D-KNFN	Schempp-Hirth Discus bT	88/425	
D-KNFU	Schempp-Hirth Discus bT	151/543	
D-KNGD	Schleicher ASH 25M (P.5.00)	25217	
D-KNGG	HpH Glasflügel 304MS	058-MS	
D-KNGS	Schempp-Hirth Ventus cM	57/507	
D-KNHB	Schleicher ASH 26E	26048	
D-KNHC(2)	Schempp-Hirth Ventus-2cM	152/. . .	
D-KNHD	Schempp-Hirth Ventus cT	136/418	
D-KNHM	Schleicher ASH 31Mi	31126	
D-KNHS-HS	Schempp-Hirth Ventus-2cxT	182	
D-KNHW	DG Flugzeugbau DG-800B	8-240B154	
D-KNIA	Scheibe SF 25C Falke 2000	44377	
D-KNIC	Scheibe SF 25C Falke 2000	44379	
D-KNID	Scheibe SF 25C Falke 2000	44380	
D-KNIF(2)	Scheibe SF 25C Falke 2000	44390	

Reg	Type	Serial	Notes
D-KNIG(2)	Scheibe SF 25C Falke 2000	44397	
D-KNIH(2)	Scheibe SF 25C Falke 2000	44398	
D-KNII (2)	Scheibe SF 25C Falke 2000	44402	
D-KNIJ(2)	Scheibe SF 25C Falke 2000	44404	
D-KNIL(2)	Scheibe SF 25C Falke 2000	44417	
D-KNIM(2)	Scheibe SF 25C Falke 2000	44418	
D-KNIN(2)	Scheibe SF 25C Falke 2000	44421	
D-KNIP	Scheibe SF 25C Falke 2000	44416	
D-KNIQ	Scheibe SF 25C Falke 2000	44403	
D-KNIS	Scheibe SF 25C Falke 2000	44424	
D-KNIT	Scheibe SF 25C Falke 2000	44427	
D-KNIU(2)	Scheibe SF 25C Falke 2000	44429	
D-KNIV	Scheibe SF 25C Falke 2000	44432	
D-KNIW	Scheibe SF 25C Falke 2000	44409	
D-KNIX	Scheibe SF 25C Falke 2000	44196	HB-2041, (D-KDAM)
D-KNJA	Technoflug Piccolo B	022	HB-2041, (D-KCTC)
D-KNJK(2)-JK	Schempp-Hirth Arcus M	1	D-KBWE
D-KNKK	Glaser-Dirks DG-400	4-141	(ZS- . . .)
D-KNKN	Scheibe SF 25K Falke	4902	
D-KNLA	Stemme S10-VT	11-105	
D-KNLB	Schleicher ASH 31Mi	31021	
D-KNLT	Stemme S12 Twin Voyager (Res .16)	12-003	D-KGBG(2)
D-KNMA(2)	Stemme S10-VT	11-003	HB-2305, D-KSTE(10)
D-KNMY	Stemme S10-VT	11-110	
D-KNNK	Schempp-Hirth Discus-2c-FES (P 17.5.16)	5	
D-KNNN	Grob G 109B	6202	OY-XNN, D-KGFB
D-KNOE	DG Flugzeugbau DG-808B	8-258B166	EC-ITE, D-KIAJ
D-KNOL	Schleicher ASK 14	14001	HB-2395, PH-1049, D-KIKY
D-KNOM	DG Flugzeugbau DG-800B	8-167B91	
D-KNOP	Scheibe SF 25C Falke 2000	44116	
D-KNOR	Scheibe SF 25C Falke	44118	
D-KNOS-OS	Schleicher ASW 28-18E (P.3.04)	28704	
D-KNOT(2)	Scheibe SF 25C Falke 2000 (P.05)	44375	HB-2106, D-KNBA
D-KNOW	Grob G 109B	6267	N713BR, N53553
D-KNOX(2)	Valentin Taifun 17E	1010	
D-KNPF	Knechtel KN-1	V-1	
D-KNRA	Glaser-Dirks DG-400 (P.3.00)	4-157	F-CFVH
D-KNRV-RV	Schempp-Hirth Duo Discus T	32/305	
D-KNSN	Diamond HK 36TC Super Dimona	36576	
D-KNTI-TBN	Schempp-Hirth Ventus-2cT	92/...	
D-KNUD	Glaser-Dirks DG-400	4-155	SX-ABH, G-WRMN
D-KNUE	Technoflug Piccolo B	062	D-MNUE, D-KNUE
D-KNUM	Valentin Taifun 17E II	1115	
D-KNUS	Schleicher ASK 16	16027	
D-KNUT(2)	Hoffmann H-36 Dimona (P.3.00)	3677	
D-KNWF	Hoffmann H-36 Dimona	36247	OE-9383, D-KITT(2)
D-KNWN	Schleicher Rhönlerche II-Storch	1	
D-KNWS	Schempp-Hirth Discus bT	56/377	
D-KOAA	Sportavia-Pützer Fournier RF5	5025	D-KORA
D-KOAB	Test Registration for Schleicher production		
D-KOAC(3)	Schempp-Hirth Janus CM	30/238	JA2404
D-KOAD	Scheibe SF 25C Falke	4457	
D-KOAF(2)	Schempp-Hirth Ventus-2cM	205	
D-KOAK(2)	Schempp-Hirth Ventus cM	73/539	
D-KOAL(2)	DG Flugzeugbau DG-808B	8-350B249	
D-KOAM(2)	Schempp-Hirth Ventus cM	81/555	
D-KOAP	Scheibe SF 28A Tandem-Falke	5727	
D-KOAS	Grob G 109	6113	
D-KOBA(3)	Grob G 102 Astir CS/TOP	1025	D-5874
D-KOBB(2)	Diamond HK 36TTC Super Dimona	36560	
D-KOBC(2)	Schleicher ASH 26E	26193	
D-KOBE(3)	Glaser-Dirks DG-400	4-69	
D-KOBG(2)	Schempp-Hirth Nimbus-3DT	7	
D-KOBI (4)	Glaser-Dirks DG-400	4-161	
D-KOBJ	Scheibe SF 25C Falke	4468	
D-KOBK	Scheibe SF 25C Falke	4469	
D-KOBM	Glaser-Dirks DG-600M	6-56M10	(D-KEJB(2))
D-KOBN	Scheibe SF 25C Rotax-Falke	44609	
D-KOBO	Raab Krähe IV (Res.)	AB.102	
D-KOBR	Glaser-Dirks DG-600M	6-71M20	
D-KOBT	Schempp-Hirth Discus bT	109/458	
D-KOCB	DG Flugzeugbau DG-808B	8-335B234	
D-KOCC	Grob G 109	6012	
D-KOCD	Scheibe SF 25C Falke 2000	44492	
D-KOCH(3)	Diamond HK 36TTC Super Dimona	36666	
D-KOCI (2)	Sportavia/ Fournier RF-5	5127	G-BJCG, (D-KOCI)
D-KOCK	Scheibe SF 25C Rotax-Falke	44534	
D-KOCM(2)-CM	Schleicher ASH 31Mi	31084	
D-KOCO(2)	Valentin Taifun 17E	1045	
D-KOCP	DG Flugzeugbau DG-800B	8-104B38	G-BXFA, D-KOCP
D-KOCS-CS	Schempp-Hirth Discus-2cT	43	
D-KODA(2)	Scheibe SF 25C Falke 2000	44422	
D-KODD	Scheibe SF 25B Falke	4615	
D-KODE(2)	Scheibe SF 25B Falke	4604	
D-KODG	Scheibe SF 25D Falke	4618D	
D-KODH-KF	Schempp-Hirth Ventus-2cM	96/201	G-OODH
D-KODI	Scheibe SF 25B Falke	4605	
D-KODO(2)	Scheibe SF 25B Falke	4614	
D-KODV-DV	Schempp-Hirth Discus-2T (P.8.00)	4/80	
D-KOEA	Scheibe SF 28A Tandem-Falke	5731	
D-KOEF	Scheibe SF 28A Tandem-Falke	5736	
D-KOEH(3)	Valentin Taifun 17E	1094	9A-DBG, D-KTAE, OE-9292, D-KEWI
D-KOEJ	Scheibe SF 28A Tandem-Falke	5740	
D-KOEN	Scheibe SF 25C Falke	4473	
D-KOEP	Scheibe SF 25C Falke	4475	
D-KOER	Scheibe SF 25C Falke	4477	
D-KOES	Sportavia/ Fournier RF-5	5047	
D-KOET	Scheibe SF 25C Falke	4478	
D-KOEU	Scheibe SF 25C Falke 2000	4479	
D-KOEV	Scheibe SF 25C Falke	4480	
D-KOEX	Scheibe SF 28A Tandem-Falke	5746	
D-KOEY(2)	Schempp-Hirth Ventus-2cxM	283	
D-KOFC(2)	Glaser-Dirks DG-400	4-278	
D-KOFE(2)	Schempp-Hirth Ventus cT	184/604	OY-XUU
D-KOFI (2)	Scheibe SF 25B Falke	4625	
D-KOFN	Glaser-Dirks DG-600M-18M	6-74M22	
D-KOFO(2)	Detmold K.8B/Lloyd	8724M	
D-KOFU	Scheibe SF 25A Motorfalke	4551	
D-KOFY(3)	Valentin Taifun 17E-II	1103	
D-KOGA	Kaiser K 12	12001M	
D-KOGB	Schleicher ASH 26E	26015	
D-KOGE(2)	SZD-45A Ogar	B-647	DDR-3501, DM-3501(2)
D-KOGM	Schempp-Hirth Nimbus-3DT	27	
D-KOGN	Scheibe SF 25C Falke 2000	44531	
D-KOGO(3)	Sportavia RF-5B Sperber	51057	D-KEAN
D-KOGR	SZD-45A Ogar	B-662	DDR-3507, DM-3507
D-KOGS	AVO 68v Samburo	027	
D-KOGY(2)	Valentin Taifun 17E (Res.11.99)	1058	(D-KBHA), F-CGAH, F-WGAH, D-KBHA
D-KOHB	Stemme S10-VT (Permit)	11-090	
D-KOHC(2)	Stemme S6 (Res as D-EAUP(2), 4.15)	6.T.10.010	(D-KCND)
D-KOHE	Sportavia/ Fournier RF-4D	4073	
D-KOHF	Schleicher ASK 14	14033	G-KOHF, D-KOHF
D-KOHG	Schleicher ASK 14	14036	
D-KOHI (2)	Sportavia/ Fournier RF-4D	4081	
D-KOHK(2)	Schempp-Hirth Ventus-2cT	24/92	
D-KOHL	Schleicher ASK 14	14046	
D-KOHO(2)	HB-Aircraft HB 23/2400SP	23044	D-KOWI
D-KOHS	Glaser-Dirks DG-400	4-287	
D-KOHW	Stemme S10-V (Originally bt as S-10 c/n 10-62)	14-009	OO-CSZ, D-KGDB, D-KSTE
D-KOIA(2)	Schleicher ASK 14 (Res .16)	14026	F-CASD, D-KOIA(2)
D-KOIG	Scheibe SF 25C Rotax-Falke	44710	
D-KOII	Scheibe SF 25C Rotax-Falke	44697	
D-KOIK	Scheibe SF 25C Rotax-Falke	44713	
D-KOIL	Schleicher ASH 26E	26131	
D-KOIM	Scheibe SF 25C Falke 2000	44659	
D-KOIN	DG Flugzeugbau DG-800B	8-122B51	HB-2308
D-KOIS	HOAC HK 36R Super Dimona	36333	
D-KOIW-IW	Schempp-Hirth Discus bT	104/449	
D-KOJB	Scheibe SF 25C Rotax-Falke	44591	
D-KOJE(2)	DG Flugzeugbau DG-500MB (Res 23.6.16)	5E213B12	(D-KORN(2)), EC-JAN, HB-2365
D-KOKB-KB	Schempp-Hirth Duo Discus xT	152	
D-KOKH	DG Flugzeugbau DG-800B	8-197B119	
D-KOKI (2)	Scheibe SF 25A Motorfalke	4553	D-KOGI (1)
D-KOKK	Glaser-Dirks DG-500M	5E87M37	
D-KOKO(2)	Sportavia/ Fournier RF-5	5042	
D-KOKS(2)	HOAC HK 36R Super Dimona	36386	OE-9400, F-CGAZ
D-KOKY	Raab Krähe IV	110	D-KAPA
D-KOLA(3)	Schleicher ASH 25E	25067	
D-KOLB(3)	Lange E1 Antares 18T (Res.9.06)	54T	
D-KOLC	Schempp-Hirth Discus bM	3/438	
D-KOLD	Sportavia-Pützer RF-5B Sperber	51061	
D-KOLE(2)	DG Flugzeugbau DG-808B	8-312B212	
D-KOLF	Technoflug Piccolo	045	PH-895, D-KGTA
D-KOLG-OLE	Schleicher ASH 26E	26091	
D-KOLI	AVO 68v Samburo	013	
D-KOLK	Technoflug Piccolo	038	
D-KOLL	Glaser-Dirks DG-400	4-1	G-KOLL, D-KOLL
D-KOLM-LM	Schleicher ASW 27-18E (ASG 29E)	29608	
D-KOLN	Schempp-Hirth Nimbus-2M	05	
D-KOLO(2)	DG Flugzeugbau DG-1000T	10-67T7	
D-KOLT	Scheibe SF 25C Falke 2000	44449	
D-KOMA	Schleicher ASK 14	14025	
D-KOMB	Brditschka HB-23/2400SP	23039-U	OE-9324
D-KOME	Schleicher ASK 14	14027	
D-KOMH	Diamond HK 36TTC Super Dimona	36593	
D-KOMI (2)	Sportavia/ Scheibe SF 25C Falke	4254	
D-KOMM(2)	Jonker Sailplanes JS1C/MD Single (P 3.15)	1C-077	
D-KOMO(2)	Glaser-Dirks DG-400	4-71	LN-GMW, G-BLCX
D-KOMS	Grob G 109	6101	
D-KOMT-MT	Schempp-Hirth Ventus-2cT	65/202	
D-KOMU	Schleicher ASK 14	14029	
D-KOMY(2)-9A	Schempp-Hirth Ventus-2cM	9/26	
D-KONB(2)	Schleicher ASK 14	14043	
D-KOND	Schleicher ASK 14	14042	
D-KONE	Schleicher ASK 14	14044	
D-KONF	Sportavia/ Fournier RF-5	5057	
D-KONG	Sportavia/ Fournier RF-5	5058	
D-KONI (2)-8X	Schleicher ASH 25M	25179	
D-KONK(2)	Fedrau Aquila	001	
D-KONO(2)	Röhrdanz JR1 Tinetta 17R/70	01	
	(Rebuild from Taifun 17E D-KONO(1) c/n 01)		
D-KONP	Schempp-Hirth Arcus M	102	
D-KONX-NX	Schleicher ASW 22BLE	22048	
D-KONY(2)	Hoffmann H-36 Dimona	36131	OE-9234
D-KONZ	Scheibe SF 25C Falke 2000	44477	
D-KOOC(2)	Scheibe SF 25C Falke 2000	44314	
D-KOOD(2)	Scheibe SF 25C Falke 2000	44313	
D-KOOE(2)	Scheibe SF 25C Falke 2000	44315	
D-KOOG(2)	Scheibe SF 25C Falke 2000	44316	
D-KOOH(3)	Scheibe SF 25C Falke 2000	44319	
D-KOOI	Scheibe SF 36R	4103	
D-KOOJ	Scheibe SF 25C Falke 2000	AB44321	
D-KOOK	Scheibe SF 25C Falke 2000	44320	
D-KOOL(2)-13	Schleicher ASH 25EB28	25258	
D-KOOM	Scheibe SF 25C Falke	4484	HB-2028, (D-KEID)
D-KOOO	Scheibe SF 36B	4106	
D-KOOS	Scheibe SF 25C Falke	44329	
D-KOOT	Scheibe SF 25C Falke	44330	
D-KOOU	Scheibe SF 25C Falke 2000	44331	
D-KOOV(2)	Scheibe SF 25C Falke 2000	44332	VH-HDM, D-KOOV(2)
D-KOOX	Scheibe SF 25C Falke	44327	
D-KOPA	Hoffmann H-36 Dimona	36267	
D-KOPC	Glaser-Dirks DG-400	4-237	
D-KOPD(3)-pi	Schempp-Hirth Ventus-2cxM	266	(D-KPIT)
D-KOPP	Hoffmann H-36 Dimona	3654	
D-KOPR	HOAC HK 36R Super Dimona	36347	
D-KOPS	Schempp-Hirth Arcus M	111	
D-KOPY	Glaser-Dirks DG-800LA	8-40A30	HB-2267
D-KOQY	Scheibe SF 25C Falke 2000	44206	(D-KDFH)
D-KORA	Nitzsche AVo 67-R Samburo (Res .10)	20	
D-KORC	Sportavia/ Fournier RF-5	5030	
D-KORD	Valentin Taifun 17E	1016	
D-KORF-WG	Schempp-Hirth Nimbus-2M	07	(D-KOKI)

Reg	Type	C/n	Previous identities
D-KORG	Glaser-Dirks DG-400	4-145	OY-XYW
D-KORK(2)	Scheibe SF 25C Falke	44328	
D-KORL	Raab Krähe IV (Ntu, now in Deutsches Museum)	14	D-KODL, (D-KOPD), D-KEDI (1)
D-KORM	Sportavia/ Fournier RF-4D	4035	F-BORM
D-KORO(2)	Schempp-Hirth Ventus cT	103/364	
D-KORT	Kortenbach Kora I	V-2	
D-KORU	Stemme S10	10-11	
D-KOSA	Sportavia/ Scheibe SF 25C Falke	4250	(D-KOJA)
D-KOSG	Scheibe SF 25D Falke	4693D	
D-KOSH(2)	Schempp-Hirth Duo Discus T	44/320	
D-KOSI	Scheibe SF 25B Falke	4695	SX-..., D-KOSI
D-KOSJ-SJ	Schleicher ASW 20L/TOP	20573	D-1646
D-KOSL	Scheibe SF 27M-A	6316	(D-KHIL)
D-KOSM	Scheibe SF 27M-A	6317	
D-KOSN	Nitsche AVO R100 Samburo	008	
D-KOSO(2)	Hoffmann H-36 Dimona	3647	HB-2065
D-KOSR	Schempp-Hirth Ventus bT	52/254	
D-KOSS	Scheibe SF 25C Falke	44675	
D-KOSY	Schempp-Hirth Ventus cT	99/354	
D-KOTO(2)	DG Flugzeugbau DG-800B	8-194B116	G-BZEM, BGA 4887, G-BZEM
D-KOTT(3)	Scheibe SF 25C Rotax-Falke	44688	
D-KOTZ(2)	Schempp-Hirth Ventus-2cxM	150	
D-KOWB(2)	Binder EB29D-MB (P 9.14)	902	(D-KUWB)
D-KOWC	Scheibe SF 25C Falke	44302	HB-2054, (D-KDGY)
D-KOWF	Glaser-Dirks DG-400	4-70	
D-KOWR	Stemme S10-VT	11-081	
D-KOWW	Scheibe SF 36R	4102	
D-KOXJ	Sportavia-Pützer Fournier RF4D (P 14.7.16)	4062	F-BOXJ
D-KOZZ	*Schempp-Hirth test registration*		
D-KPAA	HOAC HK 36R Super Dimona	36378	
D-KPAB	HOAC HK 36R Super Dimona	36379	
D-KPAC(2)	DG Flugzeugbau DG-808C	8-427B326X86	
D-KPAF	Scheibe SF 25C Falke 2000	44513	
D-KPAH-17	Schleicher ASW 27-18E (ASG 29E)	29586	
D-KPAI(2)	Jonker JS/MD Single (P 29.6.16)	1C-104	
D-KPAJ	Binder EB28	22	
D-KPAK	Schempp-Hirth Ventus-2cM	50/104	
D-KPAL-VX	Schleicher ASH 26E	26176	
D-KPAM-AM	Binder EB29 (P. 2.14)	28	
D-KPAN	Nitsche AVO 68-R100 Samburo	003	
D-KPAR	Glaser-Dirks DG-400 (P.06)	4-11	PH-1003, D-KLAA(1)
D-KPAS(4)-61	Schleicher ASH 25Mi	25264	
D-KPAT	Diamond HK 36TC Super Dimona	36835	HA-1273, OE-9998
D-KPAU	Scheibe SF 25B Falke (Res .10)	4682	I-PAIU, D-KBAH(1)
D-KPAX-61	Schempp-Hirth Arcus M	37	
D-KPBG	Schempp-Hirth Duo Discus T	25/286	
D-KPBM	Schleicher ASH 26E	26223	
D-KPBW-BW	Lange E1 Antares	27	(D-KOLB(2))
D-KPCB	DG Flugzeugbau DG-808C	8-387B286X48	
D-KPCC	Diamond HK-36TTC Super Dimona	36694	
D-KPCH	Scheibe SF 25C Falke 2000	44334	PH-725, (D-KOOZ(1))
D-KPDC	Schempp-Hirth Ventus bT	69/284	PH-1254, BGA 3204
D-KPDG-HB	DG Flugzeugbau DG-800B	8-174B98	
D-KPDH	Schleicher ASH 31Mi	31024	
D-KPDJ	Schempp-Hirth Ventus-2cM	133/ . . .	
D-KPDS	DG Flugzeugbau DG-1001M	10-221M26	
D-KPEB	Schleicher ASW 27-18E (ASG 29E)	29691	
D-KPEL	Hoffmann H 36 Dimona (Res .07)	3672	OE-9238
D-KPER-RP	Schempp-Hirth Ventus-2cxT	127	
D-KPEX	Schempp-Hirth Ventus bT (Res. 10)	15/152	OY-PEX, D-KAUY, N3YC
D-KPEZ-SDI	Schempp-Hirth Ventus-2cxT	192	
D-KPFH-FH	Schleicher ASH 25E (Res .11)	25129	PH-1333, D-KMKK, N125BW, OO-ZYW
D-KPFI	Stemme S10-V	14-043M	OO-OSI, D-KGCU
D-KPFM-BL	Schleicher ASW 22BLE	22084	
D-KPGC-BT	Schempp-Hirth Duo Discus T	26/288	
D-KPGI	Schleicher ASK 14	14056	HB-2014, D-KISY(2)
D-KPGM	Schempp-Hirth Ventus-2cxM	226	
D-KPGS-2L	Schempp-Hirth Ventus-2cT	71/226	
D-KPGV-PG	DG Flugzeugbau DG-808C	8-383B282X44	
D-KPHG-HG	Schempp-Hirth Ventus-2cxM	258	
D-KPHJ	Schempp-Hirth Nimbus-3DM	26/59	LX-CHJ
D-KPHW-HW	Schempp-Hirth Ventus-2cxM	208	
D-KPIA-HK	DG Flugzeugbau DG-1000T	10-160T51	
D-KPIB	Schempp-Hirth Ventus cM	96/587	
D-KPIF	Scheibe SF 25C Rotax-Falke	44701	
D-KPII	DG Flugzeugbau DG-800B	8-250B163	
D-KPIK-PI	Eiriavion PIK-20E2F	710	F-CFPD
D-KPIN-CM	Schempp-Hirth Ventus cM	65/527	F-CGLR
D-KPIR	Hoffmann H-36 Dimona	3624	OE-9210
D-KPIT(2)-Pit	Schempp-Hirth Ventus-2cxM	228	
D-KPJC	Schempp-Hirth Discus-2T (Res .10)	14/127	G-TWOT, BGA5156/KKG, OY-XSY, D-KKAH
D-KPJF	Schleicher ASH 30Mi (P. 2.14)	30008	
D-KPJJ	Schleicher ASW 27-18E (ASG 29E)	29528	D-9757
D-KPJS-QM	Schempp-Hirth Nimbus-4M	7/23	
D-KPJX	Jonker Sailplanes JS/MD Single (P 7.15; w/o 7.8.15)	1C-084	
D-KPKK-KK	Lange E1 Antares 18T (P. 2.14)	65T07	D-KDEF
D-KPLA	Schleicher ASW 24E	24815	I-KKFA, D-KKFA(2)
D-KPLG	Schempp-Hirth Ventus-2cxM	163/382	G-KPLG, (BGA 5302), D-KPLG
D-KPLH	Schempp-Hirth Ventus-2cM	85/178	
D-KPLL	Schleicher ASW 27-18E	29622	
D-KPMA	Schempp-Hirth Ventus-2cxM	221	
D-KPMB-MB	DG Flugzeugbau DG-1000T	10-104T33	
D-KPMC	Grob G 109B (Res. .14)	6315	PH-746
D-KPMH-CK	Schempp-Hirth Nimbus-3DM	7/23	G-BPMH
D-KPML	Glaser-Dirks DG-400	4-33	PH-723
D-KPMM-MM	Schempp-Hirth Duo Discus T	37/312	
D-KPMS-OS	Schempp-Hirth Ventus-2cT	23/88	
D-KPMW	Grob G 102 Astir CS/TOP	1008	D-6504
D-KPOL	Scheibe SF 25C Falke 2000	44536	
D-KPOP	Stemme S6-RT	020	
D-KPOS-OS	Schempp-Hirth Ventus-2cxM	282	
D-KPPC-PC	Schleicher ASW 27-18E (ASG 29E)	29655	
D-KPPK	Schempp-Hirth Discus-2cT	29	D-2203
D-KPPP	Glaser-Dirks DG-400	4-188	OE-9273
D-KPPR	DG Flugzeugbau DG-808C	8-409B308	
D-KPRD	Schempp-Hirth Arcus M	151	(D-KDUE)
D-KPRG	Schempp-Hirth Discus-2cT	64	
D-KPRO-RO	Schleicher ASW 27-18E (ASG 29E)	29580	
D-KPRW-RW	Schleicher ASH 25M	25164	D-5547
D-KPSA(2)-EL	Schleicher ASG 32EL (P 23.3.16, electric engine prototype)	32002	
D-KPSC	Schleicher ASW 27-18E (ASG 29E)	29565	
D-KPSM-EA	Schleicher ASW 27-18E (ASG 29E)	29669	
D-KPSN	Scheibe SF 25C Rotax-Falke (Built as Falke 2000)	44518	
D-KPSP-SP	Schleicher ASW 27-18E (ASG 29E)	29697	
D-KPSV	Diamond HK 36TTC Super Dimona	36820	(D-KHCA), OE-9997
D-KPSW	Schempp-Hirth Ventus-2cM	109/224	
D-KPTB-TB	Schempp-Hirth Discus-2cT	75	
D-KPTL	Grob G 109B	6216	OO-DPC
D-KPTZ-99	Schempp-Hirth Nimbus-4DM	25/35	
D-KPUA	Glaser-Dirks DG-800LA	8-22A19	
D-KPUK	Aerotechnik L-13SL Vivat	940521	OK-4100
D-KPUR	Schleicher ASH 25M (P.7.99)	25213	
D-KPWB-WB	Binder EB28 (P 26.7.16) (C/n derived from ASH 25 c/n 25901)	901	D-KOWB(1)
D-KPWD-II	Glaser-Dirks DG-600/18M	6-88M34	
D-KPWG	Schempp-Hirth Nimbus-3DT	4/15	OE-9345, OE-5445, D-0962
D-KPXA-XP	Schleicher ASH 31Mi	31029	
D-KPYB-F2	Schempp-Hirth Ventus-2cxT	140/ . . .	
D-KQAC-AS	Schempp-Hirth Quintus M (P.5.12)	10	
D-KQAS-AS	Schempp-Hirth Ventus-2cxT	128	
D-KQCB-FG	Schempp-Hirth Ventus-2cxT	236	
D-KQCD-CD	Schempp-Hirth Quintus M (P.5.12)	8	
D-KQIN-V	Schempp-Hirth Quintus M (P. 11.11)	1	(D-KUIN)
D-KQMA-MA	Schempp-Hirth Arcus M	94	
D-KQQQ	Fournier RF3 (Res .13)	51	G-BIIA, F-BMTA
D-KQUI	Schempp-Hirth Quintus (P.4.12)	4	
D-KQWB	Schleicher ASH 25EB 28	25911	
D-KQWG	Schempp-Hirth Quintus M (P.7.12)	12	
D-KRAB	Diamond HK 36TTC Super Dimona	36678	
D-KRAD	Schleicher ASW 27-18E (ASG 29E)	29602	
D-KRAI	Schempp-Hirth Discus bT	74/402	
D-KRAJ-IT	Schempp-Hirth Ventus-2cxM	288	
D-KRAK-AK	Schempp-Hirth Discus bM	6/463	
D-KRAM	Scheibe SF 25C Rotax-Falke	44582	
D-KRAN	Scheibe SF 25C Rotax-Falke	44652	D-KIEP
D-KRAP	Schempp-Hirth Discus bT	102/444	
D-KRAR	Schleicher ASH 31Mi	31043	
D-KRAS-AS	Schleicher ASH 25M	25183	
D-KRAT	Schleicher ASW 27-18E (ASG 29E)	29557	D-9829
D-KRAU-SS	Schempp-Hirth Arcus M	136	
D-KRAW	Schleicher ASH 26E	26103	
D-KRBA	Binder EB28	19	
D-KRBB-BB	Schleicher ASG 29E	?	
D-KRBH-BH	Schempp-Hirth Ventus-2cT	31/103	
D-KRBM	Diamond HK 36 TC Super Dimona	36834	OE-9997
D-KRBP	Schleicher ASH 25M	25177	
D-KRCF-CF	Schleicher ASH 31Mi	31016	
D-KRDG	DG Flugzeugbau DG-505MB	5E193MB8	
D-KRDL-DL	Schempp-Hirth Duo Discus XLT	239	
D-KRDP	Diamond HK 36TC-100 Super Dimona	36802	OE-9997
D-KREB	Schempp-Hirth Ventus-2cM	93/582	
D-KREH-4D	Schempp-Hirth Nimbus-4DM	1/4	
D-KREM-YT	Schleicher ASH 25EB	25178	
D-KRES	Diamond HK 36TTC Super Dimona	36602	
D-KREW-63	Schempp-Hirth Arcus M	47	
D-KRFP-PR	Schleicher ASH 25E	21805	
D-KRGD	Nitsche AVO 68-R100 Samburo	007	
D-KRGO	Schleicher ASH 25EB28	25246	
D-KRGS	Schleicher ASH 31Mi	31115	
D-KRGT	Schempp-Hirth Arcus M	2	
D-KRGW-GW	Schempp-Hirth Ventus cM	100/591	
D-KRHA	Grob G 109B	6406	G-BNAY, N920BG
D-KRHB	Schempp-Hirth Ventus-2cM	153/ . . .	
D-KRHG-HG	Schleicher ASH 25Mi	25211	
D-KRHH-RB	Schempp-Hirth Arcus M	12	
D-KRHL	Rolladen-Schneider LS9	9005	
D-KRHP	Schempp-Hirth Arcus M	17	
D-KRHT	Schleicher ASH 26E (Formerly ASH-26)	26071	D-9426
D-KRIB-RI	Schleicher ASW 27-18E (ASG 29E)	29613	
D-KRID(2)	MAG Carat A	CA034	
D-KRII	DG Flugzeugbau DG-800B	8-172B96	
D-KRIL	Schempp-Hirth Discus-2T	16/131	PH-1248, D-KGBC
D-KRIT	DG Flugzeugbau DG-505MB	5E237B17	N689RN
D-KRJB	Diamond HK 36TC Super Dimona	36860	
D-KRJP	Schleicher ASH 25E	25061	HB-2359, D-KOGH(1)
D-KRJR-JR	Schleicher ASH 31Mi	31005	
D-KRJS	Schleicher ASH 26E	26025	D-8839
D-KRKA(2)-ARK	Schempp-Hirth Arcus M	126	
D-KRLA-LA	Schempp-Hirth Duo Discus XT (P.7.06)	147	
D-KRLD-LN	Schleicher ASH 25Mi	25223	
D-KRLH	Schleicher ASH 26E	26119	
D-KRLL	Schleicher ASH 31Mi	31009	
D-KRLM-ML	Lange Antares 23T (P 24.5.16)	79B04	
D-KRMA-EVE	Schempp-Hirth Ventus-2cxM	213	
D-KRMB	Schempp-Hirth Arcus M	142	
D-KRME	Schempp-Hirth Nimbus-4DM	67	
D-KRMH	Schempp-Hirth Ventus cT (Res .12)	141/435	D-KNBE, D-5092
D-KRMO	Schleicher ASH 26E	26047	OY-JXH, D-KALH, OO-LAU

Reg	Type	C/n	Previous identities
D-KRMP	Hoffmann H 36 Dimona	36214	HA-1276, EC-EFP, OE-9270
D-KRMR(2)	Glaser-Dirks DG-400	4-147	N105EE
D-KROB	Schempp-Hirth Duo Discus XLT	250/646	
D-KROD	Aerojaen/Fournier RF5-AJ1 Serrania (R .12)	E-005	EC-FOJ
D-KROG	Schempp-Hirth Discus bT	126/484	
D-KROH	Groh Piuma Twin S (P.01)	0001	
D-KROP	Grob G 109	6124	PH-948, N3837S
D-KRPM-MX	Schleicher ASW 27-18E (ASG 29E)	29607	OH-994
D-KRPS-MR	Schleicher ASH 26E	26151	D-KZZZ
D-KRPT-PT	Schempp-Hirth Arcus M	83	
D-KRRK(2)	Valentin Taifun 17E-II/2400	1128	OE-9330, D-KHVA
D-KRRR	DG Flugzeugbau DG-800B	8-132B61	
D-KRSA	Schleicher ASH 25M	25238	
D-KRSF	Rolladen-Schneider LS6-18M (P. 4.11)	6279	D-1462
D-KRSG	Schempp-Hirth Ventus-2cM (Res .16)	293	
D-KRST	Stemme S10-V (Res 11.15)	14-047M	D-KGCB
D-KRTS-JR	Schempp-Hirth Ventus-2cT	19/81	
D-KRUG-OK	Schleicher ASH 26E	26006	
D-KRUK	Stemme S6 (C/n previously quoted as 6.T.10.016)	16	
D-KRUM	Scheibe SF 25C Rotax-Falke	44566	
D-KRWA	Aeromot AMT-200 Super Ximango	200.093	PP-XAD
D-KRWK	Schleicher ASH 26E	26216	
D-KRXT-XT	Jonker JS/MD Single (P 5.4.16)	1C-088	(D-KKXI)
D-KRYS	Schempp-Hirth Duo Discus XLT	217	
D-KSAB(3)	Stemme S10-VT	11-131	
D-KSAC	Schempp-Hirth Discus-2cT	?	
D-KSAG(3)	Schleicher ASH 25EB	25247	
D-KSAM	Nitsche AVO 68-R115 Samburo Turbo (P.6.99)	001	
D-KSAN-AN	Schempp-Hirth Duo Discus XLT	218	
D-KSAP-8T	Schempp-Hirth Duo Discus xT	135	
D-KSAS-AS	Schleicher ASW 22BLE 50R	22071	D-KKUH
D-KSBA-BA	Schempp-Hirth Arcus T	38	
D-KSBC	Grob G 103C Twin IIISL	35038	
D-KSBD	Diamond HK 36TTC Super Dimona	36522	OE-9422
D-KSBG-BG	Schempp-Hirth Ventus-2cxM	235	SE-UUR
D-KSBH	Stemme S10-V	14-028	G-JULS, D-KGDC(3)
D-KSBM-BM	Schleicher ASH 31Mi	31068	
D-KSBN-BN	Schempp-Hirth Arcus T	56	
D-KSBS-S2	Schleicher ASH 26E	26145	
D-KSBX-BX	Schleicher ASW 27-18E (ASG 29E)	29662	
D-KSBY	Stemme S10-VT	11-101	
D-KSCB	DG Flugzeugbau DG-808C	8-421B320X80	
D-KSCC	Schempp-Hirth Discus-2cT	17	
D-KSCE(2)	Schempp-Hirth Discus-2c-FES (P 11.7.16)	6	
D-KSCH	HOAC HK-36R Super Dimona	36327	OE-9365
D-KSCL-1D	Schleicher ASW 27-18E (ASG 29E)	29712	
D-KSCM-SCM	DG Flugzeugbau DG-1000T	10-142T48	
D-KSCR-POL	Schempp-Hirth Duo Discus XLT	246	
D-KSCS-S5	Schleicher ASW 28-18E	28702	D-8428
D-KSCT	Glaser-Dirks DG-400	4-135	HB-2109
D-KSDB	Grob G 103C Twin IIISL	35004	
D-KSDD-DD	Schempp-Hirth Duo Discus XLT	202	
D-KSDF(2)	Valentin Taifun 17E-II	1111	OE-9497, D-KRRK(1), OE-9297, D-KHVA
D-KSDG(3)-YH	DG Flugzeugbau DG-1000T	10-93T27	SE-UTM
D-KSDI-GA	Schleicher ASH 26E	26198	
D-KSDL	Aerotechnik L-13SDL Vivat	910428	OK- . . . .
D-KSDU	Schempp-Hirth Ventus-2cT	104/ . . .	
D-KSDW-DW	Schempp-Hirth Discus-2cT	111	
D-KSEB	Binder EB28	20	
D-KSEE	Schempp-Hirth Discus bT	123/481	OE-9386
D-KSEF-EF	Schempp-Hirth Duo Discus T	1/187	
D-KSEG-EG	Schempp-Hirth Arcus M	73	
D-KSEI-AS	Schempp-Hirth Duo Discus XLT	189	T7-CAS
D-KSEJ	Helwan/Sportavia RF5B Sperber	1010	D-KMRW, EAF
D-KSEL	Schempp-Hirth Duo Discus T	10/256	
D-KSEM	Diamond HK 36TTS Super Dimona	36515	
D-KSEP-BS	Schempp-Hirth Ventus cT	162/526	
D-KSEX	Schleicher ASH 25Mi	25221	D-8320
D-KSFC	HOAC HK 36R Super Dimona	36342	
D-KSFE	Stemme S10-V (C/n also quoted as 14-006)	14-059M	OE-9397, D-KGCZ(2)
D-KSFF-63	Schleicher ASG 32Mi	32035	
D-KSFL	Schempp-Hirth Ventus-2cxM	276	
D-KSFM	Glaser-Dirks DG-500M	5E98M44	OE-9388
D-KSFN-FN	Schempp-Hirth Discus-2T	15/128	
D-KSFO	Diamond HK 36TTC Super Dimona	36636	OE-9436
D-KSFS	Schempp-Hirth Duo Discus T (Res .12)	118	OY-RTX
D-KSFT-FT	Schleicher ASH 31Mi	31063	
D-KSFU	Diamond HK 36TC Super Dimona	36648	
D-KSFW-KK	Schempp-Hirth Duo Discus T	78/390	
D-KSGA	Schleicher ASW 27-18E	29605	
D-KSGB	Grob G 109B	6386	OE-9256
D-KSGC	DG Flugzeugbau DG-808B	8-344B243	
D-KSGI-2A	Schempp-Hirth Arcus T	30	
D-KSGJ	Schleicher ASH 26E	26136	
D-KSGM	HOAC HK 36R Super Dimona	36301	I-SEGI, OE-9350
D-KSGS(2)-S1	Schempp-Hirth Duo Discus T	67/360	
D-KSGW	Schempp-Hirth Ventus-2cxM	277	
D-KSHA	Schempp-Hirth Nimbus-4DM	13/22	
D-KSHB	HOAC HK 36R Super Dimona		OE-9403, (D-KAIB(2))
D-KSHI	DG Flugzeugbau DG-1000T	10-205T55	
D-KSHK	Schempp-Hirth Arcus M	129	
D-KSHL	Aerotechnik L-13SL Vivat	920426	
D-KSHS	Schempp-Hirth Discus bT	130/495	
D-KSHW	Schleicher ASW 24E	24838	HB-2195
D-KSHX-HX	Schleicher ASH 25M	25140	D-9525, OE-5525
D-KSID	Stemme S6	019	
D-KSIE(2)	Stemme S10-V	14-012	PH-1055, D-KGDE(1)
D-KSIG	Glaser-Dirks DG-800LA	8-15A12	
D-KSIN	Scheibe SF 25C Falke 2000	44475	D-KIAX
D-KSIM-KS	Schempp-Hirth Ventus-2cxM	220	
D-KSIS-IS	Schleicher ASH 26E	26149	D-1619
D-KSIX(3)	Stemme S6-RT	024	
D-KSIZ	Stemme S12 Twin Voyager (Res 4.15, P .16)	12-001	(D-KAZW)
D-KSJA	Schempp-Hirth Discus-2cT	107	
D-KSJG	Schleicher ASH 25Mi	25242	D-KKLY
D-KSJH	DG Flugzeugbau DG-1000M (P. 11.10)	10-156M6	
D-KSJM-JM	Schempp-Hirth Ventus-2cM	47/97	
D-KSJW	Valentin Taifun 17E	1079	EC-ECV, D-KLPA
D-KSKA-SG	DG Flugzeugbau DG-800B	8-260B168	
D-KSKL	Schleicher ASH 31Mi	31004	
D-KSKS	DG Flugzeugbau DG-800B	8-89B25	
D-KSKX	Schempp-Hirth Ventus-2cxaj (P 4.15)	26J	
D-KSLA	DG Flugzeugbau DG-800B	8-91B27	
D-KSLH-Q	Lange E1 Antares	06	
D-KSLL-LL	Schempp-Hirth Arcus T	32	
D-KSLM	Glaser-Dirks DG-400	4-244	HB-2153
D-KSLQ	Schempp-Hirth Duo Discus T	36/310	
D-KSLS	Schempp-Hirth Discus bT (Res .01)	148/535	
D-KSLT	Stemme S6-RT	23	N566P, D-KSIX
D-KSMA(2)-MA	Schempp-Hirth Arcus M	7	
D-KSMB-MB	Schleicher ASW 28-18E	28724	
D-KSMC	Schleicher ASH 26E	26023	
D-KSMF-XV	Schleicher ASW 27-18E (ASG 29E)	29610	
D-KSMH	Schleicher ASH 25M	25160	D-0541
D-KSMS(2)	Schempp-Hirth Duo Discus T	278	
D-KSMW	Schleicher ASG 32Mi	32026	
D-KSOB	Glaser-Dirks DG-800B	8-81B18	PH-1100, (PH-1097), D-KDIL
D-KSOE	DG Flugzeugbau DG-1000T	10-98T30	
D-KSOR	Eiriavion PIK-20E	20211	PH-630
D-KSPC	Schleicher ASH 26E	26120	D-KSUT(1)
D-KSPE	Scheibe SF 25C Rotax-Falke	44709	D-KEOZ
D-KSPF	Schempp-Hirth Ventus-2cxM	193	
D-KSPK	Scheibe SF 25C Rotax-Falke	44635	
D-KSPL(2)	Glaser-Dirks DG-400	4-286	
D-KSPP-MR	Schleicher ASH 25Mi	25231	
D-KSPR	Glaser-Dirks DG-500M	5E80M33	
D-KSRF	DG Flugzeugbau DG-1001M	10-219M25	
D-KSRJ	Schleicher ASH 26E	26021	D-5771
D-KSRV-L4	Schempp-Hirth Discus bT	138/514	
D-KSRW	Schleicher ASH 26E	26101	
D-KSSB	Diamond HK-36TTC Super Dimona	36732	
D-KSSI-Si	Schleicher ASW 27-18E (ASG 29E)	29598	
D-KSSK(2)-7	Schleicher ASH 25EB28	25232	
D-KSSS	Scheibe SF 25C Rotax-Falke	44598	D-KSAH(2), OE-9442, D-KTIU(1)
D-KSSW	Schempp-Hirth Ventus cM	61/523	
D-KSTA-STA	Schleicher ASH 31Mi	31114	
D-KSTD	Hoffmann H 36 Dimona II	36228	F-CGAR, F-WGAR

D-KSTE to D-KSTI *Test Registrations for Stemme production*

Reg	Type	C/n	Previous identities
D-KSTL	Binder EB28	11	
D-KSTN-4K	Schempp-Hirth Discus-2cT	85	
D-KSTO	Schempp-Hirth Ventus bT	9/136	HB-2098, HB-1658
D-KSTS	Schleicher ASH 26E	26005	
D-KSTY	Studeny STY-1	1	
D-KSUB	HOAC HK 36R Super Dimona	36390	
D-KSUT(3)	Schleicher ASH 26E	26220	
D-KSVA	Glaser-Dirks DG-400	4-215	F-CGRE
D-KSWB	Diamond HK 36TTC Super Dimona	36558	F-CHQB
D-KSWE	Schempp-Hirth Ventus-2cxM	165	
D-KSWG	SZD-45A Ogar	B-753	D-KLHP, DDR-3508, DM-3508
D-KSWH	Schempp-Hirth Ventus cM	97/587	OH-861
D-KSWJ	Schleicher ASH 26E	26098	
D-KSWM-WM	Schleicher ASH 31Mi	31058	
D-KSWR-WR	Schleicher ASW 22BLE 50R	22083	(D-KSSK(1))
D-KSWS	Technoflug Piccolo B	096	
D-KSYL-72	Schempp-Hirth Quintus M (P.5.12)	7	
D-KSZF-ZF	Lange E1 Antares	26	
D-KSZX	Schleicher ASW 22BLE 50R	22080	VH-ZBB, D-KMOL
D-KTAA-2A	Schempp-Hirth Arcus T	57	
D-KTAB-BRA	Schempp-Hirth Arcus T	8	
D-KTAC(2)	Schleicher ASG 32Mi (P 10.15)	32010	
D-KTAJ-AJ	Schleicher ASH 31Mi	31027	
D-KTAK(3)-K	Schleicher ASW 27-18E (ASG 29E)	29546	
D-KTAL	Stemme S10-V (Built as Stemme S10 c/n 10-49)	14-049M	G-LINA, D-KFDF
D-KTAS-LS	Schempp-Hirth Ventus-2cT	21/85	
D-KTAW	Technoflug Piccolo B	073	
D-KTBA-LS	Schempp-Hirth Ventus-2cxM	239	
D-KTBB	Glaser-Dirks DG-800B	8-67B12	
D-KTBC	Glaser-Dirks DG-400	4-67	(D-KXCB(1)), OE-9225
D-KTBL	Schempp-Hirth Duo Discus XLT	261	
D-KTBM	DG Flugzeugbau DG-808B	8-339B238	
D-KTBT	Schempp-Hirth Discus bT	141/516	
D-KTBY-2Y	Schempp-Hirth Ventus-2cxT	149	
D-KTCA	DG Flugzeugbau LS8-t	8513	
D-KTCB-U	Schleicher ASH 26E	26128	(D-5222)
D-KTCC	Schempp-Hirth Ventus-2cM	33/57	G-KTCC, D-KTCC
D-KTCH	Technoflug Piccolo B	099	
D-KTCJ-CJ	Schempp-Hirth Duo Discus T	74/377	
D-KTDB-DB	Schleicher ASH 30Mi (P 4.13)	30002	(D-KWHG)
D-KTDD-OS	Glaser-Dirks DG-800LA	8-52A34	
D-KTDH-DH	Schempp-Hirth Duo Discus T	96/422	
D-KTDM-DM	Schempp-Hirth Ventus-2cM	15/32	D-4486
D-KTEC	DG Flugzeugbau DG-808C Competition	8-404B303X65	
D-KTEE	DG Flugzeugbau DG-808C Competition	8-343B242X10	
D-KTEG	Schleicher ASH 26E	26129	
D-KTEL-EL	Binder EB 29	16	
D-KTEN	DG Flugzeugbau DG-800B	8-155B79	
D-KTET	Brditschka HB-21-V2 (P.10.06)	21004	OE-9246, OE-9105
D-KTEX-TEX	Schempp-Hirth Nimbus-4M	21	
D-KTFS	Schempp-Hirth Ventus-2cxM	243	
D-KTFW	Glaser-Dirks DG-600/18M	6-89M35	(D-KGBD), EC-FJC, D-1245
D-KTGE-A8	DG Flugzeugbau DG-800B	8-232B146	

Registration	Type	Serial	Notes
D-KTGM-JB	HpH Glasflügel 304S-JET (P 6.15)	043-MS	
D-KTGR	Technoflug Piccolo B	074	
D-KTGS-DA	Rolladen-Schneider LS8-t	8466	
D-KTGT-TG	Schleicher SF 26E	26139	HB-2304
D-KTHA-WII	Schempp-Hirth Ventus-2cM	35/62	
D-KTHB	Schempp-Hirth Ventus-2cM	38/68	
D-KTHG(2)	Schleicher ASW 27-18E (ASG 29E)	29704	
D-KTHK	Schleicher ASH 26E	26086	
D-KTHL	Schempp-Hirth Arcus M	100	
D-KTHN-HN	Schempp-Hirth Discus bT	160/564	
D-KTHO	Lange E1 Antares 18T (P. 2.11)	66T08	
D-KTHT	Diamond HK 36TTS Super Dimona	36513	
D-KTHW	DG Flugzeugbau DG-800B	8-265B173	
D-KTIA	Scheibe SF 25C Rotax-Falke	44560	
D-KTIB	Scheibe SF 25C Rotax-Falke	44572	
D-KTID	Scheibe SF 25C Rotax-Falke	44575	
D-KTIE	Scheibe SF 25C Rotax-Falke	44568	
D-KTIF	Scheibe SF 25C Rotax-Falke	44549	
D-KTIG	Scheibe SF 25C Rotax-Falke	44552	
D-KTIH(2)	Scheibe SF 25C Rotax-Falke	44593	
D-KTIJ	Scheibe SF 25C Rotax-Falke	44594	
D-KTIL	Scheibe SF 25C Rotax-Falke	44562	
D-KTIM	Scheibe SF 25C Rotax-Falke	44564	
D-KTIO	Scheibe SF 25C Rotax-Falke	44559	
D-KTIP	Scheibe SF 36R	4107	
D-KTIQ	Scheibe SF 25C Rotax-Falke	44597	
D-KTIR	Scheibe SF 25C Rotax-Falke	44590	
D-KTIS	Scheibe SF 25C Rotax-Falke	44584	
D-KTIT(2)	Scheibe SF 25C Rotax-Falke	44599	
D-KTIU(3)	Scheibe SF 25C Falke	44225	OE-9142, D-KDFN(3)
D-KTIV(2)	Scheibe SF 25C Rotax-Falke	44614	
D-KTIX	Scheibe SF 25C Falke	44624	
D-KTIY	Scheibe SF 25C Falke	44681	
D-KTJM	Valentin Kiwi	K3017	HB-2220, D-KEGX(5)
D-KTJX	Schempp-Hirth Discus-2cT	6	D-8023
D-KTKL-29L	Schleicher ASW 27-18E (ASG 29E)	29601	
D-KTKM	Glaser-Dirks DG-600/18M	6-103M46	
D-KTKO-KWI	Schempp-Hirth Ventus-2cxM	241	
D-KTLB-53	Schleicher ASH 31Mi	31025	
D-KTLL(2)	DG Flugzeugbau DG-800B	8-152B76	
D-KTLT	Schempp-Hirth Ventus-2cxM	159	
D-KTMB-MB	Schempp-Hirth Arcus M	9	
D-KTMC	Schempp-Hirth Duo Discus T	240	
D-KTMD	DG Flugzeugbau DG-800B	8-281B189	
D-KTME-ME	Schempp-Hirth Ventus-2cT	47/147	
D-KTMG(3)	Schleicher ASG 32Mi	32013	
D-KTMH	Schleicher ASH 26E	26009	D-5961
D-KTMI	Scheibe SF 28A Tandem-Falke	5764	SE-TME, D-KACQ
D-KTMM-2M	DG Flugzeugbau DG-800B	?	
D-KTMS	Schempp-Hirth Ventus-2cM	158/ . . .	
D-KTMT-ZY	Schempp-Hirth Nimbus-4DT	14	
D-KTMW	Glaser-Dirks DG-800B	8-69B14	
D-KTOA, B, C	*Test registrations for DG Flugzeugbau production*		
D-KTOF	Schempp-Hirth Discus 2c-FES (P 29.1.16)	3	
D-KTOH	Schempp-Hirth Nimbus-4DM	47/64	
D-KTOL	Diamond HK 36TTC Super Dimona	36600	
D-KTOM-HE	Schempp-Hirth Ventus-2cM	91/190	
D-KTOP	Schleicher ASW 29CL/TOP (Res .16)	20757	F-CMOZ, D-KHGN, HB-2178, HB-1740
D-KTOY	DG Flugzeugbau DG-800B	8-263B171	
D-KTPC-32	Schleicher ASG 32Mi	32017	
D-KTPE-PE	Schempp-Hirth Ventus-2cxM	251	
D-KTPR	Technoflug Piccolo B	072	
D-KTRB	DG Flugzeugbau DG-800B	8-119B48	
D-KTRI-RI	Schempp-Hirth Duo Discus XLT	197	D-KKPG
D-KTSA	Stemme S6/8 (Res 4.15)	6.T.06.001	
D-KTSB-PW	Schleicher ASW 27-18E (ASG 29E)	29521	
D-KTSC-DT	Schleicher ASW 27-18E (ASG 29E)	29617	
D-KTSF	Scheibe SF 25B Falke (P 7.15)	46138	SE-TSF, D-KCAE
D-KTSG-SG	Schempp-Hirth Discus bT	100/442	
D-KTSH	Schempp-Hirth Arcus M	15	
D-KTSP-SP	Schempp-Hirth Arcus T	4	
D-KTSS	Schempp-Hirth Ventus-2cxT	198	
D-KTTC	HOAC HK-36TTC Super Dimona	36676	PH-1205
D-KTTH	Schleicher ASH 31Mi	31067	
D-KTTK(3)	Schempp-Hirth Arcus M	128	
D-KTTM-3T	Schempp-Hirth Nimbus-3T	4/51	G-LYDS, D-KTFP, HB-2147, D-KAPE, VH-GAA
D-KTTT	Schempp-Hirth Nimbus-3DM (P.3.00)	18/42	OH-840
D-KTVB-VB	Schempp-Hirth Quintus M (P.3.12)	5	
D-KTVR	Schempp-Hirth Ventus-2cxM	186	
D-KTVS	Schleicher ASH 26E	26069	
D-KTVX	Jonker JS/MD Single (P 28.7.16)	1C-108	
D-KTWG	DG Flugzeugbau DG-800B	8-146B70	
D-KTWM	Schempp-Hirth Arcus M	120	
D-KTWO-TWO	Schempp-Hirth Arcus M	59	
D-KTWR	Glaser-Dirks DG-800LA	8-80A41	
D-KTWS	Schleicher ASH 26E	26140	
D-KUAD-AD	Schleicher ASH 30Mi	30010	
D-KUAS-25M	Schleicher ASH 25Mi (Permit)	25204	
D-KUAX-Q2	DG Flugzeugbau DG-1001M	10-145M2	
D-KUBA-2C	Schleicher ASW 27-18E (ASG 29E)	29604	
D-KUBI	Lange Antares 18T (P 7.9.16)	81T75	
D-KUBM-9X	Schleicher ASG 29E	?	
D-KUBR	Schempp-Hirth Nimbus-4M	16/40	OK-1000, D-KOZX
D-KUBO	Schempp-Hirth Discus 2M	131/498	
D-KUCB	Schempp-Hirth Ventus-2cT	130/ . . .	
D-KUCI	Schempp-Hirth Ventus-2cxM	261	
D-KUCK	Scheibe SF 25C Falke 2000	44376	HB-2107, (D-KNBB)
D-KUDL	HOAC HK 36R Super Dimona	36398	
D-KUDO	Valentin Taifun 17E-II	1114	(D-KMLC), D-KATK, HB-2137, D-KHVA
D-KUDU	DG Flugzeugbau DG-808C Competition	8-334B233X4	
D-KUEL	Schempp-Hirth Ventus-2cM (Formerly Ventus-2c c/n 53/160)	77/160	D-5048
D-KUEN	Schempp-Hirth Duo Discus XLT	205	
D-KUEP	Alpavia/ Fournier RF-3	82	F-BMTQ
D-KUFO	Scheibe SF 25C Rotax-Falke	44663	
D-KUFP	HOAC HK-36R Super Dimona	36331	F-CGAY
D-KUGK	DG Flugzeugbau DG-800B	8-257B165	
D-KUHE	DG Flugzeugbau DG-800B	8-103B37	
D-KUHH	Scheibe SF 25C Falke	44150	OE-9320, D-KDEH(1)
D-KUHL	Schempp-Hirth Ventus cM	90/575	
D-KUHM	Schempp-Hirth Arcus T	12	
D-KUHN	Diamond HK 36TTC Super Dimona	36693	
D-KUHR	Schempp-Hirth Discus bM	2/423	
D-KUHU	Scheibe SF 25C Falke	44660	
D-KUKA-KA	Schempp-Hirth Arcus T	26	
D-KUKI	Glaser-Dirks DG-400 (Res.11.99)	4-156	I-KFAP, D-KFAP
D-KUKK	Diamond HK 36TC Super Dimona	36861	OE-9998
D-KULA-VFR	Schleicher ASH 25M	25180	D-KGGO(1)
D-KULE	Glaser-Dirks DG-800LA	8-7A6	
D-KULI	Schleicher ASH 25M (Crashed as D-KSAG 24.3.01, rebuilt)	25220	D-KSAG(1)
D-KULM	Technoflug Piccolo B	085	
D-KULS(2)-LS	Lange E1 Antares 23E (P 9.13)	71A01	
D-KULT(3)	DG Flugzeugbau DG-808B	8-304B204	
D-KULY	Valentin Taifun 17E-II (Res.04)	1106	OE-9293, D-KHVA(31)
D-KUMB-MB	Schempp-Hirth Arcus M	148	
D-KUML-ML	Schempp-Hirth Ventus cM	105/602	SE-UML, HB-2246
D-KUMO	Glaser-Dirks DG-400	4-211	G-BYTG, D-KBBP
D-KUMS	Stemme S10-VT (P.08)	11-116	
D-KUNG-REX	Schempp-Hirth Duo Discus XLT	177	
D-KUNI	Scheibe SF 25C Rotax-Falke	44667	
D-KUNK(2)	Schempp-Hirth Duo Discus xT	151	
D-KUNO(2)-CH	Schempp-Hirth Discus bT	146	
D-KUNT(2)-HM	Rolladen-Schneider LS8-t	8432	D-3361
D-KUNX(2)-BW	Binder EB28 (P. 4.07)	2	
D-KUPC	Schleicher ASH 26E	26049	D-KLHB
D-KUPE	Schempp-Hirth Ventus bT (Res .16)	43/233	S5-KKE, PH-1351, D-KSPT, HB-2104
D-KUPO	DG Flugzeugbau DG-1001M	10-163M12	
D-KUPR-PR	Schempp-Hirth Nimbus-4DM	58/78	
D-KURA	Technoflug Piccolo B	060	
D-KURK	Grob G 109B	6339	OH-716
D-KURO	Diamond HK 36TTC Super Dimona	36715	
D-KURS	Sportavia/ Fournier RF-5	5036	N555VM, OE-9030
D-KURT(3)	Scheibe SF 25C Rotax-Falke	44693	
D-KURZ	Scheibe SF 25C Rotax-Falke	44612	
D-KUSA-VX	Schleicher ASH 31Mi	31001	
D-KUSS	Glaser-Dirks DG-500M	5E147M59	
D-KUSU	Scheibe SF 25C Rotax-Falke	44645	
D-KUTE	Schempp-Hirth Duo Discus XLT	260	
D-KUTT-CM	Binder EB28	4	
D-KUUU	Schempp-Hirth Ventus-2cxM	237	
D-KUWE	Schempp-Hirth Ventus-2cM	129	
D-KUWO-WO	Schempp-Hirt Ventus-3T (P 31.8.16)	5	
D-KUXS	Schempp-Hirth Discus-2cT	30	OY-MXJ, D-KMXJ
D-KUYH	Schempp-Hirth Janus CM	23/216	JA2360
D-KUYY	Schempp-Hirth Discus-2cT	67	
D-KVAB	Schleicher ASW 27-18E	29509	
D-KVAS-26	Schleicher ASH 26E	26001	
D-KVBO	Schempp-Hirth Ventus bT (Res .16)	12/147	D-3143, SE-TYY
D-KVBR	DG Flugzeugbau DG-808C	8-392B291X53	
D-KVBS	Lange E1 Antares	17	
D-KVCB	DG Flugzeugbau DG-800B	8-235B149	
D-KVCM	Schempp-Hirth Ventus-2cxM	227	
D-KVCT	Schempp-Hirth Ventus cT	118/392	OO-YGI, OY-PHX, LX-CDT, D-KHUM
D-KVDC	Schempp-Hirth Ventus-2cM	289	
D-KVDG-DG	DG Flugzeugbau DG-1001M	10-158M8	
D-KVDS-DS	Schleicher ASH 26E	26227	
D-KVEB	Binder EB28D (W/o 14.9.16)	36	
D-KVEL-FC	Schleicher ASH 26E	26174	D-5634
D-KVES	DG Flugzeugbau DG-808C Competition	8-414B313X74	
D-KVFF	Schempp-Hirth Discus-2cT	61	
D-KVFL	Scheibe SF 25C Rotax-Falke	44613	
D-KVIE-MK	Stemme S10-VT	11-044	
D-KVII	Schempp-Hirt Ventus-3T (P 16.6.16)	2	
D-KVIO	Schleicher ASW 20BL/TOP	20955	SE-UTB, HB-2140
D-KVKA	Schempp-Hirth Discus bT	159/561	
D-KVKV	Schempp-Hirth Arcus T	36	
D-KVLB-LB	Schempp-Hirth Ventus cT	166/543	OO-YRZ, (PH-1339), OY-XRZ, D-KNMA(1)
D-KVLS(2)	Lange Antares 23E (Res .16)	82A04	
D-KVMC	Grob G 109B	6352	N109KC
D-KVMO	Schempp-Hirth Quintus M (P 7.13)	16	(D-KCJB)
D-KVOE	Schempp-Hirth Discus bT	119/475	OE-9385
D-KVOK	Diamond HK 36TTC Super Dimona (Dbr 7.5.16)	36566	
D-KVOY	Stemme S12 Twin Voyager (Res 10.5.16)	12-002	(D-KXOS)
D-KVSA-3L	Schleicher ASW 27-18E (ASG 29E)	29575	OH-986
D-KVSL-SL	Glaser-Dirks DG-400	4-89	HB-2092
D-KVTT	Schleicher ASW 27-18E (ASG 29E)	29651	
D-KVTX	Stemme S10-VT	11-043	C-FPAE
D-KVVB-VB	Binder EB29	29	
D-KVVE	DG Flugzeugbau LS8-t	8522	
D-KVVJ-VJ	Schempp-Hirth Discus bT	90/427	
D-KVVR	DG Flugzeugbau DG-808B	8-315B215	
D-KVVV-PO	Schempp-Hirth Janus CM	6	OE-9229, D-KBOS, OO-BPC, (D-KIBC)
D-KVWB-3E	Schempp-Hirth Ventus-2cxT	245	
D-KVWR	Schempp-Hirth Nimbus-4DM	74	
D-KVXX-3V	Schempp-Hirth Ventus-3 (P 13.1.16)	1	
D-KVYY-Y4	Schempp-Hirth Arcus M	3	

Registration	Type	Serial	Notes
D-KVZC	Glaser-Dirks DG-800B	8-68B13	
D-KWAB(2)-XAB	Schempp-Hirth Quintus M	9	(P.5.12)
D-KWAC	Sportavia-Pützer Fournier RF4D	4023	(D-KUAX), F-BORL (P. 1.11)
D-KWAE-1	Schempp-Hirth Discus-2cT	?	
D-KWAG	Glaser-Dirks DG-800LA	8-5A4	
D-KWAH	DG Flugzeugbau DG-808C	8-379B278X40	
D-KWAI	Schleicher ASH 26E	26053	HB-2270, D-KMML, D-2270
D-KWAK	Sportavia-Pützer Fournier RF4D	4097	(D-KQAX), HB-2004
D-KWAL	Schleicher ASH 26E	26106	
D-KWAM	Binder EB28	08	
D-KWAP-30	DG Flugzeugbau DG-800B	8-272B180	
D-KWAS-BM	Schempp-Hirth Ventus-2cM	127/...	
D-KWAT	Watzlawek M76	001	(D-KFHR)
D-KWAX	Diamond HK 36TS Super Dimona	36501	
D-KWAY	Schleicher ASH 26E	26231	D-8826
D-KWAZ	Diamond HK 36TS Super Dimona	36509	
D-KWBB-31	Schleicher ASH 31Mi	31127	
D-KWBE	DG Flugzeugbau DG-800B	8-247B160	
D-KWBM	Schempp-Hirth Discus bM	1/384	
D-KWCB	DG Flugzeugbau DG-808C	8-424B323X83	
D-KWDE-3E	Schempp-Hirth Discus-2cT	41	
D-KWDG(2)	DG Flugzeugbau DG-800B	8-148B72	
D-KWEB-EB	Binder EB29	12	
D-KWED	Schleicher ASH 31Mi	31042	
D-KWEI-W92	Schempp-Hirth Duo Discus XLT	245	
D-KWEK	MAG Carat A	CA036	
D-KWEL	Scheibe SF 25C Rotax-Falke	44666	
D-KWEM	Diamond HK 36TTC Super Dimona	36823	OE-9998
D-KWEN	Nitsche AVO 68-R100 Samburo	002	
D-KWER	Diamond HK 36TTC Super Dimona	36578	
D-KWES-1E	Schleicher ASW 22BLE	22069	D-6822
D-KWFG	Scheibe SF 25C Rotax-Falke	44576	
D-KWFS-WK	Schempp-Hirth Duo Discus XT	130	
D-KWFW	Lange E1 Antares 18T	59T05	
D-KWGC-EL	Schempp-Hirth Duo Discus XLT	207	
D-KWGL	Schempp-Hirth Nimbus-4M	18/42	(W/o 3.10.13)
D-KWGW	Schempp-Hirth Ventus-2cxM	280	
D-KWHA-HA	Schempp-Hirth Arcus M	10	
D-KWHB	Schleicher ASH 26E	26030	
D-KWHJ	Technoflug Piccolo B	115	
D-KWHT-2Y	Schempp-Hirth Arcus M	76	
D-KWIK	Valentin Taifun 17E	1098	PH-816, D-KHVA
D-KWIL-NJ	Schleicher ASH 26E	26004	
D-KWIM	Stemme S10-VT	11-108	
D-KWIN	Huber Windex 1200C	AB001	(P.8.04)
D-KWIR-IR	Schleicher ASH 31Mi	31142	
D-KWIT	Scheibe SF 25C Falke	44297	OE-9177, (D-KDGQ)
D-KWIX	Schempp-Hirth Discus-2cT	90	
D-KWKA	Binder EB29DE	21	(P. 8.11.12)
D-KWKS	Schempp-Hirth Duo Discus XT	163	
D-KWKU	Schempp-Hirth Arcus E	1	(D-KWET) (P. 4.10)
D-KWKW	Schleicher ASH 26E	26019	D-1807
D-KWLA	Schleicher ASH 31Mi	31074	
D-KWLF	Schempp-Hirth Arcus M	54/100	
D-KWMB-MB	Schleicher ASH 31Mi	31083	
D-KWMG(2)-4Y	Schempp-Hirth Arcus M	65	
D-KWMH	Schleicher ASG 32Mi	32006	(P 7.15)
D-KWMI	Schleicher ASK 21Mi	21854	
D-KWML(2)	Schleicher ASH 26E	26054	
D-KWMR-MR	Schempp-Hirth Arcus M	107	
D-KWMW	Schempp-Hirth Nimbus-4DM	28/42	PH-1120
D-KWMZ	Diamond HK 36TC Super Dimona	36867	OE-9998
D-KWNW	Schempp-Hirth Discus bT	71/398	
D-KWOB-WN	Schempp-Hirth Duo Discus xT	169	
D-KWOK	Schleicher ASH 26E	26179	
D-KWOR-OR	Binder EB28	18	
D-KWOS	DG Flugzeugbau DG-1000T	10-169T52	
D-KWPG-PG	Schempp-Hirth Discus bT	113/466	
D-KWPP-PP	Schempp-Hirth Arcus T	7	
D-KWRA(2)	AMS-Flight Carat A	CA032	
D-KWRR	Schempp-Hirth Ventus cM	109/608	
D-KWSC	Hoffmann H-36 Dimona	36233	OE-9286
D-KWSE	Glaser-Dirks DG-600/18M	6-114M54	
D-KWSF	Grob G 109B	6224	HB-2209, D-KGFK
D-KWSJ	Aerotechnik L-13SL Vivat	930510	
D-KWSZ-W2	Schempp-Hirth Duo Discus xT	136	
D-KWTR	Schempp-Hirth Duo Discus T	15/263	(P.3.01)
D-KWTT	Eiri PIK-20E	20232	LX-CWC, D-KEHI (2)
D-KWUB	Schleicher ASH 26E	26163	(D-KLPA), D-KIFH
D-KWUG	Schempp-Hirth Duo Discus T	51/335	
D-KWUN	DG Flugzeugbau DG-1000T	10-141T47	
D-KWVE	Scheibe SF 25C Rotax-Falke	44553	
D-KWWB	Lange E1 Antares	55E46	D-KHAK
D-KWWE-2E	Schempp-Hirth Ventus-2cM	1/5	
D-KWWF	Diamond HK 36TTS Super Dimona	36622	
D-KWWG	Schleicher ASH 31Mi	31077	
D-KWWJ	Schempp-Hirth Discus-2T	5/92	(P.1.01)
D-KWWM	Schleicher ASH 26E	26020	
D-KWWS	Grob G 109B	6363	G-BMCM, (EAF-674)
D-KWWW	Diamond HK 36TTC Super Dimona	36569	
D-KWYS	Glaser-Dirks DG-800A	8-4A3	
D-KWZE	Diamond HK 36TC-100 Super Dimona	36803	OE-9997
D-KXAA	Schleicher ASW 27-18E	29687	
D-KXAB-AB	Rolladen-Schneider LS6-18M	6351	D-0531 (P. 4.11)
D-KXAG	DG Flugzeugbau DG-808C	8-372B271X35	
D-KXAI	Schempp-Hirth Ventus 2cT	246	(Res .16)
D-KXAT-AT	Schleicher ASW 27-18E (ASG 29E)	29653	
D-KXBB-BB	Schempp-Hirth Duo Discus T	145	
D-KXBE-BX	Sportine Aviacija LAK-17B FES	238	
D-KXBS	DG Flugzeugbau DG-808C	8-353B252X17	
D-KXCB(2)	Schempp-Hirth Duo Discus T	83/397	
D-KXCM	Schempp-Hirth Ventus-2cM	67/138	
D-KXCZ(2)	Stemme S10-VT	11-074	(D-KLCC(1))
D-KXDD-DD	Schleicher ASH 25M	25101	D-6093
D-KXDG-DG	DG Flugzeugbau DG-808C	8-373B272X36	
D-KXDH	DG Flugzeugbau DG-808C	8-365B264X28	
D-KXDX-DX	Schempp-Hirth Arcus T	37	
D-KXEX	Schempp-Hirth Arcus T	45	(D-KTTK)
D-KXFF-SKY	Schleicher ASH 31Mi	31002	
D-KXFT	Schempp-Hirth Arcus M	144	
D-KXGS	DG Flugzeugbau DG-800B	8-307B207	
D-KXGT-GT2	Schempp-Hirth Duo Discus XLT	247	
D-KXGX-GX	Schempp-Hirth Discus-2cT	15	D-9515
D-KXHB-HB	Schleicher ASW 27-18E (ASG 29E)	29711	
D-KXHG	Glaser-Dirks DG-400	4-118	HB-2101 (Res .09)
D-KXHI-HI	Schleicher ASW 27-18E (ASG 29E)	29695	
D-KXHW-HW	Schempp-Hirth Arcus M	27	
D-KXII	Schempp-Hirth Ventus-2cxM	229	
D-KXIK-IK	Schempp-Hirth Ventus-2cxT	108	
D-KXKX	DG Flugzeugbau DG-808C	8-325B225X2	
D-KXLH	Schempp-Hirth Ventus-2cM	53/107	
D-KXLL-7L	Schempp-Hirth Ventus-2cxT	207	
D-KXLS-10	DG Flugzeugbau LS10-st	L10-003	
D-KXLW-WK	Schempp-Hirth Duo Discus XLT	236	
D-KXMO-MO	Schempp-Hirth Arcus T	9	
D-KXMP	DG Flugzeugbau DG-808C Competition	8-348B247X14	
D-KXMX	DG Flugzeugbau DG-1001M	10-147M4	(P. 7.10)
D-KXOV	Schempp-Hirth Arcus M	143	
D-KXPB	Glaser-Dirks DG-400	4-248	G-BPXB
D-KXPP	Schleicher ASH 26E	26061	D-KORR
D-KXPS	DG Flugzeugbau DG-808B	8-259B167	PH-1249
D-KXPT	Schempp-Hirth Duo Discus XLT	257	
D-KXSA-29	Schleicher ASW 27-18E (ASG 29E)	29603	
D-KXSH-SH	HpH Glasflügel 304S-JET	007-S	OK-1931 (P.3.12)
D-KXSW-SW	Schleicher ASW 27-18E (ASG 29E)	29619	
D-KXTC-XTC	Schempp-Hirth Ventus-2cxaj	8J	D-4760 (P. 4.10)
D-KXTW	Schleicher ASH 31Mi	31085	
D-KXUM-UM	Schempp-Hirth Discus-2T	28/172	OY-XUM
D-KXVG	Grob G103C Twin III SL	35014	OY-XVG, OE-9374
D-KXVH	DG Flugzeugbau DG-808C Competition	8-341B240X8	
D-KXWH-K2	Schempp-Hirth Arcus T	11	
D-KXWW	Schempp-Hirth Discus-2T	20	HB-2389, (D-KLLS)
D-KXXA	Schempp-Hirth Ventus-2cxM	189	
D-KXXB-1C	DG Flugzeugbau DG-808C Competition	8-316B216X1	
D-KXXC(2)	Schempp-Hirth Ventus-2cxM	183	
D-KXXE-I7	Schempp-Hirth Ventus-2cxT	145	OY-XXE, D-KEIT
D-KXXH-H	Schleicher ASH 26E	26160	N10ZQ (P.05)
D-KXXK	DG Flugzeugbau DG-808C Competition	8-388B287X49	
D-KXXL	Akaflieg Stuttgart Icaré	2	(P.10.09)
D-KXXM-XM	Schempp-Hirth Ventus-2cxM	242	
D-KXXX-KX	Schempp-Hirth Nimbus-4DT	?	
D-KXXY	Schempp-Hirth Nimbus-4DM	71	OY-XXY, D-KXXY (Res .14)
D-KXYA	Aerotechnik L-13SEH Vivat	940520	PH-1238, D-KXYA
D-KXYZ	Schempp-Hirth Ventus-2cxM	260	
D-KYAA	DG Flugzeugbau DG-800B	8-292B197	
D-KYAK(2)-Y8	Lange E1 Antares	38E36	
D-KYAS	Schleicher ASH 26E	26175	
D-KYBB-2B	Schempp-Hirth Ventus-2cxT	188	D-9112
D-KYBG	Sportine Aviacija LAK-17AT	157	OE-9600, (D-KLAV), LY-GIS
D-KYBL	Scheibe SF 25C Rotax-Falke	44413	D-KEGL(1)
D-KYBS-BS	Schleicher ASH 31Mi	31023	
D-KYBY	Schempp-Hirth Discus-2cT	128	
D-KYCB	DG Flugzeugbau DG-800B	8-187B111	D-KERG(2)
D-KYCT-CT	Schempp-Hirth Ventus-2cT	58/188	OO-YCT
D-KYDM-45	Schempp-Hirth Ventus-2cM	132	
D-KYDS	Schleicher ASH 26E	26133	OO-YDS
D-KYES	DG Flugzeugbau DG-800B	8-294B199	
D-KYGG	DG Flugzeugbau DG-1000T	10-125T44	
D-KYGI	Scheibe SF 25C Falke 2000	44408	OY-XYG, (D-KNIN)
D-KYHF-LSJ	Schempp-Hirth Nimbus-4M	5/20	
D-KYHL	Scheibe SF 25C Rotax-Falke	44655	(P.06)
D-KYHN	Scheibe SF 25C Rotax-Falke	44630	
D-KYKY	Schempp-Hirth Duo Discus T	119	
D-KYLA-9T	Schleicher ASH 26E	26211	
D-KYLI-9T	Schleicher ASH 31Mi	31091	
D-KYLJ-LJ	Sportine Aviacija LAK-17AT	167	LY-YLJ
D-KYLO-LO	Schempp-Hirth Ventus-2cM	119/255	HB-2383
D-KYLS	Rolladen-Schneider LS8-t	8474	(D-KUTC), SP-3768, HB-3368 (Res 1.10)
D-KYMG	Schempp-Hirth Ventus-2cxT	112	OO-YVT, D-KSAC
D-KYNG	Scheibe SF 25C Rotax-Falke	44699	(P.4.04)
D-KYNT	Scheibe SF 25C Heubacher-Falke	44718	
D-KYPI	Schleicher ASW 27-18E (ASG 29E)	29654	
D-KYRJ	Schempp-Hirth Nimbus-3DT	62	OO-YRJ, F-CFUQ
D-KYSA	DG Flugzeugbau DG-800B	8-114B43	
D-KYSI	HOAC HK-36TC Super Dimona	36730	
D-KYSS	Nitsche AVO 68-R115 Samburo Turbo	005	
D-KYTH	Stemme S10-VT	11-106	N9TH
D-KYTT	Schempp-Hirth Ventus-2cT	28/98	
D-KYVG	Schleicher ASW 20C	20758	D-9744, OO-YVG, D-8123
D-KYXL-XL	Schempp-Hirth Nimbus-4DM	24/34	D-KCGG
D-KYYA-YA	Schempp-Hirth Arcus T	24	(D-KTTK)
D-KYYX	Schempp-Hirth Arcus M	57/105	
D-KYYY(2)	Hoffmann H-36 Dimona	3615	OE-9206
D-KZAC-52	Schleicher ASW 22BLE 50R	22079	G-CDII, BGA 4656
D-KZAR-AR	Schleicher ASH 26E	26155	
D-KZAS-21	Schleicher ASK 21Mi	21784	
D-KZBY	Schempp-Hirth Arcus M	40	(D-KSWK)
D-KZCB	DG Flugzeugbau DG-808C	8-426B325X85	
D-KZCE	Stemme S6	6.T.10.012	(P. 4.15)
D-KZCZ	Schempp-Hirth Discus bT	22/314	OO-ZCZ, D-KGBF
D-KZDS-DS	Schleicher ASH 31Mi	31057	
D-KZEM	Diamond HK 36 TC Super Dimona	36.815	F-CHQI, OE-9998
D-KZEN	Lange E1 Antares	45E41	
D-KZGH	Scheibe SF 25C Heubacher-Falke	44723	

D-KZHS	Schempp-Hirth Duo Discus XLT	256	
D-KZMR	Schleicher ASW 22BLE 50R	22087	OK-2277
D-KZOB	Schempp-Hirth Nimbus-4DM	35/50	OO-NKD, (OO-NDH)
D-KZPG-KZP	Schempp-Hirth Arcus T	17	
D-KZSF	Glaser-Dirks DG-400	4-284	
D-KZWU	Stemme S10-VT	11-068	

CLASS L : Airships

D-LDFO	WDL-1 (PL4360A) Airship 'Fuji Film'	101A	JA1002, D-LDFN
D-LDFQ	WDL-1B Airship 'König Pilsner' (Dismantled)	106	JA1007, D-LDFQ
D-LDFR	WDL-1B Airship 'Sparkasse'	107	
D-LJOE	Cargo-Lifter Joey B	1	
D-LZFN(1)	Zeppelin LZ N07-100 Airship "Friedrichshafen" (W/o 20.9.07, Botswana)	01	
D-LZFN(2)	Zeppelin LZ NT N07-100 Airship "Wagner"	001	
D-LZGA	Zeppelin LZ NT N07-101 Airship (Res. 11.14, for USA)	008	
D-LZGY	Zeppelin LZ NT N07-101 Airship "Wingfoot One" (Regd in USA as N1A)	006	
D-LZGZ	Zeppelin LZ NT N07-101 Airship (Export permit 4.4.16; regd in USA as N2A)	007	
D-LZZF	Zeppelin LZ-NT N07-100 Airship "Baden-Wurttemberg"	003	(D-LION)
D-LZZR	Zeppelin LZ NT N07-100 Airship "Bodensee" (To Japan, 2005, returned 2010)	002	
D-LZNT	Zeppelin LZ-NT N07-100 Airship "Eureka"	004	N704LZ, D-LZNT

CLASS M : Microlights

In the listings below we have retained details of duplicated registrations to help in the identification of aircraft seen in the past. In some cases the order of the aircraft identified could be incorrect as dates are not always available. Most of those marked (1) may be presumed to have been cancelled although details are often unknown. However, weight-shift and three-axis microlights are certified by different authorities and there are examples of registration marks apparently being used by both simultaneously. To save space, further entries now known to have been cancelled prior to 29.11.16 without specific information are marked # and may be expected to be re-used.

D-MAAA(1)	Flight Team Spider D	049	
D-MAAA(2)	Autogyro Europe MT-03	D07G20	
D-MAAB	Fresh Breeze 112 AL2F	764	
D-MAAC(1)	NST Minimum Nimbus 62	M527	
D-MAAC(2)	NST Minimum Zephir CX M	M583	
D-MAAD	Plätzer Kiebitz-B	144	
D-MAAE	Fresh Breeze 112 AL2F	784	
D-MAAF(1)	Ultra-Vector F 610	1399	
D-MAAG(1)	Behlen Power-Trike Euro III	8400100	
D-MAAG(2)	Bautek Eagle V / Ghost 12	02 W015	
D-MAAH(1)	UPM Funplane	19002	
D-MAAH(2)	B&F Funk FK-9 Mk.III (To EC-049(2), EC-GQI) (Original c/n 09-04-252)	002-190	
D-MAAH(3)	Flight Design CT	08-04-03	
D-MAAI	Fresh Breeze 112 AL2F	326	
D-MAAJ	Fresh Breeze Snap 120	unkn	
D-MAAK	Cosmos Bi90 Phase III / Chronos 14	B963	
D-MAAL	Fresh Breeze 110 AL2F	1478	
D-MAAM	Comco Ikarus C-42B (W/o 18.4.08)	0208-6485	
D-MAAN	Fresh Breeze Flyke Monster	278	
D-MAAO	Zenair CH-601D Zodiac	6-9877	
D-MAAP(1)	Alpi Aviation Pioneer 300	66	
D-MAAP(2)	Alpi Aviation Pioneer 300UL	167	
D-MAAQ(1)	UPM Funplane	86006	
D-MAAQ(2)	Fresh Breeze SportiX 122	1371	
D-MAAR(1)	Impulse (To OO-F03)	030	
D-MAAR(2)	Bautek Eagle V/ Pico S	04 B 08	
D-MAAS(1)	Fresh Breeze 110 AL2F	356	
D-MAAS(2)	Nirvana Instinct NS200/Dudek Hadron	unkn	
D-MAAT	Schönleber trike 47 Vento	V01/01/05	
D-MAAU(1)	Fresh Breeze XCitor / XWing	XC2006/26	
D-MAAU(2)	Autogyro Europe MT-03	unkn	
D-MAAV	B&F Funk FK-14 Polaris (t/w)	014-039	
D-MAAW	Fresh Breeze Monster 4	394	
D-MAAX	Schönleber trike 47 Vento	V01/1002	
D-MAAY	Fresh Breeze Simo 122	3302.629.36250	
D-MAAZ	Schmidtler Enduro 582 / Mild 16	02-027	
D-MABA	Sky Service Pagojet M4	RB9909	
D-MABB	Ful Graffiti MA30 Maverick II	046/152	
D-MABC(2)	Cosmos Bi 90 / Ghost 14.9	21226	
D-MABD(1)	Aviasud Mistral BA-53	003	
D-MABD(2)	Fresh Breeze Bulli-X Monster	1111	
D-MABE	Fresh Breeze 4 Monster	96	
D-MABF	Interplane Skyboy ZK	004.03.03.TD	
D-MABG	Flight Team Twister / iXess	D011-T	
D-MABH(1)	B&F Funk F-14 Polaris (To OO-E09, 4.03)	014-023	
D-MABH(2)	Pioneer Flightstar	061002	
D-MABI	Bautek Eagle V/ Ipsos 14.9	05 B 09	
D-MABJ(1)	Roland Z-602XL (W/o 27.6.11)	Z-9527	
D-MABJ(2)	Technoflug Piccolo	075	
D-MABK(1)	UPM Funplane	86007	
D-MABK(2)	Fly Products Max 130 Simo Mini 2+	061536	
D-MABL #	Fresh Breeze 110 AL 4H	27	
D-MABM	Fresh Breeze 122 AL 2F	606	
D-MABN(1)	Albatros	109	
D-MABN(2)	Autogyro Europe Calidus	D10C07	
D-MABO	Comco Fox D	8505-FD27	
D-MABP(1)	Mini-Fly-Set Zephir CX	127591-5	
D-MABP(2)	Autogyro Europe MTOsport	unkn	
D-MABR(1)	Power Trike Evolution / Pico	unkn	
D-MABR(2)	Aerostyle Breezer B400	UL123	
D-MABS	Comco Ikarus C-42	0203-6464	
D-MABT(1)	Ultra-Vector H	1758	
D-MABT(2)	Comco Ikarus C-42B	0807-7002	
D-MABU	HFL Stratos	014	
D-MABV	Autogyro Europe MTOsport	OE08S02	
D-MABW	Comco Ikarus C-42	unkn	
D-MABX	Moyes Dragonfly floatplane	D02002	
D-MABY(1)	Warnke Euro III Trike	SI 030	
D-MABY(2)	Fresh Breeze Simo 122	1261	
D-MABZ	Fisher FP-202 Koala	2183	
D-MACA	Aeroprakt A-22 Vision	0033-011	
D-MACB(1)	UPM Funplane Trike	86010	
D-MACB(2)	Power Trike 582 / Ghost 12	unkn	
D-MACB(3)	Fresh Breeze 122 AL 2F	1611	
D-MACC(1)	NST Minimum	46/85-1501	
D-MACC(2)	Comco Ikarus C-42B	0211-6502	
D-MACD	Sky-Craft AJS-2000	033	
D-MACE	Behlen Power-Trike Vampir II	85013	
D-MACF(1)	Avio Delta Swan 1 582/Ipsos 12.9	unkn	
D-MACF(2)	Autogyro Europe MTOsport	D08S20	
D-MACG(1)	NST Minimum Focus 18	M184	
D-MACG(2)	Technoflug Piccolo	114	
D-MACH	Fresh Breeze 122 AL 2F	750	
D-MACI (1)	Klüver Kaiman Trike	080706	
D-MACI(2)	Fresh Breeze Simo 122	M2 3586	
D-MACJ	Fresh Breeze Simo 122	unkn	
D-MACK	Fresh Breeze 122 AL 2F	584	
D-MACL(1)	Comco Ikarus Fox-C22	8705-3059	
D-MACL(2)	Autogyro Europe MT-03	D06G32	
D-MACM	Cosmos Phase II / Top 14.9	B21509	
D-MACN	Fresh Breeze Snap 120	unkn	
D-MACO(1)	Ultraleichtverbund Bi 90	993	
D-MACO(2)	Rans S-6 Coyote II	01061723-S	
D-MACP	Sky-Walker II	202	
D-MACQ	Plätzer Kiebitz A	052	
D-MACR	NST Minimum Saphir 16	M307	
D-MACS	Evektor EV-97 Eurostar 2000R	2004-2015	
D-MACT	Flight Design CT	08-02-22	
D-MACU	Fresh Breeze Simo 122	609	
D-MACV	Fresh Breeze Skip One Simo 122	unkn	
D-MACW	Fresh Breeze Simo 122	unkn	
D-MACX	Comco Ikarus Fox-C22	8901-3163	
D-MACY	Comco Ikarus Fox-C22	8904-3171	
D-MACZ	Aviasud AE209 Albatros (Re-regd D-MQJB)	121	
D-MADA	Autogyro Europe MT-03	04G02	
D-MADC(1)	Ultraleichtverbund Bi 90 /Chronos 14	21002	
D-MADC(2)	Autogyro Europe Calidus	C00146	
D-MADD(1)	Fair Fax Euro III Trike	026	
D-MADD(2)	Dova DV-1 Skylark (To OO-G09)	07/10	
D-MADE	Schmidtler Ranger M	M1817	
D-MADF(1)	Autogyro Europe MTOsport	M01000	
D-MADF(2)	Autogyro Europe Calidus	unkn	
D-MADG(1)	NST Minimum	M576	
D-MADG(2)	TL Ultralight TL-96 Sting	11ST359	
D-MADH	Sky-Walker II	211	
D-MADI	Fresh Breeze 122 AL 2F	1636	
D-MADJ	Autogyro Europe MTOsport	OE08S04	
D-MADK	Aerostyle Breezer	034	
D-MADL (1)	NST Schwarze Mimimum	462	
D-MADL(2)	Flight Design CT LS	07-12-01	
D-MADM (1)	Take Off Maximum Lotus 16	027020	
D-MADM(2)	Roland Z602Z	Z-9535	
D-MADN	Sky-Walker II	208	
D-MADO	Flight Design CT LS	08-04-04	
D-MADP	Klüver Racer 462 / XP II	371903	
D-MADR	ATEC Zephyr 2000C (C/n also reported as Z 351202 TU, 2 aircraft ?)	Z 710103S	
D-MADS(1)	Wisch Star-Trike Hazard 15M	127.04.898	
D-MADS(2)	Euro-Fly Viper 462/Hazard 15	unkn	
D-MADS(3)	Comco Ikarus C-42B	1406-7335	
D-MADT	Sky-Walker II	218	
D-MADU(1)	Comco Ikarus Fox II Doppel	8604-3013	
D-MADU(2)	Autogyro Europe MTOsport	unkn	
D-MADV(1)	Fair Fax Trike	27	
D-MADV(2)	Fresh Breeze 122 AL 2F	1469	
D-MADW	Fisher FP-202 Koala	001	
D-MADX	Sunny Light	020/0407	
D-MADZ	Ultraleichtverbund Bi 90 / Chronos 12	21003	
D-MAEA	Walkerjet RR W200	041	
D-MAEB(1)	ASO Viper 462 / Hazard 15	15/16791	
D-MAEB(2)	paramotor / Relax wing	unkn	
D-MAEC	Schönleber DS Enduro / Vento	03/0489	
D-MAED(1)	Fair Fax Euro III Trike	029	
D-MAED(2)	Fresh Breeze Snap 120	116	
D-MAEE	Ultraleichtverbund Bi 90 / Chronos 12	21043	
D-MAEF(1)	Cosmos Bi 90 / Chronos 12	unkn	
D-MAEF(2)	Technoflug Piccolo	006	D-KATT
D-MAEG	ASO Viper 462 / Hazard 15	15/18290	
D-MAEH(1)	Mosquito IB	004	
D-MAEH(2)	Fresh Breeze Simo 122	940	
D-MAEI	Sky-Walker II	235	
D-MAEJ	Fisher FP-404 Classic	Schmidt 1/ 014	
D-MAEK	Comco Ikarus Fox-C22	9003-3222	
D-MAEL	Comco Ikarus Fox D	014	
D-MAEM	Comco Ikarus Fox-C22	9003-3224	
D-MAEN	Aeroprakt A-22L Vision	331	
D-MAEO	Fresh Breeze Simo 122	186	
D-MAEP(2)#	Kümmerle Mini-Fly-Set	44465	
D-MAEQ	Aeros-2 912 / Profi 14.5	112	
D-MAER	Ultraleichtverbund Bi 90 / Chronos 12	21000	
D-MAES(2)#	Kümmerle Mini-Fly-Set	73085-3	
D-MAET	Behlen Power-Trike 582 / Falcon	90026	
D-MAEU(1)	Sky-Walker II	246	
D-MAEU(2)	Aeros-2 912 / Profi	036	
D-MAEV(1)	Fair Fax DR Hazard Trike	D009	
D-MAEV(2)	Fresh Breeze 122 AL 2F	453	
D-MAEW	HFL Stratos 300K	300-019K	
D-MAEX	Schmidtler Enduro Focus 18	010885	
D-MAEY	Air-Light Wild Thing	091	
D-MAFA	Fantasy Air Allegro	02-414	
D-MAFB	Sky-Walker II	248	
D-MAFC(1)	Sky-Walker II	unkn	
D-MAFC(2)	Remos G.3 Mirage	092	
D-MAFD	Ultraleichtverbund Bi 90 / Chronos 12	21010	
D-MAFE(1)	UPM Cobra Raven Trike	910113	
D-MAFE(2)	Skyrider Sonic Smart / Hazard 12s	G005/SM/12	
D-MAFF	Comco Ikarus C-42B	0705-6891	
D-MAFG	NST Minimum Milan	M689	
D-MAFH(1)	Fisher FP-202 Koala	002 Wachter	
D-MAFH(2)	Fresh Breeze Simo 122	1687	
D-MAFI	Dallach Sunrise IIA	027	
D-MAFJ #	Ultraleichtverbund Bi 90	3957004	
D-MAFK	Sky-Walker II	253	

Reg	Type	c/n	Notes
D-MAFL(1)	Flight Design CT-2K	03-06-06-31	
	(W/o 22.12.04 in USA)		
D-MAFL(2)	Fresh Breeze Simo 122	1220	
D-MAFM(1)	Klüver Twin Racer Quartz SX 16	834910	
D-MAFM(2)	Pipistrel Apis BEE 15 MB	053 ABF 33	
D-MAFN #	Klüver Twin Racer Quartz SX 16	835910	
D-MAFO(1)	NST Minimum	M525	
D-MAFO(2)	Fresh Breeze Flyke Simo 122	396/2007	
D-MAFP(1)	Comco Ikarus Fox-C22	8911-3247	
D-MAFP(2)	Autogyro Europe MTOsport	D10S25	
D-MAFQ	Ultraleichtverbund Bi 90 / Chronos 12	21049	
D-MAFR	Fresh Breeze122 AL 2F	566	
D-MAFS(1)	Pioneer Flightstar	672	
	(Re-regd D-MPFS)		
D-MAFS(2)	Skyjam Airmaster / Profi 430 Sport	432 M02/AM802030	
D-MAFT(1)	Aviasud Mistral 53	006	
D-MAFT(2)	Plätzer Kiebitz-B	340	
D-MAFU(1)	Sky-Walker II	250	
D-MAFU(2)	UPM Funplane	unkn	
D-MAFW(1)	NST Minimum	M324	
D-MAFW(2)	Avio Delta Swan I 582 / Ipsos 12.9	MK05 070301	
D-MAFX	Dallach Sunrise II	028	
D-MAFY(1)	Autogyro Europe MTOsport	M00162	
D-MAFZ(1)	Behlen Power-Trike	90016	
D-MAFY(2)	Breezer B400 Club	unkn	
D-MAFZ(2)	Fresh Breeze Monster 4	742	
D-MAGA	Behlen Power-Trike Vampir II	89040	
D-MAGB(1)	Ultraleichtverbund Bi 90 / Chronos 12	21093	
D-MAGB(2)	NST Minimum Astir M	1261254	
D-MAGC	Ultraleichtverbund Bi 90 / Chronos 12	21080	
D-MAGE	Comco Ikarus Fox-C22	042	
D-MAGF	Fresh Breeze SportiX 122 Simo 122	1387 1/03-11	
D-MAGG	Dallach Sunrise II	018	
D-MAGH	Fresh Breeze122 AL 2F	1522	
D-MAGI (1)	UPM Cobra Trike	920119	
D-MAGI(2)	Flight Design CT SW	07-10-24	
D-MAGJ	Magni M-24 Orion	24116344	
D-MAGK(2)	Tandem Air Sunny Sport	045-93	
D-MAGL	TVS 700 Tandem Air Sunny Sport	08.91	
D-MAGM(1)	Autogyro Europe MT-03	D06G13	
D-MAGM(2)	ELA Aviacion ELA-09 Junior	130162681	EC-XLT
D-MAGN(1)	Magni M-14 Scout	14011753	Ex or to I-5282
D-MAGN(2)	Autogyro Europe MTOsport	D08S09	
D-MAGO(1)	Fresh Breeze122 AL 2F	1911	
D-MAGO(2)	Aero East Europe Sila 450C	unkn	
D-MAGP	Fresh Breeze122 AL 2F	1915	
D-MAGQ(1)	Fresh Breeze Simo 122	1091	
D-MAGQ(2)	Breezer CR	82	
	(Sold as 95-AAV)		
D-MAGS	Tecnam P.96S Golf 100	310	
D-MAGT(1)	Fresh Breeze Simo 122	unkn	
D-MAGT(2)	Autogyro Europe Cavalon	V00029	
	(Re-regd D-MCVN)		
D-MAGU	Flight Design CT SW	07-02-02	N244CT ?
	(Damaged 12.5.08, to SP-SWCT 2011)		
D-MAGW	Bautek Eagle V/ Pico	04815	
D-MAGX	Remos GX Mirage	363	
D-MAGY	Remos G.3/600 Mirage	151	
D-MAGZ	Autogyro Europe MTOsport	D09S37	
D-MAHA	Behlen Power Trike Vampir II	85/029	
D-MAHB(1)	Fair Fax DR Trike	D026	
D-MAHB(2)	Per Il Volo Miniplane 125	19/73	
D-MAHC	PAP-ROS 125 Parapente	02	
D-MAHD	Autogyro Europe MTOsport	D09S30	
D-MAHE	B&F Funk FK-9 Mk.IV	09-244	
D-MAHF(1)	Enduro DS	20KS20	
D-MAHF(2)	Breezer Aircraft Breezer	035	
D-MAHG	Take Off Merlin 1100 / Avant	87.703	
D-MAHH	Fresh Breeze Simo 122	673	
D-MAHI(1)	Aeroaviation Airo 1	A004	(N163AA)
D-MAHI(2)	AirLony Skylane UL	unkn	
D-MAHJ(1)	Fresh Breeze Snap 120	85	
D-MAHJ(2)	Remos GX	322	
D-MAHK	Keller Mosquito NRG Atos	3002	
D-MAHL(1)	Fresh Breeze 110 AL 4H	24	
D-MAHL(2)	ATEC Zephyr 2000C	Z 550402A	
D-MAHN (1)	Comco Ikarus Fox II Doppel	8605-3016	
D-MAHN(2)	Flight Design CT-2K	unkn	
D-MAHN(3)#	Flight Design CT LS	09-11-02	
D-MAHO	Fresh Breeze Flyke Simo 122	762	
D-MAHP(1)	Autogyro Europe MTOsport	unkn	
D-MAHP(2)	Fresh Breeze Flyke Monster	539	
D-MAHR	Flight Design CT SW	05-04-11	
D-MAHS	Buttner Crazy Flyer	43	
D-MAHU	Fresh Breeze XCitor / XWing	XC140/2009	
D-MAHV	Fresh Breeze Simo 122	M2 7951	
D-MAHW(1)	Behlen Power-Trike 582 / Falcon	92002	
D-MAHW(2)	Ekolot KR-010 Elf	01-01-02	
D-MAHX	Fresh Breeze XCitor / XWing	XC40/2006	
D-MAHY(1)	Buttner Crazy Flyer	41	
D-MAHY(2)	Comco Ikarus C-42B	1207-7212	
D-MAHZ	Solid Air Twin Diamant / Chronos 12	T-011	
D-MAIA(1)	Aeros-2 / Profi 14.5	02.09.152	
D-MAIA(2)	Avio Delta Swan I 582/ Ghost 12	unkn	
D-MAIB	Kummerle Mini-Fly-Set Zerphir CX	90483	
D-MAIC(1)	Comco Ikarus C-42	0005-6253	
	(To D-MOFL)		
D-MAIC(2)	Evektor EV-97R Eurostar	2007 2942	
	(Same c/n as D-MAIK(2), re-regd as such?)		
D-MAIC(3)	Avio Delta Swan I 582 / Pico	unkn	
D-MAID(1)	Behlen Power-Trike	830025	
D-MAID(2)	Fresh Breeze122 AL 2F	657	
D-MAIE	Ultraleichtverbund Bi 90 / Chronos 14	4105552-8907	
D-MAIF	Keller Mosquito NRG Atos	010 227-096	
D-MAIG	Aeros trike	027-08	
D-MAIH(1)	Tandem Air Sunny Sport	13.91	
D-MAIH(2)#	Fair Fax Trike Euro III	005	
D-MAII (1)	Take Off Maximum Trike	75109	
D-MAII(2)	Comco Ikarus C-42B	1101-7134	
D-MAIK(1)	Take Off Merlin 1100	7503	
D-MAIK(2)	Evektor EV-97 Eurostar 2000	2007 2942	
	(Same c/n as D-MAIC(2), ex?)		
D-MAIL	Schmidtler Enduro / XP 15	02-026	
D-MAIM	Fresh Breeze SportiX 122 Simo 122	1338	
D-MAIN	Flight Design CT SW	06-02-03	
D-MAIO	Comco Ikarus C-42B	1102-7128	
D-MAIP(1)	Roland Z-602DX	DX 9515	
D-MAIP(2)	Roland Z-602DX	DX 9536	
D-MAIQ	Zlin Savage Cruiser	unkn	
D-MAIR	Fresh Breeze122 AL 2F	1894	
D-MAIS	Tandem Air Sunny Sport	42.92	
D-MAIT	Flight Team Twister 912 / iXess	D004	
D-MAIV	Autogyro Europe MTOsport	M01155	
D-MAIW #	Klüver Twin Racer SX 16	542008	
D-MAIZ	Parasport Fun Simo 125	M2-2871	
D-MAJA(1)	Drachenstudio Piccolo	01/92	
D-MAJA(2)	Autogyro Europe Calidus 912	D10C09	
D-MAJB	Klüver Racer SX 12	443904	
D-MAJE	Fresh Breeze Simo 122	119	
D-MAJG	Schmidtler Enduro 1150 / Kiss 450	unkn	
D-MAJH(2)	Aerostyle Breezer UL	008	
D-MAJJ	FUL Graffiti MA30 / Stranger	067/2008	
	(W/o 14.9.14)		
D-MAJK	Fresh Breeze Skip One Monster 4B	820	
D-MAJM	Ultraleichtverbund Bi 90 / Chronos 12	21347	
D-MAJN	Vetterl Raven Atos	RAV 03101601	
D-MAJO	Zenair CH-601DX Zodiac	6-9478	
D-MAJP	Keller Mosquito NRG Atos	509	
D-MAJR #	Fresh Breeze122 AL 2F	1433	
D-MAJS	Scheibe Uli 1	5208	
D-MAJU	Junkers Profly JUL / Ghost 12	94/1061	
D-MAJV	unidentified paramotor	unkn	
D-MAJW	Spacek SD-1 Minisport TD	035	
D-MAKA	Tandem Air Sunny Sport	013.08.04	
D-MAKB #	Fresh Breeze122 AL 2F	1292	
D-MAKC	Fläming Air FA-01 Smaragd	5025018	
D-MAKD	Remos GX	266	
D-MAKE(1)	Comco Ikarus Fox II Doppel	8607-3024	
D-MAKE(2)	Autogyro Europe MTOsport	D09S55	
D-MAKF(1)	Sky Walker II	252	
D-MAKF(2)	Aerostyle Breezer CR	066	
D-MAKG	Cosmos Bi 90 / Chronos 14.9	B21461	
D-MAKI	Cosmos Phase II / Top 12.9	B21377	
D-MAKJ	Kümmerle Mini-Fly-Set	1279 91-5	
D-MAKK	Albatros	165	
D-MAKL	NST Minimum	M319	
D-MAKM	Schmidtler Enduro 582 / Mild 16	02-014	
D-MAKN	Tandem Air Sunny Targa	TA 009.94	
D-MAKO	Autogyro Europe MT-03	D07G63	A22NIS [USA]
D-MAKP(1)	UPM Cobra BF 52UL Trike	940126	
D-MAKP(2)	Evektor EV-97R Eurostar 2000	2007 2901	
	(W/o 3.6.16)		
D-MAKQ	Autogyro Europe MTOsport	M00850	
D-MAKR(1)	Aerostyle Breezer	068	
D-MAKR(2)	Aerostyle Breezer CR	076	
D-MAKS	Warnke-Trike Lightning	007	
D-MAKT	Flight Design CT LS	F-08-07-19	
D-MAKU	Fresh Breeze 122 AL 2F	88	
D-MAKV	Fresh Breeze Snap SportiX 120	73	
D-MAKW(2)	Aerostyle Breezer C	031	
D-MAKX #	SBM Cloud Dancer II	061 Z1 ZZZ3	
D-MAKY	Fresh Breeze Simo 122	unkn	
D-MAKZ	Eurofly Viper 582 / ASO 12	VIII 62048308	
D-MALA(1)	AS0 Viper 582 / Hazard 15	11039208	
D-MALA(2)	Zenair CH-601XL Zodiac	6-9903	PH-THO
D-MALB(1)	Comco Ikarus Sherpa II	8407-1072	
D-MALB(2)	Schmidtler Enduro 1150 / Kiss 450	03-004	
D-MALC	Fresh Breeze Simo 122	29408	
D-MALD	Fair Fax DR / Hazard 15	D029	
D-MALE	FUL Graffiti MA30 / Stranger	031/0097	
D-MALF	B&F Funk FK-9 Mk.III	09-03U-210	
D-MALG	Fair Fax Trike Euro III	021	
D-MALH	Comco Ikarus C-42B	0205-6440	
D-MALI	Aeroprakt A-22 Vision	unkn	
D-MALJ	Flyitalia MD-3 Rider	24	
D-MALK	Autogyro Europe MTOsport	OE09S01	
D-MALL(1)	Fresh Breeze 110 AL 4B	107	
D-MALL(2)	Fresh Breeze Monster	749	
D-MALM	Plätzer Kiebitz-B8	115	
D-MALN	Comco Ikarus Fox-C22	002	
D-MALO	Take Off Maximum Hazard 15M	T055051	
D-MALP	Alpi Avn Pioneer 200	167	
D-MALQ	Fresh Breeze Simo 122	406	
D-MALR	Behlen Power-Trike Light	007 L	
D-MALS	Light Aero Avid Flyer	618	
D-MALT	Best Off Sky Ranger	399	
D-MALU	NST Minimum Saphir 17	M163	
D-MALV(1)	Fair Fax AH Trike	25	
D-MALV(2)	Fresh Breeze Flyke Simo 122	488	
D-MALW	Flight Team Spider D / Hazard 13	D022	
D-MALX(1)	Autogyro Europe Calidus	unkn	
D-MALX(2)	Aerospool WT-9 Dynamic	022	PH-3S2
D-MALY #	Keller Mosquito A-10 Ghostbuster	NRG-010112-070	
D-MALZ	Büttner Crazyplane III Solo	78	
D-MAMB	Fresh Breeze 122 AL 2F	426	
D-MAMC	WDFL Dallach D4 Fascination BK	130	
D-MAMD	Autogyro Europe MTOsport	D09S27	
D-MAME	Comco Ikarus Fox-C22	9103-3323	
D-MAMF	Bautek Eagle V/ Hazard 15S	03W08	
D-MAMF(2)	Lucknair	unkn	
D-MAMG(1)	Schönleber Enduro KS Speed 14	3585491	
D-MAMG(2)	Aerospool WT-9 Dynamic	DY183/2007	T7-MPA
D-MAMH	Aeros / Profi Athlet	520	
D-MAMI(1)	Comco Ikarus Fox-C22	021	
D-MAMI(2)	B&F Funk FK-9 Mk.4	04-371	
D-MAMJ	Rans S-6 Coyote t/w	08061757 S	
D-MAMK	Fresh Breeze XCitor / XWing	XC2008/100	
D-MAML(1)	B&F Funk FK-14 Polaris	unkn	
	(W/o 28.7.11, Spain)		
D-MAML(2)	Autogyro Europe MTOsport	unkn	
D-MAML(3)	Autogyro Europe Calidus	unkn	
D-MAMM	Fresh Breeze 122 AL 2F	2499	
D-MAMN	Avio Delta Swan I 912 / Ipsos 14.9	MK 04 111 001	
D-MAMO	Alpi Avn Pioneer 300UL	274	
D-MAMR	Steinbach Austro-Trike Euro III	108/85	
D-MAMS	Comco Ikarus C-42B	0304-6541	
D-MAMU	Flight Design CT SW	06-11-03	
D-MAMV #	Flight Design CT-2K	02.05.04.23	
	(Re-registered D-MBDM)		
D-MAMX	Pro.Mec. Freccia 912 ULS	FR 012	
D-MAMY	Fresh Breeze Simo 122	unkn	

Regn	Type	c/n	Notes
D-MAMZ	Autogyro Europe Cavalon	V00019	
D-MANA(1)	FUL Graffiti MA30 / Stranger	unkn	
D-MANA(2)	BRM Aero Bristell UL	081/2014	
D-MANB #	B&F Funk FK-12 Comet	12-081	
D-MANC	Avio Delta Swan I 582 / Ghost 12	02.07.01	
D-MAND	Eurofly Viper / Hazard 15	V15/T17791	
D-MANE(1)	Fresh Breeze 110 AL 2F	57	
D-MANE(2)	Roll-Flight MR V Duo	0105	
D-MANF	Fresh Breeze Bulli-X Monster	BX 503	
D-MANG	Fresh Breeze XCitor / XWing	XC285/2011	
D-MANH #	Keller Mosquito A-10 Zephir	110/696	
D-MANI	Eurofly Viper / Hazard 15	15/12291	
D-MANJ(1)	Behlen Power-Trike	86017	
D-MANJ(2)	PAP 1400 PA parapente	A11 P094-02	
D-MANK	Comco Ikarus C-42B	0204-6471	
D-MANL	Celier Xenon	CAG12Z1B02AA0046	
D-MANN(1)	Scheibe Ultra (Status unknown)	3404	
D-MANN(2)	Firebird Avant (trike)	unkn	
D-MANN(3)	Drachenstudio Royal 912	5508210	
D-MANO	Fair Fax DR / Hazard 15M	D022	
D-MANP	PAP-ROS 125 parapente	56	
D-MANR(1)	Pago Jet M4	951102	
D-MANR(2)	Fresh Breeze Simo 122	SI32.126.17156	
D-MANS #	Fresh Breeze Flyke Simo 122	434	
D-MANT	ATEC Zephyr 2000	ZP 630903	
D-MANU	Roland Z601DX	DX-9517	
D-MANW	Roland Z602XL	Z-9551	
D-MANX	Autogyro Europe MTOsport (Re-regd D-MRWZ)	unkn	
D-MANY(1)	Klüver Bison II Trike	247901	
D-MANY(2)	Flight Design CT SW	06-02-01	
D-MANZ	Schmidtler Enduro / XP 15	02-005	
D-MAOA	Autogyro Europe MTOsport	D09S49	
D-MAOB(1)	Kappa KP-2U Sova (W/o 30.5.11)	8400 I	
D-MAOB(2)	Aerospool WT-9 Dynamic	DY452/2012	
D-MAOC	Pago Jet M4	RB97002	
D-MAOD	Fresh Breeze Super ThoriX	BX780/118	
D-MAOE(1)	NST Minimum Nimbus	M295	
D-MAOE(2)	Magni M-24 Orion	24127034	
D-MAOG	Tecnam P.92S Echo	1033	
D-MAOH	Autogyro Europe MT-03	D07G54	
D-MAOI	Aerospool WT-9 Dynamic	DY169/2007	OM-ALM
D-MAOL	Aerospool WT-9 Dynamic	DY051/2004	OK-JUU 19
D-MAOM	Autogyro Europe MTOsport	D09S24	
D-MAOO	Fresh Breeze XCitor / XWing	XC2008/118	
D-MAOP	Autogyro Europe MTOsport	unkn	
D-MAOR(2)	Comco Ikarus Fox II Doppel	8605-3017	
D-MAOS	Flight Team Twister / Kiss 13	D-002	
D-MAOT(1)	Aeroprakt A-22L-2 Vision (To SP-SAOT)	345	
D-MAOT(2)	Celier Xenon	unkn	
D-MAOW	Rans S-6 Coyote II	0105379	
D-MAOX	Quicksilver GT	unkn	
D-MAPA	Pioneer Flightstar	008 or 383	
D-MAPB	UPM Cobra / Raven	900101	
D-MAPC	AJS Sky-Craft	2000-37	
D-MAPD	Fantasy Air Allegro 2000	02-415	
D-MAPE	WDFL Dallach D4 Fascination BK	117	
D-MAPF	Fresh Breeze 122 AL 2F	516	
D-MAPG	Light Aero Avid Flyer IV	1305	
D-MAPH	NST Minimum Saphir 16	M621	
D-MAPI	Schmidtler Enduro	18/40	
D-MAPK	Drachenstudio Royal / Eos 15	401026	
D-MAPL	Comco Ikarus C-42C	1402-7303	
D-MAPN	Roland Z701 STOL	7-9424	OO-F42, D-MAPN
D-MAPO(1)	NST Minimum Saphir	M86	
D-MAPO(2)	B&F Funk FK-9 ELA	09-05-448	
D-MAPP(1)	NST Minimum	M548	
D-MAPP(2)	Roland Z602XL	Z-9526	
	(Previously quoted as Z-9535 which is D-MADM)		
D-MAPR	Fresh Breeze 122 AL 2F	unkn	
D-MAPS	Fresh Breeze Simo 122	1185	
D-MAPT(1)	Ultraleichtverbund Bi 90 / Chronos 14	553	
D-MAPT(2)	Flight Design CT SW	07-01-19	OE-7122
D-MAPU	Autogyro Europe MTOsport	M00820	
D-MAPV	Remos GX	312	D-MRGX
D-MAPX	Roland S-STOL Sky Jeep	S-9779	
D-MAPY	Autogyro Europe MTOsport	D08S34	
D-MAPZ	Autogyro Europe MTOsport	M00837	
D-MAQB #	NST Minimum Saphir 17	128850	
D-MAQS	Comco Ikarus C-42B	1002-7087	
D-MARA	Fresh Breeze 122 AL 2F	751	
D-MARB	Ultralight Flight Phantom	0311-041001	
D-MARD	Steinbach Austro Trike Euro III	134	
D-MARE	Fresh Breeze 122 AL 2F	1564	
D-MARF(2)	Comco Ikarus Sherpa II	8503-1093	
D-MARF(3)	Fresh Breeze SportiX 122 Simo 122	1500	
D-MARG	Bautek Eagle III / XP12	00 B 03	
D-MARH	Flight Team Spider / Hazard 13M	D005	
D-MARI	FUL Graffiti MA30 / Stranger	0340/0106	
D-MARJ(1)	Klüver Racer SX 12 (To LN-YNN(4))	444904	
D-MARJ(2)	B&F Funk FK-14A Polaris	014-127	
D-MARJ(3)	Roland Z602	D-9578	
D-MARK(1)	Scheibe ULI-1 Rastatt	unkn	
D-MARK(2)	Schmidtler Enduro	unkn	
D-MARK(3)	Solid Air Diamant LP	903388	
D-MARL	Sky-Walker II	322	
D-MARM	Fresh Breeze Simo 122	351	
D-MARN	Comco Ikarus Fox-C22	9004-3262	
D-MARO	Magni M-24 Orion	24138054	
D-MARP(1)	Fresh Breeze Simo 122	unkn	
D-MARP(2)	Nirvana Instinct Simo Mini 2+	376	
D-MARR(2)	ARCO Spacer L	665	
D-MARS	B&F Funk FK-12 Comet (To Z3-UA-005)	12-055	
D-MART #	Fresh Breeze 110 AL 2F	36	
D-MARU	Behlen Power-Trike	91025	
D-MARV	Behlen Power-Trike 582/ Ghost 14.9	unkn	
D-MARW	Ultraleichtverbund Bi 90 / Ipsos 12.9	21216	
D-MARX	Flight Team Spider / XP 15	005	
D-MARY	Aerostyle Breezer	018	
D-MARZ	Comco Ikarus Fox-C22	9110-3369	
D-MASA(1)	Comco Ikarus Fox D	012	
D-MASA(2)	Bautek Eagle V/ Pico	unkn	
D-MASB	Zenair CH-601XL Zodiac	6-9782	
D-MASC	Comco Ikarus Fox-C22	9205-3375	
D-MASD	Buttner Crazy Flyer	26	
D-MASE	Behlen Power-Trike 582 / Ghost 12	980014	
D-MASF(1)	Warnke Skylight Trike	031	
D-MASF(2)#	Comco Ikarus C-42B	0604-6813	
D-MASG(1)	Comco Ikarus C-42B	0407-6616	
	(To SE-VOY, 3.11)		
D-MASG(2)	Flight Design CT SW	07-08-26	
D-MASH(2)	Comco Ikarus C-42B	0404-6599	
D-MASI	Fresh Breeze 122 AL 2F	377	
D-MASJ	Flight Team Twister / iXess	D003	
D-MASK	Fresh Breeze 110 AL 2F	451	
D-MASM(1)	Schmidtler Ranger M	1813	
D-MASM(2)	Comco Ikarus C-42	unkn	
D-MASM(3)	Autogyro Europe Cavalon	V00018	
D-MASN	Comco Ikarus C-42B	0903-7031	
D-MASO(1)	Sonic	unkn	
D-MASO(2)	Vidor Asso V Champion	003	
D-MASP(1)	Sonic	unkn	
D-MASP(2)	Alpi Avn Pioneer 300	329	
D-MASQ	Zenair CH-601D Zodiac	6-9931	
D-MASR	Comco Ikarus Fox-C22	9009-3293	
D-MASS	Scheibe Ultra	3401	
D-MAST	Flight Team Twister / XP 15	01	
D-MASU	Plätzer Kiebitz	unkn	
D-MASV	Flight Design CT SW	07-03-22	
D-MASW(1)	Sky-Walker II	167	
D-MASW(2)	Remos GX	unkn	
D-MASX	Comco Ikarus Fox-C22	9106-3327	
D-MASY	Aerostyle Breezer C	022	
D-MASZ	Comco Ikarus C-42B	0310-6573	
D-MATA	Kluver Racer Quartz / SX 12	080303	
D-MATB #	Krampen Ikarus S	53	
D-MATC(1)	Dallach D4 Sunwheel	unkn	
D-MATC(2)	Avio Delta Swan I 582 / Pico	unkn	
D-MATC(3)	BRM Aero Bristell UL	034/2012	
D-MATD	Fresh Breeze Skip One 122 AL 2F	314	
D-MATE	Sky-Walker II		
D-MATF	ATEC Zephyr 2000	Z 750403 S	
D-MATG	B&F Funk Fk-9 Utility MkIV	09-04U-288	
D-MATH	Sky Rider NDA	unkn	
D-MATI	Best Off Sky Ranger	469	
D-MATJ	Raj Hamsa X'Air F	003	
D-MATK #	Schönleber DS Lotus / Vento	01/0190	
D-MATL	ARCO Spacer L	11812	
D-MATM	Fresh Breeze Monster	1095	
D-MATN	Flight Design CT-2K	04-04-04	
D-MATO	Keller Mosquito NRG Atos	010829-155	
D-MATP	Klüver Racer Quartz SX 12	080303	
D-MATR	Fläming Air FA-01 Smaragd	01/03	
D-MATR(2)	Aerostyle Breezer	069	
D-MATS	Remos G-3	212	LY-BIZ, D-MRPJ
D-MATT	NST Minimum	M416	
D-MATU	Fresh Breeze Flyke Monster	812	
D-MATV	Nirvana Rodeo 125 Simo Mini 2+	612472	
D-MATW	Albatros	116	
D-MATX	Comco Ikarus C-42B	0906-7053	
D-MATY	Plätzer Kiebitz B	236	
D-MATZ(1)	Scheibe Uli 1	5207	
D-MATZ(2)	Air Création / Kiss	A01145-1148	
D-MATZ(3)	Schmidtler Enduro / Mild 16	02-018	
D-MAUA(1)	Fresh Breeze Simo 122	unkn	
D-MAUA(2)	Cosmos Phase II / Top 14.9	B21453	
D-MAUD	TL Ultralight TL-3000 Sirius	12Si61	
D-MAUG	Fresh Breeze Simo 122	1064	
D-MAUI	Aériane Sirocco II	031	
D-MAUL	Take Off Merlin 1100 / EOS	112804	
D-MAUM	Drachenstudio Royal / Avant 17	12-0496	
D-MAUN #	Behlen Power Trike Vampir II	89016	
D-MAUS	Flight Team Spider / XP 12	D045	
D-MAUT(1)	Autogyro Europe MT-03	05G09	
D-MAUT(2)	Autogyro Europe MTOsport (W/o 16.7.11)	unkn	
D-MAUZ	Fresh Breeze Monster 4	7	
D-MAVA	Schmidtler Enduro 582 / BioniX 15	02-028	
D-MAVB	Comco Ikarus Fox-C22	9109-3335	
D-MAVE	Comco Ikarus C-42B	1309-7274	
D-MAVG	Autogyro Europe MTOsport	M00873	
D-MAVH	Löbenstein Racer / Quartz SX 12	001	
D-MAVI	Light Aero Avid Flyer IV	441	
D-MAVJ	Cosmos Phase II / Top 12.9	2 15 10	
D-MAVK	Rans S-6 Coyote II	0792329	
D-MAVL	Autogyro Europe Cavalon	V00040	
D-MAVM	Blackshape Prime CF300	14	I-X010(1)
D-MAVR #	Solid Air Diamant LP / Pico L	LP31	
D-MAVS(1)	Kümmerle Mini-Fly-Set	1270/91-5	
D-MAVS(2)	Drachenstudio Royal 912 / Pico S	250921	
D-MAVU	Roland Z602	Z-9580	
D-MAVV	Autogyro Europe Calidus	C00134	
D-MAVY	Light Aero Avid Speedwing	645	F-WRFU
D-MAWA #	Corvus CA-21 Phantom	034	
	(Now reported as Corvus Fusion with same c/n)		
D-MAWB	Fresh Breeze 110 AL 2F	219	
D-MAWC	Autogyro Europe MT-03	unkn	
D-MAWD	ASO Viper 582 / Ghost 12	10504	
D-MAWE(1)	UL-F Jochum Eagle III	970502	
	(Possibly re-regd, same c/n quoted for D-MKME)		
D-MAWE(2)	Fresh Breeze Simo 122	897	
D-MAWF(1)	Remos GX NXT	412	
	(W/o 7.7.12)		
D-MAWF(2)	Remos GX	425	
D-MAWG	Apis BEE 15 MB	A034MB07	
D-MAWH	Eurofly Viper 582 / Hazard 13	12033206	
D-MAWI	Comco Ikarus Fox-C22	8807-3140	
D-MAWK	Autogyro Europe MT-03	D08G09	
D-MAWL #	Sky-Walker II	391	
D-MAWM	Rans S-6 Coyote II	1011 1949 S	
D-MAWN	Fresh Breeze SportiX 122 Simo 122	1286	
D-MAWO #	Comco Ikarus Fox-C22	8907-3198	
D-MAWP	Avio Delta Swan I 582 / Pico	MK 05 08 07 01	
D-MAWR	Comco Ikarus C-42B	0305-6528	
D-MAWS	Fresh Breeze 110 AL2F	152	
D-MAWT(1)	NST Minimum SierrAIIM	151	
D-MAWT(2)	Silent Glider M	unkn	
D-MAWW	Behlen Power-Trike 582 / Pico	9800015	

Reg	Type	c/n	Notes
D-MAWX	AirLony Skylane UL	47	
D-MAWZ #	Fresh Breeze 122 AL 2F	1106	
D-MAXA	Autogyro Europe MT-03	05G10	
D-MAXB	Comco Ikarus C-42B	0611-6858	
D-MAXC	Vagabund	unkn	
D-MAXD	Fresh Breeze Simo 122	1066	
D-MAXE(1)	Cosmos / Top 14.9	21313	
D-MAXE(2)	Fresh Breeze XCitor / XWing	XC2010/162	
D-MAXG	B&F Funk FK-12 Comet	12-087	
	(To 95-IL, 57-AXT, PH-4P5)		
D-MAXH	Fresh Breeze SportiX 122 Simo 122	unkn	
D-MAXI	Fresh Breeze 110 AL 2F	408	
D-MAXJ	Fresh Breeze Simo 110	M21155	
D-MAXK	Flight Design CT LS	F-09-09-15	
D-MAXL	Tecnam P.92 Echo 100S	663	
	(W/o 23.3.12)		
D-MAXM	Phönix Skywalker 210	0037	
D-MAXN	Fresh Breeze 122 AL 2F	857	
D-MAXO	Fresh Breeze 122 AL 2F	509	
D-MAXP	Fly Products Race C Fly 100 EVO	061091	
D-MAXQ	Aeros Nanolight Trike Combat 12T	04.14.028/024.14	
D-MAXR	EDM Aerotec CoAX 2D	3	
D-MAXS	Comco Ikarus Fox-C22	9303-3496	
D-MAXT	WDFL Sunwheel R	003	
D-MAXU	Flyitalia MD-3 Rider	101	
D-MAXV(1)	Autogyro Europe Calidus 912	D10C01	
D-MAXV(2)	Shark Aero Shark UL	039/2015	(LN-YNR)
D-MAXW #	Behlen Power-Trike	85012	
D-MAXX(1)	Alpha Aero Tech Spotter G97	unkn	
D-MAXX(2)	Flight Design CT SW	07.10.23	
D-MAXY(2)	Flight Design CT SW	04.03.03	
D-MAYA(1)	Kümmerle Mini-Fly-Set Saphir 17	258/86-4	
D-MAYA(2)	Tecnam P.92 Echo SW	1502	
D-MAYB	Alpi Avn Pioneer 300UL	269	
D-MAYC	Zlin Savage Cruiser	206	
D-MAYD	Autogyro Europe MTOsport	unkn	
D-MAYG	Comco Ikarus C-42	1206-7209	
D-MAYI	Flight Design CT SW	06-05-03	
D-MAYK	Drachenstudio Regal 912ULS / EOS-15	530210	
D-MAYM	ELA Aviacion ELA-07/S	03.123.560.722	
D-MAYO	Comco Ikarus C-42B	0502-6658	
D-MAYP	Magni M-24 Orion	24116834	
D-MAYR	Roland S-STOL Sky Jeep	7-9607	
D-MAYS	Evektor EV-97R Eurostar 2000	2006 2819	
D-MAYT	Junkers L582 / Pico S	094002/II	
D-MAYW	Comco Ikarus C-42B	0702-6870	
D-MAYZ	Autogyro Europe MTOsport	D08G08	
D-MAZA	Comco Ikarus Fox-C22	9208-3386	
D-MAZD(1)	UPM Funplane Lotus 18	003	
D-MAZD(2)	Fresh Breeze Simo 122	0783139680	
D-MAZE	Fresh Breeze 122 AL 2F	2158	
D-MAZF	Fresh Breeze Simo 122	1368	
D-MAZH	Kümmerle Mini-Fly-Set Saphir 17M	127950	
D-MAZI	Fresh Breeze 122 AL 2F	2274	
D-MAZL	Comco Ikarus C-42B	0809-7011	
D-MAZM	Fresh Breeze 122 AL 2F	6	
D-MAZP #	Schmidtler Enduro / XP 15	02-25/A01010-1007	
D-MAZR	Drachenstudio Royal 912 / EOS	360825	
D-MAZS #	Zlin Savage Classic	094	
D-MAZT	Kümmerle Mini-Fly-Set	1312916	
D-MAZW	Fresh Breeze 122 AL 2F	unkn	
D-MAZY	Plätzer Kiebitz B	345	
D-MAZZ	Schmidtler Enduro / Mild 16	02-008	
D-MBAA	Silent Glider M	04	
D-MBAB	TL Ultralight TL-96 Sting	08ST295	
D-MBAC	Sky-Walker II	205	
D-MBAD	Behlen Power-Trike	89000109	
D-MBAE(1)	Klüver Racer SX 12	834012	
D-MBAE(2)	Fresh Breeze Flyke Monster	22	
D-MBAF	ASO Viper 462 / Hazard 15	unkn	
D-MBAG	Aquilair Swing 582 / Ghost 14.9	400-3201	
D-MBAH	Aeroprakt A-22L2 Vision	448	
D-MBAI	Fresh Breeze Simo 122	1052	
D-MBAJ	NST Minimum Atos	M967	
D-MBAK	Bek ME 109R replica	001	
D-MBAL	Comco Ikarus Fox-C22	9110-3384	
D-MBAM	Remos G-3-600	unkn	
	(W/o 21.5.11)		
D-MBAN(1)	Dallach Sunrise II	010	
D-MBAN(2)	Drachenstudio Royal 912S / EOS	470428	
	(W/o 22.7.12)		
D-MBAN(3)	Remos GX	434	
	(To N434GX, 7.16)		
D-MBAN(4)	Comco Ikarus C-42	unkn	
D-MBAO(1)	Behlen Trike Vampir II	87027	
D-MBAO(2)	Autogyro Europe MTOsport	M01188	
D-MBAP	Drachenstudio Royal 912 / EOS	510429	
D-MBAR	Ultralight Flight Phantom	410	
D-MBAS(1)	HFL Stratos 300K	300-009K	
D-MBAS(2)	Take Off Merlin 1200 / EOS	47401	
D-MBAT	UPM Funplane / Profil 19M	900085	
D-MBAU(1)	Büttner Crazyplane III	003	
D-MBAU(2)	Büttner Crazy Flyer	61	
D-MBAW	Plätzer Kiebitz-B	033	
D-MBAY	Take Off Merlin 1100 / Avant	45201	
D-MBAZ	Fresh Breeze Monster	377	
D-MBBA(1)	Comco Ikarus Fox-C22	9202-3377	
D-MBBA(2)	Autogyro Europe MTOsport	D07G10	
D-MBBC	Plätzer Kiebitz-B	100	
	(Dbr 7.11.15)		
D-MBBD	Evektor EV-97 Eurostar SLW Sport	2014 4112	
D-MBBE	LO-120	EB 001	
D-MBBF	Autogyro Europe MTOsport	D06G06	
D-MBBG	Fresh Breeze XCitor	XC 2006/22	
D-MBBH	Krampen Ikarus S	65	
D-MBBI	Fresh Breeze 110 AL 2F	40	
D-MBBJ	Flight Design CT SW	07-10-16	
D-MBBK	FD Composites Arrowcopter AC20	005	OE-XAB, OE-VXR
D-MBBL	Take Off Merlin / Titan	21193	
D-MBBM	Plätzer Kiebitz-B6	023	
D-MBBN	HFL Stratos IIe	002	
D-MBBO	Fresh Breeze 110 AL2F	96	
D-MBBP	Fresh Breeze Simo 122	1536	
D-MBBQ	Autogyro Europe MTOsport	D09S50	
D-MBBR(1)	Scheibe Uli 1	5205	
D-MBBR(2)	Drachenstudio Royal 912 / Avant	190598	
D-MBBS	Comco Ikarus Fox-C22	9206-3412	
D-MBBT(1)	FUL Graffiti Trike	036/0102	
D-MBBT(2)	Autogyro Europe MTOsport	D10S33	
D-MBBU	Fresh Breeze 122 AL2F	961	
D-MBBV	Fresh Breeze Monster	47	
D-MBBW(1)	Comco Ikarus Fox-C22	9201-3372	
D-MBBW(2)	Tecnam P.92S Echo 100	518	
D-MBBX	Tecnam P.96 Golf 100	020	
	(Same c/n quoted as D-MRKD)		
D-MBBY	Autogyro Europe MTOsport	unkn	
D-MBBZ	Keller Mosquito NRG Atos	NR5030310-298/04	
D-MBCA(2)	Schmidtler Enduro / XP 15	02-015	
D-MBCB(1)	Albatros 64	166	
D-MBCB(2)	Fresh Breeze 122 AL2F	1117	
D-MBCC	Zlin Savage Classic	102	
	(Also reported as a Magni gyro, cld?)		
D-MBCD(2)	Dallach Sunrise IIA	030	
	(Same c/n as D-MMDB but different aircraft)		
D-MBCE	Büttner Crazyplane III Solo	86	
D-MBCG(1)	Aeroprakt A-22L Vision	264	
	(To OK-PUR 08)		
D-MBCG(2)	Aeroprakt A-22L Vision	335	SP-SIEK
D-MBCH	Scheibe Ultra	3409	
D-MBCI	Fly Synthesis Storch HS	FACF 4700 A13C	
D-MBCK	Alpi Aviation Pioneer 200UL	108	(F)55-SA/F-JUKR, D-MPTF
D-MBCL	Flight Design CT LS	07-12-17	I-9282
D-MBCM	B&F Funk FK-9 Mk.IV ELA	431-TG	
D-MBCN	Take Off Merlin / Avant	205093	
D-MBCO	Aerostyle Breezer	042	
	(Also marked T2B04529)		
D-MBCP	Autogyro Europe MT-03	D06G35	
D-MBCR(1)	Magni M-16 Tandem Trainer	unkn	
D-MBCR(2)	Aeropilot Legend 540	1418	
D-MBCS(1)	Magni M-14 Scout	14-02-1953	
D-MBCS(2)	Zenair CH-601D Zodiac	1402195372002	
D-MBCT(1)	Behlen Power-Trike	89014	
D-MBCT(2)	Flight Design CT SL	E-12-01-04	
D-MBCV	Fläming Air Peregrine SL	122/11	
D-MBCW	Autogyro Europe Cavalon	V00025	
D-MBCX	Remos GX	403	
D-MBCY(1)	Magni M-16 Tandem Trainer	16053274	
D-MBCY(2)	Magni M-24TT Orion	unkn	
D-MBCZ	Magni M-14 Scout	14-04-2713	
D-MBDA	Adventure Funflyer Tiger 160	QHTM 4913	
D-MBDB	Comco Ikarus Fox D	005	
D-MBDC	Bautek Eagle III/ Ipsos 14.9	2000/04/09	
D-MBDD(1)	Kümmerle Mini-Fly-Set	1084-1	
D-MBDD(2)	Fresh Breeze Simo 122	415	
D-MBDE	NST Minimum Saphir 17	34765	
D-MBDF	Zenair CH-701 STOL	7-9479	
D-MBDG	Dyn'Aéro MCR-01 ULC	194	
D-MBDH(1)	Comco Ikarus C-42B	unkn	
D-MBDH(2)	Motorparafly X-Max	48713	
D-MBDI	Next Aircraft MD-3 Rider	unkn	
D-MBDJ	Comco Ikarus Fox-C22C	9606-3709	PH-2W8
D-MBDK	Autogyro Europe MT-03	D07G14	
D-MBDM	Flight Design CT-2K	02.05.04.23	D-MAMV
D-MBDN	Ekolot JK-05 Junior	unkn	
D-MBDP	Ekolot KR-030 Topaz	30-05-08	
D-MBDQ	Fresh Breeze Simo 122	2529	
D-MBDR	Ekolot JK-05 Junior	05-09-06	
D-MBDS	Rans S-6 Coyote II	0293446	
D-MBDW	Fresh Breeze 122 AL2F	1455	
D-MBEA(1)	MKB Ranger M	0100785	
D-MBEA(2)	Flight Design CT SW	07-02-19	
D-MBEB	Fresh Breeze Monster	unkn	
D-MBEC	Light Aero Avid Flyer	808	
D-MBED	Fresh Breeze XCitor	XC 308/2013	
D-MBEE	Behlen Power-Trike 582 / Pico S	980021	
D-MBEF	HFL Stratos 300	300-002	
D-MBEG	Me 109 Scale Replica	003	
D-MBEH	AirLony Skylane C100	unkn	
D-MBEI	Schmidtler Enduro 582 / Speed 14	010293	
D-MBEJ	EEL ULF-2	17	
D-MBEK(2)	Behlen Power-Trike 582 / Ghost 14.9	980022	
D-MBEL	Cosmos Phase II / Top 12.9	21298	
D-MBEM	Take Off Merlin 1100 / Avant	181.064	
D-MBEN	Fresh Breeze 122 AL 2F	241	
D-MBEO	Plätzer Kiebitz-B	048	
D-MBEP #	Fresh Breeze 122 AL 2F	1710	
D-MBER	Fresh Breeze 122 AL 2F	207	
D-MBES(1)	Fisher FP-202 Koala	1988/1/1	
D-MBES(2)	Tecnam P.92 Echo 100S	662	
D-MBET(1)	Tandem Air Sunny Sport	22.91	
D-MBET(2)	Steyr Redstar	H125/44	
D-MBEU	Alisport Silent Club	22	
D-MBEW(1)	Behlen Power-Trike	877947/900/12	
D-MBEW(2)	Fair Fax Trike Euro III	unkn	
D-MBEX	Comco Ikarus C-42B	0206-6466	
D-MBEZ	WDFL D4BK Fascination	066	PH-3J2
D-MBFA(1)	UPM Cobra Raven Trike	91108	
	(Correct c/n may be 910108)		
D-MBFA(2)	WDFL Sunwheel	011	OE-7022
D-MBFC(1)	Ultraleichtverbund Bi 90	21312	
D-MBFC(2)	Behlen Power-Trike / Vampir II	91025	
D-MBFE	Autogyro Europe Cavalon	V00156	
D-MBFF	Konsuprod Mosquito IB	016	
D-MBFH	Flight Design CT SW	04-07-04	PH-3V4
D-MBFI(1)	Autogyro Europe MT-03	unkn	
D-MBFI(2)	Flight Design CT SW	06-10-26	T7-MAX
D-MBFJ	Comco Ikarus C-42B	0404-6606	
D-MBFK	Comco Ikarus Fox-C22	9208-3437	
D-MBFL	Fresh Breeze XCitor	XC 2005/07	
D-MBFM	Rans S-10 Sakota	0189040	
D-MBFN	Ekolot JK-05 Junior	05-09-04	
D-MBFO	Fresh Breeze Simo 122	923	
D-MBFR	Light Aero Avid Flyer IV	1103	
D-MBFS	Fresh Breeze Bulli-X Monster	unkn	
D-MBFU	Autogyro Europe MTOsport	M01012	
D-MBFW	Light Aero Avid Flyer IV	1102	
D-MBFZ	Evektor EV-97R Eurostar 2000	2007 2922	
D-MBGB	Silent Glider M	015	
D-MBGD	Best Off Sky Ranger Swift	916/988	
D-MBGE	Nando Groppo Trail	59/18	
D-MBGG	Comco Ikarus C-42B	0208-6497	
D-MBGH	Behlen Power-Trike 582 / Ghost 12	950002	

Regn	Type	C/n	Notes
D-MBGL	Vagabund	14	
D-MBGM	Autogyro Europe Calidus	C00136	
D-MBGO	Autogyro Europe MTOsport	D09S11	
D-MBGP	Autogyro Europe MTOsport	M01109	
D-MBGR(1)	FUL Graffiti Trike	027/0093	
D-MBGR(2)	Ekolot KR.030 Topaz	30-04-07	
	(Now known as Galaxy High Technology KR-30 Topaz)		
D-MBGR(3)	Galaxy KR-30 Topaz	unkn	
	(W/o 23.4.14 Leutkirch)		
D-MBGS	Autogyro Europe MTOsport	D09S52	
D-MBGT	Remos G.3 Mirage	056	
D-MBGW	Flight Design CT-2K	02.05.01.20	
D-MBGX	Remos GX Voyager	323	
D-MBHA	Remos G.3 Mirage	140	
D-MBHB(1)	ICP MXP-640 Amigo !	001	
D-MBHB(2)	Podesva Chico		
D-MBHD	Comco Ikarus C-42B	0909-7062	
D-MBHE	B&F Funk FK-9 Mk.IV	09-367	
	(To LN-YMQ(2), 7.09)		
D-MBHF	B&F Funk FK-14B2 Polaris	014-119	
D-MBHG(1)	Aériane Sirocco	140	
D-MBHG(2)	B&F Funk FK-9 Mk.IV	09-04-408	
D-MBHH(1)	Pioneer Flightstar	384	
	(Sold as N269KT)		
D-MBHH(2)	B&F Funk FK-9 ELA Professional	09-05-467	
D-MBHI	Fresh Breeze Simo 122	M22570	
D-MBHJ	Comco Ikarus Fox-C22	9309-3508	
D-MBHK	NST Minimum Twister	M 1005	
D-MBHL	Flight Design CT-2K	02.03.06.15	
	(Damaged 29.4.12)		
D-MBHM(1)	UPM Funplane	850001	
D-MBHM(2)	Aeroprakt A-22L2 Vision	518	
D-MBHO	Flight Team Spider / XP 15	D016	
D-MBHP	Magni M-24 Orion	24148444	
D-MBHR	Air Création GT 582S / XP 15	0494	
D-MBHS	Ital-Festa Fly Angel Walkerjet RR	M23239	
D-MBHT	Fresh Breeze 110 AL 2F	158	
D-MBHU	Flylight Dragonfly	228	
D-MBHV	Autogyro Europe MT-03	D07G15	
D-MBHW(1)	Fresh Breeze 122 AL 2F	420	
D-MBHW(2)	Autogyro Europe MTOsport	M00926	
D-MBHX	Air Création Tanarg 912 / BioniX 13	T14023	
D-MBIA	Comco Ikarus Fox-C22	9202-3385	
D-MBIB	Aeropro Eurofox	15604	
D-MBIC	Fresh Breeze 110 AL 2F	151	
D-MBIE(1)	Aeroprakt A-22L Vision	unkn	
D-MBIE(2)	Magni M-24 Orion	24148774	
D-MBIG	Pipistrel Virus SW 100	388	
D-MBIH	Aeropro Eurofox	10201	PH-3L4
D-MBII	Comco Ikarus C-42B	0207-6495	
D-MBIK	Comco Ikarus C-42B	0612-6859	
D-MBIL	Plätzer Kiebitz-B4	082	
D-MBIM #	Keller Mosquito NRG Atos	060705-256	
D-MBIN	ICP MXP-740 Savannah S	S11-02-54-0074	
D-MBIO	Roland CH-701 S-STOL	S-9782	
D-MBIP	Fresh Breeze XCitor	XC 2010/169	
D-MBIR #	Fresh Breeze 110 AL 2F	361	
D-MBIS #	Behlen Power-Trike Light	2002/002L	
D-MBIT	Plätzer Kiebitz-B	201	
D-MBIW	Behlen Power-Trike 582 / Pico	2011	
D-MBIX #	Breezer UL	unkn	
D-MBIZ	Comco Ikarus C-42B	0504-6680	
D-MBJE	AirLony Skylane	68	
D-MBJH	ASO Viper / Bautek wing	unkn	
D-MBJJ	Behlen Power-Trike II	2008-001 B	
D-MBJK #	Klüver Bison Trike	089706	
D-MBJM	Adventure A4	2604	
D-MBJR(1)	Take Off Maximum Karat 13	083121	
D-MBJR(2)	B&F Funk FK-14 Polaris	14-107	
D-MBJS(1)	Rans S-10 Sakota	unkn	
D-MBJS(2)	Fresh Breeze ThoriX Thor 100	91	
D-MBJU	Junkers Profly JUL / Ghost 14.9	95/1201	
D-MBJW #	Fresh Breeze 122 AL 2F	1783	
D-MBKA	B&F Funk Fk-9 Mk.III	09-03-200	
D-MBKD	Evektor EV-97 Eurostar SLW	2011 3917	
D-MBKE(1)	Air Création GTE 582S	7954557569	
D-MBKE(2)	ICP MXP-740 Savannah S	10-07-54-0013	
D-MBKF	Aerostyle Breezer	065	
D-MBKG #	Ultraleichtverbund Bi 90	21090	
D-MBKH	Aerostyle Breezer	051	
D-MBKI	Autogyro Europe MTOsport	unkn	
D-MBKK	Eagle Air Ghostbuster / Ghost 12R	95001	
D-MBKL	Fly Synthesis Storch HS	282	
D-MBKM	Flight Design CT LS	F-11-05-10	
D-MBKN	Fresh Breeze Simo 122	909	
D-MBKO	BOT Speed Cruiser SC07	006	
D-MBKP #	Fresh Breeze Flyke Monster	595	
D-MBKS #	NST Minimum Zephir	M548	
D-MBKT	Fresh Breeze 122 AL 2F	1625	
D-MBKU	Tecnam P.92 Echo S100	484	D-MYXY
D-MBKV	Autogyro Europe MTOsport	M00907	
D-MBKW	Wezel Flug. Apis 2	004	
D-MBKY	Celier Xenon XL	CAL10574R	
D-MBLA	BRM Aero Bristell UL	128/2015	
D-MBLB	Plätzer Kiebitz B	250	
D-MBLC	Vogt LO-120S	006	
D-MBLF	Sky-Service Pago Jet M4	95302	
D-MBLG	Flight Design CT SW	04-07-02	
D-MBLH	Autogyro Europe MTOsport	unkn	
D-MBLI	Behlen Power-Trike	94001	
D-MBLK	Celier Xenon	CAL09773R	
D-MBLL	Drachenstudio Royal 912 / Eos	unkn	
D-MBLN	Plätzer Motte B2	32	
D-MBLP	Ultraleichtverbund Bi 90	21239	
D-MBLR	B&F Funk FK-9 Mk.IV	09-04-248	
D-MBLS #	ASO Viper Trike	VIII 22071503	
D-MBLU	Tecnam P.92 Echo Super	unkn	
D-MBLV	Fresh Breeze Simo 122	unkn	
D-MBLW	NST Minimum Zephir	M440	
D-MBMA	Ultraleichtverbund Bi 90	7894016045	
D-MBMB	NST Skylark	0474	
D-MBME	Comco Ikarus C-42B	0306-6560	
D-MBMG	Behlen Power-Trike Vampir II	89023	
D-MBMH	Ultraleichtverbund Bi 90	927	
D-MBMI	Rans S-12 Airaile	1092298	
D-MBML	Flight Design CT SL	E-11-12-01	
D-MBMM	Dova DV-1 Skylark	7/40	
D-MBMW(1)	Schmidtler Enduro Focus 18	M868086	
D-MBMW(2)	BRM Aero NG5 Bristell	unkn	
D-MBND(1)	Autogyro Europe MTOsport	unkn	
D-MBND(2)	Comco Ikarus C-42C	1403-7308	
D-MBNK	Magni M-16 Tandem Trainer	16021874	
D-MBNN(1)	Ultraleicht Wildente-2	unkn	
	(Now in Meseburg museum)		
D-MBNN(2)	Impulse 100	17	
D-MBNS #	Büttner Crazyplane III	7	
D-MBNX	B&F Funk FK-9 Mk.IV ELA (t/w)	unkn	
D-MBNY	Light Aero Avid Flyer IV	1228	
D-MBOA	Aerospool WT-9 Dynamic	DY402/2011	
D-MBOC	HFL Stratos 300	300-007	
D-MBOD #	NST Minimum Saphir	M159	
D-MBOE	Flight Design CT Supralight	E-10-08-15	
D-MBOF	Autogyro Europe MTOsport	unkn	
D-MBOG	CzAW/Zenair CH-601XL Zodiac	6-7405	PH-4D4
D-MBOK	Alpi Avn Pioneer 200	unkn	
D-MBOL	Sky-Walker II	263	
D-MBON	Aeropro Eurofox	16804	OE-7111
D-MBOP(1)	Schönleber DS Speed KS 14	L04/0489	
D-MBOP(2)	Zlin Savage Classic	unkn	
D-MBOS	J-3 Kitten	8610-3	
D-MBOX	Plätzer Kiebitz-B	219	OO-F64, D-MUAT
	(To 83-GAA/F-JGAA)		
D-MBOY	UPM Cobra Raven Trike	900092	
	(Same c/n also quoted for D-MULB)		
D-MBOZ(1)	WDFL Dallach F100 Fascination	17	
D-MBOZ(2)	WD4 Fascination Fasbo 100	01	
D-MBPA(1)	Autogyro Europe MTOsport	unkn	
D-MBPA(2)	Autogyro Europe Calidus	D10C21	
D-MBPB(1)	Fresh Breeze Simo 122	unkn	
D-MBPB(2)	PAP Marabella 1400PA	unkn	
D-MBPC(1)	Drachenstudio Royal 912 / Avant 15	unkn	
D-MBPC(2)	Aero Bristell E-LSA	052	
D-MBPH	FUL Graffiti MA 30 Maverick II	042/01421	
D-MBPM	Fresh Breeze Simo 122	49.129.17481	
D-MBPO	Fresh Breeze Simo 122	265	
D-MBPP #	Fresh Breeze 122 AL 2F	780	
D-MBPQ	Fresh Breeze 122 AL 2F	463	
D-MBPR #	Behlen Power-Trike	88017	
D-MBPS	Tecnam P.92 Echo De Luxe	1315	PH-4F6
D-MBPT	Rans S-6 Coyote II	07971140	
D-MBPU #	Blackshape Prime	unkn	
D-MBPV #	MKB Enduro Focus 18M	00187	
D-MBPW	Tandem Air Sunny Sport	006	
D-MBPY	Fresh Breeze 122 AL 2F	421	
D-MBPZ	Rans S-12 Airaile	0395568	
D-MBRA(1)	Cosmos Trike	B21514	
D-MBRA(2)	Ultraleichtverbund Bi 90/Ghost 14.9	2 15 11	
D-MBRB	Ultralight Flight Phantom T-44	328	
D-MBRD	Comco Ikarus C-42B	0207-6468	
D-MBRE(1)	Flight Team Spider	D041	
D-MBRE(2)	Aerospool WT-9 Dynamic	DY492/2014	
D-MBRF	Mosquito NRG Atos	573	
D-MBRG	Aerostyle Breezer	047	D-MOBC, D-MBRG, G-90-2, D-MBRG
D-MBRH	Air Création GTE / iXess 15	S4173187195	
D-MBRI	Autogyro Europe Cavalon	V00048	
D-MBRK	Rans S-6 Coyote II	0992357	
D-MBRP(1)	Fresh Breeze 110 AL4H	21	
D-MBRP(2)	Autogyro Europe MTOsport	D08S18	
D-MPRR	Fresh Breeze Zcitor	XC2006/23	
D-MBRT	Drachenstudio Royal Trike	01-9610	
D-MBRU	Tomark Skyper GT9	0006	
D-MBRW	Bautek Eagle V/Pico	04 B 13	
D-MBRZ	Aerostyle Breezer	033	
D-MBSA	Fresh Breeze Simo 122	346	
D-MBSB	Behlen Power-Trike / Ghost 12	940023	
D-MBSC	Plätzer Kiebitz B9	315	
D-MBSD	Fresh Breeze Simo 122	1408-17015	
D-MBSE	ARCO Spacer L	1178	
D-MBSF	Behlen Power-Trike /Rotax 582	97006	
D-MBSG(1)	Flight Design CT SW	04-05-03	
D-MBSG(2)	Flight Design CT SW	05-07-03	
D-MBSH	Flight Design CT SW	06-08-16	
D-MBSI	Fresh Breeze Simo 122	5211/0311	
D-MBSJ	UL-F Jochum Eagle III / Pico	980907	
D-MBSK	Comco Ikarus Fox-C22	9105-3325	
D-MBSL	Comco Ikarus C-42B	0702-6869	
D-MBSM	Dallach Sunrise II	005	
D-MBSN	Fresh Breeze 122 AL 2F	1781	
D-MBSO(1)	NST Minimum	M551	
D-MBSO(2)	Fresh Breeze Simo 122	86	
D-MBSP	Autogyro Europe Cavalon	unkn	
D-MBSR #	NST Minimum Zephir	421	
D-MBSS(1)	Comco Ikarus C-42B	0308-6549	
D-MBSS(2)	Autogyro Europe MT-03	unkn	
D-MBSS(3)	Flight Design CT SW	D-11-07-08	
D-MBST	Comco Ikarus Fox-C22	9308-3516	
D-MBSU	FUL Graffiti Trike	024/0090	
D-MBSV #	Drachenstudio Royal Trike	150996	
D-MBSW	Sky Walker II	161	
D-MBSX	Albatros SX	200	
D-MBSY	Bautek Eagle V / Profi 14.5 TL	12 W 12	
D-MBSZ	Fresh Breeze Bulli-X Monster Big Wheel	1176	
D-MBTA	Trixy G4-2R	003-12	
	Trixy G4-2 Liberty	049-16	
	(Test & demo registration for Trixy Avn Products GmbH, various users)		
D-MBTB #	Drachenstudio Royal Karat 13	02-9308	
	(Regn now used as test marks for Trixy Avn G4s)		
D-MBTD	Flight Design CT SW	07-09-07	
D-MBTF	Autogyro Europe MTOsport	M01006	
D-MBTG	B&F Funk FK-14 Polaris	14-126	
D-MBTI	Sunny	unkn	
D-MBTK	Fresh Breeze Simo 122	1568	
D-MBTL #	NST Minimum	M221	
D-MBTM	Trixy G4-2 R	037-14	
D-MBTN	Trixy G4-2 Liberty	unkn	D-MBTB
D-MBTP	Dova DV-1 Skylark	154/12	
D-MBTR	Trixy Former	unkn	
D-MBTS	Solid Air Diamant Twin	T-009	
D-MBTT	Tandem Air Sunny Targa	TA 008.93	
D-MBTU	Rans S-6 Coyote II	1293572	
D-MBTV	Adventure A4 Puissance	DMM23428	

Registration	Type	C/n	Notes
D-MBTW	Pipistrel Sinus	788SNLTF912	
D-MBTX #	Warnke Trike	SI 033	
D-MBTY	Flight Design CT LS	F-11-01-04	
D-MBTZ(1)	Autogyro Europe MTOsport	unkn	
D-MBTZ(2)	Trixy Spirit	unkn	
D-MBUB	Comco Ikarus C-42B	0906-7048	
D-MBUC	Comco Ikarus C-42	unkn	
D-MBUD	Drachenstudio Royal 912 / Avant	220521	
D-MBUF #	Schmidtler Enduro Lotus 16	020993	
D-MBUG	Fresh Breeze 122 AL 2F	1940	
D-MBUH	Flying Machines FM250 Vampire II	unkn	
D-MBUL	Cosmos / Top 14.9	B21311	
D-MBUM	Bäumer Racer (Homebuilt)	01/90	
D-MBUR #	Flight Team Spider	D042	
D-MBUS	Bautek Eagle III / Chronos 12	2000/02/08	
D-MBUT(1)	Solid Air Diamant Sierra Trike	014	
D-MBUT(2)	Autogyro Europe MT-03	unkn	
D-MBUW	FUL Graffiti MA 30 Stranger	069/2610	
D-MBUX	Fresh Breeze Bulli-X Monster Big Wheel	471	
D-MBVB	Comco Ikarus Fox-C22	9108-3337	
D-MBVG	Flight Design CT SW	07-03-25	OE-7123
D-MBVJ	Cosmos Phase III / Top 12.9	1000	
D-MBVL(1)	Comco Ikarus C-42B	0206-6483	
	(Re-regd D-MCLL)		
D-MBVL(2)	Comco Ikarus C-42B	1103-7140	
D-MBVM	Fresh Breeze Simo 122	464	
D-MBVO	Take Off Merlin Karat 13	22344	
D-MBVU	Autogyro Europe MTOsport	M01232	
D-MBVV	Dova DV-1 Skylark	150/11	
D-MBVW	VierWerke Aerolite 120	unkn	
D-MBWB	Seiffert Mini II	10	
D-MBWC	Tandem Air Sunny Sport	005.05.02SP	
D-MBWE	ATEC 321 Faeta	F860714A	
D-MBWF #	PAP Marabella ROS 125	07028	
D-MBWG	Pago Jet M4	96701	
D-MBWH	Pioneer Flightstar II	100601	
D-MBWI	Mosquito NRG Space 16	NRG 128518	
D-MBWJ	Autogyro Europe MT-03	04G14	
D-MBWK	Comco Ikarus C-42B	0506-6675	
D-MBWL	Evektor EV-97 Eurostar SL	2008 3509	
	(Same c/n as 49-RQ / F-JWLS)		
D-MBWO	Drachenstudio Royal Trike	170/879	
D-MBWP #	Behlen Trike	83/1	
D-MBWR	Direct Fly Alto	025	
D-MBWS	Light Aero Avid Flyer IV	939	
	(W/o 8.11.15)		
D-MBWT	Air-Light Wild Thing	082	
	(W/o 22.10.11)		
D-MBWW	Fresh Breeze 122 AL 2F	2084	
D-MBXS	Schmidtler Enduro / Kiss	unkn	
D-MBXX	UL-F Jochum Eagle III	970803	
D-MBYE	Klüver Twin Racer SX 16	950103891 S	
D-MBYH	TL Ultralight TL-3000 Sirius	unkn	
D-MBYI	Flight Team Spider XL / Pico	D 061	
D-MBYO	Flight Design CT LS	F-12-06-04	
D-MBYS	Light Aero Avid Flyer	443C	
D-MBYT	Flying Machines FM250 Vampire II TOW	V31Z012	
D-MBYV	Light Aero Avid Flyer	1101D	
D-MBYY	Behlen Power-Trike / Pico S	2004-003	
D-MBYZ #	Flight Team Spider Trike	D032	
D-MBZA	Walkerjet RR W200	51.629.22973	
D-MBZB	Fresh Breeze Simo 122	44	
D-MBZF	Autogyro Europe MTOsport	M00984	
D-MBZT	Breezer CR	084	
D-MBZZ	Tandem Air Sunny Sport	25.91	
D-MCAA(1)	UPM Cobra Trike	91107	
	(Correct c/n may be 910107)		
D-MCAA(2)	BRM Aero Bristell UL	181/2016	
D-MCAB(1)	Fair Fax DR Hazard 15	D015	
D-MCAB(2)	Comco Ikarus C-42B	0408-6615	
D-MCAC	Klüver Twin Racer SX 16	616205	
D-MCAD	Fresh Breeze 110 AL2F	30	
D-MCAE	Comco Ikarus Fox-D	004	
D-MCAG	Bautek Eagle V/ Pico S	unkn	
D-MCAH #	Comco Ikarus Fox-C22	9009-3272	
D-MCAK	Fresh Breeze 122 AL 2F	341	
D-MCAL(1)	Ultraleichtverband Bi 90	B21152	
D-MCAL(2)	Autogyro Europe Calidus	unkn	
D-MCAM	Sky Walker II	387	
D-MCAN	ARCO Spacer L	689	
D-MCAO #	Mini Twin	unkn	
D-MCAP(1)	Fresh Breeze Simo 122	unkn	
D-MCAP(2)	Trixy G 4-2R	013-12	
D-MCAS	Solid Air Diamant Euro III	016	
D-MCAT(1)	Behlen Power Trike II	980020	
D-MCAT(2)	Zlin Savage	250	
D-MCAV(1)	Autogyro Europe MT-03	unkn	
D-MCAV(2)	Autogyro Europe Cavalon	V00004	G-2389 (Australia)
D-MCAW	Behlen Power-Trike /Rotax 582	93003	
D-MCAX	NST Minimum Saphir	M530	
D-MCAY #	Autogyro Europe Calidus	D10C16	
D-MCAZ	Fresh Breeze Simo 122	unkn	
D-MCBA	Dyn' Aero MCR-01 UL	241	
D-MCBB	Schönleber DS Trike	5153	
D-MCBC	UL-F Jochum Eagle III	980405	
D-MCBD	Autogyro Europe MTOsport	M01065	
D-MCBG	Freash Breeze	unkn	
D-MCBL	FUL Graffiti MA 30 Maverick II	unkn	
D-MCBO	Trixy G 4-2R Princess	008-12	
D-MCBP	Aerospool WT-9 Dynamic	DY455/2012	
D-MCBQ	Fresh Breeze 110 AL 2F	105	
D-MCBR #	Klüver Bison II / Quartz SX 16	unkn	
D-MCBS	ASO Viper Trike	V III 22071807	
D-MCBT	Autogyro Europe Cavalon	unkn	
D-MCBV	Autogyro Europe Calidus	C00157	
D-MCBW	Zlin Savage Cruiser	unkn	
D-MCBY	Autogyro Europe Calidus	unkn	
D-MCCB	B&F Funk FK-14 Polaris (t/w)	014-035	
D-MCCC	B&F Funk FK-9 Mk.III	09-04-406	
D-MCCE	Sky-Walker II	237	
D-MCCF	Best Off Sky Ranger	unkn	
D-MCCG(1)	Autogyro Europe Calidus	unkn	
D-MCCG(2)	Breezer C	unkn	
D-MCCH	Pipistrel Sinus NW	unkn	
D-MCCI #	Büttner Crazyplane III	86	
D-MCCK	Air Création Tanarg 912ES / BioniX 15	unkn	
D-MCCL #	Comco Ikarus Fox-C22	9107-3368	
	(Possible c/n error: PH-2F5 = 9109-3368, to Lithuania)		
D-MCCP	Behlen Power-Trike	95003	
D-MCCR(1)	Plätzer Kiebitz B	084	
D-MCCR(2)	Autogyro Europe MTOsport	unkn	
D-MCCS	Ultraleichtverbund Bi 90	985	
D-MCCT	Flight Design CT SW	unkn	
D-MCCV	B&F Funk FK-9 Mk.IV	09-215	D-MOGC
D-MCCW	B&F Funk FK-9	unkn	
D-MCCX(2)	B&F Funk FK-14A Polaris	014-025	
D-MCCY(1)	B&F Funk FK-9 Mk.IV SW ELA	unkn	
D-MCCY(2)	Autogyro Europe Calidus	unkn	
D-MCCY(3)	Roko Aero NG6 UL	unkn	
D-MCDC	UL-F Jochum Eagle III	970501	
D-MCDD	Dova DV-1 Skylark	07/36	
D-MCDE	Fresh Breeze Simo 122	unkn	
D-MCDF	Take Off Merlin Trike	23135	
D-MCDH	Remos G.3 Mirage	142	
D-MCDI(1)	Sky-Service Pago Jet	95201	
D-MCDI(2)	Autogyro Europe Calidus	unkn	
D-MCDJ	NST Minimum	M541	
D-MCDL	FUL Graffiti MA 30 / Profi	unkn	
D-MCDM	Pipistrel Virus SW	389VSW100	
D-MCDP(2)	Büttner Crazyplane III	82	
D-MCDR #	Kilb Air Création GTE 5	AC 004	
D-MCDS	Kappa KP-2U Sova Rapid	2103 119J	
D-MCDV	Comco Ikarus Fox-C22	9109-3356	
D-MCDW	Ultraleichtverbund Bi 90	21053	
D-MCDX	Schönleber Trike	TK 01/0395	
D-MCDY	Autogyro Europe Cavalon	unkn	
D-MCDZ	Fresh Breeze Simo 122	unkn	
D-MCEA	Remos G3-600 Gemini	unkn	
D-MCEC(1)	NST Minimum	M569	
D-MCEC(2)	Comco Ikarus C-42B	unkn	
D-MCEE	Vidor Asso V Champion	ULBB-A	
D-MCEG #	Autogyro Europe Calidus	unkn	
D-MCEH(1)	Cosmos / Top 12.9	21297	
D-MCEH(2)	Comco Ikarus C-42B	unkn	
D-MCEJ	Autogyro Europe Calidus	unkn	
D-MCEK	Comco Ikarus Fox-C22	9106-3331	
D-MCEM	Aerospool WT-9 Dynamic	DY516/2014	
D-MCES(2)	HFL Stratos 300K	300-028K	
D-MCET #	Flight Team Spider Hazard 15	002	
D-MCEY	Autogyro Europe Calidus	unkn	
D-MCFA	Light Aero Avid Flyer SW	1304D	
D-MCFB	Tecnam P.92 Echo 2000S	633	
D-MCFD	Flight Design CT SW	unkn	
D-MCFF	Comco Ikarus C-42B	0601-6780	
D-MCFG	Aerostyle Breezer CL	UL109	
D-MCFH	Corvus Fusion	unkn	
D-MCFI(1)	Autogyro Europe MT-03 914 Turbo	05G02	
D-MCFI(2)	Autogyro Europe MT-03	D06G12	
	(Re-registered D-MZZM ?)		
D-MCFI(3)	Autogyro Europe MTOsport	M00897	
D-MCFK	B&F Funk FK-9TG Mk.II Smart	013	
D-MCFL	Plätzer Kiebitz B	322	
D-MCFM	Fresh Breeze Simo 122	unkn	
D-MCFR	Light Aero Avid Flyer	418	
D-MCFT	Vidor Asso V Champion	2001	
D-MCGB	Drachenstudio Royal Trike	03-03039	
D-MCGE #	Ultraleichtverbund Bi 90	690	
D-MCGG	Autogyro Europe MT-03	05G04	
D-MCGH	Fresh Breeze Simo 122	unkn	
D-MCGI	Roko Aero NG6	unkn	
	(Crashed, Kempten, 13.8.16)		
D-MCGL	Drachenstudio Royal 912 / Avant 15	unkn	
D-MCGM	Remos G3 Mirage RS	095	
D-MCGN	Flight Design CT2SW	04.08.02	
D-MCGS	Aeroprakt A-22L Vision	310	
D-MCGX(2)	Remos GX	367	
	(To HB-WYF, 6.10)		
D-MCGX(3)	Remos GX	378	
D-MCHA	Fisher FP-404 Classic	001	
D-MCHB	NST Minimum	120623	
D-MCHC	Schmidtler Enduro / Mild 16	unkn	
D-MCHF	Rans S-10 Sakota	0491128	
D-MCHG	Aeropro Eurofox	14404	
D-MCHH	Plätzer Kiebitz B	243	
D-MCHK	Dallach Sunrise IIA	032	
D-MCHL	Comco Ikarus C-42B	0307-6566	
	(Sold as EW-454SL)		
D-MCHM(1)	ASO Viper Trike	VIII 122070503	
D-MCHM(2)	Alpi Avn Pioneer 300	unkn	
D-MCHO	Bautek Eagle V/Pico	unkn	
D-MCHP (1)	Albatros 52	131	
D-MCHP(2)	Fresh Breeze Simo 122	unkn	
D-MCHR	NST Minimum	M577	
D-MCHS	ASO Viper Trike	VII 2049309	
D-MCHV	Autogyro Europe MTO Sport	unkn	
D-MCHW	NST Minimum	M567	
D-MCIA	Autogyro Europe MTOsport	unkn	
D-MCIB	NST Minimum Saphir 17	M297	
D-MCIC	Autogyro Europe MT-03	unkn	
D-MCID	Comco Ikarus C-42B	0902--7023	
D-MCIH	ELA Aviacion ELA-07 Cougar	unkn	
D-MCII(1)	Schmidtler Enduro Trike	865186	
D-MCII(2)	Schönleber DS Speed 14	unkn	
D-MCIK	Comco Ikarus C-42B	1104-7151	
D-MCIL	UPM Cobra BF 52 UL Trike	950134	
D-MCIM	Magni M-24 Orion	24127074	
D-MCIN	Schönleber DS Trike	11290	
D-MCIO	Magni M-24 Orion	24106024	
D-MCIS	Magni M-16 Tandem Trainer	16116604	
D-MCIT(1)	B&F Funk FK-14 Polaris	014-096	
	(W/o 8.10.12)		
D-MCIT(2)	Comco Ikarus C-42C	unkn	
D-MCIW	Comco Ikarus C-42B	1203-7196	
D-MCIX	Comco Ikarus C-42C	unkn	
	(W/o 23.8.16)		
D-MCJA(1)	Fresh Breeze 110 AL 2F	38	
D-MCJA(2)	Autogyro Europe Calidus	unkn	
D-MCJJ #	Behlen Power-Trike /Rotax 582	980016	
D-MCJN #	Behlen Power Trike II	97010	
D-MCJW #	FUL Graffiti Trike	037/0103	
D-MCJX	Zlin Savage Cub	0224	
D-MCKA	Flight Design CT LS	F-11-03-10	

Reg	Type	c/n	Notes
D-MCKC	Fresh Breeze Simo 122	unkn	
D-MCKF	Take Off Merlin 1100 / XP 15	unkn	
D-MCKG	Remos	unkn	
D-MCKH	Autogyro Europe MTOsport	unkn	
D-MCKK	TL Ultralight TL-2000 Sting	03ST60	
D-MCKL	Fly Synthesis Storch HS	410 or 450?	
D-MCKO	Air Création / iXess	unkn	
D-MCKP	B&F Funk FK-9 Mk.IV	09-04-384	
D-MCKS(1)	Apis BEE 15 MB	A028MB4	
D-MCKS(2)	Roland Z602		
D-MCKT	Comco Ikarus Fox-C22	9207-3428	
D-MCKW	Technoflug Piccolo	120	
D-MCLA	Fresh Breeze 110 AL 2F	213	
D-MCLG	unidentified weightshift	unkn	
D-MCLL	Comco Ikarus C-42B	0206-6483	D-MBVL(1)
D-MCLM	Fresh Breeze Simo 122	unkn	
D-MCLS	Zlin Savage	90	
D-MCLU #	Albatros Milan	08085	
D-MCLW	Flight Design CT-2K	unkn	
D-MCMA	NST Minimum Zephir CX	M524	
D-MCMB	Flight Design CT SW	05-06-05	D-MFSW(2)
D-MCMC	Tandem Air Sunny Sport	2-91	
D-MCMD	Autogyro Europe MTOsport	unkn	
D-MCMI	Autogyro Europe MTOsport	unkn	
D-MCMK	FUL Graffiti Trike	001/0045	
D-MCML	Comco Ikarus C-42B	0705-6884	
D-MCMM	TL Ultralight TL-96 Sting	07ST260	
D-MCMP #	Ultraleichtverbund Bi 90	21060	
D-MCMR	Autogyro Europe Calidus	unkn	
D-MCMY	Flight Design CT LS	unkn	
D-MCNA	B&F Funk FK-9 Mk.IV ELA	unkn	
D-MCNC	Autogyro Europe Calidus	unkn	
D-MCNK #	Magni M-16 Tandem Trainer	16-02-1914	
	(Same c/n as D-MDTV)		
D-MCNO	Fresh Breeze 122 AL 2F	212	
D-MCOB	Tandem Air Sunny Sport	1-91	
D-MCOC	Bautek Eagle V/Pico S	unkn	
D-MCOD	Dova DV-1 Skylark	unkn	
D-MCOE	B&F Funk FK-9 Mk.IV	387	
D-MCOG #	Fresh Breeze 110 AL 4H	25	
D-MCOH(1)	Comco Ikarus C-42B	1005-7109	
D-MCOH(2)	Comco Ikarus C-42CS	1504-7335	
	(C/n incorrect, possibly 1504-7385?)		
D-MCOI	Comco Ikarus C-42B	0711-6928	
	(To 9-336, OY-9336)		
D-MCOL	Kümmerle Mini-Fly-Set	73185-3	
D-MCOM	Comco Ikarus C-42B	0304-6532	
D-MCON(1)	Sky-Walker II	264	
D-MCON(2)	Comco Ikarus C-52	unkn	
	(Stored, Mengen, noted 9.16)		
D-MCOO	Comco Ikarus C-42	unkn	
D-MCOP	Comco Ikarus C-42C	1303-7253	
	(Re-regd D-MIKB)		
D-MCOQ	Warnke Trike	S1/009	
D-MCOR	Fresh Breeze 122 AL 2F	389	
D-MCOV	Corvus CA-21 Corone Mk.II	CNE02/001	HA-YCAB, HA-Y08, 35-05
D-MCOW	Sky-Walker II	236	
D-MCOX	Aerostyle Breezer CR	77	
D-MCOY	Rans S-6ES Coyote II	0392280	
D-MCPA(1)	Autogyro Europe MT-03	unkn	
D-MCPA(2)	Autogyro Europe MTOsport	unkn	
D-MCPA(3)	Trixy G 4-2R	033-14	
D-MCPC	Air Création Skypper / NuviX	unkn	
D-MCPE	Impulse 100B/TD	37	
D-MCPI	Büttner Crazyplane I	103	
D-MCPK(1)	B&F Funk FK-14B Polaris	014-036	
	(Crashed, 25.8.08)		
D-MCPK(2)	B&F Funk FK-14B Polaris	014-090	
D-MCPL	TL Ultralight TL-96 Sting carbon	05ST135	
D-MCPM(2)#	Büttner Easy Plane	8	
D-MCPP	Comco Ikarus C-42B	unkn	
D-MCPR	Roland Z602	Z-9555	
D-MCPS	Flight Design CT LS	F-08-07-22	
D-MCPW	Evektor EV-97 Eurostar SLW	2009 3618	
D-MCPY	Comco Ikarus C-42B	unkn	
D-MCQX	Comco Ikarus C-42B	1003-7104	
D-MCQY	Comco Ikarus C-42B	1105-7150	
D-MCQZ	Comco Ikarus C-42C	1309-7273	
	(W/0 15.5.16)		
D-MCRA(1)	TL Ultralight TL-2000 Sting	03ST39	
	(W/o 24.5.10)		
D-MCRA(2)	Corvus CA-21 Phantom	unkn	
D-MCRB(1)	Ultralight Flight Phantom	402	
D-MCRB(2)	Corvus CA-41 Racer 312	0009	
D-MCRC	Light Aero Avid Flyer IV	870	
D-MCRG	Alpi Avn Pioneer 300UL	unkn	
D-MCRH	NST Schwarze Trike	MT66	
D-MCRI	Dyn'Aero MCR-01 ULC	111	
D-MCRJ	Dyn'Aero MCR-01	404	
D-MCRK	Magni M-16 Tandem Trainer	16 11 6404	
D-MCRL	Kappa KP-2U Sova	unkn	
D-MCRN	Comco Ikarus C-42C	1310-7281	
D-MCRP	Flight Design CT SW	unkn	
D-MCRS(1)	Rans S-10S Sakota	1191140	
D-MCRS(2)	Corvus Fusion	unkn	
D-MCRT	TL Ultralight TL-96 Sting	07ST218	
D-MCRU	Take Off Merlin 1200 / Eos	unkn	
D-MCRV	Dyn'Aero MCR-01 ULC	unkn	
D-MCRW(1)	Autogyro Europe MTOsport	unkn	
D-MCRW(2)	Aerospool WT-9 Dynamic	DY401/2011	D-MHIS(3)
D-MCRY #	Flight Design CT LS	F-08-03-09	
D-MCSA	Light Aero Avid Flyer	1154D	
D-MCSB	Schmidtler Enduro Trike	01-002	
D-MCSC(1)	Rans S-6 Coyote II	unkn	
D-MCSC(2)	Autogyro Europe MTOsport	unkn	
D-MCSD	B&F Funk FK-9 Mk.IV	09-04U-291	
D-MCSE	Pipistrel Spider / Hazard 13	D007	
D-MCSG	Evektor EV-97 Eurostar SL	unkn	
D-MCSK	Plätzer Kiebitz B	347	
D-MCSL	Fläming Air Peregrine SL	120/10	
D-MCSM	Remos G3/600 Mirage	unkn	
D-MCSN #	WDFL Dallach D4B Fascination	unkn	
D-MCSP	Scheibe ULI-1	unkn	
D-MCSW	Sky-Walker II	162	
D-MCTA	Flight Design Supralight	unkn	
D-MCTF	Fresh Breeze Simo 122	unkn	
D-MCTI	unidentified autogyro	unkn	
D-MCTK	Flight Design CT-2K	01-09-05-29	
D-MCTL	Flight Design CT SW	07-04-24	
D-MCTM	Flight Design CT LS	unkn	
D-MCTO #	Warnke Trike	034	
D-MCTP	Flight Design CT SL	E-12-04-02	
D-MCTR	Fresh Breeze 110 AL 2F	42	
D-MCTS	Warnke Skylight Trike	2	
D-MCTT	Tecnam P.92 Echo S-100	574	
D-MCTW #	Flight Design CT LS	unkn	
D-MCTX	Flight Design CT	unkn	
D-MCUB	Zlin Savage Classic	unkn	
D-MCUG	B&F Funk FK-9 Mk.IV	182	
	(Probably ex D-MGDP Mk.3 c/n 09-03-182)		
D-MCUI	Tecnam P.92 Echo	unkn	
D-MCUL	Ultraleichtverbund Bi 90	21178	
D-MCUP	WDFL Dallach D4 Fascination BK	116	
D-MCUS	Autogyro Europe Calidus	C00147	
D-MCUT	Magni M-24 Orion	24127404	
D-MCUU(1)	Autogyro Europe MT-03	unkn	
D-MCUU(2)	Autogyro Europe MTOsport	unkn	
D-MCVB	Autogyro Europe MTOsport	unkn	
D-MCVC	Autogyro Europe MT-03	unkn	
D-MCVI	Fresh Breeze Simo 122	unkn	
D-MCVK	Pipistrel Virus SW	523SWN100	
D-MCVN	Autogyro Europe Cavalon	V00029	D-MAGT
D-MCVP	Fresh Breeze Simo 122	unkn	
D-MCVR	Autogyro Europe Cavalon	unkn	
D-MCVW	B&F Funk FK-12 Comet	12-052	
D-MCWA	Albatros 64	130	
D-MCWB	Roman-Weller UW 9 Sprint	03	
D-MCWC	Comco Ikarus C-42B	unkn	
D-MCWE(1)	Ultraleichtverbund Bi 90	21036	
D-MCWE(2)	Comco Ikarus C-42B	0307-6559	
	(Same c/n quoted for D-MCWR)		
D-MCWF #	Autogyro Europe Calidus	unkn	
D-MCWG	Comco Ikarus C-42B	1003-7096	
D-MCWH	TL Ultralight TL-96 Sting	07ST232	
D-MCWI	Comco Ikarus C-42B	unkn	
D-MCWK	Comco Ikarus C-42	0203-6457	
D-MCWM	FUL Graffiti Trike	38/0104	
D-MCWO	Comco Ikarus C-42B	unkn	
D-MCWR	Comco Ikarus C-42B	0307-6559	
	(Same c/n quoted for D-MCWE(2))		
D-MCWT	Comco Ikarus C-42B	0301-6530	
	(Damaged 18.4.15)		
D-MCWW	Fair Fax DR Trike	1022	
D-MCXI	Autogyro Europe Calidus	C00227	
D-MCXL	Celier Xenon IV	J.14.5.013	
D-MCXT	Celier Xenon IV	CAM14M3E19AA021L	
	(Re-regd D-MFGP)		
D-MCYB	B&F Funk FK-9 Mk.IV	323	
D-MCYR	Autogyro Europe MTOsport	unkn	
D-MCYZ #	Fresh Breeze 110 AL 2F	93	
D-MCZZ	Comco Ikarus C-42B	0708-6913	
D-MDAA	Klüver Twin Racer SX 16	555203	
D-MDAB	Schönleber DS Lotus 18 Trike	020490	
D-MDAC	Celier Xenon	CAH09173R	
D-MDAD	Flight Design CT LS	F-08-08-03	
D-MDAE	Comco Ikarus C-42B	unkn	
D-MDAF	Autogyro Europe Cavalon	unkn	
D-MDAG(1)	Behlen Trike	unkn	
D-MDAG(2)	Bautek Eagle V/ Pico	unkn	
D-MDAL	Dallach Sunrise IIA	033	
D-MDAM	ASO Viper Trike	12059404	
D-MDAN	Sky-Walker II	232	
D-MDAO	Aeroprakt A22L2 Vision	441	
D-MDAS	Tandem Air Sunny Targa	TA 07.93	
D-MDAS	Comco Ikarus C-42	unkn	
D-MDAT(1)	Take Off Merlin 1100	28368	
D-MDAT(2)	Pipistrel Alpha Trainer	unkn	
D-MDAU	Comco Ikarus C-42B	0903-7028	
D-MDAV	Behlen Power Trike II	89044	
D-MDAW	Flight Design CT SW	07-07-21	
D-MDAX	Sunny Side-by-Side	unkn	
D-MDAY	Autogyro Europe MTOsport	unkn	
D-MDBA	Apis BEE 15 MB	A040MB10	
D-MDBB	Dallach Sunrise IIA	020	
D-MDBC	Flight Design CT SW	unkn	
D-MDBE	Magni M-24 Orion	24148764	
D-MDBG	Fresh Breeze 110 AL2F	33	
D-MDBH	WDFL Sunwheel	008	
D-MDBI	Flight Team Spider	D038	
D-MDBK	Pago Jet M4	961201	
D-MDBL	Take Off Merlin Trike	22114	
D-MDBO	B&F Funk FK-9 Mk.III Utility	09-03U-220	
D-MDBR	Aerostyle Breezer	075	
D-MDBS(1)	Mantel Mono-Dragster	2248410002	
D-MDBS(2)	Comco Ikarus C-42B	0909-7061	
D-MDBT	Bautek / Pico	unkn	
D-MDBU	Fresh Breeze Monster / Silex	unkn	
D-MDBW	Autogyro Europe MT-03	unkn	
D-MDBX(2)	HFL Stratos IIe	11e/005	
D-MDBY	Autogyro Europe MTOsport	unkn	
D-MDCA	Comco Ikarus C-42B	0207-6450	
D-MDCC(1)	Comco Ikarus Fox-C22CS	0301-3750	
	(To YL-PIF, D-MEAP)		
D-MDCC(2)	Comco Ikarus C-42B	0609-6849	
D-MDCD	Zenair CH-701D STOL	7-9305	
D-MDCF #	Comco Ikarus C-42B	unkn	
D-MDCK	BOT Speed Cruiser SC07	016	
D-MDCL	Behlen Power-Trike	88023	
D-MDCM	NST Minimum Sierra	SN 105	
D-MDCS #	Schmidtler Enduro Trike	02-003	
D-MDCT	Flight Design CTSW	unkn	
D-MDCW	NST Minimum	M323	
D-MDCY	Autogyro Europe MTOsport	unkn	
D-MDDA	Autogyro Europe MT-03	unkn	
	(W/o 3.10.07)		
D-MDDB	B&F Funk FK-9	09-022	
D-MDDD(1)	Aviasud Mistral BRD	085	
D-MDDD(2)	Remos G3 Mirage	129	
D-MDDF(1)	Autogyro Europe MT-03	04G13	
	(Same c/n as D-MDEM(1))		
D-MDDF(2)	Autogyro Europe MTOsport	unkn	
D-MDDK	Aerostyle Breezer	074	

Registration	Type	C/n	Note
D-MDDM	Remos G.3-600 Mirage	159	
D-MDDO	Remos GX	379	
D-MDDP	Sky-Walker II	392	
D-MDDT	Behlen Power Trike II	98011	
D-MDDY	Autogyro Europe MTOsport	unkn	
D-MDEA(1)	Wisch Star-Trike	12601	
D-MDEA(2)	Magni M-16 Tandem Trainer	16105854	
D-MDEB	Behlen Power-Trike	95001	
D-MDEC(2)	Fresh Breeze 110 AL 2F	421	
D-MDEC(3)	TL Ultralight TL-3000 Sirius	13SI90	
D-MDED	ICP MXP-740 Savannah	083	
D-MDEE	Fresh Breeze 110 AL 2F	411	
D-MDEF	Behlen Power-Trike	94003	
D-MDEG	Magni M-14 Scout 2000 gyro	214042723	
D-MDEH	Dova DV-1 Skylark	unkn	
D-MDEI	Take Off Merlin Trike	25125	
D-MDEJ	B&F Funk FK-14B Polaris	unkn	
D-MDEL(1)	Seiffert Mini-Speed Trike	unkn	
D-MDEL(2)	Delphin	unkn	
D-MDEM(1)	Autogyro Europe MT-03 (Same c/n as D-MDDF(1))	04G13	
D-MDEM(2)	Autogyro Europe MTOsport	unkn	
D-MDEN	TL Ultralight TL-96 Sting	14ST420	
D-MDEO	Comco Ikarus Fox-C22	9104-3334	
D-MDEP	Fresh Breeze Simo 122	unkn	
D-MDET(1)	NST Minimum Pamir	M523	
D-MDET(2)	B&F Funk FK-9 Mk4 Utility	09-04U-268	
D-MDEU	EDM Aerotec CoAx 2D	AEH0002	
D-MDEW #	Fresh Breeze 110 AL 2F	12	
D-MDEY	Autogyro Europe MTOsport	unkn	
D-MDFA	Fantasy Air Allegro	02-416	
D-MDFC #	Ultraleichtverbund Bi 90	976-4105546	
D-MDFD	Fresh Breeze 110 AL2F	35	
D-MDFF	Comco Ikarus C-42B	0403-6596	
D-MDFG	NST Minimum	MT81	
D-MDFI #	Ultraleichtverbund Bi 90	B21122	
D-MDFK	B&F Funk FK-9 Mk.IV	unkn	
D-MDFN #	ATEC Zephyr 2000	Z800603S	
D-MDFO	Gyrotec DF-02	001	
D-MDFR(1)	LO-120S	011	
D-MDFR(2)	unidentified weightshift	unkn	
D-MDFS(1)	Remos G.3 Mirage	145	
D-MDFS(2)	Celier Xenon	unkn	
D-MDFT	Celier Xenon 2	unkn	
D-MDFY	Autogyro Europe MTOsport	unkn	
D-MDGB	Fresh Breeze Simo 122	unkn	
D-MDGC	unidentified paramotor	unkn	
D-MDGF	Comco Ikarus C-42A	1501-7365	
D-MDGG	Flight Design CT SW	05-02-04	
D-MDGK	Urban Air Lambada	unkn	
D-MDGO	Autogyro Europe MTOsport (W/o 11.9.16)	unkn	
D-MDGP	Aerostyle Breezer	014	
D-MDGS(1)	UPM Cobra Trike	900099	
D-MDGS(2)	Trixy G 4-2R	002-12	
D-MDGV(1)	Aerostyle Breezer	026	
D-MDGV(2)	Aerostyle Breezer	055	
D-MDGW	Flight Design CT SW	unkn	
D-MDGX	Autogyro Europe MTOsport	unkn	
D-MDGY	Autogyro Europe MTOsport	M01209	
D-MDHA	Trixy G4-2	010-12	
D-MDHC	Comco Ikarus C-42C	1301-7232	
D-MDHE	Comco Ikarus Fox-C22	9303-3481	
D-MDHF #	Tandem Air Sunny	46.93	
D-MDHG	Behlen Power-Trike	97011	
D-MDHH	Kümmerle Mini-Fly-Set	1278/91-5	
D-MDHK	Comco Ikarus C-42B (W/o 13.5.15)	0904-7036	
D-MDHM	Autogyro Europe Calidus	unkn	
D-MDHO #	Fresh Breeze Simo 122	unkn	
D-MDHP	Ultralight Flight Phantom	327	
D-MDHR	Corvus CA-21 Phantom	unkn	
D-MDHS	Autogyro Europe MT-03	unkn	
D-MDHW	Tecnam P.92 Echo Short Wing S	858	
D-MDHX	Büttner Crazyplane IV	14	
D-MDIC	Autogyro Europe MT-03	unkn	
D-MDID	Autogyro Europe MTOsport	unkn	
D-MDIE	Flight Design CT SW	unkn	
D-MDIF	Flight Design CT LS	unkn	
D-MDIG	Aerospool WT-9 Dynamic	unkn	
D-MDII	FUL Graffiti Trike	030/0096	
D-MDIL	Autogyro Europe Calidus	D10C33	
D-MDIM	Take Off Merlin 1100 / Avant	unkn	
D-MDIN	Dallach Sunrise IIA	026	
D-MDIP	Zenair CH-602XL Zodiac	unkn	
D-MDIS(1)	MKB Ranger M	01/006/85	
D-MDIS(2)	AirLony Skylane	56	
D-MDIW	Roland Z601DX	6-9299	
D-MDIY	Peak Aerospace Bf 109R R2	2-004	
D-MDJF	Behlen Power-Trike / Avant 17	unkn	
D-MDJJ	B&F Funk FK-14 Polaris	014-106	
D-MDJU #	Remos G-3-600 Mirage	unkn	
D-MDKB(1)	Flight Design CT 2K	03-03-02-09	D-MFSW(1)
D-MDKB(2)	Flight Design CT Supralight	unkn	
D-MDKE	Drachenstudio Piccolo II Trike	099306	
D-MDKE(2)	Aerospool WT-9 Dynamic	DY088/2005	
D-MDKF	Best Off Sky Ranger SW	unkn	
D-MDKG	Comco Ikarus C-42B	0912-7079	
D-MDKH	Comco Ikarus Fox-C22	8705-3062	
D-MDKI	Aerospool WT-9 Dynamic	unkn	
D-MDKK	Remos G.3 Mirage	144	
D-MDKL	NST Minimum SierrAll	558	
D-MDKM(1)	Behlen Power-Trike Hazard 15M	91034	
D-MDKM(2)	Autogyro Europe Cavalon	unkn	
D-MDKP	Pipistrel Taurus	060T503	
D-MDKR #	Comco Ikarus Fox II Doppel	8608-3029	
D-MDKT	Comco Ikarus Fox-C22	9103-3315	PH-2G8
D-MDKU	Light Aero Avid Heavy Hauler	1155C	
D-MDKV	Aerospool WT-9 Dynamic	unkn	
D-MDKW	Albastar Apis 2.2	unkn	
D-MDLB	Interplane Skyboy ZK	69/2003	
D-MDLE #	Flight Design CT SW	unkn	
D-MDLF #	Tandem Air Sunny Sport	007.03.03 SP	
D-MDLH	Comco Ikarus C-42B	0702-6873	
D-MDLS	Technoflug Piccolo	116	
D-MDLT	Sky-Service Pago Jet M4	95303	
D-MDLU	Trixy G 4-2 R	012-12	
D-MDLW	Comco Ikarus Fox-C22	9111-3357	
D-MDMA	Behlen Power-Trike	86027	
D-MDMC(1)	Behlen Power-Trike	M878502	
D-MDMC(2)	B&F Funk FK-12 Comet	012-096	
D-MDMD	Comco Ikarus C-42B	0302-6506	
D-MDME	Autogyro Europe MT-03	unkn	
D-MDMJ	Behlen Power-Trike Vampir II	88018	
D-MDMK	Behlen Power-Trike	7017	
D-MDMM	Impulse 2200 BR	35	
D-MDMO	Flight Design CT SW	06-12-04	
D-MDMR	Behlen Power-Trike Vampir II	M876642	
D-MDMT #	Comco Ikarus Fox-C22	8905-3201	
D-MDMV	Fresh Breeze 110 AL 2F	413	
D-MDMW	Tecnam P.92 Echo	1460	
D-MDMX #	Take Off Merlin 1200 / Eos	unkn	
D-MDMY(1)	Comco Ikarus Fox-C22	9008-3292	
D-MDMY(2)	Flight Design CT LS	F-11-01-01	
D-MDNA	Autogyro Europe Cavalon	unkn	
D-MDNK	Pago Jet M4	960501	
D-MDNS	Remos GX	225	
D-MDOB #	Behlen Power-Trike	93002	
D-MDOC(1)	Tandem Air Sunny	30.92	
D-MDOC(2)	BRM Aero Bristell	099/2014	
D-MDOE	FD Composites Arrowcopter AC20	033	
D-MDOG(2)	B&F Funk FK-9 Mk.II	006	
D-MDOH	Pegasus Quasar II	unkn	
D-MDOK	Breezer B400	unkn	
D-MDOL #	Junkers Profly JUL Trike	00594	
D-MDON	Behlen Power-Trike / Pico	unkn	
D-MDOR	Plätzer Kiebitz B2	186	
D-MDOT	Airtrike	unkn	
D-MDOX(1)	Steinbach Austro Trike Spot IIM	1915	
D-MDOX(2)	Autogyro Europe MTOsport	unkn	
D-MDOZ	Autogyro Europe MTOsport	unkn	
D-MDPA(1)	Schmidtler Ranger M	18-24	
D-MDPA(2)	TL Ultralight TL-3000 Sirius	15SI119	
D-MDPC	Pipistrel Taurus M	unkn	
D-MDPD	Zenair CH-601DX Zodiac (Damaged 17.9.11)	6-9298	
D-MDPG #	Take Off Merlin Karat 13	20573	
D-MDPI	Pipistrel Taurus 503	078T503	
D-MDPK	Autogyro Europe MTOsport	unkn	
D-MDPL	Behlen Power-Trike / Ghost 12	unkn	
D-MDPM	Alpi Avn Pioneer 300	unkn	
D-MDPT	Behlen Power-Trike / Ghost 12	unkn	
D-MDPW	Drachenstudio Royal Trike	13-0696	
D-MDRA	Cosmos /Chromos 12	unkn	
D-MDRB	Ultralight Flight Phantom T44	0293	
D-MDRF	Remos G.3 Mirage	097	
D-MDRM	Take Off Merlin Trike	25516	
D-MDRN	Pegasus Quantum 15 Super Sport	unkn	
D-MDRO	Flight Design CT SW	unkn	
D-MDRP(1)	WDFL Sunwheel (To F-JSRR, by 5.2011)	002	
D-MDRP(2)	Comco Ikarus C-42B	unkn	
D-MDRR	Pegasus QuikR 912 ULS	unkn	
D-MDRS	Air-Light Wild Thing	083	
D-MDRT #	Plätzer Kiebitz-B4	099	
D-MDRU #	Autogyro Europe MT-03	unkn	
D-MDRW	AirLony Skylane	unkn	
D-MDSB	Take Off Merlin Trike/La Mouette	26356	
D-MDSC	UPM Funplane	860016	
D-MDSD	B&F Funk FK-14B Polaris	unkn	
D-MDSF(1)	Behlen Power-Trike Vampir II	89014	
D-MDSF(2)	Drachenstudio Royal 912 / Eos	unkn	
D-MDSH	Bautek Eagle V/ iXess 15	unkn	
D-MDSI	B&F Funk FK-14 Polaris	unkn	
D-MDSK(1)	Flight Team Spider Hazard 13	D013	
D-MDSK(2)	Celier Xenon	unkn	
D-MDSK(3)	Comco Ikarus C-42B	unkn	
D-MDSL	Comco Ikarus Fox-C22B	9202-3389	
D-MDSM(1)	Kilb Air Création GTE 5	AC 005	
D-MDSM(2)	Autogyro Europe MTO Sport	unkn	
D-MDSM(3)	Pipistrel Taurus 503	unkn	
D-MDSO	Ultraleichtverbund Bi 90	529	
D-MDSR	Flight Team Spider Trike	D023	
D-MDSS	HFL Stratos IIe	IIe-008	
D-MDST	Air Création GTE 582S / XP 15	unkn	
D-MDSV	Autogyro Europe Calidus	unkn	
D-MDSW	Flight Team Spider Trike	D039	
D-MDSY	Autogyro Europe MTOsport	unkn	
D-MDSZ	Autogyro Europe MT-03	unkn	
D-MDTA	FUL Graffiti Trike	002/0049	
D-MDTB	Fresh Breeze Simo 122	unkn	
D-MDTC	Vidor Asso V Champion	013	
D-MDTF	Autogyro Europe MTOsport	unkn	
D-MDTG #	Fresh Breeze 110 AL 2A	140	
D-MDTI	Pipistrel Taurus 503	026T503	
D-MDTK	Corvus CA-21 Phantom	CP 05.002	
D-MDTL(1)	Seiffert Mini II	774	
D-MDTL(2)	TL Ultralight TL-3000 Sirius	unkn	
D-MDTM	Comco Ikarus C-42	unkn	
D-MDTP	Pipistrel Taurus 503	unkn	
D-MDTR	Aerospool WT-9 Dynamic	DY489/2013	
D-MDTT	Air Light Wild Thing (To ZK-DTT(2), 10.10)	52	
D-MDTV	Magni M-16 Tandem Trainer (Same c/n as D-MCNK)	16-12-1914	
D-MDTW	Behlen Power-Trike /Rotax 582	980017	
D-MDUC	UPM / Raven	unkn	
D-MDUD	Fresh Breeze 110 AL 2F	200	
D-MDUF	Comco Ikarus C-42B	0309-6562	
D-MDUG(1)	Wildente	109	
D-MDUG(2)	Magni M-24 Orion	24137734	
D-MDUK(1)	Comco Ikarus Fox II Doppel	001/85	
D-MDUK(2)	Autogyro Europe MTOsport	unkn	
D-MDUO	Comco Ikarus Fox-C22 II	unkn	
D-MDUP #	Ultraleichtverbund Bi 90	623	
D-MDUS(1)	Sky-Walker II	350	
D-MDUS(2)	Autogyro Europe Calidus	C00353	
D-MDUT	Aerospool WT-9 Dynamic	DY581/2016	
D-MDUV	Pipistrel Sinus NW	unkn	
D-MDUW #	Fresh Breeze Simo 122	unkn	
D-MDVD	Flight Design CT SW (Previously 07-05-10, to YR- ?)	07-05-18	

Registration	Type	c/n	Notes
D-MDVH	Magni M-24 Orion VIP	unkn	
D-MDVK #	Behlen Power-Trike	91021	
D-MDVP	Pipistrel Virus SW	unkn	
D-MDVV	Silent Glider M	unkn	
D-MDVZ	Fresh Breeze Simo 122	unkn	
D-MDWA	FUL Graffiti MA 30 / Stranger	unkn	
D-MDWB(1)	Autogyro Europe MTOsport	unkn	
D-MDWB(2)	Comco Ikarus C-42B	unkn	
D-MDWD	Dallach Sunrise II	017	D-MHOB(1)
D-MDWE #	Eurofly Viper / Hazard 13	unkn	
D-MDWG	Fresh Breeze Simo 122	unkn	
D-MDWL	Air Création Twin 582SL / iXess 15	unkn	
D-MDWO #	WDFL Sunrise II	unkn	
D-MDWR	Celier Xenon 2	unkn	
D-MDWT	Aerospool WT-9 Dynamic	DY069/2004	
D-MDWW	Comco Ikarus Fox-C22	9305-3501	
D-MDXD	Comco Ikarus C-42B	unkn	
D-MDXE	Celier Xenon IV	CAJ14M3F11AA016L	
D-MDXL	Celier Xenon 2	unkn	
D-MDYA	Aerospool WT-9 Dynamic	DY124/2006	
D-MDYB	Aerospool WT-9 Dynamic	DY232/2008	
D-MDYC	Aerospool WT-9 Dynamic	DY171/2007	
D-MDYG	Aerospool WT-9 Dynamic	unkn	
D-MDYH	Dynali H3 EasyFlyer	unkn	
D-MDYL	Aerospool WT-9 Dynamic	DY141/2006	
D-MDYN	Aerospool WT-9 Dynamic	DY076	
	(Re-regd D-MFRB)		
D-MDYR	Autogyro Europe MTOsport	unkn	
D-MDYY	Aerospool WT-9 Dynamic	DY206/2007	
D-MDZR #	Fresh Breeze 122 AL 2F	170	
D-MDZZ	Sky-Service Pago Jet	95308	
D-MEAA(1)	Sky-Service Pago Jet	95301	
D-MEAA(2)	Aerostyle Breezer	027	
D-MEAB(1)	Solid Air Diamant Trike	18	
D-MEAB(2)	Magni M-24 Orion	24148264	
D-MEAC	Behlen Power-Trike /Rotax 582	980023	
D-MEAE	Alpi Avn Pioneer 300	unkn	
D-MEAF(1)	Klüver Racer SX 12	14007	
D-MEAF(2)	Aerocopter Futura	unkn	
D-MEAG(1)	Autogyro Europe MT-03	unkn	
D-MEAG(2)	Autogyro Europe MTOsport	unkn	
D-MEAJ	Autogyro Europe Calidus	unkn	
D-MEAL	FUL Graffiti Trike	014/0074	
D-MEAM #	Flight Design CTSW	06-08-01	
D-MEAP	Comco Ikarus Fox-C22CS	0301-3750	YL-PIF, D-MDCC(1)
D-MEAS	Ultraleichtverbund Bi 90	609	
D-MEAT	Warnke Puma Sprint DS	D003	
D-MEBA(1)	Behlen Power-Trike	86026	
D-MEBA(2)	Aerostyle Breezer LSA	73	
	(To G-OLSA, 3.11, but regd with c/n 014LSA)		
D-MEBA(3)	Aerostyle Breezer 400 Club	UL 127	
D-MEBB	Comco Ikarus C-42B	0203-6470	
D-MEBC	Cosmos / Chronos 14	B21542	
D-MEBE	Flight Team Spider Trike	D011	
D-MEBG	Fresh Breeze Simo 122	unkn	
D-MEBH	Tecnam P.92 Echo Super	904	
D-MEBI	Flight Team Spider Trike	D029	
D-MEBL	Take Off Merlin Karat 13	22544	
D-MEBM	WDFL Dallach D4 Fascination BK	125	
D-MEBO	Dragonfly	unkn	
D-MEBP	JMB VL-3 Evolution	174	
D-MEBR(1)	Ultraleichtverbund Bi 90	21065	
D-MEBR(2)	Aerostyle Breezer	087	
D-MEBS	Comco Ikarus Fox D	8410-FD21	
D-MEBY #	Sky-Walker II	257	
D-MECA(1)	Solid Air Diamant Sierra	003	
D-MECA(2)	Comco Ikarus C-42B	0907-7049	
	(Similar c/n to D-MNFB(2))		
D-MECB #	Tecnam P.92 Echo Super	unkn	
D-MECC	NST Minimum Zephir	M353	
D-MECD	Zlin Savage	288	
D-MECF	Plätzer Kiebitz B	343	
D-MECG	Evektor EV-97R Eurostar 2000	unkn	
D-MECH(1)	Evektor EV-97 Eurostar	2002 1409	
	(To D-ENOA as VLA c/n 2011 1409)		
D-MECH(2)	Autogyro Europe MTOsport	unkn	
D-MECI	Evektor EV-97 Eurostar	unkn	
D-MECK	Evektor EV-97 Eurostar 2000	2002 1409	
	(Same c/n quoted as D-MECH(1) – error?)		
D-MECL	Trixy G4-2	. . .-15	
D-MECM	Aerospool WT-9 Dynamic	DY521/2014	
D-MECO	Autogyro Europe MTO Sport	unkn	
D-MECQ	Flight Design CTSW	unkn	
D-MECS	B&F Funk FK-9 Mk.IV	09-04-228	
D-MECT	Flight Design CT-2K	01-04-06-15	
D-MECW	Bautek Eagle V/ Pico	unkn	
D-MEDB	Bautek Eagle V/ Pico	unkn	
D-MEDC	Autogyro Europe MT-03	unkn	
D-MEDD	NST Minimum	1449	
D-MEDE	Comco Ikarus Fox-C22	9107-3365	
	(Same c/n as D-MNAO)		
D-MEDE(2)	Fläming Air FA-01 Smaragd	unkn	
D-MEDH	Evektor EV-97 Eurostar SL	unkn	
D-MEDI (2)	WDFL Dallach D4 Fascination BK	101	
D-MEDJ #	Autogyro Europe MTOsport	unkn	
D-MEDL	Comco Ikarus C-42B	0506-6686	
	(W/o 8.8.14 Kulmbach)		
D-MEDM	Evektor EV-97 Eurostar SL	unkn	
D-MEDO(1)	NST Minimum	M535	
D-MEDO(2)	Flight Design CT LS	F-08-07-14	
	(W/o 26.4.12)		
D-MEDP #	NST Minimum	M521	
D-MEDR	Celier Xenon 44 Medevac	CAC14M9E08AA013L	
D-MEDS #	Behlen Power-Trike	002583	
D-MEDT	Kümmerle Mini-Fly-Set	1273/91-5	
D-MEDU	Roland Z602	Z-9569	
D-MEDV	Comco Ikarus C-42 Cyclone	9610-6010	OE-7037
D-MEDX	Celier Xenon	CAF08273R	
D-MEDY(1)	B&F Funk FK-9 Mk.IV	unkn	
D-MEDY(2)	Silent 2 Electro	unkn	
D-MEDZ	Autogyro Europe MTOsport	unkn	
	(Cancelled)		
D-MEEA	ATEC 321 Faeta	UNKN	
D-MEEB	Pottier P.130UL	1	
D-MEEC(1)	Ultraleichtverbund Bi 90	168308471	
D-MEEC(2)	Cosmos / Chronos 12	unkn	
D-MEED	Plätzer Kiebitz	unkn	
D-MEEF	Aeropro Eurofox	unkn	
D-MEEG	Tecnam P.96S Golf 100	unkn	
D-MEEH	Autogyro Europe Calidus	unkn	
D-MEEI	Aerospool WT-9 Dynamic	DY383/2010	
D-MEEJ	B&F Funk FK-9 Mk.IV ELA	09-05-416	
D-MEEK	Plätzer Kiebitz-B	320	
	(Damaged 5.6.16)		
D-MEEL(1)	Comco Ikarus Fox-C22	9207-3440	
D-MEEL(2)	Autogyro Europe MTOsport	unkn	
D-MEEM	Fresh Breeze 110 AL 2F	113	
D-MEEN	Bautek Eagle III/ Chronos 12	unkn	
D-MEEO	Pipistrel Virus	unkn	
D-MEES	Rans S-6 Coyote II	11041620-ES	
D-MEEU	Pipistrel Virus SW	unkn	
D-MEEV	Sky-Walker II	283	
D-MEEW	Fresh Breeze Simo 122	unkn	
D-MEEX	Fresh Breeze BulliX	unkn	
D-MEEY	Fresh Breeze Simo 122	unkn	
D-MEEZ	Aerostyle Breezer	054	
	(Previously quoted as 055)		
D-MEFA(1)	Schönleber DS Speed KS 14 Trike	KS01/0192	
D-MEFA(2)	Fläming Air FA-04 Peregrine SL	unkn	
D-MEFB	Flight Team Spider Trike	D033	
D-MEFC	Aeropro Eurofox	25408	
D-MEFD	Fresh Breeze Simo 122	unkn	
D-MEFE(1)	Ultraleichtverbund Bi 90	6480	
D-MEFE(2)	Trixy G 4-2 R	011-12	
D-MEFF	Aerostyle Breezer	016	
D-MEFG #	Fair Fax Trike	024	
D-MEFH	Schmidtler Enduro Trike	01-003	
D-MEFI	Comco Ikarus C-42B	0303-6521	
D-MEFK	Fresh Breeze 110 AL 2F	163	
D-MEFL	Ultraleichtverbund Bi 90	552	
D-MEFM	Aerostyle Breezer	044	
	(To OH-U486, 4.06)		
D-MEFR	Fresh Breeze Simo 110	unkn	
D-MEFS	Alpi Avn Pioneer 300UL	unkn	
D-MEFU	Aerospool WT-9 Dynamic	unkn	
D-MEFW #	NST Minimum Zephir	M520/23670	
D-MEFY	Comco Ikarus C-42	unkn	
D-MEGA	Air Création	unkn	
D-MEGB	Take Off Merlin / Avant	unkn	
D-MEGD	WDFL Dallach D4 Fascination BK	133	
D-MEGE	Aerospool WT-9 Dynamic	DY440/2012	
D-MEGF #	Comco Ikarus Fox-D	unkn	
D-MEGG	Tandem Air Sunny Sport	33.92	
D-MEGH	Pipistrel Virus	unkn	
D-MEGI (2)	B&F Funk FK-9 Mk.II	09-005	
D-MEGL	Magni M-24 Orion	24138134	
D-MEGO	Aerostyle Breezer CL	091	
D-MEGP	Comco Ikarus C-42C	1503-7367	
D-MEGS	unidentified weightshift	unkn	
D-MEGW	Plätzer Kiebitz-B	074	
D-MEGX	Remos GX	400	
D-MEHC	Fresh Breeze 110 AL2F	39	
D-MEHE	Behlen Power-Trike	92001	
D-MEHF	Comco Ikarus Fox-C22	8906-3197	
D-MEHG	HFL Stratos 300K	300-011K	
D-MEHH	Pipistrel Taurus 503	unkn	
D-MEHI	AirLony Skylane	51	
D-MEHJ	Autogyro Europe MT-03	unkn	
D-MEHK	Fresh Breeze 110 AL 2F	156	
D-MEHL(2)	Pago Jet M4	970401	
D-MEHL(3)	Zenair CH-701D STOL	7-9479	
D-MEHL(4)	Roland Skyjeep	unkn	
	(May be D-MEHL(3) converted)		
D-MEHM #	Evektor EV-97 Eurostar SL	unkn	
D-MEHN	AirLony Skylane UL	unkn	
D-MEHO	Unidentified flexwing	unkn	
D-MEHP(1)	Autogyro Europe MT-03	unkn	
D-MEHP(2)	Autogyro Europe MTOsport	unkn	
D-MEHR	Scheibe Uli-2	3304	
D-MEHS	APIS	W009	
D-MEHT	AirLony Skylane UL	55	
D-MEHU #	Fisher FP-202 Koala	2322	
D-MEHV #	Behlen Power-Trike	875022	
D-MEHW(1)	Behlen Power-Trike II Hazard 15M	910604	
D-MEHW(2)	AirLony Skylane	77	
D-MEHX	AirLony Skylane	unkn	
D-MEHZ	AirLony Skylane	60/2013	
D-MEIA	Flight Team Spider Hazard 13	D021	
D-MEIB	Aeropilot Legend 540	1419	
D-MEIC	Alpi Aviation Pioneer 300S	unkn	
D-MEID	B&F Funk FK-9 ELA	05-441	
D-MEIF	Comco Ikarus C-42	0202-6416	
D-MEIG	Moyes Dragonfly	D05006	
D-MEIH	Aerospool WT-9 Dynamic	DY164/2007	
D-MEII	Fisher FP-202 Koala	JE 001	
D-MEIK	Zenair CH-602XL Zodiac	9521	
D-MEIL	Autogyro Europe MTOsport	unkn	
D-MEIN(1)	Büttner Crazyplane I	118	
D-MEIN(2)	Autogyro Europe MTO Sport	unkn	
D-MEIO #	Silent 2 Electro	unkn	
D-MEIQ #	Speed	unkn	
D-MEIR	UPM Funplane Trike	870027	
D-MEIS	Behlen Power-Trike	1000683	
D-MEIT #	Wisch Star-Trike Vampir II	12603895	
D-MEJB	Jihlavan KP-2U Rapid 200	2143160N	
D-MEJF	Herringhausen Vagabund	11	
D-MEJH	B&F Funk FK-12 Comet	12-070	
D-MEJK #	Behlen Power-Trike Vampir II	88020	
D-MEJP	Fresh Breeze Simo 122	unkn	
D-MEJS	B&F Funk FK-14 Polaris	014-103	
D-MEKA	Comco Ikarus Fox I	054	
D-MEKB	Pipistrel Virus SW	unkn	
D-MEKE	Flight Team Spider	D047	
D-MEKF	Dallach D4B Fascination	unkn	
	(Cancelled)		
D-MEKH	EEL ULF-2	022	
D-MEKI	Plätzer Kiebitz-B8	031	
D-MEKL	Alpi Avn Pioneer 300UL	unkn	
D-MEKN	Comco Ikarus C-42B	0211-6499	
D-MEKO	Ekolot JK-05 Junior	05-06-10	
D-MEKS	Aerostyle Breezer	036	
D-MEKU	Plätzer Motte B	047	

Reg	Type	c/n	
D-MEKW(1)	Comco Ikarus Fox D	8505-FD20	
D-MEKW(2)#	Bautek Eagle V/ Profi	unkn	
D-MEKZ	Comco Ikarus C-42C	unkn	
D-MELA(1)	Magni M-16 Tandem Trainer (?)	unkn	
D-MELA(2)	ELA Aviacion ELA-10 Eclipse	02164681014	
D-MELB(1)	Plätzer Kiebitz P5	unkn	
D-MELB(2)	Aeropilot Legend 540	1312	
D-MELD	P&M Pegasus Quantum 15-912	unkn	
D-MELE(1)	Klüver Bison Trike	982704	
D-MELE(2)	AirLony Skylane	unkn	
D-MELF(2)	Schmidtler Enduro Trike	M3557747	
D-MELF(3)	Autogyro Europe MTOsport	unkn	
D-MELG	Take Off Maximum Karat 13 Trike	035100	
D-MELH	Remos G3 Mirage RS	125	
D-MELI(1)	TL Ultralight TL-96 Star	unkn	
D-MELI(2)	Comco Ikarus C-42B	0211-6512	
D-MELJ	B&F Funk FK-9 ELA	09-05-438	
D-MELK	Spacek SD-1 Minisport TD	024	
D-MELL	LO-120S	010-A	
D-MELM	Behlen Power-Trike Falcon	1718	
D-MELN	Solar World Elektra One	unkn	
D-MELO	Autogyro Europe MT-03	D06G04	
D-MELQ	PC-Aero Elektra One	unkn	
D-MELR(1)	Schmidtler Ranger M	14/49	
D-MELR(2)	Autogyro Europe MTOsport	unkn	
D-MELT	Tecnam P.96 Golf 100	unkn	
D-MELV	Flight Design CT-2K	unkn	
D-MELW	Air-Light Wild Thing	07.090	
D-MELX(1)	Fresh Breeze 122 AL 2F	410	
D-MELX(2)	ParaZoom Trio-Star/Swing/Scorpio	unkn	
D-MELY	Light Aero Avid Flyer Mk.4	936	
D-MELZ	Flight Design CTSW	unkn	
D-MEMA	Alpi Aviation Pioneer 300	185	
D-MEMB	Take Off Merlin Trike	25726	
D-MEMC	Fläming Air Smaragd 100	119/09	
D-MEMD	Remos GX	314	
D-MEME	Flight Design CT SW	04-09-04	
	(To LN-YAA)		
D-MEMF	Plätzer Kiebitz B	255	
D-MEMI	Fresh Breeze Simo 122	unkn	
D-MEMJ	Fresh Breeze 110 AL 2F	201	
D-MEMK #	ASO Viper Hazard 15 Trike	11290	
D-MEMM	Autogyro Europe MT-03	unkn	
D-MEMO(1)	Scheibe Ultra	3409	
D-MEMO(2)	Zenair CH-701D STOL	7-9507	
	(To ZK-STK, 11.12)		
D-MEMP	Aeropro Eurofox 2K	unkn	
D-MEMR	Schmidtler Enduro Trike	02-007	
D-MEMS	Kappa KP-2U Sova	013J	
D-MEMY(1)	Aerospool WT-9 Dynamic	19	
D-MEMY(2)	Aerospool WT-9 Dynamic	DY289/2008	
D-MENA	Tecnam P.92 Echo 2000S	unkn	
D-MENB(1)	Light Aero Avid Flyer	905	
D-MENB(2)	Comco Ikarus C-42B	1203-7188	
D-MENC	Aerostyle Breezer	049	
D-MEND	Sky-Walker II	358	
D-MENE	Flight Design CT LS	07.11.25	
D-MENG	Sky-Walker II	234	
D-MENK	Flight Design CT-2K	03.03.05.12	
D-MENN	Autogyro Europe MTOsport	unkn	
D-MENO #.	UPM Cobra BF 52UL Trike	950133	
D-MENP	Comco Ikarus C-42B	1502-7369	
D-MENS	B&F Funk FK-9Mk.IV Utility Club	04U-266	
D-MENT	Comco Ikarus C-42B	0903-7030	
D-MENU	Behlen Power-Trike II Hazard 15	90020	
D-MENW	Alpi Aviation Pioneer 300	unkn	
D-MENZ	Fisher FP.404	4079	
D-MEOB	Breezer Aircraft Breezer CL	UL069	
D-MEON	Autogyro Europe MTOsport	unkn	
D-MEOP	Autogyro Europe MTOsport	unkn	
D-MEOW	Zenair CH-602	unkn	
D-MEPA	ASO Viper 13/582 Hazard 13 Trike	122020108	
D-MEPC(1)	DPM (trike)	unkn	
D-MEPC(2)#	Magni M-24 Orion	24148474	
D-MEPG(1)	Albatros AN-22	8332	
D-MEPG(2)	Comco Ikarus C-42B	0803-6949	
D-MEPH	Comco Ikarus Fox-C22	9003-3261	
	(To 01-IV)		
D-MEPI	Fair Fax DR Trike	D012	
D-MEPK	Remos G3-600 Mirage	175	
D-MEPM	Roland Z602	Z-9577	
D-MEPO	B&F Funk FK-9 ELA	09-418	
D-MEPP	Autogyro Europe MTOsport	unkn	
D-MEPS(1)	ASO Viper Trike	22038208	
D-MEPS(2)	Fly Synthesis Storch CL	ST11004304	PH-2L8
	(To Australia as 24-8067, 2.12)		
D-MEPS(3)	Flight Design CT LS	08-05-17	T7-MGL
D-MEPU	Pioneer Flightstar	678	
D-MEPW(1)	Comco Ikarus Fox-C22	8906-3204	
D-MEPW(2)	Flight Design CT2SW	04.12.03	
D-MEPY	CzAW/Zenair CH-601XL Zodiac	6-9897	
D-MERA	Kiggen/Heiland Air Création GTE 582S	9954557785	
D-MERB	Ultralight Flight Phantom	0294	
D-MERC	Enduro Trike (Homebuilt)	12/92	
D-MERD(1)	UPM Omega Focus 20	880032	
D-MERD(2)	Flight Design CT SW	unkn	
D-MERE	ATEC 321 Faeta	unkn	
D-MERF #	Comco Ikarus Fox D	8710-FD41	
D-MERG(2)	Zlin Savage	114	
D-MERH(2)	Aerostyle Breezer	025	
D-MERI	Saphir (Trike)	unkn	
D-MERK(1)	Fresh Breeze 110 AL2F	7439	
D-MERK(2)	Aerospool WT-9 Dynamic	DY426/2011	
D-MERL	Behlen Trike	86023	
D-MERN #	Flight Design CT LS	unkn	
D-MERO	Scheibe UL-1 Coach IIS	003	
D-MERP	Alpi Avn Pioneer 300	unkn	
D-MERR	Loehle P-51 Mustang	unkn	
D-MERS	Comco Ikarus Fox-C22	9204-3395	
D-MERT#	Albatros SX	503	
D-MERW	Alpi Avn Pioneer 200	unkn	
D-MERY	Celier Xenon	unkn	
D-MERZ	Scheibe Uli 1	5216	
D-MESA	ASO Viper Hazard 15 Trike	11024201	
D-MESB(2)	Fläming Air FA-01 Smaragd	07/04	
D-MESC	Aerospool WT-9 Dynamic	DY465/2013	
D-MESD	Spacek SD-1 Minisport TD	034	
D-MESE	Pipistrel Taurus 503	unkn	
D-MESG #	Behlen Power-Trike	87028	
D-MESH	Autogyro Europe MT-03	unkn	
D-MESK	Fresh Breeze Simo 122	unkn	
D-MESL	Comco Ikarus Fox-C22	9203-3392	
D-MESN	B&F Funk FK Mk.IV Executive	unkn	
D-MESP(1)	UPM Cobra Trike	900105	
D-MESP(2)	Comco Ikarus C-42B	unkn	
D-MESR	FUL Graffiti Trike	018/0076	
D-MESS	Comco Ikarus C-42B	unkn	
D-MEST	Ultraleichtverbund Bi 90	4926438690	
D-MESU	Zenair CH-701 STOL	7-9068	
D-MESW	Sky-Walker II	169	
D-MESX	Autogyro Europe Cavalon	V00131	
D-MESY	Comco Ikarus C-42B	unkn	
D-METB	Alpi Avn Pioneer 300STD	330	
D-METC	Plätzer Kiebitz-B	372	
D-METD	Pipistrel Taurus Electro	unkn	S5-P1104
D-METE	Comco Ikarus Fox-C22	9207-3417	
D-METH	Plätzer Kiebitz-B4	019	
D-METI	Comco Ikarus C-42B	0902-7024	
D-METL	Schmidtler Enduro Trike	01001	
D-METO	Aeropro Eurofox	unkn	
D-METP	Autogyro Europe MT-03	D06G29	
D-METT	Light Aero Avid Flyer IV	1153 D	
D-METU	Aériane Sirocco II	116	
D-METY #	Drachenstudio Royal Trike	14-0896	
D-METZ #	Schmidtler Enduro Trike	02-018	
D-MEUB #	Junkers Profly JUL Trike	0001	
D-MEUD	B&F Funk FK-9 Mk.IV Utility	09-04U-315	
D-MEUE	FUL Graffiti MA-30 / Aeros	unkn	
D-MEUL	FUL Graffiti Trike	034/0100	
D-MEUR	Flight Team Spider Hazard 15	D011	
D-MEUT	Blackshape Prime BS100	unkn	
D-MEVA	HFL Stratos IIe	IIe-OO9	
D-MEVB	Alpi Avn Pioneer 300	unkn	
D-MEVC #	Büttner Crazyplane III	5	
D-MEVE	Alpi Avn Pioneer 200	unkn	
D-MEVI	Light Aero Avid Flyer Mk.4	972	
D-MEVL	Arrow Copter AC20	043	
D-MEVO	Zlin Savage Cruiser	97	
D-MEVT(1)	Kümmerle Mini-Fly-Set	251864	
D-MEVT(2)	Autogyro Europe MTOsport	M00868	
D-MEVV	Autogyro Europe MTOsport	unkn	
D-MEWE	Albatros 52	115	
D-MEWH	Urban Air Samba XXL	unkn	
D-MEWJ	Autogyro Europe MT-03	unkn	
D-MEWK	ICP MXP-740V Savannah	02-07-51-152	
D-MEWL	Flight Team Spider Trike	D030	
D-MEWM	Pioneer Flightstar II	090501	
D-MEWO	NST Minimum Sierra II	231	
D-MEWP	Plätzer Kiebitz-B	89	
	(Same c/n as OE-7016)		
D-MEWR	NST Minimum	unkn	
D-MEWS	WDFL Dallach Sunrise	015	
	(Same c/n as D-MWSI)		
D-MEWU	Klüver Kaiman Trike	701612	
D-MEXI	Autogyro Europe MT-03	unkn	
D-MEXY	B&F Funk FK-14 Polaris	147	
D-MEYE	Autogyro Europe MTOsport	unkn	
	(Cancelled)		
D-MEYN	Autogyro Europe MTOsport	unkn	
D-MEYR	Drachenstudio Royal 912	unkn	
D-MEYZ	Comco Ikarus C-42B	0703-6879	
D-MEZE(1)	UPM Cobra BF 52UL Trike	950132	
D-MEZE(2)	Air Light WT-01 Wild Thing	095	
D-MEZI	Zenair CH-602XL Zodiac	unkn	
D-MEZO	B&F Funk FK-9 Mk.IV	389	
D-MEZZ	TL Ultralight TL-96 Sting	07ST238	
D-MFAA(1)	Comco Ikarus Fox-C22	8703-3036	
D-MFAA(2)	Vidor Asso V Champion	AP1	
D-MFAB(1)	Comco Ikarus Fox II Doppel	8612-3051	
D-MFAB(2)	trike / Firebird	unkn	
D-MFAB(3)	Flight Design CT SW	07-05-21	
D-MFAC(1)	Comco Ikarus Fox II Doppel	8609-3033	
D-MFAC(2)	Evektor EV-97 Eurostar SL	2010 3904	
D-MFAD #	Comco Ikarus Fox II Doppel	8611-3034	
D-MFAE	Flight Design CT SW	unkn	
D-MFAF	Comco Ikarus Fox-C22	8701-3034	
D-MFAG	Bautek Eagle III/Ghost 14.9	99B00	
D-MFAH	Fläming Air FA-01 Smaragd	unkn	
D-MFAK	Fläming Air FA-01 Smaragd	08/04	
D-MFAL #	Celier Xenon	CAF05972R	
D-MFAN(1)	Comco Ikarus Fox-C22	8703-3039	
D-MFAN(2)	Dyn'Aero MCR-01 UL	223	
D-MFAO	Comco Ikarus Fox II Doppel	8703-3037	
D-MFAP	Comco Ikarus Fox II Doppel	8706-3040	
D-MFAQ	Comco Ikarus Fox II Doppel	8703-3038	
D-MFAR	Comco Ikarus C-42B	unkn	
D-MFAS	Solid Air Twin Diamant Trike	T-010	
D-MFAT #	Comco Ikarus Fox II Doppel	8706-3041	
D-MFAU	Comco Ikarus Fox-C22	8707-3091	
D-MFAX	Comco Ikarus Fox D	8512-FD37	
D-MFAZ	Autogyro Europe MTOsport	unkn	
D-MFBA	Comco Ikarus Fox-C22	8907-3175	
D-MFBB	Comco Ikarus C-42B	0307-6558	
D-MFBC	Comco Ikarus Fox-C22	8907-3176	
D-MFBD	Comco Ikarus Fox-C22	8905-3178	
D-MFBE	Comco Ikarus Fox-C22	8907-3177	
D-MFBG	Flight Design CT-2K	01.09.04.28	
D-MFBH(1)	Comco Ikarus C-42B	0310-6582	
D-MFBH(2)	Comco Ikarus C-42B	0806-6979	
D-MFBJ	Comco Ikarus Fox-C22	unkn	
D-MFBL #	MKB Enduro Focus 18	0300185	
D-MFBM	Plätzer Kiebitz-B8	121	
D-MFBO	AirLony Skylane	unkn	
D-MFBP	ASO Viper 15 Hazard Trike	15/ 2690	
D-MFBS	B&F Funk FK-9 Mk3 Utility	09-04U-281	
D-MFBT	Fresh Breeze 110 AL2F	103	
D-MFBW(1)	Ultraleichtverbund Bi 90	994	
D-MFBW(2)	B&F Funk FK-9 ELA Professional	09-05-468	
D-MFBY	Best Off Sky Ranger	unkn	
D-MFCA	Comco Ikarus Fox-C22	9308-3525	
D-MFCB	Magni M-24 Orion	24137644	
D-MFCC	Autogyro Europe Cavalon	unkn	

Reg	Type	C/n	Notes
D-MFCE	Drachenstudio Royal 912 ULS / Eos	unkn	
D-MFCG	Celier Xenon	CAI06472R	
D-MFCI	Tecnam P.92 Echo Light	1480	
D-MFCJ	Fresh Breeze X-One 4T	unkn	
D-MFCO	Zenair CH-601XL Zodiac	6-9883	
D-MFCS	Autogyro Europe MTOsport	unkn	
D-MFCT	Flight Design CT SW	05-12-03	
	(To N375CT)		
D-MFCW	Bautek Eagle V/ Ghost 14.9	unkn	
D-MFDA #	Aeropro Eurofox	unkn	
D-MFDC	FD Composites Arrowcopter AC20 test marks	-	
D-MFDF	WDFL Dallach D4 Fascination BK	112	
D-MFDH	Behlen Power-Trike	92012	
D-MFDI #	Flight Design CT Supralight	E-12-09-08	
D-MFDK	Fresh Breeze 110 AL2F	72	
D-MFDS	Autogyro Europe MTOsport	unkn	
D-MFDT	Aquilair Swing 14 Trike	unkn	
D-MFDX	Flight Design CT LS	F-09-05-11	
D-MFEA #	Comco Ikarus Fox-C22	8711-3098	
D-MFEC	Comco Ikarus Fox-C22	8709-3093	
D-MFED	Comco Ikarus Fox-C22	8709-3094	
D-MFEE	Comco Ikarus Fox II Doppel	8707-3046	
D-MFEF	Schmidtler Enduro XP / XP 15	unkn	
D-MFEG	Flight Design CT SW	07-03-23	
D-MFEH	Tandem Air Sunny Sport	29.92	
D-MFEI (2)	Comco Ikarus Fox-C22	8709-3095	
D-MFEJ	Magni M-24 Orion	unkn	
D-MFEL	Comco Ikarus Fox-C22	8710-3097	
D-MFEM	Comco Ikarus Fox II Doppel	8604-3014	
D-MFEN	Comco Ikarus Fox-C22	8711-3099	
D-MFEP #	Firebird M-1	59092	
D-MFEQ #	Comco Ikarus Fox-C22	8805-3100	
D-MFER(1)	Comco Ikarus Fox-C22	8804-3103	
D-MFER(2)	Aerospool WT-9 Dynamic	DY481/2013	
D-MFES	Comco Ikarus Fox-C22	8808-3102	
D-MFET	Comco Ikarus Fox-C22	8807-3101	
D-MFEU	Comco Ikarus C-42	0805-6977	
D-MFEZ	Autogyro Europe MTOsport	unkn	
D-MFEZ(2)?	Celier Xenon	unkn	
D-MFFA	Rans S-6 Coyote II	0193422	
D-MFFC	Aeroprakt A-22L Vision	306	
D-MFFD #	Fair Fax Trike	011	
D-MFFE	Trixy G 4-2R	020-13	
D-MFFI	Autogyro Europe MTOsport	unkn	
D-MFFK(1)	Fair-Fax Euro III Trike	045	
D-MFFK(2)	B&F Funk FK-14B Polaris	014-093	
D-MFFM(1)	Fair Fax Trike	042	
D-MFFM(2)	Aeropro Eurofox Pro (n/w)	unkn	
D-MFFN	Fair Fax DR Trike	D028	
D-MFFO(1)	B&F Funk FK-9 Mk.IV	09-04-231	
	(W/o 25.7.08, replaced with (2), 3.09)		
D-MFFO(2)	B&F Funk FK-9 Mk.IV	386	
D-MFFS	Pipistrel/Zen Sinus	unkn	
D-MFFT	Comco Ikarus Fox-C22	8809-3152	
D-MFFW(1)	Fair Fax DR Hazard 15M Trike	D017	
D-MFFW(2)	Comco Ikarus C-42B	0303-6540	
D-MFFZ	Autogyro Europe MTOsport	unkn	
D-MFGB	Alpi Avn Pioneer 200STD	unkn	
D-MFGD #	Flight Design CT-2K	02.01.05.05	
D-MFGF	Aerospool WT-9 Dynamic	DY384/2010	
D-MFGG	Albatros 52	141	
D-MFGH	Albatros 64	302	
D-MFGI	Fresh Breeze 110AL2F	55	
D-MFGK #	Fresh Breeze Simo 122	unkn	
D-MFGL	Fresh Breeze 110 AL 2F	343	
D-MFGM #	ASO Viper Trike	12044 503	
D-MFGN	Flight Design CT2SW	04-02-05	
D-MFGO	Aeropro Eurofox	20906	
D-MFGP	Celier Xenon 4	CAM14M3E14AA021L	D-MCXT
D-MFGS	Eurofly Viper 582 / Hazard 12S	unkn	
D-MFGT	Albatros SX	502	
D-MFGW	Bautek Eagle V / Pico S	unkn	
D-MFHB	Autogyro Europe MT-03	unkn	
D-MFHC	Fresh Breeze Simo 122	unkn	
D-MFHD	Flight Design CT SL	unkn	
D-MFHE	TL Ultralight TL-232 Condor Plus	99C03	
D-MFHG	Comco Ikarus Fox-C22	9010-3295	
D-MFHJ(1)	NST Minimum	M540	
D-MFHJ(2)	Comco Ikarus C-42B	1501-7270	
D-MFHL	Autogyro Europe MTOsport	unkn	
D-MFHM	Bautek Eagle V / Pico	unkn	
D-MFHP	PAP ROS 125 / Fusion paramotor	unkn	
D-MFHR	Air Light WT-02 Wild Thing	07.086	
D-MFHT	Tecnam P.92 Echo Super	unkn	
D-MFHW	Best Off Sky Ranger	532	
D-MFHX	Aerostyle Breezer	060	
D-MFHY	Tecnam P.92 Echo Classic	925	
D-MFHZ	FD Composites Arrowcopter AC20	036	
D-MFIA	Tecnam P.92 Echo Classic De Luxe	1324	
D-MFIB	Comco Ikarus Fox-C22	8809-3161	
D-MFIC	Fresh Breeze Simo 122	unkn	
D-MFID	Comco Ikarus Fox-C22	8811-3162	
D-MFIE	Evektor EV-97 Eurostar SL	2011 3911	OK-FUU 09
D-MFIH	Comco Ikarus Fox-C22	8903-3165	
D-MFII	Comco Ikarus C-42B	0209-6500	
D-MFIK	Strike Cub	unkn	
D-MFIM	Comco Ikarus Fox-C22	8903-3167	
D-MFIN	Comco Ikarus Fox-C22	8904-3168	
D-MFIO	Einzelstück Nemesis N1 UL	001	
D-MFIP	Comco Ikarus Fox II Doppel	8706-3042	
D-MFIR #	Comco Ikarus Fox-C22	8905-3169	
D-MFIS #	Comco Ikarus Fox-C22	8905-3170	
D-MFIT	Aerostyle Breezer CR	073	
D-MFIV #	Comco Ikarus Fox-C22	8904-3172	
D-MFIW #	Comco Ikarus Fox-C22	8906-3173	
D-MFIX	Dallach Sunrise IIA	004	
D-MFIZ	Comco Ikarus Fox-C22	8908-3174	
D-MFJB	ATEC 321 Faeta	F230606A	
D-MFJH #	Fläming Air FA-01 Smaragd	unkn	
D-MFJK	Plätzer Kiebitz	unkn	
D-MFJP	Rotortec Cloud Dancer II	unkn	
D-MFJR	Fresh Breeze BulliX	unkn	
D-MFJS	Fair Fax DR Trike	D019	
D-MFKA	Klüver Bison Trike	883806	
D-MFKB	Alpi Avn Pioneer 300	unkn	
D-MFKC	Comco Ikarus C-42B	1204-7192	
D-MFKD	B&F Funk FK-12 Comet	12-060	
D-MFKE	Comco Ikarus Fox-C22	8805-3109	
D-MFKF	Point Aviation Albatros AN-22	09	
D-MFKG	Comco Ikarus C-42B	0603-6796	
D-MFKH	J-3 Kitten	01	
D-MFKJ	B&F Funk FK-12 Comet	012-098	
D-MFKK(1)	Plätzer Kiebitz-B2	102	
	(Same c/n as (to?) D-MZHR)		
D-MFKK(2)	Dova DV-1 Skylark	07/33	
D-MFKL	Seiffert Mini II	0101/89-1	
D-MFKM	B&F Funk FK-14A Polaris	014-028	
D-MFKN	Best Off Sky Ranger	unkn	
D-MFKO(1)	Sky-Walker 1+1	26122	
D-MFKO(2)	Best Off Sky Ranger	unkn	
D-MFKP	B&F Funk FK-9 Mk IV	04-361	
D-MFKR #	Fresh Breeze Simo 122	unkn	
D-MFKS	Comco Ikarus C-42B	0412-6644	
D-MFKT	B&F FK-14B Polaris	14-085	
D-MFKU	B&F Funk FK-9 Mk.3	09-03-209	PH-3U2
D-MFKV	B&F Funk FK-9 Mk.IV	434	
D-MFKW #	Comco Ikarus Fox II Doppel	8603-3012	
D-MFKY	B&F Funk FK-9 Mk.IV ELA SW	unkn	
D-MFLA	Light Aero Avid Flyer IV C	1325C	
D-MFLB	ASO Viper Trike/Royal 912	15181090	
D-MFLD	Bautek Eagle V/ Pico	unkn	
D-MFLE	Comco Ikarus Fox-C22B	8809-3110	
D-MFLF	Fresh Breeze Simo 122	unkn	
D-MFLH(1)	Comco Ikarus Fox II Doppel	8606-3020	
	(To Hungary as 06-80)		
D-MFLH(2)	B&F Funk FK-14B Polaris	014-122	
D-MFLL	Comco Ikarus C-42B	1403-7305	
D-MFLM	Comco Ikarus C-42B	0212-6517	PH-3S4
D-MFLO	Take Off Maximum Trike	109013	
D-MFLP	AirEnergy AE-1 Silent	unkn	
D-MFLS	ASO Viper Hazard 15 Trike	15I 6990	
D-MFLT(1)	Comco Ikarus C-42	unkn	
D-MFLT(2)	Flight Design CT LS	F-09-03-02	
D-MFLU	Aviasud Albatros 64	303	
D-MFLW	Fly Whale	unkn	
D-MFLY	Behlen Power-Trike /Rotax 582	88027	
D-MFMA	Comco Ikarus Fox-C22	8701-3031	
D-MFMB(1)	Firebird	unkn	
D-MFMB(2)	B&F Funk FK-9 Mk IV	09-04-322	
D-MFMD	Comco Ikarus C-42B	0406-6600	
D-MFME	Take Off Merlin 1100	unkn	
D-MFMF(1)	Tandem Air Sunny	15.91	
D-MFMF(2)	Aerospool WT-9 Dynamic	DY275/2008	67-BEK/F-JWFR
D-MFMK	Flight Design CT SW	05-03-08	
D-MFML	Drachenstudio Royal 912 / Eos	unkn	
D-MFMM #	Flight Design CT LS	F-09-07-03	
D-MFMN	Fresh Breeze 110 AL 2F	10	
D-MFMO	AirLony Skylane UL	unkn	OK-PUO 81
	(Identity unconfirmed – see PH-4F4)		
D-MFMS	Autogyro Europe MT-03	unkn	
D-MFMV	Schönleber Trike	V070198	
D-MFMW #	ARCO Spacer L	966	
D-MFND	Aerospool WT-9 Dynamic	DY195/2007	
D-MFNH #	Plätzer Kiebitz A/B9	unkn	
D-MFNJ #	FUL Graffiti MA 30 / Stranger	unkn	
D-MFNL(1)	Magni M-24 Orion	24 13 7874	
D-MFNL(2)	Alpi Avn Pioneer 300 Kite	unkn	
D-MFNY	B&F Funk FK-9 Mk.4	09-04SW-388	
D-MFNZ #	Autogyro Europe MT-03	unkn	
D-MFOB #	Krampen Ikarus S	59	
D-MFOO #	Magni M-24 Orion	24 12 7524	
D-MFOQ #	Klüver Twin Racer Quartz SX 16	236004	
D-MFOR	Trixy G 4-2 R Princess	004-12	
D-MFOS #	Comco Ikarus Fox-C22	8707-3044	
D-MFOW	Aerospool WT-9 Dynamic	DY469/2013	
D-MFOX	Comco Ikarus Fox D	023	
D-MFPA(1)	Fantasy Air Allegro 2000	unkn	
D-MFPA(2)	Albastar Apis 2	W006	
D-MFPB #	NST Minimum	M430	
D-MFPC	Aeropro Eurofox	unkn	
D-MFPE	Fresh Breeze Simo 122	unkn	
D-MFPF	FUL Graffiti	028/0094	
D-MFPG	B&F Funk FK-9 Mk,III	09-04U-251	
D-MFPI	Pipistrelle Sinus	unkn	
D-MFPK	Plätzer Kiebitz-B2	103	
D-MFPL	Magnus MG-11 Fusion	unkn	
D-MFPM #	WDFL Dallach D4 Fascination BK	107	
D-MFPS	Autogyro Europe MT-03	unkn	
D-MFPW	Autogyro Europe MTOsport	unkn	
D-MFPY	Zlin Savage	284	
D-MFRA(1)	Fresh Breeze 110 AL 2F	63	
D-MFRA(2)	Comco Ikarus C-42B	unkn	
D-MFRB	Aerospool WT-9 Dynamic	DY076/2005	D-MDYN
D-MFRC	FUL Maverick Trike	unkn	
D-MFRD	Schönleber DS Lotus KS 16 Trike	KS01/0191	
D-MFRE	NST Minimum	M231	
D-MFRG	Fair Fax DR Trike	001	
D-MFRI	Comco Ikarus Sherpa 1	8306-1029	
D-MFRI(2)	Platzer Kiebitz B	205	
	(painted D-MFRitz)		
D-MFRK	Light Aero Avid Flyer	809	
D-MFRL	Autogyro Europe MTOsport	unkn	
D-MFRM	Autogyro Europe MT-03	unkn	
D-MFRR	Air-Light Wild Thing	084	
D-MFRW	T2	N33931534	
D-MFRZ	Plätzer Kiebitz-B8	135	
D-MFSA(1)	Comco Ikarus Fox-C22	8805-3108	
D-MFSA(2)	Plätzer Kiebitz	277	
D-MFSG(1)	ASO Viper Trike	VI 12037207	
D-MFSG(2)	Plätzer Kiebitz	56	
D-MFSH	Comco Ikarus C-42B	unkn	
D-MFSI #	Fresh Breeze 110 AL2F	87	
D-MFSJ	Remos G.3 Mirage	119	
D-MFSK	Plätzer Kiebitz	unkn	
D-MFSL(1)	B&F Funk FK-9 Mk.III	09-184	
	(To 85-AGK/F-JTQM)		
D-MFSL(2)	Comco Ikarus C-42	unkn	
D-MFSO	Aerospool WT-9 Dynamic	DY079/2005	
D-MFSS(1)	Schmidtler Ranger M Trike	1832	
D-MFSS(2)	Comco Ikarus C-42	unkn	
D-MFST(1)	Plätzer Motte B-2	039	
D-MFST(2)	TL Ultralight TL-96 Star	unkn	

Reg	Type	C/n	Note
D-MFSV	TL Ultralight TL-2000 Sting	08ST267	
D-MFSW(1)	Flight Design CT-2K	03.03.02.09	
	(Same c/n as D-MDKB(1))		
D-MFSW(2)	Flight Design CT-2K	05-06-05	
D-MFSW(3)	Gramex Song 120	unkn	
D-MFSZ #	Comco Ikarus C-42B	0309-6563	
D-MFTA	Comco Ikarus Fox-C22	8808-3104	
	(To SP-SMTA)		
D-MFTC	Aerostyle Breezer	089	
D-MFTE	Comco Ikarus Fox-C22	8808-3105	
D-MFTF	B&F Funk FK-14B Polaris	014-087	
D-MFTH	Solid Air Diamant Twin / Pico S	unkn	
D-MFTL	Aerospool WT-9 Dynamic	DY431/2012	
D-MFTN #	NST Minimum	10873	
D-MFTO	Comco Ikarus Fox-C22	8808-3106	
D-MFTP	Pipistrel Taurus	144T503	
D-MFTT	Dova DV-1 Skylark	07/34	
D-MFUA #	ASO Viper Trike	V 15 I 14491	
D-MFUD	Drachenstudio Royal 912 / Avant 15	unkn	
D-MFUE	Klüver Twin Racer SX 16	554203	
D-MFUF	Klüver Twin Racer SX 16	773209	
D-MFUH	Comco Ikarus C-42B	0303-6548	
D-MFUI #	FUL Maverick T2	4	
D-MFUL	FUL Graffiti Trike	042/0142	
D-MFUM	Autogyro Europe MTOsport	unkn	
D-MFUN(1)	UPM Funplane	86009	
D-MFUN(2)	Autogyro Europe MTOsport	unkn	
D-MFUP	Plätzer Kiebitz B	334	
D-MFUR	Aquilair Swing 582S / Ghost 14.9	unkn	
D-MFUS #	Comco Ikarus Fox-C22	9211-3483	
D-MFUX	Comco Ikarus Fox-C22	8705-3043	
D-MFVB	Comco Ikarus C-42	9701-6022	PH-2Y5
D-MFVC	Comco Ikarus C-42B	unkn	
D-MFVD	Magnus MG-11 Fusion Vantage	unkn	
D-MFVE	Comco Ikarus C-42B	unkn	
D-MFWA	Autogyro Europe MTOsport	unkn	
D-MFWB	Autogyro Europe MT-03	unkn	
D-MFWC	Magni M-24 Orion	24127084	
	(Previously reported as Calidus – in error?)		
D-MFWD	Dallach Sunrise II	009	
D-MFWE	Wempe / Pico S	unkn	
D-MFWF	Remos G.3/600 Mirage	135	
D-MFWG	Autogyro Europe MTO Sport	unkn	
D-MFWH	Light Aero Avid Flyer IV	1295	
D-MFWI #	Autogyro Europe MTOsport	unkn	
D-MFWJ	Autogyro Europe MTOsport	D10S55	
D-MFWK	Autogyro Europe MTOsport	unkn	
D-MFWL	Autogyro Europe MTOsport	unkn	
D-MFWM	Autogyro Europe Calidus	C00167	
D-MFWN	Autogyro Europe MTOsport	unkn	
D-MFWO	Comco Ikarus C-42B	0412-6643	
D-MFWQ #	Autogyro Europe Cavalon	V00031	
	(W/o 23.6.12)		
D-MFWR(1)	Trixy G 4-2 R	023-13	
D-MFWR(2)	Fly Whale Aircraft Adventure iS Sport	unkn	
D-MFWS(1)	Aerospool WT-9 Dynamic	unkn	
D-MFWS(2)	Autogyro Europe MTOsport	unkn	
D-MFWT	Celier Xenon 2	CAB07373R	
	(Cancelled)		
D-MFWU	Autogyro Europe MTOsport	unkn	
D-MFWW	Comco Ikarus C-42B	0803-6963	
D-MFWZ	Remos G3/600 Mirage	unkn	
D-MFZA	B&F Funk FK-9 Mk.III Utility	09-185	
D-MFZB	Evektor EV-97 Eurostar	2005-2419	
D-MFZR	Jihlavan Skyleader 150	unkn	
	(Cancelled)		
D-MFZZ	TL Ultralight TL-96 Star	unkn	
D-MGAA	Autogyro Europe Cavalon	unkn	
	(Severely damaged, Bobenheim 8.9.16)		
D-MGAB	Fresh Breeze Simo 122	unkn	
D-MGAC(1)	Flight Design CT-2K	03.01.04.03	
D-MGAC(2)	Flight Design CT SW	05-06-06	D-MRLD
D-MGAD #	Sky-Walker II	209	
D-MGAE	Autogyro Europe Cavalon	unkn	
D-MGAF	Pioneer Flightstar	373	
D-MGAG	Bautek Eagle III/ Hazard 12S	unkn	
D-MGAH	Behlen Power Trike II	96007	
D-MGAI #	Flight Team Spider	D019	
D-MGAK	Tandem Air Sunny Sport	13.91	
D-MGAL	Fly Synthesis Storch HS	unkn	
D-MGAM	Drachenstudio Royal 912 / Eos	unkn	
D-MGAN	Remos G.3 Mirage	198	
D-MGAP	Comco Ikarus Fox-C22	9108-3355	
D-MGAQ	Zlin Savage Cruiser	unkn	
D-MGAR	Light Aero Avid Flyer	811	
D-MGAS(1)	Zenair CH-701D STOL	7-9270	
D-MGAS(2)	Tecnam P.96S Golf 100	unkn	
D-MGAT	Flight Team Spider Trike	D008	
D-MGAV	Flaming Air Saphir 100	unkn	
	(Crashed 28.3.04)		
D-MGAW	Comco Ikarus C-42B	0905-7039	
D-MGAY #	ARCO Spacer L	361	
D-MGBB	Klüver Racer SX 12	094002	
D-MGBC #	Büttner Crazyplane III	106	
D-MGBD	Trixy G4-2	unkn	
D-MGBE	Autogyro Europe MTOsport	unkn	
D-MGBI	Pipistrel Sinus NW	unkn	
D-MGBK #	Klüver Twin Racer Quartz SX	838910	
D-MGBL (1)	Scheibe Ultra	3412	
D-MGBM	Fresh Breeze Simo 122	unkn	
D-MGBN	TL Ultralight TL-2000 Sting	04ST87	
D-MGBP	Fresh Breeze 110 AL 2F	240	
D-MGBR	Aeropro Eurofox	12702	
D-MGBT #	B&F Funk FK-9 Mk.III	09-03-183	
D-MGBU	Plätzer Kiebitz B	335	
D-MGBW	Flight Team Spider Hazard 13M	D007	
D-MGBY	NST Minimum Saphir	1128	
D-MGCA(1)	Autogyro Europe MT-03	D06G01	
D-MGCA(2)	Autogyro Europe MTOsport	unkn	
D-MGCB	Sky-Walker II	261	
D-MGCC	Light Aero Avid Flyer Heavy Hauler IV C	942C	
	(Presumed ex (PH-2E8) cld in Netherlands 2000)		
D-MGCD	Ekolot KR-030 Topaz	unkn	
D-MGCE	Autogyro Europe MT-03	unkn	
D-MGCE	Autogyro Europe MTOsport	unkn	
D-MGCH	Comco Ikarus C-42B	0911-7073	
D-MGCK	Autogyro Europe MTOsport	unkn	
D-MGCL	Aerostyle Breezer CL	106	
D-MGCO	ES-Trike Carbon ATOS VQ Elektro	0020	
	(ATOS wing c/n is 13090202)		
D-MGCR	Autogyro Europe MTOsport	unkn	
D-MGCS	Tecnam P.92 Echo 2000S	unkn	
D-MGCT(1)	Flight Design CT SW	unkn	
D-MGCT(2)	Autogyro Europe MTOsport	unkn	
D-MGDA	Autogyro Europe Calidus	unkn	
	(Destroyed 10.9.12)		
D-MGDB	Comco Ikarus C-42C	1206-7206	
	(W/o 30.6.15)		
D-MGDC	AirLony Skylane	unkn	
D-MGDE	Celier Xenon 2	unkn	
D-MGDF	Aerospool WT-9 Dynamic	DY058/2004	
D-MGDI	Autogyro Europe Calidus	unkn	
D-MGDJ	unidentified paramotor	unkn	
D-MGDL	B&F Funk FK-14B Polaris	unkn	
D-MGDO	Autogyro Europe MTOsport	unkn	
D-MGDP #	B&F Funk FK-9 Mk.III	09-03-182	
	(Cld by 5.11, probably to D-MCUG)		
D-MGDW	TL Ultralight TL-96 Sting	unkn	
D-MGDX	Autogyro Europe Calidus	unkn	
D-MGEA	Comco Ikarus C-42B	0801-6944	
D-MGEB	TL Ultralight TL-96 Sting	unkn	
D-MGEC	Comco Ikarus C-42	unkn	
D-MGED	Comco Ikarus Fox II Doppel	8607-3030	
D-MGEE	Aeropro Eurofox	unkn	
	(Crashed nr Messkirch 24.9.13)		
D-MGEF	ATEC 321 Faeta	F870914A	
D-MGEG(1)	Ultraleichtverbund Bi 90	6363951644	
D-MGEG(2)	Fresh Breeze Simo 122	unkn	
D-MGEH #	Kümmerle Mini-Fly-Set	483/86-4	
D-MGEK	Autogyro Europe MT-03	unkn	
D-MGEL	Autogyro Europe Calidus	unkn	
D-MGEO	Warnke Skylight Trike	SI 035	
D-MGER	Rans S-12 Airaile	1292339	
D-MGET	Comco Ikarus Fox-C22	9205-3402	
D-MGEW #	Behlen Power-Trike / Ghost 14.9	unkn	
D-MGEY	Flight Design CT SW	07-09-06	
D-MGFA	Schönleber DS Lotus KS 18 Trike	KS02/0389	
D-MGFB	Autogyro Europe MTOsport	unkn	
D-MGFC #	Ultraleichtverbund Bi 90	21296	
D-MGFE	Schmidtler Ranger M Trike	1821	
D-MGFF	Comco Ikarus C-42B	1105-7153	
D-MGFH #	Seiffert Mini II	M-SC88646	
D-MGFK	B&F Funk FK-12 Comet	12-062	
D-MGFL	Light Aero Avid Flyer	683	
D-MGFR #	NST Minimum	M562	
D-MGFT	Trixy G 4-2 R	021-12	
D-MGFU(1)	Behlen Power-Trike	88025	
D-MGFU(2)	AirLony Skylane	59	
D-MGFX(1)	Swift	SA020	
D-MGFX(2)	Comco Ikarus C-42	1412-7357	
D-MGFY #	Swift	SA034	
D-MGGB	Tandem Air Sunny Sport	14.91	
D-MGGC(1)	Rotorvox C2A	C2A-13000	
D-MGGC(2)	Rotorvox C2A	C2A-15002	
D-MGGF	Behlen Power Trike II	878188	
D-MGGG	Plätzer Kiebitz-B2	035	
D-MGGH	Comco Ikarus C-42B	1107-7156	
D-MGGK	Ultraleichtverbund Bi 90	96974171166	
D-MGGL	Pipistrel Sinus	unkn	
D-MGGM	Plätzer Kiebitz-B9	021	
D-MGGN	Flight Design CT Supralight	E-12-04-08	
D-MGGO	Autogyro Europe Calidus	unkn	
D-MGGP	FUL Graffiti Trike	011/0072	
D-MGGX	Remos GX	368	
D-MGGZ	Comco I*karus C-42C	unkn	
D-MGHA	NST Minimum Zephir	2378	
D-MGHB(1)	Pioneer Flightstar	682	
D-MGHB(2)	Comco Ikarus C-42	0002-6255	D-MTBZ
D-MGHD	Behlen Power-Trike	463	
D-MGHE	Comco Ikarus Fox II Doppel	8606-3021	
D-MGHF	Ultraleichtverbund Bi 90	21278	
D-MGHG	Autogyro Europe MTOsport	unkn	
D-MGHH	Aviasud Albatros 64	301	
D-MGHI	Klüver Twin Racer SX 16	543008	
D-MGHK	Büttner Crazyplane II	51	
D-MGHL	Ultraleichetverbund Bi 90	635	
D-MGHM	Dallach Sunrise IIA	036	
D-MGHP	trike / Bautek (Pico?)	unkn	
D-MGHR	Corvus CA-21 Phantom	CA21/025	
D-MGHS	Light Aero Avid Flyer IV	810	
D-MGHT #	Take Off Merlin Trike	24565	
D-MGHW	Tecnam P.96 Golf 100S	228	
	(Re-regd D-MPIL)		
D-MGIE	Alpi Svn Pioneer 300UL	unkn	
D-MGIH #	Ikarus Comco Fox-C22	unkn	
D-MGII (1)	Comco Ikarus C-42B	0310-6583	
	(Dbr 24.9.11)		
D-MGII (2)	Comco Ikarus C-42B	1111-7179	
D-MGIL	Best Off Sky Ranger	unkn	
D-MGIN	Ultraleichtverbund Bi 90	595	
D-MGIO	Fresh Breeze Simo 122	unkn	
D-MGIS	Kümmerle Mini-Fly-Set	12897-8	
D-MGJB(1)	NST Minimum Santana	M503	
D-MGJB(2)#	Autogyro Europe MTOsport	unkn	
D-MGJE	B&F Funk FK-12 Comet	unkn	
D-MGJH	Fresh Breeze 122 AL 2F	357	
D-MGJR #	Autogyro Europe MTOsport	unkn	
D-MGJT #	Klüver Bison Trike	427711	
D-MGKA	Evektor EV-97 Eurostar	2007 2904	
D-MGKB	Remos GX	270	
D-MGKC	Autogyro Europe MT-03	unkn	
D-MGKK	Behlen Trike	90028	
D-MGKL #	Sky-Walker II	238	
D-MGKM	Dova DV-1 Skylank	unkn	
	(To YR-5200)		
D-MGKP	Cosmos Phase 2	21199	
D-MGKS	Apis BEE 15MB	AP030MB06	
D-MGKU	LO-120	007 A	
D-MGLA	Zenair CH-601 Zodiac	unkn	
D-MGLB	Silent Club	unkn	
D-MGLC	Eagle II / Pico Trike	unkn	
D-MGLD	Silent Club	unkn	

Regn	Type	c/n	Notes
D-MGLE	Fresh Breeze Simo 122	unkn	
D-MGLG	TL Ultralight TL-96 Sting	07ST240	
D-MGLH	Denney Kitfox III	1025	
	(To OH-U579)		
D-MGLI	B&F Funk FK-14B Polaris	014-114	
D-MGLK	Ghostbuster	199651	
D-MGLL	Tecnam P.96 Golf 100S	205	
D-MGLM #	Rans S-6 Coyote II	0293436	
	(To OO-G77, 11.10)		
D-MGLR #	Seiffert Mini II	100	
D-MGLS	FD Composites Arrowcopter AC20	028	
D-MGLT	Fresh Breeze Simo 122	unkn	
D-MGLU #	Klüver Bison Trike	645802	
D-MGLV	DB Aerospace Airbus FK10	02	
D-MGLW	Fresh Breeze Simo 122	unkn	
D-MGMA	Zlin Savage Classic	0106	
D-MGMB(1)	Sky-Walker II	181	
D-MGMB(2)	Remos G.3 Mirage	150	
D-MGMC	Schmidtler Enduro Trike	02-017	
D-MGME	Plätzer Kiebitz	unkn	
D-MGMF	B&F Funk FK-9 Mk.IV Utility	09-04U-287	
D-MGMG	Air-Light Wild Thing	073	
D-MGMK #	Flight Design CT SW	unkn	
D-MGML	Autogyro Europe MT-03	unkn	
D-MGMM(1)	Comco Ikarus Fox-C22	9307-3528	
D-MGMM(2)	Pipistrel Sinus	unkn	
D-MGMP #	Comco Ikarus Fox-C22	9206-3404	
D-MGMT	Alpi Avn Pioneer 300	206	D-MGUM
	(To I-B629, 6.13)		
D-MGMW	Comco Ikarus C-42B	1501-7363	
D-MGMZ	Bautek Eagle V/Avaint	unkn	
D-MGNC	ICP MXP-740V Savannah	02-10-51-171	
D-MGNE	Klüver Twin Racer / Pico S	unkn	
D-MGNI	ARCO Spacer L	877	
D-MGOD	Solid Air Diamant 55db(A) Trike	023	
D-MGOE	B&F Funk FK-9 Mk.IV	unkn	
D-MGOH	ASO Viper Trike	12022001	
D-MGOL	Comco Ikarus C-42B	0704-6890	
	(Reserved as SE-VUT 3.16)		
D-MGOO	Rans S-10 Sakota	0290093	
	(To OO-G94, 10.11)		
D-MGOS	Magni M-24 Orion	24126934	
D-MGPA	Evektor EV-97 Eurostar	2006-2702	
D-MGPB	Air-Light Wild Thing	unkn	
D-MGPC(1)	Kiggen/Heiland Air Création GTE 582 S	4317124295	
D-MGPC(2)	BOT Speed Cruiser SC07	018	
D-MGPD #	Fresh Breeze 110 AL 2F	471	
D-MGPG	Take Off Maximum Trike	016/0077	
D-MGPH	Zlin Savage Cruiser	unkn	
D-MGPI	Spider	unkn	
D-MGPJ	Fresh Breeze Simo 122	unkn	
D-MGPK	Magni M-16 Tandem Trainer	16106124	
D-MGPL	TL Ultralight TL-3000 Sirius	12SI68	
D-MGPN	FUL Graffiti MA 30 / Stranger	unkn	
D-MGPP #	Büttner Crazyplane II	97	
D-MGPR	Solar Wings Pegasus Quasar IITC	SW-WQT-0551/SW-TQD-0111	
D-MGPS	Krampen Ikarus S	62	
D-MGRA	Grossklaus Silent Racer 12	06	
D-MGRB	Silent Racer / Ghost 14.9	unkn	
D-MGRC #	Blankert (Homebuilt)	E25	
D-MGRD #	Comco Ikarus Fox C-22	9008-3291	
D-MGRE	Ultraleichtverbund Bi 90	999	
	(Reported as Cosmos; wing?)		
D-MGRG(1)	FUL Graffiti Trike	003/0053	
D-MGRG(2)	Autogyro Europe MTOsport	unkn	
D-MGRI	FUL Graffiti Trike	0055	
D-MGRJ	FUL Graffiti Trike	0046	
D-MGRK(1)	FUL Graffiti Trike	010/0048	
D-MGRK(2)	Millenium Master	unkn	
D-MGRL	FUL Graffiti Trike	019/0079	
D-MGRM	Schönleber DS Lotus KS 16 Trike	KS01/1190	
D-MGRO	Ultraleichtverbund Bi 90	21018	
D-MGRP	NST Minimum	M539	
D-MGRR	FUL Graffiti Trike	200080	
D-MGRS	Ultraleichtverbund Bi 90	794	
D-MGRT(1)	Comco Ikarus Fox-C22	9211-3422	
D-MGRT(2)	Zenair CH-601 Zodiac	6-9851	
D-MGRU	ASO Viper Hazard 15 Trike	15791	
D-MGRV	Comco Ikarus Fox-C22	9108-3350	
D-MGRW #	Sky-Walker II	278	
D-MGRX #	ASO Viper Trike	12052402	
D-MGRY #	FUL Graffiti Trike	009/0047	
D-MGRZ	FUL Graffiti Trike	0050	
D-MGSA	NST Schwarze Trike	M564	
D-MGSC	Behlen Power-Trike	91029	
D-MGSE	Behlen Power-Trike / Pico	unkn	
D-MGSG	Comco Ikarus C-42B	0403-6591	
D-MGSH(1)	Seiffert Mini-Speed Trike	1000000	
D-MGSH(2)	Autogyro Europe MTOsport	unkn	
D-MGSK	Plätzer Kiebitz B6	276	
D-MGSL(1)	NST Minimum	010205	
D-MGSL(2)	Flyitalia MD-3 Rider	44	
D-MGSM	HFL Stratos IIe	IIe-011	
D-MGSO	Behlen Power-Trike II	91022	
D-MGSP(1)	Büttner Crazyplane I	105	
D-MGSP(2)	TL Ultralight TL-96 Sting SP4	11ST352	
D-MGSR	Pago Jet M4	RB 98008	
D-MGSS	Behlen Power-Trike	1715	
D-MGST	HFL Stratos 300K	300-006	
D-MGSU	Evektor EV-97 Eurostar SL	unkn	
D-MGSW	Fresh Breeze Xcitor	unkn	
D-MGSY	Schönleber Trike 4	TK01/0296	
D-MGSZ	Fresh Breeze Simo 122	unkn	
D-MGTA	Quicksilver GT	unkn	
D-MGTB	Remos GX	359	
D-MGTC	Autogyro Europe MTOsport	unkn	
D-MGTD	Autogyro Europe Cavalon	unkn	
D-MGTE	UPM Cobra Trike	920114	
D-MGTF #	Take Off Maximum Trike	13079	
D-MGTH	Zenair CH-602XL Zodiac	unkn	
D-MGTI	Fresh Breeze	unkn	
D-MGTJ #	Comco Ikarus Fox-C22	9106-3339	
D-MGTL	Comco Ikarus Fox-C22	9106-3338	
	(To D-MTTC (2))		
D-MGTR	Ultraleichtverbund Bi 90	3762057	
D-MGTS	Autogyro Europe MT-03	unkn	
D-MGTT	Comco Ikarus Fox-C22	unkn	
D-MGTW	NST Minimum	M1454	
D-MGTX	Pegasus	unkn	
D-MGTZ	Roland Z602 Economy	unkn	
D-MGUD	ASO Viper Trike	VIII 22072506	
D-MGUE	Albatros SX	501	
D-MGUH #	Air Command Elite Tandem	unkn	
D-MGUI	Warnke Skylight Trike	SI 037	
D-MGUL	Kiggen/Heiland Air Création GTE 5	4954433118	
D-MGUM(1)	Alpi Aviation Pioneer 300	206	
	(Re-regd D-MGMT then I-B629)		
D-MGUM(2)	Alpi Aviation Pioneer 300	241	
	(W/o 26.11.14)		
D-MGUN	Roland Z602	Z-9562	
D-MGUS	Flight Team Spider Trike	D031	
D-MGUT	Flight Team Spider Trike	D036	
D-MGUW	Aerostyle Breezer CL	093	
D-MGUZ #	Klüver Twin Racer SX 16	235004	
D-MGVA	Plätzer Kiebitz-B8	055	
D-MGVH	Konsuprod Moskito Ib	020	
D-MGVK	Kappa KP-2U Skyleader 150	2523 E	I-6019
D-MGVL	Ultraleichtverbund Bi 90	21041	
D-MGVM	TL Ultralight TL-96 Sting	unkn	
D-MGVR #	Comco Ikarus Fox-C22	unkn	
D-MGWB	Aerostyle Breezer	020	
D-MGWC	Autogyro Europe MTOsport	unkn	
D-MGWD	Comco Ikarus C-42B	1105-7144	
D-MGWI	Autogyro Europe MT-03	unkn	
D-MGWL	Trixy G 4-2 R	019-12	
D-MGWM	Plätzer Motte B-2	11	
D-MGWP	Flight Design CT SW	unkn	
D-MGWR	Behlen Power-Trike /Rotax 582	98010	
D-MGWU	Greenwing ESpyder	0006	
D-MGWY	Greenwing ESpyder E280	unkn	
D-MGXH	Cosmos / Chronos 12	unkn	
D-MGXR	Celier Xenon 2	CA714475R	
D-MGXX	Remos GX	369	
D-MGYL	Autogyro Europe MT-03	D06G27	
	(To SE-VJC)		
D-MGYR(2)	Autogyro Europe MT-03	04G03	
D-MGZI	Kümmerle Mini-Fly-Set	67986-4	
D-MGZZ(1)	Comco Ikarus C-42B	0905-7042	
	(To OH-U639, 5.11)		
D-MGZZ(2)	Comco Ikarus C-42B	1401-7296	
D-MHAA	Tecnam P.92 Echo 100S	614	
D-MHAC	Sky-Walker II	390	
D-MHAD(2)	ASO Sonic Trike	5954173091	
D-MHAD(3)	Autogyro Europe Calidus	D10C39	
D-MHAE	Corvus CA-21 Corone	unkn	
	(Also reported as Corvus Phantom)		
D-MHAF	ASO Viper Trike	10504	
D-MHAG	Comco Ikarus Fox II Doppel	8603-3011	
D-MHAH	Kümmerle Mini-Fly-Set Thalhofer GT	1304/91-6	
D-MHAI(1)	ASO Viper Trike	12060405	
D-MHAI(2)	Alpi Aviation Pioneer 300	186	
D-MHAJ	FUL Graffiti Trike	033/0099	
D-MHAL	Comco Ikarus Fox-C22	9008-3280	
D-MHAM	Autogyro Europe Calidus	unkn	
D-MHAN	ASO Viper Trike	VIII 22064408	
D-MHAO	Kiggen/Heiland Air Création GTE 582 S	5954173091	
D-MHAP	Kiggen/Heiland Air Création GTE 582 S	3954317120	
D-MHAQ	Kiggen/Heiland Air Création GTE 582 S	5954173195	
D-MHAS(1)	Comco Ikarus Sherpa II	8505-1098	
D-MHAS(2)	Apis BEE 15 MB	AO41MB11	
D-MHAT #	Comco Ikarus C-42	0507-6751	
	(Reserved as SE-VSM, 12.12)		
D-MHAU	Air-Light Wild Thing	2001-06-077	
D-MHAW	Air Création GTE	unkn	
D-MHAX	Aerospool WT-9 Dynamic	DY299/2009	
D-MHAY	Flight Design CT LS	09-06-01	
D-MHAZ(1)	NST Minimum	1147	
D-MHAZ(2)	Comco Ikarus C-42C	1402-7302	
D-MHBA	Flight Design CT SW	06-04-05	
D-MHBB	Flight Design CT SW	03.04.05.19	
D-MHBC	Alpi Avn Pioneer 200	unkn	
D-MHBE	Comco Ikarus C-42B	0210-6507	
D-MHBG	ATEC 321 Faeta	F390108A	
D-MHBJ	Sky-Walker II	328	
D-MHBK	Comco Ikarus Fox-C22	9304-3498	
D-MHBL	Take Off Merlin 1100 / Avant	unkn	
D-MHBO(1)	Ultraleichtverbund Bi 90	21123	
D-MHBO(2)	ICP MXP-740 Savannah	02-09-51-169	
D-MHBP	Sky-Walker II	272	
	(Wfu)		
D-MHBR(1)	Behlen Power-Trike / Pico	unkn	
D-MHBR(2)	Autogyro Europe MTOsport	MO1111	
D-MHBS(1)	Eipper Quicksilver	unkn	
D-MHBS(2)	WDFL Dallach D4 Fascination BK	109	
D-MHBS(3)	Comco Ikarus C-42	unkn	
D-MHBW(1)	Klüver Racer Quartz SX 16	247004	
D-MHBW(2)	P&M QuikR – 912S	8530	
D-MHBX	Fresh Breeze Xcitor	unkn	
D-MHCB	Aero East Europe Sila 450C	unkn	
D-MHCC	Air Light Wild Thing	unkn	
D-MHCD	Unidentified flexwing	unkn	
D-MHCE	Ultraleichtverbund Bi 90	unkn	
D-MHCH	Tecnam P.92 Echo	185	D-MNIT
D-MHCJ	Magni M-24 Orion VIP	unkn	
D-MHCL	UPM Cobra Falcon	unkn	
D-MHCP #	Büttner Crazyplane III	90	
D-MHCQ(1)	Evektor EV-97 Eurostar	2007-2939	
	(Crashed in North Sea 3.8.08)		
D-MHCQ(2)	Evektor EV-97R Eurostar 2000	2008 3309	
D-MHCR	Plätzer Kiebitz-B9	065	
D-MHDD	Fresh Breeze Simo 122	unkn	
D-MHDE	Skystar S34	002	
D-MHDF	Autogyro Europe MTOsport	unkn	
D-MHDG	FUL Graffiti MA 30 / Stranger	unkn	
D-MHDH #	Solid Air Diamant Trike	017	
D-MHDK	Fresh Breeze Simo 122	unkn	

Registration	Type	C/n	Previous id.
D-MHDO	Solid Air Diamant 55dB(A) Trike	019	
D-MHDP	Comco Ikarus C-42B	0609-6850	
D-MHDS(1)	Flight Team Spider / Hazard 15	D024	
D-MHDS(2)	Air Création / Kiss	A01003-0204	
D-MHDT	Aurogyro Europe MTOsport	unkn	
D-MHDU #	Evektor EV-97 Eurostar	unkn	
D-MHDV(2)	Silent Flyer	unkn	
D-MHDW	FUL Graffiti Trike	95	
D-MHDY	Buggy (Air Création ?)	unkn	
D-MHDZ	Pegasus Quasar II	6637	
D-MHEB	Magni M-24 Orion	24127304	
D-MHEC	Cosmos / Chronos 12	unkn	
D-MHED	Comco Ikarus Fox-C22	8809-3154	
D-MHEE	Comco Ikarus C-42B	0307-6557	
D-MHEF	Tecnam P.92 Echo-S 100	857	
D-MHEI	Comco Ikarus C-42	unkn	
D-MHEJ	Comco Ikarus C-42B	0411-6638	
D-MHEL	Flight Team Spider Trike	D015	
D-MHEM	WDFL Sunwheel	007	
D-MHEN	Fresh Breeze 110 AL2F	88	
D-MHET (1)	Flight Team Spider	D052	
D-MHET (2)	Plätzer Kiebitz-B3	004	
D-MHEU	Comco Ikarus C-42B	0608-6844	
D-MHEX(1)	Autogyro Europe Calidus	unkn	
D-MHEX(2)	Autogyro Europe Cavalon	unkn	
D-MHEY	Shark Aero Shark	004-2011	OK-QUR 07
D-MHEZ	Zlin Savage	191	
D-MHFA	Pipistrel Sinus	unkn	
D-MHFB	Junkers Profly JUL Trike	94/1062	
D-MHFD #	Flight Design CT SL	unkn	
D-MHFG	Cosmos / Chronos 12	21052	
D-MHFK #	Behlen Power-Trike	90011	
D-MHFL	HFL Stratos IIe	004	
D-MHFM	NST Minimum Zephir	438	
D-MHFN	Comco Ikarus C-42B	0506-6693	
D-MHFU	Cosmos / Chronos 12	unkn	
D-MHFW	Kümmerle Mini-Fly-Set	1284/91-5	
D-MHFX	Cellier Xenon	CAG12Z1B01AA002L	
D-MHGA	Sky-Service Pago Jet	95602	
D-MHGB	Evektor EV-97R Eurostar 2000 (W/o 23.7.08)	unkn	
D-MHGD	Cosmos / Chronos 12	21231	
D-MHGE	Fresh Breeze 122 AL 2F	354	
D-MHGF	Autogyro Europe MT-03	unkn	
D-MHGG	Remos GX	324	
D-MHGH	Comco Ikarus C-42B	0209-6501	
D-MHGJ	Profe Banjo MH	unkn	
D-MHGK	Cosmos / Chronos 14	5323804244	
D-MHGL	Aquilair Swing 582 / Ghost 14.9	unkn	
D-MHGP	Comco Ikarus Fox-C22	9102-3317	
D-MHGR #	Bautek Eagle III / Ghost 14.9	980506	
D-MHGS(1)	T2	2	
D-MHGS(2)	Autogyro Europe MTOsport	unkn	
D-MHGT	Comco Ikarus Fox-C22	9204-3405	
D-MHGW	Sky-Walker II	199	
D-MHGZ	Magni M-24 Orion	24148514	
D-MHHA	Behlen Power Trike	99005	
D-MHHB(1)	Comco Ikarus Fox-C22	9305-3507	
D-MHHB(2)	ATEC 321 Faeta	F381207A	
D-MHHC(1 ?)	Flight Design CT-2K	unkn	
D-MHHC(2)	Flight Design CT SW	04-03-05	
D-MHHD #	Take Off Maximum Trike	095052	
D-MHHE	Remos G3 Mirage	169	
D-MHHG	Kümmerle Mini-Fly-Set	1275/91-5	
D-MHHK(1)	Light Aero Avid Flyer Speedwing	1229	
D-MHHK(2)	Aeropro Eurofox	18305	
D-MHHL	Aerospool WT-9 Dynamic	DY068/2004	
D-MHHO	Kiggen/Hieland Air Création GTE 582 S	7954557566	
D-MHHS(1)	MKB Ranger M Trike	1835	
D-MHHS(2)	B&F Funk FK-14A Polaris	014-004	D-MORC
D-MHHT	Comco Ikarus Fox-C22	9301-3423	
D-MHHW(1)	Remos G3-600 Gemini (W/o 15.5.10)	unkn	
D-MHHW(2)	Ekolot JK-05 Junior	05-08-10	
D-MHHY	Pipistrel Taurus 503	unkn	
D-MHHZ	Schönleber Trike Speed 14	010893	
D-MHIA(1)	KP-2U Sova	unkn	
D-MHIA(2)	Jihlavan Skyleader 200	2 196 217 Q	
D-MHIB	Kilb Air Création GTE 582 S Trike	AC 006	
D-MHIC	BRM Aero NG-5 Bristell	unkn	
D-MHID	BRM Aero NG-5 Bristell	unkn	
D-MHIE #	Büttner Crazyplane II	96	
D-MHIG	Take Off Merlin 1200 / Avant	unkn	
D-MHII(1)	Fisher FP-404 Classic	JE-02	
D-MHII(2)	FAMA Helicopters Kiss 209M	unkn	
D-MHIJ	Aerospool WT-9 Dynamic	DY349/2010	D-MHIS(2)
D-MHIK	Aerospool WT-9 Dynamic	DY490/2014	
D-MHIN	Take Off Merlin Trike	23955	
D-MHIO	Aerospool WT-9 Dynamic	DY303/2009	D-MHIS(1)
D-MHIP	Air-Light Wild Thing	72	
D-MHIS(1)	Aerospool WT-9 Dynamic (Re-regd D-MHIO)	DY303/2009	
D-MHIS(2)	Aerospool WT-9 Dynamic (Re-regd D-MHIJ)	DY349/2010	
D-MHIS(3)	Aerospool WT-9 Dynamic	DY401/2011	
D-MHIS(4)	Aerospool WT-9 Dynamic	DY504/2014	
D-MHIS(5)	Aerospool WT-9 Dynamic	DY540/2015	
D-MHIT(1)	Ultraleichtverbund Bi 90	21237	
D-MHIT(2)	Autogyro Europe MTOsport	unkn	
D-MHIW	Magni M-24 Orion	24148394	
D-MHIX	Comco Ikarus C-42B	unkn	
D-MHJA	Remos G.3 Mirage	131	
D-MHJD #	Roland Z602XL	Z-9553	
D-MHJE	NST Minimum	031205	
D-MHJF(1)	Schönleber DS Speed KS 14 Trike	14010992	
D-MHJF(2)	Comco Ikarus C-42B	unkn	
D-MHJH	Remos G.3 Mirage	unkn	
D-MHJI #	Warnke Skylight Trike	026	
D-MHJK #	Comco Ikarus C-42B	unkn	
D-MHJM	Aveko VL-3D-1 Sprint (W/o 13.4.08)	unkn	
D-MHJR	Zenair Z601XL	Z-9512	
D-MHJS	Cosmos / Chronos 12	21054	
D-MHJT	Roland Z701 S-STOL	unkn	
D-MHJU	Profe Banjo MH	unkn	
D-MHJV	Fresh Breeze 110 AL2F	92	
D-MHJZ	Autogyro Europe Calidus	C00206	
D-MHKA	Air Création GTE 582 S	5964559925	
D-MHKB	Dallach Sunrise IIA	021	
D-MHKE	Behlen Power-Trike	91024	
D-MHKF	Rans S-6 Coyote II	1292404	
D-MHKG	Best Off Sky Ranger (Cancelled)	505	
D-MHKH	Sky-Walker II	216	
D-MHKJ	WDFL Sunwheel	005	
D-MHKK #	Kümmerle Mini-Fly-Set Windfex II	9841	
D-MHKL	Kiggen/Hieland Air Création GTE	S 4954433120	
D-MHKM	Sky-Walker II	316	
D-MHKO	Autogyro Europe MT-03	unkn	
D-MHKP	Bautek Eagle V/ Profi 14.5	unkn	
D-MHKS	Fair Fax Euro II Trike	012	
D-MHKV	Schönleber DS Speed KS 14 Trike TK	02/0893	
D-MHKZ	Comco Ikarus Fox-C22	0208-3749	
D-MHLA(1)	FUL Graffiti Trike	170078	
D-MHLA(2)	Comco Ikarus C-42C	1209-7217	
D-MHLB(1)	Fair Fax DR Trike	D014	
D-MHLB(2)	BOT Speed Cruiser SC07	028	
D-MHLC	Take Off Merlin Trike	10564	
D-MHLD	TL Ultralight TL-3000 Sirius (Damaged 12.4.15)	14SI101	
D-MHLE	Autogyro Europe MTOsport	unkn	
D-MHLG	Aerospool WT-9 Dynamic	DY416/2011	
D-MHLK	Fair Fax DR Trike	D027	
D-MHLL	Fair Fax DR Trike	D024	
D-MHLL(2)	Alpi Aviation Pioneer 200	unkn	
D-MHLM	Behlen Trike	830037	
D-MHLN	Alpi Helicopter 130 Syton	unkn	
D-MHLO	Take Off Merlin 1100 / Avant	unkn	
D-MHLP	ICP MXP-740 Savannah	07-05-51--598	
D-MHLR	Take Off Merlin Trike	26146	
D-MHLS(1)	Behlen Power Trike II	96004	
D-MHLS(2)	Magni M-16 Tandem Trainer	unkn	
D-MHLU	Wezel/Albastar Apis-2	W008	
D-MHLW(2)	Pegasus Quik 912S	8112	
D-MHLW(3)	P&M QuikR 912S	8609	
D-MHLX	Take Off Merlin Trike	26957	
D-MHMA	UPM Cobra Raven Trike	900096	
D-MHMB	Cosmos Chronos 12	unkn	
D-MHMD	TL Ultralight TL-3000 Sirius (Severely damaged, Kufstein, Austria 12.4.15)	14SI101	
D-MHME	Comco Ikarus C-42	unkn	
D-MHMI	Comco Ikarus C-42B	1402-7295	
D-MHMJ #	Büttner Crazyplane IV	4	
D-MHMK	Zlin Savage Classic	unkn	
D-MHMM(1)	Sky-Walker II	249	
D-MHMM(2)	Comco Ikarus C-42B	unkn	
D-MHMN	Autogyro Europe MTOsport	unkn	
D-MHMR(1)	Pegasus Quantum 15 912	7969	
D-MHMR(2)	Autogyro Europe MT-03	D06G11	
D-MHMS	Fair Fax DR Trike	D025	
D-MHNC	Evektor EV-97 Eurostar SL	2008 3508	
D-MHNE	Remos G.3 Mirage	126	
D-MHNG	Comco Ikarus Fox-C22	9304-3500	
D-MHNH	Autogyro Europe Cavalon	V00186	
D-MHNM	Bautek Eagle V/ Pico	unkn	
D-MHNP #	FUL Graffiti Trike	005/0052	
D-MHNW #	Seiffert Mini-Speed Trike	73	
D-MHNZ	EEL ULF-2	unkn	
D-MHOB(1)	Dallach Sunrise II (Re-regd D-MDWD)	017	
D-MHOB(2)	Fläming Air FA-01 Smaragd	118/07	
D-MHOD	Fresh Breeze Simo 122	unkn	
D-MHOE	Flight Team Spider XL	unkn	
D-MHOF(1)	WDFL Sunwheel	004	
D-MHOF(2)	Comco Ikarus C-42B	1105-7154	
D-MHOH	Take Off Maximum Trike	039110	
D-MHOI	Roland Z.602 Economy	unkn	
D-MHOL #	Rotortec Cloud Dancer II	10202-04	
D-MHON	Aeropro Eurofox	12202	
D-MHOO	DF Helicopters DF334 Dragonfly	unkn	
D-MHOP	Comco Ikarus C-42 "3"	unkn	
D-MHOR(1)	Fresh Breeze 110 AL2F	49	
D-MHOR(2)	Autogyro Europe MTOsport	unkn	
D-MHOS #	NST Minimum	M301	
D-MHOT	Fair Fax DR Hazard 15M Trike	D020	
D-MHOW(1)	Klüver Twin Racer SX 16 Trike	541008	
D-MHOW(2)	Comco Ikarus C-42B	unkn	
D-MHPA(1)	Behlen Power-Trike	08/020	
D-MHPA(2)	Flight Design CT LS	unkn	
D-MHPB #	Behlen Power-Trike 582 / Pico	unkn	
D-MHPD(1)	Autogyro Europe MT-03	unkn	
D-MHPD(2)	Autogyro Europe MTOsport	unkn	
D-MHPE	WDFL Sunwheel	006	
D-MHPF	Comco Ikarus Fox-C22	9104-3324	
D-MHPG(1)	Aerospool WT-9 Dynamic RG (To YL-AVL 11.08, c/n quoted DY085/2005 but w/o 10.5.16)	DY085/2005	
D-MHPG(2)	Aerospool WT-9 Dynamic (Fixed-gear version. C/n DY085/2005 also quoted, presumably in error. Crashed 24.12.15)	DY085/2005	
D-MHPH	B&F Funk FK-9 Mk.III Utility	09-03U-196	
D-MHPK	Tecnam P.92 Echo	unkn	
D-MHPL	Zenair CH-601XL Zodiac	6-9757	
D-MHPM	B&F Funk FK-12 Comet	12-007	57-ADB/F-JGCO, D-MSUF
D-MHPV	Evektor EV-97 Eurostar SL	2008 3310	
D-MHPW	Remos G-3 Mirage	114	OE-7001
D-MHPX	Autogyro Europe Calidus	unkn	
D-MHPZ #	Behlen Power-Trike 582 / Pico	unkn	
D-MHRA	Solid Air Diamant Trike	006	
D-MHRB(1)	Comco Ikarus Fox-C22	8512-FD36	
D-MHRB(2)	Air Light Wild Thing	078	
D-MHRC #	Fresh Breeze Simo 122	unkn	
D-MHRD	Alpi Helicopter 130 Syton	unkn	
D-MHRE	Comco Ikarus C-42B	unkn	
D-MHRF	Sky-Walker II	352	
D-MHRG(1)	Fisher FP-202 Koala	St-004	
D-MHRG(2)	TL Ultralight TL-232 Condor Plus	AB09	
D-MHRK	TL Ultralight TL-96 Sting	unkn	
D-MHRL	Solar Wings Pegasus Quasar IITC	SW-WQT-0585/SW-TQD-0125	
D-MHRM #	Rans S-6 Coyote II	unkn	

Reg	Type	C/n	Notes
D-MHRO	Flight Design CT LS	F-09-05-16	
D-MHRS	Schönleber DS Trike	16020692	
D-MHRT #	Ultraleichtverbund Bi 90	21008	
D-MHRW	Cosmos / Chronos 12	21099	
D-MHSA	Autogyro Europe Calidus 09	unkn	
D-MHSB	ASO Viper Hazard Trike	VI 22027202	
D-MHSC	J-3 Kitten	01033	
D-MHSD(1)	Behlen Trike	850026	
D-MHSD(2)	Alpi Avn Pioneer 300	unkn	
D-MHSE	Fly Synthesis Storch HS	290	
D-MHSF	Zlin Savage Cub	312	
D-MHSH	Dallach Sunrise II	002	
D-MHSI	Cosmos Phase II / Top 12.9	21287	
D-MHSJ #	Autogyro Europe Calidus	unkn	
D-MHSK	Take Off Maximum Trike	T079191	
D-MHSM	BVL Speedy Mouse	01/ID	
D-MHSO	Take Off Merlin 1100	27958	
D-MHSP	FUL Graffiti Trike	012/0073	
D-MHSR	Behlen Power-Trike 582 / Pico	unkn	
D-MHSS	Behlen Power-Trike II Hazard 15M	90025	
D-MHST(1)	Behlen Power-Trike /Rotax 582	980012	
D-MHST(2)	Comco Ikarus C-42	unkn	
D-MHSU	Rans S-7 Courier	0598244	
D-MHSV	Schönleber Trike Speed	14020993	
D-MHSX	Schilling autogyro	unkn	
D-MHTA	Flight Design CT SW	A-03-80-24	
	(C/n '80' incorrect)		
D-MHTB	Bautek Eagle V/ Pico	unkn	
D-MHTC	Kiggen/Heiland Air Création GTE 582 S		
		9954559387	
D-MHTE	Kiggen/Heiland Air Création GTE 582 S		
		3964655068	
D-MHTG #	MKB Enduro Trike	04/003/85	
D-MHTL	ASO Viper Trike	22034206	
D-MHTM	Take Off Merlin / Karat 13	unkn	
D-MHTN	Autogyro Europe MTOsport	unkn	
D-MHTS	Breezer	unkn	
D-MHTT	Comco Ikarus C-42B	unkn	
D-MHTV	Autogyro Europe MTOsport	unkn	
D-MHUB	Fresh Breeze 122 AL 2F	112	
D-MHUC	Aerostyle Breezer CL	107	
D-MHUE #	Plätzer Motte B-2	005	
	(Dbf 15.8.16)		
D-MHUG	Soarma Libre II LO-120	002A	
D-MHUH #	Parsons Gyrocopter	unkn	
D-MHUI (1)	Autogyro Europe MTOsport	unkn	
D-MHUI (2)	Comco Ikarus C-42C	1404-7328	
D-MHUM #	Sky-Service Pago Jet	94003	
D-MHUN	Magnus MG-11 Fusion	unkn	
D-MHUP	Flight Design CT SW	03.06.04.29	
D-MHUR(1)	Autogyro Europe MT-03	unkn	
D-MHUR(2)	Autogyro Europe MTOsport	unkn	
D-MHUS	Plätzer Kiebitz-B	037	
D-MHUU	Cosmos / Chronos 12	21036	
D-MHUW #	trike / Ghost 14.9	unkn	
D-MHVA	Pipistrel Virus SW	633SWN100	
D-MHVK #	Fresh Breeze 110 AL2F	37	
D-MHVL	HFL Stratos 300	300-010K	
D-MHVN	Roland Z601	unkn	
D-MHVV	Flight Team Spider	D 18	
D-MHWA	Albatros Milan	07085	
D-MHWD	Flight Design CT-2K	02-05-03-22	
D-MHWE	Comco Ikarus Fox-C22	9202-3374	
D-MHWH	Comco Ikarus Fox-C22	9211-3448	
D-MHWK	Plätzer Kiebitz-B2	040	
D-MHWL	Warnke Skylight Trike	027	
D-MHWM	Apis BEE 15 MB	064	
D-MHWN	Autogyro Europe MTO Sport	unkn	
D-MHWO #	Gyrotec DF-02	002	
D-MHWR	Aerospool WT-9 Dynamic	DYK 19/2007	
D-MHWS #	Comco Ikarus Fox	043	
D-MHWT	Vidor Asso V Champion	unkn	
D-MHWY	Roko Aero NG6 UL	unkn	
D-MHWZ	Rans S-10 Sakota	0404817	
D-MHXX	ICP MXP-740 Savannah	unkn	
D-MHYD	Flight Design CT SW	07-05-25	
	(C/n may be -26 or -28. 07-05-25 = ZU-JPB)		
D-MHYD	Ramphos FIB	unkn	
D-MHYF #	Behlen Power-Trike	88041	
D-MHYU	JMB VL-3i Evolution	132	
D-MHZH	Solid Air Twin Diamant Trike	T005	
D-MHZI(1)	Pegasus Quasar II	6717	
D-MHZI(2)	P&M Quik GT450-912S	8389	
D-MHZT #	UPM Omega Trike	88006	
D-MIAA	Flight Team Spider	D 048	
	(W/o 15.8.16)		
D-MIAB	NST Minimum	M549	
D-MIAC(1)	Comco Ikarus Fox-C22	9006-3281	
D-MIAC(2)	Aerospool WT-9 Dynamic	DY112/2005	
D-MIAD	Plätzer Kiebitz-B9	143	
	(Wears code '143')		
D-MIAE(1)	Firebird Tri CX	288	
D-MIAE(2)	Autogyro Europe MT-03	unkn	
D-MIAG	Bautek Eagle III / XP 15	unkn	
D-MIAH	Aeroprakt A-22L Vision	323	
D-MIAI	Drachenstudio Royal 912 / Avant 17	unkn	
D-MIAK	Aeroprakt A-22L Vision	313	
D-MIAL(2)	Flight Team Spider	51	
D-MIAM	Light Aero Avid Flyer IV	1010	
D-MIAN	Comco Ikarus Fox D	022	
D-MIAO	Comco Ikarus Fox-C22	unkn	
D-MIAP	Aeroprakt A22L2 Vision	432	
D-MIAR(1)	Take Off Maximum Trike	070591	
D-MIAR(2)#	Air-Light Wild Thing	unkn	
D-MIAS	Ultra-Vector H	1424	
D-MIAT(1)	Aeroprakt A-22L Vision	287	
	(To OO-H01, 3.12)		
D-MIAT(2)	Pipistrel Alpha Trainer	unkn	
D-MIAU	Plätzer Kiebitz-B	072	
D-MIAV	Zlin Savage Cruiser	243	
D-MIAW(1)	Krampen Ikarus S	63	
D-MIAW(2)	Aeroprakt A-22L Vision	303	
D-MIAX(1)	Aeroprakt A-22L Vision	unkn	
D-MIAX(2)	Aeroprakt A-22L Vision	350	
D-MIAZ	EEL ULF-2	06	
D-MIBA	Kümmerle Mini-Fly-Set	127591-5	
D-MIBA(2)	Bautek Eagle V/ Pico	unkn	
D-MIBB	Flight Team Spider / Fun 18	unkn	
D-MIBC	Comco Ikarus Fox-C22	9009-3282	
D-MIBD	Flight Team Spider XL / XP 15	unkn	
D-MIBE	Fair Fax Trike Euro III	040	
D-MIBF	Flight Team Spider XL / Kiss 450	unkn	
D-MIBG	Flight Team Spider XL	unkn	
D-MIBH	BRM Aero NG5 Bristell	155	
D-MIBI #	Fresh Breeze 110 AL 2F	153	
D-MIBJ #	Comco Ikarus Fox-C22	9301-3463	
D-MIBL	Air Création Buggy / XP	unkn	
D-MIBM	Air Création / Kiss	A01002-0202	
D-MIBN #	Flight Team Spider XL / Kiss 13	unkn	
D-MIBR	Flight Team Spider XL / iXess	unkn	
D-MIBT	Rans S-6 Coyote II (t/w)	10061771-8	
D-MICA	Comco Ikarus Fox-C22	8907-3216	
D-MICB(1)	Comco Ikarus Fox-C22	8907-3217	
D-MICB(2)	Best Off Sky Ranger	unkn	
D-MICC	Dallach Sunrise II	022	
D-MICD	Comco Ikarus Fox-C22	8907-3220	
D-MICE	Comco Ikarus Fox-C22	8909-3218	
D-MICG	Comco Ikarus Fox-C22	9003-3221	
D-MICH	Schmidtler Enduro Trike	180485	
D-MICI(1)	B&F Funk FK-12 Comet	unkn	
D-MICI(2)	Pipistrel Taurus	122	
D-MICK	Comco Ikarus Sherpa I	8306-1026	
D-MICL	Comco Ikarus Fox-C22	9003-3225	
D-MICM #	Comco Ikarus Fox-C22	9003-3226	
D-MICN #	Comco Ikarus Fox-C22	9004-3227	
D-MICO	Comco Ikarus Fox-C22	8908-3228	
D-MICP	Comco Ikarus Fox-C22	9005-3229	
D-MICQ #	Comco Ikarus Fox-C22	9004-3230	
D-MICR	Comco Ikarus Fox-C22	9004-3231	
D-MICS	Comco Ikarus Fox-C22	9008-3232	
D-MICT	Comco Ikarus Fox-C22	9004-3233	
D-MICU	Comco Ikarus Fox-C22	9002-3234	
D-MICV	Comco Ikarus Fox D	8410-FD15	
D-MICW	Comco Ikarus Fox-C22	9005-3235	
D-MICX	Comco Ikarus Fox-C22	9103-3314	
D-MICY	Aerospool WT-9 Dynamic	unkn	
D-MICZ #	Comco Ikarus Fox-C22	9104-3313	
D-MIDB	Comco Ikarus C-42B	0804-6955	
D-MIDC	Comco Ikarus Fox-C22	9009-3285	
D-MIDD	Dova DV-1 Skylark	unkn	
D-MIDI	Alpi Aviation Pioneer 200	48	
D-MIDN	Tecnam P.92 Echo 2000S	690	
D-MIDO	Pioneer Flightstar	617	
D-MIDR	Fresh Breeze Simo 122	unkn	
D-MIDY	Technoflug Piccolo	083	
D-MIEB	Autogyro Europe MTO Sport	unkn	
D-MIEC	Comco Ikarus Fox-C22	9008-3283	
D-MIEE	Comco Ikarus C-42B	unkn	
D-MIEF	Tandem Air Sunny Sport	21-91	
D-MIEG	UPM Cobra Trike	900090	
D-MIEH	Comco Ikarus Fox-C22	9209-3424	
D-MIEK	AS0 Viper Hazard 15 Trike	041302	
D-MIEL	Flight Design CT SW	05-04-10	
D-MIEM	Flight Design CT SW	E-10-08-02	
D-MIEN	Pipistrel Alpha Trainer	667AT912	
D-MIEP	Evektor EV-97R Eurostar 2000	2008 3228	OK-FUU 09
D-MIER	Profe Banjo MH	14/2012	
D-MIES	Behlen Power-Trike	90014	
D-MIET	Roland Z602	Z-9534	
D-MIEW	Pipistrel Virus SW	unkn	
D-MIEX #	Comco Ikarus Fox-C22	unkn	
D-MIEZ	Scheibe Uli 1	5201	
D-MIFA	Fresh Breeze Simo 122	unkn	
D-MIFC(1)	Comco Ikarus Fox-C22	9009-3284	
D-MIFC(2)	BRM Aero Bristell	068-2013	
D-MIFD #	Behlen Power-Trike Focus 20	89012	
D-MIFF(1)	Magni M-16 Tandem Trainer	D-9302	
	(To G-BXEJ 4.97)		
D-MIFF(2)	Comco Ikarus C-42	0710-6925	
D-MIFG	Fresh Breeze Simo 122	unkn	
D-MIFI	Aerostyle Breezer	017	
D-MIFK	B&F Funk FK-12 Comet	12-050	
D-MIFL(1)	Ultraleichtverbund Bi 90	B21154	
D-MIFL(2)	Autogyro Europe MTOsport	unkn	
D-MIFR	Autogyro Europe MTOsport	M00825	
D-MIFS	Aeropro Eurofox	13703	
	(Has been reported as "Ikarus Eurofox" c/n 210520044)		
D-MIFT	Comco Ikarus Fox-C22	8902-3188	
D-MIFU	Schmidtler Enduro Trike	02-019	
D-MIGA	Remos G.3 Mirage	134	
D-MIGB	Aeroprakt A-22 Vision	unkn	
D-MIGE	Remos GX	413	
D-MIGH	Cosmos / Chronos 12	941	
D-MIGK	Trixy G4-2R	unkn	
D-MIGL	Bautek Eagle V/ Pico	unkn	
D-MIGR	Tecnam P.92 Echo Super	unkn	
D-MIGS	Flight Design CT-2K	03.01.05.04	
D-MIGT	Eipper Quicksilver GT	2801032	
D-MIGW	BOT Speed Cruiser SC07	004	
D-MIGX	Dyn'Aéro MCR-01 ULC	243	
D-MIHA (1)	Comco Ikarus Fox-C22	9302-3491	
D-MIHA(2)	Autogyro Europe MT-03	unkn	
D-MIHB(1)	Comco Ikarus Fox-C22	8807-3138	
D-MIHB(2)	Autogyro Europe MTOsport	unkn	
D-MIHC	Comco Ikarus Fox-C22	9009-3286	
	(Same c/n as PH-2D2, LZ- . . .)		
D-MIHG #	Behlen Power Trike II	615205	
D-MIHH	Tandem Air Sunny	028.11.07 SPL	
D-MIHI	Kümmerle Mini-Fly-Set	67886-4	
D-MIHK	Comco Ikarus Sherpa I	8308-1038	
D-MIHL	Rans S-6S Coyote II	050920617-S	
D-MIHN(1)	Aero East Europe SILA 450C	120608-AEE-0005	
D-MIHN(2)	Aero East Europe SILA 450C	140211-AEE-0023	
	(To France as 27-AGI/F-JSFM)		
D-MIHR	Autogyro Europe MTOsport	unkn	
D-MIHS	Aeropro Eurofox	13403	
D-MIHT	Zlin Savage Cruiser	92	
D-MIHV #	Fresh Breeze 122 AL 2F	382	
D-MIHY	Plätzer Motte B-3	43	
D-MIIB	Autogyro Europe MTOsport	unkn	
D-MIIC	Fresh Breeze Simo 122	unkn	
D-MIIH	Fresh Breeze Simo 122	unkn	

Registration	Type	C/n	Notes
D-MIII	Comco Ikarus Fox-C22	8908-3215	
D-MIIL	Plätzer Motte B-3	27	
D-MIIM	Ultraleichtverbund / Ghost 14.9	unkn	
D-MIIN	Denney Kitfox 4	1735	
D-MIIO	Nando Groppo Trial	unkn	
D-MIIP	Remos GX NXT	414	
D-MIIS	Zenair CH-601XL Zodiac	6-9700	
D-MIIT	Rotortec Cloud Dancer II	unkn	
D-MIIU	Rotortec Cloud Dancer II	1114 X1 ZZZ4	
D-MIIW	NST Minimum	M572/92	
D-MIIZ	Scheibe ULI	unkn	
D-MIJB	Apis BEE 15 MB	A039 MB09	
D-MIJF	FUL Graffiti Trike	043/0149	
D-MIJG	Comco Ikarus C-42B	1206-7207	
D-MIJH	Aerospool WT-9 Dynamic	DY319/2009	
D-MIJI #	NST Minimum	M555	
D-MIJK	Comco Ikarus C-42C	1311-7290	
D-MIJN	Flight Design CT Supralight	unkn	
D-MIJR	Take Off Merlin Trike	24155	
D-MIJT	NST Minimum Santana	M532	
D-MIKB(1)	Autogyro Europe Calidus	unkn	
D-MIKB(2)	Comco Ikarus C-42C	1303-7253	D-MCOP
D-MIKC	Comco Ikarus Fox-C22	9010-3287	
D-MIKD	Comco Ikarus C-42B	unkn	
D-MIKE	Cosmos / Chronos 12	21227	
D-MIKF	Evektor EV-97 Eurostar SL	unkn	
D-MIKG	Take Off Maximum Trike	001049	
D-MIKH(1)	Zenair CH-601 Zodiac	unkn	
D-MIKH(2)	Autogyro Europe Calidus	unkn	
D-MIKI	Schmidtler Enduro Trike	02-013	
D-MIKK	Drachenstudio Royal 912 / iXess 15	390926	
D-MIKL	Plätzer Motte B2	60	
D-MIKO	Scheibe ULI NG	UW100210	
D-MIKP	Comco Ikarus C-42B	0403-6587	D-MULI(2)
D-MIKR(1)	Behlen Trike	84012	
D-MIKR(2)	Aeropro Eurofox	unkn	
D-MIKS	Ultraleichtverbund Bi 90	530380431167	
D-MIKY(1)	MKB Ranger M	0100284	
D-MIKY(2)	Aerospool WT-9 Dynamic	DY063/2004	
D-MILA(2)	Pago Jet M4	RB 97000	
D-MILA(3)	Aeropilot SRO Legend 540	1308	
D-MILB	Zlin Savage	233	
D-MILC	Comco Ikarus Fox-C22	9010-3288	
D-MILD	Aviasud Mistral BRD	088	
D-MILD	B&F Funk FK-9 Mk.IV Utility	09-04U-233	
D-MILE	Scheibe Uli 1	5226	
	(W/o 5.8.15)		
D-MILF	Schönleber Trike	010794	
D-MILG	Aerospool WT-9 Dynamic	DY018 02	
D-MILH(1)	Autogyro Europe MT-03	05G15	
D-MILH(2)	Autogyro Europe Calidus	unkn	
D-MILI (1)	Pipistrel Sinus	unkn	
D-MILI(2)	Flight Design CT LS	08-01-21	
D-MILJ #	Behlen Power-Trike II	90024	
D-MILK	Remos G.3 Mirage	117	
D-MILL(1)	Autogyro Europe MT-03	04G12	
D-MILL(2)	Autogyro Europe MTOsport	M01229	
D-MILM	Comco Ikarus Fox-C22	9005-3265	
	(To S5-PAK)		
D-MILO(1)	Dallach Sunrise IIB	031	
D-MILO(2)	Aerostyle Breezer CR	085	
D-MILP	B&F Funk FK-14 Polaris	14B-049	
D-MILR	Pagotto Brako-GT Turbo	unkn	
D-MILT(1)	Seiffert Mini-Speed Trike	001	
D-MILT(2)	Comco Ikarus C-42B	0807-6985	
D-MILU	Cosmos / Chronos 12	21151	
D-MILV	Aerostyle Breezer CL	092	
D-MILY	Zlin Savage Cruiser	196	
D-MILZ	Klüver Racer SX 12 Trike	652907	
D-MIMB	Comco Ikarus Fox-C22	9103-3321	
D-MIMC #	Comco Ikarus Fox-C22	9009-3289	
D-MIME	Fresh Breeze Simo 122	unkn	
D-MIMG	Flight Design CT 2K	02-02-06-11	
D-MIMI (1)	Comco Ikarus Fox-C22	9209-3441	
D-MIMI(2)	B&F Funk FK-9 Mk.IV (t/w)	unkn	
D-MIML	Fisher FP-202 Koala	20290	
D-MIMM	Comco Ikarus Fox-C22	9208-3416	
D-MIMN #	Ultraleichtverbund Bi 90	21074	
D-MIMP	Fresh Breeze Simo 122	unkn	
D-MIMS	Plätzer Kiebitz B	297	
D-MIMW	TL Ultralight TL-96 Sting	07ST219	
D-MIMY	Avid Flyer Mk.IV Heavy Hauler	1050D	
	(C/n as officially recorded, NB c/n 1050A is 59-CQG)		
D-MINA	Junkers Profly JU L 2002 / Pico	unkn	
D-MIND	Bautek Eagle V/ Ghost 14.9	unkn	
D-MINE	Fresh Breeze 110 AL2A	352	
D-MING	Plätzer Motte-B2	013	
D-MINI	Scheibe Uli 1	5209	
D-MINK	NST Minimum	M447	
D-MINL	OMM M-7 Servator	353-1003	
D-MINN #	Tecnam P.92 Echo	unkn	
D-MINO	Nando Groppo Trial	00050	
D-MINR	Air Création Tanarg 912ES / iXess 13	unkn	
D-MINT	Remos G.3 Mirage	141	
D-MINU	HFL Stratos 300	300-004	
D-MINX	Tandem Air Sunny Sport	006.07.02SP	
D-MINY	Fresh Breeze Simo 122	unkn	
D-MINZ(1)	Scheibe UL-1 Coach	3202	
D-MINZ(2)	Fresh Breeze Simo 122	unkn	
D-MIOA	Comco Ikarus Fox-C22	9101-3302	
D-MIOC	Comco Ikarus Fox-C22	9009-3290	
D-MIOD	Comco Ikarus Fox D	8806-FD43	
D-MIOG	Fresh Breeze 110 AL 2F	332	
D-MIOK	Aerostyle Breezer CL	UL104	
D-MIOL #	Autogyro Europe MT-03	unkn	
D-MIOO	Light Aero Avid Flyer D	1230	
D-MIOP	Aerostyle Breezer	unkn	
D-MIOR	Aerostyle Breezer CL	UL112	
D-MIOS	Fläming Air FA-01 Smaragd TD	117/07n	
D-MIOX	Nando Groppo Trial	unkn	
D-MIPA(1)	Tandem Air Sunny Sport	010.01.04SP	
D-MIPA(2)	Autogyro Europe MTOsport	unkn	
D-MIPB	Aerostyle Breezer	012	
D-MIPC	Comco Ikarus Fox-C22	9012-3303	
D-MIPD	Roland CH-701D Amphibian	unkn	
D-MIPF	Aeroprakt A-22L2 Vision	unkn	
D-MIPL	Roland Z602XL	Z-9531	
D-MIPP #	Alpi Aviation Pioneer 200	unkn	
D-MIPR	Flight Design CT SW	unkn	
D-MIPS	Light Aero Avid Flyer C	943 C	
D-MIPU	Aerospool WT-9 Dynamic	DYK 18/2007	
D-MIPV	Comco Ikarus Fox-C22	9106-3362	
D-MIPW	Schmidtler Enduro Trike	02-016	
D-MIPY	Air Light Wild Thing	unkn	
D-MIPZ	Aerospool WT-9 Dynamic	DY074/2005	
D-MIQC	Comco Ikarus Fox-C22	9101-3304	
D-MIQI	Bautek Eagle V/ Pico	unkn	
D-MIRA(1)	Flight Design CT-2K	unkn	
D-MIRA(2)	Roland Z602	Z-9566	
D-MIRB #	Comco Ikarus Fox-C22	9106-3305	
D-MIRC	Albatros 52	129	
D-MIRE	WDFL Sunwheel	033	OE-7030
D-MIRG	Zlin Savage Cruiser	149	
	(Cancelled)		
D-MIRH	Technoflug Piccolo	126	
D-MIRI	Behlen Power-Trike	97003	
D-MIRJ	Comco Fox D	045	
D-MIRK	B&F Funk FK-12 Comet	12-018	
D-MIRL	Tecnam P.92 Echo	unkn	
D-MIRM	AirLony Skylane	64	
D-MIRO	Schmidtler Enduro / Mild 16	unkn	
D-MIRR	Aurogyro Europe MTOsport	unkn	
D-MIRT #	Schönleber DS Trike	030492	
D-MIRU	Tomark SD-4 Viper	unkn	
D-MIRY	Magni M-24 Orion	24148574	
D-MIRZ	Autogyro Europe MTOsport	unkn	
D-MISA (1)	Schmidtler Ranger M	18/37	
D-MISA(2)	Zenair CH-601XL Zodiac	unkn	
D-MISA(3)	B&F Funk FK-9 Mk.IV	unkn	
D-MISB	Pipistrel Taurus 503	unkn	
D-MISC	Comco Ikarus Fox-C22	9102-3306	
D-MISE #	Light Aero Avid Flyer D	1231	
D-MISF #	Autogyro Europe MTOsport	unkn	
D-MISG	Zlin Savage Classic	unkn	
D-MISH	B&F Funk FK-9 Mk.III Utility	09-03U-212	
D-MISI(2) #	B&F Funk FK-14B-2 Polaris	014-060	
	(To CS-URO, 4.10; w/o 6.2.15 still as D-MISI)		
D-MISI(3)	Pipistrel Virus SW	unkn	
D-MISL	Comco Ikarus Sherpa I	8305-1017	
D-MISR	Rans S-6 Coyote II	unkn	
D-MISS	Air Création/	unkn	
D-MIST (1)	Comco Ikarus Fox D	008	
D-MIST(2)	Autogyro Europe MTOsport	unkn	
D-MISU	Flight Design CT SW	07-04-25	
D-MISY	Alpi Aviation Pioneer 300	unkn	
D-MITA	Tecnam P.92 Echo 2000S	991	
D-MITB	Seiffert Mini II	4392	
D-MITC	Comco Ikarus Fox-C22	9102-3307	
D-MITE	B&F Funk FK-12 Comet	12-063	
D-MITF(1)	Rans S-12 Airaile	0192168	
	(To Hungary as 35-34)		
D-MITF(2)	Aeroprakt A-22 Vision	173	
D-MITG	Comco Ikarus Fox-C22	9207-3388	
D-MITH	EEL ULF-2	6	
D-MITI	NST Minimum	unkn	
D-MITK	Flight Design CT LS	F-12-02-01	
D-MITL	Schönleber DS Trike	020794	
D-MITP	Pipistrel Taunus 503	130T503	
D-MITR	Flight Design CT LS	F-09-03-07	
D-MITT	Fresh Breeze 110 AL 2F	160	
D-MITV	Plätzer Kiebitz B6-450	12	
D-MITY	Evektor EV-97 Eurostar SL	2012 4001	
D-MITZ	Rans S-6S Coyote II	unkn	
D-MIUB	Cosmos / Chronos 12	B21155	
D-MIUC #	Comco Ikarus Fox-C22	9102-3308	
D-MIUL	Autogyro Europe MT-03	05G06	
D-MIUR	Eurofly Viper 582 / Hazard 13	unkn	
D-MIUS	Pioneer Flightstar	539	D-MTAF
D-MIUU	Roland Z602XL	Z-9556	
D-MIVA	BRM Aero NG5 Bristell	unkn	
D-MIVC #	Comco Ikarus Fox-C22	9104-3309	
D-MIVF	Bautek Eagle V/ Pico	unkn	
D-MIVK #	Behlen Power-Trike Vampir II	85-027	
D-MIVO	Autogyro Europe Calidus	unkn	
D-MIVP	Pipistrel Virus SW100	663SWN100	
D-MIWA	Zlin Savage Cruiser	221	
D-MIWB	Zenair CH-701D STOL	7-9539	
D-MIWC	Comco Ikarus Fox-C22	9105-3310	
D-MIWH	Alpi Avn Pioneer 300UL	unkn	
D-MIWM	Zlin Savage	074	
D-MIWN	Flight Team Spider XL / iXess	unkn	
D-MIWR	Comco Ikarus C-42B	0907-7058	
D-MIWS	Wezel Apis 2	W003	
D-MIWT	TL Ultralight TL-3000 Sirius	12Si70	
D-MIWU	Flight Design CT-2K	unkn	
D-MIWV	Flight Team Spider	D050	
D-MIWW	Flight Team Spider	D043	
D-MIXA	Pipistrel Sinus 912NW	288SNLD912	
D-MIXC #	Comco Ikarus Fox-C22	9102-3311	
D-MIXI	Twister / Pico S Valve	unkn	
D-MIXL(2)	Zenair CH-601XL Zodiac	6-9803	
D-MIXO	Roman-Weller UW-9 Sprint	2	
D-MIXR	Trixy G4-2R	016	
	(Cr 8.3.13)		
D-MIXS	Denney Kitfox IV-1200	unkn	
D-MIXX	Schmidtler Enduro 1150 / iXess 15	unkn	
D-MIYT	Plätzer Kiebitz B	235	
D-MIYZ	Autogyro Europe MTOsport	unkn	
D-MIZA	Pioneer Flightstar	377	
D-MIZC #	Comco Ikarus Fox-C22	9102-3312	
D-MIZE (1)	MKB Ranger M Trike	01/009/86	
D-MIZE(2)	Flight Design CT SW	unkn	
D-MIZG #	NST Minimum Pamir	443	
D-MIZP #	Comco Ikarus Fox-C22	9009-3316	
D-MIZY	Flight Design CT LS	F-08-05-04	
D-MIZZ	Flight Team Spider	D044	
D-MJAA	JMB/Aveko VL-3	114/2013	
D-MJAB	Jabiru 450C	0538	
D-MJAC	Zlin Savage Cruiser	unkn	
D-MJAE	Klüver Twin Racer Quartz SX 16	228004	
D-MJAG(2)	B&F Funk FK-9 Mk.2	007	
D-MJAH	Flight Design CT LS	unkn	

Reg	Type	c/n	Notes
D-MJAI #	Kümmerle Mni-Fly-Set	1305916	
D-MJAK	Fresh Breeze Simo 122	unkn	
D-MJAL	Fair Fax DR Trike	D016	
D-MJAM	Plätzer Kiebitz-B6	020	
D-MJAN(1)	Behlen Power-Trike II	90027	
D-MJAN(2)	Comco Ikarus C-42B	1101-7126	
D-MJAR	Dova DV-1 Skylark	07/21	
D-MJAS	Ultraleichtverbund Bi 90	736	
D-MJAT	TVS 700 Tandem Air Sunny	991	
D-MJAU	Light Aero Avid Flyer	491	
D-MJAY	Flight Design CT SW	unkn	
D-MJAZ	Ekolot JK-05 Junior	unkn	
D-MJBH	NST Minimum Saphir 17	976	
D-MJBL	J.Blank Trike (Homebuilt)	unkn	
D-MJBM	Comco Ikarus C-42B	0707-6908	
D-MJBR	Comco Ikarus C-42B		
D-MJBU	Comco Ikarus Fox-C22	9002-3253	
D-MJBV	Aveko VL-3	VL-3-128	
D-MJCA	FD Composites Arrowcopter AC20S	035	
D-MJCE #	Behlen Power-Trike /Rotax 582	980019	
D-MJCT(1)	Ultraleichtverbund Bi 90	1055508906	
D-MJCT(2)	Flight Design CT LS	07-11-12	
D-MJCW	Autogyro Europe MTOsport	unkn	
D-MJDC	Comco Ikarus C-42	0909-7063	
D-MJDO	Schmidtler Ranger M Trike	1812	
D-MJDS #	Magni M-24 Orion	24116484	
D-MJDT	Air Light Wild Thing 2200	102	
D-MJEA	Remos G-3 600	unkn	
D-MJEE(1)	Autogyro Europe MT-03	05G26	
D-MJEE(2)	Autogyro Europe MTOsport	unkn	
D-MJEF #	Sky Walker II	240	
	(same c/n quoted for D-MJFE)		
D-MJEH #	Take Off Maximum Trike	T057061	
D-MJEJ	unidentified paramotor	unkn	
D-MJEK	Dallach D4B Fascination BK	128	
D-MJEL	Autogyro Europe Cavalon	unkn	
D-MJEM	Silent 2 Electro	2032K	
D-MJET	TVS 700 Tandem Air Sunny	006	
D-MJEU	Aerospool WT-9 Dynamic	unkn	
D-MJEV	Vector Ultra-Vector	unkn	
D-MJEW	Flight Team Spider Trike	D037	
D-MJFA	IBIS GS-700 Jet Magic	GS-10-10-700-106	
D-MJFC #	UPM Cobra BF 52UL Trike	930123	
D-MJFE	Sky Walker	240	
	(see D-MJEF, ex?)		
D-MJFF(1)	Comco Ikarus C-42B	1310-7279	
D-MJFF(2)	Comco Ikarus C-42B	1502-7373	
D-MJFH	Platzer Kiebitz B	253	
D-MJFK(1)	B&F Funk FK-9 Club	unkn	
D-MJFK(2)	B&F Funk FK-14A Polaris	unkn	
D-MJFN	Drachenstudio Royal 912 / Avant 15	unkn	
D-MJFO #	Take Off Maximum Trike	107013	
D-MJFP	Aeropilot Legend 540	1523	
D-MJFS	Remos G-3 Mirage	157	
D-MJGG	TL Ultralight TL-96 Sting	unkn	
	(W/o 2.8.11)		
D-MJGH	Comco Ikarus Fox-C22	8604-3015	
	(To 68-BO)		
D-MJGS	Magni M-24 Orion	24137774	
D-MJGX	Remos GX	404	
D-MJHA	Behlen Power-Trike	unkn	
D-MJHB	Behlen Power-Trike II	90022	
D-MJHE	Remos G3 Mirage	133	
D-MJHG	Comco Ikarus C-42C	1210-7225	
D-MJHH #	Konsuprod Moskito Ib	012	PH-2D5
D-MJHI	Fresh Breeze Simo 122	unkn	
D-MJHM	Take Off Maximum Trike	063071	
D-MJHO	Bautek Eagle V/ Avant	unkn	
D-MJHP	Rans S-10 Sakota	206203	
D-MJHR	Aerostyle Breezer	037	
D-MJHS	Plätzer Kiebitz-B2	068	
D-MJHW	Autogyro Europe MT-03	unkn	
D-MJIT	Rotortec Cloud Dancer 2		
	RCD2 DEU ROT 0613Z1 ZZ11	006	
D-MJIY #	Dallach Sunrise II	006	
D-MJJA	TVS 700 Tandem Air Sunny Sport	004	
D-MJJC	Behlen Power-Trike	960002	
D-MJJJ	Solid Air Twin Diamant	7	
D-MJJM	Aerostyle Breezer CL		
D-MJJP #	WDFL Dallach D4 Fascination BK	122	
D-MJJY #	TVS 700 Tandem Air Sunny	003	
D-MJJZ	TVS 700 Tandem Air Sunny	002	
D-MJKA	Ekolot JK—05 Junior	unkn	
D-MJKB(1)	Fair Fax AH Euro III Trike	32	
D-MJKB(2)	Drachenstudio Royal 912 / Eos	unkn	
D-MJKE	Büttner Crazyplane III	2	
D-MJKG #	Fresh Breeze 110 AL2F	98	
D-MJKH(1)	Comco Ikarus Fox-C22	9006-3271	
D-MJKH(2)	Ekolot JK-05 Junior	05-07-08	
	(To PH-4M3, 6.15)		
D-MJKI #	UPM Funplane	870.023	
D-MJKK	B&F Funk FK-9 Mk.IV	unkn	
D-MJKO #	Behlen Power Trike II	89038	
D-MJKP	Behlen Power-Trike /Rotax 582	97002	
D-MJKS	Autogyro Europe MTOsport	unkn	
D-MJKU	B&F Funk FK-9 Classic	unkn	
D-MJKW(1)	Fair Fax DR Trike	D005	
D-MJKW(2)	Comco Ikarus C-42B	unkn	
D-MJLC #	Solid Air Diamant 55dB(A) Trike	011	
D-MJLL(1)	Autogyro Europe MT-03	unkn	
D-MJLL(2)	Autogyro Europe MTOsport	unkn	
D-MJLP	J-3 Kitten	12-8-88	
D-MJLS #	Kiggen/Heiland Air Création GTE 582 S		
		6954556835	
D-MJLY	Scheibe ULI NG	UW100512	
D-MJMA	Skywalker 1+1	26127	
D-MJMB(1)	Behlen Power-Trike	91027	
D-MJMB(2)	Tecnam P.92S Echo	unkn	
D-MJMJ	UPM Cobra BF 52UL Trike	940128	
D-MJMK	Fresh Breeze 110 AL 2F	332	
D-MJMM	Comco Ikarus Fox-C22	9703-3722	LX-XAE, D-MXAE
D-MJMO #	UPM Cobra Trike	900094	
D-MJMS	Corvus CA-21 Phantom	unkn	
D-MJMW	Breezer CL	UL96	
D-MJMX	Pipistrel Alpha Trainer	unkn	
	(W/o 18.3.15, Klagenfurt)		
D-MJNA	ARCO Spacer L	463	
D-MJND #	Drachenstudio Piccolo II	089-94/04	
D-MJNL	Comco Ikarus C-42B	1404-7321	
D-MJNN	Kilb Air Création GTE 5	AC 009	
D-MJNP	Comco Ikarus C-42B	unkn	
D-MJNV	Aerospool WT-9 Dynamic	unkn	
D-MJOA #	Behlen Power-Trike	87019	
D-MJOB	Behlen Power-Trike	92002	
D-MJOC	Fresh Breeze Simo 122	unkn	
D-MJOE(1)	NST Minimum Pamir	503	
D-MJOE(2)	Autogyro Europe Calidus	D10C12	
	(To SE-VRR 8.11)		
D-MJOG	Fresh Breeze Simo 122	unkn	
D-MJOH(1)	Klüver Twin Racer SX 16 Trike	449007	
D-MJOH(2)	Remos Cruiser	232	
D-MJOK	FUL Graffiti MA 30 / Stranger	301	
	(To PH-4J6)		
D-MJOS #	Bautek Eagle V/ Pico	unkn	
D-MJOY	Evektor EV-97R Eurostar 2000	2002-1402	
D-MJPA	NST Minimum	M542	
D-MJPC	Fresh Breeze 110 AL 2F	222	
D-MJPD	Profe Banjo MH	08	
D-MJPE	B&F Funk FK-9SW Mk.IV	09-04-293	
D-MJPG(2)	Rans S-12 Airaile	1091138	
D-MJPH	Aerostyle Breezer CR	070	
D-MJPJ	Comco Ikarus C-42B	1009-7118	
D-MJPK(1)	Light Aero Avid Flyer IV	868	
	(To OY-9440)		
D-MJPK(2)	Gramex Song LW 120	14/2014	
D-MJPL	Fresh Breeze Xcitor	09XCR1282BF63299	
D-MJPW #	Seiffert Mini-Speed Trike	7	
D-MJRB(1)	Fresh Breeze 110 AL 2F	951105	
D-MJRB(2)	Spacek SD-1 Minisport	unkn	
D-MJRN	Fresh Breeze 110 AL 2F	951103	
D-MJRR(1)	Mantel Mono-Dragster	M508	
D-MJRR(2)	Dova DV-1 Skylark	152/12	
D-MJSA(1)	B&F Funk FK-9 Mk.2	unkn	
D-MJSA(2)	Aerostyle Breezer CL	unkn	
D-MJSC	Fresh Breeze Simo 122	unkn	
D-MJSF	Comco Ikarus C-42B	0307-6555	
D-MJSG	Quicksilver MX	13744	
D-MJSH	Fisher FP-202 Koala	2302	
D-MJSJ	FUL Graffiti Trike	015/0075	
D-MJSL	Air Création XP GT 582 ES	17/511994	
D-MJSN	Plätzer Kiebitz-B6	034	
D-MJSS(1)	Plätzer Motte D	01	
D-MJSS(2)	Evektor EV-97 Eurostar SL	2009 3511	
D-MJST	Tandem Air Sunny Sport	032-92	
D-MJSV #	Plätzer Kiebitz	unkn	
D-MJSW	Comco Ikarus Fox-C22	9010-3301	
D-MJTA	B&F Funk FK-9 Mk.IV ELA Professional	unkn	
D-MJTC	Comco Ikarus C-42	unkn	
D-MJTM	Autogyro Europe Calidus	unkn	
D-MJTR	UPM Funplane	950050	
D-MJTS	Pipistrel Taurus 503	unkn	
D-MJUA	Steinbach Austro-Trike	101	
D-MJUA(2)	Alisport Silent	2026	
D-MJUG	LO-120	003A	
D-MJUH	Behlen Power-Trike /Rotax 582	98009	
D-MJUK #	Take Off Maximum Trike	47041	
D-MJUN #	Junkers Profly JUL Trike	094/003	
D-MJUR #	Comco Ikarus Fox-C22	910 .-3326	
D-MJUS #	Avio Delta Swan I / Ghost 12	unkn	
D-MJUT	NST Minimum	M547	
D-MJUV	Junkers Profly JUL Trike	58294003	
D-MJUX	Comco Ikarus C-42B	unkn	
D-MJVG #	Dallach D4B Fascination	unkn	
D-MJVS	J.van Stappen (Homebuilt)	SC 89746	
D-MJWB	HFL Stratos IIe	007	
D-MJWD	Ultraleichtverbund Bi 90	6118903	
D-MJWF #	Alpi Aviation Pioneer 200	unkn	
	(W/o 5.5.11)		
D-MJWH	Comco Ikarus C-42B	unkn	
D-MJWS	NST Minimum	M537	
	(Also listed, probably in error, as a UPM Funplane with this c/n)		
D-MJWT	Aerostyle Breezer	040	
D-MJWW	Flight Team Spider Trike	D028	
D-MJXC	Aerostyle Breezer CL	UL131	
D-MJXI	Drachenstudio Royal 912 / Avant 15	unkn	
D-MJXX	Autogyro Europe MT-03	unkn	
D-MJYY	Sky Walker 1+1	26129	
D-MJZD #	Flight Design CT-2K	unkn	
D-MKAA(1)	Ultraleichtverbund Bi 90	21064	
D-MKAA(2)	Spacek SD-1 Minisport TG	unkn	
D-MKAB	TL Ultralight TL-96 Star	02 S 128	
D-MKAC	Air Création SX GT 582ES Quartz SX 16	AC 001	
D-MKAE(2)#	Sky Walker II	193	
D-MKAF #	Take Off Maximum Trike	87022	
D-MKAG(1)	Eagle	unkn	
D-MKAG(2)	Autogyro Europe MTOsport	E08G03	
D-MKAH #	Büttner Crazyplane III	106	
D-MKAK	Fresh Breeze BulliX	2098	
D-MKAL	Autogyro Europe MTOsport	unkn	
D-MKAM	Flight Design CT SW	04.03.01	
D-MKAN #	Flight Design CT SW	unkn	
D-MKAO	B&F Funk FK-14B2 Polaris	unkn	
D-MKAP	Drachenstudio Royal 912 / Avant	180997	
D-MKAR #	Fresh Breeze Simo 122	unkn	
D-MKAS(1)	Behlen Power-Trike	91033	
D-MKAS(2)	Impulse turbo	unkn	
D-MKAT	Tecnam P.92 Echo 2000S	655	
D-MKAU	Best Off Sky Ranger Swift	unkn	
D-MKAV	Aviomania G1sB Genesis Solo	unkn	
D-MKAW	Flight Design CT SW	06-04-06	(SP-SGEL)
D-MKBA	Behlen Power-Trike /Rotax 582	980018	
D-MKBB	Plätzer Kiebitz-B6	174	
D-MKBC	Zenair CH-601 Zodiac	6-9906	
D-MKBE(1)	Comco Ikarus Sherpa I	8306-1028	
D-MKBE(2)	ICP MXP-740 Savannah S	unkn	
D-MKBF	Plätzer Kiebitz	248	
D-MKBG	Ultraleichtverbund Bi 90	701	
D-MKBH	Apis BEE 15 MB	A052MB14	
D-MKBK	HFL Stratos	300-012K	
D-MKBL	Comco Ikarus C-42B	0206-6473	
D-MKBM	Behlen Power-Trike II	95005	
D-MKBR	NST Minimum	M531	

Registration	Type	C/n	Notes
D-MKBT	Drachenstudio Royal 912 / Avant	unkn	
D-MKBV	Zlin Savage Cruiser	unkn	
D-MKBZ	Bautek Eagle V/ Avant	unkn	
D-MKCC	Evektor EV-97 Eurostar SL W	unkn	
D-MKCH(1)	Sky-Walker II	383	
D-MKCH(2)	Technoflug Piccolo	098	
D-MKCK	Autogyro Europe MTOsport	M01204	
D-MKCL	Aerospool WT-9 Dynamic	unkn	
D-MKCM #	Point Avn/Albatros AN-22	01	
D-MKCP	Autogyro Europe MT-03	unkn	
D-MKCS	Roland Z602	Z-9548	
D-MKCT	Flight Design CT-2K	03.07.05.36	
D-MKDA	Cloud Dancer / Atos-VX	unkn	
	(Also reported as Aeros Air)		
D-MKDB	Airsport Song	unkn	
	(Crashed Gruibingen 14.9.16)		
D-MKDE	Fantasy Air Allegro	04-417	
D-MKDI #	Behlen Power-Trike II	90021	
D-MKDL #	NST Minimum	C2483	
D-MKDM	Behlen Power-Trike	91028	
D-MKDS	Aeroprakt A-22 Vision	007	
D-MKDT #	Rans S-6 Coyote II	unkn	
D-MKEA #	Behlen Power-Trike	89042	
D-MKEC	Tecnam P.92S Echo	unkn	
D-MKED	Comco Ikarus C-42B	unkn	
D-MKEE	Comco Ikarus C-42B	0203-6459	
D-MKEF	B&F Funk FK-14B Polaris	870026	
D-MKEH	UPM Funplane	90009	
D-MKEJ(1)	Behlen Power-Trike	90009	
D-MKEJ(2)	B&F Funk FK-14 Le Mans	unkn	
D-MKEK	Pipistrel Virus SW	443	
D-MKEL	Air-Light Wild Thing	071	
D-MKEN	BOT Speed Cruiser SC07	008	
D-MKER	Fisher FP-202 Koala	ST-005	
D-MKES	Tandem Air Sunny Sport	26-91	
D-MKET	Comco Ikarus C-42	9904-6153	OE-7055
D-MKEY	Roland CH602XL	Z-9526	
D-MKFA(1)	Ultraleichtverbund Bi 90	6613917738	
D-MKFA(2)	EEL ULF-2	003	
D-MKFC	Comco Ikarus C-42B	0812-7019	
D-MKFD(1)	Fresh Breeze Simo 122	unkn	
D-MKFD(2)	Plätzer Kiebitz	375	
D-MKFE	Comco Ikarus C-42B	0506-6684	
D-MKFF	Comco Ikarus C-42B	0301-6475	
D-MKFG	Best Off Sky Ranger	unkn	
D-MKFH #	Take Off Maximum Karat 13 Trike	081111	
D-MKFK(1)	BRM Aero Bristell UL	067/2013	
	(Re-regd D-MMRP(2))		
D-MKFK(2)	BRM Aero Bristell UL	071/2013	D-MTYP
D-MKFL	Fresh Breeze Simo 122	unkn	
D-MKFM	Vidor Asso V Champion	002	
D-MKFS #	Fresh Breeze 122 AL 2F	349	
D-MKFU	Flight Design CT SW	unkn	
D-MKFW	Behlen Power-Trike	94002	
D-MKGA(2#	Ultraleichtverband Bi 90	331-7740	
D-MKGB(1)	Ultraleichtverbund Bi 90	908	
D-MKGB(2)	Autogyro Europe MT-03	unkn	
D-MKGC	Ultraleichtverbund Bi 90	3950478	
D-MKGG	Celier Xenon	CAL10273 R	
D-MKGH	Kilb Air Création GTE 5	AC 007	
D-MKGI	Comco Ikarus Fox II Doppel	8607-3025	
D-MKGM	Exxtacy Elektro Minimum	unkn	
D-MKGR #	Comco Ikarus Fox-C22	9205-3432	
D-MKGS	Rans S-6 Coyote II	unkn	
	(Cr 3.9.11)		
D-MKGW	Flight Design CT LS	F-09-08-02	SE-MBV
D-MKHA #	Flight Team Spider	D046	
D-MKHB	Behlen Power-Trike	89015	
D-MKHC(1)	Merlin	unkn	
D-MKHC(2)	Drachenstudio Royal 912 / Eos	unkn	
D-MKHD(1)	AirLony Skylane UL	42/2011	
	(Re-registered D-MMNC)		
D-MKHD(2)	Celier Xenon	unkn	
D-MKHD(3)	Magni M-24 Orion	24148324	
D-MKHE	Comco Ikarus Fox-C22	9102-3318	
D-MKHG(1)	Behlen Power-Trike	92015	
D-MKHG(2)	Tecnam P.92S Echo Super	unkn	
D-MKHH(1)	NST Minimum	M590	
D-MKHH(2)	Autogyro Europe MTOsport	unkn	
D-MKHK	HFL Stratos 300	300-018K	
D-MKHL(1)	Comco Ikarus Fox-C22	8706-3071	
D-MKHL(2)	Comco Ikarus C-42	9710-6058	D-MYKA
D-MKHM #	Sky-Walker II	329	
D-MKHP	Tandem Air Sunny	007	
D-MKHR	Behlen Power-Trike /Rotax 582	86013	
D-MKHS(2)	Rans S-6 Coyote II	0192263	
D-MKHT	Schmidtler Enduro Trike	02-012	
D-MKHW(1)	Behlen Power-Trike	84229	
D-MKHW(2)	B&F Funk FK-14B Polaris	unkn	
D-MKHZ #	Comco Ikarus Fox-C22	unkn	
D-MKIC	Take Off Merlin Titan	unkn	
D-MKID	Ultraleichtverbund Bi 90	79282054016042	
D-MKIE	Plätzer Kiebitz-B	323	
D-MKIH	Aero East Europe Sila 450C	unkn	
D-MKII	Remos G.3 Mirage	unkn	
D-MKIJ	Tecnam P.92S Echo	unkn	
D-MKIK	Plätzer Kiebitz-B	119	
D-MKIL	Comco Ikarus C-42B	0807-6968	
D-MKIM(1)	Flight Design CT SW	unkn	
D-MKIM(2)	Aveko VL-3	VL-3-121	
D-MKIO	Autogyro Europe MTOsport	unkn	
D-MKIS	Ultraleichtverbund Bi 90	9604171161	
D-MKIT	Denney Kitfox IV	1839	D-EPHS
D-MKIW	Evektor EV-97 Eurostar	2002 1501	
D-MKIY	Aerospool WT-9 Dynamic	DY015 02	
D-MKJA	Fresh Breeze 110 AL 2F	51	
D-MKJA(2)	Autogyro Europe MTOsport	unkn	
D-MKJB	Plätzer Kiebitz-B	079	
D-MKJC	Fresh Breeze 110 AL 2F	66	
D-MKJD	Fresh Breeze 110 AL 2F	65	
D-MKJE	Fresh Breeze 110 AL 2F	64	
D-MKJF	Fresh Breeze 110 AL 2F	195	
D-MKJG	Fresh Breeze 110 AL 2F	56	
D-MKJH	Fresh Breeze 110 AL 2F	203	
D-MKJJ	Plätzer Kiebitz B	352	
D-MKJK	Spacek SD-1 Minisport TD	unkn	
D-MKJU	Flight Design CT LS	F-09-12-09	
D-MKKC	Kilb Air Création GTE 582 S Trike	AC 008	
D-MKKD(1)	Evektor EV-97R Eurostar SL	2008 0002	
D-MKKD(2)	Evektor EV-97 Eurostar SLW	2009 3608	
D-MKKD(3)	Evektor EV-97 Eurostar SLW Sport	2013 4105	
D-MKKE	Evektor EV-97 Eurostar SL	2008 3404	
D-MKKF	Evektor EV-97 Eurostar SL	2008 3413	
D-MKKG	Evektor EV-97 Eurostar SLW	2009 3623	
D-MKKH(1)	Tandem Air Sunny Sport	48.93	
D-MKKH(2)	B&F Funk FK-14B Polaris	14-040	
	(W/o 13.2.16)		
D-MKKI	Autogyro Europe MT-03	unkn	
D-MKKJ	B&F Funk FK-12 Comet	12-077	
D-MKKK(1)	Remos G.3 Mirage	130	
D-MKKK(2)	Comco Ikarus C-42	unkn	
D-MKKL	Air-Light Wild Thing	2001-06-080	
D-MKKM	Evektor EV-97R Eurostar 2000	2004-2204	
D-MKKN	Fresh Breeze Simo SportiX / Skywalk Tequila M	unkn	
D-MKKO	Take Off Merlin Trike	24705	
D-MKKP	Evektor EV-97R Eurostar 2000	2007 3101	
D-MKKQ	Evektor EV-97 Eurostar SLW Sport	2014 4110	
D-MKKR	Stratos 300	unkn	
D-MKKS	Apis BEE 15 MB	A014M06	
D-MKKT(1)	Autogyro Europe MT-03	D06G03	
	(Crashed 31.3.09 Bonn-Hangelar)		
D-MKKT(2)	Autogyro Europe MT0sport	unkn	
D-MKKU	Shark Aero Shark	005/2012	D-MYBE, OK-RUR 01
	(To D-MMKV)		
D-MKKV(1)	Plätzer Kiebitz	unkn	
D-MKKV(2)	Evektor EV-97 Eurostar SL	2011 3922	
D-MKKW #	Behlen Ladas M Trike	M041120200	
D-MKKY	Evektor EV-97 Eurostar SL	2012 3934	
D-MKKZ	Evektor EV-97 Eurostar SLW	2012 4106	
D-MKLA	Klüver Kaiman Profil 17 Trike	269916703	
D-MKLB	B&F Funk FK-9 Mk.IV	unkn	
D-MKLC	Klüver Bison Trike	917703	
D-MKLE(1)	Solid Air Diamant Trike	009	
D-MKLE(2)	Fresh Breeze Simo 122	unkn	
D-MKLG	Fresh Breeze Simo 122	unkn	
D-MKLI	ASO Viper Hazard 13 Trike	22047307	
D-MKLJ	B&F Funk FK-9 FI A	409	
D-MKLK	Light Aero Avid Flyer IV D	1271D	
D-MKLL	B&F Funk FK-9 Mk IV	04-337	
	(Same c/n as D-MLLL, or typing error?)		
D-MKLM	Solid Air Diamant Twin / Ghost 14.9	unkn	
D-MKLN	Comco Ikarus Fox-C22	9007-3278	
D-MKLO	ICP MXP-740V Savannah S	11-06-54-0107	
D-MKLR	Alpi Aviation Pioneer 200UL	103	
D-MKLS	Take Off Maximum Trike	093052	
D-MKLU	Comco Icarus C-42B	unkn	
	(Damaged 13.5.10)		
D-MKLV	Ultralight Flight Phantom	312	
D-MKLW	Bautek Eagle V/ Pico	unkn	
D-MKLY	B&F Funk FK-9	09-05-425	
D-MKMB	Zenair CH-601XL Zodiac	unkn	
D-MKME	UL-F Jochum Eagle III	970502	
	(Possibly ex D-MAWE, same c/n quoted)		
D-MKMF	Comco Ikarus C-42B	0302-6476	
D-MKMG	Fresh Breeze 110 AL 2F	211	
D-MKMH	Zlin Savage Classic	105	
D-MKMI	Comco Ikarus Fox D	8410-FD16	
D-MKMK	Roland Z602XL	Z-9525	
D-MKML	Autogyro Europe MT-03	unkn	
D-MKMN	TL Ultralight TL-96 Sting	07ST245	
D-MKMS	Plätzer Kiebitz B	026	
D-MKMU	Unidentified flexwing	unkn	
D-MKNA	Aerostyle Breezer CL	UL 119	
D-MKNE	Kümmerle Mini-Fly-Set	1265/91-4	
D-MKNF	Tandem Sunny Sport	unkn	
D-MKNI	Best Off Sky Ranger	unkn	
D-MKNL	Best Off Sky Ranger Swift	unkn	
D-MKNO	Flight Design CT2SW	04.08.03	
D-MKNS	Flight Design CT-2K	99.06.04.57/1	
D-MKNU	Light Aero Avid Flyer C	938 C	
D-MKNY	Dova DV-1 Skylark	08/2006	
D-MKOA	Fisher FP-202 Koala	001	
D-MKOB #	Take Off Maximum Chronos 14	101072	
D-MKOC(1)	Comco Ikarus Fox-C22	9304-3467	
	(To PH-3J5)		
D-MKOC(2)	Flight Design CT SW	unkn	
D-MKOF	Comco Ikarus Fox-C22	9308-3477	
D-MKOG	Comco Ikarus Fox-C22	9307-3476	
	(To SE-YJV)		
D-MKOH	ATEC 321 Faeta	F490709A	
	(To PH-4H7 9.00, wfu 9.04)		
D-MKOI	Comco Ikarus Fox-C22	9308-3474	
D-MKOK	Comco Ikarus Fox-C22	9307-3473	
D-MKOL	Plätzer Kiebitz-B2	076	
D-MKOM	Comco Ikarus Fox-C22	8909-3240	
D-MKON	Fresh Breeze Simo 122	unkn	
D-MKOO	Comco Ikarus Fox-C22	9307-3472	
D-MKOP	Comco Ikarus Fox-C22	9303-3471	
D-MKOQ	Comco Ikarus Fox-C22	9307-3470	
D-MKOS	Comco Ikarus Fox-C22	9304-3469	
D-MKOX	Air Création GTE 582 S	7974656039	
D-MKPA(1)	Evektor EV-97 Eurostar	2002-1407	
D-MKPA(2)	Skyranger SW	unkn	
D-MKPB(1)	Behlen Power-Trike	85010	
D-MKPB(2)#	Tandem Sunny Sport	030.06.08.SPL	
D-MKPC(1)	UPM Cobra BF 52UL Trike	950135	
D-MKPC(2)#	B&F Funk FK-9 ELA SW	unkn	
D-MKPF	Eipper Quicksilver	4603	
D-MKPG	Flight Team Spider Trike	D027	
D-MKPI (1)	Flight Team Spider Trike	D035	
D-MKPI(2)	Autogyro Europe MT-03	unkn	
D-MKPK	Comco Ikarus C-42B	unkn	
D-MKPM	Autogyro Europe Cavalon	unkn	
D-MKPN	Comco Ikarus C-42B	0511-6775	
D-MKPP	Comco Ikarus Fox-C22	9305-3421	
D-MKPS	Deewald Sunny Sport	03.06.08.SPL	
	(W/o 6.5.16 – possibly D-MKPS(2) unkn)		
D-MKPT	Flight Team Spider Trike	D034	
D-MKPW #	Backes Mini-Speed Trike (Homebuilt)	15/94	
D-MKRA(1)	Aeroprakt A-22 Vision	120	
	(Sold as YL-CCR)		

Registration	Type	C/n	Notes
D-MKRA(2)	Aeroprakt A-22 Vision	143	
	(Sold as SP-SKRA)		
D-MKRA(3)	Autogyro Europe MTOsport	unkn	
D-MKRB(1)	Comco Ikarus Fox-C22	9305-3459	
D-MKRB(2)	Behlen Power-Trike /Rotax 582	97012	
D-MKRC(1)	Comco Ikarus Fox-C22	9304-3458	
	(To LY-UAE)		
D-MKRC(2)#	B&F Funk FK-9 ELA SW	unkn	
D-MKRD	Comco Ikarus Fox-C22	9308-3457	
D-MKRE	Comco Ikarus Fox-C22	9305-3456	
D-MKRF	Comco Ikarus Fox-C22	9305-3455	
D-MKRG #	Comco Ikarus Fox-C22	9305-3454	
D-MKRH	Comco Ikarus Fox-C22	9305-3453	
D-MKRI	Comco Ikarus Fox-C22	9210-3452	
D-MKRJ	Comco Ikarus Fox-C22	9303-3451	
D-MKRK	Comco Ikarus Fox-C22	9304-3450	
D-MKRL	Comco Ikarus Fox-C22	9303-3449	
D-MKRM #	Comco Ikarus Fox-C22	9303-3497	
D-MKRN	Comco Ikarus Fox-C22	9210-3447	
D-MKRO	Tecnas P.92S Echo	unkn	
D-MKRP	Comco Ikarus Fox-C22	9210-3445	
D-MKRQ	Comco Ikarus Fox-C22	9210-3444	
D-MKRR #	Comco Ikarus Fox-C22	9209-3443	
D-MKRS(1)	Comco Ikarus Fox-C22	9209-3442	
	(Cld by 12.09)		
D-MKRS(2)	Zlin Savage	44	
	(To 01-XC)		
D-MKRT	Ultraleichtverbund Bi 90	21204	
D-MKRU(1)	Comco Ikarus Fox D	8810-FD44	
D-MKRU(2)	Comco Ikarus C-42	unkn	
D-MKRV #	B&F Funk FK-14 Polaris	unkn	
D-MKRW	Sky-Walker II	252	
D-MKRZ	Fresh Breeze Simo 122	unkn	
D-MKSA(1)	Klüver Bison	16807002	
D-MKSA(2)	Roland Z602	Z-9516	
D-MKSB	Star-Trike	unkn	
D-MKSD	Spacek SD-1 Minisport TD	unkn	
D-MKSE	Take Off Merlin 1100	28568	
D-MKSF	B&F Funk FK-9 Mk.III	09-044-269	
D-MKSG	Aerostyle Breezer	061	
D-MKSH	Fresh Breeze Simo 122	unkn	
D-MKSI	Comco Ikarus C-42B	unkn	
D-MKSJ	Dova DV-1 Skylark	unkn	
D-MKSK	Autogyro Europe MTOsport	unkn	
D-MKSL	Comco Ikarus C-42B	0207-6474	
D-MKSM	Comco Ikarus Fox-C22	9207-3426	
D-MKSN	Plätzer Kiebitz-B	unkn	
	(W/o 25.6.10)		
D-MKST	ASO Viper / Hazard 15	VIII 12063408	
D-MKSW	Remos GX	325	
D-MKSY(2)	Comco Ikarus C-42C	1210-7230	
	(W/o 9.5.16)		
D-MKSZ	Evektor EV-97 Eurostar	2006 2810	
	(W/o 7.5.11)		
D-MKTB	Aerospool WT-9 Dynamic	unkn	
D-MKTC #	Remos G3 Mirage	107	D-MUTC
D-MKTE	Dova DV-1 Skylark	unkn	
D-MKTF	Autogyro Europe Cavalon	unkn	
D-MKTG	Fresh Breeze 122 AL 2F	400	
D-MKTH	Zenair CH-701D STOL	7-9426	
D-MKTI	Flight Design CT LS	unkn	
D-MKTK	Autogyro Europe MT-03	unkn	
D-MKTM	Comco Ikarus Fox-C22	9107-3346	
D-MKTN	Remos G.3 Mirage	096	
D-MKTO #	NST Minimum	M331	
D-MKTP	Plätzer Kiebitz	unkn	
D-MKTS(1)	Fresh Breeze 110 AL 2F	195	
D-MKTS(2)	Flying Machines FM250 Vamjpire II	FM250V27	
D-MKTT	TL Ultralight TL-96 Sting	10ST348	
D-MKTV	Autogyro Europe MTOsport	unkn	
D-MKTZ #	MKB Enduro Trike	08/85	
D-MKUB #	Evektor EV-97 Eurostar	unkn	
D-MKUD	Comco Ikarus C-42B	0403-6590	
	(W/o in mid-air collision 24.8.09)		
D-MKUE	NST Minimum	M194	
D-MKUK	Tandem Air Sunny Targa	TA-015	
D-MKUL	Ultraleichtverbund Bi 90	601	
D-MKUM	Dallach Sunrise IIA	031	
D-MKUN	Comco Ikarus C-42B	0504-6668	
D-MKUP	Comco Ikarus C-42B	unkn	
D-MKUR	Schönleber Trike Speed 14	01/1293	
D-MKUS	Flight Team Spider / Hazard 15	D025	
D-MKUU	Parasport Nirvana Rodeo / Infinity II U-turn	unkn	
D-MKVF #	Plätzer Kiebitz	unkn	
D-MKVK	Cosmos Phase II	unkn	
D-MKVL	Alpi Avn Pioneer 300UL	unkn	
D-MKVR	TL Ultralight TL-232 Condor Plus	AB 06	
D-MKWB	B&F Funk FK-12 Comet	12-054	
D-MKWE	Apic BEE 15 MB	AO27MB3	
D-MKWH	Ultralight Flight Phantom	420	
D-MKWL	Flight Team Spider XL / iXess	unkn	
D-MKWM #	FUL Graffiti Trike	024/0081	
D-MKWP	Solid Air Twin Diamant	T006	
D-MKWR(1)	Flight Team Spider	D020	
D-MKWR(2)	Weller/ULI V3 Rebell	UW 110214	
D-MKWS(1)	Comco Ikarus Fox-C22	9008-3279	
	(To Hungary as 35-26)		
D-MKWS(2)	Aerospool WT-9 Dynamic	unkn	
D-MKWT	Autogyro Europe MTOsport	D10S14	
D-MKXK	Robin HR.200/160	unkn	
	(Noted 8.13 at Nizhny-Novgorod, Russia also wearing I-B135, which may be ex OH-RAA c/n 75)		
D-MKXX	Roland Z602 Economy	Z-9586	
D-MKYB #	Autogyro Europe MTOsport	unkn	
D-MKYF #	Fresh Breeze Simo 122	unkn	
D-MKYY	Evektor EV-97 Eurostar 2000R	2004 2115	
D-MLAA #	Klüver Racer SX 12 Trike	624009	
D-MLAB	Rans S-12 Airaile	0892256	
	(Believed w/o 30.5.98)		
D-MLAD	Plätzer Kiebitz-B	059	
D-MLAG	Bautek Eagle V/ Pico	unkn	
D-MLAI	Urban Air UFM-13 Lambada	130/13	
D-MLAJ	Pipistrel Virus SW	unkn	
D-MLAK	Zlin Savage Classic	unkn	
D-MLAL	Bautek Pico	unkn	
D-MLAO	Comco Ikarus C-42B	0303-6525	
D-MLAP (1)	Vidor Asso V Champion	unkn	
D-MLAP(2)	Technoflug Piccolo	100	
D-MLAR	Rans S-6 Coyote II	0904 1608 S	
	(W/o 16.6.16)		
D-MLAT	Comco Ikarus C-42B	0604-6801	
D-MLAU #	NST Minimum	M283	
D-MLAX	B&F Funk FK-9 Mk.IV	09-04-354	
D-MLAZ	Schmidtler Enduro 582 / Kiss	unkn	
D-MLBA	Plätzer Kiebitz B	281	
D-MLBB	ASO-Storch 503	11002206	
D-MLBC	Rans S-6 Coyote II	0791209	
D-MLBG	Plätzer Kiebitz B9	unkn	
D-MLBH	Comco Ikarus Fox-C22	9208-3461	
D-MLBI	Autogyro Europe MT-03	unkn	
D-MLBK	Comco Ikarus Fox-C22	9311-3522	
D-MLBL	Take Off Merlin 1200 / Eos	unkn	
D-MLBM	B&F Funk FK-9 Mk.III Club	09-03-213	
D-MLBP	Drachenstudio Royal R1100 RS / Eos	unkn	
D-MLBR	ATEC Zephyr 200QC	Z 190300S	
D-MLBS	Pipistrel Taurus 503	unkn	
D-MLBV	Magni M-24 Orion	unkn	
D-MLBW	Plätzer Kiebitz-B	280	
D-MLBY	Comco Ikarus C-42C	1604-7445	
D-MLCB #	Take Off Merlin Trike	22744	
D-MLCH	Sky-Walker II	395	
D-MLCL	Alisport Silent	unkn	
D-MLCM	unidentified paramotor	unkn	
D-MLCQ	unidentified paramotor	unkn	
D-MLCR	Evektor EV-97 Eurostar SL	2009 3611	
D-MLCS	Remos G-3 -600 Mirage	165	
D-MLCT	Flight Design CT SW	05-11-09	
D-MLDB	Light Aero Avid Flyer	unkn	
D-MLDE #	Fläming Air FA-01 Smaragd	02-03	
D-MLDG	Autogyro MTOsport	M01201	
D-MLDK(1)	NST Minimum	M544	
D-MLDK(2)	Fresh Breeze Simo 122	unkn	
D-MLDL	Autogyro Europe MTOsport	unkn	
D-MLDM	Magni M-24 Orion	24126944	
D-MLDT	B&F Funk FK-14 Polaris Club (t/w)	014-051	
D-MLEA(1)	ASO Viper Hazard 15	13451	
D-MLEA(2)	Rans S-7 mod Hermes 1	0210538	
D-MLEC	B&F Funk FK-12 Comet	12-091	
D-MLEE	Rans S-6 Coyote II	0992351	
D-MLEF	Ultraleichtverbund Bi 90	4559418	
D-MLEG	Evektor EV-97 Eurostar SLW	unkn	
D-MLEI	Behlen Power Trike Vampir II	88018	
D-MLEK	Cosmos / Top 12.9	21167	
D-MLEM	B&F Funk FK-9 Mk.II	09-02-051	
D-MLEN	Aeropilot Legend 540	unkn	OK-RUL 91
D-MLEO	Take-Off Avant	unkn	
D-MLES(1)	Comco Ikarus Fox-C22	9204-3391	
D-MLES(2)	Comco Ikarus C-42C	unkn	
D-MLET	Zlin Savage Cruiser	164	
D-MLEU(1)	Autogyro Europe MTOsport	unkn	
D-MLEU(2)	Autogyro Europe Calidus	unkn	
D-MLEV	Sky-Walker 1 + 1	26139	
D-MLFA	TL Ultralight TL-96 Sting	unkn	
D-MLFE #	Ultraleichtverbund Bi 90	703	
D-MLFF	Comco Ikarus C-42B	0405-6604	
D-MLFI	Ultraleichtverbund Bi 90	21048	
D-MLFL	Dallach Sunrise IIA	039	
D-MLFM	Zenair 601DX Zodiac	6-9478	
D-MLFO	B&F Funk FK-9 Mk.V WB	unkn	
D-MLFP	Air Energy Silent Club 2AE	005	
D-MLFZ	Air-Light Wild Thing	2003-07-085	
D-MLGA	Aeropilot Legend 540	unkn	
D-MLGE	Aerospool WT-9 Dynamic	unkn	
D-MLGG(1)	Schmidtler Ranger M	18-25	
D-MLGG(2)	Comco Ikarus C-42	1107-7167	
	(W/o 7.3.15 Iserlohn)		
D-MLGG(3)	Comco Ikarus C-42B	unkn	
D-MLGH	Autogyro Europe MT-03	unkn	
D-MLGI	B&F Funk FK-12 Comet	12-069	
	(To 59-DJK)		
D-MLGN	Fresh Breeze Simo 122	unkn	
D-MLGP	Autogyro Europe MTOsport	unkn	
D-MLGR	Bautek Eagle V/ Pico	unkn	
D-MLGS	Flight Design CT SW	unkn	
D-MLGT	Flight Design CT LS	F-10-05-08	
D-MLGX	Remos GX	417	
D-MLHH(1)	Autogyro Europe MT-03	unkn	
D-MLHH(2)	Autogyro Europe MTOsport	unkn	
D-MLHI	Urban Air UFM-13 Lambada	134/13	
D-MLHJ	Drachenstudio Royal Trike	05-9506	
D-MLHL	Autogyro Europe MT-03	unkn	
D-MLHM	UPM Cobra BF 52UL Raven	930121	
D-MLHO	Rotortech Cloud Dancer II	unkn	
D-MLHS	Fresh Breeze Simo 122	unkn	
D-MLHW	Behlen Power-Trike / Ghost 12	unkn	
D-MLIA(1)	Behlen Power-Trike II	95006	
D-MLIA(2)	B&F Funk FK-9	unkn	
D-MLIB #	FUL Graffiti MA 30 / Stranger	unkn	
D-MLIC #	Solid Air Diamant / Pico L	unkn	
D-MLIG	Plätzer Kiebitz-B	286	
D-MLII	Ultraleichtverbund Bi 90	41055519681	
D-MLIL	Comco Ikarus C-42B	0608-6846	
D-MLIM #	Fresh Breeze 110 AL2F	69	
D-MLIN	Tandem Air Sunny Sport	10-91	
D-MLIP(1)	Comco Ikarus Fox-C22	9105-3336	
D-MLIP(2)	Bilsam Sky Cruiser	unkn	
D-MLIP(3)	BOT SC07 Speed Cruiser	unkn	
D-MLIR	BOT SC07 Speed Cruiser	unkn	
D-MLIS #	Klüver Bison II Quartz SX 16	567801	
D-MLIT	Schönleber 47KW / Vento	unkn	
D-MLIU #	NST Minimum	M313	
D-MLIV	Autogyro Europe MTOsport	unkn	
D-MLIW	Zenair CH-601XL Zodiac	6-9821	
D-MLIX(1)	Celier Xenon	unkn	
D-MLIX(2)	Autogyro Europe Calidus	unkn	
D-MLIX(3)	ELA Aviacion ELA-07S	0711 337 0724	
	(Identification (2) in error?)		
D-MLIY	Plätzer Kiebitz-B	153	
D-MLIZ	Comco Ikarus Fox-C22	9306-3510	
D-MLJA(1)	Klüver Bison	982704	
D-MLJA(2)	Roland Z602	Z-9528	
D-MLJL	Rans S-6S Coyote II	12062782-S	

Reg	Type	C/N	Notes
D-MLJN	Tecnam P.92 Echo	1431	
D-MLJP	Kümmerle Mini-Fly-Set	1274/91-5	
D-MLKA	Autogyro Europe MTOsport	unkn	
D-MLKC	Fresh Breeze Simo 122	unkn	
D-MLKF	Air Création Mild GT 582 ES	2	
D-MLKG	Aeroprakt A-22L2 Vision	unkn	
D-MLKH	Comco Ikarus Sherpa II Doppel	8501-1087	
D-MLKK #	Klüver Racer SX 12	442904	
D-MLKL	Tecnam P.92 Echo Super	unkn	
D-MLKP	Evektor EV-97 Eurostar SL	2008 3407	
D-MLKR(1)	Junkers Profly Junka UL	unkn	
	(Type unconfirmed)		
D-MLKR(2)	Alpi Avn Pioneer 200	unkn	
D-MLKS	Comco Ikarus Fox-C22	9202-3390	
D-MLKV #	Celier Xenon	CAK06772 R	
D-MLKW(1)	Comco Ikarus Fox-C22	9104-3333	
D-MLKW(2)	BRM Aero Bristell	102/2014	D-MMRA(2), OK-QUU 06
D-MLLA	Tandem Air Sunny Sport	035-92	
D-MLLB	Take Off Maximum	027040	
D-MLLC(1)	Tandem Air Sunny Sport	032-92	
D-MLLC(2)	Behlen Power Trike Vampir II	M877829	
D-MLLE	Flight Design CT Supralight	E-09-02-11	D-MPCT
D-MLLF	Fresh Breeze Simo 122	unkn	
D-MLLG	Bautek Eagle V/ Ipsos 14.9	unkn	
D-MLLH	B&F Funk FK-14 Polaris	unkn	
D-MLLI	Autogyro Europe MT-03	unkn	
D-MLLL	B&F Funk FK-9 Mk IV	04-337	
	(Same c/n as D-MKLL or typing error?)		
D-MLLM(1)	Büttner Crazyplane IV	2	
D-MLLM(2)	Autogyro Europe MT-03	unkn	
D-MLLM(3)	Autogyro Europe Calidus	unkn	
D-MLLO #	Tandem Air Sunny	unkn	
D-MLLP	Autogyro Europe MTOsport	unkn	
D-MLLS	Evektor EV-97 Eurostar SL	2012 4002	
D-MLLT	Remos GX	300	
D-MLLU	Cosmos Phase II / Top 12.9	unkn	
D-MLLV	Fresh Breeze Snap / Mojito M	unkn	
D-MLLW	Aerospool WT-9 Dynamic	DY362/2010	
D-MLLY	Pipistrel Taurus	unkn	
D-MLLZ	Evektor EV-97 Eurostar SLW	2009 3721	
D-MLMD	Aerostyle Breezer C	057	PH-3Z1
D-MLME	Zlin Savage Bobber	212	
D-MLMG	Dova DV-1 Skylark	07/46	
D-MLMI	Autogyro Europe MTOsport	unkn	
D-MLMK	Schönleber DS Speed 14	9010891	
D-MLML	Schmidtler Enduro	1004	
D-MLMM	Eipper Quicksilver GT	1250	
D-MLMS	Alpi Aviation Pioneer 300	unkn	
D-MLMT #	Sky-Walker 1+1	26123	
D-MLMU	Schmidtler Enduro 1150 / Kiss 450	unkn	
D-MLMW	Murphy Renegade Spirit	unkn	
D-MLNF	Aerostyle Breezer UL	102	
D-MLNO	Rans S-9 Chaos	unkn	
D-MLNT	Comco Ikarus C-42B	unkn	
D-MLOA	Autogyro Europe MT-03	05G19	
D-MLOE	Plätzer Kiebitz-B	094	
D-MLOH	Solid Air Twin Diamant	801-02-825-440	
D-MLOK	Urban Air Samba XXL	unkn	
D-MLOM	Comco Ikarus Fox-C22	9207-3414	
	(Cld 1996. To D-MNUM, N5454C)		
D-MLOO	Autogyro Europe MT-03	04G05	
	(To SE-VRE 8.15. Same c/n as D-MSEX)		
D-MLOP #	UPM Funplane Trike	870019	
D-MLOR	Kümmerle Mini-Fly-Set	1306/91-6	
D-MLOS	Aeroprakt A-22L2 Vision	500	
D-MLOT(1)	Aviasud Mistral 53	011	
D-MLOT(2)	Fresh Breeze Simo 122	unkn	
D-MLOV	Autogyro Europe MTOsport	unkn	
D-MLOZ #	Fresh Breeze 110 AL 2F	333	
D-MLPA	WDFL Dallach D4 Fascination BK	123	
D-MLPB #	Fläming Air FA-01 Smaragd	unkn	
D-MLPC	Plätzer Kiebitz-B	337	
D-MLPF	Apis BEE 15 MB	A047 MB12	
D-MLPG	Spacek SD-1 Minisport	134	
D-MLPH	Zlin Savage	63	
D-MLPJ	Zlin Savage Cruiser	unkn	
D-MLPK	NST Minimum	unkn	
D-MLPL	Comco Ikarus C-42B	1108-7146	
D-MLPM	Autogyro Europe Calidus	unkn	
D-MLPP	Pipistrel Virus SW100	unkn	
D-MLPR	Air Création Tanarg 912ES / BioniX 15		
		A11020/110012	
D-MLPS(1)	Rans S.12 Airaile	unkn	
D-MLPS(2)	Aerospool WT-9 Dynamic	DY150/2006	67-ABL/F-JZVK
D-MLPT	Flyitalia MD-3 Rider	MD3-102	
D-MLPW	Schönleber Trike Speed KS 14	TK 01/0395	
D-MLPX	Fresh Breeze 110 AL 2F	112	
D-MLRA	Schmidtler Enduro 1150 / iXess 15	unkn	
D-MLRC(1)	Dyn'Aéro MCR-01	unkn	
D-MLRC(2)	Comco Ikarus C-42	unkn	
D-MLRD	Remos GX	384	
D-MLRE	Alisport Silent 2 Targa	2041	
D-MLRG #	Pago Jet M4	960503	
D-MLRH	Fläming Air FA-01 Smaragd	unkn	
D-MLRK	Scheibe ULI	unkn	
D-MLRL	NST Minimum Zephir CX	M436	
D-MLRP	Comco Ikarus C-42C	1505-7391	
D-MLRW	LO-120 S	027	
D-MLSA	Fresh Breeze Simo 122	unkn	
D-MLSB	Flight Design CT LS	unkn	
D-MLSC	Roland Z602	6-9271	
D-MLSD	Comco Ikarus Fox-C22	9106-3340	
D-MLSE	Comco Ikarus Fox-C22	9107-3343	
D-MLSG	B&F Funk FK-9 Mk.III	09-181	
D-MLSH	Remos GX eLite	393	
D-MLSJ	Air Création GTE 582 S	2974656186	
D-MLSM	Evektor EV-97R Eurostar 2000	2006 2905	
D-MLSR	Flight Design CT SW	06-09-17	
D-MLSS #	Comco Ikarus C-42B	unkn	
D-MLST(1)	NST Minimum Zephir	M528	
D-MLST(2)	Flight Design CT SW	07-08-20	
D-MLSU	Fieseler Werke Kassel Storch 156A	unkn	
D-MLSV	B&F Funk FK-9 Mk.III Utility	09-03U-204	
D-MLSW(1)	UPM Cobra Raven Trike	90007	
D-MLSW(2)	Remos G.3 Mirage	115	
D-MLSZ	Comco Ikarus Fox-C22	9010-3294	
D-MLTA #	Cosmos / Chronos 14	unkn	
D-MLTB	ParaZoom Trio-Star/Dudek Nucleon	unkn	
D-MLTF(1)	Autogyro Europe MT-03	D06G09	
D-MLTF(2)	Autogyro Europe MTOsport	unkn	
D-MLTG	Comco Ikarus Fox-C22	9208-3387	
D-MLTH	Fresh Breeze Simo 122	unkn	
D-MLTI	Kümmerle Mini-Fly-Set	734 85-3	
D-MLTK	Fresh Breeze Simo 122	unkn	
D-MLTM	Rans S-6 Coyote II	11061781-S	
D-MLTP	Sky-Walker II	unkn	
D-MLTR	Comco Ikarus Fox-C22	9206-3397	
D-MLTS	B&F Funk FK-9 Mk.IV	09-04-329	
D-MLTT	Fair Fax DR / Hazard 15	unkn	
D-MLTU	FUL Graffiti Trike	023/0083	
D-MLTW	Bautek Eagle V / Ghost 14.9	unkn	
D-MLUA	Plätzer Kiebitz-B	049	
D-MLUE	Comco Ikarus C-42C	1409-7339	
D-MLUF	Comco Ikarus C-42B	0205-6482	
D-MLUI	Behlen Power-Trike	92/014	
D-MLUM	Aerospool WT-9 Dynamic	DY447/2012	
D-MLUN	Schönleber 47kw / Vento	unkn	
D-MLUP #	Behlen Ladas M Trike	04-001-82	
D-MLUR	DS Speed 14	unkn	
D-MLUU	Fresh Breeze Simo 122	unkn	
D-MLUW	Fresh Breeze 110 AL2F	77	
D-MLUX	Comco Ikarus Fox-C22	9308-3509	
D-MLVA #	Fresh Breeze 122 AL 2F	242	
D-MLVB	Pipistrel Alpha Trainer	639	
D-MLVE #	Sky-Walker II	310	
D-MLVG	Fresh Breeze Simo 122	unkn	
D-MLVK	B&F Funk FK-131	008	
D-MLVL	Comco Ikarus C-42B	0703-6875	
D-MLVM(2)	B&F Funk FK-9 Mk.III Utility	09-03U203	
D-MLVT(1)	Tandem Air Sunny Sport	11-91	
D-MLVT(2)	B&F Funk DK-9	09-05-456	
D-MLVW	Tecnam P.92 Echo 100S	648	
D-MLWB #	ASO Viper Trike	3690	
D-MLWC	Comco Ikarus C-42B	0307-6561	
D-MLWD	Bautek Eagle III/ Ghost 14.9	unkn	
D-MLWG	B&F Funk FK-9 Mk.IV Utility	09-04U-256	
D-MLWM(1)	NST Minimum	M563	
D-MLWM(2)#	B&F Funk FK-12 Comet	12-067	
	(To F-JTOO)		
D-MLWO	B&F Funk FK-14 Polaris (t/w)	unkn	
D-MLWP	Hirt / Denney Kitfox IV-1200	1733	D-ELWP
	(C/n also quoted as DCU-025)		
D-MLWR	Autogyro Europe Cavalon	V00033	
D-MLWS	Krampen Ikarus S	52	
D-MLWT	TL Ultralight TL-3000 Sirius	unkn	
	(W/o 30.11.12)		
D-MLWU	Roko Aero NG4	unkn	
D-MLWW	WDFL Dallach D4 Fascination BK	126	
D-MLYD	B&F Funk FK-14 Polaris	unkn	
D-MLZV	Solid Air Twin Diamant Trike	T004	
D-MLZZ	Autogyro Europe MTOsport	unkn	
D-MMAA	Konsuprod Moskito	005	
D-MMAB #	Kümmerle Mini-Fly-Set	1276/91-5	
D-MMAC	P&M Pegasus Quantum 15-912	unkn	
D-MMAD	Evektor EV-97 Eurostar	2004-2218	
D-MMAE	Comco Ikarus C-42B	0910-7064	
D-MMAG	Sky-Walker II	357	
D-MMAH	Tecnam P.92S Echo	unkn	
D-MMAI(1)	Warnke Puma Sprint	D002	
D-MMAI(2)	Comco Ikarus C-42B	unkn	
D-MMAI(3)	Aerospool WT-9 Dynamic	DY405/2011	T7-MFG
D-MMAJ	Sky-Service Pago Jet	941001	
D-MMAL(1)	Ultraleichtverbund Bi 90	21205	
D-MMAL(2)#	Autogyro Europe MTOsport	unkn	
D-MMAM	ATEC Zephyr 2000	Z820703A	
D-MMAN(1)	Fresh Breeze 110 AL 2F	234	
D-MMAN(2)	Autogyro Europe Calidus	unkn	
D-MMAR	Behlen Power Trike II	97005	
D-MMAS(1)	Solid Air Diamant	013	
D-MMAS(2)	Vidor Asso V Champion	009	
D-MMAT	Kümmerle Mini-Fly-Set	1278/91-5	
D-MMAU	Solid Air Twin Diamant Hazard	T008	
D-MMAV	P&M Pegasus Quantum 15 – 912	unkn	
D-MMAW(1)	Kümmerle Mini-Fly-Set	1285/91-5	
D-MMAW(2)	Magni M-16 Tandem Trainer	16011804	
D-MMAX	Fresh Breeze 110 AL 2F	43	
D-MMAY(1)	Pegasus Quantum Super Sport	7444	
D-MMAY(2)	B&F Funk FK-9 Mk,III	unkn	
D-MMAZ(1)	Autogyro Europe MTOsport	unkn	
D-MMAZ(2)	Scmidtler Enduro / Fun 18	unkn	
D-MMAZ(3)	Spacek SD-1 Minisport TD	unkn	
D-MMBA	Flight Design CT-2K	99-09-03-67	
D-MMBB	Cosmos Bi 90 Phase II/ Chronos 12	977	
D-MMBD	Impulse 100	unkn	
D-MMBE	Tecnam P.92 Echo	unkn	
D-MMBE(2)	Aerostyle Breezer	029	
D-MMBG	B&F Funk FK-9 Utility	unkn	
D-MMBH	BRM Aero Bristell NG5 UL	084/2014	
	(To N96HA, 8.15, but may be a different acft as D-MMBH still		
	reported 7.16. This and D-MVMR of 6.16 have same owner)		
D-MMBI	Take Off Merlin 1100 / Avant	unkn	
D-MMBJ	NST Minimum	M580	
D-MMBL	Bautek Eagle V/ Ghost 14.9	unkn	
D-MMBN	Behlen Power Trike Vampir II	86017	
D-MMBP	B&F Funk FK-14B2 Le Mans	unkn	
D-MMBR	Pegasus Quantum 15	6683	
D-MMBT #	Behlen Power Trike II	97001	
D-MMBU	Best Off Sky Ranger SW	10121021	
D-MMBV #	ASO Viper Hazard 15	18991	
D-MMBW	Seiffert Mini II	F020890	
D-MMCB	Flight Design CT SW	06-02-04	
D-MMCC	B&F Funk FK-9 Mk.IV	unkn	
D-MMCD(1)	Zenair CH-701D STOL	7-9383	
D-MMCD(2)	Spacek SD-1 Minisport TD	unkn	
D-MMCE	Autogyro Europe Cavalon	unkn	
D-MMCH	Fresh Breeze Simo 122	unkn	
D-MMCI	Fisher FP-202 Koala	003	
D-MMCK	Comco Ikarus C-42B	unkn	
D-MMCL	Autogyro Europe MTOsport	unkn	
D-MMCM	Behlen Power-Trike / Pico	unkn	
D-MMCN	Autogyro Europe MTOsport	unkn	
D-MMCO(1)	FUL Graffiti Trike	032/0098	

Regn	Type	C/n	Prev id
D-MMCO(2)	Corvus CA-21 Phantom	CA21/035	
D-MMCP	Urban Air Samba XXL	unkn	
D-MMCS(1)	Melos 3000	unkn	
D-MMCS(2)	Tecnam P.92 Echo Light	1495	
D-MMCT	Flight Design CT SW	07-06-19	
D-MMCV	FD Composites Arrowcopter AC20	038	
D-MMCY	BRM Aero NG5 Bristell	217/2016	
D-MMDB	Dallach Sunrise	030	
	(Same c/n as D-MBCD but different aircraft)		
D-MMDC	Alpi Avn Pioneer 200STD	unkn	
D-MMDD	Flight Design CT SW	unkn	
D-MMDH(2)	B&F Funk FK-9	010	
D-MMDH(3)	Airsport Song	unkn	
D-MMDK	Autogyro Europe MTOsport	unkn	
D-MMDM	Autogyro Europe MTOsport	unkn	
D-MMDR(1)	Schmidtler Enduro Trike	02-006	
D-MMDR(2)	TUL-02 Tandem Tulak	unkn	
D-MMDW	B&F Funk FK-9	011	
D-MMEB	Comco Ikarus C-42B	0308-6556	
D-MMEC	Remos G.3 Mirage	111	
D-MMED	Remos G.3 Mirage	109	
D-MMEF	Fresh Breeze Simo 122	unkn	
D-MMEH #	Kluver Twin Racer / Ghost 12	unkn	
D-MMEJ	Aerostyle Breezer CL	UL132	
D-MMEN	Roland Z602 Economy	Z-9559	
D-MMEP	Autogyro Europe Cavalon	unkn	
D-MMER	Fresh Breeze Simo 122	unkn	
D-MMES	Aerospool WT-9 Dynamic	DY186/2007	
D-MMEY	Autogyro Europe MTOsport	unkn	
D-MMFA	Evektor EV-97 Eurostar 2000R	2003 1812	
D-MMFB	Remos GX	422	
D-MMFH	Evektor EV-97 Eurostar 2000R	2005 2413	
D-MMFI	Autogyro Europe MT-03	unkn	
D-MMFK	B&F Funk FK-9 Mk.II	012	
D-MMFM(1)	Remos GX	unkn	
	(W/o 5.4.09)		
D-MMFM(2)	Autogyro Europe MT-03	unkn	
D-MMFR	Autogyro Europe MTOsport	unkn	
D-MMFS	Autogyro Europe MT-03	unkn	
D-MMFW	Comco Ikarus C-42B	0502-6659	
D-MMGB	Comco Ikarus Fox-C22	9208-3436	
D-MMGD	ASO Viper Trike	4590	
D-MMGE	Rans S-6 Coyote II	unkn	
	(W/o 21.9.11)		
D-MMGF	Remos GX	281	D-MPGB(1)
D-MMGH	Plätzer Kiebitz-B9-450	125	
D-MMGL	Pipistrel Sinus NW	unkn	
D-MMGM	Take Off Maximum	17099	
D-MMGO	Autogyro Europe MT-03	unkn	
D-MMGR(1)	Fresh Breeze 110 AL2F	31	
D-MMGR(2)	Autogyro Europe MTOsport	unkn	
D-MMGT	P&M Quik GT450 912S	8454	
D-MMGW	Flight Design CT LS	08.01.20	
D-MMGZ	NST Minimum	M464	
D-MMHA	Flight Design CT SW	06-12-07	
D-MMHB	Behlen Power-Trike	87001	
D-MMHE	Fresh Breeze 110 AL 2F	71	
D-MMHF	Denney Kitfox IV	1841	
	(C/n recorded on aircraft as 11176, 5.02)		
D-MMHG	B&F Funk FK-9	09-04U-257	
D-MMHH	Comco Ikarus Fox-C22	8905-3200	
D-MMHI #	Comco Ikarus Fox D	8410-FD17	
D-MMHK(1)	Behlen Trike	85024	
D-MMHK(2)	Vidor Asso V Champion	unkn	
D-MMHL	Autogyro Europe MTOsport	unkn	
D-MMHM	Schönleber Trike 40kw	TK 02/0198	
D-MMHR	Spacek SD-1 Minisport	unkn	
D-MMHT	Fläming Air FA-01 Smaragd	05/04	
D-MMHW	B&F Funk FK-9 Mk.III	09-03-190	
D-MMHZ	Behlen Trike	83033	
D-MMIA	Alpi Avn Pioneer 300	unkn	
D-MMIB	NST Minimum	M545	
D-MMIG	Tandem Air Sunny Sport	24.91	
D-MMIH	Millenium Master	unkn	
D-MMII	Klüver Bison	646802	
D-MMIK(1)	Bobcat	146 EB	
D-MMIK(2)	Rans S-6 Coyote II	08031516-S	
D-MMIL #	Behlen Power Trike Vampir II	89016	
D-MMIM(1)	Alpi Aviation Pioneer 200	unkn	
D-MMIM(2)	Autogyro Europe MT-03	unkn	
D-MMIO	Best Off Sky Ranger	unkn	
D-MMIP	Bristell UL	065/2013	
D-MMIS	Behlen Power Trike Vampir II	89011	
D-MMIX	Light Aero Avid Flyer IV C	1104 C	
D-MMJA(1)	ASO Viper Trike	VIII 12067501	
D-MMJA(2)	Remos GX	383	
D-MMJD	Autogyro Europe Calidus	unkn	
D-MMJF	Flight Design CT SW	unkn	
D-MMJJ	Aerostyle Breezer CL	097	
	(W/o 8.11.15)		
D-MMJK(1)	B&F Funk FK-14 Polaris	unkn	
	(W/o 15.9.07)		
D-MMJK(2)	Comco Ikarus C-42E	1105-7152	
D-MMJM	Alpi Aviation Pioneer 200	unkn	
D-MMJS	FUL Graffiti Trike	025/0091	
D-MMJT	Sky-Service Pago Jet M4	94002	
D-MMJU	Fresh Breeze Simo 122	unkn	
D-MMJV #	FUL Graffiti Trike	026/0092	
D-MMKB	MKB Ranger	028841	
D-MMKG	MKB Ranger M	01/005/85	
D-MMKK	Comco Ikarus C-42B	1207-7208	
D-MMKL	Remos G.3 Mirage	104	
D-MMKM	Autogyro Europe MTOsport	unkn	
D-MMKN	Autogyro Europe MTOsport	unkn	
D-MMKR(2)	Evektor EV-97 Eurostar SL	unkn	
D-MMKS	Aero East Europe Sila 450C	unkn	
D-MMKT	Flight Team Spider Trike	D040	
D-MMKU	Fresh Breeze 110 AL 2F	61	
D-MMKV(1)	Shark Aero Shark	2012-005	
	(Ex D-MMKU, D-MYBR, OK-RUR 01, all same c/n)		
D-MMKV(2)	Aero East Europe SILA 450C	130509-AEE-0012	
	(Same c/n quoted as D-MSPR(2))		
D-MMKW	Comco Ikarus C-42B	0207-6489	
D-MMLA	Comco Ikarus Fox-C22	9209-3430	
D-MMLB	UPM Cobra BF 52 UL Trike	930122	
D-MMLC	Plätzer Kiebitz-B	145	
D-MMLF	PAP-ROS 125 / Arcus L	unkn	
D-MMLH #	Flight Team Spider Trike	D014	
D-MMLI	Behlen Power-Trike /Rotax 582	980025	
D-MMLK	Remos G.3 Mirage	127	
D-MMLL	Sky-Walker II	274	
D-MMLN	Fresh Breeze Simo 122	unkn	
D-MMLO	Comco Ikarus Fox-C22	9205-3403	
D-MMLT	Fresh Breeze Simo 122	unkn	
D-MMLU	Take Off Maximum	097062	
D-MMMB(1)	Albatros 64	304	
D-MMMB(2)	Autogyro Europe MTOsport	unkn	
D-MMMC	Flight Design CT LS	F-08-10-25	
D-MMMD(1)	Ultraleichtverbund Bi 90	702	
D-MMMD(2)	JMB VL-3 Junior	unkn	
D-MMME	Autogyro Europe MTOsport	unkn	
D-MMMG	Alpi Aviation Pioneer 300	unkn	
D-MMMH(1)	Autogyro Europe MT-03	05G13	
D-MMMH(2)	Comco Ikarus C-42C	unkn	
D-MMMI (1)	Comco Ikarus Fox-C22	9306-3506	
	(Re-regd D-MMNI)		
D-MMMI(2)	Autogyro Europe Cavalon	unkn	
D-MMMJ	Autogyro Europe MTOsport	unkn	
D-MMMK	Evektor EV-97 Eurostar	unkn	
D-MMMM	T2	5	
	(Regn worn by a WDFL Fascination, Friedrichshafen 4.99, and by Dallach Evolution 4.01. Mock-ups?)		
D-MMMN	Denney Kitfox IV	1758	D-EEUX
D-MMMO(1)	Autogyro Europe MT-03	unkn	
D-MMMO(2)	JMB VL-3 Sprint	unkn	
D-MMMQ	Autogyro Europe MTOsport	unkn	
D-MMMS	UPM Cobra BF 52 UL / Raven	unkn	
D-MMMT	Behlen Power-Trike II	95008	
D-MMMU	B&F Funk FK-9	09-04-381	
D-MMMV	Autogyro Europe Calidus	unkn	
D-MMMW	Platzer Kiebitz B-450	128	
D-MMMX	Pipistrel Taurus 503	unkn	
D-MMMY	Autogyro Europe Cavalon	unkn	
D-MMMZ	ATEC 321 Faeta	unkn	
D-MMNC	AirLony Skylane	42/2011	D-MKHD
D-MMND(1)	Fresh Breeze 122 AL 2F	233	
D-MMND(2)	Autogyro Europe MTOsport	D10S52	
	(Cld to G-CINW 4.15, with UK c/n RSUK/MTOS/058)		
D-MMNI #	Comco Ikarus Fox-C22	9306-3506	D-MMMI(1)
D-MMNM	Zlin Savage Classic	unkn	
D-MMNN	B&F Funk FK-9	360	
D-MMNS #	Comco Ikarus Fox-C22	8812-3184	
D-MMOC #	Cosmos/Top 14.9	21079	
D-MMOE	Comco Ikarus C-42B	0206-6462	
D-MMOG	Comco Ikarus C-42	unkn	
D-MMOK	Take Off Merlin 1200 / Eos	unkn	
D-MMOL	Fresh Breeze Simo 122	unkn	
D-MMON	Kaiman Focus 18	unkn	
D-MMOP	B&F Funk FK-9	unkn	
D-MMOR	Comco Ikarus C-42B	0906-7041	
D-MMOZ	ATEC 122 Zephyr 2000	ZP671003	
D-MMPA(1)	Fresh Breeze 110 AL 2F	951104	
D-MMPA(2)	Drachenstudio Royal 912	unkn	
D-MMPC #	Fresh Breeze Simo 122	unkn	
D-MMPD	Flight Design CT-2K	03.02.03.07A	
D-MMPE	NST Minimum	M441	
D-MMPF	Pretty Flight	unkn	
D-MMPG	Fresh Breeze 110 AL 2F	54	
D-MMPH	AirLony Skylane	50	
D-MMPK	ASO Viper Trike	VIII 12069502	
D-MMPL	Sky-Walker II	267	
D-MMPO #	Bautek Eagke V/ Pico	unkn	
D-MMPR	NST Schwarze-Trike	010	
D-MMPS(1)	Solar Wings Pegasus Quantum 15	6738	D-MMTT
D-MMPS(2)	Fresh Breeze Simo 122	unkn	
D-MMPW	Bautek Eagle V/ Pico	unkn	
D-MMPY	Comco Ikarus C-42B	0804-6962	
D-MMQQ	Tandem Air Sunny	022.10.06.Sbs	
D-MMRA(1)	Ultraleichtverbund Bi 90	4017031	
D-MMRA(2)	BRM Aero Bristell UL	102/2014	OK-QUU 06
	(Re-regd D-MLKW(2))		
D-MMRB(1)	Ultralight Flight Phantom	403	
D-MMRB(2)	NST Minimum	M556	
D-MMRE	Rans S-6 Coyote II	08031514	
D-MMRH	Ultraleichtverbund Bi 90	21254	
D-MMRK	Magni M-24 Orion	24127224	
D-MMRL(1)	Behlen Power-Trike /Rotax 582	91026	
D-MMRL(2)	Weller Uli V3 Rebell	unkn	
D-MMRM	Pegasus Quantum	7611	
D-MMRP(1)	Kümmerle Mini-Fly-Set	67686-4	
D-MMRP(2)	BRM Aero Bristell UL	067/2013	D-MKFK(1)
D-MMRR	Enduro Lotus/Air Création XP	02/003	
D-MMRS	Fresh Breeze 122 AL 2F	391	
D-MMRT	Pipistrel Taurus 503	unkn	
D-MMSB	Rans S-12 Airaile	1292359	
	(W/o 30.8.08)		
D-MMSD	Pipistrel Taurus	unkn	
D-MMSE	Aerostyle Breezer CL	111	
D-MMSG(1)	Comco Ikarus Fox-C22	9110-3361	
D-MMSG(2)	Apis BEE 15 MB	061ABF33	
D-MMSK #	Bautek Eagle V/ Ghost 14.9	unkn	
D-MMSL #	Take Off Merlin Trike	G20363	
D-MMSM(1)	Konsuprod Moskito 1b	019	
D-MMSM(2)	NST Minimum	M462	
D-MMSN	Pioneer Flightstar 385		
D-MMSO	Flight Design CT	unkn	
D-MMSP(1)	Großklaus Silent Racer	3	
D-MMSP(2)	Autogyro Europe MT-03	05G11	
	(Crashed 29.5.09)		
D-MMSR	NST Minimum	M517	
D-MMST	Klüver Bison	0168	
D-MMSU	Plätzer Kiebitz-B	111	
D-MMSW	Kümmerle Mini-Fly-Set	67786-4	
D-MMSY	ASO Viper Trike	VIII 12068501	
D-MMTB	Roland Z602	Z-9573	
D-MMTC	Comco Ikarus Fox-C22	9205-3396	
D-MMTG	Roko Aero NG6	unkn	
D-MMTH	Autogyro Europe MTOsport	unkn	
D-MMTI	Fresh Breeze 110 AL2F	102	
D-MMTK #	Behlen Trike Vampir II 18M	9002A785	
D-MMTM	Alpi Avn Pioneer 300	unkn	
D-MMTO	Autogyro Europe MTOsport	unkn	

Reg	Type	c/n	Notes
D-MMTR	Behlen Power Trike Ghost	unkn	
D-MMTT	Autogyro Europe MTOsport	unkn	
D-MMTV	Comco Ikarus C-42	unkn	
D-MMTW(1)	Comco Ikarus Sherpa II Doppel	8505-1099	
D-MMTW(2)	Fresh Breeze 110 AL 2F	159	
D-MMTZ	unidentified paramotor	unkn	
D-MMUC	Aerostyle Breezer CL	UL124	
	(W/0 21.5.16)		
D-MMUF	Fresh Breeze Simo 122	unkn	
D-MMUH	Kappa KPD-2U Sova	07/98	
D-MMUL	Drachenstudio Royal 912 / Eos	unkn	
D-MMUM	NST Minimum	M508	
D-MMUP #	Autogyro Europe MTOsport	unkn	
D-MMUR #	Fresh Breeze 110 AL 2F	338	
D-MMUT	Nando Groppo Trial	unkn	
D-MMUU	Comco Ikarus C-42	9801-6060	D-MTDC, OE-7050
D-MMUW #	NST Minimum	M554	
D-MMUZ	B&F Funk FK-9	unkn	
D-MMVB #	Comco Ikarus Fox-C22	8808-3149	
D-MMVI	Comco Ikarus C-42	9908-6201	PH-3F9
D-MMVK	Flight Design CT SW	06-03-12	
D-MMVM #	Autogyro Europe MTOsport	unkn	
D-MMVS	Eagle / Avant Trike	unkn	
D-MMVV	PAP-ROS 125 / Powerplay Sting 140	unkn	
D-MMWA(1)	Dallach Sunrise II	034	
D-MMWA(2)	Comco Ikarus C-42	1410-7349	
D-MMWB	ASO Viper Trike	12061405	
D-MMWC	NST Minimum	M560	
D-MMWD	B&F Funk FK-9 Mk.II	009	
D-MMWE	ASO Viper Trike	12066408	
D-MMWF #	Fresh Breeze	unkn	
D-MMWG	UL-F Jochum Eagle III	970804	
D-MMWH	TL Ultralight TL-96 Sting	04ST82	
D-MMWK	Evektor EV-97 Eurostar	unkn	
D-MMWL	Fresh Breeze 110 AL 2F	443	
D-MMWM	TL Ultralight TL-96 Star	unkn	
D-MMWN	Take Off Merlin Karat 13	20993	
D-MMWP	Alpi Avn Pioneer 200	unkn	
D-MMWR	Aquilair Trike	unkn	
D-MMWS(1)	Fresh Breeze 110 AL 2F	76	
D-MMWS(2)	Zlin Savage	unkn	
D-MMWT	Autogyro Europe Calidus	C00175	
D-MMWW(1)	Ultraleichtverbund Bi 90	21238	
D-MMWW(2)	Plätzer Kiebitz-B2	105	
D-MMWY	Fresh Breeze PM Swiss	unkn	
D-MMWZ	B&F Funk FK-14B Polaris (t/w)	unkn	
D-MMXG	Euro-ALA Jet Fox 97	0026BIS	
D-MMXM(1)	Autogyro Europe MT-03	unkn	
D-MMXM(2)	Autogyro Europe Cavalon	unkn	
D-MMXN	Autogyro Europe MTOsport	unkn	
D-MMXX	Remos GX	unkn	
D-MMXY	Bautek Eagle V /	07W12	
D-MMYG	Autogyro Europe MTOsport	M01192	
D-MMYM	Autogyro Europe MTOsport	M01061	
D-MMYY(1)	Schmidtler Enduro Trike	02-011	
D-MMYY(2)	Evektor EV-97 Eurostar	unkn	
D-MMYZ(1)	Air Création GTE 582	unkn	
D-MMYZ(2)	Air Light Wild Thing	97 02 017	D-MWAR
D-MMZA	B&F Funk FK-9 Mk.IV ELA Professional	09-05-446	
D-MMZB #	B&F Funk FK-9 Mk.IV ELA Professional	09-05-460	
D-MMZC	B&F Funk FK-9 Mk.IV ELA Professional	09-05-470	
D-MMZD	Aerospool WT-9 Dynamic	unkn	
D-MMZM	Autogyro Europe MTOsport	unkn	
D-MMZY #	Kiggen/Heiland Air Création GTE 582 S	9954557782	
D-MMZZ	Kiggen/Heiland Air Création GTE 582 S	7954557571	
D-MNAA	Rans S-6 Coyote II	0693514	
D-MNAB	Rans S-6ES Coyote II	0391168	
D-MNAC	Rans S-6 Coyote II	0393460	
D-MNAD	Comco Ikarus Fox-C22	9309-3530	
D-MNAE	Zenair CH-601D Zodiac	unkn	
D-MNAF	Comco Ikarus Fox-C22	9310-3532	
D-MNAG	Comco Ikarus Fox-C22	93 . .-3535	
D-MNAH	Comco Ikarus Fox-C22	9311-3537	
D-MNAI #	Klüver Bison Profil 19	557801	
D-MNAJ (1)	Comco Ikarus Fox-C22	9101-3299/3538	
D-MNAJ (2)	Fisher FP-202 Koala	HO.001.1	
D-MNAK(2)	Rans S-6 Coyote II	0596990	
D-MNAL	Comco Ikarus C-42 Cyclone	9807-6107	
D-MNAM #	Behlen Power-Trike	84009	
D-MNAO #	Comco Ikarus Fox-C22	9107-3365	
	(Same c/n as D-MEDE)		
D-MNAP	Light Aero Avid Flyer IV	1273D	
D-MNAQ #	Rans S-6 Coyote II	0192261	OO-A52, 59-MO
D-MNAR	Rans S-6 Coyote II	0992352	
D-MNAS(1)	Aviasud Mistral BRD	191	
D-MNAS(2)	Evektor EV-97 Eurostar	2001-1204	
D-MNAT	Air-Light Wild Thing	076	
D-MNAU	Rans S-6 Coyote II	0593493	
D-MNAV	Rans S-6 Coyote II	0393464	
D-MNAW #	Plätzer Kiebitz-B	148	
D-MNAX	Fisher FP-404 Classic	4169	
D-MNAY #	Aviasud Albatros	306	
D-MNAZ(1)	Aviasud Albatros	305	
D-MNAZ(2)	B&F Funk FK-12S Comet	012-095	
	(To 67-BQI, w/o)		
D-MNBA(2)	Remos Gemini Ultra B	E22-23	
D-MNBB	WDFL Sunwheel	015	
D-MNBC	B&F Funk FK-9 Mk.II	024	
D-MNBD #	Klüver Bison	202708	
D-MNBE(1)	Tandem Air Sunny Targa	TA-017	
D-MNBE(2)	Tecnam P.92 Echo Classic	unkn	
D-MNBF #	Trixy G 4-2 R	007	
D-MNBG	Comco Ikarus Fox-C22	9310-3541	
D-MNBH	Scheibe Uli 1	5223	
D-MNBI(1)	Rans S-12 Airaile	1292356	
	(Registered as 68-GH in France)		
D-MNBI(2)	ICP MXP-740V Savannah S	11-03-54-0083	
D-MNBJ	Rans S-6 Coyote II	0693515	
D-MNBK	Rans S-6 Coyote II	0593508	
D-MNBL #	Comco Ikarus Fox-C22	9402-3546	
D-MNBM(2)#	WDFL Dallach D4 Fascination	015	
D-MNBN	Rans S-12 Airaile	1092299	
D-MNBO #	Klüver Kaiman Trike	945703	
D-MNBP #	Bek ME.109R Replica	003	
D-MNBQ	Tandem Air Sunny Targa	TA-003	
D-MNBR(1)	B&F Funk FK-14 Polaris	014-019	
	(To Belgium 2.11 as OO-G74)		
D-MNBR(2)	Aerostyle Breezer CL	103	
D-MNBT	Comco Ikarus Fox-C22	9208-3434	
D-MNBU	Comco Ikarus Fox-C22CS	9409-3597	
D-MNBV #	Murphy Renegade	530	
D-MNBW	WDFL Sunwheel	028	
D-MNBX	Tandem Air Sunny	58.94	
D-MNBY	Light Aero Avid Flyer	499	
D-MNBZ	Plätzer Kiebitz-B9	155	
D-MNCA	Comco Ikarus C-42 Cyclone	9702-6024	
D-MNCB	Tandem Air Sunny s.b.s.	11.94	
	(2) same type 2005 or change of c/n?015.10.04 S-S		
D-MNCC	Rans S-6 Coyote II	0994676	
D-MNCD	Murphy Renegade	521	
D-MNCE #	Autogyro Europe Calidus	unkn	
D-MNCF	Jet Fox	D-0016	
D-MNCG	Plätzer Kiebitz-B	unkn	
D-MNCH	Comco Ikarus Fox-C22	8909-3219	
D-MNCI #	Autogyro Europe Calidus	unkn	
D-MNCJ	Fisher Super Koala	001	
D-MNCL	Light Aero Avid Flyer	947	
D-MNCM(1)	Eipper Quicksilver MX	1133	D-MASB
D-MNCM(2)#	Comco Ikarus Fox-C22B	unkn	
D-MNCN	Tecnam P.92S Echo	unkn	
D-MNCO	Light Aero Avid Flyer	1427	
D-MNCP	ICP MXP-740V Savannah	07-98-50-091	
D-MNCR	Plätzer Kiebitz B	113	
D-MNCS	Remos G-3 Mirage	unkn	
	(Cancelled)		
D-MNCU	Tecnam P.92 Echo	373	
D-MNCW	Tecnam P.92 Echo	556	
D-MNDB	B&F Funk FK-9 Mk.II	034	
D-MNDD	Comco Ikarus Fox-C22B	9408-3619	
D-MNDE #	Comco Ikarus Fox-C22B	-3686	
D-MNDF	Flight Design CT-2K	98.12.01.42	
D-MNDG	Dyn'Aéro MCR-01	73	
D-MNDJ	Remos G.3 Mirage	079	
D-MNDK	Fantasy Air Allegro 2000	99-401	
D-MNDM	Comco Ikarus C-42 Cyclone	9803-6085	
D-MNDP #	Comco Ikarus C-42 Cyclone	9809-6122	
D-MNDR	Comco Ikarus Fox-C22B	9509-3671	
D-MNDS	Rans S-12 Airaile	1292347	
D-MNDT	Comco Ikarus Fox-C22	9206-3410	
D-MNEA	Fisher FP-404 Classic	4128	
D-MNEB	Light Aero Avid Flyer IV	975	
D-MNEC	Comco Ikarus Fox-C22	9502-3653	
D-MNED #	Murphy Renegade II	409	
D-MNEE(1)	ASO-Storch	11015506	
D-MNEE(2)	Autogyro Europe MT-03	unkn	
D-MNEF	Comco Ikarus C-42 Cyclone	9806-6104	
D-MNEG #	Flight Design CT-2K	02.02.04.09	
D-MNEH #	Rans S-6 Coyote II	0293449	
D-MNEK	Comco Ikarus Fox-C22	9201-3360	
D-MNEL	Behlen Power-Trike	86022	
D-MNEM	EEL ULF-2	8	
D-MNEP	TEAM Airbike	002	
D-MNER	Scheibe SF-40B	3105	
D-MNES #	Scout	D 012-84	
D-MNEU	Comco Ikarus C-42	0203-6428	
D-MNEV	Evektor EV.97 Eurostar	98 01 01	OK-FUU 09
D-MNEW	Schönleber DS Lotus KS 16	010790	
D-MNEZ	III Sky Arrow 450TG	058	
D-MNFA	Fantasy Air Allegro 2000	02-413	
D-MNFB(1)	Comco Ikarus C-42 Cyclone	9901-6105	
D-MNFB(2)	Comco Ikarus C-42B Cyclone	0905-7049	
	(Similar c/n to D-MECA(2))		
D-MNFC #	Comco Ikarus Fox-C22C	9807-3740	
D-MNFF	Rans S-6 Coyote II	0698-1241	
D-MNFG	Tecnam P.92S Echo	unkn	
D-MNFH #	Sky-Service Pago Jet	95603	
D-MNFJ #	Comco Ikarus Fox II Doppel	8605-3019	
D-MNFK	B&F Funk FK-9 Mk.II	025	
D-MNFL	Fisher FP-202 Koala	Ho 001	
D-MNFM	Plätzer Kiebitz-B9	003	
D-MNFN	TEAM Airbike	D-003	
D-MNFR	III Sky Arrow 450TG	047	
D-MNFT	Rans S-6 Coyote II	1092363	N7010L
D-MNFW	WDFL Sunwheel	026	
D-MNFZ	Tecnam P.92 Echo	245	
D-MNGB #	Jaguar	1001	
D-MNGD	LO-120S	012A	
D-MNGE	Pioneer Flightstar	546	
D-MNGF	HFL Stratos 300	300-005	
D-MNGG	Comco Ikarus C-42 Cyclone	9901-6171	
	(To OY-9445, 1.13)		
D-MNGH	Tecnam P.92 Echo	167	
	(Same c/n as OK-GUU 26 but different aircraft)		
D-MNGI #	B&F Funk FK-9 Mk.II	058	
D-MNGK #	WDFL D4 Fascination	020	
D-MNGM	Comco Ikarus C-42 Cyclone	9804-6125	
D-MNGP	Flight Design CT2K	unkn	
D-MNGR	TL Ultralight TL-2000 Sting S3	unkn	
D-MNGS	Murphy Renegade Spirit	TC032004	C-FIHP
D-MNGT	HIF Albatros	104	
D-MNGV #	Rotortec Cloud Dancer	unkn	
	(Company test marks for Cloud Dancers)		
D-MNGX	Remos GX	415	
D-MNHA	Scheibe SF-40	3102	
D-MNHB(1)	Kümmerle Mini-Fly-Set	1269/91-51 66	
D-MNHB(2)#	WDFL Dallach D4 Fascination	063	
D-MNHD	WDFL Dallach D4 Fascination	035	
D-MNHE	Comco Ikarus C-42 Cyclone	9710-6036	
D-MNHF	Rans S-12 Airaile	0691098	
D-MNHG #	Pioneer Flightstar	950501	
	(To Denmark 9-409, 2010)		
D-MNHH(2)	Comco Ikarus C-42 Cyclone	unkn	
D-MNHI #	Kappa KPD-2U Sova	5259G	
D-MNHK #	LO-120S	014A	
D-MNHL #	B&F Funk FK-12 Comet	012-016	
	(To ZU-EDV, SE-VLJ)		
D-MNHO	Tandem Air Sunny s.b.s.	SuS 01.96	
D-MNHP	Remos G-3 Mirage	158	
D-MNHR #	Rans S-6 Coyote II	0594626	
D-MNHS(1)	Rans S-6TD Coyote II	0994672	

Registration	Type	c/n	Notes
D-MNHS(2)	Magni gyro	unkn	
D-MNHW	B&F Funk FK-12 Comet	12-026	
D-MNHZ	Zenair CH-601D Zodiac	6-3413/015 0097	
D-MNIC	Aviasud BA-83 Mistral	004	
D-MNIE	ASO Viper Trike	15 I7990	
D-MNIG #	Autogyro Europe MT-03	unkn	
D-MNII	Tandem Air Sunny Targa	005/92	
D-MNIJ	Tandem Air Sunny	unkn	
D-MNIK	NST Minimum	503	
D-MNIL	Aerospool WT-9 Dynamic	DY00601	
D-MNIN	Fresh Breeze Simo 122	unkn	
D-MNIR #	NST Minimum	081593	
D-MNIS #	Tandem Air Sunny s.b.s.	036/92	
D-MNIT #	Tecnam P.92 Echo	185	
	(Re-regd D-MHCH)		
D-MNIU #	B&F Funk FK-9	065	
D-MNIV	Dallach Sunrise II	003	
D-MNIW	Dallach Sunrise II	007	
D-MNIX	Plätzer Kiebitz B	237	
D-MNIZ #	Zenair CH-601D Zodiac	6-8027/009 0397	
D-MNJA	WDFL Dallach D4 Fascination BK	076	
D-MNJB #	Euro-ALA Jet Fox 91D	004	
D-MNJC	Tecnam P.92 Echo	284	
D-MNJE	Alpi Avn Pioneer 200	206	
D-MNJJ	Tecnam P.92 Echo	180	
D-MNJL	Aeropro Eurofox	12102	
D-MNJS #	WDFL Sunwheel	014	
D-MNJU	Junkers Profly Ultima	JU 001 97	
D-MNKA	NST Minimum	M515	
D-MNKB	Comco Ikarus Fox-C22C	9704-3725	
D-MNKC	Comco Ikarus C-42 Cyclone	9803-6084	
D-MNKD	Comco Ikarus C-42 Cyclone	9901-6146	
D-MNKE	B&F Funk FK-9 Mk.II	091	
D-MNKF	Comco Ikarus C-42 Cyclone	9709-6048	
D-MNKG #	Flight Design CT-2K	unkn	
D-MNKH	Tecnam P.92 Echo	126	
D-MNKI	Comco Ikarus C-42 Cyclone	9804-6081	
D-MNKJ	Rans S-6 Coyote II	"4172285"	
	(Quoted c/n is actually Rotax engine number)		
D-MNKK	Ikarusflug Eurofox	040097	
D-MNKL(2)	Flight Design CT-2K	03.01.03.03	
D-MNKM	Light Aero Avid Flyer IV	1458	
D-MNKN	TL Ultralight TL-96 Star	unkn	
D-MNKP	Comco Ikarus C-42B	0206-6460	
D-MNKR	Albatros SX	504	
D-MNKS	Rans S-12 Airaile	1092341	
D-MNKT	Comco Ikarus C-42	0502-6663	
D-MNKU	Ultravia Pelican Sport 450S	721	
D-MNKW	Technoflug Piccolo	035	
D-MNKX #	Comco Ikarus C-42B	0210-6493	
D-MNKY	Comco Ikarus C-42 Cyclone	9906-6190	
	(W/o 14.6.15)		
D-MNKZ	Comco Ikarus C-42B	0210-6511	
D-MNLA(1)	Aerospool WT-9 Dynamic	DY014 02	
	(Re-regd D-MNMA)		
D-MNLA(2)	Millenium Master	unkn	
D-MNLC #	Comco Ikarus Fox-C22B	9407-3606	
D-MNLE #	Light Aero Avid Flyer IV	1493	
D-MNLF	Euro-ALA Jet Fox 91D	014	
D-MNLG	B&F Funk FK-9 TG Mk.II	077	
D-MNLH	Tandem Air Sunny	025.05.07.SPL	
D-MNLI	Autogyro Europe MTOsport	unkn	
D-MNLJ	Comco Ikarus C-42C	1212-7243	
D-MNLK #	Comco Ikarus Fox-C22	9108-3349	
D-MNLL	Zenair CH-601D Zodiac	6-3648	
D-MNLN	Comco Ikarus C-42C	1407-7337	
D-MNLP #	WDFL Dallach D4 Fascination BK	067	
D-MNLR	Air-Light Wild Thing	004	
D-MNLT	Rans S-6 Coyote II XL	1294712	
D-MNLY #	Aerostyle Breezer	004	
D-MNMA	Aerospool WT-9 Dynamic	DY014 02	D-MNLA(1)
D-MNMB	WDFL Dallach D4 Fascination BK	077	
D-MNMC	Flight Design CT LS	09-09-04	
D-MNMF	Tandem Air Sunny Sport	64.96	
D-MNMG	Zenair CH-601D Zodiac	6-3789	
D-MNMH	Fläming Air Trener Baby	02	
D-MNMM	Tecnam P.96 Golf 100S	059	
D-MNMN(1)	Pico Trike	unkn	
D-MNMN(2)	Autogyro Europe MTOsport	unkn	
D-MNMP #	Comco Ikarus Fox-C22	9411-3636	
D-MNMS	Air-Light Wild Thing	036	
D-MNNA #	Albatros 64	311	
D-MNNB	Albatros 64	501	
D-MNNF	Air-Light Wild Thing	054	
D-MNNK	Technoflug Piccolo	028	
D-MNNL	Comco Ikarus C-42B	0905-7046	
D-MNNM(1)	Behlen Power-Trike	023	
D-MNNM(2)	Tecnam P.96 Golf	unkn	
D-MNNM(3)	Autogyro Europe MTOsport	unkn	
D-MNNN(1)	Comco Ikarus Fox-C22	9002-3254	
D-MNNN(2)	Flight Design CT SW	04.10.06	
D-MNNO	Light Aero Avid Flyer STOL	1401C	
D-MNNP	B&F Funk FK-9 Mk.II	043	
D-MNNQ	B&F Funk FK-9 Mk.II	042	
D-MNNS	Eurostar EV-97 Eurostar	2006-2718	
D-MNNZ	Comco Ikarus C-42 Cyclone	9701-6023	
D-MNOA	Euro-ALA Jet Fox 97	023	
D-MNOB	Comco Ikarus Fox-C22	9706-3731	
D-MNOC	Comco Ikarus Fox-C22B	9602-3693	
D-MNOD	Kümmerle Mini-Fly-Set	25986-4	
D-MNOE	Comco Ikarus C-42 Cyclone	9804-6078	
D-MNOF	Light Aero Avid Flyer IV	501	
	(To SE-VOT)		
D-MNOG(2)	WDFL Dallach D4 Fascination	055	D-ELOG
D-MNOH(1)	Flight Design CT-2K		
D-MNOH(2)#	Flight Design CT SW	07-06-15	
	(Damaged 27.7.12)		
D-MNOK	Rans S-6ES Coyote II	unkn	
D-MNOM	B&F Funk FK-9 Mk.II	057	
D-MNON	B&F Funk FK-9 Mk.II	056	
D-MNOO	Light Aero Avid Flyer IV	1272	
D-MNOP	Konsuprod Mosquito IB	011	
D-MNOR(1)	NST Minimum	1783	
D-MNOR(2)	Flight Design CT-2K	99.10.02.72	
D-MNOW	B&F Funk FK-9 Mk.IV	unkn	
D-MNOX	Rans S-10 Sakota	0488010	N70301
D-MNPC	Eipper Quicksilver MXL	1148	
D-MNPE	Comco Ikarus C-42 Cyclone	9810-6144	
D-MNPF	PC Flight Pretty Flight	01	
D-MNPG	Plätzer Kiebitz	218	
D-MNPL	TL Ultralight TL-96 Star	01 S 103	
D-MNPP	TL Ultralight TL-96 Star	02 S 115	
D-MNPR	Remos Gemini Ultra B	031	
D-MNPS	Tecnam P.92 Echo	321	
D-MNPU	Remos G.3 Mirage	044	
D-MNPW	ATEC Zephyr 2000	ZP 480900	
D-MNRA	Ikarusflug Eurofox	051098	
D-MNRB #	Tecnam P.92 Echo	182	
D-MNRC	Zenair CH-601D Zodiac	6-3519	
D-MNRD	TL Ultralight TL-232 Condor Plus	AB05 / 198	
D-MNRE	Comco Ikarus C-42 Cyclone	0106-6342	
D-MNRF #	Ferrari Tucano A	308	
D-MNRH	Comco Ikarus Fox-C22	94 . . -3572	
D-MNRL	WDFL Sunwheel R	025	
D-MNRM	B&F Funk FK-9 Mk.II	027	
	(To France 13 RG/F-JJTT)		
D-MNRO	B&F Funk FK-9 Mk.II	033	
D-MNRR	Ultravia Pelican Sport 450S	720	
D-MNRS	Euro-ALA Jet Fox 91D	007	
D-MNRT	Comco Ikarus C-42B	0005-6258	
D-MNRU	Comco Ikarus C-42 Cyclone	9804-6132	
D-MNRV	Tecnam P.92 Echo	338	
D-MNRW	Comco Ikarus Fox-C22B	9602-3692	
D-MNSB	Zenair CH-601D Zodiac	003	
D-MNSD	Tecnam P.92 Echo Light	unkn	
D-MNSE	EEL ULF-2	016	
D-MNSH #	Tandem Air Sunny Sport	56.93	
D-MNSI	Rans S-6 Coyote II	1294714F	
D-MNSJ	Comco Ikarus C-42 Cyclone	9807-6106	
D-MNSK #	Aviasud Albatros 64	308	
D-MNSL	WDFL Dallach D4 Fascination BK	097	
D-MNSM	Comco Ikarus Fox-C22B	9406-3595	
D-MNSO	Swing MA 12	unkn	
D-MNSP #	Tecnam P.92S Echo 100S	473	
D-MNSR	Euro-ALA Jet Fox 91D	005	
D-MNSS #	Euro-ALA Jet Fox 91D	006	
D-MNST #	Euro-ALA Jet Fox 91D	008	
D-MNSU	Tecnam P.92 Echo	537	
D-MNTB	Comco Ikarus Fox-C22B	9407-3596	
D-MNTE	WDFL Dallach D4 Fascination	014	
D-MNTH	Zenair CH-601D Zodiac	6-3457	
D-MNTK	B&F Funk FK-14 Polaris Le Mans	014-132	
D-MNTL	ATEC Zephyr 2000	ZP 270700	
D-MNTM	Comco Ikarus C-42 Cyclone	9710-6017	
D-MNTS	Remos G.3 Mirage	051	
D-MNTT	B&F Funk FK-9 Mk.II	047	
D-MNTV	Autogyro Europe MT-03	unkn	
D-MNTW	Tecnam P.92 Echo	187	
D-MNTZ	Zenair CH-701D STOL	unkn	
D-MNUC	EEL ULF-2	unkn	
D-MNUF	B&F Funk FK-9 Mk.IV	385	
D-MNUI	Cosmos / Top 14.9	B21541	
D-MNUL	B&F Funk FK-9 ELA Professional	unkn	
D-MNUM	Comco Ikarus Fox-C22	9207-3414	D-MLOM
	(To N5454C)		
D-MNUN	Rans S-6 Coyote II	0193420	N6183Z, D-MNUN, N6183Z
D-MNUR	Kappa KPD-2U Sova	050	
D-MNUT	Aerospool WT-9 Dynamic Club	DY520/2014	
D-MNVA	Autogyro Europe Calidus	unkn	
D-MNVB	Murphy Renegade Spirit	414	
D-MNVC	WDFL Dallach D4 Fascination BK	079	
D-MNVF	SFS Vagabund	004	
D-MNVH #	ASO Storch	11017508	
D-MNVM	Light Aero Avid Flyer IV	1294D	
D-MNVV	Zenair CH-601D Zodiac	6-3652	
D-MNWA	Urban Air UFM-13 Lambada	unkn	
D-MNWB	Aeroprakt A-22 Vision	031/009	
D-MNWC	Light Aero Avid Flyer IV	1354	
D-MNWD	Comco Ikarus C-42 Cyclone	0011-6259	
D-MNWE #	Tecnam P.92 Echo	324	
	(Possibly to Australia as 24-3783)		
D-MNWH	B&F Funk FK-9 Mk.II	021	
D-MNWI	Comco Ikarus C-42 Cyclone	9609-6006	
D-MNWJ	Plätzer Kiebitz-B9	060	
D-MNWK #	Pago (or D-MMWK?)	unkn	
D-MNWL	Comco Ikarus C-42 Cyclone	9803-6089	
D-MNWN	NST Minimum	04911	
D-MNWO	Comco Ikarus C-42 Cyclone	0003-6260	
	(To OH-U397)		
D-MNWR #	EEL ULF-2	11	
D-MNWS	TL Ultralight TL-232 Condor Plus	98 C 09	
D-MNWT	Air-Light Wild Thing	unkn	
D-MNWW	Air-Light Wild Thing	002	
D-MNWZ	Comco Ikarus C-42 Cyclone	9804-6126	
D-MNXI	Quicksilver Sprint II	000778	
D-MNXT	3XTrim 3XLS Navigator 600	E63	
	(To SP-SAFE 21.6.11)		
D-MNXU(1)	Elisport CH-7 Angel	unkn	
D-MNXU(2)	Jihlavan Skyleader 200	2 187189 Q	
D-MNXY	Kappa KPD-2U Sova	88103 I	
D-MNYA	Best Off Nynja	unkn	
D-MNYC	Autogyro Europe Calidus	unkn	
D-MNYT	Skystar S-34	012	
D-MNZB	Air-Light Wild Thing	027	
D-MNZI	Comco Ikarus C-42 Cyclone	0007-6265	
D-MNZZ	Comco Ikarus C-42 Cyclone	9806-6119	
D-MOAA	Rans S-6 Coyote II	unkn	
D-MOAB	Tandem Air Sunny Sport	17.91	
D-MOAC(1)	Technoflug Piccolo BM	109	
D-MOAC(2)	SG Aviation Storm	unkn	
D-MOAD	Tecnam P.92 Echo Light	unkn	
D-MOAE	Technoflug Piccolo BM	110	
D-MOAF	Tecnam P.92 Echo	226	
D-MOAG(1)	WDFL Fascination	025	
D-MOAG(2)	Bautek Eagle V/ Pico	unkn	
D-MOAI	Tecnam P.96 Golf	10	
D-MOAJ	Zenair CH-601D Zodiac	6-3484	
D-MOAK #	Rans S-6 Coyote II	1294713	
D-MOAL	Comco Ikarus C-42 Cyclone	9704-6029	
D-MOAM	Tecnam P.96 Golf	13	
D-MOAN	Plätzer Kiebitz-B-450	187	

Registration	Type	Serial	Notes
D-MOAO	Air-Light Wild Thing	040	
D-MOAP	Tandem Air Sunny Sport	38.92	
D-MOAS	Euro-ALA Jet Fox 91D	012	
D-MOAT	TEAM Airbike Tandem	AT-001	
D-MOAU	Comco Ikarus C-42 Cyclone	9909-6210	
D-MOAW	Tecnam P.92 Echo	300	
D-MOAX	Plätzer Kiebitz	406	
D-MOAZ	Konsuprod Moskito 1b	015	
D-MOBA	Tecnam P.96 Golf	031	
D-MOBB	Aerostyle Breezer	002	
D-MOBC	Aerostyle Breezer	047	D-MBRG, G-90-2, D-MBRG
D-MOBE	Comco Ikarus C-42 Cyclone	9908-6205	
D-MOBF	B&F Funk FK-9 Mk.II	038	
D-MOBG	Aerostyle Breezer UL	003	
D-MOBG(2)	Tecnam P.92 Echo	unkn	
D-MOBH	Pretty Flight	003	
D-MOBI (2)	B&F Funk FK-9 Mk.II	075	
D-MOBK	B&F Funk FK-9 TG Mk.II	046	
D-MOBL	Fisher FP-404 Classic	AB 001	
D-MOBM	Comco Ikarus C-42 Cyclone	0103-6318	
D-MOBN	Urban Air UFM-13 Lambada	1/13	
D-MOBO	B&F Funk FK-9 Mk.II	09-02-132	
D-MOBP(1)	Fresh Breeze Simo 122	unkn	
D-MOBP(2)	Autogyro Europe MTOsport	unkn	
D-MOBS(1)	UPM Cobra Raven Trike	900102	
D-MOBS(2)	B&F FunkFK-12 Comet	12-031	
D-MOBT	Light Aero Avid Flyer	617	
D-MOBU	Drachenstudio Royal 912 / Eos	unkn	
D-MOBW #	Autogyro Europe MT-03 (W/o 13.9.09)	unkn	
D-MOBY(1)	Take Off Maximum Karat 13	005059	
D-MOBY(2)	Rans S-6 Coyote II	0893532	
D-MOCA(1)	Warnke Skylight Trike	038	
D-MOCA(2)	Remos G.3 Mirage	063	
D-MOCB	WDFL Sunwheel	036	
D-MOCC	Comco Ikarus C-42 Cyclone	9707-6016	
D-MOCD	Fantasy Air Allegro	00-404	
D-MOCF	Comco Ikarus Fox-C22C	9606-3710	
D-MOCG	Evektor EV-97 Eurostar	2001 1205	
D-MOCH	Vidor Asso V Champion	unkn	
D-MOCI	Evektor EV-97 Eurostar	2001 1002	
D-MOCK	Fisher FP.202 Koala	unkn	
D-MOCO	Flight Design CT	97.08.02.06	
D-MOCS	Comco Ikarus C-42 Cyclone	9902-6165	
D-MOCT #	Flight Design CT	CT 006/97	
D-MOCV	NST Minimum	1781	
D-MOCZ	Shark Aero Shark	030-2014	
D-MODA	Rans S-9 Chaos	1287033	
D-MODC	Flight Design CT-2K	99.06.01.54	
D-MODD	Schönleber DS Trike	04/0989	
D-MODE(2)	Tandem Air Sunny	47.93	
D-MODE(2)	Remos G-3 Mirage	156	
D-MODF	MAI 890-1	142	
D-MODG	WDFL Sunwheel R	023	
D-MODI	Comco Ikarus C-42 Cyclone	9704-6018	
D-MODK #	Aerostyle Breezer CL	068	
D-MODL (1)	NST Minimum Zephir CX	M456	
D-MODL(2)	Aerospool WT-9 Dynamic	DY348/2010	
D-MODM(1)	Dess/ WDFL D4/B Fascination (W/o 22.3.00)	038	(D-EWSB)
D-MODM(2)	Pipistrel Alpha Trainer	unkn	
D-MODR	Apis BEE 15 MB	A038MB08	
D-MODS	Comco Ikarus C-42 Cyclone (W/o 17.2.13)	0001-6223	
D-MODU	Aerostyle Breezer CR	UL88	
D-MODW	ATEC Zephyr	SF060201	
D-MODY	Murphy Renegade Spirit	unkn	
D-MODZ	Remos G3 Mirage	105	
D-MOEA	Tecnam P.92 Echo 100S	372	
D-MOEB	Tecnam P.92 Echo 2000 Super	1212	
D-MOEC	Comco Ikarus C-42 Cyclone	9611-6030	
D-MOEE	Flight Design CT	97.12.01.16	
D-MOEG	Comco Ikarus C-42 Cyclone	0106-6343	
D-MOEH	Air-Light Wild Thing	066	
D-MOEK	Plätzer Kiebitz B6	unkn	
D-MOEN #	Comco Ikarus Fox-C22	9403-3579	
D-MOEP	TL Ultralight TL-96 Sting	08ST300	
D-MOER	Evektor EV-97 Eurostar	2006 2710	
D-MOES	Euro-ALA Jet Fox 91D	003	
D-MOET	Comco Ikarus Fox-C22	94083608	
D-MOEU	Tecnam P.92 Echo	083	
D-MOEW	Flight Design CT-2K	unkn	
D-MOEZ	AMF Chevvron 2-32	037	
D-MOFA	ATEC Zephyr	ZP 340200	
D-MOFB	Technoflug Piccolo	021	
D-MOFC	Comco Ikarus C-42B	0506-6685	HB-WAE
D-MOFD	Autogyro Europe MT-03	unkn	
D-MOFE	Comco Ikarus C-42	0012-6297	
D-MOFF	Comco Ikarus Fox-C22B	9506-3670	
D-MOFG	Evektor EV-97 Eurostar 2000R	2006 2701	
D-MOFH	Euro-ALA Jet Fox 91D	022/00	
D-MOFI	Tecnam P.92 Echo	595	
D-MOFK	B&F Funk FK-9 Mk.II	061	
D-MOFL #	Comco Ikarus C-42 Cyclone	0005-6253	D-MAIC(1)
D-MOFP	Alpi Avn Pioneer 200	180	
D-MOFS	Celier Xenon	CAD07973R	
D-MOFT	Plätzer Kiebitz-B6	171	
D-MOFU	Rans S-10 Sakota	0697184	
D-MOGA	WDFL Sunwheel R	021	
D-MOGB	ATEC Zephyr	SF 101199	
D-MOGC #	B&F Funk FK-9 Mk.IV Utility (Re-regd D-MCCV)	09-03U-215	
D-MOGG	B&F Funk FK-9 Mk.IV	unkn	
D-MOGH	ASO 26 Storch	160	
D-MOGI	Tecnam P.92S Echo	unkn	
D-MOGK	Zenair CH-601 Zodiac	6-2008	
D-MOGL	Murphy Renegade Spirit	518	
D-MOGR	TL Ultralight TL-96 Sting	07ST224	
D-MOGS	WDFL Dallach D4 Fascination	016	
D-MOHA	Rans S-12 Airaile (W/o 6.5.16)	1292346	
D-MOHB	Remos G.3 Mirage	047	
D-MOHE	TL Ultralight TL-232 Condor Plus	98 C 08	
D-MOHF	Denney Kitfox IV	1876	
D-MOHG	Pioneer Flightstar	960701	
D-MOHI	Ikarusflug Eurofox	026096	
D-MOHK	Malchow HK-12	001	
D-MOHL	Comco Ikarus C-42	0109-6360	
D-MOHM	Comco Ikarus C-42 Cyclone	9809-6131	
D-MOHN	Scheibe Uli 1	5222	
D-MOHP	III Sky Arrow 450	086 S	
D-MOHR	Sky-Walker II	147	
D-MOHS	Weedhopper	0998	
D-MOHW(1)	Behlen Power-Trike /Rotax 582	92028	
D-MOHW(2)	Genesis MT120	unkn	
D-MOHY	Jet Fox 91D	00122	
D-MOHZ	Autogyro Europe MTOsport	unkn	
D-MOIC #	ASO Viper Hazard 15	11031204	
D-MOIG	Plätzer Kiebitz B	152	
D-MOII	Comco Ikarus C-42	0103-6345	
D-MOIK	WDFL Dallach D4 Fascination	010	
D-MOIL	Comco Ikarus C-42 Cyclone	9804-6101	
D-MOIN(1)	Warnke Skylight Trike	S2005	
D-MOIN(2)	Zenair CH-602XL Zodiac	9518	
D-MOIO	Me 108UL Taifun scale replica (Flies as 'D-IOIO')	1	
D-MOIS #	Pretty Flight	02	
D-MOIX #	Autogyro Europe MTOsport (Accident 7.7.12)	M00839	
D-MOJA	Zenair CH-701D STOL	7-3519	
D-MOJB #	Euro-ALA Jet Fox 91D	D 0013	
D-MOJE	B&F Funk FK-12 Comet	12-004	
D-MOJH(1)	Tandem Air Sunny Targa	TA 014	
D-MOJH(2)	Aerostyle Breezer	021	
D-MOJJ	B&F Funk FK-9 Mk.III	09-170	
D-MOJN	Aerospool WT-9 Dynamic	unkn	
D-MOJO	Flightworks FW2 C-80XLS Capella	061962	
D-MOJS	Comco Ikarus C-42 Cyclone	9811-6152	
D-MOJU	Comco Ikarus C-42 Cyclone	0003-6240	
D-MOKA	Scheibe Ultra	3411	
D-MOKB	Evektor EV-97 Eurostar	99 05 03	
D-MOKC #	Klüver Racer / Quartz SX12	unkn	
D-MOKE(1)	Racer (Homebuilt)	004/90	
D-MOKE(2)	Tecnam P.92 Echo 100S	664	
D-MOKF	B&F Funk FK-9 Mk.III	098	
D-MOKG	Rans S-6ES Coyote II	0496966	
D-MOKH	Comco Ikarus C-42 Cyclone	9911-6214	
D-MOKI (1)	Zephir CX	unkn	
D-MOKI(2)	Evektor EV-97R Eurostar 2000	unkn	
D-MOKK	Comco Ikarus C-42 Cyclone	9712-6072	
D-MOKL(1)	Rans S-9 Chaos	10961045	
D-MOKL(2)	B&F Funk FK-9 Mk.I Smart	09-01-095	
D-MOKM	Tecnam P.92 Echo	225	
D-MOKN #	Plätzer Kiebitz-B6	195	
D-MOKO	Konsuprod Moskito	006	
D-MOKS	Tecnam P.92 Echo (Same c/n as CS-UHC)	135	
D-MOKT	Tandem Air Sunny Sport	57.94	
D-MOKU	B&F Funk FK-12 Comet	12-072	
D-MOKV	Fresh Breeze Simo 122	unkn	
D-MOKW	ATEC Zephyr	ZO 32	
D-MOKY	Rans S-7 Courier	unkn	
D-MOLA(1)	Fair Fax Trike	21	
D-MOLA(2)	Solair II	unkn	
D-MOLB	Flight Team Spider Trike	DOO9	
D-MOLC	Comco Ikarus Fox-C22 (To PH-4C1)	9405-3603	
D-MOLD	Konsuprod Moskito	002	
D-MOLE(1)	NST Minimum Santana	100378	
D-MOLE(2)	Comco Ikarus C-42	0101-6290	
D-MOLF	Fresh Breeze Simo 122	unkn	
D-MOLG	Flight Design CT (W/o Bad Solgau 5.5.13)	98.04.05.32	
D-MOLH #	Tecnam P.92 Echo 100S	399	
D-MOLI #	Pioneer Flightstar	545	D-MTAM
D-MOLJ	Fresh Breeze Simo 122	unkn	
D-MOLK	Flight Design CT-2K	00-06-03-99	
D-MOLL	Scheibe UL-1 Coach	3201	
D-MOLM	Comco Ikarus Fox-C22	9108-3352	
D-MOLO	LO-120S	021	
D-MOLR	B&F Funk FK-9 Mk.III (W/o 4.10.09)	09-03-118	
D-MOLS	Tecnam P.92 Echo	252	
D-MOLT	ASO Viper Hazard 15	12023103	
D-MOLV	B&F Funk FK-9 Mk.III	09-03-101	
D-MOLW	Plätzer Kiebitz-B	066	
D-MOLY(1)	Light Aero Avid Flyer	867	
D-MOLY(2)	Tecnam P-96 Golf 100S	110	
D-MOLZ	Plätzer Kiebitz B	183	
D-MOMA	Dyn'Aéro MCR-01 ULC	137	
D-MOMB	TL Ultralight TL-96 Star	02 S 120	
D-MOMC	B&F Funk FK-9 Mk.III (Damaged 28.6.15)	09-03-107	
D-MOMD #	Comco Ikarus C-42 Cyclone	9803-6087	
D-MOME	Me.109 Replica	005	
D-MOMF	WDFL Dallach D4 Fascination	042	
D-MOMI	ATEC Zephyr	ZP 130100	
D-MOMK	Aveko VL-3	VL-3-113	
D-MOMM	Rans S-7 Courier	0798251	
D-MOMN	Comco Ikarus C-42 Cyclone	9703-6032	
D-MOMO	Scheibe Ultra	3414	
D-MOMP	Klüver Racer Quartz SX 12	309005	
D-MOMR	BRM Aero Bristell UL	057/2013	
D-MOMS	Ikarusflug Eurofox	024096	
D-MOMT	Tecnam P.92 Echo	480	
D-MOMU	B&F Funk FK-9 Mk.IV	unkn	
D-MONA	Ultra-Vector H	1401	
D-MONB	Comco Ikarus Fox-C22	9407-3574	
D-MONC	Rans S-6 Coyote II	0494609	
D-MOND(1)	Warnke Puma Sprint	D001	
D-MOND(2)	B&F Funk FK-12 Comet	12-024	
D-MOND(3)	Rans S-6 Coyote II	unkn	
D-MONE (1)	Comco Ikarus Fox D	015	
D-MONE(2)	Tecnam P.92S Echo	922	
D-MONG	Albatros 64	502	
D-MONI (1)	Power Power-Trike Euro III	84018	
D-MONI(2)	Remos G-3 Mirage	170	
D-MONJ	UPM Omega Trike	880045	
D-MONK(1)	Rans S-6ES Coyote II	unkn	
D-MONK(2)	B&F Funk FK-9 Mk.IV SW	09-04SW-358	
D-MONL	Comco Ikarus Fox-C22	9407-3575	

Registration	Type	C/n	
D-MONM	Plätzer Kiebitz	016	
D-MONN(1)	Impulse 100	100-3	
D-MONN(2)	Remos GX	419	
D-MONO	Scheibe Uli 1	5211	
D-MONP	Tecnam P.96 Golf 100	unkn	
D-MONT	Air-Light Wild Thing	057	
	(Same c/n as 57-QF)		
D-MONW	Comco Ikarus Fox-C22B	9603-3678	
D-MONY	Aeroprakt A-22 Vision	032/010	
D-MONZ	Tecnam P.96 Golf 100S	117	
D-MOOB	Kümmerle Mini Fly Set Bullet C	73285-4	
D-MOOC	Aerostyle Breezer C	005	
D-MOOD	Fisher FP-404 Classic	014	
D-MOOE	Pipistrel Virus SW	unkn	
D-MOOF #	Comco Ikarus Fox-C22C	9605-3708	
D-MOOG	Flight Design CT	99.08.03.63	
D-MOOH	WDFL Dallach D4 Fascination	unkn	
D-MOOI	Pretty Flight Mikron	001	
D-MOOJ	Aerostyle Breezer	038	
D-MOOK	Aerostyle Breezer	009	
D-MOOL	SG Aviation Storm 280	G 003	
D-MOOM(1)	Magni M-14 Scout	unkn	
D-MOOM(2)	Autogyro Europe MT-03	05G05	
D-MOON	WDFL Dallach D4B Fascination	104	
D-MOOO	Moyes Dragonfly	D 01001	
D-MOOP	Tecnam P.92ES-100 Echo	482	
D-MOOQ #	Rans S-6 Coyote II	0295739XL	
D-MOOR	Flight Design CT-2K	00.06.03.10	
D-MOOS(1)	SG Aviation Storm 200G	508G	
D-MOOS(2)	Aerostyle Breezer	043	
D-MOOS(3)	Flight Design CT LS	F-13-01-04	
D-MOOT	Tandem Air Sunny s.b.s.	SuS 03.96	
D-MOOU	SG Aviation Storm 280	G 008	
D-MOOV	Aerostyle Breezer	001	
D-MOOW	Aerostyle Breezer	006	
D-MOOX	TL Ultralight TL-96 Sting	09ST317	
D-MOOY(1)	Aerostyle Breezer	unkn	
D-MOOY(2)	Aerospool WT-9 Dynamic	DY174/2007	I-8927
D-MOOZ	Aerostyle Breezer	015	
D-MOPA	Fantasy Air Allegro 2000	01-411	
D-MOPB	Fresh Breeze Simo 122	unkn	
D-MOPC	UPM Omega Lotus 18	069/883	
D-MOPD	Remos G.3 Mirage	100	
D-MOPE	Scheibe SF-40	3101	
D-MOPF	Rans S-6 Coyote II	0895864	
D-MOPG	Comco Ikarus C-42 Cyclone	9611-6026	
D-MOPH	Tecnam P.92 Echo	214	
D-MOPI	B&F Funk FK-9 Mk.II	060	
D-MOPL	Comco Ikarus Fox-C22	9502-3657	
D-MOPM	TL Ultralight TL-96 Star	02 S 122	
D-MOPO(2)	B&F Funk FK-9 Mk.III	09-142	
D-MOPP(1)	Take Off Maximum	7069	
D-MOPP(2)	Solid Air Twin Diamant/ Pico	T-018	
D-MOPT	Zenair CH-601D Zodiac	6-3530/013 0897	
D-MOPU	Rans S-6SXL Coyote II	0396956	
D-MOPV	B&F Funk FK-9 Mk.III	09-092	
D-MOPW	Ferrari Tucano A	328	
D-MOPY	ICP MXP-740V Savannah	01-04-51-070	
D-MOPZ	Comco Ikarus Fox-C22B	9505-3677	
D-MORA	Evektor EV-97 Eurostar 2000R	2001-0908	
	(To TC-UMS)		
D-MORB	TL Ultralight TL-96 Sting Carbon	05ST131	
D-MORC	B&F Funk FK-14 Polaris	014-004	
	(Re-regd D-MHHS(2))		
D-MORD	Seiffert Mini II	296	
D-MORE(1)	Warnke Skylight Trike	028	
D-MORE(2)	B&F Funk FK-12 Comet	12-032	
D-MORG #	B&F Funk FK-9 Mk.III	09-176	
D-MORH	Comco Ikarus C-42	unkn	
D-MORJ	WDFL Sunwheel	030	
D-MORK	Plätzer Kiebitz-B9	129	
D-MORL	Tecnam P.92 Echo	136	
D-MORM	Comco Ikarus C-42 Cyclone	0003-6231	
D-MORN	Plätzer Kiebitz	211	
D-MORO	Light Aero Avid Flyer IV	1495	
D-MORP	Fresh Breeze Simo 122	unkn	
D-MORR	B&F Funk FK-9 Mk.IV	09-245	
D-MORS(1)	Ultra-Vector F 610	1402	
D-MORS(2)	Autogyro Europe MTO Sport	unkn	
D-MORT	Tecnam P.92S Echo	unkn	
D-MORV	B&F Funk FK-14 Polaris	014-007	
D-MORW	WDFL Dallach D4B Fascination	008	
D-MORY	Fair Fax DR Trike	004	
D-MORZ	Dallach Sunrise IIA	035	
D-MOSA	Air-Light Wild Thing	033	
D-MOSB	Interplane Skyboy ZK	26/97	
D-MOSC	Tecnam P.92 Echo 100S	500	
D-MOSD	WDFL Dallach D4 Fascination BK	062	
	(Ditched 20.7.14, Austria)		
D-MOSE(2)	B&F Funk FK-9 Mk.IV	09-04-321	
D-MOSG(2)	Comco Ikarus C-42 Cyclone	9909-6212	
D-MOSH	B&F Funk FK-9 Mk.II	078	
D-MOSI	Urban Air UFM-13/15 Lambada	24/13	
D-MOSK(1)	NST Minimum Saphir 17	345	
D-MOSK(2)	Skyrider Storm 280	unkn	
D-MOSL	Avid Flyer Mk.IV Heavy Hauler	1104	HB-YFP
D-MOSM(1)	Comco Ikarus Fox-C22B	940 .-3605	
D-MOSM(2)#	Sky-Walker II	249	
D-MOSN	Fresh Breeze Simo 122	unkn	
D-MOSO	Air Création Tanarg 912ES	unkn	
D-MOSP	Fantasy Air Allegro	01-701	
D-MOSS	Rans S-6 Coyote II XL	1095886	
D-MOST	Scheibe Ultra	3407	
D-MOSV #	Sky-Walker 1+1	unkn	
D-MOSW(1)	Sky-Walker 1+1	26118	
D-MOSW(2)	Rans S-6 Coyote II	0803151	
	(Now reported as 11061777 S)		
D-MOSX	Maximum R100 / Karat 13	unkn	
D-MOSY	Plätzer Kiebitz	216	
D-MOTA	Plätzer Motte B2	04	
D-MOTB	Light Aero Avid Flyer IV	1522	
D-MOTC	B&F Funk FK-14 Polaris	014-003	
	(Damaged 14.11.10)		
D-MOTE(1)	WDFL Dallach D4 Fascination BK	065	
	(Crashed)		
D-MOTE(2)	Comco Ikarus Fox-C22	unkn	
D-MOTF	Autogyro Europe MTOsport	unkn	
D-MOTG(2)	Evektor EV-97 Eurostar SL	2015 4207	
D-MOTH	Plätzer Kiebitz B9	203	
D-MOTI	Point Aviation Albatros AN-22	8327	
D-MOTL	Magnii M-24 Orion	24116704	
D-MOTO(1)	Behlen Trike	87011	
D-MOTO(2)	Aerostyle Breezer	052	
D-MOTP #	Tecnam P.92 Echo	319	
D-MOTR(1)	Fisher FP-404 Classic	001	
D-MOTR(2)	TL Ultralight TL-96 Sting	07ST242	
D-MOTS	WDFL Dallach D4 Fascination BK	103	
D-MOTT	B&F Funk FK-9 Mk.III	09-113	
D-MOTU	Capella FW1 C50	691055	
D-MOTV	Comco Ikarus C-42 Cyclone	9706-6070	
D-MOTY	Flightworks FW2 C-80XLS Capella	061941	
D-MOTZ(1)	ASO Viper Hazard 15	11026202	
D-MOTZ(2)	Plätzer Kiebitz	unkn	
D-MOUG	B&F Funk FK-9 Mk.II	018	
D-MOUL(1)	Tandem Air Sunny s.b.s.	SuS-05.94	
D-MOUL(2)	Aerostyle Breezer CR	UL90	
D-MOUO	ICP MXP-740V Savannah	12-11-51-955	
D-MOUS	Pioneer Flightstar	370	
D-MOUT	B&F Funk FK-12 Comet	12-019	
D-MOUZ	Plätzer Motte B2/B3	48	
D-MOVA	Zenair CH-601DX Zodiac	6-8061/008 0297	
D-MOVE(1)	Pipistrel Sinus	199	
D-MOVE(2)	B&F Funk FK-12 Comet	12-043	
	(To France aa 60-RJ, 2011)		
D-MOVF	Pipistrel Virus SW 100	unkn	
D-MOVG	Zenair CH-601D Zodiac	6-3406/017 0097	
D-MOVI	Comco Ikarus Fox-C22	9210-3429	
D-MOVO(1)	Remos Gemini Ultra	015	
D-MOVO(2)	Rotortec Cloud Dancer II	unkn	
D-MOVW	Air-Light Wild Thing	030	
D-MOVY	Rans S-12 Airaile	0794508	
D-MOWA(1)	Aerotechnik Cobra S1A	001	
D-MOWA(2)	Fresh Breeze Simo 122	unkn	
D-MOWB	Rans S-6 Coyote II	10971168	
D-MOWE(1)	Schmidtler Ranger M	18/22	
D-MOWE(2)	ASO Viper 582 /	122020108	
D-MOWG	TL Ultralight TL-3000 Sirius	unkn	
D-MOWH	Euro-ALA Jet Fox 97	013	
D-MOWI (3)	Drifter	001	
D-MOWK	Comco Ikarus C-42 Cyclone	9812-6139	
D-MOWL	Plätzer Kiebitz B	077	
D-MOWO	Comco Ikarus Fox-C22B	9604-3699	
D-MOWR	Plätzer Motte BR	18	
D-MOWS	B&F Funk FK-9 Mk.II	085	
D-MOWT	Comco Ikarus C-42 Cyclone	0004-6251	
D-MOWZ #	Aerotechnik Cobra S1	unkn	
D-MOXE #	Comco Ikarus Fox-C22	9404-3560	
D-MOXI	Impulse 3300TD	15	
D-MOXL	B&F Funk FK-12 Comet	12-036	
D-MOXX	B&F Funk FK-9 Mk.III	09-117	
D-MOYA	Cosmos trike	unkn	
D-MOYN	Autogyro Europe Calidus	unkn	
D-MOYO(1)	WDFL Sunwheel	035	57-AAF
D-MOYO(2)	Comco Ikarus C-42A	1409-7345	
D-MOYS	Plätzer Kiebitz-B	053	
D-MOYY	TL Ultralight TL-96 Star	01 S 109	
D-MOYZ	Air-Light Wild Thing	016	
D-MOZD	Roland 602XL (Zodiac)	9529	
D-MOZE	Moyes Dragonfly	D04003	
D-MOZI	B&F Funk FK-9 Mk.II	039	
D-MOZO	Comco Ikarus Fox-C22	9503-3646	
D-MOZR	Comco Ikarus Fox-C22	940 .-3551	
D-MOZT	Plätzer Kiebitz	268	
D-MOZY	Urban Air UFM-13/15 Lambada	18/13	
D-MOZZ(1)	Klüver Twin Racer Quartz SX 16	229004	
D-MOZZ(2)	Autogyro Europe MTOsport	unkn	
D-MPAA	Remos Gemini Ultra	E11.012	
D-MPAB	WDFL Dallach D4 Fascination	075	
D-MPAC(1)	Comco Ikarus Fox-C22C	9310-3542	
D-MPAC(2)	Platzer Kiebitz B	unkn	
D-MPAD	Mantel Mono-Dragster	857	
D-MPAE	Bobcat		Bü-002
D-MPAF	Roland Z602 (t/w)	Z-9550	
D-MPAG	Air-Light Wild Thing	060	
D-MPAH(2)	Behlen Power Trike II	91125	
D-MPAH(3)	Comco Ikarus C-42 Cyclone	0102-6314	
D-MPAI	TL Ultralight TL-96 Star	unkn	
D-MPAJ (1)	Mantel Mono-Dragster	874225	
D-MPAJ(2)	Autogyro Europe MT-03	unkn	
D-MPAK	TL Ultralight TL-232 Condor Plus	AB-08/C0201	
D-MPAL	TL Ultralight TL-96 Star	unkn	
D-MPAM(1)	Comco Ikarus Fox-C22B	9404-3556	
D-MPAM(2)	Comco Ikarus C-42B	0907-7052	
D-MPAN(1)	NST Minimum Zephir CX	M467	
D-MPAN(2)	Tecnam P.92 Echo 100S	488	
D-MPAO	B&F Funk FK-12 Comet	012-025	
D-MPAP(1)	Comco Ikarus Fox-C22	9209-3406	
	(To OE-7027)		
D-MPAP(2)	Remos G.3 Mirage	057	
D-MPAQ #	Comco Ikarus Fox-C22B	9407-3598	
D-MPAR	Comco Ikarus Fox-C22	9403-3578	
D-MPAS	Remos G.3 Mirage	98	
D-MPAU	B&F Funk FK-9 Mk.IV	09-427	
D-MPAV	Autogyro Europe Calidus 914	unkn	
D-MPAW	Kolb Twinstar Mk.III	M3-100	
D-MPAY	Aerostyle Breezer	041	
D-MPAZ	Flight Design CT SW	07-11-10	
D-MPBA	EEL ULF-2	002	
D-MPBB	Light Aero Avid Flyer	1290	
D-MPBC #	Fresh Breeze Simo 122	unkn	
D-MPBE	B&F Funk FK-9 Mk.IV ELA	09-05-426	
	(Same c/n quoted for YR-5307)		
D-MPBF #	B&F Funk FK-9	040	
	(W/o 31.8.08)		
D-MPBG	Tecnam P.96 Golf 100S	097	
D-MPBH #	Plätzer Kiebitz-B	173	
D-MPBI	B&F Funk FK-14 Polaris	014-026	
D-MPBK	B&F Funk FK-9 Mk.III	09-105	
D-MPBL #	Ultrastar	018	
D-MPBM	Comco Ikarus C-42 Cyclone	9912-6227	
D-MPBO	B&F Funk FK-9 Mk.II Classic	066	
D-MPBS	Dallach Sunrise II	012	

Registration	Type	c/n	Other marks
D-MPBT(1)	Fair Fax DR Trike	34	
D-MPBT(2)	Tecnam P.92 Echo Super	661	S5-PBT
D-MPBV	Tecnam P.92 Echo 100S	432	
D-MPBW #	Air-Light Wild Thing	051	
D-MPCB(1)	Albatros	114	
D-MPCB(2)	TEAM Airbike Tandem	AB 002	
D-MPCC	Rans S-6 Coyote II	0495805	
D-MPCD	Flight Design CT	05-01-04	D-MPCT(1)
D-MPCD(2)	Flight Design CT SW	unkn	
D-MPCF	Rans S-6 Coyote II	0396963	
D-MPCH	Fisher Super Koala	B291248	
D-MPCI	Remos G.3 Mirage	061	
D-MPCJ	Remos G.3 Mirage	069	
D-MPCL	ATEC Zephyr 2000	SF 091101	
D-MPCM(1)	B&F Funk FK-9 Mk.III	094	
	(To 85-MR/F-JHAQ)		
D-MPCM(2)	Plätzer Kiebitz	160 ?	
D-MPCN	Comco Ikarus C-42 Cyclone	9704-6025	
D-MPCO	Flyitalia MD-3 Rider	33	
D-MPCP	Remos G.3 Mirage	059	
D-MPCR #	Plätzer Kiebitz-B2	007	
D-MPCT	Flight Design CT Supralight	E-09-02-11	
	(Marks re-used on company demonstrators, latest noted above)		
D-MPCV	Autogyro Europe MTOsport	unkn	
D-MPCW	Rans S-7 Courier	0698249	
D-MPCX	Zlin Trener Baby UL	03A/2002	03
D-MPDA	Aeropro Eurofox	unkn	
D-MPDB	EEL ULF-2	044	
D-MPDD	Comco Ikarus C-42	0101-6292	
D-MPDG	Plätzer Kiebitz-B2	041	
D-MPDH #	Tandem Air Sunny Sport	31.92	
D-MPDK	Air-Light Wild Thing	045	
D-MPDL	Tecnam P.96 Golf 100S	047	
D-MPDM	Moyes Dragonfly	D04005	
D-MPDP	Remos G.3 Mirage	078	
D-MPDS(1)	B&F Funk FK-9 Mk.II	unkn	
D-MPDS(2)	Shark Aero Shark	007	OK-RUR 02
D-MPDU	Autogyro Europe MTOsport	unkn	
D-MPDW	Flight Design CT SW	unkn	
D-MPEA (1)	Schönleber DS Lotus KS 18	010490	
D-MPEA(2)	ATEC Zephyr 2000	SF 040101	
D-MPEB #	UPM Funplane	890059	
D-MPEC(1)	Homebuilt, possibly Enduro	8/90	
D-MPEC(2)#	Fly Synthesis Storch	160.6	
D-MPED	Tecnam P.92 Echo 100S	573	
D-MPEE	Comco Ikarus Fox-C22B	9501-3642	
D-MPEF	Aeropro Eurofox	080099	
D-MPEG(1)	Scheibe Uli 1	5217	
D-MPEG(2)	Remos G.3 Mirage	160	
D-MPEI	Tecnam P.96 Golf	076	
D-MPEJ	Comco Ikarus C-42 Cyclone	9807-6116	
D-MPEK	Tecnam P.92 Echo Light	1478	
D-MPEL	Remos G.3 Mirage	unkn	
D-MPEM	Fresh Breeze Simo 122	unkn	
D-MPEN	Alpi Avn Pioneer 300	unkn	
	(Multiple use ferry marks)		
D-MPEP	Comco Ikarus Fox-C22B	9603-3697	
D-MPER	Scheibe Uli 1	5225	
D-MPES	Euro-ALA Jet Fox 91D	010	
D-MPET	Tandem Air Sunny Sport	0031001S,S	
D-MPEU	Comco Ikarus Fox-C22	9 . . .-3544	
D-MPEV	Evektor EV.97 Eurostar	98 03 01	
D-MPEW #	B&F Funk FK-9 Mk.II	064	
D-MPEZ	Comco Ikarus Fox-C22	9311-3545	
D-MPFA(1)	ASO Viper Trike	22035206	
D-MPFA(3)	Fantasy Air Allegro	03-417	
D-MPFB	ATEC Zephyr	SF 050301	
D-MPFC	Comco Ikarus C-42 Cyclone	0006-6264	
D-MPFD #	Autogyro Europe MT-03	unkn	
D-MPFF	Rans S-6 Coyote II	04981223	
D-MPFG	Comco Ikarus C-42B	0507-6694	
D-MPFI	Sky-Walker II	504	
D-MPFJ	WDFL Fascination	unkn	
D-MPFK	J-3 Kitten	001	
D-MPFN	Magni M-24 Orion	24138194	
D-MPFS	Pioneer Flightstar	672	D-MAFS
D-MPFU	WDFL Dallach D4 Fascination BK	119	
D-MPFW	Plätzer Motte BR	unkn	
D-MPGA	Firebird Sierra Trike	unkn	
D-MPGB(1)	Remos GX	281	
	(Re-regd D-MMGF)		
D-MPGB(2)	ProFe Banjo-MH	16	
D-MPGE	Remos G.3 Mirage	062	
D-MPGG	Tecnam P.92 Echo S100	513	
D-MPGH	Tecnam P.92 Echo	243	
D-MPGI	Dallach Sunrise II	011	
D-MPGK	Ikarusflug Eurofox Pro	039097	
D-MPGL	Plätzer Kiebitz B	383	
D-MPGM	Flight Design CT-2K	unkn	
D-MPGN	Comco Ikarus Fox-C22	8707-3045	
D-MPGO	Flight Design CT SL	E-12-03-06	
D-MPGS	TL Ultralight TL-96 Star	01 S 82	
D-MPGT	Evektor EV-97 Eurostar SLW	unkn	
D-MPGW #	Flight Design CT	99-07-03-60	
	(Re-registered D-MRRI)		
D-MPHA	Euro-ALA Jet Fox 97	00134	
D-MPHB	HB Cubby	unkn	
D-MPHC	Plätzer Kiebitz B	180	
D-MPHD	Skystar S-34	013	
D-MPHE	Comco Ikarus Fox-C22B	9511-3679	
D-MPHF	Comco Ikarus C-42 Cyclone	9803-6088	
D-MPHG	Comco Ikarus C-42 Cyclone	9906-6189	
D-MPHI	Behlen Power-Trike	830002	
D-MPHK	B&F Funk FK-12 Comet	012-030	
D-MPHL	Comco Ikarus C-42B	unkn	
D-MPHM(1)	B&F Funk FK-12 Comet	012-020	
	(To OO-F67)		
D-MPHM(2)	Aerospool WT-9 Dynamic	DY153/2006	PH4A5
D-MPHN(1)	Comco Ikarus C-42 Cyclone	0008-6274	
	(Probably re-regd D-MUMY(2))		
D-MPHN(2)	Flight Design CT SL	unkn	
D-MPHO	Aeropro Eurofox	unkn	
D-MPHP	Comco Ikarus C-42B	0412-6641	
	(Same c/n as D-MPHV, presumed re-regd)		
D-MPHR	Flightworks FW2 C80 Capella	61941-1	
D-MPHS	WDFL Sunwheel R	042	
D-MPHT	Comco Ikarus C-42C	unkn	
D-MPHV	Comco Ikarus C-42B	0412-6641	D-MPHP
D-MPHW(1)	WDFL Dallach D4 Fascination	023	
D-MPHW(2)	Pipistrel Virus	unkn	
D-MPHX	Tecnam P.96 Golf	unkn	
D-MPHZ #	Comco Ikarus C-42C	1308-7280	
D-MPIA	Rans S-7 Courier	unkn	
D-MPIB	Technoflug Piccolo	27	
D-MPIC	Remos G.3 Mirage	106	
D-MPIE	Comco Ikarus Fox-C22E	9507-3669	
D-MPII	ICP MXP-740V Savannah	01-00-51-004	
D-MPIK	Fresh Breeze Simo 122	unkn	
D-MPIL	Tecnam P.96 Golf S100	228	D-MGHW
D-MPIN	Alpi Avn Pioneer 200	unkn	
	(Multiple use ferry marks)		
D-MPIO	Alpi Avn Pioneer 300	20	I-7099
D-MPIP	Tecnam P.92 Echo 100S (floatplane)	390	
D-MPIR #	Comco Ikarus Fox-C22	9208-3427	
D-MPIT	Remos G.3 Mirage	unkn	
D-MPIU	Fresh Breeze Simo 122	unkn	
D-MPIW	Flight Design CT	97.11.03.15	
	(To PH-3A5)		
D-MPIX	Scheibe SF 40B	3107	
D-MPJA	Remos G.3 Mirage	120	
D-MPJF(1)	Plätzer Kiebitz-B	038	
D-MPJF(2)	Celier Xenon	CAF08373R	
D-MPJH	ParaZoom Trio-Star/Dudek Nucleon		
D-MPJK	Light Aero Avid Flyer	5115	
D-MPJL	Ikarusflug Eurofox	029097	
D-MPJM	Plätzer Kiebitz	88	
D-MPKA	ICP MXP-740V Savannah	01-03-51-060	
D-MPKB	Zenair CH-601 Zodiac	unkn	
D-MPKC	Tecnam P.92S Echo 100	unkn	
D-MPKD	Wezel Apis 2	003	
D-MPKE	Letov LK-2M Sluka	unkn	
D-MPKF	Comco Ikarus C-42	unkn	
D-MPKG	Flight Design CT	98.05.01.33	
D-MPKH	Dyn'Aéro MCR-01 UL	056	
D-MPKI	LO-120S	016-A	
D-MPKK	Comco Ikarus C-42	0203-6420	
D-MPKL	Wezel Apis 2	unkn	
D-MPKL(2)	B&F Funk FK-14B2 Polaris	014-080	
D-MPKM	B&F Funk FK-9 TG Mk.II	063	
D-MPKN	Aerospool WT-9 Dynamic	DY518/2014	
D-MPKO	Wezel Apis 2	W001	
D-MPKP	Aviasud Mistral BRD	182/92	
D-MPKS	Comco Ikarus C-42 Cyclone	9707-6050	
D-MPKW	Comco Ikarus Fox-C22 Seaplane	9303-3344	
D-MPLA	Rans S-6S Coyote II	0196922	
D-MPLC	Aquilair Swing 582 / Ghost 12.9	unkn	
D-MPLE	Take Off Maximum Hazard 15 Trike	019109	
D-MPLF	Comco Ikarus C-42 Cyclone	9906-6193	
D-MPLH	WDFL Dallach D4 Fascination	027	
D-MPLI(1)	B&F Funk FK.12 Comet	012-001	
	(Sold to France)		
D-MPLI(2)	Shark Aero Shark	021	
D-MPLK	Remos G-3 Mirage	122	
	(To Denmark, 9-250)		
D-MPLL	ASO Storch	ST 11014503	
D-MPLM	Bautek Eagle V/ Pico	unkn	
D-MPLO	Comco Ikarus C-42 Cyclone	9801-6077	
D-MPLR	Light Aero Avid Flyer IV	1435D	
D-MPLS #	Ultravia Pélican Sport 450S	714	
D-MPLT	Flight Design CT-2K	00.08.02.14	
D-MPLV	Comco Ikarus Fox-C22	9203-3401	
D-MPLW	Sky Craft 2000	2000-39	
D-MPLZ #	Best Off Sky Ranger	unkn	
D-MPMA(1)	Behlen Power-Trike II	91030	
D-MPMA(2)	Fly Synthesis Storch	94	
D-MPMB	Comco Ikarus C-42 Cyclone	9707-6066	
D-MPMC	Flight Design MC	unkn	
D-MPMG	Tecnam P.92 Echo 100S	443	
D-MPMK	B&F Funk FK-9 Mk.III	09-146	
D-MPML	B&F Funk FK-14B Polaris Professional (t/w)	138	
D-MPMM	WDFL Dallach D5 Evolution	001	
D-MPMN	Comco Ikarus C-42 Cyclone	9803-6086	
D-MPMO	Breezer	079	
D-MPMR	Alpi Aviation Pioneer 300	118	
D-MPMS	B&F Funk FK-9 Mk.II (t/w)	unkn	
D-MPMW	TL Ultralight TL-2000 Sting	21ST02	
D-MPMZ #	P&M Pegasus Quantum 15 912	unkn	
D-MPNK	Jetfoxair Jet Magic	GS-10-10-900-107	
D-MPNN #	WDFL Fascination D4	unkn	
D-MPNR	Tecnam P.92 Echo	325	
D-MPNS(1)	Tecnam P.92 Echo	unkn	
D-MPNS(2)	Plätzer Kiebitz B	350	
D-MPNT #	Tecnam P.92 Echo	378	
	(Damaged, rebuild project?)		
D-MPNX	Phenix Aero Phenix autogyro	unkn	
D-MPOA	TL Ultralight TL-96 Star	00 S 71	
D-MPOE	NST Minimum	M347	
D-MPOH	Drachenstudio Royal 912 ULS / Eos	unkn	
D-MPOJ	Tandem Air Sunny s.b.s.	SUS 05 96	
D-MPOK	Jodel D.18	unkn	
D-MPOL	Schmidtler Ranger M Trike	1819	
D-MPOO(1)	Flight Design CT	unkn	
D-MPOO(2)	Herringhausen Vagabund	014	
D-MPOP	Tecnam P.92 Echo	165	
D-MPOR	Comco Ikarus C-42 Cyclone	9903-6170	
D-MPOW	Remos G.3 Mirage	050	
D-MPOZ	Comco Ikarus Sherpa II	8512-1112	D-MWLF(1)?
D-MPPB	Air-Light Wild Thing	021	
D-MPPC	Remos G.3 Mirage	046	
D-MPPD #	Take Off Merlin / Karat 13	unkn	
D-MPPF	Aero East Europe SILA 450C	131203 AEE 0019	
D-MPPG	Flight Design CT2SW	04.10.05	
D-MPPH(1)	WDFL Sunwheel	019	
D-MPPH(2)	Aerostyle Breezer C	UL13	
D-MPPI	Remos GX	421	
D-MPPJ	Tecnam P.96 Golf 100S	125	
D-MPPK	Plätzer Kiebitz	unkn	
D-MPPL	Autogyro Europe MT-03	D07G24	
D-MPPM	ATEC Zephyr 2000	ZP 511200	
D-MPPO	Comco Ikarus C-42C	1303-7242	
D-MPPP	Murphy Renegade Spirit	506	
D-MPPR	Comco Ikarus Fox-C22	9201-3382	

Reg	Type	C/n	Notes
D-MPPS	Comco Ikarus C-42 Cyclone	9809-6129	
D-MPPV	EEL ULF-2	89/2090	
D-MPPW(1)	Klüver Twin Racer Trike	574008	
D-MPPW(2)	Remos GX	440	
D-MPPX	Raj Hamsa X'Air	unkn	
D-MPPY(1)	TUL-2 Tandem Tulak	031	
D-MPPY(2)	HB Cubby	unkn	
D-MPPZ	Drachenstudio Royal 912 / Eos	unkn	
D-MPQA	Plätzer Kiebitz-B	321	
D-MPQR	Comco Ikarus Fox-C22	9407-3581	
D-MPRA	TL Ultralight TL-96 Star	99 C 04	
D-MPRB	Tecnam P.96 Golf 100S	065	
D-MPRC	TL Ultralight TL-3000 Sirius	10SI32	
D-MPRD	Comco Ikarus C-42B	1205-7201	
D-MPRE	Comco Ikarus Fox-C22	9104-3345	
D-MPRG	Comco Ikarus C-42 Cyclone	9702-6068	
D-MPRH	Flight Design CT	98.02.04.24	D-MWFP
D-MPRI(1)	Tecnam P.92 Echo 100S	554	
D-MPRI(2)	Fresh Breeze Simo 122	unkn	
D-MPRK	Comco Ikarus Fox-C22	9307-3520	
D-MPRL	Autogyro Europe MTOsport	unkn	
D-MPRM	Comco Fox	037	
D-MPRO(1)	Albatros	102	
D-MPRO(2)	B&F Funk FK-9 Mk.II TG	048	PH-2U4, D-MRTB
D-MPRP	Comco Ikarus Fox-C22	9705-3726	
D-MPRR	Alpi Aviation Pioneer 300	unkn	
D-MPRS(1)	Jet Fox	015	
D-MPRS(2)	Breezer C	046	
D-MPRU	Comco Ikarus C-42 Cyclone	9704-6015	
D-MPRV #	Flight Design CT	01.06.06.16	
D-MPRW	Comco Ikarus Fox-C22C	9608-3716	
D-MPSA	Air-Light Wild Thing	023	
D-MPSB	Air-Light Wild Thing	047	
	(Was c/n 010, 2 acft?)		
D-MPSC	Comco Ikarus Fox	039	
D-MPSD	B&F Funk FK-14 Polaris	014-015	
D-MPSE	Urban Air UFM-13 Lambada	unkn	
D-MPSF	Flight Design CT SW	07-02-25	
D-MPSG	Zenair CH-601 Zodiac	6-3209/012 0097	
D-MPSH	Dova DV-1 Skylark	07/09	
D-MPSJ	Bilsam Sky Cruiser	unkn	
D-MPSK #	Let Mont Tulak	unkn	
D-MPSL	Autogyro Europe Calidus	unkn	
D-MPSM	Comco Ikarus C-42	unkn	
D-MPSN	Comco Ikarus Fox-C22	9404-3518	
D-MPSR	Light Aero Avid Flyer IV	941	
D-MPSS	Comco Ikarus C-42 Cyclone	9806-6124	
D-MPST	Air-Light Wild Thing	06 074	
D-MPSU	Magni M-24 Orion	24148294	
D-MPSV	Autogyro Europe MTOsport	unkn	
D-MPSW	Comco Ikarus C-42 Cyclone	9809-6123	
D-MPSY	Autogyro Europe MTOsport	unkn	
D-MPSZ	Comco Ikarus C-42 Cyclone	0004-6245	
D-MPTA(1)	Dallach D4 Fascination	unkn	
D-MPTA(2)	Aerospool WT-9 Dynamic	DY081/2005	
	(N81BT current in USA quoted as c/n 081 – possibly kit?)		
D-MPTB	Remos G-3 Gemini Mirage	unkn	
D-MPTC #	Ultraleichtverbund Bi 90	942	
D-MPTD	Autogyro Europe MT-03	unkn	
D-MPTF	Zenair CH-601 Zodiac	unkn	
D-MPTF(1?)	Alpi Aviation Pioneer 200UL	108	
	(Sold as 55-SA/F-JUKR, D-MBCK)		
D-MPTH	Tecnam P.92 Echo 100S	528	
D-MPTK	Comco Ikarus C-42 Cyclone	0005-6262	
D-MPTL	Plätzer Kiebitz	230	
D-MPTR	Urban Air Samba XXL	unkn	
D-MPTS	Comco Ikarus Fox-C22	9307-3515	
D-MPTU	Comco Ikarus C-42 Cyclone	9611-6019	
D-MPTW	Fresh Breeze Simo 122	unkn	
D-MPUA	Tecnam P.92 Echo 2000 Super	1211	
D-MPUB	Tecnam P.92 Echo 2000 Super	1037	
D-MPUC	Comco Ikarus C-42 Cyclone	0006-6256	
D-MPUD	ATEC 122 Zephyr 2000	Z741201	
D-MPUE	Urban Air UFM-11 Lambada	07/11	
D-MPUF	TL Ultralight TL-232 Condor Plus	98C02	PH-3A8
D-MPUK	Comco Ikarus Fox-C22B	9503-3643	
D-MPUL(1)	Comco Ikarus Sherpa	8403-1059	LX-XPS
D-MPUL(2)	Impulse Aircraft Impulse 100UL	1	
D-MPUR	Comco Ikarus Fox-C22	9111-3381	
D-MPUT	Aerostyle Breezer	unkn	
D-MPVG	Autogyro Europe MTOsport	unkn	
D-MPVM	Plätzer Kiebitz-B6	11/2	
D-MPVP	Tecnam P.92 Echo	158	
D-MPVY	Remos G.3 Mirage	71	
D-MPWA	Kappa KP-2U Sova	625/98	
D-MPWE	B&F Funk FK-9 Mk.II	030	
D-MPWF	Fresh Breeze Simo 122	unkn	
D-MPWG	Tecnam P.92S Echo	unkn	
D-MPWH	Flight Design CT-2K	unkn	
D-MPWK	Tecnam P.92 Echo	157	
D-MPWM	Alpi Avn Pioneer 300	unkn	
D-MPWN	Aerospool WT-9 Dynamic	unkn	
D-MPWP	Tandem Air Sunny Sport	60.95	
D-MPWR	Aeropro Eurofox	10101	
D-MPWS	Flight Design CT	98.04.04.31	
	(Re-regd D-MXTF)		
D-MPWT	Air-Light Wild Thing	047	
D-MPWW	Autogyro Europe Calidus	unkn	
D-MPWY	LTD LO-120S	013	
D-MPWZ(1)	Flight Design CT-2K	01.02.01.04	
	(To SE-VMG 6.09)		
D-MPWZ(2)	Flight Design CT LS	F-09-07-12	
D-MPXX	Raj Hamsa X'Air F	unkn	
D-MPYA	Plätzer Kiebitz-B6	008	
D-MPYR	Autogyro Europe Calidus	unkn	
D-MPYY #	Comco Ikarus Fox-C22	8612-3055	
D-MPYY #	TL Ultralight TL-2000 Sting carbon	04ST97	
	(TL-96 titles; probably now YL-LKD "04SL97")		
D-MPYZ	B&F Funk FK-9 Mk.III	unkn	
D-MPZE #	Air Création Tanarg 912ES / BioniX 15	unkn	
D-MPZI	Aero East Europe SILA 450c	140513-AEE-0025	
D-MPZZ(1)	Comco Ikarus C-42 Cyclone	0002-6241	
	(To SE-VMZ, 1.11)		
D-MPZZ(2)	Aero East Europe SILA 450c	130708-AEE-0014	
D-MQAB	unidentified weightshift	unkn	
D-MQAC	SG Aviation Storm Century	G 006	
D-MQAG	HTC Eagle / Pico	unkn	
D-MQAK	Schmidtler Enduro XP-15	01-005	
D-MQAL	Alpi Avn Pioneer 300S	55	
D-MQAS	Plätzer Kiebitz B	207	
D-MQAX(1)	B&F Funk FK-12 Comet	012-042	
	(Re-regd D-MSPI)		
D-MQAX(2)	Aerospool WT-9 Dynamic	unkn	
D-MQBA	Aerostyle Breezer C	UL072	
D-MQBB(1)	Comco Ikarus C-42B	0905-7047	
	(To LN-YWZ(2) 7.11)		
D-MQBB(2)	Dova DV-1 Skylark	155/12	
D-MQBF	B&F Funk FK-9 Mk.II	036	
	(To France as 91 AHR)		
D-MQBG	Tecnam P.96 Golf 100	unkn	
D-MQBK	Light Aero Avid Flyer IV	1293	
D-MQBR	Aerostyle Breezer	110	
D-MQBT	HFL Stratos 300K	300-014K	D-MJBT(1)
D-MQCC	Flight Design CT	97.08.03.07	
D-MQCT	Flight Design CT SW	07-01-16	
D-MQDM	Moyes Dragonfly	D04004	
D-MQFF	WDFL Dallach D4 Fascination	EB 011	D-EWMG
D-MQFK	Comco Ikarus C-42 Cyclone	9708-6064	
D-MQHG(1)	Pioneer Flightstar II SL	970501	
D-MQHG(2)	Pioneer Flightstar II	020401	
D-MQII	WDFL Sunwheel	46	
	(To 17-LY)		
D-MQIK(1)	Flight Design CT	98.06.01.34	
	(Re-regd D-MSSB(2))		
D-MQIK(2)	Pegasus GT450-912S	8259	
D-MQIS	Aerostyle Breezer CL 912iS	UL118	
D-MQJB	Aviasud Albatros AE 209	121	D-MACZ
D-MQJC #	Trixy G4-2R gyrocopter	005-12	
D-MQJK	Ekolot JK-05 Junior	unkn	
D-MQKM	SFS Vagabund	07	
D-MQLC	EEL ULF-2	unkn	
D-MQLD #	Sunny Light	unkn	
D-MQLL	Alpi Avn Pioneer 300UL	unkn	
D-MQMM	Flight Design CT LS	F-10-06-06	
	(C/n also quoted as F-10-06-16)		
D-MQNH	Pipistrel Taurus 503	unkn	
D-MQOP	LET-Mont Tandem Tulak UL	37	
D-MQPA	Autogyro Europe MTOsport	unkn	
D-MQPG	Comco Ikarus C-42 Cyclone	0010-6229	
D-MQQQ	Rans S-12 Airaile	1292340	N7082C
D-MQQR	Comco Ikarus C-42B	0112-6369	
D-MQRF	EEL ULF-2 Prototype	001	
D-MQRL	Autogyro Europe Cavalon	unkn	
D-MQRP	Air-Light Wild Thing	025	D-MYHL(1)
D-MQRS	Tecnam P.92 Echo	096	
D-MQTA #	Autogyro Europe MT-03	05G23	
D-MQTT	Flight Design CT LS	F-11-11-07	
D-MQWT	WDFL Dallach D4 Fascination	061	
D-MQWW	Tecnam P.96 Golf 100S	140	
D-MQXA	Air Light Wild Thing	081	
D-MQXZ	Tecnam P.92 Echo	127	
D-MQYJ	Plätzer Kiebitz-B	010	
D-MQYK #	Ekolot JK-05 Junior	05-06-04	
	(Sold as 54-AGS)		
D-MQYV	WDFL Sunwheel R	020	
D-MQZZ	Comco Ikarus C-42	unkn	
D-MRAA	Comco Ikarus C-42 Cyclone	unkn	
D-MRAB	Fisher FP-202 Koala	2183-1	
D-MRAC(3)	Plätzer Kiebitz-B9	142	
D-MRAD	Comco Ikarus C-42 Cyclone	9606-6008	
D-MRAE	Remos G.3-500 Mirage	172	
D-MRAF	Comco Ikarus C-42	unkn	
D-MRAG	Denney Kitfox	C94100072	
D-MRAH	Plätzer Kiebitz-B2	178	
D-MRAI	Denney Kitfox IV-1200	JCU-114	
D-MRAJ	SG Aviation Storm 280	D002	
D-MRAK	Comco Ikarus Fox-C22	8812-3185	
D-MRAL	Sky-Walker II	321	
D-MRAM	Light Aero Avid Flyer	1274	
D-MRAN	Rans S-6 Coyote II	1192390	
D-MRAO	Comco Ikarus Fox-C22	9 . . .-3609	
D-MRAP	Plätzer Kiebitz-B9	090	
D-MRAQ	Comco Ikarus Fox-C22	9407-3549	
D-MRAR	Flight Design CT	unkn	
D-MRAS #	Sky-Walker II	323	
D-MRAU	Comco Ikarus Fox-C22	8808-3139	
D-MRAV	Zenair CH-602XL Zodiac	unkn	
D-MRAW(1)	B&F Funk FK-12 Comet	012-006	
D-MRAW(2)	Ultravia Pélican Sport 450S	774	
D-MRAX	B&F Funk FK-9 Mk.III	09-102	
D-MRAY	Comco Ikarus C-42 Cyclone	9709-6035	
D-MRAZ	Light Aero Avid Flyer	"989952-199" or "9999"	
D-MRBA	Aerostyle Breezer	100	
D-MRBB	Flight Design CT	97.06.02.00	
D-MRBC	Rans S-6 Coyote II	0293435	
D-MRBD	Comco Ikarus C-42 Cyclone	9801-6037	
D-MRBF	Air-Light Wild Thing	012	
D-MRBG	Flight Design CT	97.11.02.14	
D-MRBH	WDFL Dallach D4 Fascination	004	
D-MRBI	Comco Ikarus C-42 Cyclone	9609-6012	
D-MRBJ	Plätzer Kiebitz-B	296	
D-MRBL(1)	Eipper Quicksilver GT	GT-280-1193	
D-MRBL(2)	Zenair CH-601D Zodiac	6-3655	
D-MRBM #	Alpi Aviation Pioneer 300	unkn	
D-MRBO	Tecnam P.92 Echo 100S	425	
D-MRBP #	Remos G.3 Mirage	049	
D-MRBT #	Aerospool WT-9 Dynamic	unkn	
D-MRBV	Tecnam P.92 Echo	unkn	
D-MRBX	Autogyro Europe MT-03	unkn	
D-MRBZ #	Flight Design CT	unkn	
D-MRCA(1)	Autogyro Europe MT-03	D06G08	
D-MRCA(2)	Autogyro Europe MTOsport	unkn	
D-MRCB(1)	Rans S-6 Coyote II	0295738	
D-MRCB(2)	Flight Design CT2 SW	04-07-03	
D-MRCD(1)	Comco Ikarus Fox-C22	8702-3048	
D-MRCD(2)	Rotortec Cloud Dancer II	unkn	
D-MRCF #	Konsuprod Moskito 1b	013	
D-MRCG	Comco Ikarus C-42B	unkn	
D-MRCH(1)	Remos GX	324	
	(Re-regd D-MHGG)		
D-MRCH(2)	Remos GX	350	
D-MRCI #	Remos G.3 Mirage	unkn	

Regn	Type	c/n	Notes
D-MRCK	Autogyro Europe Calidus	unkn	
D-MRCM #	Albatros 52	133	
D-MRCO	Remos GX	265	
D-MRCP	ICP MX-740V Savannah	05-96-50-042	
D-MRCR #	Autogyro Europe MT-03	unkn	
D-MRCT(1)	Flight Design CT	98.01.03.20	
D-MRCT(2)	Comco Ikarus Fox-C22	9110-3371	PH-2G1
D-MRCU	Comco Ikarus Fox-C22B	9407-3602	
D-MRCX	B&F Funk FK-14 Polaris	14-123	
D-MRDA	Fresh Breeze Simo 122	unkn	
D-MRDB	Fresh Breeze Simo 122	unkn	
D-MRDC	Comco Ikarus Fox-C22	9502-3656	
D-MRDE	Comco Ikarus C-42B	0905-7050	
D-MRDF	WDFL Dallach D4 Fascination	018	
D-MRDG	B&F Funk FK-9 Mk.II	037	
D-MRDI	Flyitalia MD-3 Rider	28	
D-MRDK	Plätzer Kiebitz-B2	132	
D-MRDL	Rans S-6E Coyote II (t/w)	1193560	
D-MRDM	B&F Funk FK-12 Comet	012-008	
	(To 17-RB/F-JXRK)		
D-MRDS	Bautek Eagle V/ Hazard 12S	unkn	
D-MRDW	Ultraleichtverbund Bi 90	704	
D-MRDX	Zenair CH-601D Zodiac	6-9197	
D-MRDZ	ICP MXP-740V Savannah	230	
D-MREA #	Remos G.3 Mirage	unkn	
D-MREB	Fresh Breeze Simo 122	unkn	
D-MREC	Comco Ikarus C-42B	0802-6952	
D-MRED	Remos Gemini Ultra	16.17/032	
D-MREE	Rans S-6 Coyote II	594630	
D-MREF	Bautek Eagle V/ Pico	unkn	
D-MREG	Tecnam P.96 Golf 100S	170	
D-MREH	Comco Ikarus C-42 Cyclone	9708-6046	
D-MREI	Plätzer Kiebitz-B2	039	
D-MREL(1)	Plätzer Motte	unkn	
D-MREL(2)	Roman-Weller UW-9 Sprint	001	
	(Morane A-1 replica) (W/o 13.8.16)		
D-MREM	Remos Gemini Ultra	E15.16/016	
D-MREP	Comco Ikarus C-42 Cyclone	9904-6157	
D-MRER #	B&F Funk FK-14 Polaris	014-006	
D-MRES	Tecnam P.96 Golf 100S	107	
D-MREU	Tandem Air Sunny	55.93	
D-MREV	Comco Ikarus C-42 Cyclone	9609-6011	
D-MREW	WDFL Dallach D4 Fascination BK	114	
D-MREX	WDFL Dallach D4 Fascination BK	078	
D-MRFA	B&F Funk FK-9 Mk.IV SW	09-04SW-373	
D-MRFB(1)	Delda-S/A Delta Dart II	002	
D-MRFB(2)	Rans S-12 Airaile	unkn	
D-MRFC	Ferrari Tucano-A	303	
D-MRFE	Ferrari Tucano-A	327	
D-MRFF	Comco Ikarus Fox-C22C	9705-3724	
D-MRFG #	Ultra-Vector H	1383	
D-MRFH	Comco Ikarus C-42	0304-6547	
D-MRFI	Autogyro Europe MTOsport	unkn	
D-MRFK(1)	B&F Funk FK-14 Polaris	unkn	
D-MRFK(2)	B&F Funk FK-9 Mk.III	09-398	
D-MRFL	Comco Ikarus C-42 Cyclone	0105-6350	
D-MRFM	Comco Ikarus C-42 Cyclone	0108-6410	
D-MRFO	Vidor Asso V Champion	008	
D-MRFP	Comco Ikarus C-42B	unkn	
D-MRFR	Comco Ikarus C-42 Cyclone	0105-"262"	
D-MRFS #	Rans S-12 Airaile	1292360	
D-MRFT	Kappa KP-2U Sova	4651 G	
D-MRFX	Remos GX	439	
D-MRGA #	Plätzer Motte B-3	033	
D-MRGB	Murphy Renegade Spirit	387	
D-MRGC	Fresh Breeze Simo 122	unkn	
D-MRGD	III Sky Arrow 450TG	018	
D-MRGE(1)	Ultraleichtverbund Bi 90	935	
D-MRGE(2)	ATEC Zephyr 2000	K 001	
D-MRGG	Comco Ikarus C-42	unkn	
D-MRGH	Murphy Renegade II	458	
D-MRGK(1)	Cosmos Phase III / Top 14.9	C1145	
D-MRGK(2)	Remos G3 Mirage	unkn	
D-MRGL	Euro-ALA Jet Fox 91D	009	
D-MRGO	Comco Ikarus C-42 Cyclone	9805-6056	
D-MRGP	Comco Ikarus C-42C	1304-7247	
D-MRGR	Fresh Breeze Solo 122 / Nova Rookie M	unkn	
D-MRGS	Tecnam P.96 Golf 100S	183	
D-MRGT	Zenair CH-601D Zodiac	6-9851	
D-MRGV	Comco Ikarus C-42 Cyclone	0010-6285	
D-MRGW(1)	Sky-Walker II	221	
D-MRGW(2)	Flight Design CT Supralight	E-10-06-07	
D-MRGX	Remos GX	316	
	(Originally c/n 250)		
D-MRHA	B&F Funk FK-9 Mk.III	110	
D-MRHB	Comco Ikarus Fox-C22	940 .-3571	
D-MRHC #	Fresh Breeze Simo 122	unkn	
D-MRHD	Plätzer Kiebitz B	147	
D-MRHE	Flight Design CT	007/97	
D-MRHF #	Behlen Power-Trike	88011	
D-MRHG	Zenair CH-601XL Zodiac	6-9687	
D-MRHH	Tecnam P.92 Echo	194	
D-MRHI	Schönleber 47KW / Vento	unkn	
D-MRHJ	B&F Funk FK-9 Mk.III	unkn	
D-MRHK	Tecnam P.92 Echo	266	
D-MRHL	Remos G.3 Mirage	041	
D-MRHM	Rans S-6ES Coyote II	0895880ES	
D-MRHN #	Comco Ikarus Fox-C22	9208-3420	D- MIAL(1)
D-MRHO	Ultraleichtverbund Bi 90	3957005	
D-MRHP	Ultraleichtverbund Bi 90	970	
D-MRHR	Comco Ikarus Fox-C22	9309-3539	
D-MRHS	Tecnam P.92 Echo	391	
D-MRHU	B&F Funk FK-9 Mk.III	09-097	
D-MRHW(1)	Schönleber DS Speed KS 14 Trike KS	01/0391	
D-MRHW(2)	B&F Funk FK-14 Polaris	014-018	
D-MRHX	Zenair CH.601DX Zodiac	6-9067	
D-MRHY #	Plätzer Kiebitz B	313	
D-MRHZ	Zenair CH-601D Zodiac	6-3521/006 0997	
	(W/o 3.10.09)		
D-MRIA	Tecnam P.92 Echo Classic	1385	
D-MRIC	Remos G.3 Mirage	121	
D-MRID	Comco Ikarus Fox-C22	9404-3555	
D-MRIE	Seiffert Mini II	F0111/88	
D-MRIF #	Aviasud Mistral 53	010	
D-MRII(1)	Plätzer Kiebitz	168	
D-MRII(2)	Aveko VL-3	VL-3-117	
D-MRIK	Tecnam P.92 Echo	265	
D-MRIL	III Sky Arrow 450	066	
D-MRIM	Remos G.3 Mirage	045	
D-MRIO	Roland Z602	Z-9571	
D-MRIP	Alpi Avn Pioneer 200	unkn	
D-MRIR(1)	Autogyro Europe MT-03	unkn	
D-MRIR(2)#	Autogyro Europe MTOsport	unkn	
D-MRIS	Tecnam P.96 Golf	16	
D-MRIT	Aviasud Albatros	037	
D-MRIW	WDFL Dallach D4 Fascination	043	
D-MRIX #	Scheibe Uli 1	5204	
D-MRIY	Scheibe Uli 1	5210	
D-MRIZ	Remos G.3 Mirage	040	
D-MRJA(1)	Seiffert Mini 1	F0209/87	
D-MRJA(2)	Autogyro Europe MTOsport	unkn	
D-MRJD #	B&F Funk FK-12 Comet	012-048	
	(To France as 86-IA /F-JRBC)		
D-MRJF	Comco Ikarus Fox-C22B	9510-3700	
D-MRJH	Comco Ikarus C-42 Cyclone	9710-6074	
D-MRJJ	Dova DV-1 Skylark	151/12	
D-MRJK	Flight Design CT	00.01.02.82	
D-MRJL	B&F Funk FK-9 Mk.III	108	
D-MRJN	Flight Design CT SW	06-11-16	
D-MRJO	Aeriane Swift E	unkn	
D-MRJR	Flight Design CT	98.11.01.40	
	(Re-regd D-MTMU)		
D-MRJS	Rans S-10 Sakota	0490104	
D-MRJU	Alisport Silent 2 Targa	2037	
D-MRJZ	Tecnam P.96 Golf	039	
D-MRKA	Konsuprod Moskito	003	
D-MRKB(1)	Comco Ikarus Fox-C22	9308-3519	
D-MRKB(2)	Bautek Eagle V/ Pico	unkn	
D-MRKD	Tecnam P.96 Golf	020	
	(Same c/n quoted as D-MBBX)		
D-MRKE	Comco Ikarus C-42 Cyclone	9612-6027	
D-MRKF	Rans S-6TD Coyote II	1294703	
D-MRKG	Aeroprakt A-22 Vision	19	
D-MRKK	Flight Design CT	01.03.02.09	
D-MRKL	Comco Ikarus C-42B	unkn	
D-MRKM	Air-Light Wild Thing	97 02 018	
D-MRKN	Tecnam P.92S Echo S 100	507	
D-MRKO	Comco Ikarus C-42 Cyclone	9709-6055	
D-MRKP	Comco Ikarus C-42 Cyclone	9707-6069	
D-MRKR	B&F Funk FK-9 Mk.II TG	053	
D-MRKS	Tecnam P.96 Golf 100S	131	
D-MRKT	Comco Ikarus C-42	0201-6405	
D-MRKW #	Light Aero Avid Flyer D	1156D	
D-MRKX	Celier Xenon 4	unkn	
D-MRLA	Behlen Power-Trike	877353	
D-MRLB	Aerospool WT-9 Dynamic	DY011 02	
D-MRLC	Dyn'Aéro MCR-01 UL	104	
D-MRLD(1)	Tecnam P.92 Echo	278	
	(Regd 6Y-JUC, 4.02)		
D-MRLD(2)	Flight Design CT SW	05-06-06	
	(Re-regd D-MGAC(2))		
D-MRLE	Comco Ikarus C-42B	0905-7037	
D-MRLH	TL Ultralight TL-232 Condor Plus	AB 03	
D-MRLI	Autogyro Europe MTOsport	unkn	
D-MRLK	Light Aero Avid Flyer IV	1400	
D-MRLL(1)	Tecnam P.96 Golf	unkn	
D-MRLL(2)	Alpi Aviation Pioneer 200	unkn	
D-MRLL(3)	Evektor EV-97 Eurostar SL	unkn	
D-MRLM(1)	Sky-Walker II	393	
D-MRLM(2)#	Flight Design CT LS	F-08-06-02	
D-MRLO(1)	Comco Ikarus C-42	unkn	
D-MRLO(2)	Flight Design CT SW	03.07.02.33	
D-MRLP	Rotortec Cloud Dancer II	CD410AS	
D-MRLR	Alpi Avn Pioneer 300	unkn	
D-MRLS #	Zenair CH-701D STOL	7-9068	
D-MRLT	Zlin Savage	45	
D-MRLW(1)	Comco Ikarus Fox-C22B	9606-3703	
D-MRLW(2)	Fresh Breeze Simo 122	unkn	
D-MRLX	Tecnam P.92 Echo 2000S	707	
D-MRMA	B&F Funk FK-9 Mk.III	09-03-100	
D-MRMC	Sky-Walker II	265	
D-MRMD	B&F Funk FK-9 TG Mk.II	059	
D-MRMF(1)	Comco Ikarus Fox-C22B	9 . . .-3681	
	(To France as 47 OU)		
D-MRMF(2)	Fläming Air FA-04 Peregrine SL	unkn	
D-MRMG	Remos Gemini Ultra B	E09.10	
D-MRMH	Aerospool WT-9 Dynamic	DYK05/2006	
D-MRMI	Remos G.3 Mirage	038	
D-MRMK(1)	Comco Ikarus Fox-C22	9109-3353	
D-MRMK(2)	Zlin Savage Cruiser Turbo	unkn	
D-MRMM(1)	B&F Funk FK-9 Mk.II	084	
D-MRMM(2)	Flight Design CT SW	unkn	
D-MRMM(3)	Dova DV-1 Skylark	unkn	
D-MRMN	Comco Ikarus Fox-C22C	9705-3715	
D-MRMP	Flight Design CT	00.11.02.23	
D-MRMR	WDFL Dallach D4 Fascination BK	111	
D-MRMS(1)	Comco Ikarus C-42	9801-6075	
D-MRMS(2)	Zlin Savage 912	72	
D-MRMU #	Warnke Trike Euro III	183001	
D-MRMW	Aerospool WT-9 Dynamic	DY264-2008	
D-MRMX	Pipistrel Alpha Trainer	unkn	
D-MRMY	Aerospool WT-9 Dynamic	DY381/2010	
D-MRMZ	Comco Ikarus C-42 Cyclone	9707-6045	
D-MRND	Rans S-6 Coyote II	unkn	
D-MRNG	Murphy Renegade	412	
D-MRNN	Flight Design CT-2K	99.12.04.78	
	(To OO-G51)		
D-MRNR	Autogyro Europe MTOsport	unkn	
D-MRNS #	Rans S-12 Airaile	unkn	
D-MROA	Aerostyle Breezer	048	
D-MROB	Comco Ikarus C-42B	0205-6447	
D-MROC	TL Ultralight TL-232 Condor Plus	00 C 04	
D-MROD	Rans S-10 Sakota	0194170	
D-MROE	Comco Ikarus Fox-C22	9406-3573	
D-MROF	Roko Aero NG6	6P040303K	
D-MROG	B&F Funk FK-9 Mk.II	unkn	
D-MROH	Rans S-6 Coyote II	0794652	
D-MROI	Zenair CH-701D STOL	7-9356	
D-MROK	NST Minimum	157	
D-MROM	Plätzer Kiebitz-B4	109	
D-MROO	Comco Ikarus C-42B	0305-6537	
D-MROP	B&F Funk FK-9 Mk.III	09-03-158	

Reg	Type	c/n	Prev/Notes
D-MROQ	Comco Ikarus C-42B	unkn	
D-MROR	ICP MXP-740 Savannah S	unkn	
D-MROS	Tandem Air Sunny Sport	23.91	
D-MROT(1)	NST Minimum	M431	
D-MROT(2)	Rotortec Cloud Dancer	unkn	
D-MROU	Comco Ikarus Fox-C22	9206-3409	
D-MROW	Comco-Ikarus C-42B	0604-6802	
D-MROY #	Comco Ikarus C-42B	9112-3298	
D-MROZ	Fly Synthesis Storch 503	unkn	
D-MRPA	Comco Ikarus C-42 Cyclone	0102-6301	
D-MRPC	TL Ultralight TL-232 Condor Plus	00 C 02	
D-MRPD	Rans S-6 Coyote II XL	08971150	
D-MRPE(1)	EAG Falcon Hawk X3	unkn	
D-MRPE(2)	Remos G-3	213	
D-MRPF	B&F Funk FK-9 Mk.III Utility	09-03U-136	
D-MRPG	Comco Ikarus C-42C	1305-7262	
D-MRPH	Fantasy Air Allegro	00-403	
D-MRPI #	Air Light Wild Thing	unkn	
D-MRPJ	Remos G-3 Mirage	212	
	(To LY-BIZ, 2010; later D-MATS))		
D-MRPK	Comco Ikarus Fox-C22	9310-3521	
D-MRPL	Air-Light Wild Thing	05-064	
D-MRPM	Sky Craft 2000	2000-31	
D-MRPP	Flight Design CT SW	unkn	
D-MRPR	Tecnam P.92 Echo 2000S	666	
D-MRPS #	Behlen Power-Trike	unkn	
D-MRPT	B&F Funk FK-9 Mk.III	09-165	
D-MRPW	B&F Funk FK-9 Mk.II	049	
D-MRRA	Aeroprakt A-22L Vision	320	
D-MRRB	Aerospool WT-9 Dynamic	DYK-04/2006	
D-MRRC	Comco Ikarus C-42C	unkn	
D-MRRF	WDFL Dallach D4 Fascination BK	096	
D-MRRG	WDFL Dallach D4 Fascination	049	
D-MRRH	UPM Funplane	870024	
D-MRRI	Flight Design CT	99-07-03-60	D-MPGW
D-MRRK	Tecnam P.92 Echo	296	
D-MRRL(1)	Tecnam P.96 Golf	17	
D-MRRL(2)	Fresh Breeze Simo 122	unkn	
D-MRRM	Sky Craft 2000	2000-38	
D-MRRM(2)	Pegasus GT-450 912S	8205	
D-MRRO	Roland Z602XL	Z-9554	
D-MRRP	B&F Funk FK-9 Mk.II	050	
	(Dbr 2.4.16)		
D-MRRR	WDFL Sunwheel	009	
D-MRRS	Comco Ikarus Sherpa II	8310-1044	PH-1M2
D-MRRT	Zlin Savage Classic	unkn	
D-MRRW	Comco Ikarus C-42 Cyclone	0110-6414	
D-MRRZ	Kümmerle Mini-Fly-Set	1268/91-5	
D-MRSA	WDFL Sunwheel R	032	
	(To Spain, 2005)		
D-MRSB	Sky Craft AJS	2000-32	
D-MRSC	Plätzer Kiebitz B	112	
D-MRSE	Rans S-6 Coyote II	12961078	
D-MRSF	Autogyro Europe MTOsport	unkn	
D-MRSG	Zenair CH-601D Zodiac UL	6-3651	
	(W/o 17.5.08)		
D-MRSH	Murphy Renegade Spirit	410	
D-MRSI	Roland Z601DX	6-9086	
D-MRSK	Comco Ikarus C-42 Cyclone	9806-6091	
D-MRSL	Comco Ikarus C-42 B	0304-6533	
D-MRSM	Comco Ikarus Fox-C22	9406-3593	
D-MRSN	Rans S-12 Airaile	1090028	
	(To RP-S56, 3.11)		
D-MRSO #	Fair Fax DR Trike	002	
D-MRSP	BRM Aero Bristell	unkn	
D-MRSR	Tecnam P.96 Golf	002	
D-MRSS	Ultraleichtverbund Bi 90	555395	
D-MRST(1)	Schmidtler Ranger M Trike	unkn	
D-MRST(2)	Plätzer Kiebitz-B6	141	
D-MRST(3)	Autogyro Europe MTOsport	unkn	
D-MRSU	NST Minimum Zephir	M497	
D-MRSW	Fresh Breeze Simo 122	unkn	
D-MRSX	Fresh Breeze Simo 122	unkn	
D-MRSY	WDFL Dallach D4B Fascination	40	
	(Same c/n as D-MWFR)		
D-MRTA	Schmidtler Ranger M Trike	18-23	
D-MRTB(1)	B&F Funk FK-9	048	
	(To PH-2U4)		
D-MRTB(2)	B&F Funk FK-9 Mk.II	026	
D-MRTD	TL Ultralight TL-96 Sting	unkn	
D-MRTE	Remos G-3 Mirage	065	
D-MRTF	Rans S-10 Sakota	0190084	
D-MRTG	Flight Design CT SW	05-10-11	
D-MRTH	Zenair CH-601D Zodiac UL	6-3485/021 0897	
D-MRTK	Tecnam P.92 Echo	unkn	
D-MRTL	Comco Ikarus Fox-C22	9107-3347	
D-MRTM	Remos G.3 Mirage	066	
D-MRTN	Tecnam P.92 Echo	188	
D-MRTR	Rans S-12 Airaile	0491064	
D-MRTS	Ferrari Tucano-A	305	
D-MRTT	Comco Ikarus C-42 Cyclone	9802-6044	
D-MRTV(1)	Comco Ikarus Fox-C22	9206-3415	
D-MRTV(2)	Autogyro Europe Cavalon	unkn	
D-MRTX	B&F Funk FK-14 Polaris Le Mans	014-145	
D-MRTZ	Blackshape Prime CF300	unkn	
D-MRUA	TL Ultralight TL-96 Star	00 S 43	
D-MRUB	Trixy G 4-2 R	035-14	
D-MRUD	B&F Funk FK131 Jungmann	unkn	
D-MRUE	Evektor EV-97 Eurostar	unkn	
	(W/o 20.5.11)		
D-MRUH	Best Off Sky Ranger	unkn	
D-MRUK	Comco Ikarus Fox-C22B	9508-3668	
D-MRUL(1)	Rans S-12 Airaile	0291054	
D-MRUL(2)	Rans S-12 Airaile	0791102	
	(To SP-SPKT)		
D-MRUN	Remos G.3 Mirage	073	
D-MRUT	Comco Ikarus Fox-C22	9212-3425	
D-MRUW #	UW-8 Rebell	23.91	
D-MRVA	Zenair CH-701D STOL	7-9063	
D-MRVB	Nando Groppo Trail	00092/51	
D-MRVE #	Plätzer Kiebitz-B1	002	
D-MRVG	Comco Ikarus C-42	0506-6688	
D-MRVH	Tandem Air Sunny s.b.s.	SuS 05.95	
D-MRVK	Air-Light Wild Thing	031	
D-MRVM	Technoflug Piccolo	037	
D-MRVR #	Autogyro Europe MTOsport	NL10S01	
	(To PH-4N9)		
D-MRVX	Rotorvox C2A	C2A-14002	
D-MRWA	Rans S-10T Sakota	1099190	
D-MRWB	Comco Ikarus Fox-C22	9211-3482	
D-MRWD #	Warnke Puma Sprint Trike	D007	
D-MRWE	WDFL Dallach D4 Fascination	006	
D-MRWG	Comco Ikarus C-42 Cyclone	9803-6095	
D-MRWH	WDFL Dallach D4 Fascination	002	
D-MRWI #	Fresh Breeze 110 AL2F	50	
D-MRWK(1)	Klüver Racer Quartz SX 12 Trike	445904	
D-MRWK(2)	Comco Ikarus C-42B	1010-7124	
D-MRWR	Remos G3-600	162	
D-MRWW	Fisher Celebrity	1039	
D-MRWZ	Autogyro Europe MTOsport	unkn	D-MANX
D-MRXL	Cellier Aviation Xenon	CAC04872R	
D-MRYC	WDFL Dallach D4 Fascination	060	
D-MRYI	Plätzer Kiebitz-B	158	
D-MRYY	Evektor EV-97 Eurostar 2000R	2002 1408	
D-MRZA	Evektor EV-97 Eurostar 2000R	2004 2110	
D-MRZJ	Comco Ikarus Fox-C22	94 . .-3590	
D-MRZW	Fresh Breeze Simo 122	unkn	
D-MSAA	Drachenstudio Royal 912 / Eos	unkn	
D-MSAB	Solid Air Diamant Twin / Pico S	unkn	
D-MSAC(1)	Comco Ikarus C-42 Cyclone	9910-6221	
D-MSAC(2)	Aeroprakt A-22L2 Vision	unkn	
D-MSAD	Schönleber DS Trike	502/0991	
D-MSAE(1)	NST Minimum	M63	
D-MSAE(2)	Comco Ikarus C-42 Cyclone	0004-6252	
D-MSAE(3)	Autogyro Europe MT-03	04G04	
D-MSAE(4)	Autogyro Europe MTOsport	unkn	
D-MSAF	Light Aero Avid Flyer IVC	869	
D-MSAG(1)	Tandem Air Sunny Sport	62.95	
D-MSAG(2)	Autogyro Europe MTOsport	unkn	
D-MSAH(1)	Ultraleichtverbund Bi 90	493	
D-MSAH(2)	B&F Funk FK-12 Comet	012-038	
D-MSAI	Tandem Air Sunny Targa	TA-013	
D-MSAJ	Comco Ikarus C-42	unkn	
D-MSAK(2)	Solid Air Diamant Twin	T-016	
D-MSAL	Schmidtler Enduro Trike	0401086	
D-MSAM	Roland CH-701D	7-9561	
D-MSAN	Vidor Asso V Champion V	001	
D-MSAO	Light Aero Avid Flyer	1520	
D-MSAQ	Shark Aero Shark	unkn	
D-MSAR	Remos G.3 Mirage	146	
D-MSAS	Comco Ikarus C-42B	0304-6538	
D-MSAT	Comco Ikarus Fox-C22C	9107-3348	
D-MSAU	Tandem Air Sunny s.b.s.	SuS-10.94	
D-MSAV	Comco Ikarus Fox-C22B	9403-3577	
D-MSAW	WDFL Sunwheel R	039	
D-MSAX(1)	Autogyro Europe MT-03	unkn	
D-MSAX(2)	Flight Design CT SL Turbo	E-14-02-02	
D-MSAY	B&F Funk FK-9 Mk.II	087	
D-MSAZ	Comco Ikarus C-42	9908-6204	
	(To EI-ELC, 5.10)		
D-MSBA	Pipistrel Taurus	085 T 503	
D-MSBB	Comco Ikarus Fox-C22	9106-3330	
D-MSBC	WDFL Dallach D4 Fascination BK	073	
D-MSBF	Aeroprakt A-22 Vision	0021	
D-MSBG	Remos G.3 Mirage	054	
D-MSBH	Tecnam P.92 Echo	257	
D-MSBI	ULFlugzeugwerk SF-45SA Spirit	unkn	
D-MSBK(1)	Take Off Merlin Karat 13 Trike	21904	
D-MSBK(2)	Comco Ikarus C-42 Cyclone	9912-6225	
D-MSBM	Comco Ikarus C-42 Cyclone	9607-6002	
D-MSBN	Tandem Air Sunny s.b.s.	01-95	
D-MSBP	Comco Ikarus Fox-C22	9304-3499	
D-MSBR	Comco Ikarus C-42 Cyclone	9909-6208	
D-MSBS	Aeropro Eurofox	053098	
D-MSBT	B&F Funk FK-9TG Mk.II	062	
D-MSBV	Comco Ikarus C-42	0202-6363	
D-MSBZ	Comco Ikarus C-42 Cyclone	9902-6163	
D-MSCB	Tecnam P.92 Echo	179	
D-MSCC	Rans S-6ES Coyote II (t/w)	1195900	
D-MSCD	Fresh Breeze Simo 122	unkn	
D-MSCE	TL Ultralight TL-96 Star	01 S 100	
D-MSCF	Comco Ikarus Fox-C22C	9706-3723	
D-MSCG	Rotortec Cloud Dancer II	1114 X1 ZZ12	
D-MSCH	TL Ultralight TL-96 Star	00 S 75	
D-MSCI	Remos G-3 Mirage	083	PH-3T6
D-MSCK	Tecnam P.92S Echo	unkn	
D-MSCL	Comco Ikarus Fox-C22	9106-3341	
D-MSCM	Comco Ikarus C-42B	0311-6478	
D-MSCN	WDFL Fascination	028	
D-MSCO	Comco Ikarus C-42 Cyclone	9906-6178	
D-MSCP	Urban UFM-11 Lambada	09/11	
D-MSCQ	Comco Ikarus C-42B	0705-6893	
D-MSCR	EEL ULF-II	unkn	
D-MSCS	Pipistrel Sinus NW	249SNL912	
D-MSCT(1)	Flight Design CT	97.09.03.09	
D-MSCT(2)	Flight Design CT	98.07.03.36	
D-MSCU	Comco Ikarus C-42 Cyclone	9711-6071	
D-MSCV	Roland Z602	Z-9546	
D-MSCW	Brack/ Denney Kitfox	613	D-ERPB
D-MSCY(2)	Flight Design CT SW	07.03.03	
D-MSCZ #	Fresh Breeze Simo 122	unkn	
D-MSDA	Aerospool WT-9 Dynamic	DY471/2013	
D-MSDB	ASO 26 Storch	160.1	
D-MSDC	Autogyro Europe MTOsport	unkn	
D-MSDD	Autogyro Europe MTOsport	unkn	
D-MSDE	Spacek SD-1 Minisport TD	021	
D-MSDG	TL Ultralight TL-3000 Sirius	14SI103	
D-MSDH	Plätzer Kiebitz-B9	224	
D-MSDI	Rans S-6 Coyote II	01991294	
D-MSDK	Aerostyle Breezer	067	
D-MSDL(1)	Remos G.3 Mirage	101	
D-MSDL(2)	Comco Ikarus C-42C	unkn	
D-MSDM	Corvus CA-21 Phantom	CA21-036	
D-MSDN #	Corvus CA-21 Phantom	unkn	
D-MSDS #	Kümmerle Mini-Fly-Set	1303/91-6	
D-MSDW	SDW Maximum Trike	1	
D-MSDY	Comco Ikarus C-42 Cyclone	0005-6268	
D-MSEA	WDFL Dallach D4 Fascination BK	091	
D-MSEB	Fläming Air FA-01 Smaragd	12/05	
D-MSEC	Tecnam P.92 Echo	173	
D-MSED	Tecnam P.92 Echo	174	

Registration	Type	Serial	Notes
D-MSEE(1)	Autogyro Europe MT-03	05G01	
D-MSEE(2)	Autogyro Europe MTOsport	unkn	
D-MSEE(3)	Autogyro Europe Calidus	unkn	
D-MSEE(4)	Autogyro Europe MTOsport	M01221	
D-MSEF	Aeropro Eurofox	076099	
D-MSEI(1)	Behlen Power-Trike Vampir II	88012	
D-MSEI(2)	Air-Light Wild Thing	039	OE-7047
D-MSEJ	Rans S-6 Coyote II	0593509	
D-MSEK	Tecnam P.92SEcho 100S	536	
D-MSEL(1)	Comco Ikarus Fox-C22	9107-3342	
D-MSEL(2)	Rans S-6 Coyote	03061735 S	
D-MSEM	Light Aero Avid Flyer	619	
D-MSEN	Kümmerle Mini-Fly-Set Zephir CX	1272/91-5	
D-MSEO #	Comco Ikarus C-42 Cyclone	9804-6097	
D-MSEP	Urban UFM-11 Lambada	08/11	
D-MSER	Scheibe SF-40	3106	
D-MSES	Fly Synthesis Storch	160.1	
D-MSET	Plätzer Motte B2	35	
D-MSEU	Murphy Renegade Spirit	411	
D-MSEV	Evektor EV.97 Eurostar	99 05 01	
D-MSEW	SFS Vagabund	08	
D-MSEX(1)	Behlen Trike	830014	
D-MSEX(2)	B&F Funk F-14 Polaris	unkn	
	(Sold to France as 73-LF)		
D-MSEX(3)	Autogyro Europe MT-03	04G05	
	(Same c/n as SE-VRE ex D-MLOO)		
D-MSEY	Fresh Breeze Simo 142	unkn	
D-MSEZ	Alpi Aviation Pioneer 200	unkn	
D-MSFA(1)	Warnke Trike	M869530	
D-MSFA(2)	B&F Funk FK-14B Polaris	124	
D-MSFB	Rans S-6 Coyote II	0393462	
D-MSFC	Warnke Europlane Euro III Trike	M867935	
D-MSFE	Warnke Trike	1028	
D-MSFF	Comco Ikarus C-42 Cyclone	9807-6115	
D-MSFG(1)	UPM Funplane	86011	
D-MSFG(2)	Comco Ikarus C-42B	0203-6477	
D-MSFH	Evektor EV-97 Eurostar	2004-1813	
D-MSFI	Aerostyle Breezer	028	
D-MSFK	B&F Funk FK-14 Polaris	014-009	
D-MSFL	Murphy Renegade Spirit	619	
D-MSFO	Steinbach Austro-Trike Euro IIIM	1200	
D-MSFP	Pipistrel Alpha Trainer	605AT912	
D-MSFR	Tecnam P.96 Golf 100S	180	
D-MSFS	Comco Ikarus Fox-C22	9401-3543	
D-MSFU	Tecnam P.96 Golf	11	
D-MSFV	Comco Ikarus C-42 Cyclone	9802-6080	
D-MSFW	Comco Ikarus C-42 Cyclone	0106-6365	
D-MSFZ	Comco Ikarus C-42B	unkn	
D-MSGA	Konsuprod Moskito	007	
D-MSGB	TL Ultralight TL-96 Star	01 S 99	
D-MSGC	ICP MXP-740 Savannah	unkn	
D-MSGD	Flight Design CT SW	04-08-01	
D-MSGE	Comco Ikarus C-42 Cyclone	9902-6175	
D-MSGF #	Comco Fox	unkn	
D-MSGG	Comco Ikarus C-42 Cyclone	9801-6057	
D-MSGH	Comco Ikarus C-42 Cyclone	9709-6059	
D-MSGI	Comco Ikarus C-42B	0303-6514	
D-MSGJ	Comco Ikarus C-42 Cyclone	unkn	
D-MSGK #	Comco Ikarus Fox-C22	9001-3250	
D-MSGL #	Behlen Power-Trike	86-015	
D-MSGM(1)	Comco Ikarus C-42 Cyclone	9806-6120	
D-MSGM(2)	Comco Ikarus C-42B Cyclone	1101-7135	
D-MSGO	Remos Gemini Ultra	036R	
D-MSGP	Remos G.3 Mirage	093	
D-MSGR	Zlin Savage Classic	unkn	
D-MSGS	Tandem Air Sunny Sport	44.93	
D-MSGU #	Tandem Air Sunny Targa	TA-018	
D-MSGW	Light Aero Avid Flyer	1011	
D-MSGX	Remos GX	unkn	
D-MSHA	Comco Ikarus C-42 Cyclone	9903-6172	
D-MSHB	ATEC 122 Zephyr 2000	ZP610404	
D-MSHE	Comco Ikarus Sherpa	8305-1019	
D-MSHF	Zlin Savage Classic	unkn	
D-MSHG	Comco Ikarus Sherpa I	8304-1021	
D-MSHH	WDFL Fascination	044	
D-MSHJ	Comco Ikarus C-42 Cyclone	9807-6111	
D-MSHK	Aeropro Eurofox	083000	
D-MSHL	Tecnam P.96 Golf 100S	182	
D-MSHM	Tecnam P.92 Echo	232	
D-MSHN #	Comco Ikarus Sherpa I	8307-1032	
D-MSHO	Comco Ikarus C-42	unkn	
D-MSHP	Comco Ikarus C-42 Cyclone	0001-6236	
D-MSHR(1)	Comco Ikarus Sherpa II	8311-02	
D-MSHR(2)	Autogyro Europe MTOsport	unkn	
D-MSHS	Remos G.3 Mirage	153	
D-MSHU	Pipistrel Taurus	unkn	
D-MSIA	Comco Ikarus Sherpa II	8408-1079	
D-MSIB(1)	Comco Ikarus Sherpa II	8410-1083	
D-MSIB(2)	Alisport Silent 2 Electro	2054	
	(To G-CIRK 5.15)		
D-MSIC	Comco Ikarus Sherpa II	8501-1088	
D-MSID #	Comco Ikarus Sherpa II	850 .-1089	
D-MSIE	Comco Ikarus C-42B	0210-6491	
D-MSIF	Comco Fox D	8507-FD30	
D-MSIG(2)	TL Ultralight TL-232 Condor Plus	97 C 04	
D-MSIH	Comco Fox D	8409-FD12	
D-MSIK	WDFL Dallach D4 Fascination BK	118	
D-MSIL(1)	Comco Fox D	8507-FD31	
D-MSIL(2)	Flight Design CT2SW	04.03.02	
D-MSIM	Comco Fox D	8508-FD32	
D-MSIN	WDFL Dallach D4 Fascination	064	
D-MSIO	Rans S-10S Sakota	0989060	
D-MSIP #	Comco Fox D	8503-FD24	
D-MSIQ	Fresh Breeze Simo 122	unkn	
D-MSIR (1)	Comco Ikarus Sherpa II	850 .-1090	
D-MSIR(2)	Sirius (TL-3000 ?)	unkn	
D-MSIS	Comco Fox II	8605-3018	
D-MSIT	WDFL Dallach D4 Fascination	022	
	(Sold as RP-S1832)		
D-MSIU	Remos G.3 Mirage	086	
D-MSIV	Comco Ikarus Sherpa II	8412-1075	
D-MSIW #	Comco Ikarus Sherpa II	8503-1092	
D-MSIX(1)	Comco Ikarus Sherpa II	850 .-1091	
D-MSIX(2)	Fresh Breeze Simo 122	unkn	
D-MSIZ	Comco Ikarus Sherpa II	8504-1094	
D-MSJA	B&F Funk FK-9 Mk.II (t/w)	073	
D-MSJB	TL Ultralight TL-96 Sting	unkn	
D-MSJE	Fresh Breeze Simo 122	unkn	
D-MSJF	Remos G3-600	224	
D-MSJH	B&F Funk FK-14A Polaris	unkn	
D-MSJL	Flight Design CT	99-12-03-77FR	
D-MSJN	Trixy G4-2	024-13	
	(Accident 30.3.14, repaired?)		
D-MSJO	Fresh Breeze Simo 122	unkn	
D-MSJR	NST Minimum Trike Profil 17M	206	
D-MSJS	Comco Ikarus C-42 Cyclone	9802-6054	
D-MSJT #	Fresh Breeze Simo 122	unkn	
D-MSKA	Comco Ikarus C-42 Cyclone	9807-6121	
D-MSKB	Comco Ikarus C-42 Cyclone	9710-6062	
D-MSKC	Comco Ikarus Sherpa I	8307-1037	
D-MSKC(2)	Best Off Sky Ranger	0409529	
D-MSKD(1)	Comco Ikarus Sherpa II	8406-1070	
D-MSKD(2)	Spacek SD-1 Minisport TD	94	
D-MSKE	Comco Ikarus Sherpa II	8402-1051	
D-MSKF	B&F Funk FK-9 Mk.II	055	
D-MSKG	Flight Design CT	99-03-01-48	
	(Re-regd D-MTKG)		
D-MSKH	III Sky Arrow 450TS	087S	
D-MSKI	Flight Design CT	97-07-02-04	
D-MSKJ	Comco Ikarus Sherpa II	8406-1068	
D-MSKJ(2)	Best Off Sky Ranger	unkn	
D-MSKK	TL Ultralight TL-96 Star	99 S 33	
D-MSKL	Comco Ikarus Sherpa II	8410-1082	
D-MSKM	Comco Ikarus Sherpa II	8409-10 . .	
D-MSKM(2)	Comco Ikarus C-42	unkn	
D-MSKN(2)	Albatros 64	309	
D-MSKO	Best Off Sky Ranger	unkn	
D-MSKP	Comco Ikarus Fox-C22B	9403-3558	
D-MSKQ	Comco Ikarus Fox-C22	9408-3585	
D-MSKR(1)	Comco Ikarus Sherpa II	8311-1048	
D-MSKR(2)	Comco Ikarus Sherpa II	8406-1068	
D-MSKS	Comco Ikarus Sherpa II	8403-1054	
D-MSKT(1)	Comco Ikarus Sherpa II	8408-1077	
D-MSKT(2)	Autogyro Europe MTOsport	D11S02	
D-MSKV #	Comco Ikarus Sherpa II	8407-1071	
D-MSKW(1)	Comco Ikarus Sherpa II	8405-1066	
D-MSKW(2)	Best Off Sky Ranger	470	
D-MSKX	Comco Ikarus Sherpa II	8407-1074	
D-MSKY(2)	III Sky Arrow 450TS	085S	
D-MSKY(3)	Best Off Sky Ranger	unkn	
D-MSKY(4)	Roland Z602XL	unkn	
D-MSKZ	Comco Ikarus Sherpa II	8407-1073	
D-MSLA(1)	Comco Ikarus Sherpa II	8506-1102	
D-MSLA(2)	BRM Aero Bristell	091/2014	
D-MSLB	Lohle Mustang 5151	213-12350	
D-MSLC	Comco Ikarus Sherpa II D	8507-1104	
D-MSLD	Comco Ikarus Sherpa II D	8511-1109	
D-MSLE	Comco Ikarus Sherpa II D	8606-1122	
D-MSLF	Autogyro Europe Calidus	unkn	
D-MSLG	Comco Fox D	038	
D-MSLH	Comco Ikarus C-42 Cyclone	9801-6079	OE-7041
D-MSLI (1)	Comco Ikarus Fox-C22	8607-3026	
D-MSLI(2)	Flight Design CT SW	04.04.02	
D-MSLJ	Tandem Air Sunny s.b.s.	SuS-08.94	
D-MSLK	B&F Funk FK-12 Comet	012-021	D-MTOT
D-MSLL(2)	Tecnam P.92 Echo	215	
D-MSLM	WDFL Sunwheel R	038	
D-MSLN	Konsuprod Moskito Ib	021	
D-MSLO	B&F Funk FK-12 Comet	012-015	
D-MSLP	B&F Funk FK-12 Comet	012-005	
D-MSLR	Evektor EV-97 Eurostar SL	unkn	
D-MSLS	Zenair CH-601D Zodiac	6-3650	
D-MSLT	Rans S-7 Courier	0301302	
D-MSLU	Comco Ikarus Fox-C22B	940 .-3600	
D-MSLZ	Sherwood Ranger	unkn	
D-MSMA	Comco-Ikarus C-42B	0505-6683	
D-MSMB	WDFL Sunwheel DZ	047	
D-MSMD	Plätzer Kiebitz-B	unkn	
D-MSME	Impulse 100	045	
D-MSMG(1)	Magni M-14 Scout	unkn	
D-MSMG(2)	BRM Aero Bristell	100/2014	
D-MSMH(2)#	WDFL Sunwheel	052	
	(Previously c/n 017)		
D MSMI	Comco Ikarus Fox-C22C	9602-3682	
D-MSMK(1)	Comco Ikarus C-42 Cyclone	0011-6296	
D-MSMK(2)	Fresh Breeze Simo 122	unkn	
D-MSML(2)	Albatros 64	310	
D-MSMM (1)	Rans S-12 Airaile	1292357	
D-MSMM(2)	Flight Design CT-2K	02.07.05.30	
D-MSMP	Aerospool WT-9 Dynamic	unkn	
D-MSMR	Zenair CH-701D STOL	7-9367	
D-MSMS(1)	Rans S-12 Airaile	0493406	
D-MSMS(2)	Comco Ikarus C-42	unkn	
D-MSMT(1)	Tandem Air Sunny Sport	53.93	
	(To YL-PIT .08)		
D-MSMT(2)	Technoflug Piccolo	048	
D-MSMV #	WDFL Dallach D4 Fascination	011	
D-MSMW	unidentified paramotor	unkn	
D-MSNB	Plätzer Kiebitz	212	
D-MSNG	Flight Design CT-2K	01.03.03.10	
D-MSNJ	Zenair CH-601D Zodiac	6-3792	
D-MSNK	TL Ultralight TL-96 Star	00 S 56	
D-MSNO #	Comco Ikarus Fox-C22B	unkn	
D-MSNP	Plätzer Kiebitz B	304	
D-MSNR	NST Minimum Saphir 17	M471	
D-MSNT	Comco Ikarus C-42B	0808-7004	
D-MSNU(1)	WDFL Sunwheel	unkn	
D-MSNU(2)	Magni M-24 Orion	unkn	
D-MSNW	Comco Ikarus Fox-C22C	9608-3711	
D-MSNX	Remos GX	420	
D-MSOA	Basic Fox	BF11001401	
D-MSOB(1)	Steinbach Austro-Trike Euro IIIM	1129	
D-MSOB(2)	B&F Funk FK-9 Mk.IV	09-04-USW-302	
D-MSOC	ASO Storch	11010408	
D-MSOD	Comco Ikarus Fox-C22B	9403-3547	
D-MSOE	Tandem Air Sunny s.b.s.	SuS-04.94	
D-MSOF	ASO Storch	11011408	
D-MSOG	ASO Storch	11012409	
D-MSOH(1)	NST Minimum	218	
D-MSOH(2)	Sunny Side-by-side	unkn	
D-MSOI (1)	Comco Ikarus Fox-C22B	9507-3667	
	(To Russia as RA-0034A)		

Regn	Type	C/n	Prev id
D-MSOI(2)	Best Off Sky Ranger SW	unkn	
D-MSOK	Fisher Super Koala	A01	
D-MSOL(2#)	Comco Ikarus C-42 Cyclone	9702-6039	
D-MSOM	Comco Ikarus C-42 Cyclone	9604-6004	
D-MSON	Comco Ikarus C-42B	0308-6553	
	(W/o 23.8.15)		
D-MSOO	Flight Design CT	98.02.01.21	
D-MSOP	Comco Ikarus C-42 Cyclone	9604-6005	
D-MSOQ	Zenair CH-601 Zodiac	6-3523	
D-MSOS	Schmidtler Ranger M Trike	M 868066	
D-MSOT(1)	Mantel Mono-Dragster	M 873089	
D-MSOT(2)	Comco Ikarus C-42B	unkn	
D-MSOV #	Comco Ikarus C-42 Cyclone	9507-0001	
D-MSOW	Solid Air Diamant 55dB(A) Trike	018	
D-MSPA	Urban Air UFM-13 Lambada	unkn	
	(Dam.28.2.06)		
D-MSPB	Flight Design CT LS	F-09-01-12	
D-MSPC	Rans S-6 Coyote II	0795856	
D-MSPD #	Flight Design CT-2K	unkn	
D-MSPE	Tandem Air Sunny s.b.s.	SuS-01.94	
D-MSPG #	Vidor Asso V Champion	unkn	
D-MSPH	WDFL Dallach D4 Fascination	036	
D-MSPI (1)	B&F Funk FK-12 Comet	12-042	D-MQAX
	(W/o 14.8.08)		
D-MSPI(2)	Aerospool WT-9 Dynamic	unkn	
D-MSPK	B&F Funk FK-11 (Prototype)	11912	
D-MSPL	Ultravia Pélican Sport 450S	20015/722	
D-MSPM	Dyn'Aéro MCR-01 UL	091	
D-MSPN	Take Off Merlin 1200	unkn	
D-MSPO	Flight Design CT	98.03.01.25	
D-MSPP	Albatros 52	128	
D-MSPR(1)	Ultraleichtverbund Bi 90	7373917708	
D-MSPR(2)	Aero East Europe SILA 450C	130509AEE0012	
	(Same c/n quoted as D-MMKV(2))		
D-MSPS	NST Minimum Saphir 17	465	
D-MSPT	Flight Design CT LS	F-11-08-02	
D-MSPW	Schmidtler Enduro Trike	02001	
D-MSPY	Fair Fax Trike Euro III	043	
D-MSPZ	Comco Ikarus C-42 Cyclone	9903-6181	
D-MSQG	Wezel APIS	W005	
D-MSRA	Roland 701D	7-9427	
D-MSRB	Zenair CH-601D Zodiac	6-3404/023 0697	
D-MSRD	TUL-03 Amigo	03	
D-MSRE	Best Off Sky Ranger Swift	SKR0805889	
D-MSRG	WDFL Sunrise II	025	D-MLOH
D-MSRH	Roland Z701D	7-8030 / 001	
D-MSRI	Best Off Sky Ranger	. 26B3206	
D-MSRJ	Tecnam P.92 Echo	233	
	(Same c/n as D-MSSE)		
D-MSRL(1)	Tecnam P.96 Golf	027	
D-MSRL(2)	Aerostyle Breezer B400	unkn	
D-MSRM	Tecnam P.92 Echo (Short wing)	unkn	
D-MSRO	Ultraleichtverbund Bi 90	674	
D-MSRP(1)	Tecnam P.92 Echo	131	
D-MSRP(2)	BRM Aero Bristell UL	014/2012	
D-MSRR	Tandem Air Sunny Targa	TA-001	
D-MSRS(1)	Aviasud Mistral 53	008	
D-MSRS(2)	Autogyro Europe MTOsport	unkn	
D-MSRT	WDFL Dallach D4 Fascination BK	095	
D-MSRU	Plätzer Kiebitz-B2	087	
D-MSRV	ATEC Zephyr 2000	SF 010202	
D-MSRW	Tecnam P.96 Golf 100	025	
D-MSSA	Fly Synthesis Storch	160.4	
	(W/o 17.9.12)		
D-MSSB(1)	Behlen Power-Trike Vampir	87023	
D-MSSB(2)	Flight Design CT-2K	98.06.01.34	D-MQIK
D-MSSC(1)	Eipper Quicksilver GT-400	GT 2801326	
D-MSSC(2)	Autogyro Europe MTOsport	D10S30	
D-MSSD	Comco Ikarus C-42	unkn	
D-MSSE(1)	Tecnam P.92 Echo	233	
	(Same c/n as D-MSRJ)		
D-MSSE(2)	ICP MXP-740 Savannah S	unkn	
D-MSSG	Klüver Twin Racer SX 16 Trike	503202	
D-MSSH	Evektor EV-97R Eurostar 2000	unkn	
D-MSSI	Evektor EV-97 Eurostar	2004-2121	
D-MSSJ	Tecnam P.96 Golf 100S	100	
D-MSSK	Tecnam P.96 Golf	034	
D-MSSL	Comco Ikarus Fox-C22C	9606-3717	
	(To Thailand as U-P31, 30.4.14)		
D-MSSM	ISON Tandem Airbike	unkn	
D-MSSN	Aerospool WT-9 Dynamic	DY231/2008	
D-MSSO	Tecnam P.92 Echo	227	
D-MSSP	Evektor EV-97 Eurostar 2000R	2005 2422	
D-MSSQ	Evektor EV-97 Eurostar SL	unkn	
D-MSSR #	Euro-ALA Jet Fox 91D	0011	
D-MSSS	B&F Funk FK-12 Comet	012-029	
D-MSST(1)	Fantasy Air Allegro SW	unkn	
D-MSST(2)	Fresh Breeze Simo 122	unkn	
D-MSSU	Evektor EV-97 Eurostar SL	unkn	
D-MSSV(1)	B&F Funk FK-9 Mk.IV Utility	09-04U-246	
D-MSSV(2)	Evektor EV-97 Eurostar SL	unkn	
D-MSSW	WDFL Sunwheel DZ	044	
D-MSSX	DEA Yuma 912S	1970535	
D-MSSY	Aerospool WT-9 Dynamic	DY225/2008	
D-MSSZ(1)	TL Ultralight TL-232 Condor II	97 C 03	
D-MSSZ(2)	Fresh Breeze Simo 122	unkn	
D-MSTA	TL Ultralight TL-96 Star	00 S 67	
D-MSTB	HFL Stratos 300K	300-024K	
D-MSTC	HFL Stratos 300K	300-025K	
D-MSTD	HFL Stratos 300K	300-026K	
D-MSTE(1)	Warnke Skylight Trike	1010	
D-MSTE(2)	Fantasy Air Allegro	00-701	
D-MSTF	Plätzer Kiebitz	unkn	
D-MSTG #	B&F Funk FK-9 TG Mk.II	083	
D-MSTH	Comco Ikarus C-42 Cyclone	9904-6166	
D-MSTI	Comco Ikarus Fox-C22	9309-3517	
D-MSTK	Ultraleichtverbund Bi 90	B987	
D-MSTM(1)	Flight Design CT	99.09.06.70	
D-MSTM(2)	Fresh Breeze Simo 122	unkn	
D-MSTO	NST Schwarze Trike	T285	
D-MSTP	Evektor EV-97 Eurostar	2001-1208	
D-MSTR	Remos G.3 Mirage	unkn	
D-MSTS	Remos G.3 Mirage	089	
D-MSTT(1)	NST Minimum	M250	
D-MSTT(2)	Autogyro Europe Calidus	unkn	
D-MSTU	Comco Ikarus Fox-C22	9504-3644	
D-MSTW	Fisher FP-404 Classic	C084	
D-MSTX(1)	Autogyro Europe MT-03	05G24	
D-MSTX(2)	Autogyro Europe MTOsport	unkn	
D-MSTZ	Loehle Sport Parasol	002	
D-MSUB(2)	Comco Ikarus Fox-C22C	9901-3741	
D-MSUE(1)	Kümmerle Mini-Fly-Set	1309/91-6	
D-MSUE(2)	B&F Funk FK-9 Mk.III	09-03-164	
D-MSUF	B&F Funk FK-12 Comet	12-007	
	(To 57-ADB, D-MHPM)		
D-MSUG	Comco Ikarus C-42 Cyclone	0002-6233	
D-MSUK	Best Off Sky Ranger	unkn	
	(W/o 8.9.16)		
D-MSUL	B&F Funk FK-9 Mk.IV Club	04-U319	
D-MSUN	Dallach Sunrise II	016	
D-MSUR(1)	Rans S-6 Coyote II	0391171	G-MWUM
D-MSUR(2)	Comco Ikarus C-42B	0410-6631	
D-MSUV	Sunny Sport	unkn	
D-MSUW	Comco Ikarus Fox-C22C	9804-3738	
D-MSVC	Fresh Breeze Simo 122	unkn	
D-MSVE	Comco Ikarus C-42B	0606-6829	
D-MSVG	Aerostyle Breezer	007	
D-MSVH	FUL Graffiti MA 30 Stranger	unkn	
D-MSVL	B&F Funk FK-9 Mk.IV	unkn	
D-MSVN	Zlin Trener Baby UL	001/2000	
D-MSVS(2)	Air Création GTE 582 S	7974656042	
D-MSVS(3)	Aerospool WT-9 Dynamic	unkn	
D-MSVT	Comco Ikarus Sherpa II	unkn	
D-MSVV	Remos GX	unkn	
D-MSWA(1)	WDFL Dallach D4 Fascination	058	
D-MSWA(2)	Spacek SD-1 Minisport	unkn	
D-MSWB	Tecnam P.92 Echo 100S	575	
D-MSWC(1)	Sky-Walker II	102	
D-MSWC(2)	Autogyro Europe MTOsport	unkn	
D-MSWD	Sky-Walker 1+1	26134	
D-MSWE	Sky-Walker 1+1	26135	
D-MSWF(1)	Sky-Walker 1+1	26136	
D-MSWF(2)	BRM Aero Bristell UL	1/2015-KIT	
D-MSWG	Sky-Walker 1+1	26137	
D-MSWG(2)	Evektor EV-97 Eurostar	unkn	
D-MSWH	B&F Funk FK-12 Comet floatplane	12-061	SP-YOA
	(Returned to Poland as SP-SLRM, 2012)		
D-MSWI	Sky-Walker 1+1	26138	
D-MSWJ	Comco Fox D	8506-FD28	
D-MSWK	Tecnam P.96 Golf	026	
D-MSWL	HFL Stratos 300K	300-016K	
D-MSWN	Sky-Walker 1+1	26141	
D-MSWO	Sky-Walker 1+1	26130	
D-MSWP	Sky-Walker II	144	
D-MSWQ	Sky-Walker II	145	
D-MSWR(1)	Sky-Walker 1+1	26146	
D-MSWR(2)	Autogyro Europe MTOsport	unkn	
D-MSWS	Tecnam P.96 Golf S	064	
D-MSWT	Sky-Walker II	157	
D-MSWU #	Sky-Walker II	212	
D-MSWW(2)	Aerostyle Breezer	045	
D-MSWX(1)	Sky-Walker 1+1	26124	
D-MSWX(2)	B&F / Scale Wings SW51 Mustang	unkn	
D-MSWY #	Sky-Walker 1+1	26125	
D-MSWZ	Sky-Walker 1+1	26126	
D-MSXS	Roland 701D STOL	7-9224	
D-MSXT	Celier Xenon	CAL09973R	
D-MSXW	Flight Design CT LS	F-11-11-03	
D-MSYG	Aeropro Eurofox	unkn	
	(To 17-YA and 85-LW, two acft?)		
D-MSYK	Plätzer Kiebitz-B6	162	
D-MSYL	Evektor EV-97 Eurostar SLW Sport	2016 4231	
D-MSYS	Aveko VL-3 Sprint	VL-3-108	
	(To 14-MT)		
D-MSYW	Sky-Walker II	185	
D-MSYY	Albatros 64	127	
D-MSYZ	Lohle Mustang 5151	001	
D-MSZC	Autogyro Europe Calidus	unkn	
D-MSZR	Plätzer Kiebitz	291	
D-MSZT	Tandem Air Sunny Sport	012.06.04 SuS	
D-MSZW #	UPM Cobra Trike	920116	
D-MSZZ	Remos GX	389	
D-MTAA(2)	Comco Ikarus Fox-C22	9706-3728	
D-MTAB(1)	Pioneer Flightstar	535	
D-MTAB(2)	Fresh Breeze Simo 122	unkn	
D-MTAC(2)	WDFL Sunwheel R	043	
D-MTAD(2)	Comco Ikarus Fox-C22C	9706-3730	
D-MTAE	Pioneer Flightstar	538	
D-MTAF(1)	Pioneer Flightstar	539	
	(Re-regd D-MIUS)		
D-MTAF(2)	B&F Funk FK-9 Mk.III	09-03-116	
	(Possibly ex 31 AI/F-JIAI, D-MXBV)		
D-MTAG	Pioneer Flightstar	540	
D-MTAH(2)	Comco Ikarus Fox-C22	9205-3398	
D-MTAH(3)	B&F Funk FK-14 Polaris	070	
D-MTAI(1)	Autogyro Europe MT-03	05G03	
D-MTAI(2)	Autogyro Europe MTOsport	unkn	
D-MTAJ	Tandem Air Sunny s.b.s.	03.94	
D-MTAK	Pioneer Flightstar	544	D-MTAL(1)
D-MTAL(1)	Pioneer Flightstar	544	
	(Re-regd D-MTAK)		
D-MTAL(2)	Comco Ikarus C-42 Cyclone	9706-6038	
D-MTAM(1)	Pioneer Flightstar	545	
	(Re-regd D-MOLI)		
D-MTAM(2)	WDFL Sunwheel	049	
D-MTAN	Pioneer Flightstar	553	
D-MTAO	Autogyro Europe Calidus	unkn	
D-MTAP	B&F Funk FK-12 Comet	012-045	
D-MTAQ	Pioneer Flightstar	549	
D-MTAR	Pioneer Flightstar	550	
D-MTAS	Pioneer Flightstar	551	
	(C/n now 030703 or change of type?)		
D-MTAT	Comco Ikarus C-42B	0405-6598	
	(To EI-ETB, 8.11)		
D-MTAU	Pioneer Flightstar	543	
D-MTAV	Tandem Air Sunny Targa	002	
D-MTAW(1)	Comco Ikarus C-42 Cyclone	unkn	
D-MTAW(2)	Autogyro Europe MTOsport	unkn	
D-MTAX	Klüver Racer SX 12 Trike	078809	
D-MTAY	Comco Ikarus Fox-C22B	9404-3576	
D-MTAZ	Klüver Twin Racer Trike	233109	

Reg	Type	C/N	Notes
D-MTBA(1)	Pioneer Flightstar IISC	374	
	(To YL-CDJ)		
D-MTBA(2)	Comco Ikarus Fox-C22C	9705-3727	
D-MTBB	B&F Funk FK-12 Comet	012-023	
D-MTBC	Warnke Skylight Trike	043	
D-MTBD	Comco Ikarus Fox-C22	9411-3616	
D-MTBE #	Comco Ikarus Fox-C22B	9409-3617	
D-MTBF	Comco Ikarus Fox-C22C	9607-3712	
D-MTBG #	LO-120S	022	
D-MTBI (1)	Autogyro Europe MTOsport	unkn	
D-MTBI (2)	Comco Ikarus C-42C	unkn	
D-MTBJ	NST Minimum	M536	
D-MTBK	Comco Ikarus Fox-C22	9306-3523	
D-MTBL	Autogyro Europe MT-03	04G06	
D-MTBO ?	Flight Design CT	unkn	
D-MTBO ?	Autogyro Europe MTOsport	unkn	
D-MTBQ	Behlen Trike	87020	
D-MTBR	Plätzer Kiebitz	226	
D-MTBS	LO-120	008A	
D-MTBT	B&F Funk FK-12 Comet	012-033	
D-MTBW	Comco Ikarus C-42 Cyclone	9809-6134	
D-MTBZ(1)	Comco Ikarus C-42 Cyclone	0002-6255	
	(Re-regd D-MGHB)		
D-MTBZ(2)	Tecnam P.92 Echo Light	unkn	
D-MTCA	Comco Ikarus Fox-C22C	9411-3615	
D-MTCB	Flight Design CT-2K	00.02.04.86	
D-MTCC	Flight Design CT	98.04.03.30	
D-MTCD	Rotortec Cloud Dancer	22922/403-08	
D-MTCF #	Tecnam P.92 Echo	546	
	(Possibly to Australia as 24-4867)		
D-MTCG	Autogyro Europe MT-03	D06G05	
D-MTCH	Behlen Power Trike Vampir II	0025/83	
D-MTCI	Air-Light Wild Thing	97 02 009	(PH-3A1(1))
D-MTCL	Trendak Tercel	unkn	
D-MTCO	Autogyro Europe MTOsport	unkn	
D-MTCR	Remos G.3/600 Mirage	148	
D-MTCS(1)	Autogyro Europe MT-03	04G15	
D-MTCS(2)	Remos Gemini Ultra B	037	
D-MTCT #	Flight Design CT	98.09.01.37	
D-MTCV	Flight Design CT	98.02.02.22	D-MWPN
	(Damaged in f/l 7.6.14)		
D-MTDB	Autogyro Europe Cavalon	V00132	
D-MTDC	Comco Ikarus C-42 Cyclone	9801-6060	OE-7050
	(Cld by 5.11, to D-MMUU)		
D-MTDD	B&F Funk FK-10	001	
D-MTDI	Flight Design CT	unkn	
D-MTDK	Aerostyle Breezer CR	72	
D-MTDL #	Flight Design CT	00.09.01.17	
D-MTDN	Comco Ikarus Fox-C22B	9110-3359	
D-MTDP	Rans S-6S Coyote II	0795860	
D-MTDX	Comco Ikarus Fox-C22B	9406-3583	
D-MTEA	Comco Ikarus Fox-C22C	9509-3680	
D-MTEB(1)	Comco Ikarus Fox-C22B	9601-3698	
D-MTEB(2)#	Autogyro Europe Calidus	D10C15	
D-MTEC	Light Aero Avid Flyer D	1358	
D-MTED	Sky-Walker II	262	
D-MTEE	Plätzer Kiebitz B	127	
D-MTEF	Ikarusflug Eurofox	048098	
D-MTEG	Comco Ikarus Fox-C22C	9804-3737	
D-MTEH	Tecnam P.96 Golf 100	120	
D-MTEI	Rans S-6 Coyote II	895879	
D-MTEJ	Rans S-6 Coyote II	10971174 S	
D-MTEK	Comco Ikarus C-42 Cyclone	9705-6028	
D-MTEN	Eurofly Viper / Hazard 10	unkn	
D-MTES(1)	Air-Light Wild Thing	024	
D-MTES(2)#	Fresh Breeze Simo 122	unkn	
D-MTET	Autogyro Europe MT-03	unkn	
D-MTEU	Murphy Renegade Spirit	unkn	
D-MTEV #	Klüver Twin Racer SX 16 Trike	836910	
D-MTEX	Plätzer Kiebitz B	341	
D-MTEZ	Comco Ikarus C-42 Cyclone	0004-6232	
D-MTFB	Autogyro Europe MT-03	unkn	
D-MTFC	Comco Ikarus Fox-C22B	9403-3557	
D-MTFD	B&F Funk FK-9 Mk.II	09-126	
D-MTFF	Comco Ikarus C-42 Cyclone	9711-6092	
D-MTFG	Fresh Breeze Simo 122	unkn	
D-MTFH	Comco Ikarus C-42 Cyclone	0010-6291	
	(W/o 5.6.16)		
D-MTFI	Autogyro Europe MTOsport	unkn	
D-MTFJ #	Warnke Skylight Trike	SI 032	
D-MTFK	B&F Funk FK-9 Mk.III Utility Smart	09-04U-299	
D-MTFL	Comco Ikarus Fox-C22C	9611-3720	
D-MTFM(1)	Autogyro Europe MT-03	unkn	
D-MTFM(2)	Autogyro Europe MTOsport	D07G28	
	(To LN-YUR, 8.12)		
D-MTFM(3)	ELA Aviacion ELA-07	unkn	
D-MTFP	Zenair CH-602XL Zodiac	9519	
D-MTFR	Autogyro Europe MTOsport	unkn	
D-MTFS	Fresh Breeze Simo 122	unkn	
D-MTFT	Rans S-12 XL Airaile	06950613	
D-MTFU	Trendak Taifun	L22115CD	
D-MTFW	Aerostyle Breezer	030	
D-MTFZ	Tecnam P.96 Golf	021	
D-MTGA	Comco Ikarus Fox-C22	9109-3354	
D-MTGB #	B&F Funk FK-9 Mk.II TG	041	
	(W/o 6.8.12)		
D-MTGE	Tecnam P.92 Echo	118	
D-MTGG	Remos G.3 Mirage	077	
D-MTGH	Comco Ikarus C-42 Cyclone	9903-6168	
D-MTGI	Comco Ikarus C-42B	1311-7291	
D-MTGJ #	Autogyro Europe MT-03	unkn	
D-MTGM	Seiffert Mini II	FO 10189	
D-MTGN	Aerospool WT-9 Dynamic	unkn	
D-MTGO	Autogyro Europe MTOsport	unkn	
D-MTGP	Fresh Breeze Simo 122	unkn	
D-MTGS	TL Ultralight TL-232 Condor Plus	02 C 01	
D-MTGT	Evektor EV-97 Eurostar 2000R	unkn	
D-MTGX	Remos GX	392	
D-MTGY	Autogyro Europe MTOsport	unkn	
D-MTGZ	Autogyro Europe Calidus 09	unkn	
	(Used as test marks including c/n SE09C01 to SE-VNE)		
D-MTHA	Plätzer Kiebitz B	086	
D-MTHB	ATEC 321 Faeta	unkn	
D-MTHC	Dova DV-1 Skylark	07/20	
D-MTHE	Dallach Sunrise IIa	024	
D-MTHG	Bek Me 109R replica	007	
D-MTHH #	Albatros SX	506	
	(To Russia, possibly RA-0191A)		
D-MTHI	Eipper Quicksilver MX	4315	
D-MTHJ	Colomban MC-30 Luciole	153	
D-MTHK	Autogyro Europe MTOsport	unkn	
D-MTHL	Comco Ikarus C-42 Cyclone	9709-6040	
D-MTHM(1)	Comco Ikarus C-42 Cyclone	9805-6083	
D-MTHM(2)	Autogyro Europe Cavalon	V00122	
D-MTHN	Aeropro Eurofox	08900	
D-MTHO(1)	Autogyro Europe MT-03	04G11	
D-MTHO(2)	Autogyro Europe MTOsport	unkn	
D-MTHR	Zenair CH-601RD Zodiac	6-8052	
D-MTHS(1)	WDFL Sunwheel R	040	
D-MTHS(2)	Mark-Flug Seahawk UL-II	unkn	
D-MTHU	Albatros SX	505	
D-MTHW	Ultraleichtverbund Bi 90	21001	
D-MTIA	Autogyro Europe MTOsport	unkn	
D-MTIB	Solid Air Diamant Twin B / Pico		
D-MTIC	WDFL Dallach D4 Fascination	052	
	(Was c/n 046 originally)		
D-MTIF	Aviasud Mistral	012	
D-MTIG	Tecnam P.92 Echo	216	
D-MTII #	Schönleber Trike Speed 14	011093	
D-MTIK	Evektor EV-97 Eurostar SL	2008 3510	
D-MTIL(1)	Comco Ikarus Fox-C22B	9406-3599	
D-MTIL(2)	Fly Synthesis Storch 503	246	I-5800
D-MTIM(1)	Kappa KP-2U Sova	unkn	
D-MTIM(2)	Comco Ikarus C-42B	0906-7043	
D-MTIP	Klüver Kaiman Trike	076809	
D-MTIR	Rans S-6ES Coyote II	11061780 S	
D-MTIS	Tecnam P.92 Echo	288	
D-MTIT	Plätzer Kiebitz-B2	080	
D-MTIW	Fantasy Air Allegro	01-408	
D-MTIY	WDFL Sunwheel R	012	
D-MTJA(1)	Autogyro Europe MT-03	unkn	
D-MTJA(2)	Autogyro Europe MTOsport	unkn	
D-MTJG	Behlen Power-Trike II Hazard 15	93001	
D-MTJK	Autogyro Europe MTOsport	unkn	
D-MTJW	Dyn'Aéro MCR-01	96	
D-MTKB	Flight Design CT	98.03.02.26	
D-MTKD	Aerospool WT-9 Dynamic	DY004 01	
D-MTKF(1)	Pioneer Flightstar I	980316	
D-MTKF(2)	Pioneer Flightstar	060201	
D-MTKG #	Flight Design CT	99.03.01.48	D-MSKG
D-MTKH	EEL ULF-2	36	
D-MTKK	Aerospool WT-9 Dynamic	DY104/2005	
D-MTKL	ATEC Zephyr 2000	ZP 540302	
D-MTKM	WDFL Dallach D4 Fascination	033	
D-MTKN	B&F Funk FK-9 Mk.II	008	
D-MTKP	B&F Funk FK-14A Polaris	14-111	
D-MTKR #	Comco Ikarus Fox-C22	9209-3431	
	(W/o 12.9.10)		
D-MTKS	Air Light Wild Thing 3300	unkn	
D-MTLB #	Flight Design CT SW	unkn	
D-MTLD	Schönleber DS Lotus KS 16 Trike	030589	
D-MTLF	Tecnam P.92 Echo	205	
D-MTLH	Autogyro Europe MT-03	unkn	
D-MTLI	HFL Stratos 300	300-029	
D-MTLL	Aeropro Eurofox	12002	
D-MTLM	Tandem Air Sunny	27-92	
D-MTLR	Autogyro Europe MTOsport	unkn	
D-MTLS	Flight Design CT LS	unkn	
D-MTLT	Comco Ikarus Fox-C22C	unkn	
D-MTLU	TL Ultralight TL-232 Condor	98 C 07	
D-MTLV #	B&F Funk FK-9 Mk IV	unkn	
D-MTLW	B&F Funk FK-12 Comet	012-27	
	(To 67-AAT/F-JZPE)		
D-MTLW(2)	Aerostyle Breezer	039	
D-MTMA	NST Minimum	M312	
D-MTMB	Comco Ikarus C-42 Cyclone	0009-6276	
D-MTMD	Aerospool WT-9 Dynamic	DY006 01	
D-MTME	Comco Ikarus C-42	unkn	
D-MTMG	Aerostyle Breezer	023	
D-MTMH(1)	Striker Silence	001	
D-MTMH(2)	Striker Silence	20	
D-MTMK	Flight Design CT SW	05-01-03	
D-MTMM(2)	Comco Ikarus C-42 Cyclone	0008-6287	
D-MTMM(3)	Dova DV-1 Skylark	153/12	
D-MTMN	Striker Silence SA.180	003	
D-MTMO	Striker Silence SA.180	002	
D-MTMR	WDFL Dallach D4 Fascination	090	
D-MTMS	ATEC Zephyr	SF 540600	
D-MTMT	Zenair CH-601D Zodiac	6-8047/004 0097	
D-MTMU	Flight Design CT	98-11-01-40	D-MRJR
D-MTMW	Sport IXX / Epsilon 5 Grosse 31	unkn	
D-MTMY	Autogyro Europe MTOsport	unkn	
D-MTMZ	Autogyro Europe MTOsport	unkn	
D-MTNN	Roland Z602	Z-6547	
	(W/o 7.9.14)		
D-MTNR(1)	Celier Xenon	unkn	
D-MTNR(2)	Aerospool WT-9 Dynamic	DY525/2015	
D-MTNS	Tecnam P.92 Echo 2000S	616	
D-MTNT	Comco Ikarus Fox-C22	950 .-3645	
D-MTOA #	Autogyro Europe MTOsport	unkn	
D-MTOB	Autogyro Europe MTOsport	unkn	
D-MTOE	Evektor EV-97 Eurostar	2002-1404	
D-MTOF(1)	Take Off Maximum Hazard 15M	T033080	
D-MTOF(2)	Drachenstudio Royal 912S	unkn	
D-MTOG	Tecnam P.92 Echo	117	
D-MTOH	Technoflug Piccolo BM	103	
D-MTOK	Autogyro Europe MTOsport	unkn	
D-MTOL	Comco Ikarus C-42 Cyclone	9904-6186	
D-MTOM	Comco Ikarus C-42 Cyclone	0007-6271	
D-MTOO	Autogyro Europe MTOsport	unkn	
D-MTOP(1)	B&F Funk FK-9 Mk.II	082	
D-MTOP(2)	B&F Funk FK-9 Mk.III Clubman	001	
D-MTOR	Fresh Breeze Simo 122	unkn	
D-MTOS(1)	Tandem Air Sunny Sport	18.91	
D-MTOS(2)	Autogyro Europe MTOsport	D08S01	
D-MTOT #	B&F Funk FK-12 Comet	12-021	
	(Re-regd D-MSLK)		
D-MTOV	Air-Light Wild Thing	041	
D-MTOW	Aeropro Eurofox	19406	
D-MTOX(1)	Autogyro Europe MT-03	04G01	
D-MTOX(2)	Autogyro Europe MTOsport	unkn	
D-MTOY(2)	Evektor EV-97 Eurostar	99 05 07	

Reg	Type	Serial	Notes
D-MTPA(1)	Sky-Walker 1+1	26117	
D-MTPA(2)	Zlin Savage Classic	155	
D-MTPB	Comco Ikarus C-42B	0409-6628	
D-MTPC	Tecnam P.92 Echo	175	
D-MTPE	Flight Design CT LS	F-10-02-02	
D-MTPH #	Tecnam P.92 Echo	unkn	
D-MTPK	B&F Funk FK-9 Mk.III	09-106	
D-MTPL	Roko Aero NG6 UL	unkn	
D-MTPP	Comco Ikarus C-42B	1304-7245	
D-MTPR	Fisher Classic	unkn	
D-MTPS	Comco Ikarus Fox-C22	9501-3655	
D-MTPT	Fresh Breeze Monster	704016 D41	
D-MTPW	Pipistrel Taurus	117	
D-MTRA	Aeropro Eurofox	09800	
D-MTRB	Comco Ikarus C-42B	0303-6518	
D-MTRC	Autogyro Europe MT-03	unkn	
D-MTRD	Comco Ikarus C-42 Cyclone	0002-6228	
D-MTRE	Fresh Breeze Simo 122	unkn	
D-MTRF #	Autogyro Europe MT-03	05G21	
D-MTRG	Comco Ikarus Fox-C22C	9401-3536	D-MWZL
D-MTRH	Comco Ikarus C-42 Cyclone	9809-6128	
D-MTRI	Ikarusflug Eurofox Pro	027096	
D-MTRK	Zlin Savage Classic	078	
D-MTRL	Comco Ikarus C-42 Cyclone	9607-6003	
D-MTRM(1)	Autogyro Europe MT-03	04G07	
D-MTRM(2)	Autogyro Europe MTOsport	unkn	
D-MTRN	Autogyro Europe MTOsport	unkn	
D-MTRO	Pipistrel Taurus	unkn	
D-MTRP(1)	Fisher Classic	unkn	
D-MTRP(2)	Autogyro Europe MTOsport	unkn	
D-MTRR	Ekolot JK-05 Junior	unkn	
D-MTRS(1)	Eipper Quicksilver	3898	
D-MTRS(2)	Autogyro Europe MT-03	unkn	
D-MTRS(3)	Trendak Tercel	unkn	
D-MTRT	Comco Ikarus Fox-C22	9407-3586	
D-MTRV	Comco Ikarus C-42B	0211-6498	
D-MTRW	B&F Funk FK-9 Mk.II	014	
D-MTRX	Trixy G 4-2 R	001-11	
D-MTRY	Autogyro Europe MTOsport	unkn	
D-MTRZ	Autogyro Europe MTOsport	unkn	
D-MTSA	Solid Air Twin Diamant Trike	002	
D-MTSB	B&F Funk FK-9 Mk.II	035	
D-MTSC	Autogyro Europe MT-03	unkn	
D-MTSD	Murphy Renegade Spirit	483	
D-MTSF	Plätzer Kiebitz B	097	
D-MTSG	Autogyro Europe MTOsport	unkn	
D-MTSH	Comco Ikarus C-42B	0404-6601	
D-MTSI	Comco Ikarus C-42 Cyclone	9905-6188	
D-MTSK	Fantasy Air Allegro	00-402	
D-MTSL	Remos G.3 Mirage	088	
D-MTSM	Comco Ikarus Fox-C22B (floatplane)	9406-3594	
D-MTSR	Celier Xenon 2	unkn	
D-MTSS	Rans S-6 Coyote II	0395782	
D-MTST	Behlen Power-Trike	84003	
D-MTSV	Air Light WT-01 Wild Thing	068	
D-MTSW	Remos G.3 Mirage	167	
D-MTSX	AirLony Skylane	46/2011	
D-MTTA(1)	Pioneer Flightstar	385	
	(To Denmark as 9-25)		
D-MTTA(2)	Plätzer Kiebitz	unkn	
D-MTTB	Remos G.3 Mirage	149	
D-MTTC(1)	Pioneer Flightstar	unkn	
D-MTTC(2)	Comco Ikarus Fox-C22	9106-3338	D-MGTL
D-MTTD	Aerospool WT-9 Dynamic	DY467/2013	
D-MTTF(1)	Pioneer Flightstar	379	
D-MTTF(2)	Autogyro Europe MT-03	unkn	
D-MTTG	Remos GX	358	
D-MTTL	Remos GX	267	
D-MTTM	Evektor EV-97 Eurostar	2000-0610	
D-MTTO(1)	Alpi Aviation Pioneer 200	155	
D-MTTO(2)	Breezer	unkn	
D-MTTP(2)	Rans S-6ES Coyote II	019811991 ES	
D-MTTR(1)	Ultraleichtverbund Bi 90	3916759	
D-MTTR(2)	Autogyro Europe MTOsport	unkn	
D-MTTS	Air-Light Wild Thing	055	
D-MTTT	Loehle P5151 Mustang	004	
	(Painted as "VF-X")		
D-MTTU	Flight Design CT SW	unkn	
D-MTTV #	Comco Ikarus Fox-C22	9208-3419	
D-MTTW	Flight Design CT SW	unkn	
D-MTTZ	Autogyro Europe MTOsport	unkn	
D-MTUA	Comco Ikarus C-42	unkn	
D-MTUB	Comco Ikarus C-42 Cyclone	0003-6247	
D-MTUC	Pipistrel Virus SW100 survey acft	unkn	
D-MTUD	B&F Funk FK-6	002	
D-MTUG	Bailey N.Moyes Dragonfly	SN106	
D-MTUH	Plätzer Kiebitz	176	
D-MTUI	Tecnam P.92 Echo	261	
D-MTUK(1)	Autogyro Europe MT-03	unkn	
D-MTUK(2)	Autogyro Europe MTOsport	unkn	
	(W/o 7.8.09)		
D-MTUL	Autogyro Europe MT-03	unkn	
D-MTUN	Zlin Savage	113	
D-MTUS	Comco Ikarus Fox-C22B	9507-3666	
D-MTUT	Aerostyle Breezer	032	
D-MTUX	unidentified paramotor	unkn	
D-MTVA	Autogyro Europe MTOsport	unkn	
D-MTVG	Comco Ikarus C-42B	0807-7003	
D-MTVM	WDFL Sunwheel R	016	
D-MTVS	Pipistrel Virus SW100	780	
D-MTVV	Comco Ikarus C-42 Cyclone	9705-6061	
D-MTVW	Comco Ikarus C-42 Cyclone	0101-6279	
D-MTWA(1)	Air Light Wild Thing	unkn	
D-MTWA(2)#	Autogyro Europe MTOsport	unkn	
D-MTWD	Ikarusflug Eurofox Pro	054098	
D-MTWE	Sky-Walker II	396	
D-MTWF	Comco Ikarus C-42 Cyclone	0109-6329	
D-MTWH	Comco Ikarus C-42	unkn	
D-MTWI	Kolb Twinstar Mk.III	M III-136	
D-MTWL	Comco Ikarus Fox-C22B	9404-3561	
D-MTWO	WDFL Sunwheel	022	
D-MTWP	Comco Ikarus C-42 Cyclone	9908-6198	
D-MTWR	Comco Ikarus C-42 Cyclone	9903-6173	
D-MTWS	Comco Ikarus C-42 Cyclone	9908-6202	
	(To EI-FGG)		
D-MTWT	Air-Light Wild Thing	001	
D-MTWX	Drachenstudio Kecur / EOS 15	unkn	
	(Crashed 27.7.13)		
D-MTWZ(2)	Drachenstudio Piccolo	003	
D-MTXL	Autogyro Europe MTOsport	unkn	
D-MTXX	Bautek Skycruiser / Pico L	unkn	
D-MTYA	Zlin Savage Cub	242	
D-MTYC	Comco Ikarus C-42B	1203-7185	
D-MTYP	BRM Aero Bristell UL	071/2013	
	(Re-regd D-MKFK(2))		
D-MTZA	Magni M-24 Orion VIP	unkn	
D-MTZZ	Comco Ikarus C-42 Cyclone	0105-6352	
D-MUAB	Sky-Walker II	500	
D-MUAC #	Fisher FP-404 Classic	4065	
D-MUAE #	Comco Ikarus Fox-C22	8812-3183	
D-MUAF	Remos G-3 Mirage	173	HB-WAF
D-MUAG	Comco Ikarus C-42 Cyclone	9803-6138	
D-MUAK	Air-Light Wild Thing	044	
D-MUAS	Aerostyle Breezer	024	
D-MUAT	Plätzer Kiebitz-B	219	
	(To OO-F64, D-MBOX, 83-GAA)		
D-MUAV	Autogyro Europe MTOsport	unkn	
D-MUAW	Aerospool WT-9 Dynamic	DY418/2011	
D-MUAZ	Behlen Power Trike II	91023	
D-MUBA	Aeropro Eurofox	unkn	
D-MUBB	Warnke Skylight Trike	036	
D-MUBF #	Rans S-10S Sakota	1189068	
D-MUBI	Rans S-12 Airaile	01970771	
D-MUBJ	Aeroprakt A-22L2 Vision	491	
D-MUBK	Comco Ikarus Fox-C22	9403-3548	
D-MUBP	Sport Parasol	inkn	
D-MUBS(1)	Air-Light Wild Thing	015	
D-MUBS(2)	Comco Ikarus C-42B	unkn	
D-MUBT #	Comco Ikarus Fox-C22B	9404-3563	
D-MUBU #	Magni gyro	unkn	
D-MUCB	Sky-Walker II	309	
D-MUCC	B&F FK-14B2 Polaris (t/w)	unkn	
D-MUCE	Air-Light Wild Thing	022	
D-MUCH	Comco Ikarus Fox-C22	9508-3687	
D-MUCI	WDFL Sunwheel R	018	
D-MUCK	Scheibe Uli 1	5215	
D-MUCL	Aerospool WT-9 Dynamic Basic	DY053/2004	
	(W/o 24.7.16)		
D-MUCS	Remos G.3 Mirage	113	
D-MUCT	Flight Design CT SW	07-05-20	C-ISEY
D-MUCX	Air Création Skypper / BioniX	unkn	
D-MUCY	Roland Z-602	unkn	
D-MUCZ	Bek Me 109 R	004	
D-MUDB	Aerostyle Breezer B400 UL	unkn	
D-MUDD	Fair Fax Trike Euro III	1712	
D-MUDI	Klüver Bison Profil 19 Trike	M3485733	
D-MUDK	Comco Ikarus C-42 Cyclone	0103-6307	
D-MUDM	UPM-Trike	880051	
D-MUDO	Plätzer Motte B-2	49	
D-MUDO(2)	B&F Funk FK-9 Mk.IV	04-365	
D-MUDP #	Comco Ikarus Fox-C22	8905-3196	
D-MUDR	Deewald Sunny Sport	026-05-07 SP	
D-MUDS	Comco Ikarus C-42B	unkn	
D-MUEC	Evektor EV-97 Eurostar 99	99 0403	
D-MUED(1)	B&F Funk FK-9 Mk.III	09-111	
	(To 41-KP, 37-XE, 72-JL, 62-ARD)		
D-MUED(2)	B&F Funk FK-12 Comet	012-022	
	(To 56-LV/F-JXQR, 71-LP)		
D-MUEE	Comco Ikarus C-42B	0407-6613	
D-MUEF	Ikarusflug Eurofox Pro	050098	
D-MUEH	Remos G-3 Mirage	unkn	
D-MUEK	Ikarusflug Eurofox Bugrad	045098	
D-MUEL	Aerospool WT-9 Dynamic	DY160/2006	
D-MUEN	Sky-Walker 1+1	156	
D-MUEP	ATEC 122 Zephyr 2000	Z070199A	
D-MUES	NST Minimum Santana Trike	M329	
D-MUFD	Comco Ikarus Fox-C22	9503-3631	
D-MUFE	Comco Ikarus Fox-C22	9303-3495	
D-MUFF	Comco Ikarus C-42 Cyclone	0010-6289	
D-MUFG	Comco Ikarus C-42 Cyclone	9704-6013	
D-MUFH	Tecnam P.92 Echo S 100	587	
D-MUFI	Comco Ikarus C-42B	1102-7145	
D-MUFK	B&F Funk FK-9TG Mk.III	09-03-096	
D-MUFL	Light Aero Avid Flyer	1457D	
D-MUFM	Tecnam P.92 Echo	320	
D-MUFN	ATEC Zephyr	Z 500202A	
D-MUFO	Comco Ikarus Fox-C22	8709-3083	
D-MUFP	Helisport CH-77 Ranabot	unkn	
D-MUFR	unidentified paramotor	unkn	
D-MUFS	B&F Funk FK-9 Mk.III	09-03-099	
D-MUFW	Comco Ikarus C-42B	0310-6579	
	(Re-regd D-MVVC)		
D-MUFY	Plätzer Kiebitz	366	
D-MUFZ	Schindler Enduro 1150 / Kiss 450	unkn	
D-MUGH	Comco Ikarus C-42 Cyclone	0106-6354	
D-MUGI	ATEC Zephyr 2000	SF 070301	
D-MUGK #	Plätzer Kiebitz-B2	117	
D-MUGL	Fantasy Air Allegro 2000	00-407	
D-MUGO	Comco Ikarus C-42	0206-6422	
D-MUGS	WDFL Sunwheel R	041	
D-MUGY	B&F Funk FK-9 Mk.III	09-03-186	
D-MUHA	Comco Ikarus C-42 Cyclone	9906-6194	
D-MUHB(1)	Pioneer Flightstar	unkn	
D-MUHB(2)	Autogyro Europe Cavalon	V00183	
D-MUHC #	Flight Design CT SW	unkn	
D-MUHE	Plätzer Kiebitz	unkn	
D-MUHF	Comco Ikarus Fox-C22	9403-3584	
D-MUHG	Remos G.3 Mirage	048	
D-MUHH	Comco Ikarus C-42B "2"	0907-7056	
	(W/o 23.8.15)		
D-MUHI	Ultraleichtverbund Bi 90	21000	
D-MUHK #	Light Aero Avid Flyer STOL	1521D	
	(Sold Thailand as U-K11, 2011)		
D-MUHL(2)	Mitchell Wing B	AB-01	
D-MUHM	Apis BEE 15 MB	A029MB05	
D-MUHR	Air-Light Wild Thing	003	
D-MUHS	Rans S-10S Sakota	0790109	OY-GJA
D-MUHU	Ultravia Pélican Sport 450S	20017	
D-MUID	Comco Ikarus C-42 Cyclone	9612-6014	
D-MUIF(2)	Ikarusflug Eurofox Basic	033097	
D-MUJF #	Euro-ALA Jet Fox 97	unkn	
D-MUJH	Comco Ikarus C-42B	0805-6973	

Reg	Type	c/n	Notes
D-MUJR	Aerostyle Breezer	011	
D-MUKA	Flight Design CT-2K	02.07.03.28	
D-MUKB	Tecnam P.92 Echo 100S	506	
D-MUKD	Comco Ikarus Fox-C22B	9702-3704	
D-MUKE(1)	Fair Fax Trike	015	
D-MUKE(2)	Comco Ikarus C-42B	0504-6667	
D-MUKF	Air-Light Wild Thing	034	
D-MUKG	Comco Ikarus C-42 Cyclone	9909-6199	
D-MUKH	Comco Ikarus C-42	0204-6415	
D-MUKI (1)	Schmidtler Ranger M Trike	18-33	
D-MUKI(2)	Comco Ikarus Fox-C22C	unkn	
D-MUKJ	Alpi Avn Pioneer 200	unkn	
D-MUKK	Warnke Puma Sprint Trike	D006	
D-MUKL(1)	Scheibe Uli 1	5212	
D-MUKL(2)	WDFL Dallach D4 Fascination BK	071	
D-MUKM	EEL ULF-2	007	
D-MUKO	Evektor EV-97 Eurostar 2000	2000-0811	
D-MUKP	Silent Targa 2	unkn	
D-MUKR	Schindler Enduro 54PS / XP15	unkn	
D-MUKS	Urban Air UFM-13 Lambada	20/13	
D-MUKU(1)	Micro Star	01	
D-MUKU(2)#	Autogyro Europe MTOsport	unkn	
D-MUKW	Rans S-6 Coyote II	1294702	N8046U
D-MUKY	Moskito Ib	018	
D-MULA(1)	Scheibe Uli I	5214	
D-MULA(2)	Autogyro Europe MT-03	unkn	
D-MULA(3)	B&F Funk FK-9 Mk.V ELA SW	09-05-464	
D-MULB(1)	UPM Cobra Trike	900092	
	(Same c/n also quoted for D-MBOY)		
D-MULB(2)	Air Light Wild Thing	unkn	
D-MULC	Comco Ikarus C-42C	1403-7288	
	(W/o 11.9.14)		
D-MULE	Light Aero Avid Flyer D	1402 D	
D-MULF	B&F Funk FK-9 Mk.IV Utility	04-U-222	
D-MULG #	Zenair CH-601D Zodiac	6-9225	
D-MULH	EDM Aerotec CoAX 2D	2	
D-MULI (1)	Scheibe Uli 1	5203	
D-MULI (2)	Comco Ikarus C-42B	0403-6587	
	(Re-regd D-MIKP)		
D-MULI(3)	Comco Ikarus C-42B	1003-7101	
D-MULJ	Plätzer Kiebitz-B4	108	
D-MULK	Comco Ikarus C-42 Cyclone	9706-6043	
D-MULL	TL Ultralight TL-232 Condor Plus	01 C 01	
D-MULM	Fresh Breeze Simo 122	unkn	
D-MULN	Klüver Twin Racer Trike	232109	
D-MULO	LO-120S	015A	
D-MULP	Comco Ikarus C-42 Cyclone	9708-6052	
D-MULR	Ultraleichtverbund Bi 90	940	
D-MULS #	Flugschule Skyrider Sonic Smart / Pico	unkn	
D-MULT	NST Minimum	359	
D-MULV	Remos G3 Mirage	072	
D-MULW	Comco Ikarus C-42 Cyclone	0001-6220	
D-MULY(2)	Tecnam P.96 Golf	163	
D-MULY(?)	Remos G-3 Mirage	unkn	
D-MULZ	Comco Ikarus C-42B	0302-6524	
D-MUMA #	Klüver Twin Racer SX 16 Trike	117106	
D-MUMD #	Comco Ikarus C-42 Cyclone	9809-6143	
D-MUMG	Air-Light Wild Thing	065	
	(W/o 7.6.08)		
D-MUMI(1)	Tecnam P.92 Echo	295	
	(For sale in Russia 7.16)		
D-MUMI(2)	Aerospool WT-9 Dynamic	DY513/2014	
D-MUML	Evektor EV-97 Eurostar	2001-1202	
D-MUMM	WDFL Dallach D4 Fascination	045	
D-MUMO #	Lohle Mustang 5151	006	
D-MUMS	Plätzer Kiebitz-B8	107	
D-MUMU	B&F Funk FK-9 Mk.II	019	
D-MUMY(1)	Behlen Power-Trike II Focus 20	85029	
D-MUMY(2)	Comco Ikarus C-42	0008-6274	
	(Same c/n quoted as D-MPHN, ex?)		
D-MUMZ	EEL ULF-2	24	
D-MUNA	Schönleber DS Speed KS 14	L01039093	
D-MUNB	Junkers Profly JU L 2002 / Pico	unkn	
D-MUNC	Aerostyle Breezer	058	
D-MUND	Plätzer Motte B3	55	
	(Dbr Jesenwang 19.7.14)		
D-MUNE	Comco Ikarus Fox-C22	9507-3665	D-MUNO(1)
D-MUNH #	Comco Ikarus C-42	unkn	
D-MUNI (1)	Bobcat	09AD91	
D-MUNI(2)	Tecnam P.96 Golf 100	unkn	
D-MUNK	Comco Ikarus C-42 Cyclone	9702-6031	
D-MUNO(1)	Comco Ikarus Fox-C22B	9507-3665	
	(Re-regd D-MUNE)		
D-MUNO(2)	Rotortec Cloud Dancer II	unkn	
D-MUNY	Air-Light Wild Thing	053	
D-MUNZ	Murphy Renegade	unkn	
D-MUON #	Klüver Twin Racer Quartz SX 16	504202	
D-MUPA	Tandem Air Sunny s.b.s.	SuS-V-4.95	
D-MUPC	Blackshape Prime BS100	unkn	
D-MUPE	Pipistrel Twister / Hazard XP15	unkn	
D-MUPF	WDFL Sunwheel R	031	
D-MUPH	Flight Design CT SW	05-01-06	
D-MUPI	UL-Eigenbau Toruk	unkn	
	(Wears code "140513")		
D-MUPL	Ultravia Pélican Sport 450S	20026/755	
D-MUPP	Fresh Breeze Simo 122	unkn	
D-MUPS	Dallach Sunrise II	unkn	
D-MUPT	Flight Design CT Supralight	E-09-12-04	
D-MUPU(1)	B&F Funk FK-9	unkn	
D-MUPU(2)	Air-Light Wild Thing	07.092	
D-MUPW	B&F Funk FK-9 Mk.II	088	
D-MUPY	Flight Design CT LS	F-10-07-04	
D-MUPZ	Tecnam P.96 Golf	022	
D-MUQI	Evektor EV.97 Eurostar	98 03 05	
D-MUQU #	Autogyro Europe MTOsport	unkn	
D-MURA(1)	Warnke Skylight Trike	S 1019	
D-MURA(2)	Aeropro Eurofox	11001	
D-MURB	Mahe Scout	013	
D-MURC #	B&F Funk FK-9 Mk.III	09-03-123	
D-MURD #	Plätzer Kiebitz-B9	160	
D-MURE	Scheibe Uli 1	5218	
D-MURF	EEL ULF-2	78	
D-MURG	TL Ultralight TL-96 Star	01 S 93	
D-MURI (1)	Scheibe Uli 1	5213	
D-MURI(2)	Zenair CH-601D Zodiac	unkn	
	(Dbf 3.10.09)		
D-MURJ	Comco Ikarus C-42 Cyclone	9803-6103	
D-MURK #	Comco Ikarus Fox-C22	9304-3494	
D-MURL	Zenair CH-601 Zodiac	unkn	
D-MURM	Bautek Eagle V/ Pico	unkn	
D-MURO(1)	Comco Ikarus C-42B	0201-6317	
D-MURO(2)	Flight Design CT SW	unkn	
D-MURR	Sky-Walker 1+1	26116	
D-MURT	Comco Ikarus Fox-C22	9202-3 . . .	
D-MURU	Tomark SD-4 Viper	unkn	
D-MURW	Bautek Eagle V/ Pico	unkn	
D-MURX	Scheibe Uli 1	5220	
D-MUSA	Rans S-12 Airaile	0294479	
	(To OO-H19)		
D-MUSB	Dyn'Aéro MCT-01 ULC	183	
D-MUSC	Comco Ikarus Fox-C22	9006-3270	
D-MUSD	Plätzer Kiebitz-B	15	
D-MUSE	Scheibe Ultra Uli 2	3303	
D-MUSF	Aviatika 890	87B 002	
D-MUSH	Comco Ikarus C-42 Cyclone	0108-6411	
D-MUSI	Tecnam P.92 Echo	339	
D-MUSJ #	ASO Viper Hazard 15M Trike	1102502	
D-MUSK	Fantasy Air Allegro	00-405	
D-MUSL	Comco Ikarus Fox-C22	9209-3464	
D-MUSM	Comco Ikarus Fox-C22	9502-3632	
D-MUSP	B&F Funk FK-14 Polaris	014-121	
D-MUSS	Behlen Power-Trike Vampir II	85031	
D-MUST	Behlen Power-Trike	88026	
D-MUSV	SFS Vagabund	6	
D-MUSW(1)	Schmidtler Enduro Trike	F03/86	
D-MUSW(2)	Tecnam P.92-S Echo	588	
D-MUSX #	Weller UW-9 Sprint	06	
D-MUSZ #	Silent Club	012	
D-MUTA	Plätzer Kiebitz-B8	042	
D-MUTB	Remos G.3 Mirage	99	
D-MUTC	Remos G.3 Mirage	107	
	(Re-regd D-MKTC)		
D-MUTF	Tandem Air Sunny s.b.s.	SuS 04.96	
D-MUTH	Flight Design CT SW	07-06-16	
D-MUTI(1)	Remos G.3 Mirage	94	
D-MUTI(2)	B&F Funk FK-9 Mk.IV	09-04-474	
D-MUTJ	Dyn'Aéro MCR-01 ULC	110	
D-MUTM	Plätzer Kiebitz B	227	
D-MUTS	Schmidtler Ranger M Trike	0021	
D-MUTT	Air-Light Wild Thing	013	
D-MUTV	Plätzer Kiebitz-B8	181, was 110	
D-MUTY	Fresh Breeze Simo 122	unkn	
D-MUTZ(1)	Zlin Savage Cruiser	unkn	
D-MUTZ(2)	B&F Funk FK-12 Comet	unkn	
D-MUUD(1)	Celier Xenon 2	unkn	
D-MUUD(2)	ATEC Zephyr	unkn	
D-MUUJ	Urban Air Samba XXL	unkn	
D-MUUL	Comco Ikarus C-42C	1405-7326	
D-MUUR #	Air-Light Wild Thing	2000-05-070	
D-MUUS	Roland S-STOL	S-9781	
D-MUUT	Cellier Xenon 2	unkn	
D-MUUU(2)	Comco Ikarus C-42 Cyclone	9810-6156	
D-MUVE	WDFL Sunwheel	051	
D-MUVH	Tecnam P.92 Echo Classic	unkn	
D-MUVI	Tecnam P.92 Echo	210	
	(Same c/n as D-MWRO)		
D-MUVL	Drachenstudio Royal 912 ULS/ EOS	unkn	
D-MUVO	Bobcat	KA-1	
D-MUVR	Plätzer Kiebitz B	137	
D-MUVW	Flight Design CT LS	F-08-08-25	
D-MUWA	TUL-02 Tandem Tulak	TP005/2010	
	(Wears USAAF c/s "480173/57")		
D-MUWB	Fresh Breeze Simo 122	unkn	
D-MUWE	ATEC Zephyr	ZP 390400	
D-MUWG	Evektor EV-97 Eurostar SL	unkn	
D-MUWH	Comco Ikarus C-42B	0104-6336	
D-MUWI	TL Ultralight TL-2000 Sting	04ST67	
D-MUWM	Comco Ikarus C-42 Cyclone	0105-6337	
D-MUWP	Urban Air UFM-13 Lambada	16/13	
D-MUWR	Remos GX	426	
D-MUWT #	Air-Light Wild Thing	049	
D-MUWW	Tecnam P.92 Echo 100S	431	
D-MUXC	Air Création Tanarg 912ES / BioniX	A10142-10134	
D-MUXF	Cosmos Phase II/ Mach 14.9	unkn	
D-MUXI	Remos Gemini Ultra	029	
D-MUXL(1)	Tecnam P.96GGolf 100S	118	
D-MUXL(2)#	Pipistrel Sinus NW		
D-MUXS	Comco Ikarus Fox-C22	9409-3589	
D-MUXX	WDFL Dallach D4 Fascination	050	
D-MUXY	Tecnam P.92 Echo	562	
D-MUYY	Comco Ikarus C-42	unkn	
D-MUZE	Schmidtler Enduro Trike	02002	
D-MUZI	WDFL Dallach D4 Fascination BK	082	
D-MUZL	Best Off Sky Ranger Swift	unkn	
D-MUZY	Comco Ikarus C-42B	1209-7222	
D-MUZZ	B&F Funk FK-12 Comet	12-056	
D-MVAA	Comco Ikarus C-42B	0906-7044	
D-MVAB	Comco Ikarus Fox-C22B	940.-3601	
D-MVAC	Comco Ikarus Fox-C22	9501-3614	
D-MVAD	Plätzer Kiebitz-B9	161	
D-MVAE	Tecnam P.92 Echo	234	
D-MVAG	Saurier Flug Vagabond	unkn	
D-MVAK	Comco Ikarus C-42 Cyclone	0010-6288	
D-MVAL	Rans S-6S Coyote II	1195897 S	
D-MVAM	Tecnam P.92 Echo 100S	487	
D-MVAN	Flight Design CT SW	05-04-04	
D-MVAR	Comco Ikarus C-42B	0004-6246	
D-MVAS	Comco Ikarus C-42 Cyclone	9906-6184	
D-MVBA	WDFL Dallach D4 Fascination	048	
D-MVBB	WDFL Dallach D4B Fascination	032	
D-MVBC	Tecnam P.96 Golf 100	unkn	
D-MVBD	ASO Viper Trike	22028202	
D-MVBF(2)#	Plätzer Kiebitz-B2	101	
D-MVBG	Aviasud AE-209 Albatros	940550812	
D-MVBJ #	Cosmos/Top 14.9	unkn	
D-MVBL #	Klüver Bison Trike	112706	
D-MVBM	WDFL Dallach D4 Fascination	041	
D-MVBO	Take Off Merlin 1200 / Eos	unkn	
D-MVBP(1)	Sky Walker II	384	
D-MVBP(2)	Autogyro Europe MT-03	05G16	
D-MVBR #	Fläming Air FA-01 Smaragd	06/04	
	(Cr 28.7.10)		

Reg	Type	c/n	Prev id
D-MVBS	Scheibe SF-40	3104	
D-MVBU	Comco Ikarus Fox-C22	9407-3588	
D-MVBY	B&F FK-131 Jungmann UL	unkn	
D-MVCA	Flight Design CT	00.06.02.00	
D-MVCB	Flight Design CT SW	unkn	
D-MVCC	Flight Design CT	01-01-01-00	
D-MVCD #	Flight Design CT SW	unkn	
D-MVCF	Flight Design CT	98.12.02.43	OE-7046
D-MVCH	Tecnam P.92 Echo Classic	unkn	
D-MVCI #	Remos G.3 Mirage	082	
D-MVCK	Flugtechnik Herringhausen Vagabund	10	
D-MVCL	Shark Aero Shark	014-2013	
D-MVCO	Urban Air UFM-10 Samba	7/10	
D-MVCS	Comco Ikarus C-42CS	1509-7412	
D-MVCT	Flight Design CT (Cancelled?)	CT 005	
D-MVCW(1)	B&F Flug FK-12 Comet	12-083	
	(To France as 11-IJ)		
D-MVCW(2)	B&F Flug FK-12 Comet	12-092	
D-MVCY	Tandem Air Sunny Targa	TA-011.93	
D-MVCZ	Autogyro Europe MTOsport	unkn	
D-MVDB #	Flight Design CT	unkn	
D-MVDC	Comco Ikarus Fox-C22	9205-3407	
D-MVDH	Flight Design CT-2K	03.05.01.20	
D-MVDO	B&F Funk FK-12 TG Mk.II	045	
D-MVDV #	TLUltralight TL-96 Star	00 S 96	
D-MVEB	Comco Ikarus C-42 Cyclone	9811-6148	
D-MVEC	Comco Ikarus C-42 Cyclone	0006-6237	
D-MVEE	TL Ultralight TL-96 Star	00 S 60	
D-MVEF	Ikarusflug Eurofox	074099	
D-MVEK	Tecnam P.92-S Echo	483	
D-MVEL	Air-Light Wild Thing	026	
D-MVEN	Aerostyle Breezer	unkn	
D-MVER(1)	Comco Ikarus Fox-C22	9101-3300/3511	
D-MVER(2)#	B&F Funk FK-9 Mk.IV	unkn	
D-MVES #	B&F Funk FK-12 Comet	012-073	
D-MVET	Comco Ikarus C-42 Cyclone	9610-6053	
D-MVEY	Alpi Avn Pioneer 200	unkn	
D-MVEZ	Autogyro Europe Calidus	unkn	
D-MVFB	Comco Ikarus Fox-C22	9105-3332	
D-MVFC	Kappa KP-2U Sova	27/99	
D-MVFF(1)	Comco Ikarus Sherpa	8403-1053	PH-1M9
D-MVFF(2)	Aerostyle Breezer	053	
D-MVFK	B&F Funk FK-14 Polaris	014-001	
D-MVFL	Comco Ikarus Fox-C22B	9506-3664	
D-MVFP	Rans S-6 Coyote II	0994675	
D-MVFR	Comco Ikarus C-42B	unkn	
D-MVFS	B&F Funk FK-9 Mk,IV	09-04-453	
D-MVGB	VierWerk Aerolite	unkn	
D-MVGG	Urban Air UFM-13 Lambada	17/13	
D-MVGH	Fresh Breeze Simo 122	unkn	
D-MVGM	Bautek Eagle V / Pico	unkn	
D-MVGS	Air-Light Wild Thing	029	
D-MVGW	SFS Vagabund	002	
D-MVHA(1)	Comco Ikarus C-42	9907-6191	
D-MVHA(2)	Remos Gemini Ultra	unkn	
D-MVHB	WDFL Dallach D4 Fascination	021	
D-MVHE(1)	WDFL Dallach D4 Fascination	026	
D-MVHE(2)	Comco Ikarus C-42	0106-6349	PH-3M5
	(To OY-9470)		
D-MVHF	Evektor EV-97 Eurostar	2001-1010	
	(W/o 11.4.10)		
D-MVHG	Pioneer Flightstar I	990601	
D-MVHH	Autogyro Europe MT-03	unkn	
D-MVHL	Aerospool WT-9 Dynamic Club	DY524/2014	
D-MVHM	Dyn'Aéro MCR-01 UL	109	
D-MVHP #	B&F Funk FK-9	090	
D-MVHR	Comco Ikarus C-42 Cyclone	9804-6133	
D-MVHS	Tecnam P.96 Golf 100S	060	
D-MVHW	Evektor EV-97 Eurostar	2001-1212	
D-MVIA	Autogyro Europe MTOsport	unkn	
D-MVIB #	Comco Ikarus C-42	unkn	
D-MVIC	Plätzer Kiebitz-B6	165	
D-MVIE	Interplane ZJ Viera	unkn	
D-MVIL #	Rans S-6 Coyote II	1295914	
D-MVIP(1)	Klüver Racer SX 12 Trike	641907	
D-MVIP(2)	Zlin Savage Classic	unkn	
D-MVIR #	Comco Ikarus Fox-C22B	9405-3564	
D-MVIS	Comco Ikarus Fox-C22	9501-3633	
D-MVIV	Comco Ikarus C-42	0507-6745	
	(To SE-VOP, 3.11)		
D-MVJB	Comco Ikarus C-42 Cyclone	9708-6049	
D-MVJL #	SG Aviation Storm	unkn	
D-MVJR	Aeropro Eurofox	078099	
D-MVKA	Comco Ikarus C-42 Cyclone	9712-6041	
D-MVKB	Plätzer Motte B2	58	
D-MVKK	B&F Funk FK-12 Comet	12-90	
D-MVKL	Fly Synthesis Storch	unkn	
D-MVKM	Remos G.3 Mirage	052	
D-MVKO	Sky-Walker II	382	
D-MVKR	Sky-Walker II	268	
D-MVKT	Evektor EV-97 Eurostar SL	unkn	
D-MVKV	Tecnam P.92 Echo	164	
D-MVLA	Aeropro Eurofox	09500	
D-MVLB	Kondor Aviatik (Aveko) VL-3	VL-3-63	
D-MVLC	JMB VL-3 Evolution	unkn	
D-MVLE	Aveko VL-3 Sprint	VL-3-54	
D-MVLG	JMB VL-3 Evolution	185	
D-MVLH	Trixy G 4-2 R	017-12	
D-MVLK	Zenair CH-601 Zodiac	6-4038	
D-MVLL	Comco Ikarus Fox-C22	9502-3647	
D-MVLO	Zenair CH-601D Zodiac	6-3790	
D-MVLP #	Comco Ikarus Fox-C22	9109-3351	
D-MVLS	JMB VL-3 Evolution	unkn	
D-MVLT	JMB VL-3 Evolution	VL-3-116	LY-VLT
D-MVLV	Fantasy Air Allegro	unkn	
D-MVLX	JMB VL-3 Evolution	189	
	(W/o 8.5.16)		
D-MVLY	JMB VL-3 Evolution	unkn	
D-MVMA	Remos GX NXT	unkn	
D-MVMC	Aeropro Eurofox	11601	
D-MVML	B&F Funk FK-12 Comet	012-002	
D-MVMM	WDFL Dallach D4 Fascination	unkn	
D-MVMR	BRM Aero NG5 Bristell RG	unkn	
	(Possible link to D-MMBH, qv)		
D-MVMS	Comco Ikarus C-42 Cyclone	0111-6344	
D-MVMV	Zenair CH-601D Zodiac	6-3788	
D-MVNA	SG Aviation Storm 280	004	
D-MVNE	Light Aero Avid Mk.IV	1496	
D-MVNO	Comco Ikarus Fox-C22C	9607-3713	
D-MVOC	Zenair CH-701-D STOL	7-3972	
D-MVOE #	WDFL Dallach D4 Fascination	003	
D-MVOF	Flight Design CT SW	07-03-04	
D-MVOG	Wisch Star-Trike Profil 17M	09870020	
D-MVOI	Comco Ikarus C-42 Cyclone	9706-6033	
D-MVOK	Rans S-12 Airaile	0593416	
D-MVOL	Rans S-7 Courier	0597219	N7210V
D-MVOM	Scheibe SF-40	3103	
D-MVOX	Autogyro Europe MTOsport	unkn	
D-MVPA	Murphy Maverick	unkn	
D-MVPG	Comco Ikarus C-42 Cyclone	0001-6239	
D-MVPI	WDFL Dallach D4 Fascination BK	089	
D-MVPP	Pipistrel Virus SW100	unkn	
D-MVPS	Comco Ikarus C-42 Cyclone	0111-6426	
D-MVPW	Remos GX	328	
D-MVQR #	P&M Quik R 912S	unkn	
D-MVRA	Comco Ikarus C-42 Cyclone	9808-6114	
D-MVRH	Zenair CH-601D Zodiac	6-9193	
D-MVRK	SFS Vagabund	003	
D-MVRL	Aerospool WT-9 Dynamic	DY010 02	
D-MVRO	Fresh Breeze Simo 122	unkn	
D-MVRP	Remos G.3 Mirage	unkn	
D-MVRR	Aeropro Eurofox	11101	
D-MVRS	Tecnam P.92 Echo	155	
D-MVSB	Aeropro Eurofox	096-00	
D-MVSC	Magni M-24 Orion VIP	unkn	
D-MVSD	Tomark SD-4 Viper	0024	
D-MVSE #	WDFL Dallach D4 Fascination	017	
D-MVSG(1)	Remos G-3 Mirage	unkn	
D-MVSG(2)	Ekolot JK-05 Junior	unkn	
D-MVSK #	ASO Viper Hazard 15 Trike	15I17791	
D-MVSL #	Comco Ikarus C-42 Cyclone	0102-6309	
D-MVSP	Comco Ikarus C-42 Cyclone	0202-6432	
D-MVSR	Tecnam P.92 Echo 2000RG	unkn	
D-MVST	Tandem Air Sunny s.b.s.	SuS 06.96	
D-MVSW	Pipistrel Virus SW 100	unkn	
D-MVTT	Tandem Air Sunny	0010301Sp	
D-MVUL	Aeroprakt A-22L2 Vision	unkn	
D-MVUS	Flight Design CT LS	unkn	
D-MVVA #	Klüver Racer Quartz SX 12 Trike	734011	
D-MVVB #	AGREX	001	
D-MVVC	Comco Ikarus C-42B	0310-6579	D-MUFW
D-MVVH #	Comco Ikarus Fox-C22B	9 . . .-3702	
D-MVVR(2)	Flight Design CT	99.02.01.45	
	(To Namibia, V5-URM)		
D-MVVS #	Tandem Air Sunny Sport	008.07.03 S-s	
D-MVVT	B&F Funk FK-14 Polaris	014-017	
D-MVVV #	Aviasud Mistral BRD	125	
D-MVVX	Schmidtler Enduro Focus 18M Trike	040385	
D-MVWB	Herringhausen Vagabund	009	
D-MVWH	Autogyro Europe MTOsport	unkn	
D-MVWK	Autogyro Europe MTOsport	unkn	
D-MVWN	Fresh Breeze Solo 122 AL / Arcus L	unkn	
D-MVWR	Comco Ikarus C-42B	0204-6438	
D-MVWS	Comco Ikarus C-42 Cyclone	9906-6169	
D-MVWW	B&F Funk FK-9 Mk.IV Diesel CDi	09-04U-298	
D-MVXY #	NST Minimum	460	
D-MVYY	Ikarusflug Eurofox	022096	
D-MVZZ(1)	B&F Funk FK-9 Mk.IV (t/w)	unkn	
D-MVZZ(2)	B&F Funk FK-14B Polaris	unkn	
D-MWAA	Remos G.3/600 Mirage	035	
D-MWAB	Comco Ikarus C-42 Cyclone	0002-6254	
	(W/o 21.5.15)		
D-MWAC(1)	Remos Gemini Ultra	004	
D-MWAC(2)	Plätzer Kiebitz-B	361	
D-MWAD	Behlen Power-Trike Hazard 15	92031	
D-MWAE	Plätzer Kiebitz-B2	133	
D-MWAF	Take Off Maximum Trike	3059	
D-MWAG	Plätzer Kiebitz-B6	030	
D-MWAH	Fisher FP-404 Classic	C087	
D-MWAI	Comco Ikarus Fox-C22C	9708-3732	
D-MWAJ	Euro-ALA Jet Fox 97	018	
D-MWAK	B&F Funk FK-9 Mk.II	052	
D-MWAL #	Ultraleichtverbund Bi 90	9234016831	
D-MWAM	Comco Ikarus C-42 Cyclone	9807-6130	
D-MWAN	Rans S-12XL Airaile	08950641	
D-MWAO	Zlin Savage Classic	075	
D-MWAP(1)	Flight Design CT SW	04.05.04	
	(To ZU-FMG, 3.11)		
D-MWAP(2)	Remos GX	385	
D-MWAR	Air-Light Wild Thing WT.01	97 02 017	
	(Re-regd D-MMYZ)		
D-MWAS	Flightstar II	030402	
D-MWAT	Comco Ikarus C-42 Cyclone	0007-6269	
D-MWAV(1)	NST Minimum	M472	
D-MWAV(2)	Aerospool WT-9 Dynamic	unkn	
D-MWAW	Comco Ikarus Fox-C22	9502-3613	
D-MWAY	Flight Design CT-2K	01.06.04.14	
D-MWBA(1)	Weedhopper	1006	D-MDJK?
D-MWBA(2)	Flight Design CT SW	unkn	
D-MWBB	Ikarusflug Eurofox	030097	
D-MWBC(1)	Weedhopper	0999	
D-MWBC(2)	Trixy G 4-2 R	038-14	
D-MWBE	Funbird	1005/84	
D-MWBF	WDFL Dallach D4 Fascination	046	
D-MWBH #	Funbird	0143/82	
D-MWBI	Comco Ikarus C-42 Cyclone	0110-6339	
D-MWBK	Comco Fox	040	
D-MWBL	Tecnam P.92 Echo 100S	489	
D-MWBM	Comco Ikarus Fox-C22C	9710-3733	
D-MWBO	Comco Ikarus C-42	0203-6448	
D-MWBR	Murphy Renegade Spirit	607	
D-MWBS	Fläming Air FA-01 Smaragd	03/04	
D-MWBT	Tecnam P.92 Echo Classic	374	
D-MWBV	Rans S-7 Courier	0193103	
D-MWBW	Comco Ikarus Fox-C22	9411-3612	
	(Sold as CS-U . . but ntu by 9.16)		
D-MWCA #	Fair Fax DR Hazard 15M Trike	D007	
D-MWCB	Comco Ikarus Fox-C22	9408-3611	
D-MWCC	Comco Ikarus Fox-C22B	9506-3675	
D-MWCF	Vidor Asso V Champion	1750	
D-MWCG	Autogyro Europe Cavalon	unkn	
D-MWCI	Remos G.3 Mirage	081	

Reg	Type	C/n	Note
D-MWCJ	Fokker EIII UL replica (Marked 422/15)	unkn	
D-MWCL	Air Light Wild Thing 3300	067	
D-MWCO	WDFL Dallach D4 Fascination	039	
D-MWCS	Aerostyle Breezer CL	117	
D-MWCW	Evektor EV-97 Eurostar 2000R	2001-0910	
D-MWCX	Magni M-24 Orion VIP	unkn	
D-MWDA	WDFL Sunwheel R	001	
D-MWDB	LO-120S	025	
D-MWDC	Ekolot KR-030 Topaz	30-06-06	
D-MWDD	Roland Z701	unkn	
D-MWDE	Comco Ikarus C-42 Cyclone	0105-6303	
D-MWDF	WDFL Dallach D4B Fascination	005	D-MWDH
D-MWDG	Rans S-6 Coyote II XL	1294707	
D-MWDH(1)	WDFL Dallach D4 Fascination (To D-MWDF)	005	
D-MWDH(2)	Aerospool WT-9 Dynamic	unkn	
D-MWDI	Plätzer Kiebitz-B4	175	
D-MWDK	Remos Gemini Ultra	E12.013	
D-MWDL	Zenair CH-601D Zodiac	6-3653	
D-MWDM #	Spacek SD-1 Minisport TD (Damaged 1.8.12)	032	
D-MWDR	Tecnam P.92 Echo	277	
D-MWDT #	TL Ultralight TL-232 Condor Plus	AB 07	
D-MWDW	Flight Design CT SW	05-01-05	
D-MWEA	Rans S-6 Coyote II	0895876	
D-MWEB	Tecnam P.92 Echo 100S	561	
D-MWEC	Comco Ikarus C-42 Cyclone	9806-6098	
D-MWED	ICP MXP-740 Savannah	06-99-50-118	
D-MWEE	Autogyro Europe MTOsport	unkn	
D-MWEF	Hummer	15184	
D-MWEG	WDFL Dallach D4 Fascination	105	
D-MWEH	Fisher Super Koala	Ei-10	
D-MWEI	Schönleber DS Trike 40kw	030389	
D-MWEJ	Bücker Jungmann UL	unkn	
D-MWEK	Aerospool WT-9 Dynamic	DY311/2009	
D-MWEL	Plätzer Kiebitz	221	
D-MWEM	Comco Ikarus C-42B	0210-6505	
D-MWEP	Comco Ikarus Fox-C22B	9...-3683	
D-MWER	Comco Ikarus Fox-C22	9010-3296	
D-MWES	B&F Funk FK-9 Mk.III	09-109	
D-MWET	Air-Light Wild Thing	WT01 99 04 048	
D-MWEU	Comco Ikarus C-42B	unkn	
D-MWEV	Evektor EV-97 Eurostar	990509	
D-MWEW	B&F Funk FK-12 Comet	012-014	
D-MWEX	Fresh Breeze Simo 122	unkn	
D-MWEZ	Remos G3 Mirage	180	
D-MWFA	Comco Ikarus C-42B (W/o 19.9.14)	1103-7148	
D-MWFB #	Scheibe Uli NG	UW100110	
D-MWFC	Autogyro Europe Calidus (Cld)	unkn	
D-MWFD	Weller Demoiselle replica	unkn	
D-MWFF	Comco Ikarus C-42B (C/n? 0905-7047 was D-MQBB, LN-YWZ)	0907-7047	
D-MWFG	Comco Ikarus C-42 Cyclone	9805-6096	
D-MWFH	Comco Ikarus C-42 Cyclone	9903-6174	
D-MWFI	Comco Ikarus C-42	0201-6427	
D-MWFK	TL Ultralight TL-3000 Sirius	unkn	
D-MWFN #	B&F Funk FK-9 Mk.III Club	unkn	
D-MWFR	WDFL Dallach D4B Fascination (Same c/n as D-MRSY)	040	
D-MWFS	Comco Ikarus C-42 Cyclone	9811-6099	
D-MWFT	Zenair CH-601D Zodiac	6-3529/014 0097	
D-MWFU	Comco Ikarus C-42B	0910-7067	
D-MWFW	Roman-Weller UW-9 Sprint (Morane A-1 replica)	001	
D-MWFY	Roman-Weller UW-9 Sprint (Morane A-1 replica)	05	
D-MWFZ	Loehle Sport Parasol	001	
D-MWGB(2)	Comco Ikarus C-42 Cyclone	9801-6063	
D-MWGC	Pipistrel Taurus 503	unkn	
D-MWGE	B&F Funk FK-9 Mk.II	069	
D-MWGF	Plätzer Kiebitz-B9	202	
D-MWGG	Remos G3 Mirage	084	
D-MWGH	B&F Funk FK-9 Mk.II	054	
D-MWGI	Comco Ikarus C-42B	1408-7334	
D-MWGJ	Comco Ikarus C-42 Cyclone	9810-6140	
D-MWGN(1)	Plätzer Kiebitz-B9	140	
D-MWGN(2)	Autogyro Europe MTOsport	unkn	
D-MWGS	Remos Gemini Ultra (W/o 6.3.02)	009	
D-MWGT	Plätzer Kiebitz-B6	182	
D-MWGW	Air-Light Wild Thing	042	
D-MWGX	Remos GX	376	
D-MWHA	Remos Gemini Ultra	030	
D-MWHB(1)	Take Off Maximum Lotus 18	021129	
D-MWHB(2)	AirLony Skylane UL Classic	unkn	
D-MWHC	Comco Ikarus C-42 Cyclone	9810-6136	
D-MWHD	UPM Cobra Trike	920117	
D-MWHE	Murphy Renegade Spirit	608	
D-MWHF	ATEC Zephyr	unkn	
D-MWHG	MKB Enduro Focus 18 Trike	030886	
D-MWHH	NST Minimum	M245	
D-MWHI (1)	Sky-Walker II	271	
D-MWHI(2)	Airoaviation Airo 5	A5-001/08	(N154AA)
D-MWHJ	Remos Gemini Ultra	E07.08	
D-MWHK	Comco Ikarus C-42 Cyclone	9809-6145	
D-MWHL	EEL ULF-2	20	
D-MWHM	ASO 26 Storch 582	160.2	
D-MWHN	TL Ultralight TL-96 Star	00 S 52	
D-MWHO	Ultraleichtverbund Bi 90	662	
D-MWHP	Roland Z601	unkn	
D-MWHR	Tandem Air Sunny Sport	49.93	
D-MWHS	ICP MXP-740V Savannah	10-99-50-132	
D-MWHT	AirLony Skylane UL	unkn	
D-MWHU	Denney Kitfox IV	1860	
D-MWHV(2)	B&F Funk FK-9 Mk.III Utility	09-03U-197	
D-MWHW	Comco Ikarus Fox-C22	9203-3373	
D-MWHX	AirLony Skylane UL	unkn	
D-MWHY	Murphy Renegade	548	
D-MWHZ(1)	Autogyro Europe MT-03	unkn	
D-MWHZ(2)#	Urban Air Samba XXL	SAXL D89	
D-MWID	EEL ULF-2	68	
D-MWIE	Plätzer Kiebitz-B2	032	
D-MWIF	Ikarusflug Eurofox	95017	
D-MWIG	Comco Ikarus C-42B (W/o 9.9.15)	1008-7116	
D-MWIH	Celier Xenon	CAJ14475R	
D-MWII	WDFL Dallach D4 Fascination	024	
D-MWIK(1)	Fair Fax Trike	016	
D-MWIK(2)#	Flight Design CT LS	F-08-06-01	
D-MWIL	Air-Light Wild Thing	056	
D-MWIN	TL Ultralight TL-96 Sting	unkn	
D-MWIP #	Tandem Air Sunny 912	TA-020	
D-MWIR(1)	Behlen Power-Trike II	95007	
D-MWIR(2)	Comco Ikarus C-42	0203-6437	
D-MWIT	Cosmos Bi 90 Phase II/ Chronos 14	4017032	
D-MWIW	Take Off Maximum Hazard 15	037110	
D-MWJA	Zenair CH-601D Zodiac	6-3520	
D-MWJB	Remos Gemini Ultra	E13.014	
D-MWJE	Technoflug Piccolo	020	
D-MWJF	Comco Ikarus Fox-C22B	9902-3742	
D-MWJH	Comco Ikarus C-42 Cyclone	9904-6179	
D-MWJM	Rans S-10 Sakota (Modified)	unkn	
D-MWJN	Ultraleichtverbund Bi 90	735	
D-MWJO #	WDFL Sunwheel	029	
D-MWKA(1)	Comco Ikarus Fox-C22B	9504-3659	
D-MWKA(2)	Tecnam P.92 Echo	unkn	
D-MWKB	HFL Stratos IIe	IIe-010	D-MMDH?
D-MWKC	Autogyro Europe MTOsport	unkn	
D-MWKD	Plätzer Kiebitz-B8	027	
D-MWKE	Comco Ikarus Fox-C22	9204-3393	
D-MWKF	Plätzer Kiebitz-B8	130	
D-MWKG #	Comco Ikarus Fox-C22B (Sold as YL-APO)	9507-3660	
D-MWKH(1)	Dallach Sunrise II	019	
D-MWKH(2)	Comco Ikarus C-42B	0206-6449	
D-MWKJ(1)	WDFL Dallach D4 Fascination	007	
D-MWKJ(2)	Aerospool WT-9 Dynamic	DY016 02	
D-MWKK	Evektor EV-97R Eurostar 2000	unkn	
D-MWKL	Comco Ikarus C-42 Cyclone	9804-6093	
D-MWKM	Rans S-6 Coyote II	11981281	
D-MWKN	Murphy Renegade	517	
D-MWKO	Comco Ikarus Fox-C22	9501-3610	
D-MWKP	Flight Design CT	99.12.02.76	
D-MWKR	TL Ultralight TL-3000 Sirius 912S	unkn	
D-MWKS(1)	ASO Viper Hazard 15 Trike	1234	
D-MWKS(2)	Euro-ALA Jet Fox 97	027-2	
D-MWKT	Comco Ikarus Fox-C22	95013626	
D-MWKU #	Comco Ikarus Fox-C22	9...-3649	
D-MWKV	Plätzer Kiebitz-B6 (Damaged 2.11.14)	46	
D-MWKW	Plätzer Kiebitz-B4	126	
D-MWLA(1)	Pioneer Flightstar	683	
D-MWLA(2)	Comco Ikarus C-42B	0410-6637	
D-MWLB	Zenair CH-601D Zodiac (W/o 13.9.15)	6-3451/019 0097	
D-MWLC	Comco Ikarus Fox-C22	9501-3627	
D-MWLD	Comco Ikarus Fox-C22	9205-3408	
D-MWLE	Aeropilot Legend 540	1528	
D-MWLF(1)	Comco Ikarus Sherpa II (Re-regd D-MPOZ ?)	8512-1112	
D-MWLF(2)	Comco Ikarus Fox-C22	9505-3651	D-MWLH(1)
D-MWLG	Remos G3 Mirage	090	
D-MWLH(1)	Comco Ikarus Fox-C22 (Re-regd D-MWLF(2))	9505-3651	
D-MWLH(2)	TL Ultralight TL-96 Star	01 S 108	
D-MWLI	Loehle Mustang 5151	009	
D-MWLK	Fresh Breeze Simo 122	unkn	
D-MWLL	ATEC Zephyr 2000	SF 080301	
D-MWLM(1)	Comco Ikarus Fox-C22	9501-3628	
D-MWLM(2)#	Remos GX	427	
D-MWLR	Comco Ikarus Fox-C22	9503-3650	
D-MWLS	Comco Ikarus C-42 Cyclone	9904-6158	
D-MWLT(1)	Klüver Bison Trike	22/708	
D-MWLT(2)	Autogyro Europe Cavalon	V00088	
D-MWLU	WDFL Dallach D4 Fascination BK	094	
D-MWLV	Comco Ikarus C-42 Cyclone	9907-6197	
D-MWLZ	Comco Ikarus Fox-C22	9310-3533	
D-MWMA(1)	Flight Design CT	97.11.03.13	
D-MWMA(2)	Rans S-6 Coyote II	12051717	
D-MWMB	Comco Ikarus C-42 Cyclone	0106-6330	
D-MWMC	Comco Ikarus C-42 Cyclone	9904-6177	
D-MWMD	Autogyro Europe MTOsport	unkn	
D-MWME	Flight Team Twister / iXess	unkn	
D-MWMF(1)	Rans S-12 Airaile	1292358	
D-MWMF(2)	Roland Z602	Z-9532	
D-MWMG	Loehle Mustang 5151	008	
D-MWMH	Sky-Walker II	511	
D-MWMI	Plätzer Kiebitz-B8	122	
D-MWMK	TL Ultralight TL-96 Star	99 S 31	
D-MWML	Plätzer Kiebitz-B9	037	
D-MWMM	Comco Ikarus C-42 Cyclone	0004-6230	
D-MWMN #	Mantel Mono-Dragster	M870226	
D-MWMO(1)	Air Light WT-01 Wild Thing	unkn	
D-MWMO(2)	Aerospool WT-9 Dynamic	unkn	
D-MWMP	Flight Design CT SW	unkn	
D-MWMR	Comco Ikarus C-42B	0810-7014	
D-MWMS(1)	NST Minimum	M504	
D-MWMS(2)	Flight Design CT	00.04.03.93	
D-MWMW	TL Ultralight TL-96 Sting	05ST105	
D-MWMZ	Light Aero Avid Flyer IV	877	
D-MWNA	Autogyro Europe MTOsport	unkn	
D-MWND	Joker SE / Profi TL	01	
D-MWNL	Comco Ikarus C-42 Cyclone	0009-6295	
D-MWNM	WDFL Sunwheel	027	
D-MWNN	Rans S-6ES Coyote II	1292414	
D-MWNO	Evektor EV-97 Eurostar SLW	2010 3727	
D-MWOB	Comco Ikarus Fox-C22	9310-3531	
D-MWOC	Comco Ikarus Fox-C22	9106-3329	
D-MWOD	Plätzer Kiebitz	206	
D-MWOF	Flight Design CT SW	04.06.04	
D-MWOI	B&F Funk FK-9 Mk IV	09-04-347	
D-MWOJ	Flight Design CT SW	07-07-19	
D-MWOK	Tecnam P.92 Echo 100S	472	
D-MWOL	WDFL Dallach D4 Fascination	001	
D-MWOM	Fresh Breeze / Simo 122	ORC 838	
D-MWOP(1)	Behlen Power-Trike	87013	
D-MWOP(2)	Comco Ikarus C-42 Cyclone	0103-6315	
D-MWOR(1)	Comco Ikarus Fox-C22	9110-3358	
D-MWOR(2)	Evektor EV-97 Eurostar SL	2010 3802	

Registration	Type	C/n	Other
D-MWOS	Evektor EV-97 Eurostar SL	2014 4201	
D-MWOT	Comco Ikarus C-42 Cyclone	9806-6109	
D-MWOW	Comco Ikarus C-42 Cyclone	0009-6270	
D-MWPA	Remos G.3 Mirage	080	
D-MWPB	Comco Ikarus Fox II Doppel	8606-3022	
D-MWPC #	Autogyro Europe MT-03	unkn	
D-MWPD	Autogyro Europe MTOsport	unkn	
D-MWPE	TL Ultralight TL-96 Star	01 S 86	
D-MWPF	Plätzer Motte	037	
D-MWPG #	Comco Ikarus C-42 Cyclone	9711-6065	
	(To OO-G79, 5.11)		
D-MWPH	Comco Ikarus C-42 Cyclone	0003-6244	PH-3J8
D-MWPI	Comco Ikarus C-42 Cyclone (floatplane)	unkn	
D-MWPK	B&F Funk FK-9 Mk.IV Utility Club	09-04U-254	
D-MWPL	Murphy Renegade II	549	
D-MWPM	TL Ultralight TL-232 Condor Plus	98 C 10	
D-MWPN	Flight Design CT	98.02.02.22	
	(Re-regd D-MTCV)		
D-MWPP	Sky-Walker II	254	
D-MWPR	Murphy Renegade Spirit	unkn	
D-MWPS	Flight Design CT	00.11.02.22	
D-MWPT	Malchow HK-12	002	
D-MWPW	Aviasud AE-209 Albatros	940550802	
D-MWRA(1)	Rans S-6ES Coyote II	595817ES	
D-MWRA(2)	TL Ultralight TL-3000 Sirius	unkn	
D-MWRB	Klüver Twin Racer Quartz SX 16	695010	
D-MWRC	Comco Ikarus C-42 Cyclone	9810-6142	
D-MWRD(1)	Tecnam P.92 Echo	204	
D-MWRD(2)	Tecnam P.96 Golf 100S	072	
D-MWRF	Comco Ikarus C-42 Cyclone	9902-6160	
D-MWRG	Murphy Renegade Spirit	592	
	(W/o 3.9.16)		
D-MWRH(1)	Evektor EV.97 Eurostar	98 0202	
D-MWRH(2)	Tecnam P.92 Echo Classic	695	
	(Possibly sold as (VH-OSK), D-MWRH, 24-3737)		
D-MWRI	Fresh Breeze	unkn	
D-MWRJ	Comco Ikarus C-42 Cyclone	0003-6248	
D-MWRK	B&F Funk FK-9 Mk.IV	unkn	
D-MWRL	Comco Ikarus C-42 Cyclone	0001-6207	
D-MWRM	Comco Ikarus C-42B	0507-6740	
D-MWRN	Comco Ikarus C-42 Cyclone	0102-6305	
D-MWRO	Tecnam P.92 Echo	210	
	(Same c/n as D-MUVI)		
D-MWRP	Comco Ikarus C-42	unkn	
D-MWRR	Comco Ikarus C-42B	unkn	
D-MWRS	Remos Gemini Ultra B	E06.07	
D-MWRT	Tecnam P.92 Echo 100S	505	
D-MWRV	ATEC Zephyr	ZF 121299	
D-MWRW	NST Minimum	unkn	
D-MWRX	Plätzer Kiebitz-B2	043	
D-MWRZ	Comco Ikarus C-42	unkn	
D-MWSA	ASO Viper Trike	15I1690	
D-MWSB	Sky-Walker II	269	
D-MWSC	Comco Ikarus C-42 Cyclone	0202-6456	
D-MWSD	Remos Gemini Ultra B	011	
D-MWSE	Rans S-6 Coyote II	0694636	D-MNDC
D-MWSF	WDFL Dallach D4B Fascination	068	
D-MWSG	B&F Funk FK-14 Polaris	014-002	
	(To 31-AO, OO-F34)		
D-MWSH	Plätzer Kiebitz-B-450	177	
D-MWSI(1)	Dallach Sunrise II	015	
	(Same c/n as D-MEWS)		
D-MWSI(2)	Schmidtler Enduro DS Trike	010987	
D-MWSJ #	Murphy Renegade Spirit	unkn	
D-MWSK(1)	ASO Viper Trike	3101	
D-MWSK(2)	Comco Ikarus Fox-C22	9509-3688	
D-MWSK(3)	Comco Ikarus C-42B	unkn	
D-MWSL	B&F Funk FK-9 Mk.IV SW	unkn	
D-MWSM	Steinbach Austro-Trike	unkn	
D-MWSN	B&F Funk FK-9 Mk.III	09-121	
D-MWSP	Behlen Power-Trike	374	
D-MWSR	Tecnam P.92 Echo 100S	361	
D-MWSS(1)	Comco Ikarus C-42 Cyclone	9901-6135	
D-MWSS(2)	Autogyro Europe MTOsport	unkn	
D-MWST	WDFL Dallach D4 Fascination BK	074	
D-MWSU	Evektor EV-97R Eurostar	2007 3004	
D-MWSV	Aerostyle Breezer	019	
D-MWSW	Take Off Maximum Trike	045021	
D-MWSY #	Tandem Air Sunny Targa	010	
D-MWSZ	Zenair CH-601D Zodiac	6-3412/007 0597	
D-MWTA	Air-Light Wild Thing	058	
D-MWTB	Air-Light Wild Thing	043	
D-MWTC	Air-Light Wild Thing	007	
D-MWTD	Air-Light Wild Thing	050	
D-MWTE	Air-Light Wild Thing	059	
	(W/o 23.6.08)		
D-MWTG	Aerospool WT-9 Dynamic	DY012/2002	PH-3T9
D-MWTH	Plätzer Kiebitz B	273	
D-MWTL	TL Ultralight TL-232 Condor Plus	96C01	
D-MWTO	Air Light WT-01 Wild Thing	093	
D-MWTR(1)	Comco Ikarus C-42 Cyclone	9810-6141	PH-3D3
	(W/o 28.6.10)		
D-MWTR(2)	Comco Ikarus C-42B	unkn	
D-MWTS	Comco Ikarus Fox-C22	9405-3552	
D-MWTT (1)	Fair Fax Trike	028	
D-MWTT(2)	Remos G.3 Mirage	102	
D-MWTV #	Aviasud Albatros 52	124	
D-MWTW #	Comco Ikarus Fox-C22	9503-3648	
D-MWUD #	Aviasud Albatros 64	307	
D-MWUF	Ekolot JK-05 Junior	05-07-06	
D-MWUG	ATEC Zephyr 2000	"ZK6911205"	
D-MWUL	Autogyro Europe MTOsport	unkn	
D-MWUM #	Light Aero Avid Flyer	1465	
D-MWUT	Comco Ikarus Fox-C22B	9506-3663	
D-MWUW	Vidor Asso V Champion	unkn	
D-MWVA	Klüver Bison Trike	253708	
D-MWVE	Autogyro Europe Cavalon	unkn	
D-MWVH	Albatros	113	65-CR
D-MWVR #	Ultraleichtverbund Bi 90	3957007	
D-MWVV #	Schönleber Minimum	LO 1/0288	
D-MWVY	Comco Ikarus C-42 Cyclone	0110-6421	
D-MWVZ	Schmidtler Enduro Trike	01-002	
D-MWWA	Evektor EV-97 Eurostar 2000R	2005 2421	
D-MWWB	Plätzer Kiebitz B	318	
D-MWWC	Fresh Breeze Simo 122	unkn	
D-MWWD	Flight Design CT	99-02-01-47	
D-MWWE	B&F Funk FK-12 Comet	12-040	
D-MWWF	Comco Ikarus C-42B	0206-6446	
D-MWWG	Flight Design CT LS	unkn	
D-MWWJ	Ekolot JK-05 Junior	unkn	
D-MWWK	Technoflug Piccolo	051	
D-MWWL(1)	Zenair CH-701 STOL	unkn	
D-MWWL(2)	Flight Design CT LS	unkn	
D-MWWM	Tecnam P.96 Golf 100	193	
D-MWWN	Tecnam P.92 Echo 100S	454	
D-MWWO	Plätzer Kiebitz-B9	261	
D-MWWR(2)	Sky-Walker II	26148	
D-MWWS	Autogyro Europe MTOsport	unkn	
D-MWWT	Air-Light Wild Thing	032	
D-MWWW(1)	Sky-Walker 1+1	26143	
D-MWWW(2)	WDFL Dallach D4 Fascination BK	085	
D-MWXB #	Comco Ikarus Fox-C22	9309-3529	
D-MWXL	Urban Air Samba XXL	unkn	
D-MWXW	Comco Ikarus Fox-C22	9501-3630	
D-MWXY	Flugschule Skyrider Sonic / Pico	unkn	
D-MWYC #	Aviasud Albatros 52	125	
D-MWYK	Air Trike Berlin Eagle V / Ghost 14.9	01B11	
	(Later with Profi 14.5 wing)		
D-MWYY	B&F Funk FK-9 Mk.II	017	
D-MWYZ	Take Off Merlin 1100	unkn	
D-MWZI #	WDFL Dallach D4 Fascination BK	unkn	
D-MWZL	Comco Ikarus Fox-C22	9401-3536	
	(Re-regd D-MTRG)		
D-MXAA	Flight Team Spider XL / iXess	unkn	
D-MXAC	Plätzer Motte B Rumpf	VO 001	
D-MXAD(1)	B&F Funk FK-12 Comet	012-046	
D-MXAD(2)	Autogyro Europe MTOsport	unkn	
D-MXAE	Comco Ikarus Fox-C22	9703-3722	
	(To LX-XAE, D-MJMM)		
D-MXAF	Plätzer Kiebitz A	001	
D-MXAG	Bautek Eagle V/ Pico	unkn	
D-MXAH	Zenair CH-601P Zodiac	unkn	
D-MXAI	Aerospool WT-9 Dynamic	DY287/2008	OM-OLI
D-MXAL	B&F Funk FK-14B2 Polaris	014-140	
D-MXAM	B&F Funk FK-14 Polaris	014-016	
D-MXAP	WDFL Dallach D4 Fascination BK	072	
D-MXAQ	Aériane Sirocco	042	
D-MXAR	Comco Ikarus C-42 Cyclone	0103-6308	
D-MXAS	Solid Air Diamant / Pico S	unkn	
D-MXAT	Spacek SD-1 Minisport TD	027	
D-MXAU #	Zenair CH-601 Zodiac	unkn	
D-MXAX	Ultravia Pelican	unkn	
D-MXAY	B&F Funk FK-9 TG Mk.II	068	
D-MXAZ	Götz 50	001	
D-MXBA(2)	ASO 26 Storch 503	FT460	
D-MXBB	Comco Ikarus C-42B	0602-6795	
D-MXBC #	Comco Ikarus Sherpa	8309-001	
D-MXBD	Aviasud Mistral 53	002	
D-MXBE(2)	Comco Ikarus Fox-C22B	9404-3562	
D-MXBE(3)	Trendak Tercel	TRSJ 219115	
D-MXBM	Aviasud Mistral 53	001	
D-MXBR	Aerostyle Breezer CR	086	
D-MXBS	B&F Funk FK-9 Mk.III Utility	09-03U-198A	
D-MXBV #	B&F Funk FK-9 Mk.III	116	
	(To 31 AI/F-JIAI, D-MTAF ?)		
D-MXBW #	Homebuilt, type unknown	1	
D-MXBX	Rans S-12 Airaile	0594493	
D-MXBY	ASO 26 Storch	FT240	
D-MXBZ	ASO 26 Storch 503	FT234	
D-MXCA	Spacek SD-1 Minisport TD	003	
D-MXCC	Light Aero Avid Flyer IV	261	
D-MXCH	Birdman Chinook	02817	
D-MXCI	Birdman Chinook	unkn	
D-MXCM #	Bobcat	001	
D-MXCT	Flight Design CT SW	05-08-09	
D-MXCX	Fresh Breeze Wedermach	W09XCR1288BF6311	
D-MXDD	WDFL Dallach D4 Fascination	070	
D-MXDE	ASO Storch/503	11001202	
D-MXDI	Solid Air Diamant Twin Hazard 13	T003	
D-MXDL	Light Aero Avid Flyer IV	419	
D-MXDM	Aerospool WT-9 Dynamic Turbo	unkn	
D-MXDR	Autogyro Europe Cavalon	unkn	A6-XDR
	(Crashed nr Scharding, Austria 18.8.16)		
D-MXEF	Aeropro Eurofox	10401	
D-MXEG	Dallach Sunrise II	014	
D-MXEL	Ballard Pelican 450 S Sport	unkn	
D-MXEN(1)	WDFL Dallach D4 Fascination	053	
D-MXEN(2)	Celier Xenon	unkn	
D-MXES	Aerospool WT-9 Dynamic	DY008 01	D-MXFW(1) ?
D-MXET	Flight Team Spider Trike	D017	
D-MXEV	Evektor EV-97 Eurostar	2000-0611	
D-MXFG	Comco Ikarus C-42B	unkn	
D-MXFK	B&F Funk FK-9 Mk.II	001	
D-MXFO #	Snoopy II	001	
D-MXFT	Rans S-6 Coyote II	0889060	
D-MXFW(1)	Aerospool WT-9 Dynamic	DY008 01	
	(Re-regd D-MXES ?)		
D-MXFW(2)	Aerospool WT-9 Dynamic	DY013 02	
D-MXGG #	Autogyro Europe MTO Sport	unkn	
D-MXGH	Comco Ikarus C-42B	0201-6423	
D-MXGI	Comco Ikarus C-42 Cyclone	9804-6090	
D-MXGM	Comco Ikarus C-42B	unkn	
D-MXGS	Trixy G4-2	unkn	
D-MXGX #	Autogyro Europe MTOsport	unkn	
D-MXHB	Comco Ikarus C-42B	0910-7065	
D-MXHE	LO-120	001	
D-MXHL(1)	Weedhopper	2214	
D-MXHL(2)	Flight Design CT LS HL	unkn	
D-MXHM	Eipper Quicksilver	1100	
D-MXHT #	HFL Stratos 300	300-001	
D-MXHW	Air-Light Wild Thing	014	
D-MXIA	Comco Ikarus C-42B	1303-7237	
D-MXIB	Comco Ikarus C-42C	1307-7269	
D-MXIC	Comco Ikarus C-42B	1407-7324	
D-MXID	Comco Ikarus C-42B	1408-7325	
D-MXIE	Flight Team Spider trike	unkn	
D-MXIF	Comco Ikarus C-42B	unkn	
D-MXII	Comco Ikarus C-42B	0503-6660	
D-MXIK	Comco Ikarus C-42B	unkn	
D-MXIL(1)	Fly Synthesis Storch	FT 231	
D-MXIL(2)	B&F Funk FK-12S Comet	012-088	
D-MXIM	Bobcat	AB-RM 001	

Reg	Type	C/n	Other
D-MXIP	Comc Ikarus Fox-C22C	unkn	
D-MXIS	ME.13B	003	
D-MXIV(1)	Celier Zenon 4	unkn	
	(To Russia)		
D-MXIV(2)	Celier Xenon 4	unkn	
D-MXIW	Fisher FP-202 Koala	001	
D-MXIX	Fresh Breeze Pegasus 2	unkn	
D-MXJR(1)	NST Minimum	M249	
D-MXJR(2)	Comco Ikarus C-42B	unkn	
D-MXKD	J-3 Kitten	AF 131285L	
D-MXKF	B&F Funk FK-9 Mk.III	09-03-166	
D-MXKG	Aveko VL-3	VL-3-142	
D-MXKK	Eipper Quicksilver Sprint II	215	
D-MXKL	Comco Ikarus C-42B	1307-7267	
D-MXKM	TL Ultralight TL-96 Star	02 S 114	
D-MXKO	JMB VL-3 Evolution RG	unkn	
	(Crashed Eisental, Austria 6.1.14)		
D-MXKS	Apis BEE 15 MB	A022MB02	
D-MXKW	S.T.A.B. Trike XP-15	unkn	
D-MXKX	BOT SC-7 Speed Cruiser	unkn	
D-MXLA	Roko Aero NG-6UL	unkn	
D-MXLF	B&F Funk FK-14B Polaris	014-044	
D-MXLH	WDFL Dallach D4 Fascination BK	108	
D-MXLL	Zenair CH-602XL Zodiac	unkn	
D-MXLR	Scheibe UL-1 Coach IIb	001	
D-MXMB	ICP MXP-740V Savannah	181	
D-MXMD #	Light Aero Avid Flyer IV	498 or 001	
D-MXMM	Mitchell Wing	P-808	
D-MXMP	Tecnam P.92 Echo 100S	406	
D-MXMS	Air-Light Wild Thing	035	
D-MXMT	BRM Aero Bristell UL	151/2015	
D-MXMU(1)	Autogyro Europe MT-03	04G08	
D-MXMU(2)	Autogyro Europe MT-03	05G17	
D-MXMU(3)	Autogyro Europe MT-03	D06G02	
D-MXMU(4)	Autogyro Europe MTOsport	unkn	
D-MXMX	Autogyro Europe MT-03	05G08	
D-MXNA	Eipper Quicksilver Sprint II	216	
D-MXNB	Fresh Breeze Simo 122	unkn	
D-MXNO	Bobcat	EI-01	
D-MXNP	Light Aero Avid Flyer IV	616	
D-MXNV #	Eipper Quicksilver	1393	
D-MXOF	B&F Funk FK-6	003	
D-MXOX #	Falter	unkn	
D-MXPA	Sky-Walker II	325	
D-MXPB	Sky-Walker II	26117	
D-MXPC	Rans S-6 Coyote II	0994677	
D-MXPD	Comco Ikarus C-42B	0910-7066	
D-MXPE	Comco Ikarus C-42B	0210-6490	
D-MXPF	Comco Ikarus C-42B	unkn	
D-MXPG(2)	Comco Ikarus C-42 Cyclone	0007-6273	
D-MXPH #	Comco Ikarus C-42B	0911-7069	
D-MXPI	Comco Ikarus C-42B	0505-6677	
D-MXPJ(1)	Bobcat	PAU-1	
D-MXPJ(2)	Comco Ikarus C-42	unkn	
D-MXPK	B&F Funk FK-9 Mk.II	031	
D-MXPL	Ultravia Pélican Super Sport 450S	98-001	C-IFTP
D-MXPM	Plätzer Motte B2/B3	05	
D-MXPN	Comco Ikarus C-42B	unkn	
D-MXPO	Comco Ikarus C-42 Cyclone	0202-6429	
D-MXPP	unidentified paramotor	unkn	
D-MXPQ	Comco Ikarus C-42B	1205-7194	
D-MXPR	Comco Ikarus C-42B	0309-6567	
D-MXPS	Comco Ikarus C-42B	0606-6793	
D-MXPT	Comco Ikarus C-42	0907-7057	
	(W/o 22.9.15)		
D-MXPU	Comco Ikarus C-42B	0601-6781	
D-MXPV	Bautek Eagle V/ Pico	unkn	
D-MXPW	Comco Ikarus C-42B	1105-7149	
D-MXPX	Comco Ikarus C-42B	unkn	
D-MXPY	Comco Ikarus C-42B	0803-6950	
D-MXPZ	Comco Ikarus C-42B	1107-7168	
D-MXRA	Remos G.3 Mirage	064	
D-MXRG	Autogyro Europe MTOsport	unkn	
D-MXRJ	Aerospool WT-9 Dynamic	unkn	
D-MXRM #	Reuter UL-Arco	unkn	
D-MXRO	Alpi Aviation Pioneer 200	225	
D-MXRS	Tecnam P.92 Echo	200	
D-MXRU	Evektor EV-97 Eurostar	unkn	
D-MXRW	PA-17	001	
D-MXRX	Autogyro Europe MTOsport	M00993	
D-MXRY	Tecnam P.96 Golf S100	159	
D-MXSA	Schmidtler Enduro / iXess	unkn	
D-MXSB	Schmidtler Enduro Trike	01-002	
D-MXSD	Spacek SD-1 Minisport TG	033	
D-MXSE	Aerospool WT-9 Dynamic	unkn	
D-MXSG	SG.38 experimental powered glider	unkn	
D-MXSL	Pipistrel/Zen ULM Sinus	unkn	
D-MXSP #	Sky Pup	01	
D-MXSS	Tecnam P.92 Echo	197	
	(C/n 703 reported)		
D-MXST	Drachenstudio Royal 912 Trike	unkn	
D-MXSX	Roland 701D STOL	7-9066 / 002	
D-MXTA	Ekolot JK-05 Junior	unkn	
D-MXTC	Evektor EV-97 Eurostar	2003-1805	
D-MXTE	AirLony Skylane	unkn	
D-MXTF	Flight Design CT	98-04-04-31	D-MPWS
D-MXTH	Comco Ikarus Fox-C22	9402-3550	
D-MXTN	J-3 Kitten	A001	
D-MXTO	Comco Fox II Doppel Prototype	02	
D-MXTP	Skywalker XXL	unkn	
D-MXTT	Flight Design CT LS	unkn	
D-MXTV	J-3 Kitten	A001	
D-MXUI	Solid Air Diamant	022	
D-MXUR	Light Aero Avid Flyer	262	
D-MXUV #	B&F Funk FK-14B Polaris	unkn	
D-MXVL #	Aeroprakt	unkn	
D-MXVO #	Impulse 300	unkn	
D-MXVW	Klüver Twin Racer	423201	
D-MXWB	Nando Groppo Trial	unkn	
D-MXWF	Remos GX	287	N103GX
D-MXWO #	Eipper Quicksilver	3962	
D-MXWS	B&F Funk FK-9 Mk.II	004	
D-MXWT	Aerospool WT-9 Dynamic	unkn	
D-MXWU	Ferrari Tucano	076	
D-MXWW	Aerostyle Breezer	059	
D-MXWX	Comco Ikarus Fox-C22B	9604-3701	
D-MXXC	Fresh Breeze Xcitor XC123W09XCR1288BF63123		
D-MXXI	III Sky Arrow 450TGS	084 S	
D-MXXM	Fresh Breeze Simo 110	unkn	
D-MXXO	Fresh Breeze Simo 122	unkn	
D-MXXS #	XS Style WAD Power Cruiser	unkn	
D-MXXT	WDFL Dallach D4 Fascination BK	099	
D-MXXW(2)	Aviation Products Star Trike DS	127.08.054	
D-MXXW(3)	Bobcat	Wi 1	
D-MXXX	Fläming Air Trener Baby	03	OK-GUD 01
D-MXXZ	Tecnam P.92 Echo	253	
D-MXYL	Autogyro Europe Calidus	unkn	
D-MXYP	Autogyro Europe Calidus	unkn	
D-MXYR	Fresh Breeze Simo 122	unkn	
D-MXYW	Comco Ikarus C-42B	unkn	
D-MXYZ(2)	Murphy Renegade II	584	
D-MXZZ	B&F Funk FK-12 Comet S2	unkn	
D-MYAA (1)	Sky-Walker II	325	
D-MYAA(2)	Flight Design CT LS	unkn	
D-MYAB	Sky-Walker II	327	
D-MYAC	Scheibe UL-1Coach IIb	002	
D-MYAE	Aeros Nanolight Trike Discus 15T		
		04.13.021/023.14	
D-MYAF	Konsuprod Moskito Ib	014	
D-MYAG	Bautek Eagle V/ Pico	unkn	
D-MYAK(1)	B&F Funk FK-9 Mk.II	016	
D-MYAK(2)	Aeroprakt A-22L2 Vision	467	
D-MYAL	Tandem Air Sunny Sport	2-91	
D-MYAL(2)	TL Ultralight TL-96 Sting	unkn	
D-MYAN	Rans S-6 Coyote II	1291243	
D-MYAQ	ASO Storch	11005305	
D-MYAR	Denney Kitfox IV	546	
D-MYAS(1)	Tandem Air Sunny	010	
D-MYAS(2)	Autogyro Europe MT-03	unkn	
D-MYAU	Rans S-12 Airaile	0192170	
D-MYAV	AMF Chevvron 2-32	035	
D-MYAW	LO-120S	005A	
D-MYAX	Technoflug Piccolo BM	068	
D-MYAY	Technoflug Piccolo BM	069	
D-MYAZ	Impulse 100	2	
D-MYBA	B&F Funk FK-9 Mk.II	015	
D-MYBB	Comco Ikarus C-42B	0502-6647	
D-MYBC	B&F Funk FK-9 Mk.II	002	
D-MYBD	Technoflug Piccolo	077	
	(Re-regd D-KYBD, D-MZWS)		
D-MYBE	Shark Aero Shark	2012-005	OK-RUR 01
	(Re-regd D-MKKU, D-MMKV)		
D-MYBF	ASO Storch	11006306	
D-MYBG	Fisher FP-404 Classic	01	
D-MYBI	Euro-ALA Jet Fox 91D	001	
D-MYBJ	ASO Storch	11008307	
D-MYBK	Konsuprod Moskito Ib	017	
D-MYBL	Euro-ALA Jet Fox 91D	002	
D-MYBM	Fisher FP-404 Classic	TM-01	
D-MYBN	ASO 26 Storch	11007307	
D-MYBO	B&F Funk FK-9 Mk.II	020	
D-MYBR	Aerostyle Breezer CR	UL80	
D-MYBS	Tecnam P.92 Echo 100S	581	
D-MYBY	ICP MXP-740V Savannah	04-01-51-263	
D-MYCA	Blackshape Prime BS100	unkn	
D-MYCB	Plätzer Kiebitz B	376	
D-MYCC	Aeropro Eurofox	11201	
D-MYCD	ICP MXP-740V Savannah	01-09-51-097	
D-MYCH	Fly Synthesis Storch HS	329A273	
	(Same c/n as 28-XW)		
D-MYCK	Aerostyle Breezer CL	UL113	
D-MYCL	Autogyro Europe Calidus 09	unkn	
D-MYCN	Autogyro Europe Cavalon	unkn	
D-MYCO	Herringhausen Vagabund	15	
D-MYCT	Flight Design CT	97.10.01.10	
D-MYDD	Comco Ikarus C-42B	unkn	
D-MYDK	Breezer CL	UL108	
D-MYDM	UPM Conra Trike	910113	
D-MYDY	Plätzer Kiebitz B	240	
D-MYEA	Remos G.3 Mirage	060	
D-MYEC	Comco Ikarus C-42	unkn	
D-MYEF	Aeropro Eurofox	10801	
D-MYEG	Autogyro Europe Calidus	C00357	
D-MYEK	Tecnam P.92 Echo	244	
D-MYEN(1)	Kappa KPD-2U Sova	6169 G	
	(Skyleader 200 titles – or new aircraft, see next entry ?)		
D-MYEN(2?)	Kappa KP-2U	2 157 179 0	
D-MYER	Kappa KPD-2U Rapid 200	2108 121 K	
D-MYES	Kappa KPD-2U Sova	8292 I	
D-MYET #	Comco Ikarus Fox-C22	9310-3514	
D-MYEV	Evektor EV-97 Eurostar 2000	2000-0802	
D-MYFB	Plätzer Kiebitz-B2	047	
D-MYFF	Rans S-12 Airaile	01990861A	
D-MYFK	B&F Funk FK-9 Mk.IV ELA	09-429	
D-MYFM	Flight Design CT SW	04-05-02	
D-MYFP	Autogyro Europe Calidus	unkn	
D-MYFR	Autogyro Europe Calidus	unkn	
D-MYGG	Impulse 100	UL-4	
D-MYGH #	B&F Funk FK-9 TG Mk.II	086	
D-MYGK	Comco Ikarus C-42 Cyclone	9612-6067	
	(Reported as "Horus II", 5.02)		
D-MYGL	Comco Ikarus C-42 Cyclone	9701-6021	
D-MYGO	Shark Aero Shark	015-2013	
D-MYGS	B&F Funk FK-12 Comet	012-089	
D-MYGW	Plätzer Kiebitz	63	
D-MYGX	Remos GX	251	
D-MYGY(1)	Autogyro Europe MT-03	unkn	
D-MYGY(2)	Autogyro Europe MTOsport	D07G02	
D-MYGZ	Remos GX	382	
	(To RA-1607G)		
D-MYHA	ASO Storch	11009408	
D-MYHB	TL Ultralight TL-96 Sting	12ST388	
D-MYHE	Light Aero Avid Flyer IV	937	
D-MYHF	Gramex Song	13/2014	
D-MYHG	Pioneer Flightstar CL	950101	
D-MYHH	WDFL Dallach D4 Fascination	034	
D-MYHI	Remos GX	348	
D-MYHK	Flight Design CT	99.06.03.56	D-MPCT
D-MYHL(1)	Air-Light Wild Thing	025	
	(Re-regd D-MQRP)		
D-MYHL(2)	Air-Light Wild Thing	101	
D-MYHR	ICP MXP-740V Savannah	01-01-51-051	

Registration	Type	c/n	Notes
D-MYHS	B&F Funk FK-12 Comet	012-035	
	(W/o 22.5.15)		
D-MYHY	ICP MXP-740V Savannah	01-09-51-098	
D-MYIA	TL Ultralight TL-96 Star	01 S 89	
D-MYIC #	Plätzer Kiebitz	unkn	
D-MYIF	Ikarusflug Eurofox	038097	
D-MYII	Comco Ikarus C-42 Cyclone	0106-6361	
D-MYIN #	Aeroprakt A-22 Vision	028008	
D-MYJB	Aerospool WT-9 Dynamic	DY356/2010	
D-MYKA	Comco Ikarus C-42 Cyclone	9710-6058	
	(Re-regd D-MKHL)		
D-MYKB	Air-Light Wild Thing	020	
D-MYKD #	Comco Ikarus Fox-C22C	9 . . .-3658	
D-MYKE	Fisher Super Koala	SK 028	
D-MYKF	Zenair CH-601D Zodiac	6-3791	
D-MYKI	Comco Ikarus Fox-C22C	9605-3707	
D-MYKL	Ikarusflug Eurofox Pro	042097	
D-MYKM	Comco Ikarus C-42 Cyclone	0109-6370	
D-MYKO(1)	Comco Ikarus Fox-C22	9305-3512	
D-MYKO(2)	Remos G.3 Mirage	152	
D-MYLA	TL Ultralight TL-96 Star	02 S 127	
D-MYLD	B&F Funk FK-14B Polaris	unkn	
D-MYLE	Shark Aero Shark Premium	008-2012	
D-MYLF	Aeroprakt A-22L2 Vision	unkn	
D-MYLG	B&F Funk FK-12 Comet	012-010	
D-MYLI (1)	Technoflug Piccolo BM	026	D-KCFC
D-MYLI(2)	Flight Design CT LS	08-02-08	
D-MYLK(1)	ATEC Zephyr 2000	unkn	
D-MYLK(2)	B&F Funk FK-14B Polaris	unkn	
D-MYLL	Comco Ikarus C-42 Cyclone	0201-6424	
D-MYLO	Remos G.3 Mirage	unkn	
D-MYLW	Autogyro Europe Cavalon	V00096	
	(To C-FGYE 10.15)		
D-MYMA	Aeroprakt A-22 Vision	unkn	
D-MYMB	Remos G.3 Mirage	075	
D-MYME	Peak Bf-109R replica	2-002	
D-MYMI	Flight Design CT	99.09.05.69	
D-MYML	Comco Ikarus C-42B	unkn	
D-MYMM	TL Ultralight TL-232 Condor Plus	AB 02	
D-MYMR	Nando Groppo Trial	unkn	
D-MYMS(1)	Ultraleichtverbund Bi 90	922	
D-MYMS(2)	Aerostyle Breezer CL	UL 115	
D-MYMU	Flight Design CT SW	unkn	
D-MYMY	Flight Design CT SW	unkn	
D-MYND	Aerospool WT-9 Dynamic	DY553/2015	
D-MYNF	Aerostyle Breezer CL	UL137	
D-MYNK	Evektor EV-97 Eurostar	2002-1109	
D-MYNL #	Aeros Nanolight Trike Fox 16T	04.14.026/039.14	
D-MYNT #	Tecnam P.92E Echo	unkn	
D-MYOB(1)	Flight Design CT	98.04.02.29	
D-MYOB(2)	Rotortec Cloud Dancer	22909/7328-07	
D-MYON	ICP MXP-740V Savannah	01-00-50-142	
D-MYOP	B&F Funk FK-9 TG Mk.III (t/w)	09-03-133	
D-MYPC	Tecnam P.96 Golf 100S	171	
D-MYPE	Evektor EV-97 Eurostar	unkn	
D-MYPI(1)	WDFL Dallach D4 Fascination	unkn	
D-MYPI(2)	Pipistrel Sinus NW	435	
D-MYPL #	B&F Funk FK-9 Mk.II	023	
D-MYPS	Pipistrel Sinus NW	unkn	
D-MYQR	P&M Quik-R 912S	8573	
D-MYRA	B&F Funk FK-14 Polaris	014-021	
	(To 974-GB/F-JMBK c/n 14-021?)		
D-MYRC	Flight Design CT LS	F-12-06-02	
D-MYRE	Zenair CH-601D Zodiac	6-3574/002 1097	
D-MYRH	Roland Z602XL	Z-9561	
D-MYRI #	Comco Ikarus Fox-C22	9402-3567	
D-MYRJ	TUL-02 Tandem Tulak	040	
D-MYRL	Remos GX	unkn	
D-MYRO	Autogyro Europe MT-03	unkn	
D-MYRR	Wezel Apis 2	W007	
D-MYRS	Tandem Air Sunny	32	
D-MYRT(2)	Tecnam P.92 Echo 100S	474	
	(Formerly c/n 244)		
D-MYRU	Tomark SD-4 Viper	unkn	
D-MYRZ	Autogyro Europe MTOsport	unkn	
D-MYSA	Evektor EV-97R Eurostar 2000	2008 3225	
D-MYSB(1)	Flight Design CT	98.10.01.39	
D-MYSB(2)	Comco Ikarus C-42C	unkn	
D-MYSC	Comco Ikarus C-42C	unkn	
D-MYSD	Spacek SD-1 Minisport TD	026	
D-MYSE	WDFL Dallach D4 Fascination	081	
D-MYSF	Comco Ikarus C-42C	1411-7356	
D-MYSK	Magni M-24 Orion	unkn	
D-MYSL	Messerschmitt Bf.108 Taifun UL	02	
D-MYSR	Evektor EV-97 Eurostar	2001-1214	
D-MYSS	Autogyro Europe MTOsport	unkn	
D-MYST	Klüver Twin Racer Quartz SX 16	419201	
D-MYSY #	Comco Ikarus C-42B	0410-6629	
	(To 9H-UNA 6.09)		
D-MYTA	Fisher FP.202 Koala	unkn	
D-MYTH	B&F Funk FK-9 Mk.II	072	
D-MYTO	Alisport Silent 2 Electro (code "ER")	unkn	
D-MYTR	Air-Light Wild Thing	006	
D-MYTS(1)	Autogyro Europe MTOsport	unkn	
D-MYTS(2)	B&F Funk FK-9 Mk.IV ELA	09-05-417	
D-MYTW	Flight Design CT	97.09.02.08	
D-MYUL	Rans S-6 Coyote II XL	0895877	
D-MYUP	Zlin Savage	unkn	
D-MYUW	Evektor EV-97 Eurostar 2000R	2006-2703	
D-MYVC	Volocopter VC200	001	
D-MYVO #	B&F Funk FK-12 Comet	012-017	
	(To France as 83 AKM)		
D-MYVW	Zenair CH-601 Zodiac	6-9297	
D-MYWE	Pipistrel Sinus	unkn	
D-MYWT	Aerospool WT-9 Dynamic	DY438/2012	
D-MYWW	Tecnam P.96 Golf 100S	150	
D-MYWY	Zenair CH-601 Zodiac	unkn	
D-MYWZ	Fresh Breeze Simo 122	unkn	
D-MYXA	WDFL Sunwheel R	024	
D-MYXB	Autogyro Europe Cavalon	unkn	
D-MYXI #	Comco Ikarus C-42	9812-6110	OE-7107
D-MYXL	Spacek SD-1 Minisport	125	
D-MYXX	Tandem Air Sunny	006.07.02 SP	
D-MYXY(1)	Tecnam P.92 Echo S100	484	
	(Re-regd D-MBKU, 2013)		
D-MYXZ	Tecnam P.92 Echo	166	
D-MYYB	WDFL Dallach D4B Fascination	031	
D-MYYM	Autogyro Europe Calidus	unkn	
D-MYYX	Zlin Savage	unkn	
D-MYYY	Plätzer Kiebitz-B4	036	
D-MYYZ	Flight Design CT-2K	97-10-02-11	
	(To OE-7117)		
D-MYZE	Aerostyle Breezer CL	UL114	
D-MYZF	Aerostyle Breezer CL	UL105	
D-MYZG	Fresh Breeze Simo 122	unkn	
D-MYZI	Aerospool WT-9 Dynamic	DY506/2014	
D-MYZY	EEL ULF-2	53	
D-MYZZ(1)	B&F Funk FK-9 Mk.IV (t/w)	unkn	
D-MYZZ(2)	Alpi Avn Pioneer 300 UL	333	
D-MZAA	Fly Synthesis Storch	160.5	
D-MZAB	TEAM Airbike	AB 104	
D-MZAC	Remos G.3 Mirage	039	
D-MZAD	WDFL Sunwheel R	045	
D-MZAE	Air Energy AE-1 Silent Club	001	
D-MZAF	Plätzer Kiebitz B	unkn	
D-MZAG	J-3 Kitten	AL-1	
D-MZAH	Comco Ikarus C-42 Cyclone	9805-6100	
D-MZAI	Roland Z602XL	Z-9538	
D-MZAK	Flight Design CT SW	07-10-02	
D-MZAL(1)	Comco Ikarus C-42 Cyclone	9903-6182	
D-MZAL(2)	VierWerk Aerolite 120	unkn	
D-MZAM	Comco Ikarus Fox-C22	9405-3587	
D-MZAN	Comco Ikarus Fox-C22B	9507-3662	
D-MZAP	Comco Ikarus C-42B	unkn	
D-MZAR	Racer (Homebuilt)	02/90	
D-MZAS	Comco Ikarus Fox-C22	9405-3582	
D-MZAT	Comco Ikarus Fox-C22	9503-3635	
D-MZAV	Comco Ikarus C-42 Cyclone	9906-6195	
D-MZAY	Aviasud Mistral BA-83	009	
D-MZAZ	Aeroprakt A-22 Vision	20	
D-MZBA(1)	JK-1 Elf	001	
D-MZBA(2)	Aerostyle Breezer CL	121	
D-MZBB(1)	Flight Design CT	99.10.03.73	
D-MZBB(2)	Comco Ikarus C-42	unkn	
D-MZBC	Comco Ikarus C-42	0107-6368	
D-MZBD #	Impulse 100	5	
D-MZBE	Comco Ikarus C-42B	unkn	
D-MZBG	Comco Ikarus Fox-C22C	9511-3685	
D-MZBH	WDFL Dallach D4 Fascination BK	086	
D-MZBK	Tecnam P.96 Golf 100S	241	
D-MZBN #	Urban UFM-13 Lambada	07/13	
D-MZBR	Comco Ikarus C-42B	unkn	
D-MZBS	Tecnam P.92 Echo 100S	617	
D-MXBV	Remos GX	unkn	
D-MZCC	B&F Funk FK-9SW Mk,IV	09-04SW-353	
D-MZCH	Comco Ikarus C-42 Cyclone	9805-6127	
D-MZCI	Remos G.3 Mirage	070	
D-MZCT #	Flight Design CT LS	unkn	
D-MZCU	Remos G.3 Mirage	087	
D-MZCW	UPM-Trike	880057	
D-MZDD	Dova DV-1 Skylark	07/08	
	(Later c/n 07/27, two aircraft?)		
D-MZDF(2)	Comco Fox	009	
D-MZDG	B&F Funk FK-9 Mk.III	09-03-119	
D-MZDM	Remos G.3 Mirage	068	
D-MZDS	Autogyro Europe MTOsport	unkn	
D-MZDY	Aerospool WT-9 Dynamic	DY009 02	
D-MZEB	Air Light WT-01 Wild Thing	075	
D-MZEC	Roland Z602 Economy	Z-9544	
D-MZEE	Air Création /	unkn	
D-MZEF	Comco Ikarus C-42B	0307-6565	
D-MZEG	Tecnam P.92 Echo	unkn	
D-MZEI	Tecnam P.92 Echo	unkn	
D-MZEL	Plätzer Kiebitz B	198	
D-MZEM	Comco Ikarus C-42B	1107-7166	
D-MZEN(1)	Light Aero Avid Flyer	1292	
D-MZEN(2)	Alpi Avn Pioneer 300UL	unkn	
D-MZEP	ATEC Zephyr 2000	ZX 010497A	
D-MZES(1)	Flight Design CT	97.10.03.12	
D-MZES(2)	Roland Z602	unkn	
D-MZFC	Comco Ikarus C-42	0103-6333	
D-MZFF	Comco Ikarus C-42 Cyclone	9903-6159	
D-MZFG #	Behlen Power-Trike	89011	
D-MZFK	B&F Funk FK-9 Mk.IV	397	
D-MZFT	Remos G.3 Mirage	055	
D-MZGA	Zenair CH-602XL Zodiac	unkn	
D-MZGF	Ikarusflug Eurofox	10601	
D-MZGG	Urban Air Lambada UFM 13/15	7/13	
D-MZGH	Loehle Mustang 5151	010	
D-MZGS	Magni M-24 Orion	24138144	
D-MZGW	Zenair CH-601XI Zodiac	6-9850	
D-MZGZ	Remos GX	291	
D-MZHH	WDFL Dallach D4 Fascination BK	100	
D-MZHK	Comco Ikarus C-42 Cyclone	9910-6209	
D-MZHM	Comco Ikarus C-42B	unkn	
D-MZHR	Plätzer Kiebitz-B	102	
	(Same c/n as (ex?) D-MFKK)		
D-MZHS	ATEC Zephyr 2000	ZP521200	
	(To France as 25-TT)		
D-MZHT #	UPM-Trike	88058	
D-MZHW	Dyn'Aéro MCR-01 ULC	140	
D-MZIA	Tecnam P.92 Echo Classic	1420	
D-MZIG	Aviad Zigolo	unkn	
D-MZIH	Pioneer Flightstar CL	950302	
D-MZII	Plätzer Kiebitz-B8	139	
D-MZIL	Autogyro Europe MT-03	unkn	
D-MZIN	Comco Ikarus Fox-C22B	9404-3559	
D-MZIO	Comco Ikarus Fox-C22	950 .-3634	
D-MZIP(1)	Air-Light Wild Thing	005	
D-MZIP(2)	Air-Light Wild Thing	103	
D-MZIS	Evektor EV.97 Eurostar	98 03 08	
D-MZIW	Tandem Air Sunny Sport	61.94	
D-MZIX	Comco Ikarus C-42C	1404-7309	
D-MZJD	Flight Design CT2SW	03.05.02.21	
	(Bt as CT-2K?)		
D-MZKA	Zlin Savage Cruiser	172	
D-MZKG	Flight Design CT-2K	01.02.03.06	
D-MZKH	Air Energy AE-1 Silent	003	
D-MZKK	B&F Funk FK-9 Mk IV	09-04U-324	
D-MZKL(1)	Tecnam P.92 Echo 2000S	660	
D-MZKL(2)	Autogyro Europe MT-03	unkn	
D-MZKM	TL Ultralight TL-96 Star	00 S 79	

Reg	Type	c/n	Prev
D-MZKS	Remos G.3 Mirage	053	
D-MZKY	Magni M-16 Tandem Trainer	16 11 6364	
D-MZKZ #	Aerospool WT-9 Dynamic	DY003	
D-MZLB	Pipistrel Taurus 503	unkn	
D-MZLC	Autogyro Europe Cavalon	unkn	
D-MZLI	Air Energy AE-1 Silent Club	002	
D-MZLL	Tecnam P.92 Echo 100S	455	
D-MZLM	Pipistrel Taurus 503	unkn	
D-MZLW (1)	Comco Ikarus Fox-C22	9312-3534	
D-MZLW(2)	Autogyro Europe MTOsport	unkn	
D-MZMH	Remos G.3 Mirage	246	
D-MZMM #	B&F Funk FK-12 Comet	012-047	
D-MZMN	Comco Ikarus C-42 Cyclone	9707-6042	
D-MZMS	ATEC Zephyr	Z 200400A	
D-MZMZ	Comco Ikarus Fox-C22	9108-3364	
D-MZNF	WDFL Sunwheel R	037	
D-MZNN	Light Aero Avid Flyer	1291	
D-MZNZ	Tecnam P.96 Golf 100S	108	
D-MZOB	Air Energy AE-1 Silent Club	004	
D-MZOD #	Zenair CH-601XL Zodiac	unkn	
D-MZOH	Typhoon Trike (Homebuilt)	T1282667L	
D-MZON	Comco Ikarus Fox-C22C	9703-3714	
D-MZOO	Murphy Renegade Spirit	221	
D-MZOZ	Autogyro Europe MTOsport	unkn	
D-MZPA	Autogyro Europe MTOsport	unkn	
D-MZPF	B&F Funk FK-14B Polaris	014-120	
D-MZPP	B&F Funk FK-9 Mk.IV Smart	09-04U-316	
D-MZPS	Tecnam P.96 Golf 100S	202	
D-MZPY	Remos G-3 Mirage RS	147	
D-MZQQ	B&F Funk FK-9 Mk.IV SW	09-04-433	
D-MZRG(1)	Roland Z602RG	Z-9523	
D-MZRG(2)	Roland Z602RG	Z-9584	
D-MZRH #	Zenair CH-601D Zodiac	001	
D-MZRK	Racer (Homebuilt)	10/91	
D-MZRL	Autogyro Europe MTOsport	unkn	
D-MZRO	Trixy Zero gyrocopter	unkn	
D-MZRR	B&F Funk FK-9 Mk.IV	09-04-383	
	(Ex D-MZZR, or error?)		
D-MZRS	Tecnam P.96 Golf	042	
D-MZRX #	Point Avn/Albatros AN-22M	001	
D-MZRZ	Zenair CH-601D Zodiac	002	
D-MZSD	Spacek SD-1 Minisport TD	028	
D-MZSE	Flight Design CT-2K	unkn	
D-MZSH	Aerostyle Breezer CL	116	
D-MZSM	Roland Z602 Economy	Z-9552	
D-MZSP	Comco Ikarus C-42 Cyclone	9905-6183	
D-MZSW(1)	Ranger M	unkn	
D-MZSW(2)	B&F Funk FK-9 Smart	09-04U-272	
D-MZSY	Aerostyle Breezer CR	unkn	
D-MZSZ	Comco Ikarus C-42 Cyclone	9910-6206	
D-MZTA #	Comco Ikarus Fox-C22B	3684	
D-MZTF #	Comco Ikarus Fox-C22C	9807-3739	
D-MZTG	Autogyro Europe Calidus	unkn	
D-MZTM	Comco Ikarus Fox-C22C	unkn	
D-MZTR #	Trixy G 4-2 R	009-12	
D-MZTS	Remos G.3 Mirage	042	
D-MZTT	Kappa KP-2U Sova	09/98	
D-MZUL	B&F Funk FK-9 Mk.III Utility	09-03U-175	
D-MZUM	Fresh Breeze Simo 122	unkn	
D-MZUS	Comco Ikarus C-42	unkn	
D-MZUU #	B&F Funk FK-14 Polaris	unkn	
D-MZUZ	Cosmos Phase III / Top 14.9	unkn	
D-MZVV #	B&F Funk FK-14 Polaris	unkn	
D-MZWD	Roland Z602XL	Z-9514	
D-MZWF	TL Ultralight TL-232 Condor Plus	99 C 05	LN-YBA, SE-YUB
D-MZWO	EEL ULF-2	unkn	
D-MZWS	Technoflug Piccolo	077	D-KYBD, D-MYBD
D-MZWT #	UPM-Trike	880059	
D-MZWW	Comco Ikarus Fox-C22C	unkn	
D-MZWZ	Urban Air UFM-10 Samba	25/10	
D-MZXI	Roland Z602	unkn	
D-MZXL #	Zenair CH-601XL Zodiac	unkn	
D-MZXX	Air-Light Wild Thing	008	
D-MZYA #	Kümmerle Mini-Fly-Set	1261/91-4	
D-MZYK	Magni M-16 Tandem Trainer	16 10 5924	
D-MZYS	Aeropro Eurofox	08600	
D-MZYX	Dyn'Aéro MCR-01 UL	98	
D-MZYY	Fresh Breeze Simo 122	unkn	
D-MZYZ(1)	Autogyro Europe MT-03	unkn	
D-MZYZ(2)	Autogyro Europe MTOsport	unkn	
D-MZZD #	Autogyro Europe MTOsport	unkn	
D-MZZE #	Autogyro Europe Calidus	unkn	
D-MZZG	Zlin Savage Classic	unkn	
D-MZZH(1)	WDFL Dallach D4B Fascination	unkn	
D-MZZH(2)	ATEC Zephyr 2000	ZP521200	
	(Same c/n as for D-MZHS, 25-TT)		
D-MZZI	Autogyro Europe MT-03	unkn	
D-MZZK	Autogyro Europe MT-03	05G14	
D-MZZL	Aero East Europe Sila 450C	120428/AEE/004	YU-A101
D-MZZM(2)#	Autogyro Europe MT-03	D06G12	D-MCFI(2)
	(Stolen Nov.07)		
D-MZZM(3)	FD Composites Arrowcopter AC20	034	
D-MZZR #	B&F Funk FK-9 Mk.IV	383	
	(Re-regd D-MZRR ?)		
D-MZZT	Autogyro Europe MTOsport	unkn	
D-MZZU	Alpi Avn Pioneer 300UL	unkn	
D-MZZV	Airector 120	unkn	
D-MZZY	Remos G.3 Mirage	076	
D-MZZZ	Rans S-10S Sakota	0790105	

Sold to Germany, not yet identified:

Reg	Type	c/n	Prev
D-M . . .	Alpi Avn Pioneer 200	130	PH-3Z9
D-M . . .	B&F Funk FK-9 Mk.III	192	OO-E02
D-M . . .	Comco Ikarus Fox-C22	9606-3709	PH-2W8
D-M . . .	Flight Design MC	A-10-07-31	G-CGRA
D-M . . .	ICP MXP-740 Savannah	01-03-51-055	PH-JGN
D-M . . .	Konsuprod Moskito IB	001	LN-YWR(1)
D-M . . .	Parsons 2-place Gyrocopter	PFA G/108-1275	G-IVYS
	(Possibly D-MHUH ?)		
D-M . . .	Rans S-6ES Coyote II	1195892	OO-C21
D-M . . .	Rans S-10 Sakota	0997186	N43783
D-M . . .	Rans S-16 MPR Sakota	0294003	N5287X
D-M . . .	Take Off Merlin	26508	PH-2Y4
D-M . . .	Take Off Merlin 1100	118405	PH-3W9
D-M . . .	Tecnam P.92 Echo	1315	PH-4F6
D-M . . .	Tecnam P.96 Golf	35	PH-3E8
D-M . . .	Winters/ RAF-2000	H2-07-17-649	N2496Z
D-M . . .	Zlin Savage Cruiser	104	PH-4A8

CLASS N : Unpowered Microlights

The D-N . . . series is used for unpowered Microlight Gliders and hang gliders. No current listing is available but the following have been reported recently for example:

Reg	Type
D-NAAY	EEL ULF-1
D-NAKD	EEL ULF-1
D-NDAJ	Pro-Fe Banjo
D-NERA	Pro-Fe Banjo
D-NFUJ	Pro-Fe Banjo
D-NGFJ	Lutz Pegasus
D-NGFQ	EEL ULF-1
D-NGFU	EEL ULF-1
D-NGFZ	VJ 23H
D-NGIP	Pro-Fe Banjo
D-NGJU	Pro-Fe Banjo
D-NGVS	Pro-Fe Banjo
D-NHHM	Pro-Fe Banjo
D-NHZI	Pro-Fe Banjo
'D-NICE'	See D-AMAJ
D-NISB	Pro-Fe Banjo
D-NJOU	EEL ULF-1
D-NJPO	Pro-Fe Banjo
D-NJPP	Pro-Fe Banjo
D-NKWZ	Pro-Fe Banjo
D-NLGC	Pro-Fe Banjo
D-NPKW	Airwave Magic
D-NPPO	Pro-Fe Banjo
D-NSBJ	EEL ULF-1
D-NSWN	Aériane Swift
D-NTCX	Pro-Fe Banjo
D-NUDI	EEL ULF-1
D-NUGW	Gerhard Wagner GFW-3
D-NULV	Pro-Fe Banjo
D-NUSV	Pro-Fe Banjo
D-NUWM	Pro-Fe Banjo
D-NWKU	Pro-Fe Banjo
D-NXRA	EEL ULF-1
D-NZJA	Luftikus-2
D-NZJH	EEL ULF-1

CLASS O : Balloons

Where a balloon has been replaced by an identical model, often only a replacement envelope, we have attempted to indicate this by quoting the earlier c/n in addition. Other re-used registrations are shown in the normal manner.

Reg	Type	c/n	Prev
D-OAAA(2)	Schröder Fire Balloons G HAFB	1478	
D-OAAE	Lindstrand LBL-120A HAFB	958	
D-OAAF	Test marks for GEFA-Flug AS.105GD Hot Air Airships		
D-OAAG(2)	GEFA-Flug AS.105GD Hot Air Airship	0061	
	(P. 8.12)		
D-OAAK(2)	Lindstrand LBL-150A HAFB	1494	
D-OAAL(2)	Schröder Fire Balloons G HAFB	1104	
	(Replacement for c/n 330)		
D-OAAM	Lindstrand LBL-150A HAFB	1132	
D-OAAR	Raven Europe S-60A HAFB	E-343	
D-OAAT	Kubicek BB-85Z HAFB	1184	
D-OABC(2)	Schröder Fire Balloons G HAFB	1053	
D-OABD(3)	Cameron GB1000 Gas Balloon	1796	
D-OABE	Schröder Fire Balloons G HAFB	983	
D-OABI	Schröder Fire Balloons G HAFB	266	
D-OABK(2)	Kubicek BB-100Z HAFB	1095	
D-OABL(2)	Kubicek BB-70Z HAFB	460	
D-OABP(2)	Schröder Fire Balloons G HAFB	946	
D-OABT(2)	Schröder Fire Balloons G HAFB	1572	
D-OABW	Schröder Fire Balloons G HAFB	1209	
D-OABZ	Lindstrand LBL-120A HAFB	833	
D-OACH	Cameron A-105 HAFB	505	D-OPIF, D-Pfiffikus, HB-BAW
D-OACK	Schröder Fire Balloons G HAFB	1668	
D-OACU	Kubicek BB-42Z HAFB	516	
D-OADA(2)	Schröder Fire Balloons G HAFB	1503	
D-OAEC(2)	Cameron Z-105 HAFB	11904	
D-OAES	Head AX7-77B HAFB	234	N8294Q
D-OAFA	Schröder Fire Balloons G HAFB	1088	
D-OAFB	Schröder Fire Balloons G HAFB	965	
D-OAFC	Thunder AX8-105 SII HAFB	3802	
D-OAFG	Kubicek BB-70Z HAFB	1052	
D-OAGA	Cameron A-105 HAFB	2329	HB-BRU
D-OAGB	Cameron O-105 HAFB	974	D-Papage I
D-OAGF	Schröder Fire Balloons G HAFB	260	
D-OAGG	Schröder Fire Balloons G HAFB	634	
D-OAGH	Wörner NL-1000/STU Gas Balloon	1069	
	(W/o 1.10.01)		
D-OAHB	Cameron Z-105 HAFB	11019	
D-OAHG	Schröder Fire Balloons G HAFB	235	D-Fireballoon(2)
D-OAHM	Schröder Fire Balloons G HAFB	650	
D-OAHO	Thunder AX8-90 SI HAFB	2545	
D-OAHR	Thunder AX8-105 HAFB	2552	
D-OAIB	Thunder AX9-120 SII HAFB	4626	
D-OAIF	Schröder Fire Balloons G HAFB	184	D-Raffeisen
D-OAIG	Cameron N-77 HAFB	10219	
D-OAIR(2)	Kubicek BB-30Z HAFB	334	OK-0334
D-OAIU	Schröder Fire Balloons G HAFB	585	
D-OAIX	Sky 220-24 HAFB (Res.)	096	G-BXPH
D-OAJG(2)	Schröder Fire Balloons G HAFB	1030	
	(Replacement for c/n 389)		
D-OAKA	Thunder Ax9-120 SII HAFB	4875	
D-OAKD	Schröder Fire Balloons G HAFB	1165	
D-OAKE	Schröder Fire Balloons G HAFB	467	
D-OAKF	Colt 160A HAFB	1731	D-Sachsen, G-BSJD
D-OAKO	Schröder Fire Balloons G HAFB	610	
D-OAKS	Schröder Fire Balloons G HAFB	410	
D-OAKT(2)	Cameron A-210 HAFB	4737	
D-OALA(2)	Schröder Fire Balloons G HAFB	1635	
D-OALB	Schröder Fire Balloons G HAFB	777	
D-OALF(2)	Schröder Fire Balloons G HAFB	1611	
	(Res. 25.2.15)		
D-OALL(2)	Kubicek BB-26E HAFB	1007	
D-OALP	Thunder AX8-84 SI HAFB	1037	D-Sonthofen

Registration	Type	c/n	Notes
D-OALZ(3)	Kubicek BB-34Z HAFB	697	
D-OAMB	Cameron O-90 HAFB	2225	D-Wegener
D-OAMC	Cameron V-77 HAFB	2176	
D-OAMD	Cameron N-90 HAFB	2478	
D-OAME(2)	Schröder Fire Balloons G HAFB	1501	
D-OAMG(2)	Schröder Fire Balloons G HAFB	1369	
D-OAMP	Kubicek BB-100Z HAFB	1257	
D-OAMR	Thunder AX10-150 SII HAFB	10122	
D-OAMW	Schröder Fire Balloons G HAFB	515	
D-OANA	Raven Europe S-66A HAFB	E-321	
D-OANR	Kubicek BB-45Z HAFB	1082	
D-OANS(2)	Schröder Fire Balloons G HAFB	1340	
D-OANT	Lindstrand LBL-90A HAFB	498	
D-OAOA	Schröder Fire Balloons G HAFB	263	
D-OAOC	Cameron A-105 HAFB	3690	
	(Res. as SP-BFA(2) .12)		
D-OAOD	Cameron A-210 HAFB	3689	
D-OAOE	Sky 180 HAFB	021	
D-OAOG	Cameron N-160 HAFB	4592	
D-OAOH	Cameron N-145 HAFB	3554	
D-OAOJ	Cameron Z-225 HAFB	11084	
D-OAOK	Cameron N-160 HAFB	10220	
D-OAOM	Cameron Z-180 HAFB	11532	
D-OAOP	Wörner FK-5500/STU Gas Balloon	6020	
D-OAOS	Cameron A-210 HAFB	4864	
D-OAPB	Thunder AX9-120 SII HAFB	10059	
D-OAPH	Kubicek BB-30Z HAFB	359	
D-OAPP(2)	Schröder Fire Balloons G HAFB	1260	
D-OAPS	Cameron N-105 HAFB	3781	
D-OARC	Schröder Fire Balloons G HAFB	37	D-Arcobrau
D-OARD	Cameron A-375 HAFB	3682	
D-OARG	Augsburg K-1050/3-RI Gas Balloon	10120	D-Ergee V
D-OARH	Wörner K-1000/3-STU Gas Balloon	0321	D-Karstadt
D-OART	Raven-Europe S-60A HAFB	E-282	
D-OARW(2)	Cameron Z-180 HAFB	10706	
D-OASA	Schröder Fire Balloons G HAFB	262	
D-OASH(2)	Wörner NL-1000/STU Gas Balloon	1053	
D-OASK	Kubicek BB-30 HAFB	237	OK-0237
D-OASP(2)	Schröder Fire Balloons G HAFB	1136	
D-OASR	Schröder Fire Balloons G HAFB	1207	
D-OASU(2)	Kubicek BB-42Z HAFB	505	
D-OASW	Schröder Fire Balloons G HAFB	369	
D-OATB	Schröder Fire Balloons G HAFB	1213	
D-OATD	Cameron O-84 HAFB	2549	D-Bauknecht(2)
D-OATE	Lindstrand LBL-120A HAFB	958	
D-OATM	Schröder Fire Balloons G HAFB	212	
D-OATS(2)	Kubicek BB-37N HAFB	620	
D-OAUC	Schröder Fire Balloons G HAFB	1486	
D-OAUN	Cameron A-140 HAFB	2680	D-OFUN(1), G-BTVZ
D-OAUR(2)	Ultramagic M-145 HAFB	145/75	
D-OAUS	Schröder Fire Balloons G HAFB	1055	
D-OAWA	Kubicek BB-30 HAFB	318	OK-0318
D-OAWF	Raven-Europe FS-57A HAFB	E-284	
D-OAWS	Sky 105 HAFB	069	
D-OAWU	Schröder Fire Balloons G HAFB	612	
D-OAWW(2)	Schröder Fire Balloons G HAFB	1436	
	(Res 8.10) (Replaces c/n 665)		
D-OAXL(2)	Lindstrand LBL-210A HAFB	988	
D-OAXW	Schröder Fire Balloons G HAFB	1084	
D-OBAA	Schröder Fire Balloons G HAFB	979	
D-OBAG	Schröder Fire Balloons G HAFB	1205	
D-OBAH	Colt 105A HAFB	3861	
D-OBAK	Schröder Fire Balloons G HAFB	1603	
D-OBAM	Lindstrand LBL-310A HAFB	190	
D-OBAS(2)	Schröder Fire Balloons G HAFB	1521	
D-OBAT	Cameron N-120 HAFB	10150	
D-OBAU(3)	Kubicek BB-42Z HAFB	1188	
D-OBAV(2)	Cameron Z-105 HAFB	11267	
D-OBAX	Aerostar S-66A HAFB	3067	
D-OBAY	Kubicek BB-85Z HAFB	694	
D-OBAZ	Raven Europe S-66A HAFB	E-283	D-Russberger(2)
D-OBBB(2)	Schröder Fire Balloons G HAFB	1291	
D-OBBC	Colt 105A HAFB	4349	
D-OBBE	Schröder Fire Balloons G HAFB	270	
D-OBBG(2)	Schröder Fire Balloons G HAFB	1513	
D-OBBK	Schröder Fire Balloons G HAFB	1109	
D-OBBL(2)	Cameron A-210 HAFB	4774	
D-OBBM(2)	Schröder Fire Balloons G HAFB	667	
D-OBBN	Schröder Fire Balloons G HAFB	690	
D-OBBO(2)	Kubicek BB-30Z HAFB	417	
D-OBBR(2)	Kubicek BB-85Z HAFB	563	CS-BBR
D-OBBW	Wörner NL-510/STU Gas Balloon	1042	
D-OBBY(3)	Kubicek BB-20XR HAFB	1024	
D-OBCD	Lindstrand LBL-120A HAFB	424	
D-OBCE	Schröder Fire Balloons G HAFB	578	
D-OBCF(2)	Schröder Fire Balloons G HAFB	1426	
	(Replaces c/n 844)		
D-OBCG(2)	Schröder Fire Balloons G HAFB	1129	
D-OBCI	Schröder Fire Balloons G HAFB	509	
D-OBCK(2)	Schröder Fire Balloons G HAFB	1531	
D-OBCS	Aerostar S-60A HAFB	S60A-3284	
D-OBCU	Lindstrand LBL-260A HAFB	1161	
D-OBCW	Wörner NL-1000/STU Gas Balloon	1059	
	(Previously listed as c/n 1051, 1996-9)		
D-OBDD(2)	Lindstrand LBL-180A HAFB	1393	
D-OBDF	Cameron A-210 HAFB	4126	
D-OBDM	Schröder Fire Balloons G HAFB	195	D-Melitta
D-OBDW	Thunder AX8-105 SII HAFB	3530	
D-OBEC	Cameron N-133 HAFB	3926	
D-OBED(3)	Lindstrand LBL-150A HAFB	784	
	(Replacement for c/n 264)		
D-OBEF	Thunder AX10-150 HAFB	10210	
D-OBEG	Thunder AX9-120 SII HAFB	4136	
D-OBEI	Schröder Fire Balloons G HAFB	1273	
D-OBEK(2)	Schröder Fire Balloons G HAFB	1512	
D-OBEM	Kubicek BB-5 BEMB SS HAFB	116	OK-9046
D-OBEO(2)	Schröder Fire Balloons G HAFB	1397	
D-OBFB(2)	Cameron Z-105 HAFB	10595	
D-OBFK	Schröder Fire Balloons G HAFB	800	OO-BFK(2), D-OTDI
D-OBGA	Ultramagic M-145 HAFB	145/76	
D-OBGC	Thunder AX10-180 SII HAFB	10846	
D-OBGT	Cameron A-120 HAFB	4999	LX-BGT, OO-BGT(2), G-BZXF
D-OBHB(2)	Kubicek BB-51Z HAFB	1005	
D-OBHG	Schröder Fire Balloons G HAFB	528	
D-OBHH	Colt 180A HAFB	2360	
D-OBHL	Kubicek BB-37Z HAFB	1219	
D-OBHS(2)	Lindstrand LBL-150A HAFB	1450	
D-OBHV	Cameron Z-105 HAFB	10352	
D-OBHW	Schröder Fire Balloons G HAFB	681	
D-OBHZ	Cameron A-315 HAFB	10719	
D-OBIB	Schröder Fire Balloons G HAFB	438	
D-OBIG(3)	Cameron A-210 HAFB	4796	
	(Replacement for c/n 3322 ex D-OERT)		
D-OBII	Schröder Fire Balloons G HAFB	368	D-OBIG
D-OBIL	Wörner K-1000/3-STU Gas Balloon	0285/2	D-Mobil IV
D-OBIM	Colt 300A HAFB	2416	
D-OBIO(2)	Schröder Fire Balloons G HAFB	1380	
D-OBIS(3)	Schröder Fire Balloons G HAFB	1160	
D-OBIX	Schröder Fire Balloons G HAFB	387	
D-OBJI	Cameron O-84 HAFB	1417	HB-BJI
D-OBJT	Schröder Fire Balloons Pig 36 HAFB	1443	
D-OBKA	Thunder AX8-105 SII HAFB	3886	
D-OBKM(3)	Kubicek BB-30Z HAFB	216	
D-OBKS	Schröder Fire Balloons G HAFB	250	
D-OBKW	Cameron N-105 HAFB	10667	
D-OBKZ	Schröder Fire Balloons G HAFB	34	OO-BKM(2), D-Mosella
D-OBLA(2)	Cameron Z-105 HAFB	10900	
D-OBLB(3)	Cameron Z-140 HAFB	10297	
D-OBLF	Kubicek BB-30N HAFB	96	OO-BLF
D-OBLG	Aerostar S-60A HAFB	3286	
D-OBLO	Cameron N-120 HAFB	4265	D-OBLB(2)
D-OBLT	Ultramagic T-180 HAFB	180/79	D-OBTL(2)
D-OBLU	Schröder Fire Balloons G HAFB	856	
D-OBLZ	Kubicek BB-42Z HAFB	383	
D-OBMB(2)	Kubicek BB-30Z HAFB	294	OK-0294
D-OBMS(2)	Schröder Fire Balloons G HAFB	1402	
D-OBMW(3)	Kubicek BB-42Z HAFB	860	
D-OBNG(2)	Schröder Fire Balloons G HAFB	974	
D-OBNW	Thunder AX8-105 SII HAFB	2164	
D-OBOE(2)	Schröder Fire Balloons G HAFB	1086	
D-OBOL	Schröder Fire Balloons G HAFB	185	D-Bolberg(2)
D-OBOM	Lindstrand LBL-105A HAFB	545	
D-OBOR(2)	Schröder Fire Balloons G HAFB	1450	
	(Replaces c/n 274)		
D-OBOS	Schröder Fire Balloons G HAFB	884	
D-OBPP(2)	Thunder AX8-105 SII HAFB	4593	
D-OBPV	Schröder Fire Balloons G HAFB	1199	
D-OBPZ	Colt 120A HAFB	1618	HB-BPZ
D-OBRB	Schröder Fire Balloons G HAFB	1319	
D-OBRE(2)	Cameron Z-105 HAFB	11130	
D-OBRG	Thunder AX9-140 SII HAFB	3659	
D-OBRP	Kubicek BB-60Z HAFB	1185	
D-OBRT(2)	Schröder Fire Balloons G HAFB	1004	
	(Replacement for c/n 309)		
D-OBRW	Schröder Fire Balloons G HAFB	1428	
D-OBRX	Schröder Fire Balloons G HAFB	1343	
D-OBSB	Cameron O-105 HAFB	1948	PH-BSP
D-OBSC	Schröder Fire Balloons G HAFB	1203	
D-OBSD	Kubicek BB-100Z HAFB	655	OK-0655
D-OBSE	Cameron O-90 HAFB	3069	HB-BST
D-OBSG	Lindstrand LBL-105A HAFB	627	
D-OBSH	Schröder Fire Balloons G HAFB	162	D-Luftschloss
D-OBSI	Lindstrand LBL-180A HAFB	1274	
D-OBSJ	Schröder Fire Balloons G HAFB	1000	
D-OBSK	Schröder Fire Balloons G HAFB	28	D-Schlossbau
D-OBSN	Cameron O-77 HAFB	894	D-Noris
D-OBSS	Schröder Fire Balloons G HAFB	418	
D-OBST(3)	Kubicek BB-60Z HAFB	1121	
D-OBSW(2)	Kubicek BB-42Z HAFB	1228	
D-OBSY	Head AX8-105 HAFB	387	
D-OBTH	Schröder Fire Balloons G HAFB	101	D-Alpinist
D-OBTS(3)	Schröder Fire Balloons G HAFB	1414	
D-OBTU	Lindstrand LBL-150A HAFB	1438	
D-OBUB	Kubicek BB-37Z HAFB	1173	
D-OBUD	Schröder Fire Balloons G HAFB	1196	
D-OBUM	Colt 300A HAFB	2411	
D-OBUS	Schröder Fire Balloons G HAFB	1010	
D-OBUZ	Schröder Fire Balloons G HAFB	847	D-OBNZ
D-OBVB(2)	Schröder Fire Balloons G HAFB	1514	
D-OBVL	Thunder AX8-105 SII HAFB	2335	
D-OBVR	Schröder Fire Balloons G HAFB	1303	
D-OBWE	Cameron A-210 HAFB	3492	
D-OBWF	Cameron A-105 HAFB	1540	D-Hammonia(1)
D-OBWI	Cameron A-250 HAFB	3708	
D-OBWJ	Lindstrand LBL-210A HAFB	334	
D-OBWK	Cameron A-160 HAFB	4201	
D-OBWM(2)	Ultramagic N-210 HAFB	210/45	
D-OBWQ	Cameron A-275 HAFB	4743	
D-OBWW(2)	GEFA-Flug AS.105GD Hot Air Airship	0007	
D-OBXX	Schröder Fire Balloons G HAFB	462	
D-OBYN	Wörner NL-1000/STU Gas Balloon	1080	
D-OBYZ	Schröder Fire Balloons G22/24 HAFB	1250	LX-BYZ
D-OBZX	Cameron Z-225 HAFB	10839	OO-BZX
D-OCAB	Schröder Fire Balloons G HAFB	932	
D-OCAC(2)	Schröder Fire Balloons G HAFB	1300	
D-OCAF	Ultramagic N-210 HAFB	210/104	
D-OCAL	Schröder Fire Balloons G HAFB	339	
D-OCAM	Thunder AX8-105 SII HAFB	2359	
D-OCAR(2)	Cameron N-90 HAFB	10161	
D-OCAT(2)	Colt 105A HAFB	3749	
D-OCBM(2)	Ultramagic M-105 HAFB	105/102	
D-OCCC(3)	Schröder Fire Balloons G HAFB	1679	
D-OCCG(2)	Cameron O-105 HAFB	10221	
	(Replacement for c/n 2379)		
D-OCCM(2)	Schröder Fire Balloons G HAFB	1431	
D-OCCO	Schröder Fire Balloons G HAFB	361	
D-OCED(2)	Schröder Fire Balloons G HAFB	1646	
D-OCEL	Raven Europe FS-57A HAFB	E-153	D-Celle
D-OCEM	Sky 140-24 HAFB	156	
D-OCEW	Head AX8-105 HAFB	354	N24239
D-OCFT	Wörner N-1000/STU Gas Balloon	1041	
D-OCGC	Lindstrand LBL-260A HAFB	1275	
D-OCGI	Thunder AX8-105 SII HAFB	2356	
D-OCHB	Schröder Fire Balloons G HAFB	1226	
D-OCHL	Ultramagic N-180 HAFB	180/49	
D-OCHY	Cameron A-105 HAFB	2985	
D-OCIO(3)	Schröder Fire Balloons G HAFB	925	
D-OCKI	Aerostar RX-8 HAFB	3241	
D-OCKM	Wörner K-780/2-STU Gas Balloon	1040	
D-OCLP	Schröder Fire Balloons G HAFB	1361	
D-OCMB	Schröder Fire Balloons G HAFB	961	

Registration	Type	c/n	Notes
D-OCMK	Schröder Fire Balloons G HAFB	1485	
D-OCNF	Ultramagic M-77 HAFB	77/266	
D-OCOA	Cameron N-133 HAFB	3455	D-OOOA(1)
D-OCOC(2)	Schröder Fire Balloons G HAFB	757	
D-OCOM(2)	Kubicek BB-60Z	839	
D-OCON	Cameron O-84 HAFB	2707	
D-OCOP	Schröder Fire Balloons G HAFB	903	
D-OCOX	Wörner NL-1000/STU Gas Balloon	1054	OO-BCX, D-OCOX
D-OCPC	Cameron N-145 HAFB	10111	
	(Originally allocated as A-140 c/n 4850)		
D-OCRA	Cameron Z-105 HAFB	11619	
D-OCRW	Cameron N-133 HAFB	10189	
D-OCSO	Schröder Fire Balloons G HAFB	1268	
D-OCST	Cameron O-120 HAFB	3090	
D-OCTA(2)	Wörner FK-5500/STU Gas Balloon	6063	
D-OCTO	Thunder AX8-105 SII HAFB	1639	D-Jonathan
D-OCTY	Cameron TR-70 HAFB	10437	G-CCTY
D-OCWH	Cameron N-105 HAFB	10015	
D-OCWU	Schröder Fire Balloons G HAFB	1489	
D-OCXE	Cameron Z-120 HAFB	10595	G-CCXE
D-ODAC	Ultramagic M-145 HAFB	145/54	
D-ODAD	Schröder Fire Balloons G HAFB	1063	
D-ODAS(2)	Kubicek BB-30 HAFB	232	OK-0232
D-ODAT	GEFA-Flug AS.105GD Hot Air Airship (P.04)	0009	
D-ODAU	Schröder Fire Balloons G HAFB	585	
D-ODBL	Schröder Fire Balloons G HAFB	1289	
D-ODBM	Schröder Fire Balloons G HAFB	908	
D-ODBW	Schröder Fire Balloons G HAFB	287	
D-ODDD(2)	Schröder Fire Balloons G HAFB	1330	
D-ODEB	Cameron A-250 HAFB	4328	G-ODEB
D-ODEG	Schröder Fire Balloons G HAFB	640	
D-ODEM(2)	Cameron TR-77 HAFB	11963	
D-ODER	Cameron Z-210 HAFB	11851	
D-ODFB	Schröder Fire Balloons G HAFB	422	D-Treveris(2)
D-ODGL	Kubicek BB-60Z HAFB	1067	
D-ODHB	Colt 105A HAFB	2621	
D-ODHM	Schröder Fire Balloons G HAFB	752	
D-ODIB	Cameron A-180 HAFB	11886	
D-ODIC	Cameron O-140 HAFB	11021	
D-ODIL(3)	Schröder Fire Balloons G HAFB	1551	
D-ODIN	Cameron O-84 HAFB	2652	
D-ODKB(2)	Schröder Fire Balloons G HAFB	1647	
D-ODKD(2)	Kubicek BB-30Z HAFB	402	
D-ODKV(4)	Schröder Fire Balloons G HAFB	1477	
D-ODKW(2)	Schröder Fire Balloons G HAFB	1126	D-ODKV(3)
D-ODLL(2)	Kubicek BB-85Z HAFB	526	
D-ODLP	Schröder Fire Balloons G HAFB	1344	
D-ODLY	Cameron Z-105 HAFB	10961	
D-ODMA(2)	Cameron Z-120 HAFB	10705	
D-ODMI	Schröder Fire Balloons G HAFB	766	
D-ODMW	Schröder Fire Balloons G HAFB	290	
D-ODNI	Thunder AX8-105 SII HAFB	2236	
D-ODOC	Raven-Europe FS-57A HAFB	E-327	
D-ODOD	Cameron Z-105 HAFB	11795	
D-ODOR	Thunder AX10-150 SII HAFB	4554	
D-ODPM	Schröder Fire Balloons G HAFB	412	
D-ODSO	Schröder Fire Balloons G34/24 HAFB	950	
D-ODTI	Ultramagic N-180 HAFB	180/89	
D-ODTM	Schröder Fire Balloons G HAFB	1578	
D-ODTS	Schröder Fire Balloons G40/24 HAFB	825	
D-ODUB	Lindstrand LBL-105A HAFB	593	
D-ODUD(2)	Cameron A-180 HAFB	4163	
D-ODUG	Kubicek BB-S Wurst s/s HAFB	1222	
D-ODUS	Wörner K-1000/3-STU Gas Balloon	1034	
D-ODWA	Ultramagic M-90 HAFB	649	
D-ODWH	Schröder Fire Balloons G HAFB	1337	
D-ODYL	Cameron A-275 HAFB	4450	G-BXYL
D-ODYN(2)	Schröder Fire Balloons G HAFB	1071	
	(Replacement for c/n 613)		
D-OEAL	Cameron Z-150 HAFB	10879	
D-OEAR	Raven-Europe FS-57A HAFB	E-217	D-Aerostar
D-OEBB	Schröder Fire Balloons G HAFB	1595	
D-OEBH(2)	Schröder Fire Balloons G HAFB	1293	
D-OEBP	Lindstrand LBL-180A HAFB	1182	
D-OEBS	Schröder Fire Balloons G HAFB	1014	
D-OEBU	Kubicek BB-30N HAFB	435	
D-OECD	Schröder Fire Balloons G HAFB	1453	
D-OECO	Schröder Fire Balloons G HAFB	393	
D-OEDE	Schröder Fire Balloons G HAFB	1493	
D-OEEE	Thunder AX8-105 SII HAFB	4569	
D-OEEJ(2)	Kubicek BB-26Z HAFB	707	
D-OEEU	Cameron A-400 HAFB	4508	
D-OEFS	Cameron Z-105 HAFB	10618	
D-OEHD(2)	Cameron A-180 HAFB	11882	
D-OEHR	Kubicek BB-42 HAFB	429	
D-OEID	Schröder Fire Balloons G HAFB	1432	
D-OEIF(2)	Schröder Fire Balloons G HAFB	1659	
D-OEIK	Cameron Z-105 HAFB	11549	
D-OEIN	Schröder Fire Balloons G HAFB	1048	
D-OEJH	Lindstrand LBL-105A HAFB	136	D-OFJH(1)
	(SP-BFF(2) Res. 13)		
D-OEJN	Ultramagic M-90 HAFB	90/124	
D-OEKB	Thunder AX8-105 SI HAFB	3753	
D-OEKD	Thunder AX8-105 SI HAFB	3757	
D-OEKO	Aerostar S-60A HAFB	3259	
D-OEKY(2)	Ultramagic M-160 HAFB	160/79	
D-OELA	Schröder Fire Balloons G HAFB	851	
D-OELC	Schröder Fire Balloons G HAFB	1360	
D-OELD	Cameron Potts Lager Bottle 2 SS HAFB	4571	
D-OELE(4)	Schröder Fire Balloons G HAFB	750/857	
	(Formerly used by c/ns 79, 234 and 750)		
D-OELG	Cameron A-160 HAFB	4253	
D-OELH	Schröder Fire Balloons G HAFB	768	
D-OELI	Schröder Fire Balloons G HAFB	842	
D-OELL	Schröder Fire Balloons G HAFB	1040	
D-OELO	Lindstrand LBL-150A HAFB	699	
D-OENA	Cameron A-210 HAFB	10108	
D-OENH	Wörner NL-STU/1000 Gas Balloon	1090	
D-OENI	Schröder Fire Balloons G HAFB	1233	
D-OEON	Schröder Fire Balloons G HAFB (Res.)	2002	
D-OEPA(2)	Kubicek BB-20SS Humpty Dumpty HAFB	400	OK-5050
D-OEPP	Schröder Fire Balloons G HAFB	827	
D-OERD	Lindstrand LBL-150A HAFB	592	
D-OERR	Cameron A-105 HAFB	2289	D-Dorr
D-OERT	Cameron A-210 HAFB	3322	(D-OBIG(2), D-OERT
D-OESI(2)	Lindstrand LBL-240A HAFB	1190	
D-OESM	Thunder AX8-90 SI HAFB	2501	
D-OESR	Thunder AX10-180 SII HAFB	10035	D-OTSR
D-OESW	Cameron A-180 HAFB	10686	
D-OEUE	Schröder Fire Balloons G HAFB	786	
D-OEUF(3)	Schröder Fire Balloons G HAFB	1600	
D-OEUL	Schröder Fire Balloons G HAFB	1415	
D-OEUR	Schröder Fire Balloons G HAFB	302	
D-OEVB	Lindstrand LBL-150A HAFB	1218	
D-OEVE	Thunder AX8-90 SII HAFB	1320	D-Oeventrop
D-OEVN	Lindstrand LBL-105A HAFB	145	
D-OEWA(2)	Schröder Fire Balloons G HAFB	1490	
D-OEWB(3)	Schröder Fire Balloons G HAFB	1198	
D-OEWI	GEFA-Flug AS.105GD Hot Air Airship	0060	D-OAAF
D-OEWV	Schröder Fire Balloons G HAFB	1101	
D-OEXC	Schröder Fire Balloons G HAFB	288	
D-OEZB	Schröder Fire Balloons G HAFB	1429	
D-OEZI	Cameron A-105 HAFB	4973	
D-OEZL	Cameron A-105 HAFB	2210	D-Spezi
D-OEZY	Cameron A-105 HAFB	10151	
D-OFAR	Schröder Fire Balloons G HAFB	629	
D-OFAS	Aerostar S-60A HAFB	3227	
D-OFAU	Schröder Fire Balloons G HAFB	1667	
D-OFAX(2)	Schröder Fire Balloons G HAFB	265	D-Schmitt (4)
D-OFAZ	Schröder Fire Balloons G HAFB	490	
D-OFBC	Schröder Fire Balloons G HAFB	943	
D-OFBG	Raven-Europe RX-7 HAFB	E-214	D-Harxheim(2)
D-OFBI	Schröder Fire Balloons G HAFB	131	
D-OFBK	Aerostar RXS-8 HAFB	3070	
D-OFBS	Schröder Fire Balloons G HAFB	1581	
	(P. 29.12.14)		
D-OFDG	Schröder Fire Balloons G HAFB	1211	
D-OFDP	Schröder Fire Balloons G HAFB	1022	
D-OFEM	Schröder Fire Balloons G HAFB	959	
D-OFEN	Schröder Fire Balloons G HAFB	11	D-Feuertute
D-OFER	Schröder Fire Balloons G HAFB	202	
D-OFES	Cameron N-105 HAFB	2697	D-Feldschlossen
D-OFEY	Schröder Fire Balloons G HAFB	1011	
D-OFFB(2)	Schröder Fire Balloons M20/24 HAFB	1433	
D-OFFE	Schröder Fire Balloons G HAFB	1270	D-OFFF
D-OFFF(2)	Schröder Fire Balloons G HAFB	1519	
D-OFFW	Ultramagic T-180 HAFB	180/94	
D-OFHA	Schröder Fire Balloons G HAFB	1555	
D-OFHB(2)	Schröder Fire Balloons G HAFB	1378	
D-OFHD	Schröder Fire Balloons G HAFB	1219	
D-OFHH	Cameron N-105 HAFB	4803	
D-OFHP	Ultramagic T-210 HAFB	210/32	
D-OFHW	Lindstrand LBL-210A HAFB	1472	
D-OFIN	Schröder Fire Balloons G HAFB	173	D-Finanzgruppe
D-OFIR	Cameron A-120 HAFB	4458	
D-OFIT	Schröder Fire Balloons G HAFB	1315	
D-OFIX	Cameron A-120 HAFB	11449	
D-OFJH(2)	Lindstrand LBL-120A HAFB	1019	
D-OFJS	Cameron N-105 HAFB	1531	D-Felsenkeller(2)
D-OFLO	Schröder Fire Balloons G HAFB	210	
D-OFLS	Cameron V-77 HAFB	1050	D-Otto
D-OFLY	Schröder Fire Balloons G HAFB	1543	
D-OFMA(2)	Thunder AX10-210 SII HAFB	4316	
D-OFMD	Schröder Fire Balloons G HAFB	868	
D-OFMG	Aerostar S-60A HAFB	3226	
D-OFOS	Colt 180A HAFB	2525	
D-OFOX	Schröder Fire Balloons G HAFB	1613	
D-OFPB	Schröder Fire Balloons G HAFB	1379	
D-OFPH	Aerostar S-55A HAFB	3087	
D-OFPP	Schröder Fire Balloons G HAFB	754	
D-OFPW	Kubicek BB-30Z HAFB	240	OK-0240
D-OFSA	Schröder Fire Balloons G HAFB	468	
D-OFTR	Cameron A-105 HAFB	3879	
D-OFUE	Cameron V-90 HAFB	10431	
D-OFUN(3)	Schröder Fire Balloons G HAFB	1146	
D-OFUX	Thunder Ax8-105 SII HAFB	4301	
D-OFVA(2)	Wörner NL-1000/STU Gas Balloon	1073	
D-OFVB	Lindstrand LBL-210A HAFB	427	
D-OFVV	Schröder Fire Balloons G HAFB	464	
D-OFWH	Schröder Fire Balloons G HAFB	1617	
D-OFYH	Ultramagic M-105 HAFB	105/27	EC-FYH
D-OFYN	Schröder Fire Balloons G HAFB	1500	
D-OFZF	Kubicek BB-120P HAFB	1063	
D-OGAB(3)	Schröder Fire Balloons G HAFB	1674	
	(Replaces c/n 1458)		
D-OGAR	Aerostar S-60A HAFB	3271	
D-OGAZ	Bronschofen K-780/2-Ri Gas Balloon	10413	
D-OGBB(2)	Schröder Fire Balloons G HAFB	1110	
D-OGBO	Colt 120A HAFB	2240	
D-OGDA	Schröder Fire Balloons G HAFB	1153	
D-OGDL	GEFA-Flug AS.105GD Hot Air Airship	0047	
D-OGDP	Schröder Fire Balloons G HAFB	466	
D-OGEG	Cameron N-77 HAFB	4070	
D-OGEO(2)	Schröder Fire Balloons G HAFB	1680	
D-OGET(2)	Kubicek BB-85Z HAFB	960	
D-OGEW	Schröder Fire Balloons G HAFB	877	
D-OGFA	Schröder Fire Balloons G HAFB	745	
D-OGFB(2)	Schröder Fire Balloons G HAFB	1246	
D-OGFP	Cameron Z-105 HAFB	10716	
D-OGFS	Schröder Fire Balloons G HAFB	1341	
D-OGGG(3)	Schröder Fire Balloons G HAFB	1541	
D-OGGO	Schröder Fire Balloons G HAFB	1093	
D-OGHC	Aerostar RXS-8 HAFB	3112	
D-OGHS	Schröder Fire Balloons G HAFB	995	
D-OGIE(2)	Schröder Fire Balloons G HAFB	1060	
D-OGIN	Balloon Works Firefly 9-056 HAFB	F9-056	N25532
D-OGKR	Lindstrand LBL-150A HAFB	1016	
D-OGLA(2)	Kubicek BB-34Z HAFB	1256	
D-OGLI	Schröder Fire Balloons G HAFB	902	
D-OGMI	Lindstrand LBL-69A HAFB	845	
D-OGMT	Kubicek BB-30Z HAFB	474	HS-SMT
D-OGMZ(2)	Cameron Z-120 HAFB	10590	
D-OGNI	Ultramagic M-160 HAFB	160/17	
D-OGOG	Schröder Fire Balloons G HAFB	716	
D-OGPK	Schröder Fire Balloons G HAFB	489	
D-OGQT	Schröder Fire Balloons G HAFB	1139	
D-OGRA	Raven Europe S-60A HAFB	E-350	
D-OGRO	Cameron O-105 HAFB	2833	
D-OGRU	Cameron A-160 HAFB	3957	PH-GRU, (D-OGRU)
D-OGSB	Kubicek BB-70Z HAFB	437	PH-GSB
D-OGSH	Schröder Fire Balloons G HAFB	1568	
D-OGST(2)	Ultramagic M-120 HAFB	120/57	

Reg	Type	c/n	Previous identities
D-OGSV	Ultramagic M-120 HAFB	120/18	
D-OGTS	Schröder Fire Balloons G HAFB	620	
D-OGUP	Schröder Fire Balloons G HAFB	1648	
D-OGUT(2)	Cameron Z-120 HAFB	11289	
D-OGVS	Cameron O-105 HAFB	1296	D-Erdgas
D-OGWG	Ultramagic N-210 HAFB	210/86	
D-OGWI	GEFA-Flug AS.105GD Hot Air Airship	0034	
D-OGYN	Wörner NL-STU/1000 Gas Balloon	1100	
D-OHAA	Schröder Fire Balloons G HAFB	1295	
D-OHAC(3)	Kubicek BB-34Z HAFB	537	
D-OHAD	Head AX8-88 HAFB	187	N45244
D-OHAH(2)	Schröder Fire Balloons G HAFB	1435	
D-OHAM	Cameron N-105 HAFB (Res.11.99)	2683	D-Hammonia(2)
D-OHAN(2)	Ultramagic M-105 HAFB	105/76	
D-OHAP	Schröder Fire Balloons G HAFB	953	
D-OHAQ	Cameron N-105 HAFB	3373	D-OHAC(1)
D-OHAS	Schröder Fire Balloons G HAFB	641	
D-OHAW	Raven RX-7 HAFB	3187	D-Bruchhausen(1)
D-OHBB	Thunder AX9-140 SII HAFB	2316	
D-OHBC(2)	Thunder AX9-140 SII HAFB	2113	D-Mercedes-Benz(2)
D-OHBE(2)	Thunder AX10-160 SII HAFB	3784	
D-OHBF	Thunder AX9-140 SII HAFB	1726	D-Lowentor(2)
D-OHBI	Thunder AX9-140 SII HAFB	3486	
D-OHBJ(2)	Cameron Z-250 HAFB	11992	
D-OHBK(2)	Cameron Z-150 HAFB	11658	
D-OHBM	Colt 240A HAFB	4094	
D-OHBS	Cameron Z-225 HAFB	11186	
D-OHBT	Schröder Fire Balloons G HAFB	1375	
D-OHCC	Aerostar S-60A HAFB	3222	
D-OHCV	Schröder Fire Balloons G HAFB	1445	
D-OHDH(2)	Cameron Z-120 HAFB	11741	
D-OHDI	Cameron A-105 HAFB	3162	
D-OHDL	Kubicek BB- HAFB	345	
D-OHDR	Raven Europe S-60A HAFB	E-...	
D-OHDV	Schröder Fire Balloons G HAFB	659	
D-OHEB	Cameron A-105 HAFB	3434	
D-OHEL(2)	Lindstrand LBL-150A HAFB	1071	
D-OHEN	Schröder Fire Balloons G HAFB	1579	
D-OHER	Schröder Fire Balloons G HAFB	1597	
D-OHES(3)	Schröder Fire Balloons G HAFB	1559	
D-OHET	Kubicek BB-30Z HAFB	363	
D-OHFA	Colt 105A HAFB	1849	D-Hagdorn(1)
D-OHFB	Schröder Fire Balloons G HAFB	1499	
D-OHFQ	Schröder Fire Balloons G HAFB	1111	
D-OHFS	Schröder Fire Balloons G HAFB	1374	
D-OHFT	Schröder Fire Balloons G HAFB	1403	
D-OHFU	Cameron O-105 HAFB	3923	
D-OHHB	Kubicek BB-30Z HAFB	557	
D-OHHH	Schröder Fire Balloons G HAFB	25	D-Super
D-OHHO	GEFA-Flug AS.105GD Hot Air Airship	0019	
D-OHIO	Schröder Fire Balloons G30/24 HAFB	356	
D-OHIT(2)	Kubicek BB-60Z HAFB	786	OO-BWK(2)
D-OHIW(3)	Kubicek BB-30Z HAFB	468	
D-OHJE	Lindstrand LBL-400A HAFB	422	
D-OHJW	Aerostar RXS-8 HAFB	3088	
D-OHKE(2)	Schröder Fire Balloons G HAFB	1023	
D-OHKF	Schröder Fire Balloons G HAFB	1243	
D-OHKM	Ultramagic S-70 HAFB	70/20	
D-OHKN	Ultramagic N-250 HAFB	250/77	
D-OHKP	Raven-Europe S-60A HAFB	E-280	
D-OHKS(2)	Schröder Fire Balloons G HAFB	1509	
D-OHKW	Lindstrand LBL-120A	1131	
D-OHKY	Cameron Z-210 HAFB	11708	
D-OHLA	Schröder Fire Balloons G HAFB	1329	
D-OHLB	Lindstrand LBL-48L HAFB	552	OE-ZOO(b)
D-OHLE(2)	Schröder Fire Balloons G HAFB	1287	
D-OHLL	GEFA-Flug AS.105GD Hot Air Airship	0039	
D-OHLM	Schröder Fire Balloons G HAFB	730	
D-OHLP	Schröder Fire Balloons G HAFB	1201	
D-OHLR(2)	Kubicek BB-70Z HAFB	783	
D-OHLS	GEFA-Flug AS.105GD Hot Air Airship	0040	HB-QLE
D-OHLW	GEFA-Flug AS.105GD Hot Air Airship	0006	HB-QSE, D-OCAC
D-OHMI	Kubicek BB-60Z HAFB	506	
D-OHMN	Schröder Fire Balloons G HAFB	865	
D-OHMW	Aerostar RX-8 HAFB	RX8-3102	N63223
D-OHOB	Lindstrand LBL-150A HAFB	619	
D-OHOF	Raven-Europe FS-57A HAFB	E-281	
D-OHOI	Schröder Fire Balloons G HAFB	443	
D-OHOL	Thunder AX8-105 SII HAFB	1896	D-Holsten
D-OHOM(2)	Schröder Fire Balloons G HAFB (Replacement for c/n 384)	859	
D-OHON	Colt Pils Bottle SS HAFB	10094	
D-OHPB	Schröder Fire Balloons G HAFB	962	
D-OHPO	Cameron Z-133 HAFB	10713	
D-OHRF(2)	Schröder Fire Balloons G HAFB	1525	
D-OHRG	Kubicek BB-42Z HAFB	1091	
D-OHRM	Schröder Fire Balloons G HAFB	697	
D-OHRS	Schröder Fire Balloons G HAFB	1215	
D-OHSI	Kubicek BB-34Z HAFB	513	
D-OHSS(2)	Schröder Fire Balloons G HAFB	1331	
D-OHST(2)	Ultramagic M-105 HAFB	105/93	
D-OHUP	Colt 140A HAFB	4053	
D-OHVR(2)	Ultramagic M-145 HAFB	145/37	
D-OHVW	Cameron N-90 HAFB	1175	SE-ZBO
D-OHWB	Kubicek BB-S Bear HAFB	382	
D-OHWK(2)	Lindstrand LBL-120A HAFB	1420	
D-OHWL	Schröder Fire Balloons G HAFB	1363	
D-OHWM	Cameron O-84 HAFB	1749	D-Tassilo(2)
D-OHWW(2)	Cameron N-105 HAFB (Replacement for c/n 2816)	10136	
D-OHXH	Raven-Europe RX-7 HAFB	E-342	
D-OIAT	Cameron A-120 HAFB	2817	D-OURS(1)
D-OIBB	Wörner NL-840/STU Gas Balloon	1048	
D-OICE	Lindstrand LBL SS Cornetto HAFB	266	PH-ICE
D-OIDO	Wörner FKP-380/STU Gas Balloon	6204	
D-OIDT	Schröder Fire Balloons G HAFB	1349	
D-OIGL	Schröder Fire Balloons G HAFB	1017	D-OWIM(2)
D-OIHR	Kubicek BB-37N HAFB	433	
D-OIIC	Schröder Fire Balloons G36/24 HAFB	392	D-OEIC(1)
D-OIKF	Colt 180A HAFB	4447	
D-OIKK	Schröder Fire Balloons G HAFB	1589	
D-OILE	Aerostar RXS-8 HAFB	RXS8-3096	
D-OILY	Cameron O-105 HAFB	2595	G-SMAX, G-MADM
D-OILZ	Cameron O-140 HAFB	2887	
D-OIMM	Schröder Fire Balloons G HAFB	500	
D-OIND	Kubicek BB-42Z HAFB	591	
D-OING	Schröder Fire Balloons G HAFB	718	
D-OINK(2)	Kubicek BB-34Z HAFB	1225	
D-OIOI (2)	Cameron N-105 HAFB	2435	D-Toshiba
D-OIPE	Schröder Fire Balloons G HAFB	1384	
D-OIRO(2)	Kubicek BB-30Z HAFB	1040	
D-OISA	Colt 105 HAFB	1686	D-Schlossquell
D-OISE(2)	Schröder Fire Balloons SS Bierglas HAFB	137	D-Isenbeck
D-OISG(2)	Schröder Fire Balloons G HAFB	1595	
D-OISN	Schröder Fire Balloons G HAFB	1068	
D-OISO	Cameron A-105 HAFB	3276	
D-OIZI	Thunder AX8-105 SI HAFB	2546	
D-OJAC	Schröder Fire Balloons G HAFB	1122	
D-OJAN(3)	Ultramagic N-180 HAFB	180/114	
D-OJCA(2)	Ultramagic M-145 HAFB	145/28	
D-OJCB(3)	Ultramagic M-145 HAFB	145/60	
D-OJFB	Ultramagic M-120 HAFB	120/83	
D-OJFK	Schröder Fire Balloons G HAFB	625	
D-OJGM	Kubicek BB-S Jäger 28 HAFB	522	OK-0525
D-OJHB	Kubicek BB-S ICE HAFB	368	
D-OJHH	Kubicek BB-S Forklift HAFB	1070	
D-OJHR	Schröder Fire Balloons G HAFB	1610	
D-OJIL	Thunder AX10-150 SII HAFB	4646	
D-OJJI	Thunder AX9-120 SII HAFB	2613	D-OJJJ(1)
D-OJJJ(2)	Schröder Fire Balloons G Joker SS HAFB	1100	
D-OJMC	Aerostar S-60A HAFB	3218	
D-OJMN	Thunder AX8-105 SII HAFB	2090	
D-OJOE	Colt 210A HAFB	2425	
D-OJOR	Schröder Fire Balloons G HAFB	1280	
D-OJPI (2)	Schröder Fire Balloons G HAFB	1324	
D-OJRD	Schröder Fire Balloons G HAFB	1409	
D-OJRW	Lindstrand LBL-150A HAFB	576	
D-OJSM	Schröder Fire Balloons G HAFB	980	
D-OJUB	Kubicek BB-37Z HAFB	616	
D-OJUC(2)	Ultramagic M-105 HAFB	105/65	
D-OJUW	Schröder Fire Balloons G HAFB	1476	
D-OJWC(3)	Schröder Fire Balloons G HAFB	1128	D-OJWO(2)
D-OJWW	Kubicek BB-34Z HAFB	508	
D-OJYH	Schröder Fire Balloons G HAFB	1588	
D-OKAB	Cameron A-250 HAFB	4289	
D-OKAE	Lindstrand LBL-150A HAFB	494	
D-OKAF	Cameron A-105 HAFB	2974	
D-OKAG	Kubicek BB-26Z HAFB	831	OK-3831
D-OKAM	Schröder Fire Balloons G HAFB	334	
D-OKAN	Lindstrand LBL-150A HAFB	1388	
D-OKAP	Lindstrand LBL-150A HAFB	770	
D-OKAY	Aerostar RXS-8 HAFB	3082	
D-OKBA(2)	Schröder Fire Balloons G HAFB	1596	
D-OKBB	Schröder Fire Balloons G HAFB	249	
D-OKBE	Thunder AX8-105 SII HAFB	3650	
D-OKBF	Thunder AX8-105 SII HAFB	3511	
D-OKBG(2)	Lindstrand LBL-120A HAFB	1264	
D-OKBJ	Thunder AX9-120 SII HAFB	10139	
D-OKBM(2)	Schröder Fire Balloons G HAFB	1227	
D-OKBQ	Thunder AX9-120 SII HAFB	10006	
D-OKCF	Thunder AX8-90 SII HAFB	2607	
D-OKEI	Lindstrand LBL-150A HAFB	1178	
D-OKEP	Kubicek BB-37Z HAFB	1258	
D-OKER	Schröder Fire Balloons G HAFB	787	
D-OKES	Cameron H-34 HAFB	2214	G-BRWY
D-OKFP	GEFA-Flug AS.105GD Hot Air Airship	15	
D-OKGA	Schröder Fire Balloons G HAFB	896	
D-OKGB	Ultramagic N-250 HAFB	250/04	
D-OKGF	Schröder Fire Balloons G HAFB	217	
D-OKGH	Ultramagic S-105 HAFB	105/58	
D-OKGS	Schröder Fire Balloons G HAFB	1186	
D-OKGV	Kubicek BB-37N HAFB	264	D-OKGW(1), OE-ZCA(1), OK-0264
D-OKHG	Schröder Fire Balloons G HAFB	32	D-Sonnenbuhl
D-OKHH	Schröder Fire Balloons G HAFB	1609	
D-OKHK(2)	Ultramagic M-145 HAFB	145/86	
D-OKHL	Cameron N-120 HAFB	10060	
D-OKHO	Kubicek BB-37N Pig SS HAFB	203	OK-2063
D-OKHP(2)	Kubicek BB-37Z HAFB	602	
D-OKHW	Schröder Fire Balloons G HAFB	426	
D-OKIA	Colt 90A HAFB	2269	
D-OKIB(2)	Schröder Fire Balloons G HAFB	1033	
D-OKID(2)	Kubicek BB-34Z HAFB	1090	
D-OKIE	Thunder AX8-90 SII HAFB	3853	
D-OKIF(2)	Cameron Z-77 HAFB	11416	G-WCUP
D-OKIT	Cameron O-84 HAFB	2172	G-BROS
D-OKKB	Schröder Fire Balloons G HAFB	1567	
D-OKKK(2)	Schröder Fire Balloons G HAFB	1616	
D-OKLD	Cameron N-133 HAFB	4722	
D-OKLE	Cameron N-90 HAFB	3448	
D-OKLO	Schröder Fire Balloons G HAFB	772	
D-OKLW	Ultramagic M-120 HAFB	120/21	
D-OKMF	Raven-Europe S-60A HAFB	E-245	
D-OKNB	Schröder Fire Balloons G HAFB	970	
D-OKOK	Thunder AX8-90 SII HAFB	2053USA	N224TC
D-OKOL	Colt 240A HAFB	2243	
D-OKOM	Colt 105A HAFB	3860	
D-OKPB(2)	Schröder Fire Balloons G HAFB (Replacement for c/n 532)	1106	
D-OKPC	Cameron A-180 HAFB	2562	G-BTKO
D-OKPF	GEFA-Flug AS.105GD Hot Air Airship	0015	
D-OKPH	Cameron A-120 HAFB	4686	
D-OKRA	Schröder Fire Balloons G HAFB	46	D-Kranich
D-OKRE(2)	Cameron O-120 HAFB	10184	
D-OKRI	Cameron A-140 HAFB	2861	
D-OKRO(2)	Lindstrand LBL-150A HAFB	794	
D-OKRU	Aerostar S-60A HAFB	3183	D-OKRO(1)
D-OKSB(2)	Schröder Fire Balloons G HAFB (Res. 12.1.15)	1624	
D-OKSC	Balloon Works Firefly F9 HAFB	F9-061	
D-OKSK(2)	Ultramagic N-180 HAFB	180/121	
D-OKSP	Aerostar S-60A HAFB	3280	
D-OKSR	Cameron 90SS Coffee Jug HAFB	3789	
D-OKSU	Kubicek BB-42Z HAFB	241	
D-OKSV	Schröder Fire Balloons G HAFB (Res. 2.3.15)	1628	
D-OKSW	Thunder AX8-90 SII HAFB	2358	
D-OKTO(4)	Lindstrand LBL-150A HAFB	1248	
D-OKTP(3)	Lindstrand LBL-150A HAFB	962	D-OKTO(3)
D-OKUB	Kubicek BB-37N HAFB	441	
D-OKUE	Raven Europe S-60A HAFB	E-345	
D-OKUH	Cameron A-105 HAFB	2918	

Reg	Type	c/n	Prev id
D-OKUR	Schröder Fire Balloons G HAFB	138	D-Wittgensteiner(3)
D-OKUS	Schröder Fire Balloons G HAFB	1488	
D-OKVB	Schröder Fire Balloons G HAFB	1370	
D-OKVR(2)	Schröder Fire Balloons G HAFB	952	
D-OKWB	Sky 120 HAFB	177	
D-OKWD	Ultramagic M-120 HAFB	120/29	
D-OKWS	Schröder Fire Balloons G HAFB	824	
D-OKXC	Cameron V-77 HAFB	973	G-BKXC
D-OKZO	Lindstrand LBL-150A HAFB	957	
D-OLAE	Schröder Fire Balloons G HAFB	1605	
D-OLAF(2)	Cameron TR-84 HAFB	11437	G-LAFF
D-OLAN(2)	Schröder Fire Balloons G HAFB	1594	
D-OLAR(2)	Schröder Fire Balloons G HAFB	64	D-Gutfried
D-OLAU(2)	Schröder Fire Balloons G HAFB	1507	
D-OLAV(2)	Schröder Fire Balloons G HAFB	1162	
D-OLAW	Kubicak BB-34Z HAFB	1190	
D-OLBB	Schröder Fire Balloons G HAFB (Permit 7.10)	455	
D-OLBC	Schröder Fire Balloons G HAFB	403	
D-OLBF	Lindstrand LBL-105A HAFB	477	
D-OLBK	Schröder Fire Balloons G HAFB	181	D-LBS(4)
D-OLBL(2)	Kubicek BB-42Z HAFB	583	OE-SAA
D-OLBM(2)	Lindstrand LBL-105A HAFB	450	D-OLBA, D-OWPG
D-OLBS(3)	Cameron A-105 HAFB	4736	
D-OLBV	Schröder Fire Balloons G HAFB	1321	
D-OLBY	Cameron A-145 HAFB	2955	
D-OLCI(2)	Kubicek BB-37 HAFB	277	OK-0277
D-OLDB	Schröder Fire Balloons G HAFB	1377	
D-OLDD	Schröder Fire Balloons G HAFB	312	
D-OLDY(2)	Schröder Fire Balloons G HAFB	971	
D-OLEE	Cameron O-120 HAFB (Res.)	3066	
D-OLEG(2)	Schröder Fire Balloons Clownkopf SS HAFB	1027	
D-OLEI	Kubicek BB-70Z HAFB	419	
D-OLEK	Ultramagic V-105 HAFB	105/72	
D-OLEM	Kubicek BB-60Z HAFB	1110	
D-OLEN	Cameron N-105 HAFB	3251	
D-OLEV(2)	Schröder Fire Balloons G HAFB (Replacement for c/n 200)	728	
D-OLEW(2)	Schröder Fire Balloons G HAFB	1267	
D-OLGA	Schröder Fire Balloons G HAFB	826	
D-OLGD	Schröder Fire Balloons G HAFB	1645	(D-OTRO)
D-OLGN	Schröder Fire Balloons G HAFB	1007	
D-OLGS	Cameron Z-120 HAFB	10619	
D-OLHG	Schröder Fire Balloons G HAFB	573	
D-OLHH	Schröder Fire Balloons G HAFB (Res 3.10)	1393	
D-OLHM(2)	Schröder Fire Balloons G HAFB	1439	
D-OLIB	Wörner NL-STU/1000 Gas Balloon	1091	
D-OLIF	Schröder Fire Balloons G HAFB	40	D-Cliff
D-OLIV(2)	Aerostar S-60A HAFB	3241	
D-OLIX	Schröder Fire Balloons G HAFB	22	D-Achalm(1)
D-OLJA	Ultramagic N-210 HAFB	210/62	
D-OLLA(3)	Lindstrand LBL-180A HAFB	1040	
D-OLLB	Thunder AX8-105 SII HAFB	4919	
D-OLLD(2)	Kubicek BB-42Z HAFB	1057	
D-OLLE(3)	Schröder Fire Balloons G HAFB	1274	D-OLLL(3)
D-OLLH	Thunder AX8-105 SII HAFB	2201	
D-OLLI(2)	Schröder Fire Balloons G HAFB	1473	
D-OLME	Kubicek BB-30Z HAFB	1043	
D-OLMT	Lindstrand LBL-150A HAFB	694	
D-OLNI(2)	Schröder Fire Balloons G HAFB (Res. 10.2.15)	1627	
D-OLNZ	Cameron A-275 HAFB	11303	
D-OLOK	Cameron Loco 105SS HAFB	11338	
D-OLOT(3)	Cameron C-90 HAFB	11641	
D-OLPB	Cameron N-90 HAFB	2601	D-Light
D-OLPE	Cameron N-120 HAFB	2311	D-Dresden, G-BSRE
D-OLPJ	Kubicek BB-30Z HAFB	597	
D-OLPS	Schröder Fire Balloons G HAFB	1526	
D-OLRE	Kubicek BB-60 HAFB	314	OK-0314
D-OLRI	Lindstrand LBL-150A HAFB	1211	
D-OLRK	Ultramagic M-120 HAFB	120/27	
D-OLTB(2)	Lindstrand LBL-150A HAFB	1083	
D-OLTJ	Schröder Fire Balloons G HAFB	1008	
D-OLTM	Schröder Fire Balloons G HAFB	1018	
D-OLTS	Ultramagic N-210 HAFB	210/10	
D-OLTT	Raven Europe S-60A HAFB	E-367	
D-OLUD(2)	Schröder Fire Balloons G HAFB (Replaces c/n 549)	1054	LX-BCO
D-OLUG(3)	Cameron Z-120 HAFB	11039	
D-OLUL	Schröder Fire Balloons G HAFB (Res 3.10)	1390	
D-OLUM	Schröder Fire Balloons G HAFB	533	
D-OLUP	Schröder Fire Balloons G HAFB	1365	
D-OLVM	Schröder Fire Balloons G HAFB	1332	
D-OLVP	Kubicek BB-85Z HAFB	672	
D-OLWB	Schröder Fire Balloons G HAFB	1571	
D-OLWL	Schröder Fire Balloons G HAFB	1558	
D-OLWM(2)	Kubicek BB-40Z HAFB	1149	
D-OLWW	Schröder Fire Balloons G HAFB	1242	PH-LWW
D-OLYM	Schröder Fire Balloons G HAFB	1297	
D-OLZL	Schröder Fire Balloons G HAFB	1575	
D-OMAA(2)	Schröder Fire Balloons "Auto" SS HAFB	741	
D-OMAC(2)	Cameron N-90 HAFB (Replacement for c/n 3062)	10239	
D-OMAI(2)	Kubicek BB-30Z HAFB	1120	
D-OMAL	Raven Europe S-60A HAFB	E-339	
D-OMAM	Schröder Fire Balloons G HAFB	400	
D-OMAR(2)	Aerostar RXS-8 HAFB	3116	
D-OMAS	Cameron N-120 HAFB	3566	
D-OMAX	Lindstrand LBL-240A HAFB	589	
D-OMAY(3)	Cameron Fire Truck 100 SS HAFB	11209	
D-OMBB	Thunder AX8-105 SI HAFB	4189	
D-OMBF	Cameron A-105 HAFB	3032	
D-OMBG	Schröder Fire Balloons G HAFB	477	
D-OMBI	Schröder Fire Balloons G HAFB	1113	
D-OMBL	Schröder Fire Balloons G HAFB	750	
D-OMBO(3)	Schröder Fire Balloons G HAFB	1663	
D-OMBT	Schröder Fire Balloons G HAFB	1484	
D-OMBZ	Lindstrand LBL-150A HAFB	398	
D-OMCC	Schröder Fire Balloons G HAFB (Res 2.10)	1399	
D-OMCG	Schröder Fire Balloons G HAFB	48	D-Germany(2)
D-OMDR(2)	Schröder Fire Balloons G HAFB (Replaces c/n 386)	810	
D-OMEE	Cameron Z-120 HAFB	10911	
D-OMEG	Kubicek BB-26E HAFB	1003	
D-OMEK	Schröder Fire Balloons G HAFB	608	
D-OMEL	Kubicek BB-34Z HAFB	931	
D-OMEN(2)	Schröder Fire Balloons G HAFB	921	
D-OMES	Schröder Fire Balloons G HAFB	709	
D-OMET(2)	Kubicek BB-30Z HAFB	430	
D-OMEW	Schröder Fire Balloons G HAFB	664	
D-OMFB(2)	Ultramagic M-56C HAFB	56/54	
D-OMFE	Wörner NL-STU/1000 HAFB	1098	
D-OMFM	Raven Europe S-60A HAFB	E-351	
D-OMFX	Cameron N-105 HAFB	3443	PH-OMF
D-OMGS	Ultramagic M-145 HAFB	145/15	
D-OMHM	Schröder Fire Balloons G HAFB	512	
D-OMHR(2)	Schröder Fire Balloons G HAFB	1292	
D-OMHS(2)	Schröder Fire Balloons G HAFB	1373	
D-OMIC	Schröder Fire Balloons G30/24 HAFB	725	
D-OMIE(2)	Schröder Fire Balloons G45/24 HAFB	1532	
D-OMII	Lindstrand LBL-105A HAFB	1261	
D-OMIX	Schröder Fire Balloons G HAFB	390	
D-OMJB	Schröder Fire Balloons G HAFB	1284	
D-OMKA	Cameron N-90 HAFB	2737	
D-OMKB	Ultramagic M-145 HAFB	145/20	
D-OMKC	Ultramagic M-105 HAFB	637	
D-OMKD	Ultramagic M-105 HAFB	105/84	
D-OMKE	Schröder Fire Balloons G HAFB	619	
D-OMKG(2)	Ultramagic M-145 HAFB	145/51	
D-OMKI	Ultramagic M-145 HAFB	145/24	
D-OMKJ	Ultramagic M-210 HAFB	210/18	
D-OMKK	Ultramagic M-145 HAFB	145/25	
D-OMKM(2)	Ultramagic N-210 HAFB	210/28	
D-OMKO	Ultramagic M-145 HAFB	145/50	
D-OMKQ	Ultramagic M-145 HAFB	145/54	
D-OMKS	Ultramagic M-145 HAFB	145/48	
D-OMKT(2)	Ultramagic M-145 HAFB	145/52	
D-OMKV	Schröder Fire Balloons G HAFB	569	
D-OMKZ	Ultramagic N-210 HAFB	210/27	
D-OMLW	Thunder AX8-105 SII HAFB	2570	
D-OMMA(2)	Colt 105A HAFB	2639	
D-OMMC	Ultramagic Z-105 HAFB	10451	
D-OMMG(2)	Ultramagic M-120 HAFB	120/26	
D-OMML	Schröder Fire Balloons G HAFB	198	
D-OMMM(3)	Cameron Z-150 HAFB	10933	
D-OMMN(2)	Schröder Fire Balloons G HAFB	1601	
D-OMMR(2)	Schröder Fire Balloons G HAFB	1352	
D-OMMS	Schröder Fire Balloons G HAFB	934	
D-OMMU	GEFA-Flug AS.105GD Hot Air Airship	0018	
D-OMMY	Balloon Works Firefly 9 HAFB	F9-070	
D-OMNG	Schröder Fire Balloons G HAFB	606	
D-OMNR	Cameron Z-120 HAFB	10233	
D-OMOG	Aerostar S-57A HAFB	3191	
D-OMOS(2)	Ultramagic M-120 HAFB	120/25	
D-OMOZ	Aerostar S-60A HAFB	3236	
D-OMPA	Schröder Fire Balloons G HAFB	518	
D-OMPC	Schröder Fire Balloons G HAFB	1185	
D-OMPD	Colt 105A HAFB	2131	
D-OMPK(3)	Schröder Fire Balloons G HAFB	1678	
D-OMPL	Cameron O-105 HAFB	11196	
D-OMRB	Schröder Fire Balloons G HAFB	722	
D-OMRE	Wörner NL-STU/1000 Gas Balloon	1096	
D-OMRM	Schröder Fire Balloons G HAFB	1248	
D-OMSA	Schröder Fire Balloons G HAFB	537	
D-OMSB	Schröder Fire Balloons G HAFB	1634	
D-OMSE	Schröder Fire Balloons G HAFB	1316	PH-MSF
D-OMSH	Kubicek BB-37N HAFB	140	OK-0040
D-OMSJ	Schröder Fire Balloons G HAFB	1281	
D-OMSS	Ultramagic M-105 HAFB	105/158	
D-OMTD	Cameron A-105 HAFB	4974	
D-OMTI(3)	Kubicek BB-45Z HAFB	1229	
D-OMTK	Kubicek BB-60Z HAFB	578	
D-OMTZ	GEFA-Flug AS.105GD Hot Air Airship (Permit 10.12)	0050	
D-OMUB	Schröder Fire Balloons G HAFB	1029	
D-OMUC	Schröder Fire Balloons G HAFB	1313	
D-OMUM	Cameron O-105 HAFB	4192	
D-OMUT	Raven-Europe S-60A HAFB	E-272	
D-OMWA(2)	Lindstrand LBL-260A HAFB	1245	
D-OMWP	Schröder Fire Balloons G HAFB	1087	
D-OMWS	Schröder Fire Balloons G HAFB	1419	
D-OMWY	Schröder Fire Balloons G HAFB	530	
D-OMZF(2)	Schröder Fire Balloons G HAFB	1223	
D-ONAA	Stuttgart K-780/2-STU Gas Balloon	0102	D-Sony
D-ONAE	Cameron Z-105 HAFB	10971	
D-ONAF	Lindstrand LBL-150A HAFB	766	
D-ONAR	Lindstrand LBL-120A HAFB	519	
D-ONBG(2)	Schröder Fire Balloons G HAFB	651	
D-ONBM	Colt 90A HAFB	912	G-BNBM
D-ONBY(3)	Cameron A-250 HAFB	11244	
D-ONCC	Cameron N-105 HAFB	3427	
D-ONCH	Cameron N-105 HAFB	3602	
D-ONCK	Cameron N-133 HAFB	3084	
D-ONDO	Cameron N-105 HAFB	2851	
D-ONDY(2)	Ultramagic F-34 Metten HAFB	F34/01	
D-ONEK	Thunder AX9-140 SII HAFB	2333	
D-ONEO	Schröder Fire Balloons G HAFB (Res.)	2001	
D-ONES(2)	Cameron N-133 HAFB	4647	
D-ONET(2)	Cameron N-105 HAFB	3669	
D-ONEW(2)	Schröder Fire Balloons G30/24 HAFB	963	
D-ONGA	Cameron N-105 HAFB	10262	
D-ONGO	Cameron N-133 HAFB	3751	
D-ONHG	Thunder AX8-105 HAFB	1907	D-Wefah(2)
D-ONIK	Schröder Fire Balloons G HAFB	295	
D-ONIL(2)	Schröder Fire Balloons G HAFB (Res. 9.11.15)	1655	
D-ONJA	Cameron N-105 HAFB	3252	
D-ONKA	Cameron O-120 HAFB	2596	D-ONKY, G-BTME
D-ONKE	Lindstrand LBL-105A HAFB	126	
D-ONKI(2)	Lindstrand LBL-180A HAFB	679	
D-ONKL(2)	Cameron Z-150 HAFB	10539	
D-ONKO	Cameron N-105 HAFB	604	
D-ONLB	Schröder Fire Balloons G HAFB	645	
D-ONLY	Cameron A-105 HAFB	2900	
D-ONMR	Colt 105A HAFB	2120	D-ORAC
D-ONNA	Cameron A-210 HAFB	3014	
D-ONNI	Cameron N-120 HAFB	3765	
D-ONNN(2)	Schröder Fire Balloons G HAFB	1479	

Reg	Type	C/n	Notes
D-ONOE	Cameron O-90 HAFB	2799	D-Nordlicht(2)
D-ONOS	Kubicek BB-45 HAFB	227	OK-0227
D-ONOW	Thunder AX8-90 SI HAFB	2268	
D-ONPM	Aerostar S-60A HAFB	3223	
D-ONRA	Colt 77A HAFB	074	LN-CBC, SE-ZVX
D-ONRJ	Lindstrand LBL-210A HAFB	555	
D-ONRW	Schröder Fire Balloons G HAFB	126	D-Sportland
D-ONRJ	Lindstrand LBL-210A HAFB	555	
D-ONRZ	Lindstrand LBL-120A HAFB	1114	
D-ONTG	Cameron O-105 HAFB	2394	D-Montgolfiere
D-ONUE	Cameron N-105 HAFB	4676	
D-ONUP	Ultramagic M-105 HAFB	105/40	
D-ONUV	Schröder Fire Balloons G HAFB	590	
D-ONWB	Stuttgart K-1000/3-STU Gas Balloon	0312	D-Hopfenblute
D-ONWS	Kubicek BB-34Z HAFB	979	
D-OOAA	Schröder Fire Balloons G HAFB	848	V5-. . ., D-OOAA
D-OOAB	Schröder Fire Balloons G HAFB	1317	
D-OOAF	GEFA-Flug AS.105GD Hot Air Airship	0045	
	(Test marks for other examples also?)		
D-OOAF(2)	Schröder Fire Balloons G HAFB	1586	
D-OOAH	Ultramagic M-120 HAFB	120/10	
D-OOAL	Ultramagic M-130 HAFB	130/. .	
D-OOAR	Ultramagic T-210 HAFB	210/88	
D-OOAS	Ultramagic S-90 HAFB	90/11	
D-OOAZ	Colt 90A HAFB	4928	
D-OOBI(2)	Cameron C-90 HAFB	11301	
D-OOBU(2)	Thunder AX9-140SII HAFB	3948	
D-OOBW(2)	Schröder Fire Balloons G HAFB	384	D-OHOM(1)
D-OOCS	Schröder Fire Balloons G HAFB	1066	
D-OOCT	Ultramagic M-90 HAFB	90/88	
D-OODD	Kubicek BB-30Z HAFB	225	OK-0225
D-OODI	Schröder Fire Balloons G HAFB	534	
D-OODL	Schröder Fire Balloons G HAFB	683	
D-OODM	Schröder Fire Balloons G HAFB	344	
D-OOEF	Aerostar S-60A HAFB	3256	
D-OOEL(2)	Schröder Fire Balloons G HAFB	628	
D-OOEM	Schröder Fire Balloons G HAFB	1262	
D-OOEN	Raven Europe S-60A HAFB	E-197	
D-OOES(2)	Schröder Fire Balloons G HAFB	1542	
	(Res. 27.11.12)		
D-OOFR	Schröder Fire Balloons G HAFB	1544	
D-OOGD	Schröder Fire Balloons G HAFB	1590	
D-OOGE(2)	Cameron N-105 HAFB	3951	D-OVEL
D-OOGS	Schröder Fire Balloons G HAFB	720	
D-OOGT	Schröder Fire Balloons G HAFB	1656	
D-OOHC	Ultramagic M-120 HAFB	120/20	
D-OOHD	Aerostar S-60A HAFB	3238	
D-OOHK	Schröder Fire Balloons G HAFB	635	V5-HKU, D-OOHK
D-OOHP	Ultramagic M-65 HAFB (Res.)	65/70	HB-QDY
D-OOIK	Schröder Fire Balloons G HAFB	1576	
D-OOIL(2)	Schröder Fire Balloons G HAFB	1392	
D-OOIN	Schröder Fire Balloons G HAFB	899	
D-OOJA	Schröder Fire Balloons G HAFB	682	
D-OOJS	Schröder Fire Balloons G HAFB	1515	
D-OOJW	Schröder Fire Balloons G HAFB	1217	
D-OOKB	Kubicek BB-30N HAFB	1056	
D-OOKW	Schröder Fire Balloons G HAFB	567	
D-OOLB	Kubicek BB-42Z HAFB	575	
D-OOLE(3)	Schröder Fire Balloons G HAFB	1423	
D-OOLI	Ultramagic T-150 HAFB	150/05	
D-OOLK	Cameron O-105 HAFB	1865	D-Wokenkratzer
D-OOLS	Schröder Fire Balloons G HAFB	351	
D-OOLU	Schröder Fire Balloons G HAFB	991	
D-OOLY	Schröder Fire Balloons G HAFB	1410	
D-OOMA(2)	Schröder Fire Balloons G HAFB	1073	
D-OOMC	Schröder Fire Balloons G HAFB	719	
D-OOMD	Schröder Fire Balloons G HAFB	1661	
D-OOMH	Schröder Fire Balloons G HAFB	1416	
D-OOMO	Colt 120A HAFB	4628	G-BYPV
D-OOMP(3)	Kubicek BB-42Z HAFB	789	OK-0224
	(Replaces c/n 224)		
D-OONB	Ultramagic S-50 HAFB	50/05	
D-OONE(2)	Kubicek BB-30Z HAFB	233	OK-0233
D-OONN	Cameron A-210 HAFB	3284	D-ONNN
D-OOOA	Kubicek BB-34Z HAFB	612	
D-OOOC	Kubicek BB-42Z HAFB	339	OK-0339
D-OOOG	Schröder Fire Balloons G HAFB	1437	
D-OOOH(3)	Schröder Fire Balloons G HAFB	1673	
D-OOOM(2)	Kubicek BB-45Z HAFB	605	
D-OOOO(2)	Schröder Fire Balloons G HAFB	1326	
D-OOOR	Colt 120A HAFB	1863	G-BTLO
D-OOOT(2)	Kubicek BB-34Z HAFB	439	
D-OOPA (2)	Colt 150A HAFB	10351	
D-OOPH(2)	Schröder Fire Balloons G HAFB	1654	
D-OOPI	Lindstrand LBL-120A HAFB	1082	
D-OOPS	Cameron V-56 HAFB	3260	
D-OOPW	Schröder Fire Balloons G HAFB	513	
D-OORB	Ultramagic M-105 HAFB	105/100	
D-OORE	Schröder Fire Balloons G HAFB	1302	
D-OORH	Schröder Fire Balloons G HAFB	140	
D-OORJ(2)	Schröder Fire Balloons G HAFB	1115	
D-OORK	Ultramagic M-120 HAFB	120/52	
D-OORL	Schröder Fire Balloons G HAFB	unkn	
D-OORM	Kubicek BB-45Z HAFB	485	
D-OORT	Cameron O-105 HAFB	2775	
D-OOSD	Lindstrand LBL-240A HAFB	1251	
D-OOSE	Kubicek BB-30Z HAFB	380	
D-OOSM(2)	Kubicek BB-42Z HAFB	477	
D-OOST	Schröder Fire Balloons G HAFB	1320	
D-OOSU	Ultramagic M-77 HAFB	77/336	
D-OOSV	Schröder Fire Balloons G HAFB	1546	
D-OOSW(2)	Schröder Fire Balloons G HAFB	1623	
D-OOTK	Kubicek BB-40Z HAFB	951	
D-OOTS	Schröder Fire Balloons G HAFB	416	
D-OOTT	Schröder Fire Balloons G HAFB	1552	
D-OOTW	Schröder Fire Balloons G HAFB	744	
D-OOUM	Ultramagic H-42 HAFB	42/04	
D-OOVB	Schröder Fire Balloons G HAFB	1434	
D-OOVI	Cameron Z-105 HAFB	10531	
D-OOVW	Schröder Fire Balloons G HAFB	406	
D-OOWE	Wörner NL-1000/STU Gas Balloon	1055	
D-OOWH	Schröder Fire Balloons Sunflower 36SS HAFB	1444	
D-OOWO	Kubicek BB-34Z HAFB	1178	
D-OOWS	Wörner NL-640/STU Gas Balloon	1067	
D-OOWW	Lindstrand LBL-150A HAFB	725	
D-OOXX	Schröder Fire Balloons G HAFB	1457	
D-OOZA	Ultramagic M-56 HAFB	56/44	
D-OOZJ(2)	Schröder Fire Balloons G HAFB	1417	
D-OOZL	Wörner NL-1000/STU Gas Balloon	1079	
D-OPAC(2)	Cameron Z-140 HAFB	10720	
D-OPAF	Schröder Fire Balloons G HAFB	1662	
D-OPAH	Schröder Fire Balloons G HAFB	56	D-Lichtenstein
D-OPAK(2)	Schröder Fire Balloons G HAFB	898	
	(Replacement for c/n 160)		
D-OPAP(2)	Schröder Fire Balloons G HAFB	475	
D-OPAS	Cameron O-105 HAFB	2653	
D-OPAT	Schröder Fire Balloons G HAFB	1179	
D-OPAX	Augsburg K-630/I-STU Gas Balloon	0134	D-Eurpoa
D-OPBF	Schröder Fire Balloons G HAFB	1607	
D-OPBP	Wörner FK-5550/STU Gas Balloon	6004	
D-OPCI	Lindstrand LBL-150A HAFB	990	
D-OPCM	Schröder Fire Balloons G HAFB	424	
D-OPEB	Thunder AX7-77A SIII HAFB	325	
D-OPEC	Thunder AX7-77 SI HAFB	1970	
D-OPEL (2)	Schröder Fire Balloons G HAFB	1154	
	(Replacement for c/n 503)		
D-OPEP	Schröder Fire Balloons G HAFB	661	
D-OPET	Schröder Fire Balloons G HAFB	1371	
D-OPGR	Schröder Fire Balloons G HAFB	1405	
D-OPHC	Cameron N-105 HAFB	2871	
D-OPHS	Ultramagic N-355 HAFB	355/06	
D-OPIE	Schröder Fire Balloons Pinguin SS HAFB	341	
D-OPIH	Aerostar S-66A HAFB	3062	
D-OPIP(3)	Kubicek BB-42Z HAFB	910	
D-OPIT(2)	Kubicek BB-37N HAFB	431	
D-OPIX	Kubicek BB-34Z HAFB	1227	
D-OPJA	Schröder Fire Balloons G HAFB	1097	
D-OPLB	Schröder Fire Balloons G HAFB	201	D-Arolsen
D-OPLK	Schröder Fire Balloons G HAFB	791	
D-OPLR	Cameron N-90 HAFB	2351	D-Höfler
D-OPMI	Cameron O-120 HAFB	2686	
D-OPMK	Schröder Fire Balloons G HAFB	95	D-Feuerzahn (1)
D-OPMN	Colt 105A HAFB	4147	
D-OPOB	Schröder Fire Balloons G HAFB	853	
D-OPON	Schröder Fire Balloons G HAFB	314	
D-OPOW	Schröder Fire Balloons G HAFB	894	
D-OPPA	Cameron A-105 HAFB	1569	D-Lloyd(2)
D-OPPE	Lindstrand LBL-150A HAFB	364	
D-OPPG	Schröder Fire Balloons G HAFB	1221	
D-OPPI(3)	Schröder Fire Balloons G HAFB	1290	
	(W/o 3.7.15)		
D-OPPL	Schröder Fire Balloons G HAFB	835	
D-OPPP(4)	Schröder Fire Balloons G HAFB	1328	
D-OPPT	Schröder Fire Balloons G HAFB	331	
D-OPRI	Schröder Fire Balloons G HAFB	359	
D-OPRO(2)	Ultramagic N-250 HAFB	250/58	
D-OPSA	Kubicek BB-100Z HAFB	1212	
D-OPSD	Thunder AX8-90 SI HAFB	4625	
D-OPTJ	Thunder AX7-77 SI HAFB	800	D-Optimist
D-OPTO(2)	Schröder Fire Balloons G HAFB	1347	
D-OPUM	Cameron A-120 HAFB	3483	
D-OPUP	Schröder Fire Balloons G HAFB	564	
D-OPUV	Stuttgart K-630/1-STU Gas Balloon	0120	(D-OSIL), D-Silentium
D-OPWI	Schröder Fire Balloons G HAFB	1420	
D-OQCL(3)	Kubicek BB-42Z HAFB	639	
D-OQCM(2)	Schröder Fire Balloons G HAFB	1520	
D-OQDQ	Ultramagic S-130 HAFB	130/12	HB-QDQ, D-OJST
D-OQEL	Colt 180A HAFB	2330	
D-OQKG	Kubicek BB-20 HAFB	242	
D-OQMC	Schröder Fire Balloons G HAFB	1536	
D-OQQQ(2)	Schröder Fire Balloons G HAFB	1577	
D-OQUA	Schröder Fire Balloons G HAFB	1138	
D-OQUE	Schröder Fire Balloons G HAFB	855	
D-ORAC(2)	Colt 180A HAFB	3497	
D-ORAI	Schröder Fire Balloons G HAFB	1599	
D-ORAS	Lindstrand LBL-150A HAFB	536	
D-ORAT(2)	Schröder Fire Balloons G HAFB	1451	
D-ORAX	Schröder Fire Balloons G HAFB	1687	
D-ORBA	Schröder Fire Balloons G HAFB	981	
D-ORBB(2)	Schröder Fire Balloons G HAFB	1621	
D-ORCK	Thunder AX9-140 SII HAFB	4312	
D-ORCO	Lindstrand LBL-150A HAFB	713	
D-ORDU	Cameron A-120 HAFB	2902	
D-OREI(2)	Kubicek BB-30Z HAFB	502	
D-ORFA(2)	Kubicek BB-45Z HAFB	895	
D-ORFF(2)	Ultramagic M-105 HAFB	105/111	
D-ORGA	Cameron N-105 HAFB	2716	
D-ORGB	Schröder Fire Balloons G HAFB	1173	
D-ORGL	Schröder Fire Balloons G HAFB	684	
D-ORHA	Raven Europe FS-57A HAFB	E-207	
D-ORHE	Schröder Fire Balloons G HAFB	360	
D-ORHF	Schröder Fire Balloons G HAFB	1298	
D-ORHL	Cameron Z-150 HAFB	11440	
D-ORHV	Colt 180A HAFB	1563	G-BRHV
D-ORHW	Schröder Fire Balloons G HAFB	675	
D-ORIA(2)	Kubicek BB-40Z HAFB	1019	
D-ORID	Schröder Fire Balloons G HAFB	994	
D-ORIE(2)	Schröder Fire Balloons G HAFB	1585	
D-ORII	Cameron N-105 HAFB	2610	D-Ariel, G-BTTC
D-ORIZ	Colt 105A HAFB	4465	
D-ORJL	Colt 105A HAFB	3488	
D-ORLA(2)	Schröder Fire Balloons G HAFB	1614	
D-ORLI (2)	Cameron Z-105 HAFB	10461	
	(Replacement for A-105 c/n 2544)		
D-ORLM	Lindstrand LBL-120A HAFB	1302	
D-ORLR	Schröder Fire Balloons G HAFB	1339	
D-ORMA(2)	Schröder Fire Balloons G HAFB	1345	
D-ORMC(2)	Cameron Z-105 HAFB	10764	
D-ORMD	Schröder Fire Balloons G HAFB	763	
D-ORNG	Kubicek BB-30Z HAFB	272	OK-0272
D-ORNI	Thunder AX8-105 SII HAFB	2179	
D-ORNS	Schröder Fire Balloons G HAFB	1310	
D-ORNU	Kubicek BB-30Z HAFB	683	
D-OROL(2)	Schröder Fire Balloons G HAFB	1413	
D-OROM(2)	Schröder Fire Balloons G HAFB	1474	
D-ORON(2)	Wörner NL-1000/STU Gas Balloon	1087	
D-OROP	Thunder AX8-105 SII HAFB	4352	
D-OROS	GEFA-Flug AS.105GD Hot Air Airship	0063	D-OAAF(9)
D-OROV	Cameron N-90 HAFB	4399	D-Rheinprovinz
D-ORPP(2)	Schröder Fire Balloons G HAFB	1367	
D-ORPR	Schröder Fire Balloons G HAFB	484	

Registration	Type	c/n	Previous identities
D-ORRJ	Schröder Fire Balloons G HAFB	712	
D-ORRR	Schröder Fire Balloons G HAFB	1240	
D-ORSB	Lindstrand LBL-150A HAFB	568	
D-ORSI	Schröder Fire Balloons G26/16 HAFB	5611	
D-ORSS	Cameron N-105 HAFB	3193	
D-ORST(3)	Kubicek BB-60Z HAFB	927	
D-ORSW(2)	Kubicek BB-70Z HAFB	1197	
D-ORTA(2)	GEFA-Flug AS.105GD Hot Air Airship	0028	
D-ORTB	Schröder Fire Balloons G HAFB	1043	
D-ORTC	Schröder Fire Balloons G HAFB	1044	
D-ORTH(2)	Schröder Fire Balloons G HAFB	1510	
D-ORTS	Cameron A-105 HAFB	3202	
D-ORUB	Cameron N-105 HAFB	10662	
D-ORUE(5)	Schröder Fire Balloons G HAFB	1495	
D-ORUI (2)	Schröder Fire Balloons G HAFB	1074	
	(Replacement for c/n 248)		
D-ORUL(4)	Kubicek BB-42Z HAFB	403	
	(Replacement for c/n 274)		
D-ORUM(2)	Cameron N-105 HAFB	"5001"	
D-ORUP(2)	Schröder Fire Balloons G HAFB	1225	
	(Replacement for c/n 648)		
D-ORUT(2)	Cameron O-105 HAFB	4484	
D-ORVB	Cameron C-90 HAFB	11227	
D-ORVS	Cameron O-105 HAFB	4600	
D-ORWB	Cameron C-90 HAFB	10402	
D-ORWL	Thunder AX8-105 SII HAFB	3825	
D-ORWN	Kubicek BB-34Z HAFB	695	
D-ORWP	Kubicek BB-34Z HAFB	696	
D-ORWU	Schröder Fire Balloons G HAFB	1168	
D-ORWY	Kubicek BB-60N HAFB	160	OE-ZZN, OK-0160
D-ORZM	Schröder Fire Balloons G HAFB	693	D-Erzgebirge (2), D-ORZG
D-OSAH	Schröder Fire Balloons G HAFB	1035	
D-OSAL	Schröder Fire Balloons G HAFB	603	
D-OSAM	Wörner FK-280/STU Gas Balloon	6001	
D-OSAN	Wörner NL-640/STU Gas Balloon	1084	
D-OSAT	Schröder Fire Balloons G HAFB	721	
D-OSAU(2)	Schröder Fire Balloons Sparkasse-Pig 30 HAFB		
		1411	
D-OSAZ	Thunder AX7-77Z HAFB	450	
D-OSBA	Thunder AX9-120 SII HAFB	2306	
D-OSBB(2)	Schröder Fire Balloons G HAFB	1583	
D-OSBF	Kubicek BB-S Forklift HAFB	452	OK-6452
D-OSBK	Kubicek BB-30N HAFB	182	
D-OSBT(3)	Kubicek BB-37N HAFB	438	
D-OSCA(2)	Schröder Fire Balloons G HAFB	860	
D-OSCB(2)	Schröder Fire Balloons G HAFB	1560	
D-OSCT	Schröder Fire Balloons G HAFB	863	
D-OSDO	Schröder Fire Balloons G HAFB	1454	
D-OSDW	Lindstrand LBL-120A HAFB	1194	
D-OSED(3)	Ultramagic M-105 HAFB	105/180	
D-OSEE(2)	Cameron A-105 HAFB	3691	
D-OSEF	Schröder Fire Balloons G HAFB	299	
D-OSEL	Schröder Fire Balloons G HAFB	830	
D-OSEN	Schröder Fire Balloons G HAFB	482	
D-OSEO	Cameron N-120 HAFB (Res .08)	unkn	
D-OSEP	Ultramagic Z-90 HAFB	90/14	
D-OSET	Kubicek BB-34Z hafb	1251	
D-OSEX(3)	Cameron Z-105 HAFB	11147	D-OPAD(2)
D-OSFD	Aerostar S-60A HAFB	3228	
D-OSFE	Thunder AX8-105 SII HAFB	2527	
D-OSFL	Kubicek BB-60Z HAFB	387	
D-OSFS	Schröder Fire Balloons G HAFB	1652	
D-OSFT	Kubicek BB-30 HAFB	228	OK-0228
D-OSGH	Aerostar S-57A HAFB	3218	
D-OSHB(2)	Schröder Fire Balloons G HAFB	1032	
D-OSHG	Ultramagic M-145 HAFB	145/06	
D-OSHR	Cameron A-210SV HAFB	3897	
D-OSHS(2)	Schröder Fire Balloons G HAFB	453	
D-OSHU	Schröder Fire Balloons G HAFB	1358	
D-OSIA	Ultramagic M-120 HAFB	120/35	
D-OSIB(2)	Ultramagic M-160 HAFB	160/59	
D-OSIC	Ultramagic N-300 HAFB	300/30	
D-OSID	Ultramagic N-300 HAFB	300/31	
D-OSIG	Schröder Fire Balloons G HAFB	150	
D-OSIL	Stuttgart K-630/1-STU Gas Balloon	0120	D-Silentium
D-OSIN	Colt 105A HAFB	2057	
D-OSJM	Schröder Fire Balloons G HAFB	1452	
D-OSKA(2)	Schröder Fire Balloons G HAFB	897	
D-OSKR	Schröder Fire Balloons G HAFB	1103	
D-OSKS	Kubicek BB-30Z HAFB	1217	
D-OSKU	Schröder Fire Balloons G HAFB	552	
D-OSKY	Cameron N-77 HAFB	749	
D-OSLA	Aerostar S-57A HAFB	3075	
D-OSLL	Schröder Fire Balloons G HAFB	1002	
D-OSLN	Schröder Fire Balloons G HAFB	1677	
D-OSLO(3)	Schröder Fire Balloons G HAFB	1574	
D-OSMC(2)	Cameron N-105 HAFB	4721	
	(Replacement for c/n 3663)		
D-OSMG	Schröder Fire Balloons G	1078	
D-OSMK	Ultramagic M-145 HAFB	145/69	
D-OSMM	Schröder Fire Balloons G HAFB	1686	
D-OSMO	Lindstrand LBL-120A HAFB	970	
D-OSMP	Thunder AX10-160 SI HAFB	1419	D-OAXL, D-Jupiter, G-BPXP
D-OSMR	Schröder Fire Balloons G HAFB	1406	
D-OSMS(2)	Schröder Fire Balloons G HAFB	1626	
	(Res. 10.3.15)		
D-OSMU	Schröder Fire Balloons M20/24 HAFB	1524	
D-OSNA(3)	Kubicek BB-45N HAFB	368	
D-OSOM	Raven Europe RX-7 HAFB	E-121	D-Sommer Traum
D-OSOS	Ultramagic M-105 HAFB	105/205	
D-OSPB(2)	Schröder Fire Balloons G HAFB	1204	
D-OSPD	Cameron O-84 HAFB	2916	
D-OSPE	Cameron A-105 HAFB	3871	
D-OSPI	Kubicek BB-30Z HAFB	317	OK-0317
D-OSPK	Schröder Fire Balloons G HAFB	1263	
D-OSPM(2)	Colt 210A HAFB	4724	
	(Replacement for c/n 3523)		
D-OSPN	Lindstrand LBL-180A HAFB	421	
D-OSPU	Lindstrand LBL-120A HAFB	1053	
D-OSPW	Schröder Fire Balloons G HAFB	1671	
D-OSRH	Kubicek BB-42Z HAFB	500	
D-OSSH(2)	Schröder Fire Balloons G HAFB	1394	
D-OSSI	Cameron V-77 HAFB	2664	
D-OSSR	Schröder Fire Balloons G HAFB	761	
D-OSST(2)	Schröder Fire Balloons G HAFB	1660	
D-OSSW	Cameron O-120 HAFB	4157	
D-OSTA	Cameron N-120 HAFB	10093	D-OSTW(2)
D-OSTC(3)	Schröder Fire Balloons G HAFB	1466	
D-OSTW(3)	Schröder Fire Balloons G HAFB	1564	
D-OSTY	Wörner NL-840/STU Gas Balloon	1063	
D-OSTZ(2)	Wörner NL-1000/STU Gas Balloon	1082	
D-OSUB(2)	Schröder Fire Balloons G HAFB	1553	
D-OSUC	Schröder Fire Balloons G HAFB	1368	
D-OSUD	Schröder Fire Balloons G HAFB	607	
D-OSUG	Schröder Fire Balloons G HAFB	1188	
D-OSUL	Cameron V-90 HAFB	2807	PH-JME
D-OSUN(2)	Lindstrand LBL-120A HAFB	793	D-OUTZ
D-OSUS(3)	Schröder Fire Balloons G HAFB	1481	
D-OSUV	Schröder Fire Balloons G HAFB	370	
D-OSUW	Schröder Fire Balloons G HAFB	1271	
D-OSVB	Schröder Fire Balloons G HAFB	1494	
D-OSVM	Schröder Fire Balloons G HAFB	1502	
D-OSVO(2)	Ultramagic M-105 HAFB	105/110	
D-OSWA	Colt 105A HAFB	2142	
D-OSWB	Cameron N-120 HAFB	3927	
D-OSWD	Schröder Fire Balloons G HAFB	1158	
D-OSWH(2)	Kubicek BB-60Z HAFB	1004	
D-OSWK	Lindstrand LBL-400A HAFB	834	
D-OSWM	Schröder Fire Balloons G HAFB	1142	
D-OSWR	Cameron O-90 HAFB	4284	
D-OSWU	Lindstrand LBL-120A HAFB	789	
D-OSWW(2)	Kubicek BB-30Z HAFB	685	
D-OSXA	Kubicek BB- HAFB	368	
D-OSYK	Cameron Z-150 HAFB	10942	
D-OSZB	Wörner K-780/2-STU Gas Balloon	1033	
D-OTAB(3)	Schröder Fire Balloons G HAFB	792	
D-OTAI	Schröder Fire Balloons G HAFB	1244	
D-OTAM	Thunder AX8-84 SI HAFB	4516	
D-OTAR	Stuttgart K-1200/3-STU Gas Balloon	0257	D-Tarkett
D-OTBG	Kubicek BB-22E HAFB	1131	
D-OTBJ	Kubicek BB-26XR HAFB	1034	
D-OTBL(2)	Cameron C-90 HAFB	11199	
D-OTCC(2)	Schröder Fire Balloons G HAFB	1137	
D-OTDI (3)	Schröder Fire Balloons G HAFB	1395	
	(Replacement for c/n 540, 800) (Res 3.10)		
D-OTEG(2)	Schröder Fire Balloons G HAFB	1178	
	(Replacement for c/n 796)		
D-OTEN	Thunder AX7-77 SI HAFB	1804	G-BTEN
D-OTGF	Schröder Fire Balloons G HAFB	1235	
D-OTGL	Kubicek BB-22Z HAFB	1267	
D-OTGV(2)	Schröder Fire Balloons G HAFB	1404	
D-OTHA	Schröder Fire Balloons G HAFB	632	
D-OTHB	Wörner FKP-380/STU Gas Balloon	6203	
D-OTHC	Ultramagic M-105 HAFB	105/125	
D-OTHE	Kubicek BB-42Z HAFB	512	
D-OTHI	Ultramagic V-90 HAFB	90/24	
D-OTHK	Kubicek BB-30Z HAFB	390	
D-OTHL(3)	GEFA-Flug AS.105GD Hot Air Airship	0057	
D-OTHS	GEFA-Flug AS.105GD Hot Air Airship	0032	
D-OTIB	Schröder Fire Balloons G HAFB	1135	
D-OTIM	Schröder Fire Balloons G HAFB	1602	
D-OTIW	Schröder Fire Balloons G HAFB	686	
D-OTKA	Colt 105A HAFB	4227	G-BXOV
D-OTKN	Lindstrand LBL-120A HAFB	1173	
D-OTLG	Kubicek BB-70Z HAFB	598	
D-OTLI	Wörner NL-STU/1000 Gas Balloon	1099	
D-OTLN	Schröder Fire Balloons G HAFB	487	
D-OTML	Kubicek BB-30Z HAFB	375	
D-OTMU	Thunder AX8-105 SII HAFB	1977	G-BTMU
D-OTMW	Kubicek BB-70Z HAFB	963	
D-OTNI(2)	Schröder Fire Balloons G HAFB	1440	
D-OTOB(2)	Colt 180A HAFB	3468	
D-OTOC	Thunder AX9-140 SII HAFB	2293	
D-OTON(3)	Schröder Fire Balloons G HAFB	1028	
D-OTOR	Colt 105A HAFB	2537	
D-OTOY	Ultramagic S-50 HAFB	50/13	
D-OTPU	Cameron N-105 HAFB	2591	G-BTPU
D-OTRB	Cameron N-105 HAFB	3368	
D-OTRK	Lindstrand LBL-150A HAFB	1191	
D-OTRU	Schröder Fire Balloons G HAFB	1561	
D-OTTA	GEFA-Flug AS.105GD Hot Air Airship	0022	
D-OTTE	GEFA-Flug AS.105GD Hot Air Airship	0041	
D-OTTL	Ultramagic M-130 HAFB	130/29	F-GJLV
D-OTTO(5)	Cameron N-120 HAFB	11501	
D-OTTS(2)	Schröder Fire Balloons G HAFB	1338	
D-OTTY(2)	Cameron C-90 Concept HAFB	10561	
D-OTTZ	Schröder Fire Balloons G HAFB	1342	
D-OTUC	Schröder Fire Balloons G HAFB	1366	
D-OTUE	Schröder Fire Balloons G HAFB	1161	
D-OTUV	Schröder Fire Balloons G HAFB	538	
D-OTVS	Lindstrand LBL-150A HAFB	1221	
D-OTWD	Lindstrand LBL-150A HAFB	659	
D-OTWG	Thunder AX10-160 SII HAFB	2062	G-BTWG
D-OTWH	Cameron Z-90 HAFB	11388	
D-OTWN	Kubicek BB-37N HAFB	420	
D-OTWS	Schröder Fire Balloons G HAFB	1675	
D-OTYM	Cameron O-84 HAFB	3211	
D-OTYT	Schröder Fire Balloons G HAFB	1143	
D-OTZC	Colt 90A HAFB	1876	G-BTZC
D-OUAK	Thunder AX8-105 SII HAFB	2080	G-BUAK
D-OUAT	Schröder Fire Balloons G HAFB	292	D-Quatro(3)
D-OUCH	Cameron A-210 HAFB	3352	G-BWAX
D-OUCS	Schröder Fire Balloons G HAFB	1157	
D-OUDP	Thunder AX8-105 SII HAFB	2178	D-Reineburg(2)
D-OUDS(2)	Kubicek BB-42Z HAFB	385	
	(Replacement for c/n 360)		
D-OUDQ	Thunder AX9-120 SII HAFB	3748	
D-OUDT	Kubicek BB-42Z HAFB	1145	
D-OUHU	Head Balloons AX8-105 HAFB	389	
D-OUKW(2)	Kubicek BB-60Z HAFB	869	
D-OULM	Cameron O-84 HAFB	1817	D-Wurttfeuer(3)
D-OUNI	Schröder Fire Balloons G HAFB	1408	
D-OUPD	Schröder Fire Balloons G HAFB	622	
D-OURI	Schröder Fire Balloons G HAFB	1651	
D-OUSA	Raven Europe S-60A HAFB	E-311	
D-OUSS	Raven Europe S-55A HAFB	E-173	D-Russberger
D-OUUS(2)	Schröder Fire Balloons G HAFB	689	
D-OVAG(2)	Schröder Fire Balloons G HAFB	1156	
D-OVAW	Kubicek BB-30Z HAFB	416	
D-OVBG	Schröder Fire Balloons G HAFB	627	

Registration	Type	c/n	Previous id
D-OVBW	Lindstrand LBL-120A HAFB	047	G-BVBW
D-OVDS(3)	Schröder Fire Balloons G HAFB	1441	
	(Replaces (2) c/n 889)		
D-OVDT	Thunder AX8-105 SII HAFB	3524	
D-OVEG	Cameron N-105 HAFB	2077	D-Grevenstein(2)
D-OVEL	Schröder Fire Balloons G HAFB	1618	(D-OLEV(3))
	(Res. 16.12.14)		
D-OVER(2)	Lindstrand LBL-150A HAFB	987	
D-OVGC	Schröder Fire Balloons G HAFB	1625	
D-OVGH	Ultramagic N-180 HAFB	180/116	
D-OVHM(2)	Schröder Fire Balloons G HAFB	1252	
D-OVID	Cameron N-105 HAFB	2687	
D-OVKA	Kubicek BB-37 HAFB	288	OK-0288
D-OVKW	Kubicek BB-30Z HAFB	287	OK-0287
D-OVMH	Schröder Fire Balloons G HAFB	510	
D-OVNI	Ultramagic S-105 HAFB	105/79	
D-OVPI	Wörner FK-5500/STU Gas Balloon	6029	
D-OVRB	Schröder Fire Balloons G HAFB	987	
D-OVRL	Kubicek BB-34Z HAFB	980	
D-OVSH	Cameron O-84 HAFB	1280	D-Ostsee
D-OVSS	Thunder AX8-105 SII HAFB	3533	
D-OVUB	Schröder Fire Balloons G HAFB	1587	
D-OVUM	Schröder Fire Balloons G HAFB	1327	
D-OVUN	Schröder Fire Balloons G HAFB	887	V5-HUV, D-OVUN
D-OVUS(2)	Cameron Z-160 HAFB	11953	
D-OVVO	Schröder Fire Balloons G36/24 HAFB	947	
D-OVWB	Ultramagic VW Beetle SS HAFB	F20/01	
D-OVWW	Thunder Ax7-77 HAFB	4338	
D-OWAB	Schröder Fire Balloons G HAFB	240	
D-OWAF(4)	Kubicek BB-30Z HAFB	945	
D-OWAG(2)	Kubicek BB-42Z HAFB	320	OK-0320
D-OWAH	Thunder AX7-65 SI HAFB	2562	
D-OWAJ	Schröder Fire Balloons G HAFB	1306	
D-OWAN	Thunder AX9-140 SII HAFB	1491	D-Löwentor
D-OWAR(2)	Schröder Fire Balloons G HAFB	1570	
D-OWAU	Cameron N-77 HAFB (Res.?)	unkn	
D-OWAX	Ultramagic M65C HAFB	65/72	
D-OWAZ	Schröder Fire Balloons G HAFB	1070	
D-OWBA(2)	Wörner NL-1000/STU Gas Balloon	1070	
D-OWBC	Wörner NL-840/STU Gas Balloon	1072	
D-OWBD	Ultramagic M-145 HAFB	145/38	
D-OWBF	Wörner NL-1000/STU Gas Balloon	1058	
D-OWBI	Wörner NL-1000/STU Gas Balloon	1081	
D-OWBJ	Ultramagic M-105 HAFB	105/120	
D-OWBL	Wörner NL-840/STU Gas Balloon	1078	
D-OWBM	Wörner NL-1000/STU Gas Balloon	1085	
D-OWBO	Wörner NL-1000/STU Gas Balloon	1086	
D-OWBP	Schröder Fire Balloons G HAFB	1351	
D-OWBS	Colt 105A HAFB	2127	
D-OWCC	Schröder Fire Balloons G HAFB	1584	
D-OWCD	Cameron A-120 HAFB (Res.)	2399	G-BWCD, G-OCBC
D-OWCW(3)	Cameron N-105 HAFB	10447	
D-OWDA	Lindstrand LBL-120A HAFB	681	
D-OWDR	Schröder Fire Balloons G HAFB	583	
D-OWEB(2)	Ultramagic M-160 HAFB	160/53	D-OWES
D-OWEF	Schröder Fire Balloons G HAFB	317	
D-OWEG(2)	Ultramagic M-105 HAFB	105/147	
D-OWEI	Cameron A-105 HAFB	3846	
D-OWEW	Schröder Fire Balloons G30/24 HAFB	551	HA-873, D-OWEW
D-OWEY(2)	Schröder Fire Balloons G HAFB	1108	
D-OWFA(2)	Schröder Fire Balloons G HAFB	1681	
D-OWFG	Lindstrand LBL-120A HAFB	1231	
D-OWFU	Colt 105A HAFB	1697	D-OWFO, D-Schatz
D-OWGE	Schröder Fire Balloons G HAFB	1640	(D-OGEO(3))
D-OWGU	Cameron A-105 HAFB	4050	
D-OWGV	Kubicek BB-70Z HAFB	868	
D-OWHB	Kubicek BB-45N HAFB	404	
D-OWHF	Schröder Fire Balloons G HAFB	1259	
D-OWHH	Schröder Fire Balloons G HAFB	1656	
D-OWHL	Schröder Fire Balloons G HAFB	1638	
D-OWHS	Ultramagic T-150 HAFB	150/11	
D-OWIE	Schröder Fire Balloons G HAFB	556	
D-OWIL(2)	Kubicek BB-70Z HAFB	1164	
D-OWIM(3)	Schröder Fire Balloons G HAFB	1563	
D-OWIR	Cameron Z-120 HAFB	11572	
D-OWIS	Colt 140A HAFB	2637	G-BVTI
D-OWIY	Schröder Fire Balloons G HAFB	29	D-OWEY(1), D-Wendelstein
D-OWKA(2)	Lindstrand LBL-150A HAFB	1344	
D-OWKL	Schröder Fire Balloons G HAFB	1396	
D-OWKM	Schröder Fire Balloons G HAFB	01	D-Trier(2)
D-OWKW	Schröder Fire Balloons G HAFB	1401	
D-OWLB	Raven-Europe S-49A HAFB	E-251	
D-OWLH	Schröder Fire Balloons G HAFB	1307	
D-OWLK	Schröder Fire Balloons G HAFB	1592	
	(Res. 11.2.14)		
D-OWLN	Schröder Fire Balloons G HAFB	929	
D-OWLS	GEFA-Flug AS.105GD Hot Air Airship	H0068	D-OAAF
D-OWML	Wörner NL-1000/STU Gas Balloon	1050	
D-OWMG(2)	Schröder Fire Balloons G HAFB	1539	
D-OWML	Wörner NL-1000/STU Gas Balloon	1050	
D-OWMM	Schröder Fire Balloons M20/24 HAFB	1353	
D-OWMP	Schröder Fire Balloons G HAFB	574	
D-OWMS	Schröder Fire Balloons M20/24 HAFB	1354	
D-OWMT	Ultramagic M-145 HAFB	145/58	
D-OWNG	Schröder Fire Balloons G HAFB	1220	
D-OWNK	Schröder Fire Balloons G HAFB	1593	
D-OWNT	Wörner NL-1000/STU Gas Balloon	1065	
D-OWOA	Schröder Fire Balloons G HAFB	1299	
D-OWOP	Schröder Fire Balloons G HAFB	1372	
D-OWOT	Cameron A-105 HAFB	1790	OE-PZM
D-OWPA	Ultramagic M-120 HAFB	120/16	
D-OWPC	Ultramagic M-120 HAFB	120/13	
D-OWPG	Lindstrand LBL-105A HAFB	450	
D-OWPH	Ultramagic M-42 HAFB	42/11	
D-OWPL	Ultramagic M-120 HAFB	120/15	
D-OWPO	Ultramagic M-120 HAFB	120/14	
D-OWPS	Schröder Fire Balloons G HAFB	1562	
D-OWPT	Schröder Fire Balloons G33/24 HAFB	714	
D-OWPV(2)	Ultramagic M-120 HAFB	120/58	
D-OWRD	Schröder Fire Balloons G HAFB	1685	
D-OWRW	Ultramagic M-77 HAFB	77/248	
D-OWSF	Lindstrand LBL-120A HAFB	1096	
D-OWSH(3)	Cameron N-105 HAFB	11500	
D-OWSI (2)	Schröder Fire Balloons G HAFB	1024	
D-OWSM	Schröder Fire Balloons G HAFB	1381	
D-OWSR	Schröder Fire Balloons G HAFB	1462	
D-OWSW(5)	Cameron Z-105 HAFB	11929	
D-OWTB	Cameron O-120 HAFB	2973	
D-OWTM(2)	Ultramagic N-210 HAFB	210/67	
D-OWTS	Schröder Fire Balloons M HAFB	1517	
D-OWUE(2)	Schröder Fire Balloons G HAFB	1480	
D-OWUG	Schröder Fire Balloons G HAFB	1210	
D-OWUM(3)	Schröder Fire Balloons M20/24 HAFB	1461	
D-OWUN	Sky 120 HAFB	051	
D-OWUS	Schröder Fire Balloons G HAFB	1334	
D-OWUX	Ultramagic M-65C HAFB	65/144	
D-OWVD	Schröder Fire Balloons G HAFB	758	
D-OWVV	Kubicek BB-37 HAFB	183	OK-0183
D-OWWA	Schröder Fire Balloons G HAFB	1069	
D-OWWC	Ultramagic M-145 HAFB	145/42	
D-OWWE	Colt 105A HAFB	2583	D-OWWL(1)
D-OWWH	Aerostar Cell SS HAFB	Cell-3001	
D-OXAM	Ultramagic F-24 Flyingman HAFB	F24/01	
D-OXFT	Cameron N-105 HAFB	3018	
D-OXID	Lindstrand LBL-105A HAFB	397	
D-OXOB	Raven-Europe FS-57A HAFB	E-279	D-OWOB
D-OXON	Ultramagic M-65 HAFB	65/160	
D-OXTT	Cameron A-120 HAFB	3267	
D-OXUS	Schröder Fire Balloons G HAFB	157	D-Limes
D-OXWH	Cameron N-120 HAFB	10358	
D-OXXA	Lindstrand LBL-105A HAFB	788	
D-OXXL	Lindstrand LBL-400A HAFB	587	
D-OYEG	Specon S90 HAFB	001	
D-OYEN	Cameron Z-150 HAFB	11292	
D-OYPO	Wörner K-1000/3-STU Gas Balloon	1038	
D-OYPQ	Colt 180A HAFB	1569	G-HYPO
D-OYPS	Schröder Fire Balloons Cat-SS HAFB	1350	
D-OYTO	Raven Europe S-60A HAFB	E-347	
D-OYYO(2)	Schröder Fire Balloons G HAFB	1682	
	(Replacement for c/n 821, 9.16)		
D-OYYY(2)	Schröder Fire Balloons G HAFB	1085	
D-OZAC	Schröder Fire Balloons G HAFB	1389	(D-OIAC)
D-OZAM	Wörner NL-1000/STU Gas Balloon	1043	
D-OZAO	Schröder Fire Balloons G HAFB	1125	
D-OZAT	Ultramagic N-250 HAFB	250/56	
D-OZDP	GEFA-Flug AS.105GD Hot Air Airship	0016	
D-OZEL(2)	Schröder Fire Balloons G HAFB	1012	
D-OZEP	Schröder Fire Balloons G HAFB	441	
D-OZET	Kubicek BB-45N HAFB	369	OE-ZET, OK-0369
D-OZGT	Lindstrand LBL-120A HAFB	1225	
D-OZIK	Kubicek BB-34Z HAFB	593	OE-ZIK
D-OZKA	Schröder Fire Balloons G HAFB	930	
D-OZPO	Schröder Fire Balloons G HAFB	917	
D-OZUG	Schröder Fire Balloons G HAFB	432	
D-OZWO	Schröder Fire Balloons G HAFB	1336	
D-OZZZ(2)	Schröder Fire Balloons G HAFB	1294	
D-O . . .	GEFA-Flug AS.105GD Hot Air Airship	0047	G-PEYO
D-O . . .	Thunder AX-10/160 SII HAFB	10648	OO-BPG(2)
D-O . . .	Ultramagic M-145	145/33	OO-BTZ

The following Balloons were identified in the former system by name only. These should have been re-registered in the D-O... sequence by 1.3.2000 but may have been unrecorded or they were probably no longer airworthy.

Gas Balloons

D-Munte	Augsburg K-1050/3-RI	45778	
D-Rosie	Stuttgart K-780/2-STU	0305	

CLASS U : Unmanned aircraft

D-UFHA	Mistral C (Aachen University test aircraft)	unkn
D-UISD	Universität Stuttgart Lotte	unkn
	(Remote-controlled airship)	

GLIDERS

The most recently reported tail codes are shown next to the registration. Additions and amendments are welcome.

Registration	Type	c/n	Previous id
D-0001	*Test registration for Schleicher ASH 25, 26, ASW 28 production*		
D-0002-CH	Rolladen-Schneider LS7-WL	7098	HB-3035
D-0003	LET L-13 Blanik	026639	OO-ZRL
D-0005	Scheibe Zugvogel IIIA	1061	
D-0006	Schleicher Ka 6E	4132	
D-0007-JB	Schempp-Hirth Nimbus-2	83	PH-1275, D-9666, OE-5019
D-0009	Schleicher ASK 21	21463	
D-0010	Rolladen-Schneider LS6-a	6042	N3SZ
D-0011	Schleicher ASW 19	19011	
D-0012	Marganski MDM-1 Fox	217	
D-0013	Rolladen-Schneider LS1-d	138	OO-YRD, D-0957
D-0015	*Test Registration for DG Flugzeugbau DG-800S production*		
D-0016-IMB	Schempp-Hirth Discus CS	233CS	
D-0018-AZ	Schempp-Hirth Duo Discus	86	
D-0019-XZ	Schleicher ASK 13	13665AB	
D-0020-M1	Glasflügel H201 Standard Libelle	11	
D-0021-BA	Schempp-Hirth Nimbus-2C	224	HB-1534
D-0022-22	Akaflieg Hannover AFH 22	V-1	
	(P.17.5.16)		
D-0023	Glaser-Dirks DG-100G Elan	E119G88	OE-5307
D-0024	Akaflieg Hannover AFH 24	1	
	(Permit)		
D-0025	Schleicher ASK 13	13190	LN-GBQ
D-0026	Glasflügel H303 Mosquito	99	
D-0027	Schleicher ASK 13	13152	D-0227
D-0028-PD	Glaser-Dirks DG-300 Elan	3E268	
D-0029	Schempp-Hirth Standard Cirrus	496G	F-CEFY
D-0030-VA	DG Flugzeugbau DG-1000S	10-21S21	
D-0032-KA	Rolladen-Schneider LS8-18	8291	
D-0033-MO	Glaser-Dirks DG-100 Elan	E33	HB-1535
D-0034	Schleicher K 8B	8203	
D-0035	Schleicher K 8B	8666	
D-0036	Grunau Baby IIB	AHAB2	
	(P. .05)		

Registration	Type	C/n	Previous identities
D-0037	Glasflügel Kestrel	119	HB-1231
D-0039-M1	Schempp-Hirth Duo Discus XL687		
D-0041	Scheibe SF 26A Standard	5033	HB-745
D-0043-TS	Glaser-Dirks DG-300 Elan	3E138	
D-0044-YS	Glaser-Dirks DG-100G Elan	E219G185	
D-0045-BU	Rolladen-Schneider LS6-c	6278	
D-0047-47	Schempp-Hirth Duo Discus	468?	
D-0048-B8	SZD-51-1 Junior	B-1851	HB-3012
D-0049	Glasflügel H301B Libelle	88	
D-0050-FD	Rolladen-Schneider LS8-a	8231	F-CGZY
D-0051	Schempp-Hirth Discus-2b	176	
D-0052	Rolladen-Schneider LS4	4605	
D-0054	Scheibe SF 27B (P 20.6.16)	6201	
D-0055	Schempp-Hirth Nimbus-2C	227	HB-1533
D-0056	Schleicher K 8B	789	D-4376
D-0057	Rolladen-Schneider LS4-a	4677	
D-0058	Schleicher Ka 6E	4180	
D-0059	Schleicher Ka 6E	4213	
D-0060	PZL PW-5 Smyk	17.06.018	
D-0061	Rolladen-Schneider LS8-18	8077	F-CGZP
D-0062-F4	Scheibe Bergfalke III	5628	
D-0063	PIK-16c Vasama	12	D-0699, LN-GGB
D-0065	Grunau Baby IIB (P. 4.99)	94	D-7215, PH-215
D-0066	Scheibe SF 27A	6108	
D-0067-TO	Grob G102 Astir CS	1346	D-7384
D-0068	Schempp-Hirth SHK-1	56	I-LJET
D-0069	Schleicher ASK 13 (P 10.15)	13088	
D-0070	PZL-Swidnik PW-5 Smyk	17.03.014	CS-PCB, EC-GLQ
D-0071	Glaser-Dirks DG-300 Elan	3E326	
D-0072	Schleicher Ka 6E	4214	
D-0074	Lange E1 Antares 18S (W/o 6.6.15)	30S01	D-KGLF
D-0075-6B	Schleicher Ka 6E	4216	
D-0076	Schempp-Hirth Gö 3 Minimoa	AB001M	(D-0037)
D-0077-M	Schleicher K 8B	8745	
D-0079	Schleicher Ka 6E	4232	
D-0080	Schleicher ASK 13	13116	
D-0081	Schleicher ASK 13	13122	
D-0082-FAY	Glasflügel H201B Standard Libelle	14	
D-0083	Rolladen-Schneider LS3	3036	HB-1361
D-0084	Focke-Wulf Weihe 50	8	LX-CAF
D-0085-RH	Glasflügel Standard Libelle 201B (P.1.05)	220	OE-0913
D-0087-YX	Glaser-Dirks DG-100	14	HB-1285
D-0088	Bölkow Phoebus C	845	
D-0089-LY	Schleicher ASW 27B	?	
D-0090-SI	Rolladen-Schneider LS8-18	8439	
D-0092	Schleicher Ka 6E	4238	
D-0094-BR	Schempp-Hirth Discus b	446	
D-0095	Schleicher ASK 13	13126	
D-0096	Schleicher ASK 13	13129	
D-0097	Schleicher ASK 13	13133	
D-0098	Schleicher Ka 6E	4253	
D-0099	Schleicher Ka 6E	4254	
D-0100	Schleicher K 8B	8127	PH-300
D-0101	Schempp-Hirth Cirrus	30	
D-0102	Schleicher K 8B	8668	
D-0103	Schleicher K 8B	8671	
D-0104-IYA	Schempp-Hirth Discus CS	045CS	
D-0105	Schempp-Hirth Standard Cirrus	43	OY-XHS, SE-TIZ
D-0106	Grob G102 Standard Astir II	5044S	HB-1746
D-0107	Glasflügel H304	211	
D-0108	Schempp-Hirth Discus CS	059CS	
D-0109-SB	Rolladen-Schneider LS8-a	8105	PH-1096
D-0110	Schleicher K 8B	8327	D-KIFA
D-0111	Glasflügel H401 Kestrel	3	
D-0112-8Z	Rolladen-Schneider LS8-18	8303	
D-0113	Schleicher Ka 6E	4154	
D-0114-IEL	Glasflügel H201B Standard Libelle	211	
D-0115-3F	Rolladen-Schneider LS4-a	4546	
D-0116-EW	Schleicher ASW 20L	20243	OO-ZXT, D-3373
D-0117	Nord 1300 (Grunau Baby IIB)	117	F-CRNX, F-CBFF
D-0118	Glaser-Dirks DG-300 Elan (Damaged 7.7.16)	3E417	
D-0119	Rolladen-Schneider LS4	4544	
D-0121-W	Rolladen-Schneider LS1-0	6	
D-0123-57	Bölkow Phoebus C	870	
D-0124-NI	Schleicher ASW 20CL	20843	D-KAMC, D-3365
D-0125	Schleicher Rhönbussard	125	
D-0126	Schleicher K 8B	219/61	
D-0127	Focke-Wulf Kranich III	87	
D-0128-28	Schleicher ASW 28	28052	
D-0129	Schleicher K 8B	8115/SH	
D-0130-K	Bölkow Phoebus B-1	722	OE-5210
D-0131-HEM	Glaser-Dirks DG-300 Club Elan	3E351C40	
D-0132	Akaflieg Braunschweig SB-5E Sperber	AB5004	
D-0135	Bölkow Phoebus C	860	
D-0136-36	Rolladen-Schneider LS1-0 (P 7.10)	11	
D-0137-R4	Rolladen-Schneider LS4	4607	
D-0138	Rolladen-Schneider LS3-a (P. 3.13)	3459	I-ORNI, D-3393
D-0139-1M	Glasflügel H201B Standard Libelle (P 9.15)	222	
D-0140	Glasflügel H201 Standard Libelle	236	
D-0141-UE	Glasflügel H201B Standard Libelle	237	
D-0142	Rolladen-Schneider LS1-b	25	
D-0143	Schleicher Ka 6E	4256	
D-0144	Schleicher ASK 13	13096	
D-0145	Schleicher ASK 13	13134	
D-0146	Schempp-Hirth Discus CS	064CS	
D-0147	Grob G102 Astir CS Jeans	2106	
D-0149	Schleicher ASK 13	13138	
D-0150	Vogt Lo-150	AB.1	
D-0151	Schleicher ASK 13	13141	
D-0152-52	Glaser-Dirks DG-202/17	2-136/1734	
D-0153	Glasflügel H303 Mosquito B	129	OE-5184
D-0155	Bölkow Phoebus C	868	
D-0156-BU	Rolladen-Schneider LS1-c	10	
D-0157-B3	Rolladen-Schneider LS4-b	4761	
D-0158-KG	Rolladen-Schneider LS4	4378	
D-0159-IMW	Glasflügel H304	212	
D-0160	Schleicher Ka 6CR Rhönsegler	204	OO-ZAB, D-8352
D-0161-1T	Schleicher ASW 15	15004	
D-0162	Schleicher K 8B	8786	
D-0163	Schleicher Ka 6E	4266	
D-0164	Schleicher Ka 6E	4274	
D-0165	Rolladen-Schneider LS4	4608	
D-0166	DG Flugzeugbau DG-500 Elan Orion	5E169X24	
D-0167	Schleicher Ka 6E (P 5.10)	4269	
D-0169-FJ	Rolladen-Schneider LS8-18	8316	
D-0170	Glaser-Dirks DG-300 Elan	3E36	CS-PCD, F-CFVK, F-WFVK
D-0171-AX	Rolladen-Schneider LS4	4609	
D-0172	Grob G 103A Twin II Acro	3625-K-12	D-3072
D-0173-HB	Rolladen-Schneider LS4	4610	
D-0174	Glasflügel H201 Standard Libelle	185	
D-0175	Bölkow Phoebus C	878	
D-0176	Glasflügel H201 Standard Libelle	51	
D-0177-31	Schempp-Hirth Standard Austria SH-1	74	
D-0178	LET L-23 Super Blanik	049201	
D-0179-06	Schempp-Hirth Duo Discus	28	
D-0180	Rolladen-Schneider LS1-0	19	
D-0181-MI	Rolladen-Schneider LS1-0	18	
D-0183-88	Schempp-Hirth Janus C	183	F-CAXA(2), OO-ZXA
D-0184	Schempp-Hirth Cirrus	43	HB-3405, D-0184
D-0185	Scheibe SF 27A (P. 5.13)	6109	
D-0187-87	Schempp-Hirth Cirrus	56	
D-0189	Grunau Baby IIB	1	OE-0189
D-0190	Schempp-Hirth Standard Cirrus	128	
D-0191	Rolladen-Schneider LS4	4583	
D-0192-T3	Grob G 102 Club Astir IIIb	5568Cb	HB-1618
D-0193	Glaser-Dirks DG-300 Club Elan	3E427C72	
D-0194	Akaflieg Braunschweig SB-5B Sperber	5048/A	
D-0195	Schleicher Ka 6E	4281	
D-0196	Schleicher Ka 6E (P. 4.13)	4265	
D-0197-W	Schleicher ASW 24	24205	
D-0199	Schleicher ASK 13	13157	
D-0200-00	Schleicher ASW 15	15179	
D-0201	Schleicher Ka 6E	4271	
D-0202	Schleicher K 8B	8779	
D-0203	Rolladen-Schneider Ls 1-f	150	D 3642, OO-ZZI, D-2427
D-0204	Glasflügel H401 Kestrel	52	
D-0205	Rolladen-Schneider LS6-c	6311	
D-0206	Schleicher K 7 Rhönadler (P 12.4.16)	AB/7281	
D-0207	Schleicher ASW 12	12003	D-0007
D-0208	Schleicher ASK 13	13071/A	
D-0209	Schleicher K 8B	05	D-KAMB, D-8877
D-0210-11	Schempp-Hirth Duo Discus	30	
D-0211-RS	Rolladen-Schneider LS4-b	4874	
D-0212	Schleicher K 8B (P 18.3.16)	8740	
D-0213-LM	Glaser-Dirks DG-500 Elan Trainer	5E21T3	
D-0215	Bölkow Phoebus B-1	877	
D-0216	Grunau Baby IIB	91	PH-212
D-0217	Schleicher K 8B	8288 EI	
D-0218-L5	Schleicher ASW 24	24186	
D-0219-CI	Glaser-Dirks DG-300 Elan Acro	3E445A8	
D-0220	Eiriavion PIK-20D-78	20627	HA-4410
D-0221-IGP	Rolladen-Schneider LS4-a	4671	
D-0222	Grob G 103 Twin II (C/n out of sequence)	3377-K-50	
D-0223	Schleicher Ka 6E	4282	
D-0225	Schleicher ASW 15	15007	
D-0228	Schleicher ASK 13	13156	
D-0229	Schleicher Ka 6E	4288	
D-0230	Schleicher Ka 6E	4280	
D-0231	Schempp-Hirth Discus CS	056CS	
D-0232	Schleicher ASK 13	13161	
D-0233	Schleicher Ka 6E	4270	
D-0234-KB	Schempp-Hirth Duo Discus	98	
D-0235-W5	Schleicher ASK 13	13165	
D-0237	Schleicher Ka 6E	4283	
D-0238	Schleicher ASK 13	13162	
D-0239	Schleicher ASK 13	13163	
D-0240	Schleicher ASK 13	13164	
D-0241-GF	DG Flugzeugbau DG-800S	8-209S39	
D-0243-H9	Glasflügel H201B Standard Libelle	56	
D-0244	Schleicher ASK 21	21667	
D-0245-45	Glaser-Dirks DG-500 Elan Trainer	5E26T6	
D-0246	Bölkow Phoebus C	881	
D-0247	Slingsby T59D Kestrel 19	1785	OM-2904, OK-2904
D-0248	Akaflieg Braunschweig SB-5E Sperber	5033A	
D-0249	Schempp-Hirth Duo Discus	124	
D-0250	Schempp-Hirth Cirrus	63	
D-0252-5X	Schempp-Hirth Discus CS	058CS	
D-0253	Schempp-Hirth Ventus c	469	OY-XTX
D-0254-31	Rolladen-Schneider LS6-b	6164	
D-0256	SZD-32A Foka 5	W-519	DDR-2255, DM-2255
D-0258-58	Schleicher ASK 21	21403	
D-0261-61	Glaser-Dirks DG-500 Elan Trainer	5E57T24	
D-0266	Schleicher ASK 13	13174	
D-0267	Schleicher ASK 13	13176	
D-0268	Glaser-Dirks DG-300 Elan	3E324	OE-5472, D-8300
D-0269	Schleicher ASK 13	13179	
D-0270	Schleicher ASK 13	13180	
D-0271	Schleicher ASK 13	13181	
D-0272	Rolladen-Schneider LS4-a	4679	
D-0273	Schleicher K 8B	8798	
D-0274-C1	Schempp-Hirth Ventus-2b	41	
D-0275	Rolladen-Schneider LS4	4101	
D-0276	Schleicher Ka 2B Rhönschwalbe	937/61	
D-0277	Glasflügel H206 Hornet	46	I-CRBV
D-0278	Glasflügel H401 Kestrel	39	
D-0279	Glasflügel 604	2	BGA 2585/ECT, I-FEVG, D-0279
D-0280	Rolladen-Schneider LS1-0	2	OY-MMX, D-4734
D-0281-MIG	Glasflügel H401 Kestrel	43	
D-0282-CLP	Glaser-Dirks DG-300/22 Elan	5E8S2	
D-0283	Scheibe L-Spatz III	806	D-2003
D-0287-D9	Rolladen-Schneider LS8-a	8182	
D-0288	PIK-16c Vasama	6	OH-288, OH-VAF
D-0290-IAA	Schempp-Hirth Cirrus	66	(OY-EXP), D-0290
D-0291	VFW Fokker FK-3	0002	
D-0294	Rolladen-Schneider LS4-b	4751	

Reg.	Type	Serial	Other marks
D-0295-HH	Akaflieg Braunschweig SB-5E Sperber	5041/A	
D-0297	Scheibe L-Spatz 55	542	OE-0299
D-0298-WI	Schempp-Hirth Discus CS	091CS	
D-0299	Schempp-Hirth Ventus c	590	
D-0300	Glasflügel H304	256	
D-0301	Focke-Wulf Weihe 50	SB.01	
D-0302	Glaser-Dirks DG-300 Club Elan	3E423C71	
D-0303	Schleicher K 8B	8684/A	
D-0304-EM	Glasflügel Standard Libelle 201B	57	
D-0305	Glaser-Dirks DG-300 Elan	3E425	
D-0306	Schleicher K 8B	8668 EI	
D-0308	Scheibe Bergfalke IV	5811	
D-0309-WS	Rolladen-Schneider LS6-b	6175	
D-0310	Glaser-Dirks DG-300 Elan	3E420	I-MERY
D-0312-BB	Glasflügel H401 Kestrel	47	
D-0313	Glasflügel H101 Salto	3	
D-0314-E4	Rolladen-Schneider LS4-b	4907	
D-0315	Schempp-Hirth Standard Cirrus	108	
D-0316	Schempp-Hirth Standard Cirrus	109	
D-0317-PV	Schleicher ASK 21	21592	
D-0318	Schempp-Hirth Standard Cirrus	111	
D-0319	Schempp-Hirth Standard Cirrus	112	
D-0320	Rolladen-Schneider LS4	4160	
D-0322	Rolladen-Schneider LS6	6177	
D-0323	Rolladen-Schneider LS3-a	3130	OO-ZWS
D-0325	Scheibe Bergfalke III	5635	
D-0326-AB	Schempp-Hirth Discus CS	170CS	
D-0328	Schempp-Hirth Standard Cirrus	135	
D-0329-OI	Centrair 101A Pégase	101A0329	OO-YVI, F-CGOI
D-0330-BW	Glaser-Dirks DG-300 Elan	3E345	HB-3005
D-0331	Rolladen-Schneider LS3-a	3142	PH-629
D-0332	Schleicher K 8B	8791AB	
D-0333-GT	Glasflügel H201 Standard Libelle	69	
D-0335	Schleicher ASK 13	13184	
D-0336	Schleicher Ka 6E	4309	
D-0337	Glaser-Dirks DG-300 Elan	3E277	
D-0338	Schleicher ASK 13	13185	
D-0339	Schleicher Ka 6E (Permit)	4306	
D-0340	Glasflügel H304	259	OH-638
D-0342	Schleicher Ka 6E	4310	
D-0343	Schleicher ASK 13	13192	
D-0344-dh	Glaser-Dirks DG-300 Club Elan	3E279C5	
D-0345	Schleicher ASK 13	13193	
D-0346	Grunau Baby IIB	31	OE-0346
D-0347	Glaser-Dirks DG-100	96	HB-1347
D-0349	Schleicher Ka 6E	4313	
D-0350	Schleicher K 8B	8807	
D-0351	Schleicher Ka 6E	4318	
D-0352	Schleicher ASK 13	13204	
D-0353-G9	Rolladen-Schneider LS4-b	4947	
D-0354	Schleicher ASK 13	13206	
D-0355-2S	Glasflügel H201B Standard Libelle	277	
D-0356	Schleicher Rhönlerche II	AB 94/59	
D-0357	Glaser-Dirks DG-300 Club Elan	3E282C7	
D-0358	Glasflügel H401 Kestrel	11	
D-0359-WL	Glaser-Dirks DG-300 Club Elan	3E283C8	
D-0360	Scheibe L-Spatz 55	507/614	
D-0361	Glaser-Dirks DG-300 Elan	3E22	
D-0362	Schempp-Hirth Standard Cirrus (P 8.7.16)	174	
D-0363	Glasflügel Standard Libelle	209	OY-MIX
D-0364-HN	Schempp-Hirth Standard Cirrus	155G	
D-0366	Schleicher ASK 21	21671	
D-0367	Schleicher ASK 13	13186	
D-0368	Glasflügel H201B Standard Libelle	77	
D-0370-BG	Glaser-Dirks DG-300 Elan	3E96	HB-3037
D-0371	Glasflügel H201 Standard Libelle	291	
D-0373	Vogt Lo-100 Zwergreiher	01	
D-0374-UX	Schempp-Hirth Discus CS	065CS	
D-0375	Scheibe Bergfalke IV	5814	("D-KAAO")
D-0376	Scheibe Bergfalke IV	5818	("D-KAAQ")
D-0377	SZD-24-4A Foka 4	W-237	OY-XEB
D-0378	FFA Diamant 16.5	068	HB-1292
D-0380	Scheibe Bergfalke II/55	367	D-1251
D-0381	Schempp-Hirth Janus Ce	301	
D-0382-DF	Rolladen-Schneider LS1-c	30	
D-0384-UH	Rolladen-Schneider LS1-c	32	
D-0385-sq	Glasflügel H303 Mosquito	14	HB-1374
D-0386	Scheibe SF 27A	6093	
D-0387	Rolladen-Schneider LS4-b	4961	
D-0388	Schempp-Hirth Standard Cirrus	3	
D-0389-PC	Schempp-Hirth Cirrus	85	
D-0390-DM	Rolladen-Schneider LS4	4115	
D-0391-SR	Schempp-Hirth Ventus-2cxR	108	
D-0392	Glasflügel H-101 Salto	2	
D-0393	Rolladen-Schneider LS4	4379	
D-0394-RH	Rolladen-Schneider LS4-b	4962	
D-0395-EBI	Rolladen-Schneider LS6	6183	
D-0396	Schleicher ASW 24	24146	I-GOST
D-0397	Glasflügel H401 Kestrel	16	
D-0398	Glasflügel H401 Kestrel	17	
D-0399-ST	Rolladen-Schneider LS1-e	92	
D-0400-6V	Schempp-Hirth Duo Discus	239	
D-0401-IST	Rolladen-Schneider LS4	4388	
D-0402	Lange E1 Antares 18S (P 6.10)	63S07	
D-0403-P5	Glaser-Dirks DG-500/22 Elan	5E17S6	
D-0404-GP	Rolladen-Schneider LS4-a	4681	
D-0405-CF	Rolladen-Schneider LS4-b	4682	
D-0406	Rolladen-Schneider LS4-a	4683	
D-0407	Grob G102 Astir CS 77	1703	D-KFSL, D-7632
D-0408-GR	Valentin Mistral-C	MC 053/84	LX-CAC
D-0409	Schempp-Hirth Duo Discus	127	
D-0410-KJ	Glasflügel Standard Libelle 201B	49	OO-ZGP
D-0411-11	Rolladen-Schneider LS4-b	4684	
D-0412-T1	Rolladen-Schneider LS4-a	4697	
D-0413	Schleicher ASK 13	13207	
D-0415-AS	Rolladen-Schneider LS4-b	4685	
D-0416	Schleicher K 8B	8812	
D-0417-MB	Schempp-Hirth Ventus-2a	100	
D-0418-RN	Schleicher ASW 15	15035	
D-0419	Schleicher ASK 13	13217	
D-0420-KI	DG Flugzeugbau DG-500 Elan Orion	5E164X19	S5-7500
D-0421	Schleicher K 8B	8813	
D-0422	Schleicher ASK 13	13218	
D-0423	Rolladen-Schneider LS1-d	42	
D-0424	Glaser-Dirks DG-200/17	2-139/1736	
D-0425	Glaser-Dirks DG-200/17	2-140/1737	
D-0427-FD	Schempp-Hirth Standard Cirrus	5	
D-0429	Schempp-Hirth Standard Cirrus	7	
D-0430	HpH Glasflügel 304C	63-C	
D-0431	Schleicher ASW 15	15183	
D-0432 -NM	Rolladen-Schneider LS1-d	44	
D-0433	Glasflügel H401 Kestrel	57	
D-0434	Schleicher Ka 6E	4387	PH-434
D-0435	Schleicher K 8B	8578/A	
D-0436-OD	SZD-48-3 Jantar Standard 3	B-1946	DDR-2436
D-0438	Glasflügel H201 Standard Libelle	91	
D-0439-39	Rolladen-Schneider LS1-d	48	
D-0440	Rolladen-Schneider LS1-d	38	
D-0441-RC	Rolladen-Schneider LS4-a	4698	
D-0442-ZM	Rolladen-Schneider LS8-18	8383	
D-0445	Glasflügel H201 Standard Libelle	285	
D-0446	Schleicher Ka 6E	4326	
D-0448	Schleicher K 8B	8601/A	
D-0449-BE	Rolladen-Schneider LS1-c	96	
D-0450	Rolladen-Schneider LS1-c	90	
D-0451-A9	Glasflügel H401 Kestrel	51	
D-0452	Schempp-Hirth Duo Discus	141	
D-0455	Grunau Baby IIB (P. 3.11)	21	
D-0456-IG	Schleicher ASW 15B	15212	BGA 3723/GCH, PH-438, D-0950
D-0458-4	Rolladen-Schneider LS1-c	109	
D-0460-SA	Schleicher ASW 15	15036	
D-0462-1T	DG Flugzeugbau DG-500 Elan Orion	5E204X48	
D-0463	Schleicher Ka 6E	4327	
D-0464	Rolladen-Schneider LS4	4052	
D-0466	Schleicher ASK 13	13223	
D-0467	Eiriavion PIK-20D-78	20603	EI-GME, OH-562
D-0468	Schleicher ASK 13	13225	
D-0469	Schleicher ASK 13	13226	
D-0470	Rolladen-Schneider LS1-c	100	
D-0472	Schleicher Ka 6E	4308	
D-0473-C6	Rolladen-Schneider LS4-a	4699	
D-0474	Glasflügel H401 Kestrel	56	
D-0475	Glasflügel H401 Kestrel	25	
D-0476	Rolladen-Schneider LS1-c	103	
D-0477	Rolladen-Schneider LS4	4248	F-CATY(2), I-GATS, D-9108
D-0478	Schleicher ASK 13	13017	OO-ZXQ, PL-61 (Belgian Air Cadets)
D-0479-79	Schempp-Hirth Cirrus	90	
D-0480	Rolladen-Schneider LS4-a	4700	
D-0481-4U	Schempp-Hirth Cirrus	92	
D-0482	Glasflügel H201B Standard Libelle	115	
D-0483-KO	Rolladen-Schneider LS4-a	4701	
D-0485	Schempp-Hirth Duo Discus	33	
D-0486-R5	Rolladen-Schneider LS4-b	4946	
D-0487-MV1	Schempp-Hirth Standard Cirrus	29	
D-0488-BL	Schleicher ASK 13	13215	
D-0489-LG	Rolladen-Schneider LS1-d	56	
D-0491	Schleicher ASK 13	13227	
D-0492	Schleicher ASK 13	13228	
D-0494-YC	Rolladen-Schneider LS4-a	4702	
D-0496	Glasflügel H401 Kestrel	50	
D-0497	Rolladen-Schneider LS4-a	4703	
D-0499	Schleicher ASK 13	13231	
D-0500	Glasflügel H201B Standard Libelle	95	
D-0503	Rolladen-Schneider LS4-a	4704	
D-0504	Schempp-Hirth Cirrus-VTC	115Y	
D-0505	Schempp-Hirth Cirrus-VTC	116Y	
D-0506	Schempp-Hirth Cirrus-VTC	117Y	
D-0508	Schleicher ASW 15 (P 4.10)	15057	
D-0509	Schleicher Ka 6E	4334	
D-0510	Glaser-Dirks DG-300 Elan	3E290	
D-0512	Allstar PZL SZD-55-1	551.A.09.008	
D-0513	Schleicher ASK 13	13233	
D-0514	Schleicher ASK 13	13234	
D-0516-S1	Schleicher ASW 15	15051	
D-0517-17	Glasflügel H401 Kestrel	20	
D-0518-WK	Schleicher ASK 21	21620	
D-0519	Rolladen-Schneider LS1-c	104	
D-0520-GW	Glasflügel H304	251	
D-0521	Glasflügel H401 Kestrel	45	
D-0522	Glasflügel H201 Standard Libelle	120	
D-0523	Scheibe Bergfalke IV	5803	
D-0524	Scheibe Bergfalke IV	5804	
D-0526	Rolladen-Schneider LS4-a	4705	
D-0527	Glasflügel H205 Club Libelle	109	PH-527
D-0528	Glasflügel H201B Standard Libelle	260	
D-0530-PT	Rolladen-Schneider LS1-f	393	F-CEKJ
D-0533	Glasflügel H401 Kestrel	38	
D-0534	Schleicher K 8B	8819	
D-0535	Schleicher ASK 13	13236	
D-0536-NK	Eiriavion PIK-20D-78	20648	OH-536
D-0538	Schleicher ASK 13	13240	
D-0539	Schleicher Ka 6E	4340	
D-0541	Glasflügel Mosquito B	156	F-CELK
D-0542-CW	Schleicher ASW 24B	24236	
D-0544-DR	Schempp-Hirth Ventus-2b	3	
D-0545	Schleicher Ka 6E	4339	
D-0547-CA	Schleicher Ka 6E	4342	
D-0548	Schleicher K 8B	8828	
D-0549	Schleicher K 8B	8829	
D-0550	Schleicher ASK 13	13248	
D-0551	Schleicher ASK 13	13249	
D-0552	Schleicher ASK 13	13250	
D-0553-2A	Glasflügel H201B Standard Libelle	271	G-DCNF, BGA1670/CNF
D-0554	Glasflügel H201 Standard Libelle	171	
D-0556	Schempp-Hirth Cirrus	93	
D-0557-EA	Schempp-Hirth Standard Cirrus	117	
D-0558-HO	Schempp-Hirth Duo Discus	204	
D-0560	Schleicher K 8B	225/61	
D-0562-5D	Schempp-Hirth Discus CS	066CS	
D-0564	Schempp-Hirth Janus Ce	294	
D-0565	Rolladen-Schneider LS1-c	99	
D-0567	Rolladen-Schneider LS4-b	4796	
D-0568	Rolladen-Schneider LS4-b (P 24.5.16)	4797	

Reg	Type	Serial	Notes
D-0570	Rolladen-Schneider LS4-b	4798	
D-0572	Siebert Sie 3	3021	
	(Res.7.99)		
D-0573-FO	Rolladen-Schneider LS4-b	4799	
D-0574-AC	FFA Diamant 16.5	067	
D-0575-BI	DG Flugzeugbau DG-505 Elan Orion	5E252X81	
D-0577	Eiri PIK-20D	20616	OY-XIZ
D-0578-N4	Rolladen-Schneider LS4-a	4800	
D-0579	Rolladen-Schneider LS4-b	4926	
D-0580	Glaser-Dirks DG-100G Elan	E145G113	
D-0581	Schempp-Hirth Standard Cirrus	54	
D-0582-VL	Schempp-Hirth Standard Cirrus	55	
D-0583	Siebert Sie 3	3004	
D-0584	Bölkow Phoebus C	953	
D-0585-BU	Schempp-Hirth Discus CS	030CS	
D-0586	Schempp-Hirth Cirrus	98	
D-0588-H2	Schempp-Hirth Standard Cirrus	185	
D-0589	Schleicher ASK 13	AB13645	
	(P. 9.14)		
D-0591	Grob G 103C Twin III	36004	
D-0592	Schleicher Ka 6CR	6535/A	D-0192
D-0593-KJ	Schempp-Hirth Standard Cirrus	58	
D-0595	Schempp-Hirth Standard Cirrus	69	
D-0596	Schempp-Hirth Discus b	175	G-CJVY, BGA 4827, RAFGSA R6
D-0597	Rolladen-Schneider LS1-d	97	CS-PCH, OO-ZMY, D-0436
D-0598	Glasflügel H401 Kestrel	26	
D-0599	Glasflügel H201 Standard Libelle	154	
D-0600	Rolladen-Schneider LS1-c	102	
D-0601-FN	Schleicher ASG 29	29022	
D-0602	DG Flugzeugbau DG-303 Elan	3E501	OM-2002
D-0603-TK	Glasflügel H203 Standard Libelle	1	
D-0604	Rolladen-Schneider LS4-b	41033	
D-0605	DG Flugzeugbau DG-505 Elan Orion	5E208X51	S5-7522
D-0606-1	Lange E1 Antares 18S	46S05	
	(P 15.3.16)		
D-0607	Rolladen-Schneider LS1-f	397	F-CEKM
D-0608	Schleicher ASW 15	15020	
D-0609-SC	Schempp-Hirth Ventus c	378	
D 0610	SZD-50-3 Puchacz	B-1327	DDR-3610
D-0611-FU	Glaser-Dirks DG-100G Elan	E144G112	
D-0612	Schleicher Ka 6E	4347	
D-0614	Schleicher K 8B	8833	
D-0615	Schleicher ASW 15	15066	
D-0616	Rolladen-Schneider LS6	6100	HB-1889
D-0617	Schleicher K 8B	8835	
	(P. 5.14)		
D-0618	Schleicher ASK 13	13258	
D-0619	Schleicher ASK 13	13259	
D-0620-VIP	Schleicher ASW 15	15087	
D-0621	Schleicher ASK 13	13262	
D-0622	Schleicher K 8B	8837	
D-0623	Rolladen-Schneider LS4	4564	D-3392
D-0624	Schleicher ASK 13	13267	
D-0625	Schempp-Hirth Standard Cirrus G	56	
D-0626	Schleicher ASK 21	21559	
D-0627	Schleicher ASW 15	15078	
D-0629	Schleicher K 8B	8842	
D-0631	Schleicher ASK 13	13270	
D-0632	Schleicher K 8B	8844	
D-0634	Scheibe SF 34	5102	4X-GGM, D-3336
D-0636-L5	Schleicher ASW 15	15083	
D-0637	Schleicher K 8B	8845	
D-0638	SZD-50-3 Puchacz	B-1403	DDR-3637
D-0639	Schleicher ASK 13	13276	
D-0640-TG	Glaser-Dirks DG-100G	88G9	HB-1339
D-0641	Schleicher ASK 21	21566	
D-0642	Schleicher ASW 15	15088	
D-0643	Schleicher ASK 13	13277	
D-0644	Schleicher ASK 13	13278	
D-0645	Schleicher ASK 13	13288	
D-0646	Schleicher ASK 13	13282	
	(P 7.4.16)		
D-0647	Glasflügel H201B Standard Libelle	157	
D-0650	Schleicher ASK 21	21567	
D-0651	Grob G 102 Standard Astir III	5637S	N102FK
D-0652-RW	Schempp-Hirth Standard Cirrus	76	
D-0653	Siebert Sie 3	3005	
D-0654	Schleicher ASW 15	15095	
D-0655	Schleicher Ka 6E	4357	
D-0656-LP	Rolladen-Schneider LS1-d	112	
D-0657-HC	Schleicher ASW 15	15101	
D-0658	Schleicher ASK 13	13289	
D-0659-MJ	Schempp-Hirth Standard Cirrus	?	
D-0660	Schleicher ASW 15	15100	
D-0661-KV	Rolladen-Schneider LS6-c	6257	
D-0663	Schleicher ASK 13	13291	
D-0664	Rolladen-Schneider LS1-d	73	
D-0665	Glaser-Dirks DG-303 Club Elan Acro	3E455C79A13	
D-0666	Glasflügel H201B Standard Libelle	167	
D-0667-T	Rolladen-Schneider LS1-c	57	
D-0668	Rolladen-Schneider LS1-d	63	
D-0669-F	Rolladen-Schneider LS1-d	62	
D-0670	Rolladen-Schneider LS1-d	64	
D-0671	Glasflügel H201 Standard Libelle	172	
D-0675	Schleicher ASK 21	21569	
D-0676-M3	Rolladen-Schneider LS1-d	76	
D-0677-21	Schempp-Hirth Standard Cirrus	82	
D-0678	Schempp-Hirth Janus C	254	SE-UHB
D-0679	Rolladen-Schneider LS1-c	116	
D-0680	Schleicher ASK 21	21555	
D-0681	Rolladen-Schneider LS1-c	71	
D-0682	Focke-Wulf Kranich III	55	
D-0683-R2	Rolladen-Schneider LS1-c	74	
D-0685-12	Rolladen-Schneider LS1-c	60	
D-0686-37	Rolladen-Schneider LS1-c	66	
D-0687-JZ	Schempp-Hirth Standard Cirrus	86	
D-0688-88	Schempp-Hirth Discus CS	329CS	
D-0689-RF	Schempp-Hirth Standard Cirrus	88	
D-0690	Pilatus B4-PC11.	105	OY-VXT
D-0691	Schempp-Hirth Standard Cirrus	92	
D-0692	Rolladen-Schneider LS4-b	4853	
D-0693	Siebert Sie 3	3007	
D-0694	Rolladen-Schneider LS1-d	65	
D-0696	Schempp-Hirth Janus	45	SE-UMC, N468F
D-0697	DG Flugzeugbau DG-1000S	10-111S76	
D-0698	Schleicher ASK 21	21556	
D-0699	Rolladen-Schneider LS4-b	4963	PH-1438, D-0699
D-0700	Focke-Wulf Weihe 50	01	HB-554
	(P 11.15)		
D-0701-PI	Glasflügel H201B Standard Libelle	184	
D-0702-CV	Schempp-Hirth Standard Cirrus	180	
D-0703	Schempp-Hirth Standard Cirrus	181	
D-0704	Schempp-Hirth Standard Cirrus	555	
D-0705	Schempp-Hirth Standard Cirrus	183	
D-0706-ICU	Schempp-Hirth Standard Cirrus	184	
D-0707	Schleicher ASK 13	13287	
D-0708	Schleicher ASW 15	15107	
D-0709-SG	Schleicher Ka 6E	4363	
D-0710	Schempp-Hirth Duo Discus	18	
D-0711-CA	Schempp-Hirth Discus CS	166CS	
D-0712	DG Flugzeugbau DG-1000S	10-106S72	
D-0713-JR	Schleicher ASW 19B	19268	BGA 2499/DZD
D-0715	Schleicher ASW 15	15114	
D-0716	Schleicher ASW 15	15115	
D-0718	Schleicher Ka 2 Rhönschwalbe	40	
D-0719	Schempp-Hirth Standard Cirrus	107	
D-0720	Schempp-Hirth Janus B	121	F-CFAC
D-0721	Schleicher ASK 21	21350	
D-0723	Rolladen-Schneider LS4-b	4802	
D-0724	Rolladen-Schneider LS4-b	4803	
D-0725-MD	Rolladen-Schneider LS1-d	153	F-CBAZ, F-CDAZ
	(See also D-1065)		
D-0727	Rolladen-Schneider LS1-c	55	
D-0728-L7	Rolladen-Schneider LS1-d	67	
D-0729-AN	Schleicher ASW 27-18 (ASG 29)	29071	
D-0730	Glaser-Dirks DG-300 Elan	3E90	HB-1789
D-0731	Glasflügel Mosquito B	165	LX-CAX, D-7521
D-0733	SZD-30 Pirat	B-316	DDR-1733, DM-1733
D-0734-TL	Glaser-Dirks DG-600/18	?	
D-0735	Schleicher ASK 21	21557	
D-0736	Schempp-Hirth Standard Cirrus	104	
D-0738	Schleicher ASK 21	21575	
D-0740	LSD Ornith	V-1	
	(P.3.99)		
D-0741-NY	Schempp-Hirth Discus-2b	54	OO-YEH
D-0742-42	Glasflügel H201B Standard Libelle	204	
D-0743	Glasflügel H201 Standard Libelle	205	
D-0744	Schleicher ASK 21	21510	
D-0745-XD	Schleicher ASW 20	20069	D-7675
D-0746-IK	Schleicher ASK 13	13303	
D-0747-AP	Schleicher ASW 15	15120	
D-0749-49	Schleicher K 8B	8861	
D-0750-G8	Rolladen-Schneider LS4-a	4646?	HB-1497?
D-0752	Schleicher ASK 13	13309	
D-0754-YX	Schleicher ASW 19B	19118	PH-754, D-7556
D-0755	Schleicher ASK 13	13310	
D-0756	Schleicher ASW 15	15125	
	(Permit)		
D-0757	Schleicher ASK 13	13311	
D-0758	Schleicher ASW 15	15126	
D-0761	Schleicher ASK 13	13318	
D-0762	Schleicher ASK 13	13321	
D-0764	Rolladen-Schneider LS1-d	85	
D-0765	Rolladen-Schneider LS1-c	78	
	(P 4.7.16)		
D-0769-Z5	Glasflügel H201B Standard Libelle	298	
D-0770	Glasflügel H201 Standard Libelle	299	
D-0771-SL	Glasflügel H201B Standard Libelle	300	
D-0772	Schempp-Hirth Standard Cirrus	159	
D-0774	Schleicher ASK 21	21096	
D-0775	Schleicher ASW 20L	20555	
D-0776-MM	Schleicher ASW 20	20556	
D-0777-FH	Glasflügel H401 Kestrel	36	
D-0778-EK	Schempp-Hirth Discus CS	077CS	
D-0780	Rolladen-Schneider LS1-c	107	
D-0781-KL	Rolladen-Schneider LS1-d	98	
D-0783-A7	Schempp-Hirth Standard Cirrus	192	
D-0785	DG Flugzeugbau DG-1000S	10-114S78	
D-0787-XN	Rolladen-Schneider LS1-d	121	
D-0789	Glasflügel H201B Standard Libelle	8	OO-ZRO
	(P 12.8.16)		
D-0790-KY	SZD-48-1 Jantar Standard 2	B-1004	SP-3176
D-0792	Schleicher ASW 15	15142	
D-0793-C2	Schleicher ASW 15	15144	
D-0795	Glasflügel H301 Libelle	36	OE-0796
D-0796	Schleicher ASW 15	15148	
D-0798	Schleicher K 8B	8871	
D-0799	Schleicher ASW 15	15150	
D-0800	Rolladen-Schneider LS4-b	4820	
D-0801	DG Flugzeugbau DG-1000S	10-68S60	
D-0802	Schleicher ASW 15	15154	
D-0803	Schleicher ASW 15	15155	
D-0804-ALS	DG Flugzeugbau DG-1000S	10-46S45	
D-0806	Schleicher ASK 13	13346	
D-0807	SZD-51-1 Junior	B-1924	DDR-2807
D-0808	Schleicher ASW 20L	20417	
D-0809	Rolladen-Schneider LS1-d	101	
D-0811	Grunau Baby IIB	29	
D-0812	Rolladen-Schneider LS1-d	120	
D-0814	Schempp-Hirth Standard Cirrus	157G	
D-0815	Glasflügel H401 Kestrel	62	
D-0817	Rolladen-Schneider LS1-c	118	
D-0818-BX	Rolladen-Schneider LS8-18	8409	
D-0819-PX	Grob G 103A Twin II Acro	3756-K-51	
D-0820	Schleicher ASW 15	15014	PH-877, D-0341
D-0821	Schleicher Ka 6CR Rhönsegler	6201	RAFGGA 529
D-0822	Scheibe SF 27A Zugvogel V	1703/E	OE-0822
D-0823	Grunau Baby III	1	
D-0824	Schleicher ASK 13	13351	
D-0825	Bölkow Phoebus C	924	OE-0820
D-0826	Schleicher ASK 13	13352	
D-0827-7W	Schempp-Hirth Discus b	93	OH-964, SE-TZO
D-0828-YH	Schleicher ASW 28-18	28728	
D-0829	Schleicher ASK 13	13345	
D-0833-FU	Rolladen-Schneider LS1-c	114	
D-0834-8W	Rolladen-Schneider LS1-d	125	
D-0835	Grunau Baby IIB	3	
D-0836	Schempp-Hirth Standard Cirrus	226	
D-0837	Rolladen-Schneider LS1-ef	106	
D-0838	Glasflügel H-101 Salto	8	

Reg	Type	c/n	Other identities
D-0841-MO	Rolladen-Schneider LS4-b	4948	
D-0844-S1	Schempp-Hirth Discus CS	169CS	
D-0845-Y6	Glasflügel H201B Standard Libelle	305	
D-0846	Schleicher K 8B (P.12.99)	8881/AB	
D-0847	Glasflügel H401 Kestrel	46	
D-0848	Schleicher K 8B	8878	
D-0849	Schleicher ASK 13	13358	
D-0850	Schleicher K 8B	8875	
D-0852	Schleicher ASK 13	13360	
D-0853	Schleicher ASK 13	13361	
D-0855	Schleicher ASK 13	13362	
D-0856-UW	Schleicher ASW 15	15175	
D-0857	Akaflieg Braunschweig SB-7A (P 9.12)	1	
D-0858	Schleicher ASK 13	13341	
D-0859	Schleicher ASW 15	15176	
D-0860	Schleicher ASW 15	15177	
D-0861-WL	Schleicher ASW 15	15178	
D-0862-R1	Schempp-Hirth Discus CS	179CS	
D-0863	SZD-30 Pirat	B-585	DDR-1863, DM-1863
D-0864	Schleicher ASW 15	15181	
D-0865	Schleicher ASK 13	13368	
D-0866	Bölkow Phoebus C-1 (P.01)	808	I-SEGL
D-0868-JR	Schleicher ASW 15B	15184	
D-0869	Schleicher K 8B	8887	
D-0870-JP	Schleicher ASW 15B	15185	
D-0871	Schleicher K 8B	8889	
D-0872-FS	DG Flugzeugbau DG-500 Elan Orion	5E183X34	
D-0874	Rolladen-Schneider LS1-c	127	
D-0876	Schleicher ASW 15B	15192	
D-0877	Schleicher ASK 21	21561	
D-0878	Neukom Elfe S4A	62	HB-1305
D-0880	Pilatus B4-PC11AF	143	HB-1148
D-0881	Schempp-Hirth Discus CS	178CS	
D-0882	SZD-30 Pirat	S-01.28	DDR-1882, DM-1882
D-0883-ZJ	Schleicher ASW 20	20559	
D-0885-TH	Schleicher ASW 20	20561	
D-0886-SL	Schleicher ASW 27	27122	
D-0887	Schempp-Hirth Discus b	193	
D-0888-YL	Glasflügel Standard Libelle	278	
D-0889-CG	Schempp-Hirth Discus b	201	
D-0891-ZZ	Glasflügel H201B Standard Libelle	313	
D-0892-H1	Rolladen-Schneider LS1-c	122	
D-0893-SH	Schempp-Hirth Discus b	203	
D-0894-4R	Rolladen-Schneider LS4	4387	
D-0897	Rolladen-Schneider LS8-18	8117	G-DHZP, BGA 4337
D-0898	Rolladen-Schneider LS4-b	4794	
D-0899-XOO	Schleicher ASW 20	20048	(YR-. . . .). SE-UOO, F-CERQ
D-0900	Schleicher Ka 2B	118	D-3169, OE-0464
D-0901	Schleicher K 8B	8895	
D-0902	Schempp-Hirth Cirrus	60	OO-ZGS, D-0189
D-0904	Schleicher K 8B	8897	
D-0905	DG Flugzeugbau DG-1000S	10-137S89	
D-0907	Schempp-Hirth Duo Discus x	500	
D-0908	Schleicher ASK 13	13392	
D-0909-BD	Schempp-Hirth Discus b	188	
D-0910	Glasflügel H303 Mosquito	101	OE-5388
D-0911-HI	Glasflügel H201B Standard Libelle	306	
D-0912	Rolladen-Schneider LS1-d	129	
D-0913-FR	Glasflügel H201B Standard Libelle	250	
D-0915	Glasflügel H401 Kestrel	65	
D-0916	Schleicher ASK 13	13286AB	
D-0917	Grob G 102 Astir CS	1131	OY-XDS
D-0918	Siebert Sie 3	3019	
D-0920-TK	Glasflügel H201B Standard Libelle	315	
D-0921-EP	Schempp-Hirth Discus b	215	
D-0923	Rolladen-Schneider LS1-c	132	
D-0924	Start & Flug H-101 Salto	10	
D-0926	Göppingen Gö 1 Wolf	138	ZS-GAD, SAAF: ZS-33
D-0927-27	Schempp-Hirth Standard Cirrus	218	
D-0928-TE	Schleicher ASW 28	28069	
D-0930	Schempp-Hirth Discus b	196	
D-0931	Schleicher Ka 6CR Rhönsegler	897	
D-0932	SZD-48-3 Jantar-Standard 3	B-1737	OY-XZB, SE-UGM
D-0933-2H	Schempp-Hirth Discus b	209	
D-0934	Schleicher K 8B	8898	
D-0935	Rolladen-Schneider LS8-18	8271	
D-0936-GJ	Glaser-Dirks DG-800S	8-26S3	
D-0937-PV	Schempp-Hirth Ventus c	382	
D-0938	Darmstadt D-38	39	
D-0940	SZD-30 Pirat	B-493	OE-0943
D-0941	Schleicher ASW 15B	15206	OE-0941
D-0942	Schleicher K 8B	8899	
D-0943	Schleicher K 8B	8901	
D-0944	Schleicher ASK 13	13395	
D-0946	Schleicher K 8B	8902	
D-0947	Glaser-Dirks DG-300 Elan Acro	3E460A16	
D-0948	Schleicher ASK 13	13397	
D-0949	Schleicher ASW 15B	15221	
D-0950	Glasflügel H304	262	
D-0951-ES	Schleicher ASW 15B	15222	
D-0952	Glasflügel H401 Kestrel	60	
D-0953-HS	Schempp-Hirth Standard Cirrus	224G	
D-0954-WI	Schempp-Hirth Standard Cirrus	230G	
D-0955	Avialsa-Scheibe A.60 Fauconnet	131K	F-CDLI
D-0956	Schempp-Hirth Standard Cirrus	232G	
D-0957	Glasflügel H401 Kestrel	69	OE-0950
D-0958	Start & Flug H-101 Salto	11	
D-0959	Vogt Lo-100 Zwergreiher	04	
D-0960-HE	Glaser-Dirks DG-800S	8-37S8	HB-3165, D-8180
D-0961	Schleicher ASK 13	13246AB	
D-0962-ID	Schleicher ASW 19B	19392	SE-UID, LN-GAN
D-0965-GF	Rolladen-Schneider LS6-18W	6340	
D-0966-MM	Glasflügel H201B Standard Libelle	330	
D-0967	Schempp-Hirth Standard Cirrus	240G	
D-0968	Schleicher K 8B	4/80/89	
D-0969-AC	Schempp-Hirth Standard Cirrus	242G	
D-0970-TK	Schempp-Hirth Discus CS	026CS	OY-XRN
D-0971	Schempp-Hirth Discus b	224	
D-0972	Rolladen-Schneider LS6-c	6341	
D-0973	Rolladen-Schneider LS4-b	4805	
D-0974	Bölkow Phoebus C	874	OE-0974, OE-0876
D-0975	Schempp-Hirth Standard Cirrus	227	
D-0976-AR	Schempp-Hirth Standard Cirrus	229	
D-0977-SA	Schempp-Hirth Ventus b/16.6	186	PH-739
D-0979-FR	Glasflügel H401 Kestrel	66	
D-0980-AC	Schempp-Hirth Discus CS	031CS	
D-0982	Schleicher ASK 13	13398	
D-0983-ZE	Schempp-Hirth Ventus c	515	
D-0984-APO	Schleicher ASW 15B	15223	
D-0985	Schleicher ASK 21	21576	
D-0986	Schleicher Ka 6E	4390	
D-0987-VE	Schleicher ASW 15B	15227	
D-0988	Schleicher Ka 6 Rhönsegler	249	HB-588
D-0989	Schleicher K 8B	8910	
D-0990-90	Schleicher ASK 21	21456	
D-0991	Rolladen-Schneider LS6-c18	6348	
D-0993	Glaser-Dirks DG-300 Elan	3E173	HB-1869
D-0994	Schleicher K 8B	8915	
D-0995	Schleicher ASW 15B	15239	
D-0997-UB	Schleicher ASW 15B	15240	
D-0999-BH	Glasflügel H401 Kestrel	54	
D-1001	Pilatus B4-PC11AF	171	S5-3045, SL-3045, YU-4222
D-1002	Scheibe SF 27A	6046	
D-1003	Rolladen-Schneider LS8-18	8306	
D-1004-MG	Schempp-Hirth Discus b	220	
D-1005	SZD-9bis Bocian 1E	P-717	DDR-3005, DM-3005
D-1007	Glasflügel H401 Kestrel	24	HB-1001
D-1008	Schleicher Ka 6E	4008	
D-1010-CM	Jastreb Glasflügel 304B (P.5.12)	324	
D-1011	Schleicher K 8B	8742	
D-1013	Grunau Baby III (P. 5.14)	76	
D-1014	Scheibe Bergfalke III	5569	
D-1015-GL	Schempp-Hirth Discus b	189	
D-1016	Schempp-Hirth Ventus b/16.6	115	HB-1742
D-1017-4T	Glaser-Dirks DG-300 Elan	3E92	OY-XLU
D-1018	Grunau Baby IIB	05	
D-1020-F	Schleicher Ka 6CR Rhönsegler	6589	
D-1021	Schleicher ASK 21	21836	
D-1022	Rolladen-Schneider LS1-c	133	
D-1023-KK	Glaser-Dirks DG-300 Club Elan	3E391C59	
D-1024	Schleicher Ka 2 Rhönschwalbe	80	
D-1025	Scheibe Zugvogel IIIA	?	
D-1026-WZ	Schempp-Hirth Discus-2c	7	
D-1027	Glaser-Dirks DG-600	6-27	
D-1028-TOM	Schempp-Hirth Discus b	198	
D-1029-1W	SZD-55-1	551192047	I-NTRE
D-1030-30	Rolladen-Schneider LS1-c	123	
D-1031	Rolladen-Schneider LS1-d	135	
D-1032-W8	Schempp-Hirth Nimbus-3D	1/3	D-KAYY
D-1033	Glasflügel H-101 Salto	18	
D-1034	Schleicher ASW 24	24141	
D-1035-MU	Schempp-Hirth Ventus-2c	44/130	
D-1036-JR	Schempp-Hirth Standard Cirrus	417	I-FOFI
D-1037	Schleicher Ka 6CR Rhönsegler	6312	
D-1038	SG-38 Schulgleiter (P. 2.13)	1NE	
D-1039-1CB	Rolladen-Schneider LS6	6101	I-FAMF, D-1094
D-1040	Schempp-Hirth Ventus c (P 15.4.16)	348	
D-1041-B4	DG Flugzeugbau DG-1000S	10-31S30	
D-1043-YD	Schempp-Hirth Duo Discus	121	
D-1046-46	Neukom Elfe S4A	75	HB-1040
D-1047-KO	Glasflügel H401 Kestrel	84	OE-0969
D-1048-A3	Schempp-Hirth Discus b	237	
D-1049	DG Flugzeugbau DG-1000S	10-41S40	
D-1050	Schleicher Ka 6CR Rhönsegler	948	
D-1051-Z	Glasflügel H201B Standard Libelle	293	HB-1054
D-1052	Grunau Baby III	E-2	
D-1053	Glasflügel H201B Standard Libelle	288	HB-1056
D-1054-BEB	DG Flugzeugbau DG-1000S	10-33S32	
D-1055	DG Flugzeugbau DG-1000S	10-38S37	
D-1056-H4	Glaser-Dirks DG-300 Club Elan	3E404C63	
D-1057-4A	Rolladen-Schneider LS4	4584	
D-1058	Rolladen-Schneider LS4	4585	
D-1060	Vogt Lo-100 Zwergreiher	AB-34	
D-1061-F3	Rolladen-Schneider LS4-b	4952	
D-1062	Schempp-Hirth Duo Discus	54	
D-1063-WP	DG Flugzeugbau DG-1000S	10-49S48	
D-1064	Schleicher K 8B (P 4.15)	8410	
D-1065-RM	Rolladen-Schneider LS1-c	"530"	
	(C/n incorrect, believed to be 153 in which case this would be ex D-0725, F-CDAZ, F-CBAZ.; but D-0725 still current as LS1-d)		
	(Other possibilities are c/ns 131 or 143)		
D-1067-9C	Rolladen-Schneider LS8-18	8312	
D-1068	Grob G102 Astir CS Jeans	2173	PH-1086, D-7755
D-1069	Schempp-Hirth Standard Cirrus	228	
D-1070-XA	Glaser-Dirks DG-300 Elan	3E5	
D-1071	DG Flugzeugbau DG-1000S	10-35S34	
D-1072	Rolladen-Schneider LS4	4575	PH-1027, D-3604
D-1073	DG Flugzeugbau DG-1000S	10-42S41	
D-1074	Schempp-Hirth Standard Cirrus	239	
D-1075	SZD-59 Acro	542.A.16.012	
D-1076-BV	Rolladen-Schneider LS4	4602	
D-1077	Schleicher Ka 6CR Rhönsegler	6340/SIE	
D-1079	Grunau Baby III	01	BGA 1663, RAFGSA 373, D-1090
D-1080	Göppingen Gö IV Gövier II	1	
D-1081-A1	Rolladen-Schneider LS8-18	8461	
D-1082	Neukom S4 Elfe	4/X	HB-1084
D-1083	Schleicher Ka 6CR Rhönsegler	6285	
D-1084	Rolladen-Schneider LS4	4603	
D-1085	Glaser-Dirks DG-200/17C	2-141CL11	
D-1086	Grob G 103 Twin Astir	3136	D-1000
D-1087-F4	Schempp-Hirth Duo Discus	58	
D-1088	Schleicher Ka 6CR Rhönsegler	6526	
D-1089-ED	Rolladen-Schneider LS4	4604	
D-1090-SE	Glasflügel H301 Libelle	57	
D-1091-FS	Schleicher ASW 27	27032	PH-1094
D-1092	Schempp-Hirth Gö 4 Gövier III (P. 5.14)	417	PH-207
D-1093	Scheibe Bergfalke IV	5825	
D-1094-SHA	Schempp-Hirth Duo Discus	140	
D-1095-V5	Centrair 101 Pegase	?	
D-1096	Glasflügel H201B Standard Libelle	349	

Regn	Type	C/n	Previous Identities
D-1097-S4	Glasflügel H201B Standard Libelle	350	
D-1098-EM	Akaflieg Braunschweig SB-5E Sperber	5027/1	
D-1099	DG Flugzeugbau DG-1000S	10-55S54	
D-1100	DG Flugzeugbau DG-1000S	10-22S22	
D-1101	Schleicher ASW 19B	19055	
D-1102	Rolladen-Schneider LS1-d	142	
D-1103	Rolladen-Schneider LS4-a	4728	BGA 4841/JWN, D-7008
D-1104	Pilatus B4-PC11AF	005	HB-1104
D-1105	Akaflieg Braunschweig SB-5B Sperber	5005	
D-1106-DU	Schempp-Hirth Nimbus-3/24.5	17	
D-1107	Grunau Baby III	001	
D-1108-DL	Rolladen-Schneider LS4-b	4953	
D-1109-B	Glasflügel H201B Standard Libelle	358	
D-1110	Schleicher ASW 20L	20150	
D-1111	Schleicher K 8B	8667/AB	
D-1112	SZD-55-1	551198104	
D-1113	DG Flugzeugbau DG-1000S	10-208S130	
D-1114	Pilatus B4-PC11AF	182	S5-3125, YU-4223
D-1115	Bölkow Phoebus B1	757	G-CKLX, BGA 5190, OE-0851
D-1116	Rolladen-Schneider LS6.	6040	OO-YHN, D-6258
D-1118	Rolladen-Schneider LS3	3195	N9TE
D-1121	Schleicher K 8B	3	
D-1122	Rolladen-Schneider LS4	4430	
D-1123-G3	Rolladen-Schneider LS4-b	41029	
D-1124	Schleicher ASW 24	24001	
D-1125	Pilatus B4-PC11	118	HB-1130
D-1126	SZD-30 Pirat	B-503	D-1626, DDR-1826, DM-1826
D-1127	Schleicher K 7 Rhönadler	7026	
D-1128	Akaflieg München Mü.28	V-1	
D-1129-71	Rolladen-Schneider LS8-a (P 22.4.16)	8124	OY-CIX
D-1130	Schleicher ASK 21	21606	
D-1131	Akaflieg Stuttgart FS.31	V-1	
D-1133	Scheibe L-Spatz III	816	
D-1134	Schleicher ASK 21	21775	
D-1135	Glaser-Dirks DG-100G Elan	E213G179	
D-1136	Scheibe Bergfalke II	163	
D-1137-LB	Rolladen-Schneider LS4-b	4806	
D-1138	Allstar PZL SZD-59 Acro	590.A.05.004	
D-1139-PG	Rolladen-Schneider LS3-17	3457	I-DUNO, D-6684
D-1140	Schempp-Hirth Standard Cirrus	270	
D-1141	Grunau Baby IIB	9	D-6170, D-6028
D-1142-DP	Schleicher ASK 21	21274	
D-1143	Glaser-Dirks DG-500 Elan Trainer	5E131T57	
D-1145	Scheibe Bergfalke II	147/U	
D-1146	Dittmar Condor IV/3	28/53	OE-0869, D-1147
D-1147-73	Schempp-Hirth Discus-2b	168	
D-1149	Pilatus B4-PC11AF	117	HB-1143
D-1150	Rolladen-Schneider LS4	4508	
D-1151	Scheibe Mü 13E Bergfalke II	310	D-1699
D-1152	Rolladen-Schneider LS8-a	8014	
D-1153	Rolladen-Schneider LS4-b	4875	
D-1154	Schleicher ASK 21	21194	N174KS
D-1155-DF	Schempp-Hirth Janus C	152	LN-GDF, BGA 2823/ENR
D-1156	Fauvel AV.36C	37	
D-1157	Schleicher K 8B	8577	
D-1158-L1	Rolladen-Schneider LS8-18	8467	
D-1159	Schempp-Hirth Duo Discus	168	
D-1160	Schempp-Hirth Duo Discus	166	
D-1161-3Y	Rolladen-Schneider LS8-a	8251	
D-1162	Rolladen-Schneider LS1-c	147	
D-1163-IBG	Rolladen-Schneider LS8-a	8204	
D-1164	Scheibe Bergfalke III	5545	
D-1165	Schleicher ASK 21	21510	
D-1166-US	Schempp-Hirth Ventus b/16.6	139	HB-1693
D-1167	Scheibe Mü13E Bergfalke II	176	(D-0759), D-1167
D-1168-WG	Schempp-Hirth Ventus-2cx (P.3.04)	87	
D-1169	Glasflügel H401 Kestrel	72	
D-1170-GE	Glasflügel H401 Kestrel	75	
D-1171	Glasflügel H205 Club Libelle	144	OE-5065
D-1172	Glaser-Dirks DG-800S	8-70S18	
D-1173-TF	Glaser-Dirks DG-500 Elan Trainer	5E39T13	
D-1174-Gi	Schempp-Hirth Discus CS	063CS	
D-1175	Schleicher K 8B	8930Br	
D-1177	Akaflieg Braunschweig SB.11	01	
D-1178-EU	Glasflügel H201B Standard Libelle (Formerly Aeberli 201M Libelle)	133	HB-2056, HB-1007
D-1179	Rolladen-Schneider LS6-c	6213	
D-1180-AB	Schempp-Hirth Discus-2a	?	
D-1181-DON	Schempp-Hirth Duo Discus	409	
D-1182	Glaser-Dirks DG-200	2-85	I-DGAM
D-1185	Glaser-Dirks DG-300 Elan	3E8	OH-789, D-1300
D-1186	Scheibe Bergfalke II	319	
D-1187	Marganski MDM-1 Fox	219	
D-1189	Glaser-Dirks DG-300 Elan	3E225	
D-1190	Schempp-Hirth Standard Cirrus	255G	
D-1191-IHE	Schempp-Hirth Standard Cirrus (P 6.15)	262G	
D-1192	Akaflieg München Mü.13E Bergfalke	1	
D-1193	Schleicher Ka 6CR Rhönsegler	6445	
D-1194	Valentin Mistral C	MC 069/86	
D-1195	Schleicher K 7 Rhönadler	7258	
D-1196	Scheibe SF 27A	6091	
D-1197	Grunau Baby IIB	3	
D-1198	Schleicher K 8B	8487	
D-1199-IFF	Glaser-Dirks DG-300 Club Elan	3E368C49	
D-1200	Glasflügel Club Libelle 205	41	I-CLAB
D-1201	Fauvel AV-36CR	86	
D-1202-GD	Schempp-Hirth Nimbus-2	68	HB-1202
D-1204	Scheibe Spatz A	1	
D-1206-3G	Schempp-Hirth Ventus-2b	17	
D-1207	Schempp-Hirth Nimbus-2	19	
D-1208-KW	Schempp-Hirth Duo Discus	91	
D-1210	Rolladen-Schneider LS1-e	155	
D-1211	Schempp-Hirth Discus-2b	103	OY-JXM
D-1212	Schleicher Ka 6CR Rhönsegler	6483	
D-1213	Glasflügel H201B Standard Libelle	538	HB-1210
D-1216-GAJ	LAK-12 Lietuva	6192	(D-1200), BGA 4488, LX-CDM
D-1217	Schleicher ASW 17	17028	G-DEGD, BGA 2667, D-2343
D-1218	Neukom Elfe S-4A	81	HB-3079
D-1219-ED	Rolladen-Schneider LS8-a	8093	OO-YIL
D-1220	Schleicher K 8B	8906/AB	
D-1222	Scheibe SF 27A	6004	
D-1223-FA	Glasflügel H401 Kestrel	13	N19GW, CF-YAW
D-1224	Scheibe L-Spatz (P .08)	531	
D-1225-HQ	Akaflieg Braunschweig SB-12	1 AB	
D-1227-KR	Neukom Elfe S-4A	51	HB-1228
D-1228-WK	Schleicher ASW 28	28071	
D-1229	Grob G 103A Twin II Acro	3757-K-52	
D-1230-SC	Grob G 103A Twin II Acro	3767-K-53	
D-1231	Schleicher Ka 6CR Rhönsegler	6025	
D-1232-1Y	Rolladen-Schneider LS4-b	4967	
D-1233-33	Schleicher Ka 6E	4175	PH-967, D-4735
D-1234	Scheibe Bergfalke II	326	
D-1235-DC	Rolladen-Schneider LS4	4622	
D-1236	Schleicher ASK 21	21514	
D-1237	Scheibe Bergfalke III	5562	
D-1238	Pilatus B4-PC11	074	
D-1240	Schleicher K 8B	8611	D-KOSV, D-1240
D-1242	Schempp-Hirth Ventus c	366	
D-1243	DG Flugzeugbau DG-303 Elan Acro	3E492A31	
D-1245-YP	Glasflügel Standard Libelle 201B	333	OE-0945
D-1246	Schleicher ASK 21	21793	
D-1247	Rolladen-Schneider LS4-a	4624	
D-1248-GO	Schleicher ASH 25	25131	
D-1249-AI	Rolladen-Schneider LS6	6128	
D-1250	Schempp-Hirth Discus b	323	I-LRIP
D-1251	Schempp-Hirth Standard Cirrus	383	HB-1212
D-1252-4B	Schleicher ASK 21	21469	
D-1253-PS	Rolladen-Schneider LS4-b	4968	
D-1254	Rolladen-Schneider LS4-b	4969	
D-1256	Schleicher ASW 24	24099	
D-1257	Schleicher ASH 25	25102	
D-1258	Schleicher ASK 21	21471	
D-1259	Scheibe L-Spatz 55	548	
D-1260	Schleicher ASK 21	21472	
D-1261-GK	Grunau Baby IIB	2	
D-1262	Glaser-Dirks DG-300 Elan	3E103	
D-1263-63	Glaser-Dirks DG-100G Elan	E182G148	
D-1266	Schleicher K 8B	8247/A	
D-1267	Glasflügel Club Libelle 205	66	PH-1261, D-8205, F-CEQA
D-1269	Schleicher ASW 19B	19361	
D-1270-WM	Schleicher ASW 20L	20562	
D-1271-4J	Schempp-Hirth Discus-2c	10	
D-1273	Rolladen-Schneider LS1-d	87	OO-ZNV, D-4440
D-1276	Glaser-Dirks DG-300 Elan	3E426	I-RYZZ
D-1277-PA	Schempp-Hirth Ventus-2bx	151	
D-1278-OP	Schleicher ASW 24	24104	
D-1279	Glaser-Dirks DG-300 Elan	3E192	OY-XYD
D-1280	Grob G 103A Twin II Acro	3769-K-55	
D-1281	Rolladen-Schneider LS4-b	4909	
D-1282	Schleicher Ka 6CR Rhönsegler	6522/Si	
D-1285-W1	Schleicher ASW 24	24110	
D-1286	Rolladen-Schneider LS4-a	4661	
D-1288	Neukom Elfe S4A	74	HB-1280
D-1290-AM	Rolladen-Schneider LS4	4590	
D-1291-7B	Rolladen-Schneider LS4-b	4753	
D-1292	Schleicher ASK 23B	23124	
D-1293	Rolladen-Schneider LS6-b	6131	
D-1294	Scheibe L-Spatz 55	552	
D-1295-9W	Neukom Elfe S4A	64	HB-1297
D-1296	Scheibe SF 27A	6080	
D-1297	Rolladen-Schneider LS4-a	4755	
D-1298-98	Rolladen-Schneider LS4-b	4756	
D-1299	Rolladen-Schneider LS4-a	4757	
D-1300	LET L-13 Blanik (P. 10.11)	026351	HB-1303
D-1302-JG	Bölkow Phoebus C	825	
D-1303	Glasflügel Mosquito	01	
D-1306	Start & Flug H101 Salto	55	
D-1307	Schleicher K 8B	8594	
D-1309	Schleicher Ka 6CR Rhönsegler	6528	D-1330
D-1310-BD	DG Flugzeugbau DG-1000S	10-135S87	
D-1311	Akaflieg München Mü 13D III (P. 5.14)	2	F-CCBT, WL-XIII-55
D-1312	Neukom Elfe S4A	77	HB-1312
D-1313	Schleicher ASK 13	13686AB	
D-1314-AI	Neukom Elfe S4A	76	HB-1311
D-1315	Pilatus B4-PC11AF	127	BGA 4755/JSY, D-3055, D-5787, PH-578
D-1316-5A	Schempp-Hirth Ventus-2a	70	OY-XXA
D-1317	Scheibe Bergfalke II	E-1	
D-1318	Schleicher K 8B (P.6.12)	8112	
D-1319	SZD-30 Pirat	B-318	DDR-1719, DM-1719
D-1320	Schleicher ASW 20L	20560	
D-1321	Rolladen-Schneider LS4-b	4954	
D-1322-AW	Schleicher ASW 19B	19360	
D-1323-MZ	Rolladen-Schneider LS7	7026	
D-1324	Scheibe Bergfalke III	5619	
D-1325	Schleicher ASH 25	25240	
D-1326	Schempp-Hirth Duo Discus	455	
D-1327	Grob G 102 Club Astir IIIB	5596CB	
D-1328-ZV	Rolladen-Schneider LS7-WL	7024	
D-1329	Rolladen-Schneider LS7-WL	7023	
D-1331	Scheibe Bergfalke III	5582	
D-1332	Grob G 103 Twin II	3749	
D-1333	Pilatus B4-PC11AF	246	SE-TXY, D-7843
D-1334	Grob G 103 Twin II	3761	
D-1335	Schleicher ASK 13	13687AB	
D-1336	Schleicher Ka 6CR Rhönsegler	6595	
D-1337	Schleicher K 7 Rhönadler	7011	
D-1338-IIX	Schleicher ASK 21	21571	
D-1340-DM	Rolladen-Schneider LS6-b	6135	
D-1341	Scheibe SF 27A	6063	
D-1342-9B	Rolladen-Schneider LS4-a	4662	
D-1343	Scheibe Bergfalke III	5620	
D-1346	Schleicher Ka 6CR Rhönsegler	6632	
D-1347	Schempp-Hirth Ventus c	613	
D-1349	Schleicher K 7 Rhönadler	7202	PH-1343, D-5698
D-1351	Bölkow Phoebus C	817	
D-1352	Schempp-Hirth Discus CS	032CS	D-1321
D-1353	Scheibe Bergfalke III	5615	
D-1354-TL	Eiri PIK-20D	20528	HB-1350
D-1355	Schleicher ASK 13	13659AB	
D-1356	Rolladen-Schneider LS3	3001	HB-1352

Reg	Type	C/n	Previous identities
D-1357	Glaser-Dirks DG-300 Elan	3E227	
D-1359	SZD-9bis Bocian 1E	P-546	DDR-3359, DM-3359
D-1360	Rolladen-Schneider LS4-a	4737	
D-1361	Schleicher ASK 13	13691AB	
D-1362	Scheibe SF 27A	6077	
D-1363	Glaser-Dirks DG-300 Elan	3E18	
D-1365	Rolladen-Schneider LS4-a	4663	
D-1366	Schleicher ASK 13	13019	
D-1367	Rolladen-Schneider LS4	4591	
D-1368	Rolladen-Schneider LS3	3057	HB-1368
D-1369-ICJ	Rolladen-Schneider LS4-a	4735	
D-1370-WJ	Rolladen-Schneider LS4-a	4734	
D-1371-IKX	Rolladen-Schneider LS4	4594	
D-1372	Glaser-Dirks DG-300 Elan	3E174	
D-1373	Glaser-Dirks DG-300 Elan	3E178	
D-1374-AI	Rolladen-Schneider LS8-a	8046	
D-1375	Schleicher ASK 13	13041	D-1378
D-1376-AG	Schempp-Hirth Ventus-2cx	?	
D-1377-LD	Schempp-Hirth Duo Discus	153	
D-1378	Glasflügel H201B Standard Libelle	414	HB-1373
D-1379	Schleicher Ka 2B Rhönschwalbe	3	
D-1380	Schempp-Hirth Nimbus-4D	12	
D-1381-KC	Rolladen-Schneider LS4-a	4730	
D-1382	Rolladen-Schneider LS4-a	4729	
D-1383-YC	Schempp-Hirth Duo Discus	230	
D-1384	Akaflieg Braunschweig SB-5B	5084	
D-1386-UG	DG Flugzeugbau DG-800S	8-256S50	
D-1387	Rolladen-Schneider LS4-a	4647	
D-1388	Glaser-Dirks DG-100G	87G8	HB-1338
D-1389	Scheibe L-Spatz III	13	D-1386
D-1390	Schleicher ASK 13	13653AB	
	(C/n same as BGA 4683/JPY, ex RAFGGA 509, which is current but was previously based at RAF Bruggen. Dual identity?)		
D-1392-C8	Rolladen-Schneider LS4-b	4759	
D-1393	Schleicher ASK 13	13683AB	
D-1394	Schempp-Hirth Standard Cirrus	67	OE-0867
D-1396-96	Scheibe SF 27A	6059	
D-1397	Rolladen-Schneider LS3-a	3239	HB-1397
D-1398	Schleicher ASH 26	unkn	
	(Museum) (Res. -cld?)		
D-1399-E6	Schempp-Hirth Ventus-2c	27/72	
D-1400	Schleicher ASW 20	20118	HB-1450
D-1401-JO	Glaser-Dirks DG-101G Elan	E164G130	D-4101
	(P. 3.15)		
D-1402	Schleicher ASK 21	21162	
D-1403-IWZ	Schleicher ASW 19B	19387	
D-1404-G2	Schleicher ASW 19B	19388	
D-1405	Glasflügel H301 Libelle	79	
D-1406	SZD-30 Pirat	S-03.49	DDR-1909, DM-1909
D-1407	Schleicher K 8B	8317/A	
D-1408-S	Glasflügel H201 Standard Libelle	18	
D-1409	Schleicher Ka 2B Rhönschwalbe	243	
D-1410-Y7	Rolladen-Schneider LS8-18	8462	
D-1411	SZD-30 Pirat	B-474	DDR-1811, DM-1811
D-1412-PS	Schempp-Hirth Duo Discus	233	
D-1414-14	Rolladen-Schneider LS1-c	105	
D-1415	Scheibe L-Spatz 55	524	
D-1416	Glaser-Dirks DG-200	2-30	HB-1415
D-1417-RT	Schempp-Hirth Ventus b/16.6	183	
D-1418-2HT	Schempp-Hirth Discus CS	067CS	
D-1420	DFS Olympia-Meise	unkn	
D-1421	Scheibe L-Spatz 55	3	
D-1422	SZD-36A Cobra 15	W-673	HB-1223
D-1423	Scheibe Specht	848	
D-1424	Glasflügel H201B Standard Libelle	10	OE-0906
D-1425	Rolladen-Schneider LS4-a	4651	
D-1427-LEO	Schleicher ASW 27B	27163	ZS-GWP, BGA 4919, D-4115
D-1428	Schleicher K 8B	8550	
D-1429-KG	Rolladen-Schneider LS8-a	8183	
D-1430-LO	Schleicher ASW 20CL	20810	ZK-GRZ, D-3430
D-1431	Schleicher ASK 21	21574	
D-1432	Schleicher ASW 20L	20240	RAFGGA 720
D-1433-J0	Schleicher ASW 19B	19213	
D-1434-4D	Bölkow Phoebus A-1	710	
D-1435-L4	Rolladen-Schneider LS4-b	4931	
D-1437	Rolladen-Schneider LS8-18	8205	
D-1439-S4	Grob G 102 Astir CS 77	1748	HB-1435
D-1442	Rolladen-Schneider LS4-a	4666	
D-1444-A9	Glaser-Dirks DG-300 Elan	3E172	OY-XOE
D-1445-T	Rolladen-Schneider LS4-a	4667	
D-1446	Schempp-Hirth Mini-Nimbus HS7	43	HB-1404
D-1447	Schleicher Ka 6CR	6568	PH-374
D-1448	Schleicher ASW 27	27083	
D-1449	Rolladen-Schneider LS4	4417	HB-1749
D-1450	Schleicher Ka 6E	4184	
D-1451-YM	Schempp-Hirth Ventus b/16.6	122	I-IILY, D-3153
	(P. 2.14)		
D-1452	Scheibe Bergfalke II	334	
D-1453-CM	Schleicher ASH 25	25015	
D-1455	Rolladen-Schneider LS8-18	8414	
D-1456	Schleicher ASK 21	21341	
D-1457	Schleicher Ka 6 Rhönsegler	306	
D-1458	Schempp-Hirth Mini Nimbus C	111	HB-1452
D-1459	Grunau Baby III	EB-02	
D-1460	Grob G 102 Speed Astir IIB	4066	HB-1498
D-1463	Schleicher ASK 21	21342	
D-1465	Scheibe Specht	AB-01	
D-1466	Scheibe Zugvogel IIIA	1031	
	(P 4.15)		
D-1467	Glaser-Dirks DG-100 Elan	E13	HB-1468
D-1468	Scheibe L-Spatz 55	536	
D-1469-AN	Glaser-Dirks DG-100G Elan	E2	HB-1465
D-1470	Schleicher K 8	351/57	
D-1472-7X	Rolladen-Schneider LS4-b	4929	
D-1473-SH	Schleicher ASK 21	21165	
D-1474	Schleicher ASK 21	21166	
D-1475-UG	Schleicher ASK 21	21167	
D-1476-GO	Schempp-Hirth Discus-2b	52	
D-1477	SZD-30 Pirat	B-406	DDR-1777, DM-1777
D-1478	Schleicher Ka 6CR Rhönsegler	6586/Si	
	(P 3.5.16)		
D-1479	Rolladen-Schneider LS4-b	4930	
D-1481	Schleicher ASK 21	21343	
D-1483-GB	Schleicher ASK 21	21127	
D-1484	Breguet 905S Fauvette	30	G-DESM, BGA 2915, F-CCJA
D-1485	Glaser-Dirks DG-200	2-16	HB-1408
D-1486-A7	Glaser-Dirks DG-500 Elan Orion	5E152X9	
D-1488-LR	Rolladen-Schneider LS4-b	4970	
D-1489	Schleicher ASK 21	21345	
D-1490	Scheibe Specht	806	
D-1492-MSL	Rolladen-Schneider LS7-WL	7057	
D-1493	Schleicher ASK 23B	23097	
D-1494-G4	Rolladen-Schneider LS4-a	4808	
D-1495-CE	Rolladen-Schneider LS4-b	4809	
D-1497-MI	Rolladen-Schneider LS4-b	4971	
D-1499	HpH Glasflügel 304C	77-C	
D-1500-II	Glasflügel Standard Libelle 201B	596	OO-ZGM, OO-NAM
D-1501	Glaser-Dirks DG-100G Elan	E149G116	
D-1502	Neukom Elfe S4A	60	HB-1205
D-1503-WN	Rolladen-Schneider LS8-18	8468	
D-1505	Glaser-Dirks DG-202	2-184	OO-ZXU, PH-722
D-1506	SG-38 Schulgleiter	AB-BL-001-BS	
D-1507-EX	Rolladen-Schneider LS8-a	8008	
D-1508-1X	Rolladen-Schneider LS8-a	8009	
D-1509-PE	Rolladen-Schneider LS4-b	4932	
D-1512	Scheibe Bergfalke II	01/53	
D-1513	Schleicher ASK 21	21288	LN-GIA
D-1514-Y12	Schempp-Hirth Ventus b/16.6	260	F-CGLD, F-WGLD
D-1515-15	Bölkow Phoebus C	839	
D-1516	Schleicher ASK 21	21358	
D-1517	Scheibe L-Spatz 55	2/A	
D-1518	Rolladen-Schneider LS4-a	4668	
D-1519	Scheibe Bergfalke III	5584	
	(P 22.7.16)		
D-1521	Schleicher ASK 21	21221	
D-1522	Olympia-Meise	E-002	
D-1523	SZD-55-1	551195065	
D-1524-KD	Schempp-Hirth Duo Discus	10	
D-1525	Scheibe L-Spatz 55	556	
D-1526-AG	Schempp-Hirth Discus b	493	
D-1527-JO	Schempp-Hirth Discus b	278	I-NEWS
D-1528	Scheibe L-Spatz III	829	
D-1529	Schleicher ASH 25	25027	
D-1530	Grunau Baby IIb	536	
D-1531	Scheibe Zugvogel IIIA	1037	
D-1532-IGW	SZD-55-1	551195074	
D-1533	Schleicher ASK 21	21355	
D-1534-5	Schempp-Hirth Discus-2a	25	
D-1539	Focke-Wulf Kranich III	80	HB-1549
	(P .08)		
D-1540-W1	Schleicher ASK 21	21359	
D-1541	Schleicher ASK 23B	23101	
D-1542	Schleicher K 8B	582	
D-1543	Glasflügel H201B Standard Libelle	309	HB-1548
D-1544-T2	Schleicher ASK 21	21613	
D-1545-45	Schleicher ASK 21	21360	
D-1547-7A	Glaser-Dirks DG-100G Elan	E40G22	HB-1547
D-1548-IJT	SZD-55-1	551195075	
D-1549	Scheibe SF 27A	6085	
D-1550	Schleicher ASK 23B	23102	
D-1551	Schleicher Ka 6CR Rhönsegler	571	
D-1552-H3	Glaser-Dirks DG-100G Elan	E110G80	HB-1652
D-1554	Grob G 103A Twin II Acro	3803-K-70	
D-1556	Grob G 102 Standard Astir III	5604S	
D-1558	Schempp-Hirth Ventus-2c	78/. . .	
D-1559-59	Schleicher ASW 27	27101	
D-1560-B9	Rolladen-Schneider LS4-a	4669	
D-1561	Scheibe Zugvogel IIIA	1045	
D-1562	Scheibe Zugvogel IIIB	1072	
D-1564	Scheibe Zugvogel IVA	1509	
D-1565-K6	Schempp-Hirth Discus CS	082CS	
D-1566	Scheibe Specht	808	SE-SVS, D-6680, D-4680, D-4320
D-1568	Schleicher Ka 6BR Rhönsegler	482	
D-1569	Schleicher K 7 Rhönadler	479	
D-1570	Glasflügel Hornet C	99	OH-570
D-1572	Glaser-Dirks DG-300 Club Elan	3E307C20	
D-1573	Schleicher K 8B	8391/A	
D-1574	Schleicher ASW 20L	20570	
D-1575-TV	Schleicher ASW 20	20571	
D-1576	Schleicher ASK 21	21107	
D-1577-3P	Schleicher ASW 19B	19364	
D-1578-JOU	Sportine Aviacija LAK-17A	102	G-CJOU, BGA 4703
D-1579-ZP	Schleicher ASK 21	21422	
D-1580	Schleicher ASW 24	24048	
D-1581	Grob G103A Twin II Acro	3654-K-23	HB-1581
D-1582	Schleicher ASW 24	24049	
D-1583	Schleicher ASK 21	21423	
D-1584-24	Schleicher ASW 24	24050	
D-1585	Schleicher ASK 21	21615	(JA2538)
D-1587-STI	Schempp-Hirth Discus CS	172CS	
D-1588	SZD-30 Pirat	B-431	DDR-1788, DM-1788
D-1589	Schleicher Ka 6CR Rhönsegler	622	
D-1590	Pilatus B4-PC11A	25	PH-448
D-1591	Rolladen-Schneider LS4	4158	HB-1594
D-1592-II	Rolladen-Schneider LS4-b	4773	
D-1593	Rolladen-Schneider LS4-b	4774	
D-1594-DE	Schempp-Hirth Ventus-2bxR	142	
	(Permit)		
D-1595-FHM	Schempp-Hirth Discus-2a	214	
	(P. 2.11)		
D-1596-LD	Schempp-Hirth Duo Discus	61	
D-1597-WP	Rolladen-Schneider LS4-b	4940	
D-1598-LSF	Rolladen-Schneider LS4-b	4777	
D-1599-IT	Rolladen-Schneider LS4-b	4778	
D-1600	Scheibe Bergfalke III	5550	
D-1601	Vogt Lo-100 Zwergreiher	015	OE-0405
D-1602	Glaser-Dirks DG-300 Club Elan	3E374C53	
D-1603-CB	Rolladen-Schneider LS4	4324	HB-1668
D-1604-G3	Rolladen-Schneider LS4	4069	HB-1603
D-1605	Scheibe L-Spatz 55	004	
D-1606-01	Schleicher ASW 24	24052	
D-1607	Schleicher ASK 21	21425	
D-1608-V1	Rolladen-Schneider LS4-b	41012	
D-1610-2V	Schleicher ASK 21	21435	
D-1612	Glaser-Dirks DG-101 Elan	E94	HB-1612
D-1613	Schleicher Ka 6CR Rhönsegler	6635/Si	
D-1614	Rolladen-Schneider LS4	4154	HB-1671
D-1615	Rolladen-Schneider LS4-b	41030	

Reg	Type	C/N	Previous identities
D-1616	Glasflügel H303 Mosquito B	187	OE-5243
D-1617	SZD-30 Pirat	B-397	D-1728, DDR-1768, DM-1768
D-1618-GJ	Schempp-Hirth Discus-2b	70	
D-1619-19	SZD-50-3 Puchacz	B-1537	EC-JCJ, SP-3691, D-4653, DDR-3653
D-1620	SZD-50-3 Puchacz	B-1337	DDR-3620
D-1621	Schleicher ASK 21	21745	
D-1622-KR	Luftsport-Club Friedrichshafen LCF 2	002	
D-1623-GB	Glasflügel Mosquito B	115	HB-1423
D-1624	SZD-48-3 Jantar Standard 3	B-1970	
D-1625	Scheibe Spatz B	696	
D-1626	Rolladen-Schneider LS4-b	41031	
D-1627	Grunau Baby IIB	621	DM-1621
D-1629	Scheibe L-Spatz 55	712	
D-1632	Schleicher ASG 32	32022	
D-1633	Glaser-Dirks DG-300 Elan	3E61/17	
	(P. 7.15)		
D-1634-SF	Schleicher ASW 19B	19026	I-LIVE
D-1635	Schleicher Ka 6CR Rhönsegler	6159	OE-0635
D-1636	Kurz Me 163BS Komet replica	1	
D-1637	Schleicher ASW 20	20602	
D-1638-BE	Schleicher ASK 21	21136	
D-1639	Rolladen-Schneider LS4	4133	HB-1633
D-1640	Schleicher ASK 21	21771	
D-1641	Schleicher K 8B	8514	
D-1642	SZD-30 Pirat	B-563	DDR-1842, DM-1842
D-1643	LET L-23 Super Blanik	948120	
D-1644-E4	Rolladen-Schneider LS4-b	4781	
D-1646-W8	Rolladen-Schneider LS8-b	8435	
D-1647	Schleicher ASK 21	21110	
D-1648-DE	Schleicher ASW 20	20575	
D-1649	Schleicher ASW 20L	20577	
D-1650	Schleicher ASK 21	21112	
D-1651	Scheibe Bergfalke III	5601	
	(P 4.5.16)		
D-1652	Schleicher ASK 21	21134	
D-1653-A5	Schempp-Hirth Duo Discus	323	
D-1654	SZD-50-3 Puchacz	B-1538	DDR-3654
	(W/o 19.8.15)		
D-1655	Schleicher Ka 3	01	
	(Permit .02)		
D-1656-IF	SZD-50-3 Puchacz	B-1541	DDR-3657
D-1657-AY	Schleicher ASW 20C	20822	
D-1658	Grunau Baby IIB	01A	
D-1659	SZD-50-3 Puchacz	B-1543	DDR-3659
D-1661-XG	Schempp-Hirth Discus b	135	
D-1662	Schleicher Ka 6CR Rhönsegler	896	
D-1663	Schleicher K 8B	816	
D-1664	SZD-30 Pirat	B-588	DDR-1864, DM-1864
D-1665	Schleicher Ka 6CR Rhönsegler	852	
D-1666-IF	Schempp-Hirth Discus-2b	84	D-8027
	(P. 4.11)		
D-1667	Glasflügel H101 Salto	67	
D-1668	Schempp-Hirth Ventus C	419	OY-XRE
D-1669	SZD-32A Foka 5	W-429	OE-0892, SP-2533
D-1670	Schleicher ASK 13	13306	OE-0911
D-1672	SZD-30 Pirat	B-401	DDR-1772, DM-1772
D-1673	Scheibe SF 26A Standard	5048	
D-1674	Rolladen-Schneider LS7-WL	7036	
D-1675	Rolladen-Schneider LS7	7037	
D-1676-63	Schempp-Hirth Ventus-2cx	100	
D-1678	Rolladen-Schneider LS7-WL	7038	
D-1679	Schleicher K 8B	909	
D-1680-SW	Schempp-Hirth Discus CS	168CS	OY-XUZ, D-1590
D-1681-CW	Rolladen-Schneider LS8-a	8085	
D-1684	Rolladen-Schneider LS7	7039	
D-1685	Grob G 102 Club Astir IIIB	5520CB	
D-1686	Scheibe L-Spatz 55	851 K	
D-1687	Scheibe L-Spatz 55	820 K	
D-1688-CM	Rolladen-Schneider LS8	8011	
D-1689	Rolladen-Schneider LS4-b	4928	
D-1690	SZD-30 Pirat	B-433	DDR-1790, DM-1790
	(Rebt from D-2787 ex DDR/DM-1787 and adopted its c/n B-430 officially)		
D-1691	Schleicher ASW 19B	19052	I-FLUG
D-1694	Scheibe SF 27A	6018	
D-1697-D1	Schleicher ASK 21	21580	
D-1698-6W	Rolladen-Schneider LS8-a	8206	
D-1699-LY	SZD-41A Jantar Standard	B-802	OE-5143
D-1701	Glaser-Dirks DG-100G Elan	E67G42	
D-1702-AF	SZD-30 Pirat	W-403	DDR-1706, DM-1706
D-1703	Glaser-Dirks DG-300 Elan	3E23	
D-1704-X5	Schleicher ASK 23	23015	HB-1790
D-1705	Grob G 102 Astir CS	1238	D-7319
D-1706	Bölkow Phoebus C	823	
D-1707	Glaser-Dirks DG-300 Elan	3E325	
D-1708	Scheibe L-Spatz 55	748	(D-8397), D-1708
D-1709	SZD-30 Pirat	W-405	DDR-1708, DM-1708
D-1710	SZD-30 Pirat	W-416	DDR-1715, DM-1715
D-1711	Scheibe SF 34	5118	
D-1712	SZD-30 Pirat	W-412	DDR-1711, DM-1711
D-1713	Rolladen-Schneider LS7	7051	
D-1714	Rolladen-Schneider LS7	7052	
D-1716-6B	Rolladen-Schneider LS4	4394	
D-1717	Akaflieg München Mü.17	03	
	(Res.)		
D-1718	SZD-30 Pirat	W-413	DDR-1712, DM-1712
D-1721	Schleicher ASK 21	21813	
D-1722-LM	Schleicher ASW 20L	20481	HB-1728, OE-5289
D-1723-6C	SZD-30 Pirat	B-305	DDR-1722, DM-1722
D-1724-Y7	Schempp-Hirth Ventus-2cxa	115	
D-1725-BD	Schempp-Hirth Discus b	343	
D-1726	SZD-30 Pirat	B-307	DDR-1726, DM-1726
D-1727-IGA	Glasflügel H304	9265	
	(Built from spares)		
D-1728-E1	Schleicher ASW 28-18	28510	
	(P.3.04)		
D-1729- IYY	Schleicher ASW 20C	20713	
D-1730	Schleicher ASW 20C	20714	
D-1731	Schleicher ASW 20CL	20728	
D-1732	Schleicher K 8B	13/117	
D-1734	SZD-30 Pirat	B-298	DDR-1724, DM-1724, SP-2531
D-1735	Scheibe Bergfalke II/55	314	
D-1737	Scheibe Bergfalke III	5554	
D-1738	Scheibe L-Spatz 55	766	
D-1739	Glaser-Dirks DG-300 Elan	3E33	HB-1739
D-1740-AS	Akaflieg München Mü.17	02	
D-1741	Schleicher K 7 Rhönadler	1030	
D-1742	Schleicher K 7 Rhönadler	1031	
D-1743-IL	Glaser-Dirks DG-101G Elan	E136G104	HB-1703
D-1744-CJ	Schempp-Hirth Duo Discus	74	
D-1746	Rolladen-Schneider LS4-b	41056	
D-1747	Rolladen-Schneider LS4	4445	
D-1748	Schleicher Ka 6CR Rhönsegler	1069	
D-1749	Schleicher K 8B	136	
D-1751	Schempp-Hirth Discus b	312	
D-1752-EA	Schempp-Hirth Discus b	322	
D-1753	Fauvel AV-36C1	V-1/250	
D-1754-AC2	Schempp-Hirth Janus C	263	
D-1755-CW	Rolladen-Schneider LS8-a	8015	
D-1756	Schleicher Ka 6BR Rhönsegler	362	
D-1757	Schleicher K 8B	8034	D-KIBO, D-1757
D-1758	Schleicher Ka 6CR Rhönsegler	6003	
D-1759-IJK	Schempp-Hirth Discus b	330	
D-1760	Schempp-Hirth Discus b	338	
D-1761	SZD-30 Pirat	B-356	D-1767, DDR-1761, DM-1761
D-1762-GH	Schempp-Hirth Duo Discus	147	
D-1763	Schleicher ASH 25	25021	
D-1764	Schempp-Hirth Discus b	39	HB-1801
D-1765	Schleicher K 8B	8040	
D-1767	Schempp-Hirth Standard Cirrus	474	I-ZANI
D-1768	SZD-30 Pirat	B-367	DDR-1764, DM-1764
D-1769	Schleicher Ka 6CR Rhönsegler	6035	
D-1770	Schempp-Hirth Ventus-2b	58	
D-1771	Grunau Baby III	01	D-1271, D-1078
D-1772-W2	Schempp-Hirth Duo Discus	122	
D-1774	Schleicher K 8B	8038	
D-1775	Glaser-Dirks DG-500 Elan Orion	5E149X7	
D-1776	SZD-30 Pirat	B-402	DDR-1773, DM-1773
D-1777	Akaflieg Braunschweig SB-5B Sperber	5047	
D-1778	SZD-30 Pirat	B-407	DDR-1778, DM-1778
D-1779	Schleicher K 8B	8572	
D-1781	Schleicher K 7 Rhönadler	1095	
D-1782	Schempp-Hirth Mini Nimbus C	99	HB-1782, D-6741
D-1783	Schleicher ASK 13	13220AB	D-0462 ?
D-1784	Scheibe L-Spatz 55	653	
D-1785-K8	Schempp-Hirth Duo Discus	92	
D-1786-BD	Schempp-Hirth Duo Discus a	158	
D-1787-BP	Rolladen-Schneider LS8-a	8156	
D-1789-I	Schempp-Hirth Ventus-2b	25	
D-1791	Rolladen-Schneider LS4-a	4399	
D-1792	Rolladen-Schneider LS4	4400	
D-1793-R6	Rolladen-Schneider LS4	4401	
D-1794	Rolladen-Schneider LS1-c	146	
D-1795	Akaflieg Braunschweig SB-5B Sperber	AB5054	
D-1796	Schleicher ASK 21	21246	HB-1793
D-1797-FH	Glasflügel H201B Standard Libelle	377	
D-1798	Rolladen-Schneider LS1-c	130	
D-1800	Schleicher ASK 13	13674AB	
D-1801	SZD-30 Pirat	S-01.27	DDR-1881, DM-1881
D-1802-HI	Schleicher ASK 21	21130	
D-1803	Schleicher ASW 20	20605	
D-1804	Schleicher ASK 21	21145	
D-1805	Rolladen-Schneider LS1-c	145	
D-1806-K	Schleicher ASW 22	22022	F-CARK, D-9394
D-1807-CG	Rolladen-Schneider LS1-f	352	OO-ZYQ, D-2744
D-1808	Schleicher Ka 6E	4204	OH-652
D-1809	SZD-30 Pirat	B-461	DDR-1805, DM-1805
D-1810-K	Schempp-Hirth Discus-2a	199	HA-4525
D-1811-G	Glasflügel H401 Kestrel	117	OE-5017
	(P 9.6.16)		
D-1812	DG Flugzeugbau DG-800S	8-110S26	HB-3250
D-1813	Rolladen-Schneider LS4	4523	HB-1818
D-1814	Schleicher K 7 Rhönadler	7207	
D-1815	Scheibe Bergfalke III	5500/V1	D-1850, D-1815
D-1816-EY	Schempp-Hirth Discus b	339	
D-1817-B6	Schleicher ASW 19B	19417	HB-1815
D-1818	Schleicher ASW 18	18017	F-CERC
D-1819	SZD-30 Pirat	B-479	DDR-1815, DM-1815
	(P. 9.6.16)		
D-1821	SZD-30 Pirat	S-01.09	DDR-1871, DM-1871
D-1822-9F	Schleicher ASK 21	21169	
D-1823-CQ	Schleicher ASK 21	21170	
D-1825	Schempp-Hirth Standard Cirrus	217	SE-TKU
D-1826	Schleicher K 8B	8165/03	
D-1829	Schleicher Ka 6CR Rhönsegler	6228	
D-1831-BG	Schempp-Hirth Duo Discus	55	
D-1832-N	Rolladen-Schneider LS8-a	8019	
D-1833	Glaser-Dirks DG-600	6-18	PH-833
D-1835	Schleicher Ka 6CR Rhönsegler	6242	
D-1836	Schleicher Ka 6CR Rhönsegler	6187	
D-1837	Schleicher K 8B	189/60	
D-1838	Schempp-Hirth Discus b	165	HB-1838
D-1839	Scheibe Spatz B	01/517	
D-1840	Schleicher K 8B	8334/A	
D-1842-RN	Rolladen-Schneider LS4-a	4744	
D-1843	SZD-30 Pirat	B-331	D-1743, DDR-1742, DM-1742
D-1844-9L	Rolladen-Schneider LS4-a	4743	
D-1845-ZG	Rolladen-Schneider LS4-a	4742	
D-1846-EA	Rolladen-Schneider LS4-a	4741	
D-1847	SZD-30 Pirat	B-531	DDR-1847, DM-1847
D-1848	Akaflieg München Mü 22B	V-3	
	(Permit)		
D-1850	Schleicher ASK 21	21850	
D-1851	Scheibe SF 27A	6001	
D-1852	Grob G 103C Twin III Acro	34111	
D-1853	Grob G 103C Twin III Acro	34124	
D-1854	Schleicher Ka 6CR Rhönsegler	6225	
D-1855	Schleicher Ka 6CR Rhönsegler	6338Si	
D-1856	Schleicher K 8B	8652	OO-YKV, PL56
	(P .08)		
D-1857-FG	Schempp-Hirth Discus b	170	SE-UFG
D-1859	Schleicher Ka 6CR Rhönsegler	6355	
D-1860	Scheibe SF 27A	6005	
D-1861	Glaser-Dirks DG-600/18	6-101S56	SE-UKP
D-1862	Grob G 103A Twin II Acro	3809-K-72	
D-1863-G1	Grob G 103A Twin II Acro	3810-K-73	
D-1865	Scheibe L-Spatz 55	765	
D-1866	Scheibe Bergfalke II/55	387	

Reg.	Type	Serial	Notes
D-1870-MH4	Grob G 103C Twin III Acro	34112	
D-1871-MH	Rolladen-Schneider LS8-a	8184	
D-1872	Glaser-Dirks DG-300 Elan	3E24	
D-1873	SZD-30 Pirat	S-01.08	DDR-1870, DM-1870
D-1874	SZD-30 Pirat	S-01.23	DDR-1877, DM-1877
D-1875-FM	Schempp-Hirth Ventus-2cx	94	
D-1876-4Z	Schempp-Hirth Ventus-2a	82	
D-1877-CT	Grob G103C Twin III Acro (P. 8.14)	34126	
D-1878-9L	Schleicher ASW 28-18	28707	
D-1879	Schempp-Hirth Discus CS	008CS	
D-1880-MB	Schempp-Hirth Janus C	262	
D-1881	Schleicher K 8B	995	
D-1882	Schleicher K 8B	8452	
D-1884	Schempp-Hirth Discus-2c	54	
D-1885	Schleicher K 8B	8456	
D-1886	Scheibe L-Spatz	201	
D-1887	Schleicher K 7 Rhönadler	7028	
D-1888	Grob G102 Astir CS	?	
D-1889-DH	Rolladen-Schneider LS4	4587	HB-1882
D-1890	Schleicher K 8B	8133	
D-1891	Glaser-Dirks DG-300 Elan	3E238	HB-1919
D-1892	Schleicher ASK 21	?	
D-1893	Scheibe SF 26A Standard	5014	
D-1895	SZD-30 Pirat	S-03.08	DDR-1893, DM-1893
D-1896-H1	Rolladen-Schneider LS8-a	8108	
D-1897	Glaser-Dirks DG-800S	8-79S22	OY-PXW, D-3899
D-1898-B2	SZD-30 Pirat	S-03.22	DDR-1897, DM-1897
D-1899-FP	Rolladen-Schneider LS4	4621	HB-1892
D-1900	Schleicher ASK 13	13678AB	
D-1901	DFS Habicht E replica	AB/KSZ1	
D-1902	Schleicher K 8B	8031	
D-1903	Scheibe Zugvogel IIIB	1078	
D-1904	SZD-30 Pirat	S-03.25	DDR-1900, DM-1900
D-1906-3F	Schleicher K 8B	8273/A	
D-1907-PR	Rolladen-Schneider LS7-WL	7020	HB-1977, D-4587
D-1908-K3	Schempp-Hirth Discus CS	128CS	
D-1909	SZD-30 Pirat	S-03.46	DDR-1906, DM-1906
D-1910	Rolladen-Schneider LS6	6123	HB-1911
D-1911	Schleicher ASW 27	27205	
D-1912	Schleicher ASK 13	13641AB	
D-1915	SZD-30 Pirat	S-04.21	DDR-1914, DM-1914
D-1917	Schleicher Ka 6E	4189	
D-1918	Schleicher Ka 6BR Rhönsegler	439	ZS-GPK, D-1918, HB-918
D-1919	Rolladen-Schneider LS8-b	8456	
D-1920	Schleicher Ka 6CR Rhönsegler	6069	
D-1922-Z2	Rolladen-Schneider LS8-b	8455	
D-1923-SM	Rolladen-Schneider LS8-18	8157	
D-1924	Schleicher ASK 21	21325	
D-1925	Schleicher K 7 Rhönadler	296	
D-1927-F1	Schleicher ASW 27 (P.3.12)	27135	
D-1928	Grunau Baby III (P.05)	AB002S	
D-1929	Scheibe Bergfalke II/55	385	
D-1931-YS	Schempp-Hirth Discus CS	040CS	
D-1932-6D	Schempp-Hirth Duo Discus	162	
D-1933	Rolladen-Schneider LS6-18W	6369	
D-1934	SZD-30 Pirat	S-03.44	
D-1935	Schleicher Ka 6CR Rhönsegler	6278	
D-1937	Schleicher Ka 6E	4193	
D-1938	Schleicher Ka 6CR Rhönsegler	6307	
D-1939	Grunau Baby IIB	0123	
D-1940	Schleicher ASK 21	21698	
D-1941	Schleicher Ka 6CR Rhönsegler	6224/A	
D-1942-D1	Schempp-Hirth Discus b	222	HB-1968
D-1944-OA	Schempp-Hirth Discus-2c	35	
D-1945	Rolladen-Schneider LS3-17	3348	PH-1088, OO-ZZH, HB-1509
D-1946	SZD-30 Pirat	S-03.43	DDR-1903, DM-1903
D-1947	Schleicher ASK 21	21363	
D-1948	DFS Olympia Meise (Permit)	09	
D-1950-LIB	Glasflügel H201B Standard Libelle	429	F-CEBO
D-1952-G1	Rolladen-Schneider LS1-f (P.1.05)	290	SE-TNG
D-1954	Schleicher Ka 6CR Rhönsegler	6277	
D-1955	Pilatus B4-PC11	019	
D-1956	Glaser-Dirks DG-100G Elan	E56G32	
D-1957	Vogt Lo-100 Zwergreiher	1	
D-1958	Rolladen-Schneider LS3-a	3339	LN-GHC, (D-3183)
D-1959	Schleicher Ka 2B Rhönschwalbe	245	D-4350
D-1961-VT	Rolladen-Schneider LS8-a	8185	
D-1963	Schleicher K 8B	8080/5	
D-1964	Glaser-Dirks DG-300 Club Elan	3E299C17	HB-1969
D-1965	Lange E1 Antares 18S (P 8.08)	55S06	
D-1966	Glaser-Dirks DG-300 Club Elan	3E356C43	
D-1967	Glaser-Dirks DG-300 Club Elan	3E357C44	
D-1968-HF	Schempp-Hirth Discus CS	302CS	
D-1970	Scheibe SF 27A	6064	
D-1972	Schempp-Hirth Standard Cirrus	269	PH-1014, OO-ZVW, D-1982
D-1973-6X	Schleicher ASW 24	24134	
D-1974	Pilatus B4-PC11	141	SE-UIY, OY-VXO
D-1975	SZD-51-1 Junior	B-2133	
D-1976-RR	Eiriavion PIK-20D	20544	OO-ZNF, OH-535
D-1977	Grunau Baby III (W/o 31.7.15)	04	
D-1980	Glaser-Dirks DG-100G	91G11	BGA 2179/DKQ
D-1981-6H	Rolladen-Schneider LS1-d	192	F-CEHA
D-1982	Grunau Baby IIB	16	
D-1983-PT	Rolladen-Schneider LS1-c	45	OY-CLX, D-0442
D-1984-SN	Schempp-Hirth Standard Cirrus	278G	
D-1985	SZD-30 Pirat (P 6.10)	S-02.41	DDR-1885, DM-1885
D-1986	Schempp-Hirth Standard Cirrus	285G	
D-1987	Schempp-Hirth Cirrus-VTC	131Y	
D-1988	Sportine Aviacija LAK-19	006	LY-GFD
D-1989-B6	Rolladen-Schneider LS1-c	152	
D-1990	Schempp-Hirth Standard Cirrus	275G	
D-1991	Rolladen-Schneider LS6-18W	6237	PH-1478, D-4063
D-1992-BX	Glasflügel H201B Standard Libelle	382	
D-1993-93	Rolladen-Schneider LS4-b	4852	
D-1994-FO	Schempp-Hirth Standard Cirrus	287G	
D-1995	Marganski MDM-1 Fox	208	OE-5625
D-1996-IY	Schempp-Hirth Standard Cirrus	307G	
D-1997	Glasflügel H201 Standard Libelle	194	HB-1006
D-1998	Glasflügel H401 Kestrel	82	
D-1999	Schempp-Hirth Duo Discus	477	
D-2000	Glaser-Dirks DG-600/18	6-37	HB-1960
D-2001	Schleicher ASK 13	13359	
D-2002	Schleicher ASK 21	21604	
D-2004	Scheibe Bergfalke III	5537	D-1001
D-2005	Vogt Lo-100 Zwergreiher	AB 103	
D-2006	Molino PIK-20D	20037	HB-1235
D-2007	Schleicher ASK 23B (P 4.5.16)	23082	PH-1296, D-5350
D-2008	Schleicher K 8B	001AB	
D-2010	Schleicher K 8B	8490	
D-2011	Focke-Wulf Kranich III	66	
D-2012	Akaflieg Braunschweig SB-5B	5022/13A	
D-2014	Pilatus B4-PC11AF (P 22.7.16)	036	G-DCVM, BGA 1841, NEJSGSA 2, BGA 1841
D-2015	Glaser-Dirks DG-100G Elan	E163G129	
D-2016-FWS	Schempp-Hirth Nimbus-2B	116	D-7258
D-2017	SZD-41A Jantar Standard	B-748	DDR-2417, DM-2417
D-2018-ZZ	Rolladen-Schneider LS8-18	8287	
D-2019	Schleicher ASW 19B	19253	LX-CAG
D-2020	Schleicher ASW 20	20327	
D-2021	Schleicher ASK 21	21810	
D-2022	Caproni Calif A21S	222	F-CIKE, Fr.AF
D-2023-CH	Schleicher ASK 23B	23138	
D-2024-IW	Glasflügel H303 Mosquito B	192	
D-2025-HR	Schleicher ASW 15B	15389	
D-2026	Glaser-Dirks DG-202/17C	2-165CL15	OY-XOZ, HB-1627
D-2027	Vogt Lo-100 Zwergreiher	12	
D-2028-D3	Schempp-Hirth Discus b	342	
D-2029	Rolladen-Schneider LS4-b	41052	
D-2031	Schleicher K 7 Rhönadler	7010	
D-2032	Start & Flug H101 Salto	9	OY-MZX
D-2033	Schempp-Hirth Cirrus	71	
D-2034	Caproni Vizzola Calif A21S	234	ZS-GPM, BGA2116
D-2035-U2	Schempp-Hirth Ventus-2b	161	
D-2036	Schleicher ASW 20C	20722	
D-2038-RZ	Schempp-Hirth Discus-2b	235	
D-2039	Schleicher ASK 13	13319AB	
D-2040-V1	Start & Flug H-101 Salto	V-1	
D-2041	Rolladen-Schneider LS1-c	51	
D-2042-SL	Bölkow Phoebus C (P.4.99)	940	
D-2043-ML	Schempp-Hirth Discus CS	242CS	
D-2044	Glasflügel H204 Standard Libelle	1	
D-2045	Rolladen-Schneider LS1-d	173	
D-2046	Rolladen-Schneider LS1-d	160	
D-2047	Schleicher K 8B	8907/AB	
D-2049	Schempp-Hirth Cirrus	7	I-ASET
D-2050	Pilatus B4-PC11	042	
D-2051	Schempp-Hirth Standard Cirrus	283G	
D-2052	Schempp-Hirth Standard Cirrus	291	
D-2053	Glasflügel Club Libelle 205	148	F-CEQE
D-2054-OX	Schempp-Hirth Standard Cirrus	293	
D-2055-55	Schempp-Hirth Janus C	261	
D-2056-S1	Schempp-Hirth Janus Ce	284	
D-2057	Rolladen-Schneider LS1-d	94	OO-ZBP
D-2058-NC	Schempp-Hirth Standard Cirrus	300	
D-2059-KP	Schempp-Hirth Standard Cirrus (Permit)	303	
D-2061-VV	Schempp-Hirth Discus-2a	7	
D-2062	SZD-24C Foka	W-148	DDR-2036, DM-2036
D-2063-7M	Eiriavion PIK-20D-78	20632	OO-YAZ, D-6584
D-2064-CB	Schempp-Hirth Duo Discus	62	
D-2066	Schleicher ASK 13	13408	
D-2068-W2	Schempp-Hirth Duo Discus	123	
D-2072	Schleicher ASW 15B	15235	
D-2073	Schleicher ASW 15B	15251	
D-2074	Schleicher ASK 13	13418	
D-2075	Schleicher K 8B	8920	
D-2077	Schleicher K 8B	8921	
D-2080-BV	Schempp-Hirth Ventus-2c	62/181	
D-2082-GH	Schempp-Hirth Duo Discus	209	
D-2083	Start & Flug H101 Salto	19	
D-2084-LV	Schempp-Hirth Ventus-2b	46	
D-2085-U2	Glasflügel 604	9	
D-2086-TX	Glasflügel H401 Kestrel	83	
D-2088	Rolladen-Schneider LS6-c	6280	
D-2089	Rolladen-Schneider LS1-d	149	
D-2090	Rolladen-Schneider LS1-d	182	
D-2091	Glasflügel Standard Libelle 201B	397	HB-1091
D-2095	SZD-24-4A Foka 4	W-306	DDR-2045, DM-2045
D-2096	Rolladen-Schneider LS1-d	169	
D-2098	Glasflügel H201B Standard Libelle	404	
D-2099	Schleicher Ka 6E	4097	
D-2100-W	HpH Glasflügel 304C	73-C	OK-2304
D-2101	Schempp-Hirth Standard Cirrus	351	
D-2102-SA	Schempp-Hirth Standard Cirrus	274	
D-2103	Schempp-Hirth Standard Cirrus	290	
D-2104	Schempp-Hirth Standard Cirrus	301	
D-2105-LH	SZD-51-1 Junior	B-1922	DDR-2805
D-2106-6B	Rolladen-Schneider LS6-c	6265	SE-URR
D-2108	Glaser-Dirks DG-300 Elan	3E162	I-JUCK
D-2109	Glasflügel 604	10	I-ALTI, D-2109
D-2110-IHO	Caproni Vizzola A.21S Calif	224	
D-2111-VV	Schempp-Hirth Ventus-2ax	1	
D-2112	Schleicher ASW 24	24020	OH-790
D-2113	Rolladen-Schneider LS4-b	41028	
D-2114 -1H	Schempp-Hirth Duo Discus	38	
D-2115	Schleicher ASK 13	13420	
D-2117	Schleicher ASW 15B	15257	
D-2118	SZD-41A Jantar Standard	B-854	DDR-2418, DM-2418
D-2119- 7	Glasflügel H201B Standard Libelle	244	OE-0919
D-2120	Schleicher ASK 13	13421	
D-2122-L70	Rolladen-Schneider LS1-f	405	F-CEKU
D-2123	Glasflügel H201B Standard Libelle	196	HB-1009
D-2124-5G	Schempp-Hirth Discus-2b	65	
D-2125	SZD-24-4A Foka 4	W-337	DDR-2225, DM-2225
D-2126-K2	Schleicher ASW 15B	15263	
D-2127	Schleicher K 8B	8924	
D-2128-28	Schempp-Hirth Duo Discus	65	
D-2129	Schleicher K 8B	8925	
D-2130	Schleicher ASW 15B	15265	
D-2133	Schleicher ASK 23B	23135	D-5676

Reg	Type	Serial	Notes
D-2134-SB	Rolladen-Schneider LS6-c18	6379	
D-2135	Schleicher ASK 13	13428	
D-2136	Schleicher K 8B	8928	
D-2137-2K	Schleicher ASK 13	13429	
D-2138	Glaser-Dirks DG-100G Elan	E166G132	
D-2139	Schleicher ASK 13	13430	
D-2140-ET	Schleicher ASK 21	21789	PH-1334
D-2141	Rolladen-Schneider LS6-c18	6330	HB-3141
D-2142	Schleicher Ka 6CR Rhönsegler	6139	OO-ZHT
D-2143	Schempp-Hirth Discus b	536	
D-2144-B5	Rolladen-Schneider LS4-b	4884	
D-2146	SZD-32A Foka 5	W-485	DDR-2246, DM-2246
D-2148-A2	Rolladen-Schneider LS4-b	4885	
D-2149-49	Schempp-Hirth Duo Discus	34	
D-2150-OLE	Schempp-Hirth Standard Cirrus	354	
D-2151	Schempp-Hirth Standard Cirrus	355	
D-2152	Schempp-Hirth Standard Cirrus	361	
D-2153	Schleicher ASK 21	21480	I-IVWG
D-2154-YX	Rolladen-Schneider LS6-c	6295	
D-2155	Schleicher ASK 21 (Permit)	21477	I-IVWD
D-2156-KR	Schempp-Hirth Ventus-2b	83	
D-2158-58	Schempp-Hirth Discus-2b	210	
D-2159	Glasflügel H201B Standard Libelle	435	
D-2160	Glasflügel H201B Standard Libelle	436	
D-2161-NG	Rolladen-Schneider LS4-b	4887	
D-2163-2J	Glasflügel H401 Kestrel	88	
D-2164	Glasflügel H401 Kestrel	89	
D-2165	Glasflügel H401 Kestrel	90	
D-2166-66	Glasflügel H401 Kestrel	91	
D-2167	Schleicher ASW 24	24209	
D-2168	Schempp-Hirth Duo Discus	36	
D-2169	Pilatus B4-PC11AF	121	HB-1137
D-2170	Schleicher ASW 28-18	28523	
D-2171-CN	Rolladen-Schneider LS4-b	41013	
D-2175	LET L-23 Super Blanik (W/o 29.5.16)	938102	OE-5561
D-2176	Schempp-Hirth Discus CS	047CS	
D-2177	PZL-Swidnik PW-5 Smyk	17.04.009	(SP-3784), OH-876
D-2178	Schleicher ASK 13	13447	
D-2180-AH	Schleicher ASW 15B	15300	
D-2181	Schleicher ASW 15B	15301	
D-2183-ZE	Schleicher ASW 15B	15302	
D-2184	Schleicher K 8B	8945	
D-2185	Schleicher ASW 15B	15303	
D-2186	Schleicher ASK 21	21911	
D-2187	Schleicher ASK 13	13453	
D-2188	Schleicher ASK 13	13454	
D-2189	Schleicher ASK 21	21935	
D-2190	Schleicher ASK 13 (P.5.12)	13456	
D-2191	Glaser-Dirks DG-200	2-4	OE-5108
D-2192	Start & Flug H-101 Salto	28	
D-2193	Start & Flug H-101 Salto	29	
D-2194	Caproni Vizzola Calif A21S	229	I-CCCP
D-2195-CD	Rolladen-Schneider LS4-b	41040	
D-2196	Glasflügel H401 Kestrel	92	
D-2198	Rolladen-Schneider LS6-c	6293	
D-2199	Glasflügel H401 Kestrel	96	
D-2200-YZ	Glaser-Dirks DG-500/22 Elan	5E11S3	
D-2201	Schleicher ASK 21	21728	
D-2202	SZD-38A Jantar 1	B-642	DDR-2402, DM-2402
D-2203-VB	Glaser-Dirks DG-300 Elan	3E-449	S5-3085
D-2204	SZD-24C Foka	W-158	OO-ZXE, SP-2376
D-2205	SZD-32A Foka 5	W-518	DDR-2255, DM-2255
D-2206	SZD-59 Acro (P.4.99)	B-2176	SP-3629
D-2207-7	SZD-32A Foka 5	W-520	DDR-2257, DM-2257
D-2208-BY	Glasflügel H401 Kestrel	97	
D-2209	Rolladen-Schneider LS8	8005	
D-2211	Start & Flug H101 Salto	31	
D-2212	Pilatus B4-PC11AF	130	
D-2213	Start & Flug H101 Salto	22	(PH-1259), D-2213
D-2214-201	Glasflügel H201B Standard Libelle	477	
D-2215	Glasflügel H201B Standard Libelle	478	
D-2216-2JB	Glasflügel H201B Standard Libelle	479	
D-2217	Pilatus B4-PC11	89	
D-2218	Start & Flug H101 Salto	33	
D-2220	Start & Flug H101 Salto	35	
D-2221	Start & Flug H101 Salto	36	
D-2222	Schempp-Hirth Duo Discus XL	672	
D-2223	Rolladen-Schneider LS1-c	170	
D-2224	Schleicher Ka 6E	4025	HB-839
D-2225-C3	Rolladen-Schneider LS1-f	251	
D-2226	Glasflügel H401 Kestrel	74	OE-0953
D-2227	Glasflügel Standard Libelle 202	169	HB-1062, D-0649
D-2228	Schleicher ASW 28-18	28528	
D-2229	SZD-32A Foka 5	W-445	DDR-2206, DM-2206
D-2230	SZD-24-4A Foka 4	W-354	DDR-2230, DM-2230
D-2231	SZD-24-4A Foka 4	W-383	DDR-2232, DM-2232
D-2232	SZD-24-4A Foka 4	W-344	DDR-2233, DM-2233
D-2233	Schleicher K 8B	994	HB-689
D-2234	Rolladen-Schneider LS1-f	195	
D-2235	Glasflügel Kestrel	100	D-2210
D-2236	Schleicher Ka 6CR Rhönsegler	6502	
D-2237	Schempp-Hirth Standard Cirrus	600	
D-2238-N4	Schempp-Hirth Standard Cirrus	422G	
D-2240	Rolladen-Schneider LS1-c	184	
D-2241-NAJ	Rolladen-Schneider LS1-d	267	
D-2242	Rolladen-Schneider LS1-f	185	
D-2244	Rolladen-Schneider LS1-f	259	
D-2245	Rolladen-Schneider LS1-f	255	
D-2246	Rolladen-Schneider LS1-f	263	
D-2247	Schleicher ASW 28	28062	
D-2248	Rolladen-Schneider LS1-f	318	
D-2249-RR	Schempp-Hirth Duo Discus	325	
D-2250-SA	Rolladen-Schneider LS1-f	283	
D-2251	Rolladen-Schneider LS1-f	308	
D-2252-RW	Rolladen-Schneider LS1-f	289	
D-2253-SF	Rolladen-Schneider LS1-f	355	
D-2254-HR	Rolladen-Schneider LS1-f	374	
D-2255-KS	Schleicher ASW 22BL	22081	
D-2256-FP	Rolladen-Schneider LS1-f	314	
D-2258-IHG	Rolladen-Schneider LS4	4538	
D-2259	Schleicher Ka 6E	4291	I-BZJR
D-2261-OXX	Rolladen-Schneider LS1-f	350	
D-2262	Rolladen-Schneider LS4	4540	
D-2263-DE	Glasflügel H401 Kestrel	87	D-KOWA, D-2263
D-2264	Glasflügel H401 Kestrel	127	
D-2265	Glasflügel H401 Kestrel	128	
D-2266	Glasflügel H401 Kestrel	129	
D-2267	Caproni-Vizzola A-21S Calif	230	
D-2268	Sportine Aviacija LAK-17A	155	LY-GMO
D-2269	Schleicher ASK 13	13601AB	
D-2271	SZD-24-4A Foka 4	W-338	DDR-2227, DM-2227
D-2272	SZD-32A Foka 5	W-525	DDR-2262, DM-2262
D-2273-MH	Schleicher ASW 20	20095	V5-GOE, HB-1628
D-2275	Grob G 102 Speed Astir II	4006	BGA 2484/DYK
D-2276	Grob G 103 Twin Astir	3203	
D-2277-TH	Rolladen-Schneider LS4-b (P. 5.14)	4896	
D-2279-V1	Rolladen-Schneider LS4	4541	
D-2280	Schleicher K 8B	8715	OY-BXW
D-2282-L4	Schempp-Hirth HS-7 Mini-Nimbus	14	OE-5122
D-2283-DB	Schleicher ASW 22	22018	
D-2286	Glaser-Dirks DG-100G Elan	E138G106	S5-3024, YU-4346
D-2287	SZD-48-3 Jantar Standard 3	B-1304	SP-3230
D-2288-TG	Schempp-Hirth Standard Cirrus	665	
D-2289	Schleicher K 7 Rhönadler (Permit 20.11.12)	7048	PH-108, D-1923
D-2290-MM	SZD-32A Foka 5	W-425	DDR-2200, DM-2200
D-2291-9W	Schempp-Hirth Ventus a	20	SE-TVP
D-2292	Schempp-Hirth Standard Cirrus	386G	
D-2295-F2	Bölkow Phoebus C	1001	
D-2296-OL	Rolladen-Schneider LS4-b	4889	
D-2297	SZD-32A Foka 5	W-486	DDR-2247, DM-2247
D-2298-RCA	Schempp-Hirth Ventus-2c	43/127	
D-2299	Rolladen-Schneider LS1-c	244	
D-2300	Pilatus B4-PC11AF	097	
D-2301	Pilatus B4-PC11AF	238	
D-2303-03	Schleicher ASW 15B	15315	
D-2304	Schleicher K 8B	8951	
D-2306	SZD-36A Cobra 15	W-646	DDR-2309, DM-2309
D-2307	Schleicher ASW 15B (P 21.7.16)	15319	
D-2308	Schleicher ASW 15B	15320	
D-2310	Schleicher ASK 21	21778	
D-2311-J	Schleicher ASW 15B	15322	
D-2312-PV	Schempp-Hirth Duo Discus	281	
D-2313	Schleicher ASW 15B	15324	
D-2314-14	Schleicher ASW 15B	15325	
D-2318-NO	Schleicher ASW 15B	15328	
D-2319	Schleicher K 8B	8960	
D-2320	Schleicher K 8B	8963	
D-2321	Schleicher K 8B	8959	
D-2322-YP	Schempp-Hirth Discus-2b	219	HB-3402
D-2323	LET L-23 Super Blanik	938101	
D-2324	Schleicher K 8B	8965	
D-2325-CK	Schempp-Hirth Discus-2b	197	
D-2326	Schleicher ASK 13	13464	
D-2327-H3	Schleicher ASW 15B	15333	
D-2328	LET L-23 Super Blanik	928004	D-8064
D-2329	Schleicher ASW 15B	15334	
D-2330-NK	Schleicher ASW 15	15172	OO-YVS, D-0851
D-2332	Schleicher ASK 13	13466	
D-2333	Schleicher ASW 24	24089	SE-UPD
D-2334	Schleicher ASW 15B	15331	
D-2335-35	Schempp-Hirth Ventus-2cx	129	
D-2336	Schleicher ASW 15B	15338	
D-2337	Schleicher ASW 15B	15339	
D-2338	Schleicher ASK 21	21374	
D-2340-B1	Schempp-Hirth Discus-2c	59	
D-2341-XY	Schleicher ASW 15B	15342	
D-2342	Schleicher ASK 13	13469	
D-2343-4Z	Rolladen-Schneider LS6-18W	6343	
D-2344	Schleicher K 8C	81001	
D-2345	Glasflügel Standard Libelle 201B	411	G-CJWV, BGA 4848, OY-XBG
D-2346-2P	Schleicher ASW 15B	15357	
D-2347	Schleicher ASK 13	13470	
D-2348	Schempp-Hirth Discus-2b	151	
D-2349	Schleicher ASW 15B	15345	
D-2350-K8	Schleicher ASW 17	17029	
D-2351	Schleicher K 8B (Res.8.99)	8964	
D-2352-XC	Schempp-Hirth Duo Discus	42	
D-2353	Schleicher ASK 13	13473	
D-2354	Schleicher ASK 23	23005	PH-1244, BGA 4662, AGA 18
D-2355	Schleicher ASW 15B	15343	
D-2356-R	Schleicher ASW 15B (P.4.12)	15351	
D-2360	Rolladen-Schneider LS4-b	41055	
D-2362	Schleicher K 8B	8969	
D-2363	Schleicher ASK 23B	23030	PH-766
D-2364	Schleicher ASK 13	13477	
D-2365-AB	Rolladen-Schneider LS8-a	8081	
D-2368-B1	Schleicher ASW 15B (P.4.12)	15360	
D-2369-YO	Rolladen-Schneider LS8-a	8158	
D-2370	Schleicher ASW 15B	15362	
D-2371	DG Flugzeugbau DG-1000S	10-7S7	OY-MXM
D-2373	Schleicher ASK 13	13481	
D-2374-MX	Rolladen-Schneider LS4-b	4891	
D-2375	Schleicher ASW 15B	15365	
D-2376-HW	Schempp-Hirth Duo Discus	53	
D-2377	Schleicher ASK 13	13483	
D-2378	SZD-9bis Bocian 1E	P-568	
D-2379-LI	Schleicher ASW 15B	15368	
D-2381	SZD-36A Cobra 15	W-651	DDR-2312, DM-2312
D-2382	Schleicher ASW 15B	15372	
D-2383	Schleicher K 8B	8971	
D-2384-WT	Schleicher ASW 17	17034	
D-2385	Schleicher ASW 15B	15373	
D-2386	Schleicher ASW 15B	15216	
D-2388-F7	Grob G 103 Twin Astir Trainer	3252-T-29	
D-2389	Rolladen-Schneider LS6-b	6126	OO-ZRQ
D-2390	Schleicher Ka 6CR	6309	OY-EDX
D-2392	Grob G 102 Astir CS 77	1833	
D-2393	Grob G 102 Astir CS 77	1834	
D-2395-FR	Grob G 102 Club Astir II	5001C	
D-2396	LET L-23 Super Blanik	938103	

Regn	Type	c/n	Notes
D-2398-3RD	SZD-48-3 Jantar Standard 3	B-1664	DOSAAF
D-2400-3B	Glasflügel H201B Standard Libelle	493	
D-2401	Glasflügel H201B Standard Libelle	494	
D-2402	Glasflügel H401 Kestrel	105	
D-2403-SH	Glasflügel H201B Standard Libelle	499	
D-2404	Glasflügel H201B Standard Libelle	500	
D-2407	Glasflügel H201B Standard Libelle	507	
D-2408	Schleicher ASK 21	21172	
D-2409-NA	Schleicher ASK 21	21191	
D-2410-BW4	Schempp-Hirth Duo Discus	199	
D-2411	Grunau Baby IIb	284	DDR-1084, DM-1084
D-2412	Glasflügel H201B Standard Libelle	518	
D-2413-4F	Glasflügel H201B Standard Libelle	521	
D-2414-VK2	Slingsby T59D Kestrel 19 (P.01)	1852	
D-2415	Glasflügel H401 Kestrel	106	
D-2416	Glasflügel H201B Standard Libelle	497	
D-2417	Glasflügel H401 Kestrel	107	
D-2418-YF	Schempp-Hirth Discus CS	150CS	
D-2419-7B	Glasflügel H201B Standard Libelle	532	
D-2420	Glasflügel H201B Standard Libelle	533	
D-2421	Glasflügel H201B Standard Libelle	534	
D-2422	Glasflügel H201B Standard Libelle	535	
D-2423-E1	Rolladen-Schneider LS4-b	4979	
D-2424	Glasflügel H201B Standard Libelle (P. 5.11)	537	
D-2425-LY	Glasflügel H401 Kestrel	108	
D-2426	Glasflügel H205 Club Libelle	169	F-CEQT
D-2427	Jastreb Standard Cirrus G/81	251	SE-TYR
D-2429-GA	SZD-42-2 Jantar 2B	B-951	DDR-2429, DM-2429
D-2430	Rolladen-Schneider LS1-f (W/o 29.5.14)	297	
D-2431-8V	Rolladen-Schneider LS8-18	8252	
D-2432	Rolladen-Schneider LS1-f	280	
D-2433-33	Glasflügel H201B Standard Libelle	502	PH-481
D-2434-DB	Glasflügel H205 Club Libelle	36	
D-2435-ZK	Rolladen-Schneider LS8-18 (P.3.99)	8025	
D-2436	Glasflügel H205 Club Libelle	38	
D-2437	Glasflügel H205 Club Libelle	39	
D-2438	Glasflügel H205 Club Libelle	40	
D-2439	Pilatus B4-PC11AF	153	
D-2440	Glasflügel H205 Club Libelle	64	
D-2441	Glasflügel H205 Club Libelle	65	
D-2442	Schleicher ASW 24	24004	
D-2443-RW	Schempp-Hirth Duo Discus	171	
D-2444	Glasflügel H205 Club Libelle	68	
D-2445	Glasflügel H205 Club Libelle	69	
D-2446	Schleicher ASW 17	17015	OY-OXL, D-2131
D-2447	Glasflügel H205 Club Libelle	77	
D-2448-AJ	Glasflügel H205 Club Libelle	78	
D-2449	Glasflügel H205 Club Libelle	79	
D-2450-W6	Glasflügel H205 Club Libelle	141	
D-2451-GU	Glasflügel H205 Club Libelle	86	
D-2452	Glasflügel H205 Club Libelle	87	
D-2453-53	Glasflügel H205 Club Libelle	90	
D-2454	SZD-38A Jantar 1	B-640	DDR-2404, DM-2404
D-2455	Glasflügel H205 Club Libelle	92	
D-2456-56	Glasflügel H205 Club Libelle	93	
D-2457	Glasflügel H205 Club Libelle	94	
D-2458	Glasflügel H201B Standard Libelle	365	I-GOUP
D-2459	Glasflügel H205 Club Libelle	96	
D-2460-TZ	Glasflügel H205 Club Libelle	124	
D-2461	Schleicher ASW 24	24129	I-SKYY
D-2462-T3	Glasflügel H205 Club Libelle	100	
D-2463	Glasflügel H205 Club Libelle	101	
D-2464	Glasflügel H205 Club Libelle	102	
D-2465	Schleicher ASW 24	24136	I-OOSO
D-2466	Glasflügel Club Libelle 205	56	I-NEWD
D-2467	Glasflügel H205 Club Libelle	113	
D-2468	Glasflügel H205 Club Libelle	114	
D-2469	Glasflügel H205 Club Libelle	115	
D-2470	Grob G103C Twin III Acro	34103	PH-1181, D-6868
D-2471-3A	Glasflügel H205 Club Libelle (W/o 18.7.15)	117	
D-2472	Glasflügel H205 Club Libelle	118	
D-2474	Glasflügel H205 Club Libelle	120	
D-2476	Rolladen-Schneider LS4-b	4893	
D-2477	Schempp-Hirth Janus	12	
D-2478	Glasflügel H205 Club Libelle	137	
D-2479-V	Schempp-Hirth Discus-2a	211	
D-2480	Schempp-Hirth Janus	55	
D-2481	Rolladen-Schneider LS6-a	6061	
D-2482	Schleicher ASW 24	24066	
D-2483	Schleicher ASW 24	24067	
D-2484-GE	SZD-30 Pirat	S-06.49	
D-2485	Schleicher ASW 24	24068	
D-2486-EW	Schleicher ASW 20L	20413	
D-2487	Schempp-Hirth Ventus-2c	74	OK-2487
D-2488-BD	Schleicher ASK 21	21050	
D-2490-2W	Schleicher ASW 20L	20424	
D-2491	Schleicher ASW 20L	20425	
D-2492-Z3	Schleicher ASK 21	21055	
D-2493	Schleicher ASW 19B	19337	
D-2495-WF	Schleicher ASK 21	21057	
D-2496-XM	Rolladen-Schneider LS8-a	8027	
D-2497-HH	SZD-42-2 Jantar 2B	B-945	HA-4419
D-2498	Schleicher ASW 20	20433	
D-2499	Schleicher ASW 20L	20414	
D-2500	Glasflügel H401 Kestrel	104	PH-477
D-2501	Vogt Lo-100 Zwergreiher	1/2	
D-2502-RP	Schempp-Hirth Duo Discus	290	
D-2503-6R	Rolladen-Schneider LS6	6062	
D-2504	Bölkow Phoebus B1	769	I-ACOS
D-2505	Glaser-Dirks DG-101G Elan	E80G55	OO-YZI, D-2505
D-2506	Glaser-Dirks DG-100G Elan	E82G57	
D-2507	Glaser-Dirks DG-100G Elan	E73G48	
D-2508	Glaser-Dirks DG-100G Elan	E84G58	
D-2509	Rolladen-Schneider LS4-b	41016	
D-2510	Schleicher ASW 20C	20749	
D-2511	Schleicher ASW 20C	20737	
D-2512	Eiriavion PIK-20D-78	20646	HB-1460
D-2513	Schleicher ASK 21	21441	
D-2514-G3	Schleicher ASW 24	24071	
D-2515	Rolladen-Schneider LS4	4252	
D-2516	Glaser-Dirks DG-300 Elan	3E340	I-KEEN
D-2518-DL	Schempp-Hirth Duo Discus	45	
D-2519-SU	Schempp-Hirth Discus CS	244CS	
D-2520	Schempp-Hirth Janus C	178	
D-2521-DD	Schempp-Hirth Discus CS	086CS	
D-2522	Schleicher ASK 21	21507	HB-3075
D-2523	Schempp-Hirth Ventus a/16.6	16	
D-2524	Schleicher ASW 24	24022	OY-XRO
D-2525	Glaser-Dirks DG-300 Elan	3E111	
D-2526	Rolladen-Schneider LS4	4348	
D-2527	Schempp-Hirth Discus CS	110CS	
D-2528	Rolladen-Schneider LS4	4373	
D-2529-JT	Schleicher ASW 27-18 (ASG 29)	29074	
D-2531	Grob G 102 Astir CS Jeans	2121	
D-2533	Grob G 102 Astir CS Jeans	2124	
D-2534	Grob G 102 Astir CS Jeans (P 14.6.16)	2125	
D-2535-8M	Rolladen-Schneider LS4-b	4980	
D-2537	Grob G 102 Astir CS Jeans	2129	
D-2540	Grob G 102 Astir CS Jeans (Dbr 7.5.16)	2133	
D-2541-SJ	Grob G 102 Astir CS Jeans	2134	
D-2542	Rolladen-Schneider LS6-c	6249	
D-2543	SZD-24-4A Foka 4	W-304	DDR-2043, DM-2043
D-2544	Grob G 102 Astir CS Jeans	2139	
D-2546	Grob G 102 Astir CS 77	1737	
D-2547	Grob G 102 Astir CS Jeans	2146	
D-2548	Grob G 102 Astir CS Jeans	2147	
D-2549	Grob G 102 Astir CS Jeans	2148	
D-2550-B5	Schempp-Hirth Discus CS	108CS	
D-2551-MT	Rolladen-Schneider LS1-d	194	OO-ZMV
D-2554	Glasflügel H303 Mosquito B	193	
D-2556	Neukom Elfe S-4D	418AB	
D-2557-L5	Glasflügel Hornet C	94	
D-2558	Glaser-Dirks DG-200	2-53	I-IBTS
D-2559	Glasflügel H303 Mosquito B	190	
D-2560	Glasflügel H303 Mosquito B	147	
D-2561-DP	LET L-13 Blanik	026017	
D-2563	Rolladen-Schneider LS3-a	3242	
D-2564-S1	Rolladen-Schneider LS3-a	3207	
D-2565	Rolladen-Schneider LS3-a	3144	
D-2566	Rolladen-Schneider LS3-a	3127	
D-2567-DX	Rolladen-Schneider LS1-a	17	HB-946
D-2568	Rolladen-Schneider LS3-a	3134	
D-2570	Rolladen-Schneider LS3-a	3101	
D-2572	Schempp-Hirth Discus b	489	
D-2573	Glaser-Dirks DG-200/17 (C/n possibly 1722 or 1723)	2-97/1725	
D-2574-OF	Schempp-Hirth Discus CS	151CS	
D-2575-FN	Schempp-Hirth Duo Discus	66	
D-2576	Glaser-Dirks DG-100	25	
D-2577	Glaser-Dirks DG-100	26	
D-2578-WZ	Schleicher ASW 27B	27233	OH-981, D-2727
D-2579	Rolladen-Schneider LS8-a	8132	
D-2581-3M	Schempp-Hirth Discus CS	107CS	
D-2582	Glaser-Dirks DG-100	54	
D-2583	Glaser-Dirks DG-100	56	
D-2584	Rolladen-Schneider LS6-c	6262	
D-2585	Glaser-Dirks DG-100	62	
D-2586-DS	Schleicher ASW 24	24076	
D-2587-IJL	Glaser-Dirks DG-100	65	
D-2588-DU	Schempp-Hirth Duo Discus	19	
D-2589	Glaser-Dirks DG-100	67	
D-2590	Schleicher ASK 21	21448	
D-2594-S1	Schempp-Hirth Discus CS	319CS	
D-2595	Glaser-Dirks DG-100 Elan	E6	
D-2596	Glaser-Dirks DG-200/17	2-65/1704	
D-2598-98	SZD-55-1	551195076	BGA 4150/HRV
D-2599	Grob G 103A Twin II Acro	3656-K-25	
D-2600-CX	Schempp-Hirth Discus-2b	34	
D-2601	Grob G 102 Standard Astir III	5538S	
D-2602	Rolladen-Schneider LS3	3124	
D-2603	Grob G 103 Twin Astir	3153	F-CFBV
D-2604-A8	Schempp-Hirth Ventus-2a	12	
D-2605	Schleicher ASW 20L	20438	
D-2606	Schleicher ASW 20CL	20760	OY-SXP, N5496S, D-3642
D-2607	Schleicher ASW 20	20439	
D-2608-KS	Schleicher ASW 20L	20442	
D-2609	Rolladen-Schneider LS3-a	3067	
D-2610-4F	Rolladen-Schneider LS3-a (Permit)	3068	
D-2611-2Y	SZD-36A Cobra 15	W-650	DDR-2311, DM-2311
D-2612-AC	Schleicher ASK 21	21404	
D-2613	SZD-50-3 Puchacz	B-1330	DDR-3613
D-2616-5H	Schleicher ASK 21	21407	
D-2617	Schleicher ASK 21	21408	
D-2618	Rolladen-Schneider LS3	3074	
D-2619-MN	Rolladen-Schneider LS3-a	3158	
D-2621	Rolladen-Schneider LS3	3093	
D-2622	Rolladen-Schneider LS3	3173	
D-2623	Schempp-Hirth Discus CS	152CS	
D-2624	Rolladen-Schneider LS3-a	3463	
D-2626-MSI	Rolladen-Schneider LS3-a	3464	
D-2627	Rolladen-Schneider LS3-17	3334	
D-2628	SZD-50-3 Puchacz	B-1389	DDR-3628
D-2629-1L	Schleicher ASK 21	21411	
D-2630-EX	Schempp-Hirth Ventus-2ax (Permit .02)	48	
D-2631	Schleicher ASK 21	21412	
D-2632	Rolladen-Schneider LS3	3237	
D-2633-KM	Schleicher ASH 25	25063	
D-2634	Rolladen-Schneider LS3	3236	
D-2635-UU	Schleicher ASK 21	21796	
D-2636	Rolladen-Schneider LS3	3317	
D-2637	Rolladen-Schneider LS3-a	3318	
D-2638-NF	Rolladen-Schneider LS8-a	8028	
D-2639	Schleicher ASW 24	24040	
D-2640	Rolladen-Schneider LS4	4429	
D-2642	Schleicher ASW 20L	20126	
D-2643-NW	Schleicher ASW 19B	19232	
D-2644	Schempp-Hirth Discus-2b	155	
D-2645	Schleicher ASW 19B	19238	
D-2647	Schleicher ASK 13	13600	
D-2648-NO	Schleicher ASW 19B	19236	
D-2649-JK	Schleicher ASW 20	20119	
D-2650	Schleicher ASW 20L	20123	
D-2651-1E	Schleicher ASW 20L	20128	

Reg.	Type	Serial	Notes
D-2652	Schleicher ASK 13	13603	
D-2653-CO	Schleicher ASW 19B	19244	
D-2654	Schleicher ASW 20	20133	
D-2655	SZD-50-3 Puchacz	B-1539	DDR-3655
D-2656-VS	Schleicher ASW 19B	19249	PH-1447, D-2656
D-2657	Schleicher ASW 20	20127	
D-2658	Schleicher ASW 20L	20137	
D-2659-DM	Schempp-Hirth Ventus-2a	90	
D-2660-H6	Glaser-Dirks DG-600 (Permit)	6-75	
D-2661	Schleicher ASW 20	20140	
D-2662-9N	Glasflügel Mosquito	98	
D-2665	Rolladen-Schneider LS3	3120	
D-2666	Rolladen-Schneider LS6-c18	6221	F-CGUM
D-2668	Grob G 103 Twin II	3563	
D-2669	Rolladen-Schneider LS4-b	4981	
D-2670-70	Grob G 103A Twin II Acro	3653-K-22	
D-2672-72	Glasflügel Standard Libelle 201B	406	OY-XBF
D-2673-2S	Schleicher ASW 19B	19207	
D-2674	Schleicher ASW 20	20084	
D-2675-FE	Schleicher ASW 20	20085	
D-2676	Schempp-Hirth Discus b	150	HB-1907
D-2677	Schleicher ASK 13	13595	
D-2678-FLO	Rolladen-Schneider LS8-a	8029	
D-2680-WO	Schleicher ASW 19	19216	
D-2681-BK	Schempp-Hirth Discus CS	155CS	
D-2683	Schleicher ASW 20	20096	
D-2684-GY	Schempp-Hirth Discus CS	062CS	
D-2685	Schleicher ASW 20	20097	
D-2686-11	Schleicher ASW 20	20098	
D-2687	Schleicher ASW 19B	19223	
D-2688	Schleicher ASW 19	19225	
D-2689-70	Schleicher ASW 20	20107	
D-2690-GM	Schempp-Hirth Ventus-2b	13	
D-2691-FL	Schempp-Hirth Discus-2a	196	G-DIIA, BGA 5093/KGZ
D-2692-BU	Schleicher ASW 20	20393	
D-2693	Schleicher ASW 20L	20394	
D-2695	Schleicher ASW 20 (P. 9.14)	20399	
D-2697	Schleicher ASW 24	24157	
D-2698-L4	Rolladen-Schneider LS4	4240	
D-2699	Rolladen-Schneider LS4	4157	
D-2700-AG	Rolladen-Schneider LS4	4165	
D-2701	Neukom S4D Elfe	410AB	
D-2702	SZD-32A Foka 5	W-427	DDR-2202, DM-2202
D-2703	Grob G103 Twin Astir	?	
D-2704-KR	SZD-36A Cobra 15	W-611	DDR-2304, DM-2304
D-2705-TC	Schempp-Hirth Ventus-2bxR	147	
D-2706	Rolladen-Schneider LS4	4265	
D-2707-C5	Rolladen-Schneider LS4	4297	
D-2708-D4	Glaser-Dirks DG-300 Club Elan	3E336C31	
D-2709	Schleicher K 7	1078	PH-270
D-2710	Schleicher Ka 6CR Rhönsegler	6372/Si	D-5428
D-2711-A1	Rolladen-Schneider LS4	4218	
D-2712	Schleicher ASW 15B	15391	PH-515
D-2714	Schleicher ASW 20	20109	
D-2715-TS	Schleicher ASW 27	27160	
D-2716-PJ	Schleicher ASW 19	19219	
D-2717-G1	Schleicher ASW 27	27086	G-CJJF, BGA 4545
D-2719	Schleicher ASK 21	21043	
D-2720	Schleicher ASW 20L	20400	
D-2721	SZD-30 Pirat	B-303	DDR-1721, DM-1721
D-2722	Schleicher ASW 24	24140	
D-2723-N4	Grob G 103 Twin II	3528	
D-2724	Schleicher ASK 21	21651	
D-2725-B9	Schleicher ASW 19B	19344	
D-2726-VA	Schleicher ASW 20	20445	
D-2727-P10	Schleicher ASW 27B	27166	G-CJZX, BGA 4923
D-2728-BA	Glasflügel H303 Mosquito B	179	
D-2729-V	Schleicher ASW 27-18 (ASG 29)	29012	
D-2730	Glasflügel H303 Mosquito B	127	
D-2731	Glasflügel H303 Mosquito B	151	
D-2732	Rolladen-Schneider LS1-f	444	
D-2733-6G	Rolladen-Schneider LS1-f	445	
D-2735	Glaser-Dirks DG-300 Elan	3E77	
D-2736-B3	Glaser-Dirks DG-300 Elan	3E78	
D-2737	Rolladen-Schneider LS1-f	316	
D-2738	Schleicher ASW 27	27016	OO-ZQQ
D-2740	Glaser-Dirks DG-300 Elan	3E79	
D-2742	Rolladen-Schneider LS1-f	346	
D-2743	Glaser-Dirks DG-300 Elan	3E83	
D-2744	Schleicher ASK 21	21599	
D-2745-7A	Rolladen-Schneider LS1-f	356	
D-2746	Glaser-Dirks DG-300 Elan	3E104	
D-2747	SZD-30 Pirat	B-341	DDR-1747, DM-1747
D-2748	Rolladen-Schneider LS1-f	414	
D-2750-WT	Glaser-Dirks DG-300 Elan	3E86	
D-2751	Glaser-Dirks DG-300 Elan	3E87	
D-2752	SZD-30 Pirat	B-352	DDR-1752, DM-1752
D-2753-27	Schleicher ASW 27	27053	
D-2755	Rolladen-Schneider LS4	4018	
D-2756-MT	Rolladen-Schneider LS3-17	3449	
D-2757-L1	Schempp-Hirth Discus b	388	
D-2758	Rolladen-Schneider LS3-17	3418	
D-2759-2M	Rolladen-Schneider LS1-f	348	
D-2760-LL	Rolladen-Schneider LS1-f	347	
D-2761-IBD	Schempp-Hirth Discus CS	035CS	
D-2762-2J	Rolladen-Schneider LS1-f	323	
D-2763	Rolladen-Schneider LS1-f (P. 4.14)	336	
D-2764-64	Rolladen-Schneider LS4-b	4784	
D-2765	Rolladen-Schneider LS6-c	6323	
D-2766	Schleicher ASW 28-18	28502	G-CKKM, BGA 5161, D-9004, D-0001
D-2767-1F	Rolladen-Schneider LS1-f	340	
D-2768-KP	Rolladen-Schneider LS1-f	341	
D-2769	Rolladen-Schneider LS1-f	343	N2234W, D-2769
D-2770-CG	Glaser-Dirks DG-100G Elan	E143G111	
D-2771-H9	Rolladen-Schneider LS1-f	315	
D-2772-7A	Rolladen-Schneider LS1-f	304	
D-2773	Rolladen-Schneider LS1-f	305	
D-2774	Rolladen-Schneider LS4-a	4786	
D-2775	Rolladen-Schneider LS4-a	4787	
D-2776-1T	Rolladen-Schneider LS1-f	301	
D-2777	Schempp-Hirth Standard Cirrus	238	CF-DMW
D-2778	Rolladen-Schneider LS4	4532	PH-778
D-2779	Schempp-Hirth Standard Cirrus	480	
D-2780	SZD-30 Pirat	B-412	
D-2781	Schleicher ASW 27	27114	G-CEUG, BGA4696/JQM
D-2784-C7	Schempp-Hirth Discus-2c	51	
D-2785-PI	Schempp-Hirth Discus b	465	
D-2787	Schleicher ASW 27B	27152	G-CJXZ, BGA 4876
D-2788-tc	SZD-51-1 Junior	B-2190	
D-2789-GE	Schempp-Hirth Nimbus-2	118	
D-2790	Schempp-Hirth Nimbus-2	119	
D-2791-GI	Rolladen-Schneider LS8-a	8235	
D-2792-BF	Schempp-Hirth Nimbus-2B	164	
D-2793	Schempp-Hirth HS-7 Mini-Nimbus	55	
D-2794	Schempp-Hirth HS-7 Mini-Nimbus	56	
D-2795-F2	Rolladen-Schneider LS4-b	4996	
D-2796-96	Schempp-Hirth Nimbus-2C	205	
D-2797	Rolladen-Schneider LS4-b	4983	
D-2798	Schempp-Hirth Nimbus-2C	217	
D-2799	Schempp-Hirth Nimbus-2C	218	
D-2801-IP	Glaser-Dirks DG-300 Elan	3E93	
D-2803-S8	Glaser-Dirks DG-100G Elan	E64G39	BGA 4920/JZU, HB-1579
D-2804	Rolladen-Schneider LS3	3038	
D-2805	Rolladen-Schneider LS3	3039	
D-2806	SZD-51-1 Junior	B-1923	DDR-2806
D-2807	SZD-51-1 Junior	B-1919	DDR-2802
D-2808	Rolladen-Schneider LS3	3042	
D-2809	SZD-51-1 Junior	W-961	DDR-2800
D-2810-AG	Rolladen-Schneider LS3	3044	
D-2811	Rolladen-Schneider LS3	3045	
D-2812	Schleicher ASW 20L	20423	I-SELZ, D-2604
D-2814-PR	Schempp-Hirth Nimbus-3/24.5	42	OY-XPR, N254E
D-2815	Schempp-Hirth Janus C	182	
D-2816	Schempp-Hirth Ventus b/16.6	179	
D-2817	Rolladen-Schneider LS3 (P 5.9.16)	3053	
D-2818	Rolladen-Schneider LS3 (P. 3.13)	3054	
D-2819-DZ	Rolladen-Schneider LS4-b	4941	
D-2820	Rolladen-Schneider LS4-b	4789	
D-2821-BA	Schempp-Hirth Discus-2c	14	
D-2822-22	Rolladen-Schneider LS4-b	4790	
D-2823	Schleicher ASK 23B	23096	PH-817
D-2824	Rolladen-Schneider LS3	3061	
D-2825	Rolladen-Schneider LS3	3117	
D-2827	Akaflieg München Mü.27 (Permit)	V1	
D-2828-28	Glaser-Dirks DG-300 Elan	3E81	HB-1791
D-2832-32	Schempp-Hirth Nimbus-2C	185	
D-2833	Rolladen-Schneider LS4	4040	
D-2834-XS	Rolladen-Schneider LS8-a	8033	
D-2836-TX	Rolladen-Schneider LS8-b	8449	
D-2837	SZD-30 Pirat	B-323	DDR-1737, DM-1737
D-2839	Rolladen-Schneider LS6-c	6269	
D-2842-42	Rolladen-Schneider LS8-a	8160	
D-2843-FN	Schempp-Hirth Discus-2c	16	
D-2844	Rolladen-Schneider LS3-a	3266	
D-2845	ICA-Brasov IS-28B2	312	
D-2846-GN	Rolladen-Schneider LS3-a	3258	
D-2847	Rolladen-Schneider LS3-a	3209	
D-2848-48	Schleicher ASW 28-18	28732	
D-2849	Rolladen-Schneider LS3-a	3171	
D-2850-TM	Rolladen-Schneider LS4-a	4792	
D-2851-8L	Rolladen-Schneider LS4-a	4793	
D-2853	Schleicher ASW 19B	19318	
D-2854-R1	Schleicher ASK 21	21021	
D-2855-K1	Schleicher ASK 21	21025	
D-2856	Schleicher ASW 19B	19319	
D-2857-A8	Rolladen-Schneider LS8-a	8161	
D-2858	Glaser-Dirks DG-300 Elan	3E129	
D-2859	SZD-30 Pirat	B-581	DDR-1859, DM-1859
D-2860-FV	Rolladen-Schneider LS3-a	3107	
D-2861-I4	Glasflügel Hornet C	96	
D-2862	Glasflügel Standard Libelle 201B	311	HB-1070
D-2863	Rolladen-Schneider LS3-a	3285	
D-2865-LR	Rolladen-Schneider LS3-a	3333	
D-2866	SZD-30 Pirat	S-01.03	DDR-1866, DM-1866
D-2867	Rolladen-Schneider LS3-17	3427	
D-2868-NRW	Schempp-Hirth Discus-2c	27	
D-2869	Rolladen-Schneider LS3-17	3340	
D-2871-XS	Glaser-Dirks DG-300 Elan	3E136	
D-2872	Glaser-Dirks DG-300 Elan	3E453	
D-2873	Schleicher ASW 20L	20446	
D-2874	Schleicher ASW 20	20447	
D-2875	Schleicher ASW 20	20449	
D-2876-OD	Schempp-Hirth Discus b	557	
D-2877-B	Glasflügel Hornet C	100	OY-XKN
D-2878-JZ	Rolladen-Schneider LS3-17	3269	OO-ZJZ, D-2868
D-2879-VX	Schempp-Hirth Nimbus-2C	204	
D-2880	Glaser-Dirks DG-800S	8-28S5	
D-2881-JA	Schempp-Hirth Mini-Nimbus C	142	
D-2882-SK	Schleicher ASW 19B	19308	
D-2883-CR	Schleicher ASW 20	20318	
D-2885	Schleicher ASK 21	21014	
D-2886	Schleicher ASW 20L	20320	
D-2887-II	Schempp-Hirth Janus B	130	I-IVDC
D-2888	Eiri PIK-20D	20570	
D-2889	Rolladen-Schneider LS3-17	3369	
D-2890-XW	Schleicher ASW 28	28066	
D-2891	Grob G 103A Twin II Acro	3811-K-74	
D-2892	Glaser-Dirks DG-300 Elan	3E371	PH-892
D-2893	Rolladen-Schneider LS3-a	3397	
D-2894-2G	Rolladen-Schneider LS3-17	3257	
D-2895	Rolladen-Schneider LS3-17	3409	
D-2896	Rolladen-Schneider LS7	4284	
D-2897	Rolladen-Schneider LS7	7091	
D-2898	Schempp-Hirth Ventus b/16.6	114	SE-TYP
D-2899	Rolladen-Schneider LS4	4300	
D-2900-T2	Glaser-Dirks DG-300 Club Elan	3E354C42	
D-2901	Grob G 102 Astir CS 77	1839	
D-2902	Grob G 102 Astir CS 77	1840	
D-2903-AF	Schempp-Hirth Duo Discus	195	
D-2904	Rolladen-Schneider LS7	7094	
D-2905	Grob G 102 Speed Astir IIB	4063	
D-2906	Grob G102 Astir CS 77 (P.6.12)	1685	G-DDRU, BGA 2327
D-2907-IBL	Grob G 102 Speed Astir IIB	4065	
D-2908-08	Schleicher ASK 21	21773	

Reg.	Type	Serial	Previous
D-2909-CZ	Schleicher ASW 27-18 (ASG 29)	29599	
D-2910	SZD-30 Pirat	S-04.11	DDR-1910, DM-1910
D-2911	Pilatus B4-PC11AF	235	
D-2912	Grob G 103 Twin II	3541	
D-2913	Eiriavion PIK-20D	20642	PH-642
D-2914	Grob G 103 Twin II	3545	
D-2915	Schleicher ASW 27-18 (ASG 29)	29015	G-OASG, BGA 5235, D-7429
D-2916-FW	Schleicher ASK 21	21417	OO-ZFW
D-2917	Grob G 102 Standard Astir II	5050S	
D-2918	Grob G 102 Club Astir II	5060C	
D-2920	Grob G 102 Standard Astir II	5051S	
D-2921	Schleicher ASK 21	21668	
D-2922-O3	Rolladen-Schneider LS4-b	41051	
D-2923	Schempp-Hirth Ventus b/16.6	187	
D-2924	Schempp-Hirth Ventus b/16.6 (P. 3.14)	185	
D-2925-4N	Schempp-Hirth Duo Discus	75	
D-2926-VZ	Schempp-Hirth Duo Discus	216	
D-2927	Schempp-Hirth Ventus b/16.6	200	
D-2928-SW	Rolladen-Schneider LS7-WL	7095	
D-2930	Scheibe SF 30A Club-Spatz	6805	
D-2931-W4	Rolladen-Schneider LS4-b	4911	
D-2934	Schleicher K 8B	AB8962	
D-2935-IOO	Schempp-Hirth Duo Discus	97	
D-2936-SG	Grob G 103C Twin III	36007	
D-2938-KP	Schleicher ASK 13	13261	OO-ZKP
D-2939-BI	Rolladen-Schneider LS1-f	268	
D-2940	Schleicher ASK 13	13478	OO-YJJ, D-2366
D-2941	Schleicher K 7 Rhönadler	EB.16	OO-ZMJ, D-5650
D-2942-B7	Rolladen-Schneider LS4	4131	
D-2943-AR	Rolladen-Schneider LS8-a	8186	
D-2944-YV	Schempp-Hirth Discus b	100	
D-2945	Schleicher K 8B	8706	OO-ZAU
D-2946	Schleicher K 8B	8494	OO-YBA, HB-825
D-2947-VM	Schleicher ASK 18	18013	OO-YVM, D-6881
D-2948-L6	Schempp-Hirth Standard Cirrus	314	
D-2949-KK	Rolladen-Schneider LS6-18W (P 6.6.16)	6354	
D-2950	Rolladen-Schneider LS6-18W	6355	
D-2951	Glasflügel H201B Standard Libelle	413	
D-2952	Schleicher K 7 Rhönadler (Permit .07)	7110	D-1952
D-2955	Schempp-Hirth Standard Cirrus	316G	
D-2956	Schempp-Hirth Standard Cirrus	317G	
D-2958	Schempp-Hirth Standard Cirrus	328G	
D-2959	Schempp-Hirth Standard Cirrus	329G	
D-2960	Schleicher K 8B	8927AB	
D-2962-BK	Glasflügel H201B Standard Libelle	410	
D-2963	Schempp-Hirth Standard Cirrus 75	614	OO-ZRR
D-2964	Glaser-Dirks DG-100G Elan	E99G69	
D-2965-WL	Schempp-Hirth Standard Cirrus	321	
D-2966-66	Schempp-Hirth Duo Discus	236	
D-2967	Schempp-Hirth Standard Austria SH1	78	OO-ZUO, D-4004, LX-CWV
D-2968-ICE	Schempp-Hirth Duo Discus	94	
D-2970	Glaser-Dirks DG-100G Elan	E212G178	
D-2971	Rolladen-Schneider LS2 (P 615)	243	
D-2972	Glasflügel H201B Standard Libelle	415	
D-2973-FZ	Glasflügel H201B Standard Libelle	417	
D-2974	Glasflügel H201B Standard Libelle	418	
D-2975	Rolladen-Schneider LS1-d	126	
D-2976	ISF Mistral-C	MC 011/78	OO-YCR, D-4911
D-2978	Schleicher ASK 13	13434	
D-2979	Schleicher ASK 13	13435	
D-2980	Schleicher ASW 15B	15277	
D-2981	Schleicher ASW 15B	15278	
D-2982-CU	Schleicher ASW 15B	15279	
D-2983	Schleicher ASK 13	13432	
D-2984-JOE	Schempp-Hirth Discus b	249	I-LMIG
D-2985-K4	Schempp-Hirth Discus b	101	
D-2986	Schleicher ASW 15B	15284	
D-2989	Schleicher ASK 13	13443	
D-2991	Schleicher ASK 21	21676	
D-2992	Jastreb Standard Cirrus G/81	258	OY-SSX, SE-TYV
D-2993-1D	Rolladen-Schneider LS8-a	8109	
D-2995	Start & Flug H-101 Salto	25	
D-2996	Start & Flug H-101 Salto	26	
D-2997	Scheibe L-Spatz III	826	D-0130
D-2998	Rolladen-Schneider LS1-c	165	
D-2999	Scheibe Zugvogel IIIB	1089	OO-ZJC
D-3001	Rolladen-Schneider LS1-c	154	
D-3002-IK	Schempp-Hirth Standard Cirrus	332	
D-3004	Schempp-Hirth Discus-2b	1	D-6111
D-3005-LI	Schempp-Hirth Standard Cirrus	347G	
D-3006	Grob G 102 Club Astir IIIB	5620CB	D-4726
D-3007	Schempp-Hirth Standard Cirrus	350	
D-3008	SZD-9bis Bocian 1E	P-720	DDR-3008, DM-3008
D-3009-XX	Schempp-Hirth Nimbus-2	37	
D-3012	Schempp-Hirth Cirrus-VTC	140Y	
D-3013	Schempp-Hirth Discus b	104	
D-3014	Vogt Lo-100 Zwergreiher	EB 01	
D-3015	Schleicher Ka 6BR-PE Rhönsegler	342	
D-3016	Grob G103C Twin III Acro	34132	HB-3018
D-3017-BW3	Glasflügel H203 Standard Libelle	2	
D-3018	SZD-9bis Bocian 1E	P-727	DDR-3014, DM-3014
D-3019	Glasflügel H201B Standard Libelle	424	
D-3020	Glasflügel Kestrel	121	OE-5020
D-3021-GR	Rolladen-Schneider LS7-WL	7072	HB-3021
D-3022	Schleicher K 8B	587	
D-3024-S1	Schempp-Hirth Discus b	105	
D-3025	Kaiser Ka 1	0101	
D-3027	Schleicher K 8B	8222	
D-3028	Schleicher K 8B	8418	
D-3029	Glasflügel H304	263	
D-3031	Glaser-Dirks DG-100G Elan	E211G177	
D-3032	DG Flugzeugbau DG-303 Club Elan Acro	3E507C87A40	
D-3033	Start & Flug H101 Salto	21	
D-3035-ZD	SZD-51-1 Junior	B-1846	HB-3013
D-3036	Schleicher K 8B	8716	
D-3037	Schleicher Ka 6CR Rhönsegler	6540	
D-3038-VH	Grob G 102 Astir CS	1178	
D-3039	Schleicher Ka 6CR Rhönsegler	6627	
D-3040	Schleicher Ka 6CR Rhönsegler	6660AB	
D-3042	Glasflügel 304	205	SE-UGB, OH-564
D-3043-43	Glaser-Dirks DG-100G Elan	E209G175	
D-3044	Schempp-Hirth Discus-2c	36	
D-3045-MR	Bölkow Phoebus C	1002	
D-3046-KB	Rolladen-Schneider LS1-f	188	
D-3047	Schempp-Hirth Discus b	410	HB-3044
D-3049-F5	Schempp-Hirth Ventus b/16.6	69	
D-3050	Akaflieg Braunschweig SB-5E Sperber (P 26.5.16)	AB5053	
D-3051-L1	Schempp-Hirth Nimbus 3/24.5	12	
D-3052	Glaser-Dirks DG-300 Elan	3E142	
D-3053	Grunau Baby IIB	1	
D-3055	Glaser-Dirks DG-300 Elan	3E358	OE-5485
D-3056-CI	Grob G 103 Twin II	3510	
D-3058	Grob G 102 Standard Astir II	5046S	
D-3059	SZD-9bis Bocian 1E	P-444	DDR-3019, DM-3019
D-3060-CZ	HpH Glasflügel 304CZ-17	44-17	
D-3061	Glaser-Dirks DG-300 Elan	3E152	
D-3062	Glaser-Dirks DG-100G Elan	E208G174	
D-3063	Pilatus B4-PC11AF	298	S5-3065, SL-3065, YU-4258
D-3065	SZD-9bis Bocian 1E	P-479	DDR-3063, DM-3063
D-3066	Grob G 103 Twin II	3516	
D-3067	Grob G 102 Standard Astir II (P. 3.14)	5049S	
D-3068-FF	Grob G 103 Twin II	3518	
D-3070	Rolladen-Schneider LS1-d	193	
D-3071-DU	Schempp-Hirth Duo Discus	72	
D-3074	Schleicher ASW 24	24139	HB-3077
D-3075	Pilatus B4-PC11AF	301	S5-3035, SL-3035, YU-4261
D-3077-AM	Rolladen-Schneider LS1-f	306	
D-3078-HC	Grob G 103A Twin II Acro	3637-K-18	
D-3080-TM	Rolladen-Schneider LS8-a	8167	SE-ULX
D-3081-HH	Schleicher ASW 20C (Permit)	20838	
D-3082	Schleicher ASK 23	23045	
D-3083	Schleicher ASK 23	23046	
D-3084-99	SZD-55-1	551191027	HB-3084
D-3085	Schempp-Hirth Standard Cirrus B	598	OO-ZCJ (1)
D-3086-LA	Rolladen-Schneider LS8-a	8016	
D-3087	Rolladen-Schneider LS3	3100	D-2859, OO-ZOZ
D-3089-H0	Schempp-Hirth Nimbus-3	11	
D-3090	Schleicher Rhönlerche II (P.04)	557	D-3021
D-3092	Schempp-Hirth Standard Cirrus (P. 16.6.16)	623	
D-3093	Schempp-Hirth Standard Cirrus	504	
D-3094-i8	Schempp-Hirth Ventus-2c	49/150	
D-3095-E8	Schempp-Hirth Standard Cirrus	557	
D-3096-ZE	Schempp-Hirth Standard Cirrus	558G	
D-3097	Glaser-Dirks DG-100G Elan	E125G93	
D-3099	Schempp-Hirth Standard Cirrus	407G	I-ACOB
D-3100	Vogt Lo-100 Zwergreiher	AB/117	
D-3101	Schempp-Hirth Standard Cirrus	435G	
D-3102	Schempp-Hirth Nimbus-2	64	
D-3103	Neukom S-4D Elfe	419AB	
D-3104	Schempp-Hirth Standard Cirrus (Permit .10)	427	
D-3105	Schempp-Hirth Standard Cirrus	428	
D-3107-TK	Schempp-Hirth Ventus-2b	87	N21TK
D-3108-M1	Schempp-Hirth Ventus c	302	
D-3109	Glasflügel H201B Standard Libelle	570	
D-3110	Rolladen-Schneider LS4	4745	OE-5459, D-1841
D-3111	SZD-50-3 Puchacz	B-1085	DDR-3601
D-3112	Schempp-Hirth Ventus c	538	I-PECK
D-3113	Schleicher ASW 27	27154	
D-3114-B2	Rolladen-Schneider LS4-b	41023	
D-3115	Glaser-Dirks DG-100G Elan	E146G114	
D-3116	Schleicher ASW 20L	20220	D-KGPF, D-3156
D-3118-8W	Rolladen-Schneider LS8-a	8133	
D-3119	SZD-9bis Bocian 1E	P-499	DDR-3219, DM-3219
D-3120	Schempp-Hirth Discus CS	310CS	
D-3121	Schempp-Hirth Janus B	145	
D-3123-2D	Schempp-Hirth Duo Discus	71	
D-3124-BG	Rolladen-Schneider LS4	4422	
D-3126-4U	Schempp-Hirth Discus CS	164CS	HB-3121
D-3127	Schleicher ASW 27B	27232	
D-3129-6J	Rolladen-Schneider LS1-f	424	
D-3130-MH	Rolladen-Schneider LS1-f	425	
D-3131-9B	Rolladen-Schneider LS1-f	426	
D-3132	Rolladen-Schneider LS1-f	427	
D-3133-UX	Rolladen-Schneider LS1-f (Permit)	299	
D-3134-PS	Rolladen-Schneider LS1-f	354	
D-3135	Rolladen-Schneider LS1-f	357	
D-3137	Schempp-Hirth Duo Discus	274	
D-3139-5K	Glaser-Dirks DG-100G Elan	E113G82	
D-3140-Y3	Schempp-Hirth Discus CS	314CS	
D-3141	Schleicher ASK 21	21284	
D-3142	Schleicher ASK 23B	23055	
D-3143-BO	Schempp-Hirth Ventus b/16.6	147	SE-TYY
D-3144-BC	Rolladen-Schneider LS4-b	4991	
D-3145-CW	Rolladen-Schneider LS1-f	411	
D-3146	Schleicher ASK 21	21628	
D-3147-MB	Schempp-Hirth Ventus-2ax	145	
D-3148	Schempp-Hirth Ventus b/16.6	111	
D-3149	Rolladen-Schneider LS1-f	441	
D-3150-G6	Schleicher ASW 20CL	20839	
D-3151	Schempp-Hirth Nimbus-3/24.5	30	
D-3152-M5	Schempp-Hirth Ventus b/16.6	117	
D-3153-BI	Rolladen-Schneider LS4-b	4992	
D-3155	Schleicher ASW 20L	20219	
D-3156	Glaser-Dirks DG-800S	8-78S21	
D-3157-PO	Schleicher ASW 20	20226	
D-3158-BK	Schleicher ASW 20	20227	
D-3160-E3	Rolladen-Schneider LS4-b	4993	
D-3162	Rolladen-Schneider LS1-c	161	OO-YDD, OE-5297
D-3163-ILO	Schleicher ASW 20	20230	
D-3164	Schempp-Hirth Janus B	113	
D-3165-BV	Schempp-Hirth Nimbus-2C	219	
D-3167-V3	Schempp-Hirth Nimbus-2B	168	
D-3168	Marganski Swift S-1	120	HB-3163
D-3169	Marganski Swift S-1	122	HB-3169
D-3170	SZD-42-2 Jantar 2B	B-875	
D-3172-ZU	Schleicher ASK 21	21280	

Reg	Type	Serial	Other
D-3173-FC	Glaser-Dirks DG-300 Elan	3E151	
D-3174-6	Schempp-Hirth Standard Cirrus G	702	
D-3175	DG Flugzeugbau DG-300 Elan	3E470	
D-3177	Glaser-Dirks DG-300 Elan	3E149	
D-3179-SB	Rolladen-Schneider LS4-b	4994	
D-3181-GR	Schleicher ASW 20	20241	
D-3183	Glaser-Dirks DG-300 Elan	3E148	
D-3184	Rolladen-Schneider LS3-a	3243	
D-3185	Schleicher ASW 24B	24235	
D-3186	Rolladen-Schneider LS3-17	3251	
D-3187-LV	Rolladen-Schneider LS6-c	6281	
D-3188-AW	Schempp-Hirth Ventus b/16.6	127	
D-3189-H2	Rolladen-Schneider LS8-a	8237	
D-3190-90	Schempp-Hirth Nimbus-3/24.5	40	
D-3191-13	Schempp-Hirth Ventus b	128	
D-3192-1C	Schempp-Hirth Ventus b/16.6	130	
D-3193	Schempp-Hirth Mini-Nimbus C	133	
D-3194-CC	Schempp-Hirth Mini-Nimbus C	134	
D-3195	Schempp-Hirth Mini-Nimbus C	135	
D-3196-FE	Glaser-Dirks DG-500/22 Elan	5E94S14	
D-3198-KB	Rolladen-Schneider LS4-b	4995	
D-3199-4	Neukom S-4D Elfe	407AB	
D-3200	LET L-13 Blanik	027068	DDR-3201, DM-3201
D-3201	Schleicher ASK 13	13091	
D-3204	Glaser-Dirks DG-100	27	
D-3205	Focke-Wulf Kranich III	70	
D-3206	SZD-9bis Bocian 1E	P-508	DDR-3226, DM-3226
D-3207	Scheibe Bergfalke III	5629	
D-3208	Schleicher ASK 21	21792	
D-3209	Schleicher ASK 13	13090	
D-3210	Schleicher Ka 6CR Rhönsegler	6005	
D-3211	Schleicher Ka 6CR Rhönsegler	6253/Si	
D-3212	Glaser-Dirks DG-300 Elan	3E147	
D-3213-SM	Glaser-Dirks DG-300 Elan	3E145	
D-3215	Schleicher K 8B	992	
D-3216	Scheibe L-Spatz 55	564	
D-3217	Schleicher Ka 6CR Rhönsegler	998	
D-3218	Scheibe L-Spatz 55	736	
D-3219	Schleicher Ka 6 Rhönsegler	221	
D-3220	Schleicher ASW 22	22026	F-CGCF, F-WGCF
D-3221	Scheibe Bergfalke II/55 (P.7.12)	273	
D-3222	Scheibe SF 27A	6023	
D-3223-BZ	Schempp-Hirth Duo Discus	205	
D-3224	Schempp-Hirth Nimbus-3D	9/44	HB-3222, D-4346
D-3225-5N	Schempp-Hirth Discus-2c	9	
D-3226	SZD-9bis Bocian 1E	P-507	DDR-3225, DM-3225
D-3227	Schleicher Ka 6BR Rhönsegler	414	
D-3228-28	Glaser-Dirks DG-300 Elan	3E144	
D-3229-1N	Schleicher ASW 28-18	28521	
D-3230-30	Schempp-Hirth Discus-2b	171	
D-3231	Schleicher ASW 20L	20406	OO-YER, D-3297
D-3232	Schleicher K 8B	635	
D-3233	Schleicher ASK 21	21868	
D-3234	Schleicher K 8B	736	
D-3235-JP	Schempp-Hirth Nimbus-3/24.5	24	
D-3236	Schleicher Ka 6CR Rhönsegler	10	
D-3237	Schleicher ASK 21	21091	
D-3238	Rolladen-Schneider LS3	3094	PH-1017, HB-1360
D-3239	SZD-51-1 Junior	B-1930	SP-3727, D-6208, I-KASB
D-3240	Glasflügel H301 Libelle	3	
D-3242	Schleicher Ka 6CR Rhönsegler	6341/Si	
D-3243	SZD-9bis Bocian 1E	P-529	DDR-3242, DM-3242
D-3245	Schleicher Ka 6CR-PE Rhönsegler	6293/Bi	
D-3246	Glasflügel H201B Standard Libelle	472	
D-3247-II	Schleicher ASK 21	21074	
D-3248	SZD-9bis Bocian 1E	P-533	DDR-3246, DM-3246
D-3249	Schleicher ASW 20L	20456	
D-3250	Schleicher ASK 13	13022	
D-3251-CT2	Schempp-Hirth Duo Discus	490	
D-3252-VS	Rolladen-Schneider LS1-f	279	
D-3253-53	Rolladen-Schneider LS1-f	273	
D-3254	Schleicher ASK 21 (P. 3.14)	21707	
D-3255-55	Rolladen-Schneider LS8-18	8440	
D-3256-OM	Glasflügel H201B Standard Libelle	543	
D-3257	Glasflügel H201B Standard Libelle	544	
D-3260-EE	Rolladen-Schneider LS1-f	265	
D-3261	Schempp-Hirth Standard Cirrus B	398	
D-3262-MI	Schempp-Hirth Standard Cirrus	420	
D-3263	Schempp-Hirth Standard Cirrus	445	
D-3264-HZ	SZD-48-3 Jantar-Standard 3	B-1958	PH-916
D-3265-TM	Schempp-Hirth Discus CS	305CS	
D-3267-DS	Schempp-Hirth Ventus-2a	28	PH-1075
D-3268-EI	Schempp-Hirth Ventus-2a	54	
D-3269	Schempp-Hirth Standard Cirrus	517G	
D-3270	Schempp-Hirth Ventus-2a	30	HB-3218
D-3271	Schempp-Hirth Standard Cirrus	575	
D-3272	Schempp-Hirth Standard Cirrus	578	
D-3273	Grob G 102 Astir CS	1033	
D-3274	Grob G 102 Astir CS	1034	
D-3275	Grob G 102 Astir CS	1035	
D-3276	Grob G 102 Astir CS	1036	
D-3277-IY	Grob G 102 Astir CS	1037	
D-3278	Schleicher ASK 21	21292	
D-3279	Grob G 102 Astir CS	1039	
D-3280	Grob G 102 Astir CS	1040	
D-3282	Grob G 102 Astir CS	1042	
D-3283	Grob G 102 Astir CS	1056	
D-3284	Grob G 102 Astir CS	1057	
D-3286-DL	Grob G 102 Astir CS	1062	
D-3287-B7	SZD-51-1 Junior	B-1785	HB-1931
D-3288-LC	Grob G 102 Astir CS	1064	
D-3289-H5	Grob G 102 Astir CS	1065	
D-3290-WF	Glaser-Dirks DG-300 Elan	3E141	
D-3291	Grob G 102 Astir CS	1067	
D-3292-BU	Grob G 102 Astir CS	1068	
D-3293	Schleicher ASW 20	20404	
D-3294-GT3	Schleicher ASK 21	21044	
D-3295-95	Schleicher ASW 20L	20402	OY-XXF, D-3295
D-3296-FSV	Schleicher ASK 21	21045	
D-3297-PE	Schempp-Hirth Ventus-2a	39	HB-3217
D-3298-S9	Glasflügel H303 Mosquito B	143	
D-3299	Glasflügel H303 Mosquito B	107	
D-3300	Glaser-Dirks DG-300 Club Elan	3E269C1	
D-3301	Grob G 102 Astir CS	1069	
D-3302	Start + Flug H 101 Salto	39	OO-ZHU, D-9239
D-3303	Grob G 102 Astir CS	1071	
D-3304-RE	HpH Glasflügel 304C Wasp	49-C	SE-URE
D-3305	Grob G 102 Astir CS	1073	
D-3306	Grob G 102 Astir CS	1074	
D-3308	SZD-9bis Bocian 1E	P-558	DDR-3368, DM-3368
D-3309-C7	Schempp-Hirth Discus b	548	
D-3310	Schleicher ASK 23B	23061	
D-3311-AB	Schempp-Hirth Discus-2b	100	
D-3312-B1	AMS Flight/Rolladen-Schneider LS4-b	41057	
D-3313	Glaser-Dirks DG-100G	90G10	
D-3314-HM	Glaser-Dirks DG-100	92	
D-3315	Glaser-Dirks DG-100	94	
D-3316	Glaser-Dirks DG-100	23	
D-3317	Glaser-Dirks DG-200/17C	2-129CL06	
D-3318	Glaser-Dirks DG-200/17C	2-131CL08	
D-3320	Glaser-Dirks DG-100G Elan	E90G62	
D-3323-JO	Schleicher ASW 20L	20138	
D-3324	Glaser-Dirks DG-300 Elan	3E69	
D-3325-iX	Schempp-Hirth Ventus-2cx	103	
D-3326-S3	Glaser-Dirks DG-500 Elan Trainer	5E84T36	
D-3327	Schleicher ASW 19B	19254	
D-3328	SZD-9bis Bocian 1E	P-510	DDR-3228, DM-3228
D-3329-3B	Schleicher ASW 19B	19256	
D-3330-DU	Schleicher ASW 20	20124	
D-3331-FLM	Schempp-Hirth Duo Discus	21	G-CHNN, D-4073
D-3332-HO	Schempp-Hirth Discus-2b	98	HA-4503, D-7072
D-3333	Start & Flug H101 Salto	51	
D-3334-JH	Schleicher ASH 25	25017	HB-3335, D-3125, HB-1920
D-3335	Pilatus B4-PC11AF	308	
D-3336	Schleicher ASW 24B	24239	
D-3337	Glasflügel H 301B Libelle	96	I-BROC
D-3338	Schempp-Hirth Standard Cirrus	461G	I-NMCV
D-3339	Scheibe SF 34	5106	
D-3340-Ac2	Schempp-Hirth Duo Discus	70	
D-3342	Scheibe SF 34	5108	
D-3344-44	Rolladen-Schneider LS3-a	3383	PH-1420, F-CESJ
D-3345	LET L-13 Blanik	025605	OY-VXH
D-3346	LET L-13 Blanik	026807	
D-3347	Schempp-Hirth Discus-2b	104	HB-3327
D-3349	SZD-9bis Bocian 1E	P-596	DDR-3389, DM-3389
D-3350	Schempp-Hirth Discus-2c	28	
D-3351-WH	Glaser-Dirks DG-300 Elan	3E73	
D-3352	Schempp-Hirth Duo Discus	253	
D-3354	Sportine Aviacija LAK-19	25	
D-3355-4S	Rolladen-Schneider LS4	4035	
D-3356	Schleicher ASW 27B	27185	OK-7272
D-3357-4A	Rolladen-Schneider LS8-a	8187	
D-3358-1A	Rolladen-Schneider LS4	4031	
D-3359-EVA	Rolladen-Schneider LS4	4036	
D-3360	Rolladen-Schneider LS4	4046	
D-3363	Schempp-Hirth Mini-Nimbus C	112	
D-3364-OM	Schempp-Hirth Duo Discus	154	
D-3365-SH	Schempp-Hirth Discus CS	304CS	OK-3305
D-3366-KH	Rolladen-Schneider LS4-b	4998	
D-3367	SZD-9bis Bocian 1E	P-547	DDR-3360, DM-3360
D-3370	Schleicher ASK 21	21295	
D-3371	Schempp-Hirth Nimbus-2C	193	
D-3372-SB	Schleicher ASK 21	21296	
D-3373-ZB	Schempp-Hirth Ventus-2c	35/91	
D-3374-ED	Schleicher ASW 20L	20244	
D-3375-OS	Schleicher ASW 19B	19283	
D-3376	SZD-9bis Bocian 1E	P-564	DDR-3374, DM-3374
D-3378	Schleicher ASW 20L	20250	
D-3379	Schleicher ASW 20	20252	
D-3380	Schleicher ASW 19B	19292	
D-3381	Schleicher Ka 6E	4034	OH-338, OH-RSX
D-3382-JOY	Schempp-Hirth Duo Discus	283	
D-3383	Schleicher ASW 20	20295	
D-3384-3G	Schleicher ASW 19B	19299	
D-3385	Glaser-Dirks DG-300 Elan	3E188	
D-3386	Schleicher ASW 20	20298	
D-3388-88	Glasflügel H303 Mosquito	84	
D-3389-CO	Glasflügel H303 Mosquito	85	
D-3391-91	Rolladen-Schneider LS4	4563	
D-3392-92	Rolladen-Schneider LS4-b	4895	
D-3393	SZD-9bis Bocian 1E	P-634	DDR-3397, DM-3397
D-3394-TU	Rolladen-Schneider LS7	7065	
D-3395	Rolladen-Schneider LS7-WL	7066	
D-3396	Rolladen-Schneider LS4-b	4810	
D-3397-BE	Rolladen-Schneider LS4-a	4811	
D-3398	Glaser-Dirks DG-300 Club Elan	3E454C78	
D-3399	Schleicher ASW 19	19095	
D-3401	Schleicher Ka 6CR Rhönsegler	6208	HB-774
D-3402	Valentin Mistral C	MC 025/81	D-4925
D-3403-MM	Glasflügel H304	245	F-CEBR
D-3404	Glaser-Dirks DG-600	6-34	
D-3405-ZI	Rolladen-Schneider LS6	6080	
D-3406-4M	Rolladen-Schneider LS4	4565	
D-3408-7H	Rolladen-Schneider LS4	4567	
D-3409	SZD-9bis Bocian 1E	P-486	DDR-3209, DM-3209
D-3410	Schleicher ASW 20CL	20768	
D-3411-23	Schleicher ASK 23B	23003	
D-3412	Schleicher ASW 20C	20769	
D-3413	Schleicher ASW 20C	20770	
D-3414	Schleicher ASK 21	21230	
D-3415	Schleicher ASK 21	21229	
D-3416-B1	Schleicher ASW 20CL	20773	
D-3417	Schleicher ASK 21	21233	
D-3418	Schleicher ASW 20C	20784	
D-3419-19	Schleicher ASW 20C	20777	
D-3420-YD	Schleicher ASW 20C	20783	
D-3421	Schleicher ASW 20CL	20788	
D-3422	SZD-36A Cobra 15	W-569	HA-4004, PH-836, D-0929
D-3423	Schleicher ASW 20C	20789	
D-3424-DT	Schempp-Hirth Duo Discus	174	
D-3425	Schleicher ASW 23	23013	
D-3426-BN	Schleicher ASW 20CL	20794	
D-3427	Schleicher ASW 23	23017	
D-3428-UF	Schleicher ASW 20C	20796	
D-3429	Schleicher ASK 21	21247	
D-3430	SZD-9bis Bocian 1E	P-490	D-7213, DDR-3213, DM-3213
D-3431	Schleicher ASW 20C	20811	
D-3432	SZD-48-3 Jantar Standard 3	B-1942	DDR-2432

Regn	Type	c/n	Previous identities
D-3433-LAU	Schleicher ASK 21	21257	
D-3435	SZD-48-3 Jantar Standard 3	B-1945	DDR-2435
D-3437	Rolladen-Schneider LS4	4443	
D-3438-38	Schleicher ASK 13	13556	OO-YBV, PL66
D-3440	Rolladen-Schneider LS4	4447	
D-3441-B4	Rolladen-Schneider LS8-a	8163	
D-3442-V7	Rolladen-Schneider LS4	4455	
D-3444-S6	Rolladen-Schneider LS4	4449	
D-3445-69	Rolladen-Schneider LS4	4457	
D-3447-L4	Rolladen-Schneider LS4-a	4814	
D-3450-L1	Schempp-Hirth Discus-2c	32	
D-3451	Schleicher ASK 21	21548	
D-3452	Rolladen-Schneider LS4	4464	
D-3453	Rolladen-Schneider LS4-b	4816	
D-3454-54	Rolladen-Schneider LS4-a	4817	
D-3455	Rolladen-Schneider LS4	4475	
D-3456-01	Glaser-Dirks DG-100G Elan	E130G98	LX-CDE(1)
D-3457-57	Schempp-Hirth Standard Cirrus	622	HB-1284
D-3458-WY	Schempp-Hirth Ventus-2c	58/169	
D-3459-AN	Rolladen-Schneider LS4	4480	
D-3460	Glaser-Dirks DG-500 Elan Trainer	5E130T56	
D-3461	Schleicher ASK 21	21386	
D-3462	Schleicher ASK 21	21387	
D-3463-RS	Schleicher ASK 21 (Ditched 19.6.16)	21550	
D-3464	Schleicher ASK 21	21388	
D-3466	Schleicher ASW 24	24018	
D-3467	Schleicher ASK 21	21389	
D-3468	Schleicher ASK 21	21390	
D-3469-SI	Schleicher ASK 21	21391	
D-3470-FL	Schleicher ASW 28-18	28522	
D-3471-FGT	Schempp-Hirth Discus CS	270CS	
D-3472	Schempp-Hirth Duo Discus	112	
D-3473-GG	Glaser-Dirks DG-300 Elan	3E412	I-MIGG
D-3474	Schleicher ASH 25	25054	
D-3475-B5	Schleicher ASK 21	21393	
D-3476	Schleicher ASK 21	21396	
D-3477-FR	Schleicher ASH 25	25049	
D-3478	Rolladen-Schneider LS4	4512	
D-3479-IEI	Rolladen-Schneider LS4 (P 4.13)	4513	
D-3480-MM	Schempp-Hirth Ventus c	546	
D-3481	Schleicher ASW 24	24214	
D-3482	Schleicher ASK 21	21584	
D-3483	Rolladen-Schneider LS6-c	6197	
D-3484-B	Rolladen-Schneider LS4	4531	
D-3485	Rolladen-Schneider LS4	4530	
D-3486	Rolladen-Schneider LS8-18	8135	
D-3487	Rolladen-Schneider LS4	4528	
D-3488-FA	Schempp-Hirth Discus CS	127CS	
D-3489-E3	Rolladen-Schneider LS4	4526	
D-3490	Schleicher ASK 21	21260	
D-3491	Schleicher ASW 20BL	20677	
D-3492	Schleicher ASK 23	23027	
D-3493-MT	Schleicher ASW 20C	20824	
D-3494	Schleicher ASW 19B	19418	
D-3495-KM	Schleicher ASW 20CL	20820	
D-3496	Schleicher ASK 23	23033	
D-3497	Schleicher ASK 23	23040	
D-3498-YP	Schleicher ASK 23	23044	
D-3499-IX	Schempp-Hirth Ventus-2c	34/90	
D-3500	Grob G 102 Speed Astir IIB	4082	
D-3501	Grob G102 Astir CS	1126	HB-1301
D-3502-02	Rolladen-Schneider LS4-b	4821	
D-3503	Rolladen-Schneider LS4-b	4822	
D-3505	Schleicher ASW 20CL	20736	
D-3506	Fauvel AV 36C	201	OE-0506
D-3507	Schleicher ASW 20C (Permit)	20724	
D-3508-F1	Rolladen-Schneider LS4	4213	
D-3509	Rolladen-Schneider LS4-b	4823	
D-3510	Grob G 103A Twin II Acro	3657-K-26	
D-3511	Grob G 102 Club Astir IIIB	5571CB	
D-3512	Grob G 102 Club Astir IIIB	5572CB	
D-3513	SZD-9bis Bocian 1E	P-726	DDR-3013, DM-3013
D-3514	Rolladen-Schneider LS3-17	3154	
D-3515-1A	Rolladen-Schneider LS4	4524	
D-3516	Rolladen-Schneider LS4	4521	
D-3517-INF	Rolladen-Schneider LS3-17	3226	OO-YPR, D-4573
D-3518-J2	Schempp-Hirth Discus b	448	
D-3519	Schempp-Hirth Janus C	148	OO-ZCE
D-3522-HM	Schleicher ASW 22	22035	
D-3523-FS	Rolladen-Schneider LS3-17	3330	
D-3525	Schleicher ASW 19B	19380	
D-3526	Rolladen-Schneider LS4-b	4824	
D-3527	Rolladen-Schneider LS4-b	4912	
D-3528-DV	Rolladen-Schneider LS4-a	4826	
D-3529-IX	Schempp-Hirth Discus b	471	
D-3530	Rolladen-Schneider LS3-17	3322	
D-3533-ZS	Schempp-Hirth Ventus b/16.6	145	
D-3534-4V	Schempp-Hirth Janus C	218	OO-ZJK, HB-1829
D-3535	Glasflügel H201B Standard Libelle	142	
D-3536	Glasflügel Standard Libelle 201B	590	F-CELE
D-3537-F1	Schempp-Hirth Discus CS	057CS	OO-ZHZ
D-3538	Rolladen-Schneider LS3-a	3434	
D-3539	Rolladen-Schneider LS4-b	4841	
D-3540	SZD-9bis Bocian 1E	P-461	DDR-3040, DM-3040
D-3541-LS	Rolladen-Schneider LS4	4570	
D-3542-VV	Rolladen-Schneider LS4	4571	
D-3544-UU	Schleicher ASK 21	21297	
D-3545-45	Rolladen-Schneider LS3-17	3282	
D-3546-DS	Schleicher ASW 20C	20805	
D-3547-IEB	Rolladen-Schneider LS8-a	8071	
D-3548	SZD-9bis Bocian 1E	P-527	DDR-3240, DM-3240
D-3549	Schleicher Ka 6 Rhönsegler	198	
D-3550	Glasflügel H303 Mosquito B	194	
D-3551-Y8	Schempp-Hirth Ventus b/16.6	76	
D-3552-1Y	Schempp-Hirth Ventus a/16.6	1	
D-3553	Rolladen-Schneider LS4	4071	
D-3554	Glasflügel H401 Kestrel	81	OE-5344
D-3555	Schleicher Ka 6CR Rhönsegler	788	
D-3556-EP	Rolladen-Schneider LS4	4360	
D-3557-MS	Rolladen-Schneider LS4	4408	
D-3558	Bölkow Phoebus C	770	OE-0718
D-3559	Rolladen-Schneider LS4	4104	
D-3560	Schleicher Ka 6BR Rhönsegler	360	
D-3561-T	Rolladen-Schneider LS4	4078	
D-3562	Schleicher ASW 20C	20750	
D-3563	Schleicher ASW 19B	19405	
D-3564	Rolladen-Schneider LS4-b	4877	
D-3565	Schleicher K 8B	480	D-KAMP, D-3565
D-3566-X2	Grob G 103A Twin II Acro	3814-K-75	
D-3567-LT	Grob G 103A Twin II Acro	3827-K-84	
D-3568	SZD-9bis Bocian 1E	P-753	DDR-3068, DM-3068
D-3569	Grob G 103A Twin II Acro	3826-K-83	
D-3571-2M	Rolladen-Schneider LS8-a	8086	
D-3572-FUN	Bölkow Phoebus B-1 (P. 11.13)	721	SE-TII
D-3573	Schleicher ASW 20C	20848	
D-3574-YX	Rolladen-Schneider LS4	4070	
D-3575	Rolladen-Schneider LS4-b	41050	
D-3577	Rolladen-Schneider LS4	4109	
D-3578-W8	Rolladen-Schneider LS4	4110	
D-3579	Grunau Baby IIB (P 13.7.16)	11	
D-3580	DG Flugzeugbau DG-300 Elan Acro	3E479A22	
D-3581-ii	Rolladen-Schneider LS4	4331	
D-3582	Rolladen-Schneider LS4-a	4818	
D-3583-11	Rolladen-Schneider LS4-b	4819	
D-3584	Schleicher Rhönlerche II (P. 6.12)	55	
D-3585	Glaser-Dirks DG-300 Elan	3E44	
D-3587-PE	Schleicher ASW 24	24210	
D-3588	SZD-50-3 Puchacz	B-2112	
D-3589	Schleicher ASK 21	21299	
D-3590	SZD-9bis Bocian 1E	P-599	DDR-3390, DM-3390
D-3592	Rolladen-Schneider LS4-b	4844	
D-3593-22	Schleicher ASW 22BL	22063	SP-3595, D-4651
D-3594	Schleicher K 8B	8510/A	D-1267
D-3595	Centrair ASW 20FL	20183	OM-3596, BGA 2722
D-3596	Rolladen-Schneider LS8-a (P 4.10)	8048	
D-3598	Rolladen-Schneider LS8-a	8042	
D-3599	Grob G 103C Twin III Acro	34149	D-KGSL
D-3600	Glasflügel Standard Libelle 201B	177	N66SC
D-3601	Schleicher K 7 Rhönadler	7043	
D-3602	Glasflügel H201B Standard Libelle	362	OO-ZJX, F-CEBL
D-3603-MF	SZD-50-3 Puchacz	B-1087	DDR-3603
D-3604-VF	Schempp-Hirth Discus-2b	16	
D-3605-70	Rolladen-Schneider LS8-a	8049	
D-3607-2V	Schempp-Hirth Duo Discus	419	
D-3608	Rolladen-Schneider LS4-b	41024	
D-3609	Rolladen-Schneider LS4-b	4828	
D-3610-TUM	DG Flugzeugbau DG-1000S	10-50S49	
D-3611	SZD-50-3 Puchacz	B-1328	DDR-3611
D-3612-ZZ	Rolladen-Schneider LS4-a	4829	
D-3613-B1	Rolladen-Schneider LS4-b	4830	
D-3614	Schleicher K 8B	8310	
D-3615	Schleicher Ka 6CR Rhönsegler	6238	
D-3616-F1	Rolladen-Schneider LS4	4580	
D-3617-76	SZD-50-3 Puchacz	B-1388	DDR-3627
D-3618-PV	Schleicher ASW 28-18	28501	
D-3619	Schleicher K 10A	10002	
D-3620	SZD-50-3 Puchacz	B-1344	DDR-3625
D-3621	Schleicher Ka 3	102	D-4047
D-3622	Schleicher K 8B	8398	
D-3623-OU	Schleicher K 8B	8408	
D-3624	Schleicher ASW 24	24035	
D-3626-GP	Rolladen-Schneider LS8-a	8087	
D-3627-5	Schleicher ASW 27	27130	
D-3628	Rolladen-Schneider LS4	4582	
D-3629	Schleicher K 10A	10012	
D-3630	SZD-50-3 Puchacz	B-1465	DDR-3639
D-3631	SZD-50-3 Puchacz	B-1400	DDR-3634
D-3632	Scheibe L-Spatz III	812	
D-3633	Schleicher K 8B	8532	
D-3633	Schempp-Hirth Duo Discus XL	635	
D-3634	Schleicher K 8B	8531	
D-3635	SZD-24-4A Foka 4	W-294	
D-3636-2V	Schempp-Hirth Ventus-2c (P.05)	80	N366DW
D-3637	Grunau Baby IIB	04304	
D-3638	Schleicher ASK 21	21282	
D-3639	SZD-24-4A Foka 4	W-239	
D-3640	Glasflügel H 301 Libelle	11	OO-ZMM, D-8897
D-3641	Schleicher ASW 20CL	20752	
D-3643	Lanaverre CS 11/75L Standard Cirrus	24	F-CEVQ
D-3644	SZD-50-3 Puchacz	B-1474	DDR-3644
D-3645	Schleicher K 8B	8635	
D-3646-EW	Bölkow Phoebus A-1	764	
D-3647	Schleicher K 8B	8633	
D-3648	Schleicher Ka 6CR Rhönsegler	6567	
D-3649	SZD-50-3 Puchacz	B-1480	DDR-3648
D-3650	Rolladen-Schneider LS6-a	6036	
D-3651	SZD-50-3 Puchacz	B-1535	DDR-3651
D-3652	SZD-50-3 Puchacz	B-1542	DDR-3658
D-3653	Rolladen-Schneider LS6-a	6039	ZK-GHH, D-3653
D-3654	Focke-Wulf Weihe 50	3	D-5097
D-3655	SZD-50-3 Puchacz	B-1540	DDR-3656
D-3656	Grob G103C Twin III Acro	34168	I-IVVQ
D-3657	Schleicher Ka 6E	4084	
D-3658	Schleicher K 8B	8711	
D-3659-BY	Rolladen-Schneider LS4	4389	
D-3660-H6	Schempp-Hirth Discus-2b	(22)/158	(D-KJSM)
D-3661	SZD-30 Pirat	W-318	
D-3662	Fauvel AV-36C	573	
D-3663-MB	Glaser-Dirks DG-100	74	HB-1327
D-3665	SZD-50-3 Puchacz	B-1552	DDR-3661
D-3666-MiO	Schempp-Hirth Discus b	503	OE-5564
D-3667-TM	Scheibe L-Spatz III	241	
D-3668	Rolladen-Schneider LS4	4572	
D-3669	Rolladen-Schneider LS4	4573	
D-3670	Schleicher ASK 13	13082	
D-3671	SZD-50-3 Puchacz	B-1394	DDR-3631
D-3672	Rolladen-Schneider LS4	4574	
D-3674	Grob G 103C Twin III Acro (Permit)	34186	
D-3675	Glaser-Dirks DG-300 Elan	3E305	I-IPER
D-3676	SZD-50-3 Puchacz	B-1387	DDR-3626
D-3678-JU	Rolladen-Schneider LS4	4166	
D-3679-WH	Schleicher ASK 21	21588	
D-3680-LW	Rolladen-Schneider LS8-a	8110	

Registration	Type	Serial	Notes
D-3681	Rolladen-Schneider LS4	4241	
D-3682-CA	Rolladen-Schneider LS6-c	6328	
D-3683-JC	Schempp-Hirth Standard Cirrus	465G	
D-3684	SZD-50-3 Puchacz	B-1331	DDR-3614
D-3685	SZD-9bis Bocian 1E	P-522	DDR-3385, DM-3385
D-3686-MK	Rolladen-Schneider LS1-f	198	
D-3687	SZD-50-3 Puchacz	B-1479	DDR-3647
D-3688-88	Schempp-Hirth Standard Cirrus	447	
D-3689-GM	Schempp-Hirth Standard Cirrus	457	
D-3690	Glaser-Dirks DG-300 Elan	3E74	HB-1776
D-3691-AV	Schempp-Hirth Standard Cirrus	464G	
D-3692	Schempp-Hirth Standard Cirrus	467G	
D-3693-I	Schleicher ASW 15B	15268	HB-1093
D-3694	Glasflügel H401 Kestrel	109	
D-3695-JG	Grob G 103C Twin III Acro	34133	
D-3696-D3	Grob G 103C Twin III Acro	34131	
D-3697-ES	Grob G 103C Twin III Acro	34127	
D-3699	Scheibe Bergfalke IV	5841	
D-3700	Scheibe Bergfalke IV	5842	
D-3701-2C	Schempp-Hirth Discus-2c	25	
D-3702-KT	Schempp-Hirth Discus CS	226CS	
D-3703	Glasflügel H401 Kestrel	110	
D-3704	Glasflügel H201B Standard Libelle	552	
D-3707-SR	Glasflügel H201B Standard Libelle	561	
D-3708-M5	Rolladen-Schneider LS4-b	4846	
D-3709	Pilatus B4-PC11A	115	
D-3710	LET L-13 Blanik	026018	
D-3711-89	Grob G102 Astir CS	1216	HA-4492, D-7289
D-3712	Glasflügel H401 Kestrel	112	
D-3713	Rolladen-Schneider LS3-a	3283	
D-3715	Glasflügel H201B Standard Libelle	568	
D-3716	Rolladen-Schneider LS8-a	8111OK-8818,	D-4518
D-3717-RP	Rolladen-Schneider LS1-f	295	
D-3718	Rolladen-Schneider LS8-s	8506	
D-3719-L	SZD-48-3 Jantar-Standard 3	B-1300	SP-3226
D-3721	Schleicher ASK 21	21723	
D-3722	Glaser-Dirks DG-300 Elan	3E232	
D-3723	Rolladen-Schneider LS4-b	4848	
D-3725-M1	Rolladen-Schneider LS8-a (P 13.4.16)	8053	
D-3728	Glaser-Dirks DG-100	10	
D-3729	Pilatus B4-PC11	137	
D-3730	Rolladen-Schneider LS4-b	4850	
D-3731	Glaser-Dirks DG-100 Elan	E162	HB-1731
D-3733	Glaser-Dirks DG-300 Elan	3E116	
D-3735	Marganski Swift S-1	115	HB-3135
D-3736	Glaser-Dirks DG-100	28	
D-3737	Glaser-Dirks DG-100	29	
D-3738-HP	Glaser-Dirks DG-300 Elan	3E49	HB-1754
D-3739	Glaser-Dirks DG-100	32	
D-3740	Glaser-Dirks DG-100	38	
D-3742	SZD-50-3 Puchacz	B-1472	DDR-3642
D-3743	Schleicher ASK 18	18016	
D-3744	Schleicher ASK 13	13524	
D-3745	Schleicher ASK 18	18018	
D-3746	Schleicher ASK 13	13525	
D-3747	Glaser-Dirks DG-300 Elan	3E-179	OO-ZZG, D-5702
D-3748-6D	Schleicher ASK 18	18020	
D-3750	Schleicher ASW 19	19003	
D-3752	Schleicher ASW 15B	15451	
D-3753	Schleicher ASK 13	13533	
D-3754	Schleicher ASW 19	19005	
D-3755	Schleicher ASW 19	19006	
D-3756	Schleicher ASK 13	13534	
D-3757-B4	Rolladen-Schneider LS4-b	4854	
D-3759	Rolladen-Schneider LS8-18	8313	
D-3760	Schleicher ASK 13	13535	
D-3763	Schleicher ASK 13	13536	
D-3764-6Z	Rolladen-Schneider LS8-a	8055	
D-3765-LL	Schleicher ASW 24	24081	
D-3766-PS	Schleicher ASK 21	21453	
D-3769	Glaser-Dirks DG-100 Elan	E29	
D-3770-2D	Schempp-Hirth Discus-2c	24	
D-3771	Glaser-Dirks DG-100G Elan	E25G189	
D-3772-DE	Schempp-Hirth Ventus-2b	84	
D-3773	Glaser-Dirks DG-100 Elan	E23	
D-3774	Glaser-Dirks DG-100G Elan	E21G11	
D-3775	Glaser-Dirks DG-100G Elan	E22G12	
D-3776-SK	Rolladen-Schneider LS4-b	4855	
D-3777-77	Glasflügel Club Libelle 205	80	
D-3778	Grob G 102 Club Astir III	5550C	
D-3779	Grob G 103 Twin II	3668	
D-3781-RO	Grob G 103 Twin II	3659	
D-3783	Schempp-Hirth Nimbus-2B	144	
D-3784	Schempp-Hirth Nimbus-2B	146	
D-3785	Schempp-Hirth Janus	39	
D-3786	SZD-30 Pirat	B-429	DDR-1786, DM-1786
D-3790	Grob G 102 Club Astir III	5577C	
D-3791	Schleicher ASK 21	21454	
D-3792	Schleicher ASW 24	24085	
D-3793-RCD	Schleicher ASK 21	21457	
D-3795-PK	Schempp-Hirth HS-7 Mini-Nimbus		
D-3796	Glaser-Dirks DG-200/17C	2-111CL03	
D-3797	Glaser-Dirks DG-200/17	2-110/1718	
D-3798	Glaser-Dirks DG-200/17C	2-108CL01	
D-3799-Y1	Schempp-Hirth Discus-2a	33	
D-3800	*Test Registration for DG Flugzeugbau production*		
D-3802-B8	Glaser-Dirks DG-100G	98G14	
D-3803-HX	Glaser-Dirks DG-100G	97G13	
D-3806	Glaser-Dirks DG-100G	101G15	
D-3807	SZD-50-3 Puchacz	B-1093	DDR-3607
D-3811	Glaser-Dirks DG-200/17	2-107/1717	
D-3812-D12	Schempp-Hirth Discus b	191	F-CGGK, F-WGGK
D-3813-HM	Grob G 102 Astir CS Jeans	2190	
D-3814	Grob G 102 Astir CS Jeans	2191	
D-3815	Grob G 102 Astir CS Jeans	2192	
D-3816-H8	Rolladen-Schneider LS4-b	41018	
D-3818	SZD-30 Pirat	B-492	DDR-1818, DM-1818
D-3819	Grob G 102 Astir CS Jeans	2199	
D-3821-HA	Schleicher ASK 21	21646	
D-3822-22	Schempp-Hirth Duo Discus	652	
D-3826-CH	Grob G 102 Astir CS Jeans	2212	
D-3827-GO	Schleicher ASW 27B	27174	G-CKRM, BGA 5304, EI-GMA, EI-151
D-3828	Grob G 102 Astir CS Jeans	2215	
D-3829	SZD-50-3 Puchacz	B-1390	DDR-3629
D-3830	Grob G 102 Astir CS Jeans	2217	
D-3831-D2	Schempp-Hirth Discus-2b	23	PH-1160
D-3834-SL	Schempp-Hirth Janus Ce	279	
D-3837	Rolladen-Schneider LS4	4363	I-FACG
D-3838-MW	Glaser-Dirks DG-300 Club Elan Acro	3E435C73A4	OE-5532
D-3839	Grob G 102 Speed Astir II	4013	
D-3840-E	Schempp-Hirth Ventus-2c	22/58	
D-3841-WD	Schleicher ASW 19B (P. 9.15)	19092	
D-3844	Glaser-Dirks DG-600	6-2	HB-1944, D-0626
D-3846	Schleicher ASW 24	24087	
D-3848	Schleicher ASW 19	19099	
D-3850	Schleicher ASW 17	17052	
D-3851-B2	Schleicher ASK 21	21459	
D-3852	Schleicher ASW 24	24093	
D-3854	Schleicher ASK 13	13570	
D-3855-55	Schleicher ASW 19B	19103	
D-3856	Grunau Baby IIB	03	D-5739
D-3857-57	Schleicher ASK 21	21047	D-8807
D-3858	Schleicher ASK 13	13571	
D-3860-BW1	Schempp-Hirth Duo Discus	46	
D-3861	Schleicher ASW 20	20005	
D-3863	Schleicher ASW 19	19107	
D-3864	Schleicher ASK 13	13572	
D-3866	Schleicher ASK 21	21173	
D-3867-67	Schleicher ASK 21	21178	
D-3868	Schleicher ASK 21	21177	
D-3869	Rolladen-Schneider LS4	4045	
D-3870-TZ	Bölkow Phoebus C	939	
D-3871	Bölkow Phoebus C-2	954	
D-3872-X2	Rolladen-Schneider LS7	7145	
D-3876	Grob G102 Astir CS Jeans	2027	
D-3877-BLC	DG Flugzeugbau DG-500 Elan Orion	5E162X17	
D-3878-W2	Schempp-Hirth Duo Discus	188	G-CKOJ, BGA 5251, OE-5583
D-3880-VC	Rolladen-Schneider LS4-b	4858	
D-3881	Grob G 102 Astir CS Jeans	2035	
D-3882	DG Flugzeugbau DG-300 Club Elan Acro	3E477C85A21	
D-3883-83	Schempp-Hirth Discus b	92	
D-3884	Grob G 102 Astir CS Jeans	2039	
D-3886	Grob G 102 Astir CS Jeans	2042	
D-3887-SD	Schempp-Hirth Duo Discus	114	HB-3260, D-3887
D-3888	Grob G 102 Astir CS Jeans	2049	
D-3889	DG Flugzeugbau DG-303 Club Elan Acro	3E504C86A38	HB-3383
D-3890-NE	Grob G 102 Astir CS Jeans	2052	
D-3891	Grob G 102 Astir CS Jeans	2063	
D-3892	Grob G 102 Astir CS Jeans	2054	
D-3895	Rolladen-Schneider LS3	3104	
D-3896	Rolladen-Schneider LS3	3078	
D-3897	Rolladen-Schneider LS7	7149	
D-3900	Rolladen-Schneider LS3	3106	
D-3902-LO	Schempp-Hirth Discus-2b	36	
D-3903-1X	Rolladen-Schneider LS7	7150	
D-3904	Glaser-Dirks DG-500 Elan Orion	5E158X15	
D-3907	SZD-30 Pirat	S-03.47	DDR-1907, DM-1907
D-3908	Rolladen-Schneider LS4	4279	
D-3909	Rolladen-Schneider LS4	4283	
D-3910-IL	Rolladen-Schneider LS4	4289	
D-3911-IRL	Schleicher ASW 19B	19367	OO-YNP, D-8630
D-3912	Rolladen-Schneider LS3	3208	
D-3913	Schleicher ASK 21	21465	
D-3914	Schleicher ASK 21	21462	
D-3915	SZD-9bis Bocian 1E	P-728	DDR-3015, DM-3015
D-3916	Rolladen-Schneider LS3-ake (P. 14.9.16)	3341	
D-3917	Rolladen-Schneider LS3-ake (P 5.12)	3342	
D-3918-IHG	Schempp-Hirth Discus CS	069CS	
D-3919-TZ	Rolladen-Schneider LS7	7152	
D-3921	Rolladen-Schneider LS3-a	3296	
D-3922	Rolladen-Schneider LS3-a	3188	
D-3923	Grob G 102 Club Astir IIIB	5652CB	
D-3925	Rolladen-Schneider LS3-a	3151	
D-3926-MR	Rolladen-Schneider LS3-a	3155	
D-3927	Rolladen-Schneider LS3-a	3161	
D-3928-DV	Schleicher ASK 21	21397	
D-3929-FC	Schleicher ASK 21	21398	
D-3930-A4	Schleicher ASK 21	21399	
D-3931-DZ	Schleicher ASK 21	21401	
D-3932	Schleicher ASK 21	21402	
D-3933	Rolladen-Schneider LS3-17	3294	
D-3934-ET	Rolladen-Schneider LS8-18	8286	
D-3935	Rolladen-Schneider LS3-a	3408	
D-3936	Rolladen-Schneider LS3-a	3407	
D-3937	Rolladen-Schneider LS3-17	3268	
D-3939	Schleicher ASW 22	22020	
D-3940-40	Darmstadt D-40 (P 7.4.16)	41	
D-3941	SZD-9bis Bocian 1E	P-464	DDR-3041, DM-3041
D-3942-B	Rolladen-Schneider LS3-a	3202	
D-3946	Grob G 103 Twin Astir	3085	
D-3947	Grob G 103 Twin Astir	3086	
D-3948	Schempp-Hirth Ventus-2a	38	
D-3949-CL	Schempp-Hirth Duo Discus X	502	
D-3952-H1	Glaser-Dirks DG-300 Elan	3E468	
D-3954	Grob G 103 Twin Astir	3084	
D-3955	Schleicher ASK 21	21909	
D-3956	Schleicher Ka 6BR	305	D-1206
D-3957	Grob G 103 Twin Astir	3100	
D-3958-LX	Schempp-Hirth Duo Discus	224	
D-3959-PC	Schleicher ASH 25	25018	
D-3960-YJ	Schempp-Hirth Discus CS	072CS	
D-3961-PR	Schempp-Hirth Discus-2b	117	
D-3962-N1	Rolladen-Schneider LS8-a	8189	
D-3963	Rolladen-Schneider LS8-a	8090	
D-3964	Grob G 103 Twin II	3597	
D-3965	Grob G 103 Twin II	3598	
D-3966	Grob G 103 Twin II (P 7.10)	3599	
D-3967	Schleicher ASK 13	13268AB	
D-3968-FE	Schempp-Hirth Duo Discus	298	

Reg.	Type	c/n	Remarks
D-3969	Schleicher ASW 15B	15421	
D-3970-GB	Schleicher ASW 15B	15422	
D-3971	Schleicher ASK 13	13503	
D-3972	Schleicher ASW 15B	15423	
D-3974	Schleicher ASW 15B	15425	
D-3975	Schleicher ASW 17	17041	
D-3976-L8	Rolladen-Schneider LS8-a	8239	
D-3977-L5	Grob G102 Astir CS 77	1650	OY-XIA
D-3978	Schleicher ASK 13	13154	D-0226
D-3979	Schleicher ASW 15	15084	
D-3980-PC	Schleicher ASW 15B	15426	
D-3981-81	Schleicher ASW 15B	15434	
D-3982	Schleicher ASK 13	13505	
D-3983-6Y	Schleicher ASW 15B	15431	
D-3984	Schleicher ASW 15B	15432	
D-3986	Schleicher ASK 13	13507	
D-3987	Schleicher ASK 13	13508	
D-3988	SZD-50-3 Puchacz	B-2110	
D-3990	Schleicher ASW 15B	15435	
D-3992-AI	Schempp-Hirth Duo Discus	176	
D-3994-Z3	Schleicher ASK 21	21509	
D-3996	Grob G 102 Club Astir IIIB	5549CB	
D-3997-MZ	Glaser-Dirks DG-300 Elan	3E322	HB-1991
D-3998-8Y	Rolladen-Schneider LS1-f	262	
D-3999-99	Schleicher K 8B	8968AB	
D-4000	Scheibe SF 27A	6022	
D-4001	Glasflügel H401 Kestrel	64	PH-400, D-0972
D-4002-Wo	Schempp-Hirth Ventus-2cx (P.6.03)	82	
D-4004-FW	Schleicher ASW 19B	19112	
D-4005	Glaser-Dirks DG-300 Elan Acro	3E451A11	S5-3333
D-4006-OK	Glasflügel H205 Club Libelle	5	
D-4007	Focke-Wulf Kranich III	56	
D-4008	Schleicher Ka 6BR	491	OE-5008
D-4010-K5	Schempp-Hirth Duo Discus	100	
D-4011	Schleicher K 8B	126	
D-4012	Glasflügel H401 Kestrel	15	I-JOJO
D-4013	Schempp-Hirth Ventus b/16.6 (P. 4.11)	270	
D-4014-S2	Schempp-Hirth Discus b	57	
D-4015-1	HpH Glasflügel 304S Shark	010-S	OK-1011
D-4016	Start & Flug H-101 Salto	49	
D-4017-CH	Schempp-Hirth Discus b	79	
D-4018	Rolladen-Schneider LS4-b	4972	
D-4019-AP	Schleicher ASW 24	?	
D-4020-GD	Schempp-Hirth Duo Discus	183	
D-4021-ZP	Schempp-Hirth Duo Discus	202	
D-4022-L9	Schleicher Ka 6CR Rhönsegler	6409	
D-4023	Schleicher ASK 23B	23039	PH-765
D-4025	Schleicher ASW 15	15145	HB-1025
D-4027	SZD-9bis Bocian 1E	P-452	DDR-3027, DM-3027
D-4028-1G	Schempp-Hirth Ventus-2b	52	
D-4029-PH	Rolladen-Schneider LS4-b	4860	
D-4030	Rolladen-Schneider LS4-b	4973	
D-4031	Schleicher K 7 Rhönadler	890	
D-4032-YF	Schleicher ASK 21	21780	
D-4033	SZD-9bis Bocian 1E	P-457	DDR-3033, DM-3033
D-4034-KY	Schempp-Hirth Discus-2a	224	
D-4035	Grob G 103C Twin III Acro (P 4.5.16)	34148	
D-4036	Schleicher Ka 6CR Rhönsegler	1110	
D-4037	Scheibe SF 27A	6016	
D-4038	Schleicher Ka 2 Rhönschwalbe (P 20.6.16)	125	
D-4039	Schleicher K 7 Rhönadler	7083	
D-4040-E5	Glaser-Dirks DG-500 Elan Trainer	5E112T46	
D-4041	Schleicher Ka 6BR Rhönsegler	358	
D-4042	Rolladen-Schneider LS1-c	84	HB-1042
D-4043-F	Rolladen-Schneider LS4	4616	
D-4044-YR	Rolladen-Schneider LS4 (P 6.10)	4274	
D-4045	Schleicher Rhönlerche II	132	
D-4046-E7	Rolladen-Schneider LS4	4617	
D-4048-48	Schempp-Hirth Discus b	18	
D-4049	Schleicher Ka 6 Rhönsegler	280	
D-4050	Glasflügel Mosquito B	181	OH-569
D-4051	Schleicher ASK 21	21491	
D-4052-DU	Schempp-Hirth Duo Discus	81	
D-4053	Scheibe SF 34B	6107	
D-4054	Schleicher Ka 6BR Rhönsegler	525	
D-4057-T5	Akaflieg Braunschweig SB-5E Sperber	5042	BGA 4302/HYC, D-2009, BGA 3447/FQS, RAFGGA 200, D-2009
D-4059	Glasflügel H201B Standard Libelle	286	HB-1059
D-4060	Glaser-Dirks DG-300 Elan	3E416	CS-PCE, OE-5510
D-4061	Schempp-Hirth Ventus b/16.6	35	
D-4062	Schleicher K 8B	8417	
D-4064-8T	Rolladen-Schneider LS8-18	8240	
D-4065-12	Siebert Sie 3 (Permit 11.99)	3013	OY-XGZ, D-0778
D-4066	Schempp-Hirth Discus b	496	SE-UKV
D-4067	Schleicher Ka 6CR Rhönsegler	6226Si	
D-4068	Schleicher K 8B	755	
D-4070	Scheibe L-Spatz 55	718	
D-4072	Rolladen-Schneider LS6-a	6076	I-LVIT, D-3398
D-4073-LA1	Rolladen-Schneider LS8-a	8017	
D-4074-FM	Grob G 103C Twin III Acro	34139	
D-4075	Schleicher Ka 6E	4140	
D-4076	Schleicher K 7 Rhönadler	833	
D-4077	Schleicher Ka 6CR Rhönsegler	1070	
D-4079	Schleicher Ka 6E	4036	
D-4080-ZZ	Schleicher ASK 23B	23145	
D-4081-LD	Schempp-Hirth Ventus-2ax	173	
D-4082-N1	Grob G 103C Twin III Acro	34137	
D-4083	Schleicher Ka 6CR Rhönsegler	1074	
D-4084-37	SZD-48-3 Jantar-Standard 3	B-1944	D-2484, DDR-2434
D-4085-WS	SZD-48-1 Jantar Standard 2	B-1221	OE-5303
D-4087	Schleicher ASW 20L	20359	
D-4088-BK	Schleicher ASK 21	21029	
D-4089	Bölkow Phoebus B1	896	D-0334, F-CDOE
D-4090-XC	Schempp-Hirth Discus-2b	?	
D-4091-91	Schempp-Hirth Discus b	562	
D-4094-XF	Schempp-Hirth Duo Discus	107	
D-4095	Rolladen-Schneider LS6-c	6240	
D-4098-8B	Rolladen-Schneider LS8-a	8320	
D-4100	Schempp-Hirth Ventus-2ax	176	
D-4101	Glaser-Dirks DG-303 Elan Acro	3E444A7	LX-CRP
D-4102-LW	Glaser-Dirks DG-100G Elan	E165G131	
D-4103-FU	Rolladen-Schneider LS4-b	4862	
D-4104-MZ	Rolladen-Schneider LS4-b	4974	
D-4105-05	Rolladen-Schneider LS4	4351	
D-4107	Rolladen-Schneider LS6-c	6241	
D-4108	Schempp-Hirth Duo Discus	143	
D-4109	Schempp-Hirth Duo Discus	194	
D-4110	Rolladen-Schneider LS4-b	4863	
D-4111-HP	Schempp-Hirth Ventus-2bxR (P.05)	128	
D-4113	PZL PW-5 Smyk	17.03.009	PH-1063
D-4114-DJ	Schempp-Hirth Discus CS	114CS	OO-ZTU
D-4115-HR	Schempp-Hirth Ventus-2a	27	D-4111 (1)
D-4116	Schleicher Rhönlerche II (Res.12.02)	3072Br	BGA 4116/HQH, (BGA 4097), HB-877
D-4117	Schleicher K 8B	8583	
D-4118	Schleicher K 8B	8606	
D-4119	Rolladen-Schneider LS8-a	8164	
D-4120	Schleicher Ka 6CR Rhönsegler	6566	
D-4121	Schleicher Ka 6CR Rhönsegler (P 12.9.16)	6593	
D-4122	Schleicher Ka 6CR	6582	
D-4123	Scheibe SF 34B	5122	
D-4124-4A	Rolladen-Schneider LS4-b	4942	
D-4125	Schleicher Ka 6CR Rhönsegler	6612	
D-4126	Schleicher Ka 6CR Rhönsegler	6610	
D-4127	Schleicher Ka 6E	4107	
D-4128	Schleicher Ka 6E	4100	
D-4129	Schleicher Ka 6CR Rhönsegler	6654	
D-4130-30	Glaser-Dirks DG-100G Elan	E189G155	
D-4132-GL	Schleicher Ka 6CR Rhönsegler	6509Si	
D-4133	Schleicher ASK 13	13067	
D-4134	Schleicher ASK 13	13066	
D-4135	Schleicher ASK 13	13075	
D-4136	Schleicher K 8B	8746	
D-4137	Glaser-Dirks DG-200	2-92	I-LUKA
D-4138	Scheibe Zugvogel IIIA	1056	
D-4139	Schempp-Hirth Discus CS	112CS	
D-4140	Schleicher ASK 13	13620AB	
D-4141-TX	Schleicher ASW 19B	19085	
D-4142	Schleicher ASK 13	13621AB	
D-4144-44	Grob G 103C Twin III Acro	34171	HB-3102
D-4145	Pilatus B4-PC11AF	197	
D-4146	Pilatus B4-PC11AF	202	
D-4147-XI	Schempp-Hirth Ventus c	285	
D-4148	Rolladen-Schneider LS4-b	41025	
D-4149	Schempp-Hirth Discus CS	247CS	
D-4150-DD	Schempp-Hirth Duo Discus	278	
D-4151	SZD-41A Jantar Standard	B-739	
D-4152	Schempp-Hirth Mini-Nimbus C	152	
D-4153	Rolladen-Schneider LS6-b	6191	HB-3019, D-5026
D-4154	Schleicher K 8B	8808	PH-413
D-4156-JO	Rolladen-Schneider LS8-a	8209	OO-YBM
D-4157	SZD-41A Jantar Standard	B-879	
D-4158-HS	Glaser-Dirks DG-100G Elan	E190G156	
D-4159-D1	Glaser-Dirks DG-100G Elan	E191G157	
D-4160	Schempp-Hirth Discus b	416	
D-4161	Schleicher Ka 6CR Rhönsegler	6299	
D-4162	SZD-41A Jantar Standard	B-857	
D-4163	Grob G 102 Astir CS	1103	
D-4164	Grob G 102 Astir CS	1104	
D-4166-D6	Grob G 102 Astir CS	1106	
D-4167-AP	HpH Glasflügel 304C	75-C	
D-4168	Grob G 102 Astir CS	1108	
D-4169-XL	Schempp-Hirth Duo Discus	179	
D-4170-T5	Grob G 102 Astir CS	1110	
D-4171	Grob G 102 Astir CS	1111	
D-4172	Scheibe SF 34B	5137	
D-4173	Glaser-Dirks DG-100G Elan (P.05)	E173G139	
D-4174-IHB	Rolladen-Schneider LS4-b	4975	
D-4175	Scheibe SF 34B	5135	
D-4176	Glaser-Dirks DG-500/20 Elan	5E159W7	
D-4177	Glaser-Dirks DG-300 Club Elan Acro	3E463C83A17	
D-4180	Grob G 102 Astir CS	1136	
D-4181	Grob G 102 Astir CS	1134	
D-4182	DG Flugzeugbau DG-500 Elan Orion	5E177X29	S5-7515
D-4183	Schleicher ASK 21	21531	
D-4184	Rolladen-Schneider LS4	4184	N29798
D-4185	Glasflügel H304	243	
D-4186	Glasflügel H304	244	
D-4187	Grob G 102 Astir CS 77	1754	I-IVBD
D-4188	Rolladen-Schneider LS4	4034	
D-4189	Rolladen-Schneider LS4-b (Dbr 7.5.16)	41014	
D-4190-DZ	Rolladen-Schneider LS4	4041	
D-4191	Schempp-Hirth Standard Cirrus	408G	HB-1191
D-4192-2H	Schleicher ASK 21	21532	
D-4194	Schleicher ASK 21	21533	
D-4196-NE	Grob G 102 Astir CS	1222	
D-4198	Grob G 102 Astir CS	1224	
D-4199-H1	Schempp-Hirth Duo Discus	387	
D-4200	SZD-55-1	551197097	
D-4201	Scheibe SF 34B	5123	
D-4203	Scheibe SF 34B	5128	
D-4204	Grob G 102 Astir CS	1230	
D-4205-SVB	Schleicher ASK 21	21536	
D-4206	Grob G 102 Astir CS	1232	
D-4207	Glaser-Dirks DG-200	2-60	I-LFOX
D-4208	Schleicher ASK 21	21537	
D-4209-GW	Grob G 102 Astir CS	1235	
D-4210	Grob G 102 Astir CS	1241	
D-4211	Grob G 102 Astir CS	1242	
D-4212-LW	Schempp-Hirth Duo Discus	12	
D-4213-SO	Schempp-Hirth Duo Discus	105	
D-4214	Grob G 102 Astir CS	1245	
D-4215	Schempp-Hirth Discus-2a	242	
D-4216	Schempp-Hirth Standard Cirrus	429	HB-1217
D-4217	Grob G 102 Astir CS	1317	
D-4218-WX	Schempp-Hirth Duo Discus	169	
D-4219	Rolladen-Schneider LS6-c	6375	HB-3219
D-4220-20	Schleicher ASK 21	21525	
D-4221	Grob G 102 Astir CS	1322	
D-4222-CG	SZD-42-2 Jantar 2B	B-1383	DOSAAF
D-4224	Schleicher ASW 20	20297	

Regn	Type	C/n	Prev. id.
D-4225-IH	Schleicher ASW 20L	20321	
D-4226	Schleicher ASW 20	20303	
D-4227	Schempp-Hirth Discus CS	279CS	
D-4228-28	Schleicher ASW 20L	20306	
D-4230	Rolladen-Schneider LS4-b	4976	
D-4231-BK	Schempp-Hirth Duo Discus	82	
D-4232	Schleicher ASK 21	21527	
D-4233	Scheibe SF 34B	5130	
D-4234	Scheibe SF 34B	5129	
D-4235-LC	Rolladen-Schneider LS4	4019	
D-4236	Akaflieg Braunschweig SB-5B Sperber	5024A	
D-4238-RF	Rolladen-Schneider LS4	4125	
D-4239-EG	Schempp-Hirth Ventus-2b	89	PH-1164, D-4207
D-4240-M3	Schempp-Hirth Discus CS	315CS	
D-4242-HW	Schleicher ASW 17	17042	OH-471
D-4243	Rolladen-Schneider LS4	4132	
D-4244-WS	Rolladen-Schneider LS4	4167	
D-4245-F2	Rolladen-Schneider LS4	4127	
D-4246	Rolladen-Schneider LS4 (P. 8.14)	4144	
D-4247-BX	Rolladen-Schneider LS4	4135	
D-4248	Rolladen-Schneider LS4	4130	
D-4249	Grunau Baby III	83	Belg: PL38
D-4250-II	Rolladen-Schneider LS4	4322	
D-4252	Rolladen-Schneider LS4	4179	
D-4253	Rolladen-Schneider LS4	4268	PH-1253, D-3501
D-4254	SZD-32A Foka 5	W-515	DDR-2254, DM-2254
D-4255	Pilatus B4-PC11AF	247	HB-1319
D-4257-WA	Schempp-Hirth Ventus-2b	81	
D-4258	Grob G 102 Astir CS	1252	
D-4259	Schleicher ASK 21	21530	
D-4260	Grob G 102 Astir CS	1254	
D-4261	SZD-32A Foka 5	W-524	DDR-2261, DM-2261
D-4262	Grob G 102 Astir CS	1385	
D-4263-KD	Schempp-Hirth Duo Discus	389	
D-4264	Grob G 102 Astir CS	1390	
D-4265	Grob G 102 Astir CS	1391	
D-4266	Rolladen-Schneider LS4	4201	N42RL
D-4267	Grob G 102 Astir CS	1401	
D-4268	Grob G 102 Astir CS	1402	
D-4269-ZN	Rolladen-Schneider LS8-18	8277	ZK-GZN, ZK-GRZ
D-4270	Grob G 102 Astir CS	1404	
D-4271	Grob G 102 Astir CS	1405	
D-4272	Schleicher ASW 22BL	22085	
D-4273	Grob G 102 Astir CS	1417	
D-4274	Grob G 102 Astir CS	1420	
D-4275-5A	Grob G 102 Astir CS	1421	
D-4276	Grob G 102 Astir CS	1422	
D-4277-EH	Grob G 102 Astir CS	1423	
D-4278	Schleicher ASK 23B	23131	
D-4279	Grob G 103C Twin III Acro	34101-K-331	
D-4280	Grob G 103A Twin II Acro	34077-K-307	
D-4281	Grob G 103A Twin II Acro	34078-K-308	
D-4282-MP	Rolladen-Schneider LS8-a	8018	
D-4283	Neukom Elfe S4A	80	HB-1283
D-4284	Rolladen-Schneider LS4-b	4831	
D-4285-BS	Schleicher ASK 21	21539	
D-4286	Rolladen-Schneider LS3-a (P 11.7.16)	3183	
D-4287-SI	Rolladen-Schneider LS4	4323	
D-4288-YN	Schempp-Hirth Nimbus-2B	141	HB-1657, D-7851
D-4289-89	Rolladen-Schneider LS4-b	4833	
D-4290-ZT	Schleicher ASK 21	21647	
D-4291	Rolladen-Schneider LS3-a	3256	
D-4292	Rolladen-Schneider LS3-17	3371	
D-4293-BJ	Rolladen-Schneider LS4	4275	
D-4294	Rolladen-Schneider LS4	4273	
D-4295	Schleicher K 8B	8947	PH-429
D-4296-ZG	Rolladen-Schneider LS4-b	4835	
D-4297-8M	Rolladen-Schneider LS4-b	4836	
D-4298	Rolladen-Schneider LS4-b (P 5.13)	4837	
D-4299	SZD-48-1 Jantar Standard 2	B-1222	
D-4300-N5	DG Flugzeugbau DG-500 Elan Orion	5E199X43	S5-7518
D-4301-ST	Schempp-Hirth Discus-2cR	23	
D-4302-H4	Glaser-Dirks DG-300 Elan	3E97	
D-4303-LI	Glaser-Dirks DG-300 Elan	3E395	
D-4304	Glasflügel H304	203	
D-4305-8N	Grob G 103C Twin III	36011	
D-4306	Schleicher K 8	481	
D-4307-FZ	Glaser-Dirks DG-300 Elan	3E380	
D-4309	Rolladen-Schneider LS6-c18	6367	
D-4310	Schleicher ASW 20	20610	
D-4311	DG Flugzeugbau DG-1000S	10-3S3	
D-4312	Schleicher Rhönlerche II	1021	
D-4314-DU	Schempp-Hirth Duo Discus	226	
D-4316	Pilatus B4-PC11 (P.3.12)	234	HB-1316
D-4317-7G	Schempp-Hirth Discus CS	142CS	
D-4319	Schleicher K 8	472	
D-4320-S4	Grob G 103C Twin III Acro	34203	
D-4321-AZ	Schempp-Hirth Discus CS	149CS	
D-4322	Schleicher Rhönlerche II	3025	
D-4323	Schleicher K 7 Rhönadler	7117	
D-4325-GT	Schempp-Hirth Ventus-2ax (P.02)	32	
D-4326-PY	Schleicher ASW 20	20611	
D-4328	Scheibe L-Spatz 55	634	
D-4329	Schleicher K 8B	920	
D-4330-KE	Schleicher ASW 24	24211	
D-4331	Rolladen-Schneider LS4-b	4839	
D-4332	Glaser-Dirks DG-500 Elan Orion	5E156X13	S5-7505
D-4333	Steinlehner/Huber SH-2H (P. 17.5.16)	01	
D-4334-ZX	Schempp-Hirth Duo Discus	511	
D-4335	Schleicher K 8B	8376	
D-4336-BY	Schempp-Hirth Arcus	6	
D-4337	Schleicher ASK 21	21542	
D-4338	Schleicher Ka 6CR Rhönsegler	6447	
D-4339	Schleicher ASK 21	21543	
D-4340-AW	Glaser-Dirks DG-100G Elan	E106G75	
D-4341	Schempp-Hirth Discus-2b	122	
D-4342-D	Schempp-Hirth Ventus-2b	77	
D-4344	Schempp-Hirth Discus CS	313CS	
D-4345	Schleicher K 8B	8444	D-KOBC, D-4345
D-4346-MZ	Schempp-Hirth Discus CS	254CS	
D-4347	Schleicher Ka 6CR Rhönsegler	6389	
D-4348-BI	Schempp-Hirth Discus CS	111CS	
D-4349	Schleicher Ka 6 Rhönsegler	187	
D-4350-WL	Schempp-Hirth Discus CS	116CS	
D-4351	Schleicher Ka 6 Rhönsegler	130	
D-4352	Schleicher K 8B	8670	
D-4353	Schleicher K 8B	8690	
D-4354-AT	Schempp-Hirth Discus b	141	
D-4355	Glaser-Dirks DG-100G Elan (C/n also quoted for I-LYNO)	E222G188	
D-4356-QE	Lange Antares 18S (P. 11.3.16) (Convtd E1 Antares c/n 68E52)	68S08	
D-4357	Glasflügel Standard Libelle 201B	560	PH-503
D-4358	Schempp-Hirth Janus C	230	
D-4359	Schempp-Hirth Discus b	155	
D-4360	Schempp-Hirth Discus b	143	
D-4363-WB	Schempp-Hirth Ventus-2c	4/7	
D-4364	Schleicher ASK 21	21727	
D-4365	Schleicher Ka 6CR Rhönsegler	618	
D-4366	Bölkow Phoebus A-1	765	
D-4367	Rolladen-Schneider LS8-a	8165	
D-4368	Schleicher Ka 6E	4114	
D-4370	Schleicher Ka 6CR Rhönsegler	6414Si	
D-4371-TE	Schleicher ASW 20	20421	I-EREL
D-4372	Schleicher Ka 6E	4155	
D-4373	Schleicher K 8B	738	
D-4374-BG	Rolladen-Schneider LS6-c	6282	
D-4375	SZD-9bis Bocian 1E	P-565	DDR-3375, DM-3375
D-4376	Rolladen-Schneider LS8-a	8241	
D-4378	Schleicher Ka 2B	01-62	PH-1318, OO-ZFA, D-6743
D-4380-80	Schempp-Hirth Discus-2b	77	
D-4381	Schleicher K 8B	918	
D-4382	Schleicher K 8B	8696	
D-4384	Schleicher Ka 6CR Rhönsegler (P 29.4.16)	967	
D-4385	Schempp-Hirth Discus-2c	34	
D-4386	Schleicher ASK 13	13016	
D-4387-ED	Rolladen-Schneider LS4-b	4878	
D-4388	Schleicher Ka 6CR Rhönsegler	1066	
D-4389	Scheibe SF 27A Zugvogel V	6047	D-4380
D-4390-MP	Schempp-Hirth Discus-2b	136	
D-4391	Schleicher K 7 Rhönadler	7001	
D-4394	Schleicher K 8B	8009	
D-4395-M4	Schempp-Hirth Discus b	174	
D-4396	Pilatus B4-PC11AF	241	
D-4398	Rolladen-Schneider LS4-b	4913	
D-4399	Schleicher Ka 6CR Rhönsegler	6221/B	
D-4401	Pilatus B4-PC11AF	044	HB-1120
D-4402-D11	Schempp-Hirth Discus b	173	
D-4405	Schleicher Ka 6CR Rhönsegler (P .6.12)	6508	
D-4406	Rolladen-Schneider LS1-d	257	
D-4407-CA	Schempp-Hirth Discus-2b	121	
D-4410	Grunau Baby IIB	AB1	
D-4411	Schleicher K 8B	8313	
D-4412-EB	Rolladen-Schneider LS4-b	4851	
D-4413-7J	Glasflügel H206 Hornet C	97	
D-4414	LET L-23 Super Blanik	917811	
D-4415	FFA Diamant 18	057	
D-4416-RA	SZD-41A Jantar Standard	B-747	DDR-2416, DM-2416
D-4417	Schleicher Ka 6E (P 10.15)	4188	
D-4418-E4	Schempp-Hirth Discus CS	113CS	
D-4419	Grob G 103C Twin III	36012	D-5291
D-4421	Schleicher ASK 21	21896	
D-4422-ZF	Schempp-Hirth Discus-2b	229	YU-4462
D-4423	Schleicher ASK 13	13076	
D-4424-IX	SZD-48-3 Jantar-Standard 3	W-903	SE-UIX, SP-3171
D-4425	Schleicher ASW 15 (P.2.13)	15001	
D-4426	Schleicher K 8B	8414	
D-4428	Grob G 103C Twin III Acro	34158	
D-4429-FG	Schempp-Hirth Discus CS	024CS	
D-4430-RV	Glasflügel H303 Mosquito	31	
D-4431	Glasflügel H303 Mosquito	30	
D-4432	Rolladen-Schneider LS4-b	41041	
D-4433	Vogt Lo-100 Zwergreiher	AB 33	
D-4434	Glasflügel H303 Mosquito B (P. 7.15)	116	
D-4435	Glasflügel H303 Mosquito B	117	
D-4436-AR	Schleicher ASK 21	21594	
D-4437-SH	Schempp-Hirth Discus-2b	169	
D-4438	Glasflügel H303 Mosquito B	124	
D-4439	Glasflügel H303 Mosquito B	144	
D-4440-Y4	Schempp-Hirth Discus-2a	3	
D-4441-ZB	Rolladen-Schneider LS8-18	8480	
D-4442-LB	Rolladen-Schneider LS4	4116	
D-4444-WR	Rolladen-Schneider LS8-18 (P 1.3.16)	8396	
D-4445-LS	Rolladen-Schneider LS6E (Permit)	6364	
D-4446	Glasflügel H303 Mosquito	13	
D-4447-SV	Glasflügel H303 Mosquito	23	
D-4448-70	Glasflügel H206 Hornet	88	
D-4449-TH	Glasflügel H206 Hornet	89	
D-4450	Rolladen-Schneider LS4-b	4876	
D-4451	Rolladen-Schneider LS4-a	4676	D-0157
D-4452-DOC	Schempp-Hirth Discus-2b	141	
D-4454	SG-38 Schulgleiter	1310/691	
D-4455	Glasflügel H303 Mosquito	100	
D-4456	Glaser-Dirks DG-300 Elan	3E196	
D-4457	Glaser-Dirks DG-300 Elan	3E198	
D-4458	Rolladen-Schneider LS3-a	3443	I-LORJ, D-6923
D-4459	Glasflügel H206 Hornet	69	
D-4460	Glasflügel H303 Mosquito B	131	
D-4461-UK	Glasflügel H206 Hornet	60	
D-4462-HK	Glasflügel H206 Hornet	61	
D-4463-63	Schleicher ASK 21	21071	
D-4464	Schleicher ASK 21	21076	
D-4465	Schleicher ASK 21	21077	
D-4466	Grob G 102 Astir CS	1167	
D-4467	Schleicher ASK 13	13554	
D-4468	Schleicher ASK 13	13555	
D-4469	Schleicher ASW 19B	19063	
D-4470-2A	Schempp-Hirth Discus b	23	
D-4471	Schleicher ASK 13	13557	

Reg.	Type	c/n	Previous id.
D-4472	Schleicher ASW 19	19071	
D-4473	Schempp-Hirth Janus B	134	I-IVDE
D-4474-JH	Schempp-Hirth Discus-2a	?	
D-4475	Schleicher ASK 13	13558	
D-4476-RH	Schempp-Hirth Discus-2b	152	
D-4477	Rolladen-Schneider LS8-a	8282	
D-4478-33	Schleicher ASW 20	20574	I-RUMA
D-4479	Schleicher ASK 13	13560	
D-4480-B10	Schleicher ASK 13	13564	
	(P. 6.14)		
D-4482	Schleicher ASW 19	19078	
D-4483	Schleicher ASK 13	13561	
D-4484-84	Schleicher ASW 19B	19079	
D-4486	Glaser-Dirks DG-100G Elan	E217G183	I-LUKO
D-4487	Rolladen-Schneider LS4-b	4943	
D-4488	Schempp-Hirth Duo Discus	50	
D-4489-B4	Pilatus B4-PC11	102	PH-489
D-4490-B1	Schempp-Hirth Ventus b/16.6	28	HA-4490, PH-704
D-4491-FK	Schleicher ASK 21	21661	
	(Permit)		
D-4492-1Z	Schleicher ASK 21	21063	
D-4493	Schleicher ASW 19B	19352	
	(P. 3.15)		
D-4494-94	Schleicher ASW 19	19087	
D-4495-S4	Schempp-Hirth Duo Discus	96	
D-4497-7	Grob G 102 Speed Astir II	4015	
	(P 24.3.16)		
D-4498-HY	Schleicher ASW 19B	19080	D-4485
D-4500	Grob G 102 Speed Astir IIB	4029	
D-4503-HT	Schempp-Hirth Discus CS	014CS	
D-4505	Grob G 102 Speed Astir II	4024	
D-4506-A4	Schleicher ASW 19B	19136	
D-4507-BM	Schempp-Hirth Duo Discus	245	
D-4508-LR	Schempp-Hirth Discus CS	022CS	
D-4509-FI	Schempp-Hirth Discus CS	013CS	
D-4510	Glaser-Dirks DG-200	2-39	
D-4511-EO	Glaser-Dirks DG-200	2-80	
D-4512	Schleicher ASK 21	21497	
D-4513	Schleicher ASK 21	21498	
D-4514-B1	Schleicher ASK 21	21496	
D-4515	SZD-48-3 Jantar Standard 3	B-1464	SP-3294
D-4516	Schempp-Hirth Duo Discus	108	
D-4518	Schempp-Hirth Discus-2c	57	
D-4519-K1	Schempp-Hirth Duo Discus	289	
D-4521	Schleicher ASK 21	21204	
D-4522	Schleicher ASW 20CL	20729	
D-4523-BZ	Schleicher ASW 20CL	20726	OO-YBZ, D-4523
	(P.1.05)		
D-4525-TD	Schleicher ASW 19B	19025	
D-4526	Schleicher ASW 19	19018	
D-4527	Schleicher K 8C	81012	
D-4528	Schleicher ASW 19	19028	
D-4529	Schempp-Hirth Discus CS	055CS	
D-4534	Schleicher ASK 13	13543	
D-4535-Z1	Schleicher ASW 24B	24234	
D-4536-AVA	Schempp-Hirth Duo Discus	584	
D-4538	Schleicher ASK 13	13546	
D-4540-AT	Grob G 102 Standard Astir III	5502S	OE-5665, D-3080
D-4541	Sportine Aviacija LAK-17A	131	F-CTRF, D-0014, LY-GEP
D-4542-42	Schempp-Hirth Discus-2b	83	
D-4543	Rolladen-Schneider LS4	4247	
D-4544	Rolladen-Schneider LS4	4478	
D-4546	Scheibe Bergfalke IV	5809	SE-TLB
D-4547-47	Schempp-Hirth Ventus-2a	55	
D-4548	Rolladen-Schneider LS4-b	41034	
D-4549-E6	Grob G 102 Club Astir IIIB	5580CB	
D-4550-FF	Grob G 102 Standard Astir II	5002S	
D-4551	Grob G 103 Twin II	3731	
D-4552	Glaser-Dirks DG-200	2-5	I-RATA, D-4509
D-4553-TK	Rolladen-Schneider LS8-a	8112	
D-4554	Schempp-Hirth Discus CS	101CS	
D-4556-OM	Glaser-Dirks DG-200	2-51	YR-1314, D-6665
D-4557-69	Grob G104 Speed Astir II	4012	(YR- . . . .), PH-1370, EC-HAZ, OO-ZKT, D-3837
D-4558-4G	Grob G 102 Astir CS 77	1741	
D-4560	Marganski MDM-1 Fox	238	
D-4561	Grob G 102 Astir CS Jeans	2165	
D-4563-Y7	Grob G 102 Astir CS 77	1756	
D-4564	Grob G 102 Astir CS Jeans	2167	
D-4566	Glaser-Dirks DG-500 Elan Orion	5E137X3	
D-4567	Grob G 102 Astir CS Jeans	2168	
D-4569	Rolladen-Schneider LS3-a	3180	PH-631, D-6944
D-4570-6B	SZD-59 Acro	X-150	SP-3570, SP-P570
D-4571-27	SZD-55-1	551196087	
D-4572-NA	Rolladen-Schneider LS8-a	8113	
D-4574-NE	Schempp-Hirth Discus CS	126CS	
D-4575-XZ	Rolladen-Schneider LS3-a	3252	
D-4576	Schleicher ASK 21	21538	
D-4578-WE	Glaser-Dirks DG-300 Club Elan	3E297C15	
D-4579	Rolladen-Schneider LS3-a	3417	
D-4580	Rolladen-Schneider LS3-17	3381	
D-4581	Glaser-Dirks DG-300 Club Elan	3E298C16	
D-4582	Schleicher ASK 23B	23126	
D-4584	Schempp-Hirth Ventus-2b	118	
D-4586-1T	Rolladen-Schneider LS7-WL	7021	
D-4587-NC	Rolladen-Schneider LS8-18	8253	
D-4588	Rolladen-Schneider LS3-17	3331	
D-4589	Schempp-Hirth Janus B	184	
D-4591-KS	Schempp-Hirth Nimbus-3/24.5	61	
	(P 29.6.16)		
D-4592	Rolladen-Schneider LS3-a	3370	
D-4593	Glaser-Dirks DG-300 Elan	3E214	
D-4594-EZ	Rolladen-Schneider LS8-a	8254	
D-4595-IBR	Glaser-Dirks DG-300 Elan	3E216	
D-4596-XW	Schleicher ASK 21	21499	
D-4597	Neukom S-4D Elfe	408AB	
D-4599	Schleicher ASK 21	21607	HB-3159
D-4600	Neukom S-4 Elfe	50	
D-4602	Schleicher Ka 6CR Rhönsegler	6503	
D-4603	Schleicher K 8	391	
D-4604	Rolladen-Schneider LS6-a	6106	I-IMRH
D-4605	Schleicher K 8B	8235	
D-4606-ZD	Glaser-Dirks DG-300 Elan	3E241	
D-4607	Schleicher Ka 6CR Rhönsegler	6523Si	
D-4608	Schleicher K 8B	107	
D-4610	Schleicher K 8B	8654	OO-ZOM, PL58
D-4611	Schleicher ASK 21	21502	
D-4612	Schleicher K 7 Rhönadler	7177	
D-4613-8H	Rolladen-Schneider LS4-b	4944	
D-4614	Schleicher Ka 6CR Rhönsegler	6056	
D-4615	Scheibe Bergfalke II/55	386	
D-4616	Glaser-Dirks DG-300 Elan Acro	3E441A6	
D-4617-CP	Rolladen-Schneider LS8-18	8255	
D-4618	Schleicher K 8B	8722	
D-4620-AY	Schempp-Hirth Ventus-2cx	114	
D-4621	Akaflieg Braunschweig SB-5E Sperber	5011A	
D-4622	SZD-50-3 Puchacz	B-1341	DDR-3622
	(Res.2.99)		
D-4623	Schleicher K 7 Rhönadler	7275	
D-4624	Schempp-Hirth Ventus-2ax	78	D-6578
D-4625	Schleicher ASK 21	21500	
D-4627	Schleicher ASW 24	24125	
D-4628	Schleicher K 8B	154/59	
D-4630-TH	Schempp-Hirth Ventus-2c	71	
D-4631	Schleicher ASK 13	13663AB	
D-4632	Schleicher ASK 13	13664AB	
D-4633-2C	Glaser-Dirks DG-100G Elan	E215G181	
D-4635	SZD-50-3 Puchacz	B-1401	DDR-3635
D-4636	SZD-50-3 Puchacz	B-1402	DDR-3636
D-4637	Glaser-Dirks DG-300 Elan	3E239	
D-4638	Schleicher ASH 25	25115	
D-4639	Schleicher ASK 21	21493	
D-4640	Schleicher K 7 Rhönadler	981	
D-4641	Schleicher K 7 Rhönadler	7034	
D-4642	Grunau Baby III	AB 01	
D-4643-C3	Rolladen-Schneider LS1-f	468	SE-TRL
D-4644	Rolladen-Schneider LS4	4067	SE-TXB
D-4645	Glaser-Dirks DG-100G Elan	E201G167	
D-4646	Schleicher Rhönlerche II	66/57	
D-4647-4H	Schempp-Hirth Duo Discus	287	
D-4649	Schleicher ASW 12BV	12007	D-0074
	(P.01)		
D-4650	Schempp-Hirth Nimbus-2C	177	VH-GLN, ZS-GKT, D-6564
D-4651-N1	Schempp-Hirth Discus CS	298CS	
D-4652-GF	Schleicher Ka 6E	4083	
D-4655	Schleicher K 8B	8270	
D-4656	Grob G103A Twin II Acro	3708-K-44	CS-PBP, D-3789
D-4657	Schleicher K 8B	8653	OO-YFJ, PL57
D-4658-MN	Schleicher ASK 21	21494	
D-4659	Schleicher Ka 6E	4030	
	(P. 4.14)		
D-4661-8Y	Rolladen-Schneider LS8-a	8013	
D-4662-BB	Glaser-Dirks DG-300 Elan	3E327	
D-4663-S3	Schempp-Hirth Discus b	131	
D-4665	Schleicher Ka 6E	4145	
D-4667	Glaser-Dirks DG-300 Club Elan	3E323C26	
D-4668	Schleicher ASK 13	13101	
D-4669	Scheibe L-Spatz 55	752	
D-4670-Y	Schempp-Hirth Ventus-2cxa	147	
D-4672	Schleicher K 8B	8137	
D-4673	Schempp-Hirth Discus b	133	
D-4674-SX	Rolladen-Schneider LS4-a	"418"	
D-4675-RE	Rolladen-Schneider LS8-a	8256	
D-4678-FB	Schempp-Hirth Discus b	132	
D-4679	Schleicher ASK 18	unkn	
	(Museum) (Res. - cld?)		
D-4680-B6	Schleicher ASK 21	21626	
D-4681	Schleicher ASK 13	13025	
D-4682-MUS	Schempp-Hirth Discus CS	195CS	
D-4685-F1	Schleicher ASK 21	21506	
D-4686	Darmstadt D-36	V-2	
	(Permit)		
D-4687	Schleicher ASW 20L	20579	
D-4688-AB	Schleicher ASW 27	27133	
D-4690-MR	Schempp-Hirth Discus CS	196CS	
D-4691-91	Schleicher ASW 20L	20581	
D-4692	Schleicher Ka 6CR Rhönsegler	6297	
D-4693-6M	Rolladen-Schneider LS8-a	8190	
D-4694-WG	Schempp-Hirth Discus-2b	78	
D-4695-JF	Schleicher ASH 25	25125	
D-4696-T6	Akaflieg Braunschweig SB-5B Sperber	5007	
D-4697	Scheibe L-Spatz 55	4	D-KONK
	(P. 5.14)		
D-4698	Schleicher Ka 6E	4150	
D-4699	Schleicher Ka 6E	4144	
D-4700	Sportine Aviacija LAK-12.	6227	LY-GDV
D-4701	Glaser-Dirks DG-100G Elan	E194G160	
D-4703	Glaser-Dirks DG-300 Club Elan	3E273C4	
D-4704	Schleicher Ka 6CR Rhönsegler	6435	
D-4705-F3	Schleicher ASW 24	24203	
D-4706	Schleicher Ka 6CR Rhönsegler	6437	
D-4707-3E	Schempp-Hirth Duo Discus	41	
D-4708	Schleicher ASK 21	21361	
D-4709	Schleicher ASK 21	21705	
D-4710	Schleicher K 8B	8614	
D-4711-701	Glasflügel Standard Libelle 201B	150	F-CDPF
D-4712	Schleicher K 8B	8756	
D-4713-E2	Glaser-Dirks DG-300 Elan	3E154	
D-4714	Schleicher K 8B	8632	
	(P. 5.14)		
D-4715	Schleicher ASK 21	21364	
D-4717	Schleicher ASW 27B	27157	PH-1217
D-4716	Schleicher Ka 6E	4060	
D-4720-PE	Schempp-Hirth Ventus-2a	92	
D-4721	DG Flugzeugbau DG-500 Elan Orion	5E238X74	
D-4722	Akaflieg Braunschweig SB-5B	5010	D-4720
D-4724	Glaser-Dirks DG-200	2-33	I-TEAM, D-7417
D-4725	Akaflieg Braunschweig SB-5B Sperber	5031A	
D-4727	Schempp-Hirth Duo Discus	270	
D-4728	Schleicher ASK 21	21674	
D-4731	Schleicher Ka 6E	4185	
D-4733	Schempp-Hirth Discus b	469	
	(W/o 28.3.15)		
D-4734	Glaser-Dirks DG-100G Elan	E197G163	
D-4735	Rolladen-Schneider LS8-a	8073	
D-4736	Schempp-Hirth Cirrus-VTC	150Y	
	(W/o 4.6.15)		
D-4737	Schempp-Hirth Cirrus-VTC	151Y	
D-4738	Schleicher ASK 21	21367	
D-4741	Scheibe Zugvogel IIIA	1098A	D-1896
D-4742	Schempp-Hirth Standard Cirrus	410G	
D-4743	Schempp-Hirth Standard Cirrus	400	

Reg	Type	Serial	Notes
D-4744	Schempp-Hirth Standard Cirrus	411	
D-4747	Schempp-Hirth Standard Cirrus K (P. 14.6.16)	437G	
D-4748	Schempp-Hirth Standard Cirrus	397	
D-4749	Schempp-Hirth Standard Cirrus	415	
D-4750	Schleicher ASK 21	21339	
D-4752-PH	Schempp-Hirth Standard Cirrus	560G	
D-4753	Start & Flug H-101 Salto	72	
D-4754	Rolladen-Schneider LS4-b	41004	
D-4756	Schempp-Hirth Discus b	29	PH-756
D-4757-LP	Glaser-Dirks DG-300 Elan	3E169	
D-4759	Scheibe Bergfalke IV	5852	
D-4761-61	Scheibe Bergfalke IV	5854	
D-4762	Schleicher ASK 21	21330	
D-4764	Grunau Baby IIB	AB Try 1	
D-4765	Eiri PIK-20D	20534	
D-4766	Eiri PIK-20D	20556	
D-4769-CT	Schleicher ASK 21	21371	
D-4770	Schempp-Hirth Ventus-2c	63/	
D-4771	Grob G102 Astir CS 77	1772	HB-1446
D-4772-LVB	Schempp-Hirth Duo Discus	150	
D-4773	Grob G 103 Twin II	3524	
D-4777	Schleicher Ka 6CR Rhönsegler	6426Si	
D-4778	Schleicher ASK 21	21331	
D-4780	Schleicher ASK 21	21332	
D-4781-BS	Eiri PIK-20D	20503	(OH-509)
D-4782	Eiri PIK-20D	20535	
D-4783	Grob G 102 Astir CS	1470	
D-4784	Grob G 102 Astir CS	1477	
D-4785-FU	Schleicher ASK 21	21372	
D-4787	Grob G 102 Astir CS	1481	
D-4790	Valentin Kiwi S	001	D-KELT
D-4792	Grob G 102 Astir CS	1489	
D-4793	Schleicher ASK 23	23056	
D-4794 -FLY	Schempp-Hirth Discus-2b	149	
D-4795	Grob G102 Astir CS (P 17.3.16)	1493	
D-4796	Grob G 102 Astir CS	1495	
D-4798	Schleicher ASK 21	21287	
D-4799-RC	Schempp-Hirth Duo Discus	93	
D-4800	Grob G 102 Astir CS 77	1624	
D-4801	Grob G 102 Astir CS 77	1623	
D-4804	Grob G 102 Astir CS 77	1603	
D-4805	Schempp-Hirth Discus b	43	HB-1805
D-4806	Grob G 102 Astir CS	1520	
D-4807	SZD-30 Pirat	B-463	DDR-1807, DM-1807
D-4808	Grob G 102 Astir CS 77	1622	
D-4809	Grob G 102 Astir CS 77	1608	
D-4810-GN	Schempp-Hirth Duo Discus	299	
D-4811	Grob G 102 Astir CS 77	1610	
D-4812-DH	Schempp-Hirth Discus-2c	53	
D-4813-F	Grob G 102 Astir CS 77	1642	
D-4814-F	Rolladen-Schneider LS8-a (P.4.12)	8091	
D-4815	Grob G 102 Astir CS 77	1619	
D-4816-16	Schleicher ASK 21	21333	
D-4817	Schempp-Hirth Janus	44	
D-4818-U1	Schempp-Hirth HS-7 Mini-Nimbus	13	
D-4820	SZD-30 Pirat	B-498	DDR-1821, DM-1821
D-4821	Schleicher ASW 20CL	20857	
D-4823	SZD-30 Pirat	B-500	DDR-1823, DM-1823
D-4824-DR	Schempp-Hirth Duo Discus	89	
D-4825	Grob G 102 Astir CS 77	1655	
D-4826	Schleicher ASK 21	21334	
D-4827	Schleicher ASW 20CL	20858	
D-4829	Grob G 102 Astir CS Jeans	2022	
D-4830	Grob G 102 Astir CS Jeans	2021	
D-4831	Glaser-Dirks DG-300 Elan	3E131	
D-4832	Grob G 102 Astir CS Jeans	2019	
D-4833-SN	Schempp-Hirth Standard Cirrus	78	VH-GSN
D-4834	Grob G 102 Astir CS Jeans	2017	
D-4836	Schleicher ASK 21	21336	
D-4837-LZ	Schempp-Hirth Discus CS	222CS	
D-4838-WL	Schempp-Hirth Discus CS	224CS	
D-4840	Grob G 103 Twin Astir	3045	
D-4843-FL	Schempp-Hirth Discus-2a	198	
D-4844-SB	Schleicher ASW 24	24063	OE-5430
D-4845	Grob G 103 Twin Astir	3054	
D-4846-1K	Schempp-Hirth Discus-2b	126	
D-4847	Schempp-Hirth Janus	194	
D-4849-GJ	Schempp-Hirth Janus B	146	D-3090
D-4850	DG Flugzeugbau DG-500 Elan Orion	5E240X76	
D-4851	Grob G 103 Twin Astir	3065	
D-4852-MO	Schempp-Hirth Discus-2c	41	
D-4853-B2	Rolladen-Schneider LS8-18	8412	
D-4854-JZD	Dittmar Condor IV (P 29.8.16)	18	BGA 4905, D-0125, LV-DHV
D-4855	Grob G 103 Twin Astir	3060	D-4850
D-4857	SZD-51-1 Junior	511199243	
D-4858-4D	Grob G 103 Twin Astir	3073	
D-4859	Schleicher ASW 20CL	20859	
D-4860	SZD-55-1	551193057	OO-ZQF
D-4864-82	Schempp-Hirth Discus b	200	I-MBIG, D-8111
D-4865-O5	Schleicher ASK 21	21265	
D-4866-B2	Grob G 103 Twin II	3593	
D-4867-20	Schempp-Hirth Discus CS	216CS	
D-4869	Grob G 102 Speed Astir IIB	4102	
D-4870-DW	Schleicher ASH 25	25010	
D-4871	Rolladen-Schneider LS3-a	3379	PH-871, D-5899
D-4872-X	Rolladen-Schneider LS8-a	8115	
D-4873	Grob G 102 Speed Astir IIB	4038	
D-4874	Grob G 102 Speed Astir IIB	4046	
D-4875-L	Grob G 102 Speed Astir IIB	4071	
D-4877-F5	Grob G 102 Speed Astir IIB	4039	
D-4878-AP	Grob G 102 Speed Astir IIB	4048	
D-4880	Rolladen-Schneider LS3	3058	LN-GGY, HB-1365
D-4881	Grob G 103 Twin II	3501	
D-4882	Schempp-Hirth Duo Discus	311	
D-4883	Grob G 102 Standard Astir II	5005S	
D-4885	Grob G 102 Standard Astir II	5006S	
D-4886	Grob G 102 Club Astir II (P. 5.14)	5008C	
D-4887	Grob G 102 Club Astir II	5009C	
D-4888	Grob G 102 Astir CS Jeans	2068	
D-4889	Schleicher ASK 21	21338	
D-4891	Grob G 102 Astir CS Jeans	2152	
D-4892	Glaser-Dirks DG-300 Elan	3E113	OE-5371
D-4895-9D	Grob G 102 Astir CS Jeans	2149	
D-4896-1B	Grob G 102 Astir CS 77	1733	
D-4897	Grob G 102 Astir CS 77	1738	
D-4898-JY	Schleicher ASK 21	21385	
D-4901	Schempp-Hirth Duo Discus	295	
D-4903	Schempp-Hirth Mini-Nimbus C	129	
D-4904	Pilatus B4-PC11AF	124	PH-490
D-4905	Valentin Mistral C	MC 002/77	
D-4907	Valentin Mistral C	MC 005/77	OO-ZJT, D-4900
D-4908	SZD-30 Pirat	S-03.48	DDR-1908, DM-1908
D-4909	Glaser-Dirks DG-100G Elan	E180G146	
D-4910	Valentin Mistral C	MC 010/77	
D-4911	DG Flugzeugbau DG-1000S	10-20S20	
D-4912	Glaser-Dirks DG-300 Elan	3E234	
D-4913-N1	Glaser-Dirks DG-300 Elan	3E120	
D-4914	Glaser-Dirks DG-300 Elan	3E236	
D-4915-JT	Schempp-Hirth Ventus-2cxa	141	
D-4916	Valentin Mistral C	MC 016/78	
D-4917-MB	Schempp-Hirth Discus-2b	125	
D-4918	DG Flugzeugbau DG-1000S	10-236S155	
D-4919	Valentin Mistral C	MC 019/79	
D-4920	Valentin Mistral C	MC 021/79	G-DKBW, BGA4725/JRS, D-4921
D-4921-21	Schempp-Hirth Discus-2a	222	
D-4923	Schleicher ASK 23B	23106	
D-4924	Schleicher ASW 24	24003	
D-4926	Valentin Mistral C	MC 026/80	
D-4927-RY	Schleicher ASK 21	21862	
D-4928	Valentin Mistral C	MC 028/81	
D-4929	Valentin Mistral C	MC 029/81	
D-4930	Valentin Mistral C (P. 1.15)	MC 030/81	
D-4931	Valentin Mistral C	MC 031/81	
D-4932-FO	Valentin Mistral C	MC 032/81	
D-4933	Schleicher ASK 21	21904	
D-4935	Schleicher ASK 21	21928	
D-4936-KF2	Schempp-Hirth Discus CS	219CS	
D-4938-VL	Valentin Mistral C	MC 038/81	
D-4939	Valentin Mistral C	MC 039/81	
D-4940	Schleicher ASK 21	21378	
D-4942-UD	Rolladen-Schneider LS6-18W	6363	
D-4943-MC	Valentin Mistral C	MC 043/81	
D-4944	Valentin Mistral C	MC 044/81	
D-4945	Valentin Mistral C	MC 045/82	
D-4946	Valentin Mistral C	MC 046/82	
D-4947-S1	Schempp-Hirth Ventus-2b	96	OY-SHX
D-4950	Schempp-Hirth Duo Discus	80	
D-4951	Valentin Mistral C	MC 051/83	
D-4952	Glaser-Dirks DG-100G Elan	E177G143	
D-4953	Valentin Mistral C	MC 055/85	
D-4954	Schleicher ASK 21	21241	
D-4955-55	Schleicher ASK 21	21242	
D-4956	Valentin Mistral C	MC 056/86	
D-4957	Schempp-Hirth Discus b	394	
D-4958	Valentin Mistral C	MC 058/85	
D-4959-GJ	Schleicher ASW 22	22017	D-1653
D-4960	Valentin Mistral C	MC 060/85	
D-4961-LT	DG Flugzeugbau DG-500 Elan Orion	5E165X20	
D-4962-FS	Valentin Mistral C	MC 062/85	
D-4963	Valentin Mistral C	MC 063/83	
D-4964	Valentin Mistral C	MC 064/85	
D-4965	Valentin Mistral C	MC 065/83	OO-YPF. D-4965
D-4966-ET	Rolladen-Schneider LS4	4490	
D-4967-YH	Rolladen-Schneider LS4	4491	
D-4968-BW	Rolladen-Schneider LS4	4492	
D-4969-NRW	Rolladen-Schneider LS4	4493	
D-4970-IB	Rolladen-Schneider LS4	4494	
D-4971	Rolladen-Schneider LS4	4496	
D-4972	Rolladen-Schneider LS4	4497	
D-4973-KHB	Schempp-Hirth Discus b	236	HB-1973
D-4974	Schleicher ASK 21	21381	
D-4975	Schempp-Hirth Ventus-2cx	131	
D-4976	Schleicher K 8B	8385/A	D-1026
D-4977-77	Glaser-Dirks DG-300 Elan	3E424	I-NYKE
D-4978	Grunau Baby III	004A	
D-4979-J8	Glaser-Dirks DG-100G Elan	E187G153	
D-4980	Glasflügel Mosquito	89	N302C, N39JH
D-4981	Schempp-Hirth Nimbus-2B	152	
D-4982-AK	Rolladen-Schneider LS4-a	4686	
D-4983-SU	Schempp-Hirth HS-7 Mini-Nimbus	20	
D-4984	Schempp-Hirth HS-7 Mini-Nimbus	21	
D-4985	Grob G 103C Twin III Acro (W/o 2.6.15)	34151	
D-4986	Schempp-Hirth HS-7 Mini-Nimbus	57	
D-4987	SZD-51-1 Junior	B-1827	HB-1987
D-4988	Schempp-Hirth HS-7 Mini-Nimbus	65	
D-4989	Rolladen-Schneider LS4	4687	
D-4990-4H	Schempp-Hirth Mini-Nimbus B	75	
D-4991	Schempp-Hirth Mini-Nimbus B	76	
D-4992	Schempp-Hirth Mini-Nimbus B	77	
D-4993-LZ	Rolladen-Schneider LS4-a	4688	
D-4994	Valentin Mistral C (P 8.2.16)	MC 007/77	
D-4995-D	Schempp-Hirth Discus CS	218CS	
D-4996	Rolladen-Schneider LS7-WL	7042	HB-1996, D-5156
D-4997-728	Glasflügel Standard Libelle 201B	428	F-CELF
D-4998	Valentin Mistral A	V-1	
D-4999-SY	Rolladen-Schneider LS4-a	4689	
D-5000	Schmetz Condor IV/2	005	
D-5001-MI	Rolladen-Schneider LS4-a	4690	
D-5002	Neukom S-4D Elfe	414AB	
D-5004-GL	Rolladen-Schneider LS4-a	4692	
D-5005-HR	Glaser-Dirks DG-500 Elan Trainer	5E48T18	
D-5006-SV	Rolladen-Schneider LS4-a	4693	
D-5007	Glaser-Dirks DG-500 Elan Trainer	5E9T1	
D-5008	Rolladen-Schneider LS4-a	4695	
D-5009	Schleicher K 7 Rhönadler	7239	
D-5010	Schleicher ASK 13	13672AB	
D-5011	LET L-13A Blanik	978503	
D-5012	Schempp-Hirth HS.7 Mini-Nimbus	12	HB-1386
D-5014-YX	Schempp-Hirth Duo Discus	412	
D-5015	Neukom Elfe S-4A (Permit)	58	HB-1097
D-5016	Schleicher Ka 6CR Rhönsegler	6067	
D-5018	Schleicher Ka 6CR Rhönsegler	904	

Reg	Type	Serial	Previous identities
D-5019	Schleicher K 8B	215/61	
D-5020	PZL-Swidnik PW-5 Smyk	17.03.007	OE-5604
D-5021	Grob G 102 Club Astir IIIB	5542CB	OH-640
D-5022-22	Glaser-Dirks DG-100G Elan	E121G90	
D-5023	Schleicher K 8B	198/60	D-KIFU, D-5023
D-5026	LET L-13 Blanik	026227	OH-491
D-5027	Schleicher K 8B	1145	
D-5028	Rolladen-Schneider LS6-c	6283	
D-5029	Schleicher K 7 Rhönadler	7027/A	BGA 3218/FFD, D-5029
D-5030	Glaser-Dirks DG-100G Elan	E161G128	
D-5031	Schleicher Ka 6CR Rhönsegler	905	
D-5032	SZD-24-4A Foka 4	W-248	
D-5033	Schleicher ASK 18	18004	OE-5039
	(P.05)		
D-5034	Schempp-Hirth Discus CS	220CS	
D-5035-35	Glaser-Dirks DG-500 Elan Trainer	5E117T49	
D-5037	Schleicher ASK 21	21706	
D-5038-ZW	Rolladen-Schneider LS6	6194	
D-5039-JB	Glaser-Dirks DG-300 Elan	3E295	
D-5040	Rolladen-Schneider LS7-WL	7053	
D-5042	Schleicher K 8B	199/60	
D-5043	Glaser-Dirks DG-100	33	OE-5048
D-5044-ZO	Schempp-Hirth Discus b	246	
D-5045	Schleicher K 8B	913	
D-5048-LZ	Schempp-Hirth Discus-2c	3	
D-5049	Schleicher ASK 21	21748	
D-5050	Schleicher ASK 23B	23150	
D-5051	Schleicher K 8B	8893/AB	OE-5041
D-5052	DG Flugzeugbau DG-505 Elan Orion	5E181X32	SE-UPN
D-5055-WW	Schempp-Hirth Ventus c	389	
D-5056	Schleicher Rhönlerche II	165	
	(P 18.7.16)		
D-5057-UB	Schempp-Hirth Discus b	273	
D-5059-ER	Schempp-Hirth Ventus c	336	F-WGLL
D-5060-L4	Schleicher Ka 6CR Rhönsegler	966	
D-5061	Rolladen-Schneider LS6-a	6035	OO-ZRY
D-5063-45	Schempp-Hirth Ventus a/16.6	82	
D-5064-AY	Schempp-Hirth Discus b	286	
D-5065	Schleicher ASW 24	24127	F-CHAE
D-5066	Glasflügel H401 Kestrel	2	
D-5067	Schleicher K 8B	8520	
D-5069-69	Glasflügel H206 Hornet	29	OE-5060
D-5070-B2	Schempp-Hirth Discus CS	071CS	OY-XXI, D-3934
D-5072	Schleicher ASK 21	21248	
D-5073-TE	Schleicher ASK 23	23018	
D-5074	Schleicher ASK 21	21249	
D-5075	Schempp-Hirth Discus b	289	
D-5076	Rolladen-Schneider LS8-a	8410	
D-5077	Glaser-Dirks DG-100	83	
D-5078-IEA	Schempp-Hirth Discus b	284	
D-5080	Schempp-Hirth Janus C	249	
D-5081	Schleicher K 8B	8509SH	
D-5082	Schempp-Hirth Discus b	285	
D-5084-GX	Schempp-Hirth Janus C	251	
D-5085-U2	Schempp-Hirth Discus-2b	93	
D-5086	Schleicher Ka 6CR Rhönsegler	1156	
D-5088-88	Schempp-Hirth Janus C	248	
D-5089	Rolladen-Schneider LS6-c	6274	
D-5090	Schleicher K 8B	8425	
D-5092-VD	Schempp-Hirth Duo Discus	249	
D-5093	Glaser-Dirks DG-300 Elan	3E139	OE-5379
D-5094	Grob G 102 Astir CS 77	1613	PH-569
D-5095	Schempp-Hirth Discus b	288	
D-5096	Schleicher K 8B	1014	
D-5097-TL	Schempp-Hirth Discus b	260	
D-5098-R4	Schempp-Hirth Discus b	239	
D-5099-W1	Schleicher Ka 6CR Rhönsegler	6454	
D-5100-HT	Schempp-Hirth Discus-2b	56	
D-5101-1B	Schempp-Hirth Discus b	501	
D-5102-SD	Rolladen-Schneider LS4-a	4708	
D-5103-03	Schleicher K 7 Rhönadler	1141	
D-5104	Rolladen-Schneider LS4-b	4709	
	(P.2.13)		
D-5105	Schleicher K 8B	131	
D-5106	Schleicher K 8B	8591	
D-5107-YZ	Rolladen-Schneider LS4-a	4710	
D-5109	Rolladen-Schneider LS4-a	4711	
D-5110	Schleicher Ka 6E	4035	
D-5111	Schleicher K 8B	8336/A	
D-5112	Glaser-Dirks DG-100G Elan	E134G102	
D-5113-R2	SZD-51-1 Junior	B-1781	
D-5114-HI	Rolladen-Schneider LS4-a	4712	
D-5115-T1	Rolladen-Schneider LS4-a	4713	
D-5116	Schleicher K 7 Rhönadler	174/60	D-5011
D-5117-PK	Schempp-Hirth Discus-2b	223	
D-5118	Schleicher K 7 Rhönadler	1036	
D-5119-5M	Rolladen-Schneider LS4-a	4714	
D-5121	Schleicher Ka 6CR Rhönsegler	993	
D-5122	Rolladen-Schneider LS4-a	4716	
D-5123	Schleicher ASK 21	21513	
D-5124-9G	Schleicher ASW 24	24114	
D-5125	Schleicher ASK 21	"40670"	
D-5127-HS	SZD-50-3 Puchacz	B-1879	SE-UHS
D-5128-L4	Schempp-Hirth Duo Discus	251	
D-5129	Schleicher ASK 21	21501	
D-5130	Schleicher K 7 Rhönadler	7252	
D-5132	Grob G 102 Astir CS Jeans	2045	OE-5138
D-5133	Schleicher ASK 21	21492	
D-5135	Schleicher K 8B	8564	
D-5136-MIG	Eiri PIK-20D	20569	OE-5132
D-5137	Schleicher ASK 21	21490	
D-5138	Schleicher K 8B	8066	
D-5139	Schleicher ASW 24	24112	
D-5141	Grob G 103A Twin II Acro	3856-K-102	
D-5142	Schleicher Ka 6E	4116	
D-5143	Glaser-Dirks DG-300 Elan	3E199	
D-5144 -FF	Glaser-Dirks DG-300 Elan	3E200	
D-5145	Schleicher Ka 6CR Rhönsegler	6009	
D-5146	Rolladen-Schneider LS6-18W	6345	BGA 4655/JNU, RAFGSA R69, RAFGGA 553, D-8037
D-5147-EF	Schleicher Ka 6CR Rhönsegler	6460	
D-5148	Glaser-Dirks DG-300 Elan	3E201	
D-5149	Grunau Baby IIB	5	
D-5150	Glaser-Dirks DG-300 Elan	3E302	
D-5152	Schleicher K 8B	8097	
D-5153	Glaser-Dirks DG-200	2-79	D-6223
	(P.07)		
D-5154	Schleicher ASK 21	21595	
D-5155	Schleicher K 8B	8107	
D-5156	Schempp-Hirth Mini-Nimbus HS-7	38	OE-5157
D-5157	Glaser-Dirks DG-100	99	OE-5128
D-5158	Bölkow Phoebus C	934	HB-1173
D-5159	PZL-Swidnik PW-6U	78.02.08	CS-PBX
D-5160-E2	Schempp-Hirth Discus CS	316CS	
D-5161	Rolladen-Schneider LS7-WL	7044	
D-5162	Rolladen-Schneider LS4-b	4985	HB-3176
D-5163-6C	Rolladen-Schneider LS7	7046	
D-5167	Schleicher ASK 13	13586	OE-5164
D-5168-B2	Rolladen-Schneider LS4-b	41042	
D-5169	Schleicher K 8B	8312	
D-5171	Schleicher K 7	1143	
D-5172-F8	Rolladen-Schneider LS4-a	4750	
D-5173	Rolladen-Schneider LS4-a	4749	
D-5175	Schempp-Hirth Standard Cirrus	331	I-MACH, D-3024
D-5177	Schleicher Ka 2B Rhönschwalbe	1134	
D-5178	Schempp-Hirth Discus CS	103CS	
D-5179-YB	Schleicher Ka 6CR Rhönsegler	1127	
D-5180-BH	Rolladen-Schneider LS4	4595	
D-5181	Schleicher Ka 6CR Rhönsegler	1129	
D-5183	Schleicher K 8B	191/60	
D-5184	Rolladen-Schneider LS1-c	124	OO-ZZQ, D-0886
D-5185	Rolladen-Schneider LS4-a	4747	
D-5186	Scheibe Zugvogel IIIA	1064	
D-5187	Rolladen-Schneider LS4-a	4746	
D-5188	Schleicher Ka 6CR Rhönsegler	6467Si	
D-5189-RW	Schempp-Hirth Discus CS	104CS	
D-5190	Glaser-Dirks DG-303 Elan Acro	3E464A18	HB-3190
D-5193	Scheibe SF 27A	6048	
D-5195	Schempp-Hirth Nimbus-2B	65	V5-GOD, HB-1204, D-3687
D-5196-OMI	Schempp-Hirth Discus-2c	43	
D-5197	Schleicher Ka 6CR Rhönsegler	552	
D-5198-3T	Grob G 103C Twin III Acro	34113	
D-5199-SU	Grob G102 Astir CS 77	1728	PH-618
D-5200-1Z	Grob G 103C Twin III Acro	34109	
D-5201	Schleicher K 7 Rhönadler	7012	
D-5202-CF	SZD-36A Cobra 15	W-563	DDR-2302, DM-2302
D-5203	Schempp-Hirth Cirrus	61	
D-5204	Grunau Baby IIB	2	
D-5205-MV	Schleicher ASH 25	25009	F-CGKY, (F-CIVH), F-CGKY, F-WGKY, D-5242
D-5206	Glasflügel Club Libelle 205	53	I-ZAVA
D-5208	Grob G 103C Twin III	36009	
D-5211	Schleicher K 8B	8092	
D-5213	Schleicher Ka 2B Rhönschwalbe	2002	
D-5215	Grob G 103C Twin III Acro	34104	
D-5218	Scheibe SF 27A	6076	
D-5221	Grunau Baby IIB	6	
D-5222-AH	Schleicher ASW 27	27071	
D-5223	Schleicher ASK 23B	23141	
D-5225	Schleicher ASH 25	25011	
D-5226	Schleicher Ka 6CR Rhönsegler	6158	
D-5227	Schempp-Hirth Standard Cirrus B	682	OE-5227, OE-5088
D-5228	Schempp-Hirth Discus b	72	
D-5229	Schleicher ASW 27-18 (ASG 29)	29080	
D-5230-5E	Schempp-Hirth Discus b	81	
D-5231-DS	Schempp-Hirth Ventus c	296	
D-5232-XV	Schempp-Hirth Discus CS	122CS	OO-YXV, (OO-ZXV)
D-5233-1W	Grob G 103C Twin III Acro	34116	
D-5234	Schleicher Ka 6CR Rhönsegler	6117	D-7181
D-5236	Schleicher K 7 Rhönadler	7260	D-5238
D-5238	Rolladen-Schneider LS1-f	258	HB-1238
D-5239	Grob G102 Standard Astir II	5033S	PH-1362, OO-ZNK, D-6265, F-WFIH
D-5240	Scheibe Bergfalke II/55	362	
D-5241-AX	Schleicher ASW 24	24091	
D-5242	Rolladen-Schneider LS1-d	79	OE-0899
D-5246	Rolladen-Schneider LS4-a	4727	
D-5247	Rolladen-Schneider LS4-a	4726	
D-5248-P8	Rolladen-Schneider LS4-b	4783	
D-5249	Rolladen-Schneider LS4-a	4724	
D-5250	Schleicher K 7 Rhönadler	7063	
D-5251	Schleicher K 8B	8237	
	(P. 10.13)		
D-5253	Rolladen-Schneider LS4	4589	
D-5254-SZ	Rolladen-Schneider LS4-a	4723	
D-5255	Rolladen-Schneider LS4-a	4739	
D-5256-LL	Rolladen-Schneider LS4	4596	
D-5258	Rolladen-Schneider LS4	4597	
D-5260-FO	Schempp-Hirth Nimbus-2C	230	OE-5260
D-5261	Schleicher Ka 6E	4011	OO-YAS, D-9362
D-5262-DT	Grob G 103C Twin III Acro	34108	
D-5263-M5	Rolladen-Schneider LS4	4598	
D-5264	Rolladen-Schneider LS4-a	4719	
D-5265-3W	Rolladen-Schneider LS4-a	4718	
D-5267-WG	Schleicher Ka 6CR Rhönsegler	6127Si	
D-5270-57	Glaser-Dirks DG-800S	8-60S17	
D-5271	Grob G103A Twin II Acro	3634-K-21	OE-5274
D-5272	Schleicher Ka 6CR Rhönsegler	6125Si	
D-5274-L3	Schempp-Hirth Duo Discus	132	
D-5280-FS	Glaser-Dirks DG-300 Elan	3E249	
D-5281	Schleicher Ka 6CR Rhönsegler	6135	
D-5282	Schleicher ASK 13	13085	
D-5284-GB	Glaser-Dirks DG-300 Club Elan	3E352C41	
D-5285	Rolladen-Schneider LS4	4414	
D-5286-AP	Rolladen-Schneider LS4	4412	
D-5287	Glaser-Dirks DG-100G Elan	E35G19	OE-5282
D-5288	Glaser-Dirks DG-300 Elan	3E367	
	(P.05)		
D-5289	Schleicher Ka 6CR Rhönsegler	6375Si	
D-5290	Glaser-Dirks DG-101G Elan	E109G79	OE-5298
D-5291	Siebert Sie 3	3024	PH-529
D-5293	Schleicher K 8B	8192-A	
D-5294	Grob G 103C Twin III	36003	
D-5295	Schleicher ASW 27	27023	
D-5297-97	Schleicher ASK 21	21643	
D-5298-LA	Schempp-Hirth Ventus-2cxa	140	
D-5299-WS	Schempp-Hirth Duo Discus	403	
D-5300	Schleicher Ka 6CR Rhönsegler	6170	
	(P. 9.15)		
D-5302	Glaser-Dirks DG-100G Elan	E220G186	

Reg	Type	C/n	Previous ids
D-5303	Schleicher K 7 Rhönadler	7272	
D-5304	HpH Glasflügel 304CZ-17	21-17	
D-5305	Schleicher K 8B	8177	
D-5306-4G	Schempp-Hirth Discus CS	074CS	PH-961
D-5308	Schleicher K 8B	8181	
D-5310	SZD-36A Cobra 15	W-647	DDR-2310, DM-2310
D-5311	Schleicher ASK 13	13040	
D-5312	Schleicher ASW 12	12010	HB-953
D-5313	Schleicher Ka 6E	4134	
D-5314	Schempp-Hirth Discus CS	042CS	
D-5315	Schempp-Hirth Duo Discus XL	631	
D-5316-XG	Schempp-Hirth Duo Discus	231	
D-5318-GA	Schleicher Ka 6CR Rhönsegler	6553	
D-5319	Schleicher Ka 6CR Rhönsegler	6152Si	
D-5320-NT	Schleicher ASW 24	24005	
D-5321	Schleicher ASK 21	21309	
D-5323	Grob G 103C Twin III Acro	34130	
D-5324	Scheibe SF 34B	5141	
D-5325	Grob G 103C Twin III Acro	34115	
D-5327	Schempp-Hirth Nimbus-3/24.5	56	
D-5328-CW	Schempp-Hirth Ventus b/16.6	180	
D-5329	Schleicher K 8B	8211	
D-5330-WM	Schempp-Hirth Nimbus-3/24.5	54	OE-5334
D-5331	Rolladen-Schneider LS7	7107	
D-5332	Schleicher Ka 6BR Rhönsegler	369	D-0409, HB-614
D-5333	Schleicher Ka 6CR Rhönsegler	6376	
D-5334	Schleicher ASW 20CL	20850	
D-5335	Schempp-Hirth Ventus b/16.6	8	
D-5336-B2	Schleicher ASK 23B	23080	
D-5337	Rolladen-Schneider LS7	7109	
D-5339	Schleicher K 8B	8085/2	(D-KABL), D-5339
D-5341	Schleicher K 8B	8492	
D-5343	Schleicher K 8B	8218/EI	
D-5344	Schleicher K 7 Rhönadler	7100	
D-5345	Schleicher ASW 20CL	20851	
D-5347-LL	Schleicher ASW 24	24142	
D-5348-HC	Schempp-Hirth Nimbus-3/24.5	64	OE-5348
D-5349-3N	Schleicher ASK 21	21312	
D-5350-50	Schempp-Hirth Duo Discus XL	634	
D-5351	Glaser-Dirks DG-300 Elan	3E394	
D-5352	Glaser-Dirks DG-300 Club Elan	3E397C61	
D-5354	SZD-48-3 Jantar Standard 3	B-1409	OE-5351
D-5355	Scheibe L-Spatz 55	763	PH-838, D-5922
D-5356	Schleicher K 8B	8242	
D-5359	Schleicher ASK 21	21208	
D-5360-HZ	Schempp-Hirth Duo Discus XL	599	
D-5363	Scheibe L-Spatz	1	
D-5365	SZD-9bis Bocian 1E	P-521	DDR-3365, DM-3365
D-5366	Schleicher ASK 13	13119	I-UFFA
D-5367	SZD-48-3 Jantar-Standard 3	B-1961	OO-ZPQ, (OO-ZCY)
D-5368	Schleicher Ka 6CR Rhönsegler	6191Si	
D-5369-KA	Schempp-Hirth Arcus	1	
D-5371-HL	Schleicher ASK 21	21214	
D-5374	Grob G103 Twin Astir	3241	F-CFHE
D-5375	Schleicher K 8B	8244	D-KANT, D-5375
D-5377	Schleicher ASK 21	21712	
D-5380	Vogt Lo-100 Zwergreiher	1	
D-5383	Schleicher ASK 21	21317	
D-5384-LB	Schempp-Hirth Discus CS	051CS	
D-5386	Glaser-Dirks DG-500 Elan Trainer	5E58T25	
D-5387	Rolladen-Schneider LS1-c	187	OY-XBY
D-5390-PL	Rolladen-Schneider LS6-c	6275	
D-5391	Doppelraab 7	2	RAFGGA589, D-5891
D-5393	SZD-9bis Bocian 1E	P-610	DDR-3393, DM-3393
D-5394	Schleicher ASK 21	21322	
D-5399	Glaser-Dirks DG-300 Club Elan	3E402C62	
D-5400-WER	Schleicher ASW 20CL	20806	PH-907, D-3547
D-5401	Schleicher ASK 21	21335	
D-5402	Schleicher Ka 2B Rhönschwalbe	272	
D-5403	Schleicher ASW 20BL	20699	
D-5404	Schleicher K 7 Rhönadler	7124/A	
D-5405	Focke-Wulf Kranich III	82	
D-5406	Vogt Lo-100 Zwergreiher	17	
D-5408-LB	Schempp-Hirth Discus CS	286CS	
D-5410-210	Schempp-Hirth Ventus-2cxa	116/513	
D-5411	DG Flugzeugbau DG-1000S	10-61S56	
	(C/n clashes with 10-58S56 current as F-CGRK)		
D-5412	Doppelraab IV	EB-1	
D-5413-2T	Glaser-Dirks DG-101G Elan	E205G171	OE-5404
D-5414	Schleicher K 7 Rhönadler	7130	
D-5416	Schleicher K 8B	8757	
D-5417	Schleicher ASK 21	21637	
D-5418	Schleicher ASK 21	21324	
D-5419	Schleicher K 8B	8285	
D-5420	Schempp-Hirth Nimbus-2B	148	OO-ZYZ
D-5421	Glasflügel H401 Kestrel	9	I-KOKI
D-5422	Schleicher ASK 21	21781	
D-5424	Schleicher Ka 6CR Rhönsegler	6436	
D-5426	Schleicher Ka 2	48	PH-1214, OY-XRD, D-8757
D-5427	Schleicher ASK 21	21340	
	(P. 4.11)		
D-5428	PZL PW-5 Smyk	17.04.014	OE-5628
D-5429	Schleicher ASK 21	21328	
D-5430-BS	Glasflügel H304	232	
D-5431	Schleicher K 8B	8470	
D-5432-E1	Schleicher ASK 23B	23092	
D-5433	Glaser-Dirks DG-300 Elan	3E228	HB-1894
D-5434	Glaser-Dirks DG-300 Club Elan	3E280C6	OE-5431
D-5435	Schleicher K 8B	8276	
D-5436	Doppelraab V	1	
D-5437	Schleicher K 8B	8302	
D-5438	SZD-24-4A Foka 4	W-305	(D-2444), DDR-2044, DM-2044
D-5439-2G	Schleicher ASK 21	21321	
D-5440	DFS Olympia-Meise 51	16	PH-734, D-5444, OE-0455
D-5441	Scheibe Bergfalke III	5539	
D-5442	Grob G 103C Twin III	36001	
D-5443-WD	Schempp-Hirth Duo Discus	260	
D-5444	Glasflügel H201B Standard Libelle	519	HB-1195
D-5445-WK	Schempp-Hirth SHK-1	27	
D-5447-Z9	Scheibe L-Spatz III	825	
D-5448	Glaser-Dirks DG-500 Elan Trainer	5E67T28	
D-5449	Schleicher Ka 6CR Rhönsegler	6633Si	
D-5450	Glaser-Dirks DG-600	6-25	OE-5450
D-5451	Rolladen-Schneider LS3	3006	PH-545
D-5452	SG-38 Schulgleiter	2	
D-5454	Schleicher Ka 6CR Rhönsegler	6261	
D-5456	Schleicher K 8B	8448	
D-5457	Grunau Baby IIB	54	
D-5458-WB	Schempp-Hirth Discus-2b	94	G-CJYN, BGA 4890
D-5459	Scheibe SF 27A	6086	
D-5460-60	Glaser-Dirks DG-500 Elan Trainer	5E108T44	
D-5461-MV	Sportine Aviacija LAK-17A	154	LY-GMN
D-5463	Rolladen-Schneider LS8-18	8314	
D-5464	Schleicher K 7 Rhönadler	7154	
D-5465	Schleicher K 7 Rhönadler	7257	
D-5466-TP	Schempp-Hirth Ventus-2b	66	
D-5467	Schempp-Hirth Nimbus-2B	158	OE-5467, D-2828
D-5468	Schleicher Ka 6 Rhönsegler	176	
D-5469-CU	SZD-36A Cobra 15	W-670	OE-5466, OE-5005
D-5470	Glasflügel Standard Libelle 201B	524	PH-470
D-5471-71	Schempp-Hirth Ventus-2b	51	
D-5472	Glaser-Dirks DG-600/18	6-47	OE-5474
D-5473	Centrair 101 Pégase	10100344	OO-YLY, PL73 Belgian Air Cadets
D-5474-D7	Schempp-Hirth Janus Ce	275	
D-5475-OS	Schempp-Hirth Discus b	390	
D-5476	Schempp-Hirth Discus b	66/392	
D-5477	Scheibe L-Spatz 55	588	
D-5480-BW2	Schempp-Hirth Discus-2b	248	
D-5481	Schleicher Ka 2B Rhönschwalbe	213	
D-5484-YL	Rolladen-Schneider LS4	4568	OY-XYL
D-5486	Scheibe L-Spatz 55	02	
D-5487	Schleicher K 8B	8321/A	D-KANC, D-5487
D-5490	Schleicher ASK 13	13290	OE-5490, D-0661
D-5491-6K	Schleicher ASK 21	21652	
D-5493-DR	Schempp-Hirth Discus CS	184CS	
D-5494-CA	Schempp-Hirth Discus CS	182CS	
D-5496	Schempp-Hirth Discus-2b	112	
D-5498-99	Schleicher ASW 27-18 (ASG 29)	?	
D-5500	Ahrens LY-542K Stösser	V-1	D-7128, D-0026, D-5440
	(P.05)		
D-5501	LET L-23 Super Blanik	938110	OK-3201
D-5503	Schleicher Ka 2B Rhönschwalbe	224	
D-5504-IS	Glasflügel 304	227	SE-UET, OH-613
D-5505	Scheibe L-Spatz 55	4/58	OO-ZVU, D-5505
	(Permit)		
D-5507	Glaser-Dirks DG-300 Club Elan	3E383C55	
D-5508-K2	Glaser-Dirks DG-300 Club Elan	3E388C57	
D-5510	Rolladen-Schneider LS4-b	4881	
D-5511	Schleicher ASK 13	13028	
D-5512	Rolladen-Schneider LS6-18W	6384	
D-5513-FY	SZD-55-1	551193051	PH-993
D-5514	Schleicher ASK 13	13205	D-0353
D-5517	Valentin Mistral C	MC 036/81	OE-5517, D-4936
D-5518	SZD-55-1	X-144	SP-3501, SP-P501
D-5519	Schleicher Ka 6CR Rhönsegler	6419	
D-5520	Schleicher Ka 6CR Rhönsegler	6515	
D-5521	Schleicher K 7 Rhönadler	7122	
D-5522-CI	Rolladen-Schneider LS1-d	136	OY-XCI, D-2048
D-5523-LR	Schempp-Hirth Discus-2a	86	BGA 4889/JYM
D-5525-BX	Jonker Sailplanes JS/MD Single	1C-098	
	(P 29.4.16)		
D-5526	Glaser-Dirks DG-300 Elan	3E321	HB-1980
D-5527	Schleicher ASW 27B	27220	
	(P.4.12)		
D-5528-28	Grob G 103C Twin III Acro	34177	
D-5529	Rolladen-Schneider LS4	4117	
D-5530-30	Schleicher ASK 23B	23146	
D-5531-LX	SZD-41A Jantar Standard	B-933	OE-5231
D-5532	Grob G 103C Twin III Acro	34147	
D-5533	Schleicher Ka 2B Rhönschwalbe	253	
D-5534	Glaser-Dirks DG-300 Elan	3E72	OE-5513, D-3350
D-5535	Schleicher Ka 6CR Rhönsegler	6505	
D-5536-OF	Schempp-Hirth Ventus-2b	35	
D-5539-R2	Schempp-Hirth Discus-2b	110	
D-5540	Rolladen-Schneider LS4-b	41049	
D-5541-6W	Schempp-Hirth Duo Discus X	473	
D-5542	Marganski Swift S-1	112	OE-5542
D-5543	Schempp-Hirth Standard Cirrus	46	PH-559, D-0566
D-5545	Schleicher Ka 6 Rhönsegler	292	
D-5546-E8	Schempp-Hirth Duo Discus	333	
D-5547	Schleicher ASK 23B	23095	PH-813
D-5548-A2	Schempp-Hirth Duo Discus	117	
D-5549	Rolladen-Schneider LS4	4569	PH-786, D-3539
D-5550	SG-38 Schulgleiter	0010	
D-5551	Scheibe Specht	02/55	D-0314, OE-0319
	(Res.)		
D-5552-XR	Schempp-Hirth Discus b	492	
D-5553-22	Rolladen-Schneider LS6-b	6138	
D-5554	Schleicher Ka 6BR Rhönsegler	355	
	(P 7.4.16)		
D-5555-XY	Schempp-Hirth Ventus-2ax	149	
D-5556-TX	Rolladen-Schneider LS8-18	8361	
D-5557	DG Flugzeugbau DG-1000S	10-238S157	
D-5559	Schleicher ASW 20L	20333	D-KENN, D-7544
D-5560	SZD-55-1	551193053	
D-5561	Glasflügel H303 Mosquito B	178	HB-1517
D-5562-AB	Rolladen-Schneider LS8-18	8362	
D-5563	Schleicher K 8B	8372	
D-5564	Glaser-Dirks DG-300 Club Elan	3E316C25	HB-1984
D-5565-KA	Glaser-Dirks DG-500 Elan Orion	5E140X5	
D-5566-R4	Glaser-Dirks DG-300 Elan	3E398	
D-5569	Schleicher K 8B	8566	
D-5570	Schleicher Ka 6E	4006	
D-5571-LL	Rolladen-Schneider LS6-b	6143	
D-5572	Schleicher ASK 23B	23034	F-CGCT, F-WGCT
D-5574-XXX	Schempp-Hirth Duo Discus CS	468CS	OK-5554, D-0047
D-5576	Schleicher Ka 6CR Rhönsegler	6313	
D-5579	Grob G 103 Twin Astir	3057	OE-5576, OE-5347, D-4847
D-5581	DG Flugzeugbau DG-1000S	10-17S17	
D-5582	SZD-59 Acro	B-2165	OE-5586
D-5583	Rolladen-Schneider LS7-WL	7158	OE-5503
	(P.05)		
D-5584-WB	Schempp-Hirth Discus b	186	
D-5585-FB	Glasflügel Standard Libelle 201B	554	I-LULU
D-5586-CH	SZD-48 Jantar-Standard 2	W-880	SP-3701, SE-TRT
D-5587	Schleicher ASK 21	21158	
D-5588	Rolladen-Schneider LS4-b	4914	
D-5589-89	Schleicher ASK 21	21159	

Reg	Type	Serial	Previous/Other
D-5590	Schleicher Ka 6	202	
D-5592-PB	SZD-55-1	551192045	HB-3107
D-5593	Schleicher K 8B	8394SH	
D-5594	Schleicher K 8B	8375	
D-5595	Marganski MDM-1 Fox	231	
D-5596	Schleicher Ka 2B Rhönschwalbe	403	
D-5599-P8	Schleicher ASW 27	27015	
D-5600	Glasflügel Standard Libelle 201B	202	HB-1010
D-5601	Schleicher Ka 6CR Rhönsegler	6428Si	
D-5603	Glaser-Dirks DG-300 Elan	3E376	
D-5604	Glaser-Dirks DG-300 Club Elan	3E381C54	
D-5605	Schleicher ASK 21	21689	
D-5606(2)-PIC	Schempp-Hirth Nimbus-4D (P. 26.9.16)	15	
D-5608-H3	Schempp-Hirth Duo Discus	246	
D-5609	Schleicher K 8B	8435/A	
D-5610	Scheibe SF 27A	6050	
D-5612	SZD-50-3 Puchacz	B-1329	DDR-3612
D-5613	Schleicher K 8B	8953	OO-ZOI, PH-476
D-5614	Glaser-Dirks DG-200	2-164	HB-1614
D-5617	Schleicher K 8B	8416	
D-5618-BA	Schleicher ASK 21	21717	
D-5620	Schleicher ASK 13	13680AB	
D-5621	Schleicher ASK 21	21883	
D-5622	Schleicher ASK 13	13679AB	
D-5623	Schleicher Ka 6CR Rhönsegler	6323	
D-5624	Schleicher ASK 13	13689AB	
D-5625	Schleicher ASK 21	21081	
D-5626-2N	Schleicher ASK 21	21082	
D-5627	Schleicher ASW 27B	27214	D-8272, OK-7272
D-5628	Schleicher ASK 21	21083	
D-5629	Schleicher ASK 21	21084	
D-5630	Schleicher K 7 Rhönadler	413	
D-5631	Schleicher Ka 6BR Rhönsegler	416	
D-5632	SZD-50-3 Puchacz	B-1396	DDR-3632
D-5633	Schleicher ASK 21	21722	
D-5636	Schleicher ASW 27	27045	OE-5636
D-5637	Schleicher Ka 6BR Rhönsegler	397	
D-5638	Schleicher K 8B	8472	
D-5641-41	Schempp-Hirth Discus-2b	88	
D-5642	Glaser-Dirks DG-100G Elan	E167G133	
D-5643	PZL-Swidnik PW-5 Smyk (P. 5.11)	17.07.024	OE-5649
D-5644	Schleicher Ka 6CR Rhönsegler	6347Si	
D-5645	Schleicher K 8	451	
D-5646	Schleicher Ka 6E	4039	
D-5647	DG Flugzeugbau DG-303 Elan Acro	3E475A20	OE-5641
D-5648	Rolladen-Schneider LS8-18 (Cld? Currently quoted as Schleicher ASW-28 28016)	8351	
D-5649	Scheibe L-Spatz 55	3	
D-5650-H7	Rolladen-Schneider LS1-f	312	
D-5651	Glaser-Dirks DG-300 Elan	3E109	D-2878
D-5652	Schleicher Ka 6CR Rhönsegler	6360	
D-5653-AH	Rolladen-Schneider LS8-a	8403	
D-5655	SZD-55-1	551197095	OE-5652
D-5656	Schleicher ASK 13 (W/o 3.9.16)	13618	
D-5657-57	Schempp-Hirth Discus CS	097CS	
D-5658	Schleicher ASK 21	21593	
D-5659	Schleicher K 7 Rhönadler	502	
D-5660	SZD-50-3 Puchacz	B-1551	DDR-3660
D-5662	Schleicher Ka 6CR Rhönsegler	6424	
D-5663	Schleicher ASK 21	21125	HB-1663
D-5664-ZL	Rolladen-Schneider LS8-a	8358	
D-5665	Schleicher K 8B	216	
D-5666-D6	Schempp-Hirth Discus CS	156CS	
D-5667	Glaser-Dirks DG-300 Elan	3E252	HB-1917
D-5669	Neukom Elfe S4D	404AB	D-6669
D-5670-D2	Schempp-Hirth Discus-2b	39	
D-5671	Schleicher K 8B	8436	
D-5673-GK	Rolladen-Schneider LS6	6144	
D-5674	Schempp-Hirth Discus CS	060CS	OE-5671, D-7114
D-5678	Scheibe L-Spatz 55	E2	(D-6354), D-1354
D-5680-82	Schleicher Ka 6CR Rhönsegler	6381	
D-5686	Schleicher K 8	512	
D-5688	Schleicher K 7 Rhönadler	548	
D-5690	Schleicher ASW 27B	27150	OE-5690
D-5692	Schleicher K 8B	545	
D-5694	Rolladen-Schneider LS4	4427	
D-5695	Bölkow Phoebus A-1	749	
D-5698-PV	Schempp-Hirth Standard Cirrus	?	
D-5700-PC	Schempp-Hirth Ventus c	334	OO-PPC
D-5701	Schleicher ASK 13	13001	
D-5702	Glaser-Dirks DG-600	6-30	
D-5703	Nord 1300 (Grunau Baby IIB)	120	F-CRLT
D-5704	Schleicher K 8B	134/59	
D-5705	Schleicher Ka 6CR	6349/Si	
D-5706	Rolladen-Schneider LS4-b	41044	
D-5707-007	Schempp-Hirth Duo Discus	285	
D-5708-GG	Rolladen-Schneider LS8-18	8363	
D-5710	Glaser-Dirks DG-300 Elan	3E180	
D-5711-CB	Schleicher ASK 21	21774	
D-5712	Schempp-Hirth Discus-2b	143	
D-5713	Schleicher ASW 19B	19395	
D-5714	ISF Mistral-C	MC 012/78	HB-1429
D-5715	Schleicher K 8B	107/58	
D-5716-IT	Glaser-Dirks DG-300 Elan	3E185	
D-5717	Schleicher K 7 Rhönadler	605	
D-5718-SL	Schleicher ASW 20	20397	OE-5718, I-ZOOW
D-5719	Allstar PZL SZD-59 Acro	590.A.05.003	OE-5714
D-5720	Glasflügel 604	6	I-ETAB
D-5721	Schleicher ASK 21	21714	
D-5722	Glaser-Dirks DG-100G Elan (P. 11.13)	E192G158	
D-5723-IHM	Schempp-Hirth Discus-2b	230	
D-5725	Glaser-Dirks DG-300 Elan	3E163	
D-5727	Schleicher K 8B (P. 4.11)	8096/A	D-5207
D-5728	Schleicher ASW 28	28072	
D-5729-NM	Glaser-Dirks DG-300 Elan	3E186	
D-5730	Rolladen-Schneider LS4-a	4722	D-7255, D-1281
D-5731	Schleicher K 8B	138/59	OE-5413, D-5731
D-5733	Glaser-Dirks DG-300 Elan	3E189	
D-5734	Schempp-Hirth Duo Discus	109	
D-5737	Schleicher Ka 6CR Rhönsegler	6562	
D-5741	Rolladen-Schneider LS4	4625	
D-5742	Grob G102 Astir CS Jeans	2172	
D-5743-RC	Rolladen-Schneider LS4	4626	
D-5747-522	Glaser-Dirks DG-500/22 Elan	5E36S8	G-CHBP, BGA 3814
D-5748	Schleicher K 8B (Res. - cld?)	737	
D-5750-RR	Grob G 103C Twin III	36010	
D-5752-B52	Schleicher ASK 21	21683	
D-5755	SZD-30 Pirat	B-359	DDR-1755, DM-1755
D-5756	Schempp-Hirth Janus C	?	
D-5757	Schleicher Ka 6CR Rhönsegler	718	
D-5758-58	Rolladen-Schneider LS4	4630	
D-5760	Schleicher K 8B	850	
D-5761	Akaflieg Braunschweig SB-5E Sperber	5016	
D-5762	SZD-30 Pirat	B-365	DDR-1762, DM-1762
D-5763-63	Schleicher ASW 28	28043	
D-5764	Schleicher K 8B	163/60	
D-5765	Schleicher K 8	110/58	
D-5766	Schleicher ASW 20	20603	OH-666
D-5767	Rolladen-Schneider LS4	4631	
D-5769	SZD-30 Pirat	B-398	DDR-1769, DM-1769
D-5770-RF	Schempp-Hirth Discus CS	043CS	
D-5771-RD	Schempp-Hirth Duo Discus XL	644	
D-5773	Schleicher K 7 Rhönadler	77/57	
D-5774-7X	Rolladen-Schneider LS8-18	8285	
D-5775-KS	Glasflügel Standard Libelle	301	OO-ZTY, F-CEBA
D-5776-RA	Schempp-Hirth Duo Discus	133	
D-5777-1	Schempp-Hirth Duo Discus XL	641	
D-5779	Schleicher K 7 Rhönadler	7218	
D-5780	Scheibe SF 27A	6087	
D-5781	Schleicher K 7 Rhönadler	832	
D-5782	Schleicher K 8B	170/60	HB-105, D-5782
D-5783	Rolladen-Schneider LS7	7061	
D-5784-IMM	Rolladen-Schneider LS7-WL	7062	
D-5787	Start & Flug H-101 Salto	68	
D-5790-GK	Schempp-Hirth Ventus c	579	OY-XSS
D-5792	Rolladen-Schneider LS7	7064	
D-5793	Vogt Lo-100 Zwergreiher	21	D-4093
D-5794	Schleicher Ka 6CR Rhönsegler	848	
D-5795	SZD-51-1 Junior	B-1770	HB-1918
D-5796	Schleicher K 7 Rhönadler	866	
D-5798	Schleicher K 8	168/60	
D-5799	Schleicher ASK 13	13032	
D-5801-Y5	Rolladen-Schneider LS8-18	8333	
D-5802-O8	Schleicher K 8B	841	
D-5803	Glaser-Dirks DG-101G Elan	E222G188	I-LYNO
D-5804	Rolladen-Schneider LS1-d	88	OO-ZRX, D-0305
D-5805-IRH	Glaser-Dirks DG-300 Elan	3E106	
D-5806	Schleicher K 8B	877	
D-5807-8	Rolladen-Schneider LS8-18	8360	
D-5808-6J	Rolladen-Schneider LS8-a	8406	
D-5809-FUN	Schempp-Hirth Duo Discus	405	
D-5810	Schleicher ASK 21	21696	
D-5812	Schleicher Ka 6CR Rhönsegler	6650	D-5818
D-5813	VEB LOM 57 Libelle	015	
D-5814	Schleicher K 8B	8428/A	
D-5815	Glaser-Dirks DG-500 Elan Trainer	5E86T37	
D-5819-AL	Schleicher ASW 27B	27179	
D-5820	Schleicher K 7 Rhönadler	7220	
D-5821-16	Schleicher Ka 6CR Rhönsegler	6425	
D-5823-C2	Schleicher K 8B	8501	
D-5825	Schleicher Ka 6CR Rhönsegler	6099Si	D-5812
D-5826-JS	Rolladen-Schneider LS8-18	8407	
D-5827-LT	Schleicher ASW 27B	27178	
D-5828	Rock Geier IIB	03	
D-5829	DG Flugzeugbau DG-500 Elan Orion	5E232X70	
D-5830	Rolladen-Schneider LS3-a	3454	F-CESS
D-5831	Glaser-Dirks DG-100G Elan	E93G64	
D-5832	Schleicher ASK 13	13012	
D-5833	SZD-30 Pirat	B-512	DDR-1833, DM-1833
D-5834	Schleicher ASW 24B	24227	
D-5835	Schleicher ASW 19B	19142	PH-583
D-5836	Schleicher Ka 6CR Rhönsegler	6579	
D-5837	Scheibe SF 27A	6067	
D-5838	Glaser-Dirks DG-100G Elan	E92G63	
D-5840	Rolladen-Schneider LS6	6108	
D-5842-AV	Glaser-Dirks DG-100G Elan	E89G61	
D-5843	Scheibe SF 27A	6068	
D-5844	Schleicher K 7 Rhönadler	7265	
D-5846-GS	Glasflügel H304 (P 16.6.16)	224	
D-5847-KC	Glasflügel H304	225	
D-5848-RS	Rolladen-Schneider LS8-18	unknown	
D-5849	Schleicher Ka 6E	4139	
D-5850	Glasflügel BS.1	6	
D-5851-B2	Schleicher ASK 21	21753	
D-5852	Schleicher K 8B	8737/A	
D-5854	Schleicher Ka 6CR Rhönsegler	6637	
D-5855-HX	Jonker Sailplanes JS1C/MD Single (P 3.15)	1C-071	
D-5856	Schleicher Ka 6CR Rhönsegler (P.02)	6290	
D-5857	Schleicher ASK 13	13068	
D-5858	Schleicher K 8B	8748	
D-5859	SZD-59 Acro	B-2160	N591AS
D-5860	Rolladen-Schneider LS6-b	6110	
D-5861	Glaser-Dirks DG-100G Elan	E88G60	
D-5862	Focke-Wulf Weihe 50 (Now in Wasserkuppe museum)	unkn	
D-5863-BZ	Schleicher Ka 6CR Rhönsegler	6378	
D-5864-64	Rolladen-Schneider LS4-b	41035	
D-5865-1A	Glasflügel H304	258	
D-5866	Grob G 103C Twin III Acro	34195	
D-5867	Glaser-Dirks DG-100G Elan	E98G68	
D-5868-B5	Rolladen-Schneider LS8-18	8364	
D-5869	Glasflügel H301 Libelle	15	HB-794
D-5870	Grob G 102 Astir CS	1021	
D-5871	Grob G 102 Astir CS	1022	
D-5872	Glaser-Dirks DG-100G Elan	E96G66	
D-5875	Grob G 102 Astir CS	1026	
D-5876	Grob G 102 Astir CS	1027	
D-5878	Grob G 102 Astir CS	1029	
D-5879-RZ	Grob G 102 Astir CS	1030	
D-5880-NX	Grob G 102 Astir CS	1031	
D-5881	Grob G 102 Astir CS	1032	
D-5882	Rolladen-Schneider LS6 (P. 6.11)	6078	OE-5383

Regn	Type	c/n	Previous identities
D-5883	SZD-30 Pirat	S-01.29	DDR-1883, DM-1883
D-5885-8X	Schempp-Hirth Ventus-2a	56	
D-5886	Rolladen-Schneider LS1-f	256	
D-5889	HBV Diamant	008	HB-889
D-5890	Rolladen-Schneider LS6-b	6111	
D-5891	Glasflügel H201B Standard Libelle	503/A	
D-5892	Glaser-Dirks DG-202/17	2-175/1758	OO-YBL, D-5892
D-5893	Rolladen-Schneider LS1-f	331	HB-1916, D-2738
D-5895-BT	Schempp-Hirth Janus B	157	
D-5896-FJ	Schempp-Hirth Nimbus-3/24.5 (W/o 2.5.15)	25	
D-5898	Rolladen-Schneider LS3-a	3284	
D-5899	Schleicher ASK 21	21711	
D-5900	Grob G 103C Twin III Acro	34185	
D-5902	Rolladen-Schneider LS4	4137	
D-5903	Rolladen-Schneider LS4	4153	
D-5904-BG	Rolladen-Schneider LS4	4118	
D-5905-PZ	Glaser-Dirks DG-300 Elan	3E233	
D-5907	Glasflügel H303 Mosquito B (P 6.15)	152	
D-5908-HJ	Schempp-Hirth Ventus-2b	116	
D-5909-ISV	Schempp-Hirth Arcus	11	
D-5910-OL	Grob G 103 Twin II	3640	
D-5911	Grob G 103 Twin II	3641	
D-5912-TB	Rolladen-Schneider LS4-b	41037	
D-5913	Grob G 102 Astir CS 77	1822	
D-5914	Grob G 102 Astir CS 77	1823	
D-5915-XE	Grob G 102 Astir CS Jeans	2232	
D-5916-L4	Grob G 102 Astir CS Jeans	2236	
D-5917-E1	Schleicher ASW 28	28027	
D-5918	Grob G 102 Astir CS Jeans	2238	
D-5919	Grob G 102 Astir CS 77	1824	
D-5920	Schleicher ASW 20CL	20816	HB-1808
D-5921	Slingsby T59D Kestrel 19	1832	G-DFDK, BGA 3176, (BGA 4927), BGA 3176, G-BBVC
D-5922-2V	Schempp-Hirth Discus-2b	105	
D-5923	Schleicher ASK 21	21108	
D-5924	Glaser-Dirks DG-100G Elan	E122G91	
D-5925	Rolladen-Schneider LS8-18	8365	
D-5926-R4	Glaser-Dirks DG-100G Elan	E124G92	
D-5927	Glasflügel H304	230	
D-5928-MK	Schempp-Hirth Discus-2a	111	OH-928
D-5929	Glasflügel H304	242	
D-5930-A4	Schempp-Hirth Ventus-2b	107	
D-5931	Glasflügel H304 (P 4.15)	236	
D-5933-L7	Schleicher ASW 20CL	20756	
D-5934-34	Schleicher ASW 19B	19407	
D-5935	Schleicher ASW 20CL	20759	
D-5936-TNt	Schleicher ASW 20BL	20647	
D-5940	Scheibe Bergfalke IV	5863	
D-5941-TY	Schempp-Hirth Discus-2b	153	
D-5942	Schleicher ASK 21	21587	
D-5944	Valentin Mistral C	MC 057/85	OO-ZHI, D-4957
D-5945	Grob G 102 Astir CS 77	1828	
D-5947	Grob G 102 Astir CS Jeans	2242	
D-5948	Grob G 102 Astir CS Jeans	2243	
D-5949	SZD-59 Acro	590.A.16.018	
D-5950	Grob G 102 Astir CS 77	1825	
D-5951	Schleicher ASK 21	21803	
D-5952	SZD-48-3 Jantar Standard 3	B-1952	CCCP-1952, DOSAAF
D-5954-54	Grob G 103 Twin Astir (P .7.12)	3194	
D-5955	SZD-55-1	551193059	SP-3602
D-5957-PY	Sportine Aviacija LAK-17A	175	
D-5958	SZD-59 Acro	B-2163	OO-ZQL
D-5960	Schempp-Hirth Mini-Nimbus HS7	54	OO-LGA
D-5963	Grob G 103 Twin Astir Trainer	3211-T-24	
D-5965	Schleicher ASW 19B	19094	PH-565
D-5966-GM	Schleicher ASG 29	?	
D-5971	Grob G 103 Twin Astir	3246	
D-5974-GC	Schleicher ASW 19B	19257	
D-5975	Schleicher ASW 20L	20145	
D-5976	Schleicher ASW 19B	19258	
D-5977	Schleicher ASW 19B	19260	
D-5978-YM	Schleicher ASW 19B	19261	
D-5983	Schleicher ASW 24	24223	ZK-GRC
D-5984-JA	Glaser-Dirks DG-300 Elan	3E312	
D-5986	Rolladen-Schneider LS4	4288	
D-5988-MP	Rolladen-Schneider LS4	4341	
D-5989-KT	Schleicher ASW 20	20301	OY-XKT
D-5990-DM	Eiri PIK-20D	20523	
D-5992-CR	Schempp-Hirth Ventus a/16.6	30	
D-5994-BB	Schleicher ASH 25	25159	
D-5995	Rolladen-Schneider LS4	4042	
D-5996	Glaser-Dirks DG-101G Elan	E58G34	HB-1576
D-5997	Rolladen-Schneider LS4	4030	
D-5998-VE	Rolladen-Schneider LS4	4214	
D-5999	Glaser-Dirks DG-101G Elan	E78G53	HB-1592
D-6000-MI	Glaser-Dirks DG-600	6-23	S5-3000, SL-3000, YU-4454
D-6001	Schempp-Hirth Mini-Nimbus B	70	
D-6002	Rolladen-Schneider LS6-18W	6381	OO-YIN, (OO-YVA), OO-YIN
D-6004	Grunau Baby III	02	
D-6005	Schleicher K 7	7071	OY-XDT, D-5265
D-6006	Schempp-Hirth Discus CS	106CS	F-CGGV
D-6007	Glasflügel H304	249	
D-6008	Glaser-Dirks DG-300 Elan	3E26	
D-6009	Pilatus B4-PC11AF (P 4.15)	125	
D-6011-H4	Schempp-Hirth Discus b	308	
D-6012	SZD-9bis Bocian 1E	P-725	DDR-3012, DM-3012
D-6015	Caproni Calif A21S	239	F-CJGM, D-6615
D-6016-M2	Schempp-Hirth Duo Discus	238	
D-6018	Focke-Wulf Kranich III	53	
D-6019-PC	Schleicher ASW 19B	19389	
D-6020	Glasflügel H201B Standard Libelle	322	G-DCNY, BGA 1686
D-6021	Schleicher K 8B	8248/2	
D-6022	Schleicher Ka 6CR Rhönsegler	6057	
D-6023	Glaser-Dirks DG-500/22 Elan	5E63S10	
D-6024	Schleicher ASW 24	24038	OE-5464
D-6025	Schleicher Ka 6CR Rhönsegler	6557Si	
D-6028	Schleicher K 8B	8224	
D-6029-57	Schempp-Hirth Ventus-2ax	146	
D-6030-Z	Schleicher ASH 25	25081	SP-3578
D-6032	Glaser-Dirks DG-100	17	HB-1276
D-6034	Schempp-Hirth Ventus c	289	
D-6035-K6	Schempp-Hirth Discus-2b	227	
D-6036	Schleicher K 8B	8215	
D-6038	Schleicher K 8B	8397	
D-6039-GAD	Schleicher K 7 Rhönadler	503	PH-1039, D-6247
D-6040-40	Rolladen-Schneider LS1-b	33	HB-983
D-6041-H2	Rolladen-Schneider LS4	4627	D-5746
D-6042-CG	Rolladen-Schneider LS7	7157	
D-6043	Dittmar Condor IV	13	LV-EHB
D-6044	Focke-Wulf Kranich III	64	
D-6045	DFS Reiher III replica	AB R2	
D-6046	Olympia-Meise	1/95	BGA 2080/DFM, D-6220
D-6047	Rolladen-Schneider LS6	6116	
D-6048	DFS Kranich 2B-1	065	BGA 1092, SE-SPN, Fv8204
	(Quoted as amateur-build c/n NIE1994) (Rebt with wings from BGA 1258)		
D-6049-H2	Rolladen-Schneider LS7	7160	
D-6052	Schleicher ASK 13	13020	
D-6053	Schleicher Ka 6CR Rhönsegler	6590	
D-6054	Grunau Baby III	AB-01-53	BGA 1754/CRU, RAFGSA, D-6054
D-6055	Schempp-Hirth Ventus b/16.6	250	
D-6056	Schleicher ASK 13	13027	
D-6057	Grob G 102 Club Astir IIIB	5515CB	
D-6058	Grob G 102 Astir CS III	5518C	
D-6059	Cumulus Cu-III F	02	
D-6060	Schleicher Ka 6CR Rhönsegler	6146	OY-FJX, D-6034
D-6061	Doppelraab V	532	D-6062
D-6062-Z	Rolladen-Schneider LS6	6118	
D-6063-3C	Schleicher ASW 19B	19014	I-ALIA
D-6064	Doppelraab V (P.8.99)	534	
D-6065-G6	Schempp-Hirth Ventus b/16.6	249	
D-6066	Schleicher K 8B	8700	
D-6067	Schleicher K 7 Rhönadler	02/62	
D-6069	Reinhard Cumulus CU-IIF	3/54	D-7110
D-6070	Schleicher K 7 Rhönadler	7074	
D-6071	Focke-Wulf Kranich III	68	
D-6073	Focke-Wulf Kranich III	71	
D-6074	Schleicher ASK 21	21467	
D-6075	Schleicher ASW 24	24094	
D-6076	Schleicher ASW 24	24097	
D-6077	DG Flugzeugbau DG-1000S	10-40S39	
D-6078	Schempp-Hirth Duo Discus	436	
D-6081	Marganski Swift S-1	124	N124XX, HB-3247
D-6085-14	Akaflieg Braunschweig SB-10 (P 3.5.16)	01	
D-6086	Rolladen-Schneider LS6	6086	SE-TYC
D-6087-NW	Schleicher ASW 24	24098	
D-6089-89	Schleicher Ka 6CR Rhönsegler	6484Si	
D-6090-CF	Glaser-Dirks DG-200/17	2-173/1756	
D-6092-N9	Schleicher ASW 24	24100	
D-6094-XY	Schempp-Hirth Nimbus-3/24.5	72	
D-6097	Schempp-Hirth Discus-2c	6	
D-6099-99	Schleicher K 8B	8071	
D-6100	Glaser-Dirks DG-100G	86G7	
D-6101	Start & Flug H-101 Salto	70	
D-6102-OM	Grob G 102 Astir CS (P 29.4.16)	1001	
D-6103-GH	Schleicher ASK 21	21772	
D-6105	Grob G 102 Standard Astir III	5535S	
D-6106	Grob G 103 Twin II	3642	
D-6107	Scheibe Bergfalke III	5570	
D-6108	SG-38 Schulgleiter	14	
D-6109	Glasflügel Standard Libelle 201B	280	I-KIRA
D-6110-PB	Grob G 103C Twin III Acro	34179	
D-6114-F1	Schempp-Hirth Discus-2c	2	
D-6115	Schleicher Ka 6E	4166	
D-6116	Grob G 102 Club Astir IIIb	5516Cb	OE-5275
D-6117	Rolladen-Schneider LS8-a	8176	OY-RBX
D-6118	Schleicher Ka 6CR Rhönsegler	6636	
D-6119-F1	Schempp-Hirth Discus-2c	?	
D-6120	Schleicher ASW 20CL	20865	
D-6121	Schleicher ASK 21	21616	(JA2539)
D-6122-ACD	Schempp-Hirth Duo Discus	68	
D-6123	Schleicher Ka 6CR Rhönsegler	6162	
D-6124	Schleicher K 8B	8331SH	
D-6125	Schleicher Ka 2 Rhönschwalbe	105	
D-6126	Schleicher ASH 26	26059	
D-6127	Schempp-Hirth Cirrus	14	
D-6128	Schleicher ASK 21	21085	
D-6129-3AB	Schleicher ASW 27-18 (ASG 29)	29011	
D-6130	Schleicher K 8B	8163	G-CHYW, BGA 4320, D-5316, D-3202
D-6132-ES	Schempp-Hirth Discus-2c	11	
D-6133-DY	Glasflügel Hornet	4	I-FLAV
D-6135	Schleicher Ka 6E	4164	
D-6136	Schleicher ASK 21	21623	
D-6137	Grob G102 Astir CS Jeans	2038	OE-5137
D-6138-DT	Schleicher ASW 24	24156	
D-6139-BB	Schleicher ASW 24	24158	
D-6140-GT1	Schleicher ASW 24	24159	
D-6142	Schleicher ASW 24	24161	
D-6144	Schleicher ASK 21	21426	
D-6146-J6	Schleicher ASK 21	21428	
D-6147	Rolladen-Schneider LS6-c	6277	
D-6148	Doppelraab 7	01	
D-6149	Schleicher ASW 24	24163	
D-6150	Doppelraab 7	0110	
D-6151-MD	Schleicher ASW 24	24164	
D-6153-NI	Schleicher ASK 21	21461	
D-6154-TT	Schempp-Hirth Ventus-2b	85	PH-1154
D-6155	Schleicher ASK 21	21633	
D-6156	Scheibe Zugvogel IIIB	1106	
D-6157	Schleicher ASW 24	24169	
D-6158	Grob G 102 Standard Astir III	5522S	
D-6159	Schempp-Hirth Discus b	80	I-AYEZ, D-5241
D-6160	Schempp-Hirth Arcus (P. 7.14)	15	
D-6161	Schempp-Hirth Discus CS	263CS	OK-9307
D-6162	Grunau Baby IIB	1	
D-6163	Schleicher Ka 6CR Rhönsegler	6026	D-KODY, D-6163
D-6164-DID	Schempp-Hirth Ventus-2cx	128	
D-6165	Glaser-Dirks DG-300 Elan	3E401	
D-6166	Rolladen-Schneider LS4-b	4955	

Regn	Type	c/n	Previous identities
D-6167-M3	Schempp-Hirth Janus B	68	PH-616
D-6168	Grunau Baby III	4	
D-6169	SZD-50-3 Puchacz	B-2053	
D-6170	Glaser-Dirks DG-600/18	6-24	OO-YGE, HB-1927
D-6171	Schempp-Hirth Discus b	42	
D-6172-D6	Schleicher ASW 24	24170	
D-6174	Schleicher K 10A	10001	
D-6176	Grunau Baby IIb	3	
D-6178	Schleicher K 8B	8046	
D-6179-M6	Schleicher ASK 21	21429	
D-6180	Schleicher ASW 24	24059	
D-6181	Bölkow Phoebus A-1	788	
D-6184-GT	Schleicher ASK 21	21432	
D-6185	Schleicher ASK 21	21433	
D-6188	Grob G 103C Twin III Acro	34143	
D-6189	Schleicher ASK 21	21701	
D-6191	Rolladen-Schneider LS6	6119	
D-6192-XA	Rolladen-Schneider LS7	7022	EC-FKP, D-1338
D-6193-7	Akaflieg Braunschweig SB 7B	1	D-6103
D-6194	Schleicher K 8B	8065	D-6121
D-6199-W3	Rolladen-Schneider LS4-b	4915	
D-6200	Fauvel AV-36 (W/o 25.9.16)	222	BGA 2500/DZE, D-6200
D-6201	Pilatus B4-PC11AF	257	OO-ZNU, LX-CVA
D-6202-2W	SZD-48-1 Jantar Standard 2	B-1209	OE-5302
D-6203-TG	Glasflügel H304	233	
D-6204	Schempp-Hirth Discus b	232	EC-EKE
D-6206-AMY	Rolladen-Schneider LS6-c	6203	PH-909
D-6207	SZD-9bis Bocian 1D	P-362	DDR-3207, DM-3207
D-6208	Grob G102 Astir CS	1396	OO-ZMO
D-6210	Rolladen-Schneider LS6-c	6204	
D-6211-OH	DG Flugzeugbau DG-1000S	10-54S53	
D-6212	Vogt Lo-100 Zwergreiher	14	
D-6213	Schleicher Rhönlerche II	311	
D-6214	SZD-36A Cobra 15	W-668	HB-1214
D-6215-GD	Schleicher ASW 24	24181	
D-6216-TZ	Rolladen-Schneider LS6-c	6207	
D-6217-DG	Glaser-Dirks DG-200/17	2-91/1708	
D-6218	Glaser-Dirks DG-200	2-76	
D-6219	Schleicher K 7	5	
D-6220	Glaser-Dirks DG-200/17	2-81/1702	
D-6221	Glaser-Dirks DG-200	2-78	
D-6222-AH	Schleicher Ka 6BR Rhönsegler	395	
D-6224	Grunau Baby III	1	
D-6225	Grunau Baby III	0001	
D-6226	Pilatus B4-PC11AF	58	G-CHDW, OY-XBH
D-6227	Schleicher ASW 27B	27237	
D-6228	Focke-Wulf Kranich III	90	
D-6229-2M	Schempp-Hirth Duo Discus	542	
D-6230	Glaser-Dirks DG-300 Elan	3E53	
D-6232	Schleicher Ka 6CR Rhönsegler	6185	
D-6233-GT	Schleicher ASW 28	28049	
D-6234	Schleicher ASK 21	21437	
D-6235	Schleicher ASK 21	21449	
D-6236	Schleicher ASK 21	21450	
D-6237	Schleicher K 7 Rhönadler (Res. - cld?)	394	
D-6238	Schleicher Ka 6CR Rhönsegler	6574	
D-6239	Schleicher ASW 24	24167	
D-6240	Schleicher K 8	510	
D-6241-MT	Schleicher ASW 24	24191	
D-6243	Schleicher K 8B (Res. - cld?)	515	
D-6248	Schleicher K 8B	1016	
D-6249	Glaser-Dirks DG-200	2-25	I-LORA, D-6782
D-6250	Schleicher Ka 6CR Rhönsegler	600	
D-6251-D	Glasflügel Club Libelle 205	4	I-INES
D-6253	Schleicher ASW 24	24042	
D-6254-54	Schempp-Hirth Discus CS	332CS	
D-6255-55	Schleicher ASK 21	21416	
D-6256	Schleicher K 7 Rhönadler	7098	
D-6259	Rolladen-Schneider LS3-a	3303	F-CESE
D-6261	Schleicher K 8B	589	
D-6262	Rolladen-Schneider LS6	6043	
D-6263-AD	Rolladen-Schneider LS6-a	6044	
D-6264	DG Flugzeugbau DG-1000S	10-244S163	D-6244
D-6270-7E	Schleicher ASW 24	24197	
D-6272-J08	Schempp-Hirth Janus	32	F-CEPG
D-6274	Focke-Wulf Kranich III	62	
D-6275	Schleicher ASW 20CL	20718	HB-1727
D-6276-AR	Grob G 103C Twin III Acro	34170	
D-6277-FB	Grob G 103C Twin III Acro	34106	
D-6279	Schleicher ASW 27B	27234	G-CKLB, BGA5173/KLB
D-6280	Schleicher Ka 6CR Rhönsegler	783	
D-6283	Grob G 103C Twin III Acro	34145	
D-6284	Grob G 103C Twin III Acro	34142	
D-6285-LS	Grob G 103C Twin III Acro	34144	
D-6286	Grob G 103C Twin III Acro	34150	
D-6287	Schleicher ASK 21	21069	
D-6288	Schleicher Ka 6CR Rhönsegler	825	
D-6289	Schempp-Hirth Discus CS	068CS	PH-1289, D-1546
D-6290	Schleicher Ka 6CR Rhönsegler	809	
D-6291	Schleicher K 7 Rhönadler	792	
D-6292	Lanaverre Standard Cirrus CS11/75L	14	F-CEVO
D-6294-RA	Schempp-Hirth Discus-2a	249	
D-6295	Scheibe L-Spatz 55	554	
D-6298-Z2	Schempp-Hirth Duo Discus	126	
D-6299	Schleicher ASW 27-18	29047	OK-2299
D-6301	Neukom S-4D Elfe (Permit .00)	402AB	
D-6302	Schleicher ASW 20L	20101	
D-6304-ST2	HpH Glasflügel 304C Wasp	65-C	HB-3375
D-6305	Schleicher K 8B	5/142/59	
D-6306	Schleicher Ka 6CR Rhönsegler	6097/Si	OO-ZFR, D-5280
D-6307	SZD-36A Cobra 15	W-628	DDR-2307, DM-2307
D-6308	SZD-36A Cobra 15	W-617	DDR-2308, DM-2308
D-6309	Glaser-Dirks DG-300 Elan Acro	3E429A1	
D-6310-KB	DG Flugzeugbau DG-1000S	10-16S16	
D-6312-X6	Schempp-Hirth Nimbus-3D	12/61	
D-6313	Rolladen-Schneider LS4	4313	
D-6316	Rolladen-Schneider LS6-18W	6316	OY-XWS, VH-XWS, OH-866, D-4518
D-6317	Schleicher Ka 6CR Rhönsegler	1068	
D-6318-EP	Schempp-Hirth Nimbus-4 (P 23.6.16)	9/28	
D-6319	Schleicher Ka 6CR Rhönsegler	1044	
D-6320	Schleicher ASW 20L	20608	HB-1679
D-6321	Schleicher ASK 21	21903	
D-6322	Schleicher Rhönlerche II (Res. - cld?)	1048	
D-6323	Schempp-Hirth Ventus-2a	43	PH-1401, BGA4340/HZS
D-6326	Schleicher K 7 Rhönadler	1135	
D-6327-HH	Schleicher ASW 27B	27229	
D-6328-7M	Schleicher ASW 28-18	28517	
D-6329	Schleicher ASW 27-18 (ASG 29)	29046	
D-6330	SZD-51-1 Junior	B-2152	
D-6331	Schleicher ASK 21	21927	
D-6332	Schleicher K 7 Rhönadler	422/58	D-5633
D-6333	Grob G103 Twin II	3612	SE-TZP, (OH-725)
D-6334	Glaser-Dirks DG-300 Elan	3E422	I-BZAR
D-6335-DS	Rolladen-Schneider LS4	4486	
D-6336-NR	Rolladen-Schneider LS3-17.	3390	HB-3336, PH-679, D-6941
D-6337-BAT	Glaser-Dirks DG-300 Elan	3E409	I-BRUT
D-6340	Grunau Baby III (P. 4.15)	75	
D-6341	Schleicher K 8B	8294	
D-6343	Glaser-Dirks DG-300 Elan	3E125	OO-ZZX, N301LA
D-6344-44	Glasflügel Hornet	86	OO-YHI, D-6599, OO-ZAD, LX-CHF
D-6346	Schleicher K 8B	8359	
D-6347	Schleicher Ka 6CR Rhönsegler	6600	
D-6348	Schleicher K 8B	223/61	
D-6351	SZD-9bis Bocian 1E	P-538	DDR-3351, DM-3351
D-6352-5F	Rolladen-Schneider LS8-a	8242	OY-FXF
D-6353	ISF Mistral-C (P 9.10)	MC 018/79	PH-644, (PH-616)
D-6354-BW	Centrair ASW 20FL	20145	BGA 2635
D-6356	Scheibe Zugvogel IIIB	1077	OO-ZPK, D-1975
D-6357-MA	Schempp-Hirth Duo Discus XL	686	
D-6358	Schleicher K 7 Rhönadler	7203	
D-6360	Schleicher K 8B	8453	
D-6361	Schleicher K 8B	8547	
D-6363	Schleicher Ka 6CR Rhönsegler	6497	
D-6364	Schempp-Hirth Discus b	517	
D-6365-37	SZD-48-3 Jantar-Standard 3	B-1753	D-6563, DOSAAF
D-6366-F6	Rolladen-Schneider LS6-18W	6356	HB-3177
D-6367	Grunau Baby III	2	
D-6370	Rolladen-Schneider LS6	6088	
D-6371-09	Rolladen-Schneider LS6	6089	
D-6373	SZD-24-4A Foka 4	W-241	
D-6374	Schleicher K 8B	8584	
D-6375	Schleicher Ka 6E	4375	OO-ZHJ, D-0759
D-6376-BZ	Rolladen-Schneider LS4-b	4965	
D-6377	Schleicher K 8B	636	HB-637
D-6378	Rolladen-Schneider LS6-a	6092	
D-6379	Glaser-Dirks DG-101G	E87	HB-1609
D-6380	Schleicher Ka 6CR Rhönsegler	857	
D-6381	Schleicher Ka 6CR Rhönsegler	6547	
D-6383	Schleicher Ka 6CR Rhönsegler	6490Si	
D-6384-1S	Rolladen-Schneider LS8-18	8454	G-CKEL, BGA 5032
D-6385	Scheibe SF 27A	6062	
D-6386	Schleicher K 7 Rhönadler	979	
D-6388	Schleicher ASK 21	21475	I-IVWB
D-6392-EI	Schleicher ASK 21	21090	
D-6396	Scheibe Bergfalke II/55	307	
D-6397-K7	Grob G 103A Twin II Acro	34041-K-272	
D-6398	Grob G 103A Twin II Acro	34039-K-270	
D-6399	Schleicher Ka 6CR Rhönsegler	1005	
D-6400	Schleicher Ka 6CR Rhönsegler	854	OO-ZBL, D-5800
D-6401	Allstar SZD-54-2 Perkoz	542.A.15.007	SP-3886
D-6402	Grob G 102 Speed Astir IIB	4085	PH-1128, D-2593, N166SS, D-2593
D-6403	Glaser-Dirks DG-200/17	2-188/1762	
D-6404	Schleicher Ka 6BR Rhönsegler	357	
D-6405-CO	DG Flugzeugbau DG-505 Elan Orion	5E253X82	
D-6406	Rolladen-Schneider LS7	7125	
D-6407	Rolladen-Schneider LS7	7126	
D-6408	Schleicher Ka 6CR Rhönsegler	6124Si	D-4671
D-6409	Glaser-Dirks DG-100G (Permit .01)	105G16	LX-CCW, D-6101
D-6411-GJ	Rolladen-Schneider LS4	4173	
D-6412	Grob G 103A Twin II Acro	34059-K-289	
D-6413	Scheibe Bergfalke II/55	244	OE-0413
D-6414	Rolladen-Schneider LS7-WL	7131	
D-6415	Rolladen-Schneider LS4	4043	
D-6416-MS	Schleicher ASW 24	24180	
D-6417-01	Schempp-Hirth Discus b	180	OO-ZZU, F-CGGJ, F-WGGJ
D-6418	Schempp-Hirth Standard Cirrus	308G	D-2062
D-6419-EX	Schempp-Hirth Ventus-2cxa	134	
D-6420	Centrair ASW 20F	20193	I-IVEA, F-CEUV
D-6421	Grob G 103A Twin II Acro	34064-K-294	
D-6422-AB	Schleicher ASW 28	28070	
D-6423-MR	Rolladen-Schneider LS6-c	6224	
D-6424-CV	Schleicher ASW 24	24126	F-CHAD
D-6425	Rolladen-Schneider LS6-c	6226	
D-6426	Glaser-Dirks DG-300 Elan	3E377	I-PBEI
D-6428	Rolladen-Schneider LS4	4023	
D-6429-BS	Schleicher ASW 27-18 (ASG 29)	29642	
D-6430-1D	Glaser-Dirks DG-100G Elan	E141G109	
D-6434	Centrair 201B1 Marianne	201018	F-CGMQ, F-WGMQ
D-6435	Schleicher Ka 6BR Rhönsegler	463	OE-0435
D-6437-DG	Grob G 103 Twin II	3610	
D-6439-39	Schempp-Hirth Ventus c	558	SE-UPK
D-6440	Grob G 103C Twin III	unkn	
D-6443	Schempp-Hirth Mini-Nimbus B	68	
D-6444-H	Glasflügel H205 Club Libelle (P 26.2.16)	45	HB-1244
D-6445	Grob G 103A Twin II Acro	34066-K-296	
D-6447	Schleicher K 8B	8290/EI	
D-6448	Schleicher ASK 21	21682	
D-6451-U2	Schleicher ASW 24	24046	
D-6452	Schleicher ASK 21	21421	
D-6454	Schleicher K 8B	8769	PH-394
D-6456	Glasflügel H401 Kestrel	122	
D-6457-B3	Schleicher ASW 27	27052	
D-6459-5D	Schleicher ASK 21	21743	
D-6460-TX	Rolladen-Schneider LS6	6001	
D-6461	Rolladen-Schneider LS4	4436	
D-6462	Caproni Vizzola A-21S Calif	217	I-VIZP
D-6463-PS	Rolladen-Schneider LS8-18	8327	
D-6464	Grob G 103 Twin Astir	3233	PH-689, PH-659

Reg.	Type	Serial	Previous identities
D-6465	Schempp-Hirth Standard Austria S	15	OO-ZLI
D-6466-HP	Luftsport-Club Friedrichshafen LCF-2	1	
D-6467	Grob G 102 Club Astir IIIB	5503CB	
D-6468-NA	Grob G 103A Twin II Acro	3638-K-19	
D-6469-69	Grob G 103A Twin II Acro	3639-K-20	
D-6471-7K	Schleicher Ka 6CR Rhönsegler	6317/Si	
D-6473-GT	Schempp-Hirth Duo Discus	203	
D-6474	Rolladen-Schneider LS1-f	364	
D-6475	Schempp-Hirth Ventus b/16.6	262	PH-773
D-6476-PM	Rolladen-Schneider LS1-f	288	
D-6477	Rolladen-Schneider LS1-f	368	
D-6478-BJ	Rolladen-Schneider LS1-f	287	
D-6479-1W	Rolladen-Schneider LS1-f	369	
D-6480-BX	Rolladen-Schneider LS1-f	373	
D-6481-AJ	Schleicher ASW 27	27017	
D-6482	Rolladen-Schneider LS1-f	407	
D-6484-OI	Schleicher ASW 28-18	28511	
D-6485	Schleicher ASK 13	13489	
D-6488-LX	Schleicher ASW 24	24166	SE-URK
D-6489	Schleicher ASK 13	13648AB	
D-6491-WS	Schempp-Hirth Standard Cirrus	586	
D-6495-GW	Schempp-Hirth Nimbus-2	99	
D-6496	Schempp-Hirth Janus	6	PH-1201, OO-ZPI, D-6496
D-6499	Schleicher ASW 20CL	20735	
D-6500	Schleicher K 8B	8086	D-KOCE, D-4047
D-6501	Rolladen-Schneider LS6-c	6232	
D-6504-CW	Glasflügel H201B Standard Libelle	559	PH-504
D-6505-AY	DG Flugzeugbau DG-500 Elan Orion	5E230X68	
D-6507-G	Schleicher ASK 21	21579	
D-6508-DL	Schempp-Hirth Duo Discus	235	
D-6509	Grob G 102 Astir CS	1013	
D-6510	DG Flugzeugbau DG-1000S	10-45S44	
D-6511-11	Rolladen-Schneider LS4-a	4812	OY-XTY, D-3398
D-6513-BB	Schleicher ASW 19B	19414	
D-6514-A2	Schempp-Hirth Ventus c	380	OY-XRX
D-6515	Schleicher ASK 23	23020	
D-6516	Schleicher ASK 21	21250	
D-6517-BF	Schleicher ASK 23	23019	
D-6518	Schleicher ASW 20C	20803	
D-6519	Schleicher ASW 20CL	20804	
D-6520-HG	Schleicher ASW 20L	20552	D-KHHG, OE-9394, OE-5294
D-6521-ISV	Rolladen-Schneider LS1-f	479	
D-6522-22	Schempp-Hirth Ventus-2c	24/65	
D-6523-TH	Rolladen-Schneider LS1-f	481	
D-6524-SC	Schleicher ASW 19B	19300	
D-6525	Schleicher ASW 20	20305	
D-6527-HF	Rolladen-Schneider LS8-b	8436	
D-6528	Schleicher ASW 28 (P. 3.14)	28065	
D-6529-9T	Schleicher ASW 19B	19306	
D-6530	Schleicher ASK 21	21013	
D-6531-AU	Schleicher ASW 19B	19307	
D-6532	Grob G 102 Astir CS	1024	D-KABB, D-5873
D-6533-NY	Schleicher ASW 20L	20307	
D-6534-DK	Schleicher ASW 20L	20283	
D-6535-R1	Schleicher ASW 20L	20281	
D-6536-2	Schleicher ASK 21	21004	
D-6537	Schleicher ASK 21	21005	
D-6538	Schleicher ASW 20L	20285	
D-6540	Scheibe Specht	862	D-1944
D-6541	Schleicher ASK 13	13617	
D-6542	Schleicher ASW 20L	20287	
D-6543	Schleicher ASW 20L	20290	
D-6544	SZD-9bis Bocian 1E	P-531	DDR-3244, DM-3244
D-6546-TL	Glaser-Dirks DG-200/17	2-135/1733	
D-6547	Glaser-Dirks DG-100G Elan	E48G27	
D-6549-2A	Schleicher ASW 19B	19298	
D-6550	Schleicher ASW 20	20231	
D-6551	Schleicher ASW 20	20291	
D-6552	Schleicher ASK 21	21011	
D-6553-53	Schleicher ASW 20CL	20808	
D-6556	Schleicher ASK 21	21122	HB-1656
D-6557-57	Rolladen-Schneider LS3-a	3234	PH-650, D-3919
D-6559-2P	Rolladen-Schneider LS1-f	410	OO-ZYS, D-3144
D-6560-H7	Rolladen-Schneider LS3-17	3368	
D-6562	Rolladen-Schneider LS3-17	3425	
D-6563-LU	Eiriavion PIK-20D-78	20658	PH-656
D-6564	Schleicher ASW 20L	20125	PH-648
D-6565	Rolladen-Schneider LS7	7134	
D-6566-6A	Rolladen-Schneider LS6-a	6140	HB-1922
D-6567	Glaser-Dirks DG-100G Elan	E52G30	
D-6568	Schempp-Hirth Ventus c	505	
D-6569-5J	Schempp-Hirth Discus b	370	
D-6571	Schempp-Hirth Janus Ce	274	
D-6573	Rolladen-Schneider LS4	4044	
D-6575-B6	Schempp-Hirth Discus CS	020CS	
D-6576-S4	Rolladen-Schneider LS4	4032	
D-6577	Schleicher ASW 20	20276	N320CF
D-6581	Rolladen-Schneider LS4	4021	
D-6582	Scheibe L-Spatz 55	302	
D-6583	Schempp-Hirth Discus CS	129CS	
D-6585	Rolladen-Schneider LS4	4432	
D-6586	Rolladen-Schneider LS4-a	4433	
D-6588	Rolladen-Schneider LS6	6021	
D-6590	Schempp-Hirth Ventus c	491	
D-6593-WX	Rolladen-Schneider LS6	6018	
D-6594	Rolladen-Schneider LS6-a	6019	
D-6595	Glaser-Dirks DG-500 Elan Orion	5E139X4	
D-6598	Pilatus B4-PC11AF	064	G-CKSO, HB-1125
D-6599-EN3	Schempp-Hirth Duo Discus XL	680	
D-6600	Caproni-Vizzola A.21S Calif	238	F-CEUD
D-6601	Schempp-Hirth Janus B	69	D-4989
D-6603-DXI	Schempp-Hirth Standard Cirrus B (P. 3.14)	687	
D-6605-AM	Glaser-Dirks DG-300 Club Elan	3E414C68	
D-6606-JK	Schempp-Hirth Mini-Nimbus B	72	
D-6607-AG	Schempp-Hirth Standard Cirrus	633	OE-5062
D-6608	SZD-50-3 Puchacz	B-1094	DDR-3608
D-6609-CT	Glaser-Dirks DG-300 Club Elan	3E406C65	
D-6611	Akaflieg Köln LS11-AFK1 (P. 4.14)	11000	
D-6612-PX	Schempp-Hirth Discus b	197	OO-ZPX
D-6613	Schleicher ASW 20C	20742	D-KFDW, D-5358
D-6615-J2	Glaser-Dirks DG-600/18	6-5	BGA 4949/KAZ, VH-GHS, D-1666
D-6616	Caproni-Vizzola A-21S Calif	246	
D-6617	Caproni-Vizzola A-21S Calif (P. 4.11)	248	
D-6618	SZD-50-3 Puchacz (W/o 6.8.15)	B-1335	DDR-3618
D-6619	SZD-50-3 Puchacz	B-1336	DDR-3619
D-6621	Schleicher ASK 21	21151	BGA 3712/GBW, ZD651, BGA 2891/ERM
D-6622	Glasflügel H303 Mosquito B	162	
D-6623-MS	DG Flugzeugbau DG-800S	8-190S36	
D-6624	Schleicher ASW 20C	20763	
D-6626	Schleicher ASW 20	20337	
D-6627	Grob G 102 Club Astir IIIB	5505CB	
D-6628	Grob G 102 Club Astir IIIB	5506CB	
D-6629	Grob G 102 Club Astir IIIB	5507CB	
D-6630-PZ	SZD-50-3 Puchacz	B-1392	DDR-3630
D-6631	LET L-33 Solo (Permit .07)	940210	D-4334
D-6632	Schleicher K 8B	97	
D-6633	Schempp-Hirth Mini-Nimbus C	114	D-3392
D-6634	Schleicher Ka 6CR Rhönsegler	826	
D-6636	SZD-50-3 Puchacz	B-1092	DDR-3606
D-6640	Schleicher ASW 19B	19385	HB-1692
D-6641	Schleicher ASK 21	21739	
D-6643	Grob G 103 Twin II	3614	
D-6644-44	Grob G 102 Astir CS Jeans	2143	
D-6645	Glaser-Dirks DG-200	2-40	
D-6646	Glaser-Dirks DG-200	2-44	
D-6647	Glaser-Dirks DG-200	2-45	
D-6648	Glaser-Dirks DG-600/18	6-60	F-CGRR
D-6649	Rolladen-Schneider LS4-b	4949	
D-6650-GY	Schleicher ASW 28-18	28508	
D-6651-PM	Rolladen-Schneider LS3	3096	
D-6652-FM	Rolladen-Schneider LS3	3088	
D-6653	Rolladen-Schneider LS3	3092	
D-6654	Schleicher ASK 21	21895	
D-6655	Scheibe Bergfalke IV	5864	SE-TSD
D-6656-56	Schleicher ASK 21	21318	
D-6657-B9	Sportine Aviacija LAK-19	032	
D-6658	Rolladen-Schneider LS3	3056	
D-6660	Marganski MDM-1 Fox	230	
D-6661-A6	Rolladen-Schneider LS6-18W	6377	
D-6662	Glaser-Dirks DG-200	2-47	
D-6663	Glaser-Dirks DG-200	2-49	
D-6664	Schleicher ASW 24	24204	
D-6666	Rolladen-Schneider LS4-b	41019	
D-6667	Schempp-Hirth Ventus b/16.6	125	BGA 4839/JWL, D-6667
D-6670	Schleicher K 8	517	
D-6671	Scheibe Zugvogel II	1022	OE-0493
D-6672	Schempp-Hirth Mini-Nimbus C	122	
D-6673-4V	Rolladen-Schneider LS4	4079	
D-6674	Rolladen-Schneider LS4	4244	
D-6675-2H	Rolladen-Schneider LS4	4272	
D-6676-MF	Rolladen-Schneider LS4	4164	
D-6678	Grob G 103C Twin III Acro	34197	
D-6679	Grob G 103C Twin III Acro	34202	
D-6680-6A	Rolladen-Schneider LS4	4000	
D-6681	Schleicher ASW 19B	19076	D-4478
D-6682	Gomolzig A.21S Calif	260GO	
D-6683	Rolladen-Schneider LS6	6017	PH-758, D-3466
D-6685	Rolladen-Schneider LS4	4403	
D-6686-AP	Rolladen-Schneider LS6-a (Permit)	6029	D-6556
D-6687-DH	Schempp-Hirth Duo Discus	272	
D-6688	Rolladen-Schneider LS8-18	8428	
D-6689	SZD-36A Cobra 15	W-663	SP-2689
D-6690	Glasflügel H303 Mosquito B	105	
D-6691-DW	Schempp-Hirth Nimbus-2C	196	
D-6692	Schempp-Hirth Janus C	87	
D-6693	Schempp-Hirth Ventus-2a	113	
D-6694	Grob G102 Astir CS Jeans	2198	PH-669
D-6695	Eiri PIK-20D	20590	
D-6696-B1	Rolladen-Schneider LS8-18	8479	
D-6697-MA	Eiri PIK-20D	20604	
D-6698	Eiri PIK-20D	20596	
D-6699-SF	Rolladen-Schneider LS8-a	8281	
D-6700	Eiri PIK-20D	20560	
D-6704	Eiri PIK-20D	20574	
D-6705	Schleicher Ka 6CR Rhönsegler	964	
D-6706	Schleicher Ka 6E	4346	LY-GSR, D-0606
D-6707-FG	SZD-32A Foka 5	W-440	DDR-2204, DM-2204
D-6708	Eiri PIK-20D	20578	
D-6709-TM	Schleicher ASK 21	21688	
D-6710-10	Schempp-Hirth Duo Discus	452	
D-6711	Schleicher ASW 19	19040	
D-6712	Schleicher ASW 19	19043	
D-6713-EL	Schleicher ASW 19	19044	
D-6714-1D	Schleicher ASW 19B	19045	
D-6715	Schleicher ASW 19	19046	
D-6716	Glaser-Dirks DG-505 Elan Orion	5E153X10	PH-1072, D-1491
D-6717-MG	Rolladen-Schneider LS8-18 (W/o 31.5.14)	8390	
D-6718-TW	Rolladen-Schneider LS8-18	8348	
D-6720	Schempp-Hirth Ventus b/16.6	70	PH-823, D-3048
D-6721-TK	Schleicher ASW 19B	19049	
D-6722	Schleicher ASK 13	13551	
D-6725	Schleicher ASW 19B	19027	
D-6726	Schleicher ASK 18	18041	
D-6727-J	Glaser-Dirks DG-600	6-13	D-8929, HB-1957
D-6728	SZD-30 Pirat	B-309	DDR-1728, DM-1728
D-6730	SZD-30 Pirat	S-03.29	
D-6731	Glasflügel H303 Mosquito	81	
D-6732	Glasflügel H303 Mosquito	86	
D-6733	Schempp-Hirth HS-7 Mini-Nimbus	51	
D-6735	Schempp-Hirth Nimbus-2B	163	
D-6739	Schempp-Hirth Janus B	78	
D-6740	Schempp-Hirth Mini-Nimbus C	98	
D-6743	Schempp-Hirth Mini-Nimbus C	101	
D-6747-77	Schleicher ASW 19B	19062	OO-YZC, D-6777
D-6748	Schleicher ASW 20L	20411	
D-6749	Schleicher ASW 20	20412	
D-6750	Schleicher Ka 6CR Rhönsegler	898	
D-6751	Grob G 103 Twin Astir Trainer	3248-T-28	
D-6753	Schleicher ASK 21	21600	
D-6757	Grob G102 Astir CS Jeans	2131	PH-609
D-6758	SZD-30 Pirat	B-362	DDR-1758, DM-1758

158

Reg	Type	c/n	Other
D-6761	Rolladen-Schneider LS4	4632	
D-6762	Grob G 102 Astir CS Jeans	2228	
D-6763-DF	Schempp-Hirth Nimbus-2C	206	
D-6764	Schempp-Hirth Mini-Nimbus C	151	
D-6766	Pilatus B4-PC11AF	297	S5-3064, SL-3064, YU-4257
D-6767	Glaser-Dirks DG-100	44	OY-XDV
D-6768	SZD-55-1	551195077	
D-6770-RM	Rolladen-Schneider LS4	4634	
D-6771	Schleicher K 8	2/60	
D-6772	Rolladen-Schneider LS4	4635	
D-6773	Rolladen-Schneider LS4	4636	
D-6774	Rolladen-Schneider LS3-17	3293	
D-6776-EI	Rolladen-Schneider LS3-a	3400	
D-6778-7W	Rolladen-Schneider LS7-WL	7123	PH-915
D-6780	Schempp-Hirth Ventus-2b	23	BGA 4780/JTZ, OO-ZQS
D-6783-HD	Schempp-Hirth Discus	?	
D-6787-HV	Glaser-Dirks DG-200	2-41	
D-6788	Glaser-Dirks DG-100 Elan	E14	
D-6789	Glaser-Dirks DG-100G Elan	E10G4	
D-6790	Schempp-Hirth Discus-2b	35	
D-6791	Glaser-Dirks DG-200	2-71	
D-6792	Glaser-Dirks DG-200	2-72	
D-6794	Glaser-Dirks DG-100G Elan	E42G23	
D-6797	SZD-50-3 Puchacz	B-2113	PH-1116
D-6798	Glasflügel H301 Libelle	47	HB-798
D-6800	Glaser-Dirks DG-300 Club Elan	3E337C32	
D-6801	Pilatus B4-PC11	170	
D-6802-PI	Rolladen-Schneider LS4	4640	
D-6803	Rolladen-Schneider LS4	4641	
D-6804-LF	Schleicher ASW 20	20206	
D-6805	Grob G102 Standard Astir III	5527S	SE-TTC
D-6806	SZD-30 Pirat	B-462	DDR-1806, DM-1806
D-6807-1R	Schleicher ASW 20L	20209	
D-6808-4H	Schleicher ASW 20L	20210	
D-6810	Schempp-Hirth Duo Discus	247	
	(For conversion to Duo Discus T c/n 6/247)		
D-6811	Schempp-Hirth Discus CS	176CS	
D-6812-OY	Schleicher ASW 19B	19273	
D-6813-OD	Schleicher ASW 20	20216	
D-6814-P9	Rolladen-Schneider LS8-a	8326	
D-6815-G8	Rolladen-Schneider LS8-a	8329	
D-6817-JH	Schleicher ASW 27	27080	
	(P. 3.14)		
D-6818	Grob G 102 Speed Astir IIB	4104	
	(C/n conflicts with OO-ZPF)		
D-6819	Schempp-Hirth Ventus-2b	143	
D-6820	Grob G 102 Speed Astir IIB	4105	
D-6821	Grob G103 Twin Astir	3090	OK-1421, HB-1421
D-6822	Schleicher ASK 13	13202	PH-411
D-6823	Schleicher ASW 20L	20251	PH-681
D-6824	Schempp-Hirth Nimbus-2	113	OO-ZBT
D-6825	Schleicher Ka 6CR Rhönsegler	6116	
D-6826	Centrair 101AP Pégase	101AP214	OO-YRL, F-CGFA
D-6827	Rolladen-Schneider LS3-a	3114	
D-6828	Rolladen-Schneider LS3-a	3125	
D-6831	Rolladen-Schneider LS3-a	3116	
D-6832-GS	Rolladen-Schneider LS3	3337	
D-6833-3Z	Rolladen-Schneider LS3	3338	
	(Permit .00)		
D-6834-EL	Schempp-Hirth Discus-2a	74	
D-6835	Rolladen-Schneider LS3-a	3143	
D-6836	Glasflügel H304	206	
D-6837	Glasflügel H304	207	
D-6838	Glasflügel H304	213	D-KBOO
D-6840	Schleicher ASW 27	27054	
D-6841-TSX	Schleicher ASW 27	27056	
D-6842-BO	Schempp-Hirth Duo Discus	191	
D-6843	Schleicher ASW 20FL	20126	F-CFFU
D-6844	Schempp-Hirth Duo Discus	359	
D-6845	Glaser-Dirks DG-100 Elan	E62	
D-6847	Glaser-Dirks DG-100G Elan	E63G38	
D-6848	Schleicher ASK 21	?	
D-6850-G3	Eiri PIK-20D	20598	
D-6853	Schleicher ASW 20	20582	
D-6854	Schleicher ASK 21	21116	
D-6855	Schleicher ASK 21	21117	
D-6856-VV	Schleicher ASW 22	22010	
D-6857-57	Schleicher ASK 21	21118	
D-6858	Schleicher ASW 20L	20590	OK-6858, D-6858
D-6859	Schleicher ASW 20	20586	
D-6861	Schleicher K 8B	140	
D-6863	Glasflügel H304/17	214	
D-6864	Schleicher ASK 13	13511	
D-6865	SZD-30 Pirat	S-01.02	DDR-1865, DM-1865
D-6866	Schleicher ASW 15B	15438	
D-6867	Schleicher ASW 15B	15439	
D-6868	DFS Habicht E replica	B003S	
D-6869-GR	Schleicher ASW 28	28034	D-1907
D-6870	Schleicher ASK 18	18008	
D-6871-RY	Rolladen-Schneider LS7-WL	7143	HB-3365, D-6193
D-6872	SZD-30 Pirat	S-01.10	DDR-1872, DM-1872
D-6873-ET	Schleicher ASK 21	21052	PH-687
D-6874	Schleicher ASK 13	13514	
D-6875	Schleicher ASK 13	13515	
D-6876	Schleicher ASK 13	13516	
D-6877-3B	Schleicher ASW 15B	15444	
D-6878	Schleicher ASW 15B	15242	I-GLOO
D-6879	Schleicher ASK 13	13517	
D-6881	Scheibe Bergfalke IV	5819	OY-XEW
D-6882	Schleicher ASK 13	13518	
D-6883	Rolladen-Schneider LS3	3014	OO-ZBO
D-6884	Schleicher K 8C	81007	
D-6885	Schleicher ASW 15B	15446	
D-6886	Schleicher ASK 13	13519	
D-6887	Grob G 102 Speed Astir IIB	4041	SE-TSO
D-6888	Schleicher ASK 18	18015	
D-6889	DG Flugzeugbau DG-1000S	10-126S81	
D-6891	Schempp-Hirth Nimbus-2	121	LN-GGM, OY-XGR
D-6893	Schleicher ASK 13	13630AB	
D-6896	Rolladen-Schneider LS6	6006	OH-689
D-6897-L	Schleicher ASW 27	27036	
D-6898	Glaser-Dirks DG-600/18	6-46	PH-898
D-6899-NA4	Schleicher ASW 15B	15346	OE-0999
D-6900	Glasflügel H201B Standard Libelle	38	
D-6901	Schleicher ASK 13	13197	OO-YDN, D-0346
	(Res. .12)		
D-6902	SZD-30 Pirat	S-03.42	DDR-1902, DM-1902
D-6903	FFA Diamant 18	076	
D-6904	Schempp-Hirth Ventus a/16.6	3	
D-6905	Grob G 103A Twin II Acro	3857-K-103	
D-6906	Schleicher Ka 6CR	6001	OO-ZNM, (OO-ZMN), D-4091
	(Res. .12)		
D-6907-RK	Rolladen-Schneider LS8-18	8139	F-CJCD
D-6908	Grob G 103 Twin II	3864	
D-6909	Grob G 103A Twin II Acro	3859-K-105	
D-6910-YG	DG Flugzeugbau DG-1000S	10-25S25	
D-6912	Schleicher AS 22-2	22201	
	(P 19.4.16)		
D-6913	Schleicher ASW 20C	20780	
D-6914	Schleicher ASW 20C	20781	
D-6915-BA	Schleicher ASW 15	15025	OO-ZBA
	(Dbr 7.5.16)		
D-6916	Rolladen-Schneider LS1-f	367	
D-6917-X	Rolladen-Schneider LS1-f	428	
D-6918-RX	Rolladen-Schneider LS1-f	429	
D-6919	Rolladen-Schneider LS1-f	430	
D-6920	Rolladen-Schneider LS1-f	431	
D-6921-2F	Rolladen-Schneider LS1-f	432	
D-6922	Rolladen-Schneider LS3-17	3359	
	(This c/n also recorded as N412H)		
D-6923-LK	Rolladen-Schneider LS8-18	8370	OH-923
D-6924-IGN	Rolladen-Schneider LS4-b	41022	
D-6925	Schleicher ASW 19B	19237	OO-YDV, PH-640
	(Res. .12)		
D-6926	Rolladen-Schneider LS8-18	8311	
D-6927	Rolladen-Schneider LS4	4361	
D-6928-2G	Schleicher ASW 28	28009	
D-6929	Schleicher ASG 29	29503	
D-6930	Rolladen-Schneider LS4	4267	OE-5300
D-6931	PZL PW-5 Smyk	17.12.004	CS-PBS, SP-3640
D-6932	Scheibe SF 34	5105	OO-YZW, D-1134
	(Res. .12)		
D-6933	Rolladen-Schneider LS3-17	3302	
D-6935	Grob G 103 Twin Astir	3087	PH-935, D-3948
D-6936-MF	Rolladen-Schneider LS8-18	8437	
D-6937	Rolladen-Schneider LS3-a	3175	
D-6938-KN	Rolladen-Schneider LS3-a	3165	
D-6939	Grob G 103A Twin II Acro	3772-K-58	
D-6940-SY	DG Flugzeugbau DG-1000S	10-15S15	
D-6941-TA	Grob G 103A Twin II Acro	3775-K-61	
D-6942	Rolladen-Schneider LS3-a	3169	
D-6943	Rolladen-Schneider LS3-a	3174	
D-6944-W	Glasflügel H201B Standard Libelle	43	HB-944
D-6945-BG	Schempp-Hirth Discus CS	119CS	
D-6946	Schleicher K 8B	8703	OO-ZAR
	(Res. .12)		
D-6947	Schempp-Hirth Discus CS	123CS	
D-6948-H2	Schempp-Hirth Discus CS	124CS	
D-6950	Grob G 102 Club Astir IIIB	5597CB	
D-6951	Schempp-Hirth Discus b	281	HB-1951
D-6952	Grob G 103 Twin II	3765	
D-6953-E8	Schleicher ASK 23B	23094	PH-809
D-6954	Schempp-Hirth Discus CS	125CS	
D-6955	Grob G102 Astir CS Jeans	2205	OO-ZMW
	(Res. .12)		
D-6956-WD	Schleicher ASW 20	20280	
D-6957	Schleicher K 8B	8073	PH-285
	(P. 7.15)		
D-6958-P1	Schleicher ASW 20	20289	
D-6960-DN	Schleicher ASW 20	20293	
D-6962	Schleicher ASW 24	24212	OY-XVE, D-6962
D-6963-WK	Schempp-Hirth Discus CS	255CS	
D-6965	Schempp-Hirth Ventus-2c	32/84	
D-6966	Schleicher Ka 6CR Rhönsegler	6544	
D-6967	Glasflügel Standard Libelle 201B	67	HB-972
D-6968	Schleicher Ka 6CR Rhönsegler	6580	C-GLHB
D-6969	Schleicher ASK 21	21503	
D-6970-70	Grob G 102 Astir CS	1116	
D-6971	DG Flugzeugbau DG-1000T	10-74T13	SE-UUU
	(R. 14)		
D-6972	Grob G 102 Astir CS	1118	
D-6975	Grob G 102 Astir CS	1121	
D-6978-GA	Grob G 102 Astir CS	1124	
D-6979	Grob G 102 Astir CS	1125	
D-6980	Grob G 102 Astir CS	1127	
D-6981	Grob G 102 Astir CS	1128	
D-6983	Grob G 102 Astir CS	1102	
D-6985	Schleicher ASW 19B	19145	OK-7573, D-7573
D-6986-44	Grob G103 Twin Astir	3172	OE-5244
D-6987	Schleicher ASK 23B	23028	OH-698
D-6988	Schleicher ASK 13	13400	OO-YDM, D-0988
	(Res. .12)		
D-6989-FD	Grob G 102 Astir CS	1089	
D-6990-ZZ	Grob G 102 Astir CS	1091	
D-6991-PH	Schleicher ASK 21	21563	PH-991
D-6992	Grob G 102 Astir CS	1093	
D-6995	Grob G 102 Astir CS	1016	
D-6996-EZ	Schempp-Hirth Ventus-2a	57	
D-6997-Y	HpH Glasflügel 304C	35-C	OK-6666
D-6998	Rolladen-Schneider LS8-a	8063	F-CGZO, D-3963
D-6999	Grob G 102 Astir CS	1020	
D-7000	Rolladen-Schneider LS6-c	6310	D-7900
D-7002	Focke-Wulf Kranich III	57	
	(Permit)		
D-7003	SZD-9bis Bocian 1E	P-714	DDR-3003, DM-3003
D-7004	SG-38 Schulgleiter	AB 002/OSC	
	(Permit .05)		
D-7005	Schempp-Hirth Ventus a	5	
D-7006	Schleicher ASH 25	25158	
D-7007	Schempp-Hirth Mini-Nimbus C	126	
D-7008-BD2	Schempp-Hirth Discus-2b	203	
D-7009	Schleicher K 8B	1108	
D-7010	SZD-9bis Bocian 1E	P-722	DDR-3010, DM-3010
D-7011	Raab Doppelraab V	545	
	(Permit .07)		
D-7013	SZD-9bis Bocian 1E	P-489	DDR-3212, DM-3212
D-7014	Greif II	V-2	
D-7015	Schleicher K 8B	8291/EI	
D-7016	Schleicher K 8B	925	
D-7017	Glasflügel H304	254	

Reg	Type	C/n	Other ids
D-7018-R2	Schempp-Hirth Duo Discus	240	
D-7019	Schleicher ASK 21 (P.3.12)	21573	
D-7021	Schleicher ASK 21	21562	
D-7020(3)-H1	Glasflügel Hornet	53	OH-504
D-7023	Rolladen-Schneider LS4-b	4898	
D-7024-4Y	Schleicher ASK 21	21015	
D-7025	Schleicher ASK 21	21016	
D-7026-5H	Rolladen-Schneider LS4-b	4899	
D-7027-RO	Schleicher ASK 21	21018	
D-7028	Schleicher ASW 19B	19310	
D-7029	Rolladen-Schneider LS4-b	4900	
D-7031-YV	Schempp-Hirth Ventus b	41	
D-7032	Schempp-Hirth Nimbus-3/24.5	4	
D-7033	DFS Reiher III replica	AB R1/OSC	
D-7034-6W	Schempp-Hirth Discus CS	050CS	
D-7035	Schempp-Hirth Nimbus-4T	4	
D-7037	Glasflügel H201B Standard Libelle	23	OE-5037
D-7038	SG-38 Schulgleiter (P.4.13)	AB-002S	
D-7039	Schleicher Ka 2B Rhönschwalbe	229	
D-7042	Schleicher Ka 2B Rhönschwalbe	2008/A	
D-7044	Rolladen-Schneider LS4-b	4902	
D-7045	Schleicher Ka 6E	4201	
D-7046	Schleicher ASK 21	21215	
D-7047-CD	Schleicher ASW 19B	19404	
D-7048	Schleicher ASK 21	21216	
D-7049-X1	Rolladen-Schneider LS4-b	4903	
D-7052	SG-38 Schulgleiter	OSC-AB003	
D-7053	Schleicher ASH 25	25133	
D-7054	Schleicher ASK 21	21518	
D-7055	SG-38 Schulgleiter	AB001/OSC	
D-7058-W1	Schempp-Hirth Discus CS	044CS	
D-7059	Schleicher Rhönbussard	485	BGA395, G-ALKY, BGA395
D-7060	Schleicher K 7 Rhönadler	7139	
D-7061	Göppingen Gö IV Gövier III	411	OE-0891, D-9009
D-7062-MA	Glaser-Dirks DG-300 Elan	3E193	HB-1878
D-7064-QAX	Schleicher ASH 25	25146	
D-7066	Schleicher ASK 23B	23132	
D-7067	Rolladen-Schneider LS4	4461	
D-7068-MB	Rolladen-Schneider LS1-c	111	HB-1068
D-7069-SP	Rolladen-Schneider LS4	4485	
D-7070	Schleicher ASK 21	21654	
D-7071	SZD-9bis Bocian 1E	P-757	DDR-3071, DM-3071
D-7073	Schempp-Hirth Ventus-2bx	136	OH-939, D-2734
D-7074	Rolladen-Schneider LS3-17	3250	OO-ZGK, D-3185
D-7075-PD	Schempp-Hirth Discus-2c	21	
D-7076-IW	Schempp-Hirth Discus b	290	LN-GIW
D-7077	Schempp-Hirth Discus CS	292CS	PH-1319, N431WA
D-7078	Grunau Baby IIb	AB-04	
D-7079	Schleicher Rhönlerche II	220	D-7070
D-7080	Focke-Wulf Weihe 50	1/A	D-7082, D-5376
D-7081	Schleicher ASK 21	21031	
D-7082	Pilatus B4-PC11AF	278	
D-7083-IPB	Schempp-Hirth Nimbus-3	10	OO-YAF, BGA 2821/ENP
D-7087	Schleicher ASK 21	21583	
D-7088	Schleicher K 8	94	
D-7089	Schleicher K 8B	563	D-5678
D-7090	Schleicher Ka 6CR Rhönsegler	6548	
D-7091	Schempp-Hirth Ventus-2bx	135	N255BM
D-7093	SZD-9bis Bocian 1E	P-483	DDR-3093, DM-3093
D-7094	Grob G 103C Twin III Acro	34193	
D-7095	Raab Doppelraab VI	02	D-7091
D-7097	Rolladen-Schneider LS4	4519	
D-7098-GB	Rolladen-Schneider LS4	4520	
D-7099	Glaser-Dirks DG-100G Elan	E104G77	
D-7100	Glaser-Dirks DG-100	1	
D-7101-NW2	Schempp-Hirth Discus-2b	48	OM-0202, D-3125, BGA 4781
D-7102	Rolladen-Schneider LS7-WL	7013	SE-UGV, D-4680
D-7103	Glaser-Dirks DG-200/17C	2-109CL02	CS-PCG, EC-GGL, D-3799
D-7104	Schleicher K 8B	8401	
D-7106	Rolladen-Schneider LS1-c	254	
D-7107	Glaser-Dirks DG-100	51	
D-7109	Schleicher ASK 21	21649	
D-7110	Schleicher ASW 15B	15270	OO-ZQJ, F-CEGF
D-7111	Schempp-Hirth Nimbus-2	21	(F-C . . .), D-1988
D-7112-E2	Glaser-Dirks DG-100	42	
D-7113	DG Flugzeugbau DG-1000S	10-210S132	
D-7114-BM	Schempp-Hirth Discus-2b	218	
D-7116-GK	SZD-50-3 Puchacz	B-1333	DDR-3616
D-7117-TJ	Schempp-Hirth Janus B	58	
D-7118	Schleicher K 7 Rhönadler	744	
D-7119-KL	Schleicher ASK 21	21686	
D-7120-AY	Schleicher ASW 27-18	29681	
D-7121	Schleicher ASK 21	21603	
D-7122	Schleicher ASW 22	22001	
D-7123-MW	Schempp-Hirth Ventus-2b	95	
D-7124	Akaflieg Braunschweig SB-5E Sperber	5019/A	
D-7125	Marganski Swift S-1	?	
D-7126	Schleicher K 8B	8229/A	
D-7128-AH	Schempp-Hirth Mini-Nimbus B	66	
D-7129	SZD-51-1 Junior	B-2151	
D-7130	Schleicher K 8B	8662	
D-7131-31	Schleicher ASK 23B	23147	
D-7132	Schleicher K 8B	688	
D-7133-DR	Schempp-Hirth Ventus-2c	81	
D-7134	Vogt Lo-100 Zwergreiher (P. 11.10)	01A AH4	
D-7135	Schleicher ASK 21	21672	
D-7136-NX	Schempp-Hirth Discus-2b	221	
D-7138	Scheibe L-Spatz 55 (C/n incorrect?)	549	
D-7142	Glasflügel H201B Standard Libelle	529	OY-VXR
D-7143	Schleicher Ka 6CR Rhönsegler	1158	
D-7144	Schleicher ASK 21	21934	
D-7147	Schleicher ASK 13	13652AB	
D-7148-YH	Schempp-Hirth Janus	29	OO-ZYH, OY-XDH
D-7149-49	Schleicher Ka 6E	4181	
D-7150	Schleicher K 7 Rhönadler	7088	
D-7152-BH	Schempp-Hirth Duo Discus	656	
D-7153	Schleicher Ka 6CR Rhönsegler	6500	
D-7154	Schleicher Ka 6CR Rhönsegler	6193Si	
D-7155	Schleicher Ka 6CR Rhönsegler	6126Si	
D-7156	Grunau Baby IIB	01	D-1356
D-7158	Schleicher Ka 6CR-PE Rhönsegler	717	
D-7159-TD	Schempp-Hirth Discus CS	092CS	
D-7160-CT	Schempp-Hirth Mini-Nimbus (P. 11.10)	42	OE-5160
D-7161	Glaser-Dirks DG-100	58	PH-539
D-7162	Schempp-Hirth Mini-Nimbus B	64	
D-7163	Vogt Lo-100 Zwergreiher	07	
D-7164-E1	Schempp-Hirth Discus CS	095CS	
D-7165	Schleicher Ka 6CR Rhönsegler	6478	
D-7166-E2	Schempp-Hirth Discus CS	096CS	
D-7167	Schempp-Hirth Discus CS	201CS	
D-7168-EC	Schempp-Hirth Discus CS	204CS	
D-7169-CF	Schempp-Hirth Discus CS	203CS	
D-7170	Scheibe L-Spatz 55	709	
D-7171	Schleicher Ka 6E	4225	
D-7172	Scheibe SF 27A	6088	
D-7173	SZD-51-1 Junior	B-2144	
D-7174-7V	Schempp-Hirth Ventus-2b	47	
D-7175-WGH	Schempp-Hirth Discus b	94	
D-7176-XD	Schempp-Hirth Discus b (W/o 7.5.16)	71	
D-7177	Glasflügel H401 Kestrel	61	OO-ZPC
D-7178-KB	Schempp-Hirth Discus b	85	
D-7179-WP	Schempp-Hirth Discus b	84	
D-7184-LR	Schleicher Ka 6CR Rhönsegler	6361	
D-7185	Schleicher Ka 6CR Rhönsegler	6374/Si	
D-7186	Scheibe Bergfalke II	327	
D-7188	Schleicher K 7 Rhönadler	7225	D-7189
D-7190	Schleicher Ka 6CR Rhönsegler (P. 6.11)	6434	
D-7191	Rolladen-Schneider LS6-c	6344	
D-7194-MT	Glaser-Dirks DG-300 Elan	3E220	
D-7196-BM	Glaser-Dirks DG-300 Elan	3E230	I-LVIP
D-7198-L3	Glaser-Dirks DG-300 Elan	3E221	
D-7199	Schleicher K 7 Rhönadler	690	
D-7201-GT4	Schempp-Hirth Discus b	459	D-0299
D-7202-EL	Glaser-Dirks DG-200/17C (P. 3.11)	2-133CL09	
D-7205	Glasflügel Club Libelle 205	108	OO-YPC, PH-524
D-7206-Y2	Schempp-Hirth Duo Discus	6	
D-7207-HZ	Schempp-Hirth Duo Discus	7	
D-7208-YZ	Schempp-Hirth Discus-2c	42	
D-7209	Scheibe L-Spatz 55	714	
D-7210	Schleicher ASK 13	13014	
D-7211	Schleicher Ka 6CR Rhönsegler	859	
D-7212	Schleicher K 8B	8717	
D-7214	Schleicher Ka 6E (P 10.15)	4195	
D-7215	Pilatus B4-PC11AF	101	D-3690, PH-488
D-7216-16	Schleicher ASK 21	21086	OO-YWT, D-6129
D-7218	Schleicher ASW 28-18	28731	
D-7219	Glaser-Dirks DG-200	2-17	
D-7220	Schleicher Ka 6E	4119	
D-7221	Schempp-Hirth Ventus b	97	
D-7222	Schleicher Ka 6CR Rhönsegler	6617	
D-7223	Grob G 102 Astir CS	1138	
D-7224	Grob G 102 Astir CS	1139	
D-7226	Grob G 102 Astir CS	1137	
D-7227-CG	Grob G 102 Astir CS	1143	
D-7228-SD	Grob G 102 Astir CS	1144	
D-7230	Grob G 102 Astir CS	1043	
D-7231	Grob G 102 Astir CS	1046	
D-7232	Grob G 102 Astir CS	1047	
D-7233	SZD-9bis Bocian 1E	P-515	
D-7234	Grob G 102 Astir CS	1050	
D-7235	Grob G 102 Astir CS	1051	
D-7239	Grob G 102 Astir CS	1055	
D-7242-KR	Schempp-Hirth Standard Cirrus	630	
D-7243	Schempp-Hirth Standard Cirrus B	631	
D-7244	Schempp-Hirth Standard Cirrus B	636	
D-7246	Schempp-Hirth Janus B	104	
D-7247-JKX	Schempp-Hirth Discus b	247	G-CJKX, BGA 4585, RAFGSA R17
D-7251-SE	Schempp-Hirth Ventus-2a	49	D-9595
D-7252	Grob G 102 Astir CS	1157	
D-7253	Grob G 102 Astir CS	1159	
D-7254-TY	Grob G 102 Astir CS	1153	
D-7256	Grob G 102 Astir CS	1158	
D-7257	Schempp-Hirth Janus	19	
D-7259-WS	Glasflügel H206 Hornet	56	
D-7260	Glasflügel H206 Hornet	57	I-DEUX, D-7260
D-7261	Glaser-Dirks DG-100	55	
D-7264	Glaser-Dirks DG-100 (Res.9.99)	60	
D-7266	Schleicher ASW 24	24144	
D-7268	Schleicher ASW 24	24151	
D-7269-MH	Schempp-Hirth Discus b	538	G-CHOW, BGA 4128
D-7270	Grob G 102 Astir CS	1146	
D-7272	Grob G 102 Astir CS	1148	
D-7273	Grob G 102 Astir CS	1149	
D-7275	Grob G 102 Astir CS	1202	
D-7277	Grob G 102 Astir CS	1204	
D-7278	Grob G 102 Astir CS	1205	
D-7279	Grob G 102 Astir CS	1206	
D-7280-HSN	Schleicher ASH 25	25138	
D-7282-VG	Glaser-Dirks DG-500 Elan Orion	5E154X11	
D-7283	Grob G 102 Astir CS	1210	
D-7284	Schleicher ASK 21	21206	PH-1284, D-5714
D-7286-J4	Grob G 102 Astir CS	1213	
D-7287	Grob G 102 Astir CS	1214	
D-7288	Schleicher K 8C	81011	OY-XME, D-3765
D-7291	Grob G 102 Astir CS	1218	
D-7295	DG Flugzeugbau DG-500/20 Elan	5E173W10	
D-7296	Grob G 102 Astir CS	1175	
D-7300	Grob G 102 Astir CS	1180	
D-7303	Grob G 102 Astir CS	1176	
D-7304	Grob G 102 Astir CS	1177	
D-7305-OT	Grob G 102 Astir CS	1188	
D-7306	Glasflügel H206 Hornet	63	HB-1306
D-7309	Marganski MDM-1 Fox	210	OE-5624
D-7310	Grob G 102 Astir CS	1193	
D-7311-DU	Schempp-Hirth Duo Discus	184	
D-7312-LV	Schempp-Hirth Ventus-2cx	85	
D-7313	Grob G 102 Astir CS	1196	
D-7314-IZ	Grob G 102 Astir CS	1197	
D-7315	Glasflügel H205 Club Libelle	164	

Reg	Type	Serial	Previous identities
D-7320-20	Grob G 102 Astir CS 77	1836	D-1520, HB-1504
D-7321	Schleicher ASK 21	21713	
D-7322	Schleicher ASW 22	22036	
D-7326	Grob G 102 Astir CS	1304	
D-7327	Schleicher ASW 19B	19355	
D-7328	Schleicher ASW 20	20497	
D-7329	Schleicher ASW 19B	19358	
D-7330	Glasflügel H206 Hornet	66	
D-7331-AN	Rolladen-Schneider LS1-f	482	
D-7333-BZ	Rolladen-Schneider LS1-f	484	
D-7334	Rolladen-Schneider LS1-f	485	
D-7335-A3	Schleicher ASK 21	21027	HB-1545
D-7336-AW	Schempp-Hirth Janus	23	
D-7337	Schleicher ASK 21	21786	
D-7338	Scheibe Bergfalke III	09	
D-7343	Schleicher Ka 6CR Rhönsegler	6661AB	
D-7344-Y7	Schempp-Hirth Standard Cirrus B	659	
D-7345	Schempp-Hirth Standard Cirrus B	604	
D-7348-B3	Schempp-Hirth Discus-2b	193	
D-7351-LD	Rolladen-Schneider LS6-c	6256	
D-7353-S3	Schempp-Hirth Janus B	61	
D-7354	Rolladen-Schneider LS4-b	4916	
D-7355	Grob G 102 Astir CS	1314	
D-7357	Grob G 102 Astir CS	1262	
D-7359	Grob G 102 Astir CS	1264	
D-7360-WS	Schempp-Hirth Ventus-2b	36	
D-7362	SZD-9bis Bocian 1E	P-549	DDR-3362, DM-3362
D-7363	Bölkow Phoebus B1	780	OE-0828
D-7365	Grob G 102 Astir CS	1270	
D-7367-ZZ	Rolladen-Schneider LS3-a	3437	I-KAZZ, D-3540
D-7368-SX	Grob G 102 Astir CS	1273	
D-7369-F2	Grob G 102 Astir CS	1274	
D-7372-HF	Grob G 102 Astir CS	1278	
D-7373	Grob G 102 Astir CS	1280	
D-7374-HF	DG Flugzeugbau DG-800S	8-113S29	
D-7375	Grob G 102 Astir CS	1275	
D-7376	Grob G 102 Astir CS	1186	OE-5255
D-7380	DFS Olympia-Meise	AB3	
D-7381	Grob G 102 Astir CS	1335	
D-7383	LET L-13A Blanik	978504	
D-7388	Grob G 102 Astir CS	1359	
D-7389	Grob G 102 Astir CS	1360	
D-7391	Grob G 102 Astir CS	1364	
D-7393	Grob G 102 Astir CS	1366	
D-7395	SZD-9bis Bocian 1E	P-612	DDR-3395, DM-3395
D-7401	Pilatus B4-PC11AF	228	
D-7404	Grob G 102 Astir CS (Permit .05)	1375	
D-7405-GT	Schleicher ASW 27	27047	
D-7406-EE	Grob G 102 Astir CS	1378	
D-7407	Grob G 102 Astir CS	1398	
D-7408-ACM	Schempp-Hirth Duo Discus	363	
D-7410	Grob G 102 Astir CS	1388	
D-7411	Grob G 102 Astir CS	1389	
D-7413-HN	Schempp-Hirth Discus CS	130CS	
D-7415	Glasflügel H206 Hornet	81	
D-7416-IWD	Glasflügel H206 Hornet	82	
D-7417-BG	Sportine Aviacija LAK-17A	125	BGA 4940/KAQ
D-7418	Glaser-Dirks DG-200	2-26	
D-7421	Schleicher ASK 21	21906	
D-7422	Neukom S-4D Elfe	417AB	
D-7423-AV	Glasflügel H401 Kestrel	79	
D-7424	Grob G 102 Club Astir IIIB	5645CB	
D-7426	Grob G 102 Astir CS	1436	
D-7427	Grob G 102 Astir CS	1437	
D-7428	Grob G 102 Astir CS	1438	
D-7432-32	Schleicher ASK 23B	23161	
D-7434	Scheibe SF 34B	5134	SE-UKD
D-7437-WS	Rolladen-Schneider LS8-a	8068	
D-7439	Grob G 102 Astir CS	1468	
D-7440	Grob G 102 Astir CS	1469	
D-7442	Grob G 102 Astir CS	1419	
D-7444	Glasflügel H303 Mosquito B	191	
D-7445	Grob G 102 Astir CS	1454	
D-7446	Grob G 102 Astir CS	1455	
D-7448	Grob G 102 Astir CS	1457	
D-7449-AZ	Grob G 102 Astir CS	1458	
D-7456-WV	Schempp-Hirth Ventus-2cx	111	
D-7457	Grob G 102 Astir CS	1516	
D-7458-WY	Schempp-Hirth Duo Discus	2	
D-7459-WK	Schleicher ASK 21	21419	PH-865
D-7460	Scheibe Bergfalke IV	5853	D-4760
D-7462	Grob G 102 Astir CS	1504	
D-7465	Grob G 102 Astir CS	1530	
D-7466-C1	Schempp-Hirth Mini-Nimbus C	116	HB-1466
D-7468	Glasflügel Standard Libelle 201B	522	PH-468
D-7470	Grob G 102 Astir CS 77	1639	
D-7471	Schleicher ASK 21	21639	
D-7472	Glasflügel Standard Libelle 201B	246	G-CJBF, BGA 4377, F-CDPV
D-7473	Glasflügel H303 Mosquito	19	PH-566
D-7474-OG	Schempp-Hirth Ventus-2b	62	
D-7475	Grob G 103 Twin Astir	3002	
D-7476-CT	DG Flugzeugbau DG-1000S	10-56S55	
D-7477-EH	Rolladen-Schneider LS4-b	4956	
D-7478	SZD-22C Mucha Standard	790	HB-747
D-7479	SZD-22C Mucha Standard	599	OE-0536
D-7481	Schleicher ASK 21	21521	
D-7482	Schleicher ASK 21 (P. 3.14)	21522	
D-7483	Schleicher ASK 21	21523	
D-7484-LL	Grob G 103 Twin Astir	3011	
D-7487	Schleicher ASK 21	21731	
D-7489	Glasflügel H303 Mosquito	44	
D-7490	Glasflügel H303 Mosquito	45	
D-7493-DB	Grob G 102 Astir CS Jeans	2003	
D-7496-D5	Grob G 102 Astir CS Jeans	2005	
D-7498-NA	Grob G 102 Astir CS 77	1661	
D-7499	Grob G 104 Speed Astir IIB	4061	HB-1499
D-7500	Pilatus B4-PC11AF	181	
D-7501	Schleicher Ka 6CR Rhönsegler	6356	
D-7502	Schleicher ASH 25	25152	
D-7503	Scheibe L-Spatz 55	670	
D-7504-A3	Schleicher ASK 21	21677	
D-7505	Glasflügel Club Libelle 205	105	OE-5541, HB-1261
D-7506	Schleicher K 8B	8460	D-5392, D-5100
D-7507	Schleicher ASK 13	13693AB	
D-7508	Schempp-Hirth HS-7 Mini-Nimbus	22	
D-7510	Pilatus B4-PC11	185	
D-7511	Grob G 102 Astir CS Jeans	2007	
D-7512	Grob G 102 Astir CS Jeans	2008	
D-7514-GA	Schempp-Hirth Nimbus-2C	190	F-CEDN, F-WEDN
D-7515-HY	Schempp-Hirth Discus-2c	12	
D-7516	Grob G 102 Astir CS Jeans	2012	
D-7517-5Y	Grob G 102 Astir CS Jeans	2013	
D-7519	Grob G 102 Astir CS Jeans	2015	
D-7520	Glasflügel H303 Mosquito B	164	
D-7521	Schleicher ASK 21	21710	
D-7522	Schleicher ASK 13	13692AB	
D-7523-7H	Grob G 103 Twin Astir	3017	
D-7524	Schleicher ASW 24	24165	OE-5507
D-7527	Schleicher ASW 27	27021	
D-7528	Grob G 103 Twin Astir	3033	
D-7529	Grob G 102 Astir CS Jeans	2087	
D-7530-AB	Grob G 102 Astir CS Jeans	2088	
D-7533-OT	Grob G 102 Astir CS Jeans	2091	
D-7534	SZD-51-1 Junior	B-1995	SP-3815, PH-933
D-7536-YA	Grob G 102 Astir CS Jeans	2095	
D-7537	Grob G 102 Astir CS Jeans	2096	
D-7538	Grob G 102 Astir CS Jeans	2097	
D-7540	Schleicher ASW 20L	20329	
D-7541-IWO	Schleicher ASW 20L	20330	
D-7542	Schleicher ASW 20L	20331	
D-7543-5D	Akaflieg Darmstadt D-43 Fuchur (P 23.8.16)	43	
D-7545-FGE	Schleicher ASW 19	19108	
D-7546-SLB	Schleicher ASW 19	19109	
D-7547	Schleicher ASW 20	20004	
D-7548-ITO	Schleicher ASW 19 (P. 7.7.16)	19111	
D-7550-CH	Schleicher ASW 19	19113	
D-7551-RD	Eiri PIK-20D	20649	OH-551
D-7553	Schleicher ASK 13	13575	
D-7554	Schleicher ASK 13	13576	
D-7555-8M	Rolladen-Schneider LS8-18	8413	
D-7557-9M	Schempp-Hirth Duo Discus	291	
D-7558	Schleicher ASK 13	13578	
D-7559-LM	Schleicher ASW 19	19127	
D-7561	Schleicher ASK 13	13580	
D-7564-ZB	Schleicher ASW 19	19132	
D-7566	Schleicher ASK 13	13581	
D-7567-L7	Schleicher ASW 19B	19134	
D-7569	Schleicher ASW 20	20021	
D-7570-HN	Schleicher ASW 19B	19114	
D-7571	Schleicher ASW 19B	19143	
D-7572	Schleicher ASW 20	20022	
D-7575	Rolladen-Schneider LS7-WL	7032	
D-7576-FI	SZD-48-3 Jantar Standard 3	B-1716	DOSAAF
D-7577	Grob G 102 Astir CS Jeans	2057	
D-7578	Grob G 102 Astir CS Jeans	2058	
D-7580	Grob G 102 Astir CS Jeans	2064	
D-7581	Grob G 102 Astir CS Jeans	2065	
D-7582	Valentin Mistral-C	MC 040/81	HB-1582
D-7584	Schempp-Hirth Discus CS	202CS	OE-5584
D-7585-85	Grob G 102 Astir CS Jeans	2072	
D-7588	Grob G 102 Astir CS Jeans	2075	
D-7590	Grob G 102 Astir CS Jeans	2077	
D-7591	Grob G102 Astir CS Jeans	2078	OE-5633, D-7591
D-7592-E2	Grob G 102 Astir CS Jeans	2082	
D-7594-E3	Grob G 102 Astir CS Jeans	2085	
D-7595-MT	Grob G 102 Astir CS Jeans	2086	
D-7597	Glasflügel Hornet C	93	
D-7598	Glasflügel H303 Mosquito B	161	
D-7600	Grob G 103A Twin II Acro	3867-K-108	
D-7601	Grob G 103 Twin II	3866	
D-7604-E4	Schempp-Hirth Duo Discus	248	
D-7605	Glasflügel Hornet C	98	PH-605
D-7606-WW	Rolladen-Schneider LS4	4315	
D-7607	Rolladen-Schneider LS4	4316	
D-7608-ZI	Rolladen-Schneider LS4	4317	
D-7611	Glaser-Dirks DG-200/17	2-87/1705	
D-7612-CB	Akaflieg Berlin B-12T (P. 15.8.16)	001	
D-7613-VV	Schempp-Hirth Duo Discus	148	
D-7614-MM	Rolladen-Schneider LS8-a	8203	
D-7615	Schleicher ASW 20C (Permit .05)	20778	
D-7616	Schleicher ASW 20	20334	
D-7617	Schleicher ASW 19B	19313	
D-7618	Schleicher ASW 20L	20335	
D-7619-RP	Schleicher ASW 19B	19311	
D-7621	SZD-50-3 Puchacz	B-1340	DDR-3621
D-7622-7W	Glaser-Dirks DG-600	6-76	
D-7623	SZD-50-3 Puchacz	B-1342	DDR-3623
D-7624-W3	Schempp-Hirth Duo Discus	192	
D-7626	Grob G 102 Astir CS 77	1700	
D-7629	Grob G 102 Astir CS Jeans	2101	
D-7634	Glaser-Dirks DG-300 Elan	3E-428	I-GRRR
D-7635	Grob G 102 Astir CS Jeans	2105	
D-7636-116	Schleicher ASK 21	21591	
D-7637	Grob G 102 Astir CS Jeans	2109	
D-7639	Grob G 102 Astir CS Jeans	2112	
D-7640	Grob G 102 Astir CS Jeans	2114	
D-7641	Grob G 102 Astir CS Jeans	2127	
D-7642	Grob G 102 Astir CS Jeans	2116	
D-7643	SZD-50-3 Puchacz	B-1478	DDR-3646
D-7644	SZD-55-1	551195066	
D-7646	Schleicher ASW 20L	20217	
D-7648	Schleicher ASW 20	20259	
D-7649-R	Schleicher ASW 20L	20260	
D-7650	Schempp-Hirth Janus C	243	HB-1899
D-7653	Eiriavion PIK-20D-78	20656	PH-653
D-7654-RS	Rolladen-Schneider LS1-f	452	(BGA 5104), F-CEKZ
D-7655-H3	Schleicher ASW 19	19183	
D-7658	Schleicher ASW 20L	20050	
D-7659	Schleicher ASW 20L	20071	
D-7660-ITT	Schleicher ASW 19	19196	
D-7661	PZL-Swidnik PW-5 Smyk	17.12.001	PH-1147
D-7662-KT	Schleicher ASW 20	20075	
D-7663	Schleicher ASW 20 (P. 11.13)	20077	
D-7664	Schleicher ASK 13	13592	

Reg.	Type	Serial	Notes
D-7666	Rolladen-Schneider LS4-a	4355	G-XCIV, BGA 3709, N220BB
D-7668-IL	Schleicher ASW 19B	19201	
D-7669-FA	Schleicher ASW 20	20081	
D-7670	Schleicher ASW 20	20070	
D-7672	Schleicher ASK 13	13589	
D-7673	Schleicher ASW 17	17054	
D-7674-7F	Schleicher ASW 20	20087	
D-7675	Grob G102 Astir CS	1152	OE-5064
D-7676	Schleicher ASW 20	20074	
D-7677-E7	Grob G 102 Astir CS 77	1844	HB-1506
D-7678-L6	Grob G102 Astir CS 77	1812	HB-1458
D-7679	Schleicher ASW 20	20094	
D-7680	Glasflügel H206 Hornet C	90	
D-7682	Glasflügel H303 Mosquito B	158	
D-7683	Glasflügel H206 Hornet C	92	
D-7684-61	Schleicher ASW 20	20051	
D-7685	Grob G 102 Astir CS 77	1752	
D-7686	Grob G 102 Astir CS 77	1760	
D-7688	Schleicher ASW 28-18	28518	
D-7690	Grob G 102 Astir CS 77	1784	
D-7691	Grob G 102 Astir CS 77	1785	
D-7692	Grob G 102 Astir CS 77	1792	
D-7694	Grob G 102 Astir CS 77	1799	
D-7696	Rolladen-Schneider LS4-a	4653	OE-5696, D-8024
D-7697-i2	Schempp-Hirth Discus b	194	
D-7698	Schleicher ASK 21	21589	
D-7699-DW	Schempp-Hirth Janus C	203	HB-1762
D-7700-EKW	Schleicher ASH 25	25170	(D-KKEW)
D-7701-OK	Neukom S-4D Elfe	406AB	
D-7702	Glaser-Dirks DG-200	2-8	
D-7703-WB	Glaser-Dirks DG-200	2-10	
D-7704-PK	Schempp-Hirth Discus CS	269CS	
D-7705-3W	SZD-48-3 Jantar Standard 3	B-1573	SP-3341
D-7708-MB	Schleicher ASK 21	21160	
D-7709	Schempp-Hirth Ventus-2bx	134	
D-7710-10	Schleicher ASW 19B	19378	
D-7712	Schleicher Ka 3	E1	D-9046
D-7714	Glasflügel H201B Standard Libelle	255	F-CDPY
D-7715	Schempp-Hirth Ventus b/16.6	176	
D-7717	Glasflügel H304	215	D-6862
D-7718-T1	Rolladen-Schneider LS8-a	8057	
D-7720	Schempp-Hirth Ventus b/16.6	174	
D-7721	Schleicher ASK 21	21762	
D-7722	Rolladen-Schneider LS3	3003	
D-7723-HG	Rolladen-Schneider LS3	3004	
D-7724-IGM	Schempp-Hirth Discus CS	276CS	
D-7725-II	Schleicher ASH 25	25032	
D-7726	Rolladen-Schneider LS3	3007	
D-7727	Neukom Elfe S4A	87	
D-7728	Schleicher ASW 28	28035	HB-3344
D-7729-O1	Schleicher ASW 28	28042	
D-7730	FFA Diamant 18	077	HB-202, HB-2020
D-7731-A3	Rolladen-Schneider LS3	3064	
D-7733	Rolladen-Schneider LS3-a	3110	
D-7734	Rolladen-Schneider LS3	3105	
D-7735	Rolladen-Schneider LS3	3108	
D-7736-B5	Schleicher ASK 21	21658	
D-7737	Rolladen-Schneider LS7-WL	7000	
D-7739-TM	Rolladen-Schneider LS3	3126	
D-7740	Neukom S-4D Elfe	405AB	
D-7742-A3	Rolladen-Schneider LS5 (P. 5.15)	5001	
D-7743	SZD-30 Pirat	B-332	DDR-1743, DM-1743
D-7744-KES	Schempp-Hirth Cirrus-VTC	177	
D-7745	Rolladen-Schneider LS3-a	3404	OO-ZLS
D-7746-M4	SZD-48-3 Jantar-Standard 3	B-1346	OO-ZPS, (OO-ZTD), SP-3232
D-7747-TB	Glasflügel H201B Standard Libelle	59	I-TRIK
D-7748-KK	Rolladen-Schneider LS6-c	6248	SE-UKK
D-7750	Rolladen-Schneider LS3-a	3075	
D-7751	Rolladen-Schneider LS4	4303	
D-7752-152	Rolladen-Schneider LS4	4183	
D-7754-FR	Rolladen-Schneider LS4	4305	
D-7755	Rolladen-Schneider LS8-a	8279	
D-7756	Grob G 102 Astir CS Jeans	2176	
D-7759	Grob G 102 Astir CS Jeans	2184	
D-7760-MY	Schempp-Hirth Standard Cirrus	545	OE-5030
D-7761-77	Grob G 102 Astir CS Jeans	2186	
D-7763	Grob G 102 Astir CS Jeans	2188	
D-7764-U2	Schempp-Hirth Discus-2b	90	
D-7766	Grob G 102 Astir CS Jeans	2221	
D-7768	Scheibe SF 27A	6020	OE-0768
D-7769-B5	Grob G 102 Astir CS Jeans	2223	
D-7770	Schleicher ASK 23B	23042	PH-770
D-7771	Akaflieg Braunschweig SB-5E	AB5043	
D-7772	Grob G 102 Astir CS 77	1796	
D-7773-JU	Glasfaser Albatros (Res.3.99)	1	
D-7775-OU	Streifeneder Falcon	1	
D-7777-HL	Glasflügel H201B Standard Libelle	547	
D-7779-WU	Schempp-Hirth Discus b (P .3.99)	574	
D-7780	Grob G 103 Twin Astir	3109	
D-7781	Grob G 103 Twin Astir Trainer	3112-T-9	
D-7786	Grob G 103 Twin Astir	3138	
D-7788-RE	Rolladen-Schneider LS4-b	4917	
D-7790-90	Schempp-Hirth Duo Discus	296	
D-7791	Grob G 103 Twin Astir	3148	
D-7792-YJ	Grob G 103 Twin Astir	3149	
D-7794	SZD-30 Pirat	B-437	DDR-1794, DM-1794
D-7797-WP	Grob G 103 Twin Astir	3167	
D-7799	Pilatus B4-PC11AF	322	
D-7800-FL	Rolladen-Schneider LS6	6073	
D-7801-2X	Rolladen-Schneider LS3-a	3206	
D-7802	Rolladen-Schneider LS6	6074	
D-7803	Rolladen-Schneider LS6-a	6075	
D-7804	Rolladen-Schneider LS4-b (P. 10.11)	41038	D-7805
D-7806	Schleicher ASK 23B (W/o 26.6.15)	23143	
D-7808-DK	SZD-55-1	551196080	
D-7809-HW	Rolladen-Schneider LS8-a	8349	
D-7810	Grob G 103 Twin Astir Trainer	3174-T-17	
D-7811-EZ	Rolladen-Schneider LS6-a	6121	
D-7812	Schleicher ASK 21	21582	
D-7813	Grob G 103 Twin Astir	3178	
D-7816	Schempp-Hirth Discus b	184	
D-7817	Glasflügel H206 Hornet	51	
D-7818-XA	Glasflügel H206 Hornet	44	
D-7820	Glasflügel H206 Hornet	42	
D-7821-AMF	Glasflügel H206 Hornet	45	
D-7822	Glasflügel H206 Hornet	41	
D-7823	Glasflügel H206 Hornet (Permit .00)	5	
D-7824	Schleicher ASK 21	21022	OE-5246
D-7825	Rolladen-Schneider LS4	4364	
D-7826	Rolladen-Schneider LS4	4365	
D-7828	Rolladen-Schneider LS4	4366	
D-7829	Rolladen-Schneider LS4	4367	
D-7830	SZD-30 Pirat	B-508	DDR-1830, DM-1830
D-7831-OK	Rolladen-Schneider LS8-a	8366	
D-7832	Grob G102 Astir CS	1096	OY-XDN
D-7833	Glasflügel H206 Hornet	26	
D-7834	Glasflügel H206 Hornet	35	
D-7835	Glasflügel H206 Hornet	36	
D-7836	Glasflügel H206 Hornet	37	
D-7837	Glasflügel H206 Hornet	34	
D-7838	Schleicher ASK 21	21238	
D-7839-JV	Schleicher ASW 19B	19412	
D-7840-AG	Schleicher ASW 20BL	20661	
D-7841	Glasflügel H206 Hornet	55	
D-7842	Schempp-Hirth Discus b	374	HB-3058
D-7844	Scheibe Bergfalke III	5654	
D-7845-ISH	Glasflügel H206 Hornet (Permit)	84	
D-7848	Schempp-Hirth Janus	36	
D-7852	Schempp-Hirth Standard Cirrus	700	
D-7854-54	Schempp-Hirth Standard Cirrus B	701	
D-7855-B6	Grob G 102 Astir CS	1532	
D-7856	Glasflügel H303 Mosquito (P. 4.11)	28	
D-7857-GZ	Glasflügel H303 Mosquito	35	
D-7858	SZD-30 Pirat	B-578	DDR-1858, DM-1858
D-7859	Glasflügel H303 Mosquito B	104	
D-7861	Schleicher ASW 27	27063	
D-7863	Schleicher Ka 6CR Rhönsegler	6120	OY-DDX
D-7865	Schempp-Hirth Mini Nimbus C	125	
D-7866-DK	Rolladen-Schneider LS8-a	8280	
D-7867	Glaser-Dirks DG-200	2-36	
D-7868-II	Glaser-Dirks DG-200	2-38	
D-7869	Glasflügel H303 Mosquito	93	
D-7870-GC	Schempp-Hirth Discus b	457	
D-7872	Rolladen-Schneider LS3-a	3109	
D-7873	Schleicher ASW 22	22039	
D-7874	SZD-30 Pirat	S-01.12	DDR-1874, DM-1874
D-7875	Rolladen-Schneider LS4-b	4882	
D-7876	Schleicher ASK 21	21198	
D-7877	Rolladen-Schneider LS3	3217	
D-7878-PP	Rolladen-Schneider LS3	3111	
D-7879-DE	Rolladen-Schneider LS3-a	3084	
D-7880-JT	Rolladen-Schneider LS4	4549	
D-7881	Rolladen-Schneider LS3-a	3097	
D-7882	Rolladen-Schneider LS4	4550	
D-7883-1P	Schleicher ASW 27	27006	
D-7884	Rolladen-Schneider LS3-a	3112	
D-7885	Rolladen-Schneider LS3-a	3113	
D-7886	Glasflügel H303 Mosquito B	114	
D-7887	Focke-Wulf Weihe 50	02	
D-7888	Schleicher K 8B	8931	OE-0972
D-7890	Rolladen-Schneider LS3-a	3304	
D-7891	Schleicher ASW 19B	19178	I-PINK
D-7892-92	Rolladen-Schneider LS3-17	3115	
D-7896-FN	Grob G 102 Club Astir IIIB	5603CB	
D-7898-P8	Rolladen-Schneider LS4	4552	
D-7899	Rolladen-Schneider LS3-a	3060	
D-7902-1A	Rolladen-Schneider LS3	3012	
D-7905	Rolladen-Schneider LS3	3015	
D-7906	Rolladen-Schneider LS3	3016	
D-7907	Rolladen-Schneider LS3	3017	
D-7908	Rolladen-Schneider LS3	3018	
D-7909	Rolladen-Schneider LS3	3019	
D-7910	Rolladen-Schneider LS3	3020	
D-7912	Schempp-Hirth Discus-2b	61	
D-7914	Grob G 103 Twin II	3789	
D-7915	Grob G 102 Club Astir IIIB	5602CB	
D-7917	Rolladen-Schneider LS3	3027	
D-7918	Rolladen-Schneider LS4	4555	
D-7919	Rolladen-Schneider LS4	4556	
D-7920-6A	Rolladen-Schneider LS3	3030	
D-7921-3A	Rolladen-Schneider LS3	3031	
D-7922	Schleicher ASK 23B	23136	
D-7923	Schleicher ASK 21	21635	
D-7925	Rolladen-Schneider LS8-18	8310	
D-7926	Schempp-Hirth HS-7 Mini-Nimbus	45	
D-7927-FA	DG Flugzeugbau DG-500 Elan Orion	5E217X57	
D-7928-27	Schleicher ASW 28	28011	
D-7930	Neukom S-4D Elfe	420AB	
D-7931-E5	Bölkow Phoebus C	931	
D-7933	Schleicher ASW 19	19148	
D-7934	Schleicher ASW 20	20031	
D-7935-IRS	Schleicher ASW 20	20057	
D-7936-WC	Schleicher ASW 19	19149	
D-7937-CG	Schempp-Hirth Discus-2b	154	
D-7939	Rolladen-Schneider LS7-WL	7047	HB-1998
D-7940-R1	Rolladen-Schneider LS8-18	8323	OY-JOX
D-7942	LET L-23 Super Blanik	917810	
D-7944-L3	Schempp-Hirth Duo Discus XL	562	
D-7945-FSB	Schleicher ASW 20 (Permit 3.11)	20036	
D-7949	Schleicher ASK 13	13584	
D-7950	Rolladen-Schneider LS4-b	4950	
D-7951-4K	Schleicher ASW 20	20039	
D-7952-FD	Schleicher ASW 20	20043	
D-7953	Schleicher ASW 19B	19165	
D-7955-W	Schempp-Hirth Discus b	452	OY-XUE, D-7955
D-7956-56	Schleicher ASW 19	19167	
D-7957	Schleicher ASK 13	13585	
D-7959-TX	Schleicher ASW 19	19170	
D-7960	Schleicher ASW 19B	19169	
D-7962	Schleicher ASK 13	13588	
D-7963	Schleicher ASW 19	19181	

Reg.	Type	W/N	Prev. ID
D-7966-B8	Schleicher ASW 19	19172	
D-7967	Schempp-Hirth Discus b	183	HB-1915
D-7970-AF	Schleicher ASW 19B	19175	
D-7971-IST	Schleicher ASW 19B	19176	
D-7972-GA	Schleicher ASW 19B	19195	
D-7975	Schleicher ASW 19	19177	
D-7976-RW	Schleicher ASW 20	20066	
D-7977-GW	Schleicher ASW 20L	20055	
D-7978-AH	Schempp-Hirth Duo Discus	394	F-CIDG
D-7979	Schleicher ASW 20	20023	
D-7981-M3	Schleicher ASW 19	19182	
D-7982-HA	Glasflügel H303 Mosquito B	122	
D-7984	Schleicher ASW 19	19197	
D-7985	Grob G 103A Twin II Acro	3623-K-10	
D-7986	Grob G 102 Club Astir IIIB	5508CB	
D-7987	Schleicher ASK 23B	23057	
D-7988	Glasflügel H303 Mosquito B	132	
D-7989	Schleicher ASK 21	21289	
D-7990	Schleicher ASW 19B	19150	
D-7991	Akaflieg Braunschweig SB-5E Sperber	5050AB	
D-7992	Schempp-Hirth Mini-Nimbus C	154	
D-7993-V7	Schempp-Hirth Nimbus-2C	213	
D-7994	Schempp-Hirth Nimbus-2C	215	
D-7995-MK	Schempp-Hirth Nimbus-2C	214	
D-7996-HR	Schempp-Hirth Mini-Nimbus C	156	
D-7998	Schleicher ASK 23B	23051	
D-8000	Vogt Lo-100 Zwergreiher	AB 38	
D-8001	SZD-9bis Bocian 1E	P-705	DDR-3000, DM-3000
D-8002	DFS Habicht E replica	ABH 1/OSC	
D-8003-800	Glaser-Dirks DG-800S	8-3S1	
D-8004	Glasflügel H304	208	
D-8005	Focke-Wulf Weihe 50	164	
D-8006-9B	Rolladen-Schneider LS3-a	3170	
D-8007-007	Glaser-Dirks DG-600	6-39	
D-8008	SZD-9bis Bocian 1E	P-721	DDR-3009, DM-3009
D-8009	Glasflügel H304	221	
D-8013	Schleicher K 8B	10	
D-8014-FM	Schempp-Hirth Ventus-2a	160	
D-8019	Glaser-Dirks DG-100G Elan	E170G136	
D-8022	Scheibe Bergfalke II/55	238	
D-8023	Schleicher ASK 23	23014	HB-1779
D-8024-PL	Schleicher ASW 27-18 (ASG 29)	29013	
D-8025	Rolladen-Schneider LS4	4599	PH-802, D-5265
D-8026	Akaflieg Braunschweig SB-5B Sperber	5012/A	
D-8028-28	Schleicher ASW 28	28001	
D-8029-TEX	DG Flugzeugbau DG-800S	8-208S38	
D-8030-B6	Rolladen-Schneider LS4-a	4655	
D-8031-6L	Rolladen-Schneider LS4-a	4656	
D-8032	Schleicher Ka 6CR Rhönsegler	556	
D-8033	Schleicher Ka 6E	4152	
D-8034	Rolladen-Schneider LS4-a	4657	
D-8035	Schleicher ASK 21	21657	
D-8036-FE	Schempp-Hirth Discus-2b	226	
D-8037-YN	Schempp-Hirth Discus-2b	108	
D-8039	SZD-9bis Bocian 1E	P-460	DDR-3039, DM-3039
D-8040-40	Glaser-Dirks DG-500 Elan Trainer	5E111T45	
D-8041	Schleicher Ka 6CR Rhönsegler	150/59	
D-8042-CH	Rolladen-Schneider LS4-a	4658	
D-8043	Schleicher Ka 6CR Rhönsegler	6190Si	
D-8044	SZD-9bis Bocian 1E	P-467	DDR-3044, DM-3044
D-8046-AC	Schleicher ASW 27	27061	
D-8047-8S	Rolladen-Schneider LS8-a	8035	
D-8048-BC	Glaser-Dirks DG-800S	8-27S4	
D-8050 -D3	Schempp-Hirth Duo Discus	5	
D-8051	Schleicher Ka 6E	4120	
D-8052-RT	Schempp-Hirth Ventus-2b	139	
D-8053	Rolladen-Schneider LS6-b	6148	
D-8054	Schempp-Hirth Ventus-2c	146	
D-8055	Glaser-Dirks DG-500 Elan Trainer	5E125T54	
D-8057-34	Glaser-Dirks DG-100	43	OE-5057
D-8059-8E	Allstar PZL SZD-59 Acro	590.A.04.002	
D-8060	Schempp-Hirth Discus b	480	
D-8062	Grob G 103A Twin II Acro	33966-K-199	
D-8064	Göppingen Gö III Minimoa	184	N2664B, HB-626, D-8064
D-8065	ICA-Brasov IS-28B2	358	SE-USS, YR-1992
D-8066-S8	Glaser-Dirks DG-300 Elan	3E182	ZK-GSS
D-8067-1D	Schempp-Hirth Discus-2c	40	
D-8068-KN	SZD-42-2 Jantar 2B	B-871	DOSAAF
D-8069-6K	Grob G 103A Twin II Acro	34013-K-246	
D-8070	Vogt Lo-100 Zwergreiher	AB-36	
D-8071-RA	Schempp-Hirth Discus b	565	
D-8072	Grob G 103A Twin II Acro	33967-K-200	
D-8073	SZD-9bis Bocian 1E	P-762	DDR-3073, DM-3073
D-8074	Grunau Baby III	AB8262	
D-8076	SZD-48-3 Jantar-Standard 3.	B-1638	(F-CIGR), OO-ZGR
D-8078-V2	Glasflügel H201B Standard Libelle	2	
D-8080-1K	Glasflügel H201B Standard Libelle	1	
D-8081-PL	Schleicher ASW 24	24077	HB-3030
D-8082	DG Flugzeugbau DG-500 Elan Orion	5E207X50	S5-7521
D-8084-ALB	Schempp-Hirth Discus-2a	28	
D-8085	Schleicher Ka 6CR Rhönsegler	6148	
D-8086-MA	Schempp-Hirth Duo Discus	110	
D-8087	Grob G 103A Twin II Acro	33973-K-206	
D-8088	Schempp-Hirth Janus Ce	292	
D-8091	Rolladen-Schneider LS4-b	4864	
D-8092-F3	Rolladen-Schneider LS4-b	4865	
D-8093	Rolladen-Schneider LS4-b	4866	
D-8094	Rolladen-Schneider LS4-b	4867	
D-8095-M6	Rolladen-Schneider LS4-b	4868	
D-8097	Grob G 103A Twin II Acro	33974-K-207	
D-8098-WL	Rolladen-Schneider LS4-b	4869	
D-8099	Rolladen-Schneider LS4-b	4870	
D-8100	Schleicher ASK 13	13058	
D-8101	Scheibe Bergfalke III	5509	
D-8102	Vogt Lo-100 Zwergreiher	AB-37	
D-8104	Rolladen-Schneider LS4-b	4872	
D-8105	Rolladen-Schneider LS4-b	4873	
D-8106-LJ	Schempp-Hirth Nimbus-2B	138	OE-5106
D-8108-K2	Schempp-Hirth Duo Discus	8	
D-8109	Scheibe Bergfalke II	172	
D-8110-19	Rolladen-Schneider LS6-b	6156	
D-8112	Grob G 102 Club Astir IIIB	5634CB	
D-8113-M7	Schleicher ASW 27-18 (ASG 29)	29089	
D-8114	Marganski Swift S-1	109	HB-3114
D-8115-M6	Schleicher ASW 27 (P. 4.11)	27051	
D-8116	Schleicher K 8B	8777	I-BAUU
D-8117	Rolladen-Schneider LS6-b	6158	
D-8118	Vogt Lo-100 Zwergreiher	11	
D-8120	Scheibe L-Spatz 55	737	
D-8121	Schleicher ASK 21	21618	
D-8123	Rolladen-Schneider LS8-18	8372	OH-922
D-8124	Schleicher ASK 21	21227	
D-8125-LV	Schempp-Hirth Discus CS	144CS	
D-8126-AX	Schempp-Hirth Discus CS	145CS	
D-8127-LS	Schempp-Hirth Discus CS	140CS	
D-8128	Schleicher ASW 28-18	28507	
D-8129-2M	Schempp-Hirth Duo Discus	196	
D-8133	Schleicher Ka 6E	4182	
D-8134	Schleicher Ka 2B Rhönschwalbe	199	
D-8136-2X	Schempp-Hirth Duo Discus	83	
D-8139	Marganski Swift S-1	105	HB-3139, SP-3573
D-8140-YB	Schempp-Hirth Discus-2b	5	
D-8141	Akaflieg Stuttgart FS.25	V-1	
D-8145	Centrair 101A Pégase	101046	OO-ZHC, F-CFQI
D-8146	Schempp-Hirth Nimbus-2	85	OH-899, D-2784
D-8147	Bölkow Phoebus B1	720	SX-147, D-9371
D-8148	Scheibe Bergfalke II	174	
D-8150	Grob G 103A Twin II Acro	33989-K-222	
D-8152	FES 530/II Lehrmeister	152	(D-3208), DM-3152
D-8153-53	Schleicher ASK 21	21473	
D-8155	Raab Doppelraab V	529	
D-8156	Slingsby T59D Kestrel 19	1728	BGA 1744/CRJ
D-8159	Scheibe Bergfalke II	4	
D-8160	Scheibe L-Spatz 55	583	
D-8161-FAY	Rolladen-Schneider LS4	4395	(PH-1233), D-8161, D-5499
D-8162	Schempp-Hirth Nimbus-2B	98	VH-WVY, D-6494
D-8164	Schleicher Ka 6CR Rhönsegler	716	
D-8166-C	Schempp-Hirth Ventus-2a	86	
D-8168-CV	Schempp-Hirth Nimbus-2C	228	D-3166
D-8170-70	Glasflügel H301B Libelle	82	
D-8171-7R	Rolladen-Schneider LS7-WL	7120	F-CGYE
D-8174-UH	Glasflügel Kestrel	95	HB-1174
D-8175	Rolladen-Schneider LS4-a	4332	HB-1705
D-8176-LT	Rolladen-Schneider LS7-WL	7084	
D-8178-FY	Rolladen-Schneider LS7	7085	
D-8179-LL	Rolladen-Schneider LS7	7086	
D-8180	Göppingen Gö III Minimoa	324	PH-848, N37JK, BGA 1738/CRC, RAFGGA
D-8181-YC	Rolladen-Schneider LS7-WL	7088	
D-8182-UG	Rolladen-Schneider LS7-WL	7089	
D-8183-7H	Schleicher ASW 24B	24242	
D-8184	Göppingen Gö IV Goevier III	409	OO-ZHW, D-5946, D-6041, D-8102
D-8187	Grunau Baby III (Res.)	"XYZ"	
D-8188	HpH Glasflügel 304C	72-C	
D-8191-LV	Schleicher ASK 21	21627	
D-8192-LB	Rolladen-Schneider LS7	7114	
D-8193-77	Rolladen-Schneider LS7-WL	7115	
D-8194-RQ	Schleicher ASW 27	27088	
D-8196	Glaser-Dirks DG-100G Elan	E132G100	
D-8197	Rolladen-Schneider LS7-WL	7118	
D-8198	Scheibe Bergfalke II/55	212	
D-8200	SZD-48-3 Jantar Standard 3	B-1971	OO-YAD, F-CBZD(2)
D-8201	Rolladen-Schneider LS7	7087	OH-820
D-8202	Glaser-Dirks DG-303 Elan	3E466	HB-3202
D-8203-7G	Grob G 103A Twin II Acro	34008-K-241	
D-8204-GH	SZD-48-1 Jantar Standard	W-893	OE-5204
D-8205	Glasflügel Club Libelle 205	149	F-CEQF
D-8206	Rolladen-Schneider LS7	7122	
D-8207	Schempp-Hirth Duo Discus	49	
D-8208-KWI	Rolladen-Schneider LS7-WL	7124	
D-8209	Scheibe L-Spatz 55	695	
D-8210	Schleicher K 8B	975	
D-8211	Schleicher ASK 21	21902	
D-8212	Rolladen-Schneider LS6-c	6286	
D-8214	Schleicher Ka 6E	4199	
D-8219-LG	Schleicher ASW 19B	19218	
D-8221	SZD-32A Foka 5	W-469	DDR-2221, DM-2221
D-8222-82	Glasflügel H201B Standard Libelle (Permit .05)	354	OY-XBD
D-8223	Hütter H.28 II replica	01	
D-8224	Schleicher ASW 24	24220	PH-1350, D-6602
D-8225-SD	Schempp-Hirth Discus b	345	
D-8226	Schempp-Hirth Discus b	356	
D-8227-71	Schempp-Hirth Ventus c	482	
D-8228-5G	Schempp-Hirth Discus b	(24)/317	
D-8230-IMK	Schempp-Hirth Discus b	329	
D-8232	SZD-24-4A Foka 4	W-347	DDR-2234, DM-2234
D-8233-IT	Schempp-Hirth Discus CS	312CS	
D-8234	SZD-9bis Bocian 1E	P-516	DDR-3234, DM-3234
D-8235	Schleicher ASK 21	21598	
D-8236-E9	Akaflieg Braunschweig SB-5E Sperber	5008	
D-8238	Schleicher ASK 21	21602	
D-8239	Jacobs Weihe 50	00266	
D-8240	Glaser-Dirks DG-300 Elan	3E258	PH-824
D-8241	Scheibe Bergfalke II/55	251	D-8240
D-8242	SZD-9bis Bocian 1E	P-534	DDR-3247, DM-3247
D-8244-D7	Grob G 102 Standard Astir III	5536S	OE-5276
D-8249-FX	SZD-32A Foka 5	W-499	DDR-2249, DM-2249
D-8250	HpH Glasflügel 304C Wasp	48-C	OK-2222
D-8251	Rolladen-Schneider LS4-b	41006	
D-8252	Rolladen-Schneider LS4-b	41007	
D-8253	Schleicher ASW 20CL	20785	
D-8255	Schleicher ASW 27B	27210	
D-8256	Vogt Lo-100 Zwergreiher	05A	
D-8257-YA	Schempp-Hirth Ventus-2b	67	HB-3257
D-8258-HB	Schempp-Hirth Discus b	552	
D-8259-6H	Schempp-Hirth Discus b	553	
D-8260-1	Schempp-Hirth Discus b	554	
D-8261-PP	Schempp-Hirth Discus-2b	207	
D-8262	Scheibe L-Spatz 55	595	
D-8263	Scheibe Spatz B	AB-01	
D-8264	SZD-32A Foka 5	W-527	DDR-2264, DM-2264
D-8266-66	Schempp-Hirth Discus-2b	17	G-CJNY, BGA 4659, D-4498
D-8268	Valentin Mistral C	MC 068/86	
D-8269	Grob G103A Twin II Acro	3624-K-11	(OY-TCX), D-5268, OE-5269
D-8270-70	Schempp-Hirth Discus-2b	45	

Reg.	Type	Serial	Previous identities
D-8271	Scheibe L-Spatz 55	1	
D-8275	Schleicher ASW 20CL	20846	
D-8277-ty	SZD-48-1 Jantar Standard 2	B-1166	OE-5277
D-8281	Schleicher Ka 6BR Rhönsegler	346	
D-8282-UT	Schempp-Hirth Discus CS	049CS	
D-8283-AT	Schempp-Hirth Discus CS	159CS	
D-8284-5W	Schempp-Hirth Discus CS	163CS	
D-8285	Schleicher Rhönlerche II	AB-08	
D-8286-KL	Rolladen-Schneider LS4-b	4883	
D-8290-29	Schempp-Hirth Ventus b/16.6	33	
D-8291-X5	Schempp-Hirth Duo Discus	136	
D-8295	Schleicher K 7 Rhönadler (P 8.10)	434	
D-8296-A	DG Flugzeugbau DG-300 Elan Acro	3E469A19	
D-8297-O	DG Flugzeugbau DG-300 Elan	3E472	
D-8298	Schleicher ASW 27-18 (ASG 29)	29079	
D-8299	Schempp-Hirth Standard Cirrus	569G	OY-XCT
D-8300	SZD-36A Cobra 15	W-558	DDR-2300, DM-2300
D-8301	Schleicher Rhönlerche II	04	
D-8302	Schempp-Hirth Nimbus-4D	2/8	
D-8303	Glaser-Dirks DG-300 Club Elan	3E462C82	
D-8304	Glasflügel 304	217	OH-608
D-8305	SZD-51-1 Junior	B-2148	
D-8306	Rolladen-Schneider LS7-WL	7146	HB-3306, D-3873
D-8308-1Y	DG Flugzeugbau DG-800S	8-100S24	
D-8310	Scheibe L-Spatz 55	AB-545	
D-8311-H1	Schleicher ASK 21	21155	
D-8312	Schleicher Ka 6BR Rhönsegler	496	
D-8314	Scheibe L-Spatz 55	666	
D-8315	Start + Flug H 101 Salto	32	OY-NYX, D-2194
D-8316	Schleicher K 8B	516	
D-8317	Rolladen-Schneider LS6-c	6215	PH-1020, D-5458, OH-793
D-8318-8C	Schleicher ASW 19B	19424	
D-8321	Schleicher ASK 21	21135	HB-1677
D-8322-L2	Glaser-Dirks DG-500/20 Elan	5E144W6	
D-8325	Schleicher ASK 23B	23144	
D-8327	Schleicher Ka 6CR Rhönsegler	6479	
D-8328-MO	Schleicher ASW 28	28021	
D-8329-KB	Schleicher ASW 27-18 (ASG 29)	29052	
D-8330	Schleicher Rhönlerche II	469	
D-8332	Scheibe Zugvogel III (P 6.15)	1038	
D-8333-38	Schempp-Hirth Ventus b/16.6	190	
D-8334	Schleicher K 8B	639	
D-8336	Glaser-Dirks DG-100	79	HB-1336
D-8338-Z2	Schempp-Hirth Duo Discus XL	623	
D-8342	Schleicher Ka 6CR Rhönsegler	679	
D-8344-LG	Schempp-Hirth Duo Discus	406	
D-8345	Schleicher ASW 15B	15376	I-FLIK
D-8347	Scheibe Sperber	2	
D-8348	Glasflügel H304	220	
D-8349-M	Schleicher ASW 15B	15358	OO-YLB, D-2348
D-8351	Scheibe Zugvogel IIIA	1052	
D-8356	Scheibe Zugvogel IIIA	1051	
D-8357	Scheibe L-Spatz 55	717	
D-8358	Doppelraab IV	02	
D-8360-HH	Schleicher ASW 27	27014	
D-8363-H1	Schempp-Hirth Duo Discus	104	
D-8365	Schleicher Rhönlerche II	3060	OB-813, OB-I-813
D-8369	Nabern FS-24 Phönix T	405	
D-8374	Schleicher Ka 6CR Rhönsegler	965	
D-8376	SZD-9bis Bocian 1E	P-566	DDR-3376, DM-3376
D-8377-77	Schempp-Hirth Discus CS	214CS	
D-8381	Schleicher Ka 6CR Rhönsegler	999	
D-8383-CT	Schleicher ASK 21	21926	
D-8384	DG Flugzeugbau DG-800S	8-109S25	
D-8386	Schleicher K 7 Rhönadler	1006	
D-8387	Schleicher Ka 6CR Rhönsegler	AB-04/201	
D-8388-RZ	Schleicher ASW 27	27001	HB-3289, D-5527
D-8389-GT2	Rolladen-Schneider LS8-18	8389	
D-8390	Schorndorf/Schleicher Ka 6BS	E1	
D-8391-EN	Rolladen-Schneider LS8-18	8391	
D-8392	Schleicher K 8B	1060	
D-8393-LR	Schleicher Ka 6CR Rhönsegler	1109	
D-8394	Scheibe Bergfalke II/55	344	
D-8397	Rolladen-Schneider LS8-18	8397	
D-8399	Schleicher ASK 21	21301	
D-8401	Schleicher K 8B	1101	
D-8402-GG	Rolladen-Schneider LS8-18	8402	
D-8403-84	Schleicher ASK 21	21302	
D-8404	Scheibe L-Spatz 55	751	
D-8405-O2	Schleicher ASK 23B	23073	
D-8406	SZD-41A Jantar Standard	B-697	DDR-2406, DM-2406
D-8408	Schleicher Ka 6CR Rhönsegler	6011	
D-8409	Schleicher Ka 6CR Rhönsegler	6031Si	
D-8411-BT	Rolladen-Schneider LS8-18	?	
D-8412-WT	Schleicher K 8B	8007	
D-8414	Schleicher ASW 24B	24248	
D-8416	Schleicher Ka 6CR Rhönsegler	6286	OE-0960, D-4673
D-8417-17	Schleicher K 8B	8041	
D-8418	Schleicher ASK 21	21678	
D-8419	Scheibe L-Spatz 55	585	
D-8421	Schleicher K 8B (P 16.2.16)	8421	D-KOCA
D-8422-S22	Schleicher ASW 22	22013	G-CHTN, BGA 4191, ZS-GLN
D-8423	Test registration for Schempp-Hirth Duo Discus		
D-8424	Schleicher Ka 6CR Rhönsegler	6045	
D-8426-6N	SZD-48-1 Jantar Standard 2	W-847	DDR-2426, DM-2426, SP-3118
D-8427-ZJ	SZD-48-1 Jantar Standard 2	W-855	DDR-2427, DM-2427, (SP-3083)
D-8433	Glaser-Dirks DG-100G	95G12	HB-3433; OE-5124
D-8434	Scheibe Bergfalke III	5507	
D-8435-9G	Schempp-Hirth Duo Discus	197	
D-8437	Schleicher ASW 20C	20841	
D-8439	Schleicher K 8B	281/A/3	
D-8440-GU	SZD-48-1 Jantar Standard 2	B-1052	DDR-2430, DM-2430
D-8441-MO	Rolladen-Schneider LS4	4536	
D-8442	Schempp-Hirth Discus-2c	18	
D-8443	Scheibe Bergfalke II/55	366	
D-8444	Schleicher Ka 6CR Rhönsegler	6063	
D-8445-TM	Schempp-Hirth Discus-2c	37	
D-8446	Schleicher K 8B	103/98	
D-8448	Nabern FS-24 Phönix T	407	
D-8449	Centrair 101AP Pegase	101041	OY-XMM
D-8450	Schleicher K 8B	8168	
D-8451-20	Schleicher Ka 6CR Rhönsegler	6113	
D-8455	Grob G 102 Astir CS	1290	PH-551
D-8456-F6	Grob G102 Astir CS 77	1782	HA-3456, HB-1456
D-8460-PM	Schleicher ASK 21	21303	
D-8462	Schleicher ASK 21	21305	
D-8463	Schleicher K 7 Rhönadler	7087	
D-8464	Schleicher ASK 21	21306	
D-8466-GT	Schleicher ASK 23B	23076	
D-8467	Schleicher K 8B	8640Gö	HB-880
D-8471	Schleicher K 8B	8262	
D-8472-MS	Schleicher ASW 19B	19401	OY-XMS
D-8475	Doppelraab VI	03	
D-8477	Schleicher Ka 6CR Rhönsegler	6181	
D-8481	Schempp-Hirth Arcus	19	
D-8482	Scheibe Zugvogel IIIB	1086	
D-8483	Schleicher Ka 6CR	6227/Si	
D-8484	Schleicher ASK 13	13151	D-0284
D-8485	Schleicher Ka 6CR Rhönsegler	6234	
D-8486	Schleicher ASK 23B	23090	HB-1901
D-8488	Grob G 102 Speed Astir IIB	4043	
D-8489	Scheibe Zugvogel IIIB	1090	
D-8490-B1	Rolladen-Schneider LS4	4534	
D-8494	Rolladen-Schneider LS4	4047	
D-8495	Scheibe Bergfalke III	5516	
D-8498	Neukom S-4D Elfe	424AB	
D-8499	Schleicher Ka 6CR Rhönsegler	6300	
D-8500-CM	Rolladen-Schneider LS8-a	8500	
D-8502-GI	Schempp-Hirth Ventus-2b	5	
D-8503	Rolladen-Schneider LS8-18	8315	
D-8504	DFS Kranich II	24	
D-8505-CX	Rolladen-Schneider LS6-a	6060	
D-8506	Focke-Wulf Kranich III	74	
D-8508	Schleicher K 7 Rhönadler	7076	
D-8509	Rolladen-Schneider LS6	6059	
D-8512	Schleicher K 8B	997	
D-8513	Rolladen-Schneider LS4	4320	HB-1687
D-8514-JB	Schempp-Hirth Discus CS	205CS	
D-8515-ST	Schempp-Hirth Discus CS	207CS	
D-8516-JE	Schempp-Hirth Discus CS	213CS	
D-8518	Schleicher ASW 27	27082	
D-8519	Schleicher Ka 6E	4138	
D-8520-IR	Schempp-Hirth Ventus-2a	63	OK-8520
D-8521	Scheibe SF 27A	6078	
D-8522	Schleicher K 8B	8019	
D-8523	Schleicher K 8B	8072	
D-8524	Glasflügel Hornet	62	PH-439, (PH-511)
D-8525	Schleicher K 8B	8236	
D-8527-E4	Schleicher ASW 28-18	28527	
D-8528	Rolladen-Schneider LS4	4474	
D-8529	Schleicher K 8B	8529	
D-8530	Schleicher K 8B	919	
D-8531	Schleicher Rhönlerche II	AB-03	
D-8533	Schleicher Rhönlerche II	01	
D-8534	Schleicher K 8B	8360	
D-8535	Schleicher Ka 6BR Rhönsegler	387	
D-8541	Schleicher K 8B	8585	
D-8543	Focke-Wulf Kranich III	59	D-3008
D-8547-BW	Schempp-Hirth Discus CS	138CS	OE-5547
D-8550	Valentin Mistral-C	MC 033/81	HB-1550
D-8551-75	Grob G 102 Astir CS Jeans	2196	OO-ZJS
D-8552	Schleicher Ka 2B Rhönschwalbe	1012	
D-8554	Scheibe Bergfalke II/55	363	
D-8555	Grob G 103C Twin III Acro	34198	
D-8556	Glasflügel H304	228	
D-8557-FI	Glasflügel H304	229	
D-8558-D5	Schempp-Hirth Ventus-2b	6	
D-8560-VY	Schempp-Hirth Discus CS	309CS	
D-8561-B2	Rolladen-Schneider LS6-18W	6378	BGA 4385/JBP
D-8565	Schleicher Ka 6E	4051	
D-8567	Schleicher K 8B	8059	
D-8568	Schleicher Ka 6CR Rhönsegler	6291	
D-8569	Olympia-Meise	3	
D-8570-GG	Bölkow Phoebus C	802	
D-8572-7	Schempp-Hirth Discus a	533	
D-8575-DB	SZD-48-3 Jantar Standard 3	B-1890	SP-3541
D-8576	Scheibe Bergfalke II/55	338	HB-524
D-8577-LD	Schempp-Hirth Ventus-2a	34	
D-8578	Schleicher K 8	115/58	
D-8579	Schleicher Ka 6CR Rhönsegler	002 AB	
D-8581-DG	Glaser-Dirks DG-200	2-61	I-CEMM, D-7776
D-8582	Schleicher ASW 20CL	20767	
D-8585	Grunau Baby III	AB 1	
D-8587	Raab Doppelraab V	533	D-8080
D-8588-ALI	Rolladen-Schneider LS8-18	8339	
D-8590	Scheibe L-Spatz (Wfu)	508B	
D-8592-51	Schempp-Hirth Discus b	223	I-RHEN
D-8593	Schleicher Ka 6CR Rhönsegler	6061	
D-8595	Schleicher ASK 23B	23134	
D-8598	Schleicher K 8B	1	
D-8600-1E	Glaser-Dirks DG-600	6-7	
D-8602	Schleicher K 8B (P 18.7.16)	8275	
D-8603	Glaser-Dirks DG-600	6-35	
D-8604	SZD-50-3 Puchacz	B-1088	DDR-3604
D-8605-SK	Schempp-Hirth Discus-2b	150	
D-8606	Schleicher Ka 6 Rhönsegler	248	
D-8607	Schleicher Ka 6CR-PE Rhönsegler	6229Bi	
D-8608	Schleicher Ka 6CR Rhönsegler	6432Si	
D-8611-PA	Schempp-Hirth Arcus	12	
D-8614	Schleicher K 8C	81009	PH-432
D-8615	Eiri PIK-20D	20635	OO-ZJA
D-8616	Schleicher K 8B	1055	
D-8618	Schleicher K 8B	8511	
D-8619	Schleicher Ka 6CR Rhönsegler	6470Si	
D-8621	Schempp-Hirth SHK-1	47	HB-862
D-8622	Schleicher Ka 6BR Rhönsegler	386	
D-8624	SZD-50-3 Puchacz	B-1343	DDR-3624
D-8626	Schleicher Ka 6CR Rhönsegler	6644	
D-8627	Schleicher K 8B	8570	
D-8628-MC	Schleicher ASK 21	21120	
D-8629	Schleicher ASK 21	21121	
D-8630-AT	Rolladen-Schneider LS6-a	6079	HB-1859

Registration	Type	Serial	Previous identities
D-8631	Schleicher ASW 20	20585	
D-8632-BAS	Schleicher ASW 20	20591	
D-8633	Bölkow Phoebus A-1	731	
D-8634-UV	Schleicher ASH 25	25008	OO-ZYK, D-4741
D-8636-M7	Glasflügel H201B Standard Libelle	307	OE-0936
D-8637	Schleicher Ka 6CR Rhönsegler	6546	
D-8638	Scheibe L-Spatz 55	750	
D-8639	Centrair 101A Pégase	101063	HB-1689
D-8640	SZD-50-3 Puchacz	B-1470	DDR-3640
D-8642	Schleicher ASW 15B	15398	
D-8643	Schleicher ASK 13	13494	
D-8644-ZZ	Schleicher ASW 15B	15409	
D-8648	Schleicher ASK 13	13501	
D-8649-R9	Rolladen-Schneider LS4-b	4918	
D-8650	Schleicher ASW 15B	15403	
D-8652	Schleicher K 8C	81004	
D-8653	Schleicher ASW 15B	15410	
D-8654	Schleicher ASW 17	17040	
D-8655	Schleicher ASW 15B	15412	
D-8657	Schleicher K 8B	8973	
D-8658-JS	Schleicher ASW 15B	15411	
D-8659	Schleicher ASK 13	13500	
D-8660	Schleicher ASW 15B	15415	
D-8661	Grob G102 Astir CS	1344	OY-XHE
D-8663	Schleicher K 8B	669	HB-663
D-8664-LE	Schempp-Hirth Ventus-2cxR	123	
D-8665	Schleicher ASW 15B	15420	
D-8666-IDA	Rolladen-Schneider LS1-f	378	
D-8667-CN	Rolladen-Schneider LS1-f	334	
D-8669-RY	Rolladen-Schneider LS1-f	327	
D-8670-EX	Schempp-Hirth Standard Cirrus	522	OE-5360, PH-509
D-8671-BV	Rolladen-Schneider LS1-f	298	
D-8672	Rolladen-Schneider LS1-f	277	
D-8676-C	Glaser-Dirks DG-100	13	
D-8677	Schleicher ASK 21	21797	
D-8678	Rolladen-Schneider LS6-c18.	6349	G-CHYA, BGA 4300, D-2162
D-8679-DK	Rolladen-Schneider LS1-f	381	
D-8681	Glasflügel Club Libelle 205	150	G-CKNI, BGA 5225, F-CEQG
D-8683	Rolladen-Schneider LS8-18	8197	G-CJHU, BGA 4534
D-8684	Glasflügel H205 Club Libelle	72	
D-8685	Glasflügel H205 Club Libelle	73	
D-8686	Glasflügel H205 Club Libelle	74	
D-8688	Scheibe Bergfalke III	5651	
D-8689	Rolladen-Schneider LS8-18	8058	G-CHUW, BGA 4223
D-8690	Glasflügel H401 Kestrel	125	
D-8694-7E	Grob G 103A Twin II Acro	3689-K-40	
D-8695	Grob G 102 Club Astir IIIB	5554CB	
D-8698	Grob G 103A Twin II Acro	3690-K-41	
D-8700	Grob G 102 Speed Astir IIB	4094	VH-IUF
D-8701-FG	Schempp-Hirth Standard Cirrus	566G	
D-8703-BY	Schempp-Hirth Duo Discus	265	
D-8704	Grob G 102 Club Astir IIIB	5566CB	
D-8708	LET L-13 Blanik	027225	OK-9700
D-8709-G3	Schempp-Hirth Discus CS	160CS	OY-XSC
D-8710-HK	DG Flugzeugbau DG-1000S	10-47S46	
D-8711-GM	Rolladen-Schneider LS4	4014	
D-8712-1R	Rolladen-Schneider LS4	4015	
D-8713-PF	Rolladen-Schneider LS4	4557	
D-8714	Rolladen-Schneider LS1-f	453	
D-8715-K8	Schempp-Hirth Discus-2b	71	
D-8716-AT	Grob G 102 Speed Astir IIB	4050	
D-8717	Grob G 102 Speed Astir IIB	4052	
D-8719	Grob G 102 Speed Astir IIB	4054	
D-8720-AW	Grob G 102 Speed Astir IIB	4055	
D-8721	Grob G 102 Speed Astir IIB	4056	
D-8722	Grob G 102 Speed Astir IIB	4072	
D-8723	Schleicher ASK 23	23152	
D-8724-55	Schleicher ASW 24	24150	I-GLID
D-8726-AK	Akaflieg München Mü.26	V-1	D-0726
D-8727-A7	Schleicher ASW 27	27100	OK-2727
D-8728	Schleicher ASW 28-18 (P. 6.14)	28752	
D-8729-BI	Grob G 103 Twin II	3535	
D-8732	SZD-30 Pirat	B-315	DDR-1732, DM-1732
D-8733-3J	Schempp-Hirth Duo Discus	156	
D-8735	Schleicher Ka 6E	4156	
D-8737	Grob G 102 Speed Astir IIB	4092	
D-8739	Grob G 102 Speed Astir IIB	4095	
D-8741	Grob G 102 Standard Astir II	5003S	
D-8745	Grob G 102 Speed Astir IIB	4099	
D-8746	Schempp-Hirth Ventus b/16.6	167	OE-5332
D-8747	Schempp-Hirth Nimbus-2C	222	
D-8750	Grob G 103 Twin II	3525	
D-8752	Grob G 103 Twin II	3527	
D-8754	Schleicher K 8B	8419	
D-8755	Grob G 103A Twin II Acro	3559-K-5	
D-8756	Grob G 103 Twin II	3532	
D-8757-AD	Schleicher ASK 23B	23066	OH-757
D-8759	Grob G 102 Club Astir II	5061C	
D-8761	Grob G 103 Twin II (P.5.12)	3554	
D-8762-M3	Grob G 103 Twin II	3555	
D-8766	Grob G 103 Twin II	3560	
D-8770	Schleicher Ka 6CR Rhönsegler	6281	
D-8772	Schempp-Hirth Ventus b/16.6	141	HA-4527, BGA 3443/FQN, D-8772, D-KHIB
D-8773	Scheibe Zugvogel I	1002	
D-8774-2W	Schempp-Hirth Cirrus	62	OM-. . . ., OO-ZLL
D-8775-51	Schleicher ASW 20L	20372	
D-8776	Schleicher Ka 2 Rhönschwalbe	106	
D-8777	Scheibe L-Spatz 55	553	
D-8778-7	Schleicher K 8B	8332SH	
D-8779	Schleicher K 8B	02	
D-8781	Schleicher ASW 20L	20377	
D-8782	Schleicher K 8B	8338/A	
D-8783	Schleicher K 8B	8356	
D-8784	Schleicher ASK 21	21640	
D-8785	Scheibe L-Spatz 55	550	
D-8787	Scheibe Zugvogel IIIB	1093	
D-8790-OO7	Glasflügel H201B Standard Libelle	4	
D-8791	Schleicher K 8B	8389/A	
D-8792-T6	Schleicher ASW 20L	20368	
D-8794	Grob G 103 Twin II	3529	
D-8795	Grob G103A Twin II Acro	34065-K-295	D-6429
D-8796	SZD-30 Pirat	B-439	DDR-1796, DM-1796
D-8797	Grob G 103 Twin II	3534	
D-8798-R1	Schleicher ASK 21	21032	
D-8800-A6	Schempp-Hirth Nimbus-2B	175	
D-8801	Schleicher ASK 21	21036	
D-8802	SZD-24-4A Foka 4	W-370	DDR-2231, DM-2231
D-8803	Schempp-Hirth Duo Discus	51	OH-1007, D-3950
D-8805	Schleicher K 8B	8278	
D-8806	Scheibe L-Spatz 55	1	
D-8808-B7	Schleicher Ka 6CR Rhönsegler	313	
D-8809-4B	Schleicher ASW 19B	19324	
D-8810-S7	Schleicher ASW 20L	20383	
D-8811-8Y	Rolladen-Schneider LS8-a	8278	
D-8812	Scheibe Bergfalke II	167	
D-8816-L2	Schleicher ASK 21	21758	SE-UNK
D-8817-17	Rolladen-Schneider LS6-18W	6374	
D-8819	Schleicher K 7	7253	
D-8820	Scheibe Zugvogel IIIB	1103	
D-8822	Schleicher ASW 20L	20389	
D-8823	Schleicher Ka 6CR Rhönsegler	6370Si	
D-8824	Scheibe Zugvogel IIIB	1028	
D-8825	Schleicher ASK 21	21037	
D-8828	Schleicher K 8B (Res.1.00)	454	
D-8829	SZD-30 Pirat	B-507	DDR-1829, DM-1829
D-8830-B25	Grob G 103C Twin III Acro	34196	
D-8831	Schleicher ASW 19B	19347	
D-8832-F1	Schleicher ASW 20	20391	
D-8833	Rolladen-Schneider LS4-b	4906	
D-8836	Schleicher K 7 Rhönadler	694	
D-8838-38	Glaser-Dirks DG-300 Elan Acro	3E437A5	HB-3111
D-8840	Schleicher Ka 6CR Rhönsegler	6100	D-6215
D-8841	Schleicher Ka 6CR Rhönsegler	1073	OO-ZMZ, OO-ZMS, D-5367
D-8842	Scheibe L-Spatz 55	700	
D-8844-ET	Glaser-Dirks DG-300 Club Elan	3E288C12	
D-8845	Grob G 102 Club Astir IIIB	5510CB	
D-8846	Grob G 102 Club Astir IIIB	5511CB	
D-8847	Grob G102 Club Astir IIIB	5512Cb	
D-8848-8Z	Glasflügel Standard Libelle 201B	405	OY-XBZ
D-8849	Vogt Lo-100/150 Zwergreiher	13	
D-8850	SZD-42-2 Jantar 2B	B-1491	
D-8852	Schleicher K 8B	03	
D-8853	Schleicher K 8B	977	
D-8855	Schleicher ASW 20L	20565	
D-8858	Scheibe L-Spatz 55	741	
D-8859-OPI	Schempp-Hirth Duo Discus	371	
D-8860-CC	Schleicher Ka 6CR Rhönsegler	1075	
D-8861-6L	Rolladen-Schneider LS4	4359	F-CFZC
D-8862	Glaser-Dirks DG-300 Elan	3E265	LN-GLU
D-8863-A5	Rolladen-Schneider LS4	4371	
D-8864-P9	Rolladen-Schneider LS4	4372	
D-8865-C5	Rolladen-Schneider LS4	4381	
D-8866	AB Flygindustri DFS Weihe	224	BGA 1297/BWR, G-ASCV, SE-STN, Fv8306
D-8867-2D	Schempp-Hirth Duo Discus x	478	
D-8868	Schleicher ASW 20	20047	OO-ZVM
D-8869	Schleicher ASK 21	21641	
D-8872	Rolladen-Schneider LS4	4450	
D-8873	Rolladen-Schneider LS4	4451	
D-8874-N3	Rolladen-Schneider LS4-a	4452	
D-8875	Rolladen-Schneider LS4	4453	
D-8876	Akaflieg München Mü.13D	1	
D-8877	Schempp-Hirth Nimbus-2B	161	
D-8878	Glaser-Dirks DG-300 Elan	3E164	
D-8879	Schleicher Ka 6CR Rhönsegler	6095Si	
D-8881	Rolladen-Schneider LS8-a	8120	OY-XSR
D-8882	Schleicher Ka 6CR Rhönsegler	6543	
D-8883-RJ	Glasflügel H201B Standard Libelle	357	HB-1089
D-8884-2D	Schempp-Hirth Duo Discus	456	
D-8886-TL	Schleicher K 7 Rhönadler	7114	
D-8888	Schleicher ASK 21	21406	
D-8889	Scheibe Bergfalke III	5543	
D-8890-i7	Schempp-Hirth Discus b	37	
D-8892	Schleicher Ka 6CR	6427Si	(D-KAIA), D-8892
D-8893	Schleicher Ka 2 Rhönschwalbe (Res.)	25	
D-8895-95	Schleicher Ka 6E (Permit .05)	4005	
D-8896-MH	Schleicher ASW 27	27005	
D-8897	Schleicher ASW 20L	20204	HB-1477
D-8898	Schleicher ASW 20	20589	HB-1659
D-8899	Schleicher Ka 1	33	
D-8900	Bölkow Phoebus C	854	XB-ABO, N8541
D-8901	Scheibe L-Spatz 55	575	
D-8902	Schleicher Ka 6CR Rhönsegler	6482	
D-8903	Schleicher ASW 27	27033	
D-8905-FV	Akaflieg Karlsruhe AK-5 (P 20.7.16)	501	
D-8906	Schleicher Ka 6CR Rhönsegler	6597	
D-8907	Bölkow Phoebus C (Res.2.99)	890	D-6964, OE-0964
D-8908	Schleicher K 8	108/58/A	
D-8909-09	Schleicher ASW 24B	24238	
D-8910	Schleicher ASK 21	21910	
D-8912	Schleicher Ka 6CR Rhönsegler	6410	
D-8913	Scheibe L-Spatz 55	675	
D-8914-B4	Rolladen-Schneider LS4-b	41036	
D-8917	Schempp-Hirth Standard Cirrus	543G	
D-8919	Glasflügel Standard Libelle 201B	601	OO-ZQV, F-CELI
D-8920-1F	Rolladen-Schneider LS1-f	281	
D-8921-BD	Schleicher ASK 21 (Dbr 17.3.16)	21834	
D-8923	Rolladen-Schneider LS1-f	300	
D-8925-3Z	Rolladen-Schneider LS4	4559	
D-8927	Glasflügel H205 Club Libelle	82	
D-8928	Schleicher ASW 28-18	28516	
D-8930-BT	Rolladen-Schneider LS8-18	8438	
D-8931	Rolladen-Schneider LS6-a	6160	PH-1476, OY-XPU
D-8933-3J	Rolladen-Schneider LS1-f	359	
D-8934	Rolladen-Schneider LS1-f (W/o 5.8.16)	417	
D-8935	Rolladen-Schneider LS1-f	307	
D-8936-LG	Rolladen-Schneider LS1-f	418	
D-8939-AY	Rolladen-Schneider LS1-f	421	
D-8941	Rolladen-Schneider LS1	454	

Reg	Type	c/n	Previous identities
D-8943-CT	Glasflügel H206 Hornet	38	
D-8946	Akaflieg Braunschweig SB-5E Sperber	AB5057	
D-8947	Akaflieg Braunschweig SB-5E Sperber	AB5058	
D-8948	Glasflügel H304	222	
D-8949-PS	Glasflügel H401 Kestrel 17	71	OE-0949
D-8952	Schleicher K 8B	8912AB	
D-8954	Schleicher ASW 20L	20416	
D-8955	Schleicher ASK 21	21061	
D-8956	Glaser-Dirks DG-300 Elan	3E206	
D-8958-IEI	Rolladen-Schneider LS4	4560	
D-8959	Allstar PZL SZD-59 Acro	590.A.06.009	
D-8960-HN	Rolladen-Schneider LS4	4562	
D-8961-HI	Rolladen-Schneider LS1-f	460	
	(P.5.12)		
D-8962-YS	Rolladen-Schneider LS1-f	461	
D-8963	Schleicher ASK 13	AB13644	
D-8964	Schleicher ASK 13	AB13649	
D-8965	Glaser-Dirks DG-300 Elan	3E208	
D-8967-LX	Glaser-Dirks DG-300 Elan	3E209	
D-8968-UT	Glaser-Dirks DG-300 Elan	3E210	
D-8969-OB	Glaser-Dirks DG-300 Elan	3E218	
D-8970-A7	Glaser-Dirks DG-300 Elan	3E213	
D-8971-CP	Rolladen-Schneider LS1-f	470	
D-8972-TW	Rolladen-Schneider LS1-f	471	
D-8973	Rolladen-Schneider LS4	4522	
D-8974	Grob G 103C Twin III Acro	34199	
D-8975	Grob G 103 Twin II	3647	
D-8976	Grob G 103 Twin II	3667	
D-8977	Schempp-Hirth Discus b	70	
D-8978	Schleicher ASK 23B	23116	
D-8979-79	Schleicher ASK 21	21451	
D-8980	Rolladen-Schneider LS1-f	487	
D-8981	Bölkow Phoebus C	950	OE-0868
D-8982-RG	Rolladen-Schneider LS1-f	489	
D-8983	Glasflügel Standard Libelle 201B	351	D-9086, HB-1086
D-8984	Schleicher ASK 13	13399	
D-8985	SG-38 Schulgleiter	E-1	
D-8986	Grob G102 Standard Astir II	5029S	I-IVBL
D-8988	Rolladen-Schneider LS8-18	8429	
D-8989	Grob G 102 Club Astir IIIB	5541CB	
D-8990-L5	Grob G102 Astir CS 77	1687	HB-1394
D-8992	Rolladen-Schneider LS4	4294	
D-8994-3L	Rolladen-Schneider LS8-18	8475	G-CKFM, BGA 5057, D-9502
	(P 12.4.16)		
D-8995	Schempp-Hirth Nimbus-2B	154	I-AKOB
D-8996	Glasflügel Mosquito	15	OO-ZDD
D-8997	Rolladen-Schneider LS6	6051	
D-8998	Rolladen-Schneider LS6	6050	
D-8999	Schleicher ASK 21	21777	
D-9000	Rolladen-Schneider LS4-b	4752	
D-9001	Schempp-Hirth Discus b	305	OK-9301
D-9002-X4	Glasflügel H303 Mosquito	40	OY-XHO
D-9003	Scheibe Spatz A	505	
D-9004-PK	Schempp-Hirth Duo Discus	494	
D-9005	Schleicher Ka 6CR Rhönsegler	6476	
D-9006-K6	Glaser-Dirks DG-300 Elan	3E257	OY-XYI
D-9007	Grob G 102 Astir CS	1443	D-9000
D-9008	Glasflügel H201B Standard Libelle	426	PH-467
D-9009	Grob G 102 Club Astir IIIB	5501CB	
D-9010	Rolladen-Schneider LS6-c	6198	
D-9011-NH	Rolladen-Schneider LS6-c	6199	
D-9012	Schleicher K 8B	8099	
D-9014-CC	Rolladen-Schneider LS4-b	4763	
	(P. 5.14)		
D-9015	Rolladen-Schneider LS4-b	4772	
D-9016	Rolladen-Schneider LS4-b	4764	
D-9017-3M	Rolladen-Schneider LS4-b	4765	
D-9018-PM	Rolladen-Schneider LS4-b	4766	
D-9019	Rolladen-Schneider LS4-b	4767	
D-9020-PI	Rolladen-Schneider LS4-a	4768	
D-9021	Schleicher ASK 21	21729	
D-9022	Glaser-Dirks DG-600/18	6-61	HB-3033
D-9023-JT	Schempp-Hirth Ventus-2bxR	141	
D-9024	Schleicher ASW 24	24075	OY-HEX, D-9022
D-9025	Schleicher Rhönsperber replica	AB-02	
D-9026	Göppingen Gö.1 Wolf replica	AB-1	
D-9027	Schleicher Rhönbussard replica	AB-004-S	
D-9028	Schleicher Ka 6E	4187	
D-9029-TS	Schempp-Hirth Duo Discus	418	
D-9030	Schleicher Ka 6CR Rhönsegler	6038	
D-9031-FH	Schempp-Hirth Ventus-2a	7	F-CGLS, D-8559
D-9035	Schleicher K 8B	8491	
D-9036	Schleicher K 8B	8753	
D-9039	Schleicher Ka 6CR Rhönsegler	6096/Si	
D-9041-YD	Schempp-Hirth Duo Discus	135	
D-9042	SZD-24-4A Foka 4	W-299	DDR-2042, DM-2042
	(Res.6.03)		
D-9044	Schleicher K 7 Rhönadler	7142	
D-9046	Glaser-Dirks DG-100G Elan	E31G16	HB-1538
D-9048	Schleicher K 8B	8104	
D-9055	Scheibe L-Spatz 55	545	
D-9057	Schleicher Ka 6CR Rhönsegler	6093Si	
D-9058	Grunau Baby III	AB-01	
D-9059	Allstar PZL SZD-59 Acro	590.A.05.006	
D-9060	Schleicher K 8B	116	
D-9062	SG-38 Schulgleiter	BWLV-15	
D-9064	Schleicher ASK 13	13098	
D-9065	Schleicher ASK 21	21638	
D-9067	SZD-30 Pirat	B-396	DDR-1767, DM-1767
D-9068-LEO	Schleicher ASW 27-18 (ASG 29)	29083	
D-9070-70	Schempp-Hirth Discus b	500	
D-9071	Schleicher K 8B	8487	D-KOPF, D-1071
	(Same c/n quoted as D-1198)		
D-9074	Scheibe L-Spatz 55	567	(D-KOHN(2))
D-9075	Schleicher Ka 6 Rhönsegler	194	
D-9076	Schleicher Ka 6CR Rhönsegler	6359	
D-9077	Schempp-Hirth Ventus c	432	
D-9079	Scheibe Bergfalke II/55	224	
D-9080	Schleicher ASK 21	21590	
D-9082	Schleicher K 8B	8042	
D-9083	Doppelraab IV	E-1	
D-9088-8T	Schempp-Hirth Duo Discus	17	
D-9089-X89	Centrair ASW 20F	20189	OO-ZJI, F-CEUT
D-9090	Schleicher K 8B	8010	
D-9093-AL	Schleicher ASW 27	27024	
D-9096-RM	Schempp-Hirth Discus-2b	138	
D-9099	Rolladen-Schneider LS7	7054	
D-9100-6H	SZD-30 Pirat	B-443	DDR-1800, DM-1800
D-9101-01	Start & Flug H-101 Salto	71	
D-9103-D2	Schempp-Hirth Ventus c	568	HB-3103
D-9104-BV	Rolladen-Schneider LS4	4156	
D-9106-C1	Rolladen-Schneider LS4	4195	
D-9109	Eiri PIK-20B	20138	SE-TXO, OH-483
D-9110	HpH Glasflügel 304CZ-17	16	OK-3737, OK-1111
D-9114-UWE	Rolladen-Schneider LS4	4424	BGA 4734/JSB, D-4541
D-9115	Scheibe L-Spatz 55	678	
D-9117	Schleicher Ka 6CR Rhönsegler	553	
D-9118	Schleicher ASW 28-18E	28745	
D-9119-VN	Schleicher ASK 21	21124	
D-9122-L72	Schempp-Hirth Discus CS	135CS	
D-9123-JB	Schempp-Hirth Discus CS	136CS	(PH-1000)
D-9124-FB	Schempp-Hirth Discus CS	133CS	
D-9125-XE	Schempp-Hirth Discus CS	137CS	
D-9127	Schempp-Hirth Discus b	12	
D-9128-BK	Schleicher ASW 28	28022	
D-9130	Glasflügel H303 Mosquito B	106	
D-9131	Schleicher Ka 6CR Rhönsegler	6564	
D-9133	Schleicher K 8B	714	
D-9140	Rolladen-Schneider LS3-a	3435	I-MIMO, D-2866
D-9141	SZD-24-4A Foka 4	W-225	
D-9142-H2	Schempp-Hirth Duo Discus	125	
D-9144-44	Schleicher ASK 21	21859	
D-9145-AR	Rolladen-Schneider LS4	4407	
D-9147	Schleicher K 8B	111	
D-9149-LI	Schempp-Hirth Duo Discus	39	
D-9150-TE	DG Flugzeugbau DG-1000S	10-150T53	D-KDTE, D-9150
D-9152-DM	Schleicher ASW 28	28060	
D-9155	Schleicher K 8B	233/1	
D-9157	Schleicher K 8B	AB.05	
D-9158	Schleicher Ka 6CR Rhönsegler	6184	
D-9159	Scheibe Bergfalke II/55	346	
D-9160	Scheibe Bergfalke II/55	380	
D-9161	Schleicher K 8B	3/8196	
D-9165	Schleicher Ka 6CR Rhönsegler	6220	
D-9167	Schleicher Ka 6CR Rhönsegler	6318Si	
D-9170	Rolladen-Schneider LS3	3040	PH-849, D-2806
D-9173	Schleicher K 8B	8358	
D-9174	Schleicher K 8B	8374	
D-9175	Schempp-Hirth Duo Discus	683	
D-9176	Focke-Wulf Kranich III	58	
D-9177	Scheibe Bergfalke III	5524	
D-9179-O6	Schempp-Hirth Arcus	9/72	
D-9180	Schleicher Ka 6E	4028	
D-9181	Schleicher ASK 21	21622	
D-9182	Schleicher Ka 6CR Rhönsegler	6504	
D-9184	Schleicher Ka 6CR Rhönsegler	6507	
D-9186	Schleicher Ka 6CR Rhönsegler	6489Si	
D-9188	Schleicher Ka 6CR Rhönsegler	6514	
D-9189	Scheibe Bergfalke III	5528	
D-9190	Neukom S-4A Elfe	66	HB-1229
D-9191	Schleicher Ka 6E	4040	
D-9192	Rock Geier II	V-2	
D-9193	Bölkow Phoebus A-1	752	
D-9195-SL	Schempp-Hirth Duo Discus	657	
D-9196	LET L-13 Blanik	173343	
D-9197	Schempp-Hirth SHK-1	30	LX-CAR, OE-5090, D-9197
D-9198-19	Sportine Aviacija LAK-19.	26	OK-9191
D-9199	Sportine Aviacija LAK-17A	197	
D-9200-7J	Rolladen-Schneider LS7-WL	7031	OO-ZGW, D-1301
D-9201-01	Schleicher Ka 6CR Rhönsegler	6578	
D-9204-RD	Schempp-Hirth Duo Discus XL	642	
D-9207	Schleicher Ka 6CR Rhönsegler	6599	
D-9208	LET L-13 Blanik	170718	DDR-3208, DM-3208, OK-0901
D-9210	DG Flugzeugbau DG-1000S	10-108S74	
D-9212-AK	Schempp-Hirth Discus-2a	4	
D-9213-LX	Glasflügel H201B Standard Libelle	412	
D-9214-T	Bölkow Phoebus C	784	
D-9216	Schleicher K 8B	8732	
D-9218	Schleicher K 8B	8300/A	
D-9220	Schleicher ASK 13	13092	
D-9221	Rolladen-Schneider LS1-d	181	
D-9222-DE	Schempp-Hirth Ventus-2ax	2	
	(Mid-air collision @ World Championships, Australia 14.1.17)		
D-9223	SZD-41A Jantar Standard	B-815	LX-CRP
D-9224-WF	Schempp-Hirth Standard Cirrus	368	
D-9227	Scheibe Bergfalke IV	5832	
D-9231-7X	Rolladen-Schneider LS1-d	246	
D-9233	Glasflügel H401 Kestrel	101	
D-9234-CZ	Glasflügel H201B Standard Libelle	491	
D-9235	Schempp-Hirth Standard Cirrus	374G	
D-9236	Glasflügel H201B Standard Libelle	484	
D-9238	Glasflügel H201B Standard Libelle	486	
D-9239	Glasflügel H401 Kestrel	70	HB-1239
D-9240	Start & Flug H101 Salto	40	
D-9241	Start & Flug H101 Salto	41	
D-9242-AH	Schleicher ASW 27	27040	HB-3242
D-9243	Start & Flug H101 Salto	38	
D-9246	Schempp-Hirth Standard Cirrus	413	
D-9250-FG	Glasflügel H201B Standard Libelle	513	
D-9251	Glasflügel H201B Standard Libelle	515	
D-9252	Glasflügel H201B Standard Libelle	516	
D-9255	Schleicher K 8B	8949/A	
D-9256-PC	Schempp-Hirth Cirrus-VTC	154Y	
D-9258	DG Flugzeugbau DG-303 Elan Acro	3E511A43	
D-9260	Start + Flug H 101 Salto	47	BGA 4778/JTX, D-9260
D-9262-EF	Rolladen-Schneider LS1-f	274	
D-9264	Glasflügel H201B Standard Libelle	569	
D-9265	Schleicher ASK 13	13479	
D-9268-IGL	Schleicher ASW 15B	15377	
D-9269-ZI	Schleicher ASW 15B	15378	
D-9270	Schleicher ASW 15B	15387	
D-9273	Schleicher ASW 15B	15381	
D-9274	Schleicher ASW 17	17036	
D-9275	Schleicher ASK 13	13490	
D-9276-1W	Schleicher ASW 15B	15386	
D-9277	Schleicher ASK 13	13491	
D-9278-NI	Schleicher ASW 15B	15379	
	(P. 16.10.14)		
D-9279	Schleicher ASW 27B	27144	G-CJWF, BGA 4834
D-9280	Schleicher ASK 18	18001	
D-9283	Schleicher ASW 15B	15392	

Regn	Type	C/n	Previous identities
D-9284-WZ	Schleicher ASW 17	17035	
D-9285-FK	Schleicher ASW 15B	15395	
D-9286-NK	Schempp-Hirth Discus-2a	9	G-DTWO, BGA5217, D-2140
D-9287-CS	Rolladen-Schneider LS6	6049	
D-9289-NRW	Schleicher ASW 28	28047	
D-9290	Rolladen-Schneider LS1-f	321	
D-9291-J	Rolladen-Schneider LS1-f	326	
D-9292	Schleicher ASW 27-18 (ASG 29)	29092	
D-9293-OZ	Rolladen-Schneider LS1-f	176	
D-9294-VS	Schempp-Hirth Ventus-2a	4	
D-9296-PM	Rolladen-Schneider LS1-f	296	
D-9297	Grunau Baby III	1	D-4684, D-5043
D-9298-98	Glasflügel H401 Kestrel	115	
D-9299	Glasflügel H401 Kestrel	116	
D-9300	SZD-50-3 Puchacz	B-1082	DDR-3600
D-9301	SZD-50-3 Puchacz	B-1634	SP-3402
D-9302	Schleicher Ka 6CR Rhönsegler	6398	
D-9303-MV	Glaser-Dirks DG-300 Elan Acro	3E452A12	
D-9304	Glasflügel H304	201	
D-9305	Glaser-Dirks DG-300 Club Elan	3E284C9	
D-9306-PJ	Glaser-Dirks DG-300 Club Elan	3E287C11	
D-9307	Scheibe Bergfalke III	5538	
D-9311	Schleicher Ka 6CR Rhönsegler	6397	
D-9312	Schleicher K 8B	8226	
D-9314	Schleicher K 8B	8392/SH	
D-9316-MO	Schleicher ASW 27	27076	
D-9317	Schleicher Rhönlerche II (Res.)	102	
D-9320	Bölkow Phoebus B-1	707	
D-9321	Scheibe Bergfalke III	5533	
D-9322	Schleicher K 8B	8617/SH	
D-9323	Glasflügel H301 Libelle	9	
D-9324	Schleicher ASK 13	13460	PH-466
D-9326	SZD-48-3 Jantar-Standard 3	B-1520	LY-GBJ, DOSAAF
D-9328	Schleicher K 8B	8174/A	
D-9330	Schleicher ASK 21	21551	
D-9331-HH	Schleicher ASH 25 (P. 4.13)	25057	
D-9333	Schleicher K 8C	AB81008	
D-9334	Scheibe SF 27A	6011	
D-9336	Glasflügel BS-1	14	
D-9337	Bölkow Phoebus B1	794	OE-5670, HB-933
D-9338	Schempp-Hirth SHK-1	21	
D-9339-LD	Schempp-Hirth Duo Discus	367	
D-9340	Schleicher Ka 6CR Rhönsegler	953	
D-9343	Scheibe SF 27A (Permit .00)	6072	
D-9348	Schleicher Ka 6CR Rhönsegler	6443	
D-9349	Glasflügel H304	204	
D-9350	Rolladen-Schneider LS3-a	3233	PH-638
D-9352-SZ	Glaser-Dirks DG-300 Elan	3E134	
D-9355-BJ	Schleicher Ka 6E	4012	
D-9357	SZD-24-4A Foka 4	W-251	
D-9359	Akaflieg Braunschweig SB-5B Sperber	5014	
D-9361	Scheibe Bergfalke III	5556	
D-9363-LM	Schempp-Hirth Discus b	38	
D-9365	Schleicher Ka 6E	4001	
D-9366	Schempp-Hirth SHK-1	06	
D-9367	SZD-9bis Bocian 1E	P-554	DDR-3367, DM-3367
D-9369	Schleicher Ka 6CR Rhönsegler	6488Si	
D-9370	Scheibe L-Spatz 55	511	
D-9372	Schleicher Ka 6CR Rhönsegler	6499	
D-9373	Glaser-Dirks DG-300 Elan	3E181	
D-9378-S7	Glasflügel H301 Libelle	20	
D-9380	SZD-9bis Bocian 1E	P-576	DDR-3380, DM-3380
D-9382	Scheibe L-Spatz III	818	
D-9383	Akaflieg Braunschweig SB-5B Sperber	5029	
D-9384	SZD-9bis Bocian 1E	P-590	DDR-3384, DM-3384
D-9385	Scheibe Bergfalke III	5575	
D-9386	Schleicher K 8B	8225/A	
D-9387-BHV	Schempp-Hirth Discus CS	227CS	
D-9388-8K	Schempp-Hirth Discus CS	228CS	
D-9390	Schempp-Hirth Discus CS	231CS	
D-9391	Schleicher ASW 20CL	20720	
D-9392	Schleicher ASK 21	21193	
D-9395	Schempp-Hirth Janus Ce	303	
D-9396-LR	Schempp-Hirth Discus CS	234CS	
D-9397	Schleicher Ka 6CR Rhönsegler	6550	
D-9399	Schleicher Ka 6CR Rhönsegler	6563	
D-9401	Schleicher Ka 6CR Rhönsegler (P 14.7.16)	6561	
D-9403	Schleicher ASK 13	13006	
D-9404	Schleicher K 8B	8691	
D-9405	Schleicher Ka 6CR Rhönsegler	6576	
D-9406	SZD-38A Jantar 1	B-639	DDR-2403, DM-2403
D-9407	SZD-41A Jantar Standard	B-696	DDR-2407, DM-2407
D-9408	Schleicher Ka 6CR Rhönsegler	6592	
D-9409	Schleicher K 8B	8698	
D-9410-AT	Glaser-Dirks DG-300 Elan	3E285	OY-XPI
D-9411-PV	Scheibe SF 27A	6081	
D-9412-RM	Glasflügel H301 Libelle	45	
D-9413	Rolladen-Schneider LS1-f	311	
D-9414	Schleicher ASK 13	13039	
D-9415	Glasflügel BS.1	10	
D-9416	Glasflügel BS.1	11	
D-9417	Scheibe Bergfalke III	5611	
D-9418	Scheibe SF 27A	6104	
D-9419	Scheibe L-Spatz III	830	
D-9420-D1	Schempp-Hirth Discus-2b (For potential conversion to Discus-2T c/n 3/69)	69	
D-9421-GW	SZD-42-1 Jantar 2	B-778	DDR-2421, DM-2421
D-9422	Schempp-Hirth Cirrus	16	
D-9424	Scheibe Bergfalke III	5610	
D-9425	SZD-41A Jantar Standard	B-899	DDR-2425, DM-2425
D-9427 -Y	Glaser-Dirks DG-200/17C	2-157CL13	
D-9428-JM	Glasflügel H201B Standard Libelle	110	SE-TIT
D-9429-VO	Glaser-Dirks DG-100G Elan	E81G56	
D-9430	Scheibe Bergfalke III	5618	
D-9431	Glasflügel H304	234	
D-9433	Schempp-Hirth Standard Cirrus	487G	
D-9435-FF	Rolladen-Schneider LS1-f	162	
D-9437	Glasflügel Standard Libelle 201B	582	HB-1556
D-9440-RH	Schempp-Hirth Duo Discus	160	
D-9442	Glasflügel H401 Kestrel	118	
D-9444-S9	Glasflügel H205 Club Libelle	6	
D-9445	Glasflügel H205 Club Libelle	7	
D-9447-M	Glasflügel H201B Standard Libelle	592	
D-9448-XV	Glasflügel H201B Standard Libelle	593	
D-9449	Glasflügel H201B Standard Libelle	594	
D-9451	Glasflügel H205 Club Libelle	8	
D-9452	Glasflügel H205 Club Libelle	9	
D-9453	Rolladen-Schneider LS1-f	302	
D-9454	Start & Flug H101 Salto (P 5.9.16)	59	
D-9455-HI	Schempp-Hirth Duo Discus	95	
D-9456-WA	Rolladen-Schneider LS1-f	174	
D-9457	Schempp-Hirth Standard Cirrus	519G	
D-9459-JU	Rolladen-Schneider LS1-f	317	
D-9461	DG Flugzeugbau DG-1000S	10-225S144	
D-9463-i6	Glasflügel H205 Club Libelle	10	
D-9464	Glasflügel H205 Club Libelle	11	
D-9465	Glasflügel H205 Club Libelle	12	
D-9467	Glasflügel H205 Club Libelle	14	
D-9468	Rolladen-Schneider LS1-f	282	
D-9470	Glasflügel H205 Club Libelle	16	
D-9471	Glasflügel H205 Club Libelle	17	
D-9472	Allstar PZL SZD-51-1 Junior	511.A.05.008	
D-9473	Glasflügel H205 Club Libelle	19	
D-9474	Glasflügel H205 Club Libelle	20	
D-9475-HY	Glasflügel H205 Club Libelle	21	
D-9478	Glasflügel H205 Club Libelle	24	
D-9479	Rolladen-Schneider LS1-f	249	
D-9480	Schempp-Hirth Nimbus-2	90	
D-9481	Glasflügel H205 Club Libelle	25	
D-9482	Glasflügel H205 Club Libelle	26	
D-9484	Rolladen-Schneider LS1-f	360	
D-9485-X7	Rolladen-Schneider LS1-f	361	
D-9486-UM	Rolladen-Schneider LS1-f	362	
D-9487	Glasflügel H205 Club Libelle	27	
D-9488	Rolladen-Schneider LS1-f	372	
D-9490	Schleicher ASK 21	21684	
D-9491	Schleicher ASW 17	17038	
D-9492-1B	Schempp-Hirth Discus CS	002CS	D-0866, OK-0366 ?
D-9493	Glasflügel H205 Club Libelle	32	
D-9494	Glasflügel H205 Club Libelle	33	
D-9495	Glasflügel H205 Club Libelle	34	
D-9497-KT	Schempp-Hirth Standard Cirrus	540G	
D-9498-PS	Rolladen-Schneider LS1-f	328	
D-9499-Y9	Schleicher ASW 24	24074	
D-9500	Start & Flug H101 Salto	64	
D-9510	Marganski MDM-1 Fox	214	
D-9511-MR	Schempp-Hirth Ventus-2c	90	
D-9512	Grob G 104 Speed Astir IIB	4076	HB-1512
D-9520	Grob G 104 Speed Astir IIB	4098	HB-1520
D-9521	Schleicher ASK 21 (P.4.12)	21630	
D-9522-WK	Schleicher ASK 21	21653	
D-9523	Schleicher ASK 21	21936	
D-9525	Eiriavion PIK-20B	20090	OY-XDF
D-9526	Schleicher ASK 21	21894	
D-9527	Schleicher ASW 27	27108	G-CJPS, BGA 4677
D-9528-1B	Schleicher ASW 28	28018	
D-9531	Grunau Baby III	1-53	HB-531, D-6344
D-9532	Glasflügel H401 Kestrel	76	OE-0958
D-9540	Glasflügel Standard Libelle 201B	335	PH-440, D-1089
D-9544-HD	Schempp-Hirth Duo Discus	567	
D-9554	Grob G 102 Astir CS	1442	PH-554
D-9555	Marganski MDM-1 Fox	209	OE-5626
D-9559	SZD-59 Acro	590.A.04.001	
D-9560-NW1	Schempp-Hirth Discus-2b	205	
D-9562-IMO	Glasflügel Mosquito	61	PH-1336, OY-XIF
D-9566-EX	Schempp-Hirth Duo Discus	601	
D-9567-FK	Rolladen-Schneider LS6-a	6064	OO-YLS, D-2567
D-9570	Rolladen-Schneider LS3-a	3249	PH-757, D-2850
D-9571	Glasflügel H304	238	HB-1571
D-9575-S5	Schempp-Hirth Ventus-2ax	177	
D-9576-MP	Schleicher ASW 20	20249	I-LAMP
D-9577-PJ	Glasflügel 304	241	HB-1577
D-9580	Rolladen-Schneider LS6	6083	HB-1813
D-9588	Schleicher Ka 6CR	1130	OE-0588
D-9589	Schempp-Hirth Nimbus-2	109	I-NEVI, D-7246
D-9590	Marganski Swift S-1	116	HB-3138
D-9596-8A	Schempp-Hirth Discus-2b	238	
D-9599	Schempp-Hirth Ventus-2c	68	
D-9600-WF	Glaser-Dirks DG-600/18	6-107	HB-3092
D-9605-FT	Akaflieg Karlsruhe AK-5B (C/n formerly 1) (P 14.7.16)	502	
D-9607-KIT	Schleicher ASG 32Mi (P 30.8.16)	32018	
D-9608-FA	Akaflieg Karlsruhe AK 8 (P 17.5.16)	801	(D-0820)
D-9609-9	SZD-48-3 Jantar Standard 3	B-1947	RA-1947, D-5647, DOSAAF
D-9610-FF	DG Flugzeugbau DG-1000S	10-89S63	
D-9611-HD	Schempp-Hirth Discus-2a	1	HB-1783, D-6111
D-9614	Schempp-Hirth Discus-2b	192	
D-9618	Rolladen-Schneider LS6-c18	6252	PH-1136, D-6436, SE-UKO
D-9620	Schleicher ASK 21	21819	
D-9621	Glasflügel Standard Libelle	203	EC-GLN, OY-MGX
D-9622	Eiri PIK-20D	20629	PH-622
D-9628-SEI	Schleicher ASW 28	28053	
D-9630	Marganski Swift S-1	114	N114EW
D-9632-PF	Grob G 102 Astir CS 77	1749	
D-9633	Schempp-Hirth Discus a	3	I-DISK, D-6095
D-9638	Schleicher ASW 15B	15427	G-DJED, BGA 4447, D-3976
D-9642-2M	DG Flugzeugbau DG-1000S	10-94S66	
D-9646	Grob G 102 Astir CS 77	1798	PH-646
D-9647-K8	Schleicher K 8B	175/60	OO-ZMV, D-6390
D-9648	Grob G102 Standard Astir III	5614S	OO-ZEV
D-9649-96	Grob G102 Astir CS 77	1736	OO-ZAI
D-9650	SZD-48-3 Jantar-Standard 3	B-1953	OO-YLJ, D-2177, I-KASA
D-9651-PW	PZL-Swidnik PW-5 Smyk	17.03.018	OO-YLH, SP-3726, LN-GWC
D-9652	Schleicher ASK 13	13063	OO-YLG, PH-367
D-9653	Centrair 201B Marianne	201B049	OO-YLF, F-CBLX
D-9654	Centrair 201B Marianne	201A037	OO-YLE, F-CBLE
D-9655	Schleicher Ka 6E	4151	OO-ZGD, LX-CBP
D-9657-EMU	Rolladen-Schneider LS4	?	
D-9660-66	Schempp-Hirth Discus-2c	45	
D-9663-LX	Schempp-Hirth Ventus-2cx	126	
D-9667	Rolladen-Schneider LS3	3066	HB-1366

D-9668	Schempp-Hirth Nimbus-2	63	OM-4668, OE-0996
D-9669	Rolladen-Schneider LS8-a	8074	
D-9680-S9	Schleicher ASW 27	27077	
D-9683-WG	Schleicher ASW 27-18 (ASG 29)	29683	
D-9685	Glasflügel Club Libelle 205	170	F-CEQU
D-9686	Fauvel AV 36R	216	OE-0687
D-9687-TA	Rolladen-Schneider LS1-f	?	
D-9688-CN	Schempp-Hirth Duo Discus xL	690	
D-9691-KS	Rolladen-Schneider LS4-a	4347	OH-691
D-9696-BK	Schempp-Hirth Ventus-2b	50	
D-9697	Rolladen-Schneider LS6-c	6247	PH-946, D-2527
D-9699	Rolladen-Schneider LS3-a	3382	PH-673, D-3188
D-9700	Rolladen-Schneider LS6-a	6124	HB-1876
D-9701-18	Schempp-Hirth Ventus-2ax	178	
D-9707-W7	Schempp-Hirth Discus-2b	146	
D-9708-Y6	Rolladen-Schneider LS8-18	8463	D-9239
D-9709	Centrair 101A Pégase	101A0259	F-CGNJ
D-9710-71	Rolladen-Schneider LS10-st	10001	
D-9711	Glasflügel H206 Hornet	47	I-ROKI
D-9713-KF1	Schempp-Hirth Duo Discus	152	HB-3193
D-9720-2S	Schempp-Hirth Discus-2b	244	
D-9721	Schleicher ASK 21	21828	
D-9725-GL	Schempp-Hirth Discus CS	015CS	PH-1251, D-8229
D-9727 -K	Schleicher ASW 27	27050	
D-9728	Schleicher ASW 28	28054	
D-9729-LT	Schleicher ASW 27-18 (ASG 29)	29091	
D-9730-6S	Schempp-Hirth Discus-2b	251	
D-9733-33	Akaflieg Stuttgart FS 33 Gavilán (P 4.10)	33-1	
D-9747-G7	Schempp-Hirth Duo Discus X	525	
D-9755	Schleicher ASK 21	21938	
D-9760-ZY	Schempp-Hirth Discus b	9	HB-1760
D-9767-CC	Schleicher ASW 27 (P. 5.14)	27008	OY-CXC, D-6642
D-9770	Grob G102 Astir CS 77	1667	G-DDOR, BGA 2300
D-9777-A1	Schleicher ASW 17	17006	OO-VAT, PL69, OO-ZUU
D-9778	Grob G102 Astir CS 77	1742	OE-5186
D-9788-CM	Glaser-Dirks DG-600/18	6-26	S5-3107, SL-3107, YU-4459
D-9789	Rolladen-Schneider LS1-f	401	F-CEKQ
D-9794	Schleicher ASG 29	29028	
D-9796	Schempp-Hirth Duo Discus	667	
D-9797-H2	Schempp-Hirth Discus-2b	58	HB-3301
D-9799	Schleicher ASK 21	21822	
D-9800	Glaser-Dirks DG-800S	8-43S12	HB-3168, D-5647
D-9801-7K	Rolladen-Schneider LS8-a	8099	
D-9802	Schleicher ASK 21	21680	
D-9804	Rolladen-Schneider LS4	4514	HB-1804
D-9805-E5	Schleicher ASK 21	21871	
D-9806-3CU	Schempp-Hirth Ventus-2ax	174	T7-DGM
D-9810	DG Flugzeugbau LS10-s	L10-005	
D-9814-10	Akaflieg Braunschweig SB14 (P 14.7.16)	1	
D-9815	Schempp-Hirth Mini Nimbus C	132	OE-5217
D-9818-TW	Rolladen-Schneider LS8-18	8266	PH-1173, D-0207
D-9820-9S	Schempp-Hirth Discus-2b	245	
D-9821	Schleicher ASK 21	21673	
D-9822-A	Schleicher ASW 22	22003	SE-UNS, D-2203
D-9823-BA	Schleicher ASK 23	23026	OH-697
D-9825	Schleicher ASH 25	25107	F-CHII, D-1272
D-9827-21	Schleicher ASW 27	27073	
D-9828-D2	Schempp-Hirth Duo Discus	362	
D-9830	Schempp-Hirth Discus-2b	255	
D-9833	Schempp-Hirth Discus-2c DLR (P 2.8.16)	1	
D-9850	Vogt Lo-100 Zwergreiher	128AB	
D-9854-DL	Schempp-Hirth Discus-2c	44	
D-9855	Schempp-Hirth Mini Nimbus HS7.	30	PH-855, D-4985
D-9865	Jonkers Sailplanes JS/MD Single (P 4.8.16)	1C-105	
D-9866-EL	Schempp-Hirth Discus-2b	101	OO-YFM
D-9867-AT	Schempp-Hirth Ventus-2cx	144	
D-9868-YC	Schleicher ASW 27	27027	HB-3199, D-7453
D-9870-KA	Schempp-Hirth Discus CS	153CS	OE-5724, HB-3142
D-9871	Schempp-Hirth Ventus a/16.6	92	OO-ZMX, D-1480
D-9876	Grob G 102 Astir CS	1358	D-7387
D-9877-KM	Schleicher ASW 28	28067	
D-9878	Grob G103 Twin II	3522	OE-5258
D-9881	Siebert Sie 3 (Permit .08)	3010	CS-PBE
D-9882-RN	Schleicher ASK 23B	23113	PH-882
D-9883	Schempp-Hirth Standard Cirrus	584G	F-CEMJ
D-9886-SKY	Schempp-Hirth Ventus-2cxa	133	
D-9888-KB	Rolladen-Schneider LS8-a	8123	
D-9889-4N	Schempp-Hirth Discus-2a	208	
D-9898	Glaser-Dirks DG-100G Elan	E9G3	OE-5203
D-9899	Marganski MDM-1 Fox		
D-9900	Grob G 103A Twin II Acro	3845-K-91	F-CFYL, PH-744
D-9902-BW1	Schempp-Hirth Duo Discus	321	
D-9903	SZD-41A Jantar Standard	B-693	D-2305, DDR-2405, DM-2405
D-9906	Schleicher ASK 21	21741	
D-9907	Glasflügel Standard Libelle 201B	65	OY-XPT, LN-GIE, SE-TIE
D-9908-EY	Schempp-Hirth Ventus-2a	144	
D-9909	Schempp-Hirth Mini Nimbus C (P. 3.11)	147	BGA 4951, HB-1508
D-9910-XN	Schempp-Hirth Discus-2b	113	
D-9912	Rolladen-Schneider LS7-WL	7005	PH-850, D-1257
D-9913	Grob G102 Astir CS	1117	OY-XIY, D-6971
D-9917	Schempp-Hirth Standard Cirrus	568G	OO-ZHD
D-9918	Schleicher ASK 13	13320	OE-0918
D-9919	Schleicher K 8B	4	D-1919
D-9920-G9	Rolladen-Schneider LS4	4128	HB-1647
D-9921-L9	Schleicher ASK 21	21276	OY-XOC
D-9923-KV	Schempp-Hirth Discus-2b	202	
D-9925-666	Schleicher ASH 25	25130	F-CILC, BGA 3800/HAZ, G-BTYJ
D-9928-LL	Schleicher ASW 28	28030	
D-9929-99	Schleicher ASW 27-18E (ASG 29E)	29522	
D-9930-ICH	DG Flugzeugbau DG-1000S	10-30S29	
D-9932	Start + Flug H 101 Salto	43	
D-9940	DG Flugzeugbau DG-1000S	10-64S58	
D-9950	SZD-50-3 Puchacz	B-1534	DDR-3650
D-9951-B5	HpH Glasflügel 304C	76-C	
D-9954	Grunau Baby III	AM007	
D-9959	SZD-59 Acro	B-2179	
D-9966	Glasflügel H201B Standard Libelle	66	SE-TIF
D-9967-CB	Centrair ASW 20F	20195	I-IVEC, F-CEUY
D-9968	Rolladen-Schneider LS3-a	3166	BGA 5090/KGW, I-MMST, HB-1362
D-9969	Schempp-Hirth Nimbus-4	10/29	N497MH
D-9971-KG	Schempp-Hirth Discus-2a	231	
D-9972-72	Schempp-Hirth Duo Discus	515	
D-9973-RR	Schempp-Hirth Discus b	228	HB-1958
D-9975	Standard Austria	4	OE-0975, OE-0555
D-9977-77	Schleicher ASW 27	27075	
D-9988	Schempp-Hirth Discus-2b	254	
D-9989	Rolladen-Schneider LS4	4459	HB-1763
D-9990-1000	DG Flugzeugbau DG-1000S	10-1S1	
D-9992	Glaser-Dirks DG-200	2-2	HB-1334
D-9994	SZD-9bis Bocian 1E	P-640	OE-0994
D-9995-i1	DG Flugzeugbau DG-1000S	10-4S4	
D-9998-TOM	Schempp-Hirth Ventus-2ax	155	
D-9999-MH	Schempp-Hirth Duo Discus	129	
D-. . . .	Grob G 102 Astir CS	1080	OY-XDO
D-. . . .	Grob G 102 Standard Astir II	5027S	I-IVBJ
D-. . . .	Schleicher ASK 21Mi	21847	SE-UUH
D-. . . .	Schleicher ASW 22	22029	G-CGBX, BGA3713/GBX, D-4325

EC - SPAIN

Regn.	Type	C/n	Prev.Id.

Most aircraft officially listed as "active registrations" are included, whatever their actual condition, often with comments regarding their real status. A number of known sales or terminal cases have however been deleted although official cancellations have actually increased of late. Status reports on those damaged, wfu or stored would be welcome.

Regn.	Type	C/n	Prev.Id.
EC-AAP	Piper L-14 Army Cruiser	5-3007	CU-P18, NC41594, (45-55531)
"EC-ABC"	Douglas DC-3 - see EC-CPO		
EC-ACA	de Havilland DH.87A Hornet Moth	8039	EC-CAI, EC-EBE, EC-W51
	(Stored)		
EC-ACB	Miles M.3 Falcon	197	EC-CAO, EC-BDD
	(Museum)		
EC-ACJ	Auster J/1 Autocrat	1960	EC-DAZ, G-AHCF
	(Stored)		
EC-ACU	Miles M.38 Messenger 2A	6360	EC-UAU, (EC-EAL), G-AJEZ
	(Stored)		
EC-ADA	Piper PA-12 Super Cruiser	12-3535	
EC-ADG	Auster J/1 Autocrat	2216	G-AJAL
	(Stored)		
EC-ADS	Piper J-3C-65 Cub Special	22467	
EC-ADU	Stinson 108-3 Voyager	4386	N6386M
EC-ADY	Stinson 108-3 Voyager	4344	N6344M
EC-AFB	Cessna 170	19169	F-OAGF, N11B, N9708A
EC-AFC	Piper PA-12 Super Cruiser	12-1641	
EC-AFF	Stinson 108-3 Voyager	5183	N4183C
EC-AFG	Stinson 108-3 Voyager	4366	N6366M
EC-AGH	Piper PA-20 Pacer 125	20-648	
EC-AGJ	North American Navion 4	4-1519	F-OAIP, N4519K
EC-AGM	Macchi MB.308	5807/34	I-MACC
	(Under restoration, 10.13)		
EC-AGZ	Slingsby T-45 Swallow	1614	
EC-AHB	Percival P.34A Proctor 3	H.463	G-AMCO, LZ681
EC-AHD	Piper J-3C-65 Cub Special	22468	NC3401N
EC-AHG	Piper PA-12 Super Cruiser	12-2451	OO-XAZ, NC2290M
EC-AHL	CASA C-1.131L Jungmann	unkn	EE.3-205
	(Rebuild)		
EC-AIA	Slingsby T-45 Swallow	1656	
	(Stored dismantled)		
EC-AIF	Boeing Stearman E75	75-5513	N4657V, 42-17350
	(Museum)		
EC-AIJ	Piper PA-18A-135 Super Cub	18-2479	N10F
EC-AIQ	Piper PA-18-150 Super Cub	18-4615	F-BHAB, N10F
EC-AIS	Auster J/1 Autocrat	2190	G-AIGH
	(Noted dismantled 10.13)		
EC-AIU	de Havilland DH.82A Tiger Moth	3657	MM30-116, F-AQJX
	(Rebuild)		
EC-AIY	Piper J-3C-65 Cub	12639	HB-ODO, 44-80343
EC-AJE	Piper PA-18A-135 Super Cub	18-2935	N10F
EC-AJF	Piper PA-18A-135 Super Cub	18-2883	N10F
EC-AJR	Auster Mk.5	1505	EC-WJR, TJ517
EC-AJU	Grumman G.44A Widgeon	734	N41971
EC-AJY	Piper J-3C-65 Cub	12965	HB-OCM, 44-80669
	(Museum)		
EC-AJZ	Fairchild F.24W-41A Argus II	663	HB-EAP, FZ723, 43-14697
EC-AKD	Piper J-3C-65 Cub	11691	G-AISP, 43-30400
EC-AKE	Auster Mk.5	1526	HB-EOB, TJ479
EC-AKK	AISA I-11B Peque	005-1-70	
EC-AKL	AISA I-11B Peque	006-1-70	
EC-AKO	de Havilland DH.89A Dragon Rapide	6345	G-AERN
	(Dismantled)		
EC-AKQ	Piper J-3C-65 Cub	11190	HB-ONR, 43-29899
EC-AKU	Auster Mk.4	865	G-ALVV, MT143
EC-ALD	Auster J/1 Autocrat	1967	G-AGXS
EC-ALK	Piper PA-18A-150 Super Cub	18-3791	N10F
	(Cr 26.3.04)		
EC-ALP	CASA C-1.133C Jungmeister	041/1023	ES1-17
	(Museum)		
EC-ALS	Aerodiffusion Jodel D.112	E.5	
EC-ALU	Aerodiffusion Jodel D.112	E.8	
EC-AMK	Piper PA-18A-150 Super Cub	18-4859	N10F
EC-ANB	Aerodiffusion Jodel D.112	E.17	
EC-AND	Aerodiffusion Jodel D.112	E.19	
	(Stored dism)		
EC-ANH	Piper PA-20 Pacer 135	20-847	F-OAKO, N10F
	(Wfu)		
EC-ANI	Auster Mk.5	1262	HB-EOG, RT635
EC-ANM	North American Navion D-16	4-753	EC-WNM, N8753H
EC-AOM	Aerodiffusion Jodel D.112	E.32	
	(Stored dism)		
EC-AOR	Aerodiffusion Jodel D.112	E.37	
EC-AOU	Aerodiffusion Jodel D.112	E.41	
	(Stored dism)		
EC-AOV	Aerodiffusion Jodel D.112	E.42	
	(Stored dism)		
EC-AOY	Jodel D.1190-S	E-56	
	(Believed b/u Sywell 4.98)		
EC-APB	Beech 35-C33A Debonair	CE-70	D-ECMO
EC-APH	Omnipol Super Aero 45	04-005	
	(Museum)		
EC-API	Cessna 182 Skylane	33615	N5615B
EC-APJ	PZL-101-G2 Gawron	101701	SP-PBK, SP-PAG
	(Wfu by 1967)		
EC-APK	Aerodiffusion Jodel D.112	E.45	
EC-APO	Aerodiffusion Jodel D.112	E.54	
EC-AQA	AISA I-11B Peque	54	L.8C-54
EC-AQB	Douglas C-47A-20-DK	12844	EC-WQB, N54705, 42-92983
EC-AQJ	PZL-101-G2 Gawron	30019	SP-CED
	(Wfu by 1967; W/o 15.8.02)		
EC-AQS	Piper PA-25-235 Pawnee	25-430	N10F
EC-AQV	Piper PA-25-235 Pawnee	25-432	N10F
EC-ARD	Piper PA-25-150 Pawnee	25-446	N6336Z
EC-ARX	Piper PA-25-150 Pawnee	25-629	N10F
	(Wfu ?)		
EC-ARY	Piper PA-25-150 Pawnee	25-645	N10F
EC-ASA	Piper PA-25-150 Pawnee	25-491	N10F
	(Dbf 8.9.01)		
EC-ASB	Piper PA-25-150 Pawnee	25-651	N10F
EC-ASJ	Beech C-45H	AF-752	N9962Z, 52-10822
	(Museum)		
EC-ASO	Edgar Percival EP-9 Prospector	25	G-APCT, G-43-4
EC-ASU	Piper PA-18A-150 Super Cub	18-4607	CN-THE, F-DAEN, N10F
	(Badly Dam 3.7.94)		
EC-ASV	Piper PA-18A-150 Super Cub	18-5408	CN-TEC, F-DAFC, N10F
EC-ASY	Piper PA-18A-135 Super Cub	18-2937	CN-TEB, F-DABP, N10F
	(Crashed 7.79 but still extant)		
EC-ATJ	Aerodiffusion Jodel D.112	.50	
EC-ATS	Aerodiffusion Jodel D.1190-S	.58	
EC-ATZ	Dornier Do.28A-1	3045	EC-WTZ
EC-AUD	Agusta-Bell 47G-3B	1520	
	(W/o 30.8.02)		
EC-AUE	Agusta-Bell 47G-3B	1521	
EC-AUK	Mooney M.20C Mark 21	2395	N6668U
EC-AUL	Aerodiffusion Jodel D.1190-S	E.59	
EC-AUO	Piper PA-25-235 Pawnee	25-2315	N10F
EC-AUQ	CEA Jodel DR.1050 Ambassadeur	421	EC-WUQ
EC-AUT	Piper PA-25-235 Pawnee	25-2327	N10F
EC-AUU	Piper PA-25-235 Pawnee	25-2330	N10F
EC-AVB	Piper PA-25-150 Pawnee	25-725	N10F
EC-AVC	Piper PA-25-150 Pawnee	25-726	N10F
EC-AVE	Aerodiffusion Jodel D.1190-S	E.60	
	(Stored dism)		
EC-AVF	Cessna 182F Skylane	18254594	N3194U
EC-AVG	Aerodiffusion Jodel D.1190-S	E.62	
EC-AVH	Tipsy T.66 Nipper Mk.2	63	OO-FOL
EC-AVI	Hughes 269A	43-0201	
	(W/o 13.6.98?)		
EC-AVJ	Cessna 170B	20573	N2421D
EC-AVK	Cessna 182F Skylane	18254426	N3526Y
EC-AVM	Dornier Do.27Q-5	2038	OE-DCA, OE-VAK
EC-AVO	Piper PA-25-235 Pawnee	25-2428	N6829Z, N10F
EC-AVQ	Aerodiffusion Jodel D.1190-S	E.68	
EC-AVR	Aerodiffusion Jodel D.1190-S	E.65	
EC-AVU	Aerodiffusion Jodel D.1190-S	E.66	
EC-AVX	Aero Commander 520	10	EC-WVX, F-BBDY, N4109B
EC-AXA	Zlin Z.326A Akrobat	861	EC-WXA
	(Actually Z.326MS Trener Master, noted 10.13)		
EC-AXG	Aerodiffusion Jodel D.1190-S	E.67	
EC-AXO	Piper PA-25-235 Pawnee	25-2582	N6886Z, N10F
EC-AXT	Aerodiffusion Jodel D.1190-S	E.73	
EC-AXV	Beech 95-B55 Baron	TC-730	
	(Wfu, stored Sabadell 10.13)		
EC-AYV	Piper PA-25-235 Pawnee B	25-3065	N10F
	(Wfu)		
EC-AYX	Aerodiffusion Jodel D.1190-S	E.78	
EC-AZE	Piper PA-25-235 Pawnee B	25-3103	N10F
EC-AZF	Piper PA-25-235 Pawnee B	25-3114	N7203Z
EC-AZJ	Piper PA-25-235 Pawnee B	25-3130	N10F
	(Dam 29.6.00)		
EC-AZL	Piper PA-25-235 Pawnee B	25-3123	N10F
EC-AZY	Cessna F172F	F172-0161	EC-WZY
EC-BAH	Aerodiffusion Jodel D.1190-S	E.86	
EC-BAI	Aerodiffusion Jodel D.1190-S	E.87	
EC-BAK	Piper PA-22-150 Tri-Pacer	22-5427	SE-CDB, N7747D
EC-BAM	Piper PA-28-180 Cherokee C	28-2206	N11C, N8107W
EC-BAN	Grumman G.164 Agcat	334	N605U
EC-BAP	Gardan GY-80 Horizon 160	95	
EC-BAS	Aerodiffusion Jodel D.1190-S	E.101	(D-ELCO)
EC-BAT	Aerodiffusion Jodel D.1190-S	E.102	
EC-BBB	Cessna F172F	F172-0175	EC-WBB
EC-BBE	Piper PA-23-250 Aztec C	27-2914	N5784Y
EC-BBG	Bölkow BO.208C Junior	512	D-ENCO
EC-BBI	Piper PA-25-235 Pawnee B	25-3280	N7332Z
EC-BBJ	Cessna F172G	F172-0193	EC-WBJ
EC-BBL	MS.886 Rallye 150	440	
EC-BBM	Aerodiffusion Jodel D.1190-S	E.83	
EC-BBO	Aerodiffusion Jodel D.1190-S	E.85	
EC-BBU	Mooney M.20E Super 21	720	
EC-BBX	Piper PA-30 Twin Comanche	30-642	N7576Y
EC-BBZ	Piper PA-23-250 Aztec C	27-2938	N5805Y
EC-BCA	Cessna F172G (Dam)	F172-0215	EC-WCA
EC-BCB	Beech D95A Travel Air	TD-635	D-GARE
EC-BCG	Piper PA-25-235 Pawnee B	25-3454	N7458Z
	(Cr 22.6.03)		
EC-BCL	Aerodiffusion Jodel D.1190-S	E.92	
EC-BCN	Slingsby T-45 Swallow	1488	
EC-BCO	Slingsby T-45 Swallow	1490	
	(Noted dismantled 5.14)		
EC-BCP	Piper PA-25-235 Pawnee B	25-3398	N7423Z
EC-BCR	Piper PA-25-235 Pawnee B	25-3487	N7479Z
EC-BCT	Beech A23 Musketeer	M-765	D-EMNE
EC-BCV	Agusta-Bell 47G-4	2513	
EC-BCX	Piper PA-25-235 Pawnee B	25-3493	N7483Z
EC-BDA	Piper PA-25-235 Pawnee B	25-3640	N7574Z
EC-BDB	Piper PA-25-235 Pawnee B	25-3414	N7431Z
EC-BDJ	SOCATA MS.893A Rallye Commodore 180	10571	
EC-BDN	Piper PA-28-180 Cherokee C	28-2816	N11C, N8852J
EC-BDP	Aerodiffusion Jodel D.1190-S	E.90	
EC-BDQ	Aerodiffusion Jodel D.1190-S	E.93	
EC-BDR	Aerodiffusion Jodel D.1190-S	E.94	
EC-BDS	Zlin Z.526A Akrobat	1001	EC-WDS
EC-BEI	Cessna 182J Skylane	18256945	N2845F
EC-BEK	Aerodiffusion Jodel D.1190-S	E.103	
EC-BEL	Aerodiffusion Jodel D.1190-S	E.109	
EC-BEM	Mooney M.20E Super 21	1081	
	(Stored unmarked 2013?)		
EC-BEP	Beech A23-19 Musketeer Sport III	MB-161	HB-ENY
	(Dam 11.2.06)		
EC-BEQ	Piper PA-28-180 Cherokee C	28-4008	N11C
EC-BEU	Fauvel AV-361	152	
	(Originally listed as Bergfalke c/n 5568 - see EC-BEY)		
EC-BEY	Scheibe Bergfalke III	5568	
	(Cr 31.5.03 Quero)		
EC-BFD	Scheibe L-Spatz 55	808	
EC-BFE	Scheibe L-Spatz 55	809	
	(Preserved)		
EC-BFG	Scheibe L-Spatz 55	811	
EC-BFN	Grumman G.164 Agcat	399	N663U
EC-BFO	Piper PA-28-180 Cherokee C	28-3077	N9046J
	(Dam 18.12.03)		
EC-BFU	Hughes 269B	116-0275	
EC-BFX	Hughes 269B	106-0268	
EC-BFZ	Aerodiffusion Jodel D.1190-S	E.104	
EC-BGA	Cessna F150G	F150-0104	
EC-BGC	Piper PA-28-180 Cherokee C	28-3254	N9186J
EC-BGD	Piper PA-25-235 Pawnee B	25-4009	N4498Y, N10F
	(Dbr 7.5.02)		
EC-BGG	Cessna A188 Agwagon	188-0172	N9722V
EC-BGH	Piper PA-28-140 Cherokee	28-22148	N11C

Reg	Type	c/n	Previous identities
EC-BGI	Piper PA-25-235 Pawnee B	25-3761	N7791Z, N10F
EC-BGJ	Piper PA-25-235 Pawnee B	25-3762	N7792Z, N10F
EC-BGK	Piper PA-25-235 Pawnee B	25-3842	N4459Y, N4495Y, N10F
EC-BGM	Piper PA-25-235 Pawnee B	25-3926	N7747Z
EC-BGN	Piper PA-25-235 Pawnee B	25-3759	N7790Z, N10F
EC-BGO	Cessna F150G	F150-0105	
EC-BGP	Piper PA-25-235 Pawnee B	25-3924	N7744Z
EC-BGQ	Piper PA-25-235 Pawnee B	25-3775	N7793Z, N10F
EC-BGS	Piper PA-25-235 Pawnee B	25-3779	N7795Z, N10F
EC-BGT	Piper PA-25-235 Pawnee B	25-4012	N4499Y, N10F
EC-BGV	Piper PA-25-235 Pawnee B	25-4015	N4500Y, N10F
EC-BGX	Piper PA-14 Family Cruiser	14-177	F-BLXZ, OO-ARY
EC-BHN	Slingsby T-45 Swallow	1549	
(Stored)			
EC-BHR	Slingsby T-45 Swallow	1552	
EC-BHV	Slingsby T-45 Swallow	1556	
(Stored)			
EC-BJE	Beech A23-24 Musketeer Super III	MA-75	D-EKWA
EC-BJJ	Cessna F172H	F172-0338	
EC-BJL	Cessna A188 Agwagon	188-0224	N9774V
EC-BJN	Scheibe Bergfalke III	5546	
EC-BJO	Scheibe Bergfalke III	5548	
(Dism)			
EC-BJP	Beech A23-19 Musketeer Sport	MB-117	D-EJVA
EC-BJR	Piper PA-30 Twin Comanche B	30-1266	N8153Y
EC-BJS	Piper PA-25-235 Pawnee C	25-4215	N4557Y
(W/o 7.94)			
EC-BJU	Piper PA-23-250 Aztec C	27-3603	N6339Y
(Wfu)			
EC-BJX	Beech D95A Travel Air	TD-696	D-GARU
(Noted wfu 1.16)			
EC-BJY	SIAI-Marchetti S.205-20/R	362	EC-WJY
EC-BKB	AISA I-11B Peque	unkn	L.8C-4
EC-BKF	AISA I-11B Peque	unkn	L.8C-14
EC-BKG	Beech D95A Travel Air	TD-689	D-GARO
EC-BKH	AISA I-11B Peque	unkn	L.8C-16
(Museum)			
EC-BKK	AISA I-11B Peque	unkn	L.8C-21
EC-BKN	Piper PA-18-150 Super Cub	18-4061	54-2661
EC-BLX	AISA I-11B Peque	unkn	L.8C-123
(W/o 2.9.94?)			
EC-BLY	AISA I-11B Peque	unkn	L.8C-132
EC-BLZ	Aerodiffusion Jodel D.1190-S	E.110	
EC-BMC	Agusta-Bell 47G-4	2520	
EC-BMF	Piper PA-25-235 Pawnee C	25-4365	N4645Y
EC-BMG	SIAI-Marchetti S.205-20/R	4-107	EC-WMG
EC-BMH	SIAI-Marchetti S.205-20/R	4-115	EC-WMH
EC-BMK	Piper PA-28-180 Cherokee C	28-3973	N9774J
EC-BMN	Piper PA-25-235 Pawnee C	25-4323	N10F
EC-BMO	Piper PA-32-300 Cherokee Six	32-40132	N4136W
EC-BMP	Bölkow Phoebus A-1	708	D-1206
EC-BMR	Cessna 182K Skylane	18258034	N3034Q
EC-BNB	Piper PA-25-235 Pawnee C	25-4369	N4649Y
EC-BND	Piper PA-32-260 Cherokee Six	32-927	N5509J
EC-BNE	Cessna F172H	F172-0460	EC-WNE, (G-AVIS)
EC-BNK	Piper PA-28R-180 Cherokee Arrow	28R-30056	N11C
EC-BNO	Beech A23-24 Musketeer Super III	MA-219	D-EJVI
(Noted wfu 1.16)			
EC-BNP	Piper PA-23-250 Aztec C	7-2963	YV-T-HTH, N10F
EC-BNV	Cessna 182L Skylane	18258852	N42099
EC-BOG	Piper PA-25-235 Pawnee C	25-4449	N4714Y
EC-BOH	Piper PA-28R-180 Cherokee Arrow	28R-30440	N11C
EC-BOI	DHC-1 Chipmunk 22	C1/0147	D-EJAN, G-AOJV, WB699
EC-BOJ	Aerodiffusion Jodel D. 1190 -S	E.115	
EC-BOK	SOCATA MS.893A Rallye Commodore 180	10749	
EC-BOR	SIAI-Marchetti S.205-20/R	4-200	
EC-BOT	Piper PA-25-260 Pawnee C	25-4514	N4756Y
EC-BOX	Bölkow Phoebus C	841	
EC-BOY	Sportavia/ Fournier RF-4D	4067	
EC-BPD	Piper PA-28R-180 Cherokee Arrow	28R-30672	N11C
EC-BPN	AISA I-11B Peque	unkn	L.8C-11
EC-BPR	AISA I-11B Peque	unkn	L.8C-87
EC-BPT	AISA I-11B Peque	unkn	L.8C-129
EC-BPY	AISA I-11B Peque	unkn	L.8C-134
EC-BPZ	Aerodiffusion Jodel D.1190-S	E.117	
EC-BQC	Piper PA-30 Twin Comanche B	30-1723	N8571Y
EC-BQD	Piper PA-28R-180 Cherokee Arrow	28R-30709	N4960J
EC-BQE	Piper PA-28-140 Cherokee	28-24604	N7260J
EC-BQN	SIAI-Marchetti S.205-20/R	4-162	
EC-BQO	SIAI-Marchetti S.205-20/F	4-163	
(Wfu)			
EC-BQP	SIAI-Marchetti S.205-20/R	4-160	
EC-BQR	Aerodiffusion Jodel D.1190-S	E.118	
EC-BRA	Piper PA-23-250 Aztec D	27-4127	N6849Y, N9667N
(Noted wfu 1.16)			
EC-BRB	Aerodiffusion Jodel D.1190-S	E.119	
EC-BRD	Beech D55 Baron	TE-689	N7856R
EC-BRE	Piper PA-23-250 Turbo Aztec D	27-4120	N6784Y
EC-BRF	Piper PA-28-140 Cherokee B	28-25164	
EC-BRI	Hughes 269C	30-0015	
EC-BRK	Aerodiffusion Jodel D.1190-S	E.125	
EC-BRM	Beech 95-B55 Baron	TC-1290	
EC-BRT	Reims FR172F Rocket	FR17200109	
EC-BRV	Piper PA-25-260 Pawnee C	25-4969	N8549L
EC-BRZ	Aerodiffusion Jodel D.1190-S	E.120	
EC-BSG	Piper PA-30 Twin Comanche C	30-1919	N8763Y
(Dam 2.3.97)			
EC-BSH	SIAI-Marchetti S.205-20/F	4-273	
EC-BSI	Piper PA-28R-200 Cherokee Arrow	28R-35215	N9494N
EC-BSJ	Piper PA-25-260 Pawnee C	25-4861	N9715N
EC-BSL	Beech E33 Bonanza	CE-279	N2887A
EC-BSM	Piper PA-25-260 Pawnee C	25-4972	N8552L
EC-BSN	Piper PA-23-250 Aztec D	27-4289	N6932Y
(Wreck noted 7.04 and 10.13)			
EC-BSO	Piper PA-30 Twin Comanche C	30-1945	N8787Y
EC-BSR	Piper PA-23-250 Aztec D	27-4301	N6997Y, N9698N
(Wfu, stored)			
EC-BSS	Aerodiffusion Jodel D.1190-S	E.121	
EC-BST	Aerodiffusion Jodel D.1190-S	E.122	
EC-BSU	Aerodiffusion Jodel D.1190-S	E.123	
EC-BSV	Piper PA-28R-200 Cherokee Arrow	28R-35343	N11C
EC-BSX	Dornier Do.27Q-5	2094	D-EFKA
(Wfu, stored)			
EC-BSZ	Piper PA-23-250 Aztec D	27-4364	N6993Y
EC-BTA	Cessna T.337D Turbo Skymaster	33701090	N86129
EC-BTD	Piper PA-28R-200 Cherokee Arrow	28R-35271	N2727R
EC-BTH(2)	Schleicher ASK 21	21323	
EC-BTK(2)	Stinson 108-3 Voyager	4226	N6226M, NC6226M
(Museum)			
EC-BTM	AISA I-11B Peque	106	L.8C-31
EC-BTN(2)	Robin DR.400/180R Remorqueur	1759	
EC-BTQ(2)	Robin DR.400/180R Remorqueur	1760	
EC-BTX	AISA I-11B Peque	unkn	L.8C-67
EC-BTY	AISA I-11B Peque	unkn	L.8C-68
EC-BUB	AISA I-11B Peque	unkn	L.8C-77
EC-BUC(2)	Schleicher ASK 21	21352	
EC-BUD	AISA I-11B Peque	unkn	L.8C-84
EC-BUF(2)	Schleicher ASK 21	21351	
EC-BUI (2)	Schleicher ASK 21	21348	
EC-BUK(2)	Schleicher ASK 21	21353	
EC-BUO(2)	Schleicher ASK 21	21347	
EC-BUR	AISA I-11B Peque	unkn	L.8C- ?
EC-BUT	AISA I-11B Peque	unkn	L.8C-121
EC-BUV	AISA I-11B Peque	unkn	L.8C-127
EC-BUY	AISA I-11B Peque	206	L.8C-128
(Dam 17.7.04)			
EC-BVE	Agusta-Bell 47G-4A	2532	
EC-BVG	Dornier Do.27Q-5	2060	D-EANL, (D-ENAH)
EC-BVH	Cessna F172H	F172-0480	F-OCLX
(Wrecked)			
EC-BVI	Piper PA-25-260 Pawnee C	25-5154	N9718N
EC-BVJ	Zlin Z.526F Trenér Master	1122	
EC-BVL	Reims/Cessna F337E Super Skymaster	F33700007	
(Reims-assembled 337E with US c/n 33701236)			
EC-BVO	Aerodiffusion Jodel D. 1190-S	E.126	
EC-BVQ	Piper PA-28-140 Cherokee B	28-26212	N11C
EC-BVS	Piper PA-25-260 Pawnee C	25-5248	N9660N
EC-BVU	SIAI-Marchetti S.205-20/R	4-274	
(Wfu, noted 1.15 Cuatro Vientos)			
EC-BVY	Piper PA-28R-200 Cherokee Arrow	28R-35711	N11C
EC-BXA	Cessna 177B Cardinal	17701478	N30813
EC-BXB	Piper PA-23-250 Aztec D	27-4530	N13896
(Wrecked)			
EC-BXH	Macchi AL.60B-2	30/6210	D-EIRF, I-MACW
EC-BXO	Piper PA-22-160 Tri-Pacer	22-4987	N7127D
EC-BXS	Reims/Cessna F150K	F15000644	F-BSIH
EC-BXT	Piper PA-25-260 Pawnee C	25-5283	N8796L
EC-BXU	Sportavia/ Fournier RF-5	5081	
(Wreck reported 5.07)			
EC-BXX	Piper PA-25-260 Pawnee C	25-5259	N8774L
(W/o 29.9.99?)			
EC-BXY	Piper PA-28-180 Cherokee F	28-7105044	N11C
(Wfu)			
EC-BXZ	Piper PA-25-260 Pawnee C	25-5256	N8771L
EC-BYA	Beech C23 Sundowner	M-1291	N9237Q
(Noted derelict, 4.11)			
EC-BYO	Cessna A188 Agwagon A	188-0443	(CN-TEM), N8193V
EC-BYP	Piper PA-28-180 Cherokee F	28-7105047	N11C
EC-BYQ	Cessna 207 Skywagon 207	20700198	N1598U
(Wfu)			
EC-BYR	LET L-13 Blanik	174802	
EC-BYS	LET L-13 Blanik	174803	
EC-BYT	Reims/Cessna F177RG Cardinal RG	F177RG0030	
(Reims-assembled 177RG with c/n 177RG0193)			
EC-BYU	SZD-30 Pirat	B-311	
EC-BYY	Piper PA-25-260 Pawnee C	25-5305	N9742N
EC-BYZ	Piper PA-25-260 Pawnee C	25-5333	N9651N
EC-BZB	Piper PA-28-140 Cherokee E	28-7225217	N11C
EC-BZC	LET L-13 Blanik	174825	
EC-BZE	LET L-13 Blanik	174827	
(W/o 26.6.99?)			
EC-BZK	Piper PA-28-140 Cherokee D	28-7125534	N11C
EC-BZM	Piper PA-25-260 Pawnee C	25-5387	N8925L
EC-CAB	Cessna A188A Agwagon	18800661	N1561M
EC-CAF	Hughes 369HS	12-0366S	
EC-CAH	Reims/Cessna F150L	F15000774	F-WLIQ
(Wreck)			
EC-CAL	Reims/Cessna F150L	F15000765	F-WLIP
(Wreck)			
EC-CAN	SAAB-Scania MFI-10B Vipan	02	SE-CPH, Fv54381
EC-CAQ	Piper PA-25-260 Pawnee C	25-5461	N9672N
EC-CAV	Piper PA-28-140 Cherokee E	28-7225329	N11C
EC-CAY	Piper PA-28R-200 Arrow	28R-7235284	N11C
EC-CAZ	Piper PA-28-140 Cherokee E	28-7225526	N11C
"EC-CBB"	see EC-KVR		
EC-CBR	Beech A24R Sierra	MC-126	N9786L
EC-CBT	Piper PA-28-235 Cherokee Charger	28-7310012	N11C
EC-CBU	Piper PA-28-180 Cherokee Challenger	28-7305015	N11C
(Damaged 10.4.04)			
EC-CCB	LET L-13 Blanik	175225	
EC-CCD	Beech 65-80 Queen Air	LD-91	D-ILDO, SE-EXU, D-ILDO
(Wfu, noted 2.01)			
EC-CCE	Cessna 414	414-0391	N1611T
EC-CCI	Reims/Cessna F150L	F15000987	
EC-CCJ	LET L-13 Blanik	025305	
EC-CCK	LET L-13 Blanik	025306	
(Wfu, noted 1.15 displayed on roadside, Cuatro Vientos)			
EC-CCM	Piper PA-28-140 Cherokee E	28-7225568	N11C
EC-CCO	Reims/Cessna F337E Super Skymaster	F33700005	G-AXWN
(Reims-assembled 337E with US c/n 33701218)			
EC-CCR	Beech 58 Baron	TH-280	
EC-CCT	Beech 65-80 Queen Air	LD-47	SE-EWU, D-ILDA, SE-EDD, D-IGWS
EC-CCV	Piper PA-28-140 Cherokee	28-7325270	N11C
EC-CCZ	Reims FR172J Rocket	FR17200405	
(Ditched 7.12.04, derelict Tenerife N)			
EC-CDD	Cessna 421B Golden Eagle	421B0348	N7563Q
(Wfu - gate guard at Vigo Airport)			
EC-CDF	Beech 95-B55 Baron	TC-1555	(Also SpAF: E20-11)
EC-CDH	Beech 95-B55 Baron	TC-1582	(Also SpAF: E20-13)
EC-CDM	Beech C90 King Air	LJ-608	(Also SpAF: E.22-3)
EC-CDM	Rockwell S.2R Thrush Commander	1729R	N5529X
EC-CDS	Piper PA-31 Turbo Navajo B	31-7300951	N7561L
(Stored)			
EC-CDU	Scheibe L-Spatz 55	674	
EC-CDX	Bell 47G-5A	25108	
EC-CDZ	Piper PA-23-250 Aztec E	27-7305111	N40296
(Wfu)			
EC-CEB	SOCATA MS.894E Minerva 220GT	12135	F-OCTF
EC-CED	Piper PA-28-140 Cherokee	28-7325505	N11C
EC-CEE	LET L-13 Blanik	025509	
EC-CEG	Bell 47G-5A	25120	

Reg	Type	c/n	Previous identities / Notes
EC-CEJ	LET L-13 Blanik	025510	
EC-CEK	SOCATA MS.893E Rallye 180GT	12307	F-OCUI
EC-CEL	SOCATA Rallye 100S Sport	2336	F-OCUF
EC-CEM	Piper PA-28-140 Cherokee	28-7325498	
EC-CEO	Piper PA-28-140 Cherokee	28-7325547	N9503N
EC-CEQ	Piper PA-36-285 Pawnee Brave	36-7360016	N9542N
EC-CES	Piper PA-28-180 Cherokee Challenger	28-7305498	N9510N
EC-CEY	Piper PA-34-200 Seneca	34-7350311	N56279
EC-CFM	Dornier Do.27A-5	122	L.9-59, 55+15, AC+916, AS+916, PA+114
EC-CFN	Dornier Do.27B-1 (Museum)	129	L.9-60, 55+21, MA+391, DE+391, PB+108, PB+105
EC-CFO	Dornier Do.27B-1	149	L.9-61, 55+30, SA+114, SA+721, PL+112, PC+106
EC-CFP	Dornier Do.27A-1	166	L.9-62, 55+39, AC+920, AS+920
EC-CFQ	Dornier Do.27B-1 (Stored)	244	L.9-63, 55+86, GB+387, PG+106
EC-CFU	Dornier Do.27A-1D (Stored)	359	L.9-67, 56+65, ND+106, AC+932, AC+938, AS+938
EC-CFV	Piper PA-28-180 Cherokee Challenger	28-7305502	N9511N
EC-CFZ	Beech 58 Baron (Noted damaged 1.16)	TH-353	N2867W
EC-CGC	LET L-13 Blanik	025521	
EC-CGD	LET L-13 Blanik (Stored)	025522	
EC-CGE	Piper PA-34-200 Seneca (Stored 10.13)	34-7350324	N56378
EC-CGI	Piper PA-28-180 Cherokee Challenger (W/o 7.12.03)	28-7305599	N9556N
EC-CGJ	CASA/SIAT 223-A1 Flamingo	056	
EC-CGL	CASA/SIAT 223-A1 Flamingo	058	
EC-CGM	CASA/SIAT 223-A1 Flamingo	059	
EC-CGT	Piper PA-28-180 Cherokee Challenger	28-7305598	N9555N
EC-CGU	Piper PA-28-180 Cherokee Challenger (Damaged 4.5.08)	28-7305576	N9549N
EC-CGV	Piper PA-28-180 Cherokee Challenger	28-7305583	N9552N
EC-CHE	Beech A100 King Air	B-195	(Also SpAF: E23-2)
EC-CHF	Piper PA-28-140 Cherokee	28-7425011	N9583N
EC-CHG	LET L-13 Blanik (Noted dismantled 5.14)	025629	
EC-CHH	SEMCO TC-4A HAFB	SEM-88	
EC-CHJ	Reims/Cessna FRA150L Aerobat	FRA1500210	F-BUUA, F-WLIQ
EC-CHM	SOCATA Rallye 100S Sport	2418	F-OCVQ
EC-CHN	Dornier Do.27A-5 (Wears SpAF serial U.9-68, code 11-90)	408	L.9-68, 56+94, PB+221
EC-CHO	Dornier Do.27A-5 (Stored)	428	L.9-69, 57+02, PK+220
EC-CHQ	Dornier Do.27A-5	445	L.9-71, 57+17, PC+221, PC+106
EC-CHY	Piper PA-28-235 Charger	28-7310100	N11C
EC-CIA	Glasflügel H201B Standard Libelle	488	
EC-CIB	SOCATA MS.893E Rallye 180GT	12383	F-OCVX
EC-CIF	Piper PA-18-150 Super Cub	18-7409029	
EC-CIG	Piper PA-23-250 Aztec E (Wfu, stored)	27-7405309	N40568
EC-CIK	Cessna A188B Agtruck	18801393T	N9149G
EC-CIL	Schempp-Hirth Cirrus VTC	149	
EC-CIN	SZD-30 Pirat (Dismantled)	S-01.13	
EC-CIO	SZD-30 Pirat	B-549	
EC-CIP	SZD-30 Pirat	S-01.19	
EC-CIQ	SOCATA MS.880B Rallye Club	2413	F-OCVO
EC-CIR	LET L-13 Blanik	025602	
EC-CIS	LET L-13 Blanik	025601	
EC-CIT	LET L-13 Blanik	025628	
EC-CIU	LET L-13 Blanik	025613	
EC-CIV	LET L-13 Blanik (Stored)	025612	
EC-CIX	SOCATA MS.893E Rallye 180GT	12382	F-OCVU
EC-CIY	Piper PA-31-350 Navajo Chieftain	31-7405181	N66875
EC-CJB	SOCATA Rallye 100S Sport	2417	F-OCVP
EC-CJC	SOCATA MS.880B Rallye Club	2412	F-OCVN
EC-CJF	Reims/Cessna F337G Skymaster (Reims-assembled 337G with US c/n 33701513)	F33700063	F-BSIH, F-WLIQ
EC-CJJ	SOCATA Rallye 100S Sport (Wfu, noted 1.15 Cuatro Vientos)	2420	F-OCYC
EC-CJK	SOCATA Rallye 100S Sport	2419	F-OCYB
EC-CJL	Piper PA-31-350 Navajo Chieftain	31-7405198	N66907
EC-CJM	Scheibe L-Spatz 55	671	
EC-CJO	SOCATA MS.880B Rallye Club (Wfu)	2459	F-OCYF
EC-CJQ	SOCATA MS.893E Rallye 180GT	12434	F-OCYE
EC-CJR	Emmert Rehaz U.L-Spatz	6	
EC-CJS	Piper PA-28-180 Cherokee Archer	28-7405089	N9516N
EC-CJT	Piper PA-28-151 Cherokee Warrior	28-7415101	N9640N
EC-CJV	Piper PA-28-140 Cherokee	28-7425246	N9510N
EC-CKC	Piper PA-18-150 Super Cub	18-7409057	N9671N
EC-CKE	LET L-13 Blanik	026005	
EC-CKF	LET L-13 Blanik	025912	
EC-CKJ	Glasflügel H201B Standard Libelle	571	
EC-CKK	Britten-Norman BN-2A-27 Islander	714	G-BBZX
EC-CKL	Britten-Norman BN-2A-27 Islander	715	G-BBZY
EC-CKN	Piper PA-23-250 Aztec E	27-7405427	N54120
EC-CKQ	SOCATA Rallye 100S Sport	2394	F-OCYZ, F-BUZU
EC-CKS	SOCATA MS.894A Minerva 220	11998	F-OCZD
EC-CKT	Schleicher ASW 17	17003	D-0877
EC-CKU	Piper PA-28-180 Cherokee Archer	28-7405086	EC-YYS, N9509N
EC-CKY	Piper PA-36-285 Pawnee Brave	36-7460025	N9532N
EC-CKZ	Cessna 182P	18262820	N52752
EC-CLA	Piper PA-28-140 Cherokee	28-7425165	N9624N
EC-CLC	Piper PA-36-285 Pawnee Brave	36-7460027	N9535N
EC-CLF	SOCATA MS.893E Rallye 180GT	12491	F-OCSZ
EC-CLG	Beech F33A Bonanza	CE-517	(Also SpAF: E.24B-30)
EC-CLK	Beech F33A Bonanza	CE-529	(Also SpAF: E.24B-34)
EC-CLM	Beech F33A Bonanza	CE-531	(Also SpAF: E.24B-36)
EC-CLT	Piper PA-28-151 Warrior (Wreck noted 1.7.04)	28-7415213	N9528N, N41435
EC-CLY	SOCATA Rallye 100S Sport	2362	F-OCYU, F-BUVY
EC-CLZ	Reims FR172J Rocket	FR17200464	F-BSGV
EC-CMA	Piper PA-28-180 Cherokee Archer	28-7405135	N9569N
EC-CMB	Aérospatiale SA.341G Gazelle	1166	F-WXFQ
EC-CMC	Reims/Cessna F150L	F15001137	F-BSGR, (HB-CEE)
EC-CMF	Cessna A188A Agtruck	18801772T	N53335
EC-CMJ	Piper PA-28-140 Cherokee (Noted wfu 1.16)	28-7525053	N9621N
EC-CMK	SOCATA Rallye 100S Sport	2367	F-OCYY, F-BUXD
EC-CML	SOCATA Rallye 100S Sport	2365	F-OCYX, F-BUXB
EC-CMM	Piper PA-28-180 Cherokee Archer	28-7405141	N9572N
EC-CMO	Piper PA-28-151 Cherokee Warrior	28-7515125	N9620N, N32320
EC-CMR	Piper PA-28R-180 Cherokee Arrow (Dismantled)	28R-30686	PH-ATU, N4944J
EC-CNC	Cessna 310Q (Wfu, noted 1.15 Cuatro Vientos)	310Q1123	N1272G
EC-CNE	Piper J-3C-65 Cub	11680	HB-OCS, D-EBYK, HB-OCS, 43-30389
EC-CNI	Reims/Cessna FRA150L Aerobat	FRA1500257	F-BJDD
EC-CNL	SZD-30 Pirat	S-02.39	
EC-CNM	LET L-13 Blanik (Stored)	026108	
EC-CNN	LET L-13 Blanik	026109	
EC-CNO	LET L-13 Blanik (Stored)	026119	
EC-CNP	LET L-13 Blanik	026120	
EC-CNQ	SZD-30 Pirat	S-01.18	
EC-CNR	SZD-30 Pirat	S-01.20	
EC-CNS	SZD-30 Pirat	S-01.38	
EC-CNU	SZD-30 Pirat (W/o 12.1.02)	S-02.06	
EC-CNV	SZD-30 Pirat	S-02.37	
EC-CNY	SZD-30 Pirat	S-02.46	
EC-CNZ	LET L-13 Blanik	025829	
EC-COA	Beech 95-B55 Baron (Crashed 24.6.02)	TC-1808	(Also SpAF: E.20-12)
EC-COD	Beech 95-B55 Baron	TC-1834	(Also SpAF: E.20-15)
EC-COF	Beech 95-B55 Baron	TC-1844	(Also SpAF: E.20-17)
EC-COG	Beech 95-B55 Baron	TC-1850	(Also SpAF: E.20-18)
EC-COH	Beech 95-B55 Baron	TC-1856	(Also SpAF: E.20-19)
EC-COQ	Beech F33A Bonanza	CE-584	(Also SpAF: E.24B-46)
EC-COS	Beech F33A Bonanza	CE-588	(Also SpAF: E.24B-48)
EC-COT	Beech F33A Bonanza	CE-590	(Also SpAF: E.24B-49)
EC-COU	Beech F33A Bonanza	CE-593	(Also SpAF: E.24B-50)
EC-COV	Beech F33A Bonanza	CE-586	(Also SpAF: E.24B-51)
EC-COX	Beech F33A Bonanza	CE-587	(Also SpAF: E.24B-52)
EC-COY	Beech F33A Bonanza	CE-589	(Also SpAF: E.24B-53)
EC-CPA	LET L-13 Blanik	025911	
EC-CPB	LET L-13 Blanik	026006	
EC-CPC	LET L-13 Blanik	026019	
EC-CPD	LET L-13 Blanik	026020	
EC-CPE	LET L-13 Blanik	026034	
EC-CPJ	LET L-13 Blanik (Stored, dam)	026033	
EC-CPK	LET L-13 Blanik	026045	
EC-CPO	Douglas C-47D (Still regd but at Luis Urilla/AENA Museum, Malaga as "EC-ABC")	17094/34361	T.3-50, N86442, 45-1091
EC-CPP	Dornier Do.28A-1	3002	D-IHIL
EC-CPR	Piper PA-36-285 Pawnee Brave	36-7560008	N9909P
EC-CPT	Reims/Cessna FRA150L Aerobat	FRA1500259	F-BJDE, (TR-LTP)
EC-CPU	Reims/Cessna FRA150L Aerobat	FRA1500252	F-BJDA, (I-AFAE)
EC-CPV	Reims/Cessna F150M	F15001181	F-BPPY
EC-CPX	Piper PA-36-285 Pawnee Brave	36-7560016	N53401, N31S, N9910P
EC-CQB	Cessna 182P	18263609	N6026J
EC-CQE	SZD-30 Pirat	S-03.39	
EC-CQN	LET L-13 Blanik (Noted dismantled 5.14)	026131	
EC-CQU	Piper PA-36-285 Pawnee Brave (Dam 13.7.04)	36-7560015	N9745N
EC-CQX	Piper PA-28-180 Cherokee Archer	28-7505183	N9627N
EC-CRI	AISA I-115	54	E.9-54
EC-CRK	Cessna 207 Skywagon 207	20700230	N1630U
EC-CRL	Reims/Cessna F177RG Cardinal RG	F177RG0096	N14499, (N14491)
EC-CRM	LET L-13 Blanik	026132	
EC-CRP	Piper PA-28-140 Cherokee	28-7525267	N9648N
EC-CRQ	Piper PA-28-151 Cherokee Warrior	28-7515356	N9619N
EC-CRT	AISA I-115	197	E.9-197
EC-CRU	Piper PA-36-285 Pawnee Brave	36-7560038	N9654N
EC-CRY	Piper PA-23-250 Aztec E (Derelict)	27-7554041	N54249
EC-CRZ	Reims FR172J Rocket (Dam 3.5.94)	FR17200446	CS-APE, F-BSGZ
EC-CSI	Cessna 310Q	310Q1043	CS-APP, N69956
EC-CSO	SZD-30 Pirat (Dismantled, wings noted 5.14)	S-04.07	
EC-CSP	SOCATA Rallye 100S Sport	2559	F-ODAR
EC-CSQ	Piper PA-28R-200 Cherokee Arrow II	28R-7535058	N32451
EC-CSR	LET L-13 Blanik	026153	
EC-CSS	LET L-13 Blanik	026152	
EC-CST	Piper PA-28R-200 Cherokee Arrow II	28R-7535319	N9580N
EC-CSU	Piper PA-28-180 Cherokee Archer	28-7505236	N9576N
EC-CSX	Piper PA-28-140 Cherokee (W/o 22.7.10)	28-7525251	N9633N
EC-CSY	Reims/Cessna F172M (Dam 27.11.94)	F17201111	CS-APF, F-BSGP
EC-CTB	Reims/Cessna FRA150L Aerobat	FRA1500212	N14492
EC-CTC	Reims FR172J Rocket	FR17200544	F-BPQQ
EC-CTF	Reims FR172J Rocket	FR17200448	EC-535, CS-APR, F-BSGR
EC-CTG	Piper PA-31P Pressurized Navajo (W/o 4.7.04)	31P-7530017	N54946
EC-CTH	Reims/Cessna F150L	F15001048	CS-APH, F-BSGN
EC-CTI	Cessna 210L Centurion	21060139	EC-532, N59169
EC-CTK	Piper PA-34-200T Seneca II	34-7670055	N4493X
EC-CTM	Reims FR172J Rocket	FR17200538	F-BJDT
EC-CTN	Piper PA-28-140 Cherokee (W/o 7.5.99?)	28-7625035	N9615N
EC-CTO	Aero Commander 680F (Dam 6.2.03)	1195-100	OE-FAI
EC-CTP	Piper PA-28-140 Cherokee Cruiser	28-7625036	N9619N
EC-CTX	Eiri PIK-20	20089	
EC-CTY	Piper PA-28-151 Cherokee Warrior	28-7515448	N9612N
EC-CUB	Piper PA-28-151 Cherokee Warrior	28-7415218	EC-YYR, N9530N
EC-CUC	Reims/Cessna F150M	F15001237	F-BJDK
EC-CUD	Piper PA-36-285 Pawnee Brave (W/o 7.8.07)	36-7560127	N9707N
EC-CUE	Piper PA-28-151 Cherokee Warrior	28-7515449	N9613N
EC-CUG	Cessna 421B Golden Eagle (Wfu, noted 1.15 Cuatro Vientos)	421B0936	EC-5310, N5386J
EC-CUI	Schempp-Hirth Standard Cirrus B	652	
EC-CUJ	Schempp-Hirth Nimbus II	104	
EC-CUK	SOCATA MS.893E Rallye 180GT	12640	F-ODAY
EC-CUL	Reims/Cessna FA150K Aerobat	FA1500069	D-ECHK
EC-CUN	Cessna A188B Agtruck	18802427T	N4909R
EC-CUO	SIAI-Marchetti S.205-18/F	216	F-BNLM

Registration	Type	C/N	Previous identities
EC-CUP	Sportavia RF-5B Sperber	51058	D-KKOA
EC-CUR	Piper PA-28R-200 Cherokee Arrow II	28R-7535243	N9618N, N3995X, YV-TAST, N9521N
EC-CUV	Piper PA-36-285 Pawnee Brave	36-7660012	
EC-CUX	Piper PA-36-285 Pawnee Brave	36-7560065	N9954P
	(W/o 25.7.02?)		
EC-CVD	Piper PA-25-260 Pawnee D	25-7405725	N9598P
	(W/o 29.5.10)		
EC-CVE	Piper PA-32R-300 Cherokee Lance	32R-7680079	N8148C
EC-CVF	Cessna 210L Centurion	21060563	N94254
EC-CVI	Schempp-Hirth Standard Cirrus	658	
EC-CVK	Sud Avn SA.318C Alouette Astazou	2415	
	(Wfu)		
EC-CVL	Piper PA-36-285 Pawnee Brave	36-7560011	N9906P
	(W/o 3.11.98?)		
EC-CVN	Reims FR172J Rocket	FR17200533	N94722
EC-CVO	Dornier Do.27B-1	151	OO-PAN, D-EKOV, 55+31, ND+205, PF+107, PD+102
	(Derelict, Cuatro Vientos 1996)		
EC-CVP	Reims/Cessna FRA150M Aerobat	FRA1500271	F-BJDF
EC-CVR	Piper PA-34-200T Seneca II	34-7570312	N7623C, N9594N
EC-CVS	SOCATA Rallye 100S Sport	2542	F-ODAV
EC-CVT	PZL-104 Wilga 35A	86282	SP-WFG
	(Dbr 25.8.84. Remains at Cordoba .91)		
EC-CVU	PZL-104 Wilga 35A	86278	SP-WFF
	(W/o 8.7.82. Remains at Oviedo .83)		
EC-CVV	Cessna 414	414-0631	ECT-555, N69816
	(W/o 9.5.98?)		
EC-CVX	Reims FR172G Rocket	FR17200218	CS-AKW
	(Wfu, noted 1.15 Cuatro Vientos)		
EC-CVY	Reims FR172J Rocket	FR17200385	CS-AJT
EC-CXB	Cessna 310R	310R0010	ECT-552, ECT-5312, N1326G
EC-CXC	Reims/Cessna F337F Super Skymaster	F33700042	CS-AHH
	(Reims-assembled 337F with US c/n 33701381)		
EC-CXE	Piper PA-25-260 Pawnee D	25-7405621	N9535P
EC-CXG	Cessna A188B Agtruck	18802553T	N4816Q
EC-CXH	Cessna A188B Agtruck	18802510T	N4758Q
EC-CXI	Cessna A188B Agtruck	18802507T	N4749Q
EC-CXK	Piper PA-28-140 Cherokee Cruiser	28-7625157	N9537N
	(Wreck stored, Tenerife)		
EC-CXL	Piper PA-25-260 Pawnee D	25-7405614	N9528P
	(W/o 11.4.03)		
EC-CXM	Piper PA-28R-200 Cherokee Arrow II	28R-7335117	CS-AOL, N11C
EC-CXN	Piper PA-28-140 Cherokee Cruiser	28-7625131	N9523N
	(Wfu)		
EC-CXO	Piper PA-25-260 Pawnee D	25-7405723	N9588P
EC-CXP	Cessna F172H	F172-0367	CS-AKU
EC-CXQ	Cessna 172C	17249438	CS-AKO, N1838Y
	(Cr 30.3.01)		
EC-CXT	LET L-13 Blanik	026305	
EC-CXU	LET L-13 Blanik	026308	
EC-CXZ	SOCATA Rallye 150T	2655	F-ODAX
	(Stored 10.13)		
EC-CYA	SOCATA Rallye 235E	12796	F-ODDY
	(Stored)		
EC-CYB	Cessna 207 Skywagon 207	20700271	ECT-551, N1671U
	(W/o 13.10.96)		
EC-CYC	Bellanca 7GCBC Citabria	832-75	OE-AOV
EC-CYD	Beech A36 Bonanza	E-788	ECT-012, N6787S
EC-CYE	Piper PA-28-151 Cherokee Warrior	28-7615281	N9573N, N75288
	(Dam 15.3.06)		
EC-CYF	Piper PA-31P Pressurized Navajo	31P-7630017	N57554
EC-CYG	Reims FR172J Rocket	FR17200537	F-BJDE
	(W/o 27.8.98?)		
EC-CYH	Rockwell Commander 112A	296	N1296J
EC-CYL	SOCATA Rallye 100S Sport	2813	F-ODDV
	(Static display)		
EC-CYO	SOCATA Rallye 235E	12801	F-ODDU
EC-CYP	LET L-13 Blanik	026245	
EC-CYR	Cessna A188B Agtruck	18802769T	N731BN
EC-CYS	Cessna A188B Agtruck	18802355T	N4836R
	(Dam 6.7.99)		
EC-CYT	LET L-13 Blanik	026646	
EC-CYV	SZD-30 Pirat	S-07.20	
EC-CYX	SZD-30 Pirat	S-07.24	
EC-CYY	SZD-30 Pirat	S-07.21	
EC-CYZ	SZD-30 Pirat	S-07.22	
EC-CZA	SZD-30 Pirat	S-07.23	
EC-CZB	SOCATA MS.893E Rallye 180GT	12741	F-ODEH
EC-CZC	Grumman G.164A Agcat	1294	
	(Dam 18.4.05)		
EC-CZD	Piper PA-25-260 Pawnee D	25-7756029	N82486
EC-CZF	Reims/Cessna F177RG Cardinal RG	F177RG0067	CS-AJH
EC-CZG	Reims FR172J Rocket	FR17200558	F-BOFC, (D-EOGV)
	(Dam 25.7.07)		
EC-CZH	Piper PA-28R-200 Cherokee Arrow II	28R-7635077	N9627N
EC-CZI	Cessna 310R	310R0638	N98895
	(Wfu, noted 1.15 Cuatro Vientos)		
EC-CZJ	Piper PA-28R-200 Cherokee Arrow II	28R-7635318	N9592N
EC-CZL	Piper PA-18-150 Super Cub	18-7709055	N83522
	(W/o 25.11.11)		
EC-CZM	Piper PA-36-300 Pawnee Brave	36-7760023	N9659N
EC-CZN	Piper PA-28-140 Cherokee Cruiser	28-7625225	N9588N
EC-CZO	Piper PA-28-181 Cherokee Archer II	28-7790353	N9605N
EC-CZQ	Piper PA-34-200T Seneca II	34-7670162	N8617E
EC-CZR	Reims FR172J Rocket	FR17200534	F-BJDD
EC-CZS	Cessna A188B Agtruck	18802882T	N731GJ
	(W/o 25.8.03)		
EC-CZT	Cessna 182P	18263956	N9895E
	(Reims-assembled with "c/n" 0023)		
EC-CZU	Zlin Z.526L	1160	
	(Wfu)		
EC-CZV	Aerotek Pitts S-2A	2135	
EC-CZX	Reims/Cessna F150M	F15001345	F-BJDH
EC-CZY	Grumman G.164A Agcat	240	N670Y
EC-CZZ	Reims FR172J Rocket	FR17200550	F-BOFB, (D-EEVQ)
EC-DAA	Cessna 310R	310R0618	ECT-538, N98855
EC-DAB	Grumman AA-5A Cheetah	AA5A-0346	
EC-DAD	Piper PA-28-140 Cherokee Cruiser	28-7725331	N9615N
EC-DAE	Reims FR172J Rocket	FR17200539	F-BJDJ
EC-DAF	Piper PA-28-161 Cherokee Warrior II	28-7716229	N9537N
EC-DAG	SOCATA Rallye 100ST	2944	F-ODHD
	(Wfu)		
EC-DAI	CASA C-1.131E Jungmann	1067	E.3B-421
EC-DAJ	CASA C-1.131E Jungmann	2061	E.3B-457
EC-DAL	CASA C-1.131E Jungmann	2065	E.3B-472
	(Noted 1.16 as SpAF c/s, coded 781-27)		
EC-DAM	CASA C-1.131E Jungmann	2160	E.3B-488
EC-DAO	CASA C-1.131E Jungmann	2107	E.3B-511
EC-DAP	CASA C-1.131E Jungmann	2147	E.3B-547
	(Cr 23.1.97)		
EC-DAQ	CASA C-1.131E Jungmann	2183	E.3B-578
	(Stored)		
EC-DAR	CASA C-1.131E Jungmann	2174	E.3B-581
EC-DAS	CASA C-1.131E Jungmann	2186	E.3B-583
	(Stored)		
EC-DAU	CASA C-1.131E Jungmann	2103	E.3B-608
	(Possibly ex E.3B-508, same c/n was quoted for EC-DAX)		
EC-DAV	CASA C-1.131E Jungmann	2217	E.3B-617
EC-DAY	Reims FR172J Rocket	FR17200545	F-BJDZ, (D-EESK)
EC-DAZ	Piper PA-28-140 Cherokee Cruiser	28-7725276	N9544N
EC-DBA	Piper PA-28-140 Cherokee Cruiser	28-7725277	N9545N
EC-DBF	SOCATA MS.893E Rallye 180GT	12980	F-ODHG
EC-DBG	SOCATA MS.893E Rallye 180GT	12981	F-ODHH
EC-DBH	Piper PA-28-140 Cherokee Cruiser	28-7725281	N9547N
EC-DBI	SOCATA Rallye 235E	12802	F-ODEG
EC-DBJ	Piper PA-28-140 Cherokee Cruiser	28-7725280	N9546N
EC-DBL	Reims/Cessna F172N	F17201562	ECT-537, F-BJDJ
EC-DBP	Piper PA-28-140 Cherokee Cruiser	28-7725100	N9552N
EC-DBQ	Piper PA-25-260 Pawnee D	25-7756026	N82479
EC-DBR	Piper PA-36-300 Pawnee Brave	36-7760139	N82667
EC-DBS	Reims/Cessna F150M	F15001369	
EC-DBT	Reims/Cessna F150M	F15001362	
EC-DBU	Piper PA-28-181 Cherokee Archer II	28-7890126	N9629N
	(Cr 10.4.04)		
EC-DBX	SOCATA Rallye 150T	2970	F-ODHF
EC-DBZ	Reims/Cessna F337F Skymaster	F33700031	G-BDVK, F-OCZZ, F-BSIZ
	(Reims-assembled 337F with US c/n 33701353)		
EC-DCA	Piper PA-28-161 Cherokee Warrior II	28-7816149	N9635N
EC-DCF	Piper PA-36-300 Pawnee Brave	36-7860015	N9666N
EC-DCG	SOCATA Rallye 180T	3091	
	(W/o 23.3.06)		
EC-DCH	SOCATA Rallye 180T	3027	
EC-DCI	Cessna A188B Agtruck	18803082T	N731QX
	(Reims-assembled with "c/n" 0001)		
EC-DCJ	SOCATA Rallye 235E	12870	
EC-DCM	SOCATA Rallye 235E	12871	
EC-DCO	Reims/Cessna FR172K Hawk XP	FR17200604	F-BNGX, (F-GAQF)
EC-DCP	Reims/Cessna FR172K Hawk XP	FR17200598	F-GAST
EC-DCR	Reims/Cessna F172N	F17201595	F-BNGY, (F-GAQJ)
	(W/o 14.6.90)		
EC-DCS	SOCATA Rallye 100ST	3002	
	(Dismantled)		
EC-DCU	Piper PA-36-285 Pawnee Brave	36-7660062	N57753
EC-DCV	SOCATA MS.893E Rallye 180GT	13052	
EC-DCX	Piper PA-25-260 Pawnee D	25-7856050	N4154E
EC-DCY	Thunder AX7-77A HAFB	145	
EC-DDB	Piper PA-28-161 Cherokee Warrior II	28-7816589	N9586N
EC-DDC	SOCATA MS.883 Rallye 115	1360	F-BRMN
EC-DDD	Morane-Saulnier MS.885 Super Rallye	153	F-BMHL, HB-EDT
EC-DDE	Piper PA-28-161 Cherokee Warrior II	28-7816588	N9585N
EC-DDF	Thunder AX7-77A HAFB	035	G-BDAZ
EC-DDG	Rockwell S.2R Thrush Commander	2456R	N8846Q
EC-DDI	SOCATA Rallye 150ST	3139	
EC-DDJ	Piper PA-28-181 Cherokee Archer II	28-7890506	N9594N
EC-DDK	Reims/Cessna F182Q Skylane II	F18200047	F-BNGT, F-BJDK
EC-DDL	Piper PA-32R-300 Lance	32R-7780238	N2267Q
EC-DDM	SOCATA MS.893E Rallye 180GT	13131	
EC-DDN	AISA I-115	196	E.9-196
	(Museum)		
EC-DDO	Grumman AA-5B Tiger	AA5B-0705	N28892
EC-DDP	Grumman AA-5A Cheetah	AA5A-0550	N26704
EC-DDT	Piper PA-28R-201T Turbo Cherokee Arrow III	28R-7703345	N44942
EC-DEC	Reims/Cessna F150M	F15001360	F-BNGV
EC-DED	Reims FR172J Rocket	FR17200567	F-BSGV, F-BJDH, F-BLIK
EC-DEE	Reims/Cessna F172N	F17201517	N96092
EC-DEF	Cessna 337D Super Skymaster	33700987	N2687S
EC-DEH	Piper PA-38-112 Tomahawk	38-78A0457	N9676N
EC-DEI	AISA I-115	53	E.9-53
	(Awaiting restoration 2013)		
EC-DEJ	AISA I-115	123	E.9-123
EC-DEL	Reims/Cessna F177RG Cardinal RG	F177RG0173	ECT-012, F-BPQQ
EC-DEO	AISA I-115	194	E.9-194
EC-DEP	Piper PA-28-161 Warrior II	28-7816661	N9622N
EC-DEQ	Cessna 401B	401B0115	D-IEPC, N7975Q
	(W/o 31.10.99?)		
EC-DER	Grumman AA-5A Cheetah	AA5A-0629	N26756
	(Wfu, noted 1.15 Cuatro Vientos)		
EC-DEU	Piper PA-38-112 Tomahawk	38-78A0589	N9664N
	(Stored)		
EC-DEV	Piper PA-36-375 Brave	36-7802017	N9727N
	(Crashed 1.10.99)		
EC-DEX	Reims/Cessna F182Q Skylane	F18200088	F-BNGR
	(Wreck noted 3.08)		
EC-DEY	Aérospatiale SA.315B Lama	2398	F-BXAX
EC-DEZ	Thunder AX7-77A HAFB	177	
EC-DFB	Robin R.1180T Aiglon	216	F-GBMR
	(W/o 21.9.05)		
EC-DFD	Cessna A188B Agtruck	18803306T	N1962J
	(Reims-assembled with "c/n" 0017)		
EC-DFF	Piper PA-25-260 Pawnee D	25-7856056	(AN-BUW)
EC-DFG	Schleicher ASW 17	17055	
EC-DFH	Cameron V-77 HAFB	470	
EC-DFI	SOCATA Rallye 180T	3203	
	(Dam.18.12.94)		
EC-DFJ	Cessna A188B Agtruck	18803305T	N1961J
	(Reims-assembled with "c/n" 0016) (Crashed 14.5.98)		
EC-DFK	Piper PA-28-161 Warrior II	28-7916041	N9506N
EC-DFM	SOCATA MS.893E Rallye 180GT	13130	
EC-DFN	Piper PA-25-260 Pawnee D	25-7956005	N9771N
EC-DFT	SZD-45A Ogar	B-818	
	(Incorrectly officially recorded as c/n B-820)		
EC-DFU	Piper PA-38-112 Tomahawk	38-78A0597	N9671N
EC-DFV	Schempp-Hirth Standard Cirrus	197	BGA1679
EC-DFX	Rolladen-Schneider LS3A	3182	
EC-DFZ	Thunder AX7-77 HAFB	191	
EC-DGA	Piper PA-38-112 Tomahawk	38-78A0767	N9686N
EC-DGG	Piper PA-34-200T Seneca II	34-7670161	HB-LHU, N8567E
EC-DGH	Piper PA-28RT-201T Turbo Arrow IV	28R-7931124	N9632N
EC-DGJ	Piper PA-28-181 Archer II	28-7990034	N9647N
EC-DGK	Agusta-Bell 47G-2	210	(F-BTSR), ALAT, Fr.AF
EC-DGM	Robin R.2100A	168	F-BXQY

Reg	Type	C/n	Previous ident
EC-DGN	Cessna T188C AgHusky	T18803334T	N2029J
EC-DGO	Piper PA-44-180 Seminole	44-7995213	N3064K
EC-DGP	Piper PA-25-235 Pawnee D	25-7856029	N9179T
EC-DGQ	Piper PA-28RT-201 Arrow IV	28R-7918056	N3050R
EC-DGR	Reims/Cessna FRA150M Aerobat	FRA1500316	F-BXXK
EC-DGS	SOCATA Rallye 180T	3204	
	(Cr 7.99)		
EC-DGT	Scheibe SF 25C Falke	44123	D-KACK
EC-DGX	Piper PA-28-181 Archer II	28-7990344	N9626N
EC-DGY	Thunder AX6-56 Bolt HAFB	188	
EC-DHC	Cameron V-56 HAFB	271	(EP-FHK)
EC-DHF	Piper PA-31T Cheyenne II	31T-7920073	N23699
EC-DHG	Piper PA-28-161 Warrior II	28-7916450	N9539N
EC-DHH	Piper PA-38-112 Tomahawk	38-78A0593	N9666N
EC-DHK	Piper PA-38-112 Tomahawk	38-79A0237	N9709N
EC-DHL	Piper PA-32-300 Cherokee Six	32-7940214	N2838A, N9592N
EC-DHN	Piper PA-28-161 Warrior II	28-7916506	N9576N
EC-DHS	Scheibe SF 28A Tandem-Falke	57106	D-KDGG
EC-DHT	Hiller UH-12E	5108	(SE-HVD), EC-DHT
EC-DHU	Aerotek Pitts S-2A	2181	
	(Museum)		
EC-DHV	Cameron V-56 HAFB	545	
EC-DHX	Cameron V-56 HAFB	546	
EC-DIC	Cessna F172H	F172-0336	
EC-DID	CASA C-1.131E Jungmann	2119	E.3B-319
EC-DIE	Schempp-Hirth Nimbus IIC	223	
EC-DIF	Grob G 102 Astir CS	1086	
EC-DIG	Scheibe Bergfalke II	164	
EC-DII	SOCATA Rallye 100ST	3039	
EC-DIJ	SOCATA Rallye 150ST	3138	(D-EEUM)
EC-DIK-JJ	Schempp-Hirth Mini-Nimbus HS-7	58	PH-606
EC-DIL	Piper PA-28-181 Archer II	28-7990486	N9621N, N2841V
EC-DIM	Thunder AX7-77 HAFB	204	
EC-DIN	Cessna 337G Skymaster	33701788	N53693, N2876P
EC-DIP	Thunder AX7-77 HAFB	201	
EC-DIQ	Sud Avn SA.318C Alouette Astazou	2416	
	(Wfu)		
EC-DIT	Piper PA-25-235 Pawnee	25-8056003	N9770N
EC-DIU	Piper PA-28RT-201 Arrow IV	28R-7918266	N8111Q, N9642N
	(W/o 17.5.08)		
EC-DIV	Piper PA-25-260 Pawnee D	25-7956035	N9772N
EC-DIZ	Thunder AX8-105 HAFB	237	
EC-DJA	Schleicher ASW 20	20294	
EC-DJB	Cameron N-77 HAFB	572	
EC-DJD	Piper PA-38-112 Tomahawk	38-79A1011	N9716N
	(Wfu)		
EC-DJG	Piper PA-36-375 Brave	36-7902047	N9742N
EC-DJH	Piper PA-25-260 Pawnee	25-8056010	N2407Q
EC-DJJ	Piper PA-28-161 Warrior II	28-8016183	N9536N
EC-DJL	CASA C-1.131E Jungmann	unkn	E.3B-534
EC-DJV	Piper PA-38-112 Tomahawk	38-79A1176	N9724N
	(W/o 28.6.97)		
EC-DJX	Piper PA-28RT-201T Turbo Arrow IV	28R-7931194	N9523N
EC-DJY	Cessna T188C AgHusky	T18803461T	N2425J
EC-DJZ	Piper PA-28-161 Warrior II	28-8016267	N9645N
EC-DKA	Piper PA-18-150 Super Cub	18-8009013	N9174T
EC-DKB	Piper PA-28-181 Archer II	28-8090248	N9504N
EC-DKC	Piper PA-28-181 Archer II	28-8090249	N9512N
EC-DKD	Cessna 337G Skymaster	33701797	N53706
EC-DKE	Bölkow Phoebus A-1	717	
EC-DKF	Scheibe SF 27A	6058	
EC-DKG	Schleicher K 8B	8396SH	
EC-DKJ	Scheibe SF 28A Tandem-Falke	57114	D-KDGV
EC-DKL	Cameron N-77 HAFB	653	
EC-DKM	ICA/Brasov IS-28M2	28	
EC-DKN	Reims/Cessna F152	F15201686	N1660C
EC-DKP	Cessna 402C	402C0275	N2757A
EC-DKX	CASA C-1.131E Jungmann	2016	E.3B-412
EC-DKZ	Cessna 210N Centurion	21063653	(N4868C)
EC-DLA	Piper PA-28RT-201T Turbo Arrow IV	28R-8031113	N82377, N9564N
EC-DLB	Piper PA-38-112 Tomahawk	38-79A1174	N24702
	(Dam 17.9.03)		
EC-DLK	Westland-Bell 47G3B1 (Soloy)	WA/329	G-BHBU, XT170
EC-DLL	Piper PA-38-112 Tomahawk	38-79A1179	N9650N
	(Wreck noted 1.7.04)		
EC-DLO	Cessna R172K Hawk XP	R1723324	N758SM
EC-DLP	Cameron N-77 HAFB	534	
EC-DLQ	Thunder-Colt 56A HAFB	065	
EC-DLR	Reims/Cessna FR172K Hawk XP	FR17200563	F-ODHP, F-GAGP
EC-DLS	Reims/Cessna F337G Skymaster	F33700078	N65327, F-BRGQ
	(Reims-assembled 337G with US c/n 33701679)		
EC-DLT	Piper PA-28-161 Warrior II	28-8016330	N9557N
EC-DLV	Zlin Z.50L	0022	
EC-DLX	Zlin Z.50L	0023	
EC-DLY	Zlin Z.50L	0024	
EC-DLZ	Cameron D-50 Hot Air Airship	752	
EC-DMB	Scheibe L-Spatz 105	1	OO-ZMG, D-5166, D-3578
EC-DMC	Reims/Cessna F152	F15201783	F-WZII
	(Damaged 30.11.16)		
EC-DMD	Scheibe SF 25E Super Falke	4319	ECT-029, OY-XGX, D-KECV
EC-DME	Reims/Cessna F152	F15201784	F-WZIJ
EC-DMI	Scheibe L-Spatz 55	747	
EC-DMK	CASA C-1.131E Jungmann	2049	E.3B-344
	(C/n now quoted as 1049) (Dism)		
EC-DMM	Cameron D-96 Hot Air Airship	675	
EC-DMO	Piper PA-36-375 Brave	36-7802058	N3921E
EC-DMQ	Grob G 103 Twin Astir	3553	
EC-DMR	Cessna 172RG Cutlass RG	172RG0547	(N5496V)
	(Wfu, stored 10.13)		
EC-DMU	Scheibe SF 25E Super Falke	4358	D-KOOA
EC-DMY	SOCATA Rallye 235E	13149	F-ODNG, N358RA
EC-DMZ	Thunder AX6-56 Bolt HAFB	294	
EC-DNA	Thunder AX7-77 HAFB	309	
EC-DND	Reims/Cessna FR182 Skylane RG	FR18200021	N9012F
EC-DNE	Schempp-Hirth Standard Cirrus	134	
EC-DNJ	Piper PA-28-161 Warrior II	28-8116142	N9512N
EC-DNN	Cessna 152-II	15284203	N4645L
EC-DNO	SOCATA TB-10 Tobago	171	ECT-040, F-ODNM
EC-DNS	Thunder AX6-56 HAFB	291	
EC-DNU	Aérospatiale AS.350B Ecureuil	1475	F-WZFH
EC-DNV	Cessna R172K Hawk	R1723401	N758VF
	(W/o 22.2.04)		
EC-DNX	Reims/Cessna F172N	F17201987	N1660C, (D-EOCT)
EC-DOA	Piper PA-36-300 Brave	36-8060006	N9740N
	(Cr 6.2.01)		
EC-DOD	Thunder AX7-77 HAFB	346	
EC-DOF	Thunder AX3-17/5C Sky Chariot HAFB	296	G-BILC
EC-DOG	Cessna 152-II	15284365	N6151L
EC-DOJ	Piper PA-32RT-300T Turbo Lance II	32R-7887284	N30693
EC-DOK	Piper PA-38-112 Tomahawk	38-81A0020	N25621
EC-DOM	Piper PA-25-260 Pawnee	25-8156002	N90831
EC-DON	AISA I-115	138	E.9-138
EC-DOP	Piper PA-38-112 Tomahawk II	38-81A0109	N26030
	(Wfu, noted 1.15 Cuatro Vientos)		
EC-DOT	Piper PA-28RT-201 Arrow IV	28R-8118020	N9610N
EC-DOU	SZD-42-2 Jantar 2B	B-1074	
EC-DOV	Thunder AX8-90 HAFB	336	SE-ZYC(2)
EC-DOX	Piper PA-28-181 Archer II	28-8190194	N9525N
EC-DOY	Scheibe SF 25C Falke	4129	D-KLDF
EC-DOZ	Thunder AX6-56Z HAFB	232	G-BGYO
EC-DPA	Grob G 103A Twin II Acro	3679-K-30	
EC-DPB	Grob G 103A Twin II Acro	3680-K-31	
EC-DPD	Grob G 103A Twin II Acro	3682-K-33	
EC-DPE	Grob G 103A Twin II Acro	3683-K-34	
EC-DPF	Grob G 103A Twin II Acro	3684-K-35	
EC-DPG	Grob G 103A Twin II Acro	3685-K-36	
EC-DPH	Grob G 103A Twin II Acro	3686-K-37	
	(Dbr 21.8.02)		
EC-DPI	SOCATA Rallye 180T Galérien	3349	F-OGLA
	(W/o 19.7.02)		
EC-DPJ	SOCATA Rallye 180T Galérien	3350	F-OGLB
EC-DPK	SOCATA Rallye 180T Galérien	3351	F-OGLC
EC-DPL	SOCATA Rallye 180T Galérien	3352	F-OGLD
EC-DPO	SOCATA Rallye 235C	13355	F-OGLG
	(Fuselage replaced with c/n "13365" which may be a spare from the end of production. Stored.)		
EC-DPP	SOCATA Rallye 235C	13356	F-OGLH
	(Wreck noted 3.05)		
EC-DPQ	Piper PA-28-181 Archer II	28-8190059	N9605N
EC-DPR	Cameron V-56 HAFB	750	
EC-DPS	Cameron D-38/50 Hot Air Airship	751	
EC-DPT	Avialsa-Scheibe A.60	27	F-CCQE
EC-DPU	ICA/Brasov IS-29-D2	150	
EC-DPV	ICA/Brasov IS-28-B2	260	
EC-DPX	ICA/Brasov IS-28-M2	36	
EC-DPY	Piper PA-25-260 Pawnee	25-8156001	N90829
EC-DQA	Hughes 369D	61-0995D	N1108N
EC-DQH	Schleicher ASW 19	19007	
EC-DQI (2)	Cessna TU206G Turbo Stationair 6-II	U20606010	N4743Z
EC-DQM	Cameron V-77 HAFB	789	
EC-DQN	Raven S-55A HAFB	835	
EC-DQS	SOCATA MS.880B Rallye Club	1954	F-BTJK
EC-DQU	Cessna L-19A Bird Dog (O-1A)	unkn	U.12-11, 51-12688
EC-DQV	Beech 95-B55 Baron	TC-2338	N3716B
EC-DQY	Cessna L-19A Bird Dog (O-1A)	unkn	U.12-6, 51-11929
EC-DQZ	Cessna L-19A Bird Dog (O-1A)	unkn	U.12-13, 51-4720
EC-DRC	SOCATA MS.893E Rallye 180GT	13128	F-GBXB, D-EEUD
	(W/o 5.9.04)		
EC-DRD	SOCATA Rallye 110ST Galopin	3357	F-OGLM
	(Wfu)		
EC-DRE	SOCATA Rallye 110ST Galopin	3358	F-OGLO
EC-DRF	SOCATA TB-9 Tampico	262	F-OGLI
EC-DRK	Robinson R22	0236	N9074F
EC-DRL	Piper PA-38-112 Tomahawk II	38-81A0021	N25622
	(W/o 2.8.07)		
EC-DRM	SOCATA MS.893E Rallye 180GT	13198	F-GBKO
EC-DRN	Cessna L-19A-1 Bird Dog (O-1A)	22613	U.12-10, L.12-10, 51-12299
	(Dam. 16.1.16)		
EC-DRP	Grob G 109	6106	D-KHAA
	(W/o 13.5.00)		
EC-DRQ	SOCATA MS.880B Rallye Club	1662	F-BSKU
EC-DRT	Cameron O-77 HAFB	784	
EC-DRV	Reims/Cessna F152	F15201916	F-WZNC
EC-DRZ	Cessna F172H	F172-0424	D-ELGT
EC-DSA	Aero Commander 680T	1564-20	I-ARBO, N1199Z
EC-DSG	Cessna T188C AgHusky	T18803923T	N9994J
	(W/o 23.8.98?)		
EC-DSK	SOCATA TB-10 Tobago	308	F-OGLQ
	(Wreck noted 3.05)		
EC-DSL	Piper PA-38-112 Tomahawk II	38-82A0088	N9659N
EC-DSM	Piper PA-28-161 Warrior II	28-8116183	N9523N
	(W/o 3.7.10)		
EC-DSN	Thunder AX7-77A HAFB	454	
EC-DSQ	Agusta-Bell 47G-2	271	F-BIND, F-OBND, I-ELIT
EC-DSR	Cameron D-50 Hot Air Airship	892	
EC-DSU	MBB Bö.105S (Catalunya "02")	S-623	D-HDSS
EC-DSY	Reims/Cessna F152	F15201789	F-WZIL
EC-DSZ	Grob G 109	6122	D-KCVO
EC-DTA	Piper PA-28RT-201 Arrow IV	28R-8118038	N8315H, N9624N
EC-DTB	SOCATA Rallye 235E	13018	F-GBXD
	(Wfu, noted 1.15 Cuatro Vientos)		
EC-DTD	Hughes 369D	1172D	
	(Dam 30.6.94)		
EC-DTE	MBB Bö.105C	S-576	D-HDPY
	(Wfu)		
EC-DTF	MBB Bö.105C	S-599	D-HDQV
	(Wfu, pod stored)		
EC-DTH	Thunder/Colt AS-90 Hot Air Airship	451	
EC-DTK	Cameron D-50 Hot Air Airship	854	
EC-DTM	PADC/ MBB Bö.105C	S.9-402	D-HDNS(3), RP-C214, (D-HDMA)
	(Wfu)		
EC-DTN	SOCATA Rallye 180T Galérien	3373	F-ODQB
	(Dam 11.8.07)		
EC-DTS	Partenavia P.68 Observer	324-17-OB	
EC-DTT	Grob G 102 Astir IIIB	5583CB	
	(Stored)		
EC-DTV	CASA C.212-200 Aviocar	301	
EC-DTX	Schleicher ASW 20	20711	
EC-DTY	Piper PA-25-260 Pawnee C	25-4509	SE-FCY
	(W/o 16.8.02?)		
EC-DTZ	Piper PA-25-260 Pawnee C	25-5301	SE-FYA
EC-DUC	Reims/Cessna F172N	F17201818	D-EJCA(2)
	(Crashed 22.6.02)		
EC-DUD	Grumman G.164B Agcat	733B	
EC-DUH	Bell 47G-2	1969	F-BUYV, 74+32, AS+387
EC-DUI	Hoffmann H-36 Dimona	3608	OE-9202, (D-KAHG)
EC-DUJ	CASA C.101CC Aviojet	98	
	(Displayed at CASA factory)		
EC-DUM	North American T.6G Harvard	182-591	E16.198, 51-14904
EC-DUN	North American T.6G Harvard	unkn	E.16-201, Fr.AF, 52-8216
	(Museum, painted as E.16-201)		
EC-DUP	MBB Bö.105C	S-614	D-HDSJ

Reg	Type	c/n	Previous identities
EC-DUQ	CASA C.212-200 Aviocar	270	
EC-DUR	Aérospatiale SA.341J Gazelle	1185	F-WTNA
EC-DUU(2)	Schleicher ASK 21	21346	
EC-DUY	MBB Bö.105C (Wfu, pod stored)	S-628	D-HDSX
EC-DUZ	MBB Bö.105C (Wfu, pod stored)	S-629	D-HDSY
EC-DVA	Hoffmann H-36 Dimona (Dam)	3536	OE-9237
EC-DVH	CAARP CAP.10B	189	
EC-DVI	SOCATA MS.893E Rallye 180GT	12122	F-BTVE
EC-DVJ	Hoffmann H-36 Dimona (Stored)	3671	D-KCED
EC-DVK	MBB Bö.105C	S-630	(N5489A), D-HDSZ
EC-DVL	MBB Bö.105C	S-631	(N5489C), D-HDTA
EC-DVP	Cameron 0-65 HAFB	1124	
EC-DVQ	CASA C.101CC Aviojet	107	
EC-DVR	Agusta A.109A	7231	
EC-DVS	Robin DR.400/180R Remorqueur	1682	
EC-DVU	Grob G 103A Twin II Acro	33919-K-154	
EC-DVV	Grob G 103A Twin II Acro	33918-K-153	
EC-DVX	Grob G 103A Twin II Acro	33920-K-155	
EC-DXA	Rockwell Commander 690A	11328	D-IHVB, N81449
EC-DXC	MBB Bö.105C	S-690	D-HDVD
EC-DXD	MBB Bö.105C	S-697	D-HDVK
EC-DXG	Aero Commander 680V (Broken up)	1711-86	N535SM
EC-DXH	MBB Bö.105C	S-698	D-HDVL
EC-DXI	MBB Bö.105C (Wfu, pod stored)	S-699	D-HDVM
EC-DXJ	Hispano HA.220D Super Saeta	22/114	A.10C-109, C.10C-109
EC-DXL	Wassmer WA.421-250	409	F-BPTL
EC-DXN	Aérospatiale AS.350B Ecureuil	1387	
EC-DXO	Ultramagic V-65 HAFB	65/04	
EC-DXP	Ultramagic V-65 HAFB	65/07	
EC-DXQ	Ultramagic V-77 HAFB	77/04	
EC-DXR	Hispano HA.200 Super Saeta (W/o 5.5.13)	20/56	A.10B-50, C.10C-50
EC-DXU	Vickers V.806 Viscount (Wfu)	264	G-AOYO
EC-DXY	Reims/Cessna F152 (Dism)	F15201793	F-WZIU
EC-DXZ	Bell 206B Jet Ranger II	1051	HB-XFH, F-BVUE, HP-1533-71, N58156
EC-DYD	Bell 47G-2	1620	D-HKBM, 74+29, AS+389, YA+028, PA+118, AS+383
EC-DYI	Ultramagic H-77 HAFB	77/13	
EC-DYJ	Ultramagic V-65 HAFB	65/06	
EC-DYK	Aérospatiale AS.350B Ecureuil	1863	
EC-DYL	Piper PA-28-140 Cherokee E	28-7225250	G-AZVZ, N11C
EC-DYM	MBB Bö.105C (W/o 25.1.02?)	S-700	D-HDVN
EC-DYN	MBB Bö.105C	S-707	D-HDVU
EC-DYQ	Agusta-Bell 206B Jet Ranger 3	8677	HB-XML
EC-DYR	Continental El Tomcat 6B (Bell OH-13H)	CCI-74-8	CS-HAS, N9026T
EC-DYS	SOCATA MS.893E Rallye 180GT	12313	F-BUNZ
EC-DYV	Ultramagic V-77 HAFB	77/06	
EC-DZD	Ultramagic F01 Bottle F56 SS HAFB	F01/01	
EC-DZE	Agusta-Bell 47G-4A	2535	I-CRIT
EC-DZF	Reims/Cessna F172M	F17201210	LN-NFE, SE-GKB
EC-DZI	Agusta-Bell 47G-4A (W/o 6.3.94)	2536	I- ITOX
EC-DZJ	Bell 47G-3B (OH-13S)	3905	FAMET/, HE.7B-29, 65-13009
EC-DZK	Agusta-Bell 47G-3B-1	1614	FAMET/, HE.7B-32
EC-DZL	Agusta-Bell 47G-3B-1	1613	FAMET/, HE.7B-31
EC-DZM	Agusta-Bell 47G-3B-1	1509	FAMET/, Z..7B-18
EC-DZN	Ultramagic H-65 HAFB	65/05	
EC-DZO	Ultramagic V-65 HAFB	65/11	
EC-DZP	Ultramagic V-77 HAFB	77/07	
EC-DZR	Piper PA-32-300 Cherokee Six D (W/o 22.10.95)	32-7140028	CS-AFV, N8635N
EC-DZS	Ultramagic V-77 HAFB	77/10	
EC-DZT	Agusta A.109A	7159	HB-XIU
EC-DZU	Valentin Taifun 17E (Stored)	1060	D-KFHA
EC-DZV	Cessna 310Q (W/o 29.4.08)	310Q0039	D-ICAA, PH-PLW, (PH-ADZ), D-ICAA, N7539Q
EC-EAA	Piper PA-36-375 Brave	36-7802020	HP-1060, YS-666A, N9741N
EC-EAB	Cessna 402	402-0167	G-BAWZ, N99JH, G-BAWZ, 5Y-ANJ, OY-AHP, N4067Q
EC-EAE	Piper PA-38-112 Tomahawk II	38-82A0090	N9661N
EC-EAG	Aero Commander 680W	680W-1776-14	N680W, N121AB, N13TV, N4988E
EC-EAI	Reims/Cessna F150K	F15000532	N8892
EC-EAJ	Ultramagic V-77 HAFB	77/09	
EC-EAL	Westland-Bell 47G-3B-1	WA/431	D-HAFH, XT542
EC-EAR	Ultramagic V-65 HAFB	65/13	
EC-EAT	Ultramagic H-77 HAFB	77/08	
EC-EAX	Agusta-Bell 47G-3B	1510	HE.7B-19, 751-9, Z..7B-19
EC-EAY	Agusta-Bell 47G-3B	1511	HE.7B-20, 751-10, Z.7B-20
EC-EBE	Grumman G.164D Turbo-Agcat	07D	G-TCAT, N816 IK
EC-EBK	Colt 56A HAFB	930	
EC-EBQ	Piper PA-36-375 Brave (Damaged 20.7.16)	36-7802031	N3863E
EC-EBS	Ultramagic V-65 HAFB	65/9	
EC-EBT	Ultramagic H-77 HAFB	77/11	
EC-EBU	Piper PA-36-300 Brave	36-8160012	N2346Y
EC-ECC	Ultramagic H-65 HAFB	65/17	
EC-ECE	Cessna T188C AgHusky (Dbr 13.3.01)	T18803935T	N9348K
EC-ECF	Grumman G.164A Agcat	1426	N8597H
EC-ECG	Ultramagic H-65 HAFB	65/15	
EC-ECH	MBB Bö.105CB (Ditched 29.10.02)	S-667	N . . . . . , (D-HDUI)
EC-ECI	MBB Bö.105CB	S-720	D-HDRH(2)
EC-ECJ	Aérospatiale AS.350B Ecureuil (W/o 13.8.94)	2031	
EC-ECK	Cessna 402	402-0284	D-IFAK, N8436F
EC-ECL	Hoffmann H-36 Dimona	36218	
EC-ECT	Bell 206B Jet Ranger II	2237	D-HIPI (2), N16824
EC-ECZ	Grumman G.164B Agcat	686B	N8401K
EC-EDA	Grumman G.164B Agcat	695B	N695GA
EC-EDB	Reims/Cessna F337G Skymaster (Reims-assembled 337G with US c/n 33701564) (Damaged 8.8.02)	F33700067	OO-EDU, F-BVSX
EC-EDC	Dassault Falcon 20	6	N750SS, N497, N65311, C-GOQG, (N21DT), N21JM, N20JM, N805F, F-BMKH, F-WMKH
EC-EDD	Grumman G.164B Agcat	116B	G-BEIJ, N48685
EC-EDH	Robinson R22	0071	N90348
EC-EDJ	Grumman G.164C Agcat	36C	N2734A
EC-EDP	Grumman G.164B Agcat	318B	G-BFJO, N6814Q
EC-EDQ	Eiri PIK-30	726	
EC-EDR	Grumman G.164B Agcat	343B	N6504K
EC-EDS	Grumman G.164B Agcat	262B	N25CD
EC-EDV	Grumman G.164 Agcat	214	N403Y
EC-EDX	Grumman G.164B Agcat	782B	N3633Z
EC-EDZ	Grumman G.164C Agcat	43C	N8085K
EC-EEA	Robin ATL	47	F-GFOX
EC-EEH	MBB-Kawasaki BK.117A-3	7091	D-HBPL
EC-EEJ	Westland-Bell 47G-3B1	WA/314	D-HFFF, XT155
EC-EEL	Ultramagic V-77 HAFB	77/12	
EC-EEQ	Bell 212	30612	D-HOBB(2), EC-DYP, D-HOBB(2), LN-OSM
EC-EER	Piper PA-36-375 Brave (W/o 1.7.98?)	36-8002029	N2453V
EC-EEV	Valentin Taifun 17E	1102	D-KFAC
EC-EEX	Piper PA-36-375 Brave (Cr 1.9.04)	36-7902028	N3983E
EC-EEZ	Bell 47G-5	7802	G-BLDF, N8558F
EC-EFC	MBB-Kawasaki BK.117A-3	7120	D-HBCO, (N9019V)
EC-EFF	Hoffmann H-36 Dimona II (Stored)	36230	OE-9289
EC-EFG	Hoffmann H-36 Dimona II	36223	OE-9291
EC-EFH	Rockwell Commander 690A	11130	N111VS, N294BC, N570H
EC-EFI (2)	Ultramagic M-160 HAFB	160/01	
EC-EFL(2)	Piper PA-34-200T Seneca II	34-7970246	N29691
EC-EFM	Piper PA-28RT-201T Turbo Arrow IV	28R-7931292	N46008, XB-BKM, N9627N
EC-EFN	Cessna 210M Centurion	21062158	N8866A
EC-EFO	Piper PA-34-200T Seneca II	34-7770092	N549BR, N73GH, N8584F
EC-EFQ	Lanaverre CS-11/75L Standard Cirrus	667	F-CEMV
EC-EFT	CASA C-1.131E Jungmann (Museum)	2226	E.3B-607
EC-EFV	Cameron N-77 HAFB	1064	
EC-EFZ	Ultramagic H-56 HAFB	56/2	
EC-EGA	Ultramagic V-65 HAFB	65/12	
EC-EGB	Ultramagic V-77 HAFB	77/15	
EC-EGC	Ultramagic H-56 HAFB	56/3	
EC-EGE	Ultramagic V-65 HAFB	65/16	
EC-EGG	Ultramagic H-56 HAFB	56/4	
EC-EGJ	Brditschka HB23/2400 (Damaged)	23023-S-5	
EC-EGK	Brditschka HB23/2400	23021-S-4	
EC-EGP	CASA C-1.131E Jungmann	2222	E.3B-603
EC-EGS	HS.125 Series 600A	256034	EC-115, N600SB, N600FL, N90BL, N90B, N39BH
EC-EGT	HS.125 Series 1A-522	25080	N23KL, C-GLEO, EI-BGW, G-BDYE, 3D-AAB, VQ-ZIL
EC-EGU	Cessna T188C AgHusky	T18803437T	N2200J
EC-EGV	Aérospatiale SA.365C Dauphin 2	5032	F-GBTB
EC-EGX	Piper PA-28RT-201T Turbo Arrow IV	28R-7931102	N2165U
EC-EGZ	Sud Avn SA.316B Alouette III	2319	HB-XRY, N9005D
EC-EHB	Piper PA-36-375 Brave	36-8102001	N2364Y
EC-EHC	Dassault Falcon 20DC	46	N46VG, (N144FE), N7FE, N23555, CF-ESO, F-WMKG
EC-EHE	Beech A36 Bonanza	E-115	OO-KRZ, D-EKRZ
EC-EHF	BAe.125 Series 600A	256011	N81D, N42622, VR-BGS, N555GB, N555CB, N6001H, N24BH
EC-EHI	Cessna T210M Turbo Centurion	21061956	N1749M
EC-EHK	Cessna TU206G Turbo Stationair 6-II (W/o 10.7.05)	U20606260	N6386Z
EC-EHL	Cessna Turbo 310R	310R0101	N134SW, G-BMHE, ZS-JCF, N69593
EC-EHN	Piper PA-36-375 Brave	36-7802022	N3830E
EC-EHP	Cessna 402B (Wfu, Valencia)	402B1232	N720J, N4186G
EC-EHR	Centrair ASW-20F	20175	F-CEUM
EC-EHV	Bell UH-1B (204)	953	N88389, 63-8728
EC-EIH	Rockwell Commander 690A	11212	N690BT, C-GIAA, N9165N
EC-EIJ	Maule MX-7-180 Star Rocket	11033C	N5672A
EC-EIL	Rockwell Commander 690	11007	N171TT, N711TT, N9207N, ZS-NHG, N9207N
EC-EIN	Air Tractor AT-502 (W/o 6.8.02?)	502-0021	
EC-EIP	Piper PA-36-375 Brave	36-8002008	N2322Y, ZK-EQJ
EC-EIQ	Reims/Cessna F150L (Wfu, dismantled)	F15000900	D-ECUD(2)
EC-EIT	Ultramagic M-65 HAFB	65/23	
EC-EIX	Rockwell S.2R Thrush Commander	2171R	N4963X
EC-EIY	Air Tractor S-501	501-0016	N10018
EC-EIZ	Air Tractor AT-401	401-0679	N73173
EC-EJA	Piper PA-36-300 Brave	36-8160022	N2393Y
EC-EJB	Douglas C-47 (Derelict .05)	4479	EC-177, (N514GL), N330, (5N-ARC), N330, F-OART, N2077A, HK-1201, C-1201, 41-18417
EC-EJC	Ayres S.2R-T34 Turbo Thrush	6017	N4009W
EC-EJD	Cessna T188C AgHusky	T18803686T	N3898J
EC-EJF	Air Tractor AT-401	401-0685	
EC-EJG	Cessna 172N Skyhawk	17273863	N6324J
EC-EJJ	Ayres S.2R-T15 Turbo Thrush (W/o 10.7.94)	T15-006	N40184
EC-EJL	Glasflügel H205 Libelle	165	F-CEQP
EC-EJO	Bell 206B Jet Ranger II	2864	HB-XLD
EC-EJP	Air Tractor AT-301	301-0665	N73120
EC-EJR	Piper PA-36-375 Brave (W/o 14.10.10)	36-8002041	N2318Y
EC-EJS	Ultramagic V-65 HAFB	65/14	
EC-EJT	Ultramagic V-65 HAFB	65/18	
EC-EJV	Piper PA-34-200T Seneca II	34-7970030	N2215D
EC-EJX	Piper PA-36-375 Brave (Dam. 27.7.02)	36-7902039	N3992E
EC-EJY	Piper PA-36-375 Brave (Dam 27.6.07)	36-7902010	N3972E
EC-EKB	Bell UH-1B (204)	345	N4991D, 61-765
EC-EKC	Bell UH-1B (204)	684	N394HP, 62-12533
EC-EKF	Reims/Cessna F172P (Dam 15.8.08)	F17202189	HB-CGP
EC-EKG	Cessna 402B Utililiner II	402B1209	N321RF, N321PC, (N4163G)
EC-EKH	Piper PA-28RT-201T Turbo Arrow IV	28R-8131008	N8277Y
EC-EKI	Cessna 150J	15069733	N51055
EC-EKJ	Cessna 172N	17270334	N738YD
EC-EKK	Dassault Falcon 20C	106	N31V, N9300M, F-GBPG, N987F, F-WJMM
EC-EKL	Ultramagic V-77 HAFB	77/16	

Reg	Type	Serial	Previous identities
EC-EKN	Cessna U206F Stationair	U20603721	N7952N
EC-EKO	Bell 206B Jet Ranger II	2406	N50006
EC-EKP	Grob G 102 Astir CS	1517	D-7453
	(Dam 30.7.04)		
EC-EKR	Piper PA-36-285 Pawnee Brave	36-7660049	N57728
	(W/o 7.8.07)		
EC-EKS	Ultramagic M-77 HAFB	77/23	
EC-EKV	Cessna T210N Turbo Centurion II	21063817	N6166C
	(Damaged 8.2.12)		
EC-EKX	Reims/Cessna F172M	F17201180	D-EDJO
EC-EKY	Maule M-5-180C	8012C	N5642T
	(Open store Valencia 7.11)		
EC-EKZ	Maule M-5-210C Strata Rocket	6007C	N51467
EC-ELB	Bell 47G-5A	25103	CS-HAG
EC-ELH	Mooney M.20J Model 201	24-1322	N1171U
EC-ELP	Cessna 172N Skyhawk	17268568	C-GSOG, N733UW
EC-ELQ	Cessna 150M	15078731	C-GYEE, (N704MY)
EC-ELR	Ultramagic H-56 HAFB	56/05	
EC-ELU	Piper PA-36-375 Brave	36-8002017	TI-APF, N9734N
EC-ELX	Piper PA-36-375 Brave	36-8002021	(F-OJMD), EC-ELX, C-GJEB, N2410V
EC-EMB	Piper PA-34-200T Seneca II	34-7870034	N9052K
EC-EME	Cessna 172N Skyhawk	17271082	D-EGGQ, N1653E
	(W/o 24.10.05)		
EC-EMF	Agusta-Bell 206B Jet Ranger 2	8715	
EC-EMH	Cessna 402B	402B0534	N101GP
EC-EMM	Cessna 172N Skyhawk	17268338	D-EGGO(2), N733JV
EC-EMQ	Ultramagic M-77 HAFB	77/26	
EC-EMR	Ultramagic S-105 HAFB	105/02	
EC-EMS	Ultramagic S-90 HAFB	90/01	
EC-EMZ	Pilatus PC-6/B1-H2 Turbo-Porter	672	F-GHAS, C-GXIK, N62149, XW-PEF, HB-FEI
EC-ENA	Ayres S.2R-R1820	001DC	N40225
EC-ENB	Ayres S.2R-R1820	015DC	N3086L
EC-ENC	Cessna T188C AgHusky	T18803697T	N3933J
	(Dam. 15.10.03)		
EC-END	Air Tractor AT-401	401-0698	N1007G
EC-ENE	Cessna 172N Skyhawk	17268844	N734GN
EC-ENF	Cessna T.188C AgHusky	T18803942T	N9414K
EC-ENG	Piper PA-28-161 Cadet	2841027	N9619N
EC-ENH	Cessna Turbo 310R	310R1309	N6171X
EC-ENI	Schempp-Hirth Ventus b/16.6	172	D-7717
EC-ENJ	Bell 47G-5	7938	N1477W
EC-ENK	Thunder AX7-77 HAFB	1174	
EC-ENM	Air Tractor AT-503	503-0001	N7309X
	(Dam 19.4.07)		
EC-ENN	Air Tractor AT-502	502-0007	N7315N
EC-ENO	Rockwell S.2R Thrush Commander	2101R	N4911X
EC-ENP	Cessna 152	15284480	N4709M
EC-ENR	Piper PA-28RT-201T Turbo Arrow IV	28R-8131137	N8385A
	(W/o 27.7.06)		
EC-ENV	Maule M-5-235C Lunar Rocket	7164C	N6129M
EC-ENX	Bell UH-1B (204)	977	N5598G, 63-12916
	(Wrecked)		
EC-ENY	Piper PA-36-375 Brave	36-8202009	N2349X
	(W/o 26.9.06)		
EC-EOA	Cessna 172P Skyhawk	17275892	N65794
EC-EOB	Maule M-5-180C	8005C	N5635U
EC-EOC	Ultramagic H-77 HAFB	77/27	
EC-EOE	Robinson R22 Beta	0695	HB-XSF
EC-EOI	Bell UH-1B (204)	408	N5023U, 62-1888
EC-EOP	Schleicher ASW 20	20020	D-7568
	(W/o 20.4.02)		
EC-EOR	Ultramagic S-105 HAFB	105/05	
EC-EOS	Piper PA-28-161 Cadet	2841064	N9629N
	(Stored)		
EC-EOT	Cessna 172N Skyhawk	17273765	N5367J
	(Dbr 6.4.00)		
EC-EOU	SOCATA TB-10 Tobago	634	F-GFFE, N20FD
	(Wreck noted 5.01)		
EC-EOV	Cessna 337G Skymaster	33701779	N53681
EC-EOX	Bell UH-1B (204)	1214	N90632, 64-14090
EC-EPC	Ultramagic M-77 HAFB	77/33	
EC-EPE	Ultramagic M-77 HAFB	77/34	
EC-EPG	Robin ATL	76	F-GFSA
EC-EPI	Ultramagic M-65 HAFB	65/29	
EC-EPJ	Cessna 152	15284583	N5408M
	(W/o 12.2.07)		
EC-EPK	Cessna 402B	1036	N98666
EC-EPO	Glaser-Dirks DG-400	4-223	(D-KIDG)
	(Dismantled)		
EC-EPP	Cessna T.337H Turbo Skymaster	01837	N1345L
	(Stored)		
EC-EPR	Piper PA-34-200T Seneca II	34-7870191	N9479C
EC-EPS	Cessna 172M	17261304	N20458
EC-EPU	Grob G 103 Astir Trainer	3237	F-CFHC
EC-EPV	Ultramagic F02 Pegaso Truck SS HAFB	F02/01	EC-197
EC-EPX	Piper PA-34-220T Seneca III	34-8233029	D-GBON, N8464B
	(Major damage 8.8.16)		
EC-EPY	Mooney M.20J Model 205	24-3112	N1010H
EC-EPZ	Piper PA-32-301T Turbo Saratoga	32-8024001	N9326C
	(Wfu)		
EC-EQA	Cessna 150J	15070498	N60683
EC-EQB	Cessna 150M	15078829	N704SC
EC-EQG	Reims/Cessna F172N	F17202008	G-WAGY
	(Dam 8.8.03)		
EC-EQJ	Cessna 411	411-0198	YV-455CP
EC-EQK	Cessna 310R	310R1610	N36873
EC-EQL	Bell 47G-3B1	6524	FAP 621, 66-621
EC-EQM	Cessna 152	15281103	N49017
EC-EQN	Cessna 152	15280727	D-EMBP, N152LK, (N25544)
	(Ditched 4.8.11)		
EC-EQP	Dassault Falcon 20	149	EC-263, N568Q, (N4359F), N1818S, N4359F, F-WNGO
EC-EQR	Robinson R22M Mariner	1043M	
EC-EQT	Cessna 172M	17261170	N20297
EC-EQV	Piper PA-34-200T Seneca II	34-7770006	N5266F
	(Noted derelict 4.11)		
EC-EQY	MBB Bö.105CBS	S-810	D-HDZT
EC-EQZ	SOCATA TB-9 Tampico	926	
EC-ERA	Piper PA-18-150 Super Cub	18-8929	N4508Y
EC-ERC	Piper PA-28-181 Cherokee Archer II	28-7790257	N8539F
EC-ERG	Cessna 152	15279563	N714ZH
EC-ERH	Cessna 402B	402B1086	N543GB, N543GA, (N1927G)
EC-ERI	Piper PA-36-285 Pawnee Brave	36-7360035	N56297
	(Dam 5.2.97)		
EC-ERK	Bell UH-1E (204)	6069	N151LC, BuA151875
EC-ERL	Beech F33A Bonanza	CE-1245	N3084D
EC-ERM	Cessna U206F Stationair	U20602291	N987CA
	(W/o 16.9.16)		
EC-ERO	CASA C-1.131E Jungmann	2012	E.3B-408
EC-ERP	CASA C-1.131E Jungmann	unkn	E.3B-321
EC-ERS	Cessna 340A	340A0524	N4277C
EC-ERT	Cessna 172N Skyhawk	17271250	N2362E
	(Wfu and stored)		
EC-ERU	Cessna 172N Skyhawk	17273475	N4928G
EC-ERV	Cessna 152	15281957	N67644
EC-ERY	Sikorsky S-76	760037	EC-364, F-GHUI, N9007F, PH-NZM, N4254S
EC-ERZ	Aérospatiale AS.350B Ecureuil	2261	
EC-ESD	Cessna 150M	15079292	N714MY
EC-ESH	Reims/Cessna FA150L Aerobat	FA1500099	D-ECPK
EC-ESI	Scheibe SF 25E Super Falke	4341	D-KDCR
	(W/o 12.12.04)		
EC-ESK	SOCATA TB-20 Trinidad	747	F-GFQN
	(W/o 16.1.16)		
EC-ESL	Piper PA-36-285 Pawnee Brave	36-7660087	C-GJIK, N57774
	(W/o 7.5.98?)		
EC-ESM	Cessna U206F Stationair	U20601902	D-EGJR, N50045
EC-ESN	Piper PA-36-285 Pawnee Brave	36-7560066	C-GUAR, N9955P
EC-ESO	Cessna 152	15281549	N65433
EC-ESP	Piper PA-38-112 Tomahawk	38-79A0460	N2463F
EC-ESU	Beech F33A Bonanza	CE-1410	N56620
EC-ESX	MBB-Kawasaki BK.117B-1	7176	D-HBHS
EC-ESY	Grob G 102 Speed Astir IIB	4106	D-6819
EC-ETC	Cessna 172N Skyhawk	17269216	D-EFZN(2), N734YG
EC-ETE	Piper PA-28-181 Cherokee Archer II	28-7790459	N3461Q
	(Accident 9.3.03 Cerdanya)		
EC-ETG	Soloy-Hiller UH-12J3	5067	N4027K
EC-ETJ	Ultramagic M-160 HAFB	160/02	
EC-ETN	Glaser-Dirks DG-200	2-86	F-CAYB, F-WAQA
EC-ETO	Grob G 102 Astir CS	1486	D-4790
EC-ETP	Ultramagic H-65 HAFB	65/27	
EC-ETQ	Ultramagic V-77 HAFB	77/35	
EC-ETR	Ultramagic M-77 HAFB	77/37	
EC-ETS	Cessna T188C AgHusky	T18803872T	N9937J
	(W/o 8.9.04)		
EC-ETT	CASA C-1.131E Jungmann	unkn	E.3B-397
EC-ETU	Cessna 337G Skymaster	33701573	N6AX
	(Stored)		
EC-ETV	SOCATA TB-20 Trinidad	743	F-GFQK
EC-ETY	Thunder AX7-77 HAFB	1360	
EC-EUA	Ultramagic S-105 HAFB	105/08	
EC-EUB	Lanaverre CS-11/75L Standard Cirrus	10	F-CEVK
EC-EUG	Air Tractor AT-501	501-0083	
	(Dam 10.9.94)		
EC-EUH	Air Tractor AT-501	501-0082	
EC-EUI	Ultramagic H-65 HAFB	65/25	
EC-EUK	Cessna 172N Skyhawk	17271869	N5441E
	(W/o 29.8.03)		
EC-EUM	Piper PA-36-285 Pawnee Brave	36-7660033	N57709
EC-EUN	Piper PA-34-200T Seneca II	34-7970213	N2193Z
EC-EUO	Cessna T210M Turbo Centurion	21062810	N6660B
EC-EUP	Reims/Cessna F150M	F15001192	D-EIWD
	(Damaged)		
EC-EUQ	Thunder AX8-105 HAFB	1644	
EC-EUR	Wassmer WA.26P	23	F-CDSB
EC-EUS	SOCATA TB-9 Tampico	1028	
EC-EUT	Bell 206L-3 Long Ranger III	51337	N8212U
EC-EUV	Cessna 172N Skyhawk	17272980	N1237F
EC-EUX	Cessna 172M	17264726	N61682
EC-EUY	Cessna 152	15283383	N48864
EC-EVA	Aérospatiale AS.350B Ecureuil	1345	HB-XMA, D-HLTH
EC-EVF	Ultramagic M-77 HAFB	77/49	
	(Quoted officially as 77/79, new canopy?)		
EC-EVG	PZL M-18A Dromader	1Z020-21	N21MX
	(W/o 15.7.97)		
EC-EVH	PZL M-18A Dromader	1Z020-10	N81695
EC-EVI	PZL M-18A Dromader	1Z020-09	N8169Q
	(W/o 2.10.11)		
EC-EVJ	Grumman G-159 Gulfstream 1	39	EC-376, N39TG, N40Y
EC-EVN	Robinson R22 Beta	0854	OY-HFA
EC-EVO	PZL M-18A Dromader	1Z020-16	N81702
EC-EVP	PZL M-18A Dromader	1Z020-12	N8170Q
	(W/o 26.7.99)		
EC-EVQ	PZL M-18A Dromader	1Z019-08	N8085K, SP-DBR
EC-EVS	Bell 204 (UH-1B)	893	EC-463, N400SD, N9378A, 63-8668
EC-EVX	SOCATA TB-10 Tobago	649	F-GENZ
EC-EXA	Ultramagic M-77 HAFB	77/52	
EC-EXE	Bell 206B Jet Ranger II	1073	HB-XXA, G-BKDD, C-FDVB, CF-DVB, N83159
EC-EXI	Ultramagic S-105 HAFB	105/09	
EC-EXJ	Mooney M.20J Model 201	24-1689	EC-447, N10882
	(Stored 10.13)		
EC-EXK	Mooney M.20J Model 201	24-1690	EC-448, N10898
	(Stored 10.13)		
EC-EXL	Cessna 152	15284055	N4980H
EC-EXO	Bell 204	202	EC-436, N18SX, N18SP, N3145F, 60-3556
	(Open storage 2.07)		
EC-EXP	Cessna U206F Stationair	U20602398	N206CT
EC-EXQ	Grumman G-159 Gulfstream 1	142	EC-461, N142TG, N10ZA, N764G
	(Wfu)		
EC-EXS	Grumman G-159 Gulfstream 1	64	EC-460, N64TG, N49401, CF-COL, N4466P, N764G
	(Wfu)		
EC-EXU	Cessna T210N Turbo Centurion II	21063389	N5360A
EC-EXZ	PZL M-18A Dromader	1Z021-06	EC-450, SP-DCC
EC-EYA	Cameron V-56 HAFB	2216	
EC-EYD	Fleet 2	324	EC-500, LV-ZCD, LV-PBC, R-69
	(Museum)		
EC-EYE	PZL M-18A Dromader	1Z022-02	SP-DCR
EC-EYG	PZL M-18A Dromader	1Z021-04	SP-DCA
EC-EYH	PZL M-18A Dromader	1Z022-01	SP-DCP
EC-EYI	PZL M-18A Dromader	1Z021-23	SP-DCG
	(W/o 6.8.94)		
EC-EYJ	PZL M-18A Dromader	1Z021-29	SP-DCN
	(Dam. 6.8.94; repaired)		
EC-EYL	Cessna 150L	15075347	N11355
	(Dam 2.1.94)		
EC-EYN	Piper PA-38-112 Tomahawk	38-79A0184	N2435C
EC-EYU	CASA C-1.131E Jungmann	unkn	E.3B-340
	(Damaged 13.11.11)		

Reg	Type	c/n	Previous identities
EC-EYV	Piper PA-34-220T Seneca III	34-8233109	OE-FYB, N8161K
EC-EZB	Avialsa-Scheibe A.60	58	F-CCVK
EC-EZC	Schempp-Hirth Discus bT	35/344	
EC-EZD	Swearingen SA.226TC Metro II	TC-314	EC-488, N232AM
EC-EZE	Swearingen SA.226TC Metro II	TC-319	EC-487, N233AM
EC-EZF	Ultramagic M-77 HAFB	77/43	
EC-EZH	Ultramagic V-65 HAFB	65/35	
EC-EZI	Ultramagic M-77 HAFB	77/42	
EC-EZL	Piper PA-32-300 Cherokee Six	32-7840113	N9709C
EC-EZM	Valentin Taifun 17E	1086	G-BMXF, D-KHVA
EC-EZN	Beech 65-A80 Queen Air	LD-205	EC-EEO(1), G-ASXV, OO-ATO, G-ASXV
	(W/o 9.1.99?)		
EC-EZO	Grumman G.159 Gulfstream 1	41	EC-494, N41TG, N9ZA, N7PG
	(Wfu, Madrid)		
EC-EZQ	Piper PA-38-112 Tomahawk	38-79A0754	N2539L
EC-EZV	Piper PA-38-112 Tomahawk	38-78A0310	N9273T
EC-EZX	Piper PA-28-181 Archer II	28-7990301	N2138R
EC-EZZ	Piper PA-28-181 Archer II	28-8190295	EC-572, N8420F
EC-FAA	SOCATA MS.893E Rallye 180GT	12605	F-BXDY
EC-FAB	Piper PA-28R-201T Turbo Cherokee Arrow III	28R-7703139	N5650V
EC-FAG	Cessna 310R	310R1255	N6056X
	(Wreck noted 2.01)		
EC-FAH	Douglas C-47A	9336	EC-530, F-BVJH, F-OCKH, F-BRGO, Fr.AF, F-BFGA, 42-23474
EC-FAI	Robinson R22 Alpha	0427	G-GAZE, N8522K
EC-FAK	Piper PA-38-112 Tomahawk	38-78A0465	N2441E
EC-FAN	Cessna T210M Turbo Centurion	21062564	N761VY
EC-FAO	Bell 206L-3 Long Ranger III	51289	N206WC, C-FFCE
EC-FAT	PZL M-18A Dromader	1Z022-03	EC-471, SP-DCS
	(Dam. 15.7.15)		
EC-FAU	PZL M-18A Dromader	1Z022-04	EC-4.., SP-DCT
EC-FAV	PZL M-18A Dromader	1Z021-27	EC-458, SP-DCL
	(Dbf 8.91)		
EC-FAX	PZL M-18A Dromader	1Z021-24	EC-4.., SP-DCH
	(W/o 9.9.95)		
EC-FAZ	Piper PA-36-375 Brave	36-7802007	N102RS, SE-GVM
EC-FBB	Ultramagic F-04 Bird SS HAFB	F04/01	
EC-FBC	CASA/Nurtanio CN.235-100	033	
	(W/o 29.8.01)		
EC-FBE	Piper PA-36-375 Brave	36-8202002	N2323X
	(Dam 18.6.97)		
EC-FBF	PZL M-18A Dromader	1Z021-28	EC-4.., SP-DCM
	(W/o 11.7.91)		
EC-FBG	PZL M-18A Dromader	1Z021-30	EC-4.., SP-DCO
EC-FBH	PZL M-18A Dromader	1Z021-22	EC-4.., SP-DCF
	(Dam 21.7.94)		
EC-FBJ	PZL M-18A Dromader	1Z021-25	EC-418, SP-DCI
	(W/o 27.8.15)		
EC-FBK	Piper PA-36-375 Brave	36-7802071	N3959E
	(W/o 5.10.01)		
EC-FBN	PZL M-18A Dromader	1Z021-20	SP-DCD
	(Dam 2.8.03, repaired)		
EC-FBO	PZL M-18A Dromader	1Z021-21	SP-DCE
EC-FBT	Robinson R22 Beta	1593	
EC-FBU	Ultramagic S-105 HAFB	105/15	
EC-FBY	Mooney M.20K Model 231	25-0290	N231KU
EC-FCA	Ultramagic N-77 HAFB	77/54	
EC-FCC	Cessna 402B	402B1013	N113JG, N87184
	(Noted probably wfu 1.16)		
EC-FCD	Rolladen-Schneider LS1D	205	F-CDVI
EC-FCF	SOCATA TB-20 Trinidad	957	F-GKUJ
EC-FCH	Cessna 152	15282310	N864WC, N68474
	(W/o 26.2.01)		
EC-FCJ	Ultramagic N-77 HAFB	77/44	
EC-FCK	Ultramagic N-77 HAFB	77/62	
EC-FCM	Agusta-Bell 47G-2	267	D-HAVO, 74+25, AS+067
	(Wrecked)		
EC-FCN	Piper PA-38-112 Tomahawk	38-78A0703	EC-FBW, N2472A
EC-FCO	Bell 206L-3 Long Ranger III	51179	N52CH
EC-FCP	Agusta-Bell 206B Jet Ranger 2	8006	G-BPIB, D-HABI, SX-HAA
	(Stored)		
EC-FCR	Cessna 150E	15060906	G-AWPX, 5N-AFR, N11B, N6206T
EC-FCS	Colt 77A HAFB	1788	
EC-FCT	Continental El Tomcat 6C	CC7.77.7	N9098T
EC-FCV	Ultramagic N-65 HAFB	65/36	
EC-FCY	Piper PA-28R-201T Turbo Arrow III	28R-7803166	N3329M
EC-FCZ	Grob G 102 Astir CS	1355	D-7394
EC-FDB	Airbus A320-211	173	EC-580, F-WWIL
EC-FDC	Schleicher ASW 15B	15330	D-2323
EC-FDE	Piper PA-34-200T Seneca II	34-7970421	N2958Y
	(Wfu, noted 1.15 Cuatro Vientos)		
EC-FDF	Piper PA-28-181 Archer II	28-8090122	N21AG, N81038
EC-FDI	Wassmer WA.26P	59	F-CDXR
EC-FDJ	Ultramagic V-65 HAFB	65/38	
EC-FDK	Piper PA-28RT-201 Arrow IV	28R-7918200	N2887W
	(Dam 9.9.02)		
EC-FDM	PZL M-18A Dromader	1Z022-16	SP-DBV
	(Dam. 30.9.10)		
EC-FDN	PZL M-18A Dromader	1Z022-18	SP-DCY
	(Accident 7.6.05, destroyed)		
EC-FDO	PZL M-18A Dromader	1Z022-20	SP-DCX
	(W/o 3.2.97)		
EC-FDQ	PZL M-18A Dromader	1Z022-21	SP-DCV
	(W/o 22.9.91)		
EC-FDR	PZL M-18A Dromader	1Z022-22	SP-DAA
	(Dbr 7.99)		
EC-FDS	PZL M-18A Dromader	1Z022-23	SP-DAB
EC-FDX	Thunder AX7-77 HAFB	1822	
EC-FDY	Thunder AX7-77 HAFB	1893	
EC-FEA	Piper PA-28R-200 Cherokee Arrow II	28R-7435239	N42682
EC-FEC	Cessna 150H	15068793	N23208
EC-FED	Cessna 152	15283528	N53272
EC-FEG	Cessna T210N Turbo Centurion II	21064713	N1639U, N17CD, N1639U
EC-FEH	Cessna 150L	15073157	N92AV, N5257Q
	(Dam 14.8.04)		
EC-FEI	Cessna 340	340-0113	EC-644, N888CW, N4569Q
	(W/o 5.9.98?)		
EC-FEJ	Cessna 152	15283173	N47118
EC-FEK	Cessna 172RG Cutlass RG	172RG1088	N9939B
EC-FEL	Agusta-Bell AB.412	25576	EC-607
EC-FEU	Robin ATL	109	F-GGHC
EC-FEX	Robinson R22 Beta	1293	C-GZAR
	(W/o 22.6.02?)		
EC-FFD	Cessna 421B Golden Eagle	421B0485	N421CC, (N41159)
	(On rebuild)		
EC-FFG	Cessna 152	15284573	N5384M
EC-FFJ	Mooney M.20J Model 205	24-3217	EC-665, N9133N
EC-FFP	Piper PA-28RT-201T Turbo Arrow IV	28R-8131043	EC-736, N83093
EC-FFR	Ultramagic N-77 HAFB	77/66	
EC-FFS	Ultramagic V-65 HAFB	65/22	
EC-FFT	Ultramagic V-65 HAFB	65/39	
EC-FFU	Ultramagic N-77 HAFB	77/67	
EC-FFV	MBB Bö.105S	S-852	D-HFHJ
EC-FFX	Cessna 411	411-0085	N7385U
EC-FGA	Ultramagic V-65 HAFB	65/40	
EC-FGB	Ultramagic 180 HAFB	180/03	
EC-FGC	Aérospatiale AS.350B Ecureuil	2250	
EC-FGF	Cessna 172N Skyhawk	17271103	N1708E
EC-FGI	Cessna 172N Skyhawk	17271255	N2374E
EC-FGJ	Cessna T210N Turbo Centurion II	21064334	N6317Y
EC-FGK	Piper PA-38-112 Tomahawk	38-78A0040	N9329T
	(W/o 11.4.01)		
EC-FGO	Piper PA-28-161 Warrior II	28-8216212	N363FT, N9600N
	(W/o 10.9.05)		
EC-FGP	Cessna 152	15281421	N49972
	(Dbr 5.4.02)		
EC-FGY	Colt 180A HAFB	1701	
EC-FGZ	Aérospatiale SA.316B Alouette III	5305	EC-738, PH-SLD, 5N-AKW, F-WTNI
EC-FHC	Piper PA-32R-300T Turbo Lance II	32R-7887193	N21156
	(W/o 24.12.98, noted derelict 12.99)		
EC-FHD	McDonnell-Douglas DC-9-87	53212	EC-638
EC-FHE	Reims/Cessna F177RG Cardinal RG	F177RG0163	OO-DFV, PH-AXS
EC-FHF	SOCATA TB-9 Tampico	1317	F-GKVL
EC-FHH	Piper PA-28R-180 Cherokee Arrow	28R-30537	N505FP, N4644J
EC-FHL	SZD-50-3 Puchacz	B-2042	
	(Dam 2.3.03)		
EC-FHM	SZD-48-3 Jantar Standard 3	B-1960	
EC-FHP	SZD-48-3 Jantar Standard 3	B-1962	
EC-FHT	Grob G 103 Twin II	3573	D-0651, D-6434
	(Dbr 5.3.05)		
EC-FHV	Piper PA-28-161 Cherokee Warrior II	28-7816361	N3610M
EC-FHX	Bell 206B Jet Ranger II	3786	G-OCAP, G-OACS, G-OCAP, N18096
	(Dam.16.1.09)		
EC-FHY	Piper PA-34-200T Seneca II	34-7870184	N9365C
EC-FHZ	Piper PA-28R-200 Cherokee Arrow B	28R-7135127	EC-757, N8591N
	(W/o 13.4.08)		
EC-FID	Piper PA-34-200T Seneca II	34-7970269	N2832Y
EC-FIF	Piper PA-34-220T Seneca III	34-8333072	OY-CEJ, N4300D, N9639N
EC-FIG	McDonnell Douglas DC-9-88	53195	EC-753
EC-FII	Colt 69A HAFB	1930	
EC-FIM	SOCATA TB-9 Tampico Club	1338	F-GKVN
	(Stored)		
EC-FIP	Britten-Norman BN-2A-26 Islander	623	EC-844, G-AYJE, CR-CAS, G-AYJE, (EI-AVE), G-AYJE
EC-FIQ	Britten-Norman BN-2A-26 Islander	161	EC-843, G-BNXB, V2-LAF, VP-LAF, G-51-161
EC-FIR	Ultramagic H-77 HAFB	77/58	
EC-FIS	Ultramagic H-77 HAFB	77/64	
EC-FIT	SZD-51-1 Junior	B-1921	
EC-FIZ	Glaser-Dirks DG-600	6-80S54	
	(W/o 2.1.04)		
EC-FJB	Beech 95-B55 Baron	TC-1689	EC-741, N25712
	(Derelict)		
EC-FJD	Ultramagic V-77 HAFB	77/71	
EC-FJE	McDonnell Douglas DC-9-88	53197	EC-755
EC-FJF	Cessna 414	414-0523	N4212C
EC-FJG	Piper PA-36-300 Pawnee Brave	36-7660118	TG-SAN
	(Dam 8.8.01)		
EC-FJH	Rolladen-Schneider LS7	7159	
EC-FJM	PZL M-18A Dromader	1Z022-17	SP-DEA
EC-FJN	Beech B95A Travel Air	TD-516	EC-828, N1570S
EC-FJO	PZL M-18A Dromader	1Z022-28	SP-DEB
EC-FJS	Cessna 172P Skyhawk	17274320	N51564
EC-FJT	Cessna 414	414-0174	N3LS, N8244Q
EC-FJU	Sportavia-Pützer RF-5B Sperber	1008	EC-650, D-KILL, EAF:660
EC-FJY	Schempp-Hirth Standard Cirrus	431G	
EC-FKA	Piper PA-28R-201 Arrow III	28R-7837054	N6136H
EC-FKK	Cessna 401	401-0279	EC-EXH(1), HI-517, N32CM, N2777, N8431F
EC-FKM	Piper PA-28RT-201T Turbo Arrow IV	28R-7931094	N2132U
EC-FKN	Piper PA-36-375 Brave	36-7802012	N3812E
EC-FKR	Piper PA-28R-200 Cherokee Arrow II	28R-7535254	N1429S
EC-FKU	Air Tractor AT-502	502-0125	N4548Y
EC-FKV	Air Tractor AT-502	502-0162	N1529N
	(W/o 1.6.99?)		
EC-FKX	Air Tractor AT-502	502-0168	N15337
EC-FKY	Thunder AX7-77 HAFB	1806	
EC-FLB	Robin R.3000/160	154	
EC-FLC	Wassmer WA.28 Espadon	108	F-CEOC
EC-FLH	American AG-5B Tiger	10091	EC-928, N1195F
	(W/o 1.3.00?)		
EC-FLI	Piper PA-36-300 Pawnee Brave	36-7760080	N59670
EC-FLJ	Piper PA-36-375 Brave	36-7902014	N3979E
EC-FLL	SOCATA MS.880B Rallye Club	2556	F-BVZY
EC-FLM	Piper PA-30 Twin Comanche	30-657	LV-IMD, LV-PCK
EC-FLN	McDonnell-Douglas DC-9-88	53303	EC-945
EC-FLO	Reims FR172J Rocket	FR17200402	EC-963, F-BUMN
EC-FLR	Robinson R22 Beta	2032	EC-951
EC-FLS	Ultramagic V-65 HAFB	65/46	
EC-FMB	Robinson R22 Beta	2045	
	(Pod noted 1.15 Cuatro Vientos)		
EC-FMD	SOCATA MS.894E Minerva 220GT	12148	F-BUVD
EC-FME	Aérospatiale AS.350B2 Ecureuil	2448	F-GKLR
EC-FMF	Grob G 102 Astir CS	1479	D-...., PH-571
EC-FMH	Piper PA-28RT-201T Turbo Arrow IV	28R-7931054	N3003N
EC-FMI	Centrair ASW-20F	20529	OO-ZYT, BGA3313/FKC, OO-ZMA
EC-FMK	Ultramagic H-77 HAFB	77/75	
EC-FMR	Robinson R22 Beta	2047	
EC-FMU	PZL M-18A Dromader	1Z021-07	SP-FCM, SP-DCW
	(W/o 15.8.02)		
EC-FMV	PZL M-18A Dromader	1Z022-30	SP-FCN
	(Badly damaged 24.4.95, repaired)		
EC-FMX	Piper PA-34-200T Seneca II	34-7970396	N606RH, N50MF, N9605N
EC-FNG	Ultramagic S-130 HAFB	130/03	
EC-FNH	SOCATA MS.893A Rallye Commodore 180	11875	F-BTID
EC-FNJ	Ultramagic V-77 HAFB	77/81	
EC-FNL	Ultramagic F-08 Church SS HAFB	F08/01	

Registration	Type	c/n	Previous identities
EC-FNM	Boeing Stearman PT-17 (Museum)	75-8089	EC-973, (LV-HDT), LQ-HDT, LV-HDT, Navy 0325 /, 1-E-74, BuA38468
EC-FNN	MBB Bö.105S	S-869	D-HMBL, (D-HFNA)
EC-FNO	MBB Bö.105S	S-870	D-HMBM, (D-HFNB)
EC-FNQ	Hughes 269C	128-0743	G-OSHE, N58204
EC-FNT	Piper PA-28-161 Warrior II	28-7916153	N2243D
EC-FNV	Colt 77A HAFB	1738	
EC-FNY	Grob G 103 Twin Astir (Dam 9.7.94)	3036	D-4838
EC-FNZ	Grob G 102 Speed Astir	4037	D-4872
EC-FOB	Ultramagic M-77 HAFB	77/78	
EC-FOD	Piper PA-36-300 Pawnee Brave	36-7760069	N59660, CF-JLO, N69897
EC-FOF	McDonnell-Douglas DC-9-88	53307	EC-966
EC-FOG	McDonnell-Douglas DC-9-88	53306	EC-965
EC-FOK	Beech 35-33 Debonair	CD-617	N260LB, N9780Y
EC-FOM	Ultramagic M-77 HAFB	77/77	
EC-FON	Mooney M.20J Model 205 (Stored 10.13)	24-3260	EC-980
EC-FOO	Cessna 172N Skyhawk	17271847	N5409E
EC-FOP	Cessna 152 (Dam 31.1.94)	15284679	N4276R, XB-CFH, (N6338M)
EC-FOQ	Aérospatiale AS.350B2 Ecureuil (Cr 16.12.06)	2639	
EC-FOR	American AG-5B Tiger (Stored 10.13)	10099	N100AG
EC-FOS	Ultramagic V-65 HAFB	65/44	
EC-FOV	Cessna 177B Cardinal (W/o 13.8.98)	17702476	N13908
EC-FOZ	McDonnell-Douglas DC-9-88	53308	EC-987
EC-FPA	Cessna 421B Golden Eagle	421B0530	EC-138, N69897, CF-JLO, N69897
EC-FPB	Piper PA-38-112 Tomahawk	38-78A0728	N801DV, N2519A
EC-FPC	Fairchild Swearingen SA.226TC Metro IV	TC-408	EC-243, N252AM, N1013F
EC-FPE	Cessna 152	15284717	N4276M, XB-CFJ, (N6416M)
EC-FPF	SOCATA TBM-700A	12	F-OHBD
EC-FPJ	McDonnell-Douglas DC-9-88	53310	EC-989
EC-FPL	SOCATA TB-10 Tobago	1483	
EC-FPM	SOCATA TB-10 Tobago	1484	
EC-FPN	SOCATA TB-10 Tobago	1485	
EC-FPO	SOCATA TB-10 Tobago	1486	
EC-FPP	SOCATA TB-10 Tobago	1492	
EC-FPQ	Cessna 150L	15074733	N7838G
EC-FPT	Ultramagic H-42 HAFB	42/01	
EC-FPU	Scheibe Bergfalke II	245	D-1211
EC-FPX	Grob G 102 Astir CS 77	1620	D-7461
EC-FPY	Ultramagic M-77 HAFB	77/84	
EC-FQA	Cessna 337G Skymaster	33701713	N53575
EC-FQE	Cessna 172N Skyhawk (Dismantled)	17273515	N4968G
EC-FQF	Ultramagic M-65 HAFB	65/43	
EC-FQL	Cessna 177RG Cardinal RG	177RG0515	EC-157, N2115Q
EC-FQM	Robinson R22 Beta	2206	EC-259
EC-FQN	American AG-5B Tiger (Damaged 2001, possibly stored unmarked 213)	10132	EC-278
EC-FQR	Cessna R172K Hawk XP	R1723167	N758KX
EC-FQS	Cessna 150L	15074851	N10421, (N45RG), N10421
EC-FQT	Grob G 103 Twin Astir (Dbr 22.7.98)	3116	D-7783
EC-FQV	Hughes 269C	35-0406	N7401F
EC-FQY	Airbus A320-211	356	EC-886, F-WWIH
EC-FQZ	Ultramagic S-160 HAFB	160/10	
EC-FRA	Westland-Bell 47G3B1 (Cr 8.7.95)	WA/396	D-HAFL, XT237
EC-FRB	Aviat Pitts S-2B	5263	N473
EC-FRC	Ultramagic M-105 HAFB	105/23	
EC-FRE	Piper PA-38-112 Tomahawk	38-79A0223	N2544C
EC-FRF	Schempp-Hirth Standard Cirrus	661	D-2286
EC-FRH	Ultramagic V-65 HAFB	65/41	
EC-FRJ	Piper PA-28-140 Cherokee	28-7325592	EC-289, N56255
EC-FRM	PZL M-18 Dromader (Dbr 31.7.96)	1Z013-02	EC-365, YN-BZJ
EC-FRN	PZL M-18 Dromader	1Z012-19	EC-364, YN-CAE
EC-FRO	Robinson R22 Beta (Cr 18.3.04)	2234	N2351P
EC-FRS	Bell 206L-1 Long Ranger II	45412	HK-3166X, C-GMFQ, N1081Y
EC-FRT	Colt 77A HAFB	2302	
EC-FSD	Cessna TR182 Turbo Skylane RG (Noted wfu 1.16)	R18201004	N739TV
EC-FSE	Robinson R22 Beta	0963	G-BPOF
EC-FSF	Piper PA-31P Pressurized Navajo	31P-7730012	N821BJ, N277BW, N82608
EC-FSG	CASA C-1.131E Jungmann (Damaged)	2124	E.3B-544
EC-FSI	CASA C-1.131E Jungmann (Damaged)	2164	E.3B-548
EC-FSJ	Air Création Safari GT BI Fun 18	94105	
EC-FSK	SOCATA TB-10 Tobago	1555	
EC-FSL	SOCATA TB-10 Tobago	1556	
EC-FSM	SOCATA TB-10 Tobago	1557	
EC-FSO	SOCATA TB-10 Tobago	1560	
EC-FSP	SOCATA TB-10 Tobago (Dam 24.2.03)	1561	
EC-FSQ	Robinson R22 Beta (Dbr 8.8.99)	2097	EC-986
EC-FSR	Cessna 172M (Wfu, noted 2.01)	17262684	N13341
EC-FSS	CASA C-1.131E Jungmann (Dam 30.1.05)	2231	E.3B-319
EC-FSU	Cessna T210N Turbo Centurion II (Dam 26.5.04, under repair)	21063741	N5404C, N109TA
EC-FTA	Cessna 414 (Dam 14.2.97)	414-0647	N414TJ, N69976
EC-FTB	Sikorsky S-61N	61741	LN-OSY, OY-HDS, LN-OSY
EC-FTC	American AG-5B Tiger (W/o 19.12.98?)	10148	EC-311
EC-FTE	SOCATA TB-10 Tobago	1566	
EC-FTF	SOCATA TB-10 Tobago (Dam. 13.2.97)	1567	EC-395
EC-FTG	SOCATA TB-10 Tobago	1570	
EC-FTH	SOCATA TB-10 Tobago	1571	
EC-FTJ	SOCATA TB-10 Tobago	1573	
EC-FTK	SOCATA TB-10 Tobago	1574	
EC-FTO	Ultramagic F-09 Water Bottle SS HAFB	F09/01	
EC-FTQ	PZL M-18A Dromader (W/o 22.7.04)	1Z023-28	SP-DDH
EC-FTR	Boeing 757-256	26239	EC-420
EC-FTZ	CASA C-1.131E Jungmann	2170	E.3B-556
EC-FUC	American AG-5B Tiger	10169	EC-488
EC-FUE	Ultramagic S-90 HAFB	90/07	
EC-FUG	Piper PA-28-140 Cherokee (W/o 11.6.99?)	28-21412	N4657R
EC-FUH	Aérospatiale AS.355N Ecureuil 2	5554	F-WYMB
EC-FUI	Ultramagic M-77 HAFB	77/89	
EC-FUJ	Beech 65-B80 Queen Air (Wreck noted 3.05)	LD-408	EC-508, N5130Q, C-FCGV, CF-CGV
EC-FUK	Ultramagic S-160 HAFB	160/12	
EC-FUN	Ultramagic M-105 HAFB	105/24	
EC-FUO	Ultramagic M-65 HAFB	65/52	
EC-FUP	Ultramagic M-65 HAFB	65/47	
EC-FUQ	Ultramagic M-77 HAFB	77/92	
EC-FUS	Cameron DP-70 Hot Air Airship	1130	G-BMEZ
EC-FUU	CASA C-1.131E Jungmann	2167	E.3B-554
EC-FUY	Agusta A.109C	7670	EC-453, N1TV
EC-FUZ	Piper PA-28-140 Cherokee (Wfu)	28-22772	G-AVGB, N11C
EC-FVD	Ultramagic S-130 HAFB	130/04	
EC-FVE	Ultramagic M-77 HAFB	77/93	
EC-FVF	Ultramagic M-77 HAFB	77/94	
EC-FVG	SOCATA MS.893A Rallye Commodore 180	11636	F-BSFI
EC-FVH	Thunder AX7-77A HAFB	2519	
EC-FVI	Rolladen-Schneider LS6C	6319	
EC-FVK	Mudry CAP.10B (To F-WQPH 7.01)	264	EC-391
EC-FVN	Robinson R22 Beta (Wreck noted 1.03)	0606	EC-562, G-DLTI, N2540J
EC-FVO	Sikorsky S-61N	61756	EC-575, LN-OSX
EC-FVP	Cessna 172N Skyhawk	17270627	N739LL
EC-FVQ	Ultramagic S-105 HAFB	105/25	
EC-FVU	Hispano HA-200	20/73	E.14A-. . .
EC-FXC	Ultramagic S-160 HAFB	160/13	
EC-FXE	Schleicher K 7 Rhönadler	930	D-6310
EC-FXF	Ultramagic M-77 HAFB	77/57	
EC-FXK	Ultramagic F-10 Bird SS HAFB	F10/01	
EC-FXL	Robinson R22 Beta	0938	EC-570, I-INTA
EC-FXM	Ultramagic M-77 HAFB	77/86	
EC-FXS	Piper PA-28-161 Warrior II	28-8316003	EC-518, N82811
EC-FXZ	Beech F33A Bonanza	CE-521	EC-683 ?, E.24B-32, EC-CLI
EC-FYD	Ultramagic S-90 HAFB	90/09	
EC-FYO	Beech F33A Bonanza	CE-532	EC-688 ?, E.24B-37, EC-CLN
EC-FYQ	Ultramagic N-180 HAFB	180/07	
EC-FYR	Ultramagic S-105 HAFB	105/26	
EC-FYS	Ultramagic M-77 HAFB	77/96	
EC-FYT	Robin ATL	35	EC-568, F-GFOK, F-WFOK
EC-FYU	Cessna 172N Skyhawk	17268333	N733JQ
EC-FYV	MBB Bö.105CBS-5 (Catalunya "01")	S-896	D-HMBT(5)
EC-FYX	Thunder AX7-77A HAFB	2590	
EC-FZB	Swearingen SA.226TC Metro	TC-221	EC-666, OO-JPI
EC-FZD	Cessna 172RG Cutlass RG	172RG0187	N6498R
EC-FZF	PZL M-18A Dromader (Ditched 22.9.99, scrapped)	1Z015-14	EC-684, D-FOHY, DDR-TKY
EC-FZG	PZL M-18A Dromader	1Z019-26	D-FOLR, DDR-TLR
EC-FZI	Cessna 172N Skyhawk (Wfu, noted 1.15 Cuatro Vientos)	17271135	N2056E
EC-FZJ	Sikorsky S-61N	61758	EC-717, LN-OQE(2)
EC-FZL	Aerojaen/Fournier RF-5-AJI Serrania (Stored)	E-008	
EC-FZM	Aerojaen/Fournier RF-5-AJI Serrania (Stored)	E-009	
EC-FZN	Colt 120A HAFB	2560	
EC-FZO	Cessna 152	15282427	N69005
EC-FZR	Ultramagic V-77 HAFB	77/80	
EC-FZS	Beech F33A Bonanza	CE-525	EC-621, EC-CLJ, E.24B-33
EC-FZU	Sport Aircraft Tango II	3901	
EC-FZV	Rans S-12 Airaile	S-12-119	
EC-FZY	Rolladen-Schneider LS3A	3230	D-4290
EC-GAC	Ultramagic M-77 HAFB	77/106	
EC-GAK	Cessna 172N Skyhawk	17269089	EC-752, N734SZ
EC-GAL	Colt 69A HAFB	1867	
EC-GAM-730	Glasflügel H201B Standard Libelle	430	F-CEBP
EC-GAN	Swearingen SA.226TC Metro II	TC-203	EC-701, OY-BYH, N5303M
EC-GAQ	PZL M-18A Dromader (W/o 6.8.05)	1Z021-08	D-FOMB, DDR-TMB
EC-GAR	PZL M-18A Dromader	1Z019-27	D-FOLS, DDR-TLS
EC-GAU	Robinson R22 Beta (Wfu 10.11.04) (Static display)	0015	EC-824, N9017K
EC-GAV	Piper PA-31 Turbo Navajo	31-579	EC-411, E.18-1, N6641L
EC-GBB	Beech 200 Super King Air	BB-182	EC-727, N922JB, N155BT, N155PT
EC-GBC	Aerojaen/Fournier RF-5-AJ1 Serrania (Stored)	E-010	
EC-GBD	SNCASE SE.3130 Alouette II	1916	F-GJLN, V-64
EC-GBI	Swearingen SA.226AT Merlin IV	AT-041	EC-867, OO-JPA, N6FJ, SAAF-14, N5362M
EC-GBL	Piper PA-28-161 Warrior II	2816113	N9252N
EC-GBM	Piper PA-28-161 Warrior II	2816114	N92516
EC-GBO	Piper PA-28-161 Warrior II	2816115	N9252K
EC-GBP	Canadair CL.215-1A10	1031	EC-957, UD.13-3
EC-GBQ	Canadair CL.215-1A10 (Cancelled?)	1033	EC-958, UD.13-5
EC-GBR	Canadair CL.215-1A10	1051	EC-983, UD.13-11
EC-GBS	Canadair CL.215-1A10	1052	EC-984, UD.13-12
EC-GBT	Canadair CL.215-1A10	1054	EC-985, UD.13-14
EC-GBZ	Thunder AX7-77 HAFB	3464	
EC-GCC	Ultramagic V-77 HAFB	77/87	
EC-GCD	Ultramagic M-77 HAFB	77/110	
EC-GCE	CASA C-1.131E Jungmann	2161	E.3B-545
EC-GCF	SOCATA MS.892A Rallye Commodore 150 (Noted wfu 1.16)	10591	EC-813, (D-EAGW), OO-ADY, F-BOVB
EC-GCP	Beech F33A Bonanza (Wfu, noted 1.15 Cuatro Vientos)	CE-530	EC-842, EC-CLL, E.24B-35
EC-GCQ	Agusta A.109C	7665	EC-895, N1ZL
EC-GCX	Cessna 177RG Cardinal RG	177RG0567	EC-814, N2167Q
EC-GDC	Piper PA-28-140 Cherokee Fliteliner	28-7125346	EC-718, N521FL
EC-GDF	Piper PA-28R-201T Turbo Arrow III	28R-7803097	EC-913, YV-1431P
EC-GDG	Swearingen SA.226TC Metro III (W/o 18.2.98?)	TC-220	EC-930, N220AT, C-GFAP, N443JA, N5370M
EC-GDH	Piper PA-28-151 Cherokee Warrior	28-7415142	EC-968, N41227
EC-GDJ	Bell UH-1H (205) (W/o 19.3.98?)	5320	EC-951, N82818, 66-00837
EC-GDL	Aérospatiale AS.350B2 Ecureuil	2879	
EC-GDN	Bell UH-1H (205) (Crashed 18.6.00)	5721	N6190P, 66-16027
EC-GDQ	Ultramagic V-90 HAFB	90/13	

Reg	Type	C/n	Previous identities / Notes
EC-GDU	Beech F33A Bonanza	CE-574	EC-935, EC-COM, E.24B-42
EC-GDX	Eipper Quicksilver MXL-II	1691	
EC-GDZ	Cessna 337G Skymaster	33701687	EC-852, N53532
	(W/o 6.96)		
EC-GEB	Cessna 152	15283355	EC-914, N48642
EC-GEG	Piper PA-28-161 Warrior II	28-8516003	EC-936, N4377F, (EC- . . .), N4377F
EC-GEI	Ultramagic V-77 HAFB	77/112	
EC-GEK	Ultramagic S-90 HAFB	90/10	
EC-GEL	Ultramagic M-77 HAFB	77/101	
EC-GEM	Cameron Beer-Mug SS Balloon	2739	
EC-GER	Wassmer WA.26P Squale	74	F-CDZI
EC-GES	Cessna 172RG Cutlass RG	172RG0008	EC-981, CS-AQZ, N4650R
	(Reims-assembled 172RG with "c/n" 0002) (Dam 31.3.99)		
EC-GET	Mainair Gemini/Flash IIA	783-0290-7/ W576	EC-BT4
EC-GEV	Sport Aircraft Tango II	6871	
EC-GEX	Ultramagic N-180 HAFB	180/08	
EC-GEY	Hispano HA.200 Saeta	20/79	A.10B-73
	(W/o 31.10.96)		
EC-GEZ	Eipper Quicksilver MX-Sprint IIR	447	
	(W/o 25.7.04)		
EC-GFA	Ultramagic S-130 HAFB	130/08	
EC-GFC	Ultramagic M-105 HAFB	105/32	EC-025
EC-GFD	Rolladen-Schneider LS6C	6251	SE-UKM
EC-GFF	Ultramagic F-13 Pig SS HAFB	F13/01	
EC-GFG	Cessna 172K	17258536	G-BVBC, N84587
	(Wfu, dismantled)		
EC-GFH	Piper PA-28-161 Cherokee Warrior II	28-7716101	EC-998, G-MERV, N2364Q
	(Wfu, noted 1.15 Cuatro Vientos)		
EC-GFI	Ultramagic H-77 HAFB	77/113	
EC-GFL	Robinson R22 Beta	1949	OY-HFN
EC-GFO	Robin HR.200/120B	296	F-WZZZ
EC-GFS	Cessna F172H	F172-0635	D-EFHD
EC-GFT	Piper PA-28-140 Cherokee	28-24823	EC-162, N1899J
EC-GFV	Ultramagic F-12 Soap Powder Box SS HAFB	F12/01	
EC-GFZ	Ultramagic N-180 HAFB	180/11	
EC-GGA	Eipper Quicksilver MX-Sprint II	238	
EC-GGB	Douglas DC-7CF	45112	EC-888, N90802, G-AOIB
	(Stored)		
EC-GGC	Douglas DC-7CF	45215	EC-889, N9734Z, SE-CCF
	(Stored)		
EC-GGF	Piper PA-23-250 Aztec E	27-4810	EC-800, E.19-4, N14240
EC-GGG	Rans S-6ES Coyote II	S-6A-106	
EC-GGH	Ultramagic H-77 HAFB	77/121	
EC-GGJ	Colt 69A HAFB	3767	EC-191
EC-GGP	Ultramagic M-77 HAFB	77/88	
EC-GGQ	Air Tractor AT-802	802-0028	N60660
EC-GGR	Ultramagic N-180 HAFB	180/09	
EC-GGS	Airbus A340-313	125	EC-154, F-WWJB
EC-GGT	Mooney M.20J Model 205	24-3076	G-BPGA
EC-GGU	Air Création Safari GT BI Mild 16S	9506084	
EC-GHG	Ultramagic M-105 HAFB	105/35	
EC-GHI	Air Tractor AT-502B	502B-0360	N6095Z
	(Dam. 8.10.09)		
EC-GHQ	Ultramagic M-77 HAFB	77/117	
EC-GHS	Partenavia P.68 Observer	329-20-OB	G-OBSV
EC-GHU	Aero Commander 680	483-153	EC-252, D-IDIH
EC-GHV	Christen Pitts S-2B	5048	EC-253, N5326C
EC-GHX	Airbus A340-313	134	EC-155, F-WWJR
EC-GHZ	Beech 200 Super King Air	BB-555	EC-795, D-IFOR
EC-GID	Bell 212	31150	OY-HCS
EC-GIG	Robinson R22 Beta	1200	N3176S, JA7785, N8054U
EC-GIH	Ultramagic S-90 HAFB	90/19	
EC-GIJ	Beech 65-B90 King Air	LJ-382	EC-939, F-WQCC, F-GLED, EC-860, N25DC, N922K
EC-GIM	Sport Aircraft Tango II-GT	8861	
EC-GIN	CASA C-1.131E Jungmann	2208	E.3B-591
EC-GIO	CASA C-1.131E Jungmann	2153	E.3B-542
EC-GIP	CASA C-1.131E Jungmann	2171	E.3B-557 ?
	(Stored)		
EC-GIQ	CASA C-1.131E Jungmann	2192	E.3B-573
EC-GIR	CASA C-1.131E Jungmann	2239	E.3B-620
	(Stored)		
EC-GIS	CASA C-1.131E Jungmann	2229	E.3B-610
	Noted 1.16 in SpAF c/s coded 791-22)		
EC-GIX	Cameron C-80 HAFB	3573	
EC-GIY	Aérospatiale AS.350B Ecureuil	2175	EC-267, OY-HEP
EC-GIZ	Bell UH-1H (205)	5631	EC-297, N6738B, 66-01148
EC-GJA	Bell UH-1H (205)	5387	EC-298, N205UD, N8154L, 66-904
	(Open storage 2.07)		
EC-GJB	Bell UH-1H (205)	9262	EC-299, N8154S, 66-17068
EC-GJF	Cessna 501 Citation I/SP	501-0107	(N75471), 3A-MTB, N54TB, N501LS, N107CC, N1UL, (N33VV), (N333BG), N3204M
EC-GJG	Robin R.1180TD Aiglon	246	EC-319, F-GCRB
EC-GJJ	Reims/Cessna F172L	F17200823	D-ECQM
EC-GJL	Agusta-Bell 205A	4010	HE.10A-5, HD.10A-5, Z.10-5, EC-SSH, EC-BDF-R
	(W/o 14.6.02?)		
EC-GJM	Fairchild SA.227BC Metro	BC-772B	EC-307, N702AM, XA-RWK, N2756T
EC-GJN	Sport Aircraft Tango II-GT	2883	
EC-GJO	Sport Aircraft Tango II-GT	2895	
EC-GJP	Robinson R44 Astro	0277	
	(W/o 14.2.99?)		
EC-GJQ	Air Création Safari GT BI / XP15S	494003	
EC-GJR	Rans S-12XL Airaile	S-12-155	
	(Dbr 14.7.12)		
EC-GJS	Beech F33A Bonanza	E-576	E24B-43, EC-CON
EC-GJT	Airbus A340-313	145	EC-156, F-WWJF
EC-GJZ	Swearingen SA.26AT Merlin IIB	T26-149	EC-202, N829HS, N329HS, N642PB, N642RB, N193G, N25AC
EC-GKA	Piper PA-23-250 Aztec E	27-4807	E.18-2
EC-GKC	Sport Aircraft Tango II	5894	
	(W/o 15.12.01)		
EC-GKN	Ultramagic M-77 HAFB	77/122	
EC-GKO	Ultramagic H-77 HAFB	77/124	
EC-GKP	Schleicher ASW 20C/TOP	20748	D-KCAS(3), D-8859
EC-GKQ	Ultramagic H-77 HAFB	77/61	
EC-GKR	Fairchild Swearingen SA.227AC Metro IV	AC-620	N174SW
	(W/o 12.4.02)		
EC-GKT	Sport Aircraft Tango II-GT	T1922	
EC-GKY	Bell UH-1H (205)	13274	HE.10A-37, 72-21575
EC-GKZ	Bell UH-1H (205)	13275	HE.10A-38, 72-21576
EC-GLA	Piper PA-23-250 Aztec E	27-4811	EC-516, E.19-5, N14241
EC-GLB	Ultramagic M-65 HAFB	65/63	
EC-GLF	Cessna 172N Skyhawk	17270201	N738SM
EC-GLJ	Piper PA-23-250 Aztec E	27-4812	E.19-6, N14242
EC-GLK	Aerotek Pitts S-2A	2009	N9WK
EC-GLL	Cessna 172N Skyhawk	17268321	N733JB
EC-GLO	Cessna 172N Skyhawk	17269275	N737AT
EC-GLP	Piper PA-28-161 Warrior II	28-8116163	G-BOPL, N8342J
EC-GLR	Bell UH-1H (205)	5881	66-16187
EC-GLV	Bell 212	30587	N605LH, JA9517, N58086
EC-GLX	Hispano HA-200D Saeta	20/88	A.10B-82, C.10B-82
	(W/o 13.5.00)		
EC-GLY	Colt 90A HAFB	2295	G-BUOU
EC-GLZ	Colt 77A HAFB	3942	
EC-GMA	Hispano HA-200A Saeta	20/65	AE.10B-59, C.10B-59, E.14B-59
	(Dam 11.99, stored)		
EC-GMB	Glaser-Dirks DG-202-17	2-145/1743	D-1159
EC-GMC	LAK-12 Lietuva	6179	DOSAAF ?
EC-GMD	Beech A45 Mentor	X-100	E.17-20
EC-GME	Piper PA-28-140 Cherokee	28-7525228	N33696
EC-GMJ	Cessna 182J Skylane	18256994	N2894F
	(W/o 24.6.00)		
EC-GMK	Cameron C-80 Concept HAFB	3717	
EC-GMN	Ultramagic M-77 HAFB	77/123	
EC-GMQ	Ultramagic N-210 HAFB	210/04	
EC-GMR	Air Création Safari GT-BI Fun 18	191004	EC-BD6
EC-GMS	Cameron A-120 HAFB	4011	
EC-GMU	Airbus A310-304 (Wfu)	451	N571SW, C-GCIV, N815PA, F-WWCY
EC-GMV	Cedimex Rans S-12XL-582 Airaile	S-12-160	
	(W/o 21.3.04)		
EC-GMX	Air Tractor AT-802A	802A-0039	N5001X
	(Dbr 13.7.99)		
EC-GMZ	Eurocopter EC.135T1	0016	D-HECG
EC-GNA	Eurocopter EC.135T1	0017	D-HECH
EC-GND-CX	Grob G 102 Astir CS	1399	D-4272
EC-GNE	Rolladen-Schneider LS3A	3200	D-7804
EC-GNF	Ultramagic M-77 HAFB	77-127	
EC-GNH	Cessna 177 Cardinal	17700244	N2844X
EC-GNN	Robinson R22B2 Beta	2679	
EC-GNP	CASA C-1.131L Jungmann	2135	E.3B-509
EC-GNS	Cessna 172N Skyhawk	17273683	N4843J
EC-GNV	Reims/Cessna F172N	F17201925	F-GCHQ
	(Wfu, stored 10.13)		
EC-GNX	Ultramagic N-210 HAFB	210/05	
EC-GOD	Bell UH-1H (205)	4787	N92820, 65-09743
	(W/o 28.7.04)		
EC-GOF	Bell UH-1H (205)	5580	N15UH, 66-01097
	(Crashed 4.8.00)		
EC-GOI	Eipper Quicksilver MX-II	5008	
EC-GOL	Cameron C-80 Concept HAFB	3563	
EC-GOP	Bell 412HP	36031	N4603T
EC-GOQ	Air Création Safari GT-BI / Fun 18	195046	EC-CA8
EC-GOS	Air Tractor AT-802	802-0042	N5005M
	(W/o 30.5.06)		
EC-GOV	Cessna 560 Citation Ultra	560-0419	N5233J
EC-GOX	Schleicher ASW 20	20134	3A-MAJ, D-3325
EC-GOY	Beech C90 King Air	LJ-527	N55SG, N55SQ, N55SC
EC-GPA	Bell 412HP	36071	N7238Y, OE-XPR, N194SP, OE-XPP, D-HHQQ, N2084D
EC-GPE	Swearingen SA.226TC Metro II	TC-273	OY-JER, N5472M
EC-GPF	Reims/Cessna F337G Skymaster	F33700059	D-IOMS, (N1877M)
	(Reims-assembled 337G with US c/n 33701477)		
EC-GPG	Ultramagic S-90 HAFB	90/25	
EC-GPH	Beech E55 Baron	TE-1188	N38287
EC-GPL	PZL PW-5 Smyk	17.05.004	
EC-GPQ	Cessna 337G Skymaster	33701815	N617L, N76L, N1323L
EC-GPR	Cessna R172K Hawk XP	R1722544	N736HR
EC-GPS	Fairchild Swearingen SA-227AC Metro III	AC-722	N439MA
EC-GPT	Ultramagic M-65C HAFB	65/65	
EC-GPU	Ultramagic M-65C HAFB	65/66	
EC-GPV	Cameron C-80 Concept HAFB	4176	
EC-GPY	Piper PA-32R-301 Saratoga	32R-8513012	HB-PIO, N81708
EC-GPZ-AJ	PZL PW-5 Smyk	17.07.023	
EC-GQA	Embraer EMB.120 Brasilia	120027	EC-GMT, N14033, LN-KOD, PT-SIW
EC-GQB	Cessna 205	205-0277	OO-SPI, OE-DHW, N8277Z
	(Dam. 22.3.14)		
EC-GQC	Piper PA-28R-200 Cherokee Arrow B	28R-7135011	C9-NPV, ZS-NBG, (ZS-MXS), N2106T, XB-POH
	(W/o 18.8.99)		
EC-GQD	Cessna 150F	15061943	N8643S
EC-GQE	Piper J-3C-65 Cub	10780	G-AKAA, 43-29489
EC-GQF	Aérospatiale/Alenia ATR-72-202	489	F-WWLJ
EC-GQG	McDonnell-Douglas DC-9-83	49577	EC-FSY, EC-463, EC-EHT, EC-147
EC-GQI	B&F Funk FK-9 Mk.IV	002-190	EC-49, EC-049, D-MAAH
	(Originally c/n 09-04-252)		
EC-GQJ	LET L-23 Super Blanik	917818	
EC-GQL	DHC-4 Caribou	258	T.9-1
	(Wfu, stored)		
EC-GQM	DHC-4 Caribou	289	T.9-11
	(Wfu, stored)		
EC-GQN	DHC-4 Caribou	290	T.9-12
	(Wfu, stored)		
EC-GQQ	Reims/Cessna F177RG Cardinal RG	F177RG0151	G-BFAC, N177AB, G-BFAC, D-EDIS
EC-GQR	Ultramagic S-105 HAFB	105/44	
EC-GQY	Ultramagic M-77 HAFB	77/137	
EC-GRB	CASA C-1.131E Jungmann	unkn	E.3B-415
EC-GRC	Piper PA-36-375 Brave	36-7802047	N3903E
EC-GRD	Ultramagic M-160 HAFB	160/09	
EC-GRH	Airbus A320-211	146	EC-FBR, EC-578, F-WWDM
EC-GRQ	Ultramagic M-105 HAFB	105/45	
EC-GRR	Cessna R172K Hawk XP	R1722270	N4077V
EC-GRS	Ultramagic F-14 Beer Bottle SS HAFB	F14/01	
EC-GRT	Reims/Cessna F172P	F17202230	HB-CID
EC-GRU	Aérospatiale/Alenia ATR-72-202	493	F-WWLN
EC-GRV	Ultramagic V-77 HAFB	77/136	
EC-GSA	Colt 77A HAFB	4214	
EC-GSB	PZL PW-5 Smyk	17.09.020	
EC-GSC	Cedimex Rans S-6ES-582 Coyote II	S-6A-118	
EC-GSK	Bell 412	33092	SE-HVL, N3205S, 5N-AQS
	(Crashed 12.3.10)		
EC-GSN	Cameron C-60 Concept HAFB	3640	
EC-GSO	Bell UH-1H (205)	5466	N1217A, 66-00983
	(Open storage 2.07)		
EC-GSP	Bell UH-1H (205)	8853	N1206P, 66-16659
EC-GSR-H	Schempp-Hirth Standard Cirrus	15	D-0454
EC-GSS	Cessna A188B	18802700T	PH-YTA, N4966Q

Registration	Type	C/n	Previous identities
EC-GST	Dynali Chickinox Kot-Kot	2797-E1W	
EC-GSV	Schleicher ASW 17	17013	OO-ZXF, D-2112
EC-GTF	Reims/Cessna F172M	F17200908	OH-CFZ, SE-FZC
EC-GTH	Grob G 109	6038	PH-789, OE- . . ., PH-789, HB-2058, D-KGRO
EC-GTL	Ultramagic H-77 HAFB	77/139	
EC-GTN	Ultramagic N-210 HAFB	210/06	
EC-GTP-Q5	Schleicher ASW 19B	19331	HB-1562
EC-GTQ	Ultramagic H-65 HAFB	65/71	
EC-GTS	Cessna 500 Citation I	500-0037	N407SC, N109AL, SE-DPL, N109AL, N7CC
EC-GTT	Cedimex Rans S-12XL-503 Airaile	S-12-198	
EC-GTU	Colt 77A HAFB	4295	
EC-GTX	SOCATA TB-10 Tobago	886	SE-KBI
EC-GTY	PZL PW-5 Smyk	17.09.010	
EC-GTZ	PZL PW-5 Smyk	17.10.005	
EC-GUA	PZL PW-5 Smyk	17.10.006	
EC-GUB	PZL PW-5 Smyk	17.10.007	
EC-GUC	Robinson R22 Beta	2222	EC-GPO
EC-GUD	Beech 1900C-1	UC-156	N156YV
EC-GUE	MBB Bö.105C	S-188	EC-234, N3531T
EC-GUN	Centrair 101A Pégase	101A-0314	F-CGSZ
EC-GUP	Airbus A340-313X	217	F-WWJG
EC-GUQ	Airbus A340-313X	221	F-WWJA
EC-GUS	Fairchild Swearingen SA.227AC Metro III	AC-648	N2685L
EC-GUU	Ultramagic H-77 HAFB	77/142	
EC-GUV	Cessna 172M	17262078	N12567
(W/o 26.12.12)			
EC-GUZ	Aérospatiale AS.355F2 Ecureuil 2	5454	N26ET, PT-HXV, N84CC
EC-GVA	Cameron N-77 HAFB	4343	
EC-GVC	Cessna 172M	17263446	N5232R
EC-GVD	Cessna 172P Skyhawk	17275947	N66010
EC-GVE	Fairchild Swearingen SA.227AC Metro III	AC-669	N2702Z
(Noted wfu 1.16)			
EC-GVF	Robinson R22 Beta	1486	G-LOGS
EC-GVG	Robinson R44 Astro	0454	
EC-GVJ	Ultramagic S-105 HAFB	105/46	
EC-GVK	Ultramagic M-77 HAFB	77/146	
EC-GVL	Ultramagic M-77 HAFB	77/147	
EC-GVM	Ultramagic N-250 HAFB	250/07	
EC-GVN	Air Tractor AT-802	802-0065	N5059X
EC-GVQ	SOCATA TB-200 Tobago XL	1770	F-OHTJ
EC-GVR	Robinson R22 Beta	1489	HB-XYZ, N40233
(Dam 16.6.04)			
EC-GVT	Ultramagic V-65 HAFB	65/78	
EC-GVX	Reims/Cessna FTB337G Super Skymaster	FTB3370004	F-GGTO, FAP 3703, CS-AKK
EC-GVY	Cameron A-180 HAFB	4365	
EC-GXA	Bell 212	30812	LN-OQJ
EC-GXB	Schempp-Hirth Janus C	110	HB-1557
EC-GXC	Reims/Cessna FTB337G Super Skymaster	FTB3370013	CS-AUX, FAP 3712, CS-APM
EC-GXD	Cedimex Rans S-12 Airaile	S-12-187	
EC-GXJ	Fairchild Swearingen SA.226TC Metro II	TC-374	OY-AUO, D-IAEF, OY-AUO, SE-IKP, LN-SAP, OY-AUO, N10104
EC-GXK	Ultramagic S-90 HAFB	90/26	
EC-GXL	Ultramagic V-77 HAFB	77/149	
EC-GXM	Ultramagic V-77 HAFB	77/150	
EC-GXO	Cedimex Rans S-6ES-503 Coyote II	S-6A-121	
EC-GXP	Fairchild 24R Argus	946	EC-AEN, OO-PET, HB708, 43-14982
(Dismantled)			
EC-GXS	Schempp-Hirth Discus CS	249CS	
(Damaged 15.3.08)			
EC-GXU	McDonnell-Douglas DC-9-83	49622	EC-FTT, EC-485, EC-FNU, EC-206, EC-EJZ, EC-382, EC-EJZ, EC-179
EC-GXV	Piper PA-28-140 Cherokee	28-20004	D-ELVU, N6004W
EC-GYA	SOCATA Rallye 180T	2774	F-GARS, F-ODEI
EC-GYC	SOCATA TB-200 Tobago XL	1811	F-GRBQ
EC-GYD	Piper PA-31P Pressurized Navajo	31P-7300123	N888PD, (N831SF), N888PD, N7650L
(W/o 1.9.04)			
EC-GYG	Ultramagic S-160 HAFB	160/20	
EC-GYH	Ultramagic S-105 HAFB	105/48	
EC-GYI	Canadair CL.600-2B19 Regional Jet 200ER	7249	C-GDDM, C-FMMQ
EC-GYJ	Thunder AX7-77 SI HAFB	4451	
EC-GYL	Fokker F.27 Friendship 500	10381	G-BVOM, PH-FND, PT-LZN, F-BPNH, PH-FND
(Wfu)			
EC-GYM	Fokker F.27 Friendship 500	10427	G-BVRN, PH-FPB, HL5211, (HL5207), PH-FPB
(Wfu)			
EC-GYN	Ultramagic M-90 HAFB	90/27	
EC-GYQ	Cessna T188C	18803490T	(N2637J)
EC-GYS	Road Air Flamingo	030	
EC-GYT	Eipper Quicksilver MX-II Sprint	209	
EC-GYU	Cessna 337E Super Skymaster	33701203	N86480
EC-GYX	Air Tractor AT-401	401-1068	
EC-GYY	Piper PA-36-300 Pawnee Brave	36-7460031	TG-LAJ
(W/o 7.7.05)			
EC-GZA	Canadair CL.600-2B19 Regional Jet 200ER	7252	C-GDDO
EC-GZB-ZB	Grob G 104 Speed Astir IIB	4044	OO-ZFY, D-3836
EC-GZC	Beech 65-B80 Queen Air	LD-228	G-WJPN, N197MC, N34LT, N6876Q, YV-TANK, N6876Q
EC-GZF	Reims/Cessna F150G	F150-0156	OE-AVS
EC-GZG	Beech 1900C	UC-161	N55635
EC-GZJ	Aerojaen/Fournier RF-5-AJ1 Serrania	E-011	
EC-GZK	Ultramagic S-130 HAFB	130/15	
EC-GZM	Ultramagic M-56 HAFB	56/14	
EC-GZN	Hispano HA.220D Super Saeta	22/103	A.10C-98, C.10C-98
EC-GZO	Air Tractor AT-802	802-0071	N5166B
EC-GZQ	Cedimex Rans S-12XL-503 Airaile	S-12-200	
EC-GZR	Ultramagic H-77 HAFB	77/156	
EC-GZS	Ultramagic V-77 HAFB	77/154	
EC-GZT	Ultramagic M-90 HAFB	90/28	
EC-GZV	Ultramagic N-210 HAFB	210/09	
EC-GZX	Ultramagic V-77 HAFB	77/56	
EC-HAK	Embraer EMB.120ER Brasilia	120008	N212AS, PT-SIC
EC-HAM	Comper CLA.7 Swift	S.32/5	G-ABUU
(Painted as EC-AAT)			
EC-HAP	CASA C.212-400 Aviocar	465	EC-011
EC-HAS	Cessna 172M	17262738	N13417
(Cr 18.4.06)			
EC-HAT	Cessna 172N Skyhawk	17269055	N81709, C-GYWU, (N734RM)
EC-HAY	Ultramagic N-300 HAFB	300/01	
EC-HBA	Ultramagic F-19 Bottle SS HAFB	F19/01	
EC-HBB	Ultramagic F-19 Bottle SS HAFB	F19/02	
EC-HBD	Schleicher ASW 19	19266	OY-XTP, D-3588, OE-5206
EC-HBE	Ultramagic H-77 HAFB	77/158	
EC-HBI	SOCATA MS.893A Rallye Commodore 180	10795	F-BPGJ
EC-HBK	Ultramagic V-77 HAFB	77/155	
EC-HBS	Ultramagic H-65 HAFB	65/73	
EC-HBY	Aérospatiale/Alenia ATR-72-212A	578	F-WWEA
EC-HCA	Piper PA-34-200 Seneca	34-7250191	9A-BPW, RC-BPW, YU-BPW, D-GEAR, N4978T
EC-HCB	Rans S-12 Airaile	S-12-138	EC-BY9
(W/o 15.1.16)			
EC-HCC	Bell 206B	4505	C-GBUQ, (N82404)
EC-HCD	Ultramagic F-21 Cepsa SS HAFB	F21/01	
EC-HCF	Embraer EMB.120RT Brasilia	120007	N211AS, PT-SIB
EC-HCH	Fairchild Swearingen SA.227AC Metro III	AC-658B	N2692P
EC-HCI	Grob G 102 Astir CS77	1708	D-3311
EC-HCJ	SOCATA TB-10 Tobago	245	F-GEFL, 6V-AFG, F-OBLK
EC-HCS	Reims FR172H Rocket	FR17200320	D-EEXP
EC-HCU	Fairchild Swearingen SA.226TC Metro II	TC-390	N19WP, C-FBWY, N244AM, N1012B (Dam)
EC-HCV	Piper PA-34-200 Seneca	34-7350268	D-GMWU, N55991
EC-HDA	Cameron N-77 HAFB	4536	
EC-HDB	Cameron C-60 Concept HAFB	4550	
EC-HDC	Cameron N-77 HAFB	4560	
EC-HDI	Grob G 102 Astir CS	1002	D-8680
EC-HDS	Boeing 757-256	26252	
EC-HDX	Ultramagic M-65 HAFB	65/88	
(Now reported current as JA-A1196)			
EC-HDZ	Schleicher ASW 15B	15215	D-0940
EC-HEB	Ultramagic H-77 HAFB	77/132	
EC-HEC	Ultramagic M-90 HAFB	90/32	
EC-HED	Ultramagic H-77 HAFB	77/165	
EC-HEE	Aérospatiale AS.355N Ecureuil 2	5645	F-OHVD
EC-HEF	Scheibe SF 28A Tandem-Falke	5768	D-KACU(2)
EC-HEI	Aérospatiale/Alenia ATR-72-212A	570	F-WWEG
EC-HEJ	Aérospatiale/Alenia ATR-72-212A	565	F-WWEE
EC-HEK	Canadair CL.600-2B19 Regional Jet 200ER	7320	C-GFCN, C-FMLQ
EC-HEL	Air Tractor AT-802	802-0068	N5066S
(W/o 28.8.05)			
EC-HEM	Cameron C-80 Concept HAFB	4535	
EC-HEN	Cameron C-60 Concept HAFB	4502	
EC-HEO	Ultramagic V-77 HAFB	77/144	
EC-HEP	Cameron C-80 Concept HAFB	4537	
EC-HEQ	Cessna 337 Super Skymaster	33700239	G-ATID, N6239F
(Believed w/o 14.4.04)			
EC-HER	Grob G 102 Astir CS	1291	D-7377
EC-HET	Canadair CL.215 1A-10	1034	I-SISB, UD.13-6
EC-HEU	Canadair CL.215 1A-10	1038	I-SISC, UD.13-10
EC-HEY	Cameron C-60 Concept HAFB	4355	
(Also quoted as EC-HEY (2) with c/n 4904 - but see EC-HTN)			
EC-HFC (2)	SOCATA MS.893A Rallye Commodore 180	12634	D-EFGN
(Dam 11.7.03)			
EC-HFF	Cessna 182M	18259371	N70805
EC-HFG	Ultramagic M-77 HAFB	77/161	
EC-HFH	Ultramagic S-130 HAFB	130/20	
EC-HFI	Ultramagic S-105 HAFB	105/54	
EC-HFJ	Air Tractor AT-402A	402A-1056	N5020A
EC-HFK	Embraer EMB.120RT Brasilia	120063	N7215U, C-FZWF, LN-KOE, PT-SKG
EC-HFL	Scheibe Bergfalke II-55	0209	D-1907
EC-HFN	Ultramagic M-77 HAFB	77/99	
EC-HFO	Ultramagic M-77 HAFB	77/166	
EC-HFP	McDonnell-Douglas DC-9-82	53148	HL7548, HL7204
(W/o 20.8.08)			
EC-HFU	Ultramagic S-130 HAFB	130/19	
EC-HGF	Reims/Cessna F172M	F17201404	D-ELJB
EC-HGG	Reims/Cessna F172N	F17201560	D-EMDU (2)
EC-HGI	Cessna 550 Citation II	550-0596	D-CAWA, N96TD, (N13026)
EC-HGL	Sukhoi SU-31	04-02	RA-0402
(Damaged)			
EC-HGM	Ultramagic M-77 HAFB	77/105	
EC-HGN	Ultramagic M-77 HAFB	77/169	
EC-HGQ	Boeing 737-85P	28386	N1786B
EC-HGR	Airbus A319-111	1154	D-AVYY
EC-HGV	Airbus A340-313X	329	F-WWJP
EC-HGZ	Airbus A320-214	1208	F-WWIM
EC-HHA	Airbus A320-214	1221	F-WWBF
EC-HHE	Ultramagic N-180 HAFB	180/16	
EC-HHI	Canadair CL.600-2B19 Regional Jet 200ER	7343	C-GFKQ
EC-HHJ	Reims/Cessna FR172H	FR1720316	D-EEXO
EC-HHL	Ultramagic S-90 HAFB	90/33	
EC-HHQ	Agusta A.109E Power	11058	
EC-HHT	Eurocopter EC.120B Colibri	1060	
EC-HHV	Canadair CL.600-2B19 Regional Jet 200ER	7350	C-GFKR
EC-HHX	Cessna 172RG Cutlass RG	172RG0006	N4631R
(Damaged 4.9.04)			
EC-HHY	Cessna 172RG Cutlass RG	172RG0393	N4827V
EC-HHZ	Aérospatiale SN.601 Corvette	15	F-GNAF, D6-ECB, F-GEQF, N17AJ, SE-DEN, F-GDUB, OO-MRE, OO-MRA, SE-DEN, F-WIFA
EC-HIB	Cessna 172N Skyhawk	17270400	D-EFSB(2), N739AY
EC-HIC	Reims/Cessna F172H	F17200721	D-ECHC
EC-HID	Cessna 172N Skyhawk	17273303	D-EBER(3), N4677G
EC-HII	Piper PA-28-180 Cherokee D	28-5389	CS-ADX, N7972N
(Stored 10.13)			
EC-HIJ	Reims/Cessna F172N	F17201827	D-EIYG
EC-HIK	Cessna 172N Skyhawk	17268670	N104ES, N733ZC
EC-HIL	Eurocopter EC.120B Colibri	1075	
EC-HIN	Cessna 525 CitationJet	525-0197	N525KH, N5151S
EC-HIY	Reims/Cessna F172P	F17202098	D-EIKK, (D-ELNU)
EC-HJA	Reims/Cessna F172H	F17200690	D-EBJK(2), HB-CYB
EC-HJC	Swearingen SA.226TC Metro II	TC-318	OY-JEO, N5476M
EC-HJF	Aérospatiale AS.355N Ecureuil 2	5660	
EC-HJI	Aérospatiale/Alenia ATR-72-512	562	F-WWLZ
EC-HJK	Road Air Flamingo	041	
EC-HJM	SOCATA TB-20 Trinidad	412	SE-IZV, N141SW, F-GDGK
EC-HJN	Piper PA-36-285 Pawnee Brave	36-7560099	N9984P
(Cr. 8.7.03)			
EC-HJR	Ultramagic M-90 HAFB	90/36	
EC-HJS	Ultramagic S-105 HAFB	105/56	
EC-HJT	Ultramagic H-77 HAFB	77/168	
EC-HJX	Piper PA-28-151 Cherokee Warrior	28-7515332	N33366
(Wfu)			
EC-HJY	Glasflügel H201B Standard Libelle	523	PH-469
(W/o 23.8.14)			
EC-HKB	Grob G 102 Astir CS Jeans	2032	D-3878
EC-HKC	Piper PA-28 Cherokee 140	28-7225484	F-BTYE
(Stored 10.13)			
EC-HKD	Piper PA-28 Cherokee 140	28-7325275	F-BUIH
(Stored 10.13)			

EC-HKE	Cessna 150L	15074858	N10432
	(W/o 2.5.04)		
EC-HKF	Ultramagic N-250 HAFB	250/10	
EC-HKO	Airbus A319-111	1362	D-AVWJ
EC HKT	Air Tractor AT-802	802-0080	N90115
EC-HKU	Cessna 414	414-0038	N43ML, D-IAML, OE-FIR, N8138Q
EC-HLA	Airbus A310-324	489	OE-LAA, F-WWCK
EC-HLE	Piper PA-28R-200 Cherokee Arrow II	28R-7235051	N4439T
EC-HLG	Grob G 102 Astir CS	1250	D-4256
EC-HLH	Ultramagic H-77 HAFB	77/172	
EC-HLJ	Ultramagic S-105 HAFB	105/62	
EC-HLK	Piper PA-18-150 Super Cub	18-5388	D-EODA, ALAT, N10F
EC-HLL	Schleicher K 7 Rhönadler	7003	HB-716
EC-HLO	Piper PA-28-140 Cherokee	28-20032	N6032W, (N141DC), (N140HY), N6032W
EC-HLQ	Piper PA-34-200T Seneca II	34-7670336	N4387F
EC-HLS	Ultramagic S-90 HAFB	90/39	
EC-HLU	Eurocopter EC.120B Colibri	1106	F-WQDQ
EC-HLV	Piper PA-28R-200 Cherokee Arrow II	28R-7435019	N794AM, C-GTOY, N111RW, N56620
EC-HLY	Glaser-Dirks DG-400	4-21	D-KOTZ
EC-HLZ	Road Air Flamingo	039	
EC-HMA	Beech C90 King Air	LJ-577	N57KA
EC-HMB	Robin DR.400/180 Régent	1094	F-BXVG
EC-HMD	Air Tractor AT-802	802-0088	N9049K
EC-HMG	Robin R.2120	350	
EC-HMH	Piper PA-28-161 Cadet	2841345	D-EJLD, N92155, N623FT, (F-GJOT), (F-GIEU)
EC-HML	Beech 65-88 Queen Air	LP-2	N88338
EC-HMM	Piper PA-28-181 Cherokee Archer II	28-7890428	D-EMFK, N9566N
EC-HMN	Ultramagic M-65 HAFB	65/93	
EC-HMP	Cessna 172M	17265188	N64356
EC-HMQ	Reims/Cessna F172N	F17201709	F-GBFS
EC-HMY	Embraer EMB.120RT Brasilia	120009	N214AS, PT-SID
EC-HMZ	Air Tractor AT-802	802-0095	N9087Y
EC-HNF	Piper PA-32R-300 Lance	32R-7680047	D-ELDH, N7538C
EC-HNI	Ultramagic S-90 HAFB	90/37	
EC-HNK	Air Tractor AT-802	802-0097	N9094Z
	(W/o 15.8.06)		
EC-HNL	Cameron N-77 HAFB	4847	
EC-HNM	Cessna 340	340-0517	N1712G
EC-HNN	Piper PA-28R-180 Cherokee Arrow	28R-30184	D-EFMF(2), N3861T
EC-HNP	Reims/Cessna F177RG Cardinal RG	F177RG0131	D-EFMW
EC-HNQ	Ultramagic H-77 HAFB	77/171	
EC-HNR	Ultramagic S-90 HAFB	90/43	
EC-HNV	SOCATA MS.893E Rallye 180GT	12523	D-EHLV, F-BVNP
EC-HNX	SOCATA MS.893E Rallye 180GT	12682	D-EBWD, F-ODDJ
EC-HOB	Dassault Falcon 900EX	43	F-WQBK, F-GSDP, F-WWFE
EC-HOC	Cessna F172G	F172-0296	D-ENSE
EC-HOD	Reims/Cessna F172M	F17201016	D-EJXB
EC-HOE	Piper PA-18-150 Super Cub	18-6629	D-EJEP, N9365D
EC-HOG	Reims/Cessna FTB337G Super Skymaster	FTB3370028	CS-DBV, FAP 3727, CS-ABL
EC-HOJ	Robinson R44 Astro	0490	G-FLYZ
EC-HOK	Piper PA-34-200 Seneca	34-7350320	F-BUTT, F-ETAP
	(Stored 10.13)		
EC-HOL	Piper PA-34-220T Seneca	34-8233172	N1982J, D-GIBI, N8245J, N9541N, N8241T
	(Cr 15.12.06)		
EC-HOM	Piper PA-28-161 Cadet	2841305	D-EJTK, N9262N, N9206B
EC-HON	Bell 206B Jet Ranger II	2201	EC-GEH, EC-972, VH-HJG, N995KP, N2276K, N77AH
EC-HOP	Cessna 172N Skyhawk	17272917	D-EGLY(2), N7370D
EC-HOR	Air Tractor AT-802	802-0098	N9107X
EC-HOS	Ultramagic M-105 HAFB	105/69	
EC-HOT	Cessna 172P Skyhawk	17274044	F-GGBU, N5284K
	(W/o 3.6.07)		
EC-HOU	Robinson R22 Beta	2077	F-GMPE
EC-HOY	Bell 212	32225	4X-BCN, 4X-BCJ, IDFAF 069
	(Damaged 7.7.06)		
EC-HOZ	Piper PA-34-200T Seneca II	34-7570092	N33127
EC-HPA	Robinson R22B2 Beta	3100	
EC-HPD	Sukhoi SU-26	06-02	HB-MST, RA-0602
EC-HPE	Air Création GTE-582S / XP	00001/SF	
EC-HPF	Cameron N-77 HAFB	4888	
EC-HPG	Ultramagic N-250 HAFB	250/09	
EC-HPH	Cessna 172N Skyhawk	17270281	N738SN
	(W/o 25.1.03)		
EC-HPI	Cameron N-77 HAFB	4738	
EC-HPL	Ultramagic S-160 HAFB	160/22	
EC-HPN	Piper PA-28-151 Cherokee Warrior	28-7415276	N41574
EC-HPQ	Cessna 500 Citation	500-0157	EC-HFY, CS-DCA, N190AB, PH-CTD
EC-HPR	Canadair CL.600-2B19 Regional Jet 200ER	7430	C-GHDM, C-FMMW
EC-HPS	SOCATA MS.893A Rallye Commodore 180	11840	D-ELLR
EC-HPT	SOCATA MS.893E Rallye 180GT	12275	F-BUNA, (D-EKHL)
EC-HPY	SOCATA TB-20 Trinidad	346	F-GDNH
EC-HPZ	SOCATA TB-9 Tampico	1387	F-GLFD
EC-HQB	SOCATA MS.893E Rallye 180GT	12233	F-BUGM
EC-HQC	SOCATA MS.893A Rallye Commodore 180	11052	F-BRKZ
	(Originally built as MS.894A Minerva 220)		
EC-HQD	Robin R.2112 Alpha	130	
EC-HQE	Robin R.2100A	126	F-GAVS
EC-HQI	Airbus A320-214	1396	F-WWIX
EC-HQJ	Airbus A320-214	1430	F-WWBR
EC-HQL	Airbus A320-214	1461	F-WWDD
EC-HQO	Cessna 310Q	310Q0286	N7786Q
	(Wfu, noted 1.15 Cuatro Vientos)		
EC-HQP	Reims/Cessna F172M	F17200978	D-EGBF
EC-HQQ	Reims/Cessna F172N	F17201970	D-EDOV
EC-HQR	Cessna 172N Skyhawk	17269265	N737AH
	(W/o 14.7.06)		
EC-HQU	Cessna 172L	17260658	N19675
EC-HQY	Beech 95-B55 Baron	TC-1248	D-IHLW, OE-FNE
EC-HQZ	Airbus A321-231	1333	D-AVZB
EC-HRA	Robinson R22	0154	F-GJHB, G-BJBR, N9041N
EC-HRC	Lindstrand LBL-90A HAFB	718	
EC-HRE	Reims/Cessna F172N	F17201832	D-EGGA(2)
EC-HRF	SOCATA MS.893A Rallye Commodore 180	10948	F-BREG
EC-HRI	Grob G 103A Acro	3632-K-14	D-3074
EC-HRJ	Piper Aerostar 602P	62P-0897-8165027	D-IFFF, N602CP, D-IFFF, N6893X
	(Dam. 19.10.04)		
EC-HRK	SOCATATB-20 Trinidad	2024	F-OILP
EC-HRM	Ultramagic S-105 HAFB	105/68	
EC-HRR	Cessna TU206G Turbo Stationair 6	U20604283	N756QY
EC-HRS	Ultramagic H-77 HAFB	77/186	

EC-HRT	Rolladen-Schneider LS7-WL	7130	BGA3738/GCZ
EC-HRU	Ultramagic S-105 HAFB	105/74	
EC-HRV	Reims/Cessna F172M	F17201375	D-EEIF
EC-HRX	Cessna F172E	F172-0053	D-EFQU
EC-HRY	Reims/Cessna FR172E	FR1720051	F-BPES
EC-HRZ	Ultramagic S-105 HAFB	105/73	
EC-HSA	Eipper Quicksilver MX-II Sprint	145	unkn
EC-HSB	Robinson R22 Beta	1704	N4063T
EC-HSC	Cessna F172H	F172-0418	D-ECEQ(2)
EC-HSG	Cessna 172RG Cutlass RG	172RG0249	D-EJMH(2), N5128U
EC-HSI	Cessna 402C	402C0409	D-IGEO, N6785Z
EC-HSJ	SOCATATB-10 Tobago	49	F-GCEA
EC-HSK	Piper PA-28-140 Cherokee	28-23488	SE-FCB, N9944W
EC-HSM	Cessna 172N Skyhawk	17268875	N302DP, (N734HW)
EC-HSN	Robinson R44 Raven	0856	
	(W/o 18.1.08)		
EC-HSP	Piper PA-28RT-201 Arrow IV	28R-7918074	D-EEJN, HB-PDM, N3048J
EC-HSQ	Piper PA-34-220T Seneca III	34-8133006	OY-CRB, N8329B
EC-HSR	Piper PA-28-161 Warrior II	28-8016286	PH-KDM, OO-HLT, N81748
	(Wfu, noted 1.15 Cuatro Vientos)		
EC-HSS	Ultramagic H-77 HAFB	77/187	
EC-HST	Rockwell Commander 114	14299	D-EIXR, N4979W
EC-HSU	Ultramagic H-77 HAFB	77/185	
EC-HSX	Mooney M.20J Model 201	24-0947	HB-DGF, SE-GXS, (N3813H)
EC-HSY	Piper PA-34-200T Seneca II	34-8170043	N8297T, (D-G . . .), N8297T
	(Wfu, noted 1.15 Cuatro Vientos)		
EC-HSZ	Piper PA-28R-200 Cherokee Arrow	28R-7235020	HB-OKH, N4370T
EC-HTD	Airbus A320-214	1550	F-WWDC
EC-HTH	Glaser-Dirks DG-400	4-5	D-KEBM(2), (D-KGGJ)
EC-HTJ	Bell 212	30648	PK-HMC, PK-DBZ, N59580
EC-HTK	Cessna 337G Skymaster	33701622	N3371M, OB-1664, YV-234P, YV-TAMH, (N53436)
EC-HTM	Glaser-Dirks DG-100	59	OE-5071
EC-HTO	Piper PA-A-36-375 Pawnee Brave	AR36-8002016	CS-AVN, LV-ODG
EC-HTP	Cessna 421C Golden Eagle	421C0261	D-IAAF, SE-LCP, N421JK, 5Y-TRI, G-DEDE, N6148G
EC-HTQ	Robinson R44 Raven	0993	
EC-HTS	Embraer EMB.120RT Brasilia	120168	N168CA, PT-SQG
EC-HTU	CASA C.212-400MP Aviocar	470	
EC-HTY	Cessna 172RG Cutlass RG	172RG0407	
EC-HUA	Reims/Cessna F172M	F17200952	D-ECWS
EC-HUD	Cessna 172N Skyhawk	17268212	D-EKGR(2), SE-GUM, N733DJ
	(Noted wfu 1.16)		
EC-HUE	Piper PA-36-285 Pawnee Brave	36-7360055	N56542
EC-HUF	Ultramagic S-160 HAFB	160/21	
EC-HUH	Airbus A321-211	1021	EC-HAC, D-AVZQ
EC-HUI	Airbus A321-211	1027	EC-HAE, D-AVZL
EC-HUM	Schempp-Hirth Ventus B	74	D-9621, HB-1621
EC-HUN	Cessna 207A Skywagon	20700367	CS-AUL, D-EDOO, N1767U
	(Wfu)		
EC-HUO	Piper J-3C-90 Cub	12068	D-EMUX(2), OO-DAA, (OO-DAB), 44-79772
	(Damaged 6.6.09)		
	(f/n 11896) (Regd with c/n 11496 ex 43-30205 with which it exchanged identities)		
EC-HUQ	Piper PA-28-161 Warrior III	2842108	N5108B, N4147U, (G-BZMU), N4147U
EC-HUU	Piper PA-28R-200 Cherokee Arrow II	28R-7535317	N1540X
	(Dam. 3.2.15, Tenerife N)		
EC-HUV	Cessna 172N Skyhawk	17270374	N738ZV
	(Damaged 3.4.10)		
EC-HUX	Robinson R44 Astro	0376	D-HIKK
EC-HUY	Piper PA-34-200T Seneca II	34-7570013	D-GATB, N32273
EC-HVE	Ultramagic S-105 HAFB	105/77	
EC-HVL	Cameron N-77HAFB	10096	
EC-HVM	Ultramagic M-65C HAFB	65/99	
EC-HVN	Ultramagic M-65C HAFB	65/100	
EC-HVQ	Cessna 525 CitationJet CJ1	525-0436	N5141F
EC-HVS	SOCATA Rallye 235E-D	13154	D-EDGR
EC-HVV	Dassault Falcon 100	193	OH-AMB, N3BY, N259FJ, F-WZGY
EC-HXB	Cessna 172N Skyhawk	17267788	TC-DBP, N416CA, N75533
EC-HXC	Cessna 172N Skyhawk	17271807	TC-DBL, (D-EUCB), N5270E
	(Dam 5.8.05)		
EC-HXF	Reims/Cessna F172N	F17202001	D-EKNF, PH-AYK
EC-HXG	Air Tractor AT-802	802-0113	N91442
EC-HXH	Robinson R44 Astro	0448	CS-HEI, G-BXXM
EC-HXI	Eurocopter EC.120B Colibri	1193	
EC-HXN	Tecnam P.92S Echo	P-92-ES-005	
EC-HXP	Ultramagic N-210 HAFB	210/16	
EC-HXQ	Piper PA-28-181 Archer II	28-7990518	OY-RLN, G-BTKY, N2877D
EC-HXV	Bell 212	30647	FAP 74-614
EC-HXX	Bell 412SP	33062	N4014U, TG-WOO, H-126, TG-WOO
	(Dam 12.3.07)		
EC-HXZ	Bell 412	33106	PK-HMT
EC-HYA	Cessna 172N Skyhawk	17270143	D-EOYY, N738PZ
EC-HYB	Yakovlev Yak-55	870302	LY-EGJ, 15 (blue) , DOSAAF
EC-HYE	Reims/Cessna FR172H Rocket	FR1720231	D-ECKZ
EC-HYH	Ultramagic N-250 HAFB	250/03	
EC-HYI	Dassault Falcon 2000	150	F-WWVH
EC-HYN	Yakovlev Yak-52	822403	LY-ZRD, DOSAAF-75
EC-HYP	Piper PA-34-200T Seneca II	34-7770343	N84SA, D-GANY, D-IANY, N38821
EC-HYR	Eurocopter EC.120B Colibri	1238	
EC-HYS	Cessna 172K	17258446	D-EHTI(2), N5132G, (N84372)
	(Wfu, stored 10.13)		
EC-HYU	Sukhoi SU-26M	04-02	RA-44542
EC-HYX	Yakovlev Yak-52	822105	LY-JDJ
EC-HYY	North American T-6G Texan	182-736	F-AZAS, F-WZBN, F-AZAS, F-BMJP, Fr.AF, 51-15049
	(Rebuilt using parts from F-BMJO - flew as a Zero Replica in 1987 as F-WZBN with c/n SAM2-049. Now painted "15049/1")		
EC-HYZ	Cessna 172P Skyhawk	17276143	G-BYEN, PH-ILU, N97003
	(Wfu, stored 10.13)		
EC-HZB	Beech 95-B55 Baron	TC-1287	SE-EXL
EC-HZC	Tecnam P.92 Echo	P-92-E-011	
EC-HZD	Bell 412SP	33056	N4031F, N911FD, N2071Y
EC-HZF	Slepcev Storch SS Mk.4	084	VH-AYQ
EC-HZH	Fairchild Swearingen SA.227AC Metro III	AC-720	N2724S, XA-TGD, N2724S
EC-HZI	Cessna 172RG Cutlass RG	172RG0247	D-EJGL, N5120U
EC-HZJ	Beech 58 Baron	TH-461	CS-ART, D-IFBF
EC-HZL	Ultramagic N-180 HAFB	180/28	
EC-HZM	Piper PA-34-200 Seneca	34-7250169	F-GFJE, TU-TFU, N4838T
EC-HZP	Robinson R22B2 Beta	2598	EC-HDY, EC-GHR
EC-HZQ	Yakovlev Yak-52	822102	LY-ROS
EC-HZT	Ultramagic H-77 HAFB	77/133	
EC-HZV	Eurocopter EC.120B Colibri	1254	
EC-HZX	Eurocopter EC.120B Colibri	1255	

EC-IAC	Cedimex Rans S-6ES-582 Coyote II	S-61-129	EC-CR5
EC-IAI	Yakovlev Yak-52	833006	LY-CRI, DOSAAF-16
EC-IAJ	Yakovlev Yak-52	855705	LY-KGB, DOSAAF-55
EC-IAK	Yakovlev Yak-55	880510	LY-DER, DOSAAF-43
EC-IAL	Yakovlev Yak-52	833903	LY-RON, DOSAAF-147
EC-IAM	Yakovlev Yak-52	844504	LY-TRO, DOSAAF-79
EC-IAN	Yakovlev Yak-52 (Destroyed 16.8.13)	844310	LY-IBL, DOSAAF-55
EC-IAO	Yakovlev Yak-52	822808	LY-NCE, DOSAAF-140
EC-IAP	Yakovlev Yak-52	822109	LY-EDU, DOSAAF-36
EC-IAQ	Yakovlev Yak-52	877912	LY-IZP, DOSAAF-99
EC-IAR	Yakovlev Yak-52	822011	LY-CAT, DOSAAF-
EC-IAS	Yakovlev Yak-52	833312	LY-CEO, DOSAAF-66
EC-IAT	Cessna 182P	18262266	D-EGFY, N58737
EC-IAU	Ultramagic M-65C HAFB	65/108	
EC-IAX	Cessna 550 Citation II	550-0156	N205SC, N205SG, (N31F), N6567C, N98784
EC-IAY	Piper PA-28-180 Cherokee C	28-2765	D-EHOV, N8813J
EC-IBA	Cessna 500 Citation (W/o 2.8.12)	500-0178	HB-VKK, D-FBCK, D-IKFJ, N178CC
EC-IBC	Sud Avn SA.316B Alouette III	1324	HB-XQD, A-324
EC-IBE	Road Air Flamingo	021	
EC-IBF	Grob G 102 Astir CS	1155	D-7251
EC-IBL	Colt 77A HAFB	10160	
EC-IBP	Ultramagic M-77 HAFB	77/198	
EC-IBQ	Ultramagic S-105 HAFB	105/94	
EC-IBR	Ultramagic S-105 HAFB	105/96	
EC-IBU	Robinson R44 Raven	1141	
EC-IBV	Aérospatiale AS.350B3 Ecureuil	3489	F-WQPQ
EC-IBX	SNCASE SE.3130 Alouette II	1474	F-GPLU, ALAT
EC-IBY	Pilatus PC-6/B2-H4 Turbo Porter	815	HB-FKF, G-OAPA
EC-IBZ	Piper PA-25 Pawnee	25-66	N6059Z
EC-ICB	Piper PA-36-375 Pawnee Brave	36-7902005	TG-VEE, N3963E
EC-ICG	Piper Aerostar 602P	62P-0628-7962386	N286CB, VH-PHC, N8226J
EC-ICH	Piper PA-34-200T Seneca II	34-7970424	SE-LAV, OH-PBK, N2965Q
EC-ICI	SOCATA Rallye 100ST (Accident 9.3.03)	2295	F-BULM
EC-ICM	Yakovlev Yak-52	833401	
EC-ICO	CASA 1-131E Jungmann	2159	E.3B- . . .
EC-ICQ	Airbus A320-211	199	EC-FGU, EC-583, F-WWDI
EC-ICY	Cessna 172RG Cutlass RG	172RG1074	D-EOMZ, N9905B
EC-IDA	Boeing 737-85Q	32773	N73791
EC-IDD	Ultramagic V-65 HAFB	65/109	
EC-IDE	Ultramagic M-65 HAFB	65/110	
EC-IDG	Aérospatiale/Alenia ATR-42-300	003	F-WQNE(2), F-OICG, F-GEGE, F-WEGE, PH-HWJ, F-GEGC, F-WEGC
EC-IDI	SOCATA Rallye 180TS	3025	D-EGYT
EC-IDJ	Cessna 172N Skyhawk	17271569	D-EADS, N3492E
EC-IDL	Piper PA-28R-200 Cherokee Arrow B	28R-7135075	D-EMDP, N5071S
EC-IDM	Aérospatiale AS.355N Ecureuil 2	5698	F-WQPS
EC-IDN	Ultramagic M-77 HAFB	77/204	
EC-IDO	Ultramagic M-105 HAFB	105/98	
EC-IDP	Piper PA-28-180 Cherokee C	28-2768	SE-EPY, N11C
EC-IDR	Piper PA-28-161 Warrior	2816070	D-EUUL, N9144D
EC-IDS	Piper PA-34-200T Seneca II	34-7870429	G-BNEI, N3058K, VP-LBC, N9646N
EC-IDT	Boeing 737-86Q	30281	N73793
EC-IDV	Piper PA-28-161 Warrior	2816023	G-BNOL
EC-IDX	Piper PA-34-220T Seneca III	3433120	G-BOCW, N9612N
EC-IDY	Piper PA-34-220T Seneca III	3433122	G-BOCY, N9614N
EC-IDZ	Air Création Safari GT BI F18	192021	
EC-IEA	Tecnam P.92ES Echo	P-92-ES-017	
EC-IEC	Ultramagic M-65 HAFB	65/111	
EC-IED	Piper PA34-200 Seneca	34-7350123	G-BASX, N15781
EC-IEE	Ultramagic N-250 HAFB	250/19	
EC-IEF	Airbus A320-214	1655	F-WWDY
EC-IEG	Airbus A320-214	1674	F-WWIL
EC-IEH	Cessna 172N Skyhawk II	17273212	D-ESMW(2), N6380F
EC-IEK	Cessna 152	15284684	D-ESBC, N6344M
EC-IEO	Cessna 172M	17265632	D-EEPS(3), N172WM, N6893H
EC-IER	Piper PA-28R-180 Cherokee Arrow	28R-30458	SE-FDG, N4587J
EC-IES	Cameron N-77 HAFB	10256	
EC-IET	Cameron N-77 HAFB	10257	
EC-IEY	Piper PA-28-161 Warrior	2842137	N53436
EC-IFA	Bell 212 (Destroyed 20.12.13)	30689	XC-GUJ
EC-IFD	Reims/Cessna F150K	F15000619	D-ECDA(2)
EC-IFE	Robinson R44 Astro	0506	PH-ESP
EC-IFF	Piper PA-28-140 Cherokee Fliteliner (Marked 'Cherokee 150'. Wfu, noted 1.15 Cuatro Vientos)	28-7125194	D-EHGL, OE-DFB, N415FL
EC-IFG	Ultramagic M-77 HAFB	77/199	
EC-IFH	Cameron N/Z-77 HAFB	10237	
EC-IFI	Cameron N-65 HAFB	10238	
EC-IFJ	Hispano HA-220	22/107	A.10C-102, C.10C-102
EC-IFL	Vulcanair P.68C	412	
EC-IFM	Ultramagic M-77 HAFB	77/205	
EC-IFO	Ultramagic M-65 HAFB	65/116	
EC-IFP	Piper PA-28-161 Warrior II	28-8116103	D-ERAC, N83079
EC-IFQ	Eurocopter EC.120B Colibri	1296	F-WQQT, F-WQDK
EC-IFU	Eurocopter EC.135P2	0223	
EC-IFX	Partenavia P.68B	204	CS-AYQ, G-BNXN, CN-TCD, HB-LLV
EC-IGA	Ultramagic M-77 HAFB	77/200	
EC-IGB	Reims/Cessna F172N	F17201717	D-EOZU
EC-IGC	Piper PA-23-250 Aztec C	27-2700	N53JM, N5593Y
EC-IGD	SEEMS MS.893A Rallye Commodore 180	10478	F-BMVE
EC-IGF	Piper PA-28R-201 Cherokee Arrow	28R-7737124	D-ENTS(2), G-BPDN, N38959
EC-IGG	Robinson R22B2 Beta (Cr 16.7.16)	3288	N83754
EC-IGH	Robinson R44 Raven	1189	N70704
EC-IGI	Piper PA-34-200 Seneca	34-7450016	G-SSFC, G-BBXG, N56647
EC-IGJ	Reims/Cessna FRA150L Aerobat (Dbr 20.10.04. Dism for spares 8.05)	FRA1500232	PH-VBI, OO-KMM, (OO-HMM), (OO-WMM), N199ER, PH-VBI, OO-WAG, (PH-VBH)
EC-IGK	Airbus A321-211	1572	EC-HTF, D-AVZI
EC-IGL	Cessna 172N Skyhawk II	17267794	G-JVMD, G-BNTV, N75539
EC-IGM	Aérospatiale SA.365N3 Dauphin 2	6616	
EC-IGP	Bell 212	30915	N5009N, HK-3899X, N1074C
EC-IGQ	Bell 212	30936	N5010F
EC-IGR	Bell 212	30989	N1074C, HK-3900X, N1074C
EC-IGT	Cessna T337G Pressurized Skymaster	P3370157	CC-CEA, CC-PDN, N60S
EC-IGU	Ultramagic N-250 HAFB	250/21	
EC-IHC	Diamond DA 20-A1 Katana	10037	OE-ADM, N10UV, C-GKAI
EC-IHF	Reims/Cessna F172N	F17201704	D-EHGY(2)
EC-IHG	Antonov An-2TP	1G238-20	J5-GAH, SP-FBH(2), SP-FBR(1)
EC-IHJ	Air Tractor AT-802	802-0138	N8505Z
EC-IHK	Cessna 152	15281456	N64873
EC-IHL	Reims FR172J Rocket	FR17200460	F-BVBA
EC-IHM	Cessna F172H	F172-0634	D-EBUO
EC-IHP	American AA-1 Yankee	AA1-0385	D-ELXC, (N6185L)
EC-IHR	Robinson R22 Beta	0897	CS-HBM, G-RCGI
EC-IHS	Piper PA-34-200 Seneca	34-7250309	N1401T
EC-IHT	Piper PA-34-200 Seneca	34-7250163	N4877T
EC-IHU	Tecnam P.92JS Echo	016	
EC-IHY	Cessna 421C Golden Eagle	421C1033	N2008K, N929AK, N442MM, D-IRRR, N6794S
EC-IID	Piper PA-28R-180 Cherokee Arrow	28R-30881	D-EAEN, F-OCRF, TR-LOA, N7514J
EC-IIE	Robinson R44 Raven	1240	
EC-III	Boeing 737-86Q	30284	
EC-IIK	Piper PA-28-161 Warrior II	2816028	G-BNOR
EC-IIL	Piper PA-28-161 Warrior II	2816033	G-BNOW
EC-IIM	Piper PA-34-220T Seneca III	3433115	G-BOCV
EC-IIN	Mooney M.20J Model 201	24-0494	N201XJ, PH-SIN, N201XJ
EC-IIO	Ultramagic M-90 HAFB	90/53	
EC-IIQ	Piper PA-28-181 Archer II (Dam 30.11.07)	28-8490038	D-ELOE, N9570N, N4334L
EC-IIS	Diamond DA 20-A1 Katana	10116	N543ND, N543SS
EC-IIT	Diamond DA 20-A1 Katana	10118	N545ND, N545SS
EC-IIU	Cameron N-77 HAFB	10337	
EC-IIV	SOCATA TB-20 Trinidad	707	F-GFQD
EC-IIX	Robinson R44 Raven (Damaged 30.8.08)	0952	D-HALZ
EC-IIY	Piper PA-34-200T Seneca II	34-7670337	ZS-MNU, "ZS-MNC", N4458F
EC-IJB	Tecnam P.92JS Echo	020	
EC-IJC	Ultramagic H-77 HAFB	77/201	
EC-IJG	Vol 9/Best Off Sky Ranger	SKR 0104112	
EC-IJI	Piper PA28R-200 Arrow II	28R-7335013	D-EEPD, N15072
EC-IJN	Airbus A321-211	1836	D-AVZN
EC-IJQ	Road Air Flamingo	043	
EC-IJR	Agusta A.109E Power	11137	
EC-IJS	Canadair CL.600-2B19 Regional Jet 200ER	7706	C-GZKD
EC-IJV	Piper PA-28-161 Warrior II	28-7716104	D-EGFF, N9624N
EC-IJY	Cameron A-210 HAFB	10054	
EC-IJZ	Piper PA-34-200T Seneca II	34-8070049	ZS-LVZ, N8131F
EC-IKB	Eurocopter EC.135T2	0250	D-HTSF, D-HECK
EC-IKC	Yakovlev Yak-52	866511	
EC-IKD	Ultramagic H-77 HAFB	77/196	
EC-IKE	Ultramagic S-105 HAFB	105/89	
EC-IKG	Piper PA-28-161 Warrior II	2816031	G-BNOU
EC-IKH	Piper PA-28-161 Warrior II	2816046	G-BOKN, N9609N
EC-IKI	Piper PA-28-161 Warrior II	2816054	G-BOKU
EC-IKJ	Cessna 172S Skyhawk SP	172S8421	F-GPPL, LN-PWN, (SE-LPY), LN-PWD, N7257R
EC-IKL	Tecnam P.96 Golf	P-96-G-016	
EC-IKR	Eurocopter EC.135P2	0235	
EC-IKS	Aérospatiale AS.355N Ecureuil 2	5710	
EC-IKV	Eurocopter EC.130B4 Ecureuil	3753	
EC-IKX	Eurocopter EC.135P2	0222	G-79-07, D-HEC .
EC-ILA	Agusta A.109E Power	11028	F-GSMP
EC-ILC	Mainair Blade 503 (Major damage 1.12.16)	1057-1195-7-W855	EC-CH2
EC-ILD	Aérospatiale AS.350B2 Ecureuil (W/o 6.10.05)	2598	HB-XUU, F-WYME
EC-ILE	Beech B200 King Air	BB-1792	N5092K
EC-ILI	Scheibe SF 25C Falke	44133	OE-9147, D-KDDH
EC-ILJ	Cessna 421C Golden Eagle	421C0272	LZ-CCA, N6390G
EC-ILL	Reims/Cessna F182Q	F1820072	SE-GYI
EC-ILM	Cessna 421C Golden Eagle	421C0045	N89Q, OY-BZN, (D-IABI), OY-BZN, SE-INC, LN-VIH, N112GA, D-ICST, N9844B
EC-ILO	Airbus A321-211	1681	D-AVZW
EC-ILP	Airbus A321-211	1716	D-AVZT
EC-ILQ	Airbus A320-214	1736	F-WWDJ
EC-ILR	Airbus A320-214	1793	F-WWIM
EC-ILS	Airbus A320-214	1809	F-WWBC
EC-ILT	Reims/Cessna FT337GP Super Skymaster (Reims assembled P337G with US c/n P3370279)	FP3370021	I-BFIZ, G-BFIZ
EC-ILU	Cessna 172RG Cutlass RG	172RG0560	D-EDMS, PH-AXE, N5534V, (N5434K)
EC-ILV	Robinson R22B2 Beta	3411	
EC-ILY	Rolladen-Schneider LS3A	3205	F-CESG
EC-ILZ	Cameron A-210 HAFB	10076	
EC-IMC	Schleicher ASH 26E	26206	
EC-IMF	Cessna 550 Citation II	550-0443	D-CGAS, OY-CYT, N777FB, N777FE, N1220S
EC-IMG	Eipper Quicksilver MXL-Sport IIR	0073	EC-CB6
EC-IMI	Ultramagic M-65 HAFB	65/119	
EC-IML	Piper PA-28-180 Cherokee D	28-4838	SE-FDN
EC-IMM	Piper PA-28RT-201 Arrow IV	28R-7918242	F-GCTI, N2969V
EC-IMN	Ultramagic T-150 HAFB	150/01	
EC-IMO	Ultramagic M-77 HAFB	77/215	
EC-IMP	BA Swallow 2	475	G-AEVZ
EC-IMQ	Piper PA-28-161 Warrior II	2816026	G-BNOO
EC-IMR	Piper PA-28-161 Warrior II	2816045	G-BOKM
EC-IMS	Cessna 170A	19097	N9536A
EC-IMT	Piper PA-28RT-201 Arrow IV	28-7918165	LX-FLY, N2839K
EC-IMV	Partenavia P.68C	290	TF-VEJ, N714G, N4496M
EC-IMX	Embraer EMB.120 Brasilia	120158	P4-RAL, N312FV, N131AM, PT-SPW
EC-IMZ	Bell 407 (W/o 7.6.11)	53547	C-GLZA, (N2531Z)
EC-INC	Beech 76 Duchess	ME-382	N7WZ, G-DUCH, N38033
EC-INH	Air Tractor AT-802	802-0139	N8507V
EC-INI	Ultramagic N-210 HAFB	210/21	
EC-INK	de Havilland DH.60GIII Moth (Damaged 6.11)	5895	EC-ADE, EC-BAZ, 30-83, EM-O . ., G-ACXK
EC-INN	Bell 212	31146	SE-JLP, HL-9213, N5756W
EC-INO	Airbus A340-642	431	F-WWCI
EC-INR	Cameron N-77 HAFB	10392	
EC-INS	Gates Learjet 55B	55B-133	N810V, N700R, N55LF, N155LJ, N155PL
EC-INV	Aérospatiale/Alenia ATR-72-201	274	N274AT, F-WWLC
EC-INX	CASA C.212-400MP Aviocar	472	
EC-INY	Eurocopter EC.135T2	0275	
EC-IOA	Manuel Perez Rainbow	MPR 02-0001	
EC-IOB	Airbus A330-642	440	F-WWCL
EC-IOC	Robinson R22 Mariner	1718M	G-PIKE
EC-IOD	Partenavia P.68C	229	G-BIFZ
EC-IOE	Air Tractor AT-802 (Cr 15.6.04, repaired. W/o 9.1.11)	802-0149	N8509Q

Regn	Type	c/n	Previous identities
EC-IOF	Tecnam P.92ES Echo	P-92-ES-02	
EC-IOG	Reims/Cessna F172N	F17201523	D-EGQD
EC-IOI	Aérospatiale AS.350B3 Ecureuil (Code '80')	3640	
EC-IOK	Cessna 421B	421B0398	HB-LRL, N205PV, N203PV, (N41010)
EC-IOL	Air Tractor AT-301 (Dam.8.6.16)	301-0652	N600AB, C-GTSE
EC-IOP	Vulcanair P.68 Observer 2	424-24/OB2	
EC-IOS	Piper PA-28-161 Warrior II	2816029	G-BNOS
EC-IOT	Piper PA-28-161 Warrior II	2816052	G-BOKS
EC-IOX	Cessna 172P Skyhawk	17275025	OO-NZB, G-BNYW, N54655
EC-IOY	Cedimax Rans S-6ES-912	S6AV-0006	
EC-IPA	SOCATA MS.893A Rallye Commodore 180	10647	F-BNSG
EC-IPB	Piper PA-34-200 Seneca	34-7350116	D-GBFW, N15992
EC-IPC	Aérospatiale AS.350B3 Ecureuil	3710	
EC-IPE	Cameron Z-210 HAFB	10258	G-LGLG
EC-IPG	Vulcanair P.68 Observer 2 (W/o 23.6.09)	421-21/OB2	
EC-IPH	Tecnam P.92JS Echo	032	
EC-IPK	Diamond DA 20-A1 Katana	20129	G-BWFE
EC-IPL	Reims/Cessna FTB337G Super Skymaster (NTU. Stored Viver 1.16)	FTB3370020	FAP 3719
EC-IPM	Bell 412	33050	C-GJKT, TG-WOL, H-123, TG-WOL
EC-IPO	Cessna 421B Golden Eagle	421B0509	N630CP, EC-FLT, EC-955, N630CP, N69860
EC-IPP	Ultramagic H-31 HAFB	31/04	
EC-IPQ	Reims/Cessna F337G Skymaster (Reims-assembled 337G with US c/n 33701465)	F33700056	G-NYTE, G-BATH, N10631
EC-IPR	Tecnam P.92 Echo Super (W/o 3.9.06)	P-92-SP-014	
EC-IPU	Air Tractor AT-802	802-0150	N8509X
EC-IPY	Ultramagic M-77 HAFB	77/227	
EC-IPZ	Piper PA-31T2 Cheyenne IIXL	31T-8166056	D-ICGA, N550TL, N550T, N9165Y, (N715CA)
EC-IQB	Air Création Safari GT BI Fun 18	194040	
EC-IQC	Air Tractor AT-802A (Amphibian)	802A-0155	N8512Q
EC-IQD	Diamond DA 40-180 Star	40229	
EC-IQE	Diamond DA 40-180 Star (Cr 23.3.04)	40239	
EC-IQF	Ultramagic T-180 HAFB (Dam. 27.3.11)	180/39	
EC-IQJ	Ultramagic M-77 HAFB	77/229	
EC-IQK	Cedimax Rans S-12XL-582	S12AV-301	
EC-IQL	Piper PA-28-161 Warrior II	2816032	G-BNOV
EC-IQM	Piper PA-28-161 Warrior II	2816049	G-BOKO, N9610N
EC-IQN	Piper PA-28-161 Warrior II	2816050	G-BOKP, N9611N
EC-IQO	Piper PA-28-161 Warrior II	2816051	G-BOKR
EC-IQQ	Ultramagic T-180 HAFB	180/37	
EC-IQR	Airbus A340-642	460	F-WWCO
EC-IQS	SOCATA MS.893A Rallye Commodore 180	10687	F-BONG
EC-IQT	Ultramagic M-77 HAFB	77/70	
EC-IQU	Tecnam P.92S Echo	P-92-ES-032	
EC-IQV	Piper PA-28R-180 Cherokee Arrow	28R-30548	D-ENBG, N4654J
EC-IQX	Piper PA-46-350P Malibu Mirage (Ditched 30.4.07)	4622181	N9255H
EC-IQY	Cessna 182H Skylane	18256192	D-ECWI, N2092X
EC-IQZ	Eurocopter EC.135P2	0293	
EC-IRE	Diamond DA 20-A1 Katana	10307	G-BXTR, N607DA
EC-IRF	Ultramagic M-77 HAFB	77/235	
EC-IRH	Piper PA-28-200 Cherokee Arrow	28R-35089	D-EBIM(2), 9XR-BM, D-EBIM(2), N9380N
EC-IRJ	Piper PA-28-181 Archer II	28-8190218	D-EIGT, N8379Z
EC-IRK	Reims/Cessna F150G (Dam 18.7.05)	F150-0088	D-EKGB, OE-AVK
EC-IRL	Robinson R44 Raven II	10157	
EC-IRN	Ultramagic M-77 HAFB	77/239	
EC-IRO	Piper PA-28-181 Archer II	28-7690103	D-ECFC(2), N8124C
EC-IRP	Cessna 172N Skyhawk (W/o 28.6.08)	17271494	PH-GVE, N3296E
EC-IRS	Fairchild Swearingen SA-227BC Metro III	BC-786B	N61AJ, XA-SCS, N3200K
EC-IRV	Cessna 208B Grand Caravan	208B1038	N5174W
EC-IRX	Diamond DA 20-A1 Katana	10075	OE-VPZ, N520SS
EC-IRY	Tecnam P.92-ES Echo	P-92-ES-033	
EC-ISB	Aérospatiale AS.355N Ecureuil 2	5715	
EC-ISF	Cameron Z-210 HAFB	10286	G-CBKX
EC-ISG	Ultramagic M-65C HAFB	65/127	
EC-ISH	Pilatus PC-12/45	498	HB-FPG
EC-ISK	Lindstrand LBL-180A HAFB	824	G-CBNS
EC-ISM	Cessna 404 Titan	404-0614	5Y-LEA, 5Y-EAG, N31PG, (N2684Y)
EC-ISN	Boeing 737-86Q	30291	
EC-ISO	Tecnam P.92S Echo	P-92-ES-013	
EC-ISP	Cessna 501 Citation I/SP	501-0084	G-CITI, VP-CDM, VR-CDM, G-CITI, (N11JC), (N463CJ), N3160M
EC-ISQ	Cessna 560XL Citation Excel	560-5353	N5250E, N678QS
EC-ISR	SOCATA TB-20 Trinidad	325	D-EPUK, OO-RDL, (D-EEKX)
EC-IST	Schweizer S.269C	S-1850	N69A
EC-ISU	Tecnam P.96 Golf	P96-G-029	
EC-ISV	DHC-6 Twin Otter Series 200	205	OY-PAE, LQ-JMM, LV-JMM, LV-PMP
EC-ISX	Aérospatiale/Alenia ATR 42-300	242	N242AT, F-WWEW
EC-ISY	Boeing 757-256	26241	N26ND, EC-FXV, EC-617, EC-FUB, EC-422
EC-ISZ	Aérospatiale AS.355N Ecureuil 2	5723	
EC-ITA	Ultramagic M-77 HAFB	77/210	
EC-ITB	Robin HR.200/100 Club	66	OO-VSC
EC-ITC	Robinson R22B2 Beta	3508	N75297
EC-ITD	Robinson R44 Raven II (W/o 20.12.04)	10201	
EC-ITF	Kubicek BB-26 HAFB	252	OK-0252
EC-ITJ	Eurocopter EC.135T2	0306	
EC-ITK	Cameron DP-80 Hot Air Airship	2344	G-BTBR
EC-ITL	Ultramagic M-77 HAFB	77/230	
EC-ITM	Tecnam P.92 Echo Super	P.92-SP-017	
EC-ITN	Airbus A321-211	2115	D-AVXG
EC-ITO	SOCATA MS.892A Rallye Commodore 150	11707	F-BSKI
EC-ITP	Fairchild Swearingen SA.227BC Metro III (W/o 10.2.11)	BC-789B	XA-SES, N3003T
EC-ITR	Westland-Bell 47G-3B1	WA/514	G-BGMU, XT807
EC-ITT	Glaser-Dirks DG-200	2-56	I-ANNC
EC-ITV	Partenavia P.68C-TC	239-05/TC	SP-KWA, VH-TCU
EC-ITX	Cessna 172R Skyhawk	17280778	N9552F
EC-ITY	Cessna 172R Skyhawk	17280546	N23862, N4115W
EC-ITZ	Ultramagic T-180 HAFB	180/40	
EC-IUD	Cessna 172N Skyhawk	17270396	G-BOMT, N739AU
EC-IUF	Ultramagic M-65C HAFB	65/128	
EC-IUG	Glaser-Dirks DG-400	4-90	HB-2082, (PH-742)
EC-IUI	Reims/Cessna FTB337G Super Skymaster	FTB3370027	FAP 3726, CS-ABJ
EC-IUJ	Air Tractor AT-802A	802A-0154	C-GYZB, N51101
EC-IUK	Piper PA-28-161 Warrior II	2842178	N53665, N53662
EC-IUL	Piper PA-28-140 Cherokee D	28-7125045	D-EHFD, N1730T
EC-IUM	Robinson R22B2 Beta	2802	CS-HEF
EC-IUN	Eurocopter EC.135T2	0317	
EC-IUR	Cessna 150M	15076120	EC-HZK, N66555
EC-IUS	Agusta A.109E Power	11229	
EC-IUT	Flight Design CT-2K	03-06-01-AR	
EC-IUU	Tecnam P.92JS Echo	035	
EC-IUX	Beech B200 King Air	BB-1840	N816LD
EC-IUY	Ultramagic M-77 HAFB	77/241	
EC-IVA	Cameron C-70 Concept HAFB	10520	
EC-IVB	Cameron C-70 Concept HAFB	10526	
EC-IVC	Partenavia P.68B	160	N200VE, YV-1538P
EC-IVI	Piper PA-28-161 Warrior II	2842172	N53532, N9512N
EC-IVJ	Cessna 525 CitationJet CJ1	525-0429	N429PK
EC-IVK	Reims/Cessna F177RG Cardinal RG	F177RG0139	HZ-VIP, N31062
EC-IVN	Ultramagic T-180 HAFB	180/41	
EC-IVP	Aérospatiale/Alenia ATR-42-300	231	F-GKND
EC-IVS	Reims/Cessna F150L	F15000889	OO-WIE
EC-IVT	Robinson R44 Raven II (W/o 3.9.12)	10307	
EC-IVU	PZL M-18A Dromader	1Z018-18	N7015H
EC-IVX	Air Tractor AT-502B	502B-0349	N60762
EC-IVY	Grob G 102 Standard Astir II	5017S	D-8407, HB-1528
EC-IVZ	Piper PA-46-500TP Malibu Meridian	4697170	N3046P
EC-IXA	Grob G-103A Twin II Acro	3544-K-1	D-2913
EC-IXB	Kubicek BB-30 HAFB	295	OK-0295
EC-IXC	Kubicek BB-30 HAFB	296	OK-0296
EC-IXD	Airbus A321-211	2220	D-AVZR
EC-IXH	Aérospatiale AS.355F1 Ecureuil 2	5009	D-HFAI(2), N5774M, HC-BFC, N5774M
EC-IXI	Aérospatiale AS.355N Ecureuil 2	5725	
EC-IXJ	Air Tractor AT-401 (W/o 24.5.10)	401-0795	N4549B
EC-IXL	Fairchild Swearingen SA.227AC Metro III (Modifed and c/n amended to AC-689B, 9.06)	AC-689	D-COLC, N706C, N689NE, N2705F
EC-IXM	SOCATA MS.893A Rallye Commodore 180	11821	D-EOBI
EC-IXN	Ultramagic M-90 HAFB	90/64	
EC-IXP	Piper PA-31 Navajo C	31-7812095	SE-IAC
EC-IXQ	Reims/Cessna FTB337G Super Skymaster	FTB3370018	CS-DPB, FAP 3717, CS-AAT
EC-IXR	Reims/Cessna FTB337G Super Skymaster	FTB3370019	CS-DPC, FAP 3718, CS-AAV
EC-IXS	Piper PA-28-161 Warrior III	2842204	N53599
EC-IXT	Piper PA-28-161 Warrior III	2842205	N30910
EC-IXU	Bell 412	33037	N177EH, N177LG, N177EH, N412S, N412SA, XC-HAN, N413CH
EC-IXV	Bell 412	33068	N422EH
EC-IXX	Bell 412	33043	N419EH
EC-IXZ	Beech A36TC	EA-31	I-CINO, N817BK, N6695Z
EC-IYA	ICP Bingo	02-09-52-074	EC-014 ?
EC-IYD	Tecnam P.96 Golf	P96-G-032	
EC-IYF	Cessna 172R Skyhawk (Cr 18.4.06)	17280057	N375ES
EC-IYH	Aérospatiale/Alenia ATR-72-202	330	F-WQUI, SX-BAP, F-GKOH, F-WWLL
EC-IYK	Reims/Cessna F172M	F17201101	D-EDXN
EC-IYL	Air Tractor AT-401	401-0739	N89KC
EC-IYM	Air Tractor AT-401	401-0836	N1518V
EC-IYO	Bell 212	30946	C-GZMZ, B-7701, B-721
EC-IYP	Bell 212	30533	C-FZPX, PK-HCK, G-BGMI, EP-HCB, VR-BEE, N2916W
EC-IYU	Piper PA-28-161 Warrior II (Dbr 18.2.09)	2816044	G-BOKL
EC-IYV	Piper PA-34-220T Seneca III	3433113	G-BOCT
EC-IYX	Piper PA-34-220T Seneca III	3433121	G-BOCX, N9613N
EC-IYY	Piper PA-34-220T Seneca III (W/o 29.4.06)	3433155	G-BSOY, OY-CEU
EC-IZA	Ultramagic M-77 HAFB	77/252	
EC-IZC	Tecnam P.92 Echo	P-92-E-014	
EC-IZE	Eurocopter EC.135T2	0309	
EC-IZF	Kubicek BB-20GP HAFB	293	OK-0293
EC-IZH	Airbus A320-214	2225	F-WWID
EC-IZI	Ultramagic N-180 HAFB	180/43	
EC-IZJ	ICP Bingo	03-04-52-104	EC-DZ3
EC-IZN	Ultramagic M-105 HAFB	105/116	
EC-IZO	Aérospatiale/Alenia ATR-72-212A	711	F-WWEK
EC-IZR	Airbus A320-214	2242	F-WWDA
EC-IZS	Robinson R22B2 Beta	2979	D-HALA(2), PH-HVZ
EC-IZT	Vol 9/Best Off Sky Ranger	SKR0306347	
EC-IZU	Ultramagic M-105 HAFB	105/117	
EC-IZV	Piper PA-28-180 Cherokee Challenger	28-7305490	OY-SVD, SE-GDK
EC-IZX	Airbus A340-642	601	F-WWCS
EC-IZY	Airbus A340-642	604	F-WWCH
EC-IZZ	Ultramagic S-105 HAFB	105/108	
EC-JAA	DG Flugzeugbau DG-1000S	10-51S50	
EC-JAC	Air Tractor AT-802A	802A-0177	N8525Z
EC-JAD	Aérospatiale/Alenia ATR-42-300	321	F-GHPY, F-WWES
EC-JAF	Cessna U206G Stationair 6	U206-06011	I-PAVR, (D-EOMG), N4746Z
EC-JAG	Ted Smith Aerostar 601	61-0307-109	N26LL
EC-JAJ	SOCATA TB-9 Tampico	227	G-BJDT
EC-JAK	Kamov KA.32A11BC	9624/8811/11	
EC-JAL	Kamov KA.32A11BC	9625/8812/12	
EC-JAN	DG Flugzeugbau DG-500MB	5E213B12	HB-2365
EC-JAO	Ultramagic M-77 HAFB	77/245	
EC-JAP	Boeing 737-85P	33971	
EC-JAQ	Aérospatiale AS.350B Ecureuil	1352	F-GKCU, N300HS, XC-HEU, N1350N
EC-JAR	Bell 407	53370	N54LM, N60419, C-GLZQ
EC-JAU	Air Tractor AT-401	401-1149	
EC-JAX	Cessna 421C Golden Eagle (W/o 7.3.06)	421C0337	HB-LQT, F-GATY, (N37396)
EC-JAY	Air Tractor AT-401	401-1150	
EC-JAZ	Airbus A319-111	2264	D-AVWQ
EC-JBA	Airbus A340-642	606	F-WWCV
EC-JBB	Dassault Falcon 900	182	N168HT, F-WWFB
EC-JBC	Ultramagic T-180 HAFB	180/46	
EC-JBD	Embraer EMB.120ER Brasilia	120012	D-CAOB(2), N120AM, PT-SIG
EC-JBE	Embraer EMB.120RT Brasilia	120013	D-CAOA(2), N122AM, PT-SII
EC-JBF	Ultramagic M-65-C HAFB	65/138	EC-041
EC-JBG	Cessna 152	15280160	D-ENGN, N24225

EC-JBI	Aérospatiale/Alenia ATR-72-212A	713	F-WWEM
EC-JBJ	Boeing 737-85P	33972	
EC-JBK	Boeing 737-85P	33973	
EC-JBL	Boeing 737-85P	33974	
EC-JBM	Air Tractor AT-502B	502B-0687	N8520K
EC-JBN	Aérospatiale/Alenia ATR-42-300	218	F-GHPK, F-WWEC
EC-JBO	Tecnam P.92 Echo	P-92-E-006	EC-DM7
	(Dam 1.10.05) (Also believed to have Italian c/n 258 ex- D-MOHT)		
EC-JBP	Piper PA-18-150 Super Cub	18-8309001	N45540, IDFAF 117
EC-JBQ	Ultramagic M-77 HAFB	77/255	
EC-JBR	Piper PA-28-161 Warrior II	2816053	G-BOKT
EC-JBS	Piper PA-34-220T Seneca III	3433089	G-BOCP
EC-JBU	Bell 407	53241	I-FREC, C-GBLC, (N42978)
EC-JBV	Bell 407	53613	C-FBXL, (N8061T)
EC-JBX	Aérospatiale/Alenia ATR-42-300	254	N255AE, N254AT, F-WWEJ
EC-JBY	Reims/Cessna F172M	F17200935	EC-ITG, D-ECUY
EC-JBZ	Reims/Cessna F172L	F17200896	EC-ITH, D-EGSB, F-BTUT
EC-JCB	Robinson R22B2 Beta	3672	
EC-JCC	Cessna 421C Golden Eagle	421C-0099	LN-BAU, OE-FCA, D-IACS, N578AC, D-IFLS, OE-FLS, N98800
EC-JCH	Ultramagic M-65 HAFB	65/130	
EC-JCI	Piper PA-28-161 Warrior II	28-8316044	PH-SVF, N4305D, N4293C
	(Major damage 9.9.16)		
EC-JCK	Cameron N-77 HAFB	10643	
EC-JCN	Flight Design CT-2K	04-03-04-AR	
EC-JCP	Robinson R22 Beta	2737	
	(Damaged 21.3.08)		
EC-JCS	Flight Design CT-2K	03-07-06-AR	
EC-JCT	Mooney M.20K Model 231	25-0827	N5763A
	(W/o 22.3.06)		
EC-JCU	Fairchild Swearingen SA.227AC Metro IV	AC-679B	N6UB, VH-UUC, N364AE
EC-JCV	Swearingen SA.226AT Merlin IVA	AT-038	SX-BGT, EC-FUX, EC-509, OO-JPN, N5FJ, SAAF:12, N5360M
EC-JCY	Airbus A340-642	617	F-WWCL
EC-JCZ	Airbus A340-642	619	F-WWCP
EC-JDA	Piper PA-34-220T Seneca III	3433114	G-BOCU
EC-JDB	Ultramagic V-77 HAFB	77/246	
EC-JDD	Piper PA-28-181 Archer II	28-8190164	D-ENCH(3), N8295H, N9518N
EC-JDE	SOCATA TB-9 Tampico	879	D-EANL(3)
EC-JDF	Bell 206B Jet Ranger	2800	CS-HEP, N27785
EC-JDG	Eurocopter EC.135T2	0354	
EC-JDI	Robin ATL	100	F-GFST
EC-JDJ	Air Tractor AT-802A	802A-0190	N85230
EC-JDL	Airbus A319-111	2365	D-AVYN
EC-JDM	Airbus A321-211	2357	D-AVZV
EC-JDP	Piper PA-28-161 Cherokee Warrior II	28-7816652	SE-IAL
EC-JDQ	Aérospatiale AS.365N3 Dauphin 2	6679	EC-IZQ, F-WWON
EC-JDR(2)	Airbus A321-211	2488	D-AVXD
EC-JDS	Ultramagic H-65 HAFB	65/139	
EC-JDY	Beech 1900C-1	UC-91	N91YV, S9-CAF, N91YV
EC-JDZ	SOCATA TB-9 Tampico	286	D-EORP, HB-EQO
EC-JEA	Aérospatiale AS.350B3 Ecureuil	3819	SE-JHX
EC-JEB	Ultramagic H-65 HAFB	65/123	
EC-JEC	Piper PA-18-150 Super Cub	18-5353	F-BSEB, ALAT, N10F
	(Damaged 28.8.11)		
EC-JEH	Aérospatiale/Alenia ATR-72-212A	716	F-WWET
EC-JEI	Airbus A319-111	2311	D-AVYG
EC-JEJ	Airbus A321-211	2381	D-AVZI
EC-JEK	Piper PA-28-151 Warrior	28-7515419	OY-TOZ
EC-JEL	SOCATA Rallye 180TS Galérien	3334	D-EFRM
EC-JEM	Ultramagic M-77 HAFB	77/257	
EC-JEO	Tecnam P.96 Golf	P96-G-036	
	(Dam 17.8.06)		
EC-JEQ	Schleicher ASK 21	21791	
EC-JER	Grob G 102 Astir CS	1293	D-7379
EC-JES	Sikorsky S-76C	760576	N576ML, EC-JES, N7107J
EC-JET	Sikorsky S-76C	760578	N578ML, EC-JET, N7105G
EC-JEU	Reims/Cessna F172F	F172-0092	D-EITZ, D-EMQU
EC-JEV	Aérospatiale/Alenia ATR-72-212A	717	
EC-JEY	Ultramagic S-90 HAFB	90/67	
EC-JEZ	Ultramagic H-42 HAFB	42/09	
EC-JFA	Schempp-Hirth Ventus b/16.6	153	OO-ZLC, D-2521
EC-JFC	Piper PA-34-220T Seneca III	3433111	G-BOCR
EC-JFE	Piper PA-28-181 Cherokee Archer II	28-7690148	SE-GNE, (OY-JAP), SE-GNE
EC-JFF	Airbus A320-214	2388	F-WWIH
EC-JFG	Airbus A320-214	2143	F-WWBV
EC-JFH	Airbus A320-214	2104	(EC-IQK), F-WWBE
EC-JFN	Airbus A320-214	2391	F-WWDB
EC-JFP	Agusta-Bell 206B Jet Ranger 2	8647	EC-FYA, I-DACF
	(Dam. 11.8.14)		
EC-JFQ	Bell 212	33126	C-FAKF, N412PK, N412PD
EC-JFT	Cessna 560 Citation Ultra	560-0506	G-OGRG, G-RIBV, N50820
EC-JFU	Piper PA-34-220T Seneca IV	3448032	HB-LSO, I-SELA, N9181G
EC-JFV	SOCATA MS.893A Rallye Commodore 180	10568	OE-DFC
EC-JFX	Airbus A340-642	672	F-WWCB
EC-JFY	Cessna 172S Skyhawk SP	172S9678	N6135G
EC-JFZ	Piper PA-28-181 Archer II	28-7990548	HB-PMZ, N2910G
EC-JGA	Diamond DA 40 Star	40067	G-MOPB
EC-JGB	Beech B200 Super King Air	BB-1478	D-IHAN(3), N8150N
EC-JGC	Agusta A.109E Power	11622	
EC-JGD	Tecnam P.92S Echo	P-92-ES-029	
EC-JGF	Ultramagic V-105 HAFB	105/122	
EC-JGI	Reims/Cessna FTB337G Super Skymaster		
	(NTU. Stored Viver 1.16)	FTB3370023	FAP3722
EC-JGJ	Reims/Cessna FTB337G Super Skymaster		
	(NTU. Stored Viver 1.16)	FTB3370022	FAP3721
EC-JGL	Reims/Cessna FTB337G Super Skymaster		
	(NTU. Stored Viver 1.16)	FTB3370024	FAP3723
EC-JGM	Airbus A320-214	2407	F-WWDC
EC-JGP	Reims/Cessna 172N	F17201519	D-EOHO
EC-JGR	Slingsby T-45 Swallow	1541	BGA5028/KEG, EC-BHG
EC-JGS	Airbus A321-211	2472	D-AVXA
EC-JGT	GEFA-Flug AS.105GD Hot Air Airship	0033	
EC-JGV	Kamov KA-32A11BC	9708	
EC-JGX	Kamov KA-32A11BC	9709	
EC-JGY	Cessna 337G Skymaster	33701538	CC-PGH, CC-CFZ, N72191,
EC-JGZ	Robinson R44 Raven II	0965	N519KD
EC-JHB	Ultramagic N-300 HAFB	300/10	
EC-JHE	SAAB-Scania SF.340A	340A-018	SE-LMV, OK-PEP, HB-AHD, SE-E18
EC-JHF	Piper PA-28-161 Warrior II	2816019	G-BNOK, N9122U
EC-JHG	Piper PA-34-220T Seneca III	3433112	G-BOCS
EC-JHK	Boeing 737-85P	33975	N1787B
EC-JHL	Boeing 737-85P	33976	
EC-JHM	SOCATA TB-20 Trinidad	858	CN-CDS
EC-JHN	Cessna 172S Skyhawk SP	172S9288	N5312W

EC-JHQ	Piper PA-34-200T Seneca II	34-7970255	D-GKHF, D-IKHF, N29545
EC-JHS	Tecnam P.2002JF Sierra	012	
EC-JHT	Eurocopter EC.135T2	0396	
EC-JHY	Robinson R44 Clipper II	10600	
EC-JIC	Air Tractor AT-802A	802A-0192	N85178
EC-JIF	Air Tractor AT-401	401-1162	
EC-JIG	Schempp-Hirth Ventus b/16.6	118	HB-1646
EC-JIL	Bombardier BD.700-1A10 Global Express	9146	C-FAHQ
EC-JIM	Bell 412EP	36191	N7015K, F-GRAK, N70722
EC-JIN	Centrair 101A Pégase	101A-0274	PH-804
EC-JIO	Robin R.1180TD Aiglon	254	F-GCRJ
	(Wfu, stored Cuatro Vientos 1.15)		
EC-JIP	Swearingen SA.226TC Metro II	TC-301	N5FY, SX-BSC, F-GCFE, N5666M
EC-JIQ	Ultramagic M-65 HAFB	65/113	
EC-JIU	Cessna 525 CitationJet CJ1	525-0486	N334BD, N5211A
EC-JIV	Air Tractor AT-502B	502B-2574	
EC-JIY	Ultramagic H-77 HAFB	77/182	
EC-JIZ	Ultramagic M-90 HAFB	90/74	
EC-JJA	Bell 206B Jet Ranger II	2299	D-HHST(2), TC-HBT, D-HKWF
EC-JJC	Eurocopter EC.130B4 Ecureuil	3539	F-GSDF, F-WQDB
EC-JJE	Bell 412	33004	N164EH, N58RC
	(Damaged 24.8.08)		
EC-JJF	Reims/Cessna FT337GP Super Skymaster		
		P3370047/FP3370003	D-ICSB, G-BAGP, F-WLIO
EC-JJK	Ultramagic M-77 HAFB	77/55	
EC-JJL	Piper PA-18A-150 Super Cub	18-5428	LV-FPF, N10F
EC-JJO	Ultramagic M-160 HAFB	160/34	
EC-JJP	Beech B200 Super King Air	BB-845	OY-GRB, N486DC, N38535
EC-JJQ	Bell 412EP	36376	N46372, C-FEOD
EC-JJR	SOCATA MS.893A Rallye Commodore 180	10619	D-EMYN(2)
EC-JJS	McDonnell-Douglas DC-9-83	49793	N827NK, N872RA, N793DG, YV-42C, D-AGWF, N511RP, C-GKMV
EC-JJT	Robin ATL	127	F-GGQS
EC-JJX	Ultramagic H-77 HAFB	77/225	
EC-JKA	Tecnam P.96 Golf	P96-G-038	
EC-JKD	Cessna 310L	310L0104	F-BOLR, N3254X
EC-JKE	Diamond DA 40-P7 Star	40007	OE-KPW, OE-VPW
EC-JKG	Bell 206L-4 Long Ranger IV	52068	OK-YIP, N2137P
EC-JKH	Embraer EMB.120ER Brasilia	120092	OM-SPY, N92GL, N281UE, PT-SMJ
EC-JKI	Air Tractor AT-802A Amphibian	802A-0205	N41012
	(Cr.3.8.06)		
EC-JKJ	Flight Design CT-2K	04-09-05-AR	
EC-JKM	Beech A45 Mentor	X-104	EC-GXQ, EC-750, E.17-24
EC-JKN	SOCATA TB-200 Tobago XL	1812	F-GRBO
EC-JKO	Fairchild SA.227DC Metro IV	DC-855B	EC-GJX, EC-362, N454LA, N3026U
	(Stored)		
EC-JKP	Agusta A.109E Power	11637	
EC-JKQ	Ultramagic M-77 HAFB	77/262	
EC-JKS	Reims FR172J Rocket	FR172-0476	F-BVBR
EC-JKX	Ultramagic N-250 HAFB	250/11	
EC-JKY	ICP Bingo	05-06-52-182	
EC-JLA	Robinson R22B2 Beta	3778	
EC-JLB	Air Tractor AT-802A	802A-0206	N41744
	(Crashed and sank, Roxo Dam, Beja, Portugal 19.7.12)		
EC-JLE	Airbus A340-642	702	F-WWCM
EC-JLF	Air Tractor AT-401	401-1160	
EC-JLG	GEFA-Flug AS.105GD Hot Air Airship	0036	
EC-JLI	Airbus A321-211	2563	D-AVZB
EC-JLJ	Piper PA-28-181 Cherokee Archer II	28-7790043	D-ELCE(2), N4550F
EC-JLL	Tecnam P.92-S Echo	P92-ES-043	
EC-JLN	Diamond DA 20-A1 Katana	10046	N230JA
EC-JLQ	Tecnam P.2002JF Sierra	021	
EC-JLR	Cirrus SR20	1524	N60758
EC-JLY	Cessna R172K Hawk XP	R1722448	N736DQ
EC-JLZ	Ultramagic H-65 HAFB	65/137	
EC-JMA	Piper PA-28-161 Warrior II	2816030	G-BNOT
EC-JMC	Piper PA-28-181 Archer II	2843236	N324MR, N324MP
EC-JMD	Cessna 421	421-0189	F-GCFV, N4589L
EC-JME	Reims/Cessna F172N	F17201654	OY-BJL
EC-JMG	Air Tractor AT-802	802-0066	N98ZL
EC-JMH	Slingsby T-67M Firefly II	2117	G-BUUG
EC-JMJ	Cessna 152	15283980	N4828H
	(Damaged 16.4.10)		
EC-JMK	Aérospatiale AS.355N Ecureuil 2	5741	F-WWPP
EC-JML	Cessna U206G Stationair 6	U20605362	5H-DTD, G-BHPV, N6169U
EC-JMM	Piper PA-28-140 Cherokee F	28-7325226	OY-DZD, LN-DBJ
EC-JMN	Ultramagic M-77 HAFB	77/222	
EC-JMO	Cessna 340A	340A-0262	N551AG, D-IHPS, (N4025G)
EC-JMP	Aérospatiale AS.350B Ecureuil	1761	OE-KXH, D-HAFP
EC-JMQ	Schweizer S.269C-1	0206	
EC-JMT	Piper PA-28-181 Cherokee Archer II	28-7790327	D-EFFV, N9597N
EC-JMU	Piper PA-28R-200 Cherokee Arrow II	28R-7435157	HB-PAD, N41219
EC-JMV	Piper PA-34-220T Seneca IV	3448018	N141JL, (EC-. . .), N141JL, VH-YSE, N92216
EC-JMY	Robinson R22 Beta	0982	G-IHSB
EC-JMZ	Diamond DA 20-C1 Katana	C0107	G-CDMB, N107CT, C-FDVA
EC-JNB	Canadair CL.600-2D24 Regional Jet 900	15057	C-. . . .
EC-JNE	Robinson R44 Raven II	10730	
EC-JNF	Boeing 737-85P	33977	
EC-JNG	Cameron C-60 HAFB	10721	
EC-JNH	Partenavia P.68 Observer 2	428/OB2	
EC-JNI	Airbus A321-211	2270	D-AVZA
EC-JNJ	Ultramagic T-180 HAFB	180/54	
EC-JNL	Cessna 152	15284799	D-EVAS(2), N4680P
EC-JNM	Tecnam P.2002JF Sierra	028	
EC-JNN	Cameron SS Phone HAFB	10766	
EC-JNO	Cameron N-90 HAFB	10767	
EC-JNP	Agusta-Bell 412HP/Hkp11	25805	SE-JIZ, Armén 11335
	(Damaged 14.8.07)		
EC-JNQ	Airbus A340-642	727	F-WWCV
EC-JNR	Mooney M.20E Super 21	1053	HB-DEU
EC-JOA	Ultramagic M-77 HAFB	77/242	
EC-JOB	Cessna 172S Skyhawk SP	172S9949	N1211D
EC-JOE	Pilatus PC-6/B1-H2 Turbo Porter	705	F-GZDO, N705SA, HS-CHV, N62162, XW-PGN, HB-FFG
EC-JOF	Aérospatiale SA.330J Puma	1571	F-GONB, F-WQPM, LX-HUC, PT-HAO, LX-HUC
	(Dbf 11.9.06)		
EC-JOK	Ultramagic M-77 HAFB	77/265	
EC-JON	Cessna 550 Citation II	550-0190	F-GZLC, F-BTEL, F-GZLC, F-BTEL, N98715
EC-JOO	Piper PA-34-220T Seneca IV	3448035	G-BXPV, A7-FCH, N9198X
EC-JOP	Piper PA-34-220T Seneca IV	3448034	G-BXPW, A7-FCG, N9171R

Reg	Type	c/n	Previous identities
EC-JOQ	Piper PA-34-200T Seneca III	34-8133177	G-BYKM, N460RB, G-BYKM, HB-LMV
EC-JOR	Tecnam P.96 Golf	P96-G-010	EC-DM4
EC-JOS	Ultramagic N-210 HAFB	210/31	
I-RAII	Agusta AB.139	31034	I-RAII
EC-JOV	Diamond DA 20-C1 Katana	C0022	N237ND
EC-JOX	SOCATA TB-9 Tampico	106	PH-CYB, D-EFOE
EC-JPA	PZL W-3 Sokol	310303	SP-SUL, CCCP04107
EC-JPB	PZL W-3 Sokol	310310	SP-SYB, CCCP04113
EC-JPC	PZL W-3 Sokol	310206	SP-SUY, CCCP04104
EC-JPD	Ultramagic F-26 HAFB	F26/01	
EC-JPF	Airbus A330-202	733	F-WWKU
EC-JPI	Centrair 101A Pégase	101A-051	F-CFQN
EC-JPJ	PZL W-3 Sokol	320210	SP-SSU, SP-SXU, SP-SUE, SP-FXA, SP-SZS
EC-JPK	Gulfstream 550	5078	N578GA
EC-JPQ	SOCATA MS.893A Rallye Commodore 180T	11771	D-EBZQ, F-BSZQ
EC-JPR	Robinson R44 Raven II	11000	
EC-JPT	Cessna 182M Skylane	18259745	CS-DAV, N71764
EC-JPU	Airbus A340-642	744	F-WWCF
EC-JPX	Manuel Perez Rainbow	MPR 0016	EC-EE9
EC-JPY	Cessna 172S Skyhawk SP	172S10010	N2096D
EC-JPZ	Piper PA-31-350 Navajo Chieftain	31-7952088	LN-ACC, SX-BNV, N112GD, C-FYZF, N35161
EC-JQB	Piper PA-28-161 Warrior II	2816015	G-BNOG, N9122D
EC-JQC	Swearingen SA.226AT Merlin IV (Wfu and stored)	AT-066	N5FY, C-FTIX, D-IBAB, YU-ALG, OO-VGC, (OY-NPC), OY-FFE, N5455M
EC-JQE	IAI-1126/Gulfstream 200	125	N221GA
EC-JQF	Aérospatiale/Alenia ATR-72-201F	147	SE-LVK, OY-CIP, EI-CBC, PH-SCY, EC-GQS, EI-CBC, F-WWET
EC-JQG	Airbus A330-202	745	F-WWYG
EC-JQH	Piper PA-28-181 Cherokee Archer II	28-7790373	SE-GPO
EC-JQJ	Ultramagic M-56 HAFB	56/29	
EC-JQK	Cessna 172R Skyhawk	17281269	N2465K
EC-JQL	Aérospatiale/Alenia ATR-72-212A	726	F-WWEG
EC-JQO	Piper PA-28-181 Archer II	2843593	G-SYDD, N5365M
EC-JQQ	Airbus A330-202	749	F-WWYJ
EC-JQS	Piper PA-28-161 Warrior II	2842254	N3113J
EC-JQV	McDonnell-Douglas DC-9-83	49526	N14879, N939MC
EC-JQY	Ultramagic T-180 HAFB	180/51	
EC-JQZ	Airbus A321-212	2736	D-AVZJ
EC-JRA	Evektor EV-97 Eurostar	2005-2616	
EC-JRD	Cameron A-315 HAFB	10831	
EC-JRE	Airbus A321-211	2756	D-AVZA
EC-JRG	Piper PA-31-325 Panther Navajo	31-7912052	CC-CWN, CC-PWM, LV-WIV, N773DR, 9Y-TIB, N773DR, N27985, (N1025N), N27985
EC-JRH	HOAC DV-20 Katana (Damaged 10.10.07)	20158	G-BWPY, OE-UDV
EC-JRK	Polikarpov I-16 Type 24	2421039	ZK-JJC, Soviet AF
EC-JRM	Air Tractor AT-802A	802A-0224	N85253
EC-JRN	SOCATA TB-9 Tampico	212	D-EKMD(2), OE-KMD, D-EBZD
EC-JRP	Aérospatiale/Alenia ATR-72-212	446	D-AEWK, F-WWEA
EC-JRQ	Sukhoi SU-26M	03-04	N215YA, 24 Black, DOSAAF
EC-JRS	Piper PA-34-200T Seneca II	34-7670105	OY-ASW, D-ILBI, N7843C
EC-JRY	Agusta-Bell 412HP (Hkp 11) (W/o 19.9.11)	25803	SE-JIY, Armén 11333
EC-JRZ	Ultramagic H-77 HAFB	77/270	
EC-JSA	Cameron Z-90 HAFB	10746	
EC-JSC	Robinson R22B2 Beta	4013	
EC-JSD	Bell 407	53687	C-FHYS
EC-JSE	Focke-Wulf FW-44J Steiglitz	143	LV-YZP
EC-JSI	Piper PA-34-200T Seneca II	34-7570164	D-GILD, N33805
EC-JSK	Airbus A320-214	2807	F-WWIN
EC-JSM	Cessna 172R Skyhawk (W/o 30.3.16)	17281309	N60089
EC-JSN	Cessna 172R Skyhawk	17281310	N2426P
EC-JSO	Robinson R22B2 Beta	3172	G-VEEE, G-REDA
EC-JSP	Kamov KA.32A11BC	9710	
EC-JSQ	Kamov KA.32A11BC	9712	
EC-JSR	SOCATA MS.893A Rallye Commodore 150	11411	F-GJLO, D-EAGQ
EC-JSX	Diamond DA 40 Star	40066	G-OPHR
EC-JSY	Airbus A320-214	2785	F-WWBU
EC-JTC	Robinson R44 Raven II (W/o 31.5.14)	11143	
EC-JTD	Agusta-Bell 412HP (Hkp 11)	25801	SE-JIX, Armén 11331
EC-JTE	Cessna 421C Golden Eagle	421C0804	LN-SPO, D-IZZY, N26563
EC-JTF	Air Tractor AT-802A	802A-0219	
EC-JTJ	Cessna 172R Skyhawk	17281312	N2427W
EC-JTL	Robinson R44 Raven II	11151	
EC-JTO	Aérospatiale AS.350B3 Ecureuil	3091	LN-OPK
EC-JTP	Aérospatiale AS.350B3 Ecureuil	3445	SE-JHK, F-WQDF
EC-JTQ	Airbus A320-214	2794	F-WWBN
EC-JTR	Airbus A320-214	2798	F-WWIF
EC-JTS	Canadair CL.600-2D24 Regional Jet 900	15071	C-FJTF
EC-JTT	Canadair CL.600-2D24 Regional Jet 900	15074	C-FJTJ
EC-JTU	Canadair CL.600-2D24 Regional Jet 900	15079	C-FJTE
EC-JTX	Aérospatiale AS.350B3 Ecureuil	3600	SE-JHC, HB-ZFF, SE-JHC, F-WQDF
EC-JTY	Reims/Cessna F172N	F17201967	D-EFJZ
EC-JTZ	Air Tractor AT-802A	802A-0230	N8516V
EC-JUB	Air Tractor AT-802A	802A-0236	N8520K
EC-JUD	Ultramagic M-105 HAFB	105/138	
EC-JUE	Eurocopter EC.135T2	0345	EC-067
EC-JUF	McDonnell-Douglas DC-9-83	53168	N802NK, B-28015, N837AU
EC-JUH	Slepcev Storch SS Mk IV	SS4-068	VH-FUQ(2)
EC-JUI	Robin DR.400/180R Remorqueur	959	HB-EXL
EC-JUK	Cameron A-250 HAFB (Dam. 21.9.14)	10872	
EC-JUM	PZL W-3AM Sokol	370707	HL9257, SP-SYL(2)
EC-JUN	PZL W-3AM Sokol (W/o 2.7.12)	370804	HL9265, VN-417, SP-SYN(2)
EC-JUO	Tecnam P.92JS Echo	051	
EC-JUP	SOCATA TB-10 Tobago	116	D-EEEA
EC-JUQ	Ultramagic N-210 HAFB	210/29	
EC-JUR	Robinson R44 Raven II	10909	G-SANP
EC-JUS	Agusta A.109E Power	11675	
EC-JUT	Ultramagic H-77 HAFB	77/228	
EC-JUU	Beech 58 Baron	TH-679	F-BXOR
EC-JUX	Piper PA-28-161 Warrior II	2842261	N3132J
EC-JUY	Piper PA-28-161 Warrior II	2842262	N3132M
EC-JUZ	Kamov KA.32A11BC	9713	
EC-JVA	Kamov KA.32A11BC	9714	
EC-JVE	Airbus A319-111	2843	D-AVYT
EC-JVG	Aérospatiale AS.365N3 Dauphin 2	6718	F-WWOQ
EC-JVH	Ultramagic V-25 HAFB	25/01	
EC-JVK	SOCATA MS.893A Rallye Commodore 180	10793	D-EGPT, F-BGPT
EC-JVL	Ultramagic M-77 HAFB	77/261	
EC-JVM	Bombardier Learjet 60	60-161	D-CDNZ
EC-JVP	Piper PA-28-140 Cherokee Fliteliner	28-7125264	N901EA, EC-FRK, EC-291, N464FL
EC-JVQ	Piper PA-28-140 Cherokee C	28-26659	N902EA, EC-FRQ, EC-302, N5828U
EC-JVR	Dassault Falcon 900B	106	N333EC, (N241AM), N333EC, N332EC, F-GJRH, 9M-BAN, F-GKDI, F-WWFL
EC-JVS	Eurocopter EC.135P2	0436	
EC-JVU	Ultramagic T-210 HAFB	210/35	
EC-JVX	Piper PA-31 Turbo Navajo	31-188	N63560, HB-LFW, N9141Y
EC-JVZ	PZL M-18BS Dromader	1Z028-25	SP-DEZ
EC-JXC	Cessna 500 Citation	500-0278	OY-PCW, N103PL, (SE-RDA), VP-BBE, N103PL, XB-UAG, XB-FQO, N278SP, ZS-LYB, (N278SR), N278SP, N278CC, (N5278J)
EC-JXF	Aérospatiale/Alenia ATR-72-211F	150	OY-CIV, EI-CBD, PH-SCZ, EC-GUL, EI-CBD, (N975NA), F-WWEI
EC-JXG	Kamov KA-32A11BC	9715	
EC-JXJ	Airbus A319-111	2889	D-AVXH
EC-JXK	Cameron Sugarbox 90SS HAFB	10906	
EC-JXL	Cirrus SR22	1863	N976CD
EC-JXM	Pilatus PC-12	177	D-FCJA, HB-FSM
EC-JXO	Tecnam P.2002JF Sierra	P2002-021	
EC-JXQ	Bell 412EP	36091	N5087V, VT-TNA, N21853
EC-JXR	Dassault Falcon 2000	55	F-GJTG(2), F-WQBK, HB-IVM, F-WWMM
EC-JXT	CASA C.1-131E Jungmann	2193	E.3B-507
EC-JXU	Schweizer S.269C-1	0254	N86G
EC-JXV	Airbus A319-111	2897	D-AVWH
EC-JXX	Ultramagic H-77 HAFB	77/268	
EC-JXY	Aérospatiale AS.365N3 Dauphin 2	6719	F-WWOI
EC-JXZ	Canadair CL-600-2D24 Regional Jet 900	15087	C-FLGI
EC-JYA	Canadair CL-600-2D24 Regional Jet 900	15090	C-FLIX
EC-JYC	Swearingen SA.226TC Metro II	TC-303	N117AR, VH-MYD, C-FWWP, N9U, C-FIIC, N235AM, TU-TXV, N5681M
EC-JYE	Aérospatiale SA.330J Puma	1241	D-HAXC
EC-JYH	Ultramagic M-77 HAFB	77/277	
FC-JYI	Ultramagic M-105 HAFB	105/143	
EC-JYJ	Aérospatiale AS.355F2 Ecureuil 2	5425	N225NR, (N910KS), N225NR
EC-JYK	Ultramagic T-210 HAFB	210/36	
EC-JYL	Ultramagic H-65 HAFB	65/157	
EC-JYM	Cirrus SR22	2054	N987SR
EC-JYN	Cessna 172S Skyhawk SP	172S10165	N60150
EC-JYP	Cessna 172M	17263417	SE-KFX, N5200R
EC-JYS	Glaser-Dirks DG-200	2-32	PH-1235, D-6785
EC-JYT	Canadair CL.600-2B16 Challenger 604	5648	C-FHDV
EC-JYU	Ultramagic S-90 HAFB	90/90	
EC-JYV	Canadair CL-600-2D24 Regional Jet 900	15106	C-FLMJ
EC-JYX	Airbus A320-214	2962	F-WWDJ
EC-JYZ	Evektor EV-97 Eurostar (Same c/n as OK-JUR 115)	2006 2813	
EC-JZD	Piper PA-28R-200 Cherokee Arrow	28R-35674	D-EEFM, N4902S
EC-JZE	Cessna 172S Skyhawk SP	172S9368	N53567
EC-JZF	Robinson R22 Beta (Wfu, cancelled)	2509	G-RICE, N93MK
EC-JZG	Piper PA-34-200T Seneca II	34-7570210	SE-GIP
EC-JZH	Ultramagic T-180 HAFB	180/61	
EC-JZI	Airbus A320-214	2988	F-WWII
EC-JZJ	Partenavia P.68C	217	G-ONCM, I-CITT, G-TELE, G-DORE, OY-CAD
EC-JZL	Airbus A330-202	814	F-WWYJ
EC-JZM	Airbus A321-211	2996	D-AVZP
EC-JZN	Ultramagic H-77 HAFB	77/279	
EC-JZR	Diamond DA 42 Twin Star	42.178	
EC-JZS	Canadair CL.600-2D24 Regional Jet 900	15111	C-FLMK
EC-JZT	Canadair CL.600-2D24 Regional Jet 900	15113	C-FLMN
EC-JZU	Canadair CL.600-2D24 Regional Jet 900	15115	C-FLMQ
EC-JZV	Canadair CL.600-2D24 Regional Jet 900	15117	C-FLMS
EC-JZY	Cedimex Rans S-12XL-582 Airaile	S-12-209	EC-DE3
EC-KAA	Cirrus SR22	1932	N923SR
EC-KAB	SOCATA TB-20 Trinidad	471	F-GDNT
EC-KAD	Aérospatiale/Alenia ATR-72-202F	171	F-GKPC, F-WWEA
EC-KAF	Aérospatiale AS.355F1 Ecureuil 2	5079	F-GJFU, G-BUZI, N57894
EC-KAH	Diamond DA 20-A1 Katana	10143	G-RIBS, G-BWWM, C-GDMY
EC-KAI	Aérospatiale/Alenia ATR-42-300F	141	EI-FXF, N141AE, N431MQ, F-WWEM
EC-KAL	Ultramagic M-77 HAFB	77/283	
EC-KAM	Ultramagic M-77C HAFB	77/286	
EC-KAN	Tecnam P.2002JF Sierra	050	
EC-KAO	Tecnam P.2002JF Sierra	051	
EC-KAP	Eurocopter EC.135P2	0462	EC-068
EC-KAQ	Eurocopter EC.135P2	0505	EC-069
EC-KAR	Cessna 421A (Wfu, noted 1.15 Cuatro Vientos)	421A-0013	OY-OBC, OH-CBC, N2213Q
EC-KAU	Tecnam P.2002JF Sierra	054	
EC-KAV	Cessna 172R Skyhawk (Res as SP-OSK .11)	17281339	N6043M
EC-KAY	Piper PA-28R-201 Arrow	2844130	N10759, N3147B
EC-KBB	Bell 412EP	36426	N94479, C-GFNU
EC-KBC	IAI-1126/Gulfstream 200	145	N645GA
EC-KBD	Piper PA-34-200T Seneca II	34-8133161	F-GOUH, D-GEUH, N8413K, ZP-TVM, N8413K
EC-KBE	Ultramagic M-65 HAFB	65/151	
EC-KBG	PZL W-3AS Sokol	310302	SP-SUK, CCCP-04106
EC-KBH	Cirrus SR20	1725	N986SR, N966SR
EC-KBK	Ultramagic N-300 HAFB	300/17	
EC-KBL	Cessna 172S Skyhawk SP	172S10349	D-EVHG, N1216A
EC-KBN	Partenavia P.68C (Res. as D-GKRE, 2012)	285	N344CC, N944CC, N3380P, YV-2380P
EC-KBP	Cirrus SR20	1213	N271CD
EC-KBR	Gulfstream V	5124	N524GA
EC-KBS	Vulcanair P.68 Observer 2	438-30/OB2	
EC-KBT	Bell 412EP	36423	C-FLOX
EC-KBX	Airbus A319-111	3078	D-AVYH
EC-KBY	Piper PA-34-200 Seneca	34-7250257	OY-SUW, G-BADF, N5446T
EC-KBZ	Cessna 550 Citation II	550-0678	SE-RCI, EC-FES, EC-777, N67750, N698GA
EC-KCA	Gulfstream 200	150	N698GA
EC-KCE	Cameron Z-77 HAFB	10987	
EC-KCG	Boeing 737-85P	33981	
EC-KCH	Beech B55 Baron	TC-2042	G-BNVZ, N17720
EC-KCJ	Ultramagic M-77 HAFB	77/282	
EC-KCM	Eurocopter EC.135P2	0452	

Reg	Type	c/n	Previous identities
EC-KCN	Bell 212	30681	5N-BEN, G-BOEP, VH-BEU, G-BOEP, VR-BFO, N18091
EC-KCO	Bell 212	30666	5N-BHE, G-BMVF, VH-BEY, G-BMVF, VR-BFL, N18093
EC-KCQ	Bell 407	53741	C-FLPB
EC-KCS	Bell 212	31200	5N-AOF, G-BJIU, N18093
EC-KCU	Airbus A320-216	3109	F-WWIR
EC-KCY	de Havilland DH.60X Moth	627	G-EBXU
EC-KDA	Eurocopter EC.135P2+	0538	
EC-KDC	Robinson R44 Raven II	11632	
EC-KDG	Airbus A320-214	3095	F-WWIY
EC-KDH	Airbus A320-214	3083	F-WWIX
EC-KDM	Ultramagic M-105 HAFB	105/152	
EC-KDN	Piper PA-23-250 Aztec E	27-7305213	F-GDRG, (D-IHBR), LX-HBR, D-IHBR, N40489
EC-KDP	Piper PA-34-200T Seneca II	34-7970149	G-BRXD, N111ED, N9618N
EC-KDQ	Agusta A.119K Koala	14031	I-CLMF, N17YC
EC-KDS	Diamond DA 20-C1 Katana (W/o 13.10.11)	C0256	D-ESGF, N162MA
EC-KDT	Airbus A320-232	3145	F-WWBM
EC-KDU	Ultramagic M-77 HAFB	77/296	
EC-KDX	Airbus A320-216	3151	F-WWBU
EC-KEA	Cirrus SR22	1399	N365CD
EC-KEB	Bell 212	30972	LX-HEP(2), N606LH, JA9545, N1071G
EC-KED	Agusta A.119K Koala	14015	N119LF
EC-KEG	Agusta A.119K Koala	14048	N325BC
EC-KEJ	Ultramagic M-77 HAFB	77/295	
EC-KEK	CASA CN.235-300MPA	C166	EC-101, EC-235
EC-KEL	CASA CN.235-300MPA	C169	EC-027
EC-KEM	CASA CN.235-300MPA	C171	EC-021
EC-KER	Colt 210A HAFB	2425	D-OJOE
EC-KES	Cessna 525A CitationJet 2	525A-0155	N105PT, N5180C
EC-KEU	Flight Design CT SW	06-09-23-AR	
EC-KFC	Cessna U206G Stationair 6	U20603556	N2049Y, C-GOUJ, N8847Q
EC-KFE	Cessna 182T Skylane	18281136	N836TW
EC-KFG	Robin DR.400/180 Régent (W/o 6.9.16)	693	D-ENKF, D-EFEE(1)
EC-KFJ	Boeing Stearman A75N1	75-4991	N62AG, OO-LEF, N778RL, N67472, BuA55754
EC-KFL	Cameron Z-105 HAFB	10917	
EC-KFN	Ultramagic M-90 HAFB	90/95	
EC-KFO	Aérospatiale AS.350B3 Ecureuil	4232	
EC-KFP	Aérospatiale AS.350B3 Ecureuil	3818	F-GYRE
EC-KFU	Aérospatiale AS.350B3 Ecureuil	4251	SE-JJU
EC-KFV	Extra EA.300/200	1038	D-EXTT
EC-KFX	Cirrus SR20	1752	N681CP
EC-KFZ	Kamov KA.32A11BC	9804	
EC-KGA	Kamov KA.32A11BC	9805	
EC-KGB	ICP MXP-740 Savannah	06-12-51-562	
EC-KGC	Flight Designs CT SW	06-09-22-AR	
EC-KGD	Pilatus PC-6/B2-H2 Turbo Porter	677	ZS-LJY, HB-FEP
EC-KGF	Reims/Cessna F172M	F17200967	D-ECZJ
EC-KGG	Reims/Cessna F172N	F17201575	D-EOFU(2)
EC-KGH	SOCATA MS.893A Rallye Commodore 180	10817	D-EOBA, F-BPHV
EC-KGI	Aérospatiale/Alenia ATR-72-212A	752	F-WWEM
EC-KGJ	Aérospatiale/Alenia ATR-72-212A	753	F-WWEN
EC-KGK	Ultramagic F-11 HAFB	F11/02	
EC-KGL	Robinson R44 Raven II	11749	
EC-KGN	Ultramagic M-65 HAFB	65/156	
EC-KGO	Ultramagic M-160 HAFB	160/51	
EC-KGP	Ultramagic M-77 HAFB	77/302	
EC-KGQ	Aérospatiale AS.350B3 Ecureuil	4253	F-WWPT
EC-KGT	PZL W-3A Sokol	37.05.15	HL9298, SP-FSU, A6-SAA, RAK-101, SP-FSU, SP-FSO, PLW-0515, SP-SYL(3)
EC-KGX	Cessna 501 Citation I/SP	501-0061	SE-RBZ, N202CF, N1401L, N34DL, N436CC, N2757A
EC-KGY	Aérospatiale AS.350B3 Ecureuil	4234	F-WWPG
EC-KHB	PZL W-3A Sokol	37.05.09	N649LH, HL9256, SP-SYH (3)
EC-KHC	Fleet 10	110	LV-ZCM, LV-CCC, R-92
EC-KHK	Cessna 172R Skyhawk	17281365	N2118F
EC-KHL	Cessna 172R Skyhawk	17281373	N14766
EC-KHM	Airbus A319-111	3209	D-AVWL
EC-KHN	Airbus A320-216	3203	F-WWIG
EC-KHP	Cessna 550 Citation Bravo	550-0955	HB-VMW, N50715
EC-KHQ	Cessna 172R Skyhawk	17281150	SE-. . ., N76LU
EC-KHV	AgustaWestland AW139	31089	
EC-KHZ	Cessna 172R Skyhawk	17280824	N2461S
EC-KIA	Flight Design CT SW	07-04-18-AR	
EC-KIB	Flight Design CT SW	07-03-27-AR	
EC-KIC	Flight Design CT SW	07-04-11-AR	
EC-KIE	Aérospatiale AS.350B3 Ecureuil	4286	
EC-KIF	Ultramagic M-77 HAFB	77-304	
EC-KIH	Cirrus SR22	2503	N861SR
EC-KII	Agusta A.119K Koala	14525	N630WB, N43TG
EC-KIJ	Eurocopter EC.135T2i	0579	
EC-KIP	Ultramagic H-77 HAFB	77/301	
EC-KIQ	Ultramagic M-77 HAFB	77/291	
EC-KIR	PZL W-3AS Sokol (Cr. 4.15)	310319	SP-SWA (2), SP-SUP, CCCP-04118
EC-KIS	Aérospatiale AS.350B3 Ecureuil	4264	F-WWPR
EC-KIT	Ultramagic T-210 HAFB	210/444	
EC-KIU-E3	Grob G.103 Twin Astir Trainer	3115	D-7782
EC-KIV	Ultramagic H-77 HAFB	77/284	
EC-KIY	Cessna 152	15281478	OO-VRM, D-EBTF, N64922
EC-KIZ	Aérospatiale/Alenia ATR-72-202	204	F-GPOA, F-ORAC, (XU-RAC), F-GKJK, F-WQAG, ZS-NDI, F-WWER, (N7270), F-WWEF
EC-KJA	Aérospatiale/Alenia ATR-72-202	207	F-GPOB, F-ORAN, (XU-RAN), F-WQAH, ZS-NDJ, F-WWEF, (N7271), F-WWEF
EC-KJD	Airbus A320-216	3237	F-WWBJ
EC-KJI	McDonnell-Douglas DC-9-87	49836	EC-EXN, EC-299
EC-KJK	Tecnam P.92S Echo	P92-ES-047	
EC-KJL	Airbus A310-324 (Wfu)	453	F-OGYQ, N817PA, F-WWCK
EC-KJM	Tecnam P.2002JF Sierra	069	
EC-KJQ	Beech B300 King Air 350	FL-255	D-CDEB, N3205M
EC-KJR	Cessna 551 Citation II/SP	551-0412	OY-PDN, N413VP, G-OMCL, N12160,
EC-KJT	AgustaWestland AW139	31104	I-EASK
EC-KJU	Agusta A.109E Power	11709	
EC-KJX	Extra EA.300/L	1264	
EC-KJZ	Aeromoragon M-1	MO1-03-014	EC-DY8, EC-060
EC-KKA	Christen Pitts S-2B	5156	F-GJEP
EC-KKD	Hawker 400XP	RK-553	N533HB, N975BD, N553XP
EC-KKG	Cameron Z-77 HAFB	11024	
EC-KKH	Cirrus SR20	1814	N708SR
EC-KKI	Cirrus SR20	1817	N798BG
EC-KKM	Tecnam P.2002JR Sierra	066	
EC-KKO	Cessna 550 Citation Bravo	550-0992	D-COFY, G-EKWS, N777NG
EC-KKP	Ultramagic H-77 HAFB	77/292	
EC-KKQ	Aérospatiale/Alenia ATR-72-212A	763	F-WWEB
EC-KKR	Ultramagic M-77 HAFB	77/312	
EC-KKS	Airbus A319-111	3320	D-AVYF
EC-KLB	Airbus A320-214	3321	F-WWDY
EC-KLC	AgustaWestland AW139	31107	
EC-KLD	Boeing 757-236	24121	N28AT, 4X-BAZ, TC-AHA, G-BPEH, G-BNSE, EC-EXH, EC-544, G-BNSE
EC-KLE	Ultramagic H-77 HAFB	77/224	
EC-KLF	Ultramagic T-210 HAFB	210/40	
EC-KLG	Ultramagic N-300 HAFB	300/25	
EC-KLH	Piper PA-28-180 Cherokee F	28-7105220	EC-KFD, HB-OHX, N11C
EC-KLI	Tecnam P.92S Echo (W/o 5.9.13)	P92-ES-04	EC-EH2
EC-KLJ	Aérospatiale AS.350B3 Ecureuil (Dam. 22.5.08)	3804	TC-HEH
EC-KLM	AgustaWestland AW139	31201	I-EASB
EC-KLN	AgustaWestland AW139	31202	
EC-KLO	Tecnam P.96 Golf	P96-G-057	
EC-KLQ	Cessna 172N Skyhawk	17270921	D-EHLT, N739YV
EC-KLR	Boeing 737-3Q8	23766	N237CP, PR-RLB, N766ST, TF-ELN, OO-ILK, VH-NJE, N101GU, N188LF, EC-EHM, EC-153, N315SC, G-BNCT, N1716B
EC-KLT	Airbus A320-214	3376	F-WWDI
EC-KLV	AgustaWestland AW139	31205	
EC-KLX	Cirrus SR22	1545	N995CD
EC-KLY	Cirrus SR22g3	2689	N548SR
EC-KLZ	Cirrus SR22	2696	N375SR
EC-KMA	Ultramagic N-180 HAFB	180/74	
EC-KMB	Ultramagic T-180 HAFB	180/75	
EC-KMC	Ultramagic N-300 HAFB	300/20	
EC-KMD	Airbus A319-111	3380	D-AVWE
EC-KMG	Diamond DA 20-C1 Katana	C0119	D-EFCG(3), N959CT, C-GKAI
EC-KMH	Diamond DA 20-C1 Katana	C0217	D-EVSE, N37SE
EC-KMI	Airbus A320-216	3400	F-WWBT
EC-KMJ	Aeorprakt A-22L Vision (Cr and dbf 28.10.11)	A22L-07-0019	
EC-KML	Ultramagic M-65 HAFB	65/161	
EC-KMN	Ultramagic M-77 HAFB	77/313	
EC-KMO	Ultramagic N-180 HAFB	180/59	
EC-KMP	Ultramagic M-77 HAFB	77/285	
EC-KMQ	Ultramagic M-77 HAFB	77/278	
EC-KMY	Ultramagic H-77 HAFB	77/308	
EC-KMZ	Ultramagic M-77C HAFB	77/307	
EC-KNA	Tecnam P.2002JF Sierra	P2002 031	
EC-KNB	Tecnam P.92 Echo	P92-E-033	
EC-KNC	Cessna 172R Skyhawk	17281480	N1729L
EC-KND	Beech B200 King Air	BB-1564	EC-KHR, G-IMGL, VP-CMA, N205JT
EC-KNF	Cessna P210N Pressurised Centurion II	P21000198	F-GIGK, N521BB, N6685P
EC-KNG	Aérospatiale AS.350B3 Ecureuil	4088	EC-KJF, SE-JJJ, F-WQDC
EC-KNI	Cessna 172R Skyhawk	17281478	N1294G
EC-KNK	Ultramagic M-77 HAFB	77/310	
EC-KNN	Ultramagic H-65 HAFB	65/149	
EC-KNP	Beech 200 Super King Air	BB-561	F-GULJ, (F-GZAT), F-GULJ, G-VICW, G-ECAV, N26GA, N963JC
EC-KNR	Cessna 172R Skyhawk	17281414	N1504B
EC-KNU	Beech 77 Skipper (Damaged landing at Santarem, Portugal 17.7.09)	WA-263	SE-IIP, N3833L
EC-KNV	Piper PA-46-350P Malibu	4622143	N193PM
EC-KNX	Ultramagic T-180 HAFB	180/77	
EC-KNZ	Eurocopter EC.135T2+	0606	EC-034
EC-KOA	Eurocopter EC.135P2+	0536	
EC-KOB	Eurocopter EC.135P2+	0596	
EC-KOF	Robinson R22 Beta II	4242	OE-UXP, N41248
EC-KOG	Cessna 172R Skyhawk	17281477	N1248V
EC-KOH	Airbus A320-214	2248	XA-UDU, F-WWIK
EC-KOL	Cessna 560XL Citation Excel	560-5088	G-WCIN, VP-BSD, N52081
EC-KOM	Airbus A330-202	931	F-WWKU
EC-KON	Bell 206L-3 Long Ranger III	51083	EC-KCB, IDFAF 203, N3184M
EC-KOO	Bell 206L-3 Long Ranger III	51088	EC-KCC, IDFAF 213
EC-KOP	Cessna 182T Skylane	18282025	N1256W
EC-KOQ	Cessna 182T Skylane	18282041	N1738D
EC-KOS	ELA Aviacion ELA 07-R100 (Destroyed 3.9.11)	0707 171 0722	
EC-KOT	Tecnam P.2002 Sierra	P2002 022	EC-EX7
EC-KOY	Airbus A319-111	3443	D-AVYN
EC-KPA	Eurocopter EC.135P2+	0634	EC-034
EC-KPB	Cessna 560XL Citation Excel	unkn	
EC-KPC	Piper PA-28RT-201T Turbo Arrow IV (W/o 28.10.13)	28R-7931245	EC-KIX, F-GCJM, OO-HCZ, N2948B, N9581N
EC-KPE	Cessna 560XL Citation Excel	560-5764	N51666
EC-KPH	Ultramagic M-120 HAFB	120/33	
EC-KPI	Cirrus SR22	2466	N761SR
EC-KPJ	Gulfstream 150	243	N443GA, 4X-WID
EC-KPK	Aeroprakt A-22-L80 Vision	A22L80-07-0005	
EC-KPM	Piper PA-34-200T Seneca II	34-7670322	F-GJRS, N3892F
EC-KPN	Cessna 172S Skyhawk SP	172S10650	N1279V
EC-KPO	Cessna 172R Skyhawk	17281479	N1250F
EC-KPQ	Aérospatiale AS.355N Ecureuil 2	9612	F-WQAH
EC-KPR	Robinson R22B2 Beta	4287	N41524
EC-KPS	Piper PA-28RT-201T Turbo Arrow IV	28R-8031126	I-LAAC, N8233X
EC-KPT	Beech B200 Super King Air	BB-753	F-GERS, N3750B
EC-KPV	Ultramagic M-105 HAFB	105/162	
EC-KQB	Ultramagic S-105 HAFB	105/163	
EC-KQC	Boeing 747-412	26549	9V-SMZ, N6018N
EC-KQD	Agusta A.119K Koala	14012	VH-RPW, OE-XSB
EC-KQE	Agusta A.119K Koala	14042	VH-RPS, VH-HFX(2)
EC-KQK	Tecnam P.92 Echo (Dam. 12.6.14)	P92-E-028	
EC-KQL	Piper PA-28RT-201T Turbo Arrow IV	28R-8131019	HB-PEU, N8287X
EC-KQM	Robinson R44 Raven II	11995	
EC-KQO	Cessna 525B CitationJet 3	525B-0234	N5214K
EC-KQT	Eurocopter EC.135T2i	0652	
EC-KQU	Diamond DA 42 Twin Star	42.357	OE-VPW
EC-KQV	Vulcanair P.68TC Observer	444-08/OTC	
EC-KQX	Agusta A.119Ke Koala	14702	N52ME
EC-KQY	Agusta A.119Ke Koala	14703	N60ME
EC-KQZ	Tecnam P.96 Golf	P96-G-059	EC-FK7
EC-KRB	Robinson R44 Raven II	1314	D-HALO(2)

Regn	Type	c/n	Previous/Notes
EC-KRC	Piper PA-34-200 Seneca	34-7250356	D-GEOS, S5-CAG, SL-CAG, N15052
EC-KRF	Air Tractor AT-802A	802A-0266	
	(Dbr 1.6.12, noted stored Viver 11.1.16)		
EC-KRG	Ultramagic N-180 HAFB	180/76	
EC-KRH	Airbus A320-214	3529	D-AVVD
EC-KRI	Kamov KA.32A-11BC	9815	
EC-KRJ	Embraer 190-200LR	19000196	PT-SGE
EC-KRK	Tecnam P.92S Echo	P92-ES-048	
EC-KRL	Ultramagic M-77 HAFB	77/317	
EC-KRM	Ultramagic T-180 HAFB	180/81	
EC-KRN	Gulfstream 200	188	N388GA
EC-KRQ	Aérospatiale AS.350B3 Ecureuil	4370	
EC-KRU	Agusta-Bell AB.412	25542	I-AGSF
EC-KRV	McDonnell-Douglas DC-9-87	49843	EC-EZS,EC-306
EC-KRY	Aérospatiale/Alenia ATR-72-212A	795	F-WWEV
EC-KSA	PZL W-3A Sokol	37.08.12	EC-KHF, N647LH, HL9264, SP-SYO
EC-KSC	Agusta A.119K Koala	14034	N873MB, N19YC
EC-KSF	McDonnell-Douglas DC-9-87	53207	EC-FEZ, EC-633
EC-KSG	Aérospatiale/Alenia ATR-72-212A	796	F-WWEW
EC-KSH	Kamov KA.32A-11BC	9814	
EC-KSI	PZL W-3A Sokol	37.08.05	EC-KHG, N646LH, HL9296, EC-JUL, HL9262, SP-SYN(2)
EC-KSJ	Bell 412EP	36467	C-FSVZ
	(W/o 2.7.12)		
EC-KSK	Aérospatiale AS.350B3 Ecureuil	4365	F-WQRA, F-WWPR
EC-KSL	Aérospatiale AS.350B3 Ecureuil	4359	EC-067, F-WQAV, F-WWXE
	(W/o 23.12.15)		
EC-KSM	Boeing 747-412	27178	9V-SMW
EC-KSN	Ultramagic M-105 HAFB	105/166	
EC-KSO	Stinson L-5E Sentinel	76-3822	EC-KCI, 44-17535
EC-KSP	Ultramagic T-150 HAFB	150/08	
EC-KSQ	PZL W-3 Sokol	37.05.08	SP-SSL, SP-PSL, (SP-SYO)
EC-KSR	Tecnam P.92S Echo	P92-ES-051	
EC-KSS	Embraer EMB-145ER	145.230	D-ACIR, PT-SHT
EC-KST	Cirrus SR22	2837	N851SR
EC-KSY	Air Tractor AT-802	802A-0288	
	(W/o 2.9.11)		
EC-KTC	Dornier Do.28D-2 Skyservant	4125	HA-ACL, D-IDRC, 58+50
	(Walter M601 Turbo Conversion)		
EC-KTD	Kubicek BB-20 HAFB	79	OK-7079
EC-KTF	Evektor EV-97 Eurostar	2007 3003	EC-FB6
	(Major damage 20.5.16)		
EC-KTG	Airbus A330-203	950	F-WWKQ
EC-KTH	Ultramagic N-180 HAFB	180/32	OO-BJQ
EC-KTJ	Ultramagic T-210 HAFB	210/53	
	(Res. as N254GS 12.15)		
EC-KTL	Aérospatiale AS.365N3 Dauphin 2	6799	F-WQDN
EC-KTO	Beech 76 Duchess	ME-85	I-BEKT, HB-GGR, F-GBRO
EC-KTS	Aérospatiale AS.365N3 Dauphin 2	6811	
EC-KTU	Aérospatiale AS.350B3 Ecureuil	4520	
EC-KUB	Airbus A319-111	3651	D-AVYR
	(Stored)		
EC-KUF	Robinson R22 Beta II	4232	CS-HGK, N41247
EC-KUG	Ultramagic M-105 HAFB	105/156	
EC-KUH	Aérospatiale AS.365N3 Dauphin 2	6803	F-WWOQ
EC-KUJ	Aérospatiale AS.350B3 Ecureuil	4524	
	(W/o Algeria 17.8.10)		
EC-KUK	Diamond DA 42 Twin Star	42.329	OE-VDN, OE-VPW
EC-KUL	Aérospatiale/Alenia ATR-72-212A	809	F-WWET
EC-KUM	Gulfstream GV-SP	5155	N550GA
EC-KUP	BRM Land Africa	04-08-0109-SP	
EC-KUQ	Eurocopter EC.135T2+	0705	D-HECP
EC-KUS	Ultramagic M-42 HAFB	42/14	
EC-KUT	ELA Aviacion ELA 07-R115	0408 220 0724	
	(W/o 26.11.11)		
EC-KUU	Piper PA-28RT-201T Turbo Arrow IV	28R-7931038	EC-KPD, D-EITH(2), N2222L
	(Ditched 25.1.16)		
EC-KUV	Agusta-Bell 412	25602	I-MAGM, Fv11338, I-LEMA
EC-KUX	Diamond DA 20-C1 Katana	C0493	
EC-KUZ	Ultramagic N-210 HAFB	210/54	
EC-KVB	Cessna T206H Stationair TC	T20608325	N988SA
EC-KVC	Bell 412EP	36469	C-FSZW
EC-KVE	Cessna 172R Skyhawk	17281522	N6256A
EC-KVF	Champion 7KCAB Citabria	202	F-AZPS, C-FDSF, CF-DSF, N5224X
EC-KVG	American Champion 8KCAB Decathlon	777-96	N717TE, N717TD
EC-KVH	MBB-Kawasaki BK.117C-2	9152	D-HMBN, D-HMBE
EC-KVI	Aérospatiale/Alenia ATR-72-212A	824	F-WWEM
EC-KVJ	Beech 76 Duchess	ME-110	N7624P, YV-1624P
EC-KVK	Robinson R44 II	12423	
EC-KVL	Ultramagic M-105 HAFB	105/165	
EC-KVM	Robin DR.400/180 Régent	2136	F-GLKT
EC-KVP	Cessna 337H Super Skymaster	33701912	CC-CYE, CC-PYE, CC-CEH, N1381S
EC-KVQ	Piper PA-46-310P Malibu	46-8608030	D-EPLK, N68JT, N62JT, N9515N, N9249A
EC-KVR	BA Eagle Mk II	138	G-AFAX, VH-CAN, G-AFAX
	(Displayed as "EC-CBB", "Santander" at Cuatro Vientos)		
EC-KVT	Ultramagic N-210 HAFB	210/58	
EC-KVV	Ultramagic M-77 HAFB	77/319	
EC-KVX	Cessna 172S Skyhawk SP	172S10203	N165MW
EC-KVY	Eurocopter EC.135P2+	0650	
EC-KVZ	Robinson R22 Beta	2536	OE-XYZ
EC-KXA	AgustaWestland AW139	31219	I-EASC
EC-KXC	Ultramagic F-29 HAFB	F29/01	
EC-KXD	Embraer 190-200LR	19000244	PT-SIP
EC-KXE	Eurocopter EC.135P2+	0721	
EC-KXG	Robinson R44 Raven II	12398	
EC-KXI	Tecnam P.2002 Sierra	P2002-048	
EC-KXJ	Cedimex Rans S-6ES Coyote II	S-6A-134	EC-CY1
EC-KXK	Tecnam P.92 Echo	P92-E-032	
	(W/o 25.10.15)		
EC-KXM	Reims/Cessna FA.337G Super Skymaster	F33700073	HA-FAA, OE-FAH, (F-BJDI)
	(Reims-assembled 337G with US c/n 33701609)		
EC-KXN	Boeing 747-4H6	25703	N703AC, VT-AIS, 9M-MPG
EC-KXO	Agusta A.109E Power	11749	
EC-KXP	Ultramagic M-145 HAFB	145/66	
EC-KXR	Tecnam P.92 Eaglet	P92-SP-044	
EC-KXT	Piper PA-28-180 Cherokee Challenger	28-7305575	HB-OMX, (LN-BKJ), HB-OMX, N9548N
EC-KXU	Aérospatiale AS.355NP Ecureuil 2	5768	
EC-KXV	ELA Aviacion ELA 07-R100	0608 217 0722	
EC-KXX	Ultramagic M-77 HAFB	77/318	EC-KPG
EC-KXZ	Tecnam P.96 Golf	P96-G-061	
EC-KYA	Schempp-Hirth Duo Discus	407	D-3501
EC-KYE	BRM Land Africa	03-08-0106-SP	
EC-KYF	Schweizer S-269C-1	0337	G-SWIZ, N86G
EC-KYG	Cirrus SR22	3318	N798PG
EC-KYH	Tecnam P.92 Eaglet	P92-SP-041	
EC-KYI	Aérospatiale/Alenia ATR-72-212A	850	F-WWET
EC-KYJ	Aérospatiale AS.355NP Ecureuil 2	5767	
	(Damaged 26.3.15)		
EC-KYL	Tecnam P.2002JF Sierra	089	
EC-KYM	Robinson R44 Raven II	11910	G-CEYB, N3061S
EC-KYO	Embraer EMB.190-200LR	19000276	PT-TLQ
EC-KYP	Embraer EMB.190-200LR	19000281	PT-TLV
EC-KYS	Diamond DA 40D Star	D4.352	EC-KRZ, OE-UDX, OE-VPU
EC-KYT	American Champion 8KCAB Super Decathlon	1044-2007	G-CEUY
EC-KYV	Tecnam P.92S Echo	P92-ES-030	EC-DU5
EC-KYX	Piper PA-38-112 Tomahawk	38-79A0751	D-EESR, N9680N
	(Damaged 6.6.10)		
EC-KYY	Vulcanair P.68TC Observer	447-09/TC	
EC-KZA	Cirrus SR22	0925	N156CD
EC-KZC	Tecnam P.2002JF Sierra	095	
EC-KZD	Piper PA-32-301FT 6X	3232001	N1326X, N9520N, N5369L
EC-KZH	Piper PA-28-236 Dakota	28-8011082	D-EDEK(2), N8143H
EC-KZI	Airbus A340-642	1017	F-WWCS
	(Stored)		
EC-KZK	Bell 407	53132	N407DL, HB-XQC, C-GFNM
EC-KZL	Aérospatiale AS.350B3 Ecureuil	4688	F-WWPS
EC-KZO	Cameron C-80 Concept HAFB	3133	G-BVEK
EC-KZR	Tecnam P.92 Echo	P92-E-037	
EC-KZS	Ultramagic M-77C HAFB	77/324	
EC-KZT	Agusta A.119Ke	14727	N106YS
EC-KZU	Agusta A.119Ke	14728	N107YS
EC-KZV	Agusta A.119Ke	14729	N108YS
EC-KZX	Agusta A.119Ke	14730	N109YS
EC-LAA	Airbus A320-214	2678	A6-ABZ, EC-JPL, F-WWIQ
EC-LAB	Airbus A320-214	2761	OE-LEV, EC-JRI, F-WWBR
EC-LAD	Aérospatiale/Alenia ATR-72-212A	864	F-WWEM
EC-LAE	Gulfstream 200	219	N619GA, 4X-CVF
EC-LAG	Eipper Quicksilver MXL Sport II	079	
EC-LAH	Grob G 103 Twin II	3862	D-6906
EC-LAI	ELA Aviacion ELA 07-R100	0209 262 0722	
EC-LAK	Agusta A.109E Power	11729	I-GIEC
EC-LAL	Eurocopter EC.135P2+	0761	EC-036
EC-LAN	Tecnam P.2002 Sierra	P2002-049	
EC-LAO	Diamond DA 20C-1 Katana	C0537	
EC-LAP	Robinson R44 Raven II	10695	N997KB
EC-LAR	Aérospatiale AS.355NP Ecureuil 2	5772	F-WEVS
EC-LAS	Tecnam P.92 Echo	P92-E-039	
EC-LAU	Pilatus PC-6/B2-H4 Turbo Porter	713	ZS-IHB, HB-FFZ
EC-LAV	Boeing 737-4Q8	24352	EC-KTM, PK-MDM, EC-IVR, OO-RMV, TF-FIA
EC-LAX	Eurocopter EC.135P2+	0743	
EC-LAZ	Ultramagic H-65 HAFB	65/171	
EC-LBB	Gulfstream 200	222	N722GA, 4X-CVG
EC-LBD	Eurocopter EC.135T2+	0711	EC-001(6)
EC-LBE	Diamond DA 42 Twin Star	42.394	OE-VPI
EC-LBH	Air Tractor AT-802A Amphibian	802A-0318	
EC-LBL	Agusta-Bell AB.412	25600	I-CGCL
EC-LBM	AgustaWestland AW139	31226	
EC-LBO	Cessna 550 Citation II	550-0634	F-HDGT, SE-DVT, N550SB, PH-MDX, (N1258B)
EC-LBP	Air Tractor AT-802A	802A-0322	
EC-LBS	Bell 407	53864	CC-CIO, C-FVSJ
EC-LBU	Aérospatiale AS.350B3 Ecureuil	4780	
EC-LBV	Aérospatiale AS.350B3 Ecureuil	4781	
EC-LBX	Eurocopter EC.130B4 Ecureuil	4817	
EC-LBY	Cameron Z-250 HAFB	11266	
EC-LBZ	Ultramagic M-77 HAFB	77/323	
EC-LCA	Air Tractor AT-802	802-0326	
	(W/o 25.5.14)		
EC-LCB	Kubicek BB-22E HAFB	710	
EC-LCD	Aérospatiale AS.355NP Ecureuil 2	5758	F-WWPA
EC-LCE	Tecnam P.92 Echo Super	P92-SP-1186	
	(W/o 9.5.12)		
EC-LCF	Piper PA-28R-200 Cherokee Arrow II	28R-7435225	EC-KYD, F-BVTN, F-ETBY
EC-LCH	AgustaWestland AW139	31257	I-RAIQ
EC-LCI	Ultramagic M-105 HAFB	105/172	
EC-LCL	Ultramagic M-180 HAFB	180/44	OO-BRQ, (OO-BQR)
EC-LCM	Cessna 525 CitationJet	525-0309	D-IBMS(3)
EC-LCN	Eurocopter EC.135P2+	0824	D-HECL
EC-LCO	Ultramagic M-77 HAFB	77/331	
EC-LCQ	Embraer ERJ-190-200LR	19000303	PT-TZR
EC-LCR	Eurocopter EC.130B4 Ecureuil	4294	C-FBRP, F-WWXV
EC-LCT	Ultramagic S-130 HAFB	130/57	
EC-LCU	Robinson R22B2 Beta	4176	G-CESN, N30667
EC-LCX	Cessna 510 Citation Mustang	510-0235	
EC-LCZ	Airbus A340-642	993	F-WWCK
EC-LDA	Ultramagic M-160 HAFB	160/35	OO-BQT
EC-LDD	Cirrus SR20	1861	N681SR
EC-LDE	Cessna 525 CitationJet CJ1	525-0644	N902DP
EC-LDF	Eurocopter EC.135T2+	0744	EC-038
EC-LDG	Ultramagic H-77 HAFB	77/327	
EC-LDH	Piper PA-34-200T Seneca II	34-7870423	SE-KOY, N39949
	(Major damage 10.6.16)		
EC-LDI	Reims/Cessna F177RG Cardinal RG	F177RG0023	D-EEYB, (F-BSHT), (N8259G)
	(Reims-assembled 177RG with c/n 177RG00159)		
EC-LDK	Cessna 510 Citation Mustang	510-0152	EC-LAF, N4085D
EC-LDL	Tecnam P.92JS Echo	050	G-CDZJ
EC-LDM	Manuel Perez Rainbow	MPR0017	
EC-LDQ	Piper PA-34-200T Seneca II	34-7970012	EC-LBA, N3044B
EC-LDU	Cameron Z-77 HAFB	11276	
EC-LDV	Ultramagic N-180 HAFB	180/92	
EC-LDX	Ultramagic N-300 HAFB	300/39	
EC-LDY	Ultramagic T-210 HAFB	210/57	
EC-LDZ	Tecnam P.92 Echo	P92-E-040	
EC-LEA	Airbus A320-214	1099	EC-HDO, F-WWDR
EC-LEB	Bombardier BD.700-1A10 Global Express	9303	C-FRKO
EC-LEC	DTA Dynamic Combo 503 / 15/430	005-ES-001	
EC-LED	Cessna 152	15282327	N68711
	(Reserved as D-EVUW, 2010)		
EC-LEE	AgustaWestland AW139	31241	
EC-LEH	Hughes 369E	0396E	EC-KRR, PT-HSC, PP-EPC, N1607G
EC-LEI	Airbus A319-111	3744	D-AVWZ
EC-LEK	Embraer ERJ-190-200LR	19000344	PT-XQG
EC-LEL	Ultramagic T-180 HAFB	180/93	

EC-LEM	Flight Design CT LS	09-07-09-AR-LS	
EC-LEO	Ultramagic M-65C HAFB	65/175	
EC-LEP	Cessna 560 Citation V	560-0153	OO-SKV, SE-DYZ, N1SN, (N153VP), N502F, N502T, N6804Y
EC-LER	Robinson R22 Beta (Wfu, noted 1.15 Cuatro Vientos)	1998	CS-HGC, EC-HYK, CS-HDL, G-BUER
EC-LEU	Airbus A340-642	960	F-WWCG
EC-LEV	Airbus A340-642	1079	F-WWCE
EC-LEX	Ultramagic T-210 HAFB	210/65	
EC-LEZ	Kubicek BB-S HAFB	730	OK-0730
EC-LFA	Aérospatiale/Alenia ATR-72-212A	902	F-WWER
EC-LFD	Robinson R44 Clipper	1469	G-OEJC
EC-LFJ	Robinson R44 Clipper II	11159	G-GEST
EC-LFK	Agusta AW.119Ke Koala	14752	N202YS
EC-LFL	Agusta AW.119Ke Koala	14753	N203YS
EC-LFO	Cameron N-77 HAFB	4269	G-OHSA
EC-LFP	AgustaWestland AW139	31296	
EC-LFQ	AgustaWestland AW139	31298	
EC-LFR	Vulcanair P.68TC Observer	456-11/OTC	
EC-LFS	Airbus A340-642	1122	F-WWCF
EC-LFV	Robinson R44 Raven II	11305	EI-FAR
EC-LFX	Ultramagic S-50 HAFB	50/01	
EC-LFZ	Embraer ERJ-190-200LR	19000357	PT-XQV
EC-LGA	Ultramagic M-65 HAFB	65/170	
EC-LGC	Aérospatiale AS.355NP Ecureuil 2	5775	EC-091 ?
EC-LGD	Aérospatiale AS.355NP Ecureuil 2	5776	EC-091 ?
EC-LGF	Aérospatiale/Alenia ATR-72-212A	907	F-WWEX
EC-LGH	Tecnam P.92 Echo Classic de luxe	P-92-E-041	
EC-LGI	Agusta A.109E Power	11124	I-ESUE
EC-LGJ	Cessna 172S Skyhawk SP	172S10054	N2464T
EC-LGM	Air Création 582S/ Kiss 450 (Cr and w/o 24.4.15)	09054-AR	
EC-LGN	Air Tractor AT-802A Fire Boss	802A-0344	N5001N
EC-LGQ	Cessna 172G	17254354	N4285L
EC-LGS	Zlin Z.50LS	0044	LZ-551
EC-LGT	Air Tractor AT-802A	802A-0342	
EC-LGV	Dassault Falcon 2000EASy	198	F-WWGR
EC-LGY	Air Tractor AT-802A Fire Boss	802A-0359	N85253
EC-LGZ	Flight Design CT LS	09-11-13-AR-LS	
EC-LHA	Ultramagic T-150 HAFB	150/13	
EC-LHB	Tecnam P.2006T	024	
EC-LHD	Aérospatiale AS.355F2 Ecureuil 2	5381	F-HDLS, Algerian AF ES-92, F-WQDT, F-WQDE, F-WYML, JA9900
EC-LHE	Aérospatiale AS.355N Ecureuil 2	5780	F-WETV
EC-LHG	Reims/Cessna FR172J Rocket	FR17200384	OY-NET, D-ECWG
EC-LHH	Aérospatiale AS.350B3 Ecureuil	4931	
EC-LHI	Air Tractor AT-802	802-0361	N8520L
EC-LHJ	Air Tractor AT-802 (Code "82")	802-0363	N8521D
EC-LHN	SOCATA MS.893E Rallye 180GT	10683	F-BOTN
EC-LHP	Aérospatiale AS.350B3 Ecureuil (W/o 15.6.11)	4916	
EC-LHR	Air Tractor AT-802A (Assigned N212FB, 2014)	802A-0368	N8523C
EC-LHV	Aérospatiale/Alenia ATR-72-202	416	F-WNUH, VN-B208, F-WWLE
EC-LHX	ICP MXP-740 Savannah	09-07-51-846	
EC-LHY	Embraer EMB-120ER	120213	F-GTSK, OO-MTD, (OO-DTM), PT-SSH
EC-LIB	Robinson R44 Clipper II (Cr and w/o 2.3.13)	11650	G-CEKF, N3016R
EC-LIC	Diamond DA 20-C1 Katana	C0043	D-EPES, N791ES, C-GKAC
EC-LID	Robin DR.500/200i Président	30	F-GUXG
EC-LIE	Tecnam P.2006T	001	I-TETW
EC-LIF	Tecnam P.2006T	030	
EC-LIG	Tecnam P.92 Echo	P92-E-042	
EC-LIL	Air Création Tanarg 912S / iXess 15	10002FS	
EC-LIM	Cessna 340A	340A0274	N340AT, F-GIVC, N4085G
EC-LIN	Embraer ERJ-190-200LR	19000401	
EC-LIQ	SOCATA TB-9 Tampico (W/o 25.12.15)	141	EI-GFC, G-BIAA
EC-LIR	Ultramagic M-65C HAFB	65/183	
EC-LIS	AgustaWestland AW139	31268	
EC-LIT	ELA Aviacion ELA 07-R115	0610 300 0714	
EC-LIU	Ultramagic T-180 HAFB	180/97	
EC-LIV	Cameron A-250 HAFB	4712	G-BYYD
EC-LIX	Air Tractor AT-802	802-0046	CS-DIW, EC-GNT, N5007H
EC-LIY	Gulfstream V-SP	5279	N579GA
EC-LIZ	B&F Funk FK-9 Mk IV	09-04-407	
EC-LJA	AgustaWestland AW139	31318	
EC-LJB	CASA C.212-200 Aviocar	323	TM.12D-79, EC-FAP, EC-616, EC-007, ECT-131
EC-LJC	Cessna 510 Citation Mustang	510-0355	
EC-LJD	Cessna 172S Skyhawk SP	172S10009	SP-HAP, G-CSSE, N16298
EC-LJE	Agusta A.109E Power	11085	F-GPPX, I-GEMI
EC-LJF	Evektor EV-97 Eurostar SL	2010 3715	EC-001(9)
EC-LJH	CASA C.212-200 Aviocar	261	TR.12D-77, EC-FAQ, EC-001, LV-AYL, LV-PAC, ECT-121
EC-LJJ	Robinson R44 Clipper II	11396	G-GENI
EC-LJM	Cessna 172R Skyhawk	17281524	D-ETRP, N6185Z
EC-LJN	Beech B200GT King Air	BY-95	N63795
EC-LJO	Schempp-Hirth Duo Discus	237	F-CHTN
EC-LJR	Canadair CL.600-2E25 Regional Jet 1000	19002	C-GCBN
EC-LJS	Canadair CL.600-2E25 Regional Jet 1000	19003	C-GIZJ
EC-LJT	Canadair CL.600-2E25 Regional Jet 1000	19005	C-GIBJ
EC-LJU	Grob G 103 Twin Astir	3157	SP-3777, SE-UFD, BGA2409/DVF
EC-LJV	Tecnam P.2002-JF Sierra (W/o 15.4.12)	134	
EC-LJX	Canadair CL.600-2E25 Regional Jet 1000	19008	C-GZQA
EC-LJY	Aeroprakt A-22L Vision	A22L-09-0037	EC-FT9
EC-LJZ	Eurocopter EC.135P2+	0846	EC-094
EC-LKA	Eurocopter EC.135P2+	0851	EC-035
EC-LKC	Robinson R22 Beta II	3928	G-ROTF, EI-DKO
EC-LKF	Canadair CL.600-2E25 Regional Jet 1000	19011	C-
EC-LKG	Airbus A320-214	1047	EC-HAF, F-WWIE
EC-LKH	Airbus A320-214	1101	EC-HDP, F-WWDB
EC-LKJ	CASA C.212-200 Aviocar	247	TR.12D-81, EC-DRO
EC-LKL	Tecnam P.92 Echo Super	P92-SP-012	EC-DT7
EC-LKM	Embraer ERJ-190-200LR	19000425	PT-TVB
EC-LKN	MBB-Kawasaki BK.117C-2	9300	D-HADF
EC-LKP	Ultramagic T-180 HAFB (Dam. 24.5.15)	180/100	
EC-LKR	Cessna U206F Stationair	U20603521	N63SJ, N8768Q
EC-LKU	Wörner NL-1000/STU Gas Balloon	1045	D-OPMB
EC-LKX	Embraer ERJ-190-200LR	19000437	PT-TCX
EC-LKY	Thunder AX10-180 SII HAFB	2086	G-BTYF
EC-LLB	Reims/Cessna F152	F15201710	G-LSMI
EC-LLE	Airbus A320-214	1119	EC-HDT, F-WWBO
EC-LLG	Tecnam P.2002 Sierra	463	
EC-LLH	Beech F33A Bonanza	CE-1161	D-EJHS, N8051H
EC-LLI	Ultramagic N-180 HAFB	180/101	
EC-LLJ	Airbus A320-216	4661	F-WWII
EC-LLK	Tecnam P.2002 Sierra	464	
EC-LLM	Airbus A320-216	4681	F-WWDX
EC-LLN	CASA C.212-200 Aviocar	359	TR.12D-76, EC-ECD
EC-LLO	Robin HR.200/100 Club	85	F-BXVQ
EC-LLP	Aeroprakt A-22L Vision	A22L-11-0043	
EC-LLQ	Tecnam P.92SP Echo Super	P-92-SP-1352	
EC-LLR	Embraer ERJ-190-200LR	19000452	PT-TCW
EC-LLS	Vol 9/Best Off Sky Ranger	SKR0911983	
EC-LLT	Air Tractor AT-802	802-0392	N8519F
EC-LLV	Dassault Falcon 7X	117	F-WWZV
EC-LLX	Airbus A320-214	4735	D-AVVD
EC-LLZ	Aérospatiale AS.350B3 Ecureuil	7177	
EC-LMA	Tecnam P.2002JF Sierra	149	
EC-LMB	Grob G.102 Astir CS Jeans	2083	D-7593
EC-LMC	PZL W-3AS Sokol	310320	SP-SUR, CCCP-04396
EC-LMD	PZL W-3AS Sokol	310321	SP-SUS, CCCP-04397
EC-LME	Ultramagic N-180 HAFB	180/98	
EC-LMF	Ultramagic N-180 HAFB	180/104	
EC-LMG	Ultramagic N-210 HAFB	210/75	
EC-LMH	Ultramagic M-56C HAFB	56/32	
EC-LMI	Piper PA-23-250 Aztec F	27-7854068	N63934
EC-LMJ	Cameron A-250 HAFB	10983	F-GXOM
EC-LMK	Aérospatiale AS.350B3 Ecureuil	7118	
EC-LML	Airbus A320-216	4742	F-WWIR
EC-LMM	PZL W-3AS Sokol	310312	SP-SYD, CCCP-04115
EC-LMN	Airbus A330-243	597	EI-EOL, I-LIVN, F-WWKQ
EC-LMO	PZL W-3AS Sokol	310205	SP-SUH, CCCP-04103, SP-PSI
EC-LMP	Marganski MDM-1 Fox	239	EC-LJK
EC-LMR	BAe.146 Series 300QT	E-3151	OO-TAA, G-TNTR, SE-DIT, G-BRGM
EC-LMS	Cirrus SR22	1330	OE-KCG, N603CD
EC-LMV	Air Tractor AT-802 (Code "84")	802-0406	N8520L
EC-LMX	Aérospatiale/Alenia ATR-42-300	115	EI-SLI, 5Y-BVD, EI-SLI, CS-TLR, PT-MTO, HK-4205, HK-4205X, XA-TPZ, XA-MAR, F-WWEL
EC-LMY	McDonnell-Douglas DC-9-83	49620	N620MD, EC-HNC, D-ALLV, EI-BTV, EC-EZU, EC-531, EI-BTV
EC-LMZ	Ultramagic T-150 HAFB	150/17	
EC-LNB	Tecnam P.92 Echo	P92-E-021	EC-EL2
EC-LNC	Boeing 737-4K5	24130	N721VX, JA8954, D-AHLQ
EC-LND	Piper PA-18A-150 Super Cub	18-6373	F-GEDJ, CN-TDB, F-DAFQ, N10F
EC-LNE	Reims FR172G Rocket	FR17200164	D-ECHM
EC-LNF	ICP MXP-740 Savannah XL	10-10-51-926	
EC-LNG	Air Tractor AT-802	802-0407	
EC-LNH	Airbus A330-243	551	EI-EON, I-LIVM, F-WWKE
EC-LNI	PZL-110 Koliber 160A	04980077	G-BXLR, SP-WGF, (N150CD)
EC-LNK	Diamond DA 20-C1 Katana	C0591	
EC-LNO	de Havilland DH.82A Tiger Moth	83839	EC-LDC, G-APPN, T7328
EC-LNQ	Aérospatiale/Alenia ATR-72-201	303	OK-XFD, F-WWLB
EC-LNR	Aérospatiale/Alenia ATR-72-212A	428	I-ADRQ, EI-CLC, F-WWEF
EC-LNT	Air Tractor AT-802	802-0411	
EC-LNU	Reims/Cessna FA152 Aerobat	FA1520385	EC-LLA, G-BLAX
EC-LNV	Cessna 152	15283322	EC-LLC, N48296
EC-LNX	Cessna 152	15284309	EC-LLD, N5393L
EC-LNY	Cessna 310	35474	F-BGTB, CN-TTB, N5274A
EC-LNZ	Cessna 510 Citation Mustang	510-0368	N4081M
EC-LOA	Vulcanair P.68C Observer 2	439-31/OB2	N87AG
EC-LOB	Airbus A320-232	4849	D-AUBJ
EC-LOC	Airbus A320-232	4855	F-WWBF
EC-LOD	Agusta A.109E Power	11121	I-MAFP
EC-LOE	B&F Funk FK-9 Mk IV	FK09 ES 002-332	EC-FO9
EC-LOF	BAe.146 Series 300QT	E-3150	OO-TAK, G-TJPM, SE-DIM, G-BRGK
EC-LOG	Cedimex Rans S-6ES-582 Coyote II	S-6A-139	EC-CQ5
EC-LOH	Ultramagic S-160 HAFB	160/23	OO-BUY
EC-LOI	Robinson R44 Clipper II	12927	EC-LHF, G-OCII
EC-LOJ	Canadair CL.600-2E25 Regional Jet 1000	19018	C-GIAO
EC-LOK	Piper PA-28-180 Cherokee C	28-2533	EC-LLF, SE-EOS
EC-LOL	B&F Funk FK-9 Mk IV	09-04-432	
EC-LOM	Robinson R44 Raven II	11582	OH-HSV, G-MDPY
EC-LON	Air Tractor AT-802	802-0419	
EC-LOO	Tecnam P.2002-JF Sierra	172	
EC-LOP	Airbus A320-214	4937	D-AXAG
EC-LOR	Eurocopter EC.135P2+	0934	EC-031
EC-LOS	Eurocopter EC.135P2+	0954	EC-036
EC-LOT	Stemme S-6 TSA-M	6.T.09.004	D-KBSP
EC-LOV	Canadair CL.600-2E25 Regional Jet 1000	19019	C-GIBT
EC-LOX	Canadair CL.600-2E25 Regional Jet 1000	19020	C-GZQV
EC-LOY	Cameron A-105 HAFB	3382	PH-RFA
EC-LOZ	Cessna 182F Skylane	18254812	EC-LKQ, HB-CML, N3412U
EC-LPA	ELA Aviacion ELA-07-R115	05113350724	
EC-LPB	Tecnam P.92 Echo	P92-E-1397	
EC-LPC	Polikarpov I-153	7027	EC-LJL, ZK-JKM, Soviet AF:75
EC-LPD	Tecnam P.92 Echo	P92-E-025	EC-EP7
EC-LPE	Ultramagic N-210 HAFB	210/79	
EC-LPF	Ultramagic N-300 HAFB	300/46	
EC-LPG	Canadair CL.600-2E25 Regional Jet 1000	19021	C-GZQW
EC-LPH	Robinson R44 Raven II	11462	G-ROGE
EC-LPI	Tecnam P.2002 Sierra	477	
EC-LPJ	Piaggio P.180 Avanti II	1223	
EC-LPK	AgustaWestland AW.119 Mk II Koala	14716	N626JP
EC-LPL	Vol 9/Best Off Sky Ranger 912 (Dam. 25.5.13)	SKR 9905019	EC-DH9
EC-LPM	Boeing 717-2BL	55185	N923ME
EC-LPN	Canadair CL.600-2E25 Regional Jet 1000	19022	C-GICB
EC-LPP	Cessna 501 Citation I	501-0232	VP-CAT, VR-CAT, VR-CHF, N35TL, N853KB, N2616C, (N2616G)
EC-LPQ	Boeing 737-85P	35496	
EC-LPR	Boeing 737-85P	36588	
EC-LPS	Aeroprakt A-22L Vision	A22L-11-0049	
EC-LPT	Schleicher ASK-13	13538	OO-YPB, Belg AF:PL-65
EC-LPV	Ultramagic M-65C HAFB	65/187	EC-LMT
EC-LPX	Ultramagic M-130 HAFB	130/82	
EC-LPY	Ultramagic N-210 HAFB	210/80	
EC-LPZ	Ultramagic H-77 HAFB	77/350	
EC-LQA	PZL W-3AS Sokol (Damaged 17.7.16)	310306	SP-SUN, CCCP-04109
EC-LQB	Agusta A.119 Koala	14529	N65TG
EC-LQE	Robinson R44 Raven	1071	G-RDEL

Regn	Type	c/n	Previous identities
EC-LQF	Cessna S550 Citation SII	S550-0007	OO-SKP, CS-DCE, N30CX, TC-SAM, N573CC, N51JH, (N1256P)
EC-LQG	Agusta A.109A-II	7388	I-SEIA
EC-LQH	Pilatus PC-6/B2-H4 Turbo Porter	882	OO-PCV, D-FSPA
EC-LQJ	Airbus A320-232	1979	EI-EUK, EC-INM, F-WWBE
EC-LQK	Airbus A320-232	2589	EI-EUP, EC-JNC, F-WWDP
EC-LQL	Airbus A320-232	1749	EI-EUF, EC-IEJ, F-WWBO
EC-LQM	Airbus A320-232	2223	EI-EUN, EC-IZK, F-WWDO
EC-LQN	Airbus A320-232	2168	EI-EUM, EC-IVG, F-WWDA
EC-LQO	Airbus A330-243	505	5B-DBS, F-WWKO
EC-LQP	Airbus A330-243	526	5B-DBT, F-WWKY
EC-LQQ	Ultramagic T-210 HAFB	210/83	
EC-LQR	Ultramagic M-77 HAFB	77/358	
EC-LQT	Evektor EV-97 Eurostar SL	2012 3940	
EC-LQU	Ultramagic T-210 HAFB	210/82	
EC-LQV	Aérospatiale/Alenia ATR-72-600	995	F-WWLT
EC-LQX	Boeing 737-85P	36589	
EC-LQY	Robinson R44 Raven	1522	CS-HHT, EI-DZI, G-CDLX
EC-LQZ	Airbus A320-232	1933	EI-EUI, EC-IMB, F-WWII
EC-LRA	Airbus A320-232	2479	EI-EUO, EC-JJD, F-WWIM
EC-LRC	Agusta A.119 Mk.II Koala	14783	N308YS
EC-LRE	Airbus A320-232	1914	EI-EUH, EC-ILH, F-WWDU
EC-LRF	Diamond DA 40 Star	40.458	D-EFMA(3), N535MA
EC-LRG	Airbus A320-214	1516	EC-HTA, F-WWIK
EC-LRH	Aérospatiale/Alenia ATR-72-600	999	F-WWLX
EC-LRI	Schleicher ASK-13	13441	PH-462
EC-LRJ	TL Ultralight TL-96 Star	TL96S-2008-06	EC-FK1
EC-LRK	Air Création Tanarg 912S	T12001	
EC-LRM	Airbus A320-232	1349	EI-EUC, EC-HRP, F-WWBD
EC-LRN	Airbus A320-214	3995	D-ABDX, F-WWDG
EC-LRO	PZL W-3A Sokol	37.05.03	SP-SYT, D-HSNA
EC-LRP	Air Tractor AT-802	802-0427	N85152
EC-LRQ	Air Tractor AT-802	802-0431	N23579
EC-LRR	Aérospatiale/Alenia ATR-72-600	1023	F-WWLQ
EC-LRU	Aérospatiale/Alenia ATR-72-600	1032	F-WWEQ
EC-LRV	Aeroprakt A-22L Vision	A22L-08-0025	EC-FK3
EC-LRX	Ultramagic M-65 HAFB	65/178	G-RANO
EC-LRY	Airbus A320-232	1862	EI-EUG, EC-IIZ, F-WWDZ
EC-LSA	Airbus A320-214	4128	D-ABFB(2), F-WWIQ
EC-LSB	Air Tractor AT-802	802-0438	N8516X
EC-LSC	Air Tractor AT-802	802-0442	N8517Q
EC-LSD	Ultramagic M-77 HAFB	77/360	
EC-LSE	Ultramagic T-180 HAFB	180/48	
EC-LSF	Aérospatiale AS.350B3 Ecureuil	7416	
EC-LSG	Ultramagic N-180 HAFB	180/111	
EC-LSH	Ultramagic M-180 HAFB	180/110	
EC-LSI	ELA Aviacion ELA-07-R115	02123520724	
EC-LSJ	Air Tractor AT-802	802-0432	
EC-LSK	CASA C.212-200 Aviocar	178	TR.12D-80, EC-DNB
EC-LSL	CASA C.212-200 Aviocar	311	TR.12D-78, EC-DTL
EC-LSN	Aérospatiale/Alenia ATR-72-202	192	PR-AZZ, F-WKVC, EC-KAE, F-GKPE, F-WWEE
EC-LSO	Colyear Freedom S-100	130-002-046	
EC-LSP	Evektor EV-97 Eurostar SL	2012 3943	
EC-LSQ	Aérospatiale/Alenia ATR-72-600	1041	F-WWED
EC-LST	Aérospatiale/Alenia ATR-72-201	234	SP-OLL, EC-JDX, F-GHPV
EC-LSU	ELA Aviacion ELA-07-R115	04123590724	
EC-LSV	Polikarpov Po-2/CSS-13	8-0518	F-AZPN, SP-APB(3), SP-AEP(2)
EC-LSX	Cessna 152	15283351	EC-LQC, N48581
EC-LSZ	ICP MXP-740 Savannah S	12-06-54-0191	
EC-LTA	Beech B200 Super King Air	BB-1116	F-GDJS, (D-ILOC)
EC-LTD	Tecnam P.2002 Sierra	P2002-054	EC-FY5
EC-LTE	Diamond DA 20-C1 Katana	C0319	D-EVMA, N396MA
EC-LTF	Bombardier BD700-1A10 Global 6000 (Res. 2012)	9464	C-GKYI
EC-LTG	Boeing 737-4K5	24129	N720VX, JA8953, D-AHLP
EC-LTI	Extra EA.300/L	090	D-EXPS
EC-LTK	Yakovlev Yak-52 (Not yet taken up)	878115	UR-BLV
EC-LTM	Boeing 737-85P	36591	
EC-LTN	Air Tractor AT-802A (Code "81")	802A-0461	N2358G
EC-LTP	Robinson R44 Raven II	10509	G-ELMO
EC-LTQ	Aeroprakt A-22L-80 Xplorer	A22L80-07-0022	EC-FG4
EC-LTR	Cessna U206A Super Skywagon	U206-0653	G-BGWR, G-DISC, G-BGWR, PH-OTD, N4953F
EC-LTS	Ultramagic M-77 HAFB	77/361	
EC-LTT	Eurocopter EC.135P2+	0981	EC-030
EC-LTU	Eurocopter EC.135P2+	1044	EC-038
EC-LTV	McDonnell-Douglas DC-9-83 (W/o 24.7.14)	53190	N190AN, LV-BHN, N190AN, HK-4137X, N190AN, SU-ZCA
EC-LTX	Ultramagic M-105 HAFB	105/190	
EC-LTY	Diamond DA 42 NG-IV Twin Star	42.N106	OE-VPY
EC-LTZ	Diamond DA 42 NG-IV Twin Star	42.N107	OE-VPW
EC-LUA	Ultramagic S-90 HAFB	90/114	
EC-LUB	Airbus A330-302E	1377	F-WWYG
EC-LUC	Airbus A320-214	1059	EC-HAG, F-WWIP
EC-LUD	Airbus A320-214	1067	EC-HDK, F-WWBF
EC-LUE	Diamond DA 42 NG-IV Twin Star	42.N108	OE-VDL
EC-LUF	Diamond DA 42 NG-IV Twin Star	42.N109	OE-VDI
EC-LUG	ICP MXP-740 Savannah XL	11-10-51-944	EC-GG8
EC-LUH	Ultramagic M-105 HAFB	105/191	
EC-LUK	Airbus A330-302E	1385	F-WWYQ
EC-LUL	Airbus A320-216	5486	F-WWDE
EC-LUM	Tecnam P.2006T	085	OE-FIN
EC-LUN	Airbus A320-232	5479	F-WWBS
EC-LUO	Airbus A320-232	5530	F-WWDG
EC-LUP	Sukhoi SU-26MX	52-05	
EC-LUQ	PZL W-3AS Sokol	310307	SP-SUT, CCCP04100
EC-LUR	Aeroprakt A22-L Vision	A22L-08-0032	EC-FQ1
EC-LUS	Airbus A320-216	5501	D-AXAG
EC-LUT	Boeing 737-85P	36592	
EC-LUU	Ultramagic S-130 HAFB	130/65	
EC-LUV	PZL W-3AS Sokol	310207	SP-SUZ, RA-04105, CCCP04105
EC-LUX	Airbus A330-302E	1405	F-WWTO
EC-LUZ	Robinson R44 Clipper II	10314	G-OSCR, G-MIKS
EC-LVD	Airbus A320-216	5570	F-WWIT
EC-LVF	Glaser-Dirks DG-500 Elan Orion	5E-134X1	D-5047
EC-LVG	SOCATA MS.893A Rallye Commodore 180	11979	F-BTJV
EC-LVH	DHC-1 Chipmunk 22	C1/0080	G-TRIC, G-AOSZ, WB635
EC-LVI	Piper PA-34-200T Seneca II	34-7570240	SE-LOD, OY-CET, D-IHGB, N1415X
EC-LVJ	Cirrus SR20	1513	(EC-LTJ), G-SRVA, N60986
EC-LVL	Airbus A330-243	461	EC-LKE, CS-TRA, EC-IDB, F-WWKL
EC-LVM	Ultramagic M-120 HAFB	120/50	
EC-LVN	Ultramagic M-160 HAFB	160/49	
EC-LVO	Airbus A320-214	5533	D-AXAS
EC-LVP	Airbus A320-214	5587	F-WWBY
EC-LVQ	Airbus A320-216	5590	D-AUBG
EC-LVR	Boeing 737-85P	36593	
EC-LVS	Airbus A320-232	5599	D-AUBK
EC-LVT	Airbus A320-232	5612	D-AUBO
EC-LVU	Airbus A320-214	5616	F-WWIU
EC-LVV	Airbus A320-232	5620	F-WWII
EC-LVX	Airbus A320-214	5673	D-AVVB
EC-LVY	Ultramagic H-77 HAFB	77/369	
EC-LVZ	Ultramagic M-77 HAFB	77/365	
EC-LXA	Airbus A330-343	670	(CS-TRM), OE-ICB, EC-JHP, F-WWKU
EC-LXB	Aeroprakt A22-L Vision	A22L-12-0056	
EC-LXC	Tecnam P.96 Golf	P96-G-040	EC-EL8
EC-LXD	Glaser-Dirks DG-500 Elan Trainer	5E-28T8	SE-UIL
EC-LXE	Flight Design CT SW	06-07-16-AR	EC-EU3
EC-LXH	Aérospatiale AS.350B3 Ecureuil	7575	
EC-LXI	Ultramagic N-180 HAFB	180/80	D-OKMH
EC-LXJ	Bell 407	53795	CC-CRA, C-FPUU
EC-LXK	Airbus A330-302E	1426	F-WWCG
EC-LXL	Ultramagic S-70 HAFB	70/04	
EC-LXM	Ultramagic T-180 HAFB	180/118	
EC-LXN	Cessna 182J Skylane	18257229	G-ATTD, (EC- . . .), G-ATTD, N3129F
EC-LXO	Aérospatiale AS.350B3 Ecureuil	7625	
EC-LXQ	Airbus A320-216	5692	D-AVVG
EC-LXR	Airbus A330-343	1097	EI-FBE, EC-LEQ, F-WWKL
EC-LXS	Aérospatiale AS.350B3 Ecureuil	7633	
EC-LXT	Airbet Girabet II Sport	IIS13037	
EC-LXU	ICP MXP-740 Savannah S	13-05-54-0264	
EC-LXV	Boeing 737-86N	36594	
EC-LXZ	Tecnam P.92 Echo	P-92-E-1458	
EC-LYA	Eurocopter EC.135P2	0414	OH-HCM, D-HECO
EC-LYB	Aérospatiale/Alenia ATR-72-212A	550	N550LL, F-WWLK
EC-LYC	Aérospatiale AS.350B3 Ecureuil	7599	F-WWXP
EC-LYD	Robinson R44 Raven II	10070	OO-SLQ
EC-LYE	Airbus A320-216	5729	F-WWIZ
EC-LYF	Airbus A330-302E	1437	F-WWKA
EC-LYG	Flightech Systems Altea-Eko UAV	1	
EC-LYI	Cameron A-120 HAFB	3203	D-OPUN
EC-LYJ	Aérospatiale/Alenia ATR-72-212A	468	OY-CIM, EC-JCR, OY-CIM, F-WWLV
EC-LYK	Gulfstream 650	6029	N629GA
EC-LYL	Cessna 560XL Citation XLS+	560-6153	
EC-LYM	Airbus A320-216	5815	F-WWBM
EC-LYN	Cameron A-250 HAFB	4504	D-OJAM
EC-LYO	Gulfstream 550	5430	N850GA
EC-LYP	Agusta-Bell 206B Jet Ranger 3	8718	OO-DOU(2), G-RNGR
EC-LYQ	Airbet Girabet II Sport	IIS12036	EC-GL2
EC-LYR	Boeing 737-85P	36595	
EC-LYS	Robin DR.400/160 Chevalier	1453	F-GCIG
EC-LYT	Aeroprakt A-22L Vision	A22L-13-0061	
EC-LYU	Aérospatiale AS.365N1 Dauphin 2	6234	CC-AHR, EC-ILN, LV-WLU, F-WQDH, F-ZVLP
EC-LYV	Ultramagic M-77 HAFB	77/371	
EC-LYX	Aeroprakt A-22L Vision	A22L-12-0053	EC-GJ2
EC-LYY	Bell 407	53727	(EC-LXP), CC-CIU, C-FLFC, (CC- . . .), C-FLFC, C-GFNN
EC-LZA	Cameron A-300 HAFB	11734	
EC-LZB	Aeroprakt A-22L Vision	A22L-11-0044	EC-GG1
EC-LZC	Ultramagic M-77 HAFB	77/373	
EC-LZD	Airbus A320-214	5642	CS-TRM, D-AUBT
EC-LZE	Airbus A320-216	5885	(JA20JJ), F-WWIK
EC-LZF	Airbus A320-232	5940	F-WWDP
EC-LZG	PZL-101A Gawron	63119	SP-YFD, SP-FGP, SP-KZG, SP-KXG
EC-LZH	Agusta A.119 Mk.II Koala	14533	N149JM
EC-LZI	Pilatus PC-6/B2-H4 Turbo Porter	924	EC-LKQ, F-OHQO
EC-LZJ	Airbus A330-302E	1490	F-WWTJ
EC-LZK	Beech 99	U-46	D-IEXE, N99LM, D-IEXE, LN-SAX, SE-FOR, N855SA
EC-LZM	Airbus A320-232	5877	F-WXAA, (JA19JJ), F-WWDS
EC-LZN	Airbus A320-214	5925	D-AUBE
EC-LZO	Boeing 767-35DER	27902	EI-FDI, SP-LPB
EC-LZP	Cessna F500 Citation I	500-0312	F-HBMS, EC-KGE, F-GJDG, N82AT, N33MQ, (N233ME), N33ME, N5312J
EC-LZQ	Cirrus SR20	1570	N696DJ
EC-LZS	Cessna 510 Citation Mustang	510-0050	PH-TXI, G-OAMB, PH-TXI
EC-LZT	Aérospatiale AS.365N1 Dauphin 2	6346	CC-AEF, EC-JLX, LN-OPL(2), F-WQDP, F-OGSV(2)
EC-LZU	Gulfstream 650	6066	N606GA
EC-LZV	Piper PA-31-350 Navajo Chieftain	31-7305117	SE-ILL, 4X-CCH, N676GL, N676LL, N6767L, N74967
EC-LZX	Airbus A330-302E	1507	F-WWKG
EC-LZY	Aérospatiale AS.350B3 Ecureuil	7433	
EC-LZZ	Airbus A320-214	2620	OE-ICT, JA01MC, F-WWDM
EC-MAA	Airbus A330-302E	1515	F-WWKR
EC-MAB	Cessna 305C Bird Dog (L-19E)	305M-0040	N191JL, E-IBD, MM612992, 61-2992
EC-MAC	Colt 120A HAFB	1618	PH-JVK, D-OBPZ, HB-BPZ
EC-MAD	Boeing 737-4Y0(F)	25261	EI-STE, N286AL, TC-JDT, N600SK
EC-MAE	Agusta A.109E Power	11619	F-HCHM, I-NIGI
EC-MAF	Aérospatiale/Alenia ATR-72-212A	568	OY-CIN, F-WWEH
EC-MAG	Ultramagic M-65C HAFB	65/200	
EC-MAH	Airbus A320-214	6039	F-WWIM
EC-MAI	Airbus A320-214	6045	F-WWIN
EC-MAJ	Airbus A330-243	992	A9C-KJ, (G-XLXC), F-WWKN
EC-MAK	Wörner NL-1000/STU Gas Balloon	1101	
EC-MAL	Ultramagic N-355 HAFB	355/28	
EC-MAM	Cessna 550 Citation II	550-0415	9H-TRT, EC-KJJ, F-GJYD, N1949M, N1948B, OH-CUT, D-CNCI, N12164
EC-MAN	Airbus A320-214	6079	F-WWIV
EC-MAO	Airbus A320-214	6081	F-WWBJ
EC-MAP	Bell 412	33041	C-GWEU(2), N412AH, XC-NCT, N7034J, G-BPEY, N7034J, XC-MAZ, N2199D
EC-MAQ	Bell 412	33032	C-GUNX, N418EH, 9Y-BHI, N418EH, N3911J
EC-MAR	Bell 412	33031	N417EH, N3911E
EC-MAS	Magni M-16C Tandem Trainer	16137634	EC-GL9
EC-MAT	Evektor EV-97 Eurostar SLW	2011 3821	

Reg	Type	C/N	Previous identities
EC-MAU	CASA C-127	45	U.9-45, L.9-45
EC-MAV	CASA C-127	6	U.9-6, L.9-6
EC-MAX	Airbus A320-214	4478	F-HDGK, D-ABFM, F-WWDJ
EC-MAY	HOAC DV 20 Katana	20016	CS-DBI
EC-MAZ	Bell 412EP	36183	CS-HHK, EC-HFD, N52247, C-FOEP
EC-MBA	Cameron Z-225 HAFB	11125	OO-BWQ
EC-MBB	Ultramagic M-77 HAFB	77/378	
EC-MBC	CEDIMEX Rans S-12 Airaille	S-12-100	EC-BK8
EC-MBD	Airbus A320-214	3444	EI-FDT, A6-ABK, F-WWIF
EC-MBE	Airbus A320-214	3476	EI-FDU, A6-ABL, F-WWDG
EC-MBF	Airbus A320-214	3492	EI-LIS, EK-32005, F-WWIU
EC-MBK	Airbus A320-214	2658	OE-ICU, JA02MC, F-WWIP
EC-MBL	Airbus A320-214	3833	EI-FEZ, CN-NMB, D-ABDV, F-WWBE
EC-MBM (2)	Airbus A320-214	4463	F-HDMF, D-ABFL, D-AXAC
EC-MBN	Aérospatiale AS.355N Ecureuil 2	5598	CC-ACW, EC-KUC, OE-XAP, OY-HOY, HB-XJI
EC-MBO	AgustaWestland AW139	41357	N611SM
EC-MBP	AgustaWestland AW139	41359	N467SH
EC-MBQ	Aérospatiale AS.350B3 Ecureuil	4934	CC-ACX, EC-LGO, F-WEAB
EC-MBR	CASA C-1.133C Jungmeister	114	EC-LPU, E.1B-42, ES.1-42
	(Noted 1.16 painted as ES.1-42, code 81-105)		
EC-MBS	Airbus A320-232	6123	F-WWDU
EC-MBT	Airbus A320-214	6128	D-AXAX
EC-MBU	Airbus A320-214	1198	EI-EZR, N267AV, I-PEKP, EI-CUK, F-WWIE
EC-MBV	Piper PA-28-161 Warrior II	2816017	EC-IKF, G-BNOI, N9122N
EC-MBX	Cameron Z-77 HAFB	11767	
EC-MBY	Airbus A320-214	4674	D-ABFT(2), D-AXAF
EC-MBZ	Ultramagic S-70 HAFB	70/07	
EC-MCB	Airbus A320-214	1125	I-EEZK, I-VLEA, I-VLEO, HB-IGZ, F-WWIH
EC-MCC	Aérospatiale AS.350B3 Ecureuil	3439	OB-1880-P, EC-HXS, F-WQDA, F-WQDH
EC-MCD	Aérospatiale AS.350B3 Ecureuil	3340	OB-1820-P, EC-HSD, F-WQOS, F-WQDQ
EC-MCE	SOCATA TB-9 Tampico	194	G-BLCM, OO-TCT, (OO-TBC)
EC-MCF	Cessna 551 Citation II/SP	551-0201	D-ISEC, N550GB, N550JB, C-GGSP, N177CJ
EC-MCG	Aérospatiale AS.350B3 Ecureuil	3612	OB-1970-P, OY-HGW, SE-JHD
EC-MCH	Air Création Safari GT BI / Fun 18	08015 JL	EC-GA3
EC-MCI	Boeing 737-4Q8(F)	26298	N156GA, G-CIBE, EI-CUD, TC-JEI
EC-MCJ	Aérospatiale AS.350B2 Ecureuil	2558	OB-1855-P, EC-FIB, EC-853
EC-MCK	BAe 146 Series 300QT	E-3153	OO-TAJ, G-TNTE, G-BRPW
EC-MCL	BAe 146 Series 300QT	E-3154	OO-TAS, EC-FFY, EC-712, G-TNTF, G-BRXI, G-6-514
EC-MCM	Aérospatiale AS.350B3 Ecureuil	7932	
EC-MCN	Aérospatiale AS.350B3 Ecureuil	3727	OB-1969-P, OY-HIZ, LN-ODM
EC-MCO	Diamond DA 42 NG Twin Star	42.N129	OE-UDK, OE-VDO
EC-MCP	Bücker Bü.131 Jungmann	203	
EC-MCR	Eurocopter EC.225LP Super Puma II	2892	EC-004
EC-MCS	Airbus A320-216	6244	D-AVVP
EC-MCT	Aeropro Eurofox 3K	35912	
EC-MCU	Airbus A320-214	3907	EI-ERX, A6-RKB, EI-ERX, 9K-AEC, D-AVVA
EC-MCV	Air Tractor AT-802A Fire Boss	802A-0210	I-SPED, EC-JLD, N41810
EC-MCX	Air Tractor AT-802A Fire Boss	802A-0286	I-SPEM, EC-KRT
EC-MCY	Grob G 109B	6297	LX-CRJ, D-KEOE
EC-MCZ	ELA Aviacion ELA 07-R115	0606 100 0724	EC-ET6
EC-MDA	Tecnam P.92 Echo	P92-E-1500	
EC-MDB	Cessna 172P Skyhawk	17276310	I-AGFE, HB-CJM, N98564
EC-MDD	Air Tractor AT-802A f/p	802A-0561	
EC-MDE	Scheibe Bergfalke II/55	334	SE-TAO
EC-MDF	Rockwell Commander 112	487	OY-GSC, SE-GSC, (N1487J)
EC-MDI	Diamond DA 40D Star	D4.083	F-HABN, OE-VPW
EC-MDJ	Cessna F150J	F150-0395	D-EKET (3)
EC-MDK	Airbus A320-214	6328	D-AVVZ
EC-MDL	ICP MXP-740 Savannah S	12-12-54-0235	EC-GM1
EC-MDM	Bell 212	30558	OB-2075, CC-CRB, EC-FBL, EC-553, LN-OQZ, (G-BGFE), LN-OQZ, N83079
EC-MDN	Air Tractor AT-802A	802A-0562	
EC-MDO	Aérospatiale AS.355NP Ecureuil 2	5807	EC-005. EC-001
EC-MDQ	Ultramagic M-77 HAFB	77/238	
EC-MDR	Tecnam P.92 Echo	P92-E-1507	
EC-MDS	Boeing 747-419	26910	N342AS, ZK-NBV
EC-MDU	Bell 212	30639	OB-1972-P, EC-HFX, G-BCMC, 9Y-THL, HK-4103X, G-BCMC, (EC-GHO), EC-294, G-BCMC, EC-GCS, EC-932, G-BCMC, 9Y-THL, G-BCMC, 9M-ATU, VR-BFI, G-BCMC, N18090
EC-MDV	Bell 212	30759	OB-1973-P, EC-GXG, N21601, C-GJDC, N21601, HC-BJQ, N49688
EC-MDX	Ultramagic M-77 HAFB	77/382	
EC-MDY	Eurocopter EC.135P2+	1177	EC-030
EC-MDZ	Airbus A320-232	6377	F-WWDK
EC-MEA	Airbus A320-232	6400	F-WWIL
EC-MEB (2)	Agusta A.109E Power	11119	CC-AEO, I-REMV
EC-MEC	Aérospatiale/Alenia ATR-72-212A	595	OY-CIO, 3B-NBK, OY-CIO, EC-JCF, OY-CIO, F-WWEB
EC-MED	Ultramagic M-105 HAFB	105/206	
EC-MEE	Aérospatiale AS.365N2 Dauphin 2	6264	CC-AHS, EC-JLV, LN-OPM, CS-HCG, F-WYMI, F-ODUZ
EC-MEF	Aeroprakt A-22L Vision	A22L-14-0066	
EC-MEG	Airbus A320-214	1439	EI-CWU, 2-PAEL, EK-32039, OE-IBT, 4L-FGC, OK-GEA, CS-TQA, EI-CWU, OO-SNI, F-WWBM
EC-MEH	Airbus A320-214	1450	EI-CWV, 2-PAEK, EK-32050, 2-PAEK, SP-AEK, 4L-FGD, OE-ICC, OK-GEB, CS-TQB, EI-CWV, OO-SNJ, F-WWBX
EC-MEI	Bell 412	33089	N167EH, VH-NSO
EC-MEJ	Bell 412	33064	N169EH, XA-BDD, N169EH, C-GBHH, N5760K, HL9233, N5760K, PT-HRI, N5760K
EC-MEK	Tecnam P.92SP Echo Super	P92-SP-1510	
EC-MEL	Airbus A320-232	6450	D-AXAT
EC-MEM(2)	Agusta AW.119Ke Koala Mk.2	14736	TC-HKZ, EC-LGR, N223SM
EC-MEN	Canadair CL.600-2D24 Regional Jet 900	15063	C-FIAP, N510AP, F-HDTB, F-WDTB, N563ES, C-FXCE, TC-ETB, C-FIIW
EC-MEO	BAe.146 Series 300QT	E-3186	OO-TAF, G-TNTK, G-BSXK, G-6-186
EC-MEP	SOCATA Rallye 180T Galérien	3307	F-BLIL
EC-MEQ	Airbus A320-232	6483	F-WWDI
EC-MER	Airbus A320-232	6510	F-WWBD
EC-MES	Airbus A320-232	6518	F-WWBU
EC-MET	SOCATA TBM-700N	1058	
EC-MEV	Ultramagic N-300 HAFB	300/13	OO-BQE
EC-MEX	Ultramagic S-50 HAFB	50/15	
EC-MEY	Boeing 737-476F	24438	N248SY, OM-SDA, N248SY, VH-TJM
EC-MEZ (2)	Boeing 717-2CM	55059	OH-BLG, SE-REN, EC-HNY, N6203U
EC-MFA	Airbus A340-313X	212	EC-MDG, (SX-TIF), A9C-LG, A4O-LG, D-ABGM, 9V-SKL, F-WWJU
EC-MFB	Airbus A340-313X	215	EC-MDH(SX-TIG), A9C-LH, A4O-LH, D-ASIJ, 9V-SKM, F-WWJV
EC-MFC	Canadair CL.600-2D24 Regional Jet 900	15065	C-GLPP(2), LV-CGW, C-GEGD, N565ES, C-FXCL, TC-ETD, C-FIIZ
EC-MFD	Ultramagic M-160 HAFB	160/75	
EC-MFE	Boeing 737-476F	24445	N245SY, XU-886, N245SY, VH-TJT
EC-MFF	Cessna 152	15285617	SP-FZW, N94187
EC-MFG (2)	Cameron Z-315 HAFB	10964	G-SKYJ
EC-MFH	Tecnam P.2002 Sierra	P2002-026	EC-EX9
EC-MFI	Cameron N-120 HAFB	4604	PH-WBN
EC-MFJ	Boeing 717-2CM	55060	OH-BLH, SE-REO, EC-HNZ, N9010L
EC-MFK (2)	Airbus A320-232	6535	F-WWBY
EC-MFL	Airbus A320-232	6557	F-WWIK
EC-MFM	Airbus A320-232	6571	F-WWIR
EC-MFN	Airbus A320-232	6594	F-WWDR
EC-MFO	Airbus A319-111	938	F-GRHA, D-AVYS
EC-MFP	Airbus A319-111	998	F-GRHC, D-AVYW
EC-MFQ	Rolladen-Schneider LS4	4410	SE-TXE
EC-MFR	Tecnam P.92 Echo Super	P-92-SP-023	EC-EF5
EC-MFS	Boeing 737-4Y0	25178	OM-AEX, D-AEFL, EC-GNZ, D-ABAD, N601TR, D-ABAD
EC-MFT	BAe.146 Series 300QT	E-3182	OO-TAE, G-TNTG, G-BSUY
EC-MFU	Bell 412SP	33172	VT-AZD(2), N63385, 9M-SSP, G-SPBA, N32072
EC-MFV	Diamond DA 42 Twin Star	42.289	OH-RSH, OE-VPI
EC-MFX	Aeroprakt A-22L Vision	A22L-14-0063	EC-GO5
EC-MFY	Partenavia P.68 Observer 2	397-06/OB2	9H-AFF, 5A-DSE
EC-MFZ	Scheibe Bergfalke III	5658	SE-TVZ
EC-MGA	Robinson R44 Raven I	2060	D-HALN(4), (D-HABN)
EC-MGC	Ultramagic S-130 HAFB	130/93	
EC-MGD	Aérospatiale AS.350B3 Ecureuil	8061	
EC-MGE	Airbus A320-232	6607	D-AVVS
EC-MGF	Airbus A319-111	3028	LZ-FBF, N950FR, D-AVWD
EC-MGG	Bell 212	30802	A6-BBK
EC-MGH	Bell 212	30942	A6-BBQ
EC-MGI	Bell 412	33102	A6-BAY, EP-. . ., A6-BAY, PK-HMP
EC-MGK	Aérospatiale AS.350B3 Ecureuil	8069	
EC-MGL	Eurocopter EC.135P2+	1184	D-HECA
EC-MGM	Eurocopter EC.135P2+	1185	
EC-MGN	PZL W-3AM Sokol	370705	I-SOKL, CS-HFA, SP-SYI
EC-MGR	PZL W-3AS Sokol	310311	SP-SYC, CCCP-04114
EC-MGS	Boeing 717-2CM	55061	OH-BLI, SE-REP, EC-HOA, N9010L
EC-MGT	Boeing 717-2S3	55066	OH-BLM, SE-REM, EC-HUZ, N6202S
EC-MGU	Aérospatiale AS.350B3 Ecureuil	8078	
EC-MGV	Cessna 182E	18253630	SX-APK, N371VU, N9230X
EC-MGX	Evektor EV-97 Eurostar	2014 4209	
EC-MGY	Airbus A321-231	6638	D-AVXX
EC-MGZ	Airbus A321-231	6660	D-AVZB
EC-MHA	Airbus A321-231	6684	D-AVZI
EC-MHB	Airbus A321-231	6691	D-AVZL
EC-MHC	Ultramagic M-77 HAFB	77/388	
EC-MHD	Ultramagic T-210 HAFB	210/102	
EC-MHE	CASA C-1.131E Jungmann	2193	(EC-IQP), E3B-594
EC-MHF	Guimbal Cabri G2	1013	SE-JNE, F-WWHZ
EC-MHG	Eurocopter EC.135P2	0460	G-CGZD, D-HHDL, EC-KKF, (G-214007 Shenyang Police)
EC-MHH	Ultramagic M-65C HAFB	65/205	
EC-MHI	Aérospatiale/Alenia ATR-72-212A	879	OY-YAI, F-ORAA, (ZA-ARB), F-WWEH
EC-MHJ	Aérospatiale/Alenia ATR-72-212A	982	OY-YAF, TC-YAF, F-WWEC
EC-MHK	Air Tractor AT-802	802-0608	N8520L
EC-MHL	Airbus A330-343	1574	OE-IDI, JA330F, F-WWKR
EC-MHM	Cameron N-133 HAFB	4642	OO-BYV
EC-MHN	Ultramagic M-130 HAFB	130/95	
EC-MHO	Air Tractor AT-802A	802A-0610	N8521E
EC-MHP	AgustaWestland AW.139	31619	
EC-MHQ	Diamond DA 40 NG	40.N270	OE-VPU
EC-MHR	BAe.146 Series 300QT	E-3166	OO-TAD, G-TNTM, RP-C480, G-TNTM, G-BSLZ, G-6-166
EC-MHS	Airbus A321-231	6740	D-AYAI
EC-MHT	Tecnam P.2006T	129	OE-FAF
EC-MHU	Aérospatiale AS.355NP Ecureuil 2	5810	EC-030
EC-MHV	Aérospatiale AS.355NP Ecureuil 2	5811	EC-032
EC-MHX	Beech C90 King Air	LJ-735	N939RK, D-IHDE
EC-MHY	ELA Aviacion ELA-07-R100	06154460722	
EC-MHZ	Gulfstream 650	6135	N635GA
EC-MIA	Boeing 777-28EER	28685	HL7500
EC-MIB	Air Tractor AT-802A	802A-0611	N8517Q
EC-MIC	Air Tractor AT-802	802-0613	N8518U
EC-MID	BAe.146 Series 300QT	E-3168	OO-TAH, G-TNTL, RP-C479, G-TNTL, G-BSGI, (RP-C479), G-BSGI/G-6-168
EC-MIE	Boeing 737-4Y0(F)	26069	N320SC, JA737E, N869DC, HA-LEN, UR-GAA, N3509J, N1787D
EC-MIF	Aérospatiale/Alenia ATR-72-600	1278	F-WWEG
EC-MIG	Boeing 787-8	36412	
EC-MIH	Boeing 787-8	36413	
EC-MII	Airbus A330-343E	1691	F-WWYQ
EC-MIJ	Ultramagic M-120 HAFB	120/80	
EC-MIK	Schröder Fire Balloons G85/24 HAFB	1557	F-HMIK
EC-MIL	Airbus A330-202	1694	F-WWCH
EC-MIM	Ultramagic M-77C HAFB	77/394	
EC-MIP	PZL W-3AS Sokol	310308	EC-MGJ, SP-SUF, CCCP-04111
EC-MIQ	Airbus A319-111	3169	EI-EPR, EC-KEV, D-AVXD
EC-MIR	Airbus A319-111	3377	EI-EPS, EC-KME, D-AVWC
EC-MIS	ICP MXP-740 Savannah S	15-06-54-0401	EC-GP8
EC-MIT	Canadair CL.600-2B16 Challenger 604	5457	D-AKBH, N325FX, C-GLXW
EC-MIU	Tecnam P.96 Golf	P-96-G-022	EC-DX5
EC-MIV	Robinson R22 Beta II	3987	LN-ODX, OY-HOA, G-ZFLY
EC-MIX	Reims/Cessna F172N	F17201986	D-EOER
EC-MIY	Aérospatiale/Alenia ATR-72-212(F)	498	F-GVZR, N498AT, F-WWLW
EC-MIZ	Agusta A.109E Power	11133	F-GPPG, I-REMR
EC-MJA	Airbus A330-202	1700	F-WWKD

Reg	Type	c/n	Previous identities
EC-MJB	Airbus A320-232	6883	F-WWBI
EC-MJC	Airbus A320-232	6841	F-WWIA
EC-MJD	Lindstrand LBL-150A HAFB	896	PH-FWJ
EC-MJE	Canadair CL-600-2B19 RJ200	7622	OY-RJK, EC-IDC, C-GJYV, C-FMLT
EC-MJF	Manuel Perez Rainbow	MPR 02-0003	EC-EG1
EC-MJG	Aérospatiale/Alenia ATR-72-600	1310	F-WWEQ
EC-MJH	PZL W-3A Sokol	371010	SP-SIS
EC-MJI	PZL W-3A Sokol	371011	
EC-MJJ	PZL W-3A Sokol	371012	
EC-MJK	Eurocopter EC.145T2 (BK.117D-2)	20055	D-HADB
EC-MJL	Robin R2160 Alpha Sport	322	G-VECG, F-GSRD
EC-MJM	Flight Design CT-2K	03-05-06-AR	EC-EB4
EC-MJN	Piper PA-32-300 Cherokee Six	32-40209	LZ-SVS, YU-BRD, N4141W
	(Major damage 24.3.16)		
EC-MJO	Canadair CL-600-2E25 RJ1000	19045	
EC-MJP	Canadair CL-600-2E25 RJ1000	19046	
EC-MJQ	Canadair CL-600-2E25 RJ1000	19047	
EC-MJR	Airbus A321-231	6933	D-AVZQ
EC-MJS	Airbus A330-243	265	G-EOMA, F-WWKU
EC-MJT	Airbus A330-202	1710	F-WWYT
EC-MJU	Boeing 737-85P	60584	
EC-MJV	Ultramagic M-120 HAFB	120/84	
EC-MJX	Canadair CL-600-2B19 RJ200	7466	LV-GIJ, EC-HSH, C-GHWD, C-FMKZ
EC-MJZ	Canadair CL-600-2B19 RJ200	7975	LV-GII, EC-JCL, C-FCID, C-FMKW
EC-MKA	Agusta A.119 Koala	14033	N803EB, N7KN
EC-MKB	Agusta A.119 Koala	14045	N907AG, N119MW
EC-MKC	Bell 412	33067	N421EH, N57413
EC-MKD	Bell 412	33058	N168EH, VH-NSI, N9104F, C-GWMX, VH-SUH, C-GRLX
EC-MKE	Aérospatiale/Alenia ATR-72-212A	494	F-GVZP, N494AE, F-WWLS
EC-MKF	Ultramagic N-300 HAFB	300/57	
EC-MKG	Piper PA-44-180 Seminole	44-7995072	G-TWIN, N30267
EC-MKH	Bombardier BD-700-1A10 Global Express	9695	C-FHSX
EC-MKI	Airbus A330-202	1719	F-WWKO
EC-MKJ	Airbus A330-202	1728	F-WWKI
EC-MKK	MBB-Kawasaki BK.117B-2	7056	D-HBND, OO-XCY, D-HBND, OO-VCY, OO-XCY, (OO-VCY), D-HBND, (N156RK), D-HBND
EC-MKL	Boeing 737-85P	60585	
EC-MKM	Airbus A320-232	7017	F-WWBQ
EC-MKN	Airbus A320-232	7026	D-AUBW
EC-MKO	Airbus A320-232	7028	F-WWDS
EC-MKP	Ultramagic N-210 HAFB	210/2015	
EC-MKQ	Zlin Z.326M Trenér Master	839	D-EUBE, SE-XFY, D-ENGA(1), OK-SNB
EC-MKR	Tecnam P.2006T	083	ZK-OBZ, VH-OBZ
EC-MKS	Bell 412HP	36027	D-HAFW(6), C-GBKT(3), VT-AZJ(2), N412HX, N412FH
EC-MKT	Airbus A330-223	802	(D-ABXG), CS-TRX, EI-EZL, I-EEZL, F-WWYD
EC-MKU	Sukhoi SU-31M	01-01	OM-LMJ, (RA-01405)
EC-MKV	Airbus A319-111	3102	EI-EPU, EC-KDI, D-AVYA
EC-MKX	Airbus A319-111	3054	EI-EPT, EC-KBJ, D-AVYS
EC-MKY	HOAC HK-36TC Super Dimona	36527	PH-1114
EC-MKZ	Eurocopter EC.145T2 (BK.117D-2)	20075	
EC-MLA	Dassault Falcon 2000S	735	
EC-MLB	Airbus A330-202	1736	
EC-MLC	Canadair CL-600-2E25 RJ1000	19048	C-GZYK(2)
EC-MLD	Airbus A321-231	7105	D-AZAL
EC-MLE	Airbus A320-232	7109	D-AVVK
EC-MLF	Aérospatiale/Alenia ATR-72-212A	570	OY-YAN, CX-LFL, F-WKVI, EC-HEI, (VT- . . .), F-WWEG
EC-MLG	Bell 412SP	33188	D-HAFT(2), ZS-ROK(2), D-HAJO(3), VT-AZA(2), 9M-SSM, N3215G
EC-MLH	Agusta A.109E Power	11606	F-GPBH
EC-MLI	Tecnam P.2002-JF Sierra	281	
EC-MLJ	Tecnam P.2002-JF Sierra	280	
EC-MLK	AgustaWestland AW139	31062	ZS-HHL(2), ZS-RPM(3), ZS-VDM(2), I-EASS
EC-MLL	Ultramagic M-65 HAFB	65/180	
EC-MLM	Airbus A321-231	7108	D-AZAN
EC-MLN	Canadair CL-600-2E25 RJ1000	19049	
EC-MLO	Canadair CL-600-2E25 RJ1000	19050	
EC-MLP	Airbus A330-202	1740	
EC-MLQ	Aérospatiale AS.350B3 Ecureuil	8198	
EC-MLR	Gulfstream VI	6184	N684GA
EC-MLS	Canadair CL-600-2B19 RJ200	7661	PH-ACQ, OY-RJL, EC-IGO, C-FVAZ
EC-MLT	Boeing 787-8	36414	N8287V, EC-MLT
EC-MLU	Cameron A-275 HAFB	4879	G-SKYK
EC-MLV	Cessna 680 Citation Sovereign	680-0215	OH-WIA(4), N5093Y
EC-MLX	MBB-Kawasaki BK-117B-2	7080	D-HMUM(2), (D-HBPA)
EC-MLY	Guimbal G2 Cabri	1145	
EC-MLZ	Ultramagic N-250 HAFB	250/88	
EC-MMA	Cameron A-140 HAFB	4354	PH-DVB
EC-MMB	Ultramagic S-90 HAFB	90/154	
EC-MMC	Bell 412SP	33209	D-HAFV(4), N412LG
EC-MMD	Bombardier BD-700-1A10 Global Express	9428	N976CB, N979CB, C-GHWD
EC-MME	Beech B200 Super King Air	BB-1607	N699AL, F-GRLF, ZS-DJA(2), N724TA
EC-MMF	Aérospatiale AS.355NP Ecureuil 2	5815	EC-035
EC-MMG	Airbus A330-202	1747	
EC-MMH	Airbus A321-231	7152	D-AVXS
EC-MMI	Eurocopter EC.130T2 Ecureuil	8238	
EC-MMJ	Eurocopter EC.130T2 Ecureuil	8252	
EC-MMK	Agusta A.109E Power	11030	F-GLEG
EC-MML	Air Tractor AT-802	802-0649	N8520K
EC-MMM	Aérospatiale/Alenia ATR-72-600	1337	F-WWEU
EC-MMN	Pilatus PC-6/B2-H2 Turbo-Porter	954	HB-FMX, F-GPPG, PH-LLL, HB-FMX
EC-MMO	Air Tractor AT-802	802-0652	N8522M
EC-MMP	Eurocopter EC.145T2 (BK.117D-2)	20031	D-HADM
EC-MMQ	Eurocopter EC.135T3	1227	D-HCBB
EC-MMR	MBB-Kawasaki BK-117B-2	7224	D-HLTB, (N8196H), D-HFDO
EC-MMS	Eurocopter EC.135T3	1225	D-HECY
EC-MMT	Tecnam P.92JS Echo	139	
EC-MMU	Airbus A321-231	7218	D-AVZW
EC-MMV	Piper PA-44-180T Turbo Seminole	44-8107045	N904FC, N62981, ZP-TUA, N8356N
EC-MMX	Boeing 787-8	36415	
EC-MMY	Boeing 787-8	36416	
EC-MMZ	Aérospatiale/Alenia ATR-72-212A	846	OY-YBJ, PP-PTT, F-WWEL
EC-MNA	AgustaWestland AW139	41509	N407JZ
EC-MNB	Canadair CL-600-2B19 RJ200	7350	5Y-WWA, EC-HHV, C-GFKR
EC-MNC	Diamond DA 42 NG	42N.216	
EC-MND	Diamond DA 42 NG	42N.217	
EC-MNE	Aéros[patiale AS.350B3	8210	
EC-MNF	Air Tractor AT-802	802-0518	CC-AKO, N1001U
EC-MNG	Tecnam P.2006T	174	
EC-MNH	Bombardier BD-700-1A10 Global Express	9360	N863BA, EC-LIP, C-FXJM
EC-MNI	Robinson R44 Raven II	12158	F-GZIP, OO-RTL
EC-MNJ	Air Tractor AT-802A	802A-0325	CC-AON, I-SPEL, EC-LGX, EC-LDO
EC-MNK	Airbus A330-202	1755	F-WWKR
EC-MNL	Airbus A330-202	1761	F-WWCR
EC-MNM	Boeing 737-4UY0	26071	N6360W, VP-BAN, N314PW, PK-KKC, HA-LEO, UR-GAB, N35108, N1784B
EC-MNN	Aérospatiale/Alenia ATR-72-600	1361	F-WWEV
EC-MNO	Cessna 152	15285960	PH-TGD, (PH-TDG), N95705
EC-MNP	Diamond DA 42 NG	42.N218	
EC-MNQ	Canadair CL-600-2E25 RJ1000ER	19051	
EC-MNR	Canadair CL-600-2E25 RJ1000ER	19052	
EC-MNS	Boeing 787-8	36417	
EC-MNT	Eurocopter EC.145 (BK.117C-2)	9076	SE-JJC, D-HMBN(13)
EC-MNU	Ultramagic H-77 HAFB	77/400	
EC-MNV	Ultramagic H-77 HAFB	77/401	
EC-MNX	Ultramagic T-150 HAFB	150/14	F-HETC
EC-MNY	Airbus A330-243	261	G-GGEN, 9M-AJL, G-SMAN, F-WWKR
EC-MNZ	Airbus A320-232	7351	F-WWDV
EC-MOA	Aérospatiale AS.350B3 Ecureuil	4424	CP-2730, EC-KQH, (F-GKCY), F-WQAH
EC-MOB	Cessna 172S Skyhawk SP	172S10378	N1172X
EC-MOC	Ultramagic N-355 HAFB	355/56	
EC-MOD	Ultramagic T-180 HAFB	180/128	
EC-MOE	Reims/Cessna F172N	F17201722	SP-GIT, D-EICP
EC-MOF	Diamond DA 20-A1 Katana	10307	5T-EDM, EC-IRE, G-BXTR, N607DA
EC-MOG	Airbus A320-232	7402	F-WWBY
EC-MOH	Tecnam P.2002-JF Sierra	302	
EC-MOI	Tecnam P.2002-JF Sierra	303	
EC-MOJ	Tecnam P.2002-JF Sierra	304	
EC-MOK	Ultramagic H-77 HAFB	77/402	
EC-MOL	Aérospatiale/Alenia ATR-72-600	1359	(G-FBXG), F-WWET
EC-MOM	Boeing 787-8	36419	
EC-MOO	Airbus A321-231	7471	D-AVZE
EC-M..	Aérospatiale AS.350B3 Ecureuil	3077	G-CJFD, EC-IYQ, SE-JFX
EC-M..	Ultramagic N-180 HAFB	180/20	F-GLEK

HOMEBUILT AIRCRAFT AND MICROLIGHTS

Many of the c/ns quoted are clearly in the form of CofR or Permit numbers, not those of manufacturers or kits. Information on 'true' c/ns would be welcome if known. The EC-Yxx and the EC-Zxx series were allocated before the more recent EX-Xxx series.

Reg	Type	c/n
EC-XAA	Plätzer Kiebitz	07076-2284
EC-XAB	Rotorway Exec 162F	05049-2055
EC-XAC	Aeropro Eurofox	07092-2300
EC-XAD	Zenair CH-601HD Zodiac	04097-1981
EC-XAE	Zlin Savage Cruiser	07075-2283
EC-XAF	ICP MXP-740 Savannah	07079-2287
EC-XAG	Rotorway Exec 162F	02120-1784
EC-XAH	Fisher Classic	08020-2294
EC-XAI	Sportsman	08008-2311
EC-XAJ	Flight Design CT LS	08-03-01
	(Officially reg'd as 08016-2319)	
EC-XAK	TL Ultralight TL-2000 Sting	08050-2351
EC-XAL	Zenair CH-701 STOL	07027-2235
EC-XAM	ATEC Zephyr 2000	08012-2315
	(Cr and destroyed 30.5.09)	
EC-XAN	Dova DV-1 Skylark	07064-2272
	(Cr and destroyed 12.4.09)	
EC-XAO	CzAW Sportcruiser	08043-2344
EC-XAP	Viper Hazard 13	95029-889
EC-XAQ	Fly Synthesis Texan 600	08027-2328
EC-XAR	SG Aviation Storm Century 04	07097-2305
EC-XAS	Zenair CH-601XL Zodiac	06093-2205
EC-XAT	Plätzer Kiebitz	07055-2263
EC-XAU	Dova DV-1 Skylark	07074-2282
EC-XAV	ICP MXP-740 Savannah	08045-2346
EC-XAX	Rans S-6 Coyote II	08044-2345
EC-XAY	Glasair Sportsman 2+2	08013-2316
	(W/o 14.10.12)	
EC-XAZ	Magni M-18 Spartan	07059-2267
EC-XBA	Europa Aviation Europa	08042-2343
	(Type confirmed, but officially listed as VM-Esqual)	
EC-XBB	Eipper Quicksilver GT-500	04004-1888
EC-XBC	ICP MXP-740 Savannah	06053-2165
EC-XBD	Zenair CH-640 Zodiac	06077-2189
	(Dam. 12.8.15)	
EC-XBE	SONEX (Tri-gear)	06070-2182
EC-XBF	Evektor EV-97R Eurostar	08064-2365
EC-XBG	Alpi Avn Pioneer 200	08030-2331
EC-XBH	Tecnam P.96 Golf	08014-2317
	(Dbr 13.3.16)	
EC-XBI	Fisher Celebrity	96036-986
EC-XBJ	Falcon	07033-2241
EC-XBK	Magni M-22 Voyager	08026-2327
EC-XBL	Vans RV-7A	08060-2361
EC-XBM	Dova DV-1 Skylark	08028-2329
	(Officially registered as a 'Sports Star')	
EC-XBN	Silent IN	08066-2367
EC-XBO	Dova DV-1 Skylark	06087-2199
	(Officially regd as Roman)	
EC-XBP	Magni M-16 Tandem Trainer	08034-2335
EC-XBQ	SK-4	08010-2313
EC-XBR	Corvus Phantom	08070-2371
EC-XBS	Vidor Asso X Jewel	05095-2101
EC-XBT	Zenair CH-601XL Zodiac	07088-2296
EC-XBU	Dova DV-1 Skylark	08059-2360
	(Officially regd as Roman)	
EC-XBV	Magni M-16 Tandem Trainer	08090-2391
EC-XBX	Alpi Aviation Pioneer 200	08029-2330
EC-XBY	Evektor EV-97 Eurostar	07046-2254
EC-XBZ	Ibis Magic GS450 Europa	05106-2112
	(Dbf 13.9.09)	
EC-XCA	Eurofly FB5 Flash	08062-2363

Reg	Type	C/n
EC-XCB	Alto TG-3300	07083-2291
EC-XCC	Aviatika MAI-890	08041-2342
EC-XCD	Evektor EV-97 Eurostar	09004-2410
EC-XCE	TL Ultralight TL-2000 Sting carbon	08095-2396
EC-XCF	Rotorway A600 Talon	08076-2377
EC-XCG	Alto TG-912	08069-2370
EC-XCH	Corvus Phantom	CNE05-12
	(Official c/n 08046-2347)	
EC-XCI	Pipistrel Apis M	08039-2340
EC-XCJ	Tecnam P.92 Echo	08057-2358
EC-XCK	Fly Synthesis Storch CL	08074-2375
EC-XCL	Autogiro AC Tandem	08077-2378
EC-XCM	Magni M-22 Voyager	08102-2403
EC-XCN	Hummelbird	96095-1045
EC-XCO	Fly Synthesis Storch HS	08098-2399
EC-XCQ	Van's RV-4	08088-2389
EC-XCR	Slepcev Storch Mk IV	08067-2368
	(Dam. 10.9.15)	
EC-XCS	Flight Design CT-2K	09005-2411
EC-XCT	Pottier P.130L	04071-1955
EC-XCU	Zenair CH-601XL Zodiac	06068-2180
EC-XCV	TL Ultralight TL-2000 Sting	08091-2392
EC-XCZ	Jabiru J430	08033-2334
EC-XDA	Sky-Walker	08061-2362
EC-XDB	ATEC Zephyr 2000	07041-2249
EC-XDC	Vol Mediterrani VM-1 Esqual	09015-2421
EC-XDD	Bleriot XI replica	07021-2229
EC-XDE	Van's RV-9	07006-2214
EC-XDF	Jabiru J450	08035-2336
EC-XDG	SG Aviation Storm 280	08031-2332
EC-XDH	Flight Design CT LS	F-09-01-13
	(Officially regd as 09011-2417)	
EC-XDI	SONEX	07054-2262
EC-XDJ	Van's RV-4	07031-2239
EC-XDK	CzAW Sportcruiser	08084-2385
EC-XDL	Ekolot JK-05 Junior	04112-1996
	(Regd as JK-05 Ecoflyer)	
EC-XDM	Cometa	06060-2172
EC-XDN	Van's RV-7	05019-2025
EC-XDP	VLA Toxo	04003-1887
EC-XDQ	Zascandil 300	09013-2419
EC-XDR	JL.D.C. Mustang P-51	99033-1307
	(Destroyed Ocana 19.10.10)	
EC-XDS	Air Command Gyro	08081-2382
EC-XDT	Urban Air UFM-10 Samba	08101-2402
	(Dam. 27.5.16)	
EC-XDU	Alpi Avn Pioneer 300 Hawk	07050-2258
EC-XDV	Piper J-3C Cub	09031-2436
EC-XDX	TL Ultralight TL-2000 Sting RG	09038-2444
EC-XDY	Rans S-9 Chaos	126-91
EC-XDZ	Mainair Gemini Mercury	08096-2397
EC-XEA	Iris Aviacion 85	09036-2442
EC-XEB	Jabiru J230	09013-2424
EC-XEC	Rans S-6ES Coyote II	08009-2312
	(Originally listed as EC-XEB)	
EC-XED	Air Création Safari GT BI	09019-2425
EC-XEE	Elisport CH-7 Kompress Charlie	09017-2423
EC-XEF	VJFR	02029-1693
EC-XEG	Preceptor Ultra Pup	0016/1405
	(Major damage 6.10.16)	
EC-XEH	Evektor EV-97 SportStar Plus	08083-2384
EC-XEI	Pendular	09063-2469
EC-XEJ	ATEC Zephyr 2000	09008-2414
EC-XEK	Ain 01	08054-2355
EC-XEL	Evektor EV-97 Eurostar	09027-2433
EC-XEM	Zenair CH-601 Zodiac	05042-2048
EC-XEN	SONEX	03086-1869
EC-XEO	Rans S-9 Chaos	95014-874
EC-XEP	CzAW Sportcruiser	08082-2383
EC-XEQ	TEAM Mini-MAX	00091-1480
EC-XES	SG Aviation Storm Century XL	09024-2430
EC-XET	Replica Plans SE5A	07095-2303
EC-XEU	Pendular	09001-2407
EC-XEV	Tornado IIS	08025-2326
EC-XEX	Jabiru J450	07034-2242
EC-XEY	Iris	09058-2464
EC-XEZ	TeST TST-10M Atlas	09037-2443
EC-XFA	SG Aviation Storm Century	05096-2102
EC-XFB	SG Aviation Storm Century 04XL	09041-2447
EC-XFC	Air Création Buggy/ Mild 16	09026-2432
EC-XFD	Cosmos Bidulum 503/ Golf 19	08047-2348
EC-XFE	Zenair CH-701 STOL	08038-2339
EC-XFF	Denney Kitfox IV	10017-2488
EC-XFG	Raj Hamsa X'Air Rainbow	08015-2318
EC-XFH	Magni M-24 Orion	10010-2481
EC-XFJ	ProFe Banjo MH	10011-2482
EC-XFK	ICP MXP-640 Amigo	09060-2466
EC-XFL	Highlander	08085-2386
EC-XFM	Raj Hamsa X' Air	10009-2480
EC-XFN	ICP MXP-740 Savannah VG XL	10004-2475
EC-XFO	Akro Pirat	99047-1321
	(Dam. 11.10.13)	
EC-XFP	ICP MXP-740 Savannah VG	07090-2298
EC-XFQ	Magni M-24 Orion	10038-2509
EC-XFR	ICP MXP-740 Savannah	09062-2463
EC-XFT	Flight Design CT-2K	10014-2485
EC-XFU	Van's RV-8	06086-2198
EC-XFV	Corvus Phantom	10007-2478
EC-XFX	Murphy Renegade Spirit	09034-2440
EC-XFY	Rans S-19	08078-2379
EC-XFZ	Tot Bipla SE.5 replica	10002-2473
EC-XGA	Magni M-18 Spartan	10028-2499
EC-XGB	DEA Yuma	10006-2477
	(Dam. 6.4.14)	
EC-XGC	Colibri 2008	08073-2374
EC-XGD	Hoffman H-36 Dimona	10019-2490
	(Dam. 17.1.15, Orgaz)	
EC-XGE	Air Command 582	09022-2428
EC-XGF	BRM Land Africa	07070-2278
EC-XGG	Halley Apollo Fox	10021-2492
EC-XGH	Fly Synthesis Storch	10024-2495
EC-XGI	CASA C-1.131E Jungmann	08053-2354
EC-XGJ	CASA C-1.131E Jungmann	08055-2356
EC-XGK	Alien	09033-2439
EC-XGL	BRM Land Africa	08040-2341
EC-XGM	Roko Aero NG4UL Speedy	10008-2479
EC-XGN	Fly Synthesis Texan 400	10023-2494
EC-XGO	ICP MXP-740 Savannah	06018-2130
EC-XGP	Fly Synthesis Texan Top Class	10039-2510
EC-XGQ	BRM Land Africa	08103-2404
EC-XGR	Fly Synthesis Texan 400	10029-2500
EC-XGS	Aeroandinas MXP-140 Tumaco	08024-2325
EC-XGT	Volero V-9	10026-2497
EC-XGU	Magni M-18 Spartan	09061-2467
EC-XGV	Aerojeep	07014-2222
EC-XGX	DTA-JG Voyageur II	10044-2515
EC-XGY	Slepcev Storch Mk.IV	05104-2110
EC-XGZ	Rutan Cozy Mk.III	10022-2493
EC-XHA	CzAW Sportcruiser	10040-2511
EC-XHB	Fly Synthesis Texan 600	10037-2508
EC-XHC	Van's RV-7	10013-2484
EC-XHD	SONEX	09056-2462
EC-XHE	Air Création Trek 700E /iXess 13	11003-2544
EC-XHF	Magni M-24 Orion	09003-2409
EC-XHG	Raj Hamsa X'Air	10036-2507
EC-XHH	Alpi Aviation Pioneer 200	10046-2517
EC-XHI	Alpi Aviation Pioneer 200	10056-2526
EC-XHJ	ATEC Zephyr 2000	10031-2502
EC-XHK	Quad City Challenger II	10035-2506
EC-XHL	Ultrabike	07037-2245
EC-XHM	ICP MXP-740 Savannah S	10057-2527
EC-XHN	Vol Mediterrani VM-1 Esqual	10062-2532
EC-XHO	Tecnam P.2008	10061-2531
EC-XHP	Tecnam P.92 Echo	11009-2550
EC-XHQ	TEAM Mini-MAX	0602802140
EC-XHR	LC-2	07028-2236
EC-XHS	Cosmos	11004-2545
EC-XHT	Zlin Savage Cruiser	07019-2227
EC-XHU	Cosmos Bidulum / Profil 19	96029-979
EC-XHV	MCRL Bingo	10051-2522
EC-XHX	Elisport CH-7 Kompress Charlie	10016-2487
EC-XHY	Tecnam P.2008	11012-2553
EC-XHZ	Zlin Savage	10064-2534
EC-XIA	Mainair Gemini/Flash IIA	11017-2558
EC-XIB	Pegasus Quantum 15-915	08065-2366
EC-XIC	Tecnam P.2002 Sierra	11022-2563
EC-XID	Cervantes XXI	11020-2561
EC-XIE	Tecnam P.2002 Sierra	11001-2542
EC-XIF	BRM Land Africa	11006-2547
EC-XIG	HFL Stratos 300	10054-2525
EC-XIH	TL Ultralight TL-2000 Sting S4	11031-2572
EC-XII	Alpi Aviation Pioneer 200	11025-2566
EC-XIJ	Autogiro Futura	11007-2548
EC-XIK	Fisher FP-202 Super Koala	11002-2543
EC-XIL	Preceptor STOL King	10012-2483
EC-XIM	Tecnam P.2008	11028-2569
EC-XIN	Zenair CH-601HD Zodiac	00134-1523
EC-XIO	Alpi Aviation Pioneer 400	10063-2533
EC-XIP	Direct Fly Alto TD	07062-2270
EC-XIQ	Pterodactyl Ascender	11057-2598
EC-XIR	Bede BD-5	09054-2460
EC-XIS	BRM Land Africa Impala	11034-2575
EC-XIT	TL Ultralight TL-3000 Sirius	11048-2589
EC-XIV	CASA C-1.131L Jungmann	07071-2279
EC-XIX	Tecnam P.92 Echo	11035-2576
EC-XIY	SG Aviation Storm Century 04	08004-2288
EC-XIZ	Tecnam P.2008	11039-2580
EC-XJA	Tecnam P.92 Echo	11047-2588
EC-XJB	Rossi Soavi Paolo Biposto/Ipsos 12	12010-2622
EC-XJC	Avid Flyer STOL	01071/1608
EC-XJD	CASA I-131E Jungmann	11013-2554
EC-XJE	Volero	11069-2610
EC-XJF	TL Ultralight TL-2000 Sting S-4	12006-2618
EC-XJG	Van's RV-8	08002-2307
EC-XJH	Colometa	11045-2586
EC-XJI	Tecnam P.2008	11046-2587
EC-XJJ	Antares MA33M HKS700E/ Air Création Kiss 15	10043-2514
EC-XJK	Trike	08032-2333
EC-XJL	Alpi Aviation Pioneer 300	11023-2564
EC-XJM	Zlin Savage	11010-2551
EC-XJN	Sonex 3300	06049-2161
EC-XJO	B&F Funk FK-9 Smart-Piolin	12013-2625
EC-XJP	Dallach D.3 Sunwheel	12022-2634
EC-XJQ	Moragon M-1 Stela	11032-2573
EC-XJR	Elisport CH-7 Kompress	12007-2619
EC-XJS	Rotorway Exec 90	10027-2498
EC-XJT	Stolp SA300 Starduster Too	11029-2570
	(Crashed 9.7.16)	
EC-XJU	Magni M-22 Voyager	12004-2616
EC-XJV	Albaviation DA-22 MagicOne	11058-2599
EC-XJX	unidentified weightshift	10005-2476
EC-XJY	Slepcev Storch SS4 UL	05050-2058
EC-XJZ	Zlin Savage	11040-2581
EC-XKA	Revolution Mini 500	12023-2635
EC-XKB	Zenair CH-601XL Zodiac	08049-2350
EC-XKC	TEAM Mini-MAX	10003-2474
EC-XKD	DGS 1	08089-2390
EC-XKE	Iris	10042-2513
EC-XKF	Zlin Savage	12001-2613
EC-XKG	Zenair CH-750	11005-2546
EC-XKH	Zlin Savage Cub	12030-2642
EC-XKI	Pioneer Flightstar	10053-2524
EC-XKJ	EISSA-1	11065-2606
EC-XKK	Tecma 21 DTA 1	09064-2470
EC-XKL	Bücker Bü.131 Jungmann	12028-2640
EC-XKM	Zenair CH-601XL Zodiac	07089-2297
EC-XKN	Direct Fly Alto TG912	12034-2646
EC-XKO	Van's RV-9A	08048-2349
EC-XKP	Air Création GTE Trek 582 / iXess 15	12046-2658
EC-XKQ	Syncro	12038-2650
EC-XKR	Direct Fly Alto TG912	12050-2662
EC-XKS	Zlin Savage Classic	13011-2676
EC-XKT	Zenair CH.601 Zodiac XL	05003-2009
EC-XKU	TL Ultralight TL-2000 Sting S4	12040-2654
EC-XKV	Avion Terrestre	12017-2629
EC-XKX	Aeropro Eurofox 912-A240	12044-3656
EC-XKY	Zlin Savage	11011-2552
EC-XKZ	Eurofly Flash Light	13013-2678
EC-XLA	Cosmos Phase II	12043-2655
EC-XLB	ATEC 321 Faeta	13010-2675
EC-XLC	Bücker Bü.131 Jungmann	13008-2673

Reg	Type	C/n	Prev.
EC-XLD	SONEX	11071-2612	
EC-XLE	Direct Fly Alto	12024-2636	
EC-XLF	Van's RV-9A	08105-2406	
EC-XLG	Micro Mong	10070-2540	
	(Cr and w/o 12.7.14)		
EC-XLH	ICP MXP-1000 Tayrona	11069-2609	
EC-XLI	Rans S-10 Sakota	12037-2649	
EC-XLJ	Stolp SA.100 Starduster	11041-2582	
EC-XLK	SE.5A Replica	13030-2695	
EC-XLL	Van's RV-8	04061-1945	
EC-XLM	Zlin Savage Cub S	13015-2680	
EC-XLN	Van's RV-7A	12019-2631	
EC-XLO	Bücker replica	13002-2667	
EC-XLP	SE.5A Replica	13003-2668	
EC-XLQ	Tecnam P.2002 Sierra IS	13033-2698	
EC-XLR	Alpi Aviation Pioneer 300	13001-2666	
EC-XLS	Vidor Asso X Jewel	0925-2431	
EC-XLT	ELA Aviacion ELA-07 Junior	13016-2681	
EC-XLU	BRM Citius Sport	13019-2684	
EC-XLV	Fantasy Air Allegro SW	01035-1590	
EC-XLX	CSA Sportcruiser	13039-2704	
EC-XLY	Staaken Z-1 Flitzer	12025-26537	
EC-XLZ	Pendular JS-5	13018-2683	
EC-XMA	Alpi Aviation Pioneer 300	13052-2717	
EC-XMB	JCV.1	13023-2688	
EC-XMC	ELA Aviacion ELA-10 Eclipse	13029-2694	
EC-XMD	Chickital	14011-2728	
EC-XME	ATEC 122 Zephyr	14005-2722	
	(W/o 3.8.15)		
EC-XMF	Direct Fly Alto TG912	13045-2710	
EC-XMG	Van's RV-12	11052-2593	
EC-XMH	JMA-01	14010-2727	
EC-XMI	Pottier P.130 Coccinelle	05041-2047	
EC-XMJ	Maluan TCE	09046-2452	
EC-XMK	BRM Land Africa	07026-2234	
EC-XML	Hummel Bird	13009-2674	
EC-XMM	Biplaza Autogiro	18/91	
EC-XMN	Helisport CH-77 Ranabot	13041-2706	
EC-XMO	Air Création Pixel 250 XC/ iFun 13	14029-2746	
EC-XMP	Tecnam Astore	14002-2719	
EC-XMQ	autogiro	14001-2718	
EC-XMR	Corvus Phantom	11024-2565	
EC-XMS	Alpi Aviation Pioneer 300	14017-2734	
EC-XMT	Cubanito	14016-2733	
EC-XMU	SG Aviation Storm Century	07072-2280	
EC-XMV	Van's RV-9	13012-2677	
EC-XMX	Dutch Condor	12005-2617	
EC-XMY	Bücker biplane replica	14008-2725	
EC-XMZ	Tecnam Astore	13034-2699	
EC-XNA	Alpi Aviation Pioneer 200	14020-2737	
EC-XNB	Eurofly FB-5 Starlight	14051-2768	
EC-XNC	CSA S Sportcruiser	13051-2716	
EC-XND	Air Création Pixel 250XC / iFun 13	14042-2759	
EC-XNE	Colomban MC-100 Banbi	99081-1355	
EC-XNF	Van's RV-7	12048-2660	
EC-XNG	Ferrari Tucano	14025-2742	
EC-XNH	Dragonfly	12053-2665	
	(Major damage 31.7.16)		
EC-XNI	Rans S-10 Sakota	10067-2537	
EC-XNJ	Air Command gyroplane	14034-2751	
EC-XNK	BRM Aero Bristell UL	15005-2782	
EC-XNL	Jabiru	14022-2739	
EC-XMN	ELA Aviacion ELA-09 Junior	14054-2771	
EC-XNN	ELA Aviacion ELA-09 Junior	14053-2770	
EC-XNO	Zlin Savage Cub	15010-2787	
EC-XNP	ICP MXP-740 Savannah	13037-2702	
EC-XNQ	Rutan LongEz	14047-2764	
EC-XNR	Trikelec	13049-2714	
EC-XNS	BRM Aero Bristell UL	14045-2762	
EC-XNT	CSA Sportcruiser	13047-2712	
EC-XNU	Dyn'Aero MCR-01 ULC	14057-2774	
EC-XNV	Alpi Avn Pioneer 300 Hawk	14055-2772	
	(Officially regd as "Tucan 14"; tail code "5")		
EC-XNX	Van's RV-9A	12009-2621	
EC-XNY	Dan Rihn DR107 Delicioso VI	14035-2752	
EC-XNZ	Direct Fly Alto TG-912	14056-2773	
EC-XOA	ICP MXP-1000 Tayrona	14058-2775	
EC-XOB	Smartfly	14007-2724	
EC-XOC	Zenair CH-650B	10058-2528	
EC-XOD	Tecnam P.92 Echo	14048-2765	
EC-XOE	Murphy Renegade Spirit	13022-2687	
EC-XOF	Mainair Gemini/Flash IIA	14032-2749	G-MTKV
	(UK c/n 565-887-5-W354)		
EC-XOG	TL Ultralight TL-2000 Sting S4	14041-2758	
EC-XOH	Eurofly Flash Light	11054-2395	
EC-XOI	WDFL Dallach D4 Fascination BK	15008-2785	
EC-XOJ	Tecnam P.2002 Sierra	15025-2791	
EC-XOK	Hat Bantam	11049-2590	
EC-XOL	Aeropilot Legend 540	15034-2794	
EC-XOM	Bücker Jungmann	15028-2792	
EC-XON	Alpi Aviation Pioneer 300ST	11063-2604	
EC-XOO	BRM Aero Bristell LSA	15035-2793	
EC-XOP	TL Ultralight TL-3000 Sirius	15012-2789	
EC-XOQ	Direct Fly Alto LSA/ELA	15013-2790	
EC-XOR	Plätzer Kiebitz	14031-2748	
EC-XOS	Slepcev Storch SS4 UL	05073-2079	
EC-XOT	Zenair CH-701 STOL	15015-2802	
EC-XOU	CSA Sportcruiser	13048-2713	
EC-XOV	EAA Acrosport I	14059-2776	
EC-XOX	Zlin Savage Cub S	15003-2780	
EC-XOY	Corby CJ-1 Starlet	15019-2804	
EC-XOZ	TEAN MiniMax	94036	
EC-XPA	Van's RV-7	15029-2803	
EC-XPB	Corby CJ-1 Starlet	15054-2800	
EC-XPC	Darm 1	05035-2041	
EC-XPD	Schleicher ASW 24E	15038-2797	
EC-XPE	BRM Aero Bristell RG	15050-2798	
EC-XPF	Zenair CH-601 Zodiac	10069-2539	
EC-XPK	Heli-Sport CH-77 Ranabot	15030-2811	
EC-XPL	Illusion 01	08079-2380	
EC-YAA	Monnet Sonerai II	1	
EC-YAB	AX-9-140 Tramontana HAFB	001	
EC-YAC	Hosta JG-50A	001	
EC-YAD	Vidal JG-77A	001	
EC-YAE	Mendez JG-77C	001	
EC-YAF	Monnet Moni	203	ECT-440
EC-YAG	Roger / Druine D.31 Turbulent	01	ECT-706
EC-YAH	Rotorway 152 Executive	3589	
	(Stored)		
EC-YAI	Rotorway Executive	31416	EC-199
EC-YAJ	Sallen 2-seat	001	
EC-YAK	Pendulaire	101	
EC-YAL	Copa	6/88	
EC-YAM	Copa	7/88	
EC-YAN	Eipper Quicksilver MXL-II	1361	
EC-YAO	Eipper Quicksilver MXL-II	1403	
EC-YAQ	Pitts S-1D Special	JFG 82/01	PP-ZZZ
EC-YAR	Eipper Quicksilver MXL-II	1521	
EC-YAS	Sallen Mach 10	16/87	
EC-YAT	Sallen Mach 15	1/89	
EC-YAU	Dynali Chickinox Kot Kot	31310417	
EC-YAV	Scheibe SF 25C Falke ? now "Singilia"	10/86	
EC-YAX	Light Aero Avid Flyer	20/88	
EC-YAY	Light Aero Avid Flyer	6/89	
EC-YAZ	Light Aero Avid Flyer	23/88	
	(Cr and dbr 26.5.10)		
EC-YBA	Light Aero Avid Flyer	44/89	
EC-YBB	Dynali Chickinox Kot Kot	6/90	
EC-YBC	Weedhopper	11/84	
EC-YBD	Rans S-6 Coyote II	79/90	
EC-YBE	Rans S-4 Coyote I	77/90	
EC-YBF	Brügger MB-2 Colibri	11/86	EC-386
EC-YBG	Flying Master	34/90	
EC-YBH	Comco Ikarus Fox-C22	10/90	
EC-YBI	Eipper Quicksilver MXL-II	70/90	
EC-YBJ	Cosmos Bidulum 50	28/90	
EC-YBK	Sallen Mach 15 Gyrocopter	29/90	ECT-444 ?
EC-YBL	LET L-13E Blanik M	28/89	EC-CQV
	(To Museo del Aire)		
EC-YBM	Air Création GT BI Safari / Quartz	8/90	
EC-YBN	Air Création Racer / 12SX	43/90	
EC-YBO	Air Création GT BI Safari	25/90	
EC-YBP	Nicollier HN.700 Ménestrel II	18/90/001E	EC-605
	(Damaged 22.2.98)		
EC-YBQ	Air Command 532 Elite	102/90	
EC-YBR	Rans S-4 Coyote I	16/91	
	(Crashed 19.9.10)		
EC-YBS	Air Création Safari GT / Quartz 16SX	38/90	EC-611
EC-YBT	Air Création Safari GT BI / Fun 18	62/90	
EC-YBU	Air Création Racer / Quartz 12SX	72/90	WAC-72
EC-YBV	Rans S-4 Coyote I	50/91	
EC-YBX	Eipper Quicksilver MXL-II	84/90	
EC-YBY	Light Aero Avid Flyer STOL	22/88	
EC-YBZ	VA-12C	21/89	
EC-YCA	Rotorway Executive	95/90	EC-656
EC-YCB	Cosmos / Chronos 14	116/90	
EC-YCC	Light Aero Avid Flyer	17/88	
EC-YCD	Chickinox Tandem	21/91	
EC-YCE	Chickinox Tandem	20/91	
EC-YCF	Chickinox Monoplaza	53/90	
EC-YCG	Denney Kitfox	17/89	EC-661
EC-YCH	Sadler Vampire SV-2	11/91	
EC-YCI	AISA I-11B Peque (Replica)	7/89	
EC-YCJ	Rans S-7 Courier	17/91	EC-837
EC-YCK	Sirocco E	1/91	
EC-YCL	Pterodactyl Ascender	29/91	EC-724
EC-YCM	Air Command 582 Gyrocopter	114/90	
EC-YCN	Circa-Nieuport L	20/87	EC-201
EC-YCO	Eipper Quicksilver MXL-II	95/90	
EC-YCP	Light Aero Avid Flyer STOL	25/88	
EC-YCQ	Kolb Mk.II Twinstar	1/90	
EC-YCR	Air Création Safari GT BI	1	
EC-YCS	Air Création Safari / Quartz 16SX	74/90	
EC-YCT	Chickinox Tandem	88/90	
EC-YCU	Air Création GT BI / Plus 20	76/90	
EC-YCV	Kolb Twinstar Mk.II	55/90	EC-405
EC-YCX	Rans S-7 Courier	78/90	
EC-YCY	Rans S-10 Sakota	80/90	
EC-YCZ	Rans S-12 Airaile	38/91	
EC-YDA	TSA10 Flying Master	66/91	
EC-YDB	Rans S-4 Coyote I	139/91	
EC-YDC	Rans S-6 Coyote II	71/91	
EC-YDD	Sallen Mach 07 Gyrocopter	27/90	
EC-YDE	Rans S-6 Coyote II	80/91	
EC-YDF	Pendular Trike	13/91	
EC-YDG	Rans S-12 Airaile	83/91	
EC-YDH	Eipper Quicksilver MX-II	97/90	
EC-YDI	Volero Trike	27/91	
EC-YDJ	Air Création GT BI / Quartz 16SX	63/91	
EC-YDK	Light Aero Avid Flyer	7/90	
EC-YDL	Zenair CH-701 STOL	154/91	EC-915 ?
EC-YDM	Air Création Safari GT BI / Fun 18	3/91	
EC-YDN	Air Création Racer / Fun 14	40/91	
EC-YDO	Eipper Quicksilver GT-500	68/91	
EC-YDP	Condor	119/90	
EC-YDQ	Rans S-6 Coyote II	58/91	
EC-YDR	Colibri JL 12SX	73/90	
EC-YDS	Dynali Chickinox Tandem	98/90	
EC-YDT	Light Aero Avid Flyer STOL	20/90	
EC-YDU	Rans S-6 Coyote II	117/91	
EC-YDV	Renegade Spirit	67/91	
EC-YDX	Aériane Sirocco	45/91	
EC-YDY	Eipper Quicksilver MX-II	22/91	
EC-YDZ	Dynali Chickinox Kot-Kot	63/90	
EC-YEA	Air Création Safari GT BI / Quartz 18 BI	64/90	
EC-YEB	Air Création Safari GT BI / Plus 20	88/91	
EC-YEC	Colomban MC-15 Cri-Cri	15/87	EC-598
EC-YED	Air Création Safari GT BI / Plus 20	113/91	
EC-YEE	Ultravia Pelican Club	33/89	EC-723
EC-YEF	Air Création Racer / Fun 14	148/91	
EC-YEG	Rans S-4 Coyote I	97/91	
EC-YEH	Quad City Challenger II	116/91	EC-921 ?
EC-YEI	Flying Master	59/90	
EC-YEJ	Aériane Sirocco	66/90	EC-645
EC-YEK	Vector 610	113/90	
EC-YEL	Light Aero Avid Flyer STOL	40/91	
EC-YEM	Light Aero Avid Flyer STOL	31/89	
	(Dam. 25.3.16)		
EC-YEN	Quad City Challenger II	62/91	EC-871 ?
EC-YEO	Light Aero Avid Flyer STOL	14/90	
EC-YEP	Light Aero Avid Flyer STOL	106/90	

Reg	Type	C/n	Prev
EC-YEQ	Air Création Racer / 12SX	42/92	
EC-YER	Quad City Challenger II Special	118/90	
EC-YES	Air Création Safari GT BI / Fun	8/91	
EC-YET	Tierra II	110/91	
EC-YEU	Air Création Safari GT BI	61/91	
EC-YEV	Dynali Chickinox Kot-Kot	163/91	
EC-YEX	Rans S-4 Coyote I	144/91	
EC-YEY	Ménestrel II	002-E/58/90	
EC-YEZ	Rans S-6 Coyote II	139/91	
EC-YFA	Rans S-6 Coyote II	84/91	
EC-YFB	Kolb Twinstar Mk.II	115/90	
EC-YFC	Murphy Renegade Spirit	2/89	
	(W/o 7.8.96)		
EC-YFD	TEAM Mini MAX	56/90	EC-910
EC-YFE	Bragg	101/90	EC-143
EC-YFF	Van's RV-6A	44/90	EC-118
EC-YFG	Fischer FP-404 Classic	22/90	EC-398
EC-YFH	Capella XS	87/91	EC-200
EC-YFI	Ultravia Pelican Club	108/91	EC-846
	(W/o 15.5.06)		
EC-YFJ	Light Aero Avid Flyer	33/91	
	(Dam 8.3.05)		
EC-YFK	Rans S-12 Airaile	23/92	
EC-YFL	Rans S-12 Airaile	158/91	
EC-YFM	Air Création GT BI / Fun 18	43/91	
EC-YFN	Air Command 582	165/91	
EC-YFO	Rans S-12 Airaile	123/91	
EC-YFP	Light Aero Avid Flyer STOL	115/91	
EC-YFQ	Rans S-6 Coyote II	33/92	
EC-YFR	Air Création GT BI / Fun 18	145/91	
EC-YFS	Rans S-12 Airaile	74/92	
EC-YFT	Air Création GT BI / Quartz SX-16	8/92	
EC-YFU	Air Création Racer / Quartz SX12	121/91	
EC-YFV	Air Création Safari GT BI / Quartz	105/91	
EC-YFX	Air Création GT BI / Fun 18	104/91	
EC-YFY	Air Création Safari GT BI / Fun 18	166/91	
EC-YFZ	Colibri JL2 Quartz SX-16	133/91	
EC-YGA	Air Création Racer / Fun 14	53/91	
EC-YGB	Air Création Safari GT BI / Quartz	131/91	
EC-YGC	Kolb Twinstar Mk.II	4/90	
EC-YGD	Kolb Twinstar Mk.II	3/90	
EC-YGE	Sport Aircraft Tango II	24/92	
EC-YGF	Air Création GT BI / Quartz SX-16	168/91	
EC-YGG	Air Création Racer / Quartz SX-12	124/91	
EC-YGH	Air Création GT BI / Fun 18	54/91	
EC-YGI	Rans S-12 Airaile	70/91	
EC-YGJ	Rans S-10 Sakota	49/91	
	(Ditched 17.5.13)		
EC-YGK	Cosmos / Atlas 21	136/92	
EC-YGL	Rans S-6 Coyote II	132/92	
EC-YGM	Rans S-14	110/92	
EC-YGN	Rans S-6 Coyote II	52/92	
EC-YGO	Air Création Racer / SX-12	2/92	
EC-YGP	Synairgie Jaguar 16	21/92	
EC-YGQ	Light Aero Avid Flyer STOL	30/89	
	(Damaged 7.04)		
EC-YGR	Eipper Quicksilver Sprint II	21/93	
EC-YGS	Air Création GT BI / Fun 18	175/92	
EC-YGT	Air Création Safari GT BI / Plus 20	2/91	
EC-YGV	Capella XSX	11/92	
EC-YGX	Minimax Fun-18	93/90	
EC-YGY	Zenair STOL	108/91	
EC-YGZ	TEAM Hi-MAX	36/90	
EC-YHA	Rans S-6 Coyote II	153/91	
EC-YHB	Rans S-12 Airaile	169/91	
EC-YHC	Cosmos / Echo-12	131/92	
EC-YHD	JN-1	57/90	
EC-YHE	Rans S-12 Airaile	106/92	
EC-YHF	Doleal DJP-03	35/89	
EC-YHG	Light Aero Avid Flyer STOL	51/90	
EC-YHH	Van's RV-4	1800	EC-447
EC-YHI	Rans S-12 Airaile	167/91	
EC-YHJ	Mainair Gemini/Flash IIA	"93088"	
	(See EC-YHO)		
EC-YHK	Dynali Chickinox Kot-Kot	82/90	
EC-YHL	Eipper Quicksilver MX-II	93062	EC-671 ?
EC-YHM	Eipper Quicksilver MX-II	125/92	EC-675 ?
EC-YHN	Denney Kitfox IV	55/92	
	(W/o 15.1.08)		
EC-YHO	Mainair Gemini/Flash IIA	"50/93"	
	(This and EC-YHJ are probably c/ns 603-1187/W391 and 604-1187/W392, order unknown)		
EC-YHP	Air Création Safari GT BI / Quartz	3/92	
EC-YHQ	Air Création Safari GT 1+1 / Plus	56/93	
EC-YHR	Rans S-6 Coyote II	140/93	
EC-YHS	Lohele Sport Parasol	93119	
EC-YHT	TEAM Mini-MAX	39/90	
EC-YHU	Light Aero Avid Flyer	40/90	
EC-YHV	Light Miniature LM-1	75/90	EC-710 ?
EC-YHX	Monnett Moni	35/88	
EC-YHY	Air Création Safari GT BI / Quartz 18	22/93	
EC-YHZ	Bidulum-50 Turbo 17	60/92	
EC-YIA	Rans S-6 Coyote II	76/92	
EC-YIB	Cosmos Bidulum	123/92	
EC-YIC	Drifter ARV-582	142/92	
EC-YID	Pelican Club	23/89	
EC-YIE	Dynali Chickinox Kot-Kot	71/90	
EC-YIF	Vector 610	140/92	
EC-YIH	Sky Walker II-300	11/93	
EC-YII	Sky Walker II-300	99/91	
EC-YIJ	Capotilo	93112	
EC-YIK	Rans S-6 Coyote II	52/93	
EC-YIL	Air Création Racer / Quartz SX12	94/92	
EC-YIM	Volero	93131	
EC-YIN	Drifter ARV-503	22/92	
EC-YIO	T-Bird II	101/91	
	(Museum)		
EC-YIP	TEAM Mini-MAX	80/92	
	(W/o 13.7.07)		
EC-YIQ	Rans S-6 Coyote II	47/93	
EC-YIR	Denney Kitfox	128/91	
EC-YIS	Tierra II	119/92	
EC-YIT	Cosmos	93087	
EC-YIU	Neico Lancair 360	9/92	EC-537
EC-YIV	Sky Walker II-300	49/92	
EC-YIX	Teulai	26/90	EC-274
EC-YIY	Light Aero Avid Master	17/92	
EC-YIZ	Light Aero Avid Master	59/92	
EC-YJA	Eipper Quicksilver Sprint II-BI	93093	
EC-YJB	Rans S-6 Coyote II	115/92	
EC-YJC	Air Création Safari GT 1+1 / Plus 17	137/92	
EC-YJD	Rans S-12 Airaile	44/92	
	(Dam. 16.9.14)		
EC-YJE	Denney Kitfox	92/91	
EC-YJF	Rans S-6 Coyote II	93073	
EC-YJG	Rans S-4 Coyote I	107/91	
EC-YJH	Air Création Safari GT BI	26/93	
EC-YJI	Fisher FP-404 Classic	37/92	
EC-YJJ	CFM Streak Shadow	K.218	
EC-YJK	Rans S-14	93081	
EC-YJL	Rans S-6 Coyote II	41/93	
EC-YJM	Cosmos / Chronos	69/92	
EC-YJN	Pelican Club	22/89	
EC-YJO	Pirriqui	93085	
EC-YJP	Preceptor Ultra-Pup	95/92	EC-108 ?
EC-YJQ	Rans S-12 Airaile	93130	
EC-YJR	Dynali Chickinox Tandem	122/92	
EC-YJS	Fisher FP-202 Super Koala	12/87	
EC-YJT	Cobra	161/91	
EC-YJU	Eipper Quicksilver Sprint II-BI	93100	
EC-YJV	Mosler N-32 Pup	23/90	
EC-YJX	Air Création Safari GT-BI / Fun 18	162/91	
EC-YJY	Denney Kitfox	72/92	
EC-YJZ	Challenger II	93108	
EC-YKA	Rans S-6ES Coyote II	93099	
EC-YKB	TEAM Mini-MAX	93127	
EC-YKC	Air Création Racer / Fun 14	93114	
EC-YKD	Dynali Chickinox Kot-Kot	40/92	
EC-YKE	Titan Tornado	144/92	
EC-YKF	Rans S-6ES Coyote II	48/93	
EC-YKG	Icaro Quartz SX16	94077	
EC-YKH	Palomo	94030	
EC-YKI	TEAM Mini-MAX	37/91	
EC-YKJ	Rans S-6ES Coyote II	27/93	
EC-YKK	Pendular Trike	94050	
EC-YKM	Rans S-4 Coyote I	93086	
EC-YKN	Aero Designs Pulsar XP	7/92	
EC-YKO	Light Aero Avid Flyer	117/92	
EC-YKP	MXP-640	93140	
EC-YKQ	Pendular Biplaza Cosmos	93134	
EC-YKR	Drifter ARV-582	93095	
	(Cr and dbr 17.1.09)		
EC-YKS	Neico Lancair 360	19/93	EC-537 ?
EC-YKT	Volero Cosmos / Chronos	94087	
EC-YKU	Mosler Ultra Pup	94061	
EC-YKV	Stolp Starduster Too	36/92	EC-373 ?
	(Dam 6.6.04) (Possibly c/n ACA-38, ex N9771A)		
EC-YKX	Burumbballeta	9/88	EC-836
EC-YKY	Rans S-6ES Coyote II	57/93	
EC-YKZ	Tope 90	28/91	
EC-YLA	Terra-Bird 1	109/92	
EC-YLB	Rans S-6 Coyote II	93071	
EC-YLC	Rans S-4 Coyote I	122/91	
EC-YLD	Rans S-6 Coyote II	93068	
EC-YLE	Rans S-10 Sakota	94024	
EC-YLF	Phase II Chronos 16	95011-871	
EC-YLG	Eipper Quicksilver MX-II	94065	
EC-YLH	Bidulum Atlas-21	94067	
EC-YLI	TEAM Mini-MAX	72/91	
EC-YLJ	Rio Profil-27	44/93	
EC-YLK	Light Aero Avid Flyer	94019	
EC-YLL	Sky Walker	94096	
EC-YLM	Rans S-6 Coyote II	45/92	
EC-YLN	Villapar	60/93	
EC-YLO	Monnett Moni	93089	EC-788
EC-YLP	Anajopi GT-BI Hermes Turbo 16	35/92	
EC-YLQ	Dynali Chickinox Kot-Kot	82/92	
EC-YLR	Rans S-14	94118	EC-280 ?
EC-YLS	Flying Ghost	107/92	
EC-YLT	Pendular / Fun 18	93125	
EC-YLU	Murphy Renegade Spirit	93133	
EC-YLV	Weedhopper	81/92	
EC-YLX	Polaris Cross Country Arie	94063	
EC-YLY	Rans S-12 Airaile	93082	
EC-YLZ	Gaviota	119/91	
EC-YMA	Weedhopper AX-3	94091	
EC-YMB	DTA / Hermes 17	95040-900	
EC-YMC	TEAM Z-Hi-MAX	41/92	
EC-YMD	Capela XSX	53/93	
EC-YME	Rans S-12 Airaile	94010	
EC-YMF	Denney Kitfox	149/91	EC-466 ?
EC-YMG	Rans S-6 Coyote II	118/91	
EC-YMH	Solar Wings Pegasus XL	95047-907	
EC-YMI	Rans S-6 Coyote II	73/92	
EC-YMJ	Air Création Safari GT BI / Fun 18	94044	
EC-YMK	Air Création Safari GT BI / Fun 18	94043	
EC-YML	Cabanas Fun 18	94108	
EC-YMM	Autogyro TM-1	93067	
EC-YMN	Rans S-10 Sakota	94023	EC-901 ?
EC-YMO	Air Création Safari GT BI / Fun 18	35/93	
EC-YMP	Denney Kitfox	6/93	
EC-YMQ	Maxair Drifter	95031-891	
EC-YMR	TEAM Mini-MAX	94057	
EC-YMS	Eipper Quicksilver MX-II	93092	
EC-YMT	Rans S-6ES Coyote II	94102	
EC-YMU	Neico Lancair 320 Mk II	94008	
EC-YMV	Barom AGC-1 Pacific Wings	93083	
EC-YMX	Preceptor N-3 Pup	95036-896	EC-108 ?
EC-YMY	Formula Uno	94042	
EC-YMZ	Formula Uno	94117	
EC-YNA	Maxair 582 Drifter	95064-924	
EC-YNB	Rans S-12 Airaile	65/92	
EC-YNC	Pegasus Quasar	94066	
EC-YND	Rans S-4 Coyote I	94069	
EC-YNE	Neico Lancair 360	124/92	
EC-YNF	Echo-12 Trike	95037-897	
EC-YNG	Cosmos / Chronos14	95017-877	
EC-YNH	Cosmos Bidulum-50	95018-878	
EC-YNI	Cosmos Bidulum-50	95043-903	
EC-YNJ	Rans S-12 Airaile	94047	
EC-YNK	Neico Lancair 360	129/92	
EC-YNL	Volairo Cosmos	94112	

Registration	Type	C/n	Notes
EC-YNM	Evans VP-1 Volksplane	4/81	
EC-YNN	Sky Jet II	94016	
EC-YNO	Sky Jet II	94015	
EC-YNP	Rutan Long-Ez	2/85	EC-676 ? (To Museo del Aire)
EC-YNQ	Eipper Quicksilver MX-II	93136	
EC-YNR	Preceptor Vagabond	96017-967	
EC-YNS	Rans S-6ES Coyote II	95068-928	
EC-YNU	AX-2 Le Guepard Autogyro	95050-910	
EC-YNV	Poisck 06A	95004-864	
EC-YNX	Commander 582 Elite gyrocopter	94026	
EC-YNY	Sport Aircraft Tango II-GT	94005-865	
EC-YNZ	Rans S-6ES Coyote II	93117	
EC-YOA	Precepter Maverick	96058-1008	
EC-YOB	TEAM Mini-MAX	96021-971	EC-748 ?
EC-YOC	Air Création Safari GT BI / Fun 18	94060	
EC-YOD	Vol 9/Best Off Sky Ranger 912	95046-906	
EC-YOE	TEAM Mini-MAX	95002-862	
EC-YOG	Van's RV-6	1/92	EC-432 ?
EC-YOH	Bragg A-3	94055	
EC-YOI	Maupin Woodstock 1	159/91	
EC-YOJ	TEAM Mini-MAX	92/90	
EC-YOK	Bifly Sport	18/93	
EC-YOL	Polaris Cross-Country	94072	
EC-YOM	Murphy Maverick	93137	
EC-YON	Dynali Chickinox Tandem	94110	
EC-YOO	Comco Ikarus Sherpa II	94011	
EC-YOP	T-Bird II	94051	
EC-YOQ	Fisher FP-404 Classic	94076	
EC-YOR	ESO Pendular	93094	
EC-YOS	Colometa	96003-953	
EC-YOT	Air Création Safari 1+1 / Plus 20	94029	
EC-YOU	Dynali Chickinox	96005-955	
EC-YOV	Air Command 582 Elite	96081-1031	
EC-YOX	Van's RV-6	95056-916	
EC-YOY	Denney Kitfox IV	78/92	(Dbr 8.3.09)
EC-YOZ	Air Création Safari GT BI / Quartz 16SX	96006-956	
EC-YPA	Rans S-6 Coyote II	96035-985	
EC-YPB	Dynali Chickinox	95042-902	
EC-YPC	Formula I	94113	
EC-YPD	Rans S-14 Airaile	96063-1013	
EC-YPE	Rans S-6 Coyote II	95057-917	
EC-YPF	Challenger II	96091-1041	
EC-YPG	Navegante Aereo Stranger 16	95026-886	
EC-YPH	Glasair II-SFT	95049-909	
EC-YPI	Rans S-6XL Coyote II	95065-925	
EC-YPJ	Polaris Skin	97017-1077	
EC-YPK	Air Création Safari GT BI / Fun 18	95058-918	
EC-YPL	TEAM Mini-MAX	94022	
EC-YPM	Air Création 1+1 / Plus	96089-1039	
EC-YPN	Light Aero Avid Flyer	94020	
EC-YPO	Kolb Twinstar Mk II	17/93	
EC-YPP	Air Command 582 Elite	96085-1035	
EC-YPQ	Rans S-6ES Coyote II	96043-993	
EC-YPR	Rans S-9 Chaos	96083-1033	
EC-YPT	Preceptor Ultra Pup	95072-932	
EC-YPU	TEAM Mini-MAX	15/90	
EC-YPV	Sky Walker II-300	96106-1056	
EC-YPX	Sport Aircraft Tango I	95053-913	
EC-YPY	Sky Walker	96015-965	
EC-YPZ	Campana	96042-992	
EC-YQA	Jodel D.18	251	EC-929?
EC-YQB	Sport Aircraft Tango II-GT	96074-1024	
EC-YQC	Albatros Gyrocopter	97024-1084	
EC-YQD	Monnett Moni	97018-1078	
EC-YQE	Synairgie	97014-1074	
EC-YQF	Rans S-6 Coyote II	93122	
EC-YQG	Rotorway Exec 162F	96008-958	
EC-YQH	VM.002	96002-970	(W/o 27.10.02)
EC-YQI	Interair F-2-55	95009-869	
EC-YQJ	Rans S-14 Airaile	97032-1092	
EC-YQK	Rans S-5 Coyote I	97033-1093	
EC-YQL	Challenger II	95052-912	
EC-YQM	Air Command 582 Elite	96051-1001	
EC-YQN	Genesis	95073-933	
EC-YQO	Titan Tornado	unkn	(Officially listed as CGS Hawk Classic c/n 96011-961 but correct type confirmed as above 8.03)
EC-YQP	Rans S-10 Sakota	94035	
EC-YQQ	Sky Jet II	97012-1072	
EC-YQR	Sport Aircraft Tango I	94097	
EC-YQS	Albatros SX	97025-1085	
EC-YQT	Rans S-6ES Coyote II	96044-994	
EC-YQU	TEAM Mini-MAX	94078	
EC-YQV	Straton D-8	96087-1037	
EC-YQX	Cedimex Rans S-12 Airaile	96067-1017	
EC-YQY	Eipper Quicksilver MXL-II Sport	96107-1057	(Originally listed as a Tecnam P.96 Golf)
EC-YQZ	Rotorway Exec 152F	97019-1079	
EC-YRA	TEAM Mini-MAX	111/91	
EC-YRB	Taylorcraft LM.2X 2P	100/91	
EC-YRC	Büttner Funplane	97029-1089	(Originally listed as a DTA Trike)
EC-YRD	Rans S-6 Coyote II	97056-1116	
EC-YRE	Terra T-Bird 2	96070-1020	
EC-YRF	Cross Country Gryps 18.5	95023-883	
EC-YRG	Sky Walker	96071-1021	
EC-YRH	Air Création GT BI / Quartz 18SX	96090-1040	
EC-YRI	Murphy Renegade Spirit	94095	
EC-YRJ	Dynali Chickinox Kot-Kot	97050-1119	
EC-YRK	Eipper Quicksilver MX-II	97039-1099	
EC-YRL	LG.1 Eclipse	97052-1112	
EC-YRM	Cosmos / Hermes 2-seat	94034	
EC-YRN	Air Création Safari GT BI / Fun 18	94100	
EC-YRO	Vol 9/Best Off Sky Ranger	96033-983	
EC-YRP	Vol 9/Best Off Sky Ranger	94120	
EC-YRQ	CGS Hawk Classic	95071-931	
EC-YRR	AER Pendular	94006	
EC-YRS	Rans S-6ES Coyote II	97006-1066	
EC-YRT	Bidulum-50 Magnum 21	2/93	
EC-YRU	Challenger II	97063-1123	
EC-YRV	Murphy Maverick	96002-952	
EC-YRX	Aviatika MAI-89	96046-996	
EC-YRY	Raven Mk.2	152/91	(W/o 2.3.16)
EC-YRZ	Murphy Maverick	96099-1049	
EC-YSA	Murphy Maverick	97007-1067	
EC-YSC	Rans S-6ES Coyote II	96032-982	
EC-YSD	Puddle Jumper	96049-999	
EC-YSE	Solar Wings Pegasus	97021-1081	
EC-YSF	Nicollier HN-700 Menestrel II	17/90	(Cr and destroyed 25.5.12)
EC-YSG	Monnett Monerai	1	
EC-YSH	Van's RV-4	95024-884	
EC-YSI	V.M. (Vol Mediterrani?)	30/91	
EC-YSJ	Rans S-6ES Coyote II	93097	
EC-YSK	Eipper Quicksilver MX-II	126/92	
EC-YSL	Capela	29/92	
EC-YSM	Cosmos / Chronos 14	96048-998	
EC-YSN	Monnett Moni	5/84	
EC-YSO	Murphy Maverick	96009-959	
EC-YSP	Brügger MB-2 Colibri	20	EC-241 (C/n now quoted as 1/82)
EC-YSQ	Eipper Quicksilver MX-II	95048-908	
EC-YSR	Cosmos Phase II / Chronos 16	97066-1126	
EC-YSS	Vol 9/Best Off Sky Ranger 912	95088-948	
EC-YST	Cosmos / Hermes 16	97053-1113	
EC-YSU	Cobra	24/93	
EC-YSV	Rans S-12 Airaile	97051-1111	
EC-YSX	Cosmos / Chronos 14	97007-1114	
EC-YSY	Cosmos / Chronos 16	95003-863	
EC-YSZ	ELA Aviacion ELA 04B	98052-1213	
EC-YTA	Capela	96105-1055	
EC-YTB	Denney Kitfox IV - 1200	1880	(Official c/n 93105)
EC-YTC	CASA C-1.131E Jungmann	98027-1188	(Built from spares)
EC-YTD	Solar Wings Pegasus XL-Q	98032-1193	
EC-YTE	Rans S-5 Coyote I	98014-1175	
EC-YTF	Colyear Martin M3-S100	98012-1173	
EC-YTG	Eipper Quicksilver MXL-IIRB Sport	98057-1218	
EC-YTH	Rans S-10 Sakota	97062-1122	
EC-YTI	Bidulum 50 / Chronos 14	98018-1179	
EC-YTJ	Eipper Quicksilver GT-500	98017-1178	
EC-YTK	Pegasus Quantum	98030-1191	(Originally listed as Solar Wings Pegasus XL-Q) (Pegasus Q2 wing only supplied, c/n 8502, 12.09)
EC-YTL	Pelican GS	93120	
EC-YTM	Dyn'Aéro MCR-01	97098-1158	(Dyn'Aéro c/n 53)
EC-YTN	Preceptor N-3 Pup	94101	
EC-YTO	Capella XS	97075-1135	
EC-YTP	Rans S-7 Courier	94028	
EC-YTQ	Pegasus Quantum II	98072-1233	
EC-YTR	Pegasus Quantum 15	98058-1219	
EC-YTS	Sky Walker II-300	97027-1087	
EC-YTT	Cosmos Bidulum II	98048-1209	
EC-YTU	Cosmos Bidulum	97091-1151	
EC-YTV	Cosmos / Chronos 14	98008-1169	
EC-YTX	Eipper Quicksilver MXL-IIRB Sport	98035-1196	
EC-YTY	Nieuport II	10/88	
EC-YTZ	Preceptor N-3 Pup	97096-1156	
EC-YUA	Challenger II	97086-1146	
EC-YUB	Raj Hamsa X'Air	98067-1228	
EC-YUC	Max Trainer	94070	
EC-YUD	Eipper Quicksilver MXL-IIRB Sport	98005-1166	
EC-YUE	Aviatika MAI-890	97070-1130	
EC-YUF	Fisher FP-404 Classic II	95015-875	
EC-YUG	Buse'Air 150	98074-1235	
EC-YUH	Aviasud Mistral	96103-1053	
EC-YUI	Pegasus Quantum Super Sport Q2	98001-1162	
EC-YUJ	RAF-2000	96050-1000	(Painted as EC-YJU in error)
EC-YUK	Taylorcraft BC-12D	98026-1187	
EC-YUL	Aviatika MAI-890	96080-1030	(Originally listed as Zenair CH-601 Zodiac)
EC-YUM	Rotorway Exec 162F	97044-1104	
EC-YUN	Rans S-7 Courier	98050-1211	(Cr and dbf 25.2.12)
EC-YUO	Bidulum 50	98079-1240	
EC-YUP	Terra T-Bird 2	98013-1174	
EC-YUQ	Denney Kitfox III	66/92	
EC-YUR	Rans S-14 Airaile	98066-1227	
EC-YUS	Rans S-6XL Coyote II	98025-1186	
EC-YUT	Cosmos	98033-1194	
EC-YUU	Dyn'Aéro MCR-01	99003-1277	
EC-YUV	Air Création Safari GT BI / Quartz 16SXS	16/93	
EC-YUX	Pelican Club	103/92	
EC-YUY	Air Création Safari GT BI / Quartz 16SXS	15/93	
EC-YUZ	Air Création Safari GT BI / Plus 17	53/92	
EC-YVA	Rans S-6ES Coyote II	93098	
EC-YVB	Colibri JL1 Quartz 12SX	64/92	
EC-YVC	JF1 SX12	96034-984	
EC-YVD	Colibri II XP15	97069-1129	
EC-YVE	Colibri JL1	52/92	
EC-YVF	Loehle Sport Parasol	98108-1269	
EC-YVG	Tecnam P.92 Echo	97085-1145	
EC-YVH	Air Création Safari GT BI / Quartz 16SX	97002-1062	
EC-YVI	TEAM Mini-MAX	146/92	
EC-YVJ	Rans S-6ES Coyote II	97028-1088	
EC-YVK	Rans S-14 Airaile	98036-1197	(W/o 6.8.10)
EC-YVM	Zenair CH-601HDS Zodiac	96102-1052	
EC-YVN	Pegasus Quasar	98084-1245	
EC-YVO	Pegasus Quantum 15	98073-1234	
EC-YVP	Pegasus Q2	98097-1258	
EC-YVR	Rans S-7 Courier	98064-1225	
EC-YVS	Slepcev Storch Mk 4	97099-1169	
EC-YVT	Rans S-14 Airaile	114/92	
EC-YVU	Love Spirit	99012-1286	
EC-YVV	Murphy Renegade Spirit	95083-943	
EC-YVX	Rans S-6-116 Coyote	94063	
EC-YVY	Madero / Corby CJ-1 Starlet	96110-1060	
EC-YVZ	Rans S-10 Sakota	98/92	
EC-YXA	Zenair CH-601 Zodiac	98054-1215	
EC-YXB	Zenair CH-601 Zodiac	98055-1216	
EC-YXC	Sport Aircraft Tango GT-i	98037-1198	
EC-YXD	VPM M-18 Spartan	98070-1231	
EC-YXE	Oroneta Racer GT	98105-1266	

Reg	Type	C/n	
EC-YXF	Rans S-14 Airaile	94013	
	(Cr and dbf 17.10.9)		
EC-YXG	ELA Aviacion ELA 05B	99016-1290	
EC-YXH	Air Création Safari GT 1+1 / Fun 18	98060-1221	
EC-YXI	Buse'Air 150	98095-1256	
EC-YXJ	Zenair CH-601 Zodiac	99023-1297	
EC-YXK	D.R.P. Trike	99071-1345	
EC-YXL	Buccaneer II-B2B	98068-1229	
EC-YXM	Mistral	98043-1204	
EC-YXN	Murphy Maverick	99060-1334	
EC-YXO	Rans S-6ES Coyote II	98015-1176	
EC-YXP	Pober Pixie	50/92	
EC-YXQ	Rans S-14 Airaile	98101-1262	
EC-YXR	Stolp SA300 Starduster Too	99050-1159	
EC-YXS	Aeros	98082-1243	
EC-YXT	Skystar Kitfox IV	97099-1159	
EC-YXU	Lancair 320	86/91	
EC-YXV	JFR Gyrocopter	99015-1289	
EC-YXX	Cosmos Bidulum / Chronos 14	97071-1131	
EC-YXY	TEAM Mini-MAX	98002-1163	
EC-YXZ	Rans S-6 Coyote II	94074	
EC-YYA	Biplano II	97092-1152	
EC-YYB	Hispano Canelas Ranger	7/87	
EC-YYC	Rans S-14 Airaile	99070-1344	
EC-YYD	Dyn'Aéro MCR-01	99069-1343	
EC-YYE	Eipper Quicksilver MXL-IIRB Sport	99100-1374	
EC-YYF	Dynali Chickinox Kot-Kot	99082-1356	
EC-YYG	Xisvi	98078-1239	
	(Also noted as "Cosmos")		
EC-YYH	JRB-2	9804901210	
EC-YYI	Vidor Asso V Champion	97064-1124	
EC-YYJ	Rans S-6 Coyote II	96072-1022	
EC-YYK	Eipper Quicksilver MXL-II Sport	98109-1270	
EC-YYL	Eipper Quicksilver MXL-II Sport	98112-1273	
EC-YYM	Eipper Quicksilver MXL-II Sport	99002-1276	
EC-YYN	Eipper Quicksilver MXL-II Sport	98110-1271	
EC-YYO	Eipper Quicksilver MXL-II Sport	99001-1275	
EC-YYP	Eipper Quicksilver MXL-II Sport	98111-1272	
EC-YYQ	Murphy Maverick	99086-1360	
EC-YYR	Echo 12 Trike	99040-1314	
EC-YYS	Aero Boero 180RVR	00021-1410	
EC-YYT	Robin ATL	97060-1120	
EC-YYU	CAG Toxo	95039-899	
EC-YYV	CAG Toxo	96014-964	
EC-YYX	Colibri JL2	128/92	
EC-YYY	Air Création Twin 503 / Fun 18	99115-1389	
EC-YYZ	Colibri I+I XPI2	99027-1301	
EC-YZA	LM-1	99039-1313	
EC-YZB	Buse'Air 150	98098-1259	
EC-YZC	Alisport Silent	99018-1382	
EC-YZD	Van's RV-6	97016-1076	
EC-YZE	Rans S-6ES Coyote II	99041-1315	
EC-YZF	Pulsar X-13	97055-1115	
EC-YZG	TL Ultralight TL-96 Star	00017-1406	
EC-YZH	Preceptor N-3 Pup	99091-1365	
EC-YZI	Buse'Air 150	99084-1358	
EC-YZJ	Tecnam P.92 Echo	97084-1144	
EC-YZK	Rans S-6ES Coyote II	98011-1172	
EC-YZL	Dynali Chickinox Tandem	98046-1207	
EC-YZM	SG Aviation Storm 300	99059-1333	
EC-YZN	Buse'Air 150	99077-1351	
	(Destroyed 31.7.11)		
EC-YZO	Buse'Air 150	99087-1361	
EC-YZP	Rans S-6ES Coyote II	96064-1014	
EC-YZQ	Tecnam P.92 Echo	99097-1371	
EC-YZR	Nike Vega	99068-1342	
EC-YZS	Sky Walker	00048-1437	
EC-YZT	Zenair CH-601 Zodiac	98069-1230	
EC-YZU	Tecnam P.92 Echo	99101-1375	
EC-YZV	Rans S-12S Super Airaile	009/1398	
EC-YZX	Eipper Quicksilver MXL-II	99088-1362	
EC-YZY	Viper Hazard-12 582	99078-1352	
EC-YZZ	Vol Mediterrani VM-1 Esqual (Prototype)	00058-1447	
EC-ZAA	M3 Gyrocopter	00033-1422	
EC-ZAB	Bidulum Fun 18	98062-1223	
EC-ZAC	ELA Aviacion ELA 07BC-125	99093-1367	
EC-ZAD	Raj Hamsa X'Air 582	00062-1451	
EC-ZAE	JS Single-seat Gyrocopter	00029-1418	
EC-ZAF	Dyn'Aéro MCR-01 VLA	00073-1462	
	(Dyn'Aéro c/n 123)		
EC-ZAG	Ultralair Weedhopper Europa II	00025-1414	
EC-ZAH	Fantasy Air Allegro ST	00050-1439	
EC-ZAI	Rans S-6ES Coyote II	99114-1388	
	(Damaged 8.3.15, Valencia)		
EC-ZAJ	Moragon UL 2	99073-1347	
EC-ZAK	Sky Jet-II	00055-1444	
EC-ZAL	Pendular Racer	99042-1316	
EC-ZAM	Aeromaster	00003-1392	
EC-ZAN	Raj Hamsa X'Air	00015-1404	
EC-ZAO	Cosmos Bidulum 50	99029-1303	
EC-ZAP	Jodel D.1120S	00053-1442	
EC-ZAQ	Zenair CH-601 Zodiac	99111-1385	
EC-ZAR	CGS Hawk Classic single seat	00075-1464	
EC-ZAS	CGS Hawk Classic two seat	00074-1463	
EC-ZAT	Tecnam P.92S Echo	00076-1465	
EC-ZAU	Tecnam P.92S Echo	99095-1369	
EC-ZAV	Tecnam P.92S Echo	00096-1485	
	(Dam 17.12.00)		
EC-ZAX	Tecnam P.92S Echo	00092-1481	
EC-ZAY	Tecnam P.92S Echo	00027-1416	
EC-ZAZ	Tecnam P.92S Echo	99098-1372	
EC-ZBA	Tecnam P.92S Echo	00093-1482	
EC-ZBB	Rans S-12XL Airaile	00071-1460	
EC-ZBC	Volero Ghost 16	00047-1436	
EC-ZBD	Joker	99090-1364	
EC-ZBE	Aviaexport MAI-89	99030-1304	
EC-ZBF	Zenair CH-601 Zodiac	98104-1265	
	(W/o 18.4.06)		
EC-ZBG	Buse'Air 150	99013-1287	
EC-ZBH	Air Command 912 two-seater	00078-1467	
EC-ZBI	TL Ultralight TL-96 Star	00081-1479	
EC-ZBJ	Air Création Racer / XP11	00031-1420	
EC-ZBK	Aero Designs Pulsar	93103	
EC-ZBL	Fly Unlimited	99036-1310	
EC-ZBM	TL Ultralight TL-96 Star	00049-1438	
EC-ZBN	Sky Walker	99083-1357	
EC-ZBO	Cosmos / Chronos 16	00085-1474	
EC-ZBP	Lockwood Drifter 912	96097-1047	
EC-ZBQ	Dyn'Aéro MCR-01	00057-1446	
	(Cr. 30.3.07)		
EC-ZBR	Comco Ikarus Fox-C22	00012-1401	
EC-ZBS	Cosmos / Chronos 16	00035-1424	
EC-ZBT	Sky Walker II	00019-1408	
EC-ZBU	Raj Hamsa X'Air	00065-1454	
EC-ZBV	YC-100 Hirondelle	99113-1387	
EC-ZBX	Dyn'Aéro MCR-01	00069-1458	
EC-ZBY	Eipper Quicksilver MXL-II	96096-1046	
EC-ZBZ	Sport Aircraft Tango I	00010-1399	
EC-ZCA	Colibri 2000	00046-1435	
EC-ZCB	Air Création Safari GT BI / Plus 20	00082-1471	
EC-ZCC	Poisk-06 Fun 18	00094-1483	
EC-ZCD	Tecnam P.96 Golf	00123-1512	
EC-ZCE	Synairgie Volero	97050-1110	
EC-ZCF	Air Création Buggy / XP12	00115-1504	
EC-ZCG	Light Aero Avid Flyer STOL	00114-1503	
EC-ZCH	Air Création Safari GT BI / SX16	00083-1472	
EC-ZCI	Murphy Renegade Spirit	99028-1302	
EC-ZCJ	Air Création Buggy / XP12	00110-1499	
EC-ZCK	Rutan Cozy Classic	95035-895	
EC-ZCL	Tecnam P.92S Echo	99096-1370	
EC-ZCM	Rans S-7 Courier	00098-1487	
EC-ZCN	CASA C-1.131E Jungmann	00040-1429	
EC-ZCO	Air Création Buggy / XP12	00109-1498	
EC-ZCP	Murphy Renegade Spirit	97082-1142	
EC-ZCQ	Vol Mediterrani VM-1 Esqual	00079-1468	
EC-ZCR	CP.301C Emeraude	41/90	
	(W/o 15.6.02)		
EC-ZCS	Capella XSX TD	98088-1249	
EC-ZCT	Eipper Quicksilver MXL-II	98099-1260	
EC-ZCU	Rans S-6-116 Coyote II	94062	
EC-ZCV	Bicicleta Aerea	99020-1294	
EC-ZCX	Raj Hamsa X'Air	00038-1427	
EC-ZCY	Light Aero Avid Flyer	01003-1540	
EC-ZCZ	Jodel D.92 Bébé	96001-951	
	(Originally listed with c/n 778)		
EC-ZDA	Vol 9/Best Off Sky Ranger	01021-1558	
EC-ZDB	Rans S-4 Coyote	00119-1508	
EC-ZDC	TL Ultralight TL-96 Star	00145-1534	
EC-ZDD	Terra Bird II	98046-1207B	
EC-ZDE	Dyn'Aéro MCR-01	00051-1440	
	(Ditched 28.8.05)		
EC-ZDF	TL Ultralight TL-96 Star	00077-1466	
EC-ZDG	Tecnam P.92 2000RG	01057-1570	
EC-ZDH	Europa Avn Europa	95025-88	
	(True c/n is 187, builder E. Sanchez)		
EC-ZDI	Moragon UL 2	01013-1550	
EC-ZDJ	Rans S-6 Coyote II	94092	
EC-ZDK	Sky Walker 300-II	00005-1394	
EC-ZDL	TL Ultralight TL-96 Star	01005-1542	
EC-ZDM	Eipper Quicksilver MXL FJC	01064-1577	
EC-ZDN	Eipper Quicksilver Sport	01008-1545	
EC-ZDO	MAI MD-20	01007-1544	
EC-ZDP	MAI MD-20	01006-1543	
EC-ZDQ	Monnet Sonerai II	98093-1254	
EC-ZDR	Vol Mediterrani VM-1 Esqual	00101-1490	
EC-ZDS	Falcon XP	97045-1105	
EC-ZDT	Light Aero Avid Flyer STOL	67/92	
EC-ZDU	Zenair CH-601 Zodiac	00099-1488	
EC-ZDV	TL Ultralight TL-96 Star	01045-1598	
EC-ZDX	Air Création Racer / Quartz 12SX	00136-1525	
EC-ZDY	Tecnam P.96 Golf	01012-1549	
EC-ZDZ	Vol 9/Best Off Sky Ranger	00013-1402	
EC-ZEA	Rans S-12 Airaile	01023-1560	
EC-ZEB	J-6 Karatoo	93078	
EC-ZEC	Light Aero Avid Flyer STOL	42/90	
	(Damaged 13.10.08)		
EC-ZED	Compac 110	97041-1101	
EC-ZEE	Light Aero Avid Flyer STOL	00102-1491	
EC-ZEF	Rans S-12XL Airaile	01019-1556	
EC-ZEG	Campana 912	96045-995	
	(W/o 30.12.06)		
EC-ZEH	Tecnam P.96 Golf	01028-1581	
EC-ZEI	Sky Walker II-300	01051-1564	
EC-ZEJ	Challenger II Special	01003-1492	
EC-ZEK	Tecnam P.96 Golf	01016-1553	
EC-ZEL	Tecnam P.92 Ilusion	01052-1565	
EC-ZEM	Magni M-14 Scout	01032-1585	
EC-ZEN	Antares Pendular-Stream 16	00121-1510	
EC-ZEO	Max Air Drifter	98006-1167	
	(Ditched 1.10.08)		
EC-ZEP	Moragon UL 2	99075-1349	
EC-ZEQ	Pottier P.180S	112/91	
EC-ZER	Tecnam P.96 Golf 100	01070-1607	
EC-ZES	Sport Aircraft Tango II-GT	01050-1563	
EC-ZET	Moragon UL 2	01076-1613	EC-001
	(Originally listed as a Moragon M1)		
EC-ZEU	Magni M-16 Tandem Trainer	01046-1599	
EC-ZEV	Zenair CH-601HD Zodiac	00146-1535	
EC-ZEX	Lucentum	01078-1615	
EC-ZEY	Moragon UL 2	01061-1574	
EC-ZEZ	Tecnam P.92 Echo	00095-1484	
	(W/o 17.3.14)		
EC-ZFA	Gemini Ultra	01026-1579	
EC-ZFB	CAG Toxo II	00127-1516	
EC-ZFC	Comco Ikarus C-42 Cyclone	01033-1586	
EC-ZFD	Comco Ikarus C-42 Cyclone	01034-1587	
	(Dam 14.3.05)		
EC-ZFE	Mignet HM-1000 Balérit	01042-1595	
EC-ZFF	Vol Mediterrani VM-1 Esqual	00100-1489	
EC-ZFG	Jodel D.18	99038-1312	
EC-ZFH	Hawk Plus single-seater	01074-1611	
EC-ZFI	Comco Ikarus C-42 Cyclone	01096-1633	
EC-ZFJ	Moragon UL 2	01073-1610	
EC-ZFK	Aeriane Swift	01069-1606	
EC-ZFL	Leza-Lockwood Drifter 912	00087-1476	
EC-ZFM	Moragon UL 2	01038-1591	
EC-ZFN	Eipper Quicksilver MXL-II Sport	00122-1511	
EC-ZFO	Comco Ikarus C-32 Fox Tristar	00139-1628	
EC-ZFP	Moragon UL 2	01092-1629	
EC-ZFQ	Fantasy Air Allegro 2000	01035-1588	
EC-ZFR	Air Création Racer / Fun 14	99110-1384	

Reg	Type	C/n	Notes
EC-ZFS	Platzer Kiebitz P-25	12/89	
EC-ZFT	Vol Mediterrani VM-1 Esqual	01030-1583	
EC-ZFU	Mignet HM-1000 Balerit	129	
	(Official c/n is 01093-1630)		
EC-ZFV	Raj Hamsa X'Air	98076-1237	
EC-ZFX	Vol Mediterrani VM-1 Esqual (RG)	01120-1657	
EC-ZFY	Eipper Quicksilver GT-500	00113-1502	
EC-ZFZ	Cosmos BI TOP 14.9	98085-1246	
EC-ZGA	Zenair CH-601 Zodiac	00014-1403	
EC-ZGB	Tecnam P.92 Super	02022-1686	
EC-ZGC	Murphy Rebel Elite	00036-1425	
EC-ZGD	Rans S-6 Coyote II	98075-1236	
EC-ZGE	Brügger MB-2 Colibri	1/81	
EC-ZGF	Volero Pendular	01106-1643	
EC-ZGG	Neico Lancair 360	97037-1097	
	(Damaged 3.3.08)		
EC-ZGH	Air Création Twin 503 / Mild	00104-1493	
EC-ZGI	Air Création Racer / SX12	00112-1501	
EC-ZGJ	Magni M-16 Tandem Trainer	01039-1592	
EC-ZGK	Tecnam P.96 Golf 100	02014-1678	
EC-ZGL	Zenair CH-701 STOL	01067-1604	
EC-ZGM	Tecnam P.92 2000RG	01048-1601	
EC-ZGN	Zenair CH-601UL Zodiac	01113-1650	
EC-ZGO	ELA Aviacion ELA 07	02016-1680	
EC-ZGP	ELA Aviacion ELA 07	02021-1685	
EC-ZGQ	Vol Mediterrani VM-1 Esqual	01031-1584	
EC-ZGR	Capella XL	95019-879	
EC-ZGS	Light Aero Avid Flyer Magnum	02041-1705	
EC-ZGT	Cosmos Pendular	01058-1571	
EC-ZGU	Moragon UL 2	02024-1688	
EC-ZGV	Magni M-16 Tandem Trainer	02030-1694	
EC-ZGX	Rans S-12 Airaile	02015-1679	
EC-ZGY	Vol Mediterrani VM-1 Esqual	02036-1700	
EC-ZGZ	Tecnam P.96 Golf 100	01124-1661	
EC-ZHA	TEAM Mini-MAX V Max	00089-1478	
EC-ZHB	Alpe 101	95080-940	
EC-ZHC	Tecnam P.96 Golf 100	01125-1662	
EC-ZHD	Pendular Trike	02005-1669	
EC-ZHE	Hummel Bird	97095-1155	
EC-ZHF	Zenair CH-601 Zodiac	00072-1461	
EC-ZHG	TI Ultralight TL-96 Star	01085-1622	
EC-ZHH	Aviasud Mistral Standard	02045-1709	
	(Major damage 24.10.16)		
EC-ZHI	Sport Aircraft Tango I	01090-1627	
EC-ZHJ	Adventure Air Adventurer	96012-962	
EC-ZHK	Zenair CH-601 Zodiac	01100-1637	
EC-ZHL	Moragon M 1	02054-1718	
EC-ZHM	Moragon M 1	02060-1724	
EC-ZHN	Nicollier HN-700 Menestral	00067-1456	
EC-ZHO	Raj Hamsa X'Air	01121-1658	
EC-ZHP	Moragon M 1	02055-1719	
EC-ZHQ	Neico Lancair 320	61/93	
EC-ZHR	Raj Hamsa X'Air	02034-1698	
EC-ZHS	Eipper Quicksilver MX-II Sprint	00108-1497	
EC-ZHT	Viper 2200/Cosmos 13	02008-1672	
EC-ZHU	Vol Mediterrani VM-1 Esqual	02023-1687	
EC-ZHV	Air Command Tomatito	00141-1530	
EC-ZHX	Rans S-4 Coyote I	02009-1673	
EC-ZHY	Tecnam P.92 Echo Super	02068-1728	
	(Dam 12.10.06)		
EC-ZIA	Robin ATL L	121	F-GGHQ, F-WGHQ
	(Official c/n quoted as 02013-1677)		
EC-ZIB	Robin ATL L	130	F-GIKT
	(Official c/n quoted as 02056-1720)		
EC-ZIC	QuikKit Glass Goose	99024-1298	
	(W/o 16.6.04)		
EC-ZID	Eipper Quicksilver MX-II	97090-1150	
EC-ZIE	Vol Mediterrani VM-1 Esqual	02091-1755	
EC-ZIF	Quad City Challenger II	102/92	
EC-ZIG	Jabiru UL	99103-1377	
EC-ZIH	Platzer Kiebitz B/450	01072-1609	
EC-ZII	Light Aero Avid Flyer STOL	97088-1148	
EC-ZIJ	Dragon Light 200	01010-1547	
	(Dam 24.7.06)		
EC-ZIK	CAG Toxo	02067-1736	
EC-ZIL	Zenair CH-601 Zodiac	01114-1651	
EC-ZIM	Monnett Moni	17/84	
EC-ZIN	Vol Mediterrani VM-1 Esqual	02093-1757	
EC-ZIO	CAG Toxo	02051-1715	
EC-ZIP	Bragg	02072-1732	
EC-ZIQ	Vol Mediterrani VM-1 Esqual	01123-1660	
EC-ZIR	Aviatika MAI-890	02105-1769	
EC-ZIS	Min-Dango Volero-Cosmos P-19	01110-1647	
EC-ZIT	ATEC Zephyr 2000	02106-1770	
	(Cr and dbf 14.10.09)		
EC-ZIU	Zenair CH-801	02050-1714	
EC-ZIV	TL Ultralight TL-96 Star	02006-1670	
EC-ZIX	ATEC Zephyr 2000	02107-1771	
	(W/o 1.8.08)		
EC-ZIY	ATEC Zephyr 2000	02122-1786	
	(Crashed 6.3.04)		
EC-ZIZ	CASA C-1.131E Jungmann	02074-1738	
EC-ZJB	TL Ultralight TL-2000 Sting	03015-1804	
EC-ZJC	Platzer Kiebitz P-5	00148-1537	
EC-ZJD	Dynali Chickinox	94105	
EC-ZJE	Evektor EV-97 Eurostar 2000R	03023-1812	
EC-ZJF	ELA Aviacion ELA 07-912	02123-1787	
EC-ZJG	ICP MXP-740 Savannah	02086-1750	
EC-ZJH	Viper / Hazard-12	03003-1792	
EC-ZJI	Viper / Hazard-12	03001-1790	
	(W/o 4.8.03 - type quoted as Colyaer Mascato S100)		
EC-ZJJ	Viper / Hazard-15	03002-1791	
EC-ZJK	Magni M-16 Tandem Trainer	03014-1803	
EC-ZJL	Flamingo	02094-1758	
EC-ZJM	Rans S-16 Shekari	01065-1578	
EC-ZJN	Dallach D-7 Fascination	03013-1802	
EC-ZJO	Gemini Thruster	02049-1713	
EC-ZJP	RAF-2000 Raptor	02100-1764	
	(W/o 17.7.07)		
EC-ZJQ	ELA Aviacion ELA 07-912	03004-1793	
EC-ZJR	ATEC Zephyr 2000	03026-1782	
EC-ZJS	Sky Walker II-300	114/91	
EC-ZJT	Leza-Lockwood Drifter ARV-582	00007-1396	
EC-ZJU	Colyaer / Martin III Freedom Amphibian	03028-1783	
EC-ZJV	Moragon UL 2	01002-1539	
EC-ZJX	ELA Aviacion ELA 07-R100	03024-1813	
EC-ZJY	Sport Aircraft Tango II two-seat	01089-1626	
EC-ZJZ	Eipper Quicksilver MXL-II	02110-1774	
	(W/o 13.4.05)		
EC-ZKA	Raj Hamsa X'Air	03032-1815	
EC-ZKB	Janowski J-1B Don Quixote	48/91	
EC-ZKC	Raj Hamsa X'Air	01004-1541	
EC-ZKD	TEAM Mini-MAX	98106-1267	
EC-ZKE	ATEC Zephyr 2000	03011-1800	
EC-ZKF	Slepcev Storch SS4UL	03031-1814	
EC-ZKG	ELA Aviacion ELA 07-912S	02087-1751	
EC-ZKH	ELA Aviacion ELA 07-912S	02082-1746	
EC-ZKI	ELA Aviacion ELA 07-914	03007-1796	
EC-ZKJ	Euroala Jet Fox 97	03012-1801	
EC-ZKK	Colibri JL I+I XP12	02113-1777	
	(Cr and destroyed 23.11.12)		
EC-ZKM	Tecnam P.96 Golf 100	03037-1820	
	(W/o 26.6.09)		
EC-ZKN	Vol Mediterrani VM-1 Esqual	02037-1701	
EC-ZKO	ATEC Zephyr 2000	03036-1819	
EC-ZKP	Cedimax Rans S-6ES Coyote II	02125-1789	
EC-ZKQ	Fly Synthesis Texan Top Class	03067-1850	
EC-ZKR	Evektor EV-97 Eurostar	03022-1811	
EC-ZKS	Piper J-3C Cub	98086-1247	
EC-ZKT	Zenair CH-601 Zodiac	02052-1716	
	(Dbr 18.6.04)		
EC-ZKU	Tecnam P-2002 Sierra	03058-1841	
EC-ZKV	ATEC Zephyr 2000	03030-1788	
EC-ZKX	TL Ultralight TL-2000 Sting carbon	03070-1853	
EC-ZKY	TL Ultralight TL-2000 Sting carbon	03064-1847	
EC-ZKZ	Tecnam P-2002 Sierra	03062-1845	
EC-ZLA	ATEC Zephyr 2000	03042-1825	
	(Major damage 30.30.16)		
EC-ZLB	Magni M-16 Tandem Trainer	03063-1846	
EC-ZLC	Air Création Twin 503 / Mild	03054-1837	
EC-ZLD	Aerotec Vampir	02053-1717	
EC-ZLE	Fantasy Air Allegro 2000	01109-1646	
EC-ZLF	Moravan Zlin Savage	03010-1799	
EC-ZLG	Aeromoragón Moragón M-1	03043-1826	
EC-ZLH	Light Aero Avid Flyer	99056-1330	
EC-ZLJ	Direct Fly Asso V Champion	02112-1776	
EC-ZLK	TL Ultralight TL-2000 Sting	03075-1858	
EC-ZLL	Muotong II	00106-1495	
EC-ZLM	Titan Tornado	02042-1706	
EC-ZLN	Rutan VariEze	03045-1828	
EC-ZLO	Monnett Sonex	01111-1648	
EC-ZLP	Fisher Super Koala	13/87	
EC-ZLQ	ATEC Zephyr 2000	03044-1827	
EC-ZLR	Aerostyle Breezer	010	
	(Cr and dbf 22.2.15)		
EC-ZLS	Zenair CH-701 STOL	03049-1832	
EC-ZLT	ATEC Zephyr 2000	03076-1859	
EC-ZLU	Bicicleta Aerea	99010-1284	
EC-ZLV	Pottier P-130 UL	03018-1807	
EC-ZLX	Eipper Quicksilver MXL-II	03081-1864	
EC-ZLY	ICP MXP-740 Savannah	03091-1874	
EC-ZLZ	Alpi Avn Pioneer 200	02080-1744	
EC-ZMA	Moravan Zlin Savage	02075-1739	
EC-ZMB	Air Création GT BI / SX-16	01017-1554	
EC-ZMC	Magni M-16 Tandem Trainer	03019-1808	
EC-ZMD	Eipper Quicksilver MXL-II Sport	03052-1835	
EC-ZME	ELA Aviacion ELA 07-115	04020-1904	
	(Cr and dbr 19.2.09)		
EC-ZMF	TL Ultralight TL-232 Condor	02032-1696	
EC-ZMG	Sport Aircraft Tango I	03048-1831	
EC-ZMH	Zenair CH-601 XL Zodiac	03093-1876	
EC-ZMI	Raj Hamsa X'Air	00124-1513	
EC-ZMJ	Zenair CH-601 XL Zodiac	03071-1854	
	(W/o 5.2.08)		
EC-ZMK	ELA Aviacion ELA 07-115	04032-1916	
EC-ZML	Vol Mediterrani VM-1 Esqual	04021-1905	
	(W/o 26.7.14 Magadouro, Portugal)		
EC-ZMM	Vol Mediterrani VM-1 Esqual	04029-1913	
EC-ZMN	Tecnam P-2002 Sierra	04015-1899	
EC-ZMO	Tecnam P-2002 Sierra	04025-1909	
EC-ZMP	Tecnam P-2002 Sierra	04030-1914	
EC-ZMQ	Bello I	04007-1891	
EC-ZMR	RLR	03053-1836	
EC-ZMS	Air Création Buggy / Kiss 450	03057-1840	
EC-ZMT	Zenair CH-601 Zodiac	03050-1833	
EC-ZMU	ELA Aviacion ELA 07-R115	04058-1942	
	(W/o 27.7.16)		
EC-ZMV	Rans S-12 Airaile	57/92	
EC-ZMX	Tecnam P-2002 Sierra	04053-1937	
EC-ZMY	F.C.B.	01014-1551	
EC-ZMZ	Tecnam P-2002 Sierra	04031-1915	
EC-ZNA	Tecnam P-2002 Sierra	04022-1906	
EC-ZNB	Tecnam P-2002 Sierra	04014-1898	
EC-ZNC	Tecnam P-2002 Sierra	04024-1908	
EC-ZND	Zenair CH-601 Zodiac	02104-1768	
EC-ZNE	Zenair CH-701 STOL	04027-1911	
EC-ZNF	Light Aero Avid Flyer STOL	03060-1843	
EC-ZNG	Autogiro B II C	04041-1925	
EC-ZNH	Neico Lancair 360	01097-1634	
EC-ZNI	Tecnam P.96 Golf 100	04052-1936	
EC-ZNJ	Zenair CH-601 XL Zodiac	04005-1889	
EC-ZNK	Raj Hamsa X'Air	03073-1856	
EC-ZNL	Capella XSX TR	02073-1737	
	(Dam. 7.10.13)		
EC-ZNM	Rans S-12XL Airaile	02018-1682	
EC-ZNN	HFL Stratos	04018-1902	
EC-ZNO	Technoflug Piccolo B	04042-1926	
EC-ZNP	ATEC Zephyr 2000	03074-1857	
EC-ZNR	Comco Ikarus C-42 Cyclone	02028-1692	
EC-ZNS	Tecnam P-2002 Sierra	04051-1935	
EC-ZNT	Van's RV-4	01068-1605	
	(W/o 28.10.07)		
EC-ZNU	Vol Mediterrani VM-1 Esqual	02003-1667	
EC-ZNV	King Cobra Biplaza	96040-990	
EC-ZNX	ATEC Zephyr	04047-1931	
EC-ZNY	Air Création Racer 503 SL / XP11	04012-1896	
EC-ZNZ	Autogiro MT-2	04039-1923	
EC-ZOA	Denney Kitfox III	03033-1816	
EC-ZOB	ATEC Zephyr 2000	04079-1963	
EC-ZOC	Loehle Mustang 5151	97097-1157	
EC-ZOD	Airbet Girabet	04050-1934	
EC-ZOE	Raj Hamsa X'Air	03072-1855	

Reg	Type	c/n	Notes
EC-ZOF	Tecnam P-2002 Sierra	04040-1924	
EC-ZOG	Air Création Safari GT BI / XP15	02111-1775	
EC-ZOH	CASA C-1.131E Jungmann	02081-1745	
EC-ZOI	Ragwing Special	03101-1884	
EC-ZOJ	Raj Hamsa X'Air	04034-1918	
EC-ZOK	ELA Aviacion ELA 07-115	04095-1979	
EC-ZOL	Evektor EV-97 Eurostar 2000R	04054-1938	
EC-ZOM	Alto Jabiru 3300	04028-1912	OK-IUD 06
EC-ZON	Kappa KP-2 UR Sova	04065-1949	
EC-ZOO	Dynali Chickinox Kot-Kot	03082-1865	
EC-ZOP	Moravan Zlin Savage	04001-1878	
EC-ZOQ	Eipper Quicksilver MXL-II Sport	02098-1762	
EC-ZOR	Ekolot JK-05 Junior	04059-1943	
	(W/o 25.3.05)		
EC-ZOS	JLA Savannah	04072-1956	
EC-ZOT	Tecnam P-2002 Sierra	04101-1985	
EC-ZOU	Zenair CH-601 XL Zodiac	04090-1974	
EC-ZOV	Eipper Quicksilver MXL-II Sport	04063-1947	
EC-ZOX	TeST Alpin 2	04062-1946	
EC-ZOY	Zenair CH-601XL Zodiac	04064-1948	
EC-ZOZ	Zenair CH-601XL Zodiac	04046-1930	
EC-ZPA	Raj Hamsa X'Air	03005-1794	
EC-ZPB	ELA Aviacion ELA 07-R115	04109-1993	
	(Dam. 7.12.14)		
EC-ZPC	Pottier P-130 UL Coccinelle	03009-1798	
EC-ZPD	ELA Aviacion ELA 07-125	04081-1965	
EC-ZPE	Road Air Flamingo	02090-1754	
EC-ZPF	Cosmos Phase II	97077-1137	
EC-ZPG	Eipper Quicksilver MXL-II	01108-1645	
EC-ZPH	Eipper Quicksilver Sport II	04036-1920	
EC-ZPI	Sky Walker II	02089-1753	
EC-ZPJ	Light Aero Avid Flyer STOL	03051-1834	
EC-ZPK	Vol Mediterrani VM-1 Esqual	04107-1991	
	(Dam. 19.5.15)		
EC-ZPL	Zephir-C	04067-1951	
EC-ZPM	Zenair CH-	02078-1742	
EC-ZPN	Pottier P.220S Koala	04026-1910	
EC-ZPO	Flightstar	03006-1795	
EC-ZPP	Light Aero Avid Flyer	04017-1901	
EC-ZPQ	Rans S-6-116 Coyote II	04060-1944	
EC-ZPR	Quad City Challenger II	02040-1704	
EC-ZPS	Tecnam P.92 Echo Super	04108-1992	
EC-ZPT	Tecnam P.2002MJF Sierra	04117-2001	
EC-ZPU	Zenair CH-601XL Zodiac	04055-1939	
EC-ZPV	Zenair CH-701 STOL	04144-1998	
EC-ZPX	ELA Aviacion ELA 07-115	04120-2004	
EC-ZPY	Aviatika MAI-890	04110-1994	
EC-ZPZ	Flyair Sting	05005-2011	
EC-ZQA	Cosmos Bidulum PAG	04119-2003	
EC-ZQB	Zenair CH-601 HD-TD Zoiac	04086-1970	
EC-ZQC	Futura	04002-1883	
EC-ZQD	Tecnam P.2002JPA Sierra	04122-2006	
EC-ZQE	Tornado II	03094-1877	
EC-ZQF	Flylab Tucano	01087-1624	
	(Dismantled, parts dumped)		
EC-ZQG	CAG Toxo	04074-1958	
EC-ZQH	JSS Mistral	05025-2031	
EC-ZQI	CAG Toxo	04077-1961	
EC-ZQJ	TEAM Mini-MAX Eros	01104-1641	
EC-ZQK	ATEC Zephyr 2000	05017-2023	
EC-ZQL	Tecnam P.92 Echo	05023-2029	
	(Registered as Tecnam Terra)		
EC-ZQM	JF-97	05018-2024	
EC-ZQN	Dallach D4B Fascination	05002-2008	
EC-ZQO	Zenair CH-601XL Zodiac	05013-2019	
EC-ZQP	Zenair CH-601X2 Zodiac	04076-1960	
EC-ZQQ	Zenair CH-601XL Zodiac	04100-1984	
EC-ZQR	Capella XS-TD	04075-1959	
EC-ZQS	Dallach D4B Fascination	05006-2012	
EC-ZQT	Stranger 97106	04056-1940	
EC-ZQU	Cases M 10	95020-880	
EC-ZQV	ICP Bingo	02048-1712	
EC-ZQX	Sergio I	04099-1983	
EC-ZQY	Airbet Girabet	04103-1987	
EC-ZQZ	Airbet Girabet	04094-1978	
EC-ZRA	Tecnam P.96 Golf 100	05034-2040	
EC-ZRB	ATEC Zephyr 2000	05020-2026	
EC-ZRC	Airbet Girabet	04078-1962	
EC-ZRD	Airbet Girabet	04093-1977	
EC-ZRE	Tecnam P.2004 Bravo	05051-2057	
EC-ZRF	RA-4	04010-1894	
EC-ZRG	RSP/Zenair CH-701 STOL	05012-2018	
EC-ZRH	Airbet Girabet	04049-1933	
EC-ZRI	Herculino	95084-944	
	(Cr 26.9.06)		
EC-ZRJ	Airbet Girabet	05016-2022	
EC-ZRK	Airbet Girabet	04089-1973	
EC-ZRL	TEAM Mini-MAX	97043-1103	
EC-ZRM	ULM Pendular	01105-642	
EC-ZRN	Airbet Girabet	04038-1922	
EC-ZRO	Tecnam P.2002 Sierra	05004-2010	
	(Officially regd as Albatross D4)		
EC-ZRP	Aviatika MAI-890	03102-1885	
EC-ZRQ	JSR/Tecnam P.2004 Bravo	05010-2016	
EC-ZRR	Aeromoragon M-1	04069-1953	
	(Dam 20.8.06)		
EC-ZRS	ICP MXP-740 Savannah	04111-1995	
EC-ZRT	Air Création Safari GT-BI 503 / Fun 18	05029-2035	
EC-ZRU	Raj Hamsa X'Air	04013-1897	
EC-ZRV	Zenair CH-601XL Zodiac	05037-2043	
EC-ZRX	TL Ultralight TL-232 Condor	05064-2070	
EC-ZRZ	Air Création GT BI	05031-2037	
EC-ZSA	Air Création GT BI	05030-2036	
EC-ZSB	Janowski J-1B Don Quixote	74/91	
	(W/o 14.5.11)		
EC-ZSC	Tecnam P.2002 Sierra	05055/2061	
EC-ZSD	Autogiro Biplaza RE	02061-1725	
EC-ZSE	Vidor Asso IV Whisky	04098-1982	
EC-ZSF	Zenair CH-601XL Zodiac	04116-2000	
EC-ZSG	Urban Air UFM-13 Lambada	05058-2064	
EC-ZSH	Pottier P.130UL Coccinelle	03069-1852	
	(Pottier c/n 1162)		
EC-ZSI	Tecnam P.2004 Bravo	05056-2062	
EC-ZSJ	Cosmos Bidulum	02043-1707	
EC-ZSK	Tecnam P.2002 Sierra	05078-2084	
EC-ZSL	BRM Land Africa	05077-2083	

Reg	Type	c/n	Notes
EC-ZSM	Tecnam P.2004 Bravo	05081-2087	
EC-ZSN	Antares 503 Stream	05033-2039	
EC-ZSO	Mainair Gemini/Flash 503 Ghost 14	02044-1708	
EC-ZSP	Cosmos Phase II	04033-1917	
EC-ZSQ	Tecnam P.2004 Bravo	05099-2105	
EC-ZSR	ATEC Zephyr 2000	05076-2082	
EC-ZSS	Fantasy Air Allegro SW912	05063-2069	
EC-ZST	Rand-Robinson KR-2SB	01063-1576	
EC-ZSU	Air Création GT BI Quartz 16SX	02116-1780	
EC-ZSV	Tecnam P.2004 Bravo	05060-2066	
EC-ZSX	Eagle V	05048-2054	
EC-ZSY	Tecnam P.2004 Bravo	05100-2106	
EC-ZSZ	Skystar Kitfox III	05046-2052	
EC-ZTA	Jodel D.1190S	05022-2028	
EC-ZTB	ATEC Zephyr 2000	05069-2075	
EC-ZTC	Fast Wind 1 (weightshift)	05075-2081	
EC-ZTD	Tecnam P.92 Echo 80	05105-2111	
EC-ZTE	Aeroandina MXP-780 Calima	05093-2099	
EC-ZTF	SG Aviation Storm 300S	06007-2119	
EC-ZTG	Vol Mediterrani VM-1C Esqual	156	
	(Official c/n 05088-2094)		
EC-ZTH	Pipistrel Sinus 912	05045-2051	
EC-ZTI	Zenair CH-701 STOL	04068-1952	
EC-ZTJ	Zenair CH-601XL Zodiac	04085-1969	
EC-ZTK	Flight Design CT-2K	02-06-04-AR	EC-EA1
	(Officially reg'd as 05098-2104)		
EC-ZTL	Tecnam P.92S Echo	05038-2044	
EC-ZTM	Air Création Buggy 582/Kiss 13	05057-2063	
EC-ZTN	Rans S-6 Coyote II	05079-2085	
EC-ZTO	Zenair CH-601XL Zodiac	06010-2122	
EC-ZTP	ICP MXP-740 Savannah	04121-2005	
EC-ZTQ	SG Aviation Storm RG	06001-2113	
EC-ZTR	Zenair CH-601XL Zodiac	05071-2077	
EC-ZTS	Fashion XL	06003-2115	
EC-ZTT	Zenair CH-601 Zodiac	05094-2100	
EC-ZTU	Junior 2000	02011-1675	
EC-ZTV	SG Aviation Storm Century 04	05087-2093	
EC-ZTX	ATEC Zephyr 2000	06002-2114	
EC-ZTY	Evektor EV-97 Eurostar 2002	03021-1810	
EC-ZTZ	SG Aviation Storm Century	05091-2097	
EC-ZUA	Comco Ikarus C-42	06012-2124	
EC-ZUB	SkyStar Kitfox Ranger	05083-2089	
EC-ZUC	Hummel UltraCruiser	05082-2088	
EC-ZUD	Zenair CH-601HD Zodiac	06058-2170	
EC-ZUE	Zenair CH-601XL Zodiac	06009-2121	
EC-ZUF	Elisport CH-7 Kompress	05072-2078	
	(Cr and destroyed 9.9.09)		
EC-ZUG	Air Création GT BI	05027-2033	
EC-ZUH	Air Création / Quartz SX16	04035-1919	
EC-ZUI	Pipistrel Sinus 912	06043-2155	
EC-ZUJ	Zenair CH-601 Zodiac	02079-1743	
EC-ZUK	C-ULM	04080-1964	
EC-ZUL	Ultraligero FAG	02092-1756	
EC-ZUM	Viper / Hazard 12	04096-1980	
EC-ZUN	JMG-28	04043-1927	
EC-ZUO	LC-1	05074-2080	
EC-ZUP	Take Off Merlin	06014-2126	
EC-ZUQ	SG Aviation Storm Century	05053-2059	
	(W/o 29.11.14)		
EC-ZUR	Ural 462 Stream 16	06042-2154	
EC-ZUS	Pietenpol Air Camper	99065-1339	
EC-ZUT	Alpi Avn Pioneer 300	06016-2128	
EC-ZUU	Pipistrel Sinus	06056-2168	
EC-ZUX	ICP MXP-740 Savannah	05052-2058	
EC-ZUX	Aeroandina MXP-780 Calima	06032-2144	
EC-ZUY	Viper HKS-700E / Piccolo	06052-2164	
EC-ZUZ	J.E.C.	01101-1638	
	(Cr and destroyed 17.3.13)		
EC-ZVA	Tecnam P.92S Echo	06033-2145	
EC-ZVB	ELA Aviacion ELA 03B	06038-2150	
EC-ZVC	SG Aviation Storm Century	05062-2068	
EC-ZVD	SG Aviation Storm Century	05092-2098	
EC-ZVE	G1-V2	04066-1950	
EC-ZVF	Aeroandinas MXP-1000 Tayrona	06015-2127	
EC-ZVG	Aviatika MAI-890	06030-2142	
EC-ZVH	MA33M Antares Trike	06022-2134	
EC-ZVI	BRM Land Africa	06073-2185	
EC-ZVJ	Eipper Quicksilver Sport IIS	05011-2017	
EC-ZVK	Zenair CH-601XL Zodiac	06059-2171	
EC-ZVL	Zenair CH-601 Zodiac	06055-2167	
EC-ZVM	DTA Dynamic	06034-2146	
EC-ZVN	TL-32HW	05001-2002	
EC-ZVO	Eden	06045-2157	
EC-ZVP	DTA Dynamic 15/430	235	
	(Official c/n 06036-2148)		
EC-ZVQ	DTA Dynamic	06048-2160	
EC-ZVR	Pegasus Trike	06005-2117	
EC-ZVS	DTA Dynamic	06047-2159	
EC-ZVT	DTA Dynamic 15/430	232	
	(Official c/n 06035-2147)		
EC-ZVU	B&F Funk FK-9 Mk IV	03065-1848	
EC-ZVV	DTA Dynamic	06067-2179	
EC-ZVX	DTA Dynamic	06054-2166	
EC-ZVY	Bicicleta Aerea	99019-1293	
EC-ZVZ	Van's RV-6A	99046-1320	
EC-ZXA	Vol Mediterrani VM-1 Esqual	05101-2107	
EC-ZXB	Eipper Quicksilver GT500	07004-2212	
EC-ZXC	Alpi Avn Pioneer 200	07002-2210	
EC-ZXD	Brugger MB-2 Colibri	03098-1881	
	(Dbr 9.10.12)		
EC-ZXE	Pegasus Q	93063	
EC-ZXF	ICP MXP-740 Savannah	06096-2208	
EC-ZXG	CzAW Sportcruiser	07SC018	
	(Officially reg'd as 07009-2217)		
EC-ZXH	Iris Aviacion 85	07001-2209	
EC-ZXI	Aeroandina MXP-1000 Tayrona	06091-2203	
EC-ZXJ	Eipper Quicksilver MXL-II	06076-2188	
EC-ZXK	Midget Mustang	06090-2202	
EC-ZXL	Airbet Girabet II	06011-2123	
EC-ZXM	Pendular	07005-2213	
EC-ZXN	Vol 9/Best Off Sky Ranger V-Max	06024-2136	
EC-ZXO	Cosmos / iXess BMW 100	05032-2032	
EC-ZXP	Colyaer / Martin III Freedom Amphibian	06046-2158	
EC-ZXQ	Alpi Avn Pioneer 300	06092-2204	
EC-ZXR	Ibis GS700 Magic	06062-2174	
EC-ZXS	SG Aviation Storm Century	06074-2186	

EC-ZXT	SG Aviation Storm 280G	06094-2206
EC-ZXU	Tot Bipla Biplano (SE-5A Replica)	07044-2252
EC-ZXV	SG Aviation Storm 300	07012-2220
EC-ZXX	Jabiru SK	07007-2215
EC-ZXY	Aerostyle Breezer	05061-2067
EC-ZXZ	Villar XL	06080-2192
EC-ZYA	Zenair CH-601XL Zodiac	06089-2201
EC-ZYB	Vol Mediterrani VM-1 Esqual	06071-2183
	(W/o 2.3.08)	
EC-ZYC	DTA Voyager 582 / Dynamic 15/430	271
	(Officially registered as c/n 07045-2253)	
	(Dbr 19.10.14)	
EC-ZYD	DTA Feeling	07051-2259
EC-ZYE	RF-9 Noel	07029-2237
EC-ZYF	Solar Wings Pegasus XL-R	SW-WA-1228 G-MTOC
	(Official c/n 07043-2251)	
EC-ZYG	Jabiru J400	06057-2169
EC-ZYH	Zenair CH-601XL Condor	05103-2109
EC-ZYI	Fox C-32	94090
EC-ZYJ	Rans S-6S Coyote II	04102-1986
EC-ZYK	Zenair CH-601XL Zodiac	06075-2187
EC-ZYL	Dynali Chickinox	03088-1871
EC-ZYM	SG Aviation Storm 280Si	07017-2225
EC-ZYN	Tecnam P.92 Echo	07018-2226
EC-ZYO	Raj Hamsa Xair	07010-2218
EC-ZYP	ICP MXP-740 Savannah	07015-2223
EC-ZYQ	Autogiro Futura	05066-2072
EC-ZYR	Tecnam P.2002 Sierra	07077-2285
EC-ZYS	Aeroprakt A-20 Vista	07025-2233
EC-ZYT	Vans RV-9A	06040-2152
	(Dam. 24.7.14)	
EC-ZYU	Flight Design CT SW	07-05-23
	(Officially reg'd as 07069-2277)	
EC-ZYV	SG Aviation Storm Century 04	07030-2238
EC-ZYX	Vol Mediterrani VM-1 Esqual	06072-2184
EC-ZYY	Air Borne 2000	07073-2281
	(Cr and destroyed 30.7.12)	
EC-ZZA	Raj Hamsa X'Air	07049-2257
EC-ZZC	Zenair CH-601XLB Zodiac	06081-2193
EC-ZZD	Fly Synthesis Storch CL	07087-2295
EC-ZZE	Zenair CH-701 STOL	03056-1839
EC-ZZF	ELA Aviacion ELA 07-125	07052-2260
EC-ZZG	MAX-1	07053-2261
EC-ZZH	Eipper Quicksilver MXL-II Sport	00023-1412
EC-ZZI	ICP MXP-780 Calima	07032-2240
EC-ZZJ	Zlin Savage Cub	05007-2013
EC-ZZK	Piper J-3C-65 Cub (L-4J)	97010-1070
EC-ZZL	Alondra Autogiro	07003-2211
EC-ZZM	Alondra Autigiro	00142-1531
EC-ZZN	Air Création Safari GT BI	07036-2244
EC-ZZO	SG Aviation Storm RG	06083-2195
EC-ZZP	Titan Tornado 912	06029-2141
EC-ZZQ	BRM Land Africa	06039-2151
EC-ZZR	Fox C-32	07082-2290
EC-ZZS	Aerojeep	07013-2221
EC-ZZT	SG Aviation Storm Century	05097-2103
EC-ZZU	Antares MA-32	99104-1378
EC-ZZV	Plätzer Kiebitz B-9	04057-1941
EC-ZZX	Airbet Girabet	07058-2266
EC-ZZY	Alpi Avn Pioneer 300	07056-2264
EC-ZZZ	DUI-Tundra	06082-2194

TEMPORARY REGISTRATIONS

The following temporary registrations are also known - many have probably been re-regd in the above sequences but others are recent sightings and confirmed tie-ups would be welcome:-

EC-001	Aeroprakt A-22 Vision (Noted 6.07)	
EC-001	Flight Design CT SW (Noted 6.5.09)	
EC-002	Vol Mediterrani VM-1 Esqual (Noted 8.03)	
EC-002(2)	Aeroprakt A-22 Vision (Noted 7.07)	
EC-003	Colyaer Martin 3 S100	
EC-003(2)	Hoffman HK-36 Super Dimona (Noted 5.08)	36735
EC-004	Pipistrel Sinus 912	
	(Type unconfirmed, noted 9.7.04)	
EC-004(2)	Avionics/Fantasy Air Allegro 2000	
EC-006	Moragon (Noted 6.07)	
EC-042	Airbet Girabet II Sport (Noted 6.5.09)	
EC-043(2)	Tecnam P.96 Golf	
	(Reported 8.07 as P.92 Echo)	
EC-044	Rans S-6 Coyote IIXL	
EC-044(2)	Tecnam P.2002 Sierra (Noted 4.09)	
EC-046	Tecnam P.96 Golf (Noted 9.07)	
EC-046(2)	Airbet Girabet (Noted 17.4.09)	
EC-047	ICP Bingo	
EC-049	Tecnam P.96 Golf	
EC-108	N-3 Pup (See EC-YMX)	
EC-150	Piper PA-32-260 Cherokee Six	
	(Noted wfu 1.16)	
EC-152	Brügger MB-2 Colibri	
EC-160	Pterodactyl Ascender	
EC-161	Pterodactyl Ascender	
	(Type unconfirmed, noted 22.8.04)	
EC-164	Juvenavia Vulcano	
	(Stored incomplete)	
EC-170	Gyrocopter	
EC-173	Rand-Robinson KR-2	
EC-175	Neico Lancair 360	
EC-249	TEAM Mini-MAX	
EC-250	Air Command Gyrocopter (to EC-ZHV?)	
EC-300	Rans S-6 Coyote II	
EC-303	Pober Pixie	
EC-365	Light Aero Avid Flyer)	
EC-369	Light Aero Avid Flyer) (Probably re-registered in EC-YE. range)	
EC-370	Light Aero Avid Flyer)	
EC-414	Christen Eagle (Type unconfirmed)	
EC-432	Van's RV-6 (See EC-YOG)	
EC-444	Aviatika 890U Mai	
EC-459	Type unknown	
EC-466	Denney Kitfox III (See EC-YMF)	
EC-506	Rans S-6 Coyote II (W/o 19.6.94)	
EC-565	Light Aero Avid Flyer	
EC-573	Type unknown	
EC-579	Rotorway Executive 90 (Dam 6.10.94)	
EC-581	Saltapraos	

EC-601	Light Aero Avid Flyer		
EC-659	Sky Walker		
EC-676	Rutan Long-Ez (See EC-YNP)		
EC-693	Consolidated PBY-5A Catalina	1960	EC-314, C-FFFW, N45998,
	(at Cuatro Vientos Museum)		CF-FFW, N6070C, BuA46596
EC-703	Rand-Robinson KR-2		
EC-711	Avid Flyer STOL (W/o 6.7.05)		
EC-718	Eipper Quicksilver MXL-II Sport	029	
EC-741	Aero Designs Pulsar (See EC-CE8)		
EC-748	TEAM Mini-MAX (See EC-YOB)		
EC-826	Rans S-6 Coyote II TD/912		
EC-847	Air Création		
EC-881	Air Tractor AT-802A	unkn	
EC-901	Rans S-10 Sakota (See EC-YMN)		
EC-914	Rans S-12 Airaile		
EC-926	Eipper Quicksilver MX		
EC-927	Rans S-12 Airaile		
EC-929	Jodel D.18		
EC-937	Cameron RX-100 HAFB	2666	G-BTXP
	(at Cuatro Vientos Museum)		
EC-1592	Magni M-16 Tandem Trainer		

MICROLIGHTS

EC-AA1	Ultralight Soaring Wizard J3	
EC-AA2	Pterodactyl Ascender 1	
EC-AA3	Pterodactyl Ascender 1	
EC-AA4	Ultralight Soaring Wizard	
EC-AA5	King Cobra	
EC-AA7	Cobra	
EC-AA8	Condor III-2	
EC-AA9	Weedhopper JC-24C	
EC-AB1	Ultralight Soaring Wizard T-38B	66023
EC-AB2	Ultralight Soaring Wizard T-38B	66024
EC-AB3	King Cobra	
EC-AB4	Eipper Quicksilver MX-II	1222
EC-AB5	Condor III 40	
EC-AB7	King Cobra	
EC-AB8	Mistral 2-seater	
EC-AB9	Dragon Light 150	016
EC-AC1	Dragon 150	
EC-AC2	Southdown Puma Sprint	
EC-AC3	Condor III 440	
EC-AC4	Eipper Quicksilver MX-IIAA	1909
EC-AC5	Wizard T-38	
EC-AC6	Eipper Quicksilver MX-II	1910
EC-AC7	Eipper Quicksilver MX-II	1940
EC-AC8	Aquillon Etoile	B-19
EC-AC9	Eipper Quicksilver MX-II	1943
EC-AD1	Terratorn Tierra II	
EC-AD2	Wizard T-38	66018
EC-AD3	Rotec Rally III	
EC-AD4	Lazair II	B0-37
EC-AD5	Jordan Aviation Duet	5
EC-AD6	Wizard T-38	66069
EC-AD7	Eipper Quicksilver MX-II	2000
EC-AD9	Pterodactyl Ascender 2+2	83042092
EC-AE1	Eipper Quicksilver MX	4261
EC-AE2	Eipper Quicksilver MX	3839
EC-AE3	Eipper Quicksilver MX-I	3829
EC-AE4	PumAll	109
EC-AE5	Eipper Quicksilver MX-II	2082
EC-AE6	Eipper Quicksilver MX	3693
EC-AE7	Eipper Quicksilver MX-L	1386
EC-AE8	Eipper Quicksilver MX	1809
EC-AE9	Wizard T-38	44013
EC-AF1	Wizard T-38B	
EC-AF2	Sport Aircraft Tango II-GT	108502
EC-AF4	Pterodactyl Ascender II	
EC-AF5	Eipper Quicksilver MX-II	1955
EC-AF6	Tango B-84	12841
EC-AF7	Pterodactyl Ascender 2+2	1376
EC-AF8	Pterodactyl Ascender 2+2	1407
EC-AF9	Eipper Quicksilver MX-II	1781
EC-AG1	Pterodactyl Ascender II	
EC-AG2	Aériane Sirocco	
EC-AG3	Eipper Quicksilver MX-II	1447
EC-AG4	Sorrell SNA-8 Hiperlight	125
EC-AG5	Sorrell SNA-8 Hiperlight	134
EC-AG6	Challenger II	
EC-AG7	Challenger II	
EC-AG8	Interair F2	15/85
EC-AG9	Wizard T-38	66036
EC-AH1	Spitfire F2/55	85/16
EC-AH2	Cosmos / Hermes	
EC-AH3	Sport Aircraft Tango II	10842
EC-AH4	Sky Jet IV	OLB/00501
EC-AH5	Luroplane 3-por-2	
EC-AH6	Humbert La Moto del Cielo	8806
EC-AH7	Interair F-2/55	SF-007
EC-AH8	Interair F-2/55	SF-001
EC-AH9	Interair F-2/55	SF-006
EC-AI1	Interair F-2/55	85/00
EC-AI2	Interair F-2/55	SF-003
EC-AI3	Challenger	100B118103
EC-AI4	Sky Jet	MLB/0512A
EC-AI5	Cosmos Bidulum 53	
EC-AI6	Sport Aircraft Tango II	5861
EC-AI7	Sky Jet II A3	0101/85
EC-AI9	Sport Aircraft Tango II-GT	10863
EC-AJ1	Interair F-2/55	87/1
EC-AJ2	Cosmos Bidulum 46	3585302
EC-AJ3	Sport Aircraft Tango II	12855
EC-AJ4	Sky Jet	00505A
EC-AJ5	Hummer B	
EC-AJ8	Eipper Quicksilver MX-II	28AD
EC-AJ9	Sport Aircraft Tango II-GT	2871
EC-AK1	Sport Aircraft Tango II-GT	4871
EC-AK3	Zodiac Twinstar	116
EC-AK4	Aviasud Mistral	06.87/042
EC-AK5	Aviasud Mistral	017
EC-AK6	Eipper Quicksilver MX-II	2240
EC-AK7	Cosmos Pendular	3585110
EC-AK8	Sport Aircraft Tango II	2872
EC-AK9	Sport Aircraft Tango II	9874

Reg.	Type	Serial	Notes
EC-AL1	Sport Aircraft Tango II-GT	6875	
EC-AL2	Sport Aircraft Tango II	1882	
EC-AL3	Eipper Quicksilver MX-II	2216	
EC-AL4	Aviasud Mistral	034	
EC-AL5	Comco Ikarus Fox-C22	8803-3120	
EC-AL6	Comco Ikarus Fox-C22	8803-3121	
EC-AL7	Air Création Safari GT BI / Plus 20	042	
EC-AL8	Humbert La Moto del Cielo	8823	
EC-AL9	Sport Aircraft Tango II	5856	
EC-AM1	Sport Aircraft Tango II	4873	
EC-AM2	Sport Aircraft Tango II	6876	
EC-AM3	Rotec Panther 2	25733	
EC-AM4	Sport Aircraft Tango II-GT	3887	
EC-AM5	Eipper Quicksilver MX-II	1225	
EC-AM6	Sport Aircraft Tango II-GT	4882	
EC-AM7	Sallen Mach-15 Gyrocopter	129	
EC-AM8	Sallen Mach-15 Gyrocopter	119	
EC-AM9	Eipper Quicksilver MX-II	1994	
EC-AN1	Eipper Quicksilver MXL-II	3721	
EC-AN3	Sallen Mach-15 Gyrocopter	123	
EC-AN4	Sallen Mach-15 Gyrocopter	134	
EC-AN5	Sallen Mach-15 Gyrocopter	121	
EC-AN6	Hispano Lights Cometa 52A	1511-8852002	
EC-AN7	Sport Aircraft Tango II-GT	9872	
EC-AN8	Sallen Mach 15 Gyrocopter	132	
EC-AN9	Eipper Quicksilver MX-II	2217	
EC-AO1	Sallen Mach-10 Gyrocopter	110	
EC-AO2	Dynali Chickinox Tandem	2944381	
EC-AO3	Sport Aircraft Tango II-GT	7871	
EC-AO4	Sallen Mach-15 Gyrocopter (Res 9.13)	15-120	
EC-AO5	Sallen Mach-15 Gyrocopter	114	
EC-AO6	Sallen Mach-15 Gyrocopter	130	
EC-AO7	Sallen Mach-15 Gyrocopter	133	
EC-AO8	Sallen Mach-15 Gyrocopter	136	
EC-AO9	Sallen Mach-15 Gyrocopter	137	
EC-AP1	Sport Aircraft Tango II-GT	6891	
EC-AP2	Sport Aircraft Tango II-GT	2885	
EC-AP4	Sport Aircraft Tango II-GT	3884	
EC-AP5	Sport Aircraft Tango II-GT	3881	
EC-AP6	Sport Aircraft Tango II-GT	3871	
EC-AP7	Hispano Lights Cometa 52A	04049052003	
EC-AP8	Hispano Lights Cometa 52A	04049052004	
EC-AP9	Sport Aircraft Tango II	3895	
EC-AQ1	Sport Aircraft Tango II	3894	
EC-AQ2	Sport Aircraft Tango II	1895	
EC-AQ3	Sport Aircraft Tango II	4893	
EC-AQ4	Sport Aircraft Tango II	6892	
EC-AQ5	Sport Aircraft Tango II	5856	
EC-AQ6	Sallen Mach-15 Gyrocopter	127	
EC-AQ7	Sport Aircraft Tango II-GT	1903	
EC-AQ8	Sport Aircraft Tango II	9877	
EC-AQ9	Sport Aircraft Tango II	1902	
EC-AR1	Sport Aircraft Tango II	4891	
EC-AR2	Sport Aircraft Tango II-GT	5891	
EC-AR3	Sport Aircraft Tango II	6893	
EC-AR4	Sport Aircraft Tango II	2901	
EC-AR5	Sport Aircraft Tango II-GT	12854	
EC-AR6	Sport Aircraft Tango II	3905	
EC-AR8	Hispano Lights Cometa 52V	09049052005	
EC-AR9	Sport Aircraft Tango II-GT	5892	
EC-AS1	Sport Aircraft Tango II	1905	
EC-AS2	Eipper Quicksilver MX-II	2327	
EC-AS3	Sport Aircraft Tango II-GT	5895	
EC-AS4	Sport Aircraft Tango II	3902	
EC-AS5	Sallen Mach 15 Gyrocopter	131	
EC-AS7	Sport Aircraft Tango II	1901	
EC-AS8	Sport Aircraft Tango II	2902	
EC-AS9	Sport Aircraft Tango II	2905	
EC-AT2	Sport Aircraft Tango II	5903	
EC-AT3	Sport Aircraft Tango II	1893	
EC-AT4	Sport Aircraft Tango II	3904	
EC-AT5	Hispano Lights Cometa 52A	05119052006	
EC-AT6	Sport Aircraft Tango II	12852	
EC-AT7	Aerial Arts Chaser S	CH-779	EC-280
EC-AT8	Dynali Chickinox Kot-Kot	31191855	
EC-AU1	Dynali Chickinox Tandem II	292796	
EC-AU2	Sport Aircraft Tango II	4903	
EC-AU3	Sport Aircraft Tango II	9842	
EC-AU4	Dynali Chickinox Kot-Kot	31139741	
EC-AU5	Sport Aircraft Tango II	1913	
EC-AU6	Sport Aircraft Tango II	6904	
EC-AU7	Sallen Mach-15 Gyrocopter	138	
EC-AU8	Sallen Mach-15 Gyrocopter (W/o 21.8.05)	118	
EC-AU9	Sallen Mach-10 Gyrocopter	115	
EC-AV1	Sport Aircraft Tango II	2882	
EC-AV2	Sport Aircraft Tango II	4905	
EC-AV3	Sport Aircraft Tango II	2904	
EC-AV4	Sport Aircraft Tango II	1912	
EC-AV5	Sport Aircraft Tango II	3876	
EC-AV6	Dynali Chickinox Kot-Kot	31256693	EC-606 ?
EC-AV7	Sallen Mach 15 Gyrocopter	15-142	
EC-AV8	Sport Aircraft Tango II	4904	
EC-AV9	Sport Aircraft Tango II	9876	
EC-AX1	Sport Aircraft Tango II	6902	
EC-AX2	Sport Aircraft Tango II-GT	5901	
EC-AX3	Dynali Chickinox Tandem	219154	
EC-AX4	Sport Aircraft Tango II-GT	2913	
EC-AX5	Sport Aircraft Tango II-GT	2911	
EC-AX6	Sport Aircraft Tango II-GT	2912	
EC-AX7	Sport Aircraft Tango II	4902	
EC-AX8	Sport Aircraft Tango II-GT	5904	
EC-AX9	Eipper Quicksilver MX-II	3876	
EC-AY1	Dynali Chickinox Kot-Kot	329846	
EC-AY2	Dynali Chickinox Tandem	2106128	
EC-AY3	Sport Aircraft Tango II	5851	
EC-AY4	Sallen Mach-15 Gyrocopter	15-143	
EC-AY6	Sport Aircraft Tango II-GT	3912	
EC-AY7	Sallen Mach 10 Gyrocopter	10-111	
EC-AY8	Sport Aircraft Tango II-GT	2915	
EC-AY9	Sport Aircraft Tango II-GT	1914	
EC-AZ1	Sallen Mach 15 Gyrocopter	128	
EC-AZ2	Sport Aircraft Tango II-GT	3911	
EC-AZ3	Sport Aircraft Tango II-GT	4911	
EC-AZ4	Sport Aircraft Tango II-GT	1885	
EC-AZ5	Sport Aircraft Tango II	3853	
EC-AZ6	Eipper Quicksilver MXL -II	140	
EC-AZ7	Dynali Chickinox Kot-Kot	31086928	
EC-AZ8	Dynali Chickinox Monoplaza	11087812	
EC-BA1	Air Création Safari GT-BI / Fun 18	191003	
EC-BA2	Air Création Safari GT-BI / Fun 18	191007	
EC-BA3	Sport Aircraft Tango II	6903	
EC-BA4	Sport Aircraft Tango II	5893	
EC-BA5	Eipper Quicksilver MXL	3722	
EC-BA6	Eipper Quicksilver MX-Sprint II	212	
EC-BA7	Eipper Quicksilver MX-Sprint II	292	
EC-BA8	Sport Aircraft Tango II	4901	
EC-BA9	Air Création Safari GT-BI / Fun 18	191006	
EC-BB1	Sport Aircraft Tango II	4894	
EC-BB2	Air Création Safari GT-BI / Fun 18	192013	
EC-BB3	Eipper Quicksilver MXL-Sport II	78	
EC-BB4	Sallen Mach-15 Gyrocopter	15-144	
EC-BB5	Eipper Quicksilver MX-Sprint II	137	
EC-BB6	Dynali Chickinox	31220684	
EC-BB7	Eipper Quicksilver MXL-II	1353	
EC-BB8	Air Création Safari GT-BI / Fun 18	192014	
EC-BB9	Sallen Mach-15 Gyrocopter	112	
EC-BC1	Eipper Quicksilver MXL-II	1212	
EC-BC2	Sallen Mach-10	140	
EC-BC3	Sallen Mach-15 Gyrocopter	15-145	
EC-BC4	Eipper Quicksilver MXL	1689	
EC-BC5	Sport Aircraft Tango II	4884	
EC-BC6	Sport Aircraft Tango II	6851	
EC-BC7	Eipper Quicksilver MX-II	237	
EC-BC8	Sport Aircraft Tango II	5912	
EC-BC9	Sport Aircraft Tango II-GT	5913	
EC-BD1	Eipper Quicksilver MX-II	210	
EC-BD2	Sallen Mach-15 Gyrocopter	15-146	
EC-BD3	Sport Aircraft Tango II-GT	2914	
EC-BD4	Sport Aircraft Tango II-GT	4912	
EC-BD5	Sport Aircraft Tango II-GT	3913	
EC-BD7	Dynali Chickinox Kot-Kot	354134	
EC-BD8	Eipper Quicksilver MXL	222	
EC-BD9	Eipper Quicksilver MX-II	1315	
EC-BE1	Air Création Safari GT-BI/ Fun 18	192017	
EC-BE2	Eipper Quicksilver MXL	1685	
EC-BE3	Sport Aircraft Tango II	5914	
EC-BE4	Eipper Quicksilver MXL-II	143	
EC-BE5	Sallen Mach-15 Gyrocopter	15-147	
EC-BE6	Air Création Safari GT-BI / Fun 18	191010	
EC-BE8	Air Création Safari GT-BI / Fun 18	191002	
EC-BE9	Air Création Safari GT-BI / Fun 18	192015	
EC-BF1	Air Création Safari GT-BI / Quartz 16 SXE	292008	
EC-BF2	Eipper Quicksilver MX Sprint II	144	
EC-BF3	Eipper Quicksilver MXL	3260	
EC-BF4	Dynali Chickinox Tandem	258186	
EC-BF5	Air Création Safari GT-BI / Quartz 16 SXE	292007	
EC-BF6	Sallen Mach-15 Gyrocopter (Dam 10.2.06)	15-126	
EC-BF7	Sallen Mach-15 Gyrocopter	15-149	
EC-BF8	Eipper Quicksilver MX	142	
EC-BF9	Sport Aircraft Tango II-GT	1891	
EC-BG1	Sport Aircraft Tango II-GT	1926	
EC-BG2	Air Création GT BI / Fun 18	19001	
EC-BG3	Air Création GT BI / Quartz 16SXE	291002	
EC-BG4	Sport Aircraft Tango II-GT	4914	
EC-BG5	Ultraligeros Espana Volero Jaguar-16	V-1921	
EC-BG6	Dynali Chickinox Kot-Kot	31060000	
EC-BG7	Sport Aircraft Tango II-GT	T2922	
EC-BG8	Sport Aircraft Tango II-GT	1921	
EC-BG9	Sport Aircraft Tango II-GT	1911	
EC-BH1	Dynali Chickinox Kot-Kot	2592E106	
EC-BH2	Dynali Chickinox Kot-Kot	32144536	
EC-BH3	Ultraligeros Espana Volero Jaguar-16	V-3922	
EC-BH4	Ultraligeros Espana Volero Jaguar-16	V-3921	
EC-BH5	Ultraligeros Espana Volero Jaguar-16	V-3924	
EC-BH6	Ultraligeros Espana Volero Jaguar-16	V-3923	
EC-BH7	Fly-Master TSA-10	003	
EC-BH8	Eipper Quicksilver MX-II	3269	
EC-BH9	Sallen Mach 15 Gyrocopter	15-148	
EC-BI1	Sport Aircraft Tango GT-II	T2921	
EC-BI2	Air Création Safari GT BI / Fun 18	192025	
EC-BI3	Ultraligeros Espana Volero Jaguar-16	V-1923	
EC-BI4	Ultraligeros Espana Volero Jaguar-16	V-4921	
EC-BI5	Ultraligeros Espana Volero Jaguar-16	V-3925	
EC-BI6	Sport Aircraft Tango II-GT	T2923	
EC-BI7	Air Création Safari GT-BI / Quartz 16 SXE	291005	
EC-BI8	Eipper Quicksilver MX-Sprint IIR	0138	
EC-BJ1	Air Création Safari GT-BI / Fun 18	192029	
EC-BJ2	Air Création Safari GT-BI / Fun 18	192024	
EC-BJ4	Air Création Safari GT-BI / Fun 18	191012	
EC-BJ5	Sport Aircraft Tango II-GT	T1925	
EC-BJ7	Air Création Safari GT-BI / Fun 18	192031	
EC-BJ8	Eipper Quicksilver MX-II	5007	
EC-BK1	Eipper Quicksilver MX-II	5009	
EC-BK2	Sallen Mach-15 Gyrocopter	15-150	
EC-BK3	Dynali Chickinox Kot-Kot	31216262	
EC-BK4	Dynali Chickinox Kot-Kot	31126409	
EC-BK5	Air Création Safari GT-BI / Fun 18	192032	
EC-BK6	Ultraligeros Espana Volero Jaguar-16	V-1915	
EC-BK7	Air Création Safari GT-BI / Fun 18	192018	
EC-BK9	Air Création Safari GT-BI / Fun 18	192020	
EC-BL1	Ultraligeros Espana Volero Jaguar-16	V-1914	
EC-BL2	Ultraligeros Espana Volero Jaguar-16	V-1924	
EC-BL3	Air Création Safari GT-BI / Fun 18	192022	
EC-BL4	Air Création Safari GT-BI / Fun 18	193033	
EC-BL5	Carlos Perez Fly-Master TSA-10	000	
EC-BL6	Eipper Quicksilver MX-Sprint IIR	0349	
EC-BL7	Eipper Quicksilver MX-Sprint II	0289	
EC-BL8	Carlos Perez Fly-Master TSA-10	016	
EC-BL9	Carlos Perez Fly-Master TSA-10	012	
EC-BM1	Carlos Perez Fly-Master TSA-10	015	
EC-BM2	Air Création Safari GT-BI / Fun 18	192028	
EC-BM3	Sport Aircraft Tango II-GT	T-2925	
EC-BM4	Sport Aircraft Tango II-GT	T-2924	
EC-BM5	Eipper Quicksilver MX	0082	
EC-BM6	Carlos Perez Fly-Master TSA-10	009	
EC-BM7	Eipper Quicksilver MX-Sprint II	0364	
EC-BM8	Carlos Perez Fly-Master TSA-10	007	
EC-BM9	Ultraligeros Espana Volero Jaguar-16	V-4923	
EC-BN1	Sallen Mach-15 Gyrocopter	15-151	

EC-BN2	Eipper Quicksilver MX-Sprint IIR	390	
EC-BN3	Ultraligeros Espana Volero Jaguar-16	V-1925	
EC-BN4	Eipper Quicksilver GT-500	0068	
EC-BN5	Eipper Quicksilver GT-500	0088	
EC-BN7	Ultraligeros Espana Volero Jaguar-16	V-2922	
EC-BN8	Ultraligeros Espana Volero Jaguar-16	V-2924	
EC-BN9	Dynali Chickinox Kot-Kot	1393-E-11	
EC-BO1	Air Création Safari GT-BI / Fun 18	193034	
EC-BO2	Eipper Quicksilver GT-500	0089	
	(W/o 14.6.08)		
EC-BO3	Cedimex Rans S-12 Airaile	S-12-115	
EC-BO4	Cedimex Rans S-12 Airaile	S-12-108	
EC-BO5	Cedimex Rans S-12 Airaile	S-12-103	
EC-BO6	Eipper Quicksilver MXL-Sport IIR	0328	
EC-BO7	Air Création Safari GT BI / Quartz 16 SXE	292003	
EC-BO8	Cedimex Rans S-12 Airaile	S-12-117	
EC-BO9	Eipper Quicksilver MX-Sprint IIR	0312	
EC-BP1	Eipper Quicksilver MX-Sprint II	0365	
EC-BP2	Eipper Quicksilver MX-Sprint IIR	0309	
EC-BP3	Ultraligeros Espana Volero Jaguar-16	V-1916	
EC-BP4	Cedimex Rans S-12 Airaile	S-12-114	
EC-BP5	Eipper Quicksilver MXL-Sport IIR	0353	
EC-BP6	Air Création Safari GT-BI / Quartz	293010	
EC-BP7	Ultraligeros Espana Volero Jaguar-16	V-4925	
EC-BP8	Cedimex Rans S-12 Airaile	S-12-112	
EC-BP9	Air Création Safari GT-BI / XP15	193036	
EC-BQ1	Air Création Safari GT-BI / Quartz 16 SXE	91004	
EC-BQ2	Eipper Quicksilver MX-Sprint IIR	350	
EC-BQ3	Eipper Quicksilver GT-500	0074	
EC-BQ4	Eipper Quicksilver MX-Sprint IIR	0388	
EC-BQ5	Cedimex Rans S-12 Airaile	S-12-118	
EC-BQ6	Carlos Perez Fly-Master TSA-10	014	
	(Cr and destroyed 5.1.10)		
EC-BQ7	Eipper Quicksilver MX-Sprint IIR	0363	
EC-BQ9	Mainair Gemini/Flash IIA	934-01937-W732	
EC-BR1	Mainair Gemini/Flash IIA	914-07927-W713	
EC-BR2	Mainair Gemini/Flash IIA	871-12917-W666	
EC-BR3	Mainair Gemini/Flash IIA	847-07917-W641	
EC-BR4	Aviasud Mistral 582	157	
EC-BR5	Eipper Quicksilver MX-Sprint II	0392	
EC-BR6	Air Création Safari GT-BI / Fun 18S	191011	
EC-BR7	Air Création Safari GT-BI / SX16	291006	
EC-BR8	Eipper Quicksilver MX-Sprint II	0391	
EC-BR9	Cedimex Rans S-12 Airaile	S-12-102	
EC-BS1	Sallen Mach-15 Gyrocopter	15-154	
EC-BS2	Air Création Safari GT-BI / Quartz 16 SXS	293012	
EC-BS3	Sport Aircraft Tango II-GT	3915	
EC-BS4	Eipper Quicksilver MXL-II	1693	
EC-BS5	Dynali Chickinox Kot-Kot	3119196	
EC-BS6	Air Création Safari GT-BI / Fun 18	193038	
EC-BS7	Eipper Quicksilver MX-Sprint IIR	0362	
EC-BS8	Cedimex Rans S-12 Airaile	S-12-113	
EC-BS9	Air Création Safari GT-BI / Fun 18	193037	
EC-BT1	Air Création Safari GT-BI / Quartz 16 SXS	294015	
EC-BT2	Air Création Safari GT-BI / Quartz 16 SXS	293013	
EC-BT3	Mainair Gemini/Flash IIA	952-06937-W747	
EC-BT5	Mainair Gemini/Flash IIA	782-02907-W575	
EC-BT7	Eipper Quicksilver MXL-Sport IIR	0409	
EC-BT8	Cedimex Rans S-12 Airaile	S-12-111	
EC-BT9	Dynali Chickinox Kot-Kot	31149060	
EC-BU1	Sport Aircraft Tango II	3862	
EC-BU2	Eipper Quicksilver MXL-Sport IIR	0354	
EC-BU3	Cedimex Rans S-12 Airaile	S-12-131	
EC-BU4	Mainair Gemini/Flash IIA	987-04947-W783	
EC-BU5	Cedimex Rans S-12 Airaile	S-12-132	
EC-BU6	Mainair 582 Blade	1005-0894/-W801	
EC-BU7	Air Création Safari GT-BI / Fun 18	194041	
EC-BU8	Ultraligeros Espana Volero Jaguar-16	V-2923	
EC-BU9	Ultraligeros Espana Volero Jaguar-16	V-1931	
EC-BV1	Eipper Quicksilver MX-Sprint IIR	446	
EC-BV2	Eipper Quicksilver MXL-Sport II	0142	
EC-BV3	Aviasud Mistral Twin	146	
EC-BV4	Weedhopper AX-2	B-3043109	
EC-BV5	Cedimex Rans S-12 Airaile	S-12-133	
EC-BV6	Cedimex Rans S-12 Airaile	S-12-105	
EC-BV7	Cedimex Rans S-12 Airaile	S-12-129	
EC-BV8	Sport Aircraft Tango II-GT	4915	
EC-BV9	Dynali Chickinox Kot-Kot	5192-E-108	
EC-BX1	Air Création Safari GT-BI / Fun 18	194044	
EC-BX2	Air Création Safari GT-BI / SX16	293011	
EC-BX3	Cedimex Rans S-12 Airaile	S-12-121	
EC-BX4	Eipper Quicksilver MXL-Sport IIR	0393	
	(Noted wrecked 1.16)		
EC-BX5	Cedimex Rans S-12 Airaile	S-12-104	
EC-BX6	Eipper Quicksilver MX-Sprint IIR	211	
EC-BX7	Cedimex Rans S-6 Coyote II	S-6A-100	
EC-BX8	Cedimex Rans S-12 Airaile	S-12-130	
EC-BX9	Eipper Quicksilver GT-500	0082	
EC-BY1	Cedimex Rans S-12 Airaile	S-12-136	
EC-BY2	Cedimex Rans S-12 Airaile	S-12-135	
EC-BY4	Carlos Perez Fly-Master TSA-10	011	
EC-BY5	Cedimex Rans S-12 Airaile	S-12-106	
EC-BY6	Cedimex Rans S-6 Coyote II	S-6A-101	
EC-BY7	Cedimex Rans S-6 Coyote II	S-6A-102	
EC-BY8	Cedimex Rans S-12 Airaile	S-12-124	
EC-BZ2	Eipper Quicksilver MXL-II	1214	
EC-BZ3	Eipper Quicksilver MX-II	3763640	
EC-BZ4	Cedimex Rans S-6 Coyote II	S-6A-104	
EC-BZ5	Eipper Quicksilver MXL-Sport IIR	0350	
EC-BZ6	Cedimex Rans S-12 Airaile	S-12-122	
EC-BZ7	Cedimex Rans S-12 Airaile	S-12-127	
	(W/o 3.6.06)		
EC-BZ8	Cedimex Rans S-6 Coyote II	S-6A-103	
EC-BZ9	Dynali Chickinox Kot-Kot	1392-E-103	
EC-CA1	Cedimex Rans S-12 Airaile	S-12-141	
EC-CA2	Eipper Quicksilver GT-500	0079	
EC-CA3	Eipper Quicksilver MXL-II	1603	
EC-CA4	Air Création Safari GT-BI / Fun 18	194045	
EC-CA5	UltraLigeros Espana Volero	V-1932	
EC-CA6	Cedimex Rans S-6 Coyote II	S-6A-105	
EC-CA7	Cedimex Rans S-12 Airaile	S-12-140	
EC-CA9	Sallen Mach-10	10-155	
EC-CB1	Sallen Mach-15 Gyrocopter	15-152	
	(Destroyed 16.1.11)		
EC-CB2	Aviasud Mistral	139	
EC-CB3	Eipper Quicksilver MXL-Sport IIR	0541	
EC-CB4	Sport Aircraft Tango II-GT	6894	
EC-CB5	Cedimex Rans S-6ES Coyote II	S-6A-108	
EC-CB7	Weedhopper AX-3	C-3123195	
EC-CB8	Eipper Quicksilver MXL Sport IIR	0583	
EC-CB9	Eipper Quicksilver MX Sprint IIR	315	
EC-CC1	Air Création Safari GT-BI / Fun 18	192019	
	(Ditched 9.3.08)		
EC-CC2	Air Création Safari GT-BI / Fun 18	194043	
EC-CC3	Air Création Safari GT-BI / Fun 18	191008	
EC-CC4	Sport Aircraft Tango II-GT	T-1951	
EC-CC5	Air Création Safari GT-BI / XP15S	494004	
EC-CC6	Carlod Perez Fly Master TSA-10	010	
EC-CC7	Carlos Perez Fly Master TSA-10	002	
EC-CC8	Cedimex Rans S-12 Airaile	S-12-142	
EC-CC9	Cedimex Rans S-12 Airaile	S-12-146	
EC-CD1	Cedimex Rans S-6ES Coyote II	S-6A-111	
EC-CD2	Eipper Quicksilver MXL Sport II	0072	
EC-CD3	Eipper Quicksilver MXL-II	1357	
EC-CD4	Rans S-12 Airaile	S-12-116	
EC-CD5	Air Création Safari GT-BI / M16	394001	
	(W/o 24.5.05)		
EC-CD6	Cedimex Rans S-12 Airaile	S-12-144	
EC-CD7	Cedimex Rans S-6ES Coyote II	S-6A-110	
EC-CD8	Hispano Aeronautica Canelas Ranger	S-93-02	
EC-CD9	Cedimex Rans S-12 Airaile	S-12-134	
EC-CE1	Cedimex Rans S-12 Airaile	S-12-137	
EC-CE2	Cedimex Rans S-6 Coyote II	S-6A-109	
EC-CE3	Cedimex Rans S-6ES Coyote II	S-6A-107	
EC-CE4	Eipper Quicksilver MXL Sport II	141	
EC-CE5	Air Création Safari GT-BI / Fun 18	194042	
EC-CE7	Eipper Quicksilver MX Sprint IIR	0463	
EC-CE8	Micro Aviation Pulsar II	0130	
EC-CE9	Mainair Blade 582	994-0694-7-W791	G-MYSH
EC-CF1	UltraLigeros Espana Volero	V-1934	
EC-CF2	Dynali Chickinox Kot-Kot	5192-E-109	
EC-CF3	Cedimex Rans S-12 Airaile	S-12-147	
EC-CF4	Mainair Blade 503	1073-0296-7-W875	
EC-CF5	UltraLigeros Espana Volero	V-2921	
EC-CF6	Eipper Quicksilver MXL Sport IIR	0327	
EC-CF7	Eipper Quicksilver MXL Sport IIR	0326	
EC-CF8	Eipper Quicksilver MXL-II	1690	
EC-CF9	Eipper Quicksilver GT-500	0043	
EC-CG1	Eipper Quicksilver GT-500	0070	
EC-CG2	Eipper Quicksilver MXL Sport IIR	0259	
EC-CG3	Eipper Quicksilver MXL Sport IIR	0593	
EC-CG4	Eipper Quicksilver MXL Sport IIR	0325	
EC-CG5	Eipper Quicksilver MXL Sport IIR	0410	
EC-CG6	Eipper Quicksilver MXL Sport IIR	0352	
EC-CG7	Dynali Chickinox Kot-Kot	2395-E-2	
EC-CG8	Dynali Chickinox Tandem	1195-E-1	
EC-CG9	Cedimex Rans S-12 XL Airaile	S-12-150	
EC-CH1	Cedimex Rans S-12 Airaile	S-12-145	
EC-CH3	Cedimex Rans S-12XL Airaile	S-12-153	
EC-CH4	Cedimex Rans S-12XL Airaile	S-12-166	
EC-CH5	Cedimex Rans S-12XL Airaile	S-12-165	
EC-CH6	Cedimex Rans S-12XL Airaile	S-12-157	
EC-CH8	Cedimex Rans S-6ES Coyote II	S-6A-117	
EC-CH9	Cedimex Rans S-12XL Airaile	S-12-172	
EC-CI1	Eipper Quicksilver Sprint II	0045	
EC-CI2	Sallen Mach-10	10-116	
EC-CI3	Cedimex Rans S-12XL Airaile	S-12-154	
EC-CI4	Cedimex Rans S-6ES Coyote II	S-6A-116	
EC-CI5	Cedimex Rans S-6ES Coyote II	S-6A-112	
EC-CI6	Eipper Quicksilver MX Sprint IIR	0492	
EC-CI7	Cedimex Rans S-12XL Airaile	S-12-159	
EC-CI8	Sport Aircraft Tango II-GT	6872	
EC-CI9	Cedimex Rans S-12XL Airaile	S-12-151	
EC-CJ1	Cedimex Rans S-12XL Airaile	S-12-173	
EC-CJ2	Cedimex Rans S-6ES Coyote II	S-6A-120	
EC-CJ3	Road Air Flamingo	004	
EC-CJ4	Road Air Flamingo	003	
EC-CJ5	Road Air Flamingo	005	
EC-CJ6	Sport Aircraft Tango II-GT	2892	
EC-CJ7	Eipper Quicksilver GT-500	0305	
EC-CJ8	Cedimex Rans S-12XL Airaile	S-12-156	
EC-CJ9	Dynali Chickinox Kot-Kot	31980	
EC-CK1	Cedimex Rans S-6ES Coyote II	S-6A-115	
EC-CK2	Cedimex Rans S-12XL Airaile	S-12-170	
EC-CK3	Sport Aircraft Tango II-GT	1881	
EC-CK4	Sport Aircraft Tango II-GT	9875	
EC-CK5	Sport Aircraft Tango II-GT	6873	
EC-CK6	Cedimex Rans S-12XL-582	S-12-171	
EC-CK7	Dynali Chickinox Kot-Kot	1392-E-104	
EC-CK8	Ultralair Weedhopper AX3	B-4033202	
EC-CK9	Cedimex Rans S-6ES-503 Coyote II	S-6A-125	
EC-CL3	Cedimex Rans S-6ES-582 Coyote II	S-6A-114	
EC-CL4	Cedimex Rans S-12XL-582	S-12-168	
EC-CL5	Cedimex Rans S-12 Airaile	S-12-174	
EC-CL6	Cedimex Rans S-6ES-582 Coyote II	S-6A-113	
EC-CL7	Eipper Quicksilver MXL-IIR Sport	673	
EC-CL8	Cedimex Rans S-12XL Airaile	S-12-176	
EC-CL9	Road Air Flamingo	009	
EC-CM1	Road Air Flamingo	010	
EC-CM2	Road Air Flamingo	002	
EC-CM3	Road Air Flamingo	007	
EC-CM4	Road Air Flamingo	006	
EC-CM5	Cedimex Rans S-6ES-582 Coyote II	S-6A-124	
EC-CM6	Sport Aircraft Tango II-GT	3896	
EC-CM7	Eipper Quicksilver MXL-II Sport	081	
EC-CM8	Road Air Flamingo	012	
EC-CM9	Road Air Flamingo	011	
EC-CN1	Cedimex Rans S-6ES-503 Coyote II	S-6A-123	
EC-CN2	Air Création Safari GT BI / Fun 18	196047	
EC-CN3	Road Air Flamingo	008	
EC-CN4	Eipper Quicksilver MXL-II Sport	123	
EC-CN5	Eipper Quicksilver MXL-II Sport	0075	
EC-CN6	Eipper Quicksilver MXL-IIR Sport	587	
EC-CN7	Road Air Flamingo	016	
EC-CN8	Cedimex Rans S-12 Airaile	S-12-126	
EC-CN9	Cedimex Rans S-6ES-503 Coyote II	S-6A-122	
	(Cr and dbf 25.5.12)		
EC-CO1	Micro Aviation Pulsar II	0133	
EC-CO2	Micro Aviation Pulsar II	0129	
EC-CO3	Cedimex Rans S-6ES-582	S-6A-135	
EC-CO4	Cedimex Rans S-6ES-503 Coyote II	S-6A-137	
EC-CO5	Cedimex Rans S-6ES-503 Coyote II	S-6A-138	

EC-CO6	Mainair Blade	1058-1195-7-W856
	(Type confirmed but regd as Gemini/Flash IIA)	
EC-CO7	Mainair Blade	1102-1296-7-W905
	(Type confirmed but regd as Gemini/Flash IIA)	
EC-CO8	Eipper Quicksilver MXL-II	1694
EC-CO9	Eipper Quicksilver MXL-II	1692
EC-CP1	Eipper Quicksilver MXL-II	1688
EC-CP2	Eipper Quicksilver MXL-II Sport	224
EC-CP3	Eipper Quicksilver MXL-IIR Sport	355
EC-CP4	Eipper Quicksilver MXL-IIR Sprint	493
EC-CP5	Cedimex Rans S-12XL-503	S-12-169
EC-CP6	Cedimex Rans S-6ES-503 Coyote II	S-6A-136
EC-CP7	Eipper Quicksilver MXL-II Sport	0223
EC-CP8	Eipper Quicksilver GT-500	0304
EC-CP9	Eipper Quicksilver MXL-IIR Sport	0584
EC-CQ1	Road Air Flamingo	015
EC-CQ2	Cedimex Rans S-12 Airaile	S-12-180
EC-CQ3	Cedimex Rans S-12 Airaile	S-12-158
EC-CQ4	UltraLigeros Espana Volero	V1918
EC-CQ7	Cedimex Rans S-12XL-582 Airaile	S-12-186
	(Cr and destroyed 25.5.12)	
EC-CQ8	Cedimex Rans S-12XL-503 Airaile	S-12-184
EC-CQ9	Cedimex Rans S-12XL-582 Airaile	S-12-177
EC-CR1	Cedimex Rans S-6ES-582 Coyote II	S-6A-127
EC-CR2	Sport Aircraft Tango II-GT	5911
EC-CR3	Vol 9/Best Off Sky Ranger	SK-1210695
EC-CR4	Cedimex Rans S-12XL-503 Airaile	S-12-181
EC-CR6	Cedimex Rans S-12XL-503 Airaile	S-12-189
EC-CR7	Eipper Quicksilver MXL-II Sport	408
EC-CR8	Cedimex Rans S-6A-503 Coyote II	S-6A-133
EC-CR9	Vol 9/Best Off Sky Ranger	SK-1210795
EC-CS1	Cedimex Rans S-12XL-582 Airaile	S-12-192
EC-CS2	Cedimex Rans S-12 Airaile	S-12-178
EC-CS3	Cedimex Rans S-12XL-582 Airaile	S-12-179
EC-CS4	Eipper Quicksilver MX-II	1882
EC-CS5	Road Air Flamingo	014
EC-CS6	Air Création Safari GT BI / Fun 18	193035
EC-CS7	Pampa's Bull Flightstar	PB-FSB046
EC-CS8	Cedimex Rans S-6ES-582 Coyote II	S-6A-145
EC-CS9	Cedimex Rans S-6ES-503 Coyote II	S-6A-146
EC-CT1	Cedimex Rans S-12XL-582 Airaile	S-12-188
EC-CT2	Dynali Chickinox Kot-Kot	4595
EC-CT3	Eipper Quicksilver MXL-IIR Sport	672
EC-CT4	Eipper Quicksilver GT-500	0039
EC-CT5	Cedimex Rans S-12XL-582 Airaile	S-12-190
EC-CT6	Sport Aircraft Tango II-GT	2903
EC-CT7	Mainair Blade	1085-0596-7-W88
	(Type confirmed but regd as Gemini/Flash IIA)	
EC-CT8	Cedimex Rans S-6ES-582 Coyote II	unkn
EC-CT9	Sport Aircraft Tango II-GT	2903
EC-CU1	Eipper Quicksilver MX-II Sprint	208
EC-CU2	Cedimex Rans S-12XL-503 Airaile	S-12-183
EC-CU3	Cedimex Rans S-12XL-503 Airaile	S-12-182
EC-CU4	Eipper Quicksilver MXL-II Sport	0585
EC-CU5	Cedimex Rans S-6ES-503 Coyote II	S-6A-141
EC-CU6	Cedimex Rans S-6ES-503 Coyote II	S-6A-148
EC-CU7	Road Air Flamingo	018
EC-CU8	Sport Aircraft Tango II-GT	4872
EC-CU9	Sport Aircraft Tango I	5864
EC-CV1	Cedimex Rans S-12XL-503 Airaile	S-12-194
EC-CV2	Micro Aviation Pulsar II	0136
EC-CV3	Cedimex Rans S-6ES-503 Coyote II	S-6A-143
EC-CV4	Cedimex Rans S-6ES-503 Coyote II	S-6A-144
EC-CV5	Air Création Clipper 582S / XP	97110
EC-CV6	Cedimex Rans S-12XL-503 Airaile	S-12-193
EC-CV7	Dynali Chickinox Kot-Kot	31061814
EC-CV8	Eipper Quicksilver GT-500	319
EC-CV9	Cedimex Rans S-12XL-582 Airaile	S-12-191
EC-CX1	Cedimex Rans S-12XL-582 Airaile	S-12-196
EC-CX2	Road Air Flamingo	023
EC-CX3	Eipper Quicksilver MXL-II Sport	324
EC-CX5	Cedimex Rans S-6ES-503 Coyote II	S-6A-132
EC-CX6	Cedimex Rans S-6ES-582 Coyote II	S-6A-149
EC-CX7	Cedimex Rans S-12XL-582 Airaile	S-12-185
EC-CX8	Eipper Quicksilver MXL-IIR Sport	0411
EC-CX9	Road Air Flamingo	001
EC-CY2	Cedimex Rans S-12XL-503 Airaile	S-12-195
EC-CY3	Cedimex Rans S-6ES-503 Coyote II	S-6A-140
EC-CY4	Cedimex Rans S-12XL-582 Airaile	S-12-202
EC-CY5	Air Création Safari GT BI / Quartz 16 SXS	292009
EC-CY6	Eipper Quicksilver MX-II Sprint	141
EC-CY7	Cedimex Rans S-6ES-582 Coyote II	S-6A-151
EC-CY8	Road Air Flamingo	017
EC-CY9	Eipper Quicksilver MX-IIR Sprint	464
EC-CZ1	Cedimex Rans S-6ES-582 Coyote II	S-6A-150
EC-CZ2	Eipper Quicksilver MX-II	2214
EC-CZ3	Cedimex Rans S-12XL-582 Airaile	S-12-206
EC-CZ4	Eipper Quicksilver MXL-II Sport	125
EC-CZ5	Eipper Quicksilver MXL-IIR Sport	674
EC-CZ7	Cedimex Rans S-12XL-503 Airaile	S-12-201
EC-CZ8	Cedimex Rans S-12XL-582 Airaile	S-12-203
EC-CZ9	Cedimex Rans S-6ES-503 Coyote II	S-6A-154
EC-DA1	Cedimex Rans S-12XL-582 Airaile	S-12-207
EC-DA2	Eipper Quicksilver MX-II Sprint	0534
EC-DA3	Cedimax Rans S-12 Airaile	S-12-109
EC-DA4	Eipper Quicksilver MXL-IIRB Sport	1687
EC-DA5	Cedimex Rans S-12XL-503 Airaile	S-12-199
	(W/o 5.8.07)	
EC-DA6	Cedimex Rans S-12XL-582 Airaile	S-12-208
EC-DA7	Dynali Chickinox Kot-Kot	2797 E2W
EC-DA8	Eipper Quicksilver MXL-II Sport	221
EC-DA9	Eipper Quicksilver MX-II Sprint	0533
EC-DB1	Road Air Flamingo	019
EC-DB2	Cedimex Rans S-6ES-582 Coyote II	S-6A-153
EC-DB4	Cedimex Rans S-12 Airaile	S-12-139
EC-DB5	Cedimex Rans S-12XL-503 Airaile	S-12-210
EC-DB6	Eipper Quicksilver GT-500	0086
EC-DB7	Air Création GTE 503S / XP	98002 SF
EC-DB8	Air Création GTE 503S / Mild	98004 SF
EC-DB9	Air Création GTE 503S / XP	98001 SF
EC-DC1	Cedimex Rans S-6ES-582 Coyote II	S-6A-142
EC-DC2	Cedimex Rans S-6ES-582 Coyote II	S-6A-119
EC-DC3	Cedimex Rans S-12XL-582 Airaile	S-12-211
EC-DC4	Road Air Flamingo	033
EC-DC5	Cedimex Rans S-12XL-582 Airaile	S-12-164
EC-DC6	Road Air Flamingo	034
EC-DC7	Cedimex Rans S-12XL-582 Airaile	S-12-205
EC-DC8	Cedimex Rans S-6ES-582 Coyote II	S-6A-128
EC-DC9	Cedimex Rans S-6ES-503 Coyote II	S-6A-157
EC-DD1	Cedimex Rans S-12 Airaile	S-12-213
EC-DD2	Eipper Quicksilver MXL-II Sport	5996
EC-DD3	Cedimex Rans S-12XL-503 Airaile	S-12-214
EC-DD4	Air Création Safari GT BI / Quartz SXS	99003 SF
EC-DD5	Cedimex Rans S-6ES-582 Coyote II	S-6A-156
EC-DD6	Vol 9/Best Off Sky Ranger	SK-0516697
	(Noted dismantled 10.13)	
EC-DD7	Road Air Flamingo	038
EC-DD8	Air Création GTE 503SL / Mild	99001 SF
EC-DD9	Cedimex Rans S-12XL-582 Airaile	S-12-215
	(Cr and destroyed 25.9.11)	
EC-DE1	Cedimex Rans S-6ES-503 Coyote II	S-6A-131
EC-DE2	Cedimex Rans S-12XL-503 Airaile	S-12-212
EC-DE4	Cedimex Rans S-12XL-582 Airaile	S-12-204
EC-DE5	Cedimex Rans S-12XL-503 Airaile	S-12-218
EC-DE6	Cedimex Rans S-6ES-582 Coyote II	S-6A-159
EC-DE7	Sport Aircraft Tango II	5905
EC-DE8	Eipper Quicksilver MXL-II Sport	782
EC-DE9	Sallen Mach-15	15-157
EC-DF1	Cedimex Rans S-12XL-582 Airaile	S-12-216
EC-DF2	Eipper Quicksilver MXL-II Sport	784
EC-DF3	Eipper Quicksilver MXL-II Sport	783
EC-DF4	Road Air Flamingo	040
EC-DF5	Cedimex Rans S-12XL-582 Airaile	S-12-217
EC-DF6	Eipper Quicksilver MX-II Sprint	139
EC-DF7	Eipper Quicksilver GT-500	318
EC-DF8	Eipper Quicksilver GT-400	1421
EC-DF9	Sport Aircraft Tango II-GT	T1924
EC-DG1	Air Création GTE 503SL / Mild	99004 SF
EC-DG2	Cedimex Rans S-6ES-582 Coyote II	S-6-AV-0001
EC-DG3	Air Création Safari GT BI / Fun 18	192023
EC-DG4	Tecnam P.92S Echo	P-92-ES-011
EC-DG5	Tecnam P.92S Echo	P-92-ES-012
EC-DG6	Tecnam P.92S Echo	P-92-ES-009
EC-DG7	Road Air Flamingo	037
EC-DG8	Road Air Flamingo	045
EC-DG9	Tecnam P.92S Echo	P-92-ES-013
EC-DH1	Cedimex Rans S-6ES-582 Coyote II	S-6-AV-0002
EC-DH2	Tecnam P.92S Echo	P-92-ES-008
EC-DH3	Road Air Flamingo	013
EC-DH5	Vol 9/Best Off Sky Ranger 912	SKR 0005057
EC-DH6	Vol 9/Best Off Sky Ranger 912	SKR 0102091
EC-DH7	Vol 9/Best Off Sky Ranger 912	SKR 0010069
EC-DH8	Vol 9/Best Off Sky Ranger 912	SKR 1215696
EC-DI1	Vol 9/Best Off Sky Ranger 912	SKR 0005047
	(Dam. 14.6.14)	
EC-DI2	Sport Aircraft Tango I	1876
EC-DI3	Air Création Safari GT BI / Fun 18	192027
EC-DI4	Eipper Quicksilver GT-500	040
EC-DI5	Eipper Quicksilver MXL-II Sport	785
EC-DI6	Eipper Quicksilver MX-II Sprint	549
EC-DI7	Micro Aviation Pulsar II	138
EC-DI8	Micro Aviation Pulsar II	137
EC-DI9	Vol 9/Best Off Sky Ranger 582	SKR 0002043
EC-DJ1	Road Air Flamingo	044
EC-DJ2	Micro Aviation Pulsar II	140
EC-DJ3	Micro Aviation Pulsar II	131
	(W/o 6.11.05)	
EC-DJ4	Tecnam P.92S Echo	P-92-ES-001
EC-DJ5	Tecnam P.92S Echo	P-92-ES-016
EC-DJ6	Tecnam P.92S Echo	P-92-ES-006
EC-DJ7	Tecnam P.92S Echo	P-92-ES-007
EC-DJ8	Cedimex Rans S-6ES-HKS-700E Coyote II	S-6A-160
EC-DJ9	Micro Aviation Pulsar II	139
EC-DK1	Tecnam P.92S Echo	P-92-ES-014
EC-DK2	Tecnam P.92 Echo	P-92-E-010
EC-DK3	Road Air Flamingo	032
EC-DK4	Tecnam P.92 Echo	P-92-E-009
EC-DK5	Tecnam P.92S Echo	P-92-ES-015
EC-DK6	Eipper Quicksilver GT-500	0085
	(W/o 14.3.15)	
EC-DK7	TL Ultralight TL-96 Star	TL-96-01-010
	(W/o 12.7.09)	
EC-DK8	TL Ultralight TL-96 Star	TL-96-01-006
EC-DK9	TL Ultralight TL-96 Star	TL-96-01-012
EC-DL1	TL Ultralight TL-96 Star	TL-96-01-004
EC-DL2	Vol 9/Best Off Sky Ranger 582	SKR 0107119
EC-DL3	Road Air Flamingo	046
EC-DL4	TL Ultralight TL-96 Star	TL-96-01-007
EC-DL5	Tecnam P.92S Echo	P-92-ES-010
	(Cr 12.12.04)	
EC-DL6	Tecnam P.92S Echo	P-92-ES-018
EC-DL7	Tecnam P.92 Echo	P-92-E-007
EC-DL8	Tecnam P.92S Echo	P-92-ES-020
EC-DL9	TL Ultralight TL-96 Star	TL-96-01-009
EC-DM1	TL Ultralight TL-96 Star	TL-96-02-014
EC-DM2	TL Ultralight TL-96 Star	TL-96-01-008
EC-DM3	Tecnam P.92S Echo	P-92-ES-019
EC-DM5	Tecnam P.96 Golf	P-96-G-012
	(Dismantled)	
EC-DM6	Tecnam P.92S Echo	P-92-ES-021
EC-DM8	Tecnam P.96 Golf	P-96-G-013
EC-DM9	Tecnam P.92S Echo	P-92-ES-022
EC-DN1	Vol 9/Best Off Sky Ranger 912	SKR 0112147
EC-DN2	TL Ultralight TL-96 Star	TL-96-01-013
EC-DN3	TL Ultralight TL-96 Star	TL-96-02-011
EC-DN5	Tecnam P.96 Golf	P-96-G-014
EC-DN6	Mainair Blade 912	1200-0699-7-W1003
EC-DN7	Tecnam P.92 Echo	P-92-E-008
EC-DN8	Albin Feito Moragon M-1	M-1-02-001
EC-DN9	Albin Feito Moragon M-1	M-1-02-002
EC-DO1	Albin Feito Moragon M-1	M-1-02-003
EC-DO2	Tecnam P.96 Golf	P-96-G-011
EC-DO3	TL Ultralight TL-96 Star	TL-96-02-017
EC-DO4	Tecnam P.96 Golf	P-96-G-015
EC-DO5	TL Ultralight TL-96 Star	TL-96-02-015
EC-DO6	Eipper Quicksilver MX-II Sprint	213
EC-DO7	TL Ultralight TL-96 Star	TL-96-02-016
EC-DO8	TL Ultralight TL-96 Star	TL-96-02-018
	(W/o 25.6.15)	
EC-DO9	TL Ultralight TL-96 Star	TL-96-01-002
EC-DP1	Micro Aviation Pulsar II	135
	(Dam. 20.1.07)	

Regn	Type	Serial	Notes
EC-DP2	Albin Feito Moragon M-1	M-1-02-004	
EC-DP3	Albin Feito Moragon M-1	M-1-02-005	
EC-DP4	Tecnam P.96 Golf	P-96-G-017	
EC-DP5	Tecnam P.92S Echo	P-92-ES-024	
EC-DP6	Manuel Perez Rainbow	MPR 02-0002	
EC-DP7	Road Air Flamingo	042	
EC-DP8	Tecnam P.92S Echo	P-92-ES-023	
EC-DP9	Cedimex Rans S-12XL-582 Airaile	S-12-AV002	
EC-DQ1	TL Ultralight TL-96 Star	TL-96-01-003	
EC-DQ2	TL Ultralight TL-96 Star	TL-96-02-021	
EC-DQ3	Tecnam P.92S Echo	P-92-ES-025	
EC-DQ4	Albin Feito Moragon M-1	M-1-02-006	
EC-DQ5	Tecnam P.96 Golf	P-96-G-018	
	(Dam 21.6.06, since repaired)		
EC-DQ6	Cedimex Rans S-12 Airaile	S-12-300	
EC-DQ7	Air Création Clipper 582S / XP	00001 JL	
EC-DQ8	Air Création Clipper 582S / XP	02005 JL	
EC-DQ9	Air Création Clipper 582S / XP	99001 JL	
EC-DR1	Cedimex Rans S-12XL-582 Airaile	S-12-AV001	
EC-DR2	Air Création Clipper 582S / XP	01001 JL	
EC-DR3	Air Création Clipper 582S / XP	02006 JL	
EC-DR4	Mainair Blade	1341-0902-7-W	
EC-DR5	Cedimex Rans S-6ES-582 Coyote II	S-6-AV-0005	
EC-DR6	Albin Feito Moragon M-1	M-1-03-008	
EC-DR8	Tecnam P.92S Echo	P-92-ES-026	
EC-DR9	Tecnam P.96 Golf	P-96-G-019	
EC-DS1	Manuel Perez Rainbow	MPR 02-0004	
EC-DS2	Tecnam P.92S Echo	P-92-ES-027	
EC-DS3	Tecnam P.92 Echo	190	
EC-DS4	Air Création Clipper 582S / XP	00004 JL	
EC-DS5	TL Ultralight TL-96 Star	TL-96-03-024	
EC-DS6	TL Ultralight TL-96 Star	TL-96-02-019	
EC-DS7	Tecnam P.96 Golf	P-96-G-021	
EC-DS8	Tecnam P.92 Echo Super	P-92-SP-011	
EC-DS9	Road Air Flamingo	031	
EC-DT1	Air Création Clipper 582S / XP	00002 JL	
EC-DT2	TL Ultralight TL-96 Star	TL-96-02-020	
EC-DT3	TL Ultralight TL-96 Star	TL-96-02-024	
	(W/o 5.10.13)		
EC-DT4	Tecnam P.96 Golf	P-96-G-020	
	(Destroyed, Lumbier 23.10.10)		
EC-DT5	TL Ultralight TL-96 Star	TL-96-02-023	
EC-DT8	Tecnam P.96 Golf	P-96-G-023	
	(W/o 9.6.07)		
EC-DU1	Tecnam P.92 Echo Super	P-96-SP-010	
EC-DU2	Tecnam P.96 Golf	P-96-G-024	
EC-DU3	Road Air Flamingo	022	
EC-DU4	Tecnam P.92 Echo Super	P-92-SP-015	
EC-DU6	Tecnam P.92S Echo	P-92-ES-031	
EC-DU7	Vol 9/Best Off Sky Ranger	SKR 0209241	
EC-DU9	Tecnam P.96 Golf	P-96-G-026	
EC-DV1	Air Création Twin 503SL / Fun 18	01002SF	
EC-DV2	Air Création Twin 503SL / Fun 18	02007JL	
EC-DV3	Aeromoragón Moragón M-1	M-1-03-011	
EC-DV4	TL Ultralight TL-96 Star	TL-96-01-005	
EC-DV6	Aeromoragón Moragón M-1	M-1-03-012	
EC-DV7	Aeromoragón Moragón M-1	M-1-03-013	
EC-DV8	Tecnam P.96 Golf	P-96-G-027	
EC-DV9	Tecnam P.92S Echo	P-92-ES-035	
EC-DX1	Tecnam P.92S Echo	P-92-ES-034	
EC-DX2	Tecnam P.96 Golf	P-96-G-025	
EC-DX3	Flight Design CT-2K	02-01-01-AR	
EC-DX4	Tecnam P.92 Echo Super	P-92-SP-016	
EC-DX6	Flight Design CT-2K	01-06-03-AR	
EC-DX7	Flight Design CT-2K	02-06-05-AR	
EC-DX8	Flight Design CT-2K	00-10-04-AR	
EC-DX9	Tecnam P.96 Golf	P-96-G-028	
EC-DY1	Tecnam P.92S Echo	P-92-ES-037	
EC-DY2	Tecnam P.92S Echo	P-92-ES-036	
EC-DY3	Manuel Perez Rainbow MPR	03-0005	
EC-DY4	Manuel Perez Rainbow MPR	03-0010	
EC-DY5	Manuel Perez Rainbow MPR	02-0007	
EC-DY6	Manuel Perez Rainbow MPR	03-0011	
EC-DY7	Manuel Perez Rainbow MPR	03-0009	
EC-DY8	Aeromoragón Moragón M-1	M-1-03-014	EC-060
	(To EC-KJZ)		
EC-DY9	TL Ultralight TL-96 Star	TL-96-03-025	
EC-DZ1	ICP Bingo	03-03-52-096	
EC-DZ2	ICP Super Bingo	03-03-52-099	
EC-DZ4	ICP Bingo	03-04-52-101	
EC-DZ5	ICP Bingo	03-04-52-102	
EC-DZ6	ICP Bingo	02-12-52-083	
EC-DZ7	ICP Bingo	02-06-52-060	
EC-DZ8	ICP Bingo	03-07-52-120	
EC-DZ9	Road Air Flamingo	047	
EC-EA2	ICP Bingo	03-03-52-098	
EC-EA3	Aeromoragón Moragón M-1	M-1-03-016	
EC-EA4	Aeromoragón Moragón M-1	M-1-03-015	
	(Dbr 30.3.07)		
EC-EA5	ICP Bingo	03-03-52-095	
EC-EA6	ICP Bingo	02-07-52-061	
EC-EA7	ICP Bingo	01-12-52-039	
EC-EA8	ICP Bingo	03-02-52-092	
EC-EA9	ICP Bingo	03-01-52-090	
EC-EB1	ICP Bingo	02-09-52-073	
EC-EB2	ICP Bingo	02-02-52-054	
EC-EB3	ICP Bingo	01-05-52-016	
EC-EB5	ICP Bingo	02-12-52-086	
EC-EB6	Tecnam P.96 Golf	P-96-G-030	
EC-EB7	ICP Bingo	03-01-52-087	
EC-EB8	ICP Bingo	03-04-52-103	
EC-EB9	Tecnam P.92 Echo	P-92-E-013	
EC-EC1	Tecnam P.92 Echo Super	P-92-SP-018	
EC-EC2	ICP Bingo	03-05-52-109	
EC-EC3	Tecnam P.96 Golf	P-96-G-031	
EC-EC4	Mainair 503 Blade	1143-0198-7-W946	
	(Registered as Mainair Gemini/Flash II but exported from UK as above in 1998)		
EC-EC5	ICP Bingo	02-11-52-081	
EC-EC6	Quicksilver MX-Sprint-IIR	552	
EC-EC7	Quicksilver MX-Sprint-IIR	550	
EC-EC8	Air Création Clipper 582S / XP	99002 SF	
EC-EC9	Air Création GTE / Kiss 450	00003 SF	
EC-ED1	Air Création GTE / Kiss 450	03001 SF	
EC-ED2	Air Création Twin 503SL / Fun 18	03004 SF	
EC-ED3	Vol 9/Best Off Sky Ranger	SKR 0309374	
EC-ED4	Tecnam P.96 Golf	P-96-G-033	
EC-ED5	ICP Bingo	01-12-52-042	
EC-ED6	Tecnam P.92 Echo Super	P-92-SP-019	
EC-ED7	Aeromoragón Moragón M-1	M1-04-018	
EC-ED8	Air Création Twin 503SL / Fun 18	03005 JL	
EC-EE1	Air Création Clipper 582S / XP	03002SF	
EC-EE2	Manuel Perez Rainbow	MPR-0013	
EC-EE3	Manuel Perez Rainbow	MPR-0015	
EC-EE4	Tecnam P.92 Echo Super	P-92-SP-020	
EC-EE5	ICP Bingo	02-02-52-048	
EC-EE6	Tecnam P.92 Echo Super	P-92-SP-022	
EC-EE7	Tecnam P.92 Echo Super	P-92-SP-021	
EC-EE8	Flight Design CT-2K	03-07-07-AR	
EC-EF1	Air Création GTE Clipper/ Kiss 450	03003 SF	
EC-EF2	Vol 9/Best Off Sky Ranger	SKR 0403465	
EC-EF3	Tecnam P.96 Golf	P-96-G-034	
EC-EF4	Aeromoragón Moragón M-1	M1-04-019	
EC-EF6	Tecnam P.92 Echo	P-92-E-015	
EC-EF7	Tecnam P.92 Echo	P-92-E-016	
EC-EF8	Vol 9/Best Off Sky Ranger	SKR 0102090	
EC-EF9	Tecnam P.92 Echo	P-92-E-017	
EC-EG2	ICP Bingo	04-01-52-140	
EC-EG3	ICP Bingo	04-01-52-142	
EC-EG4	ICP Bingo	04-01-52-160	
	(Damaged 4.5.10)		
EC-EG5	Quicksilver MXL-Sport-II	0124	
EC-EG6	Tecnam P.92S Echo	P-92-ES-039	
EC-EG7	ICP Bingo	04-05-52-152	
EC-EG8	Tecnam P.96 Golf	P-96-G-035	
EC-EG9	ICP Bingo	04-10-52-161	
EC-EH1	Tecnam P.92S Echo	P-92-ES-038	
EC-EH3	Quicksilver MX-Sprint II	0553	
EC-EH4	Aeromoragón Moragón M-1	M1-04-020	
EC-EH5	Road Air Flamingo	048	
	(W/o 21.9.08)		
EC-EH6	Tecnam P.92 Echo Super	P92-ES-041	
EC-EH7	ICP Bingo	04-10-52-162	
EC-EH9	ICP Bingo	05-01-52-168	
EC-EI1	ICP Bingo	04-11-52-163	
EC-EI2	Aeromoragón Moragón M-1	M1-04-021	
EC-EI3	Aeromoragón Moragón M-1	M1-04-022	
	(Dam. 8.6.14)		
EC-EI4	Tecnam P.92 Echo Super	P92-ES-042	
EC-EI5	Cedimax Rans S-6ES-912 Coyote II	S6AV-0004	
EC-EI6	Tecnam P.96-G Golf	P-96-G-037	
EC-EI7	TL Ultralight TL-96 Star	TL-96-02-022	
EC-EI8	ICP Bingo	05-04-52-176	
EC-EI9	Tecnam P.2002 Sierra	P2002-011	
EC-EJ1	Evektor EV-97 Eurostar	2005 2409	
EC-EJ2	Tecnam P.2002 Sierra	P2002-014	
EC-EJ3	Tecnam P.2002 Sierra	P2002-013	
EC-EJ4	Tecnam P.2002 Sierra	P2002-012	
EC-EJ5	Evektor EV-97 Eurostar	2005 2515	
EC-EJ6	Evektor EV-97 Eurostar	2005 2505	
EC-EJ7	Tecnam P.92 Echo	P92-E-018	
EC-EJ8	ICP Bingo	05-06-52-183	
EC-EJ9	Tecnam P.92 Echo Super	P92-SP-026	
EC-EK1	Tecnam P.2002 Sierra	P2002-010	
EC-EK2	ICP Bingo	05-04-52-175	
EC-EK3	TL Ultralight TL-96 Star	TL-96-05-001	
EC-EK4	Tecnam P.92 Echo	P92-E-020	
EC-EK6	ICP Bingo	05-04-52-178	
EC-EK7	Quicksilver GT-500	0084	
EC-EK8	Tecnam P.92 Echo Super	P92-SP-025	
EC-EK9	Tecnam P.96 Golf	P96-G-041	
EC-EL1	Tecnam P.96 Golf	P96-G-039	
EC-EL3	ICP Bingo	05-04-52-177	
EC-EL4	Road Air Flamingo	035	
EC-EL5	Vol 9 / Best Off Sky Ranger	SKR 0402440	
EC-EL6	Tecnam P.2002 Sierra	P2002-015	
EC-EL7	Tecnam P.92 Echo Super	P92-SP-027	
EC-EL9	Evektor EV-97 Eurostar	2005 2524	
	(W/o 4.8.13)		
EC-EM1	Tecnam P.92 Echo	P92-E-022	
EC-EM2	Air Création GTE 582S / Kiss 450	05007JL	
EC-EM3	Air Création Clipper 582S / XP	05008JL	
EC-EM4	Air Création Clipper 582S / XP	00003JL	
EC-EM5	Evektor EV-97 Eurostar	2005 2523	
EC-EM6	Tecnam P.2002 Sierra	P2002-017	
EC-EM7	Air Création GTE 582S / Kiss 450	05001SF	
EC-EM8	ELA Aviacion ELA 07	0605 062 0724	
EC-EM9	Evektor EV-97 Eurostar	2005 2607	
EC-EN1	Tecnam P.92 Echo	P92-E-024	
EC-EN2	Tecnam P.96 Golf	P96-G-044	
EC-EN3	Tecnam P.2002 Sierra	P2002-018	
EC-EN4	Manuel Perez Rainbow	MPR 0017	
EC-EN5	TL Ultralight TL-96 Star	TL-96-05-002	
EC-EN6	Flight Design CT SW	05-07-11-AR	
EC-EN7	Flight Design CT SW	05-11-01-AR	
EC-EN8	Flight Design CT SW	05-10-07-AR	
EC-EN9	Tecnam P.96 Golf	P96-G-043	
EC-EO1	ELA Aviacion ELA 07	1105 079 0724	
EC-EO2	ELA Aviacion ELA 07	1105 080 0724	
	(W/o 19.7.08)		
EC-EO3	Tecnam P.2002 Sierra	P2002-016	
EC-EO4	Tecnam P.96 Golf	P-96-G-045	
	(W/o 29.5.06)		
EC-EO5	ELA Aviacion ELA 07	0405 061 0724	
EC-EO6	Vol 9/Best Off Sky Ranger	SKR 0506613	
EC-EO7	ELA Aviacion ELA 07	0505 066 0724	
	(Cr and dbr 24.7.10)		
EC-EO8	ELA Aviacion ELA 07	0505 060 0724	
EC-EO9	ELA Aviacion ELA 07	1105 090 0724	
	(W/o 2.10.06)		
EC-EP1	Mainair Blade 503	1370-1104-7-W1165	
EC-EP2	ICP Bingo	05-01-52-190	
EC-EP3	ELA Aviacion ELA 07-R115	1205 081 0724	
EC-EP4	Colyear Martin 3-S100	110-001-013	
EC-EP5	Eipper Quicksilver MXL-III Sport	077	
EC-EP8	ELA Aviacion ELA 07-R115	0406 093 0724	
EC-EP9	Tecnam P.92S Echo	P92-ES-044	
EC-EQ1	Fantasy Air Allegro 2000	05/12	
EC-EQ3	Tecnam P.92 Echo	P92-E-026	
EC-EQ4	Tecnam P.92 Echo	P92-E-023	
EC-EQ5	Air Création Safari GT BI / F18	191005	
EC-EQ6	Evektor EV-97 Eurostar	2006 2621	
EC-EQ7	Evektor EV-97 Eurostar	2005 2618	

Reg	Type	c/n	Notes
EC-EQ8	Evektor EV-97 Eurostar	2006 2706	
EC-EQ9	Fantasy Air Allegro 2000	05/103	
EC-ER1	Fantasy Air Allegro 2000	05/101	
EC-ER2	Evektor EV-97 Eurostar	2003 1803	CS-UMU
	(W/o 31.5.07)		
EC-ER3	Tecnam P.2002 Sierra	P2002-019	
EC-ER4	Vol 9/Best Off Sky Ranger	SK0402443	
EC-ER5	Tecnam P.96 Golf	P-96-G-048	
EC-ER6	Tecnam P.92 Echo Super	P-92-SP-028	
EC-ER7	Tecnam P.2002 Sierra	P2002-020	
	(Destroyed 5.9.14)		
EC-ER8	ICP MXP-740 Savannah	05-06-51-405	
EC-ER9	Airbet Girabet	05002	
EC-ES1	ICP MXP-740 Savannah	05-09-51-424	
EC-ES2	ICP MXP-740 Savannah	05-06-51-421	
EC-ES3	ICP MXP-740 Savannah	06-01-51-463	
EC-ES4	Tecnam P.96 Golf	P-96-G-046	
EC-ES5	TL Ultralight TL-96 Star	TL-96-06-003	
EC-ES6	Fantasy Air Allegro 2000	05/104	
EC-ES7	Fantasy Air Allegro 2000	05/105	
EC-ES8	Evektor EV-97 Eurostar	2006 2801	
EC-ES9	Evektor EV-97 Eurostar	2006 2804	
EC-ET1	Evektor EV-97 Eurostar	2006 2722	
EC-ET2	Manuel Perez Rainbow	MPR-0006	
EC-ET3	Tecnam P.92S Echo	P-92-ES-045	
	(Damaged 20.10.06)		
EC-ET4	ELA Aviacion ELA 07-R115	0706 118 0724	
	(Cr and dbf 23.9.10)		
EC-ET5	Tecnam P.96 Golf	P-96-G-052	
	(Tecnam c/n 289)		
EC-ET7	Tecnam P.2002 Sierra	P2002-023	
EC-ET8	Tecnam P.96 Golf	P-96-G-050	
EC-ET9	Fantasy Air Allegro 2000	06/102	
EC-EU1	ELA Aviacion ELA 07-R115	0706 113 0724	
	(Cr and dbr 27.9.09)		
EC-EU2	Tecnam P.92 Echo Super	P-92-SP-029	
EC-EU4	Flight Design CT SW	05-07-10-AR	
EC-EU5	ICP MXP-740 Savannah	06-03-51-481	
EC-EU6	ICP MXP-740 Savannah	06-03-51-480	
EC-EU7	Flight Design CT SW	06-08-13-AR	
EC-EU8	Tecnam P.96 Golf	P-96-G-049	
EC-EU9	ELA Aviacion ELA 07-R115	0906 121 0724	
	(Cr and destroyed 26.1.13)		
EC-EV1	ELA Aviacion ELA 07-R100	1006 142 0722	
EC-EV2	ELA Aviacion ELA 07-R115	0906 038 0724	
EC-EV3	Evektor EV-97 Eurostar	2006 2817	
EC-EV4	Flight Design CT SW	06-10-03-AR	
EC-EV5	Flight Design CT SW	06-10-23-AR	
EC-EV6	Tecnam P.96 Golf	P-96-G-051	
EC-EV7	Tecnam P.92 Echo Super	P-92-SP-030	
EC-EV8	Tecnam P.92 Echo Super	P-92-SP-031	
EC-EV9	Evektor EV-97 Eurostar	2007 2908	
EC-EX1	TL Ultralight TL-96 Star	TL-96S-2006-04	
EC-EX2	ICP MXP-740 Savannah	06-09-51-525	
	(Also reported as Tecnam P.2002JF Sierra)		
EC-EX3	Airbet Girabet	06006	
EC-EX4	Airbet Girabet	06005	
EC-EX5	ELA Aviacion ELA 07-R115	0107 137 0724	
	(W/o 24.7.08)		
EC-EX6	Road Air Flamingo	055	
EC-EY1	Tecnam P.96 Golf	P-96-G-053	
EC-EY2	Tecnam P.92 Echo Super	P-92-SP-024	
EC-EY3	Evektor EV-97 Eurostar	2007 2912	
EC-EY4	ELA Aviacion ELA 07-R115	0407 154 0724	
EC-EY5	Airbet Girabet	06004	
EC-EY6	Tecnam P.96 Golf	P-96-G-055	
EC-EY7	TL Ultralight TL-96 Star	TL-96-2007-05	
EC-EY8	Flight Design CT SW	07-02-05-AR	
EC-EY9	ELA Aviacion ELA 07-R115	0607 162 0724	
EC-EZ1	ELA Aviacion ELA 07-R115	0607 161 0724	
EC-EZ2	Tecnam P.2002 Sierra	P2002-025	
EC-EZ3	Evektor EV-97 Eurostar	2007 2932	
	(W/o 25.7.07)		
EC-EZ4	Tecnam P.2002 Sierra	P2002-024	
EC-EZ5	Flight Design CT SW	07-04-08-AR	
EC-EZ6	Tecnam P.96 Golf	P96-G-054	
EC-EZ7	Flight Design CT SW	06-12-05-AR	EC-007
EC-EZ8	Flight Design CT SW	07-04-09-AR	
EC-EZ9	Vol 9/Best Off Sky Ranger	SKR 0307359	
EC-FA1	Tecnam P.96 Golf 100	P96-G-056	
	(Tecnam c/n 293)		
EC-FA2	Aviakit XL	07/001	
EC-FA3	Evektor EV-97 Eurostar	2007 2935	
EC-FA4	Flight Design CT SW	07-04-19-AR	
EC-FA5	Flight Design CT SW	07-05-24-AR	
EC-FA6	Tecnam P.2002 Sierra	P2002-027	
EC-FA7	ICP MXP-740 Savannah	07-02-51-576	
EC-FA8	ICP MXP-740 Savannah	06-09-51-523	
EC-FB1	ELA Aviacion ELA 07-R115	0507 164 0724	
EC-FB2	Evektor EV-97 Eurostar	2007 3002	
EC-FB3	Tecnam P.92 Echo	P92-E-030	
EC-FB4	ELA Aviacion ELA 07-R115	0407 159 0724	
EC-FB5	Tecnam P.92S Echo Super	P92-SP-034	
EC-FB7	Flight Design CT SW	07-06-26-AR	
EC-FB8	Tecnam P.2002 Sierra	P2002-029	
	(W/o 11.1.14)		
EC-FB9	Tecnam P.92 Echo Super	P92-SP-033	
EC-FC1	ELA Aviacion ELA 07S-R100	0507 173 0712	
EC-FC3	Fantasy Air Allegro 2000	07/101	
EC-FC4	Tecnam P.96 Golf	P96-G-058	
EC-FC5	Tecnam P.92 Echo	P92-E-031	
EC-FC6	Aviakit XL	07/002	
EC-FC7	ELA Aviacion ELA 07S-R115	0607 178 0724	
EC-FC8	Air Création Twin 503 SL / Fun 18	06010JL	
EC-FC9	Air Création GTE Clipper 912 / Kiss 450	07012JL	
EC-FD1	ELA Aviacion ELA 07-R115	0607 172 0724	
EC-FD2	ICP MXP-740 Savannah	07-02-51578	
EC-FD3	Tecnam P.2002 Sierra	P2002-028	
EC-FD4	Air Création Twin 503 SL/ Fun 18	07013JL	
EC-FD5	Tecnam P.92S Echo	P92-ES-046	
EC-FD6	Fantasy Air Allegro 2000	07/102	
	(Dam. 30.1.16)		
EC-FD7	Flight Design CT SW	07-06-27-AR	
EC-FD8	Aeroprakt A-22L Vision	A22L-07-0002	
EC-FD9	Aeroprakt A-22L Vision	A22L-07-0012	
EC-FE1	Aeroprakt A-22L Vision	A22L-07-0008	
EC-FE2	ICP MXP-740 Savannah	07-05-51-604	
EC-FE3	Evektor EV-97 Eurostar	2007 3012	
EC-FE4	Evektor EV-97 Eurostar	2007 3111	
EC-FE6	Aeroprakt A-22L Vision	A22L-07-0007	
EC-FE7	Tecnam P.2002 Sierra	P2002-030	
	(Cr and w/o 11.2.15)		
EC-FE8	Aeroprakt A-22L Vision	A22L-07-0010	
	(Dam.29.12.07)		
EC-FE9	Aeroprakt A-22L Vision	A22L-07-0011	
EC-FF2	Aeroprakt A-22L80 Vision	A22L80-07-0001	
EC-FF3	ELA Aviacion ELA 07-R115	1007 199 0724	
EC-FF4	Aeroprakt A-22L Vision	A22L-07-0014	
EC-FF5	Aeroprakt A-22L80 Vision	A22L80-07-0003	
EC-FF6	Aeroprakt A-22L Vision	A22L-07-0017	
EC-FF7	Aeroprakt A-22L Vision	A22L-07-0013	
	(Dam.29.4.16)		
EC-FF8	Tecnam P.2002 Sierra	P2002-035	
EC-FF9	Tecnam P.2002 Sierra	P2002-033	
EC-FG1	Tecnam P.2002 Sierra	P2002-036	
EC-FG2	Tecnam P.92 Echo Super	P92-SP-037	
	(Damaged 13.6.08)		
EC-FG3	Air Création Clipper 582S / XP	07014JL	
EC-FG5	Tecnam P.92 Echo Super	P92-SP-035	
EC-FG6	Tecnam P.92 Echo Super	P92-SP-036	
	(Dam.12.5.16)		
EC-FG7	Air Création Twin 582 SL / XP12	07009JL	
EC-FG8	Vol 9/Best Off Sky Ranger	SKR 0604713	
EC-FG9	Vol 9/Best Off Sky Ranger	SKR 0702778	
EC-FH1	Tecnam P.92 Echo Super	P92-SP-038	
EC-FH2	Tecnam P.2002 Sierra	P2002-032	
EC-FH3	Tecnam P.2002 Sierra	P2002-034	
EC-FH4	Tecnam P.2002 Sierra	P2002-038	
EC-FH5	ELA Aviacion ELA 07S-R115	1107 195 0724	
EC-FH6	Flight Design CT SW	07-12-16-AR	
EC-FH7	Aeroprakt A-22L Vision	A22L-07-0020	
	(Cr and dbr 23.8.09)		
EC-FH8	Aeroprakt A-22L Vision	A22L-07-0021	
EC-FH9	Tecnam P.92 Echo Super	P92-SP-032	
EC-FI1	Aeroprakt A-22L Vision	A22L-07-0009	
EC-FI2	Aeroprakt A-22L Vision	A22L-07-0015	
EC-FI3	Tecnam P.2002 Sierra	P2002-039	
EC-FI4	BRM Land Africa	01/08/0101-SP	
EC-FI5	BRM Land Africa	07/07/0023-SP	
EC-FI6	BRM Land Africa	03/08/0107-SP	
EC-FI8	Eipper Quicksilver MXL Sport II	000786	
EC-FI9	Tecnam P.92S Echo	P92-ES-049	
EC-FJ1	ICP MXP-740 Savannah	07-10-51-649	
EC-FJ3	Aeroprakt A-22L Vision	A22L-08-0023	
EC-FJ4	Tecnam P.92S Echo	P92-ES-050	
EC-FJ5	ELA Aviacion ELA 07S	1007 198 0724	
EC-FJ6	ELA Aviacion ELA 07S	0308 214 0724	
EC-FJ7	ICP MXP-740 Savannah	08-02-51-677	
EC-FJ8	Jihlavan JA200 Rapid	2002B022/E	
EC-FJ9	Jihlavan JA200 Rapid	2003A032/E	EC-005
EC-FK2	Tecnam P.2002 Sierra	P2002-042	
EC-FK4	ICP MXP-740 Savannah	07-07-51-625	
EC-FK5	Tecnam P.2002 Sierra	P2002-041	
EC-FK6	Tecnam P.92 Echo	P92-E-034	
EC-FK8	Aeroprakt A-22L80 Vision	A22L80-07-0018	
EC-FK9	ELA Aviacion ELA 07-R115	0907 193 0724	
EC-FL1	Tecnam P.92 Echo	P92-E-0035	
EC-FL2	Tecnam P.96 Golf	P96-G-060	
	(Tecnam c/n 305)		
EC-FL3	Tecnam P.2002 Sierra	P2002-037	
EC-FL4	TL Ultralight TL-96 Star	TL96S-2008-07	
EC-FL5	Aeroprakt A-22L Vision	A22L-08-0027	
EC-FL6	Fantasy Air Allegro 2000	08/102	
EC-FL7	ELA Aviacion ELA 07-R115	0308 215 0724	
EC-FL8	Eipper Quicksilver MXL Sport IIR	000787	
	(W/o 8.8.14)		
EC-FL9	Airbet Girabet	07007	
EC-FM1	Aeroprakt A-22L Vision	A22L-07-0016	
EC-FM2	Manuel Perez Rainbow	MPR 02-0018	
EC-FM3	Tecnam P.2002 Sierra	P2002-044	
EC-FM4	Aviakit XL	08/003	
	(Dam. 30.8.14)		
EC-FM5	BRM Land Africa	06/08/0117-SP	
EC-FM6	Fantasy Air Allegro 2000	08/101	
EC-FM7	Airbet Girabet	08008	
EC-FM8	Tecnam P.2002 Sierra	P2002-321(?)	
EC-FM9	ICP MXP-740 Savannah	08-02-51-682	
EC-FN1	Tecnam P.92 Eaglet Light Sport	P92-SP-040	
EC-FN2	Flight Design CT SW	08-04-01-AR	
EC-FN3	Aeroprakt A-22L Vision	A22L-08-0028	
	(W/o 23.8.09)		
EC-FN4	Tecnam P.2002 Sierra	P2002-043	
	(Cr and destroyed 5.12.11)		
EC-FN5	Tecnam P.92S Echo	P92-ES-052	
	(Dam. 27.4.14)		
EC-FN6	Tecnam P.92 Echo	P92-E-036	
EC-FN7	Tecnam P.92 Echo Super	P92-SP-039	
EC-FN8	Aeroprakt A-22L Vision	A22L-08-0026	
EC-FN9	Tecnam P.96 Golf	P96-G-062	
EC-FO1	Vol 9/Best Off Sky Ranger	SKR 0503569	
EC-FO2	BRM Land Africa	07/08/0120-SP	
EC-FO3	Tecnam P.2002 Sierra	P2002-045	
	(Cr. 22.12.13)		
EC-FO4	ICP MXP-740 Savannah	08-02-51-681	
EC-FO5	Tecnam P.92 Echo Super	P92-SP-043	
EC-FO6	Aeroprakt A-22L Vision	A22L-08-0024	
EC-FO7	Tecnam P.96 Golf	P96-G-063	
	(Cr and destroyed 30.1.11)		
EC-FO8	BRM Land Africa	11/07/0025S-SP	
EC-FP1	BRM Land Africa	11/07/0026S-SP	
EC-FP2	Tecnam P.2002 Sierra	P2002-050	
EC-FP3	Tecnam P.96 Golf	P96-G-063	
EC-FP4	ICP MXP-740 Savannah	08-07-51-739	
EC-FP5	Tecnam P.92 Echo	P92-E-038	
EC-FP6	Tecnam P.2002 Sierra	P2002-047	
EC-FP7	Tecnam P.92 Echo Super	P92-SP-045	
EC-FP8	ICP MXP-740 Savannah	08-07-51-736	
EC-FP9	Aeroprakt A-22L Vision	A22L-09-0035	
EC-FQ2	Tecnam P.92S Echo	P92-ES-053	
EC-FQ3	ICP MXP-740 Savannah	08-06-51-733	
EC-FQ4	Tecnam P.2002 Sierra	P2002-046	
EC-FQ5	Airbet Girabet II	11S08013	

Regn	Type	C/n	Prev id
EC-FQ7	Airbet Girabet II	11S08021	
EC-FQ8	ELA Aviacion ELA 07-R100	1208 250 0722	
EC-FQ9	Air Création GTE 503 SL	07011JL	
EC-FR1	Micro Aviation Pulsar II	150	
EC-FR2	ELA Aviacion ELA 07-R100	1108 251 0722	
EC-FR3	Vol 9/Best Off Sky Ranger 912	SKR 0803871	
EC-FR4	ELA Aviacion ELA 07-R100	1208 253 0712	
EC-FR5	Airbet Girabet II	11S08009	
EC-FR6	BRM Land Africa	01/09/0127S-SP	
EC-FR7	BRM Land Africa	10/09/0123S-SP	
EC-FR8	Manuel Perez Rainbow	MPR 0019	
EC-FR9	Aeroprakt A-22L80 Vision	A22L80-09-003420	
EC-FS1	BRM Land Africa	11/07/0024S-SP	
EC-FS2	BRM Land Africa	0023/07	
EC-FS3	Aeroprakt A-22L Vision	A22L-08-0031	
EC-FS4	ELA Aviacion ELA 07-R115	0109 254 0724	
EC-FS5	Aeroprakt A-22L Vision	A22L-08-0030	
EC-FS6	Vol 9/Best Off Sky Ranger 912	SKR 0803856	
EC-FS7	Pipistrel Sinus 912	209SN9120906	
EC-FS8	ICP MXP-740 Savannah	08-09-51-765	
EC-FS9	Aeroprakt A-22L80 Vision	A22L80-09-0036	
EC-FT1	Tecnam P.92 Echo Super	P92-SP-048	
EC-FT2	ELA Aviacion ELA 07-R115	0209 261 0722	
EC-FT3	Tecnam P.2002 Sierra	P2002-052	
EC-FT4	Air Création Safari GTBI F18	191009	
EC-FT5	Xavier Llobet Escobar Girabet II Sport	11S08019	
EC-FT6	Flight Design CT LS	08-04-02-AR-LS	
EC-FT7	Tecnam P.92 Eaglet	P92-SP-047	
EC-FT8	Pipistrel Sinus 912	089S9121202	
EC-FU1	Pipistrel Sinus 912	080S9121002	
EC-FU2	Pipistrel Sinus 912	156SN9121104	
	(W/o 23.8.15)		
EC-FU3	Tecnam P.2002 Sierra	P2002-053	
EC-FU4	ICP Vimana	06-07-53-003	
EC-FU5	Tecnam P.92 Eaglet	P92-SP-049	
EC-FU6	ELA Aviacion ELA 07-R115	0209 258 0724	
EC-FU7	ELA Aviacion ELA 07-R100	0409 265 0722	
EC-FU8	Tecnam P.2002 Sierra	P2002-053	
EC-FU9	Pipistrel Sinus 912	233SN9120507	
	(Major damage 4.9.16)		
EC-FV1	ELA Aviacion ELA 07-R115	0709 269 0724	
EC-FV2	Tecnam P.92 Echo Classic de luxe	P92-ES-054	
EC-FV3	Air Création Clipper 582S XP	09016JL	
EC-FV4	Aeroprakt A-22L-80 Vision	A22L80-09-0038	
EC-FV5	Aeroprakt A-22L Vision	A22L-09-0039	
EC-FV6	Mainair Gemini / Flash IIA	1175-0998-7-W978	G-MZSD
	(Regd as Mainair Blade 912 Gemini)		
EC-FV7	ICP Vimana	08-05-53-009	
EC-FV8	Ultralair Weedhopper AX-3	B-4103223	
EC-FV9	TL Ultralight TL-96 Star	TL-96S-2009-08	
	(Cr and destroyed 20.6.12)		
EC-FX1	Airbet Girabet II Sport	IIS09024	
EC-FX2	Airbet Girabet II Sport	IIS09016	
EC-FX3	ELA Aviacion ELA 07-R115	1009 273 0724	
EC-FX4	ELA Aviacion ELA 07-R115	0909 272 0724	
EC-FX5	Airbet Girabet II Sport	IIS09022	
EC-FX6	Vol 9 / WT-9 Dynamic Speed	EDY/219/S	
EC-FX7	ELA Aviacion ELA 07-R115	1109 275 0714	
EC-FX9	Pipistrel Sinus 912	252SN9121207	
EC-FY1	Aeroprakt A-22L-80 Vision	A22L-80-08-0033	
EC-FY2	ICP MXP-740 Savannah	09-03-51-813	
EC-FY3	Tecnam P.2002 Sierra	P2002-055	
EC-FY4	Tecnam P.2002 Sierra	P2002-058	
EC-FY6	Tecnam P.2002 Sierra	P2002-057	
EC-FY7	Tecnam P.2002 Sierra	P2002-056	
EC-FY8	Tecnam P.92 Echo Classic de luxe	P92-ES-055	
EC-FY9	Vol 9/Best Off Sky Ranger	SKR0807908	
EC-FZ1	DTA Feeling 582-15/430	036-ES-002	
EC-FZ2	Flight Design CT LS	09-10-15-AR-LS	
EC-FZ3	B&F Funk FK-9 Mk IV	09-04-349	EC-049(3)
	(C/n also quoted as 003-349)		
EC-FZ4	Airbet Girabet II Sport	IIS10010	
EC-FZ5	Airbet Girabet II 582	582-10025	
EC-FZ6	ICP MXP-740 Savannah	09-04-51-817	
EC-FZ7	Air Création Clipper/ XP 582S	10017JL	
EC-FZ8	Airbet Girabet II Sport	IIS10011	
EC-FZ9	ICP MXP-740 Savannah	09-07051-847	
EC-GA1	ELA Aviacion ELA 07-R115	0310 286 0724	
EC-GA2	Flight Design CT-2K	00-02-03-85	
EC-GA4	Magni M-16C Tandem Trainer	16-10-5734	
EC-GA5	ELA Aviacion ELA 07-R115	0510 294 0714	
EC-GA6	ELA Aviacion ELA 07-R100	0510 296 0712	
EC-GA7	Magni M-16C Tandem Trainer	16-10-5844	
EC-GA8	ELA Aviacion ELA 07-R100	0610 298 0722	
EC-GA9	Airbet Girabet II Sport	IIS10028	
EC-GB1	Pipistrel Sinus 912	335S912	
EC-GB2	Evektor EV-97 Eurostar SL	2010 3811	
EC-GB3	ICP MXP-740 Savannah	10-07-51-914	
EC-GB4	Manuel Perez Rainbow	MPR020	
EC-GB5	BRM Land Africa	05/10/0159-SP	
EC-GB6	Tecnam P.92 Echo Super	P92-SP-1325	
EC-GB7	Tecnam P.92 Echo	P92-E-1322	
EC-GB8	Tecnam P.92S Echo	P92-ES-1308	
EC-GB9	Air Création GTE 582S / Kiss 450	10001 SF	
EC-GC1	Airbet Girabet II Sport	IIS10030	
	(W/o 11.9.13)		
EC-GC2	Tecnam P.96 Golf	030	CS-UIY
EC-GC3	Aeroprakt A-22L Vision	A22L-10-0042	
EC-GC4	ELA Aviacion ELA-07-R115	0910 308 0724	
EC-GC5	Flight Design CT LS	F-10-08-04	
EC-GC6	ELA Aviacion ELA-07-R115	0910 306 0724	
EC-GC7	ELA Aviacion ELA-07-R115	0710 304 0724	
EC-GC8	Aeroprakt A-22L Vision	A22L-10-0041	
EC-GC9	ELA Aviacion ELA-07-R100	0910 309 0712	
EC-GD1	ELA Aviacion ELA-07-R115	1010 310 0714	
EC-GD2	Tecnam P.92 Echo	P92-E-1320	
EC-GD3	Tecnam P.92S Echo	P92-ES-1351	
EC-GD4	Tecnam P.92S Echo Super	P92-SP-1353	
EC-GD5	Jihlavan KP-2U Skyleader 200	2173194P	
EC-GD6	Tecnam P.92S Echo	P92-ES-1364	
EC-GD7	Tecnam P.92S Echo	P92-ES-1365	
EC-GD8	Aeroprakt A-22L Vision	A22L-10-0040	
EC-GD9	Airbet Girabet II Sport	IIS10031	
EC-GE2	DTA Feeling 582 / Magic	248-ES-012	
	(Dbr 23.4.16)		
EC-GE3	DTA Combo 582 / Magic	608-ES-013	
EC-GE4	DTA Feeling 912 / Magic	619-ES-015	
EC-GE5	DTA Feeling 582 / 15/430	035-ES-004	
EC-GE6	Aeroprakt A-22L2 Vision	A22L-11-045	
EC-GE8	DTA Combo 912 / Magic	618-ES-014	
	(Cr and destroyed 13.6.12)		
EC-GE9	Magni M-16C Tandem Trainer	16116354	
	(W/o 7.10.13)		
EC-GF1	ELA Aviacion ELA-07-R115	01113170724	
EC-GF2	ELA Aviacion ELA-07-R115	02113190724	
EC-GF3	ELA Aviacion ELA-07-R100	06071240722	
EC-GF4	Tecnam P.92 Echo Super	P92-SP-1378	
EC-GF5	ELA Aviacion ELA-07-R115	03113260724	
	(Cr and destroyed 14.10.12)		
EC-GF6	ELA Aviacion ELA-07-R100	02113220712	
EC-GF7	Air Création Tanarg 912S / iXess 15	08025	
EC-GF8	Pipistrel Sinus 912	253SN9120108	
	(W/o 20.7.13)		
EC-GF9	Tecnam P.92S Echo	P92-ES-1387	
EC-GG2	Evektor EV-97 Eurostar SL	2011 3910	
	(Cr and destroyed 8.1.12)		
EC-GG3	ICP MXP-740 Savannah XL	11-06-51-939	
EC-GG4	ICP MXP-740 Savannah XL	11-06-51-940	
EC-GG5	Tecnam P.2002 Sierra	P2002-475	
EC-GG6	Aeroprakt A-22L2 Vision	A22L-11-0046	
EC-GG7	Aeroprakt A-22L2 Vision	A22L-11-0047	
EC-GG8	ICP MXP-740 Savannah XL	11-10-51-944	
	(Re-regd EC-LUG)		
EC-GG9	BRM Land Africa	09/10/T0172-SP	
EC-GH1	Aeropro Eurofox 3K	32911	
EC-GH2	Tecnam P.2002 Sierra	P2002-471	
EC-GH3	Aeroprakt A-22L2 Vision	A22L-11-0048	
EC-GH4	Air Création Tanarg 912S / iXess 15	T11042	
EC-GH5	Tecnam P.92 Echo	P92-E-1368	
EC-GH6	Vol 9/Best Off Sky Ranger 912	SKR 0501552	
EC-GH7	BRM Land Africa	10/11/0196-SP	
EC-GH8	ICP MXP-740 Savannah XL	11-10-51-945	
EC-GH9	Magni M-16C Tandem Trainer	22116784	
	(C/n indicates type should be M-22 Voyager)		
EC-GI1	Evektor EV-97 Eurostar SL	2012 3939	
EC-GI3	Aeroprakt A-22L Vision	A22L-12-0050	
EC-GI4	Mainair Blade 912	1140-0198-7-W943	G-MZKK
EC-GI5	DTA Voyageur 912 / Magic	665-ES-018	
EC-GI6	Airbet Girabet II Sport	IIS12027	
EC-GI7	Aeroprakt A-22L Vision	A22L-12-0051	
EC-GI8	BRM Land Africa	12/11/T0201-SP	
EC-GJ1	Aeroprakt A-22L2 Vision	A22L-12-0052	
EC-GJ3	ELA Aviacion ELA-07-R100	03123530712	
EC-GJ4	ELA Aviacion ELA-07-R100	02123510722	
	(Dam. 11.7.14)		
EC-GJ5	Pipistrel Virus SW100	358VSW100	
EC-GJ6	Tecnam P.92 Echo Super	P92-SP-1416	
EC-GJ7	Airbet Girabet II Sport	IIS12035	
EC-GJ8	Pipistrel Virus SW100	412SWN100	
EC-GJ9	Air Création Tanarg 912S / iXess 15	T07027	
EC-GK1	Evektor EV-97 Eurostar SL	2012 3944	
EC-GK2	CEDIMEX Rans S-12 Airaile	S-12-143	
EC-GK3	ELA Aviacion ELA-07-R100	06123600722	
EC-GK4	Aeroprakt A-22L Vision	A22L-12-0055	
EC-GK5	Jihlavan KP-2U Skyleader 200	2154177O	OK-OUU 40
EC-GK6	Aeroprakt A-22L Vision	A22L-12-0054	
EC-GK7	Tecnam p.92 Echo Super	P92-SP-1435	
EC-GK8	Magni M-16C Tandem Trainer 912S	16127093	
EC-GK9	ELA Aviacion ELA-07 R115	06123730714	
EC-GL1	Aeroprakt A-22L Vision	A22L-12-0057	
EC-GL3	Mainair Gemini / Flash IIA	865-1191-7-W660	G-MWWJ
EC-GL4	ICP MXP-740 Savannah S	12-09-54-209	
EC-GL5	Aeroprakt A-22L Vision	A22L-12 0059	
EC-GL6	Air Création Tanarg 912S / iXess 15	T07082	
EC-GL7	Aeropro Eurofox Space Pro 3K	20406	CS-UPC
EC-GL8	Aeropro Eurofox 3K	26708	CS-UQV
EC-GM2	BRM Land Africa 100 HP	04/11/0187S-SP	
EC-GM3	Aeropro Eurofox 3K	23507	CS-UPZ
EC-GM4	Aeroprakt A-22L Vision	A22L-12-0058	
EC-GM5	DTA Combo 912 / Magic	688-ES-017	
EC-GM6	DTA Voyageur 912S / Magic	688-ES-018	
EC-GM7	Aeroprakt A-22L-80 Vision	A22L80-0060	
EC-GM8	P&M Quik R	8489	
EC-GM9	Aeropro Eurofox Space Pro 3K	28409	CS-USG
EC-GN1	P&M Quik GT450	8213	G-MASI
EC-GN2	Vol 9/ Skyranger Nynja 80	SYK0908955	
EC-GN3	Vol 9/ Skyranger Nynja 80	SYK0908956	
EC-GN4	Aeroprakt A-22L Vision	A22L-13-0062	
EC-GN5	ELA Aviacion ELA-07-R100	12123850722	
EC-GN6	ELA Aviacion ELA-07-R115	091237600714	
EC-GN7	BRM Land Africa 100HP	04/13/0223-SP	
EC-GN8	Tecnam P.92 Echo	P92-E-1484	
EC-GN9	ELA Aviacion ELA-07-R115	090134050714	
EC-GO1	Vol 9/ Skyranger Nynja 80	SYK0908957	
EC-GO2	Jihlavan KP-2U Skyleader 200	2152M	
EC-GO3	B&F Funk FK.9 Mk IV	09-04-78	
EC-GO4	Aeroprakt A-22L Vision	A22L-14-0064	EC-045
EC-GO6	Magni M-16C Tandem Trainer	22148434	
EC-GO7	Tecnam P.92 Echo S	P92-ES-1491	
EC-GO8	Aeroprakt A-22L Vision	A22L-14-0065	
EC-GO9	Aeropro Eurofox 3K	19706	CS-UPB, OM-FOXY
EC-GP1	BRM Land Africa 100HP	02/14/0231S-SP	
EC-GP2	ELA Aviacion ELA-07-R115	07144200714	
EC-GP3	BRM Land Africa 100HP Sport	12/13/T0229S-SP	
EC-GP4	Eipper Quicksilver GT-500	0121	
EC-GP5	ELA Aviacion ELA-07-R115	03154390724	
EC-GP6	Aeroprakt A-22L Vision	A-22L-15-0068	
EC-GP7	Aeroprakt A-22L-80 Vision	A-22L80-15-0067	
	(Dam.28.5.16)		
EC-GP9	Mainair Gemini/Flash IIA	826-0191-7-W620	G-MWPC
EC-GQ2	Aerospool WT-9 Dynamic Speed	DY-548/2015	
EC-GQ3	Magni M-16C Tandem Trainer	16159414	
EC-GQ4	Tecnam P.92 Echo	P92-E-1534	
EC-GQ6	Air Création GTE 582S/ Kiss 450	08001SF	
EC-GQ7	Eipper Quicksilver GT-500	0087	
EC-GQ8	Tecnam P.2002 Sierra	P2002-256	
EC-GQ9	Pipistrel Virus SW100	751SWN100	
EC-GR1	Aerospool WT-9 Dynamic	DY-547/2016	
EC-GR2	Vol 9 Sky Ranger	SYK 1510958	
EC-GR3	Tecnam P.92 Echo	P92-E-1541	
EC-GR4	BRM Land Africa 80Hp Sport	08/14/T-0235/SP	
EC-GR5	Aeroprakt A-22L Vision	A22L-15-0069	

Regn.	Type	C/n	Prev.Id.
EC-GR6	Tecnam P.92 Echo	P92-E-047	
EC-GR7	P&M Quik R	8744	
EC-GR8	ICP MXP-740 Savannah S	16-02-54-0455	
EC-GR9	Magni Gyro M-16C	22169664	
EC-GS1	Magni Gyro M-16C	22169854	
EC-GS3	Aeroprakt A-22L	AQ22L-16-0070	
EC-GS6	Flight Design CT SW	unkn	OE-7112 ?
EC-...	Cyclone AX3/503	C 203072	G-MYIJ
EC-...	Kitfox Classic IV	C96120180	N893
EC-...	Mainair Gemini/Flash IIA	291-285-3-W27	G-MMUY
EC-...	Mainair Gemini/Flash II	504-1286-4-W307	G-MTAR
EC-...	Mainair Gemini/Flash IIA	1175-0998-7-W978	G-MZSD
EC-...	Pegasus Quantum 15-915	7629	G-BZDL
EC-...	Powerchute Kestrel	00366	G-MWGS
EC-...	Quad City Challenger II	CH2-0402-2207	N130JW
EC-...	Raj Hamsa X'Air V2	588/BMAA/HB/155	G-CBDY
EC-...	Rans S-9 Chaos	1288068	N2153F
EC-...	Rans S-10 Sakota	0791134	N773H
EC-...	Solar Wings Pegasus XL-R	SW-WA-1379	G-MVGP
EC-...	Solar Wings Pegasus XL-R		
		SW-WA-1496/SW-TE-0323	G-MWSE
EC-...	Solar Wings Pegasus Quasar IITC	6564	G-MYJV
EC-...	Solar Wings Pegasus Quantum 15	6651	G-MYLM
EC-...	Tecnam P.96 Echo	unkn	
	(Built using parts from EC-DM5)		
EC-...	Titan Tornado 1	G9744COHK0290	N7026
EC-...	Van's RV-9	90497	N434PM
EC-...	Velocity XL RG	SLL 1	N67AG
EC-...	WDFL Sunwheel R (EC-XJP?)	032	D-MRSA

Note: Tecnam models built in Spain use the following c/n batches:
P.92 Echo   P.92-E-001 to -042
P.92-S Echo   P-92-ES-001 to -055
P.92 Echo Super   P-92-SP-001 to 049
P.96 Golf   P-96-G-001 to 063
P.2002 Sierra   P2002 001 to 058
Later c/n series on the EC-register are Italian-built aircraft.

EI - IRISH REPUBLIC

Regn.	Type	C/n	Prev.Id.
EI-ABI (2)	de Havilland DH.84 Dragon 2	6105	EI-AFK, G-AECZ, AV982, G-AECZ
EI-AED	Cessna 120	11783	N77342, NC77342
EI-AEE	Auster J/1 Autocrat	1873	G-AGVN, EI-CKC, G-AGVN
EI-AEF	Cessna 120	12692	N4221N, NC4221N
EI-AEH	Luscombe 8F Silvaire	1821	G-BSHI, N39060, NC39060
EI-AEI	Aeronca 65TC	C1661TA	G-BTUV, N36816, NC36816
EI-AEJ	Piper PA-16 Clipper	16-451	N5829H, NC5829H
EI-AEL	Piper PA-16 Clipper	16-186	G-BSVI, N5379H
EI-AEM	Cessna 140	13744	G-BYCD, N4273N, NC4273N
EI-AFE	Piper J-3C-90 Cub	16687	OO-COR, D-ELAB, N9954F, EI-AFE, NC79076
EI-AGD	Taylorcraft Plus D	108	G-AFUB, HL534, G-AFUB
EI-AGJ	Auster V J/1 Autocrat	2208	G-AIPZ
EI-AHI (2)	DH.82A Tiger Moth	85347	G-APRA, DE313
EI-AII	Cessna 150F	15064509	N3109X
EI-AKM	Piper J-3C-65 Cub	15810	N88194, NC88194
EI-ALP	Avro 643 Cadet (Stored)	848	G-ADIE
EI-AMK	Auster J/1 Autocrat	1838	G-AGTV
EI-ANT	Champion 7ECA Citabria	7ECA-38	
EI-ANY	Piper PA-18 Super Cub 95	18-7152	G-AREU, N3096Z
EI-AOB	Piper PA-28-140 Cherokee	28-20667	
EI-APS (2)	Schleicher ASK14	14008	(EI-114), G-AWVV, D-KOBB
EI-ARW	Jodel DR.1050	118	
EI-ATJ	Beagle B.121 Pup Series 2	B121-029	G-35-029
EI-AUM	Auster J/1 Autocrat (Dismantled)	2612	G-AJRN
EI-AUO	Reims/Cessna FA150K Aerobat	FA1500074	
EI-AVM	Reims/Cessna F150L	F15000745	
EI-AWH	Cessna 210J Centurion	21059067	G-AZCC, (EI-AWH), G-AZCC, 5N-AIE, N1734C, (N6167F)
EI-AWP	de Havilland DH.82A Tiger Moth (Regd with c/n 19577)	85931	F-BGCL, French AF, DF195
EI-AWR	Malmö MFI-9 Junior	010	LN-HAG, (SE-EBW)
EI-AXT	Piper J-5A Cub Cruiser	5-498	G-BSXT, N33409, NC33409
EI-AYB	Gardan GY-80-180 Horizon	156	F-BNQP
EI-AYI	Morane-Saulnier MS.880B Rallye Club	189	F-OBXE
EI-AYN	Britten-Norman BN-2A-8 Islander	704	G-BBFJ
EI-AYR	Schleicher ASK 16	16022	(EI-119)
EI-AYT	SOCATA MS.894A Rallye Minerva 220 (Wreck stored but still regd)	11065	G-AXIU
EI-AYY	Evans VP-1	MD01	
EI-BAJ	SNCAN Stampe SV-4C (On rebuild)	171	F-BBPN
EI-BAT	Reims/Cessna F150M	F15001196	
EI-BAV	Piper PA-22-108 Colt	22-8347	G-ARKO
EI-BBC	Piper PA-28-180 Cherokee B	28-1049	G-ASEJ
EI-BBE	Champion 7FC Tri-Traveller (Tail-wheel conversion to 7EC Traveller status)	7FC-393	G-APZW
EI-BBI	SOCATA Rallye 150ST	2663	
EI-BBV	Piper J-3C-65 Cub (L-4J-PI) (F/n 12888) (As "480762" in USAAF c/s)	13058	D-ELWY, F-BEGB, 44-80762
EI-BCE	Britten Norman BN-2A-26 Islander	519	G-BDUV
EI-BCF	Bensen B-8M Gyrocopter (Stored)	47941	N ....
EI-BCJ (2)	Aeromere F.8L Falco III (On rebuild)	204	G-ATAK, D-ENYB
EI-BCK	Reims/Cessna F172N Skyhawk II	F17201543	
EI-BCM	Piper J-3C-65 Cub (L-4H-PI)	11983	F-BNAV, N9857F, 44-79687
EI-BCN	Piper J-3C-65 Cub (L-4H-PI)	12335	F-BFQE, OO-PIE, 44-80039
EI-BCP	Rollason/Druine D.62B Condor	RAE 618	G-AVCZ
EI-BDL	Evans VP-2	V2-2101	
EI-BDR	Piper PA-28-180 Cherokee C	28-3980	G-BAAO, LN-AEL, SE-FAG
EI-BDX	Rollason/Druine D.62B Condor	RAE/608	G-ASRB
EI-BEN	Piper J-3C-65 Cub (L-4J-PI) (F/n 12376)	12546	G-BCUC, F-BFMN, 44-80250
EI-BHV	Aeronca 7EC Traveler	7EC-739	G-AVDU, N9837Y
EI-BIB	Reims/Cessna F152 II	F15201724	
EI-BID	Piper PA-18 Super Cub 95 (L-18C-PI)	18-1524	D-EAES, French Army 18-1524, 51-15524
EI-BIK	Piper PA-18-180 Super Cub (Built as PA-18-150)	18-7909088	N82276
EI-BIO	Piper J-3C-65 Cub (L-4J-PI)	12657	F-BGXP, OO-GAE, 44-80361
EI-BIR	Reims/Cessna F172M Skyhawk II	F17201225	F-BVXI
EI-BIV	Bellanca 8KCAB Super Decathlon	464-79	N5032Q
EI-BJB	Aeronca 7DC Champion (Stored)	7AC-925	G-BKKM, EI-BJB, N82296, NC82296
EI-BJC	Aeronca 7AC Champion (Crashed 9.82)	7AC-4927	N1366E, NC1366E, SE-FBW, OY-DKN
EI-BJK	SOCATA Rallye 110ST	3226	F-GBKY
EI-BJM	Cessna A152 Aerobat	A1520936	N761CC
EI-BJO	Cessna R172K Hawk XP II	R1723340	N758TD
EI-BKC	Aeronca 15AC Sedan	15AC-467	N1394H
EI-BKK	Taylor JT.1 Monoplane	PFA 1421	G-AYYC
EI-BMI	SOCATA TB-9 Tampico	203	F-GCOV
EI-BMJ	SOCATA MS.880B Rallye 100T	2594	F-BXTG
EI-BMM	Reims/Cessna F152 II	F15201899	
EI-BMN	Reims/Cessna F152 II	F15201912	
EI-BMU	Monnett Sonerai IIL	01224	
EI-BNL	Rand-Robinson KR-2 (Wfu and b/u but still on register)	SAAC 012	
EI-BNU	SOCATA MS.880B Rallye Club	1204	F-BPQV
EI-BOE	SOCATA TB-10 Tobago	301	F-GDBL
EI-BOV	Rand Robinson KR-2 (Damaged Carnmore 3.91 on rebuild 1999: current status unknown)	unkn	
EI-BPL	Reims Cessna F172K	F17200758	G-AYSG
EI-BPP	Eipper Quicksilver MX (Stored)	3207	
EI-BRS	Cessna P172D	P17257173	G-WPUI, G-AXPI, 9M-AMR, N11B, (N8573X)
EI-BRU	Evans VP-1	V-12-84-CQ	
EI-BSB	Wassmer Jodel D.112	1067	G-AWIG, F-BKAA
EI-BSG	Bensen B-80 Gyrocopter (Stored)	HB	
EI-BSK	SOCATA TB-9 Tampico	618	
EI-BSL	Piper PA-34-220T Seneca III	34-8233041	N8468X
EI-BSN	Cameron O-65 HAFB	1278	
EI-BSO	Piper PA-28-140 Cherokee B	28-25449	C-GOBL, N8241N
EI-BSW	Solar Wings Pegasus XL-R		
		SW-TB-1124/SW-WA-1122	

Reg	Type	c/n	Previous identities
EI-BUC	Jodel D.9 Bébé	PFA 929	G-BASY
EI-BUF	Cessna 210N Centurion II	21063070	G-MCDS, G-BHNB, N6496N
EI-BUG	SOCATA ST-10 Diplomate	125	G-STIO, OH-SAB
	(Derelict)		
EI-BUL	Whittaker MW.5 Sorcerer	1	
	(Current status unknown)		
EI-BUN	Beech 76 Duchess	ME-371	(EI-BUO), N37001
EI-BUT	GEMS MS.893A Rallye Commodore 180	10559	SE-IMV, F-BNBU
EI-BVJ (2)	AMF Chevvron 2-32	009	
	(Current status unknown)		
EI-BVK	Piper PA-38-112 Tomahawk	38-79A0966	OO-FLG, OO-HLG, N9705N
EI-BVT	Evans VP-2	V2-2129	G-BEIE
	(Originally PFA.72221, Under construction: current status unknown)		
EI-BVY	Heintz Zenith CH.200AA-RW	2-582	
	(Current status unknown)		
EI-BXO	Valmet / Fouga CM-170 Magister	213	N18FM, Finnish AF FM-28
	(Stored)		
EI-BYL	Heintz Zenith CH-250	2866	(EI-BYD(1))
EI-BYX	Champion 7GCAA Citabria	7GCAA-40	N546DS
EI-BYY	Piper J-3C-85 Cub	12494	EC-AQZ, HB-OSG, 44-80198
	(F/n 12322) (Regd with c/n 22288 and officially ex G-AKTJ, N3595K, NC3595K)		
EI-CAC	Grob G 115A	8092	
EI-CAD	Grob G 115A	8104	G-WIZB, EI-CAD
EI-CAE	Grob G 115A	8105	
EI-CAN	Aerotech MW.5(K) Sorcerer	5K-0011-02	(G-MWGH)
EI-CAP	Cessna R182 Skylane RG II	R18200056	G-BMUF, N7342W
EI-CAU	AMF Chevvron 2-32C	022	
EI-CAX	Cessna P210N Pressurized Centurion II	P21000215	(EI-CAS), G-OPMB, N4553K
	(Stored)		
EI-CBK	Aérospatiale/Alenia ATR 42-310	199	F-WWEM
EI-CCF	Aeronca 11AC Chief	11AC-S-40	N3826E, NC3826E
EI-CCM	Cessna 152 II	15282320	N68679
EI-CDP	Cessna 182L	18258955	G-FALL, OY-AHS, N4230S
EI-CDV	Cessna 150G	15066677	N2777S
EI-CEG	SOCATA MS.893E Rallye 180GT	13083	SE-GTS
EI-CES	Taylorcraft BC-65	2231	G-BTEG, N27590, NC27590
EI-CFF	Piper PA-12 Super Cruiser	12-3928	N78544, NC78544
EI-CFG	Rousseau Piel CP.301B Emeraude	112	G-ARIW, F-BIRQ
	(Stored as "G-ARIW")		
EI CFH	Piper PA-12 Super Cruiser	12-3110	(EI-CCE), N4214M, NC4214M
EI-CFO	Piper J-3C-65 Cub (L-4H-PI)	11947	OO-RAZ, OO-RAF, 44-79651
	(As "479651" in USAAF c/s)		
EI-CFY	Cessna 172N Skyhawk II	17268902	N734JZ
EI-CGF	Phoenix Luton LA-5 Major	PAL-1124	G-BENH
	(Built as 'PFA 1208')		
EI-CGH	Cessna 210N Centurion II	21063524	N6374A
EI-CGP	Piper PA-28-140 Cherokee C	28-26928	G-MLUA, G-AYJT, N11C
EI-CHR	CFM Shadow Series BD	063	G-MTKT
EI-CIF	Piper PA-28-180 Cherokee C	28-2853	G-AVVV, N8880J
EI-CIG	Piper PA-18-150 Super Cub	18-7203	G-BGWF, ST-AFJ, ST-ABN
	(Frame No.18-7360)		
EI-CIM	Avid Flyer Model IV	1125D	
EI-CIN	Cessna 150K	15071728	G-OCIN, EI-CIN, G-BSXG, N6228G
EI-CJJ	Slingsby T-31M Motor Tutor	907	XE794
EI-CJR	SNCAN Stampe SV-4A	318	G-BKBK, OO-CLR, F-BCLR
EI-CJS	Jodel Wassmer D.120A Paris-Nice	339	F-BOYF
EI-CJT	Slingsby T.31 Cadet III	830	G-BPCW, XA288
	(Stored)		
EI-CJX	Boeing 757-2YOF	26160	N135CA, C-FCLJ, N160GE, EI-CJX, N3519M, N1786B
EI-CJY	Boeing 757-2YO	26161	N153CA, C-FCLK, N161GE, EI-CJY, N3521N
EI-CKH	Piper PA-18 Super Cub 95	18-7248	G-APZK, N10F
EI-CKI	Thruster TST Mk 1	8078-TST-091	G-MVDI
EI-CKJ	Cameron N-77 HAFB	3305	
EI-CKZ	Jodel D.18	229	
EI-CLA	HOAC DV-20 Katana	20106	
EI-CLQ	Reims Cessna F172N Skyhawk II	F17201653	G-BFLV
EI-CMB	Piper PA-28-140 Cherokee Cruiser	28-7725094	G-BELR, N9541N
EI-CMD	Boeing 767-324ER	27392	N838TM, G-OOBK, VN-A762, S7-RGV, EI-CMD, N1785B, N48901
EI-CML	Cessna 150M	15076786	G-BNSS, N45207
EI-CMN	Piper PA-12 Super Cruiser	12-1617	N2363M, NC2363M
EI-CMR	Rutan LongEz	1716	
EI-CMT	Piper PA-34-200T Seneca II	34-7870088	G-BNER, N2590M
EI-CMU	Mainair Mercury	1071-0296-7 and W873	
EI-CMW	Rotorway Executive	3550	
	(Current status unknown)		
EI-CNG	Air and Space 18-A Gyroplane	18-75	G-BALB, N6170S
EI-CNU	Pegasus Quantum 15-912	7326	
EI-COT	Reims/Cessna F172N Skyhawk II	F17201884	D-EIEF
EI-COY	Piper J-3C-65 Cub Special	22519	N3319N, NC3319N
EI-CPE	Airbus A321-211	926	D-AVZQ
EI-CPG	Airbus A321-211	1023	D-AVZR
EI-CPH	Airbus A321-211	1094	F-WWDD, D-AVZA
EI-CPI	Rutan LongEz	17	
EI-CPP	Piper J-3C-65 Cub (L-4H-PI)	12052	G-BIGH, F-BFQV, OO-GAS, OO-GAZ, 44-79756
EI-CPX	III Sky Arrow 650T	K.122	
EI-CRB	Lindstrand LBL 90A HAFB	550	
EI-CRG	Robin DR400/180 Régent	2021	D-EHEC
EI-CRR	Aeronca 11AC Chief	11AC-1605	OO-ESM, (OO-DEL), OO-ESM
EI-CRV	Hoffman H.36 Dimona	3674	OE-9319 , HB-2081
EI-CRX	SOCATA TB-9 Tampico	1170	F-GKUL
EI-CSG	Boeing 737-8AS	29922	N1786B
EI-CSI	Boeing 737-8AS	29924	VP-BPG, EI-CSI
EI-CTL	Aerotech MW-5B Sorcerer	SR102-R440B-07	G-MTFH
EI-CUJ	Cessna 172N Skyhawk II	17271985	G-BJGO, N6038E
EI-CUS	Agusta-Bell 206B-3 Jet Ranger III	8721	G-BZKA, (EI-...), G-OONS, G-LIND, G-OONS
EI-CUW	Pilatus Britten-Norman BN-2B-20 Islander	2293	G-BWYW
EI-CVA	Airbus A320-214	1242	F-WWIT
EI-CVB	Airbus A320-214	1394	F-WWIV
EI-CVC	Airbus A320-214	1443	F-WWBG
EI-CVL	Ercoupe 415CD	4754	G-ASNF, PH-NCF, NC94647
EI-CVW	Bensen B.8M Gyrocopter	FK-199801	
EI-CXC	Raj Hamsa X'Air 502T	333	(44 SU)
EI-CXN	Boeing 737-329	23772	OO-SDW, N506GX, OO-SDW
EI-CXR	Boeing 737-329	24355	OO-SYA, (OO-SQA)
EI-CXV	Boeing 737-8CX	32364	
EI-CXY	Evektor EV-97 Eurostar	2000 0701	OK-FUR
EI-CXZ	Boeing 767-216ER	24973	N502GX, VH-RMM, N483GX, CC-CEF
EI-CZA	ATEC Zephyr 2000	Z580602A	
EI-CZC	CFM Streak Shadow	K269SA11	G-BWHJ
EI-CZK	Boeing 737-4YO	24519	N519AP, TC-ACA, VR-CAB
EI-CZP	Schweizer 269C-1	0149	
EI-DAA	Airbus A330-202	397	F-WWKX
EI-DAC	Boeing 737-8AS	29938	
EI-DAD	Boeing 737-8AS	33544	
EI-DAE	Boeing 737-8AS	33545	
EI-DAF	Boeing 737-8AS	29939	
EI-DAG	Boeing 737-8AS	29940	
EI-DAH	Boeing 737-8AS	33546	
EI-DAI	Boeing 737-8AS	33547	
EI-DAJ	Boeing 737-8AS	33548	
EI-DAK	Boeing 737-8AS	33717	
EI-DAL	Boeing 737-8AS	33718	
EI-DAM	Boeing 737-8AS	33719	
EI-DAN	Boeing 737-8AS	33549	
EI-DAO	Boeing 737-8AS	33550	N1800B
EI-DAP	Boeing 737-8AS	33551	N6066U
EI-DAR	Boeing 737-8AS	33552	(EI-DAQ)
EI-DAS	Boeing 737-8AS	33553	(EI-DAR)
EI-DBI	Raj Hamsa X'Air Mk.2 Falcon	671	
EI-DBJ	Huntwing Pegasus XL Classic	unkn	G-MZCZ
EI-DBK	Boeing 777-243ER	32783	
EI-DBL	Boeing 777-243ER	32781	
EI-DBM	Boeing 777-243ER	32782	
EI-DBO	Air Création 582 / Kiss 400	Wing A03034-3033	
EI-DBP	Boeing 767-35H	26389	C-GGBJ, (VH-BZN), ZK-NCM, N800CZ, N60659
EI-DBV	Raj Hamsa X'Air 602T	516	44 AEE
EI-DBW	Boeing 767-201ER	23899	N647US, N607P
EI-DCA	Raj Hamsa X'Air	742	
EI-DCF	Boeing 737-8AS	33804	
EI-DCG	Boeing 737-8AS	33805	
EI-DCH	Boeing 737-8AS	33566	
EI-DCI	Boeing 737-8AS	33567	
EI-DCJ	Boeing 737-8AS	33564	
EI-DCK	Boeing 737-8AS	33565	
EI-DCL	Boeing 737-8AS	33806	
EI-DCM	Boeing 737-8AS	33807	
EI-DCN	Boeing 737-8AS	33808	N60436
EI-DCO	Boeing 737-8AS	33809	
EI-DCP	Boeing 737-8AS	33810	
EI-DCR	Boeing 737-8AS	33011	
EI-DCW	Boeing 737-8AS	33568	
EI-DCX	Boeing 737-8AS	33569	
EI-DCY	Boeing 737-8AS	33570	
EI-DCZ	Boeing 737-8AS	33815	
EI-DDC	Reims Cessna F.172M	1082	G-BCEC
EI-DDD	Aeronca 7AC Champion	7AC-1877	G-BTRH, N84204, NC84204
EI-DDH	Boeing 777-243ER	32784	
EI-DDJ	Raj Hamsa X'Air 582	863	
EI-DDK	Boeing 737-4S3	24165	N758BC, VT-SIH, VT-JAI, N690MA, G-BPKC
EI-DDP	Southdown Puma Sprint	1121/0031	G-MMYJ
EI-DDR	Bensen B.8V gyrocopter	SAAC 037	
	(Cld 11.12, restored 6.13) (Sometime incorrectly reported as EI-DOR = Boeing 737)		
EI-DDX	Cessna 172S Skyhawk SP	172S8313	G-UFCA, N2461P
EI-DEA	Airbus A320-214	2191	F-WWBX
EI-DEB	Airbus A320-214	2206	F-WWBP
EI-DEC	Airbus A320-214	2217	F-WWBH
EI-DEE	Airbus A320-214	2250	F-WWBE
EI-DEF	Airbus A320-214	2256	F-WWBK
EI-DEG	Airbus A320-214	2272	F-WWIB
EI-DEH	Airbus A320-214	2294	F-WWDF
EI-DEI	Airbus A320-214	2374	F-WWDU
EI-DEJ	Airbus A320-214	2364	F-WWDI
EI-DEK	Airbus A320-214	2399	F-WWIZ
EI-DEL	Airbus A320-214	2409	F-WWDE
EI-DEM	Airbus A320-214	2411	F-WWDG
EI-DEN	Airbus A320-214	2432	F-WWBK
EI-DEO	Airbus A320-214	2486	F-WWIV
EI-DEP	Airbus A320-214	2542	F-WWIU
EI-DER	Airbus A320-214	2583	F-WWDE
EI-DES	Airbus A320-214	2635	F-WWDZ
EI-DFM	Evektor EV-97 Eurostar	2003-1706	
EI-DFO	Airbus A.320-211	0371	A6-ABX, C-FTDD, SU-LBA, TC-OND, N531LF, C-FLSJ, F-WWIQ
EI-DFS	Boeing 767-33A	25346	ET-AKW, V8-RBE
EI-DFX	Air Création 582 / Kiss 400	(Wing A04007-4007)	
EI-DFY	Raj Hamsa X'Air R100	430	G-BYLN
EI-DGA	Urban Air UFM-11UK Lambada	16/11	
EI-DGG	Raj Hamsa X'Air 133	899	
EI-DGH	Raj Hamsa X'Air 582	861	
EI-DGJ	Raj Hamsa X'Air 582	707	G-CCEV
EI-DGK	Raj Hamsa X'Air 133	856	
EI-DGP	Urban Air UFM-11UK Lambada	15/11	OK-IUA-68
EI-DGT	Urban Air UFM-11UK Lambada	14/11	OK-FUA-09
EI-DGU	Airbus A300B4-622RF	557	N109CL, TF-ELK, EI-DGU, F-WQTL, SU-GAR, F-WWAQ
EI-DGV	ATEC Zephyr 2000	Z509702A	
EI-DGW	Cameron Z-90 HAFB	10607	
EI-DGX	Cessna 152	15281296	G-BPJL, N49473
EI-DGY	Urban Air UFM-11 Lambada	10/11	OK-EUU-55
EI-DHA	Boeing 737-8AS	33571	
EI-DHB	Boeing 737-8AS	33572	
EI-DHC	Boeing 737-8AS	33573	
EI-DHD	Boeing 737-8AS	33816	
EI-DHE	Boeing 737-8AS	33574	
EI-DHF	Boeing 737-8AS	33575	
EI-DHG	Boeing 737-8AS	33576	N1787B
EI-DHH	Boeing 737-8AS	33817	
EI-DHN	Boeing 737-8AS	33577	
EI-DHO	Boeing 737-8AS	33578	
EI-DHP	Boeing 737-8AS	33579	
EI-DHR	Boeing 737-8AS	33822	
EI-DHS	Boeing 737-8AS	33580	
EI-DHT	Boeing 737-8AS	33581	
EI-DHV	Schweizer 269C-1	33582	
EI-DHW	Boeing 737-8AS	33823	N1786B
EI-DHX	Boeing 737-8AS	33585	
EI-DHY	Boeing 737-8AS	33824	N1781B
EI-DHZ	Boeing 737-8AS	33583	
EI-DIA	Solar Wings Pegasus XL-Q	SW-WQ-0503	G-MYAD
	(Trike c/n SW-TE-0379) (Current status unknown)		
EI-DIF	Piper PA-31-350 Navajo Chieftain	31-7752105	G-OAMT, G-BXKS, N350RC, EC-EBN, N27230

Reg	Type	C/N	Previous identities
EI-DIP	Airbus A330-202	339	A6-EYW, EI-DIP, I-VLEF, C-GGWD, F-WWYZ
EI-DIR	Airbus A330-202	272	A6-EYV, EI-DIR, I-VLEE, F-WQQL, C-GGWC, F-WWKE
EI-DIY	Van's RV-4	3254	
EI-DJM	Piper PA-28-161 Warrior II	28-8316106	HB-POV, N4314K
EI-DKE	Air Création 582 / Kiss 400	Wing AO4172-4187	
EI-DKI	Robinson R22 Beta II	3882	N74703
EI-DKJ	Thruster T600N	0047-T600N-105	G-CDBN
EI-DKK	Raj Hamsa X'Air Jabiru 3	857	
EI-DKT	Raj Hamsa X'Air 582	798	
EI-DKU	Air Création 582 / Kiss 400	Wing A05036-5040	
EI-DKW	Evektor EV-97 Eurostar	2005-2513	
EI-DKY	Raj Hamsa X'Air 582	720	G-CBTY
EI-DKZ	Reality Escapade 912	JAESC0040	G-CDFH
EI-DLB	Boeing 737-8AS	33584	N1786B
EI-DLC	Boeing 737-8AS	33586	N1786B
EI-DLD	Boeing 737-8AS	33825	
EI-DLE	Boeing 737-8AS	33587	
EI-DLF	Boeing 737-8AS	33588	
EI-DLG	Boeing 737-8AS	33589	N1786B
EI-DLH	Boeing 737-8AS	33590	
EI-DLI	Boeing 737-8AS	33591	N1786B
EI-DLJ	Boeing 737-8AS	34177	
EI-DLK	Boeing 737-8AS	33592	N1786B
EI-DLN	Boeing 737-8AS	33595	
EI-DLO	Boeing 737-8AS	34178	
EI-DLR	Boeing 737-8AS	33596	
EI-DLV	Boeing 737-8AS	33598	
EI-DLW	Boeing 737-8AS	33599	
EI-DLX	Boeing 737-8AS	33600	
EI-DLY	Boeing 737-8AS	33601	
EI-DMA	SOCATA MS892E Rallye 150GT	12376	G-BVAN, F-BVAN
EI-DMB	Best Off Sky Ranger 912S	SKR0503588	
EI-DMG	Cessna 441 Conquest	441-0165	N140MP, N27214
EI-DMU	Whittaker MW6S	PFA 164-12235	
EI-DNM	Boeing 737-4S3	24166	EC-JHX, VT-SIY, N768BC, VT-SII, VT-JAJ, N691MA, G-BPKD
EI-DNN	Bede BD-5G (W/o 25.7.15)	HJC.4523	G-BCOX
EI-DNR	Raj Hamsa X'Air 582	791	G-CCAX
EI-DNV	Urban Air UFM-11 Lambada	12/11	OK-EUU 56
EI-DOB	Zenair CH.701 STOL	7-9272	
EI-DOW	Mainair Blade 912	1361-0104-7-W1156	G-CCPB
EI-DOY	PZL 110 Koliber 150A	04940072	N150AZ
EI-DPB	Boeing 737-8AS	33603	N1787B
EI-DPC	Boeing 737-8AS	33604	N1786B
EI-DPD	Boeing 737-8AS	33623	N1786B
EI-DPF	Boeing 737-8AS	33606	
EI-DPG	Boeing 737-8AS	33607	
EI-DPH	Boeing 737-8AS	33624	
EI-DPI	Boeing 737-8AS	33608	
EI-DPJ	Boeing 737-8AS	33609	
EI-DPK	Boeing 737-8AS	33610	
EI-DPL	Boeing 737-8AS	33611	
EI-DPM	Boeing 737-8AS	33640	N1786B
EI-DPN	Boeing 737-8AS	35549	N1787B
EI-DPO	Boeing 737-8AS	33612	
EI-DPP	Boeing 737-8AS	33613	
EI-DPR	Boeing 737-8AS	33614	N1786B
EI-DPT	Boeing 737-8AS	35550	N1787B
EI-DPV	Boeing 737-8AS	35551	N1779B
EI-DPW	Boeing 737-8AS	35552	
EI-DPX	Boeing 737-8AS	35553	
EI-DPY	Boeing 737-8AS	33615	
EI-DPZ	Boeing 737-8AS	33616	
EI-DRA	Boeing 737-852/W	35114	N1779B
EI-DRC	Boeing 737-852/W	35116	
EI-DRD	Boeing 737-752/W	35117	N1786B
EI-DRE	Boeing 737-752/W	35787	N1786B
EI-DRH	Mainair Blade	1320-0402-7-W1115	G-CBOL
EI-DRL	Raj Hamsa X'Air Jabiru	1005	
EI-DRM	Urban Air UFM-10 Samba	3/10	OK-FUU-31
EI-DRT	Air Création Tanarg 912S/iXess 15	A060826078	
EI-DRU	Tecnam P92/EM Echo	543	I-6351
EI-DRW	Evektor EV-97R Eurostar	2006-2814	
EI-DRX	Raj Hamsa X'Air 582	1048	
EI-DSA	Airbus A320-216	2869	F-WWBE
EI-DSB	Airbus A320-216	2932	F-WWBX
EI-DSC	Airbus A320-216	2995	F-WWIY
EI-DSD	Airbus A320-216	3076	F-WWIP
EI-DSE	Airbus A320-216	3079	F-WWIL
EI-DSG	Airbus A320-216	3115	F-WWIZ
EI-DSL	Airbus A320-216	3343	F-WWBO
EI-DSU	Airbus A320-216	3563	F-WWBI
EI-DSV	Airbus A320-216	3598	F-WWDJ
EI-DSW	Airbus A320-216	3609	F-WWIE
EI-DSX	Airbus A320-216	3643	F-WWBT
EI-DSY	Airbus A320-216	3666	F-WWDY
EI-DSZ	Airbus A320-216	3695	F-WWBI
EI-DTA	Airbus A320-216	3732	F-WWDM
EI-DTB	Airbus A320-216	3815	F-WWIF
EI-DTD	Airbus A320-216	3846	F-WWBY
EI-DTE	Airbus A320-216	3885	F-WWIY
EI-DTF	Airbus A320-216	3906	F-WWIM
EI-DTG	Airbus A320-216	3921	F-WWBK
EI-DTH	Airbus A320-216	3956	F-WWBZ
EI-DTI	Airbus A320-216	3976	F-WWIV
EI-DTJ	Airbus A320-216	3978	F-WWIX
EI-DTK	Airbus A320-216	4075	F-WWBN
EI-DTL	Airbus A320-216	4108	F-WWDS
EI-DTM	Airbus A320-216	4119	F-WWIE
EI-DTN	Airbus A320-216	4143	F-WWBB
EI-DTO	Airbus A320-216	4152	F-WWBJ
EI-DTR	Robinson R44 Raven (W/o 2.10.11)	1652	
EI-DTS	Piper PA18-95 Super Cub	18-5822	OO-VIK, N7484D
EI-DTT	ELA Aviacion ELA 07 R100	0406 105 0722	
EI-DUH	Scintex CP.1310-C3 Super Emeraude	921	F-BJMK
EI-DUJ	Evektor EV-97 Eurostar	2006-2814	
EI-DUL	Alpi Aviation Pioneer	181-UK	
EI-DUO	Airbus A330-203	0841	F-WWYT
EI-DUV	Beech 95 B55 Baron	TC-1618	N3045W
EI-DUZ	Airbus A330-203	0847	F-WWKM
EI-DVE	Airbus A320-214	3129	F-WWBJ
EI-DVG	Airbus A320-214	3318	F-WWIV
EI-DVH	Airbus A320-214	3345	F-WWBP
EI-DVI	Airbus A320-214	3501	F-WWBQ
EI-DVJ	Airbus A320-214	3857	F-WWDL
EI-DVK	Airbus A320-214	4572	D-AUBY
EI-DVL	Airbus A320-214	4678	F-WWFR
EI-DVM	Airbus A320-214	4634	F-WWDV
EI-DVN	Airbus A320-214	4715	D-AUBH
EI-DVO	Barnett J4B2	227	C-FRKB
EI-DVZ	Robinson R44 Raven II	11629	
EI-DWA	Boeing 737-8AS	33617	
EI-DWB	Boeing 737-8AS	36075	
EI-DWC	Boeing 737-8AS	36076	
EI-DWD	Boeing 737-8AS	33642	
EI-DWE	Boeing 737-8AS	36074	
EI-DWF	Boeing 737-8AS	33619	
EI-DWG	Boeing 737-8AS	33620	
EI-DWH	Boeing 737-8AS	33637	
EI-DWI	Boeing 737-8AS	33643	
EI-DWJ	Boeing 737-8AS	36077	
EI-DWK	Boeing 737-8AS	36078	
EI-DWL	Boeing 737-8AS	33618	
EI-DWM	Boeing 737-8AS	36080	
EI-DWO	Boeing 737-8AS	36079	
EI-DWP	Boeing 737-8AS	36082	
EI-DWR	Boeing 737-8AS	36081	N1786B
EI-DWS	Boeing 737-8AS	33625	N1786B
EI-DWT	Boeing 737-8AS	33626	
EI-DWV	Boeing 737-8AS	33627	
EI-DWW	Boeing 737-8AS	33629	
EI-DWX	Boeing 737-8AS	33630	N1781B
EI-DWY	Boeing 737-8AS	33638	N1781B
EI-DWZ	Boeing 737-8AS	33628	N1796B
EI-DXA	Comco Ikarus C42	0604-6809	
EI-DXL	CFM Shadow Series CD	K.232	PH-2S5
EI-DXM	Raj Hamsa X'Air 582	402	G-BYTT
EI-DXN	Zenair CH.601HD Zodiac	9-9095	
EI-DXP	Cyclone AX3/503	7252	G-MZDO
EI-DXS	CFM Shadow Series C	K.023	G-MYNA
EI-DXT	Urban Air UFM-10 Samba	10/10	OK-GUA 19
EI-DXV	Thruster T.600NT	9067-T600T-009	G-MZHC
EI-DXX	Raj Hamsa X'Air 582	685	G-CBFT
EI-DXZ	Urban Air UFM-10 Samba	20/10	OK-GUA 27
EI-DYA	Boeing 737-8AS	33631	
EI-DYB	Boeing 737-8AS	33633	
EI-DYC	Boeing 737-8AS	36567	
EI-DYD	Boeing 737-8AS	33632	N1786B
EI-DYE	Boeing 737-8AS	36568	
EI-DYF	Boeing 737-8AS	36569	
EI-DYL	Boeing 737-8AS	36574	
EI-DYM	Boeing 737-8AS	36575	
EI-DYN	Boeing 737-8AS	36576	
EI-DYO	Boeing 737-8AS	33636	
EI-DYP	Boeing 737-8AS	37515	
EI-DYR	Boeing 737-8AS	37513	
EI-DYV	Boeing 737-8AS	37512	
EI-DYW	Boeing 737-8AS	33635	
EI-DYX	Boeing 737-8AS	37517	
EI-DYY	Boeing 737-8AS	37521	N1787B
EI-DYZ	Boeing 737-8AS	37518	
EI-DZA	Colt 14A Cloudhopper HAFB	527	
EI-DZB	Colt 14A Cloudhopper HAFB	2580	G-BVKX
EI-DZE	Urban Air UFM-10 Samba	14/10	OK-GUA 24
EI-DZF	Pipistrel Sinus 912	254	
EI-DZK	Robinson R22B2 Beta	3179	G-FEBY
EI-DZL	Urban Air UFM-10 Samba XXL	SAXL64	
EI-DZM	Robinson R44 Raven II	12207	
EI-DZN	Bell 222	47071	CS-HDX,
EI-DZO	Dominator Gyroplane Ultrawhite	SAAC 112	
EI-DZS	BRM Land Africa	4/08	
EI-EAJ	Rotary Air Force RAF 2000GTX-SE	095264	G-BYDW
EI-EAK	AirBorne Windsports Edge XT	E-619	N30192
EI-EAM	Cessna 172R Skyhawk II	17280781	G-TAIT, G-DREY, N23726
EI-EAP	Mainair Blade	1327-0502-7-W1122	G-CBOV
EI-EAV	Airbus A330-302	985	F-WWKF
EI-EAY	Raj Hamsa X'Air 582 (BMAA c/n BMAA/HB/139)	525	G-CBHV
EI-EAZ	Cessna 172R Skyhawk	17281146	N74LU
EI-EBA	Boeing 737-8AS	37516	
EI-EBC	Boeing 737-8AS	37520	
EI-EBD	Boeing 737-8AS	37522	
EI-EBE	Boeing 737-8AS	37523	
EI-EBF	Boeing 737-8AS	37524	N60697, N1786B
EI-EBG	Boeing 737-8AS	37525	
EI-EBH	Boeing 737-8AS	37526	
EI-EBI	Boeing 737-8AS	37527	
EI-EBK	Boeing 737-8AS	37528	
EI-EBL	Boeing 737-8AS	37529	
EI-EBM	Boeing 737-8AS	35002	
EI-EBN	Boeing 737-8AS	35003	
EI-EBO	Boeing 737-8AS	35004	
EI-EBP	Boeing 737-8AS	37531	
EI-EBR	Boeing 737-8AS	37530	
EI-EBS	Boeing 737-8AS	35001	
EI-EBV	Boeing 737-8AS	35009	
EI-EBW	Boeing 737-8AS	35010	
EI-EBX	Boeing 737-8AS	35007	
EI-EBY	Boeing 737-8AS	35006	
EI-EBZ	Boeing 737-8AS	35008	
EI-ECC	Cameron Z-90 HAFB	11213	
EI-ECG	BRM Land Africa	114/912/K4/08	
EI-ECK	Raj Hamsa X'Air Hawk	1158	
EI-ECL	Boeing 737-86N	32655	LN-NOP(3), EI-ECL, EC-JDU
EI-ECM	Boeing 737-86N	32658	LN-NOQ(3), EI-ECM, EC-KKU, D-ALIG, EC-JFB
EI-ECP	Raj Hamsa X'Air Hawk	934	44-ALU
EI-ECR	Cessna 525A CitationJet CJ2	525A-0438	N438TA, N5026Q
EI-ECZ	Raj Hamsa X'Air Hawk	1163	
EI-EDB	Cessna 152	15282903	G-BTIK, N46068
EI-EDC	Reims/Cessna FA152 Aerobat	FA1520376	G-BILJ
EI-EDI	Comco Ikarus C-42FB	0009-6272	I-7501
EI-EDJ	CzAW Sportcruiser	700796	
EI-EDP	Airbus A320-214	3781	(D6-CAU), F-WWIR
EI-EDR	Piper PA-28R-200 Cherokee Arrow II	28R-7435265	G-BCGD, N9628N
EI-EDS	Airbus A320-214	3755	(D6-CAT), F-WWBU
EI-EDY	Airbus A330-202	1025	F-WWYU
EI-EEH	BRM Land Africa	0115-912ULS-K4-08LA	

Reg	Type	C/n	Previous identities
EI-EEO	Van's RV-7	71700	
EI-EES	ELA Aviacion ELA-07R	0604 048 0712	G-CEHO
EI-EEU	Pereira Osprey II	304	
EI-EFC	Boeing 737-8AS	35015	N1787B
EI-EFD	Boeing 737-8AS	35011	N1787B
EI-EFE	Boeing 737-8AS	35733	
EI-EFF	Boeing 737-8AS	35016	N1786B
EI-EFG	Boeing 737-8AS	35014	N1786B
EI-EFH	Boeing 737-8AS	35012	N1787B
EI-EFI	Boeing 737-8AS	35013	N1786B
EI-EFJ	Boeing 737-8AS	37536	N1786B
EI-EFK	Boeing 737-8AS	37537	N1786B
EI-EFN	Boeing 737-8AS	37538	
EI-EFO	Boeing 737-8AS	37539	
EI-EFP	Boeing 737-8AS	37540	
EI-EFR	Boeing 737-8AS	37541	
EI-EFT	Boeing 737-8AS	37543	N1787B
EI-EFV	Boeing 737-8AS	35017	N1787B, N60659
EI-EFX	Boeing 737-8AS	35019	N1787B
EI-EFY	Boeing 737-8AS	35020	N1786B
EI-EFZ	Boeing 737-8AS	38489	N1787B
EI-EGA	Boeing 737-8AS	38490	N1787B
EI-EGB	Boeing 737-8AS	38491	N1787B
EI-EGC	Boeing 737-8AS	38492	N1786B
EI-EGD	Boeing 737-8AS	34981	
EI-EGH	Robinson R22 Beta II	3509	N75302
EI-EHH	Aérospatiale/Alenia ATR 42-300	196	G-SSEA, OY-CIT, C-FZVZ, C-GITI, F-WWEK
EI-EHK	Magni M-22 Voyager	22-07-4384	
EI-EHL	Air Création Tanarg 912S / iXess 15	BMAA BH/504	G-CEBY
EI-EHM	Rand KR-2T	1554	C-GQKW
EI-EHV	CzAW Sportcruiser	OC4092	
EI-EHY	Urban Air UFM-10 Samba XXL	SA XL-36	OK-NUA 22
EI-EIA	Airbus A320-216	4195	F-WWIL
EI-EIB	Airbus A320-216	4249	F-WWDX
EI-EIC	Airbus A320-216	4520	D-AXAI
EI-EID	Airbus A320-216	4523	D-AUBU
EI-EIE	Airbus A320-216	4536	D-AXAL
EI-EJG	Airbus A330-202	1123	F-WWKY
EI-EJH	Airbus A330-202	1135	F-WWYU
EI-EJI	Airbus A330-202	1218	F-WWYT
EI-EJJ	Airbus A330-202	1225	F-WWKV
EI-EJK	Airbus A330-202	1252	F-WWKP
EI-EJL	Airbus A330-202	1283	F-WWKA
EI-EJM	Airbus A330-202	1308	F-WWKH
EI-EJN	Airbus A330-202	1313	F-WWYM
EI-EJO	Airbus A330-202	1327	F-WWTN
EI-EJP	Airbus A330-202	1354	F-WWCT
EI-EKA	Boeing 737-8AS	35022	N1786B
EI-EKB	Boeing 737-8AS	38494	N1786B
EI-EKC	Boeing 737-8AS	38495	N1786B
EI-EKD	Boeing 737-8AS	35024	N1786B
EI-EKE	Boeing 737-8AS	35023	N1787B
EI-EKF	Boeing 737-8AS	35025	N1786B
EI-EKG	Boeing 737-8AS	35021	
EI-EKH	Boeing 737-8AS	38493	N1787B
EI-EKI	Boeing 737-8AS	38496	N1786B
EI-EKJ	Boeing 737-8AS	38497	N1796B
EI-EKK	Boeing 737-8AS	38500	N1787B
EI-EKL	Boeing 737-8AS	38498	N1796B
EI-EKM	Boeing 737-8AS	38499	N1786B
EI-EKN	Boeing 737-8AS	35026	N1787B
EI-EKO	Boeing 737-8AS	35027	N1795B
EI-EKP	Boeing 737-8AS	35028	N1786B
EI-EKR	Boeing 737-8AS	38503	N1786B
EI-EKS	Boeing 737-8AS	38504	N1786N
EI-EKT	Boeing 737-8AS	38505	N1786B
EI-EKV	Boeing 737-8AS	38507	
EI-EKW	Boeing 737-8AS	38506	N1786B
EI-EKX	Boeing 737-8AS	35030	N1786N
EI-EKY	Boeing 737-8AS	35031	
EI-EKZ	Boeing 737-8AS	38058	
EI-ELA	Airbus A330-302	1106	F-WW YH
EI-ELB	Raj Hamsa X'Air 582 (Also c/n BMAA/HB/160)	561	G-BZVH
EI-ELC	Comco Ikarus C-42B	9908-6204	D-MSAZ
EI-ELL	Medway EclipseR	157/136	
EI-ELM	Piper PA-18-95 Super Cub	18-1533	G-AYPT, (D-EALX), ALAT, 51-15533
EI-ELZ	Boeing 737-4Q8	26308	SX-BGV, HL7235
EI-EMA	Boeing 737-8AS	35032	
EI-EMB	Boeing 737-8AS	38511	
EI-EMC	Boeing 737-8AS	38510	
EI-EMD	Boeing 737-8AS	38509	N1786B
EI-EME	Boeing 737-8AS	35029	
EI-EMF	Boeing 737-8AS	34978	N1786B
EI-EMH	Boeing 737-8AS	34974	
EI-EMI	Boeing 737-8AS	34979	
EI-EMJ	Boeing 737-8AS	34975	N1786B
EI-EMK	Boeing 737-8AS	38512	
EI-EML	Boeing 737-8AS	38513	N1786B
EI-EMM	Boeing 737-8AS	38514	N1786B
EI-EMN	Boeing 737-8AS	38515	
EI-EMO	Boeing 737-8AS	40283	
EI-EMP	Boeing 737-8AS	40285	
EI-EMR	Boeing 737-8AS	40284	
EI-EMT	Piper PA-16 Clipper	16-29	G-BBUG, F-BFMC
EI-EMU	Reims/Cessna F152 II	F15201882	G-BJNF
EI-EMV	CzAW Sportcruiser	07SC053	PH-IRL
EI-ENA	Boeing 737-8AS	34983	N1796B
EI-ENB	Boeing 737-8AS	40289	
EI-ENC	Boeing 737-8AS	34980	
EI-ENE	Boeing 737-8AS	34976	
EI-ENF	Boeing 737-8AS	35034	
EI-ENG	Boeing 737-8AS	34977	N1787B
EI-ENH	Boeing 737-8AS	35033	N1796B
EI-ENI	Boeing 737-8AS	40300	N1796B
EI-ENJ	Boeing 737-8AS	40301	N1796B
EI-ENK	Boeing 737-8AS	40303	
EI-ENL	Boeing 737-8AS	35037	N1786B
EI-ENM	Boeing 737-8AS	35038	N1786B
EI-ENN	Boeing 737-8AS	35036	
EI-ENO	Boeing 737-8AS	40302	
EI-ENP	Boeing 737-8AS	40304	
EI-ENR	Boeing 737-8AS	35041	N1786B
EI-ENS	Boeing 737-8AS	40307	
EI-ENT	Boeing 737-8AS	35040	N1786B
EI-ENV	Boeing 737-8AS	35039	N1786B
EI-ENW	Boeing 737-8AS	40306	N1786B
EI-ENX	Boeing 737-8AS	40305	
EI-ENY	Boeing 737-8AS	35042	
EI-ENZ	Boeing 737-8AS	40308	N1786B
EI-EOA	Raj Hamsa X'Air Jabiru	575	G-CBDW
EI-EOB	Cameron Z-69 HAFB	11432	
EI-EOC	Van's RV-6	23830	G-TEXS
EI-EOF	Jabiru SP-430	232	G-BZDZ, ZU-BVB
EI-EOH	BRM Land Africa	0162/912ULS/10-LA	
EI-EOI	Take Off Merlin 1100	119405	
EI-EOO	Comco Ikarus C-42 FB UK	PFA/322-13975	G-CCCT
EI-EOU	Evektor EV-97 Eurostar	2009 3615	
EI-EOW	Flight Design CT SW	8317 / 07-07-17	G-CETH
EI-EPA	Boeing 737-8AS	34987	
EI-EPB	Boeing 737-8AS	34986	N1787B
EI-EPC	Boeing 737-8AS	40312	
EI-EPD	Boeing 737-8AS	40310	
EI-EPE	Boeing 737-8AS	34984	
EI-EPF	Boeing 737-8AS	40309	
EI-EPG	Boeing 737-8AS	34985	
EI-EPH	Boeing 737-8AS	40311	
EI-EPI	Medway Hybred 44XLR	MR058/66	G-MVVR
EI-EPJ	Mainair Gemini / Flash IIA	551-687-5-W339	G-MTJA
EI-EPK	Pegasus Quantum 15-912	7430	G-MGMC
EI-EPN	SAN Jodel DR.1050 Ambassadeur	179	G-AYEV, F-BERH, F-OBTH, F-OBRH
EI-EPP	Piper PA-22-160 Tri-Pacer	22-7421	G-ARAI, N10F
EI-EPW	ICP MXP-740 Savannah (Jabiru) (BMAA c/n BMAA/HB/534)	04-11-51-344	G-CENU
EI-EPY	Urban Air UFM-11 Lambada	5/11	OK-DUU 15
EI-EPZ	CEA Jodel DR.1050M1 Sicile Record	02	OO-IPZ, F-BIPZ, F-WIPZ
EI-ERE	Pegasus Quantum 15 – 912	7909	G-CBTZ
EI-ERH	Airbus A320-232	2157	G-TTOJ, F-WWDE
EI-ERI	Air Création Clipper 582 / Kiss 400	BMAA/HB/225	G-CBSX
EI-ERJ	Southdown Raven X	2232/0157	G-MNTY
EI-ERL	Best Off Sky Ranger 912	0130103	I-7038
EI-ERM	Comco Ikarus C-42B	0802-6941	YR-5155
EI-ERO	Solar Wings Pegasus XL-R	SW-WA-1124	G-MTCH
EI-ERZ	Flight Design CT-2K (Assembled by Mainair with c/n 7964)	03-02-04-07	G-KKCW
EI-ESB	Urban Air Samba XXL	SAXL53	OK-MUA 78
EI-ESC	BRM Land Africa	0190/912ULS/11-LA	
EI-ESD	Mainair Blade	1008-0994-7-W804	G-MYTG
EI-ESE	Zenair CH-601XL Zodiac	6-9666	PH-3W6
EI-ESF	Piper PA-22-160 Tri-Pacer	22-6685	G-BUXV, N9769D
EI-ESL	Boeing 737-8AS	34988	N7235C
EI-ESM	Boeing 737-8AS	34992	N441BA
EI-ESN	Boeing 737-8AS	34991	N742BA
EI-ESO	Boeing 737-8AS	34989	N734BA
EI-ESP	Boeing 737-8AS	34990	N751BA
EI-ESR	Boeing 737-8AS	34995	N759BA
EI-ESS	Boeing 737-8AS	35043	N760BA
EI-EST	Boeing 737-8AS	34994	N761BA
EI-ESV	Boeing 737-8AS	34993	N762BA
EI-ESW	Boeing 737-8AS	34997	N1795B
EI-ESX	Boeing 737-8AS	34998	
EI-ESY	Boeing 737-8AS	34999	
EI-ESZ	Boeing 737-8AS	34996	
EI-ETB	Comco Ikarus C42B	0405-6598	D-MTAT, OE-7100
EI-ETD	Raj Hamsa X'Air Hawk	949	44-AFX
EI-ETE	SOCATA MS.880B Rallye Club	1733	G-BXZT, OO-EDG, D-EBDG, F-BSVL
EI-ETF	Urban Air Samba XXL	28/XXL	OK-KUA 26
EI-ETL	Airbus A321-231	954	TC-OAK, D-ALAI, D-AVZD
EI-ETV	Raj Hamsa X'Air Hawk	1247	
EI-EUA	Airbus A320-232 (Stored, Shannon 2.12)	2210	EC-IYG, F-WWBG
EI-EVA	Boeing 737-8AS	40288	
EI-EVB	Boeing 737-8AS	34982	
EI-EVC	Boeing 737-8AS	40286	
EI-EVD	Boeing 737-8AS	40287	
EI-EVE	Boeing 737-8AS	35035	
EI-EVF	Boeing 737-8AS	40291	
EI-EVG	Boeing 737-8AS	40292	
EI-EVH	Boeing 737-8AS	40290	
EI-EVI	Boeing 737-8AS	38502	
EI-EVJ	Boeing 737-8AS	38501	
EI-EVK	Boeing 737-8AS	40298	
EI-EVL	Boeing 737-8AS	40299	
EI-EVM	Boeing 737-8AS	40296	
EI-EVN	Boeing 737-8AS	40294	
EI-EVO	Boeing 737-8AS	40297	
EI-EVP	Boeing 737-8AS	40293	
EI-EVR	Boeing 737-8AS	40295	
EI-EVS	Boeing 737-8AS	40313	
EI-EVT	Boeing 737-8AS	40315	
EI-EVV	Boeing 737-8AS	40314	
EI-EVW	Boeing 737-8AS	40318	
EI-EVX	Boeing 737-8AS	40317	
EI-EVY	Pegasus Boeing 737-8AS	40319	N1796B
EI-EVZ	Boeing 737-8AS	40316	
EI-EWB	Comco Ikarus C42B	0301-6523	SX-UBP
EI-EWC	Beech 76 Duchess	ME-227	G-BZPJ, N6630Z
EI-EWI	Boeing 717-2BL	55170	N906ME
EI-EWJ	Boeing 717-2BL	55171	N907ME
EI-EWR	Airbus A330-202	330	9M-XAD, EI-EWR, PK-YVI, EI-EWR, F-WWKV
EI-EWT	Boeing 757-28A	29381	N754NA
EI-EWV	Comco Ikarus C42 FB100-VLA (Project no. PFA/322-13900)	0202-6454	G-CBRF
EI-EWX	Aeropro Eurofox 912	13002	I-6929
EI-EWY	Van's RV-6A (Swedish EAA no. 1065)	60390	SE-XVM
EI-EWZ	Brugger MB-2 Colibri	232	
EI-EXA	Boeing 717-2BL	55172	N908ME
EI-EXB	Boeing 717-2BL	55173	N909ME
EI-EXD	Boeing 737-8AS	40320	
EI-EXE	Boeing 737-8AS	40321	
EI-EXF	Boeing 737-8AS	40322	
EI-EXI	Boeing 717-2BL	55174	N910ME
EI-EXJ	Boeing 717-2BL	55176	N913ME
EI-EXR	Airbus A300B4-622RF (Stored, 7.12)	677	B-MBJ, (TC-ACM), B-MBJ, TC-OAY N461LF, PK-KDP, B-18577, N8888B, PK-GAT, F-WWAF

Reg	Type	c/n	Previous identities
EI-EXY	Urban Air Samba XXL	86XXL	OK-NUA 22
EI-EYI	Piper PA-28-181 Archer II	28-7990106	D-EFLD, N2125A
EI-EYJ	Reims/Cessna F172N	F17201696	D-EOWY
EI-EYL	Airbus A319-111	2465	N940FR, D-AVWW
EI-EYM	Airbus A319-111 (Stored, 10.12)	2497	N942FR, D-AVYT
EI-EYN	Murphy Renegade Spirit UK	PFA/188-11438	G-MWAJ
EI-EYT	Comco Ikarus C42	0805-6964	SX-UBO
EI-EYW	Thruster T600N Sprint	9039-T600N-033	G-INGE
EI-EZC	Airbus A319-112 (Stored, 2.13)	2879	B-6232, D-AVXN
EI-EZD	Airbus A319-112	2913	B-6233, D-AVWZ
EI-EZU	Reims/Cessna FR172K Hawk XP	FR17200597	D-EBXR, HB-CXO
EI-EZV	Airbus A320-214	2001	I-EEZG, F-WWBB
EI-EZW	Airbus A320-214	1983	I-EEZF, F-WWDM
EI-EZX	Piper PA-22-108 Colt	22-8199	G-ARJF
EI-EZY	Dominator Ultrawhite gyrocopter	I132	
EI-FAB	Eurocopter EC.120B Colibri	1155	F-HIAN, VP-BRD, F-WQDK
EI-FAD	Van's RV-7A	71464	
EI-FAM	Rans S-6ES Coyote II (PFA c/n PFA/204-13864)	1201.1426	G-CBOK
EI-FAS	Aérospatiale/Alenia ATR 72-212A	1083	F-WWET
EI-FAT	Aérospatiale/Alenia ATR 72-600	1097	F-WWEJ
EI-FAU	Aérospatiale/Alenia ATR 72-600	1098	F-WWEK
EI-FAV	Aérospatiale/Alenia ATR 72-600	1105	F-WWER
EI-FAW	Aérospatiale/Alenia ATR 72-600	1122	F-WWEK
EI-FAX	Aérospatiale/Alenia ATR 72-600	1129	F-WWER
EI-FAZ	Urban Air UFM-10 Samba	9/10	OK-GUA 16
EI-FBC	Cessna 172N Skyhawk	17273474	D-EAAY(3), N4927G
EI-FBJ	Boeing 717-2BL	55177	N409BC, XA-CLF, N914ME
EI-FBL	Boeing 717-2BL	55183	N921ME
EI-FBM	Boeing 717-2BL	55192	N926ME
EI-FBU	Airbus A330-322	120	D-AERK, F-WWKN
EI-FBW	BRM Land Africa	0165/912ULS/10-LA	CS-USC
EI-FBX	BRM Citius Sport	0112/Kit/08-CT	I-9631
EI-FBY	BRM Citius	0118/Kit/08-CT	I-9772
EI-FBZ	Thruster T600N	0122-T600N-074	G-PVST
EI-FCA	Urban Air UFM-11 Lambada	13/11	OK-FUA 05, OK-EUU 02
EI-FCB	Boeing 717-2BL	55191	N925ME
EI-FCH	Boeing 737-83N	32576	M-ABFV, TC-SKR, PR-GIC, PH-HST, PR-GIC, N302TZ, N1787B
EI-FCI	Zenair CH-601HD Zodiac	4074	
EI-FCU	Boeing 717-2BL	55190	N799BC, XA-CLD, N924ME
EI-FCV	Boeing 767-3X2ER	26260	N531CL, DQ-FJC
EI-FCY	Aérospatiale/Alenia ATR 72-600	1139	F-WWED
EI-FCZ	Aérospatiale/Alenia ATR 72-600	1159	F-WWEX
EI-FDC	PZL-110 Koliber 150	03930051	D-EIVF
EI-FDD	Cameron Z-105 HAFB	11777	
EI-FDF	Urban Air Samba XXL	SAXL73	OK-NUA 19
EI-FDO	Jabiru UL-D	668	G-CFIS
EI-FDR	BFC Challenger II	PFA/177A-12877	G-MYXK
EI-FDS	Boeing 737-86N	28595	OK-TVD, CN-RNO, N1784D, (TC-IAK), N1795B
EI-FDY	Comco Ikarus C-42	0101-6298	PH-3L3
EI-FEE	Boeing 737-8AS	44686	
EI-FEF	Boeing 737-8AS	44687	
EI-FEG	Boeing 737-8MD	44688	
EI-FEH	Boeing 737-8MD	44689	
EI-FEI	Boeing 737-8AS	44690	
EI-FEJ	Pipistrel Virus 912	513SW912UL	
EI-FEO	ELA Aviacion ELA-07S	03061030722	G-CENR
EI-FEP	Aviatika MAI-890	040	(F) 78-MK
EI-FET	Raj Hamsa X'Air 502T	523	
EI-FEU	Aviatika MAI-890	069	
EI-FEV	Raj Hamsa X'Air 582 (Kit c/n 790)	BMAA/HB/245	G-CBXA
EI-FEW	Van's RV-7	73242	
EI-FFK	Boeing 737-81Q	29051	C-FXGG, N290AN, G-XLAC, N904MA, G-XLAC, N904MA, G-XLAC, N904MA, G-XLAC, G-LFJB, N8254G, N1786B
EI-FFM	Boeing 737-73S	29082	D-AHIA, D-ASKH, N1787B
EI-FFN	Raj Hamsa X'Air (Kit c/n 400)	BMAA/HB/099	G-BZGX
EI-FFV	Grumman AA-5 Traveler	AA5-0645	D-EFDL
EI-FFW	Boeing 737-85F	30477	N477MQ, PR-GIO, N477GX, PP-VSB, N1782B, N1786B
EI-FFZ	Magni M-16 Tandem Trainer	16116314	
EI-FGB	BRM Land Africa	BRM/0226/K2/13-LA	
EI-FGF	Comco Ikarus C-42	9907-6192	PH-3F6
EI-FGG	Comco Ikarus C-42	9908-6202	D-MTWS
EI-FGH	Boeing 717-2BL	55169	EC-LQS, N796BC, XA-CLC, N905ME
EI-FGI	Boeing 717-2BL	55167	EC-LQI, N408BC, XA-CLG, N903ME
EI-FGN	Boeing 767-3BGER	30564	ET-ALL, OO-IHV, HB-IHV
EI-FGU	Best Off Sky Ranger 912S (Project no. BMAA/HB/429)	SKR0407507	G-CDIP
EI-FGW	Piper PA-22-108 Colt	22-8327	G-ARKN, N10F
EI-FGX	Boeing 737-3Q8	28054	N54AU, G-TOYI, YJ-AV18
EI-FHA	Boeing 737-8JP	39012	LN-DYY
EI-FHC	Boeing 737-8Q8	37159	LN-NOL, (OY-SEN)
EI-FHD	Boeing 737-8JP	39011	LN-DYX
EI-FHE	Boeing 737-8Q8	35280	LN-NOD(2)
EI-FHG	Boeing 737-86N	37884	LN-NOJ, N1796B
EI-FHH	Boeing 737-8FZ	31713	LN-NOV
EI-FHJ	Boeing 737-8JP	42069	
EI-FHK	Boeing 737-8JP	41140	
EI-FHL	Boeing 737-8JP	42078	
EI-FHM	Boeing 737-8JP	42070	
EI-FHN	Boeing 737-8JP	39046	LN-DYK, N1786B
EI-FHO	Boeing 737-8JP	35647	LN-NOG, N1786B
EI-FHP	Boeing 737-8JP	39021	LN-DYH
EI-FHR	Boeing 737-8JP	39021	LN-DYJ
EI-FHS	Boeing 737-8JP	39021	LN-NGJ
EI-FHT	Boeing 737-8JP	39021	LN-DYL
EI-FHU	Boeing 737-8JP	39019	LN-NGH
EI-FHV	Boeing 737-8JP	40870	LN-DYR, (LN-DYS)
EI-FHW	Boeing 737-8JP	39007	LN-DYS(2), N1787B
EI-FHX	Boeing 737-8JP	40866	LN-DYI
EI-FHY	Boeing 737-8JP	39021	LN-NGI
EI-FHZ	Boeing 737-8JP	39005	LN-DYM, N1786B
EI-FIA	Boeing 737-8AS	44691	
EI-FIB	Boeing 737-8AS	44692	
EI-FIC	Boeing 737-8AS	44693	
EI-FID	Boeing 737-8AS	44694	
EI-FIE	Boeing 737-8AS	44695	
EI-FIF	Boeing 737-8AS	44696	
EI-FIG	Boeing 737-8AS	44698	
EI-FIH	Boeing 737-8AS	44697	
EI-FII	Cessna 172RG Cutlass RG II	172RG0550	G-BHVC, N9048K, G-BHVC, N372SA, G-BHVC, N5515V
EI-FIJ	Boeing 737-8AS	44699	
EI-FIK	Boeing 737-8AS	44700	
EI-FIL	Boeing 737-8AS	44701	
EI-FIM	Boeing 737-8AS	61576	
EI-FIN	Boeing 737-8AS	44701	
EI-FIO	Boeing 737-8AS	61579	
EI-FIP	Boeing 737-8AS	61577	
EI-FIR	Boeing 737-8AS	61578	
EI-FIS	Boeing 737-8AS	44704	
EI-FIT	Boeing 737-8AS	44703	
EI-FIV	Boeing 737-8AS	44705	
EI-FIW	Boeing 737-8AS	44706	
EI-FIY	Boeing 737-8AS	44707	
EI-FIZ	Boeing 737-8AS	44709	
EI-FJA	Boeing 737-8JP	39419	LN-NOY
EI-FJB	Boeing 737-8JP	42081	
EI-FJC	Boeing 737-81D	39412	LN-NOR
EI-FJD	Boeing 737-8JP	41143	
EI-FJE	Boeing 737-8JP	39420	LN-NOZ
EI-FJF	Boeing 737-86N	36814	LN-NOH
EI-FJG	Boeing 737-8JP	37818	LN-NOX
EI-FJH	Boeing 737-8JP	42071	
EI-FJI	Boeing 737-8JP	37817	LN-NOW
EI-FJJ	Boeing 737-8JP	41148	
EI-FJK	Boeing 737-8JP	42072	
EI-FJL	Boeing 737-8JP	42073	
EI-FJM	Boeing 737-8JP	42074	
EI-FJN	Boeing 737-8JP	41152	
EI-FJO	Boeing 737-8JP	42076	
EI-FJP	Boeing 737-8JP	42077	
EI-FJR	Boeing 737-86N	36820	LN-NOI
EI-FJS	Boeing 737-8JP	41153	
EI-FJT	Boeing 737-8JP	42079	
EI-FJU	Boeing 737-8JP	42273	
EI-FJV	Boeing 737-8JP	42080	
EI-FJW	Boeing 737-8JP	42286	
EI-FJX	Boeing 737-8JP	42271	
EI-FJY	Boeing 737-8JP	42272	
EI-FJZ	Boeing 737-8JP	42082	
EI-FLA	Rotor Flight Dominator	PF2012	
EI-FLE	Boeing 777-212ER	32318	9V-SRN
EI-FLH	BRM Land Africa	012/05/KF2	I-8730
EI-FLI	Urban Air Samba XXL	SAXL72	OK-NUA 18
EI-FLK	BRM Land Africa	0018/05	CS-UOM
EI-FLL	Comco Ikarus C-42	9907-6200	PH-3F8
EI-FLM	Boeing 737-85F	30571	N571MQ, PR-GIP, N571GX, PP-VSA, N1795B
EI-FLO	De Angelis / Denney Kitfox 4	1702	G-CIKY, I-5863
EI-FLS	Comco Ikarus C-42B	1110-7072	PH-4K1
EI-FLU	Piper PA-22-108 Colt	22-8484	G-ARND, N10F
EI-FLW	Comco Ikarus C-42	9912-6234	PH-3H6
EI-FLX	Raj Hamsa X'Air 582	BMAA/HB/484	G-CDWL
EI-FMA	Aeropro Eurofox 912 3K	11301	I-6570
EI-FMF	Bellanca 7GCAA Citabria	339-77	G-BUGE, N4165Y
EI-FMG	Solar Wings Pegasus XL-R (Trike c/n SW-TB-1072)	SW-WA-1076	G-MNUX
EI-FMH	Airbus A330-343	1635	F-WWYM
EI-FMI	Airbus A330-343	1651	(JA330N), F-WWCE
EI-FMJ	Aérospatiale/Alenia ATR 72-600	1295	F-WWEZ
EI-FMK	Aérospatiale/Alenia ATR 72-600	1297	F-WWEC
EI-FML	Airbus A319-111	2240	N929FR, D-AVWP
EI-FMO	BRM Land Africa	06-00014	I-8035
EI-FMR	Boeing 767-304ER	28042	VP-BOQ, G-OBYD, SE-DZG, G-OBYD
EI-FMT	Airbus A319-112	2113	9H-AEG, C-GAEG, 9H-AEG, C-GAEG, 9H-AEG, D-AVWQ
EI-FMU	Airbus A319-112	2122	9H-AEH, D-AVWA
EI-FMV	Airbus A319-111	2332	9H-AEL, D-AVYZ
EI-FMY	Airbus A319-111	2253	N934FR, D-AVYR
EI-FMZ	Boeing 777-312ER	33375	9V-SYK
EI-FNA	Aérospatiale/Alenia ATR 72-600	1325	F-WWEH
EI-FNC	BRM Citius Sport	0119/KIT/08-CT	I-9885
EI-FNE	Javron PA-18	JA1009065	
EI-FNG	Airbus A330-302	1742	F-WWYM
EI-FNH	Airbus A330-302	1744	F-WWKH
EI-FNI	Boeing 777-2Q8ER	28688	VN-A141
EI-FNJ	Airbus A320-214	3174	EC-KFI, F-WWIP
EI-FNO	Aeropro Eurofox	12902	PH-3S1
EI-FNP	Aérospatiale/Alenia ATR 72-212A	715	HS-PGC, F-WWEO
EI-FNS	Comco Ikarus C-42	9904-6147	PH-3F3
EI-FNT	AgustaWestland AW169	69013	I-EASJ
EI-FNU	Boeing 737-86N	28608	HL8214, D-ABBQ, EC-HHG, N1786B
EI-FNW	Boeing 737-86N	28642	LN-NOM, SE-RHA, (LN-NOD), TC-APF, N1787B
EI-FNX	Airbus A330-243	283	A6-EKS, F-WWKH
EI-FNY	Airbus A330-343	1483	N113NT, JA330A, F-WWKH
EI-FNZ	Airbus A330-343	1491	N114NT, JA330B, F-WWTK
EI-FOA	Boeing 737-8AS	44708	
EI-FOB	Boeing 737-8AS	44710	
EI-FOC	Boeing 737-8AS	44714	
EI-FOD	Boeing 737-8AS	44715	
EI-FOE	Boeing 737-8AS	44713	
EI-FOF	Boeing 737-8AS	44716	
EI-FOG	Boeing 737-8AS	44711	
EI-FOH	Boeing 737-8AS	44717	
EI-FOI	Boeing 737-8AS	44712	
EI-FOJ	Boeing 737-8AS	44722	
EI-FOK	Boeing 737-8AS	44719	
EI-FOL	Boeing 737-8AS	61580	
EI-FOM	Boeing 737-8AS	44720	
EI-FON	Boeing 737-8AS	44721	
EI-FOO	Boeing 737-8AS	44724	
EI-FOP	Boeing 737-8AS	44723	
EI-FOR	Boeing 737-8AS	44718	
EI-FOS	Boeing 737-8AS	44727	
EI-FOT	Boeing 737-8AS	44730	
EI-FOV	Boeing 737-8AS	44725	
EI-FOW	Boeing 737-8AS	44729	
EI-FOY	Boeing 737-8AS	44728	

Reg	Type	Serial	Previous identities
EI-FOZ	Boeing 737-8AS	44731	
EI-FPA	Canadair CL-600-2D24 CRJ-900LR	15398	C-GWFX
EI-FPB	Canadair CL-600-2D24 CRJ-900LR	15399	C-GWFL
EI-FPC	Canadair CL-600-2D24 CRJ-900LR	15400	C-GWFQ
EI-FPD	Canadair CL-600-2D24 CRJ-900LR	15401	C-GZSJ(2)
EI-FPE	Canadair CL-600-2D24 CRJ-900LR	15402	C-GZYJ(2)
EI-FPF	Canadair CL-600-2D24 CRJ-900LR	15403	C-GZVR
EI-FPG	Canadair CL-600-2D24 CRJ-900LR	15406	C-GZWO(2)
EI-FPH	Canadair CL-600-2D24 CRJ-900LR	15409	C-GZUY(2)
EI-FRB	Boeing 737-8AS	44726	
EI-FRC	Boeing 737-8AS	62690	
EI-FRD	Boeing 737-8AS	44738	
EI-FRE	Boeing 737-8AS	62691	
EI-FRF	Boeing 737-8AS	44732	
EI-FRG	Boeing 737-8AS	44737	
EI-FRH	Boeing 737-8AS	44736	N1787B
EI-FRI	Boeing 737-8AS	44733	N1781B
EI-FRJ	Boeing 737-8AS	44737	
EI-FRK	Boeing 737-8AS	44735	
EI-FRL	Boeing 737-8AS	44741	
EI-FRM	Boeing 737-8AS	44743	
EI-FRN	Boeing 737-8AS	44744	
EI-FRO	Boeing 737-8AS	44742	
EI-FRP	Boeing 737-8AS	62692	
EI-FRR	Boeing 737-8AS	44739	
EI-FRS	Boeing 737-8AS	44745	
EI-FRT	Boeing 737-8AS	44740	
EI-FRV	Boeing 737-8AS	44747	
EI-FRW	Boeing 737-8AS	44748	
EI-FRX	Boeing 737-800	44746	
EI-FRY	Boeing 737-800	44750	N1786B
EI-FRZ	Boeing 737-800	44749	
EI-FSA	TL Ultralight TL-3000 Sirius	16SI140	
EI-FSC	Airbus A330-343	1542	N115NT, JA330D, F-WWCS
EI-FSD	Airbus A330-343	1554	N116NT, JA330E, F-WWYF
EI-FSE	Airbus A330-243	293	A6-EKT, F-WWKR
EI-FSF	Airbus A330-243	295	A6-EKU, F-WWYF
EI-FSH	Airbus A330-243	328	A6-EKY, F-WWYX
EI-FSI	Airbus A330-243	392	A6-EAF, F-WWYX
EI-FSJ	Boeing 737-86N	29888	N546CC, B-2673, N1786B
EI-FSK	Aérospatiale/Alenia ATR 72-600	1326	F-WWEI
EI-FSL	Aérospatiale/Alenia ATR 72-600	1339	F-WWEW
EI-FSP	Airbus A330-322	096	CS-TMT, OO-SFX, 9M-MKZ, F-WWKP
EI-FSR	ELA Aviacion ELA-07S	090611400724	ZK-CEJ(2), G-CEJH
EI-FSS	Boeing 777-2Q8ER	32701	VN-A142
EI-FST	Comco Ikarus C-42	1605-7454	
EI-FSU	Airbus A321-231	1843	N843AG, VQ-BRN, D-ALAB, (N843AG), EC-IJU, D-AVZR
EI-FSX	Pegasus Quantun 15	8065	G-CDCY
EI-FSZ	Pipistrel Virus 912	132VN912	I-9020
EI-FTA	Boeing 737-800	44751	
EI-FTB	Boeing 737-800	44752	
EI-FTC	Boeing 737-800	44753	
EI-FTD	Boeing 737-800	44754	
EI-FTE	Boeing 737-800	44755	N1786B
EI-FTF	Boeing 737-800	44756	
EI-FTG	Boeing 737-800	44757	N1795B
EI-FTH	Boeing 737-800	44758	
EI-FTI	Boeing 737-800	44759	N1786B
EI-FTJ	Boeing 737-800	44760	
EI-FTX	Rans S-6ES Coyote II (PFA No. PFA/204-14143)	1003.1524	G-CCTX
EI-FVA	Boeing 737-4Q8	24706	G-CIPH, N916SK, SP-LLI, F-GRNH, EC-FXP, EC-644, 9M-MJD
EI-FWA	Sukhoi RRJ95B Superjet	95102	I-PDVZ
EI-FWB	Sukhoi RRJ95B Superjet	95108	I-PDVW
EI-FWC	Sukhoi RRJ95B Superjet	95111	(RA)97011
EI-FXA	Aérospatiale/Alenia ATR 42-300	282	N282AT, (N281AE), N282AT, F-WWLI
EI-FXB	Aérospatiale/Alenia ATR 42-300	243	(N927FX), N246AE, N243AT, F-WWEQ
EI-FXC	Aérospatiale/Alenia ATR 42-300	310	N310DK, (N925FX), N271AT, N273AT, F-WWEC
EI-FXD	Aérospatiale/Alenia ATR 42-300	273	N271AT, N273AT, F-WWEQ
EI-FXE	Aérospatiale/Alenia ATR 42-320	327	N327AT, (N926FX), N327AT, F-WWLM
EI-FXG	Aérospatiale/Alenia ATR 72-202	224	(N814FX), D-ANFA, F-WWEQ
EI-FXH	Aérospatiale/Alenia ATR 72-212	229	N815FX, D-ANFB, F-WWEX
EI-FXI	Aérospatiale/Alenia ATR 72-202F	294	N818FX, D-ANFE, F-WWLS
EI-FXJ	Aérospatiale/Alenia ATR 72-202F	292	N813FX, D-ANFF, F-WWLT
EI-FXK	Aérospatiale/Alenia ATR 72-202F	256	N817FX, D-ANFD, F-WWEE
EI-FXL	Robinson R44 Raven	1089	G-CJJM
EI-FXN	Airbus A319-111	1684	N906FR, D-AVWK
EI-FXO	Airbus A320-214	5240	PR-MYW, F-WWBT
EI-FXP	Airbus A319-111	2258	N932FR, D-AVYW
EI-FXR	Airbus A340-313	163	A6-ERO, D-ASIB, 9V-SJG, F-WWJR
EI-FXS	Airbus A321-231	7206	B-22615, D-AVZR
EI-FXT	Airbus A321-231	7375	B-22616, D-AZAG
EI-GDJ	Piper J-4E Cub Coupe	4-1456	G-BSDJ, N35975, NC35975
EI-GER	Maule MX-7-180A Star Rocket (t/w)	20006C	
EI-GJL	Aérospatiale AS.365N3 Dauphin 2	6785	G-CEUK, F-WWOZ
EI-GLA	Schleicher ASK 21	21002	EI-150, D-6597
EI-GLB	Schleicher ASK 21	21060	EI-164, D-4089
EI-GLC-ZC	Centrair 101A Pégase	101-102	EI-163, PH-738
EI-GLD	Schleicher ASK 13	13131	EI-142
EI-GLF-08	Schleicher K 8B	8468	EI-108
EI-GLG	Schleicher Ka 6CR Rhönsegler	662	EI-127, PH-259
EI-GLH-T8	Sportine Aviacija LAK-17A	136	EI-169, HA-4511
EI-GLL-DS	Glaser-Dirks DG-200	2-22	EI-147, D-6780
EI-GLM-11	Schleicher Ka 6CR	6565	EI-111, IGA 9
EI-GLO-TK	Scheibe Zugvogel IIIB	1085	EI-146, D-4096
EI-GLP	EoN AP.5 Olympia 2B	EoN/O/155	EI-115, BGA 1097
EI-GLT	Schempp-Hirth Discus b	219	EI-149, BGA 3320/FKK
EI-GLU	Schleicher Ka 6CR Rhönsegler	808	EI-161, BGA 3536/FUM, D-6289
EI-GLV-53	Schleicher ASW 19B	19316	EI-153, BGA 4274-HWZ, HB-1524
EI-GMB-TK	Schleicher ASW 17	17031	EI-132, D-2365
EI-GMC	Schleicher ASK 18	18007	EI-136, BGA 2945/ETT, D-6868
EI-GMD	Bölkow Phoebus C	908	EI-158, BGA 4202/HTZ, OO-ZDJ, BGA 1573
EI-GMF	Schleicher ASK 13	13189	EI-113
EI-GMH	Wag-Aero Sport Trainer	PFA/108-12647	G-BVMH
EI-GML	Grob G 103 Twin Astir	3103-T-6	EI-160, EC-EKU, D3960
EI-GPT	Robinson R22 Beta II	3317	N70637
EI-GSM	Cessna 182S Skylane	18280188	N9541Q
EI-GVM	Robinson R22 Beta	2711	G-ERBL
EI-GWY	Cessna 172R Skyhawk	17280162	N9497F
EI-HFA	DHC-1 Chipmunk 22 (Painted as IAC-168)	C1/0464	IAC-168
EI-HFB	DHC-1 Chipmunk 22 (Painted as "IAC-169")	C1/0247	G-ARGG, WD305
EI-HFC	DHC-1 Chipmunk 22 (Painted as "IAC-170")	C1/0742	G-BDRJ, WP857
EI-HFD	Boeung Stearman E75	75-5736A	G-THEA, (EI-RYR), G-THEA, N1733B, BuA38122
EI-HUM	Van's RV-7	70588-1	
EI-IAL	Agusta AW.109SP Grand New	22343	I-EASU
EI-IAN	Pilatus PC-6/B2-H4 Turbo Porter	810	HB-FGI
EI-ICA	Sikorsky S-92A	920045	G-SARB, N80562
EI-ICD	Sikorsky S-92A	920052	G-SARC, N45168
EI-ICG	Sikorsky S-92A	920150	N150AL
EI-ICR	Sikorsky S-92A	920051	G-CGOC, N45165
EI-ICU	Sikorsky S-92A	920034	G-CGMU, N8010S
EI-IGU	Boeing 737-73V	32422	G-EZKA, (G-ESYA)
EI-IKB	Airbus A320-214	1226	I-BIKB, F-WWIG
EI-IKF	Airbus A320-214	1473	I-BIKF, F-WWDP
EI-IKG	Airbus A320-214	1480	I-BIKG, F-WWDT
EI-IKL	Airbus A320-214	1489	I-BIKL, F-WWDN
EI-IKU	Airbus A320-214	1217	I-BIKU, F-WWBD
EI-IMB	Airbus A319-112	2033	I-BIMB, D-AVYP
EI-IMC	Airbus A319-112	2057	I-BIMC, D-AVYC
EI-IMD	Airbus A319-112	2074	I-BIMD, D-AVYM
EI-IME	Airbus A319-112	1740	I-BIME, D-AVWW
EI-IMF	Airbus A319-112	2083	I-BIMF, D-AVYZ
EI-IMG	Airbus A319-112	2086	I-BIMG, D-AVWD
EI-IMH	Airbus A319-112	2101	I-BIMH, D-AVYY
EI-IMI	Airbus A319-112	1745	I-BIMI, D-AVWZ
EI-IMJ	Airbus A319-112	1779	I-BIMJ, D-AVYG
EI-IML	Airbus A319-112	2127	I-BIML, D-AVWN
EI-IMM	Airbus A319-111	4759	D-AVYE
EI-IMN	Airbus A319-111	4764	D-AVYG
EI-IMO	Airbus A319-112	1770	I-BIMO, D-AVWC
EI-IMP	Airbus A319-111	4859	D-AVWR
EI-IMR	Airbus A319-111	4875	D-AVYB
EI-IMS	Airbus A319-111	4910	D-AVYC
EI-IMT	Airbus A319-111	5018	F-WXAJ, D-AVYI
EI-IMU	Airbus A319-111	5130	D-AVYA
EI-IMV	Airbus A319-111	5294	D-AVWB
EI-IMW	Airbus A319-111	5383	D-AVWJ
EI-IMX	Airbus A319-111	5424	D-AVWN
EI-ING	Reims Cessna F172P	F17202084	G-BING
EI-ISA	Boeing 777-243ER	32855	I-DISA
EI-ISB	Boeing 777-243ER	32859	I-DISB, N5016R
EI-ISD	Boeing 777-243ER	32860	I-DISD
EI-ISE	Boeing 777-243ER	32856	I-DISE
EI-ISO	Boeing 777-243ER	32857	I-DISO
EI-ITN	Bombardier BD-700-1A10 Global Express XRS	9159	OE-ITN, (D-AZNF), OH-TNR, D-ATNR, C-FCOI
EI-IXH	Airbus A321-112	940	I-BIXH, D-AVZS
EI-IXJ	Airbus A321-112	959	I-BIXJ, D-AVZP
EI-IXV	Airbus A321-112	819	I-BIXV, D-AVZU
EI-IXZ	Airbus A321-112	848	I-BIXZ, D-AVZC
EI-JIM	Urban Air UFM-10 Samba XLA	43	
EI-JOR	Robinson R44 Raven II	12426	
EI-JPK	Tecnam P.2002-JF Sierra	079	
EI-JSK	Gulfstream VI	6070	N670GA
EI-KDH	Piper PA-28-181 Archer III	2843422	N301PA, N41870
EI-KEL	Eurocopter EC.135T2+	0848	G-CGHP, D-HCBK
EI-KEV	Raj Hamsa X'Air 133	567	G-BZLD
EI-KMA	Canadair CL-600-2B16 Challenger IV	5585	SX-KMA, D-AAOK, OE-IMB, (D-ARTN), N585BD, C-GLXO
EI-LAD	Robinson R44 Raven II	10779	G-CDMI
EI-LAX	Airbus A330-202	269	F-WWKV
EI-LBR	Boeing 757-2Q8	28167	OH-LBR
EI-LBS	Boeing 757-2Q8	27623	OH-LBS, N5573K
EI-LBT	Boeing 757-2Q8	28170	OH-LBT
EI-LCM	SOCATA TB-850	436	N850JS
EI-LEM	SOCATA TB-9 Tampico Club	1384	G-INIT, I-IAFS
EI-LEO	Cessna 750 Citation X	750-0232	OE-HAC, N232CX, N5120U
EI-LFC	Tecnam P.2002-JF Sierra	63	
EI-LID	AgustaWestland AW169	69015	G-CJHA
EI-LIM	AgustaWestland AW139	31541	I-EASY
EI-LNI	Boeing 787-8	37307	
EI-LNJ	Boeing 787-9	37308	
EI-LOW	Aérospatiale AS.355N Ecureuil 2	5685	LN-OGP, 5Y-EXD, F-WQDI, F-WQDB
EI-LSA	Cub Crafters CC11-160	CC11-00096	N298A
EI-LSN	Gulfstream VI	6092	SX-GSB, N692GA
EI-LSW	Gulfstream V-SP	5350	SX-GJJ, N750GA
EI-MCF	Cessna 172R Skyhawk	17280799	N2469D
EI-MCG	Cessna 172R Skyhawk	17281539	N6311Y
EI-MIK	Eurocopter EC.120B Colibri	1104	G-BZIU
EI-MIR	Roko Aero NG 4HD	017/2009	
EI-MPW	Robinson R44 Raven	1554	
EI-MRB	Denney Kitfox 2	449 / PFA/172-11752	G-BSHK
EI-MTZ	Urban Air Samba XXL	SAXL68	
EI-NFW	Cessna 172S Skyhawk SP	172S9861	G-CDOU, N1538W
EI-NJA	Robinson R44 Raven II	11945	N155N
EI-NVL	JORA Jora	C129	
EI-ODD	Bell 206B-3 Jet Ranger III	3627	G-CDES, N22751
EI-OFM	Reims/Cessna F172N	F17201988	G-EOFM, D-EDFM
EI-OOR	Cessna 172S Skyhawk SP	172S10374	N11688
EI-OZL	Airbus A300B4-622R	717	UK-31004, HL7299, F-WWAY
EI-OZM	Airbus A300B4-622R	722	UK-31005, HL7244, F-WWAH
EI-PGA	Dudek Hadron XX paramotor	P-127451	
EI-PGH	Dudek Synthesis LT paramotor	P-07518	
EI-PGJ	Swing Sting 2 paramotor	ST2 11-52628066	
EI-PGK	Ozone Power Spyder 26 paramotor	SD26-R-26B-047	
EI-PGL	Dudek Synthesis 34 paramotor	P-08129	
EI-PMI	Agusta-Bell 206B-3 Jet Ranger III	8614	EI-BLG, G-BIGS
EI-POK	Robinson R44 Raven 1	2374	D-HALS(2)
EI-POP	Cameron Z-90 HAFB	10753	
EI-PRO	Aérospatiale AS.365N2 Dauphin	6443	I-PCFL, PT-YRM, F-WYMN
EI-PWC	Magni M-24 Orion	24169754	
EI-RCA	Roko Aero NG 4UL	019/2009	OK-TUR 22, EI-RCA, OK-PUR 04
EI-RDA	Embraer ERJ-170-200LR	17000330	PT-TPD
EI-RDB	Embraer ERJ-170-200LR	17000331	PT-TPR
EI-RDC	Embraer ERJ-170-200LR	17000333	PT-TSA

Reg	Type	C/n	Previous identities
EI-RDD	Embraer ERJ-170-200LR	17000334	PT-TSP
EI-RDE	Embraer ERJ-170-200LR	17000335	PT-TUH
EI-RDF	Embraer ERJ-170-200LR	17000337	PT-TUW
EI-RDG	Embraer ERJ-170-200LR	17000338	PT-TVD
EI-RDH	Embraer ERJ-170-200LR	17000339	PT-TZV
EI-RDI	Embraer ERJ-170-200LR	17000340	PT-TAY
EI-RDJ	Embraer ERJ-170-200LR	17000342	PT-TBT
EI-RDK	Embraer ERJ-170-200LR	17000343	PT-TBY
EI-RDL	Embraer ERJ-170-200LR	17000345	PT-TDO
EI-RDM	Embraer ERJ-170-200LR	17000346	PT-TDW
EI-RDN	Embraer ERJ-170-200LR	17000347	PT-TGA
EI-RDO	Embraer ERJ-170-200LR	17000348	PT-THB
EI-REJ	Aérospatiale/Alenia ATR 72-201	126	ES-KRA, OH-KRA, F-WWEM
EI-REL	Aérospatiale/Alenia ATR 72-212A	748	F-WWEI
EI-REM	Aérospatiale/Alenia ATR 72-212A	760	F-WWEW
EI-RJC	Avro 146-RJ85	E2333	G-CEHA, N515XJ, G-6-333
EI-RJD	Avro 146-RJ85	E2334	G-CEFL, N516XJ, G-6-334
EI-RJE	Avro 146-RJ85	E2335	G-CEBU, N517XJ, G-6-335
EI-RJF	Avro 146-RJ85	E2337	G-CEFN, N518XJ, G-6-337
EI-RJG	Avro 146-RJ85	E2344	G-CEHB, N519XJ, G-6-344
EI-RJH	Avro 146-RJ85	E2345	G-CEIC, N520XJ, G-6-345
EI-RJI	Avro 146-RJ85	E2346	(G-CDZP), N521XJ, G-6-346
EI-RJN	Avro 146-RJ85	E2351	N526XJ, G-6-351
EI-RJO	Avro 146-RJ85	E2352	N527XJ, G-6-352
EI-RJR	Avro 146-RJ85	E2364	N530XJ, G-6-364
EI-RJT	Avro 146-RJ85	E2366	N532XJ, G-6-366
EI-RJU	Avro 146-RJ85	E2367	N533XJ, G-6-367
EI-RJW	Avro 146-RJ85	E2371	N535XJ, G-6-371
EI-RJX	Avro 146-RJ85	E2372	N536XJ, G-6-372
EI-RJY	Avro 146-RJ85	E2307	N502XJ, G-6-307
EI-RJZ	Avro 146-RJ85	E2326	N512XJ, G-6-326
EI-RNA	Embraer ERJ-190-100STD	19000470	PT-TOQ
EI-RNB	Embraer ERJ-190-100STD	19000479	PT-TPC
EI-RNC	Embraer ERJ-190-100STD	19000503	PT-TRL
EI-RND	Embraer ERJ-190-100STD	19000512	PT-TPC
EI-RNE	Embraer ERJ-190-100STD	19000520	PT-TUI
EI-ROB	Robin R.1180TD Aiglon	270	PH-AIG
EI-ROK	Roko Aero NG 4UL	004/2008	OK-NUR 40
EI-RUA	Boeing 737-86J	30498	D-ABAV(2), N1787B
EI-RUC	Boeing 737-85R	30494	ET-ANA, B-2660, N1786B
EI-RUD	Boeing 737-85R	30495	ET-ANB, B-2665, N1784B
EI-RUG	Boeing 737-86N	28610	VT-SJF, EI-DIS, EC-HHH, N1786B
EI-RUH	Boeing 737-8K5	28228	LX-LGT, D-AHFN, N1786B
EI-RUI	Boeing 737-85P	28387	EC-HJQ, N1786B
EI-RUJ	Boeing 737-81Q	29049	N982CQ, VT-SIJ, N8253J, N1786B
EI-RUK	Boeing 737-86N	28621	VT-SPE, EI-DIT, EC-HMJ, N1786B
EI-RUN	Boeing 737-808	34702	B-5168
EI-RUO	Boeing 737-808	34703	B-5169, N1795B
EI-SAC	Cessna 172P Skyhawk	17276263	N98149
EI-SEA	Progressive Aerodyne SeaRey	1DK359C	
EI-SEV	Boeing 737-73S	29078	N278KA, HK-4627, OY-MLW, PR-SAE, EI-CRP, PR-SAE, EI-CRP, N1014S, N60436, N1787B
EI-SKS	Robin R.2160 Acrobin	307	OO-OBC
EI-SKV	Robin R.2160D Acrobin	171	PH-BLO
EI-SKW	Piper PA-28-161 Warrior II	28-8216115	D-EIBV, N9630N
EI-SLA	Aérospatiale/Alenia ATR 42-300	149	SE-LST, F-WQNP, G-WFEP, N4210G, F-WWEV
EI-SLF	Aérospatiale/Alenia ATR 72-202	210	OY-RUA, B-22703, F-WWEH
EI-SLG	Aérospatiale/Alenia ATR 72-201	183	F-WQNI, EC-EYK, EC-515, F-WWES
EI-SLH	Aérospatiale/Alenia ATR 72-202	157	OY-RTG, F-WQNH, EC-EUJ, EC-384, F-WWEL
EI-SLJ	Aérospatiale/Alenia ATR 72-201	324	LY-PTK, HL5233, ES-KRF, OH-KRF, F-WWEU
EI-SLK	Aérospatiale/Alenia ATR 72-212	395	N642AS, F-WWLJ
EI-SLO	Aérospatiale/Alenia ATR 42-320	121	HB-AFD, (LZ-ATA), F-WQNA, D-BEEE, F-WWER
EI-SLP	Aérospatiale/Alenia ATR 72-212	461	EC-LKK, F-GVZF, F-OGXF, F-WWLP
EI-SLS	Aérospatiale/Alenia ATR 72-201F	198	HB-AFS, P2-KXZ, HB-AFS, F-WKVJ, EC-IKK, F-WQND, F-WQOG, SX-BSX, F-WQJU, EC-GQU, F-WQGC, B-22702, F-WWEL
EI-SLT	Aérospatiale/Alenia ATR 72-202F	389	HB-AFN, B-22716, F-WWEH
EI-SMK	Zenair CH.701 STOL	7-3551	
EI-SOO	Aérospatiale/Alenia ATR 72-212A	577	HB-ACE, 4X-AVZ, F-WWEN
EI-SOP	Aérospatiale/Alenia ATR 72-212	583	4X-AVW, F-WWER
EI-STA	Boeing 737-31S	29057	G-THOG, D-ADBM
EI-SYM	Van's RV-7	72940	
EI-TAT	Canadair CL.600-2B16 Challenger	5940	C-GVFI
EI-TIM	Piper J-5A Cub Cruiser	5-36	N27151, NC27151
EI-TKI	Robinson R22 Beta	1195	G-OBIP
EI-TOM	Bell 407	53744	N5080N, C-FLVT
EI-TON	Raj Hamsa X'Air 582	718	G-CCCZ
EI-TVG	Boeing 737-7ZF	60406	LY-TVG
EI-UFO	Piper PA-22-150 Tri-Pacer (T/w conversion)	22-4942	G-BRZR, N7045D
EI-UNA	Boeing 767-3P6ER	26233	A4O-GU
EI-UNB	Boeing 767-3P6ER	26234	A4O-GY
EI-UND	Boeing 767-3P6ER	26236	A4O-GS
EI-UNF	Boeing 767-3P6ER	26238	A4O-GT
EI-UNH	Boeing 737-524	28916	N14655
EI-UNL	Boeing 777-312	28515	9V-SYA
EI-UNM	Boeing 777-312	28534	9V-SYD
EI-UNN	Boeing 777-312	28517	9V-SYC
EI-UNP	Boeing 777-312	28516	9V-SYB
EI-UNR	Boeing 777-212ER	28523	9V-SRE
EI-UNT	Boeing 777-222ER	28999	9V-SRC
EI-UNU	Boeing 777-222ER	28998	9V-SRB
EI-UNW	Boeing 777-222	30214	N208UA
EI-UNX	Boeing 777-222	30213	N207UA
EI-UNY	Boeing 777-222	26918	N767UA
EI-UNZ	Boeing 777-222	26925	N770UA
EI-VII	Van's RV-7	73114	
EI-VLN	Piper PA-18A-150 Super Cub	18-6797	G-ASCU, VP-JBL
EI-WAC	Piper PA-23-250 Aztec E	27-4683	G-AZBK, N14077
EI-WAT	Tecnam P.2002-JF Sierra	086	
EI-WFD	Tecnam P.2002-JF Sierra	080	
EI-WFI	Canadair CL.600-2B16 Challenger	5812	C-FYUS
EI-WIG	Best Off Sky Ranger 912	SKR0504608	
EI-WMN	Piper PA-23-250 Aztec F	27-7954063	G-ZSFT, G-SALT, G-BGTH, N2551M, N9731N
EI-WOT	Currie Wot	PFA/3019	G-CWOT
EI-WWI	Robinson R44 Raven II	11799	
EI-WXA	Avro 146-RJ85	E2310	N503XJ, G-6-310
EI-WXP	Hawker 800XP	258382	SE-DYE, N23451
EI-XLB	Boeing 747-446	26359	N913UN, JA8913
EI-XLC	Boeing 747-446	27100	N919UN, JA8919
EI-XLD	Boeing 747-446	26360	N914UN, JA8914
EI-XLE	Boeing 747-446	26362	N916UN, JA8916
EI-XLF	Boeing 747-446	27645	N921MM, JA8921, N747BA
EI-XLG	Boeing 747-446	29899	N917UN, JA8917, N6009F
EI-XLH	Boeing 747-446	27650	N918UN, JA8918
EI-XLI	Boeing 747-446	27648	N920UN, JA8920, N6005C
EI-XLJ	Boeing 747-446	27646	N922UN, JA8922, N747BJ
EI-XLK	Boeing 747-412	29950	N747NB, 9V-SPM
EI-XLL	Boeing 747-412	28031	N747NP, 9V-SPN
EI-XLM	Boeing 747-412	28028	N747WV, 9V-SPO
EI-XLN	Boeing 747-412	28029	9V-SPP
EI-XLO	Boeing 747-412	28025	N747KD, 9V-SPQ
EI-XLP	Boeing 777-312	28531	9V-SYE
EI-XLZ	Boeing 747-444	29119	N747ZA, ZS-SAZ
EI-YLG	Robin HR200/120B	336	G-BYLG
EI-ZMA	Dassault Falcon 900EX	134	VP-CFR, VP-CEZ, F-WWFL
EI-ZZZ	Bell 222	47061	(EI-MED), N40EA, SE-HTN, G-DMAF, G-BLSZ, D-HCHS, (D-HAAD)

Reportedly sold or transferred to Ireland, the following are mostly no longer current in their last country of registration:

Reg	Type	C/n	Previous identities
EI-. . .	Aérospatiale SA.315B Lama	2661	I-EPEP
EI-. . .	Autogyro Europe Calidus	RSUK/CALS/004	G-CGJD
EI-. . .	Bensen B.8M	PFA G/01-1170	G-BSMG
EI-. . .	Bensen B.8M	PFA G/01-1196	G-BTAH
EI-. . .	Campbell Cricket replica	PFA G/03-1267	G-BWUZ
EI-. . .	Cessna 150M	15077093	G-BSBZ, N63086
EI-. . .	CFM Starstreak Shadow	K 288	G-OLGA
EI-. . .	Champion 7KCAB Citabria	124	N93SA
EI-. . .	DHC-1 Chipmunk 22	C1/0659	G-BXDP, WK642
EI-. . .	Eurowing Goldwing	GW-001	G-MJDP
EI-. . .	Flylight Dragonfly/Discus 15T	025	G-CFSO
EI-. . .	Gardan GY-80-180 Horizon	228	G-GYBO, OY-DTN, SE-FGL, OY-DTN
EI-. . .	ICP MXP-740 Savannah VG	03-12-51-261	G-CCSV
EI-. . .	Isaacs Fury	PFA/011-10742	G-BKZM
EI-. . .	Jodel D.120A	295	G-BMLB, F-BNCI
EI-. . .	Light Aero Avid Flyer	PFA/189-12037	G-BTKG
EI-. . .	Piper J-3C-65 Cub	16108	C-FLEI, CF-LEI, N88484, NC88484
EI-. . .	Piper PA-22-108 Colt	22-8199	G-ARJF
EI-. . .	Quad City Challenger II	PFA/177-12167	G-MYAG
EI-. . .	Raj Hamsa X'Air 133	675/BMAA/HB/331	G-CCWF
EI-. . .	Rans S-4 Coyote	89-098	G-MVXW
EI-. . .	Rans S-6ES Coyote II	PFA/204-12580	G-MYMR
EI-. . .	Rans S-6ESD Coyote II	1291.250 / PFA/204-12581	G-MYMP
EI-. . .	Rans S-6ESD Coyote II	0696.1001	G-MZEO
EI-. . .	Raven Aircraft Raven X	SN2232/0257	G-MTHC
EI-. . .	Rotorway Exec	3827	G-PURS
EI-. . .	Solar Wings Pegasus XL-Q (Trike c/n SW-TE-0022)	SW-WX-0013	G-MTJS
EI-. . .	Solar Wings Pegasus XL-R (Trike c/n SW-TB-1230)	SW-WA-1235	G-MTOJ
EI-. . .	Solar Wings Pegasus XL-R (Trike c/n SW-TB-1412)	SW-WA-1449	G-MWCU
EI-. . .	Solar Wings Pegasus XL-Q (Trike c/n SW-TE-0355)	SW-WQ-0468	G-MWWG
EI-. . .	Thruster TST Mk.1	8028-TST-061	G-MTVV
EI-. . .	Van's RV-6	PFA/181-12845	G-KELL
EI-. . .	Wassmer WA-81 Piranha	804	F-GAIF
EI-. . .	Whittaker MW-5B Sorcerer	SR102-R440B-02	G-MTBP

EK - ARMENIA

Regn.	Type	C/n	Prev.Id.
EK-RA01	Airbus A319-132CJ (Now flies as Government '701')	0913	HZ-NAS, VP-CAJ, G-OMAK, F-WWIF, G-OMAK, F-WWIF, G-OMAK, D-AVYL
EK-2042	Beech B200C King Air	BL-42	C-GIND, N819CD, N500BX
EK-2809	Antonov An-28	1AJ009-09	ST-TRC, YL-KAF, RA-28943, CCCP28943
EK-2815	Antonov An-28	1AJ004-15	ST-BRY, EX-916, 9L-LFS, 9XR-KG, 9U-BHR, UR-ZAN, 28766, UR-28766, RA-28766, CCCP28766
EK-4104	LET 401UVP-E	861606	UP-L4104, UN-67566, HA-LAK, UN-67566. RA-67566, CCCP67566
EK-11418	Antonov An-12BP	7344705	EX-166, EX-022, 3C-QRN, ER-AXB, UR-11418, CCCP11418
EK-12755	Antonov An-12 (Noted 8.15)	unkn	
EK-12908	Antonov An-12B (Wfu at Yerevan, stored)	7344908	EK-11029, RA-11029, CCCP11029
EK-20014	Canadair CL-600-2B19 Regional Jet 200LR (Wfu 2013)	7282	D-ACJI, C-FNMY
EK 26005	Antonov An-26B	12205	SP-FDS, RA-26116, CCCP26116
EK-26050	Antonov An-26B (Stored)	173109-05	ER-AFE, RA-26050, CCCP26050
EK-26310	Antonov An-26B (Wfu 8.15)	13310	UR-CFX, RA-26597, CCCP26597
EK-26407	Antonov An-26	6407	4L-BKA, LZ-MNH, YR-ITA, LZ-MNH, UR-26504, CCCP26504
EK-26710	Antonov An-26B-100 (Wfu 8.15)	12710	ER-AZU, RomAF;710, YR-ADH
EK-26804	Antonov An-26 (Wfu 8.15)	8004	ER-AUW, ER-AWW, RA-26246, CCCP26165
EK-26819	Antonov An-26	4507	3X-GFG, 3X-GDP, EK-26442, ER-AZQ
EK-26878	Antonov An-26	8303	3X-GFH, 3X-GEL, EX-106, RA-26185, CCCP26185
EK-28019	Antonov An-28	1AJ010-19	ER-AJD, SP-DFA, C5-GAD, SP-DDF
EK-28925	Antonov An-28 (Carries 'fake' c/n plate 1AJ008-13)	1AJ001-03	S9-PSV, ER-AKO, CCCP28801
EK-30018	Airbus A300B4-605R (Wfu, Stored)	518	HS-TAH, F-WWAE
EK-30064	Airbus A300B4-605R (Wfu, Stored)	464	HS-TAG, F-WWAL
EK-30068	Airbus A300B4-601 (Wfu, Stored)	368	HS-TAA, F-WWAG
EK-30098	Airbus A300B4-601 (Wfu, Stored)	398	HS-TAF, F-WWAN
EK-32008	Airbus A320-211	0229	N229AN, VH-HYL, F-WWIN
EK-32109	Antonov An-32B	2109	ST-NSP, ER-AZW, S9-BOI, ER-AEU, 4K-66756, 66756, CCCP66756
EK-32120	Antonov An-32A	1604	EK-32604, 9L-LFO, RA-29120, CCCP29120
EK-32458	Antonov An-32B	2410	EK-32410, 9L-LFU, RA-48121, CCCP48121
EK-32500	Antonov An-32B	2009	9L-LFP, ST-AQU, RA-69344, CCCP69344
EK-32703	Antonov An-32B	1703	3X-GHC, 4L-GSI, 3X-GES, 4L-GSI, 4L-OVE, S9-GBC, 9Q-CAF, EL-WCB, RA48094, CCCP48094
EK-32803	Antonov An-32B (Stored by 2.15)	2803	S9-PSE, UR-48053, CCCP48053
EK-32805	Antonov An-32B (Stored by 2.15)	2805	S7-GSM, ER-AZI, UR-48055, CCCP48055
EK-32968	BAe Jetstream 3201	968	ZK-ECR, ZK-JSQ, ZK-REW, N968AE, G-31-968
EK-42470	Yakovlev Yak-42D	4520424116677	RA-42444, CU-T1249, RA-42444, YL-LBY, B-2753
EK-47835	Antonov An-24B (For museum, Thailand)	17307307	47835, RA-47835, CCCP47835
EK-65072	Tupolev Tu-134A-3 (Stored)	49972	CCCP65072, ES-AAL
EK-72101	Antonov An-72 100	36572040548	4L-VAS, RA-72918, CCCP72928
EK-72903	Antonov An-72	36572020385	D2-MBP, EK-72903, RA-72903, CCCP72903
EK-72928	Antonov An-72-100	36572060640	UR-CFI, EK-72102, 4L-AAL, RA-72928, CCCP72928
EK-73733	Boeing 737-275 (Wfu)	21819	EX-127, AP-BHU, EX-015, C-GKPW
EK-73755	Boeing 737-229C	21139	EX-050, TJ-AIO, G-BYZN, OO-SDP
EK-73772	Boeing 737-55S	28472	OK-DGL
EK-73775	Boeing 737-55S	28475	OK-EGO
EK-73797	Boeing 737-505	26297	VP-BEW, N371LF, B-2529, LN-BUA
EK-74036	Antonov An-74-200	36547098965	RA-74036
EK-74043	Antonov An-74-200	36547098944	RA-74043
EK-74045	Antonov An-74-200	36547098966	RA-74060
EK-74052	Antonov An-74-200	36547098444	RA-74052
EK-74711	Boeing 747-SR81F (Damaged at Abuja 12.13)	22711	SX-DCB, N146RF, JA8158
EK-74786	Boeing 747-281F	25171	4L-MRK, VP-BIJ, JA8194
EK-74787	Boeing 747-281F	24576	4L-TZS, VP-BII, JA8191
EK-74798	Boeing 747-281F (Damaged 2013, stored)	23698	N288RF, JA8181, N6055C
EK-74923	Antonov An-74-200	36547096923	EK-74043, RA-74043, UR-74043
EK-76155	Ilyushin Il-76TD (Stored)	093421637	EK-75754, RA-76754, CCCP76754, YI-AKU
EK-76992	Ilyushin Il-76TD	073410292	EK-76292, EK-76707, RA-76495, ST-SFT, RA-76495, CCCP76495, YI-AIK
EK-85403	Tupolev Tu-154B2 (Stored as '85403')	80A-403	CCCP85403
EK-86117	Ilyushin Il-86 (Stored)	51483209085	CCCP86117
EK-86724	Ilyushin Il-76M	073410284	EP-TPZ, EK-86724, CCCP86724
EK-87662	Yakovlev Yak-40 (Last noted as '87662')	9240625	RA-87662, UN-87662, CCCP87662
EK-88167	Yakovlev Yak-40 (Preserved beside Lake Sevan)	9610147	CCCP88167
EK-88250	Yakovlev Yak-40 (Stored)	9640452	RA-88250
EK-88256	Yakovlev Yak-40 (Preserved at Ashtarak)	9711152	CCCP88256
EK-.	Diamond DA 40D Star	D4.225	G-OCCD

ER - MOLDOVA

Regn.	Type	C/n	Prev.Id.
ER-AEJ	Antonov An-72	36572094889	ER-ACA(1), ER-72977, HK-3808X, CCCP72977
ER-AFZ	Antonov An-72	36572070698	ER-72933, CCCP72933
ER-AIR	Antonov An-2V (floatplane)	1G131-25	UR-50583, CCCP50583
ER-AIX	Ilyushin Il-76TD	0063470088	ER-AIP, EY-701, EY-660, EK-76485, UP-I7637, EW-258TH, UN-76485, RA-76485, 76485, CCCP76485
ER-AUB	Antonov An-26	12409	CzAF:2409
ER-AUC	Antonov An-26	13209	CzAF:3209
ER-AUD	Antonov An-26	12408	CzAF:2408
ER-AUE	Antonov An-26B	14201	CzAF:4201, UN-26206, CCCP26206
ER-AVA	Antonov An-26B-100	11409	UR-26072, RA-26072, CCCP26072
ER-AVB	Antonov An-26B-100	3204	RA-26556, 26556, CCCP26556
ER-AVK	Antonov An-26	13808	RomAF:808, YR-ADL
ER-AVL	Antonov An-26	13809	RomAF:809, YR-ADM
ER-AWF	Antonov An-72	36572070696	ER-72932, CCCP72932
ER-AWZ	Antonov An-30A (Stored by2.15)	1103	RomAF:1103, RomAF:103
ER-AXJ	Airbus A320-231	2295	C5-AAH, EY-626, XY-AGM, 5B-DBC, F-WWIE
ER-AXL	Airbus A319-112	2849	B-6156, D-AVXJ
ER-AXO	Airbus A320-231	0357	EX-32004, XA-UCZ, G-BVYB, OO-TCB, G-BVYB, F-WWBH
ER-AXP	Airbus A320-233	0741	N452TA, F-WWBK
ER-AXU	Airbus A320-231	424	RP-C5323, C5-AAR, F-WTDF, G-CRPH, F-WQBB, F-WWIV
ER-AXV	Airbus A320-211	0622	F-WQSG, VH-HYR, F-WWBU
ER-AZB	Antonov An24RV	27307507	RA-47690, CCCP47690
ER-AZO	Antonov An-26B	10606	EX-26001, ER-AZO, EX-26036, CCCP26036
ER-AZP	Antonov An-24RV	17307002	RA-47810, CCCP47810
ER-AZX	Antonov An-24RV	47309804	RA-46687, CCCP46687
ER-BAM	Boeing 747-409SF	24312	4L-BCC, D-ACGB, N482AT, B-18275, B-164
ER-COS	Cessna 182P	0006/18263805	HA-TUP, F-BXAL, N6702M
ER-COT	Cessna 172N	17268025	D-EDAO, N75900
ER-CSA	Reims/Cessna F150L	F15000790	OE-AUA, OE-BUA, OE-ATA
ER-DOT	Diamond DA 42 Twin Star	42.273	OE-UDO
ER-ECB	Embraer ERJ-190-100LR	19000325	PT-TXN
ER-ECC	Embraer ERJ-190-100LR	19000130	F-OSUD, PT-SQZ
ER-ECD	Embraer ERJ-190-100LR	19000310	PH-IAM, TC-YAK, D-AEMF, PT-TZY
ER-EMA	Embraer EMB-120RT Brasilia	120223	N246CA, PT-SSS
ER-IAE	Ilyushin Il-76TD	0073479367	ER-IAW, EY-702, EY-680, EK-76111, EK, 76487, UN-76487, RA-76487, CCCP76487
ER-IAF	Ilyushin Il-76T	0003423699	4L-SKL, UP-I7627, ER-IBV, RA-76521, CCCP76521
ER-IAV	Ilyushin Il-76TD	0064571150	UR-76704, RA-76704, CCCP76704
ER-IAX	Ilyushin Il-76TD	0063470088	ER-IAR, ER-IAP, EY-701, EY-660, EK-76485, UP-17637, EW-258TH, UN-76485, RA76485, 76485, CCCP76485
ER-IAY	Ilyushin Il-76MD	1033418596	ER-IAI, EK-76381, ST-ATI, RA-76381
ER-IAZ	Ilyushin Il-76TD	1023412399	ER-IAK, EK-76401, RA-76401, CCCP76401
ER-IBI	Ilyushin Il-76TD	1013409303	ER-IAM, UP-I7626, YU-AMJ, UN-78734, RA-78734, UR-78734, (HA-TCA), CCCP78734
ER-IBR	Ilyushin Il-76TD	0043454623	UR-CBR, UR-76603, CCCP76603
ER-IBU	Ilyushin Il-76TD	1023414450	ER-IAH, EK-76450, EK-76442 UP-I7634, UN-76442, CCCP76442
ER-ICS	Ilyushin Il-18D	187009903	UR-CEO, D2-FDL, UR-TMD, ER-ICL, YR-IML
ER-JAI	Boeing 747-412F	26562	N743WA, N265MS, 9V-SPG
ER-JIL	Airbus A300B4-605R	626	A6-JIL, N77080, F-WWAR
ER-KGA	Kamov Ka.32T	5235002991101	HA-HSB, UR-CBK
ER-KGB	Kamov Ka.32T	523001788613	HA-HSD, UR-CBM
ER-KGE	Kamov Ka.32A	8708	RA-31586, CCCP31586
ER-KGF	Kamov Ka.32T	523001583602	UR-AAC, ER-KGF
ER-KKL	Embraer EMB-135BJ Legacy 650	14501191	PR-LBE
ER-LSA	Roko Aero NG-4 Via	unkn	
ER-MGH	Mil Mi-8MTV-1	93507	N507SL, LZ-MOY
ER-MGJ	Mil Mi-8PS	10734	MoldAF, RomAF: 08
ER-MGL	Mil Mi-17-1V	498M01	
ER-MGQ	Mil Mi-8 MTV-1	95603	EX-08012, YA-MGA, 9N-ADS, RA-25459, CCCP-25459
ER-MGR	Mil Mi-8T	98308422	EX-40002, ER-MGR, UR-AAD, UR-22715, CCCP22715
ER-MGY	Mil Mi-8PS	10735	YR-MLB, RomAF:735
ER-MHD	Mil Mi-8 MTV-1	95864	Mold.AF:02black, LZ-..., CCCP27030
ER-MHE	Mil Mi-8 MTV-1	95865	CCCP27031
ER-MHF	Mil Mi-8 MTV-1	95862	CCCP27028
ER-MHG	Mil Mi-8 MTV-1	95861	CCCP27027
ER-MHH	Mil Mi-8 MTV-1	96121	RA-25746(2)
ER-MHK	Mil Mi-8 MTV-1	95863	UR-CIN, ER-MHK, MoldAF, ER-MHK, MoldAF 01, CCCP27029
ER-MHN	Mil Mi-8PS	8562	UR-AAV, TC-HDK, UR-24636
ER-MHR	Mil Mi-8 MTV-1	95952	RA-27125, CCCP27125
ER-MHS	Mil Mi-17	103M11	BulgAF:410
ER-MHU	Mil Mi-8 MTV-1	95617	EX-921, ST-BDH, RA-24029, CCCP25473
ER-MHV	Mil Mi-17	103M13	BulgAF:412
ER-MHY	Mil Mi-8 MTV-1	95533	EX-08005, UK-25423, RA25-423,CCCP25423
ER-MHZ	Mil Mi-8 MTV-1	96078	RA-22503
ER-MYA	Mil Mi-8 MTV-1	95637	ER-MHW, RA-25492, CCCP25492
ER-MYB	Mil Mi-8 MTV-1	93309	ER-MGW, 9Q-CXD, LZ-CDN, UN-....., RA-....., CCCP ....
ER-RPA	Robinson R44 Astro	0164	YR-ADV
ER-WOA	PZL-104 Wilga 35A (Wfu)	128456	DOSAAF '14'red
ER-XTA	Lilienthal X-32 Bekas	3217	
ER-XVA	Lilienthal X-32 Bekas	3216	
ER-XVR	Lilienthal X-32 Bekas	3226	
ER-YGD	Yakovlev Yak-40 (Stored)	9831458	RA-87970, CCCP87970
ER-YOC	Yakovlev Yak-18T	22202034090	LZ-527
ER-07206	Antonov An-2TP	1G146-35	CCCP07206
ER-07351	Antonov An-2P	1G149-55	YR-SRH, ER-07351, CCCP07351
ER-07863	Antonov An-2	1G170-22	CCCP07863
ER-19316	Kamov Ka-26 (To museum)	7203105	YR-CYV, ER-19316, YR-CZM, YR-19316, CCCP19316
ER-19622	Kamov Ka-26 (Stored)	7405110	CCCP19622
ER-20121	Mil Mi-2	543022063	CCCP20121
ER-20727	Mil Mi-2	527544032	CCCP20727
ER-20739	Mil Mi-2	547636052	EW-20739, ER-20739, CCCP20739
ER-20830	Mil Mi-2	548103033	CCCP20830
ER-23237	Mil Mi-2	5210238057	CCCP23237
ER-23334	Mil Mi-2	529223055	CCCP23334
ER-65036	Tupolev Tu-134A (Preserved at Chisinau Airport)	48700	CCCP65036
ER-65094	Tupolev Tu-134A-3 (Wfu)	60255	CCCP65094
ER-65140	Tupolev Tu-134A-3 (Wfu ?)	60932	CCCP65140
ER-75929	Ilyushin Il-18D (Wfu)	187010505	CCCP75929, CCCP74251

BALLOONS

ER-CRA	Cameron O-105 HAFB	4311	D-OALI(3)
ER-KPO	AT-104 90A HAFB	1430814	
ER-KPX	AT-104 90A HAFB	1050514	
ER-KRA	AT-104 HAFB	1710609	
ER-KRB	Kubicek BB-30Z HAFB	764	

ULTRALIGHTS

0007	Aerostar 01F Festival	unkn
0008	Aerostar 01F Festival	unkn
0029	TL Ultralight TL-2000 Sting	unkn
0031	TL Ultralight TL-2000 Sting Carbon	unkn
0040	Unknown type	unkn

ES - ESTONIA

Regn.	Type	C/n	Prev.Id.
ES-ACA	Aero Commander 500	803-80	OH-ACA, N8464C
ES-ACB	Canadair CL-600-2D24 Regional Jet 900	15261	C-GIBH(2)
ES-ACC	Canadair CL-600-2D24 Regional Jet 900	15262	C-GIBQ
ES-ACD	Canadair CL-600-2D24 Regional Jet 900	15276	C-GZQK
ES-ACE	Canadair CL-600-2C10 Regional Jet 700	10083	D-ACPN, C-GIAU
ES-ACF	Canadair CL-600-2C10 Regional Jet 700	10085	D-ACPO, C-FZYS
ES-ACG	Canadair CL-600-2D24 Regional Jet 900	15277	N666RD, N151MN, C-GIAZ
ES-ACL	Aero Grand Commander 680FL	1373-46	OH-ACO, OY-DLL, N899NA, N414N
ES-AEB	Embraer ERJ-170-100STD	17000106	OH-LEF, PT-SAO
ES-AEC	Embraer ERJ-170-100STD	17000107	OH-LEG, PT-SAP
ES-ANS	Cessna 172R Skyhawk	17280581	N7274K
ES-ASO	SAAB-Scania SF.340B	223	SE-KSI, D-CASB, SE-KSI, VH-EKK, SE-KSI, SE-G23
ES-BAB	Antonov An-2D	1G160-38	EstAF 42 yel, ES-BAB, DOSAAF 09 red
ES-BAH	Antonov An-2R	1G172-34	RA-40726, CCCP40762
ES-BHB	Beech C33 Debonair	unkn	
ES-CAB	Antonov An-2R	1G219-07	CCCP32608
ES-CAC	Antonov An-2R	1G206-45	CCCP17940
ES-CAD	Antonov An-2R (Painted as DDR-SKA)	1G194-36	CCCP68096
ES-CAG(2)	Antonov An-2T	1G160-28	ES-BAG, DOSAAF
ES-CLS	Flight Design CT LS ELA	unkn	
ES-CMK	Beech 400XT Beechjet	RK-209	N413LX, (N439LX), N799TA
ES-ECA	Cessna 310K	310K0161	SE-GTY, LN-TSA, N7061L
ES-ECB	Cessna F150J	F150-0452	OH-CBO
ES-ECD	Cessna F172G	F172-0254	OH-CEM
ES-ECE	Reims/Cessna F172P	F17202196	OH-BFO, SE-IPN, G-BKWH
ES-ECF	Cessna 172R Skyhawk	17281519	N61843
ES-ECG	Reims/Cessna F172L	F17200873	OH-CFP
ES-ECH	Cessna 172P Skyhawk	17276046	N96229
ES-ECM	Cessna 150J	15069492	N50699
ES-ECN	Reims/Cessna F150L	F15000891	OH-CFT
ES-ECP	Cessna 150M	15076454	ES-FCB, OH-CMZ, N8AZ, (N3302V)
ES-ECR	Reims/Cessna F172N	F17201950	OE-DHV
ES-ECY	Cessna 172R Skyhawk	17281530	N62737
ES-ELI	Cessna 750 Citation X	750-0115	OH-PPI, N5085E
ES-EPA	Piper PA-31 Navajo C	31-7612088	SE-KZA, PH-TUR, D-IBRU, N62859
ES-ESA	SOCATA MS.893A Rallye Commodore 180	11891	OY-ANS, SE-FSH
ES-FCC	Cessna 172M	17262412	OH-CVX, C-FIGO, N12967
ES-FPC	Piper PA-28-140 Cherokee B	28-26267	OH-PCC, N5544U
ES-FPM	Piper PA-34-200T Seneca II	34-8070191	D-GLHW, N14EG, N8191J
ES-FPW	Piper PA-28R-200 Cherokee Arrow	28R-35289	OH-PJW
ES-FSR	Cirrus SR22	3214	HA-CID, N486CT
ES-GCE	Autogyro Europe Calidus	C00312	
ES-GMR	Magni M22 Voyager	22074324	
ES-HEL	Enstrom 480B	5118	XA-UKO
ES-HOG	Eurocopter EC.130T2 Ecureuil	8236	
ES-HPK	Robinson R-22 Beta	0639	OH-HBG, ES-HPK, G-LAND
ES-HRA	Robinson R44 Astro	0242	ZS-RHD
ES-HRE	Rotorway Exec 162F	KR-162F-001	N436BB
ES-HRG	Robinson R44 Raven I	1917	G-WCOM
ES-HRH	Robinson R44 Raven I	1913	YL-HHB, EI-EHP, G-LNAD
ES-HRK	Robinson R44 Raven I	1900	OK-MIS(1)
ES-HRM	Robinson R44 Raven I	2176	D-HLYT
ES-III	Bombardier Learjet 60	60-303	OH-III, OE-GTO, (OH-GVI), (OE-GJA), N40075
ES-JFA	Fairchild Swearingen SA.227AC Metro III	AC-657	SX-BBX(2), N26902
ES-JPL	CEA Jodel DR.1050 Ambassadeur (Modified)	204	OH-JOB
ES-JRS	SAN Jodel D.117 Grand Tourisme	B729	F-BIDV
ES-KRB	Aérospatiale/Alenia ATR-72-201	140	OH-KRB, F-WWER
ES-LSA	SAAB-Scania SF.340A	055	LY-NSA, SE-KPE, PH-KJH, LN-NVE, SE-E55
ES-LSB	SAAB-Scania SF.340A	045	LY-NSB, SE-ISV, SE-E45
ES-LSC	SAAB-Scania SF.340A	037	LY-NSC, SE-KPD, PH-KJL, LN-NVD, SE-E37
ES-LSD	SAAB-Scania SF.340A	080	SE-ISY, SE-E45
ES-LSE	SAAB-Scania SF.340A	132	ES-ASM, SE-LMT, ZK-NLC, SE-LMT, OK-TOP, OM-BAA, OK-TOP, SE-KFA, EC-GGK, EC-229, SE-F32, HB-AHS, SE-F32
ES-LSF	SAAB-Scania SF.340A	144	D-COLE, LV-WTF, LV-PMG, ZK-NSM, D-CHBB, SE-F44
ES-LSG	SAAB-Scania SF.340A	007	HA-TAE, S5-BAT, S5-BAN, G-CDYE, SE-LBP, EC-JPH, SE-LBP, OY-SCF, (OY-GMS), SE-LBP, OH-SAG, YL-BAG, SE-LBP, HB-AHB, SE-E07
ES-LSH	SAAB-Scania SF.340A	011	HA-TAF, LZ-SAC, S5-BAD, VH-KEQ, 9M-MSB, N342AM, SE-E11
ES-LVA	Bombardier Learjet 60	60-372	N50153
ES-LVC	Bombardier Learjet 60	60-281	OH-GVE, D-CGTF, OE-GTF, "OE-GTS", N5013U
ES-MAA	Cessna 208B Grand Caravan	208B1279	D-FAAA, N5225K
ES-MHG	Beech A36AT Bonanza	E-2661	D-EAYQ
ES-MPV	Piper PA-23-250 Aztec E	27-7304983	OH-PNJ, N14388
ES-NXT	Beech 400A Beechjet	RK-268	N789TA, (N489FL), (N453LX), N789TA,
ES-PCO	Cessna 172R Skyhawk	17281181	N21283
ES-PEG	Enstrom 480B	5094	N4924
ES-PHR	Hawker 750	HB-33	N63633
ES-PJA	BAe Jetstream 3102	749	G-NOSS, LN-FAZ, C-GJPU, (N839JS), G-31-749
ES-PJB	BAe Jetstream 3102	622	G-LOVB, VH-HSW, G-31-622, G-BLCB, G-31-622
ES-PJD	BAe Jetstream 3102	773	G-EIGG, SE-LGH, OY-SVO, C-FAMK, G-31-773
ES-PJG	BAe Jetstream 3103	701	ES-LJD, OY-SVR, D-CONA(3), (PH-KJH), G-31-701
ES-PJR	BAe Jetstream 3201	949	SE-LNU, VH-XFC, N949AE, G-31-949
ES-PLB	LET L-410UVP	851413	LY-AVY, RA-67509, CCCP67509
ES-PLW	LET L-410UVP (T)	810726	ES-EPA, 53+01, LSK 313
ES-PLY	LET L-410UVP	810727	ES-EPI, 53+02, LSK-316
ES-PSF	Schweizer 269C	S-1774	SE-JCZ, N69A
ES-PVH	Gates Learjet 31A	31A-162	N125GP, N162LJ, N525GP
ES-PVI	Bombardier Learjet 60	60-275	N101UD
ES-PVP	Bombardier Learjet 60	60-302	OE-GJA, N5012H
ES-PWA	AgustaWestland AW139	31069	I-EASV
ES-PWB	AgustaWestland AW139	31144	I-RAIU
ES-PWC	AgustaWestland AW139	31333	
ES-RAB	PZL-104 Wilga 35A (Dismantled)	107370	DOSAAF
ES-RAC	PZL-104 Wilga 35A	128435	DOSAAF
ES-RAF	PZL-104 Wilga 35A	17820668	DOSAAF
ES-RAZ	Aero L-39C Albatros	931523	G-OALB, ES-ZLD, Soviet AF
ES-RID	SOCATA MS.894A Minerva 220	11939	D-EDCJ
ES-RWE	PZL-104 Wilga 35A	17820681	DOSAAF
ES-SAK	Airbus A320-214	0888	EI-EZA, D-AHHF, EA-EZA, HB-JIW, F-HBAC, EC-GZE, F-HBAC, EC-GZE, F-WWDG
ES-SAM	Airbus A320-232	1896	D-ANNJ, N553JB, F-WWBY
ES-SHB	Aviat A-1B Husky	2291	G-JJDC, N96HY
ES-SLS	Dassault Falcon 900EX	264	OY-SLS, F-WWFK
ES-TAC	PZL-104 Wilga 35A	17830694	EstAF 50 black, ES-TAC, DOSAAF 26
ES-TAD	PZL-104 Wilga 35A	128433	DOSAAF 15
ES-TAE	PZL-104 Wilga 35A (Wfu?)	18840779	DOSAAF
ES-TLB	Aero L-39C Albatros	031824	
ES-TLC	Aero L-39C Albatros	533223	
ES-TLF	Aero L-39C Albatros	132114	
ES-TLG	Aero L-39C Albatros	131849	
ES-TLH	Aero L-39C Albatros	132042	
ES-TLM '4'	Aero L-39C Albatros	530431	
ES-TLN '2'	Aero L-39C Albatros	530432	
ES-TLP '3'	Aero L-39C Albatros	530515	
ES-TLQ '5'	Aero L-39C Albatros	530523	
ES-TLS	Aero L-39C Albatros	031826	LithAF 08, LithAF 04, Soviet AF
ES-TLU	Aero L-39C Albatros	unkn	
ES-TWG	PZL-104 Wilga 35A	18840781	DOSAAF
ES-UBC	Evektor EV-97R Eurostar (on floats)	2002 1506	
ES-UBS	Evektor EV-97 Eurostar SL	2010 3716	
ES-UCA	Comco Ikarus C-42 Cyclone	0107-6367	
ES-UCB	Comco Ikarus C-42 Cyclone	0208-6469	
ES-UFM	Urban Air UFM-13 Lambada	39/13	
ES-UHA	X-32 Bekas	346	
ES-UIN	Ekolot JK-05L Junior	05-05-10	
ES-ULM	Aeroprakt A-22 Vision	114	ES-LTL
ES-UNU	Murphy Renegade Spirit	108	
ES-URA	Rans S-12 Airaile	4655274	
ES-URB	Aeros powered hang glider	086	
ES-URV	Quad City Challenger II	CH2-0109-LSSLW-0155	
ES-VCW	Cessna 172M	17260805	OH-CTZ, C-GEXJ, N19852
ES-VLE	Dyn'Aero MCR-4S	102	OO-151
ES-VPM	Piper PA-28-180 Cherokee Archer	28-7505177	OY-TOS
ES-YLF	Aero L-39C Albatros	433141	
ES-YLI	Aero L-39C Albatros	433142	
ES-YLP	Aero L-39C Albatros	533620	
ES-YLR	Aero L-39C Albatros	533628	
ES-YLS	Aero L-39C Albatros	533638	
ES-YLX	Aero L-39C Albatros	432905	Khyrg.AF 105
ES-...	Aero L-39C Albatros	031612	N2399X
ES-...	Aero L-39C Albatros	432845	N39EP
ES-U..	Beaver RX-650	0003	OH-U211
ES-U..	Beaver RX-650	0009	OH-U268
ES-...	Beech 35 Bonanza	D-302	N2895V, NC2895V
ES-...	Comco Ikarus Fox C-22	8903-3194	OH-U132
ES-...	Extra EA.300/L	1202	N202FU
ES-...	Hoffman H-36 Dimona	36262	SE-UCY, (SE-UCX), D-KCCC, OE-9305
ES-...	Monnett Sonerai IIL	921	N942RP
ES-...	Rotorway Scorpion 133	1342	N613EL
ES-...	SOCATA MS.893A Rallye Commodore 180	11030	D-E..., F-BRDZ
ES-...	Super Aero 45	03-007	OH-EFC, OY-EFC, G-BFAZ, D-GGAM, D-EGAM

BALLOONS

ES-HAB	Thunder AX9-120 SII HAFB	2337	LY-OSB, D-OSBD
ES-HAC	Cameron A-180 HAFB	2251	SE-ZEO
ES-HAD	Cameron N-77 HAFB	2152	SE-ZEM
ES-HAE	Cameron A-120 HAFB	1943	SE-ZDU
ES-HAF	Cameron A-210 HAFB	2633	SE-ZFM
ES-HAH	Interavia 80TA HAFB	0260292	
ES-HAL	Lindstrand HiFlyer	unkn	
ES-HAS	Interavia 80TA HAFB	0270999	
ES-H..	Cameron A-120 HAFB	1860	SE-ZDM
ES-H..	Colt 240A HAFB	1408	SE-ZDV
ES-H..	Colt 105A HAFB	1619	SE-ZEG

MICROLIGHTS (Weightshift)

ES-KAK	Bogdola Janos Powered Hang Glider	BB	
ES-KAN	Ferrari Tirelli II	unkn	
ES-KAR	Ferrari Tirelli 1	unkn	
ES-KAS	Poisk-06 Hang Glider	R-1205	
ES-KAT	Powered Hang Glider	unkn	
ES-KAU	Air Création Clipper / Kiss 450	A04080-4079	
ES-KEK	Aeros Powered Hang Glider	unkn	
ES-KEV	Powered Hang Glider MD-20	3139	
ES-KHK	Poisk-06 Powered Hang Glider	R-0210	
ES-KIA	Powered Hang Glider	unkn	
ES-KIP	Powered Hang Glider	unkn	
ES-KLM	Powered Hang Glider	unkn	
ES-KLY	Powered Hang Glider MD-20	3033	
ES-KMP	Powered Hang Glider (Homebuilt)	unkn	
ES-KNB	Grats P2 Powered Hang Glider	043	
ES-KRG	Poisk-06 Hang Glider	R-2518	
ES-KUS	Airborne Edge XT912 /	XT912-0196	
ES-KVP	VP Magni Powered Hang Glider	unkn	
ES-K..	Pegasus Quantum 15	6917	G-MYUU
ES-K..	Solar Wings Pegasus XL-R/Se	SW-WA-1231	G-MTDF
ES-K..	Southdown Puma Sprint	T45	OH-U151

GLIDERS

ES-1000	LAK-12 Lietuva	653	
ES-1001	LAK-12 Lietuva	6165	
ES-1002	LAK-12 Lietuva	6156	
ES-1004	SZD-48-3 Jantar Standard 3	B-1454	DOSAAF
ES-1005-EV	SZD-48-1 Jantar Standard 2	B-1225	DOSAAF
ES-1006	SZD-48-1 Jantar Standard 2	B-1164	DOSAAF
ES-1007	SZD-41A Jantar Standard	B-912	DOSAAF
ES-1009	SZD-48-3 Jantar Standard 3	B-1702	DOSAAF
ES-1010	Schleicher ASW 15	15092	
ES-1019	LET L-13 Blanik	172307	
ES-1021	LET L-13 Blanik	173614	
ES-1025	LET L-13 Blanik	026439	
ES-1602	SZD-30 Pirat	S-05.22	DOSAAF
ES-2001	LET L-13 Blanik	026437	
ES-2003	LET L-13 Blanik	026706	
ES-2006	LET L-13 Blanik	174518	
ES-2010	LET L-13 Blanik	026951	
ES-2011	Type unknown	unkn	
ES-2024	SZD-48-3 Jantar Standard 3	B-1884	DOSAAF
	(W/o 22.5.15)		
ES-2025	LET L-13 Blanik	174309	
ES-3008	ICA-Brasov IS.30	08	G-DFDP, BGA3180/FDP
ES-3117	LET L-13 Blanik	027317	
ES-3119	LET L-13 Blanik	027319	
ES-3120	LET L-13 Blanik	027320	
ES-3276	SZD-48-3 Jantar Standard 3	B-1576	ES-2022, DOSAAF
ES-4112	LET L-13 Blanik	026919	ES-2012
ES-5075	Scheibe SF-25C Falke	4481	OE-9075, (D-KEIA)
ES-5423	LET L-33 Solo	950318	OK-5423
ES-5304	Amateur Powered Sailplane	20122.01H (4276)	
ES-5832	SZD-50-3 Puchacz	B-2027	OH-832
ES-20 . .	SZD-48-1 Jantar Standard 2	B-1229	DOSAAF

EW - BELARUS

Regn.	Type	C/n	Prev.Id.
EW-001DA(2)	Mil Mi-8MTV-1	unkn	
EW-001PA	Boeing 737-8EV	33079	N375BC
EW-001PB	Boeing 767-32K	33968	EZ-A700
EW-002PE	Mil Mi-8PS	98525049	EW-25049
EW-003DA	Mil Mi-17-2	456C01	EW-02DA(1)
EW-002SL	Aviatika MAI-890	unkn	
EW-003SL	Weightshift, type unknown	unkn	
EW-004DE	Ilyushin IL-76MD	0093490721	EW-304TH, EW-004DE, EW-78793, CCCP78793
EW-004SL	Weightshift, type unknown	unkn	
EW-005DE	Ilyushin IL-76MD	0093492771	EW-78802, CCCP78802
EW-009DD	Antonov An-26SLK	6604	09red
EW-012SL	Yakovlev Yak-52	unkn	
EW-014SL	Yakovlev Yak-18T	unkn	
EW-019SL	Comco Ikarus C-42	unkn	
EW-020SL	Comco Ikarus C-42	unkn	
EW-024SL	Busel	unkn	
EW-025BP	Mil Mi-8T	unkn	
EW-029AO	Mil Mi-2	549713056	Bel.AF 24yel
EW-029SL	Mara	unkn	
EW--030AO	Mil Mi-2	549714046	DOSAAF
EW-031AO	Mil Mi-2	549712036 ?	DOSAAF
EW-031SL	Delfin	unkn	
EW-032AB	Antonov An-2	1G236-03	Sov AF 28
EW-032SL	Phoenix	unkn	
EW-034SL	Contact	unkn	
EW-036SL	Kontur	unkn	
EW-037SL	Cessna 150	unkn	
EW-038AL	PZL-104 Wilga 35A	16820649	DOSAAF 07bl
EW-039SL	PZL-104 Wilga 35A	16820658	DOSAAF
	(Also reported as Altair homebuilt)		
EW-040AL	PZL-104 Wilga 35A	18840782	DOSAAF
	(Crashed 12.7.08)		
EW-041AL	PZL 104 Wilga 35A	85262	DOSAAF
EW-041LL	Ilyushin IL-103	03-06	
	(Crashed 6.15)		
EW-042LL	Ilyushin IL-103	03-12	
EW-043LL	Ilyushin IL-103	03-13	
EW-044LL	Ilyushin IL-103	03-14	
EW-045AB	Antonov An-2	1G237-52	Sov AF 42wh
EW-046AM	Yakovlev Yak-52	unkn	
EW-047AM	Yakovlev Yak-52	unkn	DOSAAF
EW-050AM	Yakovlev Yak-52	unkn	
EW-051AM	Yakovlev Yak-52	unkn	
EW-051SL	Aviatika MAI-890U	unkn	
	(Damaged 16.6.05)		
EW-052AM	Yakovlev Yak-52	8910013	DOSAAF
EW-052SL	Aviatika MAI-890U	unkn	
EW-053AM	Yakovlev Yak-52	unkn	
EW-053SL	Comco Ikarus C-42	unkn	
EW-054AM	Yakovlev Yak-52	889108	
EW-055AM	Yakovlev Yak-52	unkn	DOSAAF
EW-056AM	Yakovlev Yak-52	8910201	DOSAAF
EW-058AN	Yakovlev Yak-55	unkn	EW-058AL, EW-058AM, DOSAAF
EW-060AM	Yakovlev Yak-55	870405	EW-060AN, DOSAAF '28blue'
EW-061AM	Yakovlev Yak-55	890808	EW-061AN, DOSAAF,'71blue'
EW-062AL	PZL-104 Wilga 35A	139473	DOSAAF
EW-062SL	Mir-07 homebuilt	unkn	
EW-063SL	NARP-1	unkn	
EW-064SL	NARP-1	unkn	
EW-065SL	NARP-1	unkn	
EW-066SL	NARP-1zhdz	unkn	
EW-067LL(2)	Cessna 172N Skyhawk	unkn	
EW-067SL	Ariel homebuilt		
EW-074SL	Halley Apollo /Aeros wing	unkn	
EW-076SL	Aeroprakt A-21 Neman	11	
EW-077SL	Aeroprakt A-23 Neman	A23N.001	
EW-078SL	Halley Apollo	unkn	
EW-081SL	Aeromechanics Sky Cruiser Gyro	unkn	
EW-082SL	Makhov M-3	unkn	
EW-083SL	Aviatika MAI-890	unkn	
EW-091SL	Lilienthal X-32 Bekas	unkn	
EW-100PJ	Canadair CL.600-2B19 Regional Jet 200LR	7309	N400MJ, C-GKIT, D-ALIT, F-GPTH, C-FMMQ
EW-121AO	Mil Mi-2	5410925059	Bel.AF 07 white
EW-123AO	Mil Mi-2	5211143060	Bel.AF 25 white, EW-14256, CCCP14256
EW-124AO	Mil Mi-2	5311127030	Bel.AF 27 yel, RF-01229, EW-14240, CCCP14240
EW-126AM	Yakovlev Yak-52	889014	DOSAAF
EW-127AM	Yakovlev Yak-452	8910014	DOSAAF
EW-128AB	Antonov An-2	1G195-59	Bel AF 61yel
EW-229CD	Antonov An-2R	1G200-11	EW-71168, CCCP71168
EW-232TF	Mil Mi-26T	34001212463	RA-06290, RA-06187
EW-233TF	Mil Mi-26T	34001212460	RA-06289, RA-06192
EW-234TE	Mil Mi-8	unkn	
EW-237CD	Antonov An-2R	1G214-16	EW-40658, CCCP40658
	(Wfu and preserved)		
EW-239EP	Mil Mi-8T	unkn	
EW-240EP	Mil Mi-8	unkn	
EW-241EP	Mil Mi-8MTV	unkn	
EW-243EQ	Mil Mi-9	98448483	Bel.AF 33 yel
EW-244TH	Ilyushin IL-76TD	1023410344	RA-76350, ST-AIY, RA-76350
EW-245TI	Antonov An-12PS	6344608	EX-096, Russian Navy
EW-248CD	Antonov An-2T	1G160-27	EW-023AB, Sov AF
EW-249LH	Robinson R44 Raven II	11485	
	(Damaged 12.15)		
EW-250PA	Boeing 737-524	26319	N427LF, XU-756, N19634
EW-251PA	Boeing 737-5Q8	27634	PT-SSC
EW-252PA	Boeing 737-524	26340	LY-AGZ, N19636
EW-252TI	Antonov An-12BP	401912	(ER-ACX), EX-098, 3X-GDM, RA-11372, RA-12121, CCCP12121
EW-253PA	Boeing 737-524	26339	LY-AGQ, N33635
EW-254PA	Boeing 737-3Q8	26294	N201LF, B-2928, N261LF
EW-256TE	Mil Mi-8 MTV	unkn	
EW-259TG	Antonov An-26B	12706	UR-26094, CCCP26094
EW-260TF	Mil Mi-26T	34001212465	Bel.AF 63 white, RA-06188, CCCP06188
EW-261SL	Aerokopter AK1-3	0007	
	(W/o)		

215

Reg	Type	c/n	Previous identities
EW-262TK	Antonov An-32B (Stored by 2.15)	2103	ER-AWY, RA-48972, CCCP48972
EW-271CD	Antonov An-2R	1G217-26	EW-306AB, EW-305AB, EW-40986, CCCP40986
EW-275TI	Antonov An-12BK	00347210	RA-13392, CCCP13392, SovAF:61red
EW-276PJ	Canadair CL-600-2B19 Regional Jet 200ER	7799	N698BR, C-FMLI
EW-277PJ	Canadair CL-600-2B19 Regional Jet 200ER	7852	N661LF, C-FMMY
EW-278TG	Antonov An-26B	13306	HA-TCZ, ER-AZV, ST-AWC, YR-ADI
EW-280LH	Robinson R44 Raven II	12368	
EW-282PA	Boeing 737-3Q8	26321	B-5024, N641LF, G-BZZJ, N17386
EW-283PA	Boeing 737-3Q8	26333	B-2604, N661LF, D4-CBN, N263LF, TU-TAJ, HB-IIF, N661LF
EW-284TI	Antonov An-12BP	4342210	EK-11830, EX-073, RA-11830, CCCP11830)
EW-286TL	Antonov An-74-200	36547098957	YL-KSA, RA-74030
EW-287SL	MAI Aviatika 890	unkn	
EW-290PA	Boeing 737-5Q8	27629	N281LF, EI-EDW, LY-AZW, PT-SSB
EW-293CM	Kamov Ka-26	unkn	
EW-294PA	Boeing 737-505	26338	B-2975
EW-298SL	Aeroprakt A-22 Vision	unkn	
EW-299TH	Ilyushin Il-76	unkn	
EW-301PJ	Canadair CL-600-2B19 Challenger 850	8057	C-GWWW(2), C-FHCN, C-FMNX
EW-302TE	Mil Mi-8 MTV	unkn	
EW-303PJ	Canadair CL-600-2B19 Regional Jet 200ER	7436	OY-MBI, G-MSKT, C-FMKZ
EW-307AO	Mil Mi-2	5410818019	Russian AF
EW-307SL	Weightshift, type unknown	unkn	
EW-308PA	Boeing 737-3K2	24338	LN-KKH, PH-HVT
EW-309BH	Aérospatiale AS.355NP Ecureuil 2	5774	F-WWXE
EW-312CM	Kamov Ka-26	7706005	LZ-6066
EW-314AB	Antonov An-2T	1G194-23	EW-270CD, EW-033AB, DOSAAF 04yellow
EW-315AM	Yakovlev Yak-52	877901	DOSAAF
EW-316AO	Mil Mi-2	5211049129	EW-238CC, Bel. AF 24 black, EW-14214, CCCP14214
EW-317LL	Zlin Z.326	unkn	
EW-318SL	Aeroprakt A-22LS Vision	unkn	
EW-319LL	Cessna 172N Skyhawk	17271441	N3095E
EW-320LH	Robinson R44 Raven I	2178	
EW-321LL	Zlin Z.142	0281	OM-MNP, OK-MNP
EW-322AO	Mil Mi-2	549711036	DOSAAF
EW-323SL	Aeroprakt A-22LS Vision	unkn	
EW-324SL	NARP-1	unkn	
EW-325AO	Antonov An-2T	1G237-03	EW-226CD, SovAF 88
EW-325LL	Zlin Z.142	0384	
EW-327AO	Mil Mi-2	548710054	EW-247CC, EW-024AO, SovAF
EW-328TG	Antonov An-26B	12806	RA-26135, CCCP26135
EW-330TF	Mil Mi-26TS	34001212609	RA-06295, HL9261
EW-331CM	Kamov Ka-26	7404107	UR-19492, CCCP19492
EW-332CM	Kamov Ka-26	7605515	UR-SUN, UR-24337, CCCP24337
EW-335LL	Cessna 172M	17263459	N5245R
EW-336AO	Mil Mi-2	5311128030	EW-14241, Bel.AF 28yel, EW-14241, CCCP14241
EW-336PA	Boeing 737-3Q8	26312	VQ-BHD, G-TOYC, G-BZZG, N14383
EW-338TI	Antonov An-12BP	1340106	UR-DWI, EW-269TI, UN-11018, LZ-VEA, RA-11976, CCCP11976
EW-343TH	Ilyushin Il-76TD	0053464934	4L-SKY, UP-I7638, EW-239TH, EX-066, RA-76666, CCCP76666
EW-340PO	Embraer ERJ-170-200LR	170000350	PT-TFE
EW-341FB	Antonov An-2R	1G204-46	EW-17845, CCCP17845
EW-341PO	Embraer ERJ-170-200LR	170000352	PT-TGL
EW-344AO	Mil Mi-2	unkn	
EW-344LL	Cessna 172 Skyhawk	unkn	
EW-348AM	Yakovlev Yak-52	9211612	(LY-ASY), RA-22541, DOSAAF 04
EW-348LH	Robinson R44 Raven I	2139	N173AZ
EW-349AO	Mil Mi-2	5411142060	EW-225CC, Bel.AF 26white, EW-14255, CCCP14255
EW-350SL	Lilienthal X-34T Bekas	unkn	
EW-354AO	Mil Mi-2U	549031015	DOSAAF
EW-354LL	Sukhoi Su-26 (Wears '23' black)	03-03	N214YA
EW-355EH	Aérospatiale AS.355NP Ecureuil 2	unkn	
EW-355TH	Ilyushin Il-76MD	0093495883	EW-78819, CCCP78819
EW-356EH	Aérospatiale AS.355NP Ecureuil 2	unkn	
EW-356TH	Ilyushin Il-76MD	1003405159	EW-78848, CCCP78848
EW-357EH	Aérospatiale AS.355NP Ecureuil 2	5785	EW-311BH, F-WWPP
EW-357LL	Diamond DA.40 NG	40.N031	
EW-358LL	Diamond DA.40 NG	40.N032	
EW-359AO	Mil Mi-2	549439105	DOSAAF
EW-360AB	Antonov An-2	unkn	DOSAAF
EW-361AB	Antonov An-2	1G237-01	DOSAAF
EW-364TG	Antonov An-26B	4206	3X-GEN, 9Q-CMS, 9U-BHQ, 9U-BNO, 9Q-CTJ, UR-26599, CCCP26599
EW-366PA	Boeing 737-31S	29058	YR-ADB, OK-CCA, G-THOH. D-ADBN
EW-366TH	Ilyushin IL-76	unkn	
EW-368BX	unidentified drone	unkn	
EW-369LL	Cessna 172N Skyhawk	17269401	N669RA
EW-370LL	Cessna 172	unkn	
EW-371SL	Lilienthal X-32SKh-100 Bekas	unkn	
EW-373SL	Lilienthal X-32 Bekas	unkn	
EW-376CD	Antonov An-2R	1G213-28	EW-40621, CCCP40621
EW-378TG	Antonov An-26B	14004	YL-RAE, UN-26200(?), CCCP26200
EW-380LL	Cessna 172 Skyhawk	unkn	
EW-382LL	PZL-101 Gawron	119296	HA-SBN
EW-383TH	Ilyushin Il-76TD	1013405177	EY-608, EK-76808, 4L-GLL, EY-602, EX-108, RA-76808, CCCP76808
EW-384LL	Reims-Cessna F172H Skyhawk	F17200663	D-EBLL
EW-385DX	Berkut-2 drone	unkn	
EW-385LL	Cessna 172	unkn	
EW-386BS	Magni M-24 Orion	unkn	also "01"black
EW-386PA	Boeing 737-3K2	24327	LY-FLJ, LN-KKG, PH-HVN
EW-387BS	Magni M-24 Orion	unkn	also "02"black
EW-387LL	Piper PA-28-160 Cherokee	28-617	D-EHTE, N5526W
EW-388CD	Antonov An-2	unkn	
EW-389CD	Antonov An-2	unkn	
EW-391LL	GEMS MS.892A Rallye Commodore 150	10529	D-ECVA
EW-395TH	Ilyushin Il-76TD	0093499986	RA-76834, EW-78836. CCCP78836
EW-396CM	Kamov Ka-26	7504906	RA-19401
EW-396LL	Cessna 172	unkn	
EW-396TE	Mil Mi-8MSB	9765118	Bel.AF
EW-399PO	Embraer ERJ-190-200LR	19000667	PR-EFO
EW-400PO	Embraer ERJ-190-200LR	19000668	PR-EFQ
EW-401LL	Cessna 172	unkn	
EW-404PA	Boeing 737-3L9	27061	LY-AZU, LY-FLE, PK-AWG, 9M-AAG, SX-BGI, D-ADBD, OY-MAN
EW-405SL	Aeroprakt A-22LS Vision	unkn	
EW-406LH	Robinson R44 Raven	1021	N71977
EW-407PA	Boeing 737-36M	28332	YR-BBA, G-TOYJ, PK-GGW, YR-BGY, OO-VEA
EW-408LL	Yakovlev Yak-12A	19003	SP-YFA, SP-FKP, SP-CXM, PLW . . .
EW-411LL	Cessna 182	unkn	
EW-412TH	Ilyushin Il-76TD	0023437090	EK-76464, EY-609, EK-76464, RA-76464, CCCP76464
EW-413LL	Maule MX-7	unkn	
EW-414LL	Diamond DA 40 Star	40.762	N727DC
EW-417LL	Reims-Cessna F177RG Cardinal RG	F177RG0014/177RG0128	SP-TTC(2, SP-FLG, OH-CFX, SE-FXH)
EW-419SL	Best Off Sky Ranger	unkn	
EW-420LL	Cessna 170B	unkn	
EW-424LL	Grob G.109	unkn	
EW-427TI	Antonov An-12A	2340806	UP-AN213, UN-11015, LZ-SFN, ER-AXM, LZ-SFN, LZ-FEA, LZ-PHA, RA-11307
EW-430TH	Ilyushin Il-76TD	0043451528	RA-76476, CCCP76476
EW-437PA	Boeing 737-8K5	27988	D-AHFP, N1786B
EW-438PA	Boeing 737-86Q	30286	D-ANNJ. N1787B
EW-439LL	Zlin Z.142	unkn	
EW-443SL	Autogyro Europe Calidus	unkn	
EW-447LL	Piper PA-28-240 Cherokee	28-20516	D-ECSU, N11C, N6444W
EW-449TH	Ilyushin Il-76TD	1003405167	YI-AQX, EK-76425, 5A-DQA, EX-105, RA-76425, CCCP76425
EW-450TR	Ilyushin Il-62MGr	4546257	RA-86576, UK-86576, UzbekAF:86576,CCCP86576, D-AOAK, DDR--SET
EW-454SL	Comco Ikarus C-42	0307-6566	D-MCHL
EW-458SL	Magni M-24 Orion	unkn	
EW-460TQ	Boeing 747-281F	23919	SX-ASO, N783SA, JA8188, N6009F
EW-461SL	TL Ultralight TL-3000 Sirius	unkn	
EW-468LL	Yakovlev Yak-52	unkn	
EW-474LL	Tomark SD-4 Viper	unkn	
EW-477SL	Ekolot KR-030 Topaz	unkn	
EW-992AS	Autogyro Europe Calidus	unkn	
EW-999AP	Mil Mi-8MSB	unkn	
EW-01406	Antonov An-2TP	1G230-46	CCCP01406
EW-07428	Antonov An-2P (Wfu ?)	1G151-03	CCCP07428
EW-07772	Antonov An-2TP	1G161-47	CCCP07772
EW-07793	Antonov An-2P	1G162-43	CCCP07793
EW-11365(2)	Antonov An-12BP	5343109	Sov.AF 09yel
EW-14126	Mil Mi-2	5210838029	CCCP14126
EW-14158	Mil Mi-2	5210443117	CCCP14158
EW-14159	Mil Mi-2	5210444117	CCCP14159
EW-14199	Mil Mi-2	5410940069	CCCP14199
EW-14213	Mil Mi-2	5211048119	CCCP14213
EW-14216	Mil Mi-2	5211101119	CCCP14216
EW-14253	Mil Mi-2	5211140050	CCCP14253
EW-15624	Mil Mi-2	5210039126	CCCP15624
EW-15633	Mil Mi-2	5210104017	CCCP15633
EW-16051	Antonov An-2R	1G164-04	CCCP16051
EW-17979	Antonov An-2R	1G210-03	CCCP17979
EW-17981	Antonov An-2R	1G210-05	CCCP17981
EW-19280	Kamov Ka-26	7001210	CCCP19280
EW-19613	Kamov Ka-26	7505112	CCCP19613
EW-20371	Mil Mi-2	529818066	CCCP20371
EW-20737	Mil Mi-2	527634052	CCCP20737
EW-20913	Mil Mi-2	528545024	CCCP20913
EW-20961	Mil Mi-2	549517115	CCCP20961
EW-23232	Mil Mi-2	5210233057	CCCP23232
EW-23291	Mil Mi-2	529112025	CCCP23291
EW-24061	Kamov Ka-26	00304	CCCP24061
EW-24082	Kamov Ka-26	6900901	CCCP24082
EW-24086	Kamov Ka-26	7000905	CCCP24086
EW-24325	Kamov Ka-26	7706117	CCCP24325
EW-32686	Antonov An-2R	1G211-45	CCCP32686
EW-33303	Antonov An-2R	1G225-20	CCCP33303
EW-33533	Antonov An-2R	1G229-25	CCCP33533
EW-33582	Antonov An-2R	1G230-19	CCCP33582
EW-33583	Antonov An-2R	1G230-20	CCCP33583
EW-40495	Antonov An-2R (Stored, no report since 2011)	1G225-12	CCCP40495
EW-40931	Antonov An-2R (No report since 2011, stored)	1G216-11	CCCP40931
EW-46304	Antonov An-24B (Stored by 2008, derelict by 2014)	97305204	CCCP46304
EW-46631	Antonov An-24RV (Stored by 2011)	37308810	CCCP46631
EW-46835	Antonov An-24RV (Wfu 2008. To ground instructional airframe at Brest)	17306802	CCCP46835
EW-47291	Antonov An-24B (Displayed at Minsk-2)	07306601	CCCP47291
EW-47808	Antonov An-24RV (Accident 16.9.04, stored by 2011)	17306910	CCCP47808
EW-54894	Antonov An-2R	1G186-42	CCCP54894
EW-54906	Antonov An-2R (Believed sold)	1G186-54	CCCP54906
EW-54924	Antonov An-2R	1G187-17	CCCP54924
EW-56412	Antonov An-2R (Derelict by 2012)	1G180-56	CCCP54612
EW-62618	Antonov An-2R	1G178-03	CCCP62618
EW-65145	Tupolev Tu-134A (Wfu, still stored 2013)	60985	65145, CCCP65145
EW-65149	Tupolev Tu-134A-3 (Displayed at Minsk-2 as 'CCCP65036')	61033	CCCP65149

EW-71170	Antonov An-2R	1G200-13	CCCP71170
"EW-76709"	Ilyushin Il-76T	0003427796	ER-IBA, EK-76602, UP-I7602,
	(Displayed at Minsk)		UN-76034, EX-039, RA-76527,
			CCCP76527
EW-76710	Ilyushin Il-76TD	0063473182	ST-ATX, EW-76710, RA-76710,
	(Displayed at Minsk-2)		EW-76710, CCCP76710
EW-76711	Ilyushin Il-76MD	0063473187	CCCP76711
	(Instructional airframe at Ulyanovsk)		
EW-76712	Ilyushin Il-76MD	0063473190	RA-76712, CCCP76712
EW-76734	Ilyushin Il-76MD	0073476312	CCCP76734
EW-76735	Ilyushin Il-76TD	0073476314	RA-76735, CCCP76735
EW-78769	Ilyushin Il-76MD	0083487607	CCCP78769
EW-78779	Ilyushin Il-76TD	0083489662	CCCP78779
EW-78787	Ilyushin Il-76TD	0083490698	CCCP78787
EW-78799	Ilyushin Il-76TD	0093491754	CCCP78799
EW-78808	Ilyushin Il-76TD	0093493794	CCCP78808
EW-78826	Ilyushin Il-76MD	1003499991	CCCP78826
	(Fire damaged 9.3.07)		
EW-78827	Ilyushin Il-76TD	1003499997	CCCP78827
EW-78828	Ilyushin Il-76MD	1003401004	CCCP78828
EW-78839	Ilyushin Il-76MD	1003402047	CCCP78839
EW-78843	Ilyushin Il-76MD	1003403082	CCCP78843
EW-85581	Tupolev Tu-154B2	83A-581	CCCP85581
	(Displayed at Minsk)		
EW-85703	Tupolev Tu-154M	91A-878	CCCP85703
	(Stored)		
EW-85706	Tupolev Tu-154M	91A-881	CCCP85706
	(Displayed at Minsk-2)		
EW-85741	Tupolev Tu-154M	91A-896	ES-LTC, EW-85741, ES-LTR,
	(Stored)		(ES-AAD), CCCP85741
EW-85748	Tupolev Tu-154M	92A-924	
	(Stored)		
EW-85815	Tupolev Tu-154M	95A-1010	
EW-88161	Yakovlev Yak-40	9611546	CCCP88161
EW-88187	Yakovlev Yak-40	9620748	88187, CCCP88187
	(Wfu and preserved, Minsk-Borovaya)		
EW-88202	Yakovlev Yak-40	9630449	CCCP88202
	(Displayed at Minsk-2)		
EW-.....	Alliant Aviation Destiny 2000	1C0201	N51352
EW-.....	Cessna 152	15280666	N25446
EW-.....	Cessna 172M	17262497	SP-AIO(4), N13103
EW-.....	Cessna 172N Skyhawk	17269809	N737ZU
EW-.....	Cessna 172N Skyhawk	17269918	N738EK
EW-.....	Cessna 172N Skyhawk	17267585	N73625
EW-.....	Cessna 177B Cardinal	17701712	N34218
EW-.....	Cessna 177B Cardinal	17702560	N19149
EW-.....	Cessna 182R Skylane	18268585	N967OX
EW-.....	Cessna 182T Skylane	18281959	N425CD
EW-...;.	Cessna T182T Turbo Skylane	T18208816	N51558
EW-.....	Cessna 421A Golden Eagle	421A0037	N1477D
EW-.....	Grumman G-44 Widgeon	1349	N62095, NC62095
EW-.....	PZL-104 Wilga 35A	21930949	
EW-.....	PZL-104 Wilga 35A	21930950	
EW-.....	Zlin Z.42M	0168	SP-WID
EW-.....	Zlin Z.142	0491	SP-ASL(3)

BALLOONS

EW-007SL	Hot Air Balloon (Velikie Luki titles)		
EW-016SL	Hot Air Balloon		
EW-035SL	Hot Air Balloon (Belcar titles)		
EW-038SL	Hot Air Balloon		
EW-059SL	Balloon, type unknown		
EW-061SL	70TA Balloon		
EW-314SL	Hot Air Balloon		
EW-428SL	Aerotour AH-10 HAFB		
EW-555SL	Hot Air Balloon		

GLIDERS

EW-022SL	Antonov A-15	unkn	
EW-030SL	LET L-13M Blanik	unkn	
EW-054SL	LET L-13J Blanik	unkn	
EW-070SL	LET L-13 Blanik	unkn	
EW-071SL	LET L-13 Blanik	026603	OH-513
EW-072SL	LET L-13J Blanik	174224	
EW-097AS	LET L-13 Blanik	unkn	
EW-098AS	LET L-13 Blanik	unkn	DOSAAF
EW-099AS	LET L-13 Blanik	unkn	
EW-100AS	LET L-13 Blanik	unkn	
EW-101AS	LET L-13 Blanik	unkn	
EW-102AS	LET L-13 Blanik	unkn	
EW-103AS	LET L-13 Blanik	unkn	
EW-104AS	LET L-13 Blanik	unkn	
EW-107AS	SZD-41A Jantar Standard	unkn	
EW-109AS	SZD-41A Jantar Standard	unkn	
EW-110AS	SZD-41A Jantar Standard	unkn	
EW-111AS	SZD-48-1 Jantar Standard 2	unkn	DOSAAF
EW-112AS	SZD-48-3 Jantar Standard 3	unkn	DOSAAF
EW-114AS	SZD-48-3 Jantar Standard 3	unkn	
EW-115AS	SZD-48-3 Jantar Standard 3	unkn	
EW-116AS	LET L-13 Blanik	unkn	
EW-117AS	LET L-13 Blanik	unkn	
EW-118AS	LET L-13 Blanik	unkn	
EW-279SL	LET L-13SW Vivat	unkn	
	(Cr 22.6.13)		
EW-285SL	LET L-13 Blanik	unkn	
EW-326SL	Pipistrel Taurus	unkn	
EW-415SL	SZD-38A Jantar I	B-673	HA-4353
EW-424LL	Grob G 109	unkn	
EW-.....	ICA-Brasov IS-32A	05	G-DFAV, BGA3114/FAV
EW-...	LET L-13 Blanik	026604	OH-514
EW-.....	LET L-13SDM Vivat	950609	OY-RFX, D-KLIH
EW-.....	SZD-30 Pirat	B-536	SE-TKE

E7 - BOSNIA-HERZEGOVINA & REPUBLIKA SRPSKA

Regn.	Type	C/n	Prev.Id.
E7-AAB	Soko/Aérospatiale SA.341 Gazelle	037	T9-AAB, JRV12809
E7-AAD	Aérospatiale/Alenia ATR-72-212	464	T9-AAD, F-WQNF, N535AS,
			F-WQKS, ZK-MCC, F-WWLR
E7-AAE	Aérospatiale/Alenia ATR-72-212	465	T9-AAE, F-WQNG, N536AS,
			F-WQLB, ZK-MCL, F-WWLT
E7-AAG	Piper PA-18-150 Super Cub	18-7809163	T9-AAG, YU-DCC, N82169
E7-AAM	Reims/Cessna FP.172D	FP172-0002/P17257166	T9-AAM, D-EKBY, (N8566X)
E7-AAN	Reims/Cessna F172M	F17201272	T9-AAN, 9A-DNB, D-EDPT
E7-AAP	Scheibe SF 25B Falke	4807	T9-AAP, D-KAHN
E7-AAQ	LET L-13SW Vivat	970610	T9-AAQ, T9-5220
E7-AAS	Fuji FA200-160 Aero Subaru	131	D-EACE
E7-AAU	Cessna 340A	340A0540	T9-AAU, D-IFPS, OE-FCF,
			(N4374A)
E7-ABI	Soko/Aérospatiale SA.341L1 Gazelle	139	JRV12925
E7-ABJ	Cessna 150G	15064767	S5-DTT, N4717X
E7-ABK	Christen A-1 Husky	1104	OE-APL, D-EBAD(5)
E7-AHA	Bell 206B Jet Ranger II	3435	T9-AHA, (T9-HBI), 9A-HAF,
			TC-HNO, N411SB, N20879
E7-BSA	Piper PA-34-200T Seneca II	34-7970340	T9-BSA, TC-SER, F-GCJJ,
			OO-HLK, N2908U
E7-CLO	Piper PA-18-150 Super Cub	18-7809162	T9-CLO, YU-DCB, N82168
E7-DBZ	Piper PA-18-150 Super Cub	18-7809158	T9-DBZ, YU-DBZ, N82084
E7-DCA	Piper PA-18-150 Super Cub	18-7809159	T9-DCA, YU-DCA, N82086
E7-DDY	SEEMS MS.880B Rallye Club	314	T9-DDY, D-EKYN(3), F-BKYN
E7-DEE	SOCATA MS.894A Minerva 220	12016	T9-DEE, OE-DRY, F-BTRY
E7-DGI	Utva-75	unkn	T9-DGI, YU-DGI, JRV53173
E7-DKY	Utva-75	unkn	YU-DKY, JRV53161
E7-DQI	SEEMS MS.885 Super Rallye	5426	T9-DQI, D-EBQI
E7-EDO	SOCATA MS.893A Rallye Commodore 180	11890	T9-EDO, D-EODL
E7-IMB	Tecnam P.2006T	175	
E7-MEL	LET L-410UVP-E20	902517	LZ-RMW, HA-LAE
E7-NOR	SOCATA MS.893A Rallye Commodore 180	12071	D-EMJK, F-BUGB
E7-PCG	Reims/Cessna FRA150L Aerobat	FRA1500166	T9-PCG, YU-CBK
E7-PDA	Utva-75	unkn	T9-PDA, RSrp 50105, YU-DIZ,
			JRV53219
E7-PDB	Utva-75	unkn	T9-PDB, YU-DGV, JRV53182
E7-PDC	Utva-75	unkn	T9-PDC, YU-DLY, JRV53238
E7-PDD	Reims FR172J Rocket	FR1720435	T9-PDD, RSrp 51103, YU-DBJ
E7-PDG	Piper PA-18-150 Super Cub	18-7809157	T9-PDG, RSrp 51102, YU-DBY,
			N82081
E7-PDH	Champion 7GCBC Citabria	278-70	T9-PDH, YU-CAE
E7-PDI	Utva-66V	0847	T9-PDI, YU-CDW, JRV51138
E7-PDJ	Utva-66	0852 ?	T9-PDJ, RVRS 51107,
			JRV51143
E7-RCA	Piper PA-25-235 Pawnee	25-2437	T9-RCA, (T9-BBC), 9A-BBC,
			RC-BBC, YU-BBC, N6830Z, N10F
E7-RDA	Utva-75	unkn	T9-RDA, RSrp 50201, YU-DKS,
			JRV53121
E7-RDB	Utva-75	unkn	T9-RDB, RSrp 50202, YU-DIW,
			JRV53212
E7-RDC	Utva-66	0836	T9-RDC, RSrp 50208,
			JRV51127
E7-SAF	Cessna 172P Skyhawk	17275262	9A-JSA, N62371
E7-SBA	Cessna 500 Citation	500-0399	T9-SBA, YU-BML, N2069A
E7-SHA	Soko/Aérospatiale SA.341H Gazelle	046	T9-SHA, RSrpska/, JRV12663
E7-SHB	Bell 206B	2978	YU-HCO, N1086S
E7-SMS	Cessna 525 CitationJet CJ1+	525-0666	T9-SMS, N7277, N5076K
E7-VIP	Cessna 177RG Cardinal RG	177RG1120	N45469
E7-...	Cessna T206H Turbo Stationair	T20608651	N6063P
E7-...	PZL-104 Wilga 80	CF15810610	YU-DHW
	(Noted 10.08, identity unconfirmed)		
E7-...	SOCATA MS.893A Rallye Commodore 180	10989	D-EASO

GLIDERS

E7-1111	Glaser-Dirks DG-300 Elan	3E-247	T9-1111, YU-4 . . .
E7-1112	Scheibe Bergfalke II-55	251	D-8241, D-8240(1)
E7-1113	LET L-13 Blanik	026808	T9-1113, D-5495
E7-1114	LET L-23 Super Blanik	917806	YU-5396(1)
E7-1115	LET L-23 Super Blanik	907630	YU-5394
E7-1116	Bölkow Phoebus C	882	OO-ZCQ, F-CDOB
E7-1117	Schleicher K.7 Rhönadler	577	D-5699
E7-1118	VTC-76 VUK-T	384	S5-3074, YU-4438
E7-1119	Schleicher K 8B	8548	HB-834
E7-1121	Pilatus B4-PC11AF	305	YU-4268
E7-1122	Scheibe Bergfalke II	114/55	OE-1298
E7-4102	VTC-76 VUK-T	373	T9-4102, YU-4427
E7-4103	VTC-75 Standard Cirrus	234	T9-4103, YU-4324
E7-4106	Schleicher K 8B	8667	T9-4106, D-0247
E7-4269	Pilatus B4-PC11AF	306	T9-4269, YU-4269
E7-4288	VTC-75 Standard Cirrus	230	T9-4288, YU-4288
E7-4309	VTC-75 Standard Cirrus	217	T9-4309, YU-4309
E7-4326	VTC-75 Standard Cirrus	117	T9-4326, YU-4326
E7-4367	VTC-76 Vuk-T	288	T9-4367, YU-4367
E7-4435	VTC-76 Vuk-T	381	T9-4435, YU-4435
E7-4462	Schleicher K 8B	186/60	T9-4432, D-5809
E7-4582	VTC-75 Standard Cirrus	224	T9-4582, YU-4317
E7-4583	Glaser-Dirks DG-101G Elan	E128G96	T9-4583, YU-4345
E7-4585	VTC-76 VUK-T	330	T9-4585, YU-4403
E7-5101	LET L-13 Blanik	026926	T9-5101, YU-5377
E7-5105	Sportavia/ Scheibe SF 25B Falke	4867	T9-5105, D-KAOB
E7-5335	LET L-13 Blanik	174914	T9-5335, YU-5335
E7-5341	LET L-13 Blanik	173344	T9-5341, OK-6835
E7-5461	LET L-13 Blanik	174010	T9-5461, OK-9714
E7-5581	LET L-13 Blanik	026254	T9-5581, YU-5361
E7-...	Wassmer WA.30 Bijave	35	F-CCRD
E7-...	Wassmer WA.30 Bijave	122	F-CCYZ

MICROLIGHTS

E7-D111	Rodaro Storch	46	T9-D111
T9-D113	Aviasud Mistral	112	PH-2T5
E7-D116	Autogyro Europe MTOsport	M00847	HA-GYB
E7-D118	Firefly Royal Kecur/EOS 15	08/210528	
E7-D119	Autogyro Europe MTOsport	M01333	

Regn.	Type	C/n	Prev.Id.
E7-D444	Halley Apollo CX Racer GT/R	MZ74/91	T9-D444, HA-YNAI
E7-M003	Halley Apollo CX 18	T-M003	T9-M003
E7-M004	Halley Apollo CX 19/Chronos 14	MZE 03589	T9-M004
E7-M005	Pipistrel C-15 TN	191	T9-M005
E7-M006	Halley Apollo CX 18 Racer GT	MZEY 71/90	T9-M006
E7-M007	Halley Apollo CX 19	MZE 05589	T9-M007
E7-SU001	Eurofly Fire Fox	001/2001	T9-SU001
E7-V002	Light Aero Avid Flyer STOL	596	T9-V002, 9A-UNG, S5-NAB, YU-ZAI
E7-. . .	Aviasud Mistral BRD	179	PH-2S6, D-MONF

F - FRANCE

Regn.	Type	C/n	Prev.Id.

CNRAC REGISTER (HISTORIC AND VINTAGE AIRCRAFT)

Regn.	Type	C/n	Prev.Id.
F-AYAA	Piper J-3C-65 Cub	14498	N42248, NC42248
F-AYAC	Cessna 305C (L-19E) Bird Dog	24566	LX-PAC, F-GHDK, ALAT
F-AYAS	Aeronca 11AC Chief	11AC-S-50	G-BPXU, N3842E, NC3842E
F-AYBF	Bristol Fighter F2B (Painted as E2262 / A-6)	C794	ZK-VTV
F-AYCG	SNCASE SE.313B Alouette II	1506	F-GUCG, ALAT
F-AYCO	Hans Bohner NUWACO 10 Taperwing	39	N8521
F-AYDJ	Crocis / Stampe SV-4C	01-JFC	F-WYDJ
F-AYDR	Fokker DR.1 replica	1178	N425CR
F-AYDS	Bellanca 14-19 Cruisemaster	2014	N6561N
F-AYEZ	Piper J-3C-65 Cub	12383	G-BDEZ, OO-SOC, OO-EPI, 44-80087
F-AYFS	Hiller UH-12B	16095	F-BIFS, Fr.AF, 51-16095
F-AYGG	Stampe SV-4C	1073	N31034, F-BAUT
F-AYGL	Great Lakes 2T-1A Sport Trainer	91	N844K
F-AYHF	Morane-Saulnier MS.317	312	F-BHHF, F-BCBR
F-AYJD	Extra EA.260	02	N91KB
F-AYJF	Ryan 4 Navion	NAV-4-1269	N4269K, NC4269K
F-AYJJ	SNCASE SE.313 Alouette II	1019	F-GIJJ(2), ALAT
F-AYLV	Stinson L-5 Sentinel	76-1348	D-ERLU, I-AEFZ, MM52970, 42-99107
F-AYMH	Piaggio FWP.149D	026	OO-VMH, 90+16, AC+402, DE+392
F-AYMI	Fairchild F.24W-41A Argus II	W41A-767	HB-EMI, FZ827, 43-14803
F-AYMS	Morane-Saulnier MS.230 ET-2	1076	N230ET, G-AVEB, N230EB, F-BGJT
F-AYPF	Cessna 305C/L-19E Bird Dog	24705	F-GDPF, ALAT
F-AYPP	Morane-Saulnier MS.733 Alcyon	15	F-BNEA, Fr.mil
F-AYQG	Piper J-3C-65 Cub (Code "K-53", "Brenda Gail IV")	13324	N8527V, N254, NC254, 45-4584
F-AYRA	Yakovlev Yak-55M	920403	N5279S
F-AYRJ	Porterfield CP-65	720	G-BVWY, N27223, NC27223
F-AYSE	Fairchild F.24W-46 Argus III	W46173	N81273
F-AYTX	Cessna 195A	7496	F-GJTX, PH-NEN, D-EVLA, N9817A
F-AYVA	Cessna 305C/L-19E Bird Dog	24522	F-GFVA, ALAT
F-AYVD	Fokker DR.1 Replica	01-CP	
F-AYVZ	Ryan Navion F	911	F-BAVZ, N8911H
F-AYZA	Piper J-3C-65 Cub	11327	G-BLPA, OO-AJL, OO-JOE, 43-30036
F-AYZN	Luscombe 8A Silvaire	1186	G-AFZN(2), N25279, NC25279
F-AZAA	Morane-Saulnier MS.130 Et-2 (Painted as French Navy "F28" - currently stored)	02	F-APEK
F-AZAB	Salmson/CFAD 7 Cri-Cri Major (Res)	9	F-BFNG
F-AZAC(2)	SNCASO SO.1221 Djinn	010/FC18	F-BNDL, F-BHHK, F-WHHK(2)
F-AZAD(2)	Procaer F-400 Cobra (Res)	02	(I-COBR)
F-AZAE(2)	Cessna UC-78 Bobcat (Res 1.3.13)(Identity as quoted during restoration, but 5253= 43-7733, or 42-38715= c/n 2924 ?)	5253	238715
F-AZAF	Morane-Saulnier MS.733 Alcyon (Res)	190	Fr.Navy
F-AZAH	Morane-Saulnier MS.315	254	F-BBZO
F-AZAJ	Morane-Saulnier MS.138 Ep-2	3220/138	F-AQDN
F-AZAK	Morane-Saulnier MS.230	403	F-BEJO, Belgian: M-21
F-AZAN	Morane A-1 Replica	01	
F-AZAO	Morane A-1 Replica	3	
F-AZAP	Morane A-1 Replica	02	
F-AZAQ	Salis Fokker Dr1 replica	01	
F-AZAT	CCF/North American T-6H Harvard IV	CCF4-550	F-BRGB, (N73687), D-FABA, AA+635, 53-4631
F-AZAU	North American T-6G Texan	182-800	F-BNAU, Fr.AF, 51-15113
F-AZAV	Albatros C-1 Replica (Constructed from de Havilland DH.82A Tiger Moth components)	005	F-WZBH
F-AZAZ	Morane-Saulnier MS.185	3672/01	F-AJRQ
F-AZBA	Bleriot XI Replica	1	F-PERV, F-WERV
F-AZBD	Latécoère Laté 17P Replica (Regn formerly used by Norseman c/n 778 ex.F-BSTC/F-OBTC/ RNoAF/44-70513. W/o in 1987 - wreck at La Ferté-Alais)	01	
F-AZBE	North American AT-6C Harvard IIA (Painted to represent NA-64 Yale)	88-12127	F-WJBI, F-BJBI, BAF:H-29, EX633, 41-33606
F-AZBG	SFCA/Peyrot Taupin G	10	F-PMEM, F-APGB
F-AZBI	Spalinger S.18-III Glider	201	OO-ZPG,HB-416
F-AZBJ	SG-38 Primary Glider (DFS 108-14)	19	F-WRRK
F-AZBK	North American T-6G Texan (Flew as a Zero Replica as F-WZBK in 1987 with c/n SAM2-367)	182-54	F-WZBK, F-AZBK, F-BVQD, (PH-. . .), F-BVQD, Fr.AF, 51-14367
F-AZBL	North American SNJ-5 Texan (Flew as a Zero Replica as F-WZBM in 1987 with c/n SAM2-669)	88-17667	F-WZBM, F-AZBL, N9801C, BuA90669, 42-85886
F-AZBM	Piper J-2 Cub (Conversion of Piper L-4H Cub c/n 12332 ex.F-BDTH/44-80036)	"1NC"	F-WZBM
F-AZBN	Noorduyn UC-64A Norseman (Stored outside at La Ferté-Alais)	774	CN-TEE, EC-ANO, I-AIAK, YE-AAD, I-AIAK, 44-70509
F-AZBO	Caudron C.635 Simoun (Res)	342	F-DADY
F-AZBP	Breguet XIVP Replica	02	
F-AZBQ	North American T-6G Texan	182-535	F-BOEO, Fr.AF, 51-14848
F-AZBS	Bücker Bü .133C Jungmeister	16	F-BOHK, HB-MIQ, U-69
F-AZBU	Bücker Bü .131 Jungmann	83	F-BOHF, HB-UTS, A-70
F-AZBZ	CASA C-1.131E Jungmann	2150?	E3B-549
F-AZCA	de Havilland DH.89A Dragon Rapide	6541	F-BGON, G-ALZF, X7381
F-AZCB	Dassault MD-311 Flamant	291	Fr.AF
F-AZCC	Pilatus P2-05	37	U-117
F-AZCE	Pilatus P2-06 (Painted in Japanese marks)	72	U-152
F-AZCF	Fairchild F.24W-41A Argus II (Identity as quoted is suspect - another possibility is that "314" as quoted is part of a serial number 314499)	314	VH-AVN, G-AKJM, EV806, 42-13578
F-AZCG	Pilatus P2-05	26	U-106

Reg	Type	C/n	Previous identities
F-AZCH	DHC-1 Chipmunk 22 (Painted as "WB557")	C1/0702	OY-ALW, RDAF P-132
F-AZCI	Fairchild F.24R-46A Argus III (Painted as "AZ-CI") (C/n quoted as "33038AC1679" - while the above is thought correct another possible identity is c/n 999 ex.F-BFPD)	998	F-BEXC, KK380, 44-83037
F-AZCK	Boeing Stearman A75-N1	75-1653	N64926, 41-8094
F-AZCM	North American/CCF T-6H Harvard 4 (Painted as Swiss AF "U-301")	CCF4-..?	G-BJMS, MM53802
F-AZCN	SE-5 Replica (Stampe conversion)	2	F-WZCN
F-AZCP	Morane-Saulnier MS.502 Criquet	320	F-BBUS
F-AZCQ	North American T-6G Texan	168-140	E.16-191, 49-3037
F-AZCT	Caudron C-275 Luciole	7474	F-BBCF, F-APLM
F-AZCV	North American T-6G Texan	182-142	E.16-193, 51-14456
F-AZCY	SE-5 Replica (Stampe conversion)	3	
F-WZCZ	Nord N.1101 Noralpha	77	CEV
F-AZDA	Morane-Saulnier MS.500 Criquet (Painted "2E+RA")	226	F-BBUG
F-AZDB	Polikarpov Po-2W	0045	YU-CNS
F-AZDD	Dassault MD.312 Flamant (Painted "312-DK")	216	Fr.AF
F-AZDE	Dassault MD.312 Flamant (Wfu)	251	Fr.AF
F-AZDG	Erco 415C Ercoupe	3782	F-WZDG, F-BDPQ, NC3157H
F-AZDI	Boeing Stearman E75/N2S-5	75-5238	N5817N, BuA61116, 42-17075
F-AZDO	Auster J/1 Autocrat (Painted "V-J1")	2202	F-BFXO, G-AIPU
F-AZDP	Douglas AD-4 Skyraider (Painted "124143/205-RM")	7449	F-WZDP, TR-KFP, (N91909), Fr.AF'14', BuA124143
F-AZDR	Dassault MD.312 Flamant (Coded "V" Fr.AF)	160	Fr.AF
F-AZDT	Bücker Bü.133E Jungmeister replica	3F	
F-AZDU	North American AT-6D Harvard III	88-14948	F-WZDU, G-AZJD, F-BJBF, H-9, SAAF7509, EX959, 41-33932
F-AZDX	Boeing B-17G-VE Fortress (Painted "48846", "Pink Lady")	8246	F-BGSP, ZS-DXM, F-BGSP, 44-8846A
F-AZDY	Dassault MD.312 Flamant (Res)	156	CEV
F-AZDZ	Auster J/2 Arrow	2354	F-BFVJ, OO-ABP
F-AZEA	Stampe SV.4B	unkn	
F-AZEB	Utva Aero 3F	40156	YU-DAJ, YU-CWA, JRV40156
F-AZEC	Utva Aero 3F	65	YU-CYF, JRV40165
F-AZEE	Boeing Stearman A75N1 (PT-17) (Painted as RAF "FK107")	75-3286	F-WZEE, C-GBLQ, N65335, BuA28011, 41-25848
F-AZEF	North American T-6G Texan	182-74	Fr.AF, 51-14387
F-AZEG	Chance Vought F4U-5NL Corsair (Painted as "P"/"22")	124-724	FAH-605, NX4901E, BuA124724
F-AZEI	de Havilland DH.82A Tiger Moth	84882	G-APIG, T6553
F-AZEJ	Beech E-18S	BA-359	F-BTCS, N23J
F-AZEK	SIPA S.903	99	F-BEJZ, F-BGHY
F-AZEL	Dassault MD.312 Flamant	177	F-WZEL, Fr.AF
F-AZEM	Bücker Bü.131D Jungmann	5	
F-AZEN	Dassault MD.312 Flamant (Cld 26.1.95. Currently stored in Cyprus)	250	Fr.AF
F-AZER	Dassault MD.311 Flamant	276	(N276DF), Fr.AF
F-AZES	Dassault MD.312 Flamant (Code: "319-CG")	226	Fr.AF
F-AZEU(2)	DHC-1 Chipmunk T.20	C1/0299	FAP1307
F-AZEX	Stampe & Renard/ Stampe SV.4B	"1194"	
F-AZEY	Nord 3202	20	F-WZBY, ALAT
F-AZEZ	North American T-6G Texan	182-361	Fr.AF, 51-14674
F-AZFA	Auster J/2 Arrow	2377	OO-ABV
F-AZFE	Dassault MD.312 Flamant	237	Fr.AF
F-AZFF	LET L-13 Blanik	026750	OO-ZHG, LX-CAH
F-AZFG	Yakovlev Yak-18A	1609	EAF-640
F-AZFH	Brooks Pitts S-1S Special	K.027	F-WZAF, N835
F-AZFJ	Yakovlev Yak C-11	25111/02	EAF- ?
F-AZFL	Nord 3202	92	ALAT
F-AZFM	Nord 3400	122	ALAT
F-AZFN	Douglas AD-4 Skyraider (Painted "125716" "22-DG")	7609	ChadAF, Fr.AF, BuA125716
F-AZFP(2)	SPAD S-XIIIC1	4371	
F-AZFR	Soko J20 Kraguj	37	(F-AZGR), JRV30153
F-AZFT	Nord 3202	34	F-WYAY, ALAT
F-AZFU	Nord 3202	37	F-WYAZ, ALAT
F-AZFZ(2)	Beech D17S	3109	N117DS, N52950, NC52950, BuA12343
F-AZGB	North American T-6D Harvard IV	CCF4-175	N175JR, CF-UNL, RCAF20384
F-AZGC	EKW C-3605 (Stored)	273	F-WZII, C-493
F-AZGD	EKW C-3605 (Stored)	330	F-WZIG, C-550
F-AZGE	Dassault MD-312 Flamant	158	Fr.AF
F-AZGF	Nord 3202	80	G-BEFH, N2255N, ALAT
F-AZGG	CASA C-1.131E Jungmann	E3B-540	E3B-540
F-AZGI	CASA C-1.131E Jungmann (Painted in Sp.AF c/s as 781/13")	E3B-532	E3B-532
F-AZGJ	Boeing Stearman E75	"75-SA28"	
F-AZGK(2)	Stinson V-77 Reliant	77-177	N77DB, NC77DB
F-AZGM	Boeing Stearman A75-N1	75-589	G-BPEX, N65D, N61304, 40-2032
F-AZGN	Fokker DR.1 Replica	MF-01	
F-AZGO	DHC-1 Chipmunk T.20	C1/0346	F-WZGO, FAP1308
F-AZGP	OGMA/DHC-1 Chipmunk T.20	OGMA-23	FAP1333
F-AZGQ	OGMA/DHC-1 Chipmunk T.20	OGMA-15	FAP1325
F-AZGR(2)	Boeing Stearman B75N1	75-2650	N62418, BuA04320
F-AZGS	North American T-6G Texan (Painted as 49-3432)	168-556	Fr.AF, 49-3432
F-AZGT	Nord 3202	94	F-WZBB, ALAT
F-AZGV(2)	Breguet 905SA Fauvette	21	BGA2768/ELJ, F-CCGU
F-AZGY	Starck AS-70	AG-01	
F-AZGZ	Pitts S-1S Special	288H	
F-AZHA	Nord NC.856A-1 Norvigie	25	F-BYCM, F-BJLH, ALAT
F-AZHC	Bücker Bü.133E Jungmeister	F5-2009	
F-AZHD	North American NA-68 (Replica) (Painted as Fr.Navy "11F2"/"79413")	SA-30	
F-AZHE	North American NA-68 (Replica) (Painted as Fr.Navy "14.F.7")	SA-31	
F-AZHG	Pilatus P3-03 (Painted as "A-805")	322-4	A-805

Reg	Type	C/n	Previous identities
F-AZHH	de Havilland DH.100 Vampire FB.6	708	J-1199
F-AZHI	de Havilland DH.100 Vampire FB.6 (Res)	652	J-1143
F-AZHJ	de Havilland DH.100 Vampire FB.6	668	J-1159
F-AZHK	Douglas AD-4N Skyraider	61/7802	N91989, Fr.AF, BuA127002
F-AZHL	Morane-Saulnier MS.315	350	F-BCNT
F-AZHM	Antonov An-2	17311	D-FONH, DDR-SKH(2), LSK453
F-AZHN	North American T-28C Trojan (Painted as "140547"/"ER")	226-124	N2800Q, BuA140547
F-AZHO	Nord 3202	95	F-WZBC, F-AZAC, ALAT, (F-BNRN), ALAT
F-AZHP	S.O.4050 Vautour IIN	348	CEV-"DP", Fr.AF
F-AZHR	Sud Avn/North American T-28A Fennec	135/174-602	Fr.AF, 51-7749
F-AZHT	Pilatus P.3-03	324-6	(F-AZGU), A-807
F-AZHU	de Havilland DH.115 Vampire T.55 (Stored as U-1210)	870	U-1210
F-AZHX	de Havilland DH.100 Vampire FB.6 (Painted as VZ192-"4-LH")	624	J-1115
F-AZHY	de Havilland DH.100 Vampire FB.6 (Coded "DY-6")	610	J-1101
F-AZIB	North American T-6G Texan	182-585	F-BMJQ, Fr.AF, 51-14898
F-AZIC	Boeing Stearman PT-13D	75-5540	G-BTZM, N4738V, 42-17377
F-AZII	Piper J-2 Cub (Identity uncertain)	5418	
F-AZIJ	Nord 3202	85	G-BRVA, G-BIZL, N2255Y, ALAT
F-AZIK	de Havilland DH.100 Vampire FB.6	700	J-1191
F-AZIM	Yakovlev Yak-3	9/04623	RomanianAF
F-AZIN	Blériot XI	225	G-AVXV
F-AZIP	Boeing Stearman PT-17	75-341	N58712, AN-BLL, N58712, 40-1784
F-AZIR	Yakovlev Yak C-11	25111/21	
F-AZIT	Nord 3202 (Painted as "AIT")	74	ALAT
F-AZIV	Nord 3400	123	ALAT
F-AZIY	Nord 3202	15	F-WZBA, ALAT
F-AZIZ	Luscombe 8A Silvaire	3071	G-OWIZ, N71644, NC71644
F-AZJA	Grumman TBM-3E Avenger (Correct c/n believed to be 2688)	"85869"	N9927Z, BuA85869
F-AZJB	Yakovlev Yak C-11	25111/03	EAF-533 ?
F-AZJC	Waco UPF-7	5495	N29998, NC29998
F-AZJD	Dewoitine D.27-SA	SA-290/322	F-AZBF, (F-AZBC), HB-RAC, U-290
F-AZJE	Aero 3F	40174	YU-CXO, JRV40174
F-AZJF	Hirth Hi.27 Akrostar II	4003	F-WZJF, HB-MSA, D-EBAZ
F-AZJI	North American T-6G Texan	182-407	Fr.AF, 51-14720
F-AZJK	Nord 3202	64	ALAT
F-AZJL	DHC-1 Chipmunk 22 (Painted WP900-"V-15")	C1/0771	G-BWRX, WP900
F-AZJO	Nord 3202	101	F-WZBE, F-AZAI, F-BNRP, ALAT
F-AZJP	Beech D-17S	6738	(F-AZGU), N1126V, N4926V, XB-LEQ, NC67718, BuA23721, 44-76056, (BuA23721)
F-AZJQ	DHC-1 Chipmunk 22	C1/0829	WP967
F-AZJR	Boeing Stearman E75 (Painted as USN "4273"/"741")	75-5656	(F-AZJS), N5358N, 42-17493
F-AZJS	Supermarine VS.390 Spitfire XIX	6S-585110	G-CDGK, N219AM, R.Thai AF:, U14-26/97, PS890
F-AZJT	Nord 3202BIB	71	F-WZBD, F-AZAD, ALAT
F-AZJU	CASA C.352L (Regd as Junkers Ju 52/3m) (Painted as Luftwaffe "N9+AA")	24	G-BECL, T2B-212
F-AZJV	DHC-1 Chipmunk 22	OGMA-65	CS-AZP, FAP1375
F-AZJX	Aero 45	4904	F-GFYA, I-CRES
F-AZJY	Caudron-Renault JN760-C1	01	(F-PNJY), F-WNJY
F-AZKA	SZD-24C Foka (Reported stored 6.13)	W-177	OO-ZJ L, SP-2093
F-AZKB	SAAB S.91B Safir	91295	F-BHAG, SE-XAE
F-AZKD	Piaggio FWP.149D (Painted as "141"/"Z-KD")	141	D-EEWR, (G-BLOW), D-EEWR, 91+20, YA+457, YA+010, KB+118
F-AZKG	Sud Avn/North American T-28 Fennec	82/174-111	N14119, Fr.AF F-SFVQ, 51-3573
F-AZKI	Scottish Aviation Bulldog T.Mk1	BH120-273	XX615
F-AZKJ	Scottish Aviation Bulldog T.Mk1	BH120-248	XX555
F-AZKM	North American OV-10B Bronco (Painted "99+24" "Ville de Ravensburg")	338-9	99+24, D-9553, BuA 158300
F-AZKN	Morane-Saulnier MS.733 Alcyon	165	Fr.Navy
F-AZKO	Yakovlev Yak-12M	169664	
F-AZKP	AIAA/Stampe SV.4A	1143	F-BANX, Fr.mil
F-AZKS	Morane-Saulnier MS.733 Alcyon	83	F-BLXN, Fr.Mil
F-AZKT	Dassault MD.312 Flamant	260	Fr.AF
F-AZKU	Curtiss-Wright P-40N5	29677	VH-KTI(3), 42-105915
F-AZKY(2)	Douglas AD-4N Skyraider (Res) (Painted as "126997")	7798	Fr.AF, BuA126998
F-AZKZ	Morane-Saulnier MS.317	6549/295	F-AZKS, F-BGUU, Fr.Mil
F-AZLA	Beech D-17S	4829	N1255N, NC221, BuA33030
F-AZLC	Waco UPF-7	5711	(F-AZJC), N32079, NC32079
F-AZLD	Stampe SV.4B (Regd with incorrect c/n "01-97" and marked 'S.V.4B No.1' on rudder. Originally an AIAA-built SV.4C)	1065	F-BHGS, Fr.Navy
F-AZLE	SNCAN/Stampe SV.4C	551	F-BDCV
F-AZLF	CASA C-1.131E Jungmann	2036	E3B-...
F-AZLH	Alpavia/Fournier RF-3	10	
F-AZLI	DHC-1 Chipmunk 22	C1/0915	WZ877
F-AZLJ	North American NA-154 Navion 4 (Regd as a model L-17A; flies as "71277")	NAV-4-277	F-BIPP, OO-DEN, OO-TWX, NC91470
F-AZLK	Scottish Aviation Bulldog T.Mk1	BH120-321	XX663
F-AZLL	Lockheed 12A	1287	F-BJJY, G-AGTL, N33615, BuA0294
F-AZLM	Fokker D.VIIF Replica	01-MF	
F-AZLN	Boeing Stearman A75-N1	75-2143	N200FH, N52292, 41-8584
F-AZLO	DHC-1 Chipmunk 22 (Stored)	C1/0529	WG479
F-AZLP	Beech-SFERMA PD-146 Marquis 60A	10	F-BLLP
F-AZLQ	ICA-Brasov IAR-823	10	N721AR, Romanian AF
F-AZLR	SNCASE SE.3130 Alouette II	1385	ALAT
F-AZLS	Mudry CAP.20LS-200	8	F-GOSL, HB-MSF, OO-BNG

Reg	Type	c/n	Previous identities
F-AZLT	Morane-Saulnier MS.760A Paris	32	Fr.Navy
F-AZLU	Glasflügel H201B Standard Libelle	52	BGA3353/FLU, D-0298
F-AZLY	Yakovlev Yak-3R	172890	
	(Permit 1.02) (Conversion from Yak-11 with original c/n)		
F-AZLZ	Scottish Aviation Bulldog T.Mk1	BH120-217	XX531
F-AZMA	Nord 3202	65	G-BMBF, N2254X, EPNER, ALAT
F-AZMB	Caudron G-III	SA-33	F-PSYL, F-WSYL
F-AZMC	OGMA/DHC-1 Chipmunk T.20	OGMA-11	FAP1321
F-AZMD	Morane-Saulnier MS.504 Criquet	600/01	F-BCME
F-AZMF	Pilatus P3-05	466-15	A-828
F-AZMG	Soko 522 Ikarus	068	JRV60168
F-AZMH	Mooney M.20B Mark 21	1778	HB-DUM
F-AZMI	Hunting Jet Provost T.3A	PAC/W/9269	G-BVBE, XM461
F-AZML	North American AT-6D Harvard III	88-15564	F-BJBD, BAF: H-6, SAAF:7555, EZ174, 41-34047
	(Stored)		
F-AZMM	Nord 3400	29	ALAT
F-AZMO	Fouga CM.175 Zephyr	14	F-WQCG, Fr.Navy
F-AZMR	Nord 1002	216	F-BFKR, Fr.Mil
F-AZMS	Morane-Saulnier H	Sams 22.01	
F-AZMT	de Havilland DH.82A Tiger Moth	85983	F-BGEK, EM752
	(Identity unconfirmed)		
F-AZMX	Cessna 305C/L-19E Bird Dog	24557	F-GFCX, F-GECD, ALAT
F-AZMY	Morane-Saulnier MS.733 Alcyon	97	F-GDRO, F-BLXQ, Fr.Mil
	(Res 12.05)		
F-AZMZ	Boeing Stearman E75	75-SA98	unkn
	(Salis rebuild, modified) (May have used parts of F-AZJR?)		
F-AZNA	Nord 2504 Noratlas	001	(F-GFTS), Fr.Navy, F- WIFU
	(Res)		
F-AZND	Nord 3202	59	ALAT
F-AZNE	DHC-1 Chipmunk T.20	C1/0255	FAP1302
	(On rebuild)		
F-AZNF	Naval Aircraft Factory N3N-3	2909	F-WZNF, OO-JUS, N45172, BuA.....
F-AZNH	Hurel-Dubois HD-34	01	F-BHOO, F-WHOO
F-AZNI	Fauvel AV-36 Monobloc	31	HB-560
F-AZNJ	Albert A-110	17	F-A . . .
	(Res 7.04)		
F-AZNK	Fouga CM.170 Magister	217	F-GLRE, Fr AF
F-AZNM	Sopwith 1½ Strutter 182	2897	
F-AZNN	Yakovlev Yak C-11	25111/05	EAF- ?
	(Painted as "14")		
F-AZNO	Ryan ST-3KR/PT-22A	1676	N33618, CF-KTD, 41-15647
F-AZNR	Nord 1110	150	F-WJDQ, Fr.Mil
F-AZNT	Boeing Stearman A75-N1	75-4572	N60M, N49777, 42-16409
F-AZNU	SNCASE SE.313B Alouette II	1568	F-GRMS, Fr.AF
F-AZNV	Breguet 905SA	24	F-CCIV
F-AZNX	Beech C-45B	5990	F.AF: 140, RCAF: HB140, 43-35553
F-AZNZ	Mudry CAP.20	5	F-GFPZ, F-TFVY, F-BTAG
F-AZOA	Scottish Aviation Bulldog T.Mk1	BH120-334	XX688
F-AZOB	Scottish Aviation Bulldog T.Mk1	BH120-218	XX532
F-AZOC	Cessna 140	8353	G-BTOS, (F-HJLK), G-BTOS, N89325, NC89325
F-AZOD	Scottish Aviation Bulldog T.Mk1	BH120-255	XX559
F-AZOE	Mudry CAP.20E	02	F-TFVV, F-BTAI, F-ZWRP, F-BOPV
F-AZOF	AIAA/Stampe SV.4C	1070	N8334, OO-SPC, F-BHGY
F-AZOG	Scottish Aviation Bulldog T.Mk1	BH120-254	XX558
F-AZOH	Morane-Saulnier MS.733 Alcyon	63	F-BKOH, Fr.AF
F-AZOI	Scottish Aviation Bulldog T.Mk1	"406"	
	(Possibly ex JordanianAF 406, c/n BH120-340)		
F-AZOK	Yakovlev Yak C-11	172503 / 25111/19	EAF- ?
	(Painted as "37")		
F-AZOL(2)	Yakovlev Yak-50	771009	N63RA, (N501YK), N63RA, DOSAAF
F-AZOM	AIAA/Stampe SV.4C	1146	F-BAOM
F-AZON	Cessna 140	12839	HB-CAF
F-AZOO	de Havilland DH.100 Vampire FB.6	636	J-1127
	(Painted "DU-J")		
F-AZOP	de Havilland DH.100 Vampire FB.6	701	J-1192
	(Painted "DU-M")		
F-AZOT	SNCAN/Stampe SV.4C	334	F-BCOT
F-AZOU	North American T-6G Texan	"AF33-038-21174"	Tunis.AF:Y-61.., Fr.AF 51-14385, 51-14385
	(Quoted c/n is conversion contract number but correct c/n believed to be182-072. Given as ex 51-14317 but this was sold to Japan and above believed correct. Painted as "51149") (Res 12.03)		
F-AZOV	Erco Ercoupe 415CD	4834	F-WZOV, EI-CIH, G-BZKS, EI-CIH, OO-AIA, (PH-NDO), N94723, NC94723
F-AZOX	Douglas C-47B	16604/33352	F-GIDK, F-GIAZ, C-GSCC, C-GGJH, CAF12965, RCAF1000, KN655, 44-77020
F-AZOY	Mudry CAP.20	3	F-TFVW, F-BTAE
F-AZOZ	Scottish Aviation Bulldog T.Mk1	BH120-221	XX535
F-AZPB	CASA C-1.131E Jungmann	1036	F-WZPB, E3B-. . .
F-AZPD	DHC-1 Chipmunk T.10	C1/0027	WB575
F-AZPE	Yakovlev Yak-18	EM-019	SP-APR(2)
F-AZPF	Fouga CM.175 Zephyr	28	Fr.Navy
F-AZPG	Blériot XII-2	SA-29	
F-AZPH	SNCAN/Stampe SV.4C	309	F-BCLI
F-AZPI	Fouga CM.175 Zephyr	5	Fr.Navy
F-AZPK	Pilatus P.2-05	31	OO-PTO, U-111, A-111
F-AZPL	Nord NC.854	10	F-BDZT, F-BZBL, F-BDZT
F-AZPO	CSS.13 (Polikarpov Po.2)	49-026	"PLW-5", SP-ANB(1)
F-AZPP	de Havilland DH.82A Tiger Moth	PH-001	
	(Painted as "T8857")		
F-AZPQ	Fokker DR1 Triplane Replica	002	G-ATJM
F-AZPT(2)	Rearwin Sportster 8500	622	LV-X210, F-WZPT
F-AZPU	Pilatus P.3-05	465-14	HB-RCC, A-827
F-AZPV	SNCASO SO.1221S Djinn	1102/FR12	F-BHZK, ALAT: 'BST', 'BSB', 'YM', 8.000.194
F-AZPX(2)	Aeronca 7AC Champion	7AC-2192	F-BFPX, OO-TWG
F-AZPY	Yakovlev Yak-18A	710	HB-RBD, EAF-710
F-AZPZ	Fouga CM.170 Magister	413	F-GNBG, Fr.AF
F-AZQC	Fouga CM.170 Magster	480	Fr.AF
F-AZQD	CASA C-1.131E Jungmann	1101/A	G-BUTA, E3B-336
	(Res 11.05)		
F-AZQK	North American T-6H Harvard IV	"53796"	
F-AZQL	Morane-Saulnier MS.131	4	
F-AZQM	DHC-1 Chipmunk 22	C1/0723	G-BXDM, WP840
F-AZQN	Holste MH.1521M Broussard	187	Fr.AF
F-AZQQ	Pilatus P.3-05	502-51	HB-RCI, A-864
F-AZQR	North American T-6C Harvard	88-12326	F-BJBC, H-4, EX660, 41-33633
F-AZQT	Breguet Br.900	01	F-CCBA
F-AZQY	Auster J/1 Autocrat	2241	OY-AUY, D-EJSA, OE-AH(1), G-AJAI
F-AZQZ	DHC-1 Chipmunk 22	C1/0916	WZ878
F-AZRA	Fieseler Fi.156C3 Storch	2039/14	F-BBAT, Fr.mil
	(Built as MS.505 Criquet. Painted as 2E+RA)		
F-AZRB	North American SNJ-5 Texan	88-17955	N3651F, BuA90747, 42-86174
	(Painted as "90747/3")		
F-AZRC	Nord N.3400	78	ALAT
F-AZRD	North American AT-6D Texan	88-14510	F-BJBM, 42-44467
	(Painted as '14906/RD')		
F-AZRG	Bücker Bü.133E Jungmeister	"JRE-1.33"	
F-AZRK	SAAB SF-91B Safir	91299	F-BHAK, SE-XAI
F-AZRH	Nord 260	3	F-BKRH
F-AZRI	CASA C-1.131E Jungmann	2125	
F-AZRM	Scottish Aviation Bulldog T.Mk1	BH120-274	XX616
F-AZRO(2)	North American T6-M0	01-CM	
F-AZRP	Morane-Saulnier MS.733 Alcyon	147	F-BNEH, Fr.Mil
F-AZRS	Cessna 195B	7980	N3095B
F-AZRV	Zlin Z.526F Trenér Master	1079	F-GKIV, F-BRNC
F-AZRY	Ryan PT-22A	1630	N53148, 41-15601
F-AZRZ	Fournier RF-2	01	F-WJSR
F-AZSA	Morane-Saulnier MS.733 Alcyon	149	F-GIQK, F-BMQK, Fr.AF
F-AZSB	North American P-51B Mustang	122-40967	N2251D, N9148R, RCAF 9592, 44-73407
	(Painted as "411622" "NookyBooky IV")		
F-AZSC	North American AT-6D-NT Texan	88-15943	SpAF:C.6-154, NC10592, 41-34672
F-AZSH	Boeing Stearman E75N1	75-8726	F-WZSH, N53545, BuA43632
F-AZSI	SIPA S.903	unkn	
	(Res)		
F-AZSK	Potez 60	4190	F-AOSK
F-AZSM	de Havilland DHC-1 Chipmunk 22	C1/0789	WP914
F-AZSN	Boeing Stearman A75-N1	75-442	OO-JEH, G-BPTB, N55581, 40-1885
F-AZSP	Morane-Saulnier MS.733 Alcyon	123	F-BLYI, Fr.Mil
F-AZSQ	Boeing Stearman E75	75-5017	N52967, 42-16854
F-AZSR	North American T-6G Texan	197-75	Fr.AF, 53-4579
	(Painted as Navy "05-SF")		
F-AZST	Boeing Stearman PT-18	75-2184	N61860, 41-8625
F-AZSX	Fouga CM.170 Magister	533	F-GUHD, Fr.AF
F-AZSY	Slingsby T.21B Sedbergh	569/MHL.006	SE-SMN, WB979
F-AZSZ	Boeing Stearman E75 Kaydet	75-5659	N5367N, 42-17496
F-AZTA	Cessna 305C (L-19E Bird Dog)	24545	F-GFVE, ALAT
F-AZTB	MS.505 Criquet V	602/23	F-BEJN, F-ZJPJ, F-BEJN, Fr.mil
	(C/n officially quoted as 23/20)		
F-AZTC	Taylorcraft BC-12D1	10176	G-BTJZ, N44376, NC44376
F-AZTE	Douglas C-47A	9172	F-WZTE, F-GDPP, (F-ODQE), TL-AAX, TL-JBB, F-BRGN, Fr.AF, G-AGZF, WZ984, G-AGZF, 42-23310
F-AZTF	Scottish Aviation Bulldog T.Mk1	BH120-309	XX639
F-AZTK	Klemm Kl.35D	1854	D-EHKO(2), D-EBIB, SE-BHR, Fv.5020
F-AZTL	North American T-6G Texan	182-789	Fr.AF, 51-15102
F-AZTM	de Havilland DH.82A Tiger Moth	85946	F-BGCS, Fr.AF, DF210
F-AZTN	Globe GC-1B Swift	1151	N969RG
F-AZTO	Fouga CM.170 Magister	331	(F-GHLO), F-WIGY, Fr.AF
F-AZTP	Mudry CAP.20	01	F-BPXU
F-AZTS	Taylorcraft Plus D	176	F-WQVL, HB-EUL, LB317
F-AZTT	CASA C-1.131E Jungmann	2241	E3B-. . .
F-AZTV	Scottish Aviation Bulldog T.Mk.1	BH100-322	G-CBCT , XX664
F-AZTY	Piper J-5C/AE-1 Cub Cruiser	5-1477	N203SA, G-BWUG, (ZK-USN), N62073, NC62073, BuA30274
F-AZTZ	Bücker Bü .131D Jungmann	56	N55JG, N88759, OE-AAE, Swiss Mil A-44, HB-UTC
F-AZUC	Morane MS.317 replica	01-PC	
F-AZUD	Boeing Stearman A75N1 Kaydet	75-1606	N59334, 41-8047
F-AZUE	SNCASE SE.3130 Alouette II	1541	F-GKGE, ALAT
F-AZUF	SNCAN/Stampe SV.4C	383	F-BCQI
F-AZUI	Cessna 305C (L-19E) Bird Dog	0008	I-EIAH, EI-18, MM61-2962, 61-2962
	(Regal Air conversion)		
F-AZUK	Yakovlev Yak-50	801807	RA-2005K
F-AZUL	CASA C-1.131E Jungmann	2114	E3B-. . .
F-AZUN	Mudry CAP.20LS-200	09	F-GAUN
F-AZUP	Fouga CM.170 Magister	527	Fr.AF
	(Stored)		
F-AZUR	de Havilland DHC-1 Chipmunk 22	C1/0580	WK562
F-AZUS	Fouga CM.170 Magister	500	F-GJJI, Fr.AF
F-AZUU	de Havilland DHC-1 Chipmunk 22	C1/0736	PH-ZWA, (PH-DET), G-BDET, (PH-RTH), G-BDET, WP851
F-AZUV	CASA C-1.131E Jungmann	2190	OE-AUV, D-EHFT(2), E3B-580
F-AZUX	Boeing A75N1 PT-17 Kaydet	75-836	N58048, 41-1076
F-AZUY	Globe GC-1B Swift	3680	N2380B
F-AZUZ	Luscombe 8E Silvaire	5457	N2730K, NC2730K
F-AZVA	de Havilland DHC-1 Chipmunk 22	C1/0188	WB739
F-AZVC	Croses B-EC9	01-JMV	F-PYBG
F-AZVF	SDA Leopoldoff L-6 Colibri	129	G-BYKS, N10LC, F-BGIT, F-WGIT, F-WFRX
F-AZVG	Dassault MD.312 Flamant	189	Fr.AF
F-AZVH	Neukom Elfe 17	31	HB-1079
F-AZVK	Bücker Bü .131D/APM-150 Jungmann	27	D-EAUK, HB-UUK, A-18
F-AZVL	Luscombe 8A Silvaire	4873	N2146K, NC2146K
F-AZVM	Nord 2501 Noratlas	105	Fr.AF
	(Coded "63-VM")		
F-AZVN	North American T-6G-NT Texan	168-87	TunisianAF: Y-61501, MoroccanAF: 49-2983, 49-2983
	(Painted as RCAF "983")		
F-AZVO	Caudron 270 Luciole	6607/32	G-BDFM, F-BBPT, Fr.AF, F-ALVO
F-AZVQ	Ryan ST-A	132	VH-UVQ, VH-BWQ, VH-UZQ, NC16043
F-AZVR	Mudry CAP.20-LS200	11	I-IZAA
F-AZVS	CASA C-1.131E Jungmann	1035	E3B-. . .
F-AZVU	Avialsa-Scheibe A.60 Fauconnet	68	F-CCVU
F-AZVV	Nord 1101 Noralpha	15	F-BYAX, CEV, F-BBAJ
F-AZVZ	Mudry CAP.20	6	F-GIPA, F-TFVZ, F-BTAH, F-TFVZ
F-AZXC	Nord 1101 Noralpha	01-PC	F-BLQJ, Fr.mil
F-AZXD	Boeing Stearman A75N1 Kaydet	75-6807	N1226V, BuA07203

Reg	Type	c/n	History
F-AZXI	Piper PA-22-150 Tri-Pacer	22-4476	F-GHXI, PH-RCH, D-EANA, N5801D
F-AZXJ	Hawker Sea Fury FB.11	37733	N56SF, Iraqi AF 316, TF987
F-AZXK	Yakovlev Yak-50	863201	
F-AZXL	Hawker Sea Fury FB.10/ISS	37514	ZU-WOW, (ZS-ORF), N21SF, Iraqi AF
F-AZXM	de Havilland DHC-1 Chipmunk 22	C1/0863	WZ845
F-AZXN	Boeing Stearman A75N1 Kaydet	75-3885	N747JR, N56839, FJ385, 42-15696
F-AZXO	Cessna 140	8069	F-GURO, G-AHRO, N89065, NC89065
F-AZXP	Piper J-3C-65 Cub	11967	F-BGTP, F-BDRT, OO-GAN, 44-79671
F-AZXR	Hawker Hurricane IIA	-	ZK-TPK, DR393, P3351
F-AZXS	North American F-51D Mustang	122-40196	N2151D, N32FF, Salvador FAS406, N5073K, 44-73656
F-AZXT	Boeing Stearman A75N1 Kaydet	75-2430	N60806, 41-8871
F-AZXU	Morane-Saulnier MS.733 Alcyon	141	F-BLXU, Fr.Mil
F-AZXV	Fouga CM.170 Magister	479	Fr.AF
F-AZXX	Mudry CAP.20LS-200	06	(F-AZVZ), F-GIPA, F-TFVZ, F-BTAH, F-TFVZ
F-AZXY	Yakovlev Yak-50	853208	SP-YDM, RA-3218K, F-AZYD, RA-44456
F-AZXZ	Yakovlev Yak-3UA	Y-337	N3YK
F-AZYA	Yakovlev Yak-11	172624	OO-YAK, EgyptAF:079
F-AZYB	SNCASE SE.313B Alouette II	1163	F-GIJE, (F-GZJF), Fr.Mil
F-AZYC	SNCASE SE.313B Alouette II	1668	F-GTMC, ALAT
F-AZYE	SNCAN/Stampe SV-4A	207	F-BHEY, F-BBLB
F-AZYF	Yakovlev Yak-11-R2000	YAK11-01M	N11MQ
F-AZYH	Morane-Saulnier MS.181	01	F-PKFX, F-AIYH
F-AZYI	Breguet Br.1050 Alizé	59	Fr.Navy
F-AZYK	Yakovlev Yak-18A	1162624	LY-XPA, (F-AZYK), LSK
F-AZYM	Yakovlev Yak-50	781309	RA-1060K, DOSAAF
F-AZYN	Indraero Aero 101	011	HB-YAN, F-PGYO
F-AZYP	Yakovlev Yak-50	812008	DOSAAF
F-AZYQ	SNCASE SE.313B Alouette II	1003	F-GIJE, ALAT
F-AZYU	Utva-66F1	0807	F-GDLI, JRV51104
F-AZYV	Nord 1101 Noralpha	13	F-BYAV, CEV
F-AZYY	CASA C-1.131E Jungmann (Also quoted as c/n 2018)	2028	F-WZYY, E3B-414
F-AZYZ	Yakovlev Yak-50	832507	LY-CBH, DOSAAF 05 Blue
F-AZZA	Yakovlev Yak-50	812103	DOSAAF
F-AZZD	Fouga CM.170 Magister	411	Fr.AF
F-AZZF(2)	CASA C-1.131E Jungmann	2128	
F-AZZG	SG-38 Schulgleiter	20.24	
F-AZZH	Piper J-3C-65 Cub (Painted as "329994")	12476	OO-AJK(2), 44-80180
F-AZZI	Piaggio FWP.149D	153	D-EGEC(2), 91+31, ND+104, KB+130
F-AZZK	Yakovlev Yak-3 UPW	003	RA-3482K
F-AZZL	PZL-101A Gawron	107231	"F-AZYL", HA-SBE
F-AZZM	North American T-6 Harvard (Modified to A-6M)	SA-32	
F-AZZO	Morane-Saulnier MS.733 Alcyon	108	F-BMMU, Fr.Mil
F-AZZP	Fouga CM.170 Magister	569	Fr.AF
F-AZZS	Fouga CM.170 Magister	206	F-WMDM, Fr.AF
F-AZZU	North American B-25J Mitchell	108-47662	HB-RDE, F-AZID, N9621C, 45-8811
F-AZZV	Yakovlev Yak-3M	0470110	D-FAFL, N20669
F-AZZY	Ryan ST3KR/PT-22	1794	N57011, NC57011, 42-57498
F-AZZZ	Morane-Saulnier MS.733 Alcyon	139	F-BKOK, Fr.AF
F-AZ . .	Auster J/1 Autocrat	2241	OY-AUY, D-EJSA, OE-AAH(1), G-AJAI
F-AZ . .	Grumman TBM-3E Avenger	3920	F-WQON, C-GFPR, N3357G, BuA53858

METROPOLITAN FRANCE

Reg	Type	c/n	History
F-AJAC	Albert 110 (Under restoration .99)	16	
F-AJFZ	Albert A.61 (Under restoration .99)	1	
F-AMJP	Potez 43.1 (Under restoration .99)	3322	
F-BAGK	AIAA/Stampe SV.4C	1110	
F-BAGY	AIAA/Stampe SV.4C	1116	
F-BAHF	AIAA/Stampe SV.4C	1121	
F-BAHG	AIAA/Stampe SV.4C	1122	
F-BAHV	AIAA/Stampe SV.4C	1130	
F-BANI	AIAA/Stampe SV.4C	1140	
F-BAOL(3)	SNCAN/Stampe SV.4C	207	F-BHEY, ALAT, F-BBLB
F-BAQC	Poullin PJ.5B (Cub Conversion)	6	F-PAQC
F-BARP	Morane-Saulnier MS.505 Criquet	496/10	
F-BASF	Beech P35 Bonanza	D-7077	F-OBSF, N9548Y
F-BASJ(3)	Morane-Saulnier MS.733 Alcyon	13	(F-BDZC(2), F-BDZY
F-BAUA	Beech D50 Twin Bonanza (Instructional airframe at Dinan)	DH-39	F-OAUA
F-BAVN	Agusta-Bell 47G-2	066	F-OAVF
F-BAYP	PA-18A-150 Super Cub (Damaged 24.6.00)	18-5486	N6192D
F-BBEG	Nord N.1203 Norécrin VI	295	
F-BBER	Nord N.1203 Norécrin VI	332	
F-BBEZ	Nord N.1203 Norécrin VI	344	
F-BBIK	Piper J-3C-65 Cub	11173	Fr.Mil, 43-29882
F-BBJZ	Nord NC.858S Norvigie	140	
F-BBON	SNCAN/Stampe SV.4C	322	
F-BBPY	Bell 47G	490	F-OAPY, OO-SHZ, OO-UBC
F-BBQP	SNCAN/Stampe SV.4C	191	
F-BBQY(2)	SNCAN/Stampe SV.4C	195	F-BBQR
F-BBQZ	Piper J-3C-65 Cub (Correct c/n is 11921, ex Fr.Mil 625, 44-79625)	"625"	
F-BBTD	Piper J-3C-65 Cub	13148	HB-OVU, 45-4408
F-BBUU	SNCAN/Stampe SV.4A	85	Fr.Mil
F-BBVI	SNCAN/Stampe SV.4A	16	Fr.Mil
F-BBXU(3)	Morane-Saulnier MS.317	6522/268	F-BBZU
F-BBZR	Morane-Saulnier MS.317	6512/258	
F-BCAP	Piper PA-18-135 Super Cub	18-2890	
F-BCBC	Morane-Saulnier MS.317	323	
F-BCBN	Piper PA-25-235 Pawnee B	25-3744	F-OCHN, N7624Z
F-BCCB	Beech S35 Bonanza	D-7345	F-OCCB
F-BCDX	Piper J-3C-65 Cub (Officially quoted with f/n 10353 as c/n)	10528	43-29237
F-BCGQ	SNCAN/Stampe SV.4A	263	
F-BCGS	SNCAN/Stampe SV.4C	281	
F-BCLH	SNCAN/Stampe SV.4C	308	
F-BCNL	Morane-Saulnier MS.317	6527/273	
F-BCNN	Morane-Saulnier MS.317	6592/338	
F-BCNV	Morane-Saulnier MS.317	352	
F-BCOP	SNCAN/Stampe SV.4C	328	
F-BCPF	Piper J-3C-65 Cub	13251	45-4511
F-BCPK	Piper J-3C-65 Cub	13147	45-4407
F-BCPN	Piper J-3C-65 Cub	11801	OO-REA, 43-30510
F-BCPY	Piper J-3C-65 Cub	11531	43-30240
F-BCPZ	Piper PA-12 Super Cruiser seaplane	12-3485	NC4057H
F-BCQB	SNCAN/Stampe SV.4C	364	
F-BCQM	SNCAN/Stampe SV.4C	398	
F-BCQT	SNCAN/Stampe SV.4C	411	
F-BCUV	SNCAN/Stampe SV.4A	419	F-BCTC
F-BCXD	SNCAN/Stampe SV.4A	438	
F-BCXZ	Nord 1203 Norécrin II	309	D-EKIC, HB-DAK
F-BCZE	SNCAN/Stampe SV.4C	262	F-BCKH
F-BCZQ	Gardan GY-80 Horizon 160 (Derelict at Lognes)	7	F-OCBQ
F-BDCM	SNCAN/Stampe SV.4C	542	
F-BDGL	SNCAN/Stampe SV.4C	493	
F-BDHC(4)	AIAA/Stampe SV.4A	1125	F-BAHN, Fr.Mil
F-BDII	SNCAN/Stampe SV.4C	487	
F-BDME	SNCAN/Stampe SV.4A	635	
F-BDMI	SNCAN/Stampe SV.4A	639	
F-BDNF	SNCAN/Stampe SV.4A	661	
F-BDNM	SNCAN/Stampe SV.4A1	668	
F-BDNN	SNCAN/Stampe SV.4C	669	
F-BDNU	SNCAN/Stampe SV.4C	676	
F-BDOX	SNCAN/Stampe SV.4C	370	
F-BDOY	Zodiac-Vernanchet HG 380 Free Balloon	205/8888	
F-BDTI	Piper J-3C-65 Cub	13181	45-4441
F-BDTS	Piper J-3C-65 Cub	12526	44-80230
F-BDTT	Piper J-3C-65 Cub	12488	44-80192
F-BDTX	Piper J-3C-65 Cub	12804	44-80508
F-BDUV	Piper J-3C-65 Cub	11653	OO-AVL, 43-30362
F-BDXM	Morane-Saulnier MS.506L Criquet (Lycoming conversion)	635	F-WDXM, F-BDHM
F-BDZP	Nord NC.854	6	
F-BEAU	Piper PA-20-135 Pacer	20-1057	N10F
F-BEBR	Nord 1203 Norécrin VI	48	
F-BEGD	Piper J-3C-65 Cub	9676	43-815
F-BEGG	Piper J-3C-65 Cub	12886	44-80590
F-BEGN	Piper PA-12 Super Cruiser	12-3472	N4041H
F-BEGU	Piper J-3C-65 Cub	10384	F-OTAN-2, F-BEGU, 43-29093
F-BEHG	Morane-Saulnier MS.733 Alcyon	6	Fr.AF
F-BEHM	Macchi MB.308	53/5826	F-OAHM, I-LAGI
F-BEJF	Morane-Saulnier MS.505 Criquet	654/4	
F-BEJZ(3)	Piper J-3C-65 Cub	11457	F-BFCX, 43-30166
F-BEKZ	Piper J-3C-65 Cub	11889	Fr.AF, 44-79593
F-BEOF	Nord N.1203 Norécrin VI	108	
F-BEOM	Nord N.1203 Norécrin VI	127	
F-BEPO	GY-30 Supercab (Stored)	01	F-WEPO
F-BEPY	AIAA/Stampe SV.4A	1056	Fr.Navy
F-BEPZ	Cessna 170B	26103	F-OAPZ
F-BERB	SAN Jodel D.140 Mousquetaire	33	F-OBRB
F-BERY	Nord N.1203 Norécrin III	353	
F-BETD	Piper PA-12 Super Cruiser	12-3557	
F-BETK	Piper J-3C-65 Cub	13241	NC74120, 45-4501
F-BETR	Piper J-3C-65 Cub	12164	44-79868
F-BETY	Piper J-3C-65 Cub	13177	45-4437
F-BEUS	Nord N.1203 Norécrin VI	180	
F-BEXD	Stinson 108-3 Voyager	108-4419	OO-UFO, HB-TRS, F-BBSV, HB-TRH, N6419M
F-BEYR	SIPA S.903	15	
F-BEZG	Nord NC.858S	100	
F-BEZX	Nord NC.858S	116	
F-BFAM	Piper PA-24-250 Comanche	24-2802	F-OCCC, N4636S, LV-PQE, N7591P
F-BFAR	Wassmer WA.41 Baladou	105	
F-BFBO	Piper J-3C-65 Cub	13153	NC74119, 45-4413
F-BFBP	Piper J-3C-65 Cub (Noted wfu Gueret-St.Laurent 8.06)	13195	NC74118, 45-4455
F-BFBQ	Piper J-3C-90 Cub (Officially quoted as c/n 12959 which is HB-OGL)	12443	44-80147
F-BFCC	Piper J-3C-65 Cub	11157	Fr.Mil, 43-29866
F-BFCF	SNCAN/Stampe SV.4C (Reserved as D-EEDQ 1.15)	58	Fr.Navy, F-BDYN, Fr.AF
F-BFCO	Piper J-3C-65 Cub	11226	Fr.Mil, 43-29935
F-BFDS	Jodel D.112 Club	485	
F-BFES	Piper PA-18A-150 Super Cub	18-3293	F-DAES, N3295B
F-BFET	Piper PA-18A-150 Super Cub	18-4095	CN-TTU, F-DAEB
F-BFFJ	Piper J-3C-65 Cub	12679	44-80383
F-BFFN	Piper J-3C-65 Cub	13348	NC74115, 45-4608
F-BFFP	Piper PA-11 Cub Special (Damaged 23.6.99)	11-867	
F-BFFU	Piper PA-11 Cub Special	11-939	
F-BFFV	Piper PA-11 Cub Special	11-940	
F-BFHH	Piper PA-18 Super Cub 95	18-1537	ALAT, 51-15537
F-BFIQ	Nord NC.858 (Restoration project)	23	
F-BFKL(3)	Holste MH.1521M Broussard	38	ALAT
F-BFLC	C.A.B .GY-20 Minicab	3	
F-BFMA	Piper PA-11 Cub Special	11-946	
F-BFMG	Piper PA-11 Cub Special	11-945	
F-BFML	Piper J-3C-65 Cub	12229	44-79933
F-BFMQ	Piper J-3C-65 Cub	12527	44-80231
F-BFOL	Beech D35 Bonanza	D-3606	F-OBOL, OO-YAC, (OO-SCF)
F-BFON	Boisavia B.601 Mercurey	01	F-WFON
F-BFOP	SNCAN/Stampe SV.4C	494	CEV
F-BFOZ	Piper J-3C-65 Cub	12696	N74123, 44-80400
F-BFPM	Stinson 108-3 Voyager	108-5080	N4080C
F-BFQD	Piper J-3C-65 Cub (Coded "YC")	13028	OO-SUD, 44-80732
F-BFQG	Piper J-3C-65 Cub	13289	45-4549
F-BFQL	Piper J-3C-65 Cub	12788	NC74124, 44-80492
F-BFQN	Piper J-3C-65 Cub	11725	N79815, 43-30434
F-BFQO	Piper PA-12 Super Cruiser (Badly damaged 29.5.03)	12-3492	N79814, NC79814, NC4059H
F-BFSY	Nord NC.858S	77	

Reg	Type	c/n	Previous identities
F-BFUB	AIAA/Stampe SV.4C	1087	Fr.Mil
F-BFYD	Piper J-3C-65 Cub	"8979"	Fr.Mil, 42-38410
	(Quoted c/n is believed in error; possibly 8335 ex Fr.Mil, 42-15216?)		
F-BFYI	Piper J-3C-65 Cub	13054	OO-AVJ, 44-80758
F-BFYO	Piper J-3C-65 Cub	10531	Fr.Mil, 43-29240
F-BFZA	Piper PA-18 Super Cub 95	18-1338	ALAT, 51-15338
F-BFZK	Morane-Saulnier MS.317	6525/271	Fr.Mil
F-BFZN	SNCAN/Stampe SV.4C	71	Fr.Mil
F-BFZU	SNCAN/Stampe SV.4C	377	Fr.Mil
F-BGGE	SNCAN/Stampe SV.4C	531	Fr.Mil
F-BGGP	SNCAN/Stampe SV.4C	41	Fr.Mil
F-BGJR	Nord N.1203 Norécrin VI	375	
F-BGKL	Jodel D.112 Club	618	
F-BGKX	Morane-Saulnier MS.317	6518/264	Fr.Mil
F-BGOF	Bell 47G-2	1319	
F-BGOS	Bell 47D-1	609	
F-BGOZ	Cessna 170A	19959	
F-BGPA	Piper J-3C-65 Cub	8531	OO-AVC, 42-36407
F-BGPP	Beech 35 Bonanza	D-677	HB-ECS, NC90572
F-BGPT	Piper PA-18 Super Cub 125	18-1137	N1327A
F-BGQC	Piper J-3C-65 Cub	9001	Fr.Mil, 42-38432
F-BGQM	Piper J-3C-65 Cub	9920	43-1059
F-BGQY	Piper PA-12 Super Cruiser	12-1118	G-AJGY
F-BGSD	Aero Commander 560A	366	
F-BGUV	Morane-Saulnier MS.317	6551/297	Fr.Mil
F-BGUZ	Morane-Saulnier MS.317	6560/306	Fr.Mil
F-BGXC	Piper J-3C-65 Cub	11446	43-30155
F-BGXR	Bell 47D-1	158	F-OAMR, I-SILT, N229B
F-BGXS	Piper J-3C-65 Cub	10535	43-29244
F-BGXY	Bell 47G-2	690	
F-BGZM(2)	Boisavia B.606 Mercurey	3	F-BHCH
F-BHCK	Jodel D.112 Club	483	
F-BHDB	Bell 47G	19	OO-CSC, N165B
F-BHDM(2)	Boisavia B.601L Mercurey	110	F-BIRF(2)
F-BHEG	Beech F35 Bonanza	D-4333	
F-BHFK(2)	Nord 1203 Norécrin	230	F-BEUU
F-BHGH	Jodel D.112 Club	377	
	(Noted dism, Le Mans 6.06)		
F-BHGJ	Bell 47G-2	1342	
F-BHGN	Jodel D.112 Club	379	
F-BHGX	Leopoldoff L.55 Colibri	5	
F-BHHD(3)	AIAA/Stampe SV.4C	1119	F-BAHC, Fr.mil
F-BHHP(2)	Piper PA-22-135 Tri-Pacer	22-2013	(F-BMXY), F-DAFE, OO-HAA, N3771A
F-BHHQ(2)	Piper J-3C-65 Cub	10272	(F-GJMQ), C-GVGM, N46784, NC46784, 43-1411, (42-60221)
F-BHHV(2)	SNCAN/Stampe SV.4C	361	F-BCOJ
F-BHHX	Beech C35 Bonanza	D-2691	HB-EBC
F-BHJM	Schröder Fire Balloons G34/24 HAFB	891	HB-QJM
F-BHKF	Wassmer Jodel D.112 Club	333	
F-BHKR	Wassmer Jodel D.112 Club	347	
F-BHLP	Nord N.1203 Norécrin VI	141	F-OBLP, CN-TYN, F-BEQI
F-BHLT	SAN Jodel D.140A Mousquetaire	25	F-OBLT
F-BHNJ	SAN Jodel D.117 Grand Tourisme	425	
F-BHOR	Rockwell Commander 112	0284	N1284J
F-BHOT	SNCASO SO.1221-S Djinn	1006/FR25	F-WHOT
F-BHOY	Rousseau Piel CP.301B Emeraude	107	
F-BHPY	Jodel D.112 Club	550	
F-BHQO	Bell 47G-2	684	F-OAQO
F-BHQP	CEA Jodel DR.1051 Sicile	538	
F-BHTF	Nord N.1203 Norécrin III	358	
	(Wfu)		
F-BHTO	Wassmer Jodel D.112 Club	518	
F-BHTP	Wassmer Jodel D.112 Club	519	
F-BHVN	Agusta-Bell 47G-2	098	
F-BHXK	SAN Jodel D.112 Club (ex D.117)	512	
F-BHXL	SAN Jodel D.117 Grand Tourisme	588	
F-BHXM	SAN Jodel D.117 Grand Tourisme	591	
F-BHYV(2)	Nord 1101 Noralpha (code"42")	42	Fr mil
F-BHYZ	Wassmer Jodel D.120 Paris-Nice	69	
F-BIAL	Beech D50 Twin Bonanza	DH-104	N4347D
	(USArmy c/s)		
F-BIAV	Passot Jodel D.112 Club	708	
F-BIBC	Jodel D.117	606	
	(Being rebuilt)		
F-BIBH	Jodel D.119D	626	
F-BIBI	SAN Jodel D.117 Grand Tourisme	612	
F-BICB	Agusta-Bell 47G-2	062	F-BHEO
F-BICE	Cessna 170B	26436	N2893C
F-BIDB	SAN Jodel D.117A Grand Tourisme	691	
F-BIDQ	SAN Jodel D.117 Grand Tourisme	721	
F-BIEI	Bell 47G-2	1275	F-ZBA ., F-BGSS
F-BIEJ	Bell 47G	1285	Fr.Mil
F-BIEQ	Bell 47G-2	1465	F-ZBAI, F-BHKZ
F-BIEV	SNCASO SO.1221-S Djinn	1019/FR58	F-WJSO, PB+158, PB+120, F-WIFG
F-BIEX	Jodel D.112 Club	568	F-BIKX
F-BIFH	Hiller UH-12B	273	Fr.AF, 51-16119
F-BIFN	Agusta-Bell 47G-2	209	Fr.Mil
F-BIFT	Aérospatiale SA.315B Lama	05	
F-BIGF	Jodel D.112D Club	850	
F-BIGH	Jodel D.119 (ex D.112 Club)	857	
F-BIHC	Dornier Do.28A-1	3024	F-OBHC, D-IDTF
F-BIHT	CEA DR.250/160 Capitaine	71	F-OCHT
F-BIKS	Wassmer Jodel D.112 Club	571	
F-BIMQ	Piel CP.301A Emeraude	244	
F-BINC	SAN Jodel D.140C Mousquetaire III	104	(D-EFVK), F-BINC
F-BINY	CEA DR.253 Régent	101	F-WINY
F-BIOE	SAN Jodel D.117 Grand Tourisme	755	F-WINY
F-WIPA	Bell 47GRP	"01"	
F-BIPJ(3)	Morane-Saulnier MS.505 Criquet	149	F-BAOU
F-BIPS	Morane-Saulnier MS.733 Alcyon	5	Fr.Mil
	(Wfu)		
F-BIPU	Jodel D.112 Club	5	F-BIRU
F-BIPY	SNCASO SO.1221-S Djinn	1033/FR83	F-WIFU
F-BIQA	Wassmer Jodel D.112 Club	572	
F-BIQL	Wassmer Jodel D.112 Club	581	
F-BIRL	Jodel D.112 Club	654	
F-BIRV	SNCAN/Stampe SV.4C	697	CEV
F-BISI	Piel CP.301A Emeraude	268	(D-EHBI)
F-BISN	Piel CP.301A Emeraude	284	
F-BITA	SAN Jodel DR.1050 Ambassadeur	52	
F-BITS	SAN Jodel DR.100A Ambassadeur	56	
F-BIUI	Jodel D.119	955	
F-BIUR	Rousseau Piel CP.301B Emeraude	116	
F-BIVI	SAN Jodel DR.100A Ambassadeur	65	
F-BIXA	Wassmer Jodel D.120 Paris-Nice	116	
F-BIXM	Wassmer Jodel D.112 Club	892	
F-BIXN	Wassmer Jodel D.112 Club	1001	
F-BIZE	SAN Jodel D.140C Mousquetaire III	01	
F-BIZF	SAN Jodel D.140 Mousquetaire	20	
F-BIZH	SAN Jodel D.140A Mousquetaire	43	
F-BIZP	SAN Jodel D.140C Mousquetaire III	29	
F-BJAC	Piper PA-22-150 Tri-Pacer	22-5147	ALAT/F-MKAD, N10F
F-BJAG	Piper PA-24-250 Comanche	24-359	N10F
F-BJAX	Scintex Piel CP.301C-1 Emeraude	567	
F-BJCL	Jodel DR100A Ambassadeur	8	
	(Damaged 22.4.03, probable write-off)		
F-BJDE	Agusta-Bell 47G	067	ALAT, F-BHPC
F-BJDR	SAN Jodel D.140C Mousquetaire III	26	
F-BJDU	Gardan GY-80 Horizon 150	01	F-WJDU
F-BJEE	Cessna 182B Skylane	52201	(N7201E)
F-BJFN	Scintex Piel CP.301C Emeraude	538	
F-BJFR	Scintex Piel CP.301C-1 Emeraude	547	
F-BJFU	Scintex Piel CP.301C-1 Emeraude	554	
F-BJGM	Wassmer WA.41 Baladou	168	
F-BJGS	Piper PA-23-235 Apache	27-516	N4924P
F-BJIC	Wassmer Jodel D.112A Club	1005	
F-BJIK	Wassmer Jodel D.112A Club	1010	
F-BJIY	Wassmer Jodel D.112A Club	1014	
F-BJJA	SAN Jodel DR.1050 Ambassadeur	92	
F-BJJG	SAN Jodel DR.1050 Ambassadeur	115	
F-BJJR	SAN Jodel DR.1050 Ambassadeur	107	
F-BJJV	Cessna 172B	17248393	N7893X
	(Dismantled)		
F-BJJX	Jodel D.127	1048	
F-BJLK	Cessna 172B	17248217	N7717X
F-BJLL	CEA Jodel DR.1050 Ambassadeur	13	
F-BJLP	CEA Jodel DR.1051-M1 Sicile Record	25	
F-BJMD	Scintex ML.250 Rubis	03	
F-BJMG	Scintex ML.250 Rubis	103	
F-BJMO	Scintex CP.1310-C3 Super Emeraude	907	
F-BJMQ	Scintex CP.1310-C3 Super Emeraude	911	
F-BJMT	Scintex CP.1315-C3 Super Emeraude	922	
F-BJOA	Jodel D.128	974	
F-BJOO	Procaer F-15A Picchio	12	
F-BJOQ	Piel CP.301A Emeraude	349	
F-BJOV	CEA Jodel DR.1050 Ambassadeur	24	
F-BJOZ	CEA Jodel DR.1050 Ambassadeur	30	
F-BJPE	Wassmer Jodel D.112 Club	1018	
F-BJPI	Wassmer Jodel D.112 Club	1020	
F-BJPV	Wassmer Jodel D.112 Club	1065	
F-BJPY	Wassmer Jodel D.112A Club	1066	
F-BJPZ	Wassmer WA.40 Super IV	6	
F-BJQZ	SAN Jodel D.140B Mousquetaire II	70	
F-BJRG	Cessna 172B	17248424	N7924X
F-BJRI	Cessna 182D Skylane	18253401	(N9001X)
F-BJRN	Cessna 210A	21057828	N9528X
F-BJRQ	Cessna 170B	26377	F-OAQV, N2834C
F-BJUB	CEA Jodel DR.1050 Ambassadeur	43	
F-BJUK	Piper PA-18-150 Super Cub	18-7549	N3812Z
F-BJUM	Procaer F.15A Picchio	11	
F-BJUN	Nord NC.858	27	F-BFIV
	(Res)		
F-BJUR	Cessna 172B	17248725	N8225X
	(Noted dismantled Montpellier-L'Or 9.06)		
F-BJVB	Scintex Piel CP.315-C2 Emeraude	571	
F-BJVD	Scintex Piel CP.301-C2 Emeraude	576	
F-BJVE	Scintex Piel CP.301-C2 Emeraude	577	
F-BJVJ	Scintex CP.1310-C3 Super Emeraude	900	
F-BJVM	Scintex Piel CP.301-C3 Emeraude	591	
F-BJVX	Scintex CP.1315-C3 Super Emeraude	912	
F-BJVZ	Scintex CP.1315-C3 Super Emeraude	914	
F-BJYP	SAN Jodel DR.1050 Ambassadeur	254	
F-BJYV	SAN Jodel DR.1050 Ambassadeur	258	
F-BJZB	CEA Jodel DR.1051 Sicile	212	
F-BJZF	CEA Jodel DR.1050 Ambassadeur	213	
F-BJZG	CEA Jodel DR.1050 Ambassadeur	214	
F-BKAF	Wassmer WA.40 Super IV	18	
F-BKAI	Wassmer Jodel D.112 Club	1069	
F-BKAU	Wassmer Jodel D.112 Club	1076	
	(Stored dismantled)		
F-BKBA	Cessna 172C	17248784	N8284X
F-BKBB	Cessna 182D Skylane	18253628	N9228X
F-BKBE	Piper PA-18-150 Super Cub	18-7658	N10F
	(Dam.14.12.99)		
F-BKCF	Wassmer Jodel D.112 Club	1080	
F-BKCQ	Wassmer Jodel D.119	1113	
F-BKCT	Wassmer WA.40 Super IV	34	
F-BKDD	Morane-Saulnier MS.880B Rallye Club	15	
F-BKDF	Morane-Saulnier MS.880B Rallye Club	17	
F-BKDV	Morane-Saulnier MS.880B Rallye Club	69	
F-BKEH	Morane-Saulnier MS.885 Super Rallye	54	
F-BKEO	Morane-Saulnier MS.885 Super Rallye	55	
F-BKEQ	Morane-Saulnier MS.885 Super Rallye	58	
F-BKFA	Beech S35 Bonanza	D-7432	HB-EFA
F-BKGL	CEA Jodel DR.1050-M1 Sicile Record	233	
F-BKGU	Cessna 172C	17249387	N1687Y
	(Dismantled)		
F-BKHC	SAN Jodel DR.1051 Sicile	385	
F-BKHD	SAN Jodel DR.1050 Ambassadeur	366	
F-BKHF	SAN Jodel DR.1050 Ambassadeur	370	
F-BKHP	SAN Jodel DR.1050 Ambassadeur	368	
F-BKII	CEA Jodel DR.1051 Sicile	316	
F-BKIJ	CEA Jodel DR.1050 Ambassadeur	305	
F-BKIT	CEA Jodel DR.1051-M1 Sicile Record	329	
F-BKIU	CEA Jodel DR.1050 Ambassadeur	313	
F-BKJE	Wassmer WA.40 Super IV	38	
F-BKJZ	Wassmer Jodel D.112 Club	1128	
F-BKKP	Morane-Saulnier MS.880B Rallye Club	172	
F-BKKU	Morane-Saulnier MS.886 Super Rallye	319	
F-BKLA	Morane-Saulnier MS.885 Super Rallye	95	
F-BKLG	Morane-Saulnier MS.885 Super Rallye	121	
F-BKLK	Morane-Saulnier MS.885 Super Rallye	131	
F-BKLN	Morane-Saulnier MS.885 Super Rallye	138	
F-BKLS	Morane-Saulnier MS.885 Super Rallye	167	
F-BKLT	Morane-Saulnier MS.885 Super Rallye	156	
F-BKLV	Morane-Saulnier MS.885 Super Rallye	162	
F-BKLZ	Morane-Saulnier MS.885 Super Rallye	157	
F-BKMP	AIAA/Stampe SV.4C	1091	Fr.Navy, Fr.AF
F-BKND	Wassmer WA.40A Super IV	50	

Reg	Type	C/n	Previous identities
F-BKNO	Piper J-3C-65 Cub	12784	F-BBOO, OO-AVT, 44-80488
F-BKNT	Wassmer Jodel D.112 Club	1169	
F-BKOD	Morane-Saulnier MS.733 Alcyon	46	Fr.AF
F-BKOG	Morane-Saulnier MS.733 Alcyon (Res)	61	Fr.Mil
F-BKOI	Morane-Saulnier MS.733 Alcyon	74	Fr.AF
F-BKOJ	Morane-Saulnier MS.733 Alcyon	138	Fr.AF
F-BKOZ	Morane-Saulnier MS.733 Alcyon	45	Fr.AF, F-BHCV, Fr.AF
F-BKPK	CEA Jodel DR.1050 Ambassadeur	332	
F-BKPN	CEA Jodel DR.1050-MI Sicile Record	336	
F-BKPS	CEA Jodel DR.1051 Sicile	324	
F-BKQN	Cessna 182F Skylane	18254493	N3593Y
F-BKQQ	Cessna 182E Skylane	18253793	N9393X
F-BKQU	Pilatus PC-6A/H2 Porter	534	
F-BKRA	Cessna 182E Skylane	18254163	N3163Y
F-BKRF	Cessna 172C	17249241	N1541Y
F-BKRL	Piper PA-23-250 Aztec B	27-2082	N5068Y
F-BKRM	Cessna 310F	310-0074	HB-LBK, N6774X
F-BKRU	Piper PA-18 Super Cub 95	18-1456	ALAT, 51-15456
F-BKRZ	Cessna 182A Skylane	51468	F-DAFU, N2168G
F-BKSB	SAN Jodel D.140B Mousquetaire II	85	
F-BKSD	SAN Jodel D.140C Mousquetaire III	91	
F-BKSH	SAN Jodel D.140B Mousquetaire II	94	
F-BKSJ	SAN Jodel D.140C Mousquetaire III	97	
F-BKSR	SAN Jodel D.140C Mousquetaire III (W/o 25.1.02)	106	
F-BKSS	SAN Jodel D.140C Mousquetaire III	107	
F-BKTK	Morane-Saulnier MS.880B Rallye Club	215	
F-BKTX	Morane-Saulnier MS.880B Rallye Club	288	
F-BKTZ	SEEMS MS.880B Rallye Club	315	
F-BKUC	Morane-Saulnier MS.885 Super Rallye	234	(D-ELVO)
F-BKUU	Morane-Saulnier MS.885 Super Rallye	268	
F-BKVN	Beech P35 Bonanza	D-7114	
F-BKVU	Bell 47J	1050	
F-BKVY	SAN DR.1050-M Excellence	394	(G-. . . .), F-BKHX
F-BKXK	Morane-Saulnier MS.885 Super Rallye	232	F-OBXK
F-BKYB	SEEMS MS.880B Rallye Club	308	
F-BKZB	SEEMS MS.880B Rallye Club	337	
F-BKZG	SEEMS MS.880B Rallye Club	341	
F-BLAD	CEA Jodel DR.1051 Sicile	404	
F-BLAO	CEA Jodel DR.1051 Sicile	416	
F-BLAS	CEA Jodel DR.1051 Sicile	420	
F-BLAT	CEA Jodel DR.1051 Sicile	425	
F-BLAY	CEA Jodel DR.1051 Sicile	427	
F-BLBN	SEEMS MS.885 Super Rallye	5352	
F-BLBU	SEEMS MS.885 Super Rallye	384	
F-BLBV	SEEMS MS.885 Super Rallye	383	
F-BLDN	SAN Jodel D.150A Mascaret	21	
F-BLDS	SAN Jodel D.150A Mascaret	23	
F-BLEB	Piper PA-23-250 Aztec B	27-2434	N5394Y, N10F
F-BLEC	Cessna 182F Skylane	18254872	N3472U
F-BLEV	Morane-Saulnier MS.733 Alcyon	68	Fr.AF
F-BLEY(3)	Piper PA-18-150 Super Cub (Dam. 6.4.02)	18-5544	ALAT
F-BLFK	Wassmer Jodel D.112 Club	1177	
F-BLFP	Wassmer WA.40A Super IV	59	
F-BLFT	Wassmer WA.40A Super IV	55	
F-BLFX	Wassmer Jodel D.112 Club	1179	
F-BLGA	SOCATA Rallye 180T Galérien	3303	
F-BLGB	SOCATA Rallye 180T Galérien	3304	
F-BLGC	SOCATA Rallye 180T Galérien	3305	
F-BLGD	Beech 35-C33 Debonair	CD-867	
F-BLGN	Agusta-Bell 47G-2	283	
F-BLGO	Procaer F.15A Picchio	10	D-EBBE
F-BLHA	Mooney M.20C Mark 21	2485	
F-BLHD	Cessna 172D	17250009	N2409U
F-BLHJ	Piper PA-24-250 Comanche	24-3507	N8253P
F-BLHP	Piper PA-18-150 Super Cub	18-5355	ALAT, N10F
F-BLIK	SOCATA Rallye 180T Galérien	3306	
F-BLIM	SOCATA Rallye 180T Galérien	3308	
F-BLIN	SOCATA Rallye 180T Galérien	3309	
F-BLIO	SOCATA Rallye 180T Galérien	3310	
F-BLIP	SOCATA Rallye 180T Galérien	3311	
F-BLIQ	SOCATA Rallye 180T Galérien	3312	
F-BLIS	SOCATA Rallye 180T Galérien	3314	
F-BLIT	SOCATA Rallye 180T Galérien	3315	
F-BLIV	SOCATA Rallye 180T Galérien	3316	
F-BLJM	SANJodel DR.1050 Ambassadeur	470	
F-BLJN	SANJodel DR.1050M Excellence	474	
F-BLJO	SANJodel DR.1050M Excellence	475	
F-BLJT	SAN Jodel DR.1050M Excellence	484	
F-BLJV	SAN Jodel DR.105-M Excellence	482	
F-BLKD	Cessna FP172D Skyhawk Powermatic	FP172-0003/P17257179	F-WLKD
F-BLKK	SAN Jodel D.140R Abeille	501	F-WLKK
F-BLKL	Morane-Saulnier MS.760C Paris III	01	F-WLKL
F-BLKM(2)	Bücker Bü 133E Jungmeister	39	F-BLGM, HB-MIB, U-92
F-BLKU	Gardan GY-80 Horizon 180	07	
F-BLKY	Moynet 360-6 Jupiter (C/n quoted officially as "360.6")	03	F-WLKY
F-BLLJ	Piper PA-23-250 Aztec C	27-3756	N6462Y
F-BLMF	CEA Jodel DR.1050 Ambassadeur	434	
F-BLMI	CEA Jodel DR.1051 Sicile	438	
F-BLMK	CEA Jodel DR.1051 Sicile	440	
F-BLMO	CEA Jodel DR.1051 Sicile	445	
F-BLMR	CEA Jodel DR.1051 Sicile	441	
F-BLMS	CEA Jodel DR.1051 Sicile	448	
F-BLNA	Wassmer Jodel D.112 Club	1204	
F-BLNM	Wassmer Jodel D.112 Club	1207	
F-BLNS	Wassmer Jodel D.112 Club	1210	
F-BLNY	Wassmer WA.40A Super IV	72	
F-BLOB	Mooney M.20C Mark 21 (Wrecked)	2613	
F-BLOD	Piper PA-22-150 Caribbean (Converted to PA-20 taildragger standard)	22-7482	G-ARFA, N3566Z
F-BLON	Cessna 206 Super Skywagon	206-0081	N5081U
F-BLOQ	Piper PA-25-235 Pawnee	25-2400	N6824Z
F-BLOU	Gardan GY-80 Horizon 160	5	
F-BLPE	Gardan GY-80 Horizon 150	20	
F-BLPJ	Gardan GY-80 Horizon 160	44	
F-BLPK	Gardan GY-80 Horizon 160 (Dismantled)	41	
F-BLPM	Gardan GY-80 Horizon 180	06	
F-BLPQ	Gardan GY-80 Horizon 160	48	
F-BLPV	Gardan GY-80 Horizon 160	59	
F-BLPY	Gardan GY-80 Horizon 160	63	
F-BLQU	Nord 1101 Noralpha	136	N6171X, F-BLQU, Fr.Mil
F-BLRB	CEA Jodel DR.1051 Sicile	507	
F-BLRK	CEA Jodel DR.1051 Sicile	518	
F-BLRL	CEA Jodel DR.1050 Ambassadeur	516	
F-BLRN	CEA Jodel DR.1051 Sicile	514	
F-BLRQ	CEA Jodel DR.1051-M1 Sicile Record	524	
F-BLRR	CEA Jodel DR.1050 Ambassadeur	522	
F-BLRU	CEA Jodel DR.1050 Ambassadeur	525	
F-BLRY	CEA Jodel DR.1051 Sicile	523	
F-BLSB	SEEMS MS.885 Super Rallye	388	
F-BLSI	SEEMS MS.892A Rallye Commodore 150	10453	
F-BLSK	SEEMS MS.892A Rallye Commodore 150	10450	
F-BLSO	SEEMS MS.892A Rallye Commodore 150	10485	
F-BLTS(2)	Aérospatiale AS.350B Ecureuil	1175	
F-BLUE	CEA Jodel DR.1051 Sicile	539	F-BLZI
F-BLVC	Gardan GY-80 Horizon 160	32	
F-BLVG	Gardan GY-80 Horizon 160	72	
F-BLVI	Gardan GY-80 Horizon 160	31	
F-BLVQ	Gardan GY-80 Horizon 160	81	
F-BLVR	Gardan GY-80 Horizon 160	82	
F-BLVS	Gardan GY-80 Horizon 160	83	
F-BLVU	Gardan GY-80 Horizon 160	85	
F-BLVV	Gardan GY-80 Horizon 160	76	
F-BLXB	Alpavia/ Fournier RF-3	19	
F-BLXC	Alpavia/ Fournier RF-3	14	
F-BLXE	Alpavia/ Fournier RF-3	13	
F-BLXG	Alpavia/ Fournier RF-3	15	
F-BLXP	Morane-Saulnier MS.733 Alcyon	95	Fr.Mil
F-BLYU	Nord 1101 Noralpha	18	Fr.Mil
F-BLZC	CEA Jodel DR.1051 Sicile	531	
F-BLZS	CEA Jodel DR.1050 Ambassadeur	550	
F-BMAC	Wassmer Jodel D.112 Club	1215	
F-BMAN	Wassmer Jodel D.112 Club	1221	
F-BMBM	SAN Jodel D.140C Mousquetaire III	129	
F-BMBS	SAN Jodel D.140C Mousquetaire III	126	
F-BMBV	SAN Jodel D.140C Mousquetaire III	134	
F-BMBX	SAN Jodel D.140C Mousquetaire III	142	
F-BMBY	SAN Jodel D.140C Mousquetaire III	137	
F-BMBZ	SAN Jodel D.140C Mousquetaire III	115	
F-BMCA	Piper PA-24-250 Comanche	24-3288	N8099P, N10F, (N8043P)
F-BMCB	Cessna 182F Skylane	18254698	N3298U
F-BMCQ	Cessna 206 Super Skywagon	206-0003	N5003U
F-BMCR	Cessna F172E	F172-0062	
F-BMCU	Piper PA-18 Super Cub 95	18-1429	OO-MJD, (OO-HNB), ALAT, 51-15429
F-BMDM	Alpavia/ Fournier RF-3	34	
F-BMDY	Alpavia/ Fournier RF-3	49	
F-BMEE	SOCATA MS.893E Rallye 180GT	12435	
F-BMEJ	SAN Jodel D.140 Mousquetaire	32	D-EHBY, F-BIZQ
F-BMFF	SAN Jodel D.140C Mousquetaire III	140	
F-BMFK	SAN Jodel D.140C Mousquetaire III	147	
F-BMFS	SAN Jodel D.140C Mousquetaire III	157	
F-BMFV	SAN Jodel D.140C Mousquetaire III	159	
F-BMFX	SAN Jodel D.140C Mousquetaire III (W/o 22.3.09)	161	
F-BMGB	CEA Jodel DR.1051-M1 Sicile Record	570	
F-BMGE	CEA Jodel DR.1051 Sicile	562	
F-BMGG	CEA Jodel DR.1051 Sicile	574	
F-BMGH	CEA Jodel DR.1051 Sicile	567	
F-BMGK	CEA Jodel DR.1050 Ambassadeur	572	
F-BMGL	CEA Jodel DR.1050-M1 Sicile Record	576	
F-BMGQ	CEA Jodel DR.1051-M1 Sicile Record	583	
F-BMHM	Piper J-3C-65 Cub	11907	Fr.Mil, 44-79611
	(Quoted officially with c/n 11157 - but f/n 11735 confirms the true c/n as 11907)		
F-BMII	Wassmer WA.40A Super IV (Exp.4.03)	80	
	(Fuselage reported scrapped by Skycraft Aviation UK)		
F-BMIL	Wassmer Jodel D.112 Club	1261	
F-BMIN	Wassmer WA.40A Super IV	81	
F-BMIT	Wassmer Jodel D.112 Club	1267	
F-BMIV	Wassmer Jodel D.112F Club	1269	
F-BMJB	Scintex CP.1310-C3 Super Emeraude	926	
F-BMJC	Scintex CP.1315-C3 Super Emeraude	930	
F-BMJD	Scintex CP.1310-C3 Super Emeraude	932	
F-BMJF	CAARP CP.1315-C3 Super Emeraude	933	
F-BMJM	CAARP CP.1330 Super Emeraude	942	
F-BMJN	Piper PA-18 Super Cub 95	18-1419	ALAT, 51-15419
F-BMJR	Piper PA-28-140 Cherokee	28-20191	5T-TJI, HB-OLF, N6174W
F-BMJU	Morane-Saulnier MS.733 Alcyon	189	Fr.Navy
F-BMJV	Piper PA-18 Super Cub 95	18-1356	ALAT, 51-15356
F-BMKB	Sportavia/ Fournier RF-4D	4005	
F-BMKD	Sportavia/ Fournier RF-4D	4007	
F-BMKL	AIAA/Stampe SV.4C	1078	Fr.Navy, F-BCDN, Fr.Navy
F-BMKP	Piper PA-28R-180 Cherokee Arrow	28R-30086	(F-GBOP), F-OCKP, N3774T
F-BMLA	Cessna F172E	F172-0066	
F-BMLC	Cessna 336 Skymaster	336-0193	N3893U
F-BMLJ	Mooney M.20E Super 21	425	
F-BMLS	Cessna F172E	F172-0073	
F-BMLT	Piper PA-24-250 Comanche	24-3573	N8322P
F-BMMA	SNCAN/Stampe SV.4A	630	ALAT, Fr.AF/CEV, F-BDGA
F-BMMG	SNCAN/Stampe SV.4A	153	ALAT, F-BBAK, CEV
F-BMMH	SNCAN/Stampe SV.4A	247	Fr.Mil
F-BMMJ	SNCAN/Stampe SV.4C	691	ALAT, Fr.AF, (F-BDOK)
F-BMMY	Morane-Saulnier MS.733 Alcyon	128	Fr.Mil
F-BMNC	SEEMS MS.881 Rallye 105	408	
F-BMNE	GEMS MS.881 Rallye 105	410	
F-BMNL	SEEMS MS.893A Rallye Commodore 180	10489	
F-BMNO	SEEMS MS.892A Rallye Commodore 150	10492	
F-BMNQ	SEEMS MS.892A Rallye Commodore 150	10494	
F-BMNS	SEEMS MS.893A Rallye Commodore 180	10496	
F-BMNT	SEEMS MS.893A Rallye Commodore 180	10497	
F-BMOE	Wassmer Jodel D.120A Paris-Nice	268	
F-BMOU	Wassmer Jodel D.112 Club	1300	
F-BMOY	Wassmer Jodel D.112 Club	1301	
F-BMPM	CEA Jodel DR.1051-M1 Sicile Record	606	
F-BMPR	CEA Jodel DR.1051-M1 Sicile Record	613	
F-BMQC	Morane-Saulnier MS.733 Alcyon	200	Fr.Mil
F-BMQQ	Zlin Z.326 Trenér Master	890	
F-BMQS	Zlin Z.326 Trenér Master	894	
F-BMQU	Zlin Z.326 Trenér Master	900	
F-BMRA	Cessna 210D Centurion	21058295	N3795Y
F-BMRC	Piper PA-28-235 Cherokee	28-10272	N8800W
F-BMRI	Cessna 310 I	310I0198	N8198M
	(Noted dismantled nr Bergerac 9.11)		
F-BMRL	Cessna F172F	F172-0108	

Reg	Type	Serial	Previous ids
F-BMRT	SNCAN/Stampe SV.4A	686	Fr.Mil
F-BMRV	Mooney M.20E Super 21	512	
F-BMSK	Dornier Do.28A-1	3055	D-IBOR
F-BMSN	Cessna 182G Skylane	18255120	N3720U
F-BMSO	Cessna 182H Skylane	18256106	N2006X
F-BMSY	Piper PA-24-260 Comanche	24-4050	N8633P, N10F
F-BMSZ	Piper PA-18-150 Super Cub	18-8156	N5409Y
F-BMTD	Alpavia/ Fournier RF-3	55	
F-BMTS	Alpavia/ Fournier RF-3	85	
F-BMUB	Gardan GY-80 Horizon 160	86	
F-BMUC	Gardan GY-80 Horizon 160	87	
F-BMUE	Gardan GY-80 Horizon 160	89	
F-BMUF	Gardan GY-80 Horizon 160 (Stored)	90	
F-BMUI	Gardan GY-80 Horizon 160 (Abandoned ?, Tunis)	103	
F-BMUT	Gardan GY-80 Horizon 180	140	
F-BMUX	Gardan GY-80 Horizon 160D	154	
F-BMUZ	Gardan GY-80 Horizon 180	146	
F-BMVC	SEEMS MS.892A Rallye Commodore 150	10461	
F-BMVK	SEEMS MS.892A Rallye Commodore 150	10509	
F-BMVS	SEEMS MS.892A Rallye Commodore 150	10511	
F-BMVV	GEMS MS.892A Rallye Commodore 150	10538	
F-BMYJ	Wassmer WA.40A Super IV	90	
F-BMYM	Wassmer WA.41 Baladou	94	
F-BMZD	CEA Jodel DR.1050-M1 Sicile Record	629	
F-BMZE	CEA DR.250 Capitaine	19	
F-BMZF	CEA DR.250 Capitaine	5	
F-BMZH	CEA DR.250/160 Capitaine	7	
F-BMZK	CEA DR.250/160 Capitaine	14	
F-BMZN	CEA DR.250/160 Capitaine	21	
F-BMZO	CEA DR.250/160 Capitaine	2	
F-BMZP	CEA DR.250/160 Capitaine	4	
F-BMZS	CEA DR.250 Capitaine	23	
F-BMZT	CEA DR.250A/160 Capitaine	3	
F-BMZU	CEA DR.250/160 Capitaine	34	
F-BMZX	CEA DR.250/160 Capitaine	26	
F-BMZY	CEA DR.250/160 Capitaine	24	
F-BMZZ	CEA DR.250 Capitaine	1	
F-BNAE	Cessna U206 Super Skywagon	U206-0403	N8003Z
F-BNAF	Piper PA-30 Twin Comanche	30-17	N7016Y
F-BNAJ	Zlin Z.326 Trenér Master	906	
F-BNBA	SEEMS MS.892A Rallye Commodore 150	10514	
F-BNBJ	GEMS MS.892A Rallye Commodore 150	10542	
F-BNBN	GEMS MS.892A Rallye Commodore 150	10549	
F-BNBT	GEMS MS.892A Rallye Commodore 150	10557	
F-BNCJ	Wassmer Jodel D.112 Club	1311	
F-BNCM	Wassmer Jodel D.112 Club	1313	
F-BNCO	Wassmer Jodel D.112 Club	1315	
F-BNCU	SNCAN/Stampe SV.4C	447	(F-GDXM), F-BCXM
F-BNDD(4)	Holste MH.1521M Broussard	240	Fr.AF
F-BNDR	Beech 35-C33 Debonair	CD-929	
F-BNDT	Cessna F172G	F172-0198	
F-BNEC	Morane-Saulnier MS.733 Alcyon	129	Fr.Mil
F-BNEK	Morane-Saulnier MS.733 Alcyon	158	Fr.Mil
F-BNEL	Morane-Saulnier MS.733 Alcyon (Dismantled)	159	Fr.Mil
F-BNEX	Holste MH.1521C Broussard	108	Fr.AF
F-BNFF	Cessna F150F	F150-0001/15062312	F-WLIK, (N3512L)
F-BNFN	Cessna F172G (Damaged, noted stored Sabadell, Spain 10.13)	F172-0256	
F-BNFQ	Piper PA-28-140 Cherokee	28-20635	N6550W, N11C
F-BNFS	Piper PA-32-260 Cherokee Six	32-191	N3376W
F-BNFX	Piper PA-28-180 Cherokee C	28-2489	N8316W
F-BNGL	Hiller UH-12B	667	ALAT
F-BNGM	Hiller UH-12B	699	ALAT
F-BNGP	CEA DR.220 2+2	01	F-WNGP
F-BNHE	Wassmer WA.41 Baladou	109	
F-BNHH	Wassmer WA.41 Baladou	111	
F-BNHO	Wassmer Jodel D.112 Club	1345	
F-BNHS	Wassmer WA.41 Baladou	113	
F-BNIA	Mooney M.20E Super 21	624	
F-BNIF	SAN Jodel D.140C Mousquetaire III	168	
F-BNII	SAN Jodel D.140C Mousquetaire III	171	
F-BNIL	SAN Jodel D.140E Mousquetaire IV	174	
F-BNIR	SAN Jodel D.140E Mousquetaire IV	177	
F-BNIZ	SAN Jodel D.140E Mousquetaire IV	184	
F-BNJE	CEA DR.250/160 Capitaine	38	
F-BNJF	CEA DR.250/160 Capitaine	39	
F-BNJI	CEA DR.250/160 Capitaine	44	
F-BNJK	CEA DR.250/160 Capitaine	45	
F-BNJO	CEA DR.250/160 Capitaine	56	
F-BNJQ	CEA DR.250/160 Capitaine	55	
F-BNKS	Piper PA-28-140 Cherokee	28-21180	N11C
F-BNLC	Cessna 185B Skywagon	185-0533	TR-LLR, F-OBZU, N2533Z
F-BNLH	Cessna T210F Turbo-System Centurion	T210-0074	N6174R
F-BNLR	Piper PA-18 Super Cub 95	18-2076	(F-BNOH), R-65, 52-2476
F-BNMG	Cessna 172C	17249164	HB-CRU, N1464Y
F-BNMJ	Beech A23-19 Musketeer Sport III	MB-116	
F-BNMP	Piper PA-18-150 Super Cub	18-1022	ALAT, 51-15325
F-BNMR	Piper PA-18 Super Cub 95	18-1388	ALAT, 51-15388
F-BNMT	Beech D95A Travel Air	TD-577	HB-GBU
F-BNMU	Zlin Z.326 Trenér-Master	910	
F-BNMY	Zlin Z.526A Akrobat	1005	
F-BNNK	SOCATA MS.892A Rallye Commodore 150	10590	
F-BNOA	Mooney M.20E Super 21	919	
F-BNOB	Mooney M.20E Super 21	960	
F-BNOF	Jodel D.112D Club	1380	
F-BNOI	Beech 35-C33A Debonair	CE-39	
F-BNOK	Beech 95-C55 Baron	TE-54	
F-BNOM	Beech 35-C33 Debonair	CD-1029	
F-BNOR	Beech 35-C33 Debonair	CD-942	HB-ENI
F-BNOS	Beech S35 Bonanza	D-7944	HB-EFG
F-BNOZ	CEA DR.250/160 Capitaine	28	
F-BNPC	CEA Jodel DR.1051 Sicile	446	HB-EBM
F-BNPI	Piper PA-18-150 Super Cub	18-5396	ALAT, N10F
F-BNPM	CEA DR.220 2+2	2	F-WNPM
F-BNPP	Agusta-Bell 47G-2	246	
F-BNPQ	Bell 47J	1425	F-OBPQ, I-AGUS
F-BNPR	Piper PA-23-250 Aztec C	27-3297	N6091Y
F-BNQA	Gardan GY-80 Horizon 180	150	
F-BNQB	Gardan GY-80 Horizon 180	169	
F-BNQC	Gardan GY-80 Horizon 180	133	
F-BNQI	Gardan GY-80 Horizon 180	158	
F-BNQL	Gardan GY-80 Horizon 180	155	
F-BNQO	Gardan GY-80 Horizon 150D	168	
F-BNQQ	Piper PA-18 Super Cub 95	18-1601	ALAT, 51-15601
F-BNQT	Gardan GY-80 Horizon 180	174	
F-BNQX	Gardan GY-80 Horizon 180	178	
F-BNQY	Gardan GY-80 Horizon 180	164	
F-BNQZ	Gardan GY-80 Horizon 180	161	
F-BNRI	Beech A23-24 Musketeer Super III	MA-105	
F-BNRM	Cessna 210E Centurion	21058693	F-OCGG, N4993U
F-WNRQ(2)	Cessna 305C Bird Dog (L-19) (Coded AJO)	24519	ALAT
F-BNRR	Zlin Z.326 Trenér Master	913	F-WNRR, F-BNRR
F-BNRX (F-GADM)	Fournier RF-6B-100 (Res)	14	HB-EZP, F-GANP, D-EGRF,
F-BNRY	Nord NC.856A Norvigie	85	ALAT
F-BNRZ(2)	SNCAN/Stampe SV.4C	357	F-BCOF
F-BNSD	SOCATA MS.893A Rallye Commodore 180	10644	
F-BNSI	SOCATA MS.893A Rallye Commodore 180	10642	
F-BNSN	SOCATA MS.893A Rallye Commodore 180	10600	
F-BNSQ	SOCATA MS.893A Rallye Commodore 180	10580	
F-BNST	SOCATA MS.893A Rallye Commodore 180	10583	
F-BNSV	SOCATA MS.893A Rallye Commodore 180	10596	
F-BNSX	SOCATA MS.893A Rallye Commodore 180	10597	
F-BNSZ	SOCATA MS.893A Rallye Commodore 180	10599	
F-BNTG	Beech A23-24 Musketeer Super III	MA-33	
F-BNTL	Beech 35-C33 Debonair	CD-1049	
F-BNUV	CEA DR.250/160 Capitaine	68	HB-EXV, F-BNJV
F-BNVA	CEA DR.250/160 Capitaine	64	
F-BNVB	CEA DR.220 2+2	3	
F-BNVC	CEA DR.250/160 Capitaine	67	
F-BNVE	CEA DR.250/160 Capitaine	61	
F-BNVO	CEA DR.220 2+2	8	
F-BNVS	CEA DR.250/160 Capitaine	78	
F-BNVT	CEA DR.220 2+2	9	
F-BNVU	CEA DR.250/160 Capitaine	80	
F-BNVY	CEA DR.220 2+2	11	
F-BNXB	SOCATA MS.893A Rallye Commodore 180	10652	
F-BNXD	AIAA/Stampe SV.4C	1090	Fr.Navy
F-BNXL	SOCATA MS.893A Rallye Commodore 180	10608	
F-BNXM	SOCATA MS.892A Rallye Commodore 150	10633	
F-BNXP	SOCATA MS.880B Rallye Club	839	
F-BNXY	SOCATA MS.880B Rallye Club	832	
F-BNYB	Gardan GY-80 Horizon 180	162	
F-BNYC	Gardan GY-80 Horizon 160D	152	
F-BNYE	Gardan GY-80 Horizon 180	185	
F-BNYI	Gardan GY-80 Horizon 180	189	
F-BNYJ	Gardan GY-80 Horizon 180	201	
F-BNYO	Gardan GY-80 Horizon 160D	219	
F-BNYQ	Gardan GY-80 Horizon 180	191	
F-BNYR	Gardan GY-80 Horizon 180	193	
F-BNYS	Gardan GY-80 Horizon 180	206	
F-BNYU	Gardan GY-80 Horizon 180	165	
F-BNZB	Wassmer Jodel D.112 Club	1348	
F-BNZH	Wassmer WA.41 Baladou	120	
F-BNZU	Wassmer Jodel D.120A Paris-Nice	323	
F-BNZV	Wassmer WA.41 Baladou	125	
F-BOAF	Piper PA-28-180 Cherokee B	28-1130	F-OCAF, N7183W
F-BOBE	Wassmer WA.41 Baladou	131	
F-BOBF	Wassmer WA.40A Super IV	132	
F-BOBK	Wassmer WA.41 Baladou	135	
F-BOBN	Wassmer WA.41 Baladou	137	
F-BOBP	Wassmer WA.41 Baladou	129	
F-BOBQ	Wassmer WA.41 Baladou	140	
F-BOBV	Wassmer WA.41 Baladou	145	
F-BOBX	Wassmer Jodel D.120 Paris-Nice	334	
F-BOCA	CEA DR.250B/160 Capitaine	82	
F-BOCG	CEA DR.250/160 Capitaine	85	
F-BOCI	CEA DR.220A 2+2	50	
F-BOCJ	CEA DR.220 2+2	16	
F-BOCL	CEA DR.220 2+2	18	
F-BOCR	CEA DR.220 2+2	24	
F-BODE	SOCATA MS.892A Rallye Commodore 150	10658	
F-BOEI	Piper PA-32-260 Cherokee Six	32-690	N3769W
F-BOER	Piper PA-18 Super Cub 95	18-1442	ALAT, 51-15442
F-BOFA	SOCATA MS.893A Rallye Commodore 180	10825	F-OCMA
F-BOFC	Wassmer Super WA.421-250	401	
F-BOFD	Wassmer WA.54 Atlantic	133	F-ODBD
F-BOFE	Cerva CE.43 Guepard	465	F-ODAI
F-BOFF	CEA DR.221 Dauphin	49	F-WOFF
F-BOFG	CEA DR.253 Régent	01	F-WOFG
F-BOFS	CEA DR.360 Chevalier	01	F-WOFS
F-BOFU	Agusta-Bell 47G-2	102	
F-BOFV	Agusta-Bell 47G-2	169	ALAT
F-BOFY	Piper PA-18 Super Cub 95	18-1378	F-BOMY, ALAT, 51-15378
F-BOGA	Cessna F150G	F150-0092	
F-BOGE	Cessna F150G	F150-0094	
F-BOGH	Cessna F150G	F150-0103	
F-BOGO	Cessna F172H	F172-0362	
F-BOGP	Cessna F172H	F172-0371	
F-BOGT	Cessna F172H	F172-0340	
F-BOGX	Cessna F150G	F150-0179	
F-BOGZ	Cessna F172H	F172-0333	
F-BOHJ	Piper PA-18-150 Super Cub	18-5324	ALAT, N10F
F-BOHK(2)	Wassmer WA.40A Super IV	127	F-BOBA
F-BOHP	Holste MH.1521C.1 Broussard	10	Fr.AF
F-BOHT	Mooney M.20F Executive	670170	N9593M
F-BOHV	Piper PA-23-250 Aztec C	27-3442	N6215Y
F-BOHX	Cessna T210G Turbo-System Centurion	T210-0241	N6841R
F-BOID	Beech M35 Bonanza	D-6434	HB-EID
F-BOIS	Cessna F172E	F172-0082	F-OCIS
F-BOJK	SIAI-Marchetti S.205-18/F	240	(OO-HAP)
F-BOJN	Mooney M.20F Executive	670026	
F-BOJU	Cessna 182K Skylane	18257740	N2540Q
F-BOJX	Piper PA-30 Twin Comanche B	30-1318	N8199Y
F-BOJZ	Cessna 401	401-0072	N3272Q
F-BOKA	CEA DR.250/160 Capitaine	89	
F-BOKF	CEA DR.220 2+2	35	
F-BOKG	CEA DR.220 2+2	36	
F-BOKH	CEA DR.220 2+2	37	
F-BOKJ	CEA DR.220 2+2	39	
F-BOKK	CEA DR.220 2+2	40	
F-BOKN	CEA DR.220 2+2	43	
F-BOKO	CEA DR.220A 2+2	52	
F-BOKS	CEA DR.220 2+2	48	
F-BOKX	CEA DR.220A 2+2	54	

Reg	Type	c/n	Previous ids
F-BOKY	CEA DR.220A 2+2	55	
F-BOKZ	CEA DR.221 Dauphin	56	
F-BOLC	Piper PA-23-250 Aztec C	27-3382	N6172Y, N10F
F-BOLN	SIAI-Marchetti S.205-20/R	363	
F-BOLO	Mooney M.20E Super 21	1177	OO-WIA
F-BOLP	Beech 35-C33A Debonair	CE-147	
F-BOLS	Aero Commander 200D	351	N2978T
	(W/o 24.9.00)		
F-BOLU	Piper PA-30 Twin Comanche B	30-1438	N8370Y, N10F
F-BOLV	Mooney M.20F Executive	670296	
F-BOLZ	Piper PA-30 Twin Comanche B	30-1233	N8135Y, (CF-U . C)
F-BOMB	Piper PA-18 Super Cub 95	18-1640	ALAT, 51-15640
F-BOMC	Piper PA-18 Super Cub 95	18-1636	ALAT, 51-15636
F-BOMF	Piper PA-18 Super Cub 95	18-1435	ALAT, 51-15435
F-BOMH	Piper PA-18 Super Cub 95	18-2097	ALAT, 52-2497
	(On rebuild)		
F-BOMI	Piper PA-18 Super Cub 95	18-1359	ALAT, 51-15359
F-BOMK	Piper PA-18 Super Cub 95	18-1455	ALAT, 51-15455
F-BOML	Piper PA-18 Super Cub 95	18-1367	ALAT, 51-15367
F-BOMM	Piper P-A-18-95 Super Cub	18-1397	ALAT, 51-15397
F-BOMP	Piper PA-18 Super Cub 95	18-1409	ALAT, 51-15409
F-BOMT	Piper PA-18 Super Cub 95	18-1506	ALAT, 51-15506
F-BOMV	Piper PA-18 Super Cub 95	18-1465	ALAT, 51-15465
F-BOMX	Piper PA-18 Super Cub 95	18-1368	ALAT, 51-15368
F-BONA	SOCATA MS.892A Rallye Commodore 150 10706		
	(Destroyed landing at Portimao, Portugal 10.8.10)		
F-BOOF	Beech V35A Bonanza	D-8635	
F-BOOR	Piper PA-18 Super Cub 95	18-2108	ALAT, 52-2508
F-BOOV	Piper PA-18 Super Cub 95	18-1594	ALAT, 51-15594
F-BOOX	Piper PA-18 Super Cub 95	18-1616	ALAT, 51-15616
F-BOPA	SAN Jodel D.140R Abeille	522	
F-BOPF	SAN Jodel D.150 Mascaret	61	
F-BOPG	SAN Jodel D.140E Mousquetaire IV	188	
F-BOPH	SAN Jodel D.140E Mousquetaire IV	191	
F-BOPK	SAN Jodel D.140R Abeille	523	
F-BOPO	SAN Jodel D.140R Abeille	526	
F-BOPS	SAN Jodel D.140E Mousquetaire IV	190	
F-BOPT	SAN Jodel D.140R Abeille	528	
F-BOPY	Beech V35 Bonanza	D-8383	N3744Q
F-BOPZ	SAN Jodel D.140E Mousquetaire IV	189	F-WOPZ
F-BOQD	Cessna F172H	F172-0369	
F-BOQF	Cessna F150G	F150-0208	
F-BOQH	Cessna F150G	F150-0210	
F-BOQJ	Cessna F150G	F150-0212	
F-BOQK	Cessna F150G	F150-0213	
F-BOQN	Cessna R172E	R172-0256	
	(Converted to Reims FR172 Rocket prototype FR1720001)		
F-BOQO	Cessna F150G	F150-0133	
F-BOQP	Cessna F172H	F172-0402	
F-BOQV	Cessna F172H	F172-0452	
F-BOQY	Cessna F172H	F172-0483	
F-BORA	Sportavia/ Fournier RF-4D	4012	
F-BORB	Sportavia/ Fournier RF-4D	4014	
F-BORC	Sportavia/ Fournier RF-4D	4015	
F-BORG	Sportavia/ Fournier RF-4D	4020	
F-BORI	Sportavia/ Fournier RF-4D	4017	
F-BORY	Zlin Z.326 Trenér Master	927	
F-BOSK	Club Aerostatique de France Free Balloon HG 600m3	8810	
F-BOSO	Piper PA-28-180 Cherokee C	28-3931	(G-AVBR), N9679J
F-BOSX	SIAI-Marchetti S.205-20/R	376	
F-BOTB	SOCATA MS.893A Rallye Commodore 180 10671		
F-BOTC	SOCATA MS.893A Rallye Commodore 180 10672		
F-BOTF	SOCATA MS.893A Rallye Commodore 180 10675		
F-BOTG	SOCATA MS.893A Rallye Commodore 180 10676		
	(Dismantled)		
F-BOTH	SOCATA MS.893A Rallye Commodore 180 10677		
F-BOTI	SOCATA MS.893A Rallye Commodore 180 10678		
F-BOTJ	SOCATA MS.893A Rallye Commodore 180 10679		
F-BOTK	SOCATA MS.893A Rallye Commodore 180 10680		
F-BOTL	SOCATA MS.893A Rallye Commodore 180 10681		
F-BOTQ	SOCATA MS.892A Rallye Commodore 150 10712		
F-BOTU	SOCATA MS.893A Rallye Commodore 180 10696		
F-BOTX	SOCATA MS.880B Rallye Club	881	
F-BOUA	Piper PA-18 Super Cub 95	18-1417	ALAT, 51-15417
F-BOUB	Piper PA-18 Super Cub 95	18-1422	ALAT, 51-15422
F-BOUE	Piper PA-18 Super Cub 95	18-1470	ALAT, 5I-15470
F-BOUH	Piper PA-18 Super Cub 95	18-1519	ALAT, 51-15519
F-BOUJ	Piper PA-18 Super Cub 95	18-1577	
F-BOUK	Piper PA-18 Super Cub 95	18-1605	ALAT, 51-15605
F-BOUY	Piper PA-18 Super Cub 95	18-1611	ALAT, 51-15611
F-BOUZ	Piper PA-18 Super Cub 95	18-1634	ALAT, 51-15634
F-BOVA	SOCATA MS.892A Rallye Commodore 150 10711		
F-BOVH	SOCATA MS.893A Rallye Commodore 180 10718		
F-BOVI	SOCATA MS.880B Rallye Club	1142	
F-BOVJ	SOCATA MS.880B Rallye Club	892	
F-BOVM	SOCATA MS.880B Rallye Club	1114	
F-BOVY	SOCATA MS.880B Rallye Club	895	
F-BOXD	Sportavia/ Fournier RF-4D	4044	
F-BOXI	Sportavia/ Fournier RF-4D	4061	
F-BOXR	Cessna T210G Turbo-System Centurion	T210-0248	N6848R
F-BOXT	Piper PA-28-140 Cherokee	28-23133	N9669W
F-BOXU	Piper PA-28R-180 Cherokee Arrow	28R-30290	N3947T
F-BOYC	Wassmer WA.40A Super IV	147	
F-BOYE	Wassmer WA.40A Super IV	150	
F-BOYG	Wassmer WA.41 Baladou	149	
	(Stored dismantled at Persan-Beaumont)		
F-BOYJ	Wassmer WA.41 Baladou	151	
F-BOYK	Wassmer WA.41 Baladou	152	
F-BOYR	Wassmer WA.41 Baladou	156	
F-BOYS	Wassmer Super WA.421-250	406	
F-BOYY	Wassmer Super WA.421-250	407	
F-BOZB	CEA DR.221 Dauphin	59	
F-BOZG	CEA DR.220A 2+2	63	
F-BOZH	CEA DR.221 Dauphin	64	
F-BOZJ	CEA DR.250/160 Capitaine	95	
F-BOZK	CEA DR.221 Dauphin	66	
F-BOZN	CEA DR.250/160 Capitaine	96	
F-BOZO	CEA DR.221 Dauphin	69	
F-BOZP	CEA DR.221 Dauphin	71	
F-BOZQ	CEA DR.221 Dauphin	72	
F-BOZT	CEA DR.220A 2+2	75	
F-BOZU	CEA DR.221 Dauphin	76	
F-BOZV	CEA DR.221 Dauphin	77	
F-BOZX	CEA DR.221 Dauphin	78	
F-BPAB	Gardan GY-80 Horizon 180	218	
F-BPAD	Gardan GY-80 Horizon 160D	137	
F-BPAI	SOCATA MS.880B Rallye Club	1253	
F-BPAJ	Gardan GY-80 Horizon 180	243	
F-BPAR	SOCATA MS.893A Rallye Commodore 180 10916		
F-BPAU	SOCATA MS.893A Rallye Commodore 180 11025		
F-BPAY	SOCATA MS.893A Rallye Commodore 180 10940		
F-BPBO	SOCATA MS.892A Rallye Commodore 150 10783		
F-BPBQ	SOCATA MS.893A Rallye Commodore 180 10733		
F-BPBT	SOCATA MS.893A Rallye Commodore 180 10730		
F-BPBX	SOCATA MS.893A Rallye Commodore 180 10738		
F-BPCA	CEA DR.253 Régent	108	
F-BPCC	CEA DR.253 Régent	109	
F-BPCE	CEA DR.253 Régent	110	
F-BPCG	CEA DR.221 Dauphin	84	
F-BPCH	CEA DR.220A 2+2	91	
F-BPCJ	CEA DR.221 Dauphin	86	
F-BPCK	CEA DR.221 Dauphin	87	
F-BPCN	CEA DR.221 Dauphin	117	
F-BPCO	CEA DR.221 Dauphin	92	
F-BPCY	CEA DR.221 Dauphin	101	
F-BPDA	SOCATA MS.893A Rallye Commodore 180 10734		
F-BPDP	SOCATA MS.893A Rallye Commodore 180 10790		
F-BPDR	SOCATA MS.880B Rallye Club	1140	
F-BPEI	Cessna F172H	F172-0501	
F-BPEJ	Cessna F150H	F150-0282	
F-BPEK	Cessna F150H	F150-0287	
F-BPEQ	Cessna F150H	F150-0305	
F-BPEU	Cessna F150H	F150-0311	
F-BPEV	Cessna F150H	F150-0385	
F-BPEX	Cessna F150H	F150-0388	
F-BPFH	Piper PA-23-250 Aztec C	27-3834	N6541Y
F-BPFJ	SIAI-Marchetti S.205-18/R	4-119	
F-BPFR	Beech 35-C33A Debonair	CE-85	HB-EKZ
F-BPFX	Piper PA-28R-180 Cherokee Arrow	28R-30434	N4571J
F-BPGA	SOCATA MS.880B Rallye Club	1147	
F-BPGU	SOCATA MS.880B Rallye Club	1176	
F-BPGV	SOCATA MS.893A Rallye Commodore 180 10796		
F-BPHG	SOCATA MS.880B Rallye Club	1169	
F-BPHK	SOCATA MS.880B Rallye Club	1186	
F-BPHL	SOCATA MS.892A Rallye Commodore 150 10784		
F-BPHN	SOCATA MS.880B Rallye Club	1134	F-BPBN
F-BPHU	SOCATA MS.880B Rallye Club	1221	
F-BPHY	SOCATA MS.893A Rallye Commodore 180 10816		
F-BPIC	Piper PA-30 Twin Comanche B	30-1251	F-OCIP, N8140Y
F-BPIF	Piper PA-18 Super Cub 95	18-1462	ALAT, 51-15462
	(Quoted officially as c/n 18-1384,but the f/n is 18-1359)		
F-BPIK	Piper PA-30 Twin Comanche B	30-1582	N8548Y, N10F
F-BPIR	Piper PA-30 Twin Comanche B	30-1412	N8549Y, N10F
F-BPIT	Beech 35-C33 Debonair	CD-852	HB-EKP
F-BPIU	Cessna 182L Skylane	18258690	N3390R
F-BPIX	Cessna 310N	310N0140	N5040Q
F-BPJC	SIAI-Marchetti S.205-20/R	4-209	
F-BPJE	Piper PA-32-300 Cherokee Six	32-40388	N4148R
F-BPJF	Beech 95-B55 Baron	TC-1143	
	(W/o 20.2.08)		
F-BPKB	CEA DR.221 Dauphin	104	
F-BPKD	CEA DR.253 Régent	114	
F-BPKE	CEA DR.221 Dauphin	106	
F-BPKF	CEA DR.221 Dauphin	107	
F-BPKG	CEA DR.221 Dauphin	90	
F-BPKH	CEA DR.221 Dauphin	108	
F-BPKI	CEA DR.221 Dauphin	109	
F-BPKP	CEA DR.221 Dauphin	115	
F-BPKQ	CEA DR.253 Régent	119	
F-BPKS	CEA DR.221 Dauphin	116	
F-BPKU	CEA DR.221 Dauphin	119	
F-BPKX	CEA DR.221 Dauphin	120	
F-BPKY	CEA DR.315 Petit Prince	302	
F-BPKZ	CEA DR.253 Régent	122	
F-BPLL	CEA DR.253 Régent	124	
F-BPLZ	Sportavia/ Fournier RF-5	5079	
F-BPMB	SOCATA MS.893A Rallye Commodore 180 10755		
F-BPME	SOCATA MS.893A Rallye Commodore 180 10760		
F-BPMG	SOCATA MS.893A Rallye Commodore 180 10762		
F-BPMI	SOCATA MS.893A Rallye Commodore 180 10764		
F-BPMJ	SOCATA MS.893A Rallye Commodore 180 10765		
F-BPMK	SOCATA MS.893A Rallye Commodore 180 10766		
F-BPML	SOCATA MS.893A Rallye Commodore 180 10767		
F-BPMM	SOCATA MS.893A Rallye Commodore 180 10770		
F-BPMN	SOCATA MS.893A Rallye Commodore 180 10771		
F-BPMV	SOCATA MS.892A Rallye Commodore 150 10778		
F-BPMZ	SOCATA MS.892A Rallye Commodore 150 10807		
F-BPNL	Ass.Aérostatique Nord H.400 Free Balloon	6	
F-BPNM	Zlin Z.326 Trenér Master	928	
F-BPNR	Zlin Z.326 Trenér Master	933	
F-BPOA	CEA DR.220A 2+2	121	
F-BPOB	CEA DR.340 Major	303	
F-BPOE	CEA DR.315 Petit Prince	305	
F-BPOH	CEA DR.315 Petit Prince	306	
F-BPOJ	CEA DR.253 Régent	127	
F-BPOL	CEA DR.253 Régent	128	
F-BPON	CEA DR.221 Dauphin	124	
F-BPOO	CEA DR.340 Major	301	
F-BPOQ	CEA DR.360 Chevalier	310	
F-BPOR	CEA DR.315 Petit Prince	309	
F-BPOZ	CEA DR.253 Régent	116	
F-BPPH	Sud Avn SA.316B Alouette III	2245	
F-BPPO	Piper PA-24-250 Comanche	24-1988	F-OBPO, N10F
F-BPQE	SOCATA MS.892A Rallye Commodore 150 10781		
F-BPRF	CEA DR.315 Petit Prince	319	
F-BPRG	CEA DR.253 Régent	134	
F-BPRI	CEA DR.315 Petit Prince	321	
F-BPRJ	CEA DR.315 Petit Prince	318	
F-BPRM	CEA DR.315 Petit Prince	325	
F-BPRO	CEA DR.315 Petit Prince	326	
F-BPRP	CEA DR.315 Petit Prince	327	
F-BPRR	CEA DR.221 Dauphin	127	
F-BPRT	CEA DR.221 Dauphin	128	
F-BPRU	CEA DR.315 Petit Prince	330	
F-BPSC	SOCATA MS.893A Rallye Commodore 180 10824		
F-BPSE	SOCATA MS.892A Rallye Commodore 150 10810		
F-BPSL	SOCATA MS.894A Minerva 220	11010	
F-BPTA	Wassmer WA.41 Baladou	160	
F-BPTC	Wassmer Super WA.421-250	411	
F-BPTF	Wassmer WA.41 Baladou	162	

Reg	Type	c/n	Notes
F-BPTG	Wassmer Super WA.421-250	417	
F-BPTK	Wassmer WA.41 Baladou	165	
F-BPTN	Wassmer Super WA.421-250	424	
F-BPTO	Wassmer Super WA.421-250	425	
F-BPTX	Wassmer WA.51 Pacific	04	
F-BPTY	Wassmer WA.51 Pacific	10	
F-BPVI	Wassmer Super WA.421-250	415	F-OCOK
F-BPVJ	Boeing 747-128B	20541	N28903, (F-BPVI)
	(Preserved, Le Bourget)		
F-BPXN	SOCATA ST-60 Rallye 7-300	01	
F-BPXV	Fournier RF-6B-100	01	F-WPXV
	(Stored dismantled)		
F-BPYH	SOCATA MS.893A Rallye Commodore 180	10917	
F-BPYJ	SOCATA MS.880B Rallye Club	1247	
F-BPYM	SOCATA MS.880B Rallye Club	1245	
F-BPYO	SOCATA MS.880B Rallye Club	1249	
F-BPYQ	SOCATA MS.894A Minerva 220	11016	
F-BPYS	SOCATA MS.880B Rallye Club	1251	
F-BPYU	SOCATA MS.893A Rallye Commodore 180	10932	
F-BPYX	SOCATA MS.893A Rallye Commodore 180	10923	
F-BPZP	Wassmer Super WA.421-250	430	
F-BRAE	Piper PA-28R-180 Cherokee Arrow	28R-30703	N4956J
F-BRAG	Bölkow BO.208C Junior	680	D-EGZN
	(Stored)		
F-BRAI	Cessna P206C Super Skylane	P206-0516	N8716Z
F-BRAJ	Agusta-Bell 206A Jet Ranger	8110	
F-BRAK	Beech 95-B55 Baron	TC-1170	
F-BRAU	Beech V35 Bonanza	D-8381	HB-EFL, N4809J
F-BRAY	Piper PA-32-260 Cherokee Six	32-265	6V-AAY, F-OCHD, N3404W
F-BRAZ	Beech 36 Bonanza	E-110	
F-BRBB	Cessna F172H	F172-0567	
F-BRBD	Cessna F172H	F172-0542	
F-BRBI	Reims FR172F Rocket	FR17200099	
F-BRBN	Cessna F150J	F150-0520	
F-BRBV	Reims/Cessna F172H	F17200682	
F-BRCD	CEA DR.315 Petit Prince	336	
F-BRCE	CEA DR.340 Major	337	
F-BRCI	CEA DR.315 Petit Prince	341	
F-BRCL	CEA DR.315 Petit Prince	344	
F-BRCN	CEA DR.315 Petit Prince	346	
F-BRCO	CEA DR.340 Major	348	
F-BRCP	CEA DR.380 Prince	356	
F-BRCY	CEA DR.340 Major	353	
F-BRCZ	CEA DR.340 Major	354	
F-BRDB	SOCATA MS.892A Rallye Commodore 150	10910	
	(Damaged 13.6.16)		
F-BRDI	Gardan GY-80 Horizon 180	250	
F-BRDL	SOCATA MS.893A Rallye Commodore 180	10754	
F-BRDQ	SOCATA MS.880B Rallye Club	1285	
F-BREB	SOCATA MS.893A Rallye Commodore 180	10964	
F-BREE	SOCATA MS.880B Rallye Club	1291	
F-BREL	SOCATA MS.893A Rallye Commodore 180	10956	
F-BREN	SOCATA MS.893A Rallye Commodore 180	10651	F-OCHZ
F-BRER	SOCATA MS.893A Rallye Commodore 180	10946	
F-BRET	SOCATA MS.893A Rallye Commodore 180	10967	
F-BRFA	CEA DR.340 Major	355	
F-BRFF	CEA DR.315 Petit Prince	359	
F-BRFP	CEA DR.315 Petit Prince	370	
F-BRFS	CEA DR.253B Régent	145	
F-BRFT	CEA DR.340 Major	373	
F-BRFU	CEA DR.315 Petit Prince	374	
F-BRFX	CEA DR.315 Petit Prince	375	
F-BRFY	CEA DR.253B Régent	140	
F-BRGB	SOCATA MS.880B Rallye Club	1296	F-BREJ
F-BRGN(4)	Gardan GY-100/135 Baghera	1	F-WRGA, F-BRGA
F-BRGQ	SIAI-Marchetti S.208	2-48	OO-BMW
F-BRGS	SOCATA MS.893A Rallye Commodore 180	11064	D-EBVQ
F-BRGV	SAN Jodel D.140C Mousquetaire III	96	5T-TJP, F-OCAN
F-BRHA	Mooney M.20E Super 21	810	F-OCHA, N5891Q
F-BRHM	Bölkow BO.208C Junior	687	D-EEAJ
F-BRIA	SOCATA Rallye 150SV Garnement	3366	F-OGLX
F-BRIB	Piper PA-28-235 Cherokee	28-10583	N9002W
F-BRIC	SEEMS MS.885 Super Rallye	5277	PH-MSC
F-BRIE	Aermacchi AL.60B-2	88/6268	
F-BRII	Cessna U206D Skywagon 206	U206-1318	N72204
F-BRIL	Mooney M.20F Executive	690050	
F-BRIO	Beech 95-B55 Baron	TC-1201	N164V
F-BRIR	Piper PA-32-300 Cherokee Six B	32-40635	N4261R
F-BRIZ	Beech E33A Bonanza	CE-271	(ZS-FLZ)
F-BRJO	Gardan GY-80 Horizon 180	240	
F-BRJX	SOCATA MS.892A Rallye Commodore 150	10970	
F-BRKA	SOCATA MS.893A Rallye Commodore 180	10937	
F-BRKB	SOCATA MS.893A Rallye Commodore 180	10949	
F-BRKD	SOCATA MS.893A Rallye Commodore 180	10958	
F-BRKE	SOCATA MS.893A Rallye Commodore 180	10959	
F-BRKH	SOCATA MS.893A Rallye Commodore 180	10965	
F-BRKI	SOCATA MS.893A Rallye Commodore 180	10998	
F-BRKK	SOCATA MS.893A Rallye Commodore 180	10977	
F-BRKL	SOCATA MS.893A Rallye Commodore 180	10978	
F-BRKP	SOCATA MS.893A Rallye Commodore 180	10985	
F-BRKR	SOCATA MS.893A Rallye Commodore 180	10987	
F-BRKS	SOCATA MS.893A Rallye Commodore 180	10995	
F-BRKT	SOCATA MS.893A Rallye Commodore 180	10996	
F-BRKU	SOCATA MS.893A Rallye Commodore 180	10997	
F-BRLB	SOCATA MS.893A Rallye Commodore 180	11054	
F-BRLI	Gardan GY-80 Horizon 180	259	
F-BRLO	SOCATA MS.892A Rallye Commodore 150	10993	
F-BRLQ	SOCATA MS.893A Rallye Commodore 180	11415	
F-BRLV	SOCATA MS.893A Rallye Commodore 180	11058	
F-BRLZ	SOCATA MS.880B Rallye Club	1347	
	(W/o)		
F-BRMG	SOCATA MS.893A Rallye Commodore 180	11413	
F-BRMJ	SOCATA MS.894A Minerva 220	11077	
F-BRMK	SOCATA MS.892A Rallye Commodore 150	11406	
F-BRMO	SOCATA MS.883 Rallye 115	1362	
F-BRNA	Zlin Z.526 Trenér Master	1063	
F-BRND	Zlin Z.526 Trenér Master	1080	
F-BRNO	Beech 65-B90 King Air	LJ-482	HB-GEE
F-BRNQ	Piper PA-28R-200 Cherokee Arrow	28R-35714	N4988S
F-BROA	CEA DR.360 Chevalier	376	
F-BROC	CEA DR.360 Chevalier	379	
F-BROE	CEA DR.315 Petit Prince	381	
F-BROJ	CEA DR.315 Petit Prince	388	
F-BROS	CEA DR.340 Major	393	
F-BROT	CEA DR.380 Prince	395	
F-BROV	CEA DR.380 Prince	399	
F-BROX	CEA DR.360 Chevalier	400	
F-BROY	CEA DR.315 Petit Prince	365	F-OCMY
F-BRPD	Piper PA-28-140 Cherokee C	28-25740	N8877N
F-BRPS	Reims FR172F Rocket	FR17200083	
F-BRPX	Piper PA-23-250 Aztec D	27-4285	N6928Y
F-BRQM	Piper PA-18-150 Super Cub	18-5322	(F-BRQH), ALAT
F-BRQN	Piper PA-18-150 Super Cub	18-5328	(F-BRQG), ALAT, N10F
F-BRRK	SOCATA MS.893A Rallye Commodore 180	11439	
F-BRRL	SOCATA MS.892A Rallye Commodore 150	11428	
	(Wfu)		
F-BRRP	SOCATA MS.893A Rallye Commodore 180	11418	
F-BRRR	SOCATA MS.880B Rallye Club	1403	(D-ECCG)
	(Wfu 7.00)		
F-BRRY	SOCATA MS.880B Rallye Club	1558	
F-BRSC	Beech 60 Duke	P-66	
F-BRSG	Cessna 182N Skylane	18260154	N92328
F-BRSV	Bellanca 17-30 Viking 300	30051	N6684V
F-BRTB	CEA DR.315 Petit Prince	401	
F-BRTD	CEA DR.380 Prince	403	
F-BRTF	CEA DR.340 Major	382	
F-BRTJ	CEA DR.220-A-B 2+2	133	
F-BRTK	CEA DR.315 Petit Prince	408	
F-BRTL	CEA DR.340 Major	413	
F-BRTM	CEA DR.253B Régent	152	
F-BRTN	CEA DR.380 Prince	410	
F-BRTO	CEA DR.315 Petit Prince	411	
F-BRTP	CEA DR.315 Petit Prince	412	
F-BRTR	CEA DR.315 Petit Prince	415	
F-BRTV	CEA DR.380 Prince	398	
F-BRTZ	CEA DR.253B Régent	150	
F-BRUB	Piper PA-28R-200 Cherokee Arrow	28R-35239	N2645R
F-BRUC	Beech 95-B55 Baron	TC-1298	
F-BRUE	Piper PA-28R-200 Cherokee Arrow	28R-35364	N2949R
F-BRUH	Beech E33 Bonanza	CD-1230	N7770R
F-BRUK	Piper PA-30 Twin Comanche C	30-1990	
F-BRUM	Cessna T210J Turbo-System Centurion	T210-0395	N2245R
F-BRUS	Piper PA-30 Twin Comanche C	30-1816	HB-LFG, N8673Y
F-BRUU	Wassmer Super WA.421-250	418	
F-BRUV	Bellanca 17-30A Viking 300	30269	
F-BRVD	CEA DR.380 Prince	418	
F-BRVH	CEA DR.220-A-B 2+2	134	
F-BRVI	CEA DR.360 Chevalier	427	
F-BRVK	CEA DR.315 Petit Prince	431	
F-BRVL	CEA DR.340 Major	432	
F-BRVP	CEA DR.340 Major	435	
F-BRVT	Robin DR.300/108 2+2 Tricycle	493	
F-BRXC	Reims FR172G Rocket	FR17200197	
F-BRXK	Reims/Cessna F150K	F15000615	
F-BRXN	Cessna U206E Stationair	U20601674	N9474G
F-BRXO	Reims/Cessna F150K	F15000624	
F-BRXU	Reims/Cessna F150K	F15000630	
F-BRXX	Reims/Cessna F150K	F15000632	
F-BRYA	SOCATA MS.893A Rallye Commodore 180	11468	
F-BRYL	SOCATA MS.880B Rallye Club	1523	
F-BRYU	SOCATA MS.880B Rallye Club	1515	(G-AXHH)
F-BRZA	CEA DR.315 Petit Prince	445	
F-BRZB	CEA DR.315 Petit Prince	441	
F-BRZE	CEA DR.315 Petit Prince	450	
F-BRZK	CEA DR.360 Chevalier	456	
F-BRZM	CEA DR.360 Chevalier	458	
F-BRZN	CEA DR.340 Major	459	
F-BRZO	CEA DR.315 Petit Prince	461	
	(Dbr 18.8.08)		
F-BRZQ	CEA DR.315 Petit Prince	463	
F-BRZT	CEA DR.253B Régent	165	
F-BRZY	CEA DR.220-A-B 2+2	139	
F-BSAE	SOCATA MS.880B Rallye Club	1537	
	(Wrecked)		
F-BSAF	SOCATA MS.880B Rallye Club	1539	
F-BSAG	SOCATA MS.880B Rallye Club	1543	
F-BSAO	SOCATA MS.883 Rallye 115	1551	(D-EDDH)
F-BSAV	SOCATA MS.893A Rallye Commodore 180	11457	
F-BSAX	SOCATA MS.880B Rallye Club	1576	
F-BSAY	SOCATA MS.880B Rallye Club	1556	(G-AXHI)
F-BSBA	CEA DR.220A-B 2+2	141	
F-BSBG	CEA DR.315 Petit Prince	472	
F-BSBM	CEA DR.253B Régent	170	
F-BSBN	CEA DR.315 Petit Prince	480	
F-BSBR	CEA DR.315 Petit Prince	488	
F-BSBS	CEA DR.315 Petit Prince	491	
F-BSBT	Robin DR.300/108 2+2 Tricycle	492	
F-BSBV	Robin DR.300/108 2+2 Tricycle	494	
F-BSBX	Robin DR.300/108 2+2 Tricycle	499	
F-BSBY	CEA DR.315 Petit Prince	495	
F-BSBZ	CEA DR.360	482	
	(Convtd from DR.340 Major .95)		
F-BSCD	SOCATA MS.893A Rallye Commodore 180	11486	
F-BSCK	SOCATA MS.893A Rallye Commodore 180	11073	
F-BSCM	SOCATA MS.880B Rallye Club	1598	
F-BSDA	SOCATA MS.893A Rallye Commodore 180	11465	
F-BSDB	SOCATA MS.893A Rallye Commodore 180	11467	
F-BSDC	SOCATA MS.893A Rallye Commodore 180	11475	
F-BSDD	SOCATA MS.893A Rallye Commodore 180	11476	
F-BSDE	SOCATA MS.893A Rallye Commodore 180	11477	
F-BSDF	SOCATA MS.893A Rallye Commodore 180	11478	
F-BSDG	SOCATA MS.893A Rallye Commodore 180	11479	
F-BSDH	SOCATA MS.893A Rallye Commodore 180	11480	
F-BSDI	SOCATA MS.893A Rallye Commodore 180	11481	
F-BSDK	SOCATA MS.893A Rallye Commodore 180	11483	
	(Noted wfu 7.08)		
F-BSDL	SOCATA MS.893A Rallye Commodore 180	11484	
F-BSDM	SOCATA MS.893A Rallye Commodore 180	11499	
F-BSDR	SOCATA MS.880B Rallye Club	1604	
F-BSEA	Beech E33A Bonanza	CE-249	HB-EHI
F-BSEC	Piper PA-18-150 Super Cub	18-5371	ALAT, N10F
F-BSEP	Cessna 150F	15062954	G-ATLS, (N8854G)
F-BSES	SNCASO SO.1221-S Djinn	1001/FR7	G-AXFO, F-BHOI, F-WHOI
F-BSEU	SNCASO SO.1221-S Djinn	1015/FR51	G-AXFS, F-BIEU, F-WJSN, PB+156, PB+124, F-WIEU
F-BSFF	SOCATA MS.880B Rallye Club	1614	
F-BSFQ	SOCATA MS.880B Rallye Club	1688	
F-BSFX	SOCATA ST-10 Diplomate	114	
F-BSFY	SOCATA ST-10 Diplomate	115	
F-BSGI	Dornier Do.27A-4	436	57+10, PA+325, QL+603
F-BSGN	Deveque Free Balloon HG RD 700	8	

226

Reg	Type	c/n	Previous identities
F-BSGS	Wassmer Super WA.421-250	428	
F-BSHB	Reims/Cessna F177RG Cardinal RG	F177RG0001/ 177RG0004	F-WLIR, N8004G
F-BSHD	Reims FR172H Rocket	FR17200255	
F-BSHM	Reims/Cessna FA150K Aerobat	FA1500077	
F-BSHQ	Reims/Cessna F177RG Cardinal RG	F177RG0016/ 177RG0133	
F-BSHV	Reims/Cessna F177RG Cardinal RG	F177RG0032/ 177RG0195	
F-BSIA	Bell 47G-2	1629	ALAT, Fr.AF, N2848B
F-BSIG	Reims/Cessna F150K	F15000643	
F-BSIH	CEA Jodel DR.1050-M1 Sicile Record	634	HB-EEU
F-BSIN	Reims/Cessna F150K	F15000649	
F-BSIO	Reims/Cessna F150K	F15000650	
F-BSIR	Reims/Cessna F150K	F15000653	
F-BSIS	Reims FR172H Rocket	FR17200242	
F-BSIT	Reims/Cessna F150K	F15000654	
F-BSIU	Reims/Cessna F150K	F15000655	
F-BSIX	Reims/Cessna F150K	F15000657	
	(Fuselage stored at Cosne-s-Loire 15.10.03)		
F-BSIY	Reims/Cessna F150K	F15000658	
F-BSJA	CEA DR.380 Prince	486	
F-BSJB	Robin DR.300/108 2+2 Tricycle	500	
F-BSJF	Robin DR.300/108 2+2 Tricycle	503	
F-BSJG	Robin DR.300/108 2+2 Tricycle	504	
F-BSJH	Robin DR.300/108 2+2 Tricycle	505	
F-BSJJ	Robin DR.300/108 2+2 Tricycle	506	
F-BSJN	Robin DR.300/108 2+2 Tricycle	512	
F-BSJQ	Robin DR.300/108 2+2 Tricycle	509	
F-BSJR	Robin DR.300/108 2+2 Tricycle	514	
F-BSJT	CEA DR.360 Chevalier	532	
F-BSJU	Robin DR.300/108 2+2 Tricycle	518	
F-BSJV	CEA DR.360 Chevalier	533	
F-BSJZ	CEA DR.315 Petit Prince	522	
F-BSKF	SOCATA MS.892A Rallye Commodore 150	11704	
F-BSKH	SOCATA MS.892A Rallye Commodore 150	11706	
F-BSKK	SOCATA MS.880B Rallye Club	1701	
	(Wrecked)		
F-BSKM	SOCATA MS.880B Rallye Club	1694	
F-BSKN	SOCATA MS.892A Rallye Commodore 150	11764	
F-BSKP	SOCATA MS.894A Minerva 220	11627	
F-BSKV	SOCATA MS.880B Rallye Club	1692	
F-BSKY	SOCATA MS.880B Rallye Club	1696	
F-BSLC	Robin DR.300/108 2+2 Tricycle	527	
F-BSLF	Robin DR.300/108 2+2 Tricycle	537	
F-BSLJ	Robin DR.300/108 2+2 Tricycle	540	
	(W/o 23.9.06)		
F-BSLQ	Robin DR.300/108 2+2 Tricycle	552	
F-BSLR	Robin DR.300/108 2+2 Tricycle	551	
F-BSLT	CEA DR.253B Régent	184	
F-BSLU	Robin DR.300/108 2+2 Tricycle	557	
F-BSLX	Robin DR.300/108 2+2 Tricycle (Wfu)	559	
	(Wreck dumped outside at Pontoise)		
F-BSLY	Robin DR.300/140 Major	560	
F-BSMA	SOCATA MS.893A Rallye Commodore 180	11768	
F-BSMB	SOCATA MS.893A Rallye Commodore 180	11769	
F-BSMC	SOCATA MS.893A Rallye Commodore 180	11770	
F-BSME	SOCATA MS.892A Rallye Commodore 150	11716	
F-BSMG	SOCATA MS.880B Rallye Club	1805	
F-BSMH	SOCATA MS.880B Rallye Club	1806	
F-BSMO	SOCATA ST-10 Diplomate	131	
F-BSMZ	SOCATA MS.892A Rallye Commodore 150	11817	
F-BSNA	Wassmer WA.51A Pacific	13	
F-BSND	Wassmer Super WA.421-250	427	
F-BSNE	Wassmer WA.51A Pacific	16	
F-BSNJ	Enstrom F-28A	264	F-GATB, 3A-MJC, (OO-BAO)
F-BSNL	Wassmer WA.52 Europa	24	
F-BSNM	Wassmer WA.51A Pacific	25	
F-BSNO	Wassmer Super WA.421-250	422	
F-BSNR	Wassmer WA.52 Europa	29	
F-BSNT	Wassmer WA.52 Europa	31	
F-BSOA	Robin DR.300/108 2+2 Tricycle	562	
F-BSOD	Robin DR.300/108 2+2 Tricycle	565	
F-BSOF	Robin DR.300/108 2+2 Tricycle	567	
F-BSOI	Robin HR.100/200B Royal	04	
F-BSOK	Robin DR.300/120 Petit Prince	574	
	(Painted as a 'Dauphin')		
F-BSON	CEA DR.315 Petit Prince	579	
F-BSOP	Robin DR.300/120 Petit Prince	580	
F-BSOR	Robin DR.300/108 2+2 Tricycle	582	
F-BSOT	Robin DR.300/120 Petit Prince	585	
F-BSOU	CEA DR.315 Petit Prince	587	
F-BSOV	Robin HR.100/200B Royal	06	
F-BSOY	Robin HR.100/200B Royal	07	
F-BSPE	Robin DR.300/120 Petit Prince	607	
F-BSPJ	Robin DR.300/108 2+2 Tricycle	612	
F-BSPK	Robin DR.300/140 Major	614	
F-BSPL	Robin DR.300/180R Remorqueur	591	
F-BSPM	Robin DR.300/120 Petit Prince	617	
F-BSPN	Robin DR.300/120 Petit Prince	618	
F-BSPO	Robin DR.300/120 Petit Prince	620	
F-BSPQ	Robin DR.300/120 Petit Prince	621	
F-BSPS	Robin DR.300/108 2+2 Tricycle	622	
F-BSPT	Robin DR.300/108 2+2 Tricycle	627	
F-BSPU	Robin HR.100/200B Royal	111	(D-EBAX)
F-BSPY	Robin DR.300/125 Petit Prince	30	
F-BSQJ	Cerva CE-43 Guepard	03/433	F-WSQF
F-BSQR	Robin HR.200/100 Club	01	F-WSQR
F-BSRE	Cessna 414	414-0156	N8226Q
F-BSRN	Agusta-Bell 206A Jet Ranger II	8278	
F-BSRQ	Cessna 185 Skywagon	185-0106	TR-LLQ, F-OBVN, N9906X
F-BSRS	Piper PA-18-150 Super Cub	18-4894	TR-LNS, F-OAYV
F-BSST	Cessna 210L Centurion	21061044	D-EARK, N2077S
	(Wreck at Montpellier-Candillargues)		
F-BSTD	Cessna 421B Golden Eagle	421B0106	N8076Q
F-BSUS	SIAI-Marchetti S.208	2-20	OO-HIJ
F-BSVO	Beech A23-19 Musketeer Sport III	MB-34	HB-ENR
F-BSVP	SOCATA MS.894A Minerva 220	11677	
F-BSVR	SOCATA MS.893A Rallye Commodore 180	11666	
F-BSVS	SOCATA MS.893A Rallye Commodore 180	11715	
F-BSVU	SOCATA MS.893A Rallye Commodore 180	11744	
F-BSVV	SOCATA MS.893A Rallye Commodore 180	11745	
F-BSVX	SOCATA MS.893A Rallye Commodore 180	11746	
F-BSVY	SOCATA MS.893A Rallye Commodore 180	11747	
F-BSVZ	SOCATA MS.893A Rallye Commodore 180	11749	
F-BSXD	SOCATA MS.880B Rallye Club	1762	
F-BSXE	SOCATA MS.894A Minerva 220	11872	
F-BSXK	SOCATA ST-10 Diplomate	133	
F-BSXL	SOCATA MS.880B Rallye Club	1799	
F-BSXP	SOCATA MS.892A Rallye Commodore 150	11818	
	(Wfu)		
F-BSXU	SOCATA MS.880B Rallye Club	1804	
F-BSXV	SOCATA MS.880B Rallye Club	1802	
F-BSYO	SOCATA MS.880B Rallye Club	1791	F-BSKO
	(Derelict)		
F-BSYU	Gardan GY-80 Horizon 180	229	OO-UIL
F-BSZG	SOCATA MS.880B Rallye Club	1858	
	(Dism. Beauvais)		
F-BSZM	SOCATA ST-10 Diplomate	134	
F-BTAN	SIAI-Marchetti S.205-18/R	4-169	OO-HED
F-BTBB	Robin DR.300/120 Petit Prince	636	
F-BTBC	Robin DR.300/120 Petit Prince	637	
F-BTBD	Robin DR.300/108 2+2 Tricycle	638	
F-BTBE	Robin DR.300/120 Petit Prince	640	
F-BTBJ	Robin DR.300/120 Petit Prince	654	
F-BTBK	Robin DR.300/120 Petit Prince	655	
F-BTBO	Robin DR.300/180R Remorqueur	660	
F-BTBS	Robin DR.300/120 Petit Prince	664	
F-BTBV	CEA DR.360 Chevalier	666	
F-BTBZ	Robin DR.300/180R Remorqueur	671	
F-BTCG	Pilatus PC-6/A-H2 Porter	551	I-SORE
F-BTCN	Piper PA-28R-200 Cherokee Arrow B	28R-7135182	N2289T
F-BTCQ	Piper PA-34-200 Seneca	34-7250019	N2396T
F-BTCZ	Cessna 182P Skylane	18260951	N7311Q
F-BTDM	Mudry CAP.10B	29	
F-BTDN	Mudry CAP.10B	30	
F-BTEM	Reims/Cessna FT337GP Super Skymaster	FP33700012	D-IAPV
	(Reims-assembled P337G Pressurized Skymaster US c/n P3370159)		
F-BTEN	Agusta-Bell 47G-2	251	74+11, AS+373, LA+102, AS+052
F-BTEX	SOCATA MS.893E Rallye 180GT	12438	D-EGHH, F-BVHX
F-BTEY	Piper PA-23 Apache	23-52	F-OCST, OO-EHG, HB-LBT, OO-CHF, N1075P
F-BTFA	Reims/Cessna FA150L Aerobat	FA1500121	F-WLIO, (G-AZBJ), F-BSHP
F-BTFH	Reims/Cessna F150L	F15000789	
F-BTFJ	Reims/Cessna F150L	F15000781	
F-BTFL	Reims/Cessna F172L	F17200864	
F-BTFN	Reims/Cessna F150L	F15000782	
F-BTFV	Reims/Cessna F172L	F17200886	
F-BTFY	Reims/Cessna F150L	F15000834	
F-BTGT	Piper PA-23-250 Aztec C	27-3270	5R-MCE, N6072Y
F-BTGU	Piper PA-28-140 Cherokee E	28-7225124	N11C
F-BTHC	SOCATA MS.880B Rallye Club	1902	
F-BTHM	SOCATA MS.883 Rallye 115	1644	
F-BTHO	SOCATA MS.883 Rallye 115	1646	
F-BTHV	SOCATA ST-10 Diplomate	142	
F-BTIA	SOCATA ST-10 Diplomate	143	
F-BTIC	SOCATA MS.880B Rallye Club	1905	
F-BTIG	SOCATA MS.893A Rallye Commodore 180	11892	
F-BTIK	SOCATA MS.880B Rallye Club	1922	
	(Wfu)		
F-BTIV	SOCATA MS.880B Rallye Club	1958	
	(Dam 10.6.03)		
F-BTJP	SOCATA MS.880B Rallye Club	1967	
F-BTKA	Robin DR.300/125 Petit Prince	670	
F-BTKC	Robin DR.400/120 Petit Prince	696	
F-BTKE	Robin DR.300/120 Petit Prince	695	
F-BTKF	CEA DR.360 Chevalier	698	
F-BTKG	Robin DR.300/120 Petit Prince	700	
F-BTKH	Robin DR.400/120 Petit Prince	701	
F-BTKK	Robin DR.300/108 2+2 Tricycle	711	
F-BTKP	Robin HR.100/210 Safari	143	
F-BTKR	Robin DR.400/180 Régent	699	(D-ENTJ)
F-BTKT	Robin DR.400/120 Petit Prince	723	
F-BTKU	Robin DR.400/120 Petit Prince	719	
F-BTKX	Robin DR.400/120 Petit Prince	732	
F-BTLD	Wassmer WA.54 Atlantic	52	
F-BTLE	Wassmer WA.52 Europa	55	
F-BTLI	Wassmer WA.52 Europa	58	
F-BTLJ	Wassmer WA.52 Europa	77	
F-BTLK	Wassmer WA.52 Europa	60	
F-BTLU	Cerva CE.43 Guepard	436	
F-BTLV	Wassmer WA.52 Europa	84	
F-BTLY	Cerva CE.43 Guepard	437	
F-BTMH	Piper PA-34-200 Seneca	34-7250135	F-BTDY, N4566T
F-BTMN	Beech 36 Bonanza	E-43	HB-EHG
F-BTMS	Piper PA-23-250 Aztec E	27-7305053	N9738N
F-BTPA	SOCATA MS.893A Rallye Commodore 180	11981	
F-BTPB	SOCATA MS.893A Rallye Commodore 180	11982	
F-BTPC	SOCATA MS.893A Rallye Commodore 180	11983	
F-BTPD	SOCATA MS.893A Rallye Commodore 180	11984	
F-BTPE	SOCATA MS.893A Rallye Commodore 180	11985	
F-BTPH	SOCATA MS.893A Rallye Commodore 180	11988	
F-BTPJ	SOCATA MS.893A Rallye Commodore 180	11990	
F-BTPM	SOCATA MS.880B Rallye Club	2047	
F-BTPS	SOCATA MS.893A Rallye Commodore 180	11993	
F-BTPY	SOCATA MS.880B Rallye Club	2111	
F-BTQF	Piper PA-28R-200 Cherokee Arrow II	28R-7235162	F-BTMU
F-BTQH	Piper PA-28R-200 Cherokee Arrow II	28R-7235174	N11C
F-BTQJ	Piper PA-28R-200 Cherokee Arrow II	28R-7235169	N11C
F-BTQM	Beech C23 Sundowner	M-1388	
F-BTQP	Beech 65-90 King Air	LJ-40	I-GNIS, HB-GCH
F-BTQY	Cessna 182P Skylane	18261517	N21249
F-BTRB	SOCATA MS.887 Rallye 125	2040	
F-BTRN	SOCATA ST-10 Diplomate	151	
F-BTRO	SOCATA MS.880B Rallye Club	2085	(D-EMJD)
F-BTRZ	SOCATA ST-10 Diplomate	155	
F-BTSE	Agusta-Bell 47G-2	483	ALAT
F-BTSF	Agusta-Bell 47G-2	080	ALAT
F-BTSJ	Agusta-Bell 47G-2	131	ALAT
F-BTSM	Agusta-Bell 47G-2	117	ALAT
F-BTSN	Agusta-Bell 47G-2	126	ALAT
F-BTSQ	Agusta-Bell 47G-2	168	ALAT
F-BTSV	Agusta-Bell 47G-2	199	ALAT
F-BTSX	Agusta-Bell 47G-2	147	ALAT
F-BTUB	Reims/Cessna F150L	F15000858	

Reg	Type	C/N	Previous identities
F-BTUF	Reims FR172H Rocket	FR17200335	
F-BTUH	Reims/Cessna F172L	F17200885	
F-BTUK	Reims/Cessna F172L	F17200888	
F-BTUL	Reims/Cessna F172L	F17200889	
F-BTUM	Reims/Cessna F172L	F17200890	
F-BTUN	Reims/Cessna F172L	F17200891	
F-BTUP	Reims/Cessna F172L	F17200894	
F-BTUQ	Reims/Cessna F150L	F15000837	
F-BTUY	Reims/Cessna F172L	F17200901	
F-BTUZ	Reims/Cessna F172L	F17200903	
F-BTVC	SOCATA MS.880B Rallye Club	2107	
F-BTVJ	SOCATA MS.893E Rallye 180GT	12127	
F-BTVN	SOCATA MS.880B Rallye Club	2120	
F-BTXD	SNCAN/Stampe SV.4A	595	CN-TTG, F-BDEP
F-BTXS	Robin DR.300/120 Petit Prince	720	F-BTKS
F-BTYI	Piper PA-34-200 Seneca	34-7350077	F-BTMY, F-BTMX
F-BTYK	Piper PA-34-200 Seneca	34-7250091	N4416T
F-BTYQ	Piper PA-23-250 Aztec E	27-7304972	F-BTMV, N9728N
F-BTYS	Beech F33A Bonanza	CE-433	(D-EHWB)
F-BTZF	Robin DR.400/160 Chevalier	754	
F-BTZI	Robin DR.400/120 Petit Prince	756	
F-BTZM	Robin DR.400/180 Régent	768	
F-BTZN	Robin DR.400/120 Petit Prince	769	
F-BTZO	Robin DR.400/140 Major	770	
F-BTZP	Robin DR.400/2+2 Tricycle	773	
F-BTZT	Robin HR.100/210 Safari	152	
F-BTZY	Robin DR.400/140 Major (Dbf 12.12.05)	799	
F-BTZZ	Robin DR.400/160 Chevalier	802	
F-BUAV	Sud Avn SA.316B Alouette III (For rebuild with parts of c/n 1281)	1683	HC-BMP, F-BUAV, FAP9345
F-BUAZ	SNCAN/Stampe SV.4A	19	F-BBAB, Fr.AF
F-BUBI	Reims/Cessna F172L	F17200892	
F-BUBK	Reims/Cessna F150L	F15000846	
F-BUBM	Reims/Cessna F150L	F15000849	
F-BUBN	Reims/Cessna F150L	F15000854	
F-BUBQ	Reims/Cessna F172L	F17200898	
F-BUBS	Reims/Cessna F150L	F15000855	
F-BUBT	Reims/Cessna FRA150L Aerobat	FRA1500199	
F-BUBX	Reims/Cessna F150L	F15000860	
F-BUCE	SOCATA MS.880B Rallye Club	2116	
F-BUCG	SOCATA MS.880B Rallye Club	2222	
F-BUCI	SOCATA MS.880B Rallye Club	2227	
F-BUCQ	SOCATA MS.880B Rallye Club	2242	
F-BUCY	SOCATA MS.880B Rallye Club	2223	
F-BUDJ	Mudry CAP.10B	41	
F-BUDL	Mudry CAP.10B	44	
F-BUDM	Mudry CAP.10B	45	
F-BUDQ	Mudry CAP.10B	49	
F-BUDZ(2)	Christen Pitts S-2B	5131	F-WVDZ
F-BUED	Reims FR172J Rocket	FR17200371	
F-BUEG	Reims/Cessna F177RG Cardinal RG	F177RG0085	
F-BUEL	Reims/Cessna F150L	F15000997	
F-BUEM	Reims/Cessna F150L	F15000998	
F-BUEO	Reims/Cessna F172M	F17201136	
F-BUEQ	Reims/Cessna F172M	F17201025	
F-BUER	Reims/Cessna F172M	F17201026	
F-BUET	Reims/Cessna F172M	F17201028	
F-BUEY	Reims/Cessna F172M	F17201032	
F-BUGK	SOCATA MS.893E Rallye 180GT	12231	
F-BUGL	SOCATA MS.893E Rallye 180GT	12232	
F-BUGO	SOCATA MS.893E Rallye 180GT	12265	
F-BUGP	SOCATA MS.893E Rallye 180GT	12266	
F-BUGU	SOCATA MS.880B Rallye Club	2258	
F-BUHA	Robin DR.400/120 Petit Prince	782	
F-BUHC	Robin DR.400/180 Régent	785	
F-BUHD	Robin DR.400/2+2 Tricycle	787	
F-BUHE	Robin DR.400/140B Major	788	
F-BUHI	Robin DR.400/120 Petit Prince	792	
F-BUHJ	Robin DR.400/140 Major	793	
F-BUHL	Robin DR.400/160 Chevalier	795	
F-BUHN	Robin DR.400/2+2 Tricycle	801	
F-BUHP	Robin DR.400/140 Major	804	
F-BUHQ	Robin DR.400/120 Petit Prince	805	
F-BUHR	Robin DR.400/125 Petit Prince	806	
F-BUHT	Robin DR.400/140 Major	808	
F-BUHU	Robin DR.400/180 Régent	809	
F-BUHX	Robin DR.400/120 Petit Prince	810	
F-BUJC	SOCATA MS.880B Rallye 100ST	2289	
F-BUJF	SOCATA MS.893E Rallye 180GT (Wfu)	12268	
F-BUJH	SOCATA MS.880B Rallye Club	2259	
F-BUJR	SOCATA MS.880B Rallye Club	2284	
F-BUKF	Wassmer WA.52 Europa	95	
F-BUKI	Wassmer WA.54 Atlantic	92	
F-BUKK	Wassmer WA.54 Atlantic	99	
F-BUKL	Wassmer WA.52 Europa	101	
F-BUKS	Wassmer WA.52 Europa	108	
F-BUKT	Wassmer WA.54 Atlantic	94	
F-BUKV	Wassmer WA.52 Europa	118	
F-BULD	SOCATA MS.893E Rallye 180GT	12305	
F-BULK	SOCATA Rallye 100S Sport	2293	
F-BULO	SOCATA Rallye 100S Sport	2297	
F-BULT	Procaer F.15A Picchio	15	I-LINV
F-BULX	SOCATA MS.893E Rallye 180GT	12274	
F-BUMA	Reims/Cessna F150L (Replacement fuselage fitted)	F15001090	
F-BUMB	Reims FR172J Rocket	FR17200423	
F-BUMC	Reims/Cessna F150L	F15000863	
F-BUMD	Reims/Cessna F172L	F17200904	
F-BUME	Reims/Cessna F150L	F15000999	
F-BUMF	Reims FR172J Rocket	FR17200403	
F-BUMJ	Reims/Cessna F177RG Cardinal RG	F177RG0091	
F-BUML	Reims/Cessna FRA150L Aerobat	FRA1500198	
F-BUMS	Reims/Cessna F150L	F15001007	
F-BUMT	Reims/Cessna F172M	F17201002	
F-BUMU	Reims/Cessna F172M	F17201004	
F-BUMV	Reims/Cessna F172M	F17201005	
F-BUMX	Piper PA-25-235 Pawnee C	25-5412	N8947L
F-BUMY	Reims/Cessna F172M (Dismantled)	F17201014	
F-BUNB	SOCATA MS.893E Rallye 180GT	12276	(D-EKHM)
F-BUND	SOCATA MS.893E Rallye 180GT	12278	
F-BUNG	SOCATA MS.893E Rallye 180GT	12306	
F-BUNL	SOCATA Rallye 100S Sport	2340	
F-BUNM	SOCATA MS.880B Rallye Club (Wfu)	2352	
F-BUNP	SOCATA Rallye 100S Sport	2337	
F-BUNQ	SOCATA Rallye 100ST	2338	
F-BUOF	Piper PA-25-235 Pawnee C	25-4382	4X-APR, N4660Y
F-BUOG	Piper PA-18-150 Super Cub	18-8057	F-OCSG, TT-BAA, F-OCCE, N4062Z
F-BUOJ	Piper PA-28-180 Cherokee Challenger	28-7305463	F-ETAE
F-BUOL	Piper PA-28-140 Cherokee E	28-7225130	HB-OML, N15778
F-BUON	Beech C23 Sundowner	M-1448	
F-BUOT	Piper PA-28-180 Cherokee Challenger	28-7305508	F-ETAK
F-BUOV	Grumman AA-5 Traveler	AA5-0410	N7110L
F-BUPA	Robin DR.400/120 Petit Prince	817	
F-BUPC	Robin DR.400/120 Petit Prince	821	
F-BUPE	Robin DR.400/140 Major	823	
F-BUPK	Robin DR.400/180 Régent	831	
F-BUPL	Robin DR.400/120 Petit Prince	832	
F-BUPO	Robin DR.400/120 Petit Prince	838	
F-BUPQ	Robin DR.400/120 Petit Prince	842	
F-BUPS	Robin DR.400/140 Major	852	
F-BUPT	Robin DR.400/140 Major	854	
F-BUPU	Robin DR.300/120 Petit Prince	635	PH-SRE
F-BUQE	Piper PA-25-235 Pawnee C	25-4445	4X-APS
F-BUQF	Robin HR.200/120B Club	04	(D-ENQF), F-BUQF, F-WUQF
F-BUQG	Robin HR.200/120	05	F-WUQG
F-BUQH	Robin HR.200/100 Club	06	F-WUQH
F-BUQL	Robin HR.200/100 Club	08	
F-BUQP	Aérospatiale SN.601 Corvette	4	F-WUQP
F-BUQY	Montgolfière Moderne MM18 O-56 HAFB	01	F-WUQY
F-BURE	Reims/Cessna F337G Skymaster (Reims-assembled 337G with US c/n 33701512)	F33700062	
F-BURL	Reims/Cessna F150L	F15001019	
F-BURM	Reims/Cessna F177RG Cardinal RG	F177RG0084	
F-BURN	Reims/Cessna F150L	F15001028	
F-BURP	Reims FR172J Rocket	FR17200443	
F-BURQ	Reims FR172J Rocket	FR17200451	
F-BURU	Reims/Cessna F177RG Cardinal RG	F177RG0087	
F-BURV	Reims/Cessna F172M	F17201068	
F-BUSB	Robin DR.400/180 Remorqueur	862	
F-BUSC	Robin HR.100/210 Safari	170	
F-BUSE	Robin DR.400/160 Chevalier	865	
F-BUSF	Robin DR.400/2+2 Tricycle	869	
F-BUSH	Robin DR.400/140 Major	872	
F-BUSM	Robin DR.400/180 Régent	878	
F-BUSN	Robin DR.400/140 Major	894	
F-BUSP	Robin HR.100/210 Safari	179	
F-BUSU	Robin DR.400/180 Régent	881	
F-BUSY	Robin DR.400/2+2 Tricycle	877	
F-BUTG	Cessna U206F Stationair (Dam. 8.10.00)	U20602123	N71140
F-BUTL	Piper PA-28R-200 Cherokee Arrow II	28R-7335010	N15063
F-BUUC	Piper PA-28-140 Cherokee F	28-7325567	N9506N
F-BUUE	Piper PA-34-200 Seneca	34-7350336	F-ETAR
F-BUUH	Piper PA-28-180 Cherokee Archer	28-7405006	F-ETAT
F-BUUI	Piper PA-28R-200 Cherokee Arrow II	28R-7435012	F-ETAU
F-BUUK	Cessna 310Q	310Q0275	N7775Q, VP-YEW, 5H-MOW, 5Y-AOF, N7775Q
F-BUUO	Rockwell S.2R-600 Thrush Commander	1902R	
F-BUVK	SOCATA MS.894A Minerva 220	12090	
F-BUVU	SOCATA MS.880B Rallye Club	2357	
F-BUVV	SOCATA MS.880B Rallye Club	2358	
F-BUXA	SOCATA Rallye 100S Sport	2364	
F-BUXB	Bell 47G-2	2445	G-BBKW, N6770D, ZK-HAQ, N6770D
F-BUXC	SOCATA Rallye 100S Sport	2366	
F-BUXI	SOCATA MS.880B Rallye Club (Written off)	2389	
F-BUXM	SOCATA MS.893E Rallye 180GT	12210	
F-BUXP	SOCATA MS.893E Rallye 180GT	12329	
F-BUYK	Piper PA-23-250 Aztec E	27-7405263	F-ETAW, N40528
F-BUYX	Bell 47G-2	2007	74+38, AS+399, YA+033 ?
F-BUYY	Beech 95-B55 Baron	TC-1700	
F-BUZB	SOCATA MS.893E Rallye 180GT	12314	
F-BUZE	Piper PA-28R-200 Cherokee Arrow	28R-35188	OO-LGH, N9472N
F-BUZG	SOCATA MS.880B Rallye Club	2401	
F-BUZH	SOCATA MS.880B Rallye Club	2402	
F-BUZK	SOCATA MS.880B Rallye Club	2405	
F-BUZL	SOCATA MS.893E Rallye 180GT	12212	
F-BUZQ	SOCATA MS.893E Rallye 180GT	12380	
F-BUZR	SOCATA MS.892E Rallye 150GT	12237	
F-BUZS	SOCATA MS.880B Rallye Club	2453	
F-BVAB	SOCATA MS.880B Rallye Club	2411	
F-BVAD	SOCATA MS.893E Rallye 180GT	12381	
F-BVAI	SOCATA MS.880B Rallye Club	2416	
F-BVAK	SOCATA MS.880B Rallye Club	2430	
F-BVAR	SOCATA MS.880B Rallye Club	2461	
F-BVAU	SOCATA MS.880B Rallye Club	2431	F-BVAL
F-BVAV	SOCATA MS.893E Rallye 180GT	12375	
F-BVAX	SOCATA MS.893E Rallye 180GT	12385	
F-BVBI	Reims/Cessna F172M	F17201109	
F-BVBK	Reims/Cessna F150L	F15001065	
F-BVBL	Reims/Cessna F150L	F15001077	
F-BVBN	Reims FR172J Rocket	FR17200480	
F-BVBP	Reims/Cessna F172M	F17201057	
F-BVBQ	Reims FR172J Rocket	FR17200488	
F-BVBU	Reims/Cessna F150L	F15001082	
F-BVBV	Reims/Cessna F150L	F15001104	
F-BVBX	Reims/Cessna F150L	F15001114	
F-BVCA	Robin DR.400/2+2 Tricycle	897	
F-BVCB	Robin DR.400/2+2 Tricycle	907	
F-BVCF	Robin DR.400/180 Régent	903	
F-BVCJ	Robin DR.400/180 Régent	898	
F-BVCK	Robin DR.400/180 Régent	912	
F-BVCN	Robin HR.200/100 Club	22	
F-BVCR	Robin DR.400/2+2 Tricycle	915	
F-BVCY	Robin DR.400/125 Petit Prince	923	
F-BVDA	Robin DR.400/180 Régent	922	
F-BVDC	Robin DR.400/140 Major	927	
F-BVDD	Robin DR.400/2+2 Tricycle	930	

Reg	Type	c/n	Previous identities
F-BVDI	Robin DR.400/140 Major	911	
F-BVDJ	Robin DR.400/180 Régent	910	
F-BVDL	Robin DR.400/2+2 Tricycle	934	
F-BVDP	Robin DR.400/180 Régent	941	
F-BVDR	Robin DR.400/140 Major	939	
F-BVEA	Beech B24R Sierra 200	MC-235	
F-BVEE	Piper PA-34-200 Seneca (Dam. 1.10.00)	34-7450060	F-ETAY
F-BVEJ	Aerotek Pitts S-2A	2067	F-WVEJ, G-BCGF, N80038
F-BVEK	Cessna F172G (Wrecked)	F172-0217	CN-TZG
F-BVFO	Agusta-Bell 47G	096	ALAT, Fr.AF
F-BVFR	Agusta-Bell 47G-2	143	F-BTSR, (F-BTSL), ALAT
F-BVFU	Bell 47G	1313	ALAT
F-BVFY	Agusta-Bell 47G-2	211	G-AWSK, AAF: 3B-XB, OE-UXA
F-BVFZ	Mooney M.20E Super 21	341	N6981U
F-BVHB	SOCATA MS.887 Rallye 125	2173	
F-BVHH	SOCATA MS.893E Rallye 180GT	12440	
F-BVHK	SOCATA MS.893E Rallye 180GT	12443	
F-BVHM	SOCATA MS.893E Rallye 180GT	12317	F-BUZE
F-BVHR	SOCATA MS.893E Rallye 180GT	12446	
F-BVHS	SOCATA MS.893E Rallye 180GT	12447	
F-BVHT	SOCATA MS.893E Rallye 180GT	12448	
F-BVHZ	SOCATA MS.880B Rallye 100S	2422	
F-BVIA	Reims/Cessna F172M	F17201128	
F-BVIB	Reims/Cessna FRA150L Aerobat	FRA1500235	
F-BVID	Reims/Cessna F172M	F17201168	
F-BVIE	Reims/Cessna F172M	F17201185	
F-BVIH	Reims/Cessna F150L	F15001087	
F-BVIJ	Reims/Cessna F177RG Cardinal RG	F177RG0081	(G-BAOR)
F-BVIK	Reims/Cessna F177RG Cardinal RG (Fuselage stored)	F177RG0103	
F-BVIP	Reims/Cessna F177RG Cardinal RG	F177RG0104	
F-BVIS	Reims FR172J Rocket	FR17200491	
F-BVIT	Reims/Cessna F337G Skymaster (Reims-assembled 337G with US c/n 33701560)	F33700066	
F-BVIX	Reims/Cessna F172M	F17201239	
F-BVIY	Reims/Cessna F177RG Cardinal RG	F177RG0107	
F-BVIZ	Reims/Cessna F177RG Cardinal RG	F177RG0110	
F-BVJA	Piper PA-28-140 Cherokee Cruiser	28-7425145	N9615N
F-BVJG	Cessna 337D Super Skymaster	33701048	OO-DMN
F-BVJN	Grumman AA-1B Trainer	AA1B-0369	N8869L
F-BVJS	Grumman AA-5 Traveler	AA5-0551	
F-BVJU	Cessna 185A Skywagon	185-0500	TR-LKR, F-OBYQ, N2500Z
F-WVKE	Aérospatiale SA.365 Dauphin	004	
F-WVKI	Aérospatiale AS.350 Ecureuil	002	
F-BVKQ	Bell 47G	722	Fr.Mil
F-BVLF	SOCATA MS.894E Minerva 220GT	12199	
F-BVLI	SOCATA MS.887 Rallye 125	2168	
F-BVLN	CEA DR.253B Régent	189	OO-RJB
F-BVLZ	SOCATA MS.894A Minerva 220	12081	
F-BVMB	Robin DR.400/2+2 Tricycle	949	
F-BVMC	Robin DR.400/180 Régent	955	
F-BVMF	Robin DR.400/120 Petit Prince	945	
F-BVMG	Robin DR.400/140 Major	887	(G-BBOG)
F-BVMH	Robin DR.400/160 Chevalier	958	
F-BVMK	Robin DR.400/120 Petit Prince	961	
F-BVMP	Robin DR.400/180 Régent	908	
F-BVMQ	Robin DR.400/140 Major	967	
F-BVMR	Robin DR.400/140 Major	882	(G-BBOF), (D-EFDC)
F-BVNE	SOCATA MS.880B Rallye Club	2520	
F-BVNK	SOCATA MS.893E Rallye 180GT	12495	
F-BVNZ	SOCATA MS.880B Rallye Club	2543	
F-BVOB	Piper PA-28-180 Cherokee Archer	28-7405113	F-ETBJ
F-BVOE	SNCAN/Stampe SV.4C	605	F-BDFA
F-BVOI	Piper PA-28-180 Cherokee Archer	28-7405131	F-ETBV, N9565N
F-BVOJ	Piper PA-28-180 Cherokee Archer	28-7405133	F-ETBW
F-BVOL	Piper PA-28-180 Cherokee Archer	28-7405149	F-ETBZ
F-BVOP	Piper PA-28-180 Cherokee Archer	28-7405117	F-ETBL
F-BVOR	SOCATA ST-10 Diplomate	109	TU-TFR, F-OCPF
F-BVOS	Beech V35B Bonanza	D-9286	TN-AEP, F-BVOS, TR-LSC, F-OCRY
F-BVOZ	Piper PA-18 Super Cub 95	18-3162	OO-FBA, OL-L84, L-84, 53-4762
F-BVRF	Enstrom F-28A	213	
F-BVRT	Beech 58 Baron	TH-488	
F-BVSA	Reims FR172J Rocket	FR17200502	
F-BVSC	Reims FR172J Rocket	FR17200506	
F-BVSD	Reims/Cessna F150L	F15001110	F-WLIT
F-BVSE	Reims/Cessna FTB.337G Super Skymaster	0001	F-WLIP
F-BVSJ	Reims/Cessna F172M	F17201187	
F-BVSK	Reims FR172J Rocket	FR17200511	
F-BVSM	Reims/Cessna F177RG Cardinal RG	F177RG0113	
F-BVSN	Reims/Cessna F177RG Cardinal RG	F177RG0102	(G-BBNW)
F-BVSO	Reims/Cessna F172M	F17201190	
F-BVSR	Reims/Cessna F172M	F17201195	
F-BVST	Reims FR172J Rocket	FR17200513	
F-BVSU	Holste MH.1521 Broussard	022	ALAT
F-BVSV	Reims/Cessna F150L	F15001117	
F-BVTF	Piper PA-28-180 Cherokee Archer	28-7405142	F-ETBP
F-BVTH	Piper PA-28-151 Cherokee Warrior	28-7415145	N9508N
F-BVTK	Piper PA-28-140 Cherokee Cruiser	28-7425255	N9549N
F-BVTL	Piper PA-28-180 Cherokee Archer	28-7405125	F-ETBM
F-BVTM	Piper PA-28-180 Cherokee Archer	28-7405147	F-ETBX
F-BVTP	Piper PA-23-250 Aztec C	27-3901	N6598Y
F-BVTQ	Piper PA-28-180 Cherokee Archer	28-7405153	F-ETBU
F-BVTT	Piper PA-28R-200 Cherokee Arrow II	28R-7435202	F-ETBO
F-BVUC	Piper PA-23-250 Aztec E	27-7305225	G-BCDX, N40495, N40504
F-BVUH	Beech C23 Sundowner	M-1408	F-BUIZ, N58156
F-BVUJ	Piper PA-28-180 Cherokee Archer	28-7405144	F-ETBQ
F-BVUK	Piper PA-28-140 Cherokee Cruiser	28-7425262	N9532N
F-BVUM	Mooney M.20E Chaparral	700032	F-OCRM
F-BVUN	Bell 206A Jet Ranger	247	D-HAMO
F-BVUP	Piper PA-34-200 Seneca	34-7450199	F-VAAC
F-BVUS	Piper PA-28-151 Cherokee Warrior	28-7415462	N9620N
F-BVUV	Cessna 310Q	310Q1095	N1244G
F-BVVA	Piper PA-28-180 Cherokee Archer	28-7505061	N9631N
F-BVVB	Piper PA-28-151 Cherokee Warrior	28-7515165	N9636N
F-BVVC	Cessna 210L Centurion	21061114	N2153S
F-BVVI	Grumman AA-5 Traveler	AA5-0686	
F-BVVJ	Grumman AA-5B Tiger	AA5B-0008	N1508R
F-BVVT	Bellanca 7GCBC Citabria	845-75	F-VPY
F-BVVY	Piper PA-28-180 Cherokee D	28-5336	6V-ADS, TU-TEW, N7925N
F-BVXB	Reims/Cessna F172M	F17201204	
F-BVXC	Reims/Cessna F150L	F15001123	
F-BVXD	Bell 47G	1458	F-SE . . /CNET
F-BVXE	Robin HR.100/250TR	502	D-EFIT, F-BVDS
F-BVXF	Reims/Cessna F150L	F15001129	
F-BVXG	Reims/Cessna F150L	F15001131	
F-BVXO	Reims FR172J Rocket	FR17200509	(D-EIQT)
F-BVXQ	Reims FR172J Rocket	FR17200528	(F-BSGY)
F-BVXT	Reims/Cessna F150M	F15001187	
F-BVXX	Reims FR172J Rocket	FR17200523	
F-BVYC	Robin HR.200/100 Club	51	
F-BVYD	Robin DR.400/2+2 Tricycle	987	
F-BVYF	Robin DR.400/160 Chevalier	980	
F-BVYI	Robin HR.100/250TR	504	
F-BVYK	Robin DR.400/140 Major	995	
F-BVYS	Robin HR.200/100 Club	60	
F-BVYT	Robin DR.400/180 Régent	993	
F-BVYU	Robin HR.200/100 Club	57	
F-BVYV	Robin HR.200/100 Club	58	
F-BVYZ	Robin DR.400/140 Major	1003	
F-BVZC	SOCATA MS.893E Rallye 180GT	12490	
F-BVZI	SOCATA MS.893E Rallye 180GT	12488	
F-BVZU	SOCATA MS.893E Rallye 180GT	12562	
F-BXAM	Cessna U206F Stationair	U20602751	N35844
F-BXAP	Beech C90 King Air	LJ-522	D-IHVB
F-BXAT	Cessna 172K (Damaged 12.2.00)	17258289	N79964
F-BXAV	SNCASE SE.313B Alouette II	1932	3D-XO
F-BXBC	Montgolfière-Moderne MM20 O-65 HAFB	9	
F-BXBF	Montgolfière-Moderne MM18 O-65 HAFB	14	
F-BXBS	Montgolfière-Moderne MM20 O-70 HAFB (Also has Cameron c/n 222)	25	
F-BXCE	Cerva CE-43 Guepard (CE-44 prototype) (Derelict Pontoise)	459	F-WXCE
F-BXCF	Wassmer WA.54 Atlantic	132	
F-BXCI	Cerva CE-43 Guepard	460	
F-BXCL	Wassmer WA.54 Atlantic	139	
F-BXCM	Wassmer WA.54 Atlantic	140	
F-BXCO	Cerva CE-43 Guepard	461	
F-BXCV	Cerva CE-43 Guepard	474	
F-BXDJ	SOCATA Rallye 100ST	2617	
F-BXDN	SOCATA MS.893E Rallye 180GT	12578	
F-BXDP	SOCATA MS.893E Rallye 180GT	12580	
F-BXDR	SOCATA MS.893E Rallye 180GT	12602	
F-BXDS	SOCATA MS.893E Rallye 180GT	12603	
F-BXEC	Robin DR.400/140 Major	954	
F-BXED	Robin DR.400/2+2 Tricycle	983	
F-BXEK	Robin DR.400/120 Petit Prince	1011	
F-BXEO	Robin DR.400/2+2 Tricycle	1017	
F-BXEQ	Robin DR.400/140 Major	1019	
F-BXET	Robin DR.400/2+2 Tricycle	1024	
F-BXEU	Robin DR.400/140 Major	1023	
F-BXEV	Robin HR.200/120B	65	
F-BXEX	Robin HR.200/120	52	(G-BCMX)
F-BXEZ	Robin DR.400/2+2 Tricycle	1026	
F-WXFK	Aérospatiale AS.332C Super Puma	2006	
F-BXGG	Robin HR.100/250TR Président	516	
F-BXGJ	Robin HR.100/250TR Président	518	
F-BXGN	Robin HR.100/250TR Président	522	
F-BXGQ	Robin HR.100/250TR Président	542	
F-BXGS	Robin HR.100/250TR Président	544	
F-BXGT	Robin HR.100/250TR Président	545	
F-BXGU	Robin HR.100/250TR Président	546	
F-BXGX	Robin HR.100/250TR Président	548	
F-BXGY	Robin HR.100/250TR Président	549	
F-BXHE	Mudry CAP.10B	61	
F-BXHF	Mudry CAP.10B	63	
F-BXHG	Mudry CAP.10B	64	
F-BXHL	Mudry CAP.10B	69	
F-BXHN	Mudry CAP.10B	71	
F-BXHO	Mudry CAP.10B	75	
F-BXHR	Mudry CAP.10B	79	
F-BXHS	Mudry CAP.10B	81	
F-BXHT	Mudry CAP.10B	82	
F-BXHU	Mudry CAP.10B	83	
F-BXHV	Mudry CAP.10B	85	
F-BXHX	Mudry CAP.10B	90	
F-BXIB	Reims/Cessna F172M	F17201307	
F-BXID	Reims/Cessna F177RG Cardinal RG	F177RG0128	
F-BXIF	Reims/Cessna F150M	F15001179	
F-BXIL	Reims/Cessna FTB.337G Super Skymaster	0034	
F-BXIN	Reims/Cessna F172M	F17201331	
F-BXIP	Reims FR172J Rocket	FR17200553	(F-BPQQ)
F-BXIV	Reims/Cessna F172M	F17201349	
F-BXIX	Reims/Cessna F172M	F17201357	
F-BXIY	Reims/Cessna F172M	F17201359	
F-BXJB	Robin DR.400/180 Régent	1032	
F-BXJF	Robin DR.400/2+2 Tricycle	1035	
F-BXJI	Robin DR.400/180 Régent	1040	
F-BXJK	Robin HR.200/120B	69	
F-BXJN	Robin DR.400/140 Major	1048	
F-BXJP	Robin DR.400/180 Régent	1045	
F-BXJQ	Robin HR.200/100 Club	71	
F-BXJR	Morane-Saulnier MS.733 Alcyon (Used parts of F-BLYB (82) and F-BMQA (144) in rebuild)	154	F-BNEI, Fr.Navy
F-BXJU	Robin DR.400/120 Petit Prince	1054	
F-BXJZ	Robin DR.400/2+2 Tricycle	1059	
F-BXLF	Beech 58 Baron	TH-647	
F-BXLM	Mooney M.20E Chaparral	21-1177	
F-BXLQ	Reims/Cessna FT337GP Super Skymaster	FP33700009	N14491
	(Reims-assembled P337G Pressurized Skymaster US c/n P3370150)		
F-BXLZ	Piper PA-34-200 Seneca	34-7450216	F-VAAF
F-BXMA	SOCATA MS.893E Rallye 180GT	12607	
F-BXMB	SOCATA MS.892E Rallye 150GT	2628	
F-BXMS	SOCATA Rallye 235E	12691	
F-BXMT	SOCATA Rallye 235E	12692	

Reg	Type	C/n	Notes
F-BXMV	SOCATA MS.892E Rallye 150GT	12500	
F-BXNB	Reims/Cessna F177RG Cardinal RG	F177RG0134	
F-BXNE	Reims/Cessna F177RG Cardinal RG	F177RG0132	
F-BXNG	Reims/Cessna F150M	F15001248	
F-BXNH	Reims/Cessna F150M	F15001244	
F-BXNM	Reims FR172J Rocket (Wrecked)	FR17200531	
F-BXNN	Reims/Cessna F150M	F15001207	(G-BDEO)
F-BXNO	Reims/Cessna F150M	F15001232	
F-BXNQ	Reims/Cessna F150M	F15001211	
F-BXNR	Reims/Cessna F150M	F15001282	
F-BXNS	Reims/Cessna F150M	F15001150	(D-EDNW)
F-BXNU	Reims/Cessna F150M	F15001246	
F-BXNX	Reims/Cessna F150M	F15001218	(I-BONJ)
F-BXNZ	Reims/Cessna F150M	F15001239	
F-BXOB	Piper PA-28R-200 Cherokee Arrow II	28R-7435198	OO-FEY, N41551
F-BXON	Beech E90 King Air	LW-161	
F-BXPF	Bell 206A Jet Ranger	306	G-AWRI
F-BXPM	Piper PA-28R-200 Cherokee Arrow II	28R-7335127	LX-SIM, N16323
F-BXPO	Cessna 340A	340A0053	N98599
F-BXPS	Rockwell Commander 112TC	13026	F-WXPS
F-BXPX	Piper PA-39 Twin Comanche C/R (W/o 22.3.16)	39-51	TR-LPH, (F-OCOO), N8894Y
F-BXPY	Beech C90 King Air	LJ-684	
F-BXQD	Reims/Cessna F172M	F17201412	
F-BXQG	Reims/Cessna F177RG Cardinal RG	F177RG0141	F-WLIO
F-BXQH	Reims/Cessna F150M	F15001253	
F-BXQI	Reims/Cessna F172M	F17201386	
F-BXQK	Reims/Cessna F172M	F17201388	
F-BXQM	Reims/Cessna F150M	F15001296	(F-BXZD)
F-BXQN	Reims/Cessna F150M	F15001300	
F-BXQO	Reims/Cessna F150M	F15001297	
F-BXQP	Reims/Cessna F150M	F15001284	
F-BXQQ	Reims/Cessna F172M	F17201434	
F-BXQT	Reims/Cessna F150M	F15001307	
F-BXQV	Reims/Cessna F172M	F17201464	
F-BXQX	Reims/Cessna F177RG Cardinal RG	F177RG0145	
F-BXQZ	Reims/Cessna F150M	F15001291	
F-BXRA	Robin DR.400/160 Chevalier	1062	
F-BXRB	Robin DR.400/140 Major	1063	
F-BXRD	Robin DR.400/140B Major	1064	
F-BXRG	Robin DR.400/160 Chevalier	1066	
F-BXRJ	Robin HR.200/100 Club	74	
F-BXRM	Robin DR.400/140 Major	1071	
F-BXRN	Robin DR.400/120 Petit Prince	1073	
F-BXRO	Robin DR.400/2+2 Tricycle	1074	
F-BXRP	Robin DR.400/160 Chevalier	1076	
F-BXRR	Robin DR.400/140B Major	1081	
F-BXRS	Robin DR.400/160 Chevalier	1082	
F-BXRU	Robin DR.400/2+2 Tricycle	1084	
F-BXRV	Robin DR.400/160 Chevalier	1086	
F-BXRY	Robin DR.400/2+2 Tricycle	1089	
F-BXRZ	Robin DR.400/140B Major	1087	
F-BXSC	Piper PA-28-181 Archer II	28-7690068	
F-BXSG	Cessna A185F Skywagon (Reims-assembled with "c/n" 0002)	18502844	N1466F
F-BXSK	Piper PA-31T Cheyenne	31T-7620020	
F-BXSM	Piper PA-32R-300 Cherokee Lance	32R-7680156	
F-BXSO	Beech A36 Bonanza	E-806	
F-BXSP	Beech V35B Bonanza	D-9615	N4372W
F-BXSS	Robin DR.400/2+2 Tricycle	1109	
F-BXTD	SOCATA Rallye 100ST	2621	
F-BXTE	SOCATA Rallye 150ST	2662	
F-BXTM	SOCATA MS.880B Rallye Club	2623	
F-BXTP	SOCATA Rallye 150ST	2668	
F-BXTS	SOCATA Rallye 150ST	2667	
F-BXTT	SOCATA MS.880B Rallye Club	2627	
F-BXTV	SOCATA MS.880B Rallye Club	2670	
F-BXTZ	SOCATA MS.893E Rallye 180GT	12676	
F-BXUD	Cameron V-56 HAFB	229	
F-BXUS	Chaize CS.2000F12 HAFB	006	
F-BXUX	Cameron O-77 HAFB	354	
F-BXUZ	Thunder AX7/65 HAFB	128	
F-BXVF	Robin DR.400/140B Major	1097	
F-BXVJ	Robin HR.100/285 Tiara	536	
F-BXVK	Robin HR.200/100 Club	80	
F-BXVO	Robin HR.200/100S Club	79	
F-BXVP	Robin DR.400/120 Petit Prince	1104	
F-BXVT	Robin DR.400/120 Petit Prince	1105	
F-BXVY	Robin DR.400/180 Régent	1111	
F-BXXH	Agusta-Bell 47G-2	055	ALAT
F-BXXJ	Agusta-Bell 47G-2	106	ALAT
F-BXXK	Agusta-Bell 47G	069	ALAT, F-BHPG
F-BXXO	Agusta-Bell 47G-2	189	ALAT
F-BXXP	Bell 47G-2	1627	ALAT, Fr.AF, N2846B
F-BXXQ	Bell 47G-2	1639	ALAT, Fr.AF, N2858B
F-BXXR	Mudry CAP.10B	32	D-EGTR, F-BUDB
F-BXXS	Agusta-Bell 47G	078	ALAT
F-BXXT	Agusta-Bell 47G-4	2517	G-AXHW, 9L-LAK
F-BXXU	Agusta-Bell 47G-2	154	ALAT
F-BXXY	Agusta-Bell 47G-2	203	F-MJAO, ALAT
F-BXXZ	Bell 47G-2	1636	D-HAFU, F-BILG, Fr.Mil, N2855B
	(Badly damaged near Fabregues, Spain 27.10.01)		F-
BXYE	SOCATA Rallye 235E	12699	
F-BXYI	SOCATA MS.880B Rallye Club	2721	
F-BXYJ	SOCATA MS.893E Rallye 180GT	12570	Fr.AF
F-BXYS	SOCATA Rallye 235E	12709	
F-BXYU	SOCATA Rallye 235E (Dam 11.3.04)	12711	
F-BXYV	SOCATA Rallye 235E	12712	
F-BXYY	SOCATA Rallye 235E	12769	
F-BXZD	Reims/Cessna F150M	F15001245	
F-BXZF	Reims/Cessna F172M	F17201268	
F-BXZG	Reims/Cessna F150M	F15001278	
F-BXZI	Cessna 182P Skylane (Reims-assembled with "c/n" 0046)	18264310	N1393M
F-BXZJ	Reims/Cessna F172M	F17201403	
F-BXZL	Reims/Cessna F172M	F17201245	
F-BXZM	Reims/Cessna F172M	F17201247	
F-BXZO	Reims/Cessna F172M	F17201274	
F-BXZP	Reims/Cessna F172M	F17201283	
F-BXZQ	Reims/Cessna F172M	F17201285	
F-BXZS	Reims/Cessna F172M	F17201301	
F-BXZT	Reims/Cessna F172M	F17201330	(G-BDEP), (OY-BIB)
F-BXZU	Bell 47G-2	1623	ALAT, Fr.AF, N2842B
F-BXZX	Reims/Cessna F172M	F17201367	
F-BXZZ	Reims/Cessna F172M	F17201383	
F-BYAJ	Aerotek Pitts S-2A	2195	G-BGSD, N31458
F-BYAS	Mooney M.20J Model 201	24-0380	
F-BYAX	Nord N.1101 Noralpha	15	CEV, F-BBJJ
F-BYCK	Wassmer WA.54 Atlantic	124	HB-DCN, F-BUKY
F-WZAV	Bede BD-5J	50005	N150BD
F-WZAZ	Stampe SV.4L (Lycoming)	01	
F-WZCG	Mudry CAP.X	02	
F-WZCH	Mudry CAP.232	001	F-WWZH, F-WZCH
F-WZCI	Mudry CAP.231EX	01	
F-WZCJ	Sukhoi SU.26MX	unkn	
F-WZCY	Sud SA.330 Puma	02	F-ZWWO
F-WZJF	Microjet 200	01	
F-WZJI	Aérospatiale AS.355 Ecureuil 2	002	
F-WZJY	Robin R.3000/140PRV	001	
F-WZLK	Aérospatiale AS.332L2 Super Puma	2298	Fr.AF
F-WZLQ(2)	Fouga CM-170 Magister	126	Fr.AF
F-BZOU	Piper PA-38-135 Super Cub	18-2543	OO-LFM, (OO-VVQ), OO-HMC, ALAT, 52-6225
F-GAAB	Reims/Cessna FRA150M Aerobat	FRA1500290	
F-GAAC	Reims/Cessna F177RG Cardinal RG	F177RG0142	
F-GAAF	Reims/Cessna F177RG Cardinal RG	F177RG0148	
F-GAAI	Aérospatiale AS.350B2 Ecureuil	9084	LN-OSL(3)
F-GAAJ	Reims/Cessna F172M	F17201462	
F-GAAK	Reims/Cessna F172M	F17201465	
F-GAAN	Reims/Cessna FT337GP Super Skymaster	FP33700016	
	(Reims-assembled P337G Pressurized Skymaster US c/n P3370229)		
F-GAAO	Reims/Cessna F177RG Cardinal RG	F177RG0150	
F-GAAR	Bell 47G-2 (H-13H)	2374	PT-HQQ, Brazil:8612, 58-5361
F-GAAV	Reims/Cessna F150M	F15001324	
F-GAAY	Reims/Cessna F150M	F15001327	
F-GABB	Robin DR.400/2+2 Tricycle	1114	
F-GABD	Robin DR.400/2+2 Tricycle	1118	
F-GABE	Robin DR.400/180 Régent	1119	
F-GABG	Robin DR.400/2+2 Tricycle	1121	
F-GABH	Robin DR.400/120 Petit Prince	1122	
F-GABJ	Robin DR.400/2+2 Tricycle	1125	
F-GABK	Robin DR.400/2+2 Tricycle	1126	
F-GABM	Robin HR.200/100S Club	94	
F-GABN	Robin DR.400/140B Major 80	1132	
F-GABQ	Robin DR.400/180 Régent	1135	
F-GABT	Robin DR.400/180 Régent	1138	
F-GABZ	Robin DR.400/160 Chevalier	1142	
F-GACF	SOCATA MS.880B Rallye Club	2780	
F-GACJ	SOCATA Rallye 100ST	2761	
F-GACK	SOCATA Rallye 100ST	2762	
F-GACO	SOCATA MS.880B Rallye Club	2778	
F-GACR	SOCATA Rallye 235E	12764	
F-GACS	SOCATA MS.893E Rallye 180GT	12724	
F-GADC	Fournier RF-6B-100	15	
F-GADE	Fournier RF-6B-100	6	
F-GADH	Fournier RF-6B-100	10	
F-GADI	Fournier RF-6B-100	9	
F-GADJ	Fournier RF-6B-100	11	
F-GADK	Fournier RF-6B-100	12	
F-GADL	Fournier RF-6B-100	13	
F-GADM	Fournier RF-6B-100	29	
F-GADN	Fournier RF-6B-100	16	
F-GADQ	Fournier RF-6B-100	19	
F-GADS	Fournier RF-6B-100	20	
F-GADT	Fournier RF-6B-100	21	
F-GADV	Fournier RF-6B-100	23	
F-GADY	Fournier RF-6B-100	25	
F-GAED	Robin DR.400/140B Major 80	1146	
F-GAEE	Robin DR.400/160 Chevalier	1147	
F-GAEF	Robin DR.400/160 Chevalier	1148	
F-GAEG	Robin DR.400/120 Petit Prince	1149	
F-GAEJ	Robin DR.400/180 Régent	1156	
F-GAEK	Robin DR.400/120 Petit Prince	1151	
F-GAEP	Robin DR.400/140B Major 80	1159	
F-GAEQ	Robin HR.200/100S Club	99	
F-GAET	Robin DR.400/140B Major 80	1164	
F-GAEX	Robin DR.400/140B Major 80	1168	
F-GAEZ	Robin DR.400/2+2 Tricycle	1170	
F-GAFG	SOCATA MS.880B Rallye Club	2815	
F-GAFN	SOCATA MS.893E Rallye 180GT	12738	
F-GAFP	SOCATA MS.880B Rallye Club	2852	
F-GAFQ	SOCATA MS.892E Rallye 150GT	12823	
F-GAFU	SOCATA MS.880B Rallye Club	2850	
F-GAFV	SOCATA MS.880B Rallye Club	2851	
F-GAGA	Reims/Cessna F177RG Cardinal RG	F177RG0154	
F-GAGD	Reims/Cessna F177RG Cardinal RG	F177RG0157	
F-GAGG	Reims/Cessna F177RG Cardinal RG	F177RG0160	
F-GAGI	Reims/Cessna F150M	F15001276	(G-BDPE)
F-GAGL	Reims/Cessna F150M	F15001337	
F-GAGN	Reims/Cessna F172M	F17201387	
F-GAGO	Reims/Cessna F150M	F15001317	
F-GAGR	Reims FR172J Rocket	FR17200583	
F-GAGS	Reims FR172J Rocket	FR17200563	
F-GAGY	Reims/Cessna FR172K Hawk XP	FR17200601	
F-GAGZ	Reims/Cessna F150L	F15001139	EC-CPQ, F-BSGO
F-GAHA	Robin DR.400/140B Major 80	1169	
F-GAHB	Robin DR.400/140B Major 80	1171	
F-GAHC	Robin DR.400/2+2 Tricycle	1172	
F-GAHE	Robin DR.400/2+2 Tricycle (Damaged 28.3.99)	1174	
F-GAHH	Robin DR.400/2+2 Tricycle	1177	
F-GAHK	Robin DR.400/140B Major 80	1180	
F-GAHM	Robin DR.400/120 (Originally DR.400/140B)	1183	

Reg	Type	c/n	Previous ids
F-GAHN	Robin DR.400/140B Major 80	1184	
F-GAHP	Robin DR.400/2+2 Tricycle	1186	
F-GAHQ	Robin DR.400/2+2 Tricycle	1187	
F-GAHR	Robin DR.400/180 Régent	1188	
F-GAHS	Robin DR.400/2+2 Tricycle	1189	
F-GAHV	Robin DP.400/2+2 Tricycle	1191	
F-GAHX	Robin DR.400/2+2 Tricycle	1192	
F-GAHY	Robin DR.400/160 Chevalier	1193	
F-GAHZ	Robin HR.200/100 Club	103	
F-GAIB	Wassmer WA.54 Atlantic	149	
F-GAIC	Wassmer WA.81 Piranha	803	F-WAIC
F-GAIE	Wassmer WA.54 Atlantic	150	
F-GAIG	Wassmer WA.80 Piranha	806	
F-GAIK	Wassmer WA.81 Piranha	808	
F-GAIL	Wassmer WA.81 Piranha	809	
F-GAIQ	Wassmer WA.81 Piranha	815	
F-GAIT	Wassmer WA.81 Piranha	820	
F-GAIU	Wassmer WA.81 Piranha	822	
F-GAJF	Piper PA-28R-200 Cherokee Arrow II	28R-7635357	
F-GAJM	Hughes 269C	114-0373	
F-GAJQ	Grumman G.164A Agcat	1277	N8903H
F-GAJU	Grumman AA-1B Trainer	AA1B-0664	
F-GAKB	SOCATA MS.880B Rallye Club	2887	
F-GAKG	SOCATA MS.893E Rallye 180GT	12790	
F-GAKK	SOCATA MS.880B Rallye Club	2946	
F-GAKO	SOCATA MS.880B Rallye Club	2894	
F-GALA	Piper PA-28-181 Cherokee Archer II	28-7690210	N9541N
F-GALC	Piper PA-28-181 Cherokee Archer II	28-7690147	N9517N
F-GALD	Piper PA-31T Cheyenne	31T-7620032	
	(Badly damaged Lille-Lesquin 14.1.05)		
F-GALH	Piper PA-28R-200 Cherokee Arrow II	28R-7635283	N75194
F-GALN	Beech 200T Super King Air	BB-186/BT-1	
F-GALP	Beech 200T Super King Air	BB-203/BT-2	
F-GALQ	Agusta-Bell 47G-2	108	I-MICO, ALAT
F-GAMC	IRMA/Sud Avn SA.316B Alouette III	5310	HC-BNU, F-GAMC
F-GAMD	Bell 47G-2	2005	G-BAZO, 9J-RAD, VP-RAD, ZS-HBE, N5187B
	(Dbr 24.5.16)		
F-GAME	Piper PA-38-112 Tomahawk	38-78A0655	PH-SRT, N9704N
F-GAMJ	Cessna U206G Stationair II	U20603638	F-WAMJ, F-GAMJ, N7369N
F-GAMO	Beech 58 Baron	TH-818	
F-GAMT	Enstrom F.280C Shark	1062	
F-GAMX	Cessna 182J Skylane	18256812	CS-AGM, F-OCKG, 5N-AFU, N2712F
F-GANC	Fournier RF-6B-100	31	
F-GAND	Fournier RF-6B-100	32	
F-GANF	Fournier RF-6B-120	44	F-WANF
F-GANG	Fournier RF-6B-100	35	
F-GANH	Fournier RF-6B-100	36	
F-GANK	Fournier RF-6B-100	41	
F-GANL	Fournier RF-6B-100	40	
	(Dismantled)		
F-GANX	Bell 47G-2	2434	G-BBUK, N6751D
	(W/o 7.6.16)		
F-GANY	Bell 47G-2	1635	G-BEUH, EP-HAW, N6765, Fr.AF, N2854B
F-GANZ	Cessna 172RG Cutlass RG	172RG0638	N6348V
F-GAOB	Robin DR.400/180 Régent	1195	
F-GAOD	Robin DR.400/2+2 Tricycle	1201	
F-GAOE	Robin HR.200/100S Club	104	
F-GAOJ	Robin HR.200/100 Club	105	
F-GAOK	Robin DR.400/2+2 Tricycle	1218	
F-GAON	Robin DR.400/140B Major 80	1238	
F-GAOP	Robin DR.400/120 Petit Prince	1540	
F-GAOQ	Robin DR.400/2+2 Tricycle	1239	
F-GAOU	Robin DR.400/160 Chevalier	1226	
F-GAOV	Robin DR.400/140B Major 80	1232	
F-GAOX	Robin DR.400/2+2 Tricycle	1240	
F-GAOY	Robin DR.400/2+2 Tricycle	1253	
F-GAPF	Piper PA-28R-201 Cherokee Arrow III	28R-7737064	N9504N
F-GAPI	Aerotek Pitts S-2A	2089	N28MC
F-GAPL	Piper PA-25-235 Pawnee C	25-4714	N4907Y
F-GAPZ	Beech A36 Bonanza	E-1086	
F-GAQB	Reims/Cessna F150M	F15001414	
F-GAQC	Reims/Cessna F150M	F15001420	
F-GAQG	Reims/Cessna FR172K Hawk XP	FR17200605	
F-GAQL	Reims/Cessna F182Q Skylane	F18200036	
F-GAQO	Reims/Cessna F172M	F17201501	
F-GAQP	Reims/Cessna F172M	F17201391	
F-GAQQ	Reims FR172J Rocket	FR17200580	
F-GAQR	Reims/Cessna F182Q Skylane	F18200053	
F-GAQT	Reims FR172J Rocket	FR17200566	
F-GAQV	Reims/Cessna F150M	F15001311	
F-GAQY	Reims/Cessna F177RG Cardinal RG	F177RG0144	
F-GAQZ	Reims/Cessna F172M	F17201496	
F-GARD	SOCATA MS.893E Rallye 180GT	12960	
F-GARH	SOCATA MS.880B Rallye Club	2919	
F-GARO	SOCATA MS.880B Rallye Club	2939	
F-GARQ	SOCATA MS.880B Rallye Club	2941	
F-GASB	Reims/Cessna F172M	F17201508	
F-GASE	Reims/Cessna F172M	F17201390	
F-GASF	Reims/Cessna F172M	F17201507	
F-GASH	Reims/Cessna F172M	F17201511	
F-GASJ	Robinson R66	0573	
F-GASK	Reims/Cessna F150M	F15001323	
F-GASM	Reims/Cessna F150M	F15001401	
F-GASO	Reims/Cessna F172N	F17201522	
F-GASS	Reims/Cessna F150M	F15001378	
F-GASV	Reims/Cessna F152	F15201435	(F-GAQH)
F-GASX	Reims/Cessna F172N	F17201574	
F-GASY	Reims/Cessna F150M	F15001386	F-WZDR
F-GATD	Piper PA-28-181 Cherokee Archer II	28-7890138	N9631N
F-GATE	Piper PA-28R-201T Turbo Arrow III	28R-7803039	N9636N
F-GATJ	Cessna 210K Centurion	21059380	OO-HGO, OO-PAG, N9480M
F-GATT	Grumman AA-5B Tiger	AA5B-0651	
F-GATU	Grumman AA-5A Cheetah	AA5A-0532	
F-GAUA	Mudry CAP.20LS-200	02	
F-GAUH	Mudry CAP.10B	106	
F-GAUM	Mudry CAP.21	2	
F-GAUR	Mudry CAP.10B	105	
F-GAUT	Mudry CAP.10B	174	
F-GAUY	Mudry CAP.10B	177	
F-GAVA	Robin DR.400/2+2 Tricycle	1254	
F-GAVC	Robin DR.400/180 Régent	1223	(F-BNPC)
F-GAVI	Robin DR.400/2+2 Tricycle	1263	
F-GAVK	Robin DR.400/2+2 Tricycle	1270	
F-GAVL	Robin DR.400/2+2 Tricycle	1271	
F-GAVM	Robin DR.400/180 Régent	1272	
F-GAVN	Robin DR.400/2+2 Tricycle	1273	
F-GAVO	Robin R.2100	125	
F-GAVP	Robin DR.400/2+2 Tricycle	1275	
F-GAVQ	Robin DR.400/2+2 Tricycle	1278	
F-GAVU	Robin DR.400/160 Chevalier	1229	
F-GAVV	Robin DR.400/120 Petit Prince	1280	
F-GAVX	Robin DR.400/2+2 Tricycle	1281	
F-GAXA	Robin R.2160 Alpha Sport	112	
F-GAXB	Robin R.2160 Alpha Sport	113	
F-GAXD	Robin R.2160 Alpha Sport	142	
F-GAXE	Robin R.2160 Alpha Sport	143	
F-GAXH	Robin R.2160 Alpha Sport	146	
F-GAXI	Robin R.2160 Alpha Sport	147	
F-GAXJ	Robin R.2160 Alpha Sport	148	
F-GAXM	Robin R.2160 Alpha Sport	151	
F-GAXN	Robin R.2160 Alpha Sport	152	
F-GAXO	Robin R.2160 Alpha Sport	153	
F-GAXP	Robin R.2160 Alpha Sport	154	
F-GAXQ	Robin R.2160 Alpha Sport	155	
F-GAXZ	Cessna 172S Skyhawk SP	172S9643	G-OAKR, N21738
F-GAYH	SOCATA MS.880B Rallye Club	2955	
F-GAYJ	SOCATA Rallye 235E	12877	
F-GAYO	SOCATA Rallye 100ST	2998	
F-GAYY	SOCATA MS.880B Rallye Club	3004	
	(Wfu) (Wreck dumped outside at Pontoise)		
F-GAYZ	SOCATA MS.880B Rallye Club	3005	
F-GAZN	Chaize CS.2000F12 HAFB	012	
F-GAZP	Cameron O-77 HAFB	462	
F-GAZS	Thunder Ax7-65Z HAFB	183	
F-GAZV	Cameron V-65 HAFB	488	
F-GAZX	Cameron V-77 HAFB	489	
F-GAZY	Cameron O-77 HAFB	416	
F-GBAI	Robin DR.400/2+2 Tricycle	1289	
F-GBAK	Robin DR.400/2+2 Tricycle	1292	
F-GBAM	Robin R.1180T Aiglon	215	F-WZAO
F-GBAQ	Robin DR.400/2+2 Tricycle	1305	
F-GBAR	Robin DR.400/2+2 Tricycle	1307	
F-GBAX	Robin DR.400/180R Remorqueur	1312	
F-GBAY	Robin DR.400/2+2 Tricycle	1316	
F-GBBY	Cessna U206G Stationair 6	U20604375	(N756UV)
	(Reims-assembled with "c/n" 0007)		
F-GBCB	SOCATA Rallye 100ST	3029	
F-GBCH	SOCATA Rallye 180T	3134	
F-GBCI	SOCATA Rallye 100ST	3032	
F-GBCJ	SOCATA MS.880B Rallye Club	3033	
F-GBCP	SOCATA MS.893E Rallye 180GT	13109	
F-GBCQ	SOCATA Rallye 100ST	3036	
F-GBCR	SOCATA MS.880B Rallye Club	3037	
F-GBCT	SOCATA Rallye 180T	3047	
F-GBCU	SOCATA Rallye 180T	3168	
F-GBCV	SOCATA Rallye 180T	3169	
F-GBCX	SOCATA Rallye 180T	3170	
F-GBCY	SOCATA Rallye 180T	3171	
F-GBDQ	Piper PA-25-235 Pawnee B	25-3984	N7782Z
F-GBDR	Beech F33A Bonanza	CE-740	N98170
F-GBDT	SNCASE SE.313B Alouette II	1744	XC-DOL
F-GBDX	Grumman AA-5B Tiger	AA5B-0936	
F-GBED	Ayres S.2R Thrush Commander	1819R	G-BCKB, N5619X
F-GBEH	Grumman AA-5B Tiger	AA5B-1092	OO-RTA, OO-HRT
F-GBEM	Reims/Cessna FR172K Hawk XP	FR17200626	LX-JED
F-GBEN	Holste MH.1521M Broussard	224M	Fr.AF
	(Plate on aircraft quotes c/n 253)		
F-GBEQ	Piper PA-28-161 Warrior II	28-8416103	
F-GBEU	Bell 47G-2	1995	N5159B
F-GBEY(2)	Cameron V-77 HAFB	630	
F-GBEZ	SOCATA MS.880B Rallye-Club	1205	F-BPQZ
F-GBFA	Reims/Cessna F152	F15201478	
F-GBFD	Reims/Cessna F150M	F15001356	
F-GBFL	Reims/Cessna F152	F15201482	
F-GBFP	Reims/Cessna F172N	F17201720	
F-GBFQ	Reims/Cessna F152	F15201488	
F-GBFT	Reims/Cessna F172N	F17201659	
F-GBFV	Reims/Cessna F172N	F17201727	
F-GBFX	Reims/Cessna F152	F15201486	
F-GBGE	SOCATA Rallye 235E	12729	F-WBGE, F-GBGE, F-OAGE, ZS-JSP, F-ODCM
F-GBGF	Cessna 210L Centurion	21059607	D-ECTP, (N5107Q)
F-GBHA	SOCATA TB-10 Tobago	5	
F-GBHE	SOCATA TB-9 Tampico	9	
F-GBHK	SOCATA TB-10 Tobago	21	
F-GBHL	SOCATA TB-10 Tobago	22	
F-GBHM	SOCATA TB-10 Tobago	28	
	(Stored in poor condition La Rochelle)		
F-GBHO	SOCATA TB-10 Tobago	31	
F-GBHS	SOCATA TB-10 Tobago	33	
F-GBHU	SOCATA TB-10 Tobago	36	
F-GBHZ	SOCATA TB-10 Tobago	77	
F-GBIA	Robin DR.400/140B Major 80	1321	
F-GBIC	Robin DR.400/2+2 Tricycle	1309	
F-GBIE	Robin DR.400/2+2 Tricycle	1313	
F-GBIF	Robin R.2100A	158	
F-GBIH	Robin DR.400/160 Major	1327	
F-GBIM	Robin DR.400/180 Régent	1337	
F-GBIO	Robin DR.400/2+2 Tricycle	1333	
F-GBIP	Robin R.1180T Aiglon	221	
F-GBIQ	Robin R.2160 Alpha Sport	162	
F-GBIR	Robin DR.400/180 Régent	1330	
F-GBIT	Robin DR.400/180 Régent	1335	
F-GBIU	Robin DR.400/140B Major 80	1338	
F-GBIV	Robin DR.400/120A Petit Prince	1339	
F-GBIX	Robin DR.400/180 Régent	1340	
	(Marked 'Major')		
F-GBIY	Robin DR.400/180 Régent	1344	
F-GBJA	Reims/Cessna F152	F15201492	
F-GBJF	Reims/Cessna F152	F15201485	
F-GBJG	Reims/Cessna F150M	F15001377	

Reg	Type	Serial	Previous
F-GBJH	Reims/Cessna F182Q Skylane (W/o 10.2.05)	F18200093	
F-GBJJ	Reims/Cessna F152	F15201544	
F-GBJK	Reims/Cessna F152	F15201548	
F-GBJQ	Reims/Cessna F172N	F17201771	
F-GBJS	Reims/Cessna F152	F15201610	
F-GBJX	Reims/Cessna F152	F15201568	
F-GBJY	Reims/Cessna F172N	F17201778	
F-GBJZ	Reims/Cessna F172N	F17201779	
F-GBKC	SOCATA Rallye 100ST	3062	
F-GBKE	SOCATA Rallye 100ST	3063	
F-GBKF	SOCATA Rallye 100ST (Dismantled)	3064	
F-GBKS	SOCATA Rallye 150ST	3142	
F-GBKT	SOCATA Rallye 110ST	3214	
F-GBLF	Beech A36 Bonanza	E-1443	
F-GBLH(2)	Robin DR.400/180 Régent	790	D-EDGP
F-GBLJ	Piper PA-28-161 Warrior II	28-7916190	
F-GBLL(4)	Piper PA-28RT-201T Turbo Arrow IV	28R-7931269	N2944N
F-GBLT	Hughes 269C	19-0757	N58205
F-GBLU	Beech C90 King Air	LJ-822	(F-GNCY), F-GBLU
F-GBLZ	Cessna TU206G Turbo Stationair 6	U20605151	(N4894U)
F-GBML	Mooney M.20J Model 201	24-0530	
F-GBMM	Piper PA-38-112 Tomahawk	38-79A0531	N2456G
F-GBMP	CEA DR.250/160 Capitaine	37	F-OCMP, SE-CIP, F-BNJP
F-GBMQ	Aérospatiale AS.350B Ecureuil	1042	F-WZFV
F-GBOB	SNCASE SE.313B Alouette II	1845	D-HOFI
F-GBOJ	Bell 47G-2	1621	D-HAIN, 74+30, AS+384
F-GBOL	Bombardier BD.700-1A10 Global Express	9500	C-GOEB
F-GBOM	Reims/Cessna F172M (Damaged 4.9.99)	F17201401	OO-WAW
F-GBOO	Bell 47G-2	2435	D-HEBA
F-GBOQ	Grumman AA-5B Tiger	AA5B-1083	
F-GBOR	Cameron O-65 HAFB	426	
F-GBPB	Beech 65-90 King Air	LJ-98	OY-ANP, N158G, N158GD
F-GBPI	Piper PA-28RT-201T Turbo Arrow IV	28R-7931145	N29214, N9640N
F-GBPK	Piper PA-44-180 Seminole	44-7995308	
F-GBPL	Mooney M.20K Model 231	25-0339	N231PJ
F-GBPN	Cessna A185F Skywagon	18503819	N4623E
F-GBPO	Bell 47G-2	2424	N6761D
F-GBPR	Bell 47G-2	2179	N5188B
F-GBPU	Piper PA-38-112 Tomahawk	38-79A1105	
F-GBPX	Piper PA-38-112 Tomahawk	38-79A1037	
F-GBQA	Reims/Cessna F182Q Skylane	F18200103	
F-GBQB	Reims/Cessna F182Q Skylane	F18200104	
F-GBQD	Reims/Cessna F152	F15201587	
F-GBQE	Reims/Cessna F152	F15201593	
F-GBQF	Reims/Cessna F152	F15201599	
F-GBQG	Reims/Cessna F152	F15201620	
F-GBQH	Reims/Cessna F172N	F17201807	
F-GBQI	Reims/Cessna F172N	F17201822	
F-GBQJ	Reims/Cessna FR182 Skylane RG	FR18200027	(PH-AYA)
F-GBQL	Reims/Cessna F150M	F15001344	
F-GBQQ	Reims/Cessna F172N	F17201848	
F-GBQU	Reims/Cessna F172N	F17201905	
F-GBQX	Reims/Cessna F172N	F17201899	
F-GBQY	Reims/Cessna F152	F15201641	
F-GBQZ	Reims/Cessna F172N	F17201902	
F-GBRK	Piper PA-28-161 Warrior II	28-7916448	
F-GBRN	Robin HR.200/100 Club	46	D-EEWJ
F-GBSB	SOCATA MS.892E Rallye 150GT	13228	
F-GBSC	SOCATA MS.893E Rallye 180GT	13229	
F-GBSF	SOCATA Rallye 110ST Galopin	3234	
F-GBSG	SOCATA Rallye 110ST Galopin	3235	
F-GBSN	SOCATA Rallye 110ST Galopin (Wreck at Pontoise)	3256	
F-GBSO	SOCATA Rallye 110ST Galopin	3257	
F-GBSS	SOCATA Rallye 110ST Galopin	3267	
F-GBST	SOCATA Rallye 110ST Galopin	3268	
F-GBSU	SOCATA Rallye 110ST Galopin	3269	
F-GBSV	SOCATA Rallye 110ST Galopin	3270	
F-GBTD	Cessna T210N Turbo Centurion II	21063179	N6970N
F-GBTJ	Piper PA-28RT-201T Turbo Arrow IV	28R-7931282	N9608N
F-GBTM	Dassault Falcon 20GF	397	F-WBTM, F-GBTM, F-WRQP
F-GBTN	Reims/Cessna F172N	F17201834	LX- III
F-GBTP	Piper PA-34-200 Seneca	34-7250286	TR-LRA, N1299T
F-GBTS	Reims/Cessna F182P Skylane	F18200004	OO-WAS, F-GAAA
F-GBTU	Piper PA-28-161 Warrior II	28-7916581	N8073S, N9603N
F-GBTX	Reims/Cessna F172M	F17201492	F-ODEK
F-GBTZ	Robin DR.400/2+2 Tricycle	1347	
F-GBUF	Robin DR.400/120A Petit Prince	1355	
F-GBUH	Robin DR.400/2+2 Tricycle	1359	
F-GBUJ	Robin DR.400/120 Petit Prince	1361	
F-GBUL	Robin DR.400/2+2 Tricycle (Dismantled)	1356	
F-GBUO	Robin DR.400/180 Régent	1370	
F-GBUQ	Robin DR.400/120A Petit Prince	1371	
F-GBUR	Robin DR.400/120 Petit Prince	1374	
F-GBUT	Robin DR.400/180 Régent	1377	
F-GBUY	Robin DR.400/2+2 Tricycle	1382	
F-GBVB	Robin R.1180T Aiglon II	226	
F-GBVF	Robin DR.400/2+2 Tricycle	1390	
F-GBVG	Robin R.1180T Aiglon II	230	
F-GBVH	Robin DR.400/120A Petit Prince	1394	
F-GBVJ	Robin DR.400/2+2 Tricycle	1399	
F-GBVK	Robin DR.400/2+2 Tricycle	1393	
F-GBVL	Robin DR.400/120A Petit Prince	1406	
F-GBVM	Robin R.1180T Aiglon II	229	
F-GBVN	Robin DR.400/180 Régent	1408	
F-GBVP	Robin DR.400/120A Petit Prince	1407	
F-GBVR	Robin DR.400/120 Petit Prince	1415	
F-GBVT	Robin DR.400/140B Major 80	1416	
F-GBVV	Robin DR.400/180R Remorqueur	1412	
F-GBXF	SOCATA Rallye 235CA Gaucho	13078	
F-GBXN	SOCATA Rallye 110ST Galopin	3291	
F-GBXO	SOCATA Rallye 110ST Galopin	3292	
F-GBXR	SOCATA Rallye 110ST Galopin	3295	
F-GBXS	SOCATA Rallye 110ST Galopin	3296	
F-GBZH	Cameron V-77 HAFB	524	
F-GBZI	Cameron N-31 HAFB	525	
F-GBZN	Thunder AX7/65 Bolt HAFB	209	
F-GBZS	Cameron V-65 HAFB	555	
F-GBZY	Cameron V-77 HAFB	566	
F-GCAA	Robin DR.400/160 Chevalier	1410	
F-GCAB	Robin R.1180T Aiglon II	233	
F-GCAG	Robin R.1180T Aiglon II	235	
F-GCAH	Robin DR.400/160 Chevalier	1423	
F-GCAL	Robin DR.400/120 Petit Prince	1424	
F-GCAO	Robin DR.400/2+2 Tricycle	1428	
F-GCAQ	Robin DR.400/120 Petit Prince	1433	
F-GCAR	Robin R.1180T Aiglon II	240	
F-GCAT	Robin DR.400/120 Petit Prince	1436	
F-GCAU	Robin R.1180T Aiglon II	241	
F-GCAV	Robin DR.400/120 Petit Prince (W/o 21.2.15, St Hérent)	1432	
F-GCBH	Boeing 747-228B	23611	N6046P
F-GCBY	Cessna 172S Skyhawk SP	172S10627	N17044
F-GCCD	Partenavia P.6BB	75	PH-RVR
F-GCCF	Piper PA-38-112 Tomahawk	38-79A0738	N9674N
F-GCCJ	Bell 47G	723	ALAT
F-GCCK	Bell 47G	1316	ALAT
F-GCCL	Agusta-Bell 47G	047	ALAT
F-GCCM	Agusta-Bell 47G (Exp.5.06, dism.)	085	ALAT
F-GCCN	Agusta-Bell 47G	087	ALAT
F-GCCT	Cessna 210N Centurion II	21062969	N6198N
F-GCCU	Piper PA-25-235 Pawnee D	25-7405726	N9591P
F-GCCV	Piper PA-28-181 Archer II	28-8090005	N8073Z, N9612N
F-GCEE	SOCATA TB-10 Tobago	75	
F-GCEI	SOCATA TB-10 Tobago	96	
F-GCEL	SOCATA TB-10 Tobago (Wrecked)	97	
F-GCEM	SOCATA TB-10 Tobago	112	
F-GCEN	SOCATA TB-10 Tobago	54	
F-GCER	SOCATA TB-10 Tobago	70	
F-GCEU	SOCATA TB-10 Tobago	93	
F-GCEX	SOCATA TB-10 Tobago (W/o 28.1.02)	98	
F-GCEZ	SOCATA TB-9 Tampico	123	
F-GCFA	Beech A36 Bonanza	E-1602	
F-GCFP	Piper PA-38-112 Tomahawk	38-79A1157	N9699N
F-GCFU	Piper PA-28-161 Warrior II	28-8016089	OO-HLD, N8097D
F-GCGA	Beech C90 King Air	LJ-894	
F-GCGD	Piper PA-38-112 Tomahawk	38-80A0074	
F-GCGJ	Cessna 210N Centurion (W/o 17.5.03)	21063941	(N7350C)
F-GCGL	SNCASE SE.313B Alouette II	1157	TR-LVA, AAF: 3D-XW
F-GCGM	SNCASE SE.313B Alouette II	1906	TR-LVB, AAF: 3D-XJ
F-GCGZ	Aérospatiale AS.350B Ecureuil	1068	TJ-AFU, F-WZFR
F-GCHA	Reims/Cessna F152	F15201648	
F-GCHB	Reims/Cessna F152	F15201649	
F-GCHC	Reims/Cessna F152	F15201650	
F-GCHD	Reims/Cessna F152	F15201651	
F-GCHE	Reims/Cessna F172N	F17201888	
F-GCHF	Reims/Cessna FR182 Skylane RG	FR18200044	
F-GCHJ	Reims/Cessna F152	F15201702	
F-GCHL	Reims/Cessna F152 (Dbr 16.9.00, stored)	F15201708	
F-GCHM	Reims/Cessna F172N	F17201913	
F-GCHO	Reims/Cessna F172N	F17201917	
F-GCHP	Reims/Cessna F152	F15201748	
F-GCHR	Reims/Cessna F172N	F17202009	
F-GCHS	Reims/Cessna F152	F15201717	
F-GCHT	Reims/Cessna F152	F15201722	
F-GCHU	Reims/Cessna F152	F15201703	
F-GCII	Robin DR.400/120 Petit Prince	1455	
F-GCIJ	Robin DR.400/120 Petit Prince	1456	
F-GCIL	Robin DR.400/160 Chevalier	1457	
F-GCIM	Robin DR.400/120 Petit Prince	1469	
F-GCIN	Robin DR.400/160 Chevalier	1467	
F-GCIP	Robin DR.400/120 Petit Prince	1458	
F-GCIQ	Robin DR.400/120 Petit Prince	1475	
F-GCIR	Robin DR.400/160 Chevalier	1473	
F-GCIS	Robin DR.400/120 Petit Prince	1468	
F-GCIT	Robin DR.400/120 Petit Prince	1474	
F-GCIU	Robin DR.400/120 Petit Prince	1479	
F-GCIX	Robin DR.400/120 Petit Prince	1480	
F-GCJB	Mooney M.20K Model 231	25-0248	N231GU
F-GCJD	Piper PA-28-161 Warrior II	28-8016251	N8148U
F-GCJE	Piper PA-44-180 Seminole	44-8095025	
F-GCJG	Piper PA-28-181 Archer II	28-8090219	N8146N
F-GCJK	Piper PA-28-181 Archer II	28-8090103	OO-HLF, N8093Z
F-GCJP	Partenavia P.68B	190	
F-GCJU	Wassmer WA.54 Atlantic	144	G-MPWA, F-GBIS, F-OBUS
F-GCKB	Cameron V-65 HAFB	594	
F-GCKE	Thunder AX7/65Z HAFB	249	
F-GCKI	Thunder AX3/21C Sky Chariot HAFB	276	
F-GCKQ	Cameron V-56 HAFB	650	
F-GCKU	Cameron V-77 HAFB	665	
F-GCKZ	Balloon Works Firefly 7 HAFB	10177	N1533Y
F-GCLI	Piper PA-28-161 Warrior II	28-8016236	OO-HLO, N8141Y
F-GCLJ	Beech 76 Duchess	ME-347	
F-GCLR	Piper PA-28-161 Warrior II	28-8016228	OO-HLL, N3578X
F-GCLT	Reims/Cessna F172N	F17201894	XT-ABM, F-ODKN
F-GCLU	Piper PA-28-181 Archer II	28-8090213	OO-HLP, N81419
F-GCLV	Piper PA-28-181 Archer II	28-8090312	N8216V
F-GCLX	Cessna 172RG Cutlass RG	172RG0553	(N5526V)
F-GCMB	Piper PA-28R-201T Turbo Cherokee Arrow III	8R-7703087	N3055Q
F-GCMC	Piper PA-28-181 Archer II	28-8090218	OO-HLS, N8146B
F-GCMI	Piper PA-28-161 Warrior II	28-8016287	OO-HLU, N81762
F-GCMP	Agusta-Bell 206B Jet Ranger 3	8592	(G-LOCK)
F-GCND	Reims/Cessna F152	F15201779	
F-GCNG	Reims/Cessna F152	F15201781	
F-GCNJ	Reims/Cessna F152	F15201751	
F-GCNK	Reims/Cessna F172N	F17202019	
F-GCNO	Reims/Cessna F152	F15201764	
F-GCNP	Reims/Cessna F152 (Dismantled)	F15201765	
F-GCNQ	Reims/Cessna F172N	F17202017	PH-AYF
F-GCNS	Reims/Cessna F152	F15201800	
F-GCNT	Reims/Cessna F172N	F17202039	
F-GCNU	Reims/Cessna F172N	F17202037	(OY-BNS)
F-GCNV	Reims/Cessna F172P	F17202076	
F-GCNZ	Reims/Cessna F182Q Skylane	F18200150	
F-GCOJ	SOCATA TB-9 Tampico	155	
F-GCOM	SOCATA TB-10 Tobago	161	

Registration	Type	c/n	Previous identities
F-GCOS	SOCATA TB-10 Tobago (Derelict)	174	
F-GCOX	SOCATA TB-9 Tampico	224	
F-GCPB	Piper PA-28RT-201T Turbo Arrow IV	28R-8031124	N82318
F-GCPF	Piper PA-28-161 Warrior II	28-7916587	OO-HCG, N8073T, N9604N
F-GCPO	Piper PA-34-200T Seneca II	34-8070358	N8266V
F-GCQA	Cessna 172RG Cutlass	172RG0007	N4648R
F-GCQB	SOCATA MS.880B Rallye Club	853	F-BODP
F-GCQE	Piper PA-28-181 Archer II	28-8090370	N9582N, N82525
F-GCQF	Reims/Cessna F172M	F17200947	LX-AIJ
F-GCQH	Cessna 335	335-0059	F-WCQH, F-GCQH, N6801C
F-GCQI	Agusta-Bell 47G-2	027	(F-GDQI), I- COLO, IDFAF, Fr.AF
F-GCQJ	Piper PA-28RT-201 Arrow IV	28R-8118023	N82910
F-GCQR	Aérospatiale SA.365C2 Dauphin 2	5054	
F-GCQZ	Aérospatiale AS.350B Ecureuil	1562	
F-GCRA	Robin R.1180TD Aiglon	245	
F-GCRF	Robin R.1180TD Aiglon	250	
F-GCRG	Robin R.1180TD Aiglon	251	
F-GCRH	Robin R.1180TD Aiglon	252	
F-GCRL	Robin R.1180TD Aiglon	256	
F-GCRM	Robin R.1180TD Aiglon	257	
F-GCRN	Robin R.1180TD Aiglon	258	
F-GCRP	Robin R.1180TD Aiglon	260	
F-GCRQ	Robin R.1180TD Aiglon	261	
F-GCRS	Robin DR.400/120 Petit Prince	1485	
F-GCRU	Robin DR.400/120 Petit Prince	1481	
F-GCRV	Robin DR.400/120 Petit Prince	1487	
F-GCRX	Robin DR.400/120 Petit Prince	1491	
F-GCRY	Robin DR.400/120 Petit Prince	1492	
F-GCSD	Cessna 172RG Cutlass RG (Reims-assembled with "c/n" 0008)	172RG0248	N5125U
F-GCSE	Cessna TU206G Turbo Stationair 6	U20605777	(N5463X)
F-GCSF	Cessna 207A Stationair 8	20700585	N73397
F-GCSM	Cessna 172RG Cutlass RG	172RG0548	(N5511V)
F-GCSP	Cessna 172RG Cutlass RG	172RG0563	N5539V
F-GCSV	Cessna P210N Pressurized Centurion II	P21000528	N731QL
F-GCTD	Piper PA-28-161 Warrior II	28-7916212	OO-WPC, OO-HCT, N9554N
F-GCTK	Cessna 172RG Cutlass RG	172RG0566	N5543V
F-GCTO	Aérospatiale AS.350B Ecureuil	1361	
F-GCTQ	Piper PA-28-181 Archer II	28-8090297	OO-HLZ, (OO-HCZ), N82002
F-GCTR	Beech E90 King Air	LA-115	
F-GCTV	Piper PA-38-112 Tomahawk	38-80A0087	N9695N
F-GCTX	Piper PA-38-112 Tomahawk	38-80A0088	N9696N
F-GCUA	Robin DR.400/120 Petit Prince	1498	
F-GCUB	Robin DR.400/180 Régent	1500	
F-GCUE	Robin DR.400/160 Chevalier	1503	
F-GCUI	Robin DR.400/160 Chevalier	1518	
F-GCUK	Robin DR.400/120 Petit Prince	1515	
F-GCUM	Robin DR.400/180 Régent	1521	
F-GCUT	Robin DR.400/120 Petit Prince	1507	
F-GCUU	Robin DR.400/120 Petit Prince	1533	
F-GCVA	Mooney M.20K Model 231	25-0508	
F-GCVF	Agusta-Bell 206B Jet Ranger 3	8607	
F-GCVV(2)	SNCASE SE.3130 Alouette II	1010/10	Fr.AF
F-GCVX(2)	Cessna A185F Skywagon (Dam.8.10.05)	18503383	N7379H
F-GCXA	Thunder AX7/65Z HAFB	293	
F-GCXC	Thunder AX7/65Z HAFB	305	
F-GCXF	Chaize CS.2200F12 HAFB	027	
F-GCXP	Thunder AX7/65 HAFB	335	
F-GCXU	Deveque HG RD 700 Free Balloon	11	
F-GCXX	Chaize CS.2200F12 HAFB	037	
F-GCYD	Reims/Cessna F152	F15201836	
F-GCYJ	Maule M.5-235C Lunar Rocket	7300C	HB-EYV, N56362
F-GCYL	Reims/Cessna F172P	F17202086	
F-GCYQ	Reims/Cessna FR182 Skylane RG	FR18200064	
F-GCYR	Reims/Cessna F172P	F17202104	
F-GCYT	Reims/Cessna F152	F15201851	
F-GCYY	Reims/Cessna F172P	F17202066	
F-GCZA	Thunder AX7/77 HAFB	371	
F-GCZB	Thunder AX6/56 HAFB	370	
F-GCZG	Thunder AX7/77 S1 HAFB	415	
F-GCZR	Cameron O-56 HAFB	840	
F-GCZX	Leys HG VL-248 Free Balloon	01	F-WCZX
F-GDAB	Cessna 172RG Cutlass RG	172RG0808	N9381B
F-GDAF	Enstrom F.280C Shark	1206	N5697T
F-GDAI	Piper PA-28-161 Warrior II	28-8116185	N8360V
F-GDAJ	Piper PA-28-181 Archer II	28-8090315	OO-HKC, N8218A
F-GDAP	Cessna U206G Stationair 6	U20605967	N6605X
F-GDAT	Piper PA-28-161 Warrior II	28-8116106	N8311V
F-GDBA	SOCATA TB-21 Trinidad TC	01	F-WDBA
F-GDBG	SOCATA TB-10 Tobago	279	
F-GDBK	SOCATA TB-10 Tobago	274	
F-GDBP	SOCATA TB-9 Tampico	347	
F-GDBS	SOCATA TB-9 Tampico	365	
F-GDBU	SOCATA TB-9 Tampico	361	F-WGPL
F-GDCE	Piper PA-28-181 Cherokee Archer II	28-7890538	OO-MLT, N39524
F-GDCJ	Aérospatiale SA.330J Puma	1665	F-GDFO
F-GDCM	Sud Avn SA.318C Alouette Astazou	1950	D-HIFO
F-GDCV	SOCATA TB-10 Tobago	204	F-ODOD, F-GDBD
F-GDDB	Reims/Cessna F152	F15201859	
F-GDDD	Reims/Cessna F152	F15201849	
F-GDDH	Reims/Cessna F172P	F17202130	
F-GDDJ	Reims/Cessna F152	F15201864	
F-GDDL	Reims/Cessna FR182 Skylane RG	FR18200062	
F-GDDM	Reims/Cessna F152	F15201834	
F-GDDN	Reims/Cessna F172P	F17202106	(G-BIYL), D-EEBT
F-GDDP	Reims/Cessna F152	F15201887	
F-GDDQ	Reims/Cessna F152	F15201888	
F-GDDR	Reims/Cessna F172P	F17202134	
F-GDDS	Reims/Cessna F152	F15201862	(D-EANL)
F-GDDT	Reims/Cessna F172P	F17202123	(D-EEJR)
F-GDDV	Reims/Cessna F152	F15201871	D-EAND
F-GDDX	Reims/Cessna F152	F15201905	
F-GDDY	Reims/Cessna F152	F15201917	
F-GDEA	Robin DR.400/120 Petit Prince	1531	
F-GDEB	Robin DR.400/180 Régent	1532	
F-GDED	Robin DR.400/180 Régent	1536	
F-GDEH	Robin DR.400/120 Petit Prince	1556	
F-GDEJ	Robin DR.400/160 Chevalier	1561	
F-GDEM	Robin DR.400/120 Petit Prince	1563	
F-GDEN	Robin DR.400/120 Petit Prince	1573	
F-GDEQ	Robin DR.400/120 Petit Prince	1566	D-EGDV
F-GDES	Robin DR.400/120 Petit Prince	1581	
F-GDET	Robin DR.400/120 Petit Prince	1539	
F-GDEU	Robin DR.400/120 Petit Prince	1567	
F-GDEV	Robin R.1180TD Aiglon	278	
F-GDEY	Robin DR.400/120 Petit Prince	1592	
F-GDEZ	Robin DR.400/120 Petit Prince	1579	
F-GDFM	Aérospatiale AS.350B Ecureuil	1007	G-BGHG, F-GBBK
F-GDFN	Piper PA-34-200T Seneca II	34-7970169	N159CB, N3066V
F-GDFP	Cessna T303 Crusader	T30300127	(N4933C)
F-GDFQ	Piper PA-38-112 Tomahawk II	38-81A0028	N25634
F-GDFU	Cessna 210N Centurion II	21064215	(N5467Y)
F-GDGC	SOCATA Rallye 110ST Galopin	3347	
F-GDGF	SOCATA Rallye 110ST Galopin	3364	
F-GDGG	SOCATA TB-20 Trinidad	422	
F-GDGJ	SOCATA Rallye 110ST Galopin	3378	
F-GDGL	SOCATA TB-9 Tampico	359	
F-GDGM	SOCATA TB-20 Trinidad	383	
F-GDGP	SOCATA TB-10 Tobago	392	
F-GDGQ	SOCATA TB-20 Trinidad	449	
F-GDGU	SOCATA TB-20 Trinidad	406	
F-GDHD	Britten-Norman BN-2A-9 Islander	591	F-WDHD, 9Q-CMJ, G-BENU
F-GDHI	Cessna 172RG Cutlass RG	172RG0819	(D-EANK), N9421B
F-GDHL	SNCASE SE.3130 Alouette II	1325	D-HHAA, 75+33, PK+201, PL+131, PH+135
F-GDHO	SNCASE SE.3130 Alouette II	1891	D-HOBY
F-GDHX	Aérospatiale AS.350B Ecureuil	1662	
F-GDHY	Piper PA-28R-201T Turbo Arrow III	28R-7803333	HB-PCD, N36688
F-GDID	Reims/Cessna F152	F15201911	
F-GDIE	Reims/Cessna F152	F15201898	
F-GDIH	Reims/Cessna F172P	F17202138	
F-GDII	Reims/Cessna F172P	F17202155	
F-GDIJ	Reims/Cessna F152	F15201902	
F-GDIK	Reims/Cessna F152	F15201817	
F-GDIO	Reims/Cessna F152	F15201892	
F-GDIQ	Reims/Cessna F152	F15201903	
F-GDIT	Reims/Cessna F172P	F17202180	
F-GDIV	Reims/Cessna F172P	F17202177	
F-GDIX	Reims/Cessna F172P	F17202162	
F-GDIY	Reims/Cessna F172P	F17202191	
F-GDIZ	Reims/Cessna F152	F15201923	F-WZND
F-GDJB	SOCATA Rallye 150SV Garnement	3330	F-ODNH
F-GDJD	SOCATA Rallye 235E Gabier	13346	TU-VBK, F-ODNZ
F-GDJE	Robin DR.400/120 Petit Prince	1527	D-EGWU
F-GDJF	Piper PA-28-161 Warrior II	28-8316042	N9631N
F-GDJN	Agusta-Bell 47G-2	269	I-ESTA
F-GDJO	Agusta-Bell 47G-2	121	I-CIDI, IDFAF, Fr.AF
F-GDJR	Bell 47G	1974	I-ONGO, SE-HBH, N2869B
F-GDJT	Cessna 172RG Cutlass RG	172RG1022	N9768B
F-GDJV	SNCASE SE.313B Alouette II	1680	D-HICU
F-GDKA	Robin DR.400/120 Petit Prince	1587	
F-GDKD	Robin DR.400/120 Petit Prince	1608	
F-GDKE	Robin DR.400/120 Petit Prince	1598	
F-GDKF	Robin DR.400/120 Petit Prince	1602	
F-GDKG	Robin DR.400/120 Petit Prince	1609	
F-GDKH	Robin DR.400/120 Petit Prince	1610	
F-GDKI	Robin DR.400/120 Petit Prince	1611	
F-GDKJ	Robin DR.400/120 Petit Prince	1612	
F-GDKL	Robin DR.400/160 Chevalier	1613	
F-GDKM	Robin DR.400/120 Petit Prince	1615	
F-GDKN	Robin DR.400/160 Chevalier	1616	
F-GDKP	Robin DR.400/120 Petit Prince	1620	
F-GDKQ	Robin DR.400/120 Petit Prince	1621	
F-GDKS	Robin DR.400/120 Petit Prince	1627	
F-GDKT	Robin DR.400/180 Régent	1624	
F-GDKX	Robin DR.400/120 Petit Prince	1636	
F-GDKZ	Robin DR.400/160 Chevalier	1637	
F-GDLC	SOCATA TB-10 Tobago	199	F-BNGQ, PH-AFM, F-BNGZ
F-GDLE	Beech 200 Super King Air	BB-230	G-BEHR
F-GDLI	CEA DR.220	29	(G- . . . .), F-BOCV
F-GDLJ	Piper PA-38-112 Tomahawk	38-80A0078	OO-TIC, PH-TMP, OO-HKF, N9660N
F-GDLK	Piper PA-44-180 Seminole	44-7995209	OO-ALK, OO-HCR, N2210K
F-GDLM	Cessna TR182 Turbo Skylane RG	R18201115	G-OAST, (N756MM)
F-GDLN	Piper PA-28RT-201 Arrow IV	28R-7918186	OO-PAR, N2871N
F-GDLS	Piper PA-38-112 Tomahawk	38-80A0093	OO-HKI, N9685N
F-GDLV	Aérospatiale AS.355F Ecureuil 2	5265	F-WZKM
F-GDLY	SOCATA Rallye 150SV Garnement	3345	TU-VBI, F-ODNY
F-GDLZ	Piper PA-28RT-201 Arrow IV	28R-8218003	G-BJXE, N8460L
F-GDMG	Bell 47G-2	1626	D-HABA, F-BBOK, F-OBOK, Fr.Mil, N2845B
F-GDMH	Agusta-Bell 47G-2	122	D-HAMG, D-HNFC, OE-AXT, (OE-AXI), G-AYOF, F-OCGB,Fr.AF
F-GDMJ	Agusta-Bell 47G-2	242	D-HANY, AAF: 3B-XI
F-GDMP	Sportavia/ Fournier RF-5	5002	D-KIGA
F-GDMQ	SOCATA TB-20 Trinidad	282	F-OGLN
F-GDMS	Aérospatiale AS.355F Ecureuil 2	5063	
F-WDMT(2)	Microjet MJ.200B	3	
F-WDMU	Nord 1101 Noralpha	132	CAN: CAN-9
F-WDMX	Microjet MJ-200B	2	
F-GDNA	SOCATA TB-20 Trinidad	320	
F-GDNC	SOCATA TB-20 Trinidad	327	
F-GDNE	SOCATA TB-20 Trinidad	332	
F-GDNF	SOCATA TB-20 Trinidad	344	
F-GDNG	SOCATA TB-20 Trinidad	345	
F-GDNJ	SOCATA TB-20 Trinidad	402	
F-GDNK	SOCATA TB-20 Trinidad	403	
F-GDNL	SOCATA TB-20 Trinidad	434	
F-GDNM	SOCATA TB-20 Trinidad	435	
F-GDNO	SOCATA TB-20 Trinidad	437	
F-GDNP	SOCATA TB-20 Trinidad	438	
F-GDNQ	SOCATA TB-20 Trinidad	439	
F-GDNU	SOCATA TB-20 Trinidad	472	
F-GDNZ	SOCATA TB-20 Trinidad	551	
F-GDOA	Reims/Cessna F152	F15201924	
F-GDOC	Reims/Cessna F152	F15201926	
F-GDOE	Reims/Cessna F152	F15201931	
F-GDOF	Reims/Cessna F152	F15201913	
F-GDOG	Reims/Cessna F152	F15201897	
F-GDOH	Reims/Cessna F172P	F17202207	

Reg	Type	c/n	Previous identities
F-GDOK	Reims/Cessna F152	F15201938	
	(Dam.29.5.07 Lognes)		
F-GDOL	Reims/Cessna F172P	F17202210	
F-GDOM	Reims/Cessna F172P	F17202216	
F-GDON	Reims/Cessna F172P	F17202203	
F-GDOR	Reims/Cessna F152	F15201948	
F-GDOX	Reims/Cessna F152	F15201946	
F-GDOY	Reims/Cessna F172P	F17202218	(F-WDOY)
F-GDPB	Piper PA-25-235 Pawnee B (Two-seat)	25-3109	F-WDPB, N7202Z
F-GDPC	Cessna 305C/L-19E Bird Dog	24728	F-WDPC, ALAT
F-GDPL	Aérospatiale AS.365N3 Dauphin	6624	I-LUXA, F-WQDL
F-GDPN	Piper PA-25-235 Pawnee B	25-3292	(F-BJQH), F-OGIG, F-BOAT, F-OCGT, N7342Z
	(Officially quoted as 25-3262)		
F-GDPO	Agusta-Bell 47G-2	265	HB-XHX, D-HEKG, 74+23, AS+065
F-GDPX	Holste MH.1521M Broussard	170	F-WDPX, F-GDPX, Fr.AF
	(Plate on aircraft quotes c/n 108)		
F-GDQB	Agusta-Bell 47G-2	158	HB-XOP, OE-AXY, (F-BXZU), Fr.AF, ALAT
F-GDQC	Bell 47G-4	3329	N1152W, HC-AXA, N1152W
F-GDQR	Sud Avn SA.318C Alouette Astazou	2262	C-FMQP, CF-MQP
F-GDRA	Reims/Cessna F152	F15201880	N9073F
F-GDRF	Agusta-Bell 47G-2	039	ALAT
F-GDRH	Piper PA-28-161 Warrior II	28-7916003	PH-SBV, N39735
F-GDRI	Morane-Saulnier MS.733 Alcyon	71	F-BLYA, Fr.AF
F-GDRQ	Aérospatiale AS.350B Ecureuil	1832	
F-GDRR	SNCASE SE.3130 Alouette II	1671	Gendarmerie/F-MJAV, F-MJBB
F-GDRS	Reims/Cessna F152	F15201460	D-EAAQ
F-GDRU	Robin DR.400/2+2	1000	F-BXEA
F-GDRV	Bell 47G-2	1968	D-HORN, 74+31, AS+386
F-GDRX	Reims/Cessna F172M	F17200969	D-ECZL
F-GDSE	Piper PA-28-181 Cherokee Archer II	28-7790451	N3336Q
F-GDSF	CEA DR.250/160 Capitaine	97	OY-DNW
F-GDSI	Cameron O-77 HAFB	1157	
F-GDSJ	Cameron O-84 HAFB	607	N389CB
F-GDSN	Holste MH.1521M Broussard	247	Fr.AF
F-GDSP	Cameron O-77 HAFB	1255	
F-GDST	Cessna 172RG Cutlass RG	172RG0831	N9469B
F-GDSV	Beech 58 Baron	TH-667	TJ-AFD, F-ODAZ
F-GDTA	Mudry CAP.10B	179	
F-GDTB	Mudry CAP.10B	180	
F-GDTF	Mudry CAP.10B	181	
F-GDTG	Mudry CAP.10B	191	
F-GDTJ	Mudry CAP.10B	204	
F-GDTM	Mudry CAP.21	14	
F-GDTN	Mudry CAP.10B	73	OO-LAT
F-GDTO	Mudry CAP.10B	218	
F-GDTQ	Mudry CAP.10B	227	
F-GDTR	Mudry CAP.21	16	
	(W/o 1.5.01)		
F-GDTT	Mudry CAP.230	05	
F-GDTV	Mudry CAP.10B	231	
F-GDTX	Mudry CAP.10B	225	
F-GDTY	Mudry CAP.10B	226	
F-GDTZ	Mudry CAP.10B	230	
F-GDUE(2)	SNCASE SE.313B Alouette II	1457/243	Fr.AF
F-GDUF(2)	SNCASE SE.313B Alouette II	1727/336	Fr.AF
	(W/o 12.6.97 ?)		
F-GDUP	Aermacchi AL.60C-5	68/6248	TL-KAO, I- MANH, CF-XKU
F-GDUQ	Aermacchi AL.60C-5	95/6275	TL-KAM, I- MANJ
F-GDUR	Chaize CS.2200F12 HAFB	062	
F-GDVY	Robin DR.400/140B Major 80	714	F-BTKM
F-GDXA	Aérospatiale AS.350B Ecureuil	1610	
F-GDXE	Cameron N-105 HAFB	1125	
F-WDXH	Fouga CM-170 Magister	2	Fr.AF
F-GDXJ	Bell 47G-2	1317	HB-XIE, (F-BVFX), Fr.Mil
F-GDXK	Thunder AX7-77Z HAFB	830	
F-GDXN	Chaize CS.3000F16 HAFB	063	
F-GDXO	Chaize CS.2200F12 HAFB	064	
F-GDXQ	Thunder AX7-77 HAFB	805	
F-GDYA	Robin DR.400/180 Régent	1639	
F-GDYE	Robin DR.400/120 Petit Prince	1643	
F-GDYF	Robin R.3000/140	002	F-WZJZ
F-GDYG	Robin DR.400/120 Petit Prince	1648	
F-GDYH	Robin DR.400/120 Petit Prince	1649	
F-GDYK	Robin DR.400/120 Petit Prince	1661	
F-GDYN	Robin DR.400/120 Petit Prince	1663	
F-GDYP	Robin DR.400/120 Petit Prince	1667	
F-GDYQ	Robin R.3000/120	105	F-WDYQ, F-WEIA(1)
F-GDYR	Robin DR.400/120 Petit Prince	1669	
F-GDYU	Robin DR.400/120 Petit Prince	1654	
F-GDYX	Robin DR.400/120 Petit Prince	1673	
F-GDYY	Robin DR.400/160 Chevalier	1674	
F-GDZB	Chaize CS.2200F12 HAFB	040	
F-WDZI	Chaize CS.2300F24 HAFB	039	
F-GDZM	Cameron V-56 HAFB	930	
F-GDZO	Cameron V-65 HAFB	946	
F-GDZR	Cameron V-77 HAFB	890	(F-GEAB)
F-GDZU	Cameron V-65 HAFB	950	
F-GEAC	Ballonfabrik Augsburg HG K.630N Gas Balloon	13336	
F-GEAG	Cameron V-77 HAFB	349	
F-GEAL(2)	Christen Pitts S-2B	5197	
F-GEAO	Balloon Works Firefly 8-24 HAFB	F8-023	N37228
F-GEAP	Chaize CS.2200F32 HAFB	047	
F-GEAS	Chaize CS.2200F12 CMM HAFB	049	
F-GEAT	Chaize CS.3000F16 HAFB	050	
F-GEAZ	Chaize CS.3000F16 HAFB	057	
F-GEBD	Beech A36 Bonanza	E-1592	D-EKBH
F-GEBI	Thunder AX7-65 HAFB	630	
F-GEBL	Thunder AX10-160 HAFB	643	
F-GEBM	Piper PA-18-150 Super Cub	18-1294	CS-ALJ, FAP3205
F-GEBO	Reims/Cessna F172M	F17201364	D-EEGN
F-GEBS	Pilatus PC-6/B1-H2 Turbo-Porter	702	HB-FFK
F-GEBT	Cessna 172RG Cutlass RG	172RG0648	N6385V
	(Dam. 25.5.02)		
F-GEBV	SAN Jodel D.140C Mousquetaire III	128	CN-TZH
F-GEBX	Thunder AX8-105 HAFB	640	
F-GEBY	Thunder AX10-160A HAFB	677	
F-GECG	Thunder AX7-77 HAFB	675	
F-GECH	Thunder AX7-65Z HAFB	676	
F-GECL	Mooney M.20J Model 201	24-1531	N57942
F-GECO	Chaize CS.3000F16 HAFB	059	
F-GECX	Thunder AX7-77 HAFB	741	
F-GECY	Robin DR.400/160 Chevalier	888	F-BUSQ
F-GECZ	Thunder AX7-77 HAFB	723	
F-GEDF	Aérospatiale AS.350B Ecureuil	1820	
F-GEDG	Piper PA-18A-150 Super Cub	18-2849	CN-TDE, F-DADF
F-GEDH(2)	Piper PA-18A-150 Super Cub	18-558	PH-AAT, R-207, 51-15672, N7187K
	(Officially quoted with f/n 18-490 - marks originally allotted to c/n 18-4606)		
F-GEDN	SNCASE SE.3130 Alouette II	1262/156	Fr.AF
F-GEDO	Piper PA-28-161 Warrior II	28-7916004	PH-SBW, N39736
F-GEDT	Deveque HG RD 700 Free Balloon	12	
F-GEDU	Piper PA-32-300 Cherokee Six	32-7440007	TZ-ACK, 5U-AAQ, 6V-ADM, N56601
F-GEEC	Cameron O-65 HAFB	967	
F-GEEI	Thunder AX7-65 HAFB	573	
F-GEEO	Pilatus PC-6/B1-H2 Turbo-Porter	676	HB-FEO
F-GEEP	Cameron O-77 HAFB	1147	
F-GEEQ	Chaize CS.2200F12 HAFB	058	
F-GEER	Chaize CS.2000F12 HAFB	065	
F-GEES	Durondeau L-180 HAFB	15	
F-GEET	Chaize CS.3000F16 HAFB	066	
F-GEEV	Chaize CS.2200F12 HAFB	068	
F-GEEX	Chaize CS.2200F32 HAFB	069	
F-GEEY	Chaize CS.3000F16 HAFB	071	
F-GEFD	Morane-Saulnier MS.880B Rallye Club	77	HB-EDF
F-GEFH	Reims/Cessna F172M	F17201258	D-EESB
F-GEFT	Piper PA-31 Turbo Navajo	31-678	N4683Y, D-IBRO, F-BRQJ, N6799L, N9714N
F-GEFU(2)	Cessna 172N Skyhawk	17272605	N6112D
F-WEGB	Aérospatiale/Alenia ATR-42-200	002	
	(Stored)		
F-GEGI	Cameron A-105 HAFB	1339	
F-GEGJ	Thunder AX7-77Z HAFB	941	
F-GEGM	Thunder AX10-160A HAFB	943	
F-GEGN	Thunder AX7-77 HAFB	985	
F-GEGO	Piper PA-28-181 Cherokee Archer II	28-7790320	TU-TMH, F-ODFO, N1639H
F-GEGP	Thunder AX8-9OA HAFB	995	
F-GEGV	Thunder AX7-77Z HAFB	1047	
F-GEGX	Thunder AX7-65Z HAFB	1046	
F-GEGZ	Thunder AX7-77Z HAFB	1041	
F-GEHB	Aérospatiale SA.341G Gazelle	1099	N266E
F-GEHM	Aérospatiale AS.350B Ecureuil	1722	
F-GEHO	SNCASE SE.313B Alouette II	1628	Gendarmerie/F-MJAO, ALAT
F-GEHV	Aérospatiale AS.350B Ecureuil	1454	N5786B
F-GEHX	Cessna 177B Cardinal	17702665	F-OGHX, N20379
F-GEHZ	Aérospatiale AS.350B Ecureuil	1291	N803DB, N3611T
F-WEIA	Robin R.3000Z	001	
F-GEIB	Robin DR.400/180 Régent	1676	
F-GEIC	Robin DR.400/120 Petit Prince	1678	
F-GEID	Robin DR.400/120 Petit Prince	1677	
F-GEIF	Robin DR.400/180 Régent	1690	
F-GEIH	Robin DR.400/180 Régent	1689	
F-GEIJ	Robin DR.400/180R Remorqueur	1709	F-WEIJ, F-BEIJ
F-WEIK	Robin R.3000/180R	107	
F-GEIL	Robin DR.400/180R Remorqueur	1693	
F-GEIM	Robin DR.400/180R Remorqueur	1694	
F-GEIO	Robin DR.400/120 Petit Prince	1699	
F-GEIR	Robin DR.400/120 Petit Prince	1704	
F-GEIS	Robin DR.400/120 Petit Prince	1705	
F-GEIT	Robin DR.400/180R Remorqueur	1710	
F-GEIU	Robin DR.400/120 Petit Prince	1712	
F-GEIV	Robin R.3000/120	111	
F-GEIY	Robin R.3000/120	113	
F-GEIZ	Robin R.3000/140	114	
F-GEJC	SNCASE SE.313B Alouette II	04	
	(Restored .01, c/n previously quoted as 1004 ex FrAF)		
F-GEJD	Cessna 172RG Cutlass RG	172RG1158	D-EBDO, N9428D
F-GEJJ	Beech A36TC Bonanza	EA-9	N6652Z
F-GEJO	Piper PA-28-181 Archer II	28-8690018	(F-GFEG), N9097C
F-GEJQ	Piper PA-28-181 Archer II	2890030	N9123P
F-GEJZ	Reims/Cessna F172M	F17201099	TU-TGT, F-OCVT
F-GEKA	Robin R.3000/120	115	
F-GEKC	Robin DR.400/120 Petit Prince	1722	
F-GEKD	Robin DR.400/120 Petit Prince	1728	
F-GEKG	Robin DR.400/180 Régent	1732	
F-GEKI	Robin DR.400/120D Petit Prince	1734	
F-GEKL	Robin DR.400/120 Petit Prince	1736	
F-GEKN	Robin DR.400/120 Petit Prince	1739	
F-GEKO	Robin DR.400/120 Petit Prince	1740	
F-GEKP	Robin DR.400/160 Chevalier	1741	
F-GEKQ	Robin R.3000/120	122	
F-GEKT	Robin DR.400/120 Petit Prince	1745	
F-GEKV	Robin DR.400/120 Petit Prince	1746	
F-GEKY	Robin DR.400/180R Remorqueur	1748	
F-GELB	Agusta-Bell 47G-2	103	D-HFLA, ALAT
F-GELC	Agusta-Bell 47G	019	ALAT
F-GELJ	SNCASE SE.313B Alouette II	85/1100	Fr.AF
F-GELK	Reims/Cessna F172N	F17201811	D-EGLC
F-GELM	Piper PA-34-200T Seneca II	34-7870040	N9833K
F-GELN	Bell 47G-4A	7668	N1438W
F-GELX(2)	Piper PA-32R-301T Turbo Saratoga SP	32R-8529005	N4385D
F-GELY	Beech A-36 Bonanza	E-458	TN-ACZ, CR-LMX, N2893W
F-GEMS	Reims/Cessna F152	F15201795	OO-HVB, D-EMSG, PH-CBE
F-GENB	SOCATA TB-20 Trinidad	460	
F-GENH	SOCATA TB-20 Trinidad	498	
F-GENJ	SOCATA TB-20 Trinidad	499	
F-GENR	SOCATA TB-20 Trinidad	513	F-OGMS
F-GENS	SOCATA TB-20 Trinidad	588	
F-GENT	SOCATA TB-9 Tampico	587	
F-GENY	SOCATA TB-10 Tobago	640	
F-GEOE	Aérospatiale AS.350B1 Ecureuil	2024	
F-GEOF	Hughes 269C	S-1183	D-HIVE
F-GEOL	Llopis Balloons MA-30 HAFB	183	
F-GEON	Piper PA-28R-201T Turbo Cherokee Arrow III	28-7703293	G-OTUX, SE-GPZ
F-GEOO	Piper PA-34-200T Seneca II	34-7870299	G-BMHP, 4X-CAW, N36160
F-GEOP	Thunder AX7-65Z HAFB	1088	
F-GEOQ	Piper PA-28R-201 Arrow III	28R-7837214	G-HIFI, G-BFTB, N9652C
F-GEOR	Mudry CAP.10B	77	G-WIXY, F-BXHQ
F-GEOS	Cameron O-65 HAFB	1517	
F-GEOT	Reims/Cessna FR172K Hawk XP	FR17200649	OO-VNX, OO-HNX
F-GEOU	Beech C90 King Air	LJ-941	N3804C
F-GEOV(2)	Piper PA-28R-201 Arrow III	28R-7837062	N4YN, N6207H

Registration	Type	C/n	Previous identities
F-GEPO	Beech 58 Baron	TH-112	G-AYGZ
F-GEPR	Wassmer WA.40A Super IV	82	OO-ROY
F-GEPT	SOCATA TB-10 Tobago	342	F-OGKD
F-GEPZ	SOCATA MS.892A Rallye Commodore 150	11948	TU-TKY, F-BTJU
	(Wfu, preserved Macon)		
F-GEQH(2)	Bell 47G-2	2420	N1044L, CF-DTR
F-GEQS(2)	SNCASE SE.3130 Alouette II	1142	ALAT, Fr.AF
F-GEQT	Cessna 172RG Cutlass RG	172RG0419	N4933V
F-GEQV	Cessna 172N Skyhawk	17271921	N5691E
F-GEQX	Piper PA-28-161 Cherokee Warrior II	28-7716080	N1038Q
F-GEQZ	SOCATA MS.880B Rallye-Club	1273	F-BRDN
F-GERB	Cessna U206D Skywagon 206	U206-1385	LN-LJQ, N72376
F-GERF	Sportavia/ Fournier RF-5	5021	D-KAHF
F-GERM	Piper PA-28RT-201T Turbo Arrow IV	28R-8131122	N8382V
F-GERR	Thunder AX7-77 HAFB	977	
F-GERX	Thunder AX7-77 HAFB	1107	
F-GERZ	Thunder AX7-77Z HAFB	1102	
F-GESF	Cameron A-105 HAFB	1549	
F-GESN	Piper PA-28-200 Cherokee Arrow II	28R-7535364	N3948X
F-GESR	SNCASE SE.3130 Alouette II	1551	LQ-HIS
F-GEST	Aérospatiale SA.341G Gazelle	1113	EC-CUA, F-BVRU
F-GESX	Piper PA-28RT-201T Turbo Arrow IV	28R-8431006	N4330Y
F-GETC	Reims/Cessna F177RG Cardinal RG	F177RG0050	F-GETZ, LX-RST, G-AZKU
F-GETG	Piper PA-28RT-201 Arrow IV	28R-8218009	N8040A
F-GETH	Piper PA-28RT-201T Turbo Arrow IV	28R-8031064	N8156Y
F-GETI	Beech F90 King Air	LA-19	N90NS, N90MT, N6686A
F-GETK	Piper PA-28-181 Archer II	28-8490059	N4350J
F-GETL	Reims/Cessna F177RG Cardinal RG	F177RG0065	F-OCTL
F-GETQ	Piper PA-34-200T Seneca II	34-7870437	N30JA
F-GETR	Aérospatiale AS.355F Ecureuil 2	5060	F-OBUU
F-GETT	Piper PA-18 Super Cub 95	18-3230	OO-ACC, OL-L56, L-156, 53-4830
F-GETV	Thunder AX6-56 HAFB	845	
F-GETY	Thunder AX7-77 HAFB	799	
F-GEUA	Reims/Cessna F172P	F17202225	
F-GEUB	Reims/Cessna F172P	F17202228	
F-GEUC	Reims/Cessna F172P	F17202231	
F-GEUR	Jodel DR.1051 Ambassadeur	249	OO-EUR, F-BKIE
F-GEVA	SOCATA TB-20 Trinidad	552	
F-GEVB	SOCATA TB-10 Tobago	561	
F-GEVC	SOCATA TB-10 Tobago	562	
F-GEVE	SOCATA TB-10 Tobago	564	
F-GEVF	SOCATA TB-10 Tobago	565	
F-GEVG	SOCATA TB-10 Tobago	566	
F-GEVI	SOCATA TB-10 Tobago	568	
F-GEVK	SOCATA TB-20 Trinidad	734	
F-GEVL	SOCATA TB-20 Trinidad	735	
F-GEVM	SOCATA TB-20 Trinidad	736	
F-GEVP	SOCATA TB-20 Trinidad	753	
F-GEVQ	SOCATA TB-20 Trinidad	796	
F-GEVR	SOCATA TB-20 Trinidad	797	
F-GEVS	SOCATA TB-20 Trinidad	798	
F-GEVU	SOCATA TB-20 Trinidad	800	
F-GEVV	SOCATA TB-20 Trinidad	801	
F-GEVX	SOCATA TB-20 Trinidad	802	
F-GEVY	SOCATA TB-20 Trinidad	803	
F-GEXN	Hughes 269C	27-0578	D-HDAN(2), D-HMAP
F-GEXO	Thunder AX7-77 HAFB	963	
F-GEXQ	Agusta-Bell 47G-2	241	D-HIFA, LN-ORT, I- LOBY
F-GEXV	Beech A100 King Air	B-199	N110TD, N600AC, G-BBVL, N85TC, G-BBVL
F-GEYB	Raven Europe S-55A HAFB	E-4	
F-GEYE	Raven Europe S-55A HAFB	E-7	
F-GEYH	Raven Europe S-55A HAFB	E-010	
F-GEYI	Raven Europe RX-65 HAFB	E-012	F-WEYI, F-GEYI, F-WEYI
F-GEYU	Raven Europe S-60A HAFB	E-023	
F-GEYV	Raven Europe S-60A HAFB	E-027	
F-GEYX	Raven Europe FS-57A HAFB	E-028	
F-GEZA	Raven Europe S-55A HAFB (Exp.7.02)	E-026	
	(Still regd 2012 but previously also quoted as Kubicek BB-20 c/n179 which is current as F-GIBT(3))		
F-GEZB	Raven Europe S-55A HAFB	E-036	
F-GEZG	Raven Europe S-60A HAFB	E-055	
F-GEZI	Raven Europe S-55A HAFB	E-060	
F-GEZJ	Raven Europe S-55A HAFB	E-061	
F-GEZK	Raven Europe S-60A HAFB	E-068	
F-GEZM	Raven Europe RX-7 HAFB	E-064	
F-GEZN	Raven Europe RX-7 HAFB	E-097	
F-GEZO	Raven Europe FS-57A HAFB	E-103	
F-GEZP	Raven Europe RX-7 HAFB	E-079	
F-GEZQ	Raven Europe S-55A HAFB	E-104	
F-GEZR	Raven Europe FS-57A HAFB	E-098	
F-GEZS	Thunder AX7-77Z HAFB	678	
F-GEZT	Raven Europe S-55A HAFB	E-091	
F-GEZU	Raven Europe RX-7 HAFB	E-075	
F-GEZX	Raven Europe FS-57A HAFB	E-101	
F-GEZZ	Raven Europe RX-7 HAFB	E-108	
F-GFAQ	Aérospatiale AS.350B1 Ecureuil	2048	
F-GFAU	Beech 58 Baron	TH-1281	N1829D
F-GFAV	Robinson R22 Beta	0560	
F-GFBH(3)	Thunder AX7-77 HAFB	1874	
F-GFBJ	Grumman G.164A Agcat	1124	N5168
F-GFBT	Beech V35B Bonanza	D-9727	N4079S
F-GFCC	Pilatus PC-6/B1-H2 Turbo-Porter	572	C-GWZO, N2852T
F-GFCF	Hughes 269C	119-0853	N58390
F-GFCG	Cessna 210N Centurion	21064148	OO-BIA, N5275Y
F-GFCI	Aérospatiale SA.341G Gazelle	1206	N3WU, N3WL, N55931
F-GFCK	Hughes 269C	104-0366	N9289F
F-GFCS	Aérospatiale AS.350B1 Ecureuil	1970	
F-GFCT	Cessna 172N Skyhawk 100	17267974	N75817
F-GFCU	Cessna 172N Skyhawk	17269612	N737RH
F-GFCZ	Cessna 172M	17267413	N73380
F-GFDC	Pilatus PC-6/B1-H2 Turbo-Porter	656	ZK-PTP, F-OCQV, VH-SMA, HB-FDC
F-GFDI	Thunder AX7-77 HAFB	1187	
F-GFDO	Agusta-Bell 206B Jet Ranger 2	8531	G-BEKH
F-GFDP	Bell 47G	D-6	G-ARIA, N4929V, YI-ABY, NC152B
F-GFDS	Robin DR.400/120 Petit Prince	1528	EC-EAU, F-OCJD
F-GFDT	Cameron O-77 HAFB	1651	
F-GFDY	Bell 206B Jet Ranger II	3600	G-OUPP, N206SH, N2261L
F-GFEE	Piper PA-28R-180 Cherokee Arrow	28R-30350	5R-MEE, N3995T
F-GFET	SOCATA TB-10 Tobago	659	N20HY
F-GFEX	Aérospatiale AS.355F Ecureuil 2	5217	ZS-HKZ
F-GFEY	Aérospatiale AS.355F Ecureuil 2	5046	N57826
F-GFFC	Grumman AA-5A Cheetah	AA5A-0573	TU-TMW, F-OCBJ, F-GBDJ
F-GFFD	Pilatus PC-6/B2-H2 Turbo-Porter	708	HB-FFD
F-GFFI	Cameron A-140 HAFB	1561	
F-GFFJ	Ultramagic V-77 HAFB	77/18	
F-GFFO	Cessna 150M	15078660	N704JZ
F-GFFT	SOCATA TB-20 Trinidad	672	N20LK
F-GFFX	Thunder AX8-90A SIII HAFB	1890	
F-GFGH	SOCATA Rallye 235E Gabier	13337	F-ODNQ
F-GFGI (2)	Hughes 269C	117-0646	F-GDCF, OE-CXN
F-GFGJ	Cessna U206G Stationair 6	U20604302	N756RT
F-GFGK(2)	Bell 47G-2	1990	CF-KAJ
F-GFGN	Piper PA-28-181 Archer II	2890056	
F-GFGO	Piper PA-28-181 Archer II	2890060	
F-GFGQ(2)	Cessna 172N Skyhawk	17271595	N3576E
F-GFGS	Cessna 182N Skylane	18260799	D-EFWG, N9255G
F-GFGX	Piper PA-28-181 Cherokee Archer II	28-7690275	N9697K
F-GFHA	Robinson R22 Beta	0591	N24702
F-GFHI	Cessna 172RG Cutlass RG	172RG0332	N4595V
F-GFHL	Bell 47G-2	2433	N5828K, C-FLMZ, CF-LMZ, N799B
F-GFHM(2)	Aérospatiale AS.350B Ecureuil	1560	F-WYMB, MAAW H-05, D-HEZE
F-GFHN(2)	Bell 47G-2	1489	N2805B, C-FHDP, N130B
F-GFHS	Sud Avn SA.318C Alouette Astazou	2233	N4683
F-GFHT	Cessna 172N Skyhawk	17271679	N4938E
F-GFHX	Piper PA-12 Super Cruiser	12-3534	CN-TBS, F-BFBK, NC4102H
F-GFIE	Piper PA-28-181 Archer II	2890071	
F-GFIO	SNCAN Stampe SV.4C	695	F-BDOO
F-GFIP	Thunder AX8-105 HAFB	1262	
F-GFIT	Piper PA-28RT-201 Arrow IV	28R-8018023	N35747
F-GFIX	Thunder AX8-90A HAFB	1239	
F-GFJG	Cessna TR182 Turbo Skylane RG	R18201854	N5306T
F-GFJH	Aérospatiale/Alenia ATR-42-300	049	
F-GFJI	Reims/Cessna FRA150L Aerobat	FRA1500139	TU-TFT, F-OCPM
F-GFJJ(2)	Piper PA-28-181 Archer II	28-7990157	N321DG
F-GFJO	Bell 47G-2	2251	C-FKMX, CF-KMX
F-GFJZ	Thunder AX8-105 HAFB	1240	
F-GFLC	Piper PA-28-181 Archer II	28-8490047	TJ-AHB, N4338E
F-GFLG	Piper PA-28RT-201 Arrow IV	28R-7918263	G-EDDY, N8079E
F-GFLJ(2)	Nord 1101 Noralpha	141	N72SL, F-BLTS, Fr.Mil
F-GFLM	Bell 47G-2	1631	F-GBLM, G-BEUE, EP-HAU, N6763, Fr.AF, N2850B
F-GFLU	CEA DR.253 Régent	113	G-AWCD
F-GFMB	Beech C23 Sundowner 180	M-1501	TU-TGL
F-GFMC	Chaize CS.3000F16 HAFB	076	
F-GFMD	Dassault Falcon 10	136	F-WZGS, I- MUDE, F-WZGH
F-GFMF	Chaize CS.2200F12 HAFB	082	
F-GFMG	Robin DR.300/120 Petit Prince	615	F-ZVMG
F-GFMK	Bell 206B Jet Ranger II	2386	N777TE
F-GFML	SOCATA MS.893E Rallye 180GT	12386	F-ZVML
F-GFMM	Robin DR.400/2+2	1451	F-ZVMM, F-GCIE
	(Damaged 11.8.00)		
F-GFMQ	SOCATA ST-10 Diplomate	147	F-BTJM
F-GFMT	Cessna 172N Skyhawk 100	17268481	N733RC
F-GFMU	Cessna F172H	F172-0404	LX-AVB, D-EMFC
F-GFMV	Beech 58 Baron	TH-745	OO-DUK, F-ODCZ
F-GFNE	Robin ATL	05	F-WFNE
F-GFNF	Robin ATL	06	F-WFNF
F-GFNG	Robin ATL	07	F-WFNG
F-GFNL	Robin ATL	12	F-WFNL
	(Stored)		
F-GFNP	Robin ATL	20	F-WFNP
F-GFNQ	Robin ATL	17	F-WFNQ
F-GFNS	Robin ATL	18	F-WFNS
F-GFNT	Robin ATL	19	F-WFNT
F-GFNY	Robin ATL	21	F-WFNY
F-GFOC	Robin ATL	27	F-WFOC
F-GFOD	Robin ATL	28	F-WFOD
F-GFOE	Robin ATL	29	F-WFOE
F-GFOG	Robin ATL	31	F-WFOG
F-GFOJ	Robin ATL	34	F-WFOJ
F-GFOM	Robin ATL	37	
F-GFOQ	Robin ATL	41	
F-GFOR	Robin ATL	42	
F-GFOT	Robin ATL	44	
F-GFPC	Chaize CS.2200F12 HAFB	085	
F-GFPD(2)	Piper PA-25-235 Pawnee	25-2685	N6940Z
F-GFPF	Dassault Falcon 10	68	N80MP, N91DH, N11DH, (N7NL), N7NP, N152FJ, F-WLCV
F-GFPH	Piper PA-23-235 Apache	27-602	F-OBYY, F-BMLL, N4319Y
F-GFPJ	Piper PA-18-135 Super Cub	18-3188	OO-WIK, OO-HBB, OL-L01, L-114, 53-4788
	(Quoted officially with f/n 18-3191 as c/n)		
F-GFPN	Robinson R22 Beta	0848	
F-GFPP	Beech A36 Bonanza	E-1454	N6027M
F-GFPQ	Sud Avn SA.318C Alouette Astazou	2247	C-FQMQ, CF-QMQ
F-GFPS	Beech 76 Duchess	ME-209	N6626W
F-GFPX	Thunder AX10-160 HAFB	1295	
F-GFPY	CEA DR.315 Petit Prince	332	F-BPRY
F-GFQA	SOCATA TB-20 Trinidad	571	F-OGMT
F-GFQE	SOCATA Rallye 180T Galérien	3386	
F-GFQF	SOCATA TB-20 Trinidad	709	
F-GFQH	SOCATA TB-10 Tobago	733	
F-GFQJ	SOCATA TB-20 Trinidad	741	
F-GFQO	SOCATA TB-10 Tobago	657	(N20HQ)
F-GFQV	SOCATA TB-10 Tobago	661	(N20JQ)
F-GFQX	SOCATA TB-10 Tobago	663	(N20JY)
F-GFQY	SOCATA TB-20 Trinidad	779	
F-GFRA	Robin ATL	50	
F-GFRF	Robin ATL	55	
F-GFRH	Robin ATL	57	
F-GFRJ	Robin ATL	59	
F-GFRK	Robin ATL	60	
F-GFRM	Robin ATL	62	
	(Now regd as ULM, 61-LQ)		
F-GFRP	Robin ATL	65	
F-GFRR	Robin ATL	67	
F-GFRT	Robin ATL	70	
F-GFSC	Robin ATL	79	

Registration	Type	Serial	Previous identities
F-GFSE	Robin ATL	85	
F-GFSF	Robin ATL	86	
F-GFSK	Robin ATL	91	
F-GFSL	Robin ATL	92	
F-GFSN	Robin ATL	94	
F-GFSR	Robin ATL	98	
F-GFSU	Robin ATL	101	
F-GFSX	Robin ATL	104	
F-GFSZ	Robin ATL	111	F-WFSZ
F-GFTE	Cessna 177B Cardinal	17702568	N19393
F-GFTN	Piper PA-28R-201T Turbo Arrow IV	28R-7931103	N3024U
F-GFTR	Robin DR.400/180 Régent	1858	
F-GFTU	Agusta-Bell 47G-2	250	EC-DXB, D-HIRT, 74+10, AS+051
F-GFTV	Beech A36 Bonanza	E-1640	N6730L
F-WFTX	Fouga CM.170 Magister	522	Fr.AF
F-GFTY	Piper PA-25-235 Pawnee	25-2741	N6991Z, (N585Z), N6991Z
F-GFTZ	Piper PA-28-161 Warrior II	28-8216093	N8053R
F-GFUF	Boeing 737-33A	24388	
F-GFUM	Pilatus PC-6/B2-H2 Turbo Porter	740	HA-YDB
F-GFUO	Piper PA-25-235 Pawnee	25-2141	N6585Z
F-GFUP	Piper PA-25-235 Pawnee	25-2841	N7061Z
F-WFUQ	Fouga CM-170 Magister	523	Fr.AF
F-GFUR	Robin ATL	80	
F-GFUY	Beech A36 Bonanza	E-2640	
F-GFVB	Cessna 305C/L-19E Bird Dog	24534	ALAT
F-GFVL	Thunder AX7-77Z HAFB	1242	
F-GFVP	Wassmer Jodel D.120A Paris-Nice	217	OO-PCJ, LX-OUF(1), F-BKNF
F-GFVQ	Hughes 269C	120-0073	N9646F
F-GFVV	Holste MH.1521M Broussard	298	Fr.AF
F-GFVZ	Robin DR.400/180 Régent	1113	F-BXVZ
F-GFXA	Robin DR.400/120 Petit Prince	1749	
F-GFXB	Robin DR.400/160 Chevalier	1750	
F-GFXC	Robin DR.400/120 Petit Prince	1752	
F-GFXD	Robin DR.400/120 Petit Prince	1751	
F-GFXE	Robin DR.400/180 Régent	1755	
F-GFXF	Robin DR.400/120 Petit Prince	1753	
F-GFXH	Robin DR.400/120 Petit Prince	1757	
F-GFXJ	Robin DR.400/120 Petit Prince	1772	
F-GFXK	Robin DR.400/180 Régent	1763	
F-GFXL	Robin DR.400/160 Major	1761	
F-GFXN	Robin DR.400/120 Petit Prince	1768	
F-GFXO	Robin DR.400/120 Petit Prince	1770	
F-GFXP	Robin DR.400/120 Petit Prince	1771	
F-GFXS	Robin DR.400/180 Régent	1774	
F-GFXT	Robin DR.400/100 Cadet	1775	F-WFXT
F-GFXV	Robin DR.400/180 Régent	1777	
F-GFXX	Robin DR.400/160 Chevalier	1779	
	(W/o 18.2.15, Sarazinière)		
F-GFXY	Robin DR.400/180 Régent	1780	
F-GFXZ	Robin DR.400/120 Petit Prince	1782	
F-GFYD	Zlin Z.526F Trenér Master	1176	F-BTGD, F-WTGD
F-GFYQ	Thunder AX7-77 HAFB	1366	
F-GFYR	Hughes 369D	39-0483D	N58262
F-GFYS	Robinson R22 Beta	1073	D-HOMA, N8038Q
F-GFYT	Piper PA-28-161 Cadet	2841060	
F-GFYV	Piper PA-28-161 Cadet	2841059	
F-GFZA	Piper PA-28-181 Archer II	28-8390074	TJ-AGW, N82608, N9516N
F-GFZC	Aérospatiale AS.350B Ecureuil	2163	
F-GFZF	Sud Avn SA.318C Alouette Astazou	2352	D-HHFS, SX-HAN
F-GFZH	Reims/Cessna FTB.337 Super Skymaster	0035	F-BXNL
	(W/o 15.4.04)		
F-GFZI	Zodiac MGZ 2-2-S Free Balloon	002	
F-GFZJ	SOCATA TB-20 Trinidad	626	(F-GFPO), N800X
F-GFZN	Robinson R22 Beta	1004	
F-GFZO	Morane-Saulnier MS.317	276	OO-JUL, (OO-MIL), F-BFZO
F-GFZP	Balloon Works Firefly 7 HAFB	F7-479	
F-GFZQ	SNCASE SE.313B Alouette II	1813	F-MJBO
F-WFZR(2)	Chaize CS.500F12 HAFB	EX-001	
F-GFZS	Thunder AX7-77 HAFB	718	
F-GFZV	Piper PA-28-181 Archer II	2890117	
F-GFZX	Piper PA-28R-201T Turbo Cherokee Arrow III	28R-7703319	N43938, (N748SB), N43938
F-GGAA	Schweizer 269C	S-1308	
F-GGAC	Piper PA-28-181 Archer II	2890067	
F-GGAD	Zlin Z.526F Trenér Master	1177	(F-GGAA), F-BTGE, F-WTGE
F-GGAE	Piper PA-28-161 Cadet	2841062	
F-GGAG	Bell 47G-2	665-10	CF-HFX
F-GGAL	Cessna 650 Citation III	650-0117	N1321N
F-GGAO	Aérospatiale AS.350B Ecureuil	2208	
F-GGAU	Reims/Cessna F172N	F17201867	D-EKAU
F-GGAX	Agusta-Bell 206B Jet Ranger 2	8020	D-HOOL, SE-HPD
F-GGAY	Piper PA-28-181 Cherokee Archer II	28-7790461	N3493Q
F-GGBA	Piper PA-28RT-201T Turbo Arrow IV	28R-8431002	N4324P, N9547N, N43230
F-GGBD	Piper PA-32R-301T Turbo Saratoga SP	32R-8129110	N8442U
F-GGBF	Piper PA-22-180 Colt	22-8914	G-GGLE, N5234Z
F-GGBN	Hughes 269C	20-0894	D-HKAG
F-GGBQ	Piper PA-28-140 Cherokee Cruiser	28-7625059	N921C, N4580X
F-GGBR(3)	SOCATA Rallye 150SV Garnement	3365	F-OGLV
F-GGBX	SNCASE SE.3130 Alouette II	1373	ALAT
F-GGBY	SNCASE SE.313B Alouette II	1332	ALAT
F-GGBZ(2)	Cessna 172N Skyhawk 100	17268486	N733RH
F-GGCD	Chaize CS.2200F12 HAFB	81	
F-GGCE	Piper PA-28RT-201T Turbo Arrow IV	28R-8031111	N45KC, N9566N
F-GGCF	Piper PA-28RT-201T Turbo Arrow IV	28R-7931310	N8094Q
F-GGCG	SNCASE SE.313B Alouette II	1172	ALAT
F-GGCI	SNCASE SE.313B Alouette II	1050	ALAT
F-GGCR	Raven Europe FS-57A HAFB	E-092	
F-GGCS	Cessna 152	15283555	N4622B
F-GGCT	Cessna 152	15280130	N757ZH
F-GGCV	Cessna 172RG Cutlass RG	172RG1111	N9997B
F-GGCX	Cessna 172RG Cutlass RG	172RG1134	N9360D
F-GGCZ	Cessna 172RG Cutlass RG	172RG0708	N6447V
F-GGDB	Piper PA-28RT-201 Arrow IV	28R-7918160	N2824R
F-GGDC	Piper PA-28-161 Cadet	2841063	
F-GGDE	Cessna A185F Skywagon	18504075	N60925
F-GGDF	Thunder AX7-65 HAFB	818	
F-GGDH	SNCASE SE.313B Alouette II	1103	ALAT
F-GGDK	Thunder AX7-77 HAFB	1342	
F-GGDL	Piper PA-28-181 Archer II	28-8190242	N83912
F-GGDN	Thunder AX7-77 HAFB	1504	
F-GGDO	Thunder AX7-77Z HAFB	1515	
F-GGDQ	Robinson R22 Beta	1042	
F-GGDS	Chaize CS.2000F12 HAFB	095	
F-GGDT	Hughes 369D	67-0154D	N81418, TG-REY, YS-1014P
F-GGDU	Bell 47G-2	1540	N5185B
F-GGDX	Cessna A185F Skywagon	18503538	(F-OMMP), F-GGDX, N767RC, N2901Q
F-GGDY	Hughes 269C	41-1043	D-HMIG
F-GGFC	Robinson R22 Beta	0822	
	(Dam. 23.11.99)		
F-GGFF	SNCAN Stampe SV.4C	610	F-BDFF
F-GGFG	Robinson R22 Beta	1055	N8045U
F-GGFK(2)	Colt Montgolfier SS HAFB	1281	G-BPHV
F-GGFL	Robinson R22 Beta	1045	
F-GGFT	Piper PA-28-161 Cadet	2841075	
F-GGFV	Piper PA-28-161 Cadet	2841077	
F-GGFY	Piper PA-28-161 Cadet	2841079	
F-GGFZ	Robinson R22 Beta	0838	3A-MTU
F-GGGA	Cessna F.550 Citation	F550-0586	N1301N
F-WGGC	Fouga CM-170 Magister	459	Fr.AF
F-WGGD	Holste MH.1521M Broussard	290	Fr.AF
F-WGGE	Mudry CAP.20	4	Fr.AF: F-TFVX, F-BTAF
F-GGGJ	Colt 90A HAFB	1553	
F-WGGK	Holste MH.1521M Broussard	127	ALAT
F-GGGL	Mooney M.20J Model 205	24-3027	
F-GGGN	Cessna T210N Turbo Centurion II	21064426	N6537Y
F-GGGO	Colt 90A HAFB	1565	
F-WGGQ	Holste MH.1521M Broussard	143	ALAT
	(Stored)		
F-GGGS	Robin HR.100/250TR	553	(F-ODSX), 6V-AEK, F-ODFX
F-GGGT	Cessna F550 Citation II	0611	
F-GGGZ	Piper PA-38-112 Tomahawk	38-81A0022	HB-PFT
F-GGHA	Robin ATL	106	
F-GGHE	Robin ATL	81	F-WZZX, (PH-ATL)
F-GGHG	Robin ATL	117	
F-GGHH	Robin ATL	118	
	(Derelict Wing Farm, UK, 5.10)		
F-GGHI	Robin DR.400/180R Remorqueur	1833	
F-GGHJ	Robin DR.400/140B Major 80	1832	
F-GGHK	Robin DR.400/140B Major 80	1834	
F-GGHL	Robin DR.400/180 Régent	1835	
F-GGHP	Robin ATL	120	
F-GGHR	Robin DR.400/180 Régent	1844	
F-GGHT	Robin DR.400/180 Régent	1846	
F-GGHV	Robin DR.400/120 Dauphin 2+2	1849	
F-GGHX	Robin DR.400/120 Dauphin 2+2	1850	
F-GGHY	Robin DR.400/160 Major	1853	
	(W/o 14.7.10)		
F-GGIB	SOCATA TB-20 Trinidad	777	
	(Wfu 14.5.09)		
F-GGIC	SOCATA TB-20 Trinidad	778	
	(Wfu 14.5.09)		
F-GGID	SOCATA TB-20 Trinidad	790	
	(Wfu 14.5.09)		
F-GGIE	SOCATA TB-20 Trinidad	854	
F-GGIF	SOCATA TB-20 Trinidad	855	
F-GGIG	SOCATA TB-20 Trinidad	859	
	(Wfu 14.5.09)		
F-GGII	SOCATA TB-20 Trinidad	991	
	(Wfu 14.5.09)		
F-GGIK	SOCATA TB-10 Tobago	785	
F-GGIO	SOCATA TB-20 Trinidad	791	
F-GGIP	SOCATA TB-20 Trinidad	794	
F-GGIR	SOCATA TB-9 Tampico	809	
F-GGIV	SOCATA TB-9 Tampico	890	
F-GGIY	SOCATA TB-10 Tobago	906	
F-GGJB	Robin DR.400/120 Petit Prince	1788	
F-GGJC	Robin DR.400/120 Petit Prince	1791	
F-GGJD	Robin DR.400/180 Régent	1789	
F-GGJG	Robin DR.400/120 Petit Prince	1799	
F-GGJH	Robin DR.400/160 Chevalier	1795	
F-GGJI	Robin DR.400/120 Dauphin 2+2	1801	
F-GGJJ	Robin DR.400/180 Régent	1804	
F-GGJL	Robin DR.400/180 Régent	1807	
F-GGJM	Robin R.3000/140	131	
F-GGJO	Robin DR.400/120 Dauphin 2+2	1814	
F-GGJP	Robin DR.400/180 Régent	1811	
F-GGJQ	Robin DR.400/120 Dauphin 2+2	1813	
F-GGJR	Robin DR.400/120 Dauphin 2+2	1815	
F-GGJS	Robin DR.400/120 Dauphin 2+2	1816	
F-GGJT	Robin DR.400/180 Régent	1820	
F-GGJU	Robin DR.400/120 Dauphin 2+2	1822	
F-GGJV	Robin DR.400/180 Régent	1840	
F-GGJX	Robin DR.400/120 Dauphin 2+2	1823	
F-GGJY	Robin DR.400/160 Major	1824	
F-GGKB	Piper J-3C-65 Cub	14986	N42690, NC42690
F-GGKC(2)	Piper J-3C-65 Cub	5037	N30655, NC30655
F-GGKH	Holste MH.1521C Broussard	32	F-WGKH, Fr.AF
F-GGKK	Holste MH.1521C-1 Broussard	211M	F-WGKK, Fr.AF
F-WGKN	Holste MH.1521M Broussard	261	Fr.AF
F-GGKU	Aérospatiale SA.342 Gazelle	1186	TT-OAG, F-WTNC
F-GGKV	Aérospatiale SA.342 Gazelle	1378	TT-OAF
F-GGKY	Aérospatiale SA.330 Puma	1200	TT-..., ALAT
F-GGKZ	Robinson R22 Beta	1146	
F-GGLB	Bell 47G-2	1056	N10194
	(Dbr 15.9.03)		
F-GGLH	Robinson R22 Beta	1065	N8046U
F-GGLL	Piper PA-28-161 Warrior II	28-8116012	N8255A
F-GGLM	Thunder AX7-77Z HAFB	1450	
F-GGLO	Piper PA-18-150 Super Cub	18-5329	TR-LBY, F-BLOV, ALAT, N10F
	(Dbr 26.2.06)		
F-GGLP	Beech A36 Bonanza	E-1595	N19WH, N66775
F-GGLS	Morane-Saulnier MS.885 Super Rallye	125	D-EMTE
F-GGLU	Morane-Saulnier MS.880B Rallye Club	68	D-EDRC, F-BKDU
F-GGLY	Cameron N-90 HAFB	2124	
F-GGLZ(2)	Holste MH.1521M Broussard	102	ALAT
F-WGMG	RJ-03A Roitelet Helicopter	unkn	
F-GGMH	Piper PA-28-181 Archer II	2890166	
F-GGMJ	Mooney M.20J Model 205	24-3045	N205DD
F-GGMK	Piper PA-18-150 Super Cub	1809051	N9522N, F-GGMK, N9522N

F-WGMO(2)	AS.300	008	
F-WGMQ	Aérospatiale AS.350Z Ecureuil	1013	F-WYMZ, N134BH, N90001
F-GGMT	Aerotek Pitts S-2A	2272	
F-GGMU	Piper PA-28RT-201T Turbo Arrow IV		
		28R-8031014	N8114P
F-GGMY	Piper PA-28-181 Archer II	28-7990375	6V-AEP, N2235X
F-GGNB	SOCATA TB-10 Tobago	808	
F-GGND	SOCATA TB-10 Tobago	817	
F-GGNE	SOCATA TB-10 Tobago	818	
F-GGNG	SOCATA TB-10 Tobago	945	G-BPZW
F-GGNH	SOCATA TB-10 Tobago	946	
F-GGNJ	SOCATA TB-10 Tobago	1172	
F-GGNK	SOCATA TB-10 Tobago	1173	
F-GGNM	SOCATA TB-10 Tobago	1175	
F-GGNO	SOCATA TB-20 Trinidad	1213	
F-GGNP	SOCATA TB-20 Trinidad	1264	
F-GGNQ	SOCATA TB-20 Trinidad	1265	
F-GGNR	SOCATA TB-20 Trinidad	1266	
F-GGNS	SOCATA TB-20 Trinidad	1267	
F-GGNT	SOCATA TB-20 Trinidad	1284	
F-GGNU	SOCATA TB-20 Trinidad	1285	
F-GGNV	SOCATA TB-20 Trinidad	1286	
F-GGNX	SOCATA TB-20 Trinidad	1287	
F-GGNY	SOCATA TB-20 Trinidad	1301	
F-GGNZ	SOCATA TB-20 Trinidad	1302	
F-GGOB	Grob G 115A	8027	F-WGOB, D-EGVV
F-GGOD	Grob G 115A	8036	F-WGOD, D-EGVV
F-GGOH	Grob G 115A	8076	D-EGVV
F-GGOK	Grob G 115A	8096	
F-GGOL	Grob G 115A	8103	
F-GGOP	Grob G 115A	8106	
F-GGOQ	Grob G 115A	8107	
F-GGPL(2)	Mooney M.20J Model 201	24-1632	
F-GGPO	Piper PA-28-161 Cadet	2841103	
F-GGPS	Aerotek Pitts S-2B	5015	N66LF, N53206
F-WGPU(2)	Fouga CM.170R Magister	014	Fr.AF
F-GGQA	Robin DR.400/120 Dauphin 2+2	1851	
F-GGQB	Robin DR.400/140B Major 80	1852	
F-GGQD	Robin DR.400/120 Dauphin 2+2	1878	
F-GGQE	Robin DR.400/120 Dauphin 2+2	1877	
	(W/o 11.1.06)		
F-GGQI	Robin ATL	125	
F-GGQL	Robin DR.400/120 Dauphin 2+2	1859	
F-GGQM	Robin DR.400/120 Dauphin 2+2	1863	
F-GGQN	Robin DR.400/180 Régent	1867	
F-GGQO	Robin DR.400/100 Cadet	1864	
F-GGQP	Robin DR.400/100 Cadet	1865	
F-GGQQ	Robin DR.400/180R Remorqueur	1868	
	(Wreck noted at St Girons 9.03)		
F-GGQU	Robin DR.400/100 Cadet	1871	
F-GGQX	Robin DR.400/120 Dauphin 2+2	1879	
F-GGQY	Robin DR.400/180 Régent	1873	
F-GGQZ	Robin DR.400/140B Major 80	1880	
F-GGRF	Cameron A-120 HAFB	2242	
F-GGRL	Mooney M.20J Model 201	24-1622	
F-GGRQ	Ultramagic H-77 HAFB	77/47	
F-GGRT	Chaize CS.3000F16 HAFB	086	
F-GGRU	Cameron N-65 HAFB	2287	
F-GGRX	Piper PA-28R-201 Arrow	2837035	N9187Z
F-GGRY	Piper PA-28-161 Cadet	2841104	
F-GGSD	Cameron O-77 HAFB	1410	
F-GGSG	Cameron O-77 HAFB	1429	
F-GGSH	Schweizer 269C	S-1271	D-HDAM
F-GGSJ	Chaize CS.3000F16 HAFB	077	
F-GGSK	Piper PA-23-250 Aztec F	27-7854125	TJ-AFR, N63996
F-GGSL	Robin DR.400/140B Major 80	1861	
F-GGSM	Aerotek Pitts S-2A	2151	N31502
F-GGSN	Robin DR.400/100 Cadet	1862	
	(Marked as '2+2')		
F-GGSP	SOCATA TB-10 Tobago	271	D-EEVU
F-GGSR(2)	Hughes 269C	28-0667	D-HMAR, D-HOYH
F-GGSY	Cessna 150M	15078308	N9359U
F-GGTB	Aerotek Pitts S-2A	2160	N31429

F-WGTF/G/H Re-useable test registrations for Falcon 20/TPE 731 modifications by Europe Falcon Service

F-GGTK	Piper PA-28R-201 Cherokee Arrow III		
		28R-7737162	N47453
F-GGTL	Piper PA-46-310P Malibu	46-8508077	N6915C
F-WGTM(2)	Aérospatiale AS.355F Ecureuil 2	5264	G-BOSK, D-HERP
F-GGTN	Reims/Cessna FTB.337G Super Skymaster		
		0003	FAP3702, CS-AAW
F-GGTR	Aerotek Pitts S-2A	2171	N31439
F-GGTS	Cameron O-77 HAFB	1460	
F-WGTX	Heli Atlas	01	
F-WGTY	Heli Atlas	02	
F-WGTZ	Heli Atlas	unkn	
F-GGUY	Cameron Concept 80 HAFB	3424	
F-GGVA	Cameron O-77 HAFB	1659	
F-GGVD	Colt 21A HAFB	1609	
F-GGVG	Swearingen SA.226TB Merlin IIIB	T-293	D-IBBB(2), N5469M
F-GGVI	SNCAN/Stampe SV.4C	429	F-BCVI
F-GGVS	Cameron N-90 HAFB	2312	
F-GGVZ	Piper PA-28-181 Archer II	28-8190289	N9195Y, HR-AIR, N8421H
F-GGXA	Robin DR.400/120 Dauphin 2+2	1897	
F-GGXB	Robin ATL	128	
F-GGXC	Robin DR.400/120 Dauphin 2+2	1888	
F-GGXD	Robin DR.400/120 Dauphin 2+2	1882	
F-GGXE	Robin DR.400/180R Remorqueur	1883	
F-GGXG	Robin DR.400/180 Régent	1891	
F-GGXI	Robin DR.400/120 Dauphin 2+2	1895	
F-GGXJ	Robin DR.400/140B Major 80	1896	
F-GGXK	Robin DR.400/120 Dauphin 2+2	1881	
	(Damaged 11.8.12)		
F-GGXO	Robin DR.400/120 Dauphin 2+2	1905	
F-GGXP	Robin DR.400/180 Régent	1907	
F-GGXQ	Robin DR.400/140B Major 80	1928	
F-GGXS	Robin DR.400/140B Major 80	1913	
F-GGXX	Robin ATL L	131	
F-GGXY	Robin DR.400/140B Major 80	1923	
F-GGXZ	Robin DR.400/180 Régent	1924	
F-GGYA	Mudry CAP.10B	232	
F-GGYB	Mudry CAP.10B	233	
F-GGYC	Mudry CAP.10B	235	
F-GGYD	Mudry CAP.10B	234	

F-GGYF	Mudry CAP.10B	238	
F-GGYJ	Mudry CAP.10B	243	
F-GGYL	Mudry CAP.10B	245	
F-GGYQ	Mudry CAP.231	14	F-WGZD
F-GGYT	Mudry CAP.10B	252	
F-GGYU	Mudry CAP.10B	253	
F-GGYV	Mudry CAP.10B	254	
F-GGYZ	Mudry CAP.231	20	
F-GGZB	Piper PA-28-181 Cherokee Archer II		
		28-7890105	N47624
F-GGZI	Gardan GY-80-160 Horizon	47	OO-GOD, F-OCCV
F-GGZJ	Cessna 172N Skyhawk	17269362	N737EN
F-GGZL	Thunder AX7-77 HAFB	1829	
F-GGZN	Piper PA-32R-301 Saratoga SP	32R-8313030	TR-LBD, N8246A
F-GGZO	Reims/Cessna F172N	F17201997	D-EIZO
F-GGZS	Thunder AX8-105 HAFB	1505	
F-GGZU	Ultramagic S-105 HAFB	105/14	
F-GGZX	Christen A-1 Husky	1159	
F-GGZY	Schweizer 269C	S-1487	
F-GGZZ	Piper PA-32-300 Cherokee Six	32-7440110	N42160
F-GHAC	Mooney M.20J Model 201	24-1637	
F-GHAF(2)	Hughes 269C	61-1060	D-HIRN, N5016R
F-WHAG	Raven Europe Aeroglobe Balloon	001	
F-GHAI	Bell 47G-2	1502	N2828B
F-GHAM	Robin ATL	103	
F-GHAV	Reims FR172J Rocket	FR17200489	N26674, F-BVBH
F-GHAX	Chaize CS.2200F12 HAFB	089	
F-GHAY	Chaize CS.2200F12 HAFB	087	
F-GHBA	Piper PA-28-161 Cadet	2841162	
F-GHBC	Chaize CS.3000F16 HAFB	073	F-WHBC
F-GHBD	Beech C90 King Air	LJ-545	D-ILHD
F-GHBN	Cessna 172N Skyhawk	17271123	N2026E
F-GHBO	Cameron N-77 HAFB	1643	
F-GHBP	Cameron D-96 Hot Air Airship	536	SE-ZAD, G-BHBJ
F-GHBQ	Piper PA-28-181 Archer II	28-8290018	N8406B
F-GHBR(2)	Aérospatiale AS.350BA Ecureuil	1600	(F-GHCO), (F-GGBR), N58030
F-GHBS	Mooney M.20F Executive	670142	D-EBBM(2), N9565M
F-GHBV	Aérospatiale AS.350B Ecureuil	1544	N323LB
F-GHBX	Thunder AX7-77 HAFB	1808	
F-GHBY	Piper J-3C-65 Cub	unkn	F-BFBY, "43-17737"
F-GHCE	Bell 206B Jet Ranger II	2092	N16701
F-GHCF	Kubicek BB-30Z HAFB	533	
F-GHCG	Mooney M.20J Model 205	24-3075	N205RS
F-GHCM	Cessna T303 Crusader	T30300003	N9335T
F-GHCX	Wassmer Jodel D.120 Paris-Nice	305	F-BNCX
F-GHDD	Piper PA-28-161 Cadet	2841262	
F-GHDE	Ultramagic V-77 HAFB	77/24	
F-GHDI	Ultramagic M77 Air Balloon	77/38	
F-GHDM	Piper PA-28-161 Cadet	2841263	
F-GHDN(2)	Cameron A-180 HAFB	2455	G-BTAO
F-GHDO	Beech 65-B90 King Air	LJ-206	3X-. . ., F-BTAK, HB-GDG
F-GHDU	Piper PA-28R-201 Cherokee Arrow III		
		28R-7703233	N38520
F-GHDV	Cameron N-77 HAFB	1773	
F-GHDY	Balloon Works Firefly F7-15 HAFB	F7-725	
F-GHEL	Mooney M.20J Model 205	24-3028	N205MJ
F-GHEN	Cessna U206G Stationair	U20603587	G-BOSC, 5N-ASU, N7256N
F-GHEO	Cessna R182 Skylane RG	R18200453	N9833C
F-GHEV	Cessna 172N Skyhawk	17269730	N737WK
F-GHFC	Cessna 172P Skyhawk	17274447	N52229
F-GHFG	Holste MH.1521M Broussard	104	Fr.AF
F-GHFI (2)	Aérospatiale SA.315B Lama	2476	D-HLEO, F-GHCN, G-BLXJ, N403AH, N47309
F-GHGB	Holste MH.1521C1 Broussard	256	Fr.AF
F-GHGM(2)	Rockwell S.2R-600 Thrush Commander	1821R	CS-APO, N5621X
F-GHGZ	Cessna 208 Caravan I	20800188	
F-GHHB	Robinson R22B Beta	0783	
F-GHHF	Aérospatiale AS.350B Ecureuil	2145	N373RE, N6024V
F-GHHT	Robinson R22 Beta	1815	
F-GHHU	Zlin Z.526 Trenér Master	1081	F-BRNE
F-GHHX	Thunder AX7-77A HAFB	1954	
F-GHHZ	Thunder AX7-77Z HAFB	1935	
F-GHIE	Robinson R22 Mariner	307M	
	(W/o 4.6.02?)		
F-GHIG	SNCASO SO.1221 Djinn	97/FR147	ALAT
F-GHIH	Piper J-3C-65 Cub Special	20546	N7242H, NC7242H
F-GHIO	Bell 206B Jet Ranger II	2895	YU-HDG, N1067F
F-GHIP	Piper L-4B Cub	9357	N1138V, 43-496, (42-59306)
F-WHIQ	Holste MH.1521M Broussard	291	Fr.AF
F-GHIS	Hughes 269C	74-0325	N58161
F-GHIX	Piper PA-28-181 Archer II	28-8390042	N42940
F-GHIY	Piper PA-28-181 Archer II	28-8490067	N131AV, N9592N, N43570
	(Wreck noted 17.7.05)		
F-GHJB	Agusta-Bell 47G-2	210	EC-DGK, F-BTSR, ALAT, Fr.AF
F-GHJC	Chaize CS.2200F12 HAFB	78	
F-GHJG	Piper PA-28-181 Archer II	28-7990073	N22244
F-GHJI	Piper PA-28-181 Archer II	28-7990023	N39958
F-GHJJ	Chaize CS.2200F12 HAFB	091	
F-GHJK	Reims/Cessna F150L	F15000819	HB-CWH
F-GHJL	Dassault Falcon 10	58	N500FF, N458A, N58AS, N76FJ, N458FJ, F-WJMM
F-GHJM	Cessna 207A Stationair 8	20700635	F-OGJM, (N75576)
	(Wrecked)		
F-GHJO	Cessna 152	15284330	C-GGEB, (N5517L)
F-GHJT	Piper PA-28-181 Archer II	28-8090087	N8086L
F-GHKD	Cessna 152	15280899	N25989
F-GHKE	Cessna 152	15280176	N24254
F-GHKG	Beech V35B Bonanza	D-9488	D-EAPM, CS-AOK, N2881W
F-GHKH	Chaize CS.2200F12 HAFB	107	
F-GHKJ	Piper PA-28-161 Warrior II	28-8216061	N8461Z
F-GHKO	Cameron N-105 HAFB	3103	OO-BBQ, G-BUYZ
F-GHKS	Cameron A-160 HAFB	11070	
F-WHKS	Bell 222A	47040	F-WQAA, F-WKHS, F-WYMA, SE-HSF, N1085G
F-GHKT(2)	Cameron A-160 HAFB	11071	
F-GHKU	Mudry CAP.10B	211	F-ZVMU
F-GHKV	Beech 58 Baron	TH-1537	N31425
F-GHKY	Cessna R182 Skylane RG	R18200728	N736GP
F-GHKZ	Robin DR.400/140B Major 80	924	F-BVCZ
F-GHLE	Piper PA-28RT-201T Turbo Arrow IV		
		28R-8431012	N4334K, N9561N

Regn	Type	c/n	Previous identities
F-GHLF	Hughes 369E	0361E	
F-GHLL	Balloon Works Firefly 7 HAFB	F7-603	N9041B
F-GHLO	Rockwell S.2R Thrush Commander	1920R	EC-CKM, N17535
F-GHLQ	Piper J-3C-65 Cub	15243	N42908, NC42908
F-GHLR	Bell 206B Jet Ranger II	2718	N2761B
F-GHLS	Aérospatiale AS.355N Ecureuil 2	5579	B-HJK, VR-HJK, F-OHNB
F-GHLU	Cessna 152	15280860	N25923
F-GHLX(2)	Bell 47G-2	1388	C-FVTS, CF-VTS, RCAF1388, RCN ....
F-GHLZ	Piper PA-38-112 Tomahawk	38-78A0642	N2327A
F-GHMB	Mooney M.20K Model 231	25-0740	N5634Q
F-GHMF	Ultramagic M-120 HAFB	120/77	
F-GHMH	Robinson R22 Beta	1144	
F-GHMM(2)	Ultramagic M-105 HAFB	105/112	
F-GHMQ	Aérospatiale AS.350B2 Ecureuil	2525	
F-GHMR	Thunder AX8-9OA3 HAFB	1428	
F-GHMS	Cessna T210L Turbo Centurion	21060012	N210ES, N59003
F-GHMV	Cameron O-65 HAFB	2112	
F-GHNB	Cameron V-90 HAFB	2502	
F-GHNP(2)	Grumman G.164B Agcat	768B	EC-EIE, N3632D
F-GHNR(2)	Piper PA-38-112 Tomahawk	38-78A0563	D-EAJZ, N9654N
F-GHNX	Chaize CS.2200F12 HAFB	109	
F-GHNY	Cessna 152	15284287	N5292L
F-GHNZ	Cessna 152	15279559	N714ZJ
F-GHOC	Beech 200 Super King Air	BB-406	G-OEMS, N222PA
F-GHOF	Raven Europe FS-57A HAFB	E-131	
F-GHOG	Cessna 172N Skyhawk	17270189	N738RY
F-GHOH	Schweizer 269C	S-1272	D-HDAS
F-GHOJ(2)	Robin DR.400/120 Dauphin 2+2	2319	LX-RCC
F-GHOK	Robinson R22 Beta	1591	
F-GHOM	SNCASE SE.3130 Alouette II	1510	ALAT
F-GHON	AIAA/ Stampe SV.4C	1147	F-BAON
F-GHOO	Schweizer 269C	S-1302	
F-GHOP	Cessna 172RG Cutlass RG	172RG0338	3A-MOP, F-GCGO, N4606V
F-GHOR	Cameron O-65 HAFB	1732	
F-GHOV	SNCAN Stampe SV.4C	341	F-BCOV
F-GHOY(2)	Aérospatiale AS.332L1 Super Puma	9005	
F-GHOZ	Cameron O-160 HAFB	1308	G-BMOZ
F-GHPD	SNCASE SE.3130 Alouette II	1319	ALAT
F-GHPH	Aérospatiale AS.350B2 Ecureuil	2365	
F-GHPJ	Robin DR.400/120 Dauphin 2+2	1874	
F-GHPM	Mooney M.20J Model 201	24-1640	
F-GHPP	Piper PA-32R-301 Saratoga SP	3213022	
F-GHPQ	Piper PA-28-161 Warrior II	28-7916492	N2867M
F-GHQL	Airbus A320-211	239	
F-GHQM	Airbus A320-211	237	
F-GHRG	Piper PA-46-310P Malibu	46-8608067	N9099N
F-GHRI(2)	Cessna 152	15281868	SP-KFG, D-EFMO(2), N67898
F-GHRK	DHC-6 Twin Otter 200	144	N202E, (N871SA), N202E
F-GHRL	Piper PA-32R-301T Turbo Saratoga SP	32R-8429011	HB-PIA, N43537
F-GHRM	Chaize CS.2200F12 HAFB	103	
F-GHRN	Chaize CS.2200F12 HAFB	102	
F-GHSH	Piper PA-25-260 Pawnee D	25-7656044	N54895
F-GHSJ	Cessna P210N Pressurized Centurion II	P21000493	(F-GFMJ), CN-TCZ, F-GCSY, N731MH
F-GHSM	SOCATA MS.880B Rallye Club	1559	F-GBSM, F-BRYV
F-GHSQ	Piper PA-25-235 Pawnee	25-2754	C-FRHP, CF-RHP, N7002Z
F-GHST	Bell 206B Jet Ranger II	1104	D-HOCH, SE-HLL, LN-OSV, G-BBES, N18092
F-GHSV	Beech 200 Super King Air	BB-622	N212BF, N7009J, N7009
F-GHSY	Robin DR.400/140B Major 80	2516	HB-KFU
F-GHSZ	Piper PA-28-151 Cherokee Warrior	28-7415698	N44663
F-GHTB	Robin HR.200/120B Club	23	HB-EXD
F-GHTC	Piper PA-28-161 Cadet	2841011	
F-GHTE	Diamond DA 20-A1-100 Katana	10257	G-BXPB
F-GHTH	Hughes 269C	47-0586	N7484F
F-GHTI	Cessna 421A	421A0158	(F-GGFI), N777GP, N3358Q
	(Wfu, stored)		
F-GHTJ(2)	CEA DR.250/160 Capitaine	41	F-OCIA
F-GHTL	Beech A36 Bonanza	E-799	N2545B
F-GHTM	Cessna TR182 Turbo Skylane RG	R18201528	N5263S
F-GHTN	SNCASE SE.3130 Alouette II	1401	ALAT
F-GHTQ(2)	Piper PA-25-235 Pawnee C	25-5074	N8637L
F-GHTR	Beech F33A Bonanza	CE-1054	N72167
F-GHTS	Cameron O-105 HAFB	1932	
F-GHTY	Piper PA-28RT-201 Arrow IV	28-8118013	N8282Z
F-GHTZ	Mooney M.20K Model 231	25-0322	N231NG
F-GHUE	Robinson R22 Beta	1831	
F-GHUH	Holste MH.1521C Broussard	275	ALAT
F-GHUJ	Holste MH.1521M Broussard	295	ALAT
F-GHUV	Beech E90 King Air	LW-278	YV-195CP, N4757C, N700MA
F-GHUY	Cessna 421B Golden Eagle	421B0417	I- MAME, N41049
	(W/o 18.2.02)		
F-GHVH	Fairchild PC-6/B2-H2 Turbo-Porter	2072	N530RQ, FAB-. ..., N5306F
F-GHVI	Piper PA-28-161 Cadet	2841161	
F-GHVJ	Mooney M.20J Model 201	24-1560	N5812Z
F-GHVP	Chaize CS2200F12 HAFB	104	HB-BSJ
F-GHVQ	SNCASE SE.313B Alouette II	1398	(F-GHSY), ALAT
F-GHVV	Beech 200 Super King Air	BB-676	N970AA, N676DP, G-ONCA, N1362B, 9Y-TGR
F-GHVX	Cessna 152	15285449	N93255
F-GHVY	Cessna 152	15284585	N5426M
F-GHVZ	Cessna 152	15285056	N4735Q
	(Dam. 9.6.07)		
F-GHXC	Aérospatiale AS.350B Ecureuil	1093	N3594N
F-GHXD	Rockwell Commander 114	14134	N5463A, (N58230), N5463X, YS-217P
F-GHXE	Christen A-1 Husky	1161	
F-GHXJ	Thunder AX8-90 HAFB	2126	
F-GHXR	Aérospatiale SA.360C Dauphin	1010	(F-GHXQ), G-BRMP, N49513
F-GHXT	Cameron A-105 HAFB	1755	
F-GHYC	Schweizer 269C	S-1532	N86G
F-GHYF	Piper PA-28-161 Warrior II	28-8516052	N69086
F-GHYG(2)	Aérospatiale SA.365C3 Dauphin 2	5013	EC-EBB, F-GBOU, LV-AIE, F-GBOU
F-WHYH	Zeppy II Airship	01	
F-GHYJ	Cameron O-77 HAFB	2632	
F-GHYQ(2)	Robin DR.400/120 Dauphin 2+2	2203	F-GMKK
F-GHYX	Piper PA-28-181 Archer II	28-8190101	N8302S
F-GHYY	Piper PA-28R-201T Turbo Arrow III	28R-7803232	
F-GHYZ	Piper PA-28-181 Archer II	28-7990370	N2229X
F-GHZA	SOCATA TB-20 Trinidad	917	
F-GHZC	SOCATA TB-20 Trinidad	953	
F-GHZG	SOCATA TB-9 Tampico	931	
F-GHZH	SOCATA TB-9 Tampico	966	
F-GHZI	SOCATA TB-9 Tampico	940	
F-GHZK	SOCATA TB-9 Tampico	944	
F-GHZM	SOCATA TB-9 Tampico	993	
F-GHZO	SOCATA TB-20 Trinidad	1017	
F-GHZU	SOCATA TB-20 Trinidad	1023	
F-GHZX	SOCATA TB-9 Tampico	1050	
F-GIAB	Piper PA-28-161 Cadet	2841066	
F-GIAQ(2)	Cessna 152	15279649	N757DD
F-GIAV	Cameron O-77 HAFB	1922	
F-GIAY	Piper PA-32R-301 Saratoga SP	32R-8313024	N4313T, N9518N
F-GIBA	Cessna 172N Skyhawk	17273006	N1470F
F-GIBD	Robin HR.100/210 Safari	154	5T-TJB, F-BUHG
F-GIBE	Piper PA-28-161 Cadet	2841132	
F-GIBF(2)	Ultramagic S-130 HAFB	130/24	
F-GIBJ	Robin DR.400/120 Petit Prince	830	6V-AFP, F-BUPJ
F-GIBK	Aérospatiale SA.315B Lama	2287/41	F-GEHY, N65181
F-GIBM	Aérospatiale AS.350B Ecureuil	1424	N5784Y
F-GIBN	Holste MH.1521C Broussard	261	Fr.AF
F-GIBO	Cameron N-90 HAFB	2560	
F-GIBT(3)	Kubicek BB-20 HAFB	179	OK-1059
F-GIBV	Pilatus PC-6/B1-H2 Turbo-Porter	651	D-FLEV(2), OH-POB, HB-FCZ, ST-ADH, HB-FCZ
F-GIBX	Piper PA-28-161 Cadet	2841323	N92155
F-GICE	Beech B90 King Air	LJ-363	N303WJ, N43TC, N81648, N95GR, N959B
F-GICJ	Cessna P210N Pressurized Centurion II	P21000678	(F-GFTY), N5358W
F-GICK	American AG-5B Tiger	10111	
F-GICP	Piper PA-28RT-201T Turbo Arrow IV	28R-8431004	N4327B
F-GICQ	Beech A36 Bonanza	E-2569	N8043C
F-GICR	Beech A36 Bonanza	E-2354	N3094T
F-GICU	Robin DR.400/180R Remorqueur	1483	EC-DKY, D-EGPE
F-GICX	Hughes 269C	95-0432	F-BXOU
F-GICZ	Maule MX-7-180 Star Rocket	11069C	G-MORL
F-GIDA	Robin DR.400/180 Régent	1838	
F-GIDD	Piper PA-28R-201 Arrow	2837060	(N181ND)
F-GIDF	Piper PA-44-180 Seminole	44-8195005	N89PG, (N256EP), N256ER, N252ER, N9628N
F-GIDG	Cessna 182P Skylane	18261311	TJ-AET, TL-AAL, N9086N
F-GIDI	Piper PA-28-181 Archer II	28-8290099	HB-PIE, D-EIIT, N9638N
F-GIDL	Beech C90A King Air	LJ-1224	N123AT, PT-OBF, N1556Z
F-GIDR	Aérospatiale AS.350B Ecureuil	1993	N350TC, N6008J
F-GIDS	Pilatus PC-6/B1-H2 Turbo-Porter	584	HB-FBZ, P2-SEA, P2-PNO, P2-PNG(1), VH-PNG, HB-FBZ
F-GIEA	Piper PA-28-161 Cadet	2841106	
F-GIEB	Piper PA-28-161 Cadet	2841107	
F-GIEC	Piper PA-28-181 Archer II	2890105	N91634
F-GIED	Piper PA-28-161 Cadet	2841108	
F-GIEE	Piper PA-28-161 Cadet	2841109	
F-GIEG	Piper PA-28-161 Cadet	2841149	(F-GIEH)
F-GIEH	Piper PA-28-161 Cadet	2841161	
F-GIEI	Piper PA-28-161 Cadet	2841164	
F-GIEJ	Piper PA-28-161 Cadet	2841169	
F-GIEK	Piper PA-28-161 Cadet	2841170	
F-GIEM	Piper PA-28-161 Cadet	2841267	
F-GIEN(2)	Rockwell S.2R Thrush Commander	2088R	EC-CMN, N17532
F-GIEO	Piper PA-28-161 Cadet	2841269	
F-GIEP	Piper PA-28-161 Cadet	2841270	
F-GIEQ	Piper PA-28-161 Cadet	2841271	
F-GIET	Cameron A-160 HAFB	4717	OO-BNK
F-GIEV	Partenavia P.68C	253	PH-EMC, G-OLES, G-JAJV, OO-TJG, (OO-XJG)
F-GIFA	Beech A36 Bonanza	E-1485	N6038M
F-GIFE	Piper PA-28R-201 Arrow III	28R-7837128	N3623M
F-GIFN	Piper PA-28-161 Cadet	2841133	
F-GIFS	Cameron N-105 HAFB	2903	
F-WIFS	Aérospatiale AS.332L2 Super Puma	2167	Fr.AF
F-GIFZ	Holste MH.1521M Broussard	315	Fr.AF
F-GIGE	Cessna 172N Skyhawk	17271560	N3473E
F-GIGF	Cessna 150L	15074507	N19585
F-GIGL	Robinson R22 Beta	0873	
F-GIGQ	Colt 105A HAFB	2280	
F-GIGS	Thunder AX7-77 HAFB	1944	
F-GIGT	Aérospatiale AS.355F1 Ecureuil 2	5023	N355F
F-GIGX	Piper PA-25-260 Pawnee C	25-4477	N4730Y
F-WIGY	Fouga CM.170 Magister	331	Fr.AF
F-GIHC	Hughes 369E	0376E	
	(Crashed into sea near Grand Turk, Turks & Caicos Islands 4.2.00)		
F-GIHD	Aérospatiale AS.350B Ecureuil	1100	N3598X
F-GIHE	Robinson R22 Beta	0905	
F-GIHJ(2)	Beech 77 Skipper	WA-95	D-EILW(2)
F-GIHM	Pilatus PC-6/B1-H2 Turbo Porter	581	HS-TFD, HS-SKE, HS-CHE, XW-PFB, N13200
F-GIHN	Hughes 269C	65-0417	F-BXOS
F-GIHO	Morane-Saulnier MS.733 Alcyon	155	F-BMQB, Fr.AF
F-GIHP	Schweizer 269C	S-1429	N429MS
F-GIHT(2)	Mudry CAP.10B	25	Fr.AF
F-GIIC(2)	Thunder AX8-90 SII HAFB	2343	
F-GIID	Cameron N-90 HAFB	2953	
F-GIII	Piper PA-31T Cheyenne II	31T-8020037	N805SW
F-GIIK(2)	CEA Jodel DR.1050 Ambassadeur	553	D-EFIK, F-BLZU
F-GIIL	Cessna 172N Skyhawk	17272705	N6300D
F-GIIM	Colt 90A HAFB	2370	
F-GIIO	Piper PA-28-181 Archer II	2890190	
F-GIIQ	Cessna 172M	17266422	N80177
F-GIIR	Cameron O-120 HAFB	4951	OO-BJW
F-WIIR	Ballon Assimilable 1840m BCB	001	
F-GIIS	Reims/Cessna F172P	F17202115	TU-TMG, F-OCGJ(2)
F-GIIT	Cameron Concept 80 HAFB	3088	
F-GIIZ	Aerotek Pitts S-2A	2112	G-ODAH, G-BDKS
F-GIJA	SNCASE SE.313B Alouette II	1570	ALAT
F-GIJB	Beech 200 Super King Air	BB-13	N83MA, N595A, N200PB
F-GIJC	Mooney M.20K Model 231	25-0555	N1022G
	(Wfu?)		
F-GIJH	Robin DR.300/125	651	F-ODJH, F-BTBH
F-GIJI	Mooney M.20J Model 205	24-3092	
F-GIJM	Agusta-Bell 206B Jet Ranger 3	8612	F-GCTJ
F-GIJO	Piper PA-28-180 Cherokee E	28-5776	TR-LWU, HB-OZY, N3673R
F-GIJP	Aérospatiale AS.350B Ecureuil	1672	HK-3152X, F-WZKH

Reg	Type	C/n	Previous identities
F-GIJQ	Aérospatiale AS.350B Ecureuil	1647	EI-BYT, (F-GIIC), EI-BYT, G-JRBI, EI-BNO, G-BKJY
F-GIJV	Balloon Works Firefly F7-15 HAFB	F7-2036	N21863
F-GIKA	Robin DR.400/140B Major 80	1911	
F-GIKD	Robin DR.400/180 Régent	1914	
F-GIKE	Robin DR.400/120 Dauphin 2+2	1929	
F-GIKG	Robin DR.400/140B Major 80	1930	
F-GIKI	Robin DR.400/120 Dauphin 2+2	1931	F-WIKI, F-GIKI
F-GIKJ	Robin DR.400/160 Major	1941	
F-GIKK	Robin DR.400/120 Dauphin 2+2	1942	
F-GIKL	Robin ATL L	132	
F-GIKM	Robin DR.400/140B Major 80	1945	
F-GIKN	Robin DR.400/140B Major 80	1946	
F-GIKO	Robin DR.400/120 Dauphin 2+2	1947	
F-GIKP	Robin DR.400/120 Dauphin 2+2	1948	
F-GIKQ	Robin DR.400/120 Dauphin 2+2	1965	
F-GIKR	Robin ATL L	134	
F-GIKS	Robin DR.400/180 Régent	1950	
F-GIKV	Robin DR.400/180 Régent	1951	
F-GIKX	Robin DR.400/180 Régent	1952	
F-GIKY	Robin DR.400/120 Dauphin 2+2	1954	
F-GIKZ	Robin DR.400/120 Dauphin 2+2	1961	
F-GILR	Robin R.2160D Acrobin	C209	HB-KBN, N216MH
F-GILS	Robinson R22 Beta	0601	G-BNBT, N2530W
F-GILT	Piper PA-28-161 Cadet	2841067	
F-GIMA	Cessna 414A Chancellor II	414A0446	N2732F
F-GIMB	Cameron V-65 HAFB	2055	
F-GIMC	Aérospatiale SA.315B Lama	2250/25	I-PHAI, F-ODLE, 5V-MAJ
F-GIMK	Llopis Balloons MA26 HAFB	194	
F-GIMM	Piper PA-28RT-201T Turbo Arrow IV	28R-8231067	N8261X, N9583N
F-WIMN	Fouga CM-170 Magister	440	Fr.AF
F-WIMQ	Fouga CM-170 Magister	438	Fr.AF
F-GINA	Aérospatiale SA.315B Lama	2642	YV-350CP, YV-428A
F-GINH	SOCATA MS.893A Rallye Commodore 180	10605	HB-EDZ
F-GINM	Robin DR.400/180 Régent	861	D-EDHN
F-GINP	Thunder AX7-65SI HAFB	446	G-LING
F-GINR	Bell 47G	32	N112B, NC112B
F-GINT	Chaize JZ.25F16 HAFB	131	
F-GINU	Piper PA-32R-301 Saratoga SP	3213035	
F-GINX	Chaize JZ.25F16 HAFB	132	
F-GIOI	Fokker F.28-0100	11433	EP-ASM, F-GIOI, PH-MXA, PH-NXA
F-GIOT	Thunder AX7-77 HAFB	1474	
F-GIPE	Mooney M.20J Model 205	24-3066	
F-GIPF	Cameron O-65 HAFB	1925	
F-GIPG	Beech 65-90 King Air	LJ-83	N827T, (YV-980P), N827F
F-GIPH	Dassault Falcon 10	194	N61FC, N100FJ, N260FJ, F-WZGZ
F-GIPM	Beech A36 Bonanza	E-2405	N3108F
F-GIPR	Piper PA-28-181 Archer II	28-8190312	N8433F
F-GIPS	Thunder AX7-77 HAFB	1807	
F-GIPT	Mooney M.20K Model 231	25-0172	N231RK
F-GIPU	Mudry CAP.10B	16	Fr.AF
F-GIPZ	SNCASE SE.313B Alouette II	"076"	Fr.AF
F-GIQI	Cameron Z-105 HAFB	10157	LX-BIQ
F-GIQM	Cessna 152	15280306	N24518
F-GIQN	Cessna 152	15282366	N68766
F-GIQO	Cessna 172N Skyhawk 100	17268742	I-NCCD, N734CD
F-GIQQ	CASA C.212	387	Fr.AF/F-ZVMR
	(Permit 6.00)		
F-GIQR	Piper PA-28R-180 Cherokee Arrow	28R-30757	HB-OZL, N7415J
F-GIQT	HOAC DV-20 Katana	20078	D-EHLK
F-GIRD	Beech 76 Duchess	ME-387	N3809N
F-GIRE	Wörner K-1000/3-Stu Gas Balloon	0323	
F-GIRG	Thunder AX8-105S2 HAFB	2402	
F-GIRH	Aérospatiale SN.601 Corvette	14	SP-FOA, F-BVPS
F-GIRP	Piper PA-28-161 Cherokee Warrior II	28-7816124	N2291F, C-GIYC, N9627N
F-GIRQ	Cessna 172R Skyhawk	17280293	N9520P
F-GIRR	Cameron V-65 HAFB	1723	
F-GIRT	Bell 206B Jet Ranger II	1924	F-OGNI, N49716
F-GIRU	Mudry CAP.10B	14	Fr.AF
F-GIRV	Piper PA-28-181 Archer II	28-8590018	G-BPRW, N43823
F-GITE	Boeing 747-428	25601	
F-GITZ	American AG-5B Tiger	10140	OO-MLA, PH-MLA
F-GIVA	Piper PA-28-181 Archer II	2890108	
F-GIVB	Maule MX.7-235 Star Rocket	10083C	N9208V
F-GIVH	Bell 206B Jet Ranger II	4176	
	(Damaged 4.9.06)		
F-GIVN	Bell 47G-2 (Wrecked)	2323	N7084M
F-GIVO	Ultramagic V-56 HAFB	56/13	
F-GIVS	Cessna U206G Stationair 6	U20604881	HB-CKO, N56HT, (N734VR)
	(Soloy Turbine Pac conversion)		
F-GIVU	SNCASE SE.3130 Alouette II	1473	Fr.AF
F-GIVZ	Robinson R22B2 Beta	2689	
F-GIXB	Boeing 737-33A	24789	F-OGSD, F-GFUI
F-GIXC	Boeing 737-38B	25124	F-OGSS, N4320B, N1792B
F-GIXE	Boeing 737-3B3	26850	N854WT, F-GIXE
F-GIXN	Boeing 737-4Y0F	25181	EI-STF, N288AL, TC-JDG
F-GIXT	Boeing 737-39M	28898	F-ODZZ, N35153, N1786B
F-GIXX	Pilatus PC-6/B2-H2 Turbo-Porter	564	N17XX, N777XX, N187H
F-GIXZ	Robin DR.315 Petit Prince	364	OO-NEW, F-BRFK
F-GIYA	Reims/Cessna F152	F15201854	HB-CKD, F-GCYO
F-GIYB	Aérospatiale AS.355F1 Ecureuil 2	5142	N5793Z
	(W/o 4.2.06)		
F-GIYC(2)	Cameron N-120 HAFB	10252	
F-GIYD	Cessna 152	15282164	C-GYRP, N68175
F-GIYE	Sud Avn SA.316B Alouette III	1452	A-452
F-GIYG	Aérospatiale AS.350B Ecureuil	1410	HB-XLZ
F-GIYL	Piper PA-28-180 Cherokee D	28-4540	HB-OZM, N5245L
F-GIYP	Robinson R22 Beta	1399	
F-GIYV	SOCATA MS.894A Minerva 220	11676	OO-DPS, F-BSKX
F-GIYZ	Cameron A-105 HAFB	2931	
F-GIZD	Reims/Cessna F172M	F17201355	I- CCAV
F-GIZE	CAARP CAP.10B	5	Fr.AF
F-GIZG	Aérospatiale AS.350B3 Ecureuil	3084	
F-GIZH	Cessna 172R Skyhawk	17280427	N9509Q
F-GIZI	Cessna 172R Skyhawk	17280435	N9328F
F-GIZJ	Cameron-Thunder AX9-140A SII HAFB	4566	G-BYLU
F-GIZL	Mudry CAP.10B	18	Fr.AF
F-GIZN(2)	Hughes 269C	100-0058	D-HART
F-GIZO	Robinson R22 Beta	1814	F-ODZO
F-GIZR	Enstrom F.28A	223	OO-NMT, G-RONT
F-GIZT	Ultramagic M-90 HAFB	90/35	
F-GIZX	Ultramagic H-77 HAFB	77/176	
F-GIZY	Ultramagic H-77 HAFB	77/162	
F-GJAC	Holste MH.1521C Broussard	180	Fr.AF
F-GJAD	Beech E90 King Air	LW-3	N888BH, N9493Q
F-GJAR	Cessna 172N Skyhawk	17269835	N738AX
F-GJAS	Aérospatiale SN.601 Corvette	8	6V-AEA, F-WPTT
F-GJAT	Piper PA-34-200T Seneca II	34-7670342	D-GIRK, D-IFFP, PH-WON, N4564F
F-GJAZ	Leys HG VL-248 Free Balloon	2	
F-GJBA	Mooney M.20J Model 205	24-3132	N10675
F-GJBC	Pilatus PC-6/B2-H2 Turbo-Porter	868	
F-GJBE	Robinson R22 Beta	1348	
	(Badly damaged La Nouvelle Heliport, Reunion 3.5.04)		
F-GJBF	Holste MH.1521C-1 Broussard	13	Fr.AF
	(Could possibly be c/n 013 ex. F-ZWTL)		
F-GJBH	Sud Avn SA.319B Alouette III	2102	(F-GGPU), Fr.AF
F-GJBK	Bell 47G-2	2428	N2883B
F-GJBM	SOCATA TB-10 Tobago	304	F-OIBM, F-GDBM
F-GJBN	SNCASE SE.313B Alouette II	1619	ALAT
F-GJBO	Robin DR.400/160 Chevalier	812	F-OHAL, F-BUHY
F-GJBP	Pilatus PC-6/B2-H4 Turbo-Porter	716	HB-FFL, 9N-AAW, HB-FFL
F-GJBQ	Nord 1101 Noralpha	177	F-ZJBQ
F-GJBS	Beech B200 Super King Air	BB-1181	N6725Y
F-GJBT	Stuttgart K-945/2-STU Gas Balloon	0283	HB-BBA
F-GJCB	Piper PA-28R-201 Arrow III	28R-7837053	HB-PBR, N6135H
F-GJCG	Cessna R182 Skylane RG	R18200340	N4234C
F-GJCI	Cessna 152	15280674	N25467
	(Damaged 21.3.09)		
F-GJCL	Piper PA-28RT-201T Turbo Arrow IV	28R-8131004	N8275A
F-GJCN	Cessna 152	15283979	N4806H
F-GJCO	Cessna 152	15281503	N64969
F-GJCQ	Aérospatiale SA.315B Lama	2526	
F-GJCR	Beech E90 King Air	LW-251	N7ZU, N483, TG-BET
F-GJCS	Piper PA-28R-201 Cherokee Arrow III	28R-7737016	N1915H
F-GJCV	SNCASE SE.3130 Alouette II	1344	ALAT
F-GJCX(2)	Chaize JZ.25F12 HAFB	139	
F-GJDA	Pilatus PC-6A/B2-H2 Turbo Porter	721	HA-YDA
F-GJDB	Dassault Falcon 20	76	(F-GGFO), N776DS, N937GC, N970F, F-WMKF
F-GJDC	Piper PA-28-161 Warrior II	2816100	N9222F
F-GJDD	Mooney M.20K Model 231	25-0776	(F-GJLU), LX-MLL, N5696U
F-GJDF	Aérospatiale AS.350B2 Ecureuil	2642	F-WYMO
F-GJDJ	Cameron A-105 HAFB	2450	
F-GJDN	Robin DR.400/120	1018	F-BXER
F-GJDT	Hughes 269C	99-0822	PH-HFH
F-GJDU	Cameron N-90 HAFB	3326	
F-GJDX	Robin DR.400/140B Major 80	781	F-BTZU
F-GJDZ	Cameron O-77 HAFB	2590	
F-GJEF	Piper PA-28-181 Archer II	2890189	N9232N
F-GJEG	SNCASE SE.3130 Alouette II	1229	V-45, HB-XBK, V-45
F-GJEH	Aviat Pitts S.2B	5255	N98AV
F-GJEI	Bell 47G-2	2426	N2889B
F-GJEJ	Beech K35 Bonanza	D-5912	HB-EGW, D-EGWA, HB-EGW
	(C/n quoted as "D-59A2")		
F-GJEL	Bell 206B Jet Ranger II	2784	G-PORT, N37AH, N39TV, N397TV, N2774R
F-WJEL	SOCATA TB-200 (Prototype)	1214	F-GKEC
F-GJEM	Piper J-3C-65 Cub	12963	HB-ONK, 44-80667
F-GJEN	Piper PA-28-181 Archer II	28-7990201	N3024H
F-GJER	Maule MX-7-235 Star Rocket	10071C	N6127Q
F-GJFA	Beech B200 Super King Air	BB-1270	N30391
F-GJFE	Beech B200 Super King Air	BB-1399	
F-GJFG	Pilatus PC-12/45	256	N141VY, HB-FSA
F-GJFH	Piper PA-32RT-300T Turbo Lance II	32R-7887073	HB-PMU, N36735
F-GJFI	Cessna 208B Grand Caravan	208B0230	N208GC, (N4909B)
F-GJFN	Beech F33A Bonanza	CE-896	HB-EWA
F-GJFO	Thunder AX7-65Z HAFB	1743	
F-GJFQ	Piper PA-32RT-300T Turbo Lance II	32R-7887288	I-LIMG, N3001A, N9532N
F-GJFR	Cessna 172P Skyhawk	17274712	N53258
F-GJFS	Chaize CS.4000F16 HAFB	101	
F-GJGG	Balloon Works Firefly F7B-15 HAFB	F7B-346	
F-GJGH	Piper PA-28R-201T Turbo Cherokee Arrow III	28R-7703396	N47548
F-GJGI	Chaize CS.2200F12 HAFB	112	
F-GJGK	Mooney M.20J Model 205	24-3178	N9119N
F-GJGN	Mooney M.20J Model 205	24-3200	
F-GJGR	Beech A36 Bonanza	E-2221	N7223R
F-GJGV	Bell 206B Jet Ranger II	913	G-BALC
F-GJGX	Chaize JZX.22F12 HAFB	152	
F-GJGY	Ultramagic M-145 HAFB	145/10	
F-GJGZ	Cameron N-77 HAFB	2705	
F-GJHA	Cessna F150G	F150-0089	OO-SIQ
F-GJHF	Piper PA-38-112 Tomahawk	38-78A0357	TJ-AHE, F-OBNV, N9667N
F-GJHP	Schweizer 269C	S-1402	N424MS
F-GJHR	Piper PA-28-181 Archer II	28-8090071	N876HR, N8077T
F-GJHT	Piper PA-38-112 Tomahawk	38-79A0278	N2340D
F-GJHU	SAN Jodel D.140C Mousquetaire III	153	D-EIFI
F-GJHY	Agusta-Bell 206B Jet Ranger 2	8426	EC-CPF, F-BXAJ
F-GJHZ	Piper PA-46-310P Malibu	46-8508090	I-LRNZ, I-DANB, N2484X
	(Dbr 1.6.08)		
F-GJIB	SNCASE SE.313B Alouette II	1627	FAP9209, 76+30
F-GJID	Aerostar S-57A HAFB	3187	
F-GJIF	Ultramagic H-77 HAFB	77/126	
F-GJII	Cameron V-77 HAFB	1915	OO-BRP, (OO-BRR)
F-GJIJ	Fouga CM.170 Magister	482	Fr.AF
F-GJIM	Aérospatiale AS.350B Ecureuil	1489	N5434T, XA-...
F-GJIN	Ultramagic M-77 HAFB	77/104	
F-GJIO	Ultramagic N-180 HAFB	180/19	
F-GJIV	Ultramagic H-77 HAFB	77/170	
F-GJIX	Chaize JZ.25F16 HAFB	149	
F-GJIZ	Chaize JZ.22F24 HAFB	151	
F-GJJA	Cameron N-77 HAFB	2473	
F-GJJC	Piper PA-28RT-201T Turbo Arrow IV	28R-8531004	N4391D, N9528N
F-GJJD	Cameron A-105 HAFB	2537	
F-GJJE	Chaize JZ.22F12 HAFB	141	
F-GJJH	Aérospatiale AS.350B2 Ecureuil	2584	
F-GJJM	Holste MH.1521M Broussard	292	Fr.AF
F-GJJQ	Lindstrand LBL-180 HAFB	051	
F-GJJR	Piper PA-28RT-201T Turbo Arrow IV	28R-8431016	N4340K

Reg	Type	C/n	Previous identities
F-GJJT	Chaize CS.2200F12 HAFB	106	
F-GJJY	Cessna U206F Stationair	U20602855	TR-LDV, TN-AET, N1170Q
F-GJKA	Cameron N-77 HAFB	527	LX-PIN
F-GJKB	Chaize JZ.30F16 HAFB	136	
F-GJKC	Llopis MA-26 HAFB	199	
F-GJKE	Cameron N-65 HAFB	1861	LX-OKE
F-GJKG	SOCATA TB-20 Trinidad	1181	PH-JED, F-GKUP
F-GJKU	Cessna 172R Skyhawk	17280869	N2432F
F-GJKX	Ultramagic H-65 HAFB	65/84	(F-GIZM)
F-GJKY	Aérospatiale AS.350B3 Ecureuil	3441	
F-GJLC(2)	Cessna F172H	F172-0441	CN-TTU(2)
F-GJLE	Colt 105A HAFB	1596	
F-GJLF	Mooney M.20M Model 257 TLS	27-0066	
F-GJLG	Cessna 172P Skyhawk	17275063	N54836
F-GJLK	SNCASE SE.3130 Alouette II	1914	V-62
	(W/o 23.7.98)		
F-GJLP	Holste MH.1521C1 Broussard	279	Fr.AF
F-GJLR	Piper PA-28-161 Warrior II	28-7916231	N2236K
F-GJLT	Holste MH.1521C Broussard	44C	F-BJLT
	(Stored) (Plate on aircraft quotes c/n 85)		
F-GJLU	Cameron V-90 HAFB	3132	OO-BFE
F-GJLV	Ultramagic M-130 HAFB	130/29	
F-GJLX	Hughes 369D	91-1058D	(F-GHLX), N16DK, N5107J
F-GJLY	Ultramagic M-105 HAFB	105/70	
F-GJLZ	Cessna P210N Pressurized Centurion II		
		P21000423	N7757K
F-GJMA	Dassault Falcon 10	116	N525RC, N925DS,
			(N927DS), N4DS, N189FJ, F-WNGL
	(Dbr 27.9.96 Madrid. Exp.10.97 but still currently registered)		
F-GJME	Cameron N-160 HAFB	4892	OO-BWO
F-GJMN	Fouga CM.170 Magister	424	F-WQCE, Fr.AF
F-GJMP	Bell 47G-2	7525	CF-CIU
F-GJMS	Piper PA-28-181 Archer II	28-8490103	N133AV
F-GJMX(2)	Piper PA-11 Cub Special	11-1060	F-BFMX
F-GJMY	Cameron A-105 HAFB	2277	
F-GJMZ	Mooney M.20M Model 257 TLS	27-0152	N9162D
F-GJOA	Lindstrand LBL-150A HAFB	772	G-IRTH, G-BZTO
F-GJOB	Cessna 551 Citation II	551-0174	EI-CIR, N60AR, EI-CIR,
	(Built as Cessna 550 c/n 550-0128)		F-WLEF, 9A-BPU, RC-BPU,
			YU-BPU, N220LA, N536M, N2631V
F-GJOC	Raven-Europe FS-57A	E-390	OO-BBK
F-GJOI	Schweizer H.269B	106-0269	EC-BFY
F-GJOL	Wassmer WA.41 Baladou	163	TU-TLY, F-OCOL
F-GJOM	Piper PA-28-181 Archer II	2890143	
F-GJON	Aérospatiale SA.330J Puma	1407	VN-8607, F-GBLS,
			PT-HUB, F-GBLS, HC-BNP,
			F-GBLS, PT-HRL
F-GJOT	Piper PA-28-161 Warrior II	28-7916388	I-PIOT, HB-PDP, N2210Z
F-GJOZ	SOCATA TB-10 Tobago	319	HB-EQU
F-GJPG	SNCASE SE.3130 Alouette II	1716	F-MJAN
F-GJPG	Kubicek BB-30Z HAFB	270	G-CCWS, OK-0270
F-GJPJ	Piper PA-28-161 Warrior II	28-8516001	N4376U
F-GJPO	Piper PA-28RT-201T Turbo Arrow IV		
		28R-7931039	N2227L
F-GJPP	Cameron N-90 HAFB	1952	
F-GJPS	Piper PA-28R-200 Cherokee Arrow II		
		28R-7635397	OO-JPW, N4209F
F-GJPV	Robinson R22 Beta	1836	(F-GIVM), N23104
F-GJQA	Robin DR.400/140B Major 80	1955	
F-GJQB	Robin DR.400/140B Major 80	1956	
F-GJQC	Robin DR.400/140B Major 80	1970	
F-GJQE	Robin DR.400/120 Dauphin 2+2	1966	
F-GJQF	Robin R.3000/140	143	
F-GJQH	Robin DR.400/180R Remorqueur	1964	
F-GJQI	Robin ATL L	133	
F-GJQJ	Robin DR.400/180 Régent	1967	
F-GJQK	Robin DR.400/120 Dauphin 2+2	1962	
F-GJQL	Robin DR.400/120 Dauphin 2+2	1968	
F-GJQN	Robin DR.400/180 Régent	1976	
F-GJQP	Robin DR.400/140B Major 80	1979	
F-GJQQ	Robin DR.400/140B Dauphin 4	1986	
	(W/o 14.8.16)		
F-GJQR	Robin DR.400/140B Major 80	1971	
F-GJQS	Robin DR.400/140B Dauphin 4	1977	
F-GJQT	Robin DR.400/120 Dauphin 2+2	1987	
F-GJQU	Robin DR.400/140B (ex -120)	1983	
F-GJQX	Robin DR.400/120 Dauphin 2+2	1993	
F-GJQZ	Robin DR.400/140B (ex -120)	1989	
F-GJRA	Holste MH.1521C Broussard	282	Fr.AF
F-GJRB	SOCATA TB-10 Tobago	228	SE-GFV, F-ODOE
F-GJRE	Piper PA-28RT-201 Arrow IV	28R-8118059	N8354D
F-GJRG	Thunder AX7-77SI HAFB	1627	OO-BTA
F-GJRJ	Piper PA-28-181 Archer II	2890144	
F-GJRM	Piper 28-236 Dakota	28-8211033	N8200K
F-GJRP	Aérospatiale AS.350B Ecureuil	1926	D-HOST
F-GJRR	Piper PA-28RT-201T Turbo Arrow IV		
		28R-7931294	N8072D
F-GJRY	Cameron N-105 HAFB	10304	
F-GJRZ	Cessna 152	15279724	D-EFRZ, N757GG
F-GJSE	Aérospatiale AS.355N Ecureuil 2	5225	(F-GTRE), N908BA,
			N5802X
F-GJSG	Piper PA-18 Super Cub 95	18-5648	HB-OPW, N10F
F-GJSI	Schweizer 269C	S-1390	
F-GJSJ	Cameron Z-105 HAFB	10429	
F-GJSL	Aérospatiale SA.342J Gazelle	1052	C-GPGO, N8350
	(Badly damaged UK, 8.5.05)		
F-GJSO	Cameron Z-105 HAFB	10376	
F-GJSR(2)	Eurocopter EC.135T2	0292	ZS-RPW
F-GJSS	Schweizer 269C	S-1578	N110LU
F-GJSU	Piper PA-23-250 Aztec E	27-4776	F-ODSU, TU-TJY, TU-TIC,
	(Wfu)		N14219
F-GJSZ	Aérospatiale AS.350B2 Ecureuil	9058	
F-GJTC	Christen Pitts S-2B	5162	
F-GJTD	Cessna 150M	15075860	TR-LTD, N66132
F-GJTM(2)	Beech 35-33 Debonair	CD-62	I-ANNJ, HB-EJB
F-GJTT	Cameron O-120 HAFB	3364	HB-BFJ
F-GJTZ	Cessna 172L	17260417	N7117Q
F-GJUM	Ultramagic S-105 HAFB	105/01	EC-EGR
F-GJUP	Cameron N-133 HAFB	2563	
F-GJUS	Cameron O-84 HAFB	175	N83CB
F-GJUV	Piper PA-28-181 Archer II	28-8490060	N4350K
F-GJUZ	Kubicek BB-34Z HAFB	629	
F-GJXA	SOCATA TB-20 Trinidad	1303	
F-GJXB	SOCATA TB-20 Trinidad	1304	
F-GJXD	SOCATA TB-10 Tobago	1497	
F-GJXE	SOCATA TB-10 Tobago	1498	
F-GJXF	SOCATA TB-10 Tobago	1500	
F-GJXG	SOCATA TB-10 Tobago	1504	
F-GJXH	SOCATA TB-10 Tobago	1505	
F-GJXI	SOCATA TB-10 Tobago	1591	
F-GJXJ	SOCATA TB-10 Tobago	1592	
F-GJXM	SOCATA TB-10 Tobago	1426	
F-GJXN	SOCATA TB-10 Tobago	1427	
F-GJXO	SOCATA TB-10 Tobago	1428	
F-GJXP	SOCATA TB-10 Tobago	1429	
F-GJXQ	SOCATA TB-10 Tobago	1430	
F-GJXR	SOCATA TB-10 Tobago	1431	
F-GJXS	SOCATA TB-10 Tobago	1432	
F-GJXT	SOCATA TB-10 Tobago	1433	
F-GJXU	SOCATA TB-10 Tobago	1491	
F-GJXV	SOCATA TB-10 Tobago	1493	
F-GJXY	SOCATA TB-10 Tobago	1494	
F-GJXZ	SOCATA TB-10 Tobago	1495	
F-GJYB	Robinson R22 Beta II	3021	G-TORS
F-GJYC(2)	Robinson R44 Raven	1260	
F-GJYF	Cameron O-90 HAFB	4001	
F-GJYL	Aerotek Pitts S-2A	2092	HB-MSD, N8ED
F-GJYN	Robinson R44 Astro	0418	
F-GJYP	SOCATA TB-20 Trinidad	2145	
F-GJYS	Kubicek BB-30Z HAFB	744	
F-GJYY	Reims/Cessna F152	F15201660	(F-GJMX), HB-CCM
F-GJZD	Robin DR.400/140 Major	1994	
F-GJZE	Robin DR.400/120 Dauphin 2+2	2005	
F-GJZF	Robin DR.400/140B Major 80	1999	
F-GJZG	Robin DR.400/120 Dauphin 2+2	2003	
F-GJZH	Robin DR.400/120 Dauphin 2+2	2002	
F-GJZI	Robin DR.400/140B Dauphin 4	2016	
F-GJZJ	Robin DR.400/120 Dauphin 2+2	2018	
F-GJZL	Robin DR.400/120 Dauphin 2+2	2009	
F-GJZM	Robin DR.400/120 Dauphin 2+2	2010	
F-GJZO	Robin DR.400/120 Dauphin 2+2	2023	
F-GJZP	Robin DR.400/120 Dauphin 2+2	2028	
F-GJZQ	Robin DR.400/160 Major	2030	
F-GJZR	Robin DR.400/120 Dauphin 2+2	2034	
F-GJZS	Robin DR.400/120 Dauphin 2+2	2033	
F-GJZT	Robin DR.400/140B Dauphin 4	2025	
F-GJZU	Robin DR.400/120 Dauphin 2+2	2031	
F-GJZV	Robin DR.400/160 Major	2032	
F-GJZX	Robin DR.400/140B Dauphin 4	2041	
F-GKAC	Cameron N-77 HAFB	1958	
F-GKAD	SOCATA TB-20 Trinidad	954	
F-GKAF(2)	Balloon Works Firefly F8B-15 HAFB	410	OO-BWK, N2523K
F-GKAJ	Mudry CAP.10B	27	Fr.AF
F-GKAM	Mudry CAP.10B	114	HB-SAM
F-GKAO	Piper PA-28-181 Cherokee Archer II		
		28-7690349	HB-PBE, N6134J
F-GKAP	Piper PA-28-161 Warrior II	28-8216072	N847AH, N84727
F-GKAV	Colt 21A HAFB	1742	
F-GKAX	Cessna 152	15285711	F-OGUT, N566V
	(Badly damaged at St Prive 21.7.04)		
F-GKBE	Aérospatiale AS.350B Ecureuil	2503	
F-GKBF	Aérospatiale AS.350B3 Ecureuil	3305	
F-GKBG	Rockwell 112 Commander	198	N1198J
F-GKBI	Cameron O-65 HAFB	2729	
F-GKBJ	Piper PA-12 Super Cruiser	12-3521	F-BFBJ, NC4084H
F-GKBL	Cessna 172RG Cutlass RG	172RG0609	N6289V
F-GKBN	Cameron A-105 HAFB	3289	
F-GKBO	Robin DR.400/140B Dauphin 4	2156	HB-KDG
F-GKBS	SNCASE SE.313B Alouette II	1442	ALAT
F-GKBU	SNCASE SE.3130 Alouette II	1743	Fr.AF
F-GKBV	Partenavia P.68B	13	F-OHCT, F-WQHL,
			G-MOET, G-HPVC, OH-PVB
F-GKBY	SOCATA TB-9 Tampico	1127	(F-GSJE), CS-DCD,
			F-GKUC
F-GKCA	Piper PA-18-150 Super Cub	18-8604	F-OCFI
F-GKCK	SNCASE SE.316V Alouette III	1256	ALAT
F-GKCM	Cameron Bouchon 116 HAFB	2021	
F-GKCO	Cessna 172R Skyhawk	17280055	F-WKCO, N374ES
F-GKCP	Robinson R22B Beta	1401	
F-GKCQ	Thunder AX10-180A HAFB	1791	
F-GKCR	Piper PA-28RT-201T Turbo Arrow IV		
		28R-8131078	N8339H
F-GKCU	Aérospatiale SA.365N Dauphin 2	6011	PH-SEC, F-GJEO, F-ZWVT,
			F-WZLG, N6003L, F-WZLG
F-GKDA	Piper PA-24-260 Comanche C	24-4847	5U-BAX, 5N-AHS, N9348P
F-GKDB	Dassault Falcon 20E	271/493	(F-GHPO), 7T-VRP,
			F-WNGN
F-GKDF	Mooney M.20M Model 257 TLS	27-0109	
F-GKDG	Cameron O-65 HAFB	4908	
F-GKDL	Cessna 172S Skyhawk SP	172S08117	N806RT, RP-C2729,
			N806RT, N860SP, N40595
F-WKDL	SOCATA TBM-700	003	
	(Also carries "221" on tail)		
F-GKDM	Pilatus PC-6/B1-H2 Turbo-Porter	670	S2-ACD, AP-AVU, HB-FES
F-GKDO	Ultramagic M-90 HAFB	90/108	
F-GKDP	Helibras HB.350B Esquilo	1522	YV-569CP, PT-HLX
	(Possible w/o 29.7.98)		
F-GKDU	Cessna R182 Skylane RG	R18200316	N182KP, (N3701C)
F-GKEA	Beech F33A Bonanza	CE-1628	
F-GKEB	SNCAN Stampe SV.4C	618	F-BDFN
F-GKEC(2)	Piper PA-28-181 Cherokee Archer II		
		28-7890218	N6221H
F-GKEF	Piper PA-28-181 Archer II	28-8290031	N8445U
F-GKEJ	Piper PA-38-112 Tomahawk II	38-82A0077	G-BPOW, N2592V
F-GKEM	Fokker F.27 Friendship 500	10596	TR-LCQ, PH-FTX,
			CN-CDC(2), PH-FTX, N272SA,
			N334MV, PH-FTX, PH-EXM
F-GKEN	Piper PA-23-250 Aztec E	27-4784	F-ODLN, F-BTMQ, F-BTDZ,
			N14224
F-GKER	Cameron A-140 HAFB	2181	
F-GKET	Robin DR.300/108	599	F-BMRQ, OO-JMM
F-GKEV	Cameron N-90 HAFB	2342	
F-GKEY	Robinson R44 Raven II	11289	
F-GKFA	Raven Europe RX-7 HAFB	E-164	
F-GKFB	Raven Europe FS57A HAFB	E-172	
F-GKFD	Raven Europe S-60A HAFB	E-185	
F-GKFE	Raven Europe S-60A HAFB	E-177	
F-GKFH	Raven Europe FS-57A HAFB	E-203	
F-GKFK	Raven Europe S-49A HAFB	E-210	
F-GKFL	Raven Europe S-49A HAFB	E-216	
F-GKFO	Raven Europe FS-57A HAFB	E-228	
F-GKFP	Raven Europe FS-57A HAFB	E-229	

Registration	Type	Serial	Previous identities
F-GKFR	Raven Europe S-66A HAFB	E-231	
F-GKFS	Raven Europe S-60A HAFB	E-232	
F-GKFT	Raven Europe FS-57A HAFB	E-237	
F-GKFU	Raven Europe S-52A HAFB	E-204	
F-GKFY	Raven Europe RX-8 HAFB	E-241	
F-GKGG	Cessna A185F Skywagon	18503341	C-GYVZ
F-GKGN	Grumman-American AA-5B Tiger	AA5B-0089	G-BDGN, N6147A
F-GKGQ	SNCAN/Stampe SV.4C	54	F-BGGQ, Fr.AF/EPAA.58
F-GKGR	Agusta-Bell 206B Jet Ranger 2	8294	YU-HAP
F-GKGU	Cessna 172R Skyhawk	17280338	
F-GKGX	Cessna 172R Skyhawk	17280343	N9512W
F-GKGZ	Aerotek Pitts S-2A	2149	TU-TNY, N31501
F-GKHB	Schweizer 269C	S-1438	(N431MS)
F-GKHG	Enstrom 280C Shark	1034	G-KLAY, G-BGZD
F-GKHH	Eurocopter EC.120B Colibri	1122	
F-GKHI	Cessna 172N Skyhawk	17272688	N6281D
F-GKHJ	Dassault Falcon 900	11	N251SJ, F-GLGY, UN-09002, F-WEFX, LX-AER, F-WWFK
F-GKHM(2)	DHC-6 Twin Otter 200	132	D-IDHB(2), RP-C1776, N501BA, CF-WZH
F-GKHT	Robin DR.400/120D Dauphin	1726	HB-KBB
F-GKHU	Robin DR.400/120D Dauphin	1723	HB-KBA
F-GKHY	Piper PA-18-150 Super Cub	18-7509081	D-EOVS, HB-PAI, N66804
F-GKIA	Pilatus PC-6/ B2-H2 Turbo Porter	689	VH-MKT, A14-689, HB-FEB
F-GKID	Cessna 500 Citation I	500-0319	N94MA, D-ICUW, N22LH, N5319J, HZ-NC1, N5319J
F-GKIE	Kubicek BB-20GP HAFB	300	OK-4010, OK-0300
F-GKIF	Kubicek BB-22 HAFB	62	OK-6062
F-GKIJ	Piper PA-44-180 Seminole	44-7995193	N3010H
F-GKIM	Robin DR.400/160 Major	2039	F-GJKM
F-GKIZ	Beech 350 Super King Air	FL-23	N1543Q
F-GKJB	Aérospatiale SN.601 Corvette	20	TR-LZT, F-BTTN, N616AC, F-WNGS
F-GKJE	Aérospatiale AS.350B Ecureuil	1144	N350AJ, N350S, N3604D
F-GKJF	Cameron A-105 HAFB	2678	
F-GKJI (2)	Mudry CAP.10B	20	Fr.AF
F-GKJJ	Cameron A-180 HAFB	2564	(F-GHMX)
F-GKJN	Chaize CS.3000F16 HAFB	098	
F-GKJT	Holste MH.1521M Broussard	106	Fr.AF
F-GKJZ	Lindstrand LBL-90A HAFB	1265	
F-GKKA	Mudry CAP.10B	257	
F-GKKC	Mudry CAP.10B	59	D-EDKG, F-BXHC
F-GKKE	Mudry CAP.10B	261	
F-GKKM	Mudry CAP.10B	270	
F-GKKZ	Mudry CAP.10B	113	HB-SAL
F-GKLB	Kubicek BB-26Z HAFB	487	
F-GKLC	Bell 206B Jet Ranger II	1246	G-CFFM, N83RH, N704SD, N37467, XC-GII
F-GKLD	Aérospatiale AS.350B3 Ecureuil	4233	
F-GKLS(2)	Agusta-Bell 206B Jet Ranger 2	8441	G-JERY, G-BDBR
F-GKLT	Piper PA-28-181 Archer II	2890124	F-ODLT
F-GKMA	Aérospatiale AS.350B Ecureuil	2285	
F-GKMB	Aérospatiale AS.350B Ecureuil	2304	F-WYMD
F-GKMF	Balloon Works Firefly F8 HAFB	F8-362	
F-GKMJ	Cameron N-77 HAFB	2530	
F-GKMM	Ultramagic M-65 HAFB	65/76	
F-GKMO	Ultramagic M-77C HAFB	77/250	
F-GKMP(2)	Aérospatiale AS.350B3 Ecureuil	3828	F-WQDD, F-WQDQ
F-GKMQ	Aérospatiale AS.350B3 Ecureuil	4847	
F-GKMR(3)	Aérospatiale AS.350B1 Ecureuil	2242	F-ODLU
F-GKMT	Chaize JZ.25F16 HAFB	119	F-WKMT
F-GKMU(2)	Aérospatiale AS.350B2 Ecureuil	2255	HB-XSD, F-WYMJ
F-GKMV	Mooney M.20J Model 205	24-3210	
F-GKMX	Piper PA-28-161 Warrior II	28-8616048	N9084Z, N9509N
F-GKOM	Dassault Falcon 900B	130	F-WHLV, HZ-SPAL, A6-SAC, G-HAAM, F-GKBQ, F-WQBN, VP-CID, VR-CID, F-WWFB, F-GOAB, F-WWFC
F-GKOR	Cameron O-105 HAFB	2171	
F-GKOT	SNCASE SE.3130 Alouette II	1243	ALAT, Fr.AF
F-GKOY	Piper PA-28-161 Cadet	2841334	(N9217N)
F-GKPA	Mooney M.20J Model 205	24-3166	N1079Y
F-WKPG	SOCATA TBM-700	002	
	(Also carries "212" on tail)		
F-GKPP	Morane-Saulnier MS.760B Paris 2	098	3A-MPP, HB-VEP, F-BOHN, D-INGA
	(W/o 10.91, used as spares but still regd.)		
F-GKPR	Christen Pitts S-2B	5120	N6033Z
F-GKPS	Piper PA-28RT-201 Arrow IV	28R-7918128	N28456
F-GKPU	SAN Jodel D.140C Mousquetaire III	162	EC-EFY, F-BMFY
F-GKQA	Robin DR.400/120 Dauphin 2+2	2040	
F-GKQB	Robin DR.400/140B Dauphin 4	2042	
F-GKQC	Robin DR.400/120 Dauphin 2+2	2043	
F-GKQE	Robin DR.400/100 Cadet	2049	
F-GKQG	Robin DR.400/160 Major	2064	
F-GKQH	Robin DR.400/120 Dauphin 2+2	2053	
F-GKQI	Robin DR.400/180 Régent	2048	
F-GKQK	Robin DR.400/140B Dauphin 4	2056	
F-GKQM	Robin DR.400/120 Dauphin 2+2	2057	
F-GKQN	Robin DR.400/160 Major	2058	
F-GKQO	Robin DR.400/180 Régent	2087	
F-GKQP	Robin DR.400/120 Dauphin 2+2	2060	
F-GKQR	Robin DR.400/120 Dauphin 2+2	2062	
F-GKQS	Robin DR.400/120 Dauphin 2+2	2068	
F-GKQU	Robin DR.400/180 Régent	2065	
F-WKQX	Robin X-4	001	
	(Experimental 4-seat glass-fibre design)		
F-GKQY	Robin DR.400/120 Dauphin 2+2	2069	
F-GKQZ	Robin DR.400/120 Dauphin 2+2	2070	
F-GKRB	Robin R.3000/160	141	
F-GKRD	Robin DR.400/120 Dauphin 2+2	1992	
F-GKRM	Balloon Works Firefly F7B HAFB	F7B-316	
F-GKRN	SOCATA TB-21 Trinidad TC	520	I- SERN, F-ODQO
	(Badly damaged, Poland 23.5.05)		
F-GKRO	Holste MH.1521C1 Broussard	154	Fr.AF
F-GKRP	Mooney M.20J Model 205	24-3211	
F-GKRQ	Reserved for Kit Aircraft		
F-GKRX	Robin DR.400/160 Major	2302	PH-JGB, F-GORX
F-GKRY	Cameron N-105 HAFB	10577	
F-GKSB	Raven-Europe RX-8 HAFB	E-220	
	(Envelope destroyed 3.9.03)		
F-GKSC	Thunder AX8-105Z HAFB	1763	
F-GKSJ	Balloon Works Firefly F7B-15 HAFB	F7B-326	
F-GKSM	Cessna 182P Skylane	18264935	N1373S
F-GKSS	Beech 58 Baron	TH-154	3A-MON, F-BSRF
F-GKTC	Robinson R22 Beta	1369	
F-GKTM	Cameron A-210 HAFB	4660	
F-GKTO	DHC-6 Twin Otter 300	523	TR-LAL, F-GAMR
F-GKTP	Cameron A-105 HAFB	4351	
F-GKTR	Bell 47G-2	2457	C-FCAD, CF-CAD
F-GKTS	Aérospatiale AS.355F1 Ecureuil 2	5081	HB-XPF, F-GDFH
F-GKUB	SOCATA TB-20 Trinidad	1124	
F-GKUD	SOCATA TB-9 Tampico Club	1128	
F-GKUF	SOCATA TB-9 Tampico Club	1147	
F-GKUG	SOCATA TB-9 Tampico Club	1148	
F-GKUH	SOCATA TB-9 Tampico Club	1149	
F-GKUI	SOCATA TB-10 Tobago	1150	
F-GKUM	SOCATA TB-20 Trinidad	1177	
F-GKUS	SOCATA TB-10 Tobago	1208	
F-GKUT	SOCATA TB-10 Tobago	1169	
F-GKUU	SOCATA TB-9 Tampico	1182	
F-GKUY	SOCATA TB-9 Tampico	1179	
F-GKVE	SOCATA TB-20 Trinidad	1245	
F-GKVH	SOCATA TB-9 Tampico Club	1270	
F-GKVI	SOCATA TB-9 Tampico Club	1311	
F-GKVK	SOCATA TB-9 Tampico Club	1290	
F-GKVS	SOCATA TB-9 Tampico Club	1310	
F-GKVT	SOCATA TB-9 Tampico Club	1312	
F-GKVU	SOCATA TB-9 Tampico Club	1313	
F-GKVV	SOCATA TB-9 Tampico Club	1314	
F-GKVY	SOCATA TB-9 Tampico Club	1347	
F-GKVZ	SOCATA TB-20 Trinidad	1329	N5559U
F-GKXA	Airbus A320-211	287	
F-GKXC	Airbus A320-214	1502	F-WWIG
F-GKXE	Airbus A320-214	1879	F-WWDX
F-GKXG	Airbus A320-214	1894	F-WWDV
F-GKXH	Airbus A320-214	1924	
F-GKXI	Airbus A320-214	1949	
F-GKXJ	Airbus A320-214	1900	
F-GKXK	Airbus A320-214	2140	F-WWBR
F-GKXL	Airbus A320-214	2705	
F-GKXM	Airbus A320-214	2721	F-WWXM
F-GKXN	Airbus A320-214	3008	F-WWBH
F-GKXO	Airbus A320-214	3420	F-WWIP
F-GKXP	Airbus A320-214	3470	F-WWBP
F-GKXQ	Airbus A320-214	3777	D-AVVH
F-GKXR	Airbus A320-214	3795	F-WWBM
F-GKXS	Airbus A320-214	3825	F-WWIV
F-GKXT	Airbus A320-214	3859	F-WWDM
F-GKXU	Airbus A320-214	4063	F-WWBF
F-GKXV	Airbus A320-214	4084	D-AVVA
F-GKXX	Aérospatiale AS.350D A-Star III	1354	N5771H, F-GKXX
F-GKXY	Airbus A320-214	4105	D-AVVR
F-GKXZ	Airbus A320-214	4137	F-WWIZ
F-GKYC	Aérospatiale SA.341G Gazelle	1414	EC-EET, F-GDFR, I- ETBA, F-WIPJ
F-GKYF	Fouga CM.170 Magister	315	F-WKYF, Fr.AF
F-GKYG	Aérospatiale AS.350B Ecureuil	1536	JA9315
F-GKYL	Piper PA-28RT-201T Turbo Arrow IV	28R-7931288	N4511U
F-GKYP	Cameron A-105 HAFB	4935	LX-BMK(1)
F-GKZA	Beech 58 Baron	TH-1401	(F-GHHA), N104MK, N6753K
F-GKZE	Beech 58 Baron	TH-1494	5V-MCB
F-GKZU	Beech 58 Baron	TH-1459	F-GMRD, 3A-MON, N851BE
F-GLAB	SOCATA TB-9 Tampico Club	1074	
F-GLAH	SOCATA TB-20 Trinidad	1076	
F-GLAL	SOCATA TB-9 Tampico Club	1091	
F-GLAO	SOCATA TB-9 Tampico Club	1106	
F-GLAP	SOCATA TB-9 Tampico Club	1034	
F-GLAQ	SOCATA TB-9 Tampico Club	1035	
F-GLAS	SOCATA TB-10 Tobago	1166	
F-GLBZ	SOCATA TBM-700A	32	N356M
F-GLCA	Raven Europe FS-57A HAFB	E-244	
F-GLCB	Raven Europe S-49A HAFB	E-252	
F-GLCD	Raven Europe FS-57A HAFB	E-256	
F-GLCF	Raven S-57S Fraise HAFB	3001	
F-GLCG	Raven Europe S-60A HAFB	E-262	
F-GLCH	Raven Europe FS-57A HAFB	E-264	
F-GLCI	Raven Europe S-60A HAFB	E-266	
F-GLCK	Raven Europe FS-57A HAFB	E-276	
F-GLCL	Raven Europe RX-7 HAFB	E-261	
F-GLCM	Raven Europe FS-57A HAFB	E-273	
F-GLCN	Raven Europe S-52A HAFB	E-259	
F-GLCO	Raven Europe S-55A HAFB	E-277	
F-GLCP	Raven Europe S-52A HAFB	E-278	
F-GLCQ	Raven Europe S-55A HAFB	E-285	
F-GLCR	Raven Europe FS-57A HAFB	E-286	
F-GLCT	Raven Europe S-60A HAFB	E-295	
F-GLCU	Raven Europe S-55A HAFB	E-299	
F-GLCZ	Raven Europe S-71A HAFB	E-290	
F-GLDA	Robin DR.400/160 Major	2074	
F-GLDC	Robin DR.400/120 Dauphin 2+2	2082	
F-GLDD	Robin DR.400/140B Dauphin 4	2083	
F-GLDE	Robin DR.400/140B Dauphin 4	2075	
F-GLDG	Robin DR.400/140B Dauphin 4	2092	
F-GLDI	Robin DR.400/140B Dauphin 4	2086	
F-GLDJ	Robin DR.400/120 Dauphin 2+2	2094	
F-GLDK	Robin DR.400/120 Dauphin 2+2	2090	
F-GLDL	Robin R.3000/160	155	
F-GLDM	Robin DR.400/180 Régent	2093	
F-GLDN	Robin DR.400/140B Dauphin 4	2096	
F-GLDO	Robin DR.400/120 Dauphin 2+2	2099	
F-GLDP	Robin DR.400/120 Dauphin 2+2	2097	
F-GLDS	Robin DR.400/100 Cadet	2101	
F-GLDT	Robin DR.400/120 Dauphin 2+2	2102	
F-GLDU	Robin DR.400/120 Dauphin 2+2	2103	
F-GLDV	Robin DR.400/180 Régent	2120	
F-GLDX	Robin DR.400/120 Dauphin 2+2	2110	
F-GLDY	Robin DR.400/180 Régent	2117	
F-GLDZ	Robin DR.400/180 Régent	2105	
F-GLEA	Cessna 172N Skyhawk	17272260	N9425E
F-GLEB	American AG-5B Tiger	10100	N100AG
F-GLED(2)	SNCASE SE.3130 Alouette II	1425	ALAT
F-GLEE(2)	Agusta A.109E Power	11603	
F-GLEF(3)	Agusta A.109E Power	11027	
F-GLEH	Agusta A.109E Power	11037	
F-GLEJ	Mooney M.20K Model 252 TSE	25-1100	N252GD, N252ZD
F-GLEL	Cameron V-77 HAFB	2467	
F-GLEM	Piper PA-28-181 Archer	28-7990494	N2852K
F-GLEO	Reims/ Cessna F172M	F17201196	OO-WAJ

Registration	Type	C/n	Previous identities
F-GLEQ	Agusta A.109E Power	11052	I-MUNA, G-TVAA
F-GLER	Cameron A-180 HAFB	4511	(F-GLEF)
F-GLET	Robinson R22 Beta	1957	
F-GLEU	Pilatus PC-6/B1-H2 Turbo-Porter	627	I- SAEZ, D-FLEV, N4229S, 9M-APQ, 5Y-AHY, HB-FDE, ST-ADJ(1), HB-FDE
F-GLEX	Chaize JZ.40F16 HAFB	160	
F-GLEY	Agusta-Bell 206B Jet Ranger 3	8558	3A-MRG, (F-GBLB)
F-GLFA	SOCATA TB-9 Tampico Club	1363	
F-GLFC	SOCATA TB-200 Tobago XL	1376	
F-GLFI	SOCATA TB-9 Tampico Club	1436	
F-GLFS	SOCATA TB-20 Trinidad	1364	
F-GLFV	SOCATA TB-9 Tampico Club	1471	
F-GLFY	SOCATA TB-9 Tampico Club	1582	
F-GLFZ	SOCATA Rallye 235C	13075	
F-GLGC	Piper PA-31-350 Chieftain	31-8052149	N3279H, V2-LCC, VP-LCC
F-GLGK	SOCATA MS.880B Rallye-Club	1584	LX-FBA, F-BSCL
F-GLGL	Piper PA-28RT-201 Arrow IV	28R-7918250	N108CC, N9624N
F-GLGR	Reims/Cessna FA152 Aerobat	FA1520384	(F-GLYB), 3A-MPC, (F-GLYB), 3A-MPC, F-GDOP
F-GLGV	SIGA MA-26 Pilatre de Rozier HAFB	128	
F-GLHA	Robin DR.400/120 Petit Prince	794	F-BUHK
F-GLHB	Reims/Cessna F182P Skylane II	F18200008	PH-HTM, D-EJCH
F-GLHD	Aérospatiale SA.315B Lama	2647	VT-VKT, F-GDJH
F-GLHF	Fouga CM.170 Magister	406	F-WLHF, Fr.AF
F-GLHG	Piper PA-28R-200 Cherokee Arrow II	28R-7635051	N4461X
F-GLHJ	Dassault Falcon 2000	12	I-SNAW, F-WWMM
F-GLHL	Agusta-Bell 47J	1135	
F-GLHN	Aérospatiale AS.350B3 Ecureuil	4732	
F-GLHO	Fouga CM.170 Magister (Res .99)	331	F-WIGY, Fr.AF
F-GLHY	Agusta-Bell 47G-4A	2544	D-HOOD
F-GLHZ	Rockwell Commander 112	173	N1184J
F-GLID	Bell 47G-2	2416	C-FLMD, CF-LMD
F-GLIE	SOCATA TB-20 Trinidad	994	G-PLYD
F-GLIF	Beech 200 Super King Air	BB-192	F-OGPQ, OY-CBV, LN-KCI, OY-CBV, (EI-BGR), SE-GRP
F-GLIL	SIGA MA-35 Pilatre de Rozier HAFB	150	
F-GLIN	Lindstrand LBL-105AHAFB	680	
F-GLIO	Cessna R182 Skylane RG	R18201815	N510DC, N5101T
F-GLIQ	Cameron C-80 HAFB	3584	
F-GLJB	SNCASE SE.3130 Alouette II	1073	ALAT
F-GLJC	Piper PA-22-150 Caribbean	22-6854	N2857Z
F-GLJF	Schweizer 269C	S-1550	N41S
F-GLJG	Extra EA.300/200	08	N149C, D-ETQA
F-GLJI	Cameron N-77 HAFB	4692	G-BYRF
F-GLJJ	Cameron N-120 HAFB	3713	
F-GLJM	Cameron N-77 HAFB	2659	
F-GLJN	SOCATA MS.880B Rallye Club	2427	EC-CJN, F-OCVV
F-GLJP	Agusta-Bell 206B Jet Ranger 2	8315	(F-GGPD), YU-HAV
F-GLJR	Cameron A-105 HAFB	3367	
F-GLJT	Cameron N-105 HAFB	10043	
F-GLJY	Robinson R44 Raven II	11600	EI-DVX, G-CEKN
F-GLKA	Robin DR.400/180R Remo 180	2108	
F-GLKB	Robin DR.400/180R Remo 180	2109	
F-GLKD	Robin DR.400/140B Dauphin 4	2121	
F-GLKF	Robin DR.400/120 Dauphin 2+2	2122	
F-GLKG	Robin DR.400/180 Régent	2116	
F-GLKH	Robin R.3000/160	158	
F-GLKI	Robin DR.400/140B Dauphin 4	2111	
F-GLKK	Robin DR.400/180 Régent	2130	
F-GLKL	Robin DR.400/160 Major	2129	
F-GLKO	Robin DR.400/120D Petit Prince	1604	HB-EQY
F-GLKP	Robin DR.400/180R Remo 180	2131	
F-GLKQ	Robin DR.400/120D Petit Prince	1605	HB-EQZ
F-GLKR	Robin DR.400/120 Dauphin 2+2	2134	
F-GLKS	Robin DR.400/120 Dauphin 2+2	2126	
F-GLKU	Robin DR.400/120 Dauphin 2+2	2140	
F-GLKV	Robin DR.400/120 Dauphin 2+2	2139	
F-GLKX	Robin DR.400/120 Dauphin 2+2	2141	
F-GLKZ	Robin DR.400/120 Dauphin 2+2 (Painted as Dauphin 4)	2128	
F-GLLB	Piper PA-28-161 Warrior III	2842005	
F-GLLF	Cessna 172S Skyhawk SP	172S8092	N681SP
F-GLLO(2)	Swearingen SA.266T Merlin IIIA	T-276	F-WQHQ(2), N132CW, N188SC, N262PC, N5111B, N5477M
F-GLLR	Piper PA-32-300 Cherokee Six	32-7640093	N75183
F-GLMA	CEA DR.250/160 Capitaine	99	OO-LIP, D-EDLC
F-GLMC	Wassmer Jodel D.120 Paris-Nice	82	F-BIKL
F-GLME	Thunder AX7-65 HAFB	2064	
F-GLMF	Holste MH.1521M Broussard (Stored)	289	ALAT
F-GLMK	Thunder AX10-180A S3 HAFB	2183	
F-GLML	Robin R.1180TD Aiglon	283	HB-KAF
F-GLMS	Piper J-3C-65 Cub (L-4H)	12192	OO-GMS, (OO-LSD), PH-CMS, D-EGUL, G-ANXP, N79819, NC79819, 44-79896
F-GLMT	Extra EA.300	036	JY-RNA, D-EKFD
F-GLND	Beech 1900D	UE-196	N3234G
F-GLNE	Beech 1900D	UE-197	N3234U
F-GLNF	Beech 1900D	UE-69	YR-RLA, YR-AAK, N82896
F-GLNH	Beech 1900D	UE-73	YR-RLB, YR-AAL, N82923
F-GLNK	Beech 1900D	UE-269	N11017
F-GLNS	Llopis MA-40 HAFB	171	
F-GLNY	Agusta-Bell 47G-2	260	9H-AAF, 74+18, AS+060
F-GLNZ	SOCATA TB-10 Tobago	179	I- ODNZ, F-GAKU, OO-DAL
F-GLOF	Schweizer 269C	S-1588	N69A
F-GLOH	Wassmer WA.54 Europa	93	F-BXOH(3), F-BUKX, F-OCUY
F-GLOK	Cessna 172P Skyhawk	17275517	N64080
F-GLOL	Ultramagic M-130 HAFB	130/37	
F-GLOM	Cameron A-105 HAFB	2956	
F-GLOO	Reims/Cessna F172N	F17201690	OO-VTG
F-GLOR(2)	Eurocopter EC.135T1	0041	
F-GLOU	Robinson R44 Astro	0032	I- OOOI
F-GLPD(2)	Robinson R22 Beta	2235	OK-XIE, N2347V
F-GLPF	Cameron O-105 HAFB	2856	
F-GLPN	Cessna 207A Stationair 8 (Soloy Pac conversion)	20700595	N73469
F-GLPR	Cessna 172N Skyhawk 100	17267672	N73778
F-GLPT	Swearingen SA.226T(B) Merlin IIIB	T-298	VH-AWU, N5495M
F-GLPV	SNCASE SE.3130 Alouette II	1443	F-MJAZ
F-GLPX	Aquila AT-01	AT01-168	
F-GLQQ	Piper J-3C-65 Cub	7396	C-GUQQ, N126RB, N40637, NC40637
F-GLRC	SNCASE SE.313B Alouette II (Cr. 23.9.02)	1117	F-MJAW
F-GLRD	Chaize CS.2200F12 HAFB	113	
F-GLRF	SIGA MA-26 Pilatre de Rozier HAFB	114	
F-GLRJ	Chaize CS.2200F12 HAFB	114	
F-GLRM	Cameron O-65 HAFB	2689	
F-GLRN	Diamond DA 20-100 Katana	10111	N537SS
F-GLRO	Robin DR.400/120D Dauphin 2+2	1688	HB-KAR
F-GLRS	SNCASE SE.313B Alouette II	1346	ALAT
F-GLRV	Piper J-3C-65 Cub	9440	N48526, NC48526, 43-579, (42-59389)
F-GLRZ	Beech C90A King Air	LJ-1296	(F-GJDK), F-OGRZ
F-GLSB	Cameron V-77 HAFB	3257	
F-GLSD	Airship Industries Skyship SKS 600BL	1215-06	N606SA, JA1004, VH-HAN, (G-SKSK)
F-GLSF	Robinson R22 Beta	1813	(F-GHJY)
F-GLSM	Mooney M.20C Ranger	20-0024	N7790M
F-GLSO	Ultramagic M-130 HAFB	130/31	
F-GLSP	Ultramagic H-77 HAFB	77/193	
F-GLSR	Beech A36 Bonanza	E-2120	OO-PBC, F-GIBC, N67578
F-GLSS	Cameron N-77 HAFB	1887	OO-BJR
F-GLST	Piper PA-28-161 Warrior II	28-7916306	N3036T
F-GLSV	Galaxy 7 HAFB	GLX-1737	
F-GLTB	Aérospatiale AS.365N3 Dauphin 2	6756	F-WWOE
F-GLTC	Cessna T210F Turbo-System Centurion	T210-0188	CN-TZS, N6788R
F-GLTD	Ultramagic S-90 HAFB	90/47	
F-GLTH	Aérospatiale AS.350B Ecureuil	2701	
F-GLTI	Ultramagic H-77 HAFB	77/ 232	
F-GLTK	Cessna 550 Citation II	550-0609	N344A, D-CHOP, N609TC, (N1242A)
F-GLTO	Fouga CM.170 Magister	471	F-WFPK, Fr.AF
F-GLTZ	Piper PA-18A-150 Super Cub	18-5136	N7062B
F-GLUB	Piper J-3C-65 Cub	16395	N92002, NC92002
F-GLUC	Raven-Europe S-55A HAFB	E-400	
F-GLUD	Robin DR.400/120 Dauphin 2+2	2165	
F-GLUE	Kubicek BB-26Z HAFB	698	
F-GLUF	Jum J'Aie	001	
F-GLVA	Robin DR.400/180 Régent	2146	
F CLVB	Robin DR.400/120 Dauphin 2+2	2148	
F-GLVD	Robin DR.400/120 Dauphin 2+2	2147	
F-GLVF	Robin DR.400/120 Dauphin 2+2	2150	
F-GLVG	Robin DR.400/120 Dauphin 2+2	2153	
F-GLVI	Robin DR.400/120 Dauphin 2+2	2138	
F-GLVJ	Robin DR.400/120 Dauphin 2+2	2142	
F-GLVK	Robin DR.400/140B Dauphin 4	2158	
F-GLVL	Robin DR.400/140B Dauphin 4	2154	
F-GLVN	Robin DR.400/140B Dauphin 4	2163	
F-GLVO	Robin DR.400/180 Régent	2155	
F-GLVQ	Robin DR.400/120 Dauphin 2+2	2166	
F-GLVR	Robin DR.400/120 Dauphin 2+2	2168	
F-GLVS	Robin DR.400/120 Dauphin 2+2	2169	
F-GLVU	Robin DR.400/140B Dauphin 4	2171	
F-GLVX	Robin DR.400/140B Dauphin 4	2175	
F-GLVY	Robin DR.400/120 Dauphin 2+2	2173	
F-GLVZ	Robin DR.400/160 Major	2174	
F-GLXD	Aérospatiale SA.315B Lama	2610	
F-GLXF	Boeing 737-219 (Stored Casablanca, wfu)	22657	G-BJXJ, N851L, N6066Z, (ZK-NAT)
F-GLXZ	SOCATA TB-200 Tobago XL	1448	F-ODXZ
F-GLYF	Robinson R44 Astro	0272	SP-GSC
F-GLYG	Robinson R22 Beta	0947	G-BPUK
F-GLYL	Aérospatiale AS.350B2 Ecureuil	9008	F-OIYL
F-GLYN	Robin DR.400/180R Remorqueur	1306	HB-EYN
F-GLYP	Wassmer WA.52 Europa	45	D-ENJB
F-GLZC	Airbus A340-311	029	
F-GLZH	Airbus A340-311	078	
F-GLZI	Airbus A340-311	084	
F-GLZJ	Airbus A340-313X	186	(F-GLZN)
F-GLZK	Airbus A340-313X	207	
F-GLZM	Airbus A340-313X	237	
F-GLZN	Airbus A340-313X	245	
F-GLZO	Airbus A340-313X	246	
F-GLZP	Airbus A340-313X	260	
F-GLZR	Airbus A340-313X	307	
F-GLZS	Airbus A340-313X	310	
F-GLZU	Airbus A340-313X	377	
F-GLZV, X, Y, Z	Reserved for A.340s for Air France, ntu		
F-GMAB	Piper PA-28-140 Cherokee Cruiser	28-7625052	C-GGVB
F-GMAF	Robin DR.400/140B Dauphin 4	2104	
F-GMAH	Balloon Works Firefly F7B HAFB	F7B-345	
F-GMAK	Cameron N-105 HAFB	3920	
F-GMAM	Reims/Cessna F172N	F17201814	EC-KBF, D-EORR
F-GMAN	Cameron A-105 HAFB	4361	
F-GMAP	Cameron C-80 Concept HAFB	3380	
F-GMAQ	Colt 210A HAFB	2083	G-BTYZ
F-GMAS	Commander Aircraft 114B	14552	N60096
F-GMAT	Aérospatiale AS.350B3 Ecureuil	3202	
F-GMAV	Cameron Z-90 HAFB	10744	
F-GMAX(2)	Aérospatiale AS.355N Ecureuil 2	5596	G-SEPC, G-BWGV
F-GMAY	Aérospatiale SA.365N Dauphin 2	6137	
F-GMBA	Aérospatiale AS.355N Ecureuil 2	5320	N35EC, YV-O-KWH-5, F-WZKO
F-GMBC	Piper PA-46-310P Malibu	46-8408039	G-BORP, N4346M
F-GMBD	Piper PA-28-181 Archer II	2890062	HB-PLK
F-GMBE	Reims/Cessna FTB.337G Super Skymaster	0017	(F-GGTP), FAP3716, CS-AAO
F-GMBF	Robinson R22M Mariner	2193M	F-OGUV, (F-GMAL)
F-GMBI	SIGA MA-30 Pilatre de Rozier HAFB	107	
F-GMBJ	Chaize CS.2200F12 HAFB	143	
F-GMBL	Aérospatiale AS.355N Ecureuil 2	5358	(N75EC), YV-O-KWH-6
F-GMBM	Robin DR.400/140B Dauphin 4	2219	
F-GMBO	Aérospatiale AS.350B2 Ecureuil	2253	SE-HUS
F-GMBP(2)	Ultramagic S-130 HAFB	130/18	
F-GMBQ	Cameron TR-77 HAFB	11899	
F-GMBS	Chaize CS.3000F16 HAFB	115	
F-GMBY	Cessna 182P Skylane	18264498	I-BLAC, N1948M
F-GMCA	Cameron N-77 HAFB	2714	
F-GMCE	Robinson R22 Beta	2071	N23263
F-GMCJ	Eurocopter EC.135T1	0020	
F-GMCM	Piper PA-28RT-201T Turbo Arrow IV	28R-8531010	N6914K

Reg	Type	C/N	Previous
F-GMCN	Piper PA-32R-301 Saratoga II HP	3213049	N9221G
F-GMCO	Thunder AX6-56A HAFB	163	G-BRNY
F-GMCY	Nord 1101 Noralpha	67	CEV
F-GMDE	Llopis Balloons MA26 HAFB	196	
F-GMDF	Lindstrand LBL-210A HAFB	068	CS-B.., G-BVXZ
F-GMDG	Lindstrand LBL-77B HAFB	1097	
F-GMDH	Eurocopter EC.120B Colibri	1405	F-WQDC
F-GMDM	Sky 105-24 HAFB	094	HB-QEM
F-GMDP	Cessna TR182 Skylane RG	R18201331	OO-TES, F-GHDQ, C-GDRF, N23303
F-GMDR	Cirrus SR22	2408	N915SR
F-GMEF	Piper PA-38-112 Tomahawk II	38-81A0057	N25701
F-GMEL	Pilatus PC-6/B2-H2 Turbo-Porter	536	N4915
F-GMEP	Colt 69A HAFB	1960	
F-GMER	Cameron C-80 Concept HAFB	4655	
F-GMES	Robin ATL (Res)	73	F-GFRV
F-GMEU	SIGA MA-26 Pilatre de Rozier HAFB	102	F-WMEU
F-GMEV	SIGA MA-30 Pilatre de Rozier HAFB	132	
F-GMEY	Beech F33A Bonanza	CE-1434	PH-MEY, N5534Y
F-GMFA	Raven Europe S-60A HAFB	E-110	
F-GMFB	Raven Europe RX-7 HAFB	E-111	
F-GMFD	Raven Europe FS-57A HAFB	E-122	
F-GMFF	Raven Europe FS-57A HAFB	E-129	
F-GMFG	Raven Europe RX-7 HAFB	E-156	
F-GMFH	Raven Europe RX-7 HAFB	E-162	
F-GMFJ	Raven Europe FS-55A HAFB	E-135	
F-GMFN	Raven Europe S-60A HAFB	E-139	
F-GMFO	Raven Europe FS-57A HAFB	E-144	
F-GMFP	Raven Europe RX-7 HAFB	E-133	
F-GMFT	Raven-Europe S-55A HAFB	E-157	
F-GMFU	Raven Europe FS-57A HAFB	E-158	
F-GMFX	Raven Europe S-52A HAFB	E-200	
F-GMFY	Raven Europe S-55A HAFB	E-161	
F-GMFZ	Raven Europe FS-57A HAFB	E-150	
F-GMGB	Beech B200 Super King Air	BB-1390	(F-GLOP), F-ODZK, N8043B
F-GMGD	Dragonfly 333	3330093003	
F-GMGE	Dragonfly 333	3330093004	
F-GMGO	Aerostar RX-8 HAFB	3296	
F-GMGP	Robin DR.400/140B Dauphin 4	2231	
F-GMGS	Aerostar RX-8 HAFB	3258	
F-GMGT	Aerostar S-60A HAFB	3221	
F-GMGU	Raven S-57A HAFB	3195	
F-GMGZ	SIGA Pilatre de Rozier MA-26 HAFB	152	
F-GMHA	Robinson R22 Beta (Accident 16.8.99)	2059	
F-GMHB	SIAI-Marchetti SF.260	358	Phil.AF
F-GMHC	Eurocopter EC.135T1	0036	
F-GMHE	Eurocopter EC.135T1	0048	
F-GMHF	Eurocopter EC.135T1	0056	
F-GMHH	Robin HR.100/210 Safari (Wfu 1.00. To UK .04, scrapped)	155	3A-MUZ, F-BUHH
F-GMHJ	Eurocopter EC.135T1	0032	
F-GMHK	Eurocopter EC.135T1	0081	D-HBYH
F-GMHM	SIGA MA-26 Pilatre de Rozier HAFB	101	
F-GMHR	Aérospatiale AS.350B Ecureuil	1921	OY-HEJ
F-GMHY	Bell 47G	673	F-GGSU, F-BMHY, Fr.Mil
F-GMIA	Mooney M.20J Model 205	24-3358	
F-GMIF	Cessna 207A Stationair 7 (Soloy Pac conversion)	20700416	HB-CJF, N7138J, N21190, C-GBUZ, N7352U
F-GMIH	Cameron Z-105 HAFB	10792	
F-GMIL	Robinson R44 Astro	0283	
F-GMIM	Schweizer 269C	S-1239	D-HJON
F-GMIN	Cameron A-210 HAFB	4258	
F-GMIP	Cessna 172S Skyhawk SP	172S11019	N5288C
F-GMIS	Cessna U206F Stationair	U20602194	F-MJAD, F-MJAJ, F-BRGM, N7411Q
F-GMIX	SOCATA TB-20 Trinidad	693	I- SDMB, F-ODRQ
F-GMIY	Cessna 152	15285378	HA-CPL, HA-ERE(1), N93021
F-GMJB	Thunder AX7-77 HAFB	2281	
F-GMJC	Eurocopter EC.135T1	0026	
F-GMJE	Robin DR.360 Chevalier	702	OO-FFI, OO-BOB, D-ENTG
F-GMJF	Robinson R44 Clipper II	10871	LX-HRM, F-GZDH
F-GMJG	Pilatus PC-6/B2-H2 Turbo Porter	659	HB-FEF, F-GIMU, HB-FEF, EC-EHK, HB-FEF
F-GMJH	Cameron Z-210 HAFB	10273	
F-GMJI	Robinson R44 Raven	0850	D-HALV
F-GMJL	Aérospatiale SA.341G Gazelle (W/o 18.6.98)	1245	G-BKLT, (F-GMJL), F-GGGB, G-BKLT, N15WC, N47261
F-GMKA	Robin HR.200/120B	263	
F-GMKB	Robin HR.200/120B	253	
F-GMKC	Robin HR.200/120B	252	
F-GMKF	Robin HR.200/120B	258	
F-GMKG	Robin HR.200/120B	259	
F-GMKH	Robin HR.200/120B	261	
F-GMKJ	Robin DR.400/180 Régent	2204	
F-GMKL	Robin R.2160 Alpha Sport	265	
F-GMKM	Robin DR.400/140B Dauphin 4	2202	
F-GMKN	Robin DR.400/120 Dauphin 2+2	2199	
F-GMKO	Robin DR.400/140B Dauphin 4	2179	
F-GMKP	Robin DR.400/120 Dauphin 2+2	2182	
F-GMKR	Robin DR.400/180 Régent	2186	
F-GMKT	Robin DR.400/180 Régent	2183	
F-GMKV	Robin DR.400/160 Major	2195	
F-GMKX	Robin DR.400/140B Dauphin 4	2194	
F-GMKY	Robin DR.400/180 Régent	2210	
F-GMLA	Cessna 172S Skyhawk SP	172S8715	N789SP
F-GMLG	Ultramagic S-105 HAFB	105/63	
F-GMLJ	Cessna 414	414-0635	I-CCEE, N69826
F-GMLL	Ultramagic H-77 HAFB	77/177	
F-GMLM	Cessna 182F Skylane	18254683	F-BKQM, N3283U
F-GMLN	Cameron N-90 HAFB	4146	
F-GMLO	Robin DR.400/180 Régent	2063	G-FILO
F-GMLQ	Cameron N-77 HAFB	3859	
F-GMLT	Beech 200T Super King Air (Converted from B200 c/n BB-1426 on production line)	BT-34	N56361
F-GMLZ	Robinson R22 Beta	0565	G-IEPF, N2419X
F-GMMA	Pilatus PC-6/B1-H2 Turbo-Porter (Damaged by fire Granville 13.11.03)	714	HA-YDC
F-GMMB	Hughes 269C	129-0874	D-HHUT, SE-HKN
F-GMMD	Cameron O-105 HAFB	3852	
F-GMMF	Chaize JZ.35F16 HAFB	133	
F-GMMG	Cameron N-105 HAFB	4318	
F-GMMJ	Chaize JZ.25F16 HAFB	121	
F-GMMK	Aérospatiale SA.365C2 Dauphin 2	5010	PH-SSK, 5N-BAO, PH-SSK, EC-800, PH-SSK, RP-C1248, PH-SSK, F-GFAP, PH-SSK, 5N-ALZ, PH-SSK, N9006N, F-WZAY
F-GMMO	Lindstrand LBL-69A HAFB	313	
F-GMMR	CEA Jodel DR.1051 Sicile	308	OO-GUY, F-BKIN
F-GMMT	Ultramagic M-90 HAFB	90/15	
F-GMMV	Libert L.3000 HAFB	325-049	
F-GMNA	Raven Europe FS-57A HAFB	E-307	
F-GMNB	Raven Europe S-71A HAFB	E-310	
F-GMND	Raven Europe S-52A HAFB	E-316	
F-GMNE	Raven Europe S-60A HAFB	E-334	
F-GMNF	Raven Europe FS-57A HAFB	E-317	
F-GMNG	Raven Europe RX-8 HAFB	E-328	
F-GMNJ	Raven Europe S-60A HAFB	E-336	
F-GMNM	Raven Europe FS-57A HAFB	E-340	
F-GMNN	Raven Europe FS-57A HAFB	E-346	
F-GMNQ	Raven Europe FS-57A HAFB	E-308	
F-GMNR	Raven Europe FS-57A HAFB	E-354	
F-GMNS	Raven Europe S-52A HAFB	E-301	
F-GMNT	Raven Europe FS-57A HAFB	E-329	
F-GMNU	Raven Europe S-60A HAFB	E-355	
F-GMNV	Raven Europe FS-57A HAFB	E-352	
F-GMNX	Raven Europe S-52A HAFB	E-359	
F-GMNY	Raven Europe RX-7 HAFB	E-366	
F-GMOA	Robin DR.400/120 Petit Prince	978	LX-RCA, F-BVMT
F-GMOH	Dassault Falcon 900	7	3B-XLA, TR-LCJ, F-WWFG
F-GMOI	Cameron A-210 HAFB	4257	
F-GMOJ	Bell 206B Jet Ranger II	1757	N206EN, N90280
F-GMON	Eurocopter EC.135T1	0024	
F-GMOR	Cameron C-60 Concept HAFB	2976	
F-GMOT	Dassault Falcon 50	111	N50AH, VR-CDF, F-GKTV, N297W, F-WZHZ
F-GMOU	Reims/Cessna F152	F15201925	HB-CKR, F-GDOB
F-GMPB	Cessna 182S Skylane	18280217	N2627A
F-GMPH	Piper PA-28-181 Archer II	2843085	
F-GMPJ	American AG-5B Tiger	10170	
F-GMPM	Beech C90B King Air	LJ-1303	(F-GIAO), N80513
F-GMPN	SOCATA MS.893E Rallye 180GT	12264	3A-MPO, F-BUGN
F-GMPO	Beech 200 Super King Air	BB-307	HB-GPG, N703HT, N921S, N23687
F-GMPP	Beech M35 Bonanza	D-6451	(F-GNTP), I- TINE, HB-EBH, D-EBBA
F-GMPV	Mudry CAP.10B	260	
F-GMPY	Piper PA-28-151 Cherokee Warrior	28-7615037	HB-PAK, N9637N
F-GMQA	SOCATA TB-10 Tobago	1594	
F-GMQB	SOCATA TB-10 Tobago	1595	
F-GMQC	SOCATA TB-20 Trinidad	1620	
F-GMQD	SOCATA TB-20 Trinidad	1621	
F-GMQE	SOCATA TB-20 Trinidad	1622	
F-GMQF	SOCATA TB-20 Trinidad	1623	
F-GMQG	SOCATA TB-20 Trinidad	1624	
F-GMQH	SOCATA TB-10 Tobago	1734	
F-GMQI	SOCATA TB-10 Tobago	1735	
F-GMQJ	SOCATA TB-10 Tobago	1736	
F-GMQK	SOCATA TB-20 Trinidad	1737	
F-GMQL	SOCATA TB-20 Trinidad	1738	
F-GMQM	SOCATA TB-20 Trinidad	1739	
F-GMQN	SOCATA TB-20 Trinidad	1740	
F-GMQO	SOCATA TB-20 Trinidad	1741	
F-GMRA	Robin DR.400/140B Dauphin 4	2253	
F-GMRB	Maule MX-7-235 Star Rocket	10119C	
F-GMRC	Robinson R22 Beta	2072	N23269
F-GMRE	Reims/Cessna FR182 Skylane RG	FR18200016	HB-CCG, D-EGTN
F-GMRF	SIAI-Marchetti SF.260C	426/29-061	LAF-426
F-GMRJ	Cameron A-120 HAFB	4477	
F-GMRL	Kubicek BB-26Z HAFB	782	
F-GMRM	Piaggio P.180 Avanti	1027	
F-GMRO	Beech F33A Bonanza	CE-1273	OO-DMC, G-JBET, N15574
F-GMRR	Robin DR.400/140B Dauphin 4	2430	
F-GMRS	SAN Jodel D.140E Mousquetaire	210	Fr.AF
F-GMRT	SIGA MA-26 Pilatre de Rozier HAFB	115	
F-GMRV	Robin DR.400/160 Major	1933	6V-AGB
F-GMSB	Mooney M.20M Model 257 TLS	27-0126	OO-LSD
F-GMSC	Aérospatiale AS.355N Ecureuil 2	5582	
F-GMSE	Piper PA-28RT-201T Turbo Arrow IV	28R-8131042	OO-GCI, N83090
F-GMSH	Hughes 269C	71-1071	D-HDEL, N5045J
F-GMSI	Schweizer 269C-1	0050	
F-GMSJ(2)	Piper PA-22-160 Tri-Pacer	22-6232	CN-TTF
F-GMSL	Robinson R22 Beta	2216	(F-GMBL)
F-GMSN	Cessna 172S Skyhawk SP	172S10826	N62152
F-GMSO	Robinson R44 Raven II	12784	
F-GMSP	Ultramagic M-90 HAFB	90/48	
F-GMST	Sky 220-24 HAFB	103	G-EGUY
F-GMSV	Sky 105-24 HAFB	081	
F-GMTB	Ultramagic M-105 HAFB	105/85	
F-GMTF	Eurocopter EC.135T1	0012	
F-GMTH	Aérospatiale AS.350B Ecureuil	2700	
F-GMTJ	Cessna 510 Citation Mustang	510-0222	
F-GMTL	Ultramagic H-77 HAFB	77/128	
F-GMTP	SIGA Pilatre de Rozier MA-26 HAFB	154	
F-GMTT	Schröder Fire Balloons G HAFB	364	
F-GMTU	Eurocopter EC.135T1	0042	D-HEUR(2)
F-GMUG	Ultramagic M-145 HAFB	145/16	
F-GMUL	CEA Jodel DR.1050 Ambassadeur	15	HB-EUF, F-BJHI
F-GMUP	Cessna F150J	F150-0431	HB-CJE, LX-AVA, D-EBML
F-GMUZ	Piper PA-28RT-201T Turbo Arrow IV	28R-8131143	N8396H
F-GMVS	Pilatus PC-6/B1-H2 Turbo Porter	518	N6251U, PH-OTB
F-GMVT	Robinson R44 Astro	0453	
F-GMXA	Robin DR.400/140B Dauphin 4	2211	
F-GMXB	Robin DR.400/120 Dauphin 2+2	2212	
F-GMXD	Robin DR.400/140B Dauphin 4	2214	
F-GMXE	Robin DR.400/180 Régent	2208	
F-GMXF	Robin DR.400/180 Régent	2218	
F-GMXG	Robin DR.400/120 Dauphin 2+2	2223	
F-GMXH	Robin DR.400/120 Dauphin 2+2	2132	F-WLKJ
F-GMXI	Robin DR.400/160 Major	2220	
F-GMXJ	Robin DR.400/120 Dauphin 2+2	2221	
F-GMXK	Robin HR.200/120B	266	
F-GMXL	Robin HR.200/120B	267	
F-GMXM	Robin DR.400/120 Dauphin 2+2	2226	
F-GMXN	Robin DR.400/180 Régent	2222	
F-GMXO	Robin DR.400/180 Régent	2224	

Regn	Type	c/n	Previous identities
F-GMXP	Robin DR.400/120 Dauphin 2+2	2227	
F-GMXQ	Robin HR.200/120B	272	
F-GMXR	Robin DR.400/120 Dauphin 2+2	2230	
F-GMXS	Robin DR.400/140B Dauphin 4	2233	
F-GMXU	Robin HR.200/120B	277	
F-GMXV	Robin DR.400/180 Régent	2237	
F-GMXX	Robin DR.400/180 Régent	2238	
F-GMXY	Robin DR.400/140B Dauphin 4	2239	

F-GMYA to Z *Reserved for Airbus A321-100s for Air France but not used*

Regn	Type	c/n	Previous identities
F-GMZA	Airbus A321-111	498	D-AVZK
F-GMZB	Airbus A321-111	509	D-AVZN
F-GMZC	Airbus A321-111	521	D-AVZW
F-GMZD	Airbus A321-111	529	D-AVZA
F-GMZE	Airbus A321-111	544	D-AVZF
F-GNAG	Beech A36 Bonanza	E-1653	CP-1566
F-GNAL	Piper PA-32R-300 Cherokee Lance	32R-7680422	N414AL, N9626N
F-GNAM	Piper PA-28-181 Archer II	2890014	N9108Z
F-GNAP	Reims/Cessna F150L	F15000843	F-BUBG
F-GNAR	Beech F33A Bonanza	CE-1735	
F-GNAS	CEA DR.253B Régent	157	CN-TAS, F-BIFA, D-EFCW
F-GNAV	Cameron Z-210 HAFB	11332	
F-GNAZ(2)	Cessna F172H	F172-0590	D-EONI
F-GNBD	Piper PA-28-181 Archer II	28-8090311	HB-PFD, N8216T
F-GNBF	Sud Avn SA.316B Alouette III	1383	A-383
F-GNBH	Eurocopter EC-120BColibri	1307	
F-GNBK	Mooney M.20J Model 201	24-0417	F-GKDC, N201AN
F-GNBM	Robinson R22 Mariner	unkn	
F-GNBN	Piper PA-38-112 Tomahawk	38-79A0582	D-ETAA, N2341K
F-GNBO	Robin DR.400/180 Régent	740	F-OCQQ
F-GNBP	Aérospatiale AS.350BA Ecureuil	1357	(F-GTBP), (F-GMLD), 3A-MLD, F-GCQD
F-GNBT	Aérospatiale AS.350B3 Ecureuil	3095	
F-GNBV	Cameron Z-105 HAFB	10554	
F-GNCA	Cameron N-77 HAFB	3035	
F-GNCB	Thunder AX7-77A HAFB	2202	
F-GNCC	Cessna U206F Stationair	U20602126	F-MJAA, F-BRGI, N71171
F-GNCE	Chaize JZX.18F12 HAFB	118	F-WNCE
F CNCH	Piper PA-28-181 Archer III	2843074	
F-GNCI	SIGA MA-30 Pilatre de Rozier HAFB	139	
F-GNCK	Wassmer WA.51A Pacific	72	HB-DCK
F-GNCL	SOCATA TB-20 Trinidad	960	G-BRIN
F-GNCM	Piper PA-28-161 Cadet	2841292	N9202H
F-GNCN	Ultramagic S-90 HAFB	90-12	
F-GNCS	Thunder AX8-90 SI HAFB	2503	G-DAFL
F-GNCT	Sud Avn SA.318C Alouette Astazou	2265	TJ-AHP, F-GBGX, VR-HGX
F-GNCV	Mudry CAP.10B	303	
F-GNDD	Ultramagic M-77 HAFB	77/189	
F-WNDF	Fournier RF-47	01	
F-GNDG	Diamond DA 20-A1-100 Katana	10073	HB-SDG, N518SS
F-GNDJ	Piper PA-25-235 Pawnee C	25-5323	N8819L
F-GNDL	Mudry CAP.10B	269	
F-GNDM	Firefly 9B-15 HAFB	F9B-2005	
F-GNDP	Robin DR.400/120 Petit Prince	2073	
F-GNDV	Sud Avn SA.318C Alouette Astazou	1988	F-GBDV, F-ZBDB
F-GNDX	Cameron C-80 HAFB	4124	
F-GNDZ	Dassault Falcon 10	17	EC-949, F-GHDZ, N33HL, N27DA, N29966, VH-FFB, OH-FFB, F-WLCS
F-GNEB	Cessna U206F Stationair II	U20603364	OO-SPA, (N8507Q)
F-GNEC	Cameron V-90 HAFB	3022	
F-GNED	Cessna 150J	15070895	C-GOMN, N61220
F-GNEE	Beech C90B King Air	LJ-1328	N90HB, N8250K
F-GNEL	Schröder Fire Balloons G36/24 HAFB	1630	
F-GNEN	Piper PA-28-161 Warrior II	28-8016245	F-ZBEN, D-EINK, N9614N
F-GNEV	Mudry CAP.10B	115	Fr.AF
F-GNEX	Lindstrand LBL-77A HAFB	706	
F-GNFA	Cameron O-77 HAFB	4449	
F-GNFB	Piper PA-14 Family Cruiser	14-133	F-BFFB
F-GNFK	Rockwell S.2R-600 Thrush Commander	1484R	CS-AGA, N8884Q
F-GNGC	Schweizer 269C	S-1632	
F-GNGD	Robin R.3000/160S	135	HB-KCO, F-GGXN
F-GNGE	Ultramagic M-77C HAFB	77/216	
F-GNGF	Cameron O-105 HAFB	3023	F-BUWW
F-GNGG	Mooney M.20J Model 205	24-3216	F-GMOC, N8VH, F-GKBT
F-GNGI	Chaize JZ.30F16 HAFB	185	
F-GNGM	Aérospatiale SA.365N Dauphin 2	6004	I-CIOH, F-WYMI, F-WZJS
F-GNGN	Schröder Fire Balloons G30/24 HAFB	1364	
F-GNGS	Schweizer 269C	S-1389	G-BRFP, N41S
F-GNGT	Ultramagic M-130 HAFB	130/70	
F-GNGU	Grumman G.159 Gulfstream 1	101	4X-ARV, F-GFGU, N300SB, N222H, N716G
F-GNGV	Cameron Z-180 HAFB	11109	(F-GNEU)

(Previously quoted in error as c/n 3364 which is F-GJTT ex HB-BFJ)

Regn	Type	c/n	Previous identities
F-GNHB	SOCATA Rallye 235F	3388	
F-GNHD	SOCATA TB-200 Tobago XL	1459	
F-GNHE	SOCATA Rallye 235F	3389	
F-GNHG	SOCATA TB-200 Tobago XL	1633	F-WNHG, F-GNHG
F-GNHI	Partenavia P.68B	169	G-WICK, G-BGFZ
F-GNHL	SOCATA Rallye 235F	3392	
F-GNHM	SOCATA Rallye 235F	3393	
F-GNHN	SOCATA Rallye 235F	3391	
F-GNHQ	SOCATA TB-9 Tampico	1450	SE-KNT
F-GNHS	SOCATA TB-200 Tobago XL	1761	
F-GNHZ	SOCATA TB-9 Tampico	1185	F-WWRH, F-WNGQ, (D-ENVY(2)), F-WNGQ, (D-ENVY(2))
F-GNII	Airbus A340-313X	399	
F-GNJA	HOAC DV-20 Katana	20011	
F-GNJB	HOAC DV-20 Katana	20076	OE-ADV
F-GNJC	HOAC DV-20 Katana	20031	OE-ASC, N25DV
F-GNJD	HOAC DV-20 Katana	20153	D-ENON
F-GNJE	Diamond DA 20-A1 Katana	10135	N202EC
F-GNJF	Diamond DA 20-A1 Katana	10119	N546SS
F-GNJG	Diamond DA 20-A1 Katana	10225	OE-AID, N225DA
F-GNJH	Diamond DA 20-A1-100 Katana	10090	OE-AAO, N527SS
F-GNJI	Diamond DA 20-A1-100 Katana	10125	OE-AIN, N553SS
F-GNJK	Diamond DA 20-A1-100 Katana	10072	N127MF, N177AA
F-GNJL	Diamond DA 40 Star	40006	OE-KPB, OE-VPB
F-GNJM	Diamond DA 40 Star	40013	OE-DAF, OE-VPN
F-GNJO	Diamond DA 40 Star	40031	
F-GNJP	Diamond DA 40 Star	40038	
F-GNJQ	Diamond DA 40 Star	40040	
F-GNJR	Diamond DA 40 Star	40064	
F-GNJS	Diamond DA 40 Star	40075	
F-GNJT	Diamond DA 40 Star	40076	
F-GNJV(2)	Diamond DA 40 Star	D4.009	
F-GNJX	Diamond DA 40D Star	40026	OE-DLF
F-GNJZ	Diamond DA 40D Star	D4.002	
	(Permit 11.02)		
F-GNLA	Aérospatiale SA.315B Lama	2165/32	F-GJRT, Fr.AF, ALAT
F-GNLG	Fokker F.28-0100	11363	D-ADFE, F-GIOF, PH-EZV
F-GNLH	Fokker F.28-0100	11311	D-ADFB, F-GIOC, PH-EZE
F-GNLM	Aérospatiale AS.350B1 Ecureuil	2021	LN-OGG, SE-JLL, OE-XRS, F-GEOD
F-GNLO	Eurocopter EC.135T1	0005	SE-JUP, D-HQQQ
F-GNLP	Aérospatiale AS.350B Ecureuil	1848	HB-XRO, D-HONY
F-GNLT	Aérospatiale AS.365N Dauphin 2	6069	JA9585
F-GNLV	SIGA MA-26 Pilatre de Rozier HAFB	103	(F-GNBR)
F-GNLZ	Sky 77-24 HAFB	183	
F-GNMA	Beech C90A King Air	LJ-1299	N8253D
F-GNMD	Piper PA-18-150 Super Cub floatplane	18-8209009	TR-LAX, N91243
F-GNML	Agusta-Bell 206B Jet Ranger 3	8402	F-BVEL
F-GNMT	Aero AT-3-R100	AT3-030	
F-GNMU	Aero AT-3-R100	AT3-031	
F-GNMV	Aero AT-3-R100	AT3-032	
F-GNMX	Aero AT-3-R100	AT3-033	
F-GNMY	Aero AT-3-R100	AT3-034	
F-GNMZ	Aero AT-3-R100	AT3-035	
F-GNNA	Robin DR.400/120 Petit Prince	2236	
F-GNNB	Robin HR.200/120B	278	
F-GNND	Robin DR.400/160 Major	2241	
F-GNNE	Robin DR.400/140B Dauphin 4	2247	
F-GNNF	Robin HR.200/120B	280	
F-GNNI	Robin DR.400/120 Dauphin 2+2	2252	
F-GNNJ	Robin DR.400/180R Remo 180	2254	
F-GNNK	Robin DR.400/125	2258	F-WNNK
F-GNNL	Robin DR.400/140B Dauphin 4	2256	
F-GNNM	Robin DR.400/160 Major	2259	
F-GNNN	Robin DR.400/180 Régent	2264	
F-GNNO	Robin HR.200/120B	283	
F-GNNQ	Robin HR.200/120B	284	
F-GNNR	Robin DR.400/180 Régent	2260	
F-GNNS	Robin DR.400/120 Dauphin 2+2	2262	
F-GNNT	Robin HR.200/120B	285	
F-GNNU	Robin DR.400/120 Dauphin 2+2	2263	
F-GNNX	Robin DR.400/120 Dauphin 2+2	2265	
F-GNNY	Robin DR.400/120 Dauphin 2+2	2267	
F-GNNZ	Robin DR.400/120 Dauphin 2+2	2270	
F-GNOE	Beech B300 King Air	FL-183	HB-GJL
F-GNOG	Aérospatiale AS.350B3 Ecureuil	4430	
F-GNOL	Agusta-Bell 47G-2	205	EC-DUK, D-HIPO, IDFAF, Fr.AF
F-GNOM	Cameron O-84 HAFB	4624	
F-GNOO	Cameron Concept C-60 HAFB	3176	
F-GNOP	Schweizer 269C-1	0277	N86G
F-GNOR	Cameron O-105 HAFB	3984	
F-GNOT	SIGA MA-26 Pilatre de Rozier HAFB	157	
F-GNOU	SIGA MA-26 Pilatre de Rozier HAFB	113	
F-GNPC	Ultramagic N-160 HAFB	160/15	
F-GNPJ	Robin DR.400/140B Dauphin 4	2261	
F-GNPP	Chaize JZ.30F16 HAFB	129	
F-GNPU(2)	Piper PA-23-250 Aztec D	27-4209	F-GFPU, N250GM, D-IFMS, N6864Y
F-GNPV	Piper PA-32R-301T Turbo Saratoga SP	32R-8329012	N4291Z
F-GNPY	SNCASE SE.313B Alouette II	1343	ALAT
F-GNPZ(2)	Robinson R22 Beta	2209	CS-HCR, N23466
F-GNQA	Diamond DA 20-A1-80 Katana	10038	N401PF, C-FWKI
F-GNQB	Diamond DA 20-A1-80 Katana	10226	N226DA
F-GNQC	Diamond DA 20-A1-80 Katana	10094	N199D
F-GNQD	Diamond DA 20-A1-80 Katana	10061	C-FCLR, N161MF, C-GKAN
F-GNRA	Raven Europe RX-7 HAFB	E-368	
F-GNRB	Raven Europe RX-8 HAFB	E-369	
F-GNRD	Raven Europe RX-7 HAFB	E-349	
F-GNRF	Raven Europe RX-8 HAFB	E-378	
F-GNRG	Raven Europe RXS-8 HAFB	E-382	
F-GNRI	Raven Europe FS-57A HAFB	E-394	
F-GNRJ	Raven Europe S-55A HAFB	E-391	
F-GNRK	Raven Europe FS-57A HAFB	E-404	
F-GNRS	Raven Europe S-55A HAFB	E-353	
F-GNRV	Raven Europe S-55A HAFB	E-380	
F-GNSA	Beech 58 Baron	TH-1701	
F-GNSB	Beech 58 Baron	TH-1702	
F-GNSC	Beech 58 Baron	TH-1703	
F-GNSD	Beech 58 Baron	TH-1704	
F-GNSE	Beech 58 Baron	TH-1705	
F-GNSF	Beech 58 Baron	TH-1706	
F-GNSG	Beech 58 Baron	TH-1734	
F-GNSH	Beech 58 Baron	TH-1736	
F-GNSI	Beech 58 Baron	TH-1510	N3178P
F-GNSJ	Beech 58 Baron	TH-1515	N3076B
F-GNSK	Beech 58 Baron	TH-2004	N4104H
F-GNSL	Beech 58 Baron	TH-2006	N3216S
F-GNSM	Beech 58 Baron	TH-2033	N51030
F-GNSN	Beech 58 Baron	TH-2062	N61732
F-GNSO	Beech 58 Baron	TH-2080	N62030
F-GNTV	Cameron N-77 HAFB	3900	
F-GNUA	Robinson R22M Mariner	2025M	F-OGUA
F-GNUJ	Robin ATL L	22	EC-FKB, F-GFNU, F-WFNU
F-GNUT	Chaize CS.2200F12 HAFB	168	
F-GNVN	Mudry CAP.10B	278	Fr.AF
F-GNVT(2)	Aérospatiale SA.365N3 Dauphin 2	6772	
F-GNVV	Chaize JZ.25F16 HAFB	126	
F-GNXT	Robin DR.400/140B Dauphin 4	2590	F-WNXT, PH-ASD
F-GNXX	Ultramagic M-105 HAFB	105/37	
F-GNYG	Raven-Europe FS-57A HAFB	E-408	
F-GNYH	Aérospatiale SA.365N3 Dauphin 2	6705	PR-SEJ, F-GOPJ
F-GNYK	Robinson R44 Clipper	0319	N7132M
F-GNYN	Fouga CM.170 Magister	532	Fr.AF
F-GNZA	Morane-Saulnier MS.885 Super Rallye	274	F-BHZA, F-OBZA
F-GNZC	Cessna R182 Skylane RG	R18201109	TR-LZC, (N756ZA)
F-GNZS	SIGA MA-30 Pilatre de Rozier HAFB	153	
F-GNZY	Piper PA-28-181 Archer III	2843536	F-ONZY, N2035, N53572
F-GOAA	Stuttgart K-1000/3-STU Gas Balloon	311	D-OABH(2), D-Kabel
F-GOAG	Pilatus PC-6/B1-H2 Turbo Porter	658	D-FDHP, HB-FDH
F-GOAM	Beech A36 Bonanza	E-2427	3A-MAR, N3084W
F-GOAP	Cessna 172R Skyhawk	17280423	N9540Q
F-GOAS	Mudry CAP.10B	133	F-WQHT, Fr.AF
F-GOAV	Reims/Cessna F152	F15201757	HB-CNT

Registration	Type	C/n	Previous identities
F-GOAZ	SIGA MA-22 Pilatre de Rozier HAFB	105	
F-GOBA	Robinson R44 Raven	1308	
F-GOBC	Cameron A-120 HAFB	4148	OO-BUA, LX-PFX
F-GOBD	Eurocopter EC.135T1	0034	SX-HVD, D-HECU, UAE AF
F-GOBI	Ultramagic S-130 HAFB	130/25	
	(Badly damaged 11.1.10)		
F-GOBJ	Mooney M.20M Model 257 TLS	27-0199	LX-PAL
F-GOBL	Robin ATL L	96	F-GFSP
F-GOBM	Cessna F150G	F150-0215	F-BOQM
F-GOBO	SIGA MA-26 Pilatre de Rozier HAFB	125	
F-GOBP	CASA C.212-CB	10	TC-AOS, EC-CRX, EC-102
	(W/o 22.6.99, still regd)		
F-GOBR(3)	Pilatus PC-6/B2-H4 Turbo Porter	944	
F-GOBS	Chaize JZ.30F16 HAFB	146	
F-GOBU	Lindstrand LBL-90A HAFB	582	D-OCLO, G-CLAG
F-GOBY	Cameron O-90 HAFB	2813	G-OREY
F-GOCB	Mudry CAP.10	28	Fr.AF
F-GOCC	Pilatus PC-6/B1-H2 Turbo Porter	667	SE-IRR, C-GXIJ, N62156, XW-PFQ, HB-FDR
F-GOCD	Chaize JZ.25F16 HAFB	127	
F-GOCE	Cameron N-77 HAFB	3630	
F-GOCF	Beech 200 Super King Air	BB-397	LX-GDB, D-IAMW, F-GFIV, PH-SLG, (N . . . .), PH-SLG, 5N-ALF, PH-SLG
F-GOCG	Cameron A-210 HAFB	10152	
F-GOCM	Aerospool WT-9 Dynamic LSA	DY366/2010	
F-WOCM(2)	Chaize JZ.15S16 HAFB	161	
F-GOCO	Cameron N-90 HAFB	10657	
F-GOCP	Cameron V-90 HAFB	3415	
F-GOCS	SOCATA MS.880B Rallye Club	1579	OO-CCS, F-BSCB
F-GOCV	Aérospatiale SA.341G Gazelle	1010	F-GFFN, D-HMTB, F-GBOP, D-HMTB
F-GODA(2)	Piper PA-18-150 Super Cub	18-4892	TR-LDA, TR-LME, F-OAXG
F-GODC	Cameron V-90 HAFB	3325	
F-GODM	Grob G 115	8067	LX-AVF, (D-EGVV)
F-GODZ	Pilatus PC-6/340 Porter	340	(N340N), ST-AFR, HB-FAR
F-GOEB	Kubicek BB-51Z HAFB	725	
F-GOEC	Robinson R44 Raven II	12513	
F-GOFA	Scintex Piel CP.301C Emeraude	511	F-BJFA
F-GOFD	Chaize JZ.25F16 HAFB	135	
F-GOFE	Robinson R22 Beta	2357	OO-CMQ
F-GOFF	SOCATA TB-20 Trinidad	306	HB-EQS
F-GOFL	Cameron A-160 HAFB	4159	
F-GOFP	Reims/Cessna F152	F15201752	6V-AGK, F-GCNL
F-GOFR	Ultramagic M-105 HAFB	105/104	
F-GOFX	Dassault Falcon 900B	145	VP-CGB, VR-CGB, F-WWFK
F-GOFY	Cameron N-77 HAFB	3052	
F-GOGC	Cameron O-84 HAFB	4379	
F-GOGG	Balloon Works Firefly 7-15 HAFB	F7-1037	
F-GOGH	SOCATA MS.880B Rallye Club	2041	LX-TPL, F-BTPL
F-GOGI	Cameron SS HAFB	"447"	
F-GOGM	Robinson R44 Raven II	10304	N7531S
F-GOGN	CASA C.212-200CB	92	(F-GOBP), TC-AOC
F-GOGO	Cameron A-105 HAFB	3207	
F-GOGR	Gippsland GA-8-TC 320 Airvan		
		GA8-TC 320-08-140	VH-BGM (4)
F-GOGT	Fouga CM.170 Magister	545	Fr.AF
F-GOGV	Cameron Z-250 HAFB	11368	
F-GOIK	SOCATA TB-10 Tobago	2203	
F-GOJE	Cameron N-56 HAFB	645	OO-CLA
F-GOJH	Cameron A-210 HAFB	2451	G-BTCK
F-GOJL	Schweizer 269C	S-1525	D-HHAK
F-GOJM	Cameron O-90 HAFB	3336	
F-GOJO	SIGA MA-35 Pilatre de Rozier HAFB	146	
F-GOJP	Chaize JZ.22F12 HAFB	157	
F-GOJR	Chaize CS.2200F12 HAFB	123	
F-GOJS(2)	Tecnam P.92JS Echo	39	
F-GOKQ	Robin DR.400/120 Dauphin 2+2	2185	3A-MKQ, F-GMKQ
F-GOKZ	Ayres S.2R-T34 Turbo Thrush	6032	EC-FKZ, N4012S, C-GDHB, N4012S
F-GOLA	Thunder AX7-77A HAFB	4230	
F-GOLB	Colt Bibendum 110 SS HAFB	4221	G-BXNR
F-GOLC	Thunder AX10-160 HAFB	4260	
F-GOLH	Eurocopter EC.130B4 Ecureuil	3882	(F-GSNB), F-WWXA
F-GOLK	Aérospatiale AS.350B3 Ecureuil	7194	
F-GOLL	Zlin Z.726K Universal	1069	OK-DXA, OK-YRB, OK-95
F-GOLM	Kubicek BB-34Z HAFB	626	
F-GOLR	Cameron N-90 HAFB	10154	
F-GOLY	Cameron N-77 HAFB	4075	LX-BIL(3)
F-GOMB	Pilatus PC-6/B2-H4 Turbo Porter	819	HB-FMG, FAC-111, HB-FHR
F-GOME	Pilatus PC-6/B2-H2 Turbo Porter	543	N4911
F-GOMH	Holste MH.1521M Broussard	64	Fr.AF
F-GOMJ	Christen Pitts S-2B	5176	EC-EXV, N6081F
F-GOML	Aviat Pitts S-2B	5213	G-GOMD, F-GOMD, N319JM
F-GOMM	Cessna 414	414-0831	I- CCMM, N98745
F-GOMP	Piper PA-28R-201 Arrow	2844001	N91855, N183ND
F-GOMR	Libert L.3000 HAFB	312-036	OO-BYF
F-GOMS	Robin DR.400/120 Dauphin 2+2	2316	
F-GONG	SAN Jodel D.140R Abeille	506	OO-VVN
F-GONH	Robinson R44 Raven II	12556	
F-GONS	Thunder AX7-77 SI HAFB	4204	F-GHHY
F-GONZ	Robinson R22B2 Beta	2693	
F-GOOB	Beech 1900C	UC-153	N153YV, F-GNPM, N153YV
F-GOOD	SOCATA TB-20 Trinidad	2142	
F-GOOF	Robin DR.400/140B Dauphin 4	2561	
F-GOOG	Cameron A-105 HAFB	4645	
F-GOOI	Cameron C-60 Concept HAFB	3160	LX-OOI
F-GOOL	Lindstrand LBL-105A HAFB	463	D-OKEL
F-GOOM	Piper PA-28-151 Cherokee Warrior	28-7515020	F-OGOM, N44739
F-GOOP	Kubicek BB-37N HAFB	17	OO-BBV, OK-3024
F-GOPA	Chaize JZ.30F16 HAFB	128	
F-GOPB(2)	Cameron A-210 HAFB	3672	
F-GOPC	Robinson R22 Mariner	1648M	3A-MBC
F-GOPE	Beech 1900D	UE-103	N82930, (F-GMSA)
F-GOPF	Chaize JZ.30F16 HAFB	163	
F-GOPG	Eurocopter EC.135T1	0062	D-HECP, D-HECK
F-GOPH	Schweizer 269C	S-1416	D-HEHE, N919FH, N7508D
F-GOPI	SIGA MA-26 Pilatre de Rozier HAFB	108	
F-GOPM	Dassault Falcon 20E	302/510	F-WQBM, N84V, OE-GDP(1), D-COMM, F-WRQP
F-GOPP	Chaize JZ.30F16 HAFB	150	
F-GOPR	Piper PA-23-250 Aztec E	27-4727	G-AZWW, N14161
F-GOPS	Cameron A-210 HAFB	10529	
F-GOPV	Robin DR.400/140B Dauphin 4	2621	
F-GOPX	CAARP CAP.10	01	F-ZAGO, F-BOPX
F-GORC	Robin DR.400/120 Dauphin 2+2	2276	
F-GORD	Robin DR.400/180 Régent	2277	
F-GORG	Robin DR.400/140B Dauphin 4	1034	F-BXJE
F-GORH	Robin DR.400/160 Major	2279	
F-GORI	Robin DR.400/120 Dauphin 2+2	2283	
F-GORJ	Robin DR.400 NGL Régent 3	2278	
	(Development aircraft for DR.500 Président)		
F-GORK	Robin DR.400/140B Dauphin 4	2286	
F-GORL	Robin DR.400/140B Dauphin 4	2288	
F-GORM	Robin DR.400/120 Dauphin 2+2	2289	
F-GORN	Robin DR.400/120 Dauphin 2+2	2300	
F-GORO	Robin DR.400/180 Régent	2292	
F-GORP	Robin DR.400/120 Dauphin 2+2	2295	
F-GORQ	Robin DR.400/120 Dauphin 2+2	2297	
F-GORS	Robin HR.200/120B	292	
F-GORT	Robin DR.400/180 Régent	2299	
F-GORU	Robin HR.200/120B	294	
F-GORY	Robin DR.400/180 Régent	2301	
F-GORZ	Robin DR.400/120 Dauphin 2+2	2284	
F-GOSA(2)	General Avia F.22 Pinguino	016	
F-GOSC	Ultramagic M-210 HAFB	210/13	
F-GOSE	Piper PA-46-310P Malibu	4608010	N770MR, N146DS, G-DODS, N9100N
F-GOSF	Beech A36 Bonanza	E-3259	N41020
F-GOSG	Lindstrand LBL-90A HAFB	1212	
F-GOSH	Cameron V-90 HAFB	10223	
F-GOSK	Robinson R22 Beta II	4364	N218AM
F-GOSN	Cessna 152	15285410	C-GOSM, N93126
F-GOSP	Pilatus PC-6/B2-H4 Turbo Porter	699	HB-FEZ
F-GOST	Cessna A152 Aerobat	A1520774	N7587B
F-GOTB	Bell 212	30584	EC-GVV, N58121, HK-3729X, N58121, YS-1003P, N58121, C-FADC, N58121
F-GOTE	Cameron A-180 HAFB	3144	G-TATE
F-GOTG	Cessna U206FStationair	U20603430	I-AMCK, N8574Q
F-GOTO	Airbus A330-323	1021	F-WWYN
F-GOTP	Piper PA-28-180 Cherokee B	28-1689	HB-OWM, N7750W
F-GOTT	Cessna T207 Turbo Skywagon	20700323	
	(Soloy Pac conversion)		
F-GOUD	Cameron Nivea SS HAFB	4576	
F-GOUE	SIGA MA-26 Pilatre de Rozier HAFB	112	
F-GOUF	Grumman AA-5B Tiger	AA5B-0275	LX-OUF(3), G-BDYB
F-GOUM	Mudry CAP.10B	122	Fr.AF
F-GOUP	Mudry CAP.10B	138	Fr.AF
F-GOVA	Robin DR.400/120 Dauphin 2+2	2303	
F-GOVB	Robin DR.400/120 Dauphin 2+2	2304	
F-GOVC	Robin HR.200/120B	297	
F-GOVD	Robin DR.400/180 Régent	2106	G-MRSL, G-BUAP
F-GOVE	Robin DR.400/120 Dauphin 2+2	2307	
F-GOVF	Robin DR.400/120 Dauphin 2+2	2315	
F-GOVG	Robin DR.400/140B Dauphin 4	2314	
F-GOVJ	Robin HR.200/120B	301	
F-GOVK	Robin HR.200/120B	303	
F-GOVL	Robin DR.400/120 Dauphin 2+2	2312	
F-GOVM	Robin DR.400/160 Chevalier	2317	
F-GOVO	Robin DR.400/120 Dauphin 2+2	2322	
F-GOVP	Robin DR.400/180 Régent	2328	
F-GOVQ	Robin DR.400/160 Chevalier	2321	
F-GOVR	Robin DR.400/140B Major 80	1345	I- GUCC, F-GBUC
F-GOVS	Robin DR.400/180 Régent	2323	
F-GOVT	Robin DR.400/140B Dauphin 4	2325	
F-GOVU	Robin DR.400/120 Dauphin 2+2	2326	
F-GOVV	Robin DR.400/180 Remo 180	2331	
F-GOVX	Robin DR.400/120 Dauphin 2+2	2330	
F-GOXA	Ultramagic N-180 HAFB	180/87	
F-GOXD	Robin DR.400/180RP Remorqueur 212	1817	OO-CXD, HB-KBU, D-EAJD
F-GOXN	Mudry CAP.10B	4	F-OGXN, Fr.AF
F-GOXT	Piper J-3C-65 Cub	8927	HB-OXT, F-PFQR, 42-36803
F-GOYE	Pilatus PC-6/B2-H2 Turbo Porter	517	N617SA, XW-PDG, HB-FCI, D-ENLJ
F-GOYF	Aquila AT-01	AT01-158	
F-GOYM	Classic Aircraft Waco YMF-5C	F5C-053	D-EOYM, N50YM
F-GOZZ	Robin DR.400/160 Chevalier	2306	
F-GPAA	Dassault Falcon 20/ CC117 ECM	103/423	G-FRAV, CAF117505, CAF20505, F-WMKH
F-GPAD	Dassault Falcon 20E	280/503	(F-GPAE(2)), G-FRAE, N910FR, I-EDIS, F-WPXK
F-GPAF	Piper PA-34-200T Seneca II	34-7670005	N3953X
F-GPAI	Ultramagic S-90 HAFB	90/17	
F-GPAJ	Christen Pitts S-2B	5286	(N98AV)
F-GPAL	SOCATA Rallye 100ST	2583	F-WQFQ, Fr.Navy 83
F-GPAP	Robin DR.400/180 Régent	741	(F-GLIG), TT-DEA, TL-AAO
F-GPAV	SIGA MA-26 Pilatre de Rozier HAFB	165	
F-GPAZ	Ultramagic S-160 HAFB	160/26	EC-HRD
F-GPBA	Cessna 172N Skyhawk	17272517	C-FEIQ, N5322D
F-GPBB	Piper PA-28-181 Archer III	2843196	N41332, N9503N
F-GPBC	SNCASE SE.313B Alouette II	1635	ALAT
F-GPBD	Cessna 172S Skyhawk SP	172S8574	N327ME
F-GPBG	Cirrus SR20	1502	OY-SNC, N54142
F-GPBI	Piper PA-32R-301T Saratoga II TC	3257098	OK-LAB, OY-JAG, N9515N
F-GPBJ	Lindstrand LBL-77A HAFB	272	
F-GPBL	Cameron C-90 HAFB	10816	
F-GPBV	Cameron Z-105 HAFB	11149	
F-GPCA	Cameron N-105 HAFB	3421	
F-GPCC	Mooney M.20K Model 231	25-0359	N231QJ
F-GPCJ	Fouga CM.170 Magister	369	Fr.AF
F-GPCM	Ultramagic M-77 HAFB	77/395	
F-GPCN	Raven-Europe RX-8 HAFB	E-190	HB-BRK
F-GPCO	Wassmer WA.54 Atlantic	128	D-EGNA(2)
F-GPCP	SNCASE SE.313B Alouette II	1046	ALAT
F-GPCS	Lindstrand LBL-105A HAFB	327	
F-GPCT	Cameron A-120 HAFB	4151	
F-GPCV	SNCASE SE.3130 Alouette II	1384	ALAT
F-GPDA	Durondeau L-300 HAFB	22	
F-GPDB	Cameron A-120 HAFB	4473	
F-GPDF	Aérospatiale AS.350B3 Ecureuil	3290	
F-GPDH	Eurocopter EC.120B Colibri	1334	
F-GPDL	Reims/Cessna F150M	F15001229	TN-ADL, F-BXNK
F-GPDM	Ultramagic S-90 HAFB	90/16	
F-GPDP	Lindstrand LBL-105A HAFB	251	
F-GPDR	SIGA MA-26 Pilatre de Rozier HAFB	100	
F-GPDU	SIGA MA-35 Pilatre de Rozier HAFB	129	
F-GPDV	Kubicek BB-37 HAFB	276	OK-0276
F-GPEB	Cessna 525 CitationJet	525-0533	D-IPMI, (D-IPMM), N5180K

Registration	Type	c/n	Previous identities
F-GPEE	Cameron N-90 HAFB	4573	
F-GPEG	SIGA MA.26 Pilatre de Rozier HAFB	158	
F-GPEH	SIGA MA.26 Pilatre de Rozier HAFB	140	
F-GPEI	Partenavia P.68C	402	N402VP, I-RAIZ
F-GPEK	Boeing 757-236	25808	G-BPEK, (G-BMRM)
F-GPEL	Piper PA-28-161 Warrior II	28-8216114	HB-PIM, D-EFFJ, N9629N
F-GPEM	Ultramagic S-160 HAFB	160/61	
F-GPEP	SNCASE SE.313B Alouette II	1322	ALAT
F-GPEV	Kubicek BB-37N HAFB	423	
F-GPFA	Cessna 172S Skyhawk SP	172S8159	N7280N
F-GPFJ	Ultramagic S-90 HAFB	90/54	
F-GPFL	Eurocopter EC.135T1	0227	
F-GPFN	Schweizer 269C	S-1627	
F-GPFQ	Llopis MA-30 HAFB	172	
F-GPFR	Llopis MA-30 HAFB	173	
F-GPFS	Llopis MA-30 HAFB	174	
F-GPFT	Llopis MA-26 HAFB	175	
F-GPFU	Llopis MA-26 HAFB	176	
F-GPGF	Cameron C-80 Concept HAFB	10416	
F-GPGG	Cameron O-90 HAFB	10074	
F-GPGH	Beech B300 Super King Air	FL-120	D-CBBB(2), N1512H
F-GPGK	Dassault Falcon 900	69	F-GXDZ, HB-JSP, F-WQBM, I-SNAX, F-WWFD
F-GPGL	Dassault Falcon 10	203	I-FJDC, F-WQBM, N54FH, N45JB, XA-TBL, N100CT, VR-CLA, N267FJ, F-WZGJ
F-GPGM	SNCASE SE.3160 Alouette III (Damaged)	1536	A-536
F-GPGO	Cameron 105 Ronald SS HAFB	4047	
F-GPGP	SNCASE SE.3130 Alouette II	1475	ALAT
F-GPGR	Agusta A.109E Power	11222	I-ISBE
F-GPGV	Robinson R44 Raven II	12710	
F-GPHA	Agusta A.109S Grand	22073	G-MUMU
F-GPHB	Balloon Works Firefly 7-15 HAFB	F7-911	
F-GPHD	Robinson R44 Raven II	10829	OK-PHD
F-GPHF(2)	Mooney M.20J Model 205	24-3290	D-ENHF(2)
F-GPHG	SIGA MA-18 Pilatre de Rozier HAFB	104	
F-GPHH	Aérospatiale SA.341J Gazelle (Res .02)	"57"	
F-GPHI	Aérophile 5500 Tethered Gas Balloon	1	
F-GPHL	Robin DR.400/120 Dauphin 2+2	2428	
F-GPHO	Cessna 208 Caravan	20800112	D-FROG(3), SE-LER, D-FILM, N9649F
F-GPHR	Mooney M.20J Model 201	24-0975	D-EEEN, N3882H
F-GPHS	Robinson R44 Astro	0124	
F-GPHT	Reims/Cessna F172M	F17201411	D-EFHT, (D-EOVO)
F-GPHV	Cameron N-77 HAFB	3821	
F-GPHZ	Cessna U206F Stationair	U20602364	OH-CAC, SE-GGI, N2387U
F-GPIC	SIGA MA-26 Pilatre de Rozier HAFB	119	
F-GPIF	Robinson R44 Raven II	10272	
F-GPJA	Beech 58 Baron	TH-1532	G-BPJA, N3102A
F-GPJB	Robin DR.400/120 Dauphin 2+2	2235	
F-GPJD	Beech E90 King Air	LW-328	N551M, N797PA, N1AM
F-GPJE	Aérospatiale SA.365N Dauphin 2	6151	HB-XDJ, F-OHCF, F-WYMB, JA9625
F-GPJK	Ultramagic M-105 HAFB	105/61	OO-BND, D-ONAP
F-GPJL	Robin DR.400/180 Régent	2349	
F-GPJN	Colt 105A HAFB	4783	
F-GPJO	SIGA MA-30 Pilatre de Rozier HAFB	130	
F-GPJR	Robinson R44 Astro	0036	HB-XZX
F-GPJS	Stinson SR-10C Reliant	3-5846	F-BBCS
F-GPKB	Aérophile 5500 Tethered Gas Balloon	3	
F-GPKC	Sud Avn SA.318C Alouette Astazou	2112	ALAT
F-GPKF	Robin DR.400/140B Dauphin 4	2385	(F-GVAB)
F-GPKL	Piper PA-46-350P Malibu Mirage	4622194	
F-GPKQ	Piaggio P.180 Avanti	res	
F-GPKR	Piaggio P.180 Avanti	res	
F-GPKU	Cessna 152	15282981	F-OGKU, N46006
F-GPLA	Aérospatiale SN.601 Corvette	28	F-BTTL, (OO-TTL), F-BTTL, F-WNGX
F-GPLB	SIGA MA-26 Pilatre de Rozier HAFB	122	
F-GPLD	Durondeau L220 HAFB	018	OO-BRS
F-GPLI	SNCASE SE.313B Alouette II	1458	ALAT
F-GPLK	Beech C90A King Air	LJ-1391	3A-MRL, HB-GJE
F-GPLL	SIGA MA-30 Pilatre de Rozier HAFB	155	
F-GPLM	Durondeau L-220 HAFB (Permit 7.00)	13	
F-GPLP	Robin R.3000/160	156	SX-ROB, F-WZZU
F-GPLS	Cameron V-90 HAFB	4439	
F-GPLX	SIGA MA-35 Pilatre de Rozier HAFB	134	
F-GPMA	Airbus A319-113	598	D-AVYD
F-GPMB	Airbus A319-113	600	D-AVYC
F-GPMC	Airbus A319-113	608	D-AVYE
F-GPMD	Airbus A319-113	618	D-AVYJ
F-GPME	Airbus A319-113	625	D-AVYQ
F-GPMF	Airbus A319-113	637	D-AVYT
F-GPMM	Cameron Z-77 HAFB	4719	LX-BMM
F-GPMP	Schröder Fire Balloons G34/24 HAFB	1356	
F-GPMS	Llopis MA-40 HAFB	191	
F-GPNA	Aérospatiale AS.355F1 Ecureuil 2	5207	N5802B
F-GPNB	Schröder Fire Balloons G45/24 HAFB	656	HB-...
F-GPNC	Cirrus SR20	1408	LX-PNC, N5347Y
F-GPNG	Piper J-3C-65 Cub	18282	OE-CUB, N98128, NC98128
F-GPNH	Schröder Fire Balloons G45/24 HAFB	1266	
F-GPNJ	Dassault Falcon 900EX	50	F-WWFS
F-GPOK	Kubicek BB-22 HAFB	46	OK-5056
F-GPOL	Kubicek BB-30Z HAFB	275	OK-0275
F-GPOM	Robin DR.400/120 Dauphin 2+2	2481	
F-GPON	Morane-Saulnier MS.880B Rallye Club	1257	F-BPAN
F-GPOP	Mudry CAP.10B	10	Fr.AF
F-GPOR	Thunder AX8-84 HAFB	853	
F-GPOS	Cameron V-65 HAFB	4271	LX-BOS
F-GPOY	Cessna 172N Skyhawk	17273327	N4705G
F-GPPB	Ultramagic S-90 HAFB	90/44	
F-GPPC	Chaize CS.2200F12 HAFB	184	
F-GPPE	Agusta A.109A	7173	F-WQBP, (F-GRMA), F-WQBP(2), F-GRMK, G-HWBK
F-GPPF	Dassault Falcon 50	65	N1EV, N50LV, D-BFFB, N65HS, N90FJ, N50FJ, F-WZHT
F-GPPH	Bell 206B Jet Ranger II	3661	(F-GNPH), 3A-MLS, C-GWPI, ZK-HSP
F-GPPJ	AIAA/Stampe SV.4C	1113	HB-UPT, F-BAGN(2)
F-GPPM	CAARP CAP.10	1	Fr.AF
F-GPPS	Mudry CAP.231	6	F-WQOK, CN-ABI
F-GPPZ	Schröder Fire Balloons G HAFB	560	

Registration	Type	c/n	Previous identities
F-GPRF	Cessna 152	15284714	N6410M
F-GPRH	Beech 300LW Super King Air	FA-226	F-OHRT, N80907
F-GPRI	Aérophile 5500 Tethered Gas Balloon	014	
F-GPRJ	Raven Europe S-40A HAFB	E-312	
F-GPRL	Robin DR.400/140B Major	2125	HB-KDB
F-GPRO	Pilatus PC-6/B1-H2 Turbo Porter	524	HB-FHL, OO-POF, F-BKRR
F-GPRT	Cessna 152	15279995	OO-GPJ, N757TQ
F-GPSB	Chaize JZ.22F12 HAFB	162	
F-GPSC	Reims/Cessna FA150K Aerobat	FA1500009	HB-CUQ
F-GPSG	Robinson R44 Astro II	12953	
F-GPSK	Cameron N-90 HAFB	4242	
F-GPSL	Cameron V-77 HAFB	4243	
F-GPSM	Schröder Fire Balloons G30/24 HAFB	759	D-OFID
F-GPSO	SOCATA Rallye 100ST	2584	Fr.Navy 84
F-GPSP	Cessna TR182 Turbo Skylane RG	R18200860	LX-GHL, N737NK
F-GPST	Cameron C-80 Concept HAFB	10004	
F-GPTO	Agusta-Bell 47G-2	111	OO-FBL, F-BXXD, (OO-FBL), F-BXXD, ALAT
F-GPUH	SNCASE SE.3130 Alouette II	1523	ALAT
F-GPUM	Aérospatiale SA.330J Puma	1652	HB-XUV, I- EHPD
F-GPUR	Cerva CE.43 Guepard	452	Fr.AF
F-GPUY	Cameron N-105 HAFB	4693	
F-GPVH	Agusta A.109E Power	11607	
F-GPVI	Mudry CAP.10B	21	Fr.AF
F-GPVL	Colt 105A HAFB	10113	HB-QHC
F-GPVN	Aérospatiale SA.365N3 Dauphin 2	6327	D2-ESE, F-GLNU, SX-HID, F-WQDA, ZS-HVI
F-GPVR	Agusta A.109E Power	11071	EI-PEL, HB-ZBK, D-HGHI, N50GH, 5B-CJS
F-GPVT	Cameron TR-70 HAFB	11127	
F-GPXL	Fokker F.28-0100	11290	EI-DFB, F-WQUG, PT-MRZ, PH-TAB, F-OLGA, (PH-TAB), PH-EZP
F-GPYB	Aérospatiale/Alenia ATR-42-512	480	F-WWLZ
F-GPYC	Aérospatiale/Alenia ATR-42-512	484	F-WWEB
F-GPYD	Aérospatiale/Alenia ATR-42-512	490	F-WWLJ
F-GPYF	Aérospatiale/Alenia ATR-42-512	495	F-WWLM
F-GPYK	Aérospatiale/Alenia ATR-42-512	537	F-WWLC
F-GPYL	Aérospatiale/Alenia ATR-42-512	542	F-WWLH
F-GPYM	Aérospatiale/Alenia ATR-42-512	520	F-WWLR
F-GPYN	Aérospatiale/Alenia ATR-42-512	539	F-WWLO
F-GPYO	Aérospatiale/Alenia ATR-42-512	544	F-WWLH
F-GPYY	Beech 1900C-1	UC-115	N115YV
F-GPZP	Cirrus SR22	2811	N849SR

TEMPORARY REGISTRATIONS:

The F-WQ . . series is used mainly for delivery or ferry flights. Some marks are often re-used. At the time of going to press the following blocks are thought to be currently in use:

F-WQB . mainly used by Dassault
F-WQD . , F-WQE . mainly used by Eurocopter
F-WQF . , H . , I . , J . , L . , M . , N . , Q . , S . , U . mainly used by Airbus and SNIAS/EADS
F-WQO . , F-WQP . used by CAP Aviation

Registration	Type	c/n	Previous identities
F-GRAA	Aérospatiale AS.350B3 Ecureuil	4957	
F-GRAC	Aérospatiale AS.350BA Ecureuil	1652	(F-GPUM), SX-HBP
F-GRAD	Piper PA-28-180 Cherokee Challenger	28-7305060	F-OGFW
F-GRAF	Cessna 172R Skyhawk	17280232	(N415ES)
F-GRAG(2)	Piper PA-18-135 Super Cub	18-2539	OO-VVP, OO-HMB, ALAT, 52-6221
F-GRAH	Durondeau L-300 HAFB	023	
F-GRAI	Reims F406 Caravan II	F406-0061	N406CT, F-GURA, F-OGVS, N3121X
F-GRAJ	Pilatus PC-12/45	406	
F-GRAL	Cameron O-105 HAFB	3908	
F-GRAM	Chaize CS.2200F12 HAFB (Wfu)	144	
F-GRAO	Cameron Z-225 HAFB	10537	OO-BZG
F-GRAS	Cameron V-77 HAFB	3930	
F-GRAT	Cameron V-90 HAFB	4771	
F-WRAV	Raven Europe EU-250 Balloon	E-309	
F-GRAZ(2)	Reims/Cessna F406 Caravan II	F406-0013	V5-MAD, ZS-MAD, F-GPRA, F-WWSR, 5Y-JJA, OO-TIY, F-WZDV
F-GRBD	SOCATA TB-9 Tampico Club	1092	EC-EYM, F-GKUK
F-GRBH	SOCATA TB-10 Tobago	1807	
F-GRBJ	SOCATA TB-20 Trinidad	1822	
F-GRBK	SOCATA TB-20 Trinidad	1825	F-WWRB
F-GRBW	SOCATA TB-20 Trinidad	1874	
F-GRBZ	SOCATA TB-20 Trinidad	2105	
F-GRCC	SIGA MA-26 Pilatre de Rozier HAFB	123	(F-GNUI)
F-GRCE	Bell 206B Jet Ranger II	1679	F-BXLG, N90070
F-GRCF	Aérospatiale AS.365N3 Dauphin 2	9000	(F-OHOD), D2-EVO, F-GHYM(3)
F-GRCL	Issoire APM-20 Lionceau	12	
F-GRCM	WDFL Dallach D4 Fascination VLA	1004	D-EALM(3)
F-GRCO	Kubicek BB-37 HAFB	85	OO-BPK
F-GRCP	Pilatus PC-6/B2-H2 Turbo Porter	2071	N392AC, N392CA, OB- . . . ., N5305F
F-GRCS	Balloon Works Firefly F9B-15 HAFB (Permit)	F9B-027	(F-GRCZ)
F-GRCT	Thunder Ax10-180A HAFB	1723	G-PICT
F-GRDA	Issoire APM-20 Lionceau	18	
F-GRDC	Chaize JZ.25F16 HAFB	147	
F-GRDD	Chaize CS.2200F12 HAFB	165	
F-GRDF	Chaize CS.2200F12 HAFB	158	
F-GRDM	Aérospatiale AS.355N Ecureuil 2	5690	
F-GRDN	Bell 206B Jet Ranger II	1172	G-SHCC, N280C
F-GRDO	Cameron Z-105 HAFB	10599	
F-GRDR	Cessna 150L	15074024	G-BSBY, N18662
F-GRDX	Aérophile 5500 Tethered Gas Balloon	4	(F-GSMA)
F-GREC	Hughes 269C	S-1711	N41S
F-GREJ	Robinson R22 Mariner	2710M	I-PECS, SX-HMR
F-GREL	Mooney M.20J Model 205	24-3403	N2138W
F-GREM	Chaize JF.30F16 HAFB	175	
F-GREN	Schröder Fire Balloons 50/24HAFB	886	
F-GREP	Robin DR.400/160 Major	2439	
F-GRES	Holste MH.1521M Broussard	124	Fr.AF
F-GRET	Cessna 510 Mustang	510-0141	LZ-AMA, N141BG
F-GREU	Aerostar S-49A HAFB	S49A-3019	
F-GRGC	Embraer EMB.145EP	145012	PT-SYI
F-GRGD	Embraer EMB.145EP	145043	PT-SZI
F-GRGE	Embraer EMB.145EP	145047	PT-SZM

Reg	Type	c/n	Previous identities
F-GRGF	Embraer EMB.145EP	145050	PT-SZP
F-GRGG	Embraer EMB.145EP	145118	PT-SCU
F-GRGH	Embraer EMB.145EP	145120	PT-SCW
F-GRGI	Embraer EMB.145EP	145152	PT-SED
F-GRGJ	Embraer EMB.145EP	145297	PT-SKO
F-GRGK	Embraer EMB.145EP	145324	PT-SMQ
F-GRGL	Embraer EMB.145EP	145375	PT-SOZ
F-GRGP	Embraer EMB.135ER	145188	PT-SFL
F-GRHB	Airbus A319-111	0985	D-AVYO
F-GRHE	Airbus A319-111	1020	D-AVYX
F-GRHF	Airbus A319-111	1025	D-AVYE
F-GRHG	Airbus A319-111	1036	D-AVYS
F-GRHH	Airbus A319-111	1151	D-AVWK
F-GRHI	Airbus A319-111	1169	D-AVYX
F-GRHJ	Airbus A319-111	1176	D-AVWN
F-GRHK	Airbus A319-111	1190	D-AVYQ
F-GRHL	Airbus A319-111	1201	D-AVWT
F-GRHM	Airbus A319-111	1216	D-AVYF
F-GRHN	Airbus A319-111	1267	D-AVWB
F-GRHO	Airbus A319-111	1271	D-AVWC
F-GRHP	Airbus A319-111	1344	D-AVYQ
F-GRHQ	Airbus A319-111	1404	D-AVYB
F-GRHR	Airbus A319-111	1415	D-AVYF
F-GRHS	Airbus A319-111	1444	D-AVWD
F-GRHT	Airbus A319-111	1449	D-AVWD
F-GRHU	Airbus A319-111	1471	D-AVYR
F-GRHV	Airbus A319-111	1505	D-AVYF
F-GRHX	Airbus A319-111	1524	D-AVWC
F-GRHY	Airbus A319-111	1616	D-AVWG
F-GRHZ	Airbus A319-111	1622	D-AVYO
F-GRID	Cirrus SR20	1347	LX-PHM, N8124E
F-GRIF	Robinson R22 Beta	0526	(F-GPPP), HB-XZZ, N999PS, TG- . . ., N23667
F-GRIL	Guimbal G2 Cabri	1006	
F-GRIM	Chaize JZ.30F16 HAFB	159	
F-GRIP	Robin DR.400/180 Régent	2527	
F-GRIS	Cameron N-90 HAFB	3811	
F-GRIV	Piper PA-28RT-201T Turbo Arrow IV	28R-8031091	D-EIIV(2), LX-FRL, N8190B
F-GRIX	SIGA MA-26 Pilatre de Rozier HAFB	118	
F-GRJG	Canadair CL.600-2B19 Regional Jet	7143	C-FMMQ
F-GRJI	Canadair CL.600-2B19 Regional Jet	7147	C-FZAL, C-FMMY(4)
F-GRJL	Canadair CL.600-2B19 Regional Jet	7221	C-FMNX
F-GRJN	Canadair CL.600-2B19 Regional Jet	7262	C-FMLT
F-GRJQ	Canadair CL.600-2B19 Regional Jet	7321	C-FMLS
F-GRKA	Issoire APM-20 Lionceau	23	
F-GRKB	Piper PA-28RT-201T Turbo Arrow IV	28R-8031042	D-EKKV(2), N600KR, N9585N
F-GRKD	Cessna 152	15279664	F-WRKD, EC-JKR, N757DU
F-GRKP	SAN Jodel D.140E Mousquetaire IV	194	EC-CKP, F-BOPJ
F-GRLA	Piper PA-28-161 Warrior III	2842239	D-EGLI(2), N3206P, N3103A, N4890U
F-GRLE	Reims/Cessna F172M Skyhawk	F17200931	G-BAIX
F-GRLL	Ultramagic S-130 HAFB	130/46	
F-GRLO	SIGA MA-30 Pilatre de Rozier HAFB	111	
F-GRLV	Cameron A-250 HAFB	4821	OO-BUI
F-GRLX	SAN Jodel D.140B Mousquetaire	66	G-ARLX
F-GRMA	Lindstrand LBL-105A HAFB	1165	
F-GRMB	Beech A36 Bonanza	E-2292	F-GRST, F-ODST, D-EBVS(2)
F-GRMF	Schweizer 269C	S-1395	D-HEYN, HB-XUP
F-GRMR	Robin DR.400/160 Major	2429	
F-GRMT	Robinson R22B2 Beta	3629	
F-GRNT	Swearingen SA.226T(B) Merlin IIIB	T-312	F-WRNT, N84GA, N90NB, (N52SJ), N90NB
F-GRNY	Aérophile 5500 Tethered Gas Balloon	2	
F-GROA	Robin DR.400/180 Régent	2423	
F-GROK	Cameron N-65 HAFB	4654	
F-GROM	Cameron N-77 HAFB	4838	
F-GROS	Cameron N-77 HAFB	4677	
F-GROT	Mudry CAP.10B	11	Fr.AF
F-GROU	Mudry CAP.10B	24	F-WQCM, Fr.AF
F-GROV	Piper PA-28RT-201T Turbo Arrow IV	28R-8131009	N8277H
F-GROY	Ultramagic S-90 HAFB	90/41	
F-GRPA	Mudry CAP.232	06	
F-GRPB	Cameron N-105 HAFB	4861	
F-GRPC	Nord 1101 Noralpha	113	F-BFNJ, F-ZJPS
F-GRPF	Robin DR.400/140B Dauphin 4	2620	
F-GRPG	Ultramagic S-90 HAFB	90/60	
F-GRPI	Aérospatiale/Alenia ATR-72-212A	722	F-WWEZ
F-GRPJ	Aérospatiale/Alenia ATR-72-212A	724	F-WWEI
F-GRPL	Ultramagic M-90 HAFB	90/46	
F-GRPN	Issoire APM-20 Lionceau	17	
F-GRPP	Cameron Z-250 HAFB	10885	
F-GRPV	Diamond DA 20-A1 Katana	10036	(F-GYBQ(1)), N236BR, C-GKAN
F-GRPX	Aérospatiale/Alenia ATR-72-212A	734	F-WWEO
F-GRPY	Aérospatiale/Alenia ATR-72-212A	742	F-WWEC
F-GRPZ	Aérospatiale/Alenia ATR-72-212A	745	F-WWEF
F-GRRB	Aérospatiale SA.315B Lama	2475	CNET/F-SEBO
F-GRRC	Aérospatiale SA.365N1 Dauphin 2	6306	I-SINS
F-GRRE	Issoire APM-20 Lionceau	5	
F-GRRF	Issoire APM-20 Lionceau	6	
F-GRRG(2)	Issoire APM-20 Lionceau	7	
F-GRRH	Issoire APM-20 Lionceau	8	
F-GRRI	Issoire APM-20 Lionceau	9	
F-GRRK	Issoire APM-20 Lionceau	10	
F-GRRL	Issoire APM-20 Lionceau	11	
F-GRRN	Issoire APM-20 Lionceau	15	
F-GRRO	Issoire APM-20 Lionceau	14	
F-GRRP	Issoire APM-20 Lionceau	16	
F-GRRR	Robinson R22M2 Mariner	3073M	
F-GRRT	Mudry CAP.10B	116	(F-GIPQ), Fr.AF
F-GRRV	Issoire APM-20 Lionceau	21	
F-GRRX	Issoire APM-20 Lionceau (Rebuild of Moniot APM-20 c/n 1)	13	
F-GRRZ	Issoire APM-20 Lionceau	22	
F-GRSF	SIGA MA-22 Pilatre de Rozier HAFB	106	
F-GRSL	Mudry CAP.231	17	HB-MSR, F-GGYX
F-GRSM	Cameron N-90 HAFB	2594	OO-BFT
F-GRSP	CEA DR.250/160 Capitaine	13	OO-BOY
F-GRSQ	Airbus A330-243	501	
F-GRTA	Euravial RF-47	3	F-WWNG
F-GRTC	Aquila AT-01	AT01-111	
F-GRTE(2)	Aérospatiale AS.350B3 Ecureuil	3978	
F-GRTJ	Christen A-1 Husky	1158	I-CGCC
F-GRTT	SIGA MA-26 Pilatre de Rozier HAFB	164	
F-GRUB	Pilatus PC-6/ B2-H4 Turbo Porter	940	HB-FMJ
F-GRUI	Lindstrand LBL-69A HAFB	761	
F-GRVB	Robinson R44 Astro	0042	D-HTUT
F-GRVC	Aérospatiale SA.341G Gazelle	1164	JRV126, JRV12013
F-GRVD	Ultramagic M-105 HAFB	105/86	
F-GRVJ	Robinson R44 Raven II	11644	EI-VIC
F-GRVL	Tecnam P.2002-JF Sierra	061	
F-GRVN	Piper J-3C-65 Cub	11343	F-BHEB, F-OAEB, 43-30052
F-GRVR	Extra EA.300/200	011	N3FD
F-GRVZ	Pilatus PC6/B2-H4 Turbo Porter	901	
F-GRXA	Airbus A319-111	1640	D-AVYJ
F-GRXB	Airbus A319-111	1645	D-AVYC
F-GRXC	Airbus A319-111	1677	D-AVWF
F-GRXD	Airbus A319-111	1699	D-AVYG
F-GRXE	Airbus A319-111	1733	D-AVWT
F-GRXF	Airbus A319-111	1938	D-AVWG
F-GRXJ	Airbus A319-115LR	2456	D-AVYX
F-GRXK	Airbus A319-115LR	2716	D-AVYX
F-GRXL	Airbus A319-111	2938	D-AVWV
F-GRXM	Airbus A319-111	2961	D-AVYI
F-GRXO to GRXZ	Reserved for Airbus A319s for Air France		
F-GRYF	Schröder Fire Balloons G26/24 HAFB	1348	
F-GRYL	Beech 1900D	UE-301	N22161
F-GRYP	SAN Jodel D.140E Mousquetaire IV	206	Fr.AF
F-GRYR	Raven Europe S-55A HAFB	E-357	
F-GRZE	Canadair CL.600-2C10 Regional Jet 701	10032	C-GIBL
F-GRZF	Canadair CL.600-2C10 Regional Jet 701	10036	C-GIBQ
F-GRZG	Canadair CL.600-2C10 Regional Jet 701	10037	C-GIBT
F-GRZH	Canadair CL.600-2C10 Regional Jet 701	10089	C-GIBI
F-GRZI	Canadair CL 600-2C10 Regional Jet 701	10093	C-G . . .
F-GRZJ	Canadair CL 600-2C10 Regional Jet 701	10096	C-G . . .
F-GRZK	Canadair CL 600-2C10 Regional Jet 701	10198	C-G . . .
F-GRZL	Canadair CL 600-2C10 Regional Jet 701	10245	C-G . . .
F-GRZM	Canadair CL 600-2C10 Regional Jet 701	10263	C-G . . .
F-GRZN	Canadair CL 600-2C10 Regional Jet 701	10264	C-G . . .
F-GRZO	Canadair CL 600-2C10 Regional Jet 701	10265	C-G . . .
F-GRZP to GRZZ	Reserved for Brit'air / Hop!		
F-GSAD	SOCATA TB-9 Tampico	1087	OO-GLA, F-GLAI
F-GSAE	Lindstrand LBL-180A HAFB	1259	
F-GSAJ	Cessna 172RG Cutlass RG	172RG0168	F-OJAB, F-GLOA, N6336R
F-GSAK	SAAB S.91B Safir	91229	F-BHAK
F-GSAM	Lindstrand LBL-120A HAFB	448	
F-GSAO	SOCATA TB-20 Trinidad	1801	
F-GSAS	Aérospatiale AS.355F1 Ecureuil 2	5159	N5796B
F-GSAT	Pilatus PC-6/B2-H4 Turbo Porter	904	HB-FLC
F-GSAV	SIGA MA-18 Pilatre de Rozier HAFB	161	
F-GSBA	Robin DR.400/140B Dauphin 4	2342	
F-GSBB	Robin DR.400/120 Dauphin 2+2	2334	
F-GSBC	Robin DR.400/180 Régent	2340	
F-GSBD	Robin DR.400/180 Régent	2329	
F-GSBE	Robin DR.400/120 Dauphin 2+2	2337	
F-GSBF	Robin DR.400/120 Dauphin 2+2	2335	
F-GSBI	Robin DR.400/120 Dauphin 2+2	2352	
F-GSBJ	Robin DR.400/140B Dauphin 4	2350	
F-GSBK	Robin DR.400/120 Dauphin 2+2	2351	
F-GSBL	Robin HR.200/120B	314	
F-GSBM	Robin DR.400/180 Régent	2353	
F-GSBN	Robin DR.400/120 Dauphin 2+2	2355	
F-GSBO	Robin DR.400/180 Régent	2358	
F-GSBP	Robin DR.400/120 Dauphin 2+2	2356	
F-GSBQ	Robin DR.400/120 Dauphin 2+2	2374	
F-GSBR	Robin DR.400/140B Major	2344	
F-GSBS	Robin DR.400/140B Major	2357	
F-GSBT	Robin DR.400/120 Dauphin 2+2	2359	
F-GSBU	Robin DR.400/140B Dauphin 4	2369	
F-GSBV	Robin DR.400/180 Régent	2364	
F-GSBX	Robin DR.400/180 Régent	2366	
F-GSBY	Robin HR.200/120B	319	
F-GSBZ	Robin DR.400/180 Régent	2362	
F-GSCB	Piper PA-18-135 Super Cub (Quoted with f/n 18-4577 as c/n)	18-4006	TC-CUB, Turkish AF, 54-2606
F-GSCC	Mudry CAP.10B	127	F-WQCN, Fr.AF
F-GSCD	SAN Jodel D.140E Mousquetaire IV	180	D-EDHL
F-GSCF	SOCATA TBM-850	383	
F-GSCG	Cameron Z-140 HAFB	11241	
F-GSCH	Schröder Fire Balloons G HAFB	480	
F-GSCI	SIGA MA-30 Pilatre de Rozier HAFB	121	
F-GSCP	Cessna 172R Skyhawk	17280170	N9890F
F-GSCR	Cessna 525B CitationJet CJ3	525B-0264	N5244W
F-GSCT	Kubicek BB-26 HAFB	503	
F-GSDB	Piper PA-28R-200 Cherokee Arrow	28R-35039	TC-BVFT, TU-TFA, N9339N
F-GSDE	Diamond DA.40D Star	D4.112	HB-SDE
F-GSDG	Aérospatiale AS.350B3 Ecureuil	4036	HB-ZHE
F-GSDJ	Grumman G.164A Agcat	1295	N9635
F-GSDR	Ultramagic M-77 HAFB	77/130	
F-GSDV	Commander Aircraft 114B	14601	N6018F
F-GSEC	Cameron Z-105 HAFB	10880	
F-GSED	Robinson R44 Raven II	10205	
F-GSEE	Robin DR.400/140B Dauphin 4	2360	
F-GSEH	Aérospatiale AS.350B3 Ecureuil	3827	
F-GSEM	Schröder Fire Balloons G30/24 HAFB	1070	
F-GSES	Lindstrand LBL-90A HAFB	1207	
F-GSEU	Airbus A330-243	635	F-WWYO
F-GSEV	Piper PA-28-181 Archer II	2890091	OO-MTW, N9151Z
F-GSEY	Worner NL-STU/12000 Gas Balloon	1092	G-JSEY
F-GSFF	Cameron C-80 Concept HAFB	4608	
F-GSFG	Cameron N-105 HAFB	4828	
F-GSFM	Cameron N-90 HAFB	4923	
F-GSFO	Reims/Cessna F152	F15201774	D-EGNW
F-GSFP	CEA Jodel DR.1051-M1 Sicile Record	626	F-BMEM, F-OCEM
F-GSFR	Cameron N-77 HAFB	3783	
F-GSFV	Chaize CS.3000F16 HAFB	116	
F-GSGB	Kubicek BB-22E HAFB	841	
F-GSGD	Robin DR.400/160 Major	2504	
F-GSGE	Cameron Z-120 HAFB	10628	
F-GSGF	Kubicek BB-45 HAFB	52	OO-BBT, OK-6052
F-GSGG	Aérospatiale SA.332C Super Puma	2033	HB-XVY, N5795P, N300US, N5795P
F-GSGL	Cessna 525B CitationJet CJ3	525B-0178	N5203S

Registration	Type	c/n	Previous identities
F-GSGM	Colt 160A HAFB	11250	
F-GSGO	Reims/Cessna F152 II	F15201977	OO-CLF, G-BMTL
F-GSGS	Piper PA-46-350P Malibu Mirage	4622154	D-EBPA, N92421
F-GSGV	Cameron Z-120 HAFB	10943	
F-GSHB	Robinson R22M Mariner	2101M	3A-MJM
F-GSHC	Piper PA-34-220TSeneca III	3433156	N300AN, N9174N
F-GSHK	Airbus A320-231	326	SU-RAB, F-WWDK
F-GSHO	Raven-Europe S-60A HAFB	E-304	D-OOHO(1)
F-GSHS	Robinson R66	0637	
F-GSIA	Lindstrand LBL-105A HAFB	935	G-CCIA
F-GSID	Cameron O-120 HAFB	3420	HB-QAI
F-GSIN	Beech 200 Super King Air	BB-239	N517JM, G-WWHL, G-BLAE, I- ELCO, N517JM, N17649
F-GSIP	Aerostar S-49A HAFB	S49A-3085	HB-BUM
F-GSIR	Thunder AX8-105SII HAFB	3591	
F-GSIS	SIGA MA-35 Pilatre de Rozier HAFB	133	
F-GSIT	SIGA MA-30 Pilatre de Rozier HAFB	124	
F-GSIU	Robin R.2000/120	312	
F-GSIX	Piper PA-32-260 Cherokee Six	32-59	HB-OLZ, N3313W
F-GSJB	Ultramagic S-105 HAFB	105/59	
F-GSJC	Piper PA-34-220TSeneca III	3433159	D-GIPA
F-GSJD	Beech 58P Baron	TJ-74	G-PAPU, G-NIPU, N1PU, N313A, N1PU, N1PT, N1899L
F-GSJF	Sky 77-24 HAFB	128	
F-GSJH	Sky 120-24 HAFB	007	G-BWJR
F-GSJO	Cameron Z-120 HAFB	10359	
F-GSJT	Aérospatiale AS.350BA Ecureuil	1192	F-ODLL, (N215EH), N3602V
F-GSKX	Robin DR.400/120 Dauphin 2+2	2415	
F-GSLB	Cameron C-80 Concept HAFB	4910	
F-GSLM	Kubicek BB-20E HAFB	638	
F-GSLT	Robinson R44 Astro	0470	
F-GSLZ	Dassault Falcon 100	208	F-WQBJ, N71M, I-OANN, F-GELS, F-WZGO
F-GSMA	Aérophile 5500 Tethered Gas Balloon	5	
	(Originally allocated to c/n 4 which is F-GRDX)		
F-GSMB	Eurocopter EC.135T1	0031	(F-GTIL), VP-CEO
F-GSMD	Piper PA-28-181 Archer III	2843066	N9282N
F-GSME	SIGA MA-26 Pilatre de Rozier HAFB	138	
F-GSMG	Cessna 525B CitationJet CJ3	525B-0230	N5068F
F-GSMK	Reims/Cessna F150K	F15000534	HB-CUR
F-GSMM	Cameron C-70 Concept HAFB	10112	
F-GSMR	Piper PA-34-200T Seneca II	34-8070208	D-GORS, N8195L
F-GSMU	Eurocopter EC.135T1	0043	
F-GSMV	Robin DR.400/180 Régent	2361	
F-GSNA	Dassault Falcon 900EX	145	
F-GSNC	Cameron C-80 Concept HAFB	11325	
F-GSNG	Cameron C-80 Concept HAFB	4911	
F-GSOE	Aérospatiale AS.350B3 Ecureuil	9100	
F-GSOI	Lindstrand LBL-90A HAFB	945	G-CCOI
F-GSOL	Cameron N-90 HAFB	3769	
F-GSOR	Cameron Z-180 HAFB	11304	
F-GSPA	Boeing 777-228ER	29002	
F-GSPB	Boeing 777-228ER	29003	
F-GSPC	Boeing 777-228ER	29004	
F-GSPD	Boeing 777-228ER	29005	
F-GSPE	Boeing 777-228ER	29006	
F-GSPF	Boeing 777-228ER	29007	
F-GSPG	Boeing 777-228ER	27609	
F-GSPH	Boeing 777-228ER	28675	
F-GSPI	Boeing 777-228ER	29008	
F-GSPJ	Boeing 777-228ER	29009	
F-GSPK	Boeing 777-228ER	29010	
F-GSPL	Boeing 777-228ER	30457	N50281
F-GSPM	Boeing 777-228ER	30456	
F-GSPN	Boeing 777-228ER	29011	
F-GSPO	Boeing 777-228ER	30614	
F-GSPP	Boeing 777-228ER	30615	
F-GSPQ	Boeing 777-228ER	28682	
F-GSPR	Boeing 777-228ER	28683	
F-GSPS	Boeing 777-228ER	32306	
F-GSPT	Boeing 777-228ER	32308	
F-GSPU	Boeing 777-228ER	32309	
F-GSPV	Boeing 777-228ER	28684	
F-GSPX	Boeing 777-228ER	32698	
F-GSPY	Boeing 777-228ER	32305	
F-GSPZ	Boeing 777-228ER	32310	
F-GSQA	Boeing 777-328ER	32723	N5017Q
F-GSQB	Boeing 777-328ER	32724	N5018Q
F-GSQC	Boeing 777-328ER	32727	
F-GSQD	Boeing 777-328ER	32726	
F-GSQE	Boeing 777-328ER	32851	
F-GSQF	Boeing 777-328ER	32849	N50217
F-GSQG	Boeing 777-328ER	32850	N5028Y
F-GSQH	Boeing 777-328ER	32711	
F-GSQI	Boeing 777-328ER	32725	N60697
F-GSQJ	Boeing 777-328ER	32852	
F-GSQK	Boeing 777-328ER	32845	N5017Q
F-GSQL	Boeing 777-328ER	32853	
F-GSQM	Boeing 777-328ER	32848	
F-GSQN	Boeing 777-328ER	32960	
F-GSQO	Boeing 777-328ER	32961	
F-GSQP	Boeing 777-328ER	35676	
F-GSQR	Boeing 777-328ER	35677	
F-GSQS	Boeing 777-328ER	32962	
F-GSQT	Boeing 777-328ER	32846	
F-GSQU	Boeing 777-328ER	32847	N5022E
F-GSQV	Boeing 777-328ER	32854	
F-GSQX	Boeing 777-328ER	32963	N5014K
F-GSQY	Boeing 777-328ER	32638	
F-GSQZ	*Was reserved for Boeing 777-328 for Air France*		
F-GSRA	Robin DR.400/140B Dauphin 4	2372	
F-GSRB	Robin R.2160 Alpha Sport	320	
F-GSRC	Robin DR.400/120 Dauphin 2+2	2370	
F-GSRE	Robin DR.400/160 Chevalier	2386	
F-GSRF	Robin DR.400/120 Dauphin 2+2	2390	
F-GSRG	Robin DR.400/120 Dauphin 2+2	2373	
F-GSRH	Robin R.2160 Alpha Sport	325	
F-GSRI	Robin DR.400/160 Chevalier	2394	
F-GSRJ	Robin DR.400/120 Dauphin 2+2	2380	
F-GSRK	Robin DR.400/120 Dauphin 2+2	2395	
F-GSRL	Robin DR.400/180 Régent	2368	
F-GSRN	Robin DR.400/120 Dauphin 2+2	2396	
F-GSRO	Robin DR.400/120 Dauphin 2+2	2377	
F-GSRP	Robin DR.400/120 Dauphin 2+2	2397	
F-GSRQ	Robin DR.400/120 Dauphin 2+2	2400	
F-GSRR	Robin DR.400/140B Dauphin 4	2393	
F-GSRS	Robin DR.400/120 Dauphin 2+2	2378	
F-GSRT	Robin DR.400/180 Régent	2399	
F-GSRU	Robin DR.400/120 Dauphin 2+2	2404	
F-GSRX	Robin HR.200/120B	330	
F-GSRY	Robin HR.200/120B	327	
F-GSRZ	Robin HR.200/120B	328	
F-GSSA(2)	Lindstrand LBL-77AHAFB	748	
F-GSSB	Thunder AX7-77A HAFB	4065	
F-GSSC	Robin DR.400/120 Dauphin 2+2	2338	
F-GSSD	Cirrus SR20	1858	N913SR
F-GSSF	Chaize JZ.40F16 HAFB	154	(F-GPSF)
F-GSSJ	Diamond DA 40D Star	D4.113	PH-XJB, OE-DJB
F-GSTA	Airbus A300-608ST Beluga "1"	001/655	F-WAST
F-GSTB	Airbus A300-608ST Beluga "2"	002/751	F-WSTB
F-GSTC	Airbus A300-608ST Beluga "3"	003/765	F-WSTC
F-GSTD	Airbus A300-608ST Beluga "4"	004/776	F-WSTD
F-GSTE	Schröder Fire Balloons G HAFB	679	
F-GSTF	Airbus A300-600ST Beluga "5"	005/796	F-WSTF
F-GSTH	Aérospatiale AS.355N Ecureuil 2	5649	
F-GSTJ	Fournier/Euravial RF.47	02	F-WWTJ
F-GSTL	FFA AS.202/15-1 Bravo	130	HB-HGB(2)
F-GSTM	Mudry CAP.10B	128	Fr.AF
F-GSTT	Robin DR.400/120 Dauphin 2+2	1906	G-BPTT
F-GSTY	Robin DR.400/120 Dauphin 2+2	1876	D-EDTY
F-GSTZ	Mauls MX-7-180 Star Rocket	11045C	OO-LVL
F-GSUP	Mudry CAP.10B	7	Fr.AF
F-GSUR	Robin DR.400/120 Dauphin 2+2	2524	
F-GSUV	Piper PA-28-161 Cherokee Warrior II	28-8116128	G-BIUV, N9506N
F-GSVA	Piper PA-28-181 Archer II	28-8190111	HB-PFX, N8309K
F-GSVB	Ultramagic T-180 HAFB	180/83	
F-GSVI	SIGA MA-26 Pilatre de Rozier HAFB	110	
F-GSVL	Robin DR.400/120 Dauphin 2+2	2379	PH-SVL
F-GSVT	Cirrus SR22	2071	N981SR
F-GSYB	Grumman G.164B Ag-Cat	7408	EC-EIF, N3629B
F-GSYD	Fouga CM.170 Magister	455	F-WSYD, Fr.AF
F-GSYI	Ultramagic M-145 HAFB	145/56	
F-GSYJ	Ultramagic N-180 HAFB	180/56	
F-GSYK	Ultramagic S-105 HAFB	105/137	
F-GSYL	Cameron N-105 HAFB	4509	
F GSYM	Ultramagic M-105 HAFB	105/141	
F-GSYN	Ultramagic M-105 HAFB	105/142	
F-GSYP	Cameron C-90 HAFB	10754	G-CDPC
F-GSYR	Cameron Z-120 HAFB	10609	
F-GSYS	Piper PA-34-220T Seneca V	3449091	G-CBOB, N9ZB, (G-CBOB), N61HB, N9500N
F-GSYT	Robinson R22 Beta	1480	OY-HFE
F-GSYZ	Aérospatiale AS.350B3 Ecureuil	7543	
F-GSZA	SOCATA TB-200 Tobago XL	1597	F-OHDL
F-GSZB	SOCATA TB-20 Trinidad	1886	
F-GSZC	SOCATA TB-10 Tobago	1823	
F-GSZD	SOCATA TB-20 Trinidad	1904	
F-GSZF	SOCATA TB-20 Trinidad	1910	
F-GSZG	SOCATA TB-20 Trinidad	1437	CS-DAM, F-GLFJ
F-GSZH	SOCATA TB-10 Tobago	1928	
F-GSZJ	SOCATA TB-20 Trinidad	1227	F-WHGQ
	(Formerly T-tail version)		
F-GSZM	SOCATA TB-9 Tampico GT	2011	
F-GSZN	SOCATA TB-20 Trinidad	2037	
F-GSZS	SOCATA TB-20 Trinidad	2138	
F-GSZU	SOCATA TB-9 Tampico	2146	
F-GSZV	SOCATA TB-9 Tampico Sprint GT	2143	
F-GSZX	SOCATA TB-9 Tampico	1833	5N- . . ., F-OIDF
F-GTAD	Airbus A321-111	777	D-AVZI
F-GTAE	Airbus A321-211	796	D-AVZN
F-GTAH	Airbus A321-211	1133	D-AVZD
F-GTAJ	Airbus A321-211	1476	D-AVZP
F-GTAK	Airbus A321-211	1658	D-AVZP
F-GTAM	Airbus A321-211	1859	D-AVZY
F-GTAO	Airbus A321-211	3098	D-AVZQ
F-GTAP	Airbus A321-211	3372	D-AVZK
F-GTAQ	Airbus A321-211	3399	D-AVZQ
F-GTAS	Airbus A321-211	3419	D-AVZE
F-GTAT	Airbus A321-211	3441	D-AVZH
F-GTAU	Airbus A321-211	3814	D-AVZE
F-GTAX	Airbus A321-231	3930	D-AZAD
F-GTAY	Airbus A321-212	4251	D-AZAG
F-GTAZ	Airbus A321-212	4901	D-AZVG
F-GTBA	Aérospatiale AS.350B2 Ecureuil	2577	F-OGRY
F-GTBB	Aerostar S-49A HAFB	S49A-3031	D-OAUR, D-Aurora
F-GTBF	Hughes 269C	77-0616	G-BXHI, G-GBHH, TF-HRH, TF-HHO, N45CD, N9250F, (N51CC)
F-GTBI	WDFL Dallach D4 Fascination VLA	1003	D-EBBI(5)
F-GTBJ	CEA Jodel DR.1050M1 Sicile	575	HB-EEM
F-GTBK	Ultramagic M-130 HAFB	130/68	
F-GTBL	Ultramagic T-180 HAFB	180/53	
F-WTBM	SOCATA TBM-700	001	
	(Listed erroneously as F-WTBN in DGAC records and marks therefore re-allocated as in next entry)		
F-GTBM(2)	Cameron C-70 Concept HAFB	10250	
F-GTBO	de Havilland DH.82A Tiger Moth	3810	G-AOBO, N6473
F-GTBP	Cameron Z-180 HAFB	10855	
F-GTBR	Robin DR.500/200i Président	0008	
F-GTBS	Thunder AX7-77A HAFB	4292	
F-GTBY	Partenavia P.68B	43	F-BXLI
F-GTCG	Chaize JZ22F12 HAFB	145	
F-GTCH	Aérospatiale AS.365N3 Dauphin 2	6710	
F-GTCI	Cirrus SR20	1768	N953SR
F-GTCK	Robinson R22M2 Mariner	3332M	G-MIKG
F-GTCM	Schweizer 300CB	0072	N69A
F-GTCP	Cameron N-90 HAFB	10271	
F-GTCS	Piper PA-32-301T Saratoga II TC	3257038	N9503N
	(Written-off 25.3.04)		
F-GTCY	Piper PA-32-260 Cherokee Six	32-7700021	PH-LMR, (PH-TES), N38982
F-GTDB	Wassmer WA.52 Europa	78	D-EINA
F-GTDD	Robin DR.400/180 Régent	2398	
F-GTDE	Reims/Cessna F172L	F17200841	PH-ADW, OK-CKB, PH-ADW
F-GTDJ	Grumman G.164A Ag Cat	1515	N50600, 7T-VUA, N8760H
F-GTDM	Cessna U206F Stationair	U20602340	OO-HPD, (F-GNMS), OO-HPD, (PH-TXM), OO-HPD, N88JP, (N2095U)
F-GTDN	SIGA MA-40 Pilatre de Rozier HAFB	109	D-OTAB(2)

Regn	Type	C/n	Previous identities
F-GTDO	Robin R.2160 Alpha Sport	310	OO-TDA
F-GTDP	Llopis MA-30 HAFB	180	
F-GTDR	Robinson R22M2 Mariner	2604M	(F-GRLB)
F-GTDX	Eurocopter EC.225LP Super Puma II	2752	
F-GTDZ	Pilatus PC-6/B2-H4 Turbo Porter	693	ZK-JMP, VH-REL, A14-693, HB-FEE
F-GTEB	Robinson R22B2 Beta	3517	
F-GTEE	Robinson R44 Raven II	12760	
F-GTEG	Aerostar S-66A HAFB	S66A-3057	HB-BRE
F-GTEJ	Robinson R44 Raven II	12624	
F-GTEK	Robinson R44 Raven II	12530	
F-GTEN	Aérospatiale SA.365N1 Dauphin 2	6229	T7-ETL, I-AGFA
F-GTES	Ultramagic M-77 HAFB	77/340	
F-GTET	Cameron Z-150 HAFB	10246	
F-GTEZ	Piper PA-28-181 Archer II	2890165	D-ETAP, N9195B
F-GTFA	Robin DR.400/160 Chevalier	2376	
F-GTFB	Cessna 510 Citation Mustang	510-0335	
F-GTFC	Tecnam P.2002-JF Sierra	036	
F-GTFD	Cameron A-210 HAFB	3181	G-TRAV, PH-GET, G-TRAV
F-GTFI	SOCATA TB-200 Tobago XL	2013	G-HEVN, D-EVHN(3)
F-GTFN	Wassmer WA.40 Super IV	45	HB-DCA
F-GTGB	Eurocopter EC.120B Colibri	1186	
F-GTGE	Cameron N-105 HAFB	4749	
F-GTGF	Cameron Z-315 HAFB	11350	
F-GTGL	Lindstrand LBL-105A HAFB	764	OO-BHV
F-GTGM	Robinson R22 Beta II	3859	N74534
F-GTGV	Raven RXS-8 HAFB	RXS8-3102	
F-GTHA	Pilatus PC-6/B2-H4 Turbo Porter	939	HB-FMF, N939WA, HB-FMF
F-GTHB	Robin DR.300/108 2+2	510	OO-FWB, F-BSLB
F-GTHC	Diamond DA 20-A1 Katana	10309	N309DA
F-GTHE	Aviat Pitts S-2B	5164	D-ETHE, N5KE
F-GTHF	Aérospatiale AS.350B3 Ecureuil	4514	
F-GTHP	Cameron Z-160 HAFB	11310	OO-BMJ(2)
F-GTHR	Aérospatiale AS.350B2 Ecureuil	2629	HB-XQU, OE-XHK
F-GTIC	Aquila AT-01	AT01-133	
F-GTIE	Aérospatiale AS.350B3 Ecureuil	3410	
F-GTIF	Ultramagic N-250 HAFB	250/40	
F-GTIM	Lindstrand LBL-69A HAFB	491	
F-GTIN	Cameron Z-120 HAFB	11830	
F-GTIS	Wörner FKP-380/STU Gas Balloon	6206	
F-GTIV	Cameron N-77 HAFB	4606	
F-GTJA	Ultramagic M-105 HAFB	105/107	
F-GTJB	Cameron A-250 HAFB	3928	
F-GTJC	Cessna 172S Skyhawk SP	172S8277	N7273H
F-GTJD	Cameron N-105 HAFB	11008	
F-GTJG	Ultramagic M-90 HAFB	90/112	
F-GTJH	Cameron Z-120 HAFB	10587	
F-GTJR	Robin DR.400/120 Dauphin 2+2	2459	
F-GTJS	Robin DR.400/180R Remorqueur	1464	HB-EQE
F-GTKA	Aérospatiale AS.355N Ecureuil 2	5141	SX-HIA, F-GOUT, N5793Y
F-GTKB	Eurocopter EC.135T1	0084	C-01, D-HECR
F-GTKJ	Beech 1900D	UE-348	N23406
F-GTLA	Aérospatiale AS.332C1e Super Puma	2938	
F-GTLC	Ultramagic N-210 HAFB	210/08	
F-GTLJ	Wassmer WA.54 Atlantic	107	D-EFWL
F-GTLL	SNCASE SE.313B Alouette II	1181	ALAT
F-GTLV	Kubicek BB-45 HAFB	93	OO-BDH
F-GTMA	Chaize JZ.25F12 HAFB	148	
F-GTMB	SNCASE SE.3160 Alouette III	1121	F-ZBFL, ALAT
F-GTME	CEA DR.253B Régent	179	F-OCQE
F-GTMF	Ultramagic M-130 HAFB	130/40	
F-GTMG	Libert L-3000 HAFB	329-053	
F-GTML	Piper PA-32-301T Turbo Saratoga SP	32R-8029109	CN-TKA, F-GDQA, OO-JSM, N82542
F-GTMP	Robin DR.400/120 Dauphin 2+2	2444	
F-GTMR	Robin DR.500/200i Président	20	
F-GTMT	Cameron Z-180 HAFB	11513	
F-GTMV	Cessna 152	15283134	D-ETMV, N46890
F-GTNC	Cirrus SR22	1701	N692SR
F-GTNI	Schröder Fire Balloons G 30/24 HAFB	906	D-OTNI
F-GTNM	Gippsland GA-8-TC 320 Airvan	GA8-TC 320-10-153	VH-CNQ (2)
F-GTNV	Cessna 172S Skyhawk SP	172S9963	N788MB
F-GTNY	Schröder Fire Balloons Gas Bottle SS HAFB	680	
F-GTOA	Robinson R22M2 Mariner	3097M	N723RC
F-GTOC	Aquila AT-01	AT01-136	
F-GTOD	Dassault Falcon 10	155	N725PA, (N110TP), D-CIEL, (N220FJ), F-WZGC
F-GTOL	Ultramagic M-145 HAFB	145/35	
F-GTOO	Piper PA-28-181 Archer III	2843320	N5959B, N4167K
F-GTOU	Cameron C-80 HAFB	4177	
F-GTOZ	Lindstrand LBL-105A HAFB	565	G-ICOZ
F-GTPA	Robin DR.400/180 Régent	2405	
F-GTPC	Robin DR.400/120 Dauphin 2+2	2402	
F-GTPD	Robin DR.400/120 Dauphin 2+2	2417	
F-GTPE	Robin DR.400/160 Major	2413	
F-GTPF	Robin DR.400/120 Dauphin 2+2	2416	
F-GTPG	Robin DR.400/160 Major	2409	
F-GTPH	Robin DR.400/180 Régent	2410	
F-GTPI	Robin DR.400/140B Dauphin 4	2422	
F-GTPJ	Robin DR.400/140B Dauphin 4	2432	
F-GTPK	Robin DR.400/140B Dauphin 4	2421	
F-GTPL	Robin DR.400/160 Major	2408	
F-GTPM	Robin DR.400/120 Dauphin 2+2	2425	
F-GTPN	Robin DR.400/180 Régent	2435	
F-GTPO	Robin HR.200/120B	340	
F-GTPP	Robin DR.400/160 Major	2411	
F-GTPR	Robin HR.200/120B	333	
F-GTPS	Robin DR.400/120 Dauphin 2+2	2427	
F-GTPT	Robin DR.400/180 Régent	2440	
F-GTPU	Robin DR.400/160 Major	2424	
F-GTPV	Robin DR.400/180 Régent	2438	
F-GTPX	Robin DR.400/180 Régent	2436	
F-GTPY	Robin DR.400/120 Dauphin 2+2	2437	
F-GTPZ	Robin DR.400/160 Major	2403	
F-GTQB	SOCATA TB-20 Trinidad	2095	N221H
F-GTQC	SOCATA TB-20 Trinidad	2130	F-OIUH
F-GTQF	SOCATA TB-10 Tobago	2094	
F-GTQG to F-GTQZ	*Reserved for SOCATA 11.02*		
F-GTRB	Fairchild Swearingen SA-227AC Metro III	AC-519	EC-GJV, F-GHVE, HB-LNE, N31083
F-GTRC	Kubicek BB-22 HAFB	278	OK-0278
F-GTRD	Aérospatiale AS.350B2 Ecureuil	9063	
F-GTRE(2)	Aérospatiale AS.355N Ecureuil 2	9610	
F-GTRG	Robinson R44 Raven II	10154	N75284
F-GTRH	Cameron Z-225 HAFB	11412	
F-GTRL	Wassmer Jodel D.112 Club	1002	OO-GLR, F-BIXO
F-GTRP	Cameron Z-225 HAFB	10676	
F-GTRT	Zlin Z.526AFS Akrobat Special	1227	SP-CSW
F-GTRY	Cessna 525 CitationJet	525-0359	
F-GTTA	Llopis MA-26 HAFB	177	
F-GTTD	Cessna 150M	15077651	OO-FSF, G-LFSF, G-BSRC, N6337K
F-GTTG	Stinson 108-1 Voyager	108-1-719	N8719K, NC8719K
F-GTTS	Robinson R44 Astro	0547	I-TTAM
F-GTTU	Schröder Fire Balloons G22/24 HAFB	1206	
F-GTUI	Boeing 747-422	26875	N186UA
F-GTUT	Robinson R44 Raven II	11874	
F-GTVB	SOCATA TB-10 Tobago	431	HB-KAJ
F-GTVC	Beech 1900D	UE-349	N23430
F-GTVF	Cameron Z-77 HAFB	11452	
F-GTVY	Robin DR.400/140B Dauphin 4	2019	F-GJZN
F-GTXA	Llopis MA-30 HAFB	170	
F-GTXR	Kubicek BB-70Z HAFB	761	
F-GTXU	Robin DR.400/120 Dauphin 2+2	2419	
F-GTXV	Robin DR.400/120 Dauphin 2+2	2420	
F-GTYA	SOCATA TB-20 Trinidad	2150	(F-GMQP)
F-GTYB	SOCATA TB-20 Trinidad	2153	
F-GTYC	SOCATA TB-20 Trinidad	2154	
F-GTYD	SOCATA TB-20 Trinidad	2157	
F-GTYE	SOCATA TB-20 Trinidad	2159	
F-GTYF	SOCATA TB-20 Trinidad	2162	
F-GTYG	SOCATA TB-20 Trinidad	2163	
F-GTYH	SOCATA TB-20 Trinidad	2170	
F-GTYI	SOCATA TB-20 Trinidad	2185	
F-GTYJ	SOCATA TB-20 Trinidad	2186	
F-GTYK to F-GTYS	*Reserved for S.E.F.A.*		
F-GTYT	Cameron N-90 HAFB	4461	
F-GTYU to F-GTYZ	*Reserved for S.E.F.A.*		
F-GTZC	Robin DR.500/200i Président	22	
F-GTZD	Robin DR.400/160 Major	2442	
F-GTZE	Robin HR.200/120B	342	
F-GTZH	Robin DR.400/120 Dauphin 2+2	2455	
F-GTZI	Robin DR.400/120 Dauphin 2+2	2443	
F-GTZK	Robin DR.400/120 Dauphin 2+2	2451	
F-GTZL	Robin DR.400/160 Major	2460	
F-GTZN	Robin HR.200/120B	351	
F-GTZO	Robin DR.400/120 Dauphin 2+2	2458	
F-GTZP	Robin DR.400/140B Dauphin 4	2461	
F-GTZQ	Robin DR.400/180 Régent	2446	
F-GTZR	Robin DR.400/140B Dauphin 4	2463	
F-GTZS	Robin DR.400/120 Dauphin 2+2	2464	
F-GTZT	Robin DR.400/180 Régent	2452	
F-GTZU	Robin DR.400/120 Dauphin 2+2 (Dismantled .03)	2486	
F-GTZX	Robin DR.400/180 Régent	2469	
F-GTZY	Robin DR.400/160 Major	2445	
F-GTZZ	Robin DR.400/180 Régent	2462	
F-GUAB	SOCATA TB-10 Tobago	1721	
F-GUAC	SOCATA TB-10 Tobago	1720	
F-GUAD	Sud Avn SA.316B Alouette III	1611	F-ZBDL, XC-FAR
F-GUAF	SOCATA TB-20 Trinidad	2181	
F-GUAG	Cameron C-90 HAFB	11034	
F-GUAN	Cessna FA150K Aerobat	FA1500019	OH-CBV
F-GUAO	Cessna 402B	402B1003	SP-KFT, N87147
F-GUAR	Piper PA-28-161 Cherokee Warrior II	28-7816576	PH-ANI, N31685
F-GUAS	Pilatus PC-6/B2-H2 Turbo Porter	557	N184L, ST-AGR, N184L
F-GUAT	Mudry CAP.10B	8	Fr.AF
F-GUAY	Cameron N-105 HAFB	4694	
F-GUBC	Embraer EMB.145MP	145556	PT-SZP
F-GUBE	Embraer EMB.145MP	145668	PT-SFC
F-GUBF	Embraer EMB.145MP	145669	PT-SFD
F-GUBG	Embraer EMB.145MP	14500890	PT-SYD
F-GUBH to F-GUBS	*Reserved for Regional Airlines /Hop!*		
F-GUBT	Grumman AA-1A Trainer	AA1A-0354	HB-UBT
F-GUCC	Cameron C-60 Concept HAFB	3880	LX-OIO
F-GUCD	Wassmer CE.43 Guepard	466	LX-ACD, F-BXCD
F-GUCE	Robinson R44 Astro	0551	
F-GUCK	Lindstrand LBL-120A HAFB	1148	
F-GUCP	Robinson R22B2 Beta	3374	EI-CZI, N71849
F-GUCT	Cessna F172H	F172-0489	D-ENFA(3)
F-GUDB(2)	Robinson R44 Clipper	1274	OO-PFB
F-GUDF	Cameron V-90 HAFB	2853	OO-BCL
F-GUDI	Robinson R44 Raven II	11483	
F-GUDJ	Piper PA-36-285/400 Pawnee Brave	36-7560109	N9993P
F-GUDM	Lindstrand LBL-120AHAFB	760	
F-GUDV	Aquila AT-01	AT01-131	
F-GUEA	Embraer EMB.145MP	145342	PT-SNI
F-GUEP	Aérospatiale AS.355F2 Ecureuil 2	5296	SX-BHT, F-WZFL
F-GUER	Ultramagic M-160 HAFB	160/52	
F-GUET	Piper PA-28-161 Cadet	2841158	G-KDET, N91842, (SE-KIR)
F-GUFB	Eurocopter EC.135T1	0087	D-HEDY, CC-CFG, D-HECG
F-GUFL	Robinson R44 Raven	1798	
F-GUFR	SIGA MA-30 Pilatre de Rozier HAFB	116	
F-GUFZ	SOCATA Rallye 235E	13022	F-ZAGN
F-GUGA	Airbus A318-111	2035	D-AUAD
F-GUGB	Airbus A318-111	2059	D-AUAF
F-GUGC	Airbus A318-111	2071	D-AUAG
F-GUGD	Airbus A318-111	2081	D-AUAH
F-GUGE	Airbus A318-111	2100	D-AUAI
F-GUGF	Airbus A318-111	2109	D-AUAJ
F-GUGG	Airbus A318-111	2317	D-AUAA
F-GUGH	Airbus A318-111	2344	D-AUAF
F-GUGI	Airbus A318-111	2350	D-AUAG
F-GUGJ	Airbus A318-111	2582	D-AUAE
F-GUGK	Airbus A318-111	2601	D-AUAF
F-GUGL	Airbus A318-111	2686	D-AUAA
F-GUGM	Airbus A318-111	2750	D-AUAB
F-GUGN	Airbus A318-111	2918	D-AUAB
F-GUGO	Airbus A318-111	2951	D-AUAD
F-GUGP	Airbus A318-111	2967	D-AUAF
F-GUGQ	Airbus A318-111	2972	D-AUAG
F-GUGR	Airbus A318-111	3009	D-AUAJ
F-GUGS to F-GUGZ	*Reserved for Airbus A318s for Air France*		

Reg	Type	C/n	Prev ID
F-GUHA	Robinson R22B2 Beta	3888	
F-GUHM	Cirrus SR22	3883	N613MT
F-GUHR	Robinson R22 Beta II	3910	I-NOZZ, N74689
F-GUIG	Lindstrand LBL-180A HAFB	932	
F-GUII	Llopis MA-22 HAFB	223	
F-GUIX	Cessna 172R Skyhawk	17280207	N9402F
F-GUJB	Robinson R44 Raven	0826	D-HALR
	(W/o 18.2.11)		
F-GUJD	Aérospatiale AS.350B3 Ecureuil	4569	
F-GUJE	Christen Pitts S-2B	5201	N141JH
F-GUJF	Sud Avn SA.318C Alouette Astazou	2096	ALAT
F-GUJH	Cameron Z-315 HAFB	11101	
F-GUJL	SIGA MA-22 Pilatre de Rozier HAFB	126	
F-GUKA	Grob G 120A	85035	
F-GUKB	Grob G 120A	85036	
F-GUKC	Grob G 120A	85037	D-EFRB(4)
F-GUKD	Grob G 120A	85038	D-EFRJ
F-GUKE	Grob G 120A	85039	
F-GUKF	Grob G 120A	85040	D-E...
F-GUKG	Grob G 120A	85041	
F-GUKH	Grob G 120A	85042	
F-GUKI	Grob G 120A	85043	
F-GUKJ	Grob G 120A	85044	
F-GUKK	Grob G 120A	85045	
F-GUKL	Grob G 120A	85046	
F-GUKM	Grob G 120A	85047	
F-GUKN	Grob G 120A	85048	
F-GUKO	Grob G 120A	85049	
F-GUKP	Grob G 120A	85050	
F-GUKQ	Robin DR.400/120 Dauphin 2+2	2453	
F-GUKR	Grob G 120A	85051	
F-GUKS	Grob G 120A	85052	
F-GUKT to F-GUKX	*Reserved for Grob G 120As for ECATS*	.06	
F-GULC	Robin HR.100-210	unkn	
F-GULF	Eurocopter EC.120B Colibri	1082	
F-GULI	Cameron N-90 HAFB	10888	
F-GULL	Robin DR.400/180 Régent	2475	
F-GULP	Aérospatiale AS.350BA Ecureuil	1737	D-HFSC(2), SE-HNF
F-GULY	Beech C90A King Air	LJ-1610	OY-LSA, N44406
F-GUMB	Tecnam P.2002-JF Sierra	055	
F-GUMC	Ultramagic N-300 HAFB	300/12	
F-GUMD	Piper PA-28-181 Archer III	2843243	N9524N
F-GUME	Beech 1900D	UE-371	CS-DOC, N371UE, HC-CAO, N31712
F-GUMF	Cameron Z-120 HAFB	10953	
F-GUMG	Cameron Z-133 HAFB	11137	
F-GUMI	Mudry CAP.10B	126	Fr.AF
F-GUMP(2)	Schröder Fire Balloons G33/24 HAFB	748	OO-BCO
F-GUMQ	Kubicek BB-26 HAFB	105	OO-BMQ, OM-8006
F-GUMR	Piper PA-32-301 Saratoga	32-8106040	(I- . . . .), F-GIMR, TJ-AHF, F-OBNX, N8334B
F-GUNS	Extra EA.300/200	1035	D-EVMM(2), OO-VMW
F-GUOB	Boeing 777-228F	32965	N5023Q
F-GUOC	Boeing 777-228F	32966	
F-GUOE	Boeing 777-228F	unkn	
	(Was res, Air France Cargo)		
F-GUPC	Robinson R22B2 Beta	3461	
F-GUPE	Beech 1900D	UE-248	N10882
F-GUPI	Robin DR.400/140B Dauphin 4	2519	
F-GUPK	Schröder Fire Balloons G60/24 HAFB	1491	
F-GUPL	Diamond DA 40D Star	D4.164	OE-KPL
F-GUPM	Diamond DA 42 Twin Star	42.252	OE-FPM (2), OE-VPW, OE-VPI
F-GUPP	Piper PA-28-161 Warrior III	2842155	N5349V, N9528N
F-GUPS	Cameron A-120 HAFB	10248	
F-GUPV	Robin DR.400/180 Régent	2478	(F-GNVP)
F-GUPY	Maule M4-180V	47005T	D-EUPY
F-GURB	Robinson R44 Raven II	10393	
F-GURC	Aero AT-3-R100	AT3-016	
F-GURD	Aero AT-3-R100	AT3-017	
F-GURG	Aero AT-3-R100	AT3-036	
F-GURI	Aero AT-3-R100	AT3-039	
F-GURJ	SNCASE SE.313B Alouette II	1741	ALAT
F-GURL	Kubicek BB-26 HAFB	904	
F-GURQ	Aero AT-3-R100	AT3-014	(SP-KUC)
F-GURT	Aero AT-3-R100	AT3-004	SP-TPF, (N55XT), (SP-TPF)
F-GURU	Sky 105-24 HAFB	152	
F-GURV	Aero AT-3-R100	AT3-015	(SP-KOX)
F-GUSA	Robinson R44 Raven II	12037	
F-GUSB	Ultramagic M-77C HAFB	77/237	
F-GUSE	Aérospatiale AS.350B3 Ecureuil	9046	
F-GUSF	SIAI-Marchetti SF.260WL	440	BF8451, LARAF-440, I-RAIG
F-WUSH	Ballon Helium Globe Trott'Air 2	001	
F-GUSK	Aviat A-1B Husky	2441	N907F
F-GUSN	Piper PA-32R-301 Saratoga II HP	3213090	N309TM, TC-DHD
F-GUSP	Robinson R22 Mariner	2316M	CN-HTU, LQ-BLP
F-GUST	Cessna 421B Golden Eagle	421B0968	OE-FMZ, D-IGPZ, G-BLAZ, ZS-JOL, N87534
F-GUSY	Aviat A-1B Husky	2442	N60FC
F-GUTB	Cessna 182S Skylane	18280745	N2459F
F-GUTM	Firefly Balloons F9 HAFB	F9-2006	
F-GUTO	Piper PA-28-151 Cherokee Warrior	28-7615020	N4495X
F-GUTS	Cessna 208 Caravan Amphibian	20800225	I-SEAB, N225WA, N8DB, N248A, (N844SB), N248A, HB-CJY, (N9821F)
F-GUTT	Cameron O-84 HAFB	1989	HB-BHR
F-GUVA	Diamond DA 40TDi Star	D4.012	
F-GUVB	Diamond DA 40D Star	D4.014	
F-GUVC	Diamond DA 40D Star	D4.015	
F-GUVD	Diamond DA 40D Star	D4.016	
F-GUVF	Diamond DA 40D Star	D4.019	
F-GUVH	Diamond DA 40D Star	D4.063	
F-GUVJ	Diamond DA 40D Star	D4.119	OE-VPY
F-GUVL	Diamond DA 40D Star	D4.110	
F-GUVM	Diamond DA 40D Star	D4.139	
F-GUVN	Diamond DA 40D Star	D4.140	
F-GUVO	Diamond DA 40D Star	D4.141	
F-GUVP	Diamond DA 40D Star	D4.149	
F-GUVQ	Diamond DA 40D Star	D4.131	
F-GUVS	Diamond DA 40D Star	D4.291	OE-VPU
F-GUVT	Diamond DA 40D Star	D4.288	OE-VPU
F-GUVU	Diamond DA 40D Star	D4.306	OE-VPU
F-GUVV	Diamond DA 40D Star	D4.311	OE-VPT
F-GUVX	Diamond DA 40D Star	D4.316	

Reg	Type	C/n	Prev ID
F-GUVY, Z	*Reserved for SCAP Aerosport for Diamond DA 40TDi s*		
F-GUXA	Robin DR.400/120 Dauphin 2+2	2467	
F-GUXB	Robin DR.400/160 Major	2468	
F-GUXC	Robin DR.400/120 Dauphin 2+2	2465	
F-GUXD	Robin DR.400/140B Dauphin 4	2484	
F-GUXF	Robin DR.400/120 Dauphin 2+2	2473	
F-GUXH	Robin DR.400/160 Major	2483	
F-GUXI	Robin DR.400/120 Dauphin 2+2	2476	
F-GUXJ	Robin DR.400/140B Dauphin 4	2489	
F-GUXK	Robin DR.400/180 Régent	2488	
F-GUXL	Robin DR.400/120 Dauphin 2+2	2491	
F-GUXN	Robin DR.400/140B Dauphin 4	2493	
F-GUXO	Robin DR.400/180 Régent	2496	
F-GUXP	Robin DR.400/180 Régent	2487	
F-GUXQ	Robin DR.400/120 Dauphin 2+2	2497	
F-GUXR	Robin DR.400/180 Régent	2498	
F-GUXS	Robin HR.200/120B	354	
F-GUXU	Robin R.2120U	368	
F-GUXV	Robin DR.400/120 Dauphin 2+2	2507	
F-GUXX	Robin R.2120U	347	F-WZZX
F-GUXZ	Robin DR.500/200i Président	34	
F-GUYA	Robin DR.400/160 Major	2492	
F-GUYC	Schröder Fire Balloons G 30/24 HAFB	964	
F-GUYS	Cameron C-90 Concept HAFB	10528	
F-GUZE	Aérospatiale AS.355N Ecureuil 2	5548	N548JR, XA-BBE, F-WYML
F-GUZS	SAN Jodel D.150 Mascaret	22	G-BHEZ, F-BLDO
F-GUZY	Wassmer Jodel D.120 Paris-Nice	118	(F-GUZI), G-BGZY, F-BIQU
F-GUZZ	Beech D-17S	4823	G-BUXU, N9113H, BuA.33024
F-GVAD	Robin DR.400/140B Major	1717	HB-KAZ
F-GVAF	Robinson R44 Raven II	10234	G-SBRB
F-GVAG	Cameron Z-160 HAFB	10567	
F-GVAH	Robinson R22M2 Mariner	3191M	
F-GVAK	Robin DR.400/180 Régent	2456	
F-GVAL	Ultramagic S-90 HAFB	90/29	
F-GVAM	Lindstrand LBL-69A HAFB	752	
F-GVAO	Ultramagic N-180 HAFB	180/84	
F-GVAQ	Aquila AT-01 (A-210)	AT01-104	F-WQQS, D-EZUM(1)
F-GVAR	Aérospatiale SA.365N1 Dauphin 2	6256	JA6694, N29TH, N6024P
F-GVAS	SNCASE SE.313B Alouette II	1060	ALAT
F-GVAT	Ultramagic N-180 HAFB	210/12	(F-GVAA)
F-GVAV	Robin DR.400/180R Remo 180	2466	
F-GVAX	Cessna 152	15279954	HA-WAX, N757RX
F-GVAY	Cessna 172N Skyhawk	17273917	(F-OVAY), (F-GKAY), CS-DAU, N7572J
F-GVAZ	Piper PA-28-181 Archer II	2890185	N158ML, HB-PNA
F-GVBA	SIGA MA-35 Pilatre de Rozier HAFB	145	
F-GVBB	SIGA MA-26 Pilatre de Rozier HAFB	142	
F-GVBC	Robinson R22B2 Beta	3139	(F-GUDB)
F-GVBD	Kubicek BB-30Z HAFB	484	
F-GVBE	Ultramagic S-130 HAFB	130/45	
F-GVBH	Robinson R22B2 Beta	3425	N71938
F-GVBJ	Swearingen SA.227TT Merlin IIIC	TT-512A	D-IHBL, N123GM, N927DC, N13JV, N3108G
F-GVBK	Raytheon 390 Premier I	RB-73	N107WR, (N107YR), N107WR, N371CE, N371CF
F-GVBL	Cameron C-80 HAFB	11044	
F-GVBM	Piper PA-23-150 Apache	23-618	(F-GXMA), I-GEMA, N6467C, YV-P-EPY, YV-T-ATP, N10F
F-GVBO	Mudry CAP.10B	271	I-IZAN
F-GVBV	Cessna 172S Skyhawk SP	172S10830	N6216M
F-GVCA	Lindstrand LBL-69A HAFB	790	
F-GVCB	SNCASE SE.313B Alouette II	1539	CN-HTL, ALAT
F-GVCC	Aquila AT-01	AT01-148	
F-GVCF	Cameron Z-90 HAFB	11091	
F-GVCG	Cameron Z-77 HAFB	10874	
F-GVCH	Lindstrand LBL-90A HAFB	697	
F-GVCL	Piper PA-32R-300 Cherokee Lance	32R-7780491	OY-CKU, N38966
F-GVCM	Ultramagic H-77 HAFB	77/174	(F-GUCM)
F-GVCO	Chaize JZ.35F16 HAFB	212	
F-GVCP	Reims/Cessna F152	F15201615	D-EGUX
F-GVDB	Cameron Z-90 HAFB	4945	
F-GVDC	Cameron Z-77 HAFB	10673	
F-GVDE	Kubicek BB-22 HAFB	143	
F-GVDF	Ultramagic M-77 HAFB	77/297	
F-GVDI	Robinson R22 Beta	2348	EC-GII, HA-MIP, N83090
F-GVDL	SIGA MA-30 Pilatre de Rozier HAFB	127	
F-GVDM	Cameron N-90 HAFB	10149	
F-GVDO	Piper PA-32R-301T Saratoga II TC	3257380	OM-ZAI, G-SYDE, N31064
F-GVDS	Chaize CS.2200F24 HAFB	218	
F-GVDT	SIGA MA-26 Pilatre de Rozier HAFB	149	
F-GVDV	Jodel D.140E Mousquetaire IV	193	D-EKGG
F-GVDY	Llopis Balloons MA-22 HAFB	225	
F-GVEA	Kubicek BB-22 HAFB	1232	
F-GVEB	Ultramagic S-105 HAFB	105/150	
F-GVEC	Bell 206B Jet Ranger II	2748	(F-GUEC), CN-HTB, F-GJLJ, YU-HCI, N27668
F-GVEF	Bell 412	33078	I-SARB
F-GVEN	Cameron V-90 HAFB	3182	G-YVET
F-GVEP	Beech C90 King Air	LJ-683	N269SC, PT-MPC, N1583L, (N711BE), N1583L
F-GVEV	Robinson R44 Raven II	10908	G-EVEV, G-FAKE
F-GVFA	Cessna 172R Skyhawk	17280868	N2448L
F-GVFE	Aérospatiale AS.365N Dauphin 2	6219	N29EH, HL9234
F-GVFF	Mudry CAP.231	23	CN-ABN
F-GVFM	Chaize CS.2200F24 HAFB	205	
F-GVFP	Aquila AT-01	AT01-119	
F-GVGC	Chaize JZ.40F16 HAFB	199	
F-GVGD	Cameron Z-120 HAFB	11322	
F-GVGG	Cameron A-160 HAFB	11482	
F-GVGH	Cessna T182T Turbo Skylane	T18208131	N51338
F-GVGL	Cameron C-90 HAFB	11439	
F-GVGR	Cameron Z-105 HAFB	11512	
F-GVGV	Aérospatiale AS.365N3 Dauphin 2	6724	F-WWOL
F-GVHB	Aérospatiale SA.315B Lama	2261	EC-EOF, F-GEJS, N13583, (N515HA), N13583
F-GVHD	Embraer EMB.145MP	145178	PT-SEZ
F-GVHM	Ultramagic S-105 HAFB	105/128	
F-GVHS	Diamond DA 20-A1 Katana	10287	N287DA
F-GVIB	Chaize JZ.25F24 HAFB	169	
F-GVIE	Lindstrand LBL-77A HAFB	712	
F-GVIG	Bell 47G-2	2018	D-HFWP, ST-AIU, D-HOCA
F-GVIH	Robinson R22 Mariner	3297M	3A-MGM

Registration	Type	c/n	Previous identities
F-GVIJ	Aérospatiale/Alenia ATR-42-500	515	(OY-RUF), F-WKVK, VT-ADP(2), I-ADLI, F-OHFN, F-WWLP
F-GVIK	Robin DR.400/180R Remorqueur	2114	D-EIET
F-GVIN	Cameron N-90 HAFB	4731	G-VINS
F-GVIT	SIGA MA-30 Pilatre de Rozier HAFB	117	
F-GVJA	Aérospatiale AS.355N Ecureuil 2	5689	
F-GVJC	Piper PA-32-300 Cherokee Six D	32-7140066	S5-DBW, SL-DBW, YU-BHM, N4897S
F-GVJD	Cameron N-90 HAFB	11320	
F-GVJH	Cameron Z-425LW HAFB	11048	
F-GVJL	SNCASE SE.3130 Alouette II (Res .00)	1620	ALAT
F-GVJM	Piper PA-28-181 Archer III	2843101	OY-JAE
F-GVJO	Cameron Z-120 HAFB	10950	
F-GVKM	Diamond DA 42 Twin Star	42.012	
F-GVKP	Diamond DA 20-A1-100 Katana	10274	OE-VPZ, C-GAYK, N281DA, C-GDMQ
F-GVLA	Hughes 269C	120-1003	C-GLTM
F-GVLD	SOCATA TB-20 Trinidad	1088	N21FR, SE-KBG
F-GVLE	Llopis MA-30 HAFB	182	
F-GVLF	Aquila AT-01	AT01-143	
F-GVLG	Cameron C-60 HAFB	4364	HB-QFA
F-GVLH	Robinson R44 Raven II	10635	
F-GVLI	Robinson R44 Raven II	12402	
F-GVLL	Sud Avn SA.316B Alouette III	1081	F-GSOS, ALAT
F-GVLM	Ultramagic M-77 HAFB	77/326	
F-GVLV	Llopis MA-35 HAFB	185	
F-GVMB	Schröder Fire Balloons G50/24 HAFB	673	D-OLEF(2)
F-GVMC	Cameron A-140 HAFB	1550	LX-BUS(2)
F-GVMD	Robinson R44 Astro	0699	
F-GVMF	Dassault Falcon 50EX	315	LX-LXL, PH-LSV, N668P, F-WWHU
F-GVMH	Robinson R22B2 Beta	2719	I-SIEL
F-GVMI	Bombardier BD.700-1A10 Global Express	9456	C-GKOH(2)
F-GVMM	Cameron C-90 HAFB	11115	
F-GVMP	Diamond DA 40D Star	D4.088	D-EDAZ(4), OE-VPY
F-GVMR	Chaize CS.3000F16 HAFB	213	
F-GVMT	SIGA MA-22 Pilatre de Rozier HAFB	147	
F-GVNP	Schröder Fire Balloons G22/24 HAFB	1566	
F-GVNT	Lindstrand LBL-180A HAFB	071	G-EVNT
F-GVNY	Ultramagic S-130 HAFB	130/58	
F-GVOB	Bell 206B Jet Ranger II	2624	N921RB, N5016G
F-GVOL	Ultramagic M-130 HAFB	130/17	
F-GVOM	Cameron Z-90 HAFB	10945	
F-GVOR	Tecnam P2002-JF Sierra	046	
F-GVOZ	Piper PA-28-181 Archer II	2890061	HB-PLJ, N9136B
F-GVPB	Ultramagic N-210 HAFB	210/48	
F-GVPC	Pilatus PC-6/B2-H4 Turbo Porter	951	HB-FMU
F-GVPF	Aquila AT-01	AT01-163	
F-GVPL	Robinson R22 Beta	2290	N678BH, LQ-BJV
F-GVPP	Robinson R44 Raven II	10104	G-ILTY
F-GVPT	Cessna 172S Skyhawk SP	172S9322	N5338D
F-GVPY	Diamond DA 40D Star	D4.292	
F-GVQB	Diamond DA 40D Star	D4.302	OE-VPU
F-GVRC	Chaize CS.2200F24 HAFB	215	
F-GVRD	Chaize JZ.22F12 HAFB	209	
F-GVRE	Cessna 152	15282930	OO-DRE, N89962
F-GVRF	CEA Jodel DR.1051 Sicile	511	OO-LRF, F-BLRF
F-GVRJ	Diamond DA 40D Star	D4.103	
F-GVRL	Cessna 172RG Cutlass RG	172RG0222	F-GKBB
F-GVRM	Beech 65-A90 King Air (W/o 24.12.04, still regd)	LJ-121	N948RM, N666FG, (D-I . . .), N666FG, F-GERH, HB-GCU, D-ILNA
F-GVRV	Cameron Z-90 HAFB	10717	
F-GVSB	Robinson R44 Raven (Damaged 10.4.16)	1258	
F-GVSF	Robin DR.400/140B Major	2266	HB-KDW
F-GVSO	Ultramagic M-130 HAFB	130/59	
F-GVSP	Cirrus SR20	1813	N833SR
F-GVSX	Kubicek BB-34Z HAFB	849	
F-GVSY	Extra EA.300/L	1219	
F-GVSZ	Cessna 206H Stationair	20608260	OO-DSL, N306CM
F-GVTA	Eurocopter EC.120B Colibri	1258	
F-GVTB	Aérospatiale AS.355N Ecureuil 2	5557	G-GONN, HB-XIQ, VR-BQM, G-BVNW, (D-HWPC)
F-GVTF	Pilatus PC-6/B2-H4 Turbo Porter	915	HB-FMI, F-OGXM
F-GVTH	McDonnell-Douglas DC-9-21	47308	"F-WTVH", F-WQPC, OY-KGF
F-GVUI	Lindstrand LBL-105A HAFB	1044	
F-GVUJ	Cessna 525B CitationJet CJ3	525B-0156	N5145V
F-GVUN	American AG-5B Tiger	10078	D-EPOS(1), N1194G
F-GVUS	Chaize JZ.25F12 HAFB	177	
F-GVVA	Llopis MA-26 HAFB	169	
F-GVVB	Cessna 525B CitationJet CJ3	525B-0256	N52059
F-GVYC	Cessna 560XL Citation XLS	560-5682	N50549
F-GVYD	Robinson R44 Raven II	10081	G-EKYD
F-GVYH	Robinson R22B2 Beta	3768	
F-GVYL	Piper J-3C-65 Cub	15659	N88043, NC88043
F-GVYM	Eurocopter EC.135T2	0252	OY-HJT, D-HECA
F-GVZB	Aérospatiale/Alenia ATR-42-500	524	F-OHQL, F-WWEF
F-GVZC	Aérospatiale/Alenia ATR-42-500	516	F-WNUA, SP-EDA, F-GPYG, F-WWLU
F-GVZD	Aérospatiale/Alenia ATR-42-500	530	F-WNUJ, SP-EDD, F-GPYJ, F-WWLH
F-GVZJ	Aérospatiale/Alenia ATR-42-320	093	F-WQNO, PH-XLK, TG-AGA, TG-MWA, F-WQCZ, N17810, F-WWES
F-GVZL	Aérospatiale/Alenia ATR-72-212A	553	F-OHJO, F-WWLC
F-GVZM	Aérospatiale/Alenia ATR-72-212A	590	F-OHJT, F-WWET
F-GVZN	Aérospatiale/Alenia ATR-72-212A	563	F-OHJU, F-WWEA
F-GVZU	Aérospatiale/Alenia ATR-72-212A	499	D-ANKA, N499AT, F-WWLY
F-GVZV	Aérospatiale/Alenia ATR-72-212A	686	I-ADLJ, F-WQMO, F-WWEI

F-WW . .)   These series are used as temporary registrations for test flights and
F-WX . .)   deliveries. As the majority of applications are likely to be short-lived
F-WZ . .)   we are not attempting to provide a 'current' list but would welcome
reports of confirmed usage.

Registration	Type	c/n	Previous identities
F-GXAA	Chaize CS.3000F16 HAFB	198	
F-GXAD	Robinson R22B2 Beta	3446	(F-HBCH), OO-WBF, N71970
F-GXAF	Reims/Cessna F182Q Skylane	F18200167	F-WKAF, F-OKAF, F-GCYP
F-GXAJ	Gardan GY-80-160 Horizon	108	G-ATJT
F-GXAL	Cameron V-90 HAFB	4818	
F-GXAM	Cameron Z-90 HAFB	10683	
F-GXAO	Cessna 207 Skywagon	20700209	6V-AHP, F-GEDM, D-EEDW, N1609U
F-GXAP	Ultramagic T-150 HAFB	150/03	LX-BVU
F-GXAR	Robinson R44 Astro	0432	D-HIAR
F-GXAS	Cessna 404 Titan	4040815	LX-TDC, (F-GSCR), F-ZBDY, F-GCVR(1), (N67664)
F-GXBA	Chaize JZ.22F12 HAFB	125	F-WMTZ
F-GXBB	Robin DR.400/180 Régent (W/o 19.5.16)	2499	
F-GXBC	Chaize JZ.22F24 HAFB	200	
F-GXBE	Cessna 182P Skylane (Reims-assembled with "c/n" 0053)	18264362	D-EDBE(4), N1520M
F-GXBG	Cameron A-250 HAFB	10785	
F-GXBJ	Reims/Cessna F150M	F15001203	F-BXIJ
F-GXBM	Cameron Z-105 HAFB	10542	
F-GXBN	Cessna R182 Skylane RG	R18200128	F-OHJP, N7363Y
F-GXBP	Aérophile 5500 Tethered Gas Balloon	028	
F-GXBR	Robin DR.400/120 Dauphin 2+2	2485	
F-GXBS	Cessna U206 Super Skywagon	U20604181	G-BOFD, N756LS
F-GXBV	Dassault Falcon 900EX	75	VP-BEH, (F-GYDP), F-WWFL
F-GXCA	Cameron A-120 HAFB	4637	OO-BKC
F-GXCC	Aérospatiale AS.355F1 Ecureuil 2	5172	SE-JDM, N302PS, N57973
F-GXCD	Ultramagic M-90 HAFB	90/82	
F-GXCE	Cameron N-105 HAFB	10727	
F-GXCF	Aquila AT-01	AT01-127	
F-GXCG	Chaize JZ.22F12 HAFB	173	
F-GXCM	Mudry CAP.232	14	
F-GXCP	Mudry CAP.232	40	
F-GXCQ	Agusta-Bell 206B Jet Ranger 2	8095	EC-GDB, F-GJAU, F-OGUL, F-GAJL, G-AWRV
F-GXCT	Lindstrand LBL-120A HAFB	994	
F-GXCV	Cameron Z-180 HAFB	10780	
F-GXDB	Mudry CAP.232	33	
F-GXDC	Arboglisseur de Montgolfier RZ-2000 HAFB (Res 10.05)	196	
F-GXDE	Fuji FA-200-180A0	FA-200-214	D-EIDE
F-GXDF	Agusta A.109E Power	11015	N109AB
F-GXDG	Piper PA-28RT-201 Arrow IV	28R-7918228	OO-VDG, N2936F, (N999EA), N2936F
F-GXDI	Sky 105-24 HAFB	059	G-BXDW
F-GXDJ	Grumman G.164A Agcat	1665	N48533
F-GXDM	Cameron N-77 HAFB	10107	
F-GXDN	Wassmer WA.51A Pacific	96	D-EKLA(2), F-BUKH
F-GXDR	Chaize CS.3000F16 HAFB	188	
F-GXDT	Lindstrand LBL-105A HAFB	1256	
F-GXEB	Chaize CS.3000F16 HAFB	110	OO-BBE
F-GXEJ	Chaize CS.3000F16 HAFB	204	
F-GXEK	Robin DR.400/120 Dauphin 2+2	2523	
F-GXES	Piper PA-42 Cheyenne III	42-8001043	D-IYES, OY-YES, N809AA, HB-LRI, N48WA, N4089T
F-GXFE	Robinson R44 Raven II	11490	
F-GXFL	Chaize JZ.30F16 HAFB	182	
F-GXFM	Cameron A-340HL HAFB	10650	
F-GXFP	Sud Avn SA.318C Alouette Astazou	2152	ALAT
F-GXFX	Lindstrand LBL-310A HAFB	746	G-BZPE
F-GXGA	Robin DR.400/180 Régent	2509	
F-GXGE	Robin DR.400/120 Dauphin 2+2	2514	
F-GXGH	Robin DR.400/120 Dauphin 2+2	2518	
F-GXGI	Robin DR.400/180 Régent	2520	
F-GXGL	Robin DR.400/140B Dauphin 4	2521	
F-GXGM	Robin DR.400/160 Major	2522	
F-GXGX	Cameron N-90 HAFB	4917	
F-GXHC	Robinson R22 Beta II	3658	G-CDDD
F-GXHD	Robin ATL	110	F-GGHD
F-GXHM	Ultramagic S-105 HAFB	105/212	
F-GXHP	Cameron Z-275 HAFB	10982	
F-GXHR	Robinson R44 Raven II	10329	G-SCAM, EI-JAL, N7530N
F-GXHV	Chaize JZ.30F16 HAFB	193	
F-GXIR	Cameron A-250 HAFB	10848	
F-GXJA	Robin DR.400/160 Major	2474	
F-GXJB	Cameron Z-90 HAFB	10836	
F-GXJD	Cameron TR-70 HAFB	11223	
F-GXJF	Robinson R22 Beta II	3452	G-EGGY, G-CCGD, N75107
F-GXJH	Bell 206L Long Ranger	45082	D-HHRW(2), N16762, (N17EA), N16762
F-GXJL	Ultramagic N-180 HAFB	180/23	
F-GXJM	Chaize JZ.30F16 HAFB	164	
F-GXJP	Aérospatiale AS.350B3 Ecureuil	9055	
F-GXJR	Robin DR.400/120 Dauphin 2+2	2525	
F-GXJT	Robinson R44 Raven II	11260	
F-GXKC	Cirrus SR22	1318	N744C
F-GXLA	Aérospatiale AS.350B3 Ecureuil	4507	
F-GXLB	Chaize JZ.22F12 HAFB	181	
F-GXLK	Cameron Z-275 HAFB	11379	
F-GXLL	Cameron N-65 HAFB	3037	LX-BCC
F-GXLS	Aérophile 5500 Tethered Gas Balloon	010	
F-GXLV	Cameron A-340 HAFB	10806	
F-GXMB	Nord 1101 Noralpha	74	74
F-GXMC	Dassault Falcon 50	190	CS-TMJ, I-CAFÉ, F-WWHG
F-GXMD	Lindstrand LBL-105AHAFB	968	
F-GXMF	Dassault Falcon 900	181	F-WHLV, EC-JNZ, N833AV, HB-IUY, F-WWFZ
F-GXMG	Chaize CS.3000F16 HAFB	190	
F-GXMH	Chaize CS.2200F24 HAFB	216	
F-GXML	Chaize JZ.40F16 HAFB	192	
F-GXMP	Cessna 208B Grand Caravan	208B0173	OO-JMP, N4659B
F-GXMQ	Hughes 269C	71-1086	OO-VMR, D-HESY
F-GXMV	Aquila AT-01	AT01-126	
F-GXNA	SIGA MA-22 Pilatre de Rozier HAFB	144	
F-GXNN	Cameron Z-90 HAFB	10649	
F-GXOI	Beech F33A Bonanza	CE-1571	EC-FDD, N81728
F-GXOK	Piper PA-28-161 Cadet	2841242	OK-SEP, D-ELZI(2), N9192J
F-GXOL	Robin DR.400/120 Dauphin 2+2	2539	
F-GXOP	Aérospatiale AS.350B2 Ecureuil	7525	
F-GXPA	Cameron A-160 HAFB	10992	
F-GXPB	Cirrus SR22	0390	LX-OBI, N905CD
F-GXPC	Ultramagic N-180 HAFB	180/96	
F-GXPE	Aérospatiale AS.350B2 Ecureuil	9031	
F-GXPF	Chaize JZ.18F24 HAFB	170	
F-GXPG	Eurocopter EC.130B4 Ecureuil	3810	EI-MET, SE-JHY, F-WQDA, F-WWPJ
F-GXPL	Ultramagic M-120 HAFB	120/37	
F-GXPM	Cirrus SR20	1410	LX-PEA, N5293W
F-GXPP	Robin DR.400/140B Dauphin 4	2500	
F-GXPZ	Cameron A-210 HAFB	10784	

Reg	Type	c/n	Previous identities
F-GXRC	Robinson R22B Beta	3419	
F-GXRD	Robinson R22B Beta	3420	
F-GXRE	Robinson R44 Raven	1301	N71957
F-GXRJ	Piper PA-34-220T Seneca III	3433130	HB-LQR
F-GXRS	Chaize JZ.30F16 HAFB	156	
F-GXRT	Cameron N-90 HAFB	10890	
F-GXSD	Chaize CS.3000F16 HAFB	202	
F-GXSF	Cameron Z-105 HAFB	10949	
F-GXSM	Ultramagic M-77C HAFB	77/325	
F-GXSP	Kubicek BB-22E HAFB	684	
F-GXTC	Cameron N-120 HAFB	3937	HB-QCH
F-GXTD	Schröder Fire Balloons G42/24 HAFB	1355	
F-GXTE	Cirrus SR20	1047	N158CD
F-GXTH	Cameron C-90 HAFB	11113	
F-GXTJ	Chaize JZ.25F24 HAFB	172	
F-GXTM	Dassault Falcon 50	165	HB-JSR, LX-FMR, HZ-SM3, F-WZHF
F-GXTO	Chaize JZ.25F12 HAFB	208	
F-GXTR	Cirrus SR20	1795	N672SR
F-GXUS	Ultramagic M-130 HAFB	130/55	
F-GXVA	Chaize CS.3000F16 HAFB	211	
F-GXVB	Cessna 152	15284883	OO-LVB, N5124P
F-GXVG	Ultramagic M-145 HAFB	145/72	
F-GXXL	Bell 206L-3 Long Ranger III	51330	EC-FRY, N43904, JA9859
F-GXYP	Cirrus SR20	1489	N54170
F-GXYZ	Robin DR.400/120 Dauphin 2+2	2545	
F-GXZC	Chaize JZ.22F12 HAFB	179	
F-GXZD	Cameron Z-250 HAFB	11141	
F-GXZF	Cessna 172S Skyhawk SP	172S10113	SE-MFL, N2457V
F-GYAA	Reims/Cessna F150M	F15001172	OO-SEW, (YU-CCW), F-BVXJ
F-GYAC	Robin DR.400/160 Major	2533	
F-GYAD	Robinson R44 Clipper II	11892	G-CEYA
F-GYAK	Robin R.2120U	377	
F-GYAV	Robin DR.400/120 Dauphin 2+2	2566	
F-GYBA	Agusta A.109E Power	11086	F-WYBA
F-GYBB	Robin DR.400/120 Dauphin 2+2	2548	
F-GYBC	Cameron Z-225 HAFB	10845	
F-GYBD	Robinson R44 Clipper II	12008	G-CEWV
F-GYBG	Schweizer 269C	S-1742	N1298, N41S
F-GYBI	Llopis MA-35 HAFB	178	
F-GYBL	SAN Jodel D.140C Mousquetaire III	127	HB-SFC, F-BMBL
F-GYBP	Cameron Z-105 HAFB	11278	
F-GYBR	Ultramagic N-180 HAFB	180/99	
F-GYBS	Cessna 172 RG Skyhawk RG	172RG0057	OO-MPK, N5359R
F-GYBX	Cessna 182R Skylane	18267960	PH-ERO, (PH-HBP), N9530H
F-GYCD	Cameron N-77 HAFB	11162	
F-GYCF	Cameron Z-225 HAFB	10847	
F-GYCG	Robin DR.400/180 Regent	2568	
F-GYCL	Aérospatiale AS.350B2 Ecureuil	9025	F-OICL
F-GYCT	Lindstrand LBL-180A HAFB	1009	
F-GYDC	Mudry CAP.10C	308	
F-GYDD	Robin DR.400/140B Dauphin 4	2571	
F-GYDF	Eurocopter EC.130B4 Ecureuil	3866	(F-GUDD), F-WQDK, F-WWXJ
F-GYDH	Robinson R44 Astro	1082	
F-GYDI	SNIAS SE.3130 Alouette II	1359	F-ODZR, (F-GTHL), F-ODZR, ALAT
F-GYDR	Maule MT-7-235 Super Rocket	18074C	N141CP
F-GYDS	Cessna 172R Skyhawk	17280191	(EC- . . .), N9914F
F-GYED	Eurocopter EC.135P2	0379	OH-HCL
F-GYEL	Ultramagic N-425 HAFB	425/06	
F-GYES	Aérospatiale AS.355F1 Ecureuil 2 (Ditched off Savona, Italy 18.10.06)	5042	G-KGMT, G-PASE, N57818
F-GYEU	Aérospatiale AS.355N Ecureuil 2	5574	G-SEPB, G-BVSE
F-GYFD	Ultramagic T-180 HAFB	180/69	
F-GYFF	Cirrus SR20	1331	LX-PMD, N1133C
F-GYFP	Reims/Cessna F172N	F17201846	D-EIGA, (D-ELFS)
F-GYFR	Ultramagic M-105 HAFB	105/129	
F-GYFS	AIAA/Stampe SV.4C	1132	OO-HOE, (OO-OEV), F-BALH
F-GYGD	SIGA MA.40 Pilatre de Rozier HAFB	156	
F-GYGG	Cameron Z-105 HAFB	11294	
F-GYGM	Diamond DA 42 Twin Star	42.023	
F-GYHB	Robinson R22B2 Beta	3248	
F-GYHC	Robinson R22 Beta (Badly damaged 5.4.09)	2779	G-ODOT
F-GYHF	Eurocopter EC.135T2	0255	EC-IKY, D-HECU, D-HECO
F-GYHR	Cameron Z-69 HAFB	11413	
F-GYIT	Mudry CAP.10C	312	
F-GYJB	Lindstrand LBL-120A HAFB	1031	
F-GYJC	Aerospool WT-9 Dynamic LSA	DY387.2010	
F-GYJH	Cameron Z-425LW HAFB	10762	
F-GYJL	Sud Avn SA.316B Alouette III	1527	ALAT
F-GYJO	Jodel D.112 Club	350	HB-SPS, F-BHKT
F-GYJP	Ultramagic M-145 HAFB	145/55	
F-GYJR	Robin DR.400/180 Régent	2526	
F-GYJV	Eurocopter EC.135T1	0085	I-HIFI
F-GYKA	Mudry CAP.10C	300	
F-GYKB	Robin DR.400/120 Dauphin 2+2	2540	
F-GYKC	Robin DR.400/140B Dauphin 4	2550	
F-GYKF	Robin DR.400/160 Major	2517	
F-GYKG	Robin DR.400/120 Dauphin 2+2	2547	
F-GYKH	Robin DR.400/160 Major	2541	
F-GYKI	Robin DR.400/140B Dauphin 4	2552	
F-GYKJ	Robin DR.400/180 Régent	2528	
F-GYKL	Robin DR.400/160 Major	2530	
F-GYKM	Robin DR.400/180 Régent	2536	
F-GYKN	Robin DR.400/120 Dauphin 2+2	2557	
F-GYKQ	Robin DR.400/120 Dauphin 2+2	2565	
F-GYKR	Mudry CAP.10C	314	
F-GYKX	Robin DR.400/120 Dauphin 2+2	2558	
F-GYKZ	Robin DR.400/140B Dauphin 4	2546	
F-GYLB	Eurocopter EC.120B Colibri	1340	
F-GYLC	Robin DR.400/140B Dauphin 4	2551	
F-GYLD	SAN Jodel DR.1050 Ambassadeur	20	D-EACL, D-EOAB, F-BJLN
F-GYLE	Eurocopter EC.120B Colibri	1182	
F-GYLH	Aérospatiale AS.365N3 Dauphin 2	6760	F-WWOP
F-GYLL	Cerva CE-43 Guepard	445	F-ZJDL
F-GYLR	Mudry CAP.10B	309	
F-GYMA	Cameron N-90 HAFB	3994	G-BWYC
F-GYMD	Colt 105A HAFB	797	HB-BLO
F-GYMF	Classic Aircraft Waco YMF-5	F5-032	N40134
F-GYMG	Lindstrand LBL-120A HAFB	1331	
F-GYMH	Cameron N-90 HAFB	3072	LX-GSM
F-GYMM	Robin DR.400/140B Major	2161	HB-KDH
F-GYMS	Cessna U206G Stationair 6	U20606858	D-ENLW, N9418R
F-GYNN	Piper PA-28-181 Archer III	2843172	OO-KJA, N4118T, C-GDGG
F-GYNS	Ultramagic M-77C HAFB	77/345	
F-GYNU	Jodel DR.105A Ambassadeur	63	SE-XUM, HB-EMS, F-BIVN
F-GYOM	Cameron Z-140 HAFB	11488	
F-GYPA	Robinson R44 Clipper II	10574	G-SSJP
F-GYPC	SAN Jodel D.140E Mousquetaire	509	Fr.AF
F-GYPE	Embraer EMB.135LR	145492	PT-SXL
F-GYPF	Mooney M.20M Model 257 TLS	27-0135	3A-MST, I-TLST, N9159D
F-GYPG	Robin DR.400/160 Major	2490	
F-GYPH	Aérospatiale AS.365N3 Dauphin 2	6694	F-WWOG
F-GYPL	Diamond DA 42 Twin Star	42.050	OE-VPY
F-GYPM	Beech A36 Bonanza 36	E-3522	N936B
F-GYPP	Chaize JZ.40F16 HAFB	194	
F-GYPQ	Piper PA-46-350P Malibu Mirage	4622013	I-OBER, N9154N
F-GYPR	Robin DR.400/160 Major	2532	
F-GYRA	Schweizer 269C	S-1604	N86G
F-GYRC	Alpavia Jodel D.117A Grand Tourisme	1060	OO-LUX, F-BJEL
F-GYRD	Ultramagic S-90 HAFB	90/75	
F-GYRH	Eurocopter EC.135T2+	0765	D-HHDF, VT-GVD, D-HABH
F-GYRL	Robin DR.400/ 140B Major	2554	
F-GYRM	Cirrus SR22	1273	N813SD
F-GYRT	SOCATA TB-10 Tobago	1078	D-EGSY(2)
F-GYRV	Cirrus SR20	1903	N909SR
F-GYRX	Robin HR.200/120B	268	D-EGBB(2)
F-GYRY	Pilatus PC-6/B2-H4 Turbo Porter	935	HB-FMP, D-FREI
F-GYSA	Kubicek BB-30Z HAFB	372	
F-GYSD	Aérospatiale AS.350B1 Ecureuil	1482	F-ORSD, ES-37, F-WQDV, SX-HBI, F-OCCF
F-GYSH	Aérospatiale AS.332L1 Super Puma	9006	
F-GYSO	Robinson R44 Raven II	10204	
F-GYSP	Chaize JZ.25F24 HAFB	228	
F-GYTC	Llopis MA-30 HAFB	198	
F-GYTE	Piper PA-22-150 Tri-Pacer	22-3215	F-BATE(2), F-OATF
F-GYTR	Cameron Z-120 HAFB	10798	
F-GYTT	Raven S-60A HAFB	3278	
F-GYVC	Robin DR.400/120 Dauphin 2+2	2563	
F-GYVE	Eurocopter EC.120B Colibri	1226	
F-GYVL	Sikorsky S-76C	760805	N805M
F-GYVM	SNCASE SE.313B Alouette II	1411	ALAT
F-GYXU	Robin DR.400/120 Dauphin 2+2	2494	
F-GYXV	Robin DR.400/120 Dauphin 2+2	2495	
F-GYYG	Diamond DA 42 Twin Star	42.021	OE-VPY
F-GYYJ	Diamond DA 42 Twin Star	42.020	OE-VPI
F-GYYM	Diamond DA 42 Twin Star	42.019	OE-VPY
F-GYZB	Mudry CAP.10B	306	
F-GYZC	Mudry CAP.10C	310	
F-GYZD to F-GYZZ	Reserved for DGAC / S.E.F.A.		
F-GZAA	Schröder Fire Balloons G26/24 HAFB	1123	
F-GZAB	Ultramagic M-130 HAFB	130/28	
F-GZAC	Aérospatiale AS.350B3 Ecureuil	9047	
F-GZAD	Aérospatiale AS.365N3 Dauphin 2	6810	
F-GZAF	Lindstrand LBL-77A HAFB	1010	
F-GZAG	Diamond DA 20-A1-80 Katana	10175	C-FCAD
F-GZAH	Robinson R44 Raven II	10870	
F-GZAL	Robin DR.400/120 Dauphin 2+2	2502	
F-GZAM	Cameron Z-90 HAFB	10589	
F-GZAP	Firefly Balloons F8 HAFB	F8-2022	
F-GZAR	Diamond DA.40D Star	D4.032	G-CCFR
F-GZBA	Wassmer Jodel D.120A Paris-Nice	273	OO-MOI, F-BMOI
F-GZBB	Robin DR.400/160 Major	2537	
F-GZBD	Robinson R44 Raven II	10353	G-WMBT
F-GZBG	Piper PA-46-350P Malibu Mirage	4622070	N7876Q, N7876C, N9183X
F-GZBI	Cessna F182Q Skylane	F18200062	D-EIBI
F-GZBL	Ultramagic 150 HAFB	150/09	
F-GZBM	Cameron Z-77 HAFB	10865	
F-GZBO	Cerva CE-43 Guepard	441	Fr.AF
F-GZBP	Robinson R44 Raven	1728	EI-NBP
F-GZBQ	Cameron Z-150 HAFB	11433	
F-GZBS	Cameron Z-105 HAFB	11298	
F-GZBV	Cessna 172R Skyhawk	17281540	N63119
F-GZCA	Airbus A330-203	422	
F-GZCB	Airbus A330-203	443	
F-GZCC	Airbus A330-203	448	
F-GZCD	Airbus A330-203	458	F-WWJH
F-GZCE	Airbus A330-203	465	F-WWKM
F-GZCF	Airbus A330-203	481	
F-GZCG	Airbus A330-203	498	F-WWKI
F-GZCH	Airbus A330-203	500	
F-GZCI	Airbus A330-203	502	F-WWKJ
F-GZCJ	Airbus A330-203	503	
F-GZCK	Airbus A330-203	516	
F-GZCL	Airbus A330-203	519	
F-GZCM	Airbus A330-203	567	F-WWYT
F-GZCN	Airbus A330-203	584	
F-GZCO	Airbus A330-203	657	F-WWYR
F-GZCQ to GZCZ	Reserved for Airbus A330s for Air France		
F-GZDB	Robinson R44 Raven II	11332	
F-GZDC	Cessna 177RG Cardinal RG	177RG1295	OO-JLM, PH-BRA, N52874
F-GZDF	Cameron Z-250 HAFB	10669	
F-GZDG	Cameron Z-140 HAFB	10755	
F-GZDK	Cerva CE-43 Guepard	444	F-ZJDK
F-GZDL	Aquila AT-01	AT01-120	
F-GZDR	Mooney M.20J Model 201	24-0811	D-EBZT, (N4700H)
F-GZDS	Ultramagic S-90 HAFB	90/77	
F-GZDV	Cameron V-90 HAFB	10887	
F-GZEB	Robinson R44 Raven II	12064	
F-GZED	Aerotek Pitts S-2A	2063	N33RS
F-GZEN	Aérospatiale AS.350B3 Ecureuil	4629	
F-GZEP	Cameron Colt 77A HAFB	10305	
F-GZER	Cameron V-90 HAFB	10786	
F-GZEU	Piper PA-28-181 Archer III	2843328	G-GFPC, G-CCWA, D-ELEM, PH-AEG, N41776
F-GZFA	Chaize JZ.22F24 HAFB	176	
F-GZFB	Chaize CS.2000F24 HAFB	226	
F-GZFD	Ultramagic M-130 HAFB	130/72	
F-GZFE	Maule MX-7-180	11076C	TR-LDS, F-GJPU
F-GZFG	Kubicek BB30Z HAFB	1143	
F-GZFJ	Aérospatiale AS.350B2 Ecureuil	7179	
F-GZFM	Ultramagic MV-77C HAFB	77/290	
F-GZGD	Cessna TR182 Turbo Skylane II	R18200766	G-OTRG, (N736SU)
F-GZGK	SAN Jodel D.140E Mousquetaire	203	Fr.AF
F-GZGM	Hughes 369E	0309E	HA-MSH

Reg	Type	Serial	Previous identities
F-GZGN	Aquila AT-01	AT01-138	
F-GZGP	Piper PA-28-181 Archer II	28-8290065	D-EDTX, N8467E
F-GZGS	SAN Jodel D.140E Mousquetaire	207	Fr.AF
F-GZGT	Cameron Z-133 HAFB	11222	
F-GZHA	Boeing 737-8GJ	34901	
F-GZHB	Boeing 737-8GJ	34902	
F-GZHC	Boeing 737-8K2	29651	N1786B
F-GZHD	Boeing 737-8K2	29650	
F-GZHE	Boeing 737-8K2	29678	
F-GZHF	Boeing 737-8K2	29677	PH-ZOM, (F-GZHF), N1796B
F-GZHG	Boeing 737-8K2	30650	PH-HZV, OY-TDB, PH-HZV
F-GZHH	Cameron Z-150 HAFB	10347	
F-GZHI	Boeing 737-8K2	36120	
F-GZHK	Boeing 737-8K2	37790	
F-GZHL	Boeing 737-8K2	37791	
F-GZHM	Boeing 737-8K2	37792	
F-GZHN	Boeing 737-85H	29445	OY-SEI, N1786B
F-GZHO	Boeing 737-8K2	43880	
F-GZHP	Boeing 737-8K2	44566	
F-GZHQ	Boeing 737-8K2	44567	
F-GZHR	Boeing 737-8K2	46913	
F-GZHS	Boeing 737-84P	35074	EI-IGN, SP-IGN, I-AIGN, N574TC, B-KBL
F-GZHT	Boeing 737-8K2	41332	
F-GZHU	Boeing 737-8K2	41352	
F-GZHV	Boeing 737-85H	29444	OY-SHE, N1787B
F-GZHX	Boeing 737-8K2	41343	
F-GZHY	Boeing 737-8K2	41344	
F-GZIF	Robin R.1180T Aiglon	244	F-GCIF
F-GZIG	SAN Jodel D.140A Mousquetaire	46	OO-LCA, F-BIZK
F-GZIM	Ultramagic T-180 HAFB	180/68	
F-GZIN	SIGA MA-26 Pilatre de Rozier HAFB	159	
F-GZIT	Cameron V-90 HAFB	4878	
F-GZJB	Lindstrand LBL-77B HAFB	1045	
F-GZJC	Mooney M.20R Ovation	29-0424	C-FSGY, N827F
F-GZJF	SNCASE SE.313B Alouette II	1865	77+13, AS+360
F-GZJL	Robin R.3000/235	107	F-WEIK
F-GZJM	Swearingen SA226-T Merlin III	T-264	N422AG, LX-LAP, BelgAF:CF-04, N5378M, (N100JB), N5378M
F-GZJX	Diamond DA 42 Twin Star	42.024	OE-VPY
F-GZJY	Lindstrand LBL-69A HAFB	715	G-BZJY
F-GZKG	SAN Jodel D.140E-1 Mousquetaire IV	38	EC-DKK, F-BIZR
F-GZKP	Sikorsky S-76C+	760806	N806K
F-GZLG	SIGA MA-30 Pilatre de Rozier HAFB	160	
F-GZLI	Cameron N-90 HAFB	10889	
F-GZLL	Colt 21A HAFB	2018	G-BTNN
F-GZLM	Eurocopter EC.120B Colibri	1546	E7-AAT, F-WQDC
F-GZLV	Cameron Z-210 HAFB	11255	
F-GZMA	Lindstrand LBL-90B HAFB	1136	
F-GZMB	SIGA MA-40 Pilatre de Rozier HAFB	131	
F-GZMC	Kubicek BB-26Z HAFB	461	OK-0461
F-GZMJ	Cameron C-60 HAFB	11208	
F-GZML	Cirrus SR20	1691	N996SR
F-GZMP	Diamond DA 40D Star	D4.185	
F-GZMS	Cirrus SR22	1565	N708CD
F-GZMY	Robinson R44 Raven II	11484	EI-ESK, G-CEFR
F-GZNA	Boeing 777-328ER	35297	N50217
F-GZNB	Boeing 777-328ER	32964	
F-GZNC	Boeing 777-328ER	35542	
F-GZND	Boeing 777-328ER	35543	
F-GZNE	Boeing 777-328ER	37432	
F-GZNF	Boeing 777-328ER	37433	N50281
F-GZNG	Boeing 777-328ER	32968	
F-GZNH	Boeing 777-328ER	35544	
F-GZNI	Boeing 777-328ER	39973	
F-GZNJ	Boeing 777-328ER	38706	
F-GZNK	Boeing 777-328ER	39971	
F-GZNL	Boeing 777-328ER	40063	
F-GZNM	SIGA MA-26 Pilatre de Rozier HAFB	141	
F-GZNN	Boeing 777-328ER	40376	
F-GZNO	Boeing 777-328ER	38665	
F-GZNP	Boeing 777-328ER	37435	
F-GZNQ	Boeing 777-328ER	40064	
F-GNZR	Boeing 777-328ER	44553	
F-GNZS	Boeing 777-328ER	39970	
F-GNZT	Boeing 777-328ER	38705	
F-GNZU	Boeing 777-328ER	61701	
F-GZNV to F-GZNZ	*Reserved for Boeing 777-300s for Air France*		
F-GZOB	Colt 69A HAFB	2601	
F-GZOC	Cameron C-70 HAFB	10682	
F-GZOL	Kubicek BB-26 HAFB	336	OK-0336
F-GZOS	Lindstrand LBL-90B HAFB	1127	
F-GZOU	Robin DR.400/120 Dauphin 2+2	2588	
F-GZPA	Bell 206B Jet Ranger III	4177	EI-CUG, N248BC, N118GC
F-GZPC	Cameron Z-105 HAFB	10678	
F-GZPE(2)	Piaggio P.180 Avanti	1064	
F-GZPF	Bell 206B Jet Ranger II	1162	EC-FEV, C-GZPX, N59388
F-GZPL	Aquila AT-01	AT01-146	
F-GZPM	Cameron Z-105 HAFB	10555	
F-GZPP	Cameron N-133 HAFB	10387	
F-GZPT	SOCATA Rallye 235C	13353	EC-DPM, F-OGLE
F-GZSA	Robin DR.400/180 Régent	2441	D-EIIO(2)
F-GZSB	Cameron O-90 HAFB	10594	
F-GZSD	Aérospatiale AS.350B1 Ecureuil	1681	F-ORTL, ES-..., F-WQDS, F-WQDL, F-WYMY, CS-HAY, F-WZFO
F-GZSF	Cirrus SR20	1487	N460CD
F-GZSH	Aérospatiale AS.350B3 Ecureuil	4918	
F-GZSP	Ultramagic T-210 HAFB	210/77	
F-GZTA	Boeing 737-33V	29333	HA-LKV, G-EZYI
F-GZTB	Boeing 737-33V	29336	HA-LKU, G-EZYL, N1787B
F-GZTD	Boeing 737-73V	32418	G-EZJW
F-GZTI	Boeing 737-408F	25063	N563AC, PR-LGR, N563AC, SX-BGR, TF-FID
F-GZTJ	Boeing 737-4S3F	25595	N595AG, PR-LGS, N595AG, EI-ELY, SX-BGJ, N280CD, TC-APA, 9M-MLG
F-GZTK	Boeing 737-4Q8F	24709	YR-UEZ, ZK-TLF, N709AG, SX-BKM, N406KW, 9M-MJG
F-GZTL	Mooney M.20M Model 257 TLS	27-0240	N424AT
F-GZTM	Boeing 737-3B3	24387	ZS-ASL(2), F-GFUE
F-GZUT	Cameron C-80 HAFB	10397	
F-GZVB	Cameron Z-77 HAFB	11469	
F-GZXK	Piper PA-28-181 Archer II	2890094	HB-PLR
F-GZXM	Bölkow BO.207	290	LX-UXM, HB-UXM, (D-ENWO)
F-GZXV	Extra EA.300/200 (W/o 15.8.16)	003	N134EE
F-GZYA	Robin DR.400/140B Dauphin 4	2124	HB-KDA
F-GZYB	SIGA MA-26 Pilatre de Rozier HAFB	163	
F-HAAB	Aquila AT-01	AT01-132	
F-HAAC	Robin DR.400/120 Dauphin 2+2	2576	
F-HAAD	Robin DR.400/120 Dauphin 2+2	2577	
F-HAAE	Robin DR.400/120 Dauphin 2+2	2578	
F-HAAH	Lindstrand LBL-105A HAFB	1055	
F-HAAI	Lindstrand LBL-69A HAFB	1056	
F-HAAJ	Lindstrand LBL-150A HAFB	1069	
F-HAAK	Lindstrand LBL-150B HAFB	1070	
F-HAAM	Cessna 172S Skyhawk SP	172S8743	N35234
F-HAAN	Schweizer S.269C	S1493	OO-VIC, G-JHAS
F-HAAQ	Robinson R44 Raven II	13705	
F-HAAR	Robin DR.400/140B Dauphin 4	2640	
F-HAAT	Aquila AT-01	AT01-130	
F-HAAU	Piper PA-28-140 Cherokee Cruiser	28-7425195	G-BBZF, N9501N
F-HAAZ	Piper PA-28RT-201 Arrow IV	28R-8118064	OH-PRK, N83730
F-HABA	Cameron Z-42 HAFB	11053	
F-HABB	Lindstrand LBL-105A HAFB	1099	
F-HABC	Mooney M.20M Model 257 TLS	27-0233	OE-KST(2), N10824
F-HABD(2)	Cessna 172S Skyhawk SP	172S10210	N6045Z
F-HABE	Cessna 172R Skyhawk	17281330	N6028Q
F-HABF	Aérospatiale AS.365N3 Dauphin 2	6751	
F-HABH	Reims/Cessna F177RG Cardinal RG	F177RG0010/ US c/n 177RG00117	D-EPEC, EI-BHC, G-AYTG
F-HABJ	Diamond DA 40D Star	D4.067	
F-HABL	Diamond DA 40D Star	D4.076	
F-HABM	Diamond DA 40D Star	D4.077	OE-VPW
F-HABO	Diamond DA 40DStar	D4.132	
F-HABP	Diamond DA 40D Star	D4.133	
F-HABQ	Diamond DA 40D Star	D4.134	
F-HABR	Diamond DA 40D Star	D4.136	OE-VPW
F-HABS	Cameron Z-90 HAFB	11906	
F-HACB	Cessna U206D Skywagon 206	U206-1384	D-ENWK, SE-FKZ, N72374
F-HACC	Cessna 172S Skyhawk SP	172S9753	N65766
F-HACD	Issoire APM-20 Lionceau	19	
F-HACE	Lindstrand HS-110 HAFB	362	OO-BDP, G-BWOD
F-HACF	Aquila AT-01	AT01-125	
F-HACH	Robin DR.400/140B Dauphin 4	2624	
F-HACK	Cameron Z-225 HAFB	11068	
F-HACM	Tecnam P.2002-JF Sierra	034	
F-HACN	Aérospatiale AS.350B2 Ecureuil	4415	
F-HACQ	Robin DR.400/160 Chevalier	1711	D-EAOI, I-DINU
F-HACR	Cessna 172S Skyhawk SP	172S10641	N1730W
F-HACS	Robin DR.400/120 Dauphin 2+2	2589	
F-HACT	Robin DR.400/160 Major	2544	
F-HACV	Robin DR.400/120 Dauphin 2+2	2572	
F-HACX	Cameron Z-225 HAFB	11471	
F-HADB	Kubicek BB-26 HAFB	549	
F-HADC	Lindstrand LBL-90A HAFB	1262	
F-HADD	Cirrus SR20	1619	N81437
F-HADE	Aérospatiale AS.350B3 Ecureuil	4066	EC-JSV, F-GSYG, F-WWPF
F-HADF	Piper PA-28-181 Archer III	2843040	OY-TEI
F-HADG	Chaize JZ.25F24 HAFB	224	
F-HADH	Dassault Falcon 50	11	F-GGVB, N5739, N501NC, N50FH, F-WZHE
F-HADI	Cirrus SR20	1549	N514LG
F-HADJ	Piper PA-18-150 Super Cub	18-7609036	EC-CXD, N54107
F-HADK	Robinson R44 Raven II	12062	I-...., N3016X
F-HADM	Chaize CS.4000F32 HAFB	227	
F-HADN	Llopis MA-22 HAFB	230	
F-HADO	Issoire APM-20 Lionceau	25	
F-HADP	Robin DR.400/180 Régent	2564	
F-HADS	Cameron Z-90 HAFB	10912	
F-HADT	Cessna 510 Mustang	510-0108	N939JC
F-HADU	Libert L-2600 HAFB	326-050	
F-HADZ	Sky 105-24 HAFB	091	HB-QDZ
F-HAEB	Cessna 182R Skylane	18268316	N182PN, G-OCJW, G-SJGM, N357WC, (N857WC), N357WC, N5417E
F-HAEC	Cessna 172S Skyhawk SP	172S10041	D-EKCJ, OE-DSP, N2455Z
F-HAEF	Cameron Z-350 HAFB	11472	
F-HAEG	Aquila AT-01	AT01-123	D-EAQA, (D-EFTT(3))
F-HAEJ	Piper PA-28-181 Archer III	2843641	PH-AEJ, N10532, PH-AEJ
F-HAEL	Reims/Cessna F152	F15201495	D-EAEL(3), HB-CXX
F-HAEM	Robinson R22 Beta II	4305	N41632
F-HAEN	Aérospatiale AS.350B3 Ecureuil	7136	
F-HAES	Chaize CS.3000F16 HAFB	217	
F-HAEV	Cessna 206H Stationair	20608234	N2206X
F-HAEY	Piper PA-28RT-201T Turbo Arrow IV	28R-8031047	D-EANI(4), HB-PIT, OY-GKF
F-HAFA	Lindstrand LBL-180A HAFB	1332	
F-HAFB	Cessna 172S Skyhawk SP	172S10863	N5222L
F-HAFF	Robin DR.400/120 Dauphin 2+2	2583	
F-HAFG	Robin DR.400/140B Dauphin 4	2580	
F-HAFI	Cessna 172S Skyhawk SP	172S9022	N5147T
F-HAFK	Robin DR.400/120 Dauphin 2+2	2614	
F-HAFL	Cessna 172S Skyhawk SP	172S8457	F-OJHG, F-GTHG, N2466G
F-HAFM	Schröder Fire Balloons G26/24 HAFB	1472	
F-HAFP	Cessna 172S Skyhawk SP	172S9384	N5358S
F-HAFR	Robin R.2120U	367	
F-HAFS	Embraer EMB-145EP	145177	UP-EM002, SX-CMC, G-EMBL
F-HAFZ	Kubicek BB-30Z HAFB	1023	
F-HAGB	Cirrus SR22T	0381	N466AD
F-HAGD	Tecnam P.2002JF Sierra	081	
F-HAGG	Llopis MA-40 HAFB	202	
F-HAGH	Cessna 525 CitationJet CJ	525-0518	D-IETZ, D-ILLL(4)
F-HAGK	Eurocopter EC.130B4 Ecureuil	4839	
F-HAGL	Beech A36 Bonanza	E-3003	OY-TFB, N821SA
F-HAGM	Lindstrand LBL-120A HAFB	650	HB-QED
F-HAGO	Schweizer 269C-1	0279	
F-HAGR	Robin DR.400/135CDI	2608	
F-HAGS	Diamond DA.40D Star	D4.211	OE-DXD(2), OY-RBB, OE-VPU
F-HAGV	Cameron Z-225 HAFB	11499	
F-HAHA	Cessna 510 Citation Mustang	510-0405	ZS-MTG(2), N93564
F-HAHE	Issoire APM-30 Lion	26	

Reg	Type	S/N	Previous identities
F-HAHH	Robinson R44 Raven II	12692	
F-HAHO	Piper PA-28-181 Cherokee Archer III	2843039	G-PALY, PH-AEC
F-HAHT	Robinson R22 Beta II	3083	G-DABS
F-HAHV	Llopis MA-30 HAFB	212	
F-HAIA	Robinson R44 Raven II	10734	
F-HAIE	Issoire APM-30 Lion	27	
F-HAIG	Robinson R22 Beta	2440	I-NAIG
F-HAIH	Grob G.115A	8108	EI-CCD, D-EIUD
F-HAIR	Dassault Falcon 50	37	F-GMCU, I-SAME, (I-CAIK), F-WZHM
F-HAIX	Robin DR.400/180 Régent	2609	
F-HAJB	Robin DR.400/120 Dauphin 2+2	2604	
F-HAJC	Robin DR.400/140B Dauphin 4	2636	
F-HAJD	Cessna 525 Citation	525-0523	N51246
F-HAJG	Cessna 172S Skyhawk SP	172S9531	N612TC
F-HAJF	Tecnam P.2002-JF Sierra	078	
F-HAJL	Piper PA-32-301FT 6X	3232055	D-EJFT, N31295, N3120X
F-HAJM	Kubicek BB-45 HAFB	472	
F-HAJO	Llopis MA-30 HAFB	208	
F-HAJR	Cameron Z-105 HAFB	11185	
F-HAJT	Robinson R22B2 Beta	4154	N3061N
F-HAJV	Cessna 550 Citation II	550-0622	LX-VAZ, HB-VKP, N826EW, N326EW, (N1255J)
F-HAKB	Kubicek BB-34Z HAFB	610	
F-HAKI	SOCATA Rallye 235ED	12873	D-EGEZ (2), F-GAKI
F-HAKX	Robin DR.400/120 Dauphin 2+2	2586	
F-HAKZ	Zlin Z.526F Trenér Master	1322	(F-GVOG), (D-EFOG(3)), SP-EHF
F-HALA	Raven-Europe RX-7 HAFB	E-289	
F-HALC	Robin HR.100/250TR	558	CEV:F-ZJPM
F-HALD	Robinson R22 Beta II	4257	N41324
F-HALG	Dassault Falcon 2000LX	290	F-WWGD
F-HALI	Ultramagic M-105 HAFB	105/146	
F-HALL	Aérospatiale AS.350B2 Ecureuil	2105	HB-ZCE, D-HUBW, G-PLME, G-BONN
F-HALM	Dassault Falcon 50	134	F-GOCT, N134FJ
F-HALN	Llopis MA-26 HAFB	203	
F-HALR	Chaize JZ.40F16 HAFB	NG-005	
F-HALT	Cameron Z-105 HAFB	10768	
F-HALU	Ultramagic S-130 HAFB	130/53	
F-HALX	Robinson R22 Mariner	2830M	I-SIBY
F-HAMA	Cameron Z-90 HAFB	10871	
F-HAMB	Robinson R44 Clipper	0943	F-OJCL
F-HAMD	Aérospatiale AS.350B3 Ecureuil	4955	
F-HAME	Boeing Stearman E75N1	75-190	OO-AME, N55389, NC55389, 40-1633
F-HAMG	Cessna 525A CitationJet CJ2	525A-0193	D-IKAL(2), N5183U
F-HAMH	Ultramagic M-120 HAFB	120/38	
F-HAMI	Beech B200 King Air	BB-1874	N6194V
F-HAML	Cameron Z-105 HAFB	11309	
F-HAMO	Kubicek BB-51Z HAFB	1054	
F-HAMP(2)	Cirrus SR22	2286	N959SR
F-HAMR	Pilatus PC-6/B2-H4 Turbo Porter	892	I-INOT, HB-FKZ
F-HAMS	Cessna U206E Stationair	U20601659	TC-..., G-BSMB, N9459G, C-GUUW, N9459G
F-HAMT	Schweizer 269C	S-1909	
F-HAMY	Issoire APM-20 Lionceau	20	
F-HAMZ	Cameron Z-105 HAFB	10459	
F-HANA	Eurocopter EC.130B4 Ecureuil	4590	
F-HANH	Schröder Fire Balloons G50/24 HAFB	1231	D-OBUG
F-HANI	Cameron V-90 HAFB	11361	
F-HANM	Cessna 208B Grand Caravan	208B0640	G-DLAC, N208PW, TI-BAE, HP-1399APP, TI-LRA, N1128P
F-HANN	Pilatus PC-12/47	887	HB-FQT(9)
F-HANO	Cameron Z-105 HAFB	11221	
F-HANS	Diamond DA 40D Star	D4.170	
F-HANX	Tecnam P.2002JF Sierra	209	
F-HANY	Llopis MA-30 HAFB	200	
F-HAOE	Robin DR.400/140B Dauphin 4	2401	OO-CZD
F-HAOL	Cameron Z-145 HAFB	11056	
F-HAOP	Aérospatiale AS.350B2 Ecureuil	2557	HB-XCJ, F-GJOK
F-HAPD	Cessna 172S Skyhawk SP	172S11402	N9531P
F-HAPE	Beech 1900D	UE-367	N30515
F-HAPG	Eurocopter EC.135T2+	0702	
F-HAPI	Diamond DA 40D Star	D4.056	D-EHOJ(2)
F-HAPL	Aérospatiale/Alenia ATR-72-212A	654	F-OIJG, F-WWEI
F-HAPN	Dassault Falcon 50EX	347	F-WWHC
F-HAPO	Piper PA-28-161 Cadet	2841105	(D-E...), F-GGVL
F-HAPQ	Evektor EV-97 SportStar RTC	2015 1737	
F-HAPR	Robin DR.400/140B Dauphin 4	2643	
F-HAPT	Cessna 172S Skyhawk SP	172S11187	N92382
F-HAPY	Cessna 182S Skylane	18280334	D-EEKB, N9510P
F-HAQG	SOCATA TB-20 Trinidad	534	G-THZL, F-GJDR, N65TB
F-HAQI	Aquila AT-01	AT01-135	
F-HAQU	Diamond DA.20-C1 Katana	C0439	
F-HARA	Robin DR.400/140B Dauphin 4	2559	
F-HARE	Cirrus SR22	1342	CN-TLM, N335CD
F-HARF	Issoire APM-30 Lion	29	
F-HARI	Cessna 172S Skyhawk SP	172S11404	N9135Q
F-HARJ	Cessna 172R Skyhawk	17280087	OY-PBS, N5260M
F-HARK	Robin DR.400/120 Dauphin 2+2	2602	
F-HARL	Robin DR.400/140B Dauphin 4	2607	
F-HARM	Aquila AT-01	AT01-157	
F-HARO	Aquila AT-01	AT01-179	
F-HARP	SOCATA Rallye 150ST	2858	G-BERC
F-HART	Lindstrand LBL-180A HAFB	1175	
F-HARV	Robin DR.400/140B Dauphin 4	2625	
F-HARY	Robinson R44 Raven II	12616	
F-HASE	Lindstrand LBL-90A HAFB	1243	
F-HASH	Robin DR.400/120 Dauphin 2+2	2645	
F-HASL	Cirrus SR20	1279	N252CD
F-HASO	Robin DR.400/140B Dauphin 4	2601	
F-HASP	Diamond DA 40D Star	D4.281	
F-HASR	Piper PA-28-181 Archer II	28-8490084	HB-PID, N4365U
F-HASU	Kubicek BB-26E HAFB	750	
F-HATA	Mudry CAP.10B	318	
F-HATC	SOCATA TB-21 Trinidad	2219	N226GA, F-GOIN, F-WWRA, N743TB
F-HATG	Cessna 525C CitationJet CJ4	525C-0115	N5076L
F-HATH	Cameron Z-105 HAFB	11251	
F-HATJ	Schröder Fire Balloons G34/24 HAFB	1169	D-OJAH(2)
F-HATM	Cameron Z-275 HAFB	10988	
F-HATN	Aquila AT-01	AT01-184	
F-HATO	Robin DR.400/120 Dauphin 2+2	2676	
F-HATR	Robinson R44 Raven	1860	
F-HATX	Cameron Obelix 90SS HAFB	11438	
F-HAUA	Ultramagic T-210 HAFB	210/66	
F-HAUD	Beech 77 Skipper	WA-293	OO-GVE, HB-EJL
F-HAUF	Aérospatiale AS.350B3 Ecureuil	7005	F-OKFL
F-HAUL	Xtremeair XA42	119	
F-HAUR	Robin DR.400/135CDI	2531	D-EPEX, D-ECDI(2)
F-HAUT	Ultramagic N-300 HAFB	300/19	
F-HAUX	Robin DR.400/135CDI	2605	
F-HAVA	Robin DR.400/120 Dauphin 2+2	2585	
F-HAVD	BAe Jetstream 4101	41022	N309UE, G-4-022
F-HAVE	Extra EA.300/200	1036	
F-HAVF	BAe Jetstream 4101	41025	N312UE, G-4-025
F-HAVI	Boeing 757-26D	24473	N473AP, B-2810
F-HAVM	Lindstrand LBL-120A HAFB	1242	
F-HAVN	Boeing 757-230WL	25140	D-ABNF
F-HAVS	Reims/Cessna F150L	F15000902	
F-HAVX	Eurocopter EC.120B Colibri	1523	UR-CLK, UR-CHGD, F-WWXR
F-HAXA	Dassault Falcon 900EX	12	F-WQBL, N912EX, (N900SB), N900EX, N913FJ, F-WWFJ
F-HAXR	Ultramagic S-90 HAFB	90/78	
F-HAYB	Cirrus SR20	1640	N50317
F-HAYL	Cessna F172G	F172-0239	D-ECTP(2), F-BNTP
F-HAYO	Issoire APM-20 Lionceau	28	
F-HAZA	Tecnam P.2002-JF Sierra	090	
F-HAZB	Tecnam P.2002-JF Sierra	096	
F-HAZC	Tecnam P.2002-JF Sierra	098	
F-HAZE	PZL-110 Koliber 160A	04010086	G-CBGA, SP-WGM
F-HAZU	Robinson R44 Raven II	11557	
F-HBAA	Kubicek AX-8 Replika SS HAFB	8	OO-BSP
F-HBAG	Reims/Cessna F177RG Cardinal RG	F177RG0051	D-EMEN(3), LX-MEN
F-HBAB	Airbus A321-211	823	F-WBAB, G-VOLH, D-AVZX
F-HBAC	Airbus A320-214	888	EC-GZE, F-WWDG
F-HBAH	Aérospatiale AS.350B2 Ecureuil	4414	
F-HBAI	Piaggio P.180 Avanti	1110	
F-HBAJ	Cameron C-90 HAFB	10840	
F-HBAL	Airbus A319-111	2870	EC-JXA, D-AVWG
F-HBAM	Kubicek BB-60Z HAFB	1072	
F-HBAO	Airbus A320-214	4589	F-WWIQ
F-HBAP	Airbus A320-214	4675	F-WWDE
F-HBAR	Robin DR.400/180 Régent (Dbr 7.10.16)	2549	
F-HBAS	Eurocopter EC.130B4 Ecureuil	4075	
F-HBAU	Aérospatiale AS.350B2 Ecureuil	4956	
F-HBAV	Piper PA-28-161 Warrior II	28-8316050	OO-NZG, G-LADN, G-BOLK, N4295C
F-HBAY	Lindstrand LBL-90A HAFB	1372	
F-HBAZ	Tecnam P.2002-JF Sierra	075	
F-HBBA	Kubicek BB-22E HAFB	648	
F-HBBC	Kubicek BB-26Z HAFB	541	
F-HBBE	Lindstrand LBL-120A HAFB	1285	
F-HBBG	Ultramagic M-145 HAFB	145/40	PH-RBG
F-HBBH	Kubicek BB-30Z HAFB	661	
F-HBBL	Llopis MA26 HAFB	197	
F-HBBP	Ultramagic N-180 HAFB	180/95	
F-HBBR	Cirrus SR20	1344	N6042K
F-HBCA	Beech 1900D	UE-188	SE-KXV, N1564J
F-HBCB	Beech 1900D	UE-390	3B-VTL, N853CA, N40729
F-HBCC	Beech 1900D	UE-350	3B-VIP, ZS-OOV, PH-RAT, ZS-OOV, N23481
F-HBCD	Diamond DA 42 Twin Star	42.067	
F-HBCE	Beech 1900D	UE-323	OY-CHU, ZS-SHB(2), 9J-MAS, N23047
F-HBCG	Beech 1900D	UE-70	PH-RNG, ZS-PZH, PH-RNG, ZS-PZH, N70ZV
F-HBCH	Piper PA-28-180 Cherokee G	28-7205261	D-EBCH, N11C
F-HBCI	Robin DR.500/200i Président (Res as D-EKWP(2) 9.16)	41	
F-HBCS	Aérospatiale/Alenia ATR-42-320	333	(CS-DVL), VT-ABE(2), F-WQNF, VT-ADC(2), F-WQNJ, D-BVIP, F-WQNO, VP-BOG, VR-BOG, (N333SG), F-WWLR
F-HBCT	Flight Design CT LS ELA	F-09-10-05	F-WBCT
F-HBDB	Cessna 172R Skyhawk	17281516	EC-KUE, N6184D
F-HBDD	Llopis MA26 HAFB	192	
F-HBDG	Tecnam P.2002-JF Sierra	170	
F-HBDM	Aerotek Pitts S-2A	2052	N6JP, N18JP
F-HBDO	Cameron O-84 HAFB	1068	HB-BDD
F-HBDP	Cessna 172S Skyhawk SP	172S10263	N6057A
F-HBDR	Ultramagic T-180 HAFB	180/91	
F-HBDT	Llopis MA-30 HAFB	222	
F-HBDV	Kubicek BB-26 HAFB	475	
F-HBDX	Embraer EMB-505 Phenom 300	50500216	LX-MAR, PR-LCF
F-HBDY	Cirrus SR22	1423	N61039
F-HBEA	Guimbal Cabri G2	1005	
F-HBEC(2)	Aérospatiale AS.350B3 Ecureuil	4730	
F-HBED	Eurocopter EC.120B Colibri	1362	
F-HBEE	Schweizer S-269C-1	0265	N86G
F-HBEF	Cameron Z-77 HAFB	10995	
F-HBEG	Robin DR.400/140B Dauphin 4	2575	
F-HBEJ	Cameron N-133 HAFB	3338	HB-BEJ
F-HBEK	Bell 429	57154	SE-JRC, C-GWEG(3)
F-HBEL	Bell 429	57207	C-FCQQ
F-HBEM	Llopis MA-22 HAFB	227	
F-HBEN	Lindstrand LBL-317A HAFB	1185	
F-HBEQ	Diamond DA 20-A1-100 Katana	10282	OE-VPZ, C-GIDA(2)
F-HBEV	Airbus A320-216	3952	(EC-...), F-WWBI
F-HBFA	Beech 390 Premier I	RB-83	LY-HER, N88EU, N88EL, N6183G
F-HBFB	Cameron V-77 HAFB	4740	G-BZBI
F-HBFC	Cessna 182Q Skylane	18267308	N1080T, N444V, N4719N
F-HBFG	Cessna 182T Skylane	18281792	N24377
F-HBFJ	Sud Aviation SA.318C Alouette Astazou	2151	I-COSS, F-GMLE, F-GMLF, 9V-..., F-GDQO, C-FBMG, CF-BMG, F-WIEN
F-HBFK	Cessna 550 Citation II	550-0625	(F-HCCN), N6846T, N625EA, PT-LYN, (N12554)
F-HBFL	Lindstrand LBL-105A HAFB	1477	
F-HBFM	Ultramagic M-77C HAFB	77/344	
F-HBFN	Chaize DC.2200 F16 HAFB	DC-001	
F-HBFO	Robin DR.400/140B Dauphin 4	2627	
F-HBFP	Hawker 800XP	258689	N36689
F-HBFR	Llopis MA-18 HAFB	205	
F-HBGB	SOCATA TBM-700	185	N700AU, N700AJ

Reg	Type	C/n	Previous ID
F-HBGE	SOCATA TBM-700	460	
F-HBGH	SOCATA TBM-700N	503	
F-HBHT	Aérospatiale AS.350B3 Ecureuil	8180	
F-HBIA	Aquila AT-01	AT01-181	
F-HBIB	Airbus A320-214	3289	D-ABDS, F-WWDS
F-HBIE	Reims/Cessna F172P Skyhawk	F17202051	G-BIIE, (PH-AXL(4))
F-HBIJ	Cessna 182M Skylane	18259877	D-EBHW, N91704
F-HBIL	Airbus A330-243	320	
F-HBIM	Aérospatiale AS.355N Ecureuil 2	5568	RP-C1710, F-OHNA
F-HBIO	Airbus A320-214	3242	D-ABDR, F-WWBP
F-HBIR	Cessna 510 Citation Mustang	510-0252	OK-LEO
F-HBIS	Airbus A320-214	3136	EI-DVF, F-WWDF
F-HBIX	Airbus A320-214	6012	F-WWBU
F-HBIZ	Robin DR.400/140B Dauphin 4	2631	
F-HBJB	Maule MX-7-180C Star Rocket	28023C	N928Z
F-HBJC	Sikorsky S-76C+	760748	N748A
F-HBJD	Cameron N-105 HAFB	11206	
F-HBJE	Schröder Fire Balloons G26/24 HAFB	1177	
F-HBJF	Diamond DA 40D Star	D4.339	OE-VPU
F-HBJM	Cessna 172S Skyhawk SP	172S9776	N66019
F-HBJP	Piper PA-34-200T Seneca II	34-7570228	G-GOGS, N1172X
F-HBJV	Mooney M.20J Model 201	24-3419	I-RJLJ, N433FM
F-HBKA	Eurocopter EC.120B Colibri	1568	
F-HBKB	Eurocopter EC.120B Colibri	1573	
F-HBKC	Eurocopter EC.120B Colibri	1600	
F-HBKD	Eurocopter EC.120B Colibri	1605	
F-HBKE	Eurocopter EC.120B Colibri	1606	
F-HBKF	Eurocopter EC.120B Colibri	1609	
F-HBKG	Eurocopter EC.120B Colibri	1610	
F-HBKH	Eurocopter EC.120B Colibri	1611	
F-HBKI	Eurocopter EC.120B Colibri	1612	
F-HBKJ	Eurocopter EC.120B Colibri	1613	
F-HBKL	Eurocopter EC.120B Colibri	1615	
F-HBKM	Eurocopter EC.120B Colibri	1616	
F-HBKN	Eurocopter EC.120B Colibri	1617	
F-HBKO	Eurocopter EC.120B Colibri	1620	
F-HBKP	Eurocopter EC.120B Colibri	1596	
F-HBKR	Eurocopter EC.120B Colibri	1601	
F-HBKS	Eurocopter EC.120B Colibri	1622	
F-HBKT	Eurocopter EC.120B Colibri	1623	
F-HBKV	Eurocopter EC.120B Colibri	1624	
F-HBKX	Eurocopter EC.120B Colibri	1625	
F-HBKY	Eurocopter EC.120B Colibri	1626	F-WWPD
F-HBKZ	Eurocopter EC.120B Colibri	1628	
F-HBLA	Embraer EMB.190-100LR	19000051	PT-SIA
F-HBLB	Embraer EMB.190-100LR	19000060	PT-SIN
F-HBLC	Embraer EMB.190-100LR	19000080	PT-SJW
F-HBLD	Embraer EMB.190-100LR	19000113	PT-SQH
F-HBLE	Embraer EMB.190-100LR	19000123	PT-SQS
F-HBLF	Embraer EMB.190-100LR	19000158	PT-SAO
F-HBLG	Embraer EMB.190-100LR	19000254	PT-SIZ
F-HBLH	Embraer EMB.190-100STD	19000266	PT-TLG
F-HBLI	Embraer EMB.190-100STD	19000298	PT-TZM
F-HBLJ	Embraer EMB.190-100STD	19000311	PT-TZZ
F-HBMC	Chaize CS.2200F24 HAFB	221	
F-HBMD	Aérospatiale AS.350B2 Ecureuil	4717	
F-HBME	Cirrus SR22	2962	N138PG
F-HBMG	Lindstrand LBL-120A HAFB	1180	
F-HBMI	Airbus A319-114	639	N573SX, C-FYJB, D-AVYU
F-HBMJ	Llopis MA-22 HAFB	207	
F-HBML	Lindstrand LBL-120A HAFB	1312	
F-HBMM	Diamond DA.20-C1 Katana	C0157	D-ETGF, N657DC, C-FDVA
F-HBMN	Lindstrand LBL-180A HAFB	1296	
F-HBMO	Kubicek BB-26E HAFB	840	
F-HBMP	CASA 212-DD	387	D-CJMP, I-DZPO, Fr.AF:387/MR/F-ZVMR
F-HBMR	Cessna 550 Citation II	550-0717	OE-GBC, SE-RBM, Fv103002, TC-SES, N600GH, XA-TCM, (N1205M)
F-HBMT	Schröder Fire Balloons G34/24 HAFB	1504	
F-HBMV	Lindstrand LBL-180A HAFB	1283	
F-HBMZ	Schröder Fire Balloons G30/24 HAFB	1622	
F-HBNA	Airbus A320-214	4335	F-WWIU
F-HBNB	Airbus A320-214	4402	F-WWBS
F-HBNC	Airbus A320-214	4601	F-WWID
F-HBND	Airbus A320-214	4604	F-WWIE
F-HBNE	Airbus A320-214	4664	F-WWIC
F-HBNF	Airbus A320-214	4714	F-WWBS
F-HBNG	Airbus A320-214	4747	F-WWIT
F-HBNH	Airbus A320-214	4800	F-WWIK
F-HBNI	Airbus A320-214	4820	F-WWIC
F-HBNJ	Airbus A320-214	4908	F-WWDK
F-HBNK	Airbus A320-214	5084	F-WWII
F-HBNL	Airbus A320-214	5129	F-WWBB
F-HBNM to Z	*Reserved for Airbus A320s for Air France*		
F-HBOB	Christen Pitts S-2B	5289	N963CB
F-HBOF	Cameron Z-105 HAFB	11017	OO-BYH
F-HBOI	Eurocopter EC.135T2+	1011	4K-AZ91, D-HCBH
F-HBON	Cameron Z-105 HAFB	11146	
F-HBOO	Cameron Z-77 HAFB	11540	
F-HBOP	Cameron N-90 HAFB	3969	OO-BQP, LX-TNT
F-HBOR	Cameron N-120 HAFB	10126	OO-BOR(3), D-OURE
F-HBOV	Piper PA-38-112 Tomahawk	38-78A0801	D-EBOY(3), F-GBOV, N9718N
F-HBOX	Diamond DA 40D Star	D4.220	
F-HBPA	Lindstrand LBL-105A HAFB	1284	
F-HBPB	Cessna 182T Skylane	18281951	N2344Y
F-HBPC	Robinson R44 Raven II	13081	
F-HBPE	Embraer EMB.145LR	145106	PH-RXC, ER-MKC, PH-RXC, EC-GZU
F-HBPF	Kubicek BB-30Z HAFB	491	
F-HBPG	Beech F33A Bonanza	CE-1370	OY-GEV
F-HBPK	Cameron Z-90 HAFB	10661	LX-BPK
F-HBPL	Kubicek BB-30Z HAFB	498	
F-HBPM	Robinson R44 Astro	0383	G-POTT
F-HBPN	Cirrus SR20	1778	N965SR
F-HBPO	Schröder Fire Balloons G30/24 HAFB	1045	LX-BPO
F-HBPP	Cessna 525 CitationJet CJ3	525B-0013	N831V, N5228Z
F-HBPR	Cessna 172N Skyhawk	17267700	TF-MAY, TF-LAX, N73821
F-HBPV	Wassmer Jodel D.120A	272	OO-FDS
F-HBPY	Mudry CAP.10B	182	HB-SAS
F-HBRB	Chaize JZ.25F16 HAFB	230	
F-HBRD	Tecnam P.2008-JC	1019	
F-HBRJ	Aquila AT-01	AT01-156	
F-HBRL	Llopis MA30 HAFB	195	
F-HBRM	Diamond DA 20-A1-100 Katana	10078	C-FGAI, N846DF
F-HBRO	Cirrus SR22T	0038	N121FR
F-HBRS	Eurocopter EC.135T2+	0994	D-HECQ
F-HBRV	Thunder AX7-77SI HAFB	11043	
F-HBSA	Airbus A320-214	3882	(EC-...), F-WWIP
F-HBSE	Robin DR.400/140B Dauphin 4	2632	
F-HBSF	Pilatus PC-6/B2-H4 Turbo Porter	949	
F-HBSG	Kubicek BB-26E HAFB	762	
F-HBSK	Tecnam P.2002-JF Sierra	057	
F-HBSL	Robin DR.401/155cdi	2619	F-GTCL
F-HBSM	Chaize CS.4000 F16 HAFB	223	
F-HBSN	Aérospatiale AS.350B3 Ecureuil	8047	
F-HBSP	Cameron Z-105 HAFB	11419	
F-HBSR	Schröder Fire Balloons G30/24 HAFB	954	OO-BAQ
F-HBST	Schröder Fire Balloons G34/24 HAFB	1038	D-OBST(2)
F-HBSU	Colt 315A HAFB	10176	G-CCIE
F-HBSV	Tecnam P.92JS Echo	097	D-EDJS(2)
F-HBSZ	Aerostar Raven S49A HAFB	S49A-3035	HB-BSZ
F-HBTF	Grumman-American AA-5B Tiger	AA5B-1078	HB-UCO
F-HBTM	Lindstrand LBL-90A HAFB	1204	
F-HBTN	Eurocopter EC.135T2+	0664	G-HBOB, D-HECU(16)
F-HBTV	Cessna 525 CitationJet	525-0918	
F-HBTY	Lindstrand LBL-180A HAFB	1119	OO-BTY
F-HBTZ	Tecnam P.2002-JF Sierra	027	
F-HBUD	Ultramagic M-105 HAFB	105/160	
F-HBUL	Ultramagic H-77 HAFB	77/274	
F-HBUR	Ballons Libert L2600 HAFB	333-057	
F-HBUT	Ultramagic T-180 HAFB	180/66	
F-HBVA	Eurocopter EC.120B Colibri	1630	
F-HBVB	Eurocopter EC.120B Colibri	1631	
F-HBVD	Eurocopter EC.120B Colibri	1635	
F-HBVE	Eurocopter EC.120B Colibri	1637	
F-HBVF	Eurocopter EC.120B Colibri	1638	
F-HBVG	Eurocopter EC.120B Colibri	1641	F-WWXP
F-HBVH	Eurocopter EC.120B Colibri	1643	
F-HBVI	Eurocopter EC.120B Colibri	1645	
F-HBVJ	Eurocopter EC.120B Colibri	1646	
F-HBVK	Eurocopter EC.120B Colibri	1647	
F-HBVL	Eurocopter EC.120B Colibri	1648	
F-HBVM	Eurocopter EC.120B Colibri	1649	
F-HBVN	Eurocopter EC.120B Colibri	1650	
F-HBVO	Eurocopter EC.120B Colibri	1482	(D-HAZU), F-GXRI, F-WQDE, F-WWXO
F-HBXA	Embraer ERJ-170-100STD	17000237	PT-SFN
F-HBXB	Embraer ERJ-170-100STD	17000250	PT-SJB
F-HBXC	Embraer ERJ-170-100STD	17000263	PT-SJR
F-HBXD	Embraer ERJ-170-100STD	17000281	PT-TQH
F-HBXE	Embraer ERJ-170-100STD	17000286	PT-TQM
F-HBXF	Embraer ERJ-170-100STD	17000292	PT-TQS
F-HBXG	Embraer ERJ-170-100STD	17000301	PT-XQA
F-HBXH	Embraer ERJ-170-100STD	17000307	PT-XQH
F-HBXI	Embraer ERJ-170-100STD	17000310	PT-XQX
F-HBXJ	Embraer ERJ-170-100STD	17000312	PT-XQY
F-HBXK	Embraer ERJ-170-100STD	17000008	EI-DFG, (I-EMCX), PT-SKA
F-HBXL	Embraer ERJ-170-100STD	17000009	EI-DFH, PT-SKB
F-HBXM	Embraer ERJ-170-100STD	17000010	EI-DFI, PT-SKC
F-HBXN	Embraer ERJ-170-100STD	17000011	EI-DFJ, PT-SKD
F-HBXO	Embraer ERJ-170-100STD	17000032	EI-DFK, PT-SUA
F-HBYA	Reims/Cessna F172N	F17201855	E7-GOC, 9A-NOR, D-EIYN
F-HBYC	Tecnam P.2010	020	
F-HBYD	Aérospatiale AS.350B2 Ecureuil	2109	F-ZBFC
F-HBYE	Aérospatiale AS.350B2 Ecureuil	2114	F-ZBFD, F-GIRO
F-HBYF	Aérospatiale AS.350B2 Ecureuil	1951	F-ZBBN(2), F-ZKBT, D-HHZZ(2)
F-HBYL	Aerospool WT-9 Dynamic LSA	DY420/2011	F-WBYL
F-HBYZ	Robin DR.400/140B Dauphin 4	2649	
F-HBZP	Schröder Fire Balloons G34/24 HAFB	1001	OO-BZP
F-HBZX	Cameron N-145 HAFB	3310	HB-BZX
F-HBZH	Robin DR.400/120 Dauphin 2+2	2646	
F-HBZL	Thunder AX9-120SII HAFB	2593	HB-BZL
F-HCAA	Robin DR.400/180 Régent	2596	
F-HCAB	Robin DR.400/180 Régent	2615	
F-HCAC	Diamond DA 42 Twin Star	42.261	OE-VP.
F-HCAD	Cameron Z-77 HAFB	11269	
F-HCAF	Cameron Z-105 HAFB	11197	
F-HCAG	Lindstrand LBL-150A HAFB	1217	
F-HCAH	Robinson R44 Raven II	10577	G-TEXT
F-HCAJ	Cameron C-80 HAFB	11328	
F-HCAL	Robinson R44 Clipper II	10797	
F-HCAM	Robin DR.400/140B Dauphin 4	2644	
F-HCAN	Diamond DA 42 Twin Star	42.035	
F-HCAP	Robin DR.400/140B Dauphin 4	2616	
F-HCAS	Cessna 172R Skyhawk	17280556	N26174
F-HCAT	Airbus A330-243	285	F-WWKB
F-HCAZ	Kubicek BB-30Z HAFB	867	
F-HCBA	Cameron Z-140 HAFB	10668	
F-HCBC	SAN Jodel D.140R Abeille	510	Fr.AF
F-HCBE	Cameron Z-120 HAFB	12002	
F-HCBF	Cameron TR-77 HAFB	11114	
F-HCBH	Aérospatiale AS.350B3 Ecureuil	4803	
F-HCBJ	Robin DR.400/140B Dauphin 4	2638	
F-HCBL	Chaize CS.2200F24 HAFB	225	
F-HCBN	Lindstrand LBL-180A HAFB	1186	
F-HCBR	Ultramagic M-120 HAFB	120/41	
F-HCBS	Boeing Stearman A75N1	75-883	N60320, 41-823
F-HCBV	Schröder Fire Balloons G50/24 HAFB	597	OO-BFL(2)
F-HCBY	Robinson R44 Raven II	12291	
F-HCCA	Lindstrand LBL-180A HAFB	1079	
F-HCCB	Lindstrand LBL-90A HAFB	1246	
F-HCCF	Cirrus SR20	1505	N387CD
F-HCCG	Schröder Fire Balloons G50/24 HAFB	1056	
F-HCCH	Schröder Fire Balloons G45/24 HAFB	1314	
F-HCCI	Schröder Fire Balloons G60/24 HAFB	1081	D-OREK
F-HCCJ	Schweizer 269C	S-1463	SE-JBB, G-WISK, N41S
F-HCCL	Cameron C-90 HAFB	11358	
F-HCCO	Robin DR.400/135CDI	2639	
F-HCCS	Llopis MA-35 HAFB	168	
F-HCDA	Robin DR.400/120 Dauphin 2+2	2634	
F-HCDB	Robinson R44 Raven	1106	I-RMLP, HB-ZDK
F-HCDC	Sikorsky S-76C++	760741	N741A
F-HCDD	Dassault Falcon 50EX	297	OE-HHH, F-WQBJ, N119AG, F-WWHY
F-HCDG	Robin DR.400/120 Dauphin 2+2	2693	
F-HCDI	Robin DR.400/140B Dauphin 4	2593	
F-HCDJ	Robinson R22B2 Beta	3751	
F-HCDL	Kubicek BB-34Z HAFB	663	

Reg	Type	C/n	Previous identities
F-HCDM	Reims/Cessna F182Q Skylane	F18200114	OY-BYA, (D-EPKB), OY-BYA, SE-IBA
F-HCDT	Kubicek BB-51Z HAFB	515	
F-HCEA	Ultramagic T-150 HAFB	150/15	
F-HCEI	Eurocopter EC.175B	5003	
F-HCEJ	Cameron A-300 HAFB	10954	
F-HCEL	Airbus A340-211	081	OE-LAH, F-WWJO
F-HCEN	Robin DR.400/140B Dauphin 4	2594	
F-HCES	Cessna 120	11725	G-OWIL, G-BTYW, N77283, NC77283
F-HCET	Tecnam P.2002-JF Sierra	214	
F-HCEV	Beech B200GT King Air	BY-91	N6351N
F-HCFA	SOCATA TB-10 Tobago	633	D-EFLO (2)
F-HCFC	Kubicek BB-30Z HAFB	619	
F-HCFD	Aérospatiale AS.350B3 Ecureuil	4914	
F-HCFG	Kubicek BB-37Z HAFB	753	
F-HCFP	Piper PA.31 Turbo Navajo	31-370	F-OCFP, VH-SVY, N9279Y
F-HCFR	Evektor EV-97 SportStar RTC	20141715	
F-HCFX	Cessna 172S Skyhawk SP	172S9747	N65744
F-HCGA	Cirrus SR20	1911	G-CIRS, N191PG
F-HCGC	Chaize JZ.30F16 HAFB	214	
F-HCGF	Cameron R-77 HAFB	11333	
F-HCGM	Tecnam P.2002-JF Sierra	108	
F-HCGO	Tecnam P.2006T	025	
F-HCGP	Chaize JZ.40F16 HAFB	220	
F-HCGR	Llopis Balloons MA-26 HAFB	189	
F-HCGT	Robinson R22 Beta	1197	G-CHYL
F-HCGV	Schröder Fire Balloons G22/24 HAFB	1422	
F-HCGY	Cameron Z-180 HAFB	11308	
F-HCHB	Aérospatiale AS.350B3 Ecureuil	7695	N151RL
F-HCHH	CEA Jodel DR.100A Ambassadeur	5	G-BTHH, F-BJCH
F-HCHL	Eurocopter EC.135P2+	0691	YR-RYC, D-HTSH
F-HCHO	Piper PA-28-181 Archer II	28-7990189	OO-BIR, N2136F
F-HCHQ	Raven-Europe S-66A HAFB	E-395	HB-BHQ
F-HCHR	Cameron N-120 HAFB	4219	HB-QDX
F-HCHT	Eurocopter EC.135T2+	0836	D-HTSA(6), EC-034
F-HCIA	Lindstrand LBL-105A HAFB	1441	
F-HCIC	Cessna 525B CitationJet CJ3	525B-0224	N5250P
F-HCIE	Boeing 757-204	27208	G-BYAT
F-HCIR	Cirrus SR20	1464	N618CD
F-HCJA	Cameron C-90 HAFB	10915	
F-HCJB	Lindstrand LBL-90B HAFB	1138	
F-HCJC	Lindstrand LBL-120A HAFB	1241	
F-HCJD	Morane-Saulnier MS.317	6565/311	(F-GOBQ), F-BCBQ
F-HCJE	Embraer EMB-500 Phenom 100	50000263	PT-TNR
F-HCJF	Libert L2600 HAFB	342-066	
F-HCJH	Lindstrand LBL-90A HAFB	1268	
F-HCJL	MD Helicopters MD.520N	LN-301	I-AGMP
F-HCJM	Robin DR.400/180 Regent	2665	
F-HCJR	Lindstrand LBL-90A HAFB	1321	
F-HCKV	Cameron Z-77 HAFB	4946	G-CBKV
F-HCLA	Cessna 182T Skylane	18282201	N52782
F-HCLB	Diamond DA20-C1 Katana	C0410	N767CC
F-HCLC	Tecnam P.2006T	027	
F-HCLE	Chaize CS.3000-F16 HAFB	229	
F-HCLG	Diamond DA 20-A1 Katana	10184	D-ECIG(3), C-GAHQ, N284DA, C-GDMY
F-HCLM	Robin DR.400/140B Dauphin 4	2618	
F-HCLO	Aérospatiale AS.355N Ecureuil 2	5570	F-GSAU, D-HSMM, CS-HDP, N888B, N6097C
F-HCLP	Aérospatiale AS.350B2 Ecureuil	4511	
F-HCLT	Aérospatiale AS.350B3 Ecureuil	7930	
F-HCLY	Robin DR.400/180S Regent	1900	HB-KCH
F-HCMA	Diamond DA 40D Star	D4.267	
F-HCMB	Diamond DA 40D Star	D4.268	
F-HCMC	Diamond DA 40D Star	D4.269	
F-HCMD	Diamond DA 40D Star	D4.270	
F-HCME	Diamond DA 40D Star	D4.276	
F-HCMF	Diamond DA 40D Star	D4.277	
F-HCMG	Diamond DA 40D Star	D4.278	
F-HCMH	Diamond DA 40D Star	D4.349	OE-VPU
F-HCMI	Diamond DA 40D Star	D4.364	OE-VDR
F-HCNA	Robin DR.400/140B Dauphin 4	2650	
F-HCNB	Lindstrand LBL-180A HAFB	1466	
F-HCNC	Piper PA-28-161 Warrior II	2841110	HB-PME
F-HCND	Libert L3400 HAFB	327-051	
F-HCNE	Robinson R44 Raven II	13396	
F-HCNN	Reims/Cessna F172N	F17201951	D-ENCN, PH-VSP, (PH-AXN(3))
F-HCNR	Robinson R44 Raven II	11610	G-FEAR
F-HCOA	Boeing 737-5L9	28084	OY-APB, G-MSKE, OY-APB
F-HCOL	Guimbal Cabri G2	1012	
F-HCOM	Reims/Cessna F337G Skymaster (US c/n 33701592)	F33700071	EC-CPG, F-BJDG
F-HCOP	Robinson R22 Beta II	4416	
F-HCOQ	Chaize DC.2200 F16 HAFB	DC-003	
F-HCOV	Robin DR.400/120 Dauphin 2+2 (Badly damaged 11.5.06)	2599	
F-HCOX	Ultramagic H-77 HAFB	77/330	
F-HCPA	Kubicek BB-20XR HAFB	881	
F-HCPC	Cessna 172F	17253259	D-EFZL, F-GFZL, TN-AAS, (F-GELD), TN-AAS, F-OCGC, (N5637R)
F-HCPB	Cessna 525 CitationJet CJ	525-0322	LX-YSL, N52LT
F-HCPE	Piaggio P.180 Avanti	1144	
F-HCPF	Extra EA.300/L	1320	
F-HCPG	Cirrus SR22	1847	N515PG
F-HCPJ	Cameron C-90 HAFB	10857	
F-HCPL	Robin DR.401/135cdi	2642	
F-HCPM	Robin DR.400/135CDI	2613	
F-HCPR	Robinson R44 Raven II	11337	
F-HCPZ	CSA PS-28 Cruiser	C0489	
F-HCRB	Aérospatiale SA.315B Lama	2621	I-PELL
F-HCRC	Ultramagic N-180 HAFB	180/90	
F-HCRH	Bell 206B Jet Ranger II	1897	EI-BYJ, N49725
F-HCRI	Agusta-Bell 206B Jet Ranger 2	8432	EI-BIJ, G-BCVZ
F-HCRJ	Llopis MA-22 HAFB	188	
F-HCRL	SIGA MA-30 Pilatre de Rozier HAFB	166	
F-HCRP	Llopis MA-26 HAFB	184	
F-HCRT	Cessna 550 Citation II	550-0257	N53RG, N187TA, XA-SQQ, XC-HEQ, N68609
F-HCRU	Schröder Fire Balloons G30/24 HAFB	1569	
F-HCSA	Extra EA.300/L	1216	D-ERHC
F-HCSB	Cirrus SR20	1461	OO-PYT, N504CD
F-HCSC	Aérospatiale AS.350B3 Ecureuil (Damaged 16.9.15)	4917	
F-HCSD	Robinson R44 Raven II	10255	G-LARY, (EI-...), G-LARY, G-CCRZ
F-HCSE	Lindstrand LBL-77A HAFB	1404	
F-HCSF	Piper PA-28-181 Archer III	28-8090369	D-EJEC(2), N8241F
F-HCSG	Llopis MA-26 HAFB	228	
F-HCSJ	Llopis MA-30 HAFB	210	
F-HCSK	Tecnam P.2002-JF Sierra	097	
F-HCSN	Lindstrand LBL-77A HAFB	1414	
F-HCSO	Llopis MA-26 HAFB	231	
F-HCSP	Cameron C-80 HAFB	11411	
F-HCST	Kubicek BB-37Z HAFB	1071	
F-HCSV	Diamond DA 42 Twin Star	42.371	
F-HCTA	Diamond DA 42 Twin Star	42.298	
F-HCTB	Diamond DA 42 Twin Star	42.299	
F-HCTC	Diamond DA 42 Twin Star	42.353	
F-HCTD	Diamond DA 42 Twin Star	42.359	OE-VDM
F-HCTE	Diamond DA 42 Twin Star	42.360	OE-VPW
F-HCTF	Tecnam P.2008JC	1036	
F-HCUB	Piper J-3C-65 Cub	17360	PH-OEI, N4210W, N21922, (PH-OEI), CF-JVX, N70376, NC70376
F-HCUP	Aérophile 5500 Tethered Gas Balloon	023	
F-HCVA	Diamond DA.42M NG Guardian	42M.N007	
F-HCVF	Cameron C-90 HAFB	11262	
F-HCVM	Tecnam P.2002-JF Sierra	128	
F-HCVO	Guimbal G2 Cabri	1129	
F-HCVP	Lindstrand LBL-120A HAFB	1267	OO-BVP(2)
F-HCVS	Robinson R44 Raven I	2308	
F-HCXD	Robinson R44 Raven II	10436	G-DGHD
F-HCYB	Chaize CS.2200F24 HAFB	222	
F-HCYF	Schröder Fire Balloons G26/24 HAFB	1356	
F-HCZI	Airbus A319-112	4268	D-AVWP
F-HDAB	Diamond DA 42 Twin Star	42.186	OE-VPW
F-HDAC	Diamond DA 20-C1 Katana	C0371	
F-HDAF	Diamond DA 40D Star	D4.264	OE-VPU
F-HDAG	Diamond DA 42 Twin Star	42.195	OE-VPI
F-HDAH	Diamond DA 42 Twin Star	42.274	OE-VPW
F-HDAI	Diamond DA 40D Star TDI	D4.227	OE-VPU
F-HDAL	Diamond DA 40D Star	D4.224	
F-HDAO	Diamond DA 42 Twin Star	42.253	OE-VPW
F-HDAP	Diamond DA 42 Twin Star	42.266	OE-VPY
F-HDAQ	Diamond DA 42 Twin Star	42.373	OE-VPW
F-HDAR	Diamond DA 42 Twin Star	42.382	OE-VDI
F-HDAS	Diamond DA 42 Twin Star	42.268	OE-VPW
F-HDAV	Diamond DA 40D Star TDI	D4.318	OE-VPU
F-HDAX	Diamond DA 40D Star	D4.358	
F-HDAZ	Diamond DA 40D Star TDI	D4.333	OE-VPT
F-HDBA	Cameron A-120 HAFB	11342	
F-HDBC	Cameron C-90 HAFB	11480	
F-HDBP	Cirrus SR22	3483	N171CS
F-HDBR	Cameron Z-105 HAFB	11417	
F-HDBS	Llopis MA-26 HAFB	224	
F-HDBV	Extra EA.300/SC	SC048	
F-HDBZ	Tecnam P.2008JC	1008	
F-HDCA	Cirrus SR22	1834	N798CD
F-HDCC	Aérospatiale AS.350B2 Ecureuil	4788	
F-HDCG	Diamond DA 20-C1 Katana	C0565	
F-HDCL	Ultramagic M-120 HAFB	120/79	
F-HDCM	Enstrom 280FX Shark	2044	G-VRTX, G-CBNH, Chile H-180
F-HDCP	Ultramagic N-210 HAFB	210/87	
F-HDCR	Morane-Saulnier MS.880B Rallye Club	1735	HB-KPF, F-BSVI
F-WDCT	Flight Design CT-LS	F-09-02-10	
F-HDDA	Robinson R22 Beta II	4302	
F-HDDC	Cameron Z-105 HAFB	11284	
F-HDDE	Diamond DA 40D Star	D4.074	G-CCLB
F-HDDF	Diamond DA 40D Star	D4.082	G-CCUS
F-HDDG	Diamond DA 40D Star	D4.180	PH-SVR, OE-VPU, OE-VPW
F-HDDH	Diamond DA 42 Twin Star	42.193	S5-DNE
F-HDDP	Dassault Falcon 900LX	277	M-TINK(2), F-HNLX, F-WWFD
F-HDEY	Pilatus PC-6/B2-H4 Turbo Porter	735	HB-FFW
F-HDFC	Ultramagic S-160 HAFB	160/139	
F-HDFI	Eurocopter EC.120B Colibri	1434	HB-ZNG, F-HDLB, F-WWXP
F-HDFJ	Eurocopter EC.120B Colibri	1488	LN-ODA(3), PH-HHL, F-WQDH
F-HDFK	Eurocopter EC.120B Colibri	1557	F-GZBE
F-HDFX	Aérospatiale AS.350B2 Ecureuil	9012	OO-RAX, F-GZOO
F-HDGF	Cameron RX-120 Replica HAFB	11364	
F-HDGK	Airbus A320-214	4478	D-ABFM(2), F-WWDJ
F-HDGM	Robinson R44 Raven II	12709	
F-HDIB	Diamond DA 40D Star TDI	D4.374	
F-HDID	Diamond DA 40D Star TDI	D4.378	OE-VPU
F-HDIE	Diamond DA 40D Star TDI	D4.382	
F-HDIV	Lindstrand LBL-90A HAFB	1352	
F-HDJC	Cessna 182T Skylane	18282152	N5234E
F-HDJD	Cameron N-77 HAFB	11645	
F-HDJE	Diamond DA 40D Star	D4.030	OE-DXI(2), D-EWWE(2)
F-HDJF	Diamond DA 40D Star	D4.393	OE-VDS
F-HDJG	Diamond DA 40D Star	D4.036	OE-KKC, (OM-HLH), OE-DDC
F-HDJH	Cameron Z-750 HAFB	11643	
F-HDJL	Dassault Falcon 2000LX	161	OY-MGO, (G-LSMB), F-WWGX
F-HDJO	Ultramagic M-145 HAFB	145/83	
F-HDJP	Piper PA.28RT-201 Arrow IV	28R-8018044	OO-CJF, F-GCJF, N8164D
F-HDKG	Diamond DA.40 Star	40.073	PH-JKG
F-HDKK	Piper PA-28-180 Cherokee C	28-3671	OY-DKK, LN-AEF, N9542J
F-HDKY	Cessna 172S Skyhawk SP	172S11038	N9138M
F-HDLA	Evektor EV-97 SportStar RTC	2014 1716	
F-HDLC	Aérospatiale AS.350B1 Ecureuil	2271	3A-MLC, EC-ERR
F-HDLE	Cameron C-90 HAFB	11200	
F-HDLI	Evektor EV-97 SportStar RTC	2014 1706	
F-HDLJ	Dassault Falcon 900EASy	165	OE-IMC, (F-GUDA), (N777SA), N165FJ, F-WWFZ
F-HDLK	Evektor EV-97 SportStar RTC	2015 1723	
F-HDLL	Evektor EV-97 SportStar RTC	2015 1724	
F-HDLM	Evektor EV-97 SportStar RTC	2015 1727	
F-HDLN	Beech B200GT King Air	BY-111	N6411X
F-HDLO	Llopis MA-30 HAFB	201	
F-HDLR	Llopis MA-30 HAFB	233	
F-HDLV	Evektor EV-97 SportStar RTC	2015 1718	
F-HDLY	Cameron A-210 HAFB	10089	
F-HDMA	Cirrus SR22	2719	N349SR

Registration	Type	Serial	Previous identities
F-HDMC	Piper PA-28-181 Archer III	2843667	D-ETFI, N60927, N9515N
F-HDME	HOAC DV-20 Katana	20214	OE-VPX
F-HDMI	Robinson R22 Beta II	4117	EI-DXI, N3013G
F-HDMJ	Cameron C-90 HAFB	11286	
F-HDMM	Diamond DA 42 Twin Star	42.175	OE-VPI
F-HDMP	Diamond DA 42 Twin Star	42.148	OE-VPW
F-HDMV	Tecnam P.2008JC	1009	
F-HDNK	Hughes 369HM	71-0213M	RDAF H-213
F-HDNP	Diamond DA 20-C1 Katana	C0432	
F-HDNT	Cessna 208B Grand Caravan	208B2060	N2140X
F-HDNY	Diamond DA 42NG Twin Star	42.N120	OE-VDL
F-HDOC	Extra EA.300/LC	LC003	OK-KUR, D-ESSP, Fr.AF 03/F-TGCH
F-HDOV	Aquila AT-01	AT01-182	
F-HDPA	Cessna 182T Skylane	18282166	N5239X
F-HDPB	Dassault Falcon 50EX	334	OE-HPS, N335EX, F-WWHP
F-HDPC	Lindstrand LBL-105A HAFB	1343	
F-HDPE	Piper PA-28-181 Archer II	2843573	N925WB, N291HP
F-HDPF	Schröder Fire Balloons G34/24 HAFB	1463	
F-HDPL	Aerospool WT-9 Dynamic Turbo LSA	DY400/2011	F-WDPL
F-HDPM	Cameron Z-105 HAFB	11102	
F-HDPN	Cessna 510 Citation Mustang	510-0163	CS-DPN
F-HDPP	Extra EA.300/L	1303	
F-HDPR	Piper PA-18-95 Super Cub	18-3202	G-CDPR, OY-AVT, D-ELFT, OL-L05, L128, 53-4802
F-HDPT	Robin DR.500/200i Président	0010	G-BYIT
F-HDPU	Llopis MA35 HAFB	193	
F-HDPY	Cessna 510 Citation Mustang	510-0149	
F-HDRB	Cameron Z-275 HAFB	11421	
F-HDRC	Robinson R44 Raven II	12546	
F-HDRD	SIGA MA-30 Pilatre de Rozier HAFB	167	
F-HDRJ	Swearingen SA.226T Merlin 111A	T-265	LX-NRJ, RBAF CF-05, N5381M
F-HDRS	Cameron Z-105 HAFB	11613	
F-HDRT	Lindstrand LBL-330A HAFB	1282	
F-HDRV	Llopis MA-26 HAFB	219	
F-HDRX	Aérospatiale AS.355F1 Ecureuil 2	5289	EC-IDU, SE-JFE, 9M-DPK, F-ODVY, 9V-BNI, (9M-AYW), F-WZFQ
F-HDRY	Eurocopter EC.130B4	4495	
F-HDSB	Kubicek BB-30Z HAFB	1294	
F-HDSD	Dassault Falcon 900C	188	PH-EDM, F-WWFZ
F-HDSN	Aérophile 5500 Tethered Gas Balloon	036	
F-HDST	Aérospatiale AS.350BA Ecureuil	2110	F-ZBFH, JA9771
F-HDUC	Robin DR.400/ 140B Major	2274	HB-KEA
F-HDUM	Chaize DC.2200F16 HAFB	DC-005	
F-HDUO	Ultramagic M-56 HAFB	56/46	
F-HDVA	Diamond DA 40 NG Star	D4.304	OE-DQH, SX-AZA, OE-UDP, OE-VPU
F-HDVD	Boeing Stearman A75N1	75-940	N4079, N64078, BuA3163
F-HDVF	Cameron Z-105 HAFB	10410	OO-BVF
F-HDVM	Llopis MA-26 HAFB	206	
F-HDYN	Piper PA-28-181 Archer II	28-8690048	HB-PIR, N9086Z, N9514N
F-HEAB	Kubicek BB-60N HAFB	497	OO-BAB(2)
F-HEAC	Schröder Fire Balloons G30/24 HAFB	760	D-OFII
F-HEAD	Eurocopter EC.135T2	0285	
F-HEAE	Tecnam P.2002-JF Sierra	255	
F-HEAF	Lindstrand LBL-90A HAFB	1370	
F-HEAI	SAN Jodel DR.1050 Ambassadeur	16	HB-EAI
F-HEAJ	Cameron Z-90 HAFB	11921	
F-HEAL	Beech B200 King Air	BB-1928	N964RT, N3728E
F-HEAM	SOCATA TB-9 Tampico	2164	
F-HEAR	Diamond DA 40D Star	D4.097	OE-DET(2), OE-VPU
F-HEAS	Cameron Z-180 HAFB	11372	
F-HEAT	Robinson R44 Clipper II	12986	
F-HEAU	Llopis MA30 HAFB	237	
F-HEAV	Ultramagic M-105 HAFB	105/140	G-CEAV
F-HEBA	Ultramagic M-42 HAFB	42/12	
F-HEBM	Cameron Z-90 HAFB	11377	
F-HEBO	Dassault Falcon 900EASy	236	TC-AZR, F-WWFW
F-HEBP	Kubicek BB-30Z HAFB	877	
F-HEBV	Mudry CAP.10C	315	F-WEBV, F-WWZC
F-HECA	Robin DR.400/140B Dauphin 4	2606	
F-HECB	Cameron Z-105 HAFB	10835	
F-HECC	Cessna 172R Skyhawk	17280306	SX-AEF, N502ES
F-HECD	Dassault Falcon 7X	134	F-WWUH
F-HECJ	Cirrus SR22	0176	N708PP
F-HECL	Llopis MA-26 HAFB	187	
F-HECM	Ultramagic M-105 HAFB	105/173	
F-HECN	SOCATA TB-20 Trinidad	1827	N227BL
F-HECO	Robin DR.400/140B Dauphin 4	2600	
F-HECT	Flight Design CT LS LSA	F-09-04-06	F-WECT
F-HEDE	SOCATA TB-21 Trinidad GT Turbo	500	G-BZLI, F-GENI
F-HEDG	Piper PA-46-500TP Malibu Meridian	4697501	N25266, (F-HEDG), N9532N
F-HEDO	Robinson R22 Beta II	4661	
F-HEDY	Robinson R44 Raven II	13732	
F-HEEA	Cameron Z-105 HAFB	11088	
F-HEED	Schröder Fire Balloons G22/24 HAFB	1505	
F-HEEP	Piper PA-28-161 Cadet	2841300	PH-SVH, (PH-VCR), N9528N
F-HEFS	Agusta-Bell 206A Jet Ranger II	8112	G-CRDY, G-WHAZ, OH-HRE, G-WHAZ, OH-HRE
F-HEGT	Eurocopter EC155B1 Dauphin	6978	
F-HEHC	Llopis MA-30 HAFB	190	
F-HEHO	Robinson R44 Raven II	11101	G-FUNY
F-HEIN	Aérospatiale AS.350B3 Ecureuil	4740	
F-HEIR	Beech A36 Bonanza 36	E-2374	
F-HEJB	Tecnam P.2002-JF Sierra	113	
F-HEJC	Cessna 172S Skyhawk SP	172S11074	N9051X
F-HEJD	Cameron N-105 HAFB	11547	
F-HEJM	Cameron N-105 HAFB	4804	D-OHFF
F-HEJP	Lindstrand LBL-90A HAFB	1371	
F-HEKA	Cessna 182T Skylane	18282126	N6194U
F-HELA	Embraer EMB-145EP	145167	SX-CMB, G-EMBK
F-HELC	Cameron TR-77 HAFB	11539	
F-HELE	SOCATA TBM-700N	511	N850LE
F-HELI	Robinson R44 Raven II	10920	
F-HELP	Ultramagic S-130 HAFB	130/91	
F-HEMA	Kubicek BB-26E HAFB	689	
F-HEMB	Piper PA-28RT-201T Turbo Arrow IV	28R-8231029	I-CMMB, N8101C
F-HEMC	Cameron Cork-105SS HAFB	11542	
F-HEMG	Llopis MA-30 HAFB	213	
F-HEMP	Ultramagic M-130 HAFB	130/76	
F-HEMR	Ultramagic M-77C HAFB	77/380	
F-HEMS	Piper PA-28-181 Archer III	28243637	N4870R
F-HEMV	Piper PA-46-500TP Malibu Meridian	4697337	N194JL, N9548N
F-HEND	Cessna 510 Citation Mustang	510-0161	G-ZJET
F-HENG	Eurocopter EC.135P2	0418	OH-HCO
F-HENO	Lindstrand LBL-105A HAFB	916	G-JENO
F-HENV	Llopis MA-30 HAFB	181	
F-HEPA	Airbus A320-214	4139	F-WWXZ
F-HEPB	Airbus A320-214	4241	F-WWDK
F-HEPC	Airbus A320-214	4267	F-WWBM
F-HEPD	Airbus A320-214	4295	F-WWIZ
F-HEPE	Airbus A320-214	4298	F-WWDF
F-HEPF	Airbus A320-214	5719	F-WWDX
F-HEPG	Airbus A320-214	5802	F-WWIX
F-HEPH	Airbus A320-214	5869	F-WWDK
F-HEPI to Z	Reserved for Airbus A320s for Air France		
F-HERA	Mudry CAP.232	35	Fr.AF/F-TGCD, F-WQPJ
F-HERB	Cameron Z-105 HAFB	11236	
F-HERE	Cessna 510 Citation Mustang	510-0194	LX-RSQ
F-HERV	Cameron O-42 HAFB	275	PH-ARA(2)
F-HESA	CSA PS-28 Cruiser	P1102024	OK-RTO
F-HESB	Aérospatiale AS.350B3 Ecureuil	7259	
F-HEST	Aérospatiale AS.350B Ecureuil	1089	EI-PDG, G-BMAV
F-HETH	Aérospatiale AS.350B3 Ecureuil	7108	
F-HETM	Eurocopter EC.120B Colibri	1560	I-MLTMYR-SYT, YR-YON, F-WANO, F-WWPZ
F-HETN	Piper PA-18-150 Super Cub	18-7909095	D-EBTN, I-LETY, N82384
F-HETS	Beech 1900D	UE-360	PH-RNH, PK-TVL, VH-FOZ, N30662
F-HEVA	Cameron C-90 HAFB	10462	
F-HEVP	Tecnam P.2010	003	
F-HEXE	Robin DR.400/120 Dauphin 2+2	2689	
F-HEXP	Cirrus SR22	1548	G-NETB, N226TS
F-HEXR	Dassault Falcon 7X	223	F-WWVY
F-HEXT	Ultramagic M-120 HAFB	120/74	
F-HEYC	Cameron Z-31 HAFB	11075	G-CESY
F-HFAA	Maule M-7-235 Star Rocket	4004C	OY-PJA, N56562
F-HFAB	Agusta-Bell 47G-2	186	F-BXXX, ALAT
F-HFAC	Robinson R44 Raven II	13224	
F-HFAD	Piper PA-28R-200 Cherokee Arrow	28R-35383	PH-PJX
F-HFAF	Agusta-Bell 206B Jet Ranger 3	8615	EC-DOL
F-HFAG	Tecnam P2002-JF Sierra	124	
F-HFAL	Robinson R44 Raven II	12651	G-WDNG
F-HFAM	Cameron V-77 HAFB	11580	
F-HFAN	HOAC DV-20 Katana	20210	OE-VPX
F-HFAR	Reims/Cessna F172M	F17201079	OY-BFI
F-HFBA	Lindstrand LBL-105A HAFB	1440	
F-HFBF	Aérospatiale AS.350B2 Ecureuil	7687	
F-HFBM	Lindstrand LBL-105A HAFB	1368	
F-HFBP	Libert L-3400 HAFB	319-043	
F-HFBS	Diamond DA 42NG	42.N220	
F-HFCA	Cameron TR-77 HAFB	11539	
F-HFCC	Cameron Z-105 HAFB	11642	
F-HFCD	Cameron Z-120 HAFB	11948	
F-HFCG	Robin DR.400/120 Petit Prince	2660	
F-HFCK	Robinson R22B Beta	3359	D-HAIR(2)
F-HFCL	Diamond DA 20-C1 Katana	C0330	EC-KEQ, OE-VPZ, N941JT
F-HFCM	Tecnam P.2002-JF Sierra	129	
F-HFCO	Robinson R44 Raven II	12401	
F-HFCT	Ultramagic M-77C HAFB	77/357	
F-HFDM	Issoire APM-30 Lion	36	
F-HFEB	Colt 120A HAFB	2206	PH-BBR, OO-BBR
F-HFEL	Aérospatiale AS.350B2 Ecureuil	7037	
F-HFFA	Llopis MA-26 HAFB	204	
F-HFFI	Partenavia P.68B	39	F-OGVX, G-BFVO, SE-FUK
F-HFGB	CSA PS-28 Cruiser	C0548	
F-HFGI	Robin DR.400/160 Major	2691	
F-HFGX	Tecnam P.2002-JF Sierra	252	
F-HFHF	SOCATA MS.893A Rallye Commodore 180	11500	EC-LDT, F-BSDN
F-HFIK	Issoire APM-30 Lion	35	
F-HFIP	Bombardier BD.700-1A10 Global 6000	9567	C-GUTP(2)
F-HFIT	Britten-Norman BN-2T Turbine Islander	2139	ES-PNW, G-WOTG, G-BJYT
F-HFJB	Lindstrand LBL-90A HAFB	1486	
F-HFJD	Cameron TR-77 HAFB	11840	
F-HFJM	Schröder Fire Balloons G30/24 HAFB	283	D-ORHB
F-HFKC	Embraer EMB-145LR	145282	UR-DNY, I-EXME, PT-SJY
F-HFKD	Embraer EMB-135BJ Legacy 600	14500933	HB-JEL, PT-SCB
F-HFKE	Embraer EMB-145LR	145299	F-WKXO, I-EXMO, PT-SKQ
F-HFKF	Embraer EMB-145LR	145286	SE-RAF, UR-DNX, F-WKXH, I-EXMI, PT-SKD
F-HFKG	Embraer EMB-145EP	145253	G-ERJC, PT-SIN
F-HFLC	Pilatus PC-6/B2-H4 Turbo Porter	798	N12LH, ST-0603, HB-FHE
F-HFLP	Cameron Z-90 HAFB	11524	
F-HFLR	Robinson R44 Raven II	12242	
F-HFLY	Cessna 152	15281403	PH-BSV, N521DG, N49932
F-HFMP	Ultramagic N-250 HAFB	250/67	
F-HFMS	Robin DR.400/160 Chevalier	774	G-BAMS
F-HFMV	Lindstrand LBL-69X HAFB	1475	
F-HFNP	Cessna 208B Grand Caravan	208B0993	N107AN
F-HFOM	Eurocopter EC.135T2+	0581	
F-HFON	Cameron A-275 HAFB	11945	
F-HFOR	Cameron Z-275 HAFB	11802	
F-HFPE	Cessna 172S Skyhawk SP	172S10692	N6223Q
F-HFPF	Cessna 172S Skyhawk SP	172S10740	N63152
F-HFPG	Cessna 172S Skyhawk SP	172S10761	N6296C
F-HFPH	Cessna 172S Skyhawk SP	172S10703	N63150
F-HFPI	Cessna 182T Skylane	18282022	N62291
F-HFPJ	Cessna 182T Skylane	18282047	N447CP
F-HFPK	Cessna 172S Skyhawk SP	172S10748	N6316Z
F-HFPL	Cessna 172S Skyhawk SP	172S10883	N50127
F-HFPM	Reims/Cessna F152	F15201799	PH-CBF
F-HFPP	Aérospatiale AS.350B Ecureuil	1207	G-PLMB, (F-....), G-PLMB, G-BMMB, C-GBEW, N36033
F-HFPR	Reims/Cessna F152	F15201701	PH-HGO, (PH-AXI(3))
F-HFPS	Reims/Cessna F152	F15201673	PH-JJM, PH-AXC(3), (D-EIVR)
F-HFPT	Cessna 182T Skylane	18282095	N6187K
F-HFRA	Cessna 501 Citation I	501-0044	N600RM, N50US, N131SY, (N122LG), N944JD, N5TC, N98675
F-HFRB	Cirrus SR20	1994	D-ECDG(2), N534PG
F-HFRD	Robin DR.400/ 140B Major	2655	
F-HFRM	Issoire APM-30 Lion	33	

Reg	Type	Serial	Previous identities
F-HFRN	Eurocopter EC.130B4 Ecureuil	4111	HB-ZJH, 3A-MOW, EI-WOW, G-CEDH, F-WQDA
F-HFRO	Cameron TR-77 HAFB	11839	
F-HFTO	Piper PA-28-151 Cherokee Warrior	28-7615220	D-ELHA(3), OE-DHA, N9560N
F-HFTR	Cessna 208B Grand Caravan	208B2041	OY-PBU, N208PB
F-HFTV	Beech B200 King Air	BB-123	PH-ATM, D-IBIC, PH-ATM, N120DA, N123YV, N911LR, N711AR, N9123S
F-HFUL	Airbus A320-214	2180	OK-HCB, G-OOPX, G-OOAX, F-WWDY
F-HFUN	HOAC DV-20 Katana	20200	OE-AEF(2), OE-VPX
F-HFVC	Aérospatiale AS.350B2 Ecureuil	7151	3A-MGR(2)
F-HFXB	Diamond DA 62	62.024	OE-VDN
F-HGAB	Llopis MA-30 HAFB	216	
F-HGAC	Robin DR.400/120 Petit Prince	2653	
F-HGAG	Piper PA-38-112 Tomahawk	38-80A0069	OO-MAG(2), F-GCLZ, N9725N
F-HGAM	Diamond DA.20-C1 Katana	C0597	
F-HGAP	Aérospatiale AS.350B3 Ecureuil	4783	
F-HGAR	Robinson R44 Raven	1192	G-CGRL
F-HGAS	Lindstrand LBL-210A HAFB	1479	
F-HGAT	Lindstrand LBL-105A HAFB	1383	
F-HGAZ	Cessna U206G Soloy PAC	U20605584	D-EONX
F-HGBA	Llopis MA-26 HAFB	209	
F-HGBB	Wörner K-1000/3-STU Gas Balloon	0253	D-OHOE, D-Höchst II (2)
F-HGBM	Lindstrand LBL-210A HAFB	1385	
F-HGBP	Ultramagic T-180 HAFB	180/119	
F-HGCA	Lindstrand LBL-160A HAFB	1419	
F-HGCJ	Robin DR.400/160 Major	2658	
F-HGCM	Aérospatiale AS.350B3 Ecureuil	4939	
F-HGDC	Kubicek BB-30Z HAFB	440	
F-HGDM	Lindstrand LBL-90A HAFB	1400	
F-HGDU	Cirrus SR20	2152	N226FR
F-HGDY	Diamond DA 62	62.017	
F-HGEB	SOCATA TB-200 Tobago XL	2046	CS-DEB, F-OJBB
F-HGEL	Robinson R22 Beta II	4456	OE-XPX
F-HGEM	Ultramagic N-250 HAFB	250/74	
F-HGEO	Diamond DA20-C1 Katana	C0527	SE-LUT
F-HGER	Chaize CS.2000F24 HAFB	23	
F-HGFA	Cirrus SR22	0352	N908CD
F-HGFR	Robin DR.400/140B Dauphin 4	2656	
F-HGGH	Sky 220-24 HAFB	172	G-CGGH, OE-ZAZ
F-HGIN	Schröder Fire Balloons G40/24 HAFB	1549	
F-HGIO	Cessna 510 Citation Mustang	510-0052	G-LEAI
F-HGJB	Lindstrand LBL-90A HAFB	1366	
F-HGJC	Robin DR.400/140B Dauphin 4	2681	
F-HGJM	Libert L3000 HAFB	288-012	OO-BJM
F-HGLB	Lindstrand LBL-90A HAFB	1358	
F-HGLC	Chaize DC1800F16 HAFB	DC-004	
F-HGLE	Cameron O-105 HAFB	10100	
F-HGLI	Ultramagic S-70 HAFB	70/15	
F-HGLO	Cessna 525C CitationJet CJ4	525C-0114	N52591
F-HGLP	Cameron TR-77 HAFB	11541	
F-HGMA	Cessna 172R Skyhawk	17280065	OO-KPW, N697SC
F-HGMB	Reims/Cessna F152	F15201586	SE-GYV, (OE-CFC)
F-HGMH	Diamond DA.40D Star	D4.066	F-HABI
F-HGMI	Diamond DA.40D Star	D4.071	F-HABK
F-HGMO	Cameron Z-90 HAFB	11731	
F-HGMP	Kubicek BB-26Z HAFB	1202	
F-HGMT	Cessna 172R Skyhawk	17281202	SE-LPL, N2014T
F-HGMU	Robinson R44 Raven II	12770	D-HDWI
F-HGOA	Eurocopter EC.135T2+	0668	G-PNTA, I-PNTA, D-HECX
F-HGOD	Piaggio P.180 Avanti II	1153	HB-LUR
F-HGOO	Diamond DA20-C1 Katana	C0287	HB-SGA, N22ZM, N287DC
F-HGPB	Robinson R44 Raven II	11750	
F-HGPC	Robin DR.400/155CDi	2684	
F-HGPF	Cessna 172R Skyhawk	17281197	SE-LPI, N21614
F-HGPG	Cessna 525 CitationJet	525-0102	HB-VWP, LX-LOV, TC-CRO, N202CJ, N52038
F-HGPL	Piper PA-28RT-201T Turbo Arrow IV	28R-8031107	G-BUND, (G-BOGF), N8219V
F-HGPM	Pilatus PC-7	319	HB-HMV, A-911
F-HGPP	Llopis MA-35 HAFB	211	
F-HGPZ	Cirrus SR22	1357	N700YD
F-HGRR	Issoire APM-40 Simba	3	F-WGRR
F-HGRU	Aérospatiale AS.350B3 Ecureuil	4912	SE-JLU
F-HGSC	Robinson R44 Raven II	10851	G-MRDC, G-ECIL
F-HGSL	Robinson R44 Raven I	2077	PH-WNW
F-HGSM	Robin DR.400/160 Major	2688	
F-HGTA	Piper PA-28R-201 Arrow	2844119	D-EGTA(3), N3119W
F-HGTI	Piper PA-28R-201 Cherokee Arrow III	2844152	D-EGTI(3), N4424V, N9517N
F-HGTL	Cirrus SR20	1646	D-ESTT, N81461
F-HGTP	Chaize JF.30F16 HAFB	NG-002	
F-HGTT	Robinson R22 Beta II	3018	G-BYZP
F-HGTX	Piper PA-28R-201 Arrow	2844143	D-EGTX(2), N2315R, N9520N
F-HGUI	Beech B200GT Super King Air	BY-155	N855EU
F-HGUY	Robin DR.400/140B Major	2657	
F-HGVI	Kubicek BB-34Z HAFB	952	
F-HGYP	Diamond DA 40 Star	40.617	G-SULI, N670DS
F-HHAA	Piper PA-28R-200 Cherokee Arrow II	28R-7335008	HB-OKL, N11C
F-HHAG	Cameron Z-105 HAFB	11682	
F-HHAM	Beech C90A King Air	LJ-1361	N5521T
F-HHBG	Aérospatiale AS.350B3 Ecureuil	8281	
F-HHBX	Cameron N-90 HAFB	10928	OO-BXH
F-HHCM	Cameron C-80 HAFB	11256	
F-HHDF	Aérospatiale AS.350B3 Ecureuil	4484	3A-MWI, F-HBRR
F-HHEJ	Cameron Z-120 HAFB	11968	
F-HHFA	Eurocopter EC.120B Colibri	1396	HB-ZFY, F-WQDK
F-HHJD	Cameron N-105 HAFB	11846	
F-HHLB	Lindstrand LBL-105A HAFB	1399	
F-HHLO	Cameron Z-90 HAFB	11670	
F-HHMA	Cameron A-180 HAFB	12033	
F-HHMB	Piper PA-18-150 Super Cub	18-7709053	N83505
F-HHMS	Lindstrand LBL-140A HAFB	1376	
F-HHOC	Cameron Z-31 HAFB	10243	G-CBIH
F-HHOP	Issoire APM-30 Lion	31	
F-HHOT	Issoire APM-20 Lionceau	34	
F-HHPC	Schröder Fire Balloons G26/24 HAFB	1639	
F-HHPL	Cameron Z-105 HAFB	11633	
F-HHPM	Aérospatiale AS.350BA Ecureuil	1833	HB-ZPM, F-GFPM
F-HHPP	Cameron A-250 HAFB	11733	
F-HHRJ	Piper PA-28-140 Cherokee B	28-26092	HB-OZT, N98188
F-HHRV	Cameron A-315 HAFB	11946	
F-HHSA	Aérospatiale AS.350B2 Ecureuil	1239	Algerian AF, ES-28, F-WQDC, C-GAYA
F-HHSB	Eurocopter EC.155B1 Dauphin	6802	PH-EUB, F-WWOE
F-HHSJ	Robinson R44 Raven II	12108	N4152G
F-HHUK	Sukhoi SU-29	76-03	HA-HUK, RA-3351K, RA-44539, ZU-AKS, RA-7603
F-HHUN	Schröder Fire Balloons G40/24 HAFB	1202	PH-HUW
F-HHVM	Lindstrand LBL-180A HAFB	1487	
F-HIAD	Robinson R44 Raven I	2203	OO-PMR
F-HIAE	Tecnam P.2002-JF Sierra	104	
F-HIAF	Tecnam P.2002-JF Sierra	105	
F-HIAG	Cameron C-90 HAFB	11653	
F-HIBC	Sud Avn SA.318C Alouette Astazou	2018	Belgium A-59, OL-A59
F-HIBF	Cessna 510 Citation Mustang	510-0262	F-HPHD, D-IEEN, M-MHBW, (D-ICMH)
F-HIBR	Dassault Falcon 900EX	271	M-ABGZ, M-ISRK, TC-IRR, F-WWFM
F-HIBU	Ultramagic H-77 HAFB	77/379	
F-HIBZ	Piper PA-46-350P Malibu Mirage	4636452	SP-CLS(2), N60947, SP-CLS, N60947
F-HICK	Rockwell Commander 114	14018	OO-SFL, N10481, D-EFWH
F-HICM	Cessna 510 Citation Mustang	510-0388	N4095H
F-HIDA	Robinson R44 Raven II	11613	I-DDDU
F-HIDL	Cameron A-300 HAFB	10947	G-CIDL, OH-IDC
F-HIFI	Piper PA-28-181 Archer III	2843494	PH-BRD, OY-SVV(2), N282PA
F-HIFM	Robinson R44 Clipper II	11375	G-CKEM
F-HIFR	Piper PA-28-161 Warrior II	28-8116036	G-BTID, N82647
F-HIGG	Gardan GY-80-160 Horizon	28	G-BJAV, OO-AJP, F-BLVB
F-HIHA	Pilatus PC-6/B2-H2 Turbo Porter	561	D-FJMO, F-GOMO, N1421Z
F-HIHH	Ultramagic M-105 HAFB	105/201	
F-HIII	Cameron Z-180 HAFB	11496	
F-HIIV	Piper PA-28-181 Archer II	28-7990028	G-BIIV, N20875
F-HIJC	Piper PA-32R-301T Turbo Saratoga SP	32R-8129098	PH-VMA, N8430F
F-HIJD	Cessna 525A CitationJet CJ2	525A-0462	OK-ILA
F-HIJF	Kubicek BB-26Z HAFB	926	
F-HIKE	Eurocopter EC.130T2 Ecureuil	7774	
F-HILF	Aérospatiale AS.350B3 Ecureuil	8076	SE-JOV
F-HILL	Aérospatiale AS.350B3 Ecureuil	7643	
F-HILS	Kubicek BB-34Z HAFB	820	
F-HILU	Boeing 767-336ER	24341	G-BNWI
F-HIMA	Piaggio P.180 Avanti	1138	I-PREE
F-HIMB	Piper PA-46-350P Malibu Mirage	4636305	D-EGAC(3), OY-LAC
F-HIMY	Diamond DA.42 Twin Star	42.092	N516KS
F-HINC	Learjet 75	45-488	N40077
F-HIND	Cessna 182T Skylane	18281767	EC-KFH, N20100
F-HINI	Jodel D.150 Mascaret	32	D-EINI
F-HINR	Eurocopter EC.135T2	0272	EC-ION
F-HINT	Ultramagic M-145 HAFB	145/65	EC-KXY
F-HIPB	Ultramagic N-180 HAFB	180/123	
F-HIPE	Embraer EMB-505 Phenom 300	50500016	PT-PVD
F-HIPI	Robin DR.400/120 Petit Prince	2662	
F-HIPK	Dassault Falcon 7X	258	F-WWHU
F-HIPS	Ultramagic M-105 HAFB	105/178	
F-HISA	Lindstrand LBL-105A HAFB	383	G-BWRZ
F-HISC	Cameron Z-180 HAFB	11903	
F-HISE	Cessna T303 Crusader	T30300160	OO-ISE, LX-YNC, N65NC, G-BPZN, G-RSUL, (G-BPZN), N6610C
F-HISI	Dassault Falcon 50	169	F-GUAJ, I-SNAB, F-WPXD
F-HISM	Cessna T207A Turbo Stationair 8/Soloy	20700553	D-EUHP, N70549
F-HITI	Cameron Z-31 HAFB	11497	
F-HITM	Beechjet 400XP	RK-501	N501XP
F-HITS	Yakovlev Yak-18T	22202034044	HA-CBG, LZ-YUL, LZ-524, RA-44490
F-HIUP	SIAI-Marchetti SF.260C	2-47	OY-SMM, OO-SMM
F-HIVA	Cessna 525 CitationJet CJ	525-0235	LX-GCA, I-ESAI, VP-BZZ, N5246Z
F-HIVE	Cirrus SR22	3962	N209CB
F-HIYA	Lindstrand LBL-105A HAFB	1320	
F-HIYE	Robin DR.400/180 Régent	2123	G-IEYE
F-HIYP	Piper PA-20 Pacer	20-802	G-BIYP, CN-TYP, F-DACJ, OO-ADP
F-HIZG	SAN Jodel D.140B Mousquetaire	27	G-TOAD, F-BIZG
F-HIZI	Boeing Stearman A75N1	75-548	N62133, 40-1991
F-HJAD	Cirrus SR20	1151	EC-KPY, N251CD
F-HJAF	Eurocopter EC.135T1	0044	D-HJAR, G-CGXK, D-HJAR
F-HJAK	Cessna 172S Skyhawk SP	172S8258	G-GFMT, C-GFMT, N341SP
F-HJAR	Robinson R44 Raven II	13371	
F-HJAS	Kubicek BB-34Z HAFB	650	
F-HJAV	Cessna 525 CitationJet CJ	525-0473	HB-VOR, LX-MRC, N5201M
F-HJAX	Cessna 550 Citation II	550-0321	D-COMK, (D-IOMK), YU-FCS, VP-CCO, N321GN, TC-COY, N321SE, N5430G
F-HJBC	Ultramagic M-145 HAFB	145/32	
F-HJBD	Ultramagic N-210 HAFB	210/17	D-OMKX
F-HJBE	Ultramagic M-145 HAFB	145/12	G-BZGI
F-HJBF	Schröder Fire Balloons G45/24 HAFB	982	PH-SBL
F-HJBM	Cessna 172S Skyhawk SP	172S11112	D-ESEX(4), N9287M
F-HJBP	Ultramagic N-210 HAFB	210/26	D-OMKP
F-HJBR	Embraer EMB-505 Phenom 300	50500278	
F-HJCB	Partenavia P.68C	226	OE-FJG, OE-FIL, HB-LPW, I-KDUE
F-HJCD	Dassault Falcon 2000LX	288	F-WWJQ
F-HJCG	Aérospatiale AS.350B3 Ecureuil	4950	EC-LGB
F-HJCQ	Tecnam P.2002-JF Sierra	005	EC-JCQ
F-HJCR	Reims/Cessna F172P	F17202169	HB-CLF, G-BKHZ
F-HJDA	Robin DR.400/ 140B Major	2654	
F-HJEM	Chaize JZ.30F16 HAFB	NG-007	
F-HJES	Evektor EV-97 SportStar RTC	2016 1904	
F-HJET	Cirrus SR22	4053	N4053M
F-HJFA	Cirrus SR22	3618	N621S
F-HJFG	Embraer EMB-505 Phenom 300	50500099	TC-KEH, PT-TRF
F-HJFK	Robinson R22 Beta II	2561	I-ZANC
F-HJLB	SAN Jodel D.140C Mousquetaire III	90	D-EXSB, SE-XNB, F-BKSI, F-BKSE
F-HJLD	Aérospatiale AS.355F2 Ecureuil 2	5064	(F-GSYG), F-WQDF, N211WC, N5780Y
F-HJLJ	Ultramagic N-300 HAFB	300/47	
F-HJLL	Aerospool WT-9 Dynamic LSA	DY428/2011	F-WJLL
F-HJLM	Embraer EMB-505 Phenom 300	50500304	

Reg	Type	Serial	Previous identities
F-HJMC	Robinson R44 Raven I	1792	OO-OVB, D-HEON
F-HJMD	Dassault Falcon 900EX	283	M-PATH, F-HVRO, TC-AOM, F-WWFG
F-HJMH	Llopis MA26 HAFB	235	
F-HJML	Cessna 172R Skyhawk	17280957	SE-LPD, N24527
F-HJMP	Cessna 208B Grand Caravan	208B2191	N1008G
F-HJMR	Cameron Z-105 HAFB	11593	
F-HJNC	Reims/Cessna F172H	F1720695	OO-YAO, G-AYAO
F-HJNO	Robin DR.400/160 Major	2392	OO-CSD
F-HJNP	Aérospatiale AS.350B3 Ecureuil	4777	
F-HJNZ	Robin HR.200/120B Acrobin	28	HB-EXH
F-HJOC	Cessna 172S Skyhawk SP	172S10505	N21927
F-HJOF	Robinson R44 Raven II	13237	
F-HJOZ	Cessna 172S Skyhawk SP	172S10658	N1320P
F-HJPC	Aérospatiale AS.350B Ecureuil	1153	F-GINV
F-HJPL	Robinson R44 Raven II	12439	I-ARBJ, N42135
F-HJPR	Robinson R44 Raven II	11064	
F-HJPS	Robin DR.400/135CDI	2612	
F-HJRB	Robinson R44 Raven II	10897	
F-HJRD	Robin DR.400/140B Major	2683	
F-HJSH	Aérospatiale AS.350B3 Ecureuil	8183	
F-HJTB	Aérospatiale AS.350B3 Ecureuil	4268	HB-ZIW
F-HJTD	Eurocopter EC.130B4 Ecureuil	4772	OO-ARI(6)
F-HJTE	Aérospatiale AS.350B3 Ecureuil	7410	
F-HJUL	Boeing 737-8Q8	38819	
F-HJYL	Dassault Falcon 20E-5	307/513	CS-DPW, F-GYMC, F-GYPB, F-GKIS, OE-GLL, I-GCAL, HB-VDV, F-WRQT
F-HJYP	Eurocopter EC.120B Colibri	1487	D-HVCG, I-HBDC, F-WQDG
F-HJYQ	Tecnam P.2008-JC	1031	
F-HJYR	Tecnam P.2008-JC	1032	
F-HKAF	Diamond DA 42 Twin Star	42.226	F-HOKD
F-HKBY	Aerospool WT-9 Dynamic LSA	DY514/2014	
F-HKCA	Cirrus SR22	3862	N120FR
F-HKCB	Cirrus SR20	2185	N125FR
F-HKCC	Cirrus SR22	4305	N308FA
F-HKCD	Cirrus SR20	2186	N126FR
F-HKCE	Cirrus SR20	2187	N130FR
F-HKCF	Cirrus SR22	3874	N132FR
F-HKCG	Cirrus SR20	2188	N133FR
F-HKCH	Cirrus SR20	2189	N134FR
F-HKCI	Cirrus SR22	3875	N135FR
F-HKCJ	Cirrus SR20	2190	N136FR
F-HKCK	Cirrus SR20	2192	N139FR
F-HKCL	Cirrus SR22	3877	N141FR
F-HKCM	Cirrus SR20	2193	N140FR
F-HKCN	Cirrus SR20	2195	N146FR
F-HKCO	Cirrus SR22	3878	N142FR
F-HKCP	Cirrus SR20	2196	N147FR
F-HKCQ	Cirrus SR20	2197	N148FR
F-HKCR	Cirrus SR22	3881	N143FR
F-HKCS	Cirrus SR22	3884	N145FR
F-HKCT	Cirrus SR20	2198	N149FR
F-HKCU	Cirrus SR20	2199	N150FR
F-HKCV	Cirrus SR20	2214	N152FR
F-HKCX	Cirrus SR20	2215	N153FR
F-HKCY	Cirrus SR20	4235	N423FA
F-HKCZ	Cirrus SR22	4304	N304FA
F-HKEB	Robin DR.400/140B Major	2275	HB-KEB
F-HKEY	Robinson R44 Clipper II	11893	9A-HDM, N998VV
F-HKID	Guimbal G2 Cabri	1011	SE-HJR(2)
F-HKIL	Cessna 510 Citation Mustang	510-0346	G-FBKD, N9166N, N4115W
F-HKIM	SAN Jodel D.140C Mousquetaire	101	G-DCXL, (G-DCXX), F-BKSM
F-HKJL	Robinson R44 Raven II	13383	
F-HKKP	Robin DR.500/200i Président	0018	D-EKKP(2)
F-HKLM	Ultramagic T-150 HAFB	150/21	
F-HKLN	Reims/Cessna F172N	F17201998	F-OKLN, D-EKLN
F-HKMO	Dassault Falcon 900	89	I-NUMI, F-WWFB
F-HKOX	Ultramagic N-355 HAFB	355/19	
F-HKPE	Jodel DR.250/160 Capitaine	35	G-BKPE, F-BNJD
F-HKPG	Robinson R44 Raven	0815	G-BZMG
F-HKRA	Cessna 525 CitationJet CJ1	525-0661	LN-RYG, N613AL
F-HKRE	Tecnam P.2006T	026	EC-LFB, F-BNJD
F-HKRO	Robin DR.400/120 Petit Prince	2685	
F-HKSS	Llopis Balloons MA-30 HAFB	215	
F-HKTB	Piper PA-28-181 Archer III	2843496	G-LKTB, (F-....), G-LKTB, N5339X, (G-LKTB), N5328Q
F-HKTE	Kubicek BB-26Z HAFB	708	HB-QTE
F-HKTN	Cameron A-120 HAFB	4659	
F-HKZZ	Romin DR.400/180R Remorqueur	909	EC-KZZ, F-BVCL
F-HLAC	Tecnam P2002-JF Sierra	197	
F-HLAK	AgustaWestland AW139	31269	
F-HLAM	Kubicek Phare SS HAFB	887	
F-HLAP	Schröder Fire Balloons G30/24 HAFB	1537	
F-HLAS	Extra EA.300SC	SC043	
F-HLAT	Robinson R44 Raven I	2078	D-HAAP(3), PH-WPW
F-HLAU	Schröder Fire Balloons G26/24 HAFB	1629	
F-HLBA	Llopis Balloons MA-30 HAFB	221	
F-HLBC	Piper PA-18-135 Super Cub	18-3986	G-BWUB, N786CS, G-BWUB, SX-AHB, EI-263, I-EIUO, MM542586, 54-2586
F-HLBE	Cameron Z-105 HAFB	11556	
F-HLBL	Kubicek BB-30Z HAFB	221	HB-QRT, D-OEHN, OK-0221
F-HLBM	Llopis MA-30 HAFB	217	
F-HLBP	Cameron Z-105 HAFB	11895	
F-HLBR	Aérospatiale AS.350B3 Ecureuil	4872	EC-LGU, F-WEVN, F-WJXG
F-HLCA	Eurocopter EC.135T2	0244	F-WLCA, D-HKBS
F-HLCB	Eurocopter EC.135T2	0268	
F-HLCC	Eurocopter EC.135T2	0291	
F-HLCD	Eurocopter EC.135T2+	0829	
F-HLCE	Eurocopter EC.135T2+	1094	
F-HLCF	Eurocopter EC.135T3	1198	
F-HLCV	Kubicek BB-30Z HAFB	954	
F-HLDB	Dassault Falcon 2000EX	136	TC-ATC(2), F-WWGF
F-HLDM	Cameron Z-77 HAFB	11620	
F-HLEA	North American T-6G-NF Texan	168-160	F-AZMP, F-WZMP, (F-AZMP), AE.6-188, 49-3056
F-HLEE	Cameron Z-120 HAFB	12018	
F-HLEG	Beech 95-B55 Baron	TC-1272	HB-GEC
F-HLEM	Piper PA-28-181 Archer III	2843588	D-EMPK(3), N30884, N9517N
F-HLEO	Cameron Z-120 HAFB	11594	
F-HLEV	Aérospatiale AS.350B3 Ecureuil	8227	
F-HLGC	Cameron Z-90 HAFB	11746	
F-HLIL	Extra EA.200	018	D-EXRR, G-XTRR, D-EVNO
F-HLIM	Cessna 560 Citation Encore	560-0683	N51042
F-HLIS	Eurocopter EC.225LP Super Puma II	2797	
F-HLJL	Piper PA-34-200 Seneca	34-7450159	D-GOTO, F-BVON, F-ETBR
F-HLLJ	Aérospatiale AS.350B3 Ecureuil	8101	
F-HLLM	Schröder Fire Balloons G26/24 HAFB	927	OO-BKX, LX-BKW
F-HLLZ	Robinson R44 Clipper II	10898	
F-HLMA	Chaize CS.3000F32 HAFB	NG-001	
F-HLMC	Piper PA-46R-350T Matrix	4692093	OE-DRE, I-STAY, N193HP, N3110B
F-HLMP	Robinson R44 Raven I	1750	OO-PMF
F-HLMS	Cameron Z-375 HAFB	11865	
F-HLNC	SOCATA Rallye 150ST	3177	PH-RNC
F-HLNV	Guimbal G2 Cabri	1134	
F-HLOC	CSA PS-28 Cruiser	C0485	
F-HLOK	Robinson R44 Raven II	11981	I-SUOS
F-HLOL	Thunder AX9-120SII HAFB	4617	HB-QFP
F-HLON	Beech B200 King Air	BB-1903	N203PT, N521RS
F-HLOR	Llopis Balloons MA-30 HAFB	226	
F-HLOS	Beech D-18S	A-963	N2913B
F-HLOU	Robinson R44 Raven I	10158	EC-LOU, G-FLBI
F-HLPB	Robinson R44 Clipper II	12701	3A-MWH, OE-XWE
F-HLPM	Dassault Falcon 2000LX	282	
F-HLPN	Dassault Falcon 2000LX	296	F-WWGX
F-HLPP	Aérophile 5500 Tethered Gas Balloon	048	
F-HLRA	Diamond DA 62	62.018	
F-HLRB	Diamond DA 62	62.022	
F-HLRC	Diamond DA 62	62.039	
F-HLRT	Aérospatiale AS.350B3 Ecureuil	4938	I-MAVC
F-HLRY	Embraer EMB-500 Phenom 100	50000354	PR-PFI
F-HLTI	Dassault Falcon 7X	108	XT-EBO, M-ABFM, VP-CMX, F-WWZS
F-HLTO	Llopis Balloons MA-20 HAFB	220	
F-HLTP	Diamond DA.40 Star	40.490	N765SL
F-HLTR	Cessna P210N Pressurised Centurion II	P21000570	D-EPRE, N731ZT
F-HLTZ	Cameron Z-90 HAFB	11648	
F-HLUD	Ultramagic N-355 HAFB	355/22	
F-HLUK	Beech 77 Skipper	WA-173	OO-GVF, D-EDLD, N806Y
F-HLUS	Cameron A-210 HAFB	11823	
F-HLYF	Cameron Apple-120SS HAFB	11750	
F-HLZL	Ultramagic M-77 HAFB	77/352	
F-HMAD	Evektor EV-97 SportStar RTC	2014 1701	
F-HMAG	Aérospatiale AS.350B3 Ecureuil	8056	
F-HMAJ	SIAI-Marchetti SF.260C	361/31-005	G-SIAI, F-GVAB(2), BF8479, OO-XCP, FAB:184
F-HMAM	Kubicek BB-30Z HAFB	992	
F-HMAN	Cirrus SR20	1718	HB-KHI, N561SR
F-HMAP	Schröder Fire Balloons G45/24 HAFB	1649	
F-HMAR	Airbus A340-211	075	OE-LAG, F-WWJR
F-HMAU	Embraer EMB-500 Phenom 100	50000367	PR-PGP
F-HMAV	Ultramagic H-77 HAFB	77/353	
F-HMAZ	Robinson R44 Raven II	2059	OO-PMN
F-HMBG	Cessna 525A CitationJet CJ2	525A-0142	OE-FPS(3), N5207A
F-HMBH	Eurocopter EC.135T2+	0407	G-PLAL
F-HMBL	Evektor EV-97 SportStar RTC	2015 1736	
F-HMBS	SOCATA TBM-700N	391	LX-JFL
F-HMBY	Bombardier BD-700-1A10 Global Express	9748	C-FLXD
F-HMCA	Robinson R44 Raven II	13858	
F-HMCC	Agusta A.109S Grand	22069	I-NAES
F-HMCE	Robinson R44 Raven	2030	
F-HMCI	Piper PA-28-181 Archer III	2843426	SE-ILV, N9514N
F-HMCL	Llopis Balloons MA-30 HAFB	214	
F-HMCM	Lindstrand LBL-90A HAFB	1457	
F-HMCO	Bell 407	53145	SE-JEX, N72243, C-GAEP
F-HMCS	Agusta A.109S Grand	22005	I-NAER, EC-JPP, I-RAIP
F-HMCT	Beech C90GTi King Air	LJ-1935	D-ISBC(2), N190EU, N890HB, N60FR
F-HMDA	Piper PA-34-220T Seneca V	3449256	G-NSUK, N126RB, N9513N
F-HMDB	Ultramagic M-105 HAFB	105/194	
F-HMDL	Cameron Z-105 HAFB	11523	
F-HMDM	Llopis Balloons MA-26 HAFB	232	
F-HMDR	Cessna U206G Stationair 6	U20606908	N206GE
F-HMEC	Ultramagic S-130 HAFB	130/79	
F-HMED	BAe.125-1000B	259026	G-GDEZ, P4-MAF, G-GDEZ, N9026, ZS-ACT(2), ZS-CCT(2), G-5-743
F-HMEG	Aérospatiale AS.350B2 Ecureuil	7414	
F-HMEL	Extra EA.300/SC	SC065	
F-HMEP	Robinson R44 Raven II	12961	D-HALO(3)
F-HMGA	Robinson R22 Beta II	4139	G-CESU, N30804
F-HMGI	Eurocopter EC.135T2+	0347	TC-HJF, G-EWRT, D-HECF
F-HMGM	Aérospatiale AS.350B Ecureuil	3934	
F-HMHL	Ultramagic M-120 HAFB	120/69	
F-HMIC	Cameron Z-90 HAFB	11950	
F-HMIG	Cameron Z-350 HAFB	11676	
F-HMIK	Schröder Fire Balloons G85/24 HAFB	1557	
F-HMIT	Reims/Cessna F152	F15201501	G-SACB, G-BRFB
F-HMIZ	Cessna T206H Turbo Stationair	T20608355	D-EGKS, N5171Z
F-HMJE	Robbinson R44 Clipper II	12315	G-ICIO
F-HMJP	Llopis Balloons MA-26 HAFB	229	
F-HMKF	Extra EA.300/SC	SC045	
F-HMLA	Canadair CL-600-2E25 Regional Jet	19004	C-GELU
F-HMLC	Canadair CL-600-2E25 Regional Jet	19006	C-GHKA(2)
F-HMLD	Canadair CL-600-2E25 Regional Jet	19007	C-GIBR
F-HMLE	Canadair CL-600-2E25 Regional Jet	19009	C-GZQJ
F-HMLF	Canadair CL-600-2E25 Regional Jet	19010	C-GZQX
F-HMLG	Canadair CL-600-2E25 Regional Jet	19012	C-GZQW
F-HMLH	Canadair CL-600-2E25 Regional Jet	19013	C-GIAH
F-HMLI	Canadair CL-600-2E25 Regional Jet	19014	C-GIBJ
F-HMLJ	Canadair CL-600-2E25 Regional Jet	19015	C-GIAV
F-HMLK	Canadair CL-600-2E25 Regional Jet	19016	C-GZQJ
F-HMLL	Canadair CL-600-2E25 Regional Jet	19017	C-GZQJ
F-HMLM	Canadair CL-600-2E25 Regional Jet	19023	C-GICL
F-HMLN	Canadair CL-600-2E25 Regional Jet	19024	C-GICP
F-HMLO	Canadair CL-600-2E25 Regional Jet	19041	C-GZYJ(2)
F-HMMD	Schröder Fire Balloons G30/24 HAFB	1550	
F-HMMH	Robinson R22 Beta II	4156	I-TALF
F-HMMK	Piper PA-32R-300 Cherokee Lance	32R-7680224	D-ESXY, F-GFJA, OO-BEL, OY-BLR
F-HMML	Embraer EMB-505 Phenom 300	50500247	PR-PEB
F-HMMM	Cameron Z-160 HAFB	10546	OO-BUK(2), PH-WJH
F-HMMS	Aérospatiale AS.350B3 Ecureuil	7630	
F-HMNI	Eurocopter EC.135T2	0420	TC-HJD, D-HMFR(3)

Regn	Type	c/n	Previous identities
F-HMNL	Piper PA-28R-200 Cherokee Arrow II	28R-7535040	G-BNML, N32280, (N18MW), N32280
F-HMOD	Dassault Falcon 7X	106	VP-CSG, M-ABGO, VP-CSG, N106FJ, PR-BTG, F-WWZK
F-HMOL	SOCATA TB-20 Trinidad GT	2103	G-TMOL, F-OJBQ
F-HMOM	Dassault Falcon 7X	109	SX-GRC, F-WWVL
F-HMPA	Schröder Fire Balloons G22/24 HAFB	1518	
F-HMPB	Agusta AW.109SP Grand New	22340	
F-HMPC	Cameron Z-90 HAFB	11985	
F-HMPJ	Piper PA-28R-180 Cherokee Arrow	28R-30769	HB-OZI, N7425J
F-HMPL	Robinson R22 Mariner II	3011M	N7183Y
F-HMPM	Cessna 152	15282983	G-BHPY, N46009
F-HMPR	Cessna 525A Citation CJ2	525A-0214	N7QM, N1DM, N51511
F-HMRD	Piper PA-28-181 Archer III	2843359	D-EEMZ, (D-EZIT), S5-DPJ, N245PA, N41613
F-HMRV	Kubicek BB-26N HAFB	780	YL-023
F-HMSB	Ultramagic M-77C HAFB	77/367	
F-HMSG	Cessna 525A CitationJet CJ2	525A-0033	EC-JJU, (D-IETZ), HB-VNO, N163PB
F-HMSM	Schröder Fire Balloons G34/24 HAFB	1565	
F-HMTA	Pilatus PC-6/B2-H4 Turbo Porter	860	D-FMTA, D-FALL
F-HMTB	Robin DR.400/160 Major	2678	
F-HMTO	Aérospatiale/Alenia ATR-42-320	078	F-WMTO, F-WQNI, HS-PGG, F-WQBQ, N31807, F-WWED
F-HMUT	Beech B350 King Air	FL-937	N5037A
F-HMVA	Cessna 208 Caravan I	20800275	OH-USI
F-HMVB	Schröder Fire Balloons G30/24 HAFB	1683	
F-WMVD	Winner B150 helicopter	unkn	
F-HMVL	Cameron C-80 HAFB	11691	
F-HMYD	Beech A36 Bonanza	E-2350	G-BMYD
F-HMYL	Aérospatiale AS.350B2 Ecureuil	3581	EC-IHH
F-HMYY	Robin DR.500/200i Président	0026	HB-KFJ, (D-EULA), F-WWMU
F-HNAK	Beech C90GTI King Air	LJ-2047	N443CA
F-HNAT	Tecnam P.2010	009	
F-HNAV	Beech B200GT King Air	BY-175	N175EU
F-HNCE	Eurocopter EC.135T2+	0762	G-PNTB, I-PNTB, D-HCBD
F-HNCL	Robinson R44 Raven II	11468	N53CL, G-GHDC
F-HNCY	Raytheon 390 Premier	RB-230	N3330S
F-HNDI	Robin DR.400/140B Major	2663	
F-HNEG	Cessna 172S Skyhawk SP	172S9507	G-UFCH, N53551
F-HNEL	Ultramagic M-90 HAFB	90/147	
F-HNEO	Robinson R44 Raven II	10583	EI-MVK, N74461
F-HNER	Ultramagic M-160 HAFB	160/67	
F-HNEZ	Robin DR.400/180 Regent	1304	G-BHFS
F-HNGA	Mudry CAP.10B	95	I-IZAF, F-WZCH
F-HNIZ	Issoire APM-30 Lion	37	
F-HNJG	Cirrus SR22	3126	D-ETCU, N257CP
F-HNJM	Cirrus SR22	4380	N218LL
F-HNJT	Cessna 152	15283956	N474RZ, (F-....), G-POCO, N6592B, G-POCO, N6592B
F-HNLM	Lindstrand LBL-90A HAFB	1435	
F-HNLO	Eurocopter EC.135T2+	0770	5B-CKR, SX-HVG, D-HABB(2), D-HCBL
F-HNLR	CSA PS-28 Cruiser	C0435	
F-HNLU	Libert L.2600 HAFB	335-059	
F-HNOA	Dassault Falcon 2000LX	1323	F-WWMJ
F-HNPB	Agusta A.109E Power	11728	I-AWCN, TC-HND
F-HNRJ	Cameron V-90 HAFB	2699	OO-BRJ
F-HNVA	Tecnam P.2006T	010	EC-LEJ
F-HNXF	Piper PA-28-161 Warrior II	2841299	D-ENXF, N9205Z
F-HNYO	Chaize DC2200 F16 HAFB	DC-006	
F-HOAA	Diamond DA 40 NG	D4.148	OE-DCM(2), F-HCAE
F-HOAG	Aérophile 5500 Tethered Gas Balloon	044	
F-HOBB	Diamond DA.40 NG	D4.145	PH-CAE, OE-VPU
F-HOBE	Robin DR.400/140B Dauphin 4	2567	OO-GTS, F-GYGA
F-HOBO	Robinson R44 Raven II	10746	OO-PTR
F-HOBS	Cirrus SR20	2234	N115RM
F-HOBY	Piper PA-18-150 Super Cub	18-7809112	YU-..., N82016
F-HOCA	Lindstrand LBL-140A HAFB	1469	
F-HOCC	Cameron Z-350 HAFB	11527	
F-HOCN	Eurocopter EC.135P2	0419	OH-HCP
F-HOCT	Cessna 177RG Cardinal RG	177RG1336	N-NFP(2), N53070
F-HODB	Piper PA-31-350 Chieftain	31-7752031	OY-BTZ, SE-GPM
F-HOFA	Cameron Z-105 HAFB	11964	
F-HOHA	Ultramagic N-180 HAFB	180/117	
F-HOHO	Libert L2200 HAFB	339-063	
F-HOIE	Piaggio P.180 Avanti	1225	I-FXRL
F-HOJA	Cameron Z-160 HAFB	11987	
F-HOJB	Cessna 208B Grand Caravan	208B-0584	LN-PBF(2), OY-PBF, G-MART, N1126L, N52642
F-HOJN	Llopis MA30 HAFB	236	
F-HOKI	Grob G 115A	8078	PH-SPD, (D-EGVV)
F-HOKM	Reims/Cessna FRA150L Aerobat	FRA1500247	PH-APE, D-EDJJ
F-HOLA	Guimbal Cabri G2	1037	
F-HOLI	Pilatus PC-12/47E	1506	HB-FQB(16)
F-HOLO	Robin DR.400/180 Régent	2308	D-EDLO(3)
F-HOLY	Agusta AW.109SP	22242	
F-HOMB	SOCATA TB-20 Trinidad	459	PH-TWT, D-EDEJ
F-HOMD	Lindstrand LBL-77A HAFB	1480	
F-HOMF	Eurocopter EC.135T3	1216	
F-HOMG	Eurocopter EC.135P2	0441	OH-HMV, (SE-JID), OH-HMV
F-HOMP	Lindstrand LBL-77X HAFB	1474	
F-HONB	Piper J-3C-65 Cub	12063	HB-ONB, 44-79767
F-HONE	SOCATA TBM-700N	649	N646XX
F-HOOK	Robin HR.100/210D Safari (Damaged 3.10.16)	160	D-EGOD(2), F-BUPY, (D-EIZA)
F-HOOO	Diamond DA 40 NG	D4.144	OE-DCK(2), G-CDEL, OE-VPW
F-HOOP	Tecnam P.2008JC	1007	
F-HOOS	Tecnam P.2008JC	1023	
F-HOOT	Tecnam P.2008JC	1024	
F-HOPC	Piper PA-28RT-201T Turbo Arrow IV	28R-8331031	PH-OPC, N42978, (PH-MMM), PH-JJJ, N42978
F-HOPF	Piper PA-46-350P Malibu Mirage	4636630	N4413E
F-HOPL	Aérospatiale/Alenia ATR-72-600	1283	F-WWEL
F-HOPN	Aérospatiale/Alenia ATR-72-600	1288	F-WWER
F-HOPP	Ultramagic T-180 HAFB	180/106	
F-HOPS	Aérospatiale AS.355N Ecureuil 2	5692	G-JPAL, F-GSJP
F-HOPX	Aérospatiale/Alenia ATR-72-600	1257	F-WWEI
F-HOPY	Aérospatiale/Alenia ATR-72-600	1237	F-WWEL
F-HOPZ	Aérospatiale/Alenia ATR-72-600	1265	F-WWER
F-HORG	Eurocopter EC.135P2	0438	OH-HMI
F-HORL	Eurocopter EC.135P2+	0165	(D-HAAW), C-GNZV(3), VH-WKK(2), D-HECC, D-HSLE, D-HECB, LN-OOB, D-HTSL, D-HECN
F-HORN	Aérospatiale AS.350B3 Ecureuil	7381	
F-HORS	Guimbal G2 Cabri	1135	
F-HORY	Bell 206B Jet Ranger	4587	C-FENU, N306PD
F-HOSB	Hawker 750	HB-27	G-ZIPR, M-INXS, N666NF, N3497J
F-HOSF	Piper PA-46-350P Malibu Mirage	4636619	N4415D, (F-HOSF), N9543N
F-HOST	Cameron Z-450 HAFB	11649	
F-HOSZ	Schröder Fire Balloons G30/24 HAFB	931	D-OOSZ
F-HOTE	Libert L.3400 HAFB	309-033	
F-HOTO	Piper PA-28-140 Cherokee Cruiser	28-7425107	OO-JPD(2), N9593N
F-HOTS	Mooney M.20J Model 205	24-3131	D-EUIL, F-GUIL, F-GJIL
F-HOTT	Kubicek BB-20XR HAFB	918	
F-HOTX	Mudry CAP.10B	136	D-ESPK, F-GNPK, Fr.AF
F-HOUA	GEFA-Flug AS.105GD Hot Air Airship	"H0067 G0034"	
F-HOUF	Issoire APM-30 Lion	30	
F-HOUI	Diamond DA 40 NG Club	D4.041	OE-DAG(2), EC-ITQ, OE-UDV, OE-VPY
F-HOUX	Schweizer S269C	S-1237	SE-HRP, N41S
F-HOVA	Llopis Balloons MA-40 HAFB	218	
F-HOYO	Cameron Z-120 HAFB	11970	
F-HPAA	Fairchild Swearingen SA.227AC Metro III	AC-754B	N754TR, D-COLB, N54NE, N2746Z
F-HPAF	Cessna 172S Skyhawk SP	172S9306	G-UFCF, N5320F
F-HPAK	HOAC DV-20 Katana	20212	OE-VPX
F-HPAP	Cessna 182S Skylane	18280736	EC-JSF, N341ME
F-HPAR	Xtremeair XA42	125	
F-HPBB	Evektor EV-97 SportStar RTC	2015 1720	
F-HPBH	Bell 429	57199	C-FAGQ
F-HBPR	Robin DR.400/120 Petit Prince	2659	
F-HPCB	Kubicek BB-30Z HAFB	880	
F-HPCD	Diamond DA.42 NG	42.N160	OE-UDO, OE-VDM
F-HPCG	Cameron Z-105 HAFB	11859	
F-HPCM	Cameron C-90 HAFB	11144	
F-HPCS	Cameron Z-133 HAFB	11784	
F-HPCV	Schröder Fire Balloons G30/24 HAFB	297	
F-HPDF	Diamond DA.40D Star	D4.348	HB-SDH, OE-VPT
F-HPDR	SIGA Pilatre de Rozier AX8-105 HAFB	409	
F-HPEB	Bombardier Learjet 40XR	45-2080	D-CPDR, N40076
F-HPEF	SOCATA TB-9 Tampico	1832	PH-PEF, F-GOID, (5N-...), F-OIDE
F-HPEI	Partenavia P.68C	231	SE-MCH, 9H-AFX, S5-CER, G-BJRZ, G-OAKP, G-BJRZ
F-HPEM	Cameron C-80 HAFB	12024	
F-HPEN	Ultramagic M-120 HAFB	120/42	
F-HPER	Reims/Cessna FRA150N Aerobat	FRA1500347	G-CLUB, OO-AWZ, F-WZAZ, (F-WZDZ)
F-HPGA	Beech B300 King Air	FL-774	9H-GTY, HB-GTY, N81474
F-HPGR	Cessna T206H Turbo Stationair (Soloy conversion)	T20608010	D-EPGR, N25AK, N9574D
F-HPGX	Cessna 172R Skyhawk	17281201	SE-LPK, N2093S
F-HPHA	Robinson R44 Astro	0359	G-OPHA, PH-WBW, G-OPHA, CS-HDW, G-OPHA
F-HPHR	Aérospatiale AS.350B Ecureuil	1003	F-ZBEA, F-GBBQ, F-WZAL
F-HPHT	Ultramagic H-77 HAFB	77/349	
F-HPIC	Eurocopter EC.120B Colibri	1466	RP-C8870, F-OISS
F-HPIT	Piper PA-28R-201 Arrow IV	28R-7918059	I-VDAC, D-EBLH(3), N818PD, N9610N
F-HPIX	PBN BN-2B-26 Islander	2103	G-SEIL, G-BIIP, 6Y-JQJ, 6Y-JKJ, N411JA, G-BIIP
F-HPJA	Airbus A380-861	033	F-WWSB
F-HPJB	Airbus A380-861	040	F-WWSE
F-HPJC	Airbus A380-861	043	F-WWAB
F-HPJD	Airbus A380-861	049	F-WWAL
F-HPJE	Airbus A380-861	052	F-WWAN
F-HPJF	Airbus A380-861	064	F-WWAU
F-HPJG	Airbus A380-861	067	F-WWSQ
F-HPJH	Airbus A380-861	099	F-WWAF
F-HPJI	Airbus A380-861	115	F-WWSL
F-HPJJ	Airbus A380-861	117	F-WWSV
F-HPJL	Embraer EMB-505 Phenom 300	50500274	PR-PEY
F-HPLA	Tecnam P.2008JC	1016	
F-HPLB	Libert L.2200 HAFB	330-054	
F-HPLM	Cameron Z-105 HAFB	11981	
F-HPMA	Cameron Z-105 HAFB	11548	
F-HPMB	Chaize DC2200 F16 HAFB	DC-006	
F-HPOL	Cameron Z-160 HAFB	11694	
F-HPOP	Guimbal G2 Cabri	1165	
F-HPOX	Ultramagic H-77 HAFB	77/396	
F-HPPG	Piper PA-28-161 Warrior II	28-8416075	PH-SVI, N4352P
F-HPPL	Evektor EV-97 SportStar RTC	2015 1712	
F-HPPM	Cirrus SR20	2000	G-TABY, N200CD
F-HPPP	Aérophile 5500 Tethered Gas Balloon	047	
F-HPPS	Mudry CAP.21	09	G-BPPS, F-GDTD
F-HPRB	Aero AT-3 R100	AT3-050	SP-GEM
F-HPRJ	Lindstrand LBL-150A HAFB	1342	
F-HPRS	Eurocopter EC.135T2+	0964	
F-HPSD	Robinson R22 Beta II	3493	I-HDOC
F-HPSE	Robinson R44 Raven	2073	OO-PMO
F-HPSM	Kubicek BB-26Z HAFB	921	
F-HPSZ	Robinson R44 Raven	0986	HB-ZCU
F-HPTC	Reims/Cessna F150K	F15000544	I-ALAV
F-HPTP	Airbus A330-343	1265	F-WWKZ
F-HPTV	Cessna 172R Skyhawk	17280907	SE-LPA
F-HPTZ	Cameron Z-180 HAFB	11967	
F-HPUJ	Airbus A330-323	1727	F-WWKA
F-HPUY	Cameron Z-90 HAFB	11889	
F-HPVG	Aérospatiale AS.350B3 Ecureuil	4894	I-MAVB
F-HPVL	Cameron Z-105 HAFB	11922	
F-HPVM	Eurocopter EC.120B Colibri	1211	G-PDGE, F-WQPD
F-HPVP	Cirrus SR22	3840	EC-LRL, N128ES
F-HPXO	Extra EA.300/LT	LT014	
F-HPYB	Diamond DA.40D Star	D4/289	YR-BIE, OE-KGS(2)
F-HPYH	Agusta-Bell 206B Jet Ranger 2	8517	OO-DOG, F-GDQX, 3A-MFC, F-BXSV
F-HPYR	Robin DR.400/120 Petit Prince	2668	
F-HRAA	Chaize JZ.25F24 HAFB	NG-004	

Registration	Type	Serial	Previous identities
F-HRAF	Piper PA-44-180T Turbo Seminole	44-8207020	OK-MAT, G-FRST, N8236B, N9615N
F-HRAL	Mudry CAP.231EX	04	F-GOJB, OO-CAP, F-GNCF, F-WZCF
F-HRAN	Robinson R44 Raven II	13677	
F-HRAT	Tecnam P.2010	010	
F-HRAY	Dassault Falcon 900LX	288	
F-HRBA	Boeing 787-9	38769	
F-HRCA	Cessna 525 Citation CJ1+	525-0650	HB-VWF, N51511
F-HRCC	Chaize CS.3000 F24 HAFB	NG-006	
F-HRCI	Robinson R44 Raven II	13186	
F-HRCR	Guimbal G2 Cabri	1170	
F-HREC	Piper PA-28-151 Cherokee Warrior	28-7615301	EC-CXR, N9583N
F-HRED	Chaize DC.2200 F16 HAFB	DC-002	
F-HREL	Cirrus SR22	3115	LX-MBA, N175CP
F-HREX	Hawker 800XP	258335	OE-GHU, OY-RAC, LN-AAA(3), N335XP
F-HREZ	Robin DR.400/200i Président	38	G-PREZ
F-HRGD	Embraer EMB-145LU	145369	LX-LGI(2), PT-SOU
F-HRGE	Piper PA-28-181 Archer II	28-88390004	OO-VFK, N82674
F-HRGO	Robin DR.400/160D Major	2024	D-ERGO
F-HRIO	Aérophile 5500 Tethered Gas Balloon	058	
F-HRIS	Cameron Z-275 HAFB	11720	
F-HRLA	Robinson R22 Beta II	3000	G-BYZZ
F-HRLI	Eurocopter EC.225LP Super Puma II	2824	
F-HRLS	SOCATA TB-20 Trinidad	1870	G-TANS, F-GRBX
F-HRMA	Cameron Z-90 HAFB	12004	
F-HRMD	Gardan GY-80-160 Horizon	180	G-BYPE, F-BNYD
F-HROC	Schröder Fire Balloons G22/24 HAFB	1506	
F-HRON	Tecnam P.2008-JC	1018	
F-HROY	Cessna 172M Skyhawk	17264490	G-ECON, G-JONE, N9724V
F-HRPC	Piper PA-28-201T Turbo Arrow III	28R-7803280	OO-DFB, F-GEPH, N9819C
F-HRPN	Cirrus SR22T	0002	N708CR
F-HRPP	Ultramagic M-130 HAFB	130/86	
F-HRSC	Cessna 525A Citation CJ2+	525A-0355	D-IWBL, N5079V
F-HRSN	Laverda F.8L Falco IV	414	I-EDGY, OY-BKC
F-HRST	Reims FR172H Rocket	FR17200300	LX-VAN, LX-PCL, D-ECRR
F-HRSY	Diamond DA.40D Star	D4.073	OE-DQC, G-CCLC, OE-VPW
F-HRTC	Evektor EV-97 Sportstar RTC	2013 1602	
F-HRTO	Robinson R44 Raven II	10859	CN-HAG, HB-ZGW
F-WRUB	Yakovlev Yak-52TW	888415	RA-3385K ?
F-WRUC	Yakovlev Yak-52	unkn	RA-1012K ?
F-WRUE	Yakovlev Yak-52	unkn	DOSAAF
F-WRUG	Yakovlev Yak-52	855712	RA-3691K , G-CDFE, LY-APU, DOSAAF 82
F-WRUH	Yakovlev Yak-52	899409	RA-1453K , RA-01453, DOSAAF 21yellow
F-WRUK	Yakovlev Yak-52	unkn	RA-3503K
F-WRUM	Yakovlev Yak-52	889109	RA-1808K, LY-AMV, DOSAAF 126
F-WRUP	Yakovlev Yak-52	unkn	RA-3508K
F-WRUQ	Yakovlev Yak-52	822109	EC-IAP, LY-EDU, DOSAAF 36
F-WRUS	Yakovlev Yak-52	889009	RA-1529K, RA-01529, RA-44529, DOSAAF 111yel
F-WRYK(2)	Yakovlev Yak-52	8910215	RA-1006K
F-HRZI	Robinson R44 Raven II	13357	
F-HSAA	CSA PS-28 Cruiser	C0502	
F-HSAB	CSA PS-28 Cruiser	C0504	
F-HSAC	CSA PS-28 Cruiser	C0531	
F-HSAE	CSA PS-28 Cruiser	C0520	
F-HSAI	Cessna T206H Turbo Stationair	T20608956	N5250Y
F-HSAL	SOCATA TBM-700 (900)	1125	
F-HSAM	Dassault Falcon 2000LX	230	TC-MAA, F-WWJO
F-HSAP	CSA PS-28 Cruiser	C0417	
F-HSAS	Dassault Falcon 7X	119	F-WWHA
F-HSAX	Tecnam P.2010	019	
F-HSBC	Cessna 172S Skyhawk SP	172S10727	N62570
F-HSBH	Aérospatiale AS.350B3 Ecureuil	7516	
F-HSBL	Embraer EMB-500 Phenom 100	50000353	PR-PFF
F-HSBT	SOCATA TB-10 Tobago	1586	PH-DFC, G-BZRK, VH-YHD
F-HSCC	Schröder Fire Balloons G34/24 HAFB	1522	
F-HSCF	Cessna U206G Stationair 6 (Soloy)	U20605691	PH-PCF, HB-CKM, N5375X
F-HSDA	Extra EA.300SC	SC034	
F-HSDE	Aérospatiale AS.350B3 Ecureuil	7563	
F-HSDG	Mooney M.20K Model 231	25-0817	PH-IMR, (PH-INR), N231VH
F-HSDZ	Robinson R44 Clipper II	12241	G-LULI
F-HSEA	Boeing 747-422	26877	F-WSEA, N188UA
F-HSEB	Lindstrand LBL-150A HAFB	1367	
F-HSEI	Eurocopter EC.135P2	0415	OH-HCN
F-HSER	Aérospatiale AS.350B3 Ecureuil	7573	EC-MBJ, F-HMFR
F-HSET	Cessna 182T Skylane	18282037	SE-LPP, N61924
F-HSFV	Ultramagic S-105 HAFB	105/196	
F-HSFX	Beech B300 King Air 350	FL-1034	N134FL
F-HSFZ	Cessna 208B Grand Caravan	208B0557	F-OGXX, (F-OHXI), N1268M, N5071M
F-HSGE	Eurocopter EC.135T2+	0311	TC-HJA, G-FEES
F-HSGF	Slingsby T-67C Firefly	2087	PH-SGF, OO-SGF, PH-SGF, G-7-141
F-HSHA	Cessna 510 Citation Mustang	510-0413	N678AB, (D-IPRO), N678AB
F-HSHB	Cessna 510 Citation Mustang	510-0259	M-MHDH, (D-IMNH)
F-HSID	Libert L3400 HAFB	344.068	
F-HSIR	Ultramagic T-150 HAFB	150/20	
F-HSJB	Cirrus SR20	1046	OY-CSD, N149CD
F-HSJP	Flight Design CT LS ELA	F-14-06-07	
F-HSKI	Vulcanair P.68TC	481-14/OTC	
F-HSKT	Diamond DA.40D Star	D4.341	SP-NII
F-HSKY	Airbus A330-343	1359	F-WWCZ
F-HSLA	Piper PA-28-181 Archer III	2843610	D-EMPA(3), N31011, OY-PHH, N9518N
F-HSLG	Aerospool WT-9 Dynamic LSA	DY500/2014	F-WSLG
F-HSLI	Beech B200GT Super King Air	BY-143	N883KA, N6403K
F-HSLR	Cameron C-90 HAFB	11949	
F-HSLT	Cessna 172S Skyhawk SP	172S10559	LY-DRS, N2417K
F-HSNO	Cessna 172R Skyhawk	17280116	N388ES
F-HSOL	Robin DR.400/140B Dauphin 4	2696	
F-HSOO	Robin DR.500/200i President	25	EC-IRM, F-GTZJ
F-HSOR	Guimbal Cabri G2	1087	
F-HSOT	Chaize CS.5000F24 HAFB	NG-003	
F-HSPC	Robin DR.300/180R Remorqueur	550	HB-EMP
F-HSPE	Piper PA-34-220T Seneca III	34-8333106	N8202Q
F-HSRV	Eurocopter EC.135T3	1176	
F-HSTI	Piper PA-31T2 Cheyenne IIXL	31T-8166033	G-CHEY, N67PD, N42NE, N42ND, N59WA, N9092Y
F-HSTL	Cessna U206G Stationair 6 (Soloy)	U20604266	PH-STL, HB-CKZ, N756QF
F-HSUD	Piper PA-44-180 Seminole	44-8095027	PH-VKA, N8230Z
F-HSUN	Boeing 747-422	26880	N191UA
F-HSUR	PBN BN-2A-26 Islander	530	G-XAXA, G-LOTO, G-BDWG, (N90255), (C-GYUF), G-BDWG
F-HSVM	Robin DR.400/120 Petit Prince	2388	PH-SVM
F-HSVS	Cessna 208 Caravan I	20800367	G-DLAA, VH-CXX, N208KP
F-HSXB	Diamond DA 40D Star	D4.079	G-SOHO
F-HSYS	Piper PA-34-220T Seneca V	3449464	N25107, (F-HSYS), N25107, N9515N
F-HTAF	SOCATA TB-20 Trinidad GT	2187	G-CCGL, F-OIMN
F-HTAG	Boeing 757-256	29307	G-POWJ, TF-IST, TC-OGS, (P4-NAS), EC-HIQ
F-HTAN	Cameron Z-120 HAFB	11528	
F-HTCH	Beech B200 Super King Air	BB-1006	CN-TPH, N680CB, (N46CE), N6300S
F-HTCR	Beech C90GT King Air	LJ-1887	N32087
F-WTDT	Boeing 737-8AL	35071	5Y-KYC
F-HTEC	Piper PA-28-161 Warrior III	2842207	I-NETA, N3066V
F-HTFI	SOCATA TB-200 Tobago XL	2017	CS-DEA, F-OJBA, F-WWRF
F-HTFS	Reims/Cessna F150L	F15000821	D-ETFS, D-EEWA
F-HTGV	Extra EA.300LC	LC022	
F-HTIN	Eurocopter EC.135T2+	1010	G-CIDJ, 4K-AZ90, D-HCBH
F-HTIO	Beech B200GT King Air	BY-142	HB-GSB, G-HCCL, N81404
F-HTJC	Evektor EV-97 SportStar RTC	2016 1912	
F-HTLI	Vulcanair P.68 Observer 2	473-37/OB2	
F-HTLN	Eurocopter EC.135T2+	0810	G-PNTC, I-PNTC
F-HTLS	Embraer EMB-500 Phenom 100	50000283	N81YA, HP1778AJQ, HP-I&&*, N1008U, N6004N
F-HTLV	Cessna 182T Skylane	18282130	D-EKJP, N6203D
F-HTML	Schröder Fire Balloons G34/24 HAFB	1487	
F-HTOF	Aérospatiale AS.350B3 Ecureuil	8105	
F-HTOP	Embraer EMB-135LR	14500886	LX-LGK, PT-SXY
F-HTOY	Robin DR.400/120 Petit Prince	1042	OO-TOY, F-BXJJ
F-HTPI	Eurocopter EC.135T2+	0630	TC-HJS, M-YCHT
F-HTRB	Aérophile 5500 Tethered Gas Balloon	053	
F-HTRD	Chaize JZ.25 F16 HAFB	NG-008	
F-HTRS	Eurocopter EC.135P2+	0125	(D-HAAV), C-GNZH(2), VH-WKJ(2), D-HECB, D-HECY, LN-OOA, D-HECF
F-HTRV	Eurocopter EC.135T3	1182	
F-HTRX	Aérospatiale AS.350B3 Ecureuil	8196	
F-HTRY	Piaggio P.180 Avanti	3004	
F-HTSY	Piper PA-28R-201 Cherokee Arrow III	28R-7737052	G-UTSY, N3346Q
F-HTTC	Cessna 177RG Cardinal RG	177RG0912	EC-EOD, N7857V
F-HTTO	Bombardier BD-700-1A11 Global 5000	9755	C-FMYG
F-HTTP	Raytheon Premier 390 I	RB-196	LY-OJB, OE-FIM(3), D-IIMC, N37346
F-HTVA	Bpeing 737-8K2	62158	
F-HTVB	Bpeing 737-8K2	62161	
F-HTVC	Bpeing 737-8K2	62150	
F-HTXS	Cameron O-120 HAFB	2141	G-BTXS
F-HUAJ	Aérospatiale AS.365N3 Dauphin 2	6879	G-REDE
F-HUAP	CSA PS28 Cruiser	C0518	
F-HUAT	Tecnam P.2008-JC	1030	
F-WUAV	SAGEM Patroller UAV	unkn	
F-HUBA	Bell 206B Jet Ranger III	3881	G-TCSM, G-CDYS, G-BOTM, N31940
F-HUBB	Dassault Falcon 900EASy	150	G-SABI, N900NS, F-WWFI
F-HUBG	Partenavia P.68C	278	HA-ACD, N147CH, PH-GRO, G-BMLR, OY-BYS, D-GOBY
F-HUBH	AgustaWestland AW139	41387	N245MM
F-HUBI	Tecnam P.2002-JF Sierra	211	9H-CFC
F-HUBJ	Tecnam P.2002-JF Sierra	212	9H-CFD
F-HUBK	Tecnam P.2002-JF Sierra	224	9H-CFA
F-HUBU	Ultramagic S-50 HAFB	50/12	
F-HUCK	Robinson R44 Raven II	13509	
F-HUCR	AgustaWestland AW139	41400	
F-HUDT	Aérospatiale AS.365N3 Dauphin 2	6745	D2-EWD, F-GTDL, F-WWOD
F-HUEF	AgustaWestland AW139	31701	I-EASI
F-HUEM	Sikorsky S-76C++	760752	5N-BNV, F-HELP, N20539
F-HUEZ	SAN Jodel D.140R Abeille	503	OO-VVK
F-HUFD	Eurocopter EC.225LP Super Puma	2897	
F-HUFG	Eurocopter EC.225LP Super Puma	2932	
F-HUGE	Cirrus SR22	1476	N442CD
F-HUGF	AgustaWestland AW139	41388	N251MM
F-HUGG	Robinson R44 Raven II	12440	T7-CAB, I-HEFS
F-HUGH	Robinson R44 Raven II	12340	OO-CVM(2)
F-HUGO	Aérospatiale SA.365N Dauphin 2	6103	N617TD, YR-SBS, LN-OXO, PH-SSW, PP-MCA, PH-SSW, V8-UDW(3)
F-HUGS	Dassault Falcon 2000LX	193	TC-MRK, F-WWGD
F-HUIP	Eurocopter EC.225LP Super Puma	2815	D2-EWZ, F-HUPM, F-WJXL
F-HUIS	Robinson R66	0059	
F-HUIT	CSA PS28 Cruiser	C0409	
F-HUJK	AgustaWestland AW139	41401	N264MM
F-HUKL	Sikorsky S-76C	760788	5N-BNW, F-GTNB, N788Y
F-HULK	SOCATA TB-10 Tobago	1901	TF-ELT, TF-AIR, N363DG, G-GINS, F-OILN
F-HUME	Extra EA.300/200	16	N97EX
F-HUMF	Lindstrand LBL-90A HAFB	190	
F-HUMM	Diamond DA.40D Star	D4.357	HB-SDX
F-HUMT	AgustaWestland AW139	41505	N278MM
F-HUNE	Cameron V-90 HAFB	11820	
F-HUON	Balloon Works Firefly 8 HAFB	F8-2023	C-FUON
F-HUPE	Piper PA-32RT-300 Lance II	32R-7885200	G-BFYC, N36645
F-HUPY	Cessna 170B	20767	D-EORB(2), G-AORB, OO-SIZ, N2615D
F-HURX	Aérospatiale AS.365N3 Dauphin 2	9001	5N-BNY, F-GXPY, D2-EXT, F-GTTZ, F-WQEG
F-HURY	Reims/Cessna FRA150M Aerobat	FRA1500277	EC-CVQ, F-BJDG
F-HUTA	Guimbal Cabri G2	1046	
F-HUTB	Guimbal Cabri G2	1054	
F-HUTC	Schweizer 269C-1	0167	
F-HUTD	Guimbal Cabri G2	1105	
F-HUXP	AgustaWestland AW139	41507	N279MM
F-HUZS	Aérospatiale AS.365N3 Dauphin 2	6726	D2-EWC, F-HMLB, F-WWOS
F-HVAA	Eurocopter EC.155B1 Dauphin	6976	
F-HVAD	Aerospool WT-9 Dynamic LSA	DY479/2013	F-WVAD
F-HVAI	Slingsby T.67M Mk.II	2122	HA-WAI, G-BUUL
F-HVAL	Mooney M.20J Model 201	24-0586	HA-JML, D-EEJH

Reg	Type	Serial	Previous ids
F-HVAP	Aerospool WT-9 Dynamic LSA	DY427/2011	F-WVAP
F-HVAR	Agusta A.109E Power	11160	I-RAPS
F-HVBH	Aérospatiale AS.350B3 Ecureuil	7642	
F-HVBL	Dassault Falcon 7X	188	F-WWHT
F-HVBR	Aerospool WT-9 Dynamic LSA	DY445/2012	F-WVBR
F-HVCS	Chaize CS.3000 F24 HAFB	NG-009	
F-HVCT	Piper PA-38-112 Tomahawk	38-82A0105	6V-. . . ., F-GVCT, HB-PGV
F-HVDM	Robinson R66	0582	
F-HVDP	Robin DR.400/160 Major	2555	PH-SVQ
F-HVDY	Aerospool WT-9 Dynamic LSA	DY464/2013	F-WVDY
F-HVEB	Cirrus SR22	0950	N950CD
F-HVEM	Diamond DA.20-C1 Katana	C0561	SE-MEV
F-HVER	Llopis Balloons MA-30 HAFB	234	
F-HVET	Aerospool WT-9 Dynamic LSA	DY485/2013	F-WVET
F-HVEY	Partenavia P.68C	415-05	G-SVEY, HB-LTQ, D-GYRO
F-HVEZ	Cameron A-315 HAFB	11944	
F-HVFA	Piper PA-38-112 Tomahawk	38-78A0120	G-CWFA, G-BTGC, N9507T
F-HVFM	Aerospool WT-9 Dynamic LSA	DY434/2012	F-WVFM
F-HVGA	Beech 58 Baron	TH-1400	N262LF
F-HVGT	Aerospool WT-9 Dynamic LSA	DY473/2013	F-WVGT
F-HVHV	Bell 47G-5A	925057	EC-EQD, FAP650, N2975W
F-HVIB	Dassault Falcon 7X	47	RA-09009, (CS-DSC), F-WWVS
F-HVIE	Cameron Z-77 HAFB	12000	
F-HVIF	Aerospool WT-9 Dynamic LSA	DY494/2014	F-WVIF
F-HVIT	Cameron Z-105 HAFB	11848	
F-WVJD	Flight Design CT-LS	unkn	
F-HVJL	Aerospool WT-9 Dynamic LSA	DY435/2012	F-WVJL
F-HVKA	Schröder Fire Balloons G40/24 HAFB	1548	
F-HVMA	Flight Design CT LS ELA	F-12-02-03	F-WVMA
F-HVMB	Flight Design MC	A-12-04-33	F-WVMB
F-HVMC	Flight Design CT LS ELA	F-11-07-03	F-WVMC
F-WVMD	Flight Design CT-LS	F-12-04-06	F-WVMD
F-HVMS	Cessna 172S Skyhawk SP	172S8976	D-EVMS, N3508L
F-HVOC	Aerospool WT-9 Dynamic LSA	DY510/2014	F-WVOC
F-HVOL	Lindstrand LBL-150A HAFB	631	OO-BQU
F-HVPM	Hughes 369E	0110E	I-MIIS, N5223X
F-HVPS	CSA PS-28 Cruiser	C0478	
F-HVPT	Pipistrel Virus SW100	426SWN100	F-WVPT
F-HVRC	Alpi Avn Pioneer 300	003	
F-HVSP	Cessna 207A Stationair 8	20700784	SE-KOZ, N1721Q
F-HVTF	Tecnam P.2008JC	1002	
F-HVTG	Tecnam P.2008JC	1005	
F-HVTL	Lindstrand LBL-105A HAFB	1468	
F-HVUL	Aérophile 5500 Tethered Gas Balloon	046	
F-HVVC	Cameron Z-140 HAFB	11888	
F-HVXA	Aerospool WT-9 Dynamic LSA	DY436/2012	F-WVXA
F-HVXB	Aerospool WT-9 Dynamic LSA	DY480/2013	F-WVXB
F-HVXC	Aerospool WT-9 Dynamic LSA	DY487/2013	F-WVXC
F-HVXD	Aerospool WT-9 Dynamic LSA	DY508/2014	F-WVXD
F-HVXE	Aerospool WT-9 Dynamic LSA	DY496/2014	F-WVXE
F-HXAF	Diamond DA 40 Star	40053	HB-SDA
F-HXAL	Extra EA.300/SC	SC047	
F-HXAM	CSA PS-28 Cruiser	C0443	
F-HXCC	Ultramagic M-77 HAFB	77/269	G-DXCC
F-HXEL	Extra EA.330SC	SC046	
F-HXHX	Robinson R44 Raven II	1444	OE-XHX
F-HXLA	Cessna TU206G Stationair II	U20604722	F-ODIN, N732TZ
F-HXLF	Airbus A330-303	1360	F-WWKA
F-HXLG	Tecnam P.2008JC	1025	
F-HXRA	Robinson R22 Beta II	3473	OO-RWC, N75170
F-HXRG	Bombardier BD.700-1A10 Global Express	9323	N679JB, OE-LGX, C-FUCV
F-HXTN	Cirrus SR22T	1062	N9AH
F-HXZM	Pitts S-2B Special	5205	N2MK
F-HYAC	Yakovlev Yak-18T	22202052122	HA-YAI, RA-44538
F-HYAK	Yakovlev Yak-18T	22202034139	RA-3628K, RA-44506, HA-JAC, FLARF02159, RA-44516
F-HYBO	Robinson R66	0700	
F-HYCB	Cessna 172R Skyhawk	17281327	D-EYCB, D-EZDF, N2434Z
F-HYDE	Aérospatiale AS.350B3 Ecureuil	7126	9N-. . ., F-OKFS
F-HYDJ	Eurocopter EC.135P2+	0522	EC-LHS, D-HTSI
F-HYES	Piper PA-28-181 Archer II	28-8190109	EC-HTG, D-EHAH(3), N8308D
F-HYEU	Eurocopter EC.135T2+	0873	HP-3011HF, XA-UPK, D-HTSF(8)
F-HYJC	Aérospatiale AS.350B3 Ecureuil	3719	EC-LHO, F-GYDJ, F-GURR
F-HYLA	Schröder Fire Balloons M22/24 HAFB	1528	
F-HYPA	Diamond DA 42	42.025	N315DR, F-GYYB
F-HYPE	Eurocopter EC.120B Colibri	1126	D-HBAV, SX-HVC, F-WQLY
F-HYRJ	Robinson R44 Raven II	11770	G-LUCI, G-CULF
F-HYSB	Republic RC-3 Seabee	421	N6218K, NC6218K
F-HYZY	Cessna 172R Skyhawk	17280419	G-IZZY, G-BXSF, N9967F
F-HZAA	Schröder Fire Balloons G34/24 HAFB	1465	
F-HZAF	Robin DR.400/180 Régent	2534	G-OACF
F-HZAP	Eurocopter EC.135P2+	0583	YR-CPC
F-HZBB	Kubicek BB-60Z HAFB	919	
F-HZCM	Piper PA-28-181 Archer III	2843657	N67SE, N3088U
F-HZDJ	Boeing Stearman B75N1 N2S-3 Kaydet	75-7515	N269N, BuA07911
F-HXDP	Airbus A320-214	3325	M-ABJC, PR-MHS, F-WWBS
F-HZEN	Airbus A330-343X	1376	F-WWYE
F-HZEV	SAN Jodel D.140R Abeille	519	FrAF 519/F-ZJOC, F-WQUA, F-WQUB, 519/F-ZJOC
F-HZFM	Airbus A320-214	5887	D-AVVY
F-HZIP	Robinson R44 Raven II	13424	OE-XYI
F-HZLL	Cessna 172S Skyhawk	172S11059	Z3-DAI, UR-NIKA, N5293F
F-HZOO	Issoire APM-20 Lionceau	32	
F-HZTH	Robinson R44 Raven II	13015	HB-ZTH

FRANCE d'OUTREMER

Reg	Type	Serial	Previous ids
F-OCEY	Piper PA-38-112 Tomahawk	38-78A0692	N2442A
F-OCFA	Piper PA-23-250 Aztec C	27-2788	N10F, (N5674Y)
F-OCFE	Cessna 150E	15061471	N4071U
F-OCFK	Cessna 310P	310P0053	N5753M
F-OCFL	Piper PA-23-250 Aztec C (Accident 16.12.03)	27-3856	VH-SVZ, N6560Y
F-OCFN	Piper PA-28-140 Cherokee	28-24166	N11C
F-OCGU	Cessna U206A Super Skywagon	U206-0492	N8092Z
F-OCLJ	Piper PA-32-260 Cherokee Six	32-1015	
F-OCMJ	Cessna 182J	18257111	N3011F
F-OCNX	Cessna 172K	17258463	N84411
F-OCPR	Piper PA-28-140 Cherokee C	28-26922	N11C
F-OCPT	SOCATA MS.893A Rallye Commodore 180	11665	
F-OCQG	Sud Avn SA.318C Alouette Astazou	2219	
F-OCQZ	DHC-6 Twin Otter Srs.300	412	
F-OCSO	Piper PA-23-160 Apache G	23-1988	CF-NMP, N4463P
F-OCUX	Reims/Cessna F172M (W/o 28.12.04)	F17201009	
F-OCXA	Cessna 177B Cardinal	17702092	ZK-DSF
F-OCXU	Piper PA-28-161 Cherokee Warrior II	28-7816534	N9572N
F-ODFC	Reims/Cessna F150M	F15001338	
F-ODGD	Cessna 152	15283539	ZK-EOZ, (N53379)
F-ODGF	Cessna 152	15283560	ZK-ETB, (N4710B)
F-ODGH	Cessna 207A Stationair 8	20700650	ZK-EOE, N85020, (N75894)
F-ODGJ	Hughes 269C	70-0937	ZK-HPM
F-ODGK	Hughes 369HS	85-0763S	ZK-HPE, (N222PF), N900Q
F-ODGQ	Aérospatiale AS.350B Ecureuil	2263	
F-ODGS	Piper PA-31T Cheyenne	31T-7720041	TS-LAZ, LN-PAE, (N82144)
F-ODGT	Piper PA-28-161 Warrior II	28-8616050	N9294A, N9511N
F-ODGV	Robin ATL L	97	F-GFSQ
F-ODHL	Robin R.2112 Alpha	123	
F-ODHS	Cessna U206G Stationair II	U20603900	N7362C
F-ODIV	Piper PA-38-112 Tomahawk	38-80A0058	N9656N
F-ODIX	Beech 58 Baron	TH-1016	
F-ODJD	SOCATA MS.893E Rallye 180GT F/p	13202	
F-ODJJ	Cessna 172G	17254376	5R-MDR, N11B, (N4307L)
F-ODLB	Cessna 150K	15071137	ZS-FXM, N5637G
F-ODLC	Aérospatiale SA.315B Lama	2635	
F-ODLF	Beech 58 Baron	TH-310	ZS-PTE, N1041W
F-ODLI	Aérospatiale AS.350B1 Ecureuil	2063	F-WYMC
F-ODNL	Mudry CAP.10B	70	HB-SAI
F-ODNR	Mudry CAP.10B	139	
F-ODPA	Centrair ASW-20F	20151	
F-ODQI	Piper PA-31-350 Navajo Chieftain	31-7305065	F-BUOI, F-ETAH
F-ODSM	Piper PA-28R-201 Cherokee Arrow III	28R-7737084	N38223
F-ODSZ	SOCATA TB-10 Tobago	660	SE-IMZ, N20HZ
F-ODTI	SNCASE SE.3130 Alouette II	1852	F-GBOC, D-HOFO
F-ODUN	Dornier 228-212 (Stored)	8197	D-CATS (1), D-CBDH (3)
F-ODUY	Piper PA-28-181 Archer II	2890092	N9152X
F-ODYJ	SOCATA TB-10 Tobago	1193	
F-ODYL	SOCATA TB-10 Tobago	1192	
F-ODYM	Robinson R22 Mariner	1908M	
F-ODYN	Cessna 152	15282982	C-GRXZ, N46008
F-ODYO	Piper PA-28-151 Cherokee Warrior	28-7515153	ZK-DUV, N9628N
F-ODYQ	SOCATA TB-20 Trinidad	1118	VH-LQJ
F-ODYU	Aérospatiale AS.350BA Ecureuil	1998	ZK-HZH
F-ODZP	SNCASE SE.3130 Alouette II	1573	ALAT
F-ODZQ	Robinson R22 Beta	2094	N23340
F-ODZT	Schweizer 269C	S-1650	N86G
F-ODZV	Aérospatiale AS.355F2 Ecureuil 2	5310	JA9611
F-ODZX	Aerotek Pitts S-2A	2122	N5SV
F-OFAP	Eurocopter EC.130B4 Ecureuil	7435	
F-OFDF	Airbus A330-223	253	HB-IQD, F-WWKM
F-OFGM	Eurocopter EC.135P2+	0572	PR-MEU, D-HDRS(2), D-HECB
F-OFML	Aérospatiale AS.350B	7984	
F-OFQQ	Hughes 369E	0604E	N488DW, ZK-IRB, N387SH, (N242MH), N5283F
F-OGBL	Piper PA-23-160 Apache G	23-2006	N4484P
F-OGDS	Cessna 150H	15067214	N6414S
F-OGEV	Cessna 150K	15071815	N6315G
F-OGFF	Piper PA-28-180 Cherokee F	28-7105138	
F-OGFR	Piper PA-28-140 Cherokee E	28-7225294	
F-OGGT	Beech 58 Baron	TH-514	
F-OGGX	Beech C23 Sundowner	M-1649	
F-OGHN	Piper PA-28R-200 Cherokee Arrow II	28R-7635342	
F-OGHQ	Cessna 177B Cardinal	17702522	N17238
F-OGHZ	Piper PA-28-181 Cherokee Archer II (Ditched 20.12.14)	28-7690351	N6142J
F-OGIC	Cessna A185F Skywagon	18503348	N6990H
F-OGJF	Piper PA-28-181 Archer II	28-8090333	
F-OGJG	Piper PA-28-236 Dakota	28-8011119	
F-OGJJ	Robin R.2160 Alpha Sport	184	
F-OGJT	Piper PA-23-250 Aztec E	27-7305050	N40245
F-OGJU	Piper PA-32-301 Saratoga	32-8106006	N8290U
F-OGKO	Piper PA-28-151 Cherokee Warrior	28-7715109	N5358F
F-OGKQ	Cessna 172P Skyhawk	17276311	N98571
F-OGNG	Cessna 152	15283030	N46319
F-OGNJ	Piper PA-28-161 Cherokee Warrior II	28-7816079	N47475
F-OGOC	Cessna 172M	17263038	N13913
F-OGOG	Reims/Cessna F406 Caravan II	F406-0026	
F-OGOL	Dornier 228-202K	8139	D-CACC, (D-CBDS)
F-OGON	Grumman G.164B AgCat	54B	- ? - , N48503
F-OGOQ	Dornier 228-201	8056	7P-LAL, D-CAMI
F-OGOU	Aérospatiale AS.355F2 Ecureuil 2	5051	N281DB, C-GLCA, N281DB, N5778C
F-OGOZ	Dornier 228-202K	8161	D-CBDR(2)
F-OGPB	Hughes 269C	76-0521	N42JW
F-OGPJ	Piper PA-28-161 Warrior II	28-7916379	V2-LCA, VP-LCA, N9507N
F-OGPM	Beech 58 Baron	TH-345	N1896W
F-OGPP	Piper PA-23-250 Aztec F	27-7654152	C-GPXX, N9701N
F-OGPS	Aérospatiale AS.350B2 Ecureuil	2412	
F-OGPV	Piper PA-28-181 Archer II	28-8190091	N82978
F-OGRA	Piper PA-28-181 Archer II	28-8090354	N8233S
F-OGRB	Piper PA-23-250 Aztec F	27-7754102	N6570X, - ? - , N63771
F-OGRH	Piper PA-28-161 Cherokee Warrior II	28-7716282	N38864
F-OGRT	Boeing 737-341	26854	(PP-VPC)
F-OGRX	SOCATA TB-9 Tampico Club	1349	
F-OGUK	Piper PA-28-180 Cherokee G	28-7305323	CF-CCP
F-OGVF	Cessna 150M	15078963	N704XU
F-OGVI (2)	Cessna U206G Stationair 6	U20604849	(N9ZE), F-OGVI(2), N734LN
F-OGVK	Cessna 150M	15078184	N9234U
F-OGVM	Cessna A188B AgTruck	18802804T	N731DA
F-OGVN	Partenavia P.68B (Stored: CofA exp)	155	F-GBLY
F-OGVO	Hughes 269C	86-0539	N911PD, TF-ELI, N911PD
F-OGVT	Cessna 172N Skyhawk 100	17268788	N143ER, N734EB
F-OGXA	Britten-Norman BN-2A-26 Islander	788	D-IHUG, PH-PFS, G-BDRV
F-OGXB	Britten-Norman BN-2A-2 Islander (Exp.10.04)	303	D-IHVH, G-AZUS, G-51-303, (N58JA)
F-OGXD	Cessna U206G Stationair 6	U20605007	N4622U

Registration	Type	c/n	Previous identities
F-OGXE	Robin R.2160 Alpha Sport	290	F-GORE
F-OGXH	Reims FR172J Rocket	FR17200408	F-BUMI
F-OGXT	Piper PA-28-236 Dakota	28-7911116	N3009T
F-OHAJ	Piper PA-28R-201 Arrow III	28R-7837014	N47911
F-OHAM	Aérospatiale AS.350BA Ecureuil	2633	F-WYMP
F-OHAO	Aérospatiale AS.355F2 Ecureuil 2 (Res.)	unkn	
F-OHAY	Cessna U206G Stationair 6	U20604683	N732JK
F-OHCB	Piper PA-28R-200 Cherokee Arrow II	28R-7635100	F-BXSD, N9642N
F-OHFK	Sud Avn SA.316B Alouette III	1510	JRV23157
F-OHGH	Robinson R44 Clipper	0446	
F-OHGT	Aérospatiale/Alenia ATR-72-212A (Stored)	698	F-WWEU
F-OHJG	DHC-6 Twin Otter Srs.300	603	Fr.AF, C-GRQZ
F-OHJR	Piper PA-23-250 Aztec E	27-7554087	VH-WJJ, N54785

F-OHKG to OHKZ Reservations for Eurocopter for deliveries

Registration	Type	c/n	Previous identities
F-OHMB	Airbus A320-231	376	F-WWIK
F-OHMC	Airbus A320-231	386	F-WWBI
F-OHMD	Airbus A320-231	433	F-WWDC
F-OHOR	Aérospatiale AS.350B3 Ecureuil (W/o 4.7.12)	3307	
F-OHQB	Ayres S.2R-T34	226	N2264K
F-OHQC	Ayres S.2R-T34	227	N2269V
F-OHQD	Ayres S.2R-T34	243DC	(F-GRIO), F-OHQD, N2045D
F-OHQI	Cessna 172R Skyhawk	17280214	N9403F
F-OHQY	Pilatus Britten-Norman BN-2B-20 Islander	2251	V2-LFE, 9M-TAC, G-BTLW
F-OHRA	Piper PA-32-300 Cherokee Six B	32-40635	F-BRIR, N4261R
F-OHRB	Nord 262C Frégate	74	F-BSUF
F-OHRX	Beech 1900D	UE-282	N11296
F-OHRY	Grumman G.164B AgCat	132B	N6605Q
F-OHSD	Airbus A330-202	507	F-WWYS
F-OHSE	Aérospatiale AS.350B2 Ecureuil	2291	VH-EEA, ZK-IWI
F-OHSF	Aérospatiale/Alenia ATR-72-212A	650	F-WWEC
F-OHSM	Aérospatiale AS.355F2 Ecureuil 2	5510	OE-BXV (3), F-WYMA
F-OHSN	Aérospatiale AS.355N Ecureuil 2	9606	
F-OHSP	Aérospatiale AS.355N Ecureuil 2	9607	
F-OHXY	Cessna 172S Skyhawk SP (Dbr 31.12.09)	172S9310	N53212
F-OIAA	Beech B200 Super King Air	BB-932	HB-GJX, SE-KKM, Fv:101004, SE-KKM, OY-CCE, D-IBCI
F-OIAB	Cessna 172N Skyhawk 100 (Damaged 24.10.13)	17268209	VH-KJJ, N1748C, (N733DF)
F-OIAC	Piper PA-34-200 Seneca	34-7350277	VH-RRS, OY-DZP, HB-LEK, N56054
F-OIAH	Aérospatiale AS.350B2 Ecureuil	9004	
F-OIAI	Robinson R44 Raven (Damaged 30.12.03)	0800	
F-OIAJ	Aérospatiale AS.350BA Ecureuil	1296	- ? - , F-OIAE, ZK-HLX, F-ODGE, F-WZKC
F-OIAK	Aérospatiale AS.350B3 Ecureuil	3653	
F-OIAN	Beech B200 Super King Air (Damaged, Fiji 26.4.10)	BB-1220	TR-LDM, N93GA, ET-AKA, N72294
F-OIAO	Aérospatiale AS.350B3 Ecureuil (W/o 4.10.15)	4308	
F-OIAP	Cessna 182P Skylane	18262717	VH-IRN, N52619
F-OIAQ	DHC-6 Twin Otter Srs.300	381	VH-RPZ, 6Y-JMV, N26KH, F-GGKA, TZ-ACD
F-OIAS	Robinson R44 Raven II	10326	
F-OIAT	Mooney M.20J Model 205	24-3370	
F-OIAU	Aérospatiale AS.350B2 Ecureuil	2978	
F-OIAV (3)	Piper PA-31T3 T-1040	31T-8475001	ZK-PFL, N2464W
F-OIAX	Cessna 172S Skyhawk SP	172S9213	ZK-JOL, N5281R
F-OIAY (2)	DHC-6 Twin Otter Srs.300	507	P2-KSR, N720CA, C-GPJB
F-OIBD	Robinson R22B2 Beta	2921	
F-OICB	Aérospatiale AS.332L1 Super Puma	2635	F-WWOL, F-WWOK
F-OICP	Robinson R22B2 Beta	3467	N75125
F-OIEA	AgustaWestland AW139	31418	C-GSBC(4), G-LOWC, I- . . . . , G-LOWC
F-OIED	Cessna 150H	15068116	N22174
F-OIEL	Aérospatiale AS.350B Ecureuil (W/o 4.8.10)	9052	

F-OIGC to OIGZ Reservations for SOCATA

Registration	Type	c/n	Previous identities
F-OIJA	Cessna 172S Skyhawk SP	172S08154	N954SP
F-OIJC	Cessna 172S Skyhawk SP	172S08303	N2461N
F-OIJD	Piper PA-28-181 Archer III	2843371	N9522N, N41848
F-OIJI	DHC-6 Twin Otter Srs.310	277	HB-LSU, VH-TGG, N8861
F-OIJK (2)	Aérospatiale/Alenia ATR-72-212A	736	F-WWEQ
F-OIJL	DHC-6 Twin Otter Srs.310 (To Dubai 8.12, to DU-SD5 but still not cld)	281	HB-LSV, N616BA, VH-TGH, N8336
F-OIJP	SOCATA TB-20 Trinidad	2127	
F-OIJQ	Cessna 150K	15071817	N6317G
F-OIJR	Piper PA-34-220T Seneca V	3449216	F-WIJR, N53272, F-OIJR, N9525N
F-OIJT	Piper PA-23-250 Aztec F	27-7854129	N6513A
F-OIJY	DHC-6 Twin Otter Srs.300	797	D-IFLY (6), 9Q-CJD, C-GDIU

F-OIKA to OIMZ Reserved / used by SOCATA for overseas deliveries

Registration	Type	c/n	Previous identities
F-OIOM	Aérospatiale SA.315B Lama	2423	EC-DNZ, N47065
F-OIPA	Robin DR.400/200R Remo 200	2375	
F-OIPB	Pilatus PC-6/B1-H2 Turbo Porter	661	HB-FKQ, A14-661, HB-FDM
F-OIPM	Robinson R44 Raven	0765	C-GMDV
F-OIPN	Aérospatiale/Alenia ATR-72-212A	735	F-WWEP
F-OIPS	Aérospatiale/Alenia ATR-72-212A	764	F-WWEC
F-OIQA	Piper PA-31-350 Navajo Chieftain	31-7952191	N9020S, N3534L
F-OIQC	Aérospatiale/Alenia ATR-42-512	627	F-WWCH
F-OIQF	DHC-6 Twin Otter Srs.300	815	N45KH, ET-AIM, C-GDCZ
F-OIQG	Extra EA.300/200	028	HB-MSY
F-OIQI	DHC-6 Twin Otter Srs.300 (Dam 10.8.07)	608	N228CS, HK-3523, N784DL, HK-2215X
F-OIQK	Beech 200C King Air	BL-149	N36949
F-OIQL	Beech 200C King Air	BL-148	N36948
F-OIQM	Beech A200 King Air	BB-1934	N37134
F-OIQP	DHC-6 Twin Otter Srs.300	715	5Y-SKL, N8489H,HK-2534X
F-OIQR	Aérospatiale/Alenia ATR-72-212A	862	F-WWEJ
F-OIQT	Aérospatiale/Alenia ATR-72-212A	829	F-WWEW
F-OIQU	Aérospatiale/Alenia ATR-72-212A	751	F-WWEL
F-OIQV	Aérospatiale/Alenia ATR-72-212A	806	

Registration	Type	c/n	Previous identities
F-OIQY	Beech B300 King Air 350	FL-566	N3366K
F-OIQZ	Piper PA-28-181 Archer III	2843405	N152YH, N4176X
F-OISZ	Aérospatiale AS.332L2 Super Puma	2672	
F-OITM	Cessna 172N Skyhawk	17271149	N123QA, N2085E

F-OIUA to OIUZ Reserved / used by SOCATA for overseas deliveries

Registration	Type	c/n	Previous identities
F-OIXD	Aérospatiale/Alenia ATR-42-500	695	F-WWLQ
F-OIXE	Aérospatiale/Alenia ATR-42-500	807	F-WWLX
F-OIXF	LET L-410UVP-E20 Turbolet	092635	OK-2635
F-OIXG	LET L-410UVP-E20 Turbolet	2734	OK-AIS
F-OIXI	LET L-410UVP-E20 Turbolet	2807	OK-ODR
F-OIXJ	Cessna 208B Grand Caravan	208B2325	
F-OIXL	Aérospatiale/Alenia ATR-72-212A	888	F-WWES
F-OIXM	Piper PA-28-161 Warrior III	2842441	N153DC, N9510N
F-OIXO	Aérospatiale/Alenia ATR-42-600	1010	F-WWLS
F-OIXP	Piper PA-28-181 Cherokee Archer II	28-7790509	N5899V
F-OIXT	LET L-410UVP-E20 Turbolet	2903	OK-JDB
F-OIZO	Robinson R22M2 Mariner	3296M	
F-OJAE	Cessna 150M	15079347	N714QH
F-OJAG	Cessna 172S Skyhawk SP	172S10249	N320CP
F-OJAM	Eurocopter EC.135P2+	0615	PR-MEV, D-HDRT(2), D-HECT(4)

F-OJBA to OJBZ Reserved / used by SOCATA for overseas deliveries

Registration	Type	c/n	Previous identities
F-OJCA	Beech C23 Sundowner 180	M-1788	N9176S
F-OJCB	Robinson R44 Raven II	12926	
F-OJCM	Cessna 172S Skyhawk SP	172S8882	N35117
F-OJFP	Extra EA.300/L	1186	
F-OJGF	Airbus A340-313X	385	(OO-SQA), F-WWJC
F-OJIJ	Piper PA-32-300 Cherokee Six	32-40451	F-BPIJ, N4134R
F-OJJC	Cessna 208B Grand Caravan	208B1156	OY-PBP, LN-PBP, N5216A
F-OJJD	Cessna 208B Grand Caravan	208B1252	N460HP, XA-UHP
F-OJRD	Piper PA-36-375 Brave	36-8002015	EC-FOE, N2370X
F-OJSB	Airbus A320-214	2152	
F-OJSE	Airbus A330-202	510	F-WWYT
F-OJSN	Piper PA-32-301 Saratoga (Damaged 7.5.13)	32-8006042	F-GCSN, (OO-HKB), N8199H
F-OJTN	Airbus A340-313X	395	C-GZIA, F-WWJF
F-OKAB	BN-2T Islander	2310	G-CEUE
F-WKAF	Reims/Cessna F182Q Skylane (Diesel engined) (P.10.02)	F18200167	F-OKAF, F-GCYP
F-OKAY	Aérospatiale SA.365N Dauphin 2	6113	N28EH, HL9229, F-WYMW
F-OKCL	Robinson R44 Raven II	11135	
F-OKCP	Robinson R44 Raven II	12030	
F-OKDV	Cessna 172S Skyhawk SP	172S10098	N2364S

F-OKEA to OKFZ Reserved / used by Eurocopter SE Asia for overseas deliveries

Registration	Type	c/n	Previous identities
F-OKLG	Aérospatiale AS.350B3 Ecureuil	3616	
F-OKMB	Gippsland GA-8 Airvan	GA8-08-135	
F-OKMX	Aérospatiale AS.350B3 Ecureuil	7717	
F-OKTB	SOCATA TB-20 Trinidad	2210	VH-ITB, F-OIMP
F-OKVL	Aérospatiale/Alenia ATR-72-201	215	(F-OHCE), F-WWEK
F-OLAG	Reims/Cessna F150L	F15001120	F-BVBY
F-OLDL	Robinson R44 Raven II	12621	
F-OLIE	Robinson R22B2 Beta	3193	
F-OLJB	Robinson R22 Beta II (Damaged 7.2.14)	4548	
F-OLOV	Airbus A340-313E	668	(F-OJET), (F-ONUI), F-WWJD
F-OLRB	Boeing 787-8	34491	N1015X, N1008S
F-OLRC	Boeing 787-8	34510	N885BA
F-OLRD	Boeing 777-39MER	61602	
F-OLRE	Boeing 777-39MER	61736	
F-OLVR	Aérospatiale AS.355N Ecureuil 2	9609	
F-OMAB	Aérospatiale AS.350B3 Ecureuil	7150	F-WJXB
F-OMPC	Cessna 172N Skyhawk	17270129	YV-81E, (N738PK)
F-OMRU	Aérospatiale/Alenia ATR-72-212A	855	F-WWEI
F-ONAT	Schröder Fire Balloons G HAFB	743	
F-ONCA	DHC-6 Twin Otter 300	840	C-FZYG, PJ-WIM, N721RA, N840ES, C-FCVY, C-GDKL
F-ONCD	Tecnam P.2008JC	1014	
F-ONCE	Agusta-Bell 206B Jet Ranger 2	8562	G-SKII, EI-BKT, D-HAFD(3), HB-XIC
F-ONCF	Tecnam P.2008JC	1015	
F-ONCL	Aérospatiale/Alenia ATR-72-212A	759	F-WNCL, M-IBAE, VT-KAL, F-WWEV
F-ONCP	Cessna 525C CitationJet CJ4	525C-0164	
F-ONCY	Aérospatiale SA.365N Dauphin 2	6026	N365NC, PK-TSI, N87SV, N365S, N58001
F-ONDA	Cessna 172S Skyhawk SP (Originally quoted as 172S8966 in error, dam 17.2.11)	172S8988	N271DA, N51159
F-ONDU	Cessna 172R Skyhawk	17280788	N7275G
F-ONGA	Boeing 737-89M	40910	
F-ONGB	Boeing 737-89M	40911	N1786B
F-ONNE	Bell 407	53804	C-FRGS, N2462B
F-ONOA	Viking DHC-6-400 Twin Otter	855	C-GNOA
F-ONOU	Boeing 777-3Q8ER	35783	
F-ONSD	Gippsland GA8-TC-320 Airvan	GA8-TC-320-13-189	VH-ZGS
F-ONYY	Cessna 525A Citationjet CJ2	525A0320	N5188A
F-OOGL	SOCATA TBM-700N	687	N900BR
F-OONE	Airbus A330-323E	965	F-WWYL
F-OOOO	Cessna 172S Skyhawk SP	172S9608	N928SB
F-OOPS	Aérospatiale AS.365N3 Dauphin 2	6636	3A-MXO, HL9268, F-WQDR
F-OORF	Cessna 150M	15076636	N3854V
F-OORV	Cessna 172S Skyhawk SP	172S9387	N387LP
F-OOSB	Cessna 172N Skyhawk	17271833	N428JL, N5309E
F-OOUI	Eurocopter EC.130T2 Ecureuil	8118	
F-OOVK	Cessna 150M	15077310	N63434
F-OPAE	Piper PA-23-250 Aztec E	27-7554162	ZS-NBM, TU-TMU, TR-LVT, N54863
F-OPAS	Eurocopter EC.130B4 Ecureuil	7471	
F-OPBG	Robinson R44 Raven II	11497	
F-OPCD	Aérospatiale AS.350B3 Ecureuil	7385	
F-OPEN	Aérospatiale AS.350B3e Ecureuil	7676	F-WWXC
F-OPLC	Cessna 172N Skyhawk (W/o 4.1.13)	17273009	N1488F
F-OPRG	Cessna 172S Skyhawk SP	172S9888	N1029Z
F-OPRM	Robinson R44 Raven II	11906	
F-OPYB	Eurocopter EC.120B Colibri	1116	
F-ORAR	Robinson R44 Raven II	11676	
F-ORAY	Robinson R44 Raven II	11377	G-LAID

Reg	Type	C/n	Previous identities
F-ORCE	Beech 200 Super King Air	BB-80	F-GGMS, N444TW, N200AL, N78LC, (N104AG), N78LC, N73LC, N925B
F-OREU	Boeing 777-39MER	37434	
F-ORGB	Robinson R22B2 Beta	3919	
	(W/o 31.5.10)		
F-ORGC	Robin R.2160 Alpha Sport	149	5R-MLU, F-GAXK
F-ORIE	Aérospatiale AS.350B3	3544	YR-CBO, F-GXCB
F-ORLY	Airbus A330-323	758	F-WWYR
F-ORPB	Aérospatiale SA.315B Lama	2463	HB-ZHT, EC-IME, XC-BOI, N47291
F-ORPH	Gippsland GA-8 Airvan	GA8-04-050	C-GNWL, VH-PWF(2)
	(W/o 6.1.14)		
F-ORSB	Aérospatiale AS.350B3 Ecureuil	4078	F-GXBH, F-WWPC
F-ORVB	Aérospatiale/Alenia ATR-72-600	1007	F-WWLP
F-ORVC	Aérospatiale/Alenia ATR-72-600	1013	F-WWLV
F-ORVN	Aérospatiale/Alenia ATR-72-600	1255	F-WWEG
F-ORVO	Aérospatiale/Alenia ATR-72-600	1289	F-WWES
F-ORVS	Aérospatiale/Alenia ATR-72-600	1192	F-WWEI
F-ORVU	Aérospatiale/Alenia ATR-72-600	1350	F-WWEJ
F-ORVV	Aérospatiale/Alenia ATR-72-600	1376	F-WWEM
F-ORVY	Tecnam P.2008JC	1020	
F-ORVZ	Tecnam P.2008JC	1021	
F-OSAH	Piper PA-32-301T Turbo Saratoga	32-8124010	N8337R
F-OSAM	Aérospatiale SA.365N Dauphin 2	6102	N798LL, N365ME, N365DU, 9V-BNN, F-WXFC
F-OSBC	Cessna 208B Grand Caravan	208B2188	N1029J
F-OSBH	Cessna 208B Grand Caravan	208B2117	N6137Y
F-OSBM	Cessna 208B Grand Caravan	208B2391	N2025M
F-OSBS	Cessna 208B Grand Caravan	208B2378	N578AL
F-OSEA	Airbus A340-313X	438	(F-GTUC), F-WWJV
F-OSGM	Gippsland GA-8 Airvan	GA8-05-085	VH-BSZ
F-OSIA	Cessna 207 Skywagon	20700042	SE-FER, LN-BIP, SE-FER, N91055
F-OSIX	Aérospatiale/Alenia ATR-72-600	1384	F-WWEV
F-OSPJ	Reims/Cessna F406 Caravan II	F406-0091	
F-OSTO	Cessna 172N Skyhawk	17271961	N971AJ, F-OGUP, N5820E
F-OSUN	Airbus A340-313X	446	(F-GTUD), F-WWJA
F-OSYD	Boeing 777-3Q8ER	35782	N5014K
F-OTAG	Britten-Norman BN-2A-21 Islander	760	F-GFID, LN-MAG, G-BCZE
F-OTDH	Cessna U206F Stationair	U20602794	N35912
F-OTLB	Robinson R44 Raven II	13220	
F-OTZA	Robin R.2160 Alpha Sport	341	F-GTZA
F-OVAL	Kubicek BB-30Z	HAFB	1245
F-OVFB	Aérospatiale AS.355N Ecureuil 2	5720	
F-OVJR	Dassault Falcon 20C-5	180/460	(F-GVJR), I-GOBJ, OY-BDS, F-WMKF
	(Dbr 15.2.06)		
F-OVLU	Robin R.2160 Alpha Sport	115	OO-VLU
F-OVNI	Eurocopter EC.130T2 Ecureuil	8263	
F-OXDB	Robinson R44 Raven II	10117	N75150
F-OYAK	Aérospatiale AS.350B3n Ecureuil	7666	
F-OZEN	Beech B330 King Air 350	FL-525	VH-EYN, VH-PYN, N7185A
F-OZIP	Aérospatiale/Alenia ATR-72-600	1355	F-WWEP
F-OZLI	Aérospatiale/Alenia ATR-72-600	1380	F-WWER
F-OZNC	Airbus A320-232	3547	VH-VQD, F-WWIV
F-OZPR	Reims/Cessna FR172K Hawk XP	FR17200663	EC-IAE, D-EINT
F-OZSE	Aérospatiale/Alenia ATR-72-212A	813	F-WWEC
F-O . . .	Cessna 172S Skyhawk SP	172S10249	N320CP
	(To France 12.11)		

CNRA REGISTER (Homebuilt Aircraft)

Reg	Type	C/n	Previous identities
F-PAAA	Brügger MB-2 Colibri	162	
	(Res.7.06)		
F-PAAC (2)	Stern ST-87 Europlane	27	
F-PAAF (2)	Cassutt IIIM	284	
F-WAAH	FM.100 Banbi	unkn	
	(Noted 6.01)		
F-PAAM	Jabiru J400	157	
F-PAAS	Piel CP.320 Super Emeraude	426	
F-PABC	Jodel DR.250	02	
F-PABD	Péna Bilouis	03	
F-PABF	Pottier P.230S Panda	443	
F-PABJ	Pottier P.220S Koala	245	
	(W/o 18.10.08)		
F-PABL	Nicollier HN.434 Super Ménestrel	17	
F-PABN	Jodel D.113	1744	
F-PABR	Morin M-85	14	
	(Res.04)		
F-PABY	RSA/Pottier P.130L Coccinelle	1030	
F-PACA	Jodel D.18	206	
F-PACB	Pottier P.230S Panda	1	
F-PACC	Piel CP.1320M Safir	71	
F-PACD	Pottier P.230S Panda	468	
F-PACF	Aeronca 11AC Chief	1602	OO-TWT
F-PACG	SNCAN/Stampe SV-4	220	CN-MAR, Fr.AF
F-PACI	Guy Paci GP.01 Caracara	01	
F-PACJ	Dyn'Aero MCR-01 Sportster	390	
F-PACK	Jodel D.113V	1802	
F-PACL	Dyn'Aéro MCR-4S 2002	23	
F-PACM	Jodel D.18	169	
F-PACO	Druine D.5 Turbi	67	
F-PACP	Jodel D.113	1812	
F-PACR	Dyn'Aéro MCR-4S 2002	42	
F-PACS	Pottier P.230S Panda	451	
F-PACT	Pietenpol Aircamper	3095	
F-WACV	Vandamme TPL-1(Blériot XI replica)	01	
F-PADB	Nicollier HN.700 Ménestrel II	79	
F-PADC	Dyn'Aéro MCR-4S 2002	166	
F-PADD	Dyn'Aéro MCR-01 Sportster	261	
F-PADE	Jodel D.18	327	
F-PADF	Dyn'Aéro MCR-4S 2002	44	
F-PADR	RotorSmart HeliSmart	01	F-WADR
F-PADS	Dyn'Aéro MCR-4S 2002	08	
F-PADU	Dyn'Aero MCR-4S 2002	162	
F-PADV	Pottier P.130L Coccinelle	1104	
F-PADY	Jodel D.112 Club	1626	
F-PAEA (2)	Sequoia F.8L Falco	1380	
F-PAEC	Van's RV-7	73507	
F-PAED	Rutan Cozy	CC-1037	
	(Res.98)		
F-PAEL	Dyn'Aéro MCR-4S 2002	6	F-WAEL
F-PAEM	Jodel D.140E Mousquetaire IV	533	
F-PAEN	FAMA K209MF Kiss	14	

Reg	Type	C/n	Previous identities
F-WAEO	Revolution Mini-500	0230	
F-PAER	Rotorway Exec 162HDF	7059	
F-PAFE	Rutan Long-Ez	1673	
F-PAFK	Kessler FK-001	01	
F-PAFL	Auster 5	1086	F-BECZ(2), G-AJIL, NJ702
F-PAFO	Mudry CAP.10B	A-1001	
F-PAFR	Murphy Rebel Elite	746	
F-PAFS	Jodel D.113	1852	
F-PAGA	Pottier P.180S	167	
F-PAGB	Jurca MJ.77 Gnatsum	15	
F-PAGD	Auster J/1 Autocrat	2218	G-AJID
	(Painted as Auster III "MZ221")		
F-PAGE	Nicollier H.434 Super Ménestrel	61	F-WAGE
F-PAGG	Gouvin GG-01 Scorpion	01	
	(Res.00)		
F-PAGI	Piel CP.320-100 Super Emeraude	446	
F-PAGJ	Rotorway Exec 162HDF	6941	F-WAGJ
F-PAHC	Jodel DR.1053MT	943	
F-PAHM	Mazel Acrolaram	01	F-WAHM
F-PAHS	Dyn'Aéro MCR-01 Sportster	180	
F-PAIA	Nicollier HN.700 Ménestrel II	124	
F-PAII	WagAero Aero Trainer	3724	
	(Res.00)		
F-PAIR	Del-Vion DVD-01 (Mod. Jodel D.20)	04	
	(Res.03)		
F-PAJB	Dyn'Aéro MCR-01	77	F-WAJB
F-PAJC	Pottier P.250S	405	
F-PAJD	Didier AH-01	02	
	(PA-22 or WagAero conversion?)		
F-PAJL	Colomban MC-100 Banbi	42	
F-PAJM	Van's RV-8	81975	
F-PAJN	Ollivier CO-04 Collivier	01	
F-PAJO	Europa Aviation Europa XS	413	
F-PAJP	Cariou CL-3	19	
F-PAJR	Pottier P.250S Xerus	410	
F-PAKB	Aerokopter AK1-3	0033	
F-PAKF	Aerokopter AK1-3	46	
F-PAKG	Aerokopter AK1-3	31	F-WAKG
F-PAKI	Aerokopter AK1-3	63	
F-PAKM	Aerokopter AK1-3	49	
F-PAKS	Aerokopter AK1-3	17	
F-PAKT	Kieger AK-01T	03	
F-PAKV	Europa Aviation Europa XS	564	
F-PAKZ	Aerokopter AK1-3	66	
	(Ditched 5.7.15)		
F-PALA	Pottier P.80SMR	20	
F-PALB	Jodel DR.1054M Ambassadeur	848	
F-PALC	Heintz CH-300 Tri-Z	3-1356	
F-PALE	Jodel D.18	335	
	(Res.01)		
F-PALF	Dyn'Aéro MCR-4S 2002	21	
F-WALG	Microcopter MC-1	01	
	(Res.04) (Now reported as Aquinea Volta electric helicopter – same aircraft?)		
F-PALI	Europa Aviation Europa	332	
F-PALL	Lajoye LL-1100 HAFB	01	
F-PALM	Dyn'Aéro MCR-01	152	
F-PALN	Colomban MC-100 Banbi	39	
F-PALP	Jodel D.140E Mousquetaire IV	407	
F-PALR	Jodel D.140E Mousquetaire IV	492	
F-PALS	Jeannet JH-01 Le Courlis	01	F-WALS ?
F-PALT	WagAero Sportsman	1506	
F-PALU	Colomban MC-100 Banbi	04	
F-PAMA	Rotorway Exec 162HDF	6682	
F-PAMB	Grinvals G-802B Gerfaut	02	
	(Res.98)		
F-PAMC	Nicollier HN.700 Ménestrel II	103	
F-PAMD	Brügger MB-2 Colibri	261	
F-PAME	Dyn'Aéro MCR-01 Sportster	339	
F-PAMI (2)	Piel CP.320 Super Emeraude	470	
F-PAML	Pottier P.180S	202	
F-PAMT	Rand-Robinson KR-1	5469	
F-PAMV	Dyn'Aéro MCR-4S 2002	38	
F-PAND	Nicollier HN.700 Ménestrel II	68	
F-PANZ	Jodel D.113	1794	
F-PAOI	Mauboussin M.202S	001	F-WAOI, F-BAOI
F-PAOL	Dyn'Aéro MCR-01 ULC	253	
F-PAOM	Clave Le Goéland	06	F-WAOM
	(W/o 16.6.08)		
F-PAPA	Colomban MC-15 Cri-Cri	224	
F-PAPC	Zenair CH-601HD Zodiac	6-1604	F-WAPC
F-PAPE	Blavier 8C2	01	F-WAPE
F-PAPF	Faure JPF-4 gyrocopter	01	F-WAPF
F-PAPH	Kieger AK-2R	02	
F-PAPI	Caudron C.272/5 Luciole	6799	F-PMMI, F-AMMI
F-PAPS	Van's RV-6	22077	
F-PAPY	Pottier P.80SM	59	
F-PAQK	Pena Bilouis	32	
F-PARA	Ameur Balbuzard	01	F-WARA
	(Became 2nd prototype c/n 02 which was then w/o 5.97)		
F-PARB	Jodel DR.1054M	862	
F-PARC	EAA Acrosport II	1913	(F-PLCR)
F-PARD	Pottier P.180S (Res.98)	21	
F-PARG	Van's RV-9A	91157	
F-PARI	Richet Cobra 200DR	01	
F-PARJ	Kieger AK-2R	01	
F-PARK	Pottier P.180S	112	F-PYZQ
F-PARL	Nicollier HN.453RL Super Ménestrel	01	
F-PARM	Nicollier HN.700 Ménestrel	27	
F-PARS	Pottier P.230S Panda	421	
	(W/o 16.8.06)		
F-PARV	Colomban MC-100 Banbi	93	
	(Res.03)		
F-PASB	Steen Aero Skybolt	341	
F-PASD	WagAero Sport Trainer	3122	
F-PASE	Saint-Ex AT-02	01	
F-PASH	Jabiru J430	452	
F-PASM	Rutan VariEze	1794	F-WASM
F-PASO	Jodel D.150/120	142	
F-PASR	Rolland RS-3000 HAFB	01	
F-PASS	Colomban MC-15 Cri-Cri	308	
F-PAST	Croses EC-6 Criquet	06	
F-PATA	Fairchild F.24R-46A Argus III	923	F-AZBY, F-BIPB, PH-NDH, HB685, 43-14959
F-PATH	WagAero Observer	2442	
F-PATM	Autogyre Libellule	01	
F-PATO	Pottier P.230S Panda	03	

Registration	Type	c/n	Previous identities / Notes
F-PATR	Feugray TR-200-260	04	F-WATR
F-PATT	CzAW Sportcruiser	700715	F-WATT
F-PATU	Piel CP.323 Super Emeraude	463	
F-PATV	Deramecourt-Declerck 2000	01	
F-PAUR	Van's RV-4	309	
F-PAVC	Notteghem Occitan Club	04	
F-PAVL	Murphy Rebel	525R	F-WAVL
F-PAVM	Jodel D.19	22T	
F-PAVO	Colomban MC-100 Banbi	40	
F-PAVU	Jodel D.112 Club	1709	(Res.98)
F-PAXF	Aero Designs Pulsar	101F	F-WRXF
F-PAXV	Jodel D.150C/120 Mascaret	149	G-BZXH, F-PBUS
F-PAYC	Pottier P.80S	68	
F-PAYE	Jodel D.113	1780	
F-PAYM	Piel CP.1320 Safir	36	(Res.99)
F-PAYS	Pottier P.60A Minacro	14	
F-PAYT	Rotorway Exec 162HDF	6841	
F-PAZA	Zenair CH-300	3-63	(Res.06) (Previously quoted as F-PAZZ)
F-PBAA	Dyn'Aéro MCR-4S 2002	18	
F-PBAB	Colomban MC-15 Cri-Cri	126	
F-PBAC	Sequoia F.8L Falco	1455	(Res.3.07)
F-PBAG	Pottier P.60 Minacro	15	
F-PBAL	Ameur MP.100 Balbuzard	MP100/01	(Project abandoned)
F-PBAM	Nicollier HN.700 Ménestrel II	02	
F-PBAR (2)	Jodel D.19	09-T	
F-PBAS	Europa Avn Europa Classic	146	F-WBAS
F-PBAT	Stampe LBP	01	
F-PBBF	Jodel D.112 Club	01	F-BBBF, F-WBBF
F-PBBG	Europa Aviation Europa	36	F-WBBG
F-PBBK	Aero 101C	01	F-BBBK
F-PBBM	Rutan Cozy	436	
F-PBBR	Piel CP.320 Super Emeraude	443	
F-WBBY	Tesson La Persévérance	01	
F-PBCB	Nicollier HN.700 Ménestrel II	116	
F-PBCD	Jodel D.113	1838	(Res.6.07)
F-PBCF	Dyn'Aéro MCR-01 Sportster	206	
F-PBCG	Quercy QCR-01	10	(Res.05)
F-PBCH	Piel CP.320 Super Emeraude	452	
F-PBCI	Nicollier HN.700 Ménestrel II	120	(Res.00)
F-PBCJ	Pottier P.130L Coccinelle	1000	
F-PBCL	Nicollier HN.700 Ménestrel II	97	
F-PBCM	Fairchild 24 Argus (UC-61)	01-1996	(Possibly a rebuild of 43-14531 c/n 495)
F-PBCO	Ollivier DR.100 Collivier	01	
F-PBCR	Stern ST-87 Europlane	19	(Res.4.06)
F-PBCT	Piel CP.751B Beryl II	37	
F-PBCZ	Midget Mustang I	2173	(Res.05)
F-PBDB	Bauer-Declerck DB-8/1650P (HAFB?)	01	
F-PBDF	Pennec Gaz'Aile SP-2	130	
F-PBDJ	Minijet J-01	01	(Res.11.07)
F-WBDO	Bulle d'Orage Montgolfiere HAFB	01	
F-PBDR	Jodel D.18	98	
F-PBDS	Aeronca 7AC Champion	2501	F-WBDS, F-BLLI, N83821, NC83821
F-PBEC	F-8L-BX Falco	233-1	F-BNAS, LX-AIY, I- LEPG, (D-EBQE) (1999 rebuild of Aeromere Falco F-8L c/n 233)
F-PBEF	Salis / Piper SA-18A-125	01	
F-PBEJ	Jacquot Véloce	01	
F-PBEK	Jodel DR.1053M	882	(Res.02)
F-PBEN	Dawn Chaser Racer 2200	1	
F-PBER	WAR FW-190A Replica	339	
F-PBFJ	Péna Bilouis	1	
F-PBFL	Rotorway Exec 162HDF/A600	8048	
F-PBFT	Nord NC.856N Norvigie	2	F-BBBY (Res.00)
F-PBGD	Starck AS.70 Jac	07	
F-PBGF	Adam RA-14 Loisirs	09	
F-PBGS	Starck AS.70L Jac	12	
F-PBGT (2)	Pietenpol Air Camper J-3 Torpedo	2533	
F-WBGX (3)	Stolp SA.300 Starduster Too	36	G-BPCE, N8HM (Res.92, from storage at Barcelona)
F-PBHC	Mauboussin 125 Corsaire	208	F-BBHC
F-PBHL	Zenair CH-640 Zodiac	104	
F-PBIG	Jodel D.140E Mousquetaire IV	466	
F-PBIO	Autier AG-01	01	
F-PBIP	Thomson Cassutt	402	(Res.04)
F-PBIS	Junqua RJ-03 Ibis	02	
F-PBIX	Druine Fradon D.60 Condor	01	F-BBIX
F-PBJC	Fournier RF-5	A-03	
F-PBJL	Rutan VariEze	1449	
F-PBJN	Pennec Gaz'Aile SP-2	108	
F-PBJP	Jodel D.112 Club	1630	
F-PBJR	Pottier P.180S	132	
F-PBKL	Van's RV-7	70925	
F-PBLA	Quercy CQR-01	18	
F-PBLB	Geronimo LB-1	01	
F-PBLJ	Dyn'Aéro MCR-4S 2002	125	
F-PBLR	Van's RV-7A	73453	
F-PBLU	Siers Barracuda	536	(Res.9.06)
F-PBLV	Pitts S-1C Special	972	(Res.9.06)
F-PBMC	WAR F-4U Corsair	559/512	
F-PBMD	Nicollier HN.700 Ménestrel II	29	
F-PBMG	Mugnier L'Embellie Balloon	01	
F-PBMJ	Rutan Long-Ez	184	
F-PBML	Van's RV-4	4220	
F-PBMS	Heintz Zenith CH250-160	2-1605	
F-PBNC	Thorp T-18	3047	(Res.12.05)
F-PBNF	Colomban MC-15 Cri-Cri	578	
F-PBNO	Jodel DR.1053M	832	
F-PBNP	Jodel DR.1050M	701	
F-PBNS	Piel CP.80	64	
F-PBNV	Max Plan MP-207 Busard	44	
F-PBOB (2)	Pottier P.80S	66	
F-PBOI	Jodel D.92 Bébé	40	
F-PBOS	Jodel D.92 Bébé	23	
F-PBOV	Jodel D.119A	27	(ex D.112)
F-PBOX	Jodel D.92 Bébé	115	
F-PBOZ	Jodel D.92 Bébé	97	
F-PBPC	Dyn'Aéro MCR-01	46	F-WBPC
F-PBPF	Jodel D.150 Mascaret	147	
F-PBPY	Jodel D.92 Bébé	38	
F-PBRD	Club des Ballons Libre du Nord XW-340	01	
F-PBRG	Apodo	01	(Res.97, stored)
F-PBRI	Bücker Bü.133C Jungmeister	2008	F-AZLB, F-AZEU(1)
F-PBRK	Colomban MC-100 Banbi	355	(W/o 9.5.14)
F-PBRL	Pottier P.230S Panda	426	(W/o 11.7.04)
F-PBRS	Deramecourt 1700 HAFB	01	
F-PBRU	Brügger MB.8	01	(Res.99)
F-PBRV	Jodel DR.1051	913	
F-PBSC	Amphibie Esperanza 4	05	
F-PBSE	Bücker 131SA Jungmann	2224	N52DM, E3B-624 (Presumably CASA C-1.131E from c/n)
F-PBSG	Viking Dragonfly Mk.2	824	
F-PBSH	Nicollier HN.700 Ménestrel II	113	
F-PBSM	Junqua RJ-03 Ibis	21	F-WBSM
F-PBST	Dyn'Aéro MCR-4S 2002	71	
F-PBSY	Adam RA-14 Loisirs	121	F-WBSY (Dismantled, stored)
F-PBTC	Canadian Home Rotors FR-001 Safari	2110	(Res 2.06)
F-PBTO	Jodel D.18	192	
F-PBUG	Jodel DH.251	1	
F-PBUL	Balatchev Centaure	01	(Res.99)
F-PBVA	Dyn'Aéro MCR-01 Sportster	383	
F-PBXM	Jodel D.921 Bébé	198	(Transferred to 91-UT but current)
F-PBXS	Druine D.31 Turbulent	03	
F-PBXU	Jodel D.92 Bébé	126	
F-PBYG	FAMA K209MF Kiss	35	
F-PBYM	Starck AS.80 Holiday	NJ-1	
F-PBYZ	Dyn'Aéro MCR Microvolt	366	
F-PBZE	Piel CP.320 Super Emeraude	429	
F-PBZH	Brändli BX-2 Cherry	94	(Res.)
F-PBZT	Jodel D.112 Club	unkn	
F-PBZZ	SAN Jodel D.140R Abeille	500	
F-PCAA	Pottier P.180S	169	
F-PCAB	WAR P-47D Thunderbolt	60	F-WCAB
F-PCAC	Nicollier HN.434 Super Ménestrel	14	F-WCAC
F-PCAD	Jodel D.18	89	
F-PCAI	Dyn'Aéro MCR-4S 2002	131	
F-PCAK	Dyn'Aéro MCR-01 Sportster	84	F-WCAK
F-PCAL	Jodel D.18	122	F-WCAL
F-PCAN	Midgy LD.261	2	F-BCAN
F-PCAO	Jodel D.18	79	
F-PCAP	Mudry CAP.10	A5	
F-PCAT	Pottier P.180S	90	F-WCAT
F-PCAZ	Waymel XW-650	01	
F-PCBA	ACBA-10 Midour III	01	
F-PCBC	Colomban MC-15 Cri-Cri	360	
F-PCBG	Rutan Mini Defiant 1	01	F-WCBG
F-PCBJ	Bachoffer BA-01	01	
F-PCBL	CBLN XW 500 HAFB	01	
F-PCBM	Autoplan CBM-01	01	
F-PCBN	Jodel D.114	4	F-WCBN (Formerly D.113, D.112, D.119D)
F-PCBY	Rutan Long-Ez	1803	
F-PCCA	Jodel DR.100T	803	
F-PCCB	Jabiru J430	396	
F-PCCC	Jungster J1	8002R	(Res.7.06)
F-PCCE	Cub Crafters Carbon Cub CCK-1865	82	F-WCCE
F-PCCL	Nicollier HN.700 Ménestrel II	33	
F-PCCM	Croibier-Muscat CCM 01	01	
F-PCCU	Jodel D.112 Club	40	
F-PCDB	Speedy RG	01	(Destroyed 9.9.95)
F-PCDE (2)	Colomban MC-15 Cri-Cri	333	(Res.11.06)
F-PCDM	Neico Lancair 320	586	
F-PCDO	Jodel D.140R Abeille	454	
F-PCDQ	Chapeau JC.1 Levrier	01	F-WCDQ
F-PCDY	Jodel D.128	973	
F-PCEB	Hatz CB-1	639	
F-PCEK	Mauboussin 123C Corsaire	179	F-BCEK
F-PCES	Mauboussin 125 Corsaire	177	F-BCES
F-PCET	Vintras ET-01	01	
F-PCEU	Piel CP.80	68	
F-PCFD	Viking Dragonfly Mk.2	572	F-WCFD
F-PCFH	Colomban MC-15 Cri-Cri	470	(Res.00)
F-PCFK	Paumier MP.02 Baladin	09	
F-PCGB	Viking Dragonfly Mk.2	802	
F-PCGG	Rutan Long-Ez	1655	
F-PCGH	Columban MC-100J Ban-bi	60	
F-PCGJ	Jodel D.19	123T	
F-PCGK	Jodel D.119	1679	
F-PCGL	Lepeintre KAP-10	01	
F-PCGO	Jodel DH.251	07	
F-PCGS	Pottier P.180S	89	
F-PCGV	Dyn'Aéro MCR-01 Club	166	
F-PCHA	Jodel D.140R Abeille	429	
F-PCHB	Brändli BX-2 Cherry	141	
F-PCHD	Rolland RS2600 Balloon	02	
F-PCHK	Jurca MJ.2P Tempête	116	(Res.12.06)
F-PCHM	Jodel D.119T	1831	
F-PCHN	Pechon JP-01 Sanplan	01	(Destroyed 19.6.95)
F-PCHP	Rutan Cozy	182	

Registration	Type	c/n	Previous/other identities
F-PCHR	SIPA S.903R	01	
	(Res.)		
F-PCHV	Borel C-RB01 Erbé	01	
	(Modified DR.1050MT)		
F-PCIM	Starck AS.57	11	F-BCIM
F-PCIO	Mauboussin 127 Corsaire	181	F-BCIO
F-PCIP	Mauboussin 123C Corsaire	183	F-BCIP
F-PCIQ	Mauboussin 123C Corsaire	185	F-BCIQ
F-PCIR	Jodel D.92 Bébé	826	
F-PCJA	Péna Bilouis	33	
	(Res.03)		
F-PCJB	C.A.B. GY-21 Minicab	27	
F-PCJC	Viking Dragonfly Mk.1	1115	
F-PCJG	Grinvalds G-801 Orion	54	
F-PCJH	Brügger MB-2 Colibri	269	
F-PCJK	Europa Aviation Europa XS	306	
F-PCJL	Jodel D.19	156T	
F-PCJM	Nicollier HN.700 Ménestrel II	147	
F-PCJP	Pocino PJ-1A Toucan	01	
F-PCJQ	Jodel D.18	202	
	(Destroyed 25.1.97)		
F-PCJS	Stern ST-87 Europlane	53	
F-PCLA	Dyn'Aéro MCR-4S	52	
	(Damaged Rimini 2.7.06)		
F-PCLB	Dyn'Aéro MCR-01	60	
F-PCLC	Colomban MC-15 Cri-Cri	241	
F-PCLD	Quaissard Monogast	5	
F-PCLF	Colomban MC-15 Cri-Cri	533	
F-PCLG	Jodel D.113	1673	
	(Res.99)		
F-PCLN	Nicollier HN.700 Ménestrel II	219	
	(Res.05)		
F-PCLO	Flitzer Z-2IR	01	
	(Res.12.07)		
F-PCLR	Croses LC-6 Criquet	60	
	(Res.97)		
F-PCLS	Nicollier HN.700 Ménestrel II	119	
F-PCMB	Jodel D.19	170-T	
F-PCMC	Péna Le Dahu	05	
F-PCME	Notteghem Occitan 01 Club	05	
F-PCMG	Ollivier CO-02 Collivier	01	
F-PCMH	Jodel D.18	105	
F-PCML	Canu 3J	01	
F-PCMM	Piper J-3C-65 Cub (Rebuilt)	S.1	
F-PCMN	Jodel D.113	1629	
F-PCMO	Jodel D.20	12	F-WCMO
F-PCMS	Jodel DR.1050M	791	
F-PCMV	Cassutt IIIM	646	
F-PCNC	Chambon PC-80	01	
F-PCOB	Jodel D.140 Mousquetaire	485	
	(Res 3.08)		
F-PCOF	Rotorway Exec 162HDF	6844	
F-PCOM	Viking Dragonfly Mk.2F	825	
F-PCOO	Grandjean DG.01 Alcyon	21	F-WCOO
F-PCOR	SNCAN/Stampe SV.4L	330	F-BCOR, F-WCOR, F-BCOR, F-WCOR, F-BCOR
F-PCOS	Jodel D.92 Bébé	141	
F-PCOU	Pecou Sartre SPA-230	01	
F-PCOZ	Rutan Cozy	CC-1042	
F-PCPA	Jodel D.18	143	
F-PCPC	Jodel D.18	240	
F-PCPD	Jodel D.18	49	
F-PCPI	Dyn'Aéro MCR-4S 2002	88	F-WWUV
F-PCPJ	Jodel D.113	1639	
F-PCPL	Pottier P.60A Minacro	17	F-WCPL
F-PCPR	Jurca MJ.5 Sirocco	25	
F-PCPS	Pottier P.70S	29	(F-PROO)
F-PCQB	Dutoit DG-04	01	
F-PCQR (2)	Val Lot JG-01	01	
F-PCRA	Van's RV-4	714	
F-PCRG	Gaillard RG Corsair	01	
	(Res.05)		
F-PCRH	Henetier Gold HCR-2900 HAFB	01	
F-PCRI	Colomban MC-15 Cri-Cri	405	
F-PCRM	Roussoulieres CR-02 Charly	01	F-WCRM
	(Modified PA-18)		
F-PCRP	Colomban MC-15Z Cri-Cri	289	
	(Res.03)		
F-PCRQ	Quercy CQR.01 Cadi	01	
F-PCRS	Brändli BX-2 Cherry	69	
F-PCRT	Jodel DR.1053MV	772	
F-PCRY	Brändli BX-2 Cherry	113	
F-PCSA	Marie JPM-01 Médoc	22	
F-PCSB	Deramecourt 1900 HAFB	01	
F-PCSC	Pecou SP-250	001	
F-PCSE	Nicollier HN.700 Ménestrel II	216	
	(Res.04)		
F-PCSG	Colomban MC-100 Banbi	89	
	(Regd as Stafler GS01 c/n 01)		
F-PCSL	Van's RV-7	72394	
F-PCSM	Stern ST-87C Europlane	18	
F-PCST	Rotorway Exec 162HDF	6035	
F-PCSV	Pena Dahu	11	
	(Res.05)		
F-PCSY	Bücker Bü.131D Jungmann	01	F-BCSY
F-PCTF	Van's RV-4	3903	
F-PCTL	Colomban MC-100 Banbi	10	
F-PCTR	Colomban MC-15 Cri-Cri	494	
	(Res.03)		
F-PCTS	Jodel D.113T	35T	
F-PCTY	Nicollier HN.433 Ménestrel	67	
F-PCUB	Wag-A-Bond	412	
	(Res.)		
F-PCUO	Jodel DR.1053M	906	
F-WCUV	Mignet HM.290	419	
F-PCVD	Van's RV-7	73609	
F-PCVJ	Rotorway Exec 162HDF	6962	
F-PCUX	Jodel D.112 Club	181	
F-PCVB	Vickers Blériot 22	02	
F-WCVD	Van's RV-	unkn	
	(Noted 11.15)		
F-PCYG	Monnett Sonerai II LS	836	
	(Res.98)		
F-PCYM	Jodel D.18	133	F-WCYM
F-PCYR	Van's RV-7A	73776	
F-PCZF	Brochet MB-72	01	F-BCZF, F-WCZF
	(Res.97)		
F-PCZO (2)	Jodel D.113T	31T	
	(Res.10.03)		
F-PCZT	Druine D.31 Turbulent	165	
F-PDAB	Rutan Cozy	E-717	
F-PDAC	Arlais-Chasle AC-210	001	
F-PDAF	Jodel D.18	71	
	(Res.)		
F-PDAG	Dyn'Aéro MCR-4S 2002	64	
	(Re-registered T7-MAT)		
F-PDAK	Aerokopter AK1-3	012	
F-PDAM	Durable RD-03 Edelweiss	47	
	(Res.00)		
F-PDAN	Jodel DH.251	05	
F-PDAP	Dyn'Aéro MCR-4S 2002	74	
F-PDAV	Dyn'Aéro MCR-4S	58	
F-PDAX	Jodel D.113	1588	
F-PDBA	Dyn'Aéro MCR-4S 2002	106	
F-PDBB	WagAero Sportsman 2+2	568	
F-PDBC	Collivier CO-04	02	
F-PDBG	Deborde-Rolland Cobra 201AC	01	F-WDBG, F-PDBG
F-PDBL	Piel CP.321 Super Emeraude	398	
F-PDBP	SNCAN/Stampe SV.4C	479	F-BDBP
F-PDCB	Jodel DR.1051M	770	
F-PDCC	Dyn'Aéro MCR-01 Club	171	
F-PDCF	Ducreux-Foulon ARS 300	01	
F-PDCM	Jodel D.113	1687	
F-PDDA	Jodel D.140E Mousquetaire IV	472	
F-PDDL	Jodel DR.100 Ambassadeur	894	
F-PDDR	Didier AH-01	01	
	(PA-22 or WagAero conversion)		
F-PDEL	Jodel D.18	05	
F-PDEM	Viking Dragonfly	1009	
	(Res.97)		
F-PDEP	Déperdussin T	01	
F-PDGL	Canadian Home Rotors Baby Belle	0361N	
	(Type now renamed CHR Safari)		
F-PDGM	Jodel D.140C Mousquetaire III	445	
F-PDHE (2)	SIPA 200 Minijet	7	F-BDHE
F-PDHF	Jodel D.92 Bébé	W6	
F-PDHI	Jodel D.92 Bébé	603	
F-PDHK	Jodel D.92 Bébé	M.11	F-WDHK
F-PDHT	Dyn'Aéro MCR-01 Sportster	197	
F-PDHV	Verhees Delta	01	F-WDHV
	(Cancelled 2013?)		
F-PDID	Aeronca O-58B-L3 Grasshopper	8092	F-BELT, 42-36123
	(Res., c/n quoted as '30123')		
F-PDIT	Pennec-Lucas PL-5 Dieselis	07	
F-PDJC	Jodel DR.1051T	875	
	(Res.98)		
F-PDJD	Jodel D.140C Mousquetaire III	493	
F-PDKG	Aurensan KG-1	01	
	(Res.99)		
F-PDKY	Jodel D.112 Club	42	
F-PDLC	Jodel D.18	14	
	(Now flying as 13-AAF		
F-PDLF	Junqua RJ-03 Ibis	31	
	(Res.99)		
F-PDLQ	Marie JPM-01 Médoc	38	
F-PDMA	Jodel DR.1051	858	
	(W/o 14.8.02)		
F-PDMI	Lorentz Stampe DL	01	
	(Believed to be rebuild of SV.4A F-BDMI c/n 639) (Res.04)		
F-PDMM	Europa Aviation Europa	257	
F-PDNE	Le Goeland	02	F-WDNE
	(Also currently marked 57-PH)		
F-PDOE	Dyn'Aéro MCR-4S 2002	09	F-WDOE
F-PDOF	Leopoldoff L-3 Colibri	127	F-BGFS
	(Res.97; became 59-CDU)		
F-PDOL	CAP Dole	01	
F-PDOM	Jodel D.140E Mousquetaire IV	488	
	(Res.03)		
F-PDPE	Dyn'Aéro MCR-4S 2002	87	
F-PDPZ	Holleville RH.1 Bambi	01	F-WDPZ
	(Stored, Angers)		
F-PDRA	Jodel-Miettaux DM02 Bébé Special	01	
F-PDRB	Elisport CH-7 Angel	137	
F-PDRJ	Andrieux JA-3 SP	01	
F-PDRV	Van's RV-4	3809	
F-PDSD	Jodel D.18	116	
F-PDSL	Van's RV-8	81963	
F-PDTA	Dyn'Aéro MCR-4S 2002	109	
F-PDTC	Jodel DR.1050M Sicile Record	781	
F-PDTI	Pennec & Lucas Dieselis PL-2	02	
F-PDTL	Brügger MB-2 Colibri	249	
F-PDUD	Zenair CH-701 STOL	7-1543	
F-PDVD	Poullin PJ.5A (Cub conversion)	1	F-WDVD
	(F/n 11614 - thus formerly L-4H c/n 11788 ex.43-30497)		
F-PDVL (2)	Delvion DVD-01	05	F-WDVL
F-PDVN	Marie JPM-01 Médoc	44	
F-PDVO	Poulin PJ.5A	03	
	(Displayed as Piper L-4 443895/E-72 at Normandy Tank Museum)		
F-PDVP	Poullin PJ.5A	4	
F-PDVR	Lucas L-9	01	
F-PDYT	Turquetil DYT-01	01	
F-PDZN	Junqua RJ-03 Ibis Canard	23	
F-PEAC	Jodel D.153D1 Mascaret	133	F-WEAC
F-PEAK(2)	BRT Eider (Murphy Rebel derivative)	02	
F-PEAL	Dyn'Aéro MCR-01	57	
F-PEAM	Jodel D.18	252	
F-PEAZ (2)	Durable RD-03	13	
F-PEBP	Jodel D.113	1707	
F-PEBT	Dyn'Aéro MCR-01 Sportster	232	
F-PEBZ	Brochet MB-50 Pipistrelle	52	F-PHBZ
F-PECA	Péna Le Joker	02	
F-PECB	Sable-Bouchon SB-2	01	
F-PECD	Piel CP.1321 Saphir	22	
F-PECH	Colomban MC-100 Banbi	01	F-WECH
F-PECM	Colomban MC-100 Banbi	87	
F-PECN	Staaken Flitzer Z-21S 1	37	
	(Res.3.06)		
F-PECO	Deramecourt 2200 HAFB	01	
F-PECP	Air Piston AP20/3000P HAFB	01	
F-PECQ	Nicollier HN.434 Super Ménestrel	02	
F-PECS	Jodel D.18	18	

Reg	Type	c/n	Previous identities
F-WECT	Flight Design CT LS	F-09-04-06	
F-PEDB	Protech PT-2	1164	PH-EDB
F-PEDP	Murphy Rebel	416	
F-PEDR	Jodel D.129F	1735	
	(Res.01)		
F-PEEP	Jodel DH.251	17	
F-PEER	Rotorway Exec 162HDF	6704	
F-PEGA	Lallemang Pégase 01	01	
	(Res.02)		
F-PEGG	Deramecourt 2600	03	
F-PEGH	Jodel D.113	1650	
F-PEGL	Jodel D.140E Mousquetaire IV	453	
F-PEGR	Jodel D.18	428	
	(Noted 12.7.08 as 34-UQ)		
F-PEGT	Dynali H2S	32	
F-PEHV	C.A.B. GY-201 Minicab	A-216	
F-PEJC	Rutan Cozy Mk.4	83	F-WEJC
F-PEJG	Rotorway Exec 162HDF 1	6875	
F-PEJH	Dyn'Aéro CR.100C	28	
F-PEJM	Enfissi EJM-002	01	
F-PEJP	Dyn'Aéro MCR-01 Sportster	270	
	(Res.12.07)		
F-PEJR	Rand-Robinson KR-2	7854	
F-PEJV	Jodel D.119	1828	
F-PELA	CzAW Sportcruiser	700-921	
F-PELB	Dyn'Aéro MCR-01 VLA	94	F-WELB
F-PELD	Jurca MJ.2H Tempête	48	
F-PELE	Jabiru J400	278	
F-PEMA	Stolp SA.750 Acroduster Too	634	
	(Res.6.03)		
F-PEMC	Pena Joker	17	
F-PEMH	Colomban MC-100 Banbi 1	59	F-WEMH
F-PEMJ	Jurca MJ.5L2 Sirocco	45	
F-PEMR	Deramecourt ADM 900	02	
F-PEMY	Jodel D.18	162	
F-PENA	Péna Bilouis	01	
F-PENO	Jodel D.19	13T	F-WENO
F-PEOO	SFAN-4	01	F-PFOO, F-WFOO
	(Res.99)		
F-PEPB	Rotorway Exec 162HDF-A600	7000	
F-PEPE	Jodel D.116T	01	F-WEPE
	(Formerly reserved as Anquetil JA-1 Kiout / D.11T c/n 30)		
F-PEPG	Safari FR-001	2171	
F-PEPM (2)	Nicollier HN.700 Ménestrel II	26	
F-PEPS	Pottier P.220D Koala	415	
F-PEPU	Dyn'Aéro MCR-4S 2002	100	
	(W/o 6.8.09)		
F-PERB	Rhone et Sud-Est J-3 Cub	01	
F-PERD	Jodel D.113T Club	202	
	(Conv from D.119T, formerly D.119 and originally D.112)		
F-PERG	C.A.B. GY-20 Minicab	A-162	
F-PERL	Jodel D.92 Bébé	213	
	(Still regd but flies as 05-FM)		
F-PERT	Jodel D.116 Club	54	
	(ex D.112)		
F-PERU	Jodel D.112 Club	47	F-WERU
F-PERZ	Jodel D.112 Club	231	
F-PESG	Jodel D.20	19	
F-PESK	Pottier P.180SP	33	
F-PESL	Nicollier HN.434 Super Ménestrel	21	
F-PESM	Jodel D.121	64	
	(ex D.11, D.115)		
F-PESR	Rolland RS-1600 HAFB	01	
F-PESV	Van's RV-4	3594	
	(Res.99)		
F-PESY	Jodel D.92 Bébé	175	F-WESY
F-PETE	Dyn'Aéro MCR-01	28	F-WETE
F-PETI	Colomban MC-100 Banbi	03	
F-PEUP	SAN B-1	101	F-PFUP, F-WFUP
	(Formerly SANB-101, modified Cub) (Res.02)		
F-PEVF	Jodel D.112 Club	275	
F-PEVH	Jodel D.92 Bébé	332	
F-PEVJ	Jodel D.112 Club	A.28	
F-PEVL	Jodel D.112 Club	221	
	(Dbr 1.12.16)		
F-PEVN	Jodel D.126	12	
	(ex D.112)		
F-PEVT	Jodel D.92 Bébé	A.8	
F-PEVX	Jodel D.112 Club	A.193	
F-PEVY (2)	Boudeau MB.16 Mickevy	01	
F-PEYA	Jodel DR.1053M	849	
F-PEYO	Jodel D.140E Mousquetaire IV	471	
F-PEZE	Rutan VariEze	2194	
F-PEZI	Lacroix LNB-12 Autoplan	01	
F-PFAB	Jodel D.19	390T	F-WFAB
F-PFAD	Nicollier HN.700 Ménestrel II	96	
F-PFAF	Super Marine Spitfire Mk.26/810	80	
F-PFAG	Notteghem Occitan Club	12	
F-PFAI	Dyn'Aéro (Company marks, may be re-used)		
F-PFAJ	Jabiru J430	757	
	(W/o 23.6.15)		
F-PFAK (2)	Péna Capena C	16	
F-PFAM	Pottier P.130L Coccinelle	1047	
F-PFAR	Bagimer II Alouette	01	F-WFAR
F-PFAX	Rand-Robinson KR-2	01	
	(Res.)		
F-PFBA	Sequoia F.8L Falco	1266	F-WFBA
F-PFBB	Adam RA-14 Loisirs	01	F-WFBB
F-PFBE	Jodel D.112 Club	1719	
F-PFBJ	Rotorway A600 Talon	8032	
F-PFBM	Rutan Cozy	E-736	
F-PFBR	Grinvalds G-801 Orion	38	
	(Wfu)		
F-PFCA	Jodel D.112 Club	1648	
F-PFCD	Pottier P.130L Coccinelle	1071	
F-PFCL	CQR-01 Quercy	05	
F-PFCM	Evra DR-01	1	
	(Rebuild of Jodel DR.250 c/n 88 F-BOCM)		
F-PFCR	Jodel D.119T	09A	
F-PFCZ	Jodel D.112 Club	32	
F-PFDA(2)	Gatard Statoplan AG 01 Alouette	01	F-WFDA
	(Now regd as Optima DFC-01)		
F-PFDB(2)	ACBA-7 Midour	04	F-WFDB
F-PFDE	Dyn'Aéro MCR Sportster	294	
	(W/o 18.7.10)		
F-PFDF	Jurca MJ.2H Tempête	57	
F-PFDP	Jurca MJ.5K1 Sirocco	112	
F-PFDT	Dyn'Aero MCR-4S 2002	136	
F-PFEN	Jodel D.112 Club	111	
F-PFET	Jodel D.112 Club	112	
F-PFEX	SFAN-2	102	F-PEEX
	(Res.01)		
F-WFFF	Dyn'Aéro MCR-01	121	
	(Res.00)		
F-PFFG	Elisport CH-7 Kompress F	108	F-WFFG, I-7853
F-PFGJ	Coupe JC-3	04	
F-PFGR	Dyn'Aéro MCR-4S 2002	33	
	(Res.04)		
F-PFGT	Europa Aviation Europa	145	F-WFGT
F-PFHC	Dyn'Aéro CR.100C	27	
F-PFHM	Nicollier HN.700 Ménestrel II	32	
F-PFHN	Nicollier HN.500 Bengali	01	
F-PFHV	Colomban MC-15 Cri-Cri	304	
F-PFIF	Rutan Cozy	597	
	(Res.)		
F-PFIH	Dynali H2S	09	
F-PFIL	CQR-01 Quercy	16	
F-PFIM	Dyn'Aéro MCR-01 Sportster	312	
F-PFIN	Jodel D.112 Club	1770	
F-PFIU	Taylorcraft BL-65	2258	N27616, NC27616
F-PFIZ	Jodel DR.1055M Enigma (n/w)	889	
F-PFJB	Freslon Omega	01	
F-PFJC	Quercy CQR-01	02	
F-PFJD	Darcissac-Grinvalds DG-87 Goeland	01	F-WFJD
F-PFJG	Grinvalds G-801 Orion	04	
	(Res.01)		
F-PFJJ	Rutan Long-Ez	1358	
F-PFJL	Colomban MC-15 Cri-Cri	175	
F-PFJP	Stolp SA.300 Starduster Too	265	
F-PFJR	Dyn'Aéro MCR-4S 2002	22	
	(W/o 12.5.05)		
F-WFKA	Allard D-40 Puck	unkn	
F-PFKC	Mignet HM.360	1	F-WFKC
F-PFKL	Dyn'Aéro MCR-01	138	
F-PFKR (2)	Replica FKD-8	01	
	(Res.01)		
F-PFKU	WAR F-4U Corsair	242	
	(Res.99)		
F-PFLB	Caudron C.601 Aiglon	7102/18	F-BFLB, F-ANXX
F-PFLC	Jodel D.113	1789	
F-PFLG	SNCAN/Stampe SV.4C 1	14	F-BFLG, CEV
	(Res.1.06)		
F-WFLL	Croses LC-6	87	
	(Res.98) (Damaged 27.1.01)		
F-PFLM	Rutan VariEze	1928	
F-PFLO	Jodel D.18	04	
	(Res.99)		
F-PFLX(2)	Trotobas Le Felix TF-01	01	
	(Res.97)		
F-PFLY	Jodel D.112 Club	1785	
F-PFMA	Jabiru J400	319	F-WFMA
F-PFMJ	Lucas L-7	01	
F-PFML	Jodel D.113	1822	
	(Res.02)		
F-PFMR	Pietenpol Aircamper	0041	
F-PFMT	Croses LC-6M Criquet	28	
F-PFMX	Jurca MJ.5F1 Sirocco	14	
	(Res.99)		
F-PFNE	Colomban MC-15 Cri-Cri	553	
	(Res.00)		
F-PFOI	Heintz Zenith 130 FLR	33	
F-PFOX (2)	Rand-Robinson KR-2	01	
F-PFPB	Fleurant-Pena Bijean	01	
	(Res.)		
F-PFPS	Viking Dragonfly Mk.3	101	
F-PFPZ	Stern ST-87 Europlane	06	
F-PFQA	Piper J-3C-65 Cub	9929	(F-BFQA), 43-1068
	(Quoted officially with f/n 9761)		
F-PFRA	SAN.01 Piper Cub	01	F-BFRA
F-PFRC	Nicollier HN.434 Super Ménestrel	82	
F-PFRE	Stark AS.80 Holiday	52	F-WFRE
	(Now c/n 01)		
F-PFRG	Dyn'Aéro MCR-4S 2002	34	
F-PFRI (2)	Canadian Home Rotors FR-001 Safari	S-2105	
	(Res.02)		
F-PFSA	Dyn'Aéro MCR-4S 2002	116	
F-PFSB	Dyn'Aéro MCR-01	41	F-WSLL
F-PFSD	Zenair CH.601XL Zodiac	6-7013	
F-PFSE	WagAero Sport Trainer	4494	
F-PFSU	EAA Acrosport II	1654	
F-PFSV	Jodel D.140E Mousquetaire IV	415	
F-PFTA	Lederer Futura AL-01	01	
	(Res.6.07)		
F-PFTN	Dyn'Aéro MCR-01 Sportster	250	
F-PFTY	Jurca MJ-12	03	
	(Res.99)		
F-PFVA	Potez 36/13	3203	F-PEVA, F-AMEI
	(Res. 6.94)		
F-PFVG	Brdischka HB-207 Alpha	207-030	
F-PFVS	Soccol VS.01 Gascon	01	
	(Damaged 23.7.00)		
F-PFVV(2)	Dyn'Aéro MCR R-180	01	F-WFVV
F-PFXG	Pottier P.220S Koala	409	
F-PFYC	Chasle YC-15 Tourbillon II	01	
F-PFYS	Nord NC.854S	146	
F-PFYU	WagAero Sport Trainer	4320	
	(Res.6.03)		
F-PFYY	Piel CP.30 Emeraude	01	F-PFVY, F-WFVY
F-PGAC	Dyn'Aéro MCR-01	03	F-WGAC
F-PGAD	SIPA S.903	40	F-PGAO, F-BGAO
F-PGAE	Elisport CH-7 Kompress F	158	
F-PGAF	Jodel D.113	1733	
	(Reserved originally as D.119A)		
F-PGAG	Colomban MC-15 Cri-Cri	571	
F-PGAH	SIPA S.903	33	F-BGAH
F-PGAJ	Stoddard-Hamilton GlaStar GS-1	5047	F-WGAJ
F-PGAK	Van's RV-6	24408	
F-PGAM	Brochet MB.80	3	F-WGAM, F-BGLC
F-PGAP	Canadian Home Rotors Safari FR-001	2108	
F-PGAR	Jodel DR.1051	910	
F-PGAS	Pottier P.180S	115	
F-PGAT	Jodel D.19	267-T	

Reg	Type	C/n	Prev/Notes
F-PGAY	Jurca MJ.77 Gnatsum	10	
F-PGBC	Stoddard-Hamilton GlaStar GS-1	5074	F-WSLC
F-PGBJ	Jodel D.112 Club	1610	
F-PGBL	Dyn'Aéro MCR-01	136	
F-PGBR	Besson GB-200 Bil'Aéro	01	F-WGBR
F-PGBS	Pottier P.60A Minacro	09	
F-WGBT	Jurca MJ.54 Silas	01	
	(Res 1.97.)		
F-PGCC	Brändli BX-2 Cherry	22	
F-PGCD	Nord NC.856A	33	ALAT
F-PGCF	Gyrostar	01	
F-PGCG	Jodel D.112 Club	1801	
F-PGCI	Guilie CAP TR	01	
F-PGCL	Nicollier HN.434 Super Ménestrel	30	(F-PSCM)
F-PGCR	Stolp SA.300 Starduster Too	254	
F-PGCS	Jodel D.18	584	
	(Res 9.08)		
F-PGCT	Adam RA-14 Loisirs	111	
F-PGDB	Dyn'Aéro MCR-01	148	F-WGDB
F-PGDF	Pottier P.230S Panda	423	
F-PGDG	Nicollier HN.700 Ménestrel II	25	
F-PGDL	DG-01 Leader	01	
F-PGDR	Guruble RD-03 Edelweiss	43	
F-PGDU	Dyn'Aéro MCR-4S 2002	05	
F-PGEC	Jodel DH.251	14	
	(Res.05)		
F-PGEL	Colomban MC-15 Cri-Cri	201	
F-PGEN	Jodel D.150CM Mascaret	155	
F-PGEV	Rutan Long-Ez	2106L	
F-WGFC	Paul Lucas Speer GreenElis	unkn	
	(Possibly ex N160XD, c/n 01)		
F-PGFO	Jodel D.92 Bébé	121	
F-PGFY	Fournet F-50 Cyrano	01	
F-PGGG	Guillaumaud GX-01	01	F-WXGX
	(Believed modified Glasair II N111XG (c/n 3071))		
F-PGGO	Coupe JC.200	4	
F-PGGP	Jodel D.18	413	
F-PGGR	Grinvalds G-801 Orion	13	
	(Res.)		
F-PGGT	Jodel DR.1053M	742	
F-PGGZ	Jodel D.92 Bébé	34	F-WGGZ
	(Current, but also regd 62-AAN)		
F-PGHG	Pottier P.230S Panda	455	
F-PGHM	Péna Joker	14	
F-PGHS	Mignet HM.293A	01	
	(Res.5.97, noted dismantled 4.14)		
F-PGIC	Aero 101	3	F-BGIC
F-PGIE	Jodel D.18	08	F-WGIE
F-PGIL	Jurca MJ.2D Tempête	82	
F-PGIM	AAIA/Stampe SV.4L	1093	F-BGIM
F-PGIR (2)	Giron PG-01	01	
F-PGJA	Tissot-Charbonnier TC-150 Océanair	11	
	(Res 11.06)		
F-PGJB	Rand-Robinson KR-2	8006	
F-PGJJ	Dyn'Aéro MCR-01 Sportster	202	
F-PGJL	Rutan Cozy Mk.4	162	F-PCOQ
F-PGJY	Rutan Cozy	337	
F-PGKA	Adam RA-14 Loisirs	15	
F-PGKH	Piper J-3 Marabout	EN2	F-BGKH , ALAT
	(f/n 8456 - L-4A c/n 8321 ex.42-15202) (CofA exp 7.00, stored)		
F-PGKL	Europa Aviation Europa XS	395	F-WGKL
F-PGKQ	Jodel D.112	108	
F-PGLA	Brochet MB-83	1	F-BGLA
F-PGLC	Jabiru J430	688	
F-PGLF	Brochet MB-83D	6	F-BGLF
F-PGLH	Brochet MB-83D	8	F-BGLH
F-PGLP	Junqua RJ-03 Ibis	39	
	(Stored, Angers museum)		
F-PGLT	CASA 1-131E Jungmann	2098	I-LISO, D-EMJN, E3B-386
F-PGLX	Jodel D.113	55	
F-PGMB	Marie JPM.01 Médoc	06	
F-PGMC	Dyn'Aéro MCR-4S 2002	113	
F-PGMF	Jodel D.18	163	
F-PGMG	Jodel D.119D	1197	
F-PGMH	Jodel D.18	75	
F-WGMI	Jurca MJ.77 Gnatsum	21	
	(W/o 12.4.04)		
F-PGML	Jurca MJ.100D Spitfire	02	F-WGML
F-PGMN	C.A.B. GY-201 Minicab	A.124	F-BGMN
	(Ex c/n 16)		
F-PGMR	Dyn'Aéro MCR-4S 2002	127	
F-PGMS	Rutan Long-Ez	358	
F-PGMT	FAMA Helicopters K209MF Kiss	28	
F-PGMZ	Dyn'Aéro MCR-4S 2002	121	
F-PGNA	Jodel D.11 T28	07A	
F-PGOA	Pottier P.180S	76	F-WGOA
F-PGOI	Aero Retro Caudron C.601	01-AR	
	(Res.05)		
F-PGOM	Pottier P.180S	200	
	(Res.99)		
F-PGPB	Jodel D.19	331T	
	(Res.04)		
F-PGPS	Pennec Gaz'Aile SP.2	01	
F-PGRA	Velocity Standard RG	179	F-WGRA
F-PGRB	Nicollier HN.434 Super Ménestrel	22	
F-PGRD	Fournier RF-47	06	
F-PGRE	Jodel D.112 Club	115	
F-PGRF	Fournier RF-47ACJ	04	
F-PGRK	Starck AS-80 Holiday	56	
F-PGRP	Jodel DB-1101	001	
F-PGRS	Stern ST-87	43	
	(Res.98)		
F-PGSG	Pottier P.230S Panda	444	
F-PGSH	Pereira Osprey GP-4	71	F-WGSH
F-PGSI	Fournier RF-47	05	
	(Res.01)		
F-PGSJ	Fisher Horizon 2	AH-0082	
F-PGSP	Marie JPM-01 Médoc	53	
F-PGSS	WagAero Sport Trainer	3361	
F-PGSY	Dyn'Aéro MCR-01	97	
F-PGTA	Pottier P.220S Koala	418	F-WGTA
F-PGTC	Piel CP.1320 Safir	05	
F-PGTE	Jodel D.112 Club	137	
F-PGTL	Guillotel DG-1	01	
	(Originally regd as Guillotel-Honsiger GH-1)		
F-PGTM	Junqua RJ-03 Ibis	01	
F-PGTU	Ambrosini F.4 Rondone 1	019	F-BGTU
F-PGTY	Jurca MJ.2 Tempête	54	
F-PGUE	Jodel DR.1054F Ambassadeur	878	
F-PGUI	Evans VP-1 Volksplane	V-1382-GD	
F-PGUY	Nicollier HN.434 Super Ménestrel	03	
F-PGVH	FAMA Helicopters K209 Kiss	unkn	
	(Dbr 13.11.14, Aubenas)		
F-PGVR	Piel CP.30A Emeraude	2	F-WGVR
F-PGYA	Mignet HM.293	JH-3/37	F-WGYA
F-PGYB	Jodel D.112 Club	122	
F-PGYN	Jodel D.92 Bébé	124	
F-PGYR	Druine D.5 Turbi	02	F-WGYR
F-PHAC	Dyn'Aéro MCR-4S 2002	35	
F-WHAD	HeliAirDesign HAD1-T	unkn	
F-PHAG	Dyn'Aéro MCR-4S 2002	142	
F-PHAL	Nord NC.856N Norvigie	03	F-BNAR(2), ALAT
	(Res.11.06)		
F-PHAM	Stolp SA.300 Starduster Too	785	N6099
F-PHAT	Van's RV-6	25304	
F-PHBE	Sequoia F.8L Falco	unkn	
	(Res.6.06)		
F-PHBJ	Dynali H2S	13	
F-PHBL	Innovator Mosquito	1005	
	(Res.04)		
F-PHBT	Feugray TR-200	06	
F-PHCB	Jodel D.19	268	
F-PHCC	Hennetier Gold 2190	01	
F-PHCD	Deschamps / Charles Dolfus HG-760 Balloon	01	
F-PHCH	Nicollier HN.700 Ménestrel II	61	
F-PHCJ	Dyn'Aero MCR-01 Minicruiser	382	
F-PHCL	Aviotecnica ES.101	02	
F-PHCM	Dyn'Aéro MCR-01 Sportster	336	
F-PHCO	FAMA Helicopters K209M Kiss	13	
F-PHDB	Breau BA-3	01	
	(Res.10.07)		
F-PHDF	Rotorway Exec 162HDF	6281	F-WHDF
F-PHDH	Hammentien DH-500	01	
F-PHDJ	Pottier P.220S Koala	410	
F-PHDP	Jurca MJ.77 Gnatsum	11	
F-PHDS	Quercy CQR-01	17	
F-PHEB	Jodel D.140E Mousquetaire IV	489	
F-PHEM	Colomban MC-15Z Cri-Cri	205	
	(W/o 14.4.07)		
F-PHEU	Rolland RS-3000 HAFB	03	
F-PHFB	Jodel D.112 Club	268	
F-PHFG	Couyaud GC-01	01	
F-PHFK	Caudron C.232	6486/7	F-AJSS
	(Reservn., probably ntu)		
F-PHFL	Jodel D.112 Club	184	
F-PHGG	Rotorway Exec 162HDF	6121	
F-PHGL	Dyn'Aéro MCR-01 Sportster	340	
	(Res.3.07)		
F-PHGP	Rotorway Exec 162HDF	3034	
F-PHGT	Leopoldoff L.55 Colibri	2	F-BHGT
F-PHHH	Dyn'Aéro MCR-4S 2002	19	
F-PHIF	Dyn'Aéro MCR-4S 2002	20	
F-PHIL	Piel CP.615A Super Diamant	55	
F-PHIM	Stoddard-Hamilton GlaStar GS-1	5525	
F-PHJB	Jodel D.112 Club	374	
F-PHJJ	Jodel D.113 Club	A.204	
	(ex D.112)		
F-PHJK	Jodel D.112 Club	212	
F-PHJL	Jodel D.112 Club	159	
F-PHJN	Jodel D.112 Club	104	F-WHJN
	(ex D.118, D.121)		
F-PHJO	Jodel D.112 Club	281	
F-PHJP	Jodel D.112 Club	211	
F-PHJX	Jodel D.112 Club	A.386	
F-PHJY	Jodel D.112 Club	328	
F-PHKV	Windex 1200C	007	F-WHKV
F-PHLA	Jodel D.112 Club	304	
	(Noted stored 7.11)		
F-PHLB	Jodel D.112 Club	A.14	F-WHLB
F-PHLC	Jodel D.119C	329	
	(ex D.112, D.113C)		
F-PHLF	Jodel D.112 Club	284	
F-PHLL	Druine Martin (D.61 Condor variant)	02	F-WHLL, F-WBIY
F-PHLM	Piel CP.30 Emeraude	4	
F-PHLN	Piel CP.301 Emeraude	5	
F-PHLO	Piel CP.30 Emeraude	10	
F-PHLP	Jodel D.112 Club	383	
F-PHLQ	Jodel D.112 Club	282	
F-PHLR	Jodel D.112 Club	290	F-WHLR, F-PHLR
F-PHLS	Jodel D.112 Club	136	F-WHLS
F-PHMC	Croses LC-6W Criquet	122	
F-PHME	Nicollier HN.700 Ménestrel II	181	
F-PHMH	Rutan Cozy	E-706	
F-PHMM	Elisport CH-7 Kompress F	121	
F-PHMN	Colomban MC-15 Cri-Cri	120	
	(W/o 14.1.06)		
F-PHMP	Pottier P.270S	432	
F-PHMR	Dyn'Aéro MCR-01 Sportster	228	
F-PHOK	Jodel D.113	1751	
	(W/o 30.10.11)		
F-PHOL	Dyn'Aéro MCR-4S 2002	50	
F-PHOQ	Rippert A.1-65 Cub	1	F-BEKV , 44-79858
	(Converted from Piper L-4 c/n 12154)		
F-PHOR	Jodel D.150T Mascaret	156	
	(Res.3.07)		
F-PHOT (2)	Dyn'Aéro MCR-01 Club 912F	103	F-WHOT , F-WWUQ
	(Originally allocated to MCR-01 c/n 172)		
F-PHPC	Piel CP.615 Super Diamant	50	
F-PHPG	Helicoptère Autour 01	01	
F-PHQA	Jodel D.92 Bébé	263	
F-PHQC	Jodel D.112 Club	317	
F-PHQD	C.A.B. GY-201 Minicab	A-207	
F-PHQE	Jodel D.119	144	
	(ex D.121)		
F-PHQG	Leopoldoff L.4 Colibri	24	F-APZN
	(Originally L.3 rebuilt as L-4, .88)		
F-PHQH	Larrieu JL.2	01	F-WHQH, F-BGMA
	(Converted from D.112 c/n 77)		
F-PHQI	Piel CP.301 Emeraude	38	
F-PHQK	Jodel D.119A	472	(F-BHAE)
F-PHQN	Delassalle-Planchais LD45-4	04	
F-PHQO	Chatelain AC.5 Bijou	01	

Registration	Type	c/n	Previous identities
F-PHQP	Jodel D.92 Bébé	390	
F-PHQS	Jodel D.112 Club	468	
F-PHQY	Morane-Saulnier MS.602	01	F-WCZU
F-PHQZ	Druine D.5 Turbi	48	
F-PHRA	Pennec Gaz'Aile SP2	27	
	(Registered 5.14 as Pegaz W100 c/n 3)		
F-PHRC	Europa Aviation Europa	108	F-PSLO, F-WSLO
F-PHRJ	Colomban MC-100 Banbi	61	F-WHRJ
	(W/o 25.9.09 still as F-WHRJ)		
F-PHRP(2)	Rotorway Exec 162HDF	6903	
F-PHRS	Piel CP.320 Super Emeraude	420	
F-PHRV	Van's RV-9A	91821	F-WHRV
F-PHSD	Rotorway Exec 162HDF	6964	
F-PHSF	Helisport CH-7 Kompress	82	
	(Res.3.06)		
F-PHSJ	OGMA/Auster D.5/160	136	CR-GAX
	(W/o 3.10.14 Moret-Episy)		
F-PHSV	Dyn'Aero MCR-4S 2002	120	
F-PHTM	Jabiru J400	298	
F-PHUD	Jodel D.112 Club	398	
F-PHUF	Camandre 1 (Cub convn)	01	
F-PHUI	Jodel D.119	460	
F-PHUL	Jodel D.112 Club	360	
	(W/o 27.7.07)		
F-PHUM	Jodel D.112 Club	404	
F-PHUP	Jodel D.112 Club	375	
F-PHUQ	Jodel D.119	291	
	(ex D.112)		
F-PHUS	Jodel D.112 Club	220	
F-PHUV	Jodel D.119	A.392	
F-PHVI	Boisavia B.601 Mercurey	23	F-BHVI
	(Res.02)		
F-PHYN	Brügger MB-2 Colibri	21	
F-PHZC	Adam RA-15/1 Major	1	
	(Possibly rebuild of F-PEPD, F-WEPD ?)		
F-PHZD	Piel CP.30 Emeraude	75	
F-PHZG	Jodel D.112 Club	213	
F-PHZM	Jodel D.113	318	
	(ex D.119)		
F-PHZN	Potez 36/14	3207	F-AMEM
	(Displayed in Albert Nord rail station)		
F-PHZO	Piel CP.301 Emeraude	11	
F-PHZP	Piel CP.301A Emeraude	55	
	(Stored 9.06)		
F-PHZX	Jodel D.113	A.97	
	(ex D.119)		
F-PHZY	Marabout M (Cub convn)	01	
	(Cr 2.74, rebt with new fuselage .89)		
F-PIAB	Rutan Cozy	45	
F-PIAC	Sequoia F.81LFalco	1394	
	(Res.02)		
F-PIAF	Viking Dragonfly Mk.2	1024	
F-PIAN	Boisavia B.601L Mercurey	25	(F-GLNA), F-BIAN
F-PIAT	Akrosport Jeep 2	1533	
F-PICC	Marie JPM-03 Médoc	74	
	(Res 12.08)		
F-PICG	Rand-Robinson KR-2	7499	
F-PICK	Dyn'Aéro MCR-01	147	F-WICK
F-PICL	Canadian Home Rotors Baby Belle	0366N	
	(Type now known as CHR Safari)		
F-PICM	ICAM 77 HAFB	1	
F-PICO	Jodel D.18	60	
	(W/o 28.4.07)		
F-PICR	Aero Designs Pulsar XP	unkn	
	(Res.04)		
F-PIDM	Dyn'Aero MCR Sportster	164	
F-PIDR	Van's RV-8	81866	F-WIDR
F-PIDZ	Jodel D.119V	1772	
F-PIED	Pottier P.180S	111	
F-PIEL	Piel CP.320 Super Emeraude	416	
	(Res.)		
F-PIEP	Dyn'Aéro MCR-4S 2002	43	
F-PIFE	Pottier P.180S	27	F-WIFE
F-PIFS	Soubrane Acro 200	01	
F-PIGC	Arietty II	01	
F-PIGE	Stoddard-Hamilton GlaStar GS-1	5336	F-WIGE
F-PIGT	Taillefer DT-01	01	
	(Modified Jodel DR.250, 180hp)		
F-PIHH	Jodel D.112 Club	279	
	(ex D.123)		
F-PIHI	Piel CP.301 Emeraude	34	
F-PIHL	Croses EC-1	02	F-WIHL
F-PIHV	Jodel D.112 Club	619	
	(ex D.119)		
F-PIHX	Jodel D.113	621	
	(ex D.119)		
F-PIHY	Jodel D.119	653	
F-PIID	Jodel D.112 Club	660	
F-PIIE	Jodel D.92 Bébé	292	
F-PIIM	Jodel D.112 Club	749	
F-PIIO	Jodel D.112 Club	319	
	(ex D.119)		
F-PIIS	Druine D.5 Turbi	26	
F-PIIT	C.A.B. GY-201 Minicab	217	
F-PIIX	Piel CP.30 Emeraude	19	
F-PIJH	Jurca MJ.5G2 Sirocco	60	
F-PIKA	Nicollier HN.700 Ménestrel II	84	
	(Res. 3.05)		
F-PILA	Guimbal G2 Cabri	01	
F-PILD	Neico Lancair 320	640	F-WILD
F-WILD(2)	Lionceau APM40	01	
F-PILI	Dyn'Aéro MCR R-180	04	
	(Based in Italy)		
	(Damaged 21.4.12)		
F-PILO	Jodel D.112 Club	1769	F-WILO
F-PILP	Jodel D.119	1746	
F-PILS	Dyn'Aéro MCR-01 Sportster	309	
F-PIMA	Jodel D.113	1760	
F-PIML	Rutan Cozy	1-737	
	(Res.00)		
F-PIMS	Dyn'Aero MCR-4S 2002	137	
F-PINA	Jodel D.112 Club	unkn	
F-PINB	Jodel D.112 Club	769	
F-PIND	Jodel D.92 Bébé	371	
F-PINE	Jodel D.112 Club	782	
	(ex D.124)		
F-PINI	Jodel D.119	57	
	(ex D.112)		
F-PINJ	Piel CP.310 Emeraude	49	
	(ex CP.301)		
F-PINK	Piel CP.301 Emeraude	08	
F-PINM	C.A.B. GY-201-90 Minicab	A144	
F-PINP	Jodel D.119	387	
	(ex D.112) (W/o 10.2.01)		
F-PINR	Piel CP.310 Emeraude	27	
	(ex CP.308, CP.30)		
F-PINY	Jodel D.119	449	
	(ex D.112)		
F-WIOI	Wadsworth PW-01	01	
	(Res.97)		
F-PIOL	Jurca MJ.2P Tempête	47	
F-PION	Colomban MC-15 Cri-Cri	362	
	(Res.01)		
F-PIOU	Rolland RS-3000 HAFB	04	
F-PIPA	Jodel D.112 Club	1814	
F-PIPC	Heli-Sport CH-7 Kompress F	10	
F-PIPE	Jodel D.113	1725	
F-PIPO	Jodel D.19	359T	
F-PIPR	Altair 2PL	01	
	(Res.97)		
F-PIRA	Pereira Osprey 2	752	F-WIRA
F-PIRC	Jodel D.1103	1774	
F-PIRD	Dynali H2S	18	
F-PIRE	Dyn'Aéro MCR-01 Sportster	238	
F-PIRI	Jodel D.150/120	146	
F-PISM	Albouy Helix	01	
F-PITR	Techaero Feugray TR-200	09	
	(Res.98)		
F-PITS	Cousin DFC-01 Optima	01	F-WITS
F-PITY	Brditschka HB-207 Alpha	57	
F-PITZ	Pottier P.130L Coccinelle	1063	
	(Res.10.04)		
F-PIUS	Dyn'Aéro CR.100	22	F-WWUV, Fr.AF:F-TGCJ
F-PIUT	Dyn'Aéro MCR-01 Club	158	
F-PIVA	Colomban MC-15 Cri-Cri	428	
F-PIVR	Deramecourt D16/1900 HAFB	02	
F-PIVS	Van's RV-4	4429	
F-PIVX	Nicollier HN.700 Ménestrel II	unkn	
F-PIXL	Dyn'Aéro MCR-4S 2002	15	F-WIXL
F-PIXX	Jodel D.140C Mousquetaire III	433	
	(Cr 21.7.05)		
F-PIXY	EAA Acro Sport II	1846	
	(Res.2.06)		
F-PIYA	Druine D.5 Turbi	46	
F-PIYB	C.A.B. GY-201 Minicab	A.159	
F-PIYC	Jodel D.113	713	
	(ex D.112)		
F-PIYF	Jodel D.92 Bébé	151	
F-PIYJ	Jodel D.119	864	
F-PIYM	Jodel D.112 Club	748	
	(W/o 25.12.15)		
F-PIYN	Piel CP.301 Emeraude	178	
F-PIYO	Jodel D.119	739	
F-PIYP	Jodel D.92 Bébé	398	
F-PIYS	Jodel D.112 Club	513	
	(Accident 14.3.03)		
F-PIYT	Jodel D.119	102	
F-PIYV	Brochet MB.76	23	
F-PIYY	Piel CP.315 Emeraude	16	
F-PIYZ	Jodel D.113	620	
	(ex D.119)		
F-PIZZ	Jodel DH.251	26	F-WIZZ
F-PJAB	Jabiru J400	102	
F-PJAC	Jodel D.92 Bébé	657	
F-PJAG	Jodel DR.1050MT	792	
F-PJAI	Jabiru J400	172	
F-PJAK	Rutan Cozy	190	F-WJAK
F-PJAL	Piel CP.751B Beryl II	41	
F-PJAM	Nicollier HN.700 Ménestrel II	65	
F-PJAN	Jabiru J400	315	
F-PJAR	Du Dognon 01	01	
F-PJAS	Dyn'Aéro MCR-01 Sportster	24	
F-PJAV	Murphy Rebel	532R	F-WJAV
F-PJAY	Jodel D.113.3L	1753	
F-PJBC	Jodel DR.1051 Ambassadeur	788	
F-PJBD	Morin M-82	02	
F-PJBG	Jurca MJ.5 Sirocco	19	
F-PJBH	Belin Zephyr	01	F-WJBH
F-PJBJ	Pottier P.230S Panda	428	
F-PJBL	Jodel D.18	11	
	(Res.98)		
F-PJBM	Dyn'Aéro MCR-01 Club	167	
F-PJBR	Jodel DR.1051M	827	
F-PJBS	WagAero Sport Trainer	3303	
F-PJBV	Jodel D.18	349	
F-PJBY	Blenet RB-1 Joze	01	F-WJBY
	(Stored, Gray)		
F-PJCA	Jodel D.112 Club	943	
F-PJCB(2)	Piel CP.750A Beryl II	06	
	(Res.98)		
F-PJCD	Jurca MJ.2 Tempête	66	
F-PJCH	Steen Skybolt	320	
F-PJCG	Jodel DR.105S	04	
	(Ex DR.100, DR.100A)		
F-PJCK	Aero Club Lons/Leglise L-400	01	
F-PJCL	Dyn'Aéro MCR-01	65	
F-PJCM	Piel CP.215 Pinocchio	01	
	(built as CP.211, CP.212)		
F-PJCN	Adam RA-14 Loisirs	110	
F-PJCX	Jodel D.119	671	
	(ex D.112)		
F-PJDD	Elisport CH-7 Kompress F	207	
F-PJDH	Mauboussin 123C Corsaire	159	F-ARDR
F-PJDL	Grinvalds G-801 Orion	16	F-WJDL
F-PJDP	Jodel D.113	1803	
F-PJDR	Dyn'Aéro MCR-01	07	F-WJDR
F-PJDS	Sauques DS250	01	
	(Res.11.07)		
F-PJDV	Van's RV-4	44062	
	(Res.97)		
F-PJDY (2)	Mignet HM.390 Auto-Ciel	1 bis	
	(Res.10.96)		

Reg	Type	c/n	Previous
F-PJDZ	Nord NC.858S	64	F-BFSK
F-PJEA	Dyn'Aéro MCR-01 VLA	80	
F-PJEB	Rutan VariEze	1962	
F-PJEJ	Jodel D.18	138	
F-PJET	Minijet CJ-01	01	
F-PJFB	Jodel DR.1051	892	
	(Res.04)		
F-PJFC	Van's RV-8	81128	
F-PJFK	Notteghem Occitan	02	
F-PJFM	Dyn'Aéro MCR-01 M	254	
F-PJFR	Rotorway Exec 162HDF	6334	
F-PJFT	Van's RV-6	22419	
F-PJGC	Jodel D.119	529	F-WJGC
F-PJGE	Piel CP.301A Emeraude	3	
F-PJGI	Adam RA-14 Loisirs	45	
F-PJGJ	Jodel D.119	952	
	(ex D.112)		
F-PJGM	Jodel D.112 Club	682	
F-PJGO	Jodel D.119	975	
F-PJGP	Gatard Statoplan AG 02 Poussin	02	
F-PJGQ	Damoure-Fabre-Lacroix DFL-6 Saphir	01	F-WJGQ
F-PJGR	Jodel D.112 Club	147	
F-PJGS	Jodel D.119	994	
F-PJGZ	Jodel D.112 Club	403	
F-PJHB	Caudron C.431 Rafale replica	01	
	(Res.00; Angers museum)		
F-PJHG	Pottier P.80S	69	
F-PJHJ	Pottier P.180S	156	
F-PJIC	Jodel DR.1056M Ambassadeur	886	
F-PJIL	Jodel D.113	1846	
F-PJIM	Stolp SA.300 Starduster Too	2105	
F-PJJB	Robin CR.100	06	
F-PJJC	Rutan Cozy	CC-1056	
F-WJJD	Jodel D.119	1848	
F-PJJG	Jurca MJ.5H1 Sirocco	52	
F-PJJL	Nicollier HN.700 Ménestrel	59	
F-PJJN	Jodel D.140E Mousequetaire IV	408	
F-PJJP	Rutan Cozy	819	
F-PJJR	Jurca MJ.55	01	
F-PJKB	Jodel D.119	790	
	(ex D.111)		
F-PJKD	Druine D.31 Turbulent	93	
F-PJKG	CEA Jodel DR.101 Ambassadeur	31	
F-PJKL	Piel CP.301 Emeraude	192	
F-PJKM	Jodel D.113L	617	
	(ex D.119L, D.112)		
F-PJKN	Jodel D.112 Club	963	
F-PJKP	Jodel D.121	191	
	(ex D.112)		
F-PJKR	Piel CP.315 Emeraude	343	
	(ex CP.301, CP.305; cancelled?)		
F-PJKV	Paumier MP-21 Baladin	01	
F-PJKY	Jodel D.112 Club	1037	
	(Cancelled?)		
F-PJLB	Rutan Long-Ez	1344	
F-PJLC	JLC-01 Abeille	01	
	(Res.97)		
F-PJLD	Jurca MJ.2H Tempête	105	
	(Stored, Angers)		
F-PJLE	Jodel D.140E Mousequetaire IV	465	
F-PJLG	Nicollier HN.700 Ménestrel II	76	
F-PJLH	Taylor Coot Amphibian	106	
F-PJLL	Van's RV-6	22822	
F-PJLM	Piel CP.1320 Saphir	1	F-WJLM
F-PJLN	Chouchen NL01	01	
F-PJLO	Nicollier HN.434 Super Ménestrel	53	
	(Wreck noted 7.10)		
F-PJLS	Jodel D.19	399T	
	(Transferred to ULM register 2.13)		
F-PJLT	Pottier P.270S	436	
	(Res.99)		
F-PJLV	Pottier P.270S	441	
F-PJMA	Dyn'Aéro MCR-01 VLA	54	F-WSLK
F-PJMB	Jodel D.140C Mousquetaire III	441	
F-PJMC	Jodel D.119	390	F-PIHO
F-PJMD	Jodel DR.1053M	726	
F-PJMF	Van's RV-8	81724	
F-PJMG	Jodel D.140E Mousequetaire IV	491	
F-PJMK	Van's RV-8	81197	
F-PJML	Colomban MC-15 Cri-Cri	297	
F-PJMN	Rotorway Exec 162HDF	6892	
F-PJMP	Nicollier HN.434 Super Ménestrel	48	
F-PJMR	EAA Acrosport II	1079	
F-PJMS	Sauval SE-5A	01	
	(Res.99)		
F-PJMV	Jodel DR.100D	907	
	(Res.7.06)		
F-PJNL	Lesavre DSL-160	01	
F-PJOB	Lucas L.5-200	2	F-WJOB
F-PJOC	Gravereau Box'Air Racer	01	F-WJOC ?
F-PJOD	Jodel DR.1054 Ambassadeur	857	
F-PJOE	Jurca MJ.2E Tempête	96	F-WJOE
F-PJOH	Rutan Cozy	CC-1021	F-PBCA
	(Res.99)		
F-PJOJ	C.A.B. GY-201 Minicab	A.204	
	(ex c/n 722)		
F-PJOK	Péna Le Joker	01	F-WJOK
F-PJON	Dyn'Aéro MCR-4S 2002	57	
F-PJOQ	Péna Super Joker	01	
F-PJOR	Nicollier HN.434 Super Ménestrel	74	
F-PJOS	Piel CP.301A Emeraude	445	
F-PJPB	Nicollier HN.434 Super Ménestrel	73	
F-PJPD	Marie JPM-01 Médoc	21	F-WJPD
F-PJPF	WAR FW-190 Replica	184	
F-PJPG	Croses EC-6 Criquet	47	
F-PJPH	Van's RV-7	73145	
F-PJPI	Pennec Gaz'Aile SP-2	251	
F-PJPL	Pottier P.70S	30	
F-PJPS	EAA Acrosport II	602	
F-PJQA	Junqua RJ.02 Volucelle	01	F-WJQA
F-PJRA	Jodel DR.1050M	760	
F-PJRC	Chalard JRC-01	01	
F-PJRD	Jodel D.20	04	
F-PJRG	Tissot-Charbonnier TC-160 Oceanair	05	
F-PJRH	Marcel 01	01	
F-PJRM	Colomban MC-15 Cri-Cri	294	
F-PJRV	Van's RV-7	72424	
F-WJRX	Aeroprakt A-22 Vision	unkn	
F-PJSA	Legrand-Simon LS.60	01	F-BJSA, F-WJSA
F-PJSB	Schepers / Magni M-16 Tandem Trainer	01	
F-PJSE	Juste JSE-18	01	
F-PJSF	Jodel D.18	371	
F-PJSL	Canadian Home Rotors Safari FR001	2127	
F-PJSM	Godbille GJJ	01	F-WJSM
F-PJST	Rand-Robinson KR-2S	447	
	(Res.99)		
F-PJSX	Jurca MJ.5K2 Sirocco	01	F-WJSX
F-PJTA	Jodel D.18	189	
F-PJUL	Jodel D.18	418	
F-PJVD	Van's RV-7A	70290	
F-PJVJ	Jodel D.11 D1	1585	
F-PJVM	Nicollier HN.700 Ménestrel II	85	
F-PJXA	Jodel D.112 Club	941	
F-PJXC	Jodel D.112 Club	971	
F-PJXD	Jodel D.112 Club	1054	
F-PJXE	Jodel D.112 Club	1041	
	(Re-registered as 03-AFT/F-JAQL)		
F-PJXF	Jodel D.119	1032	
F-PJXG	Jodel D.119	984	
F-PJXH	Jodel DR.100A Ambassadeur	202	
F-PJXJ	Jodel D.112 Club	1034	
F-PJXO	Jodel D.119	1087	F-WJXO
F-PJXP	Piel CP.60 Diamant	01	F-WJXP
F-PJXR	Jodel D.112 Club	1107	
F-PJXS	Jodel D.112 Club	214	
F-PJXV	Jodel D.112 Club	1104	
F-PJXX	Jodel D.119	451	F-WJXX
F-PJXZ	Piel CP.301 Emeraude	200	
F-PJYA	Baulouet JNB-01 Natur	01	
F-PJYB	Colomban MC-15 Cri-Cri	57	
	(W/o 22.5.04)		
F-PJZC	Pottier P.230B2 Panda	499	
F-PJZG	Nicollier HN.700 Ménestrel II	89	
F-PKAD	Rutan Long-Ez	1059	
F-PKAE	Pennec-Lucas PL-5 Dieselis	22	
F-PKAF	Dyn'Aéro MCR-4S 2002	144	
F-PKAM	Fournier RF-47	07	
	(Res.04)		
F-PKAS	Deramecourt D20/3000P HAFB	01	
F-PKAT	Jodel D.119A	1699	(F-PURG)
	(Including parts of F-PHUG c/n 306)		
F-PKAZ	Péna Capena	17	
	(Res.9.06)		
F-PKBM	Flamme PF-01	01	
	(Modified Cub, painted as '236389')		
F-PKCF	Piel CP.1320 Saphir	57	
F-PKEN	Jodel D.119	1551	
F-PKFC	Jodel D.112 Club	972	
F-PKFG	Jodel D.112 Club	950	
F-PKFI	Druine D.31 Turbulent	115	
F-PKFJ	Piel CP.301 Emeraude	32	
F-PKFL	Jodel D.112 Club	391	
F-PKFN	Mignet HM.380B	12	F-WKFN
F-PKFO	Jodel D.92 Bébé	446	
F-PKFT	Jodel D.112 Club	985	
F-PKFU	Lucas L.4 Baby	01	F-WKFU
F-PKFY	Jodel D.112 Club	1050	
F-PKFZ	C.A.B. GY-201-90 Minicab	A.233	
F-PKGQ	Jodel DRM	01	F-BKGQ
	(Converted DR.1050 c/n 239)		
F-PKIS	FAMA Kiss 209M	26	
F-PKIT	Dyn'Aéro MCR-01	01	
F-PKJP	Helisport CH-7 Kompress	175	
	(Res.11.07)		
F-PKJR	Wheeler Express	70	F-WKJR
F-PKLE	Pottier P.220S Koala	461	F-WKLE
F-PKMB	Jodel D.112 Club	1085	
F-PKMD	Jodel D.119	1044	
F-PKMF	Jodel D.112 Club	986	
F-PKMG	Piel CP.301A Emeraude	353	
F-PKMH	Jodel D.119	777	
	(ex D.112, D-111)		
F-PKMJ	Jodel D.113	1135	
	(ex D.119, D.112)		
F-PKMK	Jodel D.119	1154	
F-PKMN	Jodel D.119	678	
F-PKMP	Jodel D.113	793	
	(ex D.112)		
F-PKMR	Jodel D.119	741	
F-PKMV	Damoure-Fabre DF-5C	01	
F-PKMX	Piel CP.316 Emeraude	352	F-WKMX
F-PKOK	Van's RV-8	82797	
F-PKOR	Fournier RF-47	08	
	(Res.04)		
F-PKPL	Jodel DR.1050 Ambassadeur	778	
F-PKRJ	Light Aero Avid Flyer	798	F-PRKJ, F-WRKJ
F-PKRL	Europa Aviation Europa XS	447	
F-PKRU	Dyn'Aéro MCR-4S 2002	85	
F-PKRZ	Rand KR-2S	1735	
	(Res.05)		
F-PKSB	Van's RV-7	73248	
	(Res 1.08)		
F-PKSE	Jodel D.112 Club	1765	
F-PKTO	Dan Rihn DR.107 One Design	94-0244	
F-PKUE	Dyn'Aéro MCR-01	72	F-WQUR
F-PKUJ	Europa Aviation Europa	297	F-WQUJ
F-PKVB	Piel CP.301 Emeraude	93	
F-PKVD	Jodel D.112 Club	1182	
F-PKVI	Jodel D.92 Bébé	460	
F-PKVH	Junca-Steiner JS	01	
	(Res.)		
F-PKVU	Druine D.31 Turbulent	96	
F-PKVX	Jodel D.112 Club	1195	
F-PKVZ	Piel CP.325 Super Emeraude	359	F-WKVZ
F-PKXA	Piel CP.301A Emeraude	322	
F-PKXC	Jodel D.119	1139	
F-PKXL	Jodel D.112 Club	1224	
F-PKXR	Jodel D.113	1142	
F-PKXV	Jodelan D.112 Club	1201	
F-PKXX	Piel CP.601 Diamant	5	
F-PKXY	Aero 20	1	F-WKXY
F-PLAB	Jodel D.19	253-T	

Registration	Type	c/n	Previous identities
F-WLAC	Europa Aviation Europa Classic (Res.03)	320	
F-PLAF	Colomban MC-15 Cri-Cri	108	TR-LAF
F-WLAG	Europa Aviation Europa (Res. .10)	unkn	
F-PLAH	OGMA/Auster D.5/160 (Res.03, on rebuild .14)	140	CR-GBI, CR-CAQ
F-PLAJ	Jaillet AJ-160	01	
F-PLAL	Leblanc L-06 (Dismantled, noted 10.03)	01	
F-PLAM	Lamaziere AL-01 (Res.99)	01	
F-PLAN	Dyn'Aéro MCR-4S 2002	32	
F-PLAR	Tipsy T.66 Nipper Mk.III (Res.02)	61	F-OBYV
F-PLAT	Ber-ge BG-180	01	
F-PLAU	Péna Bilouis	27	
F-PLAV	SNCAN/Stampe SV.4L	528	F-BDIG
F-PLAY	Piel CP.320 Super Emeraude	439	
F-PLBC	Pottier P.220S Koala	469	
F-PLBG	Pottier P.230S Panda	453	
F-PLBM	Jodel D.119 (W/o 14.3.16)	1763	(F-PBPM)
F-PLBT	Wittman W8 Tailwind	522	
F-PLCA	Druine-Lucas D.31 LP1 Turbulent (Originally regd as Druine-Colombier D.31 Turbulent c/n 392)	01	F-WLCA
F-PLCD	Ollivier CO-03 Collivier	01	
F-PLCL	Piel CP.90 Pinocchio II	7	
F-PLCM	Colomban MC-15 Cri-Cri	11	
F-PLCO	Van's RV-9A	90847	
F-PLDA	CAP X-2 (Res.3.04)	01	
F-PLDH	Dyn'Aéro MCR-01 Sportster	71	
F-PLDJ	Dyn'Aéro MCR-4S 2002	27	
F-PLDM	Pottier P.130 Coccinelle (Res.12.07)	1232	
F-PLDS	Rutan Cozy (Res.)	CC-1038	
F-PLDV	Pottier P.240S Saiga	01	
F-PLEA	Dyn'Aéro CR.100	26	
F-PLEC	Jodel DR.1056M	817	
F-PLEF	Brügger MB-2 Colibri	242	
F-PLEG	Nicollier HN.800	01	
F-PLEJ	Godbille JG.IB	01	
F-PLEM	Dyn'Aéro MCR-01 Sportster	216	
F-PLEO	Viking Dragonfly Mk.I	1116	F-WLEO
F-PLEZ	Rutan Long-Ez	1580	
F-PLFD	Denney Kitfox III	1095	
F-PLFG	CQR-01 Quercy	15	(F-PQFG)
F-PLFM	Pena Montagnard	01	
F-PLGC	Tormancy LR-01	01	
F-PLGJ	Steen Skybolt	173	
F-PLGL	Jurca MJ.2 Tempête	44	F-WLGL
F-PLGO	Nicollier HN.700 Ménestrel II	128	
F-PLGP	Pereira Osprey GP-4	323	
F-PLGR	ARSA Club LGR-61	01	
F-PLGZ	Jodel D.18	402	
F-PLHB	Brditschka HB-207 Alpha (Res.98)	207-019	
F-PLHF	Pottier P.220S Koala	413	
F-PLHM	Viking Dragonfly Mk3	372	F-WLHM
F-PLHR	Jodel D.112	1779	
F-PLIC	Rolland RS-3000 HAFB	02	
F-PLIG	Delarue GD1050J (Previously reserved 8.08 as Jodel DR.1050 Ambassadeur c/n 934)	01	
F-PLII	Bonsergent Bons-77 HAFB?	01	
F-PLIL	Lilles JCL-01 Laser 2000 (Rebuild of DR.380 c/n 572 F-BSOJ)	01	
F-PLIO	Colomban MC-15 Cri-Cri	646	F-WLIO
F-PLIZ	Dyn'Aéro MCR-4S 2002	29	
F-PLJB	Nicollier HN.434 Super Ménestrel	31	F-WLJB
F-PLJC	Jodel D.113	1635	
F-PLJD	Deramecourt 2000	01	
F-PLJH	Elisport CH-7 Kompress F	174	
F-PLJM	Jodel D.19	424-T	
F-PLJP	Jodel D.140E Mousquetaire IV	452	
F-PLJR	Stern ST-87 Europlane	34	
F-PLKE	Europa Aviation Europa XS	389	F-WLKE
F-PLKP	Jodel DR.200P	01	F-BLKP, F-WLKP
F-PLKQ	Pierre-Georges CPG 150 (Res.99)	01	
F-PLLB	Jodel D.18 (Res.4.04)	211	
F-PLLL	Colomban MC-100 Banbi	15	
F-PLMA	Jodel D.126	1777	
F-PLMB	Leopoldoff LMB	04.98	
F-PLMC	Lucas L-5	61	F-WLMC, (F-PLFC)
F-PLMD	Péna Bilouis	34	
F-PLMJ	Pottier P.270S	438	
F-PLMK	Laigniel-Mathely-Klinka LMK-1 Oryx	01	F-WLMK
F-PLMO	Jabiru J430	593	
F-PLMP	Heintz Zenith 100	2-128	
F-PLMS	Lucas L-5	46	
F-PLMV	Rotorway Exec 162HDF	6872	
F-PLMZ	Marie JPM-01 Médoc (Res.1.05)	03	
F-PLNA	Colomban Monobi MC-210	01	
F-PLNE	Pegaz W100	01	
F-PLOB	Jodel D.103	01	
F-PLOC	Canadian Home Rotors Safari FR-001	2109	
F-PLOI	Bauer-Declerck DB-8/1650 HAFB	2	
F-PLOL	Deramecourt 2200 HAFB	2	
F-PLOO	Jodel DH.251 (Res.3.06)	20	
F-PLPG	Denize RD-20 Raid-Driver	27	F-WLPG
F-PLPH	EAA Acrosport II	1222	
F-PLPJ	Dyn'Aero MCR-4S 2002	123	
F-PLPL	Lusley PL16/2000	01	
F-PLPP	Jodel D.18	106	
F-PLPR	Pottier P.180S	135	
F-PLRJ	Gombert Péna "Le Dahu"	01	
F-PLRL	LRL-01 Sanglier (Modified EAA Acrosport)	01	
F-PLRV	Van's RV-7A	72128	
F-WLRY	Jodel D.20 Jubilé (Res.5.04)	007	
F-PLSD	Nicollier HN.700 Ménestrel II	104	
F-PLSG	Nicolas NG-01	01	
F-PLTB	Sequoia F.8L Falco	1234	
F-PLTC	Dyn'Aéro MCR-4S 2002	155	
F-PLTS	Neico Lancair IV	338 / 320-97-1P	
F-PLUA	Druine D.31B Turbulent	249	
F-PLUB	Jurca MJ.2D Tempête	3	
F-PLUC	Dyn'Aéro MCR-4S 2002	26	
F-PLUF	Jodel D.119	1132	
F-PLUG (2)	Akrotech Giles G-202	029	F-WLUG
F-PLUI	Jodel D.119	1226	
F-PLUK	Jodel D.113 (ex D.112)	1186	
F-PLUL	Jodel D.119-3L (ex D.113, D-119)	1027	
F-PLUM	Jodel D.113V (ex D.119V, D-119, D.112)	187	
F-PLUN	Piel CP.301D Emeraude	361	
F-PLUP	Jodel D.112 Club	1193	
F-PLUQ	Jodel D.119	995	
F-PLUR	Jodel D.113E (ex D.119A)	1230	
F-PLUS	Jodel D.119	530	
F-PLUU	Jodel D.112 Club	1244	
F-WLUV	Bensen B.8ML Gyrocopter (Originally regd as B.7M)	01	
F-PLUX	Piel CP.301A Emeraude	348	
F-PLVD	Jodel DR.100D	901	
F-PLVM	Oceanair TC-180	13	
F-PLYG	C.A.B. GY-20 Minicab	A-240	
F-PLVR	Dyn'Aéro MCR-01	08	F-WSLD
F-PLYM	Durable RD-03 Edelweiss (Previously listed as Durable RD-02 Edelweiss c/n 02)	23	
F-PLYT	Heintz Zenith	122	
F-PLZE	Piel CP.1320 Saphir	77	
F-PMAA	Piel CP.323 Super Emeraude	428	
F-PMAB	Jodel D.112	163	HB-SUF
F-PMAC	Jodel D.114 3L	1670	
F-PMAE	Aerokopter AK1-3	65	
F-PMAF	Laurent Lynx PL-01	01	F-WMAF
F-PMAG	Colomban MC-15 Cri-Cri	356	
F-PMAH	Dyn'Aéro MCR-01 (Res.02)	144	
F-PMAJ	Rotorway 162HDF-A600 Talon	8009	
F-PMAK	Jodel DR.1050M1 Sicile Record (Res.99)	887	
F-PMAL	Pennec-Lucas PL-5 Dieselis (Res.6.07)	05	
F-PMAN	Wright Flyer 111A Replica	01-SAR	F-WMAN
F-PMAQ	Colomban MC-100 Banbi (Res.6.05)	128	
F-PMAR	Nicollier HN.700 Ménestrel II	14	
F-PMAT	Rutan Cozy	E-707	
F-PMAV	Dyn'Aéro CR.100C	33	
F-PMAX	Stolp SA.750 Acroduster Too	529	
F-PMAY	Colomban MC-15 Cri-Cri	499	
F-PMAZ	Jodel D.18	53	
F-PMBC	Nord NC.856G Norvigie (Res.00) (Rebuilt by GPPA, Angers from c/n 38 F-MMCB)	02	
F-PMBE	Jodel D.140C Mousquetaire III (Res.01)	462	
F-PMBG	Jodel D.18 (Res.3.04)	151	
F-PMBS	WagAero Sport Trainer	2196	
F-PMCA	Pitts S-1D Special	7-0342	
F-PMCB	Nord NC.854CM	01	
F-PMCC	Piel CP.320 Super Emeraude	431	
F-PMCD	Luscombe 8A Silvaire	895	C-FRNJ, CF-RNJ, NC22069
F-PMCF	Laigniel-Mathely-Klinka LMK-1	01-LPCA	
F-PMCG	WagAero Wagabond (Res.99)	1007	
F-PMCH	Nicollier HN.700 Ménestrel II	180	
F-PMCL	Nicollier HN.700 Ménestrel II	133	
F-PMCM	Jodel D.140E Mousquetaire IV	460	
F-PMCN	Pennec Gaz'Aile SP-2	08	
F-PMCR	Pottier P.180S	176	(F-PEUG)
F-PMCS	Jurca MJ.5 Sirocco	127	
F-PMDA	Jodel DA-01 (Res.97)	01	
F-PMDC	Dyn'Aéro MCR-01 Sportster	133	
F-PMDJ	Barry Lavrande BL-1E Electra (Originally res.00 as F-PMDJ for Barry Souricette MB-2 c/n 192, but aircraft converted to electric power and re-designated as above 12.07)	1	F-WMDJ
F-WMDK	WAR F-4U Corsair (Res.1.97)	477	
F-PMDL	Jodel DR.1053 Ambassadeur	852	F-WMDL
F-PMDS	de Havilland DH.82A Tiger Moth	83741	F-WMDS, F-BGZY, (G-ATWI), F-BGZY, (F-OAPT), T7400
F-PMDV	Pennec Gaz'Aile SP-2	208	
F-PMEB	Jodel D.119 (Originally D.112; officially registered with c/n "7400")	1245	
F-PMED	Jodel D.119	1092	
F-PMEE	Jodel D.113	1235	
F-PMEH	Croses EC-6 Criquet	37	
F-PMEN	Jodel D.119	219	
F-PMEO	Jodel D.119C (W/o 10.2.01)	1249	
F-PMEQ	Piel CP.703 Béryl	01	
F-PMER	Jodel D.112 Club	1136	
F-PMES	Leger RL-3	01	
F-PMET	Lederlin 380L (HM.380L)	01	
F-PMEU	Jodel D.112 Club	1328	
F-PMEZ	Jodel D.119	718	
F-PMFH	Viking Dragonfly Mk 2	MH-5015-V	
F-PMGA	Nicollier HN.700 Ménestrel II	71	
F-PMGE	Mayence MP-01	01	
F-PMGG	Nicollier HN.700 Ménestrel II	125	
F-PMGT	Rutan Cozy	627	
F-PMGV	Jodel D.140E Mousquetaire IV (Damaged 24.7.12)	463	
F-PMHJ	Van's RV-8A	82638	
F-PMIA	Colomban MC-15 Cri-Cri	665	
F-PMIC	BRT Eider (Murphy Rebel derivative) (W/o 15.9.07)	01	

Reg	Type	c/n	Previous
F-PMIE	Péna Bilouis	30	
	(Res.99)		
F-PMIG	Piel CP.320 Super Emeraude	unkn	
	(Res.)		
F-PMIK	Péna Bilouis	31	
	(Res.03)		
F-PMIL	Junqua RJ-03	25	
F-PMIT	Jabiru J400	202	
F-PMJC	Jodel D.140R Abeille	416	
F-PMJD	Europa Aviation Europa XS	571	
F-PMJG	Kelly Hatz CB-1	326	
F-PMJL	Brügger MB.2 Colibri	22	
F-PMJM	Jodel D.113	1686	
F-PMJP	Rutan Cozy Mk IV	32	
F-PMJR	Jodel D.19	279-T	
F-PMJS	Sequoia F.8L Falco	965	
F-PMKA	Dyn'Aero MCR-01 Club	149	
F-PMKI	Dickey E Racer Mk.1	ER-263	F-WMKI
F-PMLB	Dyn'Aéro MCR-4S 2002	97	
F-PMLC	Pottier P.230S Panda	448	
F-PMLD	Jodel DH.251	06	
F-PMLG	Fournier RF-5	A-04	F-WMLG, F-BSGA
	(Originally c/n 5084)		
F-PMLO	Colomban MC-15 Cri-Cri	482	
F-PMLR	Van's RV-8	80592	
F-PMLS	Melos DFB-1A	01	
F-PMLT	Nicollier HN.701TM Ménestrel II	166-01	
F-PMMB	Stern ST-87 Europlane	35	
F-PMMC	Jodel D.112 Club	1784	
F-PMMM	Jurca MJ-2H Tempête	22	
F-PMMP	Rotorway Exec 162HDF	6934	
F-PMMR	Jodel DR.1050 Ambassadeur	861	
F-PMNA	Hubert GH-2600 HAFB	01	
F-PMNC	Rolland RS2200 HAFB	01	
F-PMOA	Jodel D.18	450	
	(Res.97)		
F-PMOD	Antoine 2700 HAFB	01	
F-PMOE	Dyn'Aéro MCR-01 Club	289	
F-PMOF	Junqua RJ-03 Ibis	34	
F-PMOH	Jodel D.112 Club	1327	
	(Res.)		
F-PMON	Jodel D.1103T	01	
	(Res.01)		
F-PMOS	Nicollier HN.700 Ménestrel II	43	
	(Res.99)		
F-PMOZ	BBC Mosquito (75% replica)	01	
	(Dbr 6.8.15)		
F-PMPF	Dyn'Aéro MCR-01 M	222	
F-PMPG	Pottier P.180S	133	
F-PMPJ	Jodel D.113-3L	1723	
	(W/o 27.2.00)		
F-PMPL	Jodel D.92 Bébé	509	
F-PMPM	Marie JPM-01 Médoc	52	
F-PMPY	Jodel DR.1051M	895	
F-PMPZ	Rutan VariEze	1736	
F-PMQJ	Jodel D.128	1764	
	(Res.99)		
F-PMQT	Duruble RD-03 Edelweiss	49	
	(Res.00)		
F-PMRA	Rotorway Exec 162HDF	6631	
	(Dbr 29.11.13)		
F-PMRD	Duruble RD-03 Edelweiss	26	
F-PMRG	Jodel DG250	01	F-WMRG
F-PMRJ	Jodel D.140E Mousquetaire IV	430	
F-PMRN	Nicollier HN.700 Ménestrel II	182	
F-PMRR	Rutan Cozy	CC-1051	
F-PMRS	Pottier P.180S	153	
	(Res.07)		
F-PMRV	Van's RV-4	3466	
F-PMRY	Nicollier HN.700 Ménestrel II	63	
F-PMSA	MSA 1800/20 HAFB	01	
F-PMSD	Jodel DR.1054M	850	
F-PMSE	Jodel D.112 Club	1700	
F-PMSG	Morane-Saulnier Type G replica	01-RA	
F-PMSJ	Molière MLR 102 Blue Djinn	01	
F-PMSV	Marcandier / Stampe SV-4L	01-CM	
F-PMSY	Dyn'Aéro MCR-M	338	
F-PMSZ	Nicollier HN.700 Ménestrel II	163	
F-PMTA	Dyn'Aéro MCR-4S 2002	98	
F-PMTB	Marie JPM-01 Médoc	34	
F-PMTF	Van's RV-7	71497	
F-PMTR	Dyn'Aéro MCR-01 Sportster	256	
F-PMTS	Stern ST-87 Europlane	30	
F-PMTY	EAA Acrosport II	2063	
F-PMUL	FAMA Kiss 209M	20	
F-PMVA	Maurel MG-100P	01	
F-PMVM	Jodel D.18	439	
F-PMVT	Maunoury DM-01	01	
	(Res.99)		
F-PMXA	Jodel D.112 Club	1291	
F-PMXB	Jodel D.119D	1337	
F-PMXF	Jodel D.119	1335	
F-PMXH	Jodel D.112 Club	1191	
F-PMXK	Chatelain AC.9	01	
F-PMXL	Vintras-Bouillier VB.20 Isard	01	F-WMXL
F-PMXO	Jurca MJ.2D Tempête	20	
F-PMXQ	Chasle YC-12 Tourbillon	01	F-WMXQ
F-PMXT	Piel CP.301 Emeraude	366	
F-PMXU	Jodel D.92 Bébé	494	
F-WMXZ	Fourneron CF-2 Gyrocopter	02	
F-PMYB	Dyn'Aéro MCR-01	68	F-WMYB
F-PMYD	Rutan Long-Ez	1797L	F-WMYD
F-PMYG	Notteghem Occitan Club	03	
	(Res.)		
F-PMYL	Van's RV-7	73874	
F-PMYV	Piel CP.605A Diamant	34	
F-PMZO	Jurca MJ-2P Tempête	88	
F-PNAB	ICAM 77 HAFB	02	
F-PNAC	Jodel D.113	1619	
F-PNAD	Gaudet/Stampe SV.4C	01-GG	
F-PNAT	Elisport CH-7 Kompress F	191	
F-PNBC	Nicollier HN.700 Ménestrel II	70	
F-PNBG	Piel CP.1321B Super Emeraude	40	
F-PNCE	Dyn'Aéro MCR-01 Club	142	
F-PNCF	Nord NC.856A Norvigie	13	F-WNCF, F-BMSD
F-PNCG	Dyn'Aéro MCR-4S 2002	53	
F-PNCM	Van's RV-8	83107	F-WNCM
F-PNDF	Fournier RF-47	01	F-WNDF
	(Dbr 8.10.16)		
F-PNEF	Jodel D.150B	165	
F-PNEP	Nicollier HN.434 Super Ménestrel	70	
	(Res.01)		
F-PNEU	Jodel D.113	1773	
	(W/o .27.7.02)		
F-PNGE	Neico Lancair 320	167	F-WNGE
F-PNGG	Rutan Cozy	469	
F-PNGM	Jodel DH.251PR	09	(F-PNGR)
F-PNGS	Nicollier HN.434 Super Ménestrel	84	
	(Res.4.06)		
F-PNGT	Leduc RL-19	1	F-PAGT
	(Res.99)		
F-PNHJ	Nicollier HN.700 Ménestrel II	137	
F-PNHP	Dynali H2S	04	
F-PNIV	Jodel D.140E Mousquetaire IV	494	
	(Suspect rebuild of F-BNIV (182) cancelled 27.2.06)		
F-PNJD	Lucas L-5	19	
F-PNJJ	Noan JN 22/29 Macareux	01	
F-PNJL	Toscas/ Neico Lancair LCT-30	01	F-WNJL
	(Originally quoted as Lancair IV-P c/n 225)		
F-PNJP	Kurun JPR-01	01	
F-PNJT	Dynali H-2S Helicopter	01	F-WNJT, F-PHII
F-PNLG	Jodel D.92	41	
F-PNLY	Coupe C-423G	02	F-WNLY
F-PNMI	Jodel D.112 Club	522	F-BHVE
F-PNOA	Murphy Rebel	524	F-WNOA
F-PNOC	Dyn'Aéro MCR-01 Sportster	195	
	(Res.03)		
F-PNOG	ACBA-8 Midour 2	01	F-PRNG
	(ACBA-7 c/n 001 modified)		
F-PNOK	Dyn'Aéro MCR-01	162	F-WNOK
F-PNRJ	Jodel D.19	110T	
	(Noted stored 5.11)		
F-PNSF	Jodel D.140E Mousquetaire IV	427	
F-PNSN	Marty JM 150	01	
F-PNTF	Nicollier HN.700 Ménestrel	55	
F-PNUB	Jodel D.119	1289	
F-PNUF	Jodel D.119A	983	
F-PNUG	Jodel D.112 Club	1155	
F-PNUH	Jodel D.113	1325	
	(ex D.119) (Danaged 28.11.13)		
F-PNUI	Jodel D.112 Club	1194	
F-PNUL	Jodel D.119D	1383	
F-PNUN	Piel CP.605B Diamant	10	F-WNUN
	(ex CP.603)		
F-PNUT	Piel CP.319 Emeraude	367	
F-PNUX	Potez 600 Sauterelle	3873	F-ANUX
F-PNVL	Dyn'Aéro MCR-01 Sportster	45	
F-PNVO	Nevereau/Stampe SV.4C	01	F-WNVO
	(Originally SNCAN-built SV.4C c/n 590 F-BDEK)		
F-PNVV	Dyn'Aéro MCR R-180	03	
F-POAD(2)	Babin BJ-3	01	
	(Piper Cub conversion, ex Swiss)		
F-WOAH	Neico Lancair	unkn	
F-POAO	Olimpio OM-05	01	
	(Res.11.07)		
F-POBG	Jodel D.18	166	F-WOBG
F-POBJ	Jodel D.18	461	
F-POBY	Jurca MJ.5 Sirocco	50	
F-POCC	Notteghem Occitan Club	01	
F-POCF	Rutan VariEze	2109	
F-POCH	Colomban MC-200 Banbi	86	
	(Res.03)		
F-POCJ	Europa Aviation Europa XS	563	
F-POCM	Jodel D.119T	1819	F-WOCM
F-POCT	Aquitain ACAAB-01	01	
F-POCU	SNCAN/Stampe SV.4C	229	F-WOCU, F-BOCU, Aéronavale, F-BEHY, Aéronavale
F-PODB	Cabrix	01	
	(Res. 00)		
F-PODR	Tissot & Charbonnier Oceanair TC-160	20	
F-POEL	Pottier P.230S Panda	456	
	(Res.98)		
F-POEM	Jodel D.113 3L	1609	
	(W/o 24.5.02)		
F-POET	Heintz CH-180 Zenith	18-841	
F-POFC	ACBM-01	01	
F-POFG	Farigoux FG-01 Origan	01	
F-POGA	Piel CP.751 Beryl II	56	
F-POGJ	WAG Aero Sport Trainer	4250	
	(Res 3.08)		
F-POIA	Jodel D.92 Bébé	466	
F-POIB	Jodel D.112 Club	1377	
F-POIC	Jodel D.113	1275	
	(ex D.112)		
F-POID	Jodel D.119	1133	
F-POIF	Jodel D.112 Club	965	
F-POIH	Jodel D.119	714	
F-POII	Jodel D.119DA	1287	
F-POIL	Jurca MJ.5G2 Sirocco	17	F-WOIL
F-POIP	Jurca MJ.5 Sirocco	11	
F-POIS	Dyn'Aéro MCR-01 Club	217	
F-POIX	Piel CP.301A Emeraude	356	
F-POIZ	Piel CP.301A Emeraude	196	
F-POJP	Pottier P.230S Panda	430	
F-POKD	Jodel DH.251PR	15	
F-POKR	Dyn'Aero MCR-4S 2002	138	
F-POLA	Stoddard-Hamilton GlaStar TD	5623	
F-POLC	Van's RV-8	81939	
	(Res.03)		
F-POLE	Bushby Midget Mustang II	1708	
F-POLI	Van's RV-6	24044	
F-POLO (2)	Jodel DR.1053	865	
F-POLU	Deramecourt D16/1600 HAFB	01	
F-POLV	Pottier P.230S Panda	431	
	(Res.98)		
F-POLY	Joly MSA 1800/20 HAFB	02	
F-POMD	Jurca MJ.5 Sirocco	189	
	(W/o 18.9.10)		
F-POME	Jodel D.113V	1732	
F-POMM	Deramecourt 2600 HAFB	01	
F-POMP	Dyn'Aero MCR R-180	02	

Regn	Type	c/n	Previous identities
F-PONC	Nord NC.858S	74	(F-PPAN), F-BFSU
F-PONG	Nicollier HN.700 Ménestrel II	189	
F-PONK	Nord NC.858S	70	F-BFSQ
F-PONT	Pontier DePonAl D-520	01	
	(Res.00)		
F-PONY	Stolp SA.750 Starduster Too	585	F-WONY
F-WOOA	Lisa L-2T Akoya	unkn	
F-POOF	Barry MB-02 Souricette	54	
	(Res.02)		
F-POOL	Dyn'Aéro MCR-4S 2002	36	F-WWUU
F-POOO	Nord NC.854S	78	F-BFSZ
F-POOS	Van's RV-4	4369	
	(Res.00)		
F-POPF	CATA LMK-1 Oryx	03-LPCA	
	(Res.04, presumed ex F-PSJM)		
F-POPG	CATA LMK-1 Oryx	02-LPCA	
F-POPI	Colomban MC-15 Cri-Cri	286	
	(Res.)		
F-POPN	Jodel D.140E Mousquetaire IV	486	
F-POQR	Jodel D.113T	1817	
F-PORM	Lucas L-5	03	
F-POSB	Helisport CH-7 Kompress F	122	
F-POSC	Dyn'Aéro MCR-4S 2002	96	
F-POSE	Potez 60 Sauterelle	4184	F-WOSE, F-AOSE
F-POSH	Rotorway Exec 162HDF	7043	
	(Res.12.07)		
F-POSM	Dyn'Aéro MCR-01 Mini Cruiser	346	F-WOSM, F-WWUU
	(Initially quoted as 001)		
F-POSO	Rutan Cozy Mk.4	443	
F-POSS	Van's RV-7	72961	F-WOSS
F-POST	Breguet 14P Replica	150-AB	F-WOST
F-POTE	Pottier P.180S	180	F-WOTE
F-POTS	Waymel XW-650 HAFB	02	
F-POTT	Bourgue PB-04 (Revolution Mini)	01	
F-POUA	Barry MB-02 Souricette	168	
F-POUF	Jodel DH.251PR	03	
F-POUL	Piel CP.751B Béryl II	15	
F-POUN	Pottier P.220S Koala	414	
F-POUS	Gatard AG-02 Poussin	53	
	(Res.99)		
F-POUT	Jodel DR.1051M1	867	
F-POUX	Mignet HM.293	796	
	(Res.7.06)		
F-POZZ	Rolland RS2000 HAFB	01	
	(Res.11.06)		
F-PPAF	Colomban MC-15 Cri-Cri	580	
	(Res.00)		
F-PPAH	Pottier P.60A Minacro	06	
	(Res.03)		
F-PPAN(2)	Nord NC.858S	142	F-BBRP
	(Previously reserved for c/n 74 ex F-BFSU, now F-PONC)		
F-PPAP	Fisher Celebrity	56	F-WPAP
	(Dismantled .99)		
F-PPAT	Jabiru SK-80	101	F-WPAT
F-PPBH	Pottier P.230S Panda	449	
F-PPCA	SIPA S.901	27	F-BGAB
	(Res 3.08)		
F-PPCC	Piel CP.301 Emeraude	338	
F-PPCF	Breand BA-5	02	
	(Modified Piper J-5 Cub Cruiser)		
F-PPCM	Zenair CH-300 Tri-Z	3.97	
F-PPCO	Rotorway Exec 162HDF	6509	F-WPCO
	(Dbr 28.6.15)		
F-PPCY	Boland 48.12 Hot Air Bag 1600m2 Balloon	01	
F-PPDG	Aérojames Isatis	01	F-WPDG, W05-HA
F-PPDI	Nicollier HN.700 Ménestrel II	123	
F-PPDM	Brändli BX-2 Cherry	147	F-WPDM
F-PPDS	Stoddard-Hamilton Glasair II-FT	1090	
	(Res.3.05)		
F-PPDY	Dyn'Aéro MCR-01	101	F-WPDY
F-PPEJ	Jodel D.113VTC	27-A	
F-PPER	Seguineau CL-2200/12 Balloon	01	
F-PPGA	Europa Aviation Europa XS	412	
	(Res.3.06)		
F-PPGB	Rolland JBG-1050	01	
F-PPGO	Pottier P.60A Minacro	28F-OIF	
F-PPHC	Nicollier HN.700 Ménestrel II	115	
F-PPHJ	Jodel D.113A	1790	
F-PPHM	Piper J-3C-65 Cub	12961	F-BCPX, 44-80665
F-PPIA	Chasle LMC-1	04	
F-PPIC	Colomban MC-100 Banbi	36	
F-PPIT	Dyn'Aéro MCR-M	321	
F-PPJB	Jodel D.18	235	
F-PPJG	Lucas L-7-160	20	
F-PPJJ	Jodel D.18	274	
	(Same c/n quoted as SE-XMF)		
F-PPJM	Jodel D.119	1599	
	(Res.97)		
F-PPJP	Piel CP.320 Super Emeraude	450	
	(Res.7.07)		
F-PPJR	Renaud 01	01	
F-PPLD	Pottier P.230S Panda	429	
F-PPLM	Stampe SV-JF4	01	
F-PPLP	Dyn'Aero MCR-4S 2002	72	
F-PPLS	Colomban MC-15 Cri-Cri	322	
	(Res.00)		
F-PPMC	Piel CP.90 Pinocchio II	16	
F-PPMD	Piel CP.1321 Saphir	70	
F-PPMF	Stern ST-87 Europlane	36	
F-PPMU	Pottier P.180S	110	
F-PPOC	Jodel DH.251-D1	13	
F-WPOL	ROS AU-30 Airship	3002	
	(W/o 22.1.08)		
F-PPOT	Rutan Long-Ez	1950-L	
F-PPOU	Mignet HM.383	112	
	(Res.5.03)		
F-PPPA	Aero 30	01	
F-PPPL	Leglaive Miniplane	1	
	(Wfu)		
F-PPPO	Druine D.31 Turbulent	316	
F-PPPP	Jurca MJ.2E Tempête	26	
F-PPPS	Jodel D.113	1427	
	(ex D.119)		
F-PPPV	Jodel D.92 Bébé	532	
	(ex D.95)		
F-PPPX	Jodel D.119	1039	
F-PPRB	Jodel D.112 Club	1767	
F-PPRC	Péna Bilouis	26	
F-PPRJ	Pottier P.230S Panda	496	
F-PPRP	Piel CP.320 Super Emeraude	434	
F-PPRQ	Jodel D.120	257	F-BMOX, F-BMAX
	(Previously rebuilt with c/n 283)		
F-PPSA	Sens AS-05	01	
F-PPSE	Leys VL1050 Le Petit Prince Balloon	01	
F-PPTC	Colomban MC-15Z Cri-Cri	666	
F-PPTL	Dyn'Aéro CR.100C	30	
F-PPUP	FAMA Helicopters K209M Kiss	32	
F-PPVD	Dufour Bil'Aero OD-01	1	
F-PPVJ	Pottier P.60A Minacro	02	
	(Res.01)		
F-PPYH	FAMA Kiss 209MF	25	
F-PPYL	Luciani PL-160	01	
F-PPYS	Jodel D.112 Club	1778	
F-WPZA	Rebaa-Courcelles gyrocopter	01	
F-PPZB	Jurca MJ.2D Tempête	13	F-WPZB
F-PPZD	Jurca MJ.5F1 Sirocco	26	
F-PPZF	Jodel D.119	1426	
F-PPZG	Barbaro RB-60	01	
	(Rebuilt 1976-86 with fuselage of Auster J/5 F-BEAV c/n 2028)		
F-PPZI	Gazuit-Valladeau GV-1031	01	F-WPZI
F-PPZK	Jodel D.112 Club	1414	
F-PPZL	Jodel D.119	1290	
F-PPZM	Croses EAC-3	5	
	(Res.: noted 9.06)		
F-PPZP	Jodel D.113	1419	
	(ex D.119)		
F-PPZX	Druine D.31B2 Turbulent	60	
F-PQAM	Jodel D.113T	1825	
	(ex D.119)		
F-PQCD	CQR-01 Quercy	19	
	(Res.11.04)		
F-PQNO	Dyn'Aéro MCR-01	14	F-WSLI
	(Re-regd 36-MC / F-JFUP)		
F-PQUA(1)	Dyn'Aéro MCR-01	21	F-WQUA
F-PQUA (2)	Aurore Souricette	168	F-WQUA
F-PQUB	KIS TR-1	034	F-WQUB
F-PQUC	Dyn'Aéro MCR-01	26	F-WQUC
F-WQUD	Dyn'Aéro MCR-01	10	
F-PQUE	Dyn'Aéro MCR-01	25	F-WQUE
F-PQUG	Dyn'Aéro MCR-01	16	F-WQUG
F-PQUI	Dyn'Aéro MCR-01	29	F-WQUI
F-PQUK	Murphy Rebel	490	F-WQUK
F-PQUL	Europa Aviation Europa	184	F-WQUL
F-PQUM	Dyn'Aéro MCR-01	70	F-WQUM
F-PQUN	Dyn'Aéro MCR-01	04	F-WQUN
	(W/o 20.12.04)		
F-PQUQ	Dyn'Aéro MCR-01	55	F-WQUQ
F-PQUS	Jodel D.20 Jubilé	11	F-WQUS
	(To 55-JT but still regd)		
F-PQUT	Jodel D.20 Jubilé	09	F-WQUT
F-PQUU	Neico Lancair 320	691	F-WQUU
F-PQUV	Dyn'Aéro MCR-01	42	F-WQUV
F-PRAA	Jodel D.19	288	
F-PRAB	Jodel D.18	90	
	(To ULM register c/s F-JERP)		
F-PRAD	Colomban MC-15 Cri-Cri	389	
F-PRAG	Rutan Cozy	279	
F-PRAH	Jurca MJ.53 Autan	01	
F-PRAI	Jodel D.18V	227	
F-PRAK	Piel CP.402 Donald	9	
F-PRAL	Pottier P.180S	195	F-WRAL
F-PRAO	Jodel D.18	315	
	(Re-registered as 26-AFU)		
F-PRAP	GR.90 Condor	01	
	(Res.)		
F-PRAR	Rutan Long-Ez	2039L	F-WRAR
F-PRAS	Viking Dragonfly Mk.3	966	
F-PRAT	Jodel D.113	1671	
F-PRAU	Jodel D.113	1550	
F-PRAV	Jodel DR.1053M	795	
F-PRAZ	C.A.B. GY-201 Minicab	A-243	
F-PRBA	Druine D.31 Turbulent	414	F-WRBA
F-PRBB	Bücker Bü.131 Jungmann	R-1	F-WRBB
	(Believed to be rebuild of CASA C-1.131E Jungmann ex E3B-459, G-BECY)		
F-PRBC	Jodel D.119	1675	
F-WRBD	Quickie Quickie Q-1	31154-84	
F-PRBE	Stolp SA.750 Acroduster Too	224	
F-PRBJ	Mazel Avaram	01	
F-PRBK	Evans VP-1 Volksplane	2344	
F-PRBL	Deborde-Rolland Cobra 200A	01	
F-PRBM	Piel CP.750A Beryl	14	
F-PRBN	Croses EC-3 Pouplume	58	
F-PRBO	Jodel D.19	309	
F-PRBP	Rutan Long-Ez	2080L	
F-PRBQ	Cassutt IIIM	169	
F-PRBR	Jodel D.18	176	
F-PRBS	Sens AS-01	01	
	(Formerly regd as Cariou LC-3 Sagittaire c/n 23)		
F-PRBT	Colomban MC-15 Cri-Cri	301	D-GLMH, F-PZIX
F-PRBU	Zenair CH-600 Zodiac	6-1008	F-WRBU
F-PRBV	Gatard AG.02 Poussin	33	
F-PRBX	Jodel D.113	1654	
F-PRCA	Jodel D.92 Bébé	692	
F-PRCB	K&S Jungster 1J1	8001-RL	
F-PRCC	Viking Dragonfly Mk.3	0538	
F-PRCD	Jurca MJ.53 Autan	02	
F-WRCE	Pottier P.180S	007	
F-PRCG	Pottier P.180S	92	
F-PRCH	Piel CP.1320 Saphir	34	F-WRCH
F-PRCJ	Jodel D.18	96	
F-PRCK	Lucas L-5-03	47	F-WRCK
F-PRCL	Brügger MB.2 Colibri	71	
F-PRCM	Piel CP.80	73	
F-PRCO	Jodel D.18	56	
F-PRCP	Stern ST-87 Europlane	01	
F-PRCQ	Colomban MC-15 Cri-Cri (electric)	171	F-WRCQ
F-PRCR	Jodel D.19	297	
F-PRCS	Taylor JT.2 Titch	F4	
F-PRCT	CAP-XB	01	F-WRCT
F-PRCU	Jeoffroy JJ-01	01	F-WRCU
	(Modified Jodel DR.1052 c/n 773)		

Reg	Type	c/n	Alt
F-PRCV	Nicollier HN.700 Ménestrel II	17	
F-PRCY	Lucas L-5	44	
F-PRDA	Jodel D.19T	318-T	
F-PRDB	Brügger MB.2 Colibri	171	F-WRDB
F-PRDC	Jodel D.18	126	
F-PRDD	Ferrière LF-04	01	
F-PRDF	Jodel D.18	281	
F-PRDG	Colomban MC-15 Cri-Cri	314	
F-PRDH	Jodel D.150/120	129	
F-PRDI	Stern ST-85 Evasion	01	F-WRDI
F-PRDJ	WagAero Sport Trainer	842	F-WRDJ
F-PRDK	Rutan Long-Ez	1197	
F-PRDL	Rutan Cozy	E-731	F-WRDL
F-PRDN	Daurelle AD-02	01	
F-PRDP	Nicollier HN.700 Ménestrel II	6	
F-PRDR	Pottier P.180S	185	
F-PRDS	Rutan Long-Ez	1859L	F-WRDS
F-WRDT	Jurca MJ.10 Spitfire	1	
F-PRDU	Denize RD-105 Raid Driver	24	
F-PRDV	Croses EC-6 Criquet	84	F-WRDV
F-PRDX	Nicollier HN.434 Super Ménestrel	29	
F-PRDY	Nicollier HN.700 Ménestrel II	38	
F-PRDZ	Jodel D.18	269	
F-WREA	Duhamel DGH-02 Gyrocopter	2	
F-WREB	Tadrent TA-01 Gyrocopter	01	
F-WREC	Quetzal Gyrocopter	01	
F-WRED	Averso AX-02 Gyrocopter	22	
F-WREE	CFB-01 Gyrocopter	01	
F-WREF(1)	Bensen-B-8 Gyrocopter	8-104-100	F-WYUV?
	(Same c/n as quoted for F-WYUV)		
F-PREG(2)	Gaz'Aile SP-2	257	
F-PREH	Druine D.5 Turbi	25	
F-WREI	Rouet JR Guêpe Gyrocopter	01	
F-WREJ	Averso AX-02 Gyrocopter	20	
F-PREK	Humbert Moto du Ciel DA	8807	
F-WREL	Fauvette Gyrocopter	01	
F-WREM(1)	Averso AX-02 Gyrocopter	23	
F-PREM(2)	Van's RV-8	82956	
F-WREN	Averso AX-02 Gyrocopter	24	
F-WREO	Averso AX-02 Gyrocopter	21	
F-WREP	Bensen B-8 Gyrocopter	104-OF	
F-WREQ	Averso AX-02 Gyrocopter	26	
F-WRER	Averso AX-02 Gyrocopter	25	
F-PRES	Jodel D.19	I99-T	
F-WRET(1)	Auque AM-01 Gyrocopter	01	
F-PRET (2)	Murphy Rebel	526R	F-WRET
F-WREU(1)	Elixir Gyrocopter	1	
F-PREU (2)	Pottier P.220S Koala	463	
F-WREV(1)	Vigneron POMV Gyrocopter	01	
F-PREV (2)	Rutan VariEze	1961	
F-WREX	Averso AX-02 Gyrocopter	28	
F-WREY(1)	TUR-1 Gyrocopter	001	
F-PREY(2)	Tissot-Charbonnier TC-120 Oceanair	10	
F-WREZ	Averso AX-02 Gyrocopter	29	
F-WRFA	Light Aero Avid Flyer	539	
F-WRFB	Light Aero Avid Amphibian	78-A	
F-PRFC	Light Aero Avid Flyer	695	F-WRFC
F-WRFD	Light Aero Avid Flyer	646	
F-WRFF	Light Aero Avid Flyer	543	
F-WRFG	Light Aero Avid Flyer	479	
F-WRFH	Aviasud Mistral Mk.10	130	
F-WRFI	Light Aero Avid Amphibian	63	
F-PRFK	Neico Lancair 235	197	F-WRFK
	(W/o 3.10.09)		
F-PRFL	Christen Eagle 2	TA-3	F-WRFL
F-WRFN	Light Aero Avid Flyer	797	
F-WRFO	Light Aero Avid Flyer	537	
F-PRFP	Light Aero Avid Flyer Mk.IV	727	F-WRFP
F-PRFR	Neico Lancair 235	195	F-WRFR
F-WRFS	Rans S-10 Sakota	05-911-33	
F-WRFT	Rans S-10 Sakota	04-911-29	
F-PRFX	Light Aero Avid Flyer	536	F-WRFX
F-PRFY	Light Aero Avid Flyer	690	F-WRFY
F-WRFZ	Christen Eagle 2	MG-2	
F-WRGA	Franck Gyrocopter	002	
F-WRGB	Doucet DP-1 Gyrocopter	01	
F-WRGC	Averso AX-02 Gyrocopter	27	
F-WRGD	Herzig HF-1 Gyrocopter	01	
F-WRGE	Averso AX-02 Gyrocopter	31	
F-WRGF	Averso AX-02 Gyrocopter	30	
F-WRGG	GA-LAPA-1 Gyrocopter	01	
F-WRGH	Radas RR-2 Gyrocopter	01	
F-WRGI	Rabillard CR-02 Gyrocopter	01	
F-WRGJ	Sagittaire Gyrocopter	02	
F-WRGK	Cartier-Traverse CT1 Gyrocopter	01	
F-WRGL	Chauvin & Changeur CHA-2 Gyrocopter	01	
F-WRGM	Playe PL-B-1 Gyrocopter	01	
F-WRGN	Flying Dream Gyrocopter	01	
F-WRGO	Averso AX-06 Guepard Gyrocopter	01	
F-WRGP	Weinbrenner J.W.Gyrocopter	004	
F-WRGQ	Nieddu NA-01 Gyrocopter	01	
F-WRGR	Averso AX-02 Gyrocopter / Snoopy	1	
F-WRGS	Ceyrat JC Gyrocopter	01	
F-WRGT	Colibri Gyrocopter	02	
F-WRGU	Averso AX-02 Gyrocopter	32	
F-WRGV	Maisonhaute MB-1 Gyrocopter	01	
F-WRGX	Max-1 Gyrocopter	1	
F-WRGY	Averso AX-06 Guepard Gyrocopter	2	
F-WRGZ	DGH-02 Gyrocopter	1	
F-WRHA	Gisquet JG-1 Gyrocopter	01	
F-PRHB	Rotorway 162HDF-A600 Talon	8007	
F-WRHC	Ledent LL-1 Gyrocopter	01	
F-WRHD	Eclair Gyrocopter	01	
F-WRHE	Soubsol S-1S Gyrocopter	01	
F-PRHF	Gyrocopter Mk.1	01	F-WRHF
F-WRHG	B.TPR Gyrocopter	01	
F-WRHH	Doleac DJP-03 Gyrocopter	02	
F-WRHI	Mehault MN-1 Gyrocopter	01	
F-WRHJ	GRB Gyrocopter	01	
F-WRHK	Averso AX-02 Gyrocopter	33	
F-WRHL	Jeanneau JC-0001 Gyrocopter	01	
F-WRHM	JG-01 Gyrocopter	01	
F-WRHN	Mammouth Gyrocopter	01	
F-WRHO	Tadrent AT-1 Gyrocopter	01	
F-WRHP	Pellefigue PJF Gyrocopter	01	
F-WRHQ	DGH-03 Gyrocopter	01	
F-WRHR	Duflos DR-01 Gyrocopter	01	
F-WRHS	Averso AX-02 Gyrocopter	34	
F-WRHT	La Gazelle Gyrocopter	01	
F-WRHU	Boillon RB-03 Gyrocopter	1	
F-WRHV	Lacoste HL-01 Gyrocopter	1	
F-WRHX	DGH-03 Gyrocopter	03	
F-WRHY	RM-02 Gyrocopter	1	
F-WRHZ	Averso AX-02 Gyrocopter	01	
F-PRIA	Pitts S-1D Special	7-0503	
F-PRIB	Brügger MB-2 Colibri	240	F-WRIB
F-PRIC	Pottier P.80S	024	
F-PRID	Heintz Zenith	2-124	
F-PRIE	Jodel D.19	1681	
F-PRIF	Jodel DR.1050	739	
F-PRIG	Nicollier HN.700 Ménestrel II	81	
F-PRIH	Rutan Long-Ez	2203	
F-PRII	Péna Capena	9	
F-PRIJ	Pottier P.60 Minacro	03	
F-PRIK	Colomban MC-15 Cri-Cri	67	F-WRIK
F-PRIL	Colomban MC-15 Cri-Cri	492	
F-PRIM	Zenair CH-600 Zodiac	6-1003	
F-PRIN	Piel CP.90 Pinocchio II	10	F-WRIN
F-PRIP	Darcissac-Grinvalds DG-87 Goëland	02	
	(Also recorded as Grivalds Orion c/n 103)		
F-PRIR	Vare JCV-24 Tangara	01	F-WRIR
F-PRIS	Rutan Long-Ez	1272	
F-PRIU	Nicollier HN.700 Ménestrel II	05	
F-PRIV	Damoure-Fabre-Lacroix DFL-6 Saphir	3	
F-PRIX	Pottier P.180S	20	F-WRIX
F-PRIZ	Jodel D.92 Bébé	811	
F-PRJA	Jodel D.18	46	
F-PRJD	Alexandre Dewoitine D-501	01	F-WRJD
	(Constructed from Mauboussin-Beaujard 130 F-PCIZ c/n 01, formerly Mauboussin 129/48 F-BCIZ c/n 226) (Damaged 18.7.09)		
F-PRJE	Jurca MJ.5H1 Sirocco	21F	
F-PRJF	Colomban MC-12 Cri-Cri	21	
F-PRJG	Piel CP.320 Super Emeraude	437	
F-PRJI	Jodel D.18	48	
F-PRJJ	Leopoldoff L-55 Colibri	LF-01-93	F-WVZR
	(Rebuild of Leopoldoff L-56 F-BHGU c/n 03)		
F-PRJL	Deborde-Rolande Cobra L-160	01	
	(Reservation)		
F-PRJM	Jess Canard	1	
	(Res .93)		
F-PRJN	Jodel DR.100MJJ	01	
F-PRJO	Jodel D.150 Mascaret	119	
F-PRJQ	Colomban MC-15 Cri-Cri	56	
F-PRJR	Max Plan MP.205 Busard	25	F-WRJR
F-PRJS	Rutan Long-Ez	2073-L	F-WRJS
F-PRJU	Viking Dragonfly Mk.3	1133	
F-PRJV	Jodel D.9 Bébé	83	
F-PRJX	Pottier P.230S Panda	409	
F-PRJY	Zenair CH-701 STOL	1302	
	(Reservation)		
F-PRJZ	Marie JPM-01 Médoc	36	F-WRJZ
F-WRKA	Light Aero Avid Flyer	696	
F-WRKB	Light Aero Avid Flyer	687	
F-WRKC	Denney Kitfox	410	
F-WRKD	Light Aero Avid Flyer	725	
F-PRKI	Neico Lancair 320	552	F-WRKI
F-PRKJ	Light Aero Avid Flyer	798	F-WRKJ
	(Alternatively quoted as reserved as F-PKRJ)		
F-PRKK	Light Aero Avid Flyer IV	1097	F-WRKK
F-WRKL	Light Aero Avid Flyer	981	
F-WRKM	Light Aero Avid Flyer	472	
F-WRKN	Light Aero Avid Flyer	726	
F-WRKO	Light Aero Avid Flyer	799	
F-WRKP	Light Aero Avid Flyer	692	
F-WRKR	Light Aero Avid Flyer	696	F-WRKR
F-WRKS	Murphy Rebel	136	
	(Appears to have become F-WSDO, F-PSDO, then C-FJCS)		
F-WRKT	Light Aero Avid Flyer	1095	
F-WRKU	Murphy Rebel	141	
F-WRKV	Light Aero Avid Flyer	1212	
F-WRKX	Light Aero Avid Flyer	724	
F-PRKY	Ultravia Pelican Club PL	438	F-WRKY
F-PRKZ	Neico Lancair 360	248	F-WRKZ
	(Same c/n quoted for PH-HAN which may be 247)		
F-PRLA	Laplace RL-221	01	
F-PRLB	Jodel D.113	1702	
F-PRLC	Brändli BX-2 Cherry	110	
	(W/o 2.8.15)		
F-PRLD	Peters PGK-1 Hirondelle	183	F-WRLD
F-PRLE	Nicollier HN.434 Super Ménestrel	27	F-WRLE
F-PRLF	Nicollier HN.700 Ménestrel II	50	
F-PRLG	Colomban MC-15 Cri-Cri	23	F-WRLG
F-PRLI	Steen Skybolt CJ-250	325	F-WRLI
F-PRLJ	CJL-100	01	
F-PRLK	Brändli BX-2 Cherry	145	
F-PRLL	Jodel D.113	1666	
F-PRLM	Pottier P.70S	38	
F-PRLN	Stolp SA.750 Acroduster Too	528	
F-PRLO	Stolp SA.300 Starduster Too ?	unkn	
	(Res. – type unconfirmed)		
F-PRLP	Marie JPM-01 Médoc	26	
F-PRLR	Brändli BX-2 Cherry	111	
F-PRLS	Zenair CH-701 STOL	7-1349	
F-PRLT	Darcissac-Grinvalds DG-87 Goëland	3	
	(Also recorded as Grivalds Orion c/n 85)		
F-PRLU	Jodel D.113	1637	
F-PRLV	Couderc Vagabond	001	
F-PRLY	Decolro DRC-01	01	
F-PRLZ	Kieger AK-01	2	
F-PRMA	Nicollier HN.434 Super Ménestrel	23	
F-PRMB	Jodel D.150	123	
F-PRMC	Microgy MK-20	01	
F-PRMD	Pottier P.230S Panda	442	
F-PRME	Rutan Cozy	455	
F-PRMG	Stern ST-87C Europlane	11	
F-PRMH	Pottier P.220S Koala	446	F-WRMH
F-PRMI	Elisport CH-7 Angel	unkn	
	(Res.)		
F-PRMJ	Jodel D.18	320	
F-PRMK	Nicollier HN.700 Ménestrel II	53	
F-PRML	Viking Dragonfly Mk.2	950	
F-PRMM	Colomban MC-15 Cri-Cri	200	

Regn	Type	c/n	Previous ident
F-PRMN	Brügger MB.2 Colibri	123	
F-PRMO	Lucas L-6B	01	
F-PRMR	Stern-Mallick SM Vega	01	
F-PRMS	Grinvalds G-801 Orion	21	F-WRMS
F-PRMT	Filcoa J-6 Karatoo	2907885	
F-PRMU	Piel CP.1320 Saphir	32	F-WRMU
F-PRMV	Piel CP.320 Super Emeraude	409	
F-PRMX	Rutan Long-Ez	2179	
F-PRMZ	WagAero Sportsman 2+2	885	
F-PRNA	Jodel D.140E Mousquetaire IV	431	
F-PRNB	Nicollier HN.434 Super Ménestrel	45	
F-PRNC	Zenair CH-600 Zodiac	6-3	
F-PRND	Protech PT-2	1070	
F-PRNE	Jodel DR.1053P	735	F-WRNE
F-PRNJ	Amicale de Voltige Aér. AVA 432 MXS	01	
F-WRNS	Taylor Monoplane	unkn	
	(Damaged on f/f 22.2.14)		
F-PRNV	Rutan Long-Ez	1486	
F-PROB	Rutan VariEze	1432	OO-101, (OO-76)
F-PROC	Pottier P.80S	65	
F-PROD	Jodel D.113	1721	
F-PROF	Salvato SVO-01	01	
F-PROI	Heintz Zenith 100	2.127	
F-PROJ	Jodel D.150/120 Mascaret	190T	
F-PROM	Tissot-Charbonnier TC-180 Océanair	02	
F-PROO (2)	Brügger MB-2 Colibri	275	
	(Res.)		
F-PROP	Dyn'Aéro MCR-01 Sportster	265	
F-PROQ	Pottier P.180S	171	
F-PROS	Lucas L.5	033	
F-PROU	Piel CP.322-120 Super Emeraude	424	
F-PROV	Colomban MC-15 Cri-Cri	311	
F-PROX	Rutan Cozy	E-714	
F-PROY	Jodel D.113	1605	
	(Regd as D.119 in error)		
F-WRPA	Berset BR-01 Gyrocopter	01	
F-PRPB	Jodel D.18	343	
F-PRPC	Pottier P.70S	15	
F-WRPH	Lacas LP-01 Gyrocopter (B-8ML)	01	
F-PRPJ	Colomban MC-12 Cri-Cri	151	
F-PRPL	Jodel DR.1055M	811	
F-PRPM	Jodel D.140R Abeille (Damaged 22.9.02)	400	
F-PRPO	Jabiru J430	453	
F-PRPR	Jodel D.113	1792	
F-PRPS	EAA Acro Sport II	864	
F-PRPT	Nicollier HN.700 Ménestrel II	16	
F-PRPY	Colomban MC-12 Cri-Cri	24	
F-WRQA	Duquenne DM-01 Gyrocopter	1	
F-WRQB	Carbonnel CR-01 Gyrocopter	1	
F-WRQC	Averso AX-02 Gyrocopter	02	
F-WRQD(1)	Averso AX-02G Gyrocopter	03	
F-PRQD(2)	Jodel D.140E Mousquetaire IV	501	
	(Reservation .10)		
F-WRQE	Vassot PV-01 Gyrocopter	001	
F-WRQF	Gyrolet 1 Gyrocopter	01	
F-WRQG	Labussiere LC-01 Gyrocopter	01	
F-WRQH	Doleac DJP-03C Gyrocopter	01	
F-WRQI	Bonnot BP-01 Gyrocopter	01	
F-WRQJ	Libellule Gyrocopter	1	
F-WRQK	Raspberry Gyrocopter	1	
F-WRQL	Doleac DJP-Max Gyrocopter	1	
F-WRQM	Hanneton Gyrocopter	1	
F-WRQN	Dupin Bizuth Gyrocopter	DD-01	
F-WRQO	Guepard Gyrocopter	01	
F-WRQP	Caylus Gyrocopter	2	
F-WRQQ	Aquila Gyrocopter	1	
F-WRQR	Pennec-Peden PP-01 Gyrcopter	01	
	(Wfu and stored)		
F-WRQS	Icarus Gyrocopter	01	
F-WRQT	Boinon GB Gyrocopter	01	
F-WRQU	Bonnafous BC Gyrocopter	02	
F-WRQV	Cherokee Gyrocopter	FK-500	
F-WRQX	Averso AX-02G Gyrocopter	GM-01	
F-WRQY	Averso AX-02 Gyrocopter	MM-01	
F-WRQZ	Bonnafous BC-2 Gyrocopter	02	
F-PRRA	Pennec Gaz'Aile SP2	26	
	(Res.11.07)		
F-PRRC	Van's RV-7A	71290	
F-PRRD	Rutan Cozy	E-751	
F-PRRG	Jodel D.18	180	
F-PRRK	Rand-Robinson KR-1	4928	
	(Res.93)		
F-PRRM	Gravereau GD-2001 Milan Royale	01	F-WRRM
F-PRRV	Vasseur Gerfan RV02	01	F-WRRV
F-PRSA	Jodel D.18	23	
F-PRSC	Rutan Cozy	593	
F-PRSG	Jodel D.119	1385	
F-PRSJ	Rolland RC-65	01	
F-PRSK	Van's RV-6	23914	
	(Res.97)		
F-PRSM	Dyn'Aéro MCR-4S 2002	28	
	(W/o 14.2.08)		
F-PRSV	Dumortier/Stampe SV.4YD	01	
	(Res.4.04) (Also reserved as F-AZSV ?)		
F-PRSZ	Piel CP.320 Super Emeraude	427	
F-PRTD	Coupe JC-380D	8	F-WRTD
F-PRTE	Dyn'Aéro MCR-4S 2002	31	
F-PRTJ	Godbille JG-03	01	
F-PRUD	Nickel-Foucard NF-02 Asterix	01	
F-PRUE	Jabiru J430	535	
F-PRUQ	Aeromarine Skyote	63	F-WRUQ
F-PRVB	Van's RV-8	82272	
F-PRVI	Pottier P.180S	94	
F-PRVJ	Rutan Cozy	384	
F-PRVM	Van's RV-6A	24431	N542BW
F-PRVN	Van's RV-9A	91587	
	(Res 10.08)		
F-PRVS	Van's RV-6	22239	
F-PRXA	Rans S-6S Coyote II	0192262	F-WRXA
F-PRXD	Stoddard-Hamilton Glasair II-RG	1060	F-WRXD
F-WRXE	Light Aero Avid Flyer	1214	
F-WRXG	Murphy Rebel	14 . ?	
	(Res.93)		
F-PRXI	Light Aero Avid Flyer	795	F-WRXI
F-PRXJ	Aero Designs Pulsar 582	255-2F	F-WRXJ
F-WRXK	Light Aero Avid Flyer	1096	
F-WRXM	Light Aero Avid Flyer Mk.IV	1094	
F-PRXN	Light Aero Avid Flyer Mk.IV	1098	F-WRXN
	(Wrecked)		
F-WRXO	Rans S-9 Chaos	0790092	
F-WRXQ	Light Aero Avid Flyer	1220-D	
F-WRXR	Denney Kitfox	785	
	(Now re-regd 28-TD)		
F-WRXS	Light Aero Avid Flyer	1372	
F-PRXT	CFM Streak Shadow SA	K192-SA	F-WRXT
F-WRXU	Light Aero Avid Flyer	800	
	(Re-regd 25-UP)		
F-WRXV	Light Aero Avid Flyer	1370	
F-PRXX	Aero Designs Pulsar	12-F	F-WRXX
F-PRXY	Murphy Rebel	263	F-WRXY
F-WRXZ	Dyn'Aéro CR.100C Banbi	05	
F-WRYA	Roitelet Gyrocopter	CA-01	
F-WRYB(1)	Averso AX-02 Gyrocopter	GC-01	
F-PRYB(2)	Zenair CH-750 STOL	75-8388	
F-WRYC	Rodriguez RH Gyrocopter	01	
F-WRYD	Ricard Jokari Gyrocopter	1	
F-WRYE	Averso AX-02 Gyrocopter	JB	
F-WRYF	Kimpe KM Gyrocopter	1	
F-PRYG	Jodel DR.1050-2P	814	
F-WRYH	Portespane Gyrocopter	03	
F-WRYI	Delsol MD Gyrocopter	2703	
F-WRYJ	Pasquier PJ Gyrocopter	01	
F-WRYK	Vimon-Hoffmann VHB-1 Gyrocopter	01	
F-WRYL	AB-01 Gyrocopter	01	
F-WRYM	REL Gyrocopter	01	
F-WRYN	Dieudonne RD Gyrocopter	01	
F-WRYO	Bimbo Gyrocopter	01	
F-PRYP	Potez 60 Sauterelle	P-1991-1	
F-WRYQ	Elite 80 Gyrocopter	01	
F-WRYR	Gyrolet 3 Gyrocopter	01	
F-WRYS	Mistral 01 Gyrocopter	01	
F-WRYT	AST-1 Gyrocopter	01	
F-WRYU	Esposito GSE-01 Gyrocopter	01	
F-WRYV	Callauzene JC Gyrocopter	01	
F-WRYX	Le Gaulois 01 Gyrocopter	01	
F-WRYY	Dal-Bor 01 Gyrocopter	01	
F-WRYZ	MS-01 Abeille Gyrocopter	01	
F-PRZB	Brochet MB-50 Pipistrelle	8	F-PHZB
F-PRZZ	Rutan Cozy	414	
F-PSAB	Jodel D.20 Jubilé	01	F-WSAB
F-PSAC	Jodel D.18	257	
	(Res.97)		
F-PSAD	Delustre DD-100	001	
	(Res.)		
F-PSAF	Mignet HM.360	166	
F-PSAG	RSA Carriou CL-3	01	
	(Res.)		
F-PSAI	Dyn'Aéro MCR-4S 2002	41	
F-PSAM	Piel CP.322 Super Emeraude	451	
	(Res.97)		
F-PSAR	Jodel D.119	1756	
F-PSAT	Murphy Rebel	523	F-WSAT
F-PSBA	Van's RV-9A	91437	F-WSBA
F-PSBC	Pottier P.230S Panda	422	
F-PSBI	Soyer-Barritault SB-1/160 Antares	01	F-WSBI
F-PSBJ	Pennec Gaz'Aile SP-2	07	
F-PSBM	Pennec Gaz'Aile SP-2	46	
F-PSBR	Marie JPM 01 Tanagra	19	
F-PSBY	Jabiru J400	316	
	(Dam. 26.7.07 on f/f)		
F-PSCA	Thebault M500 CR	01	
F-PSCB	Dyn'Aéro MCR-4S 2002	101	
F-PSCC	Cassutt 3M	582	
F-PSCF	Rutan Cozy	128	
F-PSCH	Pottier P.190S Castor	01	
F-PSCJ	Pottier P.180S	52	
F-PSCK	Chudzik CC-02	01	
F-PSCR	Rutan Cozy	CC-1054	
F-PSCZ	Europa Aviation Europa	192	F-WSCZ
F-PSDA	Light Aero Avid Amphibian	75	F-WSDA
F-WSDB	Light Aero Avid Flyer	1371	
F-WSDC	Light Aero Avid Flyer	423	
	(Also marked 25-MN)		
F-WSDD	Light Aero Avid Flyer	1369	
F-WSDE	Rans S-6ES Coyote II	0193428	
F-WSDF	Light Aero Avid Flyer	980	
	(To 35-DP)		
F-PSDG	Light Aero Avid Flyer IV	1210	F-WSDG
F-WSDI	Light Aero Avid Flyer	481	HB-YEP
F-WSDJ	Light Aero Avid Flyer	540	
F-WSDK	Light Aero Avid Flyer	1405	
F-WSDL	Light Aero Avid Flyer	1406	
F-PSDM	Fisher Celebrity	054	F-WSDM
F-PSDN	Light Aero Avid Magnum	26	F-WSDN
F-PSDO	Murphy Rebel	0136-R	F-WSDO, F-WRKS?
	(To C-FJCS)		
F-PSDP	Light Aero Avid Magnum	07	F-WSDP
F-PSDQ	Aero Designs Pulsar 582	111-F	F-WSDQ
F-PSDR	Aero Designs Pulsar 582	106-F	F-WSDR
F-WSDS	Light Aero Avid Flyer Bandit	1403	
F-PSDT(2)	Jodel D.20 Jubilé	14	F-WSDT(2)
F-PSDU	Murphy Rebel	269	F-WSDU
F-PSDV	Neico Lancair 320	651	F-WSDV
F-PSDX	Denney Kitfox IV Speedster	ACS-093/4152518	F-WSDX
F-PSDY	Murphy Rebel	352	F-WSDY
F-PSDZ	Aero Designs Pulsar	114-F	F-WSDZ
F-PSEA	Tissot-Charbonnier TC-160 Océanair	01	
F-PSEC	Jodel-Hugueney DH-251	11	
F-PSED	Van's RV-7	74389	
F-PSER	Jodel DR.1053	720	F-WSER
F-PSFE	Jodel D.112 Club	1729	
F-PSFG	Tech'Aero Feugray TR-200	05	F-WSFG
F-PSFS	Bonnet BLJ-01	01	
F-PSFV	Rotorway Exec 162HDF	6980	
F-PSGA	Van's RV-7	72588	
F-PSGG	Grinvalds G-801 Orion	48	
F-PSGN	Rotorway Exec 162HDF	6879	
F-PSGT	Dyn'Aéro MCR-01 M	372	
F-PSHB	Jurca MJ-51 Sperocco	01	
	(Res.03)		
F-PSHK	Monnet Sonerai 2S	3169023	F-WSHK
F-PSHR	Dyn'Aéro MCR-01	119	

Reg	Type	c/n	Prev id
F-PSIC	Jodel DR.1050M	821	
F-PSII	Pitts S-1.11B Special	4001	
	(Res.5.07)		
F-PSIR	Fournier RF-7	03	
F-PSIT	Europa Aviation Europa XS	289	F-WSIT
F-PSJB	Croses LC-6 Criquet	63	
F-PSJC	Sens JCS-01	001	
	(Res.10.03)		
F-PSJH	JR-01 Mancha	01	
F-PSJM	LMK-1 Oryx	LPCA-03	
	(Res. cancelled) (Project presumed restored as F-POPF .04)		
F-PSJP	DRL S.250	01	
F-WSKA	Light Aero Avid Flyer	1404	
F-PSKC	Murphy Rebel	415	F-WSKC
F-WSKD	Wheeler Express	1133	
F-WSKE	Denney Kitfox	4156	
F-PSKF	Light Aero Avid Flyer IV	1218	F-WSKF
F-WSKH	Light Aero Avid Flyer	1502	
F-PSKI	Murphy Rebel	434	F-WSKI
F-WSKK	Stoddard-Hamilton Glasair II-FT	2249-FT	
F-PSKL	Stoddard-Hamilton Glasair IIS-RG	2250-RG	F-WSKL
F-WSKM	Stoddard-Hamilton Glasair II-RG	unkn-RG	
F-PSKN	Stoddard-Hamilton Glasair IIS-FT	2305-FT	F-WSKN
F-WSKP	Rans S-10 Sakota	988030	
F-PSKQ	Murphy Rebel	262	F-WSKQ
F-WSKS	Light Aero Avid Flyer Speedwing	1415	
F-PSKT	Ultravia Pélican PL-914	624	F-WSKT
F-WSKU	Light Aero Avid Flyer	978	
F-PSKV	Colomban-Robin CR.100C	25	F-WSKV
F-PSKX	Murphy Rebel	538	F-WSKX, C-FPNT
	(Rebuild of c/n 256) (W/o 20.8.03)		
F-WSKY	Akrotech Giles G-202	030	
F-WSLB	Akrotech Giles G-202	27	
	(W/o 3.5.98)		
F-PSLF	Dyn'Aéro MCR-01	17	F-WSLF
F-PSLH	Europa Aviation Europa	273	F-WSLH
F-PSLJ	Stoddard-Hamilton GlaStar GS-1	5079	F-WSLJ
F-PSLM	Rand-Robinson KR-2	66	
F-PSLN	Europa Aviation Europa	98	F-WSLN
F-PSLP	Pottier P.230S Panda	427	
	(Damaged 22.7.12)		
F-PSLQ	Dyn'Aéro MCR-01	30	F-WSLQ
F-PSLR	Dyn'Aéro MCR-01	33	F-WSLR
F-PSLS	Dyn'Aéro MCR-01	44	F-WSLS
F-WSLT	Rans S-7 Courier	1295167	
	(Res.)		
F-PSLU	Light Aero Avid Magnum	97	F-WSLU
F-PSLX	Dyn'Aéro MCR-01	37	F-WSLX
F-PSLY	Europa Aviation Europa	275	F-WSLY
F-PSLZ	Dyn'Aéro MCR-01	39	F-WSLZ
F-PSMB	Nicollier HN.700 Ménestrel II	88	
F-PSMC	Rolland RS2600/20 HAFB	01	
	(Res.7.05)		
F-PSMD	Jodel DR.1051M	930	F-WSMD
F-PSMJ	Piel CP.1320 Saphir	25	
	(Res.97)		
F-PSML	Jodel DR.1050M1	893	
	(Res.00)		
F-PSMR	Jodel D.20 Jubilé	06	F-WSMR
F-PSNE	Dyn'Aéro MCR-4S 2002	73	
F-PSOF	Jodel D.113V	1636	
F-PSOK	Mraz M.1D Sokol	298	HB-TAY
	(Res.01)		
F-PSOL	Dyn'Aero MCR-4S	114	
F-PSOM	Jodel DR.1053M	890	
F-PSPA	Alexandre SPAD VII	01	
	(Res.7.04)		
F-PSPF	Rouet MR-01	01	
	(Res.)		
F-PSPL	Druine D.5 Turbi	77	
F-PSRA	Dyn'Aero MCR-4S 2002	163	
F-PSRD	Nicollier HN.700 Ménestrel II	127	
F-PSRE	Aerokopter AK1-3	53	
F-PSRG	EAA Acrosport II	964	
F-PSRJ	Dyn'Aéro MCR-4S 2002	55	
F-PSRV	Van's RV-7	72382	
	(Res.11.05)		
F-PSSA	Jodel D.119	1278-1	
F-WSSB	Bensen B-8MV Gyrocopter	unkn	
F-WSSC	Bensen B-8 Gyrocopter	unkn	
F-WSSE	Laboye-Bensen Gyrocopter	1	
F-PSSF	Druine D.31 Turbulent	182	
F-WSSG	Bensen-Testa 70 Gyrocopter	001	
F-PSSH	Jodel D.119V	1428	
F-WSSL	Raybout D-2 Autogyre	01	
F-PSSN	Jodel D.119	1399	
F-PSSO	Leblanc L.52	1	
F-WSSP	Bensen/Nuville JN-2 Gyrocopter	01	
F-PSSQ	Duranton DE Junior	01	
F-PSSR	Druine D.5 Turbi	50	F-WSSR, F-PSSR
F-PSSS(2)	Seckler SS-02	01	
	(Res.98)		
F-WSSU	Bensen B.8MC Gyrocopter	01	
F-PSSV	Jodel D.119	1413	
F-PSSX	Gazuit-Valladeau GV-1031	02	F-BSSX, F-WSSX
	(Dismantled)		
F-WSTA	Ameur Aviation Altania	001	
F-PSTB	Aerokopter AK1-3	64	
F-WSTC	Ultimate 20.300T	130393 004	
F-PSTE	Dyn'Aéro MCR-01 Club	128	F-WSTE, F-WWUV
F-PSTF	Dyn'Aéro MCR-4S 2002	39	F-WWUU
F-PSTL	Timiris BC253	01	
	(Res.5.06)		
F-PSTN	Pennec-Lucas PL-5 Dieselis	01	
F-PSTO	Jodel D.113T	01	F-WSTO
F-PSUA	Europa Aviation Europa	310	F-WSUA
F-PSUD	Dyn'Aéro MCR-01 Club	157	F-WSUD
F-PSUN	Jurca MJ.77 Gnatsum	09	
	(Damaged 02.9.11)		
F-PSUR	Brugger MB.2 Colibri	177	
F-PSUZ	Stoddard-Hamilton Glasair II-TD	1109TD	F-WSKO
F-PSVC	SNCAN/Stampe SV.4C	536	F-BDCG
	(Res.7.06)		
F-PSVE	Jodel DR.1053MT	947	
F-PSVJ	Pennec Gaz'Aile SP-2	188	

Reg	Type	c/n	Prev id
F-PSVO	Gasnier Kerdonis GG-01	02	
	(Res. 10.07)		
F-PSVR	Jodel DR.100	843	
F-PSXP	Pitts S-1S	2098	
F-WSYB	Gyrol G-2 Autogyro	002	
F-PSYD	Jodel D.112 Club	1472	
	(Stored)		
F-PSYE	Starck AS.80 Holiday	58	
F-PSYH	Druine D.5 Turbi	27	
F-WSYJ	Bensen B.8M Gyrocopter	01	
F-PSYN	Mignet HM.360	128	F-WSYN
F-PSYP	Jodel D.112 Club	1447	
F-PSYQ	Fleury RF	01	
F-WSYR	Campbell Cricket Gyrocopter	CA/342	G-AYHJ
	(Stored)		
F-WSYS	Bensen B-8M Gyrocopter	01	
F-WSYZ	Bensen B-8M Gyrocopter	01	
F-WSZA	Bouget-Capdeville BC-1 Gyrocopter	01	
F-WSZB	Scheila Gyrocopter	001	
F-WSZC	Fardeau Gyrocopter	001	
F-WSZD	Colin CX Gyrocopter	01	
F-WSZE	Gamin H-16 Gyrocopter	001	
F-WSZF	Lion Gyrocopter	001	
F-WSZG	Cobra Gyrocopter	01	
F-WSZH	Marquion-Dreyer MD-05B Gyrocopter	001	
F-WSZI	Bouilin BJM-III Gyrocopter	001	
F-WSZJ	Averso AX-02 Gyrocopter	LJS-01	
F-WSZK	Averso AX-02 Gyrocopter	unkn	
F-WSZL	Rapetout Gyrocopter	01	
F-WSZM	Albatros Gyrocopter	02	
F-WSZN	Arc-en-Ciel Gyrocopter	01	
F-WSZO	Dieudonne RD-02 Gyrocopter	01	
F-WSZP	Schoettel GS-01 Gyrocopter	01	
F-WSZQ	Maury M-1 Gyrocopter	001	
F-WSZR	Martins OM Gyrocopter	01	
F-WSZS	Rivollier-Bernardi RB Gyrocopter	01	
F-WSZU	Averso AX-02 Gyrocopter	001	
F-WSZV	Faure JPF-002 Gyrocopter	002	
F-WSZX	Libellule Gyrocopter	01	
F-WSZY	Colibri Gyrocopter	01	
F-WSZZ	Palombe Gyrocopter	01	
F-PTAA	Jabiru J400	312	
F-PTAC	Aerotek Pitts S-2SI	2081	
F-PTAH	Startrap FG-01	01	
	(Dismantled)		
F-PTAJ	Piel CP.615 Super Diamant	57	
F-PTAK	Chatelain 2000	01	
F-PTAL	Nicollier HN-700 Menestrel	10	
F-PTAM(2)	Van's RV-8	80946	
F-PTAO	Pottier P.130L Coccinelle	1017	
F-PTAT	W.A.R. FW.190A Replica	117	F-WTAT
F-PTAU	Grinvalds G-802B Gerfaut	07	
	(Res.3.06)		
F-PTAV	Pottier P.230S Panda	452	
F-PTAY	Jabiru J-160C	166	
F-PTAZ	Chatelain 2000	01	F-WTAZ
	(Constructed with fuselage of Chatelain AC-12 F-PYBO c/n 01)		
F-PTBA	Steen Skybolt	704	
F-PTBG	Van's RV-4	2841	
F-PTBM	Colomban MC-100 Banbi	141	
F-WTBS	Steen Skybolt	478	
F-PTCA	Stern ST-87 Europlane	47	
	(Res.99)		
F-PTCC	Stern ST-87 Europlane	32	
F-PTCD	Ameur Avn Baljims 1A	01	
F-PTCM	Jurca MJ.77 Gnatsum	02	
	(Res.4.88)		
F-PTCR	Colomban-Robin CR.120	02	
F-PTDD	Grinvalds G-802B Gerfaut	04	F-WTDD
F-PTDM	Jurca MJ.2H Tempête	10	
F-PTDS	Colomban MC-15 Cri-Cri	607	
	(Res.9.06)		
F-PTDZ	AM.01 Buffalo	01	
F-WTEA	Queniet QG-01 Gyrocopter	04	
F-WTEB	Descatha DB Gyroglider	01	
F-WTEC(1)	Goutel/Bensen B-8M Gyrocopter	01	
	(Presumed cancelled)		
F-PTEC(2)	Pitts S-1S Special	2082	
F-WTED	Danis DB Giroplaneur	01	
F-WTEE	Danis DB Giroplaneur Nautic	03	
F-WTEF	Danis DB Giroplaneur Nautic	02	
F-WTEG	Danis DB Autogire	01	
F-PTEJ	Jurca MJ.5-K2 Sirocco	16	
F-PTEK	Jodel D.112 Club	1459	
F-WTEM	Bensen B.8MG Gyrocopter	1	
F-PTER	Jurca MJ.2D Tempête	34	
F-WTEY	Bensen B8.MB Gyrocopter	01	
	(Stored .97)		
F-WTEZ(1)	Bensen B.8MT Gyrocopter	01	
	(Presumed cancelled)		
F-PTEZ (2)	Potez 60-EF	01	
F-PTGI	Dyn'Aéro MCR-01 VLA-100SP	115	F-WTGI
F-PTGJ	Pottier P.130L Coccinelle	1106	
F-PTGL	Dyn'Aéro MCR ULC	315	
F-PTGV	Van's RV-8	82513	
	(Res.1.06)		
F-PTHM	Helisport CH-7 Kompress F	230	
F-PTIC	SECAT S-5 Mouette	F-1	F-WTIC, F-PIIC, F-WCDS
F-PTIM	Bartoli BR-01	01	
F-PTIO	Dyn'Aéro MCR-01 Sportster	186	
F-PTIS	Tissot-Charbonnier TC-120 Oceanair	1	
F-PTIT	Dyn'Aéro MCR-01 Club GD	02	
F-PTJB	Grinvalds G-802B Gerfaut	03	
	(Res.99) (Formerly Orion c/n 10)		
F-PTJC	Rutan Cozy	E-716	
	(Res.)		
F-PTJD	Pottier P.70S	42	
	(Res.01)		
F-PTJM	Rutan VariEze	1756	
F-PTLC	WagAero Sport Trainer	1240	
F-PTLF	Grinvalds G-802L Gypaete	01	
	(Res.99) (Formerly Orion c/n 140)		
F-PTLM	Rutan Cozy	CC-1025	
	(Res.1.05)		
F-PTLR	Taillefer DT-01	02	
	(Res.3.07)		

Reg	Type	c/n		
F-PTMC	Colomban MC-15 Cri-Cri	478		
F-PTMF	Van's RV-7	unkn		
F-PTMJ	Colomban MC-100 Banbi	25		
F-PTML	Pennec SP-2 Gaz'Aile	12		
F-PTMV	Rutan Cozy	CC-1058		
F-PTND	Dautreppe WD-01	01		
	(Res.8.07)			
F-PTNF	Tipsy Nipper Marquis	01		
	(Damaged 13.7.03)			
F-PTOC	Rutan Cozy	452	(F-PJET)	
F-PTOP	Jodel DR.1053M	783		
	(Res.)			
F-PTOR	Aviotecnica ES 101	01		
F-PTOY	Clenet DC-01 Baboo	01		
	(Res.98)			
F-PTOZ	Dyn'Aero MCR-4S 2002	48	F-WTOZ	
F-PTPL	Druine D.5 Turbi	72		
F-PTRA	Jodel DH.251	08		
F-PTRB(2)	Dyn'Aéro MCR-01 UL	27		
	(Builder R Bodenan) (Previously listed as Bodenan CRD-01 c/n 01)			
F-PTRC	Parker Teenie Two	15-1838		
F-PTRD	Rotorway Exec 162HDF	6792		
F-PTRL	Colomban MC-15 Cri-Cri	433		
F-PTRO	Tissot-Charbonnier TC-160 Oceanair	15		
F-PTRR	Robin Twin-R	01		
F-PTSH	Jodel D.140R Abeille	434		
	(Damaged 11.7.09)			
F-PTSL	Sequoia F.8L Falco	1350	(F-PFSL)	
F-PTSM	Pennec-Lucas PL-5 Dieselis	14		
	(Res.04)			
F-PTTL	Stampe JCL-4	01		
	(Res1.07)			
F-PTUN	Dyn'Aero MCR-01 Sportster	420		
F-PTUT	Aviotecnica ES.101	03		
F-PTVC	Tissot -Charbonnier TC-160 Océanair	04		
	(W/o 17.10.09)			
F-PTVH	Colomban-Robin CR.100C	29		
F-PTXA	Jodel D.119	1276		
F-PTXC	Croses EC.8 Tourisme	18	F-WTXC	
F-PTXE	Vintras JPV.30 Joker	01	F-WTXE	
F-PTXG	Heintz Zenith	16		
F-WTXI	Bensen B.8M Gyroplaneur	01		
F-PTXL	Calvel Piel Zeff CPM	01		
	(Wfu 7.80; intended rebuild)			
F-PTXM	Jurca MJ.2D Tempête	21		
F-WTXN	Bensen-Sica SP-01 Gyrocopter	01		
F-PTXO	Druine D.31 Turbulent	359		
F-PTXP	Jodel D.119A	1341		
F-WTXQ	Bensen B.8MB Gyrocopter	01		
F-PTXR	Jodel D.119	1502		
	(w/o 03.6.10)			
F-PTXU	Piel CP.320A Super Emeraude	83	F-WTXU	
F-WTXV	Bensen JC-01 Gyrocopter	01		
F-WTXZ	Rouaux RB-01 Gyrocopter	01		
F-WTYB	Bonnafous B-5 Gyrocopter	01		
F-WTYC	Le Roitelet Gyrocopter	01		
F-WTYE	FGA Gyrocopter	01		
F-WTYF	Flying Dream Gyrocopter	02		
F-WTYG	Vignan JPV Corfou Gyrocopter	01		
F-WTYH	Despaux DR Gyrocopter	01		
F-WTYI	BMW Gyrocopter	01		
F-WTYJ	Lacombe Gyrocopter	01		
F-WTYK	Colibri Gyrocopter	01		
F-WTYL	Mondary JM Gyrocopter	01		
F-WTYM	Zéphir Gyrocopter	01		
F-WTYN	Tête Brûlée Gyrocopter	01		
F-WTYO	Averso AX-02 Gyrocopter	01		
F-WTYP	Tigre Opter Gyrocopter	07		
F-WTYQ	Phénix Gyrocopter	01		
F-WTYR	OK Gyrocopter	01		
F-WTYS	AG-15 Gyrocopter	15		
F-WTYT	Puente PR Gyrocopter	01		
F-WTYU	Aubin DA Gyrocopter	01		
F-WTYV	Ousset OA Gyrocopter	01		
F-WTYX	Galaxy Gyrocopter	01		
F-WTYY	Averso AX-02 Gyrocopter	01		
F-WTYZ	Weinbrenner Gyrocopter	05		
F-WTZA	Mila 01 Gyrocopter	01		
F-WTZB	Beltrando BD-01 Gyrocopter	01		
F-WTZC	Python Gyrocopter	01		
F-WTZD	Dilal Gyrocopter	01		
F-WTZE	Picsou Gyrocopter	01		
F-WTZF	GJ Gyrocopter	02		
F-WTZG	Glemet GJL Gyrocopter	01		
F-WTZH	Dessart-Larioze DL Gyrocopter	01		
F-WTZI	Enfossi EJM Gyrocopter	01		
F-WTZJ	VHM Gyrocopter	01		
F-WTZK	Averso AX-02 Gyrocopter	01		
F-WTZL	Evenot EL-02 Gyrocopter	01		
F-WTZM	Derlan Gyrocopter	01		
F-WTZN	Michelot DM Gyrocopter	01		
F-WTZO	Kloeti RK Gyrocopter	01		
F-PTZP	Magni M-18 Gyrocopter	01	F-WTZP	
F-WTZQ	Colombie OC Gyrocopter	01		
F-WTZR	Raoul Gyrocopter	01		
F-WTZS	Berger BX Guepard Gyrocopter	01		
F-WTZT	Romaneli RJ Gyrocopter	01		
F-PTZU	Le Loup Gyrocopter	01	F-WTZU	
	(Stored.08)			
F-WTZV	Maffre Gyrocopter	01		
F-WTZX	Tiercelin GT Gyrocopter	01		
	(Noted marked as Averso AX07, 8.99)			
F-WTZY	Navarro Gyrocopter	01		
F-WTZZ(1)	Ducos G-3 Gyrocopter	01		
	(Presumed cancelled)			
F-PTZZ(2)	Pennec SP-2 Gaz'Aile	44		
F-PUAA	Dan Rihn One Design DR107	485		
F-PUAV	Dyn'Aéro MCR-4S 2002	46	F-WUAV, F-WWUU, F-WWUY	
F-PUCE	Dyn'Aéro MCR-01	36	F-WUCE	
F-PUCH	Brändli BX-2 Cherry	151		
	(Res)			
F-PUCK	Red Wing Biplane	01		
	(Regd 4.14 but res.97 as Motopompe to same owner)			
F-PUCY	Bonnavaud LB-01	01		
F-PUDI	Dyn'Aéro MCR-4S 2002	153		
F-PUFB	Nicollier HN.343 Ménestrel	unkn		
	(Noted 7.01)			
F-PUIG	Brügger MB-2 Colibri	102		
F-PUIL	Jodel D.140E Mousquetaire IV	505		
F-PUIM	Joaquim Machaon	01		
	(Res.05)			
F-PUJG	Colomban MC-15 Cri-Cri	110		
F-PULC	Nicollier HN.700 Ménestrel II	37		
F-PULL	Piel CP.323 Super Emeraude	460		
F-PULM	Elisport CH-7 Kompress F	132		
F-PULP	Ferrier AAL-01	01		
F-PULS	Aero Designs Pulsar	109-F	F-WSKB	
F-PULY	Quercy CQR-01	22		
F-PUMA	Piel CP.320 Super Emeraude	440		
F-PUNK	Jurca MJ.52 Zephyr	01		
	(Res.99)			
F-PUNS	Deramecourt 2600 HAFB	02		
F-PUNU	Oldfield Baby Lakes	02-1026		
F-PUPY	Preceptor Ultra Pup	129		
	(Res.)			
F-WUQQ	Scorpion helicopter	01		
F-WURE	LISA L-2T Akoya	01		
F-PURL	Rutan Long-Ez	127		
F-PURR	Murphy Rebel	268R	F-WURR	
F-PURU	Dyn'Aéro MCR-01 Sportster	218		
F-WUSA	Bervat Gyrocopter	01		
F-WUSB	Ferrie FB Gyrocopter	01		
F-WUSC	Durand DC Gyrocopter	01		
F-WUSD	Gurau GG Gyrocopter	01		
F-WUSE	Gayaud GR Gyrocopter	01		
F-WUSF	Kerchaun KD Gyrocopter	01		
F-WUSG	Palavadeau Bensen 002 Gyrocopter	02		
F-WUSH	Delfour DC Gyrocopter	01F		
F-WUSI	Averso AX Gyrocopter	06		
F-WUSJ	Max Gyrocopter	001		
F-WUSK	Averso Guepard Gyrocopter	01		
F-WUSL	Fior Gyrocopter	01		
F-WUSM	Averso AX-02 Gyrocopter	01		
F-WUSN	Averso AX-02 Gyrocopter	01		
F-WUSO	Hoffmann VHB-1 Supercopter	01		
F-WUSP	Bonnafous BC03 Gyrocopter	01		
F-WUSQ	Daubert DF Gyrocopter	01		
F-WUSR	Magni Gyrocopter	01		
F-WUSS(1)	Aerogi Gyrocopter	01		
	(Presumed cancelled)			
F-PUSS(2)	Dyn'Aero MCR-4S 2002	99		
F-WUST	Snoopy Gyrocopter	01		
F-WUSU	Equilibre 2 Gyrocopter	01		
F-WUSV	Odorico R-003 Gyrocopter	03		
F-WUSX	Delawind Gyrocopter	01		
F-WUSY	Rangers Gyrocopter	001		
F-WUSZ	Pisoni P-01 Gyrocopter	01		
F-WUTA	Soriano GSXR Gyrocopter	01		
F-WUTB	Moustique Gyrocopter	001		
F-WUTC	Averso Guepard Gyrocopter	01		
F-WUTD	Lopez Gyrocopter	001		
F-WUTE	Faulcon Gyrocopter	01		
F-WUTF	Averso AX-2 Guepard Gyrocopter	01		
F-WUTG	Averso AX-2 Guepard Gyrocopter	01		
F-WUTH	Progressor Pou Gyrocopter	01		
F-WUTI	Maya Gyrocopter	001		
F-WUTJ	Jacquelin JMJ Gyrocopter	001		
F-WUTK	Lignac J'Ai s'Quim Faut Gyrocopter	001		
F-WUTL	Butaille BG Gyrocopter	01		
F-WUTM	Creusot HC Gyrocopter	01		
F-WUTN	Martins OM-02 Gyrocopter	unkn		
F-WUTO	Benus Gyrocopter	002		
F-WUTP	Techer JYT Gyrocopter	01		
F-WUTQ	Petitgirard VP-01 Gyrocopter	01		
F-WUTR	Kloeti RK-02 Gyrocopter	02		
F-WUTS	Averso AX-02 Guepard Gyrocopter	01		
F-WUTT	Schaeffer MS-01 Gyrocopter	01		
F-WUTU	Magni M-16 Tandem Trainer	01		
F-WUTV	Averso AX-02 Guepard Gyrocopter	01		
F-WUTX	Air Command 582	KC-164		
F-WUTY	Cena CP-003 Gyrocopter	03		
F-WUTZ	Averso AX-02 Guepard Gyrocopter	01		
F-WUUA	Bensen B-8 Gyrocopter	01		
F-WUUB	Berva Gyrocopter	03		
F-WUUC	Colibri 2 Gyrocopter	01		
F-WUUD	Sundarp MS-1 Gyrocopter	01		
F-WUUE	(Agnelet) Autogyre	01		
F-WUUF	Mosquito Killer Gyrocopter	001		
F-WUUG	Fourlade JF Dominator Gyrocopter	01		
F-WUUH	Gabi Gyrocopter	02		
F-WUUI	X2 Gyrocopter	001		
F-WUUJ	Vil Coyote Gyrocopter	unkn		
F-WUUK	Magni M-14 Scout	01		
F-WUUL	Magni M-18 Spartan	01		
	(Badly damaged 21.5.00)			
F-WUUM	Magni M-16 Tandem Trainer	01		
F-WUUN	Baquiast Monoplane CB Gyrocopter	01		
F-WUUO	Gisquet JG Gyrocopter	01		
F-WUUP	Magni M-16 Tandem Trainer	01		
F-WUUQ	Mourier Gyrocopter	01		
F-WUUR	Polge Gyrocopter	01		
F-PUYJ	Dyn'Aéro MCR-4S 2002	40		
F-PUZL	Light Aero Avid Amphibian	61	F-WRFE	
F-PVAC	Van's RV-6A	25387	F-WVAC	
F-PVAJ	Jodel D.113	1669		
F-PVAL	Disdier JD-01	01		
	(Res.)			
F-PVAM	Boisavia B.601L	03	F-BAIL ?	
	(Res.2.08 for Vannes museum)			
F-PVAN	Van's RV-7	73193		
	(Res 5.08)			
F-PVAO	Van's RV-7	72121		
	(Res.11.05)			
F-PVAP	Jodel DR.1052M	851		
	(Res.99)			
F-PVAR	Van's RV-6A	60542		
	(Res.5.04)			
F-PVAS	Rotorway Exec 162HDF	6890		
	(Res.10.06)			
F-PVAT	Van's RV-6A	60542		
F-PVAV	ACBA-7 Midour	05		

Reg	Type	c/n	Prev
F-PVBB	Van's RV-9A	91585	
F-PVBG	Van's RV-6	22593	
F-PVBN	Pamany PL-4A	420	
	(Res.)		
F-PVBR	Weinbrenner HJW-01	001	
	(Res.02)		
F-PVBT	Jodel DR.1051	873	
F-PVDB	Vandenbrock VDB-01 Gyrocopter	01	
	(Res.)		
F-PVDD	Stern ST-87 Europlane	12	
	(Res.02)		
F-PVDG	Piel CP.322 Super Emeraude	442	
F-PVDM	Piel CP.618A Super Diamant	59	
F-PVDN	Colomban-Robin CR.100	14	
F-PVDV	Delvion DV Diesel	01	
F-PVET	Van's RV-9A	91684	
F-PVGB	Autogyre PVGB-01	01	
	(Res.)		
F-PVGC	Dyn'Aéro MCR-01 Club	358	
F-PVGD	Van's RV-7	73804	
F-PVGR	WAR FW.190A Replica	368	
F-PVGS	Changeur-Gianinetti Cg-01 gyrocopter	01	
F-PVIB	Jodel D.140C Mousquetaire	457	
F-PVIC	Dyn'Aéro MCR-4S 2002	30	
F-PVIL	Velocity Standard RG	046	
F-PVIN	Stolp SA.750 Acroduster Too	150	
F-PVIO	Cassutt IIIM	540	
F-PVIP	Van's RV-4	730	F-WVIP
F-PVIR	Quercy CQR-01	07	
	(W/o 22.9.10)		
F-PVIT	Beck BK Sut Eleisson	03	
	(W/o 17.7.05)		
F-PVIV	Albouy M5PA/ Revolution Mini 500	01	
F-PVJB	Wittmann W-10 Tailwind	1212	
F-PVJF	Viking Dragonfly Mk 1	1017	
F-PVJM	Piel CP.615C Super Diamant	75	
	(Res.04)		
F-PVLS	Piel CP.320 Super Emeraude	435	
F-PVLT	Notteghem Occitan Club	06	F-WVLT
F-PVMA	Jurca MJ.5L2 Sirocco (Res.97)	113	
F-PVMC	Rutan Cozy	E-747	
F-PVMD	Van's RV-8	83143	
F-PVMG	Van's RV-7	71037	F-WVMG
F-PVMM	Lucas L-8	01	F-WVMM ?
F-PVMR	Dyn'Aéro MCR-01	139	F-WVMR
F-PVMT	Marie JPM-01 Médoc	50	
F-PVNK	Dyn'Aéro MCR-01 Sportster	201	
F-PVOL	Dyn'Aero MCR-4S 2002	108	
F-PVON	Jodel DR.100D	877	
F-PVQB	Delattre/Potez 60 Sauterelle	1	
F-PVQE	Piel CP.310 Emeraude	364	
F-PVQG	Pottier P.70B	01	
F-WVQH	Laboye-Bensen HL-01 Gyrocopter	01, or 2 ?	
F-PVQN	Druine D.5 Turbi	9	
F-PVQP	Jurca MJ.2D Tempête	17	
F-PVQQ	Chatelain AC.11	01	
F-PVQR	Roloff RLU-1 Breezy	FE1/01	
F-PVQT	Heintz Zenith	7	
F-PVQU	Heintz Zenith 130	22MF	
F-PVQV	Heintz Zenith 125 FLR	04	
F-PVQX	Leger JCL 01	1	F-WVQX
	(To 37- . .)		
F-WVQZ	Geiser G-10 Motodelta	01	
F-PVRB	Van's RV-8	83040	
F-PVRJ	Dyn'Aéro MCR-4S 2002	69	
F-PVSG	Dyn'Aéro MCR-4S 2002	25	F-WVSG
F-PVSM	Dyn'Aéro MCR-01	89	F-WJPY
F-PVTB	Van's RV-8	82013	
	(Res.4.05)		
F-PVTZ	Dyn'Aero MCR-01 Sportster	376	
F-PVVA	ACBA-7 Midour	03	
F-PVVP	ACBA-7 Midour	02	
F-PVYN	Jodel D.19T	483-T	
F-WWHG,X,Y	Hélicoptères Guimbal G2 Cabri test marks	-	
F-WWMU	Ameur Avn Altania 120RG	unkn	
	(Damaged 16.7.04)		
F-WWMV	LH-10 Ellipse	001	
	(P.12.07)		
F-WWNA	Murphy Rebel 912	485	
F-WWNB	Murphy Rebel 912	486	
F-WWNO	Sauper ADV.01 Papango	01	
F-WWUU, V	Dyn'Aéro MCR- series temporary registrations	-	
F-WWXZ	ATE Pulsatrix	001	
F-WWXY	Ameur/UCA Carbon Bird CB-200	001	
	(P.11.07)		
F-PXAD	Jodel D.140E Mousquetaire	428	F-WXAD ?
F-PXAK	Jodel D.112 Club	1660	
	(Rebuild of D.11A C-GABH c/n AB.18)		
F-PXAV	BK Sut Eleisson	01	
F-PXDT	Rotorway Exec 162HDF	6842	
F-PXDV	Landray GL.1	01	F-WXDV
F-PXEC	Rotorway Exec 162HDF	6651	
F-PXIV	Van's RV-8	82589	
F-PXJB	Rutan VariEze	1763	
F-PXJJ	Nicollier HN.700 Ménestrel II (Res.02)	172	
F-PXJP	Nicollier HN.700 Ménestrel II	172	(F-PXJJ)?
F-PXKA	Jurca MJ.2F Tempête	8	
	(Cr with F-PXKU 23.5.04)		
F-PXKB	Gatard Statoplan AG-02 Poussin	19	F-WXKB
F-PXKC (2)	Jurca MJ.2A Tempête	42	F-WXKC, (F-PYBR (1))
	(W/o 13.6.99)		
F-PXKE	Mudry CAP.10B	A-1	
F-PXKI	Jurca MJ.5 Sirocco	27	
F-PXKJ	Jodel D.112 Club	1488	
F-PXKK	Croses LC.10 Criquet	01	F-WXKK
F-WXKM	Eysseric F Gyrocopter	01	
	(Res.7.75)		
F-WXKN	Bos AB-01 Gyrocopter	01	
	(Res.7.75)		
F-PXKO	Brügger MB-2 Colibri	46	
F-WXKP	Rigaud RD Gyrocopter	06	
	(Stored, Angers)		
F-PXKQ	Heintz Zenith 90LR	20	F-WXKQ
F-PXKS	Jodel D.92 Bébé	486	
F-WXKT	Averso Epervier XA Gyrocopter	01	
F-PXKU	Jurca MJ.2 Tempête	4	F-WXKU
	(Cr with F-PXKA 23.5.04)		
F-PXKV	Coupe JC-01	001	
F-PXMC	Dyn'Aéro MCR-01	40	
F-PXPY	Junqua RJ-03 Ibis	041	(F-PDPY)
F-PXSM	Jabiru J400	203	
F-PXTA	Stoddard-Hamilton GlaStar GS-1	5719	F-WASK
F-PXVM	Tissot & Charbonnier TC-160 Océanair	06	
F-WXWS	Jabiru	unkn	
F-PXXL	Gatard AG-02 Poussin	35	
	(Res.97)		
F-PXXS	Dyn'Aéro MCR Club	160	
F-PXXX	Heurtevant RH19	01	
	(Res.12.05)		
F-PXYZ	Jurca MJ.2N Tempête	101	
F-PYAE	Jodel D.113V	1026	F-POAE
	(ex D.113, D.119)		
F-PYAF	Jodel D.18	248	
	(Res.)		
F-PYAM	Colomban MC-15 Cri-Cri	513	
F-PYAN(2)	ACVR 1050 J	1	
F-PYAS	Max Plan MP-207 Busard	19	
F-PYAT	Dyn'Aéro MCR-01	92	
F-PYAV	Quercy CQR-01	06	
F-PYBA	Jodel D.92 Bébé	658	
F-PYBB	Gatard AG 04 Pigeon	1	F-WYBB
F-PYBC	Heintz Zenith 100	28	
F-PYBD	Heintz Zenith 100BF	47	
F-PYBE	Lucas L-5	02	F-WYBE
F-PYBH	Piel CP.80	08	
F-PYBJ	Jodel D.119	1517	
F-PYBK	Piel CP.80	12	
F-PYBL	Jodel D.92 Bébé	638	
F-PYBN	Heintz Zenith 105	21	
F-PYBP	Piel CP.80	06	F-WYBP
F-PYBQ	Starck Nickel SN.01	1	F-WYBQ
	(Conversion of Starck AS.37 c/n 14, to La Baule Museum)		
F-PYBR (2)	Heintz Zenith 100MF	5	
F-PYBV	Terrade AT Diamant	01	
	(Jodel derivative built from D.120s F-BHYD and F-BNHK)		
F-PYBX	Jurca MJ.5G1 Sirocco	15	
F-PYBZ	Dyke JD-2 Manta	1239	F-WYBZ
F-PYCA	Dyn'Aéro MCR-4S	126	
F-PYCC	Quercy CQR-01	08	F-WYCC
F-PYCD	Rotorway Exec 162HDF	6461	
F-PYCG	Pottier P.180S	209	F-WYCG
F-PYCL	Colomban MC-100 Banbi	5	
F-PYCR	Dyn'Aéro MCR-01 Sportster	49	
F-WYDA	Megret-Amy ML-02 Gyrocopter	02	
F-WYDB	Ferrer La Darnaga Gyrocopter	01	
F-WYDC	Faure Bensen B.8 JPF Gyrocopter	01	
F-WYDE	Py MP-01 Alouette Gyrocopter	01	
F-WYDF	Chamanier AC-01 Gyrocopter	01	
F-WYDG	Sudres GS PPMB Gyrocopter	01	
F-WYDH	Faure AF-01 Gyrocopter	01	
F-WYDJ	Massemin JM-01 Gyrocopter	01	
F-WYDK	Debout AD-01 Gyrocopter	01	
F-WYDL	Callauzene JC-01 Gyrocopter	01	
F-WYDM	Lapierre Bensen RL-01 Gyroglider	01	
F-WYDN	Clerc JMC-01 Gyrocopter	01	
F-WYDO	Audrouhin AAG Gyrocopter	01, later 3	
F-WYDP	Bastet RB-01 Gyrocopter	01	
F-WYDQ	Bensen B.8MS Gyrocopter	01	
F-WYDR(1)	Lix-01 Gyrocopter	01	
F-PYDR(2)	Dickey E-Racer Mk.1	ER-326	
F-WYDS	Bensen B.8MH Gyrocopter	01	
F-WYDT	Henric CH-01 Gyrocopter	01	
F-WYDU	Bensen AR-01 Gyrocopter	01	
F-WYDV	Schleiss PS-01 Gyrocopter	01	
F-WYDX	Daubian GD-01 Gyrocopter	01	
F-WYDZ	Canville JMC-01 Gyrocopter	01	
F-PYEA	Colomban MC-15 Cri-Cri	4	F-WYEA
	(Formerly MC-11, MC-12B)		
F-PYEB	Pottier P.80S	01	F-WYEB
F-PYEC	Rand-Robinson KR-2	4391	F-WYEC
F-PYEE	Jurca MJ.5H2 Sirocco	35	
F-PYEF	Pottier P.70S	25	F-WYEF
F-PYEG	Heintz Zenith 125	31	
F-PYEI	Evans VP-1 Volksplane	2069	
F-PYEJ	Jurca MJ.5K1 Sirocco	41	
F-WYEN	Mignet HM.293	31	
	(Res.10.77)		
F-PYEP	Jodel D.112 Club	1401	
F-PYEQ	Evans VP-1 Volksplane	V-2251	
	(To museum at Lyon-Corbas)		
F-PYER	Jodel D.119	1434	
	(Marked as D.113)		
F-PYET	Jodel DR.1051M1	700	
F-PYEU	Druine D.31 Turbulent	379	
F-PYEZ	Brügger MB-2 Colibri	100	
	(Accident 30.8.87)		
F-PYFA	Jurca MJ.2 Tempête	29	
F-PYFB	Piel CP.70 Béryl	03	
F-PYFD	Jurca MJ.2D Tempête	52	
F-PYFE	Brügger MB-2 Colibri	88	F-WYFE
F-PYFH	Delaunay JDA-01	01	
	(Res.8.78)		
F-PYFO	Milon PMB-78 Faucon	01	
F-PYFP	Rutan Vari-Viggen SP	072	F-WYFP
F-PYFQ	Max Plan MP.205 Busard	17	
F-PYFR	Jodel D.119	1514	
F-PYFS	Jodel D.92 Bébé	686	
F-PYFT	Croses LC-6 Criquet	72	
F-PYFU	Delemontez-Cauchy DC-01	01	
F-PYFV	Croses LC-6 Criquet	22	
F-PYFX	Jurca MJ.2 Tempête	59	
F-PYFZ	Croses LC-6 Criquet	42	
F-WYGA	Carayon LC-01 Gyrocopter	01	
F-WYGB	Dedieu DF-01 Gyrocopter	01	
F-WYGD	St.Lary ISL-01 Gyrocopter	01	
F-WYGF	Laugier AL-01 Gyroglider	01	
F-WYGH	Audrouhin AAG-01 Gyrocopter	01	
F-WYGI	Daubian GD-02 Roitelet Gyrocopter	01	
F-WYGJ	Bordes RB-01 Gyrocopter	01	
F-WYGK	Odorico RO-01 Eole Gyrocopter	01	
F-WYGL	Bex DB-01 Gyrocopter	01	
F-WYGM	Rodriguez JCR-01 Gyrocopter	01	

Registration	Type	C/n	Prev. reg.
F-WYGO	Durieux MD-01 Gyrocopter	01	
F-WYGP	Bensen B.8MP Gyrocopter	577	
F-WYGQ	Bor BJ-01 Gyrocopter	01	
F-WYGR	Bounery DB-47 Gyrocopter	01	
F-WYGS	Pequignot MP-01 Gyrocopter	01	
F-WYGT	Forich JCF-01 Gyrocopter	01	
F-WYGU	Bensen B.8MP Gyrocopter	01	
F-WYGV	Averso-Loupiac AL-01 Gyrocopter	01	
F-WYGX (2)	Montbazon BLVM-01 Gyrocopter	01	
F-WYGY	Bouchiba JB-01 Gyrocopter	01	
F-WYGZ	Meyrou JBM-01 Gyrocopter	01	(F-WYGX)
F-PYHB	Jurca MJ.5K1 Sirocco	7	
F-PYHI	Croses LC-6 Criquet	23	
F-PYHK	Jurca MJ.2D Tempête	49	
F-PYHM	Piel CP.751 Béryl	4	F-WYHM
F-PYHO	Jodel DR.1051M1 Sicile Record	713	
F-PYHQ	Croses-Noel CN-1	01	
F-PYHR	Rutan VariEze	1991	
	(C/n also quoted for HB-YDE)		
F-PYHS	Rutan VariEze	1697	F-WYHS
F-PYHT	Rutan VariEze	1384	
F-PYHV	Jodel D.119	1573	
F-PYHX	St Germain Raz-Mut	55	
F-PYHY	Jodel D.119-3L	1504	F-WYHY
F-PYHZ	Rutan VariEze	1694	(F-PHYG(1))
F-PYIB	Rutan VariEze	1609	F-WYIB
F-PYIC	Heintz Zenith 100LR	84	
F-PYIE	Piel CP.1320 Saphir	3	F-WYIE
F-PYIF	Mudry CAP.10A	A.2	
F-PYIG	Pottier P.80S	8	
F-PYIH	Heintz Zenith 125	15	
F-PYII	Pottier P.70S	02	F-WYII
F-PYIJ	Colomban MC-15 Cri-Cri (ex MC-12)	14	F-WYIJ
F-PYIK	Pottier P.170S (Wfu)	004	
F-PYIM	Lucas LL-5	1	F-WYIM, F-PYIM, F-WYIM
F-PYIN	Tsilefski TG-01 Malech	01	
F-PYIP	Rutan VariEze	1457	
F-PYIS	Pottier P.70S	32	
F-PYIT	Durable RD-03 Edelweiss 150	1	F-WYIT
F-PYIV	Brügger MB-2 Colibri	107	
F-PYIX	Piel CP.607 Diamant	11	
F-PYIY	Cassutt IIIM	548	
F-PYIZ	Cassutt IIIM	585	
F-PYJA	Croses LC-6 Criquet	75	
F-PYJC	Pottier P.100TS	01	F-WYJC
F-PYJF	Fere F.3	1	
F-PYJG	Jurca MJ.2 Tempête	7W6	
F-PYJI	Dessevres-Coupe JCD	1	F-WYJI
F-PYJJ	Brügger MB-2 Colibri	149	
F-PYJK	Heintz Zenith 120	77	
F-PYJM	Minina MG.2	1	
F-PYJN	Jodel D.119D	1555	
F-PYJO	Rutan VariEze	1775	
F-PYJP	Piel CP.80	51	
F-PYJQ	Nicollier HN.433 Ménestrel	02	
	(cld .93 but current from 2003)		
F-PYJR	Pottier P.80S	23	
F-PYJS	Piel CP.1320 Saphir	14	
F-PYJU	Pottier P.80S	19	
F-PYJV	Brügger MB-2 Colibri (Accident 10.8.03)	114	
F-PYJX	Boyer BF	02	F-WYJX
F-PYJY	Gardan-Laverlochere GL.10	01	
F-PYKA	Nicollier HN.433 Ménestrel	43	F-WYKA
F-PYKB	Brügger MB-2 Colibri	145	
F-PYKC	Jodel D.112 Club	1570	
F-PYKD	Croses LC.6 Criquet	83	
F-PYKK	Piel CP.801 Racer	17	
F-PYKO	Colomban MC-15 Cri-Cri	08	
F-PYKP	Pottier P.70S	011	
F-PYKQ	Rutan VariEze	1989	
F-PYKR	Piel CP.80	15	
F-PYKS	Brügger MB-2 Colibri	66	
F-PYKT	Pottier P.180S	012	F-WYKT
F-PYKU	Jodel DR.1052	704	
F-PYKX	Jodel D.92 Bébé	615	
F-PYLD	Jodel D.113	1574	
F-PYLF	Croses LC.6 Criquet	79	
F-PYLG	Pottier P.170B	012	
	(ex P.170S)		
F-PYLH	Colomban MC-15 Cri-Cri	6	
	(ex MC-12)		
F-PYLJ	Piel CP.80	66	
F-PYLK	Piel CP.70 Beryl	06	F-WYLK
F-PYLL	Jodel D.92 Bébé	713	
F-PYLM	Stark AS-37B	36	
	(Originally c/n '77')		
F-PYLP	Jodel DR.1050M Excellence	718	
F-PYLQ	Jurca MJ5-G2 Sirocco	47	F-WYLQ
F-PYLX	Pottier P.180S	06	
F-PYLY	Rutan VariEze	2043	
F-PYLZ	Pottier P.80S	44	F-WYLZ
F-PYMD	Dyn'Aéro MCR-01C	102	F-WWUU
	(W/o 30.9.07)		
F-PYMI	DH.82A Tiger Moth	"T-3969"	
	(Built from spares in UK originally as film prop")		
F-PYMV	Stern ST-87 Europlane	33	
F-PYNA	Grinvalds G-801ST Orion	28	F-WYNA
F-PYNC	Jodel D.92 Bébé	729	
F-PYND	Cavarroc RC-01 Mini Shinden	01	
	(Res.)		
F-PYNE	Jodel D.92 Bébé	766	
F-PYNH	Brügger MB-2 Colibri	116	
F-PYNJ	Jodel D.18	20	
F-PYNK	Colomban MC-15 Cri-Cri	135	
	(W/o 21.9.91)		
F-PYNL	Jodel D.112 Club	1645	
F-PYNM	Cassutt IIIM	282	
F-PYNN	Colomban MC-15 Cri-Cri	269	
	(W/o 9.10.09)		
F-PYNO	Rutan Long-Ez	1595	
F-PYNP	Jodel D.18	137	
F-PYNQ	Jodel DR.1051M	753	
	(ex DR.1050M)		
F-PYNR	Colomban MC-15 Cri-Cri	262	
F-PYNS	Feugray TR-200	1	
	(Accident 5.6.93)		
F-PYNT	Colomban MC-15 Cri-Cri	47	
F-PYNU	Jodel D.112 Club	1616	
F-PYNY	Piel CP.320A Super Emeraude	412	
F-PYNZ	Pottier P.180S	139	F-WYNZ
F-PYOB	Pottier P.80S	38	
F-PYOC	Collard CSR-1 Tsétsé	01	F-WYOC
F-PYOD	Rutan VariEze	1385	
F-PYOF	Rutan Long-Ez	1047	
F-PYOG	Evans VP-1 Volksplane	V-2589	
F-PYOL	Gros-Bredelet GB-01	01	
F-PYOM	Pottier P.70S	40	
F-PYON	Jodel DR.1050 Ambassadeur	723	
F-PYOP	Rutan VariEze	2042	
F-PYOQ	Rutan Long-Ez	355	F-WYOQ
F-PYOT	Piel CP.320 Super Emeraude	386	
F-PYOU	Jodel D.113	1386	
	(ex D.112)		
F-PYOX	Jodel D.113	1444	
F-PYOY	Heintz Zenith 100	52	
F-PYPB	Pottier P.80S	40	
F-PYPC	Pottier P.180S	36	F-WYPC
F-PYPD	Marquion RM-01 Helicopter	01	
F-PYPE	Courtes JCC-01	1	
F-PYPF	Stolp SA.750 Acroduster Too	359	
F-PYPI	Pottier P.180S	41	F-WYPI
F-PYPJ	Pottier P.180S	51	
F-PYPK	Mudry-Canu CAP.10B	A-4	F-WYPK
	(Built using parts of CAP.10B F-BUDN c/n 46, 1983)		
F-PYPL	Fournier RF-7	02	
F-PYPM	Colomban MC-15 Cri-Cri	20	
F-PYPN	Colomban MC-15 Cri-Cri	74	
F-PYPO	Brügger MB-2 Colibri	87	
	(Now flying as 33-NL)		
F-PYPP	Evans VP-1 Volksplane	2258	F-WYPP
F-PYPR	Jurca MJ.5L2 Sirocco	37	
F-PYPT	Jodel D.119	1563	
F-PYPY	Rutan Long-Ez	1163	F-WYPY
F-PYPZ	Piel CP.605C Diamant	45	
F-PYQA	Stern/Staudt ST-80 Balade	01	
F-PYQC	Proust Lespace Helicopter	001	F-WYQC
F-PYQD	Colomban MC-15 Cri-Cri	177	
F-PYQE	Rutan Long-Ez	809	
F-PYQF	Jodel D.92 Bébé	725	
F-PYQG	Croses LC-6 Criquet	69	
F-PYQI	Pottier P.180S	34	
	(W/o 30.4.90)		
F-PYQJ	Jodel D.112 Club	1521	
F-PYQK	Colomban MC-15 Cri-Cri	46	
F-PYQN (2)	Rutan VariEze	2134	
F-PYQO	Piel CP.605B Super Diamant	21	
F-PYQP	Colomban MC-15 Cri-Cri	10	
F-PYQQ	WAR P-47 Thunderbolt	71	
	(Accident 24.4.99)		
F-PYQS	Lendepergt LP-01 Sibylle	01	
F-PYQT	Quaissard GQ Monogast	01	F-WYQT
F-WYQU	Quickie Q2	01	
	(Res.10.83)		
F-PYQV	Brochet MB-72	9	F-BGTG
F-PYQX	Mignet HM-384	1235	
	(Stored in Pou museum, Marennes)		
F-PYQY	Jodel D.119TK	04	

The following registration batches, suffixed (2), were originally used by ULMs but were re-allocated as shown from 1985 onwards:

Registration	Type	C/n	Prev. reg.
F-WYRA (2)	Bensen-Francois B-PF Gyrocopter	1	
F-WYRB (2)	Averso AAD La Guepe Gyrocopter	01	
F-WYRC (2)	Gros GG-01 Gyrocopter	01	
F-WYRD (2)	Phoenix Gyrocopter	01	
F-WYRE (2)	Lejeune RL Gyrocopter	02	
F-WYRF (2)	Raymond RR-01 Gyrocopter	01	
F-WYRG (2)	Varga VJM-01 Gyrocopter	01	
F-WYRH (2)	Bensen-Germain BG Gyrocopter	1	
F-WYRI (2)	Rameil RF-01 Gyrocopter	01	
F-WYRJ (2)	Rodrigue-Souza SDDS Gyrocopter	001	
F-WYRK (2)	Bensen-SENA CP Gyrocopter	01	
F-WYRL (2)	Roy RJ-01 Gyrocopter	01	
F-WYRM (2)	Santos Marques SM Gyrocopter	1	
F-WYRN (2)	Castagnet SLC-11 Gyrocopter	1	
F-WYRO (2)	Beillard Avril Gyrocopter	001	
F-PYRO(3)	Boufflert B8-1800 Balloon	01	
F-WYRP (2)	Bouchiba JB Gyrocopter	03	
F-WYRQ (2)	Bensen-Ruchonnet B.8M-BR Gyrocopter	1	
F-WYRR (2)	Doleac DJP-01 Space Gyrocopter	01	
F-WYRS (2)	Averso AX Le Guepard Gyrcopter	02	
F-WYRT (2)	Bot BF-2 Gyrocopter	1	
F-WYRU (2)	Fournier FAA Gyrocopter	01	
F-WYRV (2)	Cros CM-01 Gyrocopter	01	
F-WYRX (2)	Dougnac CD-01 Libellule Gyrocopter	01	
F-WYRY (2)	Labit LR Gyrocopter	2	
F-WYRZ (2)	Baudry-Bourgon-Bouchet-Lachaise BBBL	1	
F-PYSA (2)	Piel CP.80	59	
F-PYSB (2)	Parker Teenie Two	5-1203	
F-PYSE (2)	Pottier P.180S	48	
	(Noted damaged/dismantled 8.11)		
F-PYSF (2)	Rutan Long-Ez	1433	
F-PYSG (2)	Brügger MB-2 Colibri	175	
F-PYSH (2)	Colomban MC-15 Cri-Cri	127	
F-PYSJ (2)	Pottier P.80S	50	
F-PYSK (2)	Colomban MC-15 Cri-Cri	336	
F-PYSL (2)	Jurca MJ.5K1 Sirocco	57	
F-PYSM (2)	Rutan VariEze	2048	
F-PYSN (2)	Colomban MC-15 Cri-Cri	65	
F-PYSO (2)	Piel CP.1320D Saphir	18	
F-PYSS (2)	Piel CP.70 Béryl	7	
F-PYST (2)	Pottier P.70S	47	
	(Res.)		
F-PYSU (2)	Jodel D.92 Bébé	746	
F-PYSV (2)	Stolp SA.300 Starduster Too	1677	
F-PYSY (2)	Rutan Long-Ez	1094	
F-PYTA (2)	Mignet HM.8	L-1	F-WYTA
F-PYTB (2)	Sauzeau Eres-II Coquin	01	F-WYTB
F-PYTC (2)	Colomban MC-15 Cri-Cri	104	
F-PYTD (2)	Lucas L-5	4	
F-PYTH (2)	Colomban MC-15 Cri-Cri	156	
F-PYTI (2)	Jodel DR.1050M	762	
	(ex DR.1051M)		

Registration	Type	c/n	Previous identities
F-PYTJ (2)	Descatoire CD-01 Astuss	01	
F-PYTL (2)	Pottier P.80S	48	
F-PYTM (2)	Jodel D.18	9	
	(Accident 18.3.90)		
F-PYTN (2)	Jurca MJ.5K1 Sirocco	92	
F-PYTO (2)	Jodel DR.1050M	745	
F-PYTP (2)	Piel CP.751B Béryl	02	
F-PYTQ (2)	Péna Capena	02	F-WYTQ
F-PYTR (2)	Brügger MB-2 Colibri	115	
F-PYTU (2)	Mudry CAP.10B	A-3	
F-PYTV (2)	Rutan VariEze	2008	F-WYTV
F-PYTX (2)	Colomban MC-15 Cri-Cri	248	
F-PYTY (2)	Colomban MC-15 Cri-Cri	278	
F-PYTZ (2)	Rutan Long-Ez	2117	
F-WYUA	Bensen B.8MJ Gyrocopter	01	
F-WYUB	Franclet PF-01 Gyrocopter	01	
F-WYUC	Soulignac BS-01 Gyrocopter	01	
F-WYUD	Loupiac AL Gyrocopter	02	
F-WYUE	Sers AS-01 Gyrocopter	01	
F-WYUF	Antome Gyrocopter	01	
F-WYUG	Durand Gyrocopter	01	
F-WYUH	Baldy LB-01 Gyrocopter	01	
F-WYUI	Ocon AO-01 Gyrocopter	01	
F-WYUJ	Idrac A-1 Gyrocopter	02	
F-WYUK	Galea BG-01 Gyrocopter	01	
F-WYUL	Jurquet JJ-01 Gyrocopter	01	
F-WYUM	Puente Gyrocopter	01	
F-WYUN	Chrysalide Gyrocopter	01	
F-WYUO	Bonnafous-Chapuis BC-1 Gyrocopter	1	
F-WYUP	Bensen-Paques PB-8 Gyrocopter	1	
F-WYUQ	Doucet DR-01 Gyrocopter	01	
F-WYUR	Bensen Dutoit D8 Gyrocopter	001	
F-WYUS	Bensen-Clisson BC-1 Gyrocopter	01	
F-WYUT	Bensen-Lascombes LG Gyrocopter	1	
F-WYUU	Bensen-Miquel B-CM Gyrocopter	1	
F-WYUV	Bensen B-8 Gyrocopter	8-104100	
	(Same c/n as F-WREF(1))		
F-WYUX	Zago AZ-01 Gyrocopter	01	
F-WYUY	Rives RR-01 Gyrocopter	01	
F-WYUZ	Andre JPA-01 Gyrocopter	001	
F-PYVB (2)	Jodel DR.1053M	765	
	(ex DR.1050M)		
F-PYVC (2)	Piel CP.321 Super Emeraude	400	
F-PYVD (2)	Colomban MC-15 Cri-Cri	16	
F-PYVE (2)	WAR P-47D Thunderbolt	95	F-WYVE
F-PYVG (2)	Jodel D.113 (ex D.112)	1231	
F-PYVH (2)	Rutan Long-Ez	1218	
F-PYVI (2)	K & S Jungster 1	J1-76003R	F-WYVI
F-PYVJ (2)	Verges VJ-01 Gringo	01	
F-PYVK (2)	Colomban MC-15 Cri-Cri	160	
	(Res.86)		
F-PYVL (2)	Pottier P.180S	97	
F-PYVM (2)	Jodel D.19	01	
F-PYVN (2)	Colomban MC-15 Cri-Cri	194	F-WYVN
F-PYVO (2)	Pottier P.180S	46	F-WYVO
F-PYVP (2)	Viking Dragonfly Mk.2	511	
F-PYVS (2)	Adam RA-14 Loisirs	17	F-PGKC
F-PYVT (2)	Jurca MJ.2E Tempête	18	LX-PUT, F-PNUD
F-PYVV (2)	Brügger MB-2 Colibri	104	
F-PYVY (2)	Jodel D.18	06	
	(W/o 1.2.01)		
F-PYVZ (2)	Colomban MC-15 Cri-Cri	400	
	(Res.10.86)		
F-PYXB (2)	Starck AS.71	32R	F-WYXB
F-PYXC (2)	Kreimendahl K-10 Shoestring	054	F-WYXC, "F-WXYC"
F-PYXD (2)	Pottier P.180S	119	
F-PYXE (2)	Nicollier HN.434 Super Ménestrel	1	
F-PYXF (2)	Pottier P.180S	24	
F-PYXG (2)	Colomban MC-15 Cri-Cri	180	
F-PYXH (2)	Jodel DR.1050M	733	
F-PYXJ (2)	Rutan VariEze	2092	
F-PYXK (2)	Jodel D.150-B3 Mascaret	106	
F-PYXM (2)	Rutan Long-Ez	1688	
F-PYXN (2)	Piel CP.320 Super Emeraude	415	
F-PYXO (2)	Piel CP.80	20	
F-PYXP (2)	Jodel D.18	80	
F-PYXQ (2)	Chudzik CC.01	01	F-WYXQ, F-WYRB(1)
	(Stored, 7.05)		
F-PYXS (2)	Heintz Zenith 150 Tri-Z	3-111	F-WYXS
F-PYXT (2)	Viking Dragonfly Mk-3TH	551	
F-PYXU (2)	Jodel DR.1050M	769	
F-PYXX (2)	Jodel D.19	2	
F-PYXY (2)	Colomban MC-15 Cri-Cri	264	F-WYXY
F-PYXZ (2)	Jodel D.92 Bébé	17	
F-PYYA (2)	Coupe-Brault JCFB 01	1	
F-PYYB (2)	Piel CP.80	62	
F-PYYC (2)	Pottier P.180S	91	F-WYYC
	(Wreck noted 9.03)		
F-PYYF (2)	Piel CP.320 Super Emeraude	383	
F-PYYG (2)	Van's RV-4	474	F-WYYG
F-PYYI (2)	Rutan Long-Ez	1575	
F-PYYJ (2)	Colomban MC-15 Cri-Cri	344	
F-PYYK (2)	Colomban MC-15 Cri-Cri	86	
F-PYYL (2)	Jodel D.92 Bébé	645	
F-PYYM (2)	Piel CP.801	72	
F-PYYN (2)	Brügger MB-2 Colibri	228	
F-WYYO (2)	Feugray TR260 Faucon	001-J	
F-PYYP (2)	Jodel D.18	82	
	(Res.8.87. Dismantled)		
F-PYYR (2)	Croses LC-6 Criquet	62	
F-WYYS (2)	HLM-01 Helicopter	01 or 02 ?	
F-PYYT (2)	Viking Dragonfly Mk2	103	F-WYYT
F-PYYY (2)	Druine D.31 Turbulent	356	
F-PYZB (2)	Rutan VariEze	2013	
F-PYZC (2)	Legallois RL	1	
	(Stored .98)		
F-PYZD (2)	Rutan Long-Ez	624	F-WYZD
F-PYZF (2)	Rutan Long-Ez	734	
F-PYZG (2)	Rutan Long-Ez	1703	
	(Accident 16.6.90)		
F-PYZH (2)	Jodel DR.1050M	766	F-WYZH
F-PYZI (2)	Stolp SA.300 Starduster Too	1690	
F-PYZJ (2)	Jodel DR.1050M	764	
F-PYZK (2)	Minina MG.3 Harmattan	001	
F-PYZL (2)	Pottier P.180S	66	F-WYZL
F-PYZO (2)	Viking Dragonfly Mk.2	1007	
F-PYZP (2)	Jodel D.119V	1569	
F-PYZR (2)	Brugger MB.2 Colibri	168	
F-PYZS (2)	Piel CP.80	18	
F-PYZT (2)	Chaboud CJC-01	01	
F-PYZU (2)	Rutan VariEze	1850	
F-PYZX (2)	Pottier P.80S	57	
F-PYZY (2)	Pottier P.180S	67	
F-PZAC	Nord NC.859S	04	F-WZAC, F-BDYO
F-PZAG	Jurca MJ.2H Tempête	30	
F-PZAM	Dyn'Aéro MCR-01 Sportster	193	F-WWUY
F-PZAR	Darcissac-Grinvalds DG-87 Goëland	04	
	(Abandonned .02))		
F-PZAV	Van's RV-4	4238	
F-PZAZ	Piel CP.320 Super Emeraude (Damaged)	454	
F-WZBC (3)	SOFCA Paramoteur Agrion	0001	
F-WZBD (3)	SOFCA Paramoteur Agrion	1	
F-WZBG (2)	SOFCA Paramoteur Agrion	002	
F-WZBH (2)	SOGCA Paramoteur Agrion	003	
F-PZBM	Colomban MC-15 Cri-Cri	429	F-WZBM
F-PZBO	Piel CP.1321 Saphir	24	
F-PZBP	Jodel D.113	1161	
F-PZBQ	Jodel D.119T	05-A	F-WZBQ, (F-PART)
F-PZBR	De La Calle CRT-01 Amphibian	01	F-WZBR
F-PZBS	Colomban MC-15 Cri-Cri	417	
F-PZBT	Pottier P.180S	44	
F-WZBU	Feugray (Tech/Aero) TR.300 (Res.)	3	
F-PZBV	Rutan VariEze	1939	F-WZBV
F-PZBX	Rutan Long-Ez	1565	F-WZBX
F-PZBY	Jodel DR.1053M	746	
F-PZBZ	Jodel D.18	183	
	(W/o 21.6.03, wreck noted 9.03)		
F-PZCH	Zenair CH-640 Zodiac	105	
F-PZCR	Rohrer RC-01	01	
	(Res.9.05)		
F-PZDR	Dyn'Aero MCR-01 Sportster	215	LX-JJH
F-WZEA	Borel JPB-30 Gyrocopter	01	
F-WZEB	Mompo AM-01 Gyrocopter	01	
F-WZEC	Le Bauzec Moustique Gyrocopter	01	
F-WZED	Combon-Bonnafous BCGyrocopter	02	
F-WZEE	Averso Train'Air XA-03 Gyrocopter	03	
F-WZEF	Doleac DJP-2 Gyrocopter	01	
F-WZEG	Revol RG Gyrocopter	01	
F-WZEH	Savez SGB Gyrocopter	01	
F-WZEI	Cobra Gyrocopter	01	
F-WZEJ	Verdan VG-1 Gyrocopter	01	
F-WZEK	Domme JD Gyrocopter	01	
F-WZEL	Naja Gyrocopter	01	
F-WZEM	Poma Gyrocopter	001	
F-WZEN	Moustic Gyrocopter	01	
F-WZEO	Strupp Gyrocopter	01	
F-WZEP	Lix Condor Gyrocopter	002	
F-WZEQ	Durant DJL Gyrocopter	03	
F-WZER	Chanet JCC.2000 Gyrocopter	1	
F-WZES	Gregnanin GE Gyrocopter	01	
F-WZET	Franck Gyrocopter	001	
F-WZEU	Mono 87 Gyrocopter	001	
F-WZEV	HRP Gyrocopter	01	
F-WZEX	Stuani SR-1 Gyrocopter	01	
F-WZEY	Weinbrenner JW Gyrocopter	03	
F-WZEZ	Bouche BB Gyrocopter	01	
F-PZGL	Valladeau RV-12	01	
	(Polikarpov 1-15 replica)		
F-WZGM	Carro- Rutan Quickie 1	C-1	
	(Res.)		
F-PZGN	Wittmann W.8 Tailwind	622	
F-PZGO	Colomban MC-15 Cri-Cri	207	
F-PZGP	Pottier P.180S	159	
F-PZGQ	Adam RA-14 Loisirs	132	F-PAHD
F-PZGR	Jodel D.112 Club	1678	
F-PZGS	Pottier P.180S	161	F-WZGS
F-PZGT	Loriot DG-01	01	
F-PZGU	Brändli BX-2 Cherry	58	
	(Res.)		
F-PZGV	Chasle YC-320	001	
	(Res.)		
F-PZGX	Rand-Robinson KR-2	7975	
F-PZGZ	Denize RD.205 Raid Driver	2	
F-WZHA	AB-53 Gyrocopter	0	
F-WZHB	Averso AX-02 Gyrocopter	17	
F-WZHC	Averso AX-02 Gyrocopter	19	
F-WZHD	Pouilles GP Gyrocopter	01	
F-WZHE	Hoffmann VHB-1 Gyrocopter	01	
F-WZHF	Huvier HR-1 Gyrocopter	02-M	
F-WZHG	AU SR Gyrocopter	01	
F-WZHH	Vandenbulke VG-1 Gyrocopter	01	
F-WZHI	Faucher PF-1 Gyrocopter	001	
F-WZHJ	Darrozes MD Gyrocopter	01	
F-WZHK	Le Bigourdin Gyrocopter	1	
F-WZHL	Colibri Gyrocopter	01	
F-WZHM	Bensen-Vandamme B-VG Gyrocopter	01	
F-WZHN	Tessier YT-1 Gyrocopter	2	
F-WZHO	Revol GR Gyrocopter	02	
F-PZHP (2)	Zenith 100LR-F-M	81	
F-WZHQ	Bonnafous BC-2 Gyrocopter	02	
F-WZHR	Krauss BK-1 Gyrocopter	1	
F-WZHS	Krauss GK-1	1	
F-WZHT	Averso AX-02 Gyrocopter	18	
F-WZHU	JF-1 Gyrocopter	01	
F-WZHV	Aubert AJL-2 Gyrocopter	001	
F-WZHX	Courgey HC-1 Gyrocopter	001	
F-WZHY	Ingrassia IS-1 Gyrocopter	1	
F-PZHZ	Mercier IX Gyrocopter	01	F-WZHZ
F-WZID	2CV'Eau Volante	unkn	
	(To museum, 2.01)		
F-PZIG	Jurca MJ.2P Tempête	28	
	(Res.)		
F-PZII	Evans VP-1 Volksplane	V-1583	F-PZIT
F-PZIK	Desjardins D-01 Ibis	01	F-WZIK
F-PZIL	Piel CP.605B Super Diamant	48	
F-PZIM	Croses LC-6 Criquet	97	
F-PZIO	Croses LC-10 Criquet	32	
F-PZIP	Piel CP.803	70	
F-PZIQ	Colomban MC-15 Cri-Cri	282	F-WZIQ
F-PZIU	Pottier PRM.180	045	
F-WZJF	Marmande Aero Microjet 200	01	

Registration	Type	c/n	Previous/Other
F-WZJG	Auricoste AA-01 Gyrocopter	unkn	
	(Regn reported on Flight Design CT LS,c/n F-10-07-07, 2015)		
F-PZLD	Salis AJBS 10 (Modified CAP 10)	01	F-WZLD
F-WZLH (3)	Rotorway Executive	938	
F-WZLI (3)	Geiser Zeppy Airship	01	
F-PZLJ	Jodel D.112 Club	125	F-PKMM
F-PZLL	Constantini STC-1 Magic	1	
F-PZLM	Serleg 225EX Amphibian	001	F-WZLM
F-WZLN (2)	Lanot Aquitain	003	
F-WZLP (2)	Lanot Aquitain	002	
F-WZLS (4)	Grillon 120	01	(F-GESP)
F-WZLU	Gardan GY-120 Microlight	001	
F-WZLY	Hornet S-10	unkn	
F-WZLZ	Loravia ULI-2	01	
F-PZMA	Heintz Zenith 90	2123	
	(Regd as Zenith 100CP)		
F-PZMB	Jodel D.92 Bébé	730	
F-PZMC	Gatard AG-02 Poussin	34	
	(Res.)		
F-PZMD	Pottier P.180S	47	
F-PZMF	Colomban MC-15 Cri-Cri	51	
F-WZMG	Rutan Defiant	119	
	(Res.)		
F-PZMH	Pottier P.180S	144	F-WZMH
	(Wfu)		
F-PZMK	Dedon- Rutan Quickie 2	02-F	
F-PZML	Colomban MC-15 Cri-Cri	440	
F-PZMM	Rutan VariEze	1847	
	(Res., ex OO-104?)		
F-PZMN	Colomban MC-15 Cri-Cri	68	
F-PZMO	Kieger AK-01	01	
F-PZMP	Grinvalds G-801 Orion	9	
	(Accident)		
F-PZMQ	Taylor JT.2 Titch	108	
F-PZMR	Colomban MC-100 Banbi	83	F-GUMR
F-PZMT	Rutan Long-Ez	7801	
F-PZMV	Nicollier HN.700 Ménestrel II	001	
F-WZNL	Capdevielle CPCL Gyrocopter	1	
F-WZNM	Sudre SRE Gyrocopter	01	
F-WZNN	Guillaume DG Gyrocopter	01	
F-WZNO	Darmanne Gyrocopter	01	
F-WZNP	Fournier FAA Gyrocopter	02	
F-WZNQ	GG-200 Gyrocopter	01	
F-WZNR	Averso AX-02 Gyrocopter	8	
F-WZNS	Lambour-Deudon LLD Gyrocopter	1	
F-WZNT	Duhamel-Greaux-Huber DGH-01 Gyrocopter	01	
F-WZNU	Duhamel-Greaux-Huber DGH-02 Gyrocopter	01	
F-PZNV(2)	Nicollier HN. (Noted 7.01)	unkn	
F-WZNX	Coqu Bensen B-8 Gyrocopter	C-1	
F-WZNY	Averso AX-02 Gyrocopter	10	
F-WZNZ	Averso AX-02 Gyrocopter	11	
F-WZOA (2)	Hard HP Gyrocopter	01	
F-PZOB (1)	Le Ventilateur ULM	01	
	(Presumed cancelled?)		
F-PZOB (2)	Van's RV-4 (Res.)	3091	
F-WZOC (2)	Mono LG Gyrocopter	01	
F-WZOD (2)	Blandy AB-1 Gyrocopter	01	
F-WZOE (2)	Lejeune RL-2 Gyrocopter	03	
F-WZOF (2)	HIR-1 Gyrocopter	01	
F-WZOG (2)	Bluebird Gyrocopter	01	
F-WZOH (2)	Deluc Redbird Gyrocopter	01	
F-WZOI (2)	Averso AX-02 Gyrocopter	1	
F-WZOJ (2)	Bensen B-8JLG Gyrocopter	1	
	(W/o 27.1.91?)		
F-WZOK (2)	HTV Gyrocopter	2	
F-WZOL (2)	Liberty Gyrocopter	01	
F-WZOM (2)	Cena CP-02 Gyrocopter	1	
F-WZON (2)	Averso AX-02 Gyrocopter	2	
F-WZOO (2)	Beart JMB-1 Gyrocopter	01	
F-WZOP (2)	Averso AX-02 Gyrocopter	4	
F-WZOQ (2)	Gil Gyrocopter	01	
F-WZOT (2)	Cros CM-2 Gyrocopter	02	
F-WZOU (2)	Chevallot Bensen B-8	CD-01	
F-WZOV (2)	Bourgue BP-01 Gyrocopter	01	
F-WZOY (2)	Barbier CB Gyrocopter	01	
F-WZOZ (2)	Averso AX-02 Gyrocopter	5	
F-PZPA (2)	Chambon-Koenig CK-01 Profil	001	F-WZPA
F-PZPE (2)	Kreimendahl K-10 Shoestring	48	F-WZPE
F-PZPF (2)	Colomban MC-15 Cri-Cri	84	
F-PZPG (2)	Jodel D.112 Club	767	F-PCDV
F-PZPH (2)	Pottier P.180S	99	
	(Accident 31.12.89)		
F-PZPI (2)	Pottier P.180S	25	
F-PZPJ (2)	Brügger MB-2 Colibri	172	
F-PZPK (2)	Colomban MC-15 Cri-Cri	81	
F-PZPM (2)	Dopouridis DV.219 (Jodel variant)	01	F-WZPM
F-PZPN (2)	Rutan Long-Ez	2115	
F-PZPO (2)	Jurca MJ.7 Gnatsum	2	F-WZPO
F-PZPQ (2)	Daurelle AD-01	01	
F-PZPR (2)	Colomban MC-15 Cri-Cri	306	
F-PZPS (2)	Jodel D.18	124	
F-PZPT (2)	Jodel DR.100 Ambassadeur	763	
F-PZPV (2)	Pottier P.180S	32	F-WZPV
F-PZPY (2)	Croses LC-6 Criquet	59	
F-WZQA (2)	Bernardeau Bensen B-8B Gyrocopter	B-1	
F-WZQB (2)	Portal-Revertegat HRP Gyrocopter	02	
F-WZQC (2)	Averso AX-02 Gyrocopter	6	
F-WZQD (2)	Bourdon B-2 Gyrocopter	01	
F-WZQE (2)	Sanchez SB-01 Gyrocopter	1	
F-WZQF (2)	Baldy LB-02 Gyrocopter	1	
F-WZQG (2)	Bastien BH-2 Gyrocopter	01	
F-WZQH (2)	Doleac Aircopter DJP Max	03	
F-WZQI (2)	Tenneguin TT-01 Gyrocopter	01	
F-WZQK (2)	Lettinger LC Gyrocopter	01	
F-WZQL (2)	Passot MP-02 Morgon Gyrocopter	2	
F-WZQM (2)	Averso AX-04 Le Guépard Gyrocopter	01	
F-WZQN (2)	Averso AX-05 Léopard Gyrocopter	01	
F-WZQO (2)	Phénix Gyrocopter	SC-01	
F-WZQP (2)	Romero JR-1 Gyrocopter	001	
F-WZQQ (2)	Kraetter AK Gyrocopter	1	
F-WZQR (2)	Tenneguin TT-02 Gyrocopter	01	
F-WZQS (2)	Bourgues BP-02 Gyrocopter	1	
F-WZQT (2)	Fortunato ERF Gyrocopter	01	
F-WZQU (2)	Averso AX-02 Gyrocopter	7	
F-WZQV (2)	Pate NP-001 Gyrocopter	001	
F-WZQX (2)	Bond Gyrocopter	007	
F-WZQY (2)	Mousticq Gyrocopter	01	
F-WZQZ (2)	Bensen B-8 Gyrocopter	104-V1	
F-PZRC	Brügger MB-2 Colibri	51	
F-PZRF	Jodel D.112 Club	1602	
F-PZRH	Croise AC-1 (1/2 scale Spitfire)	01	
F-PZRJ	Christen Eagle II	01	
F-PZRM	Brügger MB-2 Colibri	108	
F-PZRN	Pottier P.80S	015	
F-PZRO	Pottier P.180S	77	
F-PZRP	Rutan Long-Ez	621	
F-PZRQ	Lucas L-5	24	F-WZRQ
F-PZRR	Croses LC-6 Criquet	104	
F-PZRT	Jodel DR.1050M	721	
	(Res.)		
F-PZRU	Rutan VariEze	1843	
F-PZRX	Rutan Long-Ez	2114	
F-PZRY	Albarde Ruty	01	F-WZRY
	(Stored .06)		
F-PZRZ	Evans VP-2 Volksplane	2201	
F-PZSF (2)	Pottier P.80S	28	
F-PZSH (2)	Jodel D.112 Club	453	
F-PZSI (2)	Max Plan MP-207 Busard	20	F-WZSI
F-WZSK (2)	Quenaud 50	01	
F-PZSL (2)	Colomban MC-15 Cri-Cri	270	
F-PZSM (2)	Jodel DR.1053M Sicile Record	737	
F-PZSN (2)	Colomban MC-15 Cri-Cri	25	
F-PZSP (2)	Colomban MC-15 Cri-Cri	39	
F-PZSS (2)	Brügger MB-2 Colibri	85	
F-PZSV (2)	Jodel DR.100A	754	
F-WZSX (2)	Averso Guepard gyrocopter	unkn	
F-PZSZ (2)	Pottier P.80S	58	
F-PZTB (2)	Jodel DR.1050M1 Sicile Record	744	
F-PZTC (2)	Péna Capena (Modified CAP-20)	01	F-WZTC
F-PZTD (2)	Colomban MC-15 Cri-Cri	64	F-WZTD
F-PZTE (2)	Jurca MJ.2E Tempête	43	
F-PZTF (2)	Pottier P.70S	49	
F-PZTG (2)	Colomban MC-15 Cri-Cri	113	
F-PZTI (2)	Colomban MC-15 Cri-Cri	63	
F-PZTL (2)	Piel CP.320A Super Emeraude	382	
F-PZTM (2)	Rutan VariEze	277	
	(Res.)		
F-PZTN (2)	Pottier P.80SR	14	F-WZTN
F-PZTO (2)	Colomban MC-15 Cri-Cri	85	
F-PZTP (2)	Colomban MC-15 Cri-Cri	66	
F-PZTQ (2)	Taylor JT-2 Titch Mk.3	CB-5	
F-PZTR (2)	Colomban MC-15 Cri-Cri	121	
F-PZTS (2)	Evans VP-2 Volksplane	V2-1521	F-WZTS
F-PZTT (2)	Watson Windwagon	JW-573	F-WZTT
F-PZTU (2)	Colomban MC-15 Cri-Cri (electric)	27	F-WZTU, F-PZTU
F-PZTV (2)	Pottier P.180S	42	
F-PZTY (2)	Pottier P.70S	28	
F-WZUA (2)	Light Aero Avid Flyer	CP84-1	
F-WZUB (2)	Light Aero Avid Flyer	263	
F-WZUE (2)	Janowski J-5 Marco	F-2	
F-WZUF (2)	Light Aero Avid Amphibian	24	
	(Now 37-QV?)		
F-WZUG (2)	Light Aero Avid Flyer	327	
F-WZUH (2)	Light Aero Avid Flyer	422	
F-WZUI (2)	Light Aero Avid Amphibian	25	
F-WZUJ (2)	Janowski J-5 Marco	6	
F-WZUK (2)	Light Aero Avid Flyer	323	
F-PZUL (2)	Janowski J-5 Marco	8	F-WZUL
F-WZUN (2)	Light Aero Avid Flyer	541	
F-WZUO (2)	Light Aero Avid Flyer	538	
F-WZUP (2)	Light Aero Avid Flyer	421	
F-WZUQ (2)	Light Aero Avid Flyer	473	
F-WZUR (2)	Light Aero Avid Flyer	471	
F-WZUS (2)	Light Aero Avid Flyer	542	
F-WZUT (2)	Light Aero Avid Flyer	424	
F-WZUU (2)	Light Aero Avid Flyer	319	
	(To S5-NAG, 9A-UVK ?)		
F-PZUV	Light Aero Avid Flyer	475	F-WZUV(2)
F-PZUY	Light Aero Avid Flyer	647	F-WZUY(2)
F-WZUZ (2)	Light Aero Avid Flyer	694	
F-WZVA (2)	Bensen GGMS Gyrocopter	01	
F-WZVB (2)	Sicard JMS-01 Gyrocopter	01	
F-WZVC (2)	Onyx Gyrocopter	01	
F-WZVD (2)	Hernando FH-1 Gyrocopter	1	
F-WZVE (2)	Condomine YC-2 Gyrocopter	1	
F-WZVF (2)	Mouchel BM-01 Gyrocopter	01	
F-WZVG (2)	Cauchy CM-01 Gyrocopter	01	
F-WZVH (2)	Flip Gyrocopter	1	
F-WZVI (2)	Hostein AH-01 Gyrocopter	01	
F-WZVJ (2)	Laboye-Meygret LMN-1 Gyrocopter	01	
F-WZVK (2)	Viala HTV Gyrocopter	1	
F-WZVL (2)	Bouchiba JB Gyrocopter	2	
F-WZVM (2)	Mace MA-01 Gyrocopter	01	
F-WZVN (2)	Proust DP-3 Gyrocopter	1	
F-WZVO (2)	Odorico OR-02 Gyrocopter	02	
F-WZVP (2)	Beaudoin GB-01 Beaugiro	01	
F-WZVQ (2)	Zamponi CZ-01 Gyrocopter (Wrecked)	01	
F-WZVR (2)	Pascal JP-01 Gyrocopter	01	
F-WZVS (2)	Seidner AS-100 Gyrocopter	01	
F-WZVT (2)	Passot MP-01 Gyrocopter	1	
F-WZVU (2)	Lejeune RL-01 Gyrocopter	01	
F-WZVV (2)	Lambelin- Bensen BML Gyrocopter	001	
F-WZVX (2)	Desauge-Bensen JD Gyrocopter	01	
F-WZVY (2)	Oudoul GO Gyrocopter	1	
F-WZVZ (2)	Dumon B-RD Gyrocopter	1	
F-PZXD (2)	ACBA-4 Pipit Véloce	01	
F-PZXE (2)	Croses EC-7 Tous Terrains	01	F-PPPM
	(Res.)		
F-PZXF (2)	Jodel D.119T	1562	
F-PZXH (2)	Nicollier HN.434 Super Ménestrel	36	
F-PZXI (2)	Lucas L-5	28	F-WZXI
F-PZXJ (2)	Colomban MC-15 Cri-Cri	268	F-WZXJ
F-PZXK (2)	Rutan Cozy	310	
F-PZXM (2)	Colomban MC-15 Cri-Cri	443	
F-PZXN (2)	Pottier P.180S	88	F-WZXN
	(W/o 16.9.12)		
F-PZXO (2)	Jodel D.18	07	
F-PZXQ (2)	Rutan VariEze	2200	
F-PZXT (2)	Descubes III	01	
F-PZXU (2)	Colomban MC-15 Cri-Cri	352	
F-PZXV (2)	Colomban MC-15 Cri-Cri	247	
F-WZXX (2)	Dirigeable DIPA Aeromodelisme Balloon	unkn	

F-WZXY (2)	Dirigeable DIPA Aeromodelisme Balloon	unkn	
F-PZXZ (2)	Viking Dragonfly Mk.2 (SB-2)	771	
F-WZYA	Portespane DP Requin Blanc Gyrocopter	01	
F-PZYB	Averso AX-02 Guepard Gyrocopter	09	F-WZYB
F-WZYC	Deluc MD-2 Black Panther Gyrocopter	01	
F-WZYE	Carletti Bensen B-8AC Gyrocopter	01	
F-WZYF	Casset RC-01 Gyrocopter	01	
F-WZYG	Lagarde AL-01 Gyrocopter	01	
F-WZYH	Laboye-Bensen B-8LH Gyrocopter	006	
F-WZYI	CD Gyrocopter	01	
F-WZYJ	Averso AX-02 Gyrocopter	12	
F-PZYK	Jodel DR.1054M (ex DR.1051, tricycle u/c)	757-13A	
F-WZYL	Telegoni ATM-01 Gyrocopter	1	
F-WZYM	Meygret CHM-2 Gyrocopter	01	
F-WZYN	Fuertes JF-1 Gyrocopter	1	
F-WZYO	Gerard- Bensen G-800MV Gyrocopter	GR-01	
F-WZYP	Averso AX-02 Gyrocopter	13	
F-WZYQ	Averso AX-02 Gyrocopter	14	
F-WZYR	Averso AX-02 Gyrocopter	15	
F-WZYS	Benoit L-1 Gyrocopter	1	
F-WZYT	Arnould JPA-001 Gyrocopter	001	
F-WZYU	Averso AX-02 Gyrocopter	16	
F-WZYV	Rabillard CR-1 Gyrocopter	01	
F-WZYX	Duhamel-Greaux-Hubert DGH-03 Gyrocopter	01	
F-WZYY	Paraire PG Gyrocopter	01	
F-WZYZ	Arnaud AR-1 Gyrocopter	01	
F-PZZE	WagAero Sport Trainer (Painted as Cub "43-29877")	4145	
F-PZZM	Jodel D.18	216	
F-PZZO	Brändli BX-2 Cherry	28	F-WZZO
F-PZZP	Jodel D.18	141	
F-PZZQ	Jurca MJ.5 Sirocco	46	
F-PZZR	Lannier LA Bengali (Res.)	01	
F-PZZS	Colomban MC-15 Cri-Cri (Res.)	94	F-WZZS
F-PZZZ	Neico Lancair 320	400	F-WZZZ

GOVERNMENT-OPERATED AIRCRAFT:

- SECURITÉ CIVILE, FIRE SERVICE AND CUSTOMS

F-ZBAA (4)	Conair Turbo-Firecat (Code "22") (Grumman US-2B Tracker conversion)	456/027	F-WEOL, C-FQCW, F-WEOL, F-ZBAA(4)/T.14, F-WEOL, C-GYQN, BuA136547
F-ZBAB (3)	Reims/Cessna F406 Vigilant	F406-0025	F-GEUL, F-WZDV
F-ZBAD (3)	Aérospatiale AS.355F2 Ecureuil 2	5156	N5796A
F-ZBAN (2)	SNCASE SE.316B Alouette III (Donated to Musée de l'Air, Paris 5.09)	1115	F-RAFQ
F-ZBAP (3)	Conair Turbo Firecat (Code "12") (Grumman US-2BTracker conversion)	567/026	F-ZBDA, F-WEOK, C-FOKN, F-WEOK, F-ZBDA/T.12, F-WEOK, C-GYQS, BuA136658
F-ZBAR (3)	Canadair CL.215 1A-10 (Code "21") (To Speyer Museum)	1021	
F-ZBAU (2)	Conair Firecat (Code "02") (Grumman CS-2F1 Tracker conversion)	DH-32/009	F-WZLQ, C-FOPW, CF-OPW, RCN1533
F-ZBAW(2)	Sud Avn SA.316B Alouette III	2306	
F-ZBAY (2)	Canadair CL.215 1A-10 (Code "23") (To Musée de l'Air, Paris)	1023	
F-ZBAZ (2)	Conair Turbo Firecat (Code "01") (Grumman CS-2F1 Tracker conversion) (Damaged 19.9.98, repair under consideration)	DH-57/008	F-WEOL, C-FVPK, F-WEOL, F-ZBAZ/T.01, F-WZLS, (F-WZLR), C-FOPZ, CF-OPZ, RCN1558
F-ZBBB (2)	Reims/Cessna F406 Vigilant	F406-0039	F-WZDS
F-ZBBH	Canadair CL.215 1A-10 (Code "26") (To Sinsheim Museum)	1021	
F-ZBBV	Canadair CL.215 1A-10 (Code "46") (Static)	1046	C-GAOS
F-ZBCE	Reims/Cessna F406 Vigilant	F406-0042	F-GKRA, F-WKRA, F-GKRA
F-ZBCF	Reims/Cessna F406 SurMar	F406-0077	F-WZDZ
F-ZBCG	Reims/Cessna F406 PolMar II	F406-0066	F-WZDT
F-ZBCH	Reims/Cessna F406 SurMar	F406-0075	
F-ZBCI	Reims/Cessna F406 Vigilant	F406-0070	
F-ZBCJ	Reims/Cessna F406 Vigilant	F406-0074	F-WZDJ
F-ZBCZ	Conair Turbo Firecat (Code "23") (Grumman CS2F-3 Tracker conversion)	DH-94/036	F-ZBCA, (F-ZBBF), C-FKUF, CAF12195, RCN1595
F-ZBDE	SNCASE SE.3160 Alouette III	1630	FAP9331
F-ZBDI	Sud Avn SA.316B Alouette III (Preserved?)	1878	FAP9388
F-ZBDJ	Sud Avn SA.316B Alouette III	1879	FAP9389
F-ZBEF	Aérospatiale AS.355F2 Ecureuil 2	5236	
F-ZBEG (2)	Canadair CL.415 6B-11 (Code "39")	2015	C-FXBH
F-ZBEH (2)	Conair Turbo Firecat (Code "20") (Grumman US-2A Tracker conversion)	410/035	F-WEOJ, C-FCAD, N435DF, BuA136501
F-ZBEK	Aérospatiale AS.355F2 Ecureuil 2	5298	
F-ZBEL	Aérospatiale AS.355F2 Ecureuil 2	5299	ALAT
F-ZBEP	Reims/Cessna F406 Vigilant	F406-0006	
F-ZBES	Reims/Cessna F406 Vigilant	F406-0017	
F-ZBET	Conair Turbo Firecat (Code "15") (Grumman US-2A Tracker conversion)	703/028	F-WEOJ(3), C-GHYH, F-ZBET/T.15, F-WEOJ, C-GHYH, BuA147559
F-ZBEU (2)	Canadair CL..4156B-11 (Code "42")	2024	C-FZDE
F-ZBEW	Conair Turbo Firecat (Code "11") (Grumman US-2B Tracker conversion)	621/025	F-WEOL, C-FSPK, F-WEOL, F-ZBEW/T.11, F-WEOJ, C-GYQY, BuA136712
F-ZBEY	Conair Turbo Firecat (Code "07") (Grumman US-2A Tracker conversion)	400/017	C-FYHB, F-WEOK, F-ZBEY/T.7, F-WDQD, C-GRXU, BuA136491
F-ZBFA	Reims/Cessna F406 PolMar I	F406-001	F-GGRA(2), F-GGAN, F-GFLT, F-WZLT
F-ZBFE	Conair Turbo Firecat (Code "17") (Grumman US-2A Tracker conversion)	656/032	F-WEOK(3), C-FFQM, N437DF, BuA136747
F-ZBFJ	Beech B200 Super King Air (Code "98")	BB-1102	(F-GKDO), D-IWAN, HB-GHI, N147D
F-ZBFK	Beech B200 Super King Air (Code "96")	BB-876	F-GHSC, N52BC
F-ZBFM	SNCASE SE.316B Alouette III	1280	ALAT
F-ZBFN	Canadair CL.415 6B-11 (Code "33")	2006	C-FVUK
F-ZBFP	Canadair CL.415 6B-11 (Code "31")	2002	C-FBET
F-ZBFS	Canadair CL.415 6B-11 (Code "32")	2001	C-GSCT
F-ZBFV	Canadair CL.415 6B-11 (Code "37")	2013	C-FWPE
F-ZBFW	Canadair CL.415 6B-11 (Code "38")	2014	C-FWZH
F-ZBFX	Canadair CL.415 6B-11 (Code "34")	2007	C-FVUJ
F-ZBFY	Canadair CL.415 6B-11 (Code "35")	2010	C-FVDY
F-ZBGA	Reims/Cessna F406 SurMar	F406-0086	F-WWSR
F-ZBGB	Cessna T206H Turbo Stationair	T20608446	F-GXRH, N2107Q
F-ZBGC	Cessna T206H Turbo Stationair	T20608445	F-GXRG, N2106R
F-ZBGD	Reims/Cessna F406 PolMar III	F406-0090	F-WWNP, (F-ZBGB)
F-ZBGE	Reims/Cessna F406 Caravan II	F406-0061	F-GRAI, N406CT, F-GURA, F-OGVS, N3121X
F-ZBGF	Eurocopter EC.135T2+	0507	D-HFCJ(2), D-HECF
F-ZBGG	Eurocopter EC.135T2+	0510	D-HFCK(2), D-HECD
F-ZBGH	Eurocopter EC.135T2+	0525	D-HECC
F-ZBGI	Eurocopter EC.135T2+	0545	D-HECO
F-ZBGJ	Eurocopter EC.135T2+	0551	D-HECG
F-ZBGK	Beech B300 King Air 350	FL-682	F-WTAE, N6382F
F-ZBGL	Beech B300 King Air 350	FL-746	N80946
F-ZBGM	Beech B300 King Air 350	FL-752	N81452
F-ZBGN	Beech B300 King Air 350	FL-781	N8061E
F-ZBGO	Beech B300 King Air 350	FL-800	N8150M
F-ZBGP	Beech B300 King Air 350	FL-802	N8049J
F-ZBMA	Conair Turbo Firecat (Code "24") (Grumman US-2B Tracker conversion)	461/021	C-GFZG, F-ZBEX, F-WEOL, F-ZBEX/T.9, F-WDSX(2), C-GQCW, N4477Z, BuA136552
F-ZBMB	Beech B200 Super King Air (Code "97")	BB-1379	F-GJFD
F-ZBMC	Bombardier DHC-8 Srs 402 (Code "73")	4040	C-FBAM, N532DS, LN-RDW, N384BC, C-FDHZ
F-ZBMD	Bombardier DHC-8 Srs 402 (Code "74")	4043	C-FBSG, N535DS, LN-RDN, C-FWBB
F-ZBME	Canadair CL-415-6B-11 (Code "44")	2057	C-GILN
F-ZBMF	Canadair CL-415-6B-11 (Code "45")	2063	C-FGZT
F-ZBMG	Canadair CL-415-6B-11 (Code "48")	2065	C-FLFW
F-ZBPA	MBB-Kawasaki BK.117C-2/ EC.145	9006	D-HMBJ, D-HJFA
F-ZBPD	MBB-Kawasaki BK.117C-2/ EC.145	9010	D-HJFE
F-ZBPE	MBB-Kawasaki BK.117C-2/ EC.145	9011	D-HJFF(3)
F-ZBPF	MBB-Kawasaki BK.117C-2/ EC.145	9012	D-HJFG
F-ZBPG	MBB-Kawasaki BK.117C-2/ EC.145	9013	D-HADY(2), F-ZBPG, D-HJFH
F-ZBPH	MBB-Kawasaki BK.117C-2/ EC.145	9015	D-HMBU, D-HJFJ
F-ZBPI	MBB-Kawasaki BK.117C-2/ EC.145	9016	D-HJFK
F-ZBPJ	MBB-Kawasaki BK.117C-2/ EC.145	9017	D-HJFL, D-HMBA(11), F-ZBPJ, D-HJFL
F-ZBPK	MBB-Kawasaki BK.117C-2/ EC.145	9020	D-HJFO
F-ZBPM	MBB-Kawasaki BK.117C-2/ EC.145	9022	D-HMBE(2), D-HJFQ
F-ZBPN	MBB-Kawasaki BK.117C-2/ EC.145	9023	D-HJFR
F-ZBPO	MBB-Kawasaki BK.117C-2/ EC.145	9025	D-HMBF(5), D-HJFS
F-ZBPP	MBB-Kawasaki BK.117C-2/ EC.145	9030	D-HJFU
F-ZBPQ	MBB-Kawasaki BK.117C-2/ EC.145	9031	(D-HIRL(3)), F-ZBPQ, D-HJFV
F-ZBPS	MBB-Kawasaki BK.117C-2/ EC.145	9042	D-HRWA
F-ZBPT	MBB-Kawasaki BK.117C-2/ EC.145	9043	D-HRWB
F-ZBPU	MBB-Kawasaki BK.117C-2/ EC.145	9045	D-HRWD
F-ZBPV	MBB-Kawasaki BK.117C-2/ EC.145	9046	D-HRWE
F-ZBPW	MBB-Kawasaki BK.117C-2/ EC.145	9048	D-HRWF
F-ZBPY	MBB-Kawasaki BK.117C-2/ EC.145	9050	D-HRWH
F-ZBPZ	MBB-Kawasaki BK.117C-2/ EC.145	9056	D-HRWI(2)
F-ZBQA	MBB-Kawasaki BK.117C-2/ EC.145	9057	D-HRWJ
F-ZBQB	MBB-Kawasaki BK.117C-2/ EC.145	9058	D-HADH, F-ZBQB, D-HMBH(10), (D-HRWO)
F-ZBQC	MBB-Kawasaki BK.117C-2/ EC.145	9059	D-HRWP
F-ZBQD	MBB-Kawasaki BK.117C-2/ EC.145	9060	D-HRWR
F-ZBQE	MBB-Kawasaki BK.117C-2/ EC.145	9062	D-HRWS
F-ZBQF	MBB-Kawasaki BK.117C-2/ EC.145	9064	D-HMBF(8), D-HRWT
F-ZBQG	MBB-Kawasaki BK.117C-2/ EC.145	9217	D-HMBG(17)
F-ZBQH	MBB-Kawasaki BK.117C-2/ EC.145	9232	(D-HAAY(2)), D-HMBK(8)
F-ZBQI	MBB-Kawasaki BK.117C-2/ EC.145	9240	D-HMBO(16)
F-ZBQJ	MBB-Kawasaki BK.117C-2/ EC.145	9323	D-HMBG(18)
F-ZBQK	MBB-Kawasaki BK.117C-2/ EC.145	9372	D-HADC(4)
F-ZBQL	MBB-Kawasaki BK.117C-2/ EC.145	9452	D-HADK(2)

GENDARMERIE AIRCRAFT

In most cases only the last 3 letters of the " Registration" are actually carried on the aircraft.

F-MCSM	Aérospatiale AS.350B1 Ecureuil	2222	F-MJCZ(1)
F-MJAA(2)	Aérospatiale AS.550U2 Fennec	2815	CEV:F-ZLAH
F-MJBA(3)	MBB-Kawasaki BK.117C-2/ EC.145	9008	D-HMBG(6), F-MJBA(3), D-HJFC
F-MJBB(4)	MBB-Kawasaki BK.117C-2/ EC.145	9014	D-HMBH(7), D-HJFI
F-MJBC(3)	MBB-Kawasaki BK.117C-2/ EC.145	9018	D-HMBF(4), D-HJFM
F-MJBD(5)	MBB-Kawasaki BK.117C-2/ EC.145	9019	D-HJFN
F-MJBE(4)	MBB-Kawasaki BK.117C-2/ EC.145	9025	D-HJFT
F-MJBF(3)	MBB-Kawasaki BK.117C-2/ EC.145	9035	D-HJFX
F-MJBG(3)	MBB-Kawasaki BK.117C-2/ EC.145	9036	D-HMBJ, D-HJFY
F-MJBJ(3)	MBB-Kawasaki BK.117C-2/ EC.145	9140	D-HMBX
F-MJBK(3)	MBB-Kawasaki BK.117C-2/ EC.145	9162	D-HMBN(18)
F-MJBM(2)	MBB-Kawasaki BK.117C-2/ EC.145	9113	D-HMBH(12)
F-MJBO(2)	MBB-Kawasaki BK.117C-2/ EC.145	9124	D-HMBT(9), F-MJBO(2), D-HMBA(10)
F-MJBR(2)	MBB-Kawasaki BK.117C-2/ EC.145	9169	D-HMBI(8)
F-MJBT(2)	MBB-Kawasaki BK.117C-2/ EC.145	9173	D-HMBC(9)
F-MJCA	Aérospatiale AS.350BA Ecureuil	1028	F-GBLQ, F-WZFL
F-MJCB	Aérospatiale AS.350BA Ecureuil	1574	
F-MJCC(2)	Aérospatiale AS.350BA Ecureuil	1916	
F-MJCD	Aérospatiale AS.350BA Ecureuil	1576	
F-MJCE(2)	Aérospatiale AS.350BA Ecureuil	1812	F-MCSC(4), F-MJCM(1)
F-MJCF(3)	Aérospatiale AS.350BA Ecureuil	1691	F-MCSC(5), F-MJCE(1)
F-MJCG	Aérospatiale AS.350BA Ecureuil	1753	
F-MJCH	Aérospatiale AS.350BA Ecureuil	1756	
F-MJCK(2)	Aérospatiale AS.350BA Ecureuil	1953	
F-MJCL	Aérospatiale AS.350BA Ecureuil	1811	
F-MJCM(2)	Aérospatiale AS.350BA Ecureuil	1952	
F-MJCN	Aérospatiale AS.350BA Ecureuil	2044	
F-MJCO	Aérospatiale AS.350BA Ecureuil	1917	
F-MJCP	Aérospatiale AS.350BA Ecureuil	2045	
F-MJCQ	Aérospatiale AS.350BA Ecureuil	2057	
F-MJCR	Aérospatiale AS.350BA Ecureuil	2088	
F-MJCS(2)	Aérospatiale AS.350BA Ecureuil	1575	F-MCSE(6), F-MJCC(1)
F-MJCT	Aérospatiale AS.350BA Ecureuil	2104	
F-MJCU	Aérospatiale AS.350BA Ecureuil	2117	
F-MJCV	Aérospatiale AS.350BA Ecureuil	2118	
F-MJCW	Aérospatiale AS.350BA Ecureuil	2218	
F-MJCX	Aérospatiale AS.350BA Ecureuil	2219	
F-MJCY	Aérospatiale AS.350BA Ecureuil	2221	
F-MJCZ(3)	Aérospatiale AS.350BA Ecureuil	1467	F-GHCO(2), (F-GHBR), LN-OTC
F-MJDA	Eurocopter EC.135T2+	0642	D-HECR(10)
F-MJDB	Eurocopter EC.135T2+	0654	D-HTSK
F-MJDC	Eurocopter EC.135T2+	0717	D-HECW(8)
F-MJDD	Eurocopter EC.135T2+	0727	D-HTSE(2)

Reg	Type	Serial	Previous identities
F-MJDE	Eurocopter EC.135T2+	0747	D-HECT(7)
F-MJDF	Eurocopter EC.135T2+	0757	D-HECH(22)
F-MJDG	Eurocopter EC.135T2+	0772	D-HECN(22)
F-MJDH	Eurocopter EC.135T2+	0787	D-HECG(16)
F-MJDI	Eurocopter EC.135T2+	0797	D-HECZ(4)
F-MJDJ	Eurocopter EC.135T2+	0806	
F-MJDK	Eurocopter EC.135T2+	0857	D-HCBL(3)
F-MJDL	Eurocopter EC.135T2+	0867	D-HECG(17)
F-MJDM	Eurocopter EC.135T2+	1055	D-HCBN(5)
F-MJDN	Eurocopter EC.135T2+	1058	D-HCBR(5)
F-MJDO	Eurocopter EC.135T2+	1086	
F-MJEB	Aérospatiale AS.350BA Ecureuil	1692	F-MCZA, F-MJCF(1)
F-MJEC	Aérospatiale AS.350BA Ecureuil	1810	F-MCSB(3), F-MJCF(2), F-MCSA(6), F-MJCK(1)
F-MJED	Aérospatiale AS.350BA Ecureuil	2096	F-MCSL, F-MJCS(1), F-ZKCP
F-MJEE	Aérospatiale AS.350BA Ecureuil	2423	F-MCSN, F-MJCZ(2)
F-MJEF	Aérospatiale AS.350B1 Ecureuil	2225	F-MCSF(3), F-MJCI(2), F-MCSF(3), F-MJBZ(2)

GLIDERS AND MOTOR GLIDERS

The most recently reported tail codes are shown next to the registration. Additions and amendments are welcome.

Reg	Type	Serial	Previous identities
F-CAAB	Scheibe SF 28A Tandem-Falke	5772	PH-635, PH-TER, D-KCLB
F-CABI	Glaser Dirks DG-200	2-117	
F-CABK-FS	Schleicher ASW 19B	19309	
(W/o 14.8.06)			
F-CABY	Breguet 900	1	
F-CACC-T73	Grob G 103 Twin Astir II	3515	OH-644, D-3063
F-CACL	Wassmer WA.22A Super Javelot	115	Fr.AF
F-CACM	Wassmer WA.22A Super Javelot	124	Fr.AF
(Wfu)			
F-CACN	ICA/Brasov IS-28B2	224	
F-CADC	Air 100	12	
F-CADN	Grob G 102/77J Astir Jeans	2099	
F-CADO	Grob G 102/77J Astir Jeans	2103	
F-CADT(2)	Rolladen-Schneider LS4	4212	BGA 2933/ETF, N3UK
F-CAEA	Wassmer WA.22A Super Javelot	126	Fr.AF
F-CAEM	Grob G 102/77J Astir CS Jeans	2061	D-7579
F-CAEN	Rolladen-Schneider LS6-a	6067	F-WAEN(2), D-1504
F-CAEO	Rolladen-Schneider LS1-c	113	D-1044
F-CAES	Wassmer WA.30 Bijave	162	Fr.AF
F-CAEU	Glaser-Dirks DG-500M	5E7M5	G-BRRG
F-CAFA	Scheibe SF 28A Tandem-Falke	5747	HB-2029, D-KOEY
F-CAFI	Carmam M.100S Mésange	57	OO-ZFE, F-CDDN
F-CAFJ-L11	Rolladen-Schneider LS1-d	137	OO-ZMH
(W/o 07.07.12)			
F-CAFK	SZD-50-3 Puchacz	B-2060	
(W/o 19.5.07)			
F-CAFL	Scheibe SF 28A Tandem-Falke	5712	OE-9069, D-KDAL(1)
F-CAFO(2)	Caudron C.800	10312/352	F-CADI
F-CAFP	Schempp-Hirth Discus bT	133/506	PH-1011
F-CAFZ	Wassmer WA.22A	151	Fr.AF
F-CAGI	Wassmer WA.22A	153	Fr.AF
F-CAGJ	Schleicher K 8B	972	D-4383
F-CAGK	Wassmer WA.30 Bijave	231	Fr.AF
F-CAGL	Fauvel AV.22S	2	F-CCGL
F-CAGU	Breguet 904S Nymphale	11	F-CCFU
F-CAHJ	Fournier RF-9	1	
F-CAHL(2)	Fournier RF-9	9	
F-CAHM(2)	Fournier RF-9	3	
F-CAHP(2)	Fournier RF-9	5	
F-CAHY	Fournier RF-9	2	
F-CAIA	Issoire D.77 Iris	01	F-WAQA
F-CAIC-IC	Schempp-Hirth Ventus c	298	F-WAIC, N125SG
F-CAID	Scheibe SF 28A Tandem-Falke	5761	HB-2007, (D-KACN)
F-CAJB-T74	Grob G 103 Twin Astir	3206	OO-ZMA
F-CAJC(2)	SZD-51-1 Junior	B-2020	
F-CAJE	Nord 2000	35	F-CAJD
F-CAJJ	Caudron C.800	9780/120	
F-CAKO-8X	Rolladen-Schneider LS4-a	4674	D-0124
F-CALB	Scheibe SF 25B Falke	46128	D-KADD
F-CALG	Schleicher ASK 14	14050	G-AYRN, (D-KISA(2))
F-CAMD	Avialsa-Scheibe A 60 Fauconnet	2	
F-CAMF	Avialsa-Scheibe A.60 Fauconnet	4	
F-CAOB(2)	Schempp-Hirth Janus CM	37/290	D-KAOK(2)
F-CAOP	Nord 2000	60	
F-CAOT	Stemme S-10	10-53	D-KGCI(3)
F-CAPF	Caudron C.800	181/9841	
(Being restored)			
F-CAPX	Wassmer WA.21 Javelot II	51	Fr.AF
F-CAPY(2)	Schempp-Hirth Ventus-2cxT	142	OM-1802
F-CAQA(4)	Scheibe SF 25C Falke 2000	44324	F-WAQA(4), D-KOOQ
F-CAQB-2A	SZD-42-1 Jantar 2A	B-784	F-WAQB, LX-CMD, F-WAQB, SP-2642
F-CAQC	Schleicher ASW 17	17051	F-WAQC
F-WAQG	Carmam C-38	25	
F-WAQH(5)	A.S.D.Glider	1	
F-WAQI	KV-3A	01	
F-CAQJ	Carmam C-38	03	F-WAQJ
F-CAQO	Grob G 109B	6333	F-WAQO
F-CAQQ	Scheibe SF 25C Falke	4483	F-WAQQ, OY-VXV, (D-KEIC(1))
F-CAQS(2)	Scheibe SF 28A Tandem-Falke	5799	OY-XJB, (D-KDCZ)
F-CAQT	Scheibe SF 28A Tandem-Falke	5741	HB-2023, (D-KOEB(2))
F-CAQU	Loravia SFL-25R Remorqueur	4813	F-WAQU(2), D-KBAV
(Converted SF 25C Falke for glider towing)			
F-CAQV(2)	Scheibe SF 25A Falke	4545	F-WAQV(2), D-KANY
(W/o 6.5.16)			
F-CAQX	Scheibe SF 25C Falke	4404	F-WAQX(2), D-KAAM
F-WAQY(2)	Centrair 201C Marianne	201C095	
F-CAQZ	Scheibe SF 25E Super Falke	4364	D-KNIY(2)
F-CARA -MV	Schempp-Hirth Nimbus IIB	162	PH-599
F-CARB	Schempp-Hirth Nimbus-3	21	Fr.AF
F-CARD	Sportavia/ Scheibe SF 25B Falke	4863	F-WARD, D-KAEB
F-CARH	Fournier RF-10	02	F-WARH
F-WARI	Fournier RF-10	03	
F-CARJ	Fournier RF-10	4	F-WARJ
F-CARL(2)	Scheibe SF 28A Tandem-Falke	5717	D-KOAI
F-CARM	Schempp-Hirth Janus C	91	D-3198
F-CARN	Grob G 102 Astir CS	1494	HB-1375
F-CARP	Scheibe SF 25B Falke	46205	F-WASW, (D-KAST)
F-CARS	Scheibe SF 25E Super Falke	4348	D-KDGA
F-CASB	Air 102	36	
F-WASE	KV-5	001	
F-CASF	Grob G 103 Twin II	3674	D-8697
F-CASH-3W	Schleicher ASH 25	25127	
F-CATA	Grob G 103 Twin Astir	3168	D-7805
F-CATC	Rolladen-Schneider LS4	4051	D-4189
F-CATE(2)	Valentin Taifun 17E	1041	HB-2099, D-KDSF
F-CATF	Schempp-Hirth Duo Discus	15	D-9194
F-CATI-4W	Rolladen-Schneider LS4	4558	D-8922
F-CATT-2	Rolladen-Schneider LS6-c	6227	D-6426
F-CATU-T72	Grob G 103 Twin Astir	3236	
F-CAVQ	Glaser-Dirks DG-300 Club Elan	3E296C14	D-4577
F-CAVT	Schempp-Hirth Duo Discus	4	D-6769
F-CAVV	HOAC HK 36R Super Dimona	36339	D-KCBN
F-CAVY	Schleicher K 8B	8170	
(Dismantled)			
F-CAYD-JB	Glaser Dirks DG-200/17	2-112/1719	
(W/o 12.8.14)			
F-CAYU	Air 102	39	
F-CBAN	Caudron C.800	9985/325	F-CBXA
F-CBAT	Sportine Aviacija LAK-17B FES	222	
F-CBBA	IAR-Brasov IS-28M2	53	
F-CBBC	IAR-Brasov IS-28M2	61	
(Stored .05)			
F-CBBD	IAR-Brasov IS-28B2	345	
F-CBBE	Glaser-Dirks DG-300 Elan	3E244	HB-3007
F-CBBF	IAR-Brasov IS-28M2	51	
F-CBBG	IAR-Brasov IS-28M2	55	
F-CBBN(2)	Schleicher K 8B	8755	D-1039
F-CBCA	Glaser Dirks DG-200/17	2-127/1729	
F-WBCB	Stralpes ST-11 Minimus	01	
F-CBCD	Stralpes CB 15 Crystal	01	F-WBCD
F-CBCE	Stralpes CB 15 Crystal	1	F-WBCE
F-CBCF	Stralpes CB 15 Crystal	2	F-WBCF
F-WBCG	Stralpes CB 15 Crystal	3	
F-CBCI	Stralpes CB 15 Crystal	8	
F-CBCJ-CJ	Stralpes CB 15 Crystal	9	
F-CBCK	Stralpes CB 15 Crystal	10	
F-CBCL	Schleicher ASK 13	13593	D-7671
F-CBCN-EM	Stralpes CB 15 Crystal	6	
F-CBCO(2)	Stralpes CB 15 Crystal	7	
F-CBDA-YV	Schleicher ASW 20L	20460	
F-CBDB	Schleicher ASW 22	22024	F-WBDB
F-CBDC(2)-DC	Schleicher ASW 20L	20319	
F-CBDD-A2	Schleicher ASW 20BL	20648	F-WBDD
F-CBDE-1Z	Schleicher ASW 22	22016	F-WBDE
F-CBDF	Schleicher ASW 20	20576	
F-CBDH	Schleicher ASW 20CL	20710	F-WBDH
F-CBDI -GP	Schleicher ASW 20CL	20744	F-WBDI
F-CBDM	Schleicher ASW 20CL	20743	F-WBDM
F-CBDN	Schleicher ASW 20C	20761	F-WBDN
F-CBDP	Schleicher ASK 21	21105	F-WBDP
F-CBDQ	Schleicher ASK 21	21209	
F-CBDR	Schleicher ASK 21	21146	F-WBDR
F-CBDS-DS	Schleicher ASK 21	21183	
F-CBDT	Schleicher ASK 21	21184	
F-CBDU	Schleicher ASK 21	21186	
F-CBDX-DX	Schleicher ASK 21	21188	
F-CBDY	Schleicher ASK 21	21202	
F-CBEC(2)-EC	Schempp-Hirth Duo Discus	293	D-2162
F-CBET(2)	Rolladen-Schneider LS6-b	6202	
F-CBFR	Nord 2000	13/10343	
F-CBGE	Nord 2000	48/10378	
F-CBGP	VMA 200 Milan	28	
F-CBGV	Wassmer WA.20 Javelot 1	3	
F-CBGZ -7	Wassmer WA.20 Javelot 1	7	
F-CBHD	Air 100	13	
F-CBHF	Air 100	7	
F-CBHN	Stralpes CB 15 Crystal	5	
F-CBIP-A54	Schleicher ASW 17B	17033	Fr.AF: A54
F-CBIZ-Y	Schempp-Hirth Ventus-2b	19	D-1443
F-CBJR(2)	Scheibe SF 25B Falke	46161	LX-CAB, D-KOXY, (D-KBIF)
F-CBLA	Centrair 201B Marianne	201A027	
F-CBLC	Centrair 201B Marianne	201A029	
F-CBLD(2)	Centrair 201B Marianne	201A032	
F-CBLG	Centrair 201B Marianne	201A033	
F-CBLH-LH	Centrair 201B Marianne	201A034	
F-CBLJ	Centrair 201B Marianne	201A036	
F-CBLK(2)-U2	Centrair 201B Marianne	201A038	
F-CBLL(2)	Centrair 201B Marianne	201A039	
F-CBLM(2)	Centrair 201B Marianne	201A040	
F-CBLN(2)	Centrair 201B Marianne	201A041	
F-CBLO	Centrair 201B Marianne	201A042	
F-CBLP	Centrair 201B Marianne	201B043	
F-CBLR(2)	Centrair 201B Marianne	201A045	
(W/o 26.7.02)			
F-CBLS(2)	Centrair 201B Marianne	201B046	
F-CBLT(2)	Centrair 201B Marianne	201B047	
F-CBLU(2)	Centrair 201B Marianne	201B048	F-WBLU
F-CBLV(2)	Centrair 201B Marianne	201B051	
F-CBLY(2)	Centrair 201B Marianne	201B050	
F-CBLZ-LZ	Centrair 201B Marianne	201B059	
F-CBMA	Castel C.310P	117	
F-CBNA	Grob G102 Astir CS Jeans	2011	D-3874
F-CBNV(2)	Schempp-Hirth Nimbus-2	52	F-CEDB
F-CBOT	Sportavia-Pützer RF-5B Sperber	51055	D-KENT
F-CBPE-FA	Schempp-Hirth Ventus-2c	5/8	OE-5597
F-CBPF(2)	Fournier RF-9	4	EC-DML, F-ODPB, F-WDPB
F-CBPJ-PJ	Glaser Dirks DG-200	2-52	
F-CBPM	Schleicher ASH 25	25038	F-WBPM, D-4756
F-CBPR	Wassmer WA.28E	117	D-4231
F-CBQO	Wassmer WA.20 Javelot 1	1	
F-CBRS	Fauvel AV.36	119	
F-CBRX	Fauvel AV.36	123	
(Being restored)			
F-CBSM	Fauvel AV.36	138	
F-CBUN	Schleicher ASW 28-18	28506	D-4071
F-CBUU	Wassmer WA.22A	152	Fr.AF
F-CBVA	Rolladen-Schneider LS1	43	OO-YAA, D-0558
F-CBVT	Schleicher ASK 13	13055	D-5340
F-CBVV	Wassmer WA.30 Bijave	175	Fr.AF
F-CBYV	Caudron C.800	9891/231	
(To museum, Lyon-Corbas)			
F-CBYY-2Y	Schempp-Hirth Janus Ce	272	D-4502
F-CBZH	SZD-51-1 Junior	W-940	HB-1847
F-CBZU	Schleicher Ka 6E	4211	
F-CBZX	Schleicher Ka 6CR Rhönsegler	6609	D-4421

Registration	Type	c/n	Previous identities
F-CCAA(2)	Schempp-Hirth Janus B	08	HB-1325, D-3115
F-CCAB	Rolladen-Schneider LS1-d	26	
F-CCAC-EP	Schempp-Hirth Ventus-2cx	89	D-5091
F-WCAF	Carmam JP.15/34	01	
F-WCAR	Carmam JP.15/36 Aiglon	02	
F-CCAV	Schleicher Ka 6CR Rhönsegler	6545	
F-CCBC	Wassmer WA.28 Espadon	01	F-WCBC
F-CCBD	Eiri PIK-20E II	20294	F-WCBD, OH-577
F-CCCB	Wassmer WA.22 Super Javelot	01	F-WCCB
F-CCCL	Breguet 901S Mouette	9	
F-CCCM	Breguet 901S Mouette	10	
F-CCCP	Breguet 901S Mouette	13	
F-CCCQ	Breguet 901S Mouette	14	
F-CCCU	Breguet 901S Mouette	18	
F-CCCX	Breguet 901S Mouette	20	
F-CCDF(2)	Schleicher ASK 21	21329	D-4745
F-CCDK	Scheibe Bergfalke II/55	207	
F-CCEA	Wassmer WA.20 Javelot	01	F-WCEA
F-CCEE	Wassmer WA.21 Javelot II	2	
F-CCEO	Wassmer WA.21 Javelot II	18	
F-CCER	Wassmer WA.21 Javelot II	24	
F-CCEU	Wassmer WA.21 Javelot II	30	
F-CCEX	Wassmer WA.21 Javelot II	32	
F-CCFA	FFA Diamant 18	70	
F-WCFC	Carmam JP.15/36 Aiglon	04	
F-CCFE	Wassmer WA.21 Javelot II	45	TU-TPB, F-CCKJ
F-CCFF	Issoire E.78 Silène	01	
F-CCFK	Breguet 904S Nymphale (Dismantled)	1	
F-CCFN	Breguet 904S Nymphale	4	
F-CCFP	Breguet 904S Nymphale (Dismantled)	6	
F-CCFQ	Breguet 904S Nymphale	7	
F-CCFR	Breguet 904S Nymphale	8	
F-CCFY	Breguet 904S Nymphale	14	
F-CCFZ	Breguet 904S Nymphale	15	
F-CCGE	Breguet 901S1	34	
F-CCGK	Fauvel AV.22S	1	
F-CCHD	Wassmer WA.21 Javelot II	8	
F-CCHG	Wassmer WA.21 Javelot II	19	
F-CCHK	Wassmer WA.21 Javelot II	28	
F-CCHR-WH	Schempp-Hirth Janus B	03	D-3110
F-CCJP	Schleicher ASK 13	13230	D-0498
F-CCJX	Schleicher ASK 21	21040	(F-CBDQ), F-WCJX
F-CCJY	Scheibe SF 28A Tandem-Falke	5763	D-KACP
F-CCKE	Wassmer WA.21 Javelot II	39	
F-CCKI	Wassmer WA.21 Javelot II	43	
F-CCKL	Wassmer WA.21 Javelot II (Dismantled)	47	
F-CCKQ	Wassmer WA.21A Javelot II	53	
F-CCLI	Avialsa-Scheibe A.60 Fauconnet (Under restoration)	13	
F-CCLL	Avialsa-Scheibe A.60 Fauconnet	16	
F-CCLM	Wassmer WA.22 Super Javelot	63	
F-CCLN	Wassmer WA.22 Super Javelot	61	
F-CCLO	Wassmer WA.22 Super Javelot	02	
F-CCLS	Wassmer WA.22 Super Javelot	66	
F-CCLZ	Wassmer WA.22 Super Javelot	70	
F-CCMH	Wassmer WA.30 Bijave	11	
F-CCMI	Wassmer WA.30 Bijave	13	
F-CCMY	Wassmer WA.30 Bijave	31	
F-CCNB	Wassmer WA.30 Bijave (Dismantled)	52	
F-CCNC	Wassmer WA.30 Bijave	53	
F-CCNH	Wassmer WA.30 Bijave	58	
F-CCNJ	Wassmer WA.30 Bijave	60	
F-CCNL	Wassmer WA.30 Bijave (Dismantled)	62	
F-CCNM	Wassmer WA.30 Bijave	63	
F-CCNP	Wassmer WA.30 Bijave	66	
F-CCNQ	Wassmer WA.30 Bijave	67	
F-CCNR	Wassmer WA.30 Bijave	68	
F-CCNU	Wassmer WA.30 Bijave	71	
F-CCNZ	Wassmer WA.30 Bijave	75	
F-CCOC	Wassmer WA.22 Super Javelot	75	
F-CCOD	Wassmer WA.22 Super Javelot (Dismantled)	76	
F-CCOH	Wassmer WA.22 Super Javelot	80	
F-CCOI	Wassmer WA.22 Super Javelot	81	
F-CCOL	Wassmer WA.22 Super Javelot	84	
F-CCOQ	Wassmer WA.30 Bijave	30	
F-CCOR	Wassmer WA.22 Super Javelot	86	
F-CCOS	Wassmer WA.22 Super Javelot	87	
F-CCOT	Wassmer WA.22 Super Javelot	88	
F-CCOU	Wassmer WA.22 Super Javelot	89	
F-CCPI	Carmam M.100S Mésange	10	
F-CCPT	Scheibe Zugvogel IIIB	1084	
F-CCQC	Avialsa-Scheibe A.60 Fauconnet	25	
F-CCQD	Avialsa-Scheibe A.60 Fauconnet	26	
F-CCQF	Avialsa-Scheibe A.60 Fauconnet	28K	
F-CCQK	Avialsa-Scheibe A.60 Fauconnet	33K	
F-CCRB	Wassmer WA.22A Super Javelot	94	
F-CCRC	Wassmer WA.30 Bijave	34	
F-CCRI	Wassmer WA.30 Bijave	38	
F-CCRJ	Wassmer WA.30 Bijave	33	
F-CCRL	Wassmer WA.30 Bijave	40	
F-CCRM	Wassmer WA.30 Bijave	41	
F-CCRN	Wassmer WA.30 Bijave	42	
F-CCRS	Wassmer WA.30 Bijave	46	
F-CCRU	Wassmer WA.30 Bijave	47	
F-CCRZ	Wassmer WA.22A Super Javelot	97	
F-CCSY	Carmam M.100S Mésange	35	
F-CCTA	Wassmer WA.30 Bijave	77	
F-CCTE	Wassmer WA.30 Bijave	80	
F-CCTH	Wassmer WA.30 Bijave	83	
F-CCTK	Wassmer WA.30 Bijave	85	
F-CCTP	Wassmer WA.30 Bijave	89	
F-CCTR	Wassmer WA.30 Bijave	91	
F-CCTZ	Wassmer WA.30 Bijave	98	
F-CCUC	Siren C.30S Edelweiss	3	
F-CCUM	Siren C.30S Edelweiss	15	
F-CCUV	Siren C.30S Edelweiss	24	
F-CCVF	Avialsa-Scheibe A.60 Fauconnet	53K	
F-CCVO	Avialsa-Scheibe A.60 Fauconnet	62	
F-CCVQ	Avialsa-Scheibe A.60 Fauconnet	64	
F-CCVX	Avialsa-Scheibe A.60 Fauconnet	70	
F-CCXJ	Carmam M.100S Mésange	45	
F-CCXX	Carmam M.200 Foehn	7	
F-CCXY	Carmam M.200 Foehn (Dismantled)	9	
F-CCXZ	Carmam M.200 Foehn	10	
F-CCYA	Wassmer WA.30 Bijave	97	
F-CCYB	Wassmer WA.30 Bijave	99	
F-CCYF	Wassmer WA.30 Bijave	103	
F-CCYO	Wassmer WA.30 Bijave	112	
F-CCYP	Wassmer WA.30 Bijave	115	
F-CCYQ	Wassmer WA.30 Bijave	114	
F-CCYS	Wassmer WA.30 Bijave	116	
F-CCYT	Wassmer WA.30 Bijave (To museum, Lyon-Corbas)	117	
F-CCYU	Wassmer WA.30 Bijave	118	
F-CCYV	Wassmer WA.30 Bijave	119	
F-CCZC	Wassmer WA.30 Bijave (Dismantled)	125	
F-CCZI	Wassmer WA.30 Bijave	130	
F-CCZJ	Wassmer WA.30 Bijave	131	
F-CCZK	Wassmer WA.30 Bijave	132	
F-CCZM	Wassmer WA.30 Bijave	133	
F-CCZO	Wassmer WA.30 Bijave	135	
F-CCZU	Wassmer WA.30 Bijave	138	
F-CCZX	Wassmer WA.22A Super Javelot	108	
F-CCZZ	Wassmer WA.22A Super Javelot	105	
F-CDAF-735	Glasflügel H201B Standard Libelle	557	
F-CDAH	Schempp-Hirth SHK-1	15	
F-CDAI	Siren C.30S Edelweiss	28	
F-CDAK	Siren C.30S Edelweiss	30	
F-CDAL	Siren C.30S Edelweiss	31	
F-CDAM	Siren C.30S Edelweiss	32	
F-CDAV	Siren C.30S Edelweiss	41	
F-CDAY	LCA-Scheibe 10 Topaze	001	F-WDAY
F-CDBG	Avialsa-Scheibe A.60 Fauconnet (Stored .05)	79K	
F-CDCB	Wassmer WA.30 Bijave	143	
F-CDCC	Wassmer WA.30 Bijave	144	
F-CDCE	Wassmer WA.30 Bijave	146	
F-CDCF	Wassmer WA.22A Super Javelot	109	
F-CDCI	Wassmer WA.22A Super Javelot	111	
F-CDCL	Wassmer WA.30 Bijave	150	
F-CDCP	Wassmer WA.30 Bijave	156	
F-CDCQ	Wassmer WA.30 Bijave	157	
F-CDCV	Wassmer WA.30 Bijave	161	
F-CDCZ	Wassmer WA.30 Bijave	166	
F-CDDC	Carmam M.200 Foehn	12	
F-CDDU	Carmam M.200 Foehn	26	
F-CDEE	Wassmer WA.22A Super Javelot	123	
F-CDEF	Wassmer WA.30 Bijave	169	
F-CDEH	Wassmer WA.30 Bijave	172	
F-CDEK	Wassmer WA.22A Super Javelot	127	
F-CDEQ	Wassmer WA.30 Bijave	177	
F-CDET	Wassmer WA.30 Bijave	180	
F-CDFK	Avialsa-Scheibe A.60 Fauconnet	108K	
F-CDFM	Avialsa-Scheibe A.60 Fauconnet	110K	
F-CDFQ	Avialsa-Scheibe A.60 Fauconnet	114	
F-CDFR	Avialsa-Scheibe A.60 Fauconnet	115K	
F-CDFT-M7	Avialsa-Scheibe A.60 Fauconnet	117	
F-CDFZ	Avialsa-Scheibe A.60 Fauconnet	122	
F-CDGA	Siren C.30S Edelweiss	42	
F-CDGC	Siren C.30S Edelweiss	44	
F-CDGN	Rocheteau-Scheibe CRA.60	12K	
F-CDHC	Carmam M.200 Foehn	30	
F-CDHE	Carmam M.200 Foehn	31	
F-CDHO	Carmam M.200 Foehn	40	
F-CDHQ	Carmam M.100S Mésange	67	
F-CDHS	Carmam M.200 Foehn	43	
F-CDHT	Carmam M.100S Mésange	69	
F-CDID	Wassmer WA.22A Super Javelot	136	
F-CDIE	Wassmer WA.30 Bijave	191	
F-CDIF	Wassmer WA.30 Bijave	192	
F-CDIJ	Wassmer WA.30 Bijave (Dismantled)	195	
F-CDIL	Wassmer WA.30 Bijave	197	
F-CDIN	Wassmer WA.22A Super Javelot	141	
F-CDIP	Wassmer WA.30 Bijave	200	
F-CDIS	Wassmer WA.30 Bijave	203	
F-CDIT	Wassmer WA.22A Super Javelot	142	
F-CDIZ	Wassmer WA.22A Super Javelot	146	
F-CDJA	Wassmer WA.30 Bijave	208	
F-CDJB	Wassmer WA.22A Super Javelot	147	
F-CDJC	Wassmer WA.30 Bijave	209	
F-CDJE	Wassmer WA.30 Bijave	211	
F-CDJF	Wassmer WA.30 Bijave	212	
F-CDJG	Wassmer WA.30 Bijave	213	
F-CDJM	Wassmer WA.30 Bijave	217	
F-CDJN	Wassmer WA.22A Super Javelot	150	
F-CDJQ	Wassmer WA.30 Bijave	220	
F-CDJR	Wassmer WA.30 Bijave	221	
F-CDJX	Wassmer WA.30 Bijave (Dismantled)	225	
F-CDKF	Carmam M.100S Mésange	74	
F-CDKI	Carmam M.200 Foehn (Dismantled)	51	
F-CDKK	Carmam M.100S Mésange	77	
F-CDKN	Carmam M.200 Foehn	53	
F-CDKV	Carmam M.200 Foehn	56	
F-CDLC	Avialsa-Scheibe A.60 Fauconnet (Being restored)	125K	
F-CDLG	Avialsa-Scheibe A.60 Fauconnet	129K	
F-CDLR	Avialsa-Scheibe A.60 Fauconnet	140	
F-CDMB	Wassmer WA.30 Bijave	234	
F-CDMC	Wassmer WA.30 Bijave	235	
F-CDMJ	Wassmer WA.30 Bijave	240	
F-CDMN	Wassmer WA.30 Bijave	242	
F-CDMP	Wassmer WA.30 Bijave	244	
F-CDMT	Wassmer WA.30 Bijave	247	
F-CDMU	Wassmer WA.26P Squale	07	
F-CDMV	Wassmer WA.30 Bijave	248	
F-CDMY	Wassmer WA.26P Squale	08	
F-CDNH	Avialsa-Scheibe A.60 Fauconnet	155K	
F-CDNX	Rocheteau-Scheibe CRA.60	08	
F-CDNY	Rocheteau-Scheibe CRA.60	09	
F-CDOC	Bölkow Phoebus C	889	
F-CDOF	Bölkow Phoebus C	902	

Registration	Type	Serial	Notes
F-CDOG	Bölkow Phoebus C	906	
F-CDOJ	Bölkow Phoebus C	915	
F-CDOL	Bölkow Phoebus CWB	925	
F-CDOO	Bölkow Phoebus C	932	
F-CDOP	Bölkow Phoebus C	926	
F-CDOR	Bölkow Phoebus CWB	941	
F-CDOS	Bölkow Phoebus B1	943	
F-CDOU-C80	Jastreb Standard Cirrus 75-VTC	227	
F-CDOV-ED	Jastreb Standard Cirrus 75-VTC	229	
F-CDOX-C82	Jastreb Standard Cirrus 75-VTC	239	
F-CDOY	Jastreb Standard Cirrus 75-VTC	240	
F-CDPC	Glasflügel H201 Standard Libelle	70	
F-CDPD	Schempp-Hirth Cirrus	29	
F-CDPF-701	Glasflügel H201 Standard Libelle	150	
F-CDPG-702	Glasflügel H201B Standard Libelle	151	
F-CDPH-703	Glasflügel H201B Standard Libelle	152	
F-CDPR	Glasflügel H201B Standard Libelle	226	
F-CDPS-707	Glasflügel H201 Standard Libelle	227	
F-CDPT-7230	Glasflügel H201B Standard Libelle	230	
F-CDPU-LiLi	Glasflügel H201 Standard Libelle	231	
F-CDPX	Glasflügel H201B Standard Libelle	247	
F-CDQA	Wassmer WA.30 Bijave	251	
F-CDQG	Wassmer WA.26P Squale	11	
F-CDQO	Wassmer WA.26P Squale	17	
F-CDQU	Wassmer WA.30 Bijave	257	
F-CDQZ	Wassmer WA.30 Bijave	261	
F-CDRA	Schleicher Ka 6E	4278	
F-CDRD	Schleicher Ka 6E	4293	
F-CDRH	Schleicher Ka 6E	4298	
F-CDRI	Schleicher Ka 6E	4299	
F-CDRK	Schleicher Ka 6E	4302	
F-CDRL	Schleicher Ka 6E	4289	
F-CDRM	Schleicher Ka 6E	4290	
F-CDRN	Schleicher Ka 6E	4303	
F-CDRT	Schleicher Ka 6E	4319	
F-CDRU	Schleicher Ka 6E	4320	
F-CDRX	Schleicher Ka 6E	4323	
F-CDSA	Wassmer WA.30 Bijave (Stored .05)	262	
F-CDSD	Wassmer WA.26P Squale	25	
F-CDSJ	Wassmer WA.26P Squale	30	
F-CDSK	Wassmer WA.30 Bijave (Stored .05)	264	
F-CDSN	Wassmer WA.26P Squale	32	
F-CDSP	Wassmer WA.26P Squale	34	
F-CDSQ	Wassmer WA.30 Bijave	266	
F-CDTC	Schleicher Ka 6E	4328	
F-CDTG	Schleicher Ka 6E	4332	
F-CDTM	Schleicher Ka 6E	4350	
F-CDTN	Schleicher Ka 6E	4351	
F-CDTQ	Schleicher ASK 13	13275	
F-CDTR	Schleicher Ka 6E	4355	
F-CDTS	Schleicher Ka 6E	4356	
F-CDTT	Schleicher Ka 6E	4358	
F-CDTU	Schleicher Ka 6E	4359	
F-CDTV	Schleicher ASW 15	15117	
F-CDTY	Schleicher Ka 6E	4361	
F-CDUA	Wassmer WA.30 Bijave	271	
F-CDUB	Wassmer WA.30 Bijave	272	
F-CDUC	Wassmer WA.30 Bijave	273	
F-CDUE	Wassmer WA.26P Squale	40	
F-CDUJ	Wassmer WA.26P Squale	44	
F-CDUN	Wassmer WA.26P Squale	47	
F-CDUO	Wassmer WA.30 Bijave	274	
F-CDUP	Wassmer WA.30 Bijave	275	
F-CDUR	Wassmer WA.26P Squale	48	
F-CDUS	Wassmer WA.26P Squale (Stored .05)	49	
F-CDUU	Wassmer WA.26CM	03	
F-CDUX	Wassmer WA.30 Bijave	278	
F-CDVC	Rolladen-Schneider LS1-c	47	
F-CDVF	Rolladen-Schneider LS1-c	202	
F-CDVJ-L7	Rolladen-Schneider LS1-d	206	D-0811
F-CDVN-L16	Rolladen-Schneider LS1-d	210	D-0815
F-CDVQ-L16	Rolladen-Schneider LS1-c	213	D-0818
F-CDVR	Rolladen-Schneider LS1-c	214	
F-CDVV	Rolladen-Schneider LS1-d	156	
F-CDVW-BP	Rolladen-Schneider LS1-c	157	
F-CDVY-L34	Rolladen-Schneider LS1-d	190	
F-CDVZ-L25	Rolladen-Schneider LS1-d	191	
F-CDXC	Wassmer WA.26P Squale (Dismantled)	54	
F-CDXH	Wassmer WA.26CM	09	
F-CDXL	Wassmer WA.26P Squale	56	
F-CDXN	Wassmer WA.30 Bijave	280	
F-CDXO	Wassmer WA.26P Squale	57	
F-CDXS	Wassmer WA.26P Squale	60	
F-CDXV	Wassmer WA.26P Squale	62	
F-CDYA	Schleicher ASK 13	13296	
F-CDYB	Schleicher ASK 13	13297	
F-CDYC	Schleicher ASK 13	13298	
F-CDYD	Schleicher ASK 13	13299	
F-CDYG	Schleicher Ka 6E	4367	
F-CDYI	Schleicher Ka 6E	4369	
F-CDYL	Schleicher Ka 6E	4372	
F-CDYM	Schleicher ASK 13	13316	
F-CDYO	Schleicher ASK 13	13322	
F-CDYS	Schleicher ASK 13	13326	
F-CDYU	Schleicher ASW 15	15123	
F-CDYX	Schleicher ASK 13	13332	
F-CDYY	Schleicher ASK 13	13336	
F-CDYZ	Schleicher ASK 13	13334	
F-CDZD	Wassmer WA.26P Squale	69	
F-CDZJ	Wassmer WA.26P Squale	75	
F-CDZK	Wassmer WA.28 Espadon	93	
F-CDZM	Wassmer WA.28 Espadon	91	
F-CDZO	Wassmer WA.28 Espadon	95	
F-CDZR	Wassmer WA.28F	98	
F-CDZT	Wassmer WA.28 Espadon	100	
F-CDZZ-W15	Wassmer WA.28 Espadon	105	
F-CEAA	Schleicher ASK 13	13337	
F-CEAB	Schleicher ASK 13	13338	
F-CEAC	Schleicher ASK 13	13339	
F-CEAD	Schleicher ASK 13	13340	
F-CEAE	Schleicher ASK 13	13343	
F-CEAF	Schleicher ASK 13	13344	
F-CEAG	Schleicher ASK 13	13347	
F-CEAI	Schleicher ASK 13	13349	
F-CEAJ	Schleicher ASK 13	13350	
F-CEAK	Schleicher ASK 13	13353	
F-CEAL	Schleicher ASK 13	13355	
F-CEAM	Schleicher ASK 13	13356	
F-CEAO-AO	Schleicher Ka 6E	4379	
F-CEAP	Schleicher ASK 13	13365	
F-CEAT	Schleicher ASK 13 (W/o 1.8.13)	13371	
F-CEAU	Schleicher Ka 6E	4380	
F-CEAV	Schleicher ASK 13	13372	
F-CEAX	Schleicher ASK 13	13373	
F-CEAY	Schleicher ASK 14	14062	D-KICI
F-CEAZ	Schleicher ASW 15	15171	
F-CEBB-715	Glasflügel H201 Standard Libelle	302	
F-CEBC-716	Glasflügel H201 Standard Libelle	303	
F-CEBE-718	Glasflügel H201B Standard Libelle	318	
F-CEBG-720	Glasflügel H201B Standard Libelle	320	
F-CEBJ-723	Glasflügel H201B Standard Libelle	360	
F-CEBK	Glasflügel H201B Standard Libelle	361	
F-CEBN	Glasflügel H201B Standard Libelle	427	
F-CEBQ	Glasflügel H201 Standard Libelle	431	
F-CEBS-M21	Glasflügel H304	246	
F-CEBU	Glasflügel H304	252	
F-CEBV	Jastreb Standard Cirrus 75-VTC	242	
F-CEBX	Jastreb Standard Cirrus 75-VTC (Dismantled)	243	
F-CECC	Schleicher ASK 13	13381	
F-CECD	Schleicher ASK 13	13382	
F-CECE	Schleicher Ka 6E	4381	
F-CECF	Schleicher Ka 6E	4382	
F-CECG	Schleicher ASW 17	17005	
F-CECH	Schleicher Ka 6E	4383	
F-CECI-R25	Schleicher ASK 13	13383	
F-CECJ	Schleicher ASK 13	13384	
F-CECK	Schleicher ASK 13	13385	
F-CECL	Schleicher ASK 13	13387	
F-CECN	Schleicher Ka 6E	4386	
F-CECO	Schleicher ASK 13	13389	
F-CECQ	Schleicher ASK 13	13390	
F-CECS-K89	Schleicher Ka 6E	4389	
F-CECT	Schleicher ASK 13	13402	
F-CECU	Schleicher ASK 13	13405	
F-CECY	Schleicher ASK 13	13407	
F-CEDC	Schempp-Hirth Nimbus II	53	
F-CEDH-N10	Schempp-Hirth Nimbus IIC	74	
F-CEDK-N14	Schempp-Hirth Nimbus IID	112	
F-CEDM-N17	Schempp-Hirth Nimbus IIB	137	F-WEDM
F-CEDO-DO	Schempp-Hirth Ventus a/16.6	25	F-WEDO
F-CEDQ-14	Schempp-Hirth Ventus b/16.6	52	F-WEDQ
F-CEDS-28	Schempp-Hirth Ventus b/16.6	44	F-WEDS
F-CEDU	Schempp-Hirth Ventus b/16.6	95	F-WEDU, D-4305
F-CEDV	Schempp-Hirth Ventus b/16.6	235	F-WEDV
F-CEDX	Glasflügel H303B Mosquito	128	
F-CEDZ-M05	Glasflügel H303B Mosquito	154	
F-CEEA	LCA-Scheibe 10 Topaze	1	
F-CEED	LCA-Scheibe 11 Topaze	4	
F-CEEE	LCA-Scheibe 11 Topaze	5	
F-CEEG	LCA-Scheibe 10 Topaze	7	
F-CEEL	LCA-Scheibe 11 Topaze	12	OO-YWM, F-CEEL
F-CEEM	LCA-Scheibe 11 Topaze	13	
F-CEEN	LCA-Scheibe 11 Topaze	14	
F-CEEO	LCA-Scheibe 11 Topaze	15	
F-CEEQ	LCA-Scheibe 11 Topaze	17	
F-CEET	LCA-Scheibe 11 Topaze	20	
F-CEEY	LCA-Scheibe 11 Topaze	24	
F-CEFB-EA	Schempp-Hirth CS-11 St.Cirrus	326G	
F-CEFF-C11	Schempp-Hirth CS-11 St.Cirrus	371G	
F-CEFG-C10	Schempp-Hirth CS-11 St.Cirrus	387G	
F-CEFH	Schempp-Hirth CS-11 St.Cirrus	401G	
F-CEFK	Schempp-Hirth CS-11 St.Cirrus	406G	
F-CEFS-C22	Schempp-Hirth CS-11 St.Cirrus	462G	
F-CEFU	Schempp-Hirth CS-11 St.Cirrus	468G	
F-CEFV	Schempp-Hirth CS-11 St.Cirrus	469G	
F-CEFZ	Schempp-Hirth CS-11 St.Cirrus	512G	
F-CEGA	Schleicher ASK 13	13404	
F-CEGC	Schleicher ASK 13	13410	
F-CEGD	Schleicher ASK 13	13412	
F-CEGE	Schleicher ASW 15B	15269	
F-CEGG	Schleicher ASW 15B	15271	
F-CEGH	Schleicher ASW 15B	15272	
F-CEGI	Schleicher ASW 15B	15273	
F-CEGN	Schleicher ASW 15B	15297	
F-CEGP-BN	Schleicher ASW 15B	15292	
F-CEGQ	Schleicher ASW 15B	15293	
F-CEGS	Schleicher ASW 15B	15295	
F-CEGT-A13	Schleicher ASW 15B	15296	
F-CEGU	Schleicher K 8B	8933	
F-CEGV	Schleicher K 8B	8934	
F-CEGX	Schleicher K 8B	8935	
F-CEGZ	Schleicher Ka 6E	4186	
F-CEHC	Rolladen-Schneider LS1-d	216	
F-CEHD	Rolladen-Schneider LS1-d	217	
F-CEHF	Rolladen-Schneider LS1-d	219	
F-CEHG-L33	Rolladen-Schneider LS1-d	220	
F-CEHI-L32	Rolladen-Schneider LS1-d	222	
F-CEHK	Rolladen-Schneider LS1-d	224	
F-CEHL	Rolladen-Schneider LS1-d	225	
F-CEHM-L35	Rolladen-Schneider LS1-d (Dismantled)	226	
F-CEHO-L39	Rolladen-Schneider LS1-d	228	
F-CEHR-L42	Rolladen-Schneider LS1-d	231	
F-CEHS-L43	Rolladen-Schneider LS1-d	232	
F-CEHT	Rolladen-Schneider LS1-d	233	
F-CEHU-L45	Rolladen-Schneider LS1-d	234	
F-CEHY	Rolladen-Schneider LS1-d	237	
F-CEIB-SB	Rolladen-Schneider LS4	4012	
F-CEIC	Rolladen-Schneider LS4	4013	
F-CEID-FL	Rolladen-Schneider LS4	4020	
F-CEIE	Rolladen-Schneider LS4	4053	
F-CEIF-SC	Rolladen-Schneider LS4	4056	
F-CEIG-V08	Rolladen-Schneider LS4	4057	
F-CEII-V10	Rolladen-Schneider LS4	4059	
F-CEIJ-V11	Rolladen-Schneider LS4	4138	
F-CEIK	Rolladen-Schneider LS4	4139	

285

Reg	Type	c/n	Prev id
F-CEIL	Rolladen-Schneider LS4	4245	
F-CEIM-RF	Rolladen-Schneider LS4	4140	
F-CEIN-FF	Rolladen-Schneider LS4	4141	
F-CEIP-V20	Rolladen-Schneider LS4	4231	
F-CEIQ-RM	Rolladen-Schneider LS4	4292	
F-CEIR-TC	Rolladen-Schneider LS4	4232	
F-CEIS-V22	Rolladen-Schneider LS4	4233	
F-CEIT-V23	Rolladen-Schneider LS4	4234	
F-CEIV-FA1	Rolladen-Schneider LS4	4236	
F-CEIX	Rolladen-Schneider LS4	4237	
F-CEIY-V27	Rolladen-Schneider LS4	4238	
F-CEIZ-V49	Rolladen-Schneider LS4	4239	
F-CEJA	Schleicher K 8B	8936	
F-CEJB	Schleicher K 8B	8937	
F-CEJC	Schleicher K 8B	8939	
F-CEJD	Schleicher K 8B	8940	
F-CEJE	Schleicher K 8B	8938	
F-CEJG-SG	Schleicher ASW 17	17022	
F-CEJH	Schleicher K 8B	8956	
F-CEJI	Schleicher K 8B	8957	
F-CEJJ	Schleicher ASK 13	13461	
F-CEJK	Schleicher ASK 13	13462	
F-CEJP	Schleicher K 8B	8976	
F-CEJQ	Schleicher K 8B	8977	
F-CEJS	Schleicher K 8B	8979	
F-CEJT	Schleicher ASK 13	13509	
F-CEJU	Schleicher ASK 13	13520	
F-CEJV	Schleicher K 8B	8982	
F-CEJW	Schleicher ASK 13	13521	
F-CEJX	Schleicher ASK 13	13522	
F-CEJY	Schleicher K 8B	8984	
F-CEJZ	Schleicher K 8B	8983	
F-CEKA	Rolladen-Schneider LS1-f	376	
F-CEKD-L53	Rolladen-Schneider LS1-f	387	
F-CEKE-L54	Rolladen-Schneider LS1-f	388	
F-CEKF-L55	Rolladen-Schneider LS1-f	389	
F-CEKL-L61	Rolladen-Schneider LS1-f	396	
F-CEKP	Rolladen-Schneider LS1-f	400	
F-CEKR	Rolladen-Schneider LS1-f	402	
F-CEKT-LT	Rolladen-Schneider LS1-f	404	
F-CEKV-L72	Rolladen-Schneider LS1-f	439	
F-CEKY	Rolladen-Schneider LS1-f	451	
F-CELB	Glasflügel H201B Standard Libelle	531	
F-CELC-758	Glasflügel H201B Standard Libelle	558	
F-CELD	Wassmer WA.26P Squale	64	F-CDXY
F-CELG	Glasflügel H201B Standard Libelle	600	
F-CELL-M07	Glasflügel H303B Mosquito	168	
F-CELM-M08	Glasflügel H303B Mosquito	169	
F-CELO	Glasflügel H303B Mosquito	176	
F-CELP-DH	Glasflügel H303B Mosquito	182	
F-CELR-738	Glasflügel H201B Standard Libelle	598	
F-CELS-M²	Glasflügel H303B Mosquito	188	
F-CELT-M14	Glasflügel H303B Mosquito	189	
F-CELU-M15	Glasflügel H303B Mosquito	197	
F-CELV	Glasflügel H303B Mosquito	198	
F-CELY	Glasflügel H303B Mosquito	202	
F-CEMC	Grob/Schempp-Hirth CS-11 St.Cirrus	552G	
F-CEMO	Schempp-Hirth CS-11/75 St.Cirrus	617	
F-CEMU-C49	Schempp-Hirth CS-11/75 St.Cirrus	657	
F-CEMZ-C53	Schempp-Hirth Standard Cirrus 75	679	
F-CENA	LCA-Scheibe 12	26	
F-CENB	LCA-Scheibe 12	27	
F-CENF	LCA-Scheibe 12	31	
F-CENN	Schleicher ASK 13	13117	I-CENN
F-CEOE	Wassmer WA.28F	110	
F-CEOF	Wassmer WA.28 Espadon	111	
F-CEOG	Wassmer WA.28 Espadon	112	
F-CEOH	Wassmer WA.28 Espadon	113	
F-CEPA	Schempp-Hirth Janus A	05	F-WEPA
F-CEPB	Schempp-Hirth Janus	14	
F-CEPC-3C	Schempp-Hirth Janus A (W/o 19.7.08)	17	
F-CEPD	Schempp-Hirth Janus A	21	
F-CEPE	Schempp-Hirth Janus A	22	
F-CEPF-33	Schempp-Hirth Janus A	33	
F-CEPG	Schempp-Hirth Janus A	32	
F-CEPH	Schempp-Hirth Janus A	38	
F-CEPI-J46	Schempp-Hirth Janus B	46	
F-CEPJ-PJ	Schempp-Hirth Janus B	67	
F-CEPL-EA	Schempp-Hirth Janus B	82	
F-CEPM-J20	Schempp-Hirth Janus B	84	
F-CEPN	Schempp-Hirth Janus B	85	
F-CEPO	Schempp-Hirth Janus B	94	
F-CEPP	Schempp-Hirth Janus B	95	
F-CEPQ	Schempp-Hirth Janus B	100	
F-CEPR-PR	Schempp-Hirth Janus B	102	
F-CEPS-J22	Schempp-Hirth Janus B	101	
F-CEPT	Schempp-Hirth Janus B	105	
F-CEPU-J107	Schempp-Hirth Janus B	107	
F-CEPX	Schempp-Hirth Janus B	109	
F-CEPY	Schempp-Hirth Janus B	114	
F-CEPZ	Schempp-Hirth Janus B	115	
F-CEQC	Glasflügel H205 Libelle	146	
F-CEQD	Glasflügel H205 Libelle	147	
F-CEQH	Glasflügel H205 Libelle	151	
F-CEQJ	Glasflügel H205 Libelle	156	
F-CEQN	Glasflügel H205 Libelle	161	
F-CEQO	Glasflügel H205 Libelle	162	
F-CEQQ	Glasflügel H205 Libelle	166	
F-CEQR	Glasflügel H205 Libelle	167	
F-CEQV-M1	Glasflügel H303 Mosquito	16	
F-CEQX-BZ	Glasflügel H303 Mosquito	41	F-WEQX
F-CEQZ	Lanaverre CS-11/75L Standard Cirrus	38	
F-CERA	Schleicher ASK 13	13523	
F-CERB	Schleicher ASK 13	13531	
F-CERD	Schleicher ASK 13	13532	
F-CERE	Schleicher ASK 13	13541	
F-CERG	Schleicher K 8B	8985	
F-CERJ	Schleicher ASK 18	18033	
F-CERL	Schleicher ASK 18	18035	
F-CERM	Schleicher ASW 19	19041	
F-CERN	Schleicher ASK 13	13544	
F-CERO	Schleicher ASK 13	13573	
F-CERP-X01	Schleicher ASW 20	20024	
F-CERS-F04	Schleicher ASW 19	19241	
F-CERU	Schleicher ASW 19B	19326	
F-CERV-X99	Centrair ASW 20FL	20500	
F-CERX-X1	Centrair ASW 20F	20513	
F-CERY-X117	Centrair ASW 20F	20517	
F-CESA	Rolladen-Schneider LS1-f	469	
F-CESB	Rolladen-Schneider LS1-f	455	
F-CESD-S1	Rolladen-Schneider LS3	3203	
F-CESF-S03	Rolladen-Schneider LS3-a	3204	
F-CESH	Rolladen-Schneider LS3-a	3157	
F-CESI-S06	Rolladen-Schneider LS3-a	3187	
F-CESL-GC	Rolladen-Schneider LS3-a	3385	
F-CESM-S10	Rolladen-Schneider LS3-a	3419	
F-CESN	Rolladen-Schneider LS3-17	3420	
F-CESO-S14	Rolladen-Schneider LS3-a	3438	
F-CESP	Rolladen-Schneider LS3-17	3439	
F-CESQ	Rolladen-Schneider LS3-a	3452	
F-CESR	Rolladen-Schneider LS3-17	3453	
F-CESU-S19	Rolladen-Schneider LS3-a	3460	
F-CESX-V60	Rolladen-Schneider LS4-b	41053	
F-CETG	Carmam JP.15/36A Aiglon	9	
F-CETL	Carmam JP.15/36A Aiglon	14	
F-CETY	Carmam JP.15/36AR Aiglon	29	
F-CEUC	Caproni A.21S Calif	237	
F-CEUF	Caproni A.21S Calif	241	
F-CEUJ	Centrair ASW 20FL	20174	
F-CEVF-C60	Lanaverre CS-11/75L Standard Cirrus	5	
F-CEVI	Lanaverre CS-11/75L Standard Cirrus	8	
F-CEVM	Lanaverre CS-11/75L Standard Cirrus	12	
F-CEVN-C68	Lanaverre CS-11/75L Standard Cirrus	13	
F-CEVU	Lanaverre CS-11/75L Standard Cirrus	29	
F-CEVV-C76	Lanaverre CS-11/75L Standard Cirrus	30	
F-CEXA-R01	Grob G 102 Astir CS	1459	
F-CEXB	Grob G 102 Astir CS	1522	
F-CEXC	Grob G 102 Astir CS	1523	
F-CEXD-R04	Grob G 102 Astir CS	1524	
F-CEXE	Grob G 102 Astir CS	1525	
F-CEXF-R06	Grob G 102 Astir CS	1526	
F-CEXG-R08	Grob G 102 Astir CS	1527	
F-CEXK	Grob G 102 Astir CS	1535	
F-CEXL	Grob G 102 Astir CS	1536	
F-CEXM-R14	Grob G 102/77 Astir CS	1688	
F-CEXN-R22	Grob G 102/77 Astir CS	1697	
F-CEXO-R20	Grob G 102/77 Astir CS	1706	
F-CEXP	Grob G 102/77 Astir CS	1699	
F-CEXQ-R26	Grob G 102/77 Astir CS	1730	
F-CEXR-R29	Grob G 102/77 Astir CS	1743	
F-CEXS-R30	Grob G 102/77 Astir CS	1759	
F-CEXT-R38	Grob G 102/77 Astir CS	1775	
F-CEXU-R31	Grob G 102/77 Astir CS	1773	
F-CEXV-R32	Grob G 102/77 Astir CS	1779	
F-CEXX	Grob G 102/77 Astir CS	1774	
F-CEXY	Grob G 102/77 Astir CS	1794	
F-CEXZ-R35	Grob G 102/77 Astir CS	1795	
F-CEYA	Scheibe SF 28A Tandem-Falke	5756	D-KMOS, (D-KMGF)
F-CEYB	Scheibe SF 28A Tandem-Falke	5781	D-KCIR(2)
F-CEYC	Scheibe SF 28A Tandem-Falke	5783	(D-KDFM(1))
F-CEYE	Scheibe SF 28A Tandem-Falke	5785	(D-KDFQ(1))
F-CEYF-L72	Scheibe SF 28A Tandem-Falke	5786	(D-KDFW(1))
F-CEYG	Scheibe SF 28A Tandem-Falke	5787	(D-KDFY(1))
F-CEYH	Scheibe SF 28A Tandem-Falke (W/o 4.12.05)	5788	(D-KDFZ(1))
F-CEYI	Scheibe SF 28A Tandem-Falke	5789	(D-KDFX(3))
F-CEYJ	Scheibe SF 28A Tandem-Falke	5790	(D-KDFY(3))
F-CEYK	Scheibe SF 28A Tandem-Falke	5792	(D-KDCJ(1))
F-CEYL	Scheibe SF 28A Tandem-Falke	5793	(D-KDCK(1))
F-CEYM	Scheibe SF 28A Tandem-Falke	5794	(D-KDOQ(1))
F-CEYN	Scheibe SF 28A Tandem-Falke	5795	(D-KDCU(2))
F-CEYO	Scheibe SF 28A Tandem-Falke	5796	(D-KDCW)
F-CEYP	Scheibe SF 28A Tandem-Falke	5797	(D-KDCX)
F-CEYQ	Scheibe SF 28A Tandem-Falke	5798	(D-KDCY)
F-CEYS	Scheibe SF 28A Tandem-Falke	57101	(D-KDBR(1))
F-CEYT	Scheibe SF 28A Tandem-Falke	57104	(D-KDBY(1))
F-CEYU	Scheibe SF 28A Tandem-Falke	57105	(D-KDBU(2))
F-CEYV	Scheibe SF 28A Tandem-Falke	5734	HB-2022, (D-KOED(1))
F-CEYY	Scheibe SF 28A Tandem-Falke	57109	(D-KDGS(1))
F-CEZA	Scheibe Bergfalke IV	5861	
F-CEZB	Scheibe Bergfalke IV	5865	
F-CFAA-JD	Schempp-Hirth HS-7 Mini-Nimbus	17	F-WFAA
F-CFAB-101	Schempp-Hirth HS-7 Mini-Nimbus	130	
F-CFAD	Schempp-Hirth Janus B	124	
F-CFAE-E	Schempp-Hirth Janus B	128	
F-CFAF-AF	Schempp-Hirth Janus B	131	
F-CFAG-AG	Schempp-Hirth Janus B	135	
F-CFAH	Schempp-Hirth Janus B	137	
F-CFAJ-J39	Schempp-Hirth Janus B (Damaged 13.3.03)	153	
F-CFAL	Schempp-Hirth Janus C	154	
F-CFAM-M	Schempp-Hirth Janus C	155	
F-CFAN-J43	Schempp-Hirth Janus C	159	
F-CFAO-PT	Schempp-Hirth Janus B	160	
F-CFAP	Schempp-Hirth Janus C	164	
F-CFAQ	Schempp-Hirth Janus C	173	
F-CFAR-IN	Schempp-Hirth Janus C	166	
F-CFAS	Schempp-Hirth Janus B	175	
F-CFAT	Schempp-Hirth Janus B	180	
F-CFAU-J50	Schempp-Hirth Janus B	192	
F-CFAV-T	Schempp-Hirth Janus CT	3/195	F-WFAV, D-KFAV, F-WFAV
F-CFAX-73	Schempp-Hirth Janus B	204	
F-CFAY -J53	Schempp-Hirth Janus B	207	
F-CFAZ-AZ	Schempp-Hirth Janus B	221	
F-CFBA-T01	Grob G 103 Twin Astir (Stored 1.11)	3055	
F-CFBB-T02	Grob G 103 Twin Astir	3082	
F-CFBC-T03	Grob G 103T Twin Astir Trainer	3124	
F-CFBD	Grob G 103 Twin Astir	3119	
F-CFBE-T05	Grob G 103 Twin Astir	3120	
F-CFBH-T08	Grob G 103 Twin Astir	3123	
F-CFBI	Grob G 103 Twin Astir	3131	
F-CFBJ-T10	Grob G 103 Twin Astir	3132	
F-CFBK-T11	Grob G 103 Twin Astir	3133	
F-CFBL	Grob G 103 Twin Astir	3114	
F-CFBO-T15	Grob G 103 Twin Astir	3128	
F-CFBT-T20	Grob G 103 Twin Astir	3125	
F-CFBX-T23	Grob G 103 Twin Astir	3281	
F-CFBZ-T25	Grob G 103T Twin Astir Trainer	3201	
F-CFCB-R15	Grob G 102/77J Astir Jeans	2079	
F-CFCC-R16	Grob G 102/77J Astir Jeans	2084	

Registration	Type	Serial	Previous/Other identities
F-CFCD-R21	Grob G 102/77J Astir Jeans	2111	
F-CFCE-R17	Grob G 102/77J Astir Jeans	2094	
F-CFCF-R18	Grob G 102/77J Astir Jeans	2098	
F-CFCH-R24	Grob G 102/77J Astir Jeans	2115	
F-CFCI -R25	Grob G 102/77J Astir Jeans	2123	
F-CFCJ -CJ	Grob G 102/77J Astir Jeans	2144	
F-CFCK-R28	Grob G 102/77J Astir Jeans	2145	
F-CFCL-R36	Grob G 102/77J Astir Jeans	2163	
F-CFCM-R37	Grob G 102/77J Astir Jeans	2177	
F-CFCO-R40	Grob G 102/77J Astir Jeans	2179	
F-CFCQ	Grob G 102/77J Astir Jeans	2200	
F-CFCR-R43	Grob G 102/77J Astir Jeans	2201	
F-CFCS-R44	Grob G 102/77J Astir Jeans	2204	
F-CFCU-R46	Grob G 102/77J Astir Jeans	2231	
F-CFCX	Grob G 102C Club Astir II	5021C	
F-CFCZ-R60	Grob G 102C Club Astir II	5023C	
F-CFDA	Jastreb Standard Cirrus G/81	256	F-WFDA
F-CFDB-SW	Jastreb Standard Cirrus G/81	257	F-WFDB
F-CFDE	Scheibe SF 34B	5140	
F-CFDF	Schempp-Hirth Discus CS	017CS	
F-CFDG-Z19	Rolladen-Schneider LS6-18W	6301	
F-CFDH	Schempp-Hirth Discus b	509	
F-CFDI-D28	Schempp-Hirth Discus b	513	
F-CFDJ-D29	Schempp-Hirth Discus CS	175CS	
F-CFDK-D30	Schempp-Hirth Discus CS	180CS	
F-CFDL-D31	Schempp-Hirth Discus CS	221CS	
F-CFDM-PM	Schempp-Hirth Discus b	139	D-4693
F-CFDN-D33	Schempp-Hirth Discus CS	235CS	
F-CFDO-LV	Schempp-Hirth Discus-2a	20	D-2778
F-CFDP-EH	Schempp-Hirth Discus-2b	31	
F-CFDQ-DA	Schempp-Hirth Discus-2a	27	D-4096
F-CFDS-ET	Schempp-Hirth Discus-2a	173	
F-CFDU-EI	Schempp-Hirth Discus-2c	38	
F-CFDV	Schempp-Hirth Discus-2c	39	
F-CFDX-CFM1	Schempp-Hirth Discus-2b	236	
F-CFEP	Scheibe SF-28A Tandem-Falke	5730	D-KEEP, (D-KOAS)
F-CFFD-X04	Centrair ASW 20F	20104	
F-CFFF	Centrair ASW 20F	20106	
F-CFFN-X18	Centrair ASW 20FL	20117	
F-CFFP	Centrair ASW 20F	20120	
F-CFFS-X24	Centrair ASW 20FL	20124	
F-CFFT	Centrair ASW 20FL	20125	
F-CFFV-X29	Centrair ASW 20F	20129	
F-CFFZ -TA	Centrair ASW 20F	20135	
F-CFGE	Pottier 15/34 Kit Club	50-38	
F-CFGI	Pottier 15/34 Kit Club	50-44	
F-CFHB-T27	Grob G 103 Twin Astir	3229	
F-CFHD	Grob G 103 Twin Astir	3234	
F-CFHH-T33	Grob G 103 Twin Astir	3250	
F-CFHJ-T35	Grob G 103T Twin Astir Trainer	3283	
F-CFHK-HK	Grob G 103T Twin Astir Trainer	3282	
F-CFHM-T38	Grob G 103 Twin Astir II	3530	
F-CFHQ-T42	Grob G 103 Twin Astir II	3568	
F-CFHR-T43	Grob G 103 Twin Astir II	3569	
F-CFHS-T44	Grob G 103 Twin Astir II	3578	
F-CFHT	Grob G 103 Twin Astir II	3579	
F-CFHU	Grob G 103 Twin Astir II	3580	
F-CFHV-T47	Grob G 103 Twin Astir II	3581	
F-CFHX-T48	Grob G 103 Twin Astir II	3582	
F-CFHY-T49	Grob G 103 Twin Astir II	3583	
F-CFHZ-T50	Grob G 103 Twin Astir II	3584	
F-CFIA	Grob G 102/77 Astir CS	1801	
F-CFIB-R51	Grob G 102/77 Astir CS	1802	
F-CFID	Grob G 102/77 Astir CS	1810	
F-CFIE-R54	Grob G 102/77 Astir CS	1811	
F-CFIG-R56	Grob G 102/77 Astir CS	1821	
F-CFII -R58	Grob G 102 Standard Astir II	5034S	
F-CFIJ-R59	Grob G 102 Standard Astir II	5035S	
F-CFIK	Grob G 102 Standard Astir II	5036S	
F-CFIL-R71	Grob G 102 Standard Astir II	5037S	
F-CFIM-R72	Grob G 102 Standard Astir II	5038S	
F-CFIN-R73	Grob G 102 Standard Astir II	5039S	
F-CFIO	Grob G 102 Standard Astir II	5042S	
F-CFIP-R75	Grob G 102 Standard Astir II	5043S	
F-CFIQ-R76	Grob G 102 Astir CS 77	1817	
F-CFIR-W	Grob G 102 Astir CS 77	1637	PH-572
F-CFIX	Fournier RF3	29	HB-2013, F-BMDG
F-CFJA	Scheibe SF 28A Tandem-Falke	57115	(D-KDGX(2))
F-CFJB	Scheibe SF 28A Tandem-Falke	57117	(D-KOOH(1))
F-CFJC-RF	Scheibe SF 28A Tandem-Falke	57119	(D-KNAU(1))
F-CFJD	Scheibe SF 28A Tandem-Falke	57121	D-KNIH
F-CFJE	Scheibe SF 28A Tandem-Falke	5769	D-KACV
F-CFJG	Scheibe SF 28A Tandem-Falke	5725	D-KOAM
F-CFJH	Scheibe SF 28A Tandem-Falke	5709	D-KHOS
F-CFJK	Scheibe SF 28A Tandem-Falke	5705	F-WFJK, D-KHOO
F-CFJL	Scheibe SF 28A Tandem-Falke	5737	D-KOEG
F-CFKB-T52	Grob G 103 Twin Astir II	3586	
F-CFKC-T53	Grob G 103 Twin Astir II	3587	
F-CFKE-T55	Grob G 103 Twin Astir II	3589	
F-CFKF-T56	Grob G 103 Twin Astir II	3590	
F-CFKG	Grob G 103 Twin Astir II	3591	
F-CFKI -T59	Grob G 103 Twin Astir II	3627	
F-CFKJ-T60	Grob G 103 Twin Astir II	3628	
F-CFKK-T61	Grob G 103 Twin Astir II	3629	
F-CFKM-T63	Grob G 103 Twin Astir II	3631	
F-CFKP-T66	Grob G 103 Twin Astir II	3695	
F-CFKQ-T67	Grob G 103 Twin Astir II	3704	
F-CFKR-T68	Grob G 103 Twin Astir II	3705	
F-CFKS-T69	Grob G 103 Twin Astir II	3706	
F-CFKT-T70	Grob G 103 Twin Astir II	3707	
F-CFKU-T71	Grob G 103 Twin Astir II	3715	
F-CFKV-T75	Grob G 103 Twin Astir II	3759	
F-CFKY-T77	Grob G 103 Twin Astir II	3834	
F-CFKZ-T78	Grob G 103 Twin Astir II	3835	
F-CFLE	Centrair ASW 20F	20142	
F-CFLF-X43	Centrair ASW 20F	20143	
F-CFLH	Centrair ASW 20FL	20146	
F-CFLI- LI	Centrair ASW 20FL	20148	
F-CFLJ	Centrair ASW 20FL	20147	
F-CFLK-X49	Centrair ASW 20F	20149	
F-CFLM	Centrair ASW 20F	20152	
F-CFLN-X53	Centrair ASW 20FL	20153	
F-CFLP-AV	Centrair ASW 20F	20157	
F-CFLQ	Centrair ASW 20F	20158	
F-CFLX-X86	Centrair ASW 20FL	20186	
F-CFMA-R61	Grob G 102C Club Astir II	5024C	
F-CFMC-R63	Grob G 102C Club Astir II	5053C	
F-CFMD-R64	Grob G 102C Club Astir II	5054C	
F-CFMF-R66	Grob G 102C Club Astir IIIB	5509CB	
F-CFMG-R67	Grob G 102C Club Astir IIIB	5544CB	
F-CFMI-R69	Grob G 102C Club Astir IIIB	5565CB	
F-CFMJ-MJ	Grob G 102C Club Astir IIIB	5582CB	
F-CFMK-FY	Grob G 102/77J Astir Jeans	2240	D-5946
F-CFML-R86	Grob G 102/77J Astir Jeans	2245	
F-CFMM-R47	Grob G 102/77J Astir Jeans	2093	D-7535
F-CFMN	Grob G 102/77J Astir Jeans	2055	D-7576
F-CFMO	Grob G 102/77J Astir Jeans	2023	D-4828
F-CFMQ	Grob G 102/77J Astir Jeans	2092	D-7534
F-CFMR-MM	Grob G 102/77J Astir Jeans	2159	D-4555
F-CFMT	Grob G 102/77J Astir Jeans	2071	HB-1399
F-CFMU	Grob G 102/77J Astir Jeans	2102	D-7630
F-CFNB	Pottier 15/34 Kit Club	50-59	
F-CFNZ	Rolladen-Schneider LS8-18	8171	G-CJCY, BGA 4418
F-CFPE	Siren PIK-30	713	
F-CFPG	Siren PIK-30	723	
F-CFPH	Siren PIK-30	724	
F-CFPJ	Siren PIK-30	727	
F-CFPO	Siren PIK-30	712	F-WFPO
F-CFQG-B43	Centrair 101A Pégase	101043	
F-CFQH	Centrair 101A Pégase	101037	
F-CFQK-B4	Centrair 101A Pégase	101047	
F-CFQL	Centrair 101A Pégase	101049	
F-CFQO-B52	Centrair 101A Pégase	101052	
F-CFQP	Centrair 101A Pégase	101053	
F-CFQS	Centrair 101A Pégase	101059	
F-CFQT	Centrair 101A Pégase	101044	
F-CFQZ	Centrair 101A Pégase	101067	
F-CFRA	Centrair 101AP Pégase	101001	F-WFRA
F-CFRB	Centrair 101AP Pégase	101005	
F-CFRC-B06	Centrair 101A Pégase	101006	
F-CFRD	Centrair 101A Pégase	101007	
F-CFRE-RE	Centrair 101A Pégase	101008	
F-CFRF	Centrair 101A Pégase	101009	
F-CFRG	Centrair 101A Pégase	101010	
F-CFRH-B14	Centrair 101A Pégase	101014	
F-CFRI	Centrair 101A Pégase	101011	
F-CFRK	Centrair 101A Pégase	101015	
F-CFRL	Centrair 101A Pégase	101018	
F-CFRM-B19	Centrair 101A Pégase	101019	
F-CFRO-B17	Centrair 101A Pégase	101017	
F-CFRQ	Centrair 101A Pégase	101021	
F-CFRT-B22	Centrair 101A Pégase	101022	
F-CFRU-B25	Centrair 101A Pégase	101025	
F-CFRV-B30	Centrair 101A Pégase	101030	
F-CFSG-SG	Centrair ASW 20F	20525	
F-CFTA-WA	Centrair ASW 20FL	20107	EI-126, F-CFFG
F-CFTB	Grob G 103 Twin Astir	3212	
F-CFTC	Schleicher K 8B	8422	
F-CFTD	Scheibe SF 28A Tandem-Falke	5719	D-KOAK
F-CFTE	Scheibe Bergfalke IV	5844	
F-CFTH	Schleicher K 8B	8450SH	HB-823
F-CFTJ	Scheibe SF 28A Tandem-Falke (W/o 11.10.15)	5738	D-KOEH
F-CFTK	Scheibe SF 28A Tandem-Falke	5758	HB-2032, D-KMGH
F-CFTL-R23	Grob G 102/77J Astir Jeans	2113	3A-MCG, F-CFCG
F-CFTM	Scheibe SF 28A Tandem-Falke	5702/V-2	D-KAOQ
F-CFTN	Scheibe SF 28A Tandem-Falke	5762	OY-XHG, D-KAWU, (D-KACO(2))
F-CFTO	Schempp-Hirth Nimbus-3/24.5	33	BGA3102/FAH, N17UF
F-CFUA	Schempp-Hirth Nimbus-3/24.5	35	
F-CFUC	Schempp-Hirth Nimbus-2	176	D-6851
F-CFUG-CLM	Schempp-Hirth Nimbus-3D	6/33	D-1753
F-CFUI-EN	Schempp-Hirth Nimbus-3D	8/41	D-4518
F-CFUJ-SFA	Schempp-Hirth Nimbus-3D	7/35	
F-CFUN-12	Schempp-Hirth Nimbus-3/24.5	50	F-WFUN
F-CFUP-UP	Schempp-Hirth Nimbus-3DT	60	
F-CFUR	Schempp-Hirth Nimbus-3/24.5	34	D-1151, N88SA
F-CFUS-US	Schempp-Hirth Nimbus-4DT	1/1	D-KFUS, D-2111
F-CFUT-EK	Schempp-Hirth Nimbus-3D	10/50	D-2872
F-CFUV-MX	Schempp-Hirth Nimbus-4D	3/11	D-8563
F-CFUX	Schempp-Hirth Nimbus-4DM	6/14	D-KLUX
F-CFUZ-EN	Schempp-Hirth Nimbus-4D	6/36	
F-CFVA-PP	Glaser-Dirks DG-400	4-52	F-WFVA
F-CFVC	Glaser-Dirks DG-400	4-109	F-WFVC
F-CFVD	Glaser-Dirks DG-400	4-110	F-WFVD
F-CFVF	Glaser-Dirks DG-400	4-122	F-WFVF
F-CFVG	Glaser-Dirks DG-400	4-140	F-WFVG
F-CFVJ	Glaser-Dirks DG-400	4-173	
F-CFVL-K31	Glaser-Dirks DG-300 Elan	3E88	F-WFVL
F-CFVM	Glaser-Dirks DG-300 Elan	3E137	F-WFVM
F-CFVN	Glaser-Dirks DG-300 Elan	3E153	F-WFVN
F-WFVO	Glaser-Dirks DG-300 Elan	3E171	
F-CFVP	Glaser-Dirks DG-300 Elan	3E170	F-WFVP
F-CFVR	Glaser-Dirks DG-300 Elan	3E212	F-WFVR
F-CFVS-K38	Glaser-Dirks DG-300 Elan	3E229	F-WFVS
F-CFVT-K27	Glaser-Dirks DG-300 Elan	3E245	F-WFVT
F-CFVU	Glaser-Dirks DG-300 Elan	3E276	F-WFVU
F-CFXC-B72	Centrair 101A Pégase	101072	
F-CFXF	Centrair 101A Pégase	101075	
F-CFXG-B76	Centrair 101A Pégase	101076	
F-CFXJ-B93	Centrair 101A Pégase	101093	
F-CFXK	Centrair 101A Pégase	101085	
F-CFXM	Centrair 101A Pégase	101A0106	
F-CFXN	Centrair 101A Pégase	101A0104	
F-CFXO-RD	Centrair 101A Pégase	101A0103	
F-CFXP	Centrair 101A Pégase	101A0101	
F-CFXQ	Centrair 101A Pégase	101A0113	
F-CFXR-B114	Centrair 101A Pégase	101A0114	
F-CFXS-B115	Centrair 101A Pégase	101A0115	
F-CFXT	Centrair 101A Pégase	101A0116	
F-CFXV-XV	Centrair 101A Pégase	101A0134	
F-CFXX	Centrair 101A Pégase	101A0133	
F-CFXY	Centrair ASW 20F	20531	
F-CFXZ-B135	Centrair 101A Pégase	101A0135	
F-CFYA-T79	Grob G 103 Twin Astir II	3838	
F-CFYB-T80	Grob G 103 Twin Astir II	3766	
F-CFYC-T82	Grob G 103A Twin II Acro	33951-K-184	
F-CFYD-T83	Grob G 103A Twin II Acro	33952-K-185	
F-CFYE-T84	Grob G 103A Twin II Acro	33963-K-196	
F-CFYG-T87	Grob G 103A Twin II Acro	34052-K-282	
F-CFYH-SH	Grob G 103A Twin II Acro	34058-K-288	
F-CFYI -ST	Grob G 103 Twin Astir II	3570	D-6640

Registration	Type	Serial	Previous identities
F-CFYJ	Grob G 103 Twin Astir II	3596	D-3963
F-CFYK-T91	Grob G 103 Twin Astir II	3556	D-8764
F-CFYM	Grob G 103A Twin II Acro	33965-K-198	D-8067
F-CFYN	Grob G 103 Twin Astir II	3594	D-4867
F-CFYR-T98	Grob G 103 Twin Astir II	3663	D-2600
F-CFYS-T99	Grob G 103 Twin Astir	3078	D-3949
F-CFYT	Grob G 103A Twin II Acro	3732-K-47	D-1604, PL90, D-6189
F-CFYU	Grob G 103 Twin Astir	3071	D-4856
F-CFZA-J	Rolladen-Schneider LS4	4336	
F-CFZB-V31	Rolladen-Schneider LS4	4358	
F-CFZD-V32	Rolladen-Schneider LS4	4397	
F-CFZE-V33	Rolladen-Schneider LS4	4409	
F-CFZF-V34	Rolladen-Schneider LS4	4425	
F-CFZH-V36	Rolladen-Schneider LS4	4476	
F-CFZI	Rolladen-Schneider LS4	4487	
F-CFZJ-V38	Rolladen-Schneider LS4	4488	
F-CFZK-V40	Rolladen-Schneider LS4	4499	
F-CFZL-34	Rolladen-Schneider LS4 (W/o 18.5.14)	4500	
F-CFZM-C43	Rolladen-Schneider LS4	4509	
F-CFZN-V43	Rolladen-Schneider LS4	4517	
F-CFZO-VM	Rolladen-Schneider LS4	4535	
F-CFZP-L1	Rolladen-Schneider LS4	4645	
F-CFZQ-V44	Rolladen-Schneider LS4	4644	
F-CFZR-V43	Rolladen-Schneider LS4	4643	
F-CFZS-AE	Rolladen-Schneider LS4	4680	
F-CFZT	Rolladen-Schneider LS4	4639	
F-CFZU-V78	Rolladen-Schneider LS4	4678	
F-CFZV-ZV	Rolladen-Schneider LS4	4707	
F-CFZX-79	Rolladen-Schneider LS4	4779	
F-CFZY-V16	Rolladen-Schneider LS4	4142	3A-MCD
F-CFZZ-V55	Rolladen-Schneider LS4-b	4938	BGA4018/HLA
F-CGAB	Valentin Taifun 17E	1027	F-WGAB, D-KCCF
F-CGAC	Valentin Taifun 17E	1037	F-WGAC, D-KDSE
F-CGAF	Valentin Taifun 17E	1073	F-WGAF, D-KHVA
F-CGAG	Valentin Taifun 17E	1100	F-WGAG, D-KHVA
F-CGAK	Hoffmann H-36 Dimona (W/o 14.7.05)	3524	F-WGAK
F-CGAM	Hoffmann H-36 Dimona	36206	F-WGAM
F-CGAN	Hoffmann H-36 Dimona	36237	F-WGAN
F-CGAP	Hoffmann H-36 Dimona	36225	F-WGAP
F-CGAQ	Hoffmann H-36 Dimona	36226	F-WGAQ
F-CGAT	Hoffmann H-36 Dimona	36258	F-WGAT
F-CGAU	Hoffmann H-36 Dimona	36260	F-WGAU
F-CGBA-B136	Centrair 101A Pégase	101A0136	
F-CGBB-TB	Centrair 101A Pégase	101A0137	
F-CGBC-TC	Centrair 101A Pégase	101A0138	
F-CGBD-BS	Centrair 101A Pégase	101A0139	
F-CGBE	Centrair 101A Pégase	101A0140	
F-CGBF	Centrair 101B Pégase	101B0143	F-WGBF
F-CGBG-B145	Centrair 101BC Pégase	101BC148	F-WGBG
F-CGBH-B144	Centrair 101A Pégase	101A0144	
F-CGBI	Centrair 101A Pégase	101A0145	
F-CGBJ-B146	Centrair 101A Pégase	101A0146	
F-CGBK-AD	Centrair 101A Pégase	101A0147	
F-CGBO	Centrair 101A Pégase	101A0153	
F-CGBP-BP	Centrair 101A Pégase	101A0171	
F-CGBQ-Q	Centrair 101A Pégase	101A0158	
F-CGBR	Centrair 101A Pégase	101A0159	
F-CGBS	Centrair 101A Pégase	101A0160	
F-CGBT	Centrair 101A Pégase	101A0162	
F-CGBV	Centrair 101A Pégase	101A0164	
F-CGBX-LY	Centrair 101A Pégase	101A0165	
F-CGBZ-B169	Centrair 101A Pégase	101A0169	
F-CGCA-BYO	Schleicher ASW 20C	20762	F-WGCA
F-CGCB	Schleicher ASW 20L	20381	
F-CGCC	Schleicher ASK 21	21244	
F-CGCD	Schleicher ASW 22	22046	F-WGCD
F-CGCE	Schleicher ASH 25	25006	F-WGCE
F-CGCG	Schleicher ASK 21	21245	
F-CGCH	Schleicher ASK 21	21269	
F-CGCI	Schleicher ASK 21	21264	
F-CGCJ	Schleicher ASK 21	21270	
F-CGCK	Schleicher ASK 21	21277	
F-CGCL	Schleicher ASK 21	21298	
F-CGCM	Schleicher ASK 21	21344	
F-CGCN	Schleicher ASW 20CL	20817	
F-CGCO	Schleicher ASW 20C	20818	
F-CGCQ-G1	Schleicher ASW 20CL	20860	
F-CGCR-S1	Schleicher ASW 20CL	20829	F-WGCR
F-CGCU	Schleicher ASK 23B	23053	F-WGCU
F-CGCV	Schleicher ASK 23B	23063	F-WGCV
F-CGCX	Schleicher ASK 23B	23064	F-WGCX
F-CGCZ	Schleicher ASK 23B	23072	F-WGCZ
F-CGDB	Aerostructure-Fournier RF-10	8	F-WGDB
F-CGDC	Aerostructure-Fournier RF-10	9	F-WGDC
F-CGDD	Aerostructure-Fournier RF-10	10	F-WGDD
F-CGDE	Aerostructure-Fournier RF-10	14	
F-CGDF	Schempp-Hirth Duo Discus	32	D-0341
F-CGDY-DY	Schempp-Hirth Duo Discus	79	D-4791
F-CGEB-B170	Centrair 101A Pégase	101A0170	
F-CGEC	Centrair 101A Pégase	101A0172	
F-CGED-E	Centrair 101A Pégase	101A0173	
F-CGEF-CS	Centrair 101A Pégase	101A0174	
F-CGEG-B180	Centrair 101A Pégase	101A0180	
F-CGEH-EZ	Centrair 101A Pégase	101A0167	
F-CGEI	Centrair 101A Pégase	101A0181	
F-CGEJ	Centrair 101A Pégase	101A0183	
F-CGEL-EL	Centrair 101A Pégase	101A0192	
F-CGEM-EM	Centrair 101A Pégase	101A0191	
F-CGEN-B196	Centrair 101A Pégase	101A0196	
F-CGEO-B194	Centrair 101A Pégase	101A0194	
F-CGEP	Centrair 101A Pégase	101A0193	
F-CGEQ-B197	Centrair 101A Pégase	101A0197	
F-CGER	Centrair 101A Pégase	101A0195	
F-CGET-B206	Centrair 101A Pégase	101A0206	
F-CGEU-B210	Centrair 101A Pégase	101A0210	
F-CGEV-B212	Centrair 101A Pégase	101A0212	
F-CGEX-ii	Centrair 101A Pégase	101A0215	
F-CGEY	Centrair 101A Pégase	101A0216	
F-CGFB-B213	Centrair 101B Pégase	101B0213	F-WGFB
F-CGFC-B217	Centrair 101A Pégase	101A0217	
F-CGFD	Centrair 101A Pégase	101A0211	
F-CGFE-E	Centrair 101A Pégase	101A0219	
F-CGFF-Z	Centrair 101A Pégase	101A0220	
F-CGFG-B222	Centrair 101A Pégase	101A0221	
F-CGFH	Centrair 101A Pégase	101A0222	
F-CGFI	Centrair 101A Pégase	101A0223	
F-CGFJ-K7	Centrair 101A Pégase	101A0226	
F-CGFK	Centrair 101 Pégase	10100232	
F-CGFL-L	Centrair 101A Pégase	101A0227	
F-CGFM-JC	Centrair 101A Pégase	101A0228	
F-CGFN-B231	Centrair 101A Pégase	101A0231	
F-CGFO	Centrair 101 Pégase	10100229	
F-CGFQ	Centrair 101A Pégase	101A0233	
F-CGFR-S06	Centrair 101A Pégase	101A0234	
F-CGFS-AA	Centrair 101A Pégase	101A0235	
F-CGFU	Centrair 101A Pégase	101A0237	
F-CGFV-ACN	Centrair 101A Pégase	101A0238	
F-CGFX	Centrair 101A Pégase	101A0239	
F-CGFY-B241	Centrair 101A Pégase	101A0241	
F-CGFZ-T	Centrair 101A Pégase	101A0242	
F-CGGA-EH	Schempp-Hirth Discus b	35	F-WGGA
F-CGGB-IL	Schempp-Hirth Discus b	36	F-WGGB
F-CGGC	Schempp-Hirth Discus b	89	F-WGGC
F-CGGE-3D	Schempp-Hirth Discus b	102	F-WGGE
F-CGGG-3G	Schempp-Hirth Discus b	129	F-WGGG
F-CGGH-D09	Schempp-Hirth Discus b	163	F-WGGH
F-CGGI-D10	Schempp-Hirth Discus b	177	F-WGGI
F-CGGL-D13	Schempp-Hirth Discus b	192	F-WGGL
F-CGGM-D14	Schempp-Hirth Discus b	213	F-WGGM
F-CGGO	Schempp-Hirth Discus b	148	F-WGGO
F-CGGP	Schempp-Hirth Discus bT	33/335	
F-CGGQ-D16	Schempp-Hirth Discus b	340	
F-CGGR-KO	Schempp-Hirth Discus b	91	D-5239
F-CGGS	Schempp-Hirth Discus CS	037CS	
F-CGGU	Schempp-Hirth Discus CS	105CS	
F-CGGY-D24	Schempp-Hirth Discus CS	117CS	
F-CGGZ	Schempp-Hirth Discus CS	118CS	
F-CGHB-E5	Centrair 101BC Pégase	101BC504	F-WGHB
F-CGHC-E507	Centrair 101BC Pégase	101BC507	
F-CGHD-E7	Centrair 101BC Pégase	101BC509	
F-CGHF	Centrair 101BC Pégase	101BC508	F-WGHF
F-CGHI	DG Flugzeugbau DG-808C	8-347B246X13	D-KKGA
F-CGHJ-E14	Centrair 101D Pégase	101D0514	
F-CGHK-E17	Centrair 101D Pégase	101D0517	
F-CGHL	Centrair 101D Pégase	101D0515	
F-CGHM	Centrair 101D Pégase	101D0516	
F-CGHO-CA	Centrair 101D Pégase	101D0521	
F-CGHQ-D	Centrair 101D Pégase	101D0522	
F-CGHR-F	Centrair 101D Pégase (W/o 24.7.02)	101D0520	
F-CGHS-HS	Centrair 101D Pégase	101D0524	
F-CGIB	Wassmer WA.30 Bijave	222	F-CDJS
F-CGIC	Wassmer WA.22A	119	Fr.AF
F-CGID	Schempp-Hirth Duo Discus	69	D-2671
F-CGIE	Rolladen-Schneider LS6-b	6122	SE-UHN, D-3711
F-CGKA-F	Schleicher ASW 20CL	20856	
F-CGKB-KB	Schleicher ASW 20CL	20847	
F-CGKC	Schleicher ASK 21	21414	
F-CGKD	Schleicher ASK 21	21427	
F-CGKF	Schleicher ASK 21	21445	
F-CGKG	Schleicher ASW 24	24007	F-WGKG
F-CGKH-AM	Schleicher ASW 24	24008	F-WGKH
F-CGKI-GN	Schleicher ASW 24	24053	F-WGKI
F-CGKK-2K	Schleicher ASW 24	24056	F-WGKK
F-CGKM-AS	Schleicher ASW 24	24102	
F-CGKN-CQ	Schleicher ASW 24	24084	F-WGKN
F-CGKO-88	Schleicher ASW 24	24088	
F-CGKQ-CB	Schleicher ASW 24	24103	
F-CGKS	Schleicher ASW 20	20583	D-4690
F-CGKT-MB	Schleicher ASH 25	25022	F-WGKT
F-CGKU	Schleicher ASH 25	25028	F-WGKU
F-CGKV-IA	Schleicher ASH 25E	25046	F-WGKV, D-KFAX(2), F-WGKV
F-CGKZ-3Z	Schleicher ASH 25	25094	
F-CGLA	Schempp-Hirth Ventus b/16.6	236	F-WGLA
F-CGLB	Schempp-Hirth Ventus b/16.6	238	F-WGLB
F-CGLC	Schempp-Hirth Ventus b/16.6	245	F-WGLC
F-CGLF-PE	Schempp-Hirth Ventus b/16.6	269	F-WGLF
F-CGLH-1W	Schempp-Hirth Ventus b/16.6	291	F-WGLH
F-CGLJ-EQ	Schempp-Hirth Ventus-2a	72	
F-CGLK-MH	Schempp-Hirth Ventus c	316	F-WGLK
F-CGLM	Schempp-Hirth Ventus c	339	F-WGLM
F-CGLN	Schempp-Hirth Ventus c	361	F-WGLN
F-CGLO-Y26	Schempp-Hirth Ventus c	433	F-WGLO
F-WGLQ	Schempp-Hirth Ventus cM	6/417	D-KGLQ
F-CGLT-1L	Schempp-Hirth Ventus-2a	08	D-8560
F-CGLX-LX	Schempp-Hirth Ventus-2b	69	
F-CGLY	Schempp-Hirth Ventus c	425	F-WGLY
F-WGMA	Centrair 201 Marianne	201001	
F-CGMB	Centrair 201 Marianne	201002	F-WGMB
F-CGMC	Centrair 201B1 Marianne	201003	F-WGMC
F-CGMD-Z04	Centrair 201B1 Marianne	201004	
F-CGME	Centrair 201B1 Marianne	201005	
F-CGMF	Centrair 201B1 Marianne	201006	
F-CGMH-E8	Centrair 201B1 Marianne (W/o 7.6.14)	201008	
F-CGMI	Centrair 201B1 Marianne	201009	
F-CGMJ	Centrair 201B1 Marianne	201010	
F-CGMO	Centrair 201B1 Marianne	201016	
F-CGMP	Centrair 201B1 Marianne	201017	F-WGMP
F-CGMR	Centrair 201B1 Marianne	201019	F-WGMR
F-CGMS	Centrair 201B1 Marianne	201020	F-WGMS
F-CGMT	Centrair 201B1 Marianne	201021	F-WGMT
F-CGMU	Centrair 201B1 Marianne	201022	F-WGMU
F-CGMX-X	Centrair 201B1 Marianne	201024	
F-CGMY	Centrair 201B1 Marianne	201025	
F-CGMZ	Centrair 201B Marianne	201026	F-WGMZ
F-CGNA	Centrair 101 Pégase	10100248	
F-CGNB-B240	Centrair 101A Pégase	101A0240	
F-CGNC	Centrair 101A Pégase	101A0256	
F-CGND	Centrair 101A Pégase	101A0246	
F-CGNE	Centrair 101 Pégase	10100249	
F-CGNF-FA	Centrair 101A Pégase	101A0247	
F-CGNH	Centrair 101A Pégase	101A0257	
F-CGNI	Centrair 101A Pégase	101A0258	
F-CGNK-LV	Centrair 101A Pégase	101A0270	
F-CGNL	Centrair 101A Pégase	101A0271	
F-CGNN	Centrair 101A Pégase	101A0263	
F-CGNO	Centrair 101A Pégase	101A0272	
F-CGNP-Y31	Centrair 101 Pégase	10100266	
F-CGNR-B903	Centrair 101C Pégase	101C0903	

Registration	Type	c/n	Previous identity
F-CGNS	Centrair 101C Pégase	101C0904	
F-CGNV	Centrair 101 Pégase	10100277	
F-CGNX-AY	Centrair 101B Pégase	101B0279	
F-CGNZ-SJ	Centrair 101A Pégase	101A0281	
F-CGOB	Centrair 101A Pégase	101A0316	
F-CGOC-U2	Centrair 101A Pégase	101A0317	
F-CGOD-OD	Centrair 101A Pégase	101A0318	
F-CGOE-F	Centrair 101A Pégase	101A0320	
F-CGOF-OF	Centrair 101A Pégase	101A0326	
F-CGOG-B327	Centrair 101A Pégase	101A0327	
F-CGOH-T	Centrair 101A Pégase	101A0328	
F-CGOJ	Centrair 101A Pégase	101A0330	
F-CGOK-SN	Centrair 101B Pégase	101B0324	
F-CGOL	Centrair 101A Pégase	101A0331	
F-CGOM-3M	Centrair 101A Pégase	101A0332	
F-CGON-AF	Centrair 101A Pégase	101A0333	
F-CGOP-B335	Centrair 101A Pégase	101A0335	
F-CGOQ-B336	Centrair 101A Pégase	101A0336	
F-CGOR-BOF	Centrair 101A Pégase	101A0337	
F-CGOS-OM	Centrair 101A Pégase	101A0338	
F-CGOT	Centrair 101A Pégase	101A0339	
F-CGOU-OV	Centrair 101A Pégase	101A0340	
F-CGOV-ED	Centrair 101A Pégase	101A0341	
F-CGOX-33	Centrair 101A Pégase	101A0342	
F-CGOZ-Z2	Centrair 101A Pégase	101A0354	
F-CGPN	Wassmer WA.22A Super Javelot	155	Fr.AF
F-CGQA-J57	Schempp-Hirth Janus C	224	
F-CGQC	Schempp-Hirth Janus CM	28/229	F-WGQC
F-CGQD	Schempp-Hirth Janus B	231	
F-CGQE-AJ	Schempp-Hirth Janus CM	29/234	F-WGQE, D-KHIA(5)
F-CGQG-FV	Schempp-Hirth Janus CM	33/250	F-WGQG, D-KGQG
F-CGQH	Schempp-Hirth Janus C	258	
F-CGQI	Schempp-Hirth Janus CM	34/259	F-WGQI, D-KGQI
F-CGQJ-VA	Schempp-Hirth Janus C	267	
F-CGQL	Schempp-Hirth Janus Ce	287	
F-CGQO-QO	Schempp-Hirth Janus Ce	293	D-7460
F-CGQP	Schempp-Hirth Janus C	219	D-4148
F-CGQQ-Q2	Schempp-Hirth Janus Ce	306	
F-CGQR	Schempp-Hirth Janus Ce	307	
F-CGQS-D34	Schempp-Hirth Discus CS	262CS	
F-CGRG	Glaser-Dirks DG-400	4-243	
F-CGRI	Glaser-Dirks DG-400	4-283	D-KSPL
F-CGRK-64	DG Flugzeugbau DG-1000S	10-58S56	
F-CGRL	PZL-Swidnik PW-5 Smyk	17.13.001	
F-CGRM	DG Flugzeugbau DG-1000S	10-88S62	
F-CGRP	Glaser-Dirks DG-600	6-59	
F-CGRT	Glaser-Dirks DG-600/18M	6-83M29	
F-CGRV	Glaser-Dirks DG-400	4-112	N62JW
F-CGRX	Glaser-Dirks DG-800A	8-23A20	D-KAPS
F-CGRY	Glaser-Dirks DG-800S	8-73S19	D-8081
F-CGRZ	Diamond HK 36TTC Super Dimona	36524	
F-CGSA	Centrair 101 Pégase	10100282	
F-CGSB	Centrair 101 Pégase	10100288	
F-CGSC-SC	Centrair 101A Pégase	101A0287	
F-CGSD	Centrair 101 Pégase	10100292	
F-CGSF	Centrair 101A Pégase	101A0291	
F-CGSG-B294	Centrair 101A Pégase	101A0294	
F-CGSH-B295	Centrair 101A Pégase	101A0295	
F-CGSJ-SF	Centrair 101A Pégase	101A0297	
F-CGSK-B298	Centrair 101A Pégase	101A0298	
F-CGSL-B300	Centrair 101A Pégase	101A0300	
F-CGSN	Centrair 101A Pégase	101A0302	
F-CGSO-B30	Centrair 101A Pégase	101A0303	
	(W/o 12.6.02)		
F-CGSP-B304	Centrair 101A Pégase	101A0304	
F-CGSQ	Centrair 101A Pégase	101A0305	
F-CGSR-ES	Centrair 101A Pégase	101A0306	
F-CGSS-S2	Centrair 101A Pégase	101A0308	
F-CGST	Centrair 101A Pégase	101A0309	
F-CGSU-DV	Centrair 101A Pégase	101A0310	
F-CGSV	Centrair 101 Pégase	10100269	
F-CGSY	Centrair 101A Pégase	101A0313	
F-CGTB	Centrair 201B Marianne	201B062	
F-CGTC	Centrair 201B Marianne	201B063	
F-CGTF	Centrair 201B Marianne	201B071	
F-CGTG-CA	Centrair 201B Marianne	201B073	
F-CGTH	Centrair 201B Marianne	201B075	
F-CGTI	Centrair 201B Marianne	201B076	
F-CGTK	Centrair 201B Marianne	201B079	
F-CGTL	Centrair 201B Marianne	201B080	
F-CGTM-P22	Centrair 201B Marianne	201B030	
F-CGTN	Centrair 201B Marianne	201B083	
F-CGTO	Centrair 201B Marianne	201B084	
F-CGTP	Centrair 201B Marianne	201B087	
F-CGTQ	Centrair 201B Marianne	201B089	
F-CGTS	Centrair 201B Marianne	201B092	
F-CGUA-Z06	Rolladen-Schneider LS6-a	6093	F-WGUA
F-CGUB	Rolladen-Schneider LS6-a	6097	F-WGUB
F-CGUD	Rolladen-Schneider LS6-b	6130	F-WGUD
F-CGUE-CA	Rolladen-Schneider LS6-b	6137	F-WGUE
F-CGUG-D	Rolladen-Schneider LS6-b	6142	F-WGUG
F-CGUH-72	Rolladen-Schneider LS6-b	6179	F-WGUH
F-CGUJ	Rolladen-Schneider LS6-c	6206	
F-CGUL-3C	Rolladen-Schneider LS6-c18	6222	
F-CGUN-Z01	Rolladen-Schneider LS6-b	6087	F-WGUN
F-CGUO-Z15	Rolladen-Schneider LS6-c	6243	
F-CGUP	Rolladen-Schneider LS6-c18	6244	
F-CGUQ	Rolladen-Schneider LS6-c	6255	
F-CGUR-3A	Rolladen-Schneider LS6-c18	6268	
F-CGUS	Rolladen-Schneider LS6-c	6312	
F-CGUT-RC	Rolladen-Schneider LS6-c	6300	
F-CGUU-Z21	Rolladen-Schneider LS6-c	6304	
F-CGUV-Z22	Rolladen-Schneider LS6-c	6305	
F-CGUX-X	Rolladen-Schneider LS6-c	6320	
F-CGUZ-Z28	Rolladen-Schneider LS6-c	6322	
F-CGVA	Grob G 102 Astir CS	1063	D-3287
F-CGVL-VL	Schempp-Hirth Ventus-2b	45	
F-CGVN	Wassmer WA.30 Bijave	206	Fr.AF
F-CGVO	Centrair 201B Marianne	201B064	
F-CGVS	Glasflügel H201B Standard Libelle	289	D-0369
F-CGXA-T101	Grob G 103C Twin III	36002	D-5443
F-CGXB-T102	Grob G 103C Twin III Acro	34119	D-5214
F-CGXC	Grob G 103C Twin III Acro	34122	D-3698
F-CGXD-TD	Grob G 103C Twin III Acro	34136	D-4034
F-CGXF	Grob G 103C Twin III Acro	34140	D-4344
F-CGXG	Grob G 103C Twin III	36008	D-8940
F-CGXH	Grob G 103C Twin III Acro	34178	
F-CGXI-T109	Grob G 103C Twin III Acro	34184	
F-CGXJ-SJ	Grob G 103C Twin III	34114	D-1833
F-CGYB	Rolladen-Schneider LS7	7014	F-WGYB, D-4644
F-CGYC	Rolladen-Schneider LS7	7015	F-WGYC, D-4643
F-CGYD	Rolladen-Schneider LS7	7103	
F-CGYF-EB	Rolladen-Schneider LS7	7155	
F-CGYG-Y55	Rolladen-Schneider LS4-b	4988	
F-CGYH-V56	Rolladen-Schneider LS4-b	4989	
F-CGYI-V57	Rolladen-Schneider LS4-b	4999	
F-CGYJ	Rolladen-Schneider LS4-b	41003	
F-CGYL-TT	Stemme S-10	10-33	D-KGCI (2)
F-CGYM	Stemme S-10V	14-055M	D-KGCU(2)
	(Originally built as S-10 c/n 10-55)		
F-CGYP	Stemme S-10VT	11-025	
	(Permit 3.00)		
F-CGZA-Z29	Rolladen-Schneider LS6-c	6327	
F-CGZB	Rolladen-Schneider LS6-c	6325	
F-CGZC	Rolladen-Schneider LS6-18W	6326	D-7141
F-CGZD	Rolladen-Schneider LS6-c18	6335	D-1681
F-CGZE	Rolladen-Schneider LS6-18W	6368	
F-CGZF-Z34	Rolladen-Schneider LS6-c18	6376	
F-CGZK-2M	Rolladen-Schneider LS8-a	8041	D-3571
F-CGZQ-LN	Rolladen-Schneider LS8-18	8082	
F-CGZR-A	Rolladen-Schneider LS8-a	8137	
F-CGZT-EC1	Rolladen-Schneider LS8-18	8143	
F-CGZU	Rolladen-Schneider LS8-a	8170	
	(W/o 1.8.13)		
F-CGZV-GA5	Rolladen-Schneider LS8-18	8191	
F-CGZX-V92	Rolladen-Schneider LS8-18	8192	
F-CGZZ-ZZ	Rolladen-Schneider LS8-18	8257	D-6597
F-CHAA-GA2	Schleicher ASW 24	24106	
F-CHAB-69	Schleicher ASW 24	24107	
F-CHAF	Schleicher ASW 24	24145	
F-CHAG-P2	Schleicher ASW 24E	24843	
F-CHAH-TT	Schleicher ASW 24E	24852	
F-CHAI	Schleicher ASW 24	24147	
F-CHAJ-GA3	Schleicher ASW 24	24148	
F-CHAL	Schleicher ASH 25	25121	
F-CHAM	Schleicher ASK 21	21504	
F-CHAN	Schleicher ASK 21	21505	
F-CHAO	Schleicher ASH 25	25092	
	(W/o 19.9.03)		
F-CHAP-AP	Schleicher ASH 25	25099	
F-CHAQ	Schleicher ASH 25	25123	
F-CHAR	Schleicher ASH 25	25137	
F-CHAS-AS	Schleicher ASK 23	23009	BGA2999/EVZ
F-CHAT-FLX	Schleicher ASH 25	25080	F-WHAT
F-CHAV-8	Schleicher ASH 25	25136	
F-CHAX-AX	Schleicher ASH 25	25065	D-5282, (D-KFAX(1))
F-CHAZ	Schleicher ASH 25	25156	
F-CHBA	Marganski Swift S-1A	108	
F-CHBC-BC	Schleicher ASH 25E	25055	F-WHBC, D-KBBC
F-CHBJ	Glaser-Dirks DG-200/17	2-122/1726	3A-MBJ
F-CHBL-VS	Rolladen-Schneider LS4	4435	D-3441
F-CHBY	Schleicher ASK 21	21619	
F-CHCA	Sportavia/ Scheibe SF 25B Falke	4827	D-KHEG
F-CHCB	Scheibe SF 25E Super Falke	4351	D-KDGK
F-CHCC	Scheibe SF 25E Super Falke	4365	D-KIOK(2)
F-CHCD	Scheibe SF 25D Falke	4825D	D-KHEE
F-CHCE	Scheibe SF 25B Falke	4630	D-KOKE, (D-KIMJ)
F-CHCF	Sportavia/ Scheibe SF 25C Falke	4242	D-KAJD
F-CHCH	Scheibe SF 25B Falke	AB46302	D-KAFI (2)
F-CHCI	Scheibe SF 25E Super Falke	4329	D-KDFO
F-CHCJ	Scheibe SF 25E Super Falke	4361	D-KLUE
F-CHCK	Scheibe SF 25B Falke	46177	D-KAGK
F-CHCL	Scheibe SF 25D Falke	AB46305	D-KOAN
F-CHCM	Scheibe SF 25B Falke	46173	D-KURT, OE-9038, D-KIBS
F-CHCN	Scheibe SF 25C Falke	44107	D-KMJG
F-CHCP	Scheibe SF 25E Super Falke	4356	D-KOOZ(2)
F-CHCR	Scheibe SFL 25R Falke	4619	D-KEGA
F-CHCS	Scheibe SF 25E Super Falke	4317	D-KLUH
F-CHCT	Scheibe SFL 25R Falke	46146	D-KCAM
F-CHCU	Scheibe SFL 25R Falke	4694	D-KOSH
F-CHCV	Scheibe SFL 25R Falke	46187	D-KASB
F-CHCY	Scheibe SFL 25R Falke	4845D	D-KHFC
F-CHDA	Centrair 101A Pégase	101A0355	
F-CHDB	Centrair 101A Pégase	101A0356	
F-CHDC-C	Centrair 101A Pégase	101A0357	
F-CHDD	Centrair 101A Pégase	101A0358	
F-CHDF	Centrair 101A Pégase	101A0360	
F-CHDG	Centrair 101A Pégase	101A0361	
F-CHDH-GP	Centrair 101A Pégase	101A0362	
F-CHDI -Si	Centrair 101A Pégase	101A0363	
F-CHDJ	Centrair 101A Pégase	101A0366	
F-CHDK-B367	Centrair 101A Pégase	101A0367	
F-CHDL-L	Centrair 101A Pégase	101A0369	
F-CHDM	Centrair 101A Pégase	101A0370	
F-CHDN-SN	Centrair 101A Pégase	101A0372	
F-CHDO-B01	Centrair 101A Pégase	101A0373	
F-CHDP-DP	Centrair 101A Pégase	101A0374	
F-CHDQ	Centrair 101A Pégase	101A0375	
F-CHDR-DR	Centrair 101A Pégase	101A0376	
F-CHDT	Centrair 101A Pégase	101A0377	
F-CHDU-B01	Centrair 101A Pégase	101A0364	
F-CHDX	Centrair 101 Pégase	10100368	
F-CHDY-SY	Centrair 101 Pégase	10100371	
F-CHDZ	Centrair 101A Pégase	101A0379	
F-CHEA-H2	Centrair 101A Pégase	101A0380	
F-CHEB	Centrair 101A Pégase	101A0378	
F-CHEC	Centrair 101A Pégase	101A0381	
F-CHED-B382	Centrair 101A Pégase	101A0382	
F-CHEE-8D	Centrair 101A Pégase	101A0383	
F-CHEF-AB	Centrair 101A Pégase	101A0384	
F-CHEG	Centrair 101A Pégase	101A0385	
F-CHEH	Centrair 101A Pégase	101A0386	
F-CHEI-EI	Centrair 101A Pégase	101A0387	
F-CHEJ-EJ	Centrair 101A Pégase	101A0388	
F-CHEK	Centrair 101A Pégase	101A0389	
F-CHEL-L	Centrair 101A Pégase	101A0390	
F-CHEM-EG	Centrair 101A Pégase	101A0391	
F-CHEN	Centrair 101A Pégase	101A0393	
F-CHEO-77	Centrair 101A Pégase	101A0395	
F-CHEP-B396	Centrair 101A Pégase	101A0396	
F-CHEQ	Centrair 101A Pégase	101A0397	
F-CHER-VO	Centrair 101A Pégase	101A0398	

Reg.	Type	c/n	Previous identities
F-CHES	Centrair 101A Pégase	101A0399	
F-CHEU-401	Centrair 101A Pégase	101A0401	
F-CHEV	Centrair 101A Pégase	101A0402	
F-CHEX-EX	Centrair 101A Pégase	101A0405	
F-CHEY	Centrair 101A Pégase	101A0406	
F-CHEZ -5	Centrair 101A Pégase	101A0407	
F-CHFA-SD	Centrair 101A Pégase	101A0466	
F-CHFD-SI	Centrair 101A Pégase	101A0469	
F-CHFE-FE	Centrair 101A Pégase	101A0470	
F-CHFF	Centrair 101A Pégase	101A0471	
F-CHFG	Centrair 101A Pégase	101A0472	
F-CHFH	Centrair 101A Pégase	101A0474	
F-CHFI	Centrair 101A Pégase	101A0473	
F-CHFK-B480	Centrair 101A Pégase	101A0480	
F-CHFL	Centrair 101A Pégase	101A0481	
F-CHFM	Centrair 101A Pégase	101A0482	
F-CHFN-N	Centrair 101A Pégase	101A0483	
F-CHFP-B486	Centrair 101A Pégase	101A0486	
F-CHFQ	Centrair 101A Pégase	101A0487	
F-CHFR-CL	Centrair 101A Pégase	101A0488	
F-CHFS-I	Centrair 101A Pégase	101A0489	
F-CHFT	Centrair 101A Pégase	101A0494	
F-CHFU-FU	Centrair 101A Pégase	101A0496	
F-CHFV	Centrair 101A Pégase	101A0497	
	(W/o 27.8.06)		
F-CHFX	Centrair 101A Pégase	101A0498	
F-CHFY-FY	Centrair 101A Pégase	101A0499	
F-CHFZ-BBX	Centrair 101A Pégase	101A0600	
F-CHGA-B601	Centrair 101A Pégase	101A0601	
F-CHGB	Centrair 101A Pégase	101A0602	
F-CHGC	Centrair 101A Pégase	101A0603	
F-CHGD-D	Centrair 101A Pégase	101A0604	
F-CHGE-GE	Centrair 101A Pégase	101A0605	
F-CHGF-GF	Centrair 101A Pégase	101A0606	
F-CHGG-G2	Centrair 101A Pégase	101A0490	
F-CHGH-GH	Centrair 101A Pégase	101A0607	
F-CHGI	Centrair 101A Pégase	101A0612	
F-CHGJ-V	Centrair 101A Pégase	101A0614	
F-CHGK-AM	Centrair 101A Pégase	101A0615	
F-CHGL-AA	Centrair 101A Pégase	101A0616	
F-CHGM-BAF	Centrair 101A Pégase	101A0617	
F-CHGN	Centrair 101A Pégase	101A0618	
F-CHGO	Centrair 101A Pégase	101A0622	
F-CHGP-1H	Centrair 101A Pégase	101A0621	
F-CHGQ-IS	Centrair 101A Pégase	101A0623	
F-CHGR-SR	Centrair 101A Pégase	101A0624	
F-CHGS-GS	Centrair 101A Pégase	101A0625	
F-CHGT-B626	Centrair 101A Pégase	101A0626	
	(W/o 25.4.02)		
F-CHGU	Centrair 101A Pégase	101A0627	
F-CHGV	Centrair 101A Pégase	101A0630	
F-CHGX-S8	Centrair 101A Pégase	101A0629	
F-CHGY	Centrair 101A Pégase	101A0631	
F-CHGZ	Centrair 101A Pégase	101A0632	
F-CHHA	Scheibe SF 25B Falke	46144	D-KJHM, OE-9138, D-KCAK
F-CHHB-Y2	Schempp-Hirth Janus C	187	D-7718
F-CHHC	Glaser-Dirks DG-800A	8-31A23	
F-CHHD	SZD-51-1 Junior	B-2138	
F-CHHE	Schleicher Ka 6E	4240	HB-961
F-CHHF-HF	Caproni A-21S Calif	218	HB-1180
F-CHHG	Schleicher K 8B	883	HB-682
F-CHHH	Grob G 102/77 Astir CS	1808	HB-1470
F-CHHI	Schleicher ASK 13	13232	D-0512
F-CHHK	Scheibe SF 28A Tandem-Falke	5749	D-KOFF
F-CHHN	Schleicher Ka 6E	4041	D-1932
F-CHHO-AG	Schleicher ASH 25	25002	D-2522
F-CHHP	Grob G 102 Astir Jeans 77J	2234	D-5949
F-CHHR	Grob G 102 Astir Jeans 77J	2237	D-5917
F-CHHS-R6	Schempp-Hirth Discus CS	210CS	OY-XUV
F-CHHU	Schleicher K 8B	8522	D-7193
	(Res. 3.01)		
F-CHHY	Glaser-Dirks DG-400	4-6	D-KINS
F-CHIA	Schleicher ASK 21	21526	
F-CHIB	Schleicher ASK 21	21540	
F-CHIC	Schleicher ASK 21	21549	
F-CHID	Schleicher ASK 21	21547	
F-CHIE	Schleicher ASK 21	21080	PH-711
F-CHIF-SA	Schleicher ASW 24	24176	
F-CHIG	Schleicher ASW 24	24178	
F-CHIL	Schleicher ASK 21	21553	
F-CHIM	Schleicher ASK 21	21614	
F-CHIN	Schleicher ASK 21	21625	
F-CHIU	Schleicher ASH 25	25157	
F-CHJB-SG	Glaser-Dirks DG-500 Elan Trainer	5E22T4	
F-CHJC	Glaser-Dirks DG-500 Elan Trainer	5E27T7	
F-CHJD-DG1	Glaser-Dirks DG-500 Elan Trainer	5E49T19	
F-CHJE-DG2	Glaser-Dirks DG-500 Elan Trainer	5E73T30	
F-CHJG-DD	Glaser-Dirks DG-500 Elan Trainer	5E88T38	
F-CHJH	Glaser-Dirks DG-500/22 Elan	5E102S15	
F-CHJI -JI	Glaser-Dirks DG-500/22 Elan	5E129T55	
F-CHJJ	DG Flugzeugbau DG-500 Elan Orion	5E168X23	(D-0168)
F-CHJK-JK	DG Flugzeugbau DG-500 Elan Orion	5E172X25	
F-CHJN-NJ	Glaser-Dirks DG-500M Elan	5E96M42	OH-857
F-CHJO-DG3	DG Flugzeugbau DG-500 Elan Orion	5E218X58	
F-CHJP-MC	DG Flugzeugbau DG-500MB	5E242B19	
F-CHKA	Centrair 101A Pégase	101A0408	
F-CHKB-KB	Centrair 101A Pégase	120A0410	
F-CHKC	Centrair 101A Pégase	101A0412	
F-CHKD	Centrair 101A Pégase	101A0411	
F-CHKE	Centrair 101A Pégase	101A0413	
F-CHKF	Centrair 101A Pégase	101A0414	
F-CHKG-B415	Centrair 101A Pégase	101A0415	
F-CHKH-I	Centrair 101A Pégase	101A0416	
F-CHKI-RI	Centrair 101A Pégase	101A0417	
F-CHKJ-AM	Centrair 101A Pégase	101A0418	
F-CHKK-K	Centrair 101A Pégase	101A0419	
F-CHKL	Centrair 101A Pégase	101A0409	
F-CHKM-W	Centrair 101A Pégase	101A0420	
F-CHKN	Centrair 101A Pégase	101A0421	
F-CHKO-B422	Centrair 101A Pégase	101A0422	
F-CHKP-B423	Centrair 101A Pégase	101A0423	
F-CHKQ	Centrair 101A Pégase	101A0424	
F-CHKR	Centrair 101A Pégase	101A0428	
F-CHKS-KS	Centrair 101A Pégase	101A0429	
F-CHKT-KT	Centrair 101A Pégase	101A0430	
F-CHKU	Centrair 101A Pégase	101A0431	
F-CHKV	Centrair 101A Pégase	101A0432	
F-CHKX	Centrair 101A Pégase	101A0433	
F-CHKY-SF1	Centrair 101A Pégase	101A0434	
F-CHLA-3A	Centrair 101A Pégase	101A0436	
F-CHLB-B43	Centrair 101A Pégase	101A0438	
F-CHLC	Centrair 101A Pégase	101A0439	
F-CHLD	Centrair 101A Pégase	101A0440	
F-CHLE-B02	Centrair 101A Pégase	101A0441	
F-CHLF-Y	Centrair 101A Pégase	101A0443	
F-CHLG-B442	Centrair 101A Pégase	101A0442	
F-CHLI	Centrair 101A Pégase	101A0446	
F-CHLJ	Centrair 101A Pégase	101A0445	
F-CHLK	Centrair 101A Pégase	101A0447	
F-CHLL	Centrair 101A Pégase	101A0452	
F-CHLM-EO	Centrair 101A Pégase	101A0453	
F-CHLN-B	Centrair 101A Pégase	101A0454	
F-CHLO-AS	Centrair 101A Pégase	101A0455	
F-CHLP	Centrair 101A Pégase	101A0456	
	(W/o 11.8.06)		
F-CHLQ	Centrair 101A Pégase	101A0457	
F-CHLR-BNO	Centrair 101A Pégase	101A0458	
F-CHLU-S1	Centrair 101A Pégase	101A0461	
F-CHLV	Centrair 101A Pégase	101A0462	
F-CHLX-SF2	Centrair 101A Pégase	101A0463	
F-CHLY	Centrair 101A Pégase	101A0464	
F-CHLZ	Centrair 101A Pégase	101A0465	
F-CHMC	Grob G 103A Twin II Acro	3768-K-54	D-1279
F-CHMD-MD	Schleicher ASH 25	25193	
F-CHME	Schleicher K 8B	8810	PH-415
F-CHMF	Schleicher ASK 21	21012	D-6526, D-6528
F-CHMG	Wassmer WA 26P Squale	71	OO-YGM, F-CDZF
F-CHML	Rolladen-Schneider LS8-18	8298	D-4408
F-CHMM	Sportine Aviacija LAK-17AT	169	LY-GMU
F-CHMP	Schleicher ASH 25	25181	
F-CHMR	Grob G102 Astir CS	1004	D-8682
F-CHMT	Schempp-Hirth Arcus	17	
F-CHMY-2L	Sportine Aviacija LAK-17A	160	
F-CHNA	Grob G 102 Astir CS	1456	D-7447
F-CHNB	Scheibe SF 25B Falke	46116	D-KABN
F-CHNC	Rolladen-Schneider LS4	4510	3A-MSS
F-CHND-J	Schempp-Hirth Janus C	165	HB-1672
	(W/o 6.8.13)		
F-CHNE-87	Bölkow Phoebus C	910	
F-CHNF	Sportine Aviacija LAK-17A	148	
F-CHNH	Marganski MDM-1 Fox	242	SP-3816
F-CHNN	Wassmer WA.30 Bijave	168	Fr.AF
F-CHNO-NO	Sportine Aviacija LAK-19	014	
F-CHNP-NP	Sportine Aviacija LAK-19	015	
F-CHNX-17	Sportine Aviacija LAK-17A	126	
F-CHOA	Grob G 103C Twin IIISL	35051	D-KPIC
F-CHOC	Schempp-Hirth Janus B	62	D-7103
F-CHOP	Schleicher Ka 6CR	6137	D-5283
F-CHOU	Rolladen-Schneider LS4-b	4920	D-6796
F-CHOZ	Glaser-Dirks DG-500 Elan Trainer	5E-45T15	D-5212
F-CHPA	Grob G 102 Astir CS	1017	D-6996
F-CHPB	Rolladen-Schneider LS4-b	41010	BGA4281/HXF
F-CHPC	Bréguet 904S Nymphale	9	F-CCFS
	(Res.99)		
F-CHPD	Schleicher ASK 13	13304	D-0754
F-CHPH	Wassmer WA.22A Super Javelot	137	Fr.AF
F-CHPT-RL	Schempp-Hirth Janus C	199	OY-XRL, N911RR
F-CHPV	Caproni Vizzola Calif A21S	46	
F-CHQE	Diamond HK 36TTC Super Dimona	36612	OE-9409
F-CHQG	Diamond HK 36TTC Super Dimona	36687	
F-CHQJ to F-CHQZ	Reserved for HK-36 Super Dimonas		
F-CHRA	Schleicher ASK 14	14023	D-KEBB
F-CHRC-A5	Schempp-Hirth Ventus c	376	F-WHRC
	(W/o 17.4.11)		
F-CHRE	Wassmer WA.22A Super Javelot	134	Fr.AF
F-CHRF	Bréguet 901S Mouette	2	F-ZABX
F-CHRG	Rolladen-Schneider LS8-a	8149	
F-CHRI	Schleicher ASK 13	13446	D-2992
F-CHRJ	Schleicher ASH 25	25089	D-6088
F-CHRK	Schleicher ASK 13	13545	F-CERK
F-CHRM	PZL-Swidnik PW-5 Smyk	17.07.016	D-8843
F-CHRS	Wassmer WA.30 Bijave	165	Fr.AF
	(Dismantled)		
F-CHRT	Rolladen-Schneider LS6-c	6273	PH-972
F-CHRY	Schempp-Hirth Janus Ce	288	HB-3087
F-CHRZ	PZL PW-6U	78.03.03	
F-CHSA	Grob G 102 Astir CS	1256	D-7350
F-CHSB	Schleicher ASK 13	13670AB	D-5800
F-CHSC	Scheibe SF 25E Super Falke	4323	G-WOLD, (G-BOVM), N250BA, (D-KECZ)
F-CHSE-GA	Schleicher ASK 13	13175	D-0265
F-CHSF	Schleicher K 8B	8206	D-8465
F-CHSG	Stralpes CB 15 Crystal	4	
F-CHSM	Rolladen-Schneider LS6-18W	6380	
F-CHSN	SZD-55-1	551191031	F-WHSN
F-CHSO-5.5	SZD-55-1	551192042	F-WHSO
F-CHTA-CHN	Schempp-Hirth Duo Discus	09	
F-CHTB	Schempp-Hirth Duo Discus	40	
F-CHTC	Schempp-Hirth Duo Discus	67	
F-CHTD	Schempp-Hirth Duo Discus	88	
F-CHTE-EC	Schempp-Hirth Duo Discus	106	
F-CHTF	Schempp-Hirth Duo Discus	120	
F-CHTG-TG	Schempp-Hirth Duo Discus	134	
F-CHTH	Schempp-Hirth Duo Discus	221	
F-CHTI	Schempp-Hirth Duo Discus	145	
F-CHTJ	Schempp-Hirth Duo Discus	151	
F-CHTK-K	Schempp-Hirth Duo Discus	155	
F-CHTL	Schempp-Hirth Duo Discus	167	
F-CHTM	Schempp-Hirth Duo Discus	190	
F-CHTO	Schempp-Hirth Duo Discus	252	
F-CHTQ-EP	Schempp-Hirth Duo Discus	264	
F-CHTR	Schempp-Hirth Duo Discus	268	
F-CHTS	Schempp-Hirth Duo Discus	276	
F-CHTT	Schempp-Hirth Duo Discus	279	
F-CHTU-TU	Schempp-Hirth Duo Discus T	34/308	D-KGBE
F-CHTV-CW	Schempp-Hirth Duo Discus	304	
F-CHTX-TX	Schempp-Hirth Duo Discus	303	
F-CHTY	Schempp-Hirth Duo Discus	331	
F-CHTZ	DG Flugzeugbau DG-800B	8-201B123	
F-CHUA	Centrair 101A Pégase	101A0633	
F-CHUB-B628	Centrair 101A Pégase	101A0628	

Reg	Type	S/N	Previous ID / Notes
F-CHUC	Centrair 101A Pégase	101A0634	
F-CHUD-DD	Centrair 101A Pégase	101A0635	
	(W/o 21.5.11)		
F-CHUE	Centrair 101A Pégase	101A0636	
F-CHUF-B22	Centrair 101A Pégase	101A0637	
F-CHVB	Sportine Aviacija LAK-17A	209	
F-CHVD	Schleicher Ka 6CR	6577	D-5841
F-CHVE-4W	Schempp-Hirth Janus C	144	BGA3857/HDG, D-3666
F-CHVU	Schempp-Hirth Janus B	66	(OH-954), F-CHVU, D-7770
F-CHVV-V2	Schempp-Hirth Duo Discus	115	
F-CHVZ	Rolladen-Schneider LS4	4489	Fr.mil
F-CHXA	Aeromot AMT.100 Ximango	100023	PT-PMV
	(W/o 17.8.02)		
F-CHXB	Aeromot AMT.100 Ximango	100022	PT-PMU
F-CHXD	Aeromot AMT.100 Ximango	100027	PT-PMZ
F-CHXE	Aeromot AMT.100 Ximango	100031	PT-POO
F-CHXF	Aeromot AMT.100 Ximango	100032	PT-POP
F-CHXG	Aeromot AMT.200 Super Ximango	200040	
F-CHYA	DG Flugzeugbau DG-800B	8-131B60	
F-CHYB-DT	DG Flugzeugbau DG-800B	8-269B177	
F-CHYD	DG Flugzeugbau DG-808B	8-349B248	
F-CHYF	DG Flugzeugbau DG-808C	8-356B255X20	
F-CHYG to CHYZ	*Reserved for Aerosport*		
F-CHZA to CHZZ	*Reserved for Centrair SNC-34C Alliance production*		
F-CIAA	Schempp-Hirth Duo Discus	266	PH-1200
F-CIAF	Bölkow Phoebus C	898	HB-960
F-CIAI	Grob G 102 Astir CS 77	1750	D-4565
F-CIAJ	Schleicher ASK 14	14051	D-KISE
F-CIAO-R	Rolladen-Schneider LS6-18W	6365	D-1049
F-CIAP	Schleicher ASW 20L	20553	OO-ZRA
F-CIAT	Schleicher ASK 21	21709	D-5421
F-CIBA-V60	Rolladen-Schneider LS8-18	8250	
F-CIBB-GA6	Rolladen-Schneider LS8-18	8262	
F-CIBC-GA7	Rolladen-Schneider LS8-18	8321	
F-CIBD	Rolladen-Schneider LS8-18	8356	
F-CIBN	Scheibe SF 25B Falke	4803	D-KBAQ
F-CIBO-6Z	Grob G 102/77J Astir Jeans	2128	D-2536
F-CIBP-BP	Schempp-Hirth Discus bT	152/544	D-KEBR, (D-KEBS)
F-CIBZ	Grob G 102 Astir CS	1381	D-7408
F-CICA	PZL PW-5 Smyk	17.02.004	
F-CICB-EZ	PZL PW-5 Smyk	17.07.012	
F-CICC-EY	PZL PW-5 Smyk	17.07.013	
F-CICD-FH	PZL PW-5 Smyk	17.09.011	
F-CICE-PW	PZL PW-5 Smyk	17.10.022	
F-CIDB-DB	Schempp-Hirth Duo Discus	337	
F-CIDC	Schempp-Hirth Duo Discus	353	
F-CIDD	Schempp-Hirth Duo Discus	341	
F-CIDE	Schempp-Hirth Duo Discus	372	
F-CIDF-DF	Schempp-Hirth Duo Discus	382	
F-CIDH	Schempp-Hirth Duo Discus	417	
F-CIDI	Schempp-Hirth Duo Discus	416	
F-CIDJ	Schempp-Hirth Duo Discus	446	
F-CIDK-EJ	Schempp-Hirth Duo Discus	462	
F-CIDL	Schempp-Hirth Duo Discus	458	
F-CIDM-DM	Schempp-Hirth Duo Discus xT	160	
F-CIDN	Schempp-Hirth Janus C	151	(F-CJDN), D-5719, PH-719
F-CIDO-CFM	Schempp-Hirth Duo Discus T	127	
F-CIDP-EX	Schempp-Hirth Duo Discus XLT	184	
F-CIDQ	Schempp-Hirth Duo Discus XLT	194	
F-CIDR	Schempp-Hirth Duo Discus XL	586	
F-CIEA	Glaser-Dirks DG-600/18	6-102	PH-964, D-3120
F-CIED	Glaser-Dirks DG-500 Elan Trainer	5E20T2	D-0262
F-CIEE	Grob G 102 Astir CS Jeans	2162	D-4557
F-CIEG-E8	Rolladen-Schneider LS8-18	8188	D-3859
F-CIEU	Schempp-Hirth Janus Ce	302	OY-LEX, SE-UKZ
F-CIFB-FB	Schleicher ASW 27-18 (ASG 29)	29066	
F-CIFF	Schempp-Hirth Arcus	14	D-4626
F-CIFM	Schleicher ASK 21	21476	I-IVWC
	(W/o 14.6.15)		
F-CIFS	Stemme S 10	10-5	D-KHFS, HB-2230, D-KHFS
F-CIGA	Glaser-Dirks DG-300 Elan	3E70	D-3325
F-CIGC	Schleicher K 8B	506	HB-620
F-CIGG-GG	Schempp-Hirth Ventus-2c	50/151	D-6777, HB-3303
F-CIGL	Siren C30S Edelweiss	53	OO-ZGG, F-CDGL
F-CIGV	Schleicher ASK 13	13422	D-2122
F-CIHB	Centrair SNC-34C Alliance	34003	
F-CIHC	Centrair SNC-34C Alliance	34001	F-WWQA
F-CIHD	Centrair SNC-34C Alliance	34004	
F-CIHE	Centrair SNC-34C Alliance	34005	
F-CIHF	Centrair SNC-34C Alliance	34006	
F-CIHG	Centrair SNC-34C Alliance	34007	
F-CIHH	Centrair SNC-34C Alliance	34008	
F-CIHI	Centrair SNC-34C Alliance	34009	
F-CIHJ-A4	Centrair SNC-34C Alliance	34010	
F-CIHK	Centrair SNC-34C Alliance	34011	
F-CIHL	Centrair SNC-34C Alliance	34012	
F-CIHM	Centrair SNC-34C Alliance	34014	
F-CIHN-A15	Centrair SNC-34C Alliance	34015	
F-CIHO	Centrair SNC-34C Alliance	34016	
F-CIHP	Centrair SNC-34C Alliance	34017	
F-CIHQ	Centrair SNC-34C Alliance	34018	
F-CIHS	Centrair SNC-34C Alliance	34020	
F-CIHU	Centrair SNC-34C Alliance	34022	
F-CIHV	Centrair SNC-34C Alliance	34023	
F-CIHX	Centrair SNC-34C Alliance	34024	
F-CIHY-RB	Centrair SNC-34C Alliance	34025	
F-CIHZ	Centrair SNC-34C Alliance	34027	
F-CIII	Schempp-Hirth Nimbus-3T	13/82	HA-4551, OO-YMA, D-KCMA
F-CIJA	Schempp-Hirth Ventus-2c	23/59	
F-CIJB-I	Schempp-Hirth Ventus-2c	26/71	
F-CIJC-Y35	Schempp-Hirth Ventus-2cM	57/113	
	(Converted from former Ventus-2c c/n 39/113)		
F-CIJD-74	Schempp-Hirth Ventus-2cT	27/96	
F-CIJF-JF	Schempp-Hirth Ventus-2cT	42/137	
F-CIJG-2Y	Schempp-Hirth Ventus-2cT	55/164	
F-CIJH	Schempp-Hirth Ventus-2cT	46/145	
	(Converted from former Ventus-2c c/n 47/145)		
F-CIJI-GA8	Schempp-Hirth Ventus-2b	122	
F-CIJJ	Schempp-Hirth Ventus-2cT	67/206	
F-CIJL	Schempp-Hirth Ventus-2cT	103	
F-CIJM	Schempp-Hirth Ventus-2cx	84	D-1219
F-CIJN-G	Schempp-Hirth Ventus-2c	77	
F-CIJO	Schempp-Hirth Ventus-2cx	86	D-2158
F-CIJP	Schempp-Hirth Ventus-2cx	91	
F-CIJS-R16	Schempp-Hirth Ventus-2cxT	161	
F-CIJT-EL	Schempp-Hirth Ventus-2b	169	
F-CIJU-EF	Schempp-Hirth Ventus-2cxa	120	D-4601
F-CILA-AM	Schempp-Hirth Duo Discus	214	
F-CILD	Schleicher K 8B	8055/A	OO-ZLD, D-5466
F-CILF	Glaser-Dirks DG-600/18	6-32	D-2800
F-CILM	Sportine Aviacija LAK-17AT	152	
F-CILS	Schleicher ASK 13	13675AB	HB-1078
F-CIMC	Schleicher ASK 21	21700	
F-CIME	Schempp-Hirth Duo Discus	218	
F-CIMJ-MJ	Schempp-Hirth Duo Discus	3	D-7459
F-CIML-ML	Schempp-Hirth Janus C	217	D-7180
F-CIMM	Rolladen-Schneider LS8-18	8270	D-0285
F-CINH	Pilatus B4-PC11AF	242	HB-1317
F-CINQ	Glaser-Dirks DG-500 Elan Trainer	5E77T33	HB-3428, D-3321
F-CIOL	Grob G 103C Twin III SL	35039	D-KSOL
F-CIPC	Centrair 101A Pégase	101028	HB-1667
F-CIPH	Schleicher ASK 14	14015	D-KILY
F-CIPP	Grob G103 Twin II	3758	I-IVVE
F-CIPV-VS	Schleicher ASK 21	21104	HB-1640
F-CIRA	Glaser-Dirks DG-300 Elan	3E253	OM-1926, HB-1926
F-CIRB-66	Schleicher ASH 25	25013	D-0766
F-CIRC	Schleicher K 8B	8384SH	(F-CLLA), HB-806
F-CIRD	Schempp-Hirth Ventus-2cxT	194	D-KARD
F-CIRF	Sportavia-Pützer Fournier RF5	5009	D-KIHA
	(Res.9.07)		
F-CIRH	Stemme S-10V	14-028M	OY-JAX, (G-CHLT), D-KGCL(1)
	(Conv. from S-10 c/n 10-28)		
F-CIRI	Rolladen-Schneider LS4	4028	D-6432
F-CIRJ	Rolladen-Schneider LS8-b	8444	D-1228
F-CIRS	Schempp-Hirth Duo Discus	130	
F-CIRV	Schleicher ASK 21	21308	I-SIRV
F-CISA-ISA	Rolladen-Schneider LS8-18	8107	D-1510
F-CISM	Schempp-Hirth Discus-2b	174	OO-YBO
F-CISO	Schleicher Ka 6E	4032	OO-ZOD
F-CITS	Schleicher ASK 21	21744	
F-CITT	Schleicher ASK 21	21779	
F-CITU	Schleicher ASK 21	21763	
F-CITV	Schleicher ASK 21	21764	
F-CITX	Schleicher ASK 21	21750	
F-CITY-TY	Schleicher ASK 21	21756	
F-CITZ	Schleicher ASK 21	21761	
F-CIUJ	Fournier RF3	6	F-BIUJ, F-BLEM
F-CIVB	Schempp-Hirth Duo Discus XL	616	
F-CIVH-VH	Schleicher ASH 25	25005	OO-ZUZ
F-CIVY	Schleicher ASK 21	21156	D-4721
F-CIZY	Scheibe SF 25C Falke	4453	D-KOZY
F-CJAA-AF	Schempp-Hirth Nimbus-4T	32	
F-CJAC-Z	Schempp-Hirth Nimbus-4D	14	
F-CJAD	Schempp-Hirth Nimbus-4DM	68	
F-CJAE-EJ	Schempp-Hirth Duo Discus XL	587	
F-CJAF	Schempp-Hirth Arcus	3	D-4683
F-CJAN	Schempp-Hirth Janus C	257	OY-XRR
F-CJAZ-32	Schempp-Hirth Nimbus-4D	8/39	(F-CIJZ), D-8157
F-CJBA	Centrair SNC-34C Alliance	34028	
F-CJBB	Centrair SNC-34C Alliance	34029	
F-CJBC	Centrair SNC-34C Alliance	34030	
F-CJBD	Centrair SNC-34C Alliance	34031	
F-CJBE	Centrair SNC-34C Alliance	34032	
F-CJBF	Centrair SNC-34C Alliance	34033	
F-CJBG	Centrair SNC-34C Alliance	34034	
F-CJBH	Centrair SNC-34C Alliance	34035	
F-CJBI	Centrair SNC-34C Alliance	34036	
F-CJBJ-S11	Centrair SNC-34C Alliance	34038	
F-CJBK	Centrair SNC-34C Alliance	34037	
F-CJBL	Centrair SNC-34C Alliance	34039	
F-CJBM	Centrair SNC-34C Alliance	34040	
F-CJBN	Centrair SNC-34C Alliance	34042	
F-CJBO-S12	Centrair SNC-34C Alliance	34043	
F-CJCA-CA	DG Flugzeugbau DG-1000S	10-36S35	PH-1294
F-CJCB	Allstar SZD-54-2 Perkoz	542.A.14.004	SP-3873
F-CJCM	Castel C.25S	160	F-CRNK, F-CBIP
	(Also reserved as F-CRMC(2))		
F-CJCN	Schleicher ASK 21	21621	HB-3178
F-CJCP	Schempp-Hirth Duo Discus	200	D-5744
F-CJCR-L38	Rolladen-Schneider LS1-d	227	D-7111, F-CEHN
F-CJCT	Breguet 901S Mouette	17	F-CCCT
F-CJCV	Schleicher ASW 20BL	20667	D-6988, OE-5363
	(W/o 2.3.12)		
F-CJDB	Grob G 102 Standard Astir II	5045S	HB-1530
F-CJDD	Schempp-Hirth Duo Discus	37	D-9148
F-CJDG	Glaser-Dirks DG-500/22 Elan	5E5S1	D-5252
F-CJDI	Schempp-Hirth Nimbus-2C	81	CX-..., F-CEDI
F-CJDJ-K6	Glaser-Dirks DG-300 Elan	3E369	I-SYBI
F-CJDR	Scheibe SF 25D Falke	AB46308D	OE-9181, (D-KDGG)
F-CJDT	Schempp-Hirth Janus C	170	D-9993, OO-YGJ, BGA 4205, (BGA 4188), D-3189
F-CJEA	Schempp-Hirth Duo Discus	154	D-3364
F-CJED	Schempp-Hirth Duo Discus	70	D-3340
F-CJEE-EE	Marganski MDM-1 Fox	236	
F-CJEF-S6	SZD-51-1 Junior	W-950	HB-1895
F-CJEK	Schempp-Hirth Duo Discus	63	D-9095
F-CJEM	Schleicher ASK 21	21439	HB-3023
F-CJER	Schleicher ASW 27-18E (ASG 29E)	29616	
F-CJFB	Avialsa-Scheibe A.60 Fauconnet	59K	OO-ZCX, F-CCVL
F-CJFF-E5	Schempp-Hirth Duo Discus	242	D-3640
F-CJFP	Schleicher ASH 30Mi	30008	
F-CJFT	Schempp-Hirth Duo Discus T	27/292	PH-1199, D-KHRC
F-CJGT-GT	Rolladen-Schneider LS6-18W	6358	D-5797
F-CJHA	Grob G 102 Astir CS	1100	D-6994
F-CJHD	Castel C.311P	16	(F-CARC), F-CALS
F-CJIM-S7	SZD-51-1 Junior	B-1500	HB-1797
F-CJJB	Glaser-Dirks DG-400	4-35	D-KAJB
F-CJJC	Schleicher ASW 27	27139	
F-CJJD	Schleicher Ka 6CR Rhönsegler	60/03	OO-YDF, D-1181
F-CJJH	Sportine Aviacija LAK-17A	159	
F-CJLC	Schleicher ASW 24	24033	OE-5538, D-2615
F-CJLD-FD	Schleicher ASW 28	28026	
F-CJLL	Sportine Aviacija LAK-17A	134	LY-GEA
F-CJLM	Schleicher ASW 27	27153	OY-SPX, D-3127
F-CJLQ	Centrair 201B Marianne	201A044	OO-YLQ, F-CBLQ
F-CJMA	Schleicher K 8	519	D-3570
F-CJMC-EI	Schempp-Hirth Discus-2a	24	
F-CJMD	Schleicher ASW 27-18E	29566	
F-CJNL	Schempp-Hirth Ventus-2cM	83	PH-1166

F-CJOD	Schleicher ASK 21	21839	D-2210
F-CJOE	Scheibe SF 25B Falke	4668	D-KAPD
F-CJPB	Rolladen-Schneider LS3-17	3450	D-6929
F-CJPC-TW2	Schleicher ASW 27	27162	
F-CJPG-PG	Schleicher ASH 25E	25119	F-CHHL, HB-2197
F-CJPH-TZ	Sportine Aviacija LAK-19	005	
F-CJPJ-JPJ	Rolladen-Schneider LS6-18W	6195	PH-913, (PH-838), (PH-828), D-3481
F-CJPK	Fournier RF5-AJI	E-004	EC-FOI
F-CJPL-LG	Schempp-Hirth Nimbus-4DM	39/55	G-IVDM, D-KABV
F-CJPV	Sportine Aviacija LAK-19	021	
F-CJRA	DG Flugzeugbau DG-1000S	10-19S19	
F-CJRC	Schleicher ASH 30Mi	30004	D-KAAC, D-KLFU
F-CJRG	Schleicher ASK 21	21734	
F-CJRP-1G	Rolladen-Schneider LS6-18W	6238	D-4084
F-CJSA	Rolladen-Schneider LS4	4120	D-4583, HB-1583
F-CJSY	Breguet 905SA Fauvette (Res.8.07)	35	F-CCJF
F-CJUB	Schempp-Hirth Duo Discus	432	
F-CJUE	Rolladen-Schneider LS8-18	8295	G-CJUE, BGA 4785
F-CJVV-SF	Scheibe SF 25C Heubacher-Falke	44720	
F-CJYB	Schempp-Hirth Duo Discus XLT	181	D-KXLT
F-CJYJ	Schleicher ASK 13	13272	
F-CJYR	CARMAM M-200 Foehn (Res.1.06)	58	OO-ZMP, F-CDPO
F-CJYS	Sportine Aviacija LAK-19	023	
F-CJZA	Start + Flug H 101 Salto	27	BGA4902/JZA, D-2997
F-CJZV	Schleicher ASW 27	27131	
F-CKAJ	Schleicher ASK 21	21286	D-4786
F-CKAH	Schempp-Hirth Discus bT	112/464	G-CKAH, BGA 4933, D-KNZZ
F-CKAN	Schempp-Hirth Janus B	93	D-6891
F-CKBC	Scheibe SF 25C Falke	44248	D-KDBC
F-CKBS	Glaser-Dirks DG-600	6-42	G-CKBS, BGA 4966, OO-YPH, D-4882
F-CKCM	Start + Flug H 101 Salto	58	OY-XXR, D-6637
F-CKEA-112	Centrair 101D Pégase	101D0112	Fr.Mil B112
F-CKFC	Schempp-Hirth Ventus-2cT	105	G-CKFC, BGA5048
F-CKID	Schempp-Hirth Ventus b/16.6	184	HB-1925, D-7721
F-CKIF-C12	Schempp-Hirth Standard Cirrus	389G	OO-ZCV
F-CKIM	Grob G 103 Twin Astir	3088	HB-1406
F-CKJN-LT	Schempp-Hirth Duo Discus	78	D-3521
F-CKLL	Grob G103 Twin II	3549	D-8748
F-CKLS	Schempp-Hirth Discus bT (Res.8.05, returned to D-KKLS)	82/415	D-KKLS
F-CKMA	Rolladen-Schneider LS6-a	6020	D-6596
F-CKPB	Sportine Aviacija LAK-17A	145	
F-CKSB-L60	Rolladen-Schneider LS1-f	394	Fr.Mil
F-CKSL	Grob G103C Twin III SL	35046	D-KWSL
F-CKTZ-KTZ	Schempp-Hirth Janus B	60	PH-595, D-7352
F-CLAB	Schleicher ASH 25	25078	D-1611
F-CLAJ	Schempp-Hirth Cirrus VTC	136Y	D-0259, OO-ZQE, D-2968
F-CLAK	Sportine Aviacija LAK-17AT	205	
F-CLAM	Schleicher ASK 13	13552	D-6727
F-CLAN	Schleicher ASK 18	18031	D-4533
F-CLAP	Centrair 101A Pégase 90	101A0477	Fr.Mil B477
F-CLAS	Schleicher ASK 13	13219	D-0461
F-CLBE	Sportavia-Pützer Fournier RF5	5044	F-GFBE, TR-LAO, F-OCOM
F-CLBF-BF	Glaser-Dirks DG-600/18	6-21	D-1913
F-CLBG	Schleicher ASK 13	13379	PH-446
F-CLBL	Schleicher ASW 27-18E (ASG 29)	29707	
F-CLBM	DG Flugzeugbau DG-1000S	10-72T11	G-DGIK, BGA 5211
F-CLBS-BK	Schleicher ASH 25	25076	D-6183
F-CLCA	Rolladen-Schneider LS8-18	8294	D-6488
F-CLCC-CC	Schleicher ASW 27	27190	
F-CLCD-I	Schleicher ASW 28	28017	D-5938
F-CLDA	Schempp-Hirth Duo Discus XL	643	
F-CLDB-28	Schempp-Hirth Arcus T	46	
F-CLDC	Schempp-Hirth Duo Discus XLT	253	
F-CLDD-CA	Schempp-Hirth Arcus	15	D-6160
F-CLDE	Schempp-Hirth Duo Discus XL	675	
F-CLDS	Glaser-Dirks DG-202/17C	2-170CL16	D-5884
F-CLEF	SZD-55-1	551194063	OE-5590
F-CLEJ	Schempp-Hirth Nimbus II	41	N2 (Fr.Mil)
F-CLEN	Fournier RF3	3	F-BLEN
F-CLEO	Glaser-Dirks DG-300 Elan	3E-321	OM-1980, D-5526, HB-1980
F-CLEP	Fournier RF3	8	F-BLEP
F-CLES	Schleicher Ka 2B	319	OO-ZRE, D-6216
F-CLFA-EW	Schleicher ASW 27-18 (ASG 29)	29038	
F-CLFK	Schempp-Hirth Nimbus-3/24.5	87	G-CFFK, BGA 3224
F-CLFM-TIF	Schleicher ASW 27	27105	D-7627
F-CLFV	Rolladen-Schneider LS4	4620	D-4056
F-CLGM	Rolladen-Schneider LS6-18W	6315	OH-865
F-CLHA	Sportine Aviacija LAK-17AT	217	
F-CLHP-T41	Grob G 103 Twin II	3567	OO-YCI, F-CFHP
F-CLIC	SZD-42-2 Jantar 2B	B-874	SP-1493, (SP-3664), HB-1493
F-CLIF	Schempp-Hirth Janus Ce	283	G-CKJK, BGA 5126, D-3666
F-CLIN	Schleicher ASK 21	21051	D-2489
F-CLIP	Schleicher ASK 13	13135	D-0148
F-CLIT	Schleicher K 8B	8528Gö	HB-829
F-CLJF	Schleicher ASK 13	13166	OO-YCU, PL62, OH-387, OH-KKP
F-CLLA	Grob G103 Twin II	3703	HB-1651
F-CLLC	Schleicher ASH 25Mi	25259	
F-CLLP	Fournier RF-3	78	F-GLLP, OO-JAZ, D-KILA
F-CLMF	Rolladen-Schneider LS4-a	4721	D-5257
F-CLMP	Schleicher ASK 21	21137	D-4311
F-CLMR	Schleicher ASH 25	25124	G-CHLX, BGA4039/HLX, D-3988
F-CLMT	Schempp-Hirth Janus C	260	OY-XSF
F-CLOE	Schleicher ASK 23B	23128	HB-3070
F-CLOL	Schleicher ASK 21	21517	D-2826
F-CLOT	Grob G102 Astir CS	1147	D-7271
F-CLOU	Grob G103C Twin III Acro	34173	D-5525, SE-URC, D-2941
F-CLPN	PZL-Swidnik PW-5 Smyk	17.05.008	LN-GWW
F-CLRC	Schleicher ASH 25	25233	
F-CLUB	Schempp-Hirth Ventus-2c	38/112	D-7453
F-CLUF-UF	Schempp-Hirth Discus b	22	D-8922, HB-1738
F-CLUI	Schempp-Hirth Janus C	240	D-1828
F-CLVA	Grob G103C Twin III SL	35002	D-KSLG
F-CLVB	Centrair 101A Pégase	101068	G-DESW, BGA 2924
F-CLXH	Fournier RF3	16	F-BLXH
F-CLZZ	Schleicher ASH 25	25003	D-2530
F-CMAD	Schempp-Hirth Ventus-2cT	183	S5-KEJ, HA-4550
F-CMAG	Glaser-Dirks DG-200/17	2-120/1725	HB-1544
F-CMAR	Schleicher ASW 20L	20498	D-2696, HB-2168, HB-1613
F-CMAX	Pilatus B4-PC11AF	207	PH-531

F-CMBE-EB	Schempp-Hirth Duo Discus	31	D-0255
F-CMCJ	Scheibe SF 25C Falke	44239	D-KDCJ
F-CMCT	Schempp-Hirth Ventus-2a	79	BGA 4695
F-CMDL	Fournier RF3	33	F-BMDL
F-CMEI	Schempp-Hirth Duo Discus	172	D-9204
F-CMET	Schempp-Hirth Standard Cirrus	392	OK-5775, PH-486
F-CMEZ	Schleicher K 8B	8228/A/SH	D-7192
F-CMFA	Schleicher ASW 27-18E (ASG 29E)	29656	
F-CMHN-4E	Schleicher ASW 27	27042	D-0414
F-CMJK	Schempp-Hirth Janus Ce	286	OY-TVX, D-9202
F-CMJL	Schleicher ASW 27	27159	D-4427
F-CMJO	Rolladen-Schneider LS4	4039	D-0039, I-LYMA, D-3356
F-CMLD	Schleicher ASK 13	13587	D-7961
F-CMLS-LS	Rolladen-Schneider LS8-18	8056	G-CHUV, BGA 4222, D-3823
F-CMNA	Schleicher K 8B	1019	D-4315
F-CMNB	Schleicher ASK 13	13300	D-0242
F-CMNC-BM	Schleicher ASK 13	13415	D-2078
F-CMOI	Schleicher K 8B	8946	D-5134, PH-402
F-CMOZ	Schleicher ASW 20CL TOP	20757	D-KHGN, HB-2178, HB-1740
F-CMPY	DG Flugzeugbau DG-1000S	10-18S18	D-8276, PH-1276
F-CMTE	Fournier RF3	60	F-BMTE
F-CMTK	Fournier RF3	70	F-BMTK
F-CMTO	Siren C30S Edelweiss (Res.3.07)	22	3A-MTO, F-CCUT
F-CMTU	Fournier RF3	87	F-BMTU
F-CNCA	Schleicher ASK 13	13280	I-ENCA
F-CNDM	Grob G103C Twin III Acro	34138	EC-JPE, F-CGXE, D-4343
F-CNEG	Schempp-Hirth Janus C	228	HB-1905
F-CNHH	Rolladen-Schneider LS4	4431	D-8548
F-CNHZ	Glaser-Dirks DG-300 Elan	3E190	D-5739
F-CNLB	Rolladen-Schneider LS8-18	8059	G-CHVF, BGA 4232, D-1683
F-CNMN	Rolladen-Schneider LS6-a	6052	D-8993
F-CNOU	Sportine Aviacija LAK-17A	184	
F-CNPU	CARMAM JP.15/36AR Aiglon	054	(F-GNPU), Fr.AF
F-CNTT	Fournier RF3	86	F-BMTT
F-CNVV	Schleicher ASW 28	28019	D-5972
F-COAG	Scheibe SF 25C Falke	4460	D-KOAG
F-COBR	SZD-36A Cobra 15	W-622	SE-TKZ, SP-2658
F-COCA	Schleicher ASK 21	21900	
F-COCI	Schempp-Hirth Janus C	208	D-6205
F-COCO	SZD-51-1 Junior	W-957	HB-1906
F-CODE	Rolladen-Schneider LS4-a (W/o 6.8.15)	4748	D-5174
F-COKE	Rolladen-Schneider LS4	4174	HB-1602
F-COLA	Schleicher ASK 13	13011	D-4717
F-COLE	Glaser-Dirks DG-600/18.	6-15	D-0134, PH-834
F-COLI	DG Flugzeugbau DG-1000S	10-138S90	
F-COLS	Schleicher ASW 27-18E	29526	
F-COLT-S10	Schempp-Hirth Duo Discus	52	D-1068
F-COMB	Rolladen-Schneider LS8-18	8146	D-5818, G-CJCP, BGA 4409
F-COMP	Schleicher ASK 21	21837	
F-COOL	Rolladen-Schneider LS8-18	8128	SE-USE
F-COOO	Schempp-Hirth Ventus C	33/467	D-1750
F-COPF	Sportavia-Pützer Fournier RF5	5082	D-KOPF, JA2127, D-KIEL
F-COQX	Avialsa-Scheibe A.60 Fauconnet	45	D- . . . ., F-CCQX
F-COSP	Stemme S 10-VT	11-092	
F-COSY	Schleicher Ka 6E	4374	D-0760
F-COUI	Schempp-Hirth Duo Discus	164	D-3159
F-CPAC	Glaser-Dirks DG-500M	5E122M52	HB-2256
F-CPAS	Schleicher ASK 13	13221	D-0465
F-CPAT	Schempp-Hirth Nimbus-2	44	HB-1496, D-1229
F-CPBA-LK	Glaser-Dirks DG-500 Elan Trainer	5E37T11	SE-ULK
F-CPCA	PZL-Swidnik PW-6U	78.03.09	SE-UUJ, LN-GCV
F-CPCV	Grob G103A Twin II Acro	3773-K-59	D-7894
F-CPDG	Glasflügel H201B Standard Libelle	319	OO-ZCU, F-CEBF
F-CPDS-S17	DG Flugzeugbau DG-1000S	10-91S64	D-4112
F-CPHR	Schempp-Hirth Nimbus-4D	1/3	OH-950, D-1211
F-CPIN	Glaser-Dirks DG-400	4-242	G-BPIN
F-CPJL	Schempp-Hirth Ventus-2cxT	174	D-KPJL
F-CPLE	Sportine Aviacija LAK-17A	110	CS-PBW
F-CPLJ	Sportavia-Pützer Fournier RF4D	4125	F-BPLJ
F-CPLM	Schleicher K 8B	8657	PH-360
F-CPLN	Schempp-Hirth Duo Discus XLT	209	D-KPLN
F-CPLR	Sportavia-Pützer Fournier RF5	5067	F-BPLR
F-CPLS-GW	Rolladen-Schneider LS8-18.	8070	D-8119, HB-3216
F-CPLU	Schleicher K 7 Rhönadler	10	OO-ZQY, D-5667
F-CPOL-H1	Glasflügel Hornet	31	I-CALM
F-CPOU	Schleicher Ka 6CR Rhönsegler	6207	OO-YCJ, PL51
F-CPPM	Scheibe SF 28A Tandem-Falke	5718	D-KEPM, HB-2034, D-KAZE(1), (D-KOAJ)
F-CPQA	Schleicher ASK 13	13480	D-9272
F-CPQB	Schleicher K 8B	8593	D-7505
F-CPQC	Schempp-Hirth Janus B	35	D-3787
F-CPQD	Schleicher ASK 13	13391	D-0905
F-CPQE	Schleicher K 8B	158/59	D-5772
F-CPQR	Schempp-Hirth Janus C	193	D-8468
F-CPRA	Glaser-Dirks DG-800S	8-41S10	D-1780
F-CPRM	Schempp-Hirth Ventus-2cM	97/204	
F-CPRN	Rolladen-Schneider LS6-18W	6287	D-6186, BGA 4427, D-9128
F-CPRS	Rolladen-Schneider LS6-a	6027	D-6336
F-CPSG	Glaser-Dirks DG-600	6-22	D-1914, (PH-837)
F-CPSL	DG Flugzeugbau DG-1000S	10-206S129	
F-CPSX	Schleicher ASK 13	13442	PH-454
F-CPVV	Rolladen-Schneider LS6-18W	6370	SP-3801, SE-UUP, D-4933
F-CPZT-AZ	Schempp-Hirth Ventus c	347	(F-CRZT), D-9438, PH-943, D-5470, D-KBHK(1)
F-CTAR	Schempp-Hirth Duo Discus	64	D-2782
F-CTBB	Grob G 102 Astir CS Jeans	2158	OO-ZNO, D-4554
F-CTDV	Grob G102 Astir CS 77	1602	D-4803
F-CTJB	Schleicher ASK 21Mi	21812	VH-JBW, D-KHAD
F-CTJD	Grob/Schempp-Hirth Std Cirrus	451G	OO-ZCC
F-CTOP	Schleicher ASW 27-18E (ASG 29E)	29692	
F-CTPG	Schleicher K 8C	81003	PH-517
F-CTVV-R	Glaser-Dirks DG-300 Elan	3E119	D-3041
F-CTZT-ZT	DG Flugzeugbau DG-808S	8-290S53X1	D-9808, HB-3374, D-9808
F-CUTA	SZD-24-4A Foka 4	W-349	PH-399
F-CUTE	Stemme S 10-VT	11-133	
F-CUVV-SF	Schempp-Hirth Duo Discus	189	OY-SFX, D-7728
F-CVAC	Schempp-Hirth Janus CT	11/270	OY-XZF, D-KDOA
F-CVAL	Schleicher K 8	514	D-5677
F-CVAT	Scheibe SF 25E Super Falke	4328	D-KVAV, OE-9127, (D-KDFF)
F-CVAV	Schempp-Hirth Duo Discus T	89/404	PH-1300
F-CVDF	Schempp-Hirth Arcus	10	D-4684
F-CVGT-4G	Schempp-Hirth Janus C	232	D-2988, HB-1897
F-CVII	Glaser-Dirks DG-600/18.	6-16	D-6260
F-CVLB	Glaser-Dirks DG-300 Elan	3E46	D-4755, HB-1757

F-CVLC	Rolladen-Schneider LS4-b	4934	D-5499
F-CVMP-MP	Schempp-Hirth Arcus	5	D-5017
F-CVNE	Schleicher ASK 21	21418	D-6449
F-CVOA	Rolladen-Schneider LS8-18	8147	OY-XDB, BGA 4406
F-CVSA	Schleicher K 8B	8536	PH-348
F-CVSL	Schempp-Hirth Janus C	123	D-6849
F-CVTG	Rolladen-Schneider LS6-18W	6371	PH-1303, BGA 4760, D-2571
F-CVVA-MX	Schleicher ASK 21	21867	
F-CVVB	Centrair 101 Pégase	10100321	Fr.AF B321
F-CVVC	Centrair 101 Pégase	10100285	Fr.AF B285
F-CVVD-E529	Centrair 101D Pégase	101D0529	Fr.AF E529
F-CVVE	Centrair 101 Pégase	10100286	Fr.AF B286
F-CVVF	Centrair 101A Pégase	101A0352	Fr.AF B352
F-CVVH	Schleicher ASK 21	21869	
F-CVVJ	Centrair 201B Marianne	201B056	
F-CVVK-Z58	Centrair 201B Marianne	201B058	Fr.AF Z58
F-CVVL-T67	Centrair 201B Marianne	201B069	Fr.AF Z67
F-CVVM	Schleicher ASK 13	13238	PH-791, OH-395, OH-KKR
F-CVVN	Centrair 201B Marianne	201B081	Fr.AF Z79, F-WQQC, Fr.AF Z79
F-CVVO-Z104	Centrair 201B Marianne	201B104	Fr.AF Z104
F-CVVP	Schleicher ASK 21	21866	
F-CVVS	Rolladen-Schneider LS8-18	8303	D-0112
F-CVVZ	Schleicher ASK 13	13170	D-1095, D-1006, D-1000
F-CXOA	Scheibe SF 25E Super Falke	4336	OY-XOA, D-KDCG
F-CXXC	Schempp-Hirth Duo Discus	101	D-6490
F-CXXD	Schempp-Hirth Discus-2cR	30	D-9557
F-CXXL-L	Schempp-Hirth Janus C	255	D-5068
F-CYAN	Schleicher ASW 20L	20408	EC-DNI
F-CYBN	Schleicher ASK 13	13476	D-2663
F-CYJD-90	Schempp-Hirth Janus C	191	D-4590
F-CYJP	Schempp-Hirth Janus C	168	OO-YJP, N806JC
F-CYPI -PL63	Schleicher ASK 13	13512	OO-YPI, (OO-YPA), Belgian Air Cadets PL63
F-CYVN	Schempp-Hirth Duo Discus	228	OO-YVN, OY-XVN
F-CZAN	Schempp-Hirth Ventus b/16.6	197	D-5277
F-CZAR	Grob G 102 Astir CS Jeans	2154	D-4890
F-CZCX-AH	Schempp-Hirth Arcus	16	
F-CZEF-U2	Schleicher ASW 27-18E (ASG 29E)	29501	G-CKNU, D-KPRC, D-2529
F-CZEN	Schempp-Hirth Ventus-2c	33/87	D-4884
F-CZRN-RN	Schempp-Hirth Ventus-2cxM	187	D-KZRN
F-CZSX-Z6	Schleicher ASW 28	28024	D-3606

GLIDERS/MOTOR-GLIDERS WITH RESTRICTED CofA

F-CRAG(2)	Pottier JP15/34R Kit Club	60-43	
F-CRAH(2)	Boulay Condor	01	
F-CRBA(2)	Rutan 77-6 Solitaire	F1	
F-CRBG(2)	Fournier RF-9	13	
F-CRBJ	Castel C.301S	1127	F-CAKD
F-CRBL	Fauvel AV.36 (Modified)	131	F-CBSF
F-CRDQ	Castel 25S	139	F-CAMX
F-CRDU(2)	ACBA 3A	01	
F-CREB	Peyronnenc PP.1	01	F-WREB
F-CREV(2)	Nord 1300	228	F-CREU, F-CBXE
F-CREZ(2)	Rolladen/Mudry LS1-SP-1	01	F-CREK(2), F-WRKE
F-CRFK	Emouchet SA.104	282	F-CCFC
F-CRFU	Nord 1300	197	F-CAXI
F-CRGC	Fauvel AV-222 Buse	07	F-WRGC
F-CRGF	Fournier RF-9	12	
F-CRGL	Nord 1300	94	F-CBXR
F-CRHL	Nord 1300	60	F-CBXV
F-CRHT	Castel C.301S	1133	F-CBXO
F-CRHX	Castel 25S	150	F-CBIK
F-CRJB	Pottier 15/34 Kit Club	60-32	F-CFGB, F-WFGB
F-CRJM(2)	Castel C.301S	1050	F-CRHQ, F-CBLA
	(Being restored)		
F-CRLA(2)	Avia 152A	301	(F-AZVI)
	(Res.02)		
F-CRLO	Nord 1300	123	F-CAGX
F-CRMB	Sablier 18	01	
	(Res.99)		
F-CRML	Castel 25S	115	F-CBOU
F-CRMU(2)	Castel 25S	172	F-CRMA, F-CBAP
F-CRND(2)	Pottier 15/34R Kit Club	60-60	
F-CRNR	Nord 1300	65	F-CAAN
F-CROF	Emouchet SA.103	94	F-CBJB
F-CROI (2)	Fouga CM.8W	01	F-WFDI
F-CROL(2)	Neukom AN-20B	7	
	(Stored)		
F-CRPI	Darry DP-01	01	
F-CRPY	Fouga Sylphe IIIB	01	F-PNKU
F-CRQS(2)	Nord 1300	112	F-CRBV, F-CAQR
F-CRQX	Fauvel AV.361	323	
F-CRRA	Scheibe Mü.13D	03	F-CAEQ
F-CRRI	Boulay Menin BM 1	01	F-WRRI
F-CRRJ	Vaysse TCV 03	PS-1	
F-CRRL	Compact 12/80	01	
F-CRRM	Fauvel AV.451	13	F-WRRM
F-CRRN	Emouchet SA.104	233	F-CRNJ, F-CBJH
F-CRRO	Mouisset AP	01	F-CCRO(2)
F-CRRP	Rambaud Fournier RF-9	03-A	F-CAHK
F-CRRY	Fauvel AV.45	01	(F-PYEY), F-WCAG
F-CRTA	Sportavia-Pützer Fournier RF5	1	F-PZTA, F-WZTA
F-CRXH	Nord 1300	88	F-CRQM, F-CAQZ

MICROLIGHTS / ULMs

Registration is by the prefix number of the Département in which the owner lives, administered on a regional basis. Département names are given below as a reference aid. It is believed that changing marks when changing owner/Département is now no longer required. The F-J... marks are portable radio call-signs rather than aircraft registrations, they may therefore remain with an owner and be transferred to other aircraft. We have moved these into the second column for ease of reference, with an alphabetical index at the end.

No complete ULM listing is as yet available and what follows is made up largely of reported sightings. As in the main register the letter W is used for test flying, although it may be applied before, after, or in the middle of the registration! A number of companies now have re-usable test marks of various types as indicated within the list. Only confirmed types are now included and the editor would welcome any additional reports and sightings. We are still recording ULMs that have been withdrawn from use or have had accidents, simply because otherwise there is as yet no other source which gives all this information in one place.

Where c/ns are quoted for weight-shift machines these usually (but not always) apply to the wings, however registrations are usually carried on the wings which in some cases may frequently be exchanged between trikes and checks should be carried out wherever possible. For Air Création types the trike unit usually has a T prefix c/n and the wing an A prefix. Where possible we quote trike details first, then wing details. A number of types now incorporate engine type into the designation – in the case of Jabiru engines this is shown in brackets in order to avoid confusion with the Jabiru aircraft.

Abbreviations: t/w = tail wheel   n/w = nose wheel   f/p = floatplane

01 : Ain

01-R		Rans S-6 Coyote II		
01-T		Zenith Baroudeur		
01-AD		Perouges X-15		
WAV-01		Murphy Rebel		
01-BK		Aerial Arts Chaser 110SX		
W01-BM		Fox Tristar		
01-BP		Air Création GT BI / Quartz		
01-CG		(Croses ?) Airplume		
01-CQ	F-JAHD	Ultralair Weedhopper		
01-CR		Weedhopper		
01-DA	F-JAFY	Dynali Chickinox		
01-DE		Aviasud Mistral		
01-DJ		Air Création		
01-DT		Aviasud Mistral		
01-DZ		Aviasud Mistral		
01-EB		Dynali Chickinox		
01-EJ		Eipper Quicksilver GT		
01-FA	F-JAGS	Denney Kitfox		
01-FT		Rans S-6 Coyote II (t/w)		
01-FY		Weedhopper AX-3		
01-GB		Denney Kitfox		
01-W-GE		Tecnam P.96 Golf		
01-GI		Dynali Chickinox		
01-GX		Air Création		
01-HC		Aviasud Mistral		
01-HF		Micro Aviation Pulsar II		
		(WHF-01 noted as Avid Champion, .00)		
01-HT		Weedhopper AX-3	C3113174	
01-HU		Air Création GTE Clipper		
01-HV		Dynali Chickinox		
01-II		Best Off Sky Ranger		
01-IJ		Arrow Caprice 21		
01-IO		Microleve (f/p)		
01-IR	F-JCOS	Rans S-6ES Coyote II		
01-IV		Comco Ikarus Fox-C22	9003-3261	D-MEPH
01-JM		Cosmos		
01-JS		Soubeyrat Albatros paramotor		
01-JT		III Sky Arrow 500TF	098/11 or 039/98	
01-KF	F-JCKL	Rans S-6ESD Coyote II		
01-KG	F-JCKM	Rans S-7 Courier		
01-KH	F-JCKO	Rans S-6ESD Coyote IIXL		
01-KI		Rans S-6 Coyote II		
01-KM	F-JCBH	Rans S-6ES Coyote II		
01-KP		Pegasus Quantum Super Sport	7279	
01-LB	F-JCUM	Tecnam P.92 Echo		
01-LG		Air Création		
01-LJ		Rans S-6 Coyote II		
01-LR		Zenith Baroudeur		
01-MB		Tecnam P.92S Echo		
01-MC	F-JEIU	Rans S-7 Courier		
01-MN	F-JEJI	Rans S-9 Chaos		
01-MO	F-JEMR	Rans S-6 Coyote (t/w)		
01-MQ		Flight Design CT		
01-MR	F-JEIK	Tecnam P.92 Echo		
01-NH		Flight Design CT		
01-NI		Flight Design CT		
01-NJ	F-JEJH	Rans S-6S Super Six	0598 1232 - 1298S	
01-NL		paramotor		
01-NM		Rans S-9 Chaos		
01-NN	F-JEJK	Flight Design CT-2K		
01-NO	F-JEJC	Flight Design CT-2K		
01-NP	F-JEKH	Tecnam P.96 Golf		
01-NS(1)	F-JBUW	Pegasus XL		
01-NS(1)	F-JZAB	Zenair CH-601XL Zodiac		
01-OD		Pipistrel Sinus		
W01-OF	F-JELH	ATEC Zephyr (see also W01-OS ??)	01	
01-OG		Tecnam P.92 Echo		
01-OI		Rans S-6 Coyote II		
01-OJ		Flight Design CT		
01-OL	F-JEKV	Tecnam P.92S Echo		
01-OQ	F-JELJ	Tecnam P.92 Echo		
01-OR	F-JELS	Tecnam P.96 Golf	18?	
W01-OS	F-JELH	ATEC Zephyr 2000		
01-OT	F-JELC	Flight Design CT		
01-OU	F-JELN	Tecnam P.96 Golf 100	062	
W-PA-01		EuroALA Jet Fox 97		
01-PE	F-JESR	Jodel D.18V	84	F-PYYQ
01-PM	F-JEML	Zenair CH-601UL Zodiac (t/w)		
01-PQ		Air Création		
01-PR	F-JENY	Tecnam P.96 Golf 100		
01-PS		Tecnam P.96 Golf (Damaged)		
01-PX		Alpaero (Noin) Sirius		
01-PY		Air Création / Quartz		
01-QB	F-JEOD	Tecnam P.96 Golf 100		
01-QC	F-JFFQ	Tecnam P.92S Echo		
		(Also carried marks 77-AHP internally 8.03)		
01-QD		Pipistrel Sinus		
01-QE		Pipistrel Sinus		
01-QI		DTA Dynamic		
		(also reported as Rans S-6ES Coyote but this probably refers to 01-OI)		

Reg	Call-sign	Type	c/n	Prev id
01-QL		Tecnam P.96 Golf 100		
01-QM	F-JBJI	Tecnam P.92 Echo		
01-QQ	F-JEPH	Tecnam P.92S Echo		
01-QR		Denney Kitfox		
01-RL	F-JERN	Flight Design CT-2K		
		(Same call-sign as 57-APE)		
01-RN		DTA Dynamic 582		
01-RP		Tecnam P.92S Echo		
01-RQ	F-JERS	Zenair CH-601UL Zodiac		
01-RT	F-JERU	Tecnam P.92S Echo	735	
01-RX	F-JESG	Rans S-6 Coyote II	0694 634	
01-RY		Air Création GTE Clipper / iXess		
W01-RZ		gyrocopter		
01-SB		Air Création GTE Clipper / iXess		
01-SC		Air Création / iXess		
01-SG	F-JAKN	Vidor Asso VI Junior		
01-SH	F-JETJ	Tecnam P.92 Echo Super (Jabiru)		
01-SK	F-JEUN	Rans S-7 Courier 912	0497 2 ..?	
01-SN		Zenair CH-601UL Zodiac (t/w)		
01-SP		Aéro Services Guépard 912	24040	
01-SS		homebuilt motorglider		W01-SS
		(forced landing 28.9.04 and 26.6.06)		
01-ST		Sauper J.300 Joker		
01-SU	F-JEVH	Tecnam P.92S Echo		
01-SW		Tecnam P.92 Echo		
01-SX		Rans S-7 Courier		
01-TD		Aviasud AE209 Albatros		
01-TE	F-JEVV	Tecnam P.2002 Sierra		
01-TG	F-JEWF	Tecnam P.92S Echo		
01-TH	F-JEKK	Tecnam P.92 Echo		
01-TJ	F-JEWR	B&F Funk FK-9 Mk.IV Club	12 03	
01-TK	F-JEXB	Tecnam P.2002 Sierra		
01-TL	F-JEXK	ICP Bingo! 4S	04-11-52-164	
01-TM	F-JEXR	Zlin Savage Classic	0048	
		(Re-regd 83-ALN)		
01-TN	F-JEYH	Tecnam P.2002 Sierra		
01-TV		Air Création GT BI 503S / Fun 450		
01-TX	F-JEYP	Tecnam P.2004 Bravo		
01-TY	F-JEJO	Rans S-6ES Coyote II	0495 808 ES	
01-UC	F-JEYZ	Tecnam P.2004 Bravo		
01-UF	F-JEZD	Jabiru		
01-UK		Air Création Tanarg 912 / iXess		
01-UL	F-JEZZ	Tecnam P.92 Echo Club		
01-UQ		DTA Combo / Dynamic		
01-UR	F-JEGL	Tecnam P.2004 Bravo		
01-UV		Air Création Tanarg 912 / iXess		
01-VA		Tecnam P.92 Echo		
01-VB	F-JYGZ	Tecnam P.2002 Sierra		
01-VG	F-JFXQ	Tecnam P.92 Echo ES	1031	
		(previously used F-JYOT)		
01-VL		Mignet HM.1000 Balerit	24	
01-VN		Tecnam P.92 Echo		
		(Accident 27.8.09)		
01-VT		Zenair CH-601UL Zodiac		
01-WE	F-JXWJ	Tecnam P.2002 Sierra		
		(also reported as F-JZWJ)		
01-WG	F-JJKV	Rans S-7 Courier		
01-WK		Tecnam P.2002 Sierra		
		(Damaged in forced landing 9.6.08)		
01-WN	F-JWHD	Air Création Tanarg / iXess 13		
01-WQ		Ultralair Espace 462 / Quartz 16		
		(W/o 28.9.08)		
01-WS		Tecnam P.2004 Bravo		
01-WX	F-JEFJ	ICP MXP-740 Savannah	05-06-51-401	26-UH
		(Damaged 19.1.11)		
01-XA	F-JWPQ	Air Création Tanarg / iXess		
01-XC		Zlin Savage Classic	0044	D-MKRS
01-XD	F-JXHI	Zlin Savage Cruiser		71-LH
01-XF		Air Création Tanarg / iXess		
01-XG		paramotor		
01-XH		paramotor		
01-XI		Flylab Tucano		
01-XL		Best Off Sky Ranger		
W01-XO		Rans S-9 Chaos		
01-XQ		Flylight Airsports Dragonfly / Aeros wing		
01-XR		Air Création iXess 15		
01-XU	F-JWOS	Zenair CH-701 STOL		
01-YA	F-JXWO	Tecnam P.92 Echo		
01-YL	F-JRKK	Tecnam P.92 Echo Classic		
01-YP		Denney Kitfox		
01-YX	F-JJDT	Aéro Services Guépard 912		
01-YY	F-JRQK	Tecnam P.2002 Sierra		
01-ZA		Alisport Silent Targa	208	
		(Re-regd G-CITK 7.15)		
01-ZL		Aeros Stream		
01-ZM		Air Création Safari GT BI 503		
01-ZQ		ICP MXP-740 Savannah VG XL	10-02-51-900	
01-ZR	F-JSYX	Plätzer Kiebitz	309	
01-ZT	F-JEZJ	Air Création Tanarg / BioniX		
01-ZY	F-JRZQ	Pipistrel Sinus	344S912	
01-AAC	F-JSEM	Tecnam P.92 Echo Classic de Luxe		
01-AAN	F-JSKE	Flight Design CT Supralight	E-10-11-03	
01-AAR	F-JSRZ	Slepcev Storch		
01-AAX		Rans S-6ES Coyote II (t/w)		
01-ABA	F-JTCU	Tecnam P.92 Echo Super		
01-ABB	F-JTCV	ICP MXP-740 Savannah S	11-05-54-0095	
01-ABC	F-JTDC	ICP MXP-740 Savannah S	11-07-54-0111	
01-ABI	F-JTJJ	Tecnam P.92 Echo Classic de Luxe	1370	
01-ABM	F-JWHD	Air Création Tanarg / NuviX	A11114-11098	
01-ABS	F-JTML	ICP MXP-740 Savvanah S	11-11-54-0133	
01-ABT		ICP MXP-740 Savannah S		
01-ACB	F-JTON	ICP MXP-740 Savannah S	12-02-54-0159	
01-ACE	F-JTTI	Tecnam P.92 Echo		74-ACE
01-ACM	F-JTVJ	ICP MXP-740 Savannah S (f/p)	12-02-54-0166	
01-ACO		Alisport Silent 2 Targa		
		(W/o 14.6.12 in mid-air collision)		
01-ACR	F-JUAY	Tecnam P.92TD	1428	
01-ACY		Murphy Renegade Spirit		
01-ADE	F-JUKE	Aerospool WT-9 Dynamic	DY458/2013	
		(W/o Ecuador during round-the-world flight 29.3.15)		
01-ADI	F-JULE	Magni M-22 Voyager		
01-ADM	F-JEJO	Jodel DD11LU		
01-ADP	F-JUYA	Pipistrel Virus SW	545SW80	
01-ADS		Best Off Sky Ranger		
01-AEE	F-JVGP	ICP MXP-740 Savannah S	12-07-54-0202	
01-AEF	F-JVJJ	Tecnam P.92 Echo Light		
01-AEM	F-JVYY	Denney Kitfox		
01-AFB	F-JWDC	ICP MXP-740 Savannah S	14-09-54-0349	
01-AFM	F-JTTC	DTA J-RO gyrocopter		
W01-AFY	F-JSIZ	ESPACE Sensation		
01-AGB		ICP MXP-740 Savannah S		
01-AGL	F-JAYS	Tecnam P.92 Ecolite		
01-AJD		ICP MXP-740 Savannah S		
WPTA-01		Aviomania G2sa Genesis gyrocopter		
01-NJT		Dynali H3 Easyflyer		
01-WUL		Twin Weedhopper		

02 : Aisne

Reg	Call-sign	Type	c/n	Prev id
02-J		Cosmos		
02-AB		Air Création		
02-AC	F-JZCM	Djicat Buse'Air 150		58-FF
02-BO		Humbert La Moto-du-Ciel		
02-BX		Mignet HM.1000 Balerit		
02-CA		La Mouette Ghost 12		
02-CN		Cosmos		
02-CO	F-JAOP	JCC Aviation J.300 Joker kit		
02-DA		Cosmos SM		
02-DE		Cosmos (trike)		
02-DG		Lascaud Bifly		
02-DJ	F-JFXW	Aéro Services Guépy (Jabiru) 80T		
02-DL		Air Création / Quartz		80-BZ
02-DM	F-JBFX	Tandem Air Sunny		
02-EF		Barry MB-04 Souris Bulle		
02-EV		Beaver AX650		
02-GH		Light Aero Avid Flyer		
02-GI		Zenair CH-701 STOL		
02-GS		Mignet HM.1000 Balerit	35	
02-GV		Piel CP.150 Onyx		
02-GY		Zenair CH-701 STOL		
02-HB	F-JCJX	III Sky Arrow 500TF		
02-HI		Light Aero Avid Flyer		
02-HQ		Rans S-12 Airaile		
02-IR	F-JBTB	Rans S-6 Coyote II		
02-IZ		TEAM Mini-MAX		
02-JB		ICP Bingo 4S	05-10-52-193	
02-JD		Djicat Buse'Air 150GT		
02-JH		Djicat Buse'Air 150		
02-JM	F-JFZK	Rans S-6 Coyote II		
02-JO	F-JFHD	Zenair CH-701 STOL		
02-JR		Lemonier Maestro FL-3		
02-JZ		Air Création / XP11		
02-KF		Cosmos Chronos		
02-KI		weightshift		
02-KJ		Air Création / Fun		
02-KN	F-JFYE	B&F Funk FK-9 Mk.III	09-149	
02-KV		Air Création Racer		
02-KY	F-JFXC	Rans S-6 Coyote II		
02-KZ	F-JFYO	ZUT Aviation TT2000 STOL		
		(Re-regd 56- . .)		
02-LE		Fantasy Air Allegro SW		
02-LN		Light Aero Avid Flyer		
02-LR		Fly Synthesis Storch CL		
		(Accident 30.9.07)		
02-LU		DTA Dynamic 450		
02-LW		Ranger 582 / La Mouette Top 12.9		
02-LZ		Air Création GTE Clipper / Mild		
02-MB		Aéro Services Guépy		
02-MF	F-JFZS	Rans S-7 Courier (t/w)		
02-MY		Zenair CH-701 STOL		
02-ND		Humbert La Moto-du-Ciel		
02-NF		Fantasy Air Allegro SW		
02-NG		Air Création / Kiss		
02-NR		DTA Dynamic 15/430		
02-NT		Air Création Buggy		
02-NX	F-JZNP	Cosmos Phase II 582 / Chronos 16		
02-NY		ICP MXP-740 Savannah	03-10-51-237	
02-OG		Magni M-18 Spartan		
02-ZC		Vidor Asso V Champion		
		(Damaged 15.6.07)		
02-ZG		Cosmos HKS700E		
02-ZR		Air Création GTE Twin 582SL		
		(Damaged 5.6.07)		
02-ZS	F-JYLL	Air Création GTE / iXess		
02-ZX	F-JFWK	ICP MXP-740 Savannah	01-10-51-100	27-PL
02-AAB		Autogyro-Europe MT-03		
02-AAF		Autogyro-Europe MT-03		
02-AAH	F-JEYR	Air Création Tanarg / iXess		
02-AAL		Autogyro-Europe MT-03		
02-AAO	F-JXWC	Tecnam P.92 Echo Club		
02-AAV	F-JQGR	Fantasy Air Allegro SW		
		(Same call-sign as 25-RN)		
02-AAW	F-JZBX	Autogyro-Europe MT-03		
02-AAX		Humbert Tetras		
02-AAY		Autogyro-Europe MTOsport		
02-AAZ		Autogyro-Europe MTOsport		
02-ABB		Autogyro-Europe MT-03		
02-ABE		gyrocopter		
02-ABF		Autogyro-Europe MTOsport		
02-ABG		Alpi Aviation Pioneer 200		
02-ABH		Air Création / Mild		
02-ABI		Fly Synthesis Storch HS		
02-ABN		Air Création GTE Clipper / iXess		
02-ABP		Magni gyrocopter		
02-ABU		Air Command Elite Tandem	912-8057-08	
02-ABY		paramotor		
02-ACA		Autogyro-Europe MTOsport		
02-ACK	F-JWZG	Autogyro-Europe Calidus 09	C09F02	
02-ACL		Autogyro-Europe Calidus 09		
02-ACO	F-JXLS	Autogyro-Europe MTOsport		
02-ACP	F-JXLU	Autogyro-Europe MTOsport		
02-ACS		Air Création GTE Clipper 582 / iXess 15		
02-ACU		Technic Moto Mustang 2		
02-ACW		Synairgie Dauphin 503 Quicky		
		(W/o 9.2.09)		
02-ACZ		Air Création GTE Clipper		
02-ADA		Air Création		
02-ADC	F-JRLV	Autogyro-Europe Calidus 09		
02-ADI		Best Off Nynja 912		
02-ADM	F-JPCO	Air Création GTE 582S / iXess 15		
02-ADN		Celier Xenon		
02-ADP		Jodel D.185	509	82-AQ
02-ADY		ITV Dakota paramotor		

Reg	F-reg	Type	Serial	Notes
02-ADZ	F-JYLN	Aviasud Mistral	184	OO-C27, D-MBTH
02-AEC	F-JSHW	Autogyro-Europe Calidus 09		
02-AEI		Autogyro-Europe Calidus 09		
02-AEL		Technic Moto Mustang 2	040	
02-AEO		Eipper Quicksilver MX IIA		
02-AEP		Murphy Renegade Spirit		
02-AEV	F-JTCC	Autogyro-Europe MT-03/MTOsport		
02-AEW	F-JIGE	Pagotto Brako gyro	65006	
02-AEY		Averso AX-02 Guépard		
02-AFC	F-JTFQ	Celier Xenon	CAL13574S	
02-AFD		Autogyro-Europe MTOsport		
02-AFE	F-JTFR	Autogyro-Europe Cavalon	V00012	F-JTHH
02-AFI		Aveko VL-3		
02-AFN		Autogyro-Europe MTOsport		
02-AFO		Autogyro-Europe MT-03		
02-AGA	F-JUNI	Helisport CH-7 Kompress		
02-AGL		Autogyro-Europe MTOsport		
02-AGN		Helisport CH-7 Kompress Charlie		
02-AGS		Autogyro-Europe MTOsport		
02-AGT	F-JVDJ	Autogyro-Europe Calidus 09	C00283	
02-AGU		Air Création Skypper / NuviX		
02-AGV		Best Off Sky Ranger floatplane		
02-AGW		Autogyro-Europe Calidus 09		
02-AGZ		JMB VL-3 Evolution RG		
02-AHC	F-JVSH	Aurogyro-Europe MTOsport	M01145	
02-AHO		Autogyro-Europe Calidus		
02-AHS	F-JSOU	Autogyro-Europe MTOfree		
02-ANV	F-JZKU	Aviasud AE209 Albatros	58	
		(out-of-sequence so possibly error)		
WUL-02		Ultravia Pelican (Special marks? Used .92)		

03 : Allier

Reg	F-reg	Type	Serial	Notes
3-B		Eipper Quicksilver MX		
03-AD		Zenith Baroudeur		
03-AF		Zenith Baroudeur		
03-AJ		Air Création GT BI / Quartz		
03-AQ	F-JABA	Aermas 386		
03-AZ		Pegasus		
03-BA	F-JECO	Aeroprakt A-22	042	
03-BC		Air Création		
03-BD		Croses Airplume		
03-BG(1)		Air Création / SX		
03-BG(2)		gyrocopter (homebuilt)		
03-BO		Cosmos / La Mouette Touring		
03-BS	F-JECR	Jodel D.19		
		(Crashed 6.10.07)		
03-BU		trike ? / La Mouette wing		
03-CB		Hipps Superbirds J-3 Kitten		
03-CG		Dynali Chickinox		
03-CI		Air Création / Mild		
03-CN	F-JEEJ	Humbert La Moto-du-Ciel		
03-CO		Air Création		
03-DD		Synairgie		
03-DE		Synairgie / Narval (wing)		
		(also reported as Eipper Quicksilver)		
03-DG		Dynali Chickinox		
03-DL		Tandem Air Sunny		
03-ET		Tandem Air Sunny		
03-FS		Aquilair Swing 14.9		
03-FV		(Tandem Air ?) Sunny (side-by-side seating)		
03-FX		Synairgie		
03-FY		Air Création GT / Fun		
03-IH		Aviasud AE209 Albatros	10	
03-II		Airwave Rave Jet Pocket paraglider		
03-IT		Air Création		
03-JE		Air Création GTE 503SL		
03-JP		Aquilair Swing		
03-JQ		Eipper Quicksilver MXL II Sport		
03-JR		Best Off Sky Ranger		
03-JT		Aquilair		
03-JU	F-JZBS	Guérin G1		F-JIGE
03-KL	F-JECU	Air Création GTE / iXess	A04176-188/465603	
		(previously Mild wing)		
03-KY		Aquilair Swing		
03-LE		Air Création / Kiss		
03-LG		Air Création GT BI 503 / Quartz		
03-LU		Air Création / iXess		
03-LV		Air Création / SX		
W03-MB		Averso AX.02 Guépard gyrocopter		
03-MP		Barry MB-02 Souricette		
		(W/o 18.6.05)		
03-NI		Rans S-6 Coyote II		
03-NK		Vidor Asso V Champion EL		
03-NM		Rapier Stecker		
		(W/o 26.6.05)		
03-NS		Air Création GTE		
03-NV		Rans S-12 Airaile		
03-NZ		Light Aero Avid Flyer		
03-PH		Fly Synthesis Storch S		
03-PY		Aquilair Swing		
03-RA		Rans S-5 Coyote		
03-RG	F-JEDO	Bela Nogrady		
		(Also reported as Alpi Aviation Pioneer 200 Ultra)		
03-RH		TEAM Mini-MAX	408	
03-RR		Magni M-16 Tandem Trainer	16-05-2944	
03-SA		Air Création / XP		
03-SB	F-JECR	Humbert Tetras		
03-VS		Voliris 900 Helium Airship	01	WAAN
03-ACL		Best Off Sky Ranger		
03-ACO	F-JWPY	Flying Machines FM250 Vampire		
03-ACP	F-JWRS	Magni M-24 Orion		
03-ACQ	F-JWVF	Flying Machines FM250 Vampire		
		(Re-regd 80-SE? Still 03-ACQ 6.16))		
03-ACW	F-JREH	Flying Machines B612		
03-ACW	F-JREH	Flying Machines FM301 Stream		
		(The above two were both noted at Vichy 16.7.10)		
03-ADA	F-JKGY	Evektor EV-97 Eurostar	2002 1603	
03-ADB	F-JWKH	Jodel D.20		
03-ADD	F-JRSZ	Comco Ikarus C-42		
03-ADE		DTA Feeling 582 / Magic		
03-ADF		Barry MB-02 Souricette		
03-ADQ	F-JSRA	Air Création Tanarg 912ES / BioniX 15		
03-ADV		Jodel D.9		
03-ADW	F-JASH	Phoenix Aircraft Maverick PA	003	
03-AEA	F-JTHK	Magni M-22 Voyager		

Reg	F-reg	Type	Serial	Notes
03-AEE	F-JTWH	Comco Ikarus C-42		
03-AEF	F-JTZI	Breezer UL	UL101	
03-AEG	F-JUKL	Didier Pti'tavion		
03-AEL	F-JUQM	Aerospool WT-9 Dynamic		
03-AEN	F-JURM	Comco Ikarus C-42C		
03-AER	F-JVGW	Magni M-22 Voyager		
03-AET	F-JVJP	Comco Ikarus C-42		
03-AEV	F-JVJU	DTA J-RO gyrocopter	020	
03-AEX	F-JVMI	Comco Ikarus C-42C		
03-AEY		Autogyro-Europe MTOsport		
03-AFB	F-JVNZ	Comco Ikarus C-42A	1404-7332	
03-AFN		weightshift		
03-AFT	F-JAQL	Jodel D.112UL	1041	F-PJXE
03-AGO	F-JBAB	G1 Aviation G1 Spyl		

04 : Alpes-de-Haute-Provence

Reg	F-reg	Type	Serial	Notes
04-AQ		Weedhopper Europa		
04-AS		Air Création		
04-AZ		Micro Aviation Pulsar		
04-BA		Cosmos Bidulm		
04-BF		Mignet HM.1000 Balerit	70	
04-BP	F-JCTJ	Mignet HM.1100 Cordouan		
04-BQ		Cosmos		
04-CC		Lascaud Bifly		
04-CD		Best Off Nynja		
04-CH		Urban Air Lambada		
04-CT		Cosmos Phase II / Chronos 16		
04-CV		Humbert Tetras		
04-CZ	F-JJWV	Best Off Sky Ranger		
04-DI	F-JYYR	Aerospool WT-9 Dynamic	DY052/2004	
		(To I-C383 .16)		
04-DJ	F-JXFI	B&F Funk FK-9 Mk.IV SW	326	
W04-DT		Dynamic 912		
04-DW	F-JZZX	Aerospool WT-9 Dynamic	DY258/2008	
04-DX	F-JWSH	ICP MXP-740 Savannah VG	07-09-51-640	
04-DY		Alisport Silent 2 Targa	2031	
		(Re-regd G-CIKD 10.14)		
04-EJ	F-JUVQ	Jodel D.92 Bébé	213	05-FM F-PERL
04-EN		Best Off Nynja		
04-EP	F-JRLV	Alpi Aviation Pioneer 300		
04-ET	F-JWVH	Aéro Services Super Guépard 912S		
04-EV	F-JWRJ	Aeropro Eurofox		
04-EW		Jodel D11UL		
04-FB		Backbone/Dudak Nucleon paramotor		
04-FF		Electravia ElectroLight 2		
		(Converted from Avialsa A60 Fauconnet)		
04-FO	F-JTXF	Aerospool WT-9 Dynamic	DY443/2012	
04-FP		Helisport CH-7 Kompress		
04-FT		Helisport CH-77 Ranabot		
04-FU		Aviasud Mistral		
04-FY		Humbert Tetras		
04-GA		Helisport CH-77 Ranabot		
04-GB		Best Off Nynja		
04-GD	F-JVHW	Pipistrel Virus SW		
04-GE		Urban Air UFM-13/15 Lambada		
04-GI	F-JVMN	Helisport CH-77 Ranabot		
04-GP		B&F Funk FK-9 Utility		
04-GS		Alpi Avn Pioneer 300		
04-HC		Helisport CH-77 Ranabot		
04-HE		ICP Zenair CH-650Ei	15-07-65ER-0022	
04-HM		Mignet HM.14 Pou-du-Ciel		
04-JB	F-JJTR	Best Off Sky Ranger		F-JFPP
04-NH		Air Création		
04-NX		Rans S-6 Coyote II		
04-SH		Eipper Quicksilver		
04-UL		Twin Weedhopper		

05 : Hautes-Alpes

Reg	F-reg	Type	Serial	Notes
05-I		Alpaero (Noin) Sirius	01	
05-AB		Alpaero (Noin) Sirius	02	
05-BD		Alpaero (Noin) Sirius		
05-BH		Alpaero (Noin) Sirius C	C15	
		(Sold as LN-YIQ)		
05-BP		Cosmus Bidulm		
05-BQ		Cosmos		
05-CG		Aquilair Swing		
05-CO	F-JBWP	Claude Noin Choucas	01	
05-DE		Air Création GTE Clipper		
05-DI		Best Off Sky Ranger		
05-DP		Raj Hamsa X'Air		
05-DX		Filcoa J-3 Kitten		
05-EH		Best Off Sky Ranger		
		(Re-regd 45-ACT)		
05-EI		Djicat Buse'Air 150		
		(Re-regd 83-AAO)		
05-EL		B&F Funk FK-9		
05-EN		Cosmos		
05-FF		Aquilair Swing		
05-FM		Jodel D.92 Ultrababy	213	F-PERL
		(Re-regd 04-EJ/F-JUVQ)		
05-FU		Zenair CH-701 STOL		
05-FX		Aero Designs Pulsar XP 912		
05-FY		Croses LC-6 U/L		
05-GA		Air Création		
05-GI		Dyn'Aéro MCR-01		
		(Accident 15.5.04)		
05-GJ		Micro Aviation Pulsar 2		
05-GL		Air Création GTE Clipper / XP		
05-GO		Air Création		
05-GS	F-JJWH	Dyn'Aéro MCR-01	165	
05-GU		B&F Funk FK-9 Mk.III		
W05-HA		Aerojames Isatis	01	
05-HB		Aquilair Swing 14.9		
05-HE		Fly Synthesis -?-		
05-HH		Alpaero (Noin) Exel	7	
		(Stolen 7.07)		
05-HK	F-JJQJ	Urban Air Lambada		
05-HL	F-JJMX	B&F Funk FK-14 Polaris		
		(Accident 20.6.04; re-regd 37-AAF)		
05-HO		Claude Noin Choucas		
05-HP		Air Création GTE Clipper / iXess		
05-HZ		ICP MXP-740 Savannah	04-06-51-307	
05-IA	F-JJTC	Dyn'Aéro MCR-01 UL		
05-IB		B&F Funk FK-9 Mk.IV Smart		
05-IE		Cosmos (trike)		

Reg	Callsign	Type	c/n	Other
05-II		Magni M-16 Tandem Trainer		
05-IK	F-JJQV	DTA Feeling / Dynamic 16		
05-IL		Air Création GTE / XP		
05-IW		Raj Hamsa X'Air		
05-IX	F-JTIZ	Air Création Tanarg 912 / iXess		
05-JA		Urban Air UFM-15 Lambada	5	
05-JC		Pingouin Turbo 912		
05-JF		Autogyro-Europe MT-03		
05-JM		Flyitalia MD-3 Rider		
05-JP		Air Création GTE Clipper 582SE / Fun 450		
05-JS	F-JYZU	Dyn'Aéro MCR Pick-Up	89	
05-JW		B&F Funk FK-12 Comet	12-079	
		(W/o 29.11.07)		
05-JZ		Flyitalia MD-3 Rider		
		(Crashed 31.8.07)		
05-KB		Take Off Merlin 1200		
		(Accident 2.12.07)		
05-KD	F-JXLN	Flight Design CT SW		
		(Re-regd 19-HT, 26-ADN)		
05-KF	F-JXMZ	B&F Funk FK-9 Mk.IV SW		
		(Same call-sign quoted for 05-KZ)		
05-KH		Guérin G1		
05-KJ	F-JXST	Air Création Tanarg 912 / iXess 13		
			A08024-8005 / T08012	
05-KQ		DTA / Ellipse Alizé (Electravia)		W05-KQ
05-KU		Humbert La Moto-du-Ciel		
		(W/o 22.8.14)		
05-KW		Beaugiro 02 gyrocopter		
05-KZ	F-JXMZ	B&F Funk FK-9 Mk.III SW	356 ?	
		(Same call-sign quoted for 05-KF)		
05-LE		B&F Funk FK-9		
05-LJ	F-JWVI	B&F Funk FK-9 ELA		
05-LP	F-JWYO	B&F Funk FK-14B Polaris		
		(Same call-sign as 56-OD)		
05-LQ		Autogyro-Europe MT-03		
05-LY		Polaris FIB		
05-MB		Best Off Sky Ranger		
05-MH		Backbone/Ozon Viper paramotor		
05-MI		weightshift		
05-MM		Air Création Tanarg / BioniX		
05-MN		Air Création trike		
05-MO	F-JHIX	DTA Dynamic 15/430	204	26-RY
05-MP		Air Création GTE 582S / XP15		
		(Crashed 19.8.06)		
05-NA		B&F Funk FK-9		
05-NH		Best Off Sky Ranger V-Max		
05-NJ	F-JSWM	Zlin Savage Cub	0213	
05-NS	F-JRKT	Jihlavan Skyleader 200		
05-OJ	F-JUGC	Zlin Savage Bobber		
05-OL		Pipistrel Alpha Trainer		
05-PF	F-JRTY	Zlin Savage Cub		
05-PO	F-JADF	Best Off Nynja		
05-PR		Weedhopper		
05-PV		Rans S-6 Coyote II		
05-QB	F-JBAK	G1 Aviation G1 Spyl		
05-QN		Zlin Savage		
05-SS		ATEC Zephyr		
05-UG		Best Off Sky Ranger		
05-VM		Colomban MC-30 Luciole		

06 : Alpes-Maritimes

Reg	Callsign	Type	c/n	Other
06-C		ULAC X-99 (2-seater)	163	
06-M		Eipper Quicksilver MX		
06-N		Ultrasport Eagle XL		
		(also reported as Pioneer Flightstar)		
06-AA		Raj Hamsa X'Air 602T		
06-AE		Arrow F.2 Foxcat		
06-AF		Skycraft AJS 2000		
06-AG		(Technic Moto ?) Mustang		
06-AI		Micro Aviation Pulsar III		
06-AJ		Weedhopper (f/p)		80-BK
06-AT		Lemonnier Maestro (f/p)		
06-AR		Weedhopper		
06-BA		Best Off Sky Ranger (f/p)		
06-BG		Dynamic 503		
06-BZ		Best Off Sky Ranger		
		(Re-regd 83-AGA)		
06-CA		PGO Aviation Cobra		
06-CB		Weedhopper Europa II		
		(Accident 24.11.04)		
06-CD		Murphy Renegade (f/p)		
06-CE		Murphy Renegade Spirit (f/p)		974-DQ
06-CR		European Aerolights Maestro II		
06-CZ		Air's Maestro		
06-DA		Rans S-6 Coyote II		
06-DD		Air's Maestro (f/p)		
06-DG		Aviasud AE209 Albatros		
06-DH		Baroudeur ?		
06-DJ		floatplane (?)		
W06-DR		Djicat Buse'Air 150		
06-DY		Best Off Sky Ranger		
06-EC	F-JJDZ	Denney Kitfox	518	
		(Same c/n as 63-EC)		
WEL-06		Espace Liberté Country		
06-FB		Best Off Sky Ranger		
06-GS	F-JJJH	Evektor EV-97 Eurostar	2000 0803	OK-FUR 09
		(Identity unconfirmed)		
06-MA		Light Aero Avid Flyer ?		
06-MB	F-JJVK	ICP MXP-740 Savannah	00-12-51-036	
06-RT		Tecnam P.92S Super Echo		
06-SW		Zenith (Baroudeur ?)		
		(W/o 29.7.01)		
06-UE		paramotor		
06-ZE		Véliplane Mosquito (trike)		
06-ZH		Blandine gyrocopter		
		(W/o 13.6.07)		
06-AAD		Guérin G1		
06-AAJ		Eipper Quicksilver GT400		
06-AAR		ELA Aviacion ELA-07S 914		
06-AAY		Zenair CH-601 Zodiac		
06-ABC		Polaris FIB		
06-ABE		Zenair CH-601UL Zodiac		
06-ABF	F-JSMI	G1 Aviation G1 Spyl		
06-ABO	F-JRDB	Didier Pti'tAvion '66'		
06-ABP		Cicaré Spirit Tandem helicopter	002	

07 : Ardèche

Reg	Callsign	Type	c/n	Other
07-B		Butterfly		
07-F		Air Création / Quartz		
07-M		Titan Tornado		
07-AA		Air Création		
07-AQ		trike / Quartz SX		
07-AX		Air Création		
07-BB		Air Création / SX		
07-BC		Air Création Racer / SX 12		
07-BL		Air Création / Quartz		
07-BM		Aviasud Mistral	50	
07-BO		Air Création		
07-CS		Air Création / SX-12		
07-CY		Air Création		
07-DC		'Pou' type		
07-DE		Eipper Quicksilver MX II Sprint		
07-DG		Butterfly		
07-DH		Air Création / Fun		
07-DT		Air Création Racer / Fun 447		
07-DU		ICP Super Bingo	02-05-52-055	
07-EC		Weedhopper Europa		
07-EI		Air Création / Fun		
07-EQ		Air Création Safari GT BI		
07-ES		Weedhopper		
07-FC		Weedhopper Europa II	C2063029	
		(Re-regd 50-LD)		
07-FI		Air Création / Mild		
07-FQ		Rans S-6 Coyote II		
07-FS		Air Création / XP		
07-FU		Air Création / Quartz		
07-GA		Air Création GTE Clipper / XP		
07-GH		Air Création / SX		
07-GL		Air Création Racer 503 / XP11		
07-GQ		Air Création GTE / XP		
07-GT		Air Création GTE / Fun	139	
		(Re-regd OO-D09 7.00)		
07-HC		Air Création Buggy / XP12		
07-HD		Air Création Buggy / Fun		
07-HI		Air Création / Kiss		
07-HJ		Air Création / XP15		
07-HM	F-JCUE	Fly Synthesis Storch		
07-HM(2 ?)		Air Création Tanarg / iXess		
		(Noted .07)		
07-HR		Air Création		
07-HZ		Weedhopper-type (f/p)		
07-IC		Air Création Racer / Fun		
07-IH		Air Création / Kiss		
07-II		Air Création Racer / Fun		
07-IM		Air Création GTE / XP15		
		(W/o 6.8.03)		
07-IP		Air Création / Kiss		
07-IV	F-JENO	Mignet HM.1000 Balerit		
07-JC		Air Création GTE / Kiss		
07-JD		Air Création Tanarg / iXess		
07-JE		Air Création GTE Clipper 912 / iXess 15		
			A03028-1075	
07-JF		Air Création GTE Clipper 912 / iXess		
			T03027/04019-4014	
		(To G-IXES, then LN-YXT)		
07-JS		Air Création GTE Clipper / iXess		
07-JX		Air Création GTE Clipper / iXess		
07-KE		Air Création		
07-KI		Air Création Tanarg / iXess	A5054-5057	
07-KJ		Air Création Tanarg / iXess		
07-KN		Air Création Tanarg		
07-KQ		Air Création Tanarg / iXess		
07-KY		Air Création / Fun		
07-LD		Air Création GTE Clipper / Kiss		
07-LF		Air Création / Fun		
07-LI		Air Création / Kiss 450		
07-LN		Mignet HM.293 Pou-du-Ciel		
07-LR		Air Création Twin Buggy / iXess		
07-LT		Air Création GTE Trek / Kiss		
07-LV		Air Création GTE Trek / Fun		
07-LW		Air Création GTE Trek HKS700E / iXess		
07-LZ		Vidor Asso IV Whisky		
		(Damaged 9.7.08)		
07-MC		Air Création Tanarg 912 / iXess		
07-ME	F-JYGS	Air Création Tanarg 912 / iXess	A09043-8073	
07-MG		Air Création Tanarg / iXess 13		
07-MH		Air Création / Kiss 450		
07-ML		Air Création Tanarg 912ES / iXess 15	T07077	
		(Re-regd PH-4G2)		
07-MV		Air Création Racer		
07-MW		Air Création Tanarg 912ES / iXess		
07-MX		Air Création GTE Trek / iXess 13		
07-MY	F-JSTX	Air Création Tanarg / iXess 13	A08076-8057	
07-MZ		Air Création Tanarg 912ES		
07-ND		Air Création GTE Trek HKS700 / Fun 450		
07-NF		Ekolot KR-030 Topaz		
07-NH	F-JWWY	Air Création Trek HKS		
07-NN	F-JXWS	Air Création Tanarg 912ES / BioniX		
07-NO		Air Création Tanarg 912ES / BioniX		
07-NQ	F-JSTX	Air Création Tanarg 912 / BioniX	A09096-9101	
07-NV		Air Création Skypper / iXess		
07-NW		Air Création Skypper / BioniX		
07-OD	F-JSQI	Air Création Skypper / BioniX		
			A11015-10140/T11014	
07-OG		Air Création Skypper 912		
07-OL		Air Création Tanarg / BioniX		
07-OO		Rans S-7ES Courrier		
07-OP		Air Création Skypper 582 / NuviX		
07-OS		Air Création GTE / XP		
07-OQ		Air Création Skypper 912 / NuviX		
07-PA		Air Création Tanarg / BioniX		
07-PC		Air Création Skypper / NuviX	A12013-1202	
07-PD		Air Création Skypper / NuviX		
07-PE		Air Création Tanarg 912ES / BioniX 13		
07-PF		Air Création Skypper / BioniX 13		
07-PS	F-JTXI	Air Création Tanarg / BioniX	A12087-12084	
07-PW		Air Création Skypper 912		
07-PY	F-JUZN	Air Création Skypper / NuviX	A13056-13058	
07-PZ	F-JUZO	Air Création Skypper / BioniX 13	A13057-13059	
07-QA	F-JUZP	Air Création Tanarg / BioniX		
			A13013-13011/T13026	
07-QB		Air Création Pixel XC / iFun 13		

Reg	Call	Type	c/n	Other
07-QC		Air Création Pixel XC / iFun 13		
07-QE		Pipistrel Sinus		
07-QG	F-JUZQ	Air Création Pixel XC / iFun	A14067-14066	
07-QH	F-JVVG	Air Création Skypper / BioniX A14068-	/T14026	
07-QI		Air Création Skypper / iFun 16 A14074-	/T14031	
07-QJ	F-JUZN	Air Création Skypper / iFun 16		
			A14063-14063	/T13025
07-QK		Air Création Pixel / iFun		
			A14078-14046	/ 61010-1306
07-QL	F-JVYE	LCA LH212 Delta		
07-QR		Air Création Skypper 912 / NuviX	15092-15075	
07-QT	F-JAAC	Air Création Skypper / iFun	A15041-15038	
07-QU		Air Création Pixel 250 / XC	T14022	
07-QZ	F-JAYO	Air Création Skypper / BioniX 2	A16064-160 . .	
07-RB	F-JUZP	Air Création Tanarg / BioniX 13 X2 A16104-16105		

08 : Ardennes

Reg	Call	Type	c/n	Other
08-D		Air Création Quartz		
08-BH		Anax Imperator		
08-BI		Cosmos Chronos		
		(Seen .03 but also reported as a Best Off Sky Ranger)		
08-BO		Air Création GT BI / XP		
08-BQ		Weedhopper AX-3	B112968	
08-BU		Rans S-12 Airaile		
08-CD		Didier Pti'avion		
08-CM		Air Création GTE Clipper / XP		
08-CR	F-JBOM	Weedhopper AX-3 Sport		
08-CT		Barry MB-02 Souricette ?		
08-CV		Air Création GT BI / XP		
08-CY		Synairgie		
08-DF		Cosmos		
08-DR		European Airwings Springbok 2000		
08-DT		Air Création GTBI / Fun		
08-DU	F-JGGI	ZUT Aviation TT2000 STOL		
08-DW	F-JGGV	Ekolot JK-03 Beetle		
08-EB	F-JGHO	ATEC Zephyr	Z281000F	51-KU
		(Re-regd 08-EZ)		
08-EE	F-JGGU	TL Ultralight TL-2000 Sting Carbon		
08-EG	F-JGHH	Morin M-85 (Dismantled .03)		
08-EH		Air Création GTE Clipper / Mild		
08-EK	F-JQAQ	Dallach D4 Fascination or UL-JIH Fascination F-80		
		(previously F-JGHA)		
08-EL		Air Création GTE / XP		
08-EM		Sauper J.300 Joker		
08-EN		Rans S-10 Sakota	0494.172	W08-EN, OO-135
08-ER		Didier Titan		
08-ET	F-JGHM	Pipistrel Sinus	100S9120303	
08-EU		weightshift		
08-EV		Air Création Racer 447 / Fun14		
		(Re-regd 84-JK)		
08-EX		Weedhopper	9102555	
08-EZ	F-JGHO	ATEC Zephyr	Z281000F	08-EB, 51-KU
08-FA		SE.5A replica		W08-FA
08-FB		Ekolot JK-05 Junior	05 02 06	
		(same c/n as 37-VI/F-JBRQ)		
08-FE		Mignet HM.293 Pou-du-Ciel		
		(Re-regd W59-DDE, based in the Netherlands)		
08-FH		Air Création / iXess		
08-FI		Air Création / iXess		
08-FO	F-JGIE	Ekolot JK-05 Junior	05 03 07	SP-SPUA
08-FP		Ekolot JK-05 Junior	05 03 06	
08-FT		Air Création		
08-FX		Ekolot JK-05 Junior	05 04 02	
08-FY		Djicat Buse'Air		
08-GA	F-JZNL	B&F Funk FK-14B Polaris	14-046	
		(Marked F-08-GA; re-regd OO-H32 3.14)		
08-GC	F-JGHC	Air Création Tanarg / iXess		
08-GD	F-JQCV	Aéro Services Guépy (Jabiru) 80T		
08-GF	F-JWED	Fly Synthesis Storch		
08-GG	F-JGAC	Humbert Tetras		
08-GJ		Aviasud Mistral		
08-GK		Wolf W-II Boredom Fighter (W/o .06?)		
08-GO	F-JXMG	Alpi Aviation Pioneer 200		
08-GP		Ekolot JK-05 Junior	05 03 05	
		(Re-regd 41-LX)		
08-GT	F-JQFH	Rans S-6ES Coyote II	0993534	OO-B66
08-GU	F-JZOY	Ekolot KR-030 Topaz	030-01-01	
08-GV	F-JYUK	Zenair CH-601XL Zodiac		
08-GW		Ekolot JK-05 Junior		
		(Accident 26.1.07)		
08-HE		Mignet HM.1000 Balerit	72	59-MD, OO-A81
08-HK		Denney Kitfox IV (t/w)		W08-HK
08-HN		Humbert Tetras		
08-HX		Slepcev Storch	SS4-099	19-3806
		(To Norway 7.07)		
08-HY	F-JZWD	Alpi Aviation Pioneer 300		59-CKR ?
08-IB		Ekolot KR-030 Topaz	030-01-02	
08-IC		Fly Synthesis Wallaby		
08-ID		Humbert Tetras 912GS		
08-IE		Rans S-6ES Coyote II (t/w)	0593502	OO-E14, 59-NJ
08-IF		Belite or Kitfox Lite		
08-IH		Air Création / iXess		
08-IK	F-JWJK	Light Aero Avid Flyer		
08-IO		Humbert Tetras 912Cs		
08-IP		Autogyro-Europe MT-03		
08-IR		Plätzer Kiebitz B-450	301	
08-IY		Aviasud Albatros		
08-JA		Croses Criquet Léger 503	16	
08-JC		Alpi Aviation Pioneer 300STD		
08-JD		Ekolot KR-030 Topaz	030-02-00	
08-JH		Rans S-6 Coyote II		
08-JI	F-JWTS	Didier Pti'avion		
08-JJ		Rans S-6 Coyote II	12081915	
		(Re-regd OO-H31 3.14; reports that this became OO-G42 8.09 are erroneous)		
08-JK		Urban Air UFM-13 Lambada		
08-JN		Rans S-6 Coyote II		
08-JQ		Alpi Aviation Pioneer 200	209	
08-JY		Didier Pti'avion		
08-JZ		Alpi Aviation Pioneer 200		
08-KB		Mignet HM.14D Pou-du-Ciel		W08-KB
08-KH	F-JRNX	Ekolot JK-05 Junior	05 08 01	
08-KJ		Ekolot KR-030 Topaz		
08-KN	F-JYYC	Air Création GTE Trek / iXess		
08-KO		Weedhopper Europa II	82022995	59-JG

Reg	Call	Type	c/n	Other
08-KP	F-JRXG	Flight Design CT Supralight	E-10-05-04	
		(Re-regd 55-PO / F-JRXG)		
08-KS	F-JWEP	Evektor EV-97 Eurostar		
08-KW	F-JTFF	Jodel D.9 Bébé	629	W08-HW, OO-45
08-KX		Alpi Aviation Pioneer 200		
08-KZ		Comco Ikarus C-42		
08-LA		Colomban MC-30 Luciole		
08-LB		Comco Ikarus Fox-C22		
08-LC	F-JSLX	Didier Pti'avion		
08-LF		Ekolot KR-030 Topaz	030-04-04	
08-LH		Corby CJ-1 Starlet		
08-LI		P&M Aviation Quik 912S	8431	
08-LJ		Didier Pti'avion		
08-LK		Doleac A3C		
08-LN	F-JVRS	BRM Aero Bristell XL-8		
		(Same call-sign as 08-NL)		
08-LO(1)		Didier Pti'avion		
		(Error for 08-LC ?)		
08-LO(2)	F-JTNX	Evektor EV-97 Eurostar SL	2011 3915	
08-LP		TEAM Mini-MAX		
08-LR	F-JRJA	Alpi Aviation Pioneer 200		26-ACT
08-LT		Stampe SV-4 replica (7/8 scale)		
		(Damaged .15, wfu)		
08-LU	F-JSXT	Alpi Aviation Pioneer 300S		
08-MD		ATEC 212 Solo		
		(Re-regd 59-DPP)		
08-ME	F-JUMS	Aveko VL-3		
08-MF		Rans S-9 Chaos		
		(Re-regd 59-CWI)		
08-MH	F-JUOO	Alpi Aviation Pioneer 200STD		
08-ML		Flight Design CT		
08-MQ	F-JUVD	Alpi Aviation Pioneer 200STD		
08-MT		ICP MXP-740 Savannah		
08-MX	F-JUYU	Didier Pti'avion	44	
08-NE		B&F Funk FK-9 ELA	480	
08-NF		B&F Funk FK-9		
08-NI		Ekolot KR-030 Topaz	030-05-05	WEK01
08-NL	F-JVRS	BRM Aero Bristell XL-8		
		(Same call-sign as 08-LN)		
08-NN		Didier Pti'tAvion		
08-NV	F-JUHJ	Autogyro Europe Cavalon		
08-NW		JMB Aircraft VL-3 Evolution		
08-NX		Dyn'Aero MCR-01 UL 912 PV50	269	OO-E32
08-NZ		Butterfly	03-04	OO-639
08-OD	F-JAAS	LCA LH212 Delta		
08-OG		B&F Funk FK-14B Polaris		
08-PI		Air Création Tanarg		
08-TA		Rans S-6 Coyote II		
08-WW		Didier Pti'tavion		

09 : Ariège

Reg	Call	Type	c/n	Other
09-AB	F-JIBB	Humbert Tetras		
09-AC		Tempest (Modified)		
09-AE		Zenair CH-701 STOL		
09-AJ		Mainair Rapier 1+1		
09-AK		Air Copter		
09-AN		Urban Air Lambada		
09-AP	F-JYTJ	Aeroprakt A-22 Vision		
		(Same call-sign as 33-ABQ)		
09-AQ		Air Création GT BI		
09-AR	F-JXPR	Scheibe SF 30 (motorised)		
09-AS	F-JXEU	Best Off Sky Ranger	SKR0704792	
09-AZ(1)		Dynali Chickinox		
		(W/o 10.08.97)		
09-AZ(2)		trike / XP		
09-BA		Humbert Tetras		
09-BC	F-JGYO	Dyn'Aéro MCR-01	239	21-VE
09-BH		gyrocopter		
09-BO	F-JRDQ	B&F Funk FK-9 ELA	400	
09-BU	F-JIFN	Denney Kitfox III		
09-BV		PAP 1250 Top 80 paramotor		
09-CD		Air Création Safari GT BI 582 / XP15		
09-CE	F-JVWX	Air Création GTE / DTA Magic		
09-CY		Best Off Nynja		
09-FC		Denney Kitfox		
09-WN		Aviasud AE209 Albatros		
09-YI		weightshift		

10 : Aube

Reg	Call	Type	c/n	Other
10-C		Huntair Pathfinder		
10-E		Huntair Pathfinder		
10-G		Vector 600		
10-R		Eipper Quicksilver MX		
10-T		Zenith (Baroudeur ?)	021	
10-Z		Dynali Chickinox		
10-AC		RP.82 Oméga		
10-AL		Aviasud Mistral		
10-AV		Eipper Quicksilver II		
10-BB		Humbert		
10-BG		Prevot Helios IV		
10-DH		(Air Création ?) Safari		
10-DP		Eipper Quicksilver GT500S		
10-DS		Prevot Helios 5TR		
10-EE		Eipper Quicksilver GT500S		
10-EK		Prevot Helios 5TR		
10-ER		Eipper Quicksilver GT500		
10-FJ		Aviakit Hermes		
10-FN		Eipper Quicksilver GT500		
10-FQ		Zenair CH-701 STOL		
10-FY	F-JBYR	Aviakit Hermes		
10-GA		Eipper Quicksilver MXL III		
10-GH	F-JGGA	Eipper Quicksilver GT500		
10-GI		Eipper Quicksilver GT500		
10-GJ		Light Aero Avid Flyer		
10-GL		Light Aero Avid Lite		
10-GM		Humbert La Moto-du-Ciel		
10-GS-W		SG Aviation Storm 300		
10-HB		Air Création		
10-HC		Aviakit Vega 2000		
10-HF		Eurofly Sky Raider		
		(actually marked W-HF-01 !)		
10-HQ		Aviakit Vega 2000		
10-HT		Aviakit Vega 2000		
10-HV		Pipistrel Sinus		
10-IB	F-JGGN	Zenair CH-701 STOL		

Reg	F-reg	Type	c/n	Prev
10-IL		Tecnam P.96 Golf 100		
10-IQ		Best Off Sky Ranger 912		
10-IS		Ecofly Norman Mini Explorer		
10-IT		Euro Sky Aero Sky Raider 447 UL IV		
		(Crashed 24.4.04)		
10-IW		Pipistrel Sinus		
10-IY		Light Aero Avid Flyer		
10-JG		Humbert Tetras 912CS		
10-JM		paramotor		
10-JV		paramotor		
10-JZ	F-JVSD	Tecnam P.92S Echo Super		
		(same c/s as 19-JZ; previously used F-JQDF)		
10-LA		Zenair CH-701 STOL (or ICP MXP-740?)		
10-LE	F-JZTZ	Zlin Savage		
10-LP		Rans S-10 Sakota		
10-MC		Zenair CH-601 Zodiac		
10-MD		paramotor		
10-NA	F-JFPN	B&F Funk FK-9 Mk.IV Club	260	
		(Same call-sign quoted for 41-JA and 41-MX)		
10-NL		Humbert Tetras		
10-NN		Urban Air UFM-13 Lambada		
10-NU		Air Création Tanarg 912 / BioniX 15		
10-NY	F-JVYZ	Comco Ikarus Fox-C22		
10-NZ		Denney Kitfox III	1079	PH-GGT
10-OJ		Air Création Tanarg / iXess Training A09068-9068		
10-OZ	F-JUXG	Pennec Gaz'Aile 2		
10-SR		Eipper Quicksilver GT500		

11 : Aude

Reg	F-reg	Type	c/n	Prev
11-AJ		Weedhopper		
11-AQ		Eipper Quicksilver Sport		
11-BY		Comco Ikarus C-22 Extreme		
11-CH		Djicat Buse'Air 150		
11-DB		WDFL Sunwheel		
11-DH		paramotor		
11-DM		Aviasud Sirocco		
11-DO	F-JCVU	DTA Dynamic		
11-DP	F-JCXQ	Eipper Quicksilver GT500		
11-DQ		Air Création GTE		
11-DR		ICP MXP-740 Savannah	02-04-51-146	
		(Re-regd 77-BAY)		
11-EA		Weedhopper AX-3	C2083041	77-MI
11-EE		gyrocopter		
11-ES		Zenair CH-701 STOL		44-RI
11-FA	F-JJIC	B&F Funk FK-9 Mk.III	09-172	
11-FD		DTA Dynamic 450		
11-FR	F-JCXS	Zenair CH-601HD Zodiac		23-MX
11-FT		Micro Aviation Pulsar II		
		(Accident 14.8.04)		
11-FU	F-JJNF	Dyn'Aéro MCR-01 ULC	001	
		(originally Jabiru engine, now ULPower engine)		
W11-FV		Delafarge (Pou-du-Ciel derivative)		
11-FZ	F-JJNO	B&F Funk FK-9 Mk.IV Club		
11-GB	F-JJRB	Zenair CH-601 Zodiac		
11-GF		Aéro Services Guépard 912-V2		
		(W/o 04.08)		
W11-GJ		gyrocopter		
11-GR		European Airwings Springbok 2000		
		(Damaged 21.07.07)		
11-GT	F-JXDN	BRM Okavango	0001/07	
11-GX	F-JXRN	Aeroprakt A-22L	221	
		(Re-regd 26-ACJ)		
11-HA	F-JXXC	DTA Combo FC / Dynamic 15/450	257	
11-HC		Aquilair Swing		
11-HG	F-JIVB	Best Off Sky Ranger	SKR0311418	
		(Re-regd 47-VX)		
11-HN	F-JWKV	Flight Design CT LS	F-08-07-24	
11-HW	F-JWXZ	Zenair CH-701 STOL		
11-IC	F-JRCZ	BRM Land Africa	0144/912/UL/09-LA	
11-IH	F-JWRM	Magni M-16 Tandem Trainer		
11-IJ		B&F Funk FK-12 Comet	12-083	D-MVCW
11-IK	F-JSCF	BRM Citius Sport	0158/912/UL/10-CT	
11-IL	F-JSES	Aeroprakt A-22L2 Vision	353	
11-IM	F-JWWK	BRM Land Africa		
11-IR	F-JSOQ	Autogyro Europe Calidus 09		
11-IS	F-JSOF	MSL Aero Type H		
		(Modified Aeroandinas A82 c/n AA-03-1-82-044)		
11-IU	F-JTCG	BRM Citius	0183/912ULS/11-CT	
11-IW	F-JSXT	BRM Land Africa	0184/912ULS/11-LA	
11-IZ	F-JTDU	BRM Citius Sport	0192/912ULS/11-CT	
11-JH	F-JTYE	BRM Citius Sport	0214/912UL/12-CT	
11-JJ		weightshift		
11-JR	F-JVFS	Halley Apollo Gyro AG1 gyrocopter		
11-JT	F-JVSR	BRM Citius Sport	0237/912UL/14-CT	
11-JV	F-JTUJ	Helisport CH-7 Kompress		
11-LA		ATEC 321 Faeta		
11-MJ		Weedhopper AX-3	C3103167	
		(Re-regd 18-LG)		
11-UG		DTA Dynamic 450		
11-BBG		Fly Synthesis Storch		
		(Probably an error for 77-BBG)		

12 : Aveyron

Reg	F-reg	Type	c/n	Prev
12-AA		Humbert Tetras		
12-AB		Aéro Services Guépard 912S		
12-AE		Aéro Services Guépy 582		
12-AF (1)		Weedhopper		
12-AF (2)		Druine D.31 Turbulent	207	F-PPPK
12-AH		Comco Ikarus Fox-C22		
12-AJ		Air Création Buggy Twin / Kiss		
12-AS		Magni M-16 Tandem Trainer		
12-AT		Aéro Services Guépy 582		
12-AU		Weedhopper		
12-BB		Ultralair Weedhopper Europa 1		
12-BD	F-JLDD	Aéro Services Guépard 912S		
12-BE (1)		Aviasud Mistral		
12-BE (2)	F-JIBE	Dallach D4 Fascination		
12-BJ		Magni M-16 Tandem Trainer		
12-BP	F-JIKE	Aéro Services Super Guépard (Jabiru)		
12-BQ		Fantasy Air Cora		
12-BU		Cosmos		
12-BV		Cosmos Echo 12		
12-BW		Magni gyrocopter		
12-BX	F-JXAK	Fly Synthesis Texan Top Class		I-7699
12-BY		Aéro Services Guépy 582		
12-CF		Weedhopper		

Reg	F-reg	Type	c/n	Prev
12-CI		Aviasud AE209 Albatros		
12-CL		Air Création / iXess		
12-CM		Aeros (trike)		
12-CO		Magni M-16 Tandem Trainer		
12-CT		Aéro Services Guépard		
12-CY		JC-31 Weedhopper Europa II		
		(W/o 16.8.05)		
12-CZ (1)		Croses Airplume		26-CL
12-CZ (2)		Best Off Sky Ranger 582		
12-DA		Djicat Buse'Air 150		
12-DD		Mignet HM.293 Pou-du-Ciel		
12-DG		Weedhopper AX-3 16 (f/p)		
12-DL	F-JIFF	Best Off Sky Ranger		
12-DM		Best Off Sky Ranger		
12-DR		Fly Synthesis Storch		
12-DT		Aéro Services Guépard 912		
12-DU	F-JWJV	Rans S-6 Coyote II		
12-DX	F-JIDX	Aéro Services Super Guépard		
12-EB		Aéro Services Super Guépard 912S		
12-EF		Magni M-24 Orion		
12-EH	F-JXKE	Aéro Services SG.10A 912SC		
12-EI	F-JWBU	UL-JIH Fascination F100		
		(Same call-sign as 12-IE and 41-PZ)		
12-EN	F-JWUZ	Impulse		
12-EW		Aéro Services Super Guépard 912		
12-FK		Averso AX-02 Guépard		
12-FU	F-JSIP	Aéro Services SG.10A		
12-GE		Magni M-14 Scout		
12-GK	F-JTKQ	Aéro Services SG.12A		
W12-GO		Helisport CH-7		
12-GQ		Helisport CH-7 Kompress Charlie		
12-GS		Air Création GTE Clipper		
12-GV		Cicaré Spirit Tandem		
12-GX	F-JUKC	Plätzer Kiebitz	367	
12-HF	F-JUZZ	Aéro Services SG10A		
12-HM	F-JVTG	Aéro Services SG.10A		
12-HP		Aéro Services SG.10A		
12-IE	F-JWBU	UL-JIH Fascination F100		
		(Same call-sign as 12-EI and 41-PZ)		
12-JC		Weedhopper AX-3		14-..
12-MB		Mignet HM.293 Pou-du-Ciel		
12-NE		Eurofly Viper		
12-OP		Evektor EV-97 Eurostar		
12-PL		Aéro Services Guépy Club 582T		
12-RJ		Aéro Services Guépard (Jabiru) 80		

13 : Bouches-du-Rhône

Reg	F-reg	Type	c/n	Prev
13-AX		Zenith Baroudeur		
13-CH		Croses Airplume	15	
13-CZ		Filcoa J-6 Karatoo		
13-DA		Best Off Sky Ranger		
13-DD		Hipps Superbirds J-3 Kitten		
13-DN		Air's Maestro		
13-DQ		Air Création / SX II		
13-DT		Aviasud Mistral		
13-DX		Air Création		
13-DZ		Cosmos Chronos		
13-EC		Zenith Baroudeur		
13-EO		Air Création		
13-FM		Anglin J-6 Karatoo		
13-GD		Oméga paraglider		
13-HK	F-JJTD	Léonard & Tocci Le Gabian		
13-HW		PGO Aviation Cobra		64-JL
13-IO		Zenith Baroudeur		
13-IR	F-JJAG	Best Off Sky Ranger (bt by Synairgie)		
		(W/o 27.9.15)		
13-IZ		Best Off Sky Ranger (f/p) (bt by Synairgie)	SK0313296	
		(sold in the Philippines as RP-S126 5.13)		
13-JF		Air Création GTE Clipper		
13-JM		Best Off Sky Ranger		
13-KD		ICP MXP-740 Savannah		
13-LD		Air Création		
13-LF		Pou-du-Ciel type		
13-LL		Zlin Savage		
13-LZ	F-JJCW	Best Off Sky Ranger		
13-MB		Zenair CH-601UL Zodiac Exclusive		
13-MD		Fantasy Air Allegro SW		
13-MH	F-JCCK	Fantasy Air Allegro SW	00-112	
		(Also reported as F-JJTL)		
13-MO	F-JJCH	Fantasy Air Allegro		
13-MW		Aviasud AE209 Albatros		
13-NT	F-JYEG	Alpi Aviation Pioneer 300		
13-NV		Alpi Aviation Pioneer 300		
13-OO	F-JJGZ	Best Off Sky Ranger		
13-OP	F-JJCD	Jodel D.18	329	F-PAON
13-OQ		Jodel D.18		
13-OU		Pipistrel Sinus		
13-PA		Alpi Aviation Pioneer 300		
13-PB	F-JJWB	Best Off Sky Ranger		
13-PM		Cosmos		
13-QC	F-JJMP	Tecnam P.92S Echo		
13-QM		Aviasud AE209 Albatros		
13-QV		gyrocopter		
13-QX	F-JJQL	Dyn'Aéro MCR-01		
13-QY	F-JJQY	Tecnam P.92 Echo		
13-QZ		Pipistrel Sinus		
13-RC		Fly Synthesis Storch		
13-RG	F-JJTT	B&F Funk FK-9 Mk.II	09-02-027	D-MNRM
13-RK	F-JJTF	Evektor EV-97 Eurostar		
13-RP		Jodel D.19	474T	F-PJDT
13-RV	F-JJBG	Evektor EV-97 Eurostar		
13-RY	F-JJMQ	Flyitalia MD-3 Rider	27/2006	
		(Same call-sign and c/n as 59-COZ)		
13-SD		Cosmos		
13-SH	F-JJWD	B&F Funk FK-9 Mk.IV		
13-SJ		DTA Dynamic 15/430		
		(Crashed 23.8.06)		
13-SQ	F-JJWU	Delpech MD.03 Transat	11	
13-ST		Snoopy gyrocopter (homebuilt)		
		(Accident 22.4.07)		
13-SU		ITV paramotor		
13-TB	F-JYGJ	Zenair CH-601UL Zodiac		
13-TE		Rans S-4 Coyote I		
13-TO	F-JYXW	B&F Funk FK-9 Mk.IV	04-314	
		(Call-sign also on 83-TO ?)		

Reg	Call-sign	Type	Serial	Notes
13-TS	F-JTWX	Pipistrel Sinus		
		(Call-sign also noted as F-JYWX)		
13-TX	F-JXDM	Tecnam P.96 Golf 100		
13-TZ		Fly Synthesis Storch HS		
13-UD		Backbone/ITV Dakota Sport paramotor		
		(parafoil changed to ITV Lapoon)		
13-UE		Aerodynos JA177 Pinguin		
		(W/o 17.5.09)		
13-UG		Best Off Sky Ranger Swift		
13-UK		Paolo Rossi trike		
13-UU		Alpi Aviation Pioneer		
W13-VK	F-JWHX	Pottier P.130UL		
13-VR	F-JXZX	Best Off Sky Ranger		
13-WC	F-JWZJ	Magni M-22 Voyager	22-09-5284	
13-WD		Best Off Sky Ranger		
13-WF		paramotor		
13-WI	F-JWBO	Flight Design CT LS	F-08-06-22	30-QP
13-WM	F-JWNE	G1 Aviation G1 SPYL		
13-WX	F-JRNW	Flight Design CT LS	F-10-02-01	
13-XA	F-JRWY	Aeroprakt A-22L Vision	337	
13-XB		DTA Combo 582		
13-XD		Adventure/Dudek Plasma paramotor		
13-XE		Tecnam P.2004 Bravo		
		(W/o 22.6.15)		
13-XH		Air Création Tanarg 582 / BioniX		
13-XJ	F-JSLD	Nando Groppo Trail	N00041	
13-ZQ	F-JURF	ICP MXP-740 Savannah S	13-02-54-0246	
13-ZT		Alpi Aviation Pioneer 300STD		
13-AAF		Jodel D.18	14	F-PDLC
13-ABR	F-JHVK	Zenair CH-601XL Zodiac		

14 : Calvados

Reg	Call-sign	Type	Serial	Notes
14-F		Condor		
14-I		Air Création		
14-K		Lega Avia		
14-AA		Weedhopper AX-3		
14-AB		Air Création / Quartz		
14-AG		Super O		
14-BC		Air Création		
14-BE		Air Création / SX		
14-BS		Air Création		33-AP
14-BV		Air Création GT BI / Fun		
14-CA		Cosmos		
14-CB		Mignet HM.1000 Balerit	51	
14-CD		Cosmos		
14-CF		JCC Aviation J.300 Joker		
14-CK		Air Création GT BI / SX		
14-CP		Mignet HM.293 Pou-du-Ciel		
14-DD		Nieuport II Replica (Coded "31")		
14-DF		Air Création GT BI		
14-DH		ACGE		
14-DI		Weedhopper AX-3		
14-DM		Weedhopper		
14-ER		Air Création		
14-FI		Weedhopper AX-3		
14-FL		Air Création / Mild		
14-FP		Mignet HM.293M Pou-du-Ciel	600	W14-FP, F-PVQM, F-WVQM
		(Re-regd 79-IV)		
14-FR	F-JHHQ	ATEC Zephyr 2000	Z480102	
14-GB	F-JHIE	ATEC Zephyr		
14-GD	F-JHIS	Rans S-6S Coyote II (t/w)		
14-GI	F-JHIK	Aeropro Eurofox	14103	
14-GM		Air Création / Fun		
14-GN		Air Création		
14-HB		Aeropro Eurofox		
14-HE		Cosmos / Mach		
14-HI		Klipo Pulma / Ellipse Titan 150		
14-HJ		Air Création GTE / iXess		
14-HK	F-JHJD	ICP MXP-740 Savannah (Jabiru)	01-10-51-101	
14-HR		Air Création Racer / Fun		
14-HT		Air Création Racer 447		
14-IC		(Corvus ?) Phantom		
14-IT	F-JXEC	Aéro Services Guépard 912		
14-IX		Alpi Aviation Pioneer 200		
14-JC	F-JXON	ELA Aviacion ELA-07S	1007 194 0724	
14-JD	F-JXOO	ELA Aviacion ELA-07		
14-JH		Micro Aviation Pulsar III		
14-JL		Mignet HM.1100 Cordouan		
14-JM	F-JHIV	Fantasy Air Allegro SW		
		(Same call-sign as 61-JE)		
14-JN	F-JVST	Autogyro-Europe Calidus 09		
		(Same call-sign as 14-NJ)		
14-JO	F-JYDY	Best Off Sky Ranger V-Max	SKR0307361	
14-JQ		ITV Dakota Sport paramotor		
14-JR	F-JHJF	Best Off Sky Ranger V-Max		
14-JS		DTA Dynamic		
		(W/o 18.8.11)		
14-JU		Fantasy Air Allegro		
14-KK		Comco Ikarus Fox-C22B		
14-KS	F-JSQH	Morin M-85		
14-LL		Raj Hamsa Hanuman		
14-LS	F-JTMX	Magni M-18 Spartan		
14-LT		G1 Aviation G1 Spyl		
14-MH		Magni M-24 Orion		
14-MQ		Cosmos Chronos II		
14-MT	F-JAOE	JMB Aircraft VL-3 Sprint	VL3-108	D-MSYS
14-NB	F-JVCG	LCA LH212 Delta		
14-NI	F-JVRM	Aéro Services Super Guépard 912		
		(W/o 11.9.16)		
14-NJ	F-JVST	Autogyro-Europe Calidus 09	C00329	
		(Same call-sign as 14-JN)		
W14-NS		Flipper-BI Canard		
14-NW		ELA Aviacion ELA-07S		
14-NY		Mosquito XE285		
14-TE		Air Création Tanarg / iXess		
14-WC		paramotor		

15 : Cantal

Reg	Call-sign	Type	Serial	Notes
15-AR		Air Création		
15-BL		weightshift		
15-BM	F-JDEP	Air Création Buggy		
15-BR		DTA Ellipse		
15-BX		Air Création		
15-CI		Air Création GT BI / Quartz		
15-CN		Air Création		
15-DA		Pipistrel Sinus		
15-FP		Air Création Twin GTE / XP15		
15-GB		Averso gyrocopter		
15-GG	F-JECM	ICP MXP-740 Savannah	01-11-51-118	
15-IT	F-JHWJ	Jodel D.18	17	72-IT, F-PRJK
W15-JC		Jodel D.11 (mod: Hirth)		
15-KM		Corsair JPX Souricette		
15-PB		Aeroprakt A-22		
		(Crashed 7.10.07)		
W15-PC		Jodel D.18		
W15-PG		Averso gyrocopter		
15-PY	F-JCCT	Evektor EV-97 Eurostar	2008 3231	
15-ACA		Evektor EV-97 Eurostar SL	2009 3518	
15-ACN		Lambert Aircraft Mission M.106	0001	OO-F47
15-ACY	F-JUIV	BRM Aero Bristell UL		

16 : Charente

Reg	Call-sign	Type	Serial	Notes
16-AC		(Kolb/Zodiac ?) Ultrastar		
16-AK		Magni M-16 Tandem Trainer		
16-AM	F-JKQI	Humbert Tetras 912BS		
16-AT		Dragon		
16-AU		Magni gyrocopter		
16-AW	F-JKSJ	Magni M-16 Tandem Trainer		
16-BF		Weedhopper AX-3		
16-BL	F-JKRH	Tecnam P.92 Echo		
16-BN		Mignet HM.360 Pou-du-Ciel	158	F-PYKI
16-BP		Air's Maestro		
16-CG		Magni M-16 Tandem Trainer		
16-CM	F-JKTL	Gatard-Farigoux GF-02T Poussin	7	87-CW, F-PYBS
		(Re-regd 77-BBC)		
16-CP(1)		Magni M-16 Tandem Trainer		
16-CP(2)		Slepcev Storch (Rotavia engine)		
16-DA		Squale		
16-DB		Magni M-14 Scout 2000		
16-DH		Micro Aviation Pulsar		
16-DI	F-JKVI	Fly Synthesis Storch HS	262	
16-DX		Piel CP.150 Onyx		
16-DZ		Magni M-16 Tandem Trainer		
16-ED		PGO Aviation Cobra		
16-EM	F-JKFE	Bermicand (homebuilt)		
		(Accident 17.7.04)		
16-EU		ITV paramotor		
16-E?		Magni M-16 Tandem Trainer		
16-FD		Micro Aviation Pulsar III		
		(W/o 20.6.15)		
16-GD	F-JBOV	Tecnam P.92 Echo		
		(also marked 55-IE)		
16-GO		Magni M-16 Tandem Trainer		
		(W/o 3.7.06)		
16-GS		Zenair CH-601 Zodiac		
16-HH		Magni M-22 Voyager		
16-HP		Magni M-16 Tandem Trainer		
16-HT		Mignet HM.1100 Cordouan		
		(Crashed 16.5.04)		
16-JE	F-JKQK	Magni M-21		W16-JE
16-JF		Eipper Quicksilver MX		
16-JG		Magni M-16 Tandem Trainer		
16-JH		Magni M-18 Spartan		
16-JK		Adventure paramotor		
16-JS		Magni M-22 Voyager		
16-JT		Aéro Services Super Guépard 912S		
		(Crashed 8.7.06)		
16-KK		Micro Aviation Pulsar III		
16-KO		Aeroandinas MXP-1000 Tayrona	AA-12-06-90-028	
16-KX	F-JXAA	Magni gyrocopter		
16-LD	F-JKQJ	Dyn'Aéro MCR-01C	145	
16-LF		Aéro Services Super Guépard 912S		
16-LN		Aéro Services Super Guépard		
16-LO		paramotor		
16-LV		Magni M-16 Tandem Trainer		
16-MG	F-JWGU	Magni M-22 Voyager	22-08-4834	
16-MH		Zenair CH-601 Zodiac		
16-MI	F-JWGY	B&F Funk FK-9 Mk.IV SW	369	
16-MK		Magni M-22 Voyager		
		(W/o 22.6.14)		
16-MN		Magni M-24 Orion		
16-MO		Magni M-16 Tandem Trainer		
16-MP		Magni M-24 Orion		
16-MR	F-JKTN	Aeroprakt A-22		
16-MS	F-JWTP	Aéro Services SG.10A		
16-MU		B&F Funk FK-9 Mk.III		
16-MW		Magni M-24 Orion	24-09-5274	
16-MX		PGO Aviation AJS 2000 Cobra		
16-NF	F-JRKH	Magni M-16 Tandem Trainer		
16-NM		Slepcev Storch (Rotavia engine)		
16-NO		Magni M-24 Orion	24-10-5764	
		(Re-regd HA-GYP)		
16-NP		Magni M-22 Voyager		
16-NT		Magni M-22 Voyager		
16-NY	F-JRHI	Magni M-16 Tandem Trainer		
16-NZ		Zenair CH-601 Zodiac	6-9555	
16-OK		Zenair CH-601 Zodiac		
16-OS		Adventure paramotor		
16-OT		Magni M-16 Tandem Trainer		
16-OY		Magni M-16 Tandem Trainer	16-11-6444	
16-PD	F-JSXF	Aeropro Eurofox (t/w)		
16-PE		Aeropro Eurofox		
16-PW		Magni M-16 Tandem Trainer		
16-PY		Magni M-22 Voyager	22-12-6914	
16-PZ		Magni M-22 Voyager		
16-QO	F-JUKN	Magni M-16 Tandem Trainer	16-12-7254	
16-QX	f-juqa	Magni M-16 Tandem Trainer		
16-RG		Magni M-16 Tandem Trainer		
16-RH	F-JUNB	Magni M-14 Scout		
16-SC		Magni M-16 Tandem Trainer		
16-SE		Magni M-16 Tandem Trainer		
16-TA		Magni M-16 Tandem Trainer		
16-TG	F-JUTB	ELA Aviacion ELA-10 Eclipse	02154311014	
16-TL		B&F Funk FK-12 Comet	12-112	
16-TN		ELA Aviacion ELA-10 Eclipse R115	09154441014	
16-TS		Magni M-22 Voyager		
16-TT		ELA Aviacion ELA-10 Eclipse R115	09154521014	
16-TU	F-JAIF	ELA Aviacion ELA-07 Cougar		
16-TZ	F-JAMA	ELA Aviacion ELA-10 Eclipse		
16-UD	F-JALR	Magni M-24 Orion		
16-UE	F-JAMA	ELA Aviacion ELA-10 Eclipse		
16-UK		ELA Aviacion ELA-10 Eclipse R115	03164821014	

Reg	Call	Type	C/n	Prev
16-UR		ELA Aviacion ELA-10 Eclipse R115 09165091014		

17 : Charente-Maritime

Reg	Call	Type	C/n	Prev
17-G		Mignet HM.1000 Balerit 3X		
17-L		Huntair Pathfinder		
17-S		Trike 44PM	8300351	
17-X		Eipper Quicksilver MX II		
17-AA		Léger Frères		
17-AC		EuroALA Jet Fox 97		
		(Arcaap Metamorphosis ?)		
17-AD		Cosmos Phase II		
17-AK		Weedhopper AX-3		
17-AS		Mignet HM.1000 Balerit 3X		
17-AU(1)		Zenith Baroudeur LS-120		
17-AU(2)		Jodel D.18	193	F-PSCG
17-AV		Cosmos / Chronos		
17-AZ		Cosmos / La Mouette		
17-BB		trike / Air Création Quartz		
17-BD		Air Création		
17-BF		Cosmos Chronos / La Mouette Top 14.9		
17-BJ		Cosmos / Chronos 16		
17-BL		weightshift		
17-BP		Cosmos / La Mouette Top 14.9		
		(W/o 17.6.05)		
17-BX		Cosmos Samba / La Mouette Topless M		
17-CB		Zenith Baroudeur		
17-CC		Weedhopper AX-3		
17-CD		Huntair Pathfinder 2 447		
17-CI		Air Création		
17-CJ		Cosmos Bidulm / Chronos 14		
17-CL		Cosmos		
17-CO		Augry/Jodel D.20	02	F-PMJA
17-CP		gyrocopter		W17-CP
17-CR		Mignet HM.1000 Balerit		
		(Crashed 11.2.04)		
17-CU		Morin M-81		
17-CV		Mignet HM.1000 Balerit 3X	24	
		(Re-regd 95-GU?)		
17-CY		Weedhopper AX-3		
17-DA		(Technic Moto ?) Mustang	044	
17-DB		Denney Kitfox		
17-DC(1)		Top Concept Hurricane		
17-DC(2)		Plätzer Kiebitz		
17-DF		La Mouette		
17-DG		Mignet HM.1000 Balerit 3X	28	
		(Re-regd 52-BF ?)		
17-DJ		Weedhopper Europa 1		
17-DL		Air Création / Mild		
17-DM(1)		Weedhopper Europa II		
17-DM(2)		Druine D.31 Turbulent	49	F-PVQC
17-DN		Weedhopper AX-3		
17-DY		Air Création / Quartz		
17-DZ		Magni M-14 Scout		
17-EA		Weedhopper AX-3		
17-EE		Weedhopper AX-3		
17-EF		Weedhopper Europa II		
17-EJ		Micro Aviation Pulsar III		
17-EP		Air Création GT BI 582 / Kiss 450		
17-ET	F-JKTO	Claude Leger Pataplume 2	01	
17-EU		Best Off Sky Ranger		
17-FA		ICP MXP-740 Savannah 912		
		(Severely damaged 15.1.06)		
17-FJ		trike / Air Création Quartz		
17-FK	F-JKSY	B&F Funk FK-12 Comet	12-057	
		(Re-regd OO-G12 9.08)		
17-FN		Mignet HM.1000 Balerit 3X	64	
17-FR		Weedhopper AX-3		
17-FU		Weedhopper AX-3		
17-GD		Le Pataplume		
17-GE		Buccaneer II (f/p)		
17-GF	F-JAMJ	Mignet HM.1000 Balerit	80	
17-GO		Adventure Xpert		
		(W/o 3.7.06)		
17-GR		Take-Off (trike)		
17-GS	F-JKTM	Kappa 77 KP-2U Sova		
17-GX	F-JKUI	Jabiru UL		
17-HC		Aquilair Swing 14		
17-HF		gyrocopter (Aircopter A3C ?)		
17-HG		Weedhopper Europa		
17-HH	F-JKUC	Schleicher Ka.6M		
17-HS		Mignet HM.1000 Balerit		
17-HU		Zenair CH-701 STOL		
17-HZ		JC-31 Weedhopper Europa II amphibian		
17-JJ		Air Création / Mild		
17-JK		Mignet HM.1000 Balerit	117	
17-JL		Mignet HM.1000 Balerit		
17-JY		Mignet HM.1000 Balerit	122	
17-KA		Jabiru		
17-KB		Air Création GTE / Mild		
17-KC		Air Création Safari GT BI 447 / Fun 18		
17-KD		Weedhopper		
W17-KS		Jodel D.9 Bébé	829	
17-KT		Airotrophy TT-2000 Trophy		
17-LE		Air's Maestro		
17-LG	F-JCIZ	Mignet HM.1100 Cordouan		
17-LK		Adventure Xpert		
17-LL (1)		Mignet HM.1100 Cordouan		
		(W/o 1.11.97)		
17-LL (2)		Adventure Speedo 27 paramotor		
		(Crashed 1.9.06)		
17-LN		Mignet HM.1100 Cordouan	04	
17-LQ		SMAN Pétrel		
17-LY		Dallach D3 Sunwheel	046	D-MQII
17-MC		JCC Aviation J.300 Joker		
17-ME	F-JCZS	Mignet HM.1100 Cordouan	8	
17-MH	F-JKVR	Flight Design CT-2K		
		(Accident 30.9.05)		
17-MJ		Weedhopper AX-3		
17-MO		Urban Air UFM-13 Lambada		
17-NM		Ellipse Alizé		
		(Crashed 28.10.08)		
17-NU		Aero Kuhlmann Scub		
		(Accident 25.8.07)		
W17-OD		Balaskovic Alizé airship		
17-OI		paramotor		
17-OL		type unknown (similar to Humbert Tetras)		

Reg	Call	Type	C/n	Prev
17-OM		Cosmos		
17-OV		Adventure Xpresso paramotor		
17-PJ		Jodel D.92 Bébé	88	F-PJKS
17-PM	F-JKTX	Jabiru		
17-PU		Best Off Sky Ranger	SKR 51-097	
		(Re-regd OO-G90)		
17-QC		Best Off Sky Ranger		
17-QH		Humbert Tetras		
17-QM	F-JIPN	Humbert Tetras		
17-QN	F-JKWL	Fly Synthesis Storch HS	418A362	
17-QZ	F-JKUO	Jodel D.18		
17-RB	F-JXRK	B&F Funk FK-12 Comet	12-008	D-MRDM
17-RQ		ICP Savannah or Bingo		
17-RR		Magni M-22 Voyager		
17-SA		paramotor		
17-SC		Sauper J.300 Joker		
17-SF	F-JWPX	Sup'Air 80		
		(MCR-01 with modifed wing & engine mounting by André Charbonnier)		
17-SG	F-JKGA	Claude Leger Pataplume 2	2	
17-SI		Adventure Fun Flyer Bi/Xpresso paramotor		
17-SY		Zenair CH-601UL Zodiac (t/w)		
17-TE		Air Création Tanarg / iXess		
17-TK	F-JRTX	MDPC JPX (homebuilt)		
17-TL		CQR Roitelet		
17-TN		Best Off Sky Ranger V-Max		
17-TS	F-JRRR	Rans S-9 Torpedo (modified)	PFA/196-11487	G-BPUS
17-TT	F-JXUC	Humbert Tetras		
17-TX		Rans S-6 Coyote II		
17-UB		Raj Hamsa X'Air		
17-UI		ICP MXP-740 Savannah		
17-UN	F-JSBI	Zenair CH-701SP		
17-UT		ICP MXP-740 Savannah		
17-UZ		La Mouette O2B / Oryx		
17-VL		paramotor		
17-VO		Pipistrel Virus		
17-VT		Nicollier HN.800	01	
17-WV		Murphy Renegade Spirit		
17-XJ		Best Off Nynja		
17-XK	F-JTZJ	Magni M-22 Voyager	22-12-..54	
17-XT		Magni M-16 Tandem Trainer		
17-XV		ITV Boxer paramotor		
17-XW	F-JUMM	Mosquito XE	MXE1125F10B	
17-YA		Aeropro Eurofox		D-MSYG
17-YG		Alpi Aviation Pioneer 300		
17-YW		Skystar Kitfox Classic IV-1200		

18 : Cher

Reg	Call	Type	C/n	Prev
18-AM		Club ASL18		
18-AS		Aériane Sirocco		
18-BB		Dynali Chickinox		
18-BL		Dynali Chickinox		
18-CB		Cosmos / La Mouette		
18-CF		Cosmos		
18-CO		Air Création		
18-CU		Air Création		
18-DC		Cosmos		
18-DF		Air Création / Quartz		
18-DN		Dynali Chickinox Kot-Kot		
18-DO		Cosmos		
18-DP		Dynali Chickinox		
18-EO	F-JART	JCC Aviation J.300 Joker		
18-ER		Eipper Quicksilver GT500		
18-EX		Rans S-6 Coyote II		
18-FA		Air Création / Fun		
18-FC		Air Création Safari GT BI 503		
		(Accident 4.6.06)		
18-FF		Air Création Racer / XP		
18-FH		Cosmos Chronos 16		
18-FX		Aquilair		
18-GH		Cosmos / La Mouette Top 14.9		
18-GM		Air Création GTE / Mild		
18-GS		Cosmos		
18-HA	F-JFRN	Sauper J.300 Joker		18-BJ
18-HE	F-JFRR	B&F Funk FK-9 Mk.III	124	
		(C/n 09-124 also on 60-UR/F-JJMB)		
18-HF	F-JFQV	Flight Design CT 180	00-05-02-96	
18-HM		Dyn'Aéro MCR-01		
18-HQ	F-JPSE	Phobos		
18-HR		Dynali Chickinox Kot-Kot		
		(Crashed 24.9.05)		
18-HS		ICP Bingo 503	01-05-52-027	
18-HU	F-JFNZ	Demos (homebuilt)		
		(Accident 27.8.07; call-sign also quoted, without dept. markings, for Phobos type)		
18-JA		Jodel D.18	177	W18-JA, F-PCEA
18-JB		Air Création / Fun		
18-JC		Murphy Renegade Spirit		
18-JE	F-JPHB	(Aéro Services ?) Guepe		
18-JJ		Light Aero Avid Flyer		
		(Re-regd 77-AHL)		
18-JM	F-JPAS	Aviasud Mistral	177	
		(Same call-sign as 90-EZ)		
18-JQ		ICP MXP-740 Savannah	09-99-50-117	
18-JT		Air Création GTE Clipper		
18-JY		Air Création / SX		
18-KD		Barry MB-02 Souricette	234	
18-KG		Cosmos / La Mouette Top 14.9		
18-KM		Jodel D.92 Bébé	UAC33	F-PBOL
18-KV	F-JPKJ	Dallach D4 Fascination		
		(Same call-sign as 91-AJO)		
18-KY		Pixel		
18-LA	F-JPSH	Aéro Services Guépard 912		
18-LE		Best Off Sky Ranger		
18-LG		Weedhopper AX-3	C3103167	11-MJ
18-LM		Raj Hamsa X'Air		
18-LW	F-JPKS	Air Création GTE Clipper / iXess	A06021	
18-LY	F-JCIK	Aviakit Hermes		
18-LZ	F-JZFI	Raj Hamsa X'Air		83-LD
18-MF	F-JCUP	Micro Aviation Pulsar II	N173	
		(Re-regd 33-ABI)		
18-MH	F-JFRR	B&F Funk FK-9 Mk.IV SW	307	
18-MM		Air Création GT BI / Fun 18		
18-MP		Jodel D.20		
18-MS		Air Création GTE Clipper / XP		

Reg	F-reg	Type	c/n	prev
18-MV		Cosmos / Bautek		
18-MW	F-JXAF	ALMS/Sauper Papango		
18-MX		ITV Dakota paramotor		
18-NF	F-JPMO	Zlin Savage Classic		
18-NG		Best Off Sky Ranger		
18-NI		Bautek Eagle / Pico		
18-NJ		Best Off Sky Ranger		
18-NN		Aviasud Albatros		
18-NO		Air Création GTE Trek / iXess		
18-NP		Raj Hamsa Hanuman		
18-NV		Fly Synthesis Storch		
18-NX		Air Création GT BI / Quartz 18		
18-OC	F-JWJD	Fly Synthesis Texan TC		
18-OF		B&F Funk FK-14 Polaris Sprinter	14-045	31-DW
18-OM		Best Off Sky Ranger V-Max		
18-OY	F-JSCY	Tecnam P.92S Echo		77-ZD
18-PT	F-JYLC	Aerospool WT-9 Dynamic	DY425/2011	
18-QF	F-JSVV	Air Création Skypper / NuviX		
			A12013-12021 / T12048	
18-RA		ICP MXP-740 Savannah S	15-11-54-0440	

19 : Corrèze

Reg	F-reg	Type	c/n	prev
19-W		weightshift		
19-AL		Extra Ultralazier		
19-AR		Alpi Aviation Pioneer 200		
19-AS		Best Off Sky Ranger		
		(Re-regd 83-AKO)		
19-AV		Delpech MD.03 Transat		
19-BG		Pegasus Quantum Sport		
19-BN		Comco Ikarus Fox-C22		
19-CC	F-JIAA	Rans S-6 Coyote II		
19-CE		Air Création Racer 447 / Fun 14		
19-CR	F-JIRC	Zenair CH-601UL Zodiac		
19-CS		Aeros LW Arrow		
19-CT		Air Création / Fun 14	A00124-0078	
19-CU		Rans S-7 Courier		
19-CV		Magni gyrocopter		
19-CZ		Jodel D.92 Bébé		
19-DA	F-JIED	Sauper J.300 Joker		
19-DE(1)		trike / Air Création Quartz		
19-DE(2)		Humbert Tétras		
		(W/o 11.6.05)		
19-DE(3)		Aéro Services Guépy		
19-DG		Zenair CH-701 STOL		
19-DH		Air Création Racer / XP11		
19-DI	F-JYYE	Zenair CH-701 STOL		
19-DL		Raj Hamsa X'Air		
19-DM		Air Création GTE		
19-DN		Best Off Sky Ranger		
19-DY		Best Off Sky Ranger		
19-EB		Delpech MD.03 Transat amphibian	01	
19-GU	F-JYPP	Aerospool WT-9 Dynamic	DY178/2007	SP-SOUL
19-GZ		Guérin G1		
		(also reported as a Zenair CH-701 STOL)		
19-HA		G1 Aviation G1 SPYL		
19-HF	F-JYLS	Best Off Sky Ranger		
19-HL	F-JPUE	Best Off Jet Ranger		
19-HM		Zlin Savage		
19-HN		Zlin Savage		
19-HO		Hipps Superbirds J-3 Kitten		
19-HP		Air Création GTE Clipper		
19-HR		Alpi Aviation Pioneer 200		
19-HT	F-JXLN	Flight Design CT SW		05-KD
		(Re-regd 26-ADN)		
19-HU		Air Création		
19-HV	F-JYNU	Pipistrel Sinus		
19-HW		trike / Zenith wing		
19-IC		Air Création / Quartz		
19-IE		DTA Combo FC 912 / Diva		
19-IG		P&M Aviation Quik		
19-IJ		Aéro Services Guépy (Jabiru) 80T		
19-IK	F-JRQC	Sauper J.300 Joker		
19-IM	F-JWPJ	Best Off Sky Ranger		
19-IO		Rans S-6ES Coyote II		
19-IP		Zenair CH-701 STOL		
19-IX		Alpi Aviation Pioneer 200		
19-JJ		P&M Aviation QuikR	8508	G-CGHO
19-JO	F-JUQO	Aéro Services Super Guepard 912S		
19-JT	F-JVPM	Dyn'Aero MCR-01 ULC	402	
19-JU		Pipistrel Virus		
19-JZ	F-JVSD	Tecnam P.92 Echo-S		
		(Same call-sign as 10-JZ ?)		
19-LA	F-JJPV	Zenair CH-701 STOL		

20 : Corse (2A :Basse-Corse, 2B :Haute-Corse)

Reg	F-reg	Type	c/n	prev
20-H		Aériane Sirocco		
20-GS	F-JBXV	SG Aviation Storm 300 Special		
20-IR		Pégase		
20-OI		Test TST-3 Alpin TM	03022201	
2A-G		Cosmos		
2A-AC		Weedhopper ?		
		(Wfu and stored, noted 1.11)		
2A-AU		Synairgie 2-seater		
2A-BP		weightshift		
2A-BQ		Djicat Buse'Air		
2A-BR	F-JJZG	Air Création GTE		
2A-BS		Air Création / XP		
2A-BT		Air Création GTE Clipper / iXess		
2A-BU		paramotor		
2A-BV		Delpech MD.03 Transat		
2A-BW		Air Création Tanarg		
2A-CC		Air Création GTE		
2A-CD		Air Création GTE Clipper 582 / iXess 15		
2A-CK		Air Création GTE Clipper		
2A-CP		Magni M-16 Tandem Trainer		
2A-CT		Air Création / iXess		
2A-LW		Air Création / iXess		
2B-H		Claude Tisserand Hydroplum I (prototype)		
2B-AA		Claude Tisserand Hydroplum II amphibian		
2B-AG		Sauper J.300 Joker		
2B-AM		Claude Tisserand Hydroplum II		
2B-AR		Claude Tisserand Amphiplane		
2B-BK		Dynali Chickinox		
		(Crashed in forced landing 15.8.04)		

Reg	F-reg	Type	c/n	prev
2B-BV		Humbert Moto-du-Ciel		
2B-CF		ELA Aviacion ELA-07S		
		(W/o 7.3.07)		
2B-CO		Remos Gemini Ultra		
2B-CP		ELA Aviacion ELA-07S		
2B-CU	F-JWYJ	Fly Synthesis Texan 450	F901123005-450	
2B-DE		Magni M-22 Voyager		
2B-DI		Zlin Savage Cub		

21 : Côte d'Or

Reg	F-reg	Type	c/n	prev
21-AH		Cosmos Profile		
21-AJ		Mono Dragster		
21-AK		Aériane Sirocco		
21-AN		Chapelet		
21-AP		JC-24 Weedhopper		
21-AR		weightshift		
21-BC		Cosmos / La Mouette		
21-BN		Croses Airplume		
21-BU		Cosmos C / La Mouette 14.9		
21-CB		Cosmos		
21-DN		Air Création		
21-DR		Rans S-6ESD Coyote II		
21-EQ		Cosmos		
21-FH		Cosmos		
21-FJ		Air Création GT BI		
21-GB		weightshift		
21-GG		Cosmos		
21-HC		weightshift		
21-HE		Dynali Chickinox		
21-HF		Cosmos Bidulm		
21-HS		Air Création		
21-HT		Air Création		
21-HU		Cosmos		
21-HV		Cosmos		
21-IM		Cosmos		
21-IU		Rans S-6 Coyote II		
21-JE		Air Création / Kiss		
21-JR		Cosmos Bi Place / Chronos 16	21100	
21-JS		Cosmos Phase II		
21-KJ		Air Création Ibis / Quartz		
21-KL		Cosmos		
21-KM		Cosmos / La Mouette		
21-LC		Cosmos / La Mouette Top 12.9		
21-LD		Cosmos / Chronos 16		
21-LH		Cosmos		
21-LI		Rans S-14 Airaile		
21-LU		Cosmos		
21-MG		Cosmos		
21-MV		Pegasus / Quasar		
21-NB		Cosmos		
21-NI		Aéro Services Super Guépard 912		
21-NJ	F-JBJH	III Sky Arrow 500TF	017	
21-NM		Cosmos Phase II		
21-NN		Cosmos Phase II		
		(W/o 17.8.02)		
21-NO	F-JCLP	Rans S-7 Courier		
21-NP		Zenair CH-601 Zodiac		
21-NQ		Cosmos	21230	
21-NU		Cosmos Phase II		
21-NY		Air Création GT BI / XP		
		(W/o 14.12.98)		
21-OF		Cosmos Phase II / Chronos 16		
21-OH		Cosmos Phase II / La Mouette Top 12.9		
21-OJ		Cosmos		
21-OR		Rans S-6ESD Coyote II		
21-OT		Raj Hamsa X'Air		
		(Reported as 'Ecolight X'Air' which is a Swiss class name for a limited number of ultralights that can be flown with Swiss markings. Believed to be a standard 'Raj Hamsa X'Air'.)		
21-OV		Eipper Quicksilver		
21-OY		Air Création Racer / Cosmos Top 12.9		
21-PG		Rans S-6 Coyote II (t/w)		
21-PJ		Cosmos		
21-PO		Cosmos		
21-PU	F-JGME	ICP MXP-740 Savannah	06-98-50-089	
21-PX	F-JGMI	DTA Combo 912 / Dynamic 450	99-33/wing159/1	
21-QD		Cosmos Bi Place / Chronos 16	B21262	
21-QF		Cosmos / La Mouette Top 12.9	B21448	
21-QG	F-JQIB	Tecnam P.92 Echo		
21-QK		Dyn'Aéro MCR-01	74	
21-QM		Cosmos Chronos		
21-QP	F-JGTP	Dyn'Aéro MCR-01	112	
		(Re-regd OO-D34 7.01)		
21-QS		Dyn'Aéro MCR-01 ULC	169	
21-RA		Cosmos Mono / Topless	M0037	
21-RK		Dyn'Aéro MCR-01		
21-RL		Janovski JS-1B Don Quixote		
21-RM		Cosmos Bi Place / Chronos 16	21399	
21-RN		Cosmos		
21-RP		Cosmos / La Mouette Ipsos 14.9		
21-RX		Dyn'Aéro MCR-01	170	
21-RY	F-JGNS	Fantasy Air Allegro SW	00-114	
21-SB		Rans S-7 Courier		
21-SC		Air Création / XP		
21-SD		Humbert Tetras		
21-SF(1)	F-JGNY	Dynali Chickinox		
21-SF(2)		Dyn'Aéro MCR-01		
21-SG	F-JGOA	Dyn'Aéro MCR-01		
21-SI		Air Création GTE Clipper / XP		
21-SJ		Cosmos Phase II	21337	
21-SM		Cosmos / La Mouette Top 14.9	B21467	
21-SO		Dynali Chickinox		
21-SP		Dyn'Aéro MCR-01E	01	
21-SR		Cosmos Bidulm 503		
21-ST		Fly Synthesis Storch		
21-SY	F-JYXA	Fly Synthesis Storch		
21-TF		Rossi / La Mouette Ghost 12		
21-TK	F-JQGD	Dyn'Aéro MCR-01 ULC	298	
		(Originally quoted as c/n 224 which was CS-XAI, F-PDAI, ZK-ORR)		
21-TL	F-JGQU	Dyn'Aéro MCR-01 ULC		
21-TM		Cosmos / La Mouette Top 12.9		
21-TN		Cosmos / La Mouette Top 14.9		
21-TU	F-JGRH	Tecnam P.92S Echo		
21-TV		Aquilair Swing L951 582		
21-TZ		Aéro Services Guépard 582		
		(Accident 28.3.04)		

Reg		Type	c/n	Other
21-UA	F-JGRL	Fantasy Air Allegro SW		
21-UB		Cosmos		
21-UE	F-JGXO	Best Off Sky Ranger		
		(Damaged 18.6.06)		
21-UG	F-JGXA	Fly Synthesis Storch HS		
21-UH		Cosmos Phase II		
		(Accident 14.3.04)		
21-UJ		Mignet HM.293 Pou-du-Ciel		
21-UO		Dyn'Aéro MCR-01	249	
		(Same c/n as 21-YT/ F-JKTN)		
21-UP		Raj Hamsa X'Air		
21-UT		Ekolot JK-05 Junior		
		(Damaged 20.5.05)		
21-UZ		Raj Hamsa X'Air		
21-VB		DTA Feeling / La Mouette Ipsos		
21-VE		Dyn'Aéro MCR-01	239	
		(Re-regd 09-BC / F-JGYO)		
21-VF	F-JGYN	Dyn'Aéro MCR-01 Diesel (Siemens VDO)		
21-VH		Pagotto Brako (trike)		
21-VK		Air Création Racer / XP11		
21-VS	F-JGYQ	Dyn'Aéro MCR-01UL		
21-VX		Cosmos / La Mouette Top 14.9		
21-XB		Sonex Aircraft Sonex		
21-XK		Tecnam P.2002 Sierra		
21-XO		Air Création Racer 503 / XP11		
		(Crashed 2.4.05)		
21-XP		Raj Hamsa Hanuman		
21-XT	F-JSRG	Humbert Tetras 912CS		
21-XX	F-JQGT	Dyn'Aéro MCR-01 ULC R912SF/PV	290	
		(Re-regd OO-G67 10.10)		
21-XZ		Magni M-16 Tandem Trainer		
21-YC		Dyn'Aéro MCR-01 UL	305	
		(Re-regd 51-VE)		
21-YD		Dyn'Aéro MCR-01 UL	303	
		(Regd LN-YWI .08)		
21-YG		ITV Tomahawk paramotor		
21-YL	F-JQHN	Best Off Sky Ranger		
21-YN		Cosmos		
21-YO		Cosmos / Mach 14.9		
21-YR	F-JQIR	Dyn'Aéro MCR-01 UL	293	
21-YT	F JKTN	Dyn'Aéro MCR-01 UL	249	21-UO
		(Re-regd 37-ACO, 85-AEY)		
21-YV	F-JQHZ	Dyn'Aéro MCR-01	314	
		(W/o 11.4.08)		
21-YW	F-JWHH	Autogyro-Europe MT-03		
21-ZD		Cosmos Phase III		
21-ZE		Sauper J.300 Joker		
21-ZF		Cosmos		
21-ZT	F-JZEN	Dyn'Aéro MCR-01		
21-ZU	F-JZCJ	Humbert Tetras 912B		
21-ZY		Air Création GTE / Kiss		
21-AAA		gyrocopter		
21-AAB		Aviasud Mistral		
		(Accident 10.10.06)		
21-AAF		Pottier P.130UL Coccinelle	1114	
21-AAG		Cosmos HKS700E / Jet 15		
21-AAI		Air Création / iXess		
21-AAN		Pipistrel Sinus		
21-AAQ		Jodel D.195T	24T	F-PRAQ
		(Re-regd 62-ATX)		
21-AAS		Dyn'Aéro MCR-01 UL	334	
		(Re-regd 83-AFK)		
21-AAT		Dyn'Aéro MCR-01 UL	89	F-PVSM ?
21-AAV		TeST TST-14 Bonus		
21-AAW		Air Création GTE Trek HKS700 / iXess		
21-AAX		Jodel D.9 Bébé	751	62-AAD, F-PFGP
21-ABE		Air Création GT BI / SX		
21-ABF	F-JYXX	Best Off Sky Ranger	SKR0701766	
21-ABI		Pegasus		
21-ABP	F-JXHC	Jabiru		
21-ABR	F-JXKK	Dyn'Aéro MCR-01	352	
21-ABS		Best Off Sky Ranger		
21-ABX		TeST TST-14M Bonus	14010806	
21-ABV		Dyn'Aéro MCR-01 ULC	277	
		(Re-regd in Australia as 24-8484)		
21-ACA		Fly Synthesis Storch HS		
		(The quoted c/n B203SF1349 is the identity card number		
		of this ULM type)		
21-ACB		DTA Dynamic 15/430		
21-ACC	F-JXOZ	Dyn'Aéro MCR-01 UL	353	
21-ACD		DTA Combo		
21-ACI	F-JXTR	Dyn'Aéro MCR-01 UL	369	
21-ACJ	f-jylt	Humbert Tetras		
21-ACK(1)		Dyn'Aéro MCR-01 UL	118	HB-YJQ
		(Reported as such 9.11 but crashed Venice lagoon 15.7.07)		
21-ACK(2)		DTA Combo / La Mouette Ipsos		
		(Regn confirmed as 21-ACK by its identity card in 2009.		
		See also 21-ACX below)		
21-ACL		Jodel D.92 Bébé	412	F-PJXB
21-ACM		DTA / La Mouette Ipsos 12		
21-ACN	F-JWJL	Dyn'Aéro MCR Pick-Up	54	89-NP/F-JQHV
21-ACR		Cosmos Phase II		
21-ACT	F-JZYB	ICP MXP-740 Savannah AVG	05-03-51-389	
		(Same c/n as 72-MJ)		
21-ACX	F-JCDL	DTA Combo 912 / La Mouette	16	
		(Reported as 21-ACK in error or re-regd?)		
21-ADB		Dyn'Aéro MCR Pick Up	119	
21-ADE	F-JUKE	Aerospool WT-9 Dynamic		
21-ADI		Jodel D.92	349	F-PHJS
21-ADJ		Air Création GTE Trek / iXess		
21-ADM	F-JEZO	Magni M-16 Tandem Trainer		
21-ADN		Magni M-16 Tandem Trainer		
21-ADO		Air Création GTE Trek HKS700E / iXess 15		
21-ADP		Humbert Tetras 912B		
21-ADQ		Dyn'Aéro MCR Pick-Up	122	
		(Re-regd 85-ADU)		
21-ADR	F-JWQI	Dyn'Aéro MCR-01 UL	386	
21-ADV		Gdecouv'R / La Mouette Ipsos 12		
21-ADX		Messer / La Mouette		
21-ADY		Aéro Services Super Guépard 912		
21-ADZ	F-JXLB	Dyn'Aéro MCR-01	396	
21-AEA	F-JIHG	Denney Kitfox II Minifox	519	74-DX
21-AEB	F-JWWB	Halley Apollo Fox		
21-AED	F-JGOG	Air Création Tanarg 912 / iXess	A04088-4087	
21-AEG		Dyn'Aéro MCR-01 UL	394	

Reg		Type	c/n	Other
21-AEL	F-JRFO	Dyn'Aéro MCR-01 ULC	284	
21-AEM	F-JRHL	Zenair CH-601XL Zodiac	6-9710	PH-4B2
21-AEP		Dyn'Aéro MCR-01 ULC	344	
21-AEQ	F-JRJN	Aéro Services SG.10A		
21-AEU		Cosmos Phase II 582 / Chronos 14		
21-AEW		CBBULM O2B / La Mouette Oryx 14.9		
21-AEX	F-JRQX	Best Off Sky Ranger V-Max 912S	877	57-ATN
21-AEY	F-JYJS	Dyn'Aéro MCR Pick-Up		
		(also reported as Dyn'Aéro MCR-01 UL)		
21-AFA		Air Création Tanarg 912ES		
21-AFB		Ellipse Alizé / Titan 14.7		
21-AFC	F-JHQP	Aéro Services Guépard 912		
21-AFD		Gdecouv'R / 14		
21-AFE		Magni M-22 Voyager	22-12-7164	
21-AFI		La Mouette		
21-AFJ		Cosmos Echo 12 / La Mouette Top 12.9		
21-AFT		APEV Scoutchel		
21-AFW		Gdecouv'R (trike) / La Mouette Oryx 14.9		
21-AGC		CBBULM O2B / La Mouette Oryx 14.9		
W21-AGJ		type unidentified (low wing, 3-axis)		
		(damaged 23.6.11)		
21-AGL	F-JWDS	SG Aviation Storm 280		
21-AGN	F-JTCO	Aerospool WT-9 Dynamic	DY419/2011	
21-AGS	F-JTFD	Dyn'Aéro MCR-01 ULC Blue Line	406	
		(Re-regd SE-VSO 7.15)		
21-AHA		Dyn'Aéro MCR-01 ULC	408	
21-AHB	F-JJDV	Dyn'Aéro MCR-01	145bis	
21-AHD		P&M Aviation Quik GT450 912S		
21-AHP	F-JTYL	Evektor EV-97 Eurostar	2012 3942	
21-AHS		trike / La Mouette wing		
21-AHY	F-JYXX	Best Off Nynja		
21-AIF	F-JUNY	Dyn'Aéro MCR Pick Up		
21-AIH		Dyn'Aéro MCR-01		
21-AIJ	F-JXTT	DTA Combo FC / Diva		
21-AIN		Aéro Services Super Guepard		
21-AIP	F-JRJN	Aéro Services SG.10A 912S		
21-AJA		Pottier P.130UL		
21-AJG		Spacek SD-1 Minisport TD	082	
21-AJN		SG Aviation Storm 280		
		(W/o 25.9.15)		
21-AJY	F-JXMC	AirLony Skylane UL		
21-AKE	F-JTZS	ICP MXP-740 Savannah S	13-10-54-0290	

22 : Côtes-d'Armor

Reg		Type	c/n	Other
W22-C		SCA Lone Ranger		
22-M		Veliplane		
22-AM		Humbert La Moto-du-Ciel		
22-AP		Weedhopper		
22-AR		Air Création		
22-BL	F-JAFZ	JCC Aviation J.300 Joker		
22-CG		Chapelet Lazer / Drachen Studio Kecur Avant 15		
22-CK		Air Création Racer		
22-DE		Humbert La Moto-du-Ciel		
22-DN		Rans S-6 Coyote II		
22-EA	F-JCDE	Rans S-6ESD Coyote II		
22-EL		Rans S-6 Coyote II		
22-FD		Best Off Sky Ranger		
22-FG		Cosmos / Chronos		
22-FI		ZUT Aviation TT2000 STOL		
22-FJ		Mignet HM.1100 Cordouan	21	
22-FO		Air Création / Kiss		
22-FT		Eipper Quicksilver GT500		
22-FX		Zenith ?		
22-GC	F-JZCY	Raj Hamsa X'Air 502T		
22-GD		Croses Criquet Léger		W22-GD
22-GE		Humbert Tetras		
22-GG		Chapelet Lazer / Drachen Studio Kecur Avant		
22-GI		ICP MXP-740 Savannah		
22-GL	F-JHPS	ICP Bingo 4S	03-08-52-159	
22-GP	F-JHQJ	Magni M-14 Scout	14-02-1934	
22-GR	F-JHQN	Kappa 77 KP-2U Sova		
		(Same call-sign as 33-ZE)		
22-GV		Mignet HM.293 Pou-du-Ciel		
22-GW	F-JHRC	Humbert Tetras		
		(Re-regd 78-ABC ?)		
22-HC		Aeroprakt A-22		
		(Crashed 7.10.06)		
22-HG	F-JHPM	Vidor Asso V Champion		
22-HI		Magni M-16 Tandem Trainer		
22-HK		Aeroprakt A-22		
22-HM	F-JYHS	Magni M-16 Tandem Trainer	16-07-4014	
22-HR	F-JHOR	Best Off Sky Ranger		
22-HW		Magni gyrocopter		
22-ID		Humbert Tetras		
22-IG	F-JXXD	B&F Funk FK-9 SW		
22-IH	F-JWSG	Mignet Pou-du-Ciel		
22-IN		Didier Pti'tavion		
22-IS	F-JXNB	Magni M-14 Scout		
22-IT		P&M Aviation Quik GT450		
22-IU		Eipper Quicksilver GT500		
22-IV		Best Off Sky Ranger		
22-IX		ICP MXP-740 Savannah	02-00-51-002 (Kit 4)	
		(Same c/n as 27-NT and 35-FM)		
22-JA	F-JZBF	Evektor EV-97 Eurostar	2007 2941	95-WF
		(Re-regd 49-UT)		
22-JD	F-JPEW	Aviasud AE209 Albatros		
22-JH		Humbert La Moto-du-Ciel		
22-JT		Tecnam P.92 Echo		
22-JU	F-JZXR	Flight Design CT SW		
22-JW		Magni M-16 Tandem Trainer		
22-KD		Ladybird HAFB		
22-KJ		Air Création Pixel QC / Fun 13		
22-KM	F-JAGK	Ekolot JK-05 Junior		
22-KQ	F-JATM	ICP MXP-740 Savannah S	16-03-54-0461	
22-SO	F-JEXP	Alpi Aviation Pioneer 200		
22-ABF		Best Off Sky Ranger		
		(believed error for 21-ABF)		

23 : Creuse

Reg		Type	c/n	Other
23-AF		Kolb Twinstar (?)		
23-AQ		Air Création / SX		
23-AW		Weedhopper		
W23-BD		Mignet Pou-du-Ciel		
23-BG		Eipper Quicksilver		
23-BH		(Weedhopper ?) AX-3		

Reg	Reg2	Type	Serial	Prev
23-BJ		Air Création Racer 447		
23-BL		Air Création / SX		
		(Earlier reported as "Joelley")		
23-BN		Air Création GT		
23-BR		Raj Hamsa X'Air		
23-BX		Raj Hamsa X'Air F		
23-BZ		Trimouille JT.XI		
23-CA		Air Création / Quartz		
23-CD	F-JIFL	Sauper J.300 Joker		
23-CH		Fly Synthesis Wallaby		
23-CI		Air Création / Kiss		
23-CK		Barry MB-02 Souricette		
W23-CM		Mignet HM.293 Pou-du-Ciel		
		(Crashed 18.6.05)		
23-CW		gyrocopter		
23-CX		Aviakit Vega 2000TR		
23-CY		Rans S-4 Coyote I		
23-CZ		Raj Hamsa X'Air		
23-DL	F-JVPN	Plätzer Kiebitz		

24 : Dordogne

Reg	Reg2	Type	Serial	Prev
24		Aériane Sirocco 377		
24-R		Zenith Baroudeur		
24-AB		Eipper Quicksilver MX II		
24-AP		Air's Maestro		
24-AS		Eipper Quicksilver MX II		
24-AX		Eipper Quicksilver MX II		
24-BD		Soprano		
24-BE		Hipps Superbirds J-3 Kitten		
24-BH		DH.82A Tiger Moth (Scale Replica)		
24-BT		Top Concept Hurricane		
24-BW		Dynali Chickinox amphibian		
24-CC		Synairgie XC		
24-CG		Toper Tielman ?		
24-CO		Delpech MD.04 Airland		
		(W/o 18.7.08)		
24-CP		Delpech MD.03 Transat amphibian		
24-CR		BMW / Bautek Sexy 14.8		
24-CT	F-JASX	TEAM Mini-MAX		
24-CY		homebuilt		
24-DF		Top Concept Hurricane		
24-DQ		Eipper Quicksilver (wing ex 24-BD)		
24-EE		Top Concept Hurricane		
24-EF		Air Création GTE / XP		
24-EV		Micro Aviation Pulsar III		
24-FE		Cosmos / La Mouette		
24-FL		Top Concept Hurricane		
24-GH		Weedhopper		
24-GI		Air's Maestro 'Lewi Special'		
24-GN		Dynali Chickinox		
24-GS		Air's Maestro		
24-GY	F-JKAH	ICP MXP-740 Savannah	12-97-50-072	
		(Re-regd 27-UO)		
24-HB		Mignet HM.1100 Corduan	17	17-NF
24-HE		Air Création / SX		
24-HF		Weedhopper		
24-HG		Weedhopper		
24-HH		Eipper Quicksilver MXL III Sport		
24-HI		Raj Hamsa X'Air		
24-HK		Eipper Quicksilver GT IE		80-IA
24-HL		Air Création GT BI		
24-HM		Magni gyrocopter		
24-HN		Cosmos / La Mouette		
24-HS		Delpech MD.03 Transat amphibian		
24-HV		Weedhopper		
24-IL		Top Concept Hurricane		
24-IN		Raj Hamsa X'Air		
24-JC		Air Création Racer 447 / La Mouette		
24-JE		Hytec Hurricane		
24-JH		Air Création / XP		
24-JM	F-JHYF	Xxtrim		
24-JV		Weedhopper		
24-JX	F-JTZW	SG Aviation Storm 280		
24-KI		Aeropro Eurofox		
24-KR(1)		Eipper Quicksilver II		
24-KR(2)		Deluc gyrocopter		W24-KR
24-KT		M.Deluc MD T2 gyrocopter		W24-KT
24-KW		Cosmos Big Bang		
24-LA	F-JWDH	Air Création GTE		
24-LE		Pagotto Brako / Bautek Pico		
24-LK		Air Création / SX		
24-LL		Air Création / iXess		
24-LM		Pegasus		
24-LN		Raj Hamsa X'Air		
24-LP		Air Création / iXess		
24-LR		Cosmos		
24-LW	F-JYAB	Air Création Tanarg / iXess		
24-MB		Comco Ikarus C-42		
24-MC		Best Off Sky Ranger		
		(Crashed 13.6.06)		
24-MJ		Best Off Sky Ranger		
		(Crashed 16.6.06)		
24-MK		Wills Wing (weightshift)		
24-MR		Bragg ulm		
24-MW(1)		Adventure M3 paramotor		
24-MW(2)		Zenair CH-701 STOL (noted 8.11)		
24-MX		Cosmos		
24-MY	F-JZDG	Flying Machines FM250 Vampire	FM250V0105	
		(Re-regd 26-ACF) (Same call-sign as 85-VY)		
24-NR		Magni M-16 Tandem Trainer (enclosed cockpit)		
24-NV		Air Création GTE / SX		
24-NZ		Magni M-22 Voyager		
24-OA		weightshift		
24-OC		Delpech Transat Aerolac		
24-OL		Aéro Services Guépy (Jabiru) 80		
24-OT		Murphy Renegade Spirit		
24-OZ		Air Création / XP		
24-PA		Air Création GTE Trek / iXess		
24-PC		Magni M-22 Voyager	22 07 4444	
24-PS		Aeroprakt A-22		
24-PT		Pagotto Brako (BMW 1100) / Bautek Pico 13.5		
24-PX		Air Création Tanarg 912S / iXess 15		
			BMAA/HB/501	G-TARG
24-PZ		weightshift		
24-QC		Delpech MD.03 Transat		
24-QM	F-JZCR	Magni M-22 Voyager		

Reg	Reg2	Type	Serial	Prev
24-QQ		Air Création GT BI		
24-QR		Eipper Quicksilver Sport 2S		
24-QY	F-JWJO	Best Off Sky Ranger		
24-RD		Magni Accordiola		
		(Believed converted from Magni M-22 Voyager)		
24-RE		Cohen 2 seat gyrocopter		
24-RJ		Air's Maestro		
24-RK		Magni M-24 Orion		
24-RM	F-JXWP	Flight Design CT LS	08-01-23	
		(Re-regd 31-KU)		
24-RR		Raj Hamsa X'Air		55-HG
		(Noted wfu at Belves 8.15)		
24-RS	F-JUCE	Air Création Twin 582SL / Kiss 450		
24-RW	F-JFTY	Denney Kitfox III Minifox	993	83-EG
24-SC	F-JZYA	Zenair CH-601 Zodiac		
24-SM		Zenair CH-601 Zodiac		
24-SP	F-JXPQ	Best Off Sky Ranger		
24-SR	F-JZDD	Humbert Tetras		
24-TC		Air Création Tanarg / BioniX		
24-TG	F-JTYY	Aviasud Albatros		
24-TV	F-JWAN	Flight Design CT SW		
24-TY	F-JSZP	Halley Apollo Fox	FR-04 05 11	
24-TZ		Magni M-22 Voyager	22-11-6434	
24-UC		Seaman Cricket Mk.6A	LAA G/16-1370	G-CFJD
24-UE		Cosmos / La Mouette		
24-UF		Micro Aviation Pulsar II		
24-UO		Layzell AV18-A Mk.6A 582 gyrocopter		
24-UP		trike / Air Création XP15		
24-UQ	F-JFSR	Aéro Services Guepard 912		
24-UR		Phoenix Air Phoenix U-15	10/U15	
24-UT		Magni M-16 Tandem Trainer		
24-UY	F-JRMU	Air Création 503SL		
24-VB		DTA / La Mouette		
24-VV		Dyn'Aéro MCR-01		
24-WI	F-JWUH	Zlin Savage Classic		
24-XX	F-JAYT	Zlin Savage Bobber		

25 : Doubs

Reg	Reg2	Type	Serial	Prev
25-J		ASW Microstar		
25-R		Kalbermatten Mini Spitfire		
25-AN		Comco Ikarus Fox-C22		
25-AR		Best Off Sky Ranger		
25-BD		SEP		
25-BM		Air Composite		
25-BX		Cosmos		
25-CD		Zenith Baroudeur		
25-CE		Air Création GT BI / XP		
25-CI		Cosmos Chronos	B025	
25-CN		Cosmos		
25-CQ		Cosmos		
25-CR		Cosmos Chronos		
25-DC		weightshift		
25-DF		Cosmos Chronos		
25-DG		Air Création		
25-DJ		Cosmos		
25-DQ		Air Création / XP Select		
25-DR		Rans S-6 Coyote II		
25-DS		Air Création / XP		
25-DV		Humbert La Moto-du-Ciel		
25-ED		Air Création		
25-EG		Airborne Australia / Cosmos Chronos		
25-EQ		Rans S-6 Coyote II		
25-FO		Air Création / Mild		
25-FP		Air Création / SX-II		
25-GE		Cosmos Chronos		
25-GS		Air Création GT BI 503		
25-GT	F-JGDU	European Airwings Springbok		
25-GV		Comco Ikarus Fox-C22		
25-HL		Air Création GTE Clipper / XP		
25-HM		Air Création GT BI 582ES		
		(Crashed 28.5.05)		
25-HN	F-JGYU	Air Création Racer / XP	A04083-4075	
25-HO		Comco Ikarus Fox-C22		
25-HS		Air Création GTE Clipper		
25-HV		Cosmos Merlin		D-MMWW ?
		(Now reported as Sun & Moon Titan or as a Magic!)		
25-IC		Rans S-6ESD Coyote II		
25-ID		Ultralair Espace 503 Turbo 17	208128	
25-IE		Rans S-6ESD Coyote II		
25-IJ	F-JQIO	Zenair CH-701 STOL		
25-IN		Humbert Tetras		
25-IS	F-JGXQ	Sauper J.300 Joker		
25-IT	F-JCLN	Air Création GTE Clipper		
25-IV	F-JUSS	B&F Funk FK-9	81	
25-JE		Air Création GTE Clipper / XP		
25-JI	F-JGNC	Comco Ikarus Fox-C22		
25-JL		European Airwings Springbok		
25-JM		Cosmos		
25-JP		weightshift		
25-JQ		Comco Ikarus Fox-C22		
25-JS		Aviakit Hermes Adventure		
25-JU		Rans S-6 Coyote II	0594618	
		(Re-regd 62-ANY)		
25-KB	F-JDFK	Humbert Tetras		
		(Re-regd 63-VD)		
25-KC		Skyfly S-34 Skystar	017	
25-KD		Best Off Sky Ranger		
25-KE		Ecolight AFM		
25-KG		type unknown		
		(Noted damaged at Besancon 2.10.05)		
25-KO		Pegasus Quantum 15-582	6876	
25-KT		Air Création / XP		
25-KY		Comco Ikarus Fox-C22		
25-LB		Air Création GT 582		
		(W/o 16.10.99)		
25-LG		Air Création / XP		
25-LN		Air Création / iXess		
25-LR		Air Création / iXess		
25-LY		DTA Dynamic 15		
25-MF		Air Création		
25-MH		DTA Evolution 503 / Dynamic (or Ghost wing)		
25-MN		Light Aero Avid Flyer	423	
		(Also marked F-WSDC)		
25-MX		Alpaero (Noin) Exel		
25-NB	F-JGZR	Rans S-6 Coyote II		F-JBRU
25-NC		Best Off Sky Ranger		

Reg	Tail	Type	C/n	Prev ID
25-NG	F-JING	SG Aviation Storm 300S		
25-NH		Djicat Buse'Air		
25-NI		Take Off Merlin / DTA Dynamic 450		
25-NO		Cosmos		
25-NQ	F-JGPH	Best Off Sky Ranger		
		(Damaged 9.9.07)		
25-NR		Air Création / XP		
25-NU		Synairgie		
25-NX		Air Création Racer / XP		
25-NY	F-JGPX	Zenair CH-701 (Dedalius Pegastol wing)		
25-OB		Cosmos Chronos 16		
		(Crashed 13.7.09)		
25-OD		Jodel D.18	33	F-PYXL
25-OE		Jodel D.18	43	F-PZPB(2),
				F-WZPB
25-OG	F-JGPJ	ATEC Zephyr		
25-OI		Test TST-3 Alpin TM	03022201	
25-OL		Air Création / Fun		
25-OR		Weedhopper AX-3		
25-OU	F-JGQO	Slepcev Storch		
25-OZ		Weedhopper AX-3		
25-PA		B&F Funk FK-9 (t/w)		
25-PF		Aero Designs Pulsar (t/w)		
25-PH		Jodel D.18	370	F-PRSB
25-PS		TeST TST-3 Alpin		
		(Crashed 23.5.05)		
25-PU		Jodel D.92 Bébé	775	
25-PV		Weedhopper AX-3	8062397	
		(Re-regd 50-LX)		
25-PY		Air Création / XP		
25-QA		Magni M-18 Spartan		
25-QC		DTA / Dynamic 15/430	209	
25-QF		Halley Apollo Fox		
25-QG		Jabiru UL3300 (t/w)	0554	
25-QI		(Aviasud ?) Sirocco GTS		
25-QJ		Air Création / iXess		
25-QN		Cosmos Bidulm		
25-QQ		Halley Apollo Fox 512		
		(Accident 19.8.07)		
25-QU	F-JQJL	Air Création GTE / iXess		
25-QW		Djicat Buse'Air 150		
25-QY	F-JGZB	Aéro Services Guépy Club 582T		
25-QZ		gyrocopter		
25-RA		DTA / Dynamic 15/430		
25-RB		Halley Apollo Fox 912		
		(Crashed 16.7.05)		
25-RM		Best Off Sky Ranger		
25-RN	F-JQGR	Fantasy Air Allegro SW		
		(Same call-sign as 02-AAV)		
W25-RO		Woopy (inflatable boat combination)		
25-RX	F-JGQU	Rans S-4 Coyote (t/w)		
25-RZ		Halley Apollo Fox		
25-SB	F-JQGX	Evektor EV-97 Eurostar	2004 2306	
25-SE	F-JQHO	Technoflug Piccolo		
25-SG		Avio Delta (trike)	MK4 020101	
25-SH		Zlin Savage Classic		
25-SI		Aéro Services Guépy Club 582T		
25-SL		Synairgie		
25-SP		Humbert Tetras		
25-ST		Aéro Services Guépy 582T		
25-SU		AC Mobil 34 Chrysalin (Buse'Air 150)		
25-SZ		Cosmos Phase II		
25-TB	F-JWAF	Halley Apollo Jet Star		
25-TC		Cosmos		
25-TF		Air Création GTE Clipper / iXess		
25-TQ		DTA Combo / Dynamic		
		(Accident 25.8.06)		
25-TS		Light Aero Avid Flyer Mk.IV Speedwing	1507	F-PQUO,
				F-WQUO
25-TT		ATEC 122 Zephyr 2000	ZP521200	D-MZHS
25-TW		TeST TST-10 Atlas M		
		(W/o 23.6.06)		
25-TX		Air Création GTE Clipper / XP15		
25-TZ		paramotor		
25-UA	F-JZMU	B&F Funk FK-12 Comet		77-ALK, 73-KD,
				28-BI
25-UE		DTA / Dynamic 450		
25-UP		Light Aero Avid Flyer	800	F-WRXU
25-UQ	F-JZPQ	Halley Apollo Fox		
25-UY	F-JXHJ	Aeropro Eurofox		
25-VH		Zlin Savage		
25-VI		Best Off Sky Ranger		
		(Forced landing 13.2.09)		
25-VM	F-JRNL	Best Off Sky Ranger		
25-VP		Evektor EV-97R Eurostar	2008 3303	
25-VW		Woopy (inflatable boat combination)		
25-VZ		DTA / Dynamic 15/430	283	
25-WH		Magni M-16 Tandem Trainer		
25-WI		Raj Hamsa X'Air F		
25-WU	F-JROO	Micro Aviation Pulsar 582		
25-XD		Air Création GTE Trek / iXess		
25-XE		Cosmos		
25-XK	F-JXVJ	Zenair CH-701 STOL		
25-XO	F-JZLQ	Best Off Nynja		
25-XS		Alisport Silent 2		
25-XT		Magni M-16 Tandem Trainer		
25-XU		DTA / Magic		
25-XV		Polaris FIB		
25-YA		Evektor EV-97 Eurostar		
25-YD		Alisport Silent 2		
		(W/o 5.5.14)		
25-YE		DTA Combo / Magic		
W25-YH		glider		
25-YO	F-JRZU	Flight Design CT SW	08-02-19	LY-USA
25-YV	F-JGZZ	Air Création Tanarg / Bionix	A14067-14066	
25-YW	F-JSBY	ICP MXP-740 Savannah S	10-04-54-0006	
25-YX	F-JSBZ	ICP MXP-740 Savannah (f/p)	09-12-54-0015	
W25-YZ		Zenair CH-601XL Zodiac		
25-ZB		Halley Apollo Fox	FR-060810	
		(W/o 27.3.13)		
25-ZG		Zlin Savage Cub		
25-ZJ	F-JSMD	ICP MXP-740 Savannah XL	09-04-51-822	
W25-ZN		gyrocopter		
25-ZX	F-JYMQ	Zenair CH-701 STOL	7-9278	
25-ZY	F-JSXL	ICP MXP-740 Savannah	10-12-54-0054	
25-AAA		Alpi Aviation Pioneer 200STD		
25-AAB		Aeros (trike)		
25-AAC		Nando Groppo Trial		
		(W/o 3.3.12)		
25-AAN		Solar / La Mouette Elektrotrike		
25-AAR	F-JTMO	ICP MXP-740 Savannah S (f/p)	11-12-54-0136	
25-ABG		Alisport Silent 2 Electro		
25-ABM	F-JUKJ	Autogyro-Europe MTOsport		
25-ABN	F-JWBM	DTA Combo / Magic		
25-ABU	F-JABU	Nando Groppo Trial	00086/45	
25-ABZ	F-JUVA	Zenair CH-650Ei		
25-ACF	F-JVQI	Colomban MC-30 Luciole	48	
25-ACT	F-JVNI	ICP MXP-740 Savannah TD		
25-ACV	F-JVOB	ICP MXP-740 Savannah S	12-12-54-0231	
25-ADO	F-JXZG	Autogyro-Europe MTOsport		
25-ADR	F-JRSR	Trixy G-4-2 Princess 914 gyrocopter	023-13	
25-AEF	F-JACO	Nando Groppo Trail	00117/76	I-A838
25-..N		Jodel D.185	567	

26 : Drôme

Reg	Tail	Type	C/n	Prev ID
26-G		Air Création		
26-AJ		Air Création / Quartz 18		
26-AP		Air Création Alpair Chariot		
26-AS		Air Création		
26-BL		Air Création		
26-BO		Air Création / XP		
26-BP		Air Création		
26-BU		Air Création / SX		
26-BZ		Denney Kitfox Speedwing		
26-CN		Humbert La Moto-du-Ciel		
26-CO		AEIM Epsilon Midi 18 paramotor		
		(Accident 1.8.04)		
26-CR		Air Création Alpair Chariot		
26-DD		Air Création / Fun		
26-DE		Air Création / SX		
26-DW	F-JWIA	Jihlavan KP-5 Skyleader		
		(Re-regd 47-TK)		
26-EC		Air Création		
26-EE		Cosmos		
26-EJ		Air Création / Fun		
26-EO		Air Création / Fun 457		
26-ER		Air Création		
26-ES		Weedhopper	B1062930	
		(Also carries c/n B3043088)		
26-EV		Eipper Quicksilver GT500		
26-FF		Air Création / S		
26-FG		Air Création / SX		
26-FK		Weedhopper		
26-FQ		Air Création		
26-FR		Air Création / Fun		
26-FS		Air Création / Fun		
26-FY		Weedhopper		
26-GB		Lascaud Bifly	1	
26-GD		Air Création / XP		
26-GE		Weedhopper		
26-GQ		Air Création Safari GT BI		
		(W/o 20.11.03)		
26-GS		Air Création / Quartz		
26-GT		Aviasud		
26-GU		Air Création GT BI / SX		
26-GV		Air Création		
26-GX		Mignet HM.1000 Balerit		
26-HG		Air Création		
26-HL		Aviasud X'Pair 65		
		(W/o 27.4.03)		
26-HP		Air Création / XP		
26-HZ		DTA Voyager II		
26-IB		Airwave		
26-IL	F-JCTY	Zenair CH-701 STOL		
26-IR		Weedhopper	B1061140	
26-IS		Air Création		
26-IV		weightshift		13-CR
26-JE		Air Création		
26-JH		Air Création / Mild		
26-JO		Alpaero (Noin) Sirius		
26-JS		Air Création / Pegasus	07-T	
26-JV		Air Création Racer / XP		
26-JX		Air Création		
26-KB		DTA / Dynamic 15		
26-KH		Magni M-16 Tandem Trainer		
26-KN		ULM Evasion		
26-KR		III Sky Arrow 500TF		
		(W/o with 26-XB 19.7.08)		
26-KV		Raj Hamsa X'Air		
26-KZ		Aviasud AE209 Albatros		
26-LA		Denney Kitfox III		
26-LB		Air Création		
26-LF		Air Création		
26-LK		Air Création / XP		
W26-LL		Air Création		
26-LO		Aéro Services Guépard		
26-LQ		Zenair CH-601 Zodiac		
26-LS		(Tandem Air ?) Sunny		
26-LT		Flight Design CT SW	D-08-04-08	
		(Same c/n as 26-ZT – error?)		
26-MD		Light Aero Avid Flyer		
26-ME	F-JAWB	Air Création GT BI / SX		
26-MO		Best Off Sky Ranger		
26-MP		DTA / Dynamic 15		
W26-MQ		Jodel D.9 (?)		
26-MQ	F-JEPT	Viking Dragonfly		
26-MR		Air Création / Kiss 450B	A01058-1051	
26-MS		Air Création		
26-MT		Air Création GT BI		
26-NB		Cosmos Bi Place	21460	
26-NE		Aviasud Mistral		
26-NH		Best Off Sky Ranger		
26-NZ		Best Off Sky Ranger		
26-OV		ATEC Zephyr 2000		
26-PE	F-JETT	RN-3 Aster XIII		
26-PI	F-JEUA	weightshift		
26-PO		Raj Hamsa X'Air		
26-PQ	F-JVGM	Raj Hamsa X'Air F	602T SP	
26-PY	F-JEXV	Best Off Sky Ranger		
26-QC		Take-Off (Merlin ?) (trike)		
26-QD		Zenair CH-601UL Zodiac (t/w)		
26-QK		Take-Off (Merlin ?) / Drachen Studio Kecur Avant		

Reg	Call-sign	Type	c/n	Other
26-QS		B&F Funk FK-9 Mk.III		
		(Damaged 1.8.05)		
26-QV		DTA Combo / Dynamic 430		
26-QW	F-JEPU	Flying K Sky Raider II		
26-RB		Air Création GTE Clipper 582 / XP15		
26-RC		Vidor Asso V Champion		
26-RI		DTA / Dynamic 15/430		
26-RJ		DTA		
26-RR		Air Création GTE / XP		
		(Damaged 3.9.05)		
26-RS		Take-Off Merlin / iXess		
26-RT	F-JEWS	Evektor EV-97 Eurostar		
26-RV		ICP MXP-740 Savannah		
26-RY		DTA Combo / Dynamic 15/430		
26-SA	F-JEFB	Jodel D.18	485	
26-SB		Weedhopper AX-3		
26-SG		Magni M-16 Tandem Trainer		
26-SK		ICP Bingo 4S		
		(Accident 22.4.07)		
26-SL		DTA / Dynamic 15/430		
26-SR		Zenair CH-601XL Zodiac		
26-SU		Jodel D.11		
26-TA		DTA / Dynamic 15/450	246	
26-TB		Raj Hamsa Hanuman		
26-TD		DTA / Dynamic 15/430		
26-TL		Air Création Racer / SX 12		
26-TM		P&M Aviation Quik 912S		
26-TO		Air Création Racer / SX 12		
		(Accident 14.1.06)		
26-TU		JC-24 Weedhopper		
		(Crashed 26.8.06)		
26-UB		B&F Funk FK-14B Polaris	14-052?	
		(Same c/n as ZU-EWD)		
26-UC		Alpi Aviation Pioneer 200		
		(Damaged 30.10.06)		
26-UE		Take-Off Merlin / iXess		
26-UG		ICP MXP-740 Savannah	02-03-51-142	
		(Same c/n as 37-UM / F-JPAR)		
26-UH	F-JEFJ	ICP MXP-740 Savannah	05-06-51-401	
		(Re-regd 01-WX)		
26-UJ		Aeropro Eurofox		
26-UL	F-JEGC	Best Off Sky Ranger V-Max		
26-UO		Jodel D.195		
26-UQ		Fantasy Air Cora Legato		
26-UU	F-JEGT	Kappa 77 KP-2U Sova		
		(Same call-sign as 47-RS, see also 47-LY)		
26-UX	F-JEGU	TL Ultralight TL-2000 Sting Carbon		83-ACT
26-VA		DTA Voyageur / Dynamic 15/430		
26-VD		Raj Hamsa X'Air		
26-VF		DTA Combo / Dynamic 15/430		
26-VG		DTA Combo / Dynamic 15/430		
26-VH		DTA Combo / Dynamic 15/430		
26-VI		DTA Combo / Dynamic 450		
		(Re-regd OK-LZF .09)		
26-VL		Best Off Sky Ranger		
26-VP		Raj Hamsa X'Air F		
26-VQ		Magni M-16 Tandem Trainer		
26-VS		weightshift		
26-VZ		Fantasy Air Cora 3		
		(Crashed 9.2.07)		
26-WD		DTA Combo		
26-WF		DTA / Dynamic 450P	238	
26-WH		Magni M-16 Tandem Trainer		
26-WM		Aviakit Vega 912T		
26-WN		ICP MXP-740 Savannah ADV	06-03-51-477	
26-WQ		DTA Combo / Dynamic	243	
26-WW		Pagotto Brako / Gryf SP		
26-WZ	F-JYUB	Aerospool WT-9 Dynamic		
26-XA		Tecnam P.92 Echo		
26-XB		Air Création GTE Trek / Kiss 450		
26-XC	F-JJQN	B&F Funk FK-9 Smart		
26-XF		Magni M-22 Voyager		
26-XG	F-JEXW	Best Off Sky Ranger		
26-XH	F-JXCD	Magni M-16 Tandem Trainer	16-07-4364	
26-XI		Comco Ikarus C-42		
26-XK	F-JUZW	ICP MXP-740 Savannah	06-10-51-535	
		(previously used F-JXDA)		
26-XL		DTA / Dynamic 450	181	
26-XM		DTA / Diva		
26-XN		DTA Combo / Diva		
26-XS		DTA / Dynamic 15/430	248	
26-YB		Light Aero Avid Flyer	728	F-WRFQ
26-YH		Best Off Sky Ranger		
26-YI		Magni M-18 Spartan		
26-YJ		Weedhopper AX-3		
		(also reported as Eipper Quicksilver)		
26-YK		Eipper Quicksilver Sport IIS		
26-YL	F-JXPJ	Alpi Aviation Pioneer 200		
26-YM		DTA / Dynamic 15/430		
26-YN		Eipper Quicksilver MX-II Sport		
26-YQ	F-JXRX	Dova DV-1 Skylark	DV07/18	
26-YR		Eurofly Firefox		
26-YS		Magni M-16 Tandem Trainer		
26-YT		Magni M-22 Voyager	22-07-4424	
26-YU		Airsport Sonata		
26-YV		ELA Aviacion ELA-07S	0406 104 0724	
		(Re-regd 34-ADM)		
26-YY		Air Création / iXess 13		
26-ZB		Light Aero Avid Flyer Mk.IV		
26-ZE		DTA Combo / Diva		
26-ZI	F-JYCU	Alpi Aviation Pioneer 200		
26-ZJ		B&F Funk FK-9 Mk.IV SW	345	
26-ZK	F-JGXI	Aéro Services Guépy (Jabiru) 80		
26-ZL		Magni M-16 Tandem Trainer		
26-ZM		Air Création GTE 912		
26-ZT		Flight Design CT SW	08-04-08	
		(Same c/n as 26-LT - error?)		
26-ZU		ICP MXP-740 Savannah	08-01-51-672	
		(Re-regd 73-OP)		
26-ZV	F-JWFA	Magni M-22 Voyager	22-06-4864	
26-ZX		Magni M-16 Tandem Trainer		
26-AAC		ICP MXP-740 Savannah VG		
26-AAO	F-JWJR	Alpi Aviation Pioneer 300STD	17	
26-AAR		ELA Aviacion ELA-07S		
26-AAS	F-JWNZ	Alpi Aviation Pioneer 200		
26-AAY		Magni M-16 Tandem Trainer		
26-ABC		DTA Combo 584 / Diva		
26-ABD		Air Création Tanarg 912 / iXess		
		A08xxx-8018 /T09022		
26-ABF		Aeros 2 HKS		
26-ABK		DTA Combo		
26-ABL		DTA Combo		
26-ABN		Magni M-16 Tandem Trainer		
26-ABO		Air Création GT BI / Fun 18		
26-ABP		Pipistrel Sinus		
26-ABW	F-JRNU	Magni M-24 Orion	24-09-5224	I-9723
26-ACA		Magni M-16 Tandem Trainer		
26-ACC		DTA / Dynamic 15/450	456 ?	
26-ACD	F-JRPU	DTA Combo Surf 912S / Dynamic 15/450 > Magic 472.5		
26-ACF	F-JZDG	Flying Machines FM250 Vampire	FM250V0105	24-MY
		(Same c/n as 85-VY)		
26-ACH	F-JRUP	Aero East Europe MXP-155 Tayrona		
		090604/AEE/0054		
26-ACJ	F-JXRN	Aeroprakt A-22L Vision	221	11-GX
26-ACN		Bautek Skycruiser / Pico L		
26-ACP		Alpi Aviation Pioneer 300		
26-ACR		DTA (trike)		
26-ACS		Zenair CH-601 Zodiac		
		(W/o 4.5.13)		
26-ACT	F-JRJA	Alpi Aviation Pioneer 200		
		(Re-regd 08-LR)		
26-ACV	F-JSEF	B&F Funk FK-14B Polaris		
26-ACY		Best Off Nynja		
26-ADH	F-JSHT	Magni M-22 Voyager		
26-ADI	F-JSMV	Murphy Renegade II		
26-ADL		DTA Voyageur 2 912S / Magic		
26-ADN	F-JXLN	Flight Design CT SW		19-HT, 05-KD
26-ADP		Magni M-16 Tandem Trainer		
26-ADQ		TeST TST-9 Junior	09020403	
26-AEB		Best Off Sky Ranger SW		
26-AEF		DTA J-RO gyrocopter (prototype)		
26-AEG		Cosmos Phase II 582 / La Mouette Top 14.9		
26-AEH		DTA J-RO gyrocopter		
26-AEM		Air Création Tanarg		
26-AEQ		ICP MXP-740 Savannah S		
26-AEX		ICP MXP-740 Savannah S	12-06-54-0189	
26-AFA		BRM Land Africa		
26-AFF		(Quad City ?) Challenger II		
26-AFH	F-JWIX	Magni M-16 Tandem Trainer		
26-AFI	F-JUAM	DTA J-RO gyrocopter		
26-AFL		DTA J-RO gyrocopter		
26-AFM		Pipistrel Apis Bee		
26-AFN		ICP MXP-740 Savannah S		
26-AFP		Helisport CH-7 Kompress		
26-AFR	F-JUAZ	Magni M-22 Voyager		
26-AFT		Eurofly Flash		
		(damaged 13.11.14)		
26-AFU	F-JUMB	Jodel D.18	315	F-PRAO
26-AGD	F-JUPJ	Alpi Aviation Pioneer 300 Kite		
26-AGJ	F-JUTE	Magni gyrocopter		
26-AGN	F-JUZK	LCA LH212 Delta		
26-AGV		LCA LH212 Delta		
26-AGY		DTA J-RO gyrocopter		
26-AHC	F-JVRI	LCA LH212 Delta		
26-AHE	F-JVXV	DTA J-RO gyrocopter	026	
26-AHF		Best Off Nynja		
26-AHG	F-JVVP	gyrocopter		
W26-AHL		Averso Guépard 2 582 gyrocopter		
26-AHT	F-JSFD	Magni M-16 Expert		
26-AHU	F-JSWG	Magni M-24 Orion		
26-AHY	F-JTQC	Aerospool WT-9 Dynamic	DY537/2015	
26-AIA		Magni M-24 Orion		
26-AIB		Mosquito XE285		
26-AIC	F-JVAL	AirLony Slylane UL		
26-AIJ	F-JABC	Dynali H3 Easyflyer		
26-AIL	F-JABJ	Spacek SD-1 Minisport TD	86	
26-AIP	F-JART	Pennec Gaz'Aile 2	210	

27 : Eure

Reg	Call-sign	Type	c/n	Other
27-H		Synairgie / Puma BI		
27-AC		Aerospecial Airpuce		
27-BG		Eipper Quicksilver MXL II		
27-BZ		weightshift		
27-CG		JPK		
27-CP		Dynali Chickinox		
27-CV		Air Création Racer 447		
27-DG		Cosmos		
27-DH		Synairgie		
27-DK		Air Création / Quartz		
27-DV		Air Création		
27-DY		Synairgie		
27-EM		Synairgie Puma		
27-ET		Air Création / Synairgie Puma		
27-EV		Dynali Chickinox Kot-Kot III		
27-EW		Air Création / SX		
27-EX		Cosmos / La Mouette		
27-FB		Synairgie		
27-FI		Synairgie / Puma		
27-FK		Mignet HM.360 Pou-du-Ciel	01	F-WNUQ
27-FO		Synairgie / Puma		
27-FS		Air's Maestro 2		
27-FT		Synairgie Puma		
27-FZ		Cosmos		
27-GA		Weedhopper		
27-GO		Air Création Safari GT BI		
		(W/o 08.07.97)		
27-GP		Allegro 1		
27-GQ		Air Création		
27-GT		Air's		
27-GU		Air Création / SX		
27-GW		Synairgie Puma		
27-GZ		Aviasud Mistral		
27-HD		Cosmos 503 / Chronos 14		
27-HE		Aviasud Sirocco		
27-HM		Weedhopper		
27-HN		Air Création		
		(Also reported as Croses Criquet .04)		
27-HO		Allegro II		
27-HS		Europa		
27-HU		Best Off Sky Ranger		
27-HZ		ICP MXP-740 Savannah	AG 07-93-50-008	
		(Same c/n as I-3415. Agrocopteros built)		

Reg	F-reg	Type	c/n	Other
27-IC		Mignet HM.1000 Balerit		
27-IH		Aviasud AE209 Albatros		
27-IK		Evasion		
27-IN		Cosmos		
27-JF		Best Off Sky Ranger		
27-JG		RC.01 Courtonne		
27-JL		Djicat Buse'Air 150		
27-JN		Zeff		
27-JR		Protoplane Campana		
		(DBR on landing 27.4.10)		
27-JV		Air Création GTE / XP		
27-KS	F-JCLG	Zenair CH-701 STOL	A6-04-91-1060	
27-KV		Chapelet Big Bang		
27-LB		Best Off Sky Ranger		
27-LE		ICP MXP-740 Savannah	06-98-50-088	
		(Re-regd I-7334, PH-4E1, F-J . . .)		
27-LH		Aviasud AE209 Albatros 582		
27-LL	F-JCSH	ICP MXP-740 Savannah	09-97-50-057	
27-LM		DTA Dynamic 15/582	20/2000/0016	
27-LP		Mignet Pou-du-Ciel		
		(W/o 25.7.04)		
27-LQ	F-JFVP	Comco Ikarus Fox-C22		
27-MA		ICP MXP-740 Savannah	12-96-50-049	
27-MB		Brügger MB.2 Colibri	180	F-PYOI
27-MC		ICP MXP-740 Savannah	01-98-50-077	
		(Same c/n as I-7482)		
27-MJ		Cosmos Echo 12		
27-ML		Rans S-6 Coyote II		
27-MO	F-JFVD	ICP MXP-740 Savannah	08-99-50-126	
27-MQ		Synairgie		
27-NA		Aquillair / Swing 14		
27-NC		Synairgie		
27-NE		Air Création		
27-NI	F-JFVJ	ICP MXP-740 Savannah	08-99-50-125	
27-NQ		Air Création / SX		
27-NR		Air Création Twin / Kiss		
27-NT		ICP MXP-740 Savannah	02-00-51-002 (Kit 4)	
		(Same c/n as 22-IX and 35-FM)		
27-NU		Synairgie Puma		
27-NW		Cosmos		
27-NX		Air Création Twin / Kiss		
27-NY	F-JHMJ	Rans S-6 Coyote II		
27-OB	F-JCLG	ICP MXP-740 Savannah	05-00-51-012	
27-OG		Micro Aviation Pulsar III		
27-OH	F-JYJJ	ICP MXP-740 Savannah	10-00-51-026	F-JFVN
27-OI		Air Création / Kiss		
27-OL		Fisher Flying Youngster		
27-OM		Aviakit Vega		
27-ON		Cosmos Chronos 16		
27-OO		Mignet HM.360 Pou-du-Ciel	97	F-PYHC
27-OR		ICP MXP-740 Savannah	10-00-51-025	
27-OV		Zenair CH-601 Zodiac		
		(Damaged 17.7.05)		
27-PB		ICP MXP-740 Savannah		
		(Damaged 5.4.11)		
27-PE		ICP MXP-740 Savannah		
27-PL		ICP MXP-740 Savannah	01-10-51-100	
		(Re-regd 02-ZX)		
27-PM	F-JFWI	Pipistrel Sinus		
27-PO		Air Création / Kiss		
27-PQ		Fly Synthesis Storch HS		
27-PT		Synairgie / Puma B1		
27-PX		ICP Super Bingo 582	01-12-52-040	to 28-ADQ
27-PY		Synairgie / Puma B1		
27-QA		Synairgie / Puma B1		
27-QE		ICP Super Bingo	01-12-52-046	
27-QF		ICP Super Bingo 582	01-12-52-045	
27-QK		Aquilair Swing / Cosmos		
27-QN		trike / Cosmos Chronos		
27-QP		Barry MB-02 Souricette		
27-QS		Djicat Buse'Air 150		
27-QV		Comco Ikarus C-42		
27-QY		ICP MXP-740 Savannah	01-12-51-127	
27-QZ	F-JRCS	ICP Super Bingo	02-11-52-079	
27-RA		ICP Super Bingo	02-11-52-080	
27-RM	F-JFVW	ICP Bingo 4S (HKS700E)	03-06-52-116	
27-RP	F-JFWM	Magni M-14 Scout		
27-RQ	F-JZWG	ICP MXP-740 Savannah VG	03-01-51-190	
27-RT		Pipistrel Sinus		
27-RX		Air Création Racer 447 / Fun 14		
27-RY		Air Création GTE Clipper / iXess		
27-SC		ICP Bingo 4S	04-01-52-135	
27-SG		DTA Feeling 582 / Dynamic 15/430	177	
27-SL		DTA Combo / Dynamic 15/430		
27-SM		Eipper Quicksilver GT500		
		(Crashed 10.8.05)		
27-SQ		paramotor with trike		
27-SU	F-JFWV	ICP MXP-740 Savannah	02-08-51-160	
27-SX		DTA Dynamic 15/430		
27-SZ		Gdecouv'R / Cosmos		
27-TC		Air Création		
27-TD		DTA / Dynamic 15		
27-TF		DTA / Dynamic 15/430		
27-TG		ICP MXP-740 Savannah	04-07-51-322	
27-TK	F-JXVV	Air Création Racer / XP II	A02198-2196	
27-TN	F-JPFW	ICP MXP-740 Savannah ADV	04-12-51-352	
		(Carried F-JZTL 9.06)		
27-TY	F-JPNF	B&F Funk FK-9 Mk.IV Club	09-04U-261	
		(Re-regd 61-LJ)		
27-UA		Best Off Sky Ranger		
27-UE		paramotor		
27-UO		weightshift		
27-UO		ICP MXP-740 Savannah	12-97-50-072	24-GY
27-UQ		ICP MXP-740 Savannah	00-07-51-014	
27-UV	F-JZAK	ICP MXP-740 Savannah ADV	05-09-51-423	
27-VA				
27-VB	F-JZGO	Best Off Sky Ranger	SKR052671	
27-VE	F-JZFD	Vol Mediterrani VM-1 Esqual		
27-VJ		ABS Aerolight Xenon		
		(Accident 24.9.06)		
27-VK	F-JZGA	Evektor EV-97 Eurostar	2006 2711	
27-VQ		Evektor EV-97 Eurostar		
27-VR	F-JZMY	ICP MXP-740 Savannah ADV	05-11-51-452	
27-WA		ICP Bingo		
27-WG	F-JYEF	Zenair CH-601XL Zodiac		
27-WH		Humbert Tetras		
27-WI	F-JYHK	ICP Bingo 4S	05-10-52-192	
27-WL	F-JYIZ	Zenair CH-701 STOL		
27-WO		Jodel D.19		
27-WP		ICP MXP-740 Savannah		
27-WU		paramotor		
27-WV		Force paramotor		
27-WZ		Force paramotor		
27-XF	F-JXDE	ELA Aviacion ELA-07S	0707 177 0724	
27-XO	F-JXIJ	Airwave / Wizard 3		
27-XQ	F-JYAS	Aéro Services Guépard Club 503		
27-XR		ICP MXP-740 Savannah	07-07-51-626	
27-XW	F-JXPS	ICP Bingo 4S	07-11-52-214	
27-XY	F-JYWT	Air Création Tanarg 912 / iXess		
27-YB		Zenair CH-601XL Zodiac		
27-YH	F-JXXO	ICP MXP-740 Savannah	08-02-51-678	
27-YI	F-JXZE	Zenair CH-601 Zodiac		
27-YK		ICP MXP-740 Savannah VG	08-02-51-680	
		(Re-regd 78-AEN)		
27-YL	F-JZMH	Autogyro-Europe MT-03		
27-YO	F-JXXB	Flight Design CT		
27-YQ		Aeros (trike)		
27-YS		ICP MXP-740 Savannah XL	08-03-51-702	
		(Re-regd 46-DW)		
27-ZC		Take Off Merlin / Air Création iXess		
27-ZG	F-JWKR	Aeropro Eurofox		
27-ZH	F-JWLU	Aeroprakt A-22L		
27-ZI	F-JPLE	TL Ultralight TL-2000 Sting Carbon	04ST99	59-CMN
27-ZJ	F-JVNH	Zenair CH-601EU Zodiac		
27-ZO		DTA Combo (HKS700E) / Dynamic 450		
27-ZP	F-JPFK	Barry MB-04 Souris Bulle		
27-ZV	F-JWWH	ICP MXP-740 Savannah XL	09-01-51-797	
27-ZZ	F-JWXE	Aerospool WT-9 Dynamic	DY312/2009	
27-AAA		P&M Aviation Quik GT450		
27-AAB	F-JWZB	Alpi Aviation Pioneer 200		
27-AAC	F-JHIA	ATEC 122 Zephyr 2000		61-HB
27-AAE		P&M Aviation Quik GT450		
27-AAF	F-JYJC	Celier Xenon		
27-AAI		ITV paramotor		
27-AAK	F-JRDM	Autogyro-Europe MTOsport	10136S	
27-AAS		Weedhopper AX-3 Ten Years		
27-AAT		paramotor		
W27-AAW		gyrocopter		
27-ABA		ELA Aviacion ELA-07S	0707 169 0722	
27-ABG		P&M Aviation Quik GT450	8204	G-LYTB
27-ABI	F-JSAZ	Marie JPM-03 Loiret	47	W27-ABI
27-ABK		ICP MXP-740 Savannah XL	09-08-51-868	
27-ABL		ICP MXP-740 Savannah S	10-09-54-0018	
		(Same c/n as 68-AAJ)		
27-ABM		Fly Synthesis Texan Club		
27-ABP		Skywalk paramotor		
27-ABR		ICP MXP-740 Savannah S		
27-ABV		P&M Aviation QuikR 912S		
27-ACE		P&M Aviation Quik		
27-ACM		Fly Synthesis Storch HS		
27-ACN		Best Off Sky Ranger		
27-ACS		P&M Aviation Quik GT450 912S	8651	
		(C/n is wing only; trike may be 8204 ex G-LTYB)		
27-ACY	F-JPJD	Zenair CH-601XL Zodiac		
27-ADC	F-JTAO	ICP MXP-740 Savannah VG XL	11-04-51-937	
27-ADD		ATEC 321 Faeta		
27-ADG	F-JTCL	ICP MXP-740 Savannah S	11-06-54-0106	
27-ADH	F-JTCN	P&M Aviation Quik		
27-ADN		Autogyro-Europe MT-03		
27-ADO	F-JTNQ	ELA Aviacion ELA-07 Cougar	0309 259 0712	
27-ADR		Autogyro-Europe MTOsport		
27-ADW		ICP MXP-740 Savannah S	11-11-54-0131	
27-ADX		ICP MXP-740 Savannah S	11-10-54-0130	
27-AEA		Mignet HM.1100 Corduan		
27-AEB		P&M Aviation QuikR 912S		
27-AEG	F-JTZT	ICP MXP-740 Savannah S	12-06-54-0187	
27-AEI	F-JUDF	BRM Aero Bristell XL-8		
27-AEL		ICP MXP-740 Savannah S		
27-AEO		ICP MXP-740 Savannah S	11-10-54-0128	
W27-AEX		P&M Aviation (type unknown)		
27-AFD		ICP MXP-740 Savannah S		
		(Accident 22.2.14)		
27-AFE		ITV paramotor		
27-AFG	F-JXXP	P&M Aviation QuikR 912S		
27-AFH	F-JUXL	Nando Groppo Trial	00093/52	
27-AFN		Platzer Kiebitz	267	OO-F90
27-AFR		Air Création GTE Clipper 912S / iXess		
			A08016- / T02112	
27-AFV		P&M Aviation Quik GT450		
27-AGI	F-JSFM	Aero East Europe SILA 450C	140211-AEE023	D-MIHN
27-AGN	F-JSJL	ICP MXP-740 Savannah S	15-02-54-0375	
27-AHB	F-JAFS	ICP MXP-740 Savannah S	14-07-54-0342	
27-AHM		ICP MXP-740 Savannah S	14-02-54-0312	I-B785
27-AHO	F-JAUK	Autogyro Europe MTOsport	M01308	
		(Same c/s as 81-CT		
27-AJX		P&M Aviation QuikR 912S		
27-AKI		Mosquito XE 285		

28 : Eure-et-Loir

Reg	F-reg	Type	c/n	Other
28-C		Langlois Eldor		
28-D		Azur (trike)		
		(Also reported as Mustang)		
28-R		Air Création		
28-U		Skycraft AJS 2000		
28-V		Eipper Quicksilver MX		
28-AC		Aiglon 01		
28-AH		P&M Aviation Quik GT450		
28-AM		Comco Ikarus Fox-C22		
28-AO		Charcoal Raven X	HN003	
28-BG		Allegro		
28-BI		B&F Funk FK-12 Comet		
		(Re-regd 73-KD, 77-ALK, 25-UA)		
28-BJ		Air's Maestro 2		
28-BL		Air's Maestro		
28-CH		Fly Synthesis Storch		
28-CT		Eipper Quicksilver		
28-DE		JC-24 Weedhopper	9072521	
28-DQ		JC-24 Weedhopper		
28-EM		Weedhopper AX-3	0082792	OO-C18
		(Restored as OO-C18)		
28-EP		Murphy Renegade 503		
		(W28-EP noted as 'Jules Special')		

Reg	F-Reg	Type	C/n	Other
28-EV		Air Création		
28-EY		Pegasus		
28-FC		Comco Ikarus Fox-C22		
28-FJ		Allegro II		
28-FM		European Airwings Springbok		91-IF
28-FN		Top Commander Tempest		
28-FP		Air Création		
28-FQ		Air Création / Cosmos		
28-FT		Comco Ikarus Fox-C22		
28-GJ	F-JALL	JCC Aviation J.300 Joker		
28-GN		Weedhopper		
28-GS		(Murphy ?) Renegade 503		
28-GT		Air Création GT / Fun		
28-GY		Flying Machines FM.250		
		(Possibly 28-AGY!)		
28-HO		Air's Maestro 2		
28-HP		Aviasud Mistral		
28-HS		Epervier		
28-HY		Aviasud AE209 Albatros		
28-IM		Weedhopper		
28-IP		Air Création		
28-JF		Air Création		
28-JL		Murphy Renegade 503		
28-JS		Aviasud Mistral		
28-KA		Weedhopper AX-3		
28-KD		Rans S-6 Coyote II		
28-KJ		Air Création Safari GT BI		
28-KM		Comco Ikarus C-42		
28-KN		Daxiwing Falcon		
28-KS		Weedhopper AX-3		
28-KW		Murphy Renegade Spirit		
28-KZ		European Airwings Springbok 3000		
28-LB		Comco Ikarus Fox-C22		
28-LE		Pagotto Brako / Bautek Pico		
28-LH		Rans S-6 Coyote II		
28-LI		Comco Ikarus Fox-C22	9411-3637	
28-LJ		Weedhopper AX-3		71-CO
28-LV		Synairgie		
28-LW	F-JBJE	Humbert Tetras		
28-ME		Rans S-6 Coyote II		
28-MM		Aviasud Albatros		
28-MO		Comco Ikarus Fox-C22		
28-MS		Aquilair Swing		
28-MZ	F-JFOK	Rans S-6 Coyote II		
28-NA		Aviasud Mistral		
28-ND		European Airwings Maestro II		
28-NE		Air Création		
28-NM		Comco Ikarus C-42		
28-NN		Air Création GTE Clipper / XP		
28-NQ		Air Création GTE Clipper / XP		
28-NR	F-JZKJ	Rans S-6 Coyote II		
		(W/o 20.4.09)		
28-NV		Air Création GT		
28-NX		B&F Funk FK-9	76	
28-NZ		B&F Funk FK-9 (t/w)	67	
		(C/n 067 is quoted for 41-NJ/F-JPSJ)		
28-OO		Mignet HM.360?		
		(Believed in error for 27-OO)		
28-PE		B&F Funk FK-9 (t/w)	74	
		(C/n 074 quoted for 50-IT)		
28-PG	F-JPNC	Rans S-6 Coyote II		
28-PL	F-JFQS	Rans S-7 Courier		
28-PM		Comco Ikarus Fox-C22	9511-3696	
28-PO		Air Création GTE Clipper		
28-PP		III Sky Arrow 500TF	040	
		(Same c/n as 45-QP and 54-QT / F-JGAY)		
28-PT		Air Création / Quartz		
28-QC		Air Création GTE Clipper		
28-QD		Air Création GTE Clipper		
28-QE		Air Création GT BI / XP		
28-QP		Rans S-6ESD Coyote IIXL		
28-QQ	F-JCQT	B&F Funk FK-9 Mk.II (t/w)	093-TG912	
28-RB	F-JPHJ	Croses LC-6 Criquet UL		
28-RC	F-JDAS	Rans S-7 Courier		
28-RJ		B&F Funk FK-9 Mk.II		
28-RL	F-JFGF	Weedhopper		
28-RR		Comco Ikarus C-42		
28-RV		Zenair CH-701 STOL		
28-RX		Air Création		
28-SA		Comco Ikarus Fox-C22	9501-3638	
28-SI		Air Création GT BI / XP15		
28-SK	F-JBGS	Comco Ikarus C-42		
28-SL	F-JFOR	Rans S-6 Coyote II		
28-SM		Air Création GTE		
28-SN		Air Création / XP		
28-SO		Air Création		
		(Also reported as Rans S-6 Coyote, .04,		
		possibly error for 28-SQ below)		
28-SQ	F-JFTK	Rans S-6 Coyote II (See above)		
		(Re-regd 30-QX)		
28-ST		Comco Ikarus Fox-C22		
28-SX		Air Création GT BI / XP15		
28-SY		Humbert Tetras		
28-SZ		Eipper Quicksilver MX		
28-TA		Rans S-6 Coyote II		72-CL
28-TC	F-JDCX	Rans S-6 Coyote II		
28-TD		Denney Kitfox	785	F-WRXR
28-TG		Air Création Racer		
28-TK		Air's Maestro 2		
28-TQ		Rans S-6 Coyote II		
28-TU		Air Création Buggy		
28-UC		Aviasud Mistral		
28-UK		Eipper Quicksilver MX		
28-UO		Fly Synthesis Storch		
28-UR		Urban Air Lambada	10/413	
28-UT		Air Création Buggy		
W28-UV	F-JFUM	Fantasy Air Allegro		
28-UW		Air Création GT BI		
28-UY		Comco Ikarus C-42		
28-VD		Air Création GTE / XP		
28-VG		Comco Ikarus C-42		
28-VI		Micro Aviation Pulsar 582		
28-VN		Cosmos		
28-VP	F-JFOU	Humbert Tetras		
28-VQ		Aeriane Swift Light		
28-VS	F-JFSV	Tecnam P.92S Echo Super		

Reg	F-Reg	Type	C/n	Other
28-VV	F-JFSW	Evektor EV-97 Eurostar	2001 1014	
		(Same c/n as 59-CEQ / F-JFKZ)		
28-WF		Comco Ikarus Fox-C22		
28-WG	F-JYSA	Air Création Buggy / XP		
28-WH	F-JFUH	Air Création GTE Clipper / iXess 15		
28-WK		Jodel (type unknown)		
28-WN		Air Création / XP		
28-WS		Aéro Services Guépy (Jabiru) 80		
28-WT		Pipistrel Sinus		
28-WX		Adventure paramotor		
		(Accident 28.5.05)		
28-XH		Cosmos / Air Création XP		
28-XL		Comco Ikarus C-42		
28-XN	F-JFNQ	Pipistrel Sinus		
28-XP		Fly Synthesis Storch HS		
28-XR	F-JFGO	Fly Synthesis Storch		
28-XV		Fly Synthesis Storch		
		(W/o 9.6.02)		
28-XW		Fly Synthesis Storch HS	329A273	
		(Same c/n as D-MYCH)		
28-XY		Fly Synthesis Storch		I-5330
28-XZ	F-JFRP	Mignet HM.1000 Balerit	127	59-UG
28-YA		Remos G.3 Mirage		
28-YE	F-JFOQ	Fly Synthesis Storch HS		
28-YI		Alpi Aviation Pioneer 300		
28-YM		Light Aero Avid Flyer		
28-YO	F-JPAO	Zenair CH-601UL Zodiac	6-9110	
		(Re-regd 58-HO)		
28-YT	F-JPKF	Air Création GTE Clipper (Chapelet mod.) / iXess	A03025-3025	
28-YV		Magni M-16 Tandem Trainer		
28-YW		Air Création / Quartz SX		
28-YX		Aviakit Vega		
28-YZ		Fly Synthesis Storch		
28-ZA		Fly Synthesis Wallaby		
28-ZB	F-JPAB	Urban Air UFM-13 Lambada		
28-ZD	F-JPAK	Aviakit Vega		
		(Also reported as F-JFAK)		
28-ZE	F-JPAF	ICP Super Bingo	03-01-52-089	
28-ZF		Weedhopper		
28-ZN	F-JPEZ	Aéro Services Guépy Club 582T		
28-ZO	F-JXCX	European Airwings Springbok Confort		
28-ZP	F-JPAV	ICP Super Bingo	01-12-52-041	
		(Re-regd 77-AYT)		
28-ZQ		Air Création / iXess		
28-ZS		Eipper Quicksilver MX		
28-ZU		Weedhopper AX-3		
28-ZV	F-JPEK	Remos G.3 Mirage RS	136	
28-ZW		Fly Synthesis Storch HS		
28-ZZ		Magni M-16 Tandem Trainer		
28-AAA		Aquilair		
28-AAD	F-JFQT	Aéro Services Guépard		
28-AAG	F-JXRC	Guérin G1		
28-AAM	F-JPEU	Impulse 100FIX	05	
		(Re-regd OO-F55 6.07)		
28-AAN	F-JFOS	Aéro Services Guépy Club 503		
28-AAO		Mignet HM.1000 Balerit	49	Fr.Mil F-MUBC
28-AAR		ICP MXP-740 Savannah	02-04-51-143	
28-AAT		Cosmos Chronos		
28-AAU	F-JKFC	Best Off Sky Ranger		
28-AAW	F-JPED	Air Création GTE / iXess		
28-AAX	F-JPHN	Remos G.3 Mirage RS	130	D-MKKK
28-AAY	F-JPHA	Fly Synthesis Storch HS	337A-281	
28-AAZ		Aquilair Swing 14		
28-ABB	F-JPHI	Alpi Aviation Pioneer 300		
28-ABC	F-JPOC	Fly Synthesis Texan Top Class		
28-ABD	F-JPHF	Fly Synthesis Storch		
28-ABE		Humbert Tetras		
28-ABF		Air Création / Aeros Stranger		
28-ABK		DTA / Dynamic 16/503		
28-ABM		ATEC 321 Faeta		
28-ABO		Air Création GT BI / XP		
28-ABT		Best Off Sky Ranger		
28-ABW		ICP MXP-740 Savannah	00-04-51-007	
		(Same c/n as 41-SE)		
28-ABZ		DTA / Dynamic 582		
		(Accident 28.9.06)		
28-ACA		Comco Ikarus C-42		
28-ACB	F-JFUH	Air Création GTE Clipper / iXess		
28-ACF	F-JFUX	Fly Synthesis Texan Top Class		
28-ACI		Cosmos Phase III / La Mouette Top 12		
		(Crashed 7.11.04)		
28-ACJ		Mignet HM.1000 Balerit	64	17-FN
28-ACN	F-JPKG	Humbert Tetras		
28-ACO		Vol Mediterrani VM-1 Esqual		
28-ACP		P&M Aviation Quik 912S	8089	
28-ACS	F-JPKL	Paille-en-Queue	304	
		(Noted as Fly Synthesis Storch 7.07)		
28-ACT	F-JFTD	Aviasud AE209 Albatros		
28-ACU	F-JPKR	Light Aero Avid Flyer	264	F-PZUD, F-WZUD(2)
		(Re-regd 78-ZZ, but still active as 28-ACU, 7.11)		
28-ACV		Light Aero Avid Flyer Mk.IV		
28-ACW		Fly Synthesis Storch		
28-ACX		Comco Ikarus C-42B		
28-ACZ		Air Création GTE Clipper 912		
28-ACY	F-JPOS	Pipistrel Virus		
28-ADB	F-JPOF	Fly Synthesis Texan Top Class	44	
28-ADC		Aeroprakt A-20R-912 Griffon	023	
28-ADE	F-JPOI	Evektor EV-97 Eurostar	2005 2402	
28-ADH		Flight Design CT		
28-ADP	F-JPUE	Best Off Sky Ranger		
28-ADQ		ICP Super Bingo 582	01-12-52-040	27-PX
28-ADR	F-JPST	Fly Synthesis Texan Top Class	57	
28-ADT	F-JZLC	Air Création GTE / XP		
28-AEF	F-JZGC	Evektor EV-97 Eurostar	2001 0914	
28-AEG	F-JFBV	Sauper J.300 Joker kit		
28-AEN		Fly Synthesis Storch		
28-AEP	F-JZIM	Klöti RK 02 gyrocopter (f/p)		
28-AEQ		Fly Synthesis Storch		
28-AET		Fly Synthesis Storch		
28-AEX		Fly Synthesis Texan Top Class		
28-AEY		Adventure Axis Vega		
28-AEZ		Aéro Services Guépy (Jabiru) 80T		
28-AFA		ITV Tomahawk paramotor		
28-AFG	F-JZRX	Aviakit Vega 3000		

Reg	Call-sign	Type	c/n	Previous
28-AFJ	F-JYBA	Fly Synthesis Texan Top Class		
28-AFM		Paramania Action paramotor		
28-AFP		Air Création Tanarg / iXess		
28-AFQ		Air Création GTE Clipper / XP		
28-AFS		Aeropro Eurofox		
28-AFT		Fly Synthesis Wallaby		
28-AGA		Fly Synthesis Storch		
28-AGB		Aéro Services Guépy 582		
28-AGC		ICP MXP-740 Savannah	10-00-51-027	
28-AGE		Micro Aviation Pulsar III		
28-AGG		Comco Ikarus C-42		
28-AGK		Murphy Renegade Spirit		
28-AGO	F-JYNK	Evektor EV-97 Eurostar	2007 2924	
		(Same c/n as 91-AMP / F-JYNK)		
28-AGP	F-JPDO	Aéro Services Guépy 582		
28-AGQ	F-JYSF	Fly Synthesis Storch HS		
28-AGT	F-JYKY	Zenair CH-601UL Zodiac		
28-AGV	F-JXIT	Jabiru J170		
		(W/o 4.2.10) (Same call-sign as 28-AGW, transferred?)		
28-AGW	F-JXIT	Jabiru J170		
28-AGZ		Aéro Services Guépard (Jabiru) 50T		
28-AHA	F-JPHJ	Croses CLP		
28-AHG		Eipper Quicksilver MXL III Sport		
28-AHI		Air Création / Quartz		
28-AHO		P&M Aviation Quik 912S		
28-AHP		Comco Ikarus C-42	9804-6094	
28-AHQ	F-JXVQ	Fly Synthesis Storch S		
28-AHR	F-JZCI	Aerospool WT-9 Dynamic	DY123/2006	
		(Re-regd 77-BFR)		
28-AHU		Fly Synthesis Storch		
28-AHV	F-JJUR	Zenair CH-601 Zodiac		
28-AHW		Alpi Aviation Pioneer 200		
28-AHX	F-JXQF	Dyn'Aéro MCR-01 UL	329	
28-AHY		Evektor EV-97R Eurostar	2008 3220	
28-AIC	F-JBYI	Fly Synthesis Storch		
28-AIG	F-JWGI	Sonex Aircraft Xenos		
28-AIK		Fly Synthesis Storch		
28-AIM		Fly Synthesis Storch		
28-AIQ		Fly Synthesis Storch S		
28-AIR	F-JWCN	Evektor EV-97 Eurostar	2008 3313	
28-AIS	F-JWHI	Fly Synthesis Storch		
28-AIV	F-JWGK	Fly Synthesis Storch		
28-AIY	F-JWCV	Flight Design CT SW	D-08-05-21	
28-AIZ	F-JWDB	Flight Design CT SW		
28-AJC		paramotor		
28-AJE		Fly Synthesis Storch S		
28-AJG	F-JJWG	Dyn'Aéro MCR-01	244	
28-AJH	F-JWII	Flight Design CT LS	F-08-07-21	
		(Re-regd 39-KX, 30-RK)		
28-AJI		Eipper Quicksilver GT400		
28-AJJ	F-JWRE	Magni M-24 Orion		
28-AJM		Aéro Services Super Guépard		
28-AJN		Eipper Quicksilver MX Sprint		
		(Type confirmed 9.13; also reported as Aéro Services Guépard but this is probably an error for 28-AJM)		
28-AJO		Fly Synthesis Storch		
28-AJP	F-JKFI	ICP MXP-740 Savannah VG	01-04-51-064	
28-AJT		Magni M-16 Tandem Trainer		
28-AJV		Eipper Quicksilver GT400		
28-AJW		Zenair CH-601 Zodiac		
28-AKB		Ekolot KR-030 Topaz	030-03-03	
W28-AKC		Dyn'Aéro MCR-01 ULC	297	
28-AKH		Aeropro Eurofox		
28-AKJ	F-JZRI	Air Création Tanarg / iXess 13		
28-AKK	F-JXQO	Comco Ikarus C-42C		
28-AKL		Comco Ikarus C-42		
28-AKM		Jodel D.18	125	F-POMF, F-WOMF 49-NF
28-AKO	F-JZDN	Fly Synthesis Storch		
28-AKR	F-JRAR	Flight Design CT SW	06-09-02	T7-MOR
28-AKS		paramotor		
28-ALG		BRM Land Africa		
28-ALH	F-JYUK	Zenair CH-601TD Zodiac (t/w)		
28-ALM		« Velos »		
28-ALN	F-JXBV	Zlin Savage Cruiser		
28-ALP	F-JRLN	Air Création Tanarg / Bionix		
W28-ALQ		Sofrec Mosquito Spad		
28-ALR	F-JSGM	Haase/Plätzer Kiebitz	168	W28-ALR, D-MRII
28-ALS		Eipper Quicksilver MX II		
28-ALT		Fly Synthesis Storch		
28-ALU		APEV e-Demoiselle (Santos Dumont Demoiselle replica)		
28-ALW		Air Création Tanarg / Bionix	A10018-10013	
28-ALX	F-JRST	Fly Synthesis Texan Club 450	F90118307-450	
28-ALY		Eipper Quicksilver MX Sport		
28-ALZ	F-JYPY	Djicat Buse'Air 150		
28-AMA		Fly Synthesis Storch	2004/344	OO-E54
28-AMB	F-JRTR	Aveko VL-3 Sprint		
28-AMD		Comco Ikarus Fox-C22		
28-AMH		Zenair CH-601XL Zodiac		
W28-AMI		Pascal Ollino OLO 01 gyrocopter		
28-AMN		Air Création GTE 503SE / Fun 450		
28-AMX		Magni M-24 Orion	24-10-6064	
28-AMZ	F-JEMC	Aviasud Mistral		
28-ANA		Fly Synthesis Storch		
28-AND		Apco Play paramotor		
28-ANF		ITV Dolpo paramotor		
28-ANG		P&M Aviation QuikR 912S		
28-ANH	F-JUBZ	Aviasud Mistral		
28-ANK	F-JFPU	Marie JPM-03 Loiret	30	
28-ANO		Pottier P.130ULS		
28-ANS	F-JFUI	ATEC 321 Faeta	F070504A	61-LN
28-ANY		Magni M-22 Voyager		
28-AOB		Autogyro-Europe MTOsport		
28-AOD		Aeroandinas A-82 (MSL Aero Type H)	AA-02-10-82-042	
28-AOF	F-JUUS	Aviasud Mistral		
28-AOG	F-JARB	Fly Synthesis Storch		
28-AOU	F-JTTR	Zenair CH-601UL Zodiac		
28-APC	F-JGSG	Fly Synthesis Storch HS (Jabiru)		
28-APG	F-JWIB	B&F Funk FK-14B Polaris	14-086	
		(Same call-sign as 57-ATZ)		
28-APJ	F-JTQV	Fly Synthesis Texan Club	F2CC1440C01B	
28-APL		APEV Demoichelle (electric power)		
28-APP	F-JTXU	P&M Aviation Quik GTR Explorer	8615	
28-AQA		Sherwood Ranger	ST49	
28-AQE	F-JVMP	Jabiru J450		
28-AQF	F-JRLN	Air Création Tanarg / BioniX	A13027-13027 / T09056	
28-ARP		Plätzer Kiebitz		
28-DNB		Aveko VL-3 Sprint		

29 : Finistère

Reg	Call-sign	Type	c/n	Previous
29-B		Therville Scout		
29-H		Eipper Quicksilver MX		
29-AA		Cosmos Bidulm		
29-AF		Air Création		
29-AX		Air Création		
29-AZ		Flipper		
29-BB		Weedhopper AX-3		
29-BI		Air Création		
29-BK		Air Création		
29-CD		Cosmos / Echo 12		
29-CF	F-JHMX	Rans S-6 Coyote II		
29-CG		Rans S-6 Coyote II		
29-CH		Rans S-12 Airaile		
29-CP		Air Création GT BI 582S		
29-CR		Air Création		
29-CS		Mignet HM.14 Pou-du-Ciel		
29-CW		Weedhopper AX-3		
29-CZ		Weedhopper AX-3		
29-DJ		Rans S-6 Coyote II		
29-DL		Synairgie Dauphin Quicky		
29-EB		Rans S-6ES Coyote II		
		(Accident 3.6.04)		
29-EC		Magni M-16 Tandem Trainer 914		
29-EG		Pennec-Lucas Navion Hydroplane	01	
29-EM		TEAM Mini-MAX		
29-EX	F-JHMS	Rans S-6 Coyote II		
29-FJ		Air Création		
		(Damaged 30.6.01)		
29-FM		JCC Aviation J.300 Joker		
29-FO	F-JHNY	Rans S-6 Coyote II		
29-FY	F-JHQI	Rans S-6 Coyote II (t/w)		
29-GH		Cosmos Phase II	916	
29-GI	F-JHRH	Aéro Services Guépy (Jabiru)		
29-GQ		JORA Jora		
29-GU		Air Création Racer 447 / Fun 14		
29-GX		Chapelet Lazer		
29-GY		Air Création Buggy		
		(Re-regd 35-HQ)		
29-HC		Rans S-6 Coyote II (Diesel)		
29-HD		Aviasud Mistral		
29-HH		Air Création / SX II		
29-HN		Cosmos Bidulm Alto 148		
		(Crashed 25.7.04)		
29-HS		Rans S-6 Coyote II		
29-IA	F-JZMR	Brugger Colibri ULM	180	F-JHOO, F-PYOI
29-IC		Zenair CH-601UL Zodiac 'Quick'		
29-IJ	F-JHPF	Zenair CH-601 Zodiac		
29-IK	F-JTMB	Best Off Sky Ranger	SKR 0216097	F-JHPC
29-IN		Pegasus Quantum 15		
29-IP		Aerotrophy TT2000 STOL		
29-IR	F-JHOO	Embree/Monnett Sonerai IIL	114389	I-4606, N348KE
29-IW		Air Création / SX		
29-IZ	F-JYFU	Urban Air UFM-13 Lambada	040/13-2004	
29-JA		Jodel D.19	108T	F-PZBB
29-JH		B&F Funk FK-12 Comet		
29-PO		Cosmos		
29-PQ		Air Création / Kiss		
29-PS	F-JHQI	Phantom Aeronautics Phantom		
29-PT		Rans S-6 Coyote II		
29-PX		Autogyro-Europe MT-03		
29-QC		Chapelet Lazer		
29-QI	F-JYKV	P&M Aviation Quik GT 912	8117	
		(Re-regd 29-VN)		
29-QL	F-JYMW	Zenair CH-601 Zodiac		
29-QO		ICP MXP-740 Savannah		
29-QQ	F-JXTX	Colomban MC-30 Luciole	1	
29-QR	F-JYVZ	Magni M-16 Tandem Trainer		
29-RL		Best Off Sky Ranger		
29-RM	F-JZSZ	Junkers Profly Junka UL		
29-RS		Weedhopper Europa II		
29-RU	F-JHNK	Aerosviluppi AS.10		
29-SO		Humbert Tétras		
29-SQ		Dudel Nucleon paramotor		
29-SR		Magni M-16 Tandem Trainer		
29-SS		Pipistrel Sinus		
29-TB	F-JXRO	Pipistrel Virus		83-ADE
29-TR		Pipistrel Virus		
		(Error for 29-TB ?)		
29-TS	F-JYKV	P&M Aviation QuikR 912S	8543	G-CGPM
		(Also reported as 39-TS)		
29-TZ	F-JHNY	Rans S-6 Coyote II		
29-UJ		ITV Boxer paramotor		
29-UM	F-JHNK	Aero Designs Pulsar (t/w)	379	LX-GER
29-UN	F-JTJT	Autogyro-Europe Calidus 09		
29-UO	F-JZMF	Didier Pti'tavion		
29-VF	F-JVDX	Pipistrel Virus	581VN912	
29-VN		P&M Aviation Quik GT 912	8117	29-QI
29-XL		DTA Combo		
29-XY		Fly Synthesis Storch HS		I-5330
		(Latest ex 95-QD / F-JBDJ ?)		
29-YD		Dyn'Aéro MCR-01 UL		

30 : Gard

Reg	Call-sign	Type	c/n	Previous
30-U		Funfly		
30-AD		Eipper Quicksilver MX II		
30-AG		Ultralair JC-31D Weedhopper	14072027	
		(W/o 10.12.05)		
30-AO		(Aviasud ?) Sirocco		
30-BM		JC-24 Weedhopper Europa II		
30-BN		Air Création / SX		
30-BP		Air Création Racer		
30-BX		Dynali Chickinox		
W30-CE	F-JAAS	Weedhopper AX-3 Ultracam		
30-CH		Pegasus		
30-CN		Dynali Chickinox		
30-CP		Tefou (trike)		17-AR
30-CT		Air Création / Quartz SX		
30-CX		Air Création		

Reg	Call-sign	Type	c/n	Notes
30-DC		Dynali Chickinox		
30-DD		Eipper Quicksilver MX		
30-DE		Air Création		
30-DF		Mignet HM.1000 Balerit	55	
30-DH		JC-24 Weedhopper Europa II		
30-DK		Air Création		
30-DN		Weedhopper	B1072931	
30-DP		Rans S-6 Coyote II		
30-DQ		Beaufils SE.5A replica	A4850	
30-DS		Air Création		
30-DU		Eipper Quicksilver MX		
30-EB		Dynali Chickinox		
30-ED		Air Création		
30-EF		Air Création Plus		
30-EG		Air Création / Quartz		
30-EH		Weedhopper		
30-EO		Ultralair Weedhopper		
30-EP		Aviasud AE209 Albatros		
30-EY		Cosmos Helios		
30-FD		Rossi 503S Pegasus		
30-FF		Weedhopper		
30-FJ		Criquet		
30-FN		Air Création GTi		
30-FT		Air Création		
30-FU		Eipper Quicksilver GT		
30-FV		Aquilair		
30-FX		Air Création GTE / XP		
30-FY		La Mouette		
30-GB		Air Création / SX		
W30-GE		Solar Wings Pegasus / Quasar IITC	6662	G-MYOD
30-GH		TEAM Mini-MAX		
30-GJ		Dynali Chickinox Kot-Kot		
30-GO		Best Off Sky Ranger		
30-GU		Best Off Sky Ranger		
30-GX		Fly Synthesis Storch		
30-GY		(Technic Moto ?) Mustang		
30-HB		Air Création / XP		
30-HF		Lascaud Bifly		
30-HH		Eipper Quicksilver MX IIA		
30-HI		Air Création Safari GT BI / Quartz SX16		
30-HL		Air Création Safari GT BI 462 / iXess		
30-HN	F-JCUO	Zenair CH-701 STOL		
30-HR		Zenair CH-701 STOL		
30-HT		Air Création Twin / XP		
30-HU		Croses EAC-3 Pouplume		
30-HV		Hipps Superbirds J-3 Kitten		
30-IE		Aviasud AE209 Albatros		
30-IF		Air Création Twin 503		
30-IG		Air Création GTE Clipper / XP		
30-IH		Eipper Quicksilver MX Sprint II		66-FC
30-JA		Jabiru UL30-KA		
30-JJ	F-JJXX	Slepcev Storch		F-JJEY
30-JL		Air Création		
30-JO		Fly Synthesis Storch		
30-JP		Raj Hamsa X'Air		
30-JS		Jodel D.92	711	F-PYKV
30-JY(1)	F-JJEW	Jabiru UL		
		(W/o 25.7.03)		
30-JY(2)	F-JJEW	Fly Synthesis Texan	2004-035	
30-JZ		Jabiru		
30-KC		Mignet Pou-du-Ciel		
30-KO	F-JJFY	Vidor Asso VI Junior		
30-KP		Dynali Chickinox Kot-Kot		
30-KT		Raj Hamsa X'Air		
30-KZ		Weedhopper AX-3		
30-LL	F-JJHH	Jabiru UL		
30-LM		Best Off Sky Ranger		
		(Forced landing 10.11.06)		
30-LV		ICP Super Bingo	03-05-52-108	
30-ME		Best Off Sky Ranger		
		(accident 31.5.12)		
30-MG	F-JJNM	Aeroprakt A-22		
30-MS		type unknown (Breezy?)		
30-NA		Best Off Sky Ranger		
30-NR		Pipistrel Sinus		
30-OC		Lobb Falco 95		
30-OG		SMAN Petrel		
30-OO		Air Création GTE / iXess		
30-OQ		Evektor EV-97 Eurostar		
30-OX		Rans S-6ES Coyote II		
30-PF		Ultralair JC-31 Weedhopper Premier AX-3		
		(Accident 1.12.07)		
30-PJ		Jabiru		
30-PO		Alpaero (Noin) Exel		
		(W/o 19.8.12)		
30-PU		Celier Xenon		
30-QI	F-JWIW	Humbert La Moto-du-Ciel		
30-QM		paramotor		
30-QO		Alpi Aviation Pioneer 300		
30-QP	F-JWBO	Flight Design CT LS	F-08-06-22	
		(Re-regd 13-WI)		
30-QQ	F-JWAR	Alpi Aviation Pioneer 200		
30-QT	F-JGSA	Murphy Maverick		
30-QX	F-JFTK	Rans S-6 Coyote II		28-SQ
30-QZ		Rans S-6ES Coyote II 0904-1610/PFA/204-14330		G-WYLE
30-RE		B&F Funk FK-9 Mk.IV Utility	09-04-301	OO-F35
		(Re-regd SE-VSZ 2.12)		
30-RI		Microlève Corsario Mk.5		
30-RK	F-JWII	Flight Design CT LS	F-08-07-21	39-KX, 28-AJH
30-RL		Air Création GTE / XP		
30-SB		Best Off Sky Ranger V-Max		
30-SK		DTA / Magic		
30-SL	F-JSHV	Microlève Corsario		
30-SN		Fisher Youngster		
30-SQ	F-JEGS	ELA Aviacion ELA-07 Cougar		
30-SS	F-JSKX	Jodel D.18		
30-SW		Air Création Safari GT BI		
		(accident 18.11.12)		
30-TB	F-JSVN	MSL Aero Type H		F-JEWN
		(W/o 25.12.15)		
30-TC		Eurofly FB5 Star Light		
30-TG		Rans S-6 Coyote II		
30-TI	F-JTKC	Flight Design CT LS	F-11-08-12	
30-TP	F-JTZR	ICP MXP-740 Savannah S	12-05-54-0182	
30-TY		trike / La Mouette Oryx 14		
30-UD	F-JUWI	Eurofly Flash Light		
30-UF		Helisport CH-77 Ranabot		
30-UN	F-JVUG	Eurofly Flash		
W30-VB		Denney Kitfox		
30-VN	F-JATU	Celier Xenon		

31 : Haute-Garonne

Reg	Call-sign	Type	c/n	Notes
31-T		Eipper Quicksilver MX		
31-AA		Pegasus Quantum		
31-AC		Aircopter A3C		
W31-AG(1)		gyrocopter		
31-AG(2)		Aircopter DJP 2000		
		(Different from the first gyrocopter to use these marks)		
31-AH		Humbert Tetras 912B		
31-AI	F-JIAI	B&F Funk FK-9	09-116	
31-AJ		Gyrotec DF-02		
31-AL		Ehroflug Coach II	015K	
31-AM		Humbert Tetras 912B		
31-AO	F-JIAO	B&F Funk FK-14 Polaris	14-002	D-MWSG
		(Re-regd OO-F34 9.06)		
31-AP		Baroudeur (trike)		
31-AQ		Ultralair Weedhopper AX-3		
		(Damaged 12.2 04)		
31-AW		gyrocopter		
31-AX		Cosmos / Aeros		
31-BA		gyrocopter		
31-BH		Urban Air UFM-13 Lambada		
31-BI	F-JIBI	B&F Funk FK-9 Mk.III	09-03-153	
		(Marks used by B&F Funk on FK-9 and FK-14 demonstrators)		
31-BK	F-JICA	Pipistrel Sinus		
31-BM		Pipistrel Sinus		
31-BO	F-JIBO	Pipistrel Virus		
31-BP	F-JIKG	B&F Funk FK-9 Mk.III (t/w, Vija XK9 engine demonstrator)		
		(Re-regd 60-TN)	09-03-152	F-JIBP
31-BQ	F-JIBQ	B&F Funk FK-9 Mk.IV Club		
31-BR		Aéro Services Guépard 912		
31-BS		B&F Funk FK-9 Mk.III		
		(Damaged 30.5.01)		
31-BU	F-JIBU	B&F Funk FK-12 Comet	12-058	
		(W/o)		
31-BV	F-JIBV	B&F Funk FK-14 Polaris	14-010	
31-BW		B&F Funk FK-9 Mk.III		
31-BY		Best Off Sky Ranger		
31-CD		Weedhopper		
31-CH		Autogyro-Europe MT-03		W31-CH
31-CI		gyrocopter		
31-CK		Cosmos HKS700E / La Mouette Ipsos 14		
31-CL		Rans S-6 Coyote II		
31-CS		Averso AX.02 Guépard gyrocopter		W31-CS
31-CU		Rans S-7 Courier		
		(W/o 10.11.08)		
31-CW	F-JIGK	Sauper J.300 Joker (Vija engine)		
31-DE	F-JIDE	B&F Funk FK-12 Comet	12-012	
		(Re-regd 77-APO)		
31-DH	F-JIDH	Flight Design CT SW		
		(Same c/n and call-sign as 82-CN)		
31-DL		Eipper Quicksilver MX		
31-DR		Delpech MD.03 Transat amphibian		
31-DS		ICP MXP-740 Savannah	12-00-51-038	
31-DT		Le Raitelet	CQR/1	
31-DV		Eipper Quicksilver MX II	1053	
31-DW	F-JIDW	B&F Funk FK-14B Polaris (t/w)	14-045	
		(Re-regd 18-OF)		
31-EJ		Eipper Quicksilver		
31-EL		TeST TST-14M Bonus		
31-EN		JC-31D Weedhopper		
31-ET		Dallach Voltige		
31-EW		Humbert Tetras		
31-EX	F-JZSI	Flight Design CT-2K		
31-FB		Azure YC 01 gyrocopter (homebuilt)		
		(Accident 14.12.07)		
W31-FE		Le Gallen LLG.24	01	
31-FK	F-JZWW	Aéro Services Super Guépard 912		
31-FN		Air Création		
31-FQ	F-JIFQ	B&F Funk FK-9 Mk.IV Club	04-U-262	
31-FS	F-JIFS	B&F Funk FK-12 Comet	12-044	
		(Re-regd 45-YP)		
31-FV	F-JZYN	B&F Funk FK-9 Mk.IV	305	
31-FZ		Fly Synthesis Storch HS		
31-GC		FDA Kit Air Copter AC Wan		
31-GJ		B&F Funk FK-9 Mk.IV	247	45-VD
		(W/o 30.5.08)		
31-GK	F-JWCH	Humbert Tetras	1124?	
31-GS		Fisher Koala		
31-GV	F-JYKY	Humbert Tetras 912B	1124?	
31-GW		Averso AX.02 Guépard gyrocopter		
		(also reported as Cosmos Phase II 582)		
31-GX		Denney Kitfox		
31-HA		Denney Kitfox		
31-HC		Dragon Light	007	
		(Dismantled .03)		
31-HD		Celier Xenon		
31-HE		AIRIC 01 gyrocopter		
31-HG		Denney Kitfox		
31-HI		Denney Minifox		
31-HK		Autogyro-Europe MT-03	F07G02	
W31-HO		Aircopter A3C		
31-HP	F-JYUM	Humbert Tetras		
31-HU		PAP 1000 / Tomahawk 2 paramotor		
31-IJ		ULM Services Frelon		
31-IQ		Micro Aviation Pulsar III		
31-IT		Delpech MD.04 Airland		
		(W/o 5.03)		
31-IW		Alpi Avn Pioneer 200		
31-IZ		Delfort gyrocopter		
31-JE		Aviasud Mistral		
		(Damaged 11.6.01)		
31-JG	F-JXOV	Flight Design CT SW	07-11-03	
31-JK	F-JXRT	Weedhopper		
31-JP		Air Création Safari GT BI 582		
		(Crashed 21.10.06)		
31-JT		ESPACE Sensation		
31-JV		Air Création / XP11		
31-JY		Aviasud AE209 Albatros		
31-JZ		Tecnam P.92 Echo		W31-JZ
31-KC	F-JXUL	B&F Funk FK-9 Mk.IV SW	356	
		(Re-regd 974-LP)		

Reg	Call-sign	Type	c/n	Other
31-KF		type unknown (high wing, 3-axis)		
31-KJ		Rans S-7 Courier		
31-KL		2-seat gyrocopter		
31-KP		Best Off Sky Ranger 503		
31-KR		Zenair CH-701 STOL (t/w)		
31-KT	F-JIKT	Humbert Tetras		
31-KU	F-JXWP	Flight Design CT LS	08-01-23	24-RM
		(Same call-sign as 31-KW below ?)		
31-KW	F-JXWP	Flight Design CT LS		
		(Same call-sign as 31-KU above ?)		
31-KX		Aeropro Eurofox		
31-LB	F-JILB	B&F Funk FK-9 Mk.III		
		(Damaged 25.9.06; also reported as Mk.IV)		
31-LD	F-JXCI	Aerospool WT-9 Dynamic		
31-LI		Celier Xenon		
W31-LJ		Air Copter Monosport		
31-LO		Best Off Sky Ranger		
31-LR		ICP MXP-740 Savannah		
31-LU		Kappa 77 KP-2U Sova		
31-LV		B&F Funk FK-9		
31-LY	F-JWMH	Alpi Aviation Pioneer 200		
31-ME		gyrocopter		
31-MF		Cosmos Echo 12		
W31-MR		Averso Guépard II XJ-01 gyrocopter		
31-MS		Averso AX.02 Guépard gyrocopter		
31-MU	F-JSRJ	AirMax SeaMax M-22		
31-MV	F-JWSY	Flight Design CT LS	F-09-02-09	
31-MW		Deramecourt 900 (balloon)		
W31-MY		Averso Guépard II XJ-01 gyrocopter		
31-NA	F-JZTF	ATEC 122 Zephyr		
31-NE	F-JXXF	ESPACE Sensation		
31-NG		Aircopter gyrocopter		
31-NJ	F-JRCW	Best Off Sky Ranger		
31-NK	F-JRCO	Autogyro-Europe MT-03		
31-NL	F-JRDL	Corvus Phantom	CA-21/024	
31-NM	F-JRDO	Flight Design CT LS Supralight	E-09-06-02	
31-NO	F-JRDP	B&F Funk FK-14B Polaris (t/w)	14-094	
31-NT	F-JRHT	Flight Design CT LS	F-09-09-03	
		(Re-regd 44-AQW)		
31-NU		gyrocopter		
31-NX	F-JRJH	Flight Design CT LS	F-09-10-06	
31-NZ	F-JRJT	B&F Funk FK-9 ELA	403	
31-OA		Celier Xenon		
31-OG		Marcellin M5 gyrocopter		W31-OG
31-OI	F-JHDK	Denney Kitfox		
31-OO		Zenith Baroudeur 2000		
31-OP	F-JIOP	B&F Funk FK-9 Explorer (t/w)	03-U-191	
31-OU		gyrocopter		
31-OV		Celier Xenon		
31-OW		Magni M-14 Scout		
31-OX		Henry Fabre Hydroplane replica		
31-OY		Averso Guépard II XJ-01 gyrocopter		W31-OY
31-PC		Air Copter A3C		
31-PG	F-JFSN	Denney Kitfox		
31-PL		Zenair CH-601UL Zodiac		
31-PQ	F-JIPQ	Humbert Tetras		
31-PR		gyrocopter		
W31-PW		gyrocopter		
31-PY		Celier Xenon		
31-QC	F-JRNP	Aveko VL-3B-3	VL3-56	83-AHH
31-QG		M'Py/Paramania Fusion paramotor		
31-QJ	F-JSPV	AirLony Skylane UL		
31-QM		Aitrbet Girabet 2 Sport gyrocopter		
31-QN	F-JSRC	Jodel D.185 (Vija engine)		
31-QO		Pipistrel Taurus		
		(Cr and destroyed in Spain 31.10.11)		
31-QS		Deramecourt 740 HAFB		
31-QW	F-JSUG	B&F Funk FK-9 ELA	05-436	
31-QZ		ELA Aviacion ELA-07		
31-Q?	F-JSMB	Flight Design CT Supralight	10-11-04	
		(Re-regd 35-MN/F-JSMB and later OO-H48 ?)		
31-RA		Alpi Aviation Pioneer 200		
31-RD(1)	F-JWOY	Aeroprakt A-22		
		(accident 15.6.12)		
31-RD(2)	F-JWOH	Guerin G1		
		(noted 7.11.15)		
31-RM	F-JTEW	Flight Design CT Supralight	E-11-05-01	
		(Same call-sign as 35-LZ)		
31-RP		gyrocopter		
		(previously reported as Humbert Tetras 912BS)		
31-SB		ICP MXP-740 Savannah	01-11-51-116	
31-SM		gyrocopter		
31-SO	F-JTRJ	Aéro Services SG.10A		
W31-SP		gyrocopter		
		(W/o 18.10.03)		
31-SQ	F-JTLZ	B&F Funk FK-9 ELA Remorqueur	459	
W31-ST		gyrocopter		
31-TA		Pagotto Brako gyro		
		(previously reported as ICP MXP-740 Savannah)		
31-TH(1)		Aviasud AE209 Albatros		
31-TH(2)	F-JUAD	B&F Funk FK-14B2 Le Mans	14-144	
31-TK		Rans S-6 Coyote II		
31-TN		Jodel D.185		
31-TU		Air Création GTE Clipper		
31-UB		Air Création Racer 447 / Fun 14		
31-UM		Weedhopper AX-3		
31-UZ		B&F Funk FK-9 Mk.III		
31-VB		Averso gyrocopter		
31-VC		DTA J-RO gyrocopter		
31-VD		Averso AX.02 Guépard gyrocopter	10	
31-VE	F-JIVE	B&F Funk FK-9 Mk.III (t/w)	09-03-112	
31-VF		Comco Ikarus C-42		
31-VG		Averso Guépard 503 gyrocopter		
31-VH		Cena 2 gyrocopter		
31-VI		Pierre Cena PC3		
31-VK		Air Copter DJP3		
31-VL	F-JIVL	Averso AX.02 Guépard 503 gyrocopter		
31-VM		gyrocopter		
31-VN		gyrocopter		
31-VP	F-JIVP	B&F Funk FK-9 Mk.III	09-03-128	
31-VT		gyrocopter		
31-VU		Georges Pouilles gyrocopter		
31-VV		A. Lagarde gyrocopter		
31-WF	F-JVAY	Corvus Fusion		
31-WI		Farrington Twinstarr gyrocopter	TS97013	
31-WM	F-JVRU	B&F Funk FK-12 Comet	108	
31-WX		BRM Citius Sport		
31-XA		Averso AX.02 Guépard gyrocopter		
31-XI		CAG Toxo		
W31-XM		Varga gyrocopter		
31-XO	F-JVTW	Flight Design CT LSi	E-13-04-01	
31-YF		Comco-Ikarus C-42		
31-YS	F-JVUY	Comco-Ikarus C-42C		
31-ZX		Aéro Services SG.10A		
31-AIL		Urban Air Lambada		
		(Confusion with 33-AIL Urban Air Lambada ?)		

32 : Gers

Reg	Call-sign	Type	c/n	Other
32-AH		Cosmos		
32-AP		Deluc gyrocopter		
32-AR		Best Off Sky Ranger		
32-AY		Raj Hamsa X'Air		
32-BN		Best Off Sky Ranger		
32-BT		Humbert La Moto-du-Ciel		
32-BW		Fly Synthesis Storch		
32-CE		DTA / Dynamnic 15/430		
W32-CK		Efil 01		
32-CL	F-JIGO	Humbert Tetras	95-26	
32-CV	F-JBCC	Ultralair JC-24 Weedhopper Sport	9122574	
32-DA		JC-31 Weedhopper		
32-DE	F-JIHQ	Aerospool WT-9 Dynamic	DY110/2005	
32-DI	F-JIAO	Pipistrel Virus		
32-DJ	F-JIAU	Best Off Sky Ranger		
32-DP		Fly Synthesis Storch CL		
32-DQ		paramotor		
32-DR		Fly Synthesis Storch		
32-ED		Pottier P.130UL		
32-EJ		Aviasud Sirocco B447		
32-EM		Eipper Quicksilver MX IIA		
32-ES	F-JYGA	B&F Funk FK-14B Polaris		
32-ET	F-JYCN	Qualt 200		
32-EX		Alpaero (Noin) Exel		
32-FA		Mignet HM.293 Pou-du-Ciel		
		(Crashed 15.7.04)		
32-FG		Eipper Quicksilver GT400		
32-FK	F-JYSM	Zlin Savage		
32-FM	F-JIFM	Zenair CH-601 Zodiac		
32-FT		Aviakit Hermes		
32-FW		Preceptor Ultra Pup		
32-GB	F-JYWU	Dyn'Aero MCR-01	182	
32-GL		Magni M-22 Voyager	22-05-3984	
		(Re-regd 66-OR)		
32-GT		Best Off Sky Ranger		
32-GV		Best Off Sky Ranger		
32-GX		Rans S-6 Coyote II (t/w)		
32-HC	F-JWMS	Marie JPM-03 Loiret	11	
		(Re-regd 40-JI)		
32-HI		ITV paramotor		
32-HL		Henri Lascombes gyrocopter		
32-HN	F-JWXM	Best Off Nynja		
32-HX		Barry MB-04 Souris Bulle		
32-IL		Leopoldoff ulm replica		
32-IN		Air Création GT BI 582 / XP15		
32-IU		paramotor		
32-JC		PIK-26 Mini-Sytky		
32-JR		Tecnam P.92 Echo		
32-JS		Barry MB-02 Souricette		
32-JZ		Aquilair / La Mouette Ipsos 14.9		44-JL
32-KF	F-JCWR	Best Off Sky Ranger		
32-KM		Fly Synthesis Storch S		
32-KX		Tecnam P.92 Echo Seasky		
32-LF	F-JTYR	Flight Design CT-2K 912S		
32-LK		Pipistrel Sinus		
32-LL	F-JUAR	Flight Design CT-2K	99-08-04-64	
32-LQ		Best off Nynja		
32-LZ	F-JUQT	Spacek SD-1 Minisport TD	042	
32-MD		M Deluc MD T2 gyrocopter		W32-MD
32-MO		ELA Aviacion ELA-07		
		(W/o 11.7.15)		
32-NG	F-JAHB	Best Off Nynja		
32-PA		Kappa 77 KP-2U Sova 912		
		(Crashed 10.3.04)		
32-PM	F-JIDM	Flight Design CT SW		
32-RE		M Deluc gyrocopter (1-seat)		

33 : Gironde

Reg	Call-sign	Type	c/n	Other
33-BL		Bombardier		
33-CO		(Technic Moto ?) Mustang		
33-CQ		Eipper Quicksilver MX		
33-CS		Eipper Quicksilver MX		
33-CU		(Technic Moto ?) Mustang		
33-CY		(Technic Moto ?) Mustang		
33-DD		Eipper Quicksilver MX II		
33-DU		Aériane Sirocco	54	
33-DX		Top Concept Hurricane		
33-EB		Air's Allegro / La Mouette Hermes 16		
33-EG		(Cosmos ?) Bidulm 43		
33-ES		JC-31 Weedhopper		
33-ET		Top Concept Hurricane		
33-FC		PGO Aviation Cobra		
33-FF		Aeronautique Systeme Hurricane		
		(W/o 2.5.04)		
33-FL		PGO Aviation Cobra		
33-FR		Eipper Quicksilver MX II	1848	
33-FT		Pou du Ciel MF-02		
33-FU		Top Concept Hurricane		
33-FZ(1)		Mignet HM.14 Pou-du-Ciel		
33-FZ(2)		SG Aviation Storm 300		
33-GJ		Aviasud Mistral		
33-GK		PGO Aviation Cobra		
33-GM		Mignet HM.1000 Balerit	14	
33-GS		JC-31 Weedhopper		
		(Crashed 15.7.04)		
33-GX		Mignet HM.1000 Balerit	23	
33-HQ		Technic Moto Mustang 2		
33-IM		Landray GL-3	01	F-PYIL, F-WYIL
33-IN		Gipsy		
		(W/o 30.10.98)		
33-KF		Top Concept Hurricane		
33-KX		Micro Aviation Pulsar III		
33-LA		Humbert Tetras		
33-LB	F-JRGN	Fantasy Air Allegro		

Reg	F-reg	Type	c/n	Other
33-LH		Cosmos / Top		
		(W/o 13.05.07)		
33-LL		DTA / Dynamic 503		
33-LM		Eipper Quicksilver MXL II		
		(Accident 1.8.05)		
33-LU	F-JKEH	Humbert Tetras		
33-LZ		Murphy Maverick	82M	C-GYSS, G-MYSS
33-MG	F-JKBK	Mignet HM.1000 Balerit	37	
33-ML	F-JKFK	Rans S-7 Courier		
		(Re-regd 40-ID, 33-AHC)		
33-MQ		Air Création GT BI		
		(Damaged 18.10.00)		
33-MT	F-JKAG	Mignet HM.1100 Cordouan	15	
33-NL		Brugger MB-2 Colibri	87	F-PYPO
33-NO	F-JYXK	Protoplane Campana L2000		
33-PC	F-JKBM	Barry MB-04 Souris Bulle		
33-PF		Rans S-6 Coyote II		
33-PM	F-JKDZ	Lucas L.11	01	W33-PM
		(Re-regd F-PLSM)		
33-PW	F-JKCI	B&F Funk FK-14 Polaris		
33-QE		Mignet HM.293 Pou-du-Ciel		
33-QH		Guerpont Autoplum		
33-QI		Best Off Sky Ranger		
		(Accident 2.7.06)		
33-QM		Humbert Tetras	"9417"?	
33-RB		Aéro Services Guépard 912S		
33-RD	F-JKDD	Jodel D.18	71	
33-RJ		Fly Synthesis Storch HS		
33-RK		Rans S-12 Airaile		
		(Damaged 12.6.03)		
33-RO		Murphy Renegade Spirit		
33-RR		Jihlavan Skyleader 150		
33-RS	F-JYPS	Aeroprakt A-22		
33-RV		Ozone paramotor		
33-SQ	F-JKET	Dyn'Aero MCR-01 ULC		
33-SW		Aeropro Eurofox		
33-SY		Djicat Buse'Air 150		
33-TB	F-JHFT	Pipistrel Sinus		
33-TG		Ozone paramotor		
33-TN	F-JKFQ	Humbert Tetras 912B	33	
33-TO		Aeroprakt A-22		
33-TP		TL Ultralight TL-2000 Sting Carbon		
33-UL		"Ela Microair M760 homebuilt gyro" / ELA-7C		
		(Accidents 9.9.04 & 29.4.05)		
33-UV		Aeroprakt A-22		
33-UX		ELA Aviacion ELA-07C		
33-VD		ZUT Aviation TT2000 STOL		
		(Damaged 20.7.06)		
33-VE		Ray Hamsa X'Air		
33-VF		Air Création GT BI 582 / XP	A01174-1181	
33-VX		Jodel D.18	301	F-PRJT
33-WA		Mignet HM.14 Pou-du-Ciel		W33-WA
33-WG		Air Création GT BI		
33-WL		ATEC Zephyr 2000		
33-WP		weightshift		
33-WR		Flight Design CT-2K		
		(W/o 20.1.08)		
33-WS		Tecnam P.96 Golf		
		(Crashed in Spain 13.9.10, w/o)		
33-WW		Technic Moto Mustang 2		
		(Crashed 21.4.07)		
33-WY		ATEC Zephyr 2000		
33-XC	F-JZDH	Laudray & Massé LM01 Galopin Bis		
		(Marked LM01; previously incorrectly reported as regn 01-LM)		
33-XQ	F-JKJG	Aeropro Eurofox (Jabiru)		
W33-XS		Volksplane VP-1		
		(Crashed 14.5.06)		
33-XY		Best Off Sky Ranger Epsilon		62-GP
33-YK		DTA Combo / Diva		
33-YR		Best Off Sky Ranger		
33-YV		Murphy Renegade Spirit		
33-YX		Dudek Reaction paramotor		
33-ZC	F-JZUB	Best Off Sky Ranger V-Max		
33-ZE	F-JHQN	Kappa 77 KP-2U Sova		
		(Same call-sign as 22-GR)		
33-ZI		Vidor Asso V Champion		
		(Damaged landing 26.9.06)		
33-ZK		Light Aero Avid Flyer		
33-ZS		SG Aviation Storm 300		
		(Forced landing 9.4.07)		
33-ZV	F-JKBK	Aeropro Eurofox		
		(Re-regd 47-VB)		
33-AAD		Eipper Quicksilver		
33-AAE		Patrick Frigeri gyrocopter		
33-AAF	F-JZII	Pagotto Brako / Bautek		
33-AAN	F-JYIH	Guérin G1		
33-AAO	F-JYJN	Rans S-6 Coyote II		
33-AAR	F-JWBX	Aéro Services Guépard 912		
33-AAS		Humbert Tetras		
		(Accident 9.11.07)		
33-AAU	F-JQBH	Zlin Savage		
33-ABB		Aeropro Eurofox		
33-ABD		Fly Synthesis Texan Top Class	37	
33-ABJ	F-JYJE	ALMS/Sauper Papango	001	71-KZ
33-ABN	F-JYUJ	Aviakit Vega 2000		
33-ABQ	F-JYTJ	Aeroprakt A-22 Vision		
		(Same call-sign as 09-AP)		
33-ABR		Aeroprakt A-22 Vision		
33-ACA		Aquilair Swing 503		
33-ACE	F-JXKT	Light Aero Avid Flyer	472	F-WRKM
33-ACF		DTA Combo		
33-ACG		Aviatec Carbone CZ 5.4		
33-ACK	F-JZEQ	Mignet HM.1000 Balerit	30	
33-ACM	F-JZYN	B&F Funk FK-9 Mk.IV SW	305	31-FV
33-ACP		DTA Combo FC		
33-ACS		Humbert Tetras 912BS		
33-ACU		Pottier P.130UL		
33-ADD		TA550		
33-ADE		Mignet HM.293 Pou-du-Ciel		
33-ADI		Pagotto Brako		
33-ADK		Eipper Quicksilver MX II Sport		
33-ADP	F-JXNM	ICP Bingo 503	01-05-52-029	
33-ADS		Best Off Sky Ranger	SK0413596	
33-ADY		Claude Léger Pataplume 2		
33-AEA		Skyeton K.10 Swift		

Reg	F-reg	Type	c/n	Other
33-AEE		Evektor EV-97 Eurostar	2008 3506	
33-AEF		Best Off Sky Ranger		
33-AEK	F-JYHG	Flight Design CT		
33-AEM		DTA Combo FC 912 / Diva		
33-AEN	F-JWVU	gyrocopter		
33-AES	F-JKFE	Fly Synthesis Storch		58-GL
33-AET		Technic Moto Mustang 2		
33-AEY	F-JYXH	Jihlavan Skyleader 150		
33-AFA		Alpi Aviation Pioneer 300		
33-AFB		MAG 01		
33-AFC	F-JBMN	Rans S-6 Coyote II		
33-AFL		ATEC Zephyr 2000		
33-AFW	F-JRJB	Magni M-16 Tandem Trainer	16-09-5584	
33-AFX	F-JXJU	Jodel D.9 Bébé		55-KQ
33-AFY		Best Off Sky Ranger		
33-AGA	F-JROL	Magni M-22 Voyager	22-10-5694	
33-AGC		Djicat Buse'Air 150		
33-AGH	F-JSBS	ToT SE.5A replica	005	
33-AGK	F-JRWA	Light Aero Avid Hauler	833	HB-YFC
33-AGO		ZUT Aviation TT2000 STOL		
33-AGP		Pagotto Brakogyro		
33-AGS	F-JRXK	ELA Aviacion ELA-07S		
33-AHB		Fly Synthesis Storch	393	OO-F21
33-AHC	F-JKFK	Rans S-7 Courier		40-ID, 33-ML
33-AHL		Air Création / iXess 13		
33-AHM		Jabiru		
33-AHQ	F-JZMZ	B&F Funk FK-9	259	
33-AHS	F-JXVO	ALMS/Sauper Papango	004	
33-AHX	F-JEQW	Take Off Merlin / Drachen Studio Kecur Eos 15		
33-AIH		Air Création GTE Clipper 582 / iXess 15		
33-AIL		Urban Air UFM-13 Lambada		
33-AIO		SE-5A replica		
33-AIS	F-JTBU	Tecnam P.92 Echo Classic		
33-AIT		Claude Leger Pataplume 2		
33-AIW	F-JREY	Halley Apollo Fox		57-SJ
33-AIZ		ITV paramotor		
33-AJD	F-JKCM	Colomban MC-30 Luciole	72	
33-AJG		B&F Funk FK-12 Comet	12-100	
33-AJH		B&F Funk FK-12 Comet	12-101	
33-AJK		Robin ATL		
33-AJT	F-JTNS	P&M Aviation QuikR 912S	8548	G-CGVL
33-AJX		Layzell AV.18A gyro		
		(This appears to be Campbell Cricket 6A c/n 006/2 ex G-CDXV, returned to UK as such 3.16)		
33-AJZ	F-JTTX	Let-Mont TUL 01 Tulak		
33-AKB		Marie JPM-03	61	
33-AKC	F-JTXJ	Flight Design CT LS	F-11-12-04	
33-AKE	F-JTZD	Best Off Nynja		
33-AKI	F-JUCQ	ICP-MXP-740 Savannah		
33-AKR		Helisport CH-7 Kompress		
33-AKV		Magni M-22 Voyager		
33-AKY		AirLony Skylane		
33-ALD		Pagotto Brakogyro		
33-ALH	F-JUSR	Zlin Savage Cub		
33-ALK		Pagotto Brakogyro		
33-ALY	F-JVJI	P&M Aviation Quik GTR Explorer		
33-AMA		JMB Aircraft VL-3 Evolution	122	
33-AMF	F-JSDW	Plätzer Kiebitz		
33-AMG	F-JAMG	Best Off Nynja		
33-ANM	F-JRBG	ESPACE Sensation		
33-ANT	F-JAJX	B&F Funk FK-9 WB		
33-ANU		JMB VL-3 Evolution	180	
33-AZK		Light Aero Avid Flyer	62-GM	
(This allocation is way out of sequence and therefore it is suspect)				

34 : Hérault

Reg	Type	Other
34-A	Mignet Pou-du-Ciel	
34-E	(Hipps Superbirds) J-3 (Kitten?)	
34-F	Humbert La Moto-du-Ciel	
34-V	Eipper Quicksilver	
34-AC	Aériane Sirocco	
34-AL	Aeropiel CP.150G Onyx	
34-AM	Mignet HM.14 Pou-du-Ciel	
34-BB	Aériane Sirocco	
34-BC	Distri Snap Epsilon paramotor	
34-BD	Mignet HM.1000 Balerit 3X	
34-BO	Weedhopper	
34-BR	Air's Maestro	
34-CC	Eipper Quicksilver MX	
34-CD	Eipper Quicksilver	
34-CE(1)	Eipper Quicksilver MX II	
34-CE(2)	ICP MXP-740 Savannah (noted 2.08)	
34-DJ	Renegade	
34-DU	Air's Allegro	
34-DV	Air's Allegro	
34-DX	Air's Maestro	
34-DY	Air's Allegro	
34-EA	Air's Maestro	
34-EB	Air's Allegro	
34-EF	Eipper Quicksilver MX	
34-EG	Hipps Superbirds J-3 Kitten	
34-EH	Eipper Quicksilver MX	
34-EL	JC-31 Weedhopper	
34-EP	Dynali Chickinox	
34-EQ	Dynali Chickinox	
34-ER	Eipper Quicksilver MX II	
34-EY	JC-24 Weedhopper Sport	
34-FB	Top Concept Hurricane	
34-FI	Eipper Quicksilver MX II	
34-FJ	Thruster TST	
34-FL	Eipper Quicksilver GT400	
34-WFM	Air Création GT BI / Quartz	
34-FP	Air Création	
34-FQ	Eipper Quicksilver MX	
34-GC	Cosmos / La Mouette	
34-GD	PGO Aviation Cobra	W34-GD
34-GG(1)	Weedhopper	
34-GG(2)	Humbert Tetras	
34-GJ	Weedhopper 1	
34-GQ	Weedhopper AX-3 Twin	
34-GU	Weedhopper AX-3	
34-GV	Eipper Quicksilver MX II	
34-G .	Air Création GT BI / SX	
34-HB	Aeriane Sirocco	
34-HC	Weedhopper AX-3 amphibian	
34-HF	Weedhopper	

Reg	F-reg	Type	Serial	Other
34-HL		Eipper Quicksilver MX II	1262	
34-HU		Tempête		
34-HX		Weedhopper AX-3		
34-IC		Weedhopper AX-3		
34-ID		Weedhopper		
34-IE		Weedhopper		
34-IH		Weedhopper AX-3		
34-II		Weedhopper AX-3		
34-IK		Weedhopper		
34-IM		Weedhopper AX-3		
34-IN		Weedhopper		
34-IT		Weedhopper AX-3		
34-JJ		Weedhopper		
W34-JP		Protoplane Campana		
34-KD	F-JJKN	Maefin Top Fun		
34-KG		Murphy Renegade Spirit		
34-KN		Air Création GTE Clipper		
34-KT		Aviasud X'Pair 582 (Damaged 19.9.04)		
34-LT		AM-1 (type uncertain)		
34-LU		Weedhopper		
34-MB		TEAM Mini-MAX		
34-ME		Technoflug Piccolo		
34-MF		Zenair CH-701 STOL		
34-MH		Best Off Sky Ranger		
34-MJ		Rans S-6ES Coyote II	0894666	
34-MN		Mignet HM.1000 Balerit (Damaged 28.05.00)		
34-MP		Air Création GTE		
34-NB		Rans S-6 Coyote II		
34-NC		Mignet HM.14 Pou-du-Ciel		
34-NF		Denney Kitfox	1037	C-FPIZ
34-NI		Weedhopper		
34-NP		Weedhopper		
34-OB		Humbert La Moto-du-Ciel (W/o 17.10.04)		
34-OO		Air Création GTE Clipper / XP		
34-OP		Eipper Quicksilver MXL II MCL 01 f/p		
34-OY		Djicat Buse'Air 150		
34-PH		Humbert Tetras		
34-PM		Djicat Buse'Air 150		
34-PN		Aviasud AE209 Albatros		
34-PU		Weedhopper AX-3-14 (Forced landing 4.7.04)		
34-PY		Humbert Tetras		
34-QJ		Fantasy Air Allegro SW		
34-QL		Michel Cros gyrocopter		
34-QM		Michel Cros gyrocopter		
34-QO		Aviasud AE209 Albatros		
34-QR		gyrocopter		
34-RB		Aviasud AE209 Albatros		
34-RC		gyrocopter (homebuilt)		
34-RD		Pipistrel Virus		
34-RE		Rans S-12 Airaile		
34-RU		Denis Chevillet Micro B		
34-RY		ProFe D-10 Tukan (W/o 28.4.07)		
34-SA		Flight Design CT		
34-SB	F-JBGD	Best Off Sky Ranger		
34-SQ		Fly Synthesis Storch HS	22A132	
W34-SX		3XTrim Trener		
34-SZ		Air Création / XP		
34-TG(1)		Weedhopper AX-3-16 (Re-regd G-CDNU 7.05)	C3103163	51-HO
34-TG(2)		Evektor EV-97 Sportstar (Re-regd 95-WE ?)	2007 0911	
34-TL		motorglider (homebuilt) (Crashed 6.6.06)		
34-UQ	F-JXJF	Jodel D.18	428	F-PEGR
34-UT		PJB Aerocomposite Vega 2000 (W/o 16.2.04)		
34-UV		Eipper Quicksilver MXL II Sport (f/p)		
34-VC		TL Ultralight TL-2000 Sting Carbon		
34-VH		Nicollier HN.700 Menestrel II	54	F-PEDF
34-VI		Raj Hamsa X'Air		
34-VL	F-JJKC	DTA Combo Voyageur / Dynamic 450	125	
34-VM	F-JJKD	Comco Ikarus C-42		
34-VN		Advance Sigma paramotor		
34-VO		Weedhopper AX-3 14 (Forced landing 2.7.04)		
34-VR		ICP MXP-740 Savannah		
34-VS		Aéro Services Guépard		
34-XF		Pottier P.320UL		
34-XG		Pottier P.320UL		
34-XI		Rans S-7 Courier		
34-XM		Vol Mediteranni VM-1 Esqual		
34-XN		ICP Bingo 4S (Re-regd 46-DO)	03-07-52-121	
34-YA		ICP Bingo 4S	03-10-52-132	
34-YB		Raj Hamsa X'Air		
34-YF		Aquilair Swing (Accident 7.8.07)		
34-YG		Humbert Tetras		
34-YH		Weedhopper II		
34-YI		Aviasud Mistral		
34-YL		Paramania Action GT paramotor		
34-YM		Sauper J.300 Joker		
34-YO		Fantasy Air Allegro SW (Accident 15.3.04)		
34-YQ		Djicat Buse'Air 150 (Accident 6.10.07)		
34-YT		Evektor EV-97 Eurostar		
W34-ZA		gyrocopter		
34-ZB		Air Création Tanarg / iXess 15		
34-ZI		Rans S-6ES Coyote II (Damaged 5.8.05)		
34-ZJ		B&F Funk FK-12 Comet (Crashed 23.9.05)		
34-ZK		ICP Super Bingo	02-11-52-082	
34-ZO		Raj Hamsa X'Air F 582		
34-ZQ		trike / Air Création Fun		
34-ZU		Magni M-16 Tandem Trainer		
34-ZW		Eipper Quicksilver Sport 2		
34-AAC		Paramania Action GT paramotor		
34-AAD		Paramania Action GT paramotor		
34-AAE		Best Off Sky Ranger		
34-AAH		Weedhopper		
34-AAI	F-JZYL	Aerospool WT-9 Dynamic		
34-AAL		Eipper Quicksilver GT500		
34-AAO		PGO Aviation Cobra		
34-AAT		Eipper Quicksilver MXL II Sport		
34-AAV		ICP MXP-740 Savannah	01-98-50-073	
34-AAW		Zenair CH-701 STOL (BMW engine)		
34-AAX		ICP MXP-740 Savannah	01-04-51-073	
34-ABC		Air Création / iXess		
34-ABD		Aéro Services Guépard 912		
34-ABE		Air Création / iXess		
34-ABF		Pipistrel Taurus 503 (W/o 13.7.15)		
34-ABG		Tecnam P.92 Echo		
34-ABH		Air Création / iXess		
34-ABL		ELA Aviacion ELA-07S		
34-ABM	F-JYRT	ELA Aviacion ELA-07S		
34-ABR		PGO Aviation Cobra		
34-ABQ	F-JYUE	Flight Design CT SW		
34-ABT		ELA Aviacion ELA-07S		
34-ABW		Zenair CH-601 Zodiac		
34-ABZ	F-JZAH	Alpi Aviation Pioneer 200	157	
34-ACB		Aéro Services Guépy		
34-ACC	F-JXCW	Zenair CH-701 STOL		
34-ACG		ELA Aviacion ELA-07S (W/o 23.6.15)		
34-ACH		ELA Aviacion ELA-07S		
34-ACI		Celier Xenon 912 RST		
34-ACM		Raj Hamsa X'Air Hawk		
34-ACP		Aéro Services SG.10A		
34-ACX		gyrocopter 2 seat		
34-ADA		Raj Hamsa X'Air		
34-ADE		Best Off Sky Ranger		
34-ADF		Air Création GTE Clipper 582 / Fun 450		
34-ADG		Ozone Viper paramotor		
34-ADI		Zenair CH-701 STOL		
34-ADL		Eipper Quicksilver		
34-ADM	F-JEGS	ELA Aviacion ELA-07S R115	0406 104 0724	26-YV
34-ADN		Flight Design CT LS (previously reported as a paramotor)		
34-ADO		gyrocopter		
34-ADS		Aéro Services Guépy		
34-ADW		Air Création Tanarg		
34-AEB	F-JWMQ	ELA Aviacion ELA-07S		
34-AEL		ELA Aviacion ELA-07S	12082290722	
34-AEO		'EC220' (Possibly 34-ABO)		
34-AEQ		ATEC 321 Faeta		
34-AEU		Miniplane/Paramania Fusion paramotor		
34-AEV		Miniplane/Paramania Fusion paramotor		
34-AEW		Air Création Buggy		
34-AFB		Dyn'Aéro MCR-01		
34-AFG	F-JWLL	Jihlavan Skyleader 200		
34-AFI	F-JXUF	Best Off Sky Ranger		
34-AFO		JC-31 Weedhopper Premier AX-3		
34-AFP		Airbet Girabet 2 Sport gyrocopter		
34-AFU	F-JEYE	ICP MXP-740 Savannah		
34-AFW	F-JROF	Magni M-24 Orion		
34-AFY		unknown biplane		
34-AGC		ICP MXP-740 Savannah		
34-AGD	F-JRQN	Magni M-24 Orion	24-10-5684	
34-AGF		Autogyro-Europe Calidus 09		
34-AGV		Raj Hamsa X'Air		
34-AGX	F-JREU	Pipistrel Virus	267 SNLD 912	
34-AGZ		Autogyro Europe Calidus		
34-AHC		Magni M-24 Orion		
34-AHF		ELA Aviacion ELA-07 (W/o 2.12.13)		
34-AHJ		Murphy Maverick		
34-AHL		Aviasud Mistral		
34-AHS		ICP MXP-740 Savannah		
34-AHV		Raj Hamsa X'Air		
34-AIC		ICP MXP-740 Savannah		
34-AID		Zenair CH-601UL Zodiac		
34-AIG	F-JTGB	Rans S-6S Coyote II (t/w)		
34-AIK	F-JWKW	Flight Design CT LS		76-SE
34-AIL	F-JTJS	Jodel D.92 UL		
34-AIQ	F-JTLO	B&F Funk FK-14B Polaris (W/o 18.7.15)	14-089	OO-G19
34-AIR		Rans S-6 Coyote II 116 (t/w)		
34-AIV	F-JJKF	Air Création Tanarg / BioniX		
34-AJB		MPY paramotor		
34-AJD	F-JTYA	Pro.Mecc. Freccia		
34-AJE	F-JTYO	ICP MXP-740 Savannah VG XL	10-04-51-908	
34-AJI		Raj Hamsa X'Air		
34-AJL		Dudek paramotor		
34-AKE		DTA J-RO gyrocopter		
34-AKH		Best Off Nynja		
34-AKT		ELA Aviacion ELA-07S		
34-AKX		Best Off Nynja		
34-ALF		Air Création Tanarg / BioniX		
34-ALI		Tecnam		
34-AMG	F-JAMG	Best Off Nynja		
34-ANJ		Sauper J.300 Joker		

35 : Ille-et-Vilaine

Reg	F-reg	Type	Serial	Other
35-E		ULM 35/Djinn 300		
35-AK		Mignet HM.14 Pou-du-Ciel		
35-AY		Air Création		
35-AZ		Air Création GT BI		
35-BC		Air Création GT BI (Re-regd 50-LA)		
35-BD		Mignet HM.1000 Balerit 3X	60	
35-BF		Weedhopper AX-3		
35-BH		Air Création GT BI		
35-BM		Weedhopper		
35-BO		Croses Criquet	60	
35-BV		Air Création GT BI / Quartz		
35-BY	F-JTBJ	Eipper Quicksilver MX III Sprint	Sprint II 416	
35-CI	F-JBGG	JCC Aviation J.300 Joker		37-..
35-CK		Air Création		
35-CP		Rans S-12 Airaile		
35-CW	F-JVAI	Air's Maestro 2		
35-DA		Air Création		
35-DB		PGO Aviation Cobra		
35-DC		Air Création		

Reg	Marks	Type	c/n	Prev ID
35-DD		Cosmos		
35-DP		Light Aero Avid Flyer	980	F-WSDF
35-DQ		Cosmos Phase II 503 / Chronos 16		
35-DR		Air Création / SX		
35-DW		Air Création / Fun 450		
35-EA		Rans S-6 Coyote II		
35-EC	F-JMHZ	Evasion		
35-EE		Air Création Racer		
35-EF		Raj Hamsa X'Air 602T AP		
		(Accident 11.8.07)		
35-EI	F-JHOK	Micro Aviation Pulsar III		
35-EO		Air Création / Fun		
35-EP		Best Off Sky Ranger (t/w)		
35-EV		Rans S-6 Coyote II		
35-EW		Raj Hamsa X'Air		
35-EZ		TL Ultralight TL-2000 Sting Carbon		
W35-FC		Barry MB-02 Souricette	177	
35-FF		Rans S-6 Coyote II		
35-FL		Rans S-4 Coyote I		
		(Damaged 1.7.04)		
35-FM	F-JHPW	ICP MXP-740 Savannah	02-00-51-002/Kit 4	
		(Same c/n as 22-IX and 27-NT)		
35-FN		Didier Pti'tavion		08-CD?
35-FO		Didier Pti'tavion		
35-FQ		Air Création / XP		
35-FS	F-JHQP	Aéro Services Guépard 912		
35-GH	F-JHRK	Pipistrel Sinus		
35-GK	F-JYAT	Colomban MC-30 Luciole	14	
35-GN	F-JHMY	Didier Pti'tavion		
35-HB		Air Création GT BI / Quartz 18		
35-HD		Raj Hamsa X'Air F		
35-HH	F-JZDK	Murphy Renegade Spirit		
35-HI	F-JZDQ	Best Off Sky Ranger		
35-HQ	F-JYTI	Air Création Buggy		29-GY
35-HX	F-JZXM	B&F Funk FK-9 Club		
		(Re-regd 37-ADX)		
35-HZ		Dyn'Aéro MCR Pick-Up		W35-HZ
		(Damaged 3.07)		
35-IA		Rans S-6 Coyote II (t/w)		
35-IC		TeST TST-9 Junior 2002	09020403	
35-II		Tagazou		
35-IS		Air Création GT BI 503 / Mild		
35-IU		Air Création GTE Clipper 582 / iXess		
		(Same c/n as 39-HL)	A04113-4122	
35-IV	F-JFKF	Aéro Services Guépard 912S		
35-IW		DTA / Dynamic		
35-JA		Zenair CH-601 Zodiac		
35-JD		Pipistrel Sinus		
35-JG	F-JXMV	Humbert Tetras		
35-JI	F-JXSG	Best Off Sky Ranger		
35-JJ	F-JXOU	Raj Hamsa X'Air		
35-JP		Maxair Drifter		
35-JR	F-JUDT	J L Gehannin JLG	001	
35-JU		Air Création 582SE / iXess 15		
35-JX		Sauper J.300 Joker		
35-KA		DTA / Diva 12M2		
35-KR		ITV Dakota paramotor		
35-KV		DTA / Diva 12M2		
35-KY		Air Création GTE Trek 582 / iXess 13		
35-LB		Fantasy Air Allegro		
35-LC		Air Création Racer 447 / Fun 14		
35-LH	F-JIBG	Humbert Tetras 912BS		
35-LK	F-JRNE	Aéro Services SG.10A 912		
35-LL	F-JSPL	Claude Nowak Bombini gyrocopter		W35-LL
35-LO		B&F Funk FK-9 ELA	415	
		(Re-regd 95-ACB)		
35-LV		DTA Combo 912S		
35-LY	F-JZIF	Vidor Asso V Champion		
35-LZ	F-JTEW	Flight Design CT Supralight		
		(Same call-sign as 31-RM)		
35-MI	F-JHCS	Air Création Skypper / NuviX		
			A11049-11033 / T11028	
35-MJ	F-JSWL	Tecnam P.92 Echo Classic		
35-MN	F-JSMB	Flight Design CT Supralight	10-11-04	
		(Re-regd OO-H48 6.15)		
35-MY	F-JSUM	Autogyro-Europe MTOsport		
35-NC		Magni M-22 Voyager		
35-NW		Magni M-16 Tandem Trainer		
35-OC	F-JVDY	Platzer Kiebitz		
35-OD	F-JVDV	Best Off Nynja		
35-OH	F-JVJC	Flight Design CT LS	F-13-11-01	
35-OP		Aéro Services Guepard 912		
35-PB		J L Gehannin JLG-2		
35-RI		ITV Dakota Sport paramotor		

36 : Indre

Reg	Marks	Type	c/n	Prev ID
36-AA		weightshift		
36-AD		weightshift		
36-AG		Air Création GT BI / Quartz		
36-AI		Humbert La Moto-du-Ciel		
36-AJ		weightshift		
36-AL		Air Création GT BI / Quartz		
36-BA		Air Création GT BI / Quartz		
36-BF		Air Création GT BI / Quartz		
36-BJ		Weedhopper AX-3		
36-BO		Air Création GT BI / Quartz		
36-BX		Breezy RLU.1		
36-CC		weightshift		
36-CE		Hovey Delta Hawk II (2-str)		
36-CI		Synairgie Puma		
36-DS		Air Création / Quartz		
36-DT		Air Création GT / Fun / Mild		
36-EJ		Air Création		
36-EK		Ikel		
36-EP		Cosmos Chronos		
36-ER		Pegasus Quantum		
36-ES		Humbert La Moto-du-Ciel		
36-EY		Cosmos		
36-FF		Synairgie / Puma		
		(Also reported as Colibri Air)		
36-FH		Synairgie		
36-FJ		Air Création / Fun		
36-FM		Syna Aero Euro		
36-FN		Synairgie Puma		
36-FO	F-JFRO	Air Création		
36-FP		Synairgie		

Reg	Marks	Type	c/n	Prev ID
36-FQ		Air Création		
36-FT		Synairgie Puma		
36-GN		Synairgie Puma B1 (now Air Création / XP ?)		
36-GT		Air Création GT BI / Cosmos Chronos 14		
36-HH		Croses L-87 Criquet		
36-HM		Synairgie		
36-HQ		Croses Criquet L		
36-HR		Air Création / SX		
36-HW		Best Off Sky Ranger		
36-HX		Synairgie		
36-HZ		Dragon Fly 2 / Air Création Fun 450		
		(W/o 3.5.08 with 36-JW)		
36-JJ		Synairgie / Puma Bi		
36-JS		Best Off Sky Ranger		
36-JW		Cosmos Bidulm / Chronos		
		(W/o 3.5.08 with 36-HZ)		
36-KB	F-JPHX	Sauper J.300 Joker		
36-KC		Air Création		
36-KE	F-JFTU	Humbert Tetras		
36-KG		Humbert La Moto-du-Ciel		
36-KI		Aviakit Hermes 2		
36-KL		TEAM Mini-MAX		
36-KM		Best Off Sky Ranger		
		(Re-regd 38-NL)		
36-KT	F-JFOW	Humbert Tetras		
36-KV		CRI 01 gyrocopter		F-WZKV
36-LB		Corrado		
36-LH		Tecnam P.92S Echo Super		
36-LK		Air Création / XP		
36-LM		gyrocopter (W/o 17.11.02)		
36-LN	F-JFQZ	Aviakit Vega 2000 (t/w)		
36-LQ		Air Création / XP		
36-LS	F-JFSL	European Airwings Maestro II		
36-LT		Raj Hamsa X'Air		
		(Reported as Air Création / XP, 5.03)		
36-LV	F-JFSM	B&F Funk FK-9 Mk.III	09-147	
36-LW		Zephr		
36-LY		III Sky Arrow 500TF		
36-MA		Raj Hamsa X'Air		
36-MC	F-JFUP	Dyn'Aéro MCR-01	14	F-PQNO,
				F-WSLI
36-ME		Humbert Tetras		
36-MH		Air Création / SX		
36-MK		Best Off Sky Ranger		
36-MU		TL Ultralight TL-2000 Sting Carbon		
36-MV	F-JWJS	Jodel D.18		
36-MW		Best Off Sky Ranger		
36-MX		Air Création / Mild		
36-MY		Barry MB-02 Souricette		
36-NR		Guérin G1		
36-NT		Air Création GTE Clipper / Kiss		
36-NV		Dyn'Aéro MCR-01 UL	287	
		(Same c/n as 82-FQ)		
36-NY		Alpaero (Noin) Sirius		
36-OC		Weedhopper AX-3		
36-OH		Hummel Bird		
36-OU		ICP MXP-740 Savannah		
36-OW		Best Off Sky Ranger		
36-PA		Best Off Sky Ranger		
36-PE		Flylab Tucano		
		(W/o 5.6.07)		
36-PF		Cosmos Phase III / La Mouette Top 14.9		
36-PN	F-JYUC	Best Off Sky Ranger		
36-PR	F-JFOW	Magni M-16 Tandem Trainer	16-06-3604	
36-PX		Dallach Sunwheel		
36-PZ		Cosmos		
36-QD		Quad City Challenger II		
36-QE		Quad City Challenger II		
36-QM		Cosmos / Chrons 14		
36-QN	F-JWXK	Quad City Challenger II		
36-QP		Dyn'Aéro MCR-01 UL	398	
36-QR		Air Création Tanarg / iXess		
36-QT		Raj Hamsa X'Air		
36-QV	F-JWOJ	Aerospool WT-9 Dynamic	DY294/2009	95-YW
36-QX		Guérin G-1		
36-RA		Best Off Nynja		
36-RG		gyrocopter		
36-RI		P&M Aviation Quik		
W36-RY		gyrocopter		
W36-RZ		Averso Guépard II XJ-01		
36-SG		Magni M-22 Voyager		
36-SN		Jodel D.185		
36-ST	F-JVKA	Colomban MC-30 Luciole	223	
36-SX	F-JVNK	Colomban MC-30 Luciole	224	

37 : Indre-et-Loire

Reg	Marks	Type	c/n	Prev ID
37-B		weightshift		
37-H		Veliplane		
37-N		weightshift		
37-X		Piel CP.150 Onyx	48	
37-AA		RH.02		93-AD
37-AD		Azur		
37-AK		Synairgie		
37-AX		Air Création GTE Trek		
37-BI		Weedhopper	8032376	
37-BP		Plus		
37-BR		Air Création / Quartz		
37-BS		Air Création		
37-BT		Air Création		
37-BU		Air Création		
37-CA		Air Création		
37-CB		Air Création GT BI / Quartz		
37-CC		JCC Aviation J.300 Joker		
37-CD		Air Création GT BI / Quartz		
37-CE		Air Création		
37-CH		France Air Ceyx 2200/18		
		(Damaged 17.4.03)		
37-CL		Air Création GT BI		
37-CO		PGO Aviation Cobra		
37-CP		Mudry Baroudeur	319	
37-CS		Air Création		
37-CU		Patrifor		
37-DC		Sauper J.300 Joker		
37-DI		(Air Création ?) Safari		
37-DJ		Air Création / Quartz		
37-DK		JCC Aviation J.300 Joker		

Reg	F-reg	Type	c/n	Other
37-DL		Denney Minifox		
37-DP		Air Création GT BI / Quartz		16-DP
37-DS		Aquilair / Cosmos Chronos		
37-DT		Air Création GT BI / Quartz (Also noted as 'CQR 1')		
37-DU	F-JFNU	Air's Maestro 2		
37-DX	F-JBRN	JCC Aviation J.300 Joker		
37-DY		Air Création / XP15		
37-EA		Kolb Twinstar		
37-EB		(Air Création ?) Safari		
37-EC		Pagojet		
37-EP		Air Création GT BI / Quartz SX		
37-ES		JCC Aviation J.300 Joker		
37-EU		Air Création / Mild		
37-FA	F-JPAC	Weedhopper AX-3		
37-FB		L.X.P.		
37-FK		Air Création / Quartz SX		
37-GB		Air Création / Cosmos Chronos		
37-GC		Air Création GT BI / Fun		
37-GP		Pagojet		
37-GQ		trike / Synairgie Midi 18		
37-GR	F-JAOU	JCC Aviation J.300 Joker		
37-GS		Air's Maestro 2		61-CA
37-HB		Aviasud Albatros		
37-HC		Air's Maestro 2		
37-HD		Air Création / Quartz		
37-HI		B&F Funk FK-9 Mk.III		
37-HL	F-JATT	JCC Aviation J.300 Joker		
37-HU		(Kolb/Zodiac ?) Ultrastar		
37-HZ	F-JPEG	Piel RF.212 Onyx Bi		
37-IQ		Air Création GTE / XP		
37-JD		Aviasud AE209 Albatros	57	
37-JE		Cosmos		
37-JF	F-JRKF	Weedhopper Europa 1	B4011...	
37-JU		Air Création GT BI		
37-JW		Colibri		
37-KA		JCC Aviation J.300 Joker		
37-KD		Weedhopper		
37-KN	F-JFOT	Air Création GTE Clipper / XP		34-SH
37-KP		Best Off Sky Ranger		
37-KS		Caprice 21		
37-KU	F-JFSC	Aviasud Mistral		
37-KY	F-JFSU	Air Création GTE Clipper / XP		
37-LA		Best Off Sky Ranger		
37-LB		Fly Synthesis Storch		
37-LE		Cosmos		
37-LH		Pelican		
37-LK		Air Création GT BI		
37-LN		Weedhopper		
37-LR		Synairgie		
37-LS		Fly Synthesis Storch (W/o 17.11.02)		
37-MH		SMAN Pétrel		
37-MK		Aviakit Vega		
37-ML	F-JFNY	European Airwings Springbok 2000		
37-MN		Air Création Racer / XP11		
37-MR		Air Création GTE Clipper		
37-MX	F-JCUF	JCC Aviation J.300 Joker		
37-MY	F-JFPY	TL Ultralight TL-232 Condor		
37-NE		European Airwings Springbok 2000		
37-NH		Aviasud Mistral		
		(Damaged 5.8.01)		
37-NJ		Dynamic IS 503		
37-NO		Air Création / XP		
37-NU		Fly Synthesis Storch		
37-NY		TL Ultralight TL-232 Condor		
37-OP		Air Création GT BI / Quartz		
37-PH		Humbert Tetras		
37-PI		gyrocopter		
37-PN	F-JFSA	Raj Hamsa X'Air 602T		
37-PQ		Synairgie / Cosmos wing		
37-PT		Raj Hamsa X'Air 602		
37-PU		Synairgie (trike)		
37-PX		DTA / Dynamic 582		
37-QA		Pegasus		
37-QB		Sauper J.300 Joker		
37-QD		ULM 17 amphibian		
37-QE		Cosmos		
37-QF		Croses Criquet L (mod)	143	
37-QI		Piel CP.462		
37-QL		Raj Hamsa X'Air		
37-QN		Synairgie		
W37-QP		Averso AX.02 Guépard gyrocopter		
37-QR	F-JSXS	Comco Ikarus Fox-C22		
37-QU		Jodel D.19	261T	F-PCSJ, F-WCSJ
37-QV		Light Aero Avid amphibian	24	F-WZUF(2)
37-QZ		Air Création GTE Clipper	A99B8-9135	
37-RC		Best Off Sky Ranger		
37-RG		Best Off Sky Ranger		
37-RH		ICP MXP-740 Savannah		
37-RI		Air Création GTE Clipper / XP		
37-RJ		Air Création GT BI / Mild		
37-RO		Best Off Sky Ranger		
37-RR		Aéro Services Guépy (Jabiru) 80		
37-RS		Sauper J.300 Joker		
37-RU		Best Off Sky Ranger		
37-RV(1)		Flight Design CT-2K		
37-RV(2)		GT BI (homebuilt)		
		(Accident 25.8.07)		
37-RX		Air Création GTE Clipper		
37-RZ		Ekolot JK-05 Junior		
37-SA	F-JFTS	Jodel D.18	333	F-PCPG
37-SC		Kolb Ultrastar FO9		
37-SF		paramotor		
37-SK	F-JPEC	DTA / Dynamic 503 / Alto 148		91-YW
37-SQ		B&F Funk FK-9		
37-SS		Aéro Services Guépy (Jabiru) 2/2		
37-SV		Sauper J.300 Joker 3		
37-TB		Sauper J.300 Joker		
W37-TF		Alpi Aviation Pioneer 300		
37-TG	F-JGXG	Sauper J.300 Joker		
		(72-GL internally)		
37-TL	F-JPEB	Anglin J-6 Karatoo-T		
37-TP		Croses LC-6		
37-TS		Air Création GTE Clipper / Kiss		
37-TV		Jodel D.18		
37-TX		Air Création Tanarg / iXess		
37-UA		Weedhopper AX-3	9042382	
37-UF	F-JPAI	Rans S-12 Airaile		
37-UM	F-JPAR	ICP MXP-740 Savannah	02-03-51-142	
		(Same c/n as 26-UG)		
37-UN		Best Off Sky Ranger 582 (built by Synairgie)		
37-UQ		Air Création GTE Clipper / iXess		
37-UW		Raj Hamsa Hanuman 602T		
		(W/o 25.7.06)		
37-UX		TL Ultralight TL-2000 Sting Carbon		
37-UZ		Impulse 100		
37-VA	F-JZER	AirLony Skylane UL		
		(Same call-sign as 78-ZK)		
37-VI	F-JVRQ	Ekolot JK-05 Junior	05 02 06	
		(Same c/n as 08-FB)		
37-VK		Air Création GTE Clipper / iXess		
37-VL		Air Création / Fun 450		
37-VT		Air Création GTE Trek / Fun 450		
37-VV		Nervures Altéa paramotor		
37-VZ		Alpi Aviation Pioneer		
37-WE		Air Création / SX		27-..
37-WG		Air Création Tanarg / iXess		
37-WH		Zenair CH-601XL Zodiac		
37-WJ	F-JFGG	Ray Hamsa Hanuman		
37-WK	F-JPAL	Fantasy Air Cora		
37-WN		Trekking Parawing paramotor		
		(Accident 28.6.05)		
37-WO		paramotor		
37-WS		Zenair CH-601 Zodiac		
37-WX		Air Création Tanarg / iXess		
37-XE		B&F Funk FK-9 Mk.III	111	41-KP, D-MUED(1)
		(Re-regd 72-JL, 62-ARD)		
37-XF		Air Création GTE Clipper / iXess		
37-XO		Jora		
37-XQ	F-JPAL	Jora		
37-XU	F-JFNK	TL Ultralight TL-2000 Sting Carbon		
37-XX		Aéro Services Guépy		
37-YG		trike / La Mouette Ipsos 16.9 > Oryx		
37-YH	F-JZHK	Sauper J.300 Joker		
37-YJ	F-JHNU	Sauper J.300 Joker		
37-YZ		La Mouette Chronos 16		
37-ZA		Airbet Girabet 1 gyrocopter		
37-ZD		Ultravia Pelican S 582 Pegass		
37-ZE		Flight Design CT		
37-ZF		AirLony Skylane UL	06C03	OK-LUO 38
37-ZH		Tecnam P.2004 Bravo		
37-ZI		Sauper J300 Joker		
37-ZJ		Magni M-22 Voyager		
37-ZL	F-JYED	Flight Design CT SW		
37-ZP	F-JFIN	Jodel D.18		59-CAN
37-ZS		Aeroprakt A-22 Vision	082	
37-ZT	F-JYRB	Magni M-22 Voyager	22-07-4194	
37-ZW		Air Création GT BI / Quartz		
37-ZZ	F-JPHX	Sauper J.300 Joker		
37-AAB	F-JFGA	Rans S-6 Coyote II		
37-AAC		Guérin G1		
37-AAD		Jodel D.9 Bébé		
37-AAF	F-JJMX	B&F Funk FK-14 Polaris		05-HL
37-AAI	F-JPLJ	Rans S-6 Coyote II		
37-AAJ	F-JPSG	Magni M-14 Scout	14-05-3173	
37-AAM		Air Création GTE Trek / Fun 450		
37-AAQ	F-JXPP	Jabiru UL450		
37-AAR		Flight Design CT		
37-ABD	F-JXYQ	Tecnam P.2004 Bravo		
37-ABE		Air Création Tanarg 582 / iXess		
37-ABP		Air Création Mild		
37-ABY	F-JPSG	Autogyro-Europe MTOsport		
37-ACM		Air Création Tanarg 912ES / iXess 13		
37-ACO	F-JXWG	Dyn'Aéro MCR-01	249	21-YT
		(Re-regd 85-AEY)		
37-ACS		(Technic Moto ?) Mustang		
37-ACY	F-JREK	Magni M-16 Tandem Trainer	16-08-4994	
37-ADA	F-JRGG	Zenair CH-601XL Zodiac	6-9920	PH-4C5
37-ADR		Air Création Tanarg / BioniX		
37-ADX	F-JZXM	B&F Funk FK-9 Club		35-HX
37-AEA		Micro Aviation Pulsar III		
37-AED	F-JSLM	ICP MXP-740 Savannah S	10-12-54-0060	
37-AEI	F-JRJW	Ekolot KR-030 Topaz	030-03-06	
37-AEJ	F-JSXZ	Pro.Mecc. Sparviero		
37-AEK	F-JSXY	Pro.Mecc. Sparviero		
37-AER	F-JUCU	Aero-Kros MP-02 Czajka	04-10	
		(Re-regd OO-H36 7.14)		
37-AES		Rans S-6ES Coyote II		
37-AFC		B&F Funk FK-9 Mk.III (t/w)		
37-AFE		Plätzer Kiebitz B9		
37-AFG	F-JZLP	ALMS/Sauper J.300 Joker		41-OI
37-AFH		Air Création Tanarg 582		
		(W/o 11.11.15)		
37-AFJ	F-JJSA	Air Création GTE Trek / iXess	A10044-10033 / T10020	
37-AFK		paramotor		
37-AFL	F-JTMH	Ekolot KR-030 Topaz	30-04-06	
37-AFQ	F-JTNE	BRM Citius Sport	0198/912ULS/11-CT	
37-AFT	F-JYRS	Rans S-6 Coyote II (t/w)		
37-AFY		Alpi Aviation Pioneer 300STD		
37-AGA	F-JTYI	Plätzer Kiebitz	300	OO-G50
37-AGM		Air Création Tanarg 912ES / BioniX 13		
37-AGT		Autogyro Europe Calidua		
37-AGU	F-JVFA	Aéro Services SG.12A		
37-AHH		Alpi Aviation Pioneer		
37-AHS		Autogyro-Europe Calidus 09		
37-AHW	F-JTPS	Magni M-16 Tandem Trainer	16-15-8994	

38 : Isère

Reg	F-reg	Type	c/n	Other
38-V		JC-31 Weedhopper		
38-AQ		Aerosport Puma	S.195/365	G-MBBU
38-AS		JC-31D Weedhopper		
38-AV		Croses Airplume	18	
38-BG		Solar Wings / Puma		55-Y
38-BH		Cosmos Elf		
38-BT		CFM Shadow		
38-CE		Cosmos Chronos		
38-CM	F-JAVL	SMAN Pétrel	045 ?	54-PL, 56-CM
38-CQ		Air Création Racer A6		
38-CR		Cosmos / Chronos		
38-CT		Dynali Chickinox		
38-DQ		Weedhopper		

Reg	Call-sign	Type	c/n	Other
38-EK		weightshift		
38-ER		Pegasus Quantum		
38-ET		Rans S-6 Coyote II		
38-EU		Rans S-6 Coyote II		
38-FC		Weedhopper	B1101148	72-ED
38-FR		Rans S-6ES Coyote II		
38-FT		weightshift		
38-FU		weightshift		
38-GK		Alpi Aviation Pioneer 200		
38-GS		Zenair CH-601 Zodiac (t/w)		
38-GY		Piel CP.152B Onyx	140	
38-HV		Rans S-6 Coyote II		
38-IA		Air's Maestro 2		
38-ID		Eipper Quicksilver MXE Sport		
38-IO		Air Création		
38-IU		Pegasus (trike)		
38-IZ		paramotor		
38-JA		TEAM Mini-MAX 1500R		
38-JG		Best Off Sky Ranger		
38-JH		Rans S-6 Coyote II		
38-JP		Rans S-6ES Coyote II (t/w)		
		(Accident 2.9.07)		
38-JR		Air Création GT BI / XP		
38-JX		Rans S-6ES Coyote II		
		(W/o 22.7.05)		
38-KA	F-JEJM	Aviakit Hermes (Code "FB")	FR977R5	
38-KC		Humbert Tetras		
38-KF		Cosmos Phase II / La Mouette Top 14.9		
38-KK		Air Création		
38-KL		Rans S-7 Courrier		
38-KM		Cosmos		
38-KQ		TEAM Mini-MAX		
38-LA	F-JEID	DTA Feeling 582		
38-LC		Rans S-6ESD Coyote II		
38-LM		Light Aero Avid Flyer	692	F-WRKP
		(Re-regd 54-UC)		
38-LR		Aerospool WT-9 Dynamic		
38-MO		Averso AX.02 Guépard gyrocopter		
38-MQ	F-JELX	Rans S-6ES Coyote II (t/w)		
38-MU	F-JEJT	Rans S-6S Super Six (t/w)	0395-761	
		(Overturned 20.3.05)		
38-MV		Averso AX.02 Guépard gyrocopter		
38-NG		Mignet HM.1000 Balerit	68	
38-NL	F-JEPL	Best Off Sky Ranger (skis)		36-KM
		(Re-regd 91-AAQ)		
38-NO		Aviakit Vega (Jabiru)		
38-OM		Cosmos		
38-OO		weightshift		
38-OU	F-JEMO	Take-Off Merlin / Drachen Studio Kecur Avant		
38-OV		Macair Merlin		
38-PE		Jora		
38-PG		Humbert Tetras 912CS		
38-PN		Air Création GTE Clipper 582S		
		(Accident 27.8.05)		
38-PW		Take-Off Merlin / Drachen Studio Kecur Avant		
38-QC		Humbert Tetras		
38-QD	F-JEUY	Guérin G1		
38-QE		Zenair CH-601 Zodiac		
38-QG		DTA / Dynamic 450		
38-QH		Aeronavis ulm dirigible		
38-QL		DTA / Dynamic 912S		
		(Crashed 23.2.07)		
38-QO		Air Création / iXess		
38-QS	F-JEWU	Aviasud AE209 Albatros		
38-QU	F-JAFA	Air Création GTE Clipper 582 / iXess		
			A05011-4255	
38-QZ		Air Création Racer / Fun 14		
		(Accident 11.10.05)		
38-RD	F-JEOM	Pipistrel Virus		
38-RN	F-JEZA	Dyn'Aéro MCR-01 UL		
38-RS	F-JAUS	Best Off Sky Ranger		
38-RX	F-JGYN	Dyn'Aéro MCR-01 Turbo Diesel	260	
		(Wreck noted 19.3.15) (Same c/n quoted for 39-RX)		
38-SA	F-JYMN	B&F Funk FK-9 Mk.III	134	OO-D25,
		(Call-sign also quoted for 83-AKE)		59-CAK
38-SJ	F-JSLG	ProFe D10 Tukan		
		(Same c/s quoted for 38-ZI)		
38-SN	F-JEZM	Light Aero Avid Hauler		
38-SQ		Air Création Racer 447 / Fun 14		
		(Accident 5.9.06)		
38-SS	F-JYHB	Sonex Aircraft Sonex		
38-SU		Dyn'Aéro MCR-01 ULC Jabiru 22 F		
		(Accident 7.10.07)		
38-SW	F-JZAG	Dyn'Aéro MCR-01 UL		
38-SY		Ventura R1200S / Air Création iXess		
		now with La Mouette Oryx 15 wing		
38-SZ		Air Création		
38-TK	F-JYHF	Avid Flyer		
38-TN	F-JYIR	ICP Bingo 4S	04-02-52-145	
		(Re-regd 91-AGZ)		
38-TW	F-JYPN	ICP MXP-740 Savannah		
38-UI		trike / Pegasus wing		
38-UO	F-JXXZ	Fantasy Air Allegro SW	02-125	
38-UV		Air Création GT BI Clipper / SX		
38-UW	F-JXPU	Best Off Sky Ranger		
38-UX		Magni gyrocopter		
38-VC		Air Création GT BI / Fun 14		
38-VF	F-JXVN	Alpi Aviation Pioneer 200 Beluga		
38-WK		Aquilair Swing 503 / Aeros Stranger		
38-WV		Air Création Tanarg / iXess		
38-WW		Aviakit Vega 3000	AFC050701R9	
38-XA		Air Création GTE Trek HKS700E / Fun 450		
38-XC		Air Création / iXess		
38-XJ		weightshift		
38-XP		Dyn'Aéro MCR-01		
38-YD		Pouchelle		
38-YE	F-JRVQ	Comco Ikarus C-42		
38-YJ		BRM Okavango		
38-YS	F-JYDA	Air Création Buggy 582		
38-ZG		Autogyro-Europe MTOsport		
38-ZH	F-JZ?S	Air Création Tanarg 912 / DTA Magic		
38-ZI	F-JSLG	Jodel D.18	277	F-PRSH
		(Same c/s quoted for 38-SJ)		
38-ZQ(1)		ICP MXP-740 Savannah VG XL	08-11-51-793	
38-ZQ(2)		ICP Bingo 4S	04-05-52-141	
		(This c/n quoted for South Korea regn HLC107 regd 6.12, active 2014)		

Reg	Call-sign	Type	c/n	Other
38-ZV		ICP MXP-740 Savannah		
38-ZW		Air Création Skypper 582 / NuviX 15		
38-ZY	F-JSVM	Pro.Mecc. Sparviero SP10	PM074	
38-AAD		Bouchara Iris Challenger II airship		
38-AAE	F-JXTC	Alpi Aviation Pioneer 200		80-XL
38-AAF		CBBULM O2B / La Mouette Top 16.9		
38-AAH		Air Création Skypper / NuviX		
38-AAV	F-JTNC	Vidor Asso X Jewel		
38-ABJ		Vidor Asso X Jewel		
38-ABR	F-JUAS	Dyn'Aéro MCR-01	410	
38-ABW		Mosquito Air helicopter		
38-ACO		Ventura 1200 / La Mouette Oryx 15		
38-ACP	F-JWKN	Ventura 1300 / La Mouette Oryx 14		
38-ACR	F-JVCW	Trixy G4 Liberty 914	029-13	D-MBTA
38-ACV		Trixy Liberty 914		
38-AED	F-JALF	Trixy G4-2 Liberty		
38-ANA		Jodel D.18		
38-…	F-JSTV	ICP MXP-740 Savannah		

39 : Jura

Reg	Call-sign	Type	c/n	Other
39-J		(Air Création ?) Safari		
39-AF		Eipper Quicksilver MX II	1776	
39-BL		JC-31 Weedhopper		
39-BP		Cosmos / Atlas		
39-BV		(Murphy ?) Renegade 503		
39-BY		(Murphy ?) Renegade 503		
39-CC		(Murphy ?) Renegade 503	328	
39-DA		Cosmos Phase II		
39-DK		Murphy Rebel		
39-ED		Koenig AK 09 Faucon		
39-ER		ICP MXP-740 Savannah		
39-FA	F-JGZS	Cosmos Chronos		
39-FC	F-JCZX	Light Aero Avid Flyer		
39-FO	F-JCYT	Humbert Tetras		
39-FR	F-JGOJ	ICP MXP-740 Savannah	06-96-50-036	
		(Reported 8.01 as 39-RF)		
39-GI		Barry MB-02 Souricette		
39-GK	F-JGZL	Mignet HM.1000 Balerit	97	F-MUMC
39-GS		Zenair CH-601UL Zodiac		
39-HC		Raj Hamsa X'Air F 602T		
39-HL	F-JQII	Air Création GTE Clipper / iXess	A04113-4122	
		(Same c/n as 35-IU)		
39-HN		Halley Apollo Fox 912		
		(Accident 17.7.05)		
39-HP		Air Création Tanarg 582 / iXess		
39-HR		DTA / Dynamic 582		
		(Accident 29.7.05)		
39-HU	F-JTIJ	Tecnam P.2002 Sierra	147	F-JQIX
39-HW		Halley Apollo Fox		
39-IA		Cosmos Chronos		
		(Re-regd 85-SL)		
39-IC		Ozone Electron paramotor		
		(Accident 18.3.06)		
39-IG		Swedish Aerosport Mosquito NRG		
		(W/o 4.8.06)		
39-IP		Alio Delta		
39-IR		Rans S-6 Coyote II		
39-IT		Dynali Chickinox		
39-IW		Best Off Sky Ranger		
39-IX		Flying Machines FM.250 Vampire		
39-JM		Urban Air Lambada		
39-JO		DTA / Dynamic 450	99/53	
39-JY		Cosmos Phase II		
39-KE		Cosmos Phase II		
39-KF		paramotor		
39-KI	F-JYAF	ICP MXP-740 Savannah	04-01-51-271	
39-KX	F-JWII	Flight Design CT LS	F-08-07-21	28-AJH
		(Re-regd 30-RK)		
39-KZ		Air Création Tanarg 912ES		
39-LA		Humbert Tetras		
39-LC		Note: A pair of Air Création Tanarg 912s referred to as 39LC and 39LD		
		were reported as sold to Russia, further details unknown.		
39-LD	F-JUDJ	Ivanov Friendship 3 (2 seat Fournier RF-3 replica)		
39-LE	F-JUCT	Flight Design CT LS amphibian		
		(Damaged 7.8.16)		
39-LP		Jodel D.11		
39-PE		Jora		
39-PH		Avio Delta Swann		
		(marked 39H9)		
39-RX	F-JGYN	Dyn'Aéro MCR-01 Diesel	260	
		(Same c/n and call-sign quoted for 38-RX)		
39-SC	F-JUAH	ICP MXP-740 Savannah	11-00-51-033	63-SC, F-JEBD
39-TS	F-JYKV	P&M Aviation QuikR 912S	8543	G-CGPM
		(Also reported as 29-TS)		

40 : Landes

Reg	Call-sign	Type	c/n	Other
40-D		Aerodyne 627SR Vector TM		
		(Re-regd 50-AF)		
40-J		Aériane Sirocco		
40-L		JC-24 Weedhopper		
40-M		Eipper Quicksilver MX		
40-S		Dynali Chickinox		
40-AP		weightshift		
40-AX		weightshift		
40-DA		Top Concept Hurricane		
40-EA		Zenair CH-701 STOL		
40-EF		Comco Ikarus C-42		
40-EG		Micro Aviation Pulsar III		
40-EJ	F-JKCH	Best Off Sky Ranger		
40-ET		DTA / Dynamic 15		
40-EU		Air Création		
40-EW		Tucan Fly		
40-EX		Jodel D.195		
40-EZ		Weedhopper (2-str)		
40-FB		Air Création		
40-FG		Air Flot Klip amphibian		
40-FI		B&F Funk FK-9 Mk.III	09-129	
40-FJ	F-JKFN	Sauper J.300 Joker		
40-FL		gyrocopter		
40-FS		Best Off Sky Ranger		
		(Crashed 20.8.04)		
40-FW		Caprice 21		
40-FX	F-JKHD	Aeroprakt A-22	086	
40-FZ	F-JCHK	SG Aviation Storm 280		
40-GD		gyrocopter		
40-GE		Aéro Services Guépy (Jabiru) 80		

Reg	F-reg	Type	C/n	Other
40-GF		B&F Funk FK-9		
40-GG		Air Création GTE Clipper 582S		
		(Crashed 30.7.06)		
40-GH		Jora LS1	C 137	
40-GI		Pagotto Brako / Bautek Sexy		
40-GJ		Magni M-22 Voyager		
40-GM		Celier Xenon	AB00200669X	
		(Now in ALAT museum, Dax)		
40-GO		Lobb Falco 95		
W40-GP		gyrocopter		
40-GQ	F-JKJP	Flight Design CT SW	05-08-06	
40-GT		Rans S-6 Coyote II		
40-HA		Zenair CH-701 STOL (f/p)		
40-HB		Zenair CH-701 STOL (f/p)		
40-HG		Aéro Services Super Guépard (Jabiru)		
40-HH		Evektor EV-97 Eurostar R 912 2 ULS FR		
		(Accident 24.11.07)		
40-HK		Ultralair Weedhopper AX-3		
		(Crashed 27.7.08)		
40-HL		Aviakit Hermes	FR974?	
40-HM	F-JJNY	Zenair CH-601UL Zodiac		
40-HO		Rans S-6ES Coyote II		
		(Accident 12.7.07)		
40-HP		Fly Synthesis Storch (f/p)		
40-HR		Fly Synthesis Texan		
		(Accident 9.8.07)		
40-HU	F-JYGE	Pipistrel Virus		
40-ID	F-JKFK	Rans S-7 Courier		33-ML
		(Re-regd 33-AHC)		
40-IO		Cosmos Chronos		
		(Re-regd 52-ET)		
40-IX	F-JRMW	Flight Design CT SW	06-03-03	T7-MAB
		(To OO-H62)		
40-JC		Eipper Quicksilver MXL II (f/p)		
40-JF		EuroALA JetFox		
40-JH	F-JKFA	Best Off Sky Ranger		
40-JI	F-JWMS	Marie JPM-03 Loiret	11	
40-JQ		Rans S-6 Coyote II		
40-JS		Fly Synthesis Catalina		
40-KD	F-JFKR	B&F Funk FK-12 Comet	12-034	85-YJ, 59-CEJ
40-KI		Le Vol des Aigles Fokker E-III 01replica		
40-KK		Magni M-16 Tandem Trainer		
40-KN		Fly Synthesis Storch	F1BC4850B13C	
40-MQ	F-JAMM	Magni M-16 Tandem Trainer		
40-UL		Twin Weedhopper		

41 : Loir-et-Cher

Reg	F-reg	Type	C/n	Other
41-G		Pelican		
41-K		Antar		
41-AH		Labasse Griffon 41		
41-AL		Synairgie Colin Epsilon (weightshift)		
41-AN		Tecnic Djins (W/o 15.8.00)		
41-AT		Fantasy		
41-AU		Air Création / Kiss		
41-BC		Ceyx 1800 (weightshift)		
41-BI		Air Création / Quartz		
41-BY		Weedhopper AX-3		
41-CD		Air Création GT BI / Quartz		
41-CK		Air Création / Kiss		
41-CO		Weedhopper AX-3		
41-DB		Air Création GT BI / Quartz		
41-DC		Biplum		
41-DJ		Synairgie		
41-DL	F-JFRX	Weedhopper AX-3		
41-EC		Synairgie / Puma		
41-ED		Air Création / Quartz		
41-EM		(Technic Moto ?) Mustang		
41-EO	F-JFRB	Denney Kitfox Lite		
41-EP		France Air ULM / Synairgie Puma 16		
41-EQ		Synairgie / Puma 16		
41-ET		Weedhopper Europa I 503		
41-EX		Weedhopper AX-3	C3083140	
41-FZ		paramotor		
41-GD		Air Création GTE Clipper / XP		
41-GE		trike / XP (Damaged 29.5.97)		
		(Later reported as Aéro Services Guépy (Jabiru) 80)		
41-GJ	F-JBWF	Sauper J.300 Joker		
		(Marked N-0323 = c/n?)		
41-GQ		Synairgie / Puma Bi 16		
41-GR		Sauper J.300 Joker		
41-GX		Rans S-7 Courier		
41-GY	F-JFGM	Air Création / Kiss	A02059-2055	
41-HA		Air's Maestro		
41-HB		European Airwings Maestro		
41-HE		ALMS/Sauper Papango		
41-HF	F-JFPW	Skystar Kitfox Mk.IV	C95030102	
41-HG		Fly Synthesis Storch HS		
41-HN		Best Off Sky Ranger		
41-HP		Croses LC-6		
41-HS		Tecnam P.92S Echo Super		
41-HT	F-JFPD	Flight Design CT	99 05 02 53	
		(Also reported 2003 as AX-3)		
41-HX	F-JFPF	Sauper J.300 Joker		
41-HY		gyrocopter		
41-JA	F-JFPN	B&F Funk FK-9 Mk.III		
		(Same call-sign quoted for 41-MX and 10-NA)		
41-JK		gyrocopter		
W41-JL		Boutin Air Copter		
		(Stored)		
41-JP		European Airwings Springbok		39-GA
41-JU	F-JFRT	Aéro Services Guépy (Jabiru) 80		
41-JX		Sauper J.300 Joker		
41-JY	F-JFNO	Raj Hamsa X'Air-F		
41-JZ		Best Off Sky Ranger		
41-KC		Air Création / SX		
41-KD		Weedhopper AX-3		
41-KM		paramotor		
41-KP		B&F Funk FK-9 Mk.III	111	D-MUED(1)
		(Re-regd 37-XE, 72-JL, 62-ARD)		
41-KS	F-JFQW	RSA Aiglon		
41-KU	F-JFUR	Comco Ikarus C-42		
41-LA	F-JPAD	Rans S-6 Coyote II		
41-LB		Air Création / iXess		
41-LD		Dyn'Aéro MCR-01 UL		
41-LE	F-JPHK	Air Création / iXess		
41-LI		TL Ultralight TL-2000 Sting Carbon		

Reg	F-reg	Type	C/n	Other
41-LJ		Flight Design CT-2K		
		(Crashed 15.7.04)		
41-LK		European Airwings Springbok 3000		
41-LL		Air Création GT BI / Fun		
41-LM		Weedhopper AX-3		
41-LO	F-JPEE	Sauper J.300 Joker		
41-LP		Weedhopper AX-3	03093148	
41-LQ		Flipper Bi Canard		
41-LR		Aéro Services Guépy (Jabiru) 80		
41-LW		Weedhopper AX-3	0032621	
41-LX(1)		European Airwings Springbok 3000		
41-LX(2)	F-JPER	Ekolot JK-05 Junior	05 03 05	08-GP
41-MB		paramotor		
41-ME	F-JPHE	ALMS/Sauper Papango		
41-MK	F-JPKA	Fantasy Air Allegro SW	04-134	
41-ML		Humbert Tetras	38	
41-MN		paramotor		
41-MQ		Sauper J.300 Joker		
41-MR		Air's Maestro		
41-MS		Micro Aviation Pulsar		
41-MV	F-JFSS	Jabiru UL450		
41-MX	F-JFPN	B&F Funk FK-9 Mk.IV Club		
		(Same call-sign quoted for 41-JA and 10-NA)		
41-ND		Micro Aviation Pulsar		
41-NE		Fly Synthesis Storch HS		
41-NF		paramotor		
41-NG	F-JPOT	Sauper J.300 Joker		
41-NH	F-JPOO	Sauper J.300 Joker		
41-NJ	F-JPSJ	B&F Funk FK-9 Mk.II	067	
		(C/n 67 quoted for 28-NZ)		
41-NM		Magni M-16 Tandem Trainer		
41-NO		paramotor		
41-NP	F-JPSS	Tecnam P.92S Echo		
41-NR		Sauper J.300 Joker		
41-NX		Ekolot JK-05 Junior		
41-OB		Air Création GTE 503 / Kiss		
41-OC	F-JZHU	Best Off Sky Ranger V-Max		
41-OE		Paramania Action GT 9 paramotor		
		(W/o 1.07)		
41-OI	F-JZLP	ALMS/Sauper J.300 Joker		
		(Accident 24.11.07; re-regd 37-AFG)		
41-OJ		Air Borne Edge XT-582 / Cruze		
41-OK		Evektor EV-97 Eurostar		
41-OO	F-JZRR	ALMS/Sauper J.300 Joker		
41-OQ		J-M Boutin JM300 gyrocopter		
41-OT		Fantasy Air Cora		
41-OY		Sauper J.300 Joker		
41-OZ		Flight Design CT		
41-PA		Magni M-22 Voyager	22-07-4184	
		(Re-regd. ...BT/F-JFTV) (Same c/n as 77-BDZ)		
W41-PB		Alain Surre gyrocopter		
41-PI		Comco Ikarus C-42		
41-PL	F-JXHB	Flight Design CT SW	07-07-23	
41-PR		ALMS/Sauper J.300 Joker		
41-PV	F-JWBB	ALMS/Jodel D.20		
41-PW		Air Création GT BI / SX		
41-PX	F-JWBC	ALMS/Sauper J.300 Joker (n/w)		
41-PZ	F-JWBU	UL-JIH Fascination F100C		
		(Same call-sign as 12-IE and 12-EI)		
41-QF		ATEC Zephyr		
41-QM	F-JEEQ	B&F Funk FK-9 Mk.IV	335	63-JD
		(Re-regd 67-BLT)		
41-QP	F-JRVF	Sauper J.300 Joker		
41-QQ		ICP Bingo 4S	07-05-52-216	
41-RB		Flight Design CT		
41-RH	F-JSJY	Antilope		
41-RK	F-JRPN	UL-JIH Fascination F100		OK-NUF 26
41-RN		Dyn'Aéro MCR-01	403	
		(Re-regd LN-YPT(2) 12.11)		
41-RO		Air Création Tanarg / Bionix		
41-RR	F-JRYH	Magni M-16 Tandem Trainer	16-10-5804	
41-RT	F-JSBN	Pro.Mecc. Sparviero	4	
41-RX		Fly Synthesis Storch S		
41-SE		ICP MXP-740 Savannah	00-04-51-007	
		(not Zenair CH-701 STOL as previously reported)		
41-SH	F-JSMY	Aerospool WT-9 Dynamic	DY403/2010	
41-SI	F-JFRP	Comco Ikarus C-42		
41-SL	F-JSTA	Humbert Tetras 912CS		
41-SQ	F-JSVU	Pro.Mecc. Sparviero		
41-TB	F-JTJP	Comco Ikarus C-42		
41-TC	F-JTKD	Alpi Aviation Pioneer 200		
41-TG	F-JTPW	Best Off Nynja	084	
41-TN	F-JUEI	Magni M-22 Voyager	22-12-7344	
41-TO		Paramania GTR paramotor		
41-TT	F-JUIA	Helisport CH-7 Kompress		
41-TU	F-JUJK	ICP MXP-740 Savannah S	12-12-54-0228	
41-TX	F-JUOC	ICP MXP-740 Savannah S	13-02-54-0244	
41-UL		Paramania paramotor		
41-VI	F-JUCW	Aerospool WT-9 Dynamic	DY539/2015	
41-VQ	F-JANM	Flight Design CT SL	E-14-03-02	
41-XX		Flight Design CT		

42 : Loire

Reg	F-reg	Type	C/n	Other
42-M		Zenith Baroudeur		
42-N		JC-31C Weedhopper		
42-O		Zenith Baroudeur		
42-AJ		Zenith Baroudeur		
42-AO		Cosmos	0059	
42-AP	F-JBNF	Cosmos Chronos		
42-BA		HFL Stratos 300		
42-BY		Weedhopper		
42-CA		Cosmos Pegasus Q (?)		
42-CK		Weedhopper		
42-CN		Humbert		
42-CY		Air Création / Quartz		
42-DM		Aviasud Mistral		
42-DX		Best Off Sky Ranger		
42-EL		Mignet HM.1000 Balerit	74	
42-EP		Air Création Buggy		
42-ET		DTA / Dynamic 503		
		(W/o 31.3.97)		
42-EU		Solar Wings Pegasus		
42-FU		TL Ultralight TL-232 Condor		
42-GI		Light Aero Avid Flyer		
42-GM	F-JETU	Morin M-85		W-42-GM
42-GZ		Croses LC UL		

Regn	Call-sign	Type	C/n	Other
42-HC		ICP MXP-740 Savannah	01-05-51-069	
42-HD		Evolution Dynamic 503		
		(Accident 9.9.04)		
42-HF		Air Création Tanarg / iXess		
42-HI		Air Création GT BI 503S		
		(Damaged 23.6.06)		
42-HJ		Air Création GTE Buggy 582SL / Kiss 450		
42-HT		Tecnam P.92 Echo		
		(Accident 20.5.05)		
42-HX		Pipistrel Sinus 912		
		(Crashed 24.2.04)		
42-IF		ICP MXP-740 Savannah	01-05-51-088	
42-IH		Aquilair SV-1 / La Mouette Top 14.9		
42-IK		Air Création / iXess 15		
42-JA	F-JEME	Dyn'Aéro MCR-01 UL	273	
42-JC		Aquilair / Cosmos Chronos 16		
42-JI	F-JEGV	DTA / Dynamic 15/430		
42-JQ	F-JEFF	Zenair CH-601XL Zodiac		
42-JU	F-JYYF	Barry MB-04 Souris Bulle	26	
42-JV		Flylab M2		
W42-KA		Mignet HM.293 Pou-du-Ciel		
42-KB	F-JYBN	Aerospool WT-9 Dynamic		
		(Same call-sign quoted for 42-LS)		
42-KE		Urban Air UFM-13 Lambada		
42-KG		Air Création GTE Trek		
42-KH		Jodel D.18		
42-KK		(Quad City ?) Challenger II		
W42-KR		gyrocopter (homebuilt)		
42-KU		Air Création Twin Buggy		
42-KX		Air Création Tanarg / iXess		
42-LE		Fly Synthesis Wallaby		
42-LF		Mignet HM.1000 Balerit	69	OO-A50
42-LM	F-JQMG	ICP MXP-740 Savannah	09-10-51-887	
42-LR		ICP MXP-740 Savannah		
42-LS	F-JYBN	Aerospool WT-9 Dynamic	DY317/2009	
		(Same call-sign quoted for 42-KB)		
42-LU		trike / La Mouette Ipsos 14		
42-LV		Air Création GTE Clipper		
42-LW		ICP MXP-740 Savannah XL		
42-LY	F-JANV	Aviasud Mistral		
42-MF		Air Création Tanarg 912ES / BioniX 15	A10087-10077	
42-MH		TeST TST-3 Alpin DM		
42-MU		Weedhopper Europa 2 582		
42-MX	F-JTCZ	Air Création Skypper 912 / NuviX 15	A11080-11064	
42-NF		Eipper Quicksilver		
42-NI	F-JTRF	ICP MXP-740 Savannah S	12-02-54-0163	
42-NY		Zenair CH-701 STOL		
42-OB		ITV Jedi paramotor		
42-OM	F-JVZK	JMB Aircraft VL-3 Evolution	141	
42-VE		Cosmos / Chronos		
42-VJ		Flylab M2		
42-ABT		La Mouette		

43 : Haute-Loire

Regn	Call-sign	Type	C/n	Other
43-J		Hipps Superbirds J-3 Kitten		
43-N		Aquila S-440		
43-BMW		Air Création GT BI / Quartz		
43-BS		Denney Kitfox		
43-BT		Helios		
		(Also noted as Air Création type)		
43-BY		Air Création / SX 16		
43-CF		Cosmos		
43-CJ		Vidor Asso V Champion		
43-DA		Aquilair Swing (also rep. as Cosmos wing)		
		(W/o 10.7.99)		
43-DD	F-JEAC	Rans S-6 Coyote II		
43-DK		Aquilair Swing		
43-DV		Fly Synthesis Storch		
43-DY		Best Off Sky Ranger		
43-DZ		Aquilair Swing 14		
43-GT		Aquilair Swing / La Mouette Ghost 16		55-GI (wing)
43-IJ		Aquilair Swing 14		
43-JI		Aquilair Swing / La Mouette Ghost 16		
43-LS		Croses LC-6 Criquet		
43-OL	F-JEBV	Best Off Sky Ranger		
43-SR		Aquilair		
43-VA		Pipistrel Sinus		
43-YT		ICP MXP-740 Savannah		
43-ZI	F-JUGH	Magni M-24 Orion	24-12-7384	

44 : Loire-Atlantique

Regn	Call-sign	Type	C/n	Other
44-L		Cosmos Chronos		
44-O		Concept		
44-S		Vector		
44-AF		Weedhopper		
44-AM		Dragon 150		
44-CD		Polaris		
44-DB		Cyclone AX-3		
44-DL		(Aviasud ?) Sirocco		
44-DU		Huiles Loto		
44-EB		wreck noted, 1.02		
44-FT		Cosmos Chronos		
44-FV		Cosmos / La Mouette		
44-GB		(Weedhopper ?) AX-3		
44-GO		Cosmos		
44-HF		Cosmos Chronos		
44-HJ		Cosmos		
44-HK		Cosmos		
44-HR		weightshift "La Poste"		
44-HS		Cosmos		
44-HY		(Weedhopper ?) AX-3		
44-IC		Cosmos		
44-IL		Cosmos		
44-IU		Cosmos		
44-JL		Aquilair / La Mouette Ipsos 14.9		
		(Re-regd 32-JZ)		
44-JM		Weedhopper AX-3		
44-WKA		Synairgie		
44-KB		Raj Hamsa X'Air		
44-KC		(Weedhopper ?) AX-3		
44-KU		Weedhopper		
44-LA		(Weedhopper ?) AX-3		
44-LF		Cosmos Chronos		
44-LK		Cosmos		
44-LO		Rans S-6 Coyote II		
44-LS		Cosmos Chronos		
44-MB		Rans S-6 Coyote II		
44-MK		Cosmos		
44-MS		Aviasud AE209 Albatros		
44-MT		Air Création / Mild		
44-ND		Raj Hamsa X'Air		
44-NP		Barry MB-02 Souricette		
44-OB		Cosmos		
44-OE	F-JHTP	Zenair CH-701 STOL		F-JBWZ
44-OK		Eipper Quicksilver GT500		
44-OL		Raj Hamsa X'Air		
		(Re-regd 45-NI)		
44-OO		(Weedhopper ?) AX-3		
44-OU		Raj Hamsa X'Air		
44-OV		Raj Hamsa X'Air		
44-PH		Raj Hamsa X'Air		
44-PN		Rans S-6 Coyote II		
44-PO		Djicat Buse'Air 150		
44-PR		(Weedhopper ?) AX-3		
44-PX		HMD.380		
44-PY		Aviasud AE209 Albatros		
44-QE		ICP MXP-740 Savannah		
44-QO		Weedhopper AX-3		
44-RH		Solar Wings Pegasus Quantum 15	6952	G-MYVF
44-RM		Cosmos		
44-RN		Aviasud AE209 Albatros		
44-RV		Raj Hamsa X'Air		
44-SF		Raj Hamsa X'Air		
44-SY		Chapelet Lazer		
44-TF		Raj Hamsa X'Air-F		
44-TT	F-JHBF	Best Off Sky Ranger		
44-TX	F-JHTM	Zenair CH-701 STOL		
44-UE		Véliplane Mosquito (trike)		
44-UH	F-JHTC	Cosmos Phase II		
44-UJ		Raj Hamsa X'Air		
44-UQ		Zenair CH-701 STOL		
44-UY		ZUT Aviation TT2000 STOL		
44-VD		Ray Hamsa X'Air		
44-VN		Air Création GTE Clipper / XP		
44-VO		KDA (trike) / First Elipse		
		(W/o 21.12.08)		
44-VT		Cosmos / La Mouette Top 12.9		
44-XD	F-JHWF	Rans S-12 Airaile		
		(New c/s F-JPAI?)		
44-XH		Raj Hamsa X'Air		
		(previously reported as Brügger MB-2 Colibri)		
44-XO	F-JHVR	Raj Hamsa X'Air 804T		
44-YD		homebuilt (Crashed 13.4.05)		
44-YH		Humbert Tetras		
44-YN		Chapelet / La Mouette Top 14		
44-ZA	F-JHCG	Weedhopper AX-3-503	9122576	
44-ZE		Raj Hamsa X'Air 602T		
		(Crashed 1.8.04)		
44-ZG		gyrocopter		
44-ZH		Magni M-16 Tandem Trainer		
44-ZJ		TL Ultralight TL-2000 Sting Carbon		
44-ZK	F-JRME	Cosmos Biplace / Top 14.9	B21245	
44-ZP		Chapelet		
44-ZR		Magni M-18 Spartan		
44-AAI		Eurowing Goldwing		
44-AAL		Fly Synthesis Storch CL		
		(W/o 17.11.02)		
44-AAM		Zenair CH-601 Zodiac		
44-AAN		TL Ultralight TL-2000 Sting Carbon		
44-AAO	F-JHWK	Chapelet		
44-AAR		weightshift		
44-AAZ		Nigrowsky gyrocopter		
44-ABB		Aero 4000		
44-ABG		3XTrim Trener		
44-ABS		Chapelet Lazer / Drachen Studio Kecur Avant		
44-ABV	F-JHYL	TL Ultralight TL-2000 Sting Carbon		
44-ABY	F-JGAZ	Light Aero Avid Flyer IV		54-QH
44-ACA		Raj Hamsa X'Air-F (Jabiru)		
44-ACB		Raj Hamsa Hanuman		W44-ACB
44-ACC		Zenair CH-601 Zodiac		
44-ACO		Raj Hamsa X'Air	714	
44-ACQ		gyrocopter		
44-ACY		Mainair Blade 912	1189-0199-7-W992	G-OHVA
44-ADC		Aeroprakt A-20		
44-ADF		Raj Hamsa X'Air-F		
44-ADJ		paramotor (W/o 3.3.13)		
44-ADR		Mignet HM.380 Pou-du-Ciel		
44-ADS		Raj Hamsa Hanuman		
44-ADU		Cosmos		
44-ADY	F-JHXD	Aeropro Eurofox	14503	
		(Also reported as Jabiru)		
44-AEG		TL Ultralight TL-2000 Sting Carbon		
44-AEH		Air Création GTE / iXess		
44-AEJ		Air Création GTE Clipper / Drachen Studion Kecur Avant		
		(Wing also noted on Chapelet Lazer trike .06)		
44-AEO	F-JHBB	Zenair CH-601 Zodiac		
44-AER		TeST TST-9 Junior 2002	09020403	
44-AEX		Magni M-16 Tandem Trainer		
44-AEY		Raj Hamsa Hanuman		
44-AEZ		Raj Hamsa Hanuman		
44-AFA	F-JHXK	Raj Hamsa X'Air		
		(Regn & c/s now reported as Zenair CH-601 Zodiac)		
44-AFD		ICP MXP-740 Savannah		
44-AFL		Raj Hamsa X'Air F		
44-AFM	F-JZJQ	Raj Hamsa X'Air		
44-AFN	F-JHBN	Raj Hamsa Hanuman		
44-AFP	F-JHBM	Raj Hamsa X'Air F (D-Motor engine)		
44-AFX		Raj Hamsa Hanuman	949	
		(Re-regd EI-ETD 8.12)		
44-AGA		Raj Hamsa Hawk		
44-AGB	F-JHBI	Raj Hamsa Hanuman		
44-AGP		Air Création GTE		
44-AGU		Corby CJ-1 Starlet		
44-AGW		Aeropro Eurofox		
44-AHC		Raj Hamsa X'Air		
44-AHH		Raj Hamsa Hanuman		
44-AHJ	F-JHDM	Aeroprakt A-22 Vision	117	
W44-AHK		Libellule (homebuilt)		
		(Crashed 9.5.06)		
44-AHL		Zenair CH-601UL Zodiac		

Reg	Call-sign	Type	c/n	Prev/Notes
44-AHM		Zenair CH-601XL Zodiac		
44-AHO	F-JHDT	Raj Hamsa Hanuman		72-NN
44-AHR		ITV Dakota paramotor		
44-AHS		DTA Combo / Dynamic		
		(Accident 8.8.06)		
44-AJS		DTA Combo / Dynamic		
44-AJT		Aéro Services Guépard 912		
44-AJW	F-JZBZ	Alpi Aviation Pioneer 200		
		(Same call-sign as 56-LF)		
44-AJZ		2-seat gyrocopter (homebuilt)		
44-AKB	F-JZFF	ATEC 321 Faeta		
44-AKG	F-JZQI	Zenair CH-601XL Zodiac	6-9663	
44-AKJ		Nigrowsky gyrocopter		
44-AKL	F-JZUH	Chapelet Lazer (BMW) / La Mouette Ipsos 16.9		
		(Dbr in forced landing 24.6.07)		
44-AKM		P&M Aviation Quik GT450	8202	
		(Re-regd G-KMAK 5.15)		
W44-AKN		Raj Hamsa Hanuman		
44-ALB		Chapelet Big Bang / Drachen Studio Kecur Eos 15		
44-ALC		Nigrowsky gyrocopter		
44-ALH		Nigrowsky Batwing 582 gyrocopter		
44-ALO	F-JYIB	Flight Design CT SW	07-01-18	
44-ALQ		Raj Hamsa Hanuman		
44-ALR		gyrocopter		
44-ALT		Autogyro-Europe MT-03		
44-ALU		Raj Hamsa X'Air Hawk	934	
		(Re-regd EI-ECP)		
44-ALV		Air Création GT BI 582S / XP15		
44-ALY	F-JXKV	Raj Hamsa Hanuman (f/p)		
44-AMB	F-JXKU	Raj Hamsa X'Air F J22	999	
44-AME		paramotor		
44-AMG		ATEC 321 Faeta		
44-AMJ	F-JHCX	DTA Combo / Dynamic 15/530	203	
44-AMM	F-JZUH	Chapelet Lazer / Drachen Studio Kecur Eos 15		
44-AMR		Chapelet		
W44-AMV		Raj Hamsa Hanuman		
44-AMY		weightshift		
		(W/o 4.7.15)		
44-ANE		trike / La Mouette Oryx		
44-ANF	F-JZHY	gyrocopter (homebuilt)		
44-ANH	F-JXSR	Quetzal / La Mouette Ipsos 14.9		W44-ANH
44-ANI		Aerola Alatus-M (motorglider)	LA-0907	
44-ANJ	F-JHDQ	Marie JPM-03 Loiret	2	49-NW, W49-NW
44-ANS		Magni M-22 Voyager		
44-ANZ		gyrocopter		
44-AOC	F-JWHY	Raj Hamsa Hanuman		
44-AOI		Aerola Alatus ME (Electric powered motorglider)		
44-AOM	F-JFCK	Best Off Sky Ranger		
44-AON	F-JZUH	P&M Aviation QuikR 912S	8439	
44-AOZ		P&M Aviation Quik		
44-APA	F-JWRG	Didier Pti'avion		
44-APC	F-JWOG	Nigrowski gyrocopter (homebuilt)		
44-APF	F-JWWF	Raj Hamsa Hanuman		
44-APK	F-JHDR	Raj Hamsa Hanuman		F-JHBN
44-APN		Air Création GTE Trek / Kiss		
44-APO	F-JHUB	Air Création GTE Trek HKS700 / iXess 13		
			A09067-9063/T09033	
44-APP		Raj Hamsa Hanuman		
44-APS	F-JXTG	Evektor EV-97R Eurostar	2007 3119	
		(Re-regd 47-UQ)		
44-APX	F-JRGI	Aveko VL-3 Sprint	VL3-53	
44-AQI	F-JDDJ	Best Off Nynja		
44-AQO	F-JPDQ	Aero Kuhlmann Scub		
44-AQR		Air Création GT BI		
44-AQV		Vol Mediterrani VM-1 Esqual		
44-AQW	F-JRHT	Flight Design CT LS	F-09-09-03	31-NT
44-AQZ		P&M Aviation QuikR 912S		
44-ARF		Ray Hamsa X'Air Hawk (D-Motor)		
44-ARH	F-JSJM	Humbert Tetras 912CSL		
44-ARJ		P&M Aviation QuikR	8606	
44-ARK		DTA Combo 582 / Diva		
44-ARN	F-JSIZ	ESPACE Sensation		
44-ARP	F-JSLF	Halley Apollo Jetstat 582		
44-ARX	F-JSSH	Aveko VL-3 Sprint		
44-ASB	F-JHAW	Raj Hamsa Hanuman		85-SK
44-ASI	F-JYDH	Javelot		
44-ASP		Polaris FIB		
44-ASR		DTA Feeling / Dynamic 450		
44-ASU	F-JXYV	Raj Hamsa Hanuman 912S SW		
44-ASW		Aeroprakt A-22L2		
44-ATJ	F-JXDW	G1 Aviation G1		
44-ATK	F-JZYJ	Fly Synthesis Storch HS		62-ALB
44-ATN		Aéro Services SG.12A		
44-ATW	F-JTWO	Aéro Services SG.12A	22117	
44-AUA	F-JUDS	Mosquito XE2		
44-AUF	F-JVGL	ESPACE Sensation	16	
44-AUI	F-JXYV	Raj Hamsa Hanuman (D-Motor)		
44-AUJ	F-JUDU	ESPACE Sensation		
44-AUK	F-JUDO	Pro.Mecc. Freccia		
44-AUR	F-JUKD	Evektor EV-97 Eurostar SL		
44-AVA	F-JHWO	Tecno trike / Halley Apollo wing		
44-AVB	F-JUPK	BRM Aero Bristell XL-8		
44-AVG		Zlin Savage Bobber		
44-AVN	F-JVBN	ELA Aviacion ELA-07S	0713 400 0712	
44-AVP	F-JSIZ	ESPACE Sensation	020	
44-AVV	F-JVKK	ESPACE Sensation	021	
44-AVX	F-JVLG	BRM Aero Bristell XL-8		
44-AVY	F-JPKJ	BRM Aero Bristell XL-8		
44-AWB	F-JVNL	Aero East Europe SILA 450C	130805-AEE015	
44-AWF	F-JVUH	TL Ultralight TL-3000 Sirius		
44-AWI	F-JVTE	Flight Design CT LS	F-13-03-06	
44-AXG		Zenair CH-601XL Zodiac		
44-AXI	F-JURH	ESPACE Sensation	023	
44-AXN	F-JVRV	Roko Aero NG6UL		
44-AYG	F-JAKK	ESPACE Sensation	026	
44-AYJ		Roko Aero NG6UL		
44-A..	F-JXKY	B&F Funk FK-9 Mk.IV SW	336?	

45 : Loiret

Reg	Call-sign	Type	c/n	Prev/Notes
45-AG		Synairgie		
45-AP		(Technic Moto ?) Mustang		
45-AY		paramotor		
45-BK		Air Création		
45-BO		Delpech MD.04 Airland		
		(W/o 1.8.99)		
45-BP		Air Création Racer / SX 12		
45-BT		(Technic Moto ?) Mustang		
45-BV		Synairgie		
45-CU		Piel CP.152B Onyx	50	
45-DB		Weedhopper AX-3	9122580	
45-DF		Trapanelle		
45-ED		Air Création		
45-EH		Cosmos		
45-EP		JCC Aviation J.300 Joker		
45-EX		SCEP Mustang		
45-FM		Air Création / Quartz		
45-FO		Air Création		
45-FX		DTA / Dynamic 450	143	
45-GC		(Technic Moto ?) Mustang		
45-GD		Cosmos		
45-GG		Weedhopper AX-3		
45-GH		CA Bidulm		
45-GQ		Air Création / Mild		
		(Re-regd 45-ZT)		
45-GR		Air Création GT BI / Quartz		
45-HG		Mignet HM.360J Pou-du-Ciel		
45-HU		Hipps Superbirds J-3 Kitten		
W-45-HY		Air Création / XP		
45-JA		Air Création		
45-JI		Air Création GTE Clipper		
45-KB		Synairgie		
45-KC		Air Création GT BI 16 / SX		
45-KG		Mignet HM.293 Pou-du-Ciel		
45-KI		Plätzer Kiebitz		
45-KL		III Sky Arrow 501TF		
45-KX		Powerchute Raider		
45-KZ		Best Off Sky Ranger		
45-LF		Air Création		
45-LG		Zenair CH-701 STOL		
45-LI		Humbert La Moto-du-Ciel		
45-LN		Cosmos		
45-LP		Aeros / Stranger		77-VE
45-LS		Cosmos		
45-MA		SE.5 replica		
45-MB		"Wild Bird"		
45-MH		Cosmos		
45-MJ		Air Création GTE Clipper		
45-MO	F-JPAT	Air Création GT BI / Kiss		
45-MS	F-JPOK	ZUT Aviation TT2000 STOL		
45-MV		Air Création GTE Clipper / XP		
45-NA		Zenair CH-701 STOL		
45-ND		III Sky Arrow 500TF	070	
		(W/o 3.5.14)		
45-NI	F-JZGN	Ray Hamsa X'Air		44-OL
45-NN		Zodiac Ultrastar	104	
45-NP	F-JFPQ	Dyn'Aéro MCR-01	121	
		(Re-regd 78-XG)		
45-NQ		Air Création Buggy Twin / Kiss		
45-PJ		Air Création GTE / Kiss		
45-PT		Cosmos Phase II	21455	
45-PW		Air Création GT BI / XP		
45-PY	F-JFUA	Rans S-6 Coyote II		
45-QF		Barry MB-02 Souricette		
45-QH		Cosmos		
45-QI		Air Création Buggy / III		
45-QJ	F-JFGH	B&F Funk FK-9 Mk.III		
W45-QK		Barry MB-02 Souricette		
45-QN	F-JFNL	TL Ultralight TL-2000 Sting Carbon		
45-QO		Micro Aviation Pulsar II		
45-QP		III Sky Arrow 500TF	040	
		(Same c/n as 28-PP and 54-QT / F-JGAY)		
45-QW		ICP Super Bingo	02-09-52-070	
45-QZ	F-JFNM	ICP MXP-740 Savannah		
45-RB	F-JPKK	Fly Synthesis Storch		
45-RF		Pipistrel Sinus		
45-RG		Air Création / iXess		
45-RL		Action paramotor		
45-RQ		ATEC Zephyr 2000C		
W45-RV		ZUT Aviation TT2000 STOL		
45-RW		Paraway 2 Seat paramotor		
45-RX		DTA / Air Création iXess		
45-SA	F-JFGV	Urban Air UFM-13 Lambda	35/13	
45-SC		Air Création GT BI / SX		
45-SG	F-JPEM	Fly Synthesis Storch HS		
45-SJ	F-JYSO	Alpi Aviation Pioneer 300		
		(Previously F-JHIZ)		
45-SL		Zenair CH-601XL Zodiac		
45-SN		Air Création Tanarg / iXess		
45-ST		DTA Combo 582 / Dynamic 15/430		
45-SW		ICP Super Bingo	02-12-52-085	
45-TK		Fly Synthesis Texan Top Class		
45-TL		ICP MXP-740 Savannah	03-05-51-229	
45-TO		trike / Synairgie		
45-TQ	F-JPHZ	ATEC Zephyr		
45-TT	F-JPFD	ICP MXP-740 Savannah	01-04-51-067	
45-TW		Cosmos		
45-UA		Best Off Sky Ranger		
45-UB		DTA / Dynamic 15/430	203	
45-UJ	F-JPKP	Humbert La Moto-du-Ciel		
45-US		DTA / Dynamic 15/430		
45-UU		Fly Synthesis Storch HS		
45-UV		paramotor		
45-UW		paramotor		
45-VA	F-JPOR	Didier Pti'avion		
45-VC		Air Création GTE Clipper / XP		
45-VD		B&F Funk FK-9 Mk.IV	247	
		(To 31-GJ and dbf 30.5.08)		
45-VE		DTA Combo / La Mouette Green 12		
45-VH	F-JPOX	Jabiru UL		
45-VL		Rans S-6 Coyote II		
45-VO	F-JZPX	Delage/Marie JPM-03 Loiret	1	W45-VO
45-WB	F-JPUA	Aviakit Vega		
		(Re-regd 77-AWU)		
45-WF		Aviasud Sirocco		
45-WL	F-JZBV	Dyn'Aéro MCR-01	327	
45-WX		ATEC 212 Solo		
45-XG	F-JZDC	Aeroprakt A-22		
45-XJ		Rans S-6 Coyote II		
45-XK		Best Off Sky Ranger V-Max (Hirth)		
45-XW	F-JZUJ	ATEC 212 Solo		
45-XX	F-JZRS	Humbert La Moto-du-Ciel		

Reg	Reg2	Type	C/n	Prev
45-YF		Air Création		
45-YI	F-JYAD	B&F Funk FK-12 Comet	12-075	
45-YJ		PAP/Ozone Viper paramotor		
45-YP	F-JIFS	B&F Funk FK-12 Comet	12-044	31-FS
45-YS		Air Création GTE Clipper / iXess		
45-YZ		PJB Aerocomposite Vega (t/w)		
45-ZA	F-JYHG	Flight Design CT SW		
45-ZB	F-JFRK	Alpi Aviation Pioneer 200		
45-ZE	F-JPOV	Flight Design CT SW		
45-ZH		type unknown (low wing, 3-axis)		
W45-ZR		Evektor EV-97 Sportstar	2007 0912	
45-ZS	F-JHVL	Rans S-7 Courier		
45-ZT		Air Création / Mild		45-GQ
45-AAJ		ELA Aviacion ELA-07		
45-AAS		paramotor		
45-AAV		Light Aero Avid Flyer		
45-ABI	F-JXVG	Flight Design CT LS	08-01-22	
45-ABL	F-JWXF	ELA Aviacion ELA-07S	0208 212 0724	
45-ABP		Best Off Sky Ranger		
45-ABZ		paramotor		
45-ACB		Aeroprakt A-22L		
45-ACF		Comco Ikarus C-42		
45-ACG	F-JXAG	Fly Synthesis Storch		
		(Same call-sign as 65-AC)		
45-ACQ		Rans S-6 Coyote II		
45-ACT		Best Off Sky Ranger		05-EH
45-ACV	F-JXAW	Halley Apollo Fox	01-02-05	
45-ACW		Ekolot KR-030 Topaz		
45-ACX	F-JZMX	Humbert Tetras		
45-ACZ	F-JXGB	Flight Design CT SW	07-07-25	
		(Same c/n and call-sign as 76-PX)		
		(not a Comco Ikarus C-42 as previously reported)		
45-ADA		Comco Ikarus C-42		
45-ADH	F-JWWS	ELA Aviacion ELA-07	0209 266 0724	
45-ADL		Ellipse Alizé (trike)		
45-ADO		Gyrojet (homebuilt gyrocopter)		
45-AEH		Nike Aeronautica 503 / Pegasus Q1		
45-AEO		Aeroandinas MXP-158 Embera		
45-AEU	F-JRXR	Comco Ikarus C-42		
45-AFK	F-JSVD	ICP MXP-740 Savannah XL	09-08-51-866	
45-AFP	F-JSGX	Pipistrel Virus		
45-AGA	F-JSPB	Nando Groppo Trial	0005/3	
45-AGH		ICP MXP-740 Savannah S		
45-AGO		Best Off Sky Ranger		
45-AGP	F-JZOW	ICP MXP-740 Savannah		
45-AGR	F-JWGW	Aerospool WT-9 Dynamic	DY280/2008	
45-AHB		Aviasud AE209 Albatros	111	
45-AHU	F-JUAL	Colomban MC-30 Luciole	32	
45-AHW		Tecnam P.92 Echo		
45-AHZ		Paramania GTR paramotor		
45-AIB		Paramania paramotor		
45-AIW		Ozone Slalom paramotor		
45-AIX		ELA Aviacion ELA-07		
45-AJA	F-JUPN	Zenair CH-650Ei (ICP-built)		
45-AJD		Ozone Slalom paramotor		
45-AJG	F-JUTO	Zlin Savage Cub	258	
45-AJT		Ozone Speedster paramotor		
45-AJV		Paramania GTX		
W45-AJX		Agrion		
45-AKH	F-JVVM	JMB Aircraft VL-3 Evolution	134	
45-ALG		unidentified paramotor		

46 : Lot

Reg	Reg2	Type	C/n	Prev
46-AC		Clavel HM.293 Pou-du-Ciel		
46-AE		Aéro Services Guépard 582		
46-AG		Air Création GTE Trek 582ES / iXess 15		
46-AK		weightshift		
46-AO	F-JIEU	Aéro Services Guépard 912		
46-AR		PGO Aviation Cobra		
		(W/o 20.7.97)		
46-AZ	F-JIHU	Fantasy Air Allegro SW		
46-BD		Aéro Services Guépard 912S		
46-BJ		weightshift		
46-BM(1)		weightshift		
46-BM(2)		Zenair CH-601 Zodiac		
46-BO		Delpech MD.04 Airland		
		(W/o 1.8.99)		
46-BS		Fly Synthesis Storch		
46-BT	F-JIBT	Aéro Services Guépard 912		
46-CI		Raj Hamsa X'Air 602T		
		(W/o 9.6.03)		
46-CS		Aéro Services Guépard 912		
46-CU		Light Aero Avid Flyer	476	F-WZUM(2)
46-CW	F-JKEO	Humbert Tetras		
46-CZ	F-JYRG	ATEC 122 Zephyr 2004C		
46-DA	F-JXEI	Raj Hamsa X'Air	1022	
46-DD	F-JXOE	Aéro Services Guépard 912S		
46-DE		Magni M-22 Voyager		
46-DM		Zlin Savage Classic		
46-DO(1)	F-JIIQ	Aéro Services Guépard		
46-DO(2)		ICP Bingo 4S	03-07-52-121	34-XN
46-DV	F-JWIF	Magni M-24 Orion	24-08-5004	
46-DW		ICP MXP-740 Savannah	08-03-51-702	27-YS
46-EA	F-JGCD	Aéro Services Guépy 582		88-FY
46-EL		Alpi Aviation Pioneer 200		
46-EQ		Top Concept Hurricane		
46-ER		Aéro Services Super Guépard 912		
46-EU		ICP MXP-740 Savannah	04-11-51-346	
46-EV		Magni M-24 Orion		
46-EW		Eipper Quicksilver		
46-EZ	F-JWLH	Magni M-22 Voyager		
46-FA	F-JIFB	Aéro Services Guépard 912		
46-FC		Synairgie		
46-FJ		Humbert Tetras		
46-FP	F-JTTZ	Pennec Gaz'Aile 2	200	
46-FU	F-JUBE	Magni M-22 Voyager	22-12-7204	
		(W/o 21.6.15)		
46-FV		Aéro Services Guépe 582		
46-GB		Plätzer Kiebitz	274	OO-F88
46-GC		Dynali H2S		
46-GJ	F-JAII	Roland Z.602RG		
46-GO		Synairgie		
46-IE		Synairgie		
46-MA	F-JIGM	Zlin Savage		
46-MB		III Sky Arrow 520TF		
46-PN		Humbert Tetras		

Reg	Reg2	Type	C/n	Prev
46-TT		DTA Dynamic 15/430		
46-AEN	F-JYAW	Weedhopper AX-3	C3113180	
		(Out of sequence. Re-regd 54-AEN, or ex?)		

47 : Lot-et-Garonne

Reg	Reg2	Type	C/n	Prev
47-P		Cosmos / La Mouette		57-AK
47-BJ		Atlas Wing		
47-BL		Air Création		
47-BY		ADR-20		
47-CK		Air Création / Kiss		
47-CR		Cosmos		
47-DF		Mignet Pou-du-Ciel		
47-DG		Mignet HM.14 Pou-du-Ciel		
47-DI		DTA / Dynamic 15		
47-DR		Cosmos Chronos		
47-DU		Comco Ikarus Fox-C22		
47-EB		Air Création GT BI / Quartz		
47-EC		Air Création GT BI / Quartz		
47-EI		Air Création Racer		
47-EO		Top Concept Hurricane		
		(W/o 9.7.01)		
47-FE		Air Création Safari GT BI 582		
		(W/o 15.7.05)		
47-FK		Humbert La Moto-du-Ciel		
47-FN	F-JBBZ	Rans S-6 Coyote II		
47-FW		Air Création GT BI / Quartz		
47-FY		Cosmos Chronos 16		
47-FZ		Air Création GT BI 503 / Fun 18		
47-GE		Synairgie / Dauphin (?)		
47-GG		Buccaneer II amphibian		
47-GH		Air Création Racer		
47-GM		Aero Designs Pulsar		
47-GN		Air Création Racer		
47-GO		Air Création Racer		
47-GU		Weedhopper	B1081143	
47-GW		Air Création GT		
47-GY		Air Création GT		
47-HB		Weedhopper	0011129	
47-HD		Air Création GT BI / SX		
47-HE		weightshift		
47-HF		Air Création		
47-HN		Synairgie Dauphin 503		
		(Crashed 8.8.04)		
47-HQ		Rans S-6 Coyote II		
47-HS		Air Création Racer		
47-HY		Rans S-6 Coyote II	0295752ES	
		(Re-regd OO-C71)		
47-IN		Buccaneer S2B		
47-JA		Rans S-6 Coyote II		
		(W/o 21.2.97)		
47-JC		Rans S-6 Coyote II		
47-JD		Air Création GT BI 462 / Fun 18		
47-JI	F-JKBG	Best Off Sky Ranger (built by Synairgie)		
47-JM		Air Création		
47-JP		Air Création		
47-JR		Jihlavan Skyleader 200		
47-KO		Mignet HM.1000 Balerit		
47-KY		Comco Ikarus C-42		
47-LA		Aquilair / Aeros Profi		
47-LF		Cosmos Bidulm		
47-LM	F-JKHM	Jihlavan Skyleader 150		
		(Same call-sign as 47-LY, see below)		
47-LR		Mignet HM.293 Pou-du-Ciel		
47-LW		Air Création GTE		
47-LY	F-JKHM	Jihlavan Skyleader 150		F-JEGT
		(Same call-sign as 47-LM – allocated to dealer for multiple use?)		
47-MA		Best Off Sky Ranger		
47-MB		Kappa 77 KP-2U Sova		
47-MC		Mignet HM.1100 Cordouan	11	
47-MF		European Airwings Springbok		
47-MJ		Best Off Sky Ranger		
47-ML		Air Création Racer	447	
47-MM	F-JYWA	Top Concept Hurricane		
		(Wing of 16-CM)		
47-MQ	F-JKCR	Kappa 77 KP-2U Sova		
47-MV		Air Création		
47-MW	F-JKDA	Vol Mediterrani VM-1 Esqual		
47-MX		DTA / Dynamic		
47-MY		Rans S-7 Courier		
47-NA		Best Off Sky Ranger		
47-NB	F-JKDB	Kappa 77 KP-2U Sova		
47-NG		Kappa 77 KP-2U Sova		
47-NH	F-JKDK	Kappa 77 KP-2U Sova	7078H	
47-NI		Buccaneer S2B		
47-NJ		Best Off Sky Ranger		
47-NL		Polaris FIB		
47-NT		Guerin G1		
47-NU		Zenair CH-601 Zodiac (t/w)		
47-NY		Top Concept Hurricane		
47-NZ		Air Création GTE / iXess		
47-OA		Air Action Quicky / Synairgie Puma		
47-OE	F-JKEH	Jihlavan Skyleader 200		
		(same call sign as 82-II)		
		(Not known which of 47-OE or 82-II is current)		
47-OF		Kappa 77 KP-2U Sova		
47-OG		Comco Ikarus C-42		
		(or 47-QG?)		
47-OI		DTA / Dynamic 16		
47-OR		Air Création Buggy 582 / XP15		
47-OU		Comco Ikarus Fox-C22B	…-3681	D-MRMF
47-OY		Aeropro Eurofox		
47-OZ		Chapelet / Dynamic		
47-PB		DTA Evolution 582 / Dynamic 16		
47-PF	F-JKHA	Zenair CH-601 Zodiac		
47-PG		Best Off Sky Ranger		
47-PK	F-JKGV	Kappa 77 KP-2U Sova		
47-PL		Aeromoragan M-1 Stela		
47-PR(1)		Aviakit Hermes		
47-PR(2)		ALMS/Sauper Papango		
47-PV		Air Création GTE 503S / Fun 450		
47-PX		Cosmos Phase 1		
47-QA	F-JKHY	Synairgie / Puma		
47-QF	F-JKID	Vol Mediterrani VM-1 Esqual		
47-QG		Evektor EV-97 Eurostar		
47-QO		Vol Mediterrani VM-1 Esqual		
47-QQ	F-JZHV	Jodel D.195		

Reg	Callsign	Type	c/n	Prev
47-QX		Best Off Sky Ranger		
		(Crashed 1.5.06)		
47-QY		Sperling biplane (homebuilt)		
47-RC		DTA / Dynamic 15/430		
47-RD	F-JZQQ	Best Off Sky Ranger "L'Afrik I"		
47-RF		Best Off Sky Ranger V-Max		
47-RN		Best Off Sky Ranger		
47-RO	F-JYFO	Rans S-6 Coyote II		
47-RS	F-JEGT	Kappa 77 KP-2U Sova		
		(Same call-sign as 26-UU, see also 47-LY))		
47-RT		Best Off Sky Ranger		
47-RU		Air Création GTE Trek		
47-RX		Air Création		
47-RZ	F-JKJE	Rans S-6 Coyote II (t/w)		
47-SA	F-JXAX	Best Off Sky Ranger V-Max		
		(Re-regd 83-AHU)		
47-SF		ELA Aviacion ELA-07		
47-SH		Rans S-6 Coyote II (t/w)		
47-SL	F-JXDX	Comco Ikarus C-42		
47-SM		DTA / Ellipse Fuji 16		
47-ST		DTA Combo 582 / Dynamic 15/430		
47-TB		Rans S-6 Coyote II		
47-TC		DTA Combo / Dynamic 15/430		
47-TF		Best Off Sky Ranger		
47-TG	F-JWDR	Jihlavan Skyleader 150		
47-TJ	F-JWEH	Zenair CH-601 Zodiac		
47-TK	F-JWIA	Jihlavan Skyleader 200		26-DW
47-TM	F-JSDO	Jihlavan KP-2U Sova	61G	PH-3V3
47-TN		Zenair CH-601XL Zodiac (t/w)		
47-TO		Synairgie Midi 18		
47-TQ		Synairgie (wing)		
		(wing noted attached to OO-A39 Microbel TD 1+1)		
47-TU		Solar Wings Pegasus XL-Q		
47-TW		Eipper Quicksilver GT400		
47-UB		Best Off Nynja		
47-UC		Autogyro-Europe MTOsport		
47-UD		Rans S-6 Coyote II		
47-UI		Jihlavan Skyleader 150		
47-UL	F-JRPQ	Best Off Nynja		
47-UN		Aéro Services SG.10A		
47-UO		Fly Synthesis Wallaby		
47-UP		Air Création Buggy 582 / XP15		
47-UQ	F-JXTG	Evektor EV-97 Eurostar	2007 3119	44-APS
47-UR	F-JRWV	Jihlavan Skyleader 200		
47-UT	F-JZHQ	Weedhopper		??-FU
47-UX	F-JIVN	unidentified gyrocopter		
47-UY		Magni M-16 Tandem Trainer		
47-VB		Aeropro Eurofox		33-ZV
47-VF		Jihlavan Skyleader 200		
47-VI		Best Off Nynja		
47-VJ		Autogyro-Europe MTOsport		
47-VO	F-JSVY	Air Création Skypper 582 / NuviX 15		
47-VQ		Campana Campana		
47-VR		Best Off Nynja		
47-VU	F-JPIW	Zenair CH-601XL Zodiac	6-1778	
47-VX	F-JIVB	Best Off Sky Ranger	SKR0311418	11-HG
47-WG	F-JYOB	Aéro Services Guepy Jabiru 80		
47-WR		Mignet HM.360 Pou-du-Ciel		
47-WS	F-JTZM	Jihlavan Skyleader 200		
47-WZ	F-JULB	Directfly Alto		
47-XB		Jihlavan Skyleader 200	2-213232S	
47-XC	F-JULY	Best Off Nynja	13010123	
47-XD	F-JUNP	Dyn'Aero MCR-01		
47-XN	F-JVMK	Jihlavan Skyleader 200RG		
47-XP	F-JVML	Best Off Nynja Remorqueur	13060143	
47-XQ	F-JVNR	Jihlavan GP One	8006006T	
47-XW		Jihlavan Skyleader 150		
47-YD		Jihlavan Skyleader 200 / KP-2U Rapid2 240261 U		
47-YU	F-JAOR	Jihlavan Skyleader 200		
47-YV		Best Off Nynja Remo		
47-ZO		trike / Drachen Studio Kecur Eos 15		

48 : Lozère

Reg	Callsign	Type	c/n	Prev
48		Dragon 150		
48-AD		Dynali Chickinox Kot-Kot		
48-AK	F-JCNQ	Aéro Services Guépard		
48-AY		Albastar Apis	A031M13	
48-AZ		ProFe D-10 Tukan		
48-BK		B&F Funk FK-14 Polaris		
48-BT	F-JAAP	ICP MXP-740 Savannah S	14-12-54-0364	
48-..	F-JXSO	TeST TST-14 Bonus		

49 : Maine-et-Loire

Reg	Callsign	Type	c/n	Prev
49-A		Air Création GT BI / Quartz		
49-AL		Air Création GT BI / Quartz		
49-AQ		Solar Wings Pegasus XL		
49-BF		Ropulcia Colt		
49-BG		Microbel Must		
49-BP		Microbel Must		
49-BV		Synairgie		
49-CH		Air Création		
49-CK		Rousseau Ropulcim		
49-CL		Tecma Ascender (Rousseau Ropulcim)		
49-CS		Air Création Racer / Fun 14		
49-DA		Chaser Microbel		
49-EU		Aerial Arts Chaser 377		
49-FO		Piel CP.152B Onyx	50	
49-FV		DTA Combo (HKS700) / Dynamic		
49-GB		Fulmar (?) (weightshift)		
		(W/o 15.4.01)		
49-GE		Air Création / Quartz		
49-GY		Air Création Safari GT BI		
		(W/o 22.7.05)		
49-HE	F-JHWX	Humbert Tetras		
		(or 49-EH ?)		
49-HF		Air Création		
49-HO		Synairgie		
49-HP		Best Off Sky Ranger		
49-IB		Best Off Sky Ranger		
49-II	F-JCWH	Tecnam P.92 Echo		
49-JF		Croses Criquet Leger		
49-JG		DTA / Dynamic 503		
		(Damaged 1.6.05)		
W49-KA		Mignet HM.293 Pou-du-Ciel		
49-KE		Cosmos / Echo 12		
49-KL		Air Création		

Reg	Callsign	Type	c/n	Prev
49-KR		Air Création		
49-KU	F-JHWS	Pipistrel Sinus		
49-KV		Mignet HM.293 Pou-du-Ciel		
49-KY		Air Création / iXess		
49-LA		DTA / Dynamic 450		
49-LE		DTA / Dynamic 450		
49-LG		Raj Hamsa X'Air		
49-LO	F-JHZC	TL Ultralight TL-2000 Sting Carbon		
49-LP		Best Off Sky Ranger		
49-LQ	F-JHKY	DTA / Dynamic 15	161	
49-LV		Pagotto Brako / Gryf CRS		
49-MF		Take Off Merlin		
49-MU		Urban Air UFM-13 Lambada		
49-NB		DTA Combo / Dynamic 15/430		
49-NF	F-JZDN	Fly Synthesis Storch		
		(To 28-AKO ?)		
49-NG		Tieleman Tommy (homebuilt)		
		(Crashed 4.9.05)		
49-NL		Véliplane Mosquito (trike)		
49-NO		Rans S-12 Airaile		
49-NU		Evektor EV-97 Eurostar	2005 2610	
49-NW		Marie JPM-03 Loiret	2	W49-NW
		(Re-regd 44-ANJ .08)		
49-NY	F-JHVA	Djicat Buse'Air		
49-OS	F-JHYE	Dyn'Aéro MCR-01 UL	316	
49-OT		Fantasy Air Allegro		
49-OU	F-JZEO	Jabiru		
49-OX		weightshift		
49-OY	F-JYKT	Best Off Sky Ranger		
49-OZ		Best Off Sky Ranger		
49-PB		Dakota Reflex paramotor		
		(Accident 14.10.07)		
49-PM	F-JZZO	Aeroprakt A-22	085	
49-PS	F-JYHP	Evektor EV-97R Eurostar	2006 2809	F-EANC
		(To 9H-UEB)		
49-PV		Magni M-22 Voyager		
49-QG		Adventure X Race / Dudek Nucleon paramotor		
49-QN	F-JGRA	Jodel D.20		
49-QX		Pagotto Brako / Gryf CRS		
49-QY		Air Création GTE Clipper		
49-QZ		Air Création GT BI / iXess		
49-RD	F-JXYO	Alpi Aviation Pioneer 200	46	
49-RJ(1)?		European Airwings Springbok 2000		
49-RJ(2)		Ekolot KR-030 Topaz		
		(W/o 29.8.08)		
49-RK		Evektor EV-97 Eurostar SLR	2008 3405	
49-RO		Humbert Tetras		
49-RQ	F-JWLS	Evektor EV-97 Eurostar	2008 3509	
		(Same c/n as D-MBWL)		
49-RR		Air Création GTE Trek		
49-RZ	F-JWUF	Evektor EV-97 Eurostar SL	2008 3504	
49-SB		Jodel (D.19 ?)		
49-SD		Adventure X Race / Dudek Nucleon paramotor		
49-SG	F-JWZS	Pipistrel Sinus	299S912	
49-SM		Evektor EV-97 Eurostar		
49-SN	F-JXWG	Evektor EV-97 Eurostar		
49-SO		ATEC 212 Solo		
49-SP	F-JRGK	Evektor EV-97 Eurostar SL	2009 3616	
49-SQ		Aeropro Eurofox		
49-SR		unidentified paramotor		
49-ST		Sherwood Ranger		
49-SY		Raj Hamsa X'Air		
49-TA	F-JXSB	ATEC 122 Zephyr		85-WE
49-TB		Aeropro Eurofox		
49-TE	F-JRMO	Evektor EV-97A Eurostar		
49-TF		Magni M-22 Voyager		
49-TN	F-JRWP	Just Outback		
49-TP	F-JRXH	TL Ultralight TL-2000 Sting Carbon RG		
49-UF	F-JHWH	Colomban MC-30 Luciole	150	
49-UH		paramotor		
49-UI		paramotor		
49-UL		Magni M-22 Voyager		
49-UN		paramotor		
49-UT	F-JZBF	Evektor EV-97 Eurostar	2007 2941	22-JA
49-UX		Colomban MC-30 Luciole	62	
49-VH	F-JTBK	Raj Hamsa Hanuman		
49-VN		Aeropro Eurofox		
49-VU		Air Création GT BI / Quartz		
49-VX		Magni M-16 Tandem Trainer		
49-WA		Best Off Sky Ranger		
49-WE		Evektor EV-97 Eurostar SL		
49-WG		Nigrowky Batwing 618 gyrocopter		
49-WW		BRM Aero Bristell XL-8		
49-XN		Pipistrel Alpha Trainer		
49-XO	F-JUOD	Celier Xenon		
49-XV	F-JVDC	Pipistrel Alpha Trainer		
49-XW	F-JVFC	Dyn'Aero MCR-01		
49-XX		Zenair CH-701 STOL		
49-ZB		JMB VL-3 Evolution	178	
49-ZE	F-JAMS	BRM Aero Bristell XL-8		
49-ZN		BRM Aero Bristell XL-8		

50 : Manche

Reg	Callsign	Type	c/n	Prev
50-L		Fantasy Air Allegro		
50-U		Aerodyne 627SR Vector		
50-AF		Aerodyne 627SR Vector TM		40-D
50-AG		Air Création / Quartz SX		
50-AI		Aerodyne 627SR Vector		
50-AJ		Air Création		
50-AN		Quartz X5		
50-AO		Air Création		
50-AQ		Quartz X5		
50-AV		Lemmonier Maestro		
50-BH		Fisher FP-202 Super Koala		
50-BI		Air Création		
50-BL		Air Création		
50-CC		Air Création		
50-CG		Aviasud Mistral		
50-CJ		Beaufils SE.5A replica		
50-CN		Air Création GT BI / SX		
50-CR		Air Création		
50-CU		Air Création		
50-CX		Air Création / SX		
50-CY		Dynali Chickinox		
50-DE		Alpaero (Noin) Sirius		
50-DF		Air Création		

Reg		Type	c/n	Prev id
50-DI		Air Création / SX		
50-DP		Air Création GT BI		
50-DU		Air Création GT		
50-DY		Air Création		
50-DZ		Air Création		
50-ED		Parapente		
50-EI		Air Création		
50-EM		Air Création GT BI / Fun		
50-EN		Humbert Tetras		
50-EP		Air Création GT BI / XP		
50-EQ		Humbert La Moto-du-Ciel		
50-EX		Air Création / SX		
50-FA		Air Création		
50-FB		Air Création		
50-FD		Croses Criquet ULM	114	
50-FH		(Technic Moto ?) Mustang		
50-FI		Pegasus		
50-FM		Air Création GT BI		
50-FN		Air Création / Mild		
50-FO		Aéro Services Guépard 912		
50-FR		Air Création / Quartz		
50-FU		Air Création		
		(Also reported as Mustang 3.04)		
50-FX		Chapelet Big Bang		
50-FZ		Air Création		76-FE
50-GA		Synairgie		
50-GB		Air Création		
50-GC		Air Création GT BI		
50-GE		Synairgie / Puma Bi		76-FA
50-GJ		Weedhopper AX-3		
50-GK		Air Création / SX		
50-GL		Air Création GT BI / SX		
		(Crashed 23.7.05)		
50-GO		Rans S-6 Coyote II		
50-GQ		Humbert Tetras		
		(Also reported as gyrocopter)		
50-GS		Air Création		
50-GT		Air Création		
50-GU		Air Création GT BI		50-DS
50-HB		Air Création		
50-HC		Air Création GT BI / Quartz (now SX)		
50-HJ		Air Création		
50-HL	F-JHGQ	Mustang	86 063	
50-HN		Air Création / Fun 450		
50-HP		Air Création		
50-HQ		Magni gyrocopter		
50-HS		Air Création GT BI		
50-HU		Dynali Chickinox		
50-HV		Air Création		
50-HX	F-JHGO	Zenair CH-601UL Zodiac		78-MT
50-HY		Air Création / Fun		
50-IA		Best Off Sky Ranger		
50-IB		Air Création Twin		
50-ID		Air Création		
50-IE		Dynamic 582 / 16		
50-II		Air Création		
50-IK		Aviasud Mistral		
		(W/o 15.2.10)		
50-IL		Air Création / SX		
50-IO		Evektor EV-97R Eurostar	2008 3227	
50-IS	F-JHHB	Dyn'Aéro MCR-01 UL	190	
50-IT		B&F Funk FK-9 Mk.II (t/w)	074	
		(Dismantled at Granville 7.05) (Ex 28-PE ?)		
50-IV		Air Création GT BI / SX		
50-IX		Air Création		
50-IY		Humbert Tetras		
50-JA		weightshift		
50-JB	F-JHHI	3XTrim		
50-JC		Air Création GTE / SX		
50-JD		Eipper Quicksilver		
		(Dismantled)		
50-JE	F-JHGU	Best Off Sky Ranger		
50-JF		Excel		
50-JH		Air Création / Quartz		
50-JK		DTA / Dynamic 15		
50-JL		Air Création / XP		
50-JM		Air Création / SX		
50-JO		Best Off Sky Ranger		
50-JQ		Air Création / XP		
50-JR		Aquilair		
50-JS	F-JHHT	Humbert Tetras		
50-JU		ProFe D-10 Tukan		
50-JY		Morin M-85		
50-KA		Croses ULM Pou du Ciel		
50-KC		DTA } both recorded 28.3.04 in		
50-KC		Air Création / SX } different locations!		
		The Air Création 50-KC may be an error for 50-KG below		
50-KG		Air Création GT BI / SX		
50-KH		Humbert Tetras 912CS		
50-KI		Mambo (trike)		
50-KK		Best Off Sky Ranger		
50-KL		Air Création / XP		
50-KN		Dynamic		
50-KP		Drachen Studio Kecur Avant		
50-KQ		Magni M-16 Tandem Trainer		
50-KS		Air Création / XP		
50-KT		Air Création GT BI / SX		
50-KU		Air Création / XP		
50-KV		Icaro 2000 Stratos		
50-LA		Air Création GT / SX		35-BC
50-LB		Air Création GTE / iXess		
50-LC		SE.5A replica		
50-LD		Weedhopper Europa II	C2063029	07-FC
50-LE	F-JHIW	ATEC Zephyr 2000		OK-DUA-04
		(W/o 20.5.12)		
50-LF		Air Création GT BI 503 / Quartz 18		
50-LI		Air's Maestro		
50-LJ	F-JKDF	DTA / Dynamic 15		
W50-LM		Seedwing Sensor 510		
		(Accident 20.4.06)		
50-LM (2)		Air Création GT BI / SX		
50-LN		Ulis	01	
50-LO		DTA / Dynamic 15		
50-LQ		DTA / Dynamic		
50-LR		Weedhopper type – modified		W50-LR
50-LU		Barry MB-04 Souris Bulle		

Reg		Type	c/n	Prev id
50-LX		Weedhopper AX-3	8062397	25-PV
50-LY		Raj Hamsa X'Air		
50-MA	F-JHJS	Fly Synthesis Storch		
50-MC	F-JZIZ	Fly Synthesis Storch HS		
50-MF	F-JGUV	Aerospool WT-9 Dynamic	DY059/2004	67-VD
50-MG		DTA / Dynamic	248	
50-MI		Eipper Quicksilver MX II		
50-MJ		Air Création / SX		
50-MO		DTA / Dynamic 15/430		
50-MP	F-JRGT	Colomban MC-30C Luciole		
50-MU		Leopold		
50-MV	F-JHHW	Colomban MC-30 Luciole		
50-MW		Best Off Sky Ranger		
50-MZ	F-JHIV	Best Off Sky Ranger		
50-NB	F-JYDY	Best Off Sky Ranger		
50-NE		Air Création		
50-NF	F-JYKC	Aerospool WT-9 Dynamic		
50-NG		Magni M-16 Tandem Trainer	16-07-4104	
50-NH		Air Création GTE Trek > Skypper 582		
50-NI		Air Création / Fun		
50-NJ	F-JYSH	Flight Design CT	99 04 03 52	
		(Same c/n as 55-IX / F-JGBR)		
50-NK		Aquilair Swing / La Mouette Ghost 15		94-GR
50-NL		Technic Moto Mustang 2		
50-NM		Air Création Twin / Fun		
50-NP		Air Création GT BI / Quartz		
50-NQ		Air Création / Fun		
50-NU		Mignet HM.1000 Balerit	111	59-PD
50-NV		Humbert La Moto-du-Ciel		
50-NW	F-JHJG	Best Off Sky Ranger		
50-NX		Air Création / Fun	A07103/7123	
50-OA		DTA / Dynamic 15/450		
50-OD		DTA / Dynamic 15/450	163	56-D.
50-OE	F-JGBE	Humbert Tetras 912BS		
50-OG		Aquilair Swing		
50-OH		Air Création Tanarg / iXess		
50-OI		Air Création GT BI / Fun		
50-OJ	F-JYFF	Flight Design CT SW		F-JWAN
		(W/o 31.1.09)		
50-OL		Weedhopper type – modified		W50-LR
50-ON	F-JWNN	Fly Synthesis Storch HS		I-5110
50-OO		DTA Combo 582 / Diva		
50-OT		Best Off Sky Ranger		
50-OU		Aerolite		
50-OX		Aviasud Mistral		
		(Reported 2011 as weightshift?)		
50-OZ		DTA Dynamic		
50-PB		Humbert La Moto-du-Ciel		
50-PE		Air Création Tanarg / BioniX		
50-PF		Evektor EV-97 Eurostar SL		
50-PG	F-JYAT	Colomban MC-30 Luciole	14	
50-PI		Aviasud Mistral		
50-PM		ELA Aviacion ELA-07 Cougar		
50-PO	F-JRPM	DTA / Magic		
50-PP		Air Création GT BI / Fun		
50-PR		DTA / Magic		
50-PS	F-JXRS	Humbert La Moto-du-Ciel		
50-PT		Fly Synthesis Catalina		
50-PU		DTA Voyageur II / Magic		
50-PV	F-JRPG	Best Off Nynja		
50-PX		DTA Combo / Dynamic 15/430		
50-PZ		DTA Combo		
50-QA		Rans S-6 Coyote II		
50-QC	F-JTNB	BRM Land Africa	0187/912UL/11-LA	
50-QE		Best Off Sky Ranger V-Max		
50-QI		Magni M-16 Tandem Trainer		
50-QL		Air Création / NuviX		
50-RC		DTA / Magic		
50-RG		DTA Dynamic 15/430		
50-UC		Zenair CH-701 STOL		
		(Error for 59-UC ?)		

51 : Marne

Reg		Type	c/n	Prev id
51-AA		Egrett Sophie		
51-AU		Jean Francois Mustang	86-055	
51-AV		(Technic Moto ?) Mustang		
51-BD		Cosmos / Profil		
51-BF		Air Création		
51-BU		(Technic Moto ?) Mustang		
51-CL		Air Création / SX		
51-CM		Air Création Safari GT BI 462		
		(Crashed 20.10.07)		
51-DC		Humbert La Moto-du-Ciel		
51-DJ		Breezy RLU.1 ("Pegase" ?)		
51-DN		Air Création GT / Fun		
		(Damaged 5.9.97)		
51-DS		Air Création		
51-EQ		Mignet HM.1000 Balerit	41	
51-ES		Weedhopper		
51-ET		Rans S-12 Airaile		
51-EW		Air Création GT BI / XP		
51-EX		Air Création GTE Racer / XP		
51-EY		Air Création Buggy		
51-FA		Aviasud AE209 Albatros	166	
51-FR		Cosmos		
51-FY	F-JBGL	Humbert Tetras		
51-GF		Aviasud AE209 Albatros		
51-GH		gyrocopter		
51-GI		Air Création Safari GT BI		
51-GK		Dédé		02-AB
51-GL		TEAM Mini-MAX		
51-GP		Mignet HM.293 Pou-du-Ciel		
51-GQ		Air Création GTE / SX		
51-GT		Interplane Skyboy		
51-GW		Curtiss Jenny replica		
		(Forced landing 19.5.04)		
51-HA		Raj Hamsa X'Air		
51-HE		Bensen B.8		
51-HK		high wing single seater		
51-HM		Jupiter		
51-HN		Helios		
51-HO		Evektor EV-97 Sportstar	2007 0911	OO-F09
		(Now re-regd 34-TG)		
51-HR		Cosmos		
51-HV		Raj Hamsa X'Air		
51-HW		Aeriane P-Swift		

Reg	Ident	Type	C/n	Previous
51-IA		Air Création / XP		
51-IB		Zenair CH-601 Zodiac		
51-IL		Ultralair JC-24 Weedhopper Sport		
51-IP	F-JGGF	Dyn'Aero MCR-01		
51-IS		Zenair CH-701 STOL		
51-IT		(Technic Moto ?) Mustang		
51-IW		Evans VP-2		
W51-IX		Magni M-16 Tandem Trainer		
51-JA		Cosmos		
51-JG		Air Création / XP		
51-JH		Air Création GT BI Buggy / XP		
51-JK		Ecolight X'Air		
51-JO	F-JGGQ	Micro Aviation Pulsar III – 912	9R	
51-JZ		Air Création GT BI	A02047-2027	
51-KE		Cosmos 503		
51-KF		Tecnam P.92S Echo		
51-KM		Cosmos		
51-KQ		Evektor EV-97 Eurostar		
51-KT	F-JGHZ	Denney Kitfox III (t/w)		
51-KU		ATEC Zephyr 2000	Z281000F	
		(Re-regd 08-EB, 08-EZ)		
51-KV	F-JFOL	Sauper J.300 Joker		
51-KW		Raj Hamsa X'Air 602T		
		(Crashed 4.9.04)		
51-KX		Zenair CH-701 STOL		
51-KY	F-JBKT	Zenair CH-701 STOL		
51-LC	F-JXXT	Raj Hamsa X'Air		
51-LI	F-JGHT	ATEC Zephyr 2000C	Z881203S	
		(Same c/n listed for 51-MF and 77-BEL)		
51-LH	F-JGIH	Didier Pti'tavion		
51-LJ	F-JFAJ	Djicat Buse'Air 150GT	41	95-KV
51-LL		Magni M-16 Tandem Trainer		
51-LO		Air Création GTE / Mild	A98-173	
51-MB	F-JGHI	Zenair CH-601UL Zodiac		
51-MF		ATEC Zephyr 2000C	Z881203S	
		(Same c/n listed for 51-LI and 77-BEL)		
51-MI	F-JYIA	Zenair CH-601XL Zodiac		
51-ML		Air Création GTE Racer / XP		
51-MO		Raj Hamsa Hanuman		
51-NS	F-JZAB	Zenair CH-601XL Zodiac (see below)		
51-NS	F-JZQI	Zenair CH-601XL Zodiac (2 a/c noted Blois 9.07 with same regn!)		
51-NU		Zenair CH-601UL Zodiac		
51-OE		gyrocopter		
51-OG	F-JZPH	Zenair CH-601XL Zodiac	6-9731	
51-OJ		Tecnam P.92 Echo		
51-OR		Raj Hamsa X'Air		
51-PF	F-JYDH	B&F Funk FK-9 Mk.III Utility	03-U-280	
51-PP		Air Création Tanarg / iXess		
51-PQ	F-JYMM	Flight Design CT SW		
		(Re-regd 61-NZ)		
51-PS		DTA Combo FC / Dynamic		
51-PX		Flight Design CT SW	07-04-23	
51-PY	F-JYXQ	Zenair CH-601XL Zodiac		
51-QE	F-JXBS	Autogyro-Europe MT-03		
51-QJ		Tecnam P.92 Echo		
51-QO	F-JXOF	Zenair CH-701 STOL		
51-QP	F-JWDK	Zenair CH-601 Zodiac (t/w)	6-9130	OO-D60, 59-VX
51-QT		Zenair CH-601 Zodiac		
51-QV		Zenair CH-601XL Zodiac		
51-QW	F-JXUM	Flight Design CT SW	08-01-17	
51-QX		Zenair CH-601 Zodiac		
51-QZ		Zenair CH-601XL Zodiac		
		(W/o 2.8.10)		
51-RA		Air Création GTE Clipper / iXess		
51-RK		Zenair CH-601 Zodiac		
51-RM		Zenair CH-701 STOL		
51-RN	F-JWER	Zenair CH-601XL Zodiac		
51-RP		Best Off Sky Ranger		
51-RS		Air Création GTE Trek		
51-RV		B&F Funk FK-14B Polaris (t/w)	14-092	
51-RW	F-JKIH	ATEC Zephyr 2000		
51-RX	F-JWDP	Zenair CH-601XL Zodiac		
51-SA	F-JWQM	Celier Xenon	CAA07073S	
51-SB	F-JWQO	Celier Xenon	CAI06372S	
51-SD		Air Création		
51-SE	F-JWSB	Zenair CH-601XL Zodiac		
51-SP	F-JRAS	Celier Xenon	CAF08473S	
51-SR		Cosmos		
51-SV	F-JYHS	Magni M-16 Tandem Trainer		
51-SW		Evans VP-2 Volksplane	0781	F-PBFD
51-TF		Air Création GTE Trek / iXess 13	A09043-8073	
51-TK	F-JWMI	Celier Xenon		
51-TU		Technic Moto Mustang 2		83-AAH
51-TZ		Chapelet Big Bang (trike)		
51-UH		Autogyro-Europe MT-03		
		(W/o 5.1.14)		
51-UP		Zenair CH-601XL Zodiac		
51-VD	F-JTGK	Directfly Alto		
51-VE		Dyn'Aéro MCR-01	305	21-YC
51-VK	F-JRBJ	Air Création Tanarg 912ES / BioniX		
		A10027-10029/T07064		
51-VL		Autogyro-Europe Calidus 09		
51-VN		Evektor EV-97 Eurostar		
51-VO		Technic Moto Mustang 2		
51-VR	F-JRRV	Autogyro-Europe Calidus 09	F10C03	
51-VS		ICP MXP-740 Savannah S	12-01-54-0150	
51-WA		PAP F200/ITV Bulldog paramotor		
51-WL	F-JULH	DTA J-RO gyrocopter	009	
51-WM		Zenair CH-701 STOL		
51-WO		Zenair CH-601 Zodiac		
51-WT		Dudek paramotor		
51-XK		Zenair CH-701 STOL		
51-XL		Autogyro Europe Calidus 09		

52 : Haute-Marne

Reg	Ident	Type	C/n	Previous
52-AD		Cosmos		
52-AH		Cosmos		
52-AL		Cosmos		
52-AP		Cosmos		
52-AT		Cosmos		
52-AW		Cosmos		
52-AX		Cosmos		
52-BC		Cosmos		
52-BE		Air Création GT BI / SX		
52-BF		Mignet HM.1000 Balerit	28	17-DG
52-BG		Air Création GT BI / SX		
52-BH		Weedhopper		
52-BL		Weedhopper		
52-BQ		Synairgie		
52-BR		Cosmos		
52-CA		Air Création		54-FV
52-CE		Air Création		
52-CI		Air Création		
52-CK		Air Création Fun		
52-CL		Cosmos		
52-CO		Air Création		
52-CQ		Air Création / SX		
52-CW		Humbert La Moto-du-Ciel		
		(W/o 13.5.04)		
52-CY		Mainair Gemini / Flash IIA		
52-DN		Pipistrel Sinus		
52-DO		DTA (trike)		
52-DW		Cosmos Phase II 582 / Chronos 12		
52-DX		Light Aero Avid Flyer IV	1097	F-PRKK, F-WRKK
52-EC		Cosmos		
52-ET		Cosmos Chronos		40-IO
52-FA		Eipper Quicksilver MXL II (f/p)		
52-GG		Cosmos		
52-GL		Rans S-6ES Coyote II		
WHM-52		Mignet HM.1100 Cordouan		

53 : Mayenne

Reg	Ident	Type	C/n	Previous
53-AJ		Mignet HM.1000 Balerit		
53-BG		Air Création		
53-CK		Weedhopper AX-3		
53-CX	F-JHTH	Djicat Buse'Air 150		
53-DB		Solar Wings Pegasus XL		
53-DD		Tertraedre (W/o 26.7.98)		
53-DF		Mainair Gemini Flash II		
53-DQ		Air Création		
53-DS		Weedhopper		
53-EB		Cosmos trike / G'Decouvr wing	B21029	
53-EH		Pegasus		
53-EU		Dynali Chickinox		
53-EV		Raj Hamsa X'Air		
53-FA		Weedhopper AX-3		
53-FC		Fly Synthesis Storch HS		
53-FD	F-JHTW	Best Off Sky Ranger		
53-FF		Pipistrel Sinus		
53-FG	F-JHBJ	ICP MXP-740 Savannah	12-97-50-070	77-YC
53-FJ		Air Création / Kiss 13		
53-FL		Aéro Services Guépy Club 582T		
53-FR		Best Off Sky Ranger 912S-1		
53-FZ	F-JHDF	Best Off Sky Ranger		
53-GB	F-JHDW	BRM Land Africa	0016/05	
53-HJ		homebuilt trike / Pegasus XL (wing)		
53-UV	F-JHZK	Rans S-6 Coyote II		
53-UX	F-JZBM	Flight Design CT		
53-VC	F-JHWS	Fantasy Air Cora		
53-VM		Air Création Tanarg 582		
53-VN		Air Création Tanarg / iXess		
53-VO		Air Création GTE Clipper		
53-VQ		DTA Combo 582 / Dynamic 15/430		
53-VV		Celier Xenon		
53-VY		Air Création / iXess		
53-VZ		weightshift		
53-WE		DTA Combo FC / Magic	260/97	
53-WL		Air Création HKS700E		
53-WO		ITV paramotor		
53-WR	F-JXMX	Celier Xenon	CAA06672S	
53-XL		ITV paramotor		
53-XM	F-JTDJ	ATEC Zephyr	Z1750610S	

54 : Meurthe-et-Moselle

Reg	Ident	Type	C/n	Previous
54-V		Cosmos 250 / Azure		
54-AC		Eipper Quicksilver MX		
54-AK		AEIM Epsilon paramotor		
54-AP		Kolb Ultrastar		
54-AR	F-JGBM	(Technic Moto ?) Mustang	920601	
54-AT		"Fujicolor"		
54-BH		Air Création GT BI / XP		
54-BX		Huntair Pathfinder		
54-CC		Rans S-6 Coyote II		
54-CK		Guerpont Biplum		
54-DT	F-JAYT	Humbert La Moto-du-Ciel		
54-EP		Eipper Quicksilver		
54-ER		Humbert La Moto-du-Ciel	9167	
54-EX		Cosmos		
54-FF	F-JGBT	Weedhopper		
54-FX		Pegasus / Air Création		
54-GI	F-JAGP	Humbert La Moto-du-Ciel		
54-GR		Murphy Renegade Spirit		
54-GS		Huntair Pathfinder (Wrecked)		
54-HD		Air Création / SX		
54-HF		Nostalgair N3 Pup		
		(Also reported as J-3 Kitten)		
54-HG		Cosmos / Echo 12		
54-HJ		SMAN Pétrel		
54-HL		JC-31 Weedhopper		
54-HN		Humbert La Moto-du-Ciel		
54-IA		Humbert La Moto-du-Ciel		
54-IB		Cosmos		
54-IR		La Mouette		
54-JE	F-JAPR	Aviasud AE209 Albatros		
54-JL		Murphy Renegade Spirit	241	
		(Re-regd 59-CTG)		
54-JM		Air Création GT / Mild		
54-JN		Piel CP.150 Onyx		
54-JS		(Weedhopper ?) AX-3		
54-KA		Ultralair Weedhopper AX-3	0062663	LX-XGK
54-KG		Air's Maestro		
54-KK		Denney Kitfox		
54-KN	F-JBWK	ASL.18		
54-KP		Guerpond Autoplum 4-01	01	
		(W/o 24.7.15)		
54-KS		Murphy Renegade Spirit		
54-KU		Air Création GTE Clipper / XP		
54-KV		Air Création		
54-KX	F-JBMJ	Rans S-6XL Coyote II		
54-LA		Air Création GTE Clipper / XP		
54-LB		Air Création GTE Clipper / XP		

Reg		Type	c/n	Notes
54-LD		Air Création GT		
54-LI		Air Création GTE Clipper		
54-LR		Air Création GTE / XP		
54-LT	F-JBRX	Denney Kitfox	1699	
54-LX		Air Création / XP		
54-ME		Air Création GTE Clipper / XP		
54-MH		Air Création / Quartz		
54-MI		Raj Hamsa X'Air		
54-MP		Air Création Racer / XP		
54-MS		Aviasud AE209 Albatros		
54-ND		Ecolight X'Air		
54-NE	F-JCCD	Tecnam P.92 Echo		
54-NN		Cosmos		
54-NO		Raj Hamsa X'Air		
54-NT		Air Création / La Mouette Ghost 14		
54-NV		Cosmos		
54-NX	F-JXML	Aviakit Vega		
54-NY		ZUT Aviation TT2000 STOL	9709007	
54-OA	F-JCPV	Micro Aviation Pulsar II		
54-OD	F-JCSK	Humbert Tetras		
		(Damaged 11.6.05)		
W54-OE		WagAero CUBy II		
		(W/o 21.6.98 Bures)		
54-OO		Air Création XB Vue 582 Max		
54-OP		Air Création GT		
		(Now reported as SE.5 replica)		
54-OR		Air Création		
54-OY		Dynali Chickinox		
54-PA		Air Création / XP		
54-PK		Cosmos		
54-PL	F-JAVL	SMAN Pétrel	045	38-CM, 56-CM
54-PY		Humbert Tetras 912BS		
54-QA		Air Création GTE Clipper 582S / XP15	T 99052	
		(Re-regd OO-E56 7.04)		
54-QB		Air Création GTE / Mild		
54-QD		Air Création GT BI / XP		
54-QH		Light Aero Avid Flyer		
		(Re-regd 44-ABY / F-JGAZ)		
54-QL		Cosmos		
54-QM	F-JGPW	Fly Synthesis Storch		
54-QP		Humbert Tetras		
54-QS		Dynamic 15		
54-QT	F-JGAY	III Sky Arrow 500TF	040	
		(Same c/n as 45-QP and 28-PP)		
54-QV		Aviakit Vega 2000		
54-QX		Humbert La Moto-du-Ciel		
		(Also reported as Patrouiller)		
54-RJ		Dynali Chickinox		
54-RO		DTA / Dynamic 582	00032	
W54-RQ		Scheibe SF-24 Motorspatz?		
54-RR	F-JGBM	Humbert La Moto-du-Ciel		
		(Call-sign previously quoted for 54-AR, a Mustang, which is not unlike the Moto-du-Ciel.)		
54-RT		DTA / Dynamic		
54-RV		SE.5A replica		
54-RY	F-JCBU	Pipistrel Sinus		
54-SA		Mignet HM.1000 Balerit	078	ALAT/F-MUCB
54-SE		Humbert Tetras		
54-SF		Croses LC-6 Criquet	38	F-PYBM
54-SG		Tecnam P.96 Golf 100		
54-SH		Cosmos / La Mouette Top 12.9		
54-SI	F-JCGF	Hipps Superbirds J-3 Kitten		
54-SK		Weedhopper 2-str		
54-SL		Pottier P.130UL Bleu Citron	1022	
54-SP		Huntair Pathfinder		57-FC
54-SR		EuroALA Jet Fox 91	121	
54-SS		Flight Design CT-2K		
54-TA		Humbert Tetras		
54-TL	F-JGCB	ZUT Aviation TT2000 STOL		
54-TN		Air Création / Mild		
54-TO		Best Off Sky Ranger		05-CF
54-TP		Rans S-6 Coyote II (t/w)	02001357S	
		(Stolen 22/23.6.04)		
54-TY	F-JGDI	Pipistrel Sinus 912	054 S912 1201	
54-UC	F-JGDE	Light Aero Avid Flyer	AF692	38-LM, F-WRKP, F-JGDM
54-UI	F-JYLU	B&F Funk FK-14 Polaris (t/w)		
54-UR	F-JGDR	B&F Funk FK-14 Polaris		
54-US	F-JGDX	B&F Funk FK-12 Comet	12-051	D-M . . .
54-UU	F-JGDP	Humbert Tetras		
54-VF		Jodel D.18	191	W54-VF
		(Re-regd 60-KB)		
54-VN		Fantasy Air Allegro		
54-VO	F-JEDJ	Rans S-6 Coyote II		
54-VP	F-JGEO	Merlin		
54-VR		Dyn'Aéro MCR-01		
54-WX		Aviakit Vega		
54-XC		Lebouder Autoplane		
54-XG		Air Création Racer		
54-XH	F-JGEM	Evektor EV-97 Eurostar	2002 1521	
54-XK		UFF-2		
54-YB	F-JCHR	Eipper Quicksilver GT500		
54-YH		Humbert La Moto-du-Ciel		
54-YI		Vidor Asso VI Junior	120	
54-YM		TEAM Mini-MAX		28-EM (?)
54-YN	F-JCMT	Pipistrel Sinus		
54-YU		Air Création Racer / Fun 14		
54-YY	F-JGFI	B&F Funk FK-9 Mk.IV Club		
54-ZA	F-JCQS	Rans S-6 Coyote II		
W54-ZC		Comco Ikarus Fox-C22		
54-ZD	F-JGFK	Best Off Sky Ranger		
54-ZI		DTA / Dynamic		
54-ZJ	F-JQBQ	Aviakit Hermes		
54-ZP	F-JZVL	Aeropro Eurofox		
54-ZS		Aquilair		
54-ZX		Humbert Tetras 912BS		
54-AAE		Comco Ikarus C-42		
		(Damaged 3.8.06)		
54-AAM		Dallach D4BK Fascination		
		(Damaged 18.4.06)		
54-AAU	F-JQBD	DTA / Dynamic 450		
54-AAY	F-JQBS	Comco Ikarus C-42		
54-ABD		ATEC Zephyr 2000C		
54-ABT		P&M Aviation Quik		
54-ABX	F-JVEB	Alpi Aviation Pioneer 300 Kite		
54-ACQ	F-JGAO	B&F Funk FK-9 Mk.III Club		
54-ACR	F-JZAX	Humbert Tetras		95-PB
54-ACT	F-JZGE	B&F Funk FK-14 Polaris		
W54-ACV		Pottier P.130UL		
		(Damaged 9.7.06)		
54-ACY		Humbert Tetras		
54-ADA		Didier Pti'tavion		
54-ADE		Light Aero Avid Flyer		
54-ADF		SE-5A replica		
54-AED	F-JZJL	Aviakit Vega		
54-AEF	F-JZDF	Zenair CH-601 Zodiac		
54-AEG		Best Off Sky Ranger		
		(Crashed 16.7.06)		
54-AEJ	F-JZTN	Dallach D4B Fascination		
		(Same call-sign as 54-AFJ below – registration misread ?)		
54-AEK		Cosmos / Jet 12	1109	
		(W/o 4.6.06)		
54-AEN		Weedhopper AX-3	C3113180	46-AEN
54-AEP	F-JZIS	SG Aviation Storm 300		
54-AEQ	F-JZKB	B&F Funk FK-12 Comet	12-074	
		(W/o 2.7.10)		
54-AES	F-JZKN	Pipistrel Sinus		
54-AET		Urban Air UFM-13 Lambada		
54-AEU(1)		Zenair CH-601UL Zodiac		EC-?
54-AEU(2)	F-JZLU	Comco Ikarus C-42		
54-AEV		Cosmos Bidulm / Mach 14.9		
54-AEZ		DTA Feeling / Dynamic 450	B202SF1075E	
		(Re-regd OO-G21 12.08)		
54-AFA	F-JJTV	Ballard Pelican Sport		
54-AFJ	F-JZTN	Dallach D4 Fascination		
54-AFP		DTA Combo / Dynamic 15/430		
54-AFX		Weedhopper AX-3		
54-AFY		Ekolot JK-05 Junior		
54-AGG		DTA Combo 582 / Dynamic 450		
54-AGH		ICP Bingo 503		
54-AGI	F-JQDM	Cyclone AX-3		
54-AGM	F-JYPL	Dyn'Aéro MCR-01 UL		
54-AGN		Best Off Sky Ranger		
54-AGQ	F-JYQD	Fly Synthesis Texan Top Class	79	
54-AGR		Dynali Chickinox		
54-AGS	F-JYVW	Ekolot JK-05 Junior	05 06 04	D-MQYK
54-AGU		Urban Air UFM-13 Lambada		
54-AGV	F-JYRO	TL Ultralight TL-2000 Sting Carbon		
54-AGW	F-JYRT	Tecnam P.96 Golf 100		
54-AHC		Comco Ikarus C-42		
54-AHH		Urban Air Samba XXL		
54-AHJ	F-JXBW	B&F Funk FK-14B2 Polaris (t/w)	14-062	
54-AHK	F-JXCR	Aéro Services Super Guépard (Jabiru)		
54-AHN		Rans S-6 Coyote II		
54-AHS	F-JUOE	Zenair CH-601XL Zodiac		
54-AHT	F-JXIA	Aerospool WT-9 Dynamic	DY203/2007	
54-AIA		ELA Aviacion ELA-07S		
54-AID	F-JXOP	B&F Funk FK-9		
54-AIE		Ekolot JK-05 Junior	05 05 02	91-PV
54-AIG		Comco Ikarus C-42		
54-AIK		Ekolot JK-05 Junior		
54-AIL		Magni M-22 Voyager		
54-AIN		Zenair CH-601HD Zodiac		
54-AIP		Air Création Tanarg 912ES / iXess 13		
54-AIQ	F-JYXG	Air Création / iXess		
		(W/o 24.6.15)		
54-AIT		Air Création Tanarg 912 / iXess 13		
54-AIV		ICP MXP-740 Savannah		
54-AIW	F-JJNY	Zenair CH-601 UL HD Zodiac		
54-AIY	F-JZVG	Aerospool WT-9 Dynamic	DY260/2008	
54-AJC		Urban Air UFM-13 Lambada		
54-AJF		Magni M-16 Tandem Trainer		
54-AJH	F-JWCB	Aerospool WT-9 Dynamic		
54-AJK		Air Création		
54-AJL		Comco Ikarus C-42		
54-AJO	F-JWFV	Aerospool WT-9 Dynamic	DY273/2008	
54-AJQ		Huntair Pathfinder		
54-AJS		Huntair Pathfinder		
54-AJW		Air Création GTE Clipper		
54-AJY	F-JWTK	Zenair CH-601XL Zodiac	6-9932	
54-AJZ		Humbert La Moto-du-Ciel		
54-AKL		Aéro Services Super Guépard 912		
54-AKT		Miniplane/Dudek Plasma paramotor		
54-ALB	F-JXGX	ICP MXP-740 Savannah		
54-ALG		Evektor EV-97 Eurostar	2002 1303	
54-ALI		Magni M-16 Tandem Trainer		
54-ALK		P&M Aviation QuikR 912S	8494	
		(Fitted 3.03 with the QuikR wing c/n 8652)		
54-ALU	F-JRLR	B&F Funk FK-14B2 Polaris		
54-ALY	F-JRPA	ATEC 122 Zephyr		
54-ALZ		Fly Products Race C/SOL Synergy paramotor		
54-AMC		Comco Ikarus C-42		
54-AMD	F-JRQQ	Air Création Tanarg / Bionix 15	A10025-10020 / T10014	
54-AMF	F-JSSE	Flugtechnik Herringhausen Vagabund		
54-AMG		Air Création Tanarg / Bionix		
54-AMK		Humbert Tetras BT		
54-AMO	F-JRYC	Aeroprakt A-22L Vision		
		(To OO-H01)		
54-AMV		Aéro Services Guépy (Jabiru)		
54-AMX	F-JSDC	Celier Xenon		
54-AMY		Ekolot JK-05 Junior	05 08 06	
54-AND		B&F Funk FK-14B Polaris		
54-ANO		Jodel D.185		
54-ANR		Mignet HM.293 Pou-du-Ciel		
54-ANX		B&F Funk FK-9		
54-AON	F-JXIF	Aerospool WT-9 Dynamic	DY421/2011	
54-AOS		Nando Groppo Trial		
54-AOT		Nervures / Aloha paramotor	M77	
		(To OO-2GU)		
54-AOW	F-JWBD	Flight Design CT SW	D-08-06-21	
54-APC	F-JTLC	Autogyro-Europe MTOsport	11102S	
54-APE		Air Création Skypper		
54-APH		Autogyro-Europe Calidus 09		
54-API		Nicollier HN.700 Menestrel II	142	F-PLSA
54-APK	F-JTOS	Autogyro-Europe Calidus 09	C00199	
54-APX		Aéro Services Guépy 912S	22116	
54-APZ		Autogyro-Europe Calidus 09		
54-AQB		Mosquito XE		
54-AQG	F-JUBQ	Aerospool WT-9 Dynamic TOW		
54-AQL		Pipistrel Virus		
54-AQQ	F-JUOG	Autogyro-Europe MTOsport		

Reg	F-reg	Type	c/n	Other
54-AQX	F-JUSU	ICP MXP-740 Savannah S	13-03-54-0258	
54-ARD		Jodel		
54-ARM	F-JAUO	Jodel D.18		
54-ARO		Aeropro Eurofox		
54-ARS	F-JVOF	Autogyro-Europe MTOsport	M01101	
54-ARX	F-JVRX	Spacek SD-1 Minisport TD	077	
54-ASC		Morane Type H replica		
54-ASH		Humbert Tetras		
54-ASJ		Zenair CH-601 Zodiac		
54-ASN		Rans S-6ES Coyote II		
54-ASR	F-JWMY	Aero Pilot Legend		
54-AST	F-JWYF	Autogyro-Europe MTOport		
54-ATA	F-JSKA	Alpi Avn Pioneer 300		
54-ATL	F-JABZ	Magni M-24 Orion	24169734	
54-ATN	F-JAEM	Humbert Tetras 912CS		
54-ATP		Autogyro Europe Calidus		
54-ATR	F-JAIU	Alpi Avn Pioneer 300STD	371	
54-AUA		Autogyro Europe MTOsport		
54-AUU		Urban Air Samba XXL		
54-AVW		Cosmos		

55 : Meuse

Reg	F-reg	Type	c/n	Other
55-N		Aviasud Sirocco		
55-AB		Weedhopper		
55-AD		Ultralair JC-31C Weedhopper		
55-AU		Huntair Pathfinder		
55-CE		Mignet HM.1000 Balerit	18	
55-CL		Aviasud Mistral		
55-CT		Ultralair JC-24 Weedhopper Sport		
55-CU		Dynali Chickinox		
55-CX		Denney Kitfox		
55-DB		Sky System		
55-DC		Aviasud Mistral	55	
		(Re-regd OO-C10 7.95)		
55-DN		Air Création		
55-DP		Weedhopper	9042500	
55-DU		Cosmos Chronos		
55-EB		Huntair Pathfinder		
55-EG		Dynali Chickinox		
55-EI		Ultralair JC-24 Weedhopper Sport	B2032997	
		("La Poste" titles)		
55-EM		Cosmos Bidulm		
		(Accident 2.8.04)		
55-EV		Mignet HM.293A Pou-du-Ciel		
55-FA		Rans S-6ESD Coyote II		
55-FC(1)	F-JBZI	Mignet HM.293 Pou-du-Ciel (DoM 1992)		
		(Repaired after accident 1995 became 55-GT)		
55-FC(2)		Mignet HM.293 Pou-du-Ciel (DoM 1996)		
55-FE		Eipper Quicksilver GT500-R582	0060	
		(Built by ULMAir Champagne)		
55-FG		Synergie		
55-FH		Air Création GT BI Fun / Quartz		
55-FJ		Air Création Safari GT BI 582		
		(Crashed 16.7.06)		
55-FM		Air Création		
55-FO	F-JAPB	Humbert Tetras		
55-FR	F-JBME	Ultravia PL-914 Pelican Super Sport		
55-FS		Humbert La Moto-du-Ciel		
55-FT		Cosmos / Chronos 12		
55-FX		Eipper Quicksilver GT500		
55-GC		Dynali Chickinox		
55-GF	F-JGEW	Rans S-6ESD Coyote II		F-JAMV
55-GG		Dynali Chickinox Kot-Kot		
		(previously reported as Air Création / La Mouette Top 12.9)		
55-GK		Cosmos		
55-GM		Micro Aviation Pulsar II		
55-GO		Cosmos		55-EH
55-GR		Cosmos		
55-GS	F-JCKR	Rans S-7 Courier		
55-GT		Mignet HM.293A Pou-du-Ciel		55-FC
55-HA		Light Aero Avid Flyer		
55-HE		Cosmos		
55-HG		Ecolight X'Air		
55-HH		Light Aero Avid Flyer	801	F-WRKH
		(Re-regd 72-KH)		
55-HN	F-JBAL	Humbert La Moto-du-Ciel		
55-HQ		Aquilair Swing 14		
55-HV		Jodel D.9 Bébé		
55-HW		Humbert La Moto-du-Ciel		
55-HX		Eipper Quicksilver MX III Sprint		
55-HY		Mignet HM.1100 Cordouan	11	
55-ID	F-JXQY	Macair Merlin		
55-IE	F-JBOV	Tecnam P.92 Echo		
		(also marked 16-GD)		
55-IG	F-JGAT	Dyn'Aéro MCR-01 ULC		
55-II		Dynali Chickinox		
55-IO		Fly Synthesis Storch		
55-IU		Air Création GTE Clipper / XP		
55-IW		Autogyro-Europe MT-03		
55-IX	F-JGBR	Flight Design CT-180	99-04-03-52	
		(Same c/n as 50-NJ / F-JYSH)		
55-IY		Ecolight X'Air		
55-JC		Best Off Sky Ranger		
55-JO		Zenair CH-701 STOL II		
55-JP		Cosmos / La Mouette		
55-JR		weightshift		
55-JT	F-JGFX	Jodel D.20	11	F-PQUS
55-JY		Aviasud Sirocco		
55-KH		Dynali Chickinox		
55-KJ		Aquilair Swing 14R		
55-KK		Cosmos		
55-KL		Air Création / iXess		
W55-KM		Barry MB-02 Souricette		
		(Accident 7.8.04)		
55-KP	F-JGGV	Ekolot JK-05 Junior		
		(Stolen 10.10)		
55-KQ	F-JXJU	Jodel D.9 Bébé		
		(Re-regd 33-AFX)		
55-KU		Zenair CH-701D STOL		
55-LC		Cosmos Phase II		
55-LF	F-JQAB	Zenair CH-701 STOL		
55-LK	F-JXSP	Zenair CH-601 Zodiac		
55-LU		Cosmos		
55-LX		Zenair CH-701 STOL (f/p)		
		(Damaged 31.12.04)		
55-MC	F-JZML	Halley Apollo trike / Air Création Kiss wing		

55-MG(2) section / right column:

Reg	F-reg	Type	c/n	Other
55-MG(1)		Micro Aviation Pulsar II		
55-MG(2)	F-JQCL	Zenair CH-601XL Zodiac		
		(Noted 9.07)		
55-MH		Magni M-16 Tandem Trainer		
55-MI		Air Création GT BI 503		
55-MM		Air Création GT BI		
55-MQ		Aerospool WT-9 Dynamic		
55-MT		Pegasus / Quantum		30-IU ?
55-OB	F-JZHW	Flyitalia MD-3 Rider		
55-OC	F-JZFL	Dyn'Aéro MCR-01 UL	324	
55-OD		Cosmos Phase II / Top 14.9		
55-OF		Fly Synthesis Storch HS		
55-OP		Air Création / SX12		
55-PA	F-JYMO	Flight Design CT SW	07-02-20	
55-PD		Aéro Services Super Guépard 912S		
55-PI		Airborne Edge		
55-PK		Fisher FP.404		59-WO
55-PL	F-JQEU	Airborne Edge XT-582		
55-PM	F-JXFS	Alpi Aviation Pioneer 200		
55-PO	F-JRXG	Flight Design CT Supralight	E-10-05-04	08-KP
55-PQ		Zenair CH-601XL Zodiac		
55-PV		Air Création Racer / XP 11		
55-QD		Cosmos Phase II / La Mouette Top 14.9		
55-QJ	F=-JZEK	Comco Ikarus C-42		
55-QS		Aeropro Eurofox	17605	PH-3X2
55-RE		Air Création Racer / Bautek Pico L		
55-RL		ICP MXP-740 Savannah		
55-RP		Air Création Racer / Bautek Pico L		
55-RR	F-JTMJ	G1 Aviation G1 SPYL	86	
55-RQ	F-JGFT	Rans S-7 Courier		
55-RS		Aériane Swift		
W55-RV		Aviasud Sirocco		
55-RX	F-JUJA	Shark Aero Shark	12/2012	
55-SA	F-JUKR	Alpi Aviation Pioneer 200UL	108	
		(Re-regd D-MBCK 10.14)		
55-SE		Pipistrel Virus	532SWN100	
55-WQ	F-JHTO	Djicat Buse'Air 150		

56 :Morbihan

Reg	F-reg	Type	c/n	Other
56		Zenith Baroudeur		
56-G		Zenith Baroudeur		
56-J		Veliplane		
56-K		Zenith Baroudeur		
56-L		Zenith Baroudeur		
56-N		SMAN (Pétrel ?)	01	
56-U		Wida		
56-X		Danis Jumbo		
56-AJ		Weedhopper		
56-AR		SMAN Pétrel	01	
56-AU		Mignet HM.293 Pou-du-Ciel		
		(Crashed 2.5.04)		
56-AV		SMAN Pétrel	001	
56-BA		SMAN Pétrel		
56-BK		Air Création (two seater)		
56-BS		Denney Kitfox		
56-CH		SMAN Pétrel	044	
56-CJ		SMAN Pétrel		
56-CQ	F-JBWG	Sauper J.300 Joker		
56-CR		Air Création		
56-DQ		Air Création / SX		
56-DR	F-JBSW	SMAN Pétrel	061	
56-DV		Air Création / SX		
56-EH		weightshift		
56-EO	F-JCNL	SMAN Petrel		
56-EW		III Sky Arrow		
56-EZ		Air Création		
56-FE		Billie Aero Marine Petrel		
56-FH		Billie Aero Marine Petrel		
56-FX		Jodel D.21		
56-GA		Rans S-6 Coyote II		
56-GD		Magni M-14 Scout 2000		
56-GI		Fly Synthesis Storch		
56-GK	F-JOAH	Tecnam P.92 Echo Super		
56-GL	F-JHQI	Raj Hamsa X'Air		
56-GP		Air Création		
56-GQ		Air Création / Kiss		
56-GR		Best Off Sky Ranger		
56-GS		Best Off Sky Ranger		
56-GT		Cosmos / Top 14.9		
56-GZ		Micro Aviation Pulsar III		
56-HA	F-JHMS	Rans S-6 Coyote II		
56-HC		Rans S-6 Coyote II		
56-HF	F-JHQA	Air Création GTE Clipper / XP		
56-HG		Ekolot JK-05 Junior	05 02 11	
56-HH	F-JHPD	Raj Hamsa X'Air		
56-HI	F-JHPQ	Djicat Buse'Air 180		
56-HM		Air Création / SX III		
56-HQ	F-JHQH	Air Création Racer / Fun		
56-HR		Remos G.3 Mirage		
56-HT		Air Création		
56-HU		Air Création / SX		
56-HX	F-JHPT	Air Création / SX		
56-HY	F-JHQR	Tecnam P.2002 Sierra		
56-IA		Air Création		
56-IB	F-JHQX	Weedhopper AX		
56-IC		Best Off Sky Ranger		
56-IH		Rans S-6 Coyote II		
56-IO	F-JHRM	Alpi Aviation Pioneer 300		
56-IP		ICP Bingo 4S	03-06-52-117	
56-IK	F-JHRF	Jodel D.20		
56-IW	F-JYEM	Autogyro-Europe MT-03	F06G02	
		(Also reported as c/n 06018)		
56-IX	F-JHGD	Humbert Tetras		
56-JA		ITV Pawnee paramotor		
56-JC		Mainair Sport Gemini Flash		
		(Crashed 4.8.06)		
56-JD		B&F Funk FK-9		
56-JE		Weedhopper AX-3		
		(Crashed 26.10.06)		
56-JH	F-JZOQ	Flight Design CT SW		
56-JK	F-JYXR	Fly Synthesis Storch		
		(Same call-sign as 56-TK)		
56-JR		Best Off Sky Ranger		
56-JU		ICP MXP-740 Savannah	01-11-51-105	
56-JZ		Zenair CH-701 SP STOL (f/p)		
56-KB		ICP MXP-740 Savannah	05-02-51-370	

Regn	Call-sign	Type	c/n	Notes
56-KC		Fly Synthesis Texan		
56-KL	F-JYWS	Flight Design CT SW		07-04-28
56-KO		Aviakit Hermes		
56-KP	F-JHMM	Aéro Services Guépard 912S		
56-KX		ITV Dakota paramotor		
56-LB	F-JRIN	Jora		
56-LD		Clemente Révolution paramotor (Crashed 24.11.07)		
56-LF	F-JZBZ	Alpi Aviation Pioneer 200 (Same call-sign as 44-AJW)		
56-LK		Zenair (Error for 55-LK/F-JXSP ?)		
56-LL		Best Off Sky Ranger		
56-LM		Autogyro-Europe MT-03		
56-LN		Croses EAC-3 Pouplume		
56-LQ	F-JXKT	Raj Hamsa X'Air		
56-LV	F-JXQR	B&F Funk FK-12 Comet (Re-regd 71-LP)	12-022	D-MUED(2)
56-LW	F-JXQT	Zlin Savage		
56-LX		Aéro Services Guépy		
56-MC	F-JHMC	Raj Hamsa X'Air		
56-MH		Comco Ikarus C-42		
56-MJ		Aquilair Swing 14		
56-MP	F-JWHP	Tecnam P.92 Echo Super		
56-MR		Air Création / Fun 18QC	A3035-3025	
56-MS		SMAM Pétrel "T-AD"	051	
56-MU	F-JZZB	Best Off Sky Ranger		
56-MW	F-JWWC	B&F Funk FK-9 Mk.IV		
56-MY		DTA Combo / Diva		
56-MZ	F-JWXU	Air Création / Fun 18QC	A3035-3220	
56-NE		Raj Hamsa X'Air		
56-NF		Raj Hamsa X'Air		
56-NG		Dudek Synthesis paramotor		
56-NH		Jodel D.18		
56-NJ		Rans S-6 Coyote II		
56-NK		Rans S-6 Coyote II		
56-NL		ITV Dakota paramotor		
56-NP		Aéro Services Super Guépard 912S		
56-NR	F-JRVD	Guérin G1		
56-NU		Flylab Tucano		
56-NW		ITV Dakota paramotor		
56-NY		Guérin G1		
56-OD	F-JWYO	B&F Funk FK-14 Polaris (Same call-sign as 05-LP)	14-095	
56-OF		Air Création Tanarg / BioniX	A10119-10108	
56-OH		Air Création GTE Clipper / iXess		
56-OV		Autogyro-Europe MTOsport		
56-OW	F-JSUQ	ICP MXP-740 Savannah S	11-03-54-0082	
56-OY		Air Création / Kiss		
56-PD	F-JTE	Rans S-6 Coyote II		
56-PG		G1 Aviation G1 SPYL		
56-PH		Vol Mediterrani VM-1 Esqual		
56-PI		Air Création Tanarg		
56-PK		B&F Funk FK-9 Mk.IV		
56-PP		Autogyro-Europe Calidus 09		
56-PQ		Best Off Sky Ranger		
56-PR		Air Création Skypper / NuviX		
56-PW		Air Création Skypper		
56-PY		Air Création Skypper / NuviX	A12056-12051	
56-QA		Autogyro-Europe Calidus 09		
56-QL		Pipistrel Alpha Trainer		
56-QS	F-JVXA	Fly Synthesis Texan Club 450	F2CC1550E0FB	
56-RF		ELA Aviacion ELA-09 Junior (W/o 13.11.15)		
56-SH		Zenair CH-601 Zodiac	6-1780	
56-TK	F-JYXR	Fly Synthesis Storch (Same call-sign as 56-JK)		
56-VM	F-JWVX	Weedhopper AX-3		

57 : Moselle

Regn	Call-sign	Type	c/n	Notes
57-F		Aériane Sirocco 377		
57-N		Lang JL-1		
57-P		Huntair Pathfinder		
57-AM		Dynali Chickinox		
57-BC	F-JBJQ	Humbert La Moto-du-Ciel		
57-BD		Huntair Pathfinder		
57-BK		Aviasud Mistral		
57-BM		Air Création / Quartz		
57-BO	F-JGEN	"Profil"		
57-BP		Huntair Pathfinder		
57-DN		(Tandem Air ?) Sunny		
57-ER		Humbert La Moto-du-Ciel		
57-EX		Air Création Racer / XP		
57-FH		Weedhopper		
57-FL		Cosmos Chronos		
57-FS		Weedhopper	B1091145	
57-GG		Synairgie		
57-GP		Air Création		
57-GQ	F-JAVT	Aviasud Mistral		
57-GV		Tandem Air Sunny Grand Raid RV (Crashed 4.9.06)		
57-HE		Synairgie		
57-HT		Rans S-14 Airaile		
57-HX	F-JAZB	Ultralair JC-24 Weedhopper Sport	C2043015	
57-IQ		Cosmos Bidulm (W/o 5.05)		
57-IT		Humbert La Moto-du-Ciel		
57-IX		Huntair Pathfinder		57-D
57-JB		Weedhopper AX-3		
57-JC		Weedhopper AX-3		
57-JD		Cosmos / Chronos 16		
57-JF		Weedhopper AX-3		
57-JJ		Weedhopper	B3013088	
57-JK		Dynali Chickinox		
57-KA		Kolb Ultrastar		
57-KC		Dynali Chickinox		
57-KF		Rans S-6 Coyote II		
57-KI		Weedhopper		
57-KL		Weedhopper AX-3 (Also reported as Dynali Chickinox)		
57-LA		Ultralair JC-24 Weedhopper Sport		
57-LI		Solar Wings Pegasus / Quasar		
57-LK		Cosmos		
57-LL		Air Création trike / Pegasus Q2 wing	8115	
57-LN		Rans S-6 Coyote II		
57-LP		Cosmos		

Regn	Call-sign	Type	c/n	Notes
57-LQ		Rans S-6 Coyote II		
57-LR	F-JBLU	Air Création GTE Clipper / XP		
57-LT		Euronef ATTL-1		
57-LX		Technoflug Piccolo	103	D-MTOH
57-LY		Air's Maestro		
57-MD		Comco Ikarus Fox-C22		
57-MJ		Rans S-6 Coyote II		
57-MK		Solar Wings Pegasus XL / Quantum 15 (Also reported as Quasar, .01)		
57-ML		Aviakit Hermes		
57-MN		Murphy Renegade Spirit		
57-MS	F-JGDT	Rans S-6 Coyote II		
57-MV		TEAM Mini-MAX 1600R SpeedMax		
57-MY		Plätzer Kiebitz		
57-NL		Rans S-6 Coyote II		
57-NM		Air Création GTE Clipper		
57-NS		Air Création / XP		
57-NX		Let-Mont Tulak		
57-OG		Mignet HM.293 Pou-du-Ciel		
57-OH		Rans S-7 Courier (W/o 10.5.98)		
57-OI		Best Off Sky Ranger		
57-OK		Comco Ikarus Fox-D	8510-FD34	LX-XOE, D-MBOE
57-OL		Fantasy Air Allegro SW		
57-ON		Air Création Racer		
57-OO		Ultralair JC-24 Weedhopper Sport	1012867	55-DM
57-OP		PGO Aviation Cobra		
57-OY		EuroALA Jet Fox 91		
57-PD		Mignet HM.1000 Balerit	13	
57-PE		Light Aero Avid Flyer		
57-PH		Le Goeland	02	F-PDNE, F-WDNE
57-PI		Dynali Chickinox		
57-PJ		"E.C.L." (Pou-type)	116	
57-PK		Aviasud AE209 Albatros		
57-PM	F-JBZG	Aerotech Storch		
57-PN		Cosmos Phase II	21086	
57-PO		Ecolight X'Air		
57-PP		Cosmos		
57-PQ		Air Création / XP		
57-PR		Cosmos		
57-PU		Humbert Tetras		
57-PX	F-JGAF	Denney Kitfox		
57-PY		Dynali Chickinox Kot-Kot		
57-QA		EuroALA Jet Fox		
57-QC	F-JGAV	Humbert Tetras		
57-QD		Aviakit Hermes		
57-QF		Air-Light Wild Thing WT-01 (Same c/n as D-MONT)	98 08 057	
57-QI		Humbert Tetras		
57-QL	F-JGAL	Best Off Sky Ranger		
57-QM	F-JGAH	TL Ultralight TL-232 Condor		
57-QP		Humbert Tetras		
57-QR		Zenair CH-701 STOL		
57-QU		DTA 582 / Dynamic 15	9/50	
57-QX		Rans S-6 Coyote II		
57-RD		Cosmos		
57-RF	F-JSTI	Rans S-6ES Coyote II		
57-RL		Humbert Tetras		
57-RN		Weedhopper	7032296	
57-RO		Raj Hamsa X'Air 502T (W/o 6.7.03)		
57-RP	F-JGRP	Let Mont Tulak (Wears regn "N4749AU" on tail)		
57-RV	F-JGEQ	Aéro Services Guépy		
57-RY		Humbert Tetras		
57-SB		Fly Synthesis Storch		
57-SH		Rans S-12 Airaile		
57-SJ	F-JREY	Halley Apollo Fox (Re-regd 33-AIW)		
57-SL		Air Création Racer		
57-SQ	F-JGCO	Humbert Tetras (Also reported as 57-SO)	791	
57-SR		Autoplum		W57-SR
57-SS	F-JGER	Stern Schmetterling 2000		W57-SS
57-TK		Plätzer Kiebitz B9		
57-TT		Raj Hamsa X'Air		
57-TY		Dynali Chickinox Kot-Kot		
57-UB		Best Off Sky Ranger		
57-UC	F-JGEP	Zenair CH-701 STOL		
57-UI		Ultralair Weedhopper AX-3 16 (Crashed 23.9.07)		
57-VC	F-JGFA	Jodel D.185		
57-VG		TEAM Mini-MAX		
57-VJ		Cosmos Phase II 582		
57-VN		(Quad City ?) Challenger		
57-VV		paramotor		
57-XE		Ekolot JK-05 Junior (Same c/n as OK-UUD 04, SP-SYAU, SP-YAU)	05 01 05	
57-XG		Best Off Sky Ranger		
57-XS		Rans S-7 Courier		
57-YH		P&M Aviation Quik 912S	7998	
57-YK	F-JQAD	B&F Funk FK-9 Mk.III Utility (Re-regd 82-BN / F-JIHO)	04-U-227	
57-YM	F-JQAS	ICP MXP-740 Savannah	03-05-51-224	
W57-YR		Wezel / AlbatarApis 2	W002	
57-YT	F-JQAR	Rans S-6ES Coyote II (t/w)	0494611	
57-ZF	F-JRAM	Best Off Sky Ranger V-Max		F-JQAT
57-ZN	F-JQBK	B&F Funk FK-9 Mk.III	241	
57-ZR	F-JQBR	Fantasy Air Allegro SW	03-124	
57-AAF	F-JQCR	Dallach Sunwheel (Re-regd D-MOYO)	035	
57-AAI		Air Création Racer 503 / XP11		
57-AAR	F-JOCI	Denney Kitfox		
57-ABB		Aveko VL-3		
57-ABD	F-JQCW	Aeropro Eurofox		
57-ABJ	F-JQDL	Comco Ikarus C-42		
57-ABM		Humbert Tetras		
57-ABO		Humbert Tetras 912BS (Accident 30.10.05, crashed 5.4.09)		
57-ABP		Dyn'Aéro MCR-01 ULC		
57-ABR	F-JYAO	Comco Ikarus C-42		
57-ABS		motor glider		
57-ABT		Cosmos Bison 447 / Mach 14.9		
57-ACB		Mignet HM-1100 Cordouan	22	

Reg	Call-sign	Type	Serial	Notes
57-ACP	F-JQEV	Aerospool WT-9 Dynamic	DY102/2005	
57-ACR	F-JQEY	Humbert Tetras VW 2L SP		
57-ADB	F-JGCO	B&F Funk FK-12 Comet	12-007	D-MSUF
		(Re-regd D-MHPM .07)		
57-ADG		Humbert Tetras		
57-AKY		Dynali Chickinox Tandem		
57-ALQ		Jodel D.18		
		(Accident 6.8.06)		
57-ALR	F-JZCV	Aerospool WT-9 Dynamic		
57-ALS		Walker W130		
57-AMS	F-JZKV	B&F Funk FK-9 Mk.IV Utility	09-04-300	
57-AMT		ICP Bingo 4S (HKS700)	06-03-52-204	
57-ANA		Didier Pti'tavion		
57-ANM		Raj Hamsa X'Air		
57-ANS	F-JZTX	Best Off Sky Ranger V-Max (Loravia mod)		
			SKR0411488	
57-APC	F-JRRL	Pietenpol Aircamper GN1	1	
57-APE	F-JYPZ	Flight Design CT SW	07-02-04	F-JERN
		(Same call-sign as 01-RL) (Also reported as F-JBLU)		
57-APJ		Ekolot JK-05 Junior	05 06 03	
57-APK	F-JYND	Flight Design CT-2K		
57-APT	F-JYPX	Comco Ikarus C-42B		
57-AQA		ULBI WT-01 Wild Thing		
57-AQE		Jodel D.92		
57-AQK	F-JXAM	Best Off Sky Ranger		
57-AQP	F-JXCE	Aerospool WT-9 Dynamic	DY191/2007	
57-AQR	F-JXCS	Fantasy Air Allegro SW	02-127	
57-AQW	F-JRJV	Autogyro-Europe MTOsport		
57-ARA		Rans S-9 Chaos		
57-ARI		paramotor		
57-ARO	F-JPJG	Best Off Sky Ranger		59-AGM
57-ARP		paramotor		
57-ARS	F-JXQV	Air Création Tanarg 912 / iXess 13		
			A08016-7209 /T06048	
57-ASM		Comco Ikarus C-42B		
57-ASV		Comco Ikarus C-42		
57-ASW	F-JZEA	Comco Ikarus C-42	0806-7000	
57-ATD		P&M Aviation Quik 912S	8392	
57-ATN	F-JRQX	Best Off Sky Ranger V-Max 912	877	
		(Re-regd 21-AEX)		
57-ATS	F-JUMY	Lipp / Denney Kitfox III	1036	D-ELIP
57-ATY	F-JQBJ	Air Création Tanarg 912 / iXess 13		
			A00100-0051 /T08007	
57-ATZ	F-JWIB	B&F Funk FK-14B Polaris	14-086	
		(Same call-sign as 28-APG)		
57-AUI	F-JWLM	Flight Design CT LS	F-08-08-01	
57-AUO		Air Création / Kiss		
57-AUT	F-JWXP	B&F Funk FK-12 Comet	12-009	D-MRKL
57-AUX		Ekolot JK-05 Junior		
57-AVB		Aveko VL-3 Sprint	VL3-37	
57-AVE		P&M Aviation QuikR 912S		
57-AVR		Pegasus		
57-AWJ		Weedhopper Europa 2	9112562	OO-933
57-AWK	F-JRDS	Zlin Savage Cub		
57-AXH		Sonex Aircraft Sonex		
57-AXM		Evektor EV-97 Eurostar	2009 3704	
57-AXT	F-JRLQ	B&F Funk FK-12 Comet	12-087	95-IL/F-JFAL,
		(To PH-4P5)		D-MAXG
57-AXV	F-JRLU	Flight Design CT SW		
57-AYD	F-JULK	Comco Ikarus C-42		F-JROG
		(Same call-sign as 57-BHC)		
57-AYF		Miniplane/ITV Lapoon paramotor		
57-AYH		Zenair CH-601XL Zodiac		
57-AYL		Humbert Tetras		
57-AYU		DTA Combo FC		
57-AYX	F-JIGM	Zlin Savage Classic		
57-AYZ		Magni gyrocopter		
57-AZF		ICP MXP-740 Savannah		
57-BAI		EEL ULF-2		
57-BAP		Flying K Sky Raider		
57-BBI		Air Création Tanarg		
57-BBJ		Air Création Tanarg		
57-BBV		Rans S-6 Coyote II		
57-BBW	F-JSWT	Rans S-6 Coyote II		
57-BCC		Rans S-6 Coyote II		
57-BCJ		Air Création Tanarg / iXess		
57-BDM		Air Création Skypper		
57-BEM	F-JTSY	Zenair CH-701 STOL		
57-BET	F-JTUZ	Humbert Tetras		
57-BEZ		ATEC 122 Zephyr		LY-UFO
57-BFA	F-JTVP	Pipistrel Alpha Trainer	458SWN100	
57-BFD		Air Création Skypper 912		
57-BHC	F-JULK	Comco Ikarus C-42B		
		(Same call-sign as 57-AYD)		
57-BHE		Air Création Tanarg / BioniX		
57-BHT	F-JRZC	Roland Z.602	Z-9560	
57-BJA		Celier Xenon		
		(damaged 25.2.14)		
57-BLT	F-JSTI	Flight Design CT SW		
57-BMI		Zenair CH-601 Zodiac	6-3182	OO-G47, 59-OK
57-BMY	F-JVVR	B&F Funk FK-14 Le Mans		
57-BNF	F-JVWH	Roland Z.602 TD		
57-BNH		Aero East Europe SILA 450C	140128-AEE-021	
57-BNY	F-JZPL	Best Off Nynja		
57-BOI	F-JUYM	Rans S-6 Coyote II		
57-BON	F-JTLE	JMB Aircraft VL-3 Evolution	VL3-154	

58 : Nièvre

Reg	Call-sign	Type	Serial	Notes
58-AA		Aeromas 386		
58-AG		Eipper Quicksilver MX	5805	
58-AH		Eipper Quicksilver MX II	1178	
58-AI		Eipper Quicksilver MX		
58-AS		Eipper Quicksilver MX		
58-AV		Zenith Baroudeur		
58-BB		Weedhopper		
58-BY		Galaxy		
58-CJ		Air Création / Quartz		
58-CN		Air Création / Quartz		
58-CX	F-JCHF	Cosmos / Air Création Mild		
58-DB		DTA 503 / Dynamic		
58-DO	F-JAID	DTA 503 / Dynamic 15		
		(or F-JATD?)		
58-DS		Air Création GT BI / Quartz 18		
58-EE		DTA 582 / Dynamic 15		
58-EI	F-JGOE	Air Création GTBI / XP 15		
58-EK		DTA 582 / Dynamic 15		

Reg	Call-sign	Type	Serial	Notes
58-EL		weightshift		
58-ER		Humbert Tetras		
58-FC		DTA Feeling 912S / Dynamic 450	00-64	
		(Re-regd OO-E31 11.03)		
58-FD		DTA 582 / Dynamic 15	00-65	
		(Re-regd OO-E42 3.04)		
58-FF		Djicat Buse'Air 150		
		(Re-regd 02-AC)		
58-FM		Sauper J.300 Joker		
58-FN	F-JGPU	Landray GL-4		
58-FQ		Micro Aviation Pulsar III		
58-FS		Rans S-6 Coyote II		
58-FT		Air Création GT BI		
58-FU	F-JGOH	Slepcev Storch		
58-GC		Air Création / Fun		
58-GD		Aviakit Vega UL		
58-GE	F-JFOK	Rans S-6 Coyote II		
58-GF	F-JQGN	Raj Hamsa X'Air		
58-GG		Zenair CH-601 Zodiac		
58-GJ	F-JQGA	Dyn'Aéro MCR-01	69	
58-GK	F-JWCI	Alpi Aviation Pioneer 200		F-JQHC
58-GL	F-JKFE	Fly Synthesis Storch		
		(Re-regd 33-AES)		
58-GM		ITV paramotor		
58-GY		ALMS/Sauper Papango		
58-HD		Air Création Tanarg / iXess		
58-HG	F-JQLU	Sauper J.300 Joker		
58-HI	F-JYQG	Vidor Asso VI Junior	121	
58-HK	F-JCOS	Rans S-6 Coyote II		
58-HL		Zlin Savage		
		(Crashed 17.9.08)		
58-HO		Zenair CH-601UL Zodiac	6-9110	28-YO
58-HR		ICP Bingo!		
58-HV		ITV Dakota paramotor		
58-HY		Alpi Aviation Pioneer		
58-IC		Jodel D.21	01	
58-ID		Air Création		
58-IE	F-JATD	Marie JPM-03 Loiret	23	
58-IH		Sky Paragliders Atis 3 paramotor		
58-IK		gyrocopter		
58-IQ	F-JWEZ	Ekolot KR-030 Topaz		
58-JE		Raj Hamsa Hanuman		
58-JV		Eipper Quicksilver		
58-MU		Rans S-6 Coyote II		
58-QL		Fly Synthesis Storch		
58-QY		Mignet Pou-du-Ciel		
58-WF		Zenair CH-601 Zodiac		

59 : Nord

Reg	Call-sign	Type	Serial	Notes
59-B		Eipper Quicksilver MX		
59-C		Air Création		
59-F		Sofrec Vélipane	248/82	
		(Re-regd OO-572 7.83)		
59-H		Dynali Chickinox Kot-Kot		
W59-AA		Rans S-6 Coyote II		
59-AM		JC-24 Weedhopper		
59-AN		JC-31C Weedhopper Europa II		
59-AR		JC-24 Weedhopper		
59-AS		JC-24 Weedhopper		
59-AW		Zenair CH-601 Zodiac		
59-BA		Zodiac Ultrastar	127	
59-BF		Cyclone AX-3		
		(The Squadron SE.5A replica "59BF" noted in the UK in 1985 and painted as "F760", is believed to have been a US-registered ultralight)		
59-BQ		Weedhopper		
59-BU		Weedhopper		
59-BZ		Lemonnier Maestro	86.102	
59-CA		Dynali Chickinox		
59-CE		Rans S-6 Coyote II		
59-CK		Weedhopper		
59-CM		Air Création / Quartz		
59-CP		paramotor		
59-DD		Kolb Twinstar		
59-DJ		Weedhopper	9041112	55-DY?
59-DP		Eipper Quicksilver GT500		
59-DR		Cosmos		
59-DT		Cosmos		
59-DV		Rans S-12 Airaile		
59-DY		Weedhopper AX-3		
59-EA		Weedhopper 1		
59-EB		Weedhopper		
59-EE		Premier Cyclone AX-3 / 503		
59-EF		Air Création		
59-EP		Aerolac MD04 Airland		
59-ES		Dynali Chickinox		
59-ET		Dynali Chickinox		
59-EU		Air Création GT BI 503 / XP 15		
59-EW		Dynali Chickinox Kot-Kot	1271886	
		(W/o 7.3.92)		
59-EX		Dynali Chickinox		
59-EZ		Marquart Charger		
		(Weedhopper 8.02?)		
59-FD		Air Création / Quartz		
59-FJ		Dynali Chickinox Kot-Kot		
59-FK		weightshift		
59-FQ		Cosmos / La Mouette Top 14.9		
		(W/o 31.7.03)		
59-FU		Weedhopper AX-3		
59-FZ		Dynali Chickinox Kot-Kot		
59-GB		Dynali Chickinox		
59-GC		Weedhopper		
59-GD		Cyclone AX-3		
59-GP		Quartz	81052901	
59-GQ		Weedhopper		
59-GT		Mignet HM.293A Pou-du-Ciel		55-FC
59-HB		Macair 1142 Merlin		
59-HC		Aviasud Mistral		
59-HG		Dynali Chickinox		OO-...
59-HI		Dynali Chickinox Kot-Kot		
59-HJ		Dynali Chickinox		
59-HM		Air Création / Fun		
59-HP		Dynali Chickinox		
59-HV		Air Création / Cosmos Chronos 16		
59-HX		JC-24D Weedhopper Sport (Stored)	B1041142	
59-IE	F-JAJQ	Humbert La Moto-du-Ciel	9178	

Regn	F-regn	Type	c/n	Other regn
59-IG		Dynali Chickinox Kot-Kot		
59-IL		Eipper Quicksilver GT500		
59-IN(1)		Eipper Quicksilver MX IIHP		
59-IN(2)		SMAN Petrel		
59-IO		Eipper Quicksilver MX		
59-IP		Mignet HM.293 Pou-du-Ciel		
59-IT		Dynali Chickinox		
59-IW	F-JAMH	SMAN Pétrel		
59-IY		Air Création GT BI / SX		
59-JE		Dynali Chickinox Kot-Kot		
59-JG		Weedhopper Europa II	82022995	
		(Re-regd 08-KO)		
59-JH		Weedhopper AX-3		
59-JO		Citizen Flyer Twin JL9		
59-JS		Dynali Ckickinox		
59-KC		Cosmos GT		
59-KG		Weedhopper		
59-KK	F-JFLR	Epervier		
59-KN		Mignet HM.1000 Balerit	46	
59-KP		Eipper Quicksilver GT500		
59-KU		Aviasud AE209 Albatros	46	PH-2M5
59-LA		Zodiac Ultrastar		
59-LH		Aviasud AE209 Albatros	024	(OO-B91)
		(Re-regd OO-E05 3.03)		
59-LJ		TEAM Mini-MAX		
59-LV		Cosmos		
59-LY		Rans S-12 Airaile	0691084	
59-LZ		Aviasud AE209 Albatros	50	
		(Re-regd OO-D37, 7.01)		
59-MB		Aviasud AE209 Albatros	51	
59-MD		Mignet HM.1000 Balerit	72	OO-A81
		(Re-regd 08-HE)		
59-MH		Zenair CH-701 STOL		
59-MI		Zenair CH-701 STOL		
59-MJ		Zenair CH-701 STOL	003	OO-B67
59-MK		Zenair CH-701 STOL	0012B	
		(W/o 3.8.95)		
59-ML		Micro Aviation Pulsar		
59-MN		Arrow F.2 Foxcat		
		(Damaged, stored)		
59-MO		Rans S-6 Coyote II	0192261	OO-A52
59-MP	F-JYPG	Rans S-6 Coyote II	0294585	
59-MQ		Cyclone AX-3 / 503		
59-MT		Zenair CH-701 STOL	7-2103	
		(Re-regd OO-E23, 8.03)		
59-MU		Zenair CH-701 STOL	7-2014	OO-B34
		(painted 59/72014)		
59-MW		Zenair CH-701 STOL		
59-MX		Fly Synthesis Storch	22?	
59-MZ		Rans S-6 Coyote II		
59-NA		Dynali Chickinox Kot-Kot		
59-NB		Dynali Chickinox Kot-Kot		
59-NE		DTA / Dynamic		
59-NG		Dynali Chickinox Kot-Kot		
59-NI		Zenair CH-701 STOL	7-3183	
59-NJ		Rans S-6 Coyote II	0593502	
		(Re-regd OO-E14, 6.03)		
59-NK		Rans S-6ESD Coyote II	0891214	OO-A60
59-NL		AMF Chevvron 2-32	031	OO-A29
59-NM		Cosmos / Chronos 16		
59-NP		Cosmos		
		(Also noted as Rans S-6ES Coyote II (t/w) 6.07; 59-MP?)		
59-NQ		Aviatika Locafly		
59-NS		Synairgie		
59-NU		Mignet HM.1000 Balerit	92	
59-NV		Rans S-6 Coyote II	0894667	
		(Re-regd OO-D28, 3.01)		
59-NW		Zenair CH-701 STOL		
59-OG		Air Création GT BI 582ES / Quartz		
59-OJ		Zenair CH-601 Zodiac		
59-OK		Zenair CH-601 Zodiac	6-3182	
		(Re-regd OO-G47, 11.09)		
59-OL		Rans S-6 Coyote II (t/w)		
59-OO		Air Création		
59-OP		Rans S-6 Coyote II (t/w)		
59-OR		Fly Synthesis Storch		
59-OS		Zenair CH-601 Zodiac		
59-OV		Rans S-12 Airaile	0792245	OO-B08
59-PB		Dynali Chickinox		
59-PD		Mignet HM.1000 Balerit	111	
		(Re-regd 50-NU)		
59-PE		Rans S-6 Coyote II (t/w)		
59-PG		Rans S-6 Coyote II		
59-PI		Fly Synthesis Storch		
59-PK		Zenair CH-701 STOL		
59-PM		Aviasud Mistral		
59-PN		Aviasud Mistral	195	OO-C22, D-MNAT
		(Also wears regn OO-C22)		
59-PP		Macair 1142 Merlin		
59-PQ		Dynali Chickinox Kot-Kot		
59-PS		Eipper Quicksilver GT500	202	OO-B01
59-PV	OQ-AYW	Rans S-6ES Coyote II (t/w)	0395772	
		(Re-regd OO-F63, 9.07)		
59-PX		Weedhopper AX-3		(OO-658)
59-QC		Zenair CH-601UL Zodiac		
		(W/o 4.6.09)		
59-QD		Rans S-6 Coyote II		
59-QE	F-JFIR	Rans S-6 Coyote II		
59-QF		Zenair CH-701 STOL		
59-QG		Air Création / Quartz		
59-QI		Solar Wings Bandit	SW-SB-0021	
59-QJ		Zenair CH-701 STOL		
59-QM		Rans S-6 Coyote II	1091222	OO-A53
		(Active again as OO-A53)		
59-QP		Zenair CH-601 Zodiac		
59-QQ		Ultravia Pelican		
59-QR		Best Off Sky Ranger		
59-QS		Rans S-6ES Coyote II	295732ES	OO-C06
		(Active again as OO-C06)		
59-QT		Zenair CH-701 STOL		
59-QX		Dynali Chickinox MX		
59-QY		Mignet HM.293 Pou-du-Ciel		
59-RA		Rans S-6 Coyote II (t/w)	0895866	
		(Re-regd OO-E58, 7.04)		
59-RB		Rans S-6ES Coyote II (t/w)	0895872ES	
		(Re-regd OO-E53, 6.04)		
59-RC		Aviasud AE209 Albatros		
59-RE		Rans S-6 Coyote II (t/w)		
59-RH		TEAM Mini-MAX		
59-RJ		Air Création GTE Clipper	103	
		(Re-regd OO-D96, 12.02)		
59-RL		Weedhopper AX-3		59-RH?
59-RN		Evans VP-2 Volksplane		
59-RR	F-JZBA	Rans S-6 Coyote II (t/w)		
59-RT		Zenair CH-701 STOL		
59-RU		Zenair CH-701 STOL		
59-RY		Mignet HM.1000 Balerit	115	
		(wfu, now at Aviodrome Museum, Lelystad, the Netherlands)		
59-RZ		Croses Criquet (Conv from Airplume .98)	23	OO-833
		(Current as OO-833)		
59-SA		Rans S-6ES Coyote II	0695842	
		(Re-regd 59-CWE,OO-G13)		
59-SE		Dynali Chickinox Kot-Kot		
59-SF		Mignet HM.1000 Balerit	119	
		(Sold in Norway)		
59-SH	F-JCPP	Zenair CH-601HD Zodiac	6-1780	C-FMXN
59-SJ		Rans S-6 Coyote II (n/w)		
59-SN		Zenair CH-701 STOL	7-2886	
		(Re-regd OO-C72 9.98, 59-CSZ)		
59-SO		Rans S-6ES Coyote II	0393468	OO-B87
59-SR		Zenair CH-601 Zodiac (t/w)		
59-SU		Air Création GT BI		
59-SW		Zenair CH-701 STOL		
59-TB		EuroALA Jet Fox 91S		
59-TD		Fly Synthesis Storch	155	
		(Re-regd OO-D59, 2.02)		
59-TF		Murphy Renegade Spirit	PFA/188-11562	G-MWHK
59-TH	F-JCBU	Rans S-7 Courier		
59-TI		Synairgie		
59-TK	F-JPQM	Mignet HM.293 Pou-du-Ciel		95-JD
59-TL		Zenair CH-601UL Zodiac		
		(Damaged 2.7.01)		
59-TM	F-JDEI	Zenair CH-601UL Zodiac		
59-TN	OQ-AXH	Rans S-6 Coyote II		
59-TP		Rans S-6 Coyote II		
59-TT		Rans S-6ES Coyote II	Co.930201	
		(Also registered OO-A98 and based in Belgium)		
59-TZ	F-JCCR	Air Création GT BI / Fun		
59-UA		Mignet Proto		
59-UB	F-JFKJ	Zenair CH-601 Zodiac		
		(Also reported as F-JFLM)		
59-UC	F-JCLU	Zenair CH-701 STOL		
59-UD		Aérianne Swift	45	
59-UE		Air Création / XP		
59-UG		Mignet HM.1000 Balerit	127	
		(Re-regd 28-XZ)		
59-UI		Air Création Racer / SX		
59-UJ	F-JFJO	Rans S-6 Coyote II		
		(also reported as F-JFJC)		
59-UK		Rans S-6 Coyote II	11961068	
		(Re-regd OO-D52 11.01)		
59-UL		Air Création GTE Clipper 582 / XP15		
59-UO		Air Création GT / Fun		
59-UN		Light Aero Avid Flyer		
59-US		Air Création GT / Fun		
59-UU		Air Création GTE Clipper /		
59-UX		Air Création / Fun		59-GR
59-VB		Cosmos Phase II / Chronos II	21225	
59-VC		TEAM Mini-MAX		
59-VF		Solar Wings Pegasus / Quantum		
59-VH		Solar Wings Pegasus / Quantum		
59-VJ		Air Création GTE Clipper		
59-VM		Rans S-12 Airaile		
59-VN		Zenair CH-601 Zodiac		
59-VO		Fly Synthesis Storch		W59-VO
59-VQ		TL Ultralight TL-132 Condor	94016	
59-VT		Zenair CH-601UL Zodiac		
59-VV		Zenair CH-601 Zodiac		
59-VX		Zenair CH-601 Zodiac (t/w)	6-9130	
		(Re-regd OO-D60, 2.02)		
59-VZ		Dynali Chickinox		74-AQ
59-WA		Rans S-6 Coyote II	07971139	
		(Re-regd OO-D06, 5.00)		
59-WB		Air Création GTE 582S / XP15	117	
		(Re-regd OO-E73, 11.04)		
59-WB		Air Création Racer 503S / XP11	147	
		(Re-regd OO-E85, 3.05)		
59-WC		Aviasud AE209 Albatros	28	
59-WD		Air Création GT BI / SX		
59-WE		Rans S-6 Coyote II	06971124	
		(Re-regd OO-D50, 11.01)		
59-WF	F-JDCH	Zenair CH-601HD Zodiac	6-3592	
59-WG		Cosmos Phase II		
59-WI	F-JDBB	Mignet HM.1100 Cordouan	05	
59-WK	F-JFKS	Rans S-7 Courier		
59-WM		Aquilair Swing 14		
59-WO		Fisher FP.404		
		(Re-regd 55-PK)		
59-WP		Dynali Chickinox Tandem		
59-WW		Zenair CH-601 Zodiac		
59-WX		Mignet HM.293A Pou-du-Ciel		(PH-MIG)
59-XA		ICP MXP-740 Savannah	09-97-50-060	
59-XC		Dynali Chickinox Tandem	2991L1	
		(W/o 14.6.99)		
59-XD		Fly Synthesis Storch		
59-XH		Aquilair Swing 14		
59-XI		Air Création GTE Clipper / XP		
59-XJ		JC-31 Weedhopper	3788844	
		(Re-regd OO-D02, 3.00)		
59-XQ		Dynali Chickinox		
59-XS		Zenair CH-701 STOL	7-9000	
		(Re-regd OO-D22, 12.00)		
59-XT		Rans S-12 Airaile		
59-XU	F-JZUC	Zenair CH-601UL Zodiac	6-9011	
59-XX		Best Off Sky Ranger		
59-XZ	F-JFJE	Zenair CH-601UL Zodiac		
		(Re-regd 83-AHO)		
59-YA		Fly Synthesis Storch		
		(W/o 23.6.05)		
59-YB		Cosmos		
59-YD		Zenair CH-601 Zodiac (t/w)	6-9009	
59-YF		Air Création	A98-101	

Reg	Marks	Type	c/n	Other
59-YI		Zenair CH-701 STOL		
59-YJ		Mignet HM.1100 Cordouan	9	
59-YK		Fly Synthesis Storch	232	
		(Re-regd OO-D74, 6.02)		
59-YM		Solar Wings Pegasus		
59-YN		Rans S-6ES Coyote II	06981238	
		(Re-regd OO-D05, 5.00)		
59-YP		Rans S-6 Coyote II		
59-YR		Aviasud AE209 Albatros	120	
		(W/o 24.4.99)		
59-YS		Rans S-12 Airaile	03960698	
		(Re-regd OO-F66, 10.07)		
59-ZB		SE.5A replica		
59-ZF		Zenair CH-601 Zodiac		
59-ZG		Zenair CH-601 Zodiac	6-6025	
		(Re-regd OO-F49 5.07)		
		(also reported as Rans S-6 Coyote II)		
59-ZI		Aviasud AE209 Albatros	129	
		(Re-regd OO-D24, 12.00)		
59-ZK		Air Création / XP		
59-ZN		Eipper Quicksilver GT500		
59-ZO		Air Création Racer 447 / Fun 14		
59-ZR		Mignet HM.293 Pou-du-Ciel		
59-ZS		SE.5A replica		
59-ZV		Fly Synthesis Storch	243	
		(Re-regd OO-D31, 5.01)		
59-ZW		Fly Synthesis Storch	245	
		(Re-regd OO-D30, 5.01)		
59-ZY		Fly Synthesis Storch		
W59-AAB	F-JFQJ	Sauper J.300 Joker		
59-AAC		Air Création / Quartz		
59-AAF		Djicat Buse'Air 150		
		(Crashed in forced landing 11.2.07)		
59-AAG	F-JFHX	Rans S-6 Coyote II		
59-AAH	F-JFHD	Zenair CH-701 STOL		
59-AAI	F-JZUO	Rans S-6S Coyote II		W59-AAI
59-AAJ		Fly Synthesis Storch	250	
		(Re-regd OO-D66, 4.02)		
59-AAM		Fly Synthesis Storch		
59-AAN		Pegasus Quantum Super Sport		
59-AAQ		Rans S-6 Coyote II		
59-AAU		Quad City Challenger		
59-AAV		Zenair CH-601 Zodiac	6-9056	
		(Re-regd OO-F79, 2.08)		
59-AAW		Zenair CH-601 Zodiac		
59-AAX		Fly Synthesis Storch		
59-AAY		Air Création / Fun		35-CC
59-ABA		Fly Synthesis Storch HS		
59-ABE		Rans S-12 Airaile		
59-ABL	F-JFIW	Rans S-6 Coyote II (t/w)		
59-ABM	F-JFHU	Barry MB-02 Souricette		
59-ABN		Rans S-12 Airaile		
		(Re-regd 59-CHY)		
59-ABO		Zenair CH-601 Zodiac		
		(W/o 17.8.03)		
59-ABT		Bierinx & Dugourd Pou-du-Ciel Bifly	JBMD-01	
		(Re-regd G-POUX 6.07)		
59-ABU	F-JAPY	Zenair CH-601 Zodiac		
59-ABW	F-JCTP	Aviasud AE209 Albatros	105	83-GO, D-MAMT, 65-CV
59-ACA	F-JABY	Zenair CH-601UL Zodiac		
59-ACB	F-JFIF	Rans S-6 Coyote II	11991346	
59-ACC		Solar Wings Pegasus Quantum	7326	
		(Re-regd OO-D27, 2.01)		
59-ACE		Fly Synthesis Storch		
59-ACG	F-JFIZ	Zenair CH-601 Zodiac		
59-ACH		Murphy Renegade Spirit		
59-ACI		Zenair CH-601UL Zodiac		
59-ACL		Zenair CH-601HD Zodiac		
59-ACQ		Fisher Celebrity		
59-ACU		Raj Hamsa X'Air		
59-ACV		Zenair CH-701 STOL		
59-ACW		Air Création Twin 582SL / XP12	E1015	
		(Re-regd OO-F04, 8.05)		
59-ARO		Fisher Celebrity		
59-ATK		Jodel D.18		
59-ATL		Jodel D.18		
59-CAB		B&F Funk FK-9 Mk.III		
59-CAC		B&F Funk FK-9 Mk.III		
59-CAD		Rans S-10 Sakota		
59-CAE		DTA / Dynamic 15		
59-CAF	F-JFHT	B&F Funk FK-9 Mk.III	09-03-130	
		(Re-regd 95-VG / F-JFHT then F-JRDE)		
59-CAI		Jodel D.9 Bébé		
59-CAJ		gyrocopter		
59-CAK		B&F Funk FK-9 Mk.III	134	
		(Re-regd OO-D25, 1.01)		
59-CAL		gyrocopter		
59-CAM		Aeropro Eurofox		W59-CAM
59-CAN	F-JFIN	Jodel D.18		
59-CAP		B&F Funk FK-9 Mk.III		
59-CAQ		Croses LC-6		
59-CAR		Dyn'Aéro MCR-01	125	
		(Re-regd OO-G40, 14.7.09)		
59-CAT		Rans S-7 Courier		59-WCAT
59-CAU		RSA / Pottier P.130UL Bleu Citron		
59-CAV		European Airwings Springbok 2000		
		(Reported as Marie JPM-03 Loiret probably in error for W59-CXV)		
59-CAW		Ultravia Pelican Sport		
		(W/o 24.5.15)		
59-CBA		Air Création Twin 582SL / Kiss 13	146	
		(Re-regd OO-D76, 19.7.02)		
59-CBD		Aviakit Vega JC		
59-CBE		ICP MXP-740 Savannah	01-00-51-001	
		(W/o 10.7.11)		
59-CBF		B&F Funk FK-9 Mk.III		
59-CBG		Best Off Sky Ranger		
59-CBI		Pegasus Quantum 582 Q2		
W59-CBJ		type unknown (biplane pusher)		
59-CBM		Zodiac Ultrastar		
59-CBO		Zenair CH-601 Zodiac		
59-CBP	F-JZKY	Pipistrel Sinus		
59-CBQ		Aeropro Eurofox		
		(Damaged, repaired 2016)		
59-CBR		Pipistrel Sinus	026S582 01 01	
		(Re-regd OO-E76, 12.04)		
59-CBS		Mignet HM.1000 Balerit	83	ALAT: F-MUCD
59-CBV		gyrocopter		
59-CBZ		B&F Funk FK-9 Mk.III	151	
		(Re-regd OO-E93, 6.05)		
59-CCA		Air Création		
59-CCB		Raj Hamsa X'Air		
59-CCC	F-JFKV	Fly Synthesis Storch		
59-CCG		Zenair CH-601 Zodiac		
59-CCI		Air Création / XP		
59-CCM		Zenair CH-601XL Zodiac		
59-CCN		Ultralair Weedhopper		
		(Accident 26.8.07)		
59-CCR	F-JDET	Aéro Services Guépy 582	98003	63-JM
59-CCU		Weedhopper		
59-CDJ		Rans S-6 Coyote II		
59-CDK		Pipistrel Sinus 582		
59-CDL		Leopoldoff L-3 Colibri	127	(F-PDOF), F-BGFS
		(Wreck noted 7.04)		
59-CDN	F-JZYI	Zenair CH-601 Zodiac (t/w)		
59-CDP		Aviasud AE209 Albatros	040	
		(W/o 3.7.05)		
59-CDU		Mignet HM.293 Pou-du-Ciel		
59-CDX		Air Création GTE 582S / Kiss	A01195-1208	
		(Re-regd OO-D97, 12.02; c/n quoted in Belgium as 145)		
59-CEC		Rans S-6 Coyote II (t/w)		
59-CEH		Air Création GTE Clipper		
59-CEI		Dynali Chickinox	5092B109	OO-A91
		(Wears both marks)		
59-CEJ	F-JFKR	B&F Funk FK-12 Comet	12-034	
		(Re-regd 85-YJ .08)		
59-CEN		Best Off Sky Ranger		
59-CEQ	F-JFKZ	Evektor EV-97 Eurostar	2001 1014	
		(Same c/n as 28-VV / F-JFSW)		
59-CER		European Airwings Springbok		
		(Damaged 30.6.02)		
59-CES		ATEC Zephyr 2000C	Z490102S	W59-CES
		(Re-regd OO-D98, 16.1.03)		
59-CET		Halley Apollo Fox	B02/2002	
		(Re-regd OO-E39, 23.12.03)		
59-CEU		Alpi Aviation Pioneer 200		W59-CEU
59-CEV		Zenair CH-601 Zodiac		
59-CEZ		Evektor EV-97 Eurostar	2002 1418	OK-DUU 33
59-CFA		Pottier P.130 Bleu Citron		
59-CFD		TL Ultralight TL-2000 Sting Carbon		
59-CFF		Zenair CH-601XL Zodiac	6-9315	
		(same c/n as 59-CFZ)		
59-CFL	F-JFLK	Urban Air UFM-13 Lambada		(OK-HUA 47)
59-CFN		Mignet HM.293 Pou-du-Ciel		
59-CFQ		Tecnam P.92 Echo		
59-CFT		DTA / Dynamic 15		
59-CFX		Zenair CH-601 Zodiac		
59-CFZ		Zenair CH-601XL Zodiac	6-9315	
		(same c/n as 59-CHY)		
59-CGA	F-JPIL	Zenair CH-601XL Zodiac		
59-CGC		Rans S-6 Coyote II		
59-CGD		weightshift		59-AJ
59-CGF		Zenair CH-601 Zodiac		
59-CGG		Zenair CH-601XL Zodiac		
59-CGI		Solar Wings Pegasus Quantum		
		(Accident 8.8.04)		
59-CGJ	F-JFLM	Kappa 77 KP-2UR Sova		
		(Same call-sign as 59-CJG, dealer?)		
59-CGK	F-JFMU	Tipsy T.66 Nipper	28	F-BMLV, OO-SRY, G-ASRY, OY-AEN
59-CGM		Aviakit Hermes		
		(W/o 2.06)		
59-CGP		Zenair CH-601XL Zodiac		
59-CGR		Air Création		
		(Also reported as Zenair CH-601 Zodiac but this may be an error for 59-CGP)		
59-CHH		P&M Aviation Pegasus		
59-CHI	F-JPBF	Zenair CH-601XL Zodiac		
59-CHM		Halley Apollo Fox (t/w)		
59-CHN		Magni M-16 Tandem Trainer		
59-CHP	F-JFMV	B&F Funk FK-12 Comet	12-059	
		(Re-regd OO-G20, 12.08)		
59-CHR		Aeroprakt A-22		
59-CHT		Raj Hamsa Hanuman		
59-CHY		Rans S-12 Airaile		59-ABN
59-CIF		TL Ultralight TL-2000 Sting Carbon		
59-CIG		Rans S-6 Coyote II		
59-CIH		Air Création / Fun 450		
59-CIL		Skyeton K-10 Swift	02-02	
59-CIN		Zenair CH-701 STOL		
59-CIO		Zenair CH-601XL Zodiac		
59-CIV		Air Création GTE Clipper / iXess		
59-CIX		Zenair CH-601UL Zodiac		
59-CIY		Zenair CH-601UL Zodiac		
59-CJA	F-JFMX	Dyn'Aéro MCR-01	200	
59-CJE		Zenair CH-601XL Zodiac (t/w)		
59-CJG	F-JFLM	Kappa 77 KP-2U Sova		
		(Same call-sign as 59-CGJ, dealer?)		
59-CJH		Rans S-9 Chaos		
59-CJK	F-JPIE	Jodel D.18V	336	F-PDGH
59-CJL	F-JXNE	Evektor EV-97 Eurostar	2007 3103	
59-CJP		Zenair CH-601 Zodiac		
59-CJT		TL Ultralight TL-2000 Sting Carbon		
59-CKA		Evektor EV-97 Eurostar		
59-CKD		Air Création GTE Clipper		
59-CKE		Air Création GTE Clipper / iXess		
59-CKF		Mignet HM.293 Pou-du-Ciel		
		(Damaged 25.4.11)		
59-CKG	F-JPBQ	ATEC Zephyr		
59-CKH		Rans S-6ES Coyote II (t/w)		
59-CKI		Aeropro Eurofox	AT9717?	
		(Re-regd 66-OI)		
59-CKJ		Zenair CH-601XL Zodiac		
59-CKM		Zenair CH-601 Zodiac		
59-CKQ		Druine D.31 Turbulent		
	F-JPBJ	also noted as Jabiru UL450 7.07		
59-CKR	F-JPIA	Alpi Aviation Pioneer 300		
59-CKS	F-JPBS	Dyn'Aéro MCR-01 UL		
59-CKU		Rans S-6 Coyote II		
		(Crashed 16.8.05)		
59-CKV	F-JBEL	Dynali Chickinox Kot-Kot		
59-CKZ	F-JPBX	ATEC Zephyr 2000	Z960304S	

Regn	F-regn	Type	c/n	Prev/Notes
59-CLD		Rans S-6 Coyote II		
59-CLI		P&M Aviation Quik 912S	8044	
	F-JPIQ	(Also noted as TL Ultralight TL-2000 Sting, 9.07 – or 59-CLP?)		
59-CLM		Aeroprakt A-22		
59-CLO		TL Ultralight TL-22 Duo		
59-CLP	F-JPIQ	TL Ultralight TL-2000 Sting Carbon RG		
59-CLZ		Dynali Chickinox		
59-CMB		Zenair CH-601 Zodiac		
59-CMD	F-JZXU	Sonex Aircraft Sonex		
59-CME		Air Création Buggy		
59-CMF		Aeropro Eurofox		
59-CMG		Aeropro Eurofox (t/w)		
59-CMH		Air Création GTE 582S / iXess	T04050	
		(Re-regd OO-G10, 9.08)		
59-CMK		Pipistrel Sinus		
59-CML	F-JPIY	Zenair CH-701SP		
59-CMM	F-JPQD	Evektor EV-97 Eurostar	2004 2217	
		(Re-regd OO-F40, 2.07)		
59-CMN	F-JPLE	TL Ultralight TL-2000 Sting Carbon	04ST99	
		(Re-regd 27-ZI)		
59-CMO		Zenair CH-701 STOL		
59-CMR		B&F Funk FK-14 Polaris	14-030	OO-D91
		(Re-regd 79-IW)		
59-CMW		ATEC Zephyr		
59-CMX		Alpi Aviation Pioneer 200		
59-CMY	F-JPLH	Morin M-80	101	
59-CNB	F-JPLO	Zenair CH-601UL Zodiac (t/w)	6-9646	
59-CNF	F-JPLJ	Rans S-6 Coyote II (t/w)		
59-CNG		Rans S-6 Coyote II		
		(Re-regd 62-AAE, 62-AME)		
59-CNI		ITV paramotor		
59-CNN		TL Ultralight TL-2000 Sting Carbon		
		(Marked 59-NNC)		
59-CNP		Aeroandinas MXP-1000 Tayrona	AA-04-05-90-005	
		(Same c/n as 59-CWN and 72-MC)		
59-CNS		B&F Funk FK-9 Mk.IV (n/w)	04-U-255	
		(To OO-H67, 8.16)		
59-CNT		Raj Hamsa Hanuman	990	
59-CNU	F-JPQL	TL Ultralight TL-2000 Sting Carbon	5ST117	
59-COB	F-JPQF	Lobb S-6 Coyote	95	
59-COJ		Rans S-6 Coyote II (t/w)		
59-CON		Zenair CH-601XL Zodiac (n/w)		
59-COP	F-JPQX	Lambert Mission M.106	02	
59-COQ	F-JPQS	Lambert Mission M.106		OM-M666
59-COR	F-JYMR	Air Création Tanarg 912 / iXess 15		
59-COU		Zenair CH-601XL Zodiac		
		(Crashed 28.9.06)		
59-COV		ProFe D.10 Tukan		
59-COW		Top Concept Hurricane		
59-COX	F-JZGS	Zenair CH-601XL Zodiac (t/w)		
59-COY		Aeroandinas MXP-1000 Tayrona		
		(Damaged 21.6.06)		
59-COZ	F-JJMQ	Flyitalia MD.3 Rider	027	
		(Same call-sign as 13-RY)		
59-CPA	F-JTPE	Aeroprakt A-22		
59-CPB		Rans S-6 Coyote II		
59-CPC		Aviasud AE209 Albatros		
59-CPE		Evektor EV-97 Eurostar		
59-CPG	F-JPTQ	Rans S-6 Coyote II (t/w)		
59-CPL	F-JPTR	Dyn'Aéro MCR-01		
59-CPS		Pegasus		
59-CPV		Air Création Buggy / Kiss		
59-CQA		DTA / Dynamic 450		
59-CQB	F-JVOO	Aeropro Eurofox		
59-CQD		Aéro Services Guépard 912		
59-CQE		TEAM Mini-MAX		
59-CQG		Light Aero Avid IV	1050A	
59-CQH		Air Création GTE Twin Buggy		
59-CQM		ProFe D-10 Tukan		
59-CQQ	F-JZLE	Evektor EV-97R Eurostar	2006 2720	
59-CQT		Dyn'Aéro MCR-01 UL		
59-CQU	F-JZMC	TL Ultralight TL-2000 Sting Carbon		
59-CQV	F-JZOE	Aéro Services Guépard 912	22024	
59-CQX		Impulse 100		
59-CRG		Aeropro Eurofox		
	F-JZQX	Also noted 7.07 as Aeroandinas MXP-1000 Tayrona AA-05-06-90-019		
59-CRI		Ekolot JK-05 Junior		
59-CRK		Air Création Tanarg 912 / iXess 15	T06054	
		(Re-regd OO-G63, 8.10)		
59-CRO		P&M Aviation Pegasus		
59-CRP		Pipistrel Taurus		
59-CRR		Preceptor N-3 Pup		W59-CRR
59-CSA	F-JYBC	B&F Funk FK-14B Polaris	14-071	
59-CSB	F-JYBZ	B&F Funk FK-14 Polaris	14-022	
59-CSC	F-JGIE	Ekolot JK-05 Junior	05 06 02	
59-CSL		B&F Funk FK-9 Mk.III		
59-CSQ	F-JYLR	Rans S-6ES Coyote II W116 (t/w)	10051669	
		(W/o 21.10.12)		
59-CSS		P&M Aviation Quik GT450		
		(Trike c/n 8258 became 59-CYK with new wing)		
59-CST	F-JYMD	B&F Funk FK-14B Polaris (t/w)		
59-CSU		Zenair CH-601 Zodiac (t/w)		
59-CSV	F-JYMF	Dova DV-1 Skylark		
59-CSW		Fly Synthesis Storch	245	OO-D30, 59-ZW
59-CSZ		Zenair CH-701 STOL	7-2886	OO-C72, 59-SN
		(current as OO-C72)		
59-CTB	F-JYZD	Didier Pti'tavion	09	
59-CTC		Halley Apollo Fox 912	B060407	
59-CTG		Murphy Renegade Spirit	241	54-JL
59-CTH	F-JXAT	Denney Kitfox III	987	?0-JX
59-CTI	F-JXBB	Lambert Mission M.106		
59-CTK	F-JXBC	Best Off Sky Ranger	159	
59-CTL		Skyeton K-10 Swift		
59-CTM		Aviasud AE209 Albatros		
59-CTN	F-JTLY	P&M Aviation Quik GT450	8297	
59-CTP		Weedhopper		
59-CTR	F-JXFP	Rans S-6ES Coyote II		
59-CTU	F-JXFU	Airflow Twinbee (prototype)		W59-CTU
59-CTV	F-JXGL	ATEC 321 Faeta		
59-CTY		P&M Aviation Quik GT450		
59-CUJ		Magni M-16 Tandem Trainer		
59-CUL		Evektor EV-97 Eurostar		
59-CUN		Rans S-6 Coyote II		
59-CUT		Pottier P.130UL	1203?	
59-CUY		P&M Aviation Quik GT450	8356	

Regn	F-regn	Type	c/n	Prev/Notes
59-CUZ		B&F Funk FK-9 Mk.IV	04-341	
59-CVA		Zlin Savage		
59-CVB		P&M Aviation QuikR 912S		
59-CVC		Fly Synthesis Storch		
59-CVD		P&M Aviation Quik GT450 912S	8451	
59-CVE	F-JXXR	Lambert Mission M.106		
59-CVF		Evektor EV-97 Eurostar		
		(W/o 31.7.15)		
59-CVJ	F-JXYR	Flight Design CT SW		
		(Also regn and c/s on Eipper Quicksilver GT500, 6.09)		
59-CVK		Jodel D.20 (model unconfirmed)		
59-CVM		Magni M-16 Tandem Trainer		
59-CVO		Air Création Tanarg / iXess 13		
W59-CVQ		Pottier P.130		
		(W/o 22.6.08)		
59-CVT	F-JRIG	Fly Synthesis Storch		
59-CVV		Pipistrel Sinus		
59-CVW		Nando Groppo Folder		
59-CWD	F-JYNN	ATEC 321 Faeta		
59-CWE		Rans S-6EWS Coyote II	0695842	59-SA
		(Re-regd OO-G13, 9.08)		
59-CWI		Rans S-9 Chaos		08-MF
59-CWN		Aeroandinas MXP-1000 Tayrona	AA-04-05-90-005	
		(Same c/n as 59-CNP and 72-MC)		
59-CWO	F-JWME	Zenair CH-650E		F-JHUW
59-CWQ		Skyeton K.10 Swift		
59-CXB		Pipistrel Virus		
59-CXG	F-JWJX	Brugger MB-2 Colibri (mod)	162	
59-CXJ		Alpi Aviation Pioneer 200		86-FR
59-CXM		Rans S-6ES Coyote II		
59-CXQ	F-JWMG	Aveko VL-3B-1 Sprint	VL3-34	
59-CXT	F-JWNP	Pipistrel Taurus	037	
59-CXU	F-JWNF	Aveko VL-3 RG Sprint	VL3-35	
59-CXV		Marie JPM-03 Loiret	21	W59-CXV
59-CXY	F-JWPR	B&F Funk FK-9 SW		
59-CYB	F-JWQG	Air Création Buggy / iXess		
		A08060-8048 / T05029		
59-CYD	F-JWSO	ICP MXP-740 Savannah XL	08-12-51-794	
59-CYE		P&M Aviation Pegasus		
59-CYF	F-JWTV	Aveko VL-3B1 Sprint	VL3-39	
59-CYI	F-JWUW	Zenair CH-701 STOL		
		(Also reported with c/s F-JWME and F-JWWW)		
59-CYJ	F-JYMR	Air Création Tanarg / iXess 13		
		(Re-regd OO-H03 5.12)		
59-CYK	F-JYMP	P&M Aviation QuikR GT450 912S	8258 / 8445	
		(Trike c/n 8258 was Quik GT450, 59-CSS) (F-JYMA also reported)		
59-CYL		P&M Aviation QuikR	8551	
59-CYM	F-JWZE	Aerospool WT-9 Dynamic	DY313/2009	
		(Reported 2011 as Zenair CH-601XL Zodiac (t/w) possibly error for 59-CYN below)		
59-CYN	F-JXHF	Zenair CH-601XL Zodiac		
		(W/o 16.11.14)		
59-CYS	F-JXFA	Skyeton K-10 Swift	0206	
59-CYT		P&M Aviation Quik GT450		
59-CYU		Aveko VL-3 Sprint		
59-CYV		Ultracraft Calypso 2a	006	
		(Re-regd OO-H33 5.14)		
59-CYW		Alisport Silent Club		
59-CYX		Fly Synthesis Texan	2002/0016A	OO-D77
		(Restored as OO-D77 1.14)		
59-CYZ		Air Création		
59-CZA	F-JYRU	Aveko VL-3 Sprint	VL3-42	
59-CZB	F-JRAT	Aveko VL-3 Sprint	VL3-47	
59-CZC	F-JRAU	Aveko VL-3 Sprint		
59-CZD	F-JRDY	Zenair CH-601HD Zodiac	6-9096	PH-3N6
59-CZH		Zenair CH-601XL Zodiac		
59-CZM		Zenair CH-601XL Zodiac		
59-CZN		Air Création / iXess		
59-CZX		P&M Aviation Pegasus Quantum 15		
59-DAA	F-JRCE	Air Création / Fun		
59-DAB	F-JRMD	Lambert Mission M106		
59-DAD		B&F Funk FK-9 Mk.III	151	OO-E93, 59-CBZ
		(Restored as OO-E93 9.11)		
59-DAE		Aveko VL-3 Sprint	VL3-52	
59-DAG		Air Création Tanarg / BioniX		
59-DAH	F-JSEA	Colomban MC-30E Luciole	1	
59-DAI	F-JEPS	Aviasud Albatros		
59-DAJ		Magni M-16 Tandem Trainer		
59-DAL		Aveko VL-3A-3 Sprint	VL3-65	
		(Re-regd OO-G66 9.10, 83-ALC)		
59-DAN	F-JRRT	Zenair CH-601XL Zodiac	6-9572	OO-F82, PH-3V7
59-DAP		AirLony Skylane UL	31	
		(Re-regd OO-G78 5.11)		
59-DAQ		Microbel trike / Air Création Quartz wing		
59-DAR	F-JRSY	AirLony Skylane UL	33	
59-DAX		AirLony Skylane UL		
59-DAY		weightshift		
59-DAZ		CFM Shadow CD	K216	OO-B39
59-DBG	F-JZIQ	Evektor EV-97 Eurostar	2004 2410	
59-DBL		Top Concept Hurricane		
59-DBM	F-JSDB	Rans S-6ES Coyote II	08051682	OO-F17
		(Restored as OO-F17 11.15)		
59-DBN		Aveko VL-3 Sprint		
59-DBY		Mignet HM.292 Pou-du-Ciel		
59-DCF	F-JSIF	Aveko VL-3 RG Sprint	VL3-78	
59-DCG	F-JSIH	Aero-Kros MP-02 Czajka	02-09	
59-DCH		Alpi Aviation Pioneer 300		
59-DCJ		Rans S-6 Coyote II		
59-DCM	F-JSMX	Aerospool WT-9 Dynamic	DY406/2011	
59-DCP		ProFe Banjo MH		OK-JUA 87
59-DCQ	F-JXTG	Evektor EV-97 Eurostar		
59-DCS		Zenair CH-601XL Zodiac		
59-DCY		Air Creation Tanarg / BioniX		
59-DDD		Zenair CH-601XL Zodiac		
W59-DDE		Mignet HM.293 Pou-du-Ciel		08-FE,55-FC(2)
59-DDO	F-JTWR	Zenair CH-650E		
59-DDU		Humbert La Moto-du-Ciel		
59-DDV		Barry MB-02 Souricette		
59-DDW		Pro.Mecc. Sparviero		
59-DDY	F-JTFY	BRM Citius Sport	0194/912ULS/11-CT	
59-DDZ		Pikalou	2018	
59-DEC		Aliport Silent 2 Targa		
59-DEP	F-JTGV	Zenair CH-601XL Zodiac		
59-DEQ		Phoenix Air Phoenix U-15	08/U15	
59-DEV	F-JTHC	Dyn'Aéro MCR-01 UL		

Reg	Call	Type	c/n	Prev
59-DEZ		Fly Product Kompress / ITV Dolpo paramotor		
59-DFA		ATEC 212 Solo		
		(Sold in UK, 2014)		
59-DFI		Rans S-6ES Coyote II	11071837	OO-F95
59-DFO	F-JTOX	Aveko VL-3 Sprint	VL3-22	OO-F94
59-DGH		Air Création GTE Clipper 503 / XP		
59-DGM	F-JTWP	Tomark SD-4 Viper	0028	
59-DGO	F-JTWR	Zenair CH.650Ei		
59-DGU	F-JTZU	Aveko VL-3 Sprint		OK-QUU 03
59-DHB	F-JUEY	Denney Kitfox		
59-DHG	F-JUGT	JMB Aircraft VL-3 Evolution	VL3-101	
59-DHJ		P&M Aviation PulsR 912	8607	G-PLSR
		(fliew marked with 59-DHJ and G-PLSR; damaged 3.9.12; reverted to G-PLSR)		
59-DHM	F-JUJY	JMB Aircraft VL-3 Sprint	VL3-103	
59-DIC		Jojowings Instinct paramotor		
59-DIH		Comco Ikarus Fox-C22	9406-3570	PH-2N9
59-DII	F-JUKQ	Zenair CH-601XL Zodiac	6-9727	OO-E96
59-DIM		AirLony Skylane UL		
59-DIR	F-JUMJ	Autogyro-Europe MTOsport	BG529-0141	
59-DIW	F-JURC	Spacek SD-1 Minisport TD	040	W59-DIW
59-DIZ	F-JUOG	Aveko VL-3 Sprint		
59-DJB	F-JUZA	Lambert Mission M.106		
59-DJH	F-JUVJ	Evektor EV-97 Eurostar	2013 4006	
59-DJI	F-JVJG	Aeropro Eurofox	10701	PH-3M4
59-DJK	F-JUYO	B&F Funk FK-12 Comet	12-069	D-MLGI
59-DJN	F-JUWZ	JMB Aircraft VL-3 Sprint	VL3-115	
59-DJO	F-JUYQ	Alpi Aviation Pioneer 300		W59-DJO
59-DJP	F-JVBJ	Pro.Mecc. Freccia		
59-DJQ		Spacek SD-1 Minisport TGC	051	
59-DKB		Kappa KP-2U Sova	9398I/2003	PH-3U9, OK-IUU 04
		(Identity unconfirmed)		
59-DKE		Pegasus		
59-DKQ		Evektor EV-97 Eurostar SL	2013 4019	
59-DLB		P&M Aviation Quik GT450		
59-DLC	F-JVJX	JMB Aircraft VL-3 Evolution	VL3-123	
59-DLI	F-JVLQ	JMB Aircraft VL-3 Evolution	VL3-118	
59-DLL		B&F Funk FK-9 ELA		
59-DLO	F-JVRT	JMB Aircraft VL-3 Evolution Remorqueur	VL3-99	
		(To OO-H47)		
59-DLP		Jodel D.18		
W59-DMC		Ludder WI	002	
59-DML	F-JVYU	Magni M-24 Orion		
59-DNF	F-JZTE	JMB Aircraft VL-3 Evolution		
59-DNI		Aviomania G2sa Genesis Duo gyrocopter		
59-DNQ		JMB Aircraft VL-3 Evolution	VL3-96	OO-G91
59-DNW	F-JTGL	ICP Zenair CH-650Ei	14-08-65ER-0014	
59-DOB		Rand KR-2S (Code"79")		
59-DOK		Magni M-16 Tandem Trainer		
59-DOR		JMB Aircraft VL-3 Evolution		
59-DOW	F-JVOY	JMB Aircraft VL-3 Evolution	VL-3-167	
		(Sold as N333VL, 12.16)		
59-DPE		JMB Aircraft VL-3 Evolution	170	
59-DPH		Vidor Asso VI Junior		
W59-DPJ		Fly Synthesis Storch HS	2006/382F326A	OO-F24
59-DPP		ATEC Solo iO		08-MD
59-DPY	F-JAQD	Comco Ikarus C-42B	1604-7448	
59-DQH		Pro.Mecc.Sparviero		
59-GTK		P&M Aviation QuikR 912S	8560	

60 : Oise

Reg	Call	Type	c/n	Prev
60-AD		Simonini Mini 2 Plus paramotor		
		(Accident 21.9.07)		
60-AO		Air Création / iXess		
60-AQ		Air Création GT BI / Quartz		
60-AU		Veliplane		
60-BC		Air Création / Fun		
60-BH		Air Création		
60-BJ		Synairgie		
60-BL		Mainair Gemini		
60-CI		Air Création / Quartz		
60-CT		Colin Epsilon / Synairgie Puma		
60-DK		Air Création GT BI / Fun		
60-DV		homebuilt trike / Synairgie Midi 18		
60-EL		weightshift		
60-FQ		Cosmos		
60-GH	F-JFTA	Air Création / XP		
60-GV		Aviasud AE209 Albatros		
60-HH	F-JZOU	Aeroprakt A-22	156	
		(W/o 11.7.07)		
60-HJ		Fantasy Air Allegro SW		
60-HX	F-JFXH	Humbert Tetras		
60-IA		Ellipse Alizé		
60-IC	F-JPHR	ICP MXP-740 Savannah		
60-IE		Brugger MB-2 Colibri		
60-IF		Air Création / iXess		
60-IT		Air Création		
60-IV		Air Création GTE		
60-JA		Aero Kuhlmann Scub		
60-JB	F-JFYV	Dyn'Aéro MCR-01		
60-JG	F-JTYX	Tecnam P.92 Echo Super		
60-KB	F-JFZI	Jodel D.18	191	54-VF, W54-VF
60-KL		Air Création / iXess		
60-KN		Djicat Buse'Air 150		
		(Crashed 4.6.04)		
60-KS	F-JPCA	TL Ultralight TL-2000 Sting Carbon	02ST25	
60-KX		DTA / Dynamic 15/450		
60-KY	F-JPRK	Aerospool WT-9 Dynamic		
60-LE		Raj Hamsa X'Air		
60-LM		Zenair CH-601XL Zodiac		
60-LN		Zenair CH-601 Zodiac		
60-LU		Advance Epsilon JPX D330 paramotor		
		(Accident 11.3.07)		
60-LY		Air Création / iXess		
60-MM		Humbert Tetras 912B		
60-MQ		Best Off Sky Ranger		
60-MS		Humbert Tetras		
60-MX		Air Création / iXess		
60-NH	F-JZOU	Aeroprakt A-22 Vision		
		(Probably an error for 60-HH which has been confirmed in an accident report)		
60-NX	F-JYXD	Aerospool WT-9 Dynamic		
60-NZ		Rans S-6 Coyote II		
60-OB	F-JXEA	Tecnam P.92 Echo Club		
60-OC	F-JHPR	ICP MXP-740 Savannah	01-05-51-090	
60-OU		Pro.Mecc.Sparviero		
60-OV		Air Création GTE 582 / iXess		
60-PC		Comco Ikarus C-42		
60-PI	F-JYAM	Autogyro-Europe MT-03		
		(Also reported as MTOsport)		
60-QD	F-JYCB	Skyeton K-10 Swift		
60-QJ		Pipistrel		
60-QP		Zenair CH-701 STOL		
60-QT	F-JZHT	Aerospool WT-9 Dynamic	DY138/2006	
60-QW	F-JFDP	Cosmos Helios		
60-QZ	F-JYVH	Tomark SD-4 Viper	026	
60-RA	F-JZAO	Tomark SD-4 Viper	025	
60-RC		Junkers Profly Junka UL		
60-RG		Dynali Chickinox ?		
60-RI		weightshift		
60-RJ		B&F Funk FK-12 Comet	12-043	D-MOVE
60-RK	F-JRIH	Aerospool WT-9 Dynamic	DY327/2009	
60-RS	F-JRMT	B&F Funk FK-14B Polaris (t/w)		
60-RV	F-JRPC	Pipistrel Sinus		
60-RW	F-JRPS	Flipper B1		
60-SE	F-JRUB	Aveko VL-3 Sprint	VL3-70	
60-SV	F-JFDS	Rans S-7 Courier		77-TK ?
60-TM		paramotor		
60-TN	F-JIKG	B&F Funk FK-9 (Vija XK9)	09-03-152	31-BP
60-TZ	F-JSZK	Aerospool WT-9 Dynamic		
60-UC		Comco Ikarus C-42		
60-UF		Aero Kuhlmann Scub		
60-UJ	F-JTGH	JMB Aircraft VL-3 Evolution		
60-UM		Dyn'Aéro MCR-01		
60-UR	F-JJMB	B&F Funk FK-9 Mk.III	09-124	
		(Same c/n as 18-HE / F-JFRR)		
60-US	F-JRMS	Aerospool WT-9 Dynamic	DY346/2010	
60-VE	F-JUDC	Colomban MC-30 Luciole	23	
60-VK	F-JTTM	ICP MXP-740 Savannah S	12-03-54-0168	
60-VL		EDRA Super Petrel		
60-VS		ELA Aviacion ELA-07S	0412 357 0712	
60-WO		Helisport CH-7 Kompress Charlie		I-B . . .
60-WW		paramotor		
60-YA	F-JTQN	ELA Aviacion ELA-07S	0914 426 07 12	
60-YB	F-JZNQ	JMB Aircraft VL-3 Evolution	VL3-144	
60-YY	F-JADH	JMB Aircraft VL-3 Evolution	169	

61 : Orne

Reg	Call	Type	c/n	Prev
61-L		Zodiac Ultrastar 500	145	
61-AE		Air Création		
61-AH		Air Création		
61-AN		Dynali Chickinox		
61-AP		Aviasud Mistral		
61-AS		Eipper Quicksilver MX II		
61-AX		Quartz		
61-BG		X5 Racer		
61-BK		JCC Aviation J.300 Joker		
61-BN		Dynali Chickinox		
61-BT		Air Création GT BI		
61-CB	F-JHGC	Dynali Chickinox		
61-CF		Aviasud Mistral		
61-CH		Air Création		
61-CK		Air Création / Fun		
61-CM		Sauper J.300 Joker		
61-DB		Dynali Chickinox		
61-DD		Air Création / Mild		
61-DH		Air Création GT		
61-DS		Air Création GT BI / Quartz		
61-EC		Biplume		
61-EF	F-JBSA	Djicat Buse'Air 150		
61-EH		Djicat Buse'Air 150		
61-EL		Dynali Chickinox		
61-EM		Powerplay Sting paramotor		
61-EP		Air's Allegro 2		
61-ER		Dynali Chickinox		
61-ET		Air Création GT / Mild		
61-EV		Air Création / SX		
61-EX	F-JHHA	Vol Mediterrani VM-1 Esqual		
61-FG	F-JHGX	Humbert Tetras		F-JCAJ
61-FJ		Humbert Tetras B		
61-FM		Air Création GT BI		
61-FO		Air Création GT / XS		
61-FR		Anglin J-6 Karatoo		
61-FU		Raj Hamsa X'Air		
61-FV		APCO paramotor		
61-GJ		ICP MXP-740 Savannah	09-98-50-094	
61-GK		Air Création / Fun		
61-GO		Air Création GTE / Mild		
61-GV		Zenair CH-601UL Zodiac		
61-GW		Air Création GTE / Mild		
61-HB	F-JHIA	ATEC Zephyr		
		(Re-regd 27-AAC)		
61-HI		Humbert Tetras		
		(Re-regd 62-ARF)		
61-HM		Synairgie / Puma B1		
61-HO		Windlass (trike)		
61-HP		ICP MXP-740 Savannah	07-00-51-015	
		(Re-regd 77-ASY)		
61-HS		Raj Hamsa X'Air		
61-IA	F-JHHY	Pipistrel Sinus		
61-IB		European Airwings Springbok		
61-IG		Air Création / Fun 450		
61-II	F-JHID	Aéro Services Guépy 582		
61-IJ		Rans S-9 Chaos		
		(W/o 4.07)		
61-IK		Comco Ikarus C-42		
61-IO		Magni gyrocopter		
61-IP	F-JHIM	Zenair CH-601 Zodiac		
61-IQ	F-JYSU	Sauper J.300 Joker		
61-IS		weighshift		
61-IX	F-JHHA	Vol Mediterrani VM-1 Esqual		
61-IY	F-JHIP	Aéro Services Guépy (Jabiru) 80	1223	
61-JA		Best Off Sky Ranger		
61-JD	F-JHIU	Air Création GT BI		
61-JE	F-JHIV	Fantasy Air Allegro SW		
		(Same call-sign as 14-JM)		
61-JG	F-JHIZ	Aviaclub Ai-10 Ikar		
61-JH		Aeropro Eurofox		
61-JI		Best Off Sky Ranger		
61-JK		Air Création / Mild		
61-JO		Pegasus / Quantum		
61-JQ		Zenair CH-601 Zodiac		

Reg	F-reg	Type	S/n	Other
61-JR	F-JHJQ	TL Ultralight TL-2000 Sting Carbon		
61-JS		Aeropro Eurofox (t/w)		
61-JT	F-JTQP	Rans S-6ES Coyote II	11991347ES	OO-D20
61-JZ	F-JZOR	Aéro Services Guépy (Jabiru) 80		
61-KC	F-JZTS	ATEC Zephyr		
61-KD	F-JZTU	Vol Mediterrani VM-1 Esqual		
61-KE	F-JYDX	Air Création GTE / Kiss		
61-KG		Air Création / SX		
61-KI	F-JYID	Fly Synthesis Storch		
61-KJ		Zenair CH-601UL Zodiac		
		(marked "H 07")		
61-KM		Air Création Tanarg / iXess		
61-KP	F-JXGG	Aéro Services Guépy Club 582		
61-KR		DTA / Dynamic 15/430		
61-KZ	F-JYMK	ICP MXP-740 Savannah	06-07-51-510	
61-LB		Fly Synthesis Storch HS		
61-LD	F-JWBH	Evektor EV-97R Eurostar 2000	2008 3304	
61-LJ	F-JPNF	B&F Funk FK-9 Mk.IV Club	09-04U-261	27-TY
61-LK		Zenair CH-601NG Zodiac		
61-LL		Aeroprakt A-22	129	
61-LN	F-JFUI	ATEC 321 Faeta	F070504A	
		(Re-regd 28-ANS)		
61-LP	F-JVLL	Zenair CH-601 Zodiac	6-9761	
61-LQ		Robin ATL	62	F-GFRM
61-LT		Quad City Challenger II		
61-LV	F-JYCG	Flight Design CT SW		
61-LW		Kappa 77 KP-2U Sova		
61-LX	F-JPEH	Aéro Services Guépy (Jabiru) 80		
61-LY		Magni M-16 Tandem Trainer		
61-MF		Aviasud AE209 Albatros		
61-MG		DTA / Dynamic		
61-MH		Synairgie Puma Bi		
		(possible error for 61-HM)		
61-MH	F-JRIE	Aerospool WT-9 Dynamic	DY330/2009	
61-MK		ITV paramotor		
61-MR		Air Création / XP		
61-MT	F-JFDF	Aéro Services Guépy (Jabiru) 80		
61-MU		Aéro Services Guépy (Jabiru) 80		
61-MZ		ITV paramotor		
61-NA		Paramania Revo 2 paramotor		
61-NG		DTA / Dynamic		
61-NI	F-JZPU	Autogyro-Europe Calidus 09		
61-NL		Air Création GTE Trek / Fun 450		
61-NN		Air Création Tanarg 582 / iXess		
61-NO	F-JTDV	ATEC 321 Faeta		
61-NQ	F-JTBO	Aéro Services Super Guépard 912		
61-NS		Aéro Services Guépy (Jabiru 2/2)		
61-NZ	F-JYMM	Flight Design CT SW		51-PQ
61-OH	F-JTXG	Robin ATL	68	F-GIHQ, HB-SCA
61-PC		Adventure Flexway 2 paramotor		
61-PD	F-JUTR	ICP MXP-740 Savannah S	15-05-54-0393	

62 : Pas-de-Calais

Reg	F-reg	Type	S/n	Other
62-P		UTA Djins 300		
62-AF		Synairgie weightshift		
62-BN		Eipper Quicksilver		
62-CD		JC-24 Weedhopper AX-3		
62-CE		Cosmos		
62-CU		Cosmos Chronos		
62-DC		Air Création / Fun		
62-DG		Weedhopper		
62-DW		Air Création / Fun		
62-ED		Rans S-6 Coyote II		
62-EE		Rans S-6 Coyote II		
62-EG		Hipps Superbirds J-3 Kitten		
62-EJ		Cosmos		
		(Later reported on Cyclone AX-3)		
62-EK	F-JFJT	Synairgie		
62-EV		Weedhopper Europa II		
62-FA	F-JWWM	Synairgie (trike)		
62-FH		Synairgie (trike)		
62-FJ		Eipper Quicksilver		
62-FQ		Dynali Chickinox		
62-FS		Weedhopper		
62-FT		Best Off Sky Ranger		
62-FU		Air Création / XP		
62-FX	F-JBUL	ICP Savannah or Bingo	"..-99-252-807"	
62-GF		Synairgie Dauphin		
62-GI	F-JFIG	Rans S-6 Coyote II		
62-GJ		Best Off Sky Ranger	SR05-17057	
62-GK		Zenair CH-601 Zodiac		
62-GM		Light Aero Avid Flyer		
		(Re-regd 33-AZK ?)		
62-GN		Rans S-6 Coyote II		
62-GP		Synairgie		
62-GS		Rans S-6ES Coyote II		
		(Damaged 4.3.07)		
62-GW		Air Création		
62-GY		Synairgie		
62-HA		Light Aero Avid Lite		
62-HB		Micro Aviation Pulsar III		
62-HC		Rans S-6 Coyote II		
62-HD		Air Création GTE / XP	E102410-ANC	
62-HH	F-JFHL	Zenair CH-601UL Zodiac	6-9113	
62-HI	F-JFLB	Zenair CH-601UL Zodiac	6-9114	
62-JM		Air Création		
62-NC	F-JZLY	type unknown		
62-NL		Aquilair Swing 14		
62-OD		DTA / Dynamic		
62-AAA		B&F Funk FK-9 Mk.III		
W62-AAB		Jodel D.92 Bébé	350	F-PHLJ
62-AAC		Jodel D.9 Bébé		F-P . . .
62-AAD		Jodel D.92 Bébé	751	F-PFGP
		(Re-regd 21-AAX)		
62-AAE	F-JPLK	Rans S-6 Coyote II		59-CNG
		(see also 62-AME)		
62-AAG		Trekking Sunbeam JPX D320 paramotor		
		(W/o 11.1.09)		
W62-AAH		Mignet HM.293 Pou-du-Ciel		
		(W/o 8.7.03)		
62-AAL		Air Création Twin SL / Kiss 13		
62-AAN		Jodel D.92 Bébé	34	F-PGGZ
62-AAT		Magni M-16 Tandem Trainer		
62-AAV		Air Création / Kiss 450B	A01026-1015	
62-AAW	F-JFJO	Zenair CH-601 Zodiac		

Reg	F-reg	Type	S/n	Other
62-ABB	F-JFKG	Djicat Buse'Air 150GT		
W62-ABD		gyrocopter		
62-ABF		Air Création / Quartz		
62-ABG		Averso AX.02 Guépard gyrocopter		
62-ABK		Air Création / Kiss		
62-ABL		Air Création GTE / Kiss		
62-ABN	F-JFKE	Zenair CH-601XL Zodiac (t/w)	6-9237	
		(Re-regd 77-AHU)		
62-ABP		Synairgie Puma		
62-ABS		Air Création / XP		
62-ABT		Humbert Tetras BS		
		(W/o 22.6.03)		
62-ABV		Best Off Sky Ranger		
62-ACE	F-JFLJ?	Aéro Services Guépard 912S		
62-ACG		Air Création GTE Clipper / XP		
62-ACH		Jodel D.92 Bébé		
62-ACI		Flight Design CT-2K	02-02-02-07	W62-ACI
		(Re-regd OO-E52, 5.04)		
62-ACJ		Zenair CH-601 Zodiac (t/w)	6-9226	
62-ACL		paramotor		
62-ACN	F-JFAP	Dyn'Aéro MCR-01 UL		
62-ACO		paramotor		
62-ACP		paramotor		
62-ACT		ExpAir 503 paramotor trike		
62-ADB	F-JFKW	Zenair CH-601UL Zodiac		
62-ADC		Air Création Twin / Kiss		
62-ADD		Air Création		
62-ADE		Averso AX.02 Guépard gyrocopter		
62-ADF		Averso Guépard G.1 Gyro		
62-ADG		Aéro Services Guépy 582		
62-ADI	F-JFLC	B&F Funk FK-9 Mk.III		
		(Now reported as Jodel D.9)		
62-ADM		Zenair CH-601 Zodiac		
62-ADS	F-JTBE	Zenair CH-601XL Zodiac (t/w) (USN c/s)		OK-HUR 99
		(previously used F-JYFJ)		
62-ADT	F-JFOU	Humbert Tetras		
62-ADX		Flight Design CT-2K		
62-ADY		ICP MXP-740 Savannah (?)		
62-ADZ		DTA / Dynamic 15	166	
62-AEA		Zenair CH-601XL Zodiac		
62-AEC		Weedhopper AX-3		
62-AED		Rans S-6ES Coyote II		
62-AEE		Rans S-6 Coyote II		
62-AEF	F-JFKE	Zenair CH-601 Zodiac		
62-AEG		Zenair CH-601XL Zodiac		
62-AEH		Zenair CH-601XL Zodiac		
62-AEK		Air Création GT BI / XP		
62-AEN		Air Création / Kiss 450		
		(Accident 15.7.07)		
62-AER		Air Création GTE 582S / iXess 15		
62-AET		Light Aero Avid Lite		
62-AEV		B&F Funk FK.IV Club		
62-AEY	F-JBPL	Vidor Asso V Champion		
62-AEZ		Cosmos Bidulm / La Mouette Top 14.9		
62-AFB		Brügger MB-2 Colibri	55	F-PYEH
62-AFC		Zenair CH-601XL Zodiac		
		(W/o 14.9.11)		
62-AFD		Zenair CH-601XL Zodiac	6-9249	
62-AFE		Air Création / Kiss 450	A03102-3095	
62-AFF		Rans S-6 Coyote II		
		(Crashed 25.12.05)		
62-AFH		Air Création GTE Clipper 582 / iXess	A04193-4190	
62-AFJ		ICP MXP-740 Savannah		
62-AFK		Zenair CH-601 Zodiac		
62-AFO	F-JPBY	Rans S-6 Coyote II		
62-AFV	F-JPIC	B&F Funk FK-9 Mk.II		
62-AFY	F-JPIC	B&F Funk FK-9 Mk.IV Club	411	
62-AFZ	F-JZLB	Zenair CH-601XL Zodiac	6-9632	
		(Previously reported as F-JPIU)		
62-AGD	F-JPIT	Zenair CH-601XL Zodiac	6-9718	
62-AGG	F-JPIK	Evektor EV-97 Eurostar	2002 1604	
62-AGH		Zenair CH-601XL Zodiac		
62-AGN		Zenair CH-601 Zodiac		
62-AGP		Humbert Tetras		
62-AGQ	F-JPIS	Zenair CH-601XL Zodiac		
62-AGS		paramotor		
62-AGV		DTA / Dynamic		
62-AGW		Zenair CH-701 STOL		
62-AHA		DTA / Dynamic 15/430		
62-AHC		Air Création / Kiss 450		
62-AHD		DTA Combo / Dynamic 15/430		
62-AHE		DTA / Dynamic 15/430	222	
		(9.10 noted with 59-CQA under the wing)		
62-AHG	F-JPLU	Zenair CH-701 STOL	7-9657	
62-AHH		Air Création Buggy / iXess	T05031 & A05010-4258	
62-AHJ	F-JPLX	Vol Mediterrani VM-1 Esqual		
62-AHL		Air Création GT BI		
62-AHM	F-JZVQ	Zenair CH-601XL Zodiac		
62-AHN		ICP Bingo 4S	04-11-52-166	
62-AHW	F-JPQI	Zenair CH-601XL Zodiac		
62-AHY	F-JPQW	Zenair CH-601XL Zodiac		
62-AID		Helite Paratrike Skydancer 582		
62-AIE		Air Création GTE Clipper / iXess 15		
62-AIG	F-JXBA	Zenair CH-601XL Zodiac		
62-AIJ		Air Création Buggy		
62-AIK	F-JYTC	Zenair CH-601UL Zodiac (t/w)		
62-AIM		ZUT Aviation TT2000 STOL		
62-AIN		B&F Funk FK-14B Polaris	14-058	
		(Re-regd OO-G68, 11.10)		
62-AIP		Raj Hamsa X'Air 502T		
		(W/o 17.4.06)		
62-AIQ		ICP MXP-740 Savannah		
62-AIV		Didier Pti'tavion		
		(Damaged 16.5.06)		
62-AIW		Rans S-6ES Coyote II	01011403ES	
		(accident in Greece 22.11.09)		
62-AIZ		DTA Combo / Dynamic 15/430	132	
		(Reported as Cosmos / Mach 14. 9 6.11)		
62-AJD		Zenair CH-601 Zodiac (t/w)		
		(F-JYFH or F-JYPH?)		
62-AJF		Best Off Sky Ranger		
62-AJG		DTA / Dynamic 450		
62-AJK		Air Création GT / Quartz		
62-AJN	F-JZFV	Air Création		
62-AJQ	F-JZGS	Zenair CH-601XL Zodiac		

Reg	F-reg	Type	C/n	Prev id
62-AJS	F-JZHE	Tecnam P.2004 Bravo		
62-AJV		Air Création Tanarg / iXess	A03197-3192	
62-AJY		Zenair CH-601 Zodiac		
62-AKB		Murphy Renegade Spirit		
62-AKC		Best Off Sky Ranger		
62-AKF	F-JZPB	Dyn'Aéro MCR Pick-Up 912 Duc	78	
		(Same c/n as 62-AQN / F-JZLI)		
62-AKI		Averso Guépard 2 gyrocopter		
62-AKM	F-JZQF	Aeroandinas MXP-1000 Tayrona		
			AA-03-06-90-018	
62-AKV	F-JUPU	Zenair CH-701 STOL		
62-AKY		DTA 582 / Dynamic		
		(Accident 14.4.07)		
62-AKZ	F-JZVX	(Piel CP.150 ?) Onyx		59-OF
62-ALA		Zenair CH-701 STOL		
62-ALB	F-JZYJ	Fly Synthesis Storch HS		
		(Re-regd 44-ATK)		
62-ALH	F-JYEJ	Rans S-6 Coyote II		
62-ALI	F-JYFA	Tecnam P.92 Echo Super		
62-ALJ		Hipps Superbirds J-3 Kitten		
62-ALK		Rans S-6 Coyote II		
62-ALM		DTA / Dynamic 450		
62-ALP		Tecnam P.92 Echo		
62-ALR		weightshift		
62-ALW		Zenair CH-601 Zodiac		
62-ALY		Air Création GTE Trek 912 / iXess		
62-ALZ	F-JWUI	Best Off Sky Ranger		
62-AMC		Cosmos		
62-AME	F-JPLK	Rans S-6 Coyote II		59-CNG
		(see also 62-AAE)		
62-AMF	F-JXMP	Pottier P.130UL Coccinelle		
62-AMG		Air Création GTE Clipper / Kiss		
62-AMJ	F-JXAC	Didier Pti'tavion		
62-AMK	F-JZBH	Zenair CH-601 Zodiac		
62-AMT		Aereos (trike)		
62-AMV		SG Aviation Storm Century		
62-AMW		Air Création Twin / Aereos		
62-AMX	F-JFMH	Fly Synthesis Storch HS	2004/292A348	OO-E55
62-ANN	F-JXPY	Zenair CH-601XL Zodiac		
62-ANO	F-JKQP	Mignet HM.1000 Balerit	82	ALAT
62-ANQ		Air Création GT BI / Kiss		
62-ANU		Rans S-6 Coyote II		
62-ANW		Zenair CH-601XL Zodiac		
62-ANX		weightshift		
62-ANY		Rans S-6 Coyote II (t/w)	0594618	25-JU
62-ANZ	F-JXZW	Zenair CH-601XL Zodiac	6-0705	
62-AOA	F-JXRL	B&F Funk FK-14B Polaris	14-079	
62-AOE	F-JXYF	Best Off Sky Ranger	SKR0801840	
62-AOF		Air Création GTE Clipper		
62-AOM		Dyn'Aéro MCR-01 UL		
62-AOO	F-JZPK	Zenair CH-701 STOL	7-8027	
62-AOP		Aeros 2 (trike)		
62-AOX		Zenair CH-601XL Zodiac		
62-AOY		Rans S-9 Chaos		
62-APC		TL Ultralight TL-22 Duo Eso	95G11	PH-2X7, (PH-2X6)
62-APK		gyrocopter		
62-APR	F-JWLZ	Plätzer Kiebitz	271	
62-APS		Rans S-6 Coyote II		
62-APT	F-JWNJ	Air Création		
62-APW		B&F Funk FK-9 Mk.IV	376	
62-APY		Air Création 912 / iXess		
		(Also reported as DTA Dynamic)		
62-AQM		Air Création Tanarg 912 / iXess 13		
62-AQN	F-JZLI	Dyn'Aéro MCR Pick-Up	78	
		(Same c/n as 62-AKF / F-JZPB) (W/o 9.10.09)		
62-ARB		Rans S-6 Coyote II		
62-ARD	F-JFSJ	B&F Funk FK-9 Mk.III	111	72-JL, 37-XE, 41-KP, D-MUED
62-ARE	F-JZZS	Evektor EV-97 Eurostar		
62-ARF	F-JHGL	Humbert Tetras		61-HI
62-ARM	F-JRBV	B&F Funk FK-14B2 Polaris	14-101	
		(Re-regd SP-SRBV 3.14)		
62-ARP		ITV paramotor		
62-ARR		Rans S-6 Coyote II		
62-ARU		weightshift		
62-ARW		Directfly Alto 912 ULS		
62-ARX	F-JTWA	Zenair CH.601XL Zodiac		
62-ASD		Zenair CH-601XL Zodiac	6-9524	PH-ZEN, PH-3V8
62-ASG		Comco Ikarus C-42		
62-ASM		Humbert Tetras 912CS		
62-ASR	F-JRCJ	Comco Ikarus Fox-C22		
62-AST		Aveko VL-3 Sprint		
62-ASU		ICP MXP-740 Savannah XL		
62-ASX		Eipper Quicksilver Sport 2S		
62-ATA		Rans S-6 Coyote II		
62-ATB		DTA Combo 912S / Diva		
62-ATD		Zenair CH-701 STOL		
62-ATG		Rans S-6 Coyote II		
62-ATK		Jodel D.19	146T	F-PCFM
62-ATL		Aeros (trike)		
62-ATM		Rans S-6 Coyote II		
62-ATR		P&M Aviation Pegasus		
62-ATS		Evektor EV-97 Eurostar		
62-ATU		Rans S-6 Coyote II		
		(W/o 17.5.14)		
62-ATX		Jodel D.195T	24	21-AAQ, F-PRAQ
62-AUB		Pro.Mecc. Sparviero		
62-AUD		Air Création / XP		
62-AUG		Dyn'Aéro MCR-01 UL		
62-AUH		Air Création Tanarg 912ES(P) / BioniX 15 T09055		
		(Re-regd OO-H10 7.12)		
62-AUK		weightshift		
62-AUO		Zenair CH-601XL Zodiac		
62-AUP	F-JFHJ	Air Création GT BI		
62-AUS	F-JSPX	Air Création Skypper / iXess	A06151-6197	
62-AUT		Air Création Safari GT BI / Mild 16		
62-AUV		Cosmos / La Mouette Oryx 14.9		
62-AUW		ELA Aviacion ELA-07S Cougar	0311 323 0712	
62-AUX		Air Création		
62-AUY		Halley Apollo Fox		
62-AVC		Aeros (trike)		
62-AVH		Autogyro-Europe MT-03		
62-AVJ	F-JPLK	Rans S-6 Coyote II		66-IQ
62-AVS		Aeros 2 (trike)		
62-AVU		CBBULM O2B (trike)		
62-AVW		unidentified weightshift		
62-AVY		Weedhopper		
62-AWG		Air Création Kiss		
62-AWP	F-JTOV	Best Off Nynja	69	
62-AXC		ITV Bulldog wing/Flanders Trike Silent Twin paramotor		
62-AXL		Rans S-6 Coyote II		
62-AXS	F-JSCV	Air Création GTE / Aeros Profi TL		
62-AXV	F-JUKX	Rans S-6ES Coyote II	12081913	OO-G39
62-AXW		Tecnam P.2004 Bravo		
62-AYF		ELA Aviacion ELA-07 Cougar	0613 395 0712	
		(W/o 30.4.15)		
62-AYM		ELA Aviacion ELA-09 Junior		
62-AZG		Rans S-6ESD Coyote II	0292271	OO-A66
62-AZZ		ELA Aviacion ELA-09 Junior		
62-BAW		Autogyro Europe MTOsport		
62-BAZ		JMB VL-3 Evolution	190	
62-BBB		ELA Aviacion ELA-07S		
62-BEE	F-JWKA	Plätzer Kiebitz B		
62-CAN		Dyn'Aéro MCR-01		
62-COR		Weedhopper AX-3		

63 : Puy-de-Dôme

Reg	F-reg	Type	C/n	Prev id
63-AH		weightshift		
63-AK		weightshift		
63-AQ		weightshift		
W63-BH		Weedhopper		
63-BX		Aeroprakt ?		
63-BZ		Atlas		
63-CB(1)		Air Création / Cosmos		
63-CB(2)	F-JECV	Humbert Tetras 912CS		
63-CC		JCC Aviation J.300 Joker		
63-CS		Air Création / Quartz		
63-DE		Light Aero Avid IV		
		(Accident 9.10.07)		
63-DF		Rans Coyote (t/w)		
63-DM		Air Création / Fun		
63-EA		Air Création / SX		
63-EC	F-JEDX	Denney Kitfox Speedster 11	518	
		(Same c/n as 06-EC) (C/n too early for Speedster model)		
63-EE(1)		Air Création GT BI		
63-EE(2)		Averso AX gyrocopter		
63-EG		Air Création		
63-EN		Titan Tornado		
63-EU		Air Création GT BI / SX		
63-FJ	F-JAZN	Denney Kitfox		
63-FK		TEAM Mini-MAX		
63-FR	F-JEAB	Cosmos		
63-GB		Air Création GT BI / Quartz		
63-GC		Technauto (trike)		
		(W/o 15.8.06)		
63-GE		Denney Kitfox		
63-GG		Rans S-6 Coyote II		
63-GQ		Air Création GT BI / Mild		
63-HF		Cosmos		
63-HS		Aviasud AE209 Albatros		
		(W/o 10.9.00)		
63-IG		Cosmos		
63-IL		Air Création GTE 582		
		(Damaged 20.6.04)		
63-IO		Air Création		
63-JC(1)		Air Création Safari GT BI 503		
		(W/o 4.10.98)		
63-JC(2)		ICP MXP-740 Savannah	07-03-51-583	
63-JD	F-JEEQ	B&F Funk FK-9 Mk.IV	335	
		(Re-regd 41-QM, 67-BLT)		
63-JM		Air Création / XP		
63-JS		trike / La Mouette 16		
63-JY		Aviasud AE209 Albatros		
63-KB		TEAM Mini-MAX		
63-KD		Light Aero Avid Flyer		
63-KF		TEAM Mini-MAX		
63-LA		homebuilt		
		(W/o 9.9.06)		
63-LF		Aéro Services Guépy 582		
63-LI		Air Création GTE Twin		
63-LJ		Flight Design CT 180		
		(Accident 24.9.07)		
63-LM		Aquilair Swing		
63-MI		Air Création Twin		
		(Also reported as Humbert Tetras W/o 26.4.02)		
63-OA		Air Création GTE Clipper / XP		
63-OM		Air Création / Fun		
63-OT	F-JEBO	Fantasy Air Allegro SW		
63-PC		Air Création Twin Buggy / Kiss	53881310	
63-PN		Rans S-12 Airaile VF		
		(Accident 20.10.07)		
63-RH		Best Off Sky Ranger		
		(W/o 23.8.04)		
63-RL	F-JGIC	Humbert Tetras		
63-SC	F-JUAH	ICP MXP-740 Savannah	11-00-51-033	F-JEBD
		(Re-regd 39-SC / F-JUAH)		
63-SO		Humbert La Moto-du-Ciel		
63-TA	F-JEBX	Humbert Tetras 912CS (Coded "949")		
W63-TO		gyrocopter		
63-TX		Zlin Savage		
63-VA		Cosmos		74-MD
63-VD	F-JDFK	Humbert Tetras		25-KB
63-VZ	F-JAVZ	Air Création / Fun 450		
63-ABL	F-JEEG	Flight Design CT SW		
63-ACX	F-JEDK	Humbert Tetras		
63-ADG		Air Création GTE 582S / Kiss		
		(Accident 12.7.07)		
63-ARU		Aquilair trike		
63-AST		JMB VL-3 Evolution		
63-ASZ		Lambert Mission M.106		
63-ATI		Adventure Funflyer Bi/Xpresso paramotor		
63-ATM		Ellipse Alizé / Ellipse Titan CX		
63-ATX		Zlin Savage Cub		
63-ATZ		Super Skyraider		
63-AUB		Adventure Funflyer Bi/Dudek Nucleon paramotor		
63-AUC	F-JSHJ	Pipistrel Sinus		
63-AUU	F-JTAY	ICP MXP-740 Savannah	06-10-51-537	I-8749
63-AUV		Cosmos / La Mouette Oryx 14.9		
63-AVF		Magni M-16 Tandem Trainer		

Reg	F-reg	Type	c/n	Other
63-AXG		JMB VL-3 Evolution		
63-AXH		G1 Aviation G1 SPYL		
63-AXQ	F-JALW	Aero Pilot Legend		

64 : Pyrénées-Atlantiques

Reg	F-reg	Type	c/n	Other
64-AX		weightshift		
64-BF		Aviakit Vega 2000	25	
64-DR		Air's Maestro 2		
64-FM		Air Création GT B		
64-GJ		Cosmos		
		(W/o 5.8.01)		
64-GN		Aériane		
64-HD		Barry MB-04 Souris Bulle		
64-HK		Ultralair JC-31 Weedhopper		
		(Accident 16.9.07)		
64-IA		SE.5A replica		
64-IO	F-JCGC	Tecnam P.92 Echo		
64-JL		PGO Aviation Cobra		
		(Re-regd 13-HW)		
64-JO	F-JKCW	B&F Funk Fk.9 Mk.III	180	
64-JP	F-JKDI	Best Off Sky Ranger		
64-JW		Air Création / SX		
64-JX		Quicky Ranger		
		(Damaged 20.11.04)		
64-KA	F-JKDQ	Tecnam P.92S Echo	675	
64-KH	F-JKFV	Hipps Superbirds J-3 Kitten		
64-KI	F-JKEP	Barry MB-02-2 Mini-Bulle		
64-KL	F-JFKB	Aviakit Vega UL		
64-KQ		gyrocopter		
64-KS		Pagotto Brako 503 / Grif Corsair 12.8		
64-KT		gyrocopter		
64-KX	F-JKGM	B&F Funk FK-9		
64-KY		gyrocopter		
64-LE	F-JKGX	B&F Funk FK-9 Mk.IV Club		
64-LJ		DTA / Dynamic 15/430		
64-LM	F-JKIG	B&F Funk FK-9 Club		
64-LP		weightshift		
64-LS		Rans S-6ES Coyote II		
64-LV		Air Création GTE / Kiss		
64-LZ		Jodel D.9 Bébé		
64-MA		Ekolot KR-010 Elf		
		(Reported flying as 64-WAN – test marks?)		
		(Sold to USA 3.08 as N307AH)		
64-NA		Air Création Racer 447 / Fun 14		
64-NF		Pagotto Brako / Bautek Pico S		
64-NJ		gyrocopter		
64-NN	F-JYWM	B&F Funk FK-9 Mk.IV	317	
		(Accident 25.10.07; re-regd 71-ME)		
64-NV		Cosmos (trike ?)		
64-NX	F-JXJD	Rans S-6 Coyote II		
64-OO	F-JZJY	Best Off Sky Ranger		
64-OW		trike / Bautek Pico		
64-OZ		gyrocopter		
64-PK		Alpi Aviation Pioneer 200	24	
64-QR		Halley Apollo Fox		
64-QU	F-JXUY	Aerospool WT-9 Dynamic	DY237/2008	
64-OY		gyrocopter (single seat)		
64-OZ		gyrocopter (two seat)		
64-QZ		ITV paramotor		
64-RQ	F-JSGD	Ekolot KR-030 Topaz	030-04-03	
		(Same c/n as 72-PP / F-JSRY)		
64-RV	F-JVAJ	gyrocopter (homebuilt)		
64-SH		B&F Funk FK-9 Mk.IV		
		(damaged 2.10.13)		
64-TD		weightshift		
64-TO		paramotor		
64-VR	F-JVLO	Dyn'Aero MCR-01		
64-WH	F-JVOI	Dyn'Aero MCR-01	416	
64-WS	F-JVSF	Dyn'Aero MCR-01	419	
64-XI		Dyn'Aero MCR-01	400	
64-AUI		Barry MB-02-2 Mini-Bulle		
64-WAU		Barry MB-02-2 Mini-Bulle (same aircraft as above?)		

65 : Hautes-Pyrénées

Reg	F-reg	Type	c/n	Other
65-N		Eipper Quicksilver MX		
65-AC	F-JXAG	Fly Synthesis Storch		
		(Same call-sign as 45-ACG)		
65-AG		Chasle YC.100 Hirondelle		
65-CO		Air Création / SX		
65-CR		Aviasud AE209 Albatros	113	
		(Re-regd D-MWVH, 86-GX)		
65-CV		Aviasud AE209 Albatros	105	83-GO,
		(Re-regd 59-ABW)		D-MAMT
W65-DY		Morin M-80 (builder Dufau)		
65-EB		Murphy Renegade Spirit		
		(Re-regd OO-B07)		
65-ED	F-JBCP	Campana Observer		
65-EM		Titan Tornado 912		
65-EN		Titan Tornado		
		(Damaged 1.4.98)		
65-FE		Air Création GT BI		
65-GE		trike / Bautek Pico		
65-GM		Djicat Buse'Air 150		
65-GU		Barry MB-02 Souricette		
		(Accident 1.7.07)		
65-GX		Pagotto Brako		
65-GZ		Eipper Quicksilver MX II Sprint		
65-HF		Raj Hamsa X'Air		
65-HG		Rans Coyote I		
65-HH		Air Création / Gryf Spyder SP		
65-HL		Air Création / Fun		
65-HN		ultralight balloon		
65-HU	F-JIHU	B&F Funk FK-9 Mk.III		
65-IA		Henri Lascombes gyrocopter		
65-IO	F-JIIO	Alpi Aviation Pioneer 200		
65-IV		Pagotto Brako		
65-JD		Aviasud Sirocco		
65-JW	F-JIHN	Flight Design CT SW	05-08-04	
65-JU		DTA Cosmos Phase II 582		
65-JY		Raj Hamsa Hanuman		
65-JZ		Rans S.6ES Coyote II		
65-KZ		Zenair CH-601XL Zodiac		
65-LE	F-JYUP	Best Off Sky Ranger		
65-LS		Fly Synthesis Storch HS		
65-MF	F-JKUV	Magni M-16 Tandem Trainer		
65-MK		Air Création / Fun 14		

Reg	F-reg	Type	c/n	Other
65-MM	F-JEGX	Tecnam P.92 Echo		
		(same call sign as 74-UG; not known which of 65-MM		
		or 74-UG is current)		
65-MS	F-JWSH	Raj Hamsa Hanuman		
65-MT		Synairgie Dauphin / Lynx 16		
65-MW	F-JWWT	Aeroprakt A-22L	308	
65-MX		trike / Bautek Pico		
65-NB		Pagotto Brako gyro	65005	ZK-ZNB, 65-NB
65-NL		PJF-001 gyrocopter		
65-NQ		Air Création Racer / La Mouette Ipsos 12		
65-NS		Jihlavan Skyleader 200		
65-NY	F-JRND	Pro.Mecc. Sparviero 100		
65-OB		Zenair CH-701 STOL		
65-OD	F-JRSG	Humbert Tetras 912CSL		
65-OL		Pagotto Brako 912 / Bautek Pico S		
65-OR		Air Création / XP		
65-OW		Micro Aviation Pulsar 582		
65-PB		Zenair CH-701 STOL	7-5186	F-PGJV
65-PC		Pagotto Brakogyro		
65-PI		Pipistrel Sinus		
65-PN	F-JTZH	Aeroprakt A-22L2	399	
65-PM		Dallach Sunwheel		
65-PP	F-JUHH	Freewind Bumble B gyrocopter		
65-PV		Pagotto Brakogyro 912 Super Turbo		
65-PW		Alpi Aviation Pioneer 300 Kite		
65-QV	F-JARN	Aeroprakt A-22L2 Vision		
		(W/o 28.8.16)		

66 : Pyrénées-Orientales

Reg	F-reg	Type	c/n	Other
66-AD		Zenith Baroudeur		
66-AJ		Weedhopper		
66-BN		Eipper Quicksilver GT		
66-BX		Weedhopper		
66-CH		Weedhopper		
66-CQ		Weedhopper		
66-CR		Air Création / Quartz		
66-CT		Weedhopper		
66-CU		Weedhopper		
66-DB	F-JAOB	Weedhopper		
66-DD		Air Création GT BI / Quartz		
66-DK	F-JBDW	Pelican (Also reported as Galaxie)		
66-DO		Ultralair JC-31 Weedhopper Premier AX-3		
		(W/o 7.8.02)		
66-DP		Best Off Sky Ranger		
66-DS		Hipps Superbirds J-3 Kitten		
W66-DT		Hélios		
66-EX		Weedhopper		
66-FC		Eipper Quicksilver MX II Sprint		
		(Re-regd 30-IH)		
66-FH		Eipper Quicksilver GT450		
66-FK		Air Création GTE Clipper / XP		
66-FW		Aviatika MAI-890U		
66-FY		Zenair CH-701 STOL		
66-GB		Zenair CH- ?		
66-GD		Best Off Sky Ranger		
66-GG		Storch		
66-GH		Denney Kitfox	693	
66-GI		Weedhopper		
66-GM		Air Création / Quartz		
66-HD		Raj Hamsa X'Air		
66-HJ		Air's Maestro 2		
66-HM		Zenair CH-601 Zodiac		
66-HN		Raj Hamsa X'Air		
66-HP		Best Off Sky Ranger		
66-HS	F-JJFB	Zenair CH-601UL Zodiac	6-9131	OK-DUU 99
66-HU		Zenair CH-701 STOL		
66-HX		Aviasud X'Pair 65		
		(Crashed 7.11.02)		
66-IA		Aviasud Mistral	79	
		(Same c/n as OO-895)		
66-IE		Zenair CH-601 Zodiac		
66-IQ		Rans S-6 Coyote II		
		(Re-regd 62-AVJ)		
66-IS		Air Création / Fun		
66-IY		Zodiac Ultrastar		
66-JA		DTA 582 / Dynamic		
		(W/o 12.7.03)		
66-JF	F-JZMB	Evektor EV-97 Eurostar		
66-JM		Raj Hamsa X'Air		
66-JN		Zenair CH-701 STOL		
66-JW		Zenair CH-701 STOL		
66-JX		DTA 503 / Dynamic		
66-JZ	F-JJIL	Zenair CH-701 STOL		
66-KA		Raj Hamsa X'Air		
66-KB		Flight Design CT SW		
66-KE		Zenair CH-601UL Zodiac		
66-KH	F-JJUG	Zenair CH-601XL Zodiac		
66-KJ		Raj Hamsa X'Air		
66-KK	F-JXKJ	Urban Air UFM-13 Lambada		
66-KL		Tandem Air Sunny Sport		
66-KM		Zenair CH-701 STOL		
		(Accident 3.5.06)		
66-KO		Zenair CH-601 Zodiac		
66-KP		Alisport Silent 2		
		(Crashed 31.10.06)		
66-KQ		Zenair CH-701 STOL		
66-KU		Pelican		OK-ZUK 01
66-KW	F-JZPU	Urban Air UFM-13 Lambada		
66-KY		Zenair CH-601 Zodiac		
66-KZ		Eipper Quicksilver MX		
66-LH	F-JYRI	Zenair CH-601XL Zodiac		
66-LL		Nikeair Delta		
66-LN		Tecnam P.92 Echo Super		
66-LV	F-JJRB	Zenair CH-601 Zodiac		
66-MK		TEAM Air-Bike	AB98	
66-MM		Magni M-18 Spartan		
66-MO		Zenair CH-701SP STOL		
66-MR	F-JWFK	Roko Aero NG4 (now labelled as BRM Aero Bristell XL-8)		
66-MV		Zenair CH-601 Zodiac (t/w)		
66-MW		Aeropro Eurofox		
66-MX		ZUT Aviation TT2000 STOL		
66-NE		Aeropro Eurofox		
66-NR	F-JRWT	Aeropro Eurofox		
66-NZ		P&M Aviation QuikR		
66-OH		PAP/ITV Lapoon paramotor		
66-OI	F-JSWI	Aeropro Eurofox	AT9717?	59-CKI

Reg	F-reg	Type	C/n	Other
66-OK		ALS/Dudek Nucleon paramotor		
66-ON		Aeropro Eurofox		
66-OO		ICP MXP-740 Savannah	11-03-51-930	
		(Reported stolen 11.11)		
66-OR		Magni M-22 Voyager	22-05-3984	32-GL
66-OT		G1 Aviation G1 SPYL		
66-OZ	F-JEVC	ICP MXP-740 Savannah	03-05-51-260	
66-PT		Fly Synthesis Storch CL		
		(Accident 9.3.14)		
66-PZ	F-JAZI	Shark Aero Shark	032	
66-QC		Weedhopper (possibly 66-CQ?)		
66-ZI		Zenair CH-701 STOL amphibian		

67 : Bas-Rhin

Reg	F-reg	Type	C/n	Other
67-V		Pioneer Flightstar		
67-AG		Falcon		
67-AK		Zenith Baroudeur		
67-AQ		(Technic Moto ?) Mustang		
67-AV		(Technic Moto ?) Mustang		
67-BG		Eipper Quicksilver Sport 2S		
67-BJ		La Mouette		
67-BK		Pioneer Flightstar		
67-BP		Eipper Quicksilver MXL		
67-CL		Pioneer Flightstar		
67-DF		Aviasud Sirocco		
		(Re-regd OO-A07 4.91)		
67-DS	F-JCOO	Rans S-6 Coyote II		
67-EF		Sky Pup		
67-EI		Denney Kitfox		
67-EK		Weedhopper AX-2		
67-EL		Koenig AK.09 Faucon		
67-EM	F-JAKQ	Rans S-6 Coyote II		
67-ES		Weedhopper		
67-FG		Epervier		
67-FK		Croses Criquet Léger	86	
67-FM		Rans S-12 Airaile		
67-GO		Airwave/CEM Rave paraglider		
67-GU		JCC Aviation J.300 Joker ?		
67-GZ	F-JBTG	Rans S-6 Coyote II		
67-HB		Rans S-12 Airaile		
67-HG		Mignet HM.1000 Balerit	114	
		(Same c/n quoted for 68-HC. Order unknown)		
67-HM		Cosmos Chronos		
67-HP		Rans S-6 Coyote II		
67-HT		Mignet HM.293 Pou-du-Ciel		
67-HV		Raj Hamsa X'Air		
67-IA		Tipsy T.66 Nipper 2	59	D-ECPU(1), LX-AIG
		(Based in Germany .13)		
67-IB		Mignet HM.293 Pou-du-Ciel		
67-IH		Interplane Skyboy		
67-IR		Interplane Skyboy		
67-IS		Rans S-6 Coyote II		
67-IY		Aéro Services Guépy (Jabiru) 80		
67-JC		Voilerie du Vent Phebus		
67-JD		Rans S-6ESD Coyote II		
67-JE		Best Off Sky Ranger		
67-JL		Mignet HM.1000 Balerit		
67-JM		Avion JC Nacelle		
67-KU		Fantasy Air Allegro ST	98-101	
67-KW		Voilerie du Vent Phebus		
67-KZ	F-JBLQ	Rans S-6 Coyote II		
67-LE		Weedhopper		
67-LG	F-JCFN	Murphy Maverick 503		
67-LQ		Pioneer Flightstar		
67-LS		Mitchell U-2 Super Wing		
67-MC		Hipps Superbirds J-3 Kitten		
67-MN	F-JGTU	Fantasy Air Allegro SW	99-107	
67-MP		Euro III		
67-MT	F-JGSI	Fantasy Air Allegro SW		
67-MV		TEAM Speed-MAX		W-67-MV
67-MY		Plätzer Kiebitz		
67-NI		Autogyro-Europe Calidus 09		
		(error for 61-NI ?)		
67-NN		Voilerie du Vent Phebus		
67-NS		Aéro Services Guépy		
67-NT		Zenair CH-701 STOL		
67-NU		Rans S-6 Coyote II		
67-OL		Fantasy Air Allegro SW	01-118	
67-OS		single-seat biplane		
67-PE	F-JGTO	Fantasy Air Allegro SW	01-120	
67-PF	F-JGTN	Mignet HM.1100 Cordouan	08	
67-PI		Bowdler Bobcat (homebuilt)		
67-PK		trike / Zenith (wing)		
67-PL	F-JGTQ	Aviakit Vega		
67-PW		DTA / Dynamic		
67-PZ		Simonini Mini 2 Plus/APCO Fista 2 paramotor		
		(Crashed 9.10.05)		
67-QE		Fantasy Air Allegro SW	02-124	
67-QI		Fantasy Air Allegro		
W67-QQ		Techoflug Piccolo		
67-QS	F-JGUC	Impulse		
67-QY	F-JGUF	Dallach D4 Fascination		
		(Re-regd D-MJJP ?)		
67-RO		Pioneer Flightstar		
		(Damaged 18.7.04)		
67-RQ		Rans S-6ES Coyote II		
		(Accident 10.7.04)		
67-RR		Humbert Tetras 912BS		
67-TH		Paraplane		
67-TP		Impulse		
67-TV		Air Création		
67-UD	F-JGUT	Aerospool WT-9 Dynamic	DY043/2004	
W67-UQ		B-87 Experimental		
67-UT	F-JGVS	Sonex Aircraft Sonex	174	
67-UU		ULM Balloon		
67-VB		Fantasy Air Allegro	04-133	
		(Same c/n as 71-OU and probably 67-ZL)		
67-VD	F-JGUV	Aerospool WT-9 Dynamic	DY059/2004	
		(Re-regd 50-MF)		
67-VN		Gyrotec DF-02		W67-VN/ 67-VNW
67-VP	F-JGVA	Aéro Services Guépard 912		
67-VR		Rans S-6 Coyote II		
W67-VS		Jodel M.S.04		
		(Crashed on test 22.10.04)		
67-VZ	F-JGVE	Fantasy Air Allegro SW	04-135	
		(Re-regd 77-BHJ)		
67-WM		Cosmos / Karat		
67-WS		Plätzer Kiebitz		
67-WV		Djicat Buse'Air 150		
		(Damaged 30.4.05)		
67-WW	F-JGVJ	Fantasy Air Allegro SW		
67-XB	F-JGVI	B&F Funk FK-14B Polaris (t/w)		
67-XD	F-JTAD	type unknown (low wing tricycle)		
67-XV		Technoflug Piccolo		
67-XZ	F-JGVP	SG Aviation Rally 105UL		
67-YM		ICP MXP-740 Savannah		
67-YU		DTA Combo		
67-ZD		Humbert Tetras		
67-ZI	F-JGVZ	Aerospool WT-9 Dynamic	DY113/2005	
67-ZL	F-JZBE	Fantasy Air Allegro SW	05-133	
		(C/n should be 04-133 ? See 67-VB)		
67-ZP		TeST TST-3 Alpin 1	01021397	
67-ZS	F-JZEM	Aerospool WT-9 Dynamic	DY129/2006	
67-ZT		Cosmos Bidulm 503 / Chronos 14		
67-ZU	F-JZJR	Zlin Savage Classic	0079	
67-AAK	F-JZTJ	Kieger AK 3 UL	01	
67-AAT	F-JZPE	B&F Funk FK-12 Comet	012-27	D-MTLW
67-ABF		DTA / Dynamic 15		
67-ABI	F-JSZN	Denney Kitfox IV TD-1		
67-ABD		Humbert Tetras		
67-ABL	F-JZVK	Aerospool WT-9 Dynamic	DY150/2006	
67-ASJ		JMB VL-3 Evilution		
67-AWS	F-JZTX	Best Off Sky Ranger 912		
67-BAC	F-JYPT	Aerospool WT-9 Dynamic	DY176/2007	
67-BAR		Comco Ikarus Fox-C22		
67-BAT		Denney Kitfox		
		(Dbr in forced landing 28.6.11)		
67-BAU	F-JYPK	Pipistrel Virus SW		
67-BAV	F-JXBF	Impulse 100	28	
67-BAY	F-JXGD	Kieger AK-3		
67-BBT		Aerospool WT-9 Dynamic	DY285/2008	
		(Same identity quoted for 67-BET ?)		
67-BCC	F-JXQI	Aerospool WT-9 Dynamic	DY223/2008	
		(Re-regd 78-ABG)		
67-BCS	F-JYIE	Air Création Tanarg / iXess		
67-BCW	F-IXYI	Aerospool WT-9 Dynamic	DY250/2008	
67-BDF	F-JWAT	Best Off Sky Ranger	SKR0712855	
67-BDX		Humbert Tetras 912CSL		
67-BEC	F-JWCW	Houdé Speedmax		
67-BEJ	F-JWFL	Aerospool WT-9 Dynamic	DY270/2009	
67-BEK	F-JWFR	Aerospool WT-9 Dynamic	DY275/2008	
		(Sold as D-MFMF)		
67-BES	F-JWHE	Aerospool WT-9 Dynamic	DY277/2008	
		(Re-regd 68-YE)		
67-BET	F-JWIC	Aerospool WT-9 Dynamic NG	DY285/2008	
		(Confirmed, but same identity quoted for 67-BBT ?)		
67-BEW	F-JWJZ	B&F Funk FK-9 Mk.III		
67-BEX	F-JGVV	DTA Combo / Dynamic 450	41	
67-BFR	F-JWUJ	Junkers Profly Junka UL		
67-BFZ	F-JWWE	Pipistrel Virus SW	298VSW100	
67-BGI		Cosmos		
67-BGL	F-JXLT	Pipistrel Sinus	307S912	
67-BGR		Adventure M/Reflexion paramotor		
67-BGU	F-JRDN	Pipistrel Taurus		
67-BHU		Per il Volo/Ozone Viper 2 paramotor		
67-BIB	F-JWYZ	Junkers Profly Junka UL		
67-BIE		BRM Land Africa	0153/912UL/10-LA	
67-BIS	F-JSDG	Houdé Bimax		
67-BIX	F-JSER	Pipistrel Virus		
67-BJO	F-JSUH	Jodel D.185		
		(Based in Germany)		
67-BKC	F-JSPH	Air Création Skypper / BioniX 15	A11008-10138	
67-BKF	F-JSPJ	Comco Ikarus C-42		
67-BKG		Paratrike Trekking ALS paramotor		
67-BKJ	F-JTFA	Denney Kitfox		
67-BKP		Air Création Skypper / BioniX		
67-BKO		AMS-Flight Apis M	A031M13	
		(Re-regd G-CIIV 6.14)		
67-BKR	F-JSTP	Urban Air Lambada		
67-BLF	F-JTEZ	Humbert Tetras 912CS		
67-BLM	F-JWOF	Aerospool WT-9 Dynamic	DY295/2009	
67-BLT	F-JEEO	B&F Funk FK-9 Mk.IV	335	41-QM, 63-JD
67-BLZ		DTA Dynamic 15/430		
67-BMC		Comco Ikarus C-42		
67-BML	F-JTRW	Pipistrel Sinus SW	459SWN80	
67-BMW		Autogyro-Europe MT-03/MTOsport		
67-BNE	F-JTYB	Pipistrel Virus		
67-BNP	F-JUCK	Pipistrel Alpha Trainer	447AT912	
67-BOG		Halley Apollo Fox	6YSZ 290904	
67-BOP		Adventure Flexway 2 paramotor		
67-BPH	F-JVBG	Aeropro Eurofox		
67-BPM		Fly Synthesis Storch		
67-BQI		B&F Funk FK-12 Comet	012-095	D-MNAZ(2)
		(Destroyed June 2014)		
67-BQA	F-JUTV	Aerospool WT-9 Dynamic		
67-BQQ		Ekolot KR-010 Elf	0001	
67-BQT		Avio Delta / La Mouette Ghost 12		
67-BRM		Junkers Profly		
67-BSI	F-JVOZ	Aerospool WT-9 Dynamic	DY498/2014	
67-BSQ		Autogyro-Europe MTOsport		
67-BSS	F-JVQU	Pipistrel Virus SW		
67-BTF		Fantasy Air Allegro 2000		
67-BTU	F-JZUU	Aerospool WT-9 Dynamic	DY519/2014	
67-BUA	F-JYPK	Pipistrel Virus		
67-BUF	F-JRUT	Pipistrel Alpha Trainer		
67-BUG	F-JRKX	Aerospool WT-9 Dynamic 912iS Sport	DY522/2015	
67-BUU	F-JTAG	Magni M-16 Expert		
67-BVA		Pipistrel Taurus		
67-BVH		B&F Funk FK-9		
67-BVX	F-JAAU	Aerospool WT-9 Dynamic	DY549/2015	
67-BWB		Fieseler Storch UL "AB+2L"		
67-BWV	F-JAKG	Aerospool WT-9 Dynamic		
W67-BWX		Aero Designs Pulsar		
67-BXM	F-JAPI	Aerospool WT-9 Dynamic	DY570/2016	

68 : Haut-Rhin

Reg	F-reg	Type	C/n	Other
68-AO		Skycraft AJS 2000		
		(Also reported as Rans S-6)		
68-BO		Comco Ikarus Fox-C22	8604-3015	D-MJGH

Reg	F-reg	Type	c/n	Prev id
68-BY		Aerotec VM18		
		(W/o 16.08.1997)		
68-CB		Humbert Tetras		
68-CE		Best Off Sky Ranger		
68-CN		Weedhopper		
68-CQ		Weedhopper		
68-DJ		Ultralair JC-24 Weedhopper Sport		
68-DQ		Ultralair JC-24 Weedhopper Sport		
68-DS		Croses Criquet Léger		
68-EB		Murphy Spirit Renegade		
		(Re-regd OO-B07, 4.93)		
68-EJ		Cosmos		
68-EL		Weedhopper		
68-FE		Weedhopper AX-3		
68-FF		Cosmos		
68-FH		Rans S-6 Coyote II		
68-FI		Aviasud AE209 Albatros		
68-FS		Croses Criquet UL		
68-GB		Aviasud AE209 Albatros		
68-GC		Humbert La Moto-du-Ciel		
		(Crashed 11.6.05)		
68-GH		Rans S-12 Airaile	1292-356	
		(Also regd D-MNBI)		
68-GK		Best Off Sky Ranger		
68-GM		Best Off Sky Ranger		
68-GP		DTA Feeling		
68-HA		Cosmos		
		(W/o 1.11.15)		
68-HC		Mignet HM.1000 Balerit	114	
		(Same c/n quoted for 67-HG. Order unknown)		
68-HK		Comco Ikarus Fox-C22		
68-HV		Weedhopper AX-3		
68-HW		Barry MB-02 Souricette		
68-HY		Cosmos		
68-IL		Air Création		
68-IN		Light Aero Avid Lite		
68-IO		Skyboy		
68-IP		Air Création / XP		
68-IQ		Best Off Sky Ranger		
68-JA		Mignet HM.293 Pou-du-Ciel		
68-JH		weightshift		
68-JM		Best Off Sky Ranger		
		(Re-regd 68-SG ?)		
68-KH		Cosmos / Phase II	21005	
68-KK		Best Off Sky Ranger		
68-KR	F-JDAB	Humbert Tetras		
68-KS		Eipper Quicksilver ?		
68-KV		Phantom 1		
68-LC		Best Off Sky Ranger		
68-LD		Aquilair XP		
68-LF		Weedhopper AX-3		
68-LM		Humbert La Moto-du-Ciel		
		(W/o 2.5.02)		
68-MS		"Petit Chef" (based on Sunwheel?)		
68-MU	F-JGBZ	Aviasud Sirocco		
68-MZ		Aéro Services Guépy 582		
68-NA	F-JGTD	Humbert Tetras		
		(Also reported as a Denney Kitfox)		
68-NG		Cosmos		
68-NK		DTA Voyager 912S /		
68-NW		Aviasud AE209 Albatros		
68-OD		Best Off Sky Ranger		
68-OH		Alisport Yuma		
68-OK	F-JGVN	Alisport Yuma		
68-ON		Rans S-6 Coyote II		
68-OP	F-JGTW	Aviakit Vega UL		
68-OT		Pipistrel Sinus 912		
		(Crashed 14.4.04)		
68-OU		DTA / Dynamic 15		
68-OY		Air Création trike / SX		
68-PH		Cosmos / Bautek Pico		
W68-PV		gyrocopter		
68-PX		Junkers Profly Allegro SW 582		
		(W/o 5.9.04)		
68-QA		Barry MB-02 Souricette		W68-QA
68-QU		Epervier 582 / Kestrel 60		
68-RJ		DTA / Dynamic 16/430		
68-RO		Fly Synthesis Wallaby		
68-RX		DTA Combo		
		(Severely damaged in accident 13.5.11)		
68-RY		Pipistrel Sinus		
68-SA		Denney Kitfox		
68-SG	F-JGSO	Best Off Sky Ranger		68-JM ?
68-SI		Air Création / XP		
68-SK		Magni M-22 Voyager		
		(also reported as Fly Synthesis Storch ?)		
68-SO		Fly Synthesis Storch FS		
68-SP		Light Aero Avid Lite		
		(Damaged 16.3.07)		
68-TB		Zenair CH-601XL Zodiac		
68-TH		Humbert Tetras 912S		
68-TK		III Sky Arrow 500TF		
		(W/o 1.8.14)		
68-TN		Light Aero Avid Flyer		
68-TU	F-JYQY	Rans S-6 Coyote II (t/w)		
68-TZ	F-JYWN	Best Off Sky Ranger V-Max		
68-UA	F-JXMW	B&F Funk FK-9 Mk.III		
68-UC		paramotor		
68-UF		Best Off Sky Ranger		
68-UM		Magni M-16C Tandem Trainer	16074444	
68-UQ		Magni M-22 Voyager		
68-UR		Weedhopper		
68-US		Aerospool WT-9 Dynamic		
68-UT		Zenair CH-601 Zodiac		
68-UU		Autogyro-Europe MT-03		
68-UY		Autogyro-Europe MT-03 912S		
68-VA		Dudek paramotor		
68-VF		Zenair CH-701 STOL		
68-VN	F-JWDE	Aerospool WT-9 Dynamic	DY214/2007	
68-VR	F-JWMJ	Alpi Aviation Pioneer 200		
68-VT		Zenith Baroudeur 582		
68-VZ	F-JWKD	Murphy Renegade Spirit		
68-WA	F-JYKF	Magni M-14 Scout		
68-WI		Dyn'Aéro MCR-01	378	
68-XG	F-JWMC	Best Off Sky Ranger Swift		
68-XW	F-JRNB	Best Off Sky Ranger V-Max		
68-YE	F-JWHE	Aerospool WT-9 Dynamic	DY277/2008	67-BES
68-YP		Air Création / XP12		
68-YT	F-JSBG	Dallach D4 Fascination		
68-ZB (1)	F-JSBT	B&F Funk FK-9 (t/w)		
68-ZB (2)	F-JSFN	Flight Design CT-2K		
W68-ZC		Ultralight Design C2 Silent		
68-ZM	F-JJPI	Air Création Racer 503SL / Fun 14		
68-ZV	F-JSPM	Magni M-24 Orion		
68-ZW		Aéro Services Guépy Club 582		
68-AAG		Zlin Savage		
68-AAJ	F-JVHR	ICP MXP-740 Savannah S	10-09-54-0018	
68-AAO		Comco Ikarus C-42		
68-AAV		B&F Funk FK-12 Comet		
68-ABH	F-JTIU	Pro.Mecc.Sparviero		
68-ABI	F-JSLT	Jihlavan Skyleader 200		
68-ABL		Magni M-24 Orion		
68-ABP		Magni M-22 Voyager		
68-ACS		BRM Citius Sport		
68-ACU		BRM Citius Sport		
68-ADH		Mosquito XE		
68-ADN		Helisport CH-7 Kompress		
68-ADQ	F-JULI	ICP MXP-740 Savannah S	13-01-54-0242	
68-AEW		Magni M-16 Tandem Trainer		
68-AFD		Air Bandit gyrocopter		
68-AGB		Zlin Savage Cruiser		
68-AGU		Spacek SD-1 Minisport	113	
68-AHR		Best Off Nynja		
68-AUG		Dyn'Aero MCR-01		

69 :Rhône

Reg	F-reg	Type	c/n	Prev id
69-M		Southdown Puma		
69-AE		JC-31 Weedhopper		
69-AK		Hipps Superbirds J-3 Kitten		
69-AR		Cosmos		
69-AU		Croses Airplume	19	
69-BI		Aerial Arts Chaser		
69-BO		Croses Airplume		
69-BX		Microbel Must		
69-CA		Colin Epsilon / Synairgie wing		
69-CX		Solar Wings Pegasus XL-Q		
69-DK		Solar Wings Pegasus XL		
			SW-TB-1399/SW-WA-1401	
69-DU		Cosmos trike	B445	
69-EG		Synairgie (trike)		
69-EI		Weedhopper		
69-EJ		Cosmos		
69-EQ		Biplum		
69-ER		Tandem Air Sunny		
69-ET		Weedhopper		
69-EX		Weedhopper		
69-GB		Aviasud AE209 Albatros		
69-GD		Weedhopper AX-3		62-DG
69-GI		TEAM Mini-MAX		
69-GV		Aviasud AE209 Albatros		
69-GX		weightshift		
69-HV		Air Création		
69-IJ		Air Création		
69-JB		Cosmos		
69-JU		Rans S-6ES Coyote II		
		(Crashed 24.10.04)		
69-KL		(Croses ?) Airplume		
69-LI		paramotor		
		(Fell into river 31.7.04)		
69-LT		trike / Air Création XP11		
69-ME		Flight Design CT		
69-MJ		DTA / Dynamic		
69-NE		Rans S-6 Coyote II		
69-NI		DTA / Dynamic 15		
69-NM		Humbert Tetras 912BS		
69-NO		Cosmos		
69-NQ		Cosmos		
69-NV		Pipistrel Sinus		
69-OD		DTA Feeling 912S / Dynamic 450		
69-OF		DTA / Dynamic 15/430		
69-OH		Exalt Air		
69-OK		DTA / Dynamic 450		
69-OU		ICP Super Bingo		
69-PA		Murphy Maverick		
69-PK	F-JETO	B&F Funk FK-9 Mk.IV Club	03-U208	
69-PM		Best Off Sky Ranger		
69-QI	F-JEZQ	Air Création Twin Buggy / iXess		
69-QO		Rans S-6 Coyote II		
69-QU	F-JYPA	Air Création Tanarg / iXess		
69-QY		ProFe D-10 Tukan		
69-RB		Air Création GT BI / iXess		
69-RK		Air Création / Kiss		
69-RQ		Murphy Renegade Spirit 912		
		(Damaged 14.8.07)		
69-RT	F-JEZS	Aéro Services Guépard 912		
69-RX	F-JEZX	Evektor EV-97 Eurostar	2003 1902	95-RV
69-SF	F-JEFO	Aviakit Vega 3000	AFC050804J8	
69-SH		Air Création Tanarg / Fun		
69-SK	F-JEGK	Fly Synthesis Storch HS (Jabiru)		
69-SR		B&F Funk FK-9 Mk.III		
69-TH		Air Création GTE		
69-TK		Dudek Reaction paramotor		
69-TL	F-JETC	Rans S-7 Courier		
69-TW	F-JEUK	Best Off Sky Ranger		
69-UE		Best Off Sky Ranger		
69-UG		Air Création Tanarg / iXess		
69-UH		Aeroandinas MXP-1000 Tayrona		
			AA-02-07-90-031	
69-UI	F-JXBU	type unknown (high wing, 3-axis, t/w)		
69-UJ		Evektor EV-97 Eurostar	2007 3009	
		(Re-regd 73-OH)		
69-UM	F-JXJY	ICP MXP-740 Savannah VG ADV		
69-UW		Best Off Sky Ranger		
69-VB		Urban Air UFM-13 Lambada		
69-VG		weightshift		
69-VM		Air Création		
69-VO		Alpi Aviation Pioneer 200		
		(W/o 10.3.11)		
69-VR		Air Création Racer		
69-VV		Dragonfly		
69-WB	F-JYSQ	DTA Combo / Dynamic 15/430		
69-WH		Dragonfly / Aeros Discus		

Reg	F-reg	Type	c/n	Extra
69-WT		Dragonfly / Aeros Discus 15		
69-WX		Air Création Tanarg 912ES / Bionix		
69-WZ		Rans S-6 Coyote II t/w		
69-XB		Aéro Servoces Guepard 912S		
69-XL		Halley Apollo Fox	FR200410	
		(Re-regd OO-H28)		
69-XY		Tecnam P.92 Echo Club		
69-XZ		ICP Bingo 582 VG		
69-YM		Air Création Skypper / NuviX		
69-YO		Air Création Skypper / Bionix 15		
69-YW		Alpi Aviation Pioneer		
69-ZD	F-JTFJ	Urban Air Samba XXL		
69-ZH		Air Création		
		(W/o 28.12.11)		
69-ZI		Jodel D.18 (Type unconfirmed)		
69-ZO		Urban Air Samba XXL		
69-ZR		Air Création Tanarg / BioniX		
69-ZZ	F-JTXO	Zenair CH-601 Zodiac		
69-AAA		Air Création GT BI / Fun		
69-AAO		Air Création Skypper		
69-AAP		Air Création		
69-AAR		Fly Synthesis Storch 912S	F1BC4970D12C	
69-ABD	F-JVNH	Best Off Nynja		
69-ABG		Air Création		
69-ABI		Air Création Pixel		
69-ABU		Air Création		
		(W/o 31.3.15)		
69-ACH		Air Création Tanarg / NuviX		
69-ACK		Fly Synthesis Storch S	F7E15070E7EC	
69-ACL		Air Création Skypper		
69-ACZ		Air Création Skypper / BioniX 15	A16050-16051	
69-ADA		Air Création Pixel XC		
69-ADC	F-JUJU	Tomark SD-4 Viper	0104	
69-ADD		unidentified paramotor		

70 : Haute-Saône

Reg	F-reg	Type	c/n	Extra
70-AB		Eipper Quicksilver MX		
70-AX		Raven		
70-BO		Cosmos		
70-BS		Cosmos Chronos		
70-BY		Weedhopper AX-3		
70-CN		Air Composite		
70-DK		Humbert La Moto-du-Ciel		
70-DR		DTA / Dynamic 15		
70-DS		Humbert La Moto-du-Ciel		
70-EH		Zenair CH-601 Zodiac		
70-EI		Air Création DT / Mild		
70-EP		Humbert Tetras		
70-EU		Aerotec 16 (trike)		
70-EX		Weedhopper		
70-EY		Air Création		
70-FG	F-JHMZ	Best Off Sky Ranger		
		(Also noted as 'Evasion')		
70-FH	F-JGQD	Jodel D.18		
70-FJ		Jodel D.20	20	
70-FN		Aéro Services Guépy (Jabiru) 80		
70-FT		B&F Funk FK-9 (t/w)		
W70-GC		Jodel D.185		
		(Damaged 25.7.04)		
70-GH		Cosmos Phase II / La Mouette Chronos 16		
70-GJ		Fly Synthesis Wallaby		
70-GY		Colomban MC-30 Luciole	6	
70-HE		DTA Combo / Dynamic		
		(Crashed 8.8.06)		
70-HH		Light Aero Avid Flyer		
70-HL		Cosmos Bidulm 503		
70-HR	F-JYVV	Pipistrel Sinus		
70-HS		DTA / Dynamic		
70-HT		DTA Combo 582 / Dynamic 450		
70-II		Jodel D.185PF		
70-IP	F-JWHK	ICP MXP-740 Savannah	08-01-51-671	
70-IQ		Eipper Quicksilver Sport IIS 582		
70-IV	F-JWNT	Zlin Savage	0157	
70-IY		Flylab Tucano		
70-JB	F-JWXJ	ICP MXP-740 Savannah	08-10-51-783	
70-JR	F-JPMT	Aerospool WT-9 Dynamic	DY072/2005	
		(Damaged 26.6.05)		
70-JT		ICP MXP-740 Savannah S		
70-KA	F-JXFX	Didier Pti'tavion		
70-KB	F-JSYW	Zenair CH-601XL Zodiac		
70-KG		Pulma Ellipse / Fuji Alizé		
70-KI		Ekolot JK-05 Junior		
70-KL	F-JTIK	ICP Bingo!	10-07-52-229	
70-KQ	F-JUIY	Jodel D.18	119	F-PYNX
70-KR	F-JTSP	DTA J-RO gyrocopter	004	
70-KT		ICP-MXP-740 Savannah		
70-KZ	F-JUDT	ICP MXP-740 Savannah S	12-10-54-0216	
70-LC	F-JUVY	Zenair CH-650Ei (ICP-built)	13-03-65EK-0007	
70-LG	F-JVIG	AirLony Skylane UL	40 ?	
70-LH	F-JVLD	AirLony Skylane UL		
70-LM	F-JVSY	J20 gyrocopter		
70-LU	F-JWWA	JMB Aircraft VL-3 Evolution	VL3-163	
70-LV	F-JABL	AirLony Skylane UL		
70-MH	F-JAUJ	AirLony Skylane UL		

71 : Saône-et-Loire

Reg	F-reg	Type	c/n	Extra
71-F		Southdown Puma		
71-N		Croses Airplume		
71-AE		(Technic Moto ?) Mustang		
71-AF		Air's Maestro		
71-AH		(Technic Moto ?) Mustang		
71-BA		Europa Malik		
71-BB		Cosmos		
71-BJ		Cosmos Bidulm / Cosmos 19 m²		
71-BK		Aviasud Mistral		
71-BL		Aviasud Mistral		
71-CJ		Aviasud Mistral	100	
71-CP		Aviasud Mistral	110	
71-CT		Croses LC-6		
71-CV		Mignet HM.1000 Balerit 3X		
71-DE		Synairgie		
71-DH		La Mouette		
71-DL		Air Création		
71-DT		Alpi Aviation Pioneer 200		
71-EA		Croses LC-6		
71-EG		Air Création GT		
71-EH		Weedhopper		
71-ES		Air Création GT BI		
71-ET		Air Création / XP		
71-FB		Air Création / Mild		
71-FC	F-JBHE	Tecnam P.92 Echo	100	
71-FG		Air Création GTE Clipper		
71-FH		Rans S-6 Coyote II		
71-FJ		Mignet Pou-du-Ciel	NK07	
71-FO		Cosmos		
71-FR		(Technic Moto ?) Mustang		
71-GH		Weedhopper	6081068	
71-GL	F-JGXE	SG Aviation Storm 300		
		(W/o 12.7.07)		
71-GO		Cosmos Phase II		
71-GP	F-JGMO	Azurlog Caprice 21		
71-HA	F-JGOY	SG Aviation Storm 300 Special		
		(Re-regd 89-UO)		
71-HE		Air Création Safari GT BI 503 / Quartz 16SX		
		(accident 1.3.12)		
71-HN		SG Aviation Storm		
71-HP		Cosmos		
71-HX		ICP MXP-740 Savannah		
71-IC	F-JGYM	ICP MX-740 Savannah	01-11-51-104	
71-ID	F-JGXZ	Pipistrel Sinus 912		
71-IF		Rans S-5 Coyote 1		
		(Damaged 13.4.05)		
71-IG		ICP MXP-740 Savannah	03-01-51-188	
71-IJ		Croses Airplume		
71-IK		Solo 210/ITV Proxima 2 paramotor		
		(W/o 24.8.07)		
71-IN	F-JGYV	Aviakit Vega 2000		
71-IP		Tecnam P.92 Echo		
71-IR		Air Création GTE 582S / XP15		
		(Crashed 26.5.06)		
71-IS		Urban Air UFM-13 Lambada		
71-IU		SE.5A replica (Marked A8898)		
71-IX	F-JGZK	SG Aviation Storm 300G		
		(Same call-sign as 80-ZD)		
71-IZ		Zenair CH-601XL Zodiac	6-9553	
71-JB		Morin M-85		
		(Forced landing 1.4.06)		
71-JF	F-JOGY	Zenair CH-601 Zodiac (t/w)		
71-JG		Zenair CH-001 Zodiac		
W71-JI		Pou-du-Ciel		
71-JK	F-JQGE	Croses CLP (prototype)		
71-JO	F-JGYF	Zenair CH-701SP STOL		
71-JS		Air Création Tanarg / iXess		
71-JY		Jodel D.92 Bébé		
		(W/o 2.7.06)		
71-JZ		Zenair CH-601 Zodiac		
71-KD		Voyageur 172		
71-KE	F-JZMW	Rans S-6 Coyote II	0593494	
71-KF		DTA / Dynamic 15/430		
71-KH		Air Création GTE 582S / Kiss		
71-KI		Dyn'Aéro MCR-01		
71-KL	F-JYBU	Dyn'Aéro MCR-01	343	
71-KN		Croses Criquet		
71-KO		DTA Combo 503 / Dynamic 15/430		
71-KS		Rans S-6 Coyote II		
71-KT		Chetverien 01 (trike)		
		(W/o 21.4.07)		
71-KV		Pottier P.320 UL		
71-KW		Croses Criquet Léger		
71-KZ		ALMS/Sauper Papango		
71-LA	F-JYVN	ATEC 321 Faeta		
71-LH	F-JXHI	Zlin Savage Cruiser		
		(Re-regd 01-XD)		
71-LL		SG Aviation Storm Century		
		(Re-regd 83-AMG)		
71-LM	F-JITM	B&F Funk FK-14 Polaris	14-034	
71-LP		B&F Funk FK-12 Comet	12-022	56-LV, D-MUED(2)
71-LR		SG Aviation Storm		
71-LU	F-JZWS	TL Ultralight TL-2000 Sting Carbon	02ST16	
71-LW		Comco Ikarus Fox-C22		
71-LX		Zenair CH-601 Zodiac		
71-MC	F-JWRY	Dyn'Aéro MCR Pick Up	135	
		(Damaged 28.8.16)		
71-ME	F-JYWM	B&F Funk FK-9 SW	317	64-NN
71-MK	F-JXLR	Pipistrel Virus		
71-MN	F-JRCL	Zlin Savage		
71-MP	F-JRZY	Hummelbird Ultra Cruiser		
71-MQ		Jodel		
71-MU	F-JBHQ	Rans S-6 Coyote II		
71-MV		Zlin Savage		
71-MZ	F-JINO	B&F Funk FK-9		
71-ND		Aveko VL-3 Sprint		
71-NH		Aero East Europe SILA 450		
71-NI		ICP MXP-740 Savannah XL		
71-NX		Dyn'Aéro MCR Pick Up	154	
71-NZ	F-JSSU	ICP MXP-740 Savannah S	11-01-54-0070	
71-OG		Humbert Tetras		
71-OK		B&F Funk FK-12 Comet		
71-ON	F-JTDM	Zlin Savage Club		
71-OU		Fantasy Air Allegro SW	04-133	
		(Same c/n as 67-VB and possibly 67-ZL)		
71-OX	F-JYKM	Flight Design CT SW	07-01-17	
		(Re-regd 77-BEP ?)		
71-PF		Aero Pilot Legend 540		
71-PH		Mignet HM.293		
		(To museum, Lyon-Corbas)		
71-PJ		Mignet HM.14 Pou	NK07	
71-PN	F-JUUV	Aero Pilot Legend 540		
71-PQ	F-JVJS	Corvus Racer 312	004	
71-PS	F-JVQO	Ekolot JK-05 Junior		
71-PU		Zenair CH-650E1		
		(W/o 7.10.16)		
71-PX		Croses ?		
71-QI		Zenair CH-601 Zodiac		
71-QU	F-JASW	DTA J'Ro	047	
71-RM		Fly Synthesis Storch		
71-XN		Dyn'Aéro MCR Pick Up	154	

72 : Sarthe

Reg	F-reg	Type	c/n	Extra
72-K		Aerokart		
72-L		JC-24 Weedhopper		

Reg	F-reg	Type	Serial	Other
72-AA		JC-24 Weedhopper		
72-AM		Air Création Safari GT BI		
72-BC		Mignet HM.1000 Balerit 3X	20	
72-BH		Air Création / Mild		
72-BJ		JC-24 Weedhopper Europa II		
72-BK		JC-24 Weedhopper Europa 1		
72-BN		Skywalker		
72-CA		Solar Wings Pegasus XL-R	SW-WA-1253 / SW-TB-1248	
72-CH		Air Création / SX		
72-CS		Air Création		
72-DJ		Air Création / Quartz		
72-EB		Air Création GT BI / 16SX		
72-EC		Cosmos / TOP		
72-EG		Air Création / SX (Or La Mouette ?)		
72-EX		Synairgie / Puma Bi		
72-FG		Solar Wings Pegasus Quasar 503		
72-FP	F-JZIM	Rans S-6 Coyote II		
72-FS	F-JBHV	Aviasud AE209 Albatros		
72-FV	F-JBIS	Humbert Tetras		
72-GA		Air Création / SX		
72-GB		Maxair Drifter XP503		
72-GL	F-JGXG	Sauper J.300 Joker (internal marking: ex or to 37-TG?)		
72-GV		Sauper J.300 Joker		
72-HB		Air Création GT BI		
72-HQ		Best Off Sky Ranger		
72-HU	F-JHUA	Raj Hamsa X'Air		
72-IB	F-JHVF	Raj Hamsa X'Air (Call sign as reported on anonymous Quasar .11)		
72-IC		Barry MB-04 Souris Bulle		
72-II		Aéro Services Guépy		
72-IO		Aeros / Stream		
72-IT	F-JHWJ	Jodel D.18 (Re-regd 15-IT)	17	F-PRJK
72-IU		Air Création / XP		
72-JB	F-JHXP	European Airwings Springbok 2000		
72-JD		Raj Hamsa X'Air		
72-JE	F-JHXU	Air Création GT BI 582 / Kiss	A00026-0028	
72-JF		Air Création		
72-JL	F-JHYV	B&F Funk FK-9 Mk.III (Re-regd 62-ARD/F-JFSJ)	09-111	37-XE, 41-KP, D-MUED(1)
72-JM		Fly Synthesis Storch HS		
72-JN		paramotor		
72-JS		Raj Hamsa X'Air 582		
72-JT		Fly Synthesis Texan Top Class		
72-JV		Cosmos Chronos / Fun		
72-JX		Fly Synthesis Storch		
72-JZ		DTA / Dynamic 15		
72-KD		Best Off Sky Ranger		
72-KF		Tecnam P.92 Echo		
72-KH	F-JHAT	Light Aero Avid Flyer	801	55-HH, F-WRKH
72-KJ	F-JHAZ	Air Création / Kiss		
72-LI		Raj Hamsa X'Air		
72-LJ		Air Création GTE Clipper / iXess		
72-LL		Pegastol		
72-LQ	F-JHDJ	ATEC Zephyr		
72-LT		Zlin Savage		
72-LU	F-JZAR	Air Création GTE Clipper / iXess	A04146-4150	
72-LV		type unknown		
72-LW		Air Création / iXess		
72-LZ	F-JHQF	Best Off Sky Ranger		
72-MC	F-JZTO	Aeroandinas MXP-1000 Tayrona (Same c/n as 59-CNP and 59-CWN)	AA-04-05-90-005	
72-MJ	F-JPJN	ICP MXP-740 Savannah ADV (Same c/n as 21-ACT)	05-03-51-389	
72-MK	F-JZYK	G1 Aviation G1 SPYL		
72-ML		Whittaker MW.6S (Accident 3.8.07)		
72-MP		Magni M-16 Tandem Trainer		
72-MQ	F-JYLH	Air Création GTE Trek / iXess	A07029-7023 / T07017	
72-MV	F-JHVA	Djicat Buse'Air 150		
72-NB	F-JPQC	Air Création Tanarg / iXess		
72-NI	F-JXVM	Aéro Services Super Guépard 912	28083	
72-NN		Raj Hamsa Hanuman (Re-regd 44-AHO)		
72-NP		Air Création Tanarg / iXess		
72-NR		Skyeton K.10 Swift		
72-NZ		ICP MXP-740 Savannah VG	07-10-51-662	
72-OB		Alpi Aviation Pioneer 200		
72-OJ		Air Création GT BI 503		
72-OP	F-JYYT	Evektor EV-97 Eurostar	2007 2923	78-YZ
72-OQ		Magni M-16 Tandem Trainer (previously quoted as Pro.Mecc. Sparviero SP10 with call sign F-JXIU)		
72-OW		Morin M.85		
72-OX		Morin M.85		
72-OZ	F-JPRD	Zenair CH-701 STOL		
72-PA	F-JRNG	Pro.Mecc. Sparviero 100		
72-PG		Pegasus Quasar 503		
72-PI	F-JRZE	Pro.Mecc. Sparviero		
72-PL		Alpi Aviation Pioneer 200		
72-PM	F-JSKF	Aerospool WT-9 Dynamic	DY396/2010	
72-PN		Magni gyrocopter		
72-PP	F-JSRY	Ekolot KR-030 Topaz (Same c/n as 64-RQ / F-JSGD)	30-04-03	
72-PS		Adventure/Dudek Plasma paramotor		
72-PU	F-JSSX	Aeroandinas MXP-850 (MSL Aero Type H)	AA-02-10-82-040	
72-PV		Ozone Viper paramotor		
72-PW	F-JFDF	Aéro Services Guepy (Jabiru 80)	99012	
72-QD		Mainair Blade 912S	1281-0401-7-W1076	G-NOOK
72-QF		Paramania Revo 2 paramotor		
72-QI	F-JHDX	Magni M-16 Tandem Trainer (C/n unconfirmed)	16-12-6974	
72-RJ	F-JVXG	Tomark SD-4 Viper	0101	OM-M337
72-RL	F-JRQR	Tomark SD-4 Viper	0102	
72-RS	F-JAEA	Aeros trike		
72-RV	F-JALV	Tomark SD-4 Viper	0107/2016	
72-RY	F-JAYD	Tomark SD-4 Viper	0110	
72-VE	F-JRPD	Aéro Services Guépard 912		
72-ADQ		Air Création		

73 : Savoie

Reg	F-reg	Type	Serial	Other
73-AB		Air's Maestro (Single-seat)		
73-AN		Air's Allegro		
73-BN		weightshift		
73-BU		Renegade 503 (noted as 'Jules Special')		
73-CG		Dynali Chickinox		
73-CI		Weedhopper		
73-CX		Weedhopper AX-3 (Re-regd OO-C07 5.95)	B3023097	
73-DG		Rans S-6 Coyote II	0293-44 .	
73-EF	F-JBEC	Rans S-6 Coyote II		
73-EK		Air Création		
73-EN	F-JBSQ	Zenair CH-701 STOL		
73-ER	F-JBOK	Rans S-6ESD Coyote II (t/w)		
73-FU	F-JCQU	Rans S-6ES Coyote II		
73-GL		P&M Aviation Quik		
73-HL		Rans S-7 Courier		
73-HR		Aviasud AE532 Mistral (W/o 18.10.00)		
73-HS	F-JEKE	Ikarusflug Eurofox	Farman No.15	
73-HX		Alpaero (Noin) Sirius		
73-IB	F-JELU	Pipistrel Sinus		
73-IK		Pipistrel Sinus		
73-IN		Pipistrel Taurus		
73-IU		Air Création Safari GT BI 503 / Kiss 450		
73-JE		Pipistrel Sinus		
73-JG		Pipistrel Sinus 912 (Damaged 3.6.05)		
73-JH		Pipistrel Virus		
73-JL		Air Création / Fun		
73-JN	F-JERF	Dyn'Aéro MCR-01 UL	175	
73-JR		Aviasud AE532 Mistral		
73-JZ		Pipistrel Sinus		
73-KB	F-JETI	Best Off Sky Ranger		
W73-KC		Mignet HM.293 Pou-du-Ciel (W/o 10.12.03)		
73-KD		B&F Funk FK-12 Comet (Re-regd 77-ALK, 25-UA)		28-BI
73-KE		Cosmos		
73-KF	F-JEUT	Pipistrel Sinus		
73-KN		Humbert Tetras B		
73-KO		Alpi Aviation Pioneer 200 (Damaged 27.10.06)		
73-KP		Pipistrel Sinus		
73-LA		Cosmos Phase 2 / Chronos 16		
73-LB		Pipistrel Sinus		
73-LC	F-JEXN	TL Ultralight TL-2000 Sting Carbon		
73-LF		B&F Funk FK-14 Polaris		D-MSEX
73-LI		Mignet HM.293 Pou-du-Ciel		
73-LJ		Mignet HM.293 Pou-du-Ciel (Mod)		
73-LM		Pipistrel Sinus		
73-LN		Pipistrel Taurus		
73-LO	F-JEGG	Pipistrel Virus (also carried F-JEZB)		
73-LP		Pipistrel Sinus		
73-LT		Zenair CH-601XL Zodiac		
73-LY		Best Off Sky Ranger		
73-MA	F-JEGD	Pipistrel Taurus 503	03	
73-MB	F-JEFY	Aerospool WT-9 Dynamic	DY126/2006	
73-MD		Rans S-4 Coyote I		
73-MN		Air Création		
73-MP		Jodel D.92 Bébé		
73-MQ	F-JYKT	Zenair CH-601UL Zodiac (t/w)		
73-MT		Aeropro Eurofox S2200j		OM-BIRD
73-MV		Pipistrel Sinus		
73-MY	F-JXMO	Pipistrel Sinus		
73-NG		Magni M-16 Tandem Trainer (Also noted as Sky Ranger (t/w))		
73-NH		SE-5A (7/8 scale replica)		
73-NO		Pipistrel Virus		
73-NQ	F-JWDA	ICP MXP-740 Savannah	08-01-51-674	
73-NR	F-JWGQ	Fly Synthesis Storch S		
73-NT	F-JPMU	Pipistrel Virus (Previously reported as Alpi Aviation Pioneer 300S)		
73-OE	F-JWRL	Pipistrel Virus 912	297V912	
73-OH	F-JXVA	Evektor EV-97 Eurostar (W/o 24.9.15)	2007 3009	69-UJ
73-OK		Pipistrel Sinus		
73-OP		ICP MXP-740 Savannah	08-01-51-672	27-ZU
73-PB		Air Création Tanarg / Bionix		
73-PF		Air Création GTE S 582 / iXess 15		
73-PJ	F-JEMZ	Autogyro-Europe Calidus 09		
73-PL		ICP MXP-740 Savannah (accident 30.4.12)		
73-PO		Magni M-24 Orion		
73-PP	F-JZWF	Tecnam P.2004 Bravo (Call-sign also quoted for 77-AWQ)		
73-PZ	F-JTSG	Alpi Aviation Pioneer 300STD		
73-QC		DTA J-RO gyrocopter		
73-QD	F-JUCA	B&F Funk FK-14B Polaris (t/w)		
73-QE	F-JUJN	Alpi Aviation Pioneer 200STD		
73-QL		Helisport CH-7 Kompress (W/o 3.12.15)		
73-QZ		Alisport Silent 2 Electro (Re-regd G-CIJE 7.14)	2062	
73-RA	F-JVNT	Humbert Tetras		
73-RJ		Helisport CH-77 Ranabot		
73-SF		Trixy G4-2		

74 : Haute-Savoie

Reg	F-reg	Type	Serial	Other
74-Y		Aériane Sirocco		
74-AM		Zodiac Ultrastar	122	
74-AU		Aviasud Sirocco (W/o 24.9.09)		
74-BT		Weedhopper Europa II		
74-CH		Weedhopper		
74-CK		Weedhopper	8032378	
74-CQ		Paraplane		
74-DC		Rans S-18 Stinger 2		
W74-DG		Paraplane		
74-DO		Alpaero (Noin) Sirius		
74-DP		Croses Airplume	21	
74-DX		Denney Kitfox II Minifox (Re-regd 21-AEA)	519	
74-EG		Denney Minifox		
74-EO		Rans S-6 Coyote II (t/w)		
74-EV		Mignet HM.14 Pou-du-Ciel		

Reg	F-reg	Type	Serial	Other
74-FH		Aviasud AE209 Albatros		
74-FL		Kolb Twinstar		
74-GB		Cosmos Profil / La Mouette		
74-GJ		Micro Aviation Pulsar III		
74-GM		Ultralair		
74-GQ		Ultralair JC-31 Weedhopper		
		(W/o 8.8.98)		
74-GU		Top Concept Hurricane		
74-HG		Synairgie		
74-HI	F-JEQC	Best Off Sky Ranger (t/w)		
74-HK		Technic'air F40GT parachute		
74-IC		Ushuaia floatplane		
74-KB		Humbert Tetras		
74-KF	F-JCWA	Rans S-6ESD Coyote II		
74-LP		Barry MB-02 Souricette		
74-MD		Cosmos		
		(Re-regd 63-VA)		
74-ME		Humbert Tetras		
74-MN		Aviasud AE209 Albatros		
74-NF		Mignet HM.1000 Balerit	102	
74-OT		Rans S-6 Coyote II		
74-OX		Air Création GTE Clipper		
74-PF		Rans S-6ESD Coyote II		
74-PG		Urban Air UFM-10 Samba		
		(W/o 11.6.02?)		
74-PT		Tecnam P.96 Golf 100		
		(W/o 25.8.07)		
74-PV	F-JESI	Pipistrel Sinus		
74-QH		B&F Funk FK-14 Polaris		
		(W/o 12.9.03)		
74-QO		Eipper Quicksilver MXL II MCL 01 amphibian		
74-QR		Air Création GTE Clipper 582SE		
		(Crashed 14.9.05)		
74-QU	F-JEVE	Air Création GTE / iXess		
74-QV	F-JEVD	Air Création Tanarg / iXess		
74-RI		B&F Funk FK-12 Comet		
		(Crashed 25.9.05)		
74-RJ		DTA / Dynamic 450		
74-RU	F-JYWP	ICP MXP-740 Savannah	04-07-51-317	
		(W/o 28.2.13)		
74-SK		Air Création		
74-SW		Air Création Tanarg / iXess		
74-SZ		Cosmos		
		(Damaged 10.7.06)		
74-TD		Air Création GT BI / iXess 13		
74-TE		Air Création GTE Clipper / iXess		
74-TK		Paramania Action GT paramotor		
74-UG	F-JEGX	Tecnam P.92 Echo	569	
		(same call sign as 65-MM; not known which of 65-MM or 74-UG is current)		
74-UH	F-JXEK	Best Off Sky Ranger		
74-UN	F-JZUY	ICP Super Bingo 582	04-01-52-136	
74-US		DTA Voyageur II / Dynamic		
		(W/o 5.08)		
74-UU		B&F Funk FK-9 Mk.IV		
74-VA		Magni M-22 Voyager		
		(W/o 14.9.07)		
74-VD	F-JYGG	DTA / Dynamic		
74-VG		DTA / Dynamic 450		
74-VI	F-JYLQ	B&F Funk FK-9 Smart	04-U-312	
74-VS	F-JEPB	Guérin G1		
74-VW		Tecnam P.92 Echo Classic		
74-VX		Tecnam P.92 Echo		
		(accident 18.11.12)		
74-WB	F-JCZS	Mignet HM.1100 Cordouan	9	
74-WC		paramotor		
74-WD		paramotor		
74-WF	F-JWMN	Guérin G1		
74-WP		Evektor EV-97 Eurostar		
74-WR		DTA / Dynamic 15		
74-WW	F-JYZX	Humbert Tetras		
74-XB	F-JZCC	Best Off Sky Ranger		28-ACI
74-XD	F-JSCX	ICP MXP-740 Savannah	01-05-51-079	F-JPQV
74-XQ		Air Création Tanarg 912S / iXess 13		
74-XR		Humbert Tetras 912CS		
74-XZ		paramotor		
74-YB		Ozone Viper 2 paramotor		
74-YE		PAP/Dudek Plasma paramotor		
74-YG		Mignet HM.293 Pou-du-Ciel		
		(W/o 19.5.09)		
74-YR		Miniplane/Ozone Viper paramotor		
74-YT	F-JWZC	ICP MXP-740 Savannah	08-04-51-711	
74-YU		Miniplane/Ozone paramotor		
74-YV		Miniplane/Ozone Viper 2 paramotor		
74-YW	F-JWTY	Tecnam P.92 Echo	1242	
74-YY	F-JWUA	Tecnam P.92 Echo Classic		
74-ZE		BRM Land Africa		
74-ZF	F-JYAI	Best Off Sky Ranger		
74-ZH		Air Création GTE Clipper / iXess		
74-ZI	F-JJDO	Tecnam P.92 Echo		
74-ZK	F-JROD	Best Off Nynja		
74-ZP		ITV Dolpo paramotor		
74-ZQ	F-JEFX	Rans S.18 Stinger II		
74-ZR		Air Création GTE Trek / iXess		
74-ZV		Dudel Nucleon paramotor		
74-ZX	F-JXMY	Autogyro-Europe MT-03	'B204SF01978E1'	
		(The c/n is the 'code d'identification' quoted on the French ULM 'carte d'identification')		
74-AAF		Air Création Tanarg 912S / BioniX 15		
74-AAS		Air Création Racer		
74-AAT	F-JFOB	Air Création Tanarg		
74-ABB		Magni M-22 Voyager		
74-ABG		MacFly/Ozone Speedster paramotor		
74-ABJ		Air Création Tanarg / BioniX 15		
74-ABK	F-JKFT	Pipistrel Sinus		
74-ABQ	F-JTEP	Autogyro-Europe Calidus 09	11014	
74-ACE		Tecnam P.92 Echo		
		(Re-regd 01-ACE)		
74-ACL		Magni M-24 Orion	24-12-6954	
74-ACU		PAP Ozone paramotor		
74-ADD	F-JUAQ	ICP MXP-740 Savannah S	12-01-54-0153	
74-AEC		Air Création Tanarg		
		(Believed sold to Russia)		
74-AED		Air Création Tanarg		
		(Believed sold to Russia)		
74-AEK		DTA J-RO gyrocopter	013	
74-AEQ		Air Création Tanarg / NuviX	A11029-11020	
74-AFH		DTA J-RO gyrocopter		
74-AGC	F-JVZG	Zlin Savage Bobber	226	
W74-AGJ		Spacek SD-1 Minisport		
74-AGZ	F-JUTS	Tecnam P.92 Echo Elite		
74-AHD		DTA J-RO gyrocopter		
74-AHF	F-JVRZ	ICP MXP-740 Savannah S	13-06-54-0273	
74-AHR		Lemmonnier Maestro		
74-AHU		ELA Aviacion ELA-10 Eclipse		
74-AHZ		Cicare 8	0008	

75 : Paris

Reg	F-reg	Type	Serial	Other
75-H		Eipper Quicksilver MX		
75-Y		Aériane Sirocco		
75-AJ		Guerpont Biplum		
75-DN		Doutart Le Chevron Volant		
75-DU		weightshift		
75-EI		Zenith Baroudeur	016	
75-FJ		Synairgie Pelican		
75-FL		Mignet HM.1000 Balerit		
75-GF		Air Création		
75-GG		Air Création Racer / SX 12		
75-GIW		Inovatic		
75-GJ		Zenith Baroudeur		
75-GV		J.2		
75-HP		Pegasus / Le Volant		
		(Previously reported as Air Création Le Volant and Synairgie Puma B1, presumably representing trike changes)		
75-HV		Synairgie		
75-HY		Zenith Baroudeur		
75-II		Air's Maestro		
75-KB		Best Off Sky Ranger		
75-KC		Cosmos		
75-KF		Pipistrel Sinus		
75-KG		JCC Aviation J.300 Joker		
75-KM		Johnathan Souricette		
75-KN		JCC Aviation J.300 Joker		
75-KT		SIT Systems Alto Paramotor		
75-KU		Adventure paraglider		
75-LG		Zenith Baroudeur		
75-LQ		Best Off Sky Ranger		
		(Re-regd 92-KW)		
75-LP		Barry MD-04 Souris Bulle		
75-MC		gyrocopter		
75-MH	F-JBVS	Aero Kuhlmann Scub	02	
75-MI		SCUB MTR-75		
75-MR	F-JPZW	Aviatika MAI-890 Petit MIG		
75-MT		Rans S-6 Coyote II		
75-NG		Cosmos		
75-NK		Weedhopper		
75-NM		III Sky Arrow 450		
75-NO		Cosmos Phase II / La Mouette Top 12.9		
75-OF		Klöti Autogiro RK-02		
75-OH		Humbert La Moto-du-Ciel		
75-OJ	F-JFDZ	Micro Aviation Pulsar III	135	
		(Re-regd 95-II)		
75-OU		Aériane Swift		
75-OV		Mignet HM.1100 Cordouan		
		(W/o 25.9.99)		
75-OY		Powerchute Raider		
75-PB		Light Aero Avid Flyer	833	33-AGK, HB-YFC
75-PV		Rans S-6 Coyote II		
75-PW		Fantasy Air Allegro		
75-PY		Aquilair		
75-PZ	F-JFDV	Rans S-6 Coyote II		
75-QC		Cosmos		
75-QG		Cosmos / La Mouette Top 14.9		
75-QL		Raj Hamsa X'Air		
75-RG		Air Création / Fun		
75-RJ		Aviasud AE209 Albatros		
75-SB		Cosmos		
75-UU		Air Création GTE / Kiss		
75-UX		Adventure Platinum paramotor		
75-VP		Air Création GTE / Mild > Kiss		
75-VT	F-JXUH	DTA Combo / La Mouette Ipsos 14.9		
75-VZ		Best Off Sky Ranger		
75-WE		DTA / La Mouette		
75-WI		trike / La Mouette		
75-WL		Cosmos / La Mouette Top 14.9		
75-WM		paramotor		
75-WN		Cosmos		
75-XH		DTA Combo / La Mouette		
75-XI	F-JEFM	Best Off Sky Ranger	0511660	
75-XL		Jojowing Instinct paramotor		
75-XN		La Mouette / Cosmos Chronos		
75-XO		Cosmos / La Mouette Top 14.9		
75-XR		Magni M-24 Orion	24-10-5894	
75-XW	F-JSJV	DTA (trike)/La Mouette wing		
75-YF	F-JTAB	ELA Aviacion ELA-07S	0511 332 0712	

76 : Seine-Maritime

Reg	F-reg	Type	Serial	Other
76-AX		Vector		
76-CC		Micro Aviation Pulsar		
76-CG	F-JAEN	Weedhopper		
76-CI		Weedhopper		
76-CM		gyrocopter		
76-DG		Air Création / SX		
76-DL		Synairgie		
76-EG		Foxi / Synairgie Puma 14		
76-EN		Synairgie / Puma Bi		
76-EO		Raj Hamsa X'Air		95-GV
76-FA		Synairgie / Puma Bi		
		(Re-regd 50-GE)		
76-FK		(Weedhopper ?) AX-3		
76-FO		Air Création / Fun 18		
76-FU		(Weedhopper ?) AX-3		
76-GD		Synairgie		
76-GH		Fly Synthesis Storch 582		
		(Crashed 6.8.08)		
76-GK		Air Création / Mild		
76-GX		Dubois / Elipse / DTA Dynamic 15/430	97/008	
76-HH	F-JZAD	Croses EC-12 Criquet	177	
76-HR		Air Création / XP		
76-HS		Weedhopper		

Reg	Call-sign	Type	c/n	Notes
76-IB		Alisport Yuma		
76-IH		Zenair CH-701 STOL		
76-IL	F-JFWP	Croses LC-6 UL		
76-IM	F-JFWY	Aviasud Mistral		
76-IR		Fly Synthesis Storch SS		
		(Damaged 23.3.06)		
76-IS		Air Création		
76-IX		Raj Hamsa X'Air 602T		
76-JB		Air Création / Kiss		
76-JC		Serval		
76-JF		ICP-MXP-740 Savannah		
76-JG		ICP MXP-740 Savannah	11-00-51-031	
76-JM		III Sky Arrow 500TF		
76-JV	F-JHTY	Rans S-6 Coyote II	0492293	
76-JX		Air Création / XP		
76-KB		Raj Hamsa X'Air		
76-KC		Liberty APL-01	01	F-PDLJ
76-KF	F-JFVU	Pipistrel Sinus		
76-KH		Raj Hamsa X'Air F		
76-KI	F-JFVR	AMF Chevron 2-32C		
76-KJ		Air Création GTE Clipper / iXess		
76-KL		Croses EC-6		
76-KN		Air Création GTE Clipper / iXess		
76-KT		Michelet gyrocopter		
76-KV		Zenair CH-601XL Zodiac		
76-KY		Mignet HM.293W Pou-du-Ciel	01	F-PYHD
76-KZ		gyrocopter		
76-LJ		European Airwings Springbok 3000		
76-LS	F-JFWU	Comco Ikarus Fox-C22		
76-LZ		Guérin G1	912SFR080411	
		(Re-regd HA-YAMP 11.08)		
76-MG		DTA / Dynamic 15/450		
76-MI		Air Création		
76-MN	F-JPFX	Pipistrel Sinus	157 S912 204	
76-MO	F-JSLA	ICP MXP-740 Savannah 912		
76-MQ	F-JPFY	Hipps Superbirds J-3 Kitten		
W76-MR		paramotor		
76-MS		Aero Kuhlmann Scub JPX		
76-MU		B&F Funk FK-9		
76-MZ	F-JPNK	Cellier Xenon		
76-NB	F-JPNM	Sauper J.300 Joker		
76-NG	F-JFQK	Magni M-16 Tandem Trainer		
76-NI		European Airwings Springbok 3000		
76-NJ		Air Création / Fun 14		
76-NT	F-JYGO	Guérin G1		
76-NW		ICP Bingo 4S	05-11-52-195	
76-NZ		European Airwings Springbok		
76-OG		Air Création		
76-OO		Air Création / iXess		
76-OQ	F-JZXG	TL Ultralight TL-2000 Sting Carbon		
76-OX	F-JYHO	Guérin G1		
76-PD		Aquilair		
76-PG		DTA / Dynamic 15/430		
76-PU		Rans S-10 Sakota		
76-PV		Ekolot JK-05 Junior	05 06 05	
76-PW	F-JXHX	Zenair CH-601XL Zodiac		
76-PX	F-JXGB	Flight Design CT SW	07-07-25	
		(Same c/n and call-sign as 45-ACZ)		
76-PY		ATEC Zephyr		
76-QB		G1 Aviation G1 SPYL		
76-QI		Jora		
76-QM	F-JXLX	ICP MXP-740 Savannah VG	07-07-51-623	
76-QP	F-JWNG	Guérin G1		F-JXXL
76-QT	F-JXSD	Best Off Sky Ranger	02/12303	OO-E38
76-QW		Pipistrel Virus		
76-QZ	F-JRCP	Jora		
76-RI		Fly Synthesis Storch		
76-RJ		Guérin G1		
76-RP		Aircopter A3C		
76-RQ		Air Création / iXess		
76-RR	F-JWQL	Fly Synthesis Storch		
76-RW		Autogyro-Europe MT-03		
76-RZ		Weedhopper Europa II		
76-SE	F-JWKW	Flight Design CT LS		
		(Re-regd 34-AIK)		
76-SN	F-JPFZ	ELA Aviacion ELA-07S		
76-SP	F-JWRR	Dyn'Aéro MCR-01	381	
76-SW		ITV paramotor		
76-SZ		ICP Bingo 4S	08-07-52-225	
76-TA	F-JRCM	Aveko VL-3 Sprint	VL3-44	
76-TE	F-JRII	DTA Combo / Diva		
76-TM		Evektor EV-97 Eurostar	2000 0812	OO-F91, PH-3R4
76-TP	F-JJPD	Best Off Sky Ranger		
76-TU	F-JRXN	Air Création Twin Buggy / iXess		
76-TX		Air Création GT BI / XP		
76-TY	F-JSAG	Best Off Nynja		
76-UA	F-JVPG	Averso AX-02 Guépard gyrocopter		
76-UB	F-JSRG	Autogyro-Europe Calidus 09		
76-UC		Phoenix Air Phoenix U-15		
76-UE		Autogyro Europe Calidus		
76-UF	F-JSXO	Pagotto Brako gyro GT912S		
76-UJ		Best Off Nynja 912S		
76-UM	F-JTHB	G1 Aviation G1 SPYL		
76-UO	F-JEZG	PJB Vega 912T		
W76-UP		Colomban MC-30 Luciole	3	
76-UT		weightshift		
76-VN		ITV paramotor		
76-WC		Aiglon		
		(W/o 8.11.15)		
76-WT		Spacek SD-1 Minisport TG	103	W76-WT
76-ACO		Celier Xenon		
		(Out of sequence)		

77 : Seine-et-Marne

Reg	Call-sign	Type	c/n	Notes
77-N		Veliplane		
77-BA		Veliplane		
77-BH		Comco Ikarus Fox-C22		
77-BJ		Falcon		
77-BN		Veliplane		
77-BS		Croses Airplume	10	
77-BT		Profile (trike)		
77-CH		Zenith Baroudeur		
77-CK		Veliplane		
77-CL		Veliplane		
77-CU		Zenith Baroudeur 2000		
77-DC		Veliplane		
77-DE		Titan / Zenith (trike)		
77-DG		Air Création		
77-DH		Dynamic		
77-DI		Veliplane		
77-DK		Rans S-7 Courier		
77-DN		Mignet HM.1000 Balerit	02	
77-DQ		Aviasud Mistral		
77-DU		Zenith Baroudeur		
77-DY		Zenith Baroudeur		
77-EA		Zenith Baroudeur		
77-EE		Zenith Baroudeur		
77-EG		Air Création		
77-ES		Etendard 493 (also reported as Air Création)		
77-FD		weightshift		
77-FH		Saphir		
77-FZ		Air Création / SX		
77-GD		Mainair Gemini / Flash IIA		
77-GK		Humbert La Moto-du-Ciel		
		(Accident 7.7.07)		
77-GN		Propulsar paramotor		
77-GP		Paraman Powerchute		
		(Now reported as Aquilair IP)		
77-GS		Mainair Gemini / Flash IIA		
77-GY		Zenith Baroudeur		
77-HH		Mainair Gemini / Flash IIA		
77-HN		SG Aviation Storm		
77-HV		Zenith Baroudeur		
77-ID		Air Création		
77-IK		Air's Maestro		
77-IM		Cosmos (Mainair wing?)		
77-IS		Powerchute		
77-JA		Zenith Baroudeur		
77-JF		Air Création GT BI / Quartz		
77-JH		Cosmos / La Mouette		
77-JV	F-JFCM	Zenith Baroudeur		
77-JZ		Zenair CH-601XL Zodiac		
77-KA		Air's Maestro		
77-KC		(Quad City ?) Challenger		
77-KD		Eipper Quicksilver GT500		
77-LB		Air Création / Cosmos		
77-LC		Zenith Baroudeur		
W77-LD		Zenith Baroudeur		
77-LF		C.Jupitor		
77-LG		Denney Kitfox		
77-LL		Rans S-6 Coyote II		
77-LQ	F-JFEC	Air Création / Cosmos Chronos		
77-LY		Air Création Safari GT BI		
77-MD		TEAM Mini-MAX		
77-MH		Air Création / Cosmos Chronos 16		
77-MK	F-JFBY	BR / Ghost 18		
77-MJ		Weedhopper		
77-MQ		paramotor		
77-MS		Air Création GT / Fun		
77-MU		Air Création GT BI / Fun		
77-MX		Air Création / Cosmos		
77-NB		Cosmos Chronos		
77-NS		Cosmos Chronos 16	B968	
77-NV		ITV Dakota Sport paramotor		
77-NX		Adventure 210 paramotor		
77-OH		Zenith (Baroudeur ?)		
77-PJ		Dynali Chickinox		
77-PK		Dynali Chickinox		
77-PV		Barry MB-02 Souricette		
77-PW		ICP MXP-740 Savannah		
77-QY		(Technic Moto ?) Mustang		
77-RK		Aviatika MAI-890		
77-RL		Air Création / Cosmos Chronos 16		
		(Re-regd 89-IU)		
77-RS		Rans S-6 Coyote II		
77-RT		Rans S-6 Coyote II		
77-SG		ITV Lampoon paramotor		
77-SK		Rans S-6 Coyote II		
77-SL		Rans S-6ESD Coyote II		
77-ST		Aviasud AE209 Albatros	107	
77-SV		Weedhopper AX-3		
77-TK	F-JFDS	Rans S-7 Courier		
		(To, or ex 60-SV)		
77-TX		Rans S-6ESD Coyote II		
77-TY		Rans S-6ESD Coyote II		
77-UD		Rans S-12 Airaile		
77-UE		Air Création Fun GT BI / Cosmos Chronos 16		
		(Damaged 1.5.04)		
77-US		Cosmos / Aeros		
77-UY		Alexandre		
77-VC	F-JCWI	Raj Hamsa X'Air		
77-VD		Humbert Tetras		
77-VE		Air Création Twin / XP		
77-VF		Cosmos		
77-VG		Raj Hamsa X'Air		
77-VH		Saphir		
77-VI		Mignet HM.293 Pou-du-Ciel		
		(Accident 27.5.06)		
77-VL	F-JCUQ	Air Création GTE Clipper		
77-VO		Aéro Services Guépard 912		
77-VQ		Raj Hamsa X'Air		
77-WJ	F-JXYB	Best Off Sky Ranger		
		(Re-regd or error 77-AWJ ?)		
77-XK		Micro Aviation Pulsar III		
77-XP		Cosmos		
77-XQ	F-JFCW	Morin M-81 Aquilon		
77-XY		Air Création / Cosmos		
77-YA		Zenith Baroudeur		
77-YE		Air Création Twin / XP		
77-YF		Cosmos		
77-YI		Nike Aeronautica / Pegasus		
77-YN		Comco Ikarus C-42		
77-YP		Cosmos		
77-YS		Aéro Services Guépy (Jabiru) 80		
		(Reported damaged 3.4.06)		
77-YZ		Air Création / XP		
77-ZD	F-JFAE	Tecnam P.92S Echo		
		(Re-regd 18-OY)		
77-ZV	F-JFAI	Tecnam P.92S Echo	383	
77-ZW		Rans S-6 Coyote II		81-BE?
77-ZY		Pocino SE.5A replica (Painted "D3540")	21	

Regn	Call-sign	Type	c/n	Other
77-AAE		Barry MB-02 Souricette		
W77-AAH		Air Création		
		(W/o 6.03)		
77-AAI		gyrocopter "Andre Terrasson"		
77-AAU		Eipper Quicksilver MX		
77-AAY		Barry MB-02 Souricette		
W77-AAZ		amphibian prototype		
77-AAZ		weightshift		
77-ABC		Gatard Statoplan (AG-02 Poussin ?)		
77-ABF	F-JFAY	Eipper Quicksilver GT500	0120	
77-ABG		Cosmos		
77-ABH		Cosmos		
77-ABK		Air Création		
77-ABP		Rans S-6 Coyote II		
77-ABT		Weedhopper AX-3	1042092	79-EX
77-ABZ	F-JZSY	Flight Design CT		
77-ACB		Fantasy Air Allegro		
77-ACC		Weedhopper AX-3		
77-ACF		Hipps Superbirds J-3 Kitten		
77-ACG	F-JPOB	European Airwings Maestro II		
77-ACH	F-JPDK	Rans S-6 Coyote II		
77-ACR		Air Création / XP		
77-ACX		Cosmos / Phase 2		
77-ADA		Advance Epsilon paramotor		
77-ADF		DTA / Dynamic 450		
77-ADH		Chapelet / DTA Dynamic		
77-ADM		Air's Maestro 2		
77-ADO	F-JFCQ	Air Création GTE Clipper / XP		
77-ADQ		DTA / Dynamic 450		
77-ADR		Aquilair		
		(Crashed 6.6.04)		
77-ADT		Rans S-9 Chaos		
77-ADU		DTA / Dynamic 450		
77-ADW	F-JFBQ	Flight Design CT-2K		
		(Same call-sign as 77-AFL)		
77-AEB	F-JFFO	DTA / Dynamic 15/450	153	
		(previously reported as F-JYPT c/n 96-14)		
77-AEC		Zenith Baroudeur		
77-AEI		Air Bulle (trike)		
77-AEK		homebuilt		
77-AEL	F-JFBO	Flight Design CT-2K 912S		68-CO
		(Also recorded 6.09 as Weedhopper AX-3)		
77-AEM		Simonini Mini 2 paramotor		
		(Crashed 10.6.06)		
77-AEP		Dynali Chickinox		
77-AES	F-JFCZ	Ekolot JK-05 Junior		
77-AEW		Magni M-16 Tandem Trainer		
77-AFE		ICP MXP-740 Savannah	01-12-51-125	
		(Re-regd 89-PA)		
77-AFI		(Quad City ?) Challenger		02-CV
77-AFJ		Light Aero Avid Flyer		
77-AFK		Pegasus Quantum 912 Super Sport		
77-AFL	F-JFBQ	Flight Design CT-2K 912S		
		(Same call-sign as 77-ADW)		
77-AFM		Cosmos Chronos		
77-AFN	F-JFET	Zenith Baroudeur 2000	098C0190	
77-AFO	F-JFDX	Fly Synthesis Storch		
77-AFP		Cosmos		
77-AFR		Piel CP.150 Onyx		
77-AFS		Force (paramotor)		
77-AFT	F-JFEN	Tecnam P.96 Golf		
77-AFW		Air Création GTE / Cosmos Chronos II		
77-AFX		Best Off Sky Ranger		
77-AGA	F-JFEK	Light Aero Avid Lite		
		(Accident 22.7.08)		
77-AGB		Cosmos		
77-AGD	F-JPRH	Eipper Quicksilver GT500		
77-AGE	F-JFEO	Humbert Tetras		
77-AGF		Air Création GT BI / Solar Wings Pegasus		
77-AGG	F-JJCP	Best Off Sky Ranger		
77-AGH		Air Création / Quartz		
77-AGJ		Comco Ikarus C-42		
77-AGL		Cosmos	B21398	
77-AGP		Air Création Safari GT BI 503 / Kiss 450		
77-AGR		Synairgie		
77-AGS		Air Création "ITIN"		
77-AGT		Air Création GTE Clipper / XP		
77-AGZ		Cosmos / Aeros		
W77-AHH		Air Création GTE / Kiss 13		
		(W/o 1.6.03)		
77-AHK	F-JFFN	Best Off Sky Ranger		
77-AHL	F-JFFL	Light Aero Avid Flyer		18-JJ
77-AHN		Druine D.31 Turbulent		W77-AHN
77-AHO		Air Création GT		
77-AHP	F-JFFQ	Tecnam P.92S Echo		01-QC
		(Carried marks internally, 01-QC externally)		
77-AHR		Cosmos		
77-AHU		Zenair CH-601XL Zodiac	6-9237	62-ABN
77-AJA		Air Création GTE Clipper / XP		
77-AJB		Cosmos		
77-AJC	F-JPDZ	Best Off Sky Ranger 582		
77-AJL	F-JPDD	Best Off Sky Ranger	SKR0206550	
77-AJO		Air Création GTE Clipper / iXess		
77-AJP	F-JFDC	Air Création GTE / Kiss		
77-AJT	F-JFBB	Rans S-6 Coyote II (t/w)		
77-AJZ		EuroALA Jet Fox		
77-AKA		Best Off Sky Ranger		
77-AKB		Aviakit Vega		
77-AKC		Fly Synthesis Storch		
77-AKH		TL Ultralight TL-2000 Sting Carbon		
77-AKJ	F-JPDP	Light Aero Avid Flyer	979	F-PRKF, F-WRKF
77-AKL		Cosmos Chronos		
77-AKO	F-JPDX	Weedhopper AX-3	B3063113	
77-AKX		Cosmos / La Mouette Top 12.9		
77-AKY		Raj Hamsa X'Air F		
77-AKZ		DTA / Dynamic 16		
77-ALA		Tecnam P.2002 Sierra		
77-ALB	F-JPGH	B&F Funk FK-9 Mk.III	235	
77-ALC		Cosmos / La Mouette Ghost 12		
77-ALG		gyrocopter		
77-ALI		Best Off Sky Ranger		
77-ALK		B&F Funk FK-12 Comet		73-KD, 28-BI
		(Re-regs 25-UA)		
77-ALL		ZUT Aviation TT2000 STOL		
		(Damaged 26.2.05)		
77-ALO	F-JPGP	Air Création GTE Clipper		
77-ALQ		Air Création / XP		
77-ALR	F-JPMH	ICP Bingo 4S	04-05-52-149	
77-ALT		Fly Synthesis Storch		
77-ALY		Pietenpol Air Camper	DC-01	
77-AMA		Fly Synthesis Storch		
		(also reported as Pipistrel)		
77-AMJ		Air Création GTE / XP		
77-AMO		paramotor		
77-AMP		paramotor		
77-AMQ	F-JPMQ	Air Borne Edge XT-912 Streak III	XT912-39	
77-AMR	F-JPMR	Dyn'Aéro MCR-01 ULC	189	
77-AMU		Pipistrel Sinus 912		
77-AMV		Air Création GTE / XP		
77-AMW		Cosmos		
77-ANF		ITV Tepee paramotor		
77-ANJ		Ozone Research paramotor		
77-ANO		Cosmos / La Mouette		
77-ANV		Gyronours gyrocopter		W77-ANV
77-ANX		Dyn'Aéro MCR-01		
77-ANY		Best Off Sky Ranger		
77-ANZ		Zenair CH-701 STOL		
77-AOH		Zenair CH-601 Zodiac		
		(W/o 1.11.06)		
77-AOR	F-JZOZ	Aéro Services Guépy 582T		
77-AOT		Air Création / iXess		
77-AOU	F-JPRM	Tecnam P.92S Echo		
77-AOZ		Magni M-16 Tandem Trainer		
77-APE		Air Création Tanarg / iXess		
77-APH	F-JZSF	Magni M-16 Tandem Trainer	16-05-3294	
77-APJ	F-JPDJ	ELA Aviacion ELA-07S		
77-APM		ATEC 212 Solo		
77-APO		B&F Funk FK-12 Comet	12-012	31-DE/F-JIDE
77-APU		Air Création Tanarg / iXess		
77-APV	F-JZLF	DTA Combo / Dynamic 430/15	241	
77-APW		Cosmos		
77-APX		Cosmos / La Mouette Top 12.9		
77-APY		Airborne Edge XT-582 / Cruze		
77-APZ		DTA / Dynamic 430/15	24 .	
		(also reported as Flight Design CT believed error for 77-ARZ)		
77-AQK		ITV Equinoxe paramotor		
		(Also reported as Cosmos / Dynamic 15/430)		
77-AQM		Autogyro-Europe MT-03		
77-AQP		Best Off Sky Ranger		
77-AQQ	F-JZKQ	Comco Ikarus C-42		
77-AQR	F-JZDP	Best Off Sky Ranger		
77-AQX	F-JZGW	Aerospool WT-9 Dynamic	DY134/2006	
77-AQZ		Cosmos		
77-ARA		Cosmos		
77-ARC	F-JZHT	Aerospool WT-9 Dynamic	DY142/2006	
		(Same details quoted as 77-ART)		
77-ARF		European Airwings Springbok 3000		
77-ARH	F-JZJO	Polaris FIB	LOMAC c/n E3555E606	
77-ARI		ELA Aviacion ELA-07	0406 106 0724	
77-ARN	F-JZOI	Aéro Services Guépard 912		F-JARN, F-JIBX
77-ARP		Air Création / Kiss		
77-ARQ	F-JZQK	Air Borne XT-582	0019	
77-ART	F-JZRC	Aerospool WT-9 Dynamic	DY142/2006	
		(Same details quoted as 77-ARC)		
77-ARU	F-JFCO	Claude Leger Pataplume 2		
77-ARV		JPP 2 Quartz 18 BI paramotor		
		(Damaged 17.6.07)		
77-ARZ		Flight Design CT-2K		
77-ASA		Aviakit Vega		
77-ASC	F-JPMG	Air Création Tanarg 582 / iXess 15	A06168 / T06083	
77-ASE	F-JZWL	Pagotto Brako / Gryf CRS		
77-ASG		Air Création GTE Clipper / iXess		
77-ASM	F-JPMJ	TL Ultralight TL-2000 Sting carbon		
77-ASX	F-JYGB	Fly Synthesis Wallaby 582		
77-ASY	F-JHHP	ICP MXP-740 Savannah	07-00-51-015	61-HP
77-ATA		Cosmos		
77-ATI		Airborne XT-582 Skyhog		
77-ATM		Cosmos / La Mouette Ipsos 14		
77-ATN		Aviakit Vega		
77-ATQ	F-JPDW	Rans S-6 Coyote II		
77-ATT	F-JYOI	TL Ultralight TL-2000 Sting carbon		
77-ATV	F-JYLK	Alpi Aviation Pioneer 200		
77-ATW	F-JYLW	Airborne Edge XT-912B / Streak III	XT912-0169	
77-ATX	F-JYLX	Zenair CH-701 STOL		
77-AUD		Cosmos / Mach 14.9		
77-AUE	F-JYTD	Aéro Services Guépy 582		
77-AUG		Remos G.3 Mirage		
		(Also reported as Fly Synthesis Wallaby)		
77-AUH	F-JXET	ELA Aviacion ELA-07S	0407 148 0722	
77-AUJ	F-JXDR	ICP Bingo		
77-AUM		Zenair CH-601 Zodiac		
77-AUO	F-JYUX	ELA Aviacion ELA-07S	0507 153 0724	
77-AUP	F-JWOE	Airborne Edge XT-582 / Cruze	XT582-0012	F-JPGC
77-AUR		Humbert Tetras		
77-AUT		Air Création GTE Clipper / XP		
77-AUV	F-JYYV	Tecnam P.92 Echo		
77-AUW		DTA Combo / Dynamic 430/15	195	
77-AUY		Averso gyrocopter		
77-AVA		Magni M-22 Voyager	22-07-4674	
77-AVB		Zenair CH601UL Zodiac		W77-AVB
77-AVC		Zlin Savage (Jabiru) 2200		
77-AVF		Best Off Sky Ranger Swift		
77-AVH		Alpi Aviation Pioneer 200		
77-AVM		European Airwings Maestro 2		
77-AVP		Airborne Edge Outback 582 / Streak II		
77-AVT		Pagotto Brako / Gryf		
77-AVV	F-JXIZ	Alpi Aviation Pioneer 300		
77-AVY		Micro Aviation Pulsar III		
77-AVZ		Humbert Tetras 912B		
77-AWD	F-JHTH	Tecnam P.92 Echo Club		
77-AWI	F-JXSO	Tecnam P.2004 Bravo		
77-AWJ	F-JXYB	Best Off Sky Ranger		77-WJ ?
77-AWQ	F-JZWF	Tecnam P.2004 Bravo		
		(Call-sign also quoted for 73-PP)		
77-AWR	F-JXTB	Magni M-16 Tandem Trainer	16-08-4664	
		(Regn also qoted for M-22 Voyager 22-07-4584)		
77-AWS		Best Off Sky Ranger		
77-AWT	F-JHBS	Tecnam P.2002 Sierra	066	
77-AWU	F-JPUA	Aviakit Vega		45-WB
77-AWY	F-JZQK	Best Off Sky Ranger		F-JIJE

Regn	Mark	Type	c/n	Notes
77-AXA	F-JHHX	Raj Hamsa X'Air		
77-AXB		Mainair Gemini/Flash IIA		
77-AXE		Denney Kitfox	4499	
77-AXG	F-JZGG	P&M Aviation GT450-912	8385	
77-AXI		Rans S-6 Coyote II		
77-AXL		Aéro Services Super Guépard		
77-AXM		Air Création / XP		
77-AXP	F-JPTB	Aeroandinas MXP-1000 Tayrona		
			AA-06-05-90-007	
77-AXV	F-JRUZ	Magni M-16 Tandem Trainer		
77-AYA	F-JWAU	Airborne Edge XT-912 Tundra / Streak III		
77-AYP	F-JWFU	Best Off Sky Ranger		
77-AYQ	F-JWGZ	Airborne Redback / Wizard 3	503:1107	
77-AYR		Magni M-16 Tandem Trainer	16-03-2414	
77-AYT	F-JPAV	ICP Bingo	01-12-52-041	28-ZP
77-AYW		Cosmos	B21197	
77-AYY		gyrocopter		
77-AZB		DTA Voyageur II / Dynamic 450	00018	
77-AZG	F-JWMT	Rans S-6S Super Six		
77-AZJ		MA-3 Shaman 2 gyrocopter		
77-AZL		Zenair CH-701 STOL		
77-AZM	F-JGIF	Zlin Savage		
77-AZQ	F-JFIX	Best Off Sky Ranger		
77-AZT		Rans S-6 Coyote II (t/w)		
77-AZX	F-JWTQ	B&F Funk FK-14B Polaris	14-100	
77-AZZ		Evektor EV-97 Eurostar		
77-BAB		Humbert Tetras		
77-BAD	F-JZTZ	Rans S-7 Courier		
77-BAK		Fly Products/Jojowing Quest II paramotor		
77-BAM	F-JYFX	Fly Synthesis Storch HS		
77-BAP		Cosmos / Dynamic 15/430	B968	
77-BAU	F-JXMU	Aeropro Eurofox		
77-BAX		DTA / Dynamic 450	226	
77-BAY	F-JJKJ	ICP MXP-740 Savannah	02-01-51-146	11-DR
77-BAZ	F-JXUE	Airborne Outback HKS700	1076	
77-BBA	F-JZUS	Aeropro Eurofox	CH-02/03	
		(severely damaged 16.1.11)		
77-BBC	F-JKTL	Gatard AG-02 Poussin	7	16-CM, 87-CW, F-PYBS
77-BBD		Airborne XT-912-SST		
		(W/o 18.8.09)		
77-BBF		Sol'R airship		W77-BBF
77-BBG		Fly Synthesis Storch		
		(See 11-BBG which was probably an error)		
77-BBS		TEAM Air-Bike		
77-BBX		Cosmos		
77-BCC	F-JRJC	ELA Aviacion ELA-07	0909 270 0712	
77-BCE		Pro.Mecc. Sparviero SP10		
77-BCH		P&M Quik GT		
77-BCK		Ekolot JK-05 Junior	05 08 03	
77-BCN	F-JROM	Air Création Tanarg / Bionix		
77-BCO	F-JROP	Aerospool WT-9 Dynamic	DY351/2010	
77-BCP	F-JRQU	Best Off Nynja		
77-BCR		Dynali Chickinox Kot-Kot		
77-BCV		Cosmos / La Mouette Top 12.9	B21189	
77-BCY	F-JRZX	European Airwings Springbok 3000		
77-BDA		Air Création GT BI / Fun 450		
77-BDB		Airborne Edge XT-912 Tundra SST	0353	
		(Wearing two call-signs 9.11: F-JPGA & F-JRUC)		
77-BDC	F-JRUF	Autogyro-Europe Calidus 09		
77-BDD	F-JPGA	Airborne Edge XT-582	0029	
77-BDF		DTA / Dynamic 16		
77-BDJ		Celier Xenon	CAC10674S	
77-BDO		weightshift		
77-BDQ		Autogyro-Europe MTOsport		
77-BDT	F-JRZL	Aveko VL-3 Sprint		
77-BDW	F-JSAD	Magni M-16 Tandem Trainer	16-10-5884	
77-BDY	F-JSAH	Humbert La Moto-du-Ciel		
77-BDZ		Magni M-22 Voyager	22-07-4184	
		(Same c/n as 41-PA)		
77-BEC		Comco Ikarus Fox-C22		
77-BEG	F-JSDU	Aeroandinas MXP-800 Calima	AA-02-10-82-039	
		(Modified by MSL Aero as MSL Type H)		
77-BEH	F-JSOH	Jodel D.92 Bébé	898	
77-BEK		La Mouette		
77-BEL	F-JGGI	ATEC 122 Zephyr 2004C	Z881203S	
		(Same c/n listed for 51-LI and 51-MF)		
77-BEO		Air Création Tanarg / BioniX 15		
77-BEP	F-JYKM	Flight Design CT SW		71-OX ?
77-BEQ	F-JSET	AirLony Skylane UL		
77-BER		Mignet HM.1000 Balerit		
77-BET		Air Création Buggy		
77-BEZ		Air Création GTE / Fun 450		
77-BFB	F-JSIN	Dyn'Aéro MCR Pick-Up	149	
77-BFD		Air Création GT		
77-BFL		Alpi Aviation Pioneer 300		
77-BFO		Air Création Tanarg / BioniX		
77-BFR	F-JZCI	Aerospool WT-9 Dynamic	DY123/2006	28-AHR
77-BFW		Celier Xenon	CAC134756	
77-BFX		Halley Apollo Fox	150509 FR	
77-BFY	F-JSUV	Air Création GTE Clipper / iXess		
77-BGE		Remos G.3/600 Mirage		
77-BGG	F-JSYK	ELA Aviacion ELA-07S	0411 329 0712	
77-BGH		Flight Design CT LS		
77-BGK	F-JRWD	Evektor EV-97 Eurostar		
77-BGP	F-JRUC	Airborne XT-912 / Cruze		
77-BGQ	F-JTDG	Zlin Savage Cruiser		
77-BGU	F-JTFO	Air Création GTE / Fun 450		
77-BGX		Aerospool WT-9 Dynamic		
77-BGZ		DTA Dynamic		
77-BHA	F-JTHJ	Aéro Services SG.10A 912S		
77-BHB		ELA Aviacion ELA-07S Cougar	0311 342 0712	
77-BHD		Best Off Sky Ranger		
77-BHE	F-JFEY	Evektor EV-97 Sportstar	2007 0911	95-WE
77-BHG	F-JTFA	B&F Funk FK-14 Polaris		
77-BHJ	F-JGVE	Fantasy Air Allegro SW	04-135	67-VZ
77-BHK	F-JROU	Best Off Sky Ranger		
77-BHN		Magni M-22 Voyager		
77-BHO		Alpi Aviation Pioneer 300STD		
77-BHV	F-JTND	Flight Design CT LS	F-11-11-01	
77-BHW	F-JTNF	Comco Ikarus C-42	1201-7184	
77-BHX	F-JTNU	DTA J-RO gyrocopter		
77-BIB		Magni M-16 Tandem Trainer		
77-BIC		Magni gyrocopter		
77-BIQ		DTA Combo / Diva		
77-BIY	F-JWIT	P&M Aviation Quik GTR Explorer	8629	
77-BJB	F-JUBL	Aviasud Mistral 582 Trainer	201	OO-B70
77-BJF		Airborne Edge		
77-BJG		Aéro Services SG.10A		
77-BJH	F-JXUE	Airborne Edge XT-912 Outback / Merlin	107609	
77-BJI	F-JUHY	ELA Aviacion ELA-07 Cougar	0912 379 0712	
77-BJK		Magni M-16 Tandem Trainer	16-07-4214	
77-BJL	F-JYLW	Airborne Edge XT / Arrow	XT912-0169	
77-BJP	F-JULX	ICP MXP-740 Savannah VG XL	10-02-51-90.	
77-BJQ		Alpi Aviation Pioneer 300		
77-BJT		ELA Aviacion ELA-07		
77-BJV	F-JUSC	Spacek SD-1 Minisport TD	061	
77-BJX		Magni M-22 Voyager		
77-BKD	F-JUWM	ELA Aviacion ELA-07S		
77-BKE	F-JXTB	Magni M-16 Tandem Trainer		
		(See also 77-AWR, same owner ?)		
77-BKT	F-JVWY	Dynali H3 Easyflyer		
77-BLC	F-JVIZ	Best Off Nynja	1311148	
77-BLM	F-JVNX	ELA Aviacion ELA-07	0314-416-0712	
77-BME		Ozone paramotor		
77-BMF	F-JVUX	Didier Pti'tavion		
77-BMG	F-JVUZ	Magni M-16 Tandem Trainer		
77-BMM		ITV paramotor		
77-BMO		Aéro Services SG.10A		
77-BMY		Autogyro-Europe MTOsport		
77-BNB		Zlin Savage Cruiser	290	
77-BNC		Aero Designs Pulsar XP		
77-BNF		Nicollier HN.433 Ménestrel	37	F-PYJZ
77-BNH		Autogyro-Europe MTOsport		
77-BNJ		DTA J'Ro		
77-BNS		Celier Xenon 2 RST	CAD05572S	LY-BBH, OK-PWA 10, OK-NWA 05
77-BOO	F-JVVC	ELA Aviacion ELA-07S	0615 443 0714	
77-BOQ	F-JVXS	Magni M-22 Voyager		
77-BPO	F-JAMQ	Trixy G4-2	051-16	
77-FNB		Ozone paramotor		
		(Regn as applied to wing, possibly 77-BNF intended?)		

78 : Yvelines

Regn	Mark	Type	c/n	Notes
78-Q		Weedhopper		
78-AI		Veliplane		
78-AS		AILE Patrilor 3		
78-BK		Jokair Maestro		
78-CM		Mignet Touraco		
78-CN		Synairgie		
78-DM		Zenith Baroudeur		
78-DN		Veliplane Mustang		
78-DS		Air's Maestro		
78-FG		(Air Création ?) Safari		
78-FN		Best Off Sky Ranger		
78-FY		Eipper Quicksilver MXL II		
78-GK		Aviasud Mistral		
F-78HV		Murphy Renegade Spirit		
78-IM	F-JPMK	Aviasud Mistral		
78-JE		Comco Ikarus Fox-C22		
78-JK		Cosmos		
78-JR		Powerchute		
78-KJ		Weedhopper		
78-KR		Zodiac Ultrastar		
78-KV		Weedhopper AX-3 (or Baroudeur?)		70-CF
78-KY		Air's Maestro		
78-LF		Djicat (Buse'Air 150?)		
		(W/o 23.1.99)		
78-MA		Kolb Twinstar		
78-MI		Rans S-6 Coyote II		
78-MK		Aviatika MAI-890	040	
		(Re-regd EI-FEP 4.14)		
78-NC		Weedhopper (f/p) (possibly Raj Hamsa X'Air)		
78-NK		GB 14 Bis		
78-PJ		Cosmos		
78-PV		ICP MXP-740 Savannah		
78-QF		Best Off Sky Ranger		
78-QV		Serval		
78-QY		Zenair CH-601 Zodiac	6-9017	
78-RE	F-JFCE	Alisport Yuma/Guérin G1	FELS 03 06 00	
78-RO	F-JFBJ	Aéro Services Guépy (Jabiru) 80		
78-RU		Vidor Asso V Champion		
78-SF		Tecma Medium 17 (trike)		
78-SG		Pulsar		
78-SM	F-JHXF	3XTrim EOL-2		
78-TJ		ITV Turquoise paramotor		
78-VA		ITV Tomahawk 2 paramotor		
		(W/o 8.05)		
78-WV		Skywalk Cayenne		
78-XG	F-JFPQ	Dyn'Aéro MCR-01 UL	121	45-NP
78-XU		Jojowing Instinct paramotor		
		(W/o in mid-air collision with 75-XL)		
78-XY		Alouette trike / Nervures Everglades paramotor		
78-XZ	F-JYIQ	Guérin G1		
78-YG	F-JYUG	Flying Machines FM250 Vampire		
78-YZ		Evektor EV-97 Eurostar	2007 2923	
		(Re-regd 72-OP)		
78-ZK	F-JZER	AirLony Skylane UL		
		(Same call-sign as 37-VA)		
78-ZL	F-JHDC	Alpi Aviation Pioneer 200		85-PG
78-ZO	F-JXPN	Celier Xenon	CAI 03171S	
78-ZW	F-JPNR	Djicat Buse'Air 150		
78-ZZ	F-JPKR	Light Aero Avid Flyer	264	28-ACU, F-PZUD, F-WZUD
		(Noted as 28-ACU, 7.2011)		
78-AAB	F-JXUT	AirLony Skylane UL		
78-AAM	F-JKDZ	Lucas L.11		
78-AAQ		Light Aero Avid Lite	1961	
78-AAS	F-JZLS	B&F Funk FK-9 Mk.III	09-135	
78-AAW	F-JCWO	Magni M-16 Tandem Trainer	16-08-4944	
78-ABA	F-JXKN	Aerospool WT-9 Dynamic	DY205/2007	
78-ABC	F-JHRC	Humbert Tetras		22-GW ?
78-ABF		Zodiac Ultrastar		
78-ABG	F-JXQI	Aerospool WT-9 Dynamic	DY223/2008	67-BCC
78-ABY	F-JWRX	Flight Design CT		
78-ACP	F-JRVV	Zenair CH-601XL Zodiac (t/w)	6-8406	
78-ACU		AEF Monotrace / Ellipse Fuji Alizé		
78-ADQ		Evektor EV-97 Eurostar SL	2009 3520	95-ZL
78-AEF		ZJ Viera		
78-AEG	F-JRNA	Zlin Savage Cruiser		
78-AEN	F-JXZO	ICP MXP-740 Savannah VG	08-02-51-680	27-YK
78-AEP	F-JXAR	Rans S-6 Coyote II		

Reg	F-reg	Type	Serial	Other
78-AEX	F-JRXV	Evektor EV-97 Eurostar SL		
		(Noted as 78-AFX, 8.14)		
78-AFH		AirMax SeaMax M-22		
78-AFQ		Aeropro Eurofox		
78-AFT		Adventure X Race/Flexway paramotor		
78-AFX		Evektor EV-97 Eurostar SL		
78-AGD		Plätzer Kiebitz : built as Pyt'Air	001	
78-AGI	F-JSYE	AirMax SeaMax M-22		
78-AGX		Aerostyle Breezer UL	UL83	95-AAL/
				F-JRWE
78-AGY	F-JWUF	Evektor EV-97 Eurostar SL		49-RZ/F-JWUF
78-AHN		Vidor Asso V Champion		
78-AJA	F-JUCF	B.O.T. SC07 Speed Cruiser		
78-AJM		BRM Aero Bristell NG5		
78-AJN		paramotor		
78-AJS		Dudek Nucleon paramotor		
78-AJX		Sonex Aircraft Sonex	1197	
78-AKB		DTA J-RO gyrocopter		
78-ALN	F-JVRL	Best Off Nynja		
78-ALT	F-JVWA	JMB Aircraft VL-3 Evolution	VL3-138	
78-AOF		Adventure Flex-Race RC18 paramotor		
78-AUM		BRM Aero Bristell UL		
		(Possibly error for 78-AJM ?)		

79 : Deux-Sèvres

Reg	F-reg	Type	Serial	Other
79-R		(Technic Moto ?) Mustang		
79-S		Quartz		
79-X		weightshift		
79-AB		Aviasud Mistral		
79-AK		Air Création / Kiss		
79-AL		Air Création Twin / Mild		
79-AO		DTA 582 Dynamic 15		
		(W/o 14.3.04)		
79-AP		Air Création / Kiss		
79-AU	F-JKRB	Anglin J-6 Karatoo		
79-AV		Air Création		
79-AX		Air Création / iXess		
79-AZ		Air Création Racer / Fun 14		
79-BC		Pottier P.320 UL	1	
79-BE		Air Création / SX		
79-BF		Air Création / SX		
79-BG		Air Création / SX		
79-BH		RS	01	
79-BJ		Air Création / Quartz		
79-BM		Air Création / Quartz		
79-BN		JC-24 Weedhopper		
79-BP	F-JKRX	Aerospool WT-9 Dynamic		
79-BQ		Zenair CH-701 STOL		
79-BS		Air Création / SX		
79-BU		Air Création		
79-BY		Air Création		
79-BZ		Air Création GT BI 503 / XP12		
79-CB(1)		Air Création / SX		
79-CB(2)		Averso AX.02 Guépard gyrocopter		
79-CD		Air Création Buggy		
79-CI		Air Création / Kiss		
79-CK		Air Création		
79-DH		Pottier P.320 UL		
79-DK		Air Création		
79-DL		Air Création / SX		
79-DR		Air Création / XP		
79-DS		Air Création / XP		
79-DU		Air Création		
79-DV		Comco Ikarus Fox-C22		
79-DY		Best Off Sky Ranger		
79-EC	F-JKVB	Magni M-16 Tandem Trainer		
79-EF		Air Création		
79-EG	F-JKTA	Pottier P.320 UL	2	
79-EK		weightshift		
79-EP		Magni M-22 Voyager	22-05-3394	
79-EQ	F-JBUE	Rans S-6 Coyote II		
79-ES		Air Création		
79-EX		Air Création / Mild		
79-EY		Weedhopper		
79-FA		TL Ultralight TL-232 Condor		
79-FC		Light Aero Avid Flyer		
79-FE		Air Création / Quartz		
79-FJ		Air Création		
79-FK		Air Création / Kiss		
79-FM		Weedhopper AX-3		
79-FR		Air Création		
79-GH		Fly Synthesis Storch 582		
		(W/o 6.8.08)		
79-GI		Rans S-6 Coyote II		
79-GJ	F-JZGJ	Aeroprakt A-22 Vision	067	
79-GK		Micro Aviation Pulsar II		
79-GL		Weedhopper AX-3		
79-GP		Fly Synthesis Storch HS		
79-GQ	F-JYAX	Aéro Services Super Guépard 912S		
79-HD	F-JKWO	DTA / Dynamic 15/450		
79-HI		Sauper J.300 Joker		
W79-HP		Boyer 2 seat gyrocopter		
79-HV	F-JKUH	Druine D.31 Turbulent		
79-HW		Magni M-24 Orion	24-08-4914	
79-IA	F-JWLJ	Aeropro Eurofox		
79-IE		Air Création Racer / Fun		
79-ID	F-JXZJ	Air Création GTE Trek HKS700 / iXess 13		
			A07140-7138/T07062	
79-IM		Air Création GTE / SX		
79-IV		Mignet HM.293M Pou-du-Ciel	600	14-FP, W14-FP,
		(Wears «Aéroports de Paris » titlles)		F-PVQM, F-WVQM
79-IW		B&F Funk FK-14A Polaris	14-030	59-CMR,
				OO-D91
79-IZ		Air Création Tanarg 912		
		(Dbr 8.2.11)		
79-JC		BRM Land Africa	0161.912UL.10-LA	
79-JD	F-JHVT	Magni M-16 Tandem Trainer	16-08-4814	
79-JE		Weedhopper (single seater)		
79-JF	F-JKTZ	EuroALA Jet Fox		
79-JJ		Flight Design CT-2K	7886/02-01-04-04	G-CBLV
79-JK	F-JWNU	Autogyro-Europe MTOsport		
79-JQ		Alizon		
		(Also reported as Humbert Tetras)		
79-KA		Weedhopper AX-3		
79-KC		Rans S-6 Coyote II		
79-KD		Rans S-6 Coyote II		

Reg	F-reg	Type	Serial	Other
79-LB		Didier Pti'tavion		
79-LQ		ATEC Zephyr 2000		
79-LX		Weedhopper AX-3		
79-LZ		Best Off Sky Ranger		
79-MY		Rans S-6 Coyote II S-116	0796/1016S	F-PSLE,
				F-WSLE
79-OI		Zenair CH-701 STOL		
79-QL		ICP MXP-740 Savannah	01-04-51-068	

80 : Somme

Reg	F-reg	Type	Serial	Other
80-C		Weedhopper		
80-D		Air Création		
80-AB		Aviasud Mistral		
80-AF		Cosmos / Comet 16	1112	
80-AI		Air Création Twin		
80-AV		Air Création		
80-AY		Eipper Quicksilver		
80-BI		Synairgie		
80-BK		Weedhopper (f/p)		
		(Re-regd 06-AJ)		
80-BO		Synairgie		
80-BU		Synairgie Puma Bi		
80-CB		Weedhopper AX-3		
80-CC		Best Off Sky Ranger		
80-CE		Synairgie Dauphin		
80-CG(1)		Synairgie/Air Action		
80-CG(2)	F-JFXU	Cosmos Fidji / Mach 14.9	1071	
80-CH		Synairgie/Air Action		
80-CK		Synairgie Dauphin		
80-CL		Cyclone AX-3		
80-CP		Synairgie Dauphin		
80-CQ		Air Création GT BI / Kiss		
80-CR		Quartz ZSX		
		(Noted 9.07 as Weedhopper AX-3)		
80-CS		Best Off Sky Ranger		
80-DD		Micro Aviation Pulsar		
80-DE		Cyclone AX-3		
80-DF		Cyclone AX-3	C3073132	
80-DI		Air Création		
80-DK		Lorafly		
80-DL		Best Off Sky Ranger		
80-DM		Air Création / SX		
80-DV		Air Création		
80-DW		Air Création GTE / Fun		
80-DX		Best Off Sky Ranger		
80-EB		Air Création GTE / Fun (or Mild?)		
80-EF		Air Création / XP		
80-EH		"Little Mouse" (Homebuilt = Souricette?)		
80-EM		Mignet HM.293 Pou-du-Ciel		
80-EO		Cyclone AX-3	C3083143	
		(Now reported as CFM Shadow)		
80-EP		Air Création / XP		
80-EQ		Air Création / Fun		
80-ER		Air Création GTE		
80-ES		Air Création GTE / Fun (or Mild?)		
80-ET		Air Création GTE / Fun (or Mild?)		
80-EU		Air Création		
80-EV	F-JBAS	Rans S-6 Coyote II		
80-FE		Ranger 582 / La Mouette Top 12.9		
80-FO		Air Création		
80-FQ		Air Création / Quartz		
80-FS		Best Off Sky Ranger		
80-FT		Air Création GTE Clipper		
80-GA		Best Off Sky Ranger		
80-GB		Cyclone AX-3	C3123184	
80-GE		Best Off Sky Ranger		
80-GF		Air Création / Quartz		
80-GI		Air Création		
80-GJ		Air Création GTE		
80-GN		Air Création Buggy		
80-GO	F-JFXA	Aéro Services Guépy 582		
80-GP		Air Création		
80-GT		Air Création GTE Clipper / Mild		
80-GV		Dallach D4 Fascination		
80-GX		Aviakit Hermes		
80-GY	F-JCMV	Cosmos	21320	
80-GZ		Air Création		
80-HD		Air Création / XP12	A98/009	
80-HF		Mignet HM.293A Pou-du-Ciel		
80-HG		Mignet HM.293A Pou-du-Ciel		
80-HI	F-JFZM	Rans S-12 Airaile		
80-HJ	F-JFXB	Cosmos / Mach 14.9	C1106	
80-HK		Cosmos		
80-HL		Air Création GTE / XP	T99078	
80-HM		Synairgie / Puma		
80-HQ		Cosmos		
80-IC		Air Création / Kiss		
80-ID	F-JFXV	ZUT Aviation TT2000 STOL	9906220	
80-IF		Air Création / Fun 18QC	A99072-9077	
80-IH	F-JSMH	Cosmos	21395	
W80-IK		gyrocopter		
80-IL		Jodel D.92 Bébé	354	F-PFRB
80-IM		Eipper Quicksilver GT500		
80-IO		Cualt 200		
80-IV	F-JFXQ	Air Création GTE / iXess XP15	A99137-9140	
80-IX		Air Création / Kiss 450B	A00185-181	
80-JA		Air Création / Kiss		
80-JF		Air Création		
80-JG		Air Création / XP		
80-JI	F-JFZD	Best Off Sky Ranger	SKR0011080	
80-JL		Air Création Dauphin		
80-JN		Air Création GTE Clipper		
80-JU		Best Off Sky Ranger		
80-JW		Air Création GTE / Kiss		
80-KB		Air Création GTE / Kiss	A02036-2026	
80-KF		Zenair CH-701 STOL		
80-KH		Air Création GTE Clipper / Kiss 450B		
			D133026-020101	
80-KI		Air Création / Kiss		
80-KL	F-JFYP	Aviakit Vega 2000C		
80-KM		Air Création / Mild		
80-KY		Air Création GTE		
80-LF		Best Off Sky Ranger		
		(W/o 11.4.09)		
80-LK		ICP Super Bingo 4S		
80-LP	F-JFZH	type unknown		

Reg	F-reg	Type	Notes	Extra
80-LR	F-JFXK	DTA / Dynamic 15		
80-LT		Air Création / XP		
80-LV		Air Création GTE Clipper / iXess		
80-LW		Air Création GTE Clipper / iXess		
80-LX		Air Création / Mild		
80-LZ		Air Création / Kiss		
80-MA		DTA / Dynamic 15		
80-MB	F-JFYG	Best Off Sky Ranger		
80-ME		Air Création / iXess		
80-MG	F-JPJG	Rans S-6 Coyote II		59-ACM
80-MI		Air Création / XP		
80-MJ		Air Création / iXess		
80-MN	F-JFYQ	ICP MXP-740 Savannah		
80-MS		Air Création / XP		
80-MU		DTA / Dynamic 15/430		
80-MZ		Cosmos		
80-NB		Cosmos		
80-NC		Cosmos / La Mouette Top 14.9		
80-ND		Air Création		
80-NK		Air Création / iXess		
80-NL		Air Création / iXess		
80-NM		Air Création / iXess		
80-NS		Air Création GTE Clipper		
80-NX		TL Ultralight TL-2000 Sting Carbon		
80-NZ		DTA / Dynamic 15/430	194	
80-PE		Air Création		
80-PH	F-JFYG	Weedhopper AX-3		
80-PJ		DTA Combo / Dynamic		
80-PK		Air Création Tanarg / iXess		
80-PN		DTA / Dynamic 15/430		
80-PO		Air Création		
80-PP		Air Création GTE Clipper / Kiss		
80-PR		Air Création Twin / Kiss		
80-PX		Air Création Tanarg 582 / iXess	T05034	
		(Re-regd OO-G06 8.08)		
80-PY		Air Création Buggy		
80-QE		Air Création Twin Buggy		
80-SE	F-JWVF	Flying Machines FM250 Vampire		03-ACQ
80-SM		Air Création GTE / iXess		
80-VA		Synairgie		
80-VJ	F-JFXQ	Best Off Sky Ranger V-Max		
80-VK	F-JZDJ	Humbert Tetras		
80-VM		Fly Synthesis Storch HS (Jabiru)		
80-VO		Alpaero (Noin) Sirius		
80-VS		Autogyro-Europe MT-03		
80-VT		DTA Combo / Dynamic 450	228	
80-VU		DTA / Dynamic 15/430		
80-VV		Air Création Tanarg / iXess		
80-VW		Fisher Koala		
80-VX		Humbert Tetras		
80-VZ		Aviasud AE209 Albatros		
80-WA	F-JZTK	Zenair CH-601XL Zodiac	6-3844	
80-WB		Fly Synthesis Storch HS	206	
		(Re-regd OO-G16 9.08)		
80-WD		TL Ultralight TL-2000 Sting Carbon		
80-WF		Air Création GTE Clipper / iXess		
80-WJ	F-JYCI	DTA Combo / Dynamic 15/430	269	
80-WK	F-JYCM	DTA Combo / Dynamic 15/430	264	
80-WP		ELA Aviacion ELA-07		
80-WQ		Air Création GTE Trek / iXess		
80-WR	F-JYOE	Alpi Aviation Pioneer 200	158	
80-WS		Air Création GTE Trek / iXess	Y011272-0703	
80-WT	F-JYQL	TL Ultralight TL-2000 Sting Carbon RG		
80-WV	F-JYTH	DTA Combo / Dynamic 15/430	232	
80-WW		DTA / Dynamic 450		
80-WZ		Celier Xenon		
80-XA		Air Création GTE Trek / Kiss		
80-XB		trike / Corsair		
80-XD	F-JXDC	DTA Combo / Dynamic 15/430	277	
80-XE		Autogyro-Europe MT-03		
80-XG		DTA Combo / Dynamic 15/430	280	
80-XK		gyrocopter		
80-XL	F-JXTC	Alpi Aviation Pioneer 200		
		(Re-regd 38-AAE)		
80-XN		DTA Combo / Dynamic 15/430	284	
80-XP		Autogyro-Europe MT-03		
80-XQ	F-JXXA	Best Off Sky Ranger	SKR0511669	
80-XR		Air Création		
80-XT	F-JWAE	Air Création Twin / Kiss		
80-XU		Air Création GTE / Kiss		
80-XX		Tecnam P.2002 Sierra		
80-XY	F-JWBA	Jabiru UL		
80-XZ	F-JWBW	DTA / Dynamic 15/430	230	
80-YA		Air Création / Kiss		
80-YB		Aéro Services Super Guépard		
80-YC	F-JWEJ	DTA Combo / Diva	261	
80-YD		Autogyro-Europe MT-03		
80-YH		Autogyro-Europe MT-03		
80-YI		DTA Combo / Diva		
80-YK	F-JWJF	Zenair CH-601 Zodiac		
80-YN		Rans S-5 Coyote I		
80-YP		Aeromax 912 / iXess		
80-YQ		Light Aero Avid Flyer		
80-YT	F-JWQQ	Air Création GTE Trek / XP		
80-YX		Autogyro-Europe MTOsport		
80-YY		Dallach D4 Fascination		
80-YZ		Rans S-6 Coyote II		
80-ZA		weightshift		
80-ZC		type unknown (high wing, 3-axis)		
80-ZD	F-JGZK	SG Aviation Storm 300G		
		(Same call-sign as 71-IX)		
80-ZE		Air Création Twin		
80-ZG	F-JTCP	DTA Combo / Dynamic 15/430	207	..-AV
80-ZI	F-JRDU	Autogyro-Europe MT-03		
80-ZK		DTA Combo JC73 / Magic		
80-ZM	F-JZED	DTA Combo		
80-ZO	F-JRMQ	Autogyro-Europe MTOsport		
80-ZP	F-JZVI	Best Off Sky Ranger		
80-ZR		weightshift		
80-ZU		Air Création GTE Clipper		
80-ZV		Rans S-6 Coyote II		
80-ZW		Autogyro-Europe MTOsport		
80-ZX		Autogyro-Europe MTOsport		
80-ZZ		Air Création GTE Trek		
80-AAA		Zenair CH-601XL Zodiac		
80-AAB	F-JSEW	DTA Combo / Magic		

Reg	F-reg	Type	Notes	Extra
80-AAC	F-JSEX	Autogyro-Europe MTOsport		
80-AAG		Jodel D.18		
80-AAH	F-JSIL	Autogyro-Europe MT-03		
80-AAI		Air Création / iXess		
80-AAR		DTA / Diva		
80-AAS		Air Création Tanarg 912 / iXess		
80-AAW	F-JSVF	DTA Combo / Diva		
80-ABB		Colomban MC-30 Luciole	158	
80-ABD		(Quad City ?) Challenger II		
80-ABE		gyrocopter		
80-ABH		Air Création GTE Clipper / iXess		
80-ABJ	F-JSKO	DTA Diva		
80-ABN		Autogyro-Europe MT-03	M00911	
80-ABP	F-JTVA	Best Off Nynja		
80-ABU	F-JUAC	Autogyro-Europe MTOsport	M00935/BG529-0043	
80-ABV	F-JUBB	Autogyro-Europe MTOsport	M00939/BG529-0045	
80-ABX	F-JUEU	Autogyro-Europe MTOsport	M00948/BG529-0057	
80-ABZ	F-JUFA	Aerospool WT-9 Dynamic		
80-ACB		Autogyro-Europe MTOsport		
80-ACD		weightshift		
80-ACI	F-JUMC	Autogyro-Europe Calidus 09		
80-ACM		Fokker DR.1 replica		
80-ACN		Pennec Gaz'Aile 2		
80-ACO	F-JUVB	Autogyro-Europe MTOsport	M01032/BG529-0156	
80-ADD		Autogyro-Europe MTOsport		
80-ADG	F-JVOS	Dynali H3 Easyflyer		
		(Danaged 3.4.16)		
80-ADH	F-JVTL	Autogyro-Europe Cavalon		
80-ADT	F-JWSI	Autogyro-Europe Calidus 09		
80-ADW	F-JSHR	Dynali H3 Easyflyer		
80-AED	F-JVTL	Autogyro-Europe Cavalon		
80-AEE		Dynali H3 Easyflyer		
80-AEH		Raid'Air Adventure		
80-AES	F-JALP	Dynali H-03 Easyflyer	H3-34-1540	
80-AEY	F-JARG	Tomark SD-4 Viper	0109/2016	

81 : Tarn

Reg	F-reg	Type	Notes	Extra
81-H		Aviasud Sirocco	16	
		(Re-regd OO-763 4.87)		
81-S		Air Création		
81-U		Air Création		
81-V		Zenith Baroudeur		
81-AB		Aviasud X'Pair 50		
		(W/o 23.7.05)		
81-AC		Aviasud AE532 Mistral		
81-AD		Aquilair		
81-AH		Air Création GTE / XP15		
81-AL		Aviasud AE209 Albatros		
81-AM		Air Création Safari GT 532 / Fun 450		
81-AX		Air Création GT BI / XP15		
81-BL		Best Off Sky Ranger		
81-BQ		Aquilair Swing 14		
81-BW		Air Action Quicky / Pegasus Q		
81-BY		weightshift		
81-CA		DTA Combo FC / Dynamic 15/430	198	
81-CH		Air Création / iXess		
81-CJ		Denney Kitfox		
81-CL		Best Off Sky Ranger		
W81-CN		gyrocopter (homebuilt)		
		(W/o 2.6.05)		
81-CT	F-JAUK	JCC Aviation J.300 Joker		
		(Same c/s as 27-AHO)		
81-CV		Bonnafous BC-2 gyrocopter		
81-CW		Bonnafous gyrocopter		
81-CY	F-JIEQ	Best Off Sky Ranger		
81-DA		Nike Aeronautica 503 / Pegasus Q		
81-DE		(Croses ?) Airplume	32	
81-DK		Aquilair / Magic		
81-DM		Air Création Racer / XP11		
81-DQ		Alpi Aviation Pioneer 200		
81-DT		Air Action Quicky 503 / Aeros Stranger 14.8		
81-EH		DTA Combo 912		
81-EM		Flipper BI	1	
81-ER		weightshift		
81-EY		Air Création GT BI / XP15		
81-EZ		Fly Synthesis Storch		
81-FC	F-JBHY	JCC Aviation J.300 Joker		
81-FE		Alpi Aviation Pioneer 300		
81-FH		Claude Leger Pataplume 2		
81-FL		Air Création GTE / XP15		
81-FM		weightshift		
81-FW		weightshift		
81-FZ		Air Création GTE 582S / XP15		
81-GB		JC-31 Weedhopper		
		(Crashed 12.6.07)		
W81-GK		Pouchel 2		
		(Damaged 20.5.07)		
W81-GM		Jean-Luc Malet gyrocopter		
81-GP		Mignet HM.1000 Balerit		
81-GV		DTA Combo		
81-GX		Marie JPM-03 Loiret	40	
81-GY	F-JXNY	Jodel D.185		
81-HC		Aviasud AE532 Mistral		
81-HH	F-JRHH	Magni M-22 Voyager	22-05-3144	
81-HP		Mignet HM.1000 Balerit		
81-HV		Best Off Sky Ranger		
81-HW		Pagotto Brako / Bautek Pico		
81-HY	F-JBHY	Sauper J.300 Joker		
81-IA		Air Création / Fun 450		
W81-IJ		Christian Bonnafous gyrocopter		
W81-JF		Montagne Noire MN800 Cocagne	01	
81-JN	F-JSEQ	ESPACE Sensation		
81-JZ	F-JUGL	Mignet HM.1100 Cordouan	11	
81-KM	F-JTQP	JMB Aircraft VL-3 Evolution	VL3-100	
81-KY		Marie JPM-03 Loiret	63	
81-LA		Best Off Nynja		
81-LG		Aquilair Swing 14		
81-LO	F-JUKV	Best Off Nynja		
81-LP	F-JUNA	Helisport CH-7 Kompress Charlie		
81-LY	F-JVKO	JMB Aircraft VL-3 Evolution	VL3-125	
81-MF	F-JFCC	Evektor EV-97 Eurostar		
		(Same call-sign as 95-TG)		
81-MH		Best Off Nynja		
81-MM	F-JSQW	Best Off Sky Ranger V-Max		
81-MS		Mignet HM.293 Pou-du-Ciel		
81-OY		Best Off Sky Ranger		

Reg	Call-sign	Type	C/n	Other
81-PT		Best Off Sky Ranger		
81-PW		Pegasus		
81-QD	F-JIQD	Tecnam P.92 Echo		
81-QE	F-JIQE	DTA / Dynamic 16		
81-QF		Raj Hamsa X'Air		
81-QR	F-JIQR	Best Off Sky Ranger		
		(marked 81-PD under left wing)		
81-SO		Jodel D.18		
81-TA		Air Action Quicky 503		
		(W/o 18.3.05)		
81-TB		weightshift		
81-TM		B&F Funk FK-14 Polaris		
		(Accident 14.8.07)		
81-UC		Air Création		

82 : Tarn-et-Garonne

Reg	Call-sign	Type	C/n	Other
82-AD		Lascaud Bifly		
W82-AE		Aviasud AE532 Mistral		
82-AF		Dynali Chickinox		
82-AG		JC-31D Weedhopper		
82-AH		Best Off Sky Ranger		
		(Also reported as Djicat Buse'Air 150)		
82-AJ		Djicat Buse'Air 150		
82-AK		Air Création Safari GT BI		
		(Damaged 5.2.06)		
82-AM		Criquet 2 (homebuilt)		
		(Crashed 31.7.05)		
82-AN	F-JTYK	Raj Hamsa X'Air		
82-AP		Zenair CH-601 Zodiac		
82-AQ	F-JIIL	Jodel D.185	509	
		(Re-regd 02-ADP)		
82-AU		Best Off Sky Ranger		
82-AW		Zenair CH-601 Zodiac		
82-AZ		Best Off Sky Ranger		
82-BB		Air Création		
82-BC		Best Off Sky Ranger		
82-BI		Best Off Sky Ranger V-Max		
82-BJ		Best Off Sky Ranger V-Max (HKS700E)	0403451	
82-BM		Lynx 14 (trike)		
82-BN	F-JIHO	B&F Funk FK-9 Mk.IV	04-U-227	57-YK
W82-BQ		Croses Criquet L		
82-BW	F-JSNM	Jodel D.185	12	
82-BX		Murphy Renegade Spirit		
		(W/o 14.11.92)		
82-CE		Best Off Sky Ranger		
82-CG		Pipistrel Sinus		
82-CK	F-JZRL	Best Off Sky Ranger		
82-CM	F-JZTT	Best Off Sky Ranger		
82-CN	F-JIDH	Flight Design CT SW		
		(Same c/n and call-sign as 31-DH)		
W82-CU		Jacques Callauzene gyrocopter		
82-DC		Jodel D.19		
		(Damaged 24.8.07)		
82-DM		Top Concept Hurricane		
82-DU		Air Création GTE Trek 582 / iXess 15		
W82-DY	F-JXAY	Aircopter A3C	2	
82-EA		Best Off Nynja Star		
82-EE (1)	F-JGMI	Best Off Sky Ranger		
82-EE (2)	F-JXIX	Best Off Sky Ranger Swift	SKR0610752	
82-EF	F-JXK-	Dallach D4 Fascination		
82-EH		Air Création Safari GT BI / Fun 450		
82-FB	F-JXZS	Best Off Sky Ranger V-Max		
82-FF		Guérin G-1 912		
82-FG		Zenith Baroudeur		
82-FO		Best Off Sky Ranger		
82-FQ		Dyn'Aéro MCR-01 UL	287	
		(Same c/n as 36-NV)		
82-FR		Guérin G-1		
82-FS	F-JCEF	Best Off Nynja		
82-FV		Air Création Racer 503 / XP11		
82-FX		Best Off Sky Ranger		
		(W/o 6.07)		
82-HA	F-JFTX	Fly Synthesis Storch HS		
82-HF		Aero Designs Pulsar		
82-HG		Aeroandinas MXP-1000 Tayrona		
82-HX	F-JYHE	Fly Synthesis Storch HS		
82-HY	F-JRLI	Best Off Nynja	0910967	
82-II	F-JKEH	Kappa 77 KP-2UR Sova		
		(same call sign as 47-OE; not known which of		
		47-OE or 82-II is current)		
82-IJ	F-JYSK	Best Off Nynja		
82-IN	F-JSCU	Best Off Nynja		
82-IW		Best Off Nynja		
82-IZ		Air Création Skypper / BioniX 15		
82-JB		Tecnam P.92 Echo		
82-JD		Cosmos Phase II		
82-JI		Vol Mediterrani VM-1 Esqual	02023-1687	EC-ZHU
82-JO		ELA Aviacion ELA-07 Cougar		
82-JU		Air Création GTE		
82-JY		Air Création		
82-KA		Magni M-16 Tandem Trainer		
82-KG		Nieuport 17 replica		
82-KZ		Paramania GTR paramotor		
82-LI	F-JUGJ	Brandli BX-2 Cherry		
82-LJ		Fly Synthesis Storch HS		
		(Crashed 30.4.06)		
82-LS		Air Création Skypper / BioniX		
82-LZ	F-JUMW	B&F Funk FK-14B Le Mans		
82-OC		B&F Funk FK-12 Comet	12-107	I-B551
82-PC		trike / Atlas (wing)		
82-PJ		CQR Roitelet		
82-PP		Best Off Sky Ranger (t/w)		
82-QM		Lemonnier Maestro		
82-WA		Zenair CH-601 Zodiac		
82-AEH		Air Création Safari GT BI 503		

83 : Var

Reg	Call-sign	Type	C/n	Other
83-D		Best Off Sky Ranger		
83-H		Aériane Sirocco		
83-T		Eipper Quicksilver MX		
83-AE		Aériane Sirocco		
		(also reported as gyrocopter 7.01)		
83-AG		CFM Shadow		
		(also reported as Storch IIS)		
83-AH	F-JJDV	Dyn'Aéro MCR-01		
		(Formerly F-JGOA)		

Reg	Call-sign	Type	C/n	Other
83-AK (3)		Best Off Sky Ranger 912UL	SKR0104098	
		(Previously reported as Aviasud Mistral & as Zenair CH-701)		
83-AP		Air's Maestro (Two-seat)		
83-AR		Vamic 450?		
83-AT		Félix		
83-AU	F-JJKJ	Ultravia Pelican Sport		
83-AW		Flight Design CT-180UL	99-07-01-58	
83-AX		Best Off Sky Ranger (f/p)		
83-BB		Aviasud Mistral		
83-BC		KFM		
83-BE		Nike Aeronautica		
83-BG		DTA Evolution		
83-BI		Jodel D.185		
83-BJ		Rans S-6 Coyote II		
		(wreck noted 4.02)		
83-BN(1)		Aviasud Sirocco	69	
		(Re-regd OO-818, 10.88)		
83-BN(2)		Rans S-6 Coyote II		
83-BP	F-JJSB	Humbert Tetras 912CS		
		(Previously Aviasud Mistral)		
83-BQ		Aviasud Mistral		
83-BV		Patrilor		
83-CB		Aviasud Mistral		
83-CC		Air's Maestro		
83-CF		Avcan		
83-CG		Cosmos		
83-CI		Aviasud Albatros		
		(Although officially an Albatros, this is a modified Sirocco,		
		used to set a world record)		
83-CJ		Aviasud Mistral		
83-CK		Air Création		
83-CL	F-JCQO	Aviasud AE209 Albatros 912		
83-CM		Best Off Sky Ranger (f/p)		
83-CP		Aviasud Mistral		
		(W/o 4.9.88)		
83-CQ		Aviasud Mistral		
83-CR(1)		Aviasud AE532 Mistral	46	
		(Re-regd OO-809, 5.88)		
83-CR(2)		Best Off Sky Ranger		
		(W/o 19.7.03)		
83-CT		Air's Maestro (Floatplane)		
83-DA		Aviasud Mistral		
83-DB		ULM Rapid		
83-DC		ICP MXP-740 Savannah	01-12-51-124	
83-DG		Weedhopper		
83-DN(1)		Aviasud Sirocco		
		(W/o 2.12.01)		
83-DN(2)		Light Aero Avid Lite		
		(Accident 26.3.06)		
83-DO		Aviasud Mistral		
83-DQ		Le Goeland amphibian		
83-DR		Le Goeland		
83-DU		Micro Aviation Pulsar (f/p)		
83-DV		PGO Aviation Cobra		
83-DY		Aviasud Mistral		
83-EA		Le Goeland amphibian		
83-EB		Murphy Renegade Spirit UK	PFA188-12791	G-BWPE
		(Wears both UK and French marks)		
83-EG		Denney Kitfox III Minifox	993	
		(Re-regd 24-RW)		
83-EP		Mignet HM.1000 Balerit	45	
83-ET	F-JVZW	Aviasud Mistral		
83-EU		Aviasud AE209 Albatros	95	
83-EV		Aviasud AE209 Albatros	32	62-CV
83-EW	F-JJJQ	B&F Funk FK-9 Mk.III Utility	09-169	
W83-FI		Croses Airplume		
W83-FJ		Fly Synthesis Storch		
83-FS		Air Création GTE Clipper / XP		
83-FY		Air Création / Kiss		
83-FZ		Magni M-16 Tandem Trainer		
83-GD		Rans S-6 Coyote II		
83-GC		ICP MXP-740 Savannah	11-00-51-032	
83-GF		Best Off Sky Ranger		
83-GJ		Zenair CH-601 Zodiac		
83-GP		Best Off Sky Ranger		
83-GR	F-JCGI	Best Off Sky Ranger		
83-HF		Air Création		
83-HJ		Dynali Chickinox Kot-Kot		
		(marked HJ83)		
83-HR	F-JDBG	Mignet HM.1100 Cordouan	07	
83-IA		Air Création 503SL		
		(W/o 8.1.98)		
83-IC		Pipistrel Sinus		
83-ID	F-JWVJ	Best Off Sky Ranger		
W83-IG		Gatard AG-02 Poussin	01	F-PHUO
83-IH		Rans S-6 Coyote II		
83-IL		Alpi Aviation Pioneer 300		
83-IM		Best Off Sky Ranger		
83-JB		Tecnam P.92 Echo		
83-JC		Raj Hamsa X'Air 582		
83-JD		Air Création / XP		
83-JF	F-JJJB	Pipistrel Sinus		
83-JG		Aviasud AE209 Albatros 582		CAP-28
83-JJ		B&F Funk FK-14 Polaris		
		(Crashed 19.1.06)		
83-JP(1)		Aéro Services Guépard 912		
83-JP(2)	F-JJAI	Dyn'Aéro MCR-01 ULC	229	
		(Re-regd OO-H57 11.15, c/s shown as ex F-JJJM)		
83-JV(1)		Dynali Chickinox Kot-Kot 3	3591F88	
		(Crashed 26.3.04)		
83-JV(2)	F-JJVB	Urban Air Lambada		
		(Reserved as SE-VOM)		
83-LA		Best Off Sky Ranger		
		(Fell into sea 19.8.04)		
83-LD		Raj Hamsa X'Air		
		(Re-regd 18-LZ)		
83-LV		Best Off Sky Ranger		
83-LW		Ekolot JK-05 Junior		
83-LX		Ultralair Weedhopper		
83-MB		Best Off Sky Ranger		
83-MD		Humbert Tetras		
83-MI		Fly Synthesis Storch HS		
83-MM		Cosmos		
83-MU		gyrocopter		
83-MZ		Dyn'Aéro MCR-01		
83-NG	F-JJHS	ICP MXP-740 Savannah	01-10-51-099	

Reg		Type		
83-NV		Flight Design CT-180		
83-OB		Fly Synthesis Storch HS		
83-PA		EVP-1		
83-PE		Best Off Sky Ranger		
83-PF		Eipper Quicksilver		
83-PM		Vidor Asso V Champion		
83-PU	F-JCMB	Kolb Firestar		
83-RB		ICP MXP-740 Savannah		
		(W/o 28.10.01)		
W83-RH		Simoun (homebuilt)		
		(Crashed 4.12.04)		
83-RM		Best Off Sky Ranger		
83-RP	F-JVZA	Best Off Sky Ranger		
83-RW		Best Off Sky Ranger		
83-SA		III Sky Arrow 500TF		
83-SB	F-JBPM	Debiazi DG01 gyrocopter		
		(marked 83-SBI)		
83-SC	F-JJWZ	Fly Synthesis Storch S		F-JJKI
83-SD		III Sky Arrow 500TF		
83-SE		III Sky Arrow 500TF	070/98.017	
83-SF	F-JWDM	III Sky Arrow 500TF	074	
83-SG		gyrocopter		
83-SJ	F-JBQT	Best Off Sky Ranger		
83-SL		Humbert Tetras		
		(W/o 6.7.03)		
83-SP	F-JJDR	Tecnam P.92 Echo		
83-SQ		Jodel D.18	96	F-PRCJ
83-SS		Celier Xenon		
83-SU		Fly Synthesis Storch		
83-SX	F-JJSR	Humbert Tetras 912CS		
83-TK		Fly Synthesis Storch		
	F-JPTK	Evektor EV-97 Eurostar (confirmed)		
83-TM	F-JJHI	Light Aero Avid IV "Tundra"		
83-TO		B&F Funk FK-9 Mk.3		
		(Quoted as F-JYXW which is 13-TO ?)		
83-TS		Cosmos Bi Bidulm		
83-TV		Flight Design CT SW		
83-TX	F-JJVI	Pipistrel Sinus	052 S912 1201	
83-UA		Slepcev Storch		
83-UD		gyrocopter		
83-UE	F-JJSI	ICP MXP-740 Savannah	05-01-51-356	
83-VD		Rans S-6 Coyote II		
83-VF		Alisport Silent Club	09	
		(Re-regd ZK-SWN 8.11)		
83-VG	F-JJDT	Aéro Services Guépard 912		
83-ZC		ICP MXP-740 Savannah		
83-ZE		Weedhopper AX-3		
83-ZH	F-JJPL	Zenair CH-601 Zodiac		
83-ZN		Raj Hamsa X'Air F (Jabiru)		
83-ZO	F-JJSG	Alpi Aviation Pioneer 200		
83-ZX		Weedhopper		
83-AAH	F-JZHX	Technic Moto Mustang 2		
		(Re-regd 51-TU)		
83-AAI		Zenair CH-601XL Zodiac	6-9752	
83-AAL		Rans S-6ES Coyote II		
		(Accident 12.8.07)		
83-AAN		Zenair CH-601 Zodiac (t/w)		
83-AAO	F-JZIS	Djicat Buse'Air 150		05-EI
		(now reported as Paramania GTR paramotor)		
83-AAP		Fresh Breeze Snap 100 paramotor		
83-AAR		Tecnam P.92 Echo		
		(Also reported as DTA Combo 582 / Dynamic)		
83-AAS	F-JZOC	Rans S-6ES Coyote II (t/w)		
83-AAV	F-JZVU	Aeroandinas MXP-1000 Tayrona		
		AA-02-06-90-016		
83-AAW		TeST TST-10 Atlas M		
		(W/o 24.4.07)		
83-ABB	F-JZXD	Tecnam P.2002 Sierra		
83-ABF		Zenair CH-601UL Zodiac		
83-ABG		B&F Funk FK-9 Mk.III		
83-ABJ		TEAM MiniMax		
83-ABL	F-JYCK	Fly Synthesis Storch CL		
83-ABW	F-JYLZ	SG Aviation Storm 280		
		(Painted 83-ABW with the '3'in the wrong direction,		
		hence reports of 38-ABW)		
83-ABY	F-JYQV	Best Off Sky Ranger		
83-ACC		Zenair CH-701 STOL		
		(Damaged 18.4.07)		
83-ACJ		Rans S-6 Coyote II		
		(W/o 30.8.09)		
83-ACN		Dyn'Aéro MCR-01	311	
		(Re-regd OO-G31, 5.09)		
W83-ACO	F-JYBO	Zlin Savage		
83-ACQ		Flying Machines FM250 Vampire		
83-ACR		Tecnam P.92 Echo		
83-ACT	F-JEGU	TL Ultralight TL-2000 Sting Carbon		
		(Re-regd 26-UX)		
83-ACU		Zenair CH-601 Zodiac		
83-ACW		Alpi Aviation Pioneer 300JS		I-8030
83-ACZ		Weedhopper AX2000		
83-ADB		Urban Air UFM-11 Lambada	53	
83-ADD	F-JXJH	Best Off Sky Ranger		
83-ADE		Pipistrel Virus		
		(Re-regd 29-TB)		
83-ADF		Raj Hamsa X'Air F		
83-ADH	F-JXBO	Aeropro Eurofox		
83-ADJ	F-JXMN	Aeropro Eurofox		
83-ADR		Light Aero Avid Flyer		
		(previously reported as Best Off Sky Ranger)		
83-ADU	F-JWGX	SG Aviation Storm Rally 105UL		
83-ADW	F-JXRY	Aeroandinas MXP-1000 Tayrona		
		AA-07-07-90-035		
83-ADY		weightshift		
83-AEA		Skyeton K.10 Swift		
83-AEC	F-JXTU	Aerospool WT-9 Dynamic	DY162/2007	
83-AEE		Alpi Aviation Pioneer 200		
83-AEG		Aviakit Vega		
83-AEH		Autogyro-Europe MT-03		
83-AEI		Zenair CH-601XL Zodiac		
83-AEK	F-JKWX	Dyn'Aéro MCR-01 UL	354	
83-AEN		Zenair CH-701 STOL		
83-AEQ		Aviasud Albatros		
83-AES		Cosmos Bidulm / La Mouette Top 14.9		
83-AEV		Aerospool WT-9 Dynamic	DY393/2010	
83-AEX		Aeroandinas MXP-1000 Tayrona		
83-AFF		Alpi Aviation Pioneer 200		

Reg		Type		
83-AFJ	F-JWTM	Slepcev Storch		
83-AFK	F-JWHC	Dyn'Aéro MCR-01	334	21-AAS
83-AFM		Rans S-12 Airaile		
83-AFT		Rans S-6 Coyote II ES (t/w)		
83-AFV		Aéro Services SG.10 912SC		
83-AFY	F-JCNQ	Aéro Services Guépard 912		
83-AGA		Best Off Sky Ranger		06-BZ
83-AGH		Best Off Sky Ranger		
83-AGM	F-JYGM	Evektor EV-97 Eurostar	2006 2906	
83-AGT		Raj Hamsa X'Air		
83-AGZ	F-JRHM	Dyn'Aéro MCR-01		
83-AHH	F-JRNP	Aveko VL-3 Sprint	VL3-56	
		(Re-regd 31-QC)		
83-AHJ		TL Ultralight TL-2000 Sting Carbon		
83-AHK	F-JAPO	Aveko VL-3		
83-AHL	F-JGSD	Best Off Sky Ranger		
83-AHN		Aveko VL-3B-3 Sprint	VL3-69	
		(Sold as PH-4F5)		
83-AHO		Zenair CH-601UL Zodiac		59-XZ
83-AHP		Zenair CH-650E		
83-AHQ		B.O.T. SC07 Speed Cruiser		
		(W/o 9.8.10)		
83-AHR	F-JSAC	B.O.T. SC07 Speed Cruiser		
83-AHS	F-JRUL	B.O.T. SC07 Speed Cruiser	SC07-007	
83-AHU	F-JXAX	Best Off Sky Ranger V-Max		47-SA
83-AHZ	F-JSQV	TL Ultralight TL-3000 Sirius		
83-AIB		gyrocopter		
83-AID		DTA/Ellipse Alizé (Electravia)		
83-AIG		Ultravia Pelican		
		(accident 31.7.12)		
83-AIH		Magni M-22 Voyageur		
83-AIN		Tecnam P.92 Echo		
83-AIR		Fly Synthesis Storch		
83-AIS		Air Création 582 / Aeros Profi TL		
83-AJH		Zlin Savage		
83-AJL		Aveko VL-3 Sprint		
83-AJR	F-JSOR	Shark Aero Shark UL	003	
		(Damaged 21.6.11, repaired)		
83-AJS		Air Création GTE Trek 582 / Fun 450		
83-AKE	F-JYMN	B&F Funk FK-9 Mk.III		
		(Call-sign also quoted for 38-SA)		
83-AKF	F-JSXI	Aveko VL-3 Sprint	VL3-90	
83-AKL		Evektor EV-97 Eurostar		
83-AKM		B&F Funk FK-12 Comet	12-017	D-MYVO
83-AKO		Best Off Sky Ranger		19-AS
83-AKQ		AirLony Skylane UL	45	
83-AKR		Halley Apollo Fox		
83-AKS	F-JTAR	Corvus CA-21 Phantom		
83-AKX		Aeropro Eurofox		
83-AKZ		Aeroparkt A22L2	375	
83-ALC	F-JRQE	Aveko VL-3A-3 Sprint	VL3-65	OO-G66,
				59-DAL
83-ALK	F-JTIR	G1 Aviation G1 SPYL		
83-ALL	F-JAKM	Alisport Silent 2 Targa		
83-ALN	F-JEXR	Zlin Savage Cub		01-TM
83-ALT		Air Création / NuviX		
83-ALW		Druine Turbulent		
83-ALX	F-JYDN	Flight Design CT-2K		
83-AMC		Aéro Services SG.12A		
83-AMG		SG Aviation Storm Century		71-LL
83-AMH	F-JCSW	ICP MXP-740 Savannah	09-97-50-058	
83-AMO	F-JTSW	Spacek SD-1 Minisport TD	037	W83-AMO
		(Company website quotes c/n as 019)		
83-AMW		Autogyro-Europe Calidus 09		
		(W/o 24.10.14)		
83-AMX		Zenair CH-601 Zodiac		
		(W/o 1.10.13)		
83-ANH	F-JUFI	ICP MXP-740 Savannah S	10-09-54-0023	
83-ANI		Humbert Teras 912CS		
83-ANW		ICP MXP-740 Savannah S	13-02-54-0248	
83-ANX	F-JUPP	Shark Aero Shark	017/2013	
83-AOA	F-JURL	Aveko VL-3B RG		
83-AOB	F-JUTC	ICP MXP-740 Savannah VG	06-10-51-536	
83-AOC		Helisport CH-7 Kompress		
83-AOV	F-JVKZ	Best Off Sky Ranger		
83-APS	F-JVVT	Shark Aero Shark	029/2014	OK-SUU 52
83-AQJ	F-JUTM	G1 Aviation G1 SPYL		
83-AQP		Phoenix Air Phoenix U-15		
83-ARC		Zenair CH.650E	15-06-65ER-0021	
83-ARL	F-JAML	Shark Aero Shark	047	
83-ARU		Aquilair Swing 14		
83-AUU		ICP-MXP-740 Savannah		
83-GAA	F-JGAA	Plätzer Kiebitz B9	219	D-MBOX,
				OO-F64, D-MUAT
83-SBI		gyrocopter		

84 : Vaucluse

Reg	Type	
84-J	Huntair	
84-O	Airplast Prima	
84-Y	Albatross Delta Pilot	
84-AE	Pipistrelle	
84-AJ	Croses Airplume	
84-AL	Aviasud Mistral	
84-AP	Weedhopper Europa II	
84-AS	Eipper Quicksilver MX	
84-AT	JC-31 Weedhopper	
84-BA	Humbert La Moto-du-Ciel	
84-BB	Croses Airplume	
84-BY	AMF Chevvron amphibian	CH005?	G-BNHY?
84-CB	Weedhopper AX-3	
84-CC	JC-31 Weedhopper	
84-CW	Air Micro	
84-DF	Aviasud AE209 Albatros	
84-DG	Air Création	
84-DI	Rans S-6 Coyote II	
84-DO	Air Création GT BI	
84-EA	Dynali Chickinox	
84-EL	Roger Marquion RM-02 gyrocopter	F-WNUC
84-EM	gyrocopter AX-06?	
84-EN	gyrocopter AX-06?	
84-EW	Aquilair Swing	
84-EX	Best Off Sky Ranger	
84-EY	Cierva C.30 gyrocopter replica	
84-FG	Pipistrel Sinus	
84-FH	Zenair CH-601UL Zodiac	
84-FK	Aviakit Vega 2000	VR0015.R9

Reg	F-reg	Type	Serial	Other
84-FS		Adventure Wheely 420 paramotor (Crashed 1.11.05)		
84-GE	F-JJQT	Dyn'Aéro MCR-01 UL	208	95-ON
84-GF		Best Off Sky Ranger		
84-GG	F-JUXQ	Airplast Micro'B ("Little Sophie")		
84-GK		ABS Aerolight Xenon (Damaged 12.9.05)		
84-GY ?		Mignet HM.14 Pou-du-Ciel		
84-GY		Jabiru UL450		
84-GZ	F-JJXB	Flight Design CT SW		
84-HC		paramotor		
84-HD		Jodel D.18	469	F-PJHM
84-HL	F-JJTH	Tecnam P.92 Echo		
84-HM		Adventure/ITV Dakota Sport paramotor		
84-HN		ITV Dakota Sport paramotor		
84-HR		B&F Funk FK-9 Mk.III		
84-HX		Mignet HM.1000 Balerit		
84-IM		Reflexion/Adventure/Dudek 29 paramotor		
84-IX		Adventure Funflyer/Flexway paramotor		
84-JD	F-JSEE	G1 Aviation G1 SPYL		
84-JE		SE.5A replica		
84-JK		Air Création Racer 447 / Fun 14		08-EV
84-JQ	F-JTSA	G1 Aviation G1 SPYL		
84-JT		Dyn'Aéro MCR-01 ULC	411	
84-JU	F-JUCN	G1 Aviation G1 SPYL	85	
		(exported to Senegal Gendarmerie as G0)		
84-JX		Ellipse Fuji Alizé 16		
84-KA	F-JUSM	ICP MXP-740 Savannah S	13-12-54-0251	
84-KB	F-JUWS	ICP MXP-740 Savannah		
84-KI	F-JVSO	G1 Aviation G1 SPYL		
84-KZ	F-JANC	Aeroprakt A-22L2 Vision	497	
84-MP		Dyn'Aéro MCR-01 (W/o 12.8.16)	88	F-PIAM(2)
84-SP	F-JPAL	G1 Aviation G1 Spyl		
84-VB		Alpi Aviation Pioneer 200		

85 : Vendée

Reg	F-reg	Type	Serial	Other
85-A		Allegro		
85-AA		Quartz		
85-AD		Agriplane Condor		
85-AE		Weedhopper		
85-AL		Quartz		
85-AT		Weedhopper Europa II		
85-AV		Weedhopper		
85-AX		Allegro		
85-BF	F-JATC	SMAN Pétrel	026	
85-BH		Synairgie / Puma		
85-BJ		Synairgie / Puma		
85-BK		Weedhopper		
85-BL		Weedhopper		
85-BT		Weedhopper		
85-BX		Weedhopper		
85-BY		Weedhopper		
85-CD		weightshift		
85-CL		Air Création		
85-CV		Air Création		
85-CX		Air Création		
85-DC		Air Création / Quartz		
85-DD		Weedhopper		
85-DG		Weedhopper		
85-DJ		Humbert La Moto-du-Ciel		
85-DS		Hermes		
85-EI		Air Création GTE / XP		
85-EL		Eipper Quicksilver GT500		
85-EN		Eipper Quicksilver MXL III Sport		
85-EP		Air Création / Quartz		
85-ES		Synairgie / Puma		
85-EU		(Weedhopper ?) AX-3		
85-EV		ALMS J.300 Joker (Crashed 3.7.05)		
85-EX		Best Off Sky Ranger		
85-FB		Synairgie (trike)		
85-FJ		Best Off Sky Ranger		
85-FN		Denney Kitfox		
85-FR		SMAN Pétrel		
85-FT		Technic' ULM (Maestro Quatro?)		
85-GA	F-JCJS	Humbert Tetras		
85-GE	F-JCPA	Raj Hamsa X'Air		
85-GL		Dyn'Aéro MCR-01 ULC	24	F-PJAS ?
85-GQ		Zlin Savage (Jabiru) 2000		
85-GT		Air Création GTE Clipper / XP		
85-GU		Humbert Tetras ?		
85-HP		Air Création / Mild		
85-HQ	F-JHVJ	Aéro Services Guépy 582		
85-HT		Fantasy Air Allegro ST		
85-IB		ZUT Aviation TT2000 STOL		
W85-IM		Evektor EV-97 Eurostar	2001 1410	
85-IQ		3XTrim		
85-IZ		Pap 1300 paramotor (Crashed 28.7.04)		
85-JB		Air Création / Kiss		
85-JH		Pegasus Quasar		
85-JJ		Eipper Quicksilver MXL III Sport		
85-JM		3XTrim		
85-JT		"TL-S"		
85-JX		ZUT Aviation TT2000 STOL		
85-KC		Humbert Tetras		
85-KE		Djicat Buse'Air 150		
85-KG		Light Aero Avid IV		
85-KH		Best Off Sky Ranger		
85-KO		Air Création / Kiss 450		
85-KQ		Aeroprakt A-22		
85-KT		TL Ultralight TL-2000 Sting Carbon		
85-LA		Pipistrel Sinus		
85-LB		Best Off Sky Ranger		
85-LL		gyrocopter		
85-LN	F-JHYC	Evektor EV-97 Eurostar	2001 1308	85-II
85-LN(2?)		Evektor EV-97 Eurostar	2003 1621	
85-LS	F-JHAA	3XTrim		
85-LU		DTA Dynamic		
85-LW	F-JHZX	Aeropro Eurofox		D-MSYG
85-ML	F-JHYA	Aéro Services Guépard 912		
85-MR	F-JHAQ	B&F Funk FK-9 Mk.III	94	D-MPCM
85-MX		Air Création GTE Clipper 582		
85-ND		Aéro Services Guépy Club 582		
85-NG	F-JHBA	ATEC 321 Faeta		

Reg	F-reg	Type	Serial	Other
85-NL		Evektor EV-97 Eurostar		
85-NQ	F-JHBU	Zlin Savage	41	
85-NU		Best Off Sky Ranger		
85-OD	F-JHCW	Sonex Aircraft Sonex	171	
85-OK		ITV Tepee paramotor		
85-OQ		Tecnam P.2002 Sierra		
85-OX	F-JXWH	Aéro Services Guépard 912	25052	F-JHVM
85-PA		Air Création (Crashed 3.7.05)		
85-PG	F-JHDC	Alpi Aviation Pioneer 200 (Re-regd 78-ZL)		
85-PK		Zenair CH-601XL Zodiac (W/o 7.7.07)		
85-PL		Air Création Tanarg		
85-PP		Air Création Tanarg 582 / iXess		
85-QA		ITV Pawnee paramotor		
85-QC		Magni M-16 Tandem Trainer		
85-QN		Zlin Savage		
85-QP	F-JHMA	Air Création		
85-QQ		ITV Dakota 25 paramotor		
85-QS		Air Création Racer 503 / XP11		
85-QZ		Guérin G1		
85-RP		Evektor EV-97 Eurostar	2006 2812	
85-RV	F-JHUW	Light Aero Avid Flyer		
85-RW		Zenair CH-601 Zodiac		
85-SK	F-JHAW	Raj Hamsa Hanuman (Re-regd 44-ASB)		
85-SL		Cosmos Chronos		39-IA
85-TF		DTA Feeling / Dynamic 15		
85-TJ		Dallach D4BK Fascination		
85-TL		Aéro Services Super Guépard 912		
85-TS		paramotor		
85-TX		Air Création GTE Trek / iXess		
85-UF		Raj Hamsa X'Air		
85-UJ		DTA / Dynamic 15/450		
85-UN		TL Ultralight TL-2000 Sting Carbon		
85-UP		Alpi Aviation Pioneer 200		
85-UT		Cosmos Chronos		
85-UV	F-JXDI	Alpi Aviation Pioneer 200 (Same call sign as 86-FG)		
85-VE		Flying Machines FM250 Vampire		
85-VO		Air Création GTE Clipper / iXess		
85-VY	F-JZDG	Flying Machines FM250 Vampire (Same call-sign as 26-ACF and 24-MY)		
85-WE	F-JXSB	ATEC 122 Zephyr (Re-regd 49-TA)		
85-WL	F-JXUP	Evektor EV-97R Eurostar	2008 3206	
85-WP	F-JXXY	Aerospool WT-9 Dynamic	DY245/2008	
85-WR	F-JISA	Fly Synthesis Storch S		
85-WW		Magni M-22 Voyager		
85-WY		ATEC 122 Zephyr		
85-XI	F-JXWI	Pottier P.130L (nosewheel)		
85-XJ		DTA 582 / Dynamic 15		
85-XN		Raj Hamsa Hanuman		
85-XS	F-JWBK	Dyn'Aéro MCR Pickup	118	
85-XZ		Ekolot KR-030 Topaz		
85-YJ	F-JFKR	B&F Funk FK-12 Comet (Re-regd 40-KD)	12-034	59-CEJ
85-ZC		ITV Lampoon paramotor		
85-ZG		Air Création Tanarg 912 / iXess 15	A05051-5093/T05056	
85-ZJ	F-JWWD	BRM Land Africa	0132/912UL/09-LA	
85-ZK	F-JWXC	Best Off Nynja		
85-ZT	F-JXHR	Aéro Services Super Guépard 912S		
85-AAG	F-JRBX	Aeropro Eurofox		
85-AAI		gyrocopter		
85-AAN		Best Off Sky Ranger		
85-AAT		Dyn'Aéro MCR-01		
85-ABB	F-JRMN	ATEC Zephyr		
85-ABJ		Aeroprakt A-22L	330	
85-ABR	F-JRQU	Evektor EV-97 Eurostar SL		
85-ABY	F-JRRP	Aerospool WT-9 Dynamic	DY354/2010	
85-ACG		PAP/ITV Lapoon Sport paramotor		
85-ACI		Magni gyrocopter		
85-ACL	F-JZRO	Flight Design CT SW (Same call-sign as 85-ACZ, one entry in error?)		
85-ACM(1)		ITV Lapoon Sport S paramotor		
85-ACM(2)	F-JZXJ	Ekolot JK-05 Junior	05 03 04	
85-ACZ	F-JZRO	Flight Design CT SW (See 85-ACL above)	1	
85-ADB		Air Création GT BI / iXess		
85-ADC		Aveko VL-3 Sprint	VL3-75	
85-ADN		Magni M-24 Orion		
85-ADU	F-JWRV	Dyn'Aéro MCR Pick-Up	122	21-ADQ
85-AEP	F-JSZI	Best Off Nynja		
85-AEY	F-JXWG	Dyn'Aéro MCR 01S	249	37-ACO, 21-YT
85-AFB	F-JTCB	ICP MXP-740 Savannah	01-04-51-066	
85-AFV		Air Création GTE / XP-15	A01030-1025	
85-AFY		Boxer M paramotor (accident 22.2.12)		
85-AGI		Air Création GTE Clipper / iXess 13		
85-AGJ		Magni M-16 Tandem Trainer		
85-AGK	F-JTQM	B&F Funk FK-9 Mk.3 Utility	09-184	D-MFSL(1)
85-AGY		paramotor		
85-AHH		Magni M-22 Voyager		
85-AHL	F-JUEK	BRM Aero Bristell XL-8		
85-AHN	F-JUFE	BRM Aero Bristell XL-8		
85-AHO		Autogyro-Europe MTOsport		
85-AID	F-JRRM	Pipistrel Virus		
85-AIL		Aeroprakt A-22L2 Vision	117	
85-AIY	F-JYZW	Air Création Tanarg / BioniX	A12110-12105 / T05084	
85-AJR	F-JVUA	Aerospool WT-9 Dynamic RG	DY054/2004	I-7602
85-AKB		Best Off Sky Ranger/Nynja		
85-ALT		Autogyro-Europe MTOsport		
85-ALX	F-JUBJ	Magni M-22 Voyager	22-13-8014	
85-ALY	F-JAEJ	Autogyro-Europe MTOsport		
85-AMK		JMB VL-3 Evolution	179	

86 : Vienne

Reg	F-reg	Type	Serial	Other
86-AA		Aile Stryker 19		
86-AC		Aéro Services Guépard		
86-AE		Air Création Buggy		
86-AL		Air Création / iXess		
86-AO		Air Création		
86-AS		Best Off Sky Ranger		

Reg	Mark	Type	Serial	Other
86-AW		Ray Hamsa X'Air		
86-AZ		Air Création / iXess		
86-BA		Air Création Buggy / iXess		
86-BI		Air Création / SX-II		
86-BJ		Zenith Baroudeur		
86-BM	F-JKSM	ICP MXP-740 Savannah		
86-BO	F-JEBY	Air Création GTE Trek / XP		
86-BR		Aéro Services Guépy 582T		
86-BS		Magni M-16 Tandem Trainer		
86-BU	F-JKSW	Magni M-14 Scout		
86-BX		Quasar		
86-CJ	F-JKUX	Humbert Tetras 912S		
86-CL		Air Création / XP11		
86-CN		Air Création / Quartz		
86-CO	F-JKVM	Synairgie / Puma Bil		
86-CS		Faucher-Jeanneau gyrocopter		
86-CT		Zodiac Ultrastar		
86-CZ		Aéro Services Guépy (Jabiru) 80T		
86-DB	F-JKUC	Denney Kitfox Lite		
86-DD		Air Création GTE BI / Quartz		
86-DO		Junkers Profly / La Mouette Ipsos 12		
86-DR		Air Création GTE 582S / Fun 450		
86-DS		Air Création Tanarg 582 / iXess 15		
		(Crashed 10.9.06)		
86-DT	F-JZHI	Alpi Aviation Pioneer 300		
86-DU		Micro Aviation Pulsar II		
		(Crashed 9.9.06)		
86-DW		Microbel / La Mouette Ipsos 12		
86-DX		ITV paramotor		
86-EC		Dynali Chickinox		
86-EF		Magni M-22 Voyager		
86-EH	F-JZYZ	Alpi Aviation Pioneer 300S	22	
86-EJ		Magni gyrocopter		
86-EL		Alpi Aviation Pioneer 200		
86-EN		X5		
86-EQ		Aides-Novis		
86-EU		Tecnam P.92-JS Echo	935	G-TECZ
86-EW		Air Création Racer / La Mouette		
86-EY	F-JYWK	BRM Okavango	0002/07	
86-EZ		Air Création 582S / Fun 450		
86-FC		CBBULM O2B / La Mouette Green 15		
86-FD		Humbert La Moto-du-Ciel		
86-FG	F-JXDI	Alpi Aviation Pioneer 200		
		(Same call-sign as 85-UV)		
86-FO		Aéro Services Super Guépard 912S		
86-FP		Alpi Aviation Pioneer 300 Hawk		
86-FQ		Alpi Aviation Pioneer 200		
86-FR		Alpi Aviation Pioneer 200		
		(Re-regd 59-CXJ)		
86-FY		Air Création GTE Clipper 582S		
86-FZ		Alpi Aviation Pioneer 200		
86-GC	F-JXTQ	Aéro Services Super Guépard 912S		
86-GE	F-JBQZ	Rans S-6 Coyote II	1001400	OO-D42
86-GI	F-JXYP	Alpi Aviation Pioneer 200		
86-GJ		Air Création Racer / XP		
86-GK		Weedhopper		
86-GL		Comco Ikarus C-42		
86-GO	F-JWCE	Alpi Aviation Pioneer 200		
86-GP		Flying Machines B612		
86-GQ		Rans S-6 Coyote II		
86-GR		Air Création / SX		
86-GU		BFC Challenger II	CH2-1093-1042	G-MYRJ
		(restored as G-MYRJ 9.15)		
86-GX		Aviasud AE209 Albatros 582	113	D-MWVH, 65-CR
86-GY	F-JWLP	Magni M-16 Tandem Trainer	16-08-5054	
86-HA	F-JWLF	Alpi Aviation Pioneer 300		
86-HB	F-JYNM	Air Création GTE Trek HKS700E / Kiss 450	AA01068-1062	
86-HE		Alpi Aviation Pioneer 200		
86-HF		Murphy Renegade Spirit		
86-HH		CBBULM O2B (HKS)		
86-HI	F-JXYP	Alpi Aviation Pioneer 200 (Sauer)		F-JWRH
86-HJ	F-JZFJ	Pipistrel Sinus		
86-HR		trike / La Mouette Ipsos		
86-HT	F-JWXT	Alpi Aviation Pioneer 200		
86-HV	F-JWZZ	Alpi Aviation Pioneer 300STD		
86-HY	F-JRBF	Alpi Aviation Pioneer 300STD		
86-IA	F-JRBC	B&F Funk FK-12 Comet	12-048	D-MRJD
86-IG		Magni M-24 Orion		
86-IJ		Tecnam P.2002 Sierra		
86-IN		Air Création GT / XP		
86-IO		Magni M-16 Tandem Trainer		
86-JC		CBBULM O2B / La Mouette Oryx 14.9		
86-JJ(1)		Synairgie		
86-JJ(2)		Air Création GTE Trek / iXess		
86-JL	F-JRZR	Alpi Aviation Pioneer 200		
86-JN		Air Création Tanarg / BioniX		
86-JQ	F-JSEC	Nando Groppo Trial		
86-JT	F-JSGG	Rans S-6 Coyote II		
86-JV	F-JKVL	Alpi Aviation Pioneer 200		
86-KA		Nando Groppo XL	00055	
86-KB		Air Création GTE 582S / Fun 450		
86-KH		Best Off Sky Ranger	185	
86-KI		Air Création Skypper 912 / NuviX		
86-KP		gyrocopter		
86-KQ		Air Création GTE Clipper / XP		
86-KY		Air Création / XP		
86-LD		Best Off Sky Ranger		
86-LI		Murphy Renegade II		
86-LM		Aéro Services Super Guépard 912S		
86-LR		CBBULM O2B / La Mouette Oryx 15		
86-MC		Eipper Quicksilver Sport 2		
86-ME		Air Création / Fun		
86-MN		Alpi Aviation Pioneer 200		
		(W/o 30.4.15)		
86-MP	F-JUBN	Alpi Aviation Pioneer 300STD		
86-MQ		Alpi Aviation Pioneer 200		
86-MR	F-JUDR	Colomban MC-30 Luciole	135	
86-NA	F-JUKZ	Aéro Services Super Guépard		
86-NJ	F-JUOQ	Alpi Aviation Pioneer 300 Kite		
86-NP	F-JUWC	DTA J-RO gyrocopter	014	
86-NV		Alpi Aviation Pioneer 200STD		
86-NW	F-JVAV	Alpi Aviation Pioneer 200STD		
86-OQ		Magni M-16 Tandem Trainer		
86-OU	F-JVVW	Alpi Aviation Pioneer 300STD		

Reg	Mark	Type	Serial	Other
86-OV	F-JVVX	Nando Groppo Trail	00108/67	
86-PC	F-JRJM	Alpi Aviation Pioneer 300 Kite		
86-PM	F-JUUD	Alpi Aviation Pioneer 300STD		
86-QF		Helisport CH-77 Ranabot		
86-QH	F-JAHI	Alpi Aviation Pioneer 300STD		
86-QR	F-JAUD	Spacek SD-1 Minisport	133	

87 : Haute-Vienne

Reg	Mark	Type	Serial	Other
87-M		Eipper Quicksilver		
87-AQ		weightshift		
87-AY		Aviasud AE209 Albatros		
87-BF	F-JIBF	III Sky Arrow 500TF	027	
87-BQ		Kitfox (?)		
87-BY	F-JIBY	Dyn'Aéro MCR-01	90	
87-CJ		Mignet HM.293 Pou-du-Ciel		W87-CJ
87-CW		Gatard-Farigoux GF-02T Poussin	7	F-PYBS
		(Re-regd 16-CM)		
87-DD		Barry MB-02 Souricette		
87-DK	F-JYYS	Raj Hamsa Hanuman		
87-DL		Mignet HM.293 Pou-du-Ciel		
87-DP		Air Création Buggy / XP		
87-DV	F-JIGJ	Humbert Tetras 912CS		
87-DX		Micro Aviation Pulsar III		
87-DY		Raj Hamsa Hanuman SP602T		
87-EJ		Air Création Buggy Twin 582SL / Fun 450		
87-ES		Guérin G1		
		(W/o 29.7.07)		
87-EU		gyrocopter		
87-FC		Best Off Sky Ranger V-Max (HKS700E)	954	
87-FI	F-JXUI	Didier Pti'tavion		
87-FJ	F-JXWQ	Air Création Tanarg / BioniX 13	A13017-13016 / T08013	
87-FO		Air Création / iXess		
87-FQ	F-JWIS	Rans S-6 Coyote II		
87-FU		Best Off Sky Ranger		
87-FZ		Aéro Services Super Guépard		
87-GH		Kangook/Paramania Action GT paramotor		
87-GI	F-JRTD	Best Off Sky Ranger V-Max		
87-GK		Rans S-12 Airaile		
87-GZ		paramotor		
87-IG		Best Off Sky Ranger Swift II		
87-JM		B&F Funk FK-9		

88 : Vosges

Reg	Mark	Type	Serial	Other
88-F		Aerokart		
88-I		Humbert La Moto-du-Ciel		
88-AJ		Humbert La Moto-du-Ciel		WHB-1
88-AK		Humbert La Moto-du-Ciel		POP-01
88-AN		Humbert La Moto-du-Ciel		
88-BD		Humbert La Moto-du-Ciel		
88-CE		Cosmos		
88-CI		Air Création / Fun		
88-CL		Weedhopper		
88-DD		Weedhopper		
88-DE		Denney Kitfox		
88-DF		Humbert La Moto-du-Ciel		
88-DM	F-JBPJ	Humbert Tetras		
88-DN		Humbert Tetras		
88-DP		Pegasus Quartz		
88-DT		Humbert Tetras		
88-EC		Humbert La Moto-du-Ciel		
		(Damaged 8.9.05)		
88-ED		Humbert La Moto-du-Ciel		
88-EE		Humbert Tetras		
88-EG		Aéro Services Guépy		
88-EQ		Humbert Tetras		
88-ES		Gemini		
88-ET	F-JASO	Humbert Tetras		
88-EX		Weedhopper		
88-FB		Humbert Tetras		
88-FE	F-JBZE	Humbert La Moto-du-Ciel		
88-FF		Air Création		
88-FY	F-JGCD	Aéro Services Guépy 582		
88-GA	F-JCXX	Humbert Tetras		
88-GB	F-JBDP	Humbert La Moto-du-Ciel		
88-GD		Humbert Tetras		
		(W/o 29.5.05)		
88-GI		Mignet HM.1000 Balerit	114	
88-GJ		Cosmos		
88-GP		Humbert La Moto-du-Ciel		
88-GS		Best Off Sky Ranger		
88-GT		Humbert Tetras		
88-GY		Aéro Services Guépy 582 (Jabiru)		
88-HE		Raj Hamsa X'Air		
88-HF		Humbert Tetras		
88-HH		DTA 582 Dynamic 15		
		(Crashed 19.5.04)		
88-HI		Humbert Tetras		
		(W/o 12.5.03; earlier reported as La Moto-du-Ciel)		
88-HJ		gyrocopter		
88-HL	F-JGCM	Alisport Yuma/Guérin G1	FELS 05 06 2001	
		(Also reported as 78-HE ?)		
88-HM	F-JGDS	Jodel D.20	17	
		(W/o 30.5.04)		
88-HP		Air Création GT BI		
88-HQ		Humbert La Moto-du-Ciel		
88-IB	F-JGEI	Humbert Tetras 912CSL		
88-IP	F-JRYG	Humbert Tetras 912CS		F-JQAU
88-JR	F-JZIO	Humbert Tetras 912BS		
88-KJ		Best Off Sky Ranger		
88-KS		Cosmos Phase III		
88-KX	F-JBDX	Guérin G1		
88-KZ		Cosmos Fidji Phase III		
88-LA	F-JZTM	Humbert Tetras	9529	
		(W/o 7.9.13)		
88-LB		Rans S-6 Coyote II		
		(W/o 24.8.11)		
88-LI		Humbert La Moto-du-Ciel		
88-LL		MacFly/Ozone Viper 2 paramotor		
88-LN	F-JZPY	Fantasy Air Allegro		
88-LT	F-JKWJ	Alpi Aviation Pioneer 200		
88-LU		Miniplane/Wings of Change Crossblade paramotor		
88-LV		ENC 200/Ozone Viper paramotor		
88-LX		Per ol Volo/Dudek Plasma paramotor		
88-MD	F-JDBP	Humbert la Moto-du-Ciel		
88-ME		Gyrotec DF-02		

Reg	F-reg	Type	C/n	Other
88-MH	F-JREV	Humbert Tetras 912CTS (n/w)		
88-MO	F-JEES	Alpi Aviation Pioneer 200		
88-MV		Cosmos Bidulm / Chronos 14		
88-NF		Miniplane/Ozone Viper 2 paramotor		
88-NJ		Celier Xenon		
88-NL	F-JAYG	Humbert Tetras 912CSL		
88-NM		Reflex/Ozone Viper 2 paramotor		
88-NN		ATEC 122 Zephyr		
88-NS		Air Création Tanarg / NuviX		
88-OI	F-JUAI	Humbert Tetras 912CS		
88-OV	F-JUSV	Aerospool WT-9 Dynamic	DY357/2010	
88-OX		Pipistrel Alpha Trainer	553AT912	
88-PC	F-JVLE	Humbert Tetras 912CS	141	
88-PI	F-JVPL	Humbert Tetras 912CS	206	
88-PP		JMB VL-3 Evolution	152	
88-WT		TL Ultralight TL-2000 Sting Carbon		

89 : Yonne

Reg	F-reg	Type	C/n	Other
89-AA		Etendard		
89-BC		Air Création / Quartz		
89-BG	F-JCQR	TEAM Mini-MAX		
89-BH		Air Création / Quartz		
89-BI		Air Création		
89-BM		Air Création		
89-BS		Air Création / Quartz		
89-CF		Air Création		
89-CM		Air Création		
89-DD		Air Création		
89-DN		Ikel / Cosmos		
89-DY		Air Création		
89-EB		Air Création		
89-EC		Air Création		
89-EH		Air Création		
89-EK		Air Création		
89-FH		Air Création GTE Clipper		
89-FJ		Weedhopper		
89-FY		Rans S-6 Coyote II		
89-GK		Djicat Buse'Air 150		
89-GN		Air Création Racer 503SL / XP II		
89-GO		Cosmos		
89-HM		Zenair CH-601 Zodiac		
89-HN		Zenair CH-601 Zodiac		
89-HO		Zenith Baroudeur		
89-HR		Djicat Buse'Air 150		
89-HV		Tecnam P.92 Echo	341-10	
89-IK		Mignet HM.293 Pou-du-Ciel		
89-IR		Djicat Buse'Air 150		
		(W/o 22.4.01)		
89-IU		Air Création / Cosmos Chronos 16		77-RL
89-IV		Djicat Buse'Air 150		
89-JA		Best Off Sky Ranger		
89-JB		Air Création / Cosmos Chronos 16		
			A202SD00250L	
		(C/n quoted is the 'code d'identification' found on the French ULM		
		'carte d'identification')		
89-JD	F-JGQF	Djicat Buse'Air 150		
89-JF		Weedhopper AX-3		
89-JG		Aviakit Vega		
89-JI		Chapelet Lazer		
89-JK		European Airwings Springbok 2000		
89-JN		Mustang III (trike)	R6413489	
89-JO	F-JGQB	Weedhopper AX-3		
89-JP		Weedhopper Europa II		
89-JR		Cosmos / La Mouette Top 14.9		
89-JT		Air Création GTE Clipper / Kiss		
89-JU		Aviakit Vega		
		(Damaged 24.6.01)		
89-KB		Air Création GT		
89-KC		Eipper Quicksilver MXL		
89-KE		Air's Maestro II		
89-KF		Air Création GT BI / Kiss 450	A08035-7059	
89-KG	F-JGPZ	Jodel D.18	214	F-PRJP
89-KJ		Air Création GTE 582 / Kiss 450		
			T01094/A01187-1199	
89-KM		Cosmos		
89-KN		ICP Bingo	02-02-52-047	
89-KO	F-JGQM	Aviakit Vega		
89-KS		ICP MXP-740 Savannah		
		(Also reported as Zenair CH-701 STOL)		
89-KT		European Airwings Springbok 3000		
89-LC		Light Aero Avid Flyer		
89-LG		Aviasud AE209 Albatros		
89-LU	F-JGZP	Clemfox CFM-01 (Kitfox)	CFX-01	W89-LU
89-MN		Dynali Chickinox		
89-MP		Air Création GT BI / XP		
89-MQ		Orenoque hydroplane		
89-MU		Flying Machines Carbone One /Aviatec CZ 15.4		
89-ND		Tecnam P.92S Echo		
89-NH		Best Off Sky Ranger V-Fun	562	
89-NI	F-JQHP	Fly Synthesis Storch		
89-NL	F-JQCP	Fly Synthesis Storch		
89-NO		Tecnam P.2004 Bravo		
		(W/o 26.6.05)		
89-NP	F-JQHV	Dyn'Aéro MCR Pick-Up	54	
		(Re-regd 21-ACN)		
89-NZ		Air Création GT BI / Kiss		
89-OB		Alpi Aviation Pioneer 200		
89-ON		Comco Ikarus C-42		
89-OS	F-JZMD	Jodel D.195	220T	F-PRAE
89-OT	F-JZOM	Alpi Aviation Pioneer 200		
		(Also reported as F-JZQM)		
89-OZ		Mignet Pou-du-Ciel		
89-PA	F-JGYX	ICP MXP-740 Savannah	01-12-51-125	77-AFE
89-PD	F-JZWX	Denney Kitfox IV-1200	1896	
89-PG		DTA / Dynamic 15/430	262	
89-PJ		Thruster (type?)		
89-PN		SE.5A scale replica "D276"		
89-PP	F-JYOP	Halley Apollo Fox		
89-PR		DTA Dynamic 582 / Synairgie Puma 14		
89-PY	F-JGHH	Sonic		
89-PZ		ICP MXP-740 Savannah	06-07-51-516	
89-QB	F-JXLZ	Flight Design CT SW	07-09-30	
89-QD		DTA / Dynamic 450		
89-QE		Quicksilver		
89-QG		Air Création GTE / Kiss		
89-QK		ELA Aviacion ELA-07	0508 222 0722	

Reg	F-reg	Type	C/n	Other
89-QM	F-JWZX	TEAM Mini-MAX 88	PFA186-12120	W89-QM, G-BYBW
89-QN		Comco Ikarus C-42		
89-QU	F-JXLP	Aviakit Vega		
89-QV		Comco Ikarus C-42		
89-QX	F-JAZF	Alpi Aviation Pioneer 300 Klte		
89-RB	F-JWWN	Best Off Nynja		
89-RD		Murphy Renegade Spirit		
89-RE	F-JKTO	Claude Leger Pataplume 2	1	
89-RI	F-JXJJ	Dyn'Aéro MCR Pick-Up	134	
89-RM		ITV paramotor		
89-RN	F-JYEO	Airborne Edge Outback 582 / Streak IIB		
89-SL	F-JZAL	Air Création GT BI 503 / Cosmos Mach 14.9		
89-SN		Air Création Tanarg / BioniX		
89-SO		gyrocopter		
89-TB		Air Création GTE / iXess		
89-TD		Fly Synthesis Storch HS		
89-TF		Air Création GT BI / Quartz 18		
89-TG		Best Off Sky Ranger		
89-TH		unidentified trike		
89-TQ	F-JTBV	Comco Ikarus C-42		
89-UF		TEAM Air Bike		
89-UI	F-JSVT	Alizon JPX		
89-UK		Quicksilver		
89-UO	F-JGOY	SG Aviation Storm 280		71-HA
89-UQ	F-JTRH	BRM Citius	0203/912UL/12-CT	
89-UX		Jodel D.18	367	F-PCBD
89-VA		Pottier P.180S	130	F-PDES
89-VC		Tipsy T-66 Nipper	7	F-PKVC, OO-NIG
89-VD	F-JUIH	ELA Aviacion ELA-07 Cougar	0912 378 0712	
89-VK		ICP MXP-740 Savannah S	14-01-54-0305	

90 : Territoire-de-Belfort

Reg	F-reg	Type	C/n	Other
90-AS		Cosmos		
90-BG		Cosmos		
90-BK		Weedhopper Europa II		
90-CC	F-JGCV	Humbert Tetras		
90-CG	F-JCGV	Humbert Tetras		
90-CI		Ikarusflug Eurofox Savane		
90-CK		Macair Merlin		
90-CL		Aviasud AE209 Albatros		
90-CR	F-JGNA	Rans S-6-116 Super Coyote II		
90-DG	F-JGNF	Rans S-6 Coyote II		
90-DH		Anglin J-6 Karatoo		
		(also reported as Let-Mont Tulak)		
90-DJ	F-JGQK	Air Création GTE Clipper / XP		
90-DK		Cosmos		
90-DM	F-JGNX	Pipistrel Sinus		
90-DN		Cosmos		
90-DP		Aviasud AE209 Albatros		
W90-DQ		gyrocopter (homebuilt)		
		(W/o 12.5.03)		
90-DS		Zenair CH-601 Zodiac		
90-DV		Halley Apollo Fox		
90-DW	F-JQGS	Humbert Tetras 912S	9960	
90-DY		Cosmos		
90-EB		Alisport Silent 2		
90-ED		ICP Bingo		
90-EH		Best Off Sky Ranger		
		(Crashed 26.7.05)		
90-EI	F-JRGF	ZUT Aviation TT2000 STOL		
		(previously used F-JQIF)		
90-EK		Rans S-6ES Coyote II	09041609	OO-F16
90-EL		Aircopter A3C	4	
90-EP		Cosmos Chronos		
90-EQ		Magni M-22 Voyager		
90-ES		Aviasud Mistral		
90-EZ	F-JPAS	Aviasud Mistral		
		(Same call-sign as 18-JM) (C/n 177 ?)		
90-FC	F-JYRY	Pipistrel Sinus		
90-FE		Magni M-18 Spartan		
90-FF		DTA Dynamic 582/16	00011	
90-FJ		Chapelet / Drachen Studio Kecur Avant		
90-FL		Magni M-14 Scout		
90-FS		Comco Ikarus Fox-C22		
90-FY		Jodel D.18	45	W90-FY, F-PJMT, F-WJMT
90-GG	F-JFRQ	Ekolot JK-05 Junior		
90-HB		Jodel D.18	368	F-PCHJ
90-RR		Best Off Sky Ranger		
90-SY		DTA Feeling / Dynamic 16		

91 : Essonne

Reg	F-reg	Type	C/n	Other
91-M		Ulac Aviation X99	169	
91-N		Landray GL.4 Visa		
91-O		Eipper Quicksilver		
91-S		Aviasud Sirocco "Antar"		
91-V		Aviasud Sirocco "Antar"		
91-X		Aviasud Sirocco "Antar"		
91-Y		Aviasud Sirocco "Antar"		
91-AD	F-JYFD	Jodel D.20		
91-BL		Veliplane		
91-BN		FT-91 Renegade		
91-CB		FT-91 Renegade		
91-CF		Eipper Quicksilver		
91-CV		Mervay		
91-DU		Air Création / iXess		
91-ED		Quartz 2 XS		
91-FN		Eipper Quicksilver MX		
91-FT		Murphy Renegade Spirit 503		
91-GF		Eipper Quicksilver MX		
91-GH		La Mouette		
91-GK		Air Création		
91-GQ		Maestro		
91-HA		Chariot		
91-HC		Aviasud AE532 Mistral		
91-HF		Papillon II		
91-HY		Allegro 2-seater		
91-IJ		Air Création / SX		
91-IO		Cyclone AX-3		
91-IQ		weightshift		
91-JE		Barry MB-02 Souricette		
91-JM		Best Off Sky Ranger		
91-JN		Barry MB-02 Souricette		
91-KB		Air Création Tanarg / BioniX		

91-KC		Ultralair Weedhopper AX-3-14		
91-KH		DTA Dynamic 503		
91-KI		Aviakit Vega 2000C		
91-KJ		Aero Kuhlmann Scub / AK		
91-KL		Air Création GTE Clipper / XP		
91-KM		Denney Kitfox		
91-KP		Best Off Sky Ranger		
91-KV		Cosmos (W/o 12.1.97 Nangis)		
91-KX		Cosmos		
91-LA		Pulsar / La Mouette		
91-LE		Synairgie Jet Ranger (tandem seat version of the Sky Ranger)		
91-LL		Aquilair Swing 14		
91-LM		Air Création / XP		
91-LN		Swift motorglider		
91-LO		Cosmos		
91-LP		Comco Ikarus Fox-C22		
91-LR		Nervures Altea paramotor		
91-LS		Aeropro Eurofox		
91-LU		Air Création GTE / Mild		
91-MI	F-JWRC	III Sky Arrow 500TF	076	
91-MJ		SE.5A replica (Painted as D3511)		
91-MO	F-JFEB	Zenith Baroudeur		
91-MP		Best Off Sky Ranger		
91-MU		paramotor		
91-NC		(Weedhopper ?) AX-3		
91-NG		ZUT Aviation TT2000 STOL		
91-NM	F-JFAH	Light Aero Avid amphibian	41	F-WZUX (2)
91-OA		Air Création / Mild		
91-OH		SMAN Pétrel		
91-OL	F-JPMD	Light Aero Avid Flyer		
91-OY		Cosmos		
91-PJ		Air Création / Mild		
91-PT		Barry MB-04 Souris Bulle		
91-PV	F-JFFV	Ekolot JK-05 Junior	05 05 02	
		(Re-regd 54-AIE)		
91-QE		Air Création GT BI		
91-QH		Zenair CH-701 STOL		
91-QI		DTA Dynamic 15		
91-QO		Air Création / Quartz		
91-QP		Zenair CH-601 Zodiac		
91-QR		Zenair CH-701 STOL		
91-QT		Zenair CH-701 STOL		
91-RB	F-JFBR	Denney Kitfox		
91-RC		Aero Kuhlmann Scub JPX (f/p)		
91-RK	F-JFBZ	Pipistrel Sinus		
91-RY	F-JFBW	Fly Synthesis Storch		
		(Same call-sign as 91-XE)		
91-SD	F-JFBI	Fantasy Air Allegro	01-119 (01-117 ?)	
91-SJ		Air Création GTE		
91-TB		Landray GL-06 Papillon		
91-TC	F-JFDO	ICP MXP-740 Savannah	01-11-51-117	
91-TN		Synairgie / Puma Bi		
91-TQ		ICP Super Bingo	02-06-52-059	
91-TR	F-JFFK	Aero Kuhlmann Scub		
91-UK		Pipistrel Sinus		
91-UM		Cosmos		
91-UT		Jodel D.921	198	F-PBXM
91-UY		Barry MB-02 Souricette		
91-VD	F-JFFV	Ekolet JK-05 Junior	05-02-02	
91-VG		Zlin Savage 912UL		
		(Crashed 2.6.05)		
91-VN		Air Création GTE		
91-WB	F-JPDY	Aero Kuhlmann Scub		
91-WC		Barry MB-02 Souricette		
91-WG		ITV Proxima paramotor		
91-WK		Rans S-10 Sakota		
91-WM		ITV Tomahawk paramotor		
91-XA		Alpi Aviation Pioneer 200		
91-XE	F-JFBW	Fly Synthesis Storch		
		(Same call-sign as 91-RY)		
91-XJ	F-JFCD	Aero Kuhlmann Scub		
	F-JWBY			
91-XU		Zlin Savage		
91-XZ	F-JPMO	ALMS Calao		
		(This is an crop sprayer version of the Zlin Savage for which ALMS was the importer for France)		
91-YC	F-JPGW	Jodel D.20	22	
91-YG		Murphy Renegade Spirit		
91-YJ		Jodel D.92 Bébé	758	
91-YO		Aéro Services Guépy		
91-YP	F-JPGZ	Flight Design CT SW		
91-YQ	F-JPMB	Aéro Services Guépy (Jabiru) 80		
91-YW		DTA Dynamic 505		
		(Re-regd 37-SK)		
91-ZO	F-JPMX	Humbert Tetras	9851	
91-ZP		ITV paramotor		
91-AAQ	F-JPRP	Best Off Sky Ranger (t/w)		38-NL, 36-KM
91-AAU		Best Off Sky Ranger		
91-ABE		Air Création GTE / iXess		
91-ABG		paramotor		
91-ABK	F-JPHD	Mignet HM.1100 Cordouan	23	
91-ABU		Magni M-22 Voyager		
91-ACD	F-JZZT	Lucas L.12		
91-ACY		paramotor		
91-ADB		Aerodynos JA177 Pinguin 912 Turbo		
91-ADY	F-JYFV	ALMS/Jodel D.20		
91-AEF		paramotor		
91-AEH		Demoiselle replica		
91-AFQ		P&M Aviation Quik GT450 912	8182	
		(Re-winged as QuikR with c/n 8423)		
91-AFA	F-JWZL	ELA Aviacion ELA-07S	0914 430 0724	
91-AFT	F-JXVI	Aéro Services Super Guépard (Jabiru)		
91-AFL		JMB Aircraft VL-3 Evolution	VL-3-160	
91-AFV		Zenair CH-601 Zodiac		
91-AFX	F-JFDE	Aero Kuhlmann Scub JPX		
91-AGF		Air Création GTE / iXess		
91-AGG		Magni M-16 Tandem Trainer		
91-AGO	F-JXCF	Aerodynos JA177 Pinguin	DTN 01 06 03	F-JXAO
91-AGZ	F-JWJC	ICP Bingo 4S	04-02-52-145	38-TN
91-AHJ	F-JWQX	Jabiru J170		
		(Also reported as 91-AHZ, 2011)		
91-AHN	F-JXAA	Magni M-22 Voyager	22-05-3284	
91-AHP		paramotor		
91-AHR	F-JUBD	B&F Funk FK-9 Mk.II	036	D-MQBF
91-AIA	F-JZIA	Raj Hamsa Hanuman		
91-AIF	F-JXQN	Aeropro Eurofox		

91-AIX		Barry MB-02 Souricette		
91-AJH		Mignet HM.1000 Balerit		
91-AJO	F-JPKJ	Dallach D4 Fascination		
		(Same call-sign as 18-KV)		
91-AKI	F-JRXX	Aerospool WT-9 Dynamic	DY360/2010	
91-AKZ		BRM Land Africa		
91-ALR		PAP/ITV Lapoon paramotor		
91-AMP	F-JYNK	Evektor EV-97 Eurostar	2007 2924	
		(Same c/n as 28-AGO, F-JYNK)		
91-AMY	F-JKEA	Vol Mediterrani VM-1 Esqual		
91-ANW		Tetra II		
91-AOO		Alpi Aviation Pioneer		
91-AOQ	F-JURE	Zenair CH-701 STOL		
91-API	F-JVEV	Shark Aero Shark	024/2013	
91-ASJ		Fokker E.III replica		
91-AXB		Air Création Tanarg / Bionix		
91-NRP		Barry MB-04 Souris Bulle		

92 : Hauts-de-Seine

92-K		(Micro Aviation ?) Pulsar III		
92-AD		Veliplane (trike)		
92-AE		Veliplane		
92-AK		Veliplane		
92-AN		Eipper Quicksilver MX		
92-AR		Kolb Ultrastar		
92-AS	F-JPMI	Aeropro Eurofox		
92-AU		Eipper Quicksilver MX II		
92-BK		Zenith Baroudeur		
92-BM		Zenith Baroudeur		
92-BS		Zenith Baroudeur		
92-BU		Zenith Baroudeur		
92-BW		Jodel D.18	12	
92-CH		Kolb Ultrastar		
92-CT		Aviasud Mistral		
92-CU		CFM Shadow Series B	010	G-MNES
92-CX		Air's Maestro		
92-DF		Zenith Baroudeur	123	
92-DN		Zenith Baroudeur		56-G
92-EB		Air Création		
92-EP		Air Création		
92-EQ		Zenith Baroudeur		
92-EV		Veliplane		
92-FF		JC-31 Weedhopper		
92-FG		Air Création GT BI / Quartz		
92-FN		Zenith Baroudeur		
92-FP		Zenith Baroudeur		
92-GA		Cosmos		
92-GD		Air's Maestro		
92-GM		Quartz		
92-GN		Air's Maestro 2		
92-GP		Cosmos		
92-GS		Air Création / Cosmos 14		
92-GU		Aviasud Mistral		83-DA
92-HD		Weedhopper		
92-HE		Air Création / Cosmos		
92-HJ		Solar Wings Pegasus Quantum		
92-HO		Jonathan (Barry MB-02 Souricette?)		
92-HQ		Weedhopper		
92-HU		Air Création GT / Fun		
92-HV		Aviasud AE209 Albatros	383	
92-II		Air Création / La Mouette Ghost 12		
92-IO		Air Plus Allegro		
		(Damaged 17.6.06)		
92-IQ		Top Concept Hurricane		
92-IR		Rans S-6ESD Coyote II		
92-IY	F-JFCO	TEAM Mini-MAX		
92-JA		Air Création / Cosmos Chronos		
92-JC		DTA Dynamic		
92-JP		Cosmos Chronos		
92-JS		Cosmos		
92-JS		Mignet HM.1000 Balerit	41	
		(destroyed in hangar fire 10.03)		
92-JV		Aviasud Albatros		
92-KJ	F-JAUM	Micro Aviation Pulsar II		
92-KM		Comco Ikarus C-42		
92-KU		Cosmos Chronos		
		(also reported as Weedhopper)		
92-KW		Best Off Sky Ranger		75-LQ
92-LK		Magni gyrocopter		
92-LS		Aeropro Eurofox		
92-MD		Paramania Action paramotor		
92-MN		Evektor EV-97 Eurostar		
92-MR		Paramania Revolution paramotor		
92-MZ	F-JZDC	Aeroprakt A-22		
92-NA	F-JWCK	trike / Zoom 19		
W92-NC		Project Dirisoft Airship (cycle power)		
92-NH	F-JYYW	Vidor Asso V Champion		
92-NQ		P&M Aviation Quik GT450	8155	G-CDVM
92-NS		Klipo Pulma (trike)		
92-NU		Dallach D4 Fascination		
92-NX		paramotor		
92-QH		Air Création Twin / iXess 13	A10134-9087	

93 : Seine-Saint-Denis

93-AJ		Mignet HM.293 Pou-du-Ciel		
93-AK		ULAC X99		
93-BB		Zenith Baroudeur ('Thompson' ?)		
93-BG		Aériane Sirocco		
93-BY		Air Création		
93-CK		Air Création / Pegasus		
93-CU		Cosmos		
93-DE		Centaure (wing)		
93-DH		Air Création / Quartz		
93-DQ		Air Création		
93-EO		Best Off Sky Ranger		
93-ET		Rans S-6ESD Coyote II		
93-FG		Cosmos		
93-FH		Cosmos Chronos		
93-FJ		Aviasud AE209 Albatros	28	65-CV
93-FK		Rans S-6 Coyote II		
93-FM		Curtiss Jenny replica		
93-FR		Cosmos		
93-FV		Best Off Sky Ranger		
93-GI		Cosmos		
93-GN		Air Création GTE Clipper		
93-HG		Cosmos / La Mouette Top 12.9	B21166	

Reg	F-reg	Type	c/n	Other
93-HJ		Mignet Pou-du-Ciel type		
W93-HV		weightshift		
93-HY	F-JPRN	ATEC 321 Faeta		
93-IA	F-JFFR	P&M Aviation Quik 912S	8094	
		(also carried F-JZCL 9.06)		
93-JH	F-JZCL	P&M Aviation QuikR 912S	8440	
93-JP		Air Création / Cosmos		
93-LO		Air Création / Quartz		
93-TA		P&M Aviation Quik GT450 912S		

94 : Val-de-Marne

Reg	F-reg	Type	c/n	Other
94-AQ		Air Création		
94-AX		Aviasud Sirocco		
94-BD		Aviasud Sirocco		
94-BE		Coutrot Pou-du-Ciel		
94-CH		Pacific		
94-CV		Aviasud Mistral		
94-DT		JCC Aviation J.300 Joker		
94-EC		Quartz X5		
94-EF		Mainair Gemini/Flash IIA		
94-EH		Veliplane		
94-EV		Air Création / Cosmos		
94-EX		Weedhopper AX-3		
94-FA		Zenith Baroudeur		
94-FB		Air Création GT BI / Fun		
94-FG		Mignet HM.1000 Balerit	71	
94-FJ		Huntair Pathfinder		
		(with Musée de l'Air reserve collection)		
94-FU		Aviasud AE209 Albatros		
94-GK		Air Création GTE / Fun		
		(Also reported as Cosmos Chronos 16, W/o 14.9.02)		
94-GP		Air Création GT BI		
94-GR		Aquilair Swing / La Mouette Ghost 16		
		(Re-regd 50-NK)		
94-HD		Cosmos		
94-HF		gyrocopter		
94-HJ		Air Création / SX		
94-HL		Air Création Racer / Fun		77-IN
94-HP		Comco Ikarus Fox-C22		
		(W/o 28.9.08)		
94-HR		Echo 12		
94-HS		Fly Synthesis Storch		
94-IJ		Tecnam P.92 Echo		
94-JC	F-JFBF	Humbert Tetras		
94-JD		Air Création / Kiss		
94-JH		Air Création / XP		
94-KG		Paramania Action paramotor		
94-KJ		Air Création Tanarg		
94-KL	F-JXGH	Light Aero Avid Flyer	723	F-WRFV
94-LW		Air Création / iXess		
94-NA		Jojowings Instinct paramotor		
94-XL		Light Aero Avid Flyer		
94-XP		Best Off Sky Ranger		

95 : Val d'Oise

Reg	F-reg	Type	c/n	Other
95-M		Veliplane		
95-O		Bee		
95-AA		B&F Funk FK-9 Utility		
95-AM		Air Création		
95-AN		Air Création		
95-BP		Zenith Baroudeur		
95-CH		ASEA 3-axis		
95-CY		Aviasud Mistral		
95-DC		Air Création		
95-DD		Quartz SX		
95-DN		Doutart Chevron Volant		
95-EA		Quartz		
95-EH		Quartz X5		
95-EV		Zenith Baroudeur		
95-FM		Aviasud Mistral	121	
95-GD		Mignet HM.293 Pou-du-Ciel		
		(Re-regd 59-TK)		
95-GJ		Air Création		
95-GS		Cyclone AX-3 / 503		
95-GU		Mignet HM.1000 Balerit	24	17-CV
95-GV		Raj Hamsa X'Air		
		(Re-regd 76-EO)		
95-HA		Air Création / Cosmos		
95-HI		Weedhopper Europa II		
95-HN	F-JPCT	Air Création / Mild		
95-HP		Air Création / Cosmos		
95-HX		Air Création / Cosmos		
95-IA	F-JFDM	Air Création / iXess	A04147-4149	
95-IH		Croses ULM Criquet		
95-II	F-JBSN	Micro Aviation Pulsar II	135	75-OJ
95-IJ		Zenair CH-701 STOL		
95-IK		Aquilair Swing 14		
95-IL(1 ?)	F-JFAL	B&F Funk FK-12 Comet Special	12-087	D-MAXG
		(Re-regd 57-AXT/F-JRLQ, then PH-4P5)		
95-IL(2)	F-JFAL	Air Création / SX		
95-IN		Air Création GT / Fun		
95-IX		Alpaero (Noin) Sirius		
95-JE		Paratech paramotor		
95-JF		Rans S-6ESD Coyote II		
95-JN		Aquilair Swing		
95-KC		Air Création / SX		
95-KD	F-JBZU	III Sky Arrow 500TF	033	
95-KJ		Urban Air UFM-13 Lambada		
		(Reporting error for 95-XJ ?)		
95-KV	F-JFAJ	Djicat Buse'Air 150GT	41	
		(Re-regd 51-LJ)		
95-LA		Air Command Autogiro		
		(W/o 29.1.01)		
95-LB		Air Command 532 Elite gyrocopter		
95-LC		Air Command 532 Elite gyrocopter		
95-LN		Air Création GTE Clipper		
95-ME		Averso AX.02 Guépard gyrocopter		
95-MG		Humbert La Moto-du-Ciel		
95-MO		Air Création / Quartz		
95-MR		PowerAssist Swift		
95-MT		paramotor		
95-MU		Cosmos Helios		
		(Damaged in forced landing 24.6.06)		
95-MU	F-JFDP	Best Off Sky Ranger		
		(also reported as Aquilair – see 95-MV)		
95-MV		Aquilair Swing		
		(Crashed 18.7.04)		
95-MX	F-JFCB	Sauper J.300 Joker		
95-MZ	F-JFEZ	Air Création Racer		
95-NA		Averso AX.02 Guépard gyrocopter		
95-NI	F-JFFF	III Sky Arrow 500TF	041	
95-NN		Zenair CH-601 Zodiac		
		(W/o 18.10.02)		
95-NP	F-JFDF	Aéro Services Guépy (Jabiru) 80		
95-NQ		Air Création GT BI / SX		
95-NU		Aero Kuhlmann Scub		
95-NX		Spratt 103		
95-NZ	F-JPOH	Light Aero Avid Flyer		
95-OB	F-JFEI	Fly Synthesis Storch HS		
95-OC		Aquilair Swing		
95-OD		Rans S-6 Coyote II		
95-OG	F-JFTX	Evektor EV-97 Eurostar		
95-OH		Air Création GT BI / La Mouette		
		(previously reported as Aquilair / La Mouette)		
95-OJ	F-JFEW	B&F Funk FK-9 Mk.III Club	03-U-202	
95-ON		Dyn'Aéro MCR-01 UL	208	
		(Re-regd 84-GE)		
95-OT	F-JFFB	B&F Funk FK-14 Polaris	14-033	
		(W/o 9.5.08)		
95-OV	F-JFFU	Humbert Tetras 912B	9418	
95-PA	F-JPMS	Fly Synthesis Storch HS		
95-PB		Humbert Tetras		
		(Re-regd 54-ACR)		
95-PJ		Aquilair Swing		
95-PK		Air Création / XP		
95-PL		Air Création Racer 447 / Fun 14		
95-PN		Flight Design CT-2K		
95-PO		Air Création GT BI / XP		
95-PY		Evektor EV-97 Eurostar	2004 2221	
95-QA		Reflex/Simoni paramotor		
		(Damaged 1.07)		
95-QB	F-JPGS	Ekolot JK-05 Junior		
95-QD	F-JBDJ	Fly Synthesis Storch HS	I-5330	
		(Same p/i quoted for 29-XY, re-regd?)		
95-QE		Alisport Yuma/Guérin G1 ?		
95-QF		Slepcev Storch SS4		
95-QL		Humbert La Moto-du-Ciel		
95-QX	F-JFAJ	B&F Funk FK-9 Mk.IV Club	243	
95-QY	F-JPGI	Aéro Services Guépard 912		
95-QZ		Air Création / XP		
95-RB	F-JPGQ	Flight Design CT SW		
95-RN		Evektor EV-97 Eurostar	2005 2503	
95-RS		Air Création		
95-RT	F-JGGT	Tandem Air Sunny		
95-RV	F-JEZX	Evektor EV-97 Eurostar	2003 1902	
		(Re-regd 69-RX)		
95-RZ	F-JPNJ	TL Ultralight TL-2000 Sting Carbon		
95-SA	F-JPMK	Jabiru J200 UL		
95-SC		Sauper J.300 Joker	008	
95-SD	F-JFCF	Evektor EV-97 Eurostar	2005 2404	
95-SF	F-JPMW	Evektor EV-97 Eurostar	2005 2416	
95-SG		Aviasud AE209 Albatros	73	
95-SH		Aquilair Swing		
95-SJ		Aerospool WT-9 Dynamic		
95-SM		ICP Bingo 4S	05-06-52-184	
95-SN	F-JFCR	TL Ultralight TL-2000 Sting Carbon		
95-SR	F-JZCX	Loic-Pochet Calamalo hydroplane		
		(SMAN Petrel derivative) (W/o 17.7.07)		
95-TC	F-JPRQ	Flight Design CT SW		
95-TG	F-JFCC	Evektor EV-97 Eurostar	2004 2201	
		(Same call-sign as 81-MF)		
95-TH		Aquilair Swing / Altitude 16.9		
95-TT		Aquilair Swing / La Mouette 14.9		
95-TY	F-JPDR	Air Création / Fun		
95-UC	F-JZIE	ATEC 321 Faeta		
		(also reported as F-JZJE)		
95-UD	F-JZJG	Aeropro Eurofox		
95-UG	F-JFCL	Best Off Sky Ranger	208	
		(Now with Aeroscopia collection, Toulouse)		
95-UN		Aeropro Eurofox		
95-US		Aquilair Swing		
95-UU	F-JZTY	Aéro Services Super Guépard (Jabiru)		
95-UV		Aquilair / La Mouette Ipsos 16.9		
95-UZ		Aquilair Swing		
95-VB		Air Création Buggy / XP		
95-VC		Aquilair Swing 582		
95-VD	F-JYBX	Flight Design CT SW		
95-VE		Pipistrel Sinus		
95-VG	F-JRDE	B&F Funk FK-9 Mk.III	09-130	95-VG / F-JFHT, 59-CAF / F-JFHT
		(Severely damaged 17.7.11, Portugal)		
95-VK	F-JYHQ	Evektor EV-97 Eurostar	2005 2528	(PH-3Y9)
95-VL		Best Off Sky Ranger		
95-VN		Best Off Sky Ranger		
95-VO	F-JFAQ	Humbert Moto-du-Ciel		
95-VR		Urban Air UFM-13 Lambada		
95-VS	F-JIBH	Urban Air UFM-11 Lambada		
95-VT	F-JYNN	ATEC 321 Faeta		
95-VU		weightshift		
95-VY		Force (paramotor)		
95-WC		Aquilair / La Mouette Ipsos		
95-WE	F-JFEY	Evektor EV-97 Sportstar	2007 0911	34-TG(2)?
		(Re-regd 77-BHE)		
95-WF	F-JZBF	Evektor EV-97 Eurostar	2007 2941	
		(Re-regd 22-JA)		
95-WS		Air Création Tanarg / iXess	A07149-7166	
95-XA	F-JXOM	Evektor EV-97 Eurostar	2007 3112	
95-XE		Paraplane		
95-XG		Air Création Tanarg / iXess	A08002-8002	
95-XI	F-JJMZ	B&F Funk FK-9 Mk.IV SW	348	
95-XJ	F-JXVU	Urban Air UFM-13 Lambada		
95-XK		Air Création GTE / Mild		
95-XP		Dyn'Aéro MCR-01		
95-XT	F-JXZH	B&F Funk FK-9 Mk.IV SW		
95-XW	F-JIPC	Celier Xenon		
95-XY		Alpi Aviation Pioneer 200		
95-YA		Paraplane		
95-YD		Aquilair		
95-YL	F-JWMW	Magni M-16 Tandem Trainer	16-08-5013	
		(stolen in the night of 9-10.10.13)		
95-YO		Flight Design CT SW		
95-YP		Adventure/Xpresso paramotor		

Reg	F-reg	Type	c/n	Other
95-YS	F-JQCA	Rans S-6 Coyote II		
95-YW	F-JWOJ	Aerospool WT-9 Dynamic	DY294/2009	
		(Re-regd 36-QV)		
95-ZA		Dyn'Aéro MCR-01	357	
95-ZD		Air Création GTE 582S / iXess 15		
95-ZL		Evektor EV-97 Eurostar	2009 3520	
		(Re-regd 78-ADQ)		
95-ZO		P&M Aviation Quik GT450	8451	
95-ZQ		gyrocopter		
95-ZT	F-JRAD	Best Off Sky Ranger		
95-ZW	F-JRCG	Flight Design CT SW	D-09-04-05	
95-AAF	F-JZSP	B&F Funk FK-9 Mk.IV Utility	09-04U-217	OO-E44
95-AAM	F-JROI	Evektor EV-97 Eurostar	2010 3709	
95-AAN	F-JRPE	Aveko VL-3 Sprint	VL3-60	
95-AAP		Evektor EV-97 Eurostar		
95-AAU	F-JRSQ	Alpi Aviation Pioneer 200		
95-AAV		Aerostyle Breezer CR	UL82	D-MAGQ(2)
95-AAY	F-JRWE	Aerostyle Breezer CR	UL83	
		(Re-regd 78-AGX)		
95-ABA	F-JRZF	Aerostyle Breezer CR	UL81	
95-ABG	F-JJWE	Pipistrel Virus		
95-ABH	F-JSCZ	Best Off Nynja 912`	561	
		(W/o 14.3.16, Kenya)		
95-ABT		Magni M-22 Voyager		
95-ABU	F-JSRB	Aeropro Eurofox	02407	
95-ACA	F-JSUN	Aveko VL-3-A Sprint	VL3-84	
95-ACB	F-JWYV	B&F Funk FK-9 Mk.IV ELA	415	35-LO
95-ACU		Airbet Girabet 503 gyrocopter		
95-ADD		Plätzer Kiebitz	54	
95-ADN	F-JZRI	Air Création Tanarg / BioniX	A13002-13003	
95-ADO	F-JROI	Aerospool WT-9 Dynamic	DY462/2013	
95-ADR		ITV Boxer paramotor		
95-ADW	F-JUTD	DTA / Magic		
95-AEI	F-JFDH	Air Création Tanarg / iXess 13	A09022-9023	
95-AEN		JMB Aircraft VL-3A	VL3-124	
		(Re-regd OO-H44 30.1.15)		
95-AEW	F-JVUR	TL Ultralight TL-2000 Sting S4	14 ST 415	
95-AFF		B&F Funk FK-9		
95-AFU		Stampe SV4-RS	1	
95-AGB	F-JAQF	Aerostyle Breezer ULM	04UL129	
		(Marked F-JAQG externally)		
95-AGF		Niki Lightning Gyro		
95-CAN		Dyn'Aero MCR Pick Up		

97 : Overseas Départements
(Part of the EU:- of those listed below, 971 is Guadeloupe, 97133 St Barthelemy, 97150 St Martin, 972 is Martinique, 973 is Guyane, 974 is La Réunion, 975 is St Pierre et Miquelon, 976 is Mayotte, 986 Wallis & Futuna Is, 987 French Polynesia and 988 New Caledonia)

Reg	F-reg	Type	c/n	Other
AD-97-1		Weedhopper amphibian		
97-BA		Air's Maestro		
97-BO		floatplane		
97-CC		Zenith Baroudeur		
97-CG		Zenair CH-701 STOL (f/p)		
971-AL		Buccaneer		
971-BA		Baulouet Frégate Hydroplane (homebuilt)		
		(Accident 27.4.05)		
971-BC		Zenair CH-701 STOL (f/p)		
971-BI		Zenair CH-601 Zodiac		
		(Damaged 30.11.04)		
971-BO		Raj Hamsa Hanuman		
		(Ditched 31.3.05)		
971-BS		Zenair CH-701 STOL (f/p)		
		(W/o 7.10.12)		
971-DL		Autogyro-Europe MTOsport		
972-CB		Evektor EV-97 Eurostar		
		(Accident 13.12.04)		
972-CC		Best Off Sky Ranger (f/p)		
		(Damaged 5.12.04)		
972-CF		Air Création Racer / Fun 450 (f/p)		
		(Accident 28.1.06)		
972-CO		Polaris FIB		
973-BY		Best Off Sky Ranger		
973-CG		Top Concept Hurricane Hydroplane		
		(Damaged in forced landing 12.11.06)		
973-ER		Best Off Sky Ranger		
W973-ES		Magny O'Taz'Gire Autogiro		
		(W/o 17.11.01)		
973-EX		Zlin Savage 912UL		
		(Damaged in forced landing 21.4.04)		
973-EY		Best Off Sky Ranger		
		(Crashed 25.8.06)		
974-D		(Technic Moto ?) Mustang		
974-J		Quartz 18		
974-AA		Quartz		
974-AB		Dewald Sunny		
		(Crashed 26.12.04)		
974-AI	F-JARI	B&F Funk FK-9 Mk.IV		
974-BS		Dynali Chickinox		
		(Damaged 21.1.05)		
974-CD	F-JXNZ	Flight Design CT SW		
974-CE		Rans S-6 Coyote II		
974-CN		Murphy Renegade Spirit		
974-CP		Air Création Safari GT BI 503		
		(Incident 15.6.06)		
974-CP ?		Rans S-6 Coyote II		
974-CT		Weedhopper Europa II		
974-DD	F-JMAT	Zenair CH-701 STOL		
		(Accident 26.2.05)		
974-DH		Zenair CH-701 STOL		
974-DM		Air Création		
		(Damaged 20.7.05)		
974-DP	F-JMDL	Flying Machines FM250 Vampyr		
974-DQ		Murphy Renegade Spirit		
		(Re-regd 06-CE)		
974-EE		Air Création GTE Clipper 582		
974-EH(1?)	F-JABI	TL Ultralight TL-132 Condor		
974-EH(2?)	F-JABI	Rans S-6 Coyote II		
		(W/o 8.5.10)		
974-EQ		Rans S-7 Courier		
		(W/o 17.9.13)		
974-ER		Best Off Sky Ranger		
		(Forced landing 16.1.06)		
974-FD		III Sky Arrow		
974-FE	F-JMAM	ICP MXP-740 Savannah		
974-FG		Rans S-7 Courier		

Reg	F-reg	Type	c/n	Other
974-FI		Best Off Sky Ranger		
974-FJ		weightshift		
974-FK	F-JMAZ	Jodel D.20	16	
974-FM		Air Création GT BI 582S		
974-FN		Best Off Sky Ranger		
974-FP	F-JMBE	B&F Funk FK-9 Mk.IV		
		(Damaged 27.11.04)		
974-FQ		B&F Funk FK-12 Comet	12-039	
		(Ditched)		
974-GA	F-JAIM	B&F Funk FK-9 ELA		
974-GB	F-JMBK	B&F Funk FK-14 Polaris	14-021	
		(D-MYRA quoted as 014-021)		
974-GC	F-JMDM	B&F Funk FK-9 Mk.IV SW		
974-GH		Pipistrel Sinus		
974-GJ	F-JMBS	B&F Funk FK-12 Comet	12-049	
		(W/o 27.8.16)		
974-GQ		Rans S-7 Courier		
		(W/o 30.3.15)		
974-GR		Air Création trike		
974-HK	F-JMCD	Alpi Aviation Pioneer 300		
974-HS		Rans S-7 Courier		
974-HT		B&F Funk FK-9		
974-HX		Rans S-6 Coyote II		
974-JA		Aeropro Eurofox		
		(Crashed 23.2.09)		
974-JN	F-JMDD	B&F Funk FK-9 Mk.IV		
974-JW		ELA Aviacion ELA-07		
974-KC	F-JMDS	Alpi Aviation Pioneer 200		
974-KD		Best Off Sky Ranger		
974-KE	F-JMDP	Best Off Nynja		
974-KL		Zenair CH-701 STOL		
974-KO		ITV paramotor		
974-KR		Ekolot KR-030 Topaz		
974-KW	F-JMDZ	B&F Funk FK-9 Mk.IV SW		
974-KX	F-JMEA	B&F Funk FK -12 Comet	12-076	
974-LK		B&F Funk FK-9 Mk.IV SW		
974-LP	F-JXUL	B&F Funk FK-9 Mk.IV	356	31-KC
974-LS		Rans S-6 Coyote II		
974-MF		Zenair CH.701 STOL		
		(Dbr 17.5.16)		
974-MR		B&F Funk FK-12 Comet	12-099	
974-MZ		ELA Aviacion ELA-07		
974-MX	F-JTMU	B&F Funk FK-9 ELA		
974-NT		Cicaré Spirit Tandem		
974-OA		DTA J-RO gyrocopter		
		(W/o 31.8.14)		
974-OS		LCA LH-212 Delta		
974-. .	F-JMCH	B&F Funk FK-9 (t/w)		
974-. .	F-JMCJ	Humbert Tetras		
974-. .	F-JMDB	(Tandem Air ?) Sunny		
974-. .	F-JRFY	B&F Funk FK-9 Mk.IV		
974-. .	F-JUZB	ATEC 21`2 Solo Racer		
975-ZZ		Rans S-6 Coyote II		
976-M		Raj Hamsa X'Air		
		(Forced landing 31.5.04)		
976-AF	F-JSIW	ELA Aviacion ELA-07S		
987-. .		B&F Funk FK-9 Mank IV	249	OO-E77
987-AZ		Flight Design CT SW		
988-BV		Ultralair JC-31 Weedhopper Premier AX-3		
		(Forced landing 8.12.07)		
988-FF		Humbert Tetras		
988-FG	F-JNAH	Slepcev Storch		
988-GC		Ekolot JK-05 Junior		
		(W/o 23.12.11)		
988-GK		Fly Synthesis Storch		
		(accident 2.9.11)		
988-GN		Dyn'Aéro MCR-01 ULC	264	
988-GO		Zenair CH-701 STOL		
		(Forced landing 28.4.07)		
988-HB		paramotor		
988-HV	F-JSUB	Aerospool WT-9 Dynamic	DY411/201.	
988-IA		Fly Synthesis Catalina NG		
		(W/o 4.1.14)		
988-IF		Fly Synthesis Storch HS		
		(accident 17.6.12)		
988-IG		Best Off Sky Ranger		

A separate series of three digits prefixed NC- has also been identified in New Caledonia.

99 : Non-Departmental
Only known use of this prefix is believed to be as a temporary registration for competition use by overseas pilots in France

Reg	Type
99-AA	Paramania Action paramotor
99-AB	Dudek Reaction paramotor

Test Registrations

Reg	F-reg	Type	c/n	Other
WAA-01		Jodel D.20	8	
WAU		Barry MB-02-2 Mini-Bulle	2	
WAAB	F-JFQJ	Sauper J.300 Joker		
WAAC		Jabiru UL/ Jabiru engines/ CAG Toxo		
WAAG		Cosmos / La Mouette Ipsos 14	trike 1087	
WAAM		Protoplane Ultra		
WAEL		Guérin G1		
WAHE01		Helisport CH-7 Kompress		
		(Damaged 25.9.05)		
WATC	F-JPSM	Aeronix Airelle		
WAVG01	F-JYMV	G1 Aviation G1 SPYL		
WC-S9		Cosmos Helios S9		
WDT 211		DTA Dynamic 15		
WDTA01	F-JAPS	DTA J'Ro	049	
WTDA01	F-JTDQ	DTA J'Ro		
WEHA		Humbert Aviation (La Moto-du-Ciel & Tetras)		
WEHA1		Humbert Tetras 912CS		
WEHA2		Humbert Tetras 912CSL		
WEK01		Ekolot KR-030 Topaz	030-05-05	
		(Regd 08-NI)		
WEL01		Espace Liberté Yuma & Guérin G1		
WEL06		Espace Liberté Country		
		(W/o 6.11.98)		
WHKW01		HKW Aero		
		(W/o 14.11.15)		
WHM52		Mignet HM.1100 Cordouan		
WPTA01		Aviomania G2sa Genesis gyrocopter	G256003	
WPTI01		Didier Pti't'Avion		
WSG-03		SG Aviation Storm 280RG		
		(Damaged 17.2.04, possibly W03-SG ?)		

WTWB01	Airflow Twinbee

Aircraft transferred from the CNRA register, new ULM registrations not yet confirmed

19- ?	Jodel D.19	120T	F-PAGM
21- ?	Jodel D.19	416T	
27- ?	Liberty APL-01	01	
38- ?	Jodel D.18	277	F-PRSH
43- ?	Zenair CH-600 Zodiac	6-1001	F-PZXL(2), F-WZXL
44- ?	Jodel D.18	311	F-PRBF
46- ?	Jodel D.19	145T	F-PCBZ
47- ?	Jodel D.18	112	F-PZPX(2)
48- ?	Zenair CH-601 Zodiac	6-2060	F-PCGT
55- ?	Jodel D.18	412	F-PLCT
56- ?	Jodel D.92 Bébé	719	F-PZRA
59- ?	Jodel D.18	91	F-PYNG
67- ?	Delvion DV-01 Zephyr	01	F-PDJV
67- ?	Dyn'Aéro MCR-01	09	F-PQUP, F-WQUP
69- ?	Light Aero Avid IV	1315	F-PSDH, F-WSDH
70- ?	Jodel D.18	388	F-PMAS
71- ?	Jodel D.92 Bébé	391	F-PINV
80- ?	Jodel D.92 Bébé	801	F-PJPR
82- ?	Jodel D.92 Bébé	648	F-PXKY, (F-PXKC)
88- ?	Jodel D.19	101	F-PEGY

Other transfers to ULM register, Department unknown

F-PBOZ	Jodel D.92 Bébé	97	
F-PDDT	Melos DFB-1A	02	
F-PHEL	Zenair CH-601HDS Zodiac	"601"	
F-PJMT	Jodel D.18	45	F-WJMT
F-PMIP	Evans VP-1 Volksplane	2315	
F-POUA	Barry MB-02 Souricette	168	
F-PRFM	Light Aero Avid IV	729	F-WRFM
F-PRKQ	Light Aero Avid IV	1099	F-WRKQ
F-PRVL	Van Lith IX bis	01	F-PYSZ, F-WYSZ
F-PRXL	Light Aero Avid IV	976	F-WRXL
F-PSKZ	Light Aero Avid IV	1501	F-WSKZ
F-PSMA	Aero Designs Pulsar XP	352	
F-PZMJ	Dupau MD-12 Papillon	01	
F-PZPD (2)	Gatard AG-02CR Poussin	40	
F-PZXR	Jodel D.18	92	

Cross-reference for observed F-J . . . tie-ups (see note at start of this section):

F-JAAC	07-QT
F-JAAP	48-BT
F-JAAS	08-OD
F-JAAU	67-BVX
F-JAAS	30-CE
F-JABA	03-AQ
F-JABC	26-AIJ
F-JABI	974-EH
F-JABJ	26-AIL
F-JABL	70-LV
F-JABU	25-ABU
F-JABY	59-ACA
F-JABZ	54-ATL
F-JACO	25-AEF
F-JADF	05-PQ
F-JADH	60-YY
F-JAEA	72-RS
F-JAEJ	85-ALY
F-JAEM	54-ATN
F-JAEN	76-CG
F-JAFA	38-QU
F-JAFS	22-BL / 27-AHB
F-JAFY	01-DA
F-JAFZ	22-BL
F-JAGK	22-KM
F-JAGP	54-GI
F-JAGS	01-FA
F-JAHB	32-NG
F-JAHD	01-CQ
F-JAHI	86-QH
F-JAID	58-DO
F-JAIF	16-TU
F-JAII	46-GJ
F-JAIU	54-ATR
F-JAJQ	59-IE
F-JAJX	33-ANT
F-JAKG	67-BWV
F-JAKK	44-AYG
F-JAKM	83-ALL
F-JAKN	01-SG
F-JAKQ	67-EM
F-JALF	38-AED
F-JALL	28-GJ
F-JALP	80-AES
F-JALR	16-UD
F-JALV	72-RV
F-JALW	63-AXQ
F-JAMA	16-TZ
F-JAMG	34-AMG
F-JAMH	59-IW
F-JAMJ	17-GF
F-JAML	83-ARL
F-JAMM	40-MQ
F-JAMQ	77-BPO
F-JAMS	49-ZE#
F-JANC	84-KZ
F-JANM	41-VQ
F-JANV	42-LY
F-JAOB	66-DB
F-JAOE	14-MT
F-JAOP	02-CO
F-JAOR	47-YU
F-JAPB	55-FO
F-JAPI	67-BXM
F-JAPO	83-AHK
F-JAPR	54-JE
F-JAPS	WDTA01
F-JAPY	59-ABU
F-JAQD	59-DPY
F-JAQF	95-AGB
F-JAQL	03-AFT
F-JARB	28-AOG
F-JARG	80-AEY
F-JARI	974-AI
F-JARN	77-ARN
F-JART	18-EO / 26-AIP
F-JASH	03-ADW
F-JASO	88-ET
F-JASW	71-QU
F-JASX	24-CT
F-JATC	85-BF
F-JATD	58-IE
F-JATM	22-KQ
F-JATT	37-HL
F-JATU	30-VN
F-JAUD	86-QR
F-JAUJ	70-MH
F-JAUK	81-CT / 27-AHO
F-JAUM	92-KJ
F-JAUN	28-AGE
F-JAUO	54-ARM
F-JAUS	38-RS
F-JAVL	38-CM / 54-PL
F-JAVT	57-GO
F-JAVZ	63-VZ
F-JAYD	72-RY
F-JAYG	88-NL
F-JAYO	07-QZ
F-JAYS	01-AGL
F-JAYT	54-DT / 24-XX
F-JAZB	57-HX
F-JAZF	89-QX
F-JAZI	66-PZ
F-JAZN	63-FJ
F-JBAB	03-AGO
F-JBAK	05-QB
F-JBAL	55-HN
F-JBAS	80-EV
F-JBBZ	47-FN
F-JBCC	32-CV
F-JBCP	65-ED
F-JBDP	88-GB
F-JPDJ	95-QD
F-JBDW	66-DK
F-JBDX	88-KX
F-JBEC	73-EF
F-JBEL	59-CKV
F-JBER	54-KK
F-JBFX	02-DM
F-JBGD	34-SB
F-JBGG	35-CI
F-JBGL	51-FY
F-JBGS	28-SK
F-JBGT	67-GZ
F-JBHE	71-FC
F-JBHQ	71-MU
F-JBHV	72-FS
F-JBHY	81-FC
F-JBIS	72-FV
F-JBJE	28-LW
F-JBJH	21-NJ
F-JBJI	01-QM
F-JBJQ	57-BC
F-JBKT	51-KY
F-JBLQ	67-JZ
F-JBLU	57-LR / 57-APE
F-JBME	55-FR
F-JBMJ	54-KX
F-JBMN	33-AFC
F-JBNF	42-AP
F-JBOK	73-ER
F-JBOM	08-CR
F-JBOV	16-GD / 55-IE
F-JBPJ	88-DM
F-JBPL	62-AEY
F-JBPM	83-SBI
F-JBQT	83-SJ
F-JBQZ	86-GE
F-JBRN	37-DX
F-JBRU	25-NB
F-JBRX	54-LT
F-JBSA	61-EF
F-JBSN	95-II
F-JBSQ	73-EN
F-JBSW	56-DR
F-JBTB	02-IR
F-JBTG	67-GZ
F-JBUE	79-EQ
F-JBUL	62-FX
F-JBUW	01-NS
F-JBVS	75-MI
F-JBWG	56-CQ
F-JBWZ	44-OE
F-JBXV	20-GS
F-JBYI	28-AIC
F-JBYR	10-FY
F-JBZE	88-FE
F-JBZG	57-PM
F-JBZI	55-FC
F-JBZU	95-KD
F-JCBH	01-KM
F-JCBU	59-TH / 54-RY
F-JCCD	54-NE
F-JCCR	59-TZ
F-JCCT	15-PY
F-JCDE	22-EA
F-JCDL	21-ACX
F-JCEF	82-FS
F-JCFN	67-LG
F-JCGC	64-IO
F-JCGI	83-GR
F-JCGV	90-CG
F-JCHF	58-CX
F-JCHK	40-FZ
F-JCHR	54-YB
F-JCIK	18-LY
F-JCJS	85-GA
F-JCJX	02-HB
F-JCKL	01-KF
F-JCKM	01-KG
F-JCKO	01-KH
F-JCKR	55-GS
F-JCLG	27-KS / 27-OB
F-JCLN	25-IT
F-JCLP	21-NO
F-JCLU	59-UC
F-JCMB	83-OU
F-JCMT	54-YN
F-JCMV	80-GY
F-JCNL	56-EO
F-JCNQ	83-AFY / 48-AK
F-JCOO	67-DS
F-JCOS	01-IR / 58-HK
F-JCPA	85-GE
F-JCPP	59-SH
F-JCPV	54-OA
F-JCQO	83-CL
F-JCQR	89-BG
F-JCQS	28-PL / 54-ZA
F-JCQT	28-QQ
F-JCQU	73-FU
F-JCSH	27-LL
F-JCSK	54-OD
F-JCTJ	04-BP
F-JCTY	26-IL
F-JCUE	07-HM
F-JCUF	37-MX
F-JCUM	01-LB
F-JCUO	30-HN
F-JCUP	18-MF
F-JCUQ	77-VL
F-JCVU	11-DO
F-JCWA	74-KF
F-JCWG	06-BZ
F-JCWH	49-II
F-JCWI	77-VC
F-JCWO	78-AAW
F-JCWR	32-KF
F-JCXQ	11-DP
F-JCXR	66-FU
F-JCXS	11-FR
F-JCXX	88-GA
F-JCYT	39-FO
F-JCZS	74-WB
F-JCZX	39-FC
F-JDAB	68-KR
F-JDAS	28-RC
F-JDBB	59-WI
F-JDBG	83-HR
F-JDBP	88-MD
F-JDCH	59-WF
F-JDCX	28-TC
F-JDDJ	44-AQI
F-JDEI	59-TM
F-JDEP	15-BM
F-JDET	59-CCR
F-JDFK	25-KB / 63-VD
F-JEAB	63-FR
F-JEAC	43-DD
F-JEBD	63-SC
F-JEBO	63-OT
F-JEBV	43-OL
F-JEBX	63-TA
F-JEBY	86-BO
F-JECM	15-GG
F-JECO	03-BA
F-JECR	03-BS / 03-SB
F-JECU	03-KL
F-JECV	63-CB
F-JEDJ	54-VO
F-JEDK	63-ACX
F-JEDO	03-RG
F-JEDX	63-EC
F-JEEG	63-ABL
F-JEEJ	03-CN
F-JEEO	67-BLT
F-JEEQ	63-JD / 41-QM
F-JEES	88-MO
F-JEFB	26-SA
F-JEFF	42-JQ
F-JEFJ	26-UH / 01-WX
F-JEFM	75-XI
F-JEFO	69-SF
F-JEFX	74-ZQ
F-JEFY	73-MB
F-JEGC	26-UL
F-JEGD	73-MA
F-JEGG	73-LO
F-JEGK	69-SK
F-JEGL	01-UR
F-JEGS	34-ADM / 30-SQ
F-JEGT	26-UU / 45-RS / 47-LY
F-JEGU	83-ACT / 26-UX
F-JEGV	42-JI
F-JEGX	74-UG / 65-MM
F-JEID	38-LA
F-JEIK	01-MR
F-JEIU	01-MC
F-JEJC	01-NO / 10-HN
F-JEJH	01-NJ
F-JEJI	01-MN
F-JEJK	01-NN
F-JEJM	38-KA
F-JEJO	01-TY / 01-ADM
F-JEJT	38-MU
F-JEKE	73-HS
F-JEKH	01-NP
F-JEKK	01-TH
F-JEKV	01-OL
F-JELC	01-OT
F-JELH	01-OF / 01-OS
F-JELJ	01-OQ
F-JELN	01-OU
F-JELS	01-OR
F-JELU	73-IB
F-JELX	38-MQ
F-JEMC	28-AMZ
F-JEME	42-JA
F-JEML	01-PM
F-JEMO	38-OU
F-JEMR	01-MO
F-JEMZ	73-PJ
F-JENO	07-IV
F-JENY	01-PR
F-JEOD	01-QB
F-JEOM	38-RD
F-JEPB	74-VS
F-JEPH	01-QQ
F-JEPL	38-NL
F-JEPR	01-QR
F-JEPS	59-DAI
F-JEPT	26-MQ
F-JEPU	26-QW
F-JEQW	33-AHX
F-JERF	73-JN
F-JERN	01-RL / (57-APE)
F-JERS	01-RQ
F-JERU	01-RT
F-JESG	01-RX
F-JESI	74-PV
F-JESR	01-PB
F-JETC	69-TL
F-JETI	73-KB
F-JETJ	01-SH
F-JETT	26-PE
F-JETU	42-GM
F-JEUA	26-PI
F-JEUK	69-TW
F-JEUN	01-SK
F-JEUT	73-KF
F-JEUY	38-QD
F-JEVC	66-OZ
F-JEVD	74-QV
F-JEVE	74-QU
F-JEVH	01-SU
F-JEVV	01-TE
F-JEWN	30-TB
F-JEWR	01-TJ
F-JEWS	26-RT
F-JEWU	39-QS
F-JEXB	01-TK
F-JEXK	01-TL
F-JEXN	73-LC
F-JEXP	22-SO ?
F-JEXR	01-TM / 83-ALN
F-JEXV	26-PY
F-JEXW	26-XG
F-JEYE	34-AFU
F-JEYH	01-TN
F-JEYP	01-TX
F-JEYR	02-AAH
F-JEYZ	01-UC
F-JEZA	38-RN
F-JEZB	73-LO
F-JEZD	01-UF
F-JEZG	76-UO
F-JEZJ	01-ZT
F-JEZM	38-SN
F-JEZO	21-ADM
F-JEZQ	69-QI
F-JEZS	69-RT
F-JEZX	95-RV / 69-RX
F-JEZZ	01-UL
F-JFAE	77-ZD
F-JFAH	91-NM
F-JFAI	77-ZV
F-JFAJ	51-LJ / 95-KV / 95-QX
F-JFAL	95-IL
F-JFAP	62-CAN
F-JFAQ	95-VO
F-JFAY	77-ABF
F-JFBB	77-AJT
F-JFBF	94-JC
F-JFBI	91-SD
F-JFBJ	78-RO
F-JFBO	77-AEL
F-JFBQ	77-ADW / 77-AFL
F-JFBR	91-RB
F-JFBV	28-AEG
F-JFBW	91-RY / 91-XE
F-JFBY	77-MK
F-JFBZ	91-RK
F-JFCB	95-MX
F-JFCC	81-MF / 95-TG
F-JFCD	91-XJ
F-JFCE	78-RE
F-JFCF	95-SD
F-JFCK	44-AOM
F-JFCL	95-UG
F-JFCM	77-JV
F-JFCO	62-AA / 92-IY / 77-ARU
F-JFCQ	77-ADO
F-JFCR	95-SN
F-JFCW	77-XQ
F-JFCZ	77-AES
F-JFDC	77-AJP
F-JFDE	91-AFX
F-JFDF	95-NP / 61-MT / 72-PW
F-JFDM	95-IA
F-JFDO	91-TC
F-JFDP	95-MU / 60-QW
F-JFDS	77-TK / 60-SV
F-JFDV	75-PZ
F-JFDX	77-AFO
F-JFDZ	75-OJ
F-JFEB	91-MO
F-JFEC	77-LQ
F-JFEI	95-OB
F-JFEK	77-AGA
F-JFEN	77-AFT
F-JFEO	77-AGE
F-JFET	77-AFN
F-JFEW	95-OJ
F-JFEY	95-WE / 77-BHE
F-JFEZ	95-MZ
F-JFFB	95-OT
F-JFFF	95-NI
F-JFFK	91-TR
F-JFFL	77-AHL
F-JFFN	77-AHK
F-JFFO	77-AEB
F-JFFQ	01-QC / 77-AHP
F-JFFR	93-IA
F-JFFU	95-OV
F-JFFV	91-VD / 91-PV
F-JFGA	37-AAB
F-JFGF	28-RL
F-JFGG	37-WJ
F-JFGH	45-QJ
F-JFGM	41-GY
F-JFGO	28-XR
F-JFGV	45-SA
F-JFHD	59-AAH / 02-JO
F-JFHJ	62-AUP
F-JFHL	62-HH
F-JFHT	59-CAF / 95-VG
F-JFHU	59-ABM
F-JFHX	59-AAG
F-JFIG	62-GI
F-JFIN	37-ZR / 59-CAN
F-JFIR	59-QE
F-JFIW	59-ABL
F-JFIX	77-AZQ
F-JFIZ	59-ACG
F-JFJE	59-XZ
F-JFJO	59-UJ / 62-AAW
F-JFJT	62-EK
F-JFKB	64-KL
F-JFKC	28-AAU
F-JFKE	62-ABN / 62-AEF
F-JFKF	35-IV
F-JFKG	62-ABB
F-JFKJ	59-UB
F-JFKR	59-CEJ / 85-YJ / 40-KD
F-JFKS	59-WK
F-JFKV	59-CCC
F-JFKW	62-ADB
F-JFKZ	59-CEQ
F-JFLB	62-HI
F-JFLJ?	62-ACE
F-JFLK	59-CFL
F-JFLM	59-UB / 59-CJG
F-JFMH	62-AMX
F-JFMU	59-CGK
F-JFMV	59-CHP
F-JFMW	95-SF
F-JFMX	59-CJA
F-JFNK	37-XU
F-JFNL	45-QN
F-JFNM	45-QZ
F-JFNO	41-JY
F-JFNQ	28-XN
F-JFNU	37-DU
F-JFNY	37-ML
F-JFNZ	18-HU
F-JFOB	74-AAT
F-JFOK	28-MZ / 58-GE
F-JFOL	51-KV
F-JFOQ	26-YE
F-JFOR	28-SL
F-JFOS	28-AAN
F-JFOT	37-KN
F-JFOU	28-VP / 62-ADT
F-JFOW	36-KT / 36-PR
F-JFPD	41-HT
F-JFPF	41-HX
F-JFPN	41-JA / 41-MX / 10-NA
F-JFPP	04-JB
F-JFPQ	45-NP / 78-XG
F-JFPR	36-KB
F-JFPU	28-ANK
F-JFPW	41-HF
F-JFPY	37-MY
F-JFQJ	59-AAB
F-JFQK	76-NG
F-JFQS	28-PL
F-JFQT	28-AAD
F-JFQV	18-HF
F-JFQW	41-KS
F-JFQZ	36-LN
F-JFRB	41-EO
F-JFRK	45-ZB
F-JFRN	18-HA
F-JFRO	36-FO
F-JFRP	28-XZ / 41-SI
F-JFRQ	90-GG
F-JFRR	18-HE / 18-MH
F-JFRT	41-JU
F-JFRX	41-DL
F-JFSA	37-PN
F-JFSC	37-KU
F-JFSJ	62-ARD
F-JFSL	36-LS
F-JFSM	36-LV
F-JFSN	31-PG
F-JFSR	24-UQ
F-JFSS	41-MV
F-JFSU	37-KY
F-JFSV	28-VS
F-JFSW	28-VV
F-JFTA	60-GH
F-JFTD	28-ACT
F-JFTK	28-SQ / 30-QX
F-JFTS	37-SA
F-JFTU	36-KE
F-JFTX	95-OG
F-JFTY	24-RW

F-JFUA	45-PY
F-JFUH	28-ACB / 28-WH
F-JFUI	61-LN / 28-ANS
F-JFUM	28-UV
F-JFUR	41-KU
F-JFUX	28-ACF
F-JFVD	27-MO
F-JFVJ	27-NI
F-JFVN	27-OH
F-JFVP	27-LQ
F-JFVR	76-KI
F-JFVU	76-KF
F-JFVW	27-RM
F-JFWI	27-PM
F-JFWK	02-ZX
F-JFWM	27-RP
F-JFWU	76-LS
F-JFWV	27-SU
F-JFWP	76-IL
F-JFWY	76-IM
F-JFXA	80-GO
F-JFXC	02-KY
F-JFXH	60-HX
F-JFXK	80-LR
F-JFXQ	80-IV / 80-VJ / 01-VG
F-JFXU	80-CG
F-JFXV	80-ID
F-JFXW	02-DJ
F-JFXZ	80-HJ
F-JFYE	02-KN
F-JFYG	80-MB / 80-PH
F-JFYO	02-KZ
F-JFYP	80-KL
F-JFYQ	80-MN
F-JFYV	60-JB
F-JFZD	80-JI
F-JFZH	80-LP
F-JFZI	60-KB
F-JFZK	02-JM
F-JFZM	80-HI
F-JFZS	02-MF
F-JGAA	83-GAA
F-JGAC	08-GG
F-JGAF	57-PX
F-JGAH	57-QM
F-JGAL	57-QL
F-JGAO	54-ACQ
F-JGAT	55-IG
F-JGAV	57-QC
F-JGAY	54-QT
F-JGAZ	44-ABY
F-JGBE	50-DE
F-JGBM	54-AR / 54-RR ?
F-JGBO	(54-ZJ)
F-JGBR	55-IX
F-JGBT	54-FF
F-JGBZ	68-MU
F-JGCB	54-TL
F-JGCD	88-FY / 46-EA
F-JGCF	54-SI
F-JGCM	88-HL
F-JGCO	57-SQ / 57-ADB
F-JGCV	90-CC
F-JGDE	54-UC
F-JGDI	54-TY
F-JGDM	54-UI
F-JGDP	54-UU
F-JGDR	54-UR
F-JGDS	88-HM
F-JGDT	57-MS
F-JGDU	25-GT
F-JGDX	54-US
F-JGEM	54-XH
F-JGEN	57-BO
F-JGEO	54-VP
F-JGEP	57-UC
F-JGEQ	57-RV
F-JGER	57-SS
F-JGEW	55-GF
F-JGFA	57-VC
F-JGFI	54-YY
F-JGFK	54-ZD
F-JGFT	55-RQ
F-JGFX	55-JT
F-JGGA	10-GH
F-JGGF	51-IP
F-JGGI	08-DU / 77-BEL
F-JGGN	10-IB
F-JGGQ	51-JO
F-JGGT	95-RT
F-JGGU	08-EE
F-JGGV	08-DW / 55-KP
F-JGHA	08-EK
F-JGHC	08-GC
F-JGHH	08-EG / 89-PY
F-JGHI	51-MB
F-JGHM	08-ET
F-JGHO	08-EB / 08-EZ
F-JGHT	51-LI
F-JGHZ	51-KT
F-JGIC	63-RL
F-JGIE	08-FO / 59-CSC
F-JGIF	77-AZM
F-JGIH	51-LH
F-JGKX	74-SF
F-JGLW	77-ATW
F-JGME	21-PU
F-JGMI	21-PX
F-JGMO	71-GP
F-JGNA	90-CR
F-JGNC	25-JI
F-JGNF	90-DG
F-JGNS	21-RY
F-JGNX	90-DM
F-JGNY	21-SF(1)

F-JGOA	21-SG / 83-AH
F-JGOE	58-EI
F-JGOG	21-AED
F-JGOH	58-FU
F-JGOJ	39-RF
F-JGOY	71-HA / 89-UO
F-JGPH	25-NQ
F-JGPJ	25-OG
F-JGPU	58-FN
F-JGPW	54-QM
F-JGPX	25-NY
F-JGPZ	89-KG
F-JGQB	89-JO
F-JGQD	70-FH
F-JGQF	89-JD
F-JGQK	90-DJ
F-JGQM	89-KO
F-JGQO	25-OU
F-JGQU	21-TL / 25-RX
F-JGRA	49-QN
F-JGRH	21-TU
F-JGRL	21-UA
F-JGRP	57-RP
F-JGSA	30-QT
F-JGSD	83-AHL
F-JGSG	28-APC
F-JGSI	67-MT
F-JGSO	68-SG
F-JGTD	68-NA
F-JGTN	67-PF
F-JGTO	67-PE
F-JGTP	21-QP
F-JGTQ	67-PL
F-JGTU	67-MN
F-JGTW	68-OP
F-JGUC	67-QS
F-JGUF	67-QY
F-JGUT	67-UD / 34-AAI
F-JGUV	67-VD / 50-MF
F-JGVA	67-VP
F-JGVE	67-VZ / 77-BHJ
F-JGVI	67-XB
F-JGVJ	67-WW
F-JGVN	68-OK
F-JGVP	67-XZ
F-JGVS	67-UT
F-JGVV	67-BEX
F-JGVZ	67-ZI
F-JGXA	21-UG
F-JGXE	71-GL
F-JGXI	26-ZK
F-JGXO	21-UE
F-JGXQ	25-IS
F-JGXZ	71-ID
F-JGYF	71-JO
F-JGYM	71-IC
F-JGYN	21-VF / 38-RX / 39-RX
F-JGYO	09-BC
F-JGYQ	21-VS
F-JGYU	25-HN
F-JGYV	71-IN
F-JGYX	89-PA
F-JGZB	25-QY
F-JGZK	71-IX / 80-ZD
F-JGZL	39-GK
F-JGZP	89-LU
F-JGZR	25-NB
F-JGZS	39-FA
F-JGZZ	25-YV
F-JHAA	85-LS
F-JHAQ	85-MR
F-JHAT	72-KH
F-JHAW	85-SK / 44-ASB
F-JHAZ	72-KJ
F-JHBA	85-NG
F-JHBB	44-AEO
F-JHBF	44-TT
F-JHBI	44-AGB
F-JHBJ	53-FG
F-JHBM	44-AFP
F-JHBN	44-AFN / 44-APK
F-JHBS	77-AWT
F-JHBU	85-NQ
F-JHCG	44-ZA
F-JHCS	35-MI
F-JHCW	85-OD
F-JHCX	44-AMJ
F-JHDC	85-PG / 78-ZL
F-JHDF	53-FZ
F-JHDJ	72-LQ
F-JHDK	31-OI
F-JHDM	44-AHJ
F-JHDQ	44-ANJ
F-JHDR	44-APK
F-JHDT	44-AHO
F-JHDW	53-GB
F-JHDX	72-QI
F-JHFT	33-TB
F-JHGC	61-CB
F-JHGD	56-IX
F-JHGL	62-ARF
F-JHGQ	50-HL
F-JHGU	50-JE
F-JHGW	77-BHH
F-JHGX	61-FG
F-JHHA	61-IX
F-JHHB	50-IS
F-JHHI	50-JB
F-JHHP	77-ASY
F-JHHQ	14-FR
F-JHHT	50-JS
F-JHHW	50-MV
F-JHHX	77-AXA
F-JHHY	61-IA

F-JHIA	61-HB / 27-AAC
F-JHID	61-II
F-JHIE	14-GB
F-JHIK	14-GI
F-JHIM	61-IP
F-JHIP	61-IY
F-JHIS	14-GD
F-JHIU	61-JD
F-JHIV	61-JE / 50-MZ / 14-JM
F-JHIW	50-LE
F-JHIX	05-MO
F-JHIZ	61-JG / 45-SJ
F-JHJD	14-HK
F-JHJF	14-JR
F-JHJG	50-NW
F-JHJQ	61-JR
F-JHJS	50-MA
F-JHMA	85-QP
F-JHMC	56-MC
F-JHMJ	27-NY
F-JHMM	56-KP
F-JHMS	29-EX / 56-HA
F-JHMX	29-CF
F-JHMY	35-GN
F-JHMZ	70-FG
F-JHNK	29-RU
F-JHNU	37-YJ
F-JHNY	29-FO / 29-TZ
F-JHOK	35-EI
F-JHOO	29-IA / 29-IR
F-JHOR	22-HR
F-JHOT	44-AHO
F-JHPC	21-IK
F-JHPF	29-IJ
F-JHPO	56-HH
F-JHPQ	56-HI
F-JHPR	60-OC
F-JHPS	22-GL
F-JHPT	56-HX
F-JHPW	35-FM
F-JHQA	56-HF
F-JHQF	72-LZ
F-JHQH	56-HQ
F-JHQI	56-GL / 29-FY / 29-PS
F-JHQJ	22-GP
F-JHQN	22-GR / 33-ZE
F-JHQP	35-FS / 21-AFC
F-JHQR	56-HY
F-JHQX	56-IB
F-JHRC	22-GW / 78-ABC
F-JHRF	56-IK
F-JHRH	29-GI
F-JHRK	35-GH
F-JHRM	56-10
F-JHTC	44-UH
F-JHTH	53-CX / 77-AWD
F-JHTM	44-TX
F-JHTO	55-WQ
F-JHTP	44-OE
F-JHTW	53-FD
F-JHTY	76-JV
F-JHUA	72-HU
F-JHUB	44-APO
F-JHUW	59-CWO / 85-RV
F-JHVA	49-NY / 72-MV
F-JHVF	72-IB
F-JHVJ	85-HQ
F-JHVK	13-ABR
F-JHVL	45-ZS
F-JHVM	85-OX
F-JHVR	44-XO
F-JHVT	79-JD
F-JHWF	44-XD
F-JHWH	49-UF
F-JHWJ	72-IT / 15-IT
F-JHWO	44-AVA
F-JHWK	44-AAO
F-JHWS	49-KU / 53-VC
F-JHWX	49-HE
F-JHXD	44-ADY
F-JHXF	78-SM
F-JHXK	44-AFA
F-JHXP	72-JB
F-JHXU	72-JE
F-JHYA	85-ML
F-JHYC	85-LN
F-JHYE	49-OS
F-JHYF	24-JM
F-JHYG	33-AEK
F-JHYL	44-ABV
F-JHYV	72-JL
F-JHZC	49-LO
F-JHZK	53-UV
F-JHZX	85-LW
F-JIAA	19-CC
F-JIAI	31-AI
F-JIAO	31-AO / 32-DI
F-JIAU	32-DJ
F-JIBB	09-AB
F-JIBE	12-BE
F-JIBF	87-BF
F-JIBG	35-LH
F-JIBH	95-VS
F-JIBI	31-BI
F-JIBO	31-BO
F-JIBP	31-BP
F-JIBQ	31-BQ
F-JIBT	46-BT
F-JIBU	31-BU
F-JIBV	31-BV
F-JIBX	(77-ARN)
F-JIBY	87-BY

F-JICA	31-BK
F-JIDE	31-DE
F-JIDH	31-DH / 82-CN
F-JIDM	32-PM
F-JIDW	31-DW
F-JIDX	12-DX
F-JIED	19-DA
F-JIEQ	81-CY
F-JIEU	46-AO
F-JIFB	46-FA
F-JIFF	12-DL
F-JIFL	23-CD
F-JIFM	32-FM
F-JIFN	09-BU
F-JIFQ	31-FQ
F-JIFS	31-FS
F-JIGE	03-JU / 02-AEW
F-JIGJ	87-DV
F-JIGK	31-CW
F-JIGM	46-MA / 57-AYX
F-JIGO	32-CL
F-JIHG	21-AEA
F-JIHN	65-JW
F-JIHO	82-BN
F-JIHQ	32-DE
F-JIHU	65-HU / 46-AZ
F-JIIL	82-AQ
F-JIIO	65-IO
F-JIIQ	46-DO
F-JIJE	77-AWY
F-JIKE	12-BP
F-JIKG	31-BP / 60-TN
F-JIKT	31-KY
F-JILB	31-LB
F-JING	25-NG
F-JINO	71-MZ
F-JIOP	31-OP
F-JIPC	95-XW
F-JIPN	17-QM
F-JIPQ	31-PQ
F-JIQD	81-QD
F-JIQE	81-QE
F-JIQR	81-QR
F-JIRC	19-CR
F-JISA	85-WR
F-JITM	71-LM
F-JIVB	11-HG / 47-VX
F-JIVE	31-VE
F-JIVL	31-VL
F-JIVN	47-UX
F-JIVP	31-VP
F-JJAG	13-IR
F-JJAI	83-JP
F-JJBG	13-RV
F-JJCD	13-OP
F-JJCH	13-MO
F-JJCK	13-MH
F-JJCP	77-AGG
F-JJCW	13-LZ
F-JJDO	74-ZI
F-JJDR	83-SP
F-JJDT	01-YX
F-JJDV	83-AH / 21-AHB
F-JJDZ	06-EC
F-JJEW	30-JY
F-JJEY	30-JJ
F-JJFB	66-HS
F-JJFY	30-KO
F-JJGZ	13-OO
F-JJHH	30-LL
F-JJHI	83-TM
F-JJHS	83-NG
F-JJIC	11-FA
F-JJIL	66-JZ
F-JJJB	83-JF
F-JJJH	06-GS
F-JJJQ	83-EW
F-JJKC	34-VL
F-JJKD	34-VM
F-JJKF	34-AIV
F-JJKI	83-SC
F-JJKJ	83-AU / 77-BAY
F-JJKN	34-KD
F-JJKV	01-WG
F-JJMB	60-UR
F-JJMP	13-QC
F-JJMQ	13-RY / 59-COZ
F-JJMX	05-HL / 37-AAF
F-JJMZ	95-XI
F-JJNF	11-FU
F-JJNM	30-MG
F-JJNO	11-FZ
F-JJNY	40-HM / 54-AIW
F-JJPD	76-TP
F-JJPI	68-ZM
F-JJPL	83-ZH
F-JJPV	19-LA
F-JJQJ	05-HK
F-JJQL	13-QX
F-JJQN	26-XC
F-JJQT	84-GE
F-JJQV	05-IK
F-JJQY	13-QY
F-JJRB	11-GB / 66-LV
F-JJSA	31-AFJ
F-JJSB	83-BP
F-JJSG	83-ZO
F-JJSI	83-UE
F-JJSR	83-SX
F-JJTC	05-IA
F-JJTD	13-HK
F-JJTF	13-RK
F-JJTH	84-HL
F-JJTL	13-MH
F-JJTR	04-JB
F-JJTT	13-RG

F-JJTV	54-AFA
F-JJUG	66-KH
F-JJUR	28-AHV
F-JJVB	83-JV
F-JJVI	83-TX
F-JJVK	06-MB
F-JJWB	13-PB
F-JJWD	13-SH
F-JJWE	95-ABG
F-JJWG	28-AJG
F-JJWH	05-GS
F-JJWU	13-SQ
F-JJWV	04-CZ
F-JJWZ	83-SC
F-JJXB	84-GZ / 27-YO
F-JJXX	30-JJ
F-JJZG	2A-BR
F-JKAG	33-MT
F-JKAH	24-GY
F-JKBG	47-JI
F-JKBK	33-MG / 33-ZV
F-JKBM	33-PC
F-JKCH	40-EJ
F-JKCI	33-PW
F-JKCM	33-AJD
F-JKCR	47-MQ
F-JKCW	64-JO
F-JKDA	47-MW
F-JKDB	47-NB
F-JKDD	33-RD
F-JKDF	50-LJ
F-JKDI	64JP
F-JKDK	47-NH
F-JKDQ	64-KA
F-JKDZ	33-PM / 78-AAM
F-JKEA	91-AMY
F-JKEH	33-LU / 47-OE / 82-II
F-JKEK	47-DE
F-JKEO	46-CW
F-JKEP	64-KI
F-JKET	33-SQ
F-JKFA	40-JH
F-JKFE	16-EM / 58-GL / 33-AES
F-JKFI	28-AJP
F-JKFK	40-ID / 33-ML / 33-AHC
F-JKFN	40-FJ
F-JKFQ	33-TN
F-JKFT	74-ABK
F-JKFV	64-KH
F-JKGA	17-SG
F-JKGM	64-KX
F-JKGV	47-PK
F-JKGX	64-LE
F-JKGY	03-ADA
F-JKHA	47-PF
F-JKHD	40-FX
F-JKHM	47-LM / 47-LY
F-JKHY	47-QA
F-JKID	47-QF
F-JKIG	64-LM
F-JKIH	51-RW
F-JKJE	47-RZ
F-JKJG	33-XQ
F-JKJP	40-GQ
F-JKQI	16-AM
F-JKQJ	16-LD
F-JKQK	16-JE
F-JKQP	62-ANO
F-JKRB	79-AU
F-JKRH	16-BL
F-JKRX	79-BP
F-JKSJ	16-AW
F-JKSM	86-BM
F-JKSW	86-BU
F-JKSY	17-FK
F-JKTA	79-EG
F-JKTL	16-CM / 77-BBC
F-JKTM	17-GS
F-JKTN	16-MR / 21-YT
F-JKTO	17-ET / 89-RE
F-JKTX	17-PM
F-JKTZ	79-JF
F-JKUC	17-HH / 86-DB
F-JKUH	79-HV
F-JKUI	17-GX
F-JKUO	17-QZ
F-JKUV	65-MF
F-JKUX	86-CJ
F-JKVB	79-EC
F-JKVI	16-DI
F-JKVL	86-JV
F-JKVM	86-CO
F-JKVR	17-MH
F-JKWJ	88-LT
F-JKWL	17-QN
F-JKWO	79-HD
F-JKWX	83-AEK
F-JLDD	12-BD
F-JMAM	974-FE
F-JMAT	974-DD
F-JMAZ	974-FK
F-JMBE	974-FP
F-JMBK	974-GB
F-JMBS	974-GJ
F-JMCD	974-HK
F-JMDB	974-..
F-JMDD	974-JN
F-JMDL	974-DP
F-JMDM	974-GC
F-JMDP	974-KE
F-JMDZ	974-KW
F-JMEA	974-..
F-JMDS	974-KC

F-JMHZ	35-EC
F-JNAH	988-FG
F-JOAH	56-GK
F-JOCI	57-AAR
F-JOGY	71-JF
F-JPAB	28-ZB
F-JPAC	37-FA
F-JPAD	41-LA
F-JPAF	28-ZE
F-JPAI	44-XD / 37-UF
F-JPAK	28-ZD
F-JPAL	37-WK / 37-XQ / 84-SP
F-JPAO	28-YO
F-JPAR	37-UM
F-JPAS	18-JM / 90-EZ
F-JPAT	45-MO
F-JPAV	28-ZP / 77-AYT
F-JPBF	59-CHI
F-JPBJ	59-CKQ
F-JPBQ	59-CKG
F-JPBS	59-CKS
F-JPBX	59-CKZ
F-JPBY	62-AFO
F-JPCA	60-KS
F-JPCO	02-ADM
F-JPCT	95-HN
F-JPDD	77-AJL
F-JPDJ	77-APJ
F-JPDK	77-ACH
F-JPDO	28-AGP
F-JPDP	77-AKJ
F-JPDQ	44-AQO
F-JPDR	95-TY
F-JPDW	77-ATQ
F-JPDX	77-AKO
F-JPDY	91-WB
F-JPDZ	77-AJC / 77-APJ
F-JPEB	37-TL
F-JPEC	37-SK
F-JPED	28-AAW
F-JPEE	41-LO
F-JPEG	37-HZ
F-JPEH	61-LX
F-JPEK	28-ZV
F-JPEM	45-SG
F-JPER	41-LX
F-JPEU	28-AAM
F-JPEW	22-JD
F-JPEZ	28-ZN
F-JPFD	45-TT
F-JPFK	27-ZP
F-JPFW	27-TN
F-JPFX	76-MN
F-JPFY	76-MQ
F-JPFZ	76-SN
F-JPGA	77-BDD
F-JPGC	(77-AUP)
F-JPGI	95-QY
F-JPGP	77-ALO
F-JPGQ	95-RB
F-JPGS	95-QB
F-JPGW	91-YC
F-JPGZ	91-YP
F-JPHA	28-AAY
F-JPHB	18-JE
F-JPHD	91-ABK
F-JPHE	41-ME
F-JPHF	28-ABD
F-JPHI	28-ABB
F-JPHJ	28-RB / 28-AHA
F-JPHK	41-LE
F-JPHN	28-AAX
F-JPHX	37-ZZ
F-JPHZ	45-TQ
F-JPIA	59-CKR
F-JPIC	62-AFV / 62-AFY
F-JPIE	59-CJK
F-JPIK	62-AGG
F-JPIL	59-CGA
F-JPIQ	59-CLP
F-JPIS	62-AGQ
F-JPIT	62-AGD
F-JPIU	62-AFZ
F-JPIW	47-VU
F-JPIY	59-CML
F-JPJD	27-ACY
F-JPJG	80-MG
F-JPJN	72-MJ
F-JPKA	41-MK
F-JPKF	28-YT
F-JPKG	28-ACN
F-JPKJ	91-AJO / 18-KV / 44-AVY
F-JPKK	45-RB
F-JPKL	28-ACS
F-JPKP	45-UJ
F-JPKR	28-ACU / 78-ZZ
F-JPKS	18-LW
F-JPLE	59-CMN / 27-ZI
F-JPLH	59-CMY
F-JPLJ	59-CNF / 37-AAI
F-JPLK	62-AME
F-JPLK	62-AAE / 62-AVJ
F-JPLO	59-CNB
F-JPLU	62-AHG
F-JPLX	62-AHJ
F-JPMB	91-YQ
F-JPMD	91-OL
F-JPMG	77-ASC
F-JPMH	77-ALR
F-JPMI	92-AS
F-JPMJ	77-ASM
F-JPMK	95-SA / 78-IM

F-JPMO	91-XZ / 18-NF
F-JPMQ	77-AMQ
F-JPMR	77-AMR
F-JPMS	95-PA
F-JPMT	70-JR
F-JPMU	73-NT
F-JPMW	95-SF
F-JPMX	91-ZO
F-JPNC	28-PG
F-JPNF	27-TY / 61-LJ
F-JPNJ	95-RZ
F-JPNK	76-MZ
F-JPNR	78-ZW
F-JPNM	76-NB
F-JPOC	41-MV
F-JPOF	28-ADB
F-JPOH	95-NZ
F-JPOI	28-ADE
F-JPOK	45-MS
F-JPOO	41-NH
F-JPOR	45-VA
F-JPOS	28-ACY
F-JPOT	41-NG
F-JPOV	45-ZE
F-JPOX	45-VH
F-JPQC	72-NB
F-JPQD	59-CMM
F-JPQF	59-COB
F-JPQI	62-AHW
F-JPQL	59-CNU
F-JPQM	59-TK / 59-TL
F-JPQV	74-XD
F-JPQW	62-AHY
F-JPQX	59-COP
F-JPRD	72-OZ
F-JPRH	77-AGD
F-JPRK	60-KY
F-JPRM	77-AOU
F-JPRN	93-HY
F-JPRP	91-AAQ
F-JPRQ	95-TC
F-JPSE	18-HQ
F-JPSG	37-AAJ / 37-ABY
F-JPSJ	41-NJ
F-JPSM	WATC
F-JPSS	41-NP
F-JPST	28-ADR
F-JPTB	77-AXP
F-JPTK	83-TK
F-JPTR	59-CPL
F-JPTQ	59-CPG
F-JPUA	45-WB / 77-AWU
F-JPUE	28-ADP / 19-HL
F-JPZW	75-MR
F-JQAB	55-LF
F-JQAD	57-YK
F-JQAQ	08-EK
F-JQAR	57-YT
F-JQAS	57-YM
F-JQAT	(57-ZF)
F-JQAU	88-IP
F-JQBD	54-AAU
F-JQBH	33-AAU
F-JQBJ	57-ATY
F-JQBK	57-ZN
F-JQBQ	54-ZJ
F-JQBR	57-ZR
F-JQBS	54-AAY
F-JQCA	95-YS
F-JQCL	55-MG
F-JQCP	89-NL
F-JQCR	57-AAF
F-JQCV	08-GD
F-JQCW	57-ABD
F-JQDF	10-JZ
F-JQDL	57-ABJ
F-JQDM	54-AGI
F-JQEU	55-PL
F-JQEV	57-ACP
F-JQEY	57-ACR
F-JQFH	08-GT
F-JQGA	58-GJ
F-JQGD	21-TK
F-JQGE	71-JK
F-JQGN	58-GF
F-JQGR	25-RN / 02-AAV
F-JQGS	90-DW
F-JQGT	21-XX
F-JQGX	25-SB
F-JQHC	58-GK
F-JQHN	21-YL
F-JQHO	25-SE
F-JQHP	89-NI
F-JQHV	89-NP / 21-ACN
F-JQHZ	21-YV
F-JQIB	21-QG
F-JQIF	90-EI
F-JQII	39-HL
F-JQIO	25-IJ
F-JQIX	39-HU
F-JQJL	25-QU
F-JQLU	58-HG
F-JQMG	42-LM
F-JQTR	21-YR
F-JRAD	95-ZT
F-JRAM	57-ZF
F-JRAR	28-AKR
F-JRAS	51-SP
F-JRAT	59-CZB
F-JRAU	59-CZC
F-JRBC	86-IA
F-JRBF	86-HY
F-JRBG	33-ANM
F-JRBJ	51-VK
F-JRBV	62-ARM
F-JRBX	85-AAG
F-JRCE	59-DAA
F-JRCG	95-ZW
F-JRCJ	66-ASR
F-JRCL	71-MN
F-JRCM	76-TA
F-JRCO	31-NK
F-JRCP	76-QZ
F-JRCS	27-QZ
F-JRCW	31-NJ
F-JRCZ	11-IC
F-JRDB	06-ABO
F-JRDE	95-VG
F-JRDL	31-NL
F-JRDM	27-AAK
F-JRDN	67-BGU
F-JRDO	31-NM
F-JRDP	31-NO
F-JRDQ	09-BO
F-JRDS	57-AWK
F-JRDU	80-ZI
F-JRDY	59-CZD
F-JREH	03-ACW
F-JREK	37-ACY
F-JREU	34-AGX
F-JREV	88-MH
F-JREY	57-SJ / 33-AIW
F-JRFO	21-AEL
F-JRGF	90-EI
F-JRGG	37-ADA
F-JRGI	44-APX
F-JRGK	49-SP
F-JRGN	33-LB
F-JRGT	50-MP
F-JRHH	81-HH
F-JRHI	16-NY
F-JRHL	21-AEM
F-JRHM	83-AGZ
F-JRHT	31-NT / 44-AQW
F-JRIE	61-MH
F-JRIG	59-CVT
F-JRIH	60-RK
F-JRII	76-TE
F-JRIN	56-LB
F-JRIW	47-VU
F-JRJA	26-ACT / 08-LR
F-JRJB	33-AFW
F-JRJC	77-BCC
F-JRJH	31-NX
F-JRJM	86-PC
F-JRJN	21-AEQ / 21-AIP
F-JRJT	31-NZ
F-JRJV	57-AQW
F-JRJW	37-AEI
F-JRKF	37-JF
F-JRKH	16-NF
F-JRKK	01-YL
F-JRKT	05-NS
F-JRKX	67-BUG
F-JRLI	82-HY
F-JRLN	28-ALP / 28-AQE
F-JRLQ	57-AXT
F-JRLR	54-ALU
F-JRLV	02-ADC / 04-EP
F-JRMD	59-DAB
F-JRME	44-ZK
F-JRMO	49-TE
F-JRMQ	80-ZO
F-JRMS	60-US
F-JRMT	60-RS
F-JRMU	24-UY
F-JRMW	40-IX
F-JRNA	78-AEG
F-JRNB	68-XW
F-JRND	65-NY
F-JRNE	35-LK
F-JRNG	72-PA
F-JRNL	25-VM
F-JRNP	83-AHH / 31-QC
F-JRNU	26-ABW
F-JRNW	13-WX
F-JRNX	08-KH
F-JROD	74-ZK
F-JROF	34-AFW
F-JROG	57-AYD
F-JROI	95-AAM
F-JROL	33-AGA
F-JROM	77-BCN
F-JROO	25-WU
F-JROP	77-BCO
F-JROU	77-BHK
F-JRPA	54-ALY
F-JRPC	60-RV
F-JRPD	72-EV
F-JRPE	95-AAN
F-JRPG	50-PV
F-JRPM	50-PO
F-JRPN	41-RK
F-JRPQ	47-UL
F-JRPS	60-RW
F-JRPU	26-ACD
F-JRQC	19-IK
F-JRQE	83-ALC
F-JRQK	01-YY
F-JRQN	34-AGD
F-JRQR	72-RL
F-JRQQ	54-AMD
F-JRQU	77-BCP / 85-ABR
F-JRQX	57-ATN / 21-AEX
F-JRRL	57-APC
F-JRRM	85-AID
F-JRRP	85-ABY
F-JRRR	17-TS
F-JRRT	59-DAN
F-JRRV	51-VR
F-JRSG	65-OD
F-JRSQ	95-AAU
F-JRSR	25-ADR
F-JRST	28-ALX
F-JRSY	59-DAR
F-JRSZ	03-ADD
F-JRTD	87-GI
F-JRTR	28-AMB
F-JRTX	17-TK
F-JRTY	05-PF
F-JRUB	60-SE
F-JRUC	77-BGP
F-JRUF	77-BDC
F-JRUL	83-AHS
F-JRUP	26-ACH
F-JRUT	67-BUF
F-JRUZ	77-AXV
F-JRVD	56-NR
F-JRVF	41-QP
F-JRVQ	38-YE
F-JRVV	78-ACP
F-JRWA	33-AGK
F-JRWD	77-BGK
F-JRWE	95-AAY / 78-AGX
F-JRWF	80-EO
F-JRWP	49-TN
F-JRWT	66-NR
F-JRWV	47-UR
F-JRWY	13-XA
F-JRXG	08-KP / 55-PO
F-JRXH	49-TP
F-JRXK	33-AGS
F-JRXR	45-AEU
F-JRXV	78-AEX
F-JRXX	91-AKI
F-JRYC	54-AMO
F-JRYG	88-IP
F-JRYH	41-RR
F-JRZC	57-BHT
F-JRZE	72-PI
F-JRZF	95-ABA
F-JRZL	77-BDT
F-JRZQ	01-ZY
F-JRZR	86-JL
F-JRZU	25-YO
F-JRZX	77-BCY
F-JRZY	71-MP
F-JSAC	83-AHR
F-JSAD	77-BDW
F-JSAG	76-TY
F-JSAH	77-BDY
F-JSAZ	27-ABI
F-JSBG	68-YT
F-JSBI	17-UN
F-JSBN	41-RT
F-JSBS	33-AGH
F-JSBT	68-ZR
F-JSBY	25-YW
F-JSBZ	25-YX
F-JSCF	11-IK
F-JSCU	82-IN
F-JSCV	62-AXS
F-JSCX	74-XD
F-JSCY	18-OY
F-JSCZ	95-ABH
F-JSDB	59-DBM
F-JSDC	54-AMX
F-JSDG	67-BIS
F-JSDO	47-TM
F-JSDU	77-BEG
F-JSDW	33-AMF
F-JSEA	59-DAH
F-JSEC	86-JQ
F-JSEE	84-JD
F-JSEF	26-ACV
F-JSEM	01-AAC
F-JSEQ	81-JN
F-JSER	67-BIX
F-JSES	11-IL
F-JSET	77-BEQ
F-JSEW	80-AAB
F-JSEX	80-AAC
F-JSFD	26-AHT
F-JSFM	27-AGI
F-JSFN	68-ZB
F-JSGD	64-RQ
F-JSGG	86-GT
F-JSGM	28-ALR
F-JSGX	45-AFP
F-JSHJ	63-AUC
F-JSHR	80-ADW
F-JSHT	26-ADH
F-JSHV	30-SL
F-JSHW	02-AEC
F-JSIF	59-DCF
F-JSIH	59-DCH
F-JSIL	80-AAH
F-JSIN	77-BFB
F-JSIP	12-FU
F-JSIW	976-AF
F-JSIZ	44-ARN / 01-AFY / 44-AUF / 44-AVP
F-JSJL	27-AGN
F-JSJM	44-ARH
F-JSJV	75-XW
F-JSJY	41-RH
F-JSKA	54-ATA
F-JSKE	01-AAN
F-JSKF	72-PM
F-JSKO	80-ABJ
F-JSKX	30-SS
F-JSLA	76-MO
F-JSLD	13-XJ
F-JSLF	44-ARP
F-JSLG	38-SJ / 38-ZI
F-JSLM	37-AED
F-JSLT	68-ABI
F-JSLX	08-LC
F-JSMB	31-Q? / 35-MN
F-JSMD	25-ZJ
F-JSMH	80-IH
F-JSMI	06-ABF
F-JSMV	26-ADI
F-JSMX	59-DCM
F-JSMY	41-SH
F-JSNM	82-BW
F-JSOF	11-IS
F-JSOH	77-BEH
F-JSOQ	11-IR
F-JSOR	83-AJR
F-JSOU	02-AHS
F-JSPB	45-AGA
F-JSPH	67-BKC
F-JSPJ	67-BKF
F-JSPL	35-LL
F-JSPM	68-ZV
F-JSPV	31-QJ
F-JSPX	62-AUS
F-JSQH	14-KS
F-JSQI	07-OD
F-JSQV	83-AHZ
F-JSQW	81-MM
F-JSRA	03-ADQ
F-JSRB	95-ABU
F-JSRC	31-QN
F-JSRG	21-XT /76-UB
F-JSRJ	31-MU
F-JSRY	72-PP
F-JSRZ	01-AAR
F-JSSE	54-AMF
F-JSSH	44-ARX
F-JSSU	71-NZ
F-JSSX	72-PU
F-JSTA	41-SL
F-JSTI	57-RF / 57-BLT
F-JSTP	67-BKR
F-JSTX	07-MY / 07-NQ
F-JSUB	988-HV
F-JSUG	31-QW
F-JSUH	67-BJO
F-JSUM	35-MY
F-JSUN	95-ACA
F-JSUQ	56-OW
F-JSUV	77-BFY
F-JSVD	45-AFK
F-JSVF	80-AAW
F-JSVM	38-ZY
F-JSVN	30-TB
F-JSVT	89-UI
F-JSVU	41-SQ
F-JSVV	18-QF
F-JSVY	47-VO
F-JSWG	26-AHU
F-JSWI	66-OI
F-JSWL	35-MJ
F-JSWM	05-NJ
F-JSWT	57-BBW
F-JSXF	16-PD
F-JSXI	83-AKF
F-JSXL	25-ZY
F-JSXO	76-UF
F-JSXS	37-QR
F-JSXT	11-IW / 08-LU
F-JSXY	37-AEK
F-JSXZ	37-AEJ
F-JSYE	78-AGI
F-JSYK	77-BGG
F-JSYW	70-KB
F-JSYX	01-ZR
F-JSZI	85-AEP
F-JSZK	60-TZ
F-JSZN	67-ABI
F-JSZP	24-TY
F-JTAB	75-YF
F-JTAD	67-XD
F-JTAG	67-BUU
F-JTAO	27-ADC
F-JTAR	83-AKS
F-JTAY	63-AUU
F-JTBE	62-ADS
F-JTBJ	35-BY
F-JTBK	49-VH
F-JTBO	61-NQ
F-JTBU	33-AIS
F-JTBV	89-TQ
F-JTCB	85-AFB
F-JTCC	02-AEV
F-JTCG	11-IU
F-JTCL	27-ADG
F-JTCN	27-ADH
F-JTCO	21-AGN
F-JTCP	80-ZG
F-JTCU	01-ABA
F-JTCV	01-ABB
F-JTCZ	42-MX
F-JTDC	01-ABC
F-JTDG	77-BGQ
F-JTDJ	53-XM
F-JTDM	71-ON
F-JTDQ	WDTA01
F-JTDU	11-IZ
F-JTDV	61-NO
F-JTDW	59-DDW
F-JTEP	74-ABQ
F-JTEW	31-RM / 35-LZ
F-JTEZ	67-BLF
F-JTFA	67-BKJ / 77-BHG
F-JTFD	21-AGS
F-JTFF	08-KW
F-JTFJ	69-ZD
F-JTFO	77-BGU
F-JTFQ	02-AFC
F-JTFR	02-AFE
F-JTFX	82-HA
F-JTFY	59-DDY
F-JTGB	34-AIG
F-JTGH	60-UJ
F-JTGK	51-VD
F-JTGL	59-DNW
F-JTGV	59-DEP
F-JTHB	76-UM
F-JTHC	59-DEV
F-JTHH	02-AFE
F-JTHJ	77-BHA
F-JTHK	03-AEA
F-JTIJ	39-HU
F-JTIK	70-KL
F-JTIR	83-ALK
F-JTIU	68-ABH
F-JTJJ	01-ABI
F-JTJP	41-TB
F-JTJS	34-AIL
F-JTJT	29-UN
F-JTKC	30-TI
F-JTKD	41-TC
F-JTKQ	12-GK
F-JTLC	54-APC
F-JTLE	57-BON
F-JTLO	34-AIQ
F-JTLY	59-CTN
F-JTLZ	31-SQ
F-JTMB	29-IK
F-JTMH	37-AFL
F-JTMJ	55-RR
F-JTML	01-ABS
F-JTMO	25-AAR
F-JTMU	974-MX
F-JTMX	14-LS
F-JTNB	50-QC
F-JTNC	38-AAV
F-JTND	77-BHV
F-JTNE	37-AFQ
F-JTNF	77-BHW
F-JTNQ	27-ADO
F-JTNS	33-AJT
F-JTNU	77-BHX
F-JTNX	08-LO
F-JTOJ	47-YD
F-JTON	01-ACB
F-JTOS	54-APK
F-JTOV	62-AWP
F-JTOX	59-DFO
F-JTPE	59-CPA
F-JTPS	37-AHW
F-JTPW	41-TG
F-JTQC	26-AHY
F-JTQM	85-AGK
F-JTQP	81-KM
F-JTQV	28-APJ
F-JTRF	42-NI
F-JTRH	89-UQ
F-JTRJ	31-SO
F-JTRW	67-BML
F-JTSA	84-JQ
F-JTSG	73-PZ
F-JTSP	70-KR
F-JTSW	83-AMO
F-JTSY	57-BEM
F-JTTC	01-AFM
F-JTTI	01-ACE
F-JTTM	60-VK
F-JTTR	28-AOU
F-JTTX	33-AJZ
F-JTTZ	46-FP
F-JTUZ	57-BET
F-JTVA	80-ABP
F-JTVJ	01-ACM
F-JTVP	57-BFA
F-JTWA	62-ARX
F-JTWH	03-AEE
F-JTWO	44-ATW
F-JTWP	59-DGM
F-JTWR	59-DGO / 59-DDO
F-JTXF	04-FO
F-JTXG	61-OH
F-JTXI	07-PS
F-JTXJ	33-AKC
F-JTXO	69-ZZ
F-JTXU	28-APP
F-JTYA	34-AJD
F-JTYB	67-BNE
F-JTYE	11-JH
F-JTYI	37-AGA
F-JTYK	82-AN
F-JTYL	21-AHP
F-JTYO	34-AJE
F-JTYR	32-LF
F-JTYX	60-JG
F-JTYY	24-TG
F-JTZD	33-AKE
F-JTZH	65-PN
F-JTZI	03-AEF
F-JTZJ	17-XK
F-JTZM	47-WS
F-JTZR	30-TP
F-JTZS	21-AKE
F-JTZT	27-AEG
F-JTZU	59-DGU
F-JUAC	80-ABU
F-JUAD	31-TH
F-JUAH	63-SC / 39-SC
F-JUAI	88-OI
F-JUAL	45-AHU
F-JUAM	26-AFI
F-JUAQ	74-ADD
F-JUAR	32-LL
F-JUAS	38-ABR
F-JUAY	01-ACR
F-JUAZ	26-AFR
F-JUBB	80-ABV
F-JUBD	91-AHR
F-JUBE	46-FU
F-JUBJ	85-ALX
F-JUBL	77-BJB
F-JUBN	86-PM
F-JUBQ	54-AQG
F-JUBZ	28-ANH
F-JUCA	73-QD
F-JUCE	24-RS
F-JUCF	78-AJA
F-JUCK	67-BNP
F-JUCN	84-JU
F-JUCQ	33-AKI
F-JUCT	39-LE
F-JUCU	37-AER
F-JUCW	41-VI
F-JUDC	60-VE
F-JUDF	27-AEI
F-JUDJ	39-LD
F-JUDO	44-AUK
F-JUDR	86-MR
F-JUDS	44-AUA
F-JUDT	70-KZ / 35-JR
F-JUDU	44-AUJ
F-JUEI	41-TN
F-JUEU	80-ABX
F-JUEY	59-DHB
F-JUFA	80-ABZ
F-JUFI	83-ANH
F-JUGC	05-OJ
F-JUGH	43-ZI
F-JUGJ	82-LI
F-JUGL	81-JZ
F-JUGT	59-DHG
F-JUHH	65-PP
F-JUHJ	08-NV
F-JUHY	77-BJI
F-JUIA	41-TT
F-JUIH	89-VD
F-JUIV	15-ACY
F-JUIY	70-KQ
F-JUJA	55-RX
F-JUJK	41-TU
F-JUJN	73-QE
F-JUJU	69-ADC
F-JUJY	59-DHM
F-JUKC	12-GX
F-JUKD	44-AUR
F-JUKE	01-ADE / 21-ADE
F-JUKH	03-ADB ?
F-JUKJ	25-ABM
F-JUKL	03-AEG
F-JUKN	16-QO
F-JUKQ	59-DII
F-JUKR	55-SA
F-JUKV	81-LO
F-JUKX	62-AXV
F-JUKZ	86-NA
F-JULB	47-WZ
F-JULE	01-ADI
F-JULH	51-WL
F-JULI	68-ADQ
F-JULK	57-BHC / 57-AYD
F-JULX	77-BJP
F-JULY	47-XC
F-JUMB	26-AFU
F-JUMC	80-ACI
F-JUMJ	59-DIR
F-JUMM	17-XW
F-JUMS	08-ME
F-JUMW	82-LZ
F-JUMY	57-ATS
F-JUNA	81-LP
F-JUNB	16-RH
F-JUNI	02-AGA
F-JUNP	47-XD
F-JUNY	21-AIF
F-JUOC	41-TX
F-JUOD	49-XO
F-JUOE	54-AHS
F-JUOG	54-AQQ / 59-DIZ
F-JUOO	08-MH
F-JUOQ	86-NJ
F-JUPJ	26-AGD
F-JUPK	44-AVP
F-JUPN	45-AJA
F-JUPP	83-ANX
F-JUPU	62-AKV
F-JUQA	16-QX
F-JUQM	03-AEL
F-JUQO	19-JO
F-JUQT	32-LZ
F-JURA	27-AEW
F-JURC	59-DIW
F-JURE	91-AOQ
F-JURF	13-ZQ
F-JURH	44-AXI
F-JURL	83-AOA
F-JURM	03-AEN
F-JUSC	77-BJV
F-JUSM	84-KA
F-JUSR	33-ALH
F-JUSS	25-IV
F-JUSU	54-AQX
F-JUSV	88-OV

F-JUTB	16-TG
F-JUTC	83-AOB
F-JUTD	95-ADW
F-JUTE	26-AGJ
F-JUTM	83-AQJ
F-JUTO	45-AJG
F-JUTR	61-PD
F-JUTS	74-AGZ
F-JUTV	67-BQA
F-JUUD	86-PM
F-JUUS	28-AOF
F-JUUV	71-PN
F-JUVA	25-ABZ
F-JUVB	80-ACO
F-JUVD	08-MQ
F-JUVJ	59-DJH
F-JUVQ	04-EJ
F-JUVY	70-LC
F-JUWC	86-NP
F-JUWI	30-UD
F-JUWM	77-BKD
F-JUWS	84-KB
F-JUWZ	59-DJN
F-JUXG	10-OZ
F-JUXL	27-AFH
F-JUXQ	84-GG
F-JUYA	01-ADP
F-JUYJ	59-DJO
F-JUYM	57-BOI
F-JUYO	59-DJK
F-JUYQ	W59-DJO
F-JUYU	08-MX
F-JUZA	59-DJB
F-JUZK	26-AGN
F-JUZN	07-PY / 07-QJ
F-JUZO	07-PZ
F-JUZP	07-QA / 07-RB
F-JUZQ	07-QG
F-JUZW	26-XK
F-JUZZ	12-HF
F-JVAI	35-CW
F-JVAJ	64-RV
F-JVAL	26-AIC
F-JVAV	86-NW
F-JVAY	31-WF
F-JVBG	67-BPH
F-JVBJ	59-DJP
F-JVBN	44-AVN
F-JVCG	14-NB
F-JVCW	38-ACR
F-JVDC	49-XV
F-JVDJ	02-AGT
F-JVDV	35-OD
F-JVDX	29-VF
F-JVDY	35-OC
F-JVEB	54-ABX
F-JVEV	91-API
F-JVFA	37-AGU
F-JVFC	49-XW
F-JVFS	11-JR
F-JVGL	44-AUF
F-JVGM	26-PQ
F-JVGW	03-AER
F-JVHR	68-AAJ
F-JVHV	04-GD
F-JVIG	70-LG
F-JVIZ	77-BLC
F-JVJC	35-OH
F-JVJG	59-DJI
F-JVJI	33-ALY
F-JVJJ	01-AEF
F-JVJP	03-AET
F-JVJS	71-PQ
F-JVJU	03-AEV
F-JVJX	59-DLC
F-JVKA	36-ST
F-JVKK	44-AVV
F-JVKO	81-LY
F-JVKZ	83-AOV
F-JVLD	70-LH
F-JVLE	88-PC
F-JVLG	44-AVX
F-JVLL	61-LP
F-JVLO	64-VR
F-JVLQ	59-DLI
F-JVMI	03-AEX
F-JVMK	47-XN
F-JVML	47-XP
F-JVMN	04-GI
F-JVMP	28-AQE
F-JVNH	69-ABD / 27-ZJ
F-JVNI	25-ACT
F-JVNK	36-SX
F-JVNL	44-AWB
F-JVNR	47-XQ
F-JVNT	73-RA
F-JVNX	77-BLM
F-JVNZ	03-AFB
F-JVOB	25-ACV
F-JVOF	54-ARS
F-JVOI	64-WH
F-JVOO	59-CQB
F-JVOS	80-ADG
F-JVOZ	67-BSI
F-JVPG	76-UA
F-JVPL	88-PI
F-JVPM	19-JT
F-JVPN	23-DL
F-JVQI	25-ACF
F-JVQO	71-PS
F-JVQU	67-BSS
F-JVRI	26-AHC
F-JVRL	78-ALN
F-JVRM	14-NI
F-JVRQ	37-VI
F-JVRS	08-LN
F-JVRT	59-DLO
F-JVRU	31-WM
F-JVRV	44-AXN
F-JVRX	54-ARX
F-JVRZ	74-AHF
F-JVSD	10-JZ
F-JVSF	64-WS
F-JVSH	02-AHC
F-JVSO	84-KI
F-JVSR	11-JT
F-JVST	14-NJ
F-JVSY	70-LM
F-JVTG	12-HM
F-JVTL	80-ADH / 80-AED
F-JVTR	21-AJN
F-JVTW	31-XO
F-JVUA	85-AJR
F-JVUG	30-UN
F-JVUH	44-AWF
F-JVUX	77-BMF
F-JVUY	31-YS
F-JVUZ	77-BMG
F-JVVC	77-BOO
F-JVVG	07-QH
F-JVVM	45-AKH
F-JVVP	26-AHG
F-JVVR	57-BMY
F-JVVT	83-APS
F-JVWA	78-ALT
F-JVWH	57-BNF
F-JVWX	09-CE
F-JVWY	77-BKT
F-JVXA	56-QS
F-JVXG	72-RJ
F-JVXS	77-BOQ
F-JVXV	26-AHE
F-JVYE	07-QL
F-JVYU	59-DML
F-JVYY	01-AEM
F-JVYZ	10-NY
F-JVZA	83-RP
F-JVZG	74-AGC
F-JVZK	42-OM
F-JWAE	80-XT
F-JWAF	25-TB
F-JWAN	50-OJ / 24-TV
F-JWAR	30-QQ
F-JWAT	67-BDF
F-JWAU	77-AYA
F-JWBA	80-XY
F-JWBB	41-PV
F-JWBC	41-PX
F-JWBD	54-AOW
F-JWBH	61-LD
F-JWBK	85-XS
F-JWBM	25-ABN
F-JWBO	30-QP / 13-WI
F-JWBU	41-PZ / 12-IE
F-JWBW	80-XZ
F-JWBX	33-AAR
F-JWBY	91-XJ
F-JWCB	54-AJH
F-JWCE	86-GO
F-JWCH	31-GK
F-JWCI	58-GK
F-JWCK	92-NA
F-JWCN	28-AIR
F-JWCV	28-AIY
F-JWCW	67-BEC
F-JWDA	73-NQ
F-JWDB	28-AIZ
F-JWDC	01-AFB
F-JWDE	68-VN
F-JWDH	24-LA
F-JWDK	51-QP
F-JWDM	83-SF
F-JWDP	51-RX
F-JWDR	47-TG
F-JWDS	21-AGL
F-JWED	08-GF
F-JWEH	47-TJ
F-JWEJ	80-YC
F-JWEP	08-KS
F-JWER	51-RN
F-JWEZ	58-IQ
F-JWFA	26-ZV
F-JWFK	66-MR
F-JWFL	67-BEJ
F-JWFR	67-BEK
F-JWFU	77-AYP
F-JWFV	54-AJO
F-JWGI	28-AIG
F-JWGK	28-AIV
F-JWGQ	73-NR
F-JWGU	16-MG
F-JWGW	45-AGR
F-JWGX	83-ADU
F-JWGY	16-MI
F-JWHC	83-AFK
F-JWHD	01-WN / 01-ABM
F-JWHE	67-BES / 68-YE
F-JWHH	21-YW
F-JWHI	28-AIS
F-JWHK	70-IP
F-JWHP	56-MP
F-JWHX	13-VK
F-JWHY	44-AOC
F-JWIA	26-DW / 47-TK
F-JWIB	57-ATZ / 28-AGP
F-JWIC	67-BET
F-JWIF	46-DV
F-JWII	28-AJH / 39-KX / 30-RK
F-JWIS	87-FQ
F-JWIT	77-BIY
F-JWIW	30-QV
F-JWIX	26-AFH
F-JWJC	91-AGZ
F-JWJD	18-OC
F-JWJF	80-YK
F-JWJK	08-IK
F-JWJL	21-ACN
F-JWJO	24-QY
F-JWJR	26-AAO
F-JWJS	36-MV
F-JWJV	12-DU
F-JWJX	59-CXG
F-JWJZ	67-BEW
F-JWKD	68-VZ
F-JWKH	03-ADB ?
F-JWKN	38-ACP
F-JWKR	27-ZG
F-JWKV	11-HN
F-JWKW	76-SE / 34-AIK
F-JWLF	86-HA
F-JWLH	46-EZ
F-JWLJ	79-IA
F-JWLL	34-AFG
F-JWLM	57-AUI
F-JWLP	86-GY
F-JWLS	49-RQ
F-JWLU	27-ZH
F-JWLZ	62-APR
F-JWMC	68-XG
F-JWME	59-CYI
F-JWMG	59-CXQ
F-JWMH	31-LY
F-JWMI	51-TK
F-JWMJ	68-VR
F-JWMN	74-WF
F-JWMQ	34-AEB
F-JWMS	40-JI / 32-HC
F-JWMT	77-AZG
F-JWMW	95-YL
F-JWMY	54-ASR
F-JWNE	13-WM
F-JWNF	54-CXU
F-JWNG	76-QP
F-JWNJ	62-APT
F-JWNN	50-ON
F-JWNP	59-CXT
F-JWNT	70-IV
F-JWNU	79-JK
F-JWNZ	26-AAS
F-JWOE	77-AUP
F-JWOG	44-APC
F-JWOH	31-RD
F-JWOJ	95-YW / 36-QV
F-JWOS	01-XU
F-JWOY	31-RD
F-JWPJ	19-IM
F-JWPQ	01-XA
F-JWPR	59-CXY
F-JWPX	17-SF
F-JWPY	03-ACO
F-JWQF	67-BLM
F-JWQG	59-CYB
F-JWQI	21-ADR
F-JWQL	76-RR
F-JWQM	51-SA
F-JWQO	51-SB
F-JWQQ	80-YT
F-JWQW	59-CYI
F-JWQX	91-AHJ
F-JWRC	91-MI
F-JWRE	28-AAJ
F-JWRG	44-APA
F-JWRH	86-HI
F-JWRJ	04-EV
F-JWRL	73-OE
F-JWRM	11-IH
F-JWRR	76-SP
F-JWRS	03-ACP
F-JWRV	85-ADU
F-JWRX	78-ABY
F-JWRY	71-MC
F-JWSB	51-SE
F-JWSG	22-IH
F-JWSH	04-DX / 65-MS
F-JWSI	80-ADT
F-JWSO	59-CYD
F-JWSY	31-MV
F-JWTK	54-AJY
F-JWTM	83-AFJ
F-JWTP	16-MS
F-JWTQ	77-AZX
F-JWTS	08-JI
F-JWTV	59-CYF
F-JWTY	74-YW
F-JWUA	74-YY
F-JWUF	49-RZ / 78-AGY
F-JWUH	24-WI
F-JWUI	62-ALZ
F-JWUJ	67-BFR
F-JWUF	78-AGY
F-JWUW	59-CYI
F-JWUZ	12-EN
F-JWVF	03-ACQ / 80-SE
F-JWVH	04-ET
F-JWVI	05-LJ
F-JWVJ	83-ID
F-JWVU	33-AEN
F-JWVX	56-VM
F-JWWA	70-LU
F-JWWB	21-AEB
F-JWWC	56-MW
F-JWWE	67-BFZ
F-JWWF	44-APF
F-JWWG	85-ZJ
F-JWWH	27-ZV
F-JWWK	11-IM
F-JWWM	62-FA
F-JWWN	89-RB
F-JWWS	45-ADH
F-JWWT	65-MW
F-JWWW	59-CYI
F-JWWY	07-NH
F-JWXC	85-ZK
F-JWXE	27-ZZ
F-JWXF	45-ABL
F-JWXJ	70-JB
F-JWXK	36-QN
F-JWXM	32-HN
F-JWXP	57-AUT
F-JWXT	86-HT
F-JWXU	56-MZ
F-JWXZ	11-HW
F-JWYF	54-AST
F-JWYJ	2B-CU
F-JWYO	05-LP / 56-OD
F-JWYV	95-ACB
F-JWYZ	67-BIB
F-JWZB	27-AAB
F-JWZC	74-YT
F-JWZE	59-CYM
F-JWZG	02-ACK
F-JWZJ	13-WC
F-JWZL	95-AFA
F-JWZS	49-SG
F-JWZX	89-QM
F-JWZZ	86-HV
F-JXAA	16-KX / 91-AHN
F-JXAC	62-AMJ
F-JXAF	18-MW
F-JXAG	65-AC / 45-ACG
F-JXAK	12-BX
F-JXAM	57-AQK
F-JXAO	(91-AGO)
F-JXAR	78-AEP
F-JXAT	59-CTH
F-JXAW	45-ACV
F-JXAX	47-SA / 83-AHU
F-JXAY	82-DY
F-JXBA	62-AIG
F-JXBB	59-CTI
F-JXBC	59-CTK
F-JXBF	67-BAV
F-JXBO	83-ADH
F-JXBS	51-QE
F-JXBU	69-UI
F-JXBV	28-ALN
F-JXBW	54-AHJ
F-JXCD	26-XH
F-JXCE	57-AQP
F-JXCF	91-AGO
F-JXCI	31-LD
F-JXCR	54-AHK
F-JXCS	57-AQR
F-JXCW	34-ACC
F-JXCX	28-ZO
F-JXDA	26-XK
F-JXDC	80-XD
F-JXDE	27-XF
F-JXDI	86-FG / 85-UV
F-JXDM	13-TX
F-JXDN	11-GT
F-JXDR	77-AUJ
F-JXDT	77-AUH
F-JXDW	44-ATJ
F-JXDX	47-SL
F-JXEA	60-OB
F-JXEC	14-IT
F-JXEI	46-DA
F-JXEK	74-UH
F-JXEU	09-JS
F-JXFA	59-CYS
F-JXFI	04-DJ
F-JXFP	59-CTR
F-JXFS	55-PM
F-JXFU	59-CTU
F-JXFX	70-KA
F-JXGB	76-PX / 45-ACZ
F-JXGG	61-KP
F-JXGH	94-KL
F-JXGL	59-CTV
F-JXGO	67-BAY
F-JXGX	54-ALB
F-JXHB	41-PL
F-JXHC	21-ABP
F-JXHF	59-CYN
F-JXHI	71-LH / 01-HD
F-JXHJ	25-UY
F-JXHR	85-ZT
F-JXHX	76-PW
F-JXIA	54-AHT
F-JXIF	54-AON
F-JXIJ	27-XO
F-JXIT	28-AGV / 28-AGW
F-JXIU	72-OQ
F-JXIZ	77-AVV
F-JXJD	64-NX
F-JXJF	34-UQ
F-JXJH	83-ADD
F-JXJJ	89-RI
F-JXJT	69-UM
F-JXJU	55-KQ / 33-AFX
F-JXK-	82-EF
F-JXKE	12-EH
F-JXKJ	66-KK
F-JXKK	21-ABR
F-JXKN	78-ABA
F-JXKT	33-ACE
F-JXKU	44-AMB
F-JXKV	44-ALY
F-JXKY	44-A..
F-JXLB	21-ADZ
F-JXLL	76-QP
F-JXLN	05-KD / 19-HT / 26-ADN
F-JXLP	89-QU
F-JXLR	71-MK
F-JXLS	02-ACO
F-JXLT	67-BGL
F-JXLU	02-ACP
F-JXLX	76-QM
F-JXLZ	89-QB
F-JXMC	21-AJY
F-JXMG	08-GO
F-JXMN	83-ADJ
F-JXMO	73-MY
F-JXMP	62-AMF
F-JXMU	77-BAU
F-JXMV	35-JG
F-JXMW	68-UA
F-JXMX	53-WR
F-JXMY	74-ZX
F-JXMZ	05-KZ / 05-KF
F-JXNB	22-IS
F-JXNE	59-CJL
F-JXNM	33-ADP
F-JXNZ	974-CD
F-JXOE	46-DD
F-JXOF	51-QO
F-JXOM	95-XA
F-JXON	14-JC
F-JXOO	14-JD
F-JXOP	54-AID
F-JXOU	35-JJ
F-JXOV	31-JG
F-JXOZ	21-ACC
F-JXPJ	26-YL
F-JXPN	78-ZO
F-JXPP	37-AAQ
F-JXPQ	24-SP
F-JXPR	09-AR
F-JXPS	27-XW
F-JXPU	38-UW
F-JXPY	62-ANN
F-JXQF	28-AHX
F-JXQI	67-BCC / 78-ABG
F-JXQN	91-AIF
F-JXQO	28-AKK
F-JXQR	56-LV
F-JXQT	56-LW
F-JXQV	57-ARS
F-JXQY	55-ID
F-JXRC	28-AAG
F-JXRK	17-RB
F-JXRL	62-AOA
F-JXRN	11-GX / 26-ACJ
F-JXRO	29-TB
F-JXRS	50-PS
F-JXRT	31-JK
F-JXRX	26-YQ
F-JXRY	83-ADW
F-JXSB	85-WE / 49-TA
F-JXSD	76-QT
F-JXSO	77-AWI / 48-??
F-JXSP	55-LK
F-JXSR	44-ANH
F-JXST	05-KJ
F-JXTB	77-AWR / 77-BKE
F-JXTC	80-XL / 38-AAE
F-JXTG	44-APS / 47-UQ / 59-DCQ
F-JXTQ	86-GC
F-JXTR	21-ACI
F-JXTT	21-AIJ
F-JXTU	83-AEC
F-JXTX	29-QQ
F-JXUC	17-TT
F-JXUE	77-BAZ / 77-BJH
F-JXUF	34-AFI
F-JXUH	75-VT
F-JXUI	87-FI
F-JXUL	31-KC / 974-LP
F-JXUM	51-QW
F-JXUP	85-WL
F-JXUY	64-QU
F-JXVA	73-OH
F-JXVG	45-ABI
F-JXVI	91-AFT
F-JXVJ	25-XK
F-JXVM	72-NI
F-JXVN	38-VF
F-JXVO	33-AHS
F-JXVQ	28-AHQ
F-JXVU	95-XJ
F-JXVV	27-TK
F-JXWC	02-AAO
F-JXWG	37-ACO / 49-SN / 85-AEY
F-JXWH	85-OX
F-JXWI	85-XI
F-JXWJ	01-WE
F-JXWO	01-YA
F-JXWP	31-KW / 24-RM / 31-KU
F-JXWQ	87-FJ
F-JXWS	07-NN
F-JXXA	80-XQ
F-JXXB	27-YO
F-JXXC	11-HA
F-JXXD	22-IG
F-JXXF	31-NE
F-JXXL	(76-QP)
F-JXXO	27-YH
F-JXXP	27-AFG
F-JXXR	59-CVE
F-JXXT	51-LC
F-JXXY	85-WP
F-JXXZ	38-UO
F-JXYB	77-WJ / 77-AWJ
F-JXYF	62-AOE
F-JXYL	67-BCW
F-JXYO	49-RD
F-JXYP	86-GI / 86-HI
F-JXYQ	37-ABD
F-JXYR	59-CVJ
F-JXYV	44-ASU / 44-AUI
F-JXZE	21-YI
F-JXZG	25-ADO
F-JXZH	95-XT
F-JXZJ	79-ID
F-JXZO	78-AEN
F-JXZS	82-FB
F-JXZW	62-ANZ
F-JXZX	13-VR
F-JYAF	39-KI
F-JYAT	35-GK
F-JYAB	24-LW
F-JYAD	45-YI
F-JYAI	74-ZF
F-JYAM	60-PI
F-JYAO	57-ABR
F-JYAS	27-XQ
F-JYAT	50-PG
F-JYAW	46-AEN
F-JYAX	79-GQ
F-JYBA	28-AFJ
F-JYBC	59-CSA
F-JYBN	42-KB / 42-LS
F-JYBO	W83-ACO
F-JYBU	71-KL
F-JYBX	95-VD
F-JYBZ	59-CSB
F-JYCB	60-QD
F-JYCG	61-LV
F-JYCI	80-WJ
F-JYCK	83-ABL
F-JYCM	80-WK
F-JYCN	32-ET
F-JYCU	26-ZI
F-JYDA	38-YS
F-JYDD	74-VD
F-JYDH	51-PF / 44-ASI
F-JYDN	83-ALX
F-JYDX	61-KE
F-JYDY	50-NB / 14-JO
F-JYED	37-ZL
F-JYEF	27-WG
F-JYEG	13-NT
F-JYEJ	62-ALH
F-JYEM	56-IW
F-JYEO	89-RN
F-JYFA	62-ALI
F-JYFF	50-OJ
F-JYFH	62-AJD
F-JYFJ	62-ADS
F-JYFO	47-RO
F-JYFU	29-IZ
F-JYFV	91-ADY
F-JYFX	77-BAM
F-JYGA	32-ES
F-JYGB	77-ASX
F-JYGE	40-HU
F-JYGJ	13-TB
F-JYGM	83-AGM
F-JYGO	76-NT
F-JYGS	07-ME
F-JYGZ	01-VB
F-JYHB	38-SS
F-JYHE	82-HX
F-JYHF	38-TK
F-JYHG	45-ZA
F-JYHK	27-WI
F-JYHO	76-OX
F-JYHP	49-PS
F-JYHQ	95-VK
F-JYHS	22-HM / 51-SV
F-JYIA	51-MI
F-JYIB	44-ALO
F-JYID	61-KI
F-JYIE	67-BCS
F-JYIH	33-AAN
F-JYIQ	78-XZ
F-JYIR	38-TN
F-JYIZ	27-WL
F-JYJC	27-AAF
F-JYJE	33-ABJ
F-JYJJ	27-OH
F-JYJN	33-AAO
F-JYJS	21-AEY
F-JYKC	50-NF
F-JYKF	68-WA
F-JYKM	71-OX / 77-BEP
F-JYKT	49-OY / 73-MQ / 56-LQ
F-JYKV	29-QI / 29-TS
F-JYKY	28-AGT / 31-GV
F-JYLC	18-PT
F-JYLH	72-MQ
F-JYLK	77-ATV
F-JYLL	02-ZS
F-JYLN	02-ADZ
F-JYLQ	74-VI
F-JYLR	59-CSQ
F-JYLS	19-HF
F-JYLT	21-ACJ
F-JYLU	54-UI
F-JYLW	77-ATW / 77-BJL
F-JYLX	77-ATX
F-JYLZ	83-ABW
F-JYMA	59-CYK ?
F-JYMD	59-CST

Reg	Code	Reg	Code	Reg	Code
F-JYMF	59-CSV / 34-CSV	F-JZAK	27-UV	F-JZOE	59-CQV
F-JYMK	61-KZ	F-JZAL	89-SL	F-JZOJ	79-GJ
F-JYMN	38-SA	F-JZAO	60-RA	F-JZOM	89-OT
F-JYMM	51-PQ / 61-NZ	F-JZBA	59-RR	F-JZOQ	56-JH
F-JYMN	38-SA / 83-AKE	F-JZBE	67-ZL	F-JZOR	61-JZ
F-JYMO	55-PA	F-JZBF	95-WF / 22-JA / 49-UT	F-JZOU	60-NH / 45-AGP
F-JYMP	59-CYK	F-JZBH	62-AMK	F-JZOW	45-AGP
F-JYMQ	25-ZX	F-JZBM	53-UX	F-JZOY	08-GU
F-JYMR	59-COR / 59-CYJ	F-JZBS	03-JU	F-JZOZ	79-GJ / 77-AOR
F-JYMV	WAVG01	F-JZBV	45-WL	F-JZPB	62-AKF
F-JYMW	29-QL	F-JZBX	02-AAW	F-JZPE	67-AAT
F-JYND	57-APK	F-JZBZ	44-AJW / 56-LF	F-JZPH	51-OG
F-JYNK	28-AGO / 91-AMP	F-JZCC	74-XB	F-JZPK	62-AOO
F-JYNN	59-CWD	F-JZCI	28-AHR / 77-BFR	F-JZPL	57-BNY
F-JYNM	86-HB	F-JZCJ	21-ZU	F-JZPQ	25-UQ
F-JYNN	95-VT	F-JZCL	93-IA / 93-JH	F-JZPU	66-KW / 61-NI
F-JYNU	19-HV	F-JZCM	02-AC	F-JZPX	45-VO
F-JYOB	47-WG	F-JZCR	24-QM	F-JZPY	88-LN
F-JYOE	80-WR	F-JZCV	57-ALR	F-JZQF	62-AKM
F-JYOI	77-ATT	F-JZCX	95-SR	F-JZQI	44-AKG / 51-NS
F-JYOP	89-PP	F-JZCY	22-GC	F-JZQJ	79-GJ
F-JYOT	(01-VG)	F-JZDC	92-MZ / 45-XG	F-JZQK	77-ARQ / 77-AWY
F-JYPA	69-QU	F-JZDD	24-SR	F-JZQQ	47-RD
F-JYPG	59-MP	F-JZDF	54-AEF	F-JZQX	59-CRG
F-JYPH	62-AJD	F-JZDG	24-MY / 85-VY / 26-ACF	F-JZRC	77-ART
F-JYPK	67-BAU	F-JZDH	33-XC	F-JZRI	28-AKJ
F-JYPL	54-AGM	F-JZDJ	80-VK	F-JZRL	82-CK
F-JYPM	77-AXI	F-JZDK	35-HH	F-JZRO	85-ACL or -ACZ
F-JYPN	38-TW	F-JZDN	49-NF / 28-AKO	F-JZRR	41-OO
F-JYPP	19-GU	F-JZDP	77-AQR	F-JZRX	28-AFG
F-JYPS	33-RS	F-JZDQ	35-HI	F-JZRS	45-XX
F-JYPT	67-BAC / 77-AEB	F-JZDW	51-MI	F-JZSF	77-APH
		F-JZEA	57-ASW	F-JZSI	31-EX
F-JYPX	57-APT	F-JZED	80-ZM	F-JZSL	78-AAQ
F-JYPY	28-ALZ	F-JZEK	55-QJ	F-JZSP	95-AAF
F-JYPZ	57-APE	F-JZEM	67-ZS	F-JZSY	77-ABZ
F-JYQD	54-AGQ	F-JZEN	21-ZT	F-JZSZ	29-RM
F-JYQG	58-HI	F-JZEO	49-OU	F-JZTE	59-DNF
F-JYQL	80-WT	F-JZEQ	33-ACK	F-JZTF	31-NA
F-JYQN	60-YA	F-JZER	37-VA / 78-ZK / 78-AAB	F-JZTI	03-AEF
F-JYQP	61-JT			F-JZTK	67-AAK
F-JYQV	83-ABY	F-JZFD	27-VE	F-JZTK	80-WA
F-JYQY	68-TU	F-JZFF	44-AKB	F-JZTL	27-TN
F-JYRB	37-ZT	F-JZFI	18-LZ	F-JZTM	88-LA
F-JYRG	46-CZ	F-JZFJ	86-HJ	F-JZTN	54-AFJ
F-JYRI	66-LH	F-JZFL	55-OC	F-JZTO	72-MC
F-JYRO	54-AGV	F-JZFV	62-AJN	F-JZTS	61-KC
F-JYRS	37-AFT	F-JZGA	27-VK	F-JZTT	82-CM
F-JYRT	34-ABM / 54-AGW	F-JZGC	28-AEF	F-JZTU	61-KD
		F-JZGE	54-ACT	F-JZTW	24-JX
F-JYRU	59-CZA	F-JZGG	77-AXG	F-JZTX	57-ANS / 67-AWS
F-JYRY	90-FC	F-JZGN	45-NI	F-JZTY	95-UU
F-JYSA	28-WG	F-JZGO	27-VB	F-JZTZ	10-LE / 77-BAD
F-JYSF	28-AGQ	F-JZGS	62-AJQ / 59-COX	F-JZUB	33-ZC
F-JYSH	50-NJ / 82-IJ			F-JZUC	59-XU
F-JYSM	32-FK	F-JZGW	77-AQX	F-JZUH	44-AMM / 44-AKL
F-JYSO	45-SJ	F-JZHE	62-AIS	F-JZUJ	45-XW
F-JYSQ	69-WB	F-JZHI	86-DT	F-JZUO	59-AAI
F-JYSU	61-IQ	F-JZHK	37-YH	F-JZUS	77-BBA
F-JYTC	62-AIK	F-JZHQ	47-UT	F-JZUU	67-BTU
F-JYTD	77-AUE	F-JZHT	77-ARC / 60-QT	F-JZUY	74-UN
F-JYTH	80-WV	F-JZHU	41-OC	F-JZVG	54-AIY
F-JYTI	35-HQ	F-JZHV	47-QQ	F-JZVI	80-ZP
F-JYTJ	09-AP / 33-ABQ	F-JZHW	55-OB	F-JZVK	67-ABL
F-JYUB	26-WZ	F-JZHX	83-AAH	F-JZVL	54-ZP
F-JYUC	36-PN	F-JZHY	44-ANF	F-JZVQ	62-AHM
F-JYUE	34-ABQ	F-JZIA	91-AIA	F-JZVU	83-AAV
F-JYUG	78-YG	F-JZIE	95-UC	F-JZVX	62-AKZ
F-JYUJ	33-ABN	F-JZIF	35-LY	F-JZWD	08-HY
F-JYUK	08-GV / 28-ALH	F-JZII	33-AAF	F-JZWF	77-AWQ / 73-PP
F-JYUM	31-HP	F-JZIM	28-AEP / 72-FP	F-JZWG	27-RQ
F-JYUP	65-LE	F-JZIO	88-JR	F-JZWL	77-ASE
F-JYUX	77-AUO	F-JZIQ	59-DBG	F-JZWS	71-LU
F-JYVH	60-QZ	F-JZIS	54-AEP	F-JZWW	31-FK
F-JYVN	71-LA	F-JZIZ	50-MC	F-JZWX	89-PD
F-JYVV	70-HR	F-JZJE	95-UC	F-JZXD	83-ABB
F-JYVW	54-AGS	F-JZJG	95-UD	F-JZXG	76-OQ
F-JYVZ	29-QR	F-JZJL	54-AED	F-JZXJ	85-ACM
F-JYWA	47-MM	F-JZJQ	44-AFM	F-JZXM	35-HX / 37-ADX
F-JYWK	86-EY	F-JZJR	67-ZU	F-JZXR	22-JU
F-JYWM	71-ME	F-JZIS	54-AEP / 83-AAO	F-JZXU	59-CMD
F-JYWN	68-TZ			F-JZYA	24-SC
F-JYWP	74-RU	F-JZJY	64-OO	F-JZYB	21-ACT
F-JYWS	56-KL	F-JZKB	54-AEQ	F-JZYI	59-CDN
F-JYWU	32-GB	F-JZKJ	28-NR	F-JZYJ	62-ALB / 44-ATK
F-JYWX	13-TS	F-JZKN	54-AES		
F-JYXA	21-SY	F-JZKQ	77-ARQ	F-JZYK	72-MK
F-JYXD	60-NX	F-JZKU	02-ANV	F-JZYL	34-AAI
F-JYXG	54-AIQ	F-JZKY	59-CBP	F-JZYN	31-FV / 33-ACM
F-JYXH	33-AEY	F-JZLB	62-AFZ	F-JZYZ	86-EH
F-JYXI	51-PX	F-JZLC	28-ADT	F-JZZB	56-MU
F-JYXK	33-NO	F-JZLE	59-CQQ	F-JZZO	49-PM
F-JYXQ	51-PY	F-JZLF	77-APV	F-JZZS	62-ARE
F-JYXR	56-TK / 56-JK	F-JZLP	41-OI / 37-AFG	F-JZZX	91-ACD
F-JYXW	13-TO / 83-TO	F-JZLQ	25-XO	F-JZZX	04-DW
F-JYXX	21-ABF / 21-AHY	F-JZLU	54-AEU ?		
F-JYYC	08-KN	F-JZLY	62-NC		
F-JYYE	19-DI	F-JZMB	66-JF		
F-JYYF	42-JU	F-JZMD	89-OS		
F-JYYR	04-DI	F-JZMF	29-UO		
F-JYYT	72-OP	F-JZMH	27-YL		
F-JYYV	77-AUV	F-JZML	55-MC		
F-JYYW	92-NH	F-JZMR	29-IA		
F-JYZD	59-CTB	F-JZMU	25-UA		
F-JYZU	05-JS	F-JZMW	71-KE		
F-JYZW	85-AIY	F-JZMX	45-ACX		
F-JYZX	74-WW	F-JZMY	27-VR		
F-JZAB	51-NS / 01-NS	F-JZMZ	33-AHQ		
F-JZAD	76-HH	F-JZNL	08-GA		
F-JZAE	72-LV	F-JZNP	02-NX		
F-JZAG	38-SW	F-JZNQ	60-YB		
F-JZAH	34-ABZ	F-JZOC	83-AAS		

Call-sign / registration tie-ups unknown, identities welcome:

Reg	Type	c/n	Prev id
F-JADA	Magni M-16 Expert		
F-JADF	Best Off Sky Ranger		
F-JAKO	Aerospool WT-9 Dynamic		
F-JAOI	Aerospool WT-9 Dynamic		
F-JAON	Pipistrel Alpha Trainer		
F-JAPW	Best Off Nynja		
F-JAQP	Pipistrel Taurus		
F-JAZF	Alpi Avn Pioneer 300 Kite		
F-JBAN	JMB VL-3 Evolution		
F-JBBO	Humbert La Moto-du-Ciel		
F-JBCF	Shark Aero Shark		
F-JBCH	Rans S-6 Coyote II		
F-JBCM	Rans S-6 Coyote II		
F-JBKQ	JMB VL-3 Evolution	219	
F-JBQI	Mignet HM.1000 Balerit	117	
F-JBTM	Halley Apollo Fox		
F-JCBN	Best Off Sky Ranger (built by Synairgie)		
F-JCEF	Best Off Sky Ranger (possibly 82-FS)		
F-JCMG	ICP MXP-740 Savannah		
F-JCQJ	Rans S-6 Coyote II		
F-JCVS	III Sky Arrow 500TF		
F-JDCM	Light Aero Avid IV STOL	1285D	
F-JEND	Humbert Tetras 912BS		
F-JEOQ	Pipistrel Sinus 912		
F-JEQS	Vidor Asso V Champion		
F-JEQW	Take Off Merlin 1100		
F-JERP	Jodel D.18	90	F-PRAB
F-JETP	B&F Funk FK-9 Mk.IV		
F-JEYM	Vol Mediterrani VM-1 Esqual		
F-JEZK	Tecnam P.92 Echo		
F-JEZY	B&F Funk FK-14B Polaris	14-053	
F-JFAQ	Humbert La Moto-du-Ciel		
F-JFLF	Cosmos		
F-JFJU	Air Création GTE Clipper		
F-JFMH	Fly Synthesis Storch HS		
F-JFMP	Magni M-16 Tandem Trainer		
F-JFNP	Magni M-16 Tandem Trainer		
F-JFOV	Magni M-16 Tandem Trainer		
F-JFTI	Rans S-6ES Coyote II		
F-JFTV	Magni M-22 Voyager (Same c/n as 77-BDZ)	22-07-4184	41-PA
F-JFVL	Fisher Youngster		
F-JFWT	ICP Super Bingo 582		
F-JFXT	Air Création GTE / Kiss		
F-JFYL	Ultralair Weedhopper 503		
F-JGBD	Aviakit Vega 2000		
F-JGBY	Zenair CH-701 STOL		
F-JGFQ	Huntair Pathfinder		
F-JGFS	Technoflug Piccolo		
F-JGNZ	European Airwings Springbok 912		
F-JGVM	Dallach D4 Fascination		
F-JGYB	B&F Funk FK-9		
F-JHAX	Aéro Services Guépy Club 582		
F-JHDZ	Jabiru J400		
F-JICQ	Best Off Sky Ranger Swift		
F-JIDO	CAG Avia Toxo		
F-JIEO	Aéro Services Guépy		
F-JIIC	Aviasud Mistral 582	118	
F-JIJH	B&F Funk FK-14 Polaris		
F-JIMW	Mitchell Wing or similar		
F-JINJ	Best Off Sky Ranger		
F-JIPF	B&F Funk FK-9 Mk.IV		
F-JITV	Rans S-6 Coyote II		
F-JIUU	Pro.Mecc. Sparviero		
F-JIYD	Fly Synthesis Storch CL 582		
F-JJFS	Zenair CH-601UL Zodiac	6-9190	
F-JJGP	Jabiru		
F-JJKA	(Weedhopper?) Europa II		
F-JJKO	Dyn'Aéro MCR-01 ULC	247	
F-JJKP	Jabiru UL450		
F-JJNC	ICP Bingo 4S		
F-JJPE	Light Aero Avid IV Heavy Hauler	1111	
F-JJPR	Jodel D.18		
F-JJTJ	Pipistrel Sinus 912		
F-JJUH	Evektor EV-97 Eurostar		
F-JJWI	Jodel D.185 (Cr in Spain 23.10.09)		
F-JJXF	Best Off Sky Ranger Swift		
F-JKCZ	Aéro Services Guépard 912		
F-JKEL	PJB Aerocomposite Vega		
F-JKGO	Light Aero Avid IV	1597	
F-JKHC	Rans S-6 Coyote II		
F-JKIH	ATEC Zephyr 2000		
F-JKIK	Flight Design CT-2K		
F-JKIO	Evektor EV-97 Eurostar		
F-JKIR	Ekolot JK-05 Junior		
F-JKIX	Cosmos		
F-JKJH	Vol Mediterrani VM-1 Esqual		
F-JKTK	Mignet HM.1100 Corduan	14	
F-JKUT	Murphy Renegade 2		
F-JKVR	Flight Design CT-2K		
F-JKWN	Best Off Sky Ranger		
F-JLAR	Zenair CH-601XL Zodiac		
F-JLCG	Evektor EV-97 Eurostar	2006 2622	
F-JLRE	Aeroprakt		
F-JNBI	Aerospool WT-9 Dynamic		
F-JOBE	Tecnam P.2002 Sierra		
F-JPCG	Flight Design CT SW		
F-JPLM	SMAN Pétrel		
F-JPOL	Aeroprakt A-22		
F-JPOW	Fly Synthesis Storch		
F-JPRO	Evektor EV-97 Eurostar		
F-JPTK	Evektor EV-97 Eurostar		
F-JQBU	Weedhopper AX-2		
F-JQFD	Magni M-16 Tandem Trainer "102"		
F-JQSM	ICP MXP-740 Savannah		
F-JRAA	Pipistrel Virus 912		
F-JRAF	Zenair CH-601 Zodiac		
F-JRDW	Freewind BumbleB gyro		
F-JREC	GN-1 Aircamper		
F-JREF	Raj Hamsa X'Air F 602T	kit no 619	
F-JRHD	Aerospool WT-9 Dynamic		
F-JRIH	Aerospool WT-9 Dynamic	DY327/....	
F-JRIN	B&F Funk FK-9		
F-JRKM	Evektor EV-97 Eurostar SL		

Reg	Type	Serial	Prev ID
F-JRLL	Jodel D.112		
F-JRSS	Denney Kitfox		
F-JRSV	Air Création Tanarg 912		
F-JRTQ	Air Création Safari GT BI 503		
F-JRXY	Aerospool WT-9 Dynamic		
F-JRYF	Flight Design CT Supralight		
F-JSDD	Aveko VL-3 Sprint		
F-JSFM	Aero East Europe SILA 450C		
F-JSGS	ICP MXP-740 Savannah		
F-JSIQ	Light Aero Avid Flyer Speedwing Mk.IV		
F-JSJS	Zenair CH-601 Zodiac (t/w)		
F-JSKR	B&F Funk FK-12 Comet SL	12-093	
F-JSND	Jodel D.112 (modified)		
F-JSNU	BRM Citius		
F-JSRR	Dallach Sunwheel	002	D-MDRP
F-JSTV	ICP MXP-740 Savannah		
F-JSXM	Evektor EV-97 Eurostar		
F-JTAJ	Zenair CH-650 Zodiac (damaged in forced landing 1.8.13)		
F-JTAX	ICP MXP-740 Savannah S	15-02-54-0377	
F-JTBM	ICP MXP-740 Savannah		
F-JTHF	TEAM Mini-MAX 1600R		
F-JTKL	ICP MXP-740 Savannah S	11-10-54-0130	
F-JTON	Fantasy Air Allegro SW		
F-JTOO	B&F Funk FK-12 Comet	12-067	D-MLWM
F-JTQR	B&F Funk FK-9 Mk.IV ELA Professional		
F-JTSA	G1 Spyl		
F-JTTS	BRM Citius		
	(W/o 27.9.14)		
F-JTVX	EDRA Super Petrel LS		
F-JTYB	Pipistrel Virus SW	415SWN100	G-MGAP
F-JTYD	ICP MXP-740 Savannah S		
F-JUAE	B&F Funk FK-14B Polaris Le Mans		
F-JUAU	Air Création Tanarg 912ES / BioniX 13	A13013-13011	
F-JUBL	Aviasud Mistral 582	201	OO-B70
F-JUCT	Flight Design CT LS		
F-JUDR	Colomban MC-30 Luciole	135	
F-JUEH	Shark Aero Shark		
F-JUIJ	Helisport CH-7 Kompress		
F-JUMG	Pipistrel Alpha Trainer		
F-JUMY	Denney Kitfox		
F-JUNS	Jodel D.18		
F-JUOT	ICP MXP-740 Savannah		
F-JUPM	Ekolot JK-05 Junior	05 01 01	
	(possibly ex SP-YAI)		
F-JUPW	Aveko VL-3 Sprint		
F-JUUB	JMB Aircraft VL-3		
F-JUUQ	Zlin Savage Bobber	0244	
F-JUZJ	ELA Aviacion ELA-07S	0108 209 0724	
F-JUZQ	Air Création Pixel XC	A14027-14016	
F-JVAY	Corvus Fusion Racer 312		
F-JVOL	DTA J-RO gyrocopter		
F-JVPA	Jodel D.9		
F-JVRE	Technoflug Piccolo		
F-JVYQ	Alpi Avn Pioneer 200	225	
F-JVZK	Ekolot JK-05 Junior		
F-JWAR	Alpi Aviation Pioneer 200		
F-JWBD	Flight Design CT SW		
F-JWDL	Alpi Aviation Pioneer 200	211	
F-JWFQ	Fly Synthesis Storch CL		
F-JWFR	Aerospool WT-9 Dynamic	DY275/2008	
F-JWGW	Aerospool WT-9 Dynamic	DY280/2008	
F-JWJX	Brügger MB-2 Colibri	162	
F-JWKC	Urban Air UFM-13 Lambada		
F-JWLB	Alpi Aviation Pioneer		
F-JWLI	Jodel D.195	564	
F-JWNI	Marie JPM-03 Loiret	21	
F-JWNQ	Flight Design CT LS		
F-JWQN	Dyn'Aéro MCR Pick-Up		
F-JWRR	Top Concept Hurricane		
F-JWRT	Aerospool WT-9 Dynamic	DY302/2009	
F-JWTC	Flight Design CT SW		
F-JWTN	Best Off Sky Ranger		
F-JWUE	BRM Land Africa		
F-JWUP	B&F Funk FK-14B Polaris		
F-JXBD	Skyeton K-10 Swift		
F-JXEF	Light Aero Avid Flyer		
F-JXGN	Alpi Avn Pioneer 300		
F-JXHA	Jabiru UL450D		
F-JXHU	Celier Xenon RST		
F-JXIF	Aerospool WT-9 Dynamic		
F-JXIK	Alpi Aviation Pioneer 300JS		
F-JXND	B&F Funk FK-9 SW		
F-JXOL	Aerospool WT-9 Dynamic		
F-JXOP	Zenair CH-601XL Zodiac		
F-JXQX	Jodel D.19	364T	F-PELR
F-JXSI	Guérin G1 912S		
F-JXTA	Aerospool WT-9 Dynamic		
F-JXTT	DTA Combo FC 912		
F-JXTX	Colomban MC-30 Luciole		
F-JXUS	Humbert Tetras BS		
F-JXVD	Rans S-6 Coyote II		
F-JXXJ	III Sky Arrow 500TF		
F-JXYG	ATEC 212 Solo		
F-JXZC	Zenair CH-601XL Zodiac		
F-JYAL	Vol Mediterrani VM-1 Esqual 912FR	180	
F-JYAR	Dyn'Aero MCR Pick Up		
F-JYCG	Flight Design CT SW		
F-JYFQ	TL Ultralight TL-2000 Sting		
F-JYGT	Zenair CH-701 STOL		
F-JYJT	Aerospool WT-9 Dynamic		
F-JYLA	Alpi Aviation Pioneer 200		
F-JYLX	Zenair CH-701 STOL		
F-JYND	Flight Design CT		
F-JYNE	Ekolot JK-05L Junior		
F-JYOA	Zenair CH-601XL Zodiac		
F-JYQI	Zenair CH-701 STOL		
F-JYQO	Fly Synthesis Texan Top Class		
F-JYRC	Dyn'Aero MCR-01	356	
F-JYRD	Humbert Tetras		
F-JYRI	Zenair		
F-JYSI	Fly Synthesis Storch CL 582		
F-JYSW	Best Off Sky Ranger Swift		
F-JYSZ	ZUT Aviation ZT610		
F-JYUY	B&F Funk FK-9 Utility		
F-JYVG	Flight Design CT SW		
F-JYVR	Guérin G1		
F-JYWC	European Airwings Springbok 3000		
F-JYXD	Aerospool WT-9 Dynamic		
F-JYXP	Jodel D.9 Bébé		
F-JYYF	Evektor EV-97 Eurostar		
	(But see 42-JU)		
F-JYZK	Ekolot JK-05 Junior		
F-JZAV	Fly Synthesis Storch		
F-JZBZ	Alpi Avn Pioneer 200		
F-JZCP	ICP Bingo 582		
F-JZEX	Fly Synthesis Storch		
F-JZFO	Denney Kitfox		
F-JZGQ	Pro Fe D-10 Tukan		
F-JZHQ	Weedhopper AX-3		
F-JZIF	Vidor Asso V Champion		
F-JZKR	Best Off Sky Ranger		
F-JZLT	Murphy Renegade Spirit		
F-JZMK	DTA Combo 582 / Dynamic 450		
F-JZOX	Fly Synthesis Storch HS		
F-JZPJ	Evektor EV-97 Eurostar		
F-JZRB	Raj Hamsa Hanuman 582		
F-JZUF	Comco Ikarus C-42		
F-JZVA	ELA Aviacion ELA-07	0607 163 0724	
F-JZVT	Weedhopper AX-3		
F-JZWC	Evektor EV-97 Eurostar		
F-JZWM	Flight Design CT SW	06-07-19	
F-JZWV	Zlin Savage Classic		
F-JZXW	Zenair CH-601XL Zodiac		
F-JZYM	B&F Funk FK-9 SW		
F-JZZI	Alpi Aviation Pioneer 200		
'QO'	Jodel D.18		

Type unidentified

Reg	Code		Reg	Code
F-JCWG	06-BZ		F-JCXR	66-FU
F-JFOQ	26-YE		F-JGKX	74-SF
F-JGVH	68-TF			

See also end of Belgian ULM section for OQ- call signs used by French aircraft.

NOTES

358

NOTES

NOTES

NOTES